Presented to

____

By

____

On

____

____

This Certifies that

____

and

____

were united in

Holy Matrimony

on ____________________ the ____________________

day of ____________________ , ______________ A.D.

at ____

in accordance with the laws of ____________________

Dated this ______________ the ______________

day of ____________________ , ______________ A.D.

Officiating ______________________________________

Witness ____

Witness ____

Births

Marriages

Deaths

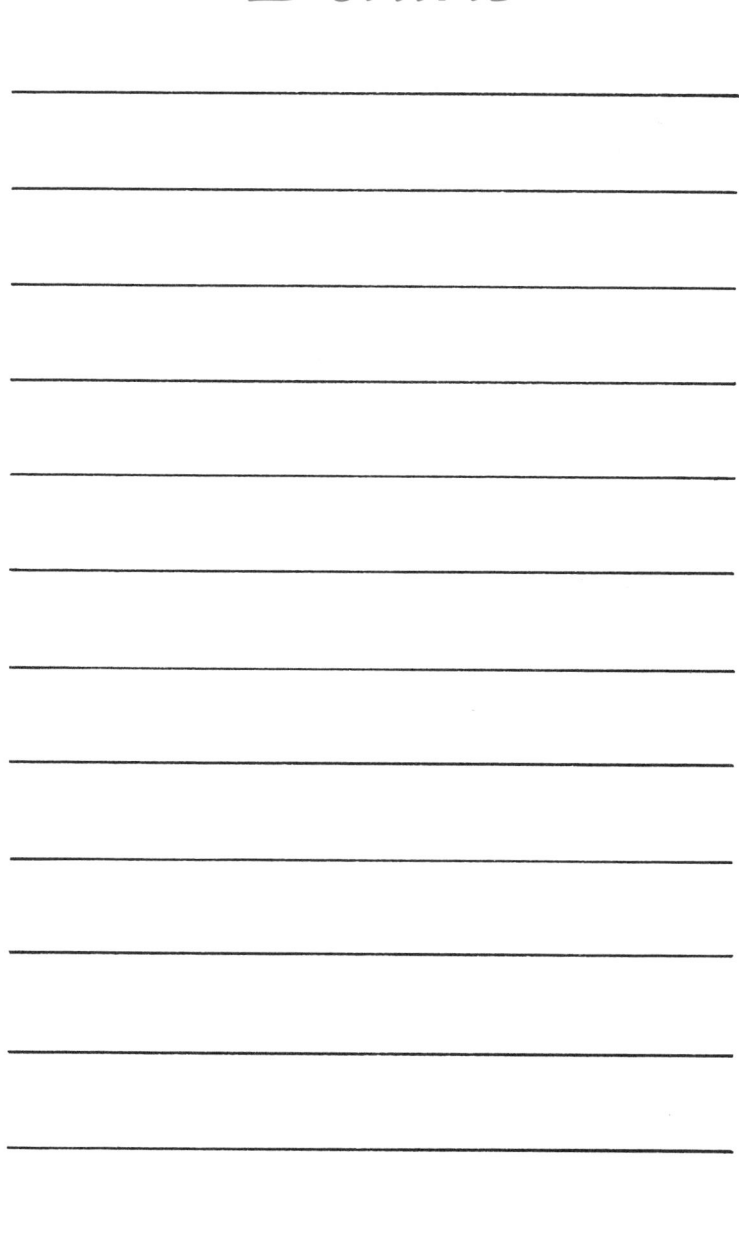

Family Record

Church Record

THE FULL LIFE STUDY BIBLE

THE FULL LIFE STUDY BIBLE

NEW INTERNATIONAL VERSION

THE NEW TESTAMENT

General Editor
DONALD C. STAMPS

Associate Editor
J. WESLEY ADAMS

ZONDERVAN
BIBLE PUBLISHERS

GRAND RAPIDS, MICHIGAN 49506, U.S.A.

The NIV Full Life Study Bible–New Testament

Library of Congress Catalog Card Number 90-081693

First printing—35,000 copies in print

Published by The Zondervan Corporation
Grand Rapids, Michigan 49506, U.S.A.
Printed in the United States of America

AG-H—5-90

You will be pleased to know that a portion of the purchase price of your new NIV Bible has been provided to the International Bible Society to help spread the Gospel of Jesus Christ around the world!

The Full Life Study Bible

General Editor

Donald C. Stamps, M.A., M. Div.
Writer of study notes and articles

Associate Editor

J. Wesley Adams, Ph.D.
Writer of introductions to books of the Bible

Editorial Committee

Stanley M. Horton, Th.D., Chairman

William W. Menzies, Ph.D., Co-chairman

French Arrington. Ph.D.

Robert Shank, A.B., D.H.L.

Roger Stronstad, M.C.S.

Richard Waters, D.Min.

Bishop Roy L. H. Winbush, M.Div., D.D.

Table of Contents

CONTENTS: MAPS AND CHARTS

CONTENTS: ARTICLES

The Full Life Study Bible

Author's Preface

The vision, call and urgency from God for this study Bible came to me while serving as a missionary in Brazil. I realized how much Christian workers needed a Bible that would give them direction in their thinking and preaching. Thus, seven years ago I began writing the notes and articles for this work. Later, when I came back to the United States for a short period of time, I discovered a similar desire among both pastors and lay people for a study Bible with notes that have a Pentecostal emphasis.

During the past number of years I have written with an increasing assurance that the Holy Spirit is not confined to the pages of Scripture, but that he wants to act today as he did in Bible times. The Spirit has come to remain personally with God's people, and his abiding presence is to be manifested in righteousness and power (Mt 6:33; Ro 4:17; 1Co 2:4; 4:20; Heb 1:8). In and through the church, God's Spirit desires to work in the same manner as he did in the earthly ministry of Jesus and continued to do in the apostolic church of the first century.

This study Bible is called *The Full Life Study Bible*. It has been so named because it is founded on three fundamental convictions:

(1) The original revelation of Christ and the apostles as recorded in the NT is fully inspired by the Holy Spirit; along with the OT, it is God's inerrant and infallible truth and the ultimate authority for the church of Christ today. All believers throughout history are dependent on the words and teachings of Biblical revelation for determining God's standard of truth and practice. In other words, we must view the NT message, standards and experience as God's preeminent pattern for the church, valid for all times.

(2) It is the task of every generation of believers not only to accept the NT as God's inspired Word, but also to sincerely seek to reproduce in their personal lives and congregations the same faith, devotion and power demonstrated in and through the faithful members of the early church. I am persuaded that the full life in the Spirit as promised by Christ and experienced by NT believers is still available for God's people today (Jn 10:10; 17:20; Ac 2:38-39; Eph 3:20-21; 4:11-13). It is the divine inheritance of all God's children to receive the fullness of Christ in the original power of the Holy Spirit.

(3) The church will fully experience the original kingdom power and life in the Holy Spirit only as it seeks with all its heart the righteousness and holiness set forth by God in the NT as his standard and will for all believers (2Co 6:14-18). Kingdom power and kingdom righteousness go together; they cannot be separated. Jesus states that we must seek both God's "kingdom and his righteousness" (Mt 6:33). The apostle Paul states that God's kingdom consists of both "power" (1Co 4:20) and "righteousness" (Ro 14:17). Thus the way to the fullness of God's kingdom with all its redemptive power is found in sincere faith in and devotion to the Lord Jesus Christ and in a separation from all unrighteousness that offends both God and the Holy Spirit whom he has poured out (Ac 2:17,38-40).

In summary, the major purpose of this study Bible is to lead you, the reader, to a deeper faith in the NT's apostolic message and to a greater expectancy for a NT experience made possible by the fullness of Christ living in the church (Eph 4:13) and by the fullness of the Holy Spirit living in the believer (Ac 2:4; 4:31).

We sincerely hope and pray that all readers will earnestly seek the NT church's devotion to God, its longing for the nearness of the risen Christ, its unshakeable trust in and love for God's Word, its zeal for truth and righteousness, its mutual care for other believers, its compassion for the lost, its dedication to a life of fervent prayer, its passion for holiness, its fullness in the Spirit, its manifestation of spiritual gifts, its urgency to preach the gospel to all nations, and its hope for the imminent return of our Lord and Savior Jesus Christ.

I gratefully acknowledge that I owe a great debt to those who served on the Editorial Committee for this study Bible. Their evaluations and suggestions have been invaluable. They gave of themselves and sacrificially took time from their own tasks to help in this work. What will be accomplished in God's kingdom through this work is in no small measure due to their help in the Lord. Also, I have benefited from the learning and labor of godly writers past and present who have produced a vast amount of literature and commentaries on the holy Scriptures. I have thankfully entered into their research and expertise and have reaped where they have sown.

Throughout these years of labor I have felt a profound sense of weakness and unworthiness to expound on God's holy Word. Many times I have been driven to my knees in need of special grace and help. I can testify that God, who is rich in mercy and whose grace is sufficient, has sustained me by his Spirit. Through all the long days and hours his Word has spoken to my heart. My desire for a full manifestation of Biblical Christianity has deepened and developed into an intense longing that is surpassed only by my longing for that day of the appearing of our Lord and Savior. With thanks to God—the Father, the Son and the Holy Spirit—for the privilege of laboring in the Scriptures, I send forth this work unto him who loves us and gave himself for us so that we may have life and have it to the full.

Donald C. Stamps

Donald C. Stamps
Easter, 1990

How to Use The Full Life Study Bible

The Full Life Study Bible is designed to help you gain a more thorough understanding of the truths of God's Word, whereby you may grow in love, purity and faith toward the Lord Jesus Christ (ITi 1:5). The special features and study helps of *The Full Life Study Bible* are the following:

Sectional headings

The entire NT contains sectional headings within the Bible text in order to help you more easily understand the subject and content of each section. NOTE: the standard New International Version sectional headings have been altered for this particular edition of the NIV. When two or more passages of Scripture are nearly identical or deal with the same event, this "parallel" is noted at the sectional headings for those passages. Identical or nearly identical passages are noted with *"pp."* Similar passages—those not dealing with the same event—are noted with *"Ref."*

Cross-reference system

The center-column cross-reference system is designed to help you connect one text of the Bible with others that have a similar theme. By using this system, difficult or obscure passages are clarified by Scripture itself. Cross references are indicated by raised light italic letters. A corresponding letter in the center column under the designated verse is followed by a list of appropriate Scripture verses.

Study Notes

The study notes at the bottom of nearly every page are written from a Pentecostal perspective and with the belief that the full message, standard and experience testified to by Christ and the apostles are forever valid and available for his people today.

The study notes fall into five classes:

(1) Expositional. The notes explain the meaning of words and phrases of many important passages in the Word of God.

(2) Theological. The notes define and explain the great doctrines and truths of the Bible, summarizing the Bible's teachings about baptism, forgiveness, perseverance, repentance, salvation, sanctification, etc.

(3) Devotional. The notes emphasize the importance of maintaining an intimate and devoted relationship with God—the Father, the Son and the Holy Spirit—through faith, obedience, prayer and the many means of grace.

(4) Ethical. The notes direct you to unreservedly commit yourself to God's kingdom and his righteousness. They emphasize the importance of Biblical principles of self-denial, godly conduct, following Christ, separation from sin, discernment of good and evil, and obligation to God and others.

(5) Practical. The notes present useful information on the believer's daily walk. They contain practical instruction about healing, the baptism in the Spirit, bringing up godly children, spiritual warfare, overcoming worry, resisting temptations, etc.

The study notes provide extensive Scripture references (usually in parentheses) that confirm comments made in the notes and help you in further in-depth Bible study. If the Scripture reference in parentheses is from the same chapter, it will normally appear first in the list, with the symbol "v." or "vv." Next will come Scripture references from the same book, usually without mention of the book's name. Last in the parentheses are passages from other Bible books, given in Bible book order. In many cases, other notes and articles are also cross-referenced.

Articles

The articles deal with important subjects more comprehensively than do the notes. They usually appear in close proximity to one of the major texts related to the subject of the article. For a complete list of the articles, see the Table of Contents for Articles on p. viii.

The articles, like the study notes, provide extensive Biblical references in parentheses. In the articles, the name of each Bible book, in Bible book order, is usually given for each reference. If there is no book mentioned before a Scripture reference, it means that that reference is found in the same book as the previous reference.

Introductions

Each book of the NT has an introduction, which includes (1) an outline of the book; (2) an explanation of the book's background and historical setting, including information about the author, circumstances and date of writing; (3) a statement about the original purpose of the book; (4) a survey of its contents; (5) a list of the book's special features and emphases; and (6) a suggested reading plan for covering the entire NT in one year. Careful reading of the introductions will help you understand each book and its applications more fully. At the end of each introduction, space is provided for you to write personal notes on that book.

Themefinders™

On many pages of this Bible you will see one of six symbols in the margin, next to a vertical line. Each of these symbols represents a specific theme of importance in the Pentecostal tradition. They are:

— Baptized in/Filled with the Holy Spirit (begin at Matthew 3:11)

— Gifts of the Holy Spirit (begin at Mark 16:17-18)

— Fruit of the Holy Spirit (begin at Matthew 7:16-20)

— Healing (begin at Matthew 4:23-24)

— Faith that moves mountains (begin at Matthew 8:10)

— Witnessing (begin at Matthew 10:18-20)

The symbol informs you which theme is contained in accompanying verses; at the bottom of each vertical line is a Bible text, directing you to the next text on that particular theme.

Charts

The Full Life Study Bible contains various charts that will help you at a glance to learn more about the Bible and its teachings, on such topics as the ministry of Jesus, the kingdom of God versus the kingdom of Satan, the last days of history, the gifts of the Holy Spirit, etc. See the Table of Contents for Maps and Charts on p. viii for a list of these charts.

Maps

Nine maps have been included within the Bible text to help you understand where the events written about in the Bible occurred. See the Table of Contents for Maps and Charts on p. viii for a list of these maps. At the back of this book are 16 full-color maps.

Subject Index

The subject index directs you to the most important notes and articles on the many topics and great doctrines of Scripture. Under each entry in this index, you will find texts of the Bible that have notes on that particular subject; next to the text is the page number on which that note is found. Articles are also included in this index.

Concordance

A concordance, compiled and edited by John R. Kohlenberger III and Edward W. Goodrick, is included to help you find Bible verses quickly and easily. By looking up key words in a Bible verse, you can find a verse for which you remember a word or two but not their location. For example, if you wanted to find out where the Bible says that the Word of God is "sharper than any double-edged sword," you could look up either "sharper," "double-edged" or "sword" in the concordance and find that the verse is located at Heb 4:12.

We trust that you will receive a rich blessing from using *The Full Life Study Bible.* It is our prayer that your knowledge of God's Word, your experience of the presence and power of the Holy Spirit, and your daily walk with Christ in truth and righteousness will increase through your use of this book.

Abbreviations

BOOKS OF THE BIBLE

Matthew	Mt	Ephesians	Eph	Hebrews	Heb
Mark	Mk	Philippians	Php	James	Jas
Luke	Lk	Colossians	Col	1 Peter	1Pe
John	Jn	1 Thessalonians	1Th	2 Peter	2Pe
Acts	Ac	2 Thessalonians	2Th	1 John	1Jn
Romans	Ro	1 Timothy	1Ti	2 John	2Jn
1 Corinthians	1Co	2 Timothy	2Ti	3 John	3Jn
2 Corinthians	2Co	Titus	Tit	Jude	Jude
Galatians	Gal	Philemon	Phm	Revelation	Rev

GENERAL

i.e.	that is
e.g.	for example
ch., chs.	chapter(s)
v., vv.	verse(s)
etc.	and so forth
Heb	Hebrew
Gk	Greek

Preface

THE NEW INTERNATIONAL VERSION is a completely new translation of the Holy Bible made by over a hundred scholars working directly from the best available Hebrew, Aramaic and Greek texts. It had its beginning in 1965 when, after several years of exploratory study by committees from the Christian Reformed Church and the National Association of Evangelicals, a group of scholars met at Palos Heights, Illinois, and concurred in the need for a new translation of the Bible in contemporary English. This group, though not made up of official church representatives, was transdenominational. Its conclusion was endorsed by a large number of leaders from many denominations who met in Chicago in 1966.

Responsibility for the new version was delegated by the Palos Heights group to a self-governing body of fifteen, the Committee on Bible Translation, composed for the most part of biblical scholars from colleges, universities and seminaries. In 1967 the New York Bible Society (now the International Bible Society) generously undertook the financial sponsorship of the project—a sponsorship that made it possible to enlist the help of many distinguished scholars. The fact that participants from the United States, Great Britain, Canada, Australia and New Zealand worked together gave the project its international scope. That they were from many denominations—including Anglican, Assemblies of God, Baptist, Brethren, Christian Reformed, Church of Christ, Evangelical Free, Lutheran, Mennonite, Methodist, Nazarene, Presbyterian, Wesleyan and other churches—helped to safeguard the translation from sectarian bias.

How it was made helps to give the New International Version its distinctiveness. The translation of each book was assigned to a team of scholars. Next, one of the Intermediate Editorial Committees revised the initial translation, with constant reference to the Hebrew, Aramaic or Greek. Their work then went to one of the General Editorial Committees, which checked it in detail and made another thorough revision. This revision in turn was carefully reviewed by the Committee on Bible Translation, which made further changes and then released the final version for publication. In this way the entire Bible underwent three revisions, during each of which the translation was examined for its faithfulness to the original languages and for its English style.

All this involved many thousands of hours of research and discussion regarding the meaning of the texts and the precise way of putting them into English. It may well be that no other translation has been made by a more thorough process of review and revision from committee to committee than this one.

From the beginning of the project, the Committee on Bible Translation held to certain goals for the New International Version: that it would be an accurate translation and one that would have clarity and literary quality and so prove suitable for public and private reading, teaching, preaching, memorizing and liturgical use. The Committee also sought to preserve some measure of continuity with the long tradition of translating the Scriptures into English.

In working toward these goals, the translators were united in their commitment to the authority and infallibility of the Bible as God's Word in written form. They believe that it contains the divine answer to the deepest needs of humanity, that it sheds unique light on our path in a dark world, and that it sets forth the way to our eternal well-being.

The first concern of the translators has been the accuracy of the translation and its fidelity to the thought of the biblical writers. They have weighed the significance of the lexical and grammatical details of the Hebrew, Aramaic and Greek texts. At the same time, they have striven for more than a word-for-word translation. Because thought patterns and syntax differ from language to language, faithful communication of the meaning of the writers of the Bible demands frequent modifications in sentence structure and constant regard for the contextual meanings of words.

A sensitive feeling for style does not always accompany scholarship. Accordingly the Committee on Bible Translation submitted the developing version to a number of stylistic consultants. Two of them read every book of both Old and New Testaments twice—once before and once after the last major revision—and made invaluable suggestions. Samples of the translation were tested for clarity and ease of reading by various kinds of people—young and old, highly educated and less well educated, ministers and laymen.

Concern for clear and natural English—that the New International Version should be idiomatic but not idiosyncratic, contemporary but not dated—motivated the translators and consultants. At the same time, they tried to reflect the differing styles of the biblical writers. In view of the international use of English, the translators sought to avoid obvious Americanisms on the one hand and obvious Anglicisms on the other. A British edition reflects the comparatively few differences of significant idiom and of spelling.

As for the traditional pronouns "thou," "thee" and "thine" in reference to the Deity, the translators judged that to use these archaisms (along with the old verb forms such as "doest," "wouldest" and "hadst") would violate accuracy in translation. Neither Hebrew, Aramaic nor Greek uses special pronouns for the persons of the Godhead. A present-day translation is not enhanced by forms that in the time of the King James Version were used in everyday speech, whether referring to God or man.

For the Old Testament the standard Hebrew text, the Masoretic Text as published in the latest editions of *Biblia Hebraica,* was used throughout. The Dead Sea Scrolls contain material bearing on an earlier stage of the Hebrew text. They were consulted, as were the Samaritan Pentateuch and the ancient scribal traditions relating to textual changes. Sometimes a variant Hebrew reading in the margin of the Masoretic Text was followed instead of the text itself. Such instances, being variants within the Masoretic tradition, are not specified by footnotes. In rare cases, words in the consonantal text were divided differently from the way they appear in the Masoretic Text. Footnotes indicate this. The translators also consulted the more important early versions—the Septuagint; Aquila, Symmachus and Theodotion; the Vulgate; the Syriac Peshitta; the Targums; and for the Psalms the *Juxta Hebraica* of Jerome. Readings from these versions were occasionally followed where the Masoretic Text seemed doubtful and where accepted principles of textual criticism showed that one or more of these textual witnesses appeared to provide the correct reading. Such instances are footnoted. Sometimes vowel letters and vowel signs did not, in the judgment of the translators, represent the correct vowels for the original consonantal text. Accordingly some words were read with a different set of vowels. These instances are usually not indicated by footnotes.

The Greek text used in translating the New Testament was an eclectic one. No other piece of ancient literature has such an abundance of manuscript witnesses as does the New Testament. Where existing manuscripts differ, the translators made their choice of readings according to accepted principles of New Testament textual criticism. Footnotes call attention to places where there was uncertainty about what the original text was. The best current printed texts of the Greek New Testament were used.

There is a sense in which the work of translation is never wholly finished. This applies to all great literature and uniquely so to the Bible. In 1973 the New Testament in the New International Version was published. Since then, suggestions for corrections and revisions have been received from various sources. The Committee on Bible Translation carefully considered the suggestions and adopted a number of them. These were incorporated in the first printing of the entire Bible in 1978. Additional revisions were made by the Committee on Bible Translation in 1983 and appear in printings after that date.

As in other ancient documents, the precise meaning of the biblical texts is sometimes uncertain. This is more often the case with the Hebrew and Aramaic texts than with the Greek text. Although archaeological and linguistic discoveries in this century aid in understanding difficult passages, some uncertainties remain. The more significant of these have been called to the reader's attention in the footnotes.

In regard to the divine name *YHWH,* commonly referred to as the *Tetragrammaton,* the translators adopted the device used in most English versions of rendering that name as "LORD" in capital letters to distinguish it from *Adonai,* another Hebrew word rendered "Lord," for which small letters are used. Wherever the two names stand together in the Old Testament as a compound name of God, they are rendered "Sovereign LORD."

Because for most readers today the phrases "the LORD of hosts" and "God of hosts" have little meaning, this version renders them "the LORD Almighty" and "God Almighty." These renderings convey the sense of the Hebrew, namely, "he who is sovereign over all the 'hosts' (powers) in heaven and on earth, especially over the 'hosts' (armies) of Israel." For readers unacquainted with Hebrew this does not make clear the distinction between *Sabaoth* ("hosts" or "Almighty") and *Shaddai* (which can also be translated "Almighty"), but the latter occurs infrequently and is always footnoted. When *Adonai* and *YHWH Sabaoth* occur together, they are rendered "the Lord, the LORD Almighty."

As for other proper nouns, the familiar spellings of the King James Version are generally retained. Names traditionally spelled with "ch," except where it is final, are usually spelled in this translation with "k" or "c," since the biblical languages do not have the sound that "ch" frequently indicates in English—for example, in *chant.* For well-known names such as Zechariah, however, the traditional spelling has been retained. Variation in the spelling of names in the original languages has usually not been indicated. Where a person or place has two or more different names in the Hebrew, Aramaic or Greek texts, the more familiar one has generally been used, with footnotes where needed.

To achieve clarity the translators sometimes supplied words not in the original texts but required by the context. If there was uncertainty about such material, it is enclosed in brackets. Also for the sake of clarity or style, nouns, including some proper nouns, are sometimes substituted for pronouns, and vice versa. And though the Hebrew writers often shifted back and forth between first, second and third personal pronouns without change of antecedent, this translation often makes them uniform, in accordance with English style and without the use of footnotes.

Poetical passages are printed as poetry, that is, with indentation of lines and with separate stanzas. These are generally designed to reflect the structure of Hebrew poetry. This poetry is normally characterized by parallelism in balanced lines. Most of the poetry in the Bible is in the Old Testament, and scholars differ regarding the scansion of Hebrew lines. The translators determined the stanza divisions for the most part by analysis of the subject matter. The stanzas therefore serve as poetic paragraphs.

As an aid to the reader, italicized sectional headings are inserted in most of the books. They are not to be regarded as part of the NIV text, are not for oral reading, and are not intended to dictate the interpretation of the sections they head.

The footnotes in this version are of several kinds, most of which need no explanation. Those giving alternative translations begin with "Or" and generally introduce the alternative with the last word preceding it in the text, except when it is a single-word alternative; in poetry quoted in a footnote a slant mark indicates a line division. Footnotes introduced by "Or" do not have uniform significance. In some cases two possible translations were considered to have about equal validity. In other cases, though the translators were convinced that the translation in the text was correct, they judged that another interpretation was possible and of sufficient importance to be represented in a footnote.

In the New Testament, footnotes that refer to uncertainty regarding the original text are introduced by "Some manuscripts" or similar expressions. In the Old Testament, evidence for the reading chosen is given first and evidence for the alternative is added after a semicolon (for example: Septuagint; Hebrew *father*). In such notes the term "Hebrew" refers to the Masoretic Text.

It should be noted that minerals, flora and fauna, architectural details, articles of clothing and jewelry, musical instruments and other articles cannot always be identified with precision. Also measures of capacity in the biblical period are particularly uncertain (see the table of weights and measures following the text).

Like all translations of the Bible, made as they are by imperfect man, this one undoubtedly falls short of its goals. Yet we are grateful to God for the extent to which he has enabled us to realize these goals and for the strength he has given us and our colleagues to complete our task. We offer this version of the Bible to him in whose name and for whose glory it has been made. We pray that it will lead many into a better understanding of the Holy Scriptures and a fuller knowledge of Jesus Christ the incarnate Word, of whom the Scriptures so faithfully testify.

The Committee on Bible Translation

June 1978
(Revised August 1983)

Names of the translators and editors may be secured
from the International Bible Society,
translation sponsors of the New International Version,
P.O. Box 62970, Colorado Springs, Colorado 80962-2970 U.S.A.

THE NEW TESTAMENT

MATTHEW

Outline

I. Introduction to the Messiah (1:1—4:11)
   A. The Jewish Lineage of Jesus (1:1–17)
   B. His Birth and Flight to Egypt (1:18—2:23)
   C. Prophetic Forerunner to the Messiah (3:1–12)
   D. Baptism of the Messiah (3:13–17)
   E. Temptation of the Messiah (4:1–11)
II. Jesus' Messianic Ministry in and Around Galilee (4:12—18:35)
   A. Summary of His Early Galilean Ministry (4:12–25)
   B. Discourse About Discipleship in the Kingdom (5:1—7:29)
   C. Narrative I: Mighty Deeds of the Kingdom (8:1—9:38)
   D. Discourse About the Proclamation of the Kingdom (10:1–42)
   E. Narrative II: The Presence of the Kingdom (11:1—12:50)
   F. Discourse About the Mystery of the Kingdom (13:1–58)
   G. Narrative III: Crisis of the Kingdom (14:1—17:27)
   H. Discourse About Membership in the Kingdom (18:1–35)
III. The Climax of Jesus' Messianic Mission in Judea/Perea and Jerusalem (19:1—26:46)
   A. Jesus' Journey to Jerusalem (19:1—20:34)
   B. Jesus' Last Week at Jerusalem (21:1—26:46)
      1. Triumphal Entry and Cleansing the Temple (21:1–22)
      2. Controversies With the Jews (21:23—22:46)
      3. Denunciations of the Teachers of the Law and the Pharisees (23:1–39)
      4. Olivet Discourse About the Future of the Kingdom (24:1—25:46)
      5. The Plot to Betray Jesus (26:1–16)
      6. The Last Supper (26:17–30)
      7. Gethsemane (26:31–46)
IV. Jesus' Arrest, Trial and Crucifixion (26:47—27:66)
   A. The Arrest (26:47–56)
   B. The Trial (26:57—27:26)
   C. The Crucifixion (27:27–56)
   D. The Burial (27:57–66)
V. The Resurrection (28:1–20)
   A. The Women's Glorious Discovery (28:1–10)
   B. False Witnesses (28:11–15)
   C. The Risen Lord's Commission (28:16–20)

Author: Matthew

Theme: Jesus, the Messianic King

Date: A.D. 60s

Background

This Gospel is appropriately placed first as an introduction to the NT and to "the Christ, the Son of the living God" (16:16). Although the author is not identified by name in the Biblical text, the unanimous testimony of all early church fathers (beginning c. A.D. 130) is that this Gospel was written by Matthew, one of Jesus' twelve disciples.

Whereas Mark's Gospel was written for the Romans (see Introduction to Mark) and Luke's Gospel for Theophilus and for all Gentile believers (see Introduction to Luke), Matthew's Gospel was written for Jewish believers. The Jewish background of this Gospel is evident in many ways, including (1) its reliance on OT revelation, promises and prophecy to prove that Jesus was the long-awaited Messiah; (2) its tracing of Jesus' lineage, starting from Abraham (1:1–17); (3) its repeated declaration that Jesus is the "Son of David" (1:1; 9:27; 12:23; 15:22; 20:30–31; 21:9,15; 22:41–45); (4) its use of preferred Jewish terminology such as "kingdom of heaven" (a synonym for "kingdom of God") because of the Jews' reverential reluctance to say the name of God directly; and (5) its reference to Jewish customs without any explanation (unlike the other Gospels).

However, this Gospel is not exclusively Jewish. Like the message of Jesus himself, Matthew's Gospel was intended ultimately for the whole church, faithfully revealing the universal scope of the gospel (e.g., 2:1–12; 8:11–12; 13:38; 21:43; 28:18–20).

The date and location of its origin are uncertain. However, there are good reasons for believing that Matthew wrote prior to A.D. 70 while in Palestine or Syrian Antioch. Some Bible scholars believe Matthew was the first of the four Gospels to be written; others ascribe that place to the Gospel of Mark.

Purpose

Matthew wrote this Gospel (1) to provide his readers with an eyewitness account of Jesus' life, (2) to assure his readers that Jesus was God's Son and the long-awaited Messiah foretold by the OT prophets, and (3) to show that God's kingdom was manifested in and through Jesus in an unprecedented way. Matthew is concerned that his readers understand (1) that Israel for the most part rejected Jesus and his kingdom, refusing to believe because he came as a spiritual rather than as a political Messiah, and (2) that only at the end of the age will Jesus come in glory as the King of kings to judge and rule the nations.

Survey

Matthew presents Jesus as the fulfillment of Israel's prophetic hope. He fulfills OT prophecy in his birth (1:22–23), birthplace (2:5–6), return from Egypt (2:15) and residence in Nazareth (2:23); as the one for whom the Messianic forerunner was sent (3:1–3); in relation to the primary location of his public ministry (4:14–16), his healing ministry (8:17), his role as God's servant (12:17–21), his teaching in parables (13:34–35), his triumphal entry into Jerusalem (21:4–5) and his arrest (26:56)

Chs. 5–25 record five major discourses by Jesus and five major narratives about his mighty deeds as Messiah. The five major discourses are: (1) Sermon on the Mount (chs. 5–7), (2) instruction for itinerant proclaimers of the kingdom (ch. 10), (3) parables about the kingdom (ch. 13), (4) the character of true disciples (ch. 18), and (5) the Olivet discourse about the end of the age (chs. 24–25). Matthew concludes with an account of Jesus' crucifixion (chs. 26–27) and resurrection (ch. 28). The last three verses of the Gospel record Jesus' "Great Commission."

Special Features

Seven major features characterize this Gospel. (1) It is the most Jewish of the NT Gospels. (2) It contains the most systematic arrangement of Jesus' teaching and ministry of healing and deliverance. This led the church already in the second century to rely heavily on it for instructing new converts. (3) The five major discourses contain the most extensive blocks of material in the Gospels on Jesus' teaching (a) during his Galilean ministry, and (b) on the subject of eschatology (the last things). (4) This Gospel specifically identifies events in Jesus' life as fulfilling the OT far more often than any other NT book. (5) It mentions the kingdom of heaven/kingdom of God twice as often as any other Gospel. (6) Matthew emphasizes (a) the righteous standards of the kingdom (chs. 5–7); (b) the present power of the kingdom over sin, sickness, demons and even death; and (c) the future triumph of the kingdom in that final victory at the end of the age. (7) It is the only Gospel to mention or predict the church as a future entity belonging to Jesus (16:18; 18:17).

Reading Matthew

In order to read the entire New Testament in one year, the book of Matthew should be read in 44 days, according to the following schedule:
☐ 1 ☐ 2 ☐ 3 ☐ 4 ☐ 5:1–20 ☐ 5:21–48 ☐ 6:1–18 ☐ 6:19—7:6 ☐ 7:7–29 ☐ 8:1–27 ☐ 8:28—9:17 ☐ 9:18–38 ☐ 10:1–23 ☐ 10:24–42 ☐ 11 ☐ 12:1–21 ☐ 12:22–50 ☐ 13:1–23 ☐ 13:24–43 ☐ 13:44—14:12 ☐ 14:13–36 ☐ 15:1–28 ☐ 15:29—16:12 ☐ 16:13—17:13 ☐ 17:14—18:14 ☐ 18:15–35 ☐ 19:1–15 ☐ 19:16—20:16 ☐ 20:17–34 ☐ 21:1–32 ☐ 21:33—22:14 ☐ 22:15–46 ☐ 23 ☐ 24:1–35 ☐ 24:36–51 ☐ 25:1–30 ☐ 25:31–46 ☐ 26:1–30 ☐ 26:31–56 ☐ 26:57–75 ☐ 27:1–26 ☐ 27:26–44 ☐ 27:45–66 ☐ 28

NOTES

The Genealogy of Jesus

1:1–17pp — Lk 3:23–38
1:3–6pp — Ru 4:18–22
1:7–11pp — 1Ch 3:10–17

1 A record of the genealogy of Jesus Christ the son of David,[a] the son of Abraham:[b]

2 Abraham was the father of Isaac,[c]
Isaac the father of Jacob,[d]
Jacob the father of Judah and his brothers,[e]
3 Judah the father of Perez and Zerah, whose mother was Tamar,[f]
Perez the father of Hezron,
Hezron the father of Ram,
4 Ram the father of Amminadab,
Amminadab the father of Nahshon,
Nahshon the father of Salmon,
5 Salmon the father of Boaz, whose mother was Rahab,[g]
Boaz the father of Obed, whose mother was Ruth,
Obed the father of Jesse,
6 and Jesse the father of King David.[h]

David was the father of Solomon, whose mother had been Uriah's wife,[i]
7 Solomon the father of Rehoboam,
Rehoboam the father of Abijah,
Abijah the father of Asa,
8 Asa the father of Jehoshaphat,
Jehoshaphat the father of Jehoram,
Jehoram the father of Uzziah,
9 Uzziah the father of Jotham,
Jotham the father of Ahaz,
Ahaz the father of Hezekiah,
10 Hezekiah the father of Manasseh,[j]
Manasseh the father of Amon,
Amon the father of Josiah,
11 and Josiah the father of Jeconiah[a] and his brothers at the time of the exile to Babylon.[k]

12 After the exile to Babylon:
Jeconiah was the father of Shealtiel,[l]
Shealtiel the father of Zerubbabel,[m]
13 Zerubbabel the father of Abiud,
Abiud the father of Eliakim,
Eliakim the father of Azor,
14 Azor the father of Zadok,
Zadok the father of Akim,
Akim the father of Eliud,
15 Eliud the father of Eleazar,
Eleazar the father of Matthan,
Matthan the father of Jacob,
16 and Jacob the father of Joseph, the husband of Mary,[n] of whom was born Jesus, who is called Christ.[o]

17 Thus there were fourteen generations in all from Abraham to David, fourteen from David to the exile to Babylon, and fourteen from the exile to the Christ.[b]

The Birth of Jesus Christ

18 This is how the birth of Jesus Christ
came about: His mother Mary was
pledged to be married to Joseph, but before they came together, she was found to
be with child through the Holy Spirit.[p]
19 Because Joseph her husband was a righ-

1:1 [a] 2Sa 7:12-16; Isa 9:6,7; 11:1; Jer 23:5,6; S Mt 9:27; Lk 1:32,69; Rev 22:16 [b] Ge 22:18; S Gal 3:16 **1:2** [c] Ge 21:3,12 [d] Ge 25:26 [e] Ge 29:35; 49:10 **1:3** [f] Ge 38:27-30 **1:5** [g] S Heb 11:31 **1:6** [h] 1Sa 16:1; 17:12 [i] 2Sa 12:24 **1:10** [j] 2Ki 20:21 **1:11** [k] 2Ki 24:14-16; Jer 27:20; 40:1; Da 1:1,2 **1:12** [l] 1Ch 3:17 [m] 1Ch 3:19; Ezr 3:2 **1:16** [n] Lk 1:27 [o] Mt 27:17 **1:18** [p] Lk 1:35

a *11* That is, Jehoiachin; also in verse 12
b *17* Or *Messiah.* "The Christ" (Greek) and "the Messiah" (Hebrew) both mean "the Anointed One."

1:1 GENEALOGY OF JESUS CHRIST. Matthew's Gospel opens with this genealogy, which traces Jesus' ancestral lineage through the paternal line (the line of Joseph), as was Jewish custom (v. 16). Although Joseph was not Jesus' biological father (v. 20), he was his legal father. Since God had promised that the Messiah would be a descendant of Abraham (Ge 12:3; 22:18; Gal 3:16) and David (2Sa 7:12–19; Jer 23:5), Matthew traces Jesus' legal lineage back to these two men in order to demonstrate to the Jews that Jesus had the proper genealogy to qualify as the Messiah.

1:1 CHRIST. The word "Christ" (Gk *christos*) means "anointed"; it is the Greek equivalent of the Hebrew term "Messiah" (Da 9:25–26). (1) From the beginning Matthew affirms that Jesus is God's Anointed One, anointed with the Holy Spirit (cf. Isa 61:1; Lk 4:18; Jn 3:34; Ac 10:38). (2) He was anointed as Prophet to bring knowledge and truth (Dt 18:15), as Priest to offer the sacrifice and cancel the guilt (Ps 110:4; Heb 10:10–14), and as King to rule, guide and establish the kingdom of righteousness (Zec 9:9).

1:1 SON OF DAVID. (1) Matthew establishes that Jesus was a legal descendant of David by tracing the genealogy of Joseph, who was from the house of David. Although Jesus was conceived by the Holy Spirit, he was still formally registered as Joseph's son and legally a son of David. (2) Luke's genealogy (see Lk 3:23, note) traces the lineage of Jesus through the males in Mary's line (she was also from the Davidic line). Luke stresses that Jesus is the flesh and blood (i.e., offspring) of Mary and therefore one of us (cf. Ro 1:3). Thus, the Gospel writers assert both Jesus' legal and biological right to the Messiahship.

1:16 MARY . . . JESUS. The virgin birth of Jesus is safeguarded in the genealogy. Notice the words "the father of" are used of all the names down to Joseph, but then the statement is altered. It is not said that Joseph "was the father of" Jesus, but rather that Joseph was the "husband of Mary, of whom was born Jesus" (see Mt 1:23, note).

teous man and did not want to expose her
to public disgrace, he had in mind to divorce[q] her quietly.
20 But after he had considered this, an
angel[r] of the Lord appeared to him in a
dream[s] and said, "Joseph son of David, do
not be afraid to take Mary home as your
wife, because what is conceived in her is
from the Holy Spirit. 21 She will give birth
to a son, and you are to give him the name
Jesus,[c][t] because he will save his people
from their sins."[u]
22 All this took place to fulfill[v] what the
Lord had said through the prophet: 23 "The
virgin will be with child and will give birth
to a son, and they will call him Immanuel"[d][w]—which means, "God with us."
24 When Joseph woke up, he did what
the angel[x] of the Lord had commanded
him and took Mary home as his wife.
25 But he had no union with her until she
gave birth to a son. And he gave him the
name Jesus.[y]

1:19 [q]Dt 24:1
1:20 [r]S Ac 5:19 [s]S Mt 27:19
1:21 [t]S Lk 1:31 [u]Ps 130:8; S Lk 2:11; S Jn 3:17; Ac 5:31; S Ro 11:14; Tit 2:14
1:22 [v]Mt 2:15,17,23; 4:14; 8:17; 12:17; 21:4; 26:54,56; 27:9; Lk 4:21; 21:22; 24:44; Jn 13:18; 19:24,28,36
1:23 [w]Isa 7:14; 8:8,10
1:24 [x]S Ac 5:19
1:25 [y]ver 21; S Lk 1:31

2:1 [z]Lk 2:4-7 [a]Lk 1:5
2:2 [b]Jer 23:5; Mt 27:11; Mk 15:2; Lk 23:38; Jn 1:49; 18:33-37 [c]Nu 24:17
2:5 [d]Jn 7:42

The Visit of the Magi

2 After Jesus was born in Bethlehem in
Judea,[z] during the time of King Herod,[a] Magi[e] from the east came to Jerusalem 2 and asked, "Where is the one who
has been born king of the Jews?[b] We saw
his star[c] in the east[f] and have come to
worship him."
3 When King Herod heard this he was
disturbed, and all Jerusalem with him.
4 When he had called together all the people's chief priests and teachers of the law,
he asked them where the Christ[g] was to
be born. 5 "In Bethlehem[d] in Judea," they
replied, "for this is what the prophet has
written:

6 " 'But you, Bethlehem, in the land of
Judah,

[c] *21 Jesus* is the Greek form of *Joshua,* which means *the LORD saves.* [d] *23* Isaiah 7:14
[e] *1* Traditionally *Wise Men* [f] *2* Or *star when it rose* [g] *4* Or *Messiah*

1:21 JESUS. Jesus is the Greek form of the Hebrew word *yeshua* (Joshua), meaning "the LORD saves." This describes the future task of Mary's son and is the initial promise of the gospel. Jesus as Savior "will save his people from their sins." Sin is the greatest enemy of the human race, destroying one's soul and life. Through the atoning death of Jesus and the sanctifying power of the Holy Spirit, those who turn to Jesus will be set free from the guilt and slavery of sin (see Jn 8:31–36; Ac 26:18; Ro 6; 8:1–16).

1:23 VIRGIN . . . GIVE BIRTH TO A SON. Both Matthew and Luke agree unequivocally that Jesus Christ was conceived by the Holy Spirit (v. 18; Lk 1:34–35) and born of a virgin mother without the intervention of a human father. The doctrine of Jesus' virgin birth has been opposed by liberal theologians for years. However, it is undeniable that the prophet Isaiah promised a virgin-born child who would be called "Immanuel," a Hebrew term meaning "God with us" (Isa 7:14). This prediction was made 700 years before the birth of Christ.

(1) The word "virgin" in Mt 1:23 is the correct translation of the Greek *parthenos* found in the Septuagint in Isa 7:14. The Hebrew word for virgin (*almah*) used by Isaiah means a virgin of marriageable age, and is never used in the OT for any state other than virginity (cf. Ge 24:43; SS 1:3; 6:8; Isa 7:14). Therefore, Isaiah in the OT and both Matthew and Luke in the NT ascribe virginity to the mother of Jesus.

(2) The importance of the virgin birth cannot be overemphasized. In order for our Redeemer to qualify to pay for our sins and bring salvation, he must be, in one person, fully human, sinless and fully divine (Heb 7:25–26). The virgin birth satisfies all three of these requirements. (a) The only way Jesus could be born a human being was to be born of a woman. (b) The only way he could be sinless was to be conceived by the Holy Spirit (1:20; cf. Heb 4:15). (c) The only way he could be divine was to have God as his Father. As a result, his conception was not by natural but by supernatural means: "the holy one to be born will be called the Son of God" (Lk 1:35). Jesus Christ is therefore revealed to us as one divine person with two natures—divine and sinless human.

(3) In living and suffering as a human person, Jesus sympathizes with our weaknesses (Heb 4:15–16). As the divine Son of God, he has the power to deliver us from sin's bondage and Satan's power (Ac 26:18; Col 2:15; Heb 2:14; 5:14–16; 7:25). As both divine and human, he qualifies to serve as a sacrifice for the sins of every person, and as a high priest to intercede for all who come to God (Heb 1:9–18; 5:1–9; 7:24–28; 10:4–12).

1:25 NO UNION WITH HER UNTIL. The word "until" draws attention to the fact that after Christ's birth, Joseph and Mary entered into the full physical union commonly associated with marriage. We are told that Jesus had brothers and sisters (12:46–47; Mk 3:31–32; 6:3; Lk 8:19–20).

2:1 MAGI. These men were probably members of a learned religious class from the region now called Iran. They specialized in astrology, medicine and natural science. Their visit occurred when Jesus was between 40 days (cf. Lk 2:22) and 2 years old (cf. v. 16). The importance of this story is that (1) Jesus is worthy of royal honor from all humanity, and (2) Gentiles as well as Jews are included in God's redemptive plan (cf. 8:11; 28:19; Ro 10:12).

2:4 CHIEF PRIESTS AND TEACHERS OF THE LAW. Chief priests were the temple ministers in charge of worship; the teachers of the law were copyists of Scripture in post-exilic times. They were trained to teach and apply OT law and were considered experts "in the Law" (22:35). Together the teachers of the law and the chief priests constituted the Sanhedrin, or the Jewish Senate and Supreme Court. This body was composed of 70 or 71 men who were in charge of the civil and religious affairs of the Jews and who were given considerable authority under the Romans.

are by no means least among the
rulers of Judah;
for out of you will come a ruler
who will be the shepherd of my
people Israel.'[h]"[e]

7Then Herod called the Magi secretly
and found out from them the exact time
the star had appeared. **8**He sent them to
Bethlehem and said, "Go and make a careful search for the child. As soon as you
find him, report to me, so that I too may
go and worship him."

9After they had heard the king, they
went on their way, and the star they had
seen in the east[i] went ahead of them until
it stopped over the place where the child
was. **10**When they saw the star, they were
overjoyed. **11**On coming to the house, they
saw the child with his mother Mary, and
they bowed down and worshiped him.[f]
Then they opened their treasures and presented him with gifts[g] of gold and of incense and of myrrh. **12**And having been
warned[h] in a dream[i] not to go back to
Herod, they returned to their country by
another route.

The Escape to Egypt

13When they had gone, an angel[j] of the
Lord appeared to Joseph in a dream.[k] "Get
up," he said, "take the child and his mother and escape to Egypt. Stay there until I
tell you, for Herod is going to search for
the child to kill him."[l]

14So he got up, took the child and his
mother during the night and left for Egypt,
15where he stayed until the death of Herod. And so was fulfilled[m] what the Lord
had said through the prophet: "Out of
Egypt I called my son."[j][n]

2:6 [e]Mic 5:2; 2Sa 5:2
2:11 [f]Isa 60:3 [g]Ps 72:10
2:12 [h]Heb 11:7 [i]ver 13,19,22; S Mt 27:19
2:13 [j]S Ac 5:19 [k]ver 12,19,22; S Mt 27:19 [l]Rev 12:4
2:15 [m]ver 17,23; S Mt 1:22 [n]Hos 11:1; Ex 4:22,23
2:17 [o]ver 15,23; S Mt 1:22
2:18 [p]Ge 35:19 [q]Jer 31:15
2:19 [r]S Ac 5:19 [s]ver 12,13,22; S Mt 27:19
2:20 [t]Ex 4:19
2:22 [u]ver 12,13, 19; S Mt 27:19 [v]Lk 2:39
2:23 [w]Mk 1:9; 6:1; S 1:24; Lk 1:26; 2:39,51; 4:16,23; Jn 1:45, 46 [x]ver 15,17; S Mt 1:22 [y]S Mk 1:24
3:1 [z]ver 13,14; Mt 9:14; 11:2-14; 14:1-12; Lk 1:13, 57-66; 3:2-19; Ac 19:3,4

16When Herod realized that he had
been outwitted by the Magi, he was furious, and he gave orders to kill all the boys
in Bethlehem and its vicinity who were
two years old and under, in accordance
with the time he had learned from the
Magi. **17**Then what was said through the
prophet Jeremiah was fulfilled:[o]

18"A voice is heard in Ramah,
weeping and great mourning,
Rachel[p] weeping for her children
and refusing to be comforted,
because they are no more."[k][q]

The Return to Nazareth

19After Herod died, an angel[r] of the
Lord appeared in a dream[s] to Joseph in
Egypt **20**and said, "Get up, take the child
and his mother and go to the land of Israel, for those who were trying to take the
child's life are dead."[t]

21So he got up, took the child and his
mother and went to the land of Israel.
22But when he heard that Archelaus was
reigning in Judea in place of his father
Herod, he was afraid to go there. Having
been warned in a dream,[u] he withdrew to
the district of Galilee,[v] **23**and he went and
lived in a town called Nazareth.[w] So was
fulfilled[x] what was said through the
prophets: "He will be called a Nazarene."[y]

John the Baptist Prepares the Way

3:1–12pp — Mk 1:3–8; Lk 3:2–17

3 In those days John the Baptist[z] came,
preaching in the Desert of Judea **2**and
saying, "Repent, for the kingdom of heav-

[h] *6* Micah 5:2 [i] *9* Or *seen when it rose*
[j] *15* Hosea 11:1 [k] *18* Jer. 31:15

2:13 ESCAPE TO EGYPT. Herod's attempt to kill Jesus and God's way of protecting the child reveal several truths about God's method of guiding and protecting his people. (1) God did not protect Joseph and Mary and their child without their cooperation (vv. 13,19–20,22). Protection required obedience to God's guidance, which in this case involved fleeing the country (v. 14).

(2) God may allow some things that are hard to understand to enter our lives in order to accomplish his will. In a real sense Christ began life as a refugee and stranger in another country (vv. 14–15). To our limited understanding it would have been easier if God had removed Herod immediately, thus avoiding the escape to Egypt and all the trials involved in that circumstance.

(3) Even after a particular trial is resolved, there may be other problems to face (vv. 19–23). God's protection and providential care will always be needed, for the believer's enemy never ceases his attack on the faithful (Eph 6:10–18; 1Pe 5:8).

2:16 KILL ALL THE BOYS. Bethlehem and its vicinity were not large. It most likely contained between one and two thousand inhabitants; in this case the number of male children slain would have been around twenty.

2:22 WARNED IN A DREAM. From the two warnings of God (vv. 12,22) we learn that God watches over those whom he loves, and that he knows best how to frustrate the plans of the wicked and how to deliver his faithful out of the hands of those who would harm them.

3:2 REPENT. The basic meaning of repentance (Gk *metanoeō*) is "to turn around." It is a turning from evil ways and a turning to Christ, and through him to God (Jn 14:1,6; Ac 8:22; 26:18; 1Pe 2:25).

(1) The decision to turn from sin and to salvation in Christ involves accepting Christ not only as Savior from the penalty of sin, but also as Lord of one's life. Thus, repentance involves a change of lords—from

en[a] is near." **3**This is he who was spoken
of through the prophet Isaiah:

"A voice of one calling in the desert,
'Prepare the way for the Lord,
make straight paths for him.' "[l][b]

4John's[c] clothes were made of camel's
hair, and he had a leather belt around his
waist.[d] His food was locusts[e] and wild
honey. **5**People went out to him from Jerusalem and all Judea and the whole region
of the Jordan. **6**Confessing their sins, they
were baptized[f] by him in the Jordan River.
7But when he saw many of the Pharisees and Sadducees coming to where he
was baptizing, he said to them: "You brood
of vipers![g] Who warned you to flee from
the coming wrath?[h] **8**Produce fruit in
keeping with repentance.[i] **9**And do not
think you can say to yourselves, 'We have
Abraham as our father.'[j] I tell you that
out of these stones God can raise up children for Abraham. **10**The ax is already at
the root of the trees, and every tree that
does not produce good fruit will be cut
down and thrown into the fire.[k]

3:2 [a] Da 7:14; Mt 4:17; 6:10; 7:21; S 25:34; Lk 11:20; 17:20, 21; 19:11; 21:31; Jn 3:3,5; Ac 1:3,6
3:3 [b] Isa 40:3; Mal 3:1; Lk 1:76; Jn 1:23
3:4 [c] S Mt 3:1 [d] 2Ki 1:8 [e] Lev 11:22
3:6 [f] ver 11; S Mk 1:4
3:7 [g] Mt 12:34; 23:33 [h] S Ro 1:18
3:8 [i] Ac 26:20
3:9 [j] S Lk 3:8
3:10 [k] Mt 7:19; Lk 3:9; 13:6-9; Jn 15:2,6
3:11 [l] ver 6; S Mk 1:4 [m] S Mk 1:8 [n] Isa 4:4; Ac 2:3,4
3:12 [o] Mt 13:30; S 25:41
3:13 [p] S Mt 3:1; S Mk 1:4
3:16 [q] Eze 1:1; Jn 1:51; Ac 7:56; 10:11; Rev 4:1; 19:11 [r] Isa 11:2; 42:1

Jesus Will Baptize in the Spirit

11"I baptize you with[m] water for repentance.[l] But after me will come one who is
more powerful than I, whose sandals I am
not fit to carry. He will baptize you with
the Holy Spirit[m] and with fire.[n] **12**His win- Mk 1:7-8
nowing fork is in his hand, and he will
clear his threshing floor, gathering his
wheat into the barn and burning up the
chaff with unquenchable fire."[o]

The Baptism of Jesus

3:13–17pp — Mk 1:9–11; Lk 3:21,22; Jn 1:31–34

13Then Jesus came from Galilee to the
Jordan to be baptized by John.[p] **14**But John
tried to deter him, saying, "I need to be
baptized by you, and do you come to me?"
15Jesus replied, "Let it be so now; it is
proper for us to do this to fulfill all righteousness." Then John consented.
16As soon as Jesus was baptized, he
went up out of the water. At that moment
heaven was opened,[q] and he saw the Spirit of God[r] descending like a dove and

[l] 3 Isaiah 40:3 [m] 11 Or *in*

the lordship of Satan (Eph 2:2) to the lordship of Christ and his Word (Ac 26:18).

(2) Repentance is a free decision on the part of sinners, made possible by the enabling grace given to them as they hear and believe the gospel (Ac 11:21; see article on FAITH AND GRACE, p. 302).

(3) The definition of saving faith as "mere trust" in Christ as Savior is wholly inadequate in the light of Christ's demand for repentance. To define saving faith in a way that does not necessarily involve a radical break with sin is to dangerously distort the Biblical view of redemption. Faith that includes repentance is always a condition for salvation (cf. Mk 1:15; Lk 13:3,5; Ac 2:38; 3:19; 11:21).

(4) Repentance was a basic message of the OT prophets (Jer 18:8; Eze 18:21; Mal 3:7), John the Baptist (Mt 3:2), Jesus Christ (Mt 4:17; 18:3; Lk 5:32) and NT Christians (Ac 2:38; 8:22; 11:18; 2Pe 3:9). The preaching of repentance must always accompany the gospel message (Lk 24:47).

3:7 PHARISEES AND SADDUCEES. Two of the most prominent religious groups in Judaism were the Pharisees and Sadducees.

(1) The Pharisees were a Jewish religious group that adhered to both the entire OT and their own human interpretations of it. They especially emphasized that salvation came by obeying the letter of God's law and their interpretations of that law. They taught that the coming Messiah would be an earthly ruler who would help Israel dominate the nations and force all people to obey God's law. However, their religion was outward in form with no inward godliness of heart (23:25), and they refused to acknowledge the depravity of their own nature. By and large they opposed Jesus and his message that religion is a matter of the heart and spirit and not simply a legalistic obedience to the commands of Scripture (cf. 9:14; 23:2–4; Lk 18:9–14).

(2) The Sadducees were the liberals and anti-supernaturalists of their day. While appearing to hold to the law of God, they really denied many of its teachings. They rejected the doctrines of the resurrection, angels, miracles, immortality and the judgment to come. Their lives were morally lax and worldly. They also were persecutors of Jesus Christ (16:1–4).

3:8 FRUIT IN KEEPING WITH REPENTANCE. Genuine repentance will be accompanied by the fruit of righteousness (cf. 23:23; Lk 3:10–14; Ac 26:20). True saving faith and conversion must become evident through lives that forsake sin and bear godly fruit (see Jn 15:16, note). Those who say they believe in Christ and are God's children, and yet do not live lives that produce good fruit, are like trees that will be cut down and thrown into the fire (vv. 8–10,12).

3:11 BAPTIZE YOU WITH THE HOLY SPIRIT. John teaches that the work of the coming Messiah will involve baptizing his followers with the Holy Spirit and fire—a baptism that gives great power to live and witness for Christ (see Lk 3:16, note on the baptism in the Holy Spirit).

3:13 JESUS . . . BAPTIZED. Jesus was baptized by John for the following reasons: (1) "To fulfill all righteousness" (v. 15; cf. Lev 16:4; Gal 4:4–5). Christ, through baptism, publicly consecrated himself to God and his kingdom and thus fulfilled God's righteous requirement. (2) To identify himself with sinners—although Jesus himself did not need to repent of sin (2Co 5:21; 1Pe 2:24). (3) To associate himself with the new movement of God that was calling everyone to repentance; note the message of John the Baptist as the forerunner of the Messiah (Jn 1:23,32–33).

3:16 SPIRIT . . . ON HIM. Everything Jesus did—

lighting on him. **17**And a voice from heav-
en[s] said, "This is my Son,[t] whom I love;
with him I am well pleased."[u]

The Temptation of Jesus

4:1–11pp — Mk 1:12,13; Lk 4:1–13

4 Then Jesus was led by the Spirit into
the desert to be tempted[v] by the devil.[w] **2**After fasting forty days and forty
nights,[x] he was hungry. **3**The tempter[y]
came to him and said, "If you are the Son
of God,[z] tell these stones to become
bread."

4Jesus answered, "It is written: 'Man
does not live on bread alone, but on every
word that comes from the mouth of
God.'[n]"[a]

5Then the devil took him to the holy
city[b] and had him stand on the highest
point of the temple. **6**"If you are the Son
of God,"[c] he said, "throw yourself down.
For it is written:

" 'He will command his angels
concerning you,
and they will lift you up in their
hands,
so that you will not strike your foot
against a stone.'[o]"[d]

7Jesus answered him, "It is also written: 'Do not put the Lord your God to the
test.'[p]"[e]

8Again, the devil took him to a very

3:17 [s]Dt 4:12; Mt 17:5; Jn 12:28 [t]Ps 2:7; Ac 13:33; Heb 1:1-5; 5:5; 2Pe 1:17,18 [u]Isa 42:1; Mt 12:18; 17:5; Mk 1:11; 9:7; Lk 3:22; 9:35; 2Pe 1:17
4:1 [v]Heb 4:15 [w]Ge 3:1-7
4:2 [x]Ex 34:28; 1Ki 19:8
4:3 [y]1Th 3:5 [z]S Mt 3:17; 14:33; 16:16; 27:54; Mk 3:11; Lk 1:35; 22:70; Jn 1:34,49; 5:25; 11:27; 20:31; Ac 9:20; Ro 1:4; 1Jn 5:10-13,20; Rev 2:18
4:4 [a]Dt 8:3; Jn 4:34
4:5 [b]Ne 11:1; Da 9:24; Mt 27:53
4:6 [c]S ver 3 [d]Ps 91:11,12
4:7 [e]Dt 6:16

[n] *4* Deut. 8:3 [o] *6* Psalm 91:11,12 [p] *7* Deut. 6:16

his preaching, his healings, his suffering, his victory over sin—he did by the power of the Holy Spirit. If Jesus could do nothing apart from the working of the Holy Spirit, how much more do we need the Spirit's enablement (cf. Lk 4:1,14,18; Jn 3:34; Ac 1:2; 10:38). The Spirit came on Jesus to equip him with power for his work of redemption (see Lk 3:22, note). Jesus himself would later baptize his followers with the Holy Spirit so that they too might have the Spirit's enablement (see Mt 3:11, notes; Ac 1:5,8; 2:4).

3:17 THE TRINITY IN EXAMPLE. The baptism of Jesus is a striking manifestation of the fact of the Trinity. (1) Jesus Christ, declared to be equal with God (Jn 10:30), is baptized in the Jordan. (2) The Holy Spirit, who is also equal with the Father (Ac 5:3–4), descends on Jesus like a dove. (3) The Father declares that he is well pleased with Jesus. Thus, we have three equal divine persons; it is contrary to the whole of Scripture to explain this event in any other manner. The trinitarian understanding of God teaches that these three divine persons exist in such unity that they are one God (see Mk 1:11, note on the Trinity; cf. Mt 28:19; Jn 15:26; 1Co 12:4–13; Eph 2:18; 1Pe 1:2).

4:1–11 JESUS . . . TEMPTED. The temptation of Jesus by Satan was an attempt to entice Jesus from the pathway of perfect obedience to the will of God. Notice that in each temptation, Jesus submitted himself to the authority of the Word of God rather than to the desires of Satan (vv. 4,7,10). What can we learn from the temptation of Christ?

(1) Satan is our greatest enemy. As Christians, we must be aware that we are engaged in a spiritual warfare with unseen but very real powers of evil (see Eph 6:12, note).

(2) Without the Holy Spirit and the proper use of God's Word, the Christian cannot overcome sin and temptation. The following are suggestions on how to use God's Word in overcoming temptation: (a) Realize that through the Word you have the power to resist any appeal Satan can make (Jn 15:3,7). (b) Engraft (i.e., memorize) the Word of God into your heart and mind (see Jas 1:21, note). (c) Meditate day and night on the verses you have memorized (Dt 6:7; Ps 1:2; 119:48). (d) Say the memorized passage to yourself and God the instant you are tempted (vv. 4,7,10). (e) Recognize and obey the prompting of the Holy Spirit to obey God's Word (Ro 8:12–14; Gal 5:18). (f) Surround all these steps with prayer (Eph 6:18).

Some passages to memorize in facing temptation: General (Ro 6 and 8); Specific: concerning immorality (Ro 13:14), lying (Jn 8:44; Col 3:9), gossiping (Jas 4:11), disobeying parents (Heb 13:17), discouragement (Gal 6:9), fear of the future (2Ti 1:7), lust (Mt 5:28; 2Ti 2:22), desire for revenge (Mt 6:15), neglect of God's Word (Mt 4:4), worry over finances (Mt 6:24–34; Php 4:6).

4:2 FASTING FORTY DAYS. After fasting "forty days and forty nights," Jesus "was hungry" and was tempted by Satan to eat. This seems to indicate that Christ abstained from food but not from water (see Lk 4:2). To abstain from water for forty days would have required a miracle. Christ, insofar as he had to encounter temptation as our human representative (cf. Heb 2:17; 4:15), could not have used any other means of resisting temptation than is available to the Spirit-filled believer (see Mt 6:16, note on fasting; cf. Ex 24:18; 34:28; 1Ki 19:8). During the forty-day fast it is reasonable to assume that he was preparing himself by means of prayer and meditation on God's Word for the work the Father sent him to do.

4:6 IT IS WRITTEN. Satan used the Word of God to tempt Christ to sin. At times worldly people will use Scripture in an attempt to persuade believers to do something they know is wrong or unwise. Some Scripture texts, when taken out of context or not compared with other passages of God's Word, may even appear to condone sinful behavior (see, e.g., 1Co 6:12). Believers must know God's Word thoroughly and beware of those who pervert Scripture in order to fulfill the desires of the sinful human nature. The apostle Peter speaks of those who distort the Scriptures to their own destruction (2Pe 3:16).

4:8 ALL THE KINGDOMS OF THE WORLD. See Lk 4:5, note.

high mountain and showed him all the
kingdoms of the world and their splendor.
9"All this I will give you," he said, "if you
will bow down and worship me."

10Jesus said to him, "Away from me,
Satan![f] For it is written: 'Worship the
Lord your God, and serve him only.'[q]"[g]

11Then the devil left him,[h] and angels
came and attended him.[i]

Jesus Begins to Preach

12When Jesus heard that John had been
put in prison,[j] he returned to Galilee.[k]
13Leaving Nazareth, he went and lived in
Capernaum,[l] which was by the lake in the
area of Zebulun and Naphtali— 14to fulfill[m] what was said through the prophet
Isaiah:

15"Land of Zebulun and land of
Naphtali,
the way to the sea, along the
Jordan,
Galilee of the Gentiles—
16the people living in darkness
have seen a great light;
on those living in the land of the
shadow of death
a light has dawned."[r][n]

17From that time on Jesus began to
preach, "Repent, for the kingdom of heav-
en[o] is near."

The Calling of the First Disciples

4:18–22pp — Mk 1:16–20; Lk 5:2–11; Jn 1:35–42

18As Jesus was walking beside the Sea
of Galilee,[p] he saw two brothers, Simon
called Peter[q] and his brother Andrew.
They were casting a net into the lake, for
they were fishermen. 19"Come, follow
me,"[r] Jesus said, "and I will make you
fishers of men." 20At once they left their
nets and followed him.[s]

21Going on from there, he saw two other brothers, James son of Zebedee and his
brother John.[t] They were in a boat with
their father Zebedee, preparing their nets.
Jesus called them, 22and immediately they
left the boat and their father and followed
him.[u]

Jesus Heals the Sick

23Jesus went throughout Galilee,[v]
teaching in their synagogues,[w] preaching
the good news[x] of the kingdom,[y] and
healing every disease and sickness among
the people.[z] 24News about him spread all
over Syria,[a] and people brought to him all
who were ill with various diseases, those
suffering severe pain, the demon-possessed,[b] those having seizures,[c] and the
paralyzed,[d] and he healed them. 25Large

Mt 8:16-17

4:10 [f] 1Ch 21:1; Job 1:6-9; Mt 16:23; Mk 4:15; Lk 10:18; 13:16; 22:3,31; Ro 16:20; 2Co 2:11; 11:14; 2Th 2:9; Rev 12:9 [g] Dt 6:13 **4:11** [h] Jas 4:7 [i] Mt 26:53; Lk 22:43; Heb 1:14 **4:12** [j] Mt 14:3 [k] Mk 1:14 **4:13** [l] Mk 1:21; 9:33; Lk 4:23,31; Jn 2:12; 4:46,47 **4:14** [m] S Mt 1:22 **4:16** [n] Isa 9:1,2; Lk 2:32; Jn 1:4,5,9 **4:17** [o] S Mt 3:2 **4:18** [p] Mt 15:29; Mk 7:31; Jn 6:1 [q] Mt 16:17,18 **4:19** [r] ver 20,22; Mt 8:22; Mk 10:21,28,52; Lk 5:28; Jn 1:43; 21:19,22 **4:20** [s] S ver 19 **4:21** [t] Mt 17:1; 20:20; 26:37; Mk 3:17; 13:3; Lk 8:51; Jn 21:2 **4:22** [u] S ver 19 **4:23** [v] Mk 1:39; Lk 4:15,44 [w] Mt 9:35; 13:54; Mk 1:21; Lk 4:15; Jn 6:59; 18:20 [x] Mk 1:14 [y] S Mt 3:2; Ac 20:25; 28:23,31 [z] Mt 8:16; 14:14; 15:30; Mk 3:10; Lk 7:22; Ac 10:38 **4:24** [a] S Lk 2:2 [b] Mt 8:16,28; 9:32; 12:22; 15:22; Mk 1:32; 5:15,16,18 [c] Mt 17:15 [d] Mt 8:6; 9:2; Mk 2:3

[q] *10* Deut. 6:13 [r] *16* Isaiah 9:1,2

4:10 SATAN. Satan (Heb, meaning "accuser" or "adversary") was a great angel created perfect and good. He was appointed to be a minister at the throne of God; yet before the world began, he rebelled and became the chief antagonist of God and humanity (Eze 28:12–15).

(1) In his rebellion against God, Satan drew with him a multitude of lesser angels (Rev 12:4) who are probably to be identified, after their fall, with demons or evil spirits (see article on POWER OVER SATAN AND DEMONS, p. 80). Satan and many of these lesser angels were exiled to the earth and the atmosphere around it, and operate within this sphere under God's permissive will.

(2) Satan, also called "the serpent," caused the fall of the human race (Ge 3:1–6; see 1Jn 5:19, note).

(3) Satan's kingdom (12:26) is a highly systematized empire of evil that has authority over the kingdom of the air (Eph 2:2), fallen angels (25:41; Rev 12:7), unregenerate humanity (vv. 8–9; Jn 12:31; Eph 2:2) and the world (Lk 4:5–6; 2Co 4:4; see 1Jn 5:19, note). Satan is not omnipresent, omnipotent or omniscient; therefore, most of his activity is delegated to demons (8:28; Rev 16:13–14).

(4) Jesus came to earth to destroy the works of Satan (1Jn 3:8), establish God's kingdom and deliver us from Satan's dominion (12:28; Lk 4:18; 13:16; Ac 26:18). By his death and resurrection, Christ initiated the defeat of Satan and thereby ensured God's ultimate victory over him (Heb 2:14).

(5) At the end of the age Satan is to be confined to the Abyss for a thousand years (Rev 20:1–3). After his release he will make a final attempt to overthrow God; this will result in Satan's final defeat and his being thrown into the lake of fire (Rev 20:7–10).

(6) Satan presently wars against God and his people (Eph 6:11–18), seeking to draw them away from loyalty to Christ (2Co 11:3) and into sin and bondage to this present world system (cf. 2Co 11:3; 1Ti 5:15; 1Jn 5:16). Believers must pray constantly for deliverance from Satan (Mt 6:13), be on the alert concerning his schemes and temptations (Eph 6:11), and resist him through spiritual warfare, while remaining firm in the faith (Eph 6:10–18; 1Pe 5:8–9).

4:19 FISHERS OF MEN. One may be a pastor, evangelist, missionary, writer, teacher, deacon or layperson, but if he or she is not actually striving to bring others to Christ, they are not fulfilling their work for God (see 28:19; Lk 5:10; Jn 15:16; Ac 1:8; 1Co 9:19).

4:23 THE KINGDOM, AND HEALING. In the Gospels, the kingdom of God is closely associated with healing, the performing of miracles and the driving out of demons (4:23–24; 9:35; 10:7–8; 12:28; Lk 9:1–2; cf. Ac 8:6–7,12). The kingdom includes blessings for the body as well as for the soul (see article on DIVINE HEALING, p. 20).

crowds from Galilee, the Decapolis,[s] Jerusalem, Judea and the region across the Jordan followed him.[e]

The Beatitudes

5:3–12pp — Lk 6:20–23

5 Now when he saw the crowds, he went up on a mountainside and sat down. His disciples came to him, 2and he began to teach them, saying:

3"Blessed are the poor in spirit,
for theirs is the kingdom of heaven.[f]
4Blessed are those who mourn,
for they will be comforted.[g]
5Blessed are the meek,
for they will inherit the earth.[h]
6Blessed are those who hunger and thirst for righteousness,
for they will be filled.[i]
7Blessed are the merciful,
for they will be shown mercy.[j]
8Blessed are the pure in heart,[k]
for they will see God.[l]
9Blessed are the peacemakers,[m]
for they will be called sons of God.[n]
10Blessed are those who are persecuted because of righteousness,[o]

4:25 [e]Mk 3:7,8; Lk 6:17 **5:3** [f]ver 10,19; S Mt 25:34 **5:4** [g]Isa 61:2,3; Rev 7:17 **5:5** [h]Ps 37:11; Ro 4:13 **5:6** [i]Isa 55:1,2 **5:7** [j]S Jas 2:13 **5:8** [k]Ps 24:3,4; 73:1 [l]Ps 17:15; 42:2; Heb 12:14; Rev 22:4 **5:9** [m]Jas 3:18; S Ro 14:19 [n]ver 44,45; S Ro 8:14 **5:10** [o]S 1Pe 3:14

[s] *25* That is, the Ten Cities

5–7 SERMON ON THE MOUNT. Chs. 5–7, commonly called Christ's Sermon on the Mount, contain a revelation of God's principles of righteousness by which all Christians are to live through faith in the Son of God (Gal 2:20) and through the power of the indwelling Spirit (cf. Ro 8:2–14; Gal 5:16–25). All who belong to the kingdom of God are to have an intense hunger and thirst for the righteousness taught in Christ's sermon (see 5:6, note).

5:3 BLESSED ... POOR IN SPIRIT. The word "blessed" refers to the well-being of those who, because of their relationship to Christ and his Word, receive God's kingdom, which includes his love, care, salvation and daily presence (see 14:19, note). There are certain requirements if we wish to receive the blessings of God's kingdom; we must be guided by God's ways and values revealed in Scripture and not by the ways and values of the world. The first of these requirements is to be "poor in spirit." We must recognize that we are not spiritually self-sufficient; we need the Holy Spirit's life, power and sustaining grace in order to inherit God's kingdom.

5:4 THOSE WHO MOURN. To "mourn" is to grieve over our own weakness in relation to God's standard of righteousness and his kingdom power (v. 6; 6:33). It is also to mourn over the things that grieve God, to have our feelings in sympathy with the feelings of God, and to be afflicted in our spirits over the sin, immorality and cruelty manifested in the world (see Lk 19:41, note; Ac 20:19; 2Pe 2:8, note). Those who mourn are comforted by receiving from the Father "righteousness, peace and joy in the Holy Spirit" (Ro 14:17).

5:5 THE MEEK. The "meek" are those who are humble and submissive before God. They find their refuge in him and commit their way entirely to him. They are more concerned about God's work and God's people than about what might happen to them personally (cf. Ps 37:11). The meek, rather than the aggressors, ultimately inherit the earth.

5:6 HUNGER AND THIRST FOR RIGHTEOUSNESS. This is one of the most important verses in the Sermon on the Mount. (1) The foundational requirement for all godly living is to "hunger and thirst for righteousness" (cf. 6:33). Such hunger is seen in Moses (Ex 33:13,18), the psalmist (Ps 42:1–2; 63:1–2) and the apostle Paul (Php 3:10). The spiritual condition of Christians all throughout their lives will depend on their hunger and thirst for (a) the presence of God (Dt 4:29), (b) the Word of God (Ps 119), (c) the communion of Christ (Php 3:8–10), (d) the fellowship of the Spirit (Jn 7:37–39; 2Co 13:14), (e) righteousness (5:6), (f) kingdom power (6:33) and (g) the return of the Lord (2Ti 4:8).

(2) The Christian's hunger for the things of God is destroyed by worldly anxiety, deceitfulness of wealth (13:22), desire for things (Mk 4:19) and life's pleasures (Lk 8:14), and failure to remain in Christ (see Jn 15:4, note). When the hunger of believers for God and his righteousness is destroyed, they will die spiritually. For this reason it is absolutely essential that we be sensitive to the Holy Spirit's convicting work in our lives (see Jn 16:8–13; Ro 8:5–16).

5:7 THE MERCIFUL. The "merciful" are full of compassion and pity toward those who are suffering either from sin or sorrow. The merciful sincerely want to make such suffering less by bringing those people to the grace and help of God through Jesus Christ (cf. 18:23–35; Lk 10:30–37; Heb 2:17). In showing mercy to others, we "will be shown mercy."

5:8 THE PURE IN HEART. The "pure in heart" are those who have been delivered from sin's power by God's grace and now strive without deceit to please and glorify God and to be like him. (1) They seek to have the same attitude of heart that God has—a love of righteousness and a hatred of evil (see Heb 1:9, note). Their heart (which includes mind, will and emotions) is in tune with the heart of God (1Sa 13:14; Mt 22:37; 1Ti 1:5). (2) Only the pure in heart "will see God." To see God means to be his child and to dwell in his presence, both now and in the future kingdom (Ex 33:11; Rev 21:7; 22:4).

5:9 THE PEACEMAKERS. The "peacemakers" are those who have been reconciled to God. They have peace with him through the cross (Ro 5:1; Eph 2:14–16). They now strive by their witness and life to bring others, including their enemies, to peace with God.

5:10 PERSECUTED BECAUSE OF RIGHTEOUSNESS. Persecution will be the lot of all who seek to live in harmony with God's Word for the sake of righteousness. (1) Those who uphold God's standards of truth, justice and purity, and who at the same time refuse to compromise with their present evil society or the lifestyles of lukewarm believers (Rev 2; 3:1–4,14–22), will undergo unpopularity, rejection

for theirs is the kingdom of
heaven.[p]

11"Blessed are you when people insult
you,[q] persecute you and falsely say all
kinds of evil against you because of me.[r]
12Rejoice and be glad,[s] because great is
your reward in heaven, for in the same
way they persecuted the prophets who
were before you.[t]

Salt and Light

13"You are the salt of the earth. But if
the salt loses its saltiness, how can it be
made salty again? It is no longer good for
anything, except to be thrown out and
trampled by men.[u]

14"You are the light of the world.[v] A
city on a hill cannot be hidden. 15Neither
do people light a lamp and put it under a
bowl. Instead they put it on its stand, and
it gives light to everyone in the house.[w]
16In the same way, let your light shine
before men,[x] that they may see your good
deeds[y] and praise[z] your Father in
heaven.

The Fulfillment of the Law

17"Do not think that I have come to
abolish the Law or the Prophets; I have
not come to abolish them but to fulfill
them.[a] 18I tell you the truth, until heaven
and earth disappear, not the smallest letter, not the least stroke of a pen, will by
any means disappear from the Law until
everything is accomplished.[b] 19Anyone
who breaks one of the least of these commandments[c] and teaches others to do the
same will be called least in the kingdom
of heaven, but whoever practices and
teaches these commands will be called
great in the kingdom of heaven. 20For I

5:10 [p]ver 3,19; S Mt 25:34
5:11 [q]Isa 51:7 [r]S Jn 15:21
5:12 [s]Ps 9:2; Ac 5:41; S 2Co 6:10; 12:10; Col 1:24; Jas 1:2; 1Pe 1:6; 4:13,16 [t]2Ch 36:16; Mt 23:31,37; Ac 7:52; 1Th 2:15; Heb 11:32-38
5:13 [u]Mk 9:50; Lk 14:34,35
5:14 [v]Jn 8:12
5:15 [w]Mk 4:21; Lk 8:16; 11:33
5:16 [x]1Co 10:31; Php 1:11 [y]S Tit 2:14 [z]S Mt 9:8
5:17 [a]Jn 10:34, 35; Ro 3:31
5:18 [b]Ps 119:89; Isa 40:8; 55:11; Mt 24:35; Mk 13:31; Lk 16:17; 21:33
5:19 [c]Jas 2:10

---

and criticism. Persecution and opposition will come from the world (10:22; 24:9; Jn 15:19) and at times from those within the professing church (Ac 20:28–31; 2Co 11:3–15; 2Ti 1:15; 3:8–14; 4:16). When they experience this suffering, Christians are to rejoice (v. 12), for to those who suffer most God imparts the highest blessing (2Co 1:5; 2Ti 2:12; 1Pe 1:7; 4:13). (2) Christians must beware of the temptation to compromise God's will in order to avoid shame, embarrassment or loss (10:33; Mk 8:38; Lk 9:26; 2Ti 2:12). The principles of God's kingdom never change: ". . . everyone who wants to live a godly life in Christ Jesus will be persecuted" (2Ti 3:12). Those who suffer and endure persecution because of righteousness are promised the kingdom and heavenly rewards.

5:13 SALT OF THE EARTH. As salt is valuable to give flavor and to preserve from corruption, believers and the church must be godly examples in the world and must resist the moral decay and corruption evident in society. (1) Churches that become lukewarm, quench the power of the Holy Spirit and cease to resist the prevailing spirit in the world will be "thrown out" by God (see Rev 3:15–16, note). (2) They consequently will be "trampled by men"; i.e., those who are lukewarm, together with their families, will be destroyed by the ways and values of an ungodly society (cf. Dt 28:13,43,48; Jdg 2:20–22).

5:17 THE LAW . . . TO FULFILL. It is Christ's intention that the spiritual requirement of God's law be fulfilled in the lives of his followers (Ro 3:31; 8:4). The believer's relation to the law of God involves the following:

(1) The law that the believer is obliged to keep consists of the ethical and moral principles of the OT (7:12; 22:36–40; Ro 3:31; Gal 5:14; see Ex 20:2) as well as the teachings of Christ and the apostles (28:20; 1Co 7:19; 9:21; Gal 6:2). These laws reveal the nature and will of God for all people and still apply today. OT laws that applied directly to the nation of Israel, such as the sacrificial, ceremonial, social or civil laws, are no longer binding (Heb 10:1–4; e.g., Lev 1:2–3; 24:10).

(2) Believers must not view the law as a system of legal commandments by which to obtain merit for forgiveness and salvation (Gal 2:16,19). Rather, the law must be seen as a moral code for those who are already in a saved relationship with God and who, by obeying it, express the life of Christ within themselves (Ro 6:15–22).

(3) Faith in Christ is the point of departure for the fulfilling of the law. Through faith in Christ, God becomes our Father (cf. Jn 1:12). Therefore, our obedience as believers is done not only out of a relationship to God as sovereign Lawgiver, but also out of a relationship of children to their Father (Gal 4:6).

(4) Through faith in Christ, believers, by God's grace (Ro 5:21) and the indwelling Holy Spirit (Ro 8:13; Gal 3:5,14), are given an inner compulsion and power to fulfill God's law (Ro 16:25–26; Heb 10:16). We fulfill it by living according to the Spirit (Ro 8:4–14). The Spirit helps us put to death the misdeeds of the body and to fulfill God's will (Ro 8:13; see Mt 7:21, note). Thus, external conformity to God's law must be accompanied by the inner transformation of our hearts and spirits (cf. vv. 21–28).

(5) Having been freed from sin's power, and now being enslaved to God (Ro 6:18–22), believers follow the principle of "faith" by being "under Christ's law" (1Co 9:21). In so doing we fulfill "the law of Christ" (Gal 6:2) and are thus faithful to the requirement of the law (see Ro 7:4, note; 8:4, note; Gal 3:19, note; 5:16–25).

(6) Jesus emphatically taught that doing the will of his heavenly Father is an ongoing condition of entering the kingdom of heaven (see 7:21, note).

5:19 GREAT IN THE KINGDOM. The position of believers in the kingdom of heaven will be determined by our attitude toward God's law and by our teaching and practice of it. Our degree of faithfulness in this respect will determine our degree of glory in heaven (see article on THE JUDGMENT OF BELIEVERS, p. 368).

5:20 UNLESS YOUR RIGHTEOUSNESS. The righteousness of the Pharisees and the teachers of the law

tell you that unless your righteousness surpasses that of the Pharisees and the teachers of the law, you will certainly not enter the kingdom of heaven.[d]

Murder

5:25,26pp — Lk 12:58,59

21 "You have heard that it was said to the people long ago, 'Do not murder,[t,e] and anyone who murders will be subject to judgment.' 22 But I tell you that anyone who is angry[f] with his brother[u] will be subject to judgment.[g] Again, anyone who says to his brother, 'Raca,[v]' is answerable to the Sanhedrin.[h] But anyone who says, 'You fool!' will be in danger of the fire of hell.[i]

23 "Therefore, if you are offering your gift at the altar and there remember that your brother has something against you, 24 leave your gift there in front of the altar. First go and be reconciled to your brother; then come and offer your gift.

25 "Settle matters quickly with your adversary who is taking you to court. Do it while you are still with him on the way, or he may hand you over to the judge, and the judge may hand you over to the officer, and you may be thrown into prison. 26 I tell you the truth, you will not get out until you have paid the last penny.[w]

Adultery

27 "You have heard that it was said, 'Do not commit adultery.'[x,j] 28 But I tell you that anyone who looks at a woman lustfully has already committed adultery with her in his heart.[k] 29 If your right eye causes you to sin,[l] gouge it out and throw it away. It is better for you to lose one part of your body than for your whole body to be thrown into hell. 30 And if your right hand causes you to sin,[m] cut it off and throw it away. It is better for you to lose one part of your body than for your whole body to go into hell.

Divorce

31 "It has been said, 'Anyone who divorces his wife must give her a certificate of divorce.'[y,n] 32 But I tell you that anyone who divorces his wife, except for marital unfaithfulness, causes her to become an adulteress, and anyone who marries the divorced woman commits adultery.[o]

Oaths

33 "Again, you have heard that it was said to the people long ago, 'Do not break your oath,[p] but keep the oaths you have made to the Lord.'[q] 34 But I tell you, Do not swear at all:[r] either by heaven, for it is God's throne;[s] 35 or by the earth, for it is his footstool; or by Jerusalem, for it is the city of the Great King.[t] 36 And do not swear by your head, for you cannot make even one hair white or black. 37 Simply let your 'Yes' be 'Yes,' and your 'No,' 'No';[u] anything beyond this comes from the evil one.[v]

An Eye for an Eye

38 "You have heard that it was said, 'Eye for eye, and tooth for tooth.'[z,w] 39 But I tell you, Do not resist an evil person. If some-

5:20 *d* Isa 26:2; Mt 18:3; Jn 3:5
5:21 *e* Ex 20:13; 21:12; Dt 5:17
5:22 *f* Ecc 7:9; 1Co 13:5; Eph 4:26; Jas 1:19,20 *g* 1Jn 3:15 *h* Mt 26:59; Jn 11:47; Ac 5:21, 27,34,41; 6:12 *i* Mt 18:9; Mk 9:43,48; Lk 16:24; Jas 3:6
5:27 *j* Ex 20:14; Dt 5:18
5:28 *k* Pr 6:25; 2Pe 2:14
5:29 *l* ver 30; Mt 18:6,8,9; Mk 9:42-47; Lk 17:2; Ro 14:21; 1Co 8:13; S 2Co 6:3; 11:29
5:30 *m* S ver 29
5:31 *n* Dt 24:1-4
5:32 *o* S Lk 16:18
5:33 *p* Lev 19:12 *q* Nu 30:2; Dt 23:21; Mt 23:16-22
5:34 *r* Jas 5:12 *s* Isa 66:1; Mt 23:22
5:35 *t* Ps 48:2
5:37 *u* Jas 5:12 *v* Mt 6:13; 13:19, 38; Jn 17:15; Eph 6:16; 2Th 3:3; 1Jn 2:13,14; 3:12; 5:18,19
5:38 *w* Ex 21:24; Lev 24:20; Dt 19:21

t *21* Exodus 20:13 u *22* Some manuscripts *brother without cause* v *22* An Aramaic term of contempt w *26* Greek *kodrantes* x *27* Exodus 20:14 y *31* Deut. 24:1 z *38* Exodus 21:24; Lev. 24:20; Deut. 19:21

was external only. They kept many rules, prayed, praised, fasted, read God's Word and attended worship services. However, they substituted the outward acts for the correct inner attitudes. Jesus said the righteousness that God requires of the believer is more. The heart and spirit, not only the outward deeds, must conform to God's will in faith and love (see Mk 7:6, note on legalism.)

5:22 ANGRY ... RACA ... FOOL. Jesus is not speaking of a righteous anger at those who are wicked and unjust (cf. Jn 2:13–17), but is condemning the vindictive anger that would unjustly desire the death of another. "Raca" is a term of contempt and probably means "empty-headed fool." To call a person a "godless fool" in anger and contempt may indicate a heart attitude that places one "in danger of the fire of hell."

5:28 LOOKS ... LUSTFULLY. What Christ condemns is not the sudden thought that Satan may place in a person's mind or an improper desire that arises suddenly. Rather it is a wrong thought or desire that is accompanied by the approval of one's will. It is having an immoral desire that would seek fulfillment if the opportunity arose. The inner desire for illicit sexual pleasure, if contemplated and not resisted, is sin.

(1) The Christian must be particularly careful to abstain from taking pleasure in scenes of immorality such as those shown in films or pornographic literature (cf. 1Co 6:15,18; Gal 5:19,21; Eph 5:5; Col 3:5; 2Ti 2:22; Tit 2:12; Heb 13:4; Jas 1:14; 1Pe 2:11; 2Pe 3:3; 1Jn 2:16).

(2) In the area of maintaining sexual purity, the woman as well as the man has a responsibility. The Christian woman must be careful not to dress in a way that attracts attention to her body, thereby creating temptation for men and encouraging lust. Dressing immodestly is sinful (1Ti 2:9; 1Pe 3:2–3).

5:29 HELL. See Mk 9:43, note.

5:32 EXCEPT FOR MARITAL UNFAITHFULNESS. See 19:9, note.

5:39 DO NOT RESIST AN EVIL PERSON. Jesus is not speaking against the administration of proper jus-

one strikes you on the right cheek, turn to
him the other also.[x] 40And if someone
wants to sue you and take your tunic, let
him have your cloak as well. 41If someone
forces you to go one mile, go with him two
miles. 42Give to the one who asks you, and
do not turn away from the one who wants
to borrow from you.[y]

Love for Enemies

43"You have heard that it was said,
'Love your neighbor[a][z] and hate your enemy.'[a] 44But I tell you: Love your enemies[b] and pray for those who persecute
you,[b] 45that you may be sons[c] of your
Father in heaven. He causes his sun to
rise on the evil and the good, and sends
rain on the righteous and the unrighteous.[d] 46If you love those who love you,
what reward will you get?[e] Are not even
the tax collectors doing that? 47And if you
greet only your brothers, what are you doing more than others? Do not even pagans
do that? 48Be perfect, therefore, as your
heavenly Father is perfect.[f]

Giving to the Needy

6 "Be careful not to do your 'acts of
righteousness' before men, to be seen
by them.[g] If you do, you will have no reward from your Father in heaven.

2"So when you give to the needy, do not
announce it with trumpets, as the hypocrites do in the synagogues and on the
streets, to be honored by men. I tell you
the truth, they have received their reward
in full. 3But when you give to the needy,
do not let your left hand know what your
right hand is doing, 4so that your giving
may be in secret. Then your Father, who
sees what is done in secret, will reward
you.[h]

Prayer

6:9–13pp — Lk 11:2–4

5"And when you pray, do not be like the
hypocrites, for they love to pray standing[i]
in the synagogues and on the street corners to be seen by men. I tell you the
truth, they have received their reward in
full. 6But when you pray, go into your
room, close the door and pray to your Father,[j] who is unseen. Then your Father,
who sees what is done in secret, will reward you. 7And when you pray, do not
keep on babbling[k] like pagans, for they
think they will be heard because of their
many words.[l] 8Do not be like them, for
your Father knows what you need[m] before
you ask him.

9"This, then, is how you should pray:

" 'Our Father[n] in heaven,

5:39 [x] Lk 6:29; Ro 12:17,19; 1Pe 3:9 **5:42** [y] Dt 15:8; Lk 6:30 **5:43** [z] Lev 19:18; Mt 19:19; 22:39; Mk 12:31; Lk 10:27; Ro 13:9; Gal 5:14; Jas 2:8 [a] Dt 23:6; Ps 139:21,22 **5:44** [b] Lk 6:27,28; 23:34; Jn 15:20; Ac 7:60; Ro 8:35; 12:14; 1Co 4:12; 1Pe 2:23 **5:45** [c] ver 9; Lk 6:35; S Ro 8:14 [d] Job 25:3 **5:46** [e] Lk 6:32 **5:48** [f] Lev 19:2; 1Pe 1:16 **6:1** [g] Mt 5:16; 23:5

6:4 [h] ver 6,18; Col 3:23,24 **6:5** [i] Mk 11:25; Lk 18:10-14 **6:6** [j] 2Ki 4:33 **6:7** [k] Ecc 5:2 [l] 1Ki 18:26-29 **6:8** [m] ver 32 **6:9** [n] Jer 3:19; Mal 2:10; 1Pe 1:17

[a] *43* Lev. 19:18 [b] *44* Some late manuscripts *enemies, bless those who curse you, do good to those who hate you*

---

tice toward those who are evil (cf. Ro 13:1–4). The verses that follow (vv. 43–48) indicate that he is referring to loving one's enemies (v. 44; Lk 6:27). When we are wronged, we are not to react in a spirit of hatred but in a way that shows we have values that are centered in Christ and his kingdom. Our actions toward those who are unkind to us should be such that it might lead them to accept Christ as their Savior. As examples of this spirit, compare Ge 13:1–13 with Ge 14:14, and Ge 50:19–21 with Ge 37:18–28; see also 1Sa 24 and 26; Lk 23:34; Ac 7:60.

6:1 'ACTS OF RIGHTEOUSNESS' BEFORE MEN. The principle stated here concerns our motives for acting righteously. (1) If believers, whether laypersons or ministers, do good for the admiration of others or for selfish reasons, they will lose their reward and praise from God. Instead they will stand exposed as hypocrites who, under the guise of giving glory to God, are really seeking glory for themselves.

(2) Jesus speaks of acts of righteousness in three areas: giving (vv. 2–4), prayer (vv. 5–8) and fasting (vv. 16–18). His condemnation of doing acts of righteousness to be seen by others challenges much of contemporary Christian activity, including competing for bigness, advertising one's success, performing and entertaining in the church, and wanting to be first (see 1Co 3:13–15; 4:5).

6:6 PRAY . . . IN SECRET. Every child of God should have some place to be alone with God. Unless such a place exists, secret prayer will not be long or consistently maintained. Jesus had his secret places (14:23; Mk 1:35; Lk 4:42; 5:16; 6:12). Secret prayer is especially important: (1) in the morning to commit our day to God (2) in the evening to give thanks for his mercies; (3) in times when the Holy Spirit prompts us to pray. Our Father promises to reward us openly—with answered prayer, with his intimate presence and with true honor for eternity (see 6:9, note on God as Father).

6:9 THIS, THEN, IS HOW YOU SHOULD PRAY. With this model prayer, Christ indicates areas of concern that should occupy a Christian's prayer. The prayer contains six petitions: three concerned with the holiness and will of God; three concerned with our personal needs. The brevity of the prayer does not mean we should pray only briefly about our concerns. At times Christ prayed all night long (Lk 6:12).

6:9 OUR FATHER IN HEAVEN. Prayer involves worship of the heavenly Father. (1) As Father, God loves us, cares for us, and welcomes our fellowship and intimacy; through Christ we have access to him at any time to worship him and communicate our needs to him (vv. 25–34). (2) God as Father does not mean that he is like an earthly father who tolerates evil in his children or fails to discipline them correctly. God is a Father of holiness who must oppose sin. He will not tolerate evil, even in those who name him as Father. His name must be "hallowed." (3) As a heav-

hallowed be your name,
10your kingdom[o] come,
your will be done[p]
on earth as it is in heaven.
11Give us today our daily bread.[q]
12Forgive us our debts,
as we also have forgiven our
debtors.[r]
13And lead us not into temptation,[s]
but deliver us from the evil one.[c][t]

14For if you forgive men when they sin
against you, your heavenly Father will
also forgive you.[u] 15But if you do not forgive men their sins, your Father will not
forgive your sins.[v]

6:10 [o]S Mt 3:2 [p]S Mt 26:39
6:11 [q]Pr 30:8
6:12 [r]Mt 18:21-35
6:13 [s]Jas 1:13 [t]S Mt 5:37
6:14 [u]Mt 18:21-35; Mk 11:25,26; Eph 4:32; Col 3:13
6:15 [v]Mt 18:35
6:16 [w]Lev 16:29, 31; 23:27-32; Nu 29:7 [x]Isa 58:5; Zec 7:5; 8:19

Fasting

16"When you fast,[w] do not look somber[x] as the hypocrites do, for they disfigure their faces to show men they are fasting. I tell you the truth, they have received

[c] *13* Or *from evil*; some late manuscripts *one, / for yours is the kingdom and the power and the glory forever. Amen.*

enly Father he can punish as well as bless, withhold as well as give, act with justice as well as with mercy. How he responds to his children depends on our faith in and obedience to him.

6:9 HALLOWED BE YOUR NAME. The greatest concern in our prayers and in our lives should be the hallowing of the name of God. It is of utmost importance that God himself be reverenced, glorified and exalted (cf. Ps 34:3). In our prayer and daily walk we must be intensely concerned with the reputation of God, his church, his gospel and his kingdom. To do something that brings scandal on the Lord's name and character is a hideous sin that puts God to open shame.

6:10 YOUR KINGDOM COME. Prayer must be concerned with the kingdom of God on earth now and with its ultimate fulfillment in the future. (1) We must pray for Christ's return and the establishment of God's eternal kingdom in the new heaven and the new earth (Rev 21:1; cf. 2Pe 3:10–12; Rev 20:11; 22:20). (2) We must pray for the spiritual presence and manifestation of the kingdom of God now. This includes asserting God's power among his people in order to destroy the works of Satan, heal the sick, save the lost, promote righteousness and pour out the Holy Spirit on his people (see article on THE KINGDOM OF GOD, p. 28).

6:10 YOUR WILL BE DONE. To pray "your will be done" means that we sincerely desire God's will and purpose to be fulfilled in our lives and the lives of our families, according to his eternal plan. We can determine what God's will is primarily in his revealed Word, the Bible, and through the Holy Spirit's leading in our hearts (cf. Ro 8:4–14). God's will is accomplished when we pray for "his kingdom and his righteousness" to come among us (v. 33; see article on THE KINGDOM OF GOD, p. 28).

6:11 DAILY BREAD. Prayer should contain requests concerned with the individual's daily needs (Php 4:19; see Lk 11:3, note).

6:12 FORGIVE . . . AS WE ALSO HAVE FORGIVEN. Prayer must be concerned with sins and a willingness to forgive those who have harmed us (vv. 14–15; Heb 9:14; 1Jn 1:9).

6:13 DELIVER US FROM THE EVIL ONE. All believers are the special object of Satan's enmity and evil purpose. For this reason, we must never forget to pray for deliverance from his power and schemes (see Lk 11:26, note; 18:1, note; 22:31; Jn 17:15; 2Co 2:11).

6:15 IF YOU DO NOT FORGIVE. Jesus here emphasizes that Christians must be ready and willing to forgive the offenses of others. If they do not forgive repenting offenders, God will not forgive them, and their prayers will be to no avail. This is an important principle by which God forgives (18:35; Mk 11:26; Lk 11:4).

6:16 WHEN YOU FAST. In the Bible fasting refers to the discipline of abstaining from food for spiritual purposes. Although it was often linked with prayer, it should be considered a spiritual exercise all its own. In fact, fasting can be called "prayer without words."

(1) There are three main forms of fasting presented in the Bible. (a) The normal fast: abstaining from all food, solid or liquid, but not from water (see 4:2, note). (b) The absolute fast: abstaining from both food and water (Est 4:16; Ac 9:9). Normally this kind of fast should not be for more than one day. The body begins to dehydrate when abstaining from water for more than two days. Moses and Elijah undertook the absolute fast for 40 days, but only under supernatural conditions (Ex 34:28; Dt 9:9,18; 1Ki 19:8). (c) The partial fast: a restriction of diet rather than complete abstention (Da 10:3).

(2) Christ himself practiced this discipline and taught that it should be a part of Christian devotion and an act of preparation for his return (see 9:15, note). The NT church practiced fasting (Ac 13:2–3; 14:23; 27:33).

(3) Fasting with prayer has several purposes: (a) to honor God (vv. 16–18; Zec 7:5; Lk 2:37; Ac 13:2); (b) to humble ourselves before God (Ezr 8:21; Ps 69:10; Isa 58:3) in order to experience more grace (1Pe 5:5) and God's intimate presence (Isa 57:15; 58:6–9); (c) to mourn over personal sin and failure (1Sa 7:6; Ne 9:1–2); (d) to mourn over the sins of the church, nation and world (1Sa 7:6; Ne 9:1–2); (e) to seek grace for a new task and to reaffirm our consecration to God (4:2); (f) to seek God by drawing near to him and persisting in prayer against opposing spiritual forces (Jdg 20:26; Ezr 8:21,23,31; Jer 29:12–14; Joel 2:12; Lk 18:3; Ac 9:10–19); (g) to show repentance and so make a way for God to change his declared intentions of judgment (2Sa 12:16,22; 1Ki 21:27–29; Jer 18:7–8; Joel 2:12–14; Jnh 3:5,10); (h) to save people from bondage to evil (Isa 58:6; Mt 17:14–21; Lk 4:18); (i) to gain revelation and wisdom concerning God's will (Isa 58:5–6,11; Da 9:3,21–22; Ac 13:2–3); (j) to discipline the body for self-control (Ps 35:13; Ro 13:14; 1Co 9:27); (k) to open the way for the outpouring of the Spirit and Christ's return to earth for his people (see 9:15, note).

their reward in full. 17But when you fast,
put oil on your head and wash your face,
18so that it will not be obvious to men that
you are fasting, but only to your Father,
who is unseen; and your Father, who sees
what is done in secret, will reward you.[y]

Treasures in Heaven

6:22,23pp — Lk 11:34–36

19"Do not store up for yourselves treasures on earth,[z] where moth and rust destroy,[a] and where thieves break in and
steal. 20But store up for yourselves treasures in heaven,[b] where moth and rust do
not destroy, and where thieves do not
break in and steal.[c] 21For where your
treasure is, there your heart will be also.[d]
22"The eye is the lamp of the body. If
your eyes are good, your whole body will
be full of light. 23But if your eyes are bad,
your whole body will be full of darkness.
If then the light within you is darkness,
how great is that darkness!
24"No one can serve two masters. Either he will hate the one and love the other, or he will be devoted to the one and
despise the other. You cannot serve both
God and Money.[e]

Do Not Worry

6:25–33pp — Lk 12:22–31

25"Therefore I tell you, do not worry[f]
about your life, what you will eat or drink;
or about your body, what you will wear. Is
not life more important than food, and the

6:18 [y]ver 4,6
6:19 [z]Pr 23:4; Lk 12:16-21; Heb 13:5
[a]S Jas 5:2,3
6:20 [b]Mt 19:21; Lk 12:33; 16:9; 18:22; 1Ti 6:19
[c]Lk 12:33
6:21 [d]Lk 12:34
6:24 [e]Lk 16:13
6:25 [f]ver 27,28, 31,34; Lk 10:41; 12:11,22
6:26 [g]Job 38:41; Ps 104:21; 136:25; 145:15; 147:9
[h]Mt 10:29-31
6:27 [i]Ps 39:5
6:29 [j]1Ki 10:4-7
6:30 [k]Mt 8:26; 14:31; 16:8; Lk 12:28
6:32 [l]ver 8
6:33 [m]S Mt 3:2
[n]Ps 37:4; Mt 19:29
7:1 [o]Lk 6:37; Ro 14:4,10,13; 1Co 4:5; 5:12; Jas 4:11,12

body more important than clothes?
26Look at the birds of the air; they do not
sow or reap or store away in barns, and
yet your heavenly Father feeds them.[g]
Are you not much more valuable than
they?[h] 27Who of you by worrying can add
a single hour to his life[d]?[i]
28"And why do you worry about
clothes? See how the lilies of the field
grow. They do not labor or spin. 29Yet I
tell you that not even Solomon in all his
splendor[j] was dressed like one of these.
30If that is how God clothes the grass of
the field, which is here today and tomorrow is thrown into the fire, will he not
much more clothe you, O you of little
faith?[k] 31So do not worry, saying, 'What
shall we eat?' or 'What shall we drink?' or
'What shall we wear?' 32For the pagans
run after all these things, and your heavenly Father knows that you need them.[l]
33But seek first his kingdom[m] and his
righteousness, and all these things will be
given to you as well.[n] 34Therefore do not
worry about tomorrow, for tomorrow will
worry about itself. Each day has enough
trouble of its own.

Judging Others

7:3–5pp — Lk 6:41,42

7 "Do not judge, or you too will be
judged.[o] 2For in the same way you
judge others, you will be judged, and with

[d] *27* Or *single cubit to his height*

6:24 MONEY. (1) To serve money is to place such a high value on it that we (a) place our trust and faith in it, (b) look to it for our ultimate security and happiness, (c) expect it to guarantee our future, and (d) desire it more than we desire God's righteousness and kingdom. (2) The accumulation of wealth soon dominates one's mind and life so that God's glory will no longer be first (see Lk 16:13, note).

6:25 DO NOT WORRY. Jesus does not mean that it is wrong to make provisions for future physical needs (cf. 2Co 12:14; 1Ti 5:8). What he does forbid is anxiety or worry that shows a lack of faith in God's fatherly care and love (Eze 34:12; 1Pe 5:7; see next note).

6:30 IF THAT IS HOW GOD CLOTHES. These words contain God's promise to all his children in this age of trouble and uncertainty. God has promised to provide for our food, clothing and necessities. We need not worry; if we seek to let God reign in our lives (v. 33), we can be sure that he will assume full responsibility for those wholly yielded to him (Php 4:6; 1Pe 5:7).

6:33 SEEK . . . KINGDOM . . . RIGHTEOUSNESS. Those who follow Christ are urged to seek above all else God's kingdom and his righteousness. The verb "seek" implies being continually absorbed in a search for something, or making a strenuous and diligent effort to obtain something (cf. 13:45). Christ refers to two objects of our seeking: (1) "His kingdom"—we must seek earnestly to have the rule and power of God demonstrated in our lives and assemblies. We must pray that God's kingdom will come in the mighty power of the Holy Spirit to save sinners, to destroy the demonic, to heal the sick and to magnify the name of the Lord Jesus (see article on THE KINGDOM OF GOD, p. 28).

(2) "His righteousness"—through the Holy Spirit we must seek to obey the commands of Christ, possess Christ's righteousness, remain separated from the world and show Christ's love toward everyone (cf. Php 2:12–13).

7:1 DO NOT JUDGE. Jesus condemns the habit of criticizing others while ignoring one's own faults. Believers must first submit themselves to God's righteous standard before attempting to examine and influence the conduct of other Christians (vv. 3–5). Judging in an unjust manner also includes condemning a wrongdoer without desiring to see the offender return to God and his ways (Lk 6:36–37).

(1) Christ is not denying the necessity of exercising a certain degree of discernment or of making value judgments with respect to sin in others. Elsewhere we are commanded to identify false ministers within the

the measure you use, it will be measured
to you.[p]
3“Why do you look at the speck of sawdust in your brother’s eye and pay no attention to the plank in your own eye?
4How can you say to your brother, ‘Let me
take the speck out of your eye,’ when all
the time there is a plank in your own eye?
5You hypocrite, first take the plank out of
your own eye, and then you will see clearly to remove the speck from your brother’s
eye.
6“Do not give dogs what is sacred; do
not throw your pearls to pigs. If you do,
they may trample them under their feet,
and then turn and tear you to pieces.

Ask, Seek, Knock

7:7–11pp — Lk 11:9–13

7“Ask and it will be given to you;[q] seek
and you will find; knock and the door will
be opened to you. 8For everyone who asks
receives; he who seeks finds;[r] and to him
who knocks, the door will be opened.

9“Which of you, if his son asks for
bread, will give him a stone? 10Or if he
asks for a fish, will give him a snake? 11If
you, then, though you are evil, know how
to give good gifts to your children, how
much more will your Father in heaven give
good gifts[s] to those who ask him! 12So in
everything, do to others what you would
have them do to you,[t] for this sums up the
Law and the Prophets.[u]

The Narrow and Wide Gates

13“Enter through the narrow gate.[v] For
wide is the gate and broad is the road that
leads to destruction, and many enter
through it. 14But small is the gate and
narrow the road that leads to life, and only
a few find it.

A Tree and Its Fruit

15“Watch out for false prophets.[w] They
come to you in sheep’s clothing, but
inwardly they are ferocious wolves.[x]

7:2 [p] Eze 35:11; Mk 4:24; Lk 6:38; Ro 2:1
7:7 [q] 1Ki 3:5; Mt 18:19; 21:22; Jn 14:13,14; 15:7, 16; 16:23,24; Jas 1:5-8; 4:2,3; 5:16; 1Jn 3:22; 5:14,15
7:8 [r] Pr 8:17; Jer 29:12,13
7:11 [s] Jas 1:17
7:12 [t] Lk 6:31 [u] Ro 13:8-10; Gal 5:14
7:13 [v] Lk 13:24; Jn 10:7,9
7:15 [w] Jer 23:16; Mt 24:24; Lk 6:26; 2Pe 2:1; 1Jn 4:1; Rev 16:13 [x] Eze 22:27; Ac 20:29

---

church (v. 15) and to evaluate the character of individuals (v. 6; cf. Jn 7:24; 1Co 5:12; see Gal 1:9, note; 1Ti 4:1, note; 1Jn 4:1).

(2) This verse must not be used as an excuse for laxity in exercising church discipline (see 18:15, note).

7:7–8 ASK . . . SEEK . . . KNOCK. Jesus encourages perseverance in prayer. The tense of the Greek verbs in v. 8 designates continued action. This means we must keep on asking, seeking and knocking. Asking implies consciousness of need and the belief that God hears our prayer. Seeking implies earnest petitioning along with obedience to God’s will. Knocking implies perseverance in coming to God even when he does not respond quickly. Christ’s assurance that those who ask will receive what they ask is based on: (1) seeking first the kingdom of God (see 6:33, note); (2) recognizing God’s fatherly goodness and love (6:8; 7:11; Jn 15:16; 16:23,26f; Col 1:9–12); (3) praying according to God’s will (Mk 11:24; Jn 21:22; 1Jn 5:14); (4) maintaining fellowship with Christ (Jn 15:7); and (5) obeying Christ (1Jn 3:22).

7:11 YOUR FATHER . . . GIVE GOOD GIFTS. Christ promises that the Father in heaven will not disappoint his children. He loves us even more than a good earthly father loves his children, and he wants us to ask him for whatever we need, promising to give us what is good. He desires to provide solutions for our problems and bread for our daily needs. And most of all, he gives the Holy Spirit to his children as their Counselor and Helper (Lk 11:13; Jn 14:16–18).

7:14 SMALL IS THE GATE . . . AND ONLY A FEW FIND IT. Christ taught that we are not to expect a majority of people to follow him on the road that leads to life.

(1) Comparatively few will enter the humble gate of true repentance and deny themselves to follow Jesus, sincerely endeavor to obey his commands, earnestly seek his kingdom and his righteousness, and persevere until the end in true faith, purity and love.

(2) Jesus in his Sermon on the Mount describes the great blessings that accompany discipleship in his kingdom (5:3–12), but he also insists that his disciples will not escape persecution (5:10–12). Furthermore, contrary to some evangelists who preach that “getting saved” is one of the easiest things in the world, Jesus taught that following him involves heavy obligations concerning righteousness, acceptance of persecution, love for enemies and self-denial.

7:15 WATCH OUT FOR FALSE PROPHETS. See article on FALSE TEACHERS, p. 98.

7:16 BY THEIR FRUIT YOU WILL RECOGNIZE THEM. False teachers who outwardly appear righteous but “inwardly . . . are ferocious wolves” (v. 15) can, at times, be identified by their “fruit.” The fruit of false teachers will be unwholesome characteristics evident in the lives of their followers (see 1Jn 4:5–6), such as those listed below.

(1) They will be professing Christians whose loyalty is more to personalities than to the Word of God (v. 21). They worship the creature more than the Creator (cf. Ro 1:25).

(2) They will be more concerned with their own desires than with God’s glory and honor. Their doctrine will be self-centered rather than God-centered (vv. 21–23; see 2Ti 4:3, note).

(3) They will accept human teachings and traditions even when those teachings contradict the Word of God (vv. 24–27; 1Jn 4:6).

(4) They will seek and respond to religious experiences and supernatural manifestations as their final authority in validating truth (vv. 22–23), rather than grounding themselves in the whole counsel of God’s Word.

(5) They will not put up with sound doctrine but will seek teachers who offer salvation with the “broad

16By their fruit you will recognize them.[y]
Do people pick grapes from thornbushes,
or figs from thistles?[z] 17Likewise every
good tree bears good fruit, but a bad tree
bears bad fruit. 18A good tree cannot bear
bad fruit, and a bad tree cannot bear good
fruit.[a] 19Every tree that does not bear
good fruit is cut down and thrown into the
fire.[b] 20Thus, by their fruit you will recog-
Mt 12:33 nize them.

The Saved Do God's Will

21"Not everyone who says to me, 'Lord,
Lord,'[c] will enter the kingdom of heav-
en,[d] but only he who does the will of my
Father who is in heaven.[e] 22Many will say
to me on that day,[f] 'Lord, Lord, did we not
prophesy in your name, and in your name
drive out demons and perform many miracles?'[g] 23Then I will tell them plainly, 'I
never knew you. Away from me, you evildoers!'[h]

7:16 [y]Mt 12:33; Lk 6:44 [z]Jas 3:12
7:18 [a]Lk 6:43
7:19 [b]S Mt 3:10
7:21 [c]Hos 8:2; Mt 25:11; S Jn 13:13; 1Co 12:3 [d]S Mt 3:2 [e]Mt 12:50; Ro 2:13; Jas 1:22; 1Jn 3:18
7:22 [f]S Mt 10:15 [g]Lk 10:20; Ac 19:13; 1Co 13:1-3
7:23 [h]Ps 6:8; Mt 25:12,41; Lk 13:25-27
7:24 [i]ver 21; Jas 1:22-25
7:28 [j]Mt 11:1; 13:53; 19:1; 26:1 [k]Mt 13:54; 22:33; Mk 1:22; 6:2; 11:18; Lk 4:32; Jn 7:46

The Wise and Foolish Builders

7:24–27pp — Lk 6:47–49

24"Therefore everyone who hears these
words of mine and puts them into practice[i] is like a wise man who built his
house on the rock. 25The rain came down,
the streams rose, and the winds blew and
beat against that house; yet it did not fall,
because it had its foundation on the rock.
26But everyone who hears these words of
mine and does not put them into practice
is like a foolish man who built his house
on sand. 27The rain came down, the
streams rose, and the winds blew and beat
against that house, and it fell with a great
crash."

28When Jesus had finished saying these
things,[j] the crowds were amazed at his
teaching,[k] 29because he taught as one
who had authority, and not as their teachers of the law.

---

road" of unrighteousness (vv. 13–14,23; see 2Ti 4:3, note).

7:21 DOES THE WILL OF MY FATHER. Jesus emphatically taught that carrying out the will of his heavenly Father was a condition of entering the kingdom of heaven (cf. vv. 22–27; 19:16–26; 25:31–46). However, this does not mean that we can gain or merit salvation by our own efforts or works. This is true for the following reasons:

(1) God's forgiveness comes to us through faith and repentance made possible by the grace and sacrificial death of Christ (see 26:28, note; Lk 15:11–32; 18:9–14).

(2) The obedience to God's will demanded by Christ is indeed an ongoing condition for salvation, but Christ also declares that it is a grace belonging to the salvation of the kingdom. As such we must continually pray for it, receive it and put it into effect by sincere faith and earnest endeavor. Note the Lord's Prayer (6:9–13) and the many admonitions directed toward believers to put sin to death and to present themselves to God as living sacrifices (cf. Ro 6:1–23; 8:1–17; 12:1–2; see Mt 5:6, note on hungering and thirsting for righteousness).

(3) We are capable of doing God's will and living righteous lives by virtue of this gift, i.e., God's grace, power and spiritual life continually given to us through Christ (Eph 2:5). Scripture declares that "by grace you have been saved, through faith—and this not from yourselves, it is the gift of God . . . . For we are God's workmanship" (Eph 2:8–10).

(4) God always makes available the obedience he demands of us. It is ascribed to God's redemptive action. "For it is God who works in you to will and to act according to his good purpose" (see Php 2:13, note). Yet God's gift of grace does not annul human responsibility or action. We must respond positively to God's gift of obedience (Eph 4:22–32; Jude 20–21,24; see Php 2:12, note), for we remain free to reject God's grace, to refuse to draw near to God through Christ (see Heb 7:25, note), and to refuse to pray for and accept the life of obedience (see 5:6, note; see article on FAITH AND GRACE, p. 302).

7:22 MANY WILL SAY . . . LORD, LORD. Jesus emphatically states that there will be "many" in the church who will minister in his name and believe they are his servants, yet in reality he never knew them (v. 23). To escape the deceit of the last days, church leaders (or any disciple) must be totally committed to the truth and the righteousness revealed in God's Word (see Rev 22:19, note) and not consider "ministerial success" as the standard by which to judge their relationship to Christ.

7:23 I NEVER KNEW YOU. These words of Christ make it unmistakably clear that preachers may proclaim the gospel in the name of Christ, drive out demons and perform miracles while they themselves have no genuine saving faith in Christ.

(1) Scripture teaches that fervent gospel preaching, an apparent zeal for righteousness and the working of miracles can be performed in this age under the influence and power of Satan. Paul warns that "Satan himself masquerades as an angel of light. It is not surprising, then, if his servants masquerade as servants of righteousness" (2Co 11:14–15; cf. Mt 24:24). Paul makes it clear that an apparent powerful anointing can be "the work of Satan" (see 2Th 2:9–10; Rev 13:3,12).

(2) Many times God overrides Satan's activity in false preachers in order to bring salvation or healing to those who sincerely respond to God's Word (see Php 1:15–18). It is always God's desire that those who proclaim the gospel be righteous (see 1Ti 3:1–7); yet when an evil or immoral person preaches God's Word, God can still work in the hearts of those who receive his Word with commitment to Christ. God does not endorse any unrighteous preacher of the gospel, but he will endorse Biblical truth and those who accept it in faith.

The Man With Leprosy

8:2–4pp — Mk 1:40–44; Lk 5:12–14

8 When he came down from the mountainside, large crowds followed him. **2**A man with leprosy[e][l] came and knelt before him[m] and said, "Lord, if you are willing, you can make me clean."

3Jesus reached out his hand and touched the man. "I am willing," he said. "Be clean!" Immediately he was cured[f] of his leprosy. **4**Then Jesus said to him, "See that you don't tell anyone.[n] But go, show yourself to the priest[o] and offer the gift Moses commanded,[p] as a testimony to them."

The Faith of the Centurion

8:5–13pp — Lk 7:1–10

5When Jesus had entered Capernaum, a centurion came to him, asking for help. **6**"Lord," he said, "my servant lies at home paralyzed[q] and in terrible suffering."

7Jesus said to him, "I will go and heal him."

8The centurion replied, "Lord, I do not deserve to have you come under my roof. But just say the word, and my servant will be healed.[r] **9**For I myself am a man under authority, with soldiers under me. I tell this one, 'Go,' and he goes; and that one, 'Come,' and he comes. I say to my servant, 'Do this,' and he does it."

10When Jesus heard this, he was astonished and said to those following him, "I tell you the truth, I have not found anyone
Mt 9:2 in Israel with such great faith.[s] **11**I say to you that many will come from the east and the west,[t] and will take their places at the feast with Abraham, Isaac and Jacob in the kingdom of heaven.[u] **12**But the subjects of the kingdom[v] will be thrown outside, into the darkness, where there will be weeping and gnashing of teeth."[w]

13Then Jesus said to the centurion, "Go! It will be done just as you believed it would."[x] And his servant was healed at that very hour.

Jesus Heals Many

8:14–16pp — Mk 1:29–34; Lk 4:38–41

14When Jesus came into Peter's house, he saw Peter's mother-in-law lying in bed with a fever. **15**He touched her hand and the fever left her, and she got up and began to wait on him.

16When evening came, many who were demon-possessed were brought to him, and he drove out the spirits with a word and healed all the sick.[y] **17**This was to fulfill[z] what was spoken through the prophet Isaiah:

> "He took up our infirmities
> and carried our diseases."[g][a] Mt 10:1

The Cost of Following Jesus

8:19–22pp — Lk 9:57–60

18When Jesus saw the crowd around him, he gave orders to cross to the other side of the lake.[b] **19**Then a teacher of the law came to him and said, "Teacher, I will follow you wherever you go."

20Jesus replied, "Foxes have holes and birds of the air have nests, but the Son of Man[c] has no place to lay his head."

21Another disciple said to him, "Lord, first let me go and bury my father."

22But Jesus told him, "Follow me,[d] and let the dead bury their own dead."

Jesus Calms the Storm

8:23–27pp — Mk 4:36–41; Lk 8:22–25
8:23–27Ref — Mt 14:22–33

23Then he got into the boat and his disciples followed him. **24**Without warning, a furious storm came up on the lake, so that the waves swept over the boat. But Jesus was sleeping. **25**The disciples went and woke him, saying, "Lord, save us! We're going to drown!"

26He replied, "You of little faith,[e] why are you so afraid?" Then he got up and rebuked the winds and the waves, and it was completely calm.[f]

27The men were amazed and asked, "What kind of man is this? Even the winds and the waves obey him!"

8:2 [l]Lev 13:45; Mt 10:8; 11:5; 26:6; Lk 5:12; 17:12 [m]Mt 9:18; 15:25; 18:26; 20:20
8:4 [n]Mt 9:30; 12:16; Mk 5:43; 7:36; S 8:30; Lk 4:41 [o]Lk 17:14 [p]Lev 14:2-32
8:6 [q]S Mt 4:24
8:8 [r]Ps 107:20
8:10 [s]Mt 15:28
8:11 [t]Ps 107:3; Isa 49:12; 59:19; Mal 1:11 [u]Lk 13:29
8:12 [v]Mt 13:38 [w]Mt 13:42,50; 22:13; 24:51; 25:30; Lk 13:28
8:13 [x]S Mt 9:22
8:16 [y]S Mt 4:23, 24
8:17 [z]S Mt 1:22 [a]Isa 53:4
8:18 [b]Mk 4:35
8:20 [c]Da 7:13; Mt 12:8,32,40; 16:13,27,28; 17:9; 19:28; Mk 2:10; 8:31
8:22 [d]S Mt 4:19
8:26 [e]S Mt 6:30 [f]Ps 65:7; 89:9; 107:29

e *2* The Greek word was used for various diseases affecting the skin—not necessarily leprosy.
f *3* Greek *made clean*
g *17* Isaiah 53:4

8:10 GREAT FAITH. The centurion's faith surpassed anything that Jesus found among the Jews, for it combined a loving concern for another person with great trust in Christ. This story, along with Christ's application to the unbelieving Jews (vv. 11–12), warns us that we may be excluded from what God is doing by adhering to human traditions or by failing to believe in the power of his kingdom.

8:16–17 HEALED ALL THE SICK. See article on DIVINE HEALING, p. 20.

8:22 LET THE DEAD BURY THEIR OWN DEAD. Christ's saying means, "Let the spiritually dead bury the physically dead." The disciple of v. 21 probably wanted to stay with his elderly father until his father died.

The Healing of Two Demon-possessed Men

8:28–34pp — Mk 5:1–17; Lk 8:26–37

28When he arrived at the other side in the region of the Gadarenes,[h] two demon-possessed[g] men coming from the tombs met him. They were so violent that no one could pass that way. **29**"What do you want with us,[h] Son of God?" they shouted. "Have you come here to torture us before the appointed time?"[i]

30Some distance from them a large herd of pigs was feeding. **31**The demons begged Jesus, "If you drive us out, send us into the herd of pigs."

32He said to them, "Go!" So they came out and went into the pigs, and the whole herd rushed down the steep bank into the lake and died in the water. **33**Those tending the pigs ran off, went into the town and reported all this, including what had happened to the demon-possessed men. **34**Then the whole town went out to meet Jesus. And when they saw him, they pleaded with him to leave their region.[j]

Jesus Heals a Paralytic

9:2–8pp — Mk 2:3–12; Lk 5:18–26

9 Jesus stepped into a boat, crossed over and came to his own town.[k] **2**Some men brought to him a paralytic,[l] lying on a mat. When Jesus saw their faith,[m] he said to the paralytic, "Take heart,[n] son; your sins are forgiven."[o]

Mt 9:29-30

3At this, some of the teachers of the law said to themselves, "This fellow is blaspheming!"[p]

4Knowing their thoughts,[q] Jesus said, "Why do you entertain evil thoughts in your hearts? **5**Which is easier: to say, 'Your sins are forgiven,' or to say, 'Get up and walk'? **6**But so that you may know that the Son of Man[r] has authority on earth to forgive sins. . . ." Then he said to the paralytic, "Get up, take your mat and go home." **7**And the man got up and went home. **8**When the crowd saw this, they were filled with awe; and they praised God,[s] who had given such authority to men.

The Calling of Matthew

9:9–13pp — Mk 2:14–17; Lk 5:27–32

9As Jesus went on from there, he saw a man named Matthew sitting at the tax collector's booth. "Follow me,"[t] he told him, and Matthew got up and followed him.

10While Jesus was having dinner at Matthew's house, many tax collectors and "sinners" came and ate with him and his disciples. **11**When the Pharisees saw this, they asked his disciples, "Why does your teacher eat with tax collectors and 'sinners'?"[u]

12On hearing this, Jesus said, "It is not the healthy who need a doctor, but the sick. **13**But go and learn what this means: 'I desire mercy, not sacrifice.'[i][v] For I have not come to call the righteous, but sinners."[w]

Jesus Questioned About Fasting

9:14–17pp — Mk 2:18–22; Lk 5:33–39

14Then John's[x] disciples came and asked him, "How is it that we and the Pharisees fast,[y] but your disciples do not fast?"

15Jesus answered, "How can the guests of the bridegroom mourn while he is with them?[z] The time will come when the bridegroom will be taken from them; then they will fast.[a]

16"No one sews a patch of unshrunk cloth on an old garment, for the patch will pull away from the garment, making the tear worse. **17**Neither do men pour new wine into old wineskins. If they do, the

8:28 [g]S Mt 4:24
8:29 [h]Jdg 11:12; 2Sa 16:10; 1Ki 17:18; Mk 1:24; Lk 4:34; Jn 2:4 [i]2Pe 2:4
8:34 [j]Lk 5:8; Ac 16:39
9:1 [k]Mt 4:13
9:2 [l]S Mt 4:24 [m]S ver 22 [n]Jn 16:33 [o]Lk 7:48
9:3 [p]Mt 26:65; Jn 10:33
9:4 [q]Ps 94:11; Mt 12:25; Lk 6:8; 9:47; 11:17; Jn 2:25
9:6 [r]S Mt 8:20
9:8 [s]Mt 5:16; 15:31; Lk 7:16; 13:13; 17:15; 23:47; Jn 15:8; Ac 4:21; 11:18; 21:20
9:9 [t]S Mt 4:19
9:11 [u]Mt 11:19; Lk 5:30; 15:2; 19:7; Gal 2:15
9:13 [v]Hos 6:6; Mic 6:6-8; Mt 12:7 [w]Lk 19:10; 1Ti 1:15
9:14 [x]S Mt 3:1 [y]Mt 11:18,19; Lk 18:12
9:15 [z]Jn 3:29 [a]Ac 13:2,3; 14:23

[h] *28* Some manuscripts *Gergesenes*; others *Gerasenes* [i] *13* Hosea 6:6

8:28 DEMON-POSSESSED MEN. See 17:17, note; see article on POWER OVER SATAN AND DEMONS, p. 80.

9:11 EAT WITH . . . 'SINNERS'. In vv. 11–13 Jesus gives the rule to guide us in our contact with nonbelievers: It should not be for pleasure or intimate friendship, but in order to do good to them and to show them the way of salvation (v. 12; Ps 1:1). At no time should a believer date or marry a nonbeliever (1Co 7:39; see article on SPIRITUAL SEPARATION FOR BELIEVERS, p. 371).

9:15 THEN THEY WILL FAST. It is clear that Jesus expected believers to fast after he was gone. This age is the time of the "bridegroom's" absence, from the time of his ascension until his return. The church awaits this return of the bridegroom (25:6; see Jn 14:3, note). Therefore, fasting in this age is (1) a sign of the believer's longing for the Lord's return, (2) a preparation for Christ's coming, (3) a mourning of Christ's absence, and (4) a sign of sorrow for the sin and decay of the world (see 6:16, note).

9:17 NEW WINE INTO OLD WINESKINS. This verse has been interpreted in various ways by commentators. Two views are: (1) The "new wine" was fresh grape juice. As it began to ferment, new wineskins would stretch and not break, whereas old wineskins would break. The "new wine" represented the gospel as fermenting change that the old forms of

DIVINE HEALING

***Mt 8:16–17** "When evening came, many who were demon-possessed were brought to him, and he drove out the spirits with a word and healed all the sick. This was to fulfill what was spoken through the prophet Isaiah: 'He took up our infirmities and carried our diseases.' "*

The problem of sickness and disease is intertwined with the problem of sin and death – i.e., the consequences of the fall. Whereas medical science views the causes of sickness and disease in physiological or psychosomatic terms, the Bible presents spiritual causes as the underlying or basic problem: (1) *sin,* which has affected our spiritual and physical makeup (e.g., Jn 5:5,14), and (2) *Satan* (e.g., Ac 10:38; cf. Mk 9:17,20,25; Lk 13:11; Ac 19:11–12).

God's provision in redemption is as extensive as the consequences of the fall. For sin, God provides forgiveness; for death, God provides eternal and resurrection life; and for sickness, God provides healing (cf. Ps 103:1–5; Lk 5:17–26). Thus, during Jesus' earthly life, his threefold ministry was *teaching* God's word, *preaching* repentance (the sin problem) and the blessings of God's kingdom (life), and *healing* every kind of sickness, disease and infirmity among the people (Mt 4:23–24).

God's will concerning healing is revealed in four main ways in Scripture.

(1) *God's own pronouncement.* In Ex 15:26 God promised health and healing for his people if they remained faithful to his covenant and commands. His pronouncement was twofold: (a) "I will not bring on you any of the diseases [as judgment] I brought on the Egyptians"; and (b) "I am the LORD, who heals you [as Redeemer]." God continued to be the doctor or healer of his OT people whenever they earnestly sought his face and obeyed his word (cf. 2Ki 20:5; Ps 103:3).

(2) *Jesus' ministry.* Jesus as the incarnate Son of God was and is the exact representation of God's nature and character (Heb 1:3; cf. Col 1:15; 2:9). In his earthly ministry (Mt 4:23–24; 8:14–16; 9:35; 15:28; Mk 1:32–34,40–41; Lk 4:40; Ac 10:38), Jesus revealed God's will in action (Jn 6:38; 14:10), proving that it is in God's heart, nature and purpose to heal all who are sick and oppressed by the devil.

(3) *The provision of Christ's atonement* (Isa 53:4–5; Mt 8:16–17; 1Pe 2:24). Jesus' atoning death was complete and adequate for redeeming the whole person—spirit, soul and body. As sin and sickness have become the twin giants designed by Satan to destroy us, so forgiveness and healing are twin blessings designed by God to redeem us and make us whole (cf. Ps 103:3; Jas 5:14–16). The believer should press on in humility and faith to possess the full provision of Christ's atonement, including the healing of the body.

(4) *The ongoing ministry of the church.* Jesus commissioned his twelve disciples to heal the sick as part of their proclamation of God's kingdom (Lk 9:1–2,6). Later, he commissioned seventy disciples to do the same (Lk 10:1,8–9,19). After Pentecost, the early church carried on Jesus' healing ministry as part of preaching the gospel (Ac 3:1–10, 4:30; 5:16; 8:7; 9:34; 14:8–10, 19:11–12; cf. Mk 16:18; 1Co 12:9,28,30; Jas 5:14–16). The NT records three ways that God's healing power and faith were imparted through the church: (a) the laying on of hands (Mk 16:15–18; Ac 9:17), (b) confession of known sin, followed by anointing the sick with oil (Jas 5:14–16), and (c) spiritual gifts of healings (1Co 12:9).

Sometimes there are hindrances to receiving divine healing, such as, (1) unconfessed sin (Jas 5:16), (2) demonic oppression or bondage (Lk 13:11–13), (3) fear or acute anxiety (Pr 3:5–8; Php 4:6–7), (4) past disappointments that undermine present faith (Mk 5:26; Jn 5:5–7), (5) people (Mk 10:48), (6) unbiblical teaching (Mk 3:1–5; 7:13), (7) unbelief (Mk 6:3–6; 9:19,23–24), and (8) self-centered behavior (1Co 11:29–30). At other times, the reason for the persistence of physical affliction in godly people is not readily apparent (e.g., Gal 4:13; 1Ti 5:23; 2Ti 4:20). In still other instances, God chooses to take his beloved saints to heaven during an illness (cf. 2Ki 13:14).

What can you do when praying and seeking for God's healing of your body?

(1) Be sure you are in a right relationship with God and others (Mt 6:33; 1Co 11:27–30; Jas 5:16; see Jn 15:7, note).

(2) Seek the presence of Jesus in your life, for it is he who will give your heart the faith you need (Ro 12:3; 1Co 12:9; Php 2:13; see Mt 17:20, note on true faith).

(3) Saturate your life with God's Word (Jn 15:7; Ro 10:17).

(4) If you are not finding healing, continue to remain in him (Jn 15:1–7). Examine your life to see what changes God is trying to work in you.

(5) Call for the prayers of the elders of the church, as well as the prayers of family members and friends (Jas 5:14–16).

(6) Attend a service where a person with a respected healing ministry is present (cf. Ac 5:15–16; 8:5–7).

(7) Expect a miracle—trust in Christ's power (Mt 7:8; 19:26).

(8) Rejoice if healing comes this day. Rejoice if it does not come in the present hour (Php 4:4,11–13).

(9) Know that God's delays in answering prayers are not denials of those requests. Sometimes God has a larger purpose in mind that, when realized, results in his greater glory (cf. Jn 9:3; 11:4,14–15,45; 2Co 12:7–10).

(10) Realize that if you are a committed Christian, in all things God will work for your good (Ro 8:28).

Note: The Bible acknowledges the proper use of medical care (Mt 9:12; Lk 10:34; Col 4:14).

skins will burst, the wine will run out and
the wineskins will be ruined. No, they
pour new wine into new wineskins, and
both are preserved."

A Dead Girl and a Sick Woman

9:18–26pp — Mk 5:22–43; Lk 8:41–56

18While he was saying this, a ruler
came and knelt before him[b] and said, "My
daughter has just died. But come and put
your hand on her,[c] and she will live."
19Jesus got up and went with him, and so
did his disciples.

20Just then a woman who had been subject to bleeding for twelve years came up
behind him and touched the edge of his
cloak.[d] 21She said to herself, "If I only
touch his cloak, I will be healed."
22Jesus turned and saw her. "Take
heart,[e] daughter," he said, "your faith has
healed you."[f] And the woman was healed
from that moment.[g]

23When Jesus entered the ruler's house
and saw the flute players and the noisy
crowd,[h] 24he said, "Go away. The girl is
not dead[i] but asleep."[j] But they laughed
at him. 25After the crowd had been put
outside, he went in and took the girl by the
hand, and she got up.[k] 26News of this
spread through all that region.[l]

Jesus Heals the Blind and Mute

27As Jesus went on from there, two
blind men followed him, calling out, "Have
mercy on us, Son of David!"[m]

9:18 [b]S Mt 8:2 [c]S Mk 5:23
9:20 [d]Mt 14:36; Mk 3:10; 6:56; Lk 6:19
9:22 [e]ver 2; Jn 16:33 [f]ver 29; Mt 8:13; Mk 10:52; Lk 7:50; 17:19; 18:42 [g]Mt 15:28
9:23 [h]2Ch 35:25; Jer 9:17,18
9:24 [i]Ac 20:10 [j]Da 12:2; Ps 76:5; Jn 11:11-14; Ac 7:60; 13:36; 1Co 11:30; 15:6, 18,20; 1Th 4:13-16
9:25 [k]S Lk 7:14
9:26 [l]ver 31; Mt 4:24; 14:1; Mk 1:28,45; Lk 4:14,37; 5:15; 7:17
9:27 [m]S Mt 1:1; 12:23; 15:22; 20:30,31; 21:9,15; 22:42; Mk 10:47
9:28 [n]Ac 14:9
9:29 [o]S ver 22
9:30 [p]S Mt 8:4
9:31 [q]S ver 26; Mk 7:36
9:32 [r]S Mt 4:24 [s]Mt 12:22-24
9:33 [t]Mk 2:12
9:34 [u]Mt 12:24
9:35 [v]S Mt 4:23
9:36 [w]Mt 14:14; 15:32; Mk 8:2 [x]Nu 27:17; 1Ki 22:17; Eze 34:5,6; Zec 10:2
9:37 [y]Jn 4:35 [z]Lk 10:2

28When he had gone indoors, the blind
men came to him, and he asked them, "Do
you believe that I am able to do this?"
"Yes, Lord," they replied.[n]
29Then he touched their eyes and said,
"According to your faith will it be done to
you";[o] 30and their sight was restored.
Jesus warned them sternly, "See that no
one knows about this."[p] 31But they went (Mt 17:20)
out and spread the news about him all
over that region.[q]

32While they were going out, a man who
was demon-possessed[r] and could not
talk[s] was brought to Jesus. 33And when
the demon was driven out, the man who
had been mute spoke. The crowd was
amazed and said, "Nothing like this has
ever been seen in Israel."[t]
34But the Pharisees said, "It is by the
prince of demons that he drives out demons."[u]

The Workers Are Few

35Jesus went through all the towns and
villages, teaching in their synagogues,
preaching the good news of the kingdom
and healing every disease and sickness.[v]
36When he saw the crowds, he had compassion on them,[w] because they were harassed and helpless, like sheep without a
shepherd.[x] 37Then he said to his disciples, "The harvest[y] is plentiful but the
workers are few.[z] 38Ask the Lord of the
harvest, therefore, to send out workers
into his harvest field."

Judaism could not contain. This view is questionable, however, because those familiar with the process of fermentation say that even the newest and strongest of wineskins, if sealed, would burst from the violent action of fermentation (see Job 32:19).

(2) A second interpretation sees the parable as emphasizing the importance of preserving both the new wine and the new wineskins. (a) The "new wine" was fresh unfermented grape juice, representing the original saving message of Jesus Christ and the power of the Holy Spirit thrust forth at Pentecost. Jesus' overriding concern was that the original gospel and redemptive power of the Spirit be preserved from all change, corruption or loss. This interpretation is supported by Christ's concern that the gospel (new wine) not be altered by the teachings (yeast) of the Pharisees and Judaism (yeast being a fermenting/altering agent, cf. 16:6,12; Ex 12:19; 1Co 5:7).

(b) In ancient times, in order to preserve the sweetness of the juice for an adequate period of time, people would strain or boil the juice, bottle it and place it in a cool area (see articles on WINE IN NEW TESTAMENT TIMES (1) and (2), p. 126 and p. 174). New wineskins were required because they would be free from all residual fermenting matter such as mature yeast cells. If placed in old wineskins, new wine would more easily begin to ferment because of the yeast cells that remained in the old wineskins. The subsequent fermentation would then cause the loss of both the new wine and the wineskins (which would burst from pressure). Columella, the great Roman authority on agriculture in the first century A.D., wrote that in order to keep new wine "always sweet" it must be put into a new sealed container (*On Agriculture*, 12.29).

9:17 NEW WINE . . . PRESERVED. Christ's emphasis here is on preserving the new wine for as long a time as possible (see previous note). For the various methods used in Bible times of keeping wine in a sweet and unfermented state, see articles on WINE IN NEW TESTAMENT TIMES (1) and (2), p. 126 and p. 174.

9:37 THE HARVEST IS PLENTIFUL. Jesus admonishes all believers to always remember that the lost have an invaluable everlasting soul and must spend eternity in heaven or in hell, and that many of them can be saved if only someone presents the gospel to them (see 10:28, note).

9:38 ASK THE LORD . . . TO SEND. This verse expresses one of God's own spiritual principles. Before he acts, he usually calls his people to prayer. Only after his people have prayed does God accomplish that work. In other words, God has limited himself to the

Jesus Sends Out the Twelve

10:2–4pp — Mk 3:16–19; Lk 6:14–16; Ac 1:13
10:9–15pp — Mk 6:8–11; Lk 9:3–5; 10:4–12
10:19–22pp — Mk 13:11–13; Lk 21:12–17
10:26–33pp — Lk 12:2–9
10:34,35pp — Lk 12:51–53

10 He called his twelve disciples to
him and gave them authority to
drive out evil[j] spirits[a] and to heal every
Mt 12:22 disease and sickness.[b]
2These are the names of the twelve
apostles: first, Simon (who is called Peter) and his brother Andrew; James son of
Zebedee, and his brother John; **3**Philip and
Bartholomew; Thomas and Matthew the
tax collector; James son of Alphaeus, and
Thaddaeus; **4**Simon the Zealot and Judas
Iscariot, who betrayed him.[c]
5These twelve Jesus sent out with the
following instructions: "Do not go among
the Gentiles or enter any town of the Samaritans.[d] **6**Go rather to the lost sheep of
Israel.[e] **7**As you go, preach this message:
'The kingdom of heaven[f] is near.' **8**Heal
the sick, raise the dead, cleanse those
who have leprosy,[k] drive out demons.
Freely you have received, freely give. **9**Do
not take along any gold or silver or copper
in your belts;[g] **10**take no bag for the journey, or extra tunic, or sandals or a staff;
for the worker is worth his keep.[h]
11"Whatever town or village you enter,
search for some worthy person there and
stay at his house until you leave. **12**As you
enter the home, give it your greeting.[i]
13If the home is deserving, let your peace
rest on it; if it is not, let your peace return
to you. **14**If anyone will not welcome you
or listen to your words, shake the dust off
your feet[j] when you leave that home or
town. **15**I tell you the truth, it will be more

10:1 [a]Mk 3:13-15; 6:7; Lk 4:36; 9:1 [b]S Mt 4:23
10:4 [c]Mt 26:14-16,25, 47; 27:3; Mk 14:10; Jn 6:71; 12:4; 13:2,26,27; Ac 1:16
10:5 [d]1Ki 16:24; 2Ki 17:24; Lk 9:52; 10:33; 17:16; Jn 4:4-26, 39,40; 8:48; Ac 8:5,25
10:6 [e]Jer 50:6; Mt 15:24
10:7 [f]S Mt 3:2
10:9 [g]Lk 22:35
10:10 [h]S 1Ti 5:18
10:12 [i]1Sa 25:6
10:14 [j]Ne 5:13; Mk 6:11; Lk 9:5; 10:11; Ac 13:51; 18:6
10:15 [k]Ge 18:20; 19:24; 2Pe 2:6; Jude 7 [l]Mt 12:36; Ac 17:31; 2Pe 2:9; 3:7; 1Jn 4:17; Jude 6 [m]Mt 11:22, 24
10:16 [n]Lk 10:3; Ac 20:29 [o]S 1Co 14:20
10:17 [p]S Mt 5:22 [q]Mt 23:34; Mk 13:9; Ac 5:40; 22:19; 26:11
10:18 [r]Ac 25:24-26
10:19 [s]Ex 4:12
10:20 [t]Lk 12:11, 12; Ac 4:8
10:21 [u]ver 35, 36; Mic 7:6 [v]Mk 13:12
10:22 [w]S Jn 15:21 [x]Mt 24:13; Mk 13:13; Lk 21:19; Rev 2:10
10:23 [y]S Lk 17:30
10:24 [z]S Jn 13:16
10:25 [a]S Mk 3:22

bearable for Sodom and Gomorrah[k] on the
day of judgment[l] than for that town.[m] **16**I
am sending you out like sheep among
wolves.[n] Therefore be as shrewd as
snakes and as innocent as doves.[o]

Discipleship and Suffering

17"Be on your guard against men; they
will hand you over to the local councils[p]
and flog you in their synagogues.[q] **18**On
my account you will be brought before
governors and kings[r] as witnesses to
them and to the Gentiles. **19**But when they
arrest you, do not worry about what to say
or how to say it.[s] At that time you will be
given what to say, **20**for it will not be you
speaking, but the Spirit of your Father[t]
speaking through you. Mt 24:14
21"Brother will betray brother to death,
and a father his child; children will rebel
against their parents[u] and have them put
to death.[v] **22**All men will hate you because of me,[w] but he who stands firm to
the end will be saved.[x] **23**When you are
persecuted in one place, flee to another. I
tell you the truth, you will not finish going
through the cities of Israel before the Son
of Man comes.[y]
24"A student is not above his teacher,
nor a servant above his master.[z] **25**It is
enough for the student to be like his
teacher, and the servant like his master.
If the head of the house has been called
Beelzebub,[l][a] how much more the members of his household!
26"So do not be afraid of them. There is
nothing concealed that will not be dis-

j *1* Greek *unclean* k *8* The Greek word was used for various diseases affecting the skin—not necessarily leprosy. l *25* Greek *Beezeboul* or *Beelzeboul*

prayers of his people. It is clear from the context (9:35—10:1,8) that the kind of workers Jesus desires in his kingdom are those who (1) teach and preach the gospel of the kingdom (9:35), (2) heal the sick (9:35; 10:1,8) and (3) drive out evil spirits (10:1,8).

10:1 AUTHORITY TO DRIVE OUT EVIL SPIRITS. Jesus wants his followers to wage war against the forces of evil by driving out evil spirits and healing the sick. This demonstration of authority in spiritual confrontation is considered a continuing manifestation of the kingdom of God on earth (see article on THE KINGDOM OF GOD, p. 28).

10:7 PREACH ... THE KINGDOM. The context (vv. 1,8) makes clear that the preaching of the kingdom is to be accompanied by God asserting his power against the forces of sin, sickness and Satan (see article on THE KINGDOM OF GOD, p. 28). It is Christ's purpose that the kingdom of heaven and its power be "near" to bring salvation, grace and healing to God's people. When the "kingdom of heaven" is not being manifested among God's people, they should turn from the spirit of the world and all that is not pleasing to God, "seek . . . first his kingdom and his righteousness" (6:33) and pray "your kingdom come, your will be done" (6:10; cf. Mk 9:29).

10:19 GIVEN WHAT TO SAY. Christ's promise is seen in operation in Ac 4:8–12,19–20; 21:39—22:21; 23:1,6; 24:10–21; 26:1–29. After Pentecost the Spirit was poured out in all his fullness to give power to witness (Ac 1:8).

10:23 CITIES OF ISRAEL. Christ may have been telling his disciples that the gospel would continue to be proclaimed to the Jews until his return.

10:26 DO NOT BE AFRAID OF THEM. The disciples' work for Christ and their battle against Satan will expose them to Satan's counterattack (vv. 16–25); yet they do not need to be afraid, because the Holy Spirit and the Father will sustain them (vv. 20,29–31). They must remain faithful to the Word of Christ, preaching openly, frankly and courageously.

closed, or hidden that will not be made
known.[b] 27What I tell you in the dark,
speak in the daylight; what is whispered
in your ear, proclaim from the roofs. 28Do
not be afraid of those who kill the body but
cannot kill the soul. Rather, be afraid of
the One[c] who can destroy both soul and
body in hell. 29Are not two sparrows sold
for a penny[m]? Yet not one of them will fall
to the ground apart from the will of your
Father. 30And even the very hairs of your
head are all numbered.[d] 31So don't be
afraid; you are worth more than many
sparrows.[e]

32"Whoever acknowledges me before
men,[f] I will also acknowledge him before
my Father in heaven. 33But whoever disowns me before men, I will disown him
before my Father in heaven.[g]

34"Do not suppose that I have come to
bring peace to the earth. I did not come to
bring peace, but a sword. 35For I have
come to turn

" 'a man against his father,
a daughter against her mother,
a daughter-in-law against her
mother-in-law[h] —
36 a man's enemies will be the
members of his own
household.'[n][i]

37"Anyone who loves his father or
mother more than me is not worthy of me;
anyone who loves his son or daughter
more than me is not worthy of me;[j] 38and
anyone who does not take his cross and
follow me is not worthy of me.[k] 39Whoev-
er finds his life will lose it, and whoever
loses his life for my sake will find it.[l]
40"He who receives you receives me,[m]
and he who receives me receives the one
who sent me.[n] 41Anyone who receives a
prophet because he is a prophet will receive a prophet's reward, and anyone who

10:26 [b] Mk 4:22; Lk 8:17
10:28 [c] Isa 8:12, 13; Heb 10:31
10:30 [d] 1Sa 14:45; 2Sa 14:11; 1Ki 1:52; Lk 21:18; Ac 27:34
10:31 [e] Mt 6:26; 12:12
10:32 [f] Ro 10:9
10:33 [g] Mk 8:38; 2Ti 2:12
10:35 [h] ver 21
10:36 [i] Mic 7:6
10:37 [j] Lk 14:26
10:38 [k] Mt 16:24; Lk 14:27
10:39 [l] S Jn 12:25
10:40 [m] Ex 16:8; Mt 18:5; Gal 4:14 [n] Lk 9:48; 10:16; Jn 12:44; 13:20

[m] *29* Greek *an assarion* [n] *36* Micah 7:6

10:28 HELL. The word translated "hell" (Gk *gehenna*) in this passage refers to a place of eternal torment reserved for the ungodly (cf. Mk 9:43,48). The Bible teaches that one's existence does not end at death but continues on forever, either in the presence of God or in a place of punishment. Concerning the state of the lost, we should note the following:

(1) Jesus teaches that there is a place of eternal punishment for those condemned before God (see 5:22,29–30; 18:9; 23:15,33; Mk 9:43,45,47; Lk 10:15; 12:5). It is the terrifying reality of continuous punishment, the place of a "fire that never goes out" (Mk 9:43), of "eternal fire, prepared for the devil and his angels" (25:41), of "weeping and gnashing of teeth" (13:42,50), of binding and darkness (22:13), and of torment and agony and separation from heaven (Lk 16:23).

(2) The teaching of the letters is essentially the same. The apostles speak of a coming judgment of God to inflict vengeance on those who disobey the gospel (2Th 1:5–9), of a separation from the presence and majesty of the Lord (2Th 1:9) and of the destruction of God's enemies (Php 3:18–19; see also Ro 9:22; 1Co 16:22; Gal 1:9; 2Ti 2:12; Heb 10:27; 2Pe 2:4; Jude 1:7; Rev 14:10; 19:20; 20:10,14).

(3) The Bible teaches that judgment on evildoers is certain. The main idea is condemnation, suffering and separation from God with no time limit. Christians may find this doctrine unpleasant or hard to understand. Yet we must submit to the authority of God's Word and trust God's decision and justice.

(4) We must always keep in mind that God sent his Son to die in order that no one should perish (Jn 3:16). It is not God's intention or desire to send anyone to hell (2Pe 3:9). Those who enter hell do so by resisting the salvation provided by God (Ro 1:16—2:10). The fact and reality of hell should cause all of God's people to hate sin fervently, to seek continually the salvation of the lost and to warn everyone of God's future righteous judgment (see Rev 20:14, note).

10:31 YOU ARE WORTH MORE. Jesus teaches that God's faithful children are of great worth to their heavenly Father. (1) God values you and your personal needs; he desires your love and fellowship so much that he sent Jesus to die on the cross for you (see Jn 3:16, note). You are never away from his presence, care and concern. He knows all your needs, trials and sorrows (6:8). (2) You are so important to God that he treasures your faithfulness, love and loyalty above all earthly things. Your unwavering faith in Christ, proved genuine in the midst of trials and trouble, is his glory and honor. Read the assurances found in Ps 91:14–16; 116:15; Isa 49:16; Mt 11:28–29; Lk 12:32; Jn 13:1; 14:3; 17:24; Ro 8:28; 1Jn 4:19.

10:32 ACKNOWLEDGES ME BEFORE MEN. To "acknowledge" (Gk *homologeō*) Christ means to confess him as Lord of one's life, and to do so openly before others, even before those who oppose him, his ways and his standards.

10:34 I DID NOT COME TO BRING PEACE. Although Jesus Christ is called the "Prince of Peace" (Isa 9:6; cf. Mt 5:9; Ro 5:1), and truth must always be proclaimed in love (Eph 4:15), there is a sense in which his coming and the proclamation of the gospel will bring division, and do so intentionally. (1) Faith in Christ separates the believer from the sinner and the world (vv. 32–37; Lk 12:51–53; see article on SPIRITUAL SEPARATION FOR BELIEVERS, p. 371). (2) The proclamation of God's Word and its truth will bring opposition, division and persecution (12:24; 14:4–12; 27:1; Ac 5:17; 7:54–60; 14:22). (3) A life lived according to Christ's righteous standards will bring ridicule and scorn (5:10–11). (4) The defense of the NT apostolic faith against heresy will bring division (2Co 11:12–15; Gal 1:9; Php 1:15–17; see 2Ti 1:15, note). (5) The teaching of Christ about peace and unity must be faithfully held in tension with the truth that he "did not come to bring peace, but a sword" (see Jn 17:21, note).

10:38 TAKE HIS CROSS. See Mk 8:34, note.

receives a righteous man because he is a
righteous man will receive a righteous
man's reward. 42And if anyone gives even
a cup of cold water to one of these little
ones because he is my disciple, I tell you
the truth, he will certainly not lose his
reward."[o]

Jesus and John the Baptist

11:2–19pp — Lk 7:18–35

11 After Jesus had finished instructing his twelve disciples,[p] he went
on from there to teach and preach in the
towns of Galilee.[o]

2When John[q] heard in prison[r] what
Christ was doing, he sent his disciples 3to
ask him, "Are you the one who was to
come,[s] or should we expect someone
else?"

4Jesus replied, "Go back and report to
John what you hear and see: 5The blind
receive sight, the lame walk, those who
have leprosy[p] are cured, the deaf hear,
the dead are raised, and the good news is
preached to the poor.[t] 6Blessed is the
man who does not fall away on account of
me."[u]

7As John's[v] disciples were leaving,
Jesus began to speak to the crowd about
John: "What did you go out into the
desert[w] to see? A reed swayed by the
wind? 8If not, what did you go out to see?
A man dressed in fine clothes? No, those
who wear fine clothes are in kings' palaces. 9Then what did you go out to see?
A prophet?[x] Yes, I tell you, and more than
a prophet. 10This is the one about whom
it is written:

> " 'I will send my messenger ahead of
> you,[y]
> who will prepare your way before
> you.'[q][z]

11I tell you the truth: Among those born
of women there has not risen anyone
greater than John the Baptist; yet he who
is least in the kingdom of heaven is greater than he. 12From the days of John the
Baptist until now, the kingdom of heaven
has been forcefully advancing, and forceful men lay hold of it. 13For all the Prophets and the Law prophesied until John.[a]
14And if you are willing to accept it, he is
the Elijah who was to come.[b] 15He who
has ears, let him hear.[c]

16"To what can I compare this generation? They are like children sitting in the
marketplaces and calling out to others:

> 17" 'We played the flute for you,
> and you did not dance;
> we sang a dirge,
> and you did not mourn.'

18For John came neither eating[d] nor
drinking,[e] and they say, 'He has a demon.' 19The Son of Man came eating and
drinking, and they say, 'Here is a glutton
and a drunkard, a friend of tax collectors
and "sinners." '[f] But wisdom is proved
right by her actions."

10:42 [o]Pr 14:31; 19:17; Mt 25:40; Mk 9:41; Ac 10:4; Heb 6:10
11:1 [p]S Mt 7:28
11:2 [q]S Mt 3:1 [r]Mt 14:3
11:3 [s]Ps 118:26; Jn 11:27; Heb 10:37
11:5 [t]Isa 35:4-6; 61:1; Mt 15:31; Lk 4:18,19
11:6 [u]Mt 13:21; 26:31
11:7 [v]S Mt 3:1 [w]Mt 3:1
11:9 [x]Mt 14:5; 21:26; Lk 1:76; 7:26
11:10 [y]Jn 3:28 [z]Mal 3:1; Mk 1:2; Lk 7:27
11:13 [a]Lk 16:16
11:14 [b]Mal 4:5; Mt 17:10-13; Mk 9:11-13; Lk 1:17; Jn 1:21
11:15 [c]Mt 13:9, 43; Mk 4:23; Lk 14:35; S Rev 2:7
11:18 [d]Mt 3:4 [e]S Lk 1:15
11:19 [f]S Mt 9:11

[o] *1* Greek *in their towns* [p] *5* The Greek word was used for various diseases affecting the skin—not necessarily leprosy. [q] *10* Mal. 3:1

10:41 PROPHET ... RIGHTEOUS MAN. Jesus speaks of receiving a prophet and a righteous man, those who are the most frequently rejected and persecuted because of their stand for godliness and their proclamation of the truth (see 5:10). For this reason those who accept prophets or righteous men and receive their messages will receive God's special reward. (1) If your commitment to truth and righteousness is so firm that you devote your life to providing for, cooperating with and encouraging God's ministers who are righteous, then your reward will be the same as that of the prophet or righteous person you help.

(2) Conversely, one should not support, encourage or cooperate with ministers and preachers who do not proclaim God's truth according to the NT revelation or who do not live godly lives according to God's righteous standards. Supporting such people will bring one into their condemnation (see 2 Jn).

11:7 JOHN. When Christ stated that John was not "a reed swayed by the wind," he was referring to John's righteous character and to his reputation as a preacher who refused to compromise his convictions. John preached God's commandments without fear of others, never yielding to popular opinion. Herod's sin was ignored in silence by all the Jewish authorities, but never for a moment by John. He rose against it as a rock, showing absolute fidelity to God and to his Word. He stood with God against sin, even though it cost him his life (14:3–12). Let every preacher of God's Word take note, for Christ will evaluate each one's ministry, character and stand against sin (see Lk 1:17, notes).

11:11 GREATER THAN HE. This statement may mean that the privileges of the least of those who belong to the age of the new covenant are greater than John the Baptist (see article on THE OLD COVENANT AND THE NEW COVENANT, p. 500). They have greater treasures of revelation given to them by God (cf. 13:16–17) and will experience greater miracles (11:5), see the death and resurrection of Christ, and receive the Pentecostal outpouring of the Holy Spirit (Ac 2:4).

11:12 FORCEFUL MEN LAY HOLD OF IT. See article on THE KINGDOM OF GOD, p. 28.

11:19 GLUTTON AND A DRUNKARD. See Lk 7:34, note.

Woe to Unrepentant Cities

11:21–23pp — Lk 10:13–15

20Then Jesus began to denounce the cities in which most of his miracles had been
performed, because they did not repent.
21"Woe to you, Korazin! Woe to you, Bethsaida![g] If the miracles that were performed in you had been performed in Tyre
and Sidon,[h] they would have repented
long ago in sackcloth and ashes.[i] **22**But
I tell you, it will be more bearable for Tyre
and Sidon on the day of judgment than for
you.[j] **23**And you, Capernaum,[k] will you
be lifted up to the skies? No, you will go
down to the depths.[r][l] If the miracles that
were performed in you had been performed in Sodom, it would have remained
to this day. **24**But I tell you that it will be
more bearable for Sodom on the day of
judgment than for you."[m]

Rest for the Weary

11:25–27pp — Lk 10:21,22

25At that time Jesus said, "I praise you,
Father,[n] Lord of heaven and earth, because you have hidden these things from
the wise and learned, and revealed them
to little children.[o] **26**Yes, Father, for this
was your good pleasure.
27"All things have been committed to
me[p] by my Father.[q] No one knows the
Son except the Father, and no one knows
the Father except the Son and those to
whom the Son chooses to reveal him.[r]
28"Come to me,[s] all you who are weary
and burdened, and I will give you rest.[t]
29Take my yoke upon you and learn from
me,[u] for I am gentle and humble in heart,
and you will find rest for your souls.[v]
30For my yoke is easy and my burden is
light."[w]

Lord of the Sabbath

12:1–8pp — Mk 2:23–28; Lk 6:1–5
12:9–14pp — Mk 3:1–6; Lk 6:6–11

12 At that time Jesus went through
the grainfields on the Sabbath. His
disciples were hungry and began to pick
some heads of grain[x] and eat them.
2When the Pharisees saw this, they said
to him, "Look! Your disciples are doing
what is unlawful on the Sabbath."[y]
3He answered, "Haven't you read what
David did when he and his companions
were hungry?[z] **4**He entered the house of
God, and he and his companions ate the
consecrated bread—which was not lawful
for them to do, but only for the priests.[a]
5Or haven't you read in the Law that on

r *23* Greek *Hades*

11:21 [g] Mk 6:45; 8:22; Lk 9:10; Jn 1:44; 12:21 [h] Joel 3:4; Am 1:9; Mt 15:21; Mk 3:8; Lk 6:17; Ac 12:20 [i] Jnh 3:5-9
11:22 [j] ver 24; Mt 10:15
11:23 [k] S Mt 4:13 [l] Isa 14:13-15
11:24 [m] S Mt 10:15
11:25 [n] Mt 16:17; Lk 22:42; 23:34; Jn 11:41; 12:27,28 [o] S Mt 13:11; 1Co 1:26-29
11:27 [p] S Mt 28:18 [q] S Jn 3:35 [r] Jn 10:15; 17:25, 26
11:28 [s] Jn 7:37 [t] Ex 33:14
11:29 [u] Jn 13:15; Php 2:5; 1Pe 2:21; 1Jn 2:6 [v] Ps 116:7; Jer 6:16
11:30 [w] 1Jn 5:3
12:1 [x] Dt 23:25
12:2 [y] ver 10; Ex 20:10; 23:12; Dt 5:14; Lk 13:14; 14:3; Jn 5:10; 7:23; 9:16
12:3 [z] 1Sa 21:6
12:4 [a] Lev 24:5,9

11:28 COME TO ME. Jesus' gracious invitation comes to all "who are weary and burdened" with the troubles of life and the sins of their own human nature. By coming to Jesus, becoming his servant and obeying his direction, he will free you from your insurmountable burdens and give you rest, peace and his Holy Spirit to lead you through life. What trials and cares you carry will be borne with his help and grace (see Heb 4:16).

12:1 SABBATH. The weekly Sabbath (Gk *sabbaton*, meaning rest, ceasing) was the seventh day of the week set apart by the Law of Moses as a day for ceasing from normal work and for giving of oneself to rest and to the worship of the Lord (Ex 20:10; Dt 5:14). There are strong reasons to believe that the principles of the Sabbath have permanent validity for Christians and that we should still set aside one day in seven as a day of rest and worship.

(1) The concept of a sacred day of rest was instituted before the Jewish law: "God blessed the seventh day and made it holy" (Ge 2:3; cf. Ex 20:11). This indicates that from the time of creation God wanted one day in seven to be a source of blessing for everyone, and not just for the Jewish race.

(2) Jesus never abrogated the principle of a day of rest, only the misuse of it by Jewish leaders (vv. 1–8; Lk 13:10–17; 14:1–6). He stated that the day of rest was given for our spiritual and physical well-being (Mk 2:27). Nowhere does the Bible indicate that this principle has been done away with.

(3) The spiritual purpose of a seventh day of rest benefits Christians. In the OT it was used as a day to rest from work and to dedicate oneself to God—a special time to get to know God, to worship him and to concentrate in private and in public on the things of God (Lev 24:8; Nu 28:9). Today it provides us an opportunity to reaffirm that our trust and delight is in the Lord and not in the world, our own selfish ways, our material goods or our pleasure (cf. Ex 20:10; 34:21; Isa 38:13). We can use this day to renew our initial commitment to Christ and our oneness with other believers, and to acknowledge that our entire lives, not just one-seventh, belong to God (see Heb 4:9–10).

(4) As the Sabbath was a covenant sign that the Israelites were the people of God (Ex 31:16–17), so the Christian day of worship (Sunday) can be seen as a sign to the world that we belong to Christ and that he is our Lord. Christians in the NT set aside the first day of the week to worship God and to commemorate the resurrection of Christ (Ac 20:7; 1Co 16:2).

(5) The Sabbath was set apart by God as a holy day (Ge 2:3; Ex 16:23; 20:11; 31:14; Isa 58:13). Thus believers who set aside one day in seven as holy are reminded that they themselves are set apart by God to live lives of holiness in the midst of a perverse generation (cf. Ex 31:13; 1Pe 2:9).

(6) Finally, the Sabbath can be seen as God's commitment to believers that he will carry out his will for them and that he is constantly available to act to meet their needs. He is always open to their prayers and devoted to their interest (cf. Ex 31:13; Eze 20:12).

the Sabbath the priests in the temple desecrate the day[b] and yet are innocent? **6**I tell you that one[s] greater than the temple is here.[c] **7**If you had known what these words mean, 'I desire mercy, not sacrifice,'[t][d] you would not have condemned the innocent. **8**For the Son of Man[e] is Lord of the Sabbath."

9Going on from that place, he went into their synagogue, **10**and a man with a shriveled hand was there. Looking for a reason to accuse Jesus,[f] they asked him, "Is it lawful to heal on the Sabbath?"[g]

11He said to them, "If any of you has a sheep and it falls into a pit on the Sabbath, will you not take hold of it and lift it out?[h] **12**How much more valuable is a man than a sheep![i] Therefore it is lawful to do good on the Sabbath."

13Then he said to the man, "Stretch out your hand." So he stretched it out and it was completely restored, just as sound as the other. **14**But the Pharisees went out and plotted how they might kill Jesus.[j]

God's Chosen Servant

15Aware of this, Jesus withdrew from that place. Many followed him, and he healed all their sick,[k] **16**warning them not to tell who he was.[l] **17**This was to fulfill[m] what was spoken through the prophet Isaiah:

18"Here is my servant whom I have chosen,
the one I love, in whom I delight;[n]
I will put my Spirit on him,[o]
and he will proclaim justice to the nations.
19He will not quarrel or cry out;
no one will hear his voice in the streets.
20A bruised reed he will not break,
and a smoldering wick he will not snuff out,
till he leads justice to victory.
21 In his name the nations will put their hope."[u][p]

Jesus and Beelzebub

12:25–29pp — Mk 3:23–27; Lk 11:17–22

22Then they brought him a demon-possessed man who was blind and mute, and Jesus healed him, so that he could both talk and see.[q] **23**All the people were astonished and said, "Could this be the Son of David?"[r] Mt 15:22-31

24But when the Pharisees heard this, they said, "It is only by Beelzebub,[v][s] the prince of demons, that this fellow drives out demons."[t]

25Jesus knew their thoughts[u] and said to them, "Every kingdom divided against itself will be ruined, and every city or household divided against itself will not stand. **26**If Satan[v] drives out Satan, he is divided against himself. How then can his kingdom stand? **27**And if I drive out demons by Beelzebub,[w] by whom do your people[x] drive them out? So then, they will be your judges. **28**But if I drive out demons by the Spirit of God, then the kingdom of God[y] has come upon you.

29"Or again, how can anyone enter a strong man's house and carry off his possessions unless he first ties up the strong man? Then he can rob his house.

30"He who is not with me is against me, and he who does not gather with me scatters.[z] **31**And so I tell you, every sin and blasphemy will be forgiven men, but the blasphemy against the Spirit will not be forgiven.[a] **32**Anyone who speaks a word against the Son of Man will be forgiven, but anyone who speaks against the Holy Spirit will not be forgiven, either in this age[b] or in the age to come.[c]

33"Make a tree good and its fruit will be

12:5 [b]Nu 28:9,10; Jn 7:22,23 **12:6** [c]ver 41,42 **12:7** [d]Hos 6:6; Mic 6:6-8; Mt 9:13 **12:8** [e]S Mt 8:20 **12:10** [f]Mk 3:2; 12:13; Lk 11:54; 14:1; 20:20 [g]S ver 2 **12:11** [h]Lk 14:5 **12:12** [i]Mt 6:26; 10:31 **12:14** [j]Ge 37:18; Ps 71:10; Mt 26:4; 27:1; Mk 3:6; Lk 6:11; Jn 5:18; 7:1,19; 11:53 **12:15** [k]S Mt 4:23 **12:16** [l]S Mt 8:4 **12:17** [m]S Mt 1:22 **12:18** [n]S Mt 3:17 [o]S Jn 3:34 **12:21** [p]Isa 42:1-4 **12:22** [q]S Mt 4:24 **12:23** [r]S Mt 9:27 **12:24** [s]S Mk 3:22 [t]Mt 9:34 **12:25** [u]S Mt 9:4 **12:26** [v]S Mt 4:10 **12:27** [w]ver 24 [x]Ac 19:13 **12:28** [y]S Mt 3:2 **12:30** [z]Mk 9:40; Lk 11:23 **12:31** [a]Mk 3:28,29; Lk 12:10 **12:32** [b]Tit 2:12 [c]Mk 10:30; Lk 20:34,35; Eph 1:21; Heb 6:5

[s] 6 Or *something*; also in verses 41 and 42
[t] 7 Hosea 6:6 [u] 21 Isaiah 42:1-4
[v] 24 Greek *Beezeboul* or *Beelzeboul*; also in verse 27

12:28 THE KINGDOM OF GOD. See article on THE KINGDOM OF GOD, p. 28.

12:29 TIES UP THE STRONG MAN. See article on POWER OVER SATAN AND DEMONS, p. 80.

12:31 BLASPHEMY AGAINST THE SPIRIT. Blasphemy against the Spirit is the continual and deliberate rejection of the Holy Spirit's witness to Christ, to his Word and to his convicting work against sin (cf. Jn 16:7–11). Those who reject and oppose the voice of the Spirit remove themselves from the only force that can lead them to forgiveness. The process leading to blasphemy against the Spirit is as follows: (1) Grieving the Spirit (Eph 4:30), if ongoing, leads to resisting the Spirit (Ac 7:51); (2) Resisting the Spirit leads to putting out the Spirit's fire (1Th 5:19); (3) Putting out the Spirit's fire leads to hardening the heart (Heb 3:8–13); (4) Hardening the heart leads to a depraved mind and to a labeling of good as evil and evil as good (Isa 5:20; Ro 1:28). When this hardening of the heart reaches a certain intensity, determined only by God, the Spirit will no longer strive to lead that person to repentance (cf. Ge 6:3). For those who are worried about having committed the unpardonable sin, the very fact of wanting to be forgiven and the willingness to repent of sin is evidence that one has not committed the unpardonable sin (see article on PERSONAL APOSTASY, p. 492).

THE KINGDOM OF GOD

***Mt 12:28** "But if I drive out demons by the Spirit of God, then the kingdom of God has come upon you."*

THE NATURE OF THE KINGDOM. The kingdom of God (or heaven) carries the idea of God coming into the world to assert his power, glory and rights against Satan's dominion and the present course of this world. It is more than salvation or the church; it is God expressing himself powerfully in all his works.

(1) The kingdom is primarily an assertion of divine power in action. God is beginning his spiritual rule on earth in hearts and among his people (Jn 14:23; 20:22). He comes into the world with power (Isa 64:1; Mk 9:1; 1Co 4:20). We must not conceive of this power as material or political, but as spiritual. The kingdom is not a religio-political theocracy; it is not a matter of social or political dominion over the kingdoms of this world (Jn 18:36). God does not intend at this time to redeem and reform the world through social or political activism, or through violent action (Mt 26:52; see Jn 18:36, note). The world throughout this age will remain an enemy of God and his people (Jn 15:19; Ro 12:1–2; Jas 4:4; 1Jn 2:15–17; 4:4). God's rule by direct judgment and force will occur only at the end of this age (Rev 19:11–21).

(2) Because God asserts himself with power, the world enters into a crisis. God's expression of power fills the devil's empire with alarm (Mt 4:3ff; 12:29; Mk 1:24), and everyone is confronted with the decision whether or not to submit to God's rule (Mt 3:1–2; 4:17; Mk 1:14–15). The necessary and fundamental condition of entry into God's kingdom is, "Repent and believe the good news" (Mk 1:15).

(3) This breaking into the world with divine power involves: (a) spiritual power over Satan's rule and dominion (Mt 12:28; Jn 18:36)—the coming of the kingdom is the beginning of the destruction of Satan's rule (Jn 12:31; 16:11) and of humanity's deliverance from the demonic (Mk 1:34,39; 3:14–15; Ac 26:18) and from sin (Ro 6); (b) power to work miracles and to heal the sick (Mt 4:23; 9:35; Ac 4:30; 8:7); (c) the preaching of the gospel, convicting in regard to sin, righteousness and judgment (Mt 11:5; Jn 16:8–11 Ac 4:33); (d) the salvation and sanctification of those who repent and believe the gospel (see Jn 3:3; 17:17; Ac 2:38–40; 2Co 6:14–18; see article on SPIRITUAL SEPARATION FOR BELIEVERS, p. 371); and (e) the baptism in the Holy Spirit for power to witness for Christ (see Ac 1:8, notes; 2:4, notes).

(4) An essential evidence that one is experiencing God's kingdom is a life of "righteousness, peace and joy in the Holy Spirit" (Ro 14:17).

(5) This kingdom has both a present and a future aspect. It is a present reality in the world today (Mk 1:15; Lk 18:16–17; Col 1:13; Heb 12:28), yet God's rule and power are not completely realized. The work and influence of Satan and evil people will continue until the end of the age (1Ti 4:1; 2Ti 3:1–5; Rev 19:19—20:10). The future manifestation of God's glory, power and kingdom will occur when Jesus returns to judge the world (Mt 24:30; Lk 21:27; Rev 19:11–20; 20:1–6). The ultimate fulfillment of the kingdom comes when Christ finally triumphs over all evil and opposition and hands over the kingdom to God the Father (1Co 15:24–28; Rev 20:7—21:8; see also Mk 1:15, note concerning the various manifestations of the kingdom in redemptive history.)

THE ROLE OF BELIEVERS IN THE KINGDOM. The NT has much to say about the role of believers in God's kingdom.

(1) It is the responsibility of believers to seek unceasingly God's kingdom in all its manifestations, hungering and thirsting for God's presence and power both in their own lives and within the Christian community (see Mt 5:10, notes; 6:33, note).

(2) In Mt 11:12 Jesus gives additional information on the nature of kingdom people. There he indicates that the kingdom of heaven is taken hold of only by forceful people who are committed to breaking away from the sinful practices of the human race and who turn to Christ, his Word and his righteous ways. No matter what the cost may be, such people vigorously seek the kingdom in all its power. In other words, experiencing the kingdom of heaven and all its blessings requires earnest endeavor and constant exertion—a fight of faith accompanied by a strong will to resist Satan, sin and an often corrupt society.

(3) The kingdom of God is not for those who seldom pray or who compromise with the world, neglect the Word and have little spiritual hunger. It is for men like Joseph (Ge 39:9), Nathan (2Sa 12:7), Elijah (1Ki 18:21), Daniel and his three friends (Da 1:8, 3:16–18), Mordecai (Est 3:4–5), Peter and John (Ac 4:19–20), Stephen (Ac 6:8, 7:51) and Paul (Php 3:13–14); it is for women like Deborah (Jdg 4:9), Ruth (Ru 1:16–18), Esther (Est 4:16), Mary (Lk 1:26–35), Anna (Lk 2:36–38) and Lydia (Ac 16:14–15,40).

JEWISH SECTS

PHARISEES

Their roots can be traced to the second century B.C. — to the Hasidim.

1. Along with the Torah, they accepted as equally inspired and authoritative, all material contained within the oral tradition.
2. On free will and determination, they held to a mediating view that made it impossible for either free will or the sovereignty of God to cancel out the other.
3. They accepted a rather developed hierarchy of angels and demons.
4. They taught that there was a future for the dead.
5. They believed in the immortality of the soul and in reward and retribution after death.
6. They were champions of human equality.
7. The emphasis of their teaching was ethical rather than theological.

SADDUCEES

They probably had their beginning during the Hasmonean period (166-63 B.C.). Their demise occurred C. A.D. 70 with the fall of Jerusalem.

1. They denied that the oral law was authoritative and binding.
2. They interpreted Mosaic law more literally than did the Pharisees.
3. They were very exacting in Levitical purity.
4. They attributed all to free will.
5. They argued there is neither resurrection of the dead nor a future life.
6. They rejected a belief in angels and demons.
7. They rejected the idea of a spiritual world.
8. Only the books of Moses were canonical Scripture.

good, or make a tree bad and its fruit will
Lk 6:43-44 be bad, for a tree is recognized by its
fruit.[d] 34You brood of vipers,[e] how can
you who are evil say anything good? For
out of the overflow of the heart the mouth
speaks.[f] 35The good man brings good
things out of the good stored up in him,
and the evil man brings evil things out of
the evil stored up in him. 36But I tell you
that men will have to give account on the
day of judgment for every careless word
they have spoken. 37For by your words
you will be acquitted, and by your words
you will be condemned."[g]

The Sign of Jonah

12:39–42pp — Lk 11:29–32
12:43–45pp — Lk 11:24–26

38Then some of the Pharisees and
teachers of the law said to him, "Teacher,
we want to see a miraculous sign[h] from
you."[i]

39He answered, "A wicked and adulterous generation asks for a miraculous
sign! But none will be given it except the
sign of the prophet Jonah.[j] 40For as Jonah
was three days and three nights in the
belly of a huge fish,[k] so the Son of Man[l]
will be three days and three nights in the
heart of the earth.[m] 41The men of Nineveh[n] will stand up at the judgment with
this generation and condemn it; for they
repented at the preaching of Jonah,[o] and
now one[w] greater than Jonah is here.
42The Queen of the South will rise at the
judgment with this generation and condemn it; for she came[p] from the ends of
the earth to listen to Solomon's wisdom,
and now one greater than Solomon is
here.

43"When an evil[x] spirit comes out of a
man, it goes through arid places seeking
rest and does not find it. 44Then it says,
'I will return to the house I left.' When it
arrives, it finds the house unoccupied,
swept clean and put in order. 45Then it
goes and takes with it seven other spirits
more wicked than itself, and they go in
and live there. And the final condition of
that man is worse than the first.[q] That is
how it will be with this wicked generation."

Jesus' Mother and Brothers

12:46–50pp — Mk 3:31–35; Lk 8:19–21

46While Jesus was still talking to the
crowd, his mother[r] and brothers[s] stood
outside, wanting to speak to him. 47Some-
one told him, "Your mother and brothers
are standing outside, wanting to speak to
you."[y]

48He replied to him, "Who is my mother,
and who are my brothers?" 49Pointing to
his disciples, he said, "Here are my mother and my brothers. 50For whoever does
the will of my Father in heaven[t] is my
brother and sister and mother."

The Parable of the Sower

13:1–15pp — Mk 4:1–12; Lk 8:4–10
13:16,17pp — Lk 10:23,24
13:18–23pp — Mk 4:13–20; Lk 8:11–15

13 That same day Jesus went out of
the house[u] and sat by the lake.
2Such large crowds gathered around him
that he got into a boat[v] and sat in it, while
all the people stood on the shore. 3Then

12:33 [d]Mt 7:16,17; Lk 6:43,44
12:34 [e]Mt 3:7; 23:33 [f]Mt 15:18; Lk 6:45
12:37 [g]Job 15:6; Pr 10:14; 18:21; Jas 3:2
12:38 [h]S Jn 2:11; S 4:48 [i]Mt 16:1; Mk 8:11,12; Lk 11:16; Jn 2:18; 6:30; 1Co 1:22
12:39 [j]Mt 16:4; Lk 11:29
12:40 [k]Jnh 1:17 [l]S Mt 8:20 [m]S Mt 16:21
12:41 [n]Jnh 1:2 [o]Jnh 3:5
12:42 [p]1Ki 10:1; 2Ch 9:1
12:45 [q]2Pe 2:20
12:46 [r]Mt 1:18; 2:11,13,14,20; Lk 1:43; 2:33,34,48,51; Jn 2:1,5; 19:25,26 [s]Mt 13:55; Jn 2:12; 7:3,5; Ac 1:14; 1Co 9:5; Gal 1:19
12:50 [t]Mt 6:10; Jn 15:14
13:1 [u]ver 36; Mt 9:28
13:2 [v]Lk 5:3

w *41* Or *something*; also in verse 42 x *43* Greek *unclean* y *47* Some manuscripts do not have verse 47.

12:36 THE DAY OF JUDGMENT. See article on THE JUDGMENT OF BELIEVERS, p. 368).

12:37 BY YOUR WORDS . . . ACQUITTED. See Lk 13:34, note.

12:40 JONAH. It is clear that Jesus accepted the OT account of Jonah as historical fact. The modern skeptics who deny the possibility of OT miracles must reckon with and be judged by the words of Jesus.

12:43 AN EVIL SPIRIT. Vv. 43–45 teach three important truths concerning demon-possession. (1) Evil spirits desire to return to one formerly possessed (v. 44). (2) Evil spirits cannot return if that person's heart is occupied by the Holy Spirit (v. 44; cf. 1Co 6:19; 2Co 6:15–16, note). (3) A whole nation or society may seek the pleasure of evil to such an extent that the society itself can become demon-possessed (v. 45; cf. Rev 16:14).

13:3 PARABLES OF THE KINGDOM. In ch. 13 we have the parables of the kingdom of heaven, describing both the results of preaching the gospel and the spiritual conditions that will prevail on earth within the visible manifestation of the kingdom of heaven (i.e., the churches) until the end of the age.

(1) In most of these parables, Christ teaches that there will be good and evil in his visible kingdom throughout the entire age. Among those who profess his name, there will be compromise and worldliness that lead to apostasy, as well as faithfulness and godliness that lead to eternal life. At the end of the age the wicked will be destroyed (vv. 41,49); "Then the righteous will shine like the sun in the kingdom of their Father" (v. 43).

(2) Christ speaks these parables in order to alert his true disciples to expect evil within the kingdom and to teach them how to overcome the influence and opposition of Satan and his followers. The only way to do so is through wholehearted devotion to Christ (vv. 44,46) and lives committed to righteousness (v. 43; see Rev 2–3 for examples of good and evil within the churches of the kingdom).

(3) Parables are stories from everyday life that relate and illustrate certain spiritual truths. Their

he told them many things in parables, saying: "A farmer went out to sow his seed.
4As he was scattering the seed, some fell
along the path, and the birds came and ate
it up. 5Some fell on rocky places, where it
did not have much soil. It sprang up quickly, because the soil was shallow. 6But
when the sun came up, the plants were
scorched, and they withered because they
had no root. 7Other seed fell among
thorns, which grew up and choked the
plants. 8Still other seed fell on good soil,
where it produced a crop—a hundred,[w]
sixty or thirty times what was sown. 9He
who has ears, let him hear."[x]

10The disciples came to him and asked,
"Why do you speak to the people in parables?"

11He replied, "The knowledge of the secrets of the kingdom of heaven[y] has been
given to you,[z] but not to them. 12Whoever
has will be given more, and he will have
an abundance. Whoever does not have,
even what he has will be taken from him.[a]
13This is why I speak to them in parables:

"Though seeing, they do not see;
though hearing, they do not hear or
understand.[b]

14In them is fulfilled[c] the prophecy of Isaiah:

" 'You will be ever hearing but never
understanding;
you will be ever seeing but never
perceiving.
15For this people's heart has become
calloused;
they hardly hear with their ears,
and they have closed their eyes.
Otherwise they might see with their
eyes,
hear with their ears,
understand with their hearts
and turn, and I would heal them.'[z][d]

16But blessed are your eyes because they
see, and your ears because they hear.[e]
17For I tell you the truth, many prophets
and righteous men longed to see what you
see[f] but did not see it, and to hear what
you hear but did not hear it.

18"Listen then to what the parable of
the sower means: 19When anyone hears
the message about the kingdom[g] and
does not understand it, the evil one[h]
comes and snatches away what was sown
in his heart. This is the seed sown along
the path. 20The one who received the seed
that fell on rocky places is the man who
hears the word and at once receives it
with joy. 21But since he has no root, he
lasts only a short time. When trouble or
persecution comes because of the word,
he quickly falls away.[i] 22The one who
received the seed that fell among the
thorns is the man who hears the word, but
the worries of this life and the deceitfulness of wealth[j] choke it, making it unfruitful. 23But the one who received the
seed that fell on good soil is the man who
hears the word and understands it. He
produces a crop, yielding a hundred, sixty
or thirty times what was sown."[k]

The Parable of the Weeds

24Jesus told them another parable:
"The kingdom of heaven is like[l] a man
who sowed good seed in his field. 25But
while everyone was sleeping, his enemy
came and sowed weeds among the wheat,
and went away. 26When the wheat sprout-
ed and formed heads, then the weeds also
appeared.

13:8 [w]Ge 26:12 **13:9** [x]S Mt 11:15 **13:11** [y]S Mt 3:2 [z]Mt 11:25; 16:17; 19:11; Jn 6:65; 1Co 2:10,14; Col 1:27; 1Jn 2:20, 27 **13:12** [a]S Mt 25:29 **13:13** [b]Dt 29:4; Jer 5:21; Eze 12:2 **13:14** [c]ver 35; S Mt 1:22 **13:15** [d]Isa 6:9, 10; Jn 12:40; Ac 28:26,27; Ro 11:8 **13:16** [e]Mt 16:17 **13:17** [f]Jn 8:56; Heb 11:13; 1Pe 1:10-12 **13:19** [g]Mt 4:23 [h]S Mt 5:37 **13:21** [i]Mt 11:6; 26:31 **13:22** [j]Mt 19:23; 1Ti 6:9,10,17 **13:23** [k]ver 8 **13:24** [l]ver 31,33, 45,47; Mt 18:23; 20:1; 22:2; 25:1; Mk 4:26,30

[z] *15* Isaiah 6:9,10

---

uniqueness is found in revealing truth to those who are spiritual while at the same time concealing it from the unbeliever (v. 11). Parables may at times demand a decision (e.g., Lk 10:30–37).

13:3 FARMER WENT OUT TO SOW. See Mk 4:3, note.

13:12 WHOEVER HAS WILL BE GIVEN MORE. See 25:29, note; Mk 4:25, note.

13:19 EVIL ONE . . . SNATCHES AWAY. See Mk 4:15, note.

13:24–25 GOOD SEED . . . WEEDS. The parable of the wheat and weeds emphasizes that Satan will sow alongside those who sow the Word of God. The "field" represents the world, and the "good seed" represents the faithful of the kingdom (v. 38).

(1) The gospel and true believers will be planted throughout the world (v. 38). Satan also will plant his followers, "the sons of the evil one" (v. 38), among God's people to counteract God's truth (vv. 25,38–39).

(2) The principal work of Satan's emissaries within the visible kingdom of heaven will be undermining the authority of God's Word (see Ge 3:4) and promoting unrighteousness and false doctrine (cf. Ac 20:29–30; 2Th 2:7,12). Christ later spoke of a great deception among his people because of these professed Christians who are really false teachers (see 24:11, note; see article on THE GREAT TRIBULATION, p. 52).

(3) The condition of Satan's people existing among God's people will terminate with God's final destruction of all the wicked at the end of the age (vv. 38–43). For other parables emphasizing the mixed condition of believers with unbelievers, see 22:11–14; 25:1–30; Lk 18:10–14; see article on CHRIST'S MESSAGE TO THE SEVEN CHURCHES, p. 576.

27"The owner's servants came to him
and said, 'Sir, didn't you sow good seed in
your field? Where then did the weeds
come from?'
28" 'An enemy did this,' he replied.
"The servants asked him, 'Do you want
us to go and pull them up?'
29" 'No,' he answered, 'because while
you are pulling the weeds, you may root
up the wheat with them. 30Let both grow
together until the harvest. At that time I
will tell the harvesters: First collect the
weeds and tie them in bundles to be
burned; then gather the wheat and bring
it into my barn.' "[m]

The Parables of the Mustard Seed and the Yeast

13:31,32pp — Mk 4:30–32
13:31–33pp — Lk 13:18–21

31He told them another parable: "The
kingdom of heaven is like[n] a mustard
seed,[o] which a man took and planted in
his field. 32Though it is the smallest of all
your seeds, yet when it grows, it is the
largest of garden plants and becomes a
tree, so that the birds of the air come and
perch in its branches."[p]
33He told them still another parable:
"The kingdom of heaven is like[q] yeast
that a woman took and mixed into a large
amount[a] of flour[r] until it worked all
through the dough."[s]
34Jesus spoke all these things to the
crowd in parables; he did not say anything
to them without using a parable.[t] 35So
was fulfilled[u] what was spoken through
the prophet:

"I will open my mouth in parables,
I will utter things hidden since the
creation of the world."[b][v]

The Parable of the Weeds Explained

36Then he left the crowd and went into
the house. His disciples came to him and
said, "Explain to us the parable[w] of the
weeds in the field."
37He answered, "The one who sowed
the good seed is the Son of Man.[x] 38The
field is the world, and the good seed
stands for the sons of the kingdom. The
weeds are the sons of the evil one,[y] 39and
the enemy who sows them is the devil.
The harvest[z] is the end of the age,[a] and
the harvesters are angels.[b]
40"As the weeds are pulled up and
burned in the fire, so it will be at the end
of the age. 41The Son of Man[c] will send
out his angels,[d] and they will weed out of
his kingdom everything that causes sin
and all who do evil. 42They will throw
them into the fiery furnace, where there
will be weeping and gnashing of teeth.[e]
43Then the righteous will shine like the
sun[f] in the kingdom of their Father. He
who has ears, let him hear.[g]

The Parables of the Hidden Treasure and the Pearl

44"The kingdom of heaven is like[h] trea-

13:30 [m]Mt 3:12 **13:31** [n]S ver 24 [o]Mt 17:20; Lk 17:6 **13:32** [p]Ps 104:12; Eze 17:23; 31:6; Da 4:12 **13:33** [q]S ver 24 [r]Ge 18:6 [s]Gal 5:9 **13:34** [t]S Jn 16:25
13:35 [u]ver 14; S Mt 1:22 [v]Ps 78:2; Ro 16:25,26; 1Co 2:7; Eph 3:9; Col 1:26 **13:36** [w]Mt 15:15 **13:37** [x]S Mt 8:20 **13:38** [y]Jn 8:44, 45; 1Jn 3:10 **13:39** [z]Joel 3:13 [a]Mt 24:3; 28:20 [b]Rev 14:15 **13:41** [c]S Mt 8:20 [d]Mt 24:31 **13:42** [e]S Mt 8:12 **13:43** [f]Da 12:3 [g]S Mt 11:15 **13:44** [h]S ver 24

[a] *33* Greek *three satas* (probably about 1/2 bushel or 22 liters) [b] *35* Psalm 78:2

13:30 LET BOTH GROW TOGETHER. Concerning the growing together of Christ's true followers and Satan's children who masquerade as believers (v. 38; cf. 2Co 11:13–15), three points should be noted.

(1) Throughout the age of the gospel such coexistence will occur. God will not command his angels to destroy the children of the evil one until the end of the age (vv. 30,38–41).

(2) The above parable does not contradict Biblical instructions found elsewhere that command believers to discipline sinning members and expel unrepentant and false members from their fellowship (see 18:15, note; Ac 20:28, note; 1Co 5:1, note). However, it must be understood that church discipline at its best will be only a partial solution to evil individuals in the kingdom. God and his angels will make the final separation.

(3) Faithful believers must always be alert to the subversive elements and individuals that Satan is planting within all parts of God's work. They will in many ways look like true children of God (see 2Co 11:13, note; see article on FALSE TEACHERS, p. 98).

13:31 MUSTARD SEED. See Lk 13:19, note.

13:33 YEAST. See Lk 13:21, note.

13:41 WEED OUT ... EVERYTHING THAT CAUSES SIN. At the return of Christ to earth after the tribulation and at the end of the age (Rev 19:11–21), there will be a time of harvest of both the wicked and the righteous living on earth (vv. 30,40–42; see article on THE GREAT TRIBULATION, p. 52). (1) The wicked are first gathered and taken out from among the righteous (vv. 30,41,49). The righteous are gathered next (vv. 30b,41–43,49); this gathering will be "out of his kingdom." (3) After the harvest and the destruction of the wicked, "then the righteous will shine like the sun in the kingdom of their Father" (v. 43; cf. 25:31–34; see Rev 20:4, notes).

13:42 THE FIERY FURNACE. Jesus describes what will happen to all who cause sin and do evil (v. 41). They will be tormented with fire and experience great suffering (cf. Rev 14:9–11; 20:10). No one accepting the Bible as the Word of God can reject this doctrine. The wicked are not annihilated, but are thrown into "the fiery furnace" (see 10:28, note).

13:44–46 KINGDOM ... TREASURE. The parables of the hidden treasure and the pearl teach two

sure hidden in a field. When a man found it, he hid it again, and then in his joy went and sold all he had and bought that field.[i]

45 "Again, the kingdom of heaven is like[j] a merchant looking for fine pearls. 46 When he found one of great value, he went away and sold everything he had and bought it.

The Parable of the Net

47 "Once again, the kingdom of heaven is like[k] a net that was let down into the lake and caught all kinds[l] of fish. 48 When it was full, the fishermen pulled it up on the shore. Then they sat down and collected the good fish in baskets, but threw the bad away. 49 This is how it will be at the end of the age. The angels will come and separate the wicked from the righteous[m] 50 and throw them into the fiery furnace, where there will be weeping and gnashing of teeth.[n]

51 "Have you understood all these things?" Jesus asked.

"Yes," they replied.

52 He said to them, "Therefore every teacher of the law who has been instructed about the kingdom of heaven is like the owner of a house who brings out of his storeroom new treasures as well as old."

A Prophet Without Honor

13:54–58pp — Mk 6:1–6

53 When Jesus had finished these parables,[o] he moved on from there. 54 Coming to his hometown, he began teaching the people in their synagogue,[p] and they were amazed.[q] "Where did this man get this wisdom and these miraculous powers?" they asked. 55 "Isn't this the carpenter's son?[r] Isn't his mother's[s] name Mary, and aren't his brothers[t] James, Joseph, Simon and Judas? 56 Aren't all his sisters with us? Where then did this man get all these things?" 57 And they took offense[u] at him.

But Jesus said to them, "Only in his hometown and in his own house is a prophet without honor."[v]

58 And he did not do many miracles there because of their lack of faith.

John the Baptist Beheaded

14:1–12pp — Mk 6:14–29

14 At that time Herod[w] the tetrarch heard the reports about Jesus,[x] 2 and he said to his attendants, "This is John the Baptist;[y] he has risen from the dead! That is why miraculous powers are at work in him."

3 Now Herod had arrested John and bound him and put him in prison[z] because of Herodias, his brother Philip's wife,[a] 4 for John had been saying to him: "It is not lawful for you to have her."[b] 5 Herod wanted to kill John, but he was afraid of the people, because they considered him a prophet.[c]

6 On Herod's birthday the daughter of Herodias danced for them and pleased Herod so much 7 that he promised with an oath to give her whatever she asked. 8 Prompted by her mother, she said, "Give me here on a platter the head of John the Baptist." 9 The king was distressed, but because of his oaths and his dinner guests, he ordered that her request be

13:44 [i] Isa 55:1; Mt 19:21; Php 3:7, 8
13:45 [j] S ver 24
13:47 [k] S ver 24 [l] Mt 22:10
13:49 [m] Mt 25:32
13:50 [n] S Mt 8:12
13:53 [o] S Mt 7:28
13:54 [p] S Mt 4:23 [q] S Mt 7:28
13:55 [r] Lk 3:23; Jn 6:42 [s] S Mt 12:46 [t] S Mt 12:46
13:57 [u] Jn 6:61 [v] Lk 4:24; Jn 4:44
14:1 [w] Mk 8:15; Lk 3:1,19; 13:31; 23:7,8; Ac 4:27; 12:1 [x] Lk 9:7-9
14:2 [y] S Mt 3:1
14:3 [z] Mt 4:12; 11:2 [a] Lk 3:19,20
14:4 [b] Lev 18:16; 20:21
14:5 [c] S Mt 11:9

---

truths: (1) The kingdom is a priceless treasure that is to be desired above all else. (2) The kingdom is to be acquired by giving up everything that would prevent our being part of it. "Selling all" means that we must transfer our whole heart from other interests to the one supreme interest, Christ (Ro 12:1).

13:47 KINGDOM . . . A NET. The parable of the net reveals once again the truth Christ has so greatly emphasized: not all who are in the visible kingdom are truly children of God. Churches and Christian organizations are not synonymous with the true people of God, who consist of all believers living in true faith and righteousness (cf. 24:11,24; Gal 5:19–21; see Lk 13:21, note).

13:49 SEPARATE THE WICKED FROM THE RIGHTEOUS. In the parable of the net, the separating of the wicked from the righteous at the end of the age is in the same order as that given in the parable of the weeds and wheat (vv. 30,41,43): all who do evil are gathered first and the righteous are gathered second (cf. Rev 19:11 — 20:4). This order clearly shows that the separation occurs at the end of the tribulation (24:29–31; Rev 19:11 — 20:4) and not at the rapture, at which time the faithful of Christ's churches are gathered from among the wicked (see 1Th 4:13–18; Rev 3:10). In this parable Christ again stresses that among God's people there will be many who are not truly loyal to him and his Word.

14:6 DANCED FOR THEM. The public dancing of an ungodly girl for Herod and his guests led to the death of one of the holiest of men. (1) Worldly parties, dancing and ungodly films lead to a forgetfulness of God, an inciting of passion, and a hardening of one's ability to discern sin, righteousness or judgment. In these things true children of God will not participate (see article on THE CHRISTIAN'S RELATIONSHIP TO THE WORLD, p. 546).

(2) According to Scripture spontaneous dancing by Hebrew women and girls was done on exceptionally joyful occasions (cf. Jer 31:4), and especially after victory in battle as they sang to the Lord (Ex 15:19–21). There is no Scriptural record, however, that Jewish men danced with women, nor is there any indication that Jewish women ever danced publicly for an audience. The dancing of the daughter of Herodias at Herod's birthday party was a pagan practice.

granted **10**and had John beheaded[d] in the
prison. **11**His head was brought in on a
platter and given to the girl, who carried
it to her mother. **12**John's disciples came
and took his body and buried it.[e] Then
they went and told Jesus.

Jesus Feeds the Five Thousand

14:13–21pp — Mk 6:32–44; Lk 9:10–17; Jn 6:1–13
14:13–21Ref — Mt 15:32–38

13When Jesus heard what had happened, he withdrew by boat privately to a
solitary place. Hearing of this, the crowds
followed him on foot from the towns.
14When Jesus landed and saw a large
crowd, he had compassion on them[f] and
healed their sick.[g]
15As evening approached, the disciples
came to him and said, "This is a remote
place, and it's already getting late. Send
the crowds away, so they can go to the
villages and buy themselves some food."
16Jesus replied, "They do not need to go
away. You give them something to eat."
17"We have here only five loaves[h] of
bread and two fish," they answered.
18"Bring them here to me," he said.
19And he directed the people to sit down
on the grass. Taking the five loaves and
the two fish and looking up to heaven, he
gave thanks and broke the loaves.[i] Then
he gave them to the disciples, and the disciples gave them to the people. **20**They all
ate and were satisfied, and the disciples
picked up twelve basketfuls of broken
pieces that were left over. **21**The number
of those who ate was about five thousand
men, besides women and children.

Jesus Walks on the Water

14:22–33pp — Mk 6:45–51; Jn 6:15–21
14:34–36pp — Mk 6:53–56

22Immediately Jesus made the disciples
get into the boat and go on ahead of him
to the other side, while he dismissed the
crowd. **23**After he had dismissed them, he
went up on a mountainside by himself to
pray.[j] When evening came, he was there
alone, **24**but the boat was already a considerable distance[c] from land, buffeted
by the waves because the wind was
against it.
25During the fourth watch of the night
Jesus went out to them, walking on the
lake. **26**When the disciples saw him walking on the lake, they were terrified.
"It's a ghost,"[k] they said, and cried out in
fear.
27But Jesus immediately said to them:
"Take courage![l] It is I. Don't be afraid."[m]
28"Lord, if it's you," Peter replied, "tell
me to come to you on the water."
29"Come," he said.
Then Peter got down out of the boat,
walked on the water and came toward
Jesus. **30**But when he saw the wind, he
was afraid and, beginning to sink, cried
out, "Lord, save me!"
31Immediately Jesus reached out his
hand and caught him. "You of little
faith,"[n] he said, "why did you doubt?"
32And when they climbed into the boat,
the wind died down. **33**Then those who
were in the boat worshiped him, saying,
"Truly you are the Son of God."[o]
34When they had crossed over, they
landed at Gennesaret. **35**And when the
men of that place recognized Jesus, they
sent word to all the surrounding country.
People brought all their sick to him **36**and
begged him to let the sick just touch the
edge of his cloak,[p] and all who touched
him were healed.

14:10 [d] Mt 17:12 **14:12** [e] Ac 8:2 **14:14** [f] S Mt 9:36 [g] S Mt 4:23 **14:17** [h] Mt 16:9 **14:19** [i] 1Sa 9:13; Mt 26:26; Mk 8:6; Lk 9:16; 24:30; Ac 2:42; 20:7,11; 27:35; 1Co 10:16; 1Ti 4:4
14:23 [j] S Lk 3:21 **14:26** [k] Lk 24:37 **14:27** [l] Mt 9:2; Ac 23:11 [m] Da 10:12; Mt 17:7; 28:10; Lk 1:13,30; 2:10; Ac 18:9; 23:11; Rev 1:17 **14:31** [n] S Mt 6:30 **14:33** [o] Ps 2:7; S Mt 4:3 **14:36** [p] S Mt 9:20

c 24 Greek *many stadia*

14:19 LOAVES AND . . . FISH. The miracle of the feeding of the five thousand is recorded in all four Gospels (Mk 6:34–44; Lk 9:10–17; Jn 6:1–14). The significance of the miracle includes the following. (1) It points to Jesus as the bread of life (cf. Jn 6), the one who provides for both body and soul. (2) It is proof of the Lord's power to perform miracles. (3) It is an example of Jesus' compassion for needy people (v. 14; cf. Ex 34:6; Mic 7:18). (4) It teaches that the little we have can be made into much if put into the Lord's hands and blessed.

14:23 PRAY . . . ALONE. While on earth, Jesus often sought time to be alone with God (cf. Mk 1:35; 6:46; Lk 5:16; 6:12; 9:18; 22:41–42; Heb 5:7). Time alone with God is essential to the spiritual well-being of every believer. The lack of desire for solitary prayer to and communion with our heavenly Father is an unmistakable sign that the spiritual life within us is in a process of decline. If this is happening, we must turn from all that offends the Lord and renew our commitment to persevere in seeking God and his saving grace (see Lk 18:1, note).

14:27 DON'T BE AFRAID. In this life there are many things to fear, yet Jesus wants us to look to him and not be afraid. His words of encouragement are founded on his limitless power and intense personal love for all who truly belong to him. Often in Scripture, God or Jesus Christ encourages his people, "do not be afraid" (see, for example, Jos 1:9; 11:6; 2Ki 19:6; 2Ch 20:15; 32:7; Ne 4:14; Ps 49:16; 91:5; Isa 10:24; 37:6; 44:8; Mt 17:7; 28:10; Mk 5:36; Lk 12:4; Jn 14:1,27; Ac 18:9; 1Pe 3:14.)

Tradition and God's Commands

15:1–20pp — Mk 7:1–23

15 Then some Pharisees and teachers of the law came to Jesus from
Jerusalem and asked, 2"Why do your disciples break the tradition of the elders?
They don't wash their hands before they
eat!"[q]
3Jesus replied, "And why do you break
the command of God for the sake of your
tradition? 4For God said, 'Honor your father and mother'[d][r] and 'Anyone who
curses his father or mother must be put to
death.'[e][s] 5But you say that if a man says
to his father or mother, 'Whatever help
you might otherwise have received from
me is a gift devoted to God,' 6he is not to
'honor his father[f]' with it. Thus you nullify the word of God for the sake of your
tradition. 7You hypocrites! Isaiah was
right when he prophesied about you:

8" 'These people honor me with their
lips,
but their hearts are far from me.
9They worship me in vain;
their teachings are but rules taught
by men.[t]'[g][u]"

Clean and Unclean

10Jesus called the crowd to him and
said, "Listen and understand. 11What
goes into a man's mouth does not make
him 'unclean,'[v] but what comes out of his
mouth, that is what makes him 'unclean.' "[w]
12Then the disciples came to him and
asked, "Do you know that the Pharisees
were offended when they heard this?"
13He replied, "Every plant that my
heavenly Father has not planted[x] will be
pulled up by the roots. 14Leave them; they
are blind guides.[h][y] If a blind man leads a
blind man, both will fall into a pit."[z]
15Peter said, "Explain the parable to
us."[a]
16"Are you still so dull?"[b] Jesus asked
them. 17"Don't you see that whatever enters the mouth goes into the stomach and
then out of the body? 18But the things that
come out of the mouth come from the
heart,[c] and these make a man 'unclean.'
19For out of the heart come evil thoughts,
murder, adultery, sexual immorality,
theft, false testimony, slander.[d] 20These
are what make a man 'unclean';[e] but eating with unwashed hands does not make
him 'unclean.' "

The Faith of the Canaanite Woman

15:21–28pp — Mk 7:24–30

21Leaving that place, Jesus withdrew to
the region of Tyre and Sidon.[f] 22A Canaanite woman from that vicinity came to
him, crying out, "Lord, Son of David,[g]
have mercy on me! My daughter is suffering terribly from demon-possession."[h]
23Jesus did not answer a word. So his
disciples came to him and urged him,
"Send her away, for she keeps crying out
after us."
24He answered, "I was sent only to the
lost sheep of Israel."[i]
25The woman came and knelt before
him.[j] "Lord, help me!" she said.
26He replied, "It is not right to take the
children's bread and toss it to their dogs."
27"Yes, Lord," she said, "but even the
dogs eat the crumbs that fall from their
masters' table."
28Then Jesus answered, "Woman, you
have great faith![k] Your request is granted." And her daughter was healed from
that very hour.

Jesus Feeds the Four Thousand

15:29–31pp — Mk 7:31–37
15:32–39pp — Mk 8:1–10
15:32–39Ref — Mt 14:13–21

29Jesus left there and went along the
Sea of Galilee. Then he went up on a
mountainside and sat down. 30Great
crowds came to him, bringing the lame,
the blind, the crippled, the mute and many
others, and laid them at his feet; and he
healed them.[l] 31The people were amazed
when they saw the mute speaking, the
crippled made well, the lame walking and

15:2 [q]Lk 11:38 **15:4** [r]Ex 20:12; Dt 5:16; Eph 6:2 [s]Ex 21:17; Lev 20:9 **15:9** [t]Col 2:20-22 [u]Isa 29:13; Mal 2:2 **15:11** [v]S Ac 10:14,15 [w]ver 18 **15:13** [x]Isa 60:21; 61:3 **15:14** [y]Mt 23:16, 24; Ro 2:19 [z]Lk 6:39 **15:15** [a]Mt 13:36 **15:16** [b]Mt 16:9 **15:18** [c]Mt 12:34; Lk 6:45; Jas 3:6 **15:19** [d]Gal 5:19-21 **15:20** [e]Ro 14:14 **15:21** [f]S Mt 11:21 **15:22** [g]S Mt 9:27 [h]S Mt 4:24 **15:24** [i]Mt 10:6, 23; Ro 15:8 **15:25** [j]S Mt 8:2 **15:28** [k]S Mt 9:22 **15:30** [l]S Mt 4:23

[d] *4* Exodus 20:12; Deut. 5:16 [e] *4* Exodus 21:17; Lev. 20:9 [f] *6* Some manuscripts *father or his mother* [g] *9* Isaiah 29:13 [h] *14* Some manuscripts *guides of the blind*

15:6 FOR THE SAKE OF YOUR TRADITION. Some Pharisees invalidated the commands of God for the sake of their traditions and the ideas of humans. Believers today must be on the alert that they do not "nullify the word of God" because of tradition, popular ideas or present-day cultural norms. To do so is to fall into this sin of the Pharisees and Jewish leaders (see Mk 7:8, note).

15:8 THEIR HEARTS ARE FAR FROM ME. See Mk 7:6, note.

15:11 THAT IS WHAT MAKES HIM 'UNCLEAN'. See Mk 7:18, note.

15:19 OUT OF THE HEART. See Mk 7:21, note.

15:28 YOU HAVE GREAT FAITH. To persevere in true faith is to trust God in all circumstances and remain true to him, even when you are in great trouble and he does not seem to answer or to care. This is "the test of faith" (Lk 18:1–7; 1Pe 1:7; see Mk 7:27, note).

Mk 2:3-12 the blind seeing. And they praised the God
of Israel.[m]
32Jesus called his disciples to him and
said, "I have compassion for these people;[n] they have already been with me
three days and have nothing to eat. I do
not want to send them away hungry, or
they may collapse on the way."
33His disciples answered, "Where could
we get enough bread in this remote place
to feed such a crowd?"
34"How many loaves do you have?"
Jesus asked.
"Seven," they replied, "and a few small
fish."
35He told the crowd to sit down on the
ground. 36Then he took the seven loaves
and the fish, and when he had given
thanks, he broke them[o] and gave them to
the disciples, and they in turn to the people. 37They all ate and were satisfied. Afterward the disciples picked up seven basketfuls of broken pieces that were left
over.[p] 38The number of those who ate was
four thousand, besides women and children. 39After Jesus had sent the crowd
away, he got into the boat and went to the
vicinity of Magadan.

The Demand for a Sign

16:1–12pp — Mk 8:11–21

16 The Pharisees and Sadducees[q]
came to Jesus and tested him by
asking him to show them a sign from
heaven.[r]
2He replied,[i] "When evening comes,
you say, 'It will be fair weather, for the
sky is red,' 3and in the morning, 'Today it
will be stormy, for the sky is red and over-
cast.' You know how to interpret the appearance of the sky, but you cannot interpret the signs of the times.[s] 4A wicked
and adulterous generation looks for a miraculous sign, but none will be given it
except the sign of Jonah."[t] Jesus then left
them and went away.

15:31 [m]S Mt 9:8
15:32 [n]S Mt 9:36
15:36 [o]S Mt 14:19
15:37 [p]Mt 16:10
16:1 [q]S Ac 4:1 [r]S Mt 12:38
16:3 [s]Lk 12:54-56
16:4 [t]Mt 12:39

The Yeast of the Pharisees and Sadducees

5When they went across the lake, the
disciples forgot to take bread. 6"Be careful," Jesus said to them. "Be on your guard
against the yeast of the Pharisees and
Sadducees."[u]
7They discussed this among themselves and said, "It is because we didn't
bring any bread."
8Aware of their discussion, Jesus
asked, "You of little faith,[v] why are you
talking among yourselves about having no
bread? 9Do you still not understand?
Don't you remember the five loaves for the
five thousand, and how many basketfuls
you gathered?[w] 10Or the seven loaves for
the four thousand, and how many basketfuls you gathered?[x] 11How is it you don't
understand that I was not talking to you
about bread? But be on your guard against
the yeast of the Pharisees and Sadducees." 12Then they understood that he
was not telling them to guard against the
yeast used in bread, but against the teaching of the Pharisees and Sadducees.[y]

Peter's Confession of Christ

16:13–16pp — Mk 8:27–29; Lk 9:18–20

13When Jesus came to the region of
Caesarea Philippi, he asked his disciples,
"Who do people say the Son of Man is?"
14They replied, "Some say John the
Baptist;[z] others say Elijah; and still others, Jeremiah or one of the prophets."[a]
15"But what about you?" he asked.
"Who do you say I am?"
16Simon Peter answered, "You are the
Christ,[j] the Son of the living God."[b]
17Jesus replied, "Blessed are you, Simon son of Jonah, for this was not revealed to you by man,[c] but by my Father
in heaven.[d] 18And I tell you that you are

16:6 [u]Lk 12:1
16:8 [v]S Mt 6:30
16:9 [w]Mt 14:17-21
16:10 [x]Mt 15:34-38
16:12 [y]S Ac 4:1
16:14 [z]S Mt 3:1 [a]Mk 6:15; Jn 1:21
16:16 [b]S Mt 4:3; Ps 42:2; Jer 10:10; Ac 14:15; 2Co 6:16; 1Th 1:9; 1Ti 3:15; Heb 10:31; 12:22
16:17 [c]1Co 15:50; Eph 6:12; Heb 2:14 [d]S Mt 13:11

i *2* Some early manuscripts do not have the rest of verse 2 and all of verse 3. j *16* Or *Messiah*; also in verse 20

16:6 BE ON YOUR GUARD AGAINST THE YEAST. Here "yeast," a symbol of evil and corruption, refers to the teaching of the Pharisees and Sadducees. Christ calls their teaching "yeast" because even a small amount can penetrate and influence a large group of people to believe the wrong thing (see Mk 8:15, note).

16:18 PETER ... ROCK ... CHURCH. In these words Christ promises to build his church on the truth of Peter's and the other disciples' confession that Jesus is the Christ, the Son of the living God (v. 16; cf. Ac 2:14–26). Jesus uses a play on words here. He calls his disciple "Peter" (Gk *Petros*, meaning a small stone), but goes on to say, "on this rock [Gk *Petra*, meaning a massive rock or a rocky cliff] I will build my church," i.e., he will build his church on Peter's solid confession.

(1) It is Jesus Christ who is the Rock, the first and great foundation of the church (1Co 3:11). Peter states in his first letter that Jesus is the "living Stone, . . . a chosen and precious cornerstone . . . the stone the builders rejected" (1Pe 2:4,6–7). At the same time, Peter and all other Christians are living stones who become part of the structure of the spiritual house that God is building (1Pe 2:5).

(2) Nowhere in Scripture is it stated that Peter

Peter,[k][e] and on this rock I will build my
church,[f] and the gates of Hades[1] will not
overcome it.[m] 19 I will give you the keys[g]
of the kingdom of heaven; whatever you
bind on earth will be[n] bound in heaven,
and whatever you loose on earth will be[n]
loosed in heaven."[h] 20 Then he warned his
disciples not to tell anyone[i] that he was
the Christ.

Jesus Predicts His Death

16:21–28pp — Mk 8:31–9:1; Lk 9:22–27

21 From that time on Jesus began to explain to his disciples that he must go to
Jerusalem[j] and suffer many things[k] at
the hands of the elders, chief priests and
teachers of the law,[l] and that he must be
killed[m] and on the third day[n] be raised to
life.[o]

22 Peter took him aside and began to
rebuke him. "Never, Lord!" he said. "This
shall never happen to you!"

23 Jesus turned and said to Peter, "Get
behind me, Satan![p] You are a stumbling
block to me; you do not have in mind the
things of God, but the things of men."

24 Then Jesus said to his disciples, "If
anyone would come after me, he must
deny himself and take up his cross and
follow me.[q] 25 For whoever wants to save
his life[o] will lose it, but whoever loses his
life for me will find it.[r] 26 What good will
it be for a man if he gains the whole world,
yet forfeits his soul? Or what can a man
give in exchange for his soul? 27 For the
Son of Man[s] is going to come[t] in his Father's glory with his angels, and then he
will reward each person according to what
he has done.[u] 28 I tell you the truth, some
who are standing here will not taste death
before they see the Son of Man coming in
his kingdom."

The Transfiguration

17:1–8pp — Lk 9:28–36
17:1–13pp — Mk 9:2–13

17 After six days Jesus took with him
Peter, James and John[v] the brother of James, and led them up a high mountain by themselves. 2 There he was transfigured before them. His face shone like
the sun, and his clothes became as white
as the light. 3 Just then there appeared before them Moses and Elijah, talking with
Jesus.

4 Peter said to Jesus, "Lord, it is good
for us to be here. If you wish, I will put up
three shelters — one for you, one for Moses and one for Elijah."

5 While he was still speaking, a bright
cloud enveloped them, and a voice from
the cloud said, "This is my Son, whom I

16:18 [e]Jn 1:42 [f]S Eph 2:20 **16:19** [g]Isa 22:22; Rev 3:7 [h]Mt 18:18; Jn 20:23 **16:20** [i]S Mk 8:30 **16:21** [j]S Lk 9:51 [k]Ps 22:6; Isa 53:3; Mt 26:67,68; Mk 10:34; Lk 17:25; Jn 18:22,23; 19:3 [l]Mt 27:1,2 [m]Ac 2:23; 3:13 [n]Hos 6:2; Mt 12:40; Lk 24:21,46; Jn 2:19; 1Co 15:3, 4 [o]Mt 17:22,23; Mk 9:31; Lk 9:22; 18:31-33; 24:6,7 **16:23** [p]S Mt 4:10 **16:24** [q]Mt 10:38; Lk 14:27 **16:25** [r]S Jn 12:25 **16:27** [s]S Mt 8:20 [t]S Lk 17:30; Jn 14:3; Ac 1:11; S 1Co 1:7; S 1Th 2:19; 4:16; S Rev 1:7; 22:7, 12,20 [u]2Ch 6:23; Job 34:11; Ps 62:12; Jer 17:10; Eze 18:20; 1Co 3:12-15; 2Co 5:10; Rev 22:12 **17:1** [v]S Mt 4:21

k 18 *Peter* means *rock.* l 18 Or *hell* m 18 Or *not prove stronger than it* n 19 Or *have been*
o 25 The Greek word means either *life* or *soul*; also in verse 26.

would be the supreme and infallible authority above all other disciples (cf. Ac 15; Gal 2:11). Nor is it stated that Peter should have infallible successors who would represent Christ and function as the official head of the church.

For a discussion of the doctrine of the church as seen here and elsewhere in Scripture, see article on THE CHURCH, p. 38.

16:18 THE GATES OF HADES WILL NOT OVERCOME IT. The "gates of Hades" represent Satan and all the world's evil striving to destroy the church of Jesus Christ. (1) This passage does not mean that any particular believer, local church, fellowship of churches, or denomination will never fall into immorality, doctrinal error or apostasy. Jesus himself predicted that many will fall from the faith, and he warns churches that are abandoning the NT faith to turn from their sins or face removal from his kingdom (24:10–11; Rev 2:5,12–29; 3:1–6,14–16; see 1Ti 4:1, note; see article on PERSONAL APOSTASY, p. 492). The promise of v. 18 does not apply to either those who deny the faith or to lukewarm churches.

(2) What Christ means is that in spite of Satan doing his worst, apostasy occurring among believers, churches becoming lukewarm, and false teachers infiltrating God's kingdom, the church will not be destroyed. By his sovereign grace, wisdom and power, God will always have a remnant of believers and churches throughout redemptive history that will remain faithful to the original gospel of Christ and the apostles and who experience his fellowship, the lordship of Christ and the power of the Holy Spirit. As God's true people, they will demonstrate the kingdom power of the Holy Spirit against Satan, sin, disease, the world and the demonic. It is this church that Satan and all his host can never destroy or resist.

16:19 KEYS OF THE KINGDOM. The "keys" represent God's delegated authority to Peter and the church. By these keys they (1) rebuke sin and carry out church discipline (18:15–18); (2) pray effectively for God's cause on earth (18:19–20); (3) tie up the demonic and set free the captives (see article on POWER OVER SATAN AND DEMONS, p. 80); (4) announce the guilt of sin, God's standard of righteousness and the judgment to come (Ac 2:23; 5:3,9); (5) proclaim salvation and the forgiveness of sin for all who repent and believe in Christ (Jn 20:23; Ac 2:37–40; 15:7–9).

16:24 TAKE UP HIS CROSS. See Mk 8:34, note.

16:28 COMING IN HIS KINGDOM. The "Son of Man coming in his kingdom" probably refers to the event of Pentecost when Christ baptized his followers with the Holy Spirit and great power (cf. Mk 9:1; Ac 1:8; 2:4).

17:2 WAS TRANSFIGURED. See Lk 9:29, note.

THE CHURCH

***Mt 16:18** "And I tell you that you are Peter, and on this rock I will build my church, and the gates of Hades will not overcome it."*

The Greek word *ekklēsia* (church) refers to a meeting of a people called out and summoned together. In the NT it designates primarily the congregation of God's people in Christ, who come together as citizens of God's kingdom (Eph 2:19) for the purpose of worshiping God. The word "church" can refer to a local church (Mt 18:17; Ac 15:4) or the universal church (Mt 16:18; Ac 20:28; Eph 2:21–22).

(1) The church is presented as the people of God (1Co 1:2; 10:32; 1Pe 2:4–10), the company of redeemed believers made possible by Christ's death (1Pe 1:18–19). It is a pilgrim people no longer belonging to this earth (Heb 13:12–14), whose first function is to stand as a community in a living, personal relationship with God (1Pe 2:5; see Heb 11:6, note).

(2) The church is a people called out (Gk *ekkaleō*) of the world and into God's kingdom. Separation from the world is inherent to the church's nature and is rewarded by having the Lord as one's God and Father (2Co 6:16–18; see article on SPIRITUAL SEPARATION FOR BELIEVERS, p. 371).

(3) The church is the temple of God and of the Holy Spirit (see 1Co 3:16, note; 2Co 6:14—7:1; Eph 2:11–22; 1Pe 2:4–10). This truth about the church demands separation from unrighteousness and from worldly immorality.

(4) The church is the body of Christ (1Co 6:15; 10:16–17; 12:12–27). This image indicates that no true church exists apart from vital union of the members with Christ. The head of the body is Christ (Eph 1:22; 4:15; 5:23; Col 1:18).

(5) The church is the bride of Christ (2Co 11:2; Eph 5:22–27; Rev 19:7–9). This marriage image emphasizes the devotion and faithfulness of the church to Christ as well as Christ's love for and intimacy with his church.

(6) The church is a spiritual fellowship (Gk *koinōnia*) (2Co 13:14; Php 2:1). This involves the indwelling of the Spirit (Lk 11:13; Jn 7:37–39; 20:22), the unity of the Spirit (Eph 4:4) and the baptism in the Spirit (Ac 1:5; 2:4; 8:14–17; 10:44; 19:1–7). The fellowship is to demonstrate observable love and care for one another (Jn 13:34–35).

(7) The church is a spiritual ministry (Gk *diakonia*). It serves through the use of gifts (Gk *charismata*) bestowed by the Holy Spirit (Ro 12:6; 1Co 1:7; 12:4–11,28–31; Eph 4:11).

(8) The church is an army involved in spiritual conflict. It fights by the sword and power of the Spirit (Eph 6:17). The church is in a spiritual struggle against Satan and sin (see article on THE KINGDOM OF GOD, p. 28). The Spirit, with which the church is filled, is like a warrior wielding the living Word of God, delivering people from Satan's dominion and conquering every power of this dark world (Ac 26:18; Eph 6:10–18; Heb 4:12; Rev 1:16; 2:16; 19:15,21).

(9) The church is the pillar and ground of the truth (1Ti 3:15), supporting the truth as a foundation supports a building. It must uphold the truth and keep it safe, defending it against distorters and false teachers (see Php 1:16, note; Jude 3, note).

(10) The church is a people with a future hope. This hope centers in Christ's return for his people (see Jn 14:3, note; 1Ti 6:14; 2Ti 4:8; Tit 2:13; Heb 9:28; see article on THE RAPTURE, p. 440).

(11) The church is both invisible and visible. (a) The church invisible is the body of true believers united by their living faith in Christ (see article on FAITH AND GRACE, p. 302). (b) The visible church consists of local congregations containing faithful overcomers (Rev 2:11,17,26; see 2:7, note) as well as those professed Christians who are false (Rev 2:2), "fallen" (Rev 2:5), spiritually "dead" (Rev 3:1), and "lukewarm" (Rev 3:16; see Mt 13:24, note; Ac 12:5, note on essential characteristics of a NT church).

love; with him I am well pleased.[w] Listen to him!"[x]

6When the disciples heard this, they fell facedown to the ground, terrified. 7But Jesus came and touched them. "Get up," he said. "Don't be afraid."[y] 8When they looked up, they saw no one except Jesus.

9As they were coming down the mountain, Jesus instructed them, "Don't tell anyone[z] what you have seen, until the Son of Man[a] has been raised from the dead."[b]

10The disciples asked him, "Why then do the teachers of the law say that Elijah must come first?"

11Jesus replied, "To be sure, Elijah comes and will restore all things.[c] 12But I tell you, Elijah has already come,[d] and they did not recognize him, but have done to him everything they wished.[e] In the same way the Son of Man is going to suffer[f] at their hands." 13Then the disciples understood that he was talking to them about John the Baptist.[g]

The Healing of a Boy With a Demon

17:14–19pp — Mk 9:14–28; Lk 9:37–42

14When they came to the crowd, a man approached Jesus and knelt before him. 15"Lord, have mercy on my son," he said. "He has seizures[h] and is suffering greatly. He often falls into the fire or into the water. 16I brought him to your disciples, but they could not heal him."

17"O unbelieving and perverse generation," Jesus replied, "how long shall I stay with you? How long shall I put up with you? Bring the boy here to me." 18Jesus rebuked the demon, and it came out of the boy, and he was healed from that moment.

19Then the disciples came to Jesus in private and asked, "Why couldn't we drive it out?"

20He replied, "Because you have so little faith. I tell you the truth, if you have faith[i] as small as a mustard seed,[j] you can say to this mountain, 'Move from here to there' and it will move.[k] Nothing will be impossible for you.[p]" Mt 21:21-22

22When they came together in Galilee, he said to them, "The Son of Man[l] is going to be betrayed into the hands of men. 23They will kill him,[m] and on the third day[n] he will be raised to life."[o] And the disciples were filled with grief.

The Temple Tax

24After Jesus and his disciples arrived in Capernaum, the collectors of the two-drachma tax[p] came to Peter and asked, "Doesn't your teacher pay the temple tax[q]?"

25"Yes, he does," he replied.

When Peter came into the house, Jesus was the first to speak. "What do you think, Simon?" he asked. "From whom do the kings of the earth collect duty and taxes[q]—from their own sons or from others?"

26"From others," Peter answered.

"Then the sons are exempt," Jesus said to him. 27"But so that we may not offend[r] them, go to the lake and throw out your

17:5 [w]S Mt 3:17 [x]Ac 3:22,23
17:7 [y]S Mt 14:27
17:9 [z]S Mk 8:30 [a]S Mt 8:20 [b]S Mt 16:21
17:11 [c]Mal 4:6; Lk 1:16,17
17:12 [d]S Mt 11:14 [e]Mt 14:3,10 [f]S Mt 16:21
17:13 [g]S Mt 3:1
17:15 [h]Mt 4:24
17:20 [i]S Mt 21:21 [j]Mt 13:31; Lk 17:6 [k]1Co 13:2
17:22 [l]S Mt 8:20
17:23 [m]Ac 2:23; 3:13 [n]S Mt 16:21 [o]S Mt 16:21
17:24 [p]Ex 30:13
17:25 [q]Mt 22:17-21; Ro 13:7
17:27 [r]Jn 6:61

p 20 Some manuscripts *you.* 21*But this kind does not go out except by prayer and fasting.*
q 24 Greek *the two drachmas*

17:17 UNBELIEVING AND PERVERSE. This text reflects Jesus' estimation of disciples and churches who fail to minister to others in the real power of God's kingdom (see article on THE KINGDOM OF GOD, p. 28). (1) Failure to deliver those oppressed by Satan or demons (vv. 15–21) demonstrates a lack of faith, understanding and spiritual authority (vv. 17,20–21; Mk 9:29). (2) The Holy Spirit's purpose in recording the narratives in vv. 14–21 emphasizes not only that Jesus drove out demons, but also that he desires his disciples to do the same thing through faith (vv. 20–21; see article on POWER OVER SATAN AND DEMONS, p. 80). Jesus is intensely disappointed and pained when his people fail to share in his ministry against the forces of Satan (see 10:1, note; 10:8; Mk 9:28–29; Lk 9:1; Jn 14:12, note).

17:20 FAITH ... NOTHING WILL BE IMPOSSIBLE. Jesus frequently comments on the nature of true faith. He speaks of a faith that can move mountains, cause miracles and healing, and accomplish great things for God. Just what is this faith that Jesus speaks of? (1) True faith is an effective faith that produces results: "it will move" mountains.

(2) True faith is not a belief in "faith" as a force or power, but it is a "faith in God" (Mk 11:22).

(3) True faith is a work of God within the hearts of Christians (Mk 9:24; Php 2:13). It involves an awareness divinely imparted to our hearts that our prayers are answered (Mk 11:23). It is created within us by the Holy Spirit; we cannot produce it in our own minds (Ro 12:3; 1Co 12:9).

(4) Since true faith is a gift imparted to us by Christ, it is important to draw near to Christ and his Word and to deepen our commitment to, and confidence in, him (Ro 10:17; Php 3:8–15). We are dependent on him for everything; "apart from me you can do nothing" (Jn 15:5; see also Jn 3:27; Heb 4:16; 7:25). In other words, we must seek Christ as the author and perfecter of our faith (Heb 12:2). His close presence and our obedience to his Word are the source and the secret of faith (9:21; Jn 15:7).

(5) True faith is under God's control. Faith is given on the basis of his love, wisdom, grace and kingdom purpose. It is given to accomplish his will and to express his love for us. It is not to be used for our own selfish interest (Jas 4:3).

line. Take the first fish you catch; open its
mouth and you will find a four-drachma
coin. Take it and give it to them for my tax
and yours."

The Greatest in the Kingdom of Heaven

18:1–5pp — Mk 9:33–37; Lk 9:46–48

18 At that time the disciples came to
Jesus and asked, "Who is the
greatest in the kingdom of heaven?"
2He called a little child and had him
stand among them. 3And he said: "I tell
you the truth, unless you change and become like little children,[s] you will never
enter the kingdom of heaven.[t] 4There-
fore, whoever humbles himself like this
child is the greatest in the kingdom of
heaven.[u]
5"And whoever welcomes a little child
like this in my name welcomes me.[v] 6But
if anyone causes one of these little ones
who believe in me to sin,[w] it would be
better for him to have a large millstone
hung around his neck and to be drowned
in the depths of the sea.[x]
7"Woe to the world because of the
things that cause people to sin! Such
things must come, but woe to the man
through whom they come![y] 8If your hand
or your foot causes you to sin,[z] cut it off
and throw it away. It is better for you to
enter life maimed or crippled than to have
two hands or two feet and be thrown into
eternal fire. 9And if your eye causes you
to sin,[a] gouge it out and throw it away. It
is better for you to enter life with one eye
than to have two eyes and be thrown into
the fire of hell.[b]

The Parable of the Lost Sheep

18:12–14pp — Lk 15:4–7

10"See that you do not look down on
one of these little ones. For I tell you that
their angels[c] in heaven always see the
face of my Father in heaven.[r]
12"What do you think? If a man owns a
hundred sheep, and one of them wanders
away, will he not leave the ninety-nine on
the hills and go to look for the one that
wandered off? 13And if he finds it, I tell
you the truth, he is happier about that one
sheep than about the ninety-nine that did
not wander off. 14In the same way your
Father in heaven is not willing that any of
these little ones should be lost.

A Brother Who Sins Against You

15"If your brother sins against you,[s] go

18:3 [s]Mt 19:14; 1Pe 2:2 [t]S Mt 3:2 **18:4** [u]S Mk 9:35 **18:5** [v]Mt 10:40 **18:6** [w]S Mt 5:29 [x]Mk 9:42; Lk 17:2 **18:7** [y]Lk 17:1 **18:8** [z]S Mt 5:29 **18:9** [a]S Mt 5:29 [b]S Mt 5:22 **18:10** [c]Ge 48:16; Ps 34:7; Ac 12:11, 15; Heb 1:14

[r] *10* Some manuscripts *heaven. 11The Son of Man came to save what was lost.* [s] *15* Some manuscripts do not have *against you.*

18:1 WHO IS THE GREATEST. See Lk 22:24–30, note.

18:3 UNLESS YOU CHANGE. The conversion or change required by Jesus consists of two parts: radically turning away from everything that is ungodly, and turning to God and doing the works of righteousness (i.e., producing fruit in keeping with repentance; see 3:8, note).

(1) It does not denote merely a single act of sorrow or penitence but an all-embracing attitude of life. This is necessary because by nature we follow a way of life that leads away from God and toward eternal death (Ro 1:18–32; Eph 2:2–3). Conversion is the human response to God's gift of salvation, accomplished by the grace and power of the Holy Spirit received through faith (Ac 11:18).

(2) Because of our new relation to God, conversion involves changes in the areas of relationships, habits, commitments, pleasures and our whole view of life. Conversion is a part of genuine saving faith and a basic requirement of salvation and sanctification (Ac 26:18).

18:6 MILLSTONE ... AROUND HIS NECK. This verse means that whoever spiritually destroys a child or a childlike believer will incur the greatest wrath of Christ. (1) Pastors, teachers and especially parents should give special attention to these words of Christ. The parents' responsibility is to instruct their children in the ways of God (see Dt 6:1–9; Lk 1:17, note; Eph 6:4; 1Ti 4:16; see article on PARENTS AND CHILDREN, p. 432) and to protect them from the influence of the world and Satan (Tit 1:10–11; 2:11–12; 1Jn 2:15–17). (2) Christian parents must not allow their children to be influenced by ungodly friends. They must be especially careful about what they allow the world to put into their children's minds and hearts by means of public education or the entertainment media (cf. Ps 101:3; Eph 6:4; Col 3:21).

18:7 WOE TO THE MAN. Jesus warns that those who are instrumental in placing sinful things before others and especially before children will receive the ultimate condemnation (vv. 2,5–7). (1) To place "things that cause people to sin" in the path of others—such as worldly entertainment, humanistic teaching, immoral films, pornographic literature, drugs, alcoholic beverages, wicked examples, false teaching and unrighteous companions—is to join oneself with Satan who is the great tempter (cf. 4:1; Ge 3:1–6; Jn 8:44; Jas 1:12). (2) The godly way of the faithful is to remove from the lives of our family, our homes, our churches and our own selves any and all things that might lead others into temptation and sin (vv. 7–9).

18:10 ANGELS. Scripture teaches that God often takes care of his faithful by means of angels. These angels carry a sincere interest and love for God's children (cf. Ps 34:7; 91:11; Lk 15:10; 16:22; Heb 1:14; Rev 5:11–12; see Heb 1:13, note).

18:15 IF YOUR BROTHER SINS. In vv. 15–17 Jesus sets forth the method of restoring or disciplining a professing Christian who sins against another mem-

and show him his fault,[d] just between the
two of you. If he listens to you, you have
won your brother over. 16But if he will not
listen, take one or two others along, so
that 'every matter may be established by
the testimony of two or three witnesses.'[t][e] 17If he refuses to listen to
them, tell it to the church;[f] and if he refuses to listen even to the church, treat
him as you would a pagan or a tax collector.[g]
18"I tell you the truth, whatever you
bind on earth will be[u] bound in heaven,
and whatever you loose on earth will be[u]
loosed in heaven.[h]
19"Again, I tell you that if two of you on
earth agree about anything you ask for, it
will be done for you[i] by my Father in
heaven. 20For where two or three come
together in my name, there am I with
them."[j]

The Parable of the Unmerciful Servant

21Then Peter came to Jesus and asked,
"Lord, how many times shall I forgive my
brother when he sins against me?[k] Up to
seven times?"[l]
22Jesus answered, "I tell you, not seven
times, but seventy-seven times.[v][m]
23"Therefore, the kingdom of heaven is
like[n] a king who wanted to settle accounts[o] with his servants. 24As he began
the settlement, a man who owed him ten
thousand talents[w] was brought to him.
25Since he was not able to pay,[p] the master ordered that he and his wife and his
children and all that he had be sold[q] to
repay the debt.
26"The servant fell on his knees before
him.[r] 'Be patient with me,' he begged,
'and I will pay back everything.' 27The
servant's master took pity on him, canceled the debt and let him go.
28"But when that servant went out, he
found one of his fellow servants who owed
him a hundred denarii.[x] He grabbed him
and began to choke him. 'Pay back what
you owe me!' he demanded.
29"His fellow servant fell to his knees
and begged him, 'Be patient with me, and
I will pay you back.'
30"But he refused. Instead, he went off
and had the man thrown into prison until
he could pay the debt. 31When the other
servants saw what had happened, they
were greatly distressed and went and told
their master everything that had happened.
32"Then the master called the servant

18:15 [d]Lev 19:17; Lk 17:3; Gal 6:1; Jas 5:19,20
18:16 [e]Nu 35:30; Dt 17:6; 19:15; Jn 8:17; 2Co 13:1; 1Ti 5:19; Heb 10:28
18:17 [f]1Co 6:1-6 [g]S Ro 16:17
18:18 [h]Mt 16:19; Jn 20:23
18:19 [i]S Mt 7:7
18:20 [j]S Mt 28:20
18:21 [k]S Mt 6:14 [l]Lk 17:4
18:22 [m]Ge 4:24
18:23 [n]S Mt 13:24 [o]Mt 25:19
18:25 [p]Lk 7:42 [q]Lev 25:39; 2Ki 4:1; Ne 5:5,8
18:26 [r]S Mt 8:2

[t] 16 Deut. 19:15 [u] 18 Or *have been* [v] 22 Or *seventy times seven* [w] 24 That is, millions of dollars [x] 28 That is, a few dollars

ber of the church in a private manner. To neglect Christ's instruction will bring spiritual compromise and ultimate destruction to the church as a holy people of God (cf. 1Pe 2:9; see Mt 5:13, note).

(1) The purpose of church discipline is to protect God's reputation (6:9; Ro 2:23–24), to guard the moral purity and doctrinal integrity of the church (1Co 5:6–7; 2Jn 7–11), and to attempt to save wayward members and restore them to full Christlikeness (1Co 5:5; Jas 5:19–20).

(2) The offender must first be dealt with and admonished in private. If he listens, he must be forgiven (v. 15). If the offender refuses to respond to his Christian brother (vv. 15–16), and after that to one or two members (v. 16) and finally to the local church, he must be treated as "a pagan," i.e., as one outside the kingdom of God, severed from Christ and fallen from grace (v. 17; cf. Gal 5:4). He has no right to church membership and must be removed from the fellowship of the church.

(3) This practice of the purity of the church is to operate not only in areas of sin and immorality, but also in cases of doctrinal heresy and unfaithfulness to the original and fundamental NT faith (see Gal 1:9, note; Jude 3, note; see articles on FALSE TEACHERS, p. 98, and OVERSEERS AND THEIR DUTIES, p. 274).

(4) Church discipline must be carried out in a spirit of humility, love, regret and self-examination (see 22:37, note; 2Co 2:6–7; Gal 6:1).

(5) Sins within the church involving sexual immorality must be dealt with according to 1Co 5:1–5 and 2Co 2:6–11. These types of grave sins require regret and mourning by the whole congregation (1Co 5:2), "punishment . . . sufficient" for the transgressor (2Co 2:6) and expulsion from the church (1Co 5:2,13). Later, after a period of evident repentance, the individual may be forgiven, receive a reaffirmation of love and be restored to fellowship (2Co 2:6–8).

(6) Sins of an elder, after being dealt with privately, must also involve public exposure and discipline, i.e., "rebuked publicly, so that the others may take warning" (Gal 2:11–18; 1Ti 5:19–20, note; see article on MORAL QUALIFICATIONS FOR OVERSEERS, p. 458).

(7) Leaders within the church and pastors of local congregations do well to remember that they are charged to "keep watch over . . . all the flock" (see article on OVERSEERS AND THEIR DUTIES, p. 274). The Lord will require of them a personal accounting of "the blood of all men" (Ac 20:26) who are lost because leaders failed to restore, discipline or expel according to God's will and purpose (cf. Eze 3:20–21; Ac 20:26–27).

18:19 IF TWO . . . AGREE. There is great authority in corporate and agreeing prayer. The reason is that where two or three are gathered together in faith and commitment to Christ, he is in their midst (v. 20). His presence will impart faith, strength, direction, grace and consolation (cf. Ps 46:5; Isa 12:6).

in. 'You wicked servant,' he said, 'I canceled all that debt of yours because you
begged me to. 33 Shouldn't you have had
mercy on your fellow servant just as I had
on you?' 34 In anger his master turned him
over to the jailers to be tortured, until he
should pay back all he owed.

35 "This is how my heavenly Father will
treat each of you unless you forgive your
brother from your heart."[s]

Divorce

19:1–9pp — Mk 10:1–12

19 When Jesus had finished saying
these things,[t] he left Galilee and
went into the region of Judea to the other
side of the Jordan. 2 Large crowds followed
him, and he healed them[u] there.

3 Some Pharisees came to him to test
him. They asked, "Is it lawful for a man to
divorce his wife[v] for any and every reason?"

4 "Haven't you read," he replied, "that at
the beginning the Creator 'made them
male and female,'[y][w] 5 and said, 'For this
reason a man will leave his father and
mother and be united to his wife, and the
two will become one flesh'[z]?[x] 6 So they
are no longer two, but one. Therefore
what God has joined together, let man not
separate."

7 "Why then," they asked, "did Moses
command that a man give his wife a certificate of divorce and send her away?"[y]

8 Jesus replied, "Moses permitted you to
divorce your wives because your hearts
were hard. But it was not this way from
the beginning. 9 I tell you that anyone who
divorces his wife, except for marital unfaithfulness, and marries another woman
commits adultery."[z]

10 The disciples said to him, "If this is
the situation between a husband and wife,
it is better not to marry."

11 Jesus replied, "Not everyone can accept this word, but only those to whom it
has been given.[a] 12 For some are eunuchs
because they were born that way; others
were made that way by men; and others
have renounced marriage[a] because of the
kingdom of heaven. The one who can accept this should accept it."

The Little Children and Jesus

19:13–15pp — Mk 10:13–16; Lk 18:15–17

13 Then little children were brought to
Jesus for him to place his hands on them[b]
and pray for them. But the disciples rebuked those who brought them.

14 Jesus said, "Let the little children
come to me, and do not hinder them, for
the kingdom of heaven belongs[c] to such
as these."[d] 15 When he had placed his
hands on them, he went on from there.

The Rich Young Man

19:16–29pp — Mk 10:17–30; Lk 18:18–30

16 Now a man came up to Jesus and
asked, "Teacher, what good thing must I
do to get eternal life[e]?"[f]

17 "Why do you ask me about what is
good?" Jesus replied. "There is only One

18:35 s S Mt 6:14; S Jas 2:13
19:1 t S Mt 7:28
19:2 u S Mt 4:23
19:3 v Mt 5:31
19:4 w Ge 1:27; 5:2
19:5 x Ge 2:24; 1Co 6:16; Eph 5:31
19:7 y Dt 24:1-4; Mt 5:31
19:9 z S Lk 16:18
19:11 a S Mt 13:11; 1Co 7:7-9,17
19:13 b S Mk 5:23
19:14 c S Mt 25:34 d Mt 18:3; 1Pe 2:2
19:16 e S Mt 25:46 f Lk 10:25

y 4 Gen. 1:27 z 5 Gen. 2:24 a 12 Or *have made themselves eunuchs*

18:35 UNLESS YOU FORGIVE. In this parable, Jesus teaches that the forgiveness of God, though freely given to repentant sinners, nevertheless remains conditional, according to a person's willingness to forgive others. In other words, one may forfeit God's forgiveness by maintaining a bitter and unforgiving heart (see 6:14–15; Heb 12:15; Jas 3:11,14; note especially Eph 4:31–32, where Paul maintains that bitterness, resentment and animosity are totally incompatible with the Christian profession and must be done away with).

19:9 EXCEPT FOR MARITAL UNFAITHFULNESS. God's will for marriage is one mate, one marriage for life (vv. 5–6; Ge 1:27; 2:24; Mk 10:6). To this Jesus gives an exception, namely, "marital unfaithfulness." Marital unfaithfulness (Gk *porneia*) includes adultery or any kind of sexual immorality (cf. 5:32). Therefore, divorce is to be permitted when sexual immorality is involved. The following are important Biblical facts concerning divorce. (1) When Jesus criticizes divorce in vv. 7–8, he is not criticizing a separation because of adultery, but a divorce permitted in the OT in those cases where a husband discovered premarital unchastity after the marriage ceremony had taken place (Dt 24:1–4). God's desire in such cases was that the two remain together. However, he permitted divorce due to premarital unchastity because of the hardness of the people's hearts (vv. 7–8).

(2) In the case of immorality after marriage, the OT law prescribed the dissolving of the marriage by executing both the offending parties (Lev 20:10; Dt 22:22). This, of course, would leave the innocent person free to remarry (Ro 7:2; 1Co 7:39).

(3) Under the new covenant the privileges of the believer are no less. Although divorce is a tragedy, marital unfaithfulness is such a cruel sin against one's mate that Christ states that the innocent party has a proper right to end the marriage by a divorce. He or she is free to remarry another believer (1Co 7:27–28).

(4) Paul's treatment of marriage and desertion in 1Co 7:12–16 indicates that a marriage also may be dissolved by the desertion of an unbelieving spouse. He further indicates that remarriage by the believer in such cases is not sin (see 1Co 7:15, note; 7:27–28).

19:13 LITTLE CHILDREN. See Mk 10:16, note.

who is good. If you want to enter life, obey the commandments."[g]

18"Which ones?" the man inquired.

Jesus replied, " 'Do not murder, do not commit adultery,[h] do not steal, do not give false testimony, 19honor your father and mother,'[b][i] and 'love your neighbor as yourself.'[c]"[j]

20"All these I have kept," the young man said. "What do I still lack?"

21Jesus answered, "If you want to be perfect,[k] go, sell your possessions and give to the poor,[l] and you will have treasure in heaven.[m] Then come, follow me."

22When the young man heard this, he went away sad, because he had great wealth.

23Then Jesus said to his disciples, "I tell you the truth, it is hard for a rich man[n] to enter the kingdom of heaven. 24Again I tell you, it is easier for a camel to go through the eye of a needle than for a rich man to enter the kingdom of God."

25When the disciples heard this, they were greatly astonished and asked, "Who then can be saved?"

26Jesus looked at them and said, "With man this is impossible, but with God all things are possible."[o]

27Peter answered him, "We have left everything to follow you![p] What then will there be for us?"

28Jesus said to them, "I tell you the truth, at the renewal of all things, when the Son of Man sits on his glorious throne,[q] you who have followed me will also sit on twelve thrones, judging the twelve tribes of Israel.[r] 29And everyone who has left houses or brothers or sisters or father or mother[d] or children or fields for my sake will receive a hundred times as much and will inherit eternal life.[s] 30But many who are first will be last, and many who are last will be first.[t]

The Parable of the Workers in the Vineyard

20 "For the kingdom of heaven is like[u] a landowner who went out early in the morning to hire men to work in his vineyard.[v] 2He agreed to pay them a denarius for the day and sent them into his vineyard.

3"About the third hour he went out and saw others standing in the marketplace doing nothing. 4He told them, 'You also go and work in my vineyard, and I will pay you whatever is right.' 5So they went.

"He went out again about the sixth hour and the ninth hour and did the same thing. 6About the eleventh hour he went out and found still others standing around. He asked them, 'Why have you been standing here all day long doing nothing?'

7" 'Because no one has hired us,' they answered.

"He said to them, 'You also go and work in my vineyard.'

8"When evening came,[w] the owner of the vineyard said to his foreman, 'Call the workers and pay them their wages, beginning with the last ones hired and going on to the first.'

9"The workers who were hired about the eleventh hour came and each received a denarius. 10So when those came who were hired first, they expected to receive more. But each one of them also received a denarius. 11When they received it, they began to grumble[x] against the landowner. 12'These men who were hired last worked only one hour,' they said, 'and you have

19:17 [g]Lev 18:5
19:18 [h]Jas 2:11
19:19 [i]Ex 20:12-16; Dt 5:16-20 [j]Lev 19:18; S Mt 5:43
19:21 [k]Mt 5:48 [l]S Ac 2:45 [m]S Mt 6:20
19:23 [n]Mt 13:22; 1Ti 6:9,10
19:26 [o]Ge 18:14; Job 42:2; Jer 32:17; Lk 1:37; 18:27; Ro 4:21
19:27 [p]S Mt 4:19
19:28 [q]Mt 20:21; 25:31 [r]Lk 22:28-30; Rev 3:21; 4:4; 20:4
19:29 [s]Mt 6:33; S 25:46
19:30 [t]Mt 20:16; Mk 10:31; Lk 13:30
20:1 [u]S Mt 13:24 [v]Mt 21:28,33
20:8 [w]Lev 19:13; Dt 24:15
20:11 [x]Jnh 4:1

[b] *19* Exodus 20:12-16; Deut. 5:16-20
[c] *19* Lev. 19:18
[d] *29* Some manuscripts *mother or wife*

19:21 GO, SELL YOUR POSSESSIONS. Jesus tested the rich young man at his weakest area, his wealth. He was not willing to put Christ above his possessions. Does Christ's statement mean that all believers should sell everything they own? No, for we must care for the needs of our families and others. However, we must be willing to give up anything that Christ asks of us. Our commitment to him can be nothing less.

19:23 A RICH MAN . . . THE KINGDOM. See article on RICHES AND POVERTY, p. 152.

19:29 RECEIVE A HUNDRED TIMES. See Mk 10:30, note.

19:30 FIRST WILL BE LAST. The "first" are those who because of their wealth, education, status or talents are held in esteem by the world and sometimes even by the church. The "last" are those who are unknown and considered unimportant. In the age to come, "many" who were thought to be great leaders in the church will be given positions behind others, and many who were unknown will be exalted to glorious positions (cf. 1Co 15:41–42). This is because God values people not by outward appearance, but by the sincerity, purity and love of their hearts (1Sa 16:7). Read the stories of the poor widow (Mk 12:42–44) and Mary of Bethany (26:7–13) to see Christ's attitude toward the humble.

20:1 MEN TO WORK IN HIS VINEYARD. The parable of the workers in the vineyard teaches that entrance into God's kingdom is a matter of privilege, not merit. Christ here warns against three wrong attitudes: (1) Do not feel superior because of a fortunate position or assignment. (2) Do not fail to share God's concern in offering his grace to all. (3) Avoid the spirit of envy toward the spiritual blessings of others.

made them equal to us who have borne the
burden of the work and the heat[y] of the
day.'
13"But he answered one of them,
'Friend,[z] I am not being unfair to you.
Didn't you agree to work for a denarius?
14Take your pay and go. I want to give the
man who was hired last the same as I gave
you. 15Don't I have the right to do what I
want with my own money? Or are you envious because I am generous?'[a]
16"So the last will be first, and the first
will be last."[b]

Jesus Again Predicts His Death

20:17–19pp — Mk 10:32–34; Lk 18:31–33

17Now as Jesus was going up to Jerusalem, he took the twelve disciples aside
and said to them, 18"We are going up to
Jerusalem,[c] and the Son of Man[d] will be
betrayed to the chief priests and the
teachers of the law.[e] They will condemn
him to death 19and will turn him over to
the Gentiles to be mocked and flogged[f]
and crucified.[g] On the third day[h] he will
be raised to life!"[i]

A Mother's Request

20:20–28pp — Mk 10:35–45

20Then the mother of Zebedee's sons[j]
came to Jesus with her sons and, kneeling
down,[k] asked a favor of him.
21"What is it you want?" he asked.
She said, "Grant that one of these two
sons of mine may sit at your right and the
other at your left in your kingdom."[l]
22"You don't know what you are asking," Jesus said to them. "Can you drink
the cup[m] I am going to drink?"
"We can," they answered.
23Jesus said to them, "You will indeed
drink from my cup,[n] but to sit at my right
or left is not for me to grant. These places
belong to those for whom they have been
prepared by my Father."
24When the ten heard about this, they
were indignant[o] with the two brothers.
25Jesus called them together and said,
"You know that the rulers of the Gentiles
lord it over them, and their high officials
exercise authority over them. 26Not so
with you. Instead, whoever wants to become great among you must be your servant,[p] 27and whoever wants to be first
must be your slave— 28just as the Son of
Man[q] did not come to be served, but to
serve,[r] and to give his life as a ransom[s]
for many."

Two Blind Men Receive Sight

20:29–34pp — Mk 10:46–52; Lk 18:35–43

29As Jesus and his disciples were leaving Jericho, a large crowd followed him.
30Two blind men were sitting by the roadside, and when they heard that Jesus was
going by, they shouted, "Lord, Son of David,[t] have mercy on us!"
31The crowd rebuked them and told
them to be quiet, but they shouted all the
louder, "Lord, Son of David, have mercy
on us!"
32Jesus stopped and called them. "What
do you want me to do for you?" he asked.
33"Lord," they answered, "we want our
sight."
34Jesus had compassion on them and
touched their eyes. Immediately they received their sight and followed him.

The Triumphal Entry

21:1–9pp — Mk 11:1–10; Lk 19:29–38
21:4–9pp — Jn 12:12–15

21 As they approached Jerusalem and
came to Bethphage on the Mount
of Olives,[u] Jesus sent two disciples, 2say-
ing to them, "Go to the village ahead of
you, and at once you will find a donkey
tied there, with her colt by her. Untie them
and bring them to me. 3If anyone says
anything to you, tell him that the Lord
needs them, and he will send them right
away."
4This took place to fulfill[v] what was
spoken through the prophet:

5"Say to the Daughter of Zion,
'See, your king comes to you,

20:12 [y]Jnh 4:8; Lk 12:55; Jas 1:11 **20:13** [z]Mt 22:12; 26:50 **20:15** [a]Dt 15:9; Mk 7:22 **20:16** [b]S Mt 19:30 **20:18** [c]S Lk 9:51 [d]S Mt 8:20 [e]Mt 27:1,2 **20:19** [f]S Mt 16:21 [g]S Ac 2:23 [h]S Mt 16:21 [i]S Mt 16:21 **20:20** [j]S Mt 4:21 [k]S Mt 8:2 **20:21** [l]Mt 19:28 **20:22** [m]Isa 51:17,22; Jer 49:12; Mt 26:39,42; Mk 14:36; Lk 22:42; Jn 18:11 **20:23** [n]Ac 12:2; Rev 1:9 **20:24** [o]Lk 22:24, 25 **20:26** [p]S Mk 9:35 **20:28** [q]S Mt 8:20 [r]Isa 42:1; Lk 12:37; 22:27; Jn 13:13-16; 2Co 8:9; Php 2:7 [s]Ex 30:12; Isa 44:22; 53:10; Mt 26:28; 1Ti 2:6; Tit 2:14; Heb 9:28; 1Pe 1:18,19 **20:30** [t]S Mt 9:27 **21:1** [u]Mt 24:3; 26:30; Mk 14:26; Lk 19:37; 21:37; 22:39; Jn 8:1; Ac 1:12 **21:4** [v]S Mt 1:22

20:26 NOT SO WITH YOU. In this world those who "lord it over" and "exercise authority" are considered great men and women. Jesus says that in the kingdom of God greatness will not be measured by authority over others, but by giving one's self in service according to the Biblical revelation of Christ. Believers must not try to reach the top in order to exert their authority or rule. Rather they must give their lives in helping others, and especially in laboring for the spiritual good of all people (v. 28; cf. Jn 13:34; 1Co 13; Col 3:14; 1Jn 3:14; 4:8).

20:28 RANSOM FOR MANY. Ransom conveys the meaning of a price paid to obtain the freedom of others. In the redemptive work of Christ, his death is the price paid for the release of men and women from sin's dominion. The release is from condemnation (Ro 3:25–26), sin (Eph 1:7) and death (Ro 8:2). "Many" is used in the sense of "all people" (1Ti 2:5–6; see Ro 3:25, note on the meaning of the cross of Christ).

gentle and riding on a donkey,
on a colt, the foal of a donkey.' "[e][w]

[6]The disciples went and did as Jesus
had instructed them. [7]They brought the
donkey and the colt, placed their cloaks
on them, and Jesus sat on them. [8]A very
large crowd spread their cloaks[x] on the
road, while others cut branches from the
trees and spread them on the road. [9]The
crowds that went ahead of him and those
that followed shouted,

"Hosanna[f] to the Son of David!"[y]

"Blessed is he who comes in the
name of the Lord!"[g][z]

"Hosanna[f] in the highest!"[a]

[10]When Jesus entered Jerusalem, the
whole city was stirred and asked, "Who is
this?"

[11]The crowds answered, "This is Jesus,
the prophet[b] from Nazareth in Galilee."

Jesus at the Temple

21:12–16pp — Mk 11:15–18; Lk 19:45–47

[12]Jesus entered the temple area and
drove out all who were buying[c] and selling there. He overturned the tables of the
money changers[d] and the benches of
those selling doves.[e] [13]"It is written," he
said to them, " 'My house will be called a
house of prayer,'[h][f] but you are making it
a 'den of robbers.'[i]"[g]

[14]The blind and the lame came to him
at the temple, and he healed them.[h] [15]But
when the chief priests and the teachers of
the law saw the wonderful things he did
and the children shouting in the temple
area, "Hosanna to the Son of David,"[i]
they were indignant.[j]

[16]"Do you hear what these children are
saying?" they asked him.

"Yes," replied Jesus, "have you never
read,

" 'From the lips of children and
infants
you have ordained praise'[j]?"[k]

[17]And he left them and went out of the
city to Bethany,[l] where he spent the
night.

The Fig Tree Withers

21:18–22pp — Mk 11:12–14,20–24

[18]Early in the morning, as he was on his
way back to the city, he was hungry.
[19]Seeing a fig tree by the road, he went up
to it but found nothing on it except leaves.
Then he said to it, "May you never bear
fruit again!" Immediately the tree withered.[m]

[20]When the disciples saw this, they
were amazed. "How did the fig tree wither
so quickly?" they asked.

[21]Jesus replied, "I tell you the truth, if
you have faith and do not doubt,[n] not only
can you do what was done to the fig tree,
but also you can say to this mountain, 'Go,
throw yourself into the sea,' and it will be
done. [22]If you believe, you will receive
whatever you ask for[o] in prayer." Mk 4:40

The Authority of Jesus Questioned

21:23–27pp — Mk 11:27–33; Lk 20:1–8

[23]Jesus entered the temple courts, and,
while he was teaching, the chief priests
and the elders of the people came to him.
"By what authority[p] are you doing these
things?" they asked. "And who gave you
this authority?"

[24]Jesus replied, "I will also ask you one
question. If you answer me, I will tell you
by what authority I am doing these things.
[25]John's baptism—where did it come
from? Was it from heaven, or from men?"

They discussed it among themselves
and said, "If we say, 'From heaven,' he
will ask, 'Then why didn't you believe
him?' [26]But if we say, 'From men'—we
are afraid of the people, for they all hold
that John was a prophet."[q]

[27]So they answered Jesus, "We don't
know."

21:5 [w]Zec 9:9; Isa 62:11
21:8 [x]2Ki 9:13
21:9 [y]ver 15; S Mt 9:27 [z]Ps 118:26; Mt 23:39 [a]Lk 2:14
21:11 [b]Dt 18:15; Lk 7:16,39; 24:19; Jn 1:21,25; 6:14; 7:40
21:12 [c]Dt 14:26 [d]Ex 30:13 [e]Lev 1:14
21:13 [f]Isa 56:7 [g]Jer 7:11
21:14 [h]S Mt 4:23
21:15 [i]ver 9; S Mt 9:27 [j]Lk 19:39
21:16 [k]Ps 8:2
21:17 [l]Mt 26:6; Mk 11:1; Lk 24:50; Jn 11:1, 18; 12:1
21:19 [m]Isa 34:4; Jer 8:13
21:21 [n]Mt 17:20; Lk 17:6; 1Co 13:2; Jas 1:6
21:22 [o]S Mt 7:7
21:23 [p]Ac 4:7; 7:27
21:26 [q]S Mt 11:9

[e] *5* Zech. 9:9 [f] *9* A Hebrew expression meaning "Save!" which became an exclamation of praise; also in verse 15 [g] *9* Psalm 118:26
[h] *13* Isaiah 56:7 [i] *13* Jer. 7:11 [j] *16* Psalm 8:2

21:12 JESUS ... OVERTURNED THE TABLES. This is the second time that Jesus entered the temple and cleansed it from unrighteousness (for the temple cleansing at the beginning of his ministry, see Lk 19:45, note; Jn 2:13–22). Those who bear Christ's name must know that hypocrisy, greed, self-serving interest, immorality and irreverence in the house of God will bring God's judgment and righteous indignation. Christ is Lord of his church and demands that it be a "house of prayer" (v. 13).

21:13 A HOUSE OF PRAYER. See Mk 11:17, note.

21:21 IF YOU HAVE FAITH. Jesus speaks of faith and prayer (v. 22), stating that answers to prayer are related to our faith. Everything that is in harmony with God's will is possible to perform or receive for those who do not doubt (see 17:20, note; Mk 11:24, note; cf. 1Ki 17:1,7; 18:42–45; Lk 17:5–6). This does not exclude other variables in receiving answers to prayer (e.g., Da 10:12–14; Jas 4:3).

Then he said, "Neither will I tell you by what authority I am doing these things.

The Parable of the Two Sons

28"What do you think? There was a man who had two sons. He went to the first and said, 'Son, go and work today in the vineyard.'[r]

29" 'I will not,' he answered, but later he changed his mind and went.

30"Then the father went to the other son and said the same thing. He answered, 'I will, sir,' but he did not go.

31"Which of the two did what his father wanted?"

"The first," they answered.

Jesus said to them, "I tell you the truth, the tax collectors[s] and the prostitutes[t] are entering the kingdom of God ahead of you. 32For John came to you to show you the way of righteousness,[u] and you did not believe him, but the tax collectors[v] and the prostitutes[w] did. And even after you saw this, you did not repent[x] and believe him.

The Parable of the Tenants

21:33–46pp — Mk 12:1–12; Lk 20:9–19

33"Listen to another parable: There was a landowner who planted[y] a vineyard. He put a wall around it, dug a winepress in it and built a watchtower.[z] Then he rented the vineyard to some farmers and went away on a journey.[a] 34When the harvest time approached, he sent his servants[b] to the tenants to collect his fruit.

35"The tenants seized his servants; they beat one, killed another, and stoned a third.[c] 36Then he sent other servants[d] to them, more than the first time, and the tenants treated them the same way. 37Last of all, he sent his son to them. 'They will respect my son,' he said.

38"But when the tenants saw the son, they said to each other, 'This is the heir.[e] Come, let's kill him[f] and take his inheritance.'[g] 39So they took him and threw him out of the vineyard and killed him.

40"Therefore, when the owner of the vineyard comes, what will he do to those tenants?"

21:28 [r] ver 33; Mt 20:1 **21:31** [s] Lk 7:29 [t] Lk 7:50 **21:32** [u] Mt 3:1-12 [v] Lk 3:12,13; 7:29 [w] Lk 7:36-50 [x] Lk 7:30 **21:33** [y] Ps 80:8 [z] Isa 5:1-7 [a] Mt 25:14,15 **21:34** [b] Mt 22:3 **21:35** [c] 2Ch 24:21; Mt 23:34,37; Heb 11:36,37 **21:36** [d] Mt 22:4 **21:38** [e] Heb 1:2 [f] S Mt 12:14 [g] Ps 2:8

21:41 [h] Mt 8:11, 12 [i] S Ac 13:46 **21:42** [j] Ps 118:22,23; S Ac 4:11 **21:43** [k] Mt 8:12 **21:44** [l] S Lk 2:34 **21:46** [m] S ver 11, 26 **22:2** [n] S Mt 13:24 **22:3** [o] Mt 21:34 **22:4** [p] Mt 21:36 **22:7** [q] Lk 19:27

41"He will bring those wretches to a wretched end,"[h] they replied, "and he will rent the vineyard to other tenants,[i] who will give him his share of the crop at harvest time."

42Jesus said to them, "Have you never read in the Scriptures:

" 'The stone the builders rejected
 has become the capstone[k];
the Lord has done this,
 and it is marvelous in our eyes'[l]?[j]

43"Therefore I tell you that the kingdom of God will be taken away from you[k] and given to a people who will produce its fruit. 44He who falls on this stone will be broken to pieces, but he on whom it falls will be crushed."[m][l]

45When the chief priests and the Pharisees heard Jesus' parables, they knew he was talking about them. 46They looked for a way to arrest him, but they were afraid of the crowd because the people held that he was a prophet.[m]

The Parable of the Wedding Banquet

22:2–14Ref — Lk 14:16–24

22 Jesus spoke to them again in parables, saying: 2"The kingdom of heaven is like[n] a king who prepared a wedding banquet for his son. 3He sent his servants[o] to those who had been invited to the banquet to tell them to come, but they refused to come.

4"Then he sent some more servants[p] and said, 'Tell those who have been invited that I have prepared my dinner: My oxen and fattened cattle have been butchered, and everything is ready. Come to the wedding banquet.'

5"But they paid no attention and went off—one to his field, another to his business. 6The rest seized his servants, mistreated them and killed them. 7The king was enraged. He sent his army and destroyed those murderers[q] and burned their city.

8"Then he said to his servants, 'The

k *42* Or *cornerstone* l *42* Psalm 118:22,23
m *44* Some manuscripts do not have verse 44.

21:33–44 THE TENANTS. This parable pictures Israel's rejection of God's beloved Son (cf. Mk 12:1, note; Lk 20:9).

21:43 KINGDOM . . . TAKEN AWAY FROM YOU. Israel rejects the Messiah and his kingdom. As a result, the kingdom of God and its power are given to others, to those who respond to the gospel, whether they are Jew or Gentile (1Pe 2:9). This principle is still in operation. The kingdom and its power will be taken away from those who fail to remain faithful to Christ, rejecting his righteous ways (Ro 11:19–22); instead, it will be given to a people who separate themselves from the world and seek first God's kingdom and righteousness (see 5:6; 6:33).

21:44 WILL BE BROKEN TO PIECES. See Lk 20:18, note.

wedding banquet is ready, but those I invited did not deserve to come. **9**Go to the street corners[r] and invite to the banquet anyone you find.' **10**So the servants went out into the streets and gathered all the people they could find, both good and bad,[s] and the wedding hall was filled with guests.

11"But when the king came in to see the guests, he noticed a man there who was not wearing wedding clothes. **12**'Friend,'[t] he asked, 'how did you get in here without wedding clothes?' The man was speechless.

13"Then the king told the attendants, 'Tie him hand and foot, and throw him outside, into the darkness, where there will be weeping and gnashing of teeth.'[u]

14"For many are invited, but few are chosen."[v]

Paying Taxes to Caesar

22:15–22pp — Mk 12:13–17; Lk 20:20–26

15Then the Pharisees went out and laid plans to trap him in his words. **16**They sent their disciples to him along with the Herodians.[w] "Teacher," they said, "we know you are a man of integrity and that you teach the way of God in accordance with the truth. You aren't swayed by men, because you pay no attention to who they are. **17**Tell us then, what is your opinion? Is it right to pay taxes[x] to Caesar or not?"

18But Jesus, knowing their evil intent, said, "You hypocrites, why are you trying to trap me? **19**Show me the coin used for paying the tax." They brought him a denarius, **20**and he asked them, "Whose portrait is this? And whose inscription?"

21"Caesar's," they replied.

Then he said to them, "Give to Caesar what is Caesar's,[y] and to God what is God's."

22When they heard this, they were amazed. So they left him and went away.[z]

22:9 [r]Eze 21:21
22:10 [s]Mt 13:47, 48
22:12 [t]Mt 20:13; 26:50
22:13 [u]S Mt 8:12
22:14 [v]Rev 17:14
22:16 [w]Mk 3:6
22:17 [x]Mt 17:25
22:21 [y]Ro 13:7
22:22 [z]Mk 12:12
22:23 [a]S Ac 4:1 [b]Ac 23:8; 1Co 15:12
22:24 [c]Dt 25:5,6
22:29 [d]Jn 20:9
22:30 [e]Mt 24:38
22:32 [f]Ex 3:6; Ac 7:32
22:33 [g]S Mt 7:28
22:34 [h]S Ac 4:1
22:35 [i]Lk 7:30; 10:25; 11:45; 14:3

Marriage at the Resurrection

22:23–33pp — Mk 12:18–27; Lk 20:27–40

23That same day the Sadducees,[a] who say there is no resurrection,[b] came to him with a question. **24**"Teacher," they said, "Moses told us that if a man dies without having children, his brother must marry the widow and have children for him.[c] **25**Now there were seven brothers among us. The first one married and died, and since he had no children, he left his wife to his brother. **26**The same thing happened to the second and third brother, right on down to the seventh. **27**Finally, the woman died. **28**Now then, at the resurrection, whose wife will she be of the seven, since all of them were married to her?"

29Jesus replied, "You are in error because you do not know the Scriptures[d] or the power of God. **30**At the resurrection people will neither marry nor be given in marriage;[e] they will be like the angels in heaven. **31**But about the resurrection of the dead—have you not read what God said to you, **32**'I am the God of Abraham, the God of Isaac, and the God of Jacob'[n]?[f] He is not the God of the dead but of the living."

33When the crowds heard this, they were astonished at his teaching.[g]

The Greatest Commandment

22:34–40pp — Mk 12:28–31

34Hearing that Jesus had silenced the Sadducees,[h] the Pharisees got together. **35**One of them, an expert in the law,[i] tested him with this question: **36**"Teacher, which is the greatest commandment in the Law?"

37Jesus replied: " 'Love the Lord your

[n] *32* Exodus 3:6

22:11 WEDDING CLOTHES. Many who claim to be members of the kingdom of heaven on earth will not be wearing wedding clothes and therefore are not among the chosen (v. 14). The "wedding clothes" symbolize a condition of readiness—present possession of true faith in Christ and continued obedience made possible through the grace of Christ (cf. 24:44; 25:21). Christ refers to the man who was not wearing wedding clothes in order to make all of us examine ourselves and ask, "Lord, is it I?"

22:14 FEW ARE CHOSEN. The call to salvation goes out to the many. However, the few who are chosen to inherit the kingdom of heaven are those who respond to God's call, repent of their sins and believe in Christ. Responding to God's grace by the free exercise of our will brings us into the chosen people of God (see article on ELECTION AND PREDESTINATION, p. 402).

22:30 PEOPLE WILL NEITHER MARRY. See Mk 12:25, note.

22:35 AN EXPERT IN THE LAW. An "expert in the law" (Gk *nomikos*) was an interpreter and teacher of the Law of Moses.

22:37 LOVE THE LORD YOUR GOD. What God asks of all those who believe in Christ and receive his salvation is devoted love (cf. Dt 6:5; Ro 13:9–10; 1Co 13). (1) This love requires an attitude of heart where God is so valued and esteemed that we truly long for his fellowship, strive to obey him, and sincerely care for his honor and will on earth. Those who truly love God will desire to share his suffering (Php 3:10), promote his kingdom (1Co 9:23), and live for his

God with all your heart and with all your
soul and with all your mind.'[o][j] 38This is
the first and greatest commandment.
39And the second is like it: 'Love your
neighbor as yourself.'[p][k] 40All the Law
and the Prophets hang on these two commandments."[l]

Whose Son Is the Christ?

22:41–46pp — Mk 12:35–37; Lk 20:41–44

41While the Pharisees were gathered
together, Jesus asked them, 42"What do
you think about the Christ[q]? Whose son is
he?"
"The son of David,"[m] they replied.
43He said to them, "How is it then that
David, speaking by the Spirit, calls him
'Lord'? For he says,

44" 'The Lord said to my Lord:
"Sit at my right hand
until I put your enemies
under your feet." '[r][n]

45If then David calls him 'Lord,' how can
he be his son?" 46No one could say a word
in reply, and from that day on no one
dared to ask him any more questions.[o]

The Sin of the Pharisees

23:1–7pp — Mk 12:38,39; Lk 20:45,46
23:37–39pp — Lk 13:34,35

23 Then Jesus said to the crowds and
to his disciples: 2"The teachers of
the law[p] and the Pharisees sit in Moses'
seat. 3So you must obey them and do everything they tell you. But do not do what
they do, for they do not practice what they
preach. 4They tie up heavy loads and put
them on men's shoulders, but they themselves are not willing to lift a finger to
move them.[q]
5"Everything they do is done for men to
see:[r] They make their phylacteries[s][s]
wide and the tassels on their garments[t]
long; 6they love the place of honor at banquets and the most important seats in the
synagogues;[u] 7they love to be greeted in
the marketplaces and to have men call
them 'Rabbi.'[v]
8"But you are not to be called 'Rabbi,'
for you have only one Master and you are
all brothers. 9And do not call anyone on
earth 'father,' for you have one Father,[w]
and he is in heaven. 10Nor are you to be
called 'teacher,' for you have one Teacher,
the Christ.[q] 11The greatest among you
will be your servant.[x] 12For whoever exalts himself will be humbled, and whoever
humbles himself will be exalted.[y]

Seven Woes

13"Woe to you, teachers of the law and

22:37 [j]Dt 6:5
22:39 [k]Lev 19:18; S Mt 5:43
22:40 [l]Mt 7:12; Lk 10:25-28
22:42 [m]S Mt 9:27
22:44 [n]Ps 110:1; 1Ki 5:3; Ac 2:34,35; 1Co 15:25; Heb 1:13; 10:13
22:46 [o]Mk 12:34; Lk 20:40
23:2 [p]Ezr 7:6,25
23:4 [q]Lk 11:46; Ac 15:10; Gal 6:13
23:5 [r]Mt 6:1,2,5,16 [s]Ex 13:9; Dt 6:8 [t]Nu 15:38; Dt 22:12
23:6 [u]Lk 11:43; 14:7; 20:46
23:7 [v]ver 8; Mt 26:25,49; Mk 9:5; 10:51; Jn 1:38,49; 3:2,26; 20:16
23:9 [w]Mal 1:6; Mt 6:9; 7:11
23:11 [x]S Mk 9:35
23:12 [y]1Sa 2:8; Ps 18:27; Pr 3:34; Isa 57:15; Eze 21:26; Lk 1:52; 14:11

o 37 Deut. 6:5 p 39 Lev. 19:18 q 42,10 Or *Messiah* r 44 Psalm 110:1 s 5 That is, boxes containing Scripture verses, worn on forehead and arm

honor and righteous standards on earth (6:9–10, 33).

(2) Our love for God must be a wholehearted and dominating love, a love inspired by his love for us whereby he gave his Son for our sake (see Jn 3:16, note; Ro 8:32). Our love is to be the kind of love expressed in Ro 12:1–2; 1Co 6:20; 10:31; 2Co 9:15; Eph 4:30; 5:1–2; Col 3:12–17.

(3) Love for God includes: (a) a personal attachment of allegiance and loyalty to him; (b) faith as a firm, unswerving adherence to the One to whom we are united by a Father-child relationship; (c) faithfulness to our commitment to him; (d) heartfelt devotion, expressed in our dedication to his righteous standards in the midst of a God-rejecting world; and (e) a desire for his presence and fellowship.

22:39 LOVE YOUR NEIGHBOR. Children of God are required to love all people (cf. Gal 6:10; 1Th 3:12), including their enemies (5:44). They are also commanded to love all true born-again Christians in a special way (see Jn 13:34, note; Gal 6:10; cf. 1Th 3:12; 1Jn 3:11). (1) The love of believers for their Christian brothers and sisters, their neighbors and their enemies must be subordinated to, and controlled and directed by, their love and devotion for God. (2) Love for God is the "first and greatest commandment" (vv. 37–38). Therefore, God's holiness, his desire for purity, and his will and standard as revealed in Scripture must never be compromised in our practice of love for all people.

23:13 WOE TO YOU . . . PHARISEES. Jesus' words in ch. 23 constitute his most severe denunciation. His words were directed against religious leaders and false teachers who had rejected at least a part of the revealed Word of God and replaced it with their own ideas and interpretations (vv. 23,28; 15:3,6–9; Mk 7:6–9). (1) The spirit of Jesus should be noted. It is not the tolerant, permissive and accommodative spirit of someone who is unconcerned about faithfulness to God and his Word. Jesus was not a weak preacher who tolerated sin. Being true to his calling caused him to be angry with evil (cf. 21:12–17; Jn 2:13–16) and to denounce sin and corruption in high places (vv. 23, 25).

(2) Jesus' love for the inspired Scriptures of his Father, as well as his concern for those who were being destroyed by its distortion (see 15:2–3; 18:6–7; 23:13,15), was so great that it caused him to use words like "hypocrites" (v. 15), "son of hell" (v. 15), "blind guides" (v. 16), "fools" (v. 17), "greed and self-indulgence" (v. 25), "whitewashed tombs . . . unclean" (v. 27), "full of . . . wickedness" (v. 28), "snakes," "brood of vipers" (v. 33) and murderers (v. 34). These words, though severe and condemning, were spoken with a broken heart (v. 37) by One who died for those to whom they were addressed (cf. Jn 3:16; Ro 5:6,8).

Pharisees, you hypocrites![z] You shut the
kingdom of heaven in men's faces. You
yourselves do not enter, nor will you let
those enter who are trying to.[t][a]
15"Woe to you, teachers of the law and
Pharisees, you hypocrites! You travel over
land and sea to win a single convert,[b] and
when he becomes one, you make him
twice as much a son of hell[c] as you are.
16"Woe to you, blind guides![d] You say,
'If anyone swears by the temple, it means
nothing; but if anyone swears by the gold
of the temple, he is bound by his oath.'[e]
17You blind fools! Which is greater: the
gold, or the temple that makes the gold
sacred?[f] 18You also say, 'If anyone
swears by the altar, it means nothing; but
if anyone swears by the gift on it, he is
bound by his oath.' 19You blind men!
Which is greater: the gift, or the altar that
makes the gift sacred?[g] 20Therefore, he
who swears by the altar swears by it and
by everything on it. 21And he who swears
by the temple swears by it and by the one
who dwells[h] in it. 22And he who swears
by heaven swears by God's throne and by
the one who sits on it.[i]
23"Woe to you, teachers of the law and
Pharisees, you hypocrites! You give a
tenth[j] of your spices—mint, dill and cum-
min. But you have neglected the more important matters of the law—justice, mercy and faithfulness.[k] You should have
practiced the latter, without neglecting
the former. 24You blind guides![l] You
strain out a gnat but swallow a camel.
25"Woe to you, teachers of the law and
Pharisees, you hypocrites! You clean the
outside of the cup and dish,[m] but inside
they are full of greed and self-indulgence.[n] 26Blind Pharisee! First clean the
inside of the cup and dish, and then the
outside also will be clean.
27"Woe to you, teachers of the law and
Pharisees, you hypocrites! You are like
whitewashed tombs,[o] which look beautiful on the outside but on the inside are full
of dead men's bones and everything unclean. 28In the same way, on the outside
you appear to people as righteous but on
the inside you are full of hypocrisy and
wickedness.
29"Woe to you, teachers of the law and
Pharisees, you hypocrites! You build
tombs for the prophets[p] and decorate the
graves of the righteous. 30And you say, 'If
we had lived in the days of our forefathers,
we would not have taken part with them
in shedding the blood of the prophets.'
31So you testify against yourselves that
you are the descendants of those who
murdered the prophets.[q] 32Fill up, then,
the measure[r] of the sin of your forefathers![s]
33"You snakes! You brood of vipers![t]
How will you escape being condemned to
hell?[u] 34Therefore I am sending you
prophets and wise men and teachers.
Some of them you will kill and crucify;[v]
others you will flog in your synagogues[w]
and pursue from town to town.[x] 35And so
upon you will come all the righteous blood
that has been shed on earth, from the
blood of righteous Abel[y] to the blood of
Zechariah son of Berekiah,[z] whom you
murdered between the temple and the altar.[a] 36I tell you the truth, all this will
come upon this generation.[b]

Jesus' Sorrow for Jerusalem

37"O Jerusalem, Jerusalem, you who kill
the prophets and stone those sent to
you,[c] how often I have longed to gather
your children together, as a hen gathers

23:13 [z] ver 15,23,25,27,29 [a] Lk 11:52
23:15 [b] Ac 2:11; 6:5; 13:43 [c] S Mt 5:22
23:16 [d] ver 24; Isa 9:16; Mt 15:14 [e] Mt 5:33-35
23:17 [f] Ex 30:29
23:19 [g] Ex 29:37
23:21 [h] 1Ki 8:13; Ps 26:8
23:22 [i] Ps 11:4; Mt 5:34
23:23 [j] Lev 27:30 [k] Mic 6:8; Lk 11:42
23:24 [l] ver 16
23:25 [m] Mk 7:4 [n] Lk 11:39
23:27 [o] Lk 11:44; Ac 23:3
23:29 [p] Lk 11:47,48
23:31 [q] S Mt 5:12
23:32 [r] 1Th 2:16 [s] Eze 20:4
23:33 [t] Mt 3:7; 12:34 [u] S Mt 5:22
23:34 [v] 2Ch 36:15,16; Lk 11:49 [w] S Mt 10:17 [x] Mt 10:23
23:35 [y] Ge 4:8; Heb 11:4 [z] Zec 1:1 [a] 2Ch 24:21
23:36 [b] Mt 10:23; 24:34; Lk 11:50,51
23:37 [c] 2Ch 24:21; S Mt 5:12

t 13 Some manuscripts *to.* [14]*Woe to you, teachers of the law and Pharisees, you hypocrites! You devour widows' houses and for a show make lengthy prayers. Therefore you will be punished more severely.*

---

(3) Jesus describes the character of false teachers and preachers as those ministers who seek to be popular, important and noticed by others (v. 5), who love honor (v. 6) and titles (v. 7), and who keep people out of heaven by their distorted gospel (v. 13). They are professional religionists who appear spiritual and godly, but are really unrighteous (vv. 14,25–27). They speak well of godly spiritual leaders of the past, but do not follow their practices or their commitment to God and his Word and righteousness (vv. 29–30).

(4) The Bible commands believers to beware of such false religious leaders (7:15; 24:11), consider them to be unbelievers (see Gal 1:9, note) and refuse to support their ministry or have fellowship with them (2Jn 9–11).

(5) Those in the church who, in the name of love, toleration or unity, refuse to share Jesus' attitude toward those who distort the original teaching of Christ and the Scriptures (7:15; Gal 1:6–7; 2Jn 9), are participating in the evil deeds of false prophets and teachers (2Jn 10–11).

23:28 ON THE OUTSIDE . . . RIGHTEOUS. Jesus continues his speech about religious leaders and ministers of his day whose public conduct appeared righteous but whose hearts were full of hypocrisy, pride, lust and wickedness. They were like painted tombs, beautiful and attractive on the outside, yet with foulness and corruption hidden inside. For more on what the Bible has to say about false teachers, see article on FALSE TEACHERS, p. 98.

23:37 O JERUSALEM, JERUSALEM. See Lk 13:34, note; Lk 19:41, note.

her chicks under her wings,[d] but you were
not willing. 38Look, your house is left to
you desolate.[e] 39For I tell you, you will
not see me again until you say, 'Blessed
is he who comes in the name of the
Lord.'[u]"[f]

Signs of the End of the Age

24:1-51pp — Mk 13:1-37; Lk 21:5-36

24 Jesus left the temple and was
walking away when his disciples
came up to him to call his attention to its
buildings. 2"Do you see all these things?"
he asked. "I tell you the truth, not one
stone here will be left on another;[g] every
one will be thrown down."
3As Jesus was sitting on the Mount of
Olives,[h] the disciples came to him privately. "Tell us," they said, "when will this
happen, and what will be the sign of your
coming[i] and of the end of the age?"[j]
4Jesus answered: "Watch out that no
one deceives you.[k] 5For many will come
in my name, claiming, 'I am the Christ,[v]'
and will deceive many.[l] 6You will hear of
wars and rumors of wars, but see to it that
you are not alarmed. Such things must
happen, but the end is still to come. 7Na-
tion will rise against nation, and kingdom
against kingdom.[m] There will be famines[n]
and earthquakes in various places. 8All
these are the beginning of birth pains.
9"Then you will be handed over to be
persecuted[o] and put to death,[p] and you

23:37 [d] Ps 57:1; 61:4; Isa 31:5 **23:38** [e] 1Ki 9:7,8; Jer 22:5 **23:39** [f] Ps 118:26; Mt 21:9 **24:2** [g] Lk 19:44 **24:3** [h] S Mt 21:1 [i] S Lk 17:30 [j] Mt 13:39; 28:20 **24:4** [k] S Mk 13:5 **24:5** [l] ver 11,23, 24; 1Jn 2:18 **24:7** [m] Isa 19:2 [n] Ac 11:28 **24:9** [o] Mt 10:17 [p] Jn 16:2

[u] *39* Psalm 118:26 [v] *5* Or *Messiah*; also in verse 23

23:39 YOU WILL NOT SEE ME AGAIN UNTIL. The city of Jerusalem repeatedly rejected Jesus' message. Therefore, in sorrow (vv. 37–38) Christ must withdraw and would not be seen by Israel again until they acknowledge their offense and call for the Messiah to come as their Deliverer. (1) This will occur only when Israel (i.e., a remnant, see Isa 10:21–22) experiences the dreadful days of the tribulation and are in their greatest peril (Hos 5:15—6:3; see article on THE GREAT TRIBULATION, p. 52).

(2) When Israel experiences intense tribulation at the end of the age (Am 9:9), the nations of the world will gather against Jerusalem (Zec 12:1–4) and two-thirds of Israel will be killed (Zec 13:8–9). At the point when Israel is nearly destroyed, the remnant will turn in repentance and mourning (Isa 26:16–17; 64:1,6; Hos 5:15; Zec 12:4–5,10; Ro 11:26; see Rev 11:2, note; 12:6, note).

24:3—25:46 THE OLIVET DISCOURSE. Jesus' prophecy was primarily a reply to the disciples' question: "What will be the sign of your coming and of the end of the age?" Jesus gave them: (1) general signs of the course of the age leading up to the last days (24:4–14); (2) special signs to indicate the final days of the age, the great tribulation (24:15–28); (3) spectacular signs to occur at his triumphant coming with power and great glory (24:29–31); (4) admonition to tribulation saints to be alert to the signs leading up to Christ's expected coming immediately after the tribulation (24:32–35); (5) admonition to believers living before the tribulation to be spiritually ready for the unexpected and unknown time of Christ's coming for his faithful (24:36–51; 25:1–30; see Jn 14:3, note; see article on THE RAPTURE, p. 440); (6) a description of the judgment of nations after his return to earth (25:31–46).

It should be observed that many details of Christ's coming are not disclosed in Mt 24. Furthermore, no one has so far deciphered all the prophecies concerning the end time with complete certainty.

24:4–51 JESUS ANSWERED. Jesus' words in the Olivet discourse are addressed to his disciples and to all of God's faithful people until the end of the age and his triumphant return to reign on earth. (1) Concerning believers living before the tribulation period, Christ tells them they cannot calculate or even estimate the time of his return for them (vv. 42–44). Therefore they must be ready at any time, for he will return to take them to heaven (i.e., his "Father's house," see Jn 14:2–3, notes) at a time when they do not think he will (see v. 44, note; see article on THE RAPTURE, p. 440).

(2) For those converted to Christ during the great tribulation, they can know the time of his coming for them with a high degree of certainty, for Christ gives them signs by which to expect and know that his return is very near (vv. 15–29). When they see these signs they will "know that it is near, right at the door" (see v. 33, note).

24:4 SIGNS OF THE END OF THIS AGE. In vv. 4–14 Jesus gives the signs (cf. v. 3) that will characterize the whole course of the last days and that will intensify as the end draws nearer. (1) False prophets and religious compromisers within the visible church will increase and deceive many (vv. 4–5,11). (2) The increase of wars, famines and earthquakes (vv. 6–7) will be "the beginning of birth pains" (v. 8) of the new Messianic age. (3) As the end draws nearer, the persecution of God's people will become more severe (v. 9), and many will forsake their loyalty to Christ (vv. 9–10). (4) Violence, crime and disregard for God's law will increase rapidly, and natural love and family affection will decrease (v. 12; cf. Mk 13:12; 2Ti 3:3). (5) In spite of this intensification of trouble, the gospel will be preached in the whole world (v. 14). (6) The saved will be those who stand firm in their faith through all the end-time distress (v. 13). (7) The faithful, as they see the intensification of these signs, will know that the day of the Lord's return for them is "approaching" (Heb 10:25; see Jn 14:3, note).

24:5 MANY WILL . . . DECEIVE MANY. This first major sign has special importance. Toward the end of this age religious deception will be rampant on the earth. Christ is so concerned that his followers be aware of the coming worldwide spiritual deception to occur just before the end that he repeats his warning twice more in the Olivet discourse (see v. 11, note; v. 24; see article on THE AGE OF THE ANTICHRIST, p. 447).

24:9 YOU WILL BE HATED. All believers in Christ

will be hated by all nations because of
me.[q] **10**At that time many will turn away
from the faith and will betray and hate
each other, **11**and many false prophets[r]
will appear and deceive many people.[s]
12Because of the increase of wickedness,
the love of most will grow cold, **13**but he
who stands firm to the end will be saved.[t]
14And this gospel of the kingdom[u] will be
preached in the whole world[v] as a testi-
Mt 28:18-20 mony to all nations, and then the end will
come.
15"So when you see standing in the holy
place[w] 'the abomination that causes desolation,'[wx] spoken of through the prophet
Daniel—let the reader understand—
16then let those who are in Judea flee to
the mountains. **17**Let no one on the roof of
his house[y] go down to take anything out
of the house. **18**Let no one in the field go
back to get his cloak. **19**How dreadful it
will be in those days for pregnant women
and nursing mothers![z] **20**Pray that your
flight will not take place in winter or on
the Sabbath. **21**For then there will be great
distress, unequaled from the beginning of
the world until now—and never to be
equaled again.[a] **22**If those days had not
been cut short, no one would survive, but
for the sake of the elect[b] those days will
be shortened. **23**At that time if anyone
says to you, 'Look, here is the Christ!' or,
'There he is!' do not believe it.[c] **24**For
false Christs and false prophets will appear and perform great signs and miracles[d] to deceive even the elect—if that
were possible. **25**See, I have told you
ahead of time.
26"So if anyone tells you, 'There he is,
out in the desert,' do not go out; or, 'Here
he is, in the inner rooms,' do not believe
it. **27**For as lightning[e] that comes from
the east is visible even in the west, so will
be the coming[f] of the Son of Man.[g]
28Wherever there is a carcass, there the
vultures will gather.[h]
29"Immediately after the distress of
those days

24:9 [q]S Jn 15:21 **24:11** [r]S Mt 7:15 [s]S Mk 13:5 **24:13** [t]S Mt 10:22 **24:14** [u]S Mt 4:23 [v]S Ro 10:18; Lk 2:1; 4:5; Ac 11:28; 17:6; Rev 3:10; 16:14 **24:15** [w]S Ac 6:13 [x]Da 9:27; 11:31; 12:11 **24:17** [y]1Sa 9:25; Mt 10:27; Lk 12:3; Ac 10:9 **24:19** [z]Lk 23:29 **24:21** [a]Eze 5:9; Da 12:1; Joel 2:2 **24:22** [b]ver 24,31 **24:23** [c]Lk 17:23; 21:8 **24:24** [d]Ex 7:11, 22; 2Th 2:9-11; Rev 13:13; 16:14; 19:20 **24:27** [e]Lk 17:24 [f]S Lk 17:30 [g]S Mt 8:20 **24:28** [h]Lk 17:37

[w] *15* Daniel 9:27; 11:31; 12:11

may expect trouble during their pilgrimage on earth. Suffering for Christ because of our loyalty to him and his Word is an intrinsic part of the Christian faith (cf. Jn 15:20; 16:33; Ac 14:22; Ro 5:3; see Mt 5:10, note).

24:11 MANY FALSE PROPHETS WILL APPEAR. As the last days draw to a close, false teachers and preachers will be exceedingly prevalent. Much of Christendom will be in an apostate condition. Those who are totally committed to the truth of God's Word and Biblical righteousness will be in the minority.

(1) Professing believers will accept "new revelation" even though it conflicts with the revealed Word of God. This will lead to opposition to Biblical truth within the churches (see 1Ti 4:1, notes; 2Ti 3:8; 4:3, note). Those who preach a distorted gospel may even gain strategic leadership positions in denominations and theological schools (see 7:22, note), enabling them to deceive and mislead many within the church (see Gal 1:9, note; 2Ti 4:3, note; 2Pe 3:3–4).

(2) Throughout the world millions will be involved in the occult, astrology, witchcraft, spiritism and Satanism. The influence of demons and evil spirits will multiply greatly (see 1Ti 4:1, note).

(3) Protection against being deceived is found in an enduring faith and love for Christ, in a commitment to the absolute authority of his Word (vv. 4,11,13,25) and in a thorough knowledge of that Word (see 1Ti 4:16, note).

24:12 INCREASE OF WICKEDNESS. An unbelievable increase in immorality, shamelessness, rebellion against God and a throwing off of moral restraint will characterize the last days. Sexual perversion, immorality, adultery, pornography, drugs, ungodly music and lustful entertainment will abound. It will be "as it was in the days of Noah" (v. 37), when the thoughts of human hearts were evil continually (see Ge 6:5). It will be as "in the days of Lot" (Lk 17:28,30), when homosexuality, lesbianism and all kinds of sexual perversion permeated society (see Ge 19:4; 1Ti 4:1, note; 2Ti 3:1–8). Jesus goes on to indicate that true love will be in short supply.

24:14 THIS GOSPEL OF THE KINGDOM . . . THE END. The end will come only after the "gospel of the kingdom" has been adequately preached in the whole world. (1) This "gospel of the kingdom" refers to the apostolic gospel preached in the power and righteousness of the Holy Spirit and accompanied by the major signs of the gospel (see article on THE KINGDOM OF GOD, p. 28).

(2) Only God will know when this is accomplished according to his purpose. The believer's task is to faithfully and continually press on "to all nations" till the Lord returns to take his church to heaven (see 28:19–20, notes; Jn 14:3, note; 1Th 4:13, note).

(3) Many interpreters believe "the end" refers to the time when "the dead in Christ will rise" and the faithful of Christ's churches "will be caught up together with them in the clouds to meet the Lord in the air" (1Th 4:16–17; see article on THE RAPTURE, p. 440). Christ gives more details about his unexpected appearance for the faithful church in vv. 37–44.

24:14 THEN THE END WILL COME. Christ speaks to the disciples as though everything he predicts could be fulfilled within their generation. This, therefore, was the hope of the NT church. It must also be the hope of all who believe in Jesus Christ throughout the ages. We are to hope that the Lord will return and that the end of the age will occur in our generation (see 1Co 15:51, note). We must live in a tension between the imminency of Christ's coming and the fact that Christ has commanded us to keep on spreading the gospel.

24:15–28 THE GREAT TRIBULATION. This entire section deals with the great tribulation. For a study of this material, see article on THE GREAT TRIBULATION, p. 52.

THE GREAT TRIBULATION

Mt 24:21 "For then there will be great distress, unequaled from the beginning of the world until now—and never to be equaled again."

Beginning with Mt 24:15, Jesus speaks about special signs that will occur during the great tribulation (Rev 7:14; cf. "great distress" in Mt 24:21—the phrase in Greek is the same), signs to indicate that the end of the age is very near (Mt 24:15–29). These signs will lead up to and signal Christ's return to earth after the tribulation (Mt 24:30–31; cf. Rev 19:11—20:4).

The major sign is "the abomination that causes desolation" (Mt 24:15), a specific observable event that tells the faithful who are alive during the tribulation that Christ's coming to earth at the end of the age will occur very shortly. This visible sign-event refers primarily to the future desecration of the Jewish temple in Jerusalem by the antichrist (see Da 9:27; 1Jn 2:18; see article on THE AGE OF THE ANTICHRIST, p. 447). The antichrist, or man of lawlessness, will set up an image of himself in God's temple, declaring himself to be God (2Th 2:3–4; Rev 13:14–15). The following are important facts concerning this pivotal event.

(1) The "abomination that causes desolation" will mark the beginning of the final stage of the tribulation, which culminates in Christ's return to earth and his judgment on the ungodly at Armageddon (Mt 24:21,29–30; see Da 9:27; Rev 19:11–21).

(2) By noting the time of this event ("So when you see" Mt 24:15), tribulation saints can know with a high degree of certainty when the tribulation will end and Christ will come to reign on earth (see Mt 24:33, note). The time span between this event and the end is given four times in Scripture as three and a half years, or 1,260 days (see Da 9:25–27; Rev 11:1–2; 12:6; 13:5–7).

(3) Because of this strong expectancy of Christ's coming (Mt 24:33), the faithful must be aware that any report that Christ has returned is deceptive (Mt 24:23–27). The "coming of the Son of Man" after the tribulation will be observable and known to all who are in the world (Mt 24:27–30).

Another sign will be the appearance of false prophets who, as ministers of Satan, will perform "great signs and miracles" (Mt 24:24).

(1) Jesus admonishes all believers to be especially alert for these professed Christian prophets, teachers and preachers who are, in reality, false, and yet who perform miracles, healings, signs and wonders and who appear to have great success in their ministries. At the same time, these false prophets will distort and reject the truth found in God's Word (see Mt 7:22, note; Gal 1:9, note; see article on THE AGE OF THE ANTICHRIST, p. 447).

(2) Elsewhere Scripture urges believers to continually test the spirits energizing all teachers, leaders and preachers (see 1Jn 4:1, note). God allows deception accompanied by miracles in order to test believers as to their love for him and their loyalty to the truth of Scripture (see Dt 13:3). This period of deception will not be easy, for Jesus states in Mt 24:24 that during the last days religious deceit will be so widespread that it will be difficult even for "the elect" (i.e., committed Christians) to discern truth from error (see 1Ti 4:16, note; Jas 1:21, note; see article on ELECTION AND PREDESTINATION, p. 402).

(3) Those among God's people who do not love the truth will be deceived. They will be given no further opportunity to believe the truth of the gospel after the antichrist comes (see 2Th 2:11, note).

Finally, the great tribulation will be a specific period of terrible suffering and distress for all the people in the world. Observe:

(1) It will be worldwide (see Rev 3:10, note). (2) It will be the worst time of affliction and distress ever to occur in the history of humanity (Da 12:1; Mt 24:21). (3) It will be a terrible time of suffering for the Jews (Jer 30:5–7). (4) The period will be dominated by the "man of lawlessness" (i.e., antichrist; cf. Da 9:27; Rev 13:12; see article on THE AGE OF THE ANTICHRIST, p. 447). (5) The faithful of Christ's churches are promised deliverance and "escape" from the tribulation time (see Lk 21:36, note; 1Th 5:8–10; Rev 3:10, note). (6) During this time, there will be both Jews and Gentiles who believe in Jesus Christ and are saved (Dt 4:30–31; Hos 5:15; Rev 7:9–17; 14:6–7). (7) It will be a time of great suffering and dreadful persecution for all who remain faithful to God (Rev 12:17; 13:15). (8) It will be a time of God's wrath and judgment upon the ungodly (1Th 5:1–11; Rev 6:16–17). (9) Jesus' statement that those days will be shortened (Mt 24:22) must not be understood to imply that there will be any reduction of the predicted three and a half years or 1,260 days. Rather, it seems to refer to the fact that the period is so awful that if it were not confined to a limited period of time, the whole human race would be destroyed. (10) The great tribulation will end with the coming of Jesus Christ in glory with his bride (Rev 19:7–8,14) to bring deliverance to the faithful and judgment and destruction to the wicked (Eze 20:34–38; Mt 24:29–31; Lk 19:11–27; Rev 19:11–21). (11) We must not confuse this coming at the end of the great tribulation with Jesus' reference to his unexpected descent from heaven in Mt 24:42,44 (see notes on those verses, which demonstrate that this coming refers to the rapture of believers occurring at a time different from that of Christ's final return at the end of the tribulation). (12) The major Scripture passage describing the whole seven-year tribulation is found in Rev 6–18.

“ ‘the sun will be darkened,
and the moon will not give its light;
the stars will fall from the sky,
and the heavenly bodies will be
shaken.’[x][i]

30“At that time the sign of the Son of
Man will appear in the sky, and all the
nations of the earth will mourn.[j] They
will see the Son of Man coming on the
clouds of the sky,[k] with power and great
glory. 31And he will send his angels[l] with
a loud trumpet call,[m] and they will gather
his elect from the four winds, from one
end of the heavens to the other.
32“Now learn this lesson from the fig
tree: As soon as its twigs get tender and
its leaves come out, you know that summer is near. 33Even so, when you see all
these things, you know that it[y] is near,
right at the door.[n] 34I tell you the truth,
this generation[z] will certainly not pass
away until all these things have happened.[o] 35Heaven and earth will pass
away, but my words will never pass
away.[p]

The Unexpected Coming of the Son of Man

24:37–39pp — Lk 17:26,27
24:45–51pp — Lk 12:42–46

36“No one knows about that day or
hour, not even the angels in heaven, nor
the Son,[a] but only the Father.[q] 37As it

24:29 [i] Isa 13:10; 34:4; Eze 32:7; Joel 2:10,31; Zep 1:15; Rev 6:12,13; 8:12
24:30 [j] Rev 1:7 [k] S Rev 1:7
24:31 [l] Mt 13:41 [m] Isa 27:13; Zec 9:14; 1Co 15:52; 1Th 4:16; Rev 8:2; 10:7; 11:15
24:33 [n] Jas 5:9
24:34 [o] Mt 16:28; S 23:36
24:35 [p] S Mt 5:18
24:36 [q] Ac 1:7

[x] *29* Isaiah 13:10; 34:4 [y] *33* Or *he* [z] *34* Or *race* [a] *36* Some manuscripts do not have *nor the Son.*

24:29 THE SUN WILL BE DARKENED. Immediately after the tribulation, there will occur spectacular cosmic signs that will precede the appearing of Christ and give clear warning of his return (v. 30). Christ's return to earth with power and great glory will not take by surprise any tribulation believer who heeds God's Word and observes the cosmic signs related to the sun, moon, stars and the shaking of the powers of the heavens (cf. Isa 13:9–11).

24:30 SON OF MAN COMING. This verse portrays Christ's appearing in the sky after the tribulation and the cosmic signs. He will come to judge the wicked (Rev 19:11—20:3), to deliver his faithful people and to establish righteousness on earth (Rev 20:4). All Christians, both the living and the dead who had been taken from the earth at the rapture (see Jn 14:3, note; see article on THE RAPTURE, p. 440), will return with Christ at his coming with power and great glory (see Rev 19:14, note). The "sign" is probably Christ himself coming on the clouds of glory, surrounded by brilliant light.

24:31 GATHER HIS ELECT. When Jesus Christ returns to earth after the tribulation, the following events will take place: (1) God's judgment on the wicked (v. 30; Rev 19:11–21), the antichrist (Rev 19:20) and Satan (Rev 20:1–3); (2) the judgment and the separation of people on earth alive at Christ's coming (see 13:41, note; 25:32, note); (3) the gathering of the saints of all ages, including the saints already in heaven (cf. Mk 13:27; see Jn 14:3, note; Rev 19:14, note; 20:4,6) and those alive on earth at Christ's advent (see 13:40); (4) the thousand-year reign of Christ on earth (see Rev 20:4, notes).

24:32 THE FIG TREE. The coming out of the leaves of the fig tree (cf. Lk 21:29–31) refers to events occurring during the tribulation (vv. 15–29). Some interpret the fig tree to represent the restoration of Israel as a political state (cf. Hos 9:10; Lk 13:6–9).

24:33 ALL THESE THINGS. This refers to all the signs that will occur during the great tribulation (vv. 15–29), the pivotal sign being the "abomination that causes desolation" (v. 15; see article on THE GREAT TRIBULATION, p. 52). As the prophetic events unfold, the tribulation faithful who search the Scriptures will "see all these things" and know that the Lord's return "is near, right at the door."

24:34 THIS GENERATION. "This generation" may refer to the generation that begins to see the intensification of the general signs of the age (vv. 4–14) that consummate with the signs of the tribulation (see v. 5, note), or it may refer to the Jewish people as a race.

24:36 ONLY THE FATHER. This verse speaks of only the Father knowing the time of Christ's return. We must understand this as referring to the time when Christ was on earth. Certainly now Jesus, who has returned to his former glory (Jn 17:5), has future knowledge of his return. Tribulation saints can also know the time of his final return by observing the signs of the tribulation that Christ described (see article on THE GREAT TRIBULATION, p. 52).

24:37 THE COMING OF THE SON OF MAN. Jesus' statements concerning "the coming of the Son of Man" have a double reference: to the first stage of his return at an unknown and unexpected time (i.e., the rapture of the church saints: see v. 42, notes; Jn 14:3, note; Rev 3:10, note; see article on THE RAPTURE, p. 440), and to the second stage of his coming after the tribulation, when he will destroy the wicked and gather all the righteous into his kingdom (Rev 19:11—20:4). We encounter this double reference when Christ describes three different categories of people in his illustration of "the days of Noah" (vv. 37–44). These three categories and their relation to Christ's coming are as follows:

(1) The tribulation unbelievers, represented by the flood victims of Noah's day. They do not know the time of Christ's return, are unprepared and are thus destroyed at the end time (vv. 38–39,43; cf. Lk 17:26–28). This is the second stage of his return, the one occurring after the tribulation.

(2) The tribulation believers, represented by Noah. Because of the signs of the end time, tribulation saints know almost the precise time of the Lord's return and are prepared and saved. Christ returns for them at the expected time (v. 27; cf. Ge 7:4; see article on THE GREAT TRIBULATION, p. 52). This too refers to the second stage of Christ's return.

(3) Present-day believers or church saints living before the tribulation, represented by Jesus' disciples. They will not know the time of Christ's return to take

was in the days of Noah,[r] so it will be at
the coming of the Son of Man. **38**For in the
days before the flood, people were eating
and drinking, marrying and giving in marriage,[s] up to the day Noah entered the
ark; **39**and they knew nothing about what
would happen until the flood came and
took them all away. That is how it will be
at the coming of the Son of Man.[t] **40**Two
men will be in the field; one will be taken
and the other left.[u] **41**Two women will be
grinding with a hand mill; one will be tak-
en and the other left.[v]

42"Therefore keep watch, because you
do not know on what day your Lord will
come.[w] **43**But understand this: If the owner of the house had known at what time
of night the thief was coming,[x] he would
have kept watch and would not have let
his house be broken into. **44**So you also
must be ready,[y] because the Son of Man
will come at an hour when you do not expect him.

45"Who then is the faithful and wise
servant,[z] whom the master has put in
charge of the servants in his household to
give them their food at the proper time?
46It will be good for that servant whose
master finds him doing so when he returns.[a] **47**I tell you the truth, he will put
him in charge of all his possessions.[b]
48But suppose that servant is wicked and

24:37 [r] Ge 6:5; 7:6-23
24:38 [s] Mt 22:30
24:39 [t] S Lk 17:30
24:40 [u] Lk 17:34
24:41 [v] Lk 17:35
24:42 [w] Mt 25:13; Lk 12:40
24:43 [x] S Lk 12:39
24:44 [y] 1Th 5:6
24:45 [z] Mt 25:21, 23
24:46 [a] Rev 16:15
24:47 [b] Mt 25:21, 23

---

them to heaven (vv. 42,44; see Jn 14:3, note; cf. 1Th 4:14). There will be no definite signs preceding the Lord's return for them, for Christ states that it will occur unexpectedly (vv. 42,44). Notice that Jesus likens the disciples (i.e., church saints) not to Noah (i.e., tribulation believers) but to the flood victims (compare "they knew nothing," v. 39, with "you do not know," v. 42). That is, the church saints will be like the flood victims in one sense: they will not know the time of Christ's return for them and will be surprised when he comes, just as the flood victims did not know the time of the flood and were surprised when it came. Therefore, church saints must be ready at any time (v. 44).

24:40 ONE ... TAKEN ... THE OTHER LEFT. Christ's statement that "one will be taken and the other left" comes before his exhortation to church saints (vv. 42–44). Therefore, these words likely refer to church saints who are taken out from among the wicked when Christ calls the faithful to himself at the rapture (see Jn 14:3, note; see article on THE RAPTURE, p. 440). He emphasizes the surprise element for the church believers (see v. 37, note).

24:42 THEREFORE KEEP WATCH. "Keep watch" (Gk *grēgoreō*) is a present imperative, indicating a constant vigil at the present time. The reason for this vigil today instead of only in the future is that present-day believers do not know when the Lord will come for them (see Jn 14:3, note). There will be no warning signs, and they may never assume that he cannot come today. In other words, they must be committed to the historical possibility of Christ returning at any time (see v. 44, note; cf. Mk 13:33–37). His return for the church is possible any day.

24:42 YOU DO NOT KNOW ON WHAT DAY. Christ's warning that his disciples must always be ready must be understood as referring to his return from heaven to take church saints out of the world, i.e., the rapture (see Jn 14:3, note; see article on THE RAPTURE, p. 440). (1) Jesus explicitly states that his coming for the saints living before the tribulation will be at an unexpected time and without warning. He declares that they not only "do not know" the time, but that he will return at a time when they "do not expect him" (v. 44). This clearly points to an element of surprise, amazement and unexpectedness for the faithful at this particular return of Christ. This is sometimes referred to as the first stage of Christ's second coming.

(2) With regard to Christ's coming with power and glory to judge the world after the tribulation (v. 30; Rev 19:11–21), his coming will be expected, anticipated and foreseen (Lk 21:28; see v. 33, note; see article on THE GREAT TRIBULATION, p. 52). The events and signs during the tribulation will create an attitude of certainty and expectancy for tribulation saints, and not the attitude of surprise that the present-day church saints will have at the time of the rapture (see v. 44, note; Jn 14:3, note). Christ's coming after the tribulation is sometimes regarded as the second stage of Christ's second coming.

24:43 THE THIEF. Christ's coming at an unknown time is to be as unexpected as that of a thief who breaks into a house. Thus the devoted disciple must be ready at any time for the Lord's appearance (v. 44).

24:44 AN HOUR WHEN YOU DO NOT EXPECT HIM. Once again Christ refers to his return for the faithful of his churches at an unexpected and unknown time. (1) This warning is not for tribulation saints (see article on THE GREAT TRIBULATION, p. 52). The only way to harmonize Christ's teaching about his unexpected coming (vv. 42,44) with his statement concerning his expected coming (v. 33) is to assume two phases to his second coming. The first stage involves Christ's return at an unexpected time to take believers from earth (cf. 1Th 4:17; see Jn 14:3, note; Rev. 3:10, note; see article on THE RAPTURE, p. 440), and the second stage is his coming at the end of the age at an expected time (i.e., after the tribulation and cosmic signs, vv. 29–30) to destroy the wicked and begin his reign on earth (see v. 42, notes; Rev 19:11–21; 20:4).

(2) This second coming of Christ as one event consisting of two phases parallels Christ's coming predicted in the OT; the OT speaks of one coming of the Messiah, but sees its fulfillment in two phases: his coming to die for sin and his coming to reign (see Isa 9:2–7; 40:3–5; compare Isa 61:1–3 with Lk 4:18–19).

(3) Christ's urgent warning to be always spiritually ready for his unexpected coming (i.e., the rapture) applies to all generations of Christians before the tribulation (vv. 15–29). It is a motive for perseverance in the faith.

24:48 MY MASTER IS STAYING AWAY. Concern-

says to himself, 'My master is staying
away a long time,' 49 and he then begins to
beat his fellow servants and to eat and
drink with drunkards.[c] 50 The master of
that servant will come on a day when he
does not expect him and at an hour he is
not aware of. 51 He will cut him to pieces
and assign him a place with the hypocrites, where there will be weeping and
gnashing of teeth.[d]

The Parable of the Ten Virgins

25 "At that time the kingdom of heav-
en will be like[e] ten virgins who
took their lamps[f] and went out to meet
the bridegroom.[g] 2 Five of them were foolish and five were wise.[h] 3 The foolish ones
took their lamps but did not take any oil
with them. 4 The wise, however, took oil in
jars along with their lamps. 5 The bridegroom was a long time in coming, and they
all became drowsy and fell asleep.[i]
6 "At midnight the cry rang out: 'Here's
the bridegroom! Come out to meet him!'
7 "Then all the virgins woke up and
trimmed their lamps. 8 The foolish ones
said to the wise, 'Give us some of your oil;
our lamps are going out.'[j]
9 " 'No,' they replied, 'there may not be
enough for both us and you. Instead, go to
those who sell oil and buy some for yourselves.'
10 "But while they were on their way to
buy the oil, the bridegroom arrived. The
virgins who were ready went in with him
to the wedding banquet.[k] And the door
was shut.
11 "Later the others also came. 'Sir!
Sir!' they said. 'Open the door for us!'
12 "But he replied, 'I tell you the truth,
I don't know you.'[l]
13 "Therefore keep watch, because you
do not know the day or the hour.[m]

The Parable of the Talents

25:14–30Ref — Lk 19:12–27

14 "Again, it will be like a man going on
a journey,[n] who called his servants and
entrusted his property to them. 15 To one
he gave five talents[b] of money, to another
two talents, and to another one talent,
each according to his ability.[o] Then he
went on his journey. 16 The man who had
received the five talents went at once and
put his money to work and gained five
more. 17 So also, the one with the two talents gained two more. 18 But the man who
had received the one talent went off, dug
a hole in the ground and hid his master's
money.
19 "After a long time the master of those
servants returned and settled accounts
with them.[p] 20 The man who had received

24:49 [c] Lk 21:34
24:51 [d] S Mt 8:12
25:1 [e] S Mt 13:24 [f] Lk 12:35-38; Ac 20:8; Rev 4:5 [g] Rev 19:7; 21:2
25:2 [h] Mt 24:45
25:5 [i] 1Th 5:6
25:8 [j] Lk 12:35
25:10 [k] Rev 19:9
25:12 [l] ver 41; S Mt 7:23
25:13 [m] Mt 24:42,44; Mk 13:35; Lk 12:40
25:14 [n] Mt 21:33; Lk 19:12
25:15 [o] Mt 18:24, 25
25:19 [p] Mt 18:23

b *15* A talent was worth more than a thousand dollars.

ing those within the church who are unfaithful to the Lord, Christ's unexpected return cannot be a motive for present vigilance if they believe it is impossible for Christ to come now. (1) Any professed believer living in sin who believes that Christ will delay his coming for a few years can be compared to the wicked servant. Such a person will feel no impending threat that the Lord's return will overtake him or her (see v. 44, note; Lk 12:45–46, notes). (2) It is significant that Jesus associates unfaithfulness and hypocrisy with the belief and desire that Christ will delay his return.

25:1 PARABLE OF THE TEN VIRGINS. The parable of the ten virgins emphasizes that all believers must constantly look to their own spiritual condition in light of Christ's coming at an unknown and unexpected time. They must persevere in faith so that when the day and hour arrive they will be received by the returning Lord (v. 10). Failure to be in a personal relationship with the Lord at his return means being excluded from his presence and kingdom.

(1) What differentiates the foolish from the wise is the failure of the foolish to recognize that the returning Lord (see Jn 14:3, note) will come at an unexpected time, a time not preceded with unmistakable and specific observable signs (v. 13; see 24:36,44, notes).

(2) Christ indicates here and elsewhere (Lk 18:8) that a large portion of the church will be unprepared at the time of his return (vv. 8–13). Thus Christ makes it clear he will not wait until all churches are prepared for his coming.

(3) It should be noticed that all the virgins (both faithful and unfaithful) were taken by surprise at the bridegroom's coming (vv. 5–7). This suggests that the parable of the ten virgins applies to believers living before the tribulation and not to those living during the tribulation, who will have adequate signs preceding Christ's return at the end of the tribulation (see article on THE GREAT TRIBULATION, p. 52).

25:4 OIL. Jesus, in a series of illustrations (ch. 25), stresses the requirement of faithfulness and watchfulness until he returns. The parable of the ten virgins stresses the necessity of perseverance in the faith and spiritual preparedness because of the danger of Christ's coming at an unforeseeable date (see Lk 21:19, note). The oil in the parable represents true faith, righteousness and the abiding presence of the Holy Spirit. Five other parables that teach the lesson of perseverance are the sower (Lk 8:4–15), the owner of the house (Lk 12:35–40), the manager (Lk 12:42–48), the tower builder (Lk 14:28–30) and the tasteless salt (Lk 14:34–35).

25:15 TALENTS. The parable of the talents warns us that our place and service in heaven will depend on the faithfulness of our lives and service here (cf. v. 29). A talent represents our abilities, time, resources and opportunities to serve God while on earth. These things are considered by God as a trust that we are responsible to administer in the wisest possible way.

the five talents brought the other five. 'Master,' he said, 'you entrusted me with five talents. See, I have gained five more.'

21"His master replied, 'Well done, good and faithful servant! You have been faithful with a few things; I will put you in charge of many things.[q] Come and share your master's happiness!'

22"The man with the two talents also came. 'Master,' he said, 'you entrusted me with two talents; see, I have gained two more.'

23"His master replied, 'Well done, good and faithful servant! You have been faithful with a few things; I will put you in charge of many things.[r] Come and share your master's happiness!'

24"Then the man who had received the one talent came. 'Master,' he said, 'I knew that you are a hard man, harvesting where you have not sown and gathering where you have not scattered seed. 25So I was afraid and went out and hid your talent in the ground. See, here is what belongs to you.'

26"His master replied, 'You wicked, lazy servant! So you knew that I harvest where I have not sown and gather where I have not scattered seed? 27Well then, you should have put my money on deposit with the bankers, so that when I returned I would have received it back with interest.

28" 'Take the talent from him and give it to the one who has the ten talents. 29For everyone who has will be given more, and he will have an abundance. Whoever does not have, even what he has will be taken from him.[s] 30And throw that worthless servant outside, into the darkness, where there will be weeping and gnashing of teeth.'[t]

25:21 [q]ver 23; Mt 24:45,47; Lk 16:10
25:23 [r]ver 21
25:29 [s]Mt 13:12; Mk 4:25; Lk 8:18; 19:26
25:30 [t]S Mt 8:12
25:31 [u]S Lk 17:30 [v]Mt 19:28
25:32 [w]Mal 3:18 [x]Eze 34:17,20
25:34 [y]S Mt 3:2; 5:3,10,19; 19:14; S Ac 20:32; 1Co 15:50; Gal 5:21; Jas 2:5 [z]Heb 4:3; 9:26; Rev 13:8; 17:8
25:35 [a]Job 31:32; Heb 13:2
25:36 [b]Isa 58:7; Eze 18:7; Jas 2:15,16 [c]Jas 1:27 [d]2Ti 1:16
25:40 [e]S Mt 10:40,42; Heb 13:2
25:41 [f]S Mt 7:23 [g]Isa 66:24; Mt 3:12; S 5:22; Mk 9:43,48; Lk 3:17; Jude 7 [h]2Pe 2:4

The Sheep and the Goats

31"When the Son of Man comes[u] in his glory, and all the angels with him, he will sit on his throne[v] in heavenly glory. 32All the nations will be gathered before him, and he will separate[w] the people one from another as a shepherd separates the sheep from the goats.[x] 33He will put the sheep on his right and the goats on his left.

34"Then the King will say to those on his right, 'Come, you who are blessed by my Father; take your inheritance, the kingdom[y] prepared for you since the creation of the world.[z] 35For I was hungry and you gave me something to eat, I was thirsty and you gave me something to drink, I was a stranger and you invited me in,[a] 36I needed clothes and you clothed me,[b] I was sick and you looked after me,[c] I was in prison and you came to visit me.'[d]

37"Then the righteous will answer him, 'Lord, when did we see you hungry and feed you, or thirsty and give you something to drink? 38When did we see you a stranger and invite you in, or needing clothes and clothe you? 39When did we see you sick or in prison and go to visit you?'

40"The King will reply, 'I tell you the truth, whatever you did for one of the least of these brothers of mine, you did for me.'[e]

41"Then he will say to those on his left, 'Depart from me,[f] you who are cursed, into the eternal fire[g] prepared for the devil and his angels.[h] 42For I was hungry and you gave me nothing to eat, I was thirsty and you gave me nothing to drink, 43I was a stranger and you did not invite me in, I needed clothes and you did not clothe me,

---

25:29 EVERYONE WHO HAS. Jesus gives an important principle with regard to the believer's reward and state in heaven. What believers receive in the future kingdom of God will depend on what they possess of it now. Their position and inheritance in heaven will be in proportion to their present commitment to God's ways and kingdom (see Lk 22:24–30, note).

25:32 SHEEP FROM THE GOATS. The sheep and goat judgment occurs after the tribulation and Christ's return to earth but before the beginning of his earthly reign (cf. Da 7:9–14; Rev 5:10; 19:11—20:4). (1) At the time of Christ's coming the saved and the lost who are living on earth and who survived the tribulation are still mingled together. (2) The judgment involves the separation of the wicked from the righteous (vv. 32–33; see 13:41, note). (3) The judgment will be based on outward works of love and kindness to those belonging to Christ and who are suffering. The expression of love and compassion is taken as an inherent part of true faith and salvation (vv. 35–46). (4) The wicked will not be allowed to enter Christ's kingdom, but will go into eternal punishment (vv. 41,46; Rev 14:11). (5) The righteous will inherit eternal life (v. 46) and the kingdom of God (v. 34; see Rev 20:4, notes).

25:41 DEVIL AND HIS ANGELS. Satan's initial rebellion against God (see 4:10, note) drew with him a third of the heavenly angels (Rev 12:4). A part of these are bound in hell (2Pe 2:4; Jude 6), while the rest are free and exist under Satan's dominion and control (12:24; 25:41; Eph 2:2; Rev 12:7). These free angels are his highly organized emissaries (Eph 6:11–12) and are probably identical with the demons referred to in the Bible (see article on POWER OVER SATAN AND DEMONS, p. 80).

I was sick and in prison and you did not look after me.'

44"They also will answer, 'Lord, when did we see you hungry or thirsty or a stranger or needing clothes or sick or in prison, and did not help you?'

45"He will reply, 'I tell you the truth, whatever you did not do for one of the least of these, you did not do for me.'[i]

46"Then they will go away to eternal punishment, but the righteous to eternal life."[j][k]

The Plot Against Jesus

26:2–5pp — Mk 14:1,2; Lk 22:1,2

26 When Jesus had finished saying all these things,[l] he said to his disciples, 2"As you know, the Passover[m] is two days away—and the Son of Man will be handed over to be crucified."

3Then the chief priests and the elders of the people assembled[n] in the palace of the high priest, whose name was Caiaphas,[o] 4and they plotted to arrest Jesus in some sly way and kill him.[p] 5"But not during the Feast," they said, "or there may be a riot[q] among the people."

Jesus Anointed at Bethany

26:6–13pp — Mk 14:3–9
26:6–13Ref — Lk 7:37,38; Jn 12:1–8

6While Jesus was in Bethany[r] in the home of a man known as Simon the Leper, 7a woman came to him with an alabaster jar of very expensive perfume, which she poured on his head as he was reclining at the table.

8When the disciples saw this, they were indignant. "Why this waste?" they asked. 9"This perfume could have been sold at a high price and the money given to the poor."

10Aware of this, Jesus said to them, "Why are you bothering this woman? She has done a beautiful thing to me. 11The poor you will always have with you,[s] but you will not always have me. 12When she poured this perfume on my body, she did it to prepare me for burial.[t] 13I tell you the truth, wherever this gospel is preached throughout the world, what she has done will also be told, in memory of her."

Judas Agrees to Betray Jesus

26:14–16pp — Mk 14:10,11; Lk 22:3–6

14Then one of the Twelve—the one called Judas Iscariot[u]—went to the chief priests 15and asked, "What are you willing to give me if I hand him over to you?" So they counted out for him thirty silver coins.[v] 16From then on Judas watched for an opportunity to hand him over.

The Lord's Supper

26:17–19pp — Mk 14:12–16; Lk 22:7–13
26:20–24pp — Mk 14:17–21
26:26–29pp — Mk 14:22–25; Lk 22:17–20; 1Co 11:23–25

17On the first day of the Feast of Unleavened Bread,[w] the disciples came to Jesus and asked, "Where do you want us to make preparations for you to eat the Passover?"[x]

18He replied, "Go into the city to a certain man and tell him, 'The Teacher says: My appointed time[y] is near. I am going to celebrate the Passover with my disciples at your house.' " 19So the disciples did as Jesus had directed them and prepared the Passover.

20When evening came, Jesus was reclining at the table with the Twelve. 21And while they were eating, he said, "I tell you the truth, one of you will betray me."[z]

22They were very sad and began to say to him one after the other, "Surely not I, Lord?"

23Jesus replied, "The one who has dipped his hand into the bowl with me will betray me.[a] 24The Son of Man will go just as it is written about him.[b] But woe to that man who betrays the Son of Man! It would be better for him if he had not been born."

25Then Judas, the one who would betray him,[c] said, "Surely not I, Rabbi?"[d]

25:45 [i]Pr 14:31; 17:5
25:46 [j]Mt 19:29; Jn 3:15,16,36; 17:2,3; Ro 2:7; Gal 6:8; 1Jn 1:2; 5:11,13,20 [k]Da 12:2; Jn 5:29; Ac 24:15; Ro 2:7, 8; Gal 6:8
26:1 [l]S Mt 7:28
26:2 [m]S Jn 11:55
26:3 [n]Ps 2:2 [o]ver 57; Lk 3:2; Jn 11:47-53; 18:13,14,24,28; Ac 4:6
26:4 [p]S Mt 12:14
26:5 [q]Mt 27:24
26:6 [r]S Mt 21:17
26:11 [s]Dt 15:11
26:12 [t]Jn 19:40
26:14 [u]ver 25, 47; S Mt 10:4
26:15 [v]Ex 21:32; Zec 11:12
26:17 [w]Ex 12:18-20 [x]Dt 16:5-8
26:18 [y]Mk 14:35,41; Jn 7:6,8,30; 8:20; 12:23; 13:1; 17:1
26:21 [z]Lk 22:21-23; Jn 13:21
26:23 [a]Ps 41:9; Jn 13:18
26:24 [b]ver 31,54, 56; Isa 53; Da 9:26; Mk 9:12; Lk 24:25-27,46; Ac 17:2,3; 26:22, 23; 1Pe 1:10,11
26:25 [c]S Mt 10:4 [d]S Mt 23:7

26:2 PASSOVER. The Passover (Gk *pascha*) was a spring festival associated with the historical episode of Israel's departure from Egypt. It celebrated the "passing over" of the Hebrews' houses by the destroying angel because of the blood of the lamb that had been put on the doorposts and frames of the houses (see Ex 12:7; Ps 78:49). Christ's crucifixion occurred on "the day of Preparation of Passover Week" (Jn 19:14). He is "our Passover . . . sacrificed" (1Co 5:7).

26:13 IN MEMORY OF HER. The Lord has ordained that this story of Mary (vv. 6–13) should always accompany the preaching of the gospel. This is because she exemplifies better than anyone else the dedication that all followers of Christ should have. Her act was the expression of her deep devotion to and profound love for the Master. The Christian faith is first of all a personal ministering to him. We learn here that our heartfelt attachment to and love for Jesus is the most valuable aspect of our relationship to him (see Jn 21:15, note).

Jesus answered, "Yes, it is you."[c]
26 While they were eating, Jesus took
bread, gave thanks and broke it,[e] and
gave it to his disciples, saying, "Take and
eat; this is my body."
27 Then he took the cup,[f] gave thanks
and offered it to them, saying, "Drink from
it, all of you. 28 This is my blood of the[d]
covenant,[g] which is poured out for many
for the forgiveness of sins.[h] 29 I tell you,
I will not drink of this fruit of the vine from
now on until that day when I drink it anew
with you[i] in my Father's kingdom."
30 When they had sung a hymn, they
went out to the Mount of Olives.[j]

Jesus Predicts Peter's Denial

26:31–35pp — Mk 14:27–31; Lk 22:31–34

31 Then Jesus told them, "This very
night you will all fall away on account of
me,[k] for it is written:

" 'I will strike the shepherd,
and the sheep of the flock will be
scattered.'[e][l]

32 But after I have risen, I will go ahead of
you into Galilee."[m]
33 Peter replied, "Even if all fall away on
account of you, I never will."
34 "I tell you the truth," Jesus answered,
"this very night, before the rooster crows,
you will disown me three times."[n]
35 But Peter declared, "Even if I have to
die with you,[o] I will never disown you."
And all the other disciples said the same.

Gethsemane

26:36–46pp — Mk 14:32–42; Lk 22:40–46

36 Then Jesus went with his disciples to
a place called Gethsemane, and he said to
them, "Sit here while I go over there and
pray." 37 He took Peter and the two sons
of Zebedee[p] along with him, and he began
to be sorrowful and troubled. 38 Then he
said to them, "My soul is overwhelmed
with sorrow[q] to the point of death. Stay
here and keep watch with me."[r]
39 Going a little farther, he fell with his
face to the ground and prayed, "My Father, if it is possible, may this cup[s] be
taken from me. Yet not as I will, but as you
will."[t]
40 Then he returned to his disciples and
found them sleeping. "Could you men not
keep watch with me[u] for one hour?" he
asked Peter. 41 "Watch and pray so that
you will not fall into temptation.[v] The
spirit is willing, but the body is weak."
42 He went away a second time and
prayed, "My Father, if it is not possible for
this cup to be taken away unless I drink
it, may your will be done."[w]
43 When he came back, he again found
them sleeping, because their eyes were
heavy. 44 So he left them and went away

26:26 [e] S Mt 14:19
26:27 [f] 1Co 10:16
26:28 [g] Ex 24:6-8; Zec 9:11; Mal 2:5; Heb 9:20; 10:29; S 13:20 [h] S Mt 20:28; Mk 1:4
26:29 [i] Ac 10:41
26:30 [j] S Mt 21:1
26:31 [k] Mt 11:6; 13:21 [l] Zec 13:7; Jn 16:32
26:32 [m] Mt 28:7, 10,16
26:34 [n] ver 75; Jn 13:38
26:35 [o] Jn 13:37
26:37 [p] S Mt 4:21
26:38 [q] S Jn 12:27 [r] ver 40,41
26:39 [s] S Mt 20:22 [t] ver 42; Ps 40:6-8; Isa 50:5; Mt 6:10; Jn 4:34; 5:30; 6:38
26:40 [u] ver 38
26:41 [v] Mt 6:13
26:42 [w] S ver 39

[c] *25* Or *"You yourself have said it"* [d] *28* Some manuscripts *the new* [e] *31* Zech. 13:7

26:26 TAKE AND EAT; THIS IS MY BODY. See 1Co 11:24–25, note on the Lord's Supper.

26:28 THE COVENANT. See article on THE OLD COVENANT AND THE NEW COVENANT, p. 500.

26:28 FORGIVENESS OF SINS. Forgiveness is necessary because we have sinned, destroyed our relationship with God and become subject to condemnation (Ro 1:18–32). Forgiveness is the means by which this relationship is restored (Eph 1:7; Col 2:13).

(1) The Hebrew and Greek words for forgiveness denote the idea of "to cover," "to pardon," "to cancel," "to send away." God's forgiveness involves making of no account the sin that has been committed (Mk 2:5; Jn 8:11), saving sinners from eternal punishment (Ro 5:9; 1Th 1:10), accepting them (Lk 15:20ff), delivering them from the dominion of sin and transferring them into Christ's kingdom (Col 1:13), and renewing the whole person and promising eternal life (Lk 23:43; Jn 14:19b).

(2) In order to receive forgiveness, there must be repentance, faith and confession of sin (Lk 17:3–4; Ac 2:38; 5:31; 20:21; 1Jn 1:9). For God to be able to extend forgiveness, the shedding of blood was required (Heb 9:22). Thus, forgiveness is based on Jesus' death on the cross (v. 28; Jn 1:29; 3:16; Ro 8:32). Divine forgiveness is an ongoing need for believers, so that we might maintain our saving relationship with God (6:12,14–15; 1Jn 1:9).

26:37 HE BEGAN TO BE SORROWFUL. The sufferings of Christ, stage one. The physical and spiritual sufferings of Christ begin in Gethsemane. "His sweat was like drops of blood" (Lk 22:44). Under great stress, the small capillaries in the sweat glands can break and mix blood with sweat (see next note for further insights into this stage of Christ's sufferings; for the second stage of Christ's sufferings, see v. 67, note).

26:39 MAY THIS CUP BE TAKEN. What Christ meant by "this cup" has been the subject of much discussion. (1) It is doubtful that Christ was praying to be saved from physical death, for he had resolutely set himself to die for the sin of humanity (cf. Mk 10:33–34; Lk 9:51; Jn 12:24,27; Heb 10:5–9).

(2) It is more probable that he was praying to be delivered from the punishment of separation from God, the ultimate penalty for sin. Christ prayed that his physical death might be accepted as full payment for the sin of sinners. However, he prayed, "yet not as I will, but as you will." He then committed himself to undergo both physical death and spiritual separation from his heavenly Father in order to achieve our salvation (cf. 27:46). His prayer was "heard," for he was strengthened by his Father to drink the appointed cup (see Heb 5:7).

once more and prayed the third time, saying the same thing.

45 Then he returned to the disciples and said to them, "Are you still sleeping and resting? Look, the hour[x] is near, and the Son of Man is betrayed into the hands of sinners. 46 Rise, let us go! Here comes my betrayer!"

Jesus Arrested

26:47–56pp — Mk 14:43–50; Lk 22:47–53

47 While he was still speaking, Judas,[y] one of the Twelve, arrived. With him was a large crowd armed with swords and clubs, sent from the chief priests and the elders of the people. 48 Now the betrayer had arranged a signal with them: "The one I kiss is the man; arrest him." 49 Going at once to Jesus, Judas said, "Greetings, Rabbi!"[z] and kissed him.

50 Jesus replied, "Friend,[a] do what you came for."[f]

Then the men stepped forward, seized Jesus and arrested him. 51 With that, one of Jesus' companions reached for his sword,[b] drew it out and struck the servant of the high priest, cutting off his ear.[c]

52 "Put your sword back in its place," Jesus said to him, "for all who draw the sword will die by the sword.[d] 53 Do you think I cannot call on my Father, and he will at once put at my disposal more than twelve legions of angels?[e] 54 But how then would the Scriptures be fulfilled[f] that say it must happen in this way?"

55 At that time Jesus said to the crowd, "Am I leading a rebellion, that you have come out with swords and clubs to capture me? Every day I sat in the temple courts teaching,[g] and you did not arrest me. 56 But this has all taken place that the writings of the prophets might be fulfilled."[h] Then all the disciples deserted him and fled.

26:45 [x]S ver 18
26:47 [y]S Mt 10:4
26:49 [z]ver 25; S Mt 23:7
26:50 [a]Mt 20:13; 22:12
26:51 [b]Lk 22:36, 38 [c]Jn 18:10
26:52 [d]Ge 9:6; Ex 21:12; Rev 13:10
26:53 [e]2Ki 6:17; Da 7:10; Mt 4:11
26:54 [f]S ver 24; S Mt 1:22
26:55 [g]Mk 12:35; Lk 21:37; Jn 7:14, 28; 18:20
26:56 [h]S ver 24; S Mt 1:22

26:57 [i]S ver 3
26:58 [j]ver 69; Mk 14:66; Lk 22:55; Jn 18:15 [k]Mk 15:16; Lk 11:21; Jn 7:32, 45,46
26:59 [l]S Mt 5:22
26:60 [m]Ps 27:12; 35:11; Ac 6:13 [n]Dt 19:15
26:61 [o]S Jn 2:19
26:63 [p]S Mk 14:61 [q]Lev 5:1 [r]S Mt 16:16 [s]Lk 22:67 [t]S Mt 4:3
26:64 [u]Mt 27:11; Lk 22:70 [v]S Mk 16:19 [w]S Rev 1:7
26:65 [x]S Mk 14:63
26:66 [y]Lev 24:16; Jn 19:7
26:67 [z]S Mt 16:21

Before the Sanhedrin

26:57–68pp — Mk 14:53–65; Jn 18:12,13,19–24

57 Those who had arrested Jesus took him to Caiaphas,[i] the high priest, where the teachers of the law and the elders had assembled. 58 But Peter followed him at a distance, right up to the courtyard of the high priest.[j] He entered and sat down with the guards[k] to see the outcome.

59 The chief priests and the whole Sanhedrin[l] were looking for false evidence against Jesus so that they could put him to death. 60 But they did not find any, though many false witnesses[m] came forward.

Finally two[n] came forward 61 and declared, "This fellow said, 'I am able to destroy the temple of God and rebuild it in three days.' "[o]

62 Then the high priest stood up and said to Jesus, "Are you not going to answer? What is this testimony that these men are bringing against you?" 63 But Jesus remained silent.[p]

The high priest said to him, "I charge you under oath[q] by the living God:[r] Tell us if you are the Christ,[g][s] the Son of God."[t]

64 "Yes, it is as you say,"[u] Jesus replied. "But I say to all of you: In the future you will see the Son of Man sitting at the right hand of the Mighty One[v] and coming on the clouds of heaven."[w]

65 Then the high priest tore his clothes[x] and said, "He has spoken blasphemy! Why do we need any more witnesses? Look, now you have heard the blasphemy. 66 What do you think?"

"He is worthy of death,"[y] they answered.

67 Then they spit in his face and struck him with their fists.[z] Others slapped him

[f] *50* Or *"Friend, why have you come?"* [g] *63* Or *Messiah*; also in verse 68

26:57 ARRESTED JESUS. A study of the events from Christ's arrest to his crucifixion can be very rewarding. The order is as follows: (1) the arrest (26:47–56; Mk 14:43–52; Lk 22:47–53; Jn 18:2–12); (2) the religious trial before Annas (Jn 18:12–14,19–24) and before Caiaphas (26:57,59–68; Mk 14:53,55–65; Lk 22:54,63–65; Jn 18:24); (3) the denial by Peter (26:58,69–75; Mk 14:54,66–72; Lk 22:54–62; Jn 18:15–18,25–27); (4) the condemnation by the Sanhedrin (27:1; Mk 15:1; Lk 22:66–71); (5) the death of Judas (27:3–10); (6) the civil trial before Pilate (27:2,11–14; Mk 15:2–5; Lk 23:1–5; Jn 18:28–38); (7) the trial before Herod (Lk 23:6–12), who sent him back to Pilate (27:11–26; Mk 15:6–15; Lk 23:11–25; Jn 18:28—19:1,4–16); (8) the mockery (27:27–30; Mk 15:16–19; Jn 19:2–3), after which he was beaten and then led away to be crucified (27:31); (9) the procession to Golgotha (27:32–34; Mk 15:20–23; Lk 23:26–33); (10) the crucifixion (27:35, note).

26:67 THEY SPIT . . . STRUCK . . . SLAPPED. The sufferings of Christ, stage two. After the arrest at night and abandonment by his disciples (vv. 55–57), Jesus is brought before Caiaphas and the Jewish council. He is blindfolded, mocked repeatedly, spat on and struck in the face. (For the third stage of Christ's sufferings, see 27:2, note.)

68 and said, "Prophesy to us, Christ. Who
hit you?"[a]

Peter Disowns Jesus

*26:69–75pp — Mk 14:66–72; Lk 22:55–62;
Jn 18:16–18,25–27*

69 Now Peter was sitting out in the
courtyard, and a servant girl came to him.
"You also were with Jesus of Galilee," she
said.

70 But he denied it before them all. "I
don't know what you're talking about," he
said.

71 Then he went out to the gateway,
where another girl saw him and said to the
people there, "This fellow was with Jesus
of Nazareth."

72 He denied it again, with an oath: "I
don't know the man!"

73 After a little while, those standing
there went up to Peter and said, "Surely
you are one of them, for your accent gives
you away."

74 Then he began to call down curses on
himself and he swore to them, "I don't
know the man!"

Immediately a rooster crowed. 75 Then
Peter remembered the word Jesus had
spoken: "Before the rooster crows, you
will disown me three times."[b] And he
went outside and wept bitterly.

Judas Hangs Himself

27 Early in the morning, all the chief
priests and the elders of the people came to the decision to put Jesus to
death.[c] 2 They bound him, led him away
and handed him over[d] to Pilate, the governor.[e]

3 When Judas, who had betrayed him,[f]
saw that Jesus was condemned, he was
seized with remorse and returned the thirty silver coins[g] to the chief priests and the
elders. 4 "I have sinned," he said, "for I
have betrayed innocent blood."

"What is that to us?" they replied.
"That's your responsibility."[h]

5 So Judas threw the money into the
temple[i] and left. Then he went away and
hanged himself.[j]

6 The chief priests picked up the coins
and said, "It is against the law to put this
into the treasury, since it is blood money."
7 So they decided to use the money to buy
the potter's field as a burial place for foreigners. 8 That is why it has been called
the Field of Blood[k] to this day. 9 Then
what was spoken by Jeremiah the prophet
was fulfilled:[l] "They took the thirty silver
coins, the price set on him by the people
of Israel, 10 and they used them to buy the
potter's field, as the Lord commanded
me."[h][m]

Jesus Before Pilate

*27:11–26pp — Mk 15:2–15; Lk 23:2,3, 18–25;
Jn 18:29–19:16*

11 Meanwhile Jesus stood before the
governor, and the governor asked him,
"Are you the king of the Jews?"[n]

"Yes, it is as you say," Jesus replied.
12 When he was accused by the chief
priests and the elders, he gave no answer.[o] 13 Then Pilate asked him, "Don't
you hear the testimony they are bringing
against you?"[p] 14 But Jesus made no reply,[q] not even to a single charge—to the
great amazement of the governor.

15 Now it was the governor's custom at
the Feast to release a prisoner[r] chosen by
the crowd. 16 At that time they had a noto-
rious prisoner, called Barabbas. 17 So
when the crowd had gathered, Pilate
asked them, "Which one do you want me
to release to you: Barabbas, or Jesus who
is called Christ?"[s] 18 For he knew it was
out of envy that they had handed Jesus
over to him.

19 While Pilate was sitting on the

26:68 [a]Lk 22:63-65 **26:75** [b]ver 34; Jn 13:38 **27:1** [c]S Mt 12:14; Mk 15:1; Lk 22:66 **27:2** [d]Mt 20:19 [e]Mk 15:1; Lk 13:1; Ac 3:13; 1Ti 6:13 **27:3** [f]S Mt 10:4 [g]Mt 26:14,15 **27:4** [h]ver 24 **27:5** [i]Lk 1:9,21 [j]Ac 1:18 **27:8** [k]Ac 1:19 **27:9** [l]S Mt 1:22 **27:10** [m]Zec 11:12,13; Jer 32:6-9 **27:11** [n]S Mt 2:2 **27:12** [o]S Mk 14:61 **27:13** [p]Mt 26:62 **27:14** [q]S Mk 14:61 **27:15** [r]Jn 18:39 **27:17** [s]ver 22; Mt 1:16

h *10* See Zech. 11:12,13; Jer. 19:1-13; 32:6-9.

27:2 HANDED HIM OVER TO PILATE. The sufferings of Christ, stage three. In the morning, Jesus, battered and exhausted, is taken across Jerusalem to be interrogated by Pilate. Barabbas is released (v. 21) and Jesus is scourged and handed over to be crucified (v. 26). (For the fourth stage of Christ's sufferings, see v. 26, note.)

27:3 JUDAS'S REMORSE. Judas learned that his sinful actions would lead to the death of Jesus. Likewise, our actions inevitably affect others for good or for evil. Many things we set in motion cannot be stopped, and their evil and destructive results will be experienced by us and others. It is of utmost importance to avoid all actions and plans that may have potentially harmful consequences.

27:5 JUDAS'S DEATH. Matthew states that Judas "hanged himself"; Ac 1:18 records that he died by falling. What Judas probably did was to throw himself on a sharpened stake. Hanging in those days was done by crucifixion or impalement.

27:9 JEREMIAH THE PROPHET. Matthew here combines and summarizes elements of prophetic symbolism, one from Jeremiah (Jer 32:6–9) and one from Zechariah (Zec 11:12–13). Then he mentions the older and more prominent prophet as the source, a custom frequently used in alluding to passages from the prophets.

judge's seat,[t] his wife sent him this message: "Don't have anything to do with that
innocent[u] man, for I have suffered a great
deal today in a dream[v] because of him."
20But the chief priests and the elders
persuaded the crowd to ask for Barabbas
and to have Jesus executed.[w]
21"Which of the two do you want me to
release to you?" asked the governor.
"Barabbas," they answered.
22"What shall I do, then, with Jesus who
is called Christ?"[x] Pilate asked.
They all answered, "Crucify him!"
23"Why? What crime has he committed?" asked Pilate.
But they shouted all the louder, "Crucify him!"
24When Pilate saw that he was getting
nowhere, but that instead an uproar[y] was
starting, he took water and washed his
hands[z] in front of the crowd. "I am innocent of this man's blood,"[a] he said. "It is
your responsibility!"[b]
25All the people answered, "Let his
blood be on us and on our children!"[c]
26Then he released Barabbas to them.
But he had Jesus flogged,[d] and handed
him over to be crucified.

The Soldiers Mock Jesus

27:27–31pp — Mk 15:16–20

27Then the governor's soldiers took
Jesus into the Praetorium[e] and gathered
the whole company of soldiers around
him. **28**They stripped him and put a scarlet
robe on him,[f] **29**and then twisted together
a crown of thorns and set it on his head.
They put a staff in his right hand and knelt
in front of him and mocked him. "Hail,
king of the Jews!" they said.[g] **30**They spit
on him, and took the staff and struck him
on the head again and again.[h] **31**After
they had mocked him, they took off the
robe and put his own clothes on him. Then
they led him away to crucify him.[i]

The Crucifixion

27:33–44pp — Mk 15:22–32; Lk 23:33–43; Jn 19:17–24

32As they were going out,[j] they met a
man from Cyrene,[k] named Simon, and
they forced him to carry the cross.[l]
33They came to a place called Golgotha
(which means The Place of the Skull).[m]
34There they offered Jesus wine to drink,
mixed with gall;[n] but after tasting it, he
refused to drink it. **35**When they had crucified him, they divided up his clothes by
casting lots.[i][o] **36**And sitting down, they
kept watch[p] over him there. **37**Above his
head they placed the written charge
against him: THIS IS JESUS, THE KING OF THE

i *35* A few late manuscripts *lots that the word spoken by the prophet might be fulfilled: "They divided my garments among themselves and cast lots for my clothing"* (Psalm 22:18)

27:19 [t]Jn 19:13 [u]ver 24 [v]Ge 20:6; Nu 12:6; 1Ki 3:5; Job 33:14-16; Mt 1:20; 2:12,13, 19,22
27:20 [w]Ac 3:14
27:22 [x]Mt 1:16
27:24 [y]Mt 26:5 [z]Ps 26:6 [a]Dt 21:6-8 [b]ver 4
27:25 [c]Jos 2:19; S Ac 5:28
27:26 [d]Isa 53:5; Jn 19:1
27:27 [e]Jn 18:28, 33; 19:9
27:28 [f]Jn 19:2
27:29 [g]Isa 53:3; Jn 19:2,3
27:30 [h]S Mt 16:21
27:31 [i]Isa 53:7
27:32 [j]Heb 13:12 [k]Ac 2:10; 6:9; 11:20; 13:1 [l]Mk 15:21; Lk 23:26
27:33 [m]Jn 19:17
27:34 [n]ver 48; Ps 69:21
27:35 [o]Ps 22:18
27:36 [p]ver 54

27:24 PILATE. Pilate's greatest sin was compromising what he knew to be true and right for the sake of position, status and personal gain. Pilate knew Christ was innocent, and declared so on several occasions (v. 18; Jn 19:4,6).

27:26 HAD JESUS FLOGGED. The sufferings of Christ, stage four. (1) The Roman flogging consisted of the victim being stripped and stretched against a pillar or bent over a low post, and the hands tied. The instrument of torture was a short wooden handle to which several leather thongs were attached, with bits of iron or bone tied to the thongs. The blows were laid on the victim's back by two men, one lashing the victim from one side, one from the other side. This resulted in the flesh being cut to such an extent that veins, arteries and sometimes even inner organs were exposed. Often the victim died during the flogging.

(2) Flogging is hideous torture. The inability of Jesus to bear his own cross is no doubt due to this severe infliction (v. 32; Lk 23:26). "But he was pierced for our transgressions, he was crushed for our iniquities; the punishment that brought us peace was upon him, and by his wounds we are healed" (Isa 53:5; 1Pe 2:24). (For the fifth stage of the sufferings of Christ, see v. 28, note.)

27:28–29 A SCARLET ROBE ... A CROWN OF THORNS. The sufferings of Christ, stage five. Jesus is untied and placed in the middle of the Roman company (v. 27). The soldiers put a robe across his shoulders, place a stick in his hand and press a circle of branches covered with long thorns on his head (v. 29). The soldiers mock him and strike him across the face and head, driving the thorns deeper into his scalp (vv. 30–31). (For the sixth stage of the sufferings of Christ, see v. 31, note.)

27:31 LED HIM AWAY TO CRUCIFY HIM. The sufferings of Christ, stage six. The heavy beam of the cross is tied to Christ's shoulder. He begins the slow journey to Golgotha. The weight of the wooden beam, together with sheer physical exhaustion, cause him to fall. He tries to rise, but cannot. Simon is then pressed into service to bear Christ's cross. (For the seventh stage of the sufferings of Christ, see v. 35, note.)

27:35 THEY ... CRUCIFIED HIM. The sufferings of Christ, stage seven. At Golgotha the cross beam is placed on the ground and Jesus is laid on it. His arms are stretched along the beams and a heavy, square, wrought-iron nail is driven through his hand (or wrist), first into the right, then into the left hand, and deep into the wood. Next Christ is lifted up by means of ropes or ladders, the cross beam is bound or nailed to the upright beam and a support for the body is fastened on it. Lastly, his feet are extended and a larger piece of iron is driven through them. (For the eighth stage of the sufferings of Christ, see v. 39, note.)

JEWS. **38**Two robbers were crucified with
him,[q] one on his right and one on his left.
39Those who passed by hurled insults at
him, shaking their heads[r] **40**and saying,
"You who are going to destroy the temple
and build it in three days,[s] save yourself![t] Come down from the cross, if you
are the Son of God!"[u]
41In the same way the chief priests, the
teachers of the law and the elders mocked
him. **42**"He saved others," they said, "but
he can't save himself! He's the King of
Israel![v] Let him come down now from the
cross, and we will believe[w] in him. **43**He
trusts in God. Let God rescue him[x] now
if he wants him, for he said, 'I am the Son
of God.' " **44**In the same way the robbers
who were crucified with him also heaped
insults on him.

The Death of Jesus

27:45–56pp — Mk 15:33–41; Lk 23:44–49

45From the sixth hour until the ninth
hour darkness[y] came over all the land.
46About the ninth hour Jesus cried out in
a loud voice, *"Eloi, Eloi,*[j] *lama sabachthani?"*—which means, "My God, my God,
why have you forsaken me?"[k][z]
47When some of those standing there
heard this, they said, "He's calling Elijah."
48Immediately one of them ran and got
a sponge. He filled it with wine vinegar,[a]
put it on a stick, and offered it to Jesus to
drink. **49**The rest said, "Now leave him
alone. Let's see if Elijah comes to save
him."
50And when Jesus had cried out again
in a loud voice, he gave up his spirit.[b]
51At that moment the curtain of the
temple[c] was torn in two from top to bottom. The earth shook and the rocks
split.[d] **52**The tombs broke open and the
bodies of many holy people who had died
were raised to life. **53**They came out of the
tombs, and after Jesus' resurrection they
went into the holy city[e] and appeared to
many people.
54When the centurion and those with
him who were guarding[f] Jesus saw the
earthquake and all that had happened,
they were terrified, and exclaimed, "Surely he was the Son[l] of God!"[g]
55Many women were there, watching
from a distance. They had followed Jesus
from Galilee to care for his needs.[h]
56Among them were Mary Magdalene,
Mary the mother of James and Joses, and
the mother of Zebedee's sons.[i]

The Burial of Jesus

27:57–61pp — Mk 15:42–47; Lk 23:50–56; Jn 19:38–42

57As evening approached, there came a
rich man from Arimathea, named Joseph,
who had himself become a disciple of
Jesus. **58**Going to Pilate, he asked for
Jesus' body, and Pilate ordered that it be
given to him. **59**Joseph took the body,
wrapped it in a clean linen cloth, **60**and
placed it in his own new tomb[j] that he

27:38 [q] Isa 53:12
27:39 [r] Ps 22:7; 109:25; La 2:15
27:40 [s] S Jn 2:19 [t] ver 42 [u] Mt 4:3,6
27:42 [v] Jn 1:49; 12:13 [w] S Jn 3:15
27:43 [x] Ps 22:8
27:45 [y] Am 8:9
27:46 [z] Ps 22:1
27:48 [a] ver 34; Ps 69:21
27:50 [b] Jn 19:30
27:51 [c] Ex 26:31-33; Heb 9:3,8; 10:19, 20 [d] ver 54
27:53 [e] S Mt 4:5
27:54 [f] ver 36 [g] S Mt 4:3; 17:5
27:55 [h] Lk 8:2,3
27:56 [i] Mk 15:47; Lk 24:10; Jn 19:25
27:60 [j] Mt 27:66; 28:2; Mk 16:4; Ac 13:29

j 46 Some manuscripts *Eli, Eli* k 46 Psalm 22:1 l 54 Or *a son*

27:39 HURLED INSULTS AT HIM. The sufferings of Christ, stage eight. Jesus is now a pathetic spectacle, blood-streaked, covered with wounds and exposed to the view of the people. He experiences hours of pain in his entire body, fatigue in his arms, great waves of cramps in the muscles and skin torn from his back. Then another agony begins—a crushing pain deep in the chest as fluid begins to compress the heart. He feels an intense thirst (Jn 19:28) and is aware of the abuse and ridicule of those who pass by the cross (vv. 39–44). (For the ninth stage of the sufferings of Christ, see v. 46, note.)

27:46 WHY HAVE YOU FORSAKEN ME? The sufferings of Christ, stage nine. These words mark the climax of the sufferings of Christ for a lost world. His cry in Aramaic, "My God, my God, why have you forsaken me," testifies that he experiences separation from God as the sinner's substitute. Here the sorrow, grief and pain are at their worst. He is pierced for our transgressions (Isa 53:5) and gives himself a "ransom for many" (20:28; 1Ti 2:6). Him who had no sin God makes "to be sin for us" (2Co 5:21); he dies forsaken, that we might never be forsaken (cf. Ps 22). Thus we are redeemed by the sufferings of Christ (1Pe 1:19). (For the tenth stage of the sufferings of Christ, see v. 50, note.)

27:50 JESUS . . . CRIED OUT AGAIN. The sufferings of Christ, stage ten. Christ utters his final words with a loud voice, "It is finished" (Jn 19:30). This cry signifies the end of his sufferings and the completion of the work of redemption. The debt for our sin has been paid in full, and the plan of salvation established. Only then does he offer a final prayer, "Father, into your hands I commit my spirit" (Lk 23:46). (For the first stage of Christ's sufferings, see 26:37, note.)

27:51 THE CURTAIN . . . WAS TORN. The tearing of the "curtain of the temple" (cf. Ex 26:31–33; 36:35) signified that a way was now open into the presence of God. The curtain separating the Holy Place from the Most Holy Place barred the way into the presence of God. Through the death of Christ, the curtain was removed and the way into the Most Holy Place (i.e., God's presence) was open for all who believe in Christ and his saving word (cf. Heb 9:1–14; 10:19–22).

27:52 MANY HOLY PEOPLE . . . WERE RAISED. The significance of this event is the prophetic indication that Christ's death and resurrection guarantee our glorious resurrection at his return. His resurrection marked the defeat of death (see 1Co 15:50–58; 1Th 4:14).

had cut out of the rock. He rolled a big
stone in front of the entrance to the tomb
and went away. **61**Mary Magdalene and
the other Mary were sitting there opposite
the tomb.

The Guard at the Tomb

62The next day, the one after Preparation Day, the chief priests and the Pharisees went to Pilate. **63**"Sir," they said, "we
remember that while he was still alive
that deceiver said, 'After three days I will
rise again.'[k] **64**So give the order for the
tomb to be made secure until the third
day. Otherwise, his disciples may come
and steal the body[l] and tell the people
that he has been raised from the dead.
This last deception will be worse than the
first."
65"Take a guard,"[m] Pilate answered.
"Go, make the tomb as secure as you
know how." **66**So they went and made the
tomb secure by putting a seal[n] on the
stone[o] and posting the guard.[p]

The Resurrection

28:1–8pp — Mk 16:1–8; Lk 24:1–10

28 After the Sabbath, at dawn on the
first day of the week, Mary Magdalene[q] and the other Mary[r] went to look
at the tomb.
2There was a violent earthquake,[s] for
an angel[t] of the Lord came down from
heaven and, going to the tomb, rolled back
the stone[u] and sat on it. **3**His appearance
was like lightning, and his clothes were
white as snow.[v] **4**The guards were so
afraid of him that they shook and became
like dead men.
5The angel said to the women, "Do not
be afraid,[w] for I know that you are looking
for Jesus, who was crucified. **6**He is not
here; he has risen, just as he said.[x] Come
and see the place where he lay. **7**Then go
quickly and tell his disciples: 'He has ris-
en from the dead and is going ahead of you
into Galilee.[y] There you will see him.'
Now I have told you."
8So the women hurried away from the
tomb, afraid yet filled with joy, and ran to
tell his disciples. **9**Suddenly Jesus met
them.[z] "Greetings," he said. They came to
him, clasped his feet and worshiped him.
10Then Jesus said to them, "Do not be
afraid. Go and tell my brothers[a] to go to
Galilee; there they will see me."

The Guards' Report

11While the women were on their way,
some of the guards[b] went into the city and
reported to the chief priests everything
that had happened. **12**When the chief
priests had met with the elders and devised a plan, they gave the soldiers a large
sum of money, **13**telling them, "You are to
say, 'His disciples came during the night
and stole him away[c] while we were
asleep.' **14**If this report gets to the governor,[d] we will satisfy him and keep you out
of trouble." **15**So the soldiers took the
money and did as they were instructed.
And this story has been widely circulated
among the Jews to this very day.

27:63 [k]S Mt 16:21
27:64 [l]Mt 28:13
27:65 [m]ver 66; Mt 28:11
27:66 [n]Da 6:17 [o]ver 60; Mt 28:2 [p]Mt 28:11
28:1 [q]Lk 8:2 [r]Mt 27:56
28:2 [s]Mt 27:51 [t]Jn 20:12; S Ac 5:19 [u]Mt 27:60
28:3 [v]Da 7:9; 10:6; Mk 9:3; S Jn 20:12
28:5 [w]ver 10; S Mt 14:27
28:6 [x]S Mt 16:21
28:7 [y]ver 10,16; Mt 26:32
28:9 [z]Jn 20:14-18
28:10 [a]Mt 12:50; 25:40; Mk 3:34; Jn 20:17; Ro 8:29; Heb 2:11-13,17
28:11 [b]Mt 27:65, 66
28:13 [c]Mt 27:64
28:14 [d]S Mt 27:2

28:6 HE HAS RISEN. The resurrection of Jesus is one of the central truths of the gospel (1Co 15:1–8). What is the importance of Christ's resurrection to those who believe in him? (1) It proves he is the Son of God (Jn 10:17–18; Ro 1:4). (2) It guarantees the efficacy of his redemptive death (Ro 6:4; 1Co 15:17). (3) It verifies the truth of Scripture (Ps 16:10; Lk 24:44–47; Ac 2:31). (4) It is proof of future judgment on the wicked (Ac 17:30–31). (5) It is the foundation for Christ's gift of the Holy Spirit and spiritual life to his people (Jn 20:22; Ro 5:10; 1Co 15:45) and for his heavenly ministry of intercession for the believer (Heb 7:23–28). (6) It assures believers of their future heavenly inheritance (1Pe 1:3–4) and of their resurrection or translation when the Lord returns (see Jn 14:3, note; 1Th 4:14ff). (7) It makes available the presence of Christ and his power over sin in our everyday experience (Gal 2:20; Eph 1:18–20).

28:9 JESUS MET THEM. The resurrection is well verified historically. After his resurrection, Christ remained on earth for forty days, appearing and talking to the apostles and many of his followers. The resurrection appearances are as follows: (1) Mary Magdalene (Jn 20:11–18); (2) the women returning from the tomb (vv. 9–10); (3) Peter (Lk 24:34); (4) two travelers on the Emmaus road (Lk 24:13–32); (5) all the disciples except Thomas, and others with them (Lk 24:36–43); (6) all the disciples on Sunday night one week later (Jn 20:26–31); (7) seven disciples by the Sea of Galilee (Jn 21:1–25); (8) five hundred people in Galilee (compare vv. 16–20 with 1Co 15:6); (9) James (1Co 15:7); (10) the disciples receiving the Great Commission (vv. 16–20); (11) the apostles at the ascension (Ac 1:3–11); and (12) the apostle Paul (1Co 15:8).

28:10 DO NOT BE AFRAID. Why were these women not to be afraid? The angel's response gives us the answer: "for I know that you are looking for Jesus" (v. 5). The women had remained loyal friends of Jesus when the world despised and crucified him. At Christ's return, his faithful will have no reason to fear if they also have remained loyal to him in the midst of a world that rejects his love, salvation and holy Word. John expresses this truth in 1Jn 2:28: "And now, dear children, continue in him, so that when he appears we may be confident and unashamed before him at his coming."

The Great Commission

16Then the eleven disciples went to
Galilee, to the mountain where Jesus had
told them to go.[e] 17When they saw him,
they worshiped him; but some doubted.
18Then Jesus came to them and said, "All
authority in heaven and on earth has been
given to me.[f] 19Therefore go and make
disciples of all nations,[g] baptizing them
in[m] the name of the Father and of the Son
and of the Holy Spirit,[h] 20and teaching[i]
them to obey everything I have commanded you. And surely I am with you[j] always,
to the very end of the age."[k] Mk 16:15-16

28:16 [e]ver 7,10; Mt 26:32 28:18 [f]Da 7:13, 14; Lk 10:22; Jn 3:35; S 13:13; 17:2; 1Co 15:27; Eph 1:20-22; Php 2:9,10 28:19 [g]Isa 49:6; Mk 16:15,16; Lk 24:47; Ac 1:8; 14:21 [h]Ac 1:8; 2:38; 8:16; Ro 6:3,4; Gal 3:27; Col 2:12 28:20 [i]Jn 14:26; Ac 2:42 [j]Dt 31:6; 1Ki 8:57; Hag 1:13; Mt 18:20; Ac 18:10 [k]Mt 13:39; 24:3

[m] *19* Or *into*; see Acts 8:16; 19:5; Romans 6:3; 1 Cor. 1:13; 10:2 and Gal. 3:27.

28:18 ALL AUTHORITY. God's people are promised authority and power to proclaim the gospel throughout the world (vv. 19–20). But first they must obey Jesus' command to wait for the promise of the Father, which is the power of the Holy Spirit at Pentecost. We cannot expect the power of Ac 1:8 to accompany our going to the nations without first following the pattern of Ac 1:4 (see Lk 24:47–49; Ac 1:8; 2:4).

28:19 GO . . . MAKE DISCIPLES . . . BAPTIZING. These words are Christ's Great Commission to all his followers of every generation. They state the goal, responsibility and commissioning of the church's missionary task. (1) The church is to go into all the world and preach the gospel to all people according to the NT revelation of Christ and the apostles (see Eph 2:20, note). This task includes the primary responsibility of sending missionaries into every nation (Ac 13:1–4).

(2) The gospel preached is centered on "repentance and forgiveness of sins" (Lk 24:47), the promise of receiving "the gift of the Holy Spirit" (Ac 2:38) and the exhortation to separate from this corrupt generation (Ac 2:40) while waiting for the return of Jesus from heaven (Ac 3:19–20; 1Th 1:10).

(3) The purpose is to make disciples who will observe Christ's commands. This is the only direct imperative in this passage. Christ does not intend that evangelism and missionary witness result only in conversion decisions. Spiritual energies must not be concentrated in merely enlarging church membership, but in making disciples who separate themselves from the world, observe the commands of Christ, and follow him with all their heart, mind and will (cf. Jn 8:31).

(4) Furthermore, it should be noted that Christ commands us to concentrate on reaching lost men and women, not on Christianizing society or taking over the world. Those who believe must come out of the current evil world system and be separated from its immorality (Ro 13:12; 2Co 6:14), while exposing its evil (Eph 5:11).

(5) Those who believe in Christ and the gospel are to be "baptized" with water. This represents their covenant pledge to renounce immorality, the world and their own sinful nature, and to unreservedly commit themselves to Christ and his kingdom purposes (see Ac 22:16, note).

(6) Christ will be with his obedient followers in the presence and power of the Holy Spirit (cf. v. 20; 1:23; 18:20). They are to go to all nations and witness only after they are "clothed with power from on high" (Lk 24:49; see Ac 1:8, notes).

28:20 I AM WITH YOU. This promise is Christ's assurance to those involved in winning the lost and teaching them to obey his righteous standards. Jesus arose, is now alive and is personally interested in each one of his children. He is with you in the person of the Holy Spirit (Jn 14:16,26) and through his Word (Jn 14:23). No matter what your condition is—weak, poor, humble, apparently unimportant—he cares for you, watches with concern every detail of life's trials and struggles, and gives both the grace that is sufficient (2Co 12:9) and his presence to lead you home (18:20; Ac 18:10). This is the Christian's answer to every fear, every doubt, every trouble, every heartache and every discouragement.

THE KINGDOM OF GOD VERSUS THE KINGDOM OF SATAN

A. The Nature of the Kingdoms

	Kingdom of God		Kingdom of Satan	
Item	**Description**	**Reference**	**Description**	**Reference**
1. Rulership	a. Rule by God—Theocracy	2Ch 20:6; Ps 95:3; Da 4:17,32; 1Ti 1:17	a. Rule by Satan—the god of this age	Jn 12:31; 14:30; 2Co 4:4; Eph 2:2; 1Jn 5:19
	b. God's rule through his Son	Ps 110:1; Isa 9:6–7; Da 7:13–14; Mt 28:18; Lk 1:32–33; Eph 1:20–22; Heb 1:3–8; Rev 1:5; 19:13–16	b. Satan assisted by principalities, powers and rulers of this dark world	Eph 1:21; 6:12; Col 1:16; 2:15; cf. Da 10:13
2. Character	a. Righteousness, peace and joy in the Holy Spirit	Mt 6:33; Jn 18:36; Ro 14:17	a. Centered in the things of this world	1Jn 2:15–17; 5:19; Rev 2:9,13
	b. Divine power	Lk 11:20–22; 1Co 2:4; 4:20; 1Th 1:5	b. Disease, sickness, slavery	Mt 10:1; Lk 9:1
	c. Truth	Jn 8:31–32; 14:6,16–17; 15:26; 16:13; 17:17	c. Deception	Ge 3:4–5,13; Jn 8:44; Ro 1:25; 2Co 4:4; 2Th 2:10–12
	d. Holiness	1Co 1:2,30; 2Co 6:17—7:1; Eph 4:24; Heb 12:10,14; 1Pe 1:15–16	d. Sin and evil	Ro 1:28–32; 1Co 6:9–10; Eph 2:1–3; 1Jn 3:7–10,12
	e. Light	Jn 1:4–9; 3:19; Ac 26:18; Col 1:12–13; 1Ti 6:16; 1Jn 1:5,7	e. Darkness	Lk 22:53; Ac 26:18; Eph 6:12; Col 1:13; 1Jn 1:6; cf. 2Co 11:14
	f. Eternal life	Jn 1:4; 3:16; Ro 5:17; 6:4,12; 8:2; 1Jn 5:12; Rev 1:18	f. Eternal death	Ro 5:12,14; 6:23; Eph 2:1; Rev 20:14–15; 21:8
3. Manifestation	a. Salvation	Mk 1:15; Ac 8:12; 1Co 5:10–11	a. Destruction	Jn 10:10; 1Pe 5:8
	b. Baptism in the Holy Spirit	Mt 3:2,11–12; Ac 1:3–8	b. Filled with the spirit of the world	1Co 2:12; Jas 4:4; 1Jn 2:15

Item	Kingdom of God		Kingdom of Satan	
	Description	Reference	Description	Reference
3. Manifestation (cont.)	c. Miracles and driving out demons	Mt 4:23–24; 10:7–8; 12:28; Lk 9:1–2,11; 11:20–22; 13:11–16	c. Counterfeit miracles and demon-possession	Mt 4:24; 8:28; 24:24; 2Th 2:9; Rev 13:13–14
	d. The presence of Jesus	Mt 3:1–3; 4:17; Mk 1:14–15	d. The presence of evil spirits	Mt 8:28; 12:22–29; Mk 5:2–5,9; 6:17; Ac 19:16; Rev 18:2
	e. Gifts of the Spirit	Ro 12:6–8; 1Co 12:1–31	e. Sorcery, witchcraft, drugs, occult activity	Ac 16:16; 19:18–19; 1Co 10:20; Gal 5:20; Rev 2:24
	f. Fruit of the Spirit	Gal 5:22–23	f. Acts of the sinful nature	Gal 5:19–21

B. The People of the Kingdoms

Item	Kingdom of God		Kingdom of Satan	
	Description	Reference	Description	Reference
1. Entrance	a. Repentance and forgiveness	Mk 1:15; Ac 2:37–38; 1Jn 1:9	a. All unregenerate humanity	Ro 3:23; 5:12; Eph 2:2–3; Col 1:13
	b. Humility	Mt 18:3; Mk 10:15	b. Pride, independence	Ps 2:1–2; Pr 16:18; Eze 16:40–50; Da 4:30; Ob 3; Ro 1:30; 2Ti 3:2; Jude 16
	c. Confession and faith	Ro 10:8–13; Heb 4:2	c. Rebellion and unbelief	Ro 1:18–32; Heb 3:19; 12:25
	d. New birth	Jn 3:3,5	d. Spiritual death	Ro 5:12,17; 6:23; Eph 2:1; Col 2:13
	e. Union with Christ	Ro 6:3–8	e. Separation from God	Eph 2:12
2. Characteristics of Members	a. Children of God	Jn 1:12–13; 3:3–5; Ro 8:15; Gal 4:5; Eph 1:5	a. Children of Satan	Jn 8:44; 1Jn 3:8–10
	b. Faith and obedience	Mt 6:25–32; Jn 14:21; Ro 1:5; 16:26; Heb 11:6	b. Unbelief and rebellion	Mt 17:17; Lk 12:46; 2Th 3:2; Tit 1:15; Rev 21:8
	c. Eternal life	Jn 3:16,36; 5:24; 6:40; 1Jn 2:25; 5:11; Rev 2:7	c. Eternal death	Jn 3:18,36; Ro 5:12; 6:23; Jas 1:15; 1Jn 5:12; Rev 20:14–15; 21:8

	Kingdom of God		Kingdom of Satan	
Item	**Description**	**Reference**	**Description**	**Reference**
2. Characteristics of Members (cont.)	d. Walk in the light	Ro 13:13; Eph 5:8; Php 2:15; 1Th 5:5,8	d. Walk in darkness	Jn 3:19; Ro 13:12–13; Eph 5:11–12; 1Jn 1:6; 2:9,11
	e. Devoted to the truth	2Th 2:13; 1Ti 3:15; 3Jn 3–5	e. Speak lies and oppose truth	Jn 8:44; Ro 1:18,25; 2Ti 2:18; 3:8; 4:4
	f. Strangers in the world	Heb 11:13; 1Pe 2:11	f. Love things of the world	1Co 6:9; 2Ti 3:4; 2Pe 2:3; Jude 11; Rev 3:17–19
	g. Live by the Spirit	Ro 8:9–11; 1Co 2:10–13; Gal 5:16–26	g. Live by the sinful nature	Ro 8:5–6; Gal 5:16–26
	h. Humble and childlike, living righteously	Mt 5:6,20; 6:33; 18:1–4; Lk 18:16–17; 1Th 2:12; Eph 4:24	h. Wicked, disobedient and immoral	Gal 5:19–21; Eph 2:2–3; 5:5–6; Jas 1:14–15; 1Jn 2:15–17; 3:8
	i. Meekness and submission	Pr 16:19; Mt 5:5; Eph 5:21–22; Jas 3:17; 1Pe 2:13—3:9	i. Arrogance and self-assertion	2Ti 3:2; Jas 4:6
	j. Freedom in Christ	Ro 6:6,18,22; 1Pe 2:16	j. Bondage to sin and Satan	Ro 7:14–24
	k. Honesty	Ex 20:15–16; Eph 4:25,28	k. Deceit	Pr 12:5,20a; Ro 1:20; Eph 4:22; Rev 21:8
	l. Love	Mt 5:43–48; 7:12; 1Co 13; Eph 5:2	l. Hatred and hostility	Lk 21:17; Jn 15:18–19; 18:14; Ro 1:30; Tit 3:3; Jas 4:4
	m. Forgiveness	Mt 5:14–15; Eph 4:32	m. Bitterness	Ro 3:14; Eph 4:31
	n. Godly influence	Mt 5:13–16; Tit 2:12; 1Pe 2:12; 2Pe 3:11	n. Corrupting influence	Ge 19:1–38; Pr 2:12–22; 1Co 15:33
	o. Sexual purity and marital faithfulness	Eph 5:3; 1Th 4:3–8	o. Lust and immorality	Ro 1:24–27; 1Co 6:9–10; Gal 5:19; Eph 5:5–6
	p. Generosity	Lk 12:33–34; 6:38; 2Co 8:2–5	p. Greed and covetousness	Lk 12:15–21; Col 3:5; 2Pe 2:14
	q. Holy	Mt 5:8; 1Pe 1:15–16; Rev 22:11	q. Unholy	2Ti 3:2; 2Pe 2:5–6; Jude 15; Rev 22:11

Item	Kingdom of God: Description	Kingdom of God: Reference	Kingdom of Satan: Description	Kingdom of Satan: Reference
2. Characteristics of Members (cont.)	r. Upright speech	Ex 20:16; Pr 10:19–21; Ecc 5:2,6–7; Eph 4:29; 5:4; Jas 1:26; 3:1–2	r. Corrupt speech	Pr 10:18; 15:28; Ro 3:13–14
	s. Inherit the kingdom	Mt 25:34–40; Jn 3:3–5; 1Co 6:11; Rev 21:7	s. Do not inherit the kingdom	1Co 6:9–11; Gal 5:21; Eph 5:5
3. Duties	a. Worship only God	Ex 20:2–6; Mt 4:10; Jn 4:23–24; 1Th 1:9	a. Idolatry; living for self; ultimately worshiping Satan and antichrist	Da 11:30–33; 2Th 2:4; Rev 13:4,8,12,15
	b. Hate sin and Satan	Ps 139:21; Ro 12:9; Heb 1:9; 1Jn 2:15	b. Hate and persecute believers; hate Christ and righteousness	Jn 15:19; 16:3; 17:14; 2Ti 3:12; Rev 12:13,17
	c. Seek to advance God's kingdom and his righteousness	Mt 6:31–33; 11:12; 28:19–20; Ac 1:6–8; 19:8; 28:23,31; Col 4:11	c. Promote evil and corrupt God's kingdom and righteousness	Mt 7:15; 13:24–28,36–43; 24:23–24; Lk 21:8; Ac 20:29–30; Gal 1:8–9; 1Jn 2:18–19; 2Jn 7–11
	d. Do not love the world	Mt 6:19–24; Jn 17:15–16; Ro 12:1–2; 1Co 10:21–22; 2Co 6:14–18; 2Ti 3:1–5; Jas 4:4; 1Jn 2:15–17	d. Love the world	Ps 17:14; Mk 8:36; Php 3:19; 2Ti 4:10; 1Jn 2:15–16
	e. Wait for Christ's return from heaven	1Th 1:10; 4:13–18; 1Ti 4:8; Tit 2:13	e. Do not watch for Christ's return	Mt 24:45–51; Lk 12:42–46; 1Th 5:4–6
4. Power and dominion	a. Personal level	Lk 10:17; Jn 16:33; Ro 6:12,14	a. Personal level	Jn 8:23; Eph 2:1; 1Jn 3:8
	b. Family level	Dt 6:1–9; 1Co 11:3; Eph 5:22—6:4	b. Family level	Lk 16:27–31; 21:16; 2Ti 3:2–3,6
	c. Church level	Mt 5:13–20; 18:15–20	c. Organizational level	Jn 12:31; Eph 6:12; Rev 13:1–11; 17—18
	d. Business level	Lk 16:1–13; Col 3:23–25	d. Business level	Ac 16:16–21; 19:23–28; Rev 18:3,11–24

C. The Warfare of the Kingdoms

Item	Kingdom of God		Kingdom of Satan	
Item	Description	Reference	Description	Reference
1. Christ's Warfare with Satan	a. Christ came to destroy Satan's kingdom	Lk 4:18–21; Jn 12:31; Ac 26:15–18; 1Jn 3:8	a. Satan intent on destroying Christ's kingdom	Mt 4:1–11; 16:22–23
	b. Christ overcame temptation	Mt 4:1–11; Lk 4:1–11; Heb 4:15	b. Satan tempted Christ	Mt 4:1–11; Lk 4:1–11; Heb 4:15
	c. Christ drove out demons	Mk 1:25–26,32–34,39; 3:12; 5:12–15; 7:24–30; 9:14–29; Lk 11:20–22	c. Demons challenged Christ	Mk 1:24,34; 3:11; 5:7
	d. All power belongs eternally to Christ	Mt 28:18; 1Jn 4:4	d. Satan has only temporary and limited power	Job 1:6–12; 2:1–6; Lk 22:53; Rev 20:7–9
	e. Deliverance from sin and disease provided through the cross	Isa 53; 1Pe 2:24	e. Satan cannot withstand the power of the cross	2Co 4:10; Rev 12:10–11
	f. Final victory belongs to Christ	2Th 2:7–8; 2Pe 3:10–13; Rev 17:14; 19:11–21	f. Satan will be finally defeated and destroyed	Mt 25:41,46; Jn 16:11; Rev 20:10,14–15
2. Believers' warfare with Satan	a. Believers hate sin and seek to destroy the works of the devil	Mt 12:29–30; Mk 3:27; Lk 11:21–23	a. Satan hates and persecutes believers	Jn 15:19; 17:14; Rev 12:13,17
	b. The weapons of believers are spiritual and not worldly	Mt 26:52; 2Co 10:4–5; Eph 6:10–17	b. Satan uses the world, the sinful nature and the demonic against believers	2Co 11:3,14–15; Gal 5:17–21; Eph 6:11–12; 1Pe 2:11; 5:8; Rev 12:13,17; 13:15–18
	c. Believers are given authority to drive out demons	Mk 3:14–15; 6:7; 16:17; Lk 9:1–2; 10:17; Ac 5:16; 8:7; 16:18; 19:12	c. Demons try to destroy believers spiritually	Mk 9:17–18; Ac 8:7; 16:16–17; 1Pe 5:8
	d. Believers must overcome the world	Gal 6:14; 1Jn 2:13–14; 4:4; 5:4; Rev 2:7,11,17,26; 3:5,12,21; 12:11; 21:7,11	d. Satan seeks to overcome believers	Jer 1:19; Lk 10:19; Ro 12:21; 1Ti 5:11; 2Pe 2:20
	e. By the cross believers are dead to the world	Gal 6:14; Heb 11:25–26	e. Satan entices to sinful pleasures of the world	Php 3:19; 2Ti 3:4; 1Jn 2:16–17

MARK

Outline

I. Preparation for Jesus' Ministry (1:1–13)
- A. The Ministry of John the Baptist (1:2–8)
- B. The Baptism of Jesus (1:9–11)
- C. The Temptation of Jesus (1:12–13)

II. Early Galilean Ministry (1:14—3:6)
- A. The First Four Disciples (1:14–20)
- B. A Sabbath in Capernaum (1:21–34)
- C. First Preaching Tour (1:35–45)
- D. Conflicts With the Pharisees (2:1—3:6)

III. Later Galilean Ministry (3:7—7:23)
- A. Withdrawal to the Seaside (3:7–12)
- B. Appointment of the Twelve Disciples (3:13–19)
- C. Friends and Foes (3:20–35)
- D. Teaching in Parables (4:1–34)
- E. Teaching Through Mighty Works (4:35—5:43)
- F. Jesus at Nazareth (6:1–6)
- G. The Mission of the Twelve (6:7–13)
- H. Herod and John the Baptist (6:14–29)
- I. Miracles and Teaching Around the Sea of Galilee (6:30–56)
- J. Conflict With Tradition (7:1–23)

IV. Ministry Beyond Galilee (7:24—9:29)
- A. Two Gentiles' Healings (7:24–37)
- B. More Miracles (8:1–26)
- C. The Caesarea Philippi Episode (8:27—9:1)
- D. The Transfiguration Episode (9:2–29)

V. The Road Toward Jerusalem (9:30—10:52)
- A. En Route Through Galilee (9:30–50)
- B. Ministry in Perea (10:1–52)

VI. Passion Week (11:1—15:47)
- A. Sunday: Triumphal Entry to Jerusalem (11:1–11)
- B. Monday: 1. Cursing the Fig Tree (11:12–14)
  - 2. Cleansing the Temple (11:15–19)
- C. Tuesday: 1. Faith and Fear (11:20–33)
  - 2. Parable and Controversy (12:1–44)
  - 3. The Olivet Discourse (13:1–37)
  - 4. The Anointing at Bethany (14:1–11)
- D. Thursday: The Last Supper (14:12–25)
- E. Friday: 1. Jesus in Gethsemane (14:26–52)
  - 2. The Jewish Trial (14:53–72)
  - 3. The Roman Trial (15:1–20)
  - 4. The Crucifixion and Burial (15:21–47)

VII. The Resurrection (16:1–20)
 A. The Resurrection Discovery (16:1–8)
 B. Post-resurrection Appearances (16:9–18)
 C. Ascension and Apostolic Mission (16:19–20)

Author: Mark

Theme: Jesus, the Servant-Son

Date: A.D. 55–65

Background

Among the four Gospels, Mark is the most concise account of "the beginning of the gospel about Jesus Christ, the Son of God" (1:1). Although the author is not identified by name in the book itself (true of all the Gospels), the early and unanimous testimony of the church is that John Mark was responsible for its writing. This man grew up in Jerusalem and was among the first generation Christians (Ac 12:12). He had the unique opportunity of being associated in ministry with three NT apostles: Paul (Ac 13:1–13; Col 4:10; Phm 24), Barnabas (Ac 15:39) and Peter (1Pe 5:13). According to Papias (c. A.D. 130) and other second-century church fathers, Mark derived the content of his Gospel from his association with Peter, wrote it in Rome and designed it for Roman believers. Although the specific date for the writing of Mark's Gospel is uncertain, most scholars date it in the late 50s or the 60s; it may have been the first of the four Gospels to be written.

Purpose

In the 60s of the first century A.D., believers in Rome were treated cruelly by the populace, and many were tortured and put to death by the Roman emperor Nero. According to tradition, among the Christian martyrs in Rome during this decade were the apostles Peter and Paul. As one of the church leaders in Rome, John Mark was moved by the Holy Spirit to write this Gospel as a prophetic anticipation of, or a pastoral response to, this time of persecution. His intention was to strengthen the foundations of faith in Roman believers and, if need be, to inspire them to suffer faithfully for the gospel, placing before them the life, suffering, death and resurrection of Jesus their Lord.

Survey

In a fast-moving narrative, Mark presents Jesus as the Son of God and the suffering servant Messiah. The watershed of the book is the episode in Caesarea Philippi, followed by the transfiguration (8:27—9:9), where both Jesus' identity and his mission of suffering are fully disclosed to his twelve disciples. The first half of Mark focuses primarily both on Jesus' mighty miracles and on his authority over sickness and demons as signs that God's kingdom is at hand. At Caesarea Philippi, however, Jesus tells his disciples openly that he "must suffer many things and be rejected by the elders, chief priests and teachers of the law, and that he must be killed and after three days rise again" (8:31). There are numerous references throughout Mark to suffering as the cost of discipleship (e.g. 3:21–22,30; 8:34–38; 10:30,33–34,45; 13:8,11–13). God's vindication, however, will follow righteous suffering, as demonstrated in Jesus' resurrection.

Special Features

Four major features characterize Mark's Gospel: (1) it is a Gospel of action, emphasizing what Jesus did rather than what he said (Mark records eighteen of Jesus' miracles but only four of his parables); (2) it is a Gospel for the Romans, explaining Jewish customs, omitting all Jewish genealogies and birth narratives, translating Aramaic words and using Latin terms; (3) it is a Gospel of urgency, beginning abruptly and proceeding rapidly from one episode to another, with 42 occurrences of the Greek adverb for "immediately"; (4) it is a Gospel of vividness, describing the events of Jesus' life succinctly, vividly and with the picturesque skill of a literary artist.

Reading Mark

In order to read the entire New Testament in one year, the book of Mark should be read in 29 days, according to the following schedule:
☐ 1:1–20 ☐ 1:21–45 ☐ 2:1–22 ☐ 2:23—3:12 ☐ 3:13–35 ☐ 4:1–20 ☐ 6:21–41 ☐ 5:1–20
☐ 5:21–43 ☐ 6:1–29 ☐ 6:30–56 ☐ 7:1–23 ☐ 7:24—8:13 ☐ 8:14–26 ☐ 8:27—9:13 ☐ 9:14–32
☐ 9:33–50 ☐ 10:1–31 ☐ 10:32–52 ☐ 11:1–26 ☐ 11:27—12:17 ☐ 12:18–44 ☐ 13 ☐ 14:1–26
☐ 14:27–52 ☐ 14:53–72 ☐ 15:1–20 ☐ 15:21–47 ☐ 16

NOTES

John the Baptist Prepares the Way

1:2–8pp — Mt 3:1–11; Lk 3:2–16

1 The beginning of the gospel about Jesus Christ, the Son of God.[a][a]

2 It is written in Isaiah the prophet:

"I will send my messenger ahead of
you,
who will prepare your way"[b][b]—
3 "a voice of one calling in the desert,
'Prepare the way for the Lord,
make straight paths for him.'"[c][c]

4 And so John[d] came, baptizing in the desert region and preaching a baptism of repentance[e] for the forgiveness of sins.[f] **5** The whole Judean countryside and all the people of Jerusalem went out to him. Confessing their sins, they were baptized by him in the Jordan River. **6** John wore clothing made of camel's hair, with a leather belt around his waist,[g] and he ate locusts[h] and wild honey. **7** And this was his message: "After me will come one more powerful than I, the thongs of whose sandals I am not worthy to stoop down and untie.[i] **8** I baptize you with[d] water, but he
Lk 1:15 will baptize you with the Holy Spirit."[j]

1:1 [a] S Mt 4:3
1:2 [b] Mal 3:1; Mt 11:10; Lk 7:27
1:3 [c] Isa 40:3; Jn 1:23
1:4 [d] S Mt 3:1 [e] ver 8; Jn 1:26,33; Ac 1:5,22; 11:36; 13:24; 18:25; 19:3,4 [f] Lk 1:77
1:6 [g] 2Ki 1:8 [h] Lev 11:22
1:7 [i] Ac 13:25
1:8 [j] Isa 44:3; Joel 2:28; Jn 1:33; Ac 1:5; 2:4; 11:16; 19:4-6

The Baptism and Temptation of Jesus

1:9–11pp — Mt 3:13–17; Lk 3:21,22
1:12,13pp — Mt 4:1–11; Lk 4:1–13

9 At that time Jesus came from Nazareth[k] in Galilee and was baptized by John[l] in the Jordan. **10** As Jesus was coming up out of the water, he saw heaven being torn open and the Spirit descending on him like a dove.[m] **11** And a voice came from heaven: "You are my Son,[n] whom I love; with you I am well pleased."[o]

12 At once the Spirit sent him out into the desert, **13** and he was in the desert forty days,[p] being tempted by Satan.[q] He was with the wild animals, and angels attended him.

The Calling of the First Disciples

1:16–20pp — Mt 4:18–22; Lk 5:2–11; Jn 1:35–42

14 After John[r] was put in prison, Jesus went into Galilee,[s] proclaiming the good news of God.[t] **15** "The time has come,"[u] he said. "The kingdom of God is near. Repent and believe[v] the good news!"[w]

1:9 [k] S Mt 2:23 [l] S Mt 3:1
1:10 [m] Jn 1:32
1:11 [n] S Mt 3:17 [o] S Mt 3:17
1:13 [p] Ex 24:18; 1Ki 19:8 [q] S Mt 4:10; Heb 4:15
1:14 [r] S Mt 3:1 [s] Mt 4:12 [t] Mt 4:23
1:15 [u] Ro 5:6; Gal 4:4; Eph 1:10 [v] S Jn 3:15 [w] Ac 20:21

[a] *1* Some manuscripts do not have *the Son of God.*
[b] *2* Mal. 3:1 [c] *3* Isaiah 40:3 [d] *8* Or *in*

1:4 REPENTANCE. See Mt 3:2, note.

1:8 BAPTIZE YOU WITH THE HOLY SPIRIT. John the Baptist was the first one who preached the good news concerning Jesus; his preaching is condensed by Mark into one single theme: the proclamation of Jesus Christ, who would come and baptize his followers in the Holy Spirit. All those who accept Christ as Lord and Savior should proclaim that Jesus is still the One who baptizes in the Holy Spirit (see Ac 1:8; 2:4,38–39; see Lk 3:16, note on the promised baptism in the Holy Spirit; Ac 1:5, note).

1:9 JESUS . . . WAS BAPTIZED. See Mt 3:13, note.

1:10 THE SPIRIT . . . DESCENDING ON HIM. See Mt 3:16, note.

1:11 MY SON, WHOM I LOVE. All three persons of the Trinity are involved in Jesus' baptism (see Mt 3:17, note). Here and elsewhere in Scripture God is revealed as one essence existing in three distinct persons who share a common nature: Father, Son and Holy Spirit (cf. Mt 3:16–17; 28:19; 2Co 13:14; Eph 4:4–6; 1Pe 1:2; Jude 20–21). Thus, God is singular (i.e., a unity) in one sense and plural (i.e., three) in another. (1) Scripture declares that God is one being—a perfect unity of one nature and essence (12:29; Dt 6:4; Gal 3:20). Of the persons in the Godhead none is God without the others and each with the others is God.

(2) The one God exists in a plurality of three identifiable and distinct, though not separate, persons. The three are not three gods, or three parts or expressions of God, but are three persons so completely united that they form the one true and eternal God. Both the Son and the Holy Spirit possess attributes that can only be true of God (see Ge 1:2; Isa 61:1; Jn 1:1,14, note; 5:18, note; 14:16; 16:8,13; 20:28, note; Ac 5:3–4; Ro 8:2,26–27; 1Co 2:10–11; 2Th 2:13; Heb 9:14). None of the three persons was ever made or created, but each exists equal in essential being, attributes, power and glory.

(3) This one God existing in three persons made possible from all eternity reciprocal love, fellowship, the exercise of divine attributes, mutual communion in knowledge, and interrelationship within the Godhead (cf. Jn 10:15; 11:27; 17:24; 1Co 2:10).

1:13 TEMPTED BY SATAN. See Mt 4:1, note.

1:14 THE GOOD NEWS. See 14:9, note.

1:15 KINGDOM OF GOD. Christ came to proclaim and bring to completion the kingdom of God. This was the theme of his earthly message (Mt 4:17). About the form of its appearing, we should be aware of several aspects of the kingdom:

(1) The kingdom in Israel. The kingdom in the OT was God's redemptive action within Israel in order to prepare the way for the salvation of the human race. Because Israel rejected Jesus, the Messiah, the kingdom was taken away from them (see Mt 21:43, note).

(2) The kingdom in Christ. The kingdom and its power were present in the person and work of Jesus the King (Lk 11:20).

(3) The kingdom in the church. This involves the present manifestation of God's power and rule in the hearts and lives of all who repent and believe the gospel (Jn 3:3,5; Ro 14:17; Col 1:13). Its presence comes with great spiritual power, asserting itself against the dominion of Satan, sin and evil. It is not a political or material kingdom, but a powerful and forceful presence and activity of God among his people (see 1:27; 9:1; see article on THE KINGDOM OF

16 As Jesus walked beside the Sea of Galilee, he saw Simon and his brother Andrew casting a net into the lake, for they were fishermen. 17 "Come, follow me," Jesus said, "and I will make you fishers of men." 18 At once they left their nets and followed him.[x]

19 When he had gone a little farther, he saw James son of Zebedee and his brother John in a boat, preparing their nets. 20 Without delay he called them, and they left their father Zebedee in the boat with the hired men and followed him.

Jesus Drives Out an Evil Spirit

1:21–28pp — Lk 4:31–37

21 They went to Capernaum, and when the Sabbath came, Jesus went into the synagogue and began to teach.[y] 22 The people were amazed at his teaching, because he taught them as one who had authority, not as the teachers of the law.[z] 23 Just then a man in their synagogue who was possessed by an evil[e] spirit cried out, 24 "What do you want with us,[a] Jesus of Nazareth?[b] Have you come to destroy us? I know who you are—the Holy One of God!"[c]

25 "Be quiet!" said Jesus sternly. "Come out of him!"[d] 26 The evil spirit shook the man violently and came out of him with a shriek.[e]

27 The people were all so amazed[f] that they asked each other, "What is this? A new teaching—and with authority! He even gives orders to evil spirits and they obey him." 28 News about him spread quickly over the whole region[g] of Galilee.

Jesus Heals Many

1:29–31pp — Mt 8:14,15; Lk 4:38,39
1:32–34pp — Mt 8:16,17; Lk 4:40,41

29 As soon as they left the synagogue,[h] they went with James and John to the home of Simon and Andrew. 30 Simon's mother-in-law was in bed with a fever, and they told Jesus about her. 31 So he went to her, took her hand and helped her up.[i] The fever left her and she began to wait on them.

32 That evening after sunset the people brought to Jesus all the sick and demon-possessed.[j] 33 The whole town gathered at the door, 34 and Jesus healed many who had various diseases.[k] He also drove out many demons, but he would not let the demons speak because they knew who he was.[l]

Jesus Prays in a Solitary Place

1:35–38pp — Lk 4:42,43

35 Very early in the morning, while it was still dark, Jesus got up, left the house and went off to a solitary place, where he prayed.[m] 36 Simon and his companions went to look for him, 37 and when they found him, they exclaimed: "Everyone is looking for you!"

38 Jesus replied, "Let us go somewhere else—to the nearby villages—so I can preach there also. That is why I have come."[n] 39 So he traveled throughout Galilee, preaching in their synagogues[o] and driving out demons.[p]

A Man With Leprosy

1:40–44pp — Mt 8:2–4; Lk 5:12–14

40 A man with leprosy[f] came to him and begged him on his knees,[q] "If you are willing, you can make me clean."

41 Filled with compassion, Jesus reached out his hand and touched the man. "I am willing," he said. "Be clean!" 42 Immediately the leprosy left him and he was cured.

43 Jesus sent him away at once with a strong warning: 44 "See that you don't tell this to anyone.[r] But go, show yourself to

1:18 [x]S Mt 4:19 **1:21** [y]ver 39; S Mt 4:23; S Mk 10:1 **1:22** [z]S Mt 7:28, 29 **1:24** [a]S Mt 8:29 [b]Jdg 13:5; S Mt 2:23; Lk 24:19; Jn 1:45, 46; Ac 4:10; 24:5 [c]Ps 16:10; Isa 41:14,16,20; Lk 1:35; Jn 6:69; Ac 3:14; 1Jn 2:20 **1:25** [d]ver 34 **1:26** [e]Mk 9:20 **1:27** [f]Mk 10:24, 32 **1:28** [g]S Mt 9:26 **1:29** [h]ver 21,23

1:31 [i]S Lk 7:14 **1:32** [j]S Mt 4:24 **1:34** [k]S Mt 4:23 [l]Mk 3:12; Ac 16:17,18 **1:35** [m]S Lk 3:21 **1:38** [n]Isa 61:1 **1:39** [o]S Mt 4:23 [p]S Mt 4:24 **1:40** [q]Mk 10:17 **1:44** [r]S Mt 8:4

e 23 Greek *unclean*; also in verses 26 and 27
f 40 The Greek word was used for various diseases affecting the skin—not necessarily leprosy.

GOD, p. 28, for a detailed description of the kingdom of God in the church age).

(4) The kingdom in the consummation. This is the Messianic kingdom foretold by the prophets (Ps 89:36–37; Isa 11:1–9; Da 7:13–14). Christ will reign on earth for a thousand years (Rev 20:4–6), and the church will reign with him over the nations (1Co 6:2–3; 2Ti 2:12; Rev 2:26–27; see 20:4, notes).

(5) The kingdom in eternity. The Messianic kingdom will terminate after a thousand years and God's eternal kingdom will be established in the new heaven and new earth (Rev 21:1–4). The center of the new earth is the Holy City, the new Jerusalem (Rev 21:9–11). Its inhabitants are the redeemed from the OT (Rev 21:12) and the NT (Rev 21:14). Their greatest blessing is, "they will see his face" (Rev 22:4; see 21:1, note).

1:17 COME, FOLLOW ME. The first calling of the disciples is to follow Jesus and to know him personally (Php 3:8–10). As a result of this relationship, they must then lead others to a saving knowledge of Jesus (cf. Pr 11:30; Da 12:3; 1Co 9:22).

1:27 EVIL SPIRITS . . . OBEY HIM. See article on POWER OVER SATAN AND DEMONS, p. 80, for comments on this text.

1:34 DROVE OUT MANY DEMONS. See article on POWER OVER SATAN AND DEMONS, p. 80.

the priest[s] and offer the sacrifices that Moses commanded for your cleansing,[t] as a testimony to them." 45Instead he went out and began to talk freely, spreading the news. As a result, Jesus could no longer enter a town openly but stayed outside in lonely places.[u] Yet the people still came to him from everywhere.[v]

Jesus Heals a Paralytic

2:3–12pp — Mt 9:2–8; Lk 5:18–26

2 A few days later, when Jesus again entered Capernaum, the people heard that he had come home. 2So many[w] gathered that there was no room left, not even outside the door, and he preached the word to them. 3Some men came, bringing to him a paralytic,[x] carried by four of them. 4Since they could not get him to Jesus because of the crowd, they made an opening in the roof above Jesus and, after digging through it, lowered the mat the paralyzed man was lying on. 5When Jesus saw their faith, he said to the paralytic, "Son, your sins are forgiven."[y]

6Now some teachers of the law were sitting there, thinking to themselves, 7"Why does this fellow talk like that? He's blaspheming! Who can forgive sins but God alone?"[z]

8Immediately Jesus knew in his spirit that this was what they were thinking in their hearts, and he said to them, "Why are you thinking these things? 9Which is easier: to say to the paralytic, 'Your sins are forgiven,' or to say, 'Get up, take your mat and walk'? 10But that you may know that the Son of Man[a] has authority on earth to forgive sins . . . ." He said to the paralytic, 11"I tell you, get up, take your mat and go home." 12He got up, took his mat and walked out in full view of them all. This amazed everyone and they praised God,[b] saying, "We have never seen anything like this!"[c]

Mk 5:25-34

The Calling of Levi

2:14–17pp — Mt 9:9–13; Lk 5:27–32

13Once again Jesus went out beside the lake. A large crowd came to him,[d] and he began to teach them. 14As he walked along, he saw Levi son of Alphaeus sitting at the tax collector's booth. "Follow me,"[e] Jesus told him, and Levi got up and followed him.

15While Jesus was having dinner at Levi's house, many tax collectors and "sinners" were eating with him and his disciples, for there were many who followed him. 16When the teachers of the law who were Pharisees[f] saw him eating with the "sinners" and tax collectors, they asked his disciples: "Why does he eat with tax collectors and 'sinners'?"[g]

17On hearing this, Jesus said to them, "It is not the healthy who need a doctor, but the sick. I have not come to call the righteous, but sinners."[h]

Jesus Questioned About Fasting

2:18–22pp — Mt 9:14–17; Lk 5:33–38

18Now John's disciples and the Pharisees were fasting.[i] Some people came and asked Jesus, "How is it that John's disciples and the disciples of the Pharisees are fasting, but yours are not?"

19Jesus answered, "How can the guests of the bridegroom fast while he is with them? They cannot, so long as they have him with them. 20But the time will come when the bridegroom will be taken from them,[j] and on that day they will fast.

21"No one sews a patch of unshrunk cloth on an old garment. If he does, the new piece will pull away from the old, making the tear worse. 22And no one pours new wine into old wineskins. If he does, the wine will burst the skins, and both the wine and the wineskins will be ruined. No, he pours new wine into new wineskins."

Lord of the Sabbath

2:23–28pp — Mt 12:1–8; Lk 6:1–5
3:1–6pp — Mt 12:9–14; Lk 6:6–11

23One Sabbath Jesus was going through the grainfields, and as his disciples walked along, they began to pick some heads of grain.[k] 24The Pharisees said to him, "Look, why are they doing what is unlawful on the Sabbath?"[l]

25He answered, "Have you never read

1:44 [s] Lev 13:49 [t] Lev 14:1-32
1:45 [u] Lk 5:15,16 [v] Mk 2:13; Lk 5:17; Jn 6:2
2:2 [w] ver 13; Mk 1:45
2:3 [x] S Mt 4:24
2:5 [y] Lk 7:48
2:7 [z] Isa 43:25
2:10 [a] S Mt 8:20
2:12 [b] S Mt 9:8 [c] Mt 9:33
2:13 [d] Mk 1:45; Lk 5:15; Jn 6:2
2:14 [e] S Mt 4:19
2:16 [f] Ac 23:9 [g] S Mt 9:11
2:17 [h] Lk 19:10; 1Ti 1:15
2:18 [i] S Mt 6:16-18; Ac 13:2
2:20 [j] Lk 17:22
2:23 [k] Dt 23:25
2:24 [l] S Mt 12:2

2:10 SON OF MAN. See Lk 5:24, note.

2:11 HEALING THE PARALYTIC. It was never God's intention that people should live with sickness, disease and infirmity. These things are the results of the sinfulness of the human race and the activity of Satan in the world. Consequently, every healing through Christ involves God invading the realm of Satan to destroy his work (1Jn 3:8; see article on DIVINE HEALING, p. 20).

2:17 TO CALL . . . SINNERS. See Mt 9:11, note.

2:20 ON THAT DAY THEY WILL FAST. See Mt 9:15, note.

2:22 NEW WINE INTO OLD WINESKINS. See Mt 9:17, note.

2:23 SABBATH. See Mt 12:1, note.

what David did when he and his companions were hungry and in need? **26**In the
days of Abiathar the high priest,[m] he entered the house of God and ate the consecrated bread, which is lawful only for
priests to eat.[n] And he also gave some to
his companions."[o]

27Then he said to them, "The Sabbath
was made for man,[p] not man for the Sabbath.[q] **28**So the Son of Man[r] is Lord even
of the Sabbath."

3 Another time he went into the synagogue,[s] and a man with a shriveled
hand was there. **2**Some of them were looking for a reason to accuse Jesus, so they
watched him closely[t] to see if he would
heal him on the Sabbath.[u] **3**Jesus said to
the man with the shriveled hand, "Stand
up in front of everyone."

4Then Jesus asked them, "Which is lawful on the Sabbath: to do good or to do evil,
to save life or to kill?" But they remained
silent.

5He looked around at them in anger
and, deeply distressed at their stubborn
hearts, said to the man, "Stretch out your
hand." He stretched it out, and his hand
was completely restored. **6**Then the Pharisees went out and began to plot with the
Herodians[v] how they might kill Jesus.[w]

Crowds Follow Jesus

3:7–12pp — Mt 12:15,16; Lk 6:17–19

7Jesus withdrew with his disciples to
the lake, and a large crowd from Galilee
followed.[x] **8**When they heard all he was
doing, many people came to him from Judea, Jerusalem, Idumea, and the regions
across the Jordan and around Tyre and
Sidon.[y] **9**Because of the crowd he told his
disciples to have a small boat ready for
him, to keep the people from crowding
him. **10**For he had healed many,[z] so that
those with diseases were pushing forward
to touch him.[a] **11**Whenever the evil[g] spirits saw him, they fell down before him and
cried out, "You are the Son of God."[b]
12But he gave them strict orders not to
tell who he was.[c]

The Appointing of the Twelve Apostles

3:16–19pp — Mt 10:2–4; Lk 6:14–16; Ac 1:13

13Jesus went up on a mountainside and
called to him those he wanted, and they
came to him.[d] **14**He appointed twelve—
designating them apostles[h][e]—that they
might be with him and that he might send
them out to preach **15**and to have authority to drive out demons.[f] **16**These are the
twelve he appointed: Simon (to whom he
gave the name Peter);[g] **17**James son of
Zebedee and his brother John (to them he
gave the name Boanerges, which means
Sons of Thunder); **18**Andrew, Philip, Bartholomew, Matthew, Thomas, James son
of Alphaeus, Thaddaeus, Simon the Zealot
19and Judas Iscariot, who betrayed him.

Jesus and Beelzebub

3:23–27pp — Mt 12:25–29; Lk 11:17–22

20Then Jesus entered a house, and
again a crowd gathered,[h] so that he and
his disciples were not even able to eat.[i]
21When his family heard about this, they

2:26 m 1Ch 24:6; 2Sa 8:17 n Lev 24:5-9 o 1Sa 21:1-6
2:27 p Ex 23:12; Dt 5:14 q Col 2:16
2:28 r S Mt 8:20
3:1 s S Mt 4:23; Mk 1:21
3:2 t S Mt 12:10 u Lk 14:1
3:6 v Mt 22:16; Mk 12:13 w S Mt 12:14
3:7 x Mt 4:25
3:8 y S Mt 11:21
3:10 z S Mt 4:23 a S Mt 9:20
3:11 b S Mt 4:3; Mk 1:23,24
3:12 c S Mt 8:4; Mk 1:24,25,34; Ac 16:17,18
3:13 d Mt 5:1
3:14 e S Mk 6:30
3:15 f S Mt 10:1
3:16 g Jn 1:42
3:20 h ver 7 i Mk 6:31

g *11* Greek *unclean;* also in verse 30
h *14* Some manuscripts do not have *designating them apostles.*

2:27 THE SABBATH WAS MADE FOR MAN. The Sabbath was instituted by God to be a blessing for humans. On this day we are to refrain from our daily work. Instead we must worship God and seek fellowship with him, in order to keep ourselves physically healthy and spiritually strong and refreshed (Isa 58:13–14). Those who ignore the principle of the Sabbath do so to their own ruin (see Mt 12:1, note).

3:5 LOOKED . . . IN ANGER. The anger of Jesus indicates his hatred and disapproval of all unrighteousness and injustice (see Heb 1:9, note). Though Christians must resist unrighteous anger (Gal 5:20; Col 3:8), it is thoroughly Christlike to be angry at evil (Ex 32:19; 1Sa 11:6; 2Sa 12:5; Ne 5:6). Indignation at the sins of one's generation is evidence of believers placing themselves on God's side against evil (Ex 32:19; 1Sa 11:6; Ps 94:16; Jer 6:11; Ac 17:16).

3:10 HEALED MANY. See article on DIVINE HEALING, p. 20.

3:15 AUTHORITY TO DRIVE OUT DEMONS. In coming to earth Jesus' purpose was to destroy the works of the devil (1:27; 1Jn 3:8) and release those oppressed by Satan and sin (Lk 4:18; see article on POWER OVER SATAN AND DEMONS, p. 80). Jesus gave his followers power and authority to continue his battle against the forces of darkness. This truth is verified by the following observations. (1) It is recorded that after Jesus appointed the twelve disciples, he gave them "authority to drive out demons" (vv. 14–15; cf. Mt 10:1). After he appointed the seventy-two, he gave them "authority . . . to overcome all the power of the enemy" (Lk 10:1,17–19; cf. Mt 10:1–8; Mk 6:7,13).

(2) The disciples were not only to go out and preach (v. 14; Mt 10:7), but also to manifest the kingdom's rule, power and authority by doing battle against Satan, driving out demons, and healing every kind of disease and sickness (Mt 10:1,7–8, notes).

(3) Mark teaches that Jesus, after his resurrection, reemphasized to his followers their task of preaching the gospel and their authority over Satan and his demons (see article on SIGNS OF BELIEVERS, p. 106).

went to take charge of him, for they said, "He is out of his mind."[j]

22And the teachers of the law who came down from Jerusalem[k] said, "He is possessed by Beelzebub[i]![l] By the prince of demons he is driving out demons."[m]

23So Jesus called them and spoke to them in parables:[n] "How can Satan[o] drive out Satan? 24If a kingdom is divided against itself, that kingdom cannot stand. 25If a house is divided against itself, that house cannot stand. 26And if Satan opposes himself and is divided, he cannot stand; his end has come. 27In fact, no one can enter a strong man's house and carry off his possessions unless he first ties up the strong man. Then he can rob his house.[p] 28I tell you the truth, all the sins and blasphemies of men will be forgiven them. 29But whoever blasphemes against the Holy Spirit will never be forgiven; he is guilty of an eternal sin."[q]

30He said this because they were saying, "He has an evil spirit."

Jesus' Mother and Brothers

3:31–35pp — Mt 12:46–50; Lk 8:19–21

31Then Jesus' mother and brothers arrived.[r] Standing outside, they sent someone in to call him. 32A crowd was sitting around him, and they told him, "Your mother and brothers are outside looking for you."

33"Who are my mother and my brothers?" he asked.

34Then he looked at those seated in a circle around him and said, "Here are my mother and my brothers! 35Whoever does God's will is my brother and sister and mother."

The Parable of the Sower

4:1–12pp — Mt 13:1–15; Lk 8:4–10
4:13–20pp — Mt 13:18–23; Lk 8:11–15

4 Again Jesus began to teach by the lake.[s] The crowd that gathered around him was so large that he got into a boat and sat in it out on the lake, while all the people were along the shore at the water's edge. 2He taught them many things by parables,[t] and in his teaching said: 3"Listen! A farmer went out to sow his seed.[u] 4As he was scattering the seed, some fell along the path, and the birds came and ate it up. 5Some fell on rocky places, where it did not have much soil. It sprang up quickly, because the soil was shallow. 6But when the sun came up, the plants were scorched, and they withered because they had no root. 7Other seed fell among thorns, which grew up and choked the plants, so that they did not bear grain. 8Still other seed fell on good soil. It came up, grew and produced a crop, multiplying thirty, sixty, or even a hundred times."[v]

9Then Jesus said, "He who has ears to hear, let him hear."[w]

10When he was alone, the Twelve and the others around him asked him about the parables. 11He told them, "The secret of the kingdom of God[x] has been given to you. But to those on the outside[y] everything is said in parables 12so that,

" 'they may be ever seeing but never
perceiving,
and ever hearing but never
understanding;
otherwise they might turn and be
forgiven!'[j]"[z]

13Then Jesus said to them, "Don't you understand this parable? How then will you understand any parable? 14The farmer sows the word.[a] 15Some people are like seed along the path, where the word is sown. As soon as they hear it, Satan[b] comes and takes away the word that was sown in them. 16Others, like seed sown on rocky places, hear the word and at once receive it with joy. 17But since they have

3:21 [j]Jn 10:20; Ac 26:24
3:22 [k]Mt 15:1 [l]Mt 10:25; 11:18; 12:24; Jn 7:20; 8:48,52; 10:20 [m]Mt 9:34
3:23 [n]Mk 4:2 [o]S Mt 4:10
3:27 [p]Isa 49:24, 25
3:29 [q]Mt 12:31, 32; Lk 12:10
3:31 [r]ver 21
4:1 [s]Mk 2:13; 3:7
4:2 [t]ver 11; Mk 3:23
4:3 [u]ver 26
4:8 [v]Jn 15:5; Col 1:6
4:9 [w]ver 23; S Mt 11:15
4:11 [x]S Mt 3:2 [y]1Co 5:12,13; Col 4:5; 1Th 4:12; 1Ti 3:7
4:12 [z]Isa 6:9,10; S Mt 13:13-15
4:14 [a]Mk 16:20; Lk 1:2; Ac 4:31; 8:4; 16:6; 17:11; Php 1:14
4:15 [b]S Mt 4:10

i *22* Greek *Beezeboul* or *Beelzeboul* j *12* Isaiah 6:9,10

3:27 TIES UP THE STRONG MAN. See article on POWER OVER SATAN AND DEMONS, p. 80.

3:29 BLASPHEMES AGAINST THE HOLY SPIRIT. See Mt 12:31, note.

4:2 PARABLES. Jesus often taught in parables. A parable is a simple story from everyday life that reveals truth about God's kingdom to those whose hearts are prepared to hear and conceals this truth from those whose hearts are unprepared (cf. Isa 6:9–10; see Mt 13:3, note).

4:3 A FARMER WENT OUT TO SOW. Jesus uses this parable to tell how the gospel will be received in the world. Three truths may be learned: (1) Conversion and fruitfulness depend on how one responds to God's Word (v. 14; cf. Jn 15:1–10). (2) There will be a mixed reaction to the gospel by the world. Some who hear will not understand (v. 15); others will believe unto salvation, but will later fall away (vv. 16–19); still others will believe unto salvation, persevere and bear fruit in varying degrees (v. 20). (3) The enemies of God's Word are Satan, worldly concerns, riches and pleasures (vv. 15,19).

4:15–17 TAKES AWAY THE WORD. Christ speaks here about an incomplete conversion—one in which individuals seek forgiveness but fall short of actual regeneration by the Holy Spirit (see article on REGENERATION, p. 178). They do not receive salvation and the new birth and never enter into fellowship

no root, they last only a short time. When trouble or persecution comes because of the word, they quickly fall away. **18**Still others, like seed sown among thorns, hear the word; **19**but the worries of this life, the deceitfulness of wealth[c] and the desires for other things come in and choke the word, making it unfruitful. **20**Others, like seed sown on good soil, hear the word, accept it, and produce a crop—thirty, sixty or even a hundred times what was sown."

A Lamp on a Stand

21He said to them, "Do you bring in a lamp to put it under a bowl or a bed? Instead, don't you put it on its stand?[d] **22**For whatever is hidden is meant to be disclosed, and whatever is concealed is meant to be brought out into the open.[e] **23**If anyone has ears to hear, let him hear."[f]

24"Consider carefully what you hear," he continued. "With the measure you use, it will be measured to you—and even more.[g] **25**Whoever has will be given more; whoever does not have, even what he has will be taken from him."[h]

The Parable of the Growing Seed

26He also said, "This is what the kingdom of God is like.[i] A man scatters seed on the ground. **27**Night and day, whether he sleeps or gets up, the seed sprouts and grows, though he does not know how. **28**All by itself the soil produces grain—first the stalk, then the head, then the full kernel in the head. **29**As soon as the grain is ripe, he puts the sickle to it, because the harvest has come."[j]

The Parable of the Mustard Seed

4:30–32pp — Mt 13:31,32; Lk 13:18,19

30Again he said, "What shall we say the kingdom of God is like,[k] or what parable shall we use to describe it? **31**It is like a mustard seed, which is the smallest seed you plant in the ground. **32**Yet when planted, it grows and becomes the largest of all garden plants, with such big branches that the birds of the air can perch in its shade."

33With many similar parables Jesus spoke the word to them, as much as they could understand.[l] **34**He did not say anything to them without using a parable.[m] But when he was alone with his own disciples, he explained everything.

Jesus Calms the Storm

4:35–41pp — Mt 8:18,23–27; Lk 8:22–25

35That day when evening came, he said to his disciples, "Let us go over to the other side." **36**Leaving the crowd behind, they took him along, just as he was, in the boat.[n] There were also other boats with him. **37**A furious squall came up, and the waves broke over the boat, so that it was nearly swamped. **38**Jesus was in the stern, sleeping on a cushion. The disciples woke him and said to him, "Teacher, don't you care if we drown?"

39He got up, rebuked the wind and said to the waves, "Quiet! Be still!" Then the wind died down and it was completely calm.

40He said to his disciples, "Why are you so afraid? Do you still have no faith?"[o] Mk 9:23-24

41They were terrified and asked each other, "Who is this? Even the wind and the waves obey him!"

The Healing of a Demon-possessed Man

5:1–17pp — Mt 8:28–34; Lk 8:26–37
5:18–20pp — Lk 8:38,39

5 They went across the lake to the region of the Gerasenes.[k] **2**When Jesus got out of the boat,[p] a man with an evil[l]

4:19 c Mt 19:23; 1Ti 6:9,10,17; 1Jn 2:15-17
4:21 d S Mt 5:15
4:22 e Jer 16:17; Mt 10:26; Lk 8:17; 12:2
4:23 f ver 9; S Mt 11:15
4:24 g S Mt 7:2
4:25 h S Mt 25:29
4:26 i S Mt 13:24
4:29 j Rev 14:15
4:30 k S Mt 13:24
4:33 l Jn 16:12
4:34 m S Jn 16:25
4:36 n ver 1; Mk 3:9; 5:2,21; 6:32,45
4:40 o Mt 14:31; Mk 16:14
5:2 p Mk 4:1

k *1* Some manuscripts *Gadarenes*; other manuscripts *Gergesenes* l *2* Greek *unclean*; also in verses 8 and 13

---

with believers; or if they do become church members, they fail to show genuine commitment to Christ and true separation from the world.

Halfway conversions result from the following: (1) The church deals with seekers quickly without communicating a proper understanding of the gospel and its demands. (2) The church fails to deal with the demonic bondage of seekers (16:15–17; Mt 10:1,8; 12:22–29). (3) Seekers believe in Christ only with their mind, not heart (i.e., with their innermost being, their whole personality; cf. Ac 2:37; 2Co 4:6). (4) They fail to repent in true sincerity or to turn from sin (cf. Mt 3:2; Ac 8:18–23). (5) Seekers want to accept Christ as Savior but not as Lord (Mt 13:20–21). (6) Their faith is based on the persuasiveness of human words rather than on the demonstration of the Spirit and the power of God (1Co 2:4–5).

4:25 EVEN WHAT HE HAS WILL BE TAKEN. Jesus states here a principle of his kingdom: believers must continue to acquire truth and grace or they will lose even what they have. Growth in grace or spiritual decline may be hardly perceptible in the lives of many. Nevertheless, it is a fact that a Christian either grows or degenerates (2Pe 3:17–18). The peril of final apostasy increases in proportion as one declines spiritually (Heb 3:12–15; 4:11; 6:11–12; 10:23–39; 12:15; see article on PERSONAL APOSTASY, p. 492).

4:31 MUSTARD SEED. See Lk 13:19, note.

POWER OVER SATAN AND DEMONS

***Mk 3:27** "No one can enter a strong man's house and carry off his possessions unless he first ties up the strong man. Then he can rob his house."*

One of the primary emphases in Mark's Gospel is Jesus' overriding concern to defeat Satan and his demonic powers; in 3:27, this is phrased as "tying up the strong man" (i.e., Satan) and "robbing his house" (i.e., setting free those who are enslaved to Satan). This power over Satan is especially evident in the driving out of demons (Gk *daimonion*) or evil spirits.

DEMONS. (1) The NT frequently refers to those who are suffering from Satan's oppression and influence because of the indwelling of an evil spirit, and to Jesus' conflict with demons. In the Gospel of Mark, for example, numerous such encounters are described: 1:23–28,32–34,39; 3:10–12,14–15; 5:1–20; 6:7,13; 7:24–30; 9:14–29; 16:17.

(2) Demons are spirit beings who have personality and intelligence. As members of Satan's kingdom and as enemies of God and humans (Mt 12:43–45), they are evil, malicious and under Satan's authority (see Mt 4:10, note).

(3) The NT presents the world as estranged from God and seized by Satan (see Jn 12:31, note; 2Co 4:4; Eph 6:10–12; see article on THE CHRISTIAN'S RELATIONSHIP TO THE WORLD, p. 546). Demons are within the hierarchy of the rulers of this age; Christians must wage continual warfare with them (see Eph 6:12, note).

(4) Demons can, and often do, live in the bodies of unbelievers (see Mk 5:15; Lk 4:41; 8:27–28; Ac 16:18) and use their voices to talk. They enslave such individuals and influence them toward evil, immorality and destruction.

(5) Demons can cause physical illness in the human body (Mt 9:32–33; 12:22; 17:14–18; Mk 9:20–22; Lk 13:11,16), although not all sicknesses and diseases are the result of evil spirits (Mt 4:24; Lk 5:12–13).

(6) Those involved in spiritism and magic (i.e., sorcery) are dealing with evil spirits; this can easily lead to demonic bondage (cf. Ac 13:8–10; 19:19; Gal 5:20; Rev 9:20).

(7) Evil spirits will be especially active in the last days of this age, promoting the occult, immorality, violence and cruelty; they will assault God's Word and sound doctrine (Mt 24:24; 2Co 11:14–15; 1Ti 4:1). The ultimate outpouring of demonic activity will be in the antichrist and his followers (2Th 2:9; Rev 13:2–8; 16:13–14).

JESUS AND DEMONS. (1) In his miracles, Jesus often attacks the power of Satan and the demonic (e.g., 1:26,34,39; 3:10–11; 5:1–20; 9:17–29; cf. Lk 13:16). One of Jesus' clearly stated purposes in coming to earth was to bind Satan and to set free those enslaved by him (Mt 12:29; Mk 1:27; Lk 4:18).

(2) Jesus' binding of Satan, accomplished in part through his driving out of demons and more completely in his death and resurrection (Jn 12:31), shatters the power of Satan's realm and restores the power of God's kingdom (see article on THE KINGDOM OF GOD, p. 28).

(3) Hell (Gk *Gehenna*), the place of torment, has been prepared by our Lord for the devil and his demons (Mt 8:29; 25:41).

BELIEVERS AND DEMONS. (1) Scripture teaches that no true believer who is indwelt by the Holy Spirit can be demon-possessed; the Spirit and demons can never live in the same body (see 2Co 6:15–16, note). Demons may, however, influence the thoughts, emotions and actions of Christians who fail to follow the leading of the Spirit (Mt 16:23; 2Co 11:3,14).

(2) Jesus promised true believers authority over the power of Satan and his cohorts. As we confront them, we must break the power they want to exert over us and others by waging intense spiritual warfare through the power of the Holy Spirit (see Lk 4:14–19). In this way we can be set free from the powers of darkness.

(3) According to the parable in Mk 3:27, spiritual conflict against Satan involves three aspects: (a) declaring war against Satan according to God's purpose (see Lk 4:14–19); (b) entering Satan's house (any place where he has a stronghold), attacking and overpowering him by prayer and proclamation of the Word and destroying his weapons of demonic deception and temptation (cf. Lk 11:20–22); (c) carrying off his possessions, i.e., delivering those who have been held captive by Satan's power and giving them over to God so that they may receive forgiveness and sanctification through faith in Christ (Lk 11:22; Ac 26:18).

(4) The following are individual steps we should take in this process: (a) Recognize that we are not in a conflict against flesh and blood but against spiritual forces and powers of evil (Eph 6:12). (b) Live before God, fervently committed to his truth and righteousness (Ro 12:1–2; Eph 6:14). (c) Have faith that Satan's power can be broken in any specific area of his domain (Ac 26:18; Eph 6:16; 1Th 5:8), and realize that the believer has powerful spiritual weapons given by God for the destruction of Satan's strongholds (2Co 10:4–5). (d) Proclaim the gospel of the kingdom in the fullness of the Holy Spirit (Mt 4:23; Lk 1:15–17; Ac 1:8; 2:4; 8:12; Ro 1:16; Eph 6:15). (e) Challenge Satan and his power directly by believing in Jesus' name (Ac 16:16–18), by using God's Word (Eph 6:17), by praying in the Spirit (Ac 6:4; Eph 6:18), by fasting (see Mt 6:16, note) and by driving out demons (see Mt 10:1, note; 12:28; 17:17–21; Mk 16:17; Lk 10:17; Ac 5:16; 8:7; 16:18; 19:12; see article on SIGNS OF BELIEVERS, p. 106). (f) Pray especially for the Holy Spirit to convict the lost concerning sin, righteousness and the coming judgment (Jn 16:7–11). (g) Pray for and eagerly desire the manifestation of the Spirit through gifts of healing, tongues, miracles, signs and wonders (Ac 4:29–33; 10:38; 1Co 12:7–11).

spirit[q] came from the tombs to meet him. **3**This man lived in the tombs, and no one could bind him any more, not even with a chain. **4**For he had often been chained hand and foot, but he tore the chains apart and broke the irons on his feet. No one was strong enough to subdue him. **5**Night and day among the tombs and in the hills he would cry out and cut himself with stones.

6When he saw Jesus from a distance, he ran and fell on his knees in front of him. **7**He shouted at the top of his voice, "What do you want with me,[r] Jesus, Son of the Most High God?[s] Swear to God that you won't torture me!" **8**For Jesus had said to him, "Come out of this man, you evil spirit!"

9Then Jesus asked him, "What is your name?"

"My name is Legion,"[t] he replied, "for we are many." **10**And he begged Jesus again and again not to send them out of the area.

11A large herd of pigs was feeding on the nearby hillside. **12**The demons begged Jesus, "Send us among the pigs; allow us to go into them." **13**He gave them permission, and the evil spirits came out and went into the pigs. The herd, about two thousand in number, rushed down the steep bank into the lake and were drowned.

14Those tending the pigs ran off and reported this in the town and countryside, and the people went out to see what had happened. **15**When they came to Jesus, they saw the man who had been possessed by the legion[u] of demons,[v] sitting there, dressed and in his right mind; and they were afraid. **16**Those who had seen it told the people what had happened to the demon-possessed man—and told about the pigs as well. **17**Then the people began to plead with Jesus to leave their region.

18As Jesus was getting into the boat, the man who had been demon-possessed begged to go with him. **19**Jesus did not let him, but said, "Go home to your family and tell them[w] how much the Lord has done for you, and how he has had mercy on you." **20**So the man went away and began to tell in the Decapolis[m][x] how much Jesus had done for him. And all the people were amazed.

5:2 [q]Mk 1:23
5:7 [r]S Mt 8:29 [s]S Mt 4:3; Lk 1:32; 6:35; Ac 16:17; Heb 7:1
5:9 [t]ver 15
5:15 [u]ver 9 [v]ver 16,18; S Mt 4:24
5:19 [w]S Mt 8:4
5:20 [x]Mt 4:25; Mk 7:31
5:21 [y]Mt 9:1 [z]Mk 4:1
5:22 [a]ver 35,36, 38; Lk 13:14; Ac 13:15; 18:8,17
5:23 [b]Mt 19:13; Mk 6:5; 7:32; 8:23; 16:18; Lk 4:40; 13:13; S Ac 6:6
5:25 [c]Lev 15:25-30
5:28 [d]S Mt 9:20
5:29 [e]ver 34
5:30 [f]Lk 5:17; 6:19
5:34 [g]S Mt 9:22 [h]S Ac 15:33

A Dead Girl and a Sick Woman

5:22–43pp — Mt 9:18–26; Lk 8:41–56

21When Jesus had again crossed over by boat to the other side of the lake,[y] a large crowd gathered around him while he was by the lake.[z] **22**Then one of the synagogue rulers,[a] named Jairus, came there. Seeing Jesus, he fell at his feet **23**and pleaded earnestly with him, "My little daughter is dying. Please come and put your hands on[b] her so that she will be healed and live." **24**So Jesus went with him.

A large crowd followed and pressed around him. **25**And a woman was there who had been subject to bleeding[c] for twelve years. **26**She had suffered a great deal under the care of many doctors and had spent all she had, yet instead of getting better she grew worse. **27**When she heard about Jesus, she came up behind him in the crowd and touched his cloak, **28**because she thought, "If I just touch his clothes,[d] I will be healed." **29**Immediately her bleeding stopped and she felt in her body that she was freed from her suffering.[e]

30At once Jesus realized that power[f] had gone out from him. He turned around in the crowd and asked, "Who touched my clothes?"

31"You see the people crowding against you," his disciples answered, "and yet you can ask, 'Who touched me?' "

32But Jesus kept looking around to see who had done it. **33**Then the woman, knowing what had happened to her, came and fell at his feet and, trembling with fear, told him the whole truth. **34**He said to her, "Daughter, your faith has healed you.[g] Go in peace[h] and be freed from your suffering." Mk 6:13

35While Jesus was still speaking, some men came from the house of Jairus, the

[m] *20* That is, the Ten Cities

5:2 A MAN WITH AN EVIL SPIRIT. Demon-possessed people suffer from satanic oppression (Ac 10:38) or influence (Mt 12:45; Ac 16:16–18) because an evil spirit dwells in them (see Lk 13:11, note). Scripture records many occasions in which Jesus drove out demons (for a full discussion on demons and the Christian's power over them, see article on POWER OVER SATAN AND DEMONS, p. 80).

5:28 JUST TOUCH HIS CLOTHES. The Gospels often speak of the sick touching Jesus (3:10; 5:27–34; 6:56) or of Jesus touching the sick (1:41–42; 7:33–35; Mt 8:3,15; 9:29–30; 20:34; Lk 5:13; 7:14–15; 22:51). It was the contact and presence of Jesus that mattered. His touch has healing power because he sympathizes with our weaknesses and is the source of life and grace (Heb 4:16). Our responsibility in seeking healing is to draw near to Jesus and to live in his presence (see Mt 17:20, note on true faith).

synagogue ruler.[i] "Your daughter is
dead," they said. "Why bother the teacher
any more?"
36Ignoring what they said, Jesus told
the synagogue ruler, "Don't be afraid; just
believe."
37He did not let anyone follow him except Peter, James and John the brother of
James.[j] 38When they came to the home of
the synagogue ruler,[k] Jesus saw a commotion, with people crying and wailing
loudly. 39He went in and said to them,
"Why all this commotion and wailing? The
child is not dead but asleep."[l] 40But they
laughed at him.
After he put them all out, he took the
child's father and mother and the disciples who were with him, and went in
where the child was. 41He took her by the
hand[m] and said to her, *"Talitha koum!"*
(which means, "Little girl, I say to you, get
up!").[n] 42Immediately the girl stood up
and walked around (she was twelve years
old). At this they were completely astonished. 43He gave strict orders not to let
anyone know about this,[o] and told them
to give her something to eat.

A Prophet Without Honor

6:1–6pp — Mt 13:54–58

6 Jesus left there and went to his hometown,[p] accompanied by his disciples.
2When the Sabbath came,[q] he began to
teach in the synagogue,[r] and many who
heard him were amazed.[s]
"Where did this man get these things?"
they asked. "What's this wisdom that has
been given him, that he even does miracles! 3Isn't this the carpenter? Isn't this
Mary's son and the brother of James, Joseph,[n] Judas and Simon?[t] Aren't his sisters here with us?" And they took offense
at him.[u]
4Jesus said to them, "Only in his hometown, among his relatives and in his own
house is a prophet without honor."[v] 5He
could not do any miracles there, except
lay his hands on[w] a few sick people and
heal them. 6And he was amazed at their
lack of faith.

Jesus Sends Out the Twelve

6:7–11pp — Mt 10:1,9–14; Lk 9:1,3–5

Then Jesus went around teaching from
village to village.[x] 7Calling the Twelve to
him,[y] he sent them out two by two[z] and
gave them authority over evil[o] spirits.[a]
8These were his instructions: "Take
nothing for the journey except a staff—no
bread, no bag, no money in your belts.
9Wear sandals but not an extra tunic.
10Whenever you enter a house, stay there
until you leave that town. 11And if any
place will not welcome you or listen to
you, shake the dust off your feet[b] when
you leave, as a testimony against them."
12They went out and preached that people should repent.[c] 13They drove out

5:35 [i]S ver 22 **5:37** [j]S Mt 4:21 **5:38** [k]S ver 22 **5:39** [l]S Mt 9:24 **5:41** [m]Mk 1:31 [n]S Lk 7:14 **5:43** [o]S Mt 8:4 **6:1** [p]S Mt 2:23 **6:2** [q]Mk 1:21 [r]S Mt 4:23 [s]S Mt 7:28

6:3 [t]S Mt 12:46 [u]Mt 11:6; Jn 6:61 **6:4** [v]Lk 4:24; Jn 4:44 **6:5** [w]S Mk 5:23 **6:6** [x]Mt 9:35; Mk 1:39; Lk 13:22 **6:7** [y]Mk 3:13 [z]Dt 17:6; Lk 10:1 [a]S Mt 10:1 **6:11** [b]S Mt 10:14 **6:12** [c]Lk 9:6

[n] 3 Greek *Joses,* a variant of *Joseph*   [o] 7 Greek *unclean*

5:36 JUST BELIEVE. The daughter of the synagogue ruler had died (v. 35). Jesus' response was to encourage the father's faith, even in this seemingly hopeless situation. Throughout redemptive history, believers have placed their trust in God even when it seemed as if all was lost. In such times, God gave the necessary faith and delivered his people according to his will and purpose (cf. Ps 22:4; Isa 26:3–4; 43:2). This was true for Abraham (Ge 22:2; Jas 2:21–22), Moses (Ex 14:10–22; 32:10–14), David (1Sa 17:44–47), Jehoshaphat (2Ch 20:1–2,12) and Jairus (vv. 21–23,35–42).

6:4 JESUS . . . A PROPHET. Jesus is portrayed in the Gospels as a prophet (vv. 4,15; Mt 21:11; Lk 4:24; cf. Ac 3:20–23). The following characteristics identify him as a prophet: (1) He was a man of the Spirit and the Word (Mt 21:42; 22:29; Lk 4:1,18; 24:27; Jn 3:34). (2) He was in intimate communion with God (see Lk 5:16, note). (3) He gave prophetic predictions (Mt 24; Lk 19:43–44). (4) He performed symbolic actions that expressed a zeal for God's honor (Mt 21:12–13; Jn 2:13–17). (5) He exposed the hypocrisy of the religious leaders and criticized their adherence to traditions rather than God's Word (7:7–9,13). (6) He shared the pathos and suffering of God over the lost condition of those who refused to repent (Lk 13:34; 19:41). (7) He emphasized the ethical teaching of God's Word (holiness, justice, righteousness, love, mercy) in contrast to ceremonial observance (12:38–40; Mt 23:1–36). (8) He proclaimed the impending reign and judgment of God (Mt 11:22,24; 10:15; Lk 10:12,14). (9) He was a preacher of repentance, calling people to turn from sin and the world to God (v. 12; Mt 4:17).

6:6 LACK OF FAITH. As lack of faith hindered the working of miracles in Jesus' hometown, so unbelief in the church still hinders the working of his power. Failure to believe Biblical truth, denial of the possibility of the gifts of the Spirit for today, or rejection of God's righteous standards will prevent our Lord from demonstrating his kingdom power among his people. Believers must maintain a hunger for the Word and pray, "increase our faith" (Lk 17:5).

6:7 EVIL SPIRITS. See 3:15, note.

6:13 ANOINTED . . . WITH OIL. Healing by anointing with oil is mentioned only here and in Jas 5:14. The oil was probably used as a symbol of the presence and power of the Holy Spirit (see Zec 4:3–6) and as a point of contact to encourage faith.

Mk 7:32-37 many demons and anointed many sick people with oil[d] and healed them.

John the Baptist Beheaded

6:14–29pp — Mt 14:1–12
6:14–16pp — Lk 9:7–9

14 King Herod heard about this, for Jesus' name had become well known. Some were saying,[p] "John the Baptist[e] has been raised from the dead, and that is why miraculous powers are at work in him."

15 Others said, "He is Elijah."[f]

And still others claimed, "He is a prophet,[g] like one of the prophets of long ago."[h]

16 But when Herod heard this, he said, "John, the man I beheaded, has been raised from the dead!"

17 For Herod himself had given orders to have John arrested, and he had him bound and put in prison.[i] He did this because of Herodias, his brother Philip's wife, whom he had married. 18 For John had been saying to Herod, "It is not lawful for you to have your brother's wife."[j] 19 So Herodias nursed a grudge against John and wanted to kill him. But she was not able to, 20 because Herod feared John and protected him, knowing him to be a righteous and holy man.[k] When Herod heard John, he was greatly puzzled[q]; yet he liked to listen to him.

21 Finally the opportune time came. On his birthday Herod gave a banquet[l] for his high officials and military commanders and the leading men of Galilee.[m] 22 When the daughter of Herodias came in and danced, she pleased Herod and his dinner guests.

The king said to the girl, "Ask me for anything you want, and I'll give it to you." 23 And he promised her with an oath, "Whatever you ask I will give you, up to half my kingdom."[n]

24 She went out and said to her mother, "What shall I ask for?"

"The head of John the Baptist," she answered.

25 At once the girl hurried in to the king with the request: "I want you to give me right now the head of John the Baptist on a platter."

26 The king was greatly distressed, but because of his oaths and his dinner guests, he did not want to refuse her. 27 So he immediately sent an executioner with orders to bring John's head. The man went, beheaded John in the prison, 28 and brought back his head on a platter. He presented it to the girl, and she gave it to her mother. 29 On hearing of this, John's disciples came and took his body and laid it in a tomb.

Jesus Feeds the Five Thousand

6:32–44pp — Mt 14:13–21; Lk 9:10–17; Jn 6:5–13
6:32–44Ref — Mk 8:2–9

30 The apostles[o] gathered around Jesus and reported to him all they had done and taught.[p] 31 Then, because so many people were coming and going that they did not even have a chance to eat,[q] he said to them, "Come with me by yourselves to a quiet place and get some rest."

32 So they went away by themselves in a boat[r] to a solitary place. 33 But many who saw them leaving recognized them and ran on foot from all the towns and got there ahead of them. 34 When Jesus landed and saw a large crowd, he had compassion on them, because they were like sheep without a shepherd.[s] So he began teaching them many things.

35 By this time it was late in the day, so his disciples came to him. "This is a remote place," they said, "and it's already very late. 36 Send the people away so they can go to the surrounding countryside and villages and buy themselves something to eat."

37 But he answered, "You give them something to eat."[t]

They said to him, "That would take eight months of a man's wages[r]! Are we to go and spend that much on bread and give it to them to eat?"

38 "How many loaves do you have?" he asked. "Go and see."

6:13 [d] S Jas 5:14
6:14 [e] S Mt 3:1
6:15 [f] Mal 4:5 [g] S Mt 21:11 [h] Mt 16:14; Mk 8:28
6:17 [i] Mt 4:12; 11:2; Lk 3:19,20
6:18 [j] Lev 18:16; 20:21
6:20 [k] S Mt 11:9
6:21 [l] Est 1:3; 2:18 [m] Lk 3:1
6:23 [n] Est 5:3,6; 7:2
6:30 [o] Mt 10:2; Lk 9:10; 17:5; 22:14; 24:10; Ac 1:2,26 [p] Lk 9:10
6:31 [q] Mk 3:20
6:32 [r] ver 45; S Mk 4:36
6:34 [s] S Mt 9:36
6:37 [t] 2Ki 4:42-44

[p] *14* Some early manuscripts *He was saying*
[q] *20* Some early manuscripts *he did many things*
[r] *37* Greek *take two hundred denarii*

6:17 JOHN . . . IN PRISON. See Mt 11:7, note.

6:22 DANCED. See Mt 14:6, note.

6:34 COMPASSION. Compassion is an emotion that moves people to the very depths of their being. It involves a sorrow felt for another's suffering and misfortune, accompanied by an intense desire to help. It is a characteristic both of God (Dt 30:3; 2Ki 13:23; Ps 78:38; 111:4) and of his Son Jesus (1:41; 8:2, note; Mt 9:36; 14:14; 15:32; Lk 7:13). In all ages, and particularly in this present age of indifference to the physical and spiritual suffering of others, Jesus wants and expects this attitude to characterize his followers (Mt 18:33; Lk 10:33).

When they found out, they said, "Five—
and two fish."[u]
39Then Jesus directed them to have all
the people sit down in groups on the green
grass. 40So they sat down in groups of
hundreds and fifties. 41Taking the five
loaves and the two fish and looking up to
heaven, he gave thanks and broke the
loaves.[v] Then he gave them to his disciples to set before the people. He also divided the two fish among them all. 42They
all ate and were satisfied, 43and the disciples picked up twelve basketfuls of broken pieces of bread and fish. 44The number of the men who had eaten was five
thousand.

Jesus Walks on the Water

6:45–51pp — Mt 14:22–32; Jn 6:15–21
6:53–56pp — Mt 14:34–36

45Immediately Jesus made his disciples
get into the boat[w] and go on ahead of him
to Bethsaida,[x] while he dismissed the
crowd. 46After leaving them, he went up
on a mountainside to pray.[y]
47When evening came, the boat was in
the middle of the lake, and he was alone
on land. 48He saw the disciples straining
at the oars, because the wind was against
them. About the fourth watch of the night
he went out to them, walking on the lake.
He was about to pass by them, 49but when
they saw him walking on the lake, they
thought he was a ghost.[z] They cried out,
50because they all saw him and were terrified.
Immediately he spoke to them and said,
"Take courage! It is I. Don't be afraid."[a]
51Then he climbed into the boat[b] with
them, and the wind died down.[c] They
were completely amazed, 52for they had
not understood about the loaves; their
hearts were hardened.[d]
53When they had crossed over, they
landed at Gennesaret and anchored
there.[e] 54As soon as they got out of the
boat, people recognized Jesus. 55They ran
throughout that whole region and carried
the sick on mats to wherever they heard
he was. 56And wherever he went—into
villages, towns or countryside—they
placed the sick in the marketplaces. They
begged him to let them touch even the
edge of his cloak,[f] and all who touched
him were healed.

Tradition and God's Commands

7:1–23pp — Mt 15:1–20

7 The Pharisees and some of the teachers of the law who had come from Jerusalem gathered around Jesus and 2saw
some of his disciples eating food with
hands that were "unclean,"[g] that is, unwashed. 3(The Pharisees and all the Jews
do not eat unless they give their hands a
ceremonial washing, holding to the tradition of the elders.[h] 4When they come from
the marketplace they do not eat unless
they wash. And they observe many other
traditions, such as the washing of cups,
pitchers and kettles.[s])[i]
5So the Pharisees and teachers of the
law asked Jesus, "Why don't your disciples live according to the tradition of the
elders[j] instead of eating their food with
'unclean' hands?"
6He replied, "Isaiah was right when he
prophesied about you hypocrites; as it is
written:

6:38 [u]Mt 15:34; Mk 8:5 **6:41** [v]S Mt 14:19 **6:45** [w]ver 32 [x]S Mt 11:21 **6:46** [y]S Lk 3:21 **6:49** [z]Lk 24:37 **6:50** [a]S Mt 14:27 **6:51** [b]ver 32 [c]Mk 4:39 **6:52** [d]Mk 8:17-21 **6:53** [e]Jn 6:24,25 **6:56** [f]S Mt 9:20 **7:2** [g]Ac 10:14,28; 11:8; Ro 14:14 **7:3** [h]ver 5,8,9,13; Lk 11:38 **7:4** [i]Mt 23:25; Lk 11:39 **7:5** [j]S ver 3; Gal 1:14; Col 2:8

[s] *4* Some early manuscripts *pitchers, kettles and dining couches*

6:41 FIVE LOAVES . . . TWO FISH. See Mt 14:19, note.

6:41 THANKSGIVING AT MEALTIMES. Before eating, Christ gave thanks to his heavenly Father for the food. Believers ought to follow his example and give thanks at every meal. To eat with thanksgiving is to recognize God's care and provision for us. Every meal should be an act of worship, done to the glory of God. On giving thanks before meals, see 1Sa 9:13; Mt 14:19; 15:36; 26:26; Ro 14:6; 1Co 10:31; 1Ti 4:4–5.

7:6 THEIR HEARTS ARE FAR FROM ME. The Pharisees and the teachers of the law were guilty of the sin of legalism. A legalist substitutes outward acts or words for proper inner attitudes that come from being born of God and the Spirit (see Mt 5:20, note; 5:27–28; 6:1–7; Jn 1:13; 3:3–6). Such people honor God with their lips, while their hearts are far from him; they appear righteous outwardly, but inwardly have no real love for God. (1) Legalism does not refer to the mere existence of laws or standards within the Christian community. Rather, it has to do with motives—the motives by which the Christian approaches God's will as expressed in his Word. Any motive for keeping commands or regulations that does not stem from a living faith in Christ, the regenerating power of the Holy Spirit, and the sincere desire to obey and please God is legalism (Mt 6:1–7; Jn 14:21).

(2) Even in this day of grace Christians remain under the instruction, discipline and duty of obeying Christ's law and his Word. The NT speaks of the "perfect law that gives freedom" (Jas 1:25), "the royal law" (Jas 2:8), the "law of Christ" (Gal 6:2) and the "law of the Spirit" (Ro 8:2). In God's Word we find (a) positive commands (1Th 5:16–18), (b) negative commands (Ro 12:2), (c) basic principles (1Co 8:13) and (d) words spoken by spiritual leaders who have been given authority to rule in spiritual matters (Eph 4:11–12; 1Ti 3:5; Heb 13:7,17).

DECAPOLIS AND LANDS BEYOND THE JORDAN

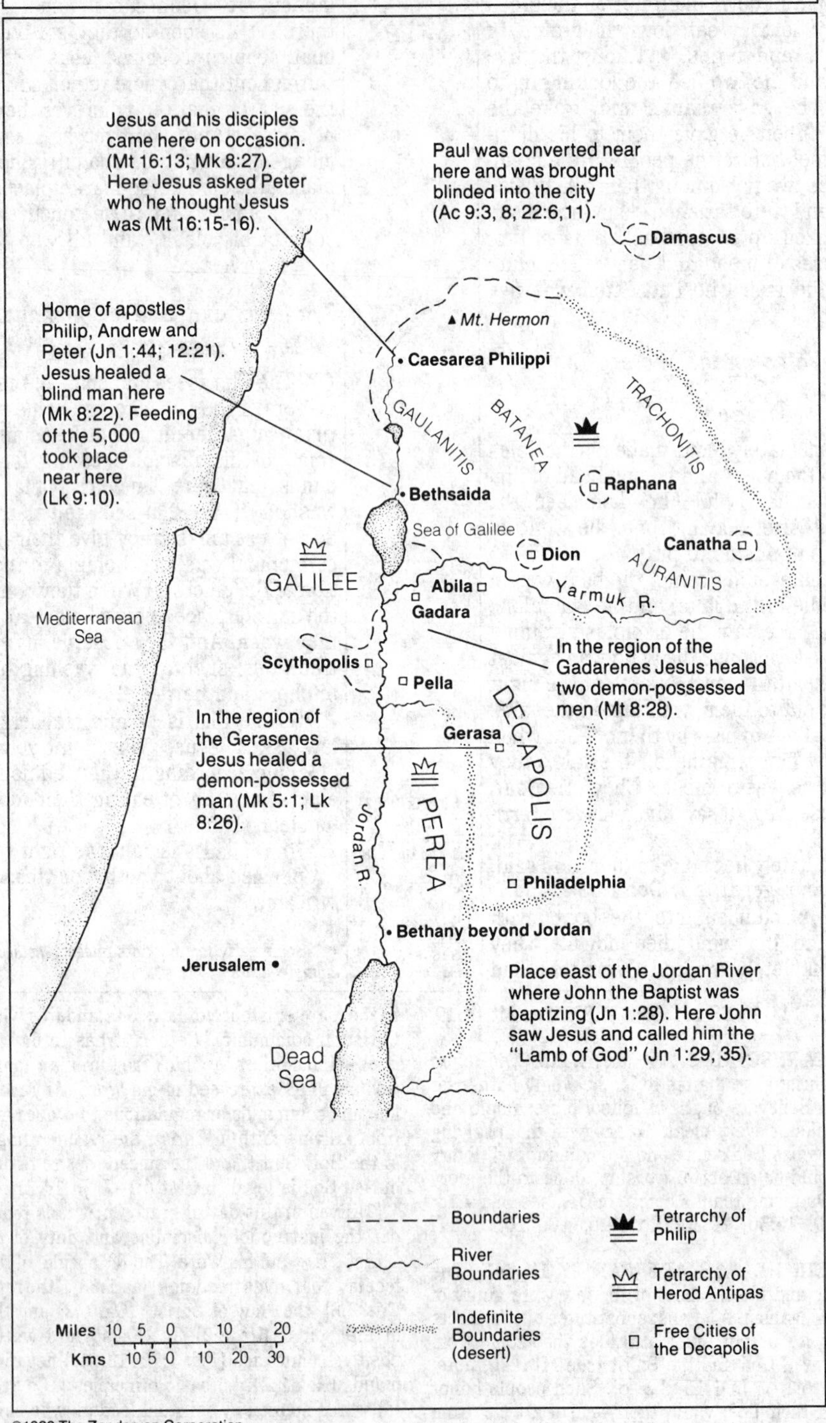

Jesus and his disciples came here on occasion. (Mt 16:13; Mk 8:27). Here Jesus asked Peter who he thought Jesus was (Mt 16:15-16).
Paul was converted near here and was brought blinded into the city (Ac 9:3, 8; 22:6,11).
Damascus
Mt. Hermon
Home of apostles Philip, Andrew and Peter (Jn 1:44; 12:21). Jesus healed a blind man here (Mk 8:22). Feeding of the 5,000 took place near here (Lk 9:10).
Caesarea Philippi
TRACHONITIS
BATANEA
GAULANITIS
Raphana
Bethsaida
Sea of Galilee
Canatha
Dion
GALILEE
AURANITIS
Abila
Yarmuk R.
Gadara
Mediterranean Sea
In the region of the Gadarenes Jesus healed two demon-possessed men (Mt 8:28).
Scythopolis
Pella
DECAPOLIS
In the region of the Gerasenes Jesus healed a demon-possessed man (Mk 5:1; Lk 8:26).
Gerasa
PEREA
Jordan R.
Philadelphia
Bethany beyond Jordan
Jerusalem
Place east of the Jordan River where John the Baptist was baptizing (Jn 1:28). Here John saw Jesus and called him the "Lamb of God" (Jn 1:29, 35).
Dead Sea
Boundaries
River Boundaries
Indefinite Boundaries (desert)
Tetrarchy of Philip
Tetrarchy of Herod Antipas
Free Cities of the Decapolis
Miles 10 5 0 10 20
Kms 10 5 0 10 20 30

" 'These people honor me with their
lips,
but their hearts are far from me.
7They worship me in vain;
their teachings are but rules taught
by men.'[t][k]

8You have let go of the commands of God
and are holding on to the traditions of
men."[l]

9And he said to them: "You have a fine
way of setting aside the commands of God
in order to observe[u] your own traditions![m]
10For Moses said, 'Honor your father and
your mother,'[v][n] and, 'Anyone who curses
his father or mother must be put to
death.'[w][o] **11**But you say[p] that if a man
says to his father or mother: 'Whatever
help you might otherwise have received
from me is Corban' (that is, a gift devoted
to God), **12**then you no longer let him do
anything for his father or mother. **13**Thus
you nullify the word of God[q] by your tradition[r] that you have handed down. And
you do many things like that."

Clean and Unclean

14Again Jesus called the crowd to him
and said, "Listen to me, everyone, and understand this. **15**Nothing outside a man
can make him 'unclean' by going into him.
Rather, it is what comes out of a man that
makes him 'unclean.'[x]"

17After he had left the crowd and entered the house, his disciples asked him[s]
about this parable. **18**"Are you so dull?" he
asked. "Don't you see that nothing that
enters a man from the outside can make
him 'unclean'? **19**For it doesn't go into his
heart but into his stomach, and then out
of his body." (In saying this, Jesus declared all foods[t] "clean.")[u]

20He went on: "What comes out of a
man is what makes him 'unclean.' **21**For
from within, out of men's hearts, come
evil thoughts, sexual immorality, theft,
murder, adultery, **22**greed,[v] malice, deceit, lewdness, envy, slander, arrogance
and folly. **23**All these evils come from inside and make a man 'unclean.' "

The Faith of a Syrophoenician Woman

7:24–30pp — Mt 15:21–28

24Jesus left that place and went to the
vicinity of Tyre.[y][w] He entered a house and
did not want anyone to know it; yet he
could not keep his presence secret. **25**In
fact, as soon as she heard about him, a
woman whose little daughter was possessed by an evil[z] spirit[x] came and fell at
his feet. **26**The woman was a Greek, born
in Syrian Phoenicia. She begged Jesus to
drive the demon out of her daughter.

27"First let the children eat all they
want," he told her, "for it is not right to
take the children's bread and toss it to
their dogs."

28"Yes, Lord," she replied, "but even
the dogs under the table eat the children's
crumbs."

29Then he told her, "For such a reply,
you may go; the demon has left your
daughter."

30She went home and found her child
lying on the bed, and the demon gone.

7:7 [k]Isa 29:13 **7:8** [l]S ver 3 **7:9** [m]S ver 3 **7:10** [n]Ex 20:12; Dt 5:16 [o]Ex 21:17; Lev 20:9 **7:11** [p]Mt 23:16, 18 **7:13** [q]S Heb 4:12 [r]S ver 3 **7:17** [s]Mk 9:28 **7:19** [t]Ro 14:1-12; Col 2:16; 1Ti 4:3-5 [u]S Ac 10:15 **7:22** [v]Mt 20:15 **7:24** [w]S Mt 11:21 **7:25** [x]S Mt 4:24

[t] *6,7* Isaiah 29:13 [u] *9* Some manuscripts *set up* [v] *10* Exodus 20:12; Deut. 5:16 [w] *10* Exodus 21:17; Lev. 20:9 [x] *15* Some early manuscripts *'unclean.' 16If anyone has ears to hear, let him hear.* [y] *24* Many early manuscripts *Tyre and Sidon* [z] *25* Greek *unclean*

7:8 THE TRADITIONS OF MEN. The Pharisees and the teachers of the law were guilty of placing human tradition above divine revelation. Jesus is not condemning all traditions here, but only those that conflict with God's Word. Traditions or rules must be based on corresponding truths found in Scripture (cf. 2Th 2:15). Churches must resist the tendency to exalt religious traditions, human wisdom or contemporary customs above the Bible. Scripture is the only infallible rule of faith and practice; it must never be nullified by human ideas (v. 13; see Mt 15:6, note).

7:18 MAKE HIM 'UNCLEAN'. Jesus is speaking of foods that enter a person but do not affect his or her heart (v. 19). This verse cannot be used to justify using harmful drugs or alcoholic beverages, for such use has resulted in all the sins listed in vv. 21–22 (see Pr 23:31).

7:20–23 MEN'S HEARTS. In this passage "makes . . . 'unclean' " (v. 20) means being separated from the life, salvation and fellowship of Christ because of sins that come from the heart. The "heart" in Scripture is the totality of intellect, emotion, desire and volition. An impure heart will corrupt one's thoughts, feelings, words and actions (Pr 4:23; Mt 12:34; 15:19). What is needed is a new, transformed heart, refashioned after the image of Christ (see Lk 6:45; see article on REGENERATION, p. 178).

7:27 CHILDREN'S BREAD. The word "children" refers to Israel. Jesus indicates that the gospel must be taken first to Israel. The woman understands this, yet responds to Christ in wisdom, perseverance and faith. She argues that it is God's purpose for Gentiles to receive blessings indirectly when he blesses Israel. Christ rewards her diligent faith by healing her child (vv. 28–30). Believers, in prayer for themselves or others, must persevere in prayer, and occasionally even reason with God (see Mt 15:28, note).

The Healing of a Deaf and Mute Man

7:31–37pp — Mt 15:29–31

31Then Jesus left the vicinity of Tyre[y] and went through Sidon, down to the Sea of Galilee[z] and into the region of the Decapolis.[a][a] **32**There some people brought to him a man who was deaf and could hardly talk,[b] and they begged him to place his hand on[c] the man.

33After he took him aside, away from the crowd, Jesus put his fingers into the man's ears. Then he spit[d] and touched the man's tongue. **34**He looked up to heaven[e] and with a deep sigh[f] said to him, *"Ephphatha!"* (which means, "Be opened!"). **35**At this, the man's ears were opened, his tongue was loosened and he began to speak plainly.[g]

36Jesus commanded them not to tell anyone.[h] But the more he did so, the more they kept talking about it. **37**People were overwhelmed with amazement. "He has done everything well," they said. "He even makes the deaf hear and the mute speak."

Lk 6:17-19

Jesus Feeds the Four Thousand

8:1–9pp — Mt 15:32–39
8:1–9Ref — Mk 6:32–44
8:11–21pp — Mt 16:1–12

8 During those days another large crowd gathered. Since they had nothing to eat, Jesus called his disciples to him and said, **2**"I have compassion for these people;[i] they have already been with me three days and have nothing to eat. **3**If I send them home hungry, they will collapse on the way, because some of them have come a long distance."

4His disciples answered, "But where in this remote place can anyone get enough bread to feed them?"

5"How many loaves do you have?" Jesus asked.

"Seven," they replied.

6He told the crowd to sit down on the ground. When he had taken the seven loaves and given thanks, he broke them and gave them to his disciples to set before the people, and they did so. **7**They had a few small fish as well; he gave thanks for them also and told the disciples to distribute them.[j] **8**The people ate and were satisfied. Afterward the disciples picked up seven basketfuls of broken pieces that were left over.[k] **9**About four thousand men were present. And having sent them away, **10**he got into the boat with his disciples and went to the region of Dalmanutha.

11The Pharisees came and began to question Jesus. To test him, they asked him for a sign from heaven.[l] **12**He sighed deeply[m] and said, "Why does this generation ask for a miraculous sign? I tell you the truth, no sign will be given to it." **13**Then he left them, got back into the boat and crossed to the other side.

The Yeast of the Pharisees and Herod

14The disciples had forgotten to bring bread, except for one loaf they had with them in the boat. **15**"Be careful," Jesus warned them. "Watch out for the yeast[n] of the Pharisees[o] and that of Herod."[p]

16They discussed this with one another and said, "It is because we have no bread."

17Aware of their discussion, Jesus asked them: "Why are you talking about having no bread? Do you still not see or understand? Are your hearts hardened?[q] **18**Do you have eyes but fail to see, and ears but fail to hear? And don't you remember? **19**When I broke the five loaves for the five thousand, how many basketfuls of pieces did you pick up?"

"Twelve,"[r] they replied.

20"And when I broke the seven loaves for the four thousand, how many basketfuls of pieces did you pick up?"

They answered, "Seven."[s]

21He said to them, "Do you still not understand?"[t]

7:31 [y]ver 24; S Mt 11:21 [z]S Mt 4:18 [a]Mt 4:25; Mk 5:20 **7:32** [b]Mt 9:32; Lk 11:14 [c]S Mk 5:23 **7:33** [d]Mk 8:23 **7:34** [e]Mk 6:41; Jn 11:41 [f]Mk 8:12 **7:35** [g]Isa 35:5,6 **7:36** [h]S Mt 8:4 **8:2** [i]S Mt 9:36

8:7 [j]Mt 14:19 **8:8** [k]ver 20 **8:11** [l]S Mt 12:38 **8:12** [m]Mk 7:34 **8:15** [n]1Co 5:6-8 [o]Lk 12:1 [p]S Mt 14:1; Mk 12:13 **8:17** [q]Isa 6:9,10; Mk 6:52 **8:19** [r]Mt 14:20; Mk 6:41-44; Lk 9:17; Jn 6:13 **8:20** [s]ver 6-9; Mt 15:37 **8:21** [t]Mk 6:52

[a] *31* That is, the Ten Cities

8:2 I HAVE COMPASSION. Jesus was touched with compassion for the needs and suffering of humanity (see 1:41). Jesus is still moved today with a deep and earnest sympathy by the needs and hurts of each child of God. This assures us that in our troubles we can come to him in prayer in order to receive grace, mercy and help (Mt 6:31–32; Heb 4:14–16; 7:25).

8:15 YEAST. In the NT "yeast" is usually a symbol for evil or corruption (see Mt 13:33; 16:6,11; Lk 12:1; 1Co 5:6–8; Gal 5:9). A small amount of yeast will ferment and affect the whole. (1) The yeast of the Pharisees refers to their preference for human-initiated ideas over the commands and righteousness of God (7:5–8, notes). (2) The yeast of Herod is identical with that of the Sadducees; it refers to a spirit of secularism and worldliness (see Mt 3:7, note). Followers of Christ must always guard against accepting the views of those who preach human ideas, unbiblical traditions or a secular, humanistic type of gospel. To accept the "yeast . . . of Herod" will cause the church to turn against Christ and his Word.

The Healing of a Blind Man at Bethsaida

22 They came to Bethsaida,[u] and some
people brought a blind man[v] and begged
Jesus to touch him. 23 He took the blind
man by the hand and led him outside the
village. When he had spit[w] on the man's
eyes and put his hands on[x] him, Jesus
asked, "Do you see anything?"
24 He looked up and said, "I see people;
they look like trees walking around."
25 Once more Jesus put his hands on the
man's eyes. Then his eyes were opened,
his sight was restored, and he saw everything clearly. 26 Jesus sent him home, saying, "Don't go into the village.[b]"

Peter's Confession of Christ

8:27–29pp — Mt 16:13–16; Lk 9:18–20

27 Jesus and his disciples went on to the
villages around Caesarea Philippi. On the
way he asked them, "Who do people say
I am?"
28 They replied, "Some say John the
Baptist;[y] others say Elijah;[z] and still others, one of the prophets."
29 "But what about you?" he asked.
"Who do you say I am?"
Peter answered, "You are the
Christ.[c]"[a]
30 Jesus warned them not to tell anyone
about him.[b]

Jesus Predicts His Death

8:31 — 9:1pp — Mt 16:21–28; Lk 9:22–27

31 He then began to teach them that the
Son of Man[c] must suffer many things[d]
and be rejected by the elders, chief priests
and teachers of the law,[e] and that he
must be killed[f] and after three days[g] rise
again.[h] 32 He spoke plainly[i] about this,
and Peter took him aside and began to
rebuke him.
33 But when Jesus turned and looked at
his disciples, he rebuked Peter. "Get behind me, Satan!"[j] he said. "You do not
have in mind the things of God, but the
things of men."
34 Then he called the crowd to him
along with his disciples and said: "If anyone would come after me, he must deny
himself and take up his cross and follow
me.[k] 35 For whoever wants to save his
life[d] will lose it, but whoever loses his life
for me and for the gospel will save it.[l]
36 What good is it for a man to gain the
whole world, yet forfeit his soul? 37 Or
what can a man give in exchange for his
soul? 38 If anyone is ashamed of me and
my words in this adulterous and sinful
generation, the Son of Man[m] will be
ashamed of him[n] when he comes[o] in his
Father's glory with the holy angels."

9 And he said to them, "I tell you the
truth, some who are standing here
will not taste death before they see the
kingdom of God come[p] with power."[q]

The Transfiguration

9:2–8pp — Lk 9:28–36
9:2–13pp — Mt 17:1–13

2 After six days Jesus took Peter, James
and John[r] with him and led them up a high
mountain, where they were all alone.
There he was transfigured before them.
3 His clothes became dazzling white,[s]

8:22 [u] S Mt 11:21 [v] Mk 10:46; Jn 9:1 **8:23** [w] Mk 7:33 [x] S Mk 5:23 **8:28** [y] S Mt 3:1 [z] Mal 4:5 **8:29** [a] Jn 6:69; 11:27 **8:30** [b] S Mt 8:4; 16:20; 17:9; Mk 9:9; Lk 9:21 **8:31** [c] S Mt 8:20 [d] S Mt 16:21 [e] Mt 27:1,2 [f] Ac 2:23; 3:13 [g] S Mt 16:21 [h] S Mt 16:21 **8:32** [i] Jn 18:20 **8:33** [j] S Mt 4:10 **8:34** [k] Mt 10:38; Lk 14:27 **8:35** [l] S Jn 12:25 **8:38** [m] S Mt 8:20 [n] Mt 10:33; Lk 12:9 [o] S 1Th 2:19 **9:1** [p] Mk 13:30; Lk 22:18 [q] Mt 24:30; 25:31 **9:2** [r] S Mt 4:21 **9:3** [s] S Mt 28:3

b *26* Some manuscripts *Don't go and tell anyone in the village* **c** *29* Or *Messiah.* "The Christ" (Greek) and "the Messiah" (Hebrew) both mean "the Anointed One." **d** *35* The Greek word means either *life* or *soul*; also in verse 36.

8:25 HIS SIGHT WAS RESTORED. This healing in Bethsaida is the only instance of a gradual cure by Jesus. It teaches that not every healing has to be instantaneous, for in some cases the victory of divine power over sickness will be gradual.

8:34 TAKE UP HIS CROSS. The cross of Christ is a symbol of suffering (1Pe 2:21; 4:13), death (Ac 10:39), shame (Heb 12:2), ridicule (Mt 27:39), rejection (1Pe 2:4) and self-denial (Mt 16:24). When we as believers take up our cross and follow Christ, we deny our own selves (Lk 14:26–27) and commit ourselves to three areas of struggle and suffering:

(1) We suffer in a lifelong battle against sin (Ro 6; 1Pe 4:1–2) by crucifying our own sinful desires (Ro 6; 8:13; Gal 2:20; 6:14; Tit 2:12; 1Pe 2:11,21–24).

(2) We suffer in a war against Satan and the powers of darkness as we advance the kingdom of God (2Co 10:4–5; 6:7; Eph 6:12; 1Ti 6:12). We experience both the hostility of the adversary with his demonic host (2Co 6:3–7; 11:23–29; 1Pe 5:8–10) and the persecution that comes from standing against false teachers who distort the true gospel (Mt 23:1–36; Gal 1:9; Php 1:15–17).

(3) We suffer the hatred and ridicule of the world (Jn 15:18–25; Heb 11:25–26) by testifying in love that its deeds are evil (Jn 7:7), by separating ourselves from it both morally and spiritually (see article on SPIRITUAL SEPARATION FOR BELIEVERS, p. 371), and by refusing to accept its standards or philosophies as our own (1Co 1:21–27).

8:38 ASHAMED OF ME AND MY WORDS. Jesus sees the world and society in which we live as an "adulterous and sinful generation." All those who seek to be popular in or accepted by their present evil generation rather than follow Christ and his righteous standards will be rejected by Christ at his return (cf. Mt 7:23; 25:41–46; Lk 9:26, note; 13:27).

9:1 KINGDOM OF GOD . . . WITH POWER. See Mt 16:28, note.

9:2 HE WAS TRANSFIGURED. See Lk 9:29, note.

whiter than anyone in the world could
bleach them. **4**And there appeared before
them Elijah and Moses, who were talking
with Jesus.

5Peter said to Jesus, "Rabbi,[t] it is good
for us to be here. Let us put up three shelters—one for you, one for Moses and one
for Elijah." **6**(He did not know what to say,
they were so frightened.)

7Then a cloud appeared and enveloped
them, and a voice came from the cloud:[u]
"This is my Son, whom I love. Listen to
him!"[v]

8Suddenly, when they looked around,
they no longer saw anyone with them except Jesus.

9As they were coming down the mountain, Jesus gave them orders not to tell
anyone[w] what they had seen until the Son
of Man[x] had risen from the dead. **10**They
kept the matter to themselves, discussing
what "rising from the dead" meant.

11And they asked him, "Why do the
teachers of the law say that Elijah must
come first?"

12Jesus replied, "To be sure, Elijah does
come first, and restores all things. Why
then is it written that the Son of Man[y]
must suffer much[z] and be rejected?[a]
13But I tell you, Elijah has come,[b] and
they have done to him everything they
wished, just as it is written about him."

The Healing of a Boy With an Evil Spirit

9:14–28; 30–32pp — Mt 17:14–19; 22,23; Lk 9:37–45

14When they came to the other disciples, they saw a large crowd around them
and the teachers of the law arguing with
them. **15**As soon as all the people saw
Jesus, they were overwhelmed with wonder and ran to greet him.

16"What are you arguing with them
about?" he asked.

17A man in the crowd answered,
"Teacher, I brought you my son, who is
possessed by a spirit that has robbed him
of speech. **18**Whenever it seizes him, it
throws him to the ground. He foams at the
mouth, gnashes his teeth and becomes
rigid. I asked your disciples to drive out
the spirit, but they could not."

19"O unbelieving generation," Jesus replied, "how long shall I stay with you?
How long shall I put up with you? Bring
the boy to me."

20So they brought him. When the spirit
saw Jesus, it immediately threw the boy
into a convulsion. He fell to the ground
and rolled around, foaming at the mouth.[c]

21Jesus asked the boy's father, "How
long has he been like this?"

"From childhood," he answered. **22**"It
has often thrown him into fire or water to
kill him. But if you can do anything, take
pity on us and help us."

23"'If you can'?" said Jesus. "Everything is possible for him who believes."[d]

24Immediately the boy's father exclaimed, "I do believe; help me overcome
my unbelief!" Mk 10:52

25When Jesus saw that a crowd was
running to the scene,[e] he rebuked the
evil[e] spirit. "You deaf and mute spirit," he
said, "I command you, come out of him
and never enter him again."

26The spirit shrieked, convulsed him violently and came out. The boy looked so
much like a corpse that many said, "He's
dead." **27**But Jesus took him by the hand
and lifted him to his feet, and he stood up.

28After Jesus had gone indoors, his disciples asked him privately,[f] "Why
couldn't we drive it out?"

29He replied, "This kind can come out
only by prayer.[f]"

30They left that place and passed

9:5 [t]S Mt 23:7
9:7 [u]Ex 24:16
[v]S Mt 3:17
9:9 [w]S Mk 8:30
[x]S Mt 8:20
9:12 [y]S Mt 8:20
[z]S Mt 16:21
[a]Lk 23:11
9:13 [b]S Mt 11:14
9:20 [c]Mk 1:26
9:23 [d]S Mt 21:21; Mk 11:23; Jn 11:40
9:25 [e]ver 15
9:28 [f]Mk 7:17

e 25 Greek *unclean*
f 29 Some manuscripts *prayer and fasting*

9:19 UNBELIEVING GENERATION. Failure to wage effective warfare against demons is seen as a spiritual weakness on the part of Christ's disciples (see Mt 17:17, note).

9:23 EVERYTHING IS POSSIBLE. Jesus' statement must not be taken as an unqualified promise. (1) The "everything" does not mean everything we can think of. The prayer of faith must be based on God's will; it never asks for anything foolish or wrong (Jas 4:3). (2) The faith required here must be received as a gift of God. He implants it in the heart of a sincere seeker who lives faithfully according to his will (see Mt 17:20, note).

9:24 HELP ME OVERCOME MY UNBELIEF. In this life our faith is often mixed with doubt. This does not mean, however, that Christ will not respond to our petitions, for he understands and sympathizes with our weaknesses (Heb 4:15). We should confess our lack of faith and pray that he would give us the faith that is needed (see Mt 17:20, note).

9:29 ONLY BY PRAYER. Jesus does not mean that a time of prayer was necessary before this kind of evil spirit could be driven out. Rather a principle is implied here: where there is little faith, there is little prayer. Where there is much prayer, founded on true commitment to God and his Word, there is much faith. Had the disciples been maintaining, as Jesus did, a life of prayer, they could have dealt successfully with this case.

through Galilee. Jesus did not want anyone to know where they were, 31because
he was teaching his disciples. He said to
them, "The Son of Man[g] is going to be
betrayed into the hands of men. They will
kill him,[h] and after three days[i] he will
rise."[j] 32But they did not understand
what he meant[k] and were afraid to ask
him about it.

Who Is the Greatest?

9:33–37pp — Mt 18:1–5; Lk 9:46–48

33They came to Capernaum.[l] When he
was in the house,[m] he asked them, "What
were you arguing about on the road?"
34But they kept quiet because on the way
they had argued about who was the greatest.[n]

35Sitting down, Jesus called the Twelve
and said, "If anyone wants to be first, he
must be the very last, and the servant of
all."[o]

36He took a little child and had him
stand among them. Taking him in his
arms,[p] he said to them, 37"Whoever welcomes one of these little children in my
name welcomes me; and whoever welcomes me does not welcome me but the
one who sent me."[q]

Whoever Is Not Against Us Is for Us

9:38–40pp — Lk 9:49,50

38"Teacher," said John, "we saw a man
driving out demons in your name and we
told him to stop, because he was not one
of us."[r]

39"Do not stop him," Jesus said. "No
one who does a miracle in my name can
in the next moment say anything bad
about me, 40for whoever is not against us
is for us.[s] 41I tell you the truth, anyone
who gives you a cup of water in my name
because you belong to Christ will certainly
not lose his reward.[t]

Causing to Sin

42"And if anyone causes one of these
little ones who believe in me to sin,[u] it
would be better for him to be thrown into
the sea with a large millstone tied around
his neck.[v] 43If your hand causes you to
sin,[w] cut it off. It is better for you to enter
life maimed than with two hands to go into
hell,[x] where the fire never goes out.[g][y]
45And if your foot causes you to sin,[z] cut
it off. It is better for you to enter life crippled than to have two feet and be thrown
into hell.[h][a] 47And if your eye causes you
to sin,[b] pluck it out. It is better for you to
enter the kingdom of God with one eye
than to have two eyes and be thrown into
hell,[c] 48where

> " 'their worm does not die,
>   and the fire is not quenched.'[i][d]

49Everyone will be salted[e] with fire.

50"Salt is good, but if it loses its saltiness, how can you make it salty again?[f]
Have salt in yourselves,[g] and be at peace
with each other."[h]

Divorce

10:1–12pp — Mt 19:1–9

10 Jesus then left that place and went
into the region of Judea and across
the Jordan.[i] Again crowds of people came
to him, and as was his custom, he taught
them.[j]

2Some Pharisees[k] came and tested him
by asking, "Is it lawful for a man to divorce his wife?"

3"What did Moses command you?" he
replied.

4They said, "Moses permitted a man to
write a certificate of divorce and send her
away."[l]

5"It was because your hearts were
hard[m] that Moses wrote you this law,"
Jesus replied. 6"But at the beginning of
creation God 'made them male and female.'[j][n] 7'For this reason a man will

9:31 [g] S Mt 8:20 [h] ver 12; Ac 2:23; 3:13 [i] S Mt 16:21 [j] S Mt 16:21
9:32 [k] Lk 2:50; 9:45; 18:34; Jn 12:16
9:33 [l] S Mt 4:13 [m] Mk 1:29
9:34 [n] Lk 22:24
9:35 [o] Mt 18:4; Mk 10:43; Lk 22:26
9:36 [p] Mk 10:16
9:37 [q] S Mt 10:40
9:38 [r] Nu 11:27-29
9:40 [s] Mt 12:30; Lk 11:23
9:41 [t] S Mt 10:42
9:42 [u] S Mt 5:29 [v] Mt 18:6; Lk 17:2
9:43 [w] S Mt 5:29 [x] Mt 5:30; 18:8 [y] S Mt 25:41
9:45 [z] S Mt 5:29 [a] Mt 18:8
9:47 [b] S Mt 5:29 [c] Mt 5:29; 18:9
9:48 [d] Isa 66:24; S Mt 25:41
9:49 [e] Lev 2:13
9:50 [f] Mt 5:13; Lk 14:34,35 [g] Col 4:6 [h] Ro 12:18; 2Co 13:11; 1Th 5:13
10:1 [i] Mk 1:5; Jn 10:40; 11:7 [j] S Mt 4:23; Mk 2:13; 4:2; 6:6, 34
10:2 [k] Mk 2:16
10:4 [l] Dt 24:1-4; Mt 5:31
10:5 [m] Ps 95:8; Heb 3:15
10:6 [n] Ge 1:27; 5:2

g *43* Some manuscripts *out,* *44where / " 'their worm does not die, / and the fire is not quenched.'*
h *45* Some manuscripts *hell,* *46where / " 'their worm does not die, / and the fire is not quenched.'*
i *48* Isaiah 66:24 j *6* Gen. 1:27

9:34 THE GREATEST. See Lk 22:24–30, note.

9:42 CAUSES . . . LITTLE ONES. One of the highest priorities for believers is to set an example for their children by life and teaching. In doing so, they demonstrate a sincere love for them. Christian parents must also do their best to keep their children from the ungodly influences of the world (see Mt 18:6, note; see article on PARENTS AND CHILDREN, p. 432).

9:43 HELL. "Hell," the place of unquenchable fire, is so terrible that every influence of sin must be opposed and rejected, whatever the cost. Sin must put to death (Col 3:5); we must never stop waging war against it through the Spirit (Ro 8:13; Eph 6:10).

9:49 SALTED WITH FIRE. This phrase probably means that those who successfully resist sin do so by means of a lifelong fiery trial involving sacrifice and self-denial. Conquering sin in the midst of this world's corrupt generation is no easy task; it requires a wholehearted effort to resist the temptation to conform to this world (Ro 12:1–2).

9:50 SALT. See Mt 5:13, note.

leave his father and mother and be united
to his wife,[k] **8**and the two will become one
flesh.'[l][o] So they are no longer two, but
one. **9**Therefore what God has joined together, let man not separate."
10When they were in the house again,
the disciples asked Jesus about this. **11**He
answered, "Anyone who divorces his wife
and marries another woman commits
adultery against her.[p] **12**And if she divorces her husband and marries another
man, she commits adultery."[q]

The Little Children and Jesus

10:13–16pp — Mt 19:13–15; Lk 18:15–17

13People were bringing little children
to Jesus to have him touch them, but the
disciples rebuked them. **14**When Jesus
saw this, he was indignant. He said to
them, "Let the little children come to me,
and do not hinder them, for the kingdom
of God belongs to such as these.[r] **15**I tell
you the truth, anyone who will not receive
the kingdom of God like a little child will
never enter it."[s] **16**And he took the children in his arms,[t] put his hands on them
and blessed them.

The Rich Young Man

10:17–31pp — Mt 19:16–30; Lk 18:18–30

17As Jesus started on his way, a man
ran up to him and fell on his knees[u] before
him. "Good teacher," he asked, "what
must I do to inherit eternal life?"[v]
18"Why do you call me good?" Jesus answered. "No one is good—except God
alone. **19**You know the commandments:
'Do not murder, do not commit adultery,
do not steal, do not give false testimony,
do not defraud, honor your father and
mother.'[m]"[w]
20"Teacher," he declared, "all these I
have kept since I was a boy."
21Jesus looked at him and loved him.
"One thing you lack," he said. "Go, sell
everything you have and give to the poor,[x]
and you will have treasure in heaven.[y]
Then come, follow me."[z]
22At this the man's face fell. He went
away sad, because he had great wealth.
23Jesus looked around and said to his
disciples, "How hard it is for the rich[a] to
enter the kingdom of God!"
24The disciples were amazed at his
words. But Jesus said again, "Children,
how hard it is[n] to enter the kingdom of
God![b] **25**It is easier for a camel to go
through the eye of a needle than for a rich
man to enter the kingdom of God."[c]
26The disciples were even more
amazed, and said to each other, "Who then
can be saved?"
27Jesus looked at them and said, "With
man this is impossible, but not with God;
all things are possible with God."[d]
28Peter said to him, "We have left everything to follow you!"[e]
29"I tell you the truth," Jesus replied,
"no one who has left home or brothers or
sisters or mother or father or children or
fields for me and the gospel **30**will fail to
receive a hundred times as much[f] in this
present age (homes, brothers, sisters,
mothers, children and fields—and with
them, persecutions) and in the age to
come,[g] eternal life.[h] **31**But many who are
first will be last, and the last first."[i]

10:8 [o] Ge 2:24; 1Co 6:16
10:11 [p] S Lk 16:18
10:12 [q] Ro 7:3; 1Co 7:10,11
10:14 [r] S Mt 25:34
10:15 [s] Mt 18:3
10:16 [t] Mk 9:36
10:17 [u] Mk 1:40 [v] Lk 10:25; S Ac 20:32
10:19 [w] Ex 20:12-16; Dt 5:16-20
10:21 [x] S Ac 2:45 [y] Mt 6:20; Lk 12:33 [z] S Mt 4:19
10:23 [a] Ps 52:7; 62:10; Mk 4:19; 1Ti 6:9,10,17
10:24 [b] Mt 7:13, 14; Jn 3:5
10:25 [c] Lk 12:16-20; 16:19-31
10:27 [d] S Mt 19:26
10:28 [e] S Mt 4:19
10:30 [f] Mt 6:33 [g] S Mt 12:32 [h] S Mt 25:46
10:31 [i] S Mt 19:30

k *7* Some early manuscripts do not have *and be united to his wife.* **l** *8* Gen. 2:24
m *19* Exodus 20:12-16; Deut. 5:16-20
n *24* Some manuscripts *is for those who trust in riches*

10:11 COMMITS ADULTERY. Anyone who divorces for other than Biblical reasons and then remarries sins against God by committing adultery (see Mt 19:9, note; 1Co 7:15). In other words, a divorce is not necessarily recognized as right or legitimate by God merely because the state (or any human institution) legalizes it.

10:14 KINGDOM OF GOD. Mark uses the term "kingdom of God" while Matthew generally uses the preferred Jewish expression "kingdom of heaven." The meaning, however, is the same; compare the following parallel passages: Mt 4:17 with Mk 1:15; Mt 5:3 with Lk 6:20; Mt 11:11 with Lk 7:28; Mt 10:7 with Lk 10:9 (see article on THE KINGDOM OF GOD, p. 28).

10:15 LIKE A LITTLE CHILD. Receiving the kingdom of God like a child means accepting it in a simple, humble, trustful and wholehearted manner so as to turn from sin and receive Christ as your Lord and Savior, and God as your heavenly Father (see Mt 18:3, note).

10:16 AND BLESSED THEM. Christ is deeply concerned about the salvation and the spiritual upbringing of children. Christian parents should use every means of grace available to bring their children to Christ, for he longs to receive them, love them and bless them (vv. 13–16; see article on PARENTS AND CHILDREN, p. 432).

10:23 THE RICH. See article on RICHES AND POVERTY, p. 152.

10:30 RECEIVE A HUNDRED TIMES. The rewards promised here are not to be understood in a literal way. Rather, the blessings and joy inherent in the relationships listed here will be experienced by the true disciple who sacrifices for Christ's sake.

10:31 FIRST WILL BE LAST. See Mt 19:30, note.

Jesus Again Predicts His Death

10:32–34pp — Mt 20:17–19; Lk 18:31–33

32 They were on their way up to Jerusalem, with Jesus leading the way, and the disciples were astonished, while those who followed were afraid. Again he took the Twelve[j] aside and told them what was going to happen to him. 33 "We are going up to Jerusalem,"[k] he said, "and the Son of Man[l] will be betrayed to the chief priests and teachers of the law.[m] They will condemn him to death and will hand him over to the Gentiles, 34 who will mock him and spit on him, flog him[n] and kill him.[o] Three days later[p] he will rise."[q]

The Request of James and John

10:35–45pp — Mt 20:20–28

35 Then James and John, the sons of Zebedee, came to him. "Teacher," they said, "we want you to do for us whatever we ask."

36 "What do you want me to do for you?" he asked.

37 They replied, "Let one of us sit at your right and the other at your left in your glory."[r]

38 "You don't know what you are asking,"[s] Jesus said. "Can you drink the cup[t] I drink or be baptized with the baptism I am baptized with?"[u]

39 "We can," they answered.

Jesus said to them, "You will drink the cup I drink and be baptized with the baptism I am baptized with,[v] 40 but to sit at my right or left is not for me to grant. These places belong to those for whom they have been prepared."

41 When the ten heard about this, they became indignant with James and John. 42 Jesus called them together and said, "You know that those who are regarded as rulers of the Gentiles lord it over them, and their high officials exercise authority over them. 43 Not so with you. Instead, whoever wants to become great among you must be your servant,[w] 44 and whoever wants to be first must be slave of all. 45 For even the Son of Man did not come to be served, but to serve,[x] and to give his life as a ransom for many."[y]

10:32 [j] Mk 3:16-19
10:33 [k] S Lk 9:51 [l] S Mt 8:20 [m] Mt 27:1,2
10:34 [n] S Mt 16:21 [o] Ac 2:23; 3:13 [p] S Mt 16:21 [q] S Mt 16:21
10:37 [r] Mt 19:28
10:38 [s] Job 38:2 [t] S Mt 20:22 [u] Lk 12:50
10:39 [v] Ac 12:2; Rev 1:9
10:43 [w] S Mk 9:35
10:45 [x] S Mt 20:28 [y] S Mt 20:28
10:47 [z] S Mk 1:24 [a] S Mt 9:27
10:51 [b] S Mt 23:7
10:52 [c] S Mt 9:22 [d] S Mt 4:19
11:1 [e] S Mt 21:17 [f] S Mt 21:1
11:2 [g] Nu 19:2; Dt 21:3; 1Sa 6:7
11:4 [h] Mk 14:16

Blind Bartimaeus Receives His Sight

10:46–52pp — Mt 20:29–34; Lk 18:35–43

46 Then they came to Jericho. As Jesus and his disciples, together with a large crowd, were leaving the city, a blind man, Bartimaeus (that is, the Son of Timaeus), was sitting by the roadside begging. 47 When he heard that it was Jesus of Nazareth,[z] he began to shout, "Jesus, Son of David,[a] have mercy on me!"

48 Many rebuked him and told him to be quiet, but he shouted all the more, "Son of David, have mercy on me!"

49 Jesus stopped and said, "Call him."

So they called to the blind man, "Cheer up! On your feet! He's calling you." 50 Throwing his cloak aside, he jumped to his feet and came to Jesus.

51 "What do you want me to do for you?" Jesus asked him.

The blind man said, "Rabbi,[b] I want to see."

52 "Go," said Jesus, "your faith has healed you."[c] Immediately he received his sight and followed[d] Jesus along the road.

Mk 11:22-24

The Triumphal Entry

11:1–10pp — Mt 21:1–9; Lk 19:29–38
11:7–10pp — Jn 12:12–15

11 As they approached Jerusalem and came to Bethphage and Bethany[e] at the Mount of Olives,[f] Jesus sent two of his disciples, 2 saying to them, "Go to the village ahead of you, and just as you enter it, you will find a colt tied there, which no one has ever ridden.[g] Untie it and bring it here. 3 If anyone asks you, 'Why are you doing this?' tell him, 'The Lord needs it and will send it back here shortly.' "

4 They went and found a colt outside in the street, tied at a doorway.[h] As they untied it, 5 some people standing there asked, "What are you doing, untying that colt?" 6 They answered as Jesus had told them to, and the people let them go. 7 When they brought the colt to Jesus and threw their cloaks over it, he sat on it. 8 Many people spread their cloaks on the road, while others spread branches they

---

10:43 WHOEVER WANTS TO BECOME GREAT. True greatness is not a matter of leadership, authority or high personal achievement (v. 42), but of an attitude of heart that sincerely desires to live for God and others. We must be so committed to God that we identify with his will on earth without desiring glory, position or material rewards. Accomplishing God's will, bringing others to salvation in Christ, and pleasing God are the rewards of the truly great (see Lk 22:24–30, note on greatness).

10:45 A RANSOM. See Mt 20:28, note; Ro 3:25, note on the meaning of Christ's death for humanity.

11:1 PASSION WEEK. At this point in the Gospel of Mark, the events of Passion Week begin (chs. 11–15), followed by the account of the resurrection (ch. 16).

had cut in the fields. **9**Those who went ahead and those who followed shouted,

"Hosanna![o]"

"Blessed is he who comes in the
name of the Lord!"[p][i]

10"Blessed is the coming kingdom of
our father David!"

"Hosanna in the highest!"[j]

11Jesus entered Jerusalem and went to the temple. He looked around at everything, but since it was already late, he went out to Bethany with the Twelve.[k]

Jesus Cleanses the Temple

11:12–14pp — Mt 21:18–22
11:15–18pp — Mt 21:12–16; Lk 19:45–47; Jn 2:13–16

12The next day as they were leaving Bethany, Jesus was hungry. **13**Seeing in the distance a fig tree in leaf, he went to find out if it had any fruit. When he reached it, he found nothing but leaves, because it was not the season for figs.[l] **14**Then he said to the tree, "May no one ever eat fruit from you again." And his disciples heard him say it.

15On reaching Jerusalem, Jesus entered the temple area and began driving out those who were buying and selling there. He overturned the tables of the money changers and the benches of those selling doves, **16**and would not allow anyone to carry merchandise through the temple courts. **17**And as he taught them, he said, "Is it not written:

" 'My house will be called
a house of prayer for all
nations'[q]?[m]

But you have made it 'a den of robbers.'[r]"[n]

18The chief priests and the teachers of the law heard this and began looking for a way to kill him, for they feared him,[o] because the whole crowd was amazed at his teaching.[p]

19When evening came, they[s] went out of the city.[q]

The Withered Fig Tree

11:20–24pp — Mt 21:19–22

20In the morning, as they went along, they saw the fig tree withered from the roots. **21**Peter remembered and said to Jesus, "Rabbi,[r] look! The fig tree you cursed has withered!"

22"Have[t] faith in God," Jesus answered. **23**"I tell you the truth, if anyone says to this mountain, 'Go, throw yourself into the sea,' and does not doubt in his heart but believes that what he says will happen, it will be done for him.[s] **24**Therefore I tell you, whatever you ask for in prayer, believe that you have received it, and it will be yours.[t] **25**And when you stand praying, if you hold anything against anyone, forgive him, so that your Father in heaven may forgive you your sins.[u]"[u]

Lk 7:50

The Authority of Jesus Questioned

11:27–33pp — Mt 21:23–27; Lk 20:1–8

27They arrived again in Jerusalem, and while Jesus was walking in the temple

11:9 [i]Ps 118:25, 26; Mt 23:39
11:10 [j]Lk 2:14
11:11 [k]Mt 21:12, 17
11:13 [l]Lk 13:6-9
11:17 [m]Isa 56:7
[n]Jer 7:11
11:18 [o]Mt 21:46; Mk 12:12; Lk 20:19
[p]S Mt 7:28
11:19 [q]Lk 21:37
11:21 [r]S Mt 23:7
11:23 [s]S Mt 21:21
11:24 [t]S Mt 7:7
11:25 [u]S Mt 6:14

[o] *9* A Hebrew expression meaning "Save!" which became an exclamation of praise; also in verse 10
[p] *9* Psalm 118:25,26 [q] *17* Isaiah 56:7
[r] *17* Jer. 7:11 [s] *19* Some early manuscripts *he*
[t] *22* Some early manuscripts *If you have*
[u] *25* Some manuscripts *sins.* *26But if you do not forgive, neither will your Father who is in heaven forgive your sins.*

11:9 BLESSED IS HE WHO COMES. The crowd believed that the Messiah would restore Israel nationally and rule the nations politically. They failed to understand the purpose that Jesus expressed regarding his coming into the world. Later the crowd shouts, "crucify him," when they see he is not the Messiah they want (15:13).

11:15 JESUS ENTERED THE TEMPLE AREA. Christ's driving out those who were buying and selling in the temple shows his zeal for true holiness and prayer among those who claim to worship God (see Lk 19:45, note).

11:17 A HOUSE OF PRAYER. Jesus makes clear that God's house was meant to be a "house of prayer," a place where God's people could meet with him in spiritual devotion, prayer and worship (see Lk 19:45, note). It must not be profaned by making it a means for social advancement, monetary gain, entertainment or showmanship. Whenever God's house is so used by worldly-minded people, it once again becomes "a den of robbers."

11:24 BELIEVE ... WILL BE YOURS. Believing that receives is not something humanly produced; rather, it is a believing faith imparted to the believer's heart by God himself (see 9:23, note). Sometimes the fulfillment that true faith desires is granted immediately; at other times it is not. Yet God gives the faith that the prayer has been heard and the request will be granted. The uncertainty concerns the time of the fulfillment, not the granting of the request (see Mt 17:20, note; 21:21, note).

11:25 WHEN YOU STAND PRAYING ... FORGIVE. Let no Christians delude themselves that they have faith sufficient for answered prayer if they secretly hold animosity or bitterness in their hearts against anyone (see Mt 18:35, note).

courts, the chief priests, the teachers of
the law and the elders came to him. 28“By
what authority are you doing these
things?” they asked. “And who gave you
authority to do this?”
29Jesus replied, “I will ask you one
question. Answer me, and I will tell you by
what authority I am doing these things.
30John’s baptism—was it from heaven, or
from men? Tell me!”
31They discussed it among themselves
and said, “If we say, ‘From heaven,’ he
will ask, ‘Then why didn’t you believe
him?’ 32But if we say, ‘From men’ ....”
(They feared the people, for everyone held
that John really was a prophet.)[v]
33So they answered Jesus, “We don’t
know.”
Jesus said, “Neither will I tell you by
what authority I am doing these things.”

The Parable of the Tenants

12:1–12pp — Mt 21:33–46; Lk 20:9–19

12 He then began to speak to them in
parables: “A man planted a vineyard.[w] He put a wall around it, dug a pit
for the winepress and built a watchtower.
Then he rented the vineyard to some farmers and went away on a journey. 2At harvest time he sent a servant to the tenants
to collect from them some of the fruit of
the vineyard. 3But they seized him, beat
him and sent him away empty-handed.
4Then he sent another servant to them;
they struck this man on the head and
treated him shamefully. 5He sent still another, and that one they killed. He sent
many others; some of them they beat, others they killed.
6“He had one left to send, a son, whom
he loved. He sent him last of all,[x] saying,
‘They will respect my son.’
7“But the tenants said to one another,
‘This is the heir. Come, let’s kill him, and
the inheritance will be ours.’ 8So they
took him and killed him, and threw him
out of the vineyard.
9“What then will the owner of the vineyard do? He will come and kill those tenants and give the vineyard to others.
10Haven’t you read this scripture:

“ ‘The stone the builders rejected
has become the capstone[v];[y]
11the Lord has done this,
and it is marvelous in our
eyes’[w]?”[z]

12Then they looked for a way to arrest
him because they knew he had spoken the
parable against them. But they were
afraid of the crowd;[a] so they left him and
went away.[b]

Paying Taxes to Caesar

12:13–17pp — Mt 22:15–22; Lk 20:20–26

13Later they sent some of the Pharisees
and Herodians[c] to Jesus to catch him[d] in
his words. 14They came to him and said,
“Teacher, we know you are a man of integrity. You aren’t swayed by men, because
you pay no attention to who they are; but
you teach the way of God in accordance
with the truth. Is it right to pay taxes to
Caesar or not? 15Should we pay or
shouldn’t we?”
But Jesus knew their hypocrisy. “Why
are you trying to trap me?” he asked.
“Bring me a denarius and let me look at
it.” 16They brought the coin, and he asked
them, “Whose portrait is this? And whose
inscription?”
“Caesar’s,” they replied.
17Then Jesus said to them, “Give to
Caesar what is Caesar’s and to God what
is God’s.”[e]
And they were amazed at him.

Marriage at the Resurrection

12:18–27pp — Mt 22:23–33; Lk 20:27–38

18Then the Sadducees,[f] who say there
is no resurrection,[g] came to him with a
question. 19“Teacher,” they said, “Moses
wrote for us that if a man’s brother dies
and leaves a wife but no children, the man
must marry the widow and have children
for his brother.[h] 20Now there were seven
brothers. The first one married and died
without leaving any children. 21The second one married the widow, but he also
died, leaving no child. It was the same
with the third. 22In fact, none of the seven
left any children. Last of all, the woman

11:32 [v]S Mt 11:9
12:1 [w]Isa 5:1-7
12:6 [x]Heb 1:1-3
12:10 [y]S Ac 4:11
12:11 [z]Ps 118:22,23
12:12 [a]S Mk 11:18 [b]Mt 22:22
12:13 [c]Mt 22:16; Mk 3:6 [d]S Mt 12:10
12:17 [e]Ro 13:7
12:18 [f]S Ac 4:1 [g]Ac 23:8; 1Co 15:12
12:19 [h]Dt 25:5

[v] *10* Or *cornerstone* [w] *11* Psalm 118:22,23

12:1 PARABLE OF THE TENANTS. This parable points out the guilt of the Jewish nation. They turned God’s kingdom into a private possession, showed contempt for his Word and refused to obey his Son, Jesus Christ. Churches today show the same attitude as the wicked landowner whenever they reject Christ’s Word and his true messengers, and create a church after their own ideas.

12:10 HAS BECOME THE CAPSTONE. Christ is the “rejected” stone, thrown away by Israel but about to become the capstone or cornerstone of God’s new people, the church (Ac 4:11–12). He is the most important stone in this new structure that God is building.

died too. 23At the resurrection[x] whose
wife will she be, since the seven were married to her?"

24Jesus replied, "Are you not in error
because you do not know the Scriptures[i]
or the power of God? 25When the dead
rise, they will neither marry nor be given
in marriage; they will be like the angels in
heaven.[j] 26Now about the dead rising—
have you not read in the book of Moses,
in the account of the bush, how God said
to him, 'I am the God of Abraham, the God
of Isaac, and the God of Jacob'[y]?[k] 27He is
not the God of the dead, but of the living.
You are badly mistaken!"

The Greatest Commandment

12:28–34pp — Mt 22:34–40

28One of the teachers of the law[l] came
and heard them debating. Noticing that
Jesus had given them a good answer, he
asked him, "Of all the commandments,
which is the most important?"

29"The most important one," answered
Jesus, "is this: 'Hear, O Israel, the Lord
our God, the Lord is one.[z] 30Love the Lord
your God with all your heart and with all
your soul and with all your mind and with
all your strength.'[a][m] 31The second is this:
'Love your neighbor as yourself.'[b][n] There
is no commandment greater than these."

32"Well said, teacher," the man replied.
"You are right in saying that God is one
and there is no other but him.[o] 33To love
him with all your heart, with all your understanding and with all your strength,
and to love your neighbor as yourself is
more important than all burnt offerings
and sacrifices."[p]

34When Jesus saw that he had answered wisely, he said to him, "You are
not far from the kingdom of God."[q] And
from then on no one dared ask him any
more questions.[r]

Whose Son Is the Christ?

12:35–37pp — Mt 22:41–46; Lk 20:41–44
12:38–40pp — Mt 23:1–7; Lk 20:45–47

35While Jesus was teaching in the temple courts,[s] he asked, "How is it that the
teachers of the law say that the Christ[c] is
the son of David?[t] 36David himself,
speaking by the Holy Spirit,[u] declared:

" 'The Lord said to my Lord:
"Sit at my right hand
until I put your enemies
under your feet." '[d][v]

37David himself calls him 'Lord.' How
then can he be his son?"

The large crowd[w] listened to him with
delight.

38As he taught, Jesus said, "Watch out
for the teachers of the law. They like to
walk around in flowing robes and be greeted in the marketplaces, 39and have the
most important seats in the synagogues
and the places of honor at banquets.[x]
40They devour widows' houses and for a
show make lengthy prayers. Such men
will be punished most severely."

The Widow's Offering

12:41–44pp — Lk 21:1–4

41Jesus sat down opposite the place
where the offerings were put[y] and
watched the crowd putting their money
into the temple treasury. Many rich people threw in large amounts. 42But a poor

12:24 [i]2Ti 3:15-17
12:25 [j]1Co 15:42,49,52
12:26 [k]Ex 3:6
12:28 [l]Lk 10:25-28; 20:39
12:30 [m]Dt 6:4,5
12:31 [n]Lev 19:18; S Mt 5:43
12:32 [o]Dt 4:35, 39; Isa 45:6,14; 46:9
12:33 [p]1Sa 15:22; Hos 6:6; Mic 6:6-8; Heb 10:8
12:34 [q]S Mt 3:2
[r]Mt 22:46; Lk 20:40
12:35 [s]S Mt 26:55 [t]S Mt 9:27
12:36 [u]2Sa 23:2 [v]Ps 110:1; S Mt 22:44
12:37 [w]Jn 12:9
12:39 [x]Lk 11:43
12:41 [y]2Ki 12:9; Jn 8:20

[x] 23 Some manuscripts *resurrection, when men rise from the dead,* [y] 26 Exodus 3:6 [z] 29 Or *the Lord our God is one Lord* [a] 30 Deut. 6:4,5 [b] 31 Lev. 19:18 [c] 35 Or *Messiah* [d] 36 Psalm 110:1

12:25 THEY WILL NEITHER MARRY. Jesus' teaching does not mean that a husband or wife will lose their particular identity and thus not recognize each other. Rather, the relationship with our earthly partners then will be a deeper, spiritual one, though no longer governed by the marriage union as on earth.

12:30 LOVE THE LORD YOUR GOD. See Mt 22:37, note.

12:31 LOVE YOUR NEIGHBOR. See Mt 22:39, note.

12:38–39 LIKE ... THE MOST IMPORTANT SEATS. Jesus warns his followers to watch out for religious leaders who seek recognition and honor from others. He calls such leaders hypocrites (Mt 23:13–15,23,25,29) and describes them as frauds and deceivers in the area of observable righteousness (cf. Mt 23:25–28). Such persons do not possess the indwelling Holy Spirit and his regenerating grace (cf. Ro 8:5–14). While remaining in this condition they cannot "escape being condemned to hell" (Mt 23:33; see Mt 23:13, note; see article on FALSE TEACHERS, p. 98).

12:40 DEVOUR WIDOWS' HOUSES. Some of the Jewish religious leaders took advantage of unsuspecting and lonely widows. They would seek and receive exorbitant offerings from them, exploiting the widows' willingness to help those whom the widows believed to be men of God. By deceit and fraud these leaders persuaded the widows to give more than they could afford, and then lived in luxury on these misguided offerings. This same pattern has occurred throughout the history of the church, right up to today; each age has its experts in the art of religious extortion.

12:42 POOR WIDOW. See Lk 7:13, note on God's special care and love for women who are alone, aban-

widow came and put in two very small
copper coins,[e] worth only a fraction of a
penny.[f]
43Calling his disciples to him, Jesus
said, "I tell you the truth, this poor widow
has put more into the treasury than all the
others. **44**They all gave out of their
wealth; but she, out of her poverty, put in
everything—all she had to live on."[z]

Signs of the End of the Age

13:1–37pp — Mt 24:1–51; Lk 21:5–36

13 As he was leaving the temple, one
of his disciples said to him, "Look,
Teacher! What massive stones! What
magnificent buildings!"
2"Do you see all these great buildings?"
replied Jesus. "Not one stone here will be
left on another; every one will be thrown
down."[a]
3As Jesus was sitting on the Mount of
Olives[b] opposite the temple, Peter,
James, John[c] and Andrew asked him privately, **4**"Tell us, when will these things
happen? And what will be the sign that
they are all about to be fulfilled?"
5Jesus said to them: "Watch out that no
one deceives you.[d] **6**Many will come in my
name, claiming, 'I am he,' and will deceive
many. **7**When you hear of wars and rumors
of wars, do not be alarmed. Such things
must happen, but the end is still to come.
8Nation will rise against nation, and kingdom against kingdom. There will be earthquakes in various places, and famines.
These are the beginning of birth pains.

12:44 [z]2Co 8:12
13:2 [a]Lk 19:44
13:3 [b]S Mt 21:1 [c]S Mt 4:21
13:5 [d]ver 22; Jer 29:8; Eph 5:6; 2Th 2:3,10-12; 1Ti 4:1; 2Ti 3:13; 1Jn 4:6

9"You must be on your guard. You will
be handed over to the local councils and
flogged in the synagogues.[e] On account of
me you will stand before governors and
kings as witnesses to them. **10**And the
gospel must first be preached to all nations. **11**Whenever you are arrested and
brought to trial, do not worry beforehand
about what to say. Just say whatever is
given you at the time, for it is not you
speaking, but the Holy Spirit.[f]
12"Brother will betray brother to death,
and a father his child. Children will rebel
against their parents and have them put to
death.[g] **13**All men will hate you because
of me,[h] but he who stands firm to the end
will be saved.[i]
14"When you see 'the abomination that
causes desolation'[g][j] standing where it[h]
does not belong—let the reader understand—then let those who are in Judea
flee to the mountains. **15**Let no one on the
roof of his house go down or enter the
house to take anything out. **16**Let no one
in the field go back to get his cloak. **17**How
dreadful it will be in those days for pregnant women and nursing mothers![k]
18Pray that this will not take place in winter, **19**because those will be days of distress unequaled from the beginning, when
God created the world,[l] until now—and
never to be equaled again.[m] **20**If the Lord
had not cut short those days, no one

13:9 [e]S Mt 10:17
13:11 [f]Mt 10:19, 20; Lk 12:11,12
13:12 [g]Mic 7:6; Mt 10:21; Lk 12:51-53
13:13 [h]S Jn 15:21 [i]S Mt 10:22
13:14 [j]Da 9:27; 11:31; 12:11
13:17 [k]Lk 23:29
13:19 [l]Mk 10:6 [m]Da 9:26; 12:1; Joel 2:2

[e] *42* Greek *two lepta* [f] *42* Greek *kodrantes*
[g] *14* Daniel 9:27; 11:31; 12:11 [h] *14* Or *he*; also in verse 29

---

doned or widowed.

12:42 TWO . . . COPPER COINS. God measures giving not by the amount but by the love, devotion and sacrifice represented in the gift (see Lk 21:1–4, note).

13:5 WATCH OUT. Jesus' Olivet discourse contains repeated warnings that, as the end draws near, his people must be on constant alert to the danger of religious deception. Jesus admonishes, "Watch out" (v. 5), "You must be on your guard" (v. 9), "So be on your guard" (v. 23), "Be on guard! Be alert!" (v. 33), "Therefore, keep watch" (v. 35), and "Watch!" (v. 37). These warnings indicate that many unbiblical teachings will be prominent among the churches. The believer, more than ever, must know and obey only the Word of God (see Mt 24:5, note).

13:6 MANY . . . WILL DECEIVE MANY. See Mt 24:11, note.

13:10 GOSPEL . . . PREACHED TO ALL NATIONS. See Mt 24:14, notes.

13:13 STANDS FIRM TO THE END. Perseverance in the faith and endurance in our loyalty to Christ is a Scriptural condition for final salvation (cf. Heb 3:14; 6:11–12; 10:36). The glory of final salvation is described in Rev 2:7,17,26–28; 3:5,12,20–21; 7:9–17; 14:13; 21:1–7.

13:14 ABOMINATION THAT CAUSES DESOLATION. The abomination that causes desolation refers to that which defames or pollutes what is holy (see Da 9:25–27). (1) Christ's statement may prophetically refer both to the Roman invasion of Jerusalem when the temple was destroyed (A.D. 70) and to the placing of the image of the antichrist in Jerusalem just before Christ returns to judge the wicked (see 2Th 2:2–3; Rev 13:14–15; 19:11–21).

(2) This is sometimes called "prophetic foreshadowing," a term used when two or more events are viewed as if they are one. Examples would be the combining of Christ's first coming with the gospel and his second coming with judgment in Isa 11:1–4 and in 61:1–2 (see Mt 24:44, note). Likewise, the Pentecostal outpouring of the Spirit and "the great and dreadful day of the LORD" are combined and spoken of as one event in Joel 2:28–31. Christ here describes Jerusalem's destruction as a type of the great tribulation that occurs at the end of the age (see article on THE GREAT TRIBULATION, p. 52).

13:19–22 DISTRESS. See article on THE GREAT TRIBULATION, p. 52, for the interpretation of these verses.

FALSE TEACHERS

Mk 13:22 "For false Christs and false prophets will appear and perform signs and miracles to deceive the elect—if that were possible."

DESCRIPTION. Believers today must be aware that within the churches there may be ministers of God's Word who are of the same spirit and life as the corrupt teachers of God's law in Jesus' day (Mt 24:11,24). Jesus warns that not everyone who professes Christ is a true believer, nor are all Christian writers, missionaries, pastors, evangelists, teachers, deacons and workers what they claim to be.

(1) These ministers will on the outside "appear to people as righteous" (Mt 23:28). They come "in sheep's clothing" (Mt 7:15). They may base their message solidly on God's Word and proclaim high righteous standards. They may appear sincerely concerned for God's work and kingdom and show great interest in the salvation of the lost while professing love for all people. They may appear to be great ministers of God, commendable spiritual leaders anointed by the Holy Spirit. They may have great success, and multitudes may follow them (see Mt 7:21–23; 24:11,24; 2Co 11:13–15).

(2) Nevertheless, these people are like the Pharisees of old. Away from the crowds and in their hidden lives, they are given over to "greed and self-indulgence" (Mt 23:25), "full of dead men's bones and everything unclean" (23:27), "full of hypocrisy and wickedness" (23:28). Their lives behind closed doors involve such things as lust, immorality, adultery, greed and self-centered indulgence.

(3) These imposters gain a place of influence in the church in two ways. (a) Some false teachers/preachers begin their ministry in sincerity, truth, purity and genuine faith in Christ. Then because of their pride and their own immoral desires, personal commitment to and love for Christ gradually die. Consequently, they are severed from God's kingdom (1Co 6:9–10; Gal 5:19–21; Eph 5:5–6) and become instruments of Satan while disguising themselves as ministers of righteousness (see 2Co 11:15). (b) Other false teachers/preachers have never been genuine believers in Christ. Satan has planted them within the church from the very beginning of their ministry (Mt 13:24–28,36–43), using their ability and charisma and aiding in their success. His strategy is to place them in influential positions so that they can undermine the genuine work of Christ. If they are discovered or exposed, Satan knows that great damage will come to the gospel and that the name of Christ will be put to open shame.

TESTING. Jesus warned his disciples fourteen times in the Gospels to watch out for leaders who would mislead (Mt 7:15; 16:6,11; 24:4,24; Mk 4:24; 8:15; 12:38–40; 13:5; Lk 12:1; 17:23; 20:46; 21:8). Elsewhere believers are exhorted to test teachers, preachers and leaders in the church (1Th 5:21; 1Jn 4:1). The following steps can be taken in testing false teachers or false prophets:

(1) Discern character. Do they have diligent prayer lives and do they show a sincere and pure devotion to God? Do they manifest the fruit of the Spirit (Gal 5:22–23), love sinners (Jn 3:16), hate wickedness and love righteousness (Heb 1:9, note), and cry out against sin (Mt 23; Lk 3:18–20)?

(2) Discern motives. True Christian leaders will seek to do four things: (a) honor Christ (2Co 8:23; Php 1:20); (b) lead the church into sanctification (Ac 26:18; 1Co 6:18; 2Co 6:16–18); (c) save the lost (1Co 9:19–22); and (d) proclaim and defend the gospel of Christ and the apostles (see Php 1:16, note; Jude 3, note).

(3) Test fruit in life and message. The fruit of false preachers will often consist in converts not totally committed to all of God's Word (see Mt 7:16, note).

(4) Discern level of reliance on Scripture. This is a key issue. Do they believe and teach that the original writings of both the OT and NT are fully inspired by God, and that we are to submit to all its teachings (2Jn 9–11; see article on THE INSPIRATION AND AUTHORITY OF SCRIPTURE, p. 474)? If not, we can be sure that they and their message are not from God.

(5) Finally, test integrity with respect to the Lord's money. Do they refuse to take large amounts for themselves, handle all finances with integrity and responsibility, and seek to promote God's work in ways consistent with NT standards for leaders (1Ti 3:3; 6:9–10)?

It must be understood that in spite of all that faithful believers do in evaluating a person's life and message, there will still be false teachers within the churches who, with Satan's help, remain undetected until God determines to expose those persons for what they are.

would survive. But for the sake of the elect, whom he has chosen, he has shortened them. 21At that time if anyone says to you, 'Look, here is the Christ[i]!' or, 'Look, there he is!' do not believe it.[n] 22For false Christs and false prophets[o] will appear and perform signs and miracles[p] to deceive the elect—if that were possible. 23So be on your guard;[q] I have told you everything ahead of time.

24"But in those days, following that distress,

" 'the sun will be darkened,
and the moon will not give its light;
25the stars will fall from the sky,
and the heavenly bodies will be shaken.'[j][r]

26"At that time men will see the Son of Man coming in clouds[s] with great power and glory. 27And he will send his angels and gather his elect from the four winds, from the ends of the earth to the ends of the heavens.[t]

28"Now learn this lesson from the fig tree: As soon as its twigs get tender and its leaves come out, you know that summer is near. 29Even so, when you see these things happening, you know that it is near, right at the door. 30I tell you the truth, this generation[k][u] will certainly not pass away until all these things have happened.[v] 31Heaven and earth will pass away, but my words will never pass away.[w]

The Day and Hour Unknown

32"No one knows about that day or hour, not even the angels in heaven, nor the Son, but only the Father.[x] 33Be on guard! Be alert[l]![y] You do not know when that time will come. 34It's like a man going away: He leaves his house and puts his servants[z] in charge, each with his assigned task, and tells the one at the door to keep watch.

35"Therefore keep watch because you do not know when the owner of the house will come back—whether in the evening, or at midnight, or when the rooster crows, or at dawn. 36If he comes suddenly, do not let him find you sleeping. 37What I say to you, I say to everyone: 'Watch!' "[a]

13:21 [n]Lk 17:23; 21:8
13:22 [o]S Mt 7:15 [p]S Jn 4:48; 2Th 2:9,10
13:23 [q]2Pe 3:17
13:25 [r]Isa 13:10; 34:4; S Mt 24:29
13:26 [s]S Rev 1:7
13:27 [t]Zec 2:6
13:30 [u]Mk 9:1 [v]Lk 17:25
13:31 [w]S Mt 5:18
13:32 [x]Ac 1:7; 1Th 5:1,2
13:33 [y]1Th 5:6
13:34 [z]Mt 25:14
13:37 [a]Lk 12:35-40
14:1 [b]S Jn 11:55 [c]S Mt 12:14
14:3 [d]S Mt 21:17 [e]Lk 7:37-39
14:7 [f]Dt 15:11
14:8 [g]Jn 19:40

Jesus Anointed at Bethany

14:1-11pp — Mt 26:2-16
14:1,2,10,11pp — Lk 22:1-6
14:3-8Ref — Jn 12:1-8

14 Now the Passover[b] and the Feast of Unleavened Bread were only two days away, and the chief priests and the teachers of the law were looking for some sly way to arrest Jesus and kill him.[c] 2"But not during the Feast," they said, "or the people may riot."

3While he was in Bethany,[d] reclining at the table in the home of a man known as Simon the Leper, a woman came with an alabaster jar of very expensive perfume, made of pure nard. She broke the jar and poured the perfume on his head.[e]

4Some of those present were saying indignantly to one another, "Why this waste of perfume? 5It could have been sold for more than a year's wages[m] and the money given to the poor." And they rebuked her harshly.

6"Leave her alone," said Jesus. "Why are you bothering her? She has done a beautiful thing to me. 7The poor you will always have with you, and you can help them any time you want.[f] But you will not always have me. 8She did what she could. She poured perfume on my body beforehand to prepare for my burial.[g] 9I tell you

[i] *21* Or *Messiah* [j] *25* Isaiah 13:10; 34:4 [k] *30* Or *race* [l] *33* Some manuscripts *alert and pray* [m] *5* Greek *than three hundred denarii*

13:22 FALSE PROPHETS. See article on FALSE TEACHERS, p. 98.
13:24 THE SUN . . . DARKENED. See Mt 24:29, note.
13:26 SON OF MAN COMING. See Mt 24:30, note.
13:27 GATHER HIS ELECT. See Mt 24:31, note.
13:28 THE FIG TREE. See Mt 24:32, note.
13:29 THESE THINGS. See Mt 24:33, note.
13:30 THIS GENERATION. See Mt 24:34, note.
13:32 NO ONE KNOWS ABOUT THAT DAY OR HOUR. See Mt 24:36, note.
13:33 BE ALERT! See Mt 24:42, notes.
13:35 IN THE EVENING . . . MIDNIGHT . . . AT DAWN. Christ affirms that his return for the faithful of his churches could occur at four possible times during the night or early morning. This points to the fact that his coming for them could be at any time and emphasizes the unexpectedness and hiddenness of the first stage of his second coming, when the faithful will be caught up from the earth (i.e., the rapture; see article on THE RAPTURE, p. 440). Since it is imminent and unexpected, all believers must be spiritually alert and faithful (see Mt 24:42, notes; 24:44, note; cf. Lk 12:35–36,38–40,46; 21:34–36).
14:9 THE GOSPEL. Gospel (Gk *euangelion*) means good news—the good news that God has acted to save the perishing human race through the incarnation, death and resurrection of Jesus Christ (Lk 4:18–21; 7:22; Jn 3:16). Wherever this is proclaimed in the power of the Spirit (1Co 2:4; Gal 1:11), (1) it comes with authority (Mt 28:18–20); (2) it reveals God's righteousness (Ro 1:16–17); (3) it demands repen-

the truth, wherever the gospel is preached
throughout the world,[h] what she has done
will also be told, in memory of her."
10Then Judas Iscariot, one of the
Twelve,[i] went to the chief priests to betray Jesus to them.[j] **11**They were delighted to hear this and promised to give him
money. So he watched for an opportunity
to hand him over.

The Lord's Supper

14:12–26pp — Mt 26:17–30; Lk 22:7–23
14:22–25pp — 1Co 11:23–25

12On the first day of the Feast of Unleavened Bread, when it was customary to
sacrifice the Passover lamb,[k] Jesus' disciples asked him, "Where do you want us to
go and make preparations for you to eat
the Passover?"
13So he sent two of his disciples, telling
them, "Go into the city, and a man carrying a jar of water will meet you. Follow
him. **14**Say to the owner of the house he
enters, 'The Teacher asks: Where is my
guest room, where I may eat the Passover
with my disciples?' **15**He will show you a
large upper room,[l] furnished and ready.
Make preparations for us there."
16The disciples left, went into the city
and found things just as Jesus had told
them. So they prepared the Passover.
17When evening came, Jesus arrived
with the Twelve. **18**While they were reclining at the table eating, he said, "I tell you
the truth, one of you will betray me—one
who is eating with me."
19They were saddened, and one by one
they said to him, "Surely not I?"
20"It is one of the Twelve," he replied,
"one who dips bread into the bowl with
me.[m] **21**The Son of Man[n] will go just as it
is written about him. But woe to that man
who betrays the Son of Man! It would be
better for him if he had not been born."
22While they were eating, Jesus took
bread, gave thanks and broke it,[o] and
gave it to his disciples, saying, "Take it;
this is my body."
23Then he took the cup, gave thanks
and offered it to them, and they all drank
from it.[p]
24"This is my blood of the[n] covenant,[q]
which is poured out for many," he said to
them. **25**"I tell you the truth, I will not
drink again of the fruit of the vine until
that day when I drink it anew in the kingdom of God."[r]
26When they had sung a hymn, they
went out to the Mount of Olives.[s]

Jesus Predicts Peter's Denial

14:27–31pp — Mt 26:31–35

27"You will all fall away," Jesus told
them, "for it is written:

" 'I will strike the shepherd,
and the sheep will be scattered.'[o][t]

28But after I have risen, I will go ahead of
you into Galilee."[u]
29Peter declared, "Even if all fall away,
I will not."
30"I tell you the truth," Jesus answered,
"today—yes, tonight—before the rooster
crows twice[p] you yourself will disown me
three times."[v]
31But Peter insisted emphatically,
"Even if I have to die with you,[w] I will
never disown you." And all the others said
the same.

Gethsemane

14:32–42pp — Mt 26:36–46; Lk 22:40–46

32They went to a place called Gethsem-

14:9 [h] S Mt 24:14; Mk 16:15
14:10 [i] Mk 3:16-19 [j] S Mt 10:4
14:12 [k] Ex 12:1-11; Dt 16:1-4; 1Co 5:7
14:15 [l] Ac 1:13
14:20 [m] Jn 13:18-27
14:21 [n] S Mt 8:20
14:22 [o] S Mt 14:19
14:23 [p] 1Co 10:16
14:24 [q] S Mt 26:28
14:25 [r] S Mt 3:2
14:26 [s] S Mt 21:1
14:27 [t] Zec 13:7
14:28 [u] Mk 16:7
14:30 [v] ver 66-72; Lk 22:34; Jn 13:38
14:31 [w] Lk 22:33; Jn 13:37

n *24* Some manuscripts *the new* o *27* Zech. 13:7 p *30* Some early manuscripts do not have *twice.*

---

tance (1:15; Mt 3:2; 4:17); (4) it convicts of sin, righteousness and judgment (Jn 16:8; cf. Ac 24:25); (5) it creates faith (Ro 10:17; Php 1:27); (6) it brings salvation, life and the gift of the Holy Spirit (Ac 2:33,38–39; Ro 1:16; 1Co 15:22; 1Pe 1:23); (7) it delivers from the dominion of sin and Satan (Mt 12:28; Ac 26:18; Ro 6); (8) it brings hope (Col 1:5,23), peace (Eph 2:17; 6:15) and immortality (2Ti 1:10); (9) it warns of judgment (Ro 2:16); and (10) it brings condemnation and eternal death when refused (Jn 3:18).

14:9 IN MEMORY OF HER. See Mt 26:13, note.

14:14 PASSOVER. See Mt 26:2, note.

14:21 HAD NOT BEEN BORN. Jesus always judges and evaluates life from a spiritual and eternal viewpoint. He affirms that it would be better that a person never be born than to come into this world, fail to accept Jesus as Lord and Savior, and consequently perish eternally in hell (see Jn 6:64, note).

14:22 BREAD . . . MY BODY. See Lk 22:20, notes; 1Co 11:24–25,27 notes.

14:24 BLOOD OF THE COVENANT. Christ's blood was shed for us in order to bring us forgiveness and salvation. His death on the cross established a new covenant between God and all who receive Christ as Lord and Savior. Those who repent and turn to God through faith in Christ will be forgiven, be delivered from the power of Satan, receive new spiritual life, be made children of God, be baptized with the Holy Spirit, and have access to God at any time in order to receive mercy, grace, strength and help (see Mt 26:28, note; Heb 4:16; 7:25).

14:32 GETHSEMANE . . . PRAY. Jesus' action is an example of what believers ought to do in times of

ane, and Jesus said to his disciples, "Sit
here while I pray." **33**He took Peter, James
and John[x] along with him, and he began
to be deeply distressed and troubled.
34"My soul is overwhelmed with sorrow to
the point of death,"[y] he said to them.
"Stay here and keep watch."

35Going a little farther, he fell to the
ground and prayed that if possible the
hour[z] might pass from him. **36**"*Abba*,[q] Father,"[a] he said, "everything is possible for
you. Take this cup[b] from me. Yet not what
I will, but what you will."[c]

37Then he returned to his disciples and
found them sleeping. "Simon," he said to
Peter, "are you asleep? Could you not
keep watch for one hour? **38**Watch and
pray so that you will not fall into temptation.[d] The spirit is willing, but the body is
weak."[e]

39Once more he went away and prayed
the same thing. **40**When he came back, he
again found them sleeping, because their
eyes were heavy. They did not know what
to say to him.

41Returning the third time, he said to
them, "Are you still sleeping and resting?
Enough! The hour[f] has come. Look, the
Son of Man is betrayed into the hands of
sinners. **42**Rise! Let us go! Here comes my
betrayer!"

Jesus Arrested

14:43–50pp — Mt 26:47–56; Lk 22:47–50; Jn 18:3–11

43Just as he was speaking, Judas,[g] one
of the Twelve, appeared. With him was a
crowd armed with swords and clubs, sent
from the chief priests, the teachers of the
law, and the elders.

44Now the betrayer had arranged a signal with them: "The one I kiss is the man;
arrest him and lead him away under
guard." **45**Going at once to Jesus, Judas
said, "Rabbi!"[h] and kissed him. **46**The
men seized Jesus and arrested him.
47Then one of those standing near drew
his sword and struck the servant of the
high priest, cutting off his ear.

48"Am I leading a rebellion," said Jesus,
"that you have come out with swords and
clubs to capture me? **49**Every day I was
with you, teaching in the temple courts,[i]
and you did not arrest me. But the Scriptures must be fulfilled."[j] **50**Then everyone deserted him and fled.[k]

51A young man, wearing nothing but a
linen garment, was following Jesus. When
they seized him, **52**he fled naked, leaving
his garment behind.

Before the Sanhedrin

14:53–65pp — Mt 26:57–68; Jn 18:12,13,19–24
14:61–63pp — Lk 22:67–71

53They took Jesus to the high priest,
and all the chief priests, elders and teachers of the law came together. **54**Peter followed him at a distance, right into the
courtyard of the high priest.[l] There he sat
with the guards and warmed himself at
the fire.[m]

55The chief priests and the whole San-

14:33 [x] S Mt 4:21 **14:34** [y] Jn 12:27 **14:35** [z] ver 41; S Mt 26:18 **14:36** [a] Ro 8:15; Gal 4:6 [b] S Mt 20:22 [c] S Mt 26:39 **14:38** [d] Mt 6:13 [e] Ro 7:22,23 **14:41** [f] ver 35; S Mt 26:18 **14:43** [g] S Mt 10:4

14:45 [h] S Mt 23:7 **14:49** [i] S Mt 26:55 [j] Isa 53:7-12; S Mt 1:22 **14:50** [k] ver 27 **14:54** [l] S Mt 26:3 [m] Jn 18:18

[q] *36* Aramaic for *Father*

---

great distress or grief. (1) Turn to God in prayer (vv. 32,35–36,39). (2) Seek the support of friends (vv. 33–34,42). (3) Affirm in your heart that God is your heavenly Father who cares for you (v. 36). (4) Trust God and commit yourself to his will (v. 36). See Mt 26:37ff, notes on the ten stages of the sufferings of Christ.

14:35 HOUR MIGHT PASS FROM HIM. See Mt 26:39, note.

14:37 KEEP WATCH FOR ONE HOUR. Peter and the disciples neglected to keep watch and pray, the only thing that could have saved them from failure at this time of testing (v. 50). Failure in our Christian life is absolutely certain without prayer (see Ac 10:9, note on the commitment to pray for one hour).

14:46 ARRESTED HIM. See Mt 26:57, note, for the order of events from Christ's arrest to his crucifixion.

14:50 EVERYONE DESERTED HIM. We should never compare the failure of Peter and the other disciples at Jesus' arrest to the spiritual and moral failure of pastors or overseers after Christ's death and resurrection. This is so for the following reasons: (1) Peter and the disciples at the time of their failure were not yet under the new covenant. The new covenant did not go into effect until Christ shed his blood on the cross (Heb 9:15–20).

(2) Peter and the disciples had not yet experienced the new birth or regeneration by the Holy Spirit in the full NT sense. The Holy Spirit was not imparted to them in his indwelling and sanctifying presence until the day of Christ's resurrection when Christ "breathed on them and said, 'Receive the Holy Spirit' " (Jn 20:22). The disciples' failure was an act of weakness rather than wickedness.

(3) When Peter and the disciples forsook Christ, they did not possess the advantage of those who are conscious of the moral implications of Christ's sacrificial death on the cross (see Ro 6), nor did they have a sustaining faith inspired by his resurrection from the dead.

In other words, this passage should not be used to justify restoring leaders to ministry who, because of their own sins and moral laxity, have voluntarily thrown aside in their personal and spiritual lives the qualifications necessary for the office of overseer (see article on MORAL QUALIFICATIONS FOR OVERSEERS, p. 458).

hedrin[n] were looking for evidence against
Jesus so that they could put him to death,
but they did not find any. **56**Many testified
falsely against him, but their statements
did not agree.

57Then some stood up and gave this
false testimony against him: **58**"We heard
him say, 'I will destroy this man-made
temple and in three days will build another,[o] not made by man.' " **59**Yet even then
their testimony did not agree.

60Then the high priest stood up before
them and asked Jesus, "Are you not going
to answer? What is this testimony that
these men are bringing against you?"
61But Jesus remained silent and gave no
answer.[p]

Again the high priest asked him, "Are
you the Christ,[r] the Son of the Blessed
One?"[q]

62"I am," said Jesus. "And you will see
the Son of Man sitting at the right hand
of the Mighty One and coming on the
clouds of heaven."[r]

63The high priest tore his clothes.[s]
"Why do we need any more witnesses?" he
asked. **64**"You have heard the blasphemy.
What do you think?"

They all condemned him as worthy of
death.[t] **65**Then some began to spit at him;
they blindfolded him, struck him with
their fists, and said, "Prophesy!" And the
guards took him and beat him.[u]

Peter Disowns Jesus

14:66–72pp — Mt 26:69–75; Lk 22:56–62; Jn 18:16–18,25–27

66While Peter was below in the courtyard,[v] one of the servant girls of the high
priest came by. **67**When she saw Peter
warming himself,[w] she looked closely at
him.

"You also were with that Nazarene,
Jesus,"[x] she said.

68But he denied it. "I don't know or understand what you're talking about,"[y] he
said, and went out into the entryway.[s]

69When the servant girl saw him there,
she said again to those standing around,
"This fellow is one of them." **70**Again he
denied it.[z]

After a little while, those standing near
said to Peter, "Surely you are one of them,
for you are a Galilean."[a]

71He began to call down curses on himself, and he swore to them, "I don't know
this man you're talking about."[b]

72Immediately the rooster crowed the
second time.[t] Then Peter remembered
the word Jesus had spoken to him: "Before
the rooster crows twice[u] you will disown
me three times."[c] And he broke down and
wept.

Jesus Before Pilate

15:2–15pp — Mt 27:11–26; Lk 23:2,3,18–25; Jn 18:29–19:16

15 Very early in the morning, the
chief priests, with the elders, the
teachers of the law[d] and the whole Sanhedrin,[e] reached a decision. They bound
Jesus, led him away and handed him over
to Pilate.[f]

2"Are you the king of the Jews?"[g] asked
Pilate.

"Yes, it is as you say," Jesus replied.

3The chief priests accused him of many
things. **4**So again Pilate asked him,
"Aren't you going to answer? See how
many things they are accusing you of."

5But Jesus still made no reply,[h] and
Pilate was amazed.

6Now it was the custom at the Feast to
release a prisoner whom the people requested. **7**A man called Barabbas was in
prison with the insurrectionists who had
committed murder in the uprising. **8**The
crowd came up and asked Pilate to do for
them what he usually did.

9"Do you want me to release to you the
king of the Jews?"[i] asked Pilate, **10**knowing it was out of envy that the chief priests
had handed Jesus over to him. **11**But the
chief priests stirred up the crowd to have
Pilate release Barabbas[j] instead.

12"What shall I do, then, with the one
you call the king of the Jews?" Pilate
asked them.

13"Crucify him!" they shouted.

14"Why? What crime has he committed?" asked Pilate.

But they shouted all the louder, "Crucify him!"

15Wanting to satisfy the crowd, Pilate
released Barabbas to them. He had Jesus

14:55 [n]S Mt 5:22 **14:58** [o]S Jn 2:19 **14:61** [p]Isa 53:7; Mt 27:12,14; Mk 15:5; Lk 23:9; Jn 19:9 [q]Mt 16:16; Jn 4:25,26 **14:62** [r]S Rev 1:7 **14:63** [s]Lev 10:6; 21:10; Nu 14:6; Ac 14:14 **14:64** [t]Lev 24:16 **14:65** [u]S Mt 16:21 **14:66** [v]ver 54 **14:67** [w]ver 54 [x]S Mk 1:24 **14:68** [y]ver 30,72 **14:70** [z]ver 30,68, 72 [a]Ac 2:7

14:71 [b]ver 30,72 **14:72** [c]ver 30,68 **15:1** [d]Mt 27:1; Lk 22:66 [e]S Mt 5:22 [f]S Mt 27:2 **15:2** [g]ver 9,12, 18,26; S Mt 2:2 **15:5** [h]S Mk 14:61 **15:9** [i]S ver 2 **15:11** [j]Ac 3:14

[r] *61* Or *Messiah* [s] *68* Some early manuscripts *entryway and the rooster crowed* [t] *72* Some early manuscripts do not have *the second time.* [u] *72* Some early manuscripts do not have *twice.*

14:65 STRUCK HIM. See Mt 26:67, note.

14:71 TO CALL DOWN CURSES ... AND HE SWORE. Peter affirmed what he was saying with an oath and called the curse of God down on himself if his statements should prove to be false.

15:1 HANDED HIM OVER TO PILATE. See Mt 27:2, note.

15:15 HAD JESUS FLOGGED. See Mt 27:26, note.

flogged,[k] and handed him over to be crucified.

The Soldiers Mock Jesus

15:16–20pp — Mt 27:27–31

16The soldiers led Jesus away into the palace[l] (that is, the Praetorium) and called together the whole company of soldiers. **17**They put a purple robe on him, then twisted together a crown of thorns and set it on him. **18**And they began to call out to him, "Hail, king of the Jews!"[m] **19**Again and again they struck him on the head with a staff and spit on him. Falling on their knees, they paid homage to him. **20**And when they had mocked him, they took off the purple robe and put his own clothes on him. Then they led him out[n] to crucify him.

The Crucifixion

15:22–32pp — Mt 27:33–44; Lk 23:33–43; Jn 19:17–24

21A certain man from Cyrene,[o] Simon, the father of Alexander and Rufus,[p] was passing by on his way in from the country, and they forced him to carry the cross.[q] **22**They brought Jesus to the place called Golgotha (which means The Place of the Skull). **23**Then they offered him wine mixed with myrrh,[r] but he did not take it. **24**And they crucified him. Dividing up his clothes, they cast lots[s] to see what each would get.

25It was the third hour when they crucified him. **26**The written notice of the charge against him read: THE KING OF THE JEWS.[t] **27**They crucified two robbers with him, one on his right and one on his left.[v] **29**Those who passed by hurled insults at him, shaking their heads[u] and saying, "So! You who are going to destroy the temple and build it in three days,[v] **30**come down from the cross and save yourself!"

31In the same way the chief priests and the teachers of the law mocked him[w] among themselves. "He saved others," they said, "but he can't save himself! **32**Let this Christ,[w][x] this King of Israel,[y] come down now from the cross, that we may see and believe." Those crucified with him also heaped insults on him.

The Death of Jesus

15:33–41pp — Mt 27:45–56; Lk 23:44–49

33At the sixth hour darkness came over the whole land until the ninth hour.[z] **34**And at the ninth hour Jesus cried out in a loud voice, *"Eloi, Eloi, lama sabachthani?"* —which means, "My God, my God, why have you forsaken me?"[x][a]

35When some of those standing near heard this, they said, "Listen, he's calling Elijah."

36One man ran, filled a sponge with wine vinegar,[b] put it on a stick, and offered it to Jesus to drink. "Now leave him alone. Let's see if Elijah comes to take him down," he said.

37With a loud cry, Jesus breathed his last.[c]

38The curtain of the temple was torn in two from top to bottom.[d] **39**And when the centurion,[e] who stood there in front of Jesus, heard his cry and[y] saw how he died, he said, "Surely this man was the Son[z] of God!"[f]

40Some women were watching from a distance.[g] Among them were Mary Magdalene, Mary the mother of James the younger and of Joses, and Salome.[h] **41**In Galilee these women had followed him and cared for his needs. Many other women who had come up with him to Jerusalem were also there.[i]

The Burial of Jesus

15:42–47pp — Mt 27:57–61; Lk 23:50–56; Jn 19:38–42

42It was Preparation Day (that is, the day before the Sabbath).[j] So as evening approached, **43**Joseph of Arimathea, a prominent member of the Council,[k] who was himself waiting for the kingdom of God,[l] went boldly to Pilate and asked for Jesus' body. **44**Pilate was surprised to hear that he was already dead. Summoning the centurion, he asked him if Jesus had already died. **45**When he learned from the centurion[m] that it was so, he gave the body to Joseph. **46**So Joseph bought some

15:15 kIsa 53:6 **15:16** lJn 18:28, 33; 19:9 **15:18** mS ver 2 **15:20** nHeb 13:12 **15:21** oS Mt 27:32 pRo 16:13 qMt 27:32; Lk 23:26 **15:23** rver 36; Ps 69:21; Pr 31:6 **15:24** sPs 22:18 **15:26** tS ver 2 **15:29** uPs 22:7; 109:25 vS Jn 2:19 **15:31** wPs 22:7 **15:32** xS Mk 14:61 yS ver 2

15:33 zAm 8:9 **15:34** aPs 22:1 **15:36** bver 23; Ps 69:21 **15:37** cJn 19:30 **15:38** dHeb 10:19,20 **15:39** ever 45 fMk 1:1,11; 9:7; S Mt 4:3 **15:40** gPs 38:11 hMk 16:1; Lk 24:10; Jn 19:25 **15:41** iMt 27:55, 56; Lk 8:2,3 **15:42** jMt 27:62; Jn 19:31 **15:43** kS Mt 5:22 lS Mt 3:2; Lk 2:25,38 **15:45** mver 39

v *27* Some manuscripts *left,* [28]*and the scripture was fulfilled which says, "He was counted with the lawless ones"* (Isaiah 53:12) w *32* Or *Messiah*
x *34* Psalm 22:1 y *39* Some manuscripts do not have *heard his cry and* z *39* Or *a son*

15:17 CROWN OF THORNS. See Mt 27:28–29, note.
15:20 LED HIM OUT TO CRUCIFY HIM. See Mt 27:31, note.
15:24 THEY CRUCIFIED HIM. See Mt 27:35, note.
15:29 HURLED INSULTS. See Mt 27:39, note.
15:34 WHY HAVE YOU FORSAKEN ME? See Mt 27:46, note.
15:36 WINE VINEGAR. See Jn 19:29, note.
15:37 BREATHED HIS LAST. See Mt 27:50, note.

linen cloth, took down the body, wrapped
it in the linen, and placed it in a tomb cut
out of rock. Then he rolled a stone against
the entrance of the tomb.[n] **47**Mary Magdalene and Mary the mother of Joses[o] saw
where he was laid.

The Resurrection

16:1–8pp — Mt 28:1–8; Lk 24:1–10

16 When the Sabbath was over, Mary
Magdalene, Mary the mother of
James, and Salome bought spices[p] so that
they might go to anoint Jesus' body. **2**Very
early on the first day of the week, just
after sunrise, they were on their way to
the tomb **3**and they asked each other,
"Who will roll the stone away from the
entrance of the tomb?"[q]

4But when they looked up, they saw
that the stone, which was very large, had
been rolled away. **5**As they entered the
tomb, they saw a young man dressed in a
white robe[r] sitting on the right side, and
they were alarmed.

6"Don't be alarmed," he said. "You are
looking for Jesus the Nazarene,[s] who was
crucified. He has risen! He is not here. See
the place where they laid him. **7**But go, tell
his disciples and Peter, 'He is going ahead
of you into Galilee. There you will see
him,[t] just as he told you.' "[u]

8Trembling and bewildered, the women
went out and fled from the tomb. They
said nothing to anyone, because they were
afraid.

[The most reliable early manuscripts and other ancient witnesses do not have Mark 16:9–20.]

15:46 [n] Mk 16:3
15:47 [o] ver 40
16:1 [p] Lk 23:56; Jn 19:39,40
16:3 [q] Mk 15:46
16:5 [r] S Jn 20:12
16:6 [s] S Mk 1:24
16:7 [t] Jn 21:1-23 [u] Mk 14:28
16:9 [v] Mk 15:47; Jn 20:11-18
16:11 [w] ver 13, 14; Lk 24:11
16:12 [x] Lk 24:13-32
16:14 [y] Lk 24:36-43
16:15 [z] Mt 28:18-20; Lk 24:47,48; Ac 1:8
16:16 [a] Jn 3:16, 18,36; Ac 16:31
16:17 [b] S Jn 4:48 [c] Mk 9:38; Lk 10:17; Ac 5:16; 8:7; 16:18; 19:13-16 [d] Ac 2:4; 10:46; 19:6; 1Co 12:10,28,30; 13:1; 14:2-39
16:18 [e] Lk 10:19; Ac 28:3-5 [f] S Ac 6:6
16:19 [g] Lk 24:50, 51; Jn 6:62; Ac 1:9-11; 1Ti 3:16 [h] Ps 110:1; Mt 26:64; Ac 2:33; 5:31; Ro 8:34; Col 3:1; Heb 1:3; 12:2
16:20 [i] S Jn 4:48

Resurrection Appearances of Jesus

9When Jesus rose early on the first day
of the week, he appeared first to Mary
Magdalene,[v] out of whom he had driven
seven demons. **10**She went and told those
who had been with him and who were
mourning and weeping. **11**When they
heard that Jesus was alive and that she
had seen him, they did not believe it.[w]

12Afterward Jesus appeared in a different form to two of them while they were
walking in the country.[x] **13**These returned and reported it to the rest; but they
did not believe them either.

14Later Jesus appeared to the Eleven as
they were eating; he rebuked them for
their lack of faith and their stubborn refusal to believe those who had seen him
after he had risen.[y]

Go and Preach

15He said to them, "Go into all the
world and preach the good news to all
creation.[z] **16**Whoever believes and is bap- Lk 24:47-48
tized will be saved, but whoever does not
believe will be condemned.[a] **17**And these
signs[b] will accompany those who believe:
In my name they will drive out demons;[c]
they will speak in new tongues;[d] **18**they
will pick up snakes[e] with their hands; and
when they drink deadly poison, it will not
hurt them at all; they will place their
hands on[f] sick people, and they will get
well." Ac 6:8

19After the Lord Jesus had spoken to
them, he was taken up into heaven[g] and
he sat at the right hand of God.[h] **20**Then
the disciples went out and preached everywhere, and the Lord worked with them
and confirmed his word by the signs[i] that
accompanied it.

16:6 HE HAS RISEN. See Mt 28:6, note.

16:9–20 JESUS' APPEARANCES. Although vv. 9–20 are omitted from two of the oldest Greek manuscripts, they do appear in other old manuscripts, as well as in the majority of Greek manuscripts from all over the ancient world. Many scholars conclude, therefore, that any reading attested to by the majority of ancient manuscripts is likely to be part of the original writing of the Biblical author; Vv. 9–20 should thus be considered part of the inspired Word of God.

16:17 THESE SIGNS WILL ACCOMPANY. See article on SIGNS OF BELIEVERS, p. 106.

16:18 PICK UP SNAKES. Picking up snakes or drinking poison is not to be ritualized and made into a "trial by ordeal" in order to prove one's spirituality. These are promises given to believers who encounter such dangers in their normal work for Christ. It is a sin to test God by initiating unnecessary danger or trials (Mt 4:5–7; 10:23; 24:16–18).

SIGNS OF BELIEVERS

Mk 16:17–18 *"And these signs will accompany those who believe: In my name they will drive out demons; they will speak in new tongues; they will pick up snakes with their hands; and when they drink deadly poison, it will not hurt them at all; they will place their hands on sick people, and they will get well."*

Scripture clearly teaches that Christ wants his followers to perform miraculous deeds as they announce the gospel of the kingdom of God (see Mt 10:1; Mk 3:14–15; Lk 9:2, note; 10:17; Jn 14:12, note).

(1) These signs (Gk *sēmeion*), done by true disciples, confirm that the gospel message is genuine, that God's kingdom has come to earth in power (see article on THE KINGDOM OF GOD, p. 28), and that the living and risen Jesus is present with his people and working through them (see Jn 10:25; Ac 10:38).

(2) Every one of these signs (except for drinking poison) occurred in the recorded history of the early church: (a) speaking in new tongues (see Ac 2:4; 10:46; 19:6; 1Co 12:30; 14; see article on SPEAKING IN TONGUES, p. 232); (b) driving out demons (Ac 5:15–16; 16:18; 19:11–12); (c) escaping death from snakebites (Ac 28:3–5); and (d) healing the sick (Ac 3:1–7; 8:7; 9:33–34; 14:8–10; 28:7–8).

(3) These spiritual manifestations are intended to continue within Christ's churches until Jesus returns. Scripture never suggests that these signs were restricted to the period immediately following Jesus' ascension (see 1Co 1:7, note; 12:28; Gal 3:5).

(4) Christ's followers were not only to preach the gospel of the kingdom and bring salvation to those who believe (Mt 28:19–20; Mk 16:15–16; Lk 24:47), but were also to bring in that kingdom, just as Jesus did (Ac 10:38), by driving out demons and healing the sick (see article on THE KINGDOM OF GOD, p. 28).

(5) Jesus indicates in Mk 16:15–20 that these signs are not special gifts for a few, but were to be given to *all* believers who, in obedience to Christ, witness to the gospel and claim his promises.

(6) The failure of these "signs" to occur in the church today is not Christ's failure to keep his promises. Failure, Jesus states, lies within the hearts of his followers (see Mt 17:17, note).

(7) Christ has promised that his authority, power and presence will accompany us as we battle Satan's kingdom (Mt 28:18–20; Lk 24:47–49). We must liberate people from their captivity by preaching the gospel, by living righteous lives (Mt 6:33; Ro 6:13; 14:17), and by performing signs and miracles through the power of the Spirit (see Mt 10:1, note; Mk 16:16–20; Ac 4:31–33; see article on POWER OVER SATAN AND DEMONS, p. 80).

LUKE

Outline

I. Preface to Luke's Gospel (1:1–4)
II. The Coming of the Savior (1:5—2:52)
   A. Announcement of John's Coming Birth (1:5–25)
   B. Announcement of Jesus' Coming Birth (1:26–56)
   C. Birth of John the Baptist (1:57–80)
   D. Birth of Jesus (2:1–20)
   E. Jesus at the Temple as an Infant (2:21–39)
   F. Jesus' Visit to the Temple as a Boy (2:40–52)
III. Preparation for the Savior's Ministry (3:1—4:13)
   A. Preaching of John the Baptist (3:1–20)
   B. Baptism of Jesus (3:21–22)
   C. Genealogy of Jesus (3:23–38)
   D. Temptation of Jesus (4:1–13)
IV. Ministry in Galilee (4:14—9:50)
   A. Jesus' Ministry and Rejection at Nazareth (4:14–30)
   B. Capernaum: Jesus' Divine Authority Manifested (4:31–44)
   C. Miraculous Catch of Fish (5:1–11)
   D. Healing the Man With Leprosy (5:12–16)
   E. Jesus' Authority Is Challenged (5:17–26)
   F. The Savior of Sinners (5:27–32)
   G. Inauguration of the New Order (5:33—6:49)
   H. Demonstration of Divine Power (7:1—8:56)
   I. Jesus Gives Power to His Disciples (9:1–7)
   J. Herod and John the Baptist (9:8–9)
   K. Feeding of the Five Thousand (9:10–17)
   L. Peter's Confession and Jesus' Response (9:18–27)
   M. The Savior's Glory Revealed (9:28–50)
V. Ministry During the Final Journey Toward Jerusalem (9:51—19:28)
   A. The Savior's Mission of Redemption (9:51—10:37)
   B. Jesus' Special Instruction on Service and Prayer (10:38—11:13)
   C. Jesus' Warnings to Both Enemies and Followers (11:14—14:35)
   D. Parables About the Lost and Found (15:1–32)
   E. Christ's Commands to His Followers (16:1—17:10)
   F. Ingratitude of Nine Men With Leprosy Who Were Healed (17:11–19)
   G. Suddenness of Christ's Return Predicted (17:20—18:14)
   H. The Savior, Little Children and the Rich Ruler (18:15–30)
   I. Toward the End of the Journey (18:31—19:28)
VI. Passion Week (19:29—23:56)
   A. Jesus Enters Jerusalem (19:29–48)
   B. Jesus Teaches Daily in the Temple (20:1—21:4)
   C. Jesus Foretells the Destruction of the Temple and His Return (21:5–38)
   D. Final Preparations and the Last Supper (22:1–38)
   E. Gethsemane and the Betrayal (22:39–53)
   F. The Jewish Trial (22:54–71)

G. The Roman Trial (23:1–25)
H. The Crucifixion (23:26–49)
I. The Burial (23:50–56)
VII. Resurrection to Ascension (24:1–53)
A. The Resurrection Morning (24:1–12)
B. The Risen Lord's Appearances (24:13–43)
C. The Farewell Instructions (24:44–53)

Author: Luke

Theme: Jesus, the Divine-Human Savior

Date: A.D. 60–63

Background

Luke's Gospel is the first of two books addressed to a man named Theophilus (1:3; Ac 1:1). Although the author is not identified by name in either book, the unanimous testimony of early Christianity and the corroborating internal evidence of the two books point to common authorship by Luke.

Apparently Luke was a Gentile convert, the only non-Jewish author of a Bible book. The Holy Spirit prompted him to write to Theophilus (whose name means "one who loves God") in order to fill a need in the Gentile church for a full account of the beginnings of Christianity. This included two parts: (1) Jesus' birth, life and ministry, death, resurrection and ascension (Luke's Gospel), and (2) the outpouring of the Spirit at Jerusalem and the subsequent development of the early church (book of Acts). These two books comprise more than one-fourth of the NT.

From Paul's letters we learn that Luke was a "dear friend . . . the doctor" (Col 4:14) and a loyal co-worker with Paul (2Ti 4:11; Phm 24; cf. "we" passages in Acts, see Introduction to Acts). From Luke's own writings we know he was well-educated, a skilled writer, a careful historian and an inspired theologian. When he wrote his Gospel, the Gentile church apparently had no complete or widely circulated Gospel about Jesus. Matthew wrote his Gospel initially for the Jews, and Mark wrote a concise Gospel for the church in Rome. The Greek-speaking Gentile world did have oral accounts about Jesus by eyewitnesses, as well as short written digests, but no complete and orderly Gospel (see 1:1–4). Thus Luke set about to investigate everything carefully "from the beginning" (1:3), probably doing research in Palestine while Paul was in prison at Caesarea (Ac 21:17; 23:23—27:21) and completing his Gospel toward the end of that time or soon after arriving in Rome with Paul (Ac 28:16).

Purpose

Luke wrote this Gospel to the Gentiles to provide a full and accurate record "about all that Jesus began to do and to teach until the day he was taken up to heaven" (Ac 1:1b-2a). Writing under the inspiration of the Holy Spirit, Luke wanted Theophilus and other Gentile inquirers and converts to know with certainty the exact truth about which they had been orally instructed (1:3–4). That Luke wrote for Gentiles is apparent throughout the Gospel; for example, he traces Jesus' human genealogy back *to Adam* (3:23–38) and not just *to Abraham*, as did Matthew (cf. Mt 1:1–17). In Luke, Jesus is clearly seen as the divine-human Savior who was God's provision of salvation for all of Adam's descendants.

Survey

Luke's Gospel begins with the most complete infancy narratives (1:5—2:40) and the only glimpse in the Gospels of Jesus' boyhood (2:41–52). After describing John the Baptist's ministry and giving Jesus' genealogy, Luke divides Jesus' ministry into three major sections: (1) his ministry in and around Galilee (4:14—9:50), (2) his ministry during the final journey to Jerusalem (9:51—19:27) and (3) his last week in Jerusalem (19:28—24:53).

While Jesus' miracles are prominent in Luke's record of the Galilean ministry, the main focus in this Gospel is on Jesus' teaching and parables during his extended ministry on the way to Jerusalem (9:51—19:27). This section comprises the greatest block of material unique to Luke, and includes many well-loved stories and parables. The pivotal verse (9:51) and the key verse (19:10) of the Gospel occur at the beginning and toward the end of this special Lukan material.

Special Features

Seven major features or emphases characterize Luke's Gospel: (1) its comprehensiveness in recording the events in Jesus' life from pre-birth to ascension; (2) its exceptional literary style, using a rich vocabulary and written with an excellent command of the Greek language; (3) its universality, pointing out how Jesus came to make salvation available for all, Jews and Gentiles alike; (4) its stress on Jesus' concern for the underprivileged, including women, children, the poor and the social outcasts; (5) its emphasis on Jesus' life of prayer and his teaching about prayer; (6) its focus on the response of joy that should characterize those who accept Jesus and his message; (7) its emphasis on the importance of the Holy Spirit in the life of Jesus and his people (e.g., 1:15,41,67; 2:25–27; 4:1,14,18; 10:21; 12:12; 24:49).

Reading Luke

In order to read the entire New Testament in one year, the book of Luke should be read in 49 days, according to the following schedule:
☐ 1:1–25 ☐ 1:26–56 ☐ 1:57–80 ☐ 2:1–20 ☐ 2:21–52 ☐ 3 ☐ 4:1–13 ☐ 4:14–44 ☐ 5:1–16 ☐ 5:17–39 ☐ 6:1–16 ☐ 6:17–49 ☐ 7:1–35 ☐ 7:36–50 ☐ 8:1–21 ☐ 8:22–39 ☐ 8:40–56 ☐ 9:1–17 ☐ 9:18–36 ☐ 9:37–62 ☐ 10:1–24 ☐ 10:25–42 ☐ 11:1–13 ☐ 11:14–36 ☐ 11:37–54 ☐ 12:1–21 ☐ 12:22–48 ☐ 12:49–59 ☐ 13:1–21 ☐ 13:22–53 ☐ 14:1–24 ☐ 14:25—15:10 ☐ 15:11–32 ☐ 16 ☐ 17:1–19 ☐ 17:20—18:14 ☐ 18:15–43 ☐ 19:1–27 ☐ 19:28–48 ☐ 20:1–19 ☐ 20:20—21:4 ☐ 21:5–38 ☐ 22:1–38 ☐ 22:39–65 ☐ 22:66—23:25 ☐ 23:26–49 ☐ 23:50—24:12 ☐ 24:13–35 ☐ 24:36–53

NOTES

Introduction

1:1–4Ref — Ac 1:1

1 Many have undertaken to draw up an account of the things that have been fulfilled[a] among us, **2**just as they were handed down to us by those who from the first[a] were eyewitnesses[b] and servants of the word.[c] **3**Therefore, since I myself have carefully investigated everything from the beginning, it seemed good also to me to write an orderly account[d] for you, most excellent[e] Theophilus,[f] **4**so that you may know the certainty of the things you have been taught.[g]

The Birth of John the Baptist Foretold

5In the time of Herod king of Judea[h] there was a priest named Zechariah, who belonged to the priestly division of Abijah;[i] his wife Elizabeth was also a descendant of Aaron. **6**Both of them were upright in the sight of God, observing all the Lord's commandments and regulations blamelessly.[j] **7**But they had no children, because Elizabeth was barren; and they were both well along in years.

8Once when Zechariah's division was on duty and he was serving as priest before God,[k] **9**he was chosen by lot,[l] according to the custom of the priesthood, to go into the temple of the Lord and burn incense.[m] **10**And when the time for the burning of incense came, all the assembled worshipers were praying outside.[n]

11Then an angel[o] of the Lord appeared to him, standing at the right side of the altar of incense.[p] **12**When Zechariah saw him, he was startled and was gripped with fear.[q] **13**But the angel said to him: "Do not be afraid,[r] Zechariah; your prayer has been heard. Your wife Elizabeth will bear you a son, and you are to give him the name John.[s] **14**He will be a joy and delight to you, and many will rejoice because of his birth,[t] **15**for he will be great in the sight of the Lord. He is never to take wine or other fermented drink,[u] and he will be filled with the Holy Spirit[v] even from birth.[b][w] **16**Many of the people of Israel will he bring back to the Lord their God. **17**And he will go on before the Lord,[x] in the spirit and power of Elijah,[y] to turn the

Lk 1:41

1:2 [a]Mk 1:1; Jn 15:27; Ac 1:21, 22 [b]Heb 2:3; 1Pe 5:1; 2Pe 1:16; 1Jn 1:1 [c]S Mk 4:14
1:3 [d]Ac 11:4 [e]Ac 24:3; 26:25 [f]Ac 1:1
1:4 [g]Jn 20:31; Ac 2:42
1:5 [h]Mt 2:1 [i]1Ch 24:10
1:6 [j]Ge 6:9; Dt 5:33; 1Ki 9:4; Lk 2:25
1:8 [k]1Ch 24:19; 2Ch 8:14
1:9 [l]Ac 1:26 [m]Ex 30:7,8; 1Ch 23:13; 2Ch 29:11; Ps 141:2
1:10 [n]Lev 16:17
1:11 [o]S Ac 5:19 [p]Ex 30:1-10
1:12 [q]Jdg 6:22, 23; 13:22
1:13 [r]ver 30; S Mt 14:27 [s]ver 60,63; S Mt 3:1
1:14 [t]ver 58
1:15 [u]Nu 6:3; Lev 10:9; Jdg 13:4; Lk 7:33 [v]ver 41,67; Ac 2:4; 4:8,31; 6:3,5; 9:17; 11:24; Eph 5:18; S Ac 10:44 [w]Jer 1:5; Gal 1:15
1:17 [x]ver 76 [y]S Mt 11:14

[a] *1* Or *been surely believed* [b] *15* Or *from his mother's womb*

1:6 UPRIGHT IN THE SIGHT OF GOD. See Lk 2:25, note.

1:15 FILLED WITH THE HOLY SPIRIT. Notice the outcome of John's Spirit-filled life and ministry. Through the power of the Holy Spirit (1) his preaching convicts people of their sins, brings them to repentance and turns them back to God (vv. 15–17; see Jn 16:8, note); (2) he preaches in the spirit and power of Elijah (v. 17; see Ac 1:8, notes); (3) he reconciles families and turns many to a life of righteousness (v. 17).

1:15 WINE . . . FERMENTED DRINK. The literal translation of the Greek text here is "He will never drink wine [*oinos*] or strong drink [*sikera*]." The word "other" ("other fermented drink") does not appear in the Greek. (1) The Greek word used for "fermented drink" is *sikera*. Its exact meaning has not been determined, but it undoubtedly corresponds to the OT word *shekar*. It may refer to sweet palm juice or syrup in its different forms, which is often fermented. Some interpreters translate *shekar* as "beer" in a number of OT passages (cf. 1Sa 1:15; Pr 20:1; 31:4,6; Isa 28:7; 56:12; Mic 2:11). (2) The 1901 *Jewish Encyclopedia* (XII.533) states that from about 200 B.C. to A.D. 200, "wine" (Heb *yayin*; Gk *oinos*) was distinguished from "fermented drink" (Heb *shekar*; Gk *sikera*) in that "wine" was diluted with water, while "fermented drink" was undiluted (see article on WINE IN NEW TESTAMENT TIMES (2), p. 174). (3) A possible understanding of *sikera* is that when the two words "wine" and "fermented drink" are used together, in the majority of cases they form a figure of speech referring to the same thing (i.e., intoxicating wine). When *oinos* is used alone, it can refer to either unfermented or fermented wine (see article on WINE IN NEW TESTAMENT TIMES (1), p. 126).

1:17 SPIRIT AND POWER OF ELIJAH. In many ways John will be like the fearless prophet Elijah. Because he is filled with the Holy Spirit (v. 15), John will be a preacher of moral righteousness (3:7–14; Mt 3:1–10). He will demonstrate the Holy Spirit's ministry by preaching about sin, righteousness and judgment (see Jn 16:8, note). He will turn the hearts of "the disobedient to the wisdom of the righteous" (see Mt 11:7, note). He will not compromise his conscience or bend Biblical principles for the sake of status or security (3:19–20; Mt 14:1–11). He will obey God and remain loyal to all truth. In short, John will be a "man of God."

1:17 THE FATHERS TO THEIR CHILDREN. This verse points to Mal 4:6, a text that reveals that one of the greatest sins of God's people in the OT had been the failure of the fathers to love their sons and daughters enough to teach them the ways and commands of God. With the coming of John and the gospel of Christ, the hearts of the fathers will return to their children.

(1) This is a clear statement that one of the key goals of the gospel is to reestablish God's will for the family in a correct relationship between fathers and children. Through the preaching of repentance and the lordship of Christ, fathers will become dedicated to their children in an attitude of righteousness.

(2) If the church today fails to become what God wants it to be, one factor may be that once again the fathers' hearts have forsaken their children by failing to love them, spend time with them, and teach them

hearts of the fathers to their children[z]
and the disobedient to the wisdom of the
righteous—to make ready a people prepared for the Lord."[a]

18Zechariah asked the angel, "How can
I be sure of this?[b] I am an old man and
my wife is well along in years."[c]

19The angel answered, "I am Gabriel.[d]
I stand in the presence of God, and I have
been sent to speak to you and to tell you
this good news. **20**And now you will be
silent and not able to speak[e] until the day
this happens, because you did not believe
my words, which will come true at their
proper time."

21Meanwhile, the people were waiting
for Zechariah and wondering why he
stayed so long in the temple. **22**When he
came out, he could not speak to them.
They realized he had seen a vision in the
temple, for he kept making signs[f] to them
but remained unable to speak.

23When his time of service was completed, he returned home. **24**After this his
wife Elizabeth became pregnant and for
five months remained in seclusion. **25**"The
Lord has done this for me," she said. "In
these days he has shown his favor and
taken away my disgrace[g] among the people."

The Birth of Jesus Foretold

26In the sixth month, God sent the angel Gabriel[h] to Nazareth,[i] a town in Galilee, **27**to a virgin pledged to be married to
a man named Joseph,[j] a descendant of
David. The virgin's name was Mary. **28**The
angel went to her and said, "Greetings,
you who are highly favored! The Lord is
with you."

29Mary was greatly troubled at his
words and wondered what kind of greeting this might be. **30**But the angel said to
her, "Do not be afraid,[k] Mary, you have
found favor with God.[l] **31**You will be with
child and give birth to a son, and you are
to give him the name Jesus.[m] **32**He will be
great and will be called the Son of the
Most High.[n] The Lord God will give him
the throne of his father David,[o] **33**and he
will reign over the house of Jacob forever;
his kingdom[p] will never end."[q]

34"How will this be," Mary asked the
angel, "since I am a virgin?"

35The angel answered, "The Holy Spirit
will come upon you,[r] and the power of the
Most High[s] will overshadow you. So the
holy one[t] to be born will be called[c] the
Son of God.[u] **36**Even Elizabeth your relative is going to have a child[v] in her old
age, and she who was said to be barren is
in her sixth month. **37**For nothing is impossible with God."[w]

38"I am the Lord's servant," Mary answered. "May it be to me as you have
said." Then the angel left her.

Mary Visits Elizabeth

39At that time Mary got ready and hurried to a town in the hill country of Judea,[x]
40where she entered Zechariah's home
and greeted Elizabeth. **41**When Elizabeth
heard Mary's greeting, the baby leaped in
her womb, and Elizabeth was filled with
the Holy Spirit.[y] **42**In a loud voice she Lk 1:67

1:17 [z]Mal 4:5,6 [a]S Mt 3:3 **1:18** [b]Ge 15:8 [c]ver 34; Ge 17:17 **1:19** [d]ver 26; Da 8:16; 9:21 **1:20** [e]Ex 4:11; Eze 3:26 **1:22** [f]ver 62 **1:25** [g]Ge 30:23; Isa 4:1 **1:26** [h]S ver 19 [i]S Mt 2:23 **1:27** [j]Mt 1:16,18, 20; Lk 2:4 **1:30** [k]ver 13; S Mt 14:27 [l]Ge 6:8 **1:31** [m]Isa 7:14; Mt 1:21,25; Lk 2:21 **1:32** [n]ver 35,76; S Mk 5:7 [o]S Mt 1:1 **1:33** [p]Mt 28:18 [q]2Sa 7:16; Ps 89:3,4; Isa 9:7; Jer 33:17; Da 2:44; 7:14,27; Mic 4:7; Heb 1:8 **1:35** [r]Mt 1:18 [s]ver 32,76; S Mk 5:7 [t]S Mk 1:24 [u]S Mt 4:3 **1:36** [v]ver 24 **1:37** [w]S Mt 19:26 **1:39** [x]ver 65 **1:41** [y]S ver 15

c *35* Or *So the child to be born will be called holy,*

God's Word and righteous standards. As a result, the children will reject God's ways (Mal 4:6).

(3) The following are important passages related to fathers and children: (a) teaching children faithfulness to God's ways: Ex 10:2; 13:8; Dt 4:9–10; 6:6–25; 11:18–21; Ps 78:5–8; Isa 38:19; Joel 1:3; Eph 6:4; 1Th 2:11; (b) loving and correcting children: Ps 103:13; Pr 3:12; 13:24; 23:13–14; Mal 4:6; Lk 11:11–13; 2Co 12:14; Eph 6:4; Col 3:21; 1Th 2:11; 1Ti 3:4–5,12; 5:8; Tit 2:4; Heb 12:7; (c) fathers praying for their children: Ge 17:18; 2Sa 12:16; 1Ch 22:11–12; 29:19; Job 1:5; Eph 3:14–19. See Jn 17:1, note on a model prayer of a father for his children; see also article on PARENTS AND CHILDREN, p. 432.

1:28 YOU WHO ARE HIGHLY FAVORED. While Mary was favored above all women in being chosen as the mother of Jesus, the NT writers never indicate that she is to be worshiped, prayed to or given special titles. Mary merits our respect, but only her son merits our worship. (1) Note that Mary was chosen because she found favor with God (cf. Ge 6:8). Her humble and godly life pleased God to such an extent that he chose her for this most important task (cf. 2Ti 2:21). (2) Mary's blessing not only brought her great joy, but also much suffering and pain (see 2:35), for her son would be rejected and crucified. In this world God's calling will always involve blessing and suffering, joy and sadness, successes and disappointments.

1:35 THE HOLY ONE. Both Luke and Matthew state explicitly and unmistakably that Jesus was born of a virgin (v. 27; Mt 1:18,23, note). The Holy Spirit would come upon Mary and the child would be conceived solely by a miraculous deed of God. As a result, Jesus would be "holy" (i.e., free from all taint of sin). For more on this, see article on JESUS AND THE HOLY SPIRIT, p. 136.

1:38 AS YOU HAVE SAID. Mary submitted herself completely to God's will and trusted his message. She willingly accepted the honor and the reproach that being the mother of the holy child would bring. Young women in the church should follow Mary's example in sexual purity, love for God, faith in his Word and a willingness to obey the Holy Spirit.

exclaimed: "Blessed are you among wom-
en,[z] and blessed is the child you will bear!
43But why am I so favored, that the mother of my Lord[a] should come to me? 44As
soon as the sound of your greeting
reached my ears, the baby in my womb
leaped for joy. 45Blessed is she who has
believed that what the Lord has said to
her will be accomplished!"

Mary's Song

1:46–53pp — 1Sa 2:1–10

46And Mary said:

"My soul glorifies the Lord[b]
47 and my spirit rejoices in God my
Savior,[c]
48for he has been mindful
of the humble state of his servant.[d]
From now on all generations will call
me blessed,[e]
49 for the Mighty One has done great
things[f] for me—
holy is his name.[g]
50His mercy extends to those who fear
him,
from generation to generation.[h]
51He has performed mighty deeds with
his arm;[i]
he has scattered those who are
proud in their inmost
thoughts.[j]
52He has brought down rulers from
their thrones
but has lifted up the humble.[k]
53He has filled the hungry with good
things[l]
but has sent the rich away empty.
54He has helped his servant Israel,
remembering to be merciful[m]
55to Abraham and his descendants[n]
forever,
even as he said to our fathers."

56Mary stayed with Elizabeth for about
three months and then returned home.

The Birth of John the Baptist

57When it was time for Elizabeth to
have her baby, she gave birth to a son.
58Her neighbors and relatives heard that
the Lord had shown her great mercy, and
they shared her joy.

1:42 [z] Jdg 5:24
1:43 [a] S Jn 13:13
1:46 [b] Ps 34:2,3
1:47 [c] Ps 18:46; Isa 17:10; 61:10; Hab 3:18; 1Ti 1:1; 2:3; 4:10
1:48 [d] ver 38; Ps 138:6
[e] Lk 11:27
1:49 [f] Ps 71:19
[g] Ps 111:9
1:50 [h] Ex 20:6; Ps 103:17
1:51 [i] Ps 98:1; Isa 40:10
[j] Ge 11:8; Ex 18:11; 2Sa 22:28; Jer 13:9; 49:16
1:52 [k] S Mt 23:12
1:53 [l] Ps 107:9
1:54 [m] Ps 98:3
1:55 [n] S Gal 3:16
1:59 [o] Ge 17:12; Lev 12:3; Lk 2:21; Php 3:5
1:60 [p] ver 13,63; S Mt 3:1
1:62 [q] ver 22
1:63 [r] ver 13,60; S Mt 3:1
1:64 [s] ver 20; Eze 24:27
1:65 [t] ver 39
1:66 [u] Ge 39:2; Ac 11:21
1:67 [v] S ver 15
[w] Joel 2:28
1:68 [x] Ge 24:27; 1Ki 8:15; Ps 72:18
[y] Ps 111:9; Lk 7:16
1:69 [z] 1Sa 2:1,10; 2Sa 22:3; Ps 18:2; 89:17; 132:17; Eze 29:21
[a] S Mt 1:1
1:70 [b] Jer 23:5; Ac 3:21; Ro 1:2
1:72 [c] Mic 7:20
[d] Ps 105:8,9; 106:45; Eze 16:60
1:73 [e] Ge 22:16-18
1:74 [f] Heb 9:14
[g] 1Jn 4:18
1:75 [h] Eph 4:24

59On the eighth day they came to circumcise[o] the child, and they were going
to name him after his father Zechariah,
60but his mother spoke up and said, "No!
He is to be called John."[p]

61They said to her, "There is no one
among your relatives who has that name."

62Then they made signs[q] to his father,
to find out what he would like to name the
child. 63He asked for a writing tablet, and
to everyone's astonishment he wrote, "His
name is John."[r] 64Immediately his mouth
was opened and his tongue was loosed,
and he began to speak,[s] praising God.
65The neighbors were all filled with awe,
and throughout the hill country of Judea[t]
people were talking about all these
things. 66Everyone who heard this wondered about it, asking, "What then is this
child going to be?" For the Lord's hand
was with him.[u]

Zechariah's Song

67His father Zechariah was filled with
the Holy Spirit[v] and prophesied:[w] Lk 4:1

68"Praise be to the Lord, the God of
Israel,[x]
because he has come and has
redeemed his people.[y]
69He has raised up a horn[d][z] of
salvation for us
in the house of his servant David[a]
70(as he said through his holy prophets
of long ago),[b]
71salvation from our enemies
and from the hand of all who hate
us—
72to show mercy to our fathers[c]
and to remember his holy
covenant,[d]
73 the oath he swore to our father
Abraham:[e]
74to rescue us from the hand of our
enemies,
and to enable us to serve him[f]
without fear[g]
75 in holiness and righteousness[h]
before him all our days.

d *69 Horn* here symbolizes strength.

1:47 GOD MY SAVIOR. In these words Mary recognizes her own need of salvation. She was a sinner who needed Christ as "Savior." The idea that Mary was immaculately conceived and lived without sin is nowhere taught in Scripture (cf. Ro 3:9,23).

1:67 FILLED WITH THE HOLY SPIRIT. Luke records how the Holy Spirit empowered many of the important people associated with the birth of Christ (vv. 15,35,41,67; 2:25). After Christ's ascension, the way was opened for all believers to be filled with the Holy Spirit (Ac 1–2).

1:75 HOLINESS AND RIGHTEOUSNESS. The ultimate aim of our redemption is to be delivered from Satan's kingdom (Ac 26:18) in order to serve God "in

76And you, my child, will be called a
prophet[i] of the Most High;[j]
for you will go on before the Lord
to prepare the way for him,[k]
77to give his people the knowledge of
salvation
through the forgiveness of their
sins,[l]
78because of the tender mercy of our
God,
by which the rising sun[m] will come
to us from heaven
79to shine on those living in darkness
and in the shadow of death,[n]
to guide our feet into the path of
peace."[o]

80And the child grew and became
strong in spirit;[p] and he lived in the desert
until he appeared publicly to Israel.

The Birth of Jesus

2 In those days Caesar Augustus[q] issued a decree that a census should be
taken of the entire Roman world.[r] 2(This
was the first census that took place while
Quirinius was governor of Syria.)[s] 3And
everyone went to his own town to register.
4So Joseph also went up from the town
of Nazareth in Galilee to Judea, to Bethlehem[t] the town of David, because he belonged to the house and line of David. 5He
went there to register with Mary, who was
pledged to be married to him[u] and was
expecting a child. 6While they were there,
the time came for the baby to be born,
7and she gave birth to her firstborn, a son.
She wrapped him in cloths and placed him
in a manger, because there was no room
for them in the inn.

The Shepherds and the Angels

8And there were shepherds living out in
the fields nearby, keeping watch over
their flocks at night. 9An angel[v] of the
Lord appeared to them, and the glory of
the Lord shone around them, and they
were terrified. 10But the angel said to
them, "Do not be afraid.[w] I bring you good
news of great joy that will be for all the
people. 11Today in the town of David a
Savior[x] has been born to you; he is
Christ[e][y] the Lord.[z] 12This will be a sign[a]
to you: You will find a baby wrapped in
cloths and lying in a manger."
13Suddenly a great company of the
heavenly host appeared with the angel,
praising God and saying,

14"Glory to God in the highest,
and on earth peace[b] to men on
whom his favor rests."

15When the angels had left them and
gone into heaven, the shepherds said to
one another, "Let's go to Bethlehem and
see this thing that has happened, which
the Lord has told us about."
16So they hurried off and found Mary
and Joseph, and the baby, who was lying
in the manger.[c] 17When they had seen
him, they spread the word concerning
what had been told them about this child,
18and all who heard it were amazed at
what the shepherds said to them. 19But
Mary treasured up all these things and
pondered them in her heart.[d] 20The shepherds returned, glorifying and praising
God[e] for all the things they had heard and
seen, which were just as they had been
told.

Jesus Presented in the Temple

21On the eighth day, when it was time
to circumcise him,[f] he was named Jesus,
the name the angel had given him before
he had been conceived.[g]
22When the time of their purification according to the Law of Moses[h] had been

1:76 [i]S Mt 11:9 [j]ver 32,35; S Mk 5:7 [k]ver 17; S Mt 3:3 **1:77** [l]Jer 31:34; Mt 1:21; Mk 1:4 **1:78** [m]Mal 4:2 **1:79** [n]Ps 107:14; Isa 9:2; 59:9; Mt 4:16; S Ac 26:18 [o]S Lk 2:14 **1:80** [p]Lk 2:40,52 **2:1** [q]Lk 3:1; Mt 22:17 [r]S Mt 24:14 **2:2** [s]Mt 4:24; Ac 15:23,41; 21:3; Gal 1:21 **2:4** [t]S Jn 7:42 **2:5** [u]Lk 1:27 **2:9** [v]S Ac 5:19 **2:10** [w]S Mt 14:27 **2:11** [x]S Mt 1:21; S Jn 3:17; 4:42; Ac 5:31; 13:23; S Ro 11:14; 1Ti 4:10; 1Jn 4:14 [y]Mt 1:16; 16:16, 20; Jn 11:27; Ac 2:36; 3:20; S 9:22 [z]S Jn 13:13 **2:12** [a]1Sa 2:34; 10:7; 2Ki 19:29; Ps 86:17; Isa 7:14 **2:14** [b]Isa 9:6; 52:7; 53:5; Mic 5:5; Lk 1:79; S Jn 14:27; Ro 5:1; Eph 2:14, 17 **2:16** [c]ver 7 **2:19** [d]ver 51 **2:20** [e]S Mt 9:8 **2:21** [f]S Lk 1:59 [g]S Lk 1:31 **2:22** [h]Lev 12:2-8

e *11* Or *Messiah.* "The Christ" (Greek) and "the Messiah" (Hebrew) both mean "the Anointed One"; also in verse 26.

holiness and righteousness before him all our days" (cf. Eph 1:4). Every child of God must aim at a life of holiness and righteousness in an evil world. This holy life is "before him," i.e., in God's presence.

2:7 A MANGER. Christ was born in a stable, a place where animals were kept. The stable was probably a cave and the manger a feeding trough for animals. The birth of the Savior, the greatest event in all history, occurred in the most humble of circumstances. Jesus was the King of kings, but he was neither born nor did he live like a king in this life. God's people are kings and priests, but in this life we must be as he was—humble and simple.

2:11 A SAVIOR . . . CHRIST THE LORD. At his birth, Jesus is called "a Savior." (1) As Savior, he has come to deliver us from sin, Satan's domain, the ungodly world, fear, death and the condemnation of our transgressions (see Mt 1:21, note). (2) The Savior is also "Christ the Lord." He has been anointed as the Messiah of God and the Lord who rules over his people (see Mt 1:1, note on the name of Christ). No person can have Jesus as Savior while not submitting to his lordship.

2:22 PRESENT HIM TO THE LORD. As Joseph and Mary presented Jesus to the Lord, so all parents should sincerely consecrate their children to the Lord. They should pray constantly that from the beginning to the end of each child's life, he or she will be found doing the Lord's will, serving and glorifying God with complete devotion.

completed, Joseph and Mary took him to
Jerusalem to present him to the Lord 23(as
it is written in the Law of the Lord, "Every
firstborn male is to be consecrated to the
Lord"[f]),[i] 24and to offer a sacrifice in
keeping with what is said in the Law of the
Lord: "a pair of doves or two young pigeons."[g][j]

Simeon and Anna Praise God

25Now there was a man in Jerusalem
called Simeon, who was righteous and devout.[k] He was waiting for the consolation
of Israel,[l] and the Holy Spirit was upon
him. 26It had been revealed to him by the
Holy Spirit that he would not die before he
had seen the Lord's Christ. 27Moved by
the Spirit, he went into the temple courts.
When the parents brought in the child
Jesus to do for him what the custom of the
Law required,[m] 28Simeon took him in his
arms and praised God, saying:

29"Sovereign Lord, as you have
promised,[n]
you now dismiss[h] your servant in
peace.[o]
30For my eyes have seen your
salvation,[p]
31 which you have prepared in the
sight of all people,
32a light for revelation to the Gentiles
and for glory to your people
Israel."[q]

33The child's father and mother marveled at what was said about him. 34Then
Simeon blessed them and said to Mary,
his mother:[r] "This child is destined to
cause the falling[s] and rising of many in
Israel, and to be a sign that will be spoken
against, 35so that the thoughts of many
hearts will be revealed. And a sword will
pierce your own soul too."

36There was also a prophetess,[t] Anna,
the daughter of Phanuel, of the tribe of
Asher. She was very old; she had lived
with her husband seven years after her
marriage, 37and then was a widow until
she was eighty-four.[i][u] She never left the
temple but worshiped night and day, fasting and praying.[v] 38Coming up to them at
that very moment, she gave thanks to God
and spoke about the child to all who were
looking forward to the redemption of Jerusalem.[w]

39When Joseph and Mary had done everything required by the Law of the Lord,
they returned to Galilee to their own town
of Nazareth.[x] 40And the child grew and
became strong; he was filled with wisdom,
and the grace of God was upon him.[y]

The Boy Jesus at the Temple

41Every year his parents went to Jerusalem for the Feast of the Passover.[z]

f *23* Exodus 13:2,12 g *24* Lev. 12:8 h *29* Or *promised, / now dismiss* i *37* Or *widow for eighty-four years*

2:23 [i]Ex 13:2,12, 15; Nu 3:13 **2:24** [j]Lev 12:8 **2:25** [k]Lk 1:6 [l]ver 38; Isa 52:9; Lk 23:51 **2:27** [m]ver 22 **2:29** [n]ver 26 [o]Ac 2:24 **2:30** [p]Isa 40:5; 52:10; Lk 3:6 **2:32** [q]Isa 42:6; 49:6; Ac 13:47; 26:23 **2:34** [r]S Mt 12:46 [s]Isa 8:14; Mt 21:44; 1Co 1:23; 2Co 2:16; Gal 5:11; 1Pe 2:7, 8 **2:36** [t]S Ac 21:9 **2:37** [u]1Ti 5:9 [v]Ac 13:3; 14:23; 1Ti 5:5 **2:38** [w]ver 25; Isa 40:2; 52:9; Lk 1:68; 24:21 **2:39** [x]ver 51; S Mt 2:23 **2:40** [y]ver 52; Lk 1:80 **2:41** [z]Ex 23:15; Dt 16:1-8; Lk 22:8

2:24 A PAIR OF DOVES. The offering of a pair of doves indicates that Joseph and Mary were poor (Lev 12:8). From the very beginning Christ was identified with the underprivileged (9:58; Mt 8:20; see Rev 2:9, note).

2:25 RIGHTEOUS AND DEVOUT. "Righteous" or "upright" (cf. 1:6) translates the Greek word *dikaios* (Heb *yasher*), meaning "straight." In the OT this word did not mean mere conformity to the commandments, but indicated a person was right with God both in heart and in action. (1) The righteousness that God sought in the OT was one that came from the heart, based on true faith in, love for and fear of God (Dt 4:10,29; 5:29). This condition of the heart was seen in the parents of John the Baptist, who observed "all the Lord's commandments and regulations blamelessly" (1:6; see Ge 7:1; 17:1; 1Ki 9:4, where the term includes "integrity of heart"). Simeon manifested the same characteristic in his life. (2) OT righteous persons were not perfect. When sin entered their lives they obtained forgiveness by presenting an animal sacrifice to God in an attitude of sincere repentance and faith (Lev 4:27–35).

2:25 WAITING FOR THE CONSOLATION. In a time of deplorable spiritual conditions righteous Simeon was devoted to God and filled with the Holy Spirit, waiting in faith, patience and great longing for the coming of the Messiah. Likewise, in the last days of this present age, when many are abandoning the NT apostolic faith and the blessed hope for the coming of Christ (Tit 2:13), there will always be the faithful Simeons. Others may place their hope in this life and this world, but the faithful will be like the loyal slave who keeps watch through the long, dark night, waiting for the return of his master (Mt 24:45–47). Our greatest blessing is to see face to face "the Lord's Christ" (v. 26; cf. Rev 22:4), to be ready when he comes and to live forever in his presence (Rev 21–22).

2:36–37 ANNA ... WORSHIPED. Anna was a prophetess who earnestly hoped for the coming of Christ. She remained a widow for many years, never remarrying, but devoting herself to the Lord, "fasting and praying" night and day. The Bible teaches that the unmarried state can be a greater blessing than the married. Paul states that the unmarried have greater opportunity to be concerned about the things of the Lord—how to please him and give him undistracted devotion (see 1Co 7:32–35).

2:40 THE CHILD GREW. As a true human child, Jesus experienced the process of physical and spiritual development. He kept increasing in wisdom as the grace of God was upon him. He was perfect in his human nature, developing perfectly as God desired.

42When he was twelve years old, they went up to the Feast, according to the custom. 43After the Feast was over, while his parents were returning home, the boy Jesus stayed behind in Jerusalem, but they were unaware of it. 44Thinking he was in their company, they traveled on for a day. Then they began looking for him among their relatives and friends. 45When they did not find him, they went back to Jerusalem to look for him. 46After three days they found him in the temple courts, sitting among the teachers, listening to them and asking them questions. 47Everyone who heard him was amazed[a] at his understanding and his answers. 48When his parents saw him, they were astonished. His mother[b] said to him, "Son, why have you treated us like this? Your father[c] and I have been anxiously searching for you."

49"Why were you searching for me?" he asked. "Didn't you know I had to be in my Father's house?"[d] 50But they did not understand what he was saying to them.[e]

51Then he went down to Nazareth with them[f] and was obedient to them. But his mother treasured all these things in her heart.[g] 52And Jesus grew in wisdom and stature, and in favor with God and men.[h]

John the Baptist Prepares the Way

3:2–10pp — Mt 3:1–10; Mk 1:3–5
3:16,17pp — Mt 3:11,12; Mk 1:7,8

3 In the fifteenth year of the reign of Tiberius Caesar—when Pontius Pilate[i] was governor of Judea, Herod[j] tetrarch of Galilee, his brother Philip tetrarch of Iturea and Traconitis, and Lysanias tetrarch of Abilene— 2during the high priesthood of Annas and Caiaphas,[k] the word of God came to John[l] son of Zechariah[m] in the desert. 3He went into all the country around the Jordan, preaching a baptism of repentance for the forgiveness of sins.[n] 4As is written in the book of the words of Isaiah the prophet:

"A voice of one calling in the desert,
'Prepare the way for the Lord,
make straight paths for him.
5Every valley shall be filled in,
every mountain and hill made low.
The crooked roads shall become straight,
the rough ways smooth.
6And all mankind will see God's salvation.' "[j][o]

7John said to the crowds coming out to be baptized by him, "You brood of vipers![p] Who warned you to flee from the coming wrath?[q] 8Produce fruit in keeping with repentance. And do not begin to say to yourselves, 'We have Abraham as our father.'[r] For I tell you that out of these stones God can raise up children for Abraham. 9The ax is already at the root of the trees, and every tree that does not produce good fruit will be cut down and thrown into the fire."[s]

10"What should we do then?"[t] the crowd asked.

11John answered, "The man with two tunics should share with him who has none, and the one who has food should do the same."[u]

12Tax collectors also came to be baptized.[v] "Teacher," they asked, "what should we do?"

13"Don't collect any more than you are required to,"[w] he told them.

14Then some soldiers asked him, "And what should we do?"

He replied, "Don't extort money and don't accuse people falsely[x]—be content with your pay."

15The people were waiting expectantly and were all wondering in their hearts if John[y] might possibly be the Christ.[k][z] 16John answered them all, "I baptize you with[l] water.[a] But one more powerful than I will come, the thongs of whose sandals

2:47 [a]S Mt 7:28 **2:48** [b]S Mt 12:46 [c]Lk 3:23; 4:22 **2:49** [d]Jn 2:16 **2:50** [e]S Mk 9:32 **2:51** [f]ver 39; S Mt 2:23 [g]ver 19 **2:52** [h]ver 40; 1Sa 2:26; Pr 3:4; Lk 1:80 **3:1** [i]S Mt 27:2 [j]S Mt 14:1 **3:2** [k]S Mt 26:3 [l]S Mt 3:1 [m]Lk 1:13 **3:3** [n]ver 16; S Mk 1:4 **3:6** [o]Isa 40:3-5; Ps 98:2; Isa 42:16; 52:10; Lk 2:30 **3:7** [p]Mt 12:34; 23:33 [q]S Ro 1:18 **3:8** [r]Isa 51:2; Lk 19:9; Jn 8:33, 39; Ac 13:26; Ro 4:1,11,12,16, 17; 9:7,8; Gal 3:7 **3:9** [s]S Mt 3:10 **3:10** [t]ver 12,14; Ac 2:37; 16:30 **3:11** [u]Isa 58:7; Eze 18:7 **3:12** [v]Lk 7:29 **3:13** [w]Lk 19:8 **3:14** [x]Ex 23:1; Lev 19:11 **3:15** [y]S Mt 3:1 [z]Jn 1:19,20; Ac 13:25 **3:16** [a]ver 3; S Mk 1:4

j 6 Isaiah 40:3-5 **k** *15* Or *Messiah* l *16* Or *in*

2:52 JESUS GREW IN WISDOM. Between 2:52 and 3:1, approximately eighteen years of Jesus' life passed without comment. What was his life like during those years? From Mt 13:55 and Mk 6:3, we learn that he grew up in a large family, that his father was a carpenter and that Jesus learned the trade. Since Joseph is never mentioned again in the Gospels, it is likely that Joseph died before Jesus began his public ministry and that Jesus provided for his mother and younger brothers and sisters. The carpenter's trade included household repairs, furniture making, and construction of agricultural implements such as plows and yokes. During all these years he grew and developed both physically and spiritually according to God's will, fully conscious that God was his Father (v. 49).

3:8 FRUIT IN KEEPING WITH REPENTANCE. See Mt 3:8, note.

3:16 BAPTIZE YOU WITH THE HOLY SPIRIT. Christ's baptizing his followers with [or in] the Holy Spirit (cf. Mt 3:11) is the new sign by which to identify God's people. (1) This was promised in Joel 2:28 and reaffirmed after Christ's resurrection (24:49; Ac 1:4–8). This prediction was initially fulfilled on the day of Pentecost (see Ac 2:4, notes).

(2) Christ's ministry of baptizing in the Holy Spirit is a continuing ministry throughout this present age. This is made clear by the Greek text of Jn 1:33 ("he who will baptize with the Holy Spirit"); this phrase

I am not worthy to untie. He will baptize
you with the Holy Spirit and with fire.[b]
17His winnowing fork[c] is in his hand to
clear his threshing floor and to gather the
wheat into his barn, but he will burn up
the chaff with unquenchable fire."[d] 18And
with many other words John exhorted the
people and preached the good news to
them.

19But when John rebuked Herod[e] the
tetrarch because of Herodias, his brother's wife, and all the other evil things he
had done, 20Herod added this to them all:
He locked John up in prison.[f]

The Baptism and Genealogy of Jesus

3:21,22pp — Mt 3:13–17; Mk 1:9–11
3:23–38pp — Mt 1:1–17

21When all the people were being baptized, Jesus was baptized too. And as he
was praying,[g] heaven was opened 22and
the Holy Spirit descended on him[h] in bodily form like a dove. And a voice came from
heaven: "You are my Son,[i] whom I love;
with you I am well pleased."[j]

23Now Jesus himself was about thirty
years old when he began his ministry.[k] He
was the son, so it was thought, of Joseph,[l]

the son of Heli, 24the son of Matthat,
the son of Levi, the son of Melki,
the son of Jannai, the son of Joseph,
25the son of Mattathias, the son of Amos,
the son of Nahum, the son of Esli,
the son of Naggai, 26the son of Maath,
the son of Mattathias, the son of Semein,
the son of Josech, the son of Joda,
27the son of Joanan, the son of Rhesa,
the son of Zerubbabel,[m] the son of Shealtiel,
the son of Neri, 28the son of Melki,
the son of Addi, the son of Cosam,
the son of Elmadam, the son of Er,
29the son of Joshua, the son of Eliezer,
the son of Jorim, the son of Matthat,
the son of Levi, 30the son of Simeon,
the son of Judah, the son of Joseph,
the son of Jonam, the son of Eliakim,
31the son of Melea, the son of Menna,
the son of Mattatha, the son of Nathan,[n]
the son of David, 32the son of Jesse,
the son of Obed, the son of Boaz,
the son of Salmon,[m] the son of Nahshon,
33the son of Amminadab, the son of Ram,[n]
the son of Hezron, the son of Perez,[o]
the son of Judah, 34the son of Jacob,
the son of Isaac, the son of Abraham,
the son of Terah, the son of Nahor,[p]
35the son of Serug, the son of Reu,
the son of Peleg, the son of Eber,
the son of Shelah, 36the son of Cainan,
the son of Arphaxad,[q] the son of Shem,
the son of Noah, the son of Lamech,[r]
37the son of Methuselah, the son of Enoch,
the son of Jared, the son of Mahalalel,
the son of Kenan,[s] 38the son of Enosh,
the son of Seth, the son of Adam,
the son of God.[t]

The Temptation of Jesus

4:1–13pp — Mt 4:1–11; Mk 1:12,13

4 Jesus, full of the Holy Spirit,[u] returned from the Jordan[v] and was led
by the Spirit[w] in the desert, 2where for
forty days[x] he was tempted by the devil.[y] Lk 24:49

3:16 [b] Jn 1:26,33; Ac 1:5; 2:3; 11:16; 19:4
3:17 [c] Isa 30:24 [d] Mt 13:30; S 25:41
3:19 [e] ver 1; S Mt 14:1
3:20 [f] S Mt 14:3,4
3:21 [g] Mt 14:23; Mk 1:35; 6:46; Lk 5:16; 6:12; 9:18,28; 11:1
3:22 [h] Isa 42:1; Jn 1:32,33; Ac 10:38 [i] S Mt 3:17 [j] S Mt 3:17
3:23 [k] Mt 4:17; Ac 1:1 [l] Lk 1:27
3:27 [m] Mt 1:12
3:31 [n] 2Sa 5:14; 1Ch 3:5
3:33 [o] Ru 4:18-22; 1Ch 2:10-12
3:34 [p] Ge 11:24, 26
3:36 [q] Ge 11:12 [r] Ge 5:28-32
3:37 [s] Ge 5:12-25
3:38 [t] Ge 5:1,2, 6-9
4:1 [u] ver 14,18; S Lk 1:15,35; 3:16,22; 10:21 [v] Lk 3:3,21 [w] Eze 37:1; Lk 2:27
4:2 [x] Ex 34:28; 1Ki 19:8 [y] Heb 4:15

m *32* Some early manuscripts *Sala* n *33* Some manuscripts *Amminadab, the son of Admin, the son of Arni*; other manuscripts vary widely.

uses the present participle (*ho baptizōn*), meaning "he who will continue to baptize." Therefore, the references in Luke and John are not only to the first outpouring of the Holy Spirit at Pentecost, but to the important role and ministry of Jesus as the Baptizer in the Holy Spirit throughout this age. "The promise is for you and your children and for all who are far off" (Ac 2:39).

3:17 HE WILL BURN UP THE CHAFF. Those who turn from sin and receive Christ and his Word will be baptized with the Holy Spirit. Those who cling to their sins will be punished with unquenchable fire (see Mt 10:28, note).

3:22 HOLY SPIRIT DESCENDED ON HIM. Jesus, who from the beginning had been conceived and indwelt by the Holy Spirit (1:35), is now personally anointed and empowered by the Spirit for his ministry. For more on the significance of Jesus' baptism in the Holy Spirit, see article on JESUS AND THE HOLY SPIRIT, p. 136.

3:23 JESUS' GENEALOGY. See Mt 1:1, notes.

4:1 JESUS, FULL OF THE HOLY SPIRIT. Jesus was empowered and led by the Spirit when he encountered Satan's temptation. For comments on the role of the Spirit in Jesus' life, see article on JESUS AND THE HOLY SPIRIT, p. 136.

4:2 TEMPTED BY THE DEVIL. One essential feature of Jesus' temptation revolved around what kind of Messiah he would be and how he would use his anointing from God. (1) Jesus was tempted to use his

He ate nothing during those days, and at
the end of them he was hungry.
3The devil said to him, "If you are the
Son of God,[z] tell this stone to become
bread."
4Jesus answered, "It is written: 'Man
does not live on bread alone.'[o]"[a]
5The devil led him up to a high place
and showed him in an instant all the kingdoms of the world.[b] 6And he said to him,
"I will give you all their authority and
splendor, for it has been given to me,[c] and
I can give it to anyone I want to. 7So if you
worship me, it will all be yours."
8Jesus answered, "It is written: 'Worship the Lord your God and serve him
only.'[p]"[d]
9The devil led him to Jerusalem and had
him stand on the highest point of the temple. "If you are the Son of God," he said,
"throw yourself down from here. 10For it
is written:

" 'He will command his angels
concerning you
to guard you carefully;
11they will lift you up in their hands,
so that you will not strike your foot
against a stone.'[q]"[e]

12Jesus answered, "It says: 'Do not put
the Lord your God to the test.'[r]"[f]
13When the devil had finished all this
tempting,[g] he left him[h] until an opportune time.

Jesus and the Power of the Spirit

14Jesus returned to Galilee[i] in the power of the Spirit, and news about him
spread through the whole countryside.[j]
15He taught in their synagogues,[k] and everyone praised him.

Jesus Rejected at Nazareth

16He went to Nazareth,[l] where he had
been brought up, and on the Sabbath day
he went into the synagogue,[m] as was his
custom. And he stood up to read.[n] 17The
scroll of the prophet Isaiah was handed to
him. Unrolling it, he found the place
where it is written:

18"The Spirit of the Lord is on me,[o]
because he has anointed me
to preach good news[p] to the poor.

4:3 [z]S Mt 4:3
4:4 [a]Dt 8:3
4:5 [b]S Mt 24:14
4:6 [c]Jn 12:31; 14:30; 1Jn 5:19
4:8 [d]Dt 6:13
4:11 [e]Ps 91:11, 12
4:12 [f]Dt 6:16
4:13 [g]Heb 4:15 [h]Jn 14:30
4:14 [i]Mt 4:12 [j]S Mt 9:26
4:15 [k]S Mt 4:23
4:16 [l]S Mt 2:23 [m]Mt 13:54 [n]S 1Ti 4:13
4:18 [o]S Jn 3:34 [p]Mk 16:15

[o] *4* Deut. 8:3 [p] *8* Deut. 6:13 [q] *11* Psalm 91:11,12 [r] *12* Deut. 6:16

anointing and position to serve his own self-interest (vv. 3–4), to attain glory and power over the nations instead of accepting the cross and the way of suffering (vv. 5–8), and to accommodate himself to the people's popular expectation for a sensational Messiah (vv. 9–11). (2) Satan still tempts Christian leaders to use their anointing, position and ability for their own self-interest, to establish their own glory and kingdom, and to please people rather than God. Those who selfishly compromise with Satan have in reality surrendered to Satan's lordship.

4:2 HE ATE NOTHING. See Mt 4:2, note on fasting.

4:4 DOES NOT LIVE ON BREAD ALONE. Jesus meets Satan's temptation by declaring that he will live by God's Word above all else (cf. Dt 8:3). (1) Jesus is saying that everything important in life depends on God and his will (Jn 4:34). To strive for success, happiness or material things apart from God's way and purpose will lead to bitter disappointment and end in failure. (2) Jesus emphasized this truth when he taught that we must seek first the kingdom of God (i.e., God's rule, activity and power in our lives); only then will other necessary things be given according to his will and way (see Mt 5:6, note; 6:33, note).

4:5 THE KINGDOMS OF THE WORLD. Satan tempts Jesus with the offer of dominion over all the kingdoms of the world, a proposal that Jesus rejects. (1) Jesus' kingdom in this age is *not* a kingdom of this world (Jn 18:36–37). He refuses to seek a kingdom for himself by the worldly methods of compromise, earthly power, political maneuvering, external violence, popularity, honor and glory. (2) Jesus' kingdom is a spiritual kingdom ruling in the hearts of his people, who have been taken out of the kingdoms of the world. As a heavenly kingdom, (a) it is gained through suffering, self-denial, humility and meekness; (b) it requires giving our bodies as living and holy sacrifices (Ro 12:1) in complete devotion and obedience to God; (c) it involves struggling with spiritual weapons against sin, temptation and Satan (Eph 6:10–20); (d) it means resisting conformity to this world (Ro 12:2). See article on THE KINGDOM OF GOD, p. 28.

4:9 THE DEVIL. See Mt 4:10, note on Satan.

4:10 SATAN'S USE OF SCRIPTURE. See Mt 4:6, note.

4:18 THE SPIRIT . . . ON ME. See article on JESUS AND THE HOLY SPIRIT, p. 136.

4:18 HE HAS ANOINTED ME. Jesus gives the purpose of his Spirit-anointed ministry here: (1) To preach the gospel to the poor, the destitute, the afflicted, the humble, those crushed in spirit, the brokenhearted and those who "tremble at his word" (cf. Isa 61:1; 66:2). (2) To heal those who are bruised and oppressed. This healing involves the whole person, both physical and spiritual. (3) To open the spiritual eyes of those blinded by the world and Satan in order that they might see the truth of God's good news (cf. Jn 9:39). (4) To proclaim the time of true freedom and salvation from Satan's domain, sin, fear and guilt (cf. Jn 8:36; Ac 26:18).

All those who are filled with the Spirit are called to share Jesus' ministry in these ways. To do so we must gain a deep realization of the terrible need and misery that has resulted from sin and the power of Satan—a condition of bondage to evil, brokenheartedness, spiritual blindness and physical distress.

He has sent me to proclaim freedom
for the prisoners
and recovery of sight for the blind,
to release the oppressed,
19 to proclaim the year of the Lord's
favor."[s][q]

20Then he rolled up the scroll, gave it back to the attendant and sat down.[r] The eyes of everyone in the synagogue were fastened on him, **21**and he began by saying to them, "Today this scripture is fulfilled[s] in your hearing."

22All spoke well of him and were amazed at the gracious words that came from his lips. "Isn't this Joseph's son?" they asked.[t]

23Jesus said to them, "Surely you will quote this proverb to me: 'Physician, heal yourself! Do here in your hometown[u] what we have heard that you did in Capernaum.' "[v]

24"I tell you the truth," he continued, "no prophet is accepted in his hometown.[w] **25**I assure you that there were many widows in Israel in Elijah's time, when the sky was shut for three and a half years and there was a severe famine throughout the land.[x] **26**Yet Elijah was not sent to any of them, but to a widow in Zarephath in the region of Sidon.[y] **27**And there were many in Israel with leprosy[t] in the time of Elisha the prophet, yet not one of them was cleansed—only Naaman the Syrian."[z]

28All the people in the synagogue were furious when they heard this. **29**They got up, drove him out of the town,[a] and took him to the brow of the hill on which the town was built, in order to throw him down the cliff. **30**But he walked right through the crowd and went on his way.[b]

Jesus Drives Out an Evil Spirit

4:31–37pp — Mk 1:21–28

31Then he went down to Capernaum,[c] a town in Galilee, and on the Sabbath began to teach the people. **32**They were amazed at his teaching,[d] because his message had authority.[e]

33In the synagogue there was a man possessed by a demon, an evil[u] spirit. He cried out at the top of his voice, **34**"Ha! What do you want with us,[f] Jesus of Nazareth?[g] Have you come to destroy us? I know who you are[h]—the Holy One of God!"[i]

35"Be quiet!" Jesus said sternly.[j] "Come out of him!" Then the demon threw the man down before them all and came out without injuring him.

36All the people were amazed[k] and said to each other, "What is this teaching? With authority[l] and power he gives orders to evil spirits and they come out!" **37**And the news about him spread throughout the surrounding area.[m]

Jesus Heals Many

4:38–41pp — Mt 8:14–17
4:38–43pp — Mk 1:29–38

38Jesus left the synagogue and went to the home of Simon. Now Simon's mother-in-law was suffering from a high fever, and they asked Jesus to help her. **39**So he bent over her and rebuked[n] the fever, and it left her. She got up at once and began to wait on them.

40When the sun was setting, the people brought to Jesus all who had various kinds of sickness, and laying his hands on each one,[o] he healed them.[p] **41**Moreover, demons came out of many people, shouting, "You are the Son of God!"[q] But he rebuked[r] them and would not allow them to speak,[s] because they knew he was the Christ.[v]

42At daybreak Jesus went out to a solitary place. The people were looking for him and when they came to where he was, they tried to keep him from leaving them. **43**But he said, "I must preach the good news of the kingdom of God[t] to the other towns also, because that is why I was sent." **44**And he kept on preaching in the synagogues of Judea.[w][u]

4:19 [q]Isa 61:1,2; Lev 25:10; Ps 102:20; 103:6; Isa 42:7; 49:8,9; 58:6
4:20 [r]ver 17; S Mt 26:55
4:21 [s]S Mt 1:22
4:22 [t]Mt 13:54, 55; Jn 6:42; 7:15
4:23 [u]ver 16; S Mt 2:23 [v]Mk 1:21-28; 2:1-12
4:24 [w]Mt 13:57; Jn 4:44
4:25 [x]1Ki 17:1; 18:1; Jas 5:17,18; Rev 11:6
4:26 [y]1Ki 17:8-16; S Mt 11:21
4:27 [z]2Ki 5:1-14
4:29 [a]Nu 15:35; Ac 7:58; Heb 13:12
4:30 [b]Jn 8:59; 10:39
4:31 [c]ver 23; S Mt 4:13
4:32 [d]S Mt 7:28 [e]ver 36; Mt 7:29
4:34 [f]S Mt 8:29 [g]S Mk 1:24 [h]Jas 2:19 [i]ver 41; S Mk 1:24
4:35 [j]ver 39,41; Mt 8:26; Lk 8:24
4:36 [k]S Mt 7:28 [l]ver 32; Mt 7:29; S Mt 10:1
4:37 [m]ver 14; S Mt 9:26
4:39 [n]ver 35,41
4:40 [o]S Mk 5:23 [p]S Mt 4:23
4:41 [q]S Mt 4:3 [r]S ver 35 [s]S Mt 8:4
4:43 [t]S Mt 3:2
4:44 [u]S Mt 4:23

[s] *19* Isaiah 61:1,2 [t] *27* The Greek word was used for various diseases affecting the skin—not necessarily leprosy. [u] *33* Greek *unclean*; also in verse 36 [v] *41* Or *Messiah* [w] *44* Or *the land of the Jews*; some manuscripts *Galilee*

4:33 AN EVIL SPIRIT. Luke records that one of Jesus' first acts after announcing his Messiahship was to enter into direct conflict with the demonic. (1) Jesus' foremost concern in his ministry was to destroy the devil's works (1Jn 3:8). There can be no realization of the kingdom of God without confronting the kingdom of Satan (see Mt 12:28; see article on THE KINGDOM OF GOD, p. 28). (2) One unmistakable sign that the kingdom has ceased to be manifested among God's people is the failure to confront directly the power of evil by setting sinners free from the bondage of sin and the demonic (see article on POWER OVER SATAN AND DEMONS, p. 80).

4:40 HEALED THEM. See Mt 4:23, note; see article on DIVINE HEALING, p. 20.

The Calling of the First Disciples

5:1–11pp — Mt 4:18–22; Mk 1:16–20; Jn 1:40–42

5 One day as Jesus was standing by the Lake of Gennesaret,[x] with the people crowding around him and listening to the word of God,[v] **2**he saw at the water's edge two boats, left there by the fishermen, who were washing their nets. **3**He got into one of the boats, the one belonging to Simon, and asked him to put out a little from shore. Then he sat down and taught the people from the boat.[w]

4When he had finished speaking, he said to Simon, "Put out into deep water, and let down[y] the nets for a catch."[x]

5Simon answered, "Master,[y] we've worked hard all night and haven't caught anything.[z] But because you say so, I will let down the nets."

6When they had done so, they caught such a large number of fish that their nets began to break.[a] **7**So they signaled their partners in the other boat to come and help them, and they came and filled both boats so full that they began to sink.

8When Simon Peter saw this, he fell at Jesus' knees and said, "Go away from me, Lord; I am a sinful man!"[b] **9**For he and all his companions were astonished at the catch of fish they had taken, **10**and so were James and John, the sons of Zebedee, Simon's partners.

Then Jesus said to Simon, "Don't be afraid;[c] from now on you will catch men." **11**So they pulled their boats up on shore, left everything and followed him.[d]

The Man With Leprosy

5:12–14pp — Mt 8:2–4; Mk 1:40–44

12While Jesus was in one of the towns, a man came along who was covered with leprosy.[z][e] When he saw Jesus, he fell with his face to the ground and begged him, "Lord, if you are willing, you can make me clean."

13Jesus reached out his hand and touched the man. "I am willing," he said. "Be clean!" And immediately the leprosy left him.

14Then Jesus ordered him, "Don't tell anyone,[f] but go, show yourself to the priest and offer the sacrifices that Moses commanded[g] for your cleansing, as a testimony to them."

15Yet the news about him spread all the more,[h] so that crowds of people came to hear him and to be healed of their sicknesses. **16**But Jesus often withdrew to lonely places and prayed.[i]

Jesus Heals a Paralytic

5:18–26pp — Mt 9:2–8; Mk 2:3–12

17One day as he was teaching, Pharisees and teachers of the law,[j] who had come from every village of Galilee and from Judea and Jerusalem, were sitting there. And the power of the Lord was present for him to heal the sick.[k] **18**Some men came carrying a paralytic on a mat and tried to take him into the house to lay him before Jesus. **19**When they could not find a way to do this because of the crowd, they went up on the roof and lowered him on his mat through the tiles into the middle of the crowd, right in front of Jesus.

20When Jesus saw their faith, he said, "Friend, your sins are forgiven."[l]

21The Pharisees and the teachers of the law began thinking to themselves, "Who is this fellow who speaks blasphemy? Who can forgive sins but God alone?"[m]

22Jesus knew what they were thinking

5:1 [v]S Mk 4:14; S Heb 4:12 **5:3** [w]Mt 13:2 **5:4** [x]Jn 21:6 **5:5** [y]Lk 8:24,45; 9:33,49; 17:13 [z]Jn 21:3 **5:6** [a]Jn 21:11 **5:8** [b]Ge 18:27; Job 42:6; Isa 6:5 **5:10** [c]S Mt 14:27 **5:11** [d]ver 28; S Mt 4:19 **5:12** [e]S Mt 8:2 **5:14** [f]S Mt 8:4 [g]Lev 14:2-32 **5:15** [h]S Mt 9:26 **5:16** [i]S Lk 3:21 **5:17** [j]Mt 15:1; Lk 2:46 [k]Mk 5:30; Lk 6:19 **5:20** [l]Lk 7:48,49 **5:21** [m]Isa 43:25

[x] *1* That is, Sea of Galilee [y] *4* The Greek verb is plural. [z] *12* The Greek word was used for various diseases affecting the skin—not necessarily leprosy.

5:10 YOU WILL CATCH MEN. See Mt 4:19, note.

5:16 PRAYERS OF JESUS. (1) Luke stresses more than the other Gospel writers the place of prayer in the life and work of Jesus. When the Holy Spirit descended upon Jesus at the Jordan, he was "praying" (3:21); at times he withdrew from the multitudes "and prayed" (5:16), and he "spent the night praying" before choosing the twelve disciples (6:12). He was "praying in private" before he asked his disciples an important question (9:18); at his transfiguration he climbed the mountain "to pray" (9:28); the actual transfiguration occurred while "he was praying" (9:29); and he "was praying" just before he taught the disciples the Lord's Prayer (11:1). In Gethsemane he "prayed more earnestly" (22:44); on the cross he prayed for others (23:34); and the last words he uttered before his death were a prayer (23:46). Luke also records that Jesus prayed after his resurrection (24:30). (2) In examining the life of Jesus in the other Gospels, we note that he prayed before extending the invitation, "Come to me, all you who are weary and burdened." (Mt 11:25–28); he prayed at Lazarus's tomb (Jn 11:41–42) and during the institution of the Lord's Supper (Jn 17). For more on prayer in Jesus' life, see Mt 14:23, note.

5:18 CARRYING A PARALYTIC. The friends of the paralyzed man had strong faith that Jesus could heal him, as seen by their determination to present him to Jesus. We too must believe that Christ can meet the needs of those we know, using every opportunity to bring them to Jesus. God's Spirit will open up such opportunities if we desire to lead others to Christ.

5:22 JESUS KNEW WHAT THEY WERE THINKING. Believers must remember that God knows and

and asked, "Why are you thinking these
things in your hearts? 23Which is easier:
to say, 'Your sins are forgiven,' or to say,
'Get up and walk'? 24But that you may
know that the Son of Man[n] has authority
on earth to forgive sins. . . ." He said to
the paralyzed man, "I tell you, get up, take
your mat and go home." 25Immediately he
stood up in front of them, took what he
had been lying on and went home praising
God. 26Everyone was amazed and gave
praise to God.[o] They were filled with awe
and said, "We have seen remarkable
things today."

The Calling of Levi

5:27–32pp — Mt 9:9–13; Mk 2:14–17

27After this, Jesus went out and saw a
tax collector by the name of Levi sitting at
his tax booth. "Follow me,"[p] Jesus said to
him, 28and Levi got up, left everything and
followed him.[q]

29Then Levi held a great banquet for
Jesus at his house, and a large crowd of
tax collectors[r] and others were eating
with them. 30But the Pharisees and the
teachers of the law who belonged to their
sect[s] complained to his disciples, "Why
do you eat and drink with tax collectors
and 'sinners'?"[t]

31Jesus answered them, "It is not the
healthy who need a doctor, but the sick.
32I have not come to call the righteous,
but sinners to repentance."[u]

5:24 [n] S Mt 8:20
5:26 [o] S Mt 9:8
5:27 [p] S Mt 4:19
5:28 [q] ver 11; S Mt 4:19
5:29 [r] Lk 15:1
5:30 [s] Ac 23:9 [t] S Mt 9:11
5:32 [u] S Jn 3:17

Jesus Questioned About Fasting

5:33–39pp — Mt 9:14–17; Mk 2:18–22

33They said to him, "John's disciples[v]
often fast and pray, and so do the disciples
of the Pharisees, but yours go on eating
and drinking."

34Jesus answered, "Can you make the
guests of the bridegroom[w] fast while he is
with them? 35But the time will come when
the bridegroom will be taken from them;[x]
in those days they will fast."

36He told them this parable: "No one
tears a patch from a new garment and
sews it on an old one. If he does, he will
have torn the new garment, and the patch
from the new will not match the old.
37And no one pours new wine into old
wineskins. If he does, the new wine will
burst the skins, the wine will run out and
the wineskins will be ruined. 38No, new
wine must be poured into new wineskins.
39And no one after drinking old wine
wants the new, for he says, 'The old is
better.' "

Lord of the Sabbath

6:1–11pp — Mt 12:1–14; Mk 2:23–3:6

6 One Sabbath Jesus was going through
the grainfields, and his disciples began to pick some heads of grain, rub them
in their hands and eat the kernels.[y]
2Some of the Pharisees asked, "Why are
you doing what is unlawful on the Sabbath?"[z]

5:33 [v] Lk 7:18; Jn 1:35; 3:25,26
5:34 [w] Jn 3:29
5:35 [x] Lk 9:22; 17:22; Jn 16:5-7
6:1 [y] Dt 23:25
6:2 [z] S Mt 12:2

---

evaluates their every thought, desire and imagination (see Ps 139; Mt 17:25; Jn 1:48; 2:25; 21:17; Heb 4:13).

5:24 SON OF MAN. The "Son of Man" is Jesus' favorite expression by which he refers to himself; Da 7:13 seems to be the background for Jesus' use of the expression. Daniel used the title to describe a person he saw in a vision, one "like a son of man" coming with the clouds of heaven, who is given an everlasting kingdom. Thus Jesus expresses the truth that he is the predicted Messiah, sent by God. Jesus uses the term (1) as a substitute for "I" (Mt 11:19); (2) when making important claims (Mt 20:28; Mk 10:45); (3) when foretelling his death on the cross (9:44; Mt 17:22; Mk 8:31); (4) when speaking about his resurrection (Mt 17:9); (5) when referring to his glorious return to earth (Mt 24:27; Mk 13:26; 14:62); (6) when speaking of his role in judgment (Mt 13:41).

5:30 EAT AND DRINK WITH . . . 'SINNERS'. See Mt 9:11, note.

5:35 IN THOSE DAYS THEY WILL FAST. See Mt 9:15, note.

5:37 NEW WINE INTO OLD WINESKINS. See Mt 9:17, notes.

5:39 'THE OLD IS BETTER'. This is probably an ironic comment about the Jews who rejected the "new wine" of the gospel and held that the "old wine" (first-century Judaism) was good enough. Jesus suggests here that those who are accustomed to drinking fermented wine acquire a desire for it and do not want unfermented wine. He recognizes the habit-forming, addictive effect of alcoholic beverages. It is not Jesus but the one drinking the old wine who thinks "the old is better."

(1) We may not interpret this verse to state that old wine (i.e., Judaism) is better than new wine (i.e., Christ's gospel), for this would invert the parable's meaning. What Jesus is stating is that the Pharisees and their followers won't even recognize the merits of the new; they feel that "the old" is good enough. The Pharisees prefer the rabbinical interpretation of the law to the pure, new, sweet wine of the gospel of Christ.

(2) The Pharisees have no desire for the best wine. They refuse to accept the fresh revelation of God and instead seek only what humans have altered (i.e., fermented). Yet for those who receive Jesus, the fresh new juice of the grape (gospel) is preferable to old fermented wine (Pharisaic religion).

6:1 SABBATH. See Mt 12:1, note on Sabbath.

6:2–10 JESUS AND THE SABBATH. Though the Pharisees accuse Jesus of breaking the Sabbath, in reality he broke only their extreme interpretation of

3Jesus answered them, "Have you never
read what David did when he and his companions were hungry?[a] 4He entered the
house of God, and taking the consecrated
bread, he ate what is lawful only for
priests to eat.[b] And he also gave some to
his companions." 5Then Jesus said to
them, "The Son of Man[c] is Lord of the
Sabbath."

6On another Sabbath[d] he went into the
synagogue and was teaching, and a man
was there whose right hand was shriveled. 7The Pharisees and the teachers of
the law were looking for a reason to accuse Jesus, so they watched him closely[e]
to see if he would heal on the Sabbath.[f]
8But Jesus knew what they were thinking[g] and said to the man with the shriveled hand, "Get up and stand in front of
everyone." So he got up and stood there.

9Then Jesus said to them, "I ask you,
which is lawful on the Sabbath: to do good
or to do evil, to save life or to destroy it?"

10He looked around at them all, and
then said to the man, "Stretch out your
hand." He did so, and his hand was completely restored. 11But they were furious[h]
and began to discuss with one another
what they might do to Jesus.

The Twelve Apostles

6:13–16pp — Mt 10:2–4; Mk 3:16–19; Ac 1:13

12One of those days Jesus went out to
a mountainside to pray, and spent the
night praying to God.[i] 13When morning
came, he called his disciples to him and
chose twelve of them, whom he also designated apostles:[j] 14Simon (whom he
named Peter), his brother Andrew, James,
John, Philip, Bartholomew, 15Matthew,[k]
Thomas, James son of Alphaeus, Simon
who was called the Zealot, 16Judas son of
James, and Judas Iscariot, who became a
traitor.

Blessings and Woes

6:20–23pp — Mt 5:3–12

17He went down with them and stood
on a level place. A large crowd of his disciples was there and a great number of people from all over Judea, from Jerusalem,
and from the coast of Tyre and Sidon,[l]
18who had come to hear him and to be
healed of their diseases. Those troubled
by evil[a] spirits were cured, 19and the people all tried to touch him,[m] because power
was coming from him and healing them
all.[n]
Lk 9:1-6

20Looking at his disciples, he said:

"Blessed are you who are poor,
for yours is the kingdom of God.[o]
21Blessed are you who hunger now,
for you will be satisfied.[p]
Blessed are you who weep now,
for you will laugh.[q]
22Blessed are you when men hate you,
when they exclude you[r] and insult
you[s]
and reject your name as evil,
because of the Son of Man.[t]

23"Rejoice in that day and leap for joy,[u]

6:3 [a] 1Sa 21:6
6:4 [b] Lev 24:5,9
6:5 [c] S Mt 8:20
6:6 [d] ver 1
6:7 [e] S Mt 12:10 [f] S Mt 12:2
6:8 [g] S Mt 9:4
6:11 [h] Jn 5:18
6:12 [i] S Lk 3:21
6:13 [j] S Mk 6:30
6:15 [k] Mt 9:9
6:17 [l] Mt 4:25; S Mt 11:21; Mk 3:7,8
6:19 [m] S Mt 9:20 [n] Mk 5:30; Lk 5:17
6:20 [o] S Mt 25:34
6:21 [p] Isa 55:1,2; Mt 5:6 [q] Isa 61:2, 3; Mt 5:4; Rev 7:17
6:22 [r] Jn 9:22; 16:2 [s] Isa 51:7 [t] S Jn 15:21
6:23 [u] S Mt 5:12

[a] 18 Greek *unclean*

it. Jesus states that Sabbath observance must not degenerate into a ritual to be kept at the cost of the essential needs of humans. Christ is the Lord of the Sabbath (v. 5); the Sabbath should be used to come away from our daily work and pursuit of material gain and turn to God as a pledge that he is Lord over all of life. Furthermore, Jesus' words and actions (vv. 6–10) teach us that the Lord's Day should be an opportunity to help those in need, spiritually as well as physically.

6:12 SPENT THE NIGHT PRAYING. Again and again Jesus sought to be alone with his Father in prayer, especially at times of momentous decisions. (1) His entire night of earnest prayer produced tremendous results (see Jas 5:16, note). Following this night of prayer, Jesus chose the twelve to become his apostles (vv. 13–16), healed many who were sick (vv. 17–19) and preached his most quoted sermon (vv. 20–49). (2) If Jesus, the perfect Son of God, spent a whole night in prayer to the Father in order to make an important decision, how much more do we, with all our weaknesses and failings, need to spend nights in prayer and in intimate communion with our heavenly Father.

6:17 SERMON ON THE PLAIN. See Mt 5–7, note on the Sermon on the Mount.

6:20 BLESSED. See Mt 5:3, note.

6:20 YOU WHO ARE POOR. See article on RICHES AND POVERTY, p. 152, for comments on this verse.

6:21 YOU WHO WEEP. See Mt 5:4, note.

6:22 WHEN MEN HATE YOU. Followers of Jesus should "rejoice" and "leap for joy" (v. 23) when, because of faithfulness to Christ and his godly standards, they are criticized and scorned. Persecution because of righteousness is proof that believers are in true fellowship with the Lord, since Jesus was also ill-treated and hated by the world (Jn 15:18–21; see Mt 5:10, note).

6:23 HOW THEIR FATHERS TREATED THE PROPHETS. The OT people of Israel rejected the prophets and their messages many times (1Ki 19:10; Mt 5:12; 23:31,37; Ac 7:51–52). (1) Churches today should bear in mind that God sends them prophets (1Co 12:28; Eph 4:11) for the purpose of calling both leaders and people to lives of righteousness, faithfulness to all Scripture, and separation from the world (see Rev 2–3).

(2) Churches can do the same thing as Israel of old

because great is your reward in heaven.
For that is how their fathers treated the
prophets.[v]

24"But woe to you who are rich,[w]
for you have already received your
comfort.[x]
25Woe to you who are well fed now,
for you will go hungry.[y]
Woe to you who laugh now,
for you will mourn and weep.[z]
26Woe to you when all men speak well
of you,
for that is how their fathers treated
the false prophets.[a]

Love for Enemies

6:29,30pp — Mt 5:39–42

27"But I tell you who hear me: Love
your enemies, do good to those who hate
you,[b] 28bless those who curse you, pray
for those who mistreat you.[c] 29If someone
strikes you on one cheek, turn to him the
other also. If someone takes your cloak,
do not stop him from taking your tunic.
30Give to everyone who asks you, and if
anyone takes what belongs to you, do not
demand it back.[d] 31Do to others as you
would have them do to you.[e]
32"If you love those who love you, what
credit is that to you?[f] Even 'sinners' love
those who love them. 33And if you do good
to those who are good to you, what credit

6:23 [v]S Mt 5:12
6:24 [w]Jas 5:1
[x]Lk 16:25
6:25 [y]Isa 65:13
[z]Pr 14:13
6:26 [a]S Mt 7:15
6:27 [b]ver 35;
Mt 5:44; Ro 12:20
6:28 [c]S Mt 5:44
6:30 [d]Dt 15:7,8,
10; Pr 21:26
6:31 [e]Mt 7:12
6:32 [f]Mt 5:46

6:34 [g]Mt 5:42
6:35 [h]ver 27
[i]S Ro 8:14
[j]S Mk 5:7
6:36 [k]Jas 2:13
[l]Mt 5:48; 6:1;
Lk 11:2; 12:32;
Ro 8:15; Eph 4:6;
1Pe 1:17; 1Jn 1:3;
3:1
6:37 [m]S Mt 7:1
[n]Mt 6:14
6:38 [o]Ps 79:12;
Isa 65:6,7
[p]S Mt 7:2
6:39 [q]Mt 15:14
6:40 [r]S Jn 13:16

is that to you? Even 'sinners' do that.
34And if you lend to those from whom you
expect repayment, what credit is that to
you?[g] Even 'sinners' lend to 'sinners,' expecting to be repaid in full. 35But love
your enemies, do good to them,[h] and lend
to them without expecting to get anything
back. Then your reward will be great, and
you will be sons[i] of the Most High,[j] because he is kind to the ungrateful and
wicked. 36Be merciful,[k] just as your Father[l] is merciful.

Judging Others

6:37–42pp — Mt 7:1–5

37"Do not judge, and you will not be
judged.[m] Do not condemn, and you will
not be condemned. Forgive, and you will
be forgiven.[n] 38Give, and it will be given
to you. A good measure, pressed down,
shaken together and running over, will be
poured into your lap.[o] For with the measure you use, it will be measured to you."[p]
39He also told them this parable: "Can
a blind man lead a blind man? Will they
not both fall into a pit?[q] 40A student is not
above his teacher, but everyone who is
fully trained will be like his teacher.[r]
41"Why do you look at the speck of sawdust in your brother's eye and pay no attention to the plank in your own eye?
42How can you say to your brother,

---

by rejecting the words of their prophets and losing the blessing and salvation of God. On the other hand, they can accept God's message, draw back from sin, deepen their loyalty to God and his Word, and continue as God's people. Those churches that reject God's true prophets will ultimately be rejected by God himself (13:34–35; Rev 2–3).

(3) Satan will deliberately send false prophets into the churches (Mt 13:24–30,36–43), prophets who reject the absolute authority of God's Word, claim to have authority equal to God's Word, and maintain that their revelation is infallible and their words immune from judgment by the churches (see article on FALSE TEACHERS, p. 98). These false prophets must be firmly rejected.

6:24 WOE TO YOU WHO ARE RICH. Jesus is speaking of those who center their lives, purpose, happiness or goals primarily in material things or in the pursuit of great wealth (see article on RICHES AND POVERTY, p. 152).

6:26 WOE TO YOU WHEN ALL MEN SPEAK WELL. When a large portion of the unbelieving world speaks well of a believer or a professed minister of God, it may be evidence that he or she is not a true follower of Christ, since false prophets are often popular with those who are not loyal to Christ. Prophets or ministers who serve God will have the same thing happen to them as happened to Christ; their lives and message will come into collision with the sins of the ungodly and will consequently be rejected by those unbelievers.

6:27 LOVE YOUR ENEMIES. In vv. 27–42, Jesus tells us how we are to live with other persons. As members of the new covenant, we are obligated to follow the demands set forth here. (1) Loving our enemies does not mean an emotional love, such as liking our enemies, but rather a genuine concern for their good and for their eternal salvation. Since we know the terrible fate awaiting those who are hostile to God and his people, we must pray for them and attempt, by repaying good for evil, to bring them to Christ and the faith of the gospel (cf. Pr 20:22; 24:29; Mt 5:39–45; Ro 12:17; 1Th 5:15; 1Pe 3:9).

(2) Loving our enemies does not mean standing by idly while evildoers continue their wicked deeds. When it is necessary for God's honor, the good or safety of others, or the ultimate good of the wicked, severe action must be taken to stop evil (see Mk 11:15; Jn 2:13–17).

6:29 DO NOT STOP HIM FROM TAKING YOUR TUNIC. See Mt 5:39, note.

6:37 DO NOT JUDGE. See Mt 7:1, note.

6:38 GIVE. In conformity with the principle of love, we must give to those in need. God himself will measure our giving and in return will give to us. The measure of blessing and reward we receive will be in proportion to our concern for and help given to others (see 2Co 9:6).

'Brother, let me take the speck out of your
eye,' when you yourself fail to see the
plank in your own eye? You hypocrite,
first take the plank out of your eye, and
then you will see clearly to remove the
speck from your brother's eye.

A Tree and Its Fruit

6:43,44pp — Mt 7:16,18,20

43"No good tree bears bad fruit, nor
does a bad tree bear good fruit. 44Each
tree is recognized by its own fruit.[s] People do not pick figs from thornbushes, or
Jn 15:1-8 grapes from briers. 45The good man
brings good things out of the good stored
up in his heart, and the evil man brings
evil things out of the evil stored up in his
heart. For out of the overflow of his heart
his mouth speaks.[t]

The Wise and Foolish Builders

6:47–49pp — Mt 7:24–27

46"Why do you call me, 'Lord, Lord,'[u]
and do not do what I say?[v] 47I will show
you what he is like who comes to me and
hears my words and puts them into practice.[w] 48He is like a man building a house,
who dug down deep and laid the foundation on rock. When a flood came, the torrent struck that house but could not
shake it, because it was well built. 49But
the one who hears my words and does not
put them into practice is like a man who
built a house on the ground without a
foundation. The moment the torrent
struck that house, it collapsed and its destruction was complete."

The Faith of the Centurion

7:1–10pp — Mt 8:5–13

7 When Jesus had finished saying all
this[x] in the hearing of the people, he
entered Capernaum. 2There a centurion's
servant, whom his master valued highly,
was sick and about to die. 3The centurion
heard of Jesus and sent some elders of the
Jews to him, asking him to come and heal
his servant. 4When they came to Jesus,
they pleaded earnestly with him, "This
man deserves to have you do this, 5be-
cause he loves our nation and has built
our synagogue." 6So Jesus went with
them.

He was not far from the house when the
centurion sent friends to say to him:
"Lord, don't trouble yourself, for I do not
deserve to have you come under my roof.
7That is why I did not even consider myself worthy to come to you. But say the
word, and my servant will be healed.[y]
8For I myself am a man under authority,
with soldiers under me. I tell this one,
'Go,' and he goes; and that one, 'Come,'
and he comes. I say to my servant, 'Do
this,' and he does it."

9When Jesus heard this, he was amazed
at him, and turning to the crowd following
him, he said, "I tell you, I have not found
such great faith even in Israel." 10Then
the men who had been sent returned to
the house and found the servant well.

Jesus Raises a Widow's Son

7:11–16Ref — 1Ki 17:17–24; 2Ki 4:32–37; Mk 5:21–24,35–43; Jn 11:1–44

11Soon afterward, Jesus went to a town
called Nain, and his disciples and a large
crowd went along with him. 12As he approached the town gate, a dead person
was being carried out—the only son of his
mother, and she was a widow. And a large
crowd from the town was with her.
13When the Lord[z] saw her, his heart went
out to her and he said, "Don't cry."

14Then he went up and touched the cof-
fin, and those carrying it stood still. He
said, "Young man, I say to you, get up!"[a]
15The dead man sat up and began to talk,
and Jesus gave him back to his mother.
16They were all filled with awe[b] and

6:44 [s]Mt 12:33
6:45 [t]Pr 4:23; Mt 12:34,35; Mk 7:20
6:46 [u]S Jn 13:13 [v]Mal 1:6; Mt 7:21
6:47 [w]Lk 8:21; 11:28; Jas 1:22-25
7:1 [x]Mt 7:28
7:7 [y]Ps 107:20
7:13 [z]ver 19; Lk 10:1; 13:15; 17:5; 22:61; 24:34; Jn 11:2
7:14 [a]Mt 9:25; Mk 1:31; Lk 8:54; Jn 11:43; Ac 9:40
7:16 [b]Lk 1:65

6:45 HIS HEART. The heart, the center of our being, determines our outward behavior and must be changed or converted (see Mk 7:20–23, note; see article on REGENERATION, p. 178). Without that inward change, no one can do God's will (cf. Jer 24:7; 31:33; 32:39; Eze 36:23,27; Mt 7:16–20; 12:33–35; 15:18–19; 21:43; Lk 1:17; Ro 6:17).

6:46 DO NOT DO WHAT I SAY. See Mt 7:21, note.

7:9 SUCH GREAT FAITH. See Mt 8:10, note.

7:13 HIS HEART WENT OUT TO HER. Jesus' compassion for this widow shows that God has a special love and care for widows or for any person who is left alone in the world. Scripture teaches the following: (1) God is a Father to the fatherless and a defender of widows (Ps 68:5). They are under his special care and protection (Ex 22:22–23; Dt 10:18; Ps 146:9; Pr 15:25). (2) By means of the tithe and the abundance of his people, God provides for the fatherless and the widows (Dt 14:28–29; 24:19–21; 26:12–13). (3) He blesses those who help and honor them (Isa 1:17,19; Jer 7:6–7; 22:3–4). (4) He is against those who take advantage of or hurt widows or ophans (Ex 22:22–24; Dt 24:17; 27:19; Job 24:3; Ps 94:6,16; Zec 7:10). (5) Widows are recipients of God's tender love and compassion (vv. 11–17; 18:2–8; 21:2–4; Mk 12:42–43). (6) The early church made it a priority to care for widows (Ac 6:1–6). (7) One aspect of true faith is to look after orphans and widows in their distress (Jas 1:27; cf. 1Ti 5:3–8).

praised God.[c] "A great prophet[d] has appeared among us," they said. "God has
come to help his people."[e] 17This news
about Jesus spread throughout Judea[b]
and the surrounding country.[f]

Jesus and John the Baptist

7:18–35pp — Mt 11:2–19

18John's[g] disciples[h] told him about all
these things. Calling two of them, 19he
sent them to the Lord to ask, "Are you the
one who was to come, or should we expect
someone else?"

20When the men came to Jesus, they
said, "John the Baptist sent us to you to
ask, 'Are you the one who was to come, or
should we expect someone else?' "

21At that very time Jesus cured many
who had diseases, sicknesses[i] and evil
spirits, and gave sight to many who were
blind. 22So he replied to the messengers,
"Go back and report to John what you have
seen and heard: The blind receive sight,
the lame walk, those who have leprosy[c]
are cured, the deaf hear, the dead are
raised, and the good news is preached to
the poor.[j] 23Blessed is the man who does
not fall away on account of me."

24After John's messengers left, Jesus
began to speak to the crowd about John:
"What did you go out into the desert to
see? A reed swayed by the wind? 25If not,
what did you go out to see? A man dressed
in fine clothes? No, those who wear expensive clothes and indulge in luxury are in
palaces. 26But what did you go out to see?
A prophet?[k] Yes, I tell you, and more than
a prophet. 27This is the one about whom
it is written:

" 'I will send my messenger ahead of
you,
who will prepare your way before
you.'[d][l]

28I tell you, among those born of women
there is no one greater than John; yet the
one who is least in the kingdom of God[m]
is greater than he."

29(All the people, even the tax collectors, when they heard Jesus' words, acknowledged that God's way was right, because they had been baptized by John.[n]
30But the Pharisees and experts in the
law[o] rejected God's purpose for themselves, because they had not been baptized by John.)

31"To what, then, can I compare the
people of this generation? What are they
like? 32They are like children sitting in
the marketplace and calling out to each
other:

" 'We played the flute for you,
and you did not dance;
we sang a dirge,
and you did not cry.'

33For John the Baptist came neither eating bread nor drinking wine,[p] and you
say, 'He has a demon.' 34The Son of Man
came eating and drinking, and you say,
'Here is a glutton and a drunkard, a friend
of tax collectors and "sinners." '[q] 35But
wisdom is proved right by all her children."

Jesus Anointed by a Sinful Woman

7:37–39Ref — Mt 26:6–13; Mk 14:3–9; Jn 12:1–8
7:41,42Ref — Mt 18:23–34

36Now one of the Pharisees invited
Jesus to have dinner with him, so he went
to the Pharisee's house and reclined at
the table. 37When a woman who had lived
a sinful life in that town learned that Jesus
was eating at the Pharisee's house, she
brought an alabaster jar of perfume, 38and

7:16 [c]S Mt 9:8 [d]ver 39; S Mt 21:11 [e]Lk 1:68 **7:17** [f]S Mt 9:26 **7:18** [g]S Mt 3:1 [h]S Lk 5:33 **7:21** [i]S Mt 4:23 **7:22** [j]Isa 29:18, 19; 35:5,6; 61:1,2; Lk 4:18 **7:26** [k]S Mt 11:9 **7:27** [l]Mal 3:1; Mt 11:10; Mk 1:2 **7:28** [m]S Mt 3:2 **7:29** [n]Mt 21:32; Mk 1:5; Lk 3:12 **7:30** [o]S Mt 22:35 **7:33** [p]Lk 1:15 **7:34** [q]Lk 5:29,30; 15:1,2

[b] *17* Or *the land of the Jews* [c] *22* The Greek word was used for various diseases affecting the skin—not necessarily leprosy. [d] *27* Mal. 3:1

7:24 A REED SWAYED. See Mt 11:7, note.
7:28 JOHN. See Mt 11:11, note.
7:33 WINE. For an examination of Biblical words for wine and for its use in NT times, see 1:15, note; see articles on WINE IN NEW TESTAMENT TIMES (1) and (2), p. 126 and p. 174.
7:34 GLUTTON AND A DRUNKARD. Wine (Gk *oinos*) in the NT referred to all kinds of wine, both unfermented and fermented (see article on WINE IN NEW TESTAMENT TIMES (1), p. 126). Jesus' statement indicates that he drank some types of wine, whereas John did not. However, it cannot be determined from this passage what types of wine he drank, for the allegation of the Pharisees concerning Jesus' character is clearly false. They accuse Jesus of being a glutton and a drunkard, but these were characteristically slanderous lies designed to destroy his influence as a teacher of righteousness (see Mt 12:24; Jn 7:20; 8:48). Jesus himself implies that those who "eat and drink with drunkards" are wicked servants who are not rightly preparing for the return of their Master (Mt 24:48–49). Therefore, it can in no way be proven from this passage that Jesus drank intoxicating wine. For a discussion on the kind of wine Jesus may have used, see articles on WINE IN NEW TESTAMENT TIMES (1) and (2), p. 126 and p. 174; cf. Pr 23:31.
7:38 WEEPING. Because of her love for Jesus, this woman wets his feet with her tears. Weeping can be an expression of sorrow and grief or of grateful love for Christ. (1) By weeping in prayer and faith, believers express to God what is in their hearts; such tears are valued as an offering and service to him (vv.

as she stood behind him at his feet weeping, she began to wet his feet with
her tears. Then she wiped them with her
hair, kissed them and poured perfume on
them.
39When the Pharisee who had invited
him saw this, he said to himself, "If this
man were a prophet,[r] he would know who
is touching him and what kind of woman
she is—that she is a sinner."
40Jesus answered him, "Simon, I have
something to tell you."
"Tell me, teacher," he said.
41"Two men owed money to a certain
moneylender. One owed him five hundred
denarii,[e] and the other fifty. **42**Neither of
them had the money to pay him back, so
he canceled the debts of both. Now which
of them will love him more?"
43Simon replied, "I suppose the one
who had the bigger debt canceled."
"You have judged correctly," Jesus
said.
44Then he turned toward the woman
and said to Simon, "Do you see this woman? I came into your house. You did not
give me any water for my feet,[s] but she
wet my feet with her tears and wiped them
with her hair. **45**You did not give me a
kiss,[t] but this woman, from the time I
entered, has not stopped kissing my
feet. **46**You did not put oil on my head,[u]
but she has poured perfume on my feet.
47Therefore, I tell you, her many sins
have been forgiven—for she loved much.
But he who has been forgiven little
loves little."
48Then Jesus said to her, "Your sins are
forgiven."[v]
49The other guests began to say among
themselves, "Who is this who even forgives sins?"
Lk 8:48 **50**Jesus said to the woman, "Your faith
has saved you;[w] go in peace."[x]

7:39 [r] ver 16; S Mt 21:11
7:44 [s] Ge 18:4; 19:2; 43:24; Jdg 19:21; Jn 13:4-14; 1Ti 5:10
7:45 [t] Lk 22:47, 48; S Ro 16:16
7:46 [u] Ps 23:5; Ecc 9:8
7:48 [v] Mt 9:2
7:50 [w] S Mt 9:22 [x] S Ac 15:33

The Parable of the Sower

8:4–15pp — Mt 13:2–23; Mk 4:1–20

8 After this, Jesus traveled about from
one town and village to another, proclaiming the good news of the kingdom of
God.[y] The Twelve were with him, **2**and
also some women who had been cured of
evil spirits and diseases: Mary (called
Magdalene)[z] from whom seven demons
had come out; **3**Joanna the wife of Cuza,
the manager of Herod's[a] household; Su-
sanna; and many others. These women
were helping to support them out of their
own means.
4While a large crowd was gathering and
people were coming to Jesus from town
after town, he told this parable: **5**"A farmer went out to sow his seed. As he was
scattering the seed, some fell along the
path; it was trampled on, and the birds of
the air ate it up. **6**Some fell on rock, and
when it came up, the plants withered because they had no moisture. **7**Other seed
fell among thorns, which grew up with it
and choked the plants. **8**Still other seed
fell on good soil. It came up and yielded
a crop, a hundred times more than was
sown."
When he said this, he called out, "He
who has ears to hear, let him hear."[b]
9His disciples asked him what this parable meant. **10**He said, "The knowledge of
the secrets of the kingdom of God has
been given to you,[c] but to others I speak
in parables, so that,

" 'though seeing, they may not see;
though hearing, they may not
understand.'[f][d]

11"This is the meaning of the parable:
The seed is the word of God.[e] **12**Those

8:1 [y] S Mt 4:23
8:2 [z] Mt 27:55,56
8:3 [a] S Mt 14:1
8:8 [b] S Mt 11:15
8:10 [c] S Mt 13:11 [d] Isa 6:9; S Mt 13:13,14
8:11 [e] S Heb 4:12

e *41* A denarius was a coin worth about a day's wages. f *10* Isaiah 6:9

37–50; Ps 126:5–6; Jer 9:1; 14:17; 31:15–16; Ac 20:19,31; 2Co 2:4). In this manner believers also participate in the sufferings of Christ (2Co 1:5; Php 3:10; 1Pe 4:13).

(2) Christ himself wept while praying and was heard (Heb 5:7); likewise, the apostle Paul served the Lord with many tears (Ac 20:19; 2Co 2:4). Even today those who weep in Christ are considered blessed (6:21). In Christ's future kingdom God will wipe away all tears from the eyes of his people (Rev 7:17; 21:4; concerning prayer and tears, read 2Ki 20:5; Ps 39:12; 56:8).

7:47 SHE LOVED MUCH. Real love for and devotion to Jesus must come from a deep awareness of the sinfulness of our past condition, his love for us revealed when he gave himself on the cross, and the inner assurance that we are now forgiven and cared for. Faith that is not based on these foundations will not endure.

8:3 HELPING TO SUPPORT THEM. These women who had received healing and special care from Jesus honored him by faithfully contributing to the support of Jesus and his disciples. Their service and devotion continue to be an example for every woman who believes in him. To the extent that you minister to him, the words of Mt 25:34–40 apply to you.

8:4 PARABLE. See Mt 13:3, note.

8:5 PARABLE OF THE SOWER. See Mk 4:3, note.

8:12 TAKES AWAY THE WORD. See Mk 4:15, note on halfway conversions.

WINE IN NEW TESTAMENT TIMES (1)

Lk 7:33–34 "For John the Baptist came neither eating bread nor drinking wine, and you say, 'He has a demon.' The Son of Man came eating and drinking, and you say, 'Here is a glutton and a drunkard, a friend of tax collectors and "sinners." ' "

WINE: FERMENTED OR UNFERMENTED? The following is an examination of the most common Biblical word for wine. The Greek word for "wine" in Lk 7:33 is *oinos*. *Oinos* can refer to two distinctly different types of juice of the grape: (1) unfermented juice, and (2) fermented or intoxicating wine. This is supported by the following data.

(1) The Greek word *oinos* was used by secular and religious authors in pre-Christian and early church times to refer to fresh grape juice (see Aristotle, *Metereologica*, 387.b.9–13). (a) Anacreon (c. 500 B.C.) writes, "Squeeze the grape, let out the wine [*oinos*]" (Ode 5). (b) Nicander (second century B.C.) writes of squeezing grapes and refers to the produced juice as *oinos* (*Georgica*, fragment 86). (c) Papias (A.D. 60–130), an early church father, mentions that when grapes are crushed they yield "jars of wine [*oinos*]" (cited by Irenaeus, *Against Heresies*, 5.33.3–4). (d) A Greek papyrus letter (P. Oxy. 729; A.D. 137) speaks of "fresh wine [*oinos*] from the treading vat" (see Moulton and Milligan, *The Vocabulary of the Greek Testament*, p. 10). (e) Athenaeus (A.D. 200) speaks of a "sweet wine [*oinos*]" that "does not make the head heavy" (Athenaeus, *Banquet*, 1.54). In another place, he writes of a man gathering grapes who "went about, and took wine [*oinos*] from the field" (1.54). For more detailed discussions on the use of *oinos* by ancient writers, see Robert P. Teachout, "The Use of 'Wine' in the Old Testament" (Th.D. dissertation, Dallas Theological Seminary, 1979).

(2) Because of the use of *oinos* in the Septuagint (the Greek version of the Hebrew OT, translated by the best Hebrew and Greek scholars in 250–131 B.C.), the authors and readers of the NT understood that this word could refer to either fermented or unfermented juice of the grape. As the OT Scriptures used by the apostles who wrote the NT, the Septuagint would have influenced their understanding and use of words for wine; it thus provides an authoritative reference for NT word studies. In the Septuagint the Greek word *oinos* was used to translate two Hebrew words.

(a) *Oinos* was normally used to translate *yayin*. *Yayin* is a generic OT term used to indicate fermented wine and unfermented wine. On the one hand, *yayin* is applied to all kinds of fermented grape juice (see Ge 9:20–21; 19:32–33; 1Sa 25:36–37; Pr 23:30–31). On the other hand, *yayin* is also used for the sweet, unfermented juice of the grape (Isa 16:10; Jer 40:10,12; 48:32–33; La 2:12); this fact is supported by *Encyclopaedia Judaica* (1971) and the Babylonian Talmud, which speaks of "the wine [*yayin*] from the press" (*Baba Bathra*, 97a).

(b) *Oinos* was also used to translate 36 of the 38 occurrences of *tirosh* (a word meaning "new wine" or "harvest wine"). *Tirosh* can refer to the unfermented fruit of the vine, grapes in a cluster, or new, sweet and unfermented grape juice. Brown, Driver, Briggs (*A Hebrew and English Lexicon of the Old Testament*) state that *tirosh* means "must, fresh or new wine," and *The Jewish Encyclopedia* of 1901 (XII.533) states that "'*tirosh*' includes all kinds of sweet juices and must, and does not include fermented wine." Thus, the NT word *oinos* may refer to either fermented or unfermented grape juice, and only the context or purpose can determine which it is.

(3) An examination of NT passages also reveals that *oinos* may mean either fermented or unfermented wine. In Eph 5:18 the command, "do not get drunk on wine [*oinos*]," refers to alcoholic wine. On the other hand, in Rev 19:15 Christ is pictured as treading the winepress. The Greek text reads: "He treads the winepress of the wine [*oinos*] "; the *oinos* that comes from the winepress would be grape juice. This verse may be compared to Jer 48:32–33, which speaks of wine (*yayin*) coming from the winepress (cf. Isa 16:10). In Rev 6:6 *oinos* refers to

grapes on the vine as a crop not to be destroyed. Thus, for believers in NT times, "wine" (*oinos*) was a general word that could be used for two distinctly different grape beverages—fermented and unfermented wine.

(4) Finally, ancient Roman writers have explained in detail various processes used in dealing with freshly squeezed grape juice, especially ways to preserve it from fermenting. (a) Columella (*On Agriculture*, 12.29), knowing that grape juice would not ferment if kept cool (under 50 degrees) and oxygen free, writes as follows: "That your grape juice may be always as sweet as when it is new, thus proceed. After you apply the press to the grapes, take the newest must [i.e., fresh juice], put it in a new container (*amphora*), bung it up, and cover it up very carefully with pitch lest any water should enter; then sink it in a cistern or pond of cold water and allow no part of the amphora to remain above the surface. After forty days take it out. It will remain sweet for a year" (see also Columella, *Agriculture and Trees*, and Cato, *On Agriculture*). The Roman writer Pliny (first century A.D.) writes: "as soon as the must [grape juice] is taken from the vat and put into casks, they plunge the casks in water till midwinter passes and regular cold weather sets in" (Pliny, *Natural History*, 14.11.83). This method would have worked well in the land of Israel (see Dt 8:7; 11:11–12; Ps 65:9–13). (b) Another method to keep grapes from fermenting was to boil them into a syrup (for more details, see article on WINE IN NEW TESTAMENT TIMES (2), p. 174). Ancient historians actually referred to this product as wine (*oinos*). Canon Farrar (*Smith's Bible Dictionary*, p. 747) states that "the wines of antiquity were more like syrups; many of them were not intoxicant." Also, *The New Bible Dictionary* (p. 1332) notes that "there were means of keeping wine sweet all year round."

USE OF WINE IN THE LORD'S SUPPER. Did Jesus use fermented or unfermented grape drink when he instituted the Lord's Supper (Mt 26:26–29; Mk 14:22–25; Lk 22:17–20; 1Co 11:23–26)? The following data support the conclusion that Jesus and his disciples drank unfermented grape juice.

(1) Neither Luke nor any other Biblical writer uses the word "wine" (Gk *oinos*) with regard to the Lord's Supper. The first three Gospel writers use "fruit of the vine" (Mt 26:29; Mk 14:25; Lk 22:18). Unfermented wine is the only truly natural "fruit of the vine," containing approximately 20 percent sugar and no alcohol. Fermentation destroys much of the sugar and alters what the vine produced. Fermented wine is not the product of the vine.

(2) The Lord's Supper was instituted when Jesus and his disciples were eating the Passover. The Passover law in Ex 12:14–20 prohibited, during Passover week, the presence and use of *seor* (Ex 12:15), a word referring to yeast or any agent of fermentation. *Seor* in the ancient world was often obtained from the thick scum on top of fermenting wine. Furthermore, all *hametz* (i.e., anything that contained any type of fermentation) was forbidden (Ex 12:19; 13:7). God had given these laws because fermentation symbolized corruption and sin (cf. Mt 16:6,12; 1Co 5:7–8). Jesus, the Son of God, fulfilled the law in every requirement (Mt 5:17). Thus, he would have followed God's law for the Passover and not used fermented wine.

(3) A rather lively debate has taken place over the centuries among Jewish rabbis and scholars as to whether fermented products of the vine were allowed in the Passover. Those who held to a stricter and more literal interpretation of the Hebrew Scriptures, especially Ex 13:7, insisted that no fermented wine could be used on this occasion.

(4) Some Jewish sources affirm that the use of unfermented wine at the Passover was common in NT times. For example, "According to the Synoptic Gospels, it would appear that on the Thursday evening of the last week of his life Jesus with his disciples entered Jerusalem in order to eat the Passover meal with them in the sacred city; if so, the wafer and the wine of . . . the communion service then instituted by him as a memorial would be the unleavened bread and the unfermented wine of the Seder service" (see "Jesus," *The Jewish Encyclopedia*, 1904 edition, V.165).

(5) In the OT, fermented drink was never to be used in the house of God, nor were the priests allowed to draw near to God in worship while drinking intoxicating beverages (Lev 10:9–11). Jesus Christ was God's high priest of the new covenant, drawing near to God for the sake of his people (Heb 3:1; 5:1–10).

(6) The value of a symbol is determined by its capacity to conceptualize the spiritual reality. Therefore, just as the bread represented Christ's pure body and had to be unleavened (i.e., uncorrupted with fermentation), the fruit of the vine, representing the incorruptible blood of Christ, would have been best represented by juice that was unfermented (cf. 1Pe 1:18–19). Since Scripture states explicitly that the process of corruption was not allowed to work in either the body or blood of Christ (Ps 16:10; Ac 2:27; 13:37), both Christ's body and blood are properly symbolized by that which is uncorrupted and unfermented.

(7) Paul instructed the Corinthians to put away spiritual yeast, i.e., the fermenting agent of "malice and wickedness," because Christ is our Passover (1Co 5:6–8). It would be inconsistent with the goal and spiritual requirement of the Lord's Supper to use something that was a symbol of evil, i.e., something with yeast.

(8) In Pr 23:29–35 God prohibited gazing at wine that has been fermented and makes one drunk. Christ would not sanction conduct that God had previously condemned. He came "to fulfill" the law (Mt 5:17).

For more on wine in NT times, see article on WINE IN NEW TESTAMENT TIMES (2), p. 174.

JESUS IN GALILEE

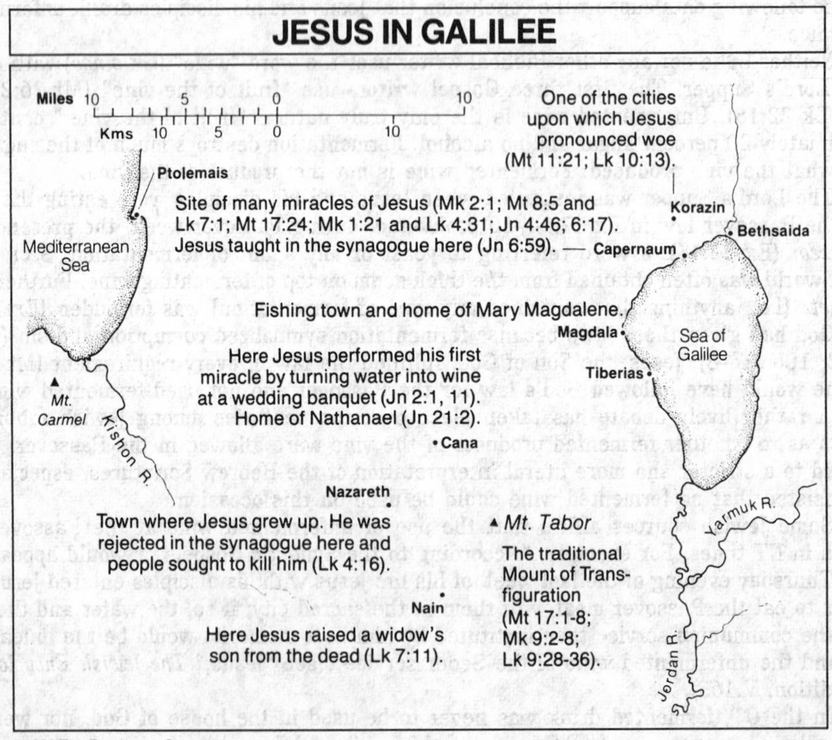
Miles 10 5 0 10
Kms 10 5 0 10
Ptolemais
Mediterranean Sea
Mt. Carmel
Kishon R.
One of the cities upon which Jesus pronounced woe (Mt 11:21; Lk 10:13).
Korazin
Bethsaida
Site of many miracles of Jesus (Mk 2:1; Mt 8:5 and Lk 7:1; Mt 17:24; Mk 1:21 and Lk 4:31; Jn 4:46; 6:17). Jesus taught in the synagogue here (Jn 6:59).
Capernaum
Fishing town and home of Mary Magdalene.
Magdala
Sea of Galilee
Tiberias
Here Jesus performed his first miracle by turning water into wine at a wedding banquet (Jn 2:1, 11). Home of Nathanael (Jn 21:2).
Cana
Nazareth
Town where Jesus grew up. He was rejected in the synagogue here and people sought to kill him (Lk 4:16).
Mt. Tabor
The traditional Mount of Transfiguration (Mt 17:1-8; Mk 9:2-8; Lk 9:28-36).
Yarmuk R.
Nain
Here Jesus raised a widow's son from the dead (Lk 7:11).
Jordan R.

along the path are the ones who hear, and
then the devil comes and takes away the
word from their hearts, so that they may
not believe and be saved. 13 Those on the
rock are the ones who receive the word
with joy when they hear it, but they have
no root. They believe for a while, but in the
time of testing they fall away.[f] 14 The
seed that fell among thorns stands for
those who hear, but as they go on their
way they are choked by life's worries,
riches[g] and pleasures, and they do not
mature. 15 But the seed on good soil
stands for those with a noble and good
heart, who hear the word, retain it, and by
persevering produce a crop.

A Lamp on a Stand

16 "No one lights a lamp and hides it in
a jar or puts it under a bed. Instead, he
puts it on a stand, so that those who come
in can see the light.[h] 17 For there is nothing hidden that will not be disclosed, and
nothing concealed that will not be known
or brought out into the open.[i] 18 Therefore consider carefully how you listen.
Whoever has will be given more; whoever
does not have, even what he thinks he has
will be taken from him."[j]

Jesus' Mother and Brothers

8:19–21pp — Mt 12:46–50; Mk 3:31–35

19 Now Jesus' mother and brothers
came to see him, but they were not able
to get near him because of the crowd.
20 Someone told him, "Your mother and
brothers[k] are standing outside, wanting
to see you."

21 He replied, "My mother and brothers
are those who hear God's word and put it
into practice."[l]

8:13 [f]Mt 11:6
8:14 [g]Mt 19:23; 1Ti 6:9,10,17
8:16 [h]S Mt 5:15
8:17 [i]Mt 10:26; Mk 4:22; Lk 12:2
8:18 [j]S Mt 25:29
8:20 [k]Jn 7:5
8:21 [l]Lk 6:47; 11:28; Jn 14:21
8:24 [m]S Lk 5:5 [n]Lk 4:35,39,41 [o]Ps 107:29; Jnh 1:15
8:28 [p]S Mt 8:29 [q]S Mk 5:7

Jesus Calms the Storm

8:22–25pp — Mt 8:23–27; Mk 4:36–41
8:22–25Ref — Mk 6:47–52; Jn 6:16–21

22 One day Jesus said to his disciples,
"Let's go over to the other side of the
lake." So they got into a boat and set out.
23 As they sailed, he fell asleep. A squall
came down on the lake, so that the boat
was being swamped, and they were in
great danger.

24 The disciples went and woke him,
saying, "Master, Master,[m] we're going to
drown!"

He got up and rebuked[n] the wind and
the raging waters; the storm subsided,
and all was calm.[o] 25 "Where is your
faith?" he asked his disciples.

In fear and amazement they asked one
another, "Who is this? He commands even
the winds and the water, and they obey
him."

The Healing of a Demon-possessed Man

8:26–37pp — Mt 8:28–34
8:26–39pp — Mk 5:1–20

26 They sailed to the region of the Gerasenes,[g] which is across the lake from Galilee. 27 When Jesus stepped ashore, he was
met by a demon-possessed man from the
town. For a long time this man had not
worn clothes or lived in a house, but had
lived in the tombs. 28 When he saw Jesus,
he cried out and fell at his feet, shouting
at the top of his voice, "What do you want
with me,[p] Jesus, Son of the Most High
God?[q] I beg you, don't torture me!" 29 For
Jesus had commanded the evil[h] spirit to
come out of the man. Many times it had
seized him, and though he was chained

[g] *26* Some manuscripts *Gadarenes*; other manuscripts *Gergesenes*; also in verse 37
[h] *29* Greek *unclean*

8:13 BELIEVE FOR A WHILE . . . FALL AWAY. In Christ's interpretation of this parable, he explicitly affirms the possibility of a person believing (i.e., making a sincere beginning in the life of faith), but subsequently falling away because of a failure to resist temptation. In contrast are those who "hear the word, retain it, and by persevering produce a crop" (v. 15). Jesus teaches that it is essential that those who hear the Word "hold firmly" to it (11:28; Jn 8:51; 1Co 15:1–2; Col 1:21–23; 1Ti 4:1,16; 2Ti 3:13–15; 1Jn 2:24–25; see Jn 15:6, note on remaining in Christ).

8:14 CHOKED BY LIFE'S WORRIES. We who believe in Jesus must always be careful that worldly responsibilities, abundance or pleasures do not absorb our thoughts until our spiritual life is altogether destroyed. These kinds of thorns/weeds can slowly but surely choke the Word from our lives. Let each of us ask: What is happening in my life? Am I being caught up more and more in the temporal things of life? Or are the Word of God and heavenly things becoming more important as time goes by?

8:18 WHOEVER HAS WILL BE GIVEN MORE. See Mt 25:29, note.

8:21 MY MOTHER AND BROTHERS. Only those who hear and obey the Word of God are personally related to Jesus and are a part of God's family. Faith without obedience is not an option in God's spiritual family.

8:27–33 A DEMON-POSSESSED MAN. Demon-possession (or the indwelling of demons within a human personality) is one of the means used by Satan and the kingdom of evil in their struggle against the kingdom of God. For more on this subject, see article on POWER OVER SATAN AND DEMONS, p. 80.

hand and foot and kept under guard, he had broken his chains and had been driven by the demon into solitary places.

30Jesus asked him, "What is your name?"

"Legion," he replied, because many demons had gone into him. **31**And they begged him repeatedly not to order them to go into the Abyss.[r]

32A large herd of pigs was feeding there on the hillside. The demons begged Jesus to let them go into them, and he gave them permission. **33**When the demons came out of the man, they went into the pigs, and the herd rushed down the steep bank into the lake[s] and was drowned.

34When those tending the pigs saw what had happened, they ran off and reported this in the town and countryside, **35**and the people went out to see what had happened. When they came to Jesus, they found the man from whom the demons had gone out, sitting at Jesus' feet,[t] dressed and in his right mind; and they were afraid. **36**Those who had seen it told the people how the demon-possessed[u] man had been cured. **37**Then all the people of the region of the Gerasenes asked Jesus to leave them,[v] because they were overcome with fear. So he got into the boat and left.

38The man from whom the demons had gone out begged to go with him, but Jesus sent him away, saying, **39**"Return home and tell how much God has done for you." So the man went away and told all over town how much Jesus had done for him.

A Dead Girl and a Sick Woman

8:40–56pp — Mt 9:18–26; Mk 5:22–43

40Now when Jesus returned, a crowd welcomed him, for they were all expecting him. **41**Then a man named Jairus, a ruler of the synagogue,[w] came and fell at Jesus' feet, pleading with him to come to his house **42**because his only daughter, a girl of about twelve, was dying.

As Jesus was on his way, the crowds almost crushed him. **43**And a woman was there who had been subject to bleeding[x] for twelve years,[i] but no one could heal her. **44**She came up behind him and touched the edge of his cloak,[y] and immediately her bleeding stopped.

45"Who touched me?" Jesus asked.

When they all denied it, Peter said, "Master,[z] the people are crowding and pressing against you."

46But Jesus said, "Someone touched me;[a] I know that power has gone out from me."[b]

47Then the woman, seeing that she could not go unnoticed, came trembling and fell at his feet. In the presence of all the people, she told why she had touched him and how she had been instantly healed. **48**Then he said to her, "Daughter, your faith has healed you.[c] Go in peace."[d] Lk 12:28

49While Jesus was still speaking, someone came from the house of Jairus, the synagogue ruler.[e] "Your daughter is dead," he said. "Don't bother the teacher any more."

50Hearing this, Jesus said to Jairus, "Don't be afraid; just believe, and she will be healed."

51When he arrived at the house of Jairus, he did not let anyone go in with him except Peter, John and James,[f] and the child's father and mother. **52**Meanwhile, all the people were wailing and mourning[g] for her. "Stop wailing," Jesus said. "She is not dead but asleep."[h]

53They laughed at him, knowing that she was dead. **54**But he took her by the hand and said, "My child, get up!"[i] **55**Her spirit returned, and at once she stood up. Then Jesus told them to give her something to eat. **56**Her parents were astonished, but he ordered them not to tell anyone what had happened.[j]

Jesus Sends Out the Twelve

9:3–5pp — Mt 10:9–15; Mk 6:8–11
9:7–9pp — Mt 14:1,2; Mk 6:14–16

9 When Jesus had called the Twelve together, he gave them power and authority to drive out all demons[k] and to cure diseases,[l] **2**and he sent them out to

8:31 [r]Rev 9:1,2, 11; 11:7; 17:8; 20:1,3
8:33 [s]ver 22,23
8:35 [t]Lk 10:39
8:36 [u]S Mt 4:24
8:37 [v]Ac 16:39
8:41 [w]ver 49; S Mk 5:22
8:43 [x]Lev 15:25-30
8:44 [y]S Mt 9:20
8:45 [z]S Lk 5:5
8:46 [a]Mt 14:36; Mk 3:10 [b]Lk 5:17; 6:19
8:48 [c]S Mt 9:22 [d]S Ac 15:33
8:49 [e]ver 41
8:51 [f]S Mt 4:21
8:52 [g]Lk 23:27 [h]S Mt 9:24
8:54 [i]S Lk 7:14
8:56 [j]S Mt 8:4
9:1 [k]S Mt 10:1 [l]S Mt 4:23; Lk 5:17

i 43 Many manuscripts *years, and she had spent all she had on doctors*

8:44 TOUCHED ... HIS CLOAK. See Mk 5:28, note.

8:50 DON'T BE AFRAID; JUST BELIEVE. See Mk 5:36, note.

9:1 AUTHORITY TO DRIVE OUT ALL DEMONS. See Mt 10:1, note.

9:2 PREACH THE KINGDOM ... HEAL THE SICK. (1) This is the first time Jesus sent out the twelve disciples to represent him by word and deed. The instruction given to the twelve, according to the parallel passage in Matthew, was to go to "the lost sheep of Israel" (Mt 10:6). After his resurrection, however, Jesus changed the scope to encompass all nations, in a commission that is to continue "to the very end of the age" (Mt 28:18–20; Mk 16:15–20).

(2) The Gospel writers make it clear that Jesus' command to preach the kingdom of God (see article on THE KINGDOM OF GOD, p. 28) was seldom

preach the kingdom of God[m] and to heal the sick. **3**He told them: "Take nothing for the journey—no staff, no bag, no bread, no money, no extra tunic.[n] **4**Whatever house you enter, stay there until you leave that town. **5**If people do not welcome you, shake the dust off your feet when you leave their town, as a testimony against them."[o] **6**So they set out and went from
Lk 13:10-17 village to village, preaching the gospel and healing people everywhere.

7Now Herod[p] the tetrarch heard about all that was going on. And he was perplexed, because some were saying that John[q] had been raised from the dead,[r] **8**others that Elijah had appeared,[s] and still others that one of the prophets of long ago had come back to life.[t] **9**But Herod said, "I beheaded John. Who, then, is this I hear such things about?" And he tried to see him.[u]

Jesus Feeds the Five Thousand

9:10–17pp — Mt 14:13–21; Mk 6:32–44; Jn 6:5–13
9:13–17Ref — 2Ki 4:42–44

10When the apostles[v] returned, they reported to Jesus what they had done. Then he took them with him and they withdrew by themselves to a town called Bethsaida,[w] **11**but the crowds learned about it and followed him. He welcomed them and spoke to them about the kingdom of God,[x] and healed those who needed healing.

12Late in the afternoon the Twelve came to him and said, "Send the crowd away so they can go to the surrounding villages and countryside and find food and lodging, because we are in a remote place here."

13He replied, "You give them something to eat."

They answered, "We have only five loaves of bread and two fish—unless we go and buy food for all this crowd." **14**(About five thousand men were there.)

But he said to his disciples, "Have them sit down in groups of about fifty each." **15**The disciples did so, and everybody sat down. **16**Taking the five loaves and the two fish and looking up to heaven, he gave thanks and broke them.[y] Then he gave them to the disciples to set before the people. **17**They all ate and were satisfied, and the disciples picked up twelve basketfuls of broken pieces that were left over.

Peter's Confession of Christ

9:18–20pp — Mt 16:13–16; Mk 8:27–29
9:22–27pp — Mt 16:21–28; Mk 8:31–9:1

18Once when Jesus was praying[z] in private and his disciples were with him, he asked them, "Who do the crowds say I am?"

19They replied, "Some say John the Baptist;[a] others say Elijah; and still others, that one of the prophets of long ago has come back to life."[b]

20"But what about you?" he asked. "Who do you say I am?"

Peter answered, "The Christ[j] of God."[c]

21Jesus strictly warned them not to tell this to anyone.[d] **22**And he said, "The Son of Man[e] must suffer many things[f] and be rejected by the elders, chief priests and teachers of the law,[g] and he must be killed[h] and on the third day[i] be raised to life."[j]

23Then he said to them all: "If anyone would come after me, he must deny himself and take up his cross daily and follow me.[k] **24**For whoever wants to save his life will lose it, but whoever loses his life for me will save it.[l] **25**What good is it for a man to gain the whole world, and yet lose or forfeit his very self? **26**If anyone is ashamed of me and my words, the Son of

9:2 [m]S Mt 3:2 **9:3** [n]Lk 10:4; 22:35 **9:5** [o]S Mt 10:14 **9:7** [p]S Mt 14:1 [q]S Mt 3:1 [r]ver 19 **9:8** [s]S Mt 11:14 [t]ver 19; Jn 1:21 **9:9** [u]Lk 23:8 **9:10** [v]S Mk 6:30 [w]S Mt 11:21 **9:11** [x]ver 2; S Mt 3:2
9:16 [y]S Mt 14:19 **9:18** [z]S Lk 3:21 **9:19** [a]S Mt 3:1 [b]ver 7,8 **9:20** [c]Jn 1:49; 6:66-69; 11:27 **9:21** [d]S Mk 8:30 **9:22** [e]S Mt 8:20 [f]S Mt 16:21 [g]Mt 27:1,2 [h]Ac 2:23; 3:13 [i]S Mt 16:21 [j]S Mt 16:21 **9:23** [k]Mt 10:38; Lk 14:27 **9:24** [l]S Jn 12:25

j 20 Or *Messiah*

---

given apart from the command to heal the sick and to drive out demons (Mt 9:35–38; 10:7–8; Mk 3:14–15; 6:7–13; 16:15,17; Lk 9:2,6; 10:1,9; cf. 4:17–19). God intends that the presentation of the gospel today be accompanied by the same demonstration of the Spirit and of power (Mt 10:1, note; Mk 16:15–18; Ac 1:8; Ro 15:18–19; 1Co 2:4–5; 4:20; see article on SIGNS OF BELIEVERS, p. 106) in order to meet Satan's challenge in these last days (1Ti 4:1; 2Ti 3:1–5).

(3) Churches today should not compare themselves with other churches, but with this NT message and pattern. Are we seeing and experiencing the kingdom of God as did the early Christians? Is the kingdom of God near us? If not, why not?

9:12–17 FEEDING OF THE FIVE THOUSAND. See Mt 14:19, note.

9:23 TAKE UP HIS CROSS DAILY. Accepting Jesus as Lord and Savior demands not only believing the truth of the gospel, but also committing ourselves to sacrificially follow him (see Mk 8:34, note). The choice between denying ourselves or living for our own selfish desires must be made daily. That choice will determine our eternal destiny.

9:24 WHOEVER LOSES HIS LIFE. Making the achievement of happiness and pleasure our goal in life instead of living in God's will and by his principles will end in disappointment and loss. To renounce our own ways and live in fellowship with Jesus, basing our lives on the teachings of his Word, is to find true life and joy, here and hereafter.

9:26 ASHAMED OF ME. To be ashamed of Jesus means to feel shame or embarrassment before the

Man will be ashamed of him[m] when he
comes in his glory and in the glory of the
Father and of the holy angels.[n] 27 I tell
you the truth, some who are standing here
will not taste death before they see the
kingdom of God."

The Transfiguration

9:28–36pp — Mt 17:1–8; Mk 9:2–8

28 About eight days after Jesus said this,
he took Peter, John and James[o] with him
and went up onto a mountain to pray.[p]
29 As he was praying, the appearance of
his face changed, and his clothes became
as bright as a flash of lightning. 30 Two
men, Moses and Elijah, 31 appeared in glorious splendor, talking with Jesus. They
spoke about his departure,[q] which he was
about to bring to fulfillment at Jerusalem.
32 Peter and his companions were very
sleepy,[r] but when they became fully
awake, they saw his glory and the two
men standing with him. 33 As the men
were leaving Jesus, Peter said to him,
"Master,[s] it is good for us to be here. Let
us put up three shelters — one for you, one
for Moses and one for Elijah." (He did not
know what he was saying.)
34 While he was speaking, a cloud appeared and enveloped them, and they
were afraid as they entered the cloud. 35 A
voice came from the cloud, saying, "This
is my Son, whom I have chosen;[t] listen to
him."[u] 36 When the voice had spoken, they
found that Jesus was alone. The disciples
kept this to themselves, and told no one
at that time what they had seen.[v]

The Healing of a Boy With an Evil Spirit

9:37–42,43–45pp — Mt 17:14–18, 22,23; Mk 9:14–27, 30–32

37 The next day, when they came down
from the mountain, a large crowd met
him. 38 A man in the crowd called out,
"Teacher, I beg you to look at my son, for
he is my only child. 39 A spirit seizes him
and he suddenly screams; it throws him
into convulsions so that he foams at the
mouth. It scarcely ever leaves him and is
destroying him. 40 I begged your disciples
to drive it out, but they could not."
41 "O unbelieving and perverse generation,"[w] Jesus replied, "how long shall I
stay with you and put up with you? Bring
your son here."
42 Even while the boy was coming, the
demon threw him to the ground in a convulsion. But Jesus rebuked the evil[k] spirit, healed the boy and gave him back to his
father. 43 And they were all amazed at the
greatness of God.

While everyone was marveling at all
that Jesus did, he said to his disciples,
44 "Listen carefully to what I am about to
tell you: The Son of Man is going to be
betrayed into the hands of men."[x] 45 But
they did not understand what this meant.
It was hidden from them, so that they did
not grasp it,[y] and they were afraid to ask
him about it.

Who Will Be the Greatest?

9:46–48pp — Mt 18:1–5
9:46–50pp — Mk 9:33–40

46 An argument started among the disciples as to which of them would be the
greatest.[z] 47 Jesus, knowing their
thoughts,[a] took a little child and had him
stand beside him. 48 Then he said to them,
"Whoever welcomes this little child in my
name welcomes me; and whoever welcomes me welcomes the one who sent
me.[b] For he who is least among you all —
he is the greatest."[c]
49 "Master,"[d] said John, "we saw a man
driving out demons in your name and we
tried to stop him, because he is not one of
us."
50 "Do not stop him," Jesus said, "for
whoever is not against you is for you."[e]

Samaritan Opposition

51 As the time approached for him to be
taken up to heaven,[f] Jesus resolutely set
out for Jerusalem.[g] 52 And he sent messengers on ahead, who went into a Samar-

9:26 [m] Mt 10:33; Lk 12:9; 2Ti 2:12 [n] S Mt 16:27 **9:28** [o] S Mt 4:21 [p] S Lk 3:21 **9:31** [q] 2Pe 1:15 **9:32** [r] Mt 26:43 **9:33** [s] S Lk 5:5 **9:35** [t] Isa 42:1 [u] S Mt 3:17 **9:36** [v] Mt 17:9

9:41 [w] Dt 32:5 **9:44** [x] S ver 22 **9:45** [y] S Mk 9:32 **9:46** [z] Lk 22:24 **9:47** [a] S Mt 9:4 **9:48** [b] S Mt 10:40 [c] S Mk 9:35 **9:49** [d] S Lk 5:5 **9:50** [e] Mt 12:30; Lk 11:23 **9:51** [f] S Mk 16:19 [g] Lk 13:22; 17:11; 18:31; 19:28

[k] *42* Greek *unclean*

---

world when we identify with the ways, values and goals that Jesus taught. It is to be ashamed of his Word, ashamed to claim its full divine inspiration, ashamed to live by it and defend it. Such people Christ will reject and condemn (Mt 10:33; Mk 8:34, note; Ro 1:16; 2Ti 1:8,12,16; Rev 3:14–16).

9:27 SEE THE KINGDOM OF GOD. See Mt 16:28, note.

9:29 THE TRANSFIGURATION. In his transfiguration, Jesus was transformed in the presence of three disciples, and they saw his heavenly glory as he really was — God in human flesh. The experience of the transfiguration was: (1) an encouragement to Jesus as he faced death on the cross (cf. Mt 16:21); (2) an announcement to the disciples that Jesus had to suffer on the cross (v. 31); (3) an endorsement by God that Jesus was his true Son qualified to redeem the human race (v. 35).

9:41 UNBELIEVING ... GENERATION. See Mt 17:17, note.

itan[h] village to get things ready for him;
[53]but the people there did not welcome
him, because he was heading for Jerusalem. [54]When the disciples James and
John[i] saw this, they asked, "Lord, do you
want us to call fire down from heaven to
destroy them[l]?"[j] [55]But Jesus turned and
rebuked them, [56]and[m] they went to another village.

The Cost of Following Jesus

9:57–60pp — Mt 8:19–22

[57]As they were walking along the
road,[k] a man said to him, "I will follow
you wherever you go."

[58]Jesus replied, "Foxes have holes and
birds of the air have nests, but the Son of
Man[l] has no place to lay his head."

[59]He said to another man, "Follow
me."[m]

But the man replied, "Lord, first let me
go and bury my father."

[60]Jesus said to him, "Let the dead bury
their own dead, but you go and proclaim
the kingdom of God."[n]

[61]Still another said, "I will follow you,
Lord; but first let me go back and say
good-by to my family."[o]

[62]Jesus replied, "No one who puts his
hand to the plow and looks back is fit for
service in the kingdom of God."

Jesus Sends Out the Seventy-two

10:4–12pp — Lk 9:3–5
10:13–15,21,22pp — Mt 11:21–23,25–27
10:23,24pp — Mt 13:16,17

10 After this the Lord[p] appointed
seventy-two[n] others[q] and sent
them two by two[r] ahead of him to every
town and place where he was about to
go.[s] [2]He told them, "The harvest is plentiful, but the workers are few. Ask the Lord
of the harvest, therefore, to send out
workers into his harvest field.[t] [3]Go! I am
sending you out like lambs among
wolves.[u] [4]Do not take a purse or bag or
sandals; and do not greet anyone on the
road.

[5]"When you enter a house, first say,
'Peace to this house.' [6]If a man of peace
is there, your peace will rest on him; if not,
it will return to you. [7]Stay in that house,
eating and drinking whatever they give
you, for the worker deserves his wages.[v]
Do not move around from house to house.

[8]"When you enter a town and are welcomed, eat what is set before you.[w] [9]Heal
the sick who are there and tell them, 'The
kingdom of God[x] is near you.' [10]But when
you enter a town and are not welcomed,
go into its streets and say, [11]'Even the
dust of your town that sticks to our feet
we wipe off against you.[y] Yet be sure of
this: The kingdom of God is near.'[z] [12]I tell
you, it will be more bearable on that day
for Sodom[a] than for that town.[b]

[13]"Woe to you,[c] Korazin! Woe to you,
Bethsaida! For if the miracles that were
performed in you had been performed in
Tyre and Sidon, they would have repented
long ago, sitting in sackcloth[d] and ashes.
[14]But it will be more bearable for Tyre and
Sidon at the judgment than for you. [15]And
you, Capernaum,[e] will you be lifted up to
the skies? No, you will go down to the
depths.[o]

[16]"He who listens to you listens to me;
he who rejects you rejects me; but he who
rejects me rejects him who sent me."[f]

[17]The seventy-two[g] returned with joy
and said, "Lord, even the demons submit
to us in your name."[h]

[18]He replied, "I saw Satan[i] fall like
lightning from heaven.[j] [19]I have given

9:52 [h]S Mt 10:5 **9:54** [i]S Mt 4:21 [j]2Ki 1:10,12 **9:57** [k]ver 51 **9:58** [l]S Mt 8:20 **9:59** [m]S Mt 4:19 **9:60** [n]S Mt 3:2 **9:61** [o]1Ki 19:20 **10:1** [p]S Lk 7:13 [q]Lk 9:1,2,51,52 [r]Mk 6:7 [s]Mt 10:1 **10:2** [t]Mt 9:37,38; Jn 4:35

10:3 [u]Mt 10:16 **10:7** [v]S 1Ti 5:18 **10:8** [w]1Co 10:27 **10:9** [x]S Mt 3:2 **10:11** [y]S Mt 10:14 [z]ver 9 **10:12** [a]S Mt 10:15 [b]Mt 11:24 **10:13** [c]Lk 6:24-26 [d]S Rev 11:3 **10:15** [e]S Mt 4:13 **10:16** [f]S Mt 10:40 **10:17** [g]ver 1 [h]S Mk 16:17 **10:18** [i]S Mt 4:10 [j]Isa 14:12; Rev 9:1; 12:8,9

[l] *54* Some manuscripts *them, even as Elijah did*
[m] *55,56* Some manuscripts *them. And he said, "You do not know what kind of spirit you are of, for the Son of Man did not come to destroy men's lives, but to save them." 56And*
[n] *1* Some manuscripts *seventy*; also in verse 17
[o] *15* Greek *Hades*

9:55 REBUKED THEM. We must be careful that our loyalty to and zeal for Christ do not conceal a spirit of revenge or violence against the unsaved who live in darkness and sin.

10:1 SENT THEM TWO BY TWO. The principle of sending out workers two by two is very important in the work of the Lord, for it provides each one with double faith and wisdom; in addition, a companion helps bolster courage. Other passages dealing with the two by two principle are: Ecc 4:9–12; Mt 18:16; Mk 6:7; 14:13; Lk 7:19; Jn 1:35–41; 8:17; Ac 9:38; 10:7; 15:36–41; 19:22; 2Co 13:1; 1Ti 5:19; Heb 10:28; Rev 11:3–6,10–12.

10:2 THE HARVEST IS PLENTIFUL. See Mt 9:37, note.

10:3 LAMBS AMONG WOLVES. Believers who faithfully follow the will of God will be threatened by many dangers. They will be like defenseless lambs among wolves. Knowing this, we must pray for God's presence, protection and provision.

10:9 HEAL THE SICK ... THE KINGDOM OF GOD. Jesus once again emphasizes that the "kingdom of God" is associated with healing the sick. For more on this, see 9:2, note.

10:19 SNAKES AND SCORPIONS. "Snakes and scorpions" are terms representing the most dangerous forces of spiritual evil. Christians have power over evil spirits because Christ has given us his authority over Satan (see article on POWER OVER SATAN AND DEMONS, p. 80).

you authority to trample on snakes[k] and
scorpions and to overcome all the power
of the enemy; nothing will harm you.
20However, do not rejoice that the spirits
submit to you, but rejoice that your names
are written in heaven."[l]

21At that time Jesus, full of joy through
the Holy Spirit, said, "I praise you, Father,
Lord of heaven and earth, because you
have hidden these things from the wise
and learned, and revealed them to little
children.[m] Yes, Father, for this was your
good pleasure.

22"All things have been committed to
me by my Father.[n] No one knows who the
Son is except the Father, and no one
knows who the Father is except the Son
and those to whom the Son chooses to
reveal him."[o]

23Then he turned to his disciples and
said privately, "Blessed are the eyes that
see what you see. 24For I tell you that
many prophets and kings wanted to see
what you see but did not see it, and to hear
what you hear but did not hear it."[p]

The Parable of the Good Samaritan

10:25–28pp — Mt 22:34–40; Mk 12:28–31

25On one occasion an expert in the law
stood up to test Jesus. "Teacher," he
asked, "what must I do to inherit eternal
life?"[q]

26"What is written in the Law?" he replied. "How do you read it?"

27He answered: " 'Love the Lord your
God with all your heart and with all your
soul and with all your strength and with
all your mind'[p];[r] and, 'Love your neighbor as yourself.'[q]"[s]

28"You have answered correctly," Jesus
replied. "Do this and you will live."[t]

29But he wanted to justify himself,[u] so
he asked Jesus, "And who is my neighbor?"

10:19 [k]Mk 16:18; Ac 28:3-5 **10:20** [l]S Rev 20:12 **10:21** [m]1Co 1:26-29 **10:22** [n]S Mt 28:18 [o]Jn 1:18 **10:24** [p]1Pe 1:10-12 **10:25** [q]Mt 19:16; Lk 18:18 **10:27** [r]Dt 6:5 [s]Lev 19:18; S Mt 5:43 **10:28** [t]S Ro 7:10 **10:29** [u]Lk 16:15 **10:31** [v]Lev 21:1-3 **10:33** [w]S Mt 10:5 **10:38** [x]Jn 11:1; 12:2 **10:39** [y]Jn 11:1; 12:3 [z]Lk 8:35 **10:40** [a]Mk 4:38 **10:41** [b]Mt 6:25-34; Lk 12:11,22

30In reply Jesus said: "A man was going
down from Jerusalem to Jericho, when he
fell into the hands of robbers. They
stripped him of his clothes, beat him and
went away, leaving him half dead. 31A
priest happened to be going down the
same road, and when he saw the man, he
passed by on the other side.[v] 32So too, a
Levite, when he came to the place and saw
him, passed by on the other side. 33But a
Samaritan,[w] as he traveled, came where
the man was; and when he saw him, he
took pity on him. 34He went to him and
bandaged his wounds, pouring on oil and
wine. Then he put the man on his own
donkey, took him to an inn and took care
of him. 35The next day he took out two
silver coins[r] and gave them to the inn-
keeper. 'Look after him,' he said, 'and
when I return, I will reimburse you for any
extra expense you may have.'

36"Which of these three do you think
was a neighbor to the man who fell into
the hands of robbers?"

37The expert in the law replied, "The
one who had mercy on him."

Jesus told him, "Go and do likewise."

At the Home of Martha and Mary

38As Jesus and his disciples were on
their way, he came to a village where a
woman named Martha[x] opened her home
to him. 39She had a sister called Mary,[y]
who sat at the Lord's feet[z] listening to
what he said. 40But Martha was distracted by all the preparations that had to be
made. She came to him and asked, "Lord,
don't you care[a] that my sister has left me
to do the work by myself? Tell her to help
me!"

41"Martha, Martha," the Lord answered, "you are worried[b] and upset

p *27* Deut. 6:5 q *27* Lev. 19:18 r *35* Greek *two denarii*

10:20 DO NOT REJOICE. Christ warns the disciples that they must not make power over demons or success in ministry a fundamental source of their joy. Their rejoicing must come from the fact that they are redeemed from sin and destined for heaven (see Mt 7:22–23, notes).

10:21 THE WISE ... LITTLE CHILDREN. Jesus rejoices that his heavenly Father has given the understanding of spiritual truths not to those who are intellectually wise in their own eyes, but to those who accept in childlike humility the truth revealed in his Word. Those who believe themselves wise enough to question the teachings of Scripture by their own "superior" knowledge, and use that as a basis for accepting or rejecting God's Word, are excluded from the fellowship and knowledge of the Son (v. 22).

10:27 LOVE THE LORD ... AND LOVE YOUR NEIGHBOR. See Mt 22:37,39, notes.

10:30 THE PARABLE OF THE GOOD SAMARITAN. This parable emphasizes that inherent in true saving faith and obedience is compassion for those in need. The call to love God is a call to love others. (1) The new life and grace that Christ gives to those who accept him will produce love, mercy and compassion for those who are distressed and afflicted. It is the responsibility of all believers to act on the Holy Spirit's love within them and not to harden their hearts. (2) Those who are professed Christians, yet whose hearts are insensitive to the suffering and needs of others, give sure evidence that they do not have eternal life in them (vv. 25–28,31–37; cf. Mt 25:41–46; 1Jn 3:16–20).

about many things, **42**but only one thing is
needed.[s][c] Mary has chosen what is better, and it will not be taken away from
her."

Jesus' Teaching on Prayer

11:2–4pp — Mt 6:9–13
11:9–13pp — Mt 7:7–11

11 One day Jesus was praying[d] in a
certain place. When he finished,
one of his disciples said to him, "Lord,[e]
teach us to pray, just as John taught his
disciples."

2He said to them, "When you pray, say:

" 'Father,[t]
hallowed be your name,
your kingdom[f] come.[u]
3Give us each day our daily bread.
4Forgive us our sins,
for we also forgive everyone who
sins against us.[v][g]
And lead us not into temptation.[w]' "[h]

5Then he said to them, "Suppose one of
you has a friend, and he goes to him at
midnight and says, 'Friend, lend me three
loaves of bread, **6**because a friend of mine
on a journey has come to me, and I have
nothing to set before him.'

7"Then the one inside answers, 'Don't
bother me. The door is already locked, and
my children are with me in bed. I can't get
up and give you anything.' **8**I tell you,
though he will not get up and give him the
bread because he is his friend, yet because
of the man's boldness[x] he will get up and
give him as much as he needs.[i]

9"So I say to you: Ask and it will be
given to you;[j] seek and you will find;
knock and the door will be opened to you.
10For everyone who asks receives; he who
seeks finds; and to him who knocks, the
door will be opened.

11"Which of you fathers, if your son
asks for[y] a fish, will give him a snake
instead? **12**Or if he asks for an egg, will
give him a scorpion? **13**If you then, though
you are evil, know how to give good gifts
to your children, how much more will your
Father in heaven give the Holy Spirit to
those who ask him!"

Jesus and Beelzebub

11:14,15, 17–22, 24–26pp — Mt 12:22,24–29, 43–45
11:17–22pp — Mk 3:23–27

14Jesus was driving out a demon that
was mute. When the demon left, the man
who had been mute spoke, and the crowd
was amazed.[k] **15**But some of them said,
"By Beelzebub,[z][l] the prince of demons,
he is driving out demons."[m] **16**Others tested him by asking for a sign from heaven.[n]

17Jesus knew their thoughts[o] and said
to them: "Any kingdom divided against itself will be ruined, and a house divided
against itself will fall. **18**If Satan[p] is divided against himself, how can his kingdom
stand? I say this because you claim that
I drive out demons by Beelzebub. **19**Now
if I drive out demons by Beelzebub, by
whom do your followers drive them out?
So then, they will be your judges. **20**But if
I drive out demons by the finger of God,[q]

10:42 [c]Ps 27:4
11:1 [d]S Lk 3:21 [e]S Jn 13:13
11:2 [f]S Mt 3:2
11:4 [g]Mt 18:35; Mk 11:25 [h]Mt 26:41; Jas 1:13
11:8 [i]Lk 18:1-6
11:9 [j]S Mt 7:7
11:14 [k]Mt 9:32, 33
11:15 [l]S Mk 3:22 [m]Mt 9:34
11:16 [n]S Mt 12:38
11:17 [o]S Mt 9:4
11:18 [p]S Mt 4:10
11:20 [q]Ex 8:19

[s] 42 Some manuscripts *but few things are needed—or only one* [t] 2 Some manuscripts *Our Father in heaven* [u] 2 Some manuscripts *come. May your will be done on earth as it is in heaven.* [v] 4 Greek *everyone who is indebted to us* [w] 4 Some manuscripts *temptation but deliver us from the evil one* [x] 8 Or *persistence* [y] 11 Some manuscripts *for bread, will give him a stone; or if he asks for* [z] 15 Greek *Beezeboul* or *Beelzeboul*; also in verses 18 and 19

10:42 ONE THING IS NEEDED. Although active, practical service to God is essential and good, our first and most important task is a love and devotion that expresses itself in quiet worship, prayer and fellowship with the Lord (see Mt 26:13, note). Are we so busy doing the work of the Lord, attending church services and performing good deeds that we forget spiritual communion with our Savior?

11:2–4 THE LORD'S PRAYER. See Mt 6:9–15, notes on the Lord's Prayer.

11:3 OUR DAILY BREAD. Believers should learn to pray for life's necessary provisions (cf. Mt 6:11) based on four principles. (1) We must pray such petitions according to God's will and his glory (Mt 6:10,33; 1Co 10:31; 1Jn 5:14–15). (2) We must want God to demonstrate his fatherly love for us (Mt 6:9,25–34). (3) The provisions we pray for must supply our basic needs and give us the ability to perform Christian service (2Co 9:8; 1Ti 6:8; Heb 13:5). (4) We may ask for things only after we have faithfully given to God and to others (2Co 9:6; see 8:2, note).

11:9 ASK . . . SEEK . . . KNOCK. See Mt 7:7, note.

11:11 GIVE HIM A SNAKE. See Mt 7:11, note on God's care for his children.

11:13 GIVE THE HOLY SPIRIT TO THOSE WHO ASK. This verse probably does not refer to the impartation of the Spirit at the new birth (Jn 3:3), since at conversion all believers are automatically given the indwelling presence of the Holy Spirit (Ro 8:9–10; 1Co 6:19–20; see article on THE REGENERATION OF THE DISCIPLES, p. 212). Rather, the verse most likely refers to the baptism in the Holy Spirit that Christ promised to his followers (see article on JESUS AND THE HOLY SPIRIT, p. 136).

11:20 DEMONS . . . THE KINGDOM OF GOD. This passage reveals three things: (1) The success of God's kingdom on earth is in direct proportion to the destruction of the devil's work and the deliverance of sinners from bondage to sin and the demonic; (2) Satan will resist the coming of Christ's kingdom on earth

JESUS AND THE HOLY SPIRIT

***Lk 11:13** "If you then, though you are evil, know how to give good gifts to your children, how much more will your Father in heaven give the Holy Spirit to those who ask him?"*

Jesus had a special relationship with the Holy Spirit, a relationship that is important for our own personal lives. This article explores that relationship and its practical implications.

JESUS' BIRTH. Both Matthew and Luke state explicitly and unmistakably that Jesus came into this world as a result of a miraculous deed of God. He was conceived by the Holy Spirit and born of the virgin Mary (Mt 1:18,23; Lk 1:27). Because of this miraculous conception, Jesus was "holy" (Lk 1:35), that is, free from all taint of sin. This made him worthy to take the guilt of our sin on himself and to make atonement (see Mt 1:23, note). Without a perfect, sinless Savior, we could not experience redemption.

JESUS' BAPTISM. When he was baptized by John the Baptist, Jesus, who would later baptize his disciples in the Spirit at Pentecost and throughout the church age (see Lk 3:16; Ac 1:4–5; 2:33,38–39), was himself personally anointed by the Spirit (Mt 3:16–17; Lk 3:21–22). The Spirit came upon him in the form of a dove, equipping him with great power to perform his ministry, including his work of redemption. When our Lord departed into the desert after his water baptism, he was "full of the Holy Spirit" (Lk 4:1). Just as with our Lord, all who have experienced a supernatural rebirth by the Holy Spirit ought to experience the baptism in the Spirit to give them power in their lives and for their ministry (see Ac 1:8, notes).

JESUS' TEMPTATION BY SATAN. Immediately after his baptism, Jesus was led by the Spirit into the desert, where he was tempted by the devil for forty days (Lk 4:1–2). It was only because he was full of the Holy Spirit that he was able to face Satan squarely and resist the temptations that came his way. Likewise, it is God's intention that we never face the spiritual forces of evil and sin without the power of the Spirit. We must be equipped with his fullness and follow his leading in order to be victorious against Satan. In God's sight we are not "normal" children of his unless we are filled with the Spirit and live by his power.

JESUS' MINISTRY. When Jesus preached for the first time in his hometown of Nazareth, he read from the prophet Isaiah: "The Spirit of the Lord is on me, because he has anointed me to preach . . . , to proclaim freedom . . . , to release . . . ." (Lk 4:16–19). He went on to assert that he personally fulfilled that prophecy spoken so many years before (Isa 61:1). Here Jesus was reaffirming the meaning and purpose of his baptism when he was anointed in the Spirit: (1) It was to empower him for his mission and ministry. Jesus was God (Jn 1:1), but he was also human (1Ti 2:5). As a human being he had to rely on the Spirit's help and power to fulfill his responsibilities before God (cf. Mt 12:28; Lk 4:1,14; Ro 8:11; Heb 9:14). (2) It was only as a Spirit-anointed man that Jesus could live, serve and proclaim the gospel (Ac 10:38). In this he is a perfect example for the Christian; each believer should receive the fullness of the Holy Spirit (see Ac 1:8, notes; 2:4, notes).

JESUS' PROMISE REGARDING THE HOLY SPIRIT. John the Baptist had prophesied that Jesus would baptize his followers in the Holy Spirit (Mt 3:11; Mk 1:8; Lk 3:16, see note; Jn 1:33), a prophecy that Jesus himself reiterated (Ac 1:5; 11:16). In Lk 11:13, Jesus promised to give the Holy Spirit to *all* who asked (see note on that verse). All of these verses refer to the fullness of the Spirit that Christ promises to give to those who are already children of the heavenly Father—a promise that was first fulfilled at Pentecost (see Ac 2:4, note), and remains a promise for all who have become his disciples and ask for the baptism in the Spirit (see Ac 1:5; 2:39, note).

JESUS' RESURRECTION. Through the power of the Holy Spirit, Jesus was raised from the grave and thereby vindicated as the true Messiah and Son of God. In Ro 1:3–4 we read that through the Spirit of holiness (i.e., the Holy Spirit) Jesus "was declared with power to be the Son of God," and in Ro 8:11, that "the Spirit . . . raised Jesus from the dead." As Jesus depended on the Holy Spirit for his resurrection, so believers depend on the Spirit for spiritual life now and bodily resurrection in the future (Ro 8:10–11).

JESUS' ASCENSION INTO HEAVEN. After Jesus' resurrection he ascended into heaven and sat down at the right hand of his Father as co-ruler of God's kingdom (Mk 16:19; Lk 24:51; Ac 1:9–11; Eph 4:8–10). In this exalted position he received the Holy Spirit from his Father and poured out the Spirit on his people at Pentecost (Ac 2:33; cf. Jn 16:5–14), thereby affirming his lordship as prophet, priest and king. This outpouring of the Holy Spirit at Pentecost and throughout this present age testifies to the exalted Savior's continual presence and authority.

JESUS' NEARNESS TO HIS PEOPLE. As one of his present tasks, the Holy Spirit takes that which is Christ's and reveals it to believers (Jn 16:14–15). That is, the redemptive benefits of salvation in Christ are mediated to us through the Spirit (cf. Ro 8:14–16; Gal 4:6). Most important is Jesus' nearness to us (Jn 14:18). The Spirit makes us aware of the personal presence of Jesus, and his love, blessing, help, forgiveness, healing and all that is ours through faith. Likewise, the Spirit draws our hearts to seek the Lord in love, prayer and worship (see Jn 4:23–24; 16:14, note).

JESUS' RETURN FOR HIS PEOPLE. Jesus has promised to return and take his faithful people to be with him always (see Jn 14:3, note; 1Th 4:13–18). This is the blessed hope of all believers (Tit 2:13), the event that we pray and long for (2Ti 4:8). Scripture reveals that the Holy Spirit directs our hearts to cry out to God for our Lord's return. It is the Spirit who testifies that our redemption remains incomplete until Christ returns (cf. Ro 8:23). At the very close of the Bible, the Holy Spirit inspired the words, "come, Lord Jesus" (Rev 22:20).

then the kingdom of God[r] has come to
you.
21“When a strong man, fully armed,
guards his own house, his possessions are
safe. 22But when someone stronger attacks and overpowers him, he takes away
the armor in which the man trusted and
divides up the spoils.
23“He who is not with me is against me,
and he who does not gather with me, scatters.[s]
24“When an evil[a] spirit comes out of a
man, it goes through arid places seeking
rest and does not find it. Then it says, ‘I
will return to the house I left.’ 25When it
arrives, it finds the house swept clean and
put in order. 26Then it goes and takes sev-
en other spirits more wicked than itself,
and they go in and live there. And the final
condition of that man is worse than the
first.”[t]
27As Jesus was saying these things, a
woman in the crowd called out, “Blessed
is the mother who gave you birth and
nursed you.”[u]
28He replied, “Blessed rather are those
who hear the word of God[v] and obey it.”[w]

The Sign of Jonah

11:29–32pp — Mt 12:39–42

29As the crowds increased, Jesus said,
“This is a wicked generation. It asks for
a miraculous sign,[x] but none will be given
it except the sign of Jonah.[y] 30For as Jonah was a sign to the Ninevites, so also
will the Son of Man be to this generation.
31The Queen of the South will rise at the
judgment with the men of this generation
and condemn them; for she came from the
ends of the earth to listen to Solomon’s
wisdom,[z] and now one[b] greater than Solomon is here. 32The men of Nineveh will
stand up at the judgment with this generation and condemn it; for they repented at
the preaching of Jonah,[a] and now one
greater than Jonah is here.

The Lamp of the Body

11:34,35pp — Mt 6:22,23

33“No one lights a lamp and puts it in
a place where it will be hidden, or under
a bowl. Instead he puts it on its stand, so
that those who come in may see the
light.[b] 34Your eye is the lamp of your
body. When your eyes are good, your
whole body also is full of light. But when
they are bad, your body also is full of darkness. 35See to it, then, that the light within you is not darkness. 36Therefore, if
your whole body is full of light, and no part
of it dark, it will be completely lighted, as
when the light of a lamp shines on you.”

11:20 [r]S Mt 3:2 **11:23** [s]Mt 12:30; Mk 9:40; Lk 9:50 **11:26** [t]2Pe 2:20 **11:27** [u]Lk 23:29 **11:28** [v]S Heb 4:12 [w]Pr 8:32; Lk 6:47; 8:21; Jn 14:21
11:29 [x]ver 16; S Mt 12:38 [y]Jnh 1:17; Mt 16:4 **11:31** [z]1Ki 10:1; 2Ch 9:1 **11:32** [a]Jnh 3:5 **11:33** [b]S Mt 5:15

[a] *24* Greek *unclean* [b] *31* Or *something*; also in verse 32

(vv. 24–26; cf. Mt 13:18–30; Rev 12:12); (3) Jesus demonstrates divine power and authority in driving out demons, overpowering Satan and plundering his possessions (vv. 20–22). For more on this, see articles on THE KINGDOM OF GOD, p. 28, and POWER OVER SATAN AND DEMONS, p. 80.

11:23 WHO IS NOT WITH ME IS AGAINST ME. It is impossible to remain neutral in the spiritual conflict between Christ's kingdom and the power of evil. (1) Those who do not, along with Christ, oppose Satan and evil have in reality set themselves against Jesus Christ. Every person is fighting either on the side of Christ and righteousness, or on the side of Satan and the ungodly. (2) Jesus' words condemn any attempted neutrality or compromise with unrighteousness, or any partial obedience.

11:26 SEVEN OTHER SPIRITS . . . LIVE THERE. The point of this passage is made clear in its parallel in Mt 12:43–45 (see note), which speaks of the house left unoccupied. (1) In conversion and salvation (Jn 3:3) believers must not only be delivered from sin, but also commit themselves to radical obedience, prayer, righteousness, the Word and being filled with the Holy Spirit (see Ac 2:4; Ro 8). (2) After conversion, Satan's power does not end but continues as a never-ceasing menace (22:31; see Mt 6:13, note). There is safety from sin and Satan only by full commitment to Christ and by using all the means of grace available through Christ (see Eph 6:11, note). (3) Believers who have been delivered from the demonic but have still not completely renounced sin or opened their lives to the Spirit of God are inviting the evil spirits to come back with renewed power to live in those persons.

11:34 YOUR EYE IS THE LAMP OF YOUR BODY. The eye is the body's means of receiving light. If the eye is healthy, then one can fully receive and use light. If the eye is defective, then darkness prevails and one cannot see in order to walk or work. (1) Likewise, when people's spiritual eyes, i.e., when their attitudes, motives and desires are directed toward God's will, then the light of his Word enters their hearts to produce blessings, fruit and salvation (Gal 5:22–23). But if their desires are not focused on the things of God, then God's revelation and truth will have no effect.

(2) We must examine our lives to make sure that our spiritual eyes are such that the gospel can really sanctify us and renew our inward lives. Do we respond to the teaching or reading of Scripture with a spirit that loves God, Christ and the Word more and more—or, in spite of all the gospel messages and Bible teaching we have received, is there deadness in our souls and are we in bondage to sin? If the latter is the case, then our spiritual eyes are still evil and our bodies full of darkness. We must then confess our sins, repent and separate ourselves from all compromise that leads to darkness.

Six Woes

37When Jesus had finished speaking, a
Pharisee invited him to eat with him; so he
went in and reclined at the table.[c] 38But
the Pharisee, noticing that Jesus did not
first wash before the meal,[d] was surprised.
39Then the Lord[e] said to him, "Now
then, you Pharisees clean the outside of
the cup and dish, but inside you are full of
greed and wickedness.[f] 40You foolish
people![g] Did not the one who made the
outside make the inside also? 41But give
what is inside ⌊the dish⌋ [c] to the poor,[h] and
everything will be clean for you.[i]
42"Woe to you Pharisees, because you
give God a tenth[j] of your mint, rue and all
other kinds of garden herbs, but you neglect justice and the love of God.[k] You
should have practiced the latter without
leaving the former undone.[l]
43"Woe to you Pharisees, because you
love the most important seats in the synagogues and greetings in the marketplaces.[m]
44"Woe to you, because you are like un-
marked graves,[n] which men walk over
without knowing it."
45One of the experts in the law[o] answered him, "Teacher, when you say
these things, you insult us also."
46Jesus replied, "And you experts in the
law, woe to you, because you load people
down with burdens they can hardly carry,
and you yourselves will not lift one finger
to help them.[p]
47"Woe to you, because you build tombs
for the prophets, and it was your forefathers who killed them. 48So you testify
that you approve of what your forefathers
did; they killed the prophets, and you
build their tombs.[q] 49Because of this, God
in his wisdom[r] said, 'I will send them
prophets and apostles, some of whom
they will kill and others they will persecute.'[s] 50Therefore this generation will be
held responsible for the blood of all the
prophets that has been shed since the beginning of the world, 51from the blood of
Abel[t] to the blood of Zechariah,[u] who
was killed between the altar and the sanctuary. Yes, I tell you, this generation will
be held responsible for it all.[v]
52"Woe to you experts in the law, because you have taken away the key to
knowledge. You yourselves have not entered, and you have hindered those who
were entering."[w]
53When Jesus left there, the Pharisees
and the teachers of the law began to oppose him fiercely and to besiege him with
questions, 54waiting to catch him in something he might say.[x]

Warnings and Encouragements

12:2–9pp — Mt 10:26–33

12 Meanwhile, when a crowd of many
thousands had gathered, so that
they were trampling on one another, Jesus
began to speak first to his disciples, saying: "Be on your guard against the yeast
of the Pharisees, which is hypocrisy.[y]
2There is nothing concealed that will not
be disclosed, or hidden that will not be
made known.[z] 3What you have said in the
dark will be heard in the daylight, and
what you have whispered in the ear in the
inner rooms will be proclaimed from the
roofs.
4"I tell you, my friends,[a] do not be
afraid of those who kill the body and after
that can do no more. 5But I will show you
whom you should fear: Fear him who, after the killing of the body, has power to
throw you into hell. Yes, I tell you, fear
him.[b] 6Are not five sparrows sold for two
pennies[d]? Yet not one of them is forgotten
by God. 7Indeed, the very hairs of your

c *41* Or *what you have* d *6* Greek *two assaria*

11:37 c Lk 7:36; 14:1
11:38 d Mk 7:3,4
11:39 e S Lk 7:13 f Mt 23:25,26; Mk 7:20-23
11:40 g Lk 12:20; 1Co 15:36
11:41 h Lk 12:33 i S Ac 10:15
11:42 j Lk 18:12 k Dt 6:5; Mic 6:8 l Mt 23:23
11:43 m Mt 23:6, 7; Lk 14:7; 20:46
11:44 n Mt 23:27
11:45 o S Mt 22:35
11:46 p S Mt 23:4
11:48 q Mt 23:29-32; Ac 7:51-53
11:49 r 1Co 1:24, 30; Col 2:3 s Mt 23:34
11:51 t Ge 4:8 u 2Ch 24:20,21 v Mt 23:35,36
11:52 w Mt 23:13
11:54 x S Mt 12:10
12:1 y Mt 16:6,11, 12
12:2 z S Mk 4:22
12:4 a Jn 15:14,15
12:5 b Heb 10:31

11:42 WOE TO YOU. See Mt 23:13, note on Christ's denunciation of the sins of the Pharisees.

12:1 HYPOCRISY. Jesus condemns the hypocrisy of the Pharisees, warning his disciples to be careful that this sin does not enter their own lives and ministry. (1) Hypocrisy means acting as if you are what you are not—for example, acting publicly as a godly and faithful believer, when in reality you harbor hidden sin, immorality, greed, lust or other unrighteousness. The hypocrite is a deceiver in the area of observable righteousness (see article on FALSE TEACHERS, p. 98).

(2) Since hypocrisy involves living a lie, it makes one a co-worker and ally with Satan, the father of lies (Jn 8:44).

(3) Jesus warns his disciples that all hypocrisy and hidden sin will be exposed, if not in this life, certainly on the day of judgment (see Ro 2:16; 1Co 3:13; 4:5; Rev 20:12). What is done secretly behind closed doors will be at some point openly revealed (vv. 2–3).

(4) Hypocrisy is a sign that one does not fear God (v. 5) and does not possess the Holy Spirit with his regenerating grace (see Ro 8:5–14; 1Co 6:9–10; Gal 5:19–21; Eph 5:5). While remaining in this condition, one cannot "escape being condemned to hell" (Mt 23:33).

12:5 FEAR HIM. The disciples of Jesus must stand in awe of God's majesty and holiness and his wrath against sin (cf. Isa 6:1–5).

head are all numbered.[c] Don't be afraid;
you are worth more than many sparrows.[d]
8“I tell you, whoever acknowledges me
before men, the Son of Man will also acknowledge him before the angels of God.[e]
9But he who disowns me before men will
be disowned[f] before the angels of God.
10And everyone who speaks a word
against the Son of Man[g] will be forgiven,
but anyone who blasphemes against the
Holy Spirit will not be forgiven.[h]
11“When you are brought before synagogues, rulers and authorities, do not
worry about how you will defend yourselves or what you will say,[i] 12for the
Holy Spirit will teach you at that time
what you should say.”[j]

The Parable of the Rich Fool

13Someone in the crowd said to him,
“Teacher, tell my brother to divide the inheritance with me.”
14Jesus replied, “Man, who appointed
me a judge or an arbiter between you?”
15Then he said to them, “Watch out! Be on
your guard against all kinds of greed; a
man's life does not consist in the abundance of his possessions.”[k]
16And he told them this parable: “The
ground of a certain rich man produced a
good crop. 17He thought to himself, ‘What
shall I do? I have no place to store my
crops.’
18“Then he said, ‘This is what I'll do. I
will tear down my barns and build bigger
ones, and there I will store all my grain
and my goods. 19And I'll say to myself,
“You have plenty of good things laid up for
many years. Take life easy; eat, drink and
be merry.” ’
20“But God said to him, ‘You fool![l] This
very night your life will be demanded from
you.[m] Then who will get what you have
prepared for yourself?’[n]

12:7 [c]S Mt 10:30 [d]Mt 12:12
12:8 [e]Lk 15:10
12:9 [f]Mk 8:38; 2Ti 2:12
12:10 [g]S Mt 8:20 [h]Mt 12:31,32; S 1Jn 5:16
12:11 [i]Mt 10:17,19; Lk 21:12,14
12:12 [j]Ex 4:12; Mt 10:20; Mk 13:11; Lk 21:15
12:15 [k]Job 20:20; 31:24; Ps 62:10
12:20 [l]Jer 17:11; Lk 11:40 [m]Job 27:8 [n]Ps 39:6; 49:10
12:21 [o]ver 33
12:24 [p]Job 38:41; Ps 147:9
12:27 [q]1Ki 10:4-7
12:28 [r]S Mt 6:30
12:30 [s]S Lk 6:36 [t]Mt 6:8
12:31 [u]S Mt 3:2 [v]Mt 19:29
12:32 [w]S Mt 14:27 [x]S Mt 25:34
12:33 [y]S Ac 2:45 [z]S Mt 6:20 [a]S Jas 5:2
12:34 [b]Mt 6:21

21“This is how it will be with anyone
who stores up things for himself but is not
rich toward God.”[o]

Do Not Worry

12:22–31pp — Mt 6:25–33

22Then Jesus said to his disciples:
“Therefore I tell you, do not worry about
your life, what you will eat; or about your
body, what you will wear. 23Life is more
than food, and the body more than
clothes. 24Consider the ravens: They do
not sow or reap, they have no storeroom
or barn; yet God feeds them.[p] And how
much more valuable you are than birds!
25Who of you by worrying can add a single
hour to his life[e]? 26Since you cannot do
this very little thing, why do you worry
about the rest?
27“Consider how the lilies grow. They
do not labor or spin. Yet I tell you, not
even Solomon in all his splendor[q] was
dressed like one of these. 28If that is how
God clothes the grass of the field, which
is here today, and tomorrow is thrown into
the fire, how much more will he clothe
you, O you of little faith![r] 29And do not set Lk 17:5-6
your heart on what you will eat or drink;
do not worry about it. 30For the pagan
world runs after all such things, and your
Father[s] knows that you need them.[t]
31But seek his kingdom,[u] and these
things will be given to you as well.[v]
32“Do not be afraid,[w] little flock, for
your Father has been pleased to give you
the kingdom.[x] 33Sell your possessions
and give to the poor.[y] Provide purses for
yourselves that will not wear out, a treasure in heaven[z] that will not be exhausted, where no thief comes near and no
moth destroys.[a] 34For where your treasure is, there your heart will be also.[b]

e 25 Or *single cubit to his height*

12:8 ACKNOWLEDGES ME BEFORE MEN. See Mt 10:32, note.

12:9 HE WHO DISOWNS ME. To disown Christ is (1) to fail to acknowledge before the ungodly that we are followers of Jesus, and (2) to refuse to stand with the gospel and Christ's principles of righteousness in the face of society's non-Christian values.

12:10 BLASPHEMES AGAINST THE HOLY SPIRIT. See Mt 12:31, note.

12:15 GUARD AGAINST ... GREED. To make earthly gain or riches the desire of one's life is a fatal error that leads to eternal loss (vv. 20–21). (1) The Greek word for greed (*pleonexia*) literally signifies the thirst for having more. (2) Covetousness does not refer to providing for one's own needs and those of one's family (cf. Pr 6:6). While we work for our needs, however, we must be rich toward God by seeking first his kingdom and his righteousness (v. 31; cf. Mt 6:33, note). (3) Each of us should heed Jesus' warning and examine whether selfishness and greed exist in our own hearts. For more on this subject, see article on RICHES AND POVERTY, p. 152.

12:22 DO NOT WORRY ABOUT YOUR LIFE. See Mt 6:25, note.

12:24 HOW MUCH MORE VALUABLE. See Mt 6:25,30, notes.

12:31 SEEK HIS KINGDOM. See Mt 6:33, note.

12:33 SELL YOUR POSSESSIONS. See Mt 19:21, note; 1Co 16:2; 2Co 8:1–5 for the meaning of what Jesus says here.

12:34 YOUR TREASURE ... YOUR HEART. A person's heart (i.e., feelings, thinking, desires, val-

Watchfulness

12:35,36pp — Mt 25:1–13; Mk 13:33–37
12:39,40; 42–46pp — Mt 24:43–51

35"Be dressed ready for service and
keep your lamps burning, **36**like men waiting for their master to return from a wedding banquet, so that when he comes and
knocks they can immediately open the
door for him. **37**It will be good for those
servants whose master finds them watching when he comes.[c] I tell you the truth,
he will dress himself to serve, will have
them recline at the table and will come
and wait on them.[d] **38**It will be good for
those servants whose master finds them
ready, even if he comes in the second or
third watch of the night. **39**But understand
this: If the owner of the house had known
at what hour the thief[e] was coming, he
would not have let his house be broken
into. **40**You also must be ready,[f] because
the Son of Man will come at an hour when
you do not expect him."

41Peter asked, "Lord, are you telling
this parable to us, or to everyone?"

42The Lord[g] answered, "Who then is
the faithful and wise manager, whom the
master puts in charge of his servants to
give them their food allowance at the
proper time? **43**It will be good for that servant whom the master finds doing so
when he returns. **44**I tell you the truth, he
will put him in charge of all his possessions. **45**But suppose the servant says to
himself, 'My master is taking a long time
in coming,' and he then begins to beat the
menservants and maidservants and to eat
and drink and get drunk. **46**The master of
that servant will come on a day when he
does not expect him and at an hour he is
not aware of.[h] He will cut him to pieces
and assign him a place with the unbelievers.

47"That servant who knows his master's will and does not get ready or does
not do what his master wants will be beat-
en with many blows.[i] **48**But the one who
does not know and does things deserving
punishment will be beaten with few
blows.[j] From everyone who has been giv-
en much, much will be demanded; and

12:37 [c]Mt 24:42, 46; 25:13 [d]S Mt 20:28
12:39 [e]Mt 6:19; 1Th 5:2; 2Pe 3:10; Rev 3:3; 16:15
12:40 [f]Mk 13:33; Lk 21:36
12:42 [g]S Lk 7:13
12:46 [h]ver 40
12:47 [i]Dt 25:2
12:48 [j]Lev 5:17; Nu 15:27-30

ues, will and decisions) is attracted to the things that are most important to him or her. (1) If you treasure earthly things, then your heart will be enslaved to such things. (2) If God's kingdom, heavenly things, his Word, his presence, his holiness and your relationship to him are your treasure, then your heart will be drawn to the things of his kingdom and your life will be directed toward heaven, waiting for the return of your Lord (vv. 35–40).

12:35–40 DRESSED READY FOR SERVICE . . . LAMPS BURNING. Concerning the Lord's coming for his people, the NT church knew no other attitude than that it was near and could happen at any time (see Mk 13:35, note). Every believer was called on to be spiritually ready at all times and to wait for the return of the Lord. This NT norm is enjoined on all true believers in Christ. (1) Believers must be so bound to the Lord as their greatest treasure (v. 34) that their hope and longing is the return of Jesus (vv. 35–37). (2) Believers must be dressed and ready, waiting for the uncertain time of Christ's coming (vv. 38,40, notes). (3) Christ's coming is imminent, i.e., he could come at any time (v. 38). The believer must be waiting and looking for Christ himself, not for a complex of events that might begin at any time (see Mt 24:42,44, notes; Jn 14:3, note; 1Co 15:51, notes).

12:36 WAITING FOR THEIR MASTER. See Mt 25:1,4, notes.

12:38 IT WILL BE GOOD FOR THOSE SERVANTS. A special blessing of Christ's presence and care is reserved for those who in full readiness and faithfulness "wait" (v. 36) and "watch" (v. 37) for their Lord's return during the interval between his ascension and second coming.

12:40 WHEN YOU DO NOT EXPECT HIM. God's servants must always be spiritually ready and obedient (v. 35) because the Lord will come at an uncertain time. Passages stressing the same truth are Mt 24:36,42–44; Lk 21:34; 1Th 5:2–4.

12:42–48 FAITHFUL AND UNFAITHFUL SERVANT. Jesus uses this parable to illustrate the two possible ways of living open to all disciples in the light of his absence and promised return. (1) They can be faithful and obedient, ever watchful and spiritually ready for the Lord's return at any time, and they will receive their Master's blessing (see v. 35, note; Mk 13:35, note; Jn 14:3, note). (2) They can grow careless and worldly-minded, believe that the Lord will delay his coming, cease to resist sin and depart from the path of faithfulness; they will then receive God's condemnation and inherit everlasting shame and ruin at his coming (vv. 45–46; cf. Mt 24:44, note; Jn 5:24, note; 15:6, note).

12:45 MY MASTER IS TAKING A LONG TIME. Denying that Christ may return at any time to judge the careless, indifferent disciple takes away the force of Christ's exhortation to persevere in faith in light of his unexpected coming (vv. 35,37–38,40). It is precisely because there is no more opportunity for spiritual repentance when he returns that his coming is so perilous for apostate believers. In other words, Christ's coming is like death: it is final and can happen at any time (see Mt 24:42,44, notes; Mk 13:35, note; 2Th 2:11, note).

12:47–48 BEATEN WITH FEW BLOWS. Just as there will be degrees of reward in heaven (1Co 15:41–42), so there will also be degrees of punishment in hell. Those who are eternally lost will undergo different grades of punishment according to their privileges and responsibility (cf. Mt 23:14; Heb 10:29).

from the one who has been entrusted with
much, much more will be asked.

Not Peace but Division

12:51–53pp – Mt 10:34–36

49“I have come to bring fire on the
earth, and how I wish it were already kindled! 50But I have a baptism[k] to undergo,
and how distressed I am until it is completed![l] 51Do you think I came to bring
peace on earth? No, I tell you, but division.
52From now on there will be five in one
family divided against each other, three
against two and two against three. 53They
will be divided, father against son and son
against father, mother against daughter
and daughter against mother, mother-in-
law against daughter-in-law and daughter-in-law against mother-in-law.”[m]

Interpreting the Times

54He said to the crowd: “When you see
a cloud rising in the west, immediately
you say, ‘It’s going to rain,’ and it does.[n]
55And when the south wind blows, you
say, ‘It’s going to be hot,’ and it is. 56Hyp-
ocrites! You know how to interpret the
appearance of the earth and the sky. How
is it that you don’t know how to interpret
this present time?[o]

57“Why don’t you judge for yourselves
what is right? 58As you are going with
your adversary to the magistrate, try hard
to be reconciled to him on the way, or he
may drag you off to the judge, and the
judge turn you over to the officer, and the
officer throw you into prison.[p] 59I tell you,
you will not get out until you have paid the
last penny.[f]”[q]

Repent or Perish

13 Now there were some present at
that time who told Jesus about the
Galileans whose blood Pilate[r] had mixed
with their sacrifices. 2Jesus answered,
“Do you think that these Galileans were
worse sinners than all the other Galileans
because they suffered this way?[s] 3I tell
you, no! But unless you repent, you too
will all perish. 4Or those eighteen who
died when the tower in Siloam[t] fell on
them — do you think they were more guilty
than all the others living in Jerusalem? 5I
tell you, no! But unless you repent,[u] you
too will all perish.”

6Then he told this parable: “A man had
a fig tree, planted in his vineyard, and he
went to look for fruit on it, but did not find
any.[v] 7So he said to the man who took
care of the vineyard, ‘For three years now
I’ve been coming to look for fruit on this
fig tree and haven’t found any. Cut it
down![w] Why should it use up the soil?’

8“ ‘Sir,’ the man replied, ‘leave it alone
for one more year, and I’ll dig around it
and fertilize it. 9If it bears fruit next year,
fine! If not, then cut it down.’ ”

A Crippled Woman Healed on the Sabbath

10On a Sabbath Jesus was teaching in
one of the synagogues,[x] 11and a woman
was there who had been crippled by a spirit for eighteen years.[y] She was bent over
and could not straighten up at all. 12When
Jesus saw her, he called her forward and
said to her, “Woman, you are set free from
your infirmity.” 13Then he put his hands
on her,[z] and immediately she straightened up and praised God.

14Indignant because Jesus had healed
on the Sabbath,[a] the synagogue ruler[b]
said to the people, “There are six days for
work.[c] So come and be healed on those
days, not on the Sabbath.”

15The Lord answered him, “You hypocrites! Doesn’t each of you on the Sabbath
untie his ox or donkey from the stall and
lead it out to give it water?[d] 16Then
should not this woman, a daughter of

12:50 [k]Mk 10:38 [l]S Jn 19:30
12:53 [m]Mic 7:6; Mt 10:21
12:54 [n]Mt 16:2
12:56 [o]Mt 16:3
12:58 [p]Mt 5:25
12:59 [q]Mt 5:26; Mk 12:42
13:1 [r]S Mt 27:2
13:2 [s]Jn 9:2,3
13:4 [t]Jn 9:7,11
13:5 [u]Mt 3:2; Ac 2:38
13:6 [v]Isa 5:2; Jer 8:13; Mt 21:19
13:7 [w]S Mt 3:10
13:10 [x]S Mt 4:23
13:11 [y]ver 16
13:13 [z]S Mk 5:23
13:14 [a]S Mt 12:2 [b]S Mk 5:22 [c]Ex 20:9
13:15 [d]Lk 14:5

f 59 Greek *lepton*

12:51 I CAME TO BRING . . . DIVISION. See Mt 10:34, note.

13:6–9 FIG TREE . . . CUT IT DOWN. The parable of the fig tree refers primarily to Israel (cf. 3:9; Hos 9:10; Joel 1:7). However, its truth applies also to all individuals who profess to believe in Jesus, yet fail to turn from sin. While God gives everyone sufficient opportunity to repent, he will not tolerate sin forever. A time will come when God’s grace will be withdrawn and the unrepentant punished without mercy (cf. 20:16; 21:20–24).

13:11 CRIPPLED BY A SPIRIT. Jesus sees some physical sickness as the direct result of demonic activity or oppression. This crippled woman was afflicted by “a spirit” (i.e., a representative of Satan; see v. 16; cf. Mt 9:32–33; 12:22; Mk 5:1–5; 9:17–18; Ac 10:38).

13:16 THIS WOMAN . . . SATAN HAS KEPT BOUND. It is a detestable sin in Christ’s eyes when a person no longer hears the sighs of suffering humanity (vv. 11–14). Jesus teaches that people are imprisoned by sin, sickness and death, and are in distress and great need (vv. 11,16; Mt 4:23; Ac 26:18). Today we are in great danger of becoming insensitive to the world’s misery and suffering because of the entertainment media that revel in showing immorality and violence for the sake of pleasure. True disciples will be like their Master, able to see the distresses of life and

Lk 17:12-19

Abraham,[e] whom Satan[f] has kept bound
for eighteen long years, be set free on the
Sabbath day from what bound her?"
17When he said this, all his opponents
were humiliated,[g] but the people were delighted with all the wonderful things he
was doing.

The Parables of the Mustard Seed and the Yeast

13:18,19pp — Mk 4:30–32
13:18–21pp — Mt 13:31–33

18Then Jesus asked, "What is the kingdom of God[h] like?[i] What shall I compare
it to? **19**It is like a mustard seed, which a
man took and planted in his garden. It
grew and became a tree,[j] and the birds of
the air perched in its branches."[k]
20Again he asked, "What shall I compare the kingdom of God to? **21**It is like
yeast that a woman took and mixed into
a large amount[g] of flour until it worked all
through the dough."[l]

The Narrow Door

22Then Jesus went through the towns
and villages, teaching as he made his way
to Jerusalem.[m] **23**Someone asked him,
"Lord, are only a few people going to be
saved?"
He said to them, **24**"Make every effort
to enter through the narrow door,[n] because many, I tell you, will try to enter
and will not be able to. **25**Once the owner
of the house gets up and closes the door,
you will stand outside knocking and
pleading, 'Sir, open the door for us.'
"But he will answer, 'I don't know you
or where you come from.'[o]
26"Then you will say, 'We ate and drank
with you, and you taught in our streets.'
27"But he will reply, 'I don't know you
or where you come from. Away from me,
all you evildoers!'[p]
28"There will be weeping there, and
gnashing of teeth,[q] when you see Abraham, Isaac and Jacob and all the prophets
in the kingdom of God, but you yourselves
thrown out. **29**People will come from east
and west[r] and north and south, and will
take their places at the feast in the kingdom of God. **30**Indeed there are those who
are last who will be first, and first who will
be last."[s]

13:16 [e] S Lk 3:8 [f] S Mt 4:10 **13:17** [g] Isa 66:5 **13:18** [h] S Mt 3:2 [i] S Mt 13:24 **13:19** [j] Lk 17:6 [k] S Mt 13:32 **13:21** [l] 1Co 5:6 **13:22** [m] S Lk 9:51 **13:24** [n] Mt 7:13 **13:25** [o] Mt 7:23; 25:10-12 **13:27** [p] S Mt 7:23 **13:28** [q] S Mt 8:12 **13:29** [r] S Mt 8:11 **13:30** [s] S Mt 19:30

g 21 Greek *three satas* (probably about 1/2 bushel or 22 liters)

hear the groaning of creation (10:33–37; Ro 8:22).

13:19 MUSTARD SEED. The parables of the mustard seed and the yeast form a pair. They speak of the growth of evil within the visible kingdom. The parable of the mustard seed illustrates the small beginning of the kingdom and its development through the ages. It began only with Jesus and a group of committed disciples (see Jn 20:22; Ac 2:4). However, the visible manifestation of the kingdom grows until it becomes large, organized and powerful. It will then accept in its "branches" (fellowship) "the birds of the air," i.e., evil imposters who take away the seed of truth. Note that in Mt 13:4,19, birds are agents of evil in Christ's parable, and in Rev 18:2, Babylon the Great (representing the apostate church) becomes a home for demons and "a haunt for every unclean and detestable bird" (see Rev 2–3 for Christ's description of how spiritual decay had permeated the majority of the seven churches; Rev 18:4, note on the false church).

13:21 THE YEAST. Yeast is normally regarded in the OT as a symbol of the presence of evil or impurity; it ferments, disintegrates or corrupts (see Ex 12:19; 13:6–8; Lev 2:11; 6:17; Dt 16:3–4; Am 4:4–5). In the NT, yeast represents the false teaching and evil doctrines of the Pharisees, Sadducees (16:12) and Herodians (Mk 8:15). In 1Co 5:6–8 yeast is regarded by Paul as representing "malice and wickedness," while the absence of yeast represents "sincerity and truth" (cf. Gal 5:9). Therefore, many understand this parable to indicate evil, false doctrine and unrighteousness existing and spreading within the visible kingdom of God.

(1) This yeast of evil will spread throughout all parts of God's work. It is found in: (a) modernism, liberalism and liberation theology, which exalt human ideas over the authority of Scripture (cf. Mt 22:23,29); (b) worldliness and immorality within the churches (cf. 1Co 5:1–2; Rev 2–3); (c) the seeking of position or power within the church by those who are concerned more for their own ambition than for God's honor (cf. Mt 23); (d) false doctrines (cf. Gal 1:9); (e) false teachers (cf. Mt 24:11,24); (f) professing Christians who appear righteous, but are not really born again (cf. Mt 23; Jude 12–19). Toward the end of this present age these evils will infiltrate God's work in Christian churches, denominations, colleges and seminaries until the NT apostolic gospel and righteous living are diluted and corrupted on a grand scale (see 18:8; Mt 24:10–12; Gal 1:9, note; 2Th 2:3; 1Ti 4:1, note; Rev 2–3; see articles on THE GREAT TRIBULATION, p. 52, and OVERSEERS AND THEIR DUTIES, p. 274).

(2) Every Christian must be careful that the yeast of evil does not affect his or her own life. The secret of victory lies in keeping our eyes fixed on Jesus in faith (Tit 2:13; Heb 12:2,15), despising the things of the world (Jas 1:27; 1Jn 2:15–17), remaining in God's Word (Jn 15:7; Jas 1:21), looking forward to Christ's return (12:35–40), continually listening to the voice of the Holy Spirit (Ro 8:12–14; Gal 5:16–18), being willing to suffer (1Pe 4:1–2), fighting against evil (1Co 10:6; 1Th 5:15; 1Pe 3:11), defending the gospel (Php 1:17) and putting on the full armor of God (Eph 6:11–18).

13:24 THE NARROW DOOR. See Mt 7:14, note.

13:30 LAST . . . WILL BE FIRST. See Mt 19:30, note.

Jesus' Sorrow for Jerusalem

13:34,35pp — Mt 23:37–39
13:34,35Ref — Lk 19:41

31 At that time some Pharisees came to
Jesus and said to him, "Leave this place
and go somewhere else. Herod[t] wants to
kill you."
32 He replied, "Go tell that fox, 'I will
drive out demons and heal people today
and tomorrow, and on the third day I will
reach my goal.'[u] 33 In any case, I must
keep going today and tomorrow and the
next day—for surely no prophet[v] can die
outside Jerusalem!
34 "O Jerusalem, Jerusalem, you who kill
the prophets and stone those sent to you,
how often I have longed to gather your
children together, as a hen gathers her
chicks under her wings,[w] but you were not
willing! 35 Look, your house is left to you
desolate.[x] I tell you, you will not see me
again until you say, 'Blessed is he who
comes in the name of the Lord.'[h]"[y]

Jesus at a Pharisee's House

14:8–10Ref — Pr 25:6,7

14 One Sabbath, when Jesus went to
eat in the house of a prominent
Pharisee,[z] he was being carefully
watched.[a] 2 There in front of him was a
man suffering from dropsy. 3 Jesus asked
the Pharisees and experts in the law,[b] "Is
it lawful to heal on the Sabbath or not?"[c]
4 But they remained silent. So taking hold
of the man, he healed him and sent him
away.
5 Then he asked them, "If one of you has
a son[i] or an ox that falls into a well on the
Sabbath day, will you not immediately pull
him out?"[d] 6 And they had nothing to say.

13:31 [t]S Mt 14:1 **13:32** [u]S Heb 2:10 **13:33** [v]S Mt 21:11 **13:34** [w]S Mt 23:37 **13:35** [x]Jer 12:17; 22:5 [y]Ps 118:26; Lk 19:38 **14:1** [z]Lk 7:36; 11:37 [a]S Mt 12:10 **14:3** [b]S Mt 22:35 [c]S Mt 12:2 **14:5** [d]Lk 13:15

7 When he noticed how the guests
picked the places of honor at the table,[e]
he told them this parable: 8 "When someone invites you to a wedding feast, do not
take the place of honor, for a person more
distinguished than you may have been invited. 9 If so, the host who invited both of
you will come and say to you, 'Give this
man your seat.' Then, humiliated, you will
have to take the least important place.
10 But when you are invited, take the lowest place, so that when your host comes,
he will say to you, 'Friend, move up to a
better place.' Then you will be honored in
the presence of all your fellow guests.
11 For everyone who exalts himself will be
humbled, and he who humbles himself will
be exalted."[f]
12 Then Jesus said to his host, "When
you give a luncheon or dinner, do not invite your friends, your brothers or relatives, or your rich neighbors; if you do,
they may invite you back and so you will
be repaid. 13 But when you give a banquet,
invite the poor, the crippled, the lame, the
blind,[g] 14 and you will be blessed. Although they cannot repay you, you will be
repaid at the resurrection of the righteous."[h]

The Parable of the Great Banquet

14:16–24Ref — Mt 22:2–14

15 When one of those at the table with
him heard this, he said to Jesus, "Blessed
is the man who will eat at the feast[i] in the
kingdom of God."[j]
16 Jesus replied: "A certain man was
preparing a great banquet and invited

14:7 [e]S Lk 11:43 **14:11** [f]S Mt 23:12 **14:13** [g]ver 21 **14:14** [h]Ac 24:15 **14:15** [i]Isa 25:6; Mt 26:29; Lk 13:29; Rev 19:9 [j]S Mt 3:2

h *35* Psalm 118:26 i *5* Some manuscripts *donkey*

13:34 THE LORD'S GREAT SORROW. Our Lord's tears (cf. 19:41) over Jerusalem's stubbornness witness to the freedom of the human will to resist the grace and will of God (see 19:41, note; Ac 7:51; Ro 1:18–32; 2:5).

14:11 EXALTS HIMSELF . . . HUMBLED. The Savior warns that those who exalt themselves in this life will be put to shame in the future kingdom of heaven. Much more important than earthly honor is our place of honor before God. Such honor cannot be secured by self-assertiveness, for it comes only through humility and servanthood (vv. 12–14), and by seeking "the praise that comes from the only God" (Jn 5:44).

14:15–24 THE PARABLE OF THE GREAT BANQUET. Although this parable originally applied to Israel and its rejection of the gospel, it also applies to the churches and every believer today. (1) The subject of this parable is the day of resurrection in its future heavenly glory (vv. 14–15; cf. 22:18), i.e., the return of Christ to bring his people into the heavenly kingdom.

(2) Those who initially accepted the invitation but then refused to come represent those who have accepted or have appeared to accept the invitation of Jesus to salvation, yet their love for him and the heavenly kingdom has grown cold (vv. 17–20).

(3) Such people have ceased to set their goals by heavenly standards (vv. 18–20). They have rejected the Biblical admonition to set their "minds on things above, not on earthly things," while waiting for the appearing of Christ (Col 3:1–4). Their hope and life are centered on the things of this world, and they no longer long for "a better country—a heavenly one" (Heb 11:16).

(4) Vv. 21–23 indicate that there will also be those whose hearts are with Christ in heaven and not fixed on their prospects in this world. They pray with the Spirit and the bride: "Amen. Come, Lord Jesus" (Rev 22:20).

many guests. 17At the time of the banquet
he sent his servant to tell those who had
been invited, 'Come, for everything is now
ready.'
18"But they all alike began to make excuses. The first said, 'I have just bought
a field, and I must go and see it. Please
excuse me.'
19"Another said, 'I have just bought five
yoke of oxen, and I'm on my way to try
them out. Please excuse me.'
20"Still another said, 'I just got married, so I can't come.'
21"The servant came back and reported
this to his master. Then the owner of the
house became angry and ordered his servant, 'Go out quickly into the streets and
alleys of the town and bring in the poor,
the crippled, the blind and the lame.'[k]
22" 'Sir,' the servant said, 'what you ordered has been done, but there is still
room.'
23"Then the master told his servant,
'Go out to the roads and country lanes and
make them come in, so that my house will
be full. 24I tell you, not one of those men
who were invited will get a taste of my
banquet.' "[l]

The Cost of Being a Disciple

25Large crowds were traveling with
Jesus, and turning to them he said: 26"If
anyone comes to me and does not hate his
father and mother, his wife and children,
his brothers and sisters—yes, even his
own life—he cannot be my disciple.[m]
27And anyone who does not carry his
cross and follow me cannot be my disciple.[n]
28"Suppose one of you wants to build a
tower. Will he not first sit down and estimate the cost to see if he has enough money to complete it? 29For if he lays the foundation and is not able to finish it, everyone
who sees it will ridicule him, 30saying,
'This fellow began to build and was not
able to finish.'
31"Or suppose a king is about to go to
war against another king. Will he not first
sit down and consider whether he is able
with ten thousand men to oppose the one
coming against him with twenty thousand? 32If he is not able, he will send a
delegation while the other is still a long
way off and will ask for terms of peace.
33In the same way, any of you who does
not give up everything he has cannot be
my disciple.[o]
34"Salt is good, but if it loses its saltiness, how can it be made salty again?[p]
35It is fit neither for the soil nor for the
manure pile; it is thrown out.[q]
"He who has ears to hear, let him
hear."[r]

The Parable of the Lost Sheep

15:4–7pp — Mt 18:12–14

15 Now the tax collectors[s] and "sinners" were all gathering around to
hear him. 2But the Pharisees and the
teachers of the law muttered, "This man
welcomes sinners and eats with them."[t]
3Then Jesus told them this parable:[u]
4"Suppose one of you has a hundred sheep
and loses one of them. Does he not leave
the ninety-nine in the open country and go
after the lost sheep until he finds it?[v]
5And when he finds it, he joyfully puts it
on his shoulders 6and goes home. Then he
calls his friends and neighbors together
and says, 'Rejoice with me; I have found
my lost sheep.'[w] 7I tell you that in the
same way there will be more rejoicing in
heaven over one sinner who repents than

14:21 [k] ver 13
14:24 [l] Mt 21:43; Ac 13:46
14:26 [m] Mt 10:37; S Jn 12:25
14:27 [n] Mt 10:38; Lk 9:23
14:33 [o] Php 3:7,8
14:34 [p] Mk 9:50
14:35 [q] Mt 5:13 [r] S Mt 11:15
15:1 [s] Lk 5:29
15:2 [t] S Mt 9:11
15:3 [u] Mt 13:3
15:4 [v] Ps 23; 119:176; Jer 31:10; Eze 34:11-16; Lk 5:32; 19:10
15:6 [w] ver 9

14:26 DOES NOT HATE HIS FATHER. The word "hate" in this passage means "love less" (compare this text with Mt 10:37; see also Ge 29:31). Jesus demands that our loyalty to and love for him be greater than every other attachment, even to our own families.

14:27 CARRY HIS CROSS. See 9:23, note; Mk 8:34, note.

14:28–33 THE COST OF DISCIPLESHIP. Jesus teaches that whoever desires to follow him and be his disciple should first decide whether he or she is prepared to pay the cost. The cost of real discipleship is to give up all relationships and possessions, i.e., all that we have: material things, family, our own lives, desires, plans and interests (v. 33). This does not mean that we must reject all we have, but that all that we have must be placed at Christ's service and under his guidance (see 13:24; Mt 7:14; cf. Jn 16:33; 2Ti 3:12).

15:4 THE LOST SHEEP. The key verse in Luke's Gospel states that "the Son of Man came to seek and to save what was lost" (19:10). The three parables in ch. 15 illustrate this purpose of Jesus' earthly mission and reveal God's desire to save the lost for time and eternity. We learn that (1) seeking lost sinners to bring them to redemption is of utmost importance to the heart of God (vv. 4,8,20,24); (2) both God and heaven rejoice when even one sinner repents (vv. 7,10); and (3) no amount of sacrifice or suffering is too great in seeking the lost and bringing them to Jesus (vv. 4,8).

15:7 REJOICING IN HEAVEN. God and the angels in heaven have such love, compassion and grief for those who have fallen into sin and spiritual death that when one sinner repents, they openly rejoice. On God's love for sinners, see Isa 62:5; Jer 32:41; Eze 18:23,32; Hos 11:8; Jn 3:16; Ro 5:6–11; 2Pe 3:9.

over ninety-nine righteous persons who
do not need to repent.[x]

The Parable of the Lost Coin

8“Or suppose a woman has ten silver
coins[j] and loses one. Does she not light
a lamp, sweep the house and search carefully until she finds it? 9And when she
finds it, she calls her friends and neighbors together and says, ‘Rejoice with me;
I have found my lost coin.’[y] 10In the same
way, I tell you, there is rejoicing in the
presence of the angels of God over one
sinner who repents.”[z]

The Parable of the Lost Son

11Jesus continued: “There was a man
who had two sons.[a] 12The younger one
said to his father, ‘Father, give me my
share of the estate.’[b] So he divided his
property[c] between them.
13“Not long after that, the younger son
got together all he had, set off for a distant
country and there squandered his wealth[d]
in wild living. 14After he had spent everything, there was a severe famine in that
whole country, and he began to be in need.
15So he went and hired himself out to a
citizen of that country, who sent him to his
fields to feed pigs.[e] 16He longed to fill his
stomach with the pods that the pigs were
eating, but no one gave him anything.
17“When he came to his senses, he said,
‘How many of my father’s hired men have
food to spare, and here I am starving to
death! 18I will set out and go back to my
father and say to him: Father, I have
sinned[f] against heaven and against you.
19I am no longer worthy to be called your
son; make me like one of your hired men.’
20So he got up and went to his father.
“But while he was still a long way off,
his father saw him and was filled with
compassion for him; he ran to his son,
threw his arms around him and kissed
him.[g]
21“The son said to him, ‘Father, I have
sinned against heaven and against you.[h]
I am no longer worthy to be called your
son.[k]’
22“But the father said to his servants,
‘Quick! Bring the best robe[i] and put it on
him. Put a ring on his finger[j] and sandals
on his feet. 23Bring the fattened calf and
kill it. Let’s have a feast and celebrate.
24For this son of mine was dead and is
alive again;[k] he was lost and is found.’ So
they began to celebrate.[l]
25“Meanwhile, the older son was in the
field. When he came near the house, he
heard music and dancing. 26So he called
one of the servants and asked him what
was going on. 27‘Your brother has come,’
he replied, ‘and your father has killed the
fattened calf because he has him back
safe and sound.’
28“The older brother became angry[m]
and refused to go in. So his father went
out and pleaded with him. 29But he an-

15:7 [x]ver 10
15:9 [y]ver 6
15:10 [z]ver 7
15:11 [a]Mt 21:28
15:12 [b]Dt 21:17 [c]ver 30
15:13 [d]ver 30; Lk 16:1
15:15 [e]Lev 11:7
15:18 [f]Lev 26:40; Mt 3:2
15:20 [g]Ge 45:14, 15; 46:29; Ac 20:37
15:21 [h]Ps 51:4
15:22 [i]Zec 3:4; Rev 6:11 [j]Ge 41:42
15:24 [k]Eph 2:1, 5; 5:14; 1Ti 5:6 [l]ver 32
15:28 [m]Jnh 4:1

j *8* Greek *ten drachmas,* each worth about a day’s wages k *21* Some early manuscripts *son. Make me like one of your hired men.*

15:8 SEARCH CAREFULLY UNTIL SHE FINDS. We should pray that the Holy Spirit may fill our hearts with an earnest desire to bring sinners to salvation.

15:13 SET OFF FOR A DISTANT COUNTRY. In this parable the Lord teaches that a life of sin and selfishness, in its deepest sense, is a separation from God’s love, fellowship and authority. The sinner or backslider is like the young son who, pursuing the pleasures of sin, wastes the physical, intellectual and spiritual gifts given by God. This results in disillusionment and sorrow, sometimes degrading personal conditions, and always the lack of a true and real life that can be found only in a right relationship with God.

15:17 HE CAME TO HIS SENSES. Before the lost can come to God, they must see their true state of slavery to sin and separation from God (vv. 14–17). They must humbly return to the Father, confess their sin and be willing to do whatever the Father requires (vv. 17–19). To bring the lost to this realization is the work of the Holy Spirit (Jn 16:7–11).

15:20 WHILE HE WAS STILL A LONG WAY OFF. Every Christian father and mother must understand that God loves their wandering child and desires his or her salvation as much as they do. Pray and trust God to seek that child until he or she returns to the heavenly Father.

15:20 HIS FATHER SAW HIM AND WAS FILLED WITH COMPASSION. Jesus’ description of the father’s response to the son’s return teaches several important truths: (1) God has compassion for the lost because of their sorrowful condition. (2) God’s love for them is so great that he never ceases to grieve over them and to wait for their return. (3) When sinners sincerely turn to God, God is more than ready to receive them with forgiveness, love, compassion, grace and the full rights of children (cf. Jn 1:12). The benefits of Christ’s death, the Holy Spirit’s influence and God’s rich grace are all made available to those who seek God. (4) God’s joy over the return of sinners is immeasurable (vv. 6–7,10,22–24).

15:24 THIS SON OF MINE . . . WAS LOST. “Lost” is used in the sense of being lost to God, like “sheep going astray” (1Pe 2:25; cf. Isa 53:6). Life away from God’s fellowship is spiritual death (Eph 2:1; 1Jn 3:14). Returning to God brings true life (Jn 11:26).

15:28 BECAME ANGRY. The “older son” represents those who have a form of religion and outwardly keep God’s commands, but inwardly they are separated from him and his purposes for the kingdom (vv. 28–30).

swered his father, 'Look! All these years
I've been slaving for you and never disobeyed your orders. Yet you never gave
me even a young goat so I could celebrate
with my friends. **30**But when this son of
yours who has squandered your property[n]
with prostitutes[o] comes home, you kill
the fattened calf for him!'
31"'My son,' the father said, 'you are
always with me, and everything I have is
yours. **32**But we had to celebrate and be
glad, because this brother of yours was
dead and is alive again; he was lost and
is found.'"[p]

The Parable of the Shrewd Manager

16 Jesus told his disciples: "There
was a rich man whose manager
was accused of wasting his possessions.[q]
2So he called him in and asked him, 'What
is this I hear about you? Give an account
of your management, because you cannot
be manager any longer.'
3"The manager said to himself, 'What
shall I do now? My master is taking away
my job. I'm not strong enough to dig, and
I'm ashamed to beg— **4**I know what I'll do
so that, when I lose my job here, people
will welcome me into their houses.'
5"So he called in each one of his master's debtors. He asked the first, 'How
much do you owe my master?'
6"'Eight hundred gallons[l] of olive oil,'
he replied.
"The manager told him, 'Take your bill,
sit down quickly, and make it four hundred.'
7"Then he asked the second, 'And how
much do you owe?'
"'A thousand bushels[m] of wheat,' he
replied.
"He told him, 'Take your bill and make
it eight hundred.'
8"The master commended the dishonest manager because he had acted
shrewdly. For the people of this world[r]
are more shrewd[s] in dealing with their
own kind than are the people of the light.[t]
9I tell you, use worldly wealth[u] to gain
friends for yourselves, so that when it is
gone, you will be welcomed into eternal
dwellings.[v]
10"Whoever can be trusted with very little can also be trusted with much,[w] and
whoever is dishonest with very little will
also be dishonest with much. **11**So if you
have not been trustworthy in handling
worldly wealth,[x] who will trust you with
true riches? **12**And if you have not been
trustworthy with someone else's property, who will give you property of your
own?
13"No servant can serve two masters.
Either he will hate the one and love the
other, or he will be devoted to the one and
despise the other. You cannot serve both
God and Money."[y]
14The Pharisees, who loved money,[z]
heard all this and were sneering at
Jesus.[a] **15**He said to them, "You are the
ones who justify yourselves[b] in the eyes
of men, but God knows your hearts.[c]
What is highly valued among men is detestable in God's sight.

Additional Teachings

16"The Law and the Prophets were proclaimed until John.[d] Since that time, the
good news of the kingdom of God is being
preached,[e] and everyone is forcing his
way into it. **17**It is easier for heaven and
earth to disappear than for the least
stroke of a pen to drop out of the Law.[f]
18"Anyone who divorces his wife and
marries another woman commits adul-

[l] 6 Greek *one hundred batous* (probably about 3 kiloliters) [m] 7 Greek *one hundred korous* (probably about 35 kiloliters)

15:30 [n] ver 12,13 [o] Pr 29:3 **15:32** [p] ver 24; Mal 3:17 **16:1** [q] Lk 15:13, 30

16:8 [r] Ps 17:14 [s] Ps 18:26 [t] Jn 12:36; Eph 5:8; 1Th 5:5 **16:9** [u] ver 11,13 [v] Mt 19:21; Lk 12:33 **16:10** [w] Mt 25:21, 23; Lk 19:17 **16:11** [x] ver 9,13 **16:13** [y] ver 9,11; Mt 6:24 **16:14** [z] S 1Ti 3:3 [a] Lk 23:35 **16:15** [b] Lk 10:29 [c] S Rev 2:23 **16:16** [d] Mt 5:17; 11:12,13 [e] S Mt 4:23 **16:17** [f] S Mt 5:18

16:8 COMMENDED THE DISHONEST MANAGER. The point of Jesus' illustration is that the worldly are earthly-minded enough to promote their own interest and welfare. In contrast, believers often are not heavenly-minded enough to use their earthly possessions to promote their spiritual and heavenly interest.

16:9 WORLDLY WEALTH. Injustice, greed and power are often involved in the accumulation and use of "worldly wealth" (see article on RICHES AND POVERTY, p. 152). We must use possessions and money in a way that promotes God's interests and the salvation of others.

16:11 IF YOU HAVE NOT BEEN TRUSTWORTHY. Those who are not trustworthy in their acquisition and use of worldly goods will be the same with spiritual things. This is why believers, and especially church leaders, must be free from the love of money (1Ti 3:1–3).

16:13 YOU CANNOT SERVE BOTH GOD AND MONEY. The world's riches make it very difficult to keep God at the center of our lives. For more on this subject, see article on RICHES AND POVERTY, p. 152.

16:14 PHARISEES . . . LOVED MONEY. The Pharisees regarded riches as a blessing from God for their faithful observance of the law. They "sneered at" Jesus, who was poor, for they regarded his poverty as a sign that God had not honored him (see article on RICHES AND POVERTY, p. 152).

16:18 COMMITS ADULTERY. Anyone who divorces (or deserts) his or her marriage partner for unscriptural reasons (see Mt 19:9, note), and then

tery, and the man who marries a divorced
woman commits adultery.[g]

The Rich Man and Lazarus

19 “There was a rich man who was
dressed in purple and fine linen and lived
in luxury every day.[h] 20 At his gate was
laid a beggar[i] named Lazarus, covered
with sores 21 and longing to eat what fell
from the rich man’s table.[j] Even the dogs
came and licked his sores.
22 “The time came when the beggar died
and the angels carried him to Abraham’s
side. The rich man also died and was buried. 23 In hell,[n] where he was in torment,
he looked up and saw Abraham far away,
with Lazarus by his side. 24 So he called to
him, ‘Father Abraham,[k] have pity on me
and send Lazarus to dip the tip of his finger in water and cool my tongue, because
I am in agony in this fire.’[l]
25 “But Abraham replied, ‘Son, remember that in your lifetime you received your
good things, while Lazarus received bad
things,[m] but now he is comforted here and
you are in agony.[n] 26 And besides all this,
between us and you a great chasm has
been fixed, so that those who want to go
from here to you cannot, nor can anyone
cross over from there to us.’
27 “He answered, ‘Then I beg you, father, send Lazarus to my father’s house,
28 for I have five brothers. Let him warn
them,[o] so that they will not also come to
this place of torment.’
29 “Abraham replied, ‘They have Moses[p] and the Prophets;[q] let them listen to
them.’
30 “ ‘No, father Abraham,’[r] he said, ‘but
if someone from the dead goes to them,
they will repent.’
31 “He said to him, ‘If they do not listen
to Moses and the Prophets, they will not
be convinced even if someone rises from
the dead.’ ”

Sin, Faith, Duty

17 Jesus said to his disciples: “Things
that cause people to sin[s] are
bound to come, but woe to that person
through whom they come.[t] 2 It would be
better for him to be thrown into the sea
with a millstone tied around his neck than
for him to cause one of these little ones[u]
to sin.[v] 3 So watch yourselves.
“If your brother sins, rebuke him,[w] and
if he repents, forgive him.[x] 4 If he sins
against you seven times in a day, and sev-
en times comes back to you and says, ‘I
repent,’ forgive him.”[y]
5 The apostles[z] said to the Lord,[a] “Increase our faith!”
6 He replied, “If you have faith as small
as a mustard seed,[b] you can say to this

16:18 [g] Mt 5:31, 32; 19:9; Mk 10:11; Ro 7:2, 3; 1Co 7:10,11 **16:19** [h] Eze 16:49 **16:20** [i] Ac 3:2 **16:21** [j] Mt 15:27; Lk 15:16 **16:24** [k] ver 30; S Lk 3:8 [l] S Mt 5:22 **16:25** [m] Ps 17:14 [n] Lk 6:21,24,25 **16:28** [o] Ac 2:40; 20:23; 1Th 4:6 **16:29** [p] S Lk 24:27,44; Jn 1:45; 5:45-47; Ac 15:21 [q] Lk 4:17; 24:27, 44; Jn 1:45 **16:30** [r] ver 24; S Lk 3:8 **17:1** [s] S Mt 5:29 [t] Mt 18:7 **17:2** [u] Mk 10:24; Lk 10:21 [v] S Mt 5:29 **17:3** [w] S Mt 18:15 [x] Eph 4:32; Col 3:13 **17:4** [y] Mt 18:21, 22 **17:5** [z] S Mk 6:30 [a] S Lk 7:13 **17:6** [b] Mt 13:31; 17:20; Lk 13:19

[n] *23* Greek *Hades*

remarries, “commits adultery.” “Commits adultery” in Greek is a present active indicative, denoting continuing action; i.e., as long as the innocent and divorced spouse desires and seeks reconciliation, the guilty party who enters into another marriage relationship is living in an adulterous union. Since God does not regard the former marriage as annulled, any other union is sexual adultery. (1) The primary moral issue in this case is whether the remarriage of the guilty partner involves disregarding the covenant obligations and parental responsibilities of the first marriage, which are still capable of fulfillment. If the innocent partner desires reconciliation, the issue is decisive. The guilty party is committing adultery if he or she marries another (cf. Mk 10:11–12).

(2) However, if the offending party (a) does not have the possibility of returning to the first marriage, (b) has already entered into the adulterous type of marriage relationship described by Jesus, and (c) sincerely repents before God and makes the commitment to build the present relationship on godly principles, then the present marriage relationship may become legitimate (i.e., accepted by God).

16:19–31 THE RICH MAN AND LAZARUS. The rich man’s life was consumed in self-centered living. He made the wrong choice and suffered eternally (vv. 22–23). Lazarus lived all his life in poverty, but his heart was right with God. His name means “God is my help,” and he never gave up his faith in God. He died and was immediately taken to paradise with Abraham (v. 22; see 23:43; Ac 7:59; 2Co 5:8; Php 1:23). The destinies of both men were irreversible at death (vv. 24–26).

17:2 MILLSTONE TIED AROUND HIS NECK. Causing someone to sin because of our example, attitude or neglect will bring such severe punishment that death before committing this sin would be preferable (see Mt 18:6, note).

17:3 IF HE REPENTS, FORGIVE. Concerning Jesus’ statement about forgiving, observe the following: (1) Jesus is concerned that we possess an attitude that desires to forgive and help those who offend us, rather than a spirit of revenge or hatred. (2) Forgiveness and reconciliation cannot truly occur until the offending person acknowledges his or her wrong action and sincerely repents. Furthermore, Jesus was not referring to the same offense constantly repeated. (3) We should be willing to persevere in forgiveness if the offender sincerely repents. Jesus’ statement concerning forgiving “seven times in a day” is not meant to condone habitual sin. Nor is he saying that the believer must allow someone to severely mistreat or abuse him or her indefinitely. Instead, he teaches that we must maintain an attitude that is always ready to help and forgive the offender.

17:6 FAITH. See Mt 17:20, note; 21:21, note; Mk 11:24, note.

mulberry tree, 'Be uprooted and planted
Jn 14:12 in the sea,' and it will obey you.[c]
7"Suppose one of you had a servant
plowing or looking after the sheep. Would
he say to the servant when he comes in
from the field, 'Come along now and sit
down to eat'? **8**Would he not rather say,
'Prepare my supper, get yourself ready
and wait on me[d] while I eat and drink;
after that you may eat and drink'? **9**Would
he thank the servant because he did what
he was told to do? **10**So you also, when you
have done everything you were told to do,
should say, 'We are unworthy servants;
we have only done our duty.' "[e]

Ten Healed of Leprosy

11Now on his way to Jerusalem,[f] Jesus
traveled along the border between Samaria and Galilee.[g] **12**As he was going into a
village, ten men who had leprosy[o][h] met
him. They stood at a distance[i] **13**and
called out in a loud voice, "Jesus, Master,[j] have pity on us!"
14When he saw them, he said, "Go,
show yourselves to the priests."[k] And as
they went, they were cleansed.
15One of them, when he saw he was
healed, came back, praising God[l] in a
loud voice. **16**He threw himself at Jesus'
feet and thanked him—and he was a Samaritan.[m]
17Jesus asked, "Were not all ten
cleansed? Where are the other nine?
18Was no one found to return and give
praise to God except this foreigner?"
Jn 4:46-53 **19**Then he said to him, "Rise and go; your
faith has made you well."[n]

The Coming of the Kingdom of God

17:26,27pp — Mt 24:37–39

20Once, having been asked by the Pharisees when the kingdom of God would
come,[o] Jesus replied, "The kingdom of
God does not come with your careful observation, **21**nor will people say, 'Here it
is,' or 'There it is,'[p] because the kingdom
of God is within[p] you."
22Then he said to his disciples, "The
time is coming when you will long to see
one of the days of the Son of Man,[q] but
you will not see it.[r] **23**Men will tell you,
'There he is!' or 'Here he is!' Do not go
running off after them.[s] **24**For the Son of
Man in his day[q] will be like the lightning,[t] which flashes and lights up the sky
from one end to the other. **25**But first he
must suffer many things[u] and be rejected[v] by this generation.[w]
26"Just as it was in the days of Noah,[x]
so also will it be in the days of the Son of
Man. **27**People were eating, drinking, marrying and being given in marriage up to
the day Noah entered the ark. Then the
flood came and destroyed them all.
28"It was the same in the days of Lot.[y]
People were eating and drinking, buying
and selling, planting and building. **29**But
the day Lot left Sodom, fire and sulfur
rained down from heaven and destroyed
them all.
30"It will be just like this on the day the
Son of Man is revealed.[z] **31**On that day no
one who is on the roof of his house, with
his goods inside, should go down to get
them. Likewise, no one in the field should
go back for anything.[a] **32**Remember Lot's
wife![b] **33**Whoever tries to keep his life will
lose it, and whoever loses his life will preserve it.[c] **34**I tell you, on that night two
people will be in one bed; one will be taken
and the other left. **35**Two women will be

17:6 [c]S Mt 21:21; Mk 9:23 **17:8** [d]Lk 12:37 **17:10** [e]1Co 9:16 **17:11** [f]S Lk 9:51 [g]Lk 9:51,52; Jn 4:3,4 **17:12** [h]S Mt 8:2 [i]Lev 13:45,46 **17:13** [j]S Lk 5:5 **17:14** [k]Lev 14:2; Mt 8:4 **17:15** [l]S Mt 9:8 **17:16** [m]S Mt 10:5 **17:19** [n]S Mt 9:22

17:20 [o]S Mt 3:2 **17:21** [p]ver 23 **17:22** [q]S Mt 8:20 [r]S Lk 5:35 **17:23** [s]Mt 24:23; Lk 21:8 **17:24** [t]Mt 24:27 **17:25** [u]S Mt 16:21 [v]Lk 9:22; 18:32 [w]Mk 13:30; Lk 21:32 **17:26** [x]Ge 6:5-8; 7:6-24 **17:28** [y]Ge 19:1-28 **17:30** [z]Mt 10:23; S 16:27; 24:3,27, 37,39; 25:31; S 1Co 1:7; S 1Th 2:19; 2Th 1:7; 2:8; 2Pe 3:4; S Rev 1:7 **17:31** [a]Mt 24:17, 18 **17:32** [b]Ge 19:26 **17:33** [c]S Jn 12:25

[o] *12* The Greek word was used for various diseases affecting the skin—not necessarily leprosy. [p] *21* Or *among* [q] *24* Some manuscripts do not have *in his day.*

17:16 THANKED HIM. We who have received from God love, grace, salvation and all his spiritual blessings must not forget to thank him. What he has done for us should cause us to come to him with grateful hearts. "We love because he first loved us" (1Jn 4:19).

17:21 THE KINGDOM OF GOD IS WITHIN YOU. According to Jesus, the present nature of the kingdom is spiritual, not material or political. The "kingdom of God does not come with your careful observation" (v. 20), i.e., it does not come as an earthly political power. Instead it is within the hearts and in the midst of God's people, consisting of "righteousness, peace and joy in the Holy Spirit" (Ro 14:17). We demonstrate it by conquering, through the power of the Spirit, the forces of sin, sickness and Satan, not by conquering kings and nations (see article on THE KINGDOM OF GOD, p. 28). When Jesus comes to earth the second time, then the kingdom will be seen in its full power and glory (v. 24; cf. Mt 24:30) as it triumphs over kings and nations (Rev 11:15–18; 19:11–21).

17:26 THE DAYS OF NOAH. See Mt 24:37, note.

17:31 ON THAT DAY. See Mk 13:14, note on the abomination that causes desolation; see article on THE GREAT TRIBULATION, p. 52.

17:32 REMEMBER LOT'S WIFE! The tragic error of Lot's wife was to place her affections on an earthly society rather than on a heavenly one (cf. Heb 11:10). She turned back because her heart was still in Sodom (Ge 19:17,26). Every believer should ask: Is my heart more attached to earthly things than to Jesus and the hope of his return?

grinding grain together; one will be taken
and the other left.[r]"[d]

37"Where, Lord?" they asked.

He replied, "Where there is a dead body,
there the vultures will gather."[e]

The Parable of the Persistent Widow

18 Then Jesus told his disciples a parable to show them that they should
always pray and not give up.[f] 2He said:
"In a certain town there was a judge who
neither feared God nor cared about men.
3And there was a widow in that town who
kept coming to him with the plea, 'Grant
me justice[g] against my adversary.'

4"For some time he refused. But finally
he said to himself, 'Even though I don't
fear God or care about men, 5yet because
this widow keeps bothering me, I will see
that she gets justice, so that she won't
eventually wear me out with her coming!'"[h]

6And the Lord[i] said, "Listen to what
the unjust judge says. 7And will not God
bring about justice for his chosen ones,
who cry out[j] to him day and night? Will
he keep putting them off? 8I tell you, he
will see that they get justice, and quickly.
However, when the Son of Man[k] comes,[l]
will he find faith on the earth?"

The Parable of the Pharisee and the Tax Collector

9To some who were confident of their
own righteousness[m] and looked down on
everybody else,[n] Jesus told this parable:
10"Two men went up to the temple to
pray,[o] one a Pharisee and the other a tax
collector. 11The Pharisee stood up[p] and
prayed about[s] himself: 'God, I thank you
that I am not like other men—robbers,
evildoers, adulterers—or even like this
tax collector. 12I fast[q] twice a week and
give a tenth[r] of all I get.'

13"But the tax collector stood at a distance. He would not even look up to heav-
en, but beat his breast[s] and said, 'God,
have mercy on me, a sinner.'[t]

14"I tell you that this man, rather than
the other, went home justified before God.
For everyone who exalts himself will be

17:35 [d] Mt 24:41 **17:37** [e] Mt 24:28 **18:1** [f] Isa 40:31; Lk 11:5-8; S Ac 1:14; S Ro 1:10; 12:12; Eph 6:18; Col 4:2; 1Th 5:17 **18:3** [g] Isa 1:17 **18:5** [h] Lk 11:8 **18:6** [i] S Lk 7:13 **18:7** [j] Ex 22:23; Ps 88:1; Rev 6:10 **18:8** [k] S Mt 8:20 [l] S Mt 16:27 **18:9** [m] Lk 16:15 [n] Isa 65:5 **18:10** [o] Ac 3:1 **18:11** [p] Mt 6:5; Mk 11:25 **18:12** [q] Isa 58:3; Mt 9:14 [r] Mal 3:8; Lk 11:42 **18:13** [s] Isa 66:2; Jer 31:19; Lk 23:48 [t] Lk 5:32; 1Ti 1:15

[r] *35* Some manuscripts *left.* *36Two men will be in the field; one will be taken and the other left.*

[s] *11* Or *to*

17:37 A DEAD BODY . . . THE VULTURES. This verse suggests the certainty of judgment on those who are spiritually dead (cf. Mt 24:28; Rev 19:17–18). Just as surely as vultures come to the corpse, so judgment will come on the wicked when Christ returns.

18:1 THEY SHOULD ALWAYS PRAY. Jesus was concerned that his followers pray continually in order to accomplish God's will for their lives. From this parable of the persistent widow we learn several things: (1) We must persevere in prayer with regard to all matters until Jesus returns (vv. 7–8; Ro 12:12; Eph 6:18; Col 4:2; 1Th 5:17). (2) In this life we have an adversary (v. 3), Satan (1Pe 5:8). Prayer can protect us from the evil one (Mt 6:13). (3) In our prayers, we should cry out against sin and for justice (v. 7). (4) Persistent prayer is counted as faith (v. 8). (5) In the final days before Christ's return, there will be increased diabolic opposition to the prayers of the faithful (1Ti 4:1). Because of Satan and the pleasures of the world, many will cease having a persistent prayer life (8:14; Mt 13:22; Mk 4:19).

18:7 CHOSEN ONES, WHO CRY OUT . . . DAY AND NIGHT. God's true chosen ones (i.e., those persevering in faith and holiness) will never cease crying out to God for Christ's return to destroy Satan's power and the present evil world system. They will persevere in prayer to "see that they get justice, and quickly" (v. 8), and for Christ to reign in righteousness, knowing that Christ's coming is the only real hope for this world (cf. Jn 14:2; 1Th 5:2–3; 2Th 2:8; Rev 19:11–21).

18:8 HE WILL SEE THAT THEY GET JUSTICE. When Jesus returns for those who cry out to him day and night (v. 7), he will put an end to the distress and suffering received at the hands of a hostile and evil world, and he will take them to himself (Jn 14:2–3, notes). At his coming, the faithful of his churches will be "caught up together with them in the clouds to meet the Lord in the air" (1Th 4:17). Then God will administer his justice and wrath on the wicked (1Th 5:2–3,9).

18:8 WILL HE FIND FAITH ON THE EARTH? Jesus' question probably indicates that as the time for his return draws near, evil will become so dominant that many in the church will fall away from genuine faith (Mt 24:11–13,24; 1Ti 4:1; see articles on THE GREAT TRIBULATION, p. 52, THE AGE OF THE ANTICHRIST, p. 447, and PERSONAL APOSTASY, p. 492). As we approach history's end, the question for each believer is: Am I persevering in faith, continuing steadfast in prayer and calling on God that justice may be done and his righteous cause may triumph completely and forever? Or am I so preoccupied with this life that I am not looking forward to Christ's return and his eternal kingdom (Rev 19–22)?

18:9–14 THE PHARISEE AND THE TAX COLLECTOR. (1) The Pharisee was self-righteous. Self-righteous people think they are righteous because of their own efforts; they are not conscious of their sinful nature, their own unworthiness and their constant need for God's help, mercy and grace. Because of their exceptional acts of piety and outward goodness, they think that they do not need God's grace. (2) The tax collector, on the other hand, was deeply conscious of his sin and guilt, and in true repentance turned from sin to God for forgiveness and mercy. He typifies the true child of God.

humbled, and he who humbles himself will
be exalted."[u]

The Little Children and Jesus

18:15–17pp — Mt 19:13–15; Mk 10:13–16

15People were also bringing babies to
Jesus to have him touch them. When the
disciples saw this, they rebuked them.
16But Jesus called the children to him and
said, "Let the little children come to me,
and do not hinder them, for the kingdom
of God belongs to such as these. **17**I tell
you the truth, anyone who will not receive
the kingdom of God like a little child[v] will
never enter it."

The Rich Ruler

18:18–30pp — Mt 19:16–29; Mk 10:17–30

18A certain ruler asked him, "Good
teacher, what must I do to inherit eternal
life?"[w]

19"Why do you call me good?" Jesus answered. "No one is good—except God
alone. **20**You know the commandments:
'Do not commit adultery, do not murder,
do not steal, do not give false testimony,
honor your father and mother.'[t]"[x]

21"All these I have kept since I was a
boy," he said.

22When Jesus heard this, he said to
him, "You still lack one thing. Sell everything you have and give to the poor,[y] and
you will have treasure in heaven.[z] Then
come, follow me."

23When he heard this, he became very
sad, because he was a man of great
wealth. **24**Jesus looked at him and said,
"How hard it is for the rich to enter the
kingdom of God![a] **25**Indeed, it is easier for
a camel to go through the eye of a needle
than for a rich man to enter the kingdom
of God."

26Those who heard this asked, "Who
then can be saved?"

27Jesus replied, "What is impossible
with men is possible with God."[b]

28Peter said to him, "We have left all we
had to follow you!"[c]

29"I tell you the truth," Jesus said to
them, "no one who has left home or wife
or brothers or parents or children for the
sake of the kingdom of God **30**will fail to
receive many times as much in this age
and, in the age to come,[d] eternal life."[e]

Jesus Again Predicts His Death

18:31–33pp — Mt 20:17–19; Mk 10:32–34

31Jesus took the Twelve aside and told
them, "We are going up to Jerusalem,[f]
and everything that is written by the
prophets[g] about the Son of Man[h] will be
fulfilled. **32**He will be handed over to the
Gentiles.[i] They will mock him, insult
him, spit on him, flog him[j] and kill him.[k]
33On the third day[l] he will rise again."[m]

34The disciples did not understand any
of this. Its meaning was hidden from
them, and they did not know what he was
talking about.[n]

A Blind Beggar Receives His Sight

18:35–43pp — Mt 20:29–34; Mk 10:46–52

35As Jesus approached Jericho,[o] a blind
man was sitting by the roadside begging.
36When he heard the crowd going by, he
asked what was happening. **37**They told
him, "Jesus of Nazareth is passing by."[p]

38He called out, "Jesus, Son of David,[q]
have mercy[r] on me!"

39Those who led the way rebuked him
and told him to be quiet, but he shouted
all the more, "Son of David, have mercy on
me!"[s]

40Jesus stopped and ordered the man to
be brought to him. When he came near,
Jesus asked him, **41**"What do you want me
to do for you?"

"Lord, I want to see," he replied.

42Jesus said to him, "Receive your
sight; your faith has healed you."[t] **43**Immediately he received his sight and followed Jesus, praising God. When all the
people saw it, they also praised God.[u]

Zacchaeus the Tax Collector

19 Jesus entered Jericho[v] and was
passing through. **2**A man was

18:14 [u]S Mt 23:12
18:17 [v]Mt 11:25; 18:3
18:18 [w]Lk 10:25
18:20 [x]Ex 20:12-16; Dt 5:16-20; Ro 13:9
18:22 [y]S Ac 2:45 [z]S Mt 6:20
18:24 [a]Pr 11:28
18:27 [b]S Mt 19:26
18:28 [c]S Mt 4:19
18:30 [d]S Mt 12:32 [e]S Mt 25:46
18:31 [f]S Lk 9:51 [g]Ps 22; Isa 53 [h]S Mt 8:20
18:32 [i]Lk 23:1 [j]S Mt 16:21 [k]S Ac 2:23
18:33 [l]S Mt 16:21 [m]S Mt 16:21
18:34 [n]S Mk 9:32
18:35 [o]Lk 19:1
18:37 [p]Lk 19:4
18:38 [q]ver 39; S Mt 9:27 [r]Mt 17:15; Lk 18:13
18:39 [s]ver 38
18:42 [t]S Mt 9:22
18:43 [u]S Mt 9:8; Lk 13:17
19:1 [v]Lk 18:35

[t] *20* Exodus 20:12-16; Deut. 5:16-20

18:22 SELL EVERYTHING YOU HAVE. See Mt 19:21, note.

18:25 A RICH MAN . . . THE KINGDOM. The disciples, holding the view generally held by the Jews, were amazed at these declarations of Jesus about the rich (vv. 24–26). For more on this topic, see RICHES AND POVERTY, p. 152.

18:30 RECEIVE MANY TIMES AS MUCH. See Mk 10:30, note.

19:1–10 CONVERSION OF ZACCHAEUS. Jesus was still seeking to save the lost (v. 10) only a few days before his crucifixion; this was the purpose of his coming (cf. 15:3–7; Eze 34:16). Zacchaeus, a tax collector, earned his living by collecting more than he should have from the people. For this reason, tax collectors were despised by the people. Jesus' concern for Zacchaeus admonishes us to bring the gospel to the undesirables of society, for all people are lost and in need of salvation.

RICHES AND POVERTY

***Lk 18:24–25** "Jesus looked at him and said, 'How hard it is for the rich to enter the kingdom of God! Indeed, it is easier for a camel to go through the eye of a needle than for a rich man to enter the kingdom of God.' "*

One of the Lord's most shocking statements is that it is virtually impossible for a rich person to enter God's kingdom. Yet this is but one of many statements he made about riches and poverty, giving a perspective repeated by the apostles in several NT letters.

RICHES. (1) The prevailing view among NT Jews was that to be wealthy was a sign of God's special favor and that to be poor was a sign of faithlessness and God's displeasure. The Pharisees, for example, thought this way and derided Jesus for his poverty (Lk 16:14). Although this false idea recurs at times in the history of the Christian church, it is soundly rejected by Christ (see Lk 6:20; 16:13; 18:24–25).

(2) The Bible identifies the pursuit of wealth with idolatry, which is demonic (cf. 1Co 10:19–20; Col 3:5). Because of the demonic power associated with possessions, the desire for wealth and the pursuit of it often bring enslavement (cf. Mt 6:24).

(3) Riches are, in Jesus' perspective, an obstacle both to salvation and to discipleship (Mt 19:24; 13:22). They give a false sense of security (Lk 12:15ff), they deceive (Mt 13:22) and they demand the total loyalty of one's heart (Mt 6:21). The rich often live as if they have no need of God. By searching for riches, their spiritual lives are choked (Lk 8:14), and they are led into temptation and harmful desires (1Ti 6:9), resulting in the abandonment of saving faith (1Ti 6:10). All too often those who are rich take advantage of the poor (Jas 2:5–6). Therefore, no Christian ought to desire to get rich (1Ti 6:9–11).

(4) Selfish amassing of material possessions is an indication that life is no longer seen from eternity's vantage point (Col 3:1). Selfish, greedy people no longer find their goals and fulfillment centered in God, but rather in themselves and their possessions. The tragedy of Lot's wife, for example, was her placing all her affections on an earthly city rather than a heavenly one (Ge 19:16,26; Lk 17:28–33; Heb 11:8–10). In other words, striving after wealth has in it the seed of total alienation from God (1Ti 6:10).

(5) True riches for a Christian consist in faith and love that express themselves in self-denial and following Jesus (1Co 13:4–7; Php 2:3–5). The truly rich are those who have gained freedom from the things of the world through confidence that God is their Father and that he will not forsake them (2Co 9:8; Php 4:19; Heb 13:5–6).

(6) With regard to the proper attitude toward, and use of, our possessions, the righteous are obligated to be faithful (Lk 16:11). Christians must not hold tightly to possessions as personal wealth or security, but they must relinquish their wealth and place their resources in the Lord's hands for use in his kingdom, for the furtherance of Christ's cause on earth, and for the salvation and need of others. Thus, those who possess wealth and material goods must see themselves as stewards of that which is God's (Lk 12:31–48), and be generous, ready to share and rich in good works (Eph 4:28; 1Ti 6:17–19).

(7) Every Christian should examine his or her own heart and desires: Am I a greedy person? Am I a selfish person? Do I yearn for abundance? Do I have a great desire for the honor, prestige and power that often come from gaining great wealth?

POVERTY. One of the tasks that Jesus saw as his Spirit-directed mission was "to preach good news to the poor" (Lk 4:18; cf. Isa 61:1). In other words, the gospel of Christ can be defined as a gospel of the poor (Mt 5:3; 11:5; Lk 7:22; Jas 2:5).

(1) The "poor" (Gk *ptōchos*) are the humble and afflicted within the world who turn to God in great need and seek his help. At the same time they are faithful to God and look forward to God's redemption of his people from the sin, suffering, hunger and hatred that are in the world. They do not seek their wealth and life in earthly things (see Ps 18:27; 22:26; 25:9; 37:11; 72:2,12–13; 74:19; 147:6; Isa 11:4; 29:19; Lk 6:20; 16:25; Jn 14:3, note).

(2) Deliverance from suffering, oppression, injustice and poverty will most certainly come to God's poor (Lk 6:20–23; 18:1–8).

(3) God sees his people in poverty and declares that they "are rich" (Rev 2:9). In no way can they be seen as spiritually or morally inferior (see Rev 2:9, note).

there by the name of Zacchaeus; he was a chief tax collector and was wealthy. **3**He wanted to see who Jesus was, but being a short man he could not, because of the crowd. **4**So he ran ahead and climbed a sycamore-fig[w] tree to see him, since Jesus was coming that way.[x]

5When Jesus reached the spot, he looked up and said to him, "Zacchaeus, come down immediately. I must stay at your house today." **6**So he came down at once and welcomed him gladly.

7All the people saw this and began to mutter, "He has gone to be the guest of a 'sinner.' "[y]

8But Zacchaeus stood up and said to the Lord,[z] "Look, Lord! Here and now I give half of my possessions to the poor, and if I have cheated anybody out of anything,[a] I will pay back four times the amount."[b]

9Jesus said to him, "Today salvation has come to this house, because this man, too, is a son of Abraham.[c] **10**For the Son of Man came to seek and to save what was lost."[d]

The Parable of the Ten Minas

19:12–27Ref – Mt 25:14–30

11While they were listening to this, he went on to tell them a parable, because he was near Jerusalem and the people thought that the kingdom of God[e] was going to appear at once.[f] **12**He said: "A man of noble birth went to a distant country to have himself appointed king and then to return. **13**So he called ten of his servants[g] and gave them ten minas.[u] 'Put this money to work,' he said, 'until I come back.'

14"But his subjects hated him and sent a delegation after him to say, 'We don't want this man to be our king.'

15"He was made king, however, and returned home. Then he sent for the servants to whom he had given the money, in order to find out what they had gained with it.

16"The first one came and said, 'Sir, your mina has earned ten more.'

17" 'Well done, my good servant!'[h] his master replied. 'Because you have been trustworthy in a very small matter, take charge of ten cities.'[i]

18"The second came and said, 'Sir, your mina has earned five more.'

19"His master answered, 'You take charge of five cities.'

20"Then another servant came and said, 'Sir, here is your mina; I have kept it laid away in a piece of cloth. **21**I was afraid of you, because you are a hard man. You take out what you did not put in and reap what you did not sow.'[j]

22"His master replied, 'I will judge you by your own words,[k] you wicked servant! You knew, did you, that I am a hard man, taking out what I did not put in, and reaping what I did not sow?[l] **23**Why then didn't you put my money on deposit, so that when I came back, I could have collected it with interest?'

24"Then he said to those standing by, 'Take his mina away from him and give it to the one who has ten minas.'

25" 'Sir,' they said, 'he already has ten!'

26"He replied, 'I tell you that to everyone who has, more will be given, but as for the one who has nothing, even what he has will be taken away.[m] **27**But those enemies of mine who did not want me to be king over them—bring them here and kill them in front of me.' "

The Triumphal Entry

19:29–38pp – Mt 21:1–9; Mk 11:1–10
19:35–38pp – Jn 12:12–15

28After Jesus had said this, he went on ahead, going up to Jerusalem.[n] **29**As he

19:4 [w] 1Ki 10:27; 1Ch 27:28; Isa 9:10 [x] Lk 18:37
19:7 [y] S Mt 9:11
19:8 [z] S Lk 7:13 [a] Lk 3:12,13 [b] Ex 22:1; Lev 6:4,5; Nu 5:7; 2Sa 12:6; Eze 33:14,15
19:9 [c] S Lk 3:8
19:10 [d] Eze 34:12,16; S Jn 3:17
19:11 [e] S Mt 3:2 [f] Lk 17:20; Ac 1:6
19:13 [g] Mk 13:34
19:17 [h] Pr 27:18 [i] Lk 16:10
19:21 [j] Mt 25:24
19:22 [k] 2Sa 1:16; Job 15:6 [l] Mt 25:26
19:26 [m] S Mt 25:29
19:28 [n] Mk 10:32; S Lk 9:51

[u] *13* A mina was about three months' wages.

19:8 I GIVE . . . TO THE POOR. True confession of sin and genuine saving faith in Christ will result in the determination to change our lives outwardly. No one can become acquainted with Jesus, accept his offer of salvation, and at the same time remain sinful, dishonest and uncharitable toward others.

19:13 UNTIL I COME BACK. The parable of the ten minas illustrates that each redeemed believer has the responsibility to use faithfully what God has given him or her. Each of us has been given the opportunity, the time and the means to live for Christ through acts of kindness, prayer, offerings and in many other ways.

19:17 YOU HAVE BEEN TRUSTWORTHY. Whoever has been faithful in service for the Lord and has shared his burden here on earth will be richly rewarded in the future kingdom. They will be given even greater tasks in the new heaven and the new earth (Rev 21:1). Those who have been faithful to a lesser degree will receive a smaller place and responsibility.

19:26 WHAT HE HAS WILL BE TAKEN AWAY. See Mt 25:29, note.

19:28 THE TRIUMPHAL ENTRY. By his entry into Jerusalem on a donkey, Jesus publicly testifies that he is Israel's predicted King and Messiah. (1) This entry was predicted by the prophet Zechariah (Zec 9:9). (2) Jesus' humble entry is a deliberate symbolic action intended to show that his kingdom is not of this world and that he did not come to rule the world with force or violence. His refusal to take action as a military conqueror demonstrates that his kingdom is spiritual.

approached Bethphage and Bethany[o] at
the hill called the Mount of Olives,[p] he
sent two of his disciples, saying to them,
30"Go to the village ahead of you, and as
you enter it, you will find a colt tied there,
which no one has ever ridden. Untie it and
bring it here. 31If anyone asks you, 'Why
are you untying it?' tell him, 'The Lord
needs it.' "

32Those who were sent ahead went and
found it just as he had told them.[q] 33As
they were untying the colt, its owners
asked them, "Why are you untying the
colt?"

34They replied, "The Lord needs it."

35They brought it to Jesus, threw their
cloaks on the colt and put Jesus on it. 36As
he went along, people spread their
cloaks[r] on the road.

37When he came near the place where
the road goes down the Mount of Olives,[s]
the whole crowd of disciples began joyfully to praise God in loud voices for all the
miracles they had seen:

38"Blessed is the king who comes in
the name of the Lord!"[v][t]

"Peace in heaven and glory in the
highest!"[u]

39Some of the Pharisees in the crowd
said to Jesus, "Teacher, rebuke your disciples!"[v]

40"I tell you," he replied, "if they keep
quiet, the stones will cry out."[w]

19:29 [o]S Mt 21:17 [p]S Mt 21:1
19:32 [q]Lk 22:13
19:36 [r]2Ki 9:13
19:37 [s]S Mt 21:1
19:38 [t]Ps 118:26; Lk 13:35 [u]S Lk 2:14
19:39 [v]Mt 21:15, 16
19:40 [w]Hab 2:11
19:41 [x]Isa 22:4; Lk 13:34,35
19:43 [y]Isa 29:3; Jer 6:6; Eze 4:2; 26:8; Lk 21:20
19:44 [z]Ps 137:9 [a]Lk 21:6 [b]1Pe 2:12
19:46 [c]Isa 56:7 [d]Jer 7:11
19:47 [e]S Mt 26:55 [f]S Mt 12:14; Mk 11:18
20:1 [g]S Mt 26:55

Jesus Weeps Over Jerusalem

41As he approached Jerusalem and saw
the city, he wept over it[x] 42and said, "If
you, even you, had only known on this day
what would bring you peace—but now it
is hidden from your eyes. 43The days will
come upon you when your enemies will
build an embankment against you and encircle you and hem you in on every side.[y]
44They will dash you to the ground, you
and the children within your walls.[z] They
will not leave one stone on another,[a] because you did not recognize the time of
God's coming[b] to you."

Jesus at the Temple

19:45,46pp — Mt 21:12–16; Mk 11:15–18; Jn 2:13–16

45Then he entered the temple area and
began driving out those who were selling.
46"It is written," he said to them, " 'My
house will be a house of prayer'[w];[c] but
you have made it 'a den of robbers.'[x]"[d]

47Every day he was teaching at the temple.[e] But the chief priests, the teachers of
the law and the leaders among the people
were trying to kill him.[f] 48Yet they could
not find any way to do it, because all the
people hung on his words.

The Authority of Jesus Questioned

20:1–8pp — Mt 21:23–27; Mk 11:27–33

20 One day as he was teaching the
people in the temple courts[g] and

[v] *38* Psalm 118:26 [w] *46* Isaiah 56:7
[x] *46* Jer. 7:11

19:41 SAW THE CITY, HE WEPT. Jesus, knowing that the people and their leaders expect a political Messiah and will ultimately reject him as God's promised Messiah, weeps in pity for the people who will soon suffer terrible judgment. The word "wept" in Greek means more than shedding tears. It suggests a lamentation, a wailing, a heaving of the bosom—the sob and the cry of a soul in agony. Jesus, as God, reveals not only his own feelings, but also God's broken heart over the lostness of the human race and their refusal to repent and accept salvation (see Mk 11:9, note).

19:43 YOUR ENEMIES ... ENCIRCLE YOU. Jesus' prediction was fulfilled forty years later (A.D. 70) when Jerusalem was destroyed by the Roman army and hundreds of thousands of Jews were killed.

19:45 DRIVING OUT THOSE WHO WERE SELLING. The cleansing of the temple was the first great public act of Jesus' ministry (Jn 2:13–22) and the last great public act of his ministry (cf. Mt 21:12–17; Mk 11:15–17). In blazing anger, he drove from God's house the ungodly, the greedy and those who were destroying its true spiritual purpose. Jesus' double cleansing of the temple during his three-year ministry indicates how important the spiritual lessons are:

(1) Christ's greatest concern is for holiness and godly sincerity within his church (cf. Jn 17:17,19). He died to "make her holy, cleansing her . . . and to present her . . . holy and blameless" (Eph 5:25–27).

(2) Worship in the church must be in spirit and in truth (Jn 4:24). The church must be a place of prayer and communion with God (cf. Mt 21:13).

(3) Christ will condemn all who use the church, the gospel or his kingdom for personal gain, glory or self-promotion.

(4) Sincere love for God and for his redemptive purposes will result in a consuming "zeal" for the righteousness of God's house and kingdom (Jn 2:17). True Christlikeness includes intolerance toward unrighteousness within the church (cf. Rev 2–3).

(5) Essential to all true Christian ministry is protest against those who profane and degrade the kingdom of God (cf. 1Co 6:9–11; Gal 1:6–10; Rev 2–3).

(6) Either we will allow Christ into our assemblies to purge out deceit, immorality, secularization and desecration (see Rev 2–3) or at his second coming, he, in divine judgment, will cleanse his churches with finality (see Mal 3:2).

19:46 HOUSE OF PRAYER. See Mk 11:17, note.

preaching the gospel,[h] the chief priests and the teachers of the law, together with the elders, came up to him. 2"Tell us by what authority you are doing these things," they said. "Who gave you this authority?"[i]

3He replied, "I will also ask you a question. Tell me, 4John's baptism[j]—was it from heaven, or from men?"

5They discussed it among themselves and said, "If we say, 'From heaven,' he will ask, 'Why didn't you believe him?' 6But if we say, 'From men,' all the people[k] will stone us, because they are persuaded that John was a prophet."[l]

7So they answered, "We don't know where it was from."

8Jesus said, "Neither will I tell you by what authority I am doing these things."

The Parable of the Tenants

20:9–19pp — Mt 21:33–46; Mk 12:1–12

9He went on to tell the people this parable: "A man planted a vineyard,[m] rented it to some farmers and went away for a long time.[n] 10At harvest time he sent a servant to the tenants so they would give him some of the fruit of the vineyard. But the tenants beat him and sent him away empty-handed. 11He sent another servant, but that one also they beat and treated shamefully and sent away empty-handed. 12He sent still a third, and they wounded him and threw him out.

13"Then the owner of the vineyard said, 'What shall I do? I will send my son, whom I love;[o] perhaps they will respect him.'

14"But when the tenants saw him, they talked the matter over. 'This is the heir,' they said. 'Let's kill him, and the inheritance will be ours.' 15So they threw him out of the vineyard and killed him.

"What then will the owner of the vineyard do to them? 16He will come and kill those tenants[p] and give the vineyard to others."

When the people heard this, they said, "May this never be!"

17Jesus looked directly at them and asked, "Then what is the meaning of that which is written:

" 'The stone the builders rejected
has become the capstone[y]'[z]?[q]

18Everyone who falls on that stone will be broken to pieces, but he on whom it falls will be crushed."[r]

19The teachers of the law and the chief priests looked for a way to arrest him[s] immediately, because they knew he had spoken this parable against them. But they were afraid of the people.[t]

Paying Taxes to Caesar

20:20–26pp — Mt 22:15–22; Mk 12:13–17

20Keeping a close watch on him, they sent spies, who pretended to be honest. They hoped to catch Jesus in something he said[u] so that they might hand him over to the power and authority of the governor.[v] 21So the spies questioned him: "Teacher, we know that you speak and teach what is right, and that you do not show partiality but teach the way of God in accordance with the truth.[w] 22Is it right for us to pay taxes to Caesar or not?"

23He saw through their duplicity and said to them, 24"Show me a denarius. Whose portrait and inscription are on it?"

25"Caesar's," they replied.

He said to them, "Then give to Caesar what is Caesar's,[x] and to God what is God's."

26They were unable to trap him in what he had said there in public. And astonished by his answer, they became silent.

The Resurrection and Marriage

20:27–40pp — Mt 22:23–33; Mk 12:18–27

27Some of the Sadducees,[y] who say

20:1 [h] Lk 8:1 **20:2** [i] Jn 2:18; Ac 4:7; 7:27 **20:4** [j] S Mk 1:4 **20:6** [k] Lk 7:29 [l] S Mt 11:9 **20:9** [m] Isa 5:1-7 [n] Mt 25:14 **20:13** [o] S Mt 3:17 **20:16** [p] Lk 19:27 **20:17** [q] Ps 118:22; S Ac 4:11 **20:18** [r] Isa 8:14, 15 **20:19** [s] Lk 19:47 [t] S Mk 11:18 **20:20** [u] S Mt 12:10 [v] Mt 27:2 **20:21** [w] Jn 3:2 **20:25** [x] Lk 23:2; Ro 13:7 **20:27** [y] S Ac 4:1

[y] 17 Or *cornerstone* [z] 17 Psalm 118:22

20:2 BY WHAT AUTHORITY? The religious leaders questioned Jesus' authority to cleanse the temple or to teach the people (19:45–48). They were offended and angered because Jesus condemned the evil practices within God's house, while they themselves tolerated and participated in those practices. Such actions demonstrate how unfit they were to be spiritual leaders. Jesus, as a true spiritual leader, used his authority for the sake of truth and righteousness, even though it cost him his life.

20:9–16 THE PARABLE OF THE TENANTS. See Mt 21:33, note.

20:16 GIVE THE VINEYARD TO OTHERS. See Mt 21:43, note on the kingdom of God taken from Israel.

20:18 THAT STONE. Those who do not accept Jesus will be broken, and those who fall under his judgment will be completely pulverized. See Isa 8:14 and Lk 2:34, where Christ is presented as a stone that causes stumbling and a rock that makes people fall; also Da 2:34–35,44–45, where the Messiah is a rock that crushes the kingdoms of the world.

20:25 THEN GIVE TO CAESAR. Believers under normal circumstances must pay taxes and submit to governmental authority (see Ro 13:1–7), even though our highest loyalty is to God. We must obey secular government except when it conflicts with the law of God; we must *never* disobey Jesus' command to "give to Caesar what is Caesar's."

there is no resurrection,[z] came to Jesus with a question. 28“Teacher,” they said, “Moses wrote for us that if a man’s brother dies and leaves a wife but no children, the man must marry the widow and have children for his brother.[a] 29Now there were seven brothers. The first one married a woman and died childless. 30The second 31and then the third married her, and in the same way the seven died, leaving no children. 32Finally, the woman died too. 33Now then, at the resurrection whose wife will she be, since the seven were married to her?”

34Jesus replied, “The people of this age marry and are given in marriage. 35But those who are considered worthy of taking part in that age[b] and in the resurrection from the dead will neither marry nor be given in marriage, 36and they can no longer die; for they are like the angels. They are God’s children,[c] since they are children of the resurrection. 37But in the account of the bush, even Moses showed that the dead rise, for he calls the Lord ‘the God of Abraham, and the God of Isaac, and the God of Jacob.’[a][d] 38He is not the God of the dead, but of the living, for to him all are alive.”

39Some of the teachers of the law responded, “Well said, teacher!” 40And no one dared to ask him any more questions.[e]

Whose Son Is the Christ?

20:41–47pp — Mt 22:41–23:7; Mk 12:35–40

41Then Jesus said to them, “How is it that they say the Christ[b] is the Son of David?[f] 42David himself declares in the Book of Psalms:

“ ‘The Lord said to my Lord:
“Sit at my right hand
43until I make your enemies
a footstool for your feet.” ’[c][g]

44David calls him ‘Lord.’ How then can he be his son?”

45While all the people were listening, Jesus said to his disciples, 46“Beware of the teachers of the law. They like to walk around in flowing robes and love to be greeted in the marketplaces and have the most important seats in the synagogues and the places of honor at banquets.[h] 47They devour widows’ houses and for a show make lengthy prayers. Such men will be punished most severely.”

The Widow’s Offering

21:1–4pp — Mk 12:41–44

21 As he looked up, Jesus saw the rich putting their gifts into the temple treasury.[i] 2He also saw a poor widow put in two very small copper coins.[d] 3“I tell you the truth,” he said, “this poor widow has put in more than all the others. 4All these people gave their gifts out of their wealth; but she out of her poverty put in all she had to live on.”[j]

Signs of the End of the Age

21:5–36pp — Mt 24; Mk 13
21:12–17pp — Mt 10:17–22

5Some of his disciples were remarking about how the temple was adorned with beautiful stones and with gifts dedicated to God. But Jesus said, 6“As for what you see here, the time will come when not one stone will be left on another;[k] every one of them will be thrown down.”

20:27 z Ac 23:8; 1Co 15:12 **20:28** a Dt 25:5 **20:35** b S Mt 12:32 **20:36** c S Jn 1:12 **20:37** d Ex 3:6 **20:40** e Mt 22:46; Mk 12:34 **20:41** f S Mt 1:1
20:43 g Ps 110:1; S Mt 22:44 **20:46** h S Lk 11:43 **21:1** i Mt 27:6; Jn 8:20 **21:4** j 2Co 8:12 **21:6** k Lk 19:44

a *37* Exodus 3:6 b *41* Or *Messiah* c *43* Psalm 110:1 d *2* Greek *two lepta*

20:36 LIKE THE ANGELS. About the believer’s life in the next age, Jesus reveals that it begins with a resurrection from the dead, involves having a glorified body that can never die, but no longer includes earthly relationships such as marriage. The fact that earthly relationships will be different does not mean we will not recognize each other. Jesus, after his resurrection, was recognized by his disciples (24:31,39; Mt 28:9).

20:44 DAVID CALLS HIM ‘LORD’. The Jews thought that the Messiah would be a descendant of David and therefore only a human ruler. Jesus shows that David’s statement in Ps 110:1, where he refers to his son as “Lord,” indicates that the Messiah is more than a human ruler; he is also the divine Son of God.

20:46 BEWARE OF THE TEACHERS OF THE LAW. See Mt 23:13, note; see article on FALSE TEACHERS, p. 98.

21:1–4 THE WIDOW’S OFFERING. Jesus gives a lesson on how God evaluates giving. (1) A person’s gift is determined not by the amount he or she gives, but by the amount of sacrifice involved in the giving. The rich at times give only out of their wealth—it involves no sacrifice. The gift of the widow cost her everything. She gave as much as she possibly could. (2) This principle can be applied to all our service for Jesus. He judges our work and ministry not by its size or influence or success, but by the amount of sincere dedication, sacrifice, faith and love involved (see 2:24–30, note; Mt 20:26, note; Mk 12:42, note).

21:6 NOT ONE STONE WILL BE LEFT ON ANOTHER. The fulfillment of this prediction occurred in A.D. 70, when the Roman general Titus and his army destroyed Jerusalem and burned the temple after a siege of 134 days. The temple was destroyed as a judgment on Israel for their rejection of God’s Son and his redemption.

PASSION WEEK

1. ARRIVAL IN BETHANY FRIDAY Jn 12:1

Jesus arrived in Bethany six days before the Passover to spend some time with his friends, Mary, Martha and Lazarus. While here, Mary anointed his feet with costly perfume as an act of humility. This tender expression indicated Mary's devotion to Jesus and her willingness to serve him.

2. SABBATH — DAY OF REST SATURDAY Not mentioned in the Gospels

Since this day was the Sabbath, the Lord spent the day in traditional fashion with his friends.

3. THE TRIUMPHAL ENTRY SUNDAY Mt 21:1-11; Mk 11:1-11; Lk 19:28-44; Jn 12:12-19

On the first day of the week Jesus rode into Jerusalem on a donkey, fulfilling an ancient prophecy (Zec 9:9). The crowd welcomed him with "Hosanna" and the words of Ps 118:25-26, thus ascribing to him a Messianic title as the agent of the Lord, the coming King of Israel.

4. CLEARING OF THE TEMPLE MONDAY Mt 21:10-17; Mk 11:15-18; Lk 19:45-48

On this day he returned to the temple and found the court of the Gentiles full of traders and money changers making a large profit as they gave out Jewish coins in exchange for "pagan" money. Jesus drove them out and overturned their tables.

5. DAY OF CONTROVERSY AND PARABLES TUESDAY Mt 21:23–24:51; Mk 11:27–13:37; Lk 20:1–21:36

In Jerusalem - Jesus evaded the traps set by the priests.
On the Mount of Olives Overlooking Jerusalem - He taught in parables and warned the people against the Pharisees. He predicted the destruction of Herod's great temple and told his disciples about future events, including his own return.

6. DAY OF REST WEDNESDAY Not mentioned in the Gospels

The Scriptures do not mention this day, but the counting of the days (Mk 14:1; Jn 12:1) seems to indicate that there was another day concerning which the Gospels record nothing.

7. PASSOVER LAST SUPPER THURSDAY Mt 26:17-30; Mk 14:12-26; Lk 22:7-23; Jn 13:1-30

In an upper room Jesus prepared both himself and his disciples for his death. He gave the Passover meal a new meaning. The loaf of bread and cup of wine represented his body soon to be sacrificed and his blood soon to be shed. And so he instituted the "Lord's Supper." After singing a hymn they went to the Garden of Gethsemane, where Jesus prayed in agony, knowing what lay ahead for him.

8. CRUCIFIXION FRIDAY Mt 27:1-66; Mk 15:1-47; Lk 22:66–23:56; Jn 18:28–19:37

Following betrayal, arrest, desertion, false trials, denial, condemnation, beatings and mockery, Jesus was required to carry his cross to "The Place of the Skull," where he was crucified with two other prisoners.

9. IN THE TOMB FRIDAY Mt 27:57-61; Mk 15:42-47; Lk 23:50-56; Jn 19:38-42

Jesus' body was placed in the tomb before 6:00 P.M. Friday night, when the Sabbath began and all work stopped, and it lay in the tomb throughout the Sabbath.

10. RESURRECTION SUNDAY Mt 28:1-13; Mk 16:1-20; Lk 24:1-49; Jn 20:1-31

Early in the morning, women went to the tomb and found that the stone closing the tomb's entrance had been rolled back. An angel told them Jesus was alive and gave them a message. Jesus appeared to Mary Magdalene in the garden, to Peter, to two disciples on the road to Emmaus, and later that day to all the disciples but Thomas. His resurrection was established as a fact.

7"Teacher," they asked, "when will
these things happen? And what will be
the sign that they are about to take
place?"
8He replied: "Watch out that you are
not deceived. For many will come in my
name, claiming, 'I am he,' and, 'The time
is near.' Do not follow them.[l] **9**When you
hear of wars and revolutions, do not be
frightened. These things must happen
first, but the end will not come right
away."
10Then he said to them: "Nation will
rise against nation, and kingdom against
kingdom.[m] **11**There will be great earthquakes, famines and pestilences in various places, and fearful events and great
signs from heaven.[n]
12"But before all this, they will lay
hands on you and persecute you. They will
deliver you to synagogues and prisons,
and you will be brought before kings and
governors, and all on account of my name.
13This will result in your being witnesses
to them.[o] **14**But make up your mind not to
worry beforehand how you will defend
yourselves.[p] **15**For I will give you[q] words
and wisdom that none of your adversaries
will be able to resist or contradict. **16**You
will be betrayed even by parents, brothers, relatives and friends,[r] and they will
put some of you to death. **17**All men will
hate you because of me.[s] **18**But not a hair
of your head will perish.[t] **19**By standing
firm you will gain life.[u]
20"When you see Jerusalem being surrounded by armies,[v] you will know that
its desolation is near. **21**Then let those
who are in Judea flee to the mountains, let
those in the city get out, and let those in
the country not enter the city.[w] **22**For this
is the time of punishment[x] in fulfillment[y]
of all that has been written. **23**How dreadful it will be in those days for pregnant
women and nursing mothers! There will
be great distress in the land and wrath
against this people. **24**They will fall by the
sword and will be taken as prisoners to all
the nations. Jerusalem will be trampled[z]
on by the Gentiles until the times of the
Gentiles are fulfilled.
25"There will be signs in the sun, moon
and stars. On the earth, nations will be in
anguish and perplexity at the roaring and
tossing of the sea.[a] **26**Men will faint from
terror, apprehensive of what is coming on
the world, for the heavenly bodies will be
shaken.[b] **27**At that time they will see the
Son of Man[c] coming in a cloud[d] with power and great glory. **28**When these things
begin to take place, stand up and lift up
your heads, because your redemption is
drawing near."[e]
29He told them this parable: "Look at
the fig tree and all the trees. **30**When they
sprout leaves, you can see for yourselves

21:8 [l] Lk 17:23
21:10 [m] 2Ch 15:6; Isa 19:2
21:11 [n] Isa 29:6; Joel 2:30
21:13 [o] Php 1:12
21:14 [p] Lk 12:11
21:15 [q] S Lk 12:12
21:16 [r] Lk 12:52, 53
21:17 [s] S Jn 15:21
21:18 [t] S Mt 10:30
21:19 [u] S Mt 10:22
21:20 [v] S Lk 19:43
21:21 [w] Lk 17:31
21:22 [x] Isa 63:4; Da 9:24-27; Hos 9:7 [y] S Mt 1:22
21:24 [z] Isa 5:5; 63:18; Da 8:13; Rev 11:2
21:25 [a] 2Pe 3:10, 12
21:26 [b] S Mt 24:29
21:27 [c] S Mt 8:20 [d] S Rev 1:7
21:28 [e] Lk 18:7

21:7–19 WHEN WILL THESE THINGS HAPPEN? Jesus' response to the disciples' question links the destruction of Jerusalem so closely with his return to earth after the tribulation that it is difficult to distinguish between the portions referring only to Jerusalem and those referring to his second coming. Jesus probably meant the destruction of Jerusalem as a type of his coming to judge the world.

21:8 WATCH OUT THAT YOU ARE NOT DECEIVED. See Mt 24:5, note.

21:9 WARS AND REVOLUTIONS. See Mt 24:4, note.

21:16 THEY WILL PUT SOME OF YOU TO DEATH. Ancient writers state that all the apostles (except John) died as martyrs at the hands of persecutors. Many believers were tortured and killed in the early days of Christianity (see Mt 24:9, note).

21:18 NOT A HAIR . . . WILL PERISH. This promise guarantees spiritual security, not physical preservation (cf. death referred to in v. 16). If believers remain faithful, in all things God works for their good (cf. Ro 8:28); nothing can separate them from his love (Ro 8:35–39).

21:19 STANDING FIRM. We must engage in the most intense devotion to Christ through the means of grace, i.e., prayer, witness, study of the Word, worship, Christian fellowship and daily resistance to sin (see Jn 15:6, note). By persevering in true faith, believers gain eternal life and are victorious in all circumstances.

21:20 JERUSALEM BEING SURROUNDED WITH ARMIES. Once again Jesus refers to the events of A.D. 70 (see note on v. 6). Those events fulfilled Jesus' prophecy that divine justice would "come upon this generation" (Mt 23:36; cf. Lk 23:27–30) for their rejection of the Messiah and refusal to turn from their sins. Jesus warns his followers to flee the city when they first see the armies (v. 21).

21:24 THE TIMES OF THE GENTILES. "The times of the Gentiles" refers to the time Israel would be under the domination or oppression of non-Jews. It began when a part of Israel was taken to Babylon in 586 B.C. (2Ch 36:1–21; Da 1:1–2). It will not end until the times are fulfilled, which probably means when Christ comes in glory and power to establish his rule over all the nations (1:32–33; Jer 23:5–6; Zec 6:13; 9:10; Ro 11:25–26; Rev 20:4).

21:25 SIGNS IN THE SUN, MOON AND STARS. Cosmic signs will precede Jesus' coming, and the world will be in utmost distress because of the great tribulation (see Mt 24:29, note; article on THE GREAT TRIBULATION, p. 52). The impenitent will be in great terror and despair.

21:27 THE SON OF MAN COMING. "Son of Man" is the term Jesus often used to refer to himself (see Mt 24:30, note on Christ's coming after the tribulation).

and know that summer is near. **31**Even so,
when you see these things happening, you
know that the kingdom of God[f] is near.
32"I tell you the truth, this generation[e][g] will certainly not pass away until
all these things have happened. **33**Heaven
and earth will pass away, but my words
will never pass away.[h]
34"Be careful, or your hearts will be
weighed down with dissipation, drunkenness and the anxieties of life,[i] and that
day will close on you unexpectedly[j] like
a trap. **35**For it will come upon all those
who live on the face of the whole earth.
36Be always on the watch, and pray[k] that
you may be able to escape all that is about
to happen, and that you may be able to
stand before the Son of Man."
37Each day Jesus was teaching at the
temple,[l] and each evening he went out[m]
to spend the night on the hill called the
Mount of Olives,[n] **38**and all the people
came early in the morning to hear him at
the temple.[o]

Judas Agrees to Betray Jesus

22:1,2pp — Mt 26:2–5; Mk 14:1,2,10,11

22 Now the Feast of Unleavened
Bread, called the Passover, was
approaching,[p] **2**and the chief priests and
the teachers of the law were looking for
some way to get rid of Jesus,[q] for they
were afraid of the people. **3**Then Satan[r]
entered Judas, called Iscariot,[s] one of the
Twelve. **4**And Judas went to the chief
priests and the officers of the temple
guard[t] and discussed with them how he
might betray Jesus. **5**They were delighted
and agreed to give him money.[u] **6**He consented, and watched for an opportunity to
hand Jesus over to them when no crowd
was present.

The Last Supper

22:7–13pp — Mt 26:17–19; Mk 14:12–16
22:17–20pp — Mt 26:26–29; Mk 14:22–25; 1Co 11:23–25
22:21–23pp — Mt 26:21–24; Mk 14:18–21; Jn 13:21–30
22:25–27pp — Mt 20:25–28; Mk 10:42–45
22:33,34pp — Mt 26:33–35; Mk 14:29–31; Jn 13:37,38

7Then came the day of Unleavened
Bread on which the Passover lamb had to
be sacrificed.[v] **8**Jesus sent Peter and
John,[w] saying, "Go and make preparations
for us to eat the Passover."
9"Where do you want us to prepare for
it?" they asked.
10He replied, "As you enter the city, a
man carrying a jar of water will meet you.
Follow him to the house that he enters,
11and say to the owner of the house, 'The
Teacher asks: Where is the guest room,
where I may eat the Passover with my
disciples?' **12**He will show you a large upper room, all furnished. Make preparations there."
13They left and found things just as

21:31 [f]S Mt 3:2 **21:32** [g]Lk 11:50; 17:25 **21:33** [h]S Mt 5:18 **21:34** [i]Mk 4:19 [j]Lk 12:40,46; 1Th 5:2-7 **21:36** [k]Mt 26:41 **21:37** [l]S Mt 26:55 [m]Mk 11:19 [n]S Mt 21:1 **21:38** [o]Jn 8:2 **22:1** [p]S Jn 11:55 **22:2** [q]S Mt 12:14 **22:3** [r]S Mt 4:10 [s]S Mt 10:4 **22:4** [t]ver 52; Ac 4:1; 5:24 **22:5** [u]Zec 11:12 **22:7** [v]Ex 12:18-20; Dt 16:5-8; S Mk 14:12 **22:8** [w]Ac 3:1,11; 4:13,19; 8:14

[e] *32* Or *race*

21:31 WHEN YOU SEE THESE THINGS HAPPENING. One can tell that the time of Jesus' glorious appearing to establish his kingdom is near by watching the signs (see Mt 24:33, note). On the other hand, Christ's return for the faithful believers of his churches at an unknown and unexpected time (i.e., the rapture or catching away of all true believers, cf. Jn 14:1–4; 1Th 4:13–18) is probably referred to in vv. 34–36 (see Mt 24:44, note).

21:31 KINGDOM OF GOD IS NEAR. See Mt 24:33, note.

21:32 THIS GENERATION. See Mt 24:34, note.

21:34 DAY WILL CLOSE ON YOU UNEXPECTEDLY. Jesus concludes his prophetic message by warning his followers not to be so preoccupied with the pleasures and cares of the world that they fail to be prepared for his coming. (1) These words are meant for all God's people of all ages, not just those living during the final days of tribulation. The demand for spiritual faithfulness is critical in the light of Jesus' teaching that he will return for the faithful believers at an unexpected time. Since the time of his coming for the church cannot be determined, believers must always be ready (see Mt 24:40,42, notes; Jn 14:3, note). (2) Christ's rapture of the faithful (1Th 4:16–17) "rescues us from the coming wrath" (1Th 1:10), in order that we "may be able to escape all that is about to happen" on earth (vv. 35–36; cf. vv. 25–26; see next note; Rev 3:10, note).

21:36 ESCAPE ALL THAT IS ABOUT TO HAPPEN. Followers of Christ must be on the watch against sin and pray that their love for Christ will not diminish, in order that they might receive strength to persevere in faith and righteousness in Jesus Christ. Only by such perseverance will they be able to "escape" all the terrible things coming on the world in the last days (see 1Th 1:10, note; Rev 3:10, note; see article on THE GREAT TRIBULATION, p. 52). Many believe that the means of "escape" for those who faithfully keep on praying is the rapture (see Jn 14:3, note; see article on THE RAPTURE, p. 440).

22:1 PASSOVER. See Mt 26:2, note.

22:3 SATAN ENTERED JUDAS. The tragic story of Judas, who at one time was in intimate fellowship with Jesus (Ps 41:9; cf. Jn 13:18) but then forsook his Lord by betraying him (see Jn 6:64, note), serves as a warning to all who follow Christ. In this life there is always the possibility that we might grow cold toward Christ, allow Satan little by little to lead us into compromise with the world, and then in the end betray the Lord and his cause.

Jesus had told them.[x] So they prepared
the Passover.
14When the hour came, Jesus and his
apostles[y] reclined at the table.[z] 15And he
said to them, "I have eagerly desired to
eat this Passover with you before I suffer.[a] 16For I tell you, I will not eat it again
until it finds fulfillment in the kingdom of
God."[b]
17After taking the cup, he gave thanks
and said, "Take this and divide it among
you. 18For I tell you I will not drink again
of the fruit of the vine until the kingdom
of God comes."
19And he took bread, gave thanks and
broke it,[c] and gave it to them, saying,
"This is my body given for you; do this in
remembrance of me."
20In the same way, after the supper he
took the cup, saying, "This cup is the new
covenant[d] in my blood, which is poured
out for you. 21But the hand of him who is
going to betray me is with mine on the
table.[e] 22The Son of Man[f] will go as it
has been decreed,[g] but woe to that man
who betrays him." 23They began to question among themselves which of them it
might be who would do this.
24Also a dispute arose among them as
to which of them was considered to be
greatest.[h] 25Jesus said to them, "The
kings of the Gentiles lord it over them;
and those who exercise authority over
them call themselves Benefactors. 26But
you are not to be like that. Instead, the
greatest among you should be like the
youngest,[i] and the one who rules like the
one who serves.[j] 27For who is greater,
the one who is at the table or the one who
serves? Is it not the one who is at the
table? But I am among you as one who
serves.[k] 28You are those who have stood
by me in my trials. 29And I confer on you
a kingdom,[l] just as my Father conferred
one on me, 30so that you may eat and
drink at my table in my kingdom[m] and sit
on thrones, judging the twelve tribes of
Israel.[n]

22:13 [x] Lk 19:32
22:14 [y] S Mk 6:30 [z] Mt 26:20; Mk 14:17,18
22:15 [a] S Mt 16:21
22:16 [b] S Lk 14:15
22:19 [c] S Mt 14:19
22:20 [d] Ex 24:8; Isa 42:6; Jer 31:31-34; Zec 9:11; 2Co 3:6; Heb 8:6; 9:15
22:21 [e] Ps 41:9
22:22 [f] S Mt 8:20 [g] Ac 2:23; 4:28
22:24 [h] Mk 9:34; Lk 9:46
22:26 [i] 1Pe 5:5 [j] S Mk 9:35
22:27 [k] S Mt 20:28
22:29 [l] S Mt 25:34; 2Ti 2:12
22:30 [m] S Lk 14:15 [n] S Mt 19:28

22:18 THE LORD'S SUPPER. See 1Co 11:24–25, note.

22:18 THE FRUIT OF THE VINE. What Jesus and the disciples drank at the Passover supper is called "the cup" or "the cup of thanksgiving" (22:17; Mt 26:27; Mk 14:23; 1Co 10:16; 11:25), and "the fruit of the vine" (22:18; Mt 26:29; Mk 14:25). Scriptural evidence supports the view that the juice of the vine was unfermented at the Lord's Supper (see article on WINE IN NEW TESTAMENT TIMES (1), p. 126).

22:20 THE NEW COVENANT IN MY BLOOD. Jesus announces the inauguration of the new covenant based on his sacrificial death (cf. Mt 26:28; 1Co 11:25). Scripture teaches that the new covenant could only become valid by the death of Christ (Heb 9:15–18). The disciples entered into this new covenant when they were regenerated and indwelt by the Holy Spirit on the evening of Jesus' resurrection (see article on THE REGENERATION OF THE DISCIPLES, p. 212). They later were baptized in the Holy Spirit on the day of Pentecost (see Ac 2:4, note; see article on BAPTISM IN THE HOLY SPIRIT, p. 228).

22:20 MY BLOOD, WHICH IS POURED OUT FOR YOU. See Mt 26:28, note.

22:24–30 TRUE GREATNESS. True greatness is a matter of inward spirit and heart. It is seen in the person who expresses his or her love for Christ in sincere humility (Php 2:3), in a desire to serve both God and fellow humans, and in a willingness to be seen as the least important in God's kingdom.

(1) We must understand that greatness is not position, office, leadership, power, influence, academic degrees, fame, ability, great accomplishments or success. It is not so much what we *do* for God as what we *are* in spirit before him (vv. 25–27; Mt 18:3–4; 20:25–28).

(2) True greatness requires that we become great in the right areas. We need to learn to be great in faith, humility, godly character, wisdom, self-control, patience and love (Gal 5:22–23). It is to have the greatness of Christ, who "loved righteousness and hated wickedness" (Heb 1:9).

(3) True greatness is a matter of heartfelt love for and commitment to God. It requires being consecrated and faithful wherever God chooses to place us. Therefore, in God's sight, the greatest in his kingdom are those with the greatest love for him and commitment to his revealed Word (21:3; Ro 12:1–2).

(4) Consecration will improve your results in God's work, but only in that area in which God has placed you and in the context of the gifts he has given you (Ro 12:3–8; 1Co 12).

22:27 THE ONE WHO SERVES. Concerning those who are chosen to lead in the church (1Ti 3:1–7), Christ says that they must lead as servants, helping others to fulfill God's will for their lives. They must never misuse or betray their position by seeking fame, power, wealth or special privilege.

22:28 STOOD BY ME. Jesus acknowledges that he is grateful for the disciples' faithfulness to him during his life and the trying circumstances that surrounded it. Our greatest concern should also be to stand by him in a world that is hostile to his cause and to his righteous standards.

22:29 CONFER ON YOU A KINGDOM. Jesus provides "a kingdom" for his faithful followers, one he has established (v. 30). The disciples must not expect earthly glory and worldly power in this age.

22:31–32 SATAN ... SIFT YOU AS WHEAT. Jesus' statement concerning Peter reveals two important truths. (1) God allows Satan to tempt us only within certain limits and by God's permission (see Job 1). The devil is not free to do what he wants with God's people. (2) Jesus prays that the faith of his people may not fail. As our heavenly intercessor, he prays for all who "come to God through him, because

31“Simon, Simon, Satan has asked[o] to
sift you[f] as wheat.[p] 32But I have prayed
for you,[q] Simon, that your faith may not
fail. And when you have turned back,
strengthen your brothers.”[r]

33But he replied, “Lord, I am ready to
go with you to prison and to death.”[s]

34Jesus answered, “I tell you, Peter, before the rooster crows today, you will deny
three times that you know me.”

35Then Jesus asked them, “When I sent
you without purse, bag or sandals,[t] did
you lack anything?”

“Nothing,” they answered.

36He said to them, “But now if you have
a purse, take it, and also a bag; and if you
don't have a sword, sell your cloak and
buy one. 37It is written: ‘And he was numbered with the transgressors’[g];[u] and I tell
you that this must be fulfilled in me. Yes,
what is written about me is reaching its
fulfillment.”

38The disciples said, “See, Lord, here
are two swords.”

“That is enough,” he replied.

Jesus Prays on the Mount of Olives

22:40–46pp — Mt 26:36–46; Mk 14:32–42

39Jesus went out as usual[v] to the
Mount of Olives,[w] and his disciples followed him. 40On reaching the place, he
said to them, “Pray that you will not fall
into temptation.”[x] 41He withdrew about a
stone's throw beyond them, knelt down[y]
and prayed, 42“Father, if you are willing,
take this cup[z] from me; yet not my will,
but yours be done.”[a] 43An angel from
heaven appeared to him and strengthened
him.[b] 44And being in anguish, he prayed
more earnestly, and his sweat was like
drops of blood falling to the ground.[h]

45When he rose from prayer and went
back to the disciples, he found them
asleep, exhausted from sorrow. 46“Why
are you sleeping?” he asked them. “Get up
and pray so that you will not fall into
temptation.”[c]

22:31 [o]Job 1:6-12 [p]Am 9:9 **22:32** [q]Jn 17:9, 15; S Ro 8:34 [r]Jn 21:15-17 **22:33** [s]Jn 11:16 **22:35** [t]Mt 10:9, 10; Lk 9:3; 10:4 **22:37** [u]Isa 53:12 **22:39** [v]Lk 21:37 [w]S Mt 21:1 **22:40** [x]Mt 6:13 **22:41** [y]Lk 18:11 **22:42** [z]S Mt 20:22 [a]S Mt 26:39 **22:43** [b]Mt 4:11; Mk 1:13 **22:46** [c]ver 40 **22:49** [d]ver 38 **22:52** [e]ver 4 **22:53** [f]S Mt 26:55 [g]Jn 12:27 [h]Mt 8:12; Jn 1:5; 3:20 **22:54** [i]Mt 26:57; Mk 14:53 [j]Mt 26:58; Mk 14:54; Jn 18:15

Jesus Arrested

22:47–53pp — Mt 26:47–56; Mk 14:43–50; Jn 18:3–11

47While he was still speaking a crowd
came up, and the man who was called Judas, one of the Twelve, was leading them.
He approached Jesus to kiss him, 48but
Jesus asked him, “Judas, are you betraying the Son of Man with a kiss?”

49When Jesus' followers saw what was
going to happen, they said, “Lord, should
we strike with our swords?”[d] 50And one
of them struck the servant of the high
priest, cutting off his right ear.

51But Jesus answered, “No more of
this!” And he touched the man's ear and
healed him.

52Then Jesus said to the chief priests,
the officers of the temple guard,[e] and the
elders, who had come for him, “Am I leading a rebellion, that you have come with
swords and clubs? 53Every day I was with
you in the temple courts,[f] and you did not
lay a hand on me. But this is your hour[g]—
when darkness reigns.”[h]

Peter Disowns Jesus

22:55–62pp — Mt 26:69–75; Mk 14:66–72; Jn 18:16–18,25–27

54Then seizing him, they led him away
and took him into the house of the high
priest.[i] Peter followed at a distance.[j]
55But when they had kindled a fire in the
middle of the courtyard and had sat down
together, Peter sat down with them. 56A
servant girl saw him seated there in the
firelight. She looked closely at him and
said, “This man was with him.”

57But he denied it. “Woman, I don't
know him,” he said.

58A little later someone else saw him
and said, “You also are one of them.”

“Man, I am not!” Peter replied.

59About an hour later another asserted,

[f] *31* The Greek is plural. [g] *37* Isaiah 53:12
[h] *44* Some early manuscripts do not have verses 43 and 44.

---

he always lives to intercede for them” (Heb 7:25). God is faithful in all our temptations to provide a way of escape (1Co 10:13). However, the fulfillment of Jesus' prayers are conditional. If a person rejects the grace of God, Christ's intercession is then of no effect (see 19:41, note).

22:36 SWORD ... BUY ONE. Jesus may be using irony here in his statement that his disciples ought to buy a sword. After all, up to this point he has been challenging them to live the life of the cross rather than choose the way of the world. Jesus then goes on to state (v. 37) his commitment to God's way of suffering and to the cross. V. 38 indicates that the disciples did not understand what Jesus meant.

22:42 THIS CUP. See Mt 26:39, note.

22:44 SWEAT WAS LIKE DROPS OF BLOOD. For the ten stages of Christ's redemptive suffering, see notes on Mt 26:37ff.

22:54 THEN SEIZING HIM. For the order of events from Christ's arrest to his crucifixion, see Mt 26:57, note.

"Certainly this fellow was with him, for he
is a Galilean."[k]
60Peter replied, "Man, I don't know
what you're talking about!" Just as he was
speaking, the rooster crowed. 61The
Lord[l] turned and looked straight at Peter. Then Peter remembered the word the
Lord had spoken to him: "Before the
rooster crows today, you will disown me
three times."[m] 62And he went outside and
wept bitterly.

The Guards Mock Jesus

22:63–65pp — Mt 26:67,68; Mk 14:65; Jn 18:22,23

63The men who were guarding Jesus began mocking and beating him. 64They
blindfolded him and demanded, "Prophesy! Who hit you?" 65And they said many
other insulting things to him.[n]

Jesus Before Pilate and Herod

22:67–71pp — Mt 26:63–66; Mk 14:61–63; Jn 18:19–21
23:2,3pp — Mt 27:11–14; Mk 15:2–5; Jn 18:29–37
23:18–25pp — Mt 27:15–26; Mk 15:6–15; Jn 18:39–19:16

66At daybreak the council[o] of the elders of the people, both the chief priests
and teachers of the law, met together,[p]
and Jesus was led before them. 67"If you
are the Christ,[i]" they said, "tell us."
Jesus answered, "If I tell you, you will
not believe me, 68and if I asked you, you
would not answer.[q] 69But from now on,
the Son of Man will be seated at the right
hand of the mighty God."[r]
70They all asked, "Are you then the Son
of God?"[s]
He replied, "You are right in saying I
am."[t]
71Then they said, "Why do we need any
more testimony? We have heard it from
his own lips."

23 Then the whole assembly rose and
led him off to Pilate.[u] 2And they
began to accuse him, saying, "We have
found this man subverting our nation.[v] He
opposes payment of taxes to Caesar[w] and
claims to be Christ,[j] a king."[x]
3So Pilate asked Jesus, "Are you the
king of the Jews?"
"Yes, it is as you say," Jesus replied.
4Then Pilate announced to the chief
priests and the crowd, "I find no basis for
a charge against this man."[y]
5But they insisted, "He stirs up the people all over Judea[k] by his teaching. He
started in Galilee[z] and has come all the
way here."
6On hearing this, Pilate asked if the
man was a Galilean.[a] 7When he learned
that Jesus was under Herod's jurisdiction,
he sent him to Herod,[b] who was also in
Jerusalem at that time.
8When Herod saw Jesus, he was greatly
pleased, because for a long time he had
been wanting to see him.[c] From what he
had heard about him, he hoped to see him
perform some miracle. 9He plied him with
many questions, but Jesus gave him no
answer.[d] 10The chief priests and the
teachers of the law were standing there,
vehemently accusing him. 11Then Herod
and his soldiers ridiculed and mocked
him. Dressing him in an elegant robe,[e]
they sent him back to Pilate. 12That day
Herod and Pilate became friends[f]—before this they had been enemies.
13Pilate called together the chief
priests, the rulers and the people, 14and

22:59 [k]Lk 23:6
22:61 [l]S Lk 7:13 [m]ver 34
22:65 [n]S Mt 16:21
22:66 [o]S Mt 5:22 [p]Mt 27:1; Mk 15:1
22:68 [q]Lk 20:3-8
22:69 [r]S Mk 16:19
22:70 [s]S Mt 4:3 [t]Mt 27:11; Lk 23:3
23:1 [u]S Mt 27:2
23:2 [v]ver 14 [w]Lk 20:22 [x]Jn 19:12
23:4 [y]ver 14,22, 41; Mt 27:23; Jn 18:38; 1Ti 6:13; S 2Co 5:21
23:5 [z]Mk 1:14
23:6 [a]Lk 22:59
23:7 [b]S Mt 14:1
23:8 [c]Lk 9:9
23:9 [d]S Mk 14:61
23:11 [e]Mk 15:17-19; Jn 19:2,3
23:12 [f]Ac 4:27

i *67* Or *Messiah* j *2* Or *Messiah*; also in verses 35 and 39 k *5* Or *over the land of the Jews*

22:62 WEPT BITTERLY. Peter denied the Lord out of weakness, not out of wickedness, for he never ceased to love his Master and to believe in him. Peter was spiritually weak and incapable of resisting great temptation since he had not yet, along with the other disciples, received the Holy Spirit and his regenerating grace in the full new covenant sense. They received the Holy Spirit's indwelling presence only on the resurrection day (see Mk 14:50, note; see article on THE REGENERATION OF THE DISCIPLES, p. 212).

22:63 MOCKING AND BEATING HIM. See Mt 26:67, note.

23:1 PILATE. Pilate was the Roman governor in Jerusalem at the time of the Passover. Jesus was brought to him because under Roman law the Jews could not legally carry out the death penalty. Pilate has become a symbol of those who make religious decisions based on political expediency rather than truth and justice. Believers must not compromise the Word of God; they must stand for what is right, and not for those things that would only serve their own selfish ambitions.

23:3 ARE YOU THE KING OF THE JEWS? See Mt 27:2, note.

23:8–11 JESUS BEFORE KING HEROD. This is the same Herod who had John the Baptist beheaded. Because Herod's heart is so hardened, Jesus refuses to speak to him. In anger Herod and his men mock Jesus' claim to be the king of the Jews.

23:11 MOCKED HIM . . . ELEGANT ROBE. See Mt 27:28–29, note.

23:14 NO BASIS FOR YOUR CHARGES. Jesus was accused of treason against Rome. Pilate comes to the conclusion that Jesus is innocent of any rebellion against the Roman government. Jesus declares that his kingdom is not a political kingdom of this world, but a spiritual kingdom (see Jn 18:36).

said to them, "You brought me this man as
one who was inciting the people to rebellion. I have examined him in your presence and have found no basis for your
charges against him.[g] 15Neither has Herod, for he sent him back to us; as you can
see, he has done nothing to deserve death.
16Therefore, I will punish him[h] and then
release him.[1]"

18With one voice they cried out, "Away
with this man! Release Barabbas to us!"[i]
19(Barabbas had been thrown into prison
for an insurrection in the city, and for murder.)

20Wanting to release Jesus, Pilate appealed to them again. 21But they kept
shouting, "Crucify him! Crucify him!"

22For the third time he spoke to them:
"Why? What crime has this man committed? I have found in him no grounds for
the death penalty. Therefore I will have
him punished and then release him."[j]

23But with loud shouts they insistently
demanded that he be crucified, and their
shouts prevailed. 24So Pilate decided to
grant their demand. 25He released the
man who had been thrown into prison for
insurrection and murder, the one they
asked for, and surrendered Jesus to their
will.

The Crucifixion

23:33–43pp — Mt 27:33–44; Mk 15:22–32; Jn 19:17–24

26As they led him away, they seized Simon from Cyrene,[k] who was on his way in
from the country, and put the cross on him
and made him carry it behind Jesus.[l] 27A
large number of people followed him, including women who mourned and wailed[m]
for him. 28Jesus turned and said to them,
"Daughters of Jerusalem, do not weep for
me; weep for yourselves and for your children.[n] 29For the time will come when you
will say, 'Blessed are the barren women,
the wombs that never bore and the breasts
that never nursed!'[o] 30Then

" 'they will say to the mountains,
"Fall on us!"
and to the hills, "Cover us!" '[m][p]

31For if men do these things when the tree
is green, what will happen when it is
dry?"[q]

32Two other men, both criminals, were
also led out with him to be executed.[r]
33When they came to the place called the
Skull, there they crucified him, along with
the criminals — one on his right, the other
on his left. 34Jesus said, "Father,[s] forgive
them, for they do not know what they are
doing."[n][t] And they divided up his clothes
by casting lots.[u]

35The people stood watching, and the
rulers even sneered at him.[v] They said,
"He saved others; let him save himself if

23:14 [g] S ver 4
23:16 [h] ver 22; Mt 27:26; Jn 19:1; Ac 16:37; 2Co 11:23,24
23:18 [i] Ac 3:13, 14
23:22 [j] ver 16
23:26 [k] S Mt 27:32 [l] Mk 15:21; Jn 19:17
23:27 [m] Lk 8:52
23:28 [n] Lk 19:41-44; 21:23,24
23:29 [o] Mt 24:19
23:30 [p] Hos 10:8; Isa 2:19; Rev 6:16
23:31 [q] Eze 20:47
23:32 [r] Isa 53:12; Mt 27:38; Mk 15:27; Jn 19:18
23:34 [s] S Mt 11:25 [t] S Mt 5:44 [u] Ps 22:18
23:35 [v] Ps 22:17

[1] *16* Some manuscripts *him." 17Now he was obliged to release one man to them at the Feast.*
[m] *30* Hosea 10:8 [n] *34* Some early manuscripts do not have this sentence.

23:22 HAVE HIM PUNISHED. See Mt 27:26, note.
23:25 SURRENDERED JESUS TO THEIR WILL. It is because of political expediency that Pilate hands Jesus over to the Jewish authorities (see v. 1, note).
23:31 TREE IS GREEN . . . DRY. If the innocent Jesus meets with such a fate, what will be the fate of guilty Jerusalem?
23:33 SKULL. Jesus was crucified in a place outside the city (cf. Heb 13:12). It was called "the Skull" for reasons that are still debated. The Greek word for skull was translated in the Latin version as *calvaria*, from which we get the word "Calvary."
23:33 THEY CRUCIFIED HIM. The crucifixion and death of Jesus are the core and foundation of God's plan of redemption (1Co 1:23–24). Jesus, who had never sinned, died in the place of sinful humanity. Through his crucifixion the penalty for our sin was paid and the work of Satan undone (cf. Ro 3:25, note). Now all people may turn to God in repentance and faith and receive forgiveness and eternal life.
23:34 SEVEN LAST SAYINGS OF CHRIST. In all probability, v. 34 is the first of the seven last sayings of Christ on the cross. The seven sayings were spoken in the following order:
(1) From 9:00 o'clock until noon: (a) The word of forgiveness: "Father, forgive them" (v. 34). (b) The word of salvation: "Today you will be with me in paradise" (v. 43). (c) The word of love: "Dear woman, here is your son, . . . Here is your mother!" (Jn 19:26–27).
(2) The three hours of darkness: from noon until 3 o'clock, no words reported.
(3) About 3 o'clock: (a) The word of spiritual suffering: "My God, my God, why have you forsaken me?" (Mk 15:34). (b) The word of physical suffering: "I am thirsty" (Jn 19:28). (c) The word of triumph: "It is finished" (Jn 19:30). (d) The word of committal: "Father, into your hands I commit my spirit" (v. 46).
23:35 THE PEOPLE STOOD WATCHING. One of the surest proofs of the depravity of the human heart is the fact that people take pleasure in violence, blood and death. (1) We see it in the Roman and Greek arenas, where spectators cheered as people fought and killed each other. We see it in the onlookers who watched Jesus die a horrible death (vv. 35–37). We see it in the history of the persecution of believers. (2) We see it in modern society as well, as millions of adults and children find pleasure and entertainment in television and other media that depict human suffering, blood, violence and death (see Ro 1:32, note). (3) Jesus died to change this attitude and to bring love and care. He wants us to see the impact of sin on human life with eyes of compassion and to hear the

he is the Christ of God, the Chosen One."[w]
36The soldiers also came up and
mocked him.[x] They offered him wine vinegar[y] 37and said, "If you are the king of the
Jews,[z] save yourself."
38There was a written notice above
him, which read: THIS IS THE KING OF THE
JEWS.[a]
39One of the criminals who hung there
hurled insults at him: "Aren't you the
Christ? Save yourself and us!"[b]
40But the other criminal rebuked him.
"Don't you fear God," he said, "since you
are under the same sentence? 41We are
punished justly, for we are getting what
our deeds deserve. But this man has done
nothing wrong."[c]
42Then he said, "Jesus, remember me
when you come into your kingdom.[o]"[d]
43Jesus answered him, "I tell you the
truth, today you will be with me in paradise."[e]

Jesus' Death

23:44–49pp — Mt 27:45–56; Mk 15:33–41

44It was now about the sixth hour, and
darkness came over the whole land until
the ninth hour,[f] 45for the sun stopped
shining. And the curtain of the temple[g]
was torn in two.[h] 46Jesus called out with
a loud voice,[i] "Father, into your hands I
commit my spirit."[j] When he had said
this, he breathed his last.[k]
47The centurion, seeing what had happened, praised God[l] and said, "Surely
this was a righteous man." 48When all the
people who had gathered to witness this
sight saw what took place, they beat their
breasts[m] and went away. 49But all those
who knew him, including the women who
had followed him from Galilee,[n] stood at
a distance,[o] watching these things.

23:35 [w]Isa 42:1 **23:36** [x]Ps 22:7 [y]Ps 69:21; Mt 27:48 **23:37** [z]Lk 4:3,9 **23:38** [a]S Mt 2:2 **23:39** [b]ver 35,37 **23:41** [c]S ver 4 **23:42** [d]S Mt 16:27 **23:43** [e]2Co 12:3, 4; Rev 2:7 **23:44** [f]Am 8:9 **23:45** [g]Ex 26:31-33; Heb 9:3,8 [h]Heb 10:19,20 **23:46** [i]Mt 27:50 [j]Ps 31:5; 1Pe 2:23 [k]Jn 19:30 **23:47** [l]S Mt 9:8 **23:48** [m]Lk 18:13 **23:49** [n]Lk 8:2 [o]Ps 38:11

Jesus' Burial

23:50–56pp — Mt 27:57–61; Mk 15:42–47; Jn 19:38–42

50Now there was a man named Joseph,
a member of the Council, a good and upright man, 51who had not consented to
their decision and action. He came from
the Judean town of Arimathea and he was
waiting for the kingdom of God.[p] 52Going
to Pilate, he asked for Jesus' body. 53Then
he took it down, wrapped it in linen cloth
and placed it in a tomb cut in the rock, one
in which no one had yet been laid. 54It was
Preparation Day,[q] and the Sabbath was
about to begin.
55The women who had come with Jesus
from Galilee[r] followed Joseph and saw
the tomb and how his body was laid in it.
56Then they went home and prepared
spices and perfumes.[s] But they rested on
the Sabbath in obedience to the commandment.[t]

The Resurrection

24:1–10pp — Mt 28:1–8; Mk 16:1–8; Jn 20:1–8

24 On the first day of the week, very
early in the morning, the women
took the spices they had prepared[u] and
went to the tomb. 2They found the stone
rolled away from the tomb, 3but when they
entered, they did not find the body of the
Lord Jesus.[v] 4While they were wondering
about this, suddenly two men in clothes
that gleamed like lightning[w] stood beside
them. 5In their fright the women bowed
down with their faces to the ground, but
the men said to them, "Why do you look
for the living among the dead? 6He is not
here; he has risen! Remember how he told

23:51 [p]Lk 2:25, 38 **23:54** [q]Mt 27:62 **23:55** [r]ver 49 **23:56** [s]Mk 16:1; Lk 24:1 [t]Ex 12:16; 20:10 **24:1** [u]Lk 23:56 **24:3** [v]ver 23,24 **24:4** [w]S Jn 20:12

o *42* Some manuscripts *come with your kingly power*

groaning of suffering humanity (see 13:16, note). (4) It is the responsibility of parents to guard themselves and their families against all influences that would desensitize them to human pain and tragedy (see Mt 18:6, note).

23:35 SNEERED AT HIM. See Mt 27:39, note.

23:43 PARADISE. The term "paradise" is used to indicate heaven or the presence of God (that "heaven" and "paradise" indicate the same place is clear from 2Co 12:2,4). Jesus' words clearly teach that after death the saved go immediately into Jesus' presence in heaven.

23:45 CURTAIN OF THE TEMPLE WAS TORN. See Mt 27:51, note.

23:46 FATHER, INTO YOUR HANDS. Jesus voluntarily gave his life over to death. At that moment he went in spirit to his Father in heaven.

23:46 I COMMIT MY SPIRIT. See Mt 27:50, note.

24:6 HE HAS RISEN! Jesus' resurrection (see Mt 28:6, note) is confirmed by the following facts. (1) The empty tomb. If the enemies of Jesus had taken his body, they surely would have displayed it to prove he had not risen. If the disciples had taken his body, they would have never sacrificed their lives and possessions for what they knew to be a lie. The empty tomb reveals that Jesus did arise and truly was the Son of God.

(2) The existence, power, joy and devotion of the early church. If Jesus had not risen and appeared to them, they would have never changed from despondency to unheard-of joy, courage and hope (vv. 52–53).

(3) The writing of the NT. The NT was written by men giving their lives for the truth and righteousness taught by Jesus. They would never have taken the trouble to write about a Messiah and his teaching if his career had ended in death and disillusionment (see

you, while he was still with you in Galilee:[x] 7'The Son of Man[y] must be delivered into the hands of sinful men, be crucified and on the third day be raised
again.' "[z] 8Then they remembered his
words.[a]

9When they came back from the tomb,
they told all these things to the Eleven
and to all the others. 10It was Mary Magdalene, Joanna, Mary the mother of James,
and the others with them[b] who told this
to the apostles.[c] 11But they did not believe[d] the women, because their words
seemed to them like nonsense. 12Peter,
however, got up and ran to the tomb.
Bending over, he saw the strips of linen
lying by themselves,[e] and he went away,[f]
wondering to himself what had happened.

On the Road to Emmaus

13Now that same day two of them were
going to a village called Emmaus, about
seven miles[p] from Jerusalem.[g] 14They
were talking with each other about everything that had happened. 15As they talked
and discussed these things with each other, Jesus himself came up and walked
along with them;[h] 16but they were kept
from recognizing him.[i]

17He asked them, "What are you discussing together as you walk along?"

They stood still, their faces downcast.
18One of them, named Cleopas,[j] asked
him, "Are you only a visitor to Jerusalem
and do not know the things that have happened there in these days?"

19"What things?" he asked.

"About Jesus of Nazareth,"[k] they replied. "He was a prophet,[l] powerful in
word and deed before God and all the people. 20The chief priests and our rulers[m]
handed him over to be sentenced to death,
and they crucified him; 21but we had
hoped that he was the one who was going
to redeem Israel.[n] And what is more, it is
the third day[o] since all this took place.
22In addition, some of our women amazed
us.[p] They went to the tomb early this
morning 23but didn't find his body. They
came and told us that they had seen a
vision of angels, who said he was alive.
24Then some of our companions went to
the tomb and found it just as the women
had said, but him they did not see."[q]

25He said to them, "How foolish you
are, and how slow of heart to believe all
that the prophets have spoken! 26Did not
the Christ[q] have to suffer these things and
then enter his glory?"[r] 27And beginning
with Moses[s] and all the Prophets,[t] he
explained to them what was said in all the
Scriptures concerning himself.[u]

28As they approached the village to
which they were going, Jesus acted as if
he were going farther. 29But they urged
him strongly, "Stay with us, for it is nearly
evening; the day is almost over." So he
went in to stay with them.

30When he was at the table with them,
he took bread, gave thanks, broke it[v] and
began to give it to them. 31Then their eyes
were opened and they recognized him,[w]
and he disappeared from their sight.
32They asked each other, "Were not our
hearts burning within us[x] while he talked
with us on the road and opened the Scriptures[y] to us?"

33They got up and returned at once to
Jerusalem. There they found the Eleven
and those with them, assembled together
34and saying, "It is true! The Lord[z] has
risen and has appeared to Simon."[a]
35Then the two told what had happened
on the way, and how Jesus was recognized
by them when he broke the bread.[b]

Jesus Appears to the Disciples

36While they were still talking about
this, Jesus himself stood among them and
said to them, "Peace be with you."[c]

37They were startled and frightened,
thinking they saw a ghost.[d] 38He said to
them, "Why are you troubled, and why do

24:6 [x]Mt 17:22, 23; Lk 9:22; 24:44 **24:7** [y]S Mt 8:20 [z]S Mt 16:21 **24:8** [a]Jn 2:22 **24:10** [b]Lk 8:1-3 [c]S Mk 6:30 **24:11** [d]Mk 16:11 **24:12** [e]Jn 20:3-7 [f]Jn 20:10 **24:13** [g]Mk 16:12 **24:15** [h]ver 36 **24:16** [i]Jn 20:14; 21:4 **24:18** [j]Jn 19:25 **24:19** [k]S Mk 1:24 [l]S Mt 21:11 **24:20** [m]Lk 23:13 **24:21** [n]Lk 1:68; 2:38; 21:28 [o]S Mt 16:21 **24:22** [p]ver 1-10 **24:24** [q]ver 12 **24:26** [r]Heb 2:10; 1Pe 1:11 **24:27** [s]Ge 3:15; Nu 21:9; Dt 18:15 [t]Isa 7:14; 9:6; 40:10,11; 53; Eze 34:23; Da 9:24; Mic 7:20; Mal 3:1 [u]Jn 1:45 **24:30** [v]S Mt 14:19 **24:31** [w]ver 16 **24:32** [x]Ps 39:3 [y]ver 27,45 **24:34** [z]S Lk 7:13 [a]1Co 15:5 **24:35** [b]ver 30,31 **24:36** [c]Jn 20:19, 21,26; S 14:27 **24:37** [d]Mk 6:49

[p] 13 Greek *sixty stadia* (about 11 kilometers)
[q] 26 Or *Messiah*; also in verse 46

1Co 15:12–19).

(4) The baptism in the Holy Spirit and his accompanying manifestations within the church. That the Holy Spirit was poured out at Pentecost as an experiential reality is proof that Jesus had risen and was exalted at God's right hand (cf. Ac 1:3–5; 2:33). If Christ had not risen, there would have been no experiential baptism in the Holy Spirit (cf. Jn 16:7).

(5) The millions of people throughout the last 2,000 years who have experienced in their own hearts and lives the presence of Jesus and the witness of the Holy Spirit.

24:15 JESUS HIMSELF CAME UP. For the post-resurrection appearances of Christ, see Mt 28:9, note.

24:19 JESUS . . . A PROPHET. The Gospel writers understood Jesus as "the prophet" sent from God (cf. Dt 18:15–16,19; Mk 6:4; Ac 3:22; see Lk 6:23, note).

24:27 HE EXPLAINED . . . THE SCRIPTURES. The Messiah and his redemptive work through suffering is a central OT theme. Christ may have cited such passages as Ge 3:15; 22:18; 49:10; Nu 24:17; Ps 22:1,18; 110:1; Isa 25:8; 52:14; 53; Jer 23:5; Da 2:24,35,44; Mic 5:2; Zec 3:8; 9:9; 13:7; Mal 3:1.

doubts rise in your minds? **39**Look at my
hands and my feet. It is I myself! Touch
me and see;[e] a ghost does not have flesh
and bones, as you see I have."
40When he had said this, he showed
them his hands and feet. **41**And while they
still did not believe it because of joy and
amazement, he asked them, "Do you have
anything here to eat?" **42**They gave him a
piece of broiled fish, **43**and he took it and
ate it in their presence.[f]
44He said to them, "This is what I told
you while I was still with you:[g] Everything must be fulfilled[h] that is written
about me in the Law of Moses,[i] the
Prophets[j] and the Psalms."[k]
45Then he opened their minds so they
could understand the Scriptures. **46**He
told them, "This is what is written: The
Christ will suffer[l] and rise from the dead
on the third day,[m] **47**and repentance and
forgiveness of sins will be preached in his
name[n] to all nations,[o] beginning at Jerusalem.[p] **48**You are witnesses[q] of these Jn 1:7
things. **49**I am going to send you what my
Father has promised;[r] but stay in the city
until you have been clothed with power Jn 1:32-33
from on high."

24:39 [e]Jn 20:27; 1Jn 1:1 **24:43** [f]Ac 10:41 **24:44** [g]Lk 9:45; 18:34 [h]S Mt 1:22; 16:21; Lk 9:22,44; 18:31-33; 22:37 [i]S ver 27 [j]S ver 27 [k]Ps 2; 16; 22; 69; 72; 110; 118 **24:46** [l]S Mt 16:21 [m]S Mt 16:21 **24:47** [n]Ac 5:31; 10:43; 13:38 [o]Mt 28:19; Mk 13:10 [p]Isa 2:3 **24:48** [q]S Jn 15:27; Ac 1:8; 2:32; 4:20; 5:32; 13:31; 1Pe 5:1 **24:49** [r]S Jn 14:16; Ac 1:4 **24:50** [s]S Mt 21:17 **24:51** [t]2Ki 2:11

The Ascension

50When he had led them out to the vicinity of Bethany,[s] he lifted up his hands
and blessed them. **51**While he was blessing them, he left them and was taken up
into heaven.[t] **52**Then they worshiped him
and returned to Jerusalem with great joy.
53And they stayed continually at the temple,[u] praising God.

24:53 [u]S Ac 2:46

24:39 A GHOST DOES NOT HAVE FLESH. Jesus has a glorified, spiritual body (Php 3:20–21), as do the saints in heaven (1Co 15:40).

24:46 THE IMPORTANCE OF THE RESURRECTION. See Mt 28:6, note.

24:47 REPENTANCE AND FORGIVENESS OF SINS. The disciples were not to preach forgiveness of sins without the demand of repentance. The preacher who offers salvation on the basis of an easy faith or by a mere acceptance of salvation without a commitment to obey Christ and his Word preaches a false gospel. Repentance involves forsaking sin; this has always been an essential element in the true gospel of the NT (see Mt 3:2, note on repentance).

24:47 WILL BE PREACHED. For comments on the Great Commission, see Mt 28:19, note.

24:47 TO ALL NATIONS. Christ himself institutes Christian missions as a holy and mandatory task of the church. Missions is a main theme in both the OT (Ge 22:18; 1Ki 8:41–43; Ps 72:8–11; Isa 2:3; 45:22–25) and the NT (Mt 28:19; Ac 1:8; 28:28; Eph 2:14–18).

24:49 WHAT MY FATHER HAS PROMISED. "What my Father has promised" that will bring "power from on high" refers to the outpouring of the Holy Spirit that began at Pentecost (see Ac 1:4, note; 2:4, note; see article on BAPTISM IN THE HOLY SPIRIT, p. 228); we find this promise recorded in the OT (Isa 32:15; 44:3; Eze 39:29; Joel 2:28) and in the NT (Jn 14:16–17,26; 15:26; 16:7; Ac 1:4–8; 2:33,38–39). The disciples devoted themselves to prayer as they waited for the fulfillment of the promise (see Ac 1:14, note). The believer today seeking the baptism in the Holy Spirit should do the same.

24:50 HE . . . BLESSED THEM. God's blessing on the lives of his followers is essential. Concerning God's blessing, Scripture teaches several things:

(1) The word "blessing" (Gk *eulogia*) has the meaning of: (a) a divine gift causing our work to succeed (Dt 28:12); (b) God's presence with us (Ge 26:3); (c) God giving us strength, power and help (Eph 3:16; Col 1:11); and (d) God working in and through us to produce good (Php 2:13).

(2) In the OT, words related to "blessing" occur more than 400 times. The first thing God did in relation to humanity was to bless them (Ge 1:28). God also sustains his work by blessing (Eze 34:26). The life and history of God's people are under the operation of blessing and cursing (Dt 11:26ff).

(3) In the NT the whole work of Christ can be summed up by the statement that God has "sent him first to you to bless you" (Ac 3:26). We see his blessing given to children (Mk 10:13–16) and to his followers during his departure from earth (vv. 50–51). Blessing likewise plays an integral part in the ministry of the apostles (Ro 15:29).

(4) The blessing of God is conditional. God's people must make a choice: either blessing through obedience or cursing through disobedience (Dt 30:15–18; Jer 17:5,7).

(5) How do we receive the Lord's blessing? Three things are required: (a) We must always look to Jesus for his blessing on our ministry, work and family (Heb 12:2). (b) We must believe in, love and obey him (cf. Mt 5:3–11; 24:45–46; Rev 1:3; 16:15; 22:7). (c) We must remove everything from our lives that would hinder the blessing (Ro 13:12; Eph 4:22; Heb 12:1).

(6) God's "blessing" may not be equated with personal material gain or the absence of suffering in our lives (see Heb 11:37–39; Rev 2:8–10).

JOHN

Outline

The Logos Prologue (1:1–18)

I. Introduction of the Christ to Israel (1:19–51)
   A. By John the Baptist (1:19–36)
   B. To the First Disciples (1:37–51)

II. Christ's Signs and Discourses to Israel and His Rejection (2:1—12:50)
   A. Christ's Revelation to Israel (2:1—11:46)
      1. First Sign: Water Into Wine (2:1–11)
         Interlude (2:12)
      2. Initial Witness to the Jews in Jerusalem (2:13–25)
         Feast in Jerusalem (Passover) (2:23–25)
      3. First Discourse: New Birth and New Life (3:1–21)
         Interlude: About John the Baptist and Jesus (3:22—4:3)
      4. Second Discourse: The Water of Life (4:4–42)
         Interlude in Galilee (4:43–45)
      5. Second Sign: Healing the Official's Son (4:46–54)
         Feast in Jerusalem (5:1)
      6. Third Sign: Healing the Paralytic at Bethesda on the Sabbath (5:2–18)
      7. Third Discourse: The Divine Sonship of Christ (5:19–47)
      8. Fourth Sign: Feeding the Five Thousand (6:1–15)
      9. Fifth Sign: Walking on the Water (6:16–21)
      10. Fourth Discourse: The Bread of Life (6:22–59)
      11. Sifting of the Disciples (6:60–71)
         Interlude (7:1)
      12. Feast in Jerusalem (Tabernacles) (7:2–52)
      13. Fifth Discourse: The Life-giving Spirit (7:37–44)
         [Woman Caught in Adultery (7:53—8:11)]
      14. Sixth Discourse: The Light of the World (8:12–30)
      15. Debate With the Jews (8:31–59)
      16. Sixth Sign: Healing the Man Born Blind (9:1–41)
      17. Seventh Discourse: The Good Shepherd (10:1–21)
         Feast in Jerusalem (Dedication) (10:22–42)
      18. Seventh Sign: The Raising of Lazarus (11:1–46)
   B. Christ's Rejection by Israel (11:47—12:50)

III. Christ and the Inception of the New Covenant People (13:1—20:29)
   A. The Last Supper (13:1—14:31)
      1. Washing the Disciples' Feet and Subsequent Conversation (13:1–38)
      2. Jesus, the Way to the Father (14:1–31)
   B. Discourse on the True Vine and Consequences of Union With Christ (15:1—16:33)
   C. Prayer of Consecration for Himself and the New Covenant People (17:1–26)
   D. The Suffering Servant (18:1—19:42)
   E. The Risen Lord (20:1–29)

The Author's Statement of Purpose (20:30–31)

The Epilogue (21:1–25)

Author: John

Theme: Jesus, the Son of God

Date: A.D. 80–95

Background

John's Gospel is unique among the four Gospels. It records much about Jesus' ministry in Judea and Jerusalem that the other three Gospels omit, and reveals more fully the mystery of Jesus' personhood. The author is identified indirectly as "the disciple whom Jesus loved" (13:23; 19:26; 20:2; 21:7,20). The testimony of ancient Christianity and the internal evidence of the Gospel itself point to authorship by John the son of Zebedee, one of the twelve original disciples and a member of Jesus' inner circle (Peter, James and John).

According to several ancient sources, the elderly apostle John, while residing at Ephesus, was requested by the elders of Asia to write this "spiritual Gospel" in order to counteract and refute a dangerous heresy about the nature, person and deity of Jesus led by a persuasive Jew named Cerinthus. John's Gospel continues to serve the church as a profound theological statement about "the truth" as it is incarnate in Jesus Christ.

Purpose

John states his purpose for writing in 20:31, namely, "that you may believe that Jesus is the Christ, the Son of God, and that by believing you may have life in his name." Ancient Greek manuscripts of John have one of two tenses for the Greek word translated "believe" (20:31): the aorist subjunctive ("that you may begin believing") and the present subjunctive ("that you may go on believing"). If John intended the former, he wrote to convince unbelievers to believe in the Lord Jesus Christ and be saved. If the latter, John wrote to strengthen the foundations of faith so that believers might go on believing in spite of false teaching, and so enter fully into fellowship with the Father and the Son (cf. 17:3). While both of these purposes find support in John, the content of the Gospel as a whole favors the latter emphasis as the overriding purpose.

Survey

The fourth Gospel presents carefully selected evidence that Jesus was Israel's Messiah and God's incarnate (not adopted) Son. The supporting evidence includes (1) seven signs (2:1–11; 4:46–54; 5:2–18; 6:1–15; 6:16–21; 9:1–41; 11:1–46) and seven discourses (3:1–21; 4:4–42; 5:19–47; 6:22–59; 7:37–44; 8:12–30; 10:1–21) by which Jesus disclosed clearly his true identity; (2) seven "I am" statements (6:35; 8:12; 10:7; 10:11; 11:25; 14:6; 15:1) by which Jesus revealed figuratively what he is redemptively for the human race; and (3) the bodily resurrection of Jesus as the ultimate sign and the climactic proof that he is "the Christ, the Son of God" (20:31).

John has two major divisions. (1) Chs. 1–12 present the incarnation and public ministry of Jesus. In spite of Jesus' seven convincing signs, seven profound discourses and seven astounding "I am" claims, the Jews rejected him as their Messiah. (2) Having been rejected by the old covenant Israel, Jesus then (chs. 13–21) focused on his disciples as the nucleus of the new covenant people (i.e., the church he founded). These chapters include Jesus' last supper (ch. 13), his last discourses (chs. 14–16) and his final prayer (ch. 17) for his disciples and for all believers. The new covenant was then initiated and established by his death (chs. 18–19) and resurrection (chs. 20–21).

Special Features

Seven major emphases characterize John's Gospel. (1) Jesus as "the Son of God": from John's prologue with its grand declaration, "we have seen his glory" (1:14), to the conclusion with Thomas's confession, "my Lord and my God" (20:28), Jesus is God's Son come in the flesh. (2) The word "believe": it occurs 98 times, is the equivalent of receiving Christ (1:12), and involves the heart in a response of total commitment. (3) "Eternal life": a key Johannine concept is Christ's life within us; this refers not so much to endless existence as to a changed quality of our present lives that comes through union with Christ, resulting in both freedom from slavery to sin and demons and a growing knowledge and fellowship with God. (4) The ministry of the Holy Spirit: he enables believers to experience Jesus' life and power in an ongoing way after Christ's death and resurrection. (5) "Truth": Jesus is the truth, the Holy Spirit is the Spirit of truth and God's Word is truth. Truth sets disciples free (8:32), makes them clean (15:3) and is the antithesis of Satan's nature and activity (8:44–47,51). (6) Prominence of the number seven: seven signs, seven discourses and seven "I am" claims testify to who Jesus is (cf. the prominence of the number "seven" in the book of Revelation by the same author). (7) Use of various other prominent words: John makes frequent use of words such as "word," "light," "flesh," "love," "witness," "know," "darkness" and "world."

Reading John

In order to read the entire New Testament in one year, the book of John should be read in 37 days, according to the following schedule:
☐ 1:1–18 ☐ 1:19–51 ☐ 2 ☐ 3:1–21 ☐ 3:22–36 ☐ 4:1–26 ☐ 4:27–54 ☐ 5:1–30 ☐ 5:31–47 ☐ 6:1–24 ☐ 6:25–59 ☐ 6:60–71 ☐ 7:1–24 ☐ 7:25—8:11 ☐ 8:12–30 ☐ 8:31–47 ☐ 8:48–59 ☐ 9 ☐ 10:1–21 ☐ 10:22–42 ☐ 11:1–16 ☐ 11:17–57 ☐ 12:1–19 ☐ 12:20–50 ☐ 13:1–30 ☐ 13:31—14:14 ☐ 14:15–31 ☐ 15:1–17 ☐ 15:18—16:16 ☐ 16:17–33 ☐ 17 ☐ 18:1–27 ☐ 18:28—19:16 ☐ 19:17–42 ☐ 20:1–18 ☐ 20:19–31 ☐ 21

NOTES

The Word Became Flesh

1 In the beginning was the Word,[a] and
the Word was with God,[b] and the
Word was God.[c] **2**He was with God in the
beginning.[d]
3Through him all things were made;
without him nothing was made that has
been made.[e] **4**In him was life,[f] and that
life was the light[g] of men. **5**The light
shines in the darkness,[h] but the darkness
has not understood**[a]** it.[i]
6There came a man who was sent from
God; his name was John.[j] **7**He came as a
witness to testify[k] concerning that light,
so that through him all men might believe.[l] **8**He himself was not the light; he
came only as a witness to the light. **9**The
true light[m] that gives light to every man[n]
was coming into the world.**[b]**
10He was in the world, and though the
world was made through him,[o] the world
did not recognize him. **11**He came to that
which was his own, but his own did not
receive him.[p] **12**Yet to all who received
him, to those who believed[q] in his name,[r]
he gave the right to become children of
God[s]— **13**children born not of natural de-

Jn 4:7-30

1:1 [a]Isa 55:11; Rev 19:13 [b]Jn 17:5; 1Jn 1:2 [c]Php 2:6 **1:2** [d]Ge 1:1; Jn 8:58; 17:5,24; 1Jn 1:1; Rev 1:8 **1:3** [e]ver 10; 1Co 8:6; Col 1:16; Heb 1:2 **1:4** [f]S Jn 5:26; 6:57; 11:25; 14:6; Ac 3:15; Heb 7:16; 1Jn 1:1,2; 5:20; Rev 1:18 [g]Ps 36:9; Jn 3:19; 8:12; 9:5; 12:46 **1:5** [h]Ps 18:28 [i]Jn 3:19 **1:6** [j]S Mt 3:1 **1:7** [k]ver 15,19, 32; Jn 3:26; 5:33 [l]ver 12; S Jn 3:15 **1:9** [m]1Jn 2:8 [n]Isa 49:6 **1:10** [o]S ver 3 **1:11** [p]Isa 53:3 **1:12** [q]ver 7; S Jn 3:15 [r]S 1Jn 3:23 [s]Dt 14:1; S Ro 8:14; 8:16,21; Eph 5:1; 1Jn 3:1,2

a 5 Or *darkness, and the darkness has not overcome*
b 9 Or *This was the true light that gives light to every man who comes into the world*

1:1 THE WORD. John begins his Gospel by calling Jesus "the Word" (Gk *logos*). In using this designation for Christ, John presents him as the personal Word of God and indicates that in these last days God has spoken to us in his Son (cf. Heb 1:1–3). Scripture declares that Jesus Christ is the manifold wisdom of God (1Co 1:30; Eph 3:10–11; Col 2:2–3) and the perfect revelation of the nature and person of God (Jn 1:3–5,14,18; Col 2:9). Just as a person's words reveal his or her heart and mind, Christ as "the Word" reveals the heart and mind of God (14:9). John gives us three main characteristics of Jesus Christ as "the Word."

(1) The Word's relation to the Father. (a) Christ was preexistent "with God" before the creation of the world (cf. Col 1:15). He was a person existing from eternity, distinct from but in eternal fellowship with God the Father. (b) Christ was divine ("the Word was God"), having the same nature and essence as the Father (Col 2:9; see Mk 1:11, note).

(2) The Word's relation to the world. It was through Christ that God the Father created and now sustains the world (v. 3; Col 1:16; Heb 1:2).

(3) The Word's relation to humanity. "The Word became flesh" (v. 14). In Jesus, God became a human being, having the same nature as humanity but without sin. This is the basic statement of the incarnation: Christ left heaven and entered the condition of human life through the gateway of human birth (see Mt 1:23, note).

1:2 WITH GOD IN THE BEGINNING. Christ was not created; he is eternal, and he has always been in loving fellowship with the Father and the Holy Spirit (see Mk 1:11, note on the Trinity).

1:4 LIFE WAS THE LIGHT OF MEN. True, genuine life is embodied in Christ (cf. 14:6; 17:3). His life was the light for everyone, i.e., God's truth, nature and power are made available to all people through him (8:12; 12:35–36,46).

1:5 LIGHT SHINES IN THE DARKNESS. The light of Christ shines in an evil and sinful world controlled by Satan. The majority of the world has not accepted his life or light, but the darkness has not "understood it" (i.e., mastered it, won over it).

1:9 GIVES LIGHT TO EVERY MAN. Christ illumines all who hear his gospel by imparting a measure of grace and understanding in order that they may freely choose to accept or reject that message. Apart from this light of Christ, there is no other light by which we may see the truth and be saved.

1:10 THE WORLD DID NOT RECOGNIZE HIM. The "world" refers to the whole of society organized and operating independently of God, his Word and his rule. The world will never recognize Christ; it will remain indifferent to or an enemy of Christ and his gospel until the end of the age (see Jas 4:4). For John the world is the great opponent of the Savior in salvation history (cf. Jas 4:4; 1Jn 2:15–17; 4:5).

1:12 RECEIVED . . . BELIEVED. This verse depicts clearly how saving faith is both the act of a single instant and an ongoing attitude of a lifetime. (1) To become a child of God, one must "receive" (Gk *elabon*, from *lambanō*) Christ. The aorist (past) tense here denotes a definite act of faith. (2) Following the act of faith, there must be a continual action of believing. The word "believed" (Gk *pisteuousin*, from *pisteuō*) is a present participle, describing continued action and indicating the need for perseverance in believing. In order for one to be finally saved, true faith must continue after the initial act of accepting Christ (Mt 10:22; 24:12–13; Col 1:21–23; Heb 3:6, 12–15).

1:12 BELIEVED. It is important to note that John never uses the noun "belief" (Gk *pistis*). Yet he uses the verb "believe" (*pisteuō*) 98 times. For John, saving faith is an activity, something that people do. True faith is not a static belief and trust in Jesus and his redeeming work, but a loving, self-abandoning commitment that constantly draws one near to him as Lord and Savior (cf. Heb 7:25).

1:12 CHILDREN OF GOD. People have the right to become the adopted children of God only if they are believing in the name of Christ. When they receive him, they are born again and become God's children (3:1–21). Not all people are "children of God."

1:13 BORN NOT OF . . . HUMAN DECISION. God was under no constraint to offer us salvation through Christ's death other than the constraint of his own love and compassion. The initiative to bring salvation is with God.

scent,[c] nor of human decision or a husband's will, but born of God.[t]
14The Word became flesh[u] and made
his dwelling among us. We have seen his
glory,[v] the glory of the One and Only,[d]
who came from the Father, full of grace[w]
and truth.[x]
15John testifies[y] concerning him. He
cries out, saying, "This was he of whom I
said, 'He who comes after me has surpassed me because he was before me.' "[z]
16From the fullness[a] of his grace[b] we
have all received one blessing after another. 17For the law was given through Moses;[c] grace and truth came through Jesus
Christ.[d] 18No one has ever seen God,[e] but
God the One and Only,[d,e][f] who is at the
Father's side, has made him known.

John the Baptist Denies Being the Christ

19Now this was John's[g] testimony
when the Jews[h] of Jerusalem sent priests
and Levites to ask him who he was. 20He
did not fail to confess, but confessed freely, "I am not the Christ.[f]"[i]
21They asked him, "Then who are you?
Are you Elijah?"[j]
He said, "I am not."
"Are you the Prophet?"[k]
He answered, "No."
22Finally they said, "Who are you? Give
us an answer to take back to those who
sent us. What do you say about yourself?"
23John replied in the words of Isaiah the
prophet, "I am the voice of one calling in
the desert,[l] 'Make straight the way for
the Lord.' "[g][m]
24Now some Pharisees who had been
sent 25questioned him, "Why then do you
baptize if you are not the Christ, nor Elijah, nor the Prophet?"
26"I baptize with[h] water,"[n] John replied, "but among you stands one you do
not know. 27He is the one who comes after
me,[o] the thongs of whose sandals I am
not worthy to untie."[p]
28This all happened at Bethany on the
other side of the Jordan,[q] where John was
baptizing.

Jesus the Lamb of God

29The next day John saw Jesus coming
toward him and said, "Look, the Lamb of
God,[r] who takes away the sin of the
world![s] 30This is the one I meant when I
said, 'A man who comes after me has surpassed me because he was before me.'[t]
31I myself did not know him, but the reason I came baptizing with water was that
he might be revealed to Israel."

Jesus Will Baptize in the Spirit

32Then John gave this testimony: "I saw
the Spirit come down from heaven as a
dove and remain on him.[u] 33I would not
have known him, except that the one who
sent me to baptize with water[v] told me,
'The man on whom you see the Spirit
come down and remain is he who will baptize with the Holy Spirit.'[w] 34I have seen Ac 1:4-5
and I testify that this is the Son of God."[x]

1:13 [t]Jn 3:6; Tit 3:5; Jas 1:18; 1Pe 1:23; 1Jn 3:9; 4:7; 5:1,4
1:14 [u]Gal 4:4; Php 2:7,8; 1Ti 3:16; Heb 2:14; 1Jn 1:1, 2; 4:2 [v]Ex 33:18; 40:34 [w]S Ro 3:24 [x]Jn 14:6
1:15 [y]ver 7 [z]ver 30; Mt 3:11
1:16 [a]Eph 1:23; Col 1:19; 2:9 [b]S Ro 3:24
1:17 [c]Dt 32:46; Jn 7:19 [d]ver 14
1:18 [e]Ex 33:20; Jn 6:46; Col 1:15; 1Ti 6:16; 1Jn 4:12 [f]Jn 3:16,18; 1Jn 4:9
1:19 [g]S Mt 3:1 [h]Jn 2:18; 5:10,16; 6:41,52; 7:1; 10:24
1:20 [i]Jn 3:28; Lk 3:15,16
1:21 [j]S Mt 11:14 [k]Dt 18:15
1:23 [l]Mt 3:1 [m]Isa 40:3
1:26 [n]S Mk 1:4
1:27 [o]ver 15,30 [p]Mk 1:7
1:28 [q]Jn 3:26; 10:40
1:29 [r]ver 36; Ge 22:8; Isa 53:7; 1Pe 1:19; Rev 5:6; 13:8 [s]S Jn 3:17
1:30 [t]ver 15,27
1:32 [u]Mt 3:16
1:33 [v]S Mk 1:4 [w]S Mk 1:8
1:34 [x]ver 49; S Mt 4:3

[c] *13* Greek *of bloods* [d] *14,18* Or *the Only Begotten* [e] *18* Some manuscripts *but the only* (or *only begotten*) *Son* [f] *20* Or *Messiah.* "The Christ" (Greek) and "the Messiah" (Hebrew) both mean "the Anointed One"; also in verse 25. [g] *23* Isaiah 40:3 [h] *26* Or *in*; also in verses 31 and 33

1:14 THE WORD BECAME FLESH. Christ, the eternal God, became a human being (Php 2:5–9). Humanity and divinity were united together in him. In a humble way he entered human life with all the limitations of human experiences (cf. 3:17; 6:38–42; 7:29; 9:5; 10:36).

1:17 GRACE AND TRUTH. For those under OT law there was a measure of grace as seen in the faith of the few (Ge 5:24; 7:1; 15:6) and in the promises of forgiveness (Ex 34:6–7; Lev 5:17–18). Now through Christ, grace and truth are available to the fullest extent (Ro 5:17–21). Truth is no longer veiled through the types (such as the sacrifices). "One blessing after another" (v. 16) means that a constant impartation of grace and power is given to believers who respond to the grace given them. Grace is the power, presence and blessing of God experienced by those who receive Christ (see article on FAITH AND GRACE, p. 302). Salvation does not come by our efforts to keep the law, but by the Holy Spirit and Christ's grace coming into our lives to regenerate our spirits and to re-create us in Christ's image.

1:29 LAMB OF GOD. Jesus is the Lamb provided by God to be sacrificed in the place of sinners (cf. Ex 12:3–17; Isa 53:7). By his death, Jesus provided for the removal of the guilt and power of sin and opened the way to God for all in the world.

1:33 WILL BAPTIZE WITH THE HOLY SPIRIT. The word "with" is a translation of the Greek preposition *en* and can be rendered "by," "with" or "in." An alternate translation would be "he who will baptize in the Holy Spirit," just as "baptize with water" may be rendered "baptize in water."

All the Gospels emphasize that Jesus is "he who will baptize with [in] the Holy Spirit" (Mt 3:11; Mk 1:8; Lk 3:16; Jn 1:33). This baptism was to be the sign and dynamic mark of the followers of Jesus. The Holy Spirit would be poured out on them so that they might carry on his saving work in all the world (cf. Ac 1:8). Jesus' task of baptizing in the Spirit is his ongoing purpose throughout this age (see Mt 3:11, note; Ac 2:39, note).

Jesus' First Disciples

1:40-42pp — Mt 4:18-22; Mk 1:16-20; Lk 5:2-11

35The next day John[y] was there again
with two of his disciples. **36**When he saw
Jesus passing by, he said, "Look, the
Lamb of God!"[z]
37When the two disciples heard him say
this, they followed Jesus. **38**Turning
around, Jesus saw them following and
asked, "What do you want?"

They said, "Rabbi"[a] (which means
Teacher), "where are you staying?"
39"Come," he replied, "and you will
see."

So they went and saw where he was
staying, and spent that day with him. It
was about the tenth hour.
40Andrew, Simon Peter's brother, was
one of the two who heard what John had
said and who had followed Jesus. **41**The
first thing Andrew did was to find his
brother Simon and tell him, "We have
found the Messiah" (that is, the Christ).[b]
42And he brought him to Jesus.

Jesus looked at him and said, "You are
Simon son of John. You will be called[c]
Cephas" (which, when translated, is Pe-
ter[i]).[d]

Jesus Calls Philip and Nathanael

43The next day Jesus decided to leave
for Galilee. Finding Philip,[e] he said to
him, "Follow me."[f]
44Philip, like Andrew and Peter, was
from the town of Bethsaida.[g] **45**Philip
found Nathanael[h] and told him, "We have
found the one Moses wrote about in the
Law,[i] and about whom the prophets also
wrote[j]—Jesus of Nazareth,[k] the son of
Joseph."[l]
46"Nazareth! Can anything good come
from there?"[m] Nathanael asked.

"Come and see," said Philip.
47When Jesus saw Nathanael approaching, he said of him, "Here is a true Israelite,[n] in whom there is nothing false."[o]
48"How do you know me?" Nathanael
asked.

Jesus answered, "I saw you while you
were still under the fig tree before Philip
called you."
49Then Nathanael declared, "Rabbi,[p]
you are the Son of God;[q] you are the King
of Israel."[r]
50Jesus said, "You believe[j] because I
told you I saw you under the fig tree. You
shall see greater things than that." **51**He
then added, "I tell you[k] the truth, you[k]
shall see heaven open,[s] and the angels of
God ascending and descending[t] on the
Son of Man."[u]

Jesus Changes Water to Wine

2 On the third day a wedding took place
at Cana in Galilee.[v] Jesus' mother[w]
was there, **2**and Jesus and his disciples
had also been invited to the wedding.
3When the wine was gone, Jesus' mother
said to him, "They have no more wine."
4"Dear woman,[x] why do you involve
me?"[y] Jesus replied. "My time[z] has not
yet come."

i *42* Both *Cephas* (Aramaic) and *Peter* (Greek) mean *rock*. j *50* Or *Do you believe . . . ?*
k *51* The Greek is plural.

1:35 [y]S Mt 3:1
1:36 [z]S ver 29
1:38 [a]ver 49; S Mt 23:7
1:41 [b]Jn 4:25
1:42 [c]Ge 17:5,15; 32:28; 35:10 [d]Mt 16:18
1:43 [e]Mt 10:3; Jn 6:5-7; 12:21,22; 14:8,9 [f]S Mt 4:19
1:44 [g]S Mt 11:21
1:45 [h]Jn 21:2 [i]S Lk 24:27 [j]S Lk 24:27 [k]S Mk 1:24 [l]Lk 3:23
1:46 [m]Jn 7:41,42, 52
1:47 [n]Ro 9:4,6 [o]Ps 32:2
1:49 [p]ver 38; S Mt 23:7 [q]ver 34; S Mt 4:3 [r]S Mt 2:2; 27:42; Jn 12:13
1:51 [s]S Mt 3:16 [t]Ge 28:12 [u]S Mt 8:20
2:1 [v]Jn 4:46; 21:2 [w]S Mt 12:46
2:4 [x]Jn 19:26 [y]S Mt 8:29 [z]S Mt 26:18

1:51 YOU SHALL SEE HEAVEN OPEN. Jesus represents himself as the ladder by which God's revelation comes to the world (cf. Ge 28:12; see also Lk 5:24, note on the term "Son of Man").

2:3 WINE. The word "wine" (Gk *oinos*) in the NT is a generic term and can refer to either fermented wine or unfermented wine (see articles on WINE IN NEW TESTAMENT TIMES (1) and (2), p. 126 and p. 174). The nature of *oinos* must be determined by context and moral likelihood.

2:3 THEY HAVE NO MORE WINE. In contrast to the position taken in this study Bible, some believe that both the wine initially provided at the wedding and the wine made by Jesus were intoxicants consumed in great quantity. If this thesis is accepted, then the following implications must be acknowledged and reckoned with: (1) The guests at the wedding would likely be drunk. (2) Mary, the mother of Jesus, would be regretting that the intoxicating drink had run out and would be asking Jesus to furnish the already drunken festivity with more fermented wine. (3) In order to oblige his mother's wishes, Jesus would be making 120–180 gallons of intoxicating wine (vv. 6–9), more than enough to keep the guests totally drunk. (4) Jesus would be making this intoxicating wine as his very first "miraculous sign" in order to "reveal his glory" (v. 11) and to persuade people to believe in him as the holy and righteous Son of God.

The above implications of the thesis in question cannot be avoided. To allege that Jesus made and used alcoholic wine is not only beyond the warrant of exegetical requirement, but leads us into conflict with moral principles embedded in the total witness of Scripture. Clearly, in light of God's nature, Christ's righteousness, his loving concern for humanity, and Mary's good character, the above implications of the view that the wine at Cana was fermented are blasphemous. An interpretation that involves such assertions and contradictions cannot be adopted. The only plausible explanation is that the wine made by Jesus to reveal his glory was the nonintoxicating pure juice of the grape. Furthermore, the initial inferior wine furnished by the one in charge of the wedding was most likely nonintoxicating as well. For further discussion of this issue, see article on WINE IN NEW TESTAMENT TIMES (2), p. 174.

WINE IN NEW TESTAMENT TIMES (2)

Jn 2:11 "This, the first of his miraculous signs, Jesus performed at Cana in Galilee. He thus revealed his glory, and his disciples put their faith in him."

In conjunction with this article, be sure to read WINE IN NEW TESTAMENT TIMES (1), p. 126.

WINE: MIXED OR FULL STRENGTH? Historical data concerning the making and use of wine by the Jews and other nations in the Biblical world indicate that it was (a) often unfermented and (b) normally mixed with water. The other article on WINE IN NEW TESTAMENT TIMES discusses one of the processes used in keeping freshly squeezed grape juice in a sweet and unfermented state. This article discusses two other processes of dealing with grapes, preparatory to mixing them with water.

(1) One method was to dehydrate the grapes, sprinkle them with olive oil to keep them moist and store them in earthenware jars (*The Zondervan Pictorial Encyclopedia of the Bible*, V.882; see also Columella, *On Agriculture*, 12.44.1–8). A very sweet grape beverage could be made from these stored grapes at any time by adding water and steeping or boiling them. Polybius indicated that the Roman women were allowed to drink this kind of grape beverage, but were forbidden to drink fermented wine (see Polybius, *Fragments*, 6.4; Pliny, *Natural History*, 14.11.81).

(2) Another method was to boil freshly squeezed grape juice until it became a thick paste or syrup (grape honey); this process made the juice storable, removed any intoxicating quality because of the high concentration of sugar, and preserved its sweetness (see Columella, 12.19.1–6 and 20.1–8; Pliny, 14.11.80). This paste was then stored in large jars or skins. The paste could be used as a jam for bread or dissolved in water to make grape juice once again (*The Zondervan Pictorial Encyclopedia of the Bible*, V.882–884). "It is probable that the grape was largely cultivated as a source of sugar: the juice expressed in the 'wine press' was reduced by boiling to a liquid . . . known as 'grape honey'" (*The International Standard Bible Encyclopedia*, V.3050). References to honey in the Bible frequently speak of grape honey (called *debash* by the Jews) rather than the honey of the bee.

(3) Water, then, could be mixed with dehydrated grapes and with grape syrup, as well as with fermented wine. Greek and Roman authors gave various ratios that were used. Homer (*Odyssey* IX.208ff) mentions a ratio of twenty parts water to one part wine. Plutarch (*Sumposiacs*, III.ix) states, "We call a mixture 'wine,' although the larger of the component parts is water." Pliny (14.6.54) mentions a ratio of eight parts water to one part wine.

(4) Among Jewish people in Bible times, social and religious customs mandated never serving unmixed wine, whether it was fermented or unfermented. The Talmud (a Jewish work that describes the traditions of Judaism from about 200 B.C. to A.D. 200) discusses in several tractates the mixture of water and wine (e.g., Shabbath 77a; Pesahim 1086). Some Jewish rabbis insisted that unless fermented wine was mixed with three parts water, it could not be blessed and would defile the drinker. Others demanded that ten parts of water must be mixed with one part of fermented wine before it would be acceptable.

(5) An interesting passage emerges in the book of Revelation: when speaking of "the wine of God's fury," an angel declares that it will be "full strength" (Rev 14:10). It was so stated because the readers normally would expect all grape beverages to be mixed with water (see Jn 2:3, notes).

In summary, the normal uses of wine by the Jews in Biblical days differed from today's uses. The wine of old was (a) freshly squeezed grape juice, (b) preserved grape juice, (c) juice from dried grapes, (d) grape wine made from grape syrup and water, and (e) unfermented or fermented stored wine diluted with water at a ratio as high as 20 to 1. If the wine was fermented and served unmixed, it was considered barbaric, defiling and incapable of being blessed by the rabbis. In the light of these facts, it is impossible to defend the modern-day practice of drinking alcoholic beverages on the basis of the Jews' use of "wine" in Biblical times. Furthermore, Christians of Biblical days were even more cautious about the various kinds of wines than the Jews (see Ro 14:21, note; 1Th 5:6, note; 1Ti 3:3, note; Tit 2:2, note).

JESUS' GLORY REVEALED THROUGH WINE. In his second chapter, John records that Jesus made "wine" out of water at a wedding at Cana. The question is, "What kind of wine?" As we have seen, it could be fermented or unfermented, full strength or diluted. We must determine our answer to this question by contextual implication and moral likelihood. The position of this study Bible is that Jesus made wine (*oinos*) that was pure unfermented grape juice. The following data supply strong rationale for rejecting the opinion that Jesus made intoxicating wine.

(1) The primary object of this miracle was to reveal his glory (Jn 2:11) in such a way as to induce personal faith in him as God's holy and righteous Son who came to save people from their sin (2:11; cf. Mt 1:21). To suggest that Christ showed his divinity as the One and Only Son of the Father (Jn 1:14) by miraculously creating gallons of intoxicating wine for a drunken party (note 2:10, which implies that the people had already drunk freely), and that this was immensely important to his Messianic mission, requires an irreverence few are willing to display. It would testify more to God's honor, and the honor and glory of Christ, to believe that Christ supernaturally created the same juice of the grape that God makes annually through the process of his natural created order (see Jn 2:3, note). This miracle, therefore, points to Christ's sovereignty over the natural world and becomes a symbol of his power to transform sinful people spiritually into God's children (Jn 3:1–15). Because of this miracle "we have seen his glory, the glory of the One and Only, who came from the Father, full of grace and truth" (Jn 1:14; cf. 2:11).

(2) It is contrary to Scriptural revelation concerning Christ's perfect obedience to his heavenly Father (cf. 2Co 5:21; Heb 4:15; 1Pe 2:22) to suppose that he disobeyed the Father's moral command, "do not gaze at wine when it is red, when it sparkles in the cup, when it goes down smoothly" i.e., when it is fermented (Pr 23:31). Indeed, Christ would have supported the Biblical passages that condemn intoxicating wine as "a mocker" and beer as "a brawler" (Pr 20:1) and the words of Hab 2:15, "woe to him who gives drink to his neighbors, pouring it . . . till they are drunk" (cf. Lev 10:8–11; Nu 6:1–5; Dt 21:20; Pr 31:4–7; Isa 28:7; Am 2:8,12; 4:1; 6:6; Ro 14:13,21).

(3) Furthermore, note the following modern medical evidence. (a) Leading medical experts have found unmistakable evidence that moderate alcoholic consumption is damaging to the reproductive systems of women of childbearing age, causing miscarriages and births of babies with incurable mental and physical defects. World authorities on early embryology maintain that women who drink even moderate amounts of alcohol around the time of conception (about a 48-hour time period) risk damaging the chromosomes of an egg preparing to leave the ovary and thus causing disastrous results to the mental and physical development of the infant. (b) It would be theologically absurd to maintain that Jesus encouraged the use of alcoholic beverages at a wedding that included many women as well as a young bride with the possibility of immediate conception. To maintain that he did not know of the potential terrible effects of intoxicating drink on unborn children is to call into question his divinity, his wisdom and his discernment of good and evil. To maintain that he knew of the potential harm and disfiguring results of alcohol, and yet promoted and encouraged its use, is to call into question his goodness, compassion and love.

The only sound conclusion rationally, theologically and Biblically is that the wine Christ made at the wedding to reveal his glory was pure, sweet, unfermented fruit of the vine.

5His mother said to the servants, "Do
whatever he tells you."[a]
6Nearby stood six stone water jars, the
kind used by the Jews for ceremonial
washing,[b] each holding from twenty to
thirty gallons.[1]
7Jesus said to the servants, "Fill the
jars with water"; so they filled them to the
brim.
8Then he told them, "Now draw some
out and take it to the master of the banquet."
They did so, **9**and the master of the banquet tasted the water that had been
turned into wine.[c] He did not realize
where it had come from, though the servants who had drawn the water knew.
Then he called the bridegroom aside
10and said, "Everyone brings out the
choice wine first and then the cheaper
wine after the guests have had too much
to drink; but you have saved the best till
now."
11This, the first of his miraculous
signs,[d] Jesus performed at Cana in Galilee. He thus revealed his glory,[e] and his
disciples put their faith in him.[f]

Jesus Cleanses the Temple

2:14–16pp — Mt 21:12,13; Mk 11:15–17; Lk 19:45,46

12After this he went down to Capernaum[g] with his mother[h] and brothers[i] and
his disciples. There they stayed for a few
days.
13When it was almost time for the Jewish Passover,[j] Jesus went up to Jerusalem.[k] **14**In the temple courts he found
men selling cattle, sheep and doves,[l] and
others sitting at tables exchanging money.[m] **15**So he made a whip out of cords, and
drove all from the temple area, both sheep
and cattle; he scattered the coins of the
money changers and overturned their tables. **16**To those who sold doves he said,
"Get these out of here! How dare you turn
my Father's house[n] into a market!"
17His disciples remembered that it is
written: "Zeal for your house will consume
me."[m][o]
18Then the Jews[p] demanded of him,
"What miraculous sign[q] can you show us
to prove your authority to do all this?"[r]
19Jesus answered them, "Destroy this
temple, and I will raise it again in three
days."[s]
20The Jews replied, "It has taken forty-
six years to build this temple, and you are
going to raise it in three days?" **21**But the
temple he had spoken of was his body.[t]
22After he was raised from the dead, his
disciples recalled what he had said.[u]
Then they believed the Scripture[v] and the
words that Jesus had spoken.
23Now while he was in Jerusalem at the
Passover Feast,[w] many people saw the
miraculous signs[x] he was doing and believed[y] in his name.[n] **24**But Jesus would
not entrust himself to them, for he knew
all men. **25**He did not need man's testimony about man,[z] for he knew what was in
a man.[a]

Jesus Teaches Nicodemus

3 Now there was a man of the Pharisees
named Nicodemus,[b] a member of the
Jewish ruling council.[c] **2**He came to Jesus
at night and said, "Rabbi,[d] we know[e] you
are a teacher who has come from God. For

2:5 [a] Ge 41:55 **2:6** [b] Mk 7:3,4; Jn 3:25 **2:9** [c] Jn 4:46 **2:11** [d] ver 23; Mt 12:38; Jn 3:2; S 4:48; 6:2,14,26, 30; 12:37; 20:30 [e] Jn 1:14 [f] Ex 14:31 **2:12** [g] S Mt 4:13 [h] S Mt 12:46 [i] S Mt 12:46 **2:13** [j] S Jn 11:55 [k] Dt 16:1-6; Lk 2:41 **2:14** [l] Lev 1:14; Dt 14:26 [m] Dt 14:25

2:16 [n] Lk 2:49 **2:17** [o] Ps 69:9 **2:18** [p] S Jn 1:19 [q] S ver 11 [r] S Mt 12:38 **2:19** [s] S Mt 16:21; 26:61; 27:40; Mk 14:58; 15:29; Ac 6:14 **2:21** [t] 1Co 6:19 **2:22** [u] Lk 24:5-8; Jn 12:16; 14:26 [v] Ps 16:10; S Lk 24:27 **2:23** [w] ver 13 [x] S ver 11 [y] S Jn 3:15 **2:25** [z] Isa 11:3 [a] Dt 31:21; 1Ki 8:39; S Mt 9:4; Jn 6:61, 64; 13:11 **3:1** [b] Jn 7:50; 19:39 [c] Lk 23:13 **3:2** [d] S Mt 23:7 [e] ver 11

[1] *6* Greek *two to three metretes* (probably about 75 to 115 liters) [m] *17* Psalm 69:9 [n] *23* Or *and believed in him*

2:10 CHOICE WINE. According to various ancient writers, the "choice" (or best) wine was the sweetest wine—one that could be drunk freely and in large quantities without harm (i.e., wine that had not had its sugar content destroyed through fermentation). The "cheaper" wine was that which had been diluted with too much water. (1) The Roman writer Pliny affirms this. He expressly states that "good wine," called *sapa*, was not fermented. *Sapa* was grape juice boiled down to one-third of its bulk to increase its sweet flavor (IV.13). He writes elsewhere that "wines are most beneficial when all their potency has been removed by the strainer" (Pliny, *Natural History*, XIV.23–24). Pliny, Plutarch and Horace all suggest that the best wine was the type that was "harmless and innocent." (2) Rabbinical witnesses affirm that some rabbis recommended boiled wine. The Mishna says: "Rabbi Yehuda permits it [boiled wine as heave-offering], because it improves it." (3) It is significant that the Greek adjective translated "choice" is not *agathos* but *kalos*, meaning "morally excellent or befitting."

2:10 HAD TOO MUCH TO DRINK. The phrase "had too much to drink" is from the Greek word *methuskō*, a word that has two meanings: (1) to be or become drunk, and (2) to be filled or satisfied (without reference to intoxication). *Methuskō* should be understood here in the second of these two meanings. (1) Regardless of how one translates this text, it cannot be used to defend the thesis that fermented wine was consumed at this wedding. The master of ceremonies is merely stating here a general policy, a policy that covers any wedding celebration regardless of the type of drink served. (2) In no way may we imply that Jesus participated in and contributed to a drunken party (see v. 3, note; also see article on WINE IN NEW TESTAMENT TIMES (2), p. 174).

2:15 DROVE ALL FROM THE TEMPLE AREA. See Lk 19:45, note.

no one could perform the miraculous
signs[f] you are doing if God were not with
him."[g]

3In reply Jesus declared, "I tell you the
truth, no one can see the kingdom of God
unless he is born again.[o]"[hi]

4"How can a man be born when he is
old?" Nicodemus asked. "Surely he cannot
enter a second time into his mother's
womb to be born!"

5Jesus answered, "I tell you the truth,
no one can enter the kingdom of God unless he is born of water and the Spirit.[jk]
6Flesh gives birth to flesh, but the Spirit[p]
gives birth to spirit.[l] 7You should not be
surprised at my saying, 'You[q] must be
born again.' 8The wind blows wherever it
pleases. You hear its sound, but you cannot tell where it comes from or where it is
going. So it is with everyone born of the
Spirit."[m]

9"How can this be?"[n] Nicodemus
asked.

10"You are Israel's teacher,"[o] said
Jesus, "and do you not understand these
things? 11I tell you the truth, we speak of
what we know,[p] and we testify to what we
have seen, but still you people do not accept our testimony.[q] 12I have spoken to
you of earthly things and you do not believe; how then will you believe if I speak
of heavenly things? 13No one has ever
gone into heaven[r] except the one who
came from heaven[s]—the Son of Man.[rt]
14Just as Moses lifted up the snake in the
desert,[u] so the Son of Man must be lifted
up,[v] 15that everyone who believes[w] in
him may have eternal life.[sx]

16"For God so loved[y] the world that he
gave[z] his one and only Son,[ta] that whoever believes[b] in him shall not perish but
have eternal life.[c] 17For God did not send
his Son into the world[d] to condemn the
world, but to save the world through
him.[e] 18Whoever believes in him is not
condemned,[f] but whoever does not believe stands condemned already because
he has not believed in the name of God's
one and only Son.[ug] 19This is the verdict:
Light[h] has come into the world, but men
loved darkness instead of light because
their deeds were evil.[i] 20Everyone who
does evil hates the light, and will not come
into the light for fear that his deeds will
be exposed.[j] 21But whoever lives by the
truth comes into the light, so that it may
be seen plainly that what he has done has
been done through God."[v]

John the Baptist's Testimony About Jesus

22After this, Jesus and his disciples
went out into the Judean countryside,

3:2 [f]S Jn 2:11 [g]Jn 10:38; 14:10, 11; Ac 2:22; 10:38 **3:3** [h]S Jn 1:13 [i]S Mt 3:2 **3:5** [j]S Ac 22:16 [k]Tit 3:5 **3:6** [l]S Jn 1:13; 1Co 15:50 **3:8** [m]1Co 2:14-16 **3:9** [n]Jn 6:52,60 **3:10** [o]Lk 2:46 **3:11** [p]Jn 1:18; 7:16,17 [q]ver 32 **3:13** [r]Pr 30:4; Ac 2:34; Eph 4:8-10 [s]ver 31; Jn 6:38, 42; Heb 4:14; 9:24 [t]S Mt 8:20 **3:14** [u]Nu 21:8,9 [v]S Jn 12:32 **3:15** [w]ver 16,36; Ge 15:6; Nu 14:11; Mt 27:42; Mk 1:15; Jn 1:7, 12; 2:23; 5:24; 7:38; 20:29; Ac 13:39; 16:31; Ro 3:22; 10:9,10; 1Jn 5:1,5,10 [x]ver 16,36; S Mt 25:46; Jn 20:31 **3:16** [y]Ro 5:8; Eph 2:4; 1Jn 4:9, 10 [z]Isa 9:6; Ro 8:32 [a]Ge 22:12; Jn 1:18 [b]S ver 15 [c]ver 36; Jn 6:29,40; 11:25, 26 **3:17** [d]Jn 6:29,57; 10:36; 11:42; 17:8,21; 20:21 [e]Isa 53:11; S Mt 1:21; S Lk 2:11; 19:10; Jn 1:29; 12:47; S Ro 11:14; 1Ti 1:15; 2:5,6; 1Jn 2:2; 3:5 **3:18** [f]Jn 5:24 [g]Jn 1:18; 1Jn 4:9 **3:19** [h]S Jn 1:4 [i]Ps 52:3; Jn 7:7 **3:20** [j]Eph 5:11,13

[o] *3* Or *born from above*; also in verse 7 [p] *6* Or *but spirit* [q] *7* The Greek is plural. [r] *13* Some manuscripts *Man, who is in heaven* [s] *15* Or *believes may have eternal life in him* [t] *16* Or *his only begotten Son* [u] *18* Or *God's only begotten Son* [v] *21* Some interpreters end the quotation after verse 15.

3:3 BORN AGAIN. For a discussion of the Biblical doctrine of regeneration (being born again), see article on REGENERATION, p. 178.

3:5 BORN OF WATER. Jesus was probably referring to the cleansing work of the Holy Spirit in the new birth. In Tit 3:5 Paul speaks of "the washing of rebirth and renewal by the Holy Spirit."

3:8 THE WIND . . . THE SPIRIT. As the wind, though unseen, is identified by its activity and sound, so also the Holy Spirit is observed by his activity in and effect on those who are born again.

3:16 GOD SO LOVED THE WORLD. This verse reveals the heart and purpose of God. (1) God's love is wide enough to embrace all persons, i.e., "the world" (cf. 1Ti 2:4).

(2) God "gave" his Son as an offering for sin on the cross. The atonement proceeds from the loving heart of God. It was not something forced on him (Ro 8:32; 1Jn 4:10).

(3) To believe (Gk *pisteuō*) includes three main elements: (a) a sure conviction that Jesus Christ is God's Son and the only Savior for lost humanity; (b) a self-surrendering fellowship with and obedience to Christ (cf. 15:1–10; see 14:21, note; 15:4, note); (c) a fully assured trust in Christ that he is both able and willing to bring you to final salvation and to fellowship with God in heaven (see article on FAITH AND GRACE, p. 302).

(4) "Perish" is often the forgotten word of v. 16. It points not to physical death but to the dreadful reality of eternal punishment (Mt 10:28, note).

(5) "Eternal life" is the gift God bestows on us when we are born again (see article on REGENERATION, p. 178). "Eternal" not only expresses perpetuity but also quality of life—a divine type of life, a life that frees us from the power of sin and Satan and removes us from what is merely earthly in order to know God (cf. 8:34–36; see 17:3, note).

3:19 LOVED DARKNESS INSTEAD OF LIGHT. A fundamental characteristic of the wicked is that they love darkness, i.e., they find their pleasure in sin and immorality (Ro 1:18–32; Php 3:19; 2Ti 3:2–5; 2Pe 2:12–15). On the other hand, truly born-again persons love righteousness and hate wickedness (Heb 1:9), and are grieved when they see the unrighteous deeds of depraved people (1Co 13:6). They take no pleasure in the sensual entertainment or the expression of sinful conduct shown so openly in contemporary society (Ps 97:10; Pr 8:13; Ro 12:9; see 2Pe 2:8, note; Rev 2:6 note).

REGENERATION

Jn 3:3 "In reply Jesus declared, 'I tell you the truth, no one can see the kingdom of God unless he is born again.'"

In Jn 3:1–8, Jesus discusses one of the fundamental doctrines of the Christian faith: regeneration (Tit 3:5), or spiritual birth. Without the new birth one cannot see the kingdom of God, i.e., receive eternal life and salvation through Jesus Christ. The following are important facts concerning the new birth.

(1) Regeneration is a re-creating and transformation of the person (Ro 12:2; Eph 4:23–24) by God the Holy Spirit (Jn 3:6; Tit 3:5; see article on THE REGENERATION OF THE DISCIPLES, p. 212). Through this process eternal life from God himself is imparted to the believer's heart (Jn 3:16; 2Pe 1:4; 1Jn 5:11), and he or she becomes a child of God (Jn 1:12; Ro 8:16–17; Gal 3:26) and a new person (2Co 5:17; Col 3:9–10). He or she no longer conforms to this world (Ro 12:2) but is now "created to be like God in true righteousness and holiness" (Eph 4:24).

(2) Regeneration is necessary because apart from Christ, all people, in their inherent natures, are sinners, incapable of obeying and pleasing God (Ps 51:5; Jer 17:9; Ro 8:7–8; 1Co 2:14; Eph 2:3).

(3) Regeneration comes to those who repent of sin, turn to God (Mt 3:2) and put their faith in Jesus Christ as Lord and Savior (see Jn 1:12, note).

(4) Regeneration involves a transition from an old life of sin to a new life of obedience to Jesus Christ (2Co 5:17; Gal 6:15; Eph 4:23–24; Col 3:10). Those who are truly born again are set free from sin's bondage (see Jn 8:36, note; Ro 6:14–23) and receive a spiritual desire and disposition to obey God and follow the leading of the Spirit (Ro 8:13–14). They live righteous lives (1Jn 2:29), love other believers (1Jn 4:7), avoid a life of sin (1Jn 3:9; 5:18) and do not love the world (1Jn 2:15–16).

(5) Those born of God cannot make sin a habitual practice in their lives (see 1Jn 3:9, note). They cannot remain born again without a sincere desire and victorious endeavor to please God and to avoid evil (1Jn 1:5–7). This is accomplished only through the grace given to believers by Christ (1Jn 2:3–11,15–17,24–29; 3:6–24; 4:7–8,20; 5:1), through a sustained relationship with Christ (see Jn 15:4, note) and through a dependence on the Holy Spirit (Ro 8:2–14).

(6) Those who live in immorality and follow the world's ways, no matter what they profess with their lips, demonstrate that they are still unregenerated children of Satan (1Jn 3:6–10).

(7) Just as one can be born of the Spirit by receiving the life of God, he or she can also extinguish that life by ungodly choices and unrighteous living, and therefore die spiritually. Scripture affirms, "if you live according to the sinful nature, you will die" (Ro 8:13). Thus, sin and the refusal to follow the Holy Spirit extinguish the life of God in the believer's soul and cause spiritual death and exclusion from God's kingdom (cf. Mt 12:31–32; 1Co 6:9–10; Gal 5:19–21; Heb 6:4–6; 1Jn 5:16).

(8) The new birth cannot be equated with physical birth, for God's relationship with the believer is a matter of spirit rather than flesh (Jn 3:6). Therefore, while the physical tie of a father and child can never be annulled, the father and child relationship that God desires with us is voluntary and not indissoluble during our probationary time on earth (see Ro 8:13, note). That relationship remains conditional on our faith in Christ throughout our earthly existence, a faith demonstrated by lives of sincere obedience and love (Ro 8:12–14; 2Ti 2:12).

where he spent some time with them, and
baptized.[k] 23Now John[l] also was baptizing at Aenon near Salim, because there
was plenty of water, and people were constantly coming to be baptized. 24(This was
before John was put in prison.)[m] 25An argument developed between some of John's
disciples and a certain Jew[w] over the matter of ceremonial washing.[n] 26They came
to John and said to him, "Rabbi,[o] that man
who was with you on the other side of the
Jordan—the one you testified[p] about—
well, he is baptizing, and everyone is going to him."

27To this John replied, "A man can receive only what is given him from heaven.
28You yourselves can testify that I said, 'I
am not the Christ[x] but am sent ahead of
him.'[q] 29The bride belongs to the bridegroom.[r] The friend who attends the bridegroom waits and listens for him, and is full
of joy when he hears the bridegroom's
voice. That joy is mine, and it is now complete.[s] 30He must become greater; I must
become less.

31"The one who comes from above[t] is
above all; the one who is from the earth
belongs to the earth, and speaks as one
from the earth.[u] The one who comes from
heaven is above all. 32He testifies to what
he has seen and heard,[v] but no one accepts his testimony.[w] 33The man who has
accepted it has certified that God is truthful. 34For the one whom God has sent[x]
speaks the words of God, for God[y] gives
the Spirit[y] without limit. 35The Father
loves the Son and has placed everything
in his hands.[z] 36Whoever believes in the
Son has eternal life,[a] but whoever rejects
the Son will not see life, for God's wrath
remains on him."[z]

3:22 [k]Jn 4:2
3:23 [l]S Mt 3:1
3:24 [m]Mt 4:12; 14:3
3:25 [n]Jn 2:6
3:26 [o]S Mt 23:7 [p]Jn 1:7
3:28 [q]Jn 1:20,23
3:29 [r]Mt 9:15 [s]Jn 16:24; 17:13; Php 2:2; 1Jn 1:4; 2Jn 12
3:31 [t]ver 13 [u]Jn 8:23; 1Jn 4:5
3:32 [v]Jn 8:26; 15:15 [w]ver 11
3:34 [x]S ver 17 [y]Isa 42:1; Mt 12:18; Lk 4:18; Ac 10:38
3:35 [z]S Mt 28:18
3:36 [a]S ver 15; Jn 5:24; 6:47

Jesus Talks With a Samaritan Woman

4 The Pharisees heard that Jesus was
gaining and baptizing more disciples
than John,[b] 2although in fact it was not
Jesus who baptized, but his disciples.
3When the Lord[c] learned of this, he left
Judea[d] and went back once more to Galilee.

4Now he had to go through Samaria.[e]
5So he came to a town in Samaria called
Sychar, near the plot of ground Jacob had
given to his son Joseph.[f] 6Jacob's well
was there, and Jesus, tired as he was from
the journey, sat down by the well. It was
about the sixth hour.

7When a Samaritan woman came to
draw water, Jesus said to her, "Will you
give me a drink?"[g] 8(His disciples had
gone into the town[h] to buy food.)

9The Samaritan woman said to him,
"You are a Jew and I am a Samaritan[i]
woman. How can you ask me for a drink?"
(For Jews do not associate with Samaritans.[a])

10Jesus answered her, "If you knew the
gift of God and who it is that asks you for
a drink, you would have asked him and he
would have given you living water."[j]

11"Sir," the woman said, "you have
nothing to draw with and the well is deep.
Where can you get this living water? 12Are
you greater than our father Jacob, who
gave us the well[k] and drank from it himself, as did also his sons and his flocks
and herds?"

13Jesus answered, "Everyone who
drinks this water will be thirsty again,
14but whoever drinks the water I give him

4:1 [b]Jn 3:22,26
4:3 [c]S Lk 7:13 [d]Jn 3:22
4:4 [e]S Mt 10:5
4:5 [f]Ge 33:19; Jos 24:32
4:7 [g]Ge 24:17; 1Ki 17:10
4:8 [h]ver 5,39
4:9 [i]S Mt 10:5
4:10 [j]Isa 44:3; 55:1; Jer 2:13; 17:13; Zec 14:8; Jn 7:37,38; Rev 7:17; 21:6; 22:1,17
4:12 [k]ver 6

[w] *25* Some manuscripts *and certain Jews*
[x] *28* Or *Messiah* [y] *34* Greek *he* [z] *36* Some interpreters end the quotation after verse 30.
[a] *9* Or *do not use dishes Samaritans have used*

3:34 GIVES THE SPIRIT WITHOUT LIMIT. See Mt 3:16 and Lk 3:22, notes on Jesus' anointing with the Holy Spirit; see article on JESUS AND THE HOLY SPIRIT, p. 136.

3:36 WHOEVER REJECTS. The Greek word translated "rejects" is *apeitheō* and means to "disobey" or "not be subject to"; it is contrasted to "whoever believes" (Gk *pisteuō*) at the beginning of the verse. For John unbelief means to "reject the Son," or to disobey him. Faith and obedience can often be used interchangeably (compare Ro 1:8 with 16:19; 1Th 1:8; also see Ro 15:18). The gospel comes as a free gift (Ro 5:15–16; 6:23), but once accepted it does not leave us free to do as we please. It requires that we enter into the way of salvation ordained by God and subject ourselves to the righteousness of God (Ro 10:3; see 1:5, note; see article on FAITH AND GRACE, p. 302).

4:7 SAMARITAN WOMAN. Jesus' conversation with the Samaritan woman reveals his commitment to his heavenly Father's purpose and his own inner desire to bring this person to eternal life. Jesus' consuming passion was to save the lost (see Lk 15; cf. Pr 11:30; Da 12:3; Jas 5:20), a goal infinitely more important to him than food and drink (v. 34). We must follow Jesus' example. All around us people are ready to hear God's Word; we must speak to them about their spiritual need and about Jesus, who can meet that need.

4:14 WATER . . . ETERNAL LIFE. The "water" given by Jesus means spiritual life (cf. Isa 12:3). To partake of this living water, one must "drink" (see 7:37). This act of drinking is not a momentary, single act, but rather a progressive or repeated drinking; note that the word "drink" (Gk *pinetō*, from *pinō*) is a present imperative, representing continuing or re-

will never thirst.[l] Indeed, the water I give
him will become in him a spring of water[m]
welling up to eternal life."[n]

15The woman said to him, "Sir, give me
this water so that I won't get thirsty[o] and
have to keep coming here to draw water."

16He told her, "Go, call your husband
and come back."

17"I have no husband," she replied.

Jesus said to her, "You are right when
you say you have no husband. **18**The fact
is, you have had five husbands, and the
man you now have is not your husband.
What you have just said is quite true."

19"Sir," the woman said, "I can see that
you are a prophet.[p] **20**Our fathers worshiped on this mountain,[q] but you Jews
claim that the place where we must worship is in Jerusalem."[r]

21Jesus declared, "Believe me, woman,
a time is coming[s] when you will worship
the Father neither on this mountain nor in
Jerusalem.[t] **22**You Samaritans worship
what you do not know;[u] we worship what
we do know, for salvation is from the
Jews.[v] **23**Yet a time is coming and has now
come[w] when the true worshipers will worship the Father in spirit[x] and truth, for
they are the kind of worshipers the Father
seeks. **24**God is spirit,[y] and his worshipers must worship in spirit and in truth."

25The woman said, "I know that Messiah" (called Christ)[z] "is coming. When he
comes, he will explain everything to us."

26Then Jesus declared, "I who speak to
you am he."[a]

The Disciples Rejoin Jesus

27Just then his disciples returned[b] and
were surprised to find him talking with a
woman. But no one asked, "What do you
want?" or "Why are you talking with her?"

28Then, leaving her water jar, the woman went back to the town and said to the
people, **29**"Come, see a man who told me
everything I ever did.[c] Could this be the
Christ[b]?"[d] **30**They came out of the town
and made their way toward him.

31Meanwhile his disciples urged him,
"Rabbi,[e] eat something."

32But he said to them, "I have food to
eat[f] that you know nothing about."

33Then his disciples said to each other,
"Could someone have brought him food?"

34"My food," said Jesus, "is to do the
will[g] of him who sent me and to finish his
work.[h] **35**Do you not say, 'Four months
more and then the harvest'? I tell you,
open your eyes and look at the fields!
They are ripe for harvest.[i] **36**Even now
the reaper draws his wages, even now he
harvests[j] the crop for eternal life,[k] so
that the sower and the reaper may be glad
together. **37**Thus the saying 'One sows
and another reaps'[l] is true. **38**I sent you
to reap what you have not worked for.
Others have done the hard work, and you
have reaped the benefits of their labor."

Many Samaritans Believe

39Many of the Samaritans from that
town[m] believed in him because of the
woman's testimony, "He told me everything I ever did."[n] **40**So when the Samaritans came to him, they urged him to stay
with them, and he stayed two days. **41**And
because of his words many more became
believers.

[b] *29* Or *Messiah*

4:14 [l]Jn 6:35 [m]Isa 12:3; 58:11; Jn 7:38 [n]S Mt 25:46
4:15 [o]Jn 6:34
4:19 [p]S Mt 21:11
4:20 [q]Dt 11:29; Jos 8:33 [r]Lk 9:53
4:21 [s]Jn 5:28; 16:2 [t]Mal 1:11; 1Ti 2:8
4:22 [u]2Ki 17:28-41 [v]Isa 2:3; Ro 3:1,2; 9:4,5; 15:8,9
4:23 [w]Jn 5:25; 16:32 [x]Php 3:3
4:24 [y]Php 3:3
4:25 [z]Mt 1:16; Jn 1:41
4:26 [a]Jn 8:24; 9:35-37
4:27 [b]ver 8
4:29 [c]ver 17,18 [d]Mt 12:23; Jn 7:26,31
4:31 [e]S Mt 23:7
4:32 [f]Job 23:12; Mt 4:4; Jn 6:27
4:34 [g]S Mt 26:39 [h]S Jn 19:30
4:35 [i]Mt 9:37; Lk 10:2
4:36 [j]Ro 1:13 [k]S Mt 25:46
4:37 [l]Job 31:8; Mic 6:15
4:39 [m]ver 5 [n]ver 29

Jn 10:25

peated action. Drinking the water of life requires regular communion with the source of the living water, Jesus Christ himself. No one can continue to drink the water of life if he or she becomes severed from its source. Such people will become, as Peter describes it, "springs without water" (2Pe 2:17).

4:23 WORSHIP . . . IN SPIRIT AND TRUTH. Jesus teaches several things here: (1) "In spirit" points to the level at which true worship occurs. One must come to God in complete sincerity and with a spirit that is directed by the life and activity of the Holy Spirit. (2) "Truth" (Gk *alētheia*) is characteristic of God (Ps 31:5; Ro 1:25; 3:7; 15:8), incarnate in Christ (14:6; 2Co 11:10; Eph 4:21), intrinsic to the Holy Spirit (14:17; 15:26; 16:13) and at the heart of the gospel (8:32; Gal 2:5; Eph 1:13). Therefore, worship must take place according to the truth of the Father that is revealed in the Son and received through the Spirit. Those who advocate a worship that sets aside the truth and doctrines of the Word of God have in reality set aside the only foundation for true worship.

4:24 TRUTH. Because Jesus Christ is the truth (1:14; 5:31; 14:6; Lk 4:25; 9:27; 12:44), to live in union with Christ requires speaking the truth (1Co 5:8; Eph 4:25). To claim to have fellowship with Christ and to possess salvation, yet not to live and speak according to the truth, is to be deceived (1Jn 1:6). Those who have no truth in them show the real condition of their hearts (8:44; Ac 5:3)—that they are in fundamental opposition to God and are outside the kingdom of heaven (Rev 21:8,27; 22:15; cf. Rev 14:5). A liar is of "the synagogue of Satan" (Rev 3:9).

4:35 LOOK AT THE FIELDS. See Mt 9:37, note.

4:36 CROP FOR ETERNAL LIFE. Those who bring others to saving faith in Jesus Christ are doing something of eternal consequence. They will one day rejoice in heaven over those who were saved because of their prayers and their witness. At the same time, they must understand that their work is often a reaping of the labors of others (v. 38). All that we do for God is in large part the result of the preceding sacrificial labor of Christ and others.

42They said to the woman, "We no longer believe just because of what you said;
now we have heard for ourselves, and we
know that this man really is the Savior of
the world."[o]

Jesus Heals the Official's Son

43After the two days[p] he left for Galilee. 44(Now Jesus himself had pointed out
that a prophet has no honor in his own
country.)[q] 45When he arrived in Galilee,
the Galileans welcomed him. They had
seen all that he had done in Jerusalem at
the Passover Feast,[r] for they also had
been there.

46Once more he visited Cana in Galilee,
where he had turned the water into wine.[s]
And there was a certain royal official
whose son lay sick at Capernaum. 47When
this man heard that Jesus had arrived in
Galilee from Judea,[t] he went to him and
begged him to come and heal his son, who
was close to death.

48"Unless you people see miraculous
signs and wonders,"[u] Jesus told him, "you
will never believe."

49The royal official said, "Sir, come
down before my child dies."

50Jesus replied, "You may go. Your son
will live."

The man took Jesus at his word and
departed. 51While he was still on the way,
his servants met him with the news that
his boy was living. 52When he inquired as
to the time when his son got better, they
said to him, "The fever left him yesterday
at the seventh hour."

53Then the father realized that this was
the exact time at which Jesus had said to
Jn 5:5-15 him, "Your son will live." So he and all his
household[v] believed.

54This was the second miraculous
sign[w] that Jesus performed, having come
from Judea to Galilee.

4:42 [o]S Lk 2:11
4:43 [p]ver 40
4:44 [q]Mt 13:57; Lk 4:24
4:45 [r]Jn 2:23
4:46 [s]Jn 2:1-11
4:47 [t]ver 3,54
4:48 [u]Da 4:2,3; S Jn 2:11; Ac 2:43; 14:3; Ro 15:19; 2Co 12:12; Heb 2:4
4:53 [v]S Ac 11:14
4:54 [w]S ver 48; S Jn 2:11

The Healing at the Pool

5 Some time later, Jesus went up to Jerusalem for a feast of the Jews. 2Now
there is in Jerusalem near the Sheep
Gate[x] a pool, which in Aramaic[y] is called
Bethesda[c] and which is surrounded by
five covered colonnades. 3Here a great
number of disabled people used to lie—
the blind, the lame, the paralyzed.[d] 5One
who was there had been an invalid for thirty-eight years. 6When Jesus saw him lying
there and learned that he had been in this
condition for a long time, he asked him,
"Do you want to get well?"

7"Sir," the invalid replied, "I have no
one to help me into the pool when the
water is stirred. While I am trying to get
in, someone else goes down ahead of me."

8Then Jesus said to him, "Get up! Pick
up your mat and walk."[z] 9At once the man
was cured; he picked up his mat and
walked.

The day on which this took place was
a Sabbath,[a] 10and so the Jews[b] said to the
man who had been healed, "It is the Sabbath; the law forbids you to carry your
mat."[c]

11But he replied, "The man who made
me well said to me, 'Pick up your mat and
walk.'"

12So they asked him, "Who is this fellow who told you to pick it up and walk?"

13The man who was healed had no idea
who it was, for Jesus had slipped away
into the crowd that was there.

14Later Jesus found him at the temple

5:2 [x]Ne 3:1; 12:39 [y]Jn 19:13, 17,20; 20:16; Ac 21:40; 22:2; 26:14
5:8 [z]Mt 9:5,6
5:9 [a]Mt 12:1-14; Jn 9:14
5:10 [b]ver 16 [c]Ne 13:15-22; Jer 17:21; S Mt 12:2

[c] 2 Some manuscripts *Bethzatha;* other manuscripts *Bethsaida* [d] 3 Some less important manuscripts *paralyzed—and they waited for the moving of the waters.* *4From time to time an angel of the Lord would come down and stir up the waters. The first one into the pool after each such disturbance would be cured of whatever disease he had.*

4:48 SIGNS AND WONDERS. Signs and wonders are an authentic work of God's kingdom. However, our faith must not be centered on them but on Jesus Christ, to whom they bear witness (see article on THE KINGDOM OF GOD, p. 28). We must believe in Jesus Christ because of who he is, God's Son, our Lord and Savior. Jesus must be worshiped and esteemed because of his love, mercy and righteous character, not just for what he can do for us in a physical or material way. Signs, wonders and miracles must lead to a deep attachment to the Lord and to a greater faith in him, as this miracle did for the official (vv. 50–53).

5:5 THIRTY-EIGHT YEARS. Having suffered for thirty-eight years, this man had experienced prolonged disappointment at not being healed, while repeatedly looking to God in expectation. Yet healing finally came. It was largely because of the length of this man's suffering that Jesus, in compassion, chose to help him. We must never give up hope that God's time to move directly on our behalf may come soon.

5:9 THE MAN WAS CURED. Normally Jesus healed as a response to the faith of individuals. Here, however, he required no faith at all; the man was cured merely at the word of Jesus. Even today people may be healed according to God's purpose even though they do not demonstrate faith in Christ. The Bible teaches that there are three contacts for healing faith: (1) the faith of the one being healed (Mt 9:27–29); (2) the faith of others on behalf of the afflicted (Mt 8:5–10; cf. 17:15–20; Jas 5:14–16); (3) the faith of one who is anointed to heal (1Co 12:9).

5:14 STOP SINNING. Jesus demands from all who

and said to him, "See, you are well again.
Stop sinning[d] or something worse may
happen to you." **15**The man went away and
told the Jews[e] that it was Jesus who had
Jn 9:1-12 made him well.

Life Through the Son

16So, because Jesus was doing these
things on the Sabbath, the Jews persecuted him. **17**Jesus said to them, "My Father[f]
is always at his work[g] to this very day,
and I, too, am working." **18**For this reason
the Jews tried all the harder to kill him;[h]
not only was he breaking the Sabbath, but
he was even calling God his own Father,
making himself equal with God.[i]
19Jesus gave them this answer: "I tell
you the truth, the Son can do nothing by
himself;[j] he can do only what he sees his
Father doing, because whatever the Father does the Son also does. **20**For the
Father loves the Son[k] and shows him all
he does. Yes, to your amazement he will
show him even greater things than
these.[l] **21**For just as the Father raises the
dead and gives them life,[m] even so the Son
gives life[n] to whom he is pleased to give
it. **22**Moreover, the Father judges no one,
but has entrusted all judgment to the
Son,[o] **23**that all may honor the Son just as
they honor the Father. He who does not
honor the Son does not honor the Father,
who sent him.[p]
24"I tell you the truth, whoever hears
my word and believes him who sent me[q]
has eternal life[r] and will not be condemned;[s] he has crossed over from death
to life.[t] **25**I tell you the truth, a time is
coming and has now come[u] when the
dead will hear[v] the voice of the Son of God
and those who hear will live. **26**For as the
Father has life in himself, so he has granted the Son to have life[w] in himself. **27**And
he has given him authority to judge[x] because he is the Son of Man.
28"Do not be amazed at this, for a time
is coming[y] when all who are in their
graves will hear his voice **29**and come out

5:14 [d]Mk 2:5; Jn 8:11
5:15 [e]S Jn 1:19
5:17 [f]Lk 2:49 [g]Jn 9:4; 14:10
5:18 [h]S Mt 12:14 [i]Jn 10:30,33; 19:7
5:19 [j]ver 30; S Jn 14:24
5:20 [k]Jn 3:35 [l]Jn 14:12
5:21 [m]Ro 4:17; 8:11; 2Co 1:9; Heb 11:19 [n]Jn 11:25
5:22 [o]ver 27; Ge 18:25; Jdg 11:27; Jn 9:39; S Ac 10:42
5:23 [p]Lk 10:16; S 1Jn 2:23
5:24 [q]S Mt 10:40; S Jn 3:15; S 3:17 [r]S Mt 25:46 [s]Jn 3:18 [t]1Jn 3:14
5:25 [u]Jn 4:23; 16:32 [v]Jn 8:43,47
5:26 [w]Dt 30:20; Job 10:12; 33:4; Ps 36:9; S Jn 1:4
5:27 [x]S ver 22
5:28 [y]Jn 4:21; 16:2

---

profess faith in his name to stop sinning; the truly saved will stop. Although not perfect or above occasional transgression, true believers will commit their lives to Christ so that, through the power of the Holy Spirit, sin will no longer be the characteristic of their lives (1Pe 1:5; 1Jn 3:6,9). Jesus' expectation for the born-again life contrasts sharply with those who emphasize that believers will continue to sin daily in thought, word and deed.

5:16 PERSECUTED HIM. At this point in his Gospel, John begins to show that in spite of Jesus' miracles, and even because of them, the religious leaders intensely opposed him.

5:18–24 MAKING HIMSELF EQUAL WITH GOD. Jesus makes several astounding claims here: (1) God is his Father in a unique way; (2) he maintains unity, communion and authority with God (vv. 19–20); (3) he has the power to give life and raise the dead (v. 21); (4) he has the right to judge all people (v. 22); (5) he has the right to divine honor (v. 23); and (6) he has the power to give eternal life (v. 24).

5:24 HEARS . . . BELIEVES. Jesus describes those who have eternal life and will not be condemned as "whoever hears . . . and believes." The verbs "hears" (Gk *akouōn*, from *akouō*) and "believes" (Gk *pisteuōn*, from *pisteuō*) are present participles, emphasizing ongoing action (i.e., "whoever is hearing and believing"). Thus, the "hearing" and "believing" are not acts of a single moment, but actions that must continue. Christ affirms that our present possession of eternal life is conditional on a present living faith rather than on a momentary decision of faith sometime in the past (see 1:12, note; 4:14, note).

5:24 WILL NOT BE CONDEMNED. "Condemned" (Gk *krisis*) is used in the sense of condemnation to eternal death. Believers will not be condemned with the world (1Co 11:32). This does not refer to their future accountability and judgment concerning their faithfulness to God's grace given to them while on earth (see article on THE JUDGMENT OF BELIEVERS, p. 368).

5:26 HAS GRANTED THE SON TO HAVE LIFE IN HIMSELF. Jesus Christ's own nature is a source of eternal life; it is inherent within him. God, however, has not given believers the power to have eternal life inherent in themselves. We have life only as we have fellowship with Christ, i.e., Christ living in us through a living faith relationship (see 15:4,6, notes; Gal 2:20).

5:29 THOSE WHO HAVE DONE GOOD. According to Scripture, judgment is always on the basis of deeds, because one's deeds are a manifestation of his or her faith and inner condition. This means that we will be judged not by our profession of faith in Christ, but by the life we have lived (Mt 12:36–37; 16:27; Ro 2:6–10; 14:12; 1Co 3:13–15; 2Co 5:10; Eph 6:8; Col 3:25; Rev 2:23; 20:12; 22:12).

5:29 RISE TO LIVE. The NT does not teach a single general simultaneous resurrection for all the dead. (1) It speaks of a resurrection of many "holy people" occurring immediately after Jesus' resurrection (Mt 27:52–53), of a resurrection occurring at the time of the rapture or catching up of the church by Christ (1Co 15:51–52; see article on THE RAPTURE, p. 440), of a "first resurrection" (see Rev 20:6, note), and of a resurrection occurring one thousand years after the "first resurrection" of Rev 20:6 (i.e., after the millennial reign of Christ on earth, Rev 20:4). (2) It is possible that "the first resurrection" includes the resurrection of *all* believers before the thousand-year reign of Christ (Rev 20:4–6). Therefore, the resurrection of Rev 20:4–6 would complete the first resurrection.

5:29 THOSE WHO HAVE DONE EVIL. Immorality, impurity, lust, evil desires, and the like have no place in the lives of believers (see Col 3:5). Those who teach, contrary to the teaching of Christ and the apostles, that a person can have eternal life while living outside of fellowship with Christ are teaching the ulti-

—those who have done good will rise to live, and those who have done evil will rise to be condemned.[z] **30**By myself I can do nothing;[a] I judge only as I hear, and my judgment is just,[b] for I seek not to please myself but him who sent me.[c]

Testimonies About Jesus

31"If I testify about myself, my testimony is not valid.[d] **32**There is another who testifies in my favor,[e] and I know that his testimony about me is valid.

33"You have sent to John and he has testified[f] to the truth. **34**Not that I accept human testimony;[g] but I mention it that you may be saved.[h] **35**John was a lamp that burned and gave light,[i] and you chose for a time to enjoy his light.

36"I have testimony weightier than that of John.[j] For the very work that the Father has given me to finish, and which I am doing,[k] testifies that the Father has sent me.[l] **37**And the Father who sent me has himself testified concerning me.[m] You have never heard his voice nor seen his form,[n] **38**nor does his word dwell in you,[o] for you do not believe[p] the one he sent.[q] **39**You diligently study[e] the Scriptures[r] because you think that by them you possess eternal life.[s] These are the Scriptures that testify about me,[t] **40**yet you refuse to come to me[u] to have life.

41"I do not accept praise from men,[v] **42**but I know you. I know that you do not have the love of God in your hearts. **43**I have come in my Father's name, and you do not accept me; but if someone else comes in his own name, you will accept him. **44**How can you believe if you accept praise from one another, yet make no effort to obtain the praise that comes from the only God[f]?[w]

45"But do not think I will accuse you before the Father. Your accuser is Moses,[x] on whom your hopes are set.[y] **46**If you believed Moses, you would believe me, for he wrote about me.[z] **47**But since you do not believe what he wrote, how are you going to believe what I say?"[a]

Jesus Feeds the Five Thousand

6:1-13pp — Mt 14:13-21; Mk 6:32-44; Lk 9:10-17

6 Some time after this, Jesus crossed to the far shore of the Sea of Galilee (that is, the Sea of Tiberias), **2**and a great crowd of people followed him because they saw the miraculous signs[b] he had

e *39* Or *Study diligently* (the imperative)
f *44* Some early manuscripts *the Only One*

5:29 z S Mt 25:46
5:30 a ver 19 b Isa 28:6; Jn 8:16 c S Mt 26:39
5:31 d Jn 8:14
5:32 e ver 37; Jn 8:18
5:33 f S Jn 1:7
5:34 g 1Jn 5:9 h Ac 16:30,31; Eph 2:8; Tit 3:5
5:35 i Da 12:3; 2Pe 1:19
5:36 j 1Jn 5:9 k Jn 14:11; 15:24 l S Jn 3:17
5:37 m Jn 8:18 n Dt 4:12; 1Ti 1:17; S Jn 1:18
5:38 o 1Jn 1:10; 2:14 p Isa 26:10 q S Jn 3:17
5:39 r Ro 2:17,18 s S Mt 25:46 t S Lk 24:27,44; Ac 13:27
5:40 u Jn 6:44
5:41 v ver 44
5:44 w S Ro 2:29
5:45 x Jn 9:28 y Ro 2:17
5:46 z Ge 3:15; S Lk 24:27,44; Ac 26:22
5:47 a Lk 16:29, 31
6:2 b S Jn 2:11

mate deception. It leads them and their followers to trust in a false doctrine of eternal security (see 1Co 6:9–10; Gal 5:19–21; Eph 5:5–6). The words of Jesus must be heeded: "those who have done evil will rise to be condemned."

5:44 ACCEPT PRAISE FROM ONE ANOTHER. Those who have true saving faith will not be motivated by the love of praise or esteem from other people. They will have as their goal to please the Father. Those who establish a habit of receiving glory from others make idols of themselves and place themselves outside God's kingdom. To love the praise of other humans more than the praise of God is to disbelieve the gospel of Christ and make genuine faith impossible (cf. Ro 2:29).

5:47 DO NOT BELIEVE WHAT HE WROTE. This passage is important in establishing Jesus' view of the OT. He indeed believed that Moses wrote the Pentateuch. The lesson the Jews needed, and one we need today, is this: if one does not believe in the inspiration and truthfulness of the OT writings, he or she will not believe or submit to the authority of Jesus' words and the NT writings that bear witness to him (see Ac 24:14, note on Paul's view of the OT).

6:2 MIRACLES. (1) What are miracles? (a) They are works of a supernatural origin and power (Gk *dunamis*; see Ac 8:13; 19:11). (b) They function as a sign or mark (Gk *semeion*) of divine authority (Lk 23:8; Ac 4:16,30,33). The central and greatest miracle of the NT faith is the resurrection of Christ (1Co 15).

(2) Miracles serve at least three purposes in the kingdom of God. (a) They witness to Jesus Christ, authenticating the truth of his message and proving his identity as the Christ of God (2:23; 5:1–21; 10:25; 11:42). (b) They express Christ's compassionate love (Mk 8:2; Lk 7:12–15; Ac 10:38). (c) They signify the age of salvation (Mt 11:2ff), the coming of the kingdom of God (see article on THE KINGDOM OF GOD, p. 28) and God's invasion into the realm of Satan (see article on POWER OVER SATAN AND DEMONS, p. 80).

(3) The Scriptures maintain that miracles are to operate throughout the entire church age. (a) Jesus sent out his followers to preach and perform miracles (Mt 10:7–8; Mk 3:14–15; see Lk 9:2, note). (b) Jesus declared that those who believed in him through the preaching of the gospel were to do the works that he did, and would do even greater things (14:12; Mk 16:15–20). (c) The book of Acts speaks of the performing of miracles in the lives of the believers (Ac 3:1ff; 5:12; 6:8; 8:6ff; 9:32ff; 15:12; 20:7ff); elsewhere in the NT these are called "signs" by which the proclamation of the gospel was confirmed (Ac 4:29–30; 14:3; Ro 15:18–19; 2Co 12:12; Heb 2:3–4). (d) The Spirit wants to give these signs to the church throughout this present age (1Co 12:8–12,28; Jas 5:14–15; see article on SIGNS OF BELIEVERS, p. 106).

(4) The NT also teaches that signs and wonders will be performed by the power of Satan through false teachers and preachers, especially by the antichrist and his false prophet (see articles on THE GREAT TRIBULATION, p. 52, and FALSE TEACHERS, p. 98).

performed on the sick. 3Then Jesus went
up on a mountainside[c] and sat down with
his disciples. 4The Jewish Passover
Feast[d] was near.
5When Jesus looked up and saw a great
crowd coming toward him, he said to Philip,[e] "Where shall we buy bread for these
people to eat?" 6He asked this only to test
him, for he already had in mind what he
was going to do.
7Philip answered him, "Eight months'
wages[g] would not buy enough bread for
each one to have a bite!"
8Another of his disciples, Andrew, Simon Peter's brother,[f] spoke up, 9"Here is
a boy with five small barley loaves and
two small fish, but how far will they go
among so many?"[g]
10Jesus said, "Have the people sit
down." There was plenty of grass in that
place, and the men sat down, about five
thousand of them. 11Jesus then took the
loaves, gave thanks,[h] and distributed to
those who were seated as much as they
wanted. He did the same with the fish.
12When they had all had enough to eat,
he said to his disciples, "Gather the pieces
that are left over. Let nothing be wasted."
13So they gathered them and filled twelve
baskets with the pieces of the five barley
loaves left over by those who had eaten.
14After the people saw the miraculous
sign[i] that Jesus did, they began to say,
"Surely this is the Prophet who is to come
into the world."[j] 15Jesus, knowing that
they intended to come and make him
king[k] by force, withdrew again to a mountain by himself.[l]

Jesus Walks on the Water

6:16–21pp — Mt 14:22–33; Mk 6:47–51

16When evening came, his disciples
went down to the lake, 17where they got
into a boat and set off across the lake for
Capernaum. By now it was dark, and
Jesus had not yet joined them. 18A strong
wind was blowing and the waters grew
rough. 19When they had rowed three or
three and a half miles,[h] they saw Jesus
approaching the boat, walking on the water;[m] and they were terrified. 20But he
said to them, "It is I; don't be afraid."[n]
21Then they were willing to take him into
the boat, and immediately the boat
reached the shore where they were heading.
22The next day the crowd that had
stayed on the opposite shore of the lake[o]
realized that only one boat had been there,
and that Jesus had not entered it with his
disciples, but that they had gone away
alone.[p] 23Then some boats from Tiberias[q] landed near the place where the people had eaten the bread after the Lord had
given thanks.[r] 24Once the crowd realized
that neither Jesus nor his disciples were
there, they got into the boats and went to
Capernaum in search of Jesus.

Jesus the Bread of Life

25When they found him on the other
side of the lake, they asked him, "Rabbi,[s]
when did you get here?"
26Jesus answered, "I tell you the truth,
you are looking for me,[t] not because you
saw miraculous signs[u] but because you
ate the loaves and had your fill. 27Do not
work for food that spoils, but for food that
endures[v] to eternal life,[w] which the Son
of Man[x] will give you. On him God the
Father has placed his seal[y] of approval."
28Then they asked him, "What must we
do to do the works God requires?"
29Jesus answered, "The work of God is
this: to believe[z] in the one he has sent."[a]
30So they asked him, "What miraculous
sign[b] then will you give that we may see
it and believe you?[c] What will you do?
31Our forefathers ate the manna[d] in the
desert; as it is written: 'He gave them
bread from heaven to eat.'[i]"[e]
32Jesus said to them, "I tell you the
truth, it is not Moses who has given you
the bread from heaven, but it is my Father
who gives you the true bread from heaven.
33For the bread of God is he who comes
down from heaven[f] and gives life to the
world."
34"Sir," they said, "from now on give us
this bread."[g]
35Then Jesus declared, "I am[h] the
bread of life.[i] He who comes to me will

6:3 [c]ver 15
6:4 [d]S Jn 11:55
6:5 [e]S Jn 1:43
6:8 [f]Jn 1:40
6:9 [g]2Ki 4:43
6:11 [h]ver 23; S Mt 14:19
6:14 [i]S Jn 2:11 [j]Dt 18:15,18; Mt 11:3; S 21:11
6:15 [k]Jn 18:36 [l]Mt 14:23; Mk 6:46
6:19 [m]Job 9:8
6:20 [n]S Mt 14:27
6:22 [o]ver 2 [p]ver 15-21
6:23 [q]ver 1 [r]ver 11
6:25 [s]S Mt 23:7
6:26 [t]ver 24 [u]ver 30; S Jn 2:11
6:27 [v]Isa 55:2 [w]ver 54; S Mt 25:46 [x]S Mt 8:20 [y]Ro 4:11; 1Co 9:2; 2Co 1:22; Eph 1:13; 4:30; 2Ti 2:19; Rev 7:3
6:29 [z]1Jn 3:23 [a]S Jn 3:17
6:30 [b]S Jn 2:11 [c]S Mt 12:38
6:31 [d]Nu 11:7-9 [e]Ex 16:4,15; Ne 9:15; Ps 78:24; 105:40
6:33 [f]ver 50; Jn 3:13,31
6:34 [g]Jn 4:15
6:35 [h]Ex 3:14; Jn 8:12; 10:7,11; 11:25; 14:6; 15:1 [i]ver 48,51

[g] *7* Greek *two hundred denarii* [h] *19* Greek *rowed twenty-five or thirty stadia* (about 5 or 6 kilometers) [i] *31* Exodus 16:4; Neh. 9:15; Psalm 78:24,25

6:5 THE FEEDING OF THE FIVE THOUSAND. See Mt 14:19, note.

6:15 JESUS PRAYS ALONE. See Mt 14:23, note.

6:20 DON'T BE AFRAID. See Mt 14:27, note.

6:35 I AM THE BREAD OF LIFE. "I am the bread of life" is the first of the seven "I am" statements recorded in John's Gospel, each one emphasizing an important aspect of the personal ministry of Jesus. This statement tells us that Christ is the sustenance that nourishes spiritual life (see v. 53). The other "I am" statements are: "the light of the world" (8:12), "the gate" (10:9), "the good shepherd" (10:11,14),

never go hungry, and he who believes[j] in
me will never be thirsty.[k] 36But as I told
you, you have seen me and still you do not
believe. 37All that the Father gives me[l]
will come to me, and whoever comes to me
I will never drive away. 38For I have come
down from heaven[m] not to do my will but
to do the will[n] of him who sent me.[o]
39And this is the will of him who sent me,
that I shall lose none of all that he has
given me,[p] but raise them up at the last
day.[q] 40For my Father's will is that everyone who looks to the Son[r] and believes in
him shall have eternal life,[s] and I will
raise him up at the last day."

41At this the Jews began to grumble
about him because he said, "I am the
bread that came down from heaven."
42They said, "Is this not Jesus, the son of
Joseph,[t] whose father and mother we
know?[u] How can he now say, 'I came
down from heaven'?"[v]

43"Stop grumbling among yourselves,"
Jesus answered. 44"No one can come to
me unless the Father who sent me draws
him,[w] and I will raise him up at the last
day. 45It is written in the Prophets: 'They
will all be taught by God.'[j][x] Everyone
who listens to the Father and learns from
him comes to me. 46No one has seen the
Father except the one who is from God;[y]
only he has seen the Father. 47I tell you
the truth, he who believes has everlasting
life.[z] 48I am the bread of life.[a] 49Your
forefathers ate the manna in the desert,
yet they died.[b] 50But here is the bread
that comes down from heaven,[c] which a
man may eat and not die. 51I am the living
bread[d] that came down from heaven.[e] If
anyone eats of this bread, he will live forever. This bread is my flesh, which I will
give for the life of the world."[f]

52Then the Jews[g] began to argue sharply among themselves,[h] "How can this
man give us his flesh to eat?"

53Jesus said to them, "I tell you the
truth, unless you eat the flesh[i] of the Son
of Man[j] and drink his blood,[k] you have no
life in you. 54Whoever eats my flesh and
drinks my blood has eternal life, and I will
raise him up at the last day.[l] 55For my
flesh is real food and my blood is real
drink. 56Whoever eats my flesh and drinks
my blood remains in me, and I in him.[m]
57Just as the living Father sent me[n] and
I live because of the Father, so the one
who feeds on me will live because of me.
58This is the bread that came down from
heaven. Your forefathers ate manna and
died, but he who feeds on this bread will
live forever."[o] 59He said this while teaching in the synagogue in Capernaum.

j *45* Isaiah 54:13

6:35 [j] S Jn 3:15 [k] Jn 4:14
6:37 [l] ver 39; Jn 17:2,6,9,24
6:38 [m] Jn 3:13,31 [n] S Mt 26:39 [o] S Jn 3:17
6:39 [p] Isa 27:3; Jer 23:4; Jn 10:28; 17:12; 18:9 [q] ver 40,44,54
6:40 [r] Jn 12:45 [s] S Mt 25:46
6:42 [t] Lk 4:22 [u] Jn 7:27,28 [v] ver 38,62
6:44 [w] ver 65; Jer 31:3; Jn 12:32
6:45 [x] Isa 54:13; Jer 31:33,34; 1Co 2:13; 1Th 4:9; Heb 8:10,11; 10:16; 1Jn 2:27
6:46 [y] S Jn 1:18; 5:37; 7:29
6:47 [z] S Mt 25:46
6:48 [a] ver 35,51
6:49 [b] ver 31,58
6:50 [c] ver 33
6:51 [d] ver 35,48 [e] ver 41,58 [f] Heb 10:10
6:52 [g] S Jn 1:19 [h] Jn 7:43; 9:16; 10:19
6:53 [i] Mt 26:26 [j] S Mt 8:20 [k] Mt 26:28
6:54 [l] ver 39
6:56 [m] Jn 15:4-7; 1Jn 2:24; 3:24; 4:15
6:57 [n] S Jn 3:17
6:58 [o] ver 49-51; Jn 3:36; 5:24

"the resurrection and the life" (11:25), "the way and the truth and the life" (14:6), and "the true vine" (15:1,5).

6:37 I WILL NEVER DRIVE AWAY. Jesus promises to welcome all who come to him in repentance and faith. Those who come to Jesus come in response to the grace given them by God (see article on FAITH AND GRACE, p. 302).

6:40 MY FATHER'S WILL. It is important to understand the relationship of the Father's will to human responsibility. (1) It is not God's will that any believer should fall from grace (cf. Gal 5:4) and subsequently be cut off from God; neither is it his will that any individual should perish (2Pe 3:9) or fail to come to the truth and be saved (1Ti 2:4). (2) However, there is a great difference between God's perfect will and his permissive will. He does not abrogate the human responsibility to repent and believe, even if it means his perfect will is not done (see Lk 19:41, note on Jesus weeping over Jerusalem). (3) God's desire that believers be raised up at the last day does not relieve them of the responsibility of obeying his voice and following him (10:27; 14:21). Jesus acknowledged on the night of his betrayal that he protected his disciples and "kept them safe by that name you gave me. None has been lost except the one doomed to destruction" (17:12).

6:44 THE FATHER . . . DRAWS HIM. The Father draws people to Jesus through the Holy Spirit. God's work of drawing covers all people, as Jesus says: "I . . . will draw all men" (12:32). But this drawing is not irresistible, for it can be rejected (see Mt 23:37, "but you were not willing").

6:54 EATS MY FLESH AND DRINKS MY BLOOD. We receive spiritual life by believing in Christ and sharing in the redemptive benefits of his death on the cross (Ro 3:24–25; 1Jn 1:7). We continue to have spiritual life as we remain in fellowship with Christ and his Word. Compare v. 53 with v. 63, where he says, "The words I have spoken to you are spirit and they are life." Thus, we partake of Christ as we continue to have faith in him and prayerfully receive his Word.

(1) Jesus is the living Word (1:1–5); the Bible is the written Word (2Ti 3:16; 2Pe 1:21). Jesus calls himself here the "bread of life" (v. 35), and elsewhere he relates this bread to the Word of God: "Man does not live on bread alone, but on every word that comes from the mouth of God" (Mt 4:4). Therefore, we eat his flesh by remaining in him and by receiving and obeying the Word of God (v. 63).

(2) We are saved by God's grace and the Spirit's regenerating power when we first hear and receive the Word (1:12; Ac 2:41). We continue to be saved and receive grace by remaining in union with Christ and partaking of the Word of God continually through reading, obeying and absorbing its words into our hearts (1Ti 4:13–16; Jas 1:21). It is fatal to withdraw from fellowship with Christ or to depart from his Word.

Many Disciples Desert Jesus

60On hearing it, many of his disciples[p]
said, "This is a hard teaching. Who can
accept it?"[q]

61Aware that his disciples were grumbling about this, Jesus said to them, "Does
this offend you?[r] 62What if you see the
Son of Man[s] ascend to where he was before![t] 63The Spirit gives life;[u] the flesh
counts for nothing. The words I have spoken to you are spirit[k] and they are life.
64Yet there are some of you who do not
believe." For Jesus had known[v] from the
beginning which of them did not believe
and who would betray him.[w] 65He went on
to say, "This is why I told you that no one
can come to me unless the Father has enabled him."[x]

66From this time many of his disciples[y]
turned back and no longer followed him.

67"You do not want to leave too, do
you?" Jesus asked the Twelve.[z]

68Simon Peter answered him,[a] "Lord,
to whom shall we go? You have the words
of eternal life.[b] 69We believe and know
that you are the Holy One of God."[c]

70Then Jesus replied, "Have I not chosen you,[d] the Twelve? Yet one of you is a
devil!"[e] 71(He meant Judas, the son of Simon Iscariot,[f] who, though one of the
Twelve, was later to betray him.)[g]

Jesus Goes to the Feast of Tabernacles

7 After this, Jesus went around in Galilee, purposely staying away from Judea because the Jews[h] there were waiting
to take his life.[i] 2But when the Jewish
Feast of Tabernacles[j] was near, 3Jesus'
brothers[k] said to him, "You ought to leave
here and go to Judea, so that your disciples may see the miracles you do. 4No one
who wants to become a public figure acts
in secret. Since you are doing these
things, show yourself to the world." 5For
even his own brothers did not believe in
him.[l]

6Therefore Jesus told them, "The right
time[m] for me has not yet come; for you any
time is right. 7The world cannot hate you,
but it hates me[n] because I testify that
what it does is evil.[o] 8You go to the Feast.
I am not yet[1] going up to this Feast, because for me the right time[p] has not yet
come." 9Having said this, he stayed in Galilee.

10However, after his brothers had left
for the Feast, he went also, not publicly,
but in secret. 11Now at the Feast the Jews
were watching for him[q] and asking,
"Where is that man?"

12Among the crowds there was widespread whispering about him. Some said,
"He is a good man."

Others replied, "No, he deceives the
people."[r] 13But no one would say anything publicly about him for fear of the
Jews.[s]

Jesus Teaches at the Feast

14Not until halfway through the Feast
did Jesus go up to the temple courts and
begin to teach.[t] 15The Jews[u] were
amazed and asked, "How did this man get
such learning[v] without having studied?"[w]

16Jesus answered, "My teaching is not
my own. It comes from him who sent me.[x]
17If anyone chooses to do God's will, he
will find out[y] whether my teaching comes
from God or whether I speak on my own.

6:60 [p]ver 66 [q]ver 52 **6:61** [r]Mt 13:57 **6:62** [s]S Mt 8:20 [t]S Mk 16:19; S Jn 3:13; 17:5 **6:63** [u]2Co 3:6 **6:64** [v]S Jn 2:25 [w]S Mt 10:4 **6:65** [x]ver 37,44; S Mt 13:11 **6:66** [y]ver 60 **6:67** [z]Mt 10:2 **6:68** [a]Mt 16:16 [b]ver 63; S Mt 25:46 **6:69** [c]S Mk 1:24; 8:29; Lk 9:20 **6:70** [d]Jn 15:16,19 [e]Jn 13:27; 17:12 **6:71** [f]S Mt 26:14 [g]S Mt 10:4 **7:1** [h]S Jn 1:19 [i]ver 19,25; S Mt 12:14 **7:2** [j]Lev 23:34; Dt 16:16 **7:3** [k]S Mt 12:46

7:5 [l]Ps 69:8; Mk 3:21 **7:6** [m]S Mt 26:18 **7:7** [n]Jn 15:18,19 [o]Jn 3:19,20 **7:8** [p]ver 6; S Mt 26:18 **7:11** [q]Jn 11:56 **7:12** [r]ver 40,43 **7:13** [s]Jn 9:22; 12:42; 19:38; 20:19 **7:14** [t]ver 28; S Mt 26:55 **7:15** [u]S Jn 1:19 [v]Ac 26:24 [w]Mt 13:54 **7:16** [x]S Jn 14:24 **7:17** [y]Ps 25:14

[k] *63* Or *Spirit* [1] *8* Some early manuscripts do not have *yet.*

6:64 JESUS HAD KNOWN FROM THE BEGINNING. This may mean that Jesus knew when Judas began to drift from his original faith and formed plans to betray him. Judas had the same choice as the other eleven disciples. He was a believer and a trusted familiar friend of Jesus (Ps 41:9; Jn 13:18), as shown by Christ's commitment to Judas (2:23–24; Mt 10:1–15). Judas later turned away by his own choice (Ac 1:25); he did not have to betray Jesus. In other words, the betrayal of Jesus was prophesied only as to its occurrence, and not to its perpetrator. The specific person to betray Christ was not predestined from all eternity. Judas's defection to the enemy and consequent tragedy should warn every follower of Christ not to reject the Spirit's warning about friendship with the world and turning away from Christ (Heb 10:29; 12:25; Jas 4:4).

7:2 FEAST OF TABERNACLES. The "Feast of Tabernacles" commemorated the post-exodus journeys of Israel and the time when they wandered in the desert, living in tabernacles (or tents) under God's care (see Lev 23:34; Zec 14:16–19).

7:7 IT HATES ME. Jesus was hated by the world because he proclaimed that all people separated from God are depraved, sinful and inherently selfish (cf. 2:14–16; 3:19–20; 5:30–47). Throughout his ministry Jesus faithfully denounced injustice, cruelty and immorality. This unfailing, forthright testimony to human sinfulness contradicts those ministers who self-righteously claim to preach a "positive gospel," i.e., one stripped of the prophetic demand for repentance and righteousness.

7:17 IF ANYONE CHOOSES TO DO GOD'S WILL. True saving faith and an experiential knowledge of his teachings require a sincere desire to do the will of God. To believe is to make a commitment to obey (see article on FAITH AND GRACE, p. 302).

18He who speaks on his own does so to
gain honor for himself,[z] but he who works
for the honor of the one who sent him is
a man of truth; there is nothing false
about him. **19**Has not Moses given you the
law?[a] Yet not one of you keeps the law.
Why are you trying to kill me?"[b]

20"You are demon-possessed,"[c] the
crowd answered. "Who is trying to kill
you?"

21Jesus said to them, "I did one miracle,[d] and you are all astonished. **22**Yet,
because Moses gave you circumcision[e]
(though actually it did not come from Moses, but from the patriarchs),[f] you circumcise a child on the Sabbath. **23**Now if
a child can be circumcised on the Sabbath
so that the law of Moses may not be broken, why are you angry with me for healing the whole man on the Sabbath? **24**Stop
judging by mere appearances, and make a
right judgment."[g]

Is Jesus the Christ?

25At that point some of the people of
Jerusalem began to ask, "Isn't this the
man they are trying to kill?[h] **26**Here he is,
speaking publicly, and they are not saying
a word to him. Have the authorities[i]
really concluded that he is the Christ[m]?[j]
27But we know where this man is from;[k]
when the Christ comes, no one will know
where he is from."

28Then Jesus, still teaching in the temple courts,[l] cried out, "Yes, you know me,
and you know where I am from.[m] I am not
here on my own, but he who sent me is
true.[n] You do not know him, **29**but I know
him[o] because I am from him and he sent
me."[p]

30At this they tried to seize him, but no
one laid a hand on him,[q] because his time
had not yet come.[r] **31**Still, many in the
crowd put their faith in him.[s] They said,
"When the Christ comes, will he do more
miraculous signs[t] than this man?"

32The Pharisees heard the crowd whispering such things about him. Then the
chief priests and the Pharisees sent temple guards to arrest him.

33Jesus said, "I am with you for only a
short time,[u] and then I go to the one who
sent me.[v] **34**You will look for me, but you
will not find me; and where I am, you cannot come."[w]

35The Jews said to one another, "Where
does this man intend to go that we cannot
find him? Will he go where our people live
scattered[x] among the Greeks,[y] and teach
the Greeks? **36**What did he mean when he
said, 'You will look for me, but you will not
find me,' and 'Where I am, you cannot
come'?"[z]

37On the last and greatest day of the
Feast,[a] Jesus stood and said in a loud
voice, "If anyone is thirsty, let him come
to me and drink.[b] **38**Whoever believes[c] in
me, as[n] the Scripture has said,[d] streams
of living water[e] will flow from within
him."[f] **39**By this he meant the Spirit,[g]
whom those who believed in him were later to receive.[h] Up to that time the Spirit

7:18 [z]Jn 5:41; 8:50,54
7:19 [a]Dt 32:46; Jn 1:17 [b]ver 1; S Mt 12:14
7:20 [c]S Mk 3:22
7:21 [d]ver 23; Jn 5:2-9
7:22 [e]Lev 12:3 [f]Ge 17:10-14
7:24 [g]1Sa 16:7; Isa 11:3,4; Jn 8:15; 2Co 10:7
7:25 [h]ver 1; S Mt 12:14
7:26 [i]ver 48 [j]Jn 4:29
7:27 [k]Mt 13:55; Lk 4:22; Jn 6:42
7:28 [l]ver 14 [m]Jn 8:14 [n]Jn 8:26, 42
7:29 [o]S Mt 11:27 [p]S Jn 3:17
7:30 [q]ver 32,44; Jn 10:39 [r]S Mt 26:18
7:31 [s]Jn 8:30; 10:42; 11:45; 12:11,42 [t]S Jn 2:11
7:33 [u]Jn 12:35; 13:33; 16:16 [v]Jn 16:5,10,17,28
7:34 [w]ver 36; Jn 8:21; 13:33
7:35 [x]S Jas 1:1 [y]Jn 12:20; Ac 17:4; 18:4
7:36 [z]ver 34
7:37 [a]Lev 23:36 [b]Isa 55:1; Rev 22:17
7:38 [c]S Jn 3:15 [d]Isa 58:11 [e]S Jn 4:10 [f]S Jn 4:14
7:39 [g]Joel 2:28; Jn 1:33; Ac 2:17, 33 [h]S Jn 20:22

[m] *26* Or *Messiah;* also in verses 27, 31, 41 and 42
[n] *37,38* Or / *If anyone is thirsty, let him come to me.* / *And let him drink,* [38]*who believes in me.* / *As*

7:18 GAIN HONOR FOR HIMSELF. Jesus emphasizes an all-important criterion for testing whether religious speakers are from God: Do they seek their own glory or advancement? In evaluating ministers, ask whether their preaching magnifies themselves or the Lord Jesus.

7:38 AS THE SCRIPTURE HAS SAID. Jesus referred to the "Scripture" because it was the very Word of his Father and therefore the supreme authority for his life and teaching. Scripture is also the supreme authority for Christians, for God alone has the right to determine our standards of conduct. He has chosen to exercise this authority by making his truth known in Scripture. The Bible, as God's revelation, carries the same authority as if God himself were speaking to us directly (see article on THE INSPIRATION AND AUTHORITY OF SCRIPTURE, p. 474).

(1) The inspired Scriptures are the believer's ultimate authority. Ecclesiastical traditions, prophecies, supposed new revelations, doctrines and human ideas must be tested against Scripture and should never be elevated to a place of equal authority with the Bible (cf. Mk 7:13; Col 2:8; 1Pe 1:18–19).

(2) To profess equal or greater allegiance to any other authority than to God and his inspired Word is to remove oneself from the Biblical faith and the lordship of Christ. To say that any person, institution, creed or church possesses equal or higher authority than God's inspired revelation is tantamount to idolatry. Thus, all those who are not willing to submit their beliefs to the authority of the NT place themselves outside of Biblical Christianity and salvation in Christ.

7:38 STREAMS OF LIVING WATER. When the gift of the Spirit is given to believers, they will experience his overflowing life. Then this "living water" will "flow" out to others with the healing message of Jesus Christ (10:10; 14:12; 15:5; see also Ps 46:4; Isa 32:15; 44:3; 58:11; Jer 31:12; Eze 47:1–12; Joel 3:18; Zec 14:8).

7:39 JESUS HAD NOT YET BEEN GLORIFIED. This refers to Jesus' glory on the cross (see 12:23–24). The Spirit cannot be fully given until sin is dealt with. "The Spirit" refers to all the work of the Holy Spirit in the believer, both regeneration (20:22) and the baptism in the Spirit (Ac 2:4).

had not been given, since Jesus had not yet been glorified.[i]

[40]On hearing his words, some of the people said, "Surely this man is the Prophet."[j]

[41]Others said, "He is the Christ."

Still others asked, "How can the Christ come from Galilee?[k] [42]Does not the Scripture say that the Christ will come from David's family[o][l] and from Bethlehem,[m] the town where David lived?" [43]Thus the people were divided[n] because of Jesus. [44]Some wanted to seize him, but no one laid a hand on him.[o]

Unbelief of the Jewish Leaders

[45]Finally the temple guards went back to the chief priests and Pharisees, who asked them, "Why didn't you bring him in?"

[46]"No one ever spoke the way this man does,"[p] the guards declared.

[47]"You mean he has deceived you also?"[q] the Pharisees retorted. [48]"Has any of the rulers or of the Pharisees believed in him?[r] [49]No! But this mob that knows nothing of the law—there is a curse on them."

[50]Nicodemus,[s] who had gone to Jesus earlier and who was one of their own number, asked, [51]"Does our law condemn anyone without first hearing him to find out what he is doing?"

[52]They replied, "Are you from Galilee, too? Look into it, and you will find that a prophet[p] does not come out of Galilee."[t]

[The earliest and most reliable manuscripts and other ancient witnesses do not have John 7:53–8:11.]

7:39 [i]Jn 12:23; 13:31,32
7:40 [j]S Mt 21:11
7:41 [k]ver 52; Jn 1:46
7:42 [l]S Mt 1:1 [m]Mic 5:2; Mt 2:5, 6; Lk 2:4
7:43 [n]Jn 6:52; 9:16; 10:19
7:44 [o]ver 30
7:46 [p]S Mt 7:28
7:47 [q]ver 12
7:48 [r]Jn 12:42
7:50 [s]Jn 3:1; 19:39
7:52 [t]ver 41

8:1 [u]S Mt 21:1
8:2 [v]ver 20; S Mt 26:55
8:5 [w]Lev 20:10; Dt 22:22; Job 31:11
8:6 [x]Mt 22:15,18 [y]S Mt 12:10
8:7 [z]Dt 17:7; Eze 16:40 [a]Ro 2:1,22
8:11 [b]Jn 3:17 [c]Jn 5:14
8:12 [d]S Jn 6:35 [e]S Jn 1:4

[53]Then each went to his own home.

8 But Jesus went to the Mount of Olives.[u] [2]At dawn he appeared again in the temple courts, where all the people gathered around him, and he sat down to teach them.[v] [3]The teachers of the law and the Pharisees brought in a woman caught in adultery. They made her stand before the group [4]and said to Jesus, "Teacher, this woman was caught in the act of adultery. [5]In the Law Moses commanded us to stone such women.[w] Now what do you say?" [6]They were using this question as a trap,[x] in order to have a basis for accusing him.[y]

But Jesus bent down and started to write on the ground with his finger. [7]When they kept on questioning him, he straightened up and said to them, "If any one of you is without sin, let him be the first to throw a stone[z] at her."[a] [8]Again he stooped down and wrote on the ground.

[9]At this, those who heard began to go away one at a time, the older ones first, until only Jesus was left, with the woman still standing there. [10]Jesus straightened up and asked her, "Woman, where are they? Has no one condemned you?"

[11]"No one, sir," she said.

"Then neither do I condemn you,"[b] Jesus declared. "Go now and leave your life of sin."[c]

The Validity of Jesus' Testimony

[12]When Jesus spoke again to the people, he said, "I am[d] the light of the world.[e] Whoever follows me will never

o 42 Greek *seed* p 52 Two early manuscripts *the Prophet*

8:7 IF ANY ONE OF YOU IS WITHOUT SIN. These words must not be taken as justification for refusing to condemn sin within the church, or for treating lightly the moral failure of professed Christians. To do so distorts the Bible's attitude toward sin among God's people. (1) The church's conduct toward sinners outside the church who have had little chance to respond to God's grace in Christ, and its conduct towards those within the church who sin and do not obey Christ, are two different situations. (2) Scripture teaches that sins committed by those within the church must not be tolerated (Rev 2:20), but ought to be sharply rebuked and exposed (Lk 17:3; 1Co 5:1–13; 2Co 2:6–8; Eph 5:11; 2Ti 4:2; Tit 1:13; 2:15; Rev 3:19; see Mt 13:30, note on church discipline).

8:11 NEITHER DO I CONDEMN YOU. Jesus' attitude reflects his redemptive purpose for the human race (Jn 3:16). He does not condemn the woman as unfit for forgiveness, but treats her with kindness and patience in order to lead her to repentance. For her there is salvation if she leaves her "life of sin," i.e., stops living in adultery and returns to her own husband (cf. Lk 7:47). (1) However, it would be blasphemous to use these words of Jesus to suggest that he looks casually at the sin of adultery and the untold heartbreak it causes for both adults and children. (2) What Jesus offers this woman is salvation and a way out of her life of sin. His condemnation awaits her if she refuses to repent and enter the kingdom of God (Ro 2:1–10).

8:12 I AM THE LIGHT OF THE WORLD. Jesus is the true light (1:9); he removes darkness and deception by illuminating the right way to God and salvation. (1) All those who follow Jesus are delivered from the darkness of sin, the world and Satan. Those who still walk in darkness do not follow him (cf. 1Jn 1:6–7). (2) "Whoever follows me" is a present participle, picturing a continuing action—"whoever keeps

walk in darkness, but will have the light
of life."[f]
13The Pharisees challenged him, "Here
you are, appearing as your own witness;
your testimony is not valid."[g]
14Jesus answered, "Even if I testify on
my own behalf, my testimony is valid, for
I know where I came from and where I am
going.[h] But you have no idea where I
come from[i] or where I am going. **15**You
judge by human standards;[j] I pass judgment on no one.[k] **16**But if I do judge, my
decisions are right, because I am not
alone. I stand with the Father, who sent
me.[l] **17**In your own Law it is written that
the testimony of two men is valid.[m] **18**I am
one who testifies for myself; my other witness is the Father, who sent me."[n]
19Then they asked him, "Where is your
father?"
"You do not know me or my Father,"[o]
Jesus replied. "If you knew me, you would
know my Father also."[p] **20**He spoke these
words while teaching[q] in the temple area
near the place where the offerings were
put.[r] Yet no one seized him, because his
time had not yet come.[s]
21Once more Jesus said to them, "I am
going away, and you will look for me, and
you will die[t] in your sin. Where I go, you
cannot come."[u]
22This made the Jews ask, "Will he kill
himself? Is that why he says, 'Where I go,
you cannot come'?"
23But he continued, "You are from below; I am from above. You are of this
world; I am not of this world.[v] **24**I told you

8:12 [f]Pr 4:18; Mt 5:14
8:13 [g]Jn 5:31
8:14 [h]Jn 13:3; 16:28 [i]Jn 7:28; 9:29
8:15 [j]S Jn 7:24 [k]Jn 3:17
8:16 [l]Jn 5:30
8:17 [m]S Mt 18:16
8:18 [n]Jn 5:37
8:19 [o]Jn 16:3 [p]S 1Jn 2:23
8:20 [q]S Mt 26:55 [r]Mk 12:41 [s]S Mt 26:18
8:21 [t]Eze 3:18 [u]Jn 7:34; 13:33
8:23 [v]Jn 3:31; 17:14
8:24 [w]Jn 4:26; 13:19
8:26 [x]Jn 7:28 [y]Jn 3:32; 15:15
8:28 [z]S Jn 12:32 [a]S Jn 14:24
8:29 [b]ver 16; Jn 16:32 [c]Isa 50:5; Jn 4:34; 5:30; 6:38
8:30 [d]S Jn 7:31
8:31 [e]Jn 15:7; 2Jn 9
8:32 [f]ver 36; Ro 8:2; 2Co 3:17; Gal 5:1,13
8:33 [g]ver 37,39; S Lk 3:8
8:34 [h]S Ro 6:16
8:35 [i]Gal 4:30
8:36 [j]ver 32

that you would die in your sins; if you do
not believe that I am ⌞the one I claim to
be⌟,[q][w] you will indeed die in your sins."
25"Who are you?" they asked.
"Just what I have been claiming all
along," Jesus replied. **26**"I have much to
say in judgment of you. But he who sent
me is reliable,[x] and what I have heard
from him I tell the world."[y]
27They did not understand that he was
telling them about his Father. **28**So Jesus
said, "When you have lifted up the Son of
Man,[z] then you will know that I am ⌞the
one I claim to be⌟ and that I do nothing on
my own but speak just what the Father
has taught me.[a] **29**The one who sent me
is with me; he has not left me alone,[b] for
I always do what pleases him."[c] **30**Even
as he spoke, many put their faith in him.[d]

The Children of Abraham

31To the Jews who had believed him,
Jesus said, "If you hold to my teaching,[e]
you are really my disciples. **32**Then you
will know the truth, and the truth will set
you free."[f]
33They answered him, "We are Abraham's descendants[r][g] and have never
been slaves of anyone. How can you say
that we shall be set free?"
34Jesus replied, "I tell you the truth,
everyone who sins is a slave to sin.[h]
35Now a slave has no permanent place in
the family, but a son belongs to it forever.[i] **36**So if the Son sets you free,[j] you

[q] *24* Or *I am he*; also in verse 28 [r] *33* Greek *seed*; also in verse 37

---

on following." Jesus recognized only a persevering discipleship (see next note).

8:31 IF YOU HOLD TO MY TEACHING. Jesus never encouraged his disciples to place confidence in past faith or past experience. It is only "if you hold to my teaching" that confidence of salvation is warranted. Genuine disciples of Christ continue to obey the words of Christ (see 15:6, note; Lk 21:19).

8:32 THE TRUTH WILL SET YOU FREE. In the context of human knowledge, many things are true. Yet there is only one truth that will set people free from sin, destruction and Satan's dominion—the truth of Jesus Christ found in God's Word. Some observations about truth are as follows: (1) Scripture, especially the original revelation of Christ and the NT apostles, testifies to the truth that frees one from sin, the world and the demonic (see Eph 2:20, note). (2) Further revelation of "truth" is not needed to complete or make more adequate the gospel of Christ. (3) Saving truth is revealed only from God "by his Spirit" (1Co 2:10) and does not originate from any person or from human wisdom (1Co 2:12–13).

8:36 YOU WILL BE FREE INDEED. Unsaved persons are slaves to sin, impurity and Satan (v. 34; Ro 6:17–20). They live according to the cravings of the sinful nature and the ways of Satan (Eph 2:1–3). (1) True believers, who possess salvation in Christ with the accompanying grace of the indwelling Holy Spirit, are set free from the power of sin and immorality (Ro 6:17–22; 8:1–17). When they face temptation to sin, they now have the power to act according to God's will. They are free to be enslaved to God and righteousness (Ro 6:18,22).

(2) Freedom from sin's bondage is one sure criterion by which all professing believers may test whether they have eternal life with its regenerating and sanctifying grace living in them. Anyone presently in bondage to immorality either has never experienced spiritual rebirth by the Holy Spirit or, having experienced spiritual regeneration, has yielded to sin and once more entered into the spiritual death that brings slavery to sin (Ro 6:16,21,23; 8:12–13; see 1Jn 3:15, note).

(3) This is not to say, however, that believers are free from spiritual warfare against sin. Throughout our lives, we will have to constantly fight against the pressures of the world, the sinful nature and the devil (see Gal 5:17, note). Full freedom from temptation

will be free indeed. 37I know you are Abraham's descendants. Yet you are ready to
kill me,[k] because you have no room for my
word. 38I am telling you what I have seen
in the Father's presence,[l] and you do
what you have heard from your father.[s]"[m]
39"Abraham is our father," they answered.
"If you were Abraham's children,"[n]
said Jesus, "then you would[t] do the things
Abraham did. 40As it is, you are determined to kill me,[o] a man who has told you
the truth that I heard from God.[p] Abraham did not do such things. 41You are
doing the things your own father does."[q]
"We are not illegitimate children," they
protested. "The only Father we have is
God himself."[r]

The Children of the Devil

42Jesus said to them, "If God were your
Father, you would love me,[s] for I came
from God[t] and now am here. I have not
come on my own;[u] but he sent me.[v]
43Why is my language not clear to you?
Because you are unable to hear what I
say. 44You belong to your father, the devil,[w] and you want to carry out your father's desire.[x] He was a murderer from
the beginning, not holding to the truth, for
there is no truth in him. When he lies, he
speaks his native language, for he is a liar
and the father of lies.[y] 45Yet because I tell
the truth,[z] you do not believe me! 46Can
any of you prove me guilty of sin? If I am
telling the truth, why don't you believe
me? 47He who belongs to God hears what
God says.[a] The reason you do not hear is
that you do not belong to God."

The Claims of Jesus About Himself

48The Jews answered him, "Aren't we
right in saying that you are a Samaritan[b]
and demon-possessed?"[c]
49"I am not possessed by a demon,"
said Jesus, "but I honor my Father and you
dishonor me. 50I am not seeking glory for
myself;[d] but there is one who seeks it,
and he is the judge. 51I tell you the truth,
if anyone keeps my word, he will never see
death."[e]
52At this the Jews exclaimed, "Now we
know that you are demon-possessed![f]
Abraham died and so did the prophets, yet
you say that if anyone keeps your word, he
will never taste death. 53Are you greater
than our father Abraham?[g] He died, and
so did the prophets. Who do you think you
are?"
54Jesus replied, "If I glorify myself,[h] my
glory means nothing. My Father, whom
you claim as your God, is the one who
glorifies me.[i] 55Though you do not know
him,[j] I know him.[k] If I said I did not, I
would be a liar like you, but I do know him
and keep his word.[l] 56Your father Abraham[m] rejoiced at the thought of seeing my
day; he saw it[n] and was glad."
57"You are not yet fifty years old," the
Jews said to him, "and you have seen
Abraham!"
58"I tell you the truth," Jesus answered,
"before Abraham was born,[o] I am!"[p] 59At
this, they picked up stones to stone him,[q]
but Jesus hid himself,[r] slipping away
from the temple grounds.

Jesus Heals a Man Born Blind

9 As he went along, he saw a man blind
from birth. 2His disciples asked him,
"Rabbi,[s] who sinned,[t] this man[u] or his
parents,[v] that he was born blind?"
3"Neither this man nor his parents
sinned," said Jesus, "but this happened so
that the work of God might be displayed

8:37 [k] ver 39,40 **8:38** [l] Jn 5:19,30; 14:10,24 [m] ver 41, 44 **8:39** [n] ver 37; S Lk 3:8 **8:40** [o] S Mt 12:14 [p] ver 26 **8:41** [q] ver 38,44 [r] Isa 63:16; 64:8 **8:42** [s] 1Jn 5:1 [t] S Jn 13:3 [u] Jn 7:28 [v] S Jn 3:17 **8:44** [w] 1Jn 3:8 [x] ver 38,41 [y] Ge 3:4; 4:9; 2Ch 18:21; Ps 5:6; 12:2 **8:45** [z] Jn 18:37 **8:47** [a] Jn 18:37; 1Jn 4:6 **8:48** [b] S Mt 10:5 [c] ver 52; S Mk 3:22

8:50 [d] ver 54; Jn 5:41 **8:51** [e] Jn 11:26 **8:52** [f] ver 48; S Mk 3:22 **8:53** [g] ver 39; Jn 4:12 **8:54** [h] ver 50 [i] Jn 16:14; 17:1,5 **8:55** [j] ver 19 [k] Jn 7:28,29 [l] Jn 15:10 **8:56** [m] ver 37,39; Ge 18:18 [n] S Mt 13:17 **8:58** [o] S Jn 1:2 [p] Ex 3:14; 6:3 **8:59** [q] Ex 17:4; Lev 24:16; 1Sa 30:6; Jn 10:31; 11:8 [r] Jn 12:36 **9:2** [s] S Mt 23:7 [t] ver 34; Lk 13:2; Ac 28:4 [u] Eze 18:20 [v] Ex 20:5; Job 21:19

[s] 38 Or *presence. Therefore do what you have heard from the Father.* [t] 39 Some early manuscripts *"If you are Abraham's children," said Jesus, "then*

---

and the pull of sin will come only with complete redemption at death or at Christ's return for his faithful. What Christ offers us now is the sanctifying power of his life, whereby those who follow the Spirit are set free from the desires of the sinful nature (Gal 5:16–24) and enabled to live holy and blameless lives before him in love (Eph 1:4).

8:42 IF GOD WERE YOUR FATHER. Here Jesus states a fundamental principle of salvation, namely, that the evidence of being a true child of God (i.e., born again of God) lies in one's attitude of love for Jesus. For this reason, one must demonstrate an attitude of sincere faith and obedience. Otherwise, the claim to be a child of God is illegitimate (cf. v. 31; 10:2–5,14,27–28; 14:15,21).

8:44 HE IS A LIAR AND THE FATHER OF LIES. Lying is specifically mentioned as a characteristic of the devil; he is the source of all falsehood (Ge 3:1–6; Ac 5:3; 2Th 2:9–11; Rev 12:9). It is a sin wholly opposed to the mind of God, who is truth (Rev 19:11). An indifference to the sin of lying is one of the most unmistakable symptoms of an ungodly condition, an indication that one is not born of the Spirit (3:6) but is under the influence of Satan as his or her spiritual father (see 4:24, note; Rev 22:15, note).

9:3 WORK OF GOD MIGHT BE DISPLAYED. Jesus corrects the disciples' erroneous belief that every serious affliction is the result of some sin. At times sickness does result from a serious sin (5:14), but not always. Sometimes suffering is permitted because of a divine purpose, i.e., to display God's mercy, love and power. Often in the world the innocent will suffer

in his life.[w] **4**As long as it is day,[x] we must
do the work of him who sent me. Night is
coming, when no one can work. **5**While I
am in the world, I am the light of the
world."[y]
6Having said this, he spit[z] on the
ground, made some mud with the saliva,
and put it on the man's eyes. **7**"Go," he
told him, "wash in the Pool of Siloam"[a]
(this word means Sent). So the man went
and washed, and came home seeing.[b]
8His neighbors and those who had formerly seen him begging asked, "Isn't this
the same man who used to sit and beg?"[c]
9Some claimed that he was.
Others said, "No, he only looks like
him."
But he himself insisted, "I am the man."
10"How then were your eyes opened?"
they demanded.
11He replied, "The man they call Jesus
made some mud and put it on my eyes. He
told me to go to Siloam and wash. So I
went and washed, and then I could see."[d]
Ac 3:1-10 **12**"Where is this man?" they asked him.
"I don't know," he said.

The Pharisees Investigate the Healing

13They brought to the Pharisees the
man who had been blind. **14**Now the day on
which Jesus had made the mud and
opened the man's eyes was a Sabbath.[e]
15Therefore the Pharisees also asked him
how he had received his sight.[f] "He put
mud on my eyes," the man replied, "and I
washed, and now I see."
16Some of the Pharisees said, "This
man is not from God, for he does not keep
the Sabbath."[g]
But others asked, "How can a sinner do
such miraculous signs?"[h] So they were
divided.[i]
17Finally they turned again to the blind
man, "What have you to say about him? It
was your eyes he opened."
The man replied, "He is a prophet."[j]
18The Jews[k] still did not believe that he
had been blind and had received his sight
until they sent for the man's parents.
19"Is this your son?" they asked. "Is this
the one you say was born blind? How is it
that now he can see?"
20"We know he is our son," the parents
answered, "and we know he was born
blind. **21**But how he can see now, or who
opened his eyes, we don't know. Ask him.
He is of age; he will speak for himself."
22His parents said this because they were
afraid of the Jews,[l] for already the Jews
had decided that anyone who acknowledged that Jesus was the Christ[u] would be
put out[m] of the synagogue.[n] **23**That was
why his parents said, "He is of age; ask
him."[o]
24A second time they summoned the
man who had been blind. "Give glory to
God,[v]"[p] they said. "We know this man is
a sinner."[q]
25He replied, "Whether he is a sinner or
not, I don't know. One thing I do know. I
was blind but now I see!"
26Then they asked him, "What did he do
to you? How did he open your eyes?"
27He answered, "I have told you already[r] and you did not listen. Why do you
want to hear it again? Do you want to
become his disciples, too?"
28Then they hurled insults at him and
said, "You are this fellow's disciple! We
are disciples of Moses![s] **29**We know that
God spoke to Moses, but as for this fellow,
we don't even know where he comes
from."[t]
30The man answered, "Now that is remarkable! You don't know where he
comes from, yet he opened my eyes. **31**We
know that God does not listen to sinners.
He listens to the godly man who does his
will.[u] **32**Nobody has ever heard of opening
the eyes of a man born blind. **33**If this man
were not from God,[v] he could do nothing."
34To this they replied, "You were
steeped in sin at birth;[w] how dare you lecture us!" And they threw him out.[x]

Spiritual Blindness

35Jesus heard that they had thrown him
out, and when he found him, he said, "Do
you believe[y] in the Son of Man?"[z]

9:3 [w]Jn 11:4 **9:4** [x]Jn 11:9; 12:35 **9:5** [y]S Jn 1:4 **9:6** [z]Mk 7:33; 8:23 **9:7** [a]ver 11; 2Ki 5:10; Lk 13:4 [b]Isa 35:5; Jn 11:37 **9:8** [c]Ac 3:2,10 **9:11** [d]ver 7 **9:14** [e]Mt 12:1-14; Jn 5:9 **9:15** [f]ver 10 **9:16** [g]S Mt 12:2 [h]S Jn 2:11 [i]S Jn 6:52 **9:17** [j]S Mt 21:11 **9:18** [k]S Jn 1:19 **9:22** [l]S Jn 7:13 [m]ver 34; Lk 6:22 [n]Jn 12:42; 16:2 **9:23** [o]ver 21 **9:24** [p]Jos 7:19 [q]ver 16 **9:27** [r]ver 15 **9:28** [s]Jn 5:45 **9:29** [t]Jn 8:14 **9:31** [u]Ge 18:23-32; Ps 34:15,16; 66:18; 145:19,20; Pr 15:29; Isa 1:15; 59:1,2; Jn 15:7; Jas 5:16-18; 1Jn 5:14,15 **9:33** [v]ver 16; Jn 3:2 **9:34** [w]ver 2 [x]ver 22,35; Isa 66:5 **9:35** [y]S Jn 3:15 [z]S Mt 8:20

[u] *22* Or *Messiah* [v] *24* A solemn charge to tell the truth (see Joshua 7:19)

when the wicked do not (cf. Ps 73:1–14).

9:34 THEY THREW HIM OUT. One of the best things that happened to the man born blind was excommunication from his former religion. If he had been allowed to stay in the synagogue, he would have been in danger of drifting back to the traditional ways of Judaism and becoming alienated from Christ and the gospel. Today the same thing can happen to those who are in lukewarm churches or unbiblical religious organizations. If they remain in that church or system, they may lose their hunger for true Biblical Christianity and return to embrace the ways of their former religion. The best thing is to be separated from what is not of God, so that Christ may come near to us in the fullest sense (vv. 35–38).

36“Who is he, sir?” the man asked. “Tell
me so that I may believe in him.”[a]
37Jesus said, “You have now seen him;
in fact, he is the one speaking with you.”[b]
38Then the man said, “Lord, I believe,”
and he worshiped him.[c]
39Jesus said, “For judgment[d] I have
come into this world,[e] so that the blind
will see[f] and those who see will become
blind.”[g]
40Some Pharisees who were with him
heard him say this and asked, “What? Are
we blind too?”[h]
41Jesus said, “If you were blind, you
would not be guilty of sin; but now that
you claim you can see, your guilt remains.[i]

The Shepherd and His Flock

10 “I tell you the truth, the man who
does not enter the sheep pen by
the gate, but climbs in by some other way,
is a thief and a robber.[j] 2The man who
enters by the gate is the shepherd of his
sheep.[k] 3The watchman opens the gate
for him, and the sheep listen to his voice.[l]
He calls his own sheep by name and leads
them out.[m] 4When he has brought out all
his own, he goes on ahead of them, and his
sheep follow him because they know his
voice.[n] 5But they will never follow a
stranger; in fact, they will run away from
him because they do not recognize a
stranger’s voice.” 6Jesus used this figure
of speech,[o] but they did not understand
what he was telling them.[p]
7Therefore Jesus said again, “I tell you
the truth, I am[q] the gate[r] for the sheep.
8All who ever came before me[s] were
thieves and robbers,[t] but the sheep did
not listen to them. 9I am the gate; whoever enters through me will be saved.[w] He
will come in and go out, and find pasture.
10The thief comes only to steal and kill
and destroy; I have come that they may
have life,[u] and have it to the full.[v]
11“I am[w] the good shepherd.[x] The good
shepherd lays down his life for the
sheep.[y] 12The hired hand is not the shepherd who owns the sheep. So when he
sees the wolf coming, he abandons the
sheep and runs away.[z] Then the wolf attacks the flock and scatters it. 13The man
runs away because he is a hired hand and
cares nothing for the sheep.
14“I am the good shepherd;[a] I know my
sheep[b] and my sheep know me— 15just
as the Father knows me and I know the
Father[c]—and I lay down my life for the
sheep.[d] 16I have other sheep[e] that are
not of this sheep pen. I must bring them
also. They too will listen to my voice, and
there shall be one flock[f] and one shepherd.[g] 17The reason my Father loves me
is that I lay down my life[h]—only to take
it up again. 18No one takes it from me, but
I lay it down of my own accord.[i] I have
authority to lay it down and authority to
take it up again. This command I received
from my Father.”[j]
19At these words the Jews were again
divided.[k] 20Many of them said, “He is demon-possessed[l] and raving mad.[m] Why
listen to him?”
21But others said, “These are not the
sayings of a man possessed by a demon.[n]
Can a demon open the eyes of the blind?”[o]

The Unbelief of the Jews

22Then came the Feast of Dedication[x]

9:36 [a]Ro 10:14 **9:37** [b]Jn 4:26 **9:38** [c]Mt 28:9 **9:39** [d]S Jn 5:22 [e]Jn 3:19; 12:47 [f]Lk 4:18 [g]Mt 13:13 **9:40** [h]Ro 2:19 **9:41** [i]Jn 15:22,24 **10:1** [j]ver 8,10 **10:2** [k]ver 11,14; Mk 6:34 **10:3** [l]ver 4,5,14, 16,27 [m]ver 4,5,14, 16,27 **10:4** [n]S ver 3 **10:6** [o]S Jn 16:25 [p]S Mk 9:32 **10:7** [q]S Jn 6:35 [r]ver 9 **10:8** [s]Jer 23:1,2; Eze 34:2 [t]ver 1

10:10 [u]S Jn 1:4; 3:15,16; 5:40; 20:31 [v]Ps 65:11; Ro 5:17 **10:11** [w]S Jn 6:35 [x]ver 14; Ps 23:1; Isa 40:11; Eze 34:11-16,23; Mt 2:6; Lk 12:32; Heb 13:20; 1Pe 2:25; 5:4; Rev 7:17 [y]ver 15, 17,18; Jn 15:13; 1Jn 3:16 **10:12** [z]Zec 11:16,17 **10:14** [a]S ver 11 [b]ver 27; Ex 33:12 **10:15** [c]Mt 11:27 [d]ver 11,17,18 **10:16** [e]Isa 56:8; Ac 10:34,35 [f]Jn 11:52; 17:20, 21; Eph 2:11-19 [g]Eze 34:23; 37:24 **10:17** [h]ver 11,15, 18 **10:18** [i]Mt 26:53 [j]Jn 15:10; Php 2:8; Heb 5:8 **10:19** [k]S Jn 6:52 **10:20** [l]S Mk 3:22 [m]2Ki 9:11; Jer 29:26; Mk 3:21 **10:21** [n]S Mt 4:24 [o]Ex 4:11; Jn 9:32, 33

[w] 9 Or *kept safe* [x] 22 That is, Hanukkah

10:1 JESUS THE GOOD SHEPHERD. The discourse about the good shepherd (vv. 1–30) displays Jesus as the true shepherd and ruler of his people in contrast to all false shepherds. (To better understand this chapter, OT passages condemning false shepherds should be read: Isa 56:9–12; Jer 23:1–4; Eze 34; Zec 11.) In vv. 7–18, Jesus applies vv. 1–5 to himself.

10:9 I AM THE GATE. Those who enter through Jesus will be “saved,” i.e., will have abundant eternal life (v. 10); they will have all they need to be delivered from sin, guilt and condemnation. Jesus is the *only* gate for salvation; none other exists (Ac 4:12).

10:11 I AM THE GOOD SHEPHERD. Jesus declares himself to be the promised good shepherd (cf. Ps 23; Isa 40:11; Eze 34:23; 37:24). (1) This metaphor illustrates Jesus’ tender and devoted care for his people. It is as if he is saying, “I am toward all who believe in me, as a good shepherd is toward his sheep—caring, watchful and loving.”

(2) The distinguishing mark of Christ as the good shepherd is his willingness to die for his sheep. This emphasizes the uniqueness of Christ the shepherd: his death on the cross saves his sheep (Isa 53:12; Mt 20:28; Mk 10:45). Christ is called the “good shepherd” here, the “great Shepherd” in Heb 13:20 and the “Chief Shepherd” in 1Pe 5:4.

(3) Be sure to note that the minister who serves merely to earn a living or to gain honor is the “hired hand” of vv. 12–13. True pastors care for their sheep, while false pastors think first of all of themselves and their position.

10:14 I KNOW MY SHEEP. God’s knowledge of and love for his children involves personal affection, faithfulness and constant providential care. We are engraved on the palms of his hands (Isa 49:16). We are never out of God’s mind, for God’s eye continually watches over us for our good (cf. Ex 33:17; Jer 1:5; see Mt 10:31, note; Ro 8:28, note).

at Jerusalem. It was winter, **23**and Jesus was in the temple area walking in Solomon's Colonnade.[p] **24**The Jews[q] gathered around him, saying, "How long will you keep us in suspense? If you are the Christ,[y] tell us plainly."[r]

Jn 15:26-27

25Jesus answered, "I did tell you,[s] but you do not believe. The miracles I do in my Father's name speak for me,[t] **26**but you do not believe because you are not my sheep.[u] **27**My sheep listen to my voice; I know them,[v] and they follow me.[w] **28**I give them eternal life,[x] and they shall never perish;[y] no one can snatch them out of my hand.[z] **29**My Father, who has given them to me,[a] is greater than all[z];[b] no one can snatch them out of my Father's hand. **30**I and the Father are one."[c]

31Again the Jews picked up stones to stone him,[d] **32**but Jesus said to them, "I have shown you many great miracles from the Father. For which of these do you stone me?"

33"We are not stoning you for any of these," replied the Jews, "but for blasphemy, because you, a mere man, claim to be God."[e]

34Jesus answered them, "Is it not written in your Law,[f] 'I have said you are gods'[a]?[g] **35**If he called them 'gods,' to whom the word of God[h] came—and the Scripture cannot be broken[i]— **36**what about the one whom the Father set apart[j] as his very own[k] and sent into the world?[l] Why then do you accuse me of blasphemy because I said, 'I am God's Son'?[m] **37**Do not believe me unless I do what my Father does.[n] **38**But if I do it, even though you do not believe me, believe the miracles, that you may know and understand that the Father is in me, and I in the Father."[o] **39**Again they tried to seize him,[p] but he escaped their grasp.[q]

40Then Jesus went back across the Jordan[r] to the place where John had been baptizing in the early days. Here he stayed **41**and many people came to him. They said, "Though John never performed a miraculous sign,[s] all that John said about this man was true."[t] **42**And in that place many believed in Jesus.[u]

The Death of Lazarus

11 Now a man named Lazarus was sick. He was from Bethany,[v] the village of Mary and her sister Martha.[w] **2**This Mary, whose brother Lazarus now lay sick, was the same one who poured perfume on the Lord and wiped his feet with her hair.[x] **3**So the sisters sent word to Jesus, "Lord, the one you love[y] is sick."

4When he heard this, Jesus said, "This sickness will not end in death. No, it is for God's glory[z] so that God's Son may be glorified through it." **5**Jesus loved Martha and her sister and Lazarus. **6**Yet when he

10:23 [p] Ac 3:11; 5:12
10:24 [q] S Jn 1:19 [r] Lk 22:67; Jn 16:25,29
10:25 [s] Jn 4:26; 8:58 [t] Jn 5:36; 14:11
10:26 [u] Jn 8:47
10:27 [v] ver 14 [w] ver 4
10:28 [x] S Mt 25:46 [y] Isa 66:22 [z] S Jn 6:39
10:29 [a] Jn 17:2,6, 24 [b] Jn 14:28
10:30 [c] Dt 6:4; Jn 17:21-23
10:31 [d] S Jn 8:59
10:33 [e] Lev 24:16; Mt 26:63-66; Jn 5:18
10:34 [f] Jn 8:17; 12:34; 15:25; Ro 3:19; 1Co 14:21 [g] Ps 82:6
10:35 [h] S Heb 4:12 [i] S Mt 5:18
10:36 [j] Jer 1:5 [k] Jn 6:69 [l] S Jn 3:17 [m] Jn 5:17,18
10:37 [n] ver 25
10:38 [o] Jn 14:10, 11,20; 17:21
10:39 [p] Jn 7:30 [q] Lk 4:30; Jn 8:59
10:40 [r] Jn 1:28
10:41 [s] S Jn 2:11 [t] Jn 1:26,27,30,34
10:42 [u] S Jn 7:31
11:1 [v] S Mt 21:17 [w] Lk 10:38
11:2 [x] Mk 14:3; Lk 7:38; Jn 12:3
11:3 [y] ver 5,36
11:4 [z] ver 40

[y] *24* Or *Messiah* [z] *29* Many early manuscripts *What my Father has given me is greater than all* [a] *34* Psalm 82:6

10:27 MY SHEEP LISTEN TO MY VOICE. Those who are true sheep of Christ obey his voice and follow him; they are in constant fellowship with the shepherd. "Listen to" and "follow" are in the present tense, denoting repeated or habitual activity. To those who are following, the shepherd gives eternal life. Those sheep who stray from the shepherd and refuse to listen prove that they are not his sheep (15:1–6).

10:28 THEY SHALL NEVER PERISH. Here is a precious promise given to all who are Christ's sheep. They will never be banished from God's love or presence, nor will any power or circumstance on earth take them from the shepherd (cf. Ro 8:35–39). There is indeed safety and security for even the weakest sheep who follow and listen to the good shepherd (see previous note).

10:34 YOU ARE GODS? In no way does this statement of Jesus teach that believers are to consider themselves gods. On the contrary, those who declare themselves to be gods will fall under God's condemnation (Jer 10:11). (1) The term "you are 'gods' " was spoken to corrupt rulers of Israel who were partial to the wicked and were cruel to children (Ps 82:1–4). These rulers, who thought they were gods, were to suffer judgment and die (Ps 82:7). (2) To declare oneself a god is the sin of the antichrist (2Th 2:4,11; see article on THE AGE OF THE ANTICHRIST, p. 447).

11:4 SICKNESS . . . FOR GOD'S GLORY. Sickness among God's people will never result in death as the final outcome. Death ultimately will be destroyed by the resurrection (vv. 25–26). The final truth is that those who believe in Christ "will never die" (v. 26).

11:5 JESUS LOVED MARTHA AND HER SISTER AND LAZARUS. Here is a family that had a genuine and strong devotion to Jesus (v. 2), enjoyed intimate fellowship with him (Lk 10:38–42) and was especially loved by him (vv. 3–5). Nevertheless, they experienced sorrow, sickness and death. Today these troubles can and will happen to God's faithful and chosen believers. Churches will have people like Mary persevering in loving devotion to the Lord, Martha faithful in good deeds, and Lazarus suffering and dying. Families like this may cry out, "How long, O Lord? Will you forget me forever?" (Ps 13:1; cf. Mt 27:46; Rev 6:10). Jesus says that his delay is not for lack of love, mercy or compassion, but for the glory of God (v. 4) and his kingdom and for the ultimate eternal good of the sufferers (vv. 15,23–26,40–44).

11:6 STAYED WHERE HE WAS TWO MORE DAYS. Jesus delayed going to the family he loved (v. 5) in order to strengthen the faith of that family and the disciples, and to perform for them a greater good.

heard that Lazarus was sick, he stayed where he was two more days.

7Then he said to his disciples, "Let us go back to Judea."[a]

8"But Rabbi,"[b] they said, "a short while ago the Jews tried to stone you,[c] and yet you are going back there?"

9Jesus answered, "Are there not twelve hours of daylight? A man who walks by day will not stumble, for he sees by this world's light.[d] **10**It is when he walks by night that he stumbles, for he has no light."

11After he had said this, he went on to tell them, "Our friend[e] Lazarus has fallen asleep;[f] but I am going there to wake him up."

12His disciples replied, "Lord, if he sleeps, he will get better." **13**Jesus had been speaking of his death, but his disciples thought he meant natural sleep.[g]

14So then he told them plainly, "Lazarus is dead, **15**and for your sake I am glad I was not there, so that you may believe. But let us go to him."

16Then Thomas[h] (called Didymus) said to the rest of the disciples, "Let us also go, that we may die with him."

Jesus Comforts the Sisters

17On his arrival, Jesus found that Lazarus had already been in the tomb for four days.[i] **18**Bethany[j] was less than two miles[b] from Jerusalem, **19**and many Jews had come to Martha and Mary to comfort them in the loss of their brother.[k] **20**When Martha heard that Jesus was coming, she went out to meet him, but Mary stayed at home.[l]

21"Lord," Martha said to Jesus, "if you had been here, my brother would not have died.[m] **22**But I know that even now God will give you whatever you ask."[n]

23Jesus said to her, "Your brother will rise again."

24Martha answered, "I know he will rise again in the resurrection[o] at the last day."[p]

25Jesus said to her, "I am[q] the resurrection and the life.[r] He who believes[s] in me will live, even though he dies; **26**and whoever lives and believes[t] in me will never die.[u] Do you believe this?"

27"Yes, Lord," she told him, "I believe that you are the Christ,[c][v] the Son of God,[w] who was to come into the world."[x]

28And after she had said this, she went back and called her sister Mary aside. "The Teacher[y] is here," she said, "and is asking for you." **29**When Mary heard this, she got up quickly and went to him. **30**Now Jesus had not yet entered the village, but was still at the place where Martha had met him.[z] **31**When the Jews who had been with Mary in the house, comforting her,[a] noticed how quickly she got up and went out, they followed her, supposing she was going to the tomb to mourn there.

32When Mary reached the place where Jesus was and saw him, she fell at his feet and said, "Lord, if you had been here, my brother would not have died."[b]

33When Jesus saw her weeping, and the Jews who had come along with her also weeping, he was deeply moved[c] in spirit and troubled.[d] **34**"Where have you laid him?" he asked.

"Come and see, Lord," they replied.

35Jesus wept.[e]

11:7 [a]Jn 10:40 **11:8** [b]S Mt 23:7 [c]Jn 8:59; 10:31 **11:9** [d]Jn 9:4; 12:35 **11:11** [e]ver 3 [f]S Mt 9:24 **11:13** [g]Mt 9:24 **11:16** [h]Mt 10:3; Jn 14:5; 20:24-28; 21:2; Ac 1:13 **11:17** [i]ver 6,39 **11:18** [j]ver 1; S Mt 21:17 **11:19** [k]ver 31; Job 2:11 **11:20** [l]Lk 10:38-42 **11:21** [m]ver 32,37 **11:22** [n]ver 41,42 **11:24** [o]Da 12:2; Jn 5:28,29; Ac 24:15 [p]Jn 6:39, 40 **11:25** [q]S Jn 6:35 [r]S Jn 1:4 [s]S Jn 3:15 **11:26** [t]S Jn 3:15 [u]S Mt 25:46 **11:27** [v]S Lk 2:11 [w]S Mt 4:3 [x]Jn 6:14 **11:28** [y]Mt 26:18; Jn 13:13 **11:30** [z]ver 20 **11:31** [a]ver 19 **11:32** [b]ver 21 **11:33** [c]ver 38 [d]S Jn 12:27 **11:35** [e]Lk 19:41

[b] *18* Greek *fifteen stadia* (about 3 kilometers)
[c] *27* Or *Messiah*

Initially, Jesus' actions appeared to indicate that he was unconcerned by their suffering. However, John repeatedly emphasizes that Jesus loved the family and shared their sorrow (vv. 3,5,35). Jesus' timing and purpose was different from what they wanted. God's timing and will, in the midst of our trials, may be different from what we want. God answers us according to his wisdom and love.

11:25–26 I AM THE RESURRECTION. For the person who believes in Jesus, physical death is not a tragic end. It is instead the gateway to abundant eternal life and fellowship with God. The ". . . will live" of v. 25 refers to the resurrection; the "will never die" of v. 26 means that resurrected believers will never die. They will have new bodies, immortal and incorruptible (1Co 15:42,54), ones that cannot die or deteriorate (cf. Ro 8:10; 2Co 4:16; see article on THE RESURRECTION OF THE BODY, p. 357).

11:33 DEEPLY MOVED IN SPIRIT. This passage reveals the heart and feelings of Jesus as he faces the heartbreak and suffering caused by all the evil in the world. (1) The word rendered "deeply moved" (Gk *embrimaomai*) pictures profound emotion involving anger. Jesus was grieved and angered by all the misery resulting from sin, Satan and death. His soul is filled not with cold unconcern, but with rage against evil, as he fights for the salvation of the human race (see 11:35, note; Mt 23:13, note; also Mt 21:12–13; Mk 11:15,17; Lk 19:45–46; Jn 2:14–16).

(2) One of the surest signs of God's work in our lives is that we begin to notice how much misery, sorrow and suffering sin has caused in the world (cf. Ge 3:16–19; Ro 5:12). As we do so, compassion for the suffering and hatred for sin will arise in our hearts. In no way can we experience pleasure in sin (see Ro 1:32, note; 2Th 2:12, note).

11:35 JESUS WEPT. These two words reveal the deep sympathy God feels for the sorrow of his people. The verb "wept" (Gk *dakruō*) indicates that Jesus burst into tears, then wept silently. Let this be a comfort to

36Then the Jews said, "See how he
loved him!"[f]

37But some of them said, "Could not he
who opened the eyes of the blind man[g]
have kept this man from dying?"[h]

Jesus Raises Lazarus From the Dead

38Jesus, once more deeply moved,[i]
came to the tomb. It was a cave with a
stone laid across the entrance.[j] 39"Take
away the stone," he said.

"But, Lord," said Martha, the sister of
the dead man, "by this time there is a bad
odor, for he has been there four days."[k]

40Then Jesus said, "Did I not tell you
that if you believed,[l] you would see the
glory of God?"[m]

41So they took away the stone. Then
Jesus looked up[n] and said, "Father,[o] I
thank you that you have heard me. 42I
knew that you always hear me, but I said
this for the benefit of the people standing
here,[p] that they may believe that you sent
me."[q]

43When he had said this, Jesus called in
a loud voice, "Lazarus, come out!"[r] 44The
dead man came out, his hands and feet
wrapped with strips of linen,[s] and a cloth
around his face.[t]

Jesus said to them, "Take off the grave
clothes and let him go."

The Plot to Kill Jesus

45Therefore many of the Jews who had
come to visit Mary,[u] and had seen what
Jesus did,[v] put their faith in him.[w] 46But
some of them went to the Pharisees and
told them what Jesus had done. 47Then
the chief priests and the Pharisees[x]
called a meeting[y] of the Sanhedrin.[z]

"What are we accomplishing?" they
asked. "Here is this man performing many
miraculous signs.[a] 48If we let him go on
like this, everyone will believe in him, and
then the Romans will come and take away
both our place[d] and our nation."

49Then one of them, named Caiaphas,[b]
who was high priest that year,[c] spoke up,
"You know nothing at all! 50You do not
realize that it is better for you that one
man die for the people than that the whole
nation perish."[d]

51He did not say this on his own, but as
high priest that year he prophesied that
Jesus would die for the Jewish nation,
52and not only for that nation but also for
the scattered children of God, to bring
them together and make them one.[e] 53So
from that day on they plotted to take his
life.[f]

54Therefore Jesus no longer moved
about publicly among the Jews.[g] Instead
he withdrew to a region near the desert,
to a village called Ephraim, where he
stayed with his disciples.

55When it was almost time for the Jewish Passover,[h] many went up from the
country to Jerusalem for their ceremonial
cleansing[i] before the Passover. 56They
kept looking for Jesus,[j] and as they stood
in the temple area they asked one another, "What do you think? Isn't he coming to
the Feast at all?" 57But the chief priests
and Pharisees had given orders that if
anyone found out where Jesus was, he
should report it so that they might arrest
him.

Jesus Anointed at Bethany

12:1–8Ref — Mt 26:6–13; Mk 14:3–9; Lk 7:37–39

12 Six days before the Passover,[k]
Jesus arrived at Bethany,[l] where
Lazarus lived, whom Jesus had raised
from the dead. 2Here a dinner was given
in Jesus' honor. Martha served,[m] while
Lazarus was among those reclining at the
table with him. 3Then Mary took about a
pint[e] of pure nard, an expensive perfume;[n] she poured it on Jesus' feet and
wiped his feet with her hair.[o] And the
house was filled with the fragrance of the
perfume.

d *48* Or *temple* e *3* Greek *a litra* (probably about 0.5 liter)

11:36 f ver 3 **11:37** g Jn 9:6,7 h ver 21,32 **11:38** i ver 33 j Mt 27:60; Lk 24:2; Jn 20:1 **11:39** k ver 17 **11:40** l ver 23-25 m ver 4 **11:41** n Jn 17:1 o S Mt 11:25 **11:42** p Jn 12:30 q S Jn 3:17 **11:43** r S Lk 7:14 **11:44** s Jn 19:40 t Jn 20:7 **11:45** u ver 19 v Jn 2:23 w Ex 14:31; S Jn 7:31 **11:47** x ver 57 y Mt 26:3 z S Mt 5:22 a S Jn 2:11 **11:49** b S Mt 26:3 c ver 51; Jn 18:13, 14 **11:50** d Jn 18:14 **11:52** e Isa 49:6; Jn 10:16 **11:53** f S Mt 12:14 **11:54** g Jn 7:1 **11:55** h Ex 12:13, 23,27; Mt 26:1,2; Mk 14:1; Jn 13:1 i 2Ch 30:17,18 **11:56** j Jn 7:11 **12:1** k S Jn 11:55 l S Mt 21:17 **12:2** m Lk 10:38-42 **12:3** n Mk 14:3 o Jn 11:2

all who experience sorrow. Christ feels the same sympathy for you that he felt for the relatives of Lazarus. He loves you that much. Note that this verse occurs in the book that stresses his divinity more than any other book. This was Jesus — the God/man, deity itself — weeping. God does have a deep, emotional and sympathetic love for you and others (Lk 19:41).

11:44 THE DEAD MAN CAME OUT. The miracle of Lazarus's resurrection was a sign pointing to Jesus as the resurrection and the life. It was a demonstration of what God will do for all believers who have died, for they too will be raised from the dead (14:3; 1Th 4:13–18). This miracle was also the final issue that caused the Jewish leaders to resolve that Jesus must be put to death (vv. 45–53).

12:3 MARY ... POURED IT ON JESUS' FEET. Mary's anointing of Jesus was an act of great sacrifice, since the perfume was very expensive. She knew that her opportunity to express devotion to Jesus would soon be over, so she took the opportunity she had. Her faith in and devotion to the Lord is the highest example of what God desires in believers. For this reason Jesus stated that her act of love would be told wherever the gospel is preached (see Mt 26:13, note).

JESUS IN JUDEA AND SAMARIA

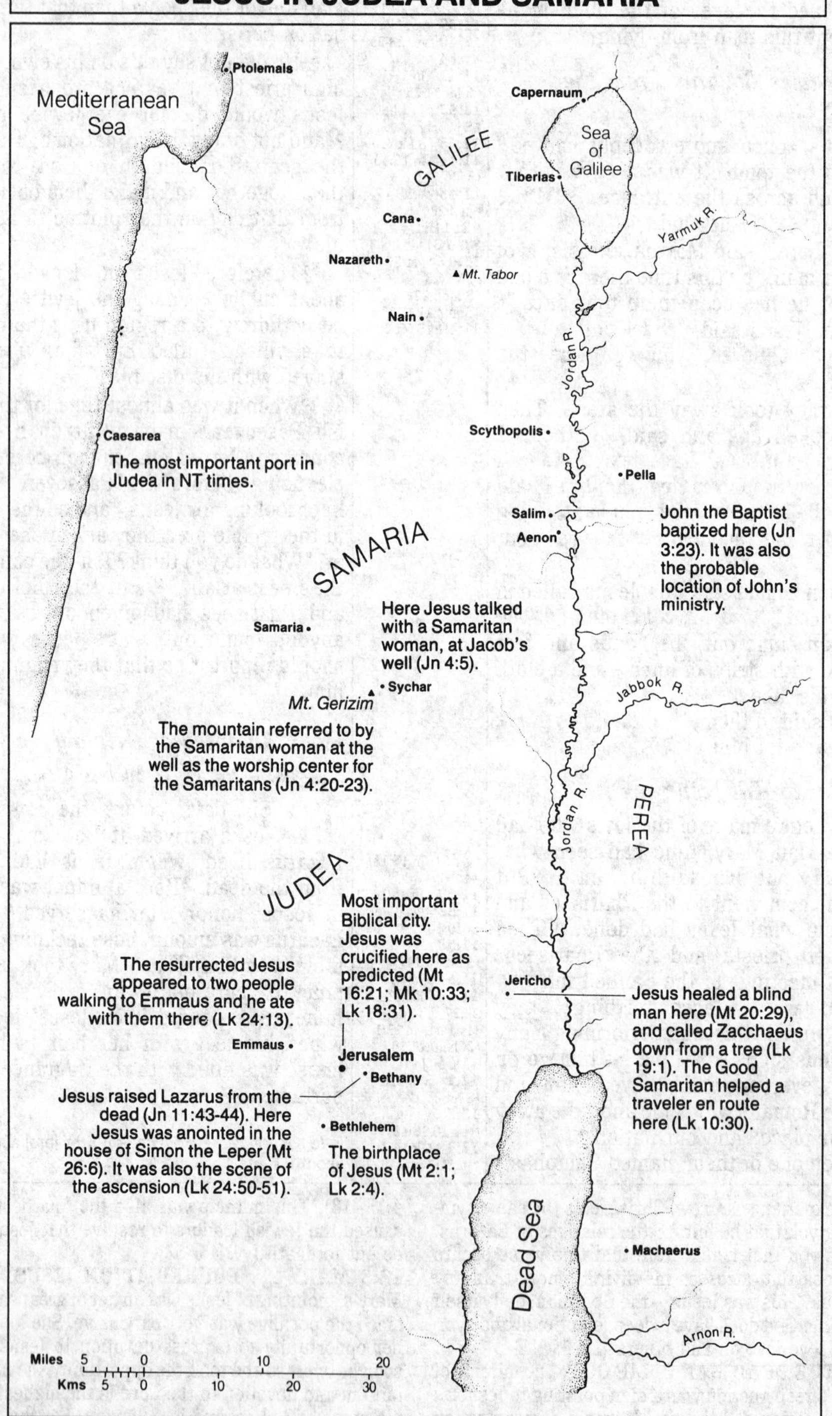

Ptolemais
Mediterranean Sea
Capernaum
Sea of Galilee
GALILEE
Tiberias
Cana
Yarmuk R.
Nazareth
Mt. Tabor
Nain
Jordan R.
Caesarea
Scythopolis
The most important port in Judea in NT times.
Pella
Salim
John the Baptist baptized here (Jn 3:23). It was also the probable location of John's ministry.
Aenon
SAMARIA
Here Jesus talked with a Samaritan woman, at Jacob's well (Jn 4:5).
Samaria
Sychar
Mt. Gerizim
Jabbok R.
The mountain referred to by the Samaritan woman at the well as the worship center for the Samaritans (Jn 4:20-23).
Jordan R.
PEREA
JUDEA
Most important Biblical city. Jesus was crucified here as predicted (Mt 16:21; Mk 10:33; Lk 18:31).
The resurrected Jesus appeared to two people walking to Emmaus and he ate with them there (Lk 24:13).
Jericho
Jesus healed a blind man here (Mt 20:29), and called Zacchaeus down from a tree (Lk 19:1). The Good Samaritan helped a traveler en route here (Lk 10:30).
Emmaus
Jerusalem
Bethany
Jesus raised Lazarus from the dead (Jn 11:43-44). Here Jesus was anointed in the house of Simon the Leper (Mt 26:6). It was also the scene of the ascension (Lk 24:50-51).
Bethlehem
The birthplace of Jesus (Mt 2:1; Lk 2:4).
Dead Sea
Machaerus
Arnon R.
Miles 5 0 10 20
Kms 5 0 10 20 30

4But one of his disciples, Judas Iscariot,
who was later to betray him,[p] objected,
5"Why wasn't this perfume sold and the
money given to the poor? It was worth a
year's wages.[f]" **6**He did not say this because he cared about the poor but because
he was a thief; as keeper of the money
bag,[q] he used to help himself to what was
put into it.

7"Leave her alone," Jesus replied. "It
was intended that she should save this
perfume for the day of my burial.[r] **8**You
will always have the poor among you,[s]
but you will not always have me."

9Meanwhile a large crowd of Jews
found out that Jesus was there and came,
not only because of him but also to see
Lazarus, whom he had raised from the
dead.[t] **10**So the chief priests made plans
to kill Lazarus as well, **11**for on account of
him[u] many of the Jews were going over to
Jesus and putting their faith in him.[v]

The Triumphal Entry

12:12–15pp — Mt 21:4–9; Mk 11:7–10; Lk 19:35–38

12The next day the great crowd that
had come for the Feast heard that Jesus
was on his way to Jerusalem. **13**They took
palm branches[w] and went out to meet
him, shouting,

"Hosanna![g]"
"Blessed is he who comes in the
name of the Lord!"[h][x]
"Blessed is the King of Israel!"[y]

14Jesus found a young donkey and sat
upon it, as it is written,

15"Do not be afraid, O Daughter of
Zion;
see, your king is coming,
seated on a donkey's colt."[i][z]

16At first his disciples did not understand all this.[a] Only after Jesus was glorified[b] did they realize that these things
had been written about him and that they
had done these things to him.

12:4 p S Mt 10:4
12:6 q Jn 13:29
12:7 r Jn 19:40
12:8 s Dt 15:11
12:9 t Jn 11:43,44
12:11 u ver 17, 18; Jn 11:45 v S Jn 7:31
12:13 w Lev 23:40 x Ps 118:25,26 y S Jn 1:49
12:15 z Zec 9:9
12:16 a S Mk 9:32 b ver 23; Jn 2:22; 7:39

17Now the crowd that was with him[c]
when he called Lazarus from the tomb and
raised him from the dead continued to
spread the word. **18**Many people, because
they had heard that he had given this miraculous sign,[d] went out to meet him.
19So the Pharisees said to one another,
"See, this is getting us nowhere. Look
how the whole world has gone after
him!"[e]

Jesus Predicts His Death

20Now there were some Greeks[f]
among those who went up to worship at
the Feast. **21**They came to Philip, who was
from Bethsaida[g] in Galilee, with a request. "Sir," they said, "we would like to
see Jesus." **22**Philip went to tell Andrew;
Andrew and Philip in turn told Jesus.

23Jesus replied, "The hour[h] has come
for the Son of Man to be glorified.[i] **24**I tell
you the truth, unless a kernel of wheat
falls to the ground and dies,[j] it remains
only a single seed. But if it dies, it produces many seeds. **25**The man who loves
his life will lose it, while the man who
hates his life in this world will keep it[k] for
eternal life.[l] **26**Whoever serves me must
follow me; and where I am, my servant
also will be.[m] My Father will honor the
one who serves me.

27"Now my heart is troubled,[n] and what
shall I say? 'Father,[o] save me from this
hour'?[p] No, it was for this very reason I
came to this hour. **28**Father, glorify your
name!"

Then a voice came from heaven,[q] "I
have glorified it, and will glorify it again."
29The crowd that was there and heard it
said it had thundered; others said an angel had spoken to him.

30Jesus said, "This voice was for your
benefit,[r] not mine. **31**Now is the time for
judgment on this world;[s] now the prince

12:17 c Jn 11:42
12:18 d ver 11; Lk 19:37
12:19 e Jn 11:47, 48
12:20 f Jn 7:35; Ac 11:20
12:21 g S Mt 11:21
12:23 h S Mt 26:18 i Jn 13:32; 17:1
12:24 j 1Co 15:36
12:25 k Mt 10:39; Mk 8:35; Lk 14:26; 17:33 l S Mt 25:46
12:26 m Jn 14:3; 17:24; 2Co 5:8; Php 1:23; 1Th 4:17
12:27 n Mt 26:38, 39; Jn 11:33,38; 13:21 o S Mt 11:25 p ver 23
12:28 q S Mt 3:17
12:30 r Ex 19:9; Jn 11:42
12:31 s Jn 16:11

f *5* Greek *three hundred denarii* **g** *13* A Hebrew expression meaning "Save!" which became an exclamation of praise **h** *13* Psalm 118:25, 26 **i** *15* Zech. 9:9

12:12 THE TRIUMPHAL ENTRY. See Mk 11:9, note; Lk 19:28, note.

12:23 SON OF MAN . . . GLORIFIED. Jesus speaks of his death as a glorification rather than a tragedy. He tells his disciples that the way to fruitfulness is through suffering and death (v. 24).

12:25 HATES HIS LIFE IN THIS WORLD. Hating one's own life points to the attitude that values heavenly interests far above those of this earth. Those who follow Christ place little importance in the pleasures, philosophies, successes, values, goals or ways of the world. These will gain "eternal life," for they count nothing in this world so dear that they will not give it up for the sake of the Lord (Mt 16:24–25; Mk 8:34–35).

12:26 WHOEVER SERVES ME. Faith in Jesus involves a personal commitment to follow him, keep his teaching and be where he is. Following Jesus includes self-denial and taking up one's cross (see Mk 8:34, note on the meaning of taking up one's cross).

12:31 PRINCE OF THIS WORLD WILL BE DRIVEN OUT. Through the cross and resurrection of Christ the defeat of Satan and all he stands for has begun. His final defeat will occur when he is thrown into the

of this world[t] will be driven out. 32But I,
when I am lifted up from the earth,[u] will
draw all men to myself."[v] 33He said this
to show the kind of death he was going to
die.[w]

34The crowd spoke up, "We have heard
from the Law[x] that the Christ[j] will remain forever,[y] so how can you say, 'The
Son of Man[z] must be lifted up'?[a] Who is
this 'Son of Man'?"

35Then Jesus told them, "You are going
to have the light[b] just a little while longer. Walk while you have the light,[c] before
darkness overtakes you.[d] The man who
walks in the dark does not know where he
is going. 36Put your trust in the light while
you have it, so that you may become sons
of light."[e] When he had finished speaking,
Jesus left and hid himself from them.[f]

The Jews Continue in Their Unbelief

37Even after Jesus had done all these
miraculous signs[g] in their presence, they
still would not believe in him. 38This was
to fulfill the word of Isaiah the prophet:

"Lord, who has believed our message
and to whom has the arm of the
Lord been revealed?"[k][h]

39For this reason they could not believe, because, as Isaiah says elsewhere:

40"He has blinded their eyes
and deadened their hearts,
so they can neither see with their
eyes,
nor understand with their hearts,
nor turn—and I would heal
them."[l][i]

41Isaiah said this because he saw Jesus'
glory[j] and spoke about him.[k]

42Yet at the same time many even
among the leaders believed in him.[l] But
because of the Pharisees[m] they would not
confess their faith for fear they would be
put out of the synagogue;[n] 43for they
loved praise from men[o] more than praise
from God.[p]

44Then Jesus cried out, "When a man
believes in me, he does not believe in me
only, but in the one who sent me.[q] 45When
he looks at me, he sees the one who sent
me.[r] 46I have come into the world as a
light,[s] so that no one who believes in me
should stay in darkness.

47"As for the person who hears my
words but does not keep them, I do not
judge him. For I did not come to judge the
world, but to save it.[t] 48There is a judge
for the one who rejects me and does not
accept my words; that very word which I
spoke will condemn him[u] at the last day.
49For I did not speak of my own accord,
but the Father who sent me commanded
me[v] what to say and how to say it. 50I
know that his command leads to eternal
life.[w] So whatever I say is just what the
Father has told me to say."[x]

Jesus Washes His Disciples' Feet

13 It was just before the Passover
Feast.[y] Jesus knew that the time
had come[z] for him to leave this world and
go to the Father.[a] Having loved his own
who were in the world, he now showed
them the full extent of his love.[m]

2The evening meal was being served,
and the devil had already prompted Judas
Iscariot, son of Simon, to betray Jesus.[b]
3Jesus knew that the Father had put all
things under his power,[c] and that he had
come from God[d] and was returning to

12:31 [t]Jn 14:30; 16:11; 2Co 4:4; Eph 2:2; 1Jn 4:4; 5:19
12:32 [u]ver 34; Isa 11:10; Jn 3:14; 8:28 [v]Jn 6:44
12:33 [w]Jn 18:32; 21:19
12:34 [x]S Jn 10:34 [y]Ps 110:4; Isa 9:7; Eze 37:25; Da 7:14 [z]S Mt 8:20 [a]Jn 3:14
12:35 [b]ver 46 [c]Eph 5:8 [d]1Jn 1:6; 2:11
12:36 [e]ver 46; S Lk 16:8 [f]Jn 8:59
12:37 [g]S Jn 2:11
12:38 [h]Isa 53:1; Ro 10:16
12:40 [i]Isa 6:10; S Mt 13:13,15
12:41 [j]Isa 6:1-4 [k]Lk 24:27
12:42 [l]ver 11; Jn 7:48 [m]S Jn 7:13 [n]Jn 9:22
12:43 [o]1Sa 15:30 [p]S Ro 2:29
12:44 [q]S Mt 10:40; Jn 5:24
12:45 [r]S Jn 14:9
12:46 [s]S Jn 1:4
12:47 [t]S Jn 3:17
12:48 [u]Jn 5:45
12:49 [v]Jn 14:31
12:50 [w]S Mt 25:46 [x]S Jn 14:24
13:1 [y]S Jn 11:55 [z]S Mt 26:18 [a]Jn 16:28
13:2 [b]S Mt 10:4
13:3 [c]S Mt 28:18 [d]Jn 8:42; 16:27, 28,30; 17:8

[j] *34* Or *Messiah* [k] *38* Isaiah 53:1
[l] *40* Isaiah 6:10 [m] *1* Or *he loved them to the last*

---

lake of burning sulfur (Rev 20:10). At this present time, however, Satan is still active as the ruler or "prince of this world" (14:30; 16:11; 2Co 4:4; cf. Eph 2:2). Satan has power and authority in the world and uses the things of the world against Christ and the church. This is why "friendship with the world is hatred toward God" (Jas 4:4; see also 1Jn 2:15–16).

12:32 DRAW ALL MEN TO MYSELF. The grace of God is not exclusive, i.e., for some people, but not for others. However, some, because of their love for sin, nullify God's grace by their decisions and actions (see Mt 23:37).

12:39 THEY COULD NOT BELIEVE. The people could not believe because their decisions about Jesus brought God's action of hardening. The gospel never leaves unchanged the person who refuses to listen, repent and believe. The apostle Paul says that the people of Israel were broken off because of their unbelief (Ro 11:20; cf. Ps 95:8; Heb 3:8). Yet the hardening was not permanent for every individual in that nation. Anyone who believed would receive eternal life (vv. 44–50). In fact, many in Israel did believe after Pentecost (Ac 2:41).

12:43 LOVED PRAISE FROM MEN. Because they love the approval of their fellow human beings, many sacrifice their convictions and act contrary to their consciences. They are ready to join the majority (cf. Da 11:32,34) and seek the favorable opinion of the powerful or the crowd. What is the secret of gaining victory over the fear of others and the desire for their praise? It is our faith (1Jn 5:4)—the faith that sees God, Christ, heaven, hell, the judgment and eternity as ultimate realities (Ro 1:20; Eph 3:16–19; Heb 11). Professing to follow Christ while loving human glory above God's glory is blatant hypocrisy.

12:50 ETERNAL LIFE. See 17:3, note.

God; 4so he got up from the meal, took off
his outer clothing, and wrapped a towel
around his waist.[e] 5After that, he poured
water into a basin and began to wash his
disciples' feet,[f] drying them with the towel that was wrapped around him.

6He came to Simon Peter, who said to
him, "Lord, are you going to wash my
feet?"

7Jesus replied, "You do not realize now
what I am doing, but later you will understand."[g]

8"No," said Peter, "you shall never
wash my feet."

Jesus answered, "Unless I wash you,
you have no part with me."

9"Then, Lord," Simon Peter replied,
"not just my feet but my hands and my
head as well!"

10Jesus answered, "A person who has
had a bath needs only to wash his feet; his
whole body is clean. And you are clean,[h]
though not every one of you."[i] 11For he
knew who was going to betray him,[j] and
that was why he said not every one was
clean.

12When he had finished washing their
feet, he put on his clothes and returned to
his place. "Do you understand what I have
done for you?" he asked them. 13"You call
me 'Teacher'[k] and 'Lord,'[l] and rightly so,
for that is what I am. 14Now that I, your
Lord and Teacher, have washed your feet,
you also should wash one another's feet.[m]
15I have set you an example that you
should do as I have done for you.[n] 16I tell
you the truth, no servant is greater than
his master,[o] nor is a messenger greater
than the one who sent him. 17Now that
you know these things, you will be blessed
if you do them.[p]

Jesus Predicts His Betrayal

18"I am not referring to all of you;[q] I
know those I have chosen.[r] But this is to
fulfill the scripture:[s] 'He who shares my
bread[t] has lifted up his heel[u] against
me.'[n][v]

19"I am telling you now before it happens, so that when it does happen you will
believe[w] that I am He.[x] 20I tell you the
truth, whoever accepts anyone I send accepts me; and whoever accepts me accepts the one who sent me."[y]

21After he had said this, Jesus was troubled in spirit[z] and testified, "I tell you the
truth, one of you is going to betray me."[a]

22His disciples stared at one another, at
a loss to know which of them he meant.
23One of them, the disciple whom Jesus
loved,[b] was reclining next to him. 24Si-
mon Peter motioned to this disciple and
said, "Ask him which one he means."

25Leaning back against Jesus, he asked
him, "Lord, who is it?"[c]

26Jesus answered, "It is the one to
whom I will give this piece of bread when
I have dipped it in the dish." Then, dipping
the piece of bread, he gave it to Judas
Iscariot,[d] son of Simon. 27As soon as Judas took the bread, Satan entered into
him.[e]

"What you are about to do, do quickly,"
Jesus told him, 28but no one at the meal
understood why Jesus said this to him.
29Since Judas had charge of the money,[f]
some thought Jesus was telling him to buy
what was needed for the Feast,[g] or to give
something to the poor.[h] 30As soon as Judas had taken the bread, he went out. And
it was night.[i]

13:4 [e] S Mt 20:28
13:5 [f] S Lk 7:44
13:7 [g] ver 12
13:10 [h] Jn 15:3 [i] ver 18
13:11 [j] S Mt 10:4
13:13 [k] Mt 26:18; Jn 11:28 [l] S Mt 28:18; Lk 1:43; 2:11; 6:46; 11:1; Ac 10:36; Ro 10:9, 12; 14:9; 1Co 12:3; Php 2:11; Col 2:6
13:14 [m] 1Pe 5:5
13:15 [n] S Mt 11:29; S 1Ti 4:12
13:16 [o] Mt 10:24; Lk 6:40; Jn 15:20
13:17 [p] Mt 7:24, 25; Lk 11:28; Jas 1:25
13:18 [q] ver 10 [r] Jn 15:16,19 [s] S Mt 1:22 [t] Mt 26:23 [u] Jn 6:70 [v] Ps 41:9
13:19 [w] Jn 14:29; 16:4 [x] Jn 4:26; 8:24
13:20 [y] S Mt 10:40
13:21 [z] S Jn 12:27 [a] Mt 26:21
13:23 [b] Jn 19:26; 20:2; 21:7,20
13:25 [c] Mt 26:22; Jn 21:20
13:26 [d] S Mt 10:4
13:27 [e] Lk 22:3
13:29 [f] Jn 12:6 [g] ver 1 [h] Jn 12:5
13:30 [i] Lk 22:53

[n] *18* Psalm 41:9

13:5 WASH HIS DISCIPLES' FEET. This dramatic act of foot washing occurred on the last night of Jesus' life on earth. Jesus did it (1) to demonstrate to his disciples how much he loved them; (2) to foreshadow his self-sacrifice on the cross; and (3) to convey the truth that he was calling his disciples to serve one another in humility. The passion to be great had continually plagued the disciples (Mt 18:1–4; 20:20–27; Mk 9:33–37; Lk 9:46–48). Christ wanted them to see that the desire to be first—to be superior and honored above fellow Christians—is contrary to the spirit of their Lord (see Lk 22:24–30, note; Jn 13:12–17; 1Pe 5:5).

13:8 UNLESS I WASH YOU. These words point to a spiritual washing from sin through the cross. Apart from this washing no one can belong to Christ (1Jn 1:7).

13:14 WASH ONE ANOTHER'S FEET. The early church appears to have followed Jesus' example and literally obeyed his admonition to humbly wash one another's feet in love. For example, in 1Ti 5:10 Paul states that widows should not be cared for by the church if they failed to qualify according to certain standards. One of those qualifications was "washing the feet of the saints."

13:22 AT A LOSS TO KNOW WHICH OF THEM HE MEANT. It is important to note that at no time did the disciples discern Judas's duplicity. He had covered his hypocrisy very well. Even today there will be those in the church who outwardly appear righteous, yet inwardly have no real faith in and devotion to Christ (see article on FALSE TEACHERS, p. 98).

13:26 PIECE OF BREAD. Jesus' giving the piece of bread to Judas was probably a final appeal to persuade him to turn from his sin. Judas, however, refused to change his mind, and Satan took control (v. 27; see Lk 22:3, note).

Jesus Predicts Peter's Denial

13:37,38pp — Mt 26:33–35; Mk 14:29–31; Lk 22:33,34

31When he was gone, Jesus said, "Now
is the Son of Man[j] glorified[k] and God is
glorified in him.[l] **32**If God is glorified in
him,[o] God will glorify the Son in himself,[m]
and will glorify him at once.

33"My children, I will be with you only
a little longer. You will look for me, and
just as I told the Jews, so I tell you now:
Where I am going, you cannot come.[n]

34"A new command[o] I give you: Love
one another.[p] As I have loved you, so you
must love one another.[q] **35**By this all men
will know that you are my disciples, if you
love one another."[r]

36Simon Peter asked him, "Lord, where
are you going?"[s]

Jesus replied, "Where I am going, you
cannot follow now,[t] but you will follow
later."[u]

37Peter asked, "Lord, why can't I follow
you now? I will lay down my life for you."

38Then Jesus answered, "Will you
really lay down your life for me? I tell you
the truth, before the rooster crows, you
will disown me three times![v]

13:31 [j]S Mt 8:20 [k]Jn 7:39; 12:23 [l]Jn 14:13; 17:4; 1Pe 4:11 **13:32** [m]Jn 17:1 **13:33** [n]S Jn 7:33, 34 **13:34** [o]Jn 15:12; 1Jn 2:7-11; 3:11 [p]Lev 19:18; 1Th 4:9; 1Pe 1:22 [q]Jn 15:12; Eph 5:2; 1Jn 4:10, 11 **13:35** [r]1Jn 3:14; 4:20 **13:36** [s]Jn 16:5 [t]ver 33; Jn 14:2 [u]Jn 21:18,19; 2Pe 1:14 **13:38** [v]Jn 18:27

Jesus Promises to Return

14 "Do not let your hearts be troubled.[w] Trust[x] in God[p];[y] trust also
in me. **2**In my Father's house are many
rooms; if it were not so, I would have told
you. I am going there[z] to prepare a place
for you. **3**And if I go and prepare a place
for you, I will come back[a] and take you to
be with me that you also may be where I
am.[b] **4**You know the way to the place
where I am going."

Jesus the Way to the Father

5Thomas[c] said to him, "Lord, we don't
know where you are going, so how can we
know the way?"

6Jesus answered, "I am[d] the way[e] and
the truth[f] and the life.[g] No one comes to
the Father except through me.[h] **7**If you
really knew me, you would know[q] my Father as well.[i] From now on, you do know
him and have seen him."

8Philip[j] said, "Lord, show us the Father and that will be enough for us."

14:1 [w]ver 27 [x]S Jn 3:15 [y]Ps 4:5 **14:2** [z]Jn 13:33, 36; 16:5 **14:3** [a]ver 18,28; S Mt 16:27 [b]S Jn 12:26 **14:5** [c]S Jn 11:16 **14:6** [d]S Jn 6:35 [e]Jn 10:9; Eph 2:18; Heb 10:20 [f]Jn 1:14 [g]S Jn 1:4 [h]Ac 4:12 **14:7** [i]Jn 1:18; S 1Jn 2:23 **14:8** [j]S Jn 1:43

o *32* Many early manuscripts do not have *If God is glorified in him.* p *1* Or *You trust in God* q *7* Some early manuscripts *If you really have known me, you will know*

13:34 LOVE ONE ANOTHER. The Christian is commanded to love, in a greater and special way, all true Christians, whether or not they are members of one's own church or followers of one's particular theological persuasion. (1) Believers must distinguish true Christians from those whose profession is false by examining their love for and obedience to Jesus Christ and their loyalty to God's holy Word (5:24; 8:31; 10:27; Mt 7:21; Gal 1:9, note).

(2) Any person who possesses a living faith in Jesus Christ and remains loyal to God's inspired and inerrant Word as he or she sincerely understands it, while standing against the prevailing popular spirit of our day, is my brother or sister in Christ and one who deserves my special love and support.

(3) Loving all true Christians, including those who are not of our church, does not mean that we must compromise or accommodate our particular Biblical beliefs or doctrinal differences. Nor does it mean we must necessarily seek organizational unity.

(4) Christians must never compromise God's holiness. Love for God and his will as revealed in his Word must control and direct our love for others. Love for God must always be first (see next note; Mt 22:37,39, notes).

13:35 KNOW THAT YOU ARE MY DISCIPLES. Love (Gk *agapē*) must be the distinguishing mark of Christ's followers (1Jn 3:23; 4:7–21). This agape love is basically a self-giving and sacrificial love that seeks the good of another (1Jn 4:9–10). Thus, the relationship among all believers must be characterized by a devoted concern that sacrificially seeks to promote the highest good of our brothers and sisters in Christ. Christians must befriend each other in trials, be careful of each other's feelings and reputation, and deny themselves to promote each other's welfare (cf. 1Co 13; Gal 6:2; 1Th 4:9; 2Th 1:3; 1Pe 1:22; 2Pe 1:7; 1Jn 3:23).

14:2 MY FATHER'S HOUSE. This phrase clearly refers to heaven, for Jesus must "go" there to prepare a place for us (Mt 6:9; cf. Ps 33:13–14; Isa 63:15). God has a home where there are many rooms and to which "God's household" now on earth (Eph 2:19) will be transferred; "here we do not have an enduring city" (Heb 13:14).

14:3 I WILL COME BACK. (1) As surely as Christ went to heaven, so he will return from his Father's presence and take his followers to be with him in heaven (see previous note; cf. 17:24), to the place prepared for them. This was the hope of NT Christians, and is the hope of all believers today. The ultimate purpose of the Lord's return is that believers may be with him forever (see articles on THE RESURRECTION OF THE BODY, p. 357, and THE RAPTURE, p. 440).

(2) The words "take you to be with me" refer to the rapture, when all living believers "will be caught up together . . . in the clouds to meet the Lord in the air. And so we will be with the Lord forever" (1Th 4:17).

(3) Christ's coming for his faithful will enable them to escape the future "hour of trial" that will come upon the world (see Lk 21:36, note; 1Th 1:10, note; 5:9; Rev 3:10, note).

(4) This glorious and eternal reunion is a comforting doctrine for all followers of Jesus who desire to "be with the Lord forever. Therefore encourage each other with these words" (1Th 4:17–18).

9Jesus answered: "Don't you know me,
Philip, even after I have been among you
such a long time? Anyone who has seen
me has seen the Father.[k] How can you
say, 'Show us the Father'? 10Don't you
believe that I am in the Father, and that
the Father is in me?[l] The words I say to
you are not just my own.[m] Rather, it is the
Father, living in me, who is doing his
work. 11Believe me when I say that I am
in the Father and the Father is in me; or
at least believe on the evidence of the miracles themselves.[n] 12I tell you the truth,
anyone who has faith[o] in me will do what
I have been doing.[p] He will do even greater things than these, because I am going
Ac 3:16 to the Father. 13And I will do whatever
you ask[q] in my name, so that the Son may
bring glory to the Father. 14You may ask
me for anything in my name, and I will
do it.

14:9 [k]Isa 9:6; Jn 1:14; 12:45; 2Co 4:4; Php 2:6; Col 1:15; Heb 1:3 **14:10** [l]ver 11,20; Jn 10:38; 17:21 [m]S ver 24 **14:11** [n]Jn 5:36; 10:38 **14:12** [o]Mt 21:21 [p]Lk 10:17 **14:13** [q]S Mt 7:7

14:15 [r]ver 21,23; Ps 103:18; Jn 15:10; 1Jn 2:3-5; 3:22,24; 5:3; 2Jn 6; Rev 12:17; 14:12 **14:16** [s]ver 26; Jn 15:26; 16:7 **14:17** [t]Jn 15:26; 16:13; 1Jn 4:6; 5:6 [u]1Co 2:14 **14:18** [v]1Ki 6:13 [w]ver 3,28; S Mt 16:27 **14:19** [x]Jn 7:33, 34; 16:16 [y]Jn 6:57 **14:20** [z]Jn 16:23, 26 [a]ver 10,11; Jn 10:38; 17:21

Jesus Promises the Holy Spirit

15"If you love me, you will obey what I
command.[r] 16And I will ask the Father,
and he will give you another Counselor[s]
to be with you forever— 17the Spirit of
truth.[t] The world cannot accept him,[u] because it neither sees him nor knows him.
But you know him, for he lives with you
and will be[r] in you. 18I will not leave you
as orphans;[v] I will come to you.[w] 19Be-
fore long, the world will not see me anymore, but you will see me.[x] Because I
live, you also will live.[y] 20On that day[z]
you will realize that I am in my Father,[a]
and you are in me, and I am in you.[b]
21Whoever has my commands and obeys
them, he is the one who loves me.[c] He

[b]S Ro 8:10 **14:21** [c]S ver 15

[r] *17* Some early manuscripts *and is*

14:12 GREATER THINGS. It is Jesus' desire that his followers do the works that he did. (1) The "greater things" include both the work of converting people to Christ and the performing of miracles. This is shown in the narratives of Acts (Ac 2:41,43; 4:33; 5:12) and in Jesus' declaration in Mk 16:17–18 (see article on SIGNS OF BELIEVERS, p. 106). (2) The reason for the "greater things" done by the disciples is that Jesus will go to his Father, send forth the power of the Holy Spirit (see v. 16; 16:7; Ac 1:8; 2:4) and answer prayer in his name (v. 14). The disciples' works will be "greater" in number and scope.

14:13 ASK IN MY NAME. Prayer in Jesus' name involves at least two things: (1) praying in harmony with his person, character and will; (2) praying with faith in him and his authority, and with the desire to glorify both the Father and the Son (Ac 3:16). Praying in the name of Jesus, therefore, means that Jesus will answer any prayer that he would have prayed himself. There is no limit to the power of prayer when addressed to Jesus or the Father in holy faith according to his desire (see Mt 17:20, note).

14:16 I WILL ASK THE FATHER. Jesus will ask the Father to give the Counselor only to those who are serious about their love for him and their devotion to his Word. Jesus uses the present tense in v. 15 ("If you love me"), thus emphasizing a continuing attitude of love and obedience.

14:16 COUNSELOR. Jesus calls the Holy Spirit a "Counselor." "Counselor" translates the Greek *paraklētos*, meaning literally "one called alongside to help." This is a rich word, meaning Counselor, Strengthener, Comforter, Helper, Adviser, Advocate, Intercessor, Ally and Friend.

(1) Jesus promises to send *another* Counselor. The Holy Spirit will do for the disciples what Christ did for them while he was with them. The Spirit will be by their side to help and strengthen them (cf. Mt 14:30–31), to teach the true course for their lives (v. 26), to comfort in difficult situations (v. 18), to intercede in prayer for them (Ro 8:26–27; cf. 8:34), to be a friend to further their best interest (v. 17) and to remain with them forever.

(2) The word *paraklētos* is applied to the Lord Jesus in 1Jn 2:1. Therefore Jesus is our helper and intercessor in heaven (cf. Heb 7:25), while the Holy Spirit is our indwelling helper and intercessor on earth (Ro 8:9,26; 1Co 3:16; 6:19; 2Co 6:16; 2Ti 1:14).

14:17 THE SPIRIT OF TRUTH. The Holy Spirit is called "the Spirit of truth" (15:26; 16:13; cf. 1Jn 4:6; 5:6), because he is the Spirit of Jesus, who is the truth. As such, he testifies to the truth (18:37), enlightens concerning the truth, exposes untruth (16:8) and guides the believer into all truth (16:13). Those who are willing to sacrifice truth for the sake of unity, love or any other reason deny the Spirit of truth, whom they claim lives in them. The church that abandons the truth abandons its Lord. The Holy Spirit will not be the Counselor of those who are indifferent to the faith or halfhearted in their commitment to the truth. He comes only to those who worship the Lord "in spirit and in truth" (4:24).

14:17 WITH YOU AND WILL BE IN YOU. The Holy Spirit now lives with the disciples, and Christ promises them that in the future he will "be in you." This promise of the indwelling of the Holy Spirit was fulfilled after Christ's resurrection when he breathed on them and said to them, "Receive the Holy Spirit" (20:22). For a discussion of the role of the Spirit in regeneration, see article on THE REGENERATION OF THE DISCIPLES, p. 212.

14:18 I WILL COME TO YOU. Jesus reveals himself to the obedient believer through the Holy Spirit, who makes known the personal presence of Jesus in and with the one who loves him (v. 21). The Spirit makes us aware of the nearness of Jesus and the reality of his love, his blessing and his help. This is one of the Spirit's primary tasks. The fact that Christ comes to us through the Spirit should cause us to respond in love, worship and devotion.

14:21 WHOEVER HAS MY COMMANDS. Obeying the commands of Christ is not optional for those who would have eternal life (3:36; 14:21,23; 15:8–10,13–14; Lk 6:46–49; Jas 1:22; 2Pe 1:5–11,

who loves me will be loved by my Father,[d]
and I too will love him and show myself to
him."
22Then Judas[e] (not Judas Iscariot)
said, "But, Lord, why do you intend to
show yourself to us and not to the
world?"[f]
23Jesus replied, "If anyone loves me, he
will obey my teaching.[g] My Father will
love him, and we will come to him and
make our home with him.[h] **24**He who does
not love me will not obey my teaching.
These words you hear are not my own;
they belong to the Father who sent me.[i]
25"All this I have spoken while still
with you. **26**But the Counselor,[j] the Holy
Spirit, whom the Father will send in my
name,[k] will teach you all things[l] and will
remind you of everything I have said to
you.[m] **27**Peace I leave with you; my peace
I give you.[n] I do not give to you as the
world gives. Do not let your hearts be
troubled[o] and do not be afraid.
28"You heard me say, 'I am going away
and I am coming back to you.'[p] If you

14:21 [d]Dt 7:13; Jn 16:27; 1Jn 2:5
14:22 [e]Lk 6:16; Ac 1:13 [f]Ac 10:41
14:23 [g]S ver 15 [h]S Ro 8:10
14:24 [i]ver 10; Dt 18:18; Jn 5:19; 7:16; 8:28; 12:49, 50
14:26 [j]ver 16; Jn 15:26; 16:7 [k]Ac 2:33 [l]Jn 16:13; 1Jn 2:20,27 [m]Jn 2:22
14:27 [n]Nu 6:26; Ps 85:8; Mal 2:6; S Lk 2:14; 24:36; Jn 16:33; Php 4:7; Col 3:15 [o]ver 1
14:28 [p]ver 2-4, 18; S Mt 16:27 [q]Jn 5:18 [r]Jn 10:29
14:29 [s]Jn 13:19; 16:4
14:30 [t]S Jn 12:31
14:31 [u]Jn 10:18; 12:49
15:1 [v]S Jn 6:35 [w]Ps 80:8-11; Isa 5:1-7
15:2 [x]ver 6; S Mt 3:10 [y]Ps 92:14; Mt 3:8; 7:20; Gal 5:22; Eph 5:9; Php 1:11

loved me, you would be glad that I am
going to the Father,[q] for the Father is
greater than I.[r] **29**I have told you now
before it happens, so that when it does
happen you will believe.[s] **30**I will not
speak with you much longer, for the
prince of this world[t] is coming. He has no
hold on me, **31**but the world must learn
that I love the Father and that I do exactly
what my Father has commanded me.[u]
"Come now; let us leave.

The Vine and the Branches

15 "I am[v] the true vine,[w] and my Father is the gardener. **2**He cuts off
every branch in me that bears no fruit,[x]
while every branch that does bear fruit[y]
he prunes[s] so that it will be even more
fruitful. **3**You are already clean because of
the word I have spoken to you.[z] **4**Remain
in me, and I will remain in you.[a] No

15:3 [z]Jn 13:10; 17:17; Eph 5:26 **15:4** [a]S Jn 6:56

[s] *2* The Greek for *prunes* also means *cleans.*

1Jn 2:3–6). (1) Obedience to Christ, though never perfect, must nevertheless be genuine. It is an essential aspect of saving faith, springing from our love for him (vv. 15,21,23–24; see Mt 7:21, note). Without love for Christ, trying to obey his commands becomes legalism. (2) To the person who loves Christ and strives to obey his commands consistently, Christ promises a special love, grace and his deepest inward presence (cf. v. 23).

14:23 WE WILL . . . MAKE OUR HOME WITH HIM. Those who truly love Jesus and obey his words will experience the immediate presence and love of the Father and the Son. The Father and the Son come to believers by means of the Holy Spirit (see v. 18, note). It should be noted that the Father's love is conditioned on our loving Jesus and being loyal to his Word.

14:24 HE WHO DOES NOT LOVE ME. Those who do not obey Christ's teachings do not have a personal love for him, and without love for Jesus true saving faith does not exist (1Jn 2:3–4). To say that people remain saved even though they cease to love Christ and begin to live lives of immorality, blasphemy, cruelty, murder, drunkenness, etc., directly contradicts these and other words of Jesus concerning love, obedience and the indwelling of the Holy Spirit.

14:26 HOLY SPIRIT. The Counselor is identified here as the "Holy Spirit." For the NT Christian the most important thing about the Spirit is not his greatness or his power (Ac 1:8), but that he is "Holy." His holy character, along with the manifestation of that holy character in the lives of believers, is what matters most (cf. Ro 1:4; Gal 5:22–26).

15:1 I AM THE TRUE VINE. In this parable or allegory, Jesus describes himself as "the true vine" and those who have become his disciples as "the branches." By remaining attached to him as the Source of life, they produce fruit. God is the gardener who takes care of the branches in order that they may bear fruit (vv. 2,8). God expects all of us to bear fruit (see next note).

15:2 EVERY BRANCH. Jesus speaks of two categories of branches: fruitless and fruitful. (1) The branches that cease to bear fruit are those who no longer have the life in them that comes from enduring faith in and love for Christ. These "branches" the Father cuts off, i.e., he separates them from vital union with Christ (cf. Mt 3:10). When they stop remaining in Christ, God then judges and rejects them (v. 6). (2) The branches that bear fruit are those who have life in them because of their enduring faith in and love for Christ. These "branches" the Father prunes so that they will become more fruitful. That is, he removes from their lives anything that diverts or hinders the vital life-flow of Christ into them. The fruit is the quality of Christian character that brings glory to God through life and witness (see Mt 3:8; 7:20; Ro 6:22; Gal 5:22–23; Eph 5:9; Php 1:11).

15:4 REMAIN IN ME. After a person believes in Christ and is forgiven, he or she receives eternal life and the power to remain in Christ. Given that power, the believer must then accept that responsibility in salvation and remain in Christ. The Greek word *menō* means to remain, continue, abide or live. Just as the branch has life only as long as the life of the vine flows into it, so believers have Christ's life only as long as Christ's life flows into them through their remaining in Christ. The conditions by which we remain in Christ are: (1) keeping God's Word continually in our hearts and minds and making it the guide for our actions (v. 7); (2) maintaining the habit of constant intimate communion with Christ in order to draw strength from him (v. 7); (3) obeying his commands, remaining in his love (v. 10) and loving each other (vv. 12,17); (4) keeping our lives clean through the Word, resisting all sin and yielding to the Spirit's direction (v. 3; 17:17;

branch can bear fruit by itself; it must remain in the vine. Neither can you bear
fruit unless you remain in me.
5“I am the vine; you are the branches.
If a man remains in me and I in him, he
will bear much fruit;[b] apart from me you
can do nothing. 6If anyone does not remain in me, he is like a branch that is
thrown away and withers; such branches
are picked up, thrown into the fire and
burned.[c] 7If you remain in me[d] and my
words remain in you, ask whatever you
wish, and it will be given you.[e] 8This is to
my Father's glory,[f] that you bear much
fruit, showing yourselves to be my disci-
Ac 13:52 ples.[g]

15:5 [b] ver 16 **15:6** [c] ver 2; Eze 15:4; S Mt 3:10 **15:7** [d] ver 4; S Jn 6:56 [e] S Mt 7:7 **15:8** [f] S Mt 9:8 [g] Jn 8:31 **15:9** [h] Jn 17:23, 24,26 **15:10** [i] S Jn 14:15 **15:11** [j] S Jn 3:29 **15:12** [k] ver 17; S Jn 13:34 **15:13** [l] Ge 44:33; Jn 10:11; Ro 5:7,8 **15:14** [m] Job 16:20; Pr 18:24; Lk 12:4 [n] Mt 12:50

Love Each Other

9“As the Father has loved me,[h] so have
I loved you. Now remain in my love. 10If
you obey my commands,[i] you will remain
in my love, just as I have obeyed my Father's commands and remain in his love.
11I have told you this so that my joy may
be in you and that your joy may be complete.[j] 12My command is this: Love each
other as I have loved you.[k] 13Greater love
has no one than this, that he lay down his
life for his friends.[l] 14You are my friends[m]
if you do what I command.[n] 15I no longer
call you servants, because a servant does
not know his master's business. Instead,
I have called you friends, for everything
that I learned from my Father I have made
known to you.[o] 16You did not choose me,
but I chose you and appointed you[p] to go
and bear fruit[q]—fruit that will last. Then
the Father will give you whatever you ask
in my name.[r] 17This is my command:
Love each other.[s]

The World Hates the Disciples

18“If the world hates you,[t] keep in
mind that it hated me first. 19If you belonged to the world, it would love you as
its own. As it is, you do not belong to the
world, but I have chosen you[u] out of the
world. That is why the world hates you.[v]
20Remember the words I spoke to you:
‘No servant is greater than his master.’[t][w]
If they persecuted me, they will persecute
you also.[x] If they obeyed my teaching,
they will obey yours also. 21They will treat
you this way because of my name,[y] for
they do not know the One who sent me.[z]
22If I had not come and spoken to them,[a]
they would not be guilty of sin. Now, however, they have no excuse for their sin.[b]

15:15 [o] Jn 8:26 **15:16** [p] ver 19; Jn 13:18 [q] ver 5 [r] S Mt 7:7 **15:17** [s] ver 12 **15:18** [t] Isa 66:5; Jn 7:7; 1Jn 3:13 **15:19** [u] ver 16 [v] Jn 17:14 **15:20** [w] S Jn 13:16 [x] 2Ti 3:12 **15:21** [y] Isa 66:5; Mt 5:10,11; 10:22; Lk 6:22; Ac 5:41; 1Pe 4:14; Rev 2:3 [z] Jn 16:3 **15:22** [a] Eze 2:5; 3:7 [b] Jn 9:41; Ro 1:20; 2:1

[t] *20* John 13:16

Ro 8:14; Gal 5:16–25; Eph 5:26; 1Pe 1:22).

15:6 LIKE A BRANCH THAT IS THROWN AWAY. The parable of the vine and branches makes it unmistakably clear that Christ did not believe “once in the vine, always in the vine.” Rather, in this parable Jesus gave his disciples a solemn but loving warning that it is indeed possible for true believers to ultimately abandon faith, turn their backs on Jesus, fail to remain in him, and thus to be thrown into the everlasting fire of hell.

(1) We have here the foundational principle governing the saving relationship of Christ and the believer, namely, that it is never a static relationship based solely on a past decision or experience. Rather, it is a progressive relationship as Christ lives in the believer and shares with him or her his divine life (see 17:3, note; Col 3:4; 1Jn 5:11–13).

(2) Three important truths are taught in this parable: (a) The responsibility of remaining in Christ is placed upon the disciples (see v. 4, note). This is our response to God's prior gift of divine life and power given at conversion. (b) Remaining in Christ results in Jesus' continued indwelling (v. 4a), the fruitfulness of the disciple (v. 5), success in prayer (v. 7) and fullness of joy (v. 11). (c) The consequences of failure to remain in Christ are fruitlessness (vv. 4–5), removal from Christ and destruction (vv. 2a,6).

15:7 ASK WHATEVER YOU WISH. The secret of answered prayer is remaining in Christ. The closer we live to Christ through meditation on and study of Scripture, the more our prayers will be in line with the nature and words of Christ, and thus the more effectual our prayers will be (see 14:13, note; 15:4, note; also Ps 66:18).

15:9–10 REMAIN IN MY LOVE. The believer must live in the atmosphere of the love of Christ. Jesus goes on to state that this is done by obeying his commands.

15:16 GO AND BEAR FRUIT. All Christians are chosen “out of the world” (v. 19) to “bear fruit” (vv. 2,4–5,8). This fruit-bearing refers to (1) spiritual virtues, such as the fruit of the Spirit mentioned in Gal 5:22–23—love, joy, peace, patience, kindness, goodness, faithfulness, gentleness, self-control (cf. Eph 5:9; Col 1:6; Heb 12:11; Jas 3:18); and (2) working for the conversion of others to Christ (4:36; 12:24).

15:20 THEY WILL PERSECUTE YOU ALSO. While Christ's followers are in this world they will be hated, persecuted and rejected for his sake. The world is the great opponent of Christ and his people throughout history. (1) True believers must understand that the world—including false religious organizations and churches—will always oppose God and the principles of his kingdom; thus the world will remain an enemy and persecutor of faithful believers until the end (Jas 4:4). (2) The reason believers suffer at the hands of the world is because they are fundamentally different; they do not “belong to the world” and have come “out of the world” (v. 19). The values, standards and direction of the faithful are in conflict with the unrighteous ways of their corrupt society. They refuse to compromise with its ungodly standards, and instead set their “minds on things above, not on earthly things” (Col 3:2).

[23]He who hates me hates my Father as
well. [24]If I had not done among them what
no one else did,[c] they would not be guilty
of sin.[d] But now they have seen these
miracles, and yet they have hated both me
and my Father. [25]But this is to fulfill what
is written in their Law:[e] 'They hated me
without reason.'[u][f]

[26]"When the Counselor[g] comes, whom
I will send to you from the Father,[h] the
Spirit of truth[i] who goes out from the
Father, he will testify about me.[j] [27]And
you also must testify,[k] for you have been
Ac 1:8 with me from the beginning.[l]

16 "All this[m] I have told you so that
you will not go astray.[n] [2]They will
put you out of the synagogue;[o] in fact, a
time is coming when anyone who kills you
will think he is offering a service to God.[p]
[3]They will do such things because they
have not known the Father or me.[q] [4]I
have told you this, so that when the time
comes you will remember[r] that I warned
you. I did not tell you this at first because
I was with you.[s]

The Work of the Holy Spirit

[5]"Now I am going to him who sent me,[t]
yet none of you asks me, 'Where are you
going?'[u] [6]Because I have said these
things, you are filled with grief.[v] [7]But I
tell you the truth: It is for your good that
I am going away. Unless I go away, the
Counselor[w] will not come to you; but if I
go, I will send him to you.[x] [8]When he
comes, he will convict the world of guilt[v]
in regard to sin and righteousness and
judgment: [9]in regard to sin,[y] because men
do not believe in me; [10]in regard to righteousness,[z] because I am going to the Father,[a] where you can see me no longer;
[11]and in regard to judgment, because the
prince of this world[b] now stands condemned.

[12]"I have much more to say to you,
more than you can now bear.[c] [13]But when

15:24 [c]Jn 5:36 [d]Jn 9:41 **15:25** [e]S Jn 10:34 [f]Ps 35:19; 69:4; 109:3 **15:26** [g]Jn 14:16 [h]Jn 14:26; 16:7 [i]S Jn 14:17 [j]1Jn 5:7 **15:27** [k]S Lk 24:48; Jn 21:24; 1Jn 1:2; 4:14 [l]S Lk 1:2 **16:1** [m]Jn 15:18-27 [n]Mt 11:6 **16:2** [o]Jn 9:22; 12:42 [p]Isa 66:5; Ac 26:9,10; Rev 6:9 **16:3** [q]Jn 15:21; 17:25; 1Jn 3:1 **16:4** [r]Jn 13:19; 14:29 [s]Jn 15:27 **16:5** [t]ver 10,17, 28; Jn 7:33 [u]Jn 13:36; 14:5 **16:6** [v]ver 22 **16:7** [w]Jn 14:16, 26; 15:26 [x]Jn 7:39; 14:26 **16:9** [y]Jn 15:22 **16:10** [z]Ac 3:14; 7:52; Ro 1:17; 3:21,22; 1Pe 3:18 [a]S ver 5 **16:11** [b]S Jn 12:31 **16:12** [c]Mk 4:33; 1Co 3:2

[u] *25* Psalms 35:19; 69:4 [v] *8* Or *will expose the guilt of the world*

16:2 PUT YOU OUT OF THE SYNAGOGUE. Jesus does not speak here of persecution from pagans, but of opposition and hostility from religious authorities and congregations. His reference earlier to the world hating believers (15:18–19) must include these religious people. (1) All professed believers or churches that do not adhere to Jesus' teaching and apostolic revelation, or that do not seek to remain separated from the corrupt systems of society, belong to the world (cf. 1Jn 4:5–6). (2) These so-called professed believers have values so different from the true NT gospel that when they persecute or kill true followers of Christ, they think they are serving God.

16:7 IF I GO, I WILL SEND HIM. The Pentecostal outpouring of the Holy Spirit will occur only after Christ goes away (cf. Ac 2:33; see article on THE REGENERATION OF THE DISCIPLES, p. 212). This outpouring at Pentecost fully ushered in the age of the Spirit.

16:8 CONVICT THE WORLD. When the Holy Spirit comes at Pentecost (see previous note; Ac 2:4), his principal work with respect to proclaiming the gospel will be that of convicting. The term "convict" (Gk *elenchō*) means to expose, refute and convince.

(1) The Spirit's ministry of convicting operates in three areas. (a) Sin. The Holy Spirit will expose sin and unbelief in order to awaken a consciousness of guilt and need for forgiveness. Conviction also makes clear the fearful results if the guilty persist in their wrongdoing. After conviction, a choice must be made. This will often lead to true repentance and a turning to Jesus as Lord and Savior (Ac 2:37–38). (b) Righteousness. The Spirit convinces people that Jesus is the righteous Son of God, resurrected, vindicated and now the Lord of all. He makes them aware of God's standard of righteousness in Christ, shows them what sin is and gives them power to overcome the world (Ac 3:12–16; 7:51–60; 17:31; 1Pe 3:18). (c) Judgment. The Spirit convinces people of Satan's defeat at the cross (12:31; 16:11), God's present judgment of the world (Ro 1:18–32) and the future judgment of the entire human race (Mt 16:27; Ac 17:31; 24:25; Ro 14:10; 1Co 6:2; 2Co 5:10; Jude 14).

(2) The Spirit's work of convicting people of sin, righteousness and judgment will be manifested in all who are baptized in the Holy Spirit and are truly Spirit-filled believers. Christ, filled with the Spirit (Lk 4:1), testified to the world that "what it does is evil" (see 7:7; 15:18) and called people to repent (Mt 4:17). John the Baptist, "filled with the Holy Spirit" from birth (see Lk 1:15, note), exposed the sin of the Jewish people and commanded them to change their ways (see Mt 11:7, note; Lk 3:1–20); Peter, "filled with the Holy Spirit" (Ac 2:4), convicted the hearts of 3,000 sinners and called them to repent and receive forgiveness (Ac 2:37–41).

(3) Clearly, any preacher or church that does not publicly expose sin and call for repentance and Biblical righteousness is not directed by the Holy Spirit. 1Co 14:24–25 explicitly states that God's presence in the congregation is recognized by the exposure of the sin of unbelievers (i.e., secrets of their hearts), and their consequent conviction and salvation.

16:13 HE WILL GUIDE YOU INTO ALL TRUTH. The convicting work of the Holy Spirit is not only directed toward the unsaved (vv. 7–8), but also operates in believers and the church in order to teach, correct and guide them into truth (Mt 18:15; 1Ti 5:20; Rev 3:19).

(1) The Holy Spirit will speak to believers concerning sin, the righteousness of Christ and the judgment of evil in order to (a) conform them to Christ and his standard of righteousness (cf. 2Co 3:18), (b) guide them into all truth, and (c) glorify Christ (v. 14). Thus, the Holy Spirit works within believers to reproduce Christ's holy life in their lives.

he, the Spirit of truth,[d] comes, he will
guide you into all truth.[e] He will not
speak on his own; he will speak only what
he hears, and he will tell you what is yet
to come. **14**He will bring glory to me by
taking from what is mine and making it
known to you. **15**All that belongs to the
Father is mine.[f] That is why I said the
Spirit will take from what is mine and
make it known to you.

16"In a little while[g] you will see me no
more, and then after a little while you will
see me."[h]

The Disciples' Grief Will Turn to Joy

17Some of his disciples said to one another, "What does he mean by saying, 'In
a little while you will see me no more, and
then after a little while you will see me,'[i]
and 'Because I am going to the Father'?"[j]
18They kept asking, "What does he mean
by 'a little while'? We don't understand
what he is saying."

19Jesus saw that they wanted to ask
him about this, so he said to them, "Are
you asking one another what I meant
when I said, 'In a little while you will see
me no more, and then after a little while
you will see me'? **20**I tell you the truth, you
will weep and mourn[k] while the world rejoices. You will grieve, but your grief will
turn to joy.[l] **21**A woman giving birth to a
child has pain[m] because her time has
come; but when her baby is born she forgets the anguish because of her joy that
a child is born into the world. **22**So with
you: Now is your time of grief,[n] but I will
see you again[o] and you will rejoice, and
no one will take away your joy.[p] **23**In that
day[q] you will no longer ask me anything.
I tell you the truth, my Father will give
you whatever you ask in my name.[r] **24**Until now you have not asked for anything in
my name. Ask and you will receive,[s] and
your joy will be complete.[t]

25"Though I have been speaking figuratively,[u] a time is coming[v] when I will no
longer use this kind of language but will
tell you plainly about my Father. **26**In that
day you will ask in my name.[w] I am not
saying that I will ask the Father on your
behalf. **27**No, the Father himself loves you
because you have loved me[x] and have believed that I came from God.[y] **28**I came
from the Father and entered the world;
now I am leaving the world and going
back to the Father."[z]

29Then Jesus' disciples said, "Now you
are speaking clearly and without figures
of speech.[a] **30**Now we can see that you
know all things and that you do not even
need to have anyone ask you questions.
This makes us believe[b] that you came
from God."[c]

31"You believe at last!"[w] Jesus answered. **32**"But a time is coming,[d] and has
come, when you will be scattered,[e] each
to his own home. You will leave me all
alone.[f] Yet I am not alone, for my Father
is with me.[g]

33"I have told you these things, so that
in me you may have peace.[h] In this world
you will have trouble.[i] But take heart! I
have overcome[j] the world."

Jesus Prays for Himself

17 After Jesus said this, he looked toward heaven[k] and prayed:

16:13 [d]S Jn 14:17 [e]Ps 25:5; Jn 14:26 **16:15** [f]Jn 17:10 **16:16** [g]S Jn 7:33 [h]ver 22; Jn 14:18-24 **16:17** [i]ver 16 [j]ver 5 **16:20** [k]Mk 16:10; Lk 23:27 [l]Jn 20:20 **16:21** [m]Isa 13:8; 21:3; 26:17; Mic 4:9; 1Th 5:3 **16:22** [n]ver 6 [o]ver 16 [p]ver 20; Jer 31:12 **16:23** [q]ver 26; Jn 14:20 [r]S Mt 7:7 **16:24** [s]S Mt 7:7 [t]S Jn 3:29 **16:25** [u]ver 29; Ps 78:2; Eze 20:49; Mt 13:34; Mk 4:33,34; Jn 10:6 [v]ver 2 **16:26** [w]ver 23,24 **16:27** [x]Jn 14:21, 23 [y]ver 30; S Jn 13:3 **16:28** [z]ver 5,10, 17; Jn 13:3 **16:29** [a]S ver 25 **16:30** [b]1Ki 17:24 [c]ver 27; S Jn 13:3 **16:32** [d]ver 2,25 [e]Mt 26:31 [f]Mt 26:56 [g]Jn 8:16,29 **16:33** [h]S Jn 14:27 [i]Jn 15:18-21 [j]Ro 8:37; 1Jn 4:4; 5:4; Rev 2:7,11, 17,26; 3:5,12,21; 21:7 **17:1** [k]Jn 11:41

[w] *31* Or *"Do you now believe?"*

(2) If Spirit-filled believers reject the Spirit's guidance and convicting work, and if they do not "by the Spirit . . . put to death the misdeeds of the body" (Ro 8:13), then they will enter into condemnation. Only those who receive the truth and are "led by the Spirit of God" are "sons of God" (Ro 8:14) and are therefore able to continue in the Spirit's fullness (see Eph 5:18, note). Sin destroys both the life and fullness of the Holy Spirit within the believer (Ro 6:23; 8:13; Gal 5:17; cf. Eph 5:18; 1Th 5:19).

16:14 TAKING FROM WHAT IS MINE. The Spirit takes that which is Christ's and reveals it to the believer. He takes the presence, love, forgiveness, redemption, sanctification, power, spiritual gifts, healing and all that is ours through our faith relationship with Christ, and makes it experientially real in our lives. Through the Spirit Jesus returns to us to disclose his love, grace and personal fellowship (cf. 14:16–23). The Spirit works within us to do what is necessary to awaken and deepen our awareness of Jesus' presence in our lives, drawing our hearts toward him in faith, love, obedience, communion, worship and praise (see article on JESUS AND THE HOLY SPIRIT, p. 136).

16:27 THE FATHER HIMSELF LOVES YOU. The Father loves all people (3:16). But it is also true that he has a special family love for those who through Jesus are reconciled to him, love him and remain loyal to him even while enduring trouble in this world (v. 33). Our affection for Jesus brings forth the Father's affection for us. Love responds to love.

17:1 CHRIST'S PRAYER FOR ALL BELIEVERS. Jesus' final prayer for his disciples shows our Lord's deepest longings for his followers, both then and now. It is also a Spirit-inspired example of how all pastors should pray for their people, and how Christian parents should pray for their children. In praying for those under our care, our greatest concerns should be: (1) that they may know Jesus Christ and his Word intimately (vv. 2–3,17,19; see v. 3, note); (2) that God

"Father, the time has come.[l] Glorify your Son, that your Son may glorify you.[m] **2**For you granted him authority over all people[n] that he
might give eternal life[o] to all those
you have given him.[p] **3**Now this is
eternal life: that they may know
you,[q] the only true God, and Jesus
Christ, whom you have sent.[r] **4**I
have brought you glory[s] on earth by
completing the work you gave me to
do.[t] **5**And now, Father, glorify me[u]
in your presence with the glory I
had with you[v] before the world began.[w]

Jesus Prays for His Disciples

6"I have revealed you[x][x] to those
whom you gave me[y] out of the
world. They were yours; you gave
them to me and they have obeyed
your word. **7**Now they know that everything you have given me comes
from you. **8**For I gave them the
words you gave me[z] and they accepted them. They knew with certainty that I came from you,[a] and
they believed that you sent me.[b] **9**I
pray for them.[c] I am not praying for
the world, but for those you have
given me,[d] for they are yours. **10**All
I have is yours, and all you have is
mine.[e] And glory has come to me
through them. **11**I will remain in the
world no longer, but they are still in
the world,[f] and I am coming to
you.[g] Holy Father, protect them by
the power of your name—the name
you gave me—so that they may be
one[h] as we are one.[i] **12**While I was
with them, I protected them and
kept them safe by that name you
gave me. None has been lost[j] except the one doomed to destruction[k]
so that Scripture would be fulfilled.[l]

13"I am coming to you now,[m] but
I say these things while I am still in
the world, so that they may have the
full measure of my joy[n] within them.
14I have given them your word and
the world has hated them,[o] for they
are not of the world any more than
I am of the world.[p] **15**My prayer is
not that you take them out of the
world but that you protect them
from the evil one.[q] **16**They are not of
the world, even as I am not of it.[r]
17Sanctify[y] them by the truth; your
word is truth.[s] **18**As you sent me
into the world,[t] I have sent them
into the world.[u] **19**For them I sanctify myself, that they too may be truly
sanctified.[v]

Jesus Prays for All Believers

20"My prayer is not for them

17:1 [l]S Mt 26:18 [m]Jn 12:23; 13:31, 32
17:2 [n]S Mt 28:18 [o]S Mt 25:46 [p]ver 6,9,24; Da 7:14; Jn 6:37, 39
17:3 [q]S Php 3:8 [r]ver 8,18,21,23, 25; S Jn 3:17
17:4 [s]Jn 13:31 [t]S Jn 19:30
17:5 [u]ver 1 [v]Php 2:6 [w]S Jn 1:2
17:6 [x]ver 26; Jn 1:18 [y]S ver 2
17:8 [z]ver 14,26; S Jn 14:24 [a]S Jn 13:3 [b]ver 3, 18,21,23,25; S Jn 3:17
17:9 [c]Lk 22:32 [d]S ver 2
17:10 [e]Jn 16:15
17:11 [f]Jn 13:1 [g]ver 13; Jn 7:33 [h]ver 21-23; Ps 133:1 [i]Jn 10:30
17:12 [j]S Jn 6:39 [k]Jn 6:70 [l]S Mt 1:22
17:13 [m]ver 11 [n]S Jn 3:29
17:14 [o]Jn 15:19 [p]ver 16; Jn 8:23
17:15 [q]S Mt 5:37
17:16 [r]ver 14
17:17 [s]S Jn 15:3; 2Sa 7:28; 1Ki 17:24
17:18 [t]ver 3,8, 21,23,25; S Jn 3:17 [u]Jn 20:21
17:19 [v]ver 17

x *6* Greek *your name*; also in verse 26
y *17* Greek *hagiazo (set apart for sacred use* or *make holy)*; also in verse 19

---

may keep them from the world, from falling away, from Satan and from false teaching (vv. 6,11,14–17); (3) that they may constantly possess the full joy of Christ (v. 13); (4) that they may be holy in thought, deed and character (see v. 17, note); (5) that they may be one in purpose and fellowship, as demonstrated by Jesus and the Father (vv. 11,21–22; see v. 21, note); (6) that they may lead others to Christ (vv. 21,23); (7) that they may persevere in the faith and finally be with Christ in heaven (v. 24); and (8) that they may constantly live in God's love and presence (v. 26).

17:3 ETERNAL LIFE. Eternal life is more than endless existence. It is a special quality of life that we as believers receive when we partake of the essential life of God through Christ; this allows us to know God in an ever-growing knowledge and fellowship with the Father, Son and Holy Spirit. In the NT eternal life is described as:

(1) A present reality (5:24; 10:27–28). The present possession of eternal life requires a living faith. Eternal life is not secured and maintained merely by an act of repentance and faith occurring in the past (see 5:24, note). It involves also a present living union and fellowship with Christ (1Jn 5:12); there is no eternal life apart from him (10:27f; 11:25f; 1Jn 5:11–13).

(2) A future hope. Eternal life is associated with the coming of Christ for his faithful (see 14:3, note; cf. Mk 10:30; 2Ti 1:1,10; Tit 1:2; 3:7) and is contingent on living by the Spirit (Ro 8:12–17; Gal 6:8).

17:6 THEY HAVE OBEYED YOUR WORD. Christ's prayer for protection, joy, sanctification, love and unity applies only to a particular people, i.e., to those who belong to God, believe in Christ (v. 8), are separated from the world (vv. 14–16), and obey the Word of Christ and accept his teachings (vv. 6,8).

17:17 SANCTIFY THEM BY THE TRUTH. "Sanctify" means to make holy, to separate or set apart. The evening before his crucifixion Jesus prays that his disciples will be a holy people, separated from the world and sin for the purpose of worshiping and serving God. They must be set apart in order to be near God, to live for him and to be like him. This sanctification is accomplished by their devotion to the truth revealed to them by the Spirit of truth (cf. 14:17; 16:13). The truth is both the living Word of God (see 1:1) and the revelation of God's written Word (see article on SANCTIFICATION, p. 526).

17:19 I SANCTIFY MYSELF. Jesus sanctifies himself by setting himself apart to do the will of God, i.e., to die on the cross. Jesus suffered on the cross in order that his followers might be separated from the world and set apart for God (see Heb 13:12).

alone. I pray also for those who will
believe in me through their message, 21that all of them may be
one,[w] Father, just as you are in me
and I am in you.[x] May they also be
in us so that the world may believe
that you have sent me.[y] 22I have
given them the glory that you gave
me,[z] that they may be one as we are
one:[a] 23I in them and you in me.
May they be brought to complete
unity to let the world know that you
sent me[b] and have loved them[c]
even as you have loved me.

24"Father, I want those you have
given me[d] to be with me where I
am,[e] and to see my glory,[f] the glory
you have given me because you
loved me before the creation of the
world.[g]

25"Righteous Father, though the
world does not know you,[h] I know
you, and they know that you have
sent me.[i] 26I have made you known
to them,[j] and will continue to make
you known in order that the love you
have for me may be in them[k] and
that I myself may be in them."

Jesus Arrested

18:3–11pp — Mt 26:47–56; Mk 14:43–50; Lk 22:47–53

18 When he had finished praying,
Jesus left with his disciples and
crossed the Kidron Valley.[l] On the other
side there was an olive grove,[m] and he and
his disciples went into it.[n]

2Now Judas, who betrayed him, knew
the place, because Jesus had often met
there with his disciples.[o] 3So Judas came
to the grove, guiding[p] a detachment of
soldiers and some officials from the chief
priests and Pharisees.[q] They were carrying torches, lanterns and weapons.

4Jesus, knowing all that was going to
happen to him,[r] went out and asked
them, "Who is it you want?"[s]

5"Jesus of Nazareth,"[t] they replied.

"I am he," Jesus said. (And Judas the
traitor was standing there with them.)
6When Jesus said, "I am he," they drew
back and fell to the ground.

7Again he asked them, "Who is it you
want?"[u]

And they said, "Jesus of Nazareth."

8"I told you that I am he," Jesus answered. "If you are looking for me, then
let these men go." 9This happened so that
the words he had spoken would be fulfilled: "I have not lost one of those you
gave me."[z][v]

10Then Simon Peter, who had a sword,
drew it and struck the high priest's servant, cutting off his right ear. (The servant's name was Malchus.)

11Jesus commanded Peter, "Put your
sword away! Shall I not drink the cup[w] the
Father has given me?"

Jesus Taken to Annas

18:12,13pp — Mt 26:57

12Then the detachment of soldiers with
its commander and the Jewish officials[x]
arrested Jesus. They bound him 13and
brought him first to Annas, who was the
father-in-law of Caiaphas,[y] the high priest
that year. 14Caiaphas was the one who
had advised the Jews that it would be good
if one man died for the people.[z]

[z] 9 John 6:39

17:21 [w]Jer 32:39 [x]ver 11; Jn 10:38 [y]ver 3,8,18,23,25; S Jn 3:17 **17:22** [z]Jn 1:14 [a]S Jn 14:20 **17:23** [b]ver 3,8, 18,21,25; S Jn 3:17 [c]Jn 16:27 **17:24** [d]S ver 2 [e]S Jn 12:26 [f]Jn 1:14 [g]ver 5; S Mt 25:34; S Jn 1:2 **17:25** [h]Jn 15:21; 16:3 [i]ver 3,8,18, 21,23; S Jn 3:17; 16:27 **17:26** [j]ver 6 [k]Jn 15:9 **18:1** [l]2Sa 15:23 [m]ver 26; S Mt 21:1 [n]Mt 26:36 **18:2** [o]Lk 21:37; 22:39 **18:3** [p]Ac 1:16 [q]ver 12 **18:4** [r]Jn 6:64; 13:1,11 [s]ver 7 **18:5** [t]S Mk 1:24 **18:7** [u]ver 4 **18:9** [v]S Jn 6:39 **18:11** [w]S Mt 20:22 **18:12** [x]ver 3 **18:13** [y]ver 24; S Mt 26:3 **18:14** [z]Jn 11:49-51

17:21 THAT ALL OF THEM MAY BE ONE. The unity that Jesus prayed for was not organizational unity but spiritual unity based on: living in Christ (v. 23); knowing and experiencing the love of the Father and the fellowship of Christ (v. 26); separation from the world (vv. 14–16); sanctification in truth (vv. 17,19); receiving and believing the truth of the Word (vv. 6,8,17); obedience to the Word (v. 6); and the desire to bring salvation to the lost (vv. 21,23). When any one of these factors is missing, the true unity that Jesus prayed for cannot exist.

(1) Jesus does not pray for his followers to "become one," but rather that they may "be one." The present subjunctive used here designates ongoing action: "continually be one," a oneness based on their common relationship to the Father and the Son, and on having the same basic attitude toward the world, the Word and the need to reach out to the lost (cf. 1Jn 1:7).

(2) To attempt to create an artificial unity by meetings, conferences or complex organization can result in a betrayal of the very unity for which Jesus prayed. What Jesus had in mind is much more than cosmetic "unity meetings." It is a spiritual unity of heart, purpose, mind and will in those who are fully devoted to Christ, the Word and holiness (see Eph 4:3, note).

17:22 THE GLORY THAT YOU GAVE ME. The "glory" of Christ was his life of self-denying service and his dying on the cross in order to redeem the human race. Likewise, the "glory" of the believer is the path of humble service and bearing his or her cross (cf. Lk 9:23, note). Humility, self-denial and the willingness to suffer for Christ will insure the true unity of believers and will lead to true glory.

18:11 THE CUP. See Mt 26:39, note on Christ's cup of sorrow.

18:12 ARRESTED JESUS. See Mt 26:57, note on the order of the events from Christ's arrest to his crucifixion.

Peter's First Denial

18:16–18pp — Mt 26:69,70; Mk 14:66–68; Lk 22:55–57

15 Simon Peter and another disciple were following Jesus. Because this disciple was known to the high priest,[a] he went with Jesus into the high priest's courtyard,[b] 16 but Peter had to wait outside at the door. The other disciple, who was known to the high priest, came back, spoke to the girl on duty there and brought Peter in.

17 "You are not one of his disciples, are you?" the girl at the door asked Peter.

He replied, "I am not."[c]

18 It was cold, and the servants and officials stood around a fire[d] they had made to keep warm. Peter also was standing with them, warming himself.[e]

The High Priest Questions Jesus

18:19–24pp — Mt 26:59–68; Mk 14:55–65; Lk 22:63–71

19 Meanwhile, the high priest questioned Jesus about his disciples and his teaching.

20 "I have spoken openly to the world," Jesus replied. "I always taught in synagogues[f] or at the temple,[g] where all the Jews come together. I said nothing in secret.[h] 21 Why question me? Ask those who heard me. Surely they know what I said."

22 When Jesus said this, one of the officials[i] nearby struck him in the face.[j] "Is this the way you answer the high priest?" he demanded.

23 "If I said something wrong," Jesus replied, "testify as to what is wrong. But if I spoke the truth, why did you strike me?"[k] 24 Then Annas sent him, still bound, to Caiaphas[l] the high priest.[a]

Peter's Second and Third Denials

18:25–27pp — Mt 26:71–75; Mk 14:69–72; Lk 22:58–62

25 As Simon Peter stood warming himself,[m] he was asked, "You are not one of his disciples, are you?"

He denied it, saying, "I am not."[n]

26 One of the high priest's servants, a relative of the man whose ear Peter had cut off,[o] challenged him, "Didn't I see you with him in the olive grove?"[p] 27 Again Peter denied it, and at that moment a rooster began to crow.[q]

Jesus Before Pilate

18:29–40pp — Mt 27:11–18,20–23; Mk 15:2–15; Lk 23:2,3,18–25

28 Then the Jews led Jesus from Caiaphas to the palace of the Roman governor.[r] By now it was early morning, and to avoid ceremonial uncleanness the Jews did not enter the palace;[s] they wanted to be able to eat the Passover.[t] 29 So Pilate came out to them and asked, "What charges are you bringing against this man?"

30 "If he were not a criminal," they replied, "we would not have handed him over to you."

31 Pilate said, "Take him yourselves and judge him by your own law."

"But we have no right to execute anyone," the Jews objected. 32 This happened so that the words Jesus had spoken indicating the kind of death he was going to die[u] would be fulfilled.

33 Pilate then went back inside the palace,[v] summoned Jesus and asked him, "Are you the king of the Jews?"[w]

34 "Is that your own idea," Jesus asked, "or did others talk to you about me?"

35 "Am I a Jew?" Pilate replied. "It was your people and your chief priests who handed you over to me. What is it you have done?"

36 Jesus said, "My kingdom[x] is not of this world. If it were, my servants would fight to prevent my arrest by the Jews.[y]

18:15 [a] S Mt 26:3 [b] Mt 26:58; Mk 14:54; Lk 22:54 **18:17** [c] ver 25 **18:18** [d] Jn 21:9 [e] Mk 14:54,67 **18:20** [f] S Mt 4:23 [g] Mt 26:55 [h] Jn 7:26 **18:22** [i] ver 3 [j] Mt 16:21; Jn 19:3 **18:23** [k] Mt 5:39; Ac 23:2-5 **18:24** [l] ver 13; S Mt 26:3

18:25 [m] ver 18 [n] ver 17 **18:26** [o] ver 10 [p] ver 1 **18:27** [q] Jn 13:38 **18:28** [r] S Mt 27:2 [s] ver 33; Jn 19:9 [t] Jn 11:55 **18:32** [u] Mt 20:19; 26:2; Jn 3:14; 8:28; 12:32,33 **18:33** [v] ver 28,29; Jn 19:9 [w] Lk 23:3; S Mt 2:2 **18:36** [x] S Mt 3:2 [y] Mt 26:53

[a] 24 Or *(Now Annas had sent him, still bound, to Caiaphas the high priest.)*

18:15 PETER'S DENIAL. See notes on Mk 14:50; 14:71; Lk 22:62.

18:28 JESUS BEFORE PILATE. See Mt 27:2, note; Lk 23:1, note.

18:36 MY KINGDOM IS NOT OF THIS WORLD. Concerning the true nature of Christ's kingdom and its redemptive purpose, three points should be noted:

(1) What Jesus' kingdom is not. It is "not of this world." It did not originate in this world, nor does it seek to take over the world's system. Jesus did not come to establish a religio-political theocracy or aspire to world dominion. Jesus states that if he had come to establish a political kingdom on earth, then "my servants would fight." Since this is not the nature of the kingdom, they do not resort to war or revolution to promote Christ's purpose on earth (cf. Mt 26:51–52). They do not ally themselves with political parties, social pressure groups or any secular organizations in order to establish God's kingdom. They refuse to turn the cross into a boastful attempt to rule society. Rather than using worldly weapons (2Co 10:4), Jesus' followers are armed only with spiritual weapons (Eph 6:10–18). This does not mean, however, that Jesus' disciples are indifferent to God's demand for just government, justice, peace or curtailing lawlessness. Christians must bring a "prophetic word" to the state concerning its moral responsibilities under God.

But now my kingdom is from another
place."[z]
37 "You are a king, then!" said Pilate.
Jesus answered, "You are right in saying I am a king. In fact, for this reason I
was born, and for this I came into the
world, to testify to the truth.[a] Everyone
on the side of truth listens to me."[b]
38 "What is truth?" Pilate asked. With
this he went out again to the Jews and
said, "I find no basis for a charge against
him.[c] 39 But it is your custom for me to
release to you one prisoner at the time of
the Passover. Do you want me to release
'the king of the Jews'?"
40 They shouted back, "No, not him!
Give us Barabbas!" Now Barabbas had
taken part in a rebellion.[d]

Jesus Sentenced to be Crucified

19:1–16pp — Mt 27:27–31; Mk 15:16–20

19 Then Pilate took Jesus and had
him flogged.[e] 2 The soldiers twisted together a crown of thorns and put it
on his head. They clothed him in a purple
robe 3 and went up to him again and again,
saying, "Hail, king of the Jews!"[f] And
they struck him in the face.[g]
4 Once more Pilate came out and said to
the Jews, "Look, I am bringing him out[h]
to you to let you know that I find no basis
for a charge against him."[i] 5 When Jesus
came out wearing the crown of thorns and
the purple robe,[j] Pilate said to them,
"Here is the man!"
6 As soon as the chief priests and their
officials saw him, they shouted, "Crucify!
Crucify!"
But Pilate answered, "You take him and
crucify him.[k] As for me, I find no basis for
a charge against him."[l]
7 The Jews insisted, "We have a law, and
according to that law he must die,[m] because he claimed to be the Son of God."[n]
8 When Pilate heard this, he was even
more afraid, 9 and he went back inside the
palace.[o] "Where do you come from?" he
asked Jesus, but Jesus gave him no answer.[p] 10 "Do you refuse to speak to me?"
Pilate said. "Don't you realize I have power either to free you or to crucify you?"
11 Jesus answered, "You would have no
power over me if it were not given to you
from above.[q] Therefore the one who handed me over to you[r] is guilty of a greater
sin."
12 From then on, Pilate tried to set Jesus
free, but the Jews kept shouting, "If you
let this man go, you are no friend of Caesar. Anyone who claims to be a king[s] opposes Caesar."
13 When Pilate heard this, he brought
Jesus out and sat down on the judge's
seat[t] at a place known as the Stone Pavement (which in Aramaic[u] is Gabbatha).
14 It was the day of Preparation[v] of Passover Week, about the sixth hour.[w]

18:36 [z] Lk 17:21; Jn 6:15
18:37 [a] Jn 3:32 [b] Jn 8:47; 1Jn 4:6
18:38 [c] S Lk 23:4
18:40 [d] Ac 3:14
19:1 [e] Dt 25:3; Isa 50:6; 53:5; Mt 27:26
19:3 [f] Mt 27:29 [g] Jn 18:22
19:4 [h] Jn 18:38 [i] ver 6; S Lk 23:4
19:5 [j] ver 2
19:6 [k] Ac 3:13 [l] ver 4; S Lk 23:4
19:7 [m] Lev 24:16 [n] Mt 26:63-66; Jn 5:18; 10:33
19:9 [o] Jn 18:33 [p] S Mk 14:61
19:11 [q] S Ro 13:1 [r] Jn 18:28-30; Ac 3:13
19:12 [s] Lk 23:2
19:13 [t] Mt 27:19 [u] S Jn 5:2
19:14 [v] Mt 27:62 [w] Mk 15:25

---

(2) What Jesus' kingdom is. Christ's kingdom, i.e., the kingdom of God, involves his rule, lordship, power and spiritual activity in the lives of all who receive him and obey his word of truth (v. 37). The kingdom of God is "righteousness, peace and joy in the Holy Spirit" (Ro 14:17). It confronts the spiritual forces of Satan with spiritual weapons (see Mt 12:28; Lk 11:20; Ac 26:18; Eph 6:12). The church's role is that of a servant of Jesus Christ, not that of a ruler of this present world. Her strength is not in worldly power but in the cross; her suffering and rejection at the hands of the world is her glory (2Co 3:7–18). Only in renouncing worldly power did the NT church find God's power. The church today faces this same choice: only by losing her life in the world will she find herself in God (see article on THE KINGDOM OF GOD, p. 28).

(3) What Jesus' kingdom will be. In the future, Christ's kingdom and rule will be the new heaven and earth; this will occur after he comes to earth to judge the nations, destroy the antichrist, rule on earth for a thousand years and then bring Satan to a final end in the lake of fire (Rev 19:11—20:15).

18:37 TESTIFY TO THE TRUTH. An essential part of Jesus' mission was to testify to the truth and point people to it, i.e., his incarnate witness to the Father and to the revealed truth of his gospel now recorded in Scripture. How strange that some ministers today compromise truth and sound doctrine, obscure the clear meaning of Scripture and promote unity at the cost of Biblical faith. Such ministers err in tolerating false doctrine and refusing to draw distinctions between right and wrong, truth and error. In the name of love and broad-mindedness, they reject this purpose of Christ's coming. Truth is one thing churches must never sacrifice (cf. 17:8,17; 2Th 2:10).

19:1 HAD HIM FLOGGED. For details concerning the method of Roman floggings, see Mt 27:26, note.

19:4 I FIND NO BASIS FOR A CHARGE. See Lk 23:14, note.

19:11 POWER . . . GIVEN TO YOU FROM ABOVE. Jesus says that all earthly power exists only as God permits it (cf. Da 4:34–35; Ro 13:1). Pilate's sin was yielding to the crowd because of political expediency. Israel's sin was greater—they were rejecting their Messiah.

19:14 THE SIXTH HOUR. John states that Jesus' trial neared completion "about the sixth hour." Mark, however, says that Jesus was crucified at "the third hour" (Mk 15:25). This apparent contradiction is resolved if we understand that John used the Roman method of computing time, while Mark used the Palestinian method. The Roman day began at midnight, and the Palestinian day began at sunrise.

"Here is your king,"[x] Pilate said to the
Jews.
15But they shouted, "Take him away!
Take him away! Crucify him!"
"Shall I crucify your king?" Pilate
asked.
"We have no king but Caesar," the chief
priests answered.
16Finally Pilate handed him over to
them to be crucified.[y]

The Crucifixion

19:17–24pp — Mt 27:33–44; Mk 15:22–32; Lk 23:33–43

So the soldiers took charge of Jesus.
17Carrying his own cross,[z] he went out to
the place of the Skull[a] (which in Aramaic[b] is called Golgotha). **18**Here they crucified him, and with him two others[c]—one
on each side and Jesus in the middle.
19Pilate had a notice prepared and fastened to the cross. It read: JESUS OF NAZA-
RETH,[d] THE KING OF THE JEWS.[e] **20**Many of the
Jews read this sign, for the place where
Jesus was crucified was near the city,[f]
and the sign was written in Aramaic, Latin and Greek. **21**The chief priests of the
Jews protested to Pilate, "Do not write
'The King of the Jews,' but that this man
claimed to be king of the Jews."[g]
22Pilate answered, "What I have written, I have written."
23When the soldiers crucified Jesus,
they took his clothes, dividing them into
four shares, one for each of them, with the
undergarment remaining. This garment
was seamless, woven in one piece from
top to bottom.
24"Let's not tear it," they said to one
another. "Let's decide by lot who will get
it."
This happened that the scripture might
be fulfilled[h] which said,

"They divided my garments among
them
and cast lots for my clothing."[b][i]

So this is what the soldiers did.
25Near the cross[j] of Jesus stood his
mother,[k] his mother's sister, Mary the
wife of Clopas, and Mary Magdalene.[l]
26When Jesus saw his mother[m] there, and
the disciple whom he loved[n] standing
nearby, he said to his mother, "Dear woman, here is your son," **27**and to the disciple, "Here is your mother." From that time
on, this disciple took her into his home.

The Death of Jesus

19:29,30pp — Mt 27:48,50; Mk 15:36,37; Lk 23:36

28Later, knowing that all was now completed,[o] and so that the Scripture would
be fulfilled,[p] Jesus said, "I am thirsty."
29A jar of wine vinegar[q] was there, so
they soaked a sponge in it, put the sponge
on a stalk of the hyssop plant, and lifted
it to Jesus' lips. **30**When he had received
the drink, Jesus said, "It is finished."[r]
With that, he bowed his head and gave up
his spirit.
31Now it was the day of Preparation,[s]
and the next day was to be a special Sabbath. Because the Jews did not want the
bodies left on the crosses[t] during the
Sabbath, they asked Pilate to have the
legs broken and the bodies taken down.
32The soldiers therefore came and broke
the legs of the first man who had been
crucified with Jesus, and then those of the
other.[u] **33**But when they came to Jesus
and found that he was already dead, they
did not break his legs. **34**Instead, one of
the soldiers pierced[v] Jesus' side with a
spear, bringing a sudden flow of blood and
water.[w] **35**The man who saw it[x] has given
testimony, and his testimony is true.[y] He
knows that he tells the truth, and he testifies so that you also may believe. **36**These
things happened so that the scripture
would be fulfilled:[z] "Not one of his bones
will be broken,"[c][a] **37**and, as another

19:14 [x]ver 19,21 **19:16** [y]Mt 27:26; Mk 15:15; Lk 23:25 **19:17** [z]Ge 22:6; Lk 14:27; 23:26 [a]Lk 23:33 [b]S Jn 5:2 **19:18** [c]Lk 23:32 **19:19** [d]S Mk 1:24 [e]ver 14,21 **19:20** [f]Heb 13:12 **19:21** [g]ver 14 **19:24** [h]ver 28,36, 37; S Mt 1:22 [i]Ps 22:18

19:25 [j]Mt 27:55, 56 [k]S Mt 12:46 [l]Lk 24:18 **19:26** [m]S Mt 12:46 [n]S Jn 13:23 **19:28** [o]S ver 30; Jn 13:1 [p]ver 24, 36,37; S Mt 1:22 **19:29** [q]Ps 69:21 **19:30** [r]Lk 12:50; Jn 4:34; 17:4 **19:31** [s]ver 14,42 [t]Dt 21:23; Jos 8:29; 10:26,27 **19:32** [u]ver 18 **19:34** [v]Zec 12:10; Rev 1:7 [w]1Jn 5:6, 8 **19:35** [x]S Lk 24:48 [y]Jn 15:27; 21:24 **19:36** [z]ver 24,28, 37; S Mt 1:22 [a]Ex 12:46; Nu 9:12; Ps 34:20

b *24* Psalm 22:18 **c** *36* Exodus 12:46; Num. 9:12; Psalm 34:20

19:16 HANDED HIM OVER ... TO BE CRUCIFIED. See Lk 23:25, note.

19:17 CARRYING HIS OWN CROSS. See Mt 27:31, note.

19:18 THEY CRUCIFIED HIM. For comments on the crucifixion, see Mt 27:35, note.

19:26 DEAR WOMAN, HERE IS YOUR SON. Even in the agony of dying, Jesus is concerned about the welfare of his mother. He appoints "the disciple whom he loved" (probably John) to take care of her. To assist needy family members is a responsibility we have until death. The emphasis here is on the responsibility of children for their dependent parents.

19:29 WINE VINEGAR. The Greek word translated "wine vinegar" is *oxos*, a sour wine or vinegar. The English word "vinegar" is from the French *vin* (wine) and *aigre* (sour), thus, sour wine. Vinegar, or sour wine, is made when alcohol changes into vinegar by the formation of acetic acid. Christ's tasting of the vinegar was a fulfillment of the prophecy of Ps 69:21, "they . . . gave me vinegar for my thirst."

19:30 IT IS FINISHED. Jesus' sufferings in providing redemption for fallen humanity were over and his work of redemption completed. He had borne the punishment for our sins and opened the way of salvation for all (see Mt 27:50, note; Lk 23:46, note).

scripture says, "They will look on the one
they have pierced."[d][b]

The Burial of Jesus

19:38–42pp — Mt 27:57–61; Mk 15:42–47; Lk 23:50–56

38Later, Joseph of Arimathea asked Pilate for the body of Jesus. Now Joseph was
a disciple of Jesus, but secretly because he
feared the Jews.[c] With Pilate's permission, he came and took the body away.
39He was accompanied by Nicodemus,[d]
the man who earlier had visited Jesus at
night. Nicodemus brought a mixture of
myrrh and aloes, about seventy-five
pounds.[e] **40**Taking Jesus' body, the two of
them wrapped it, with the spices, in strips
of linen.[e] This was in accordance with
Jewish burial customs.[f] **41**At the place
where Jesus was crucified, there was a
garden, and in the garden a new tomb, in
which no one had ever been laid. **42**Because it was the Jewish day of Preparation[g] and since the tomb was nearby,[h]
they laid Jesus there.

The Empty Tomb

20:1–8pp — Mt 28:1–8; Mk 16:1–8; Lk 24:1–10

20 Early on the first day of the week,
while it was still dark, Mary Magdalene[i] went to the tomb and saw that the
stone had been removed from the entrance.[j] **2**So she came running to Simon
Peter and the other disciple, the one Jesus
loved,[k] and said, "They have taken the
Lord out of the tomb, and we don't know
where they have put him!"[l]

3So Peter and the other disciple started
for the tomb.[m] **4**Both were running, but
the other disciple outran Peter and
reached the tomb first. **5**He bent over and
looked in[n] at the strips of linen[o] lying
there but did not go in. **6**Then Simon Peter, who was behind him, arrived and went
into the tomb. He saw the strips of linen
lying there, **7**as well as the burial cloth
that had been around Jesus' head.[p] The
cloth was folded up by itself, separate
from the linen. **8**Finally the other disciple,
who had reached the tomb first,[q] also
went inside. He saw and believed. **9**(They
still did not understand from Scripture[r]
that Jesus had to rise from the dead.)[s]

Jesus Appears to Mary Magdalene

10Then the disciples went back to their
homes, **11**but Mary stood outside the tomb
crying. As she wept, she bent over to look
into the tomb[t] **12**and saw two angels in
white,[u] seated where Jesus' body had
been, one at the head and the other at the
foot.

13They asked her, "Woman, why are
you crying?"[v]

"They have taken my Lord away," she
said, "and I don't know where they have
put him."[w] **14**At this, she turned around
and saw Jesus standing there,[x] but she
did not realize that it was Jesus.[y]

15"Woman," he said, "why are you crying?[z] Who is it you are looking for?"

Thinking he was the gardener, she said,
"Sir, if you have carried him away, tell me
where you have put him, and I will get
him."

16Jesus said to her, "Mary."

She turned toward him and cried out in
Aramaic,[a] "Rabboni!"[b] (which means
Teacher).

17Jesus said, "Do not hold on to me, for
I have not yet returned to the Father. Go
instead to my brothers[c] and tell them, 'I
am returning to my Father[d] and your Father, to my God and your God.' "

18Mary Magdalene[e] went to the disciples[f] with the news: "I have seen the
Lord!" And she told them that he had said
these things to her.

Jesus Appears to His Disciples

19On the evening of that first day of the
week, when the disciples were together,
with the doors locked for fear of the
Jews,[g] Jesus came and stood among them
and said, "Peace[h] be with you!"[i] **20**After

19:37 [b]Zec 12:10; Rev 1:7 **19:38** [c]S Jn 7:13 **19:39** [d]Jn 3:1; 7:50 **19:40** [e]Lk 24:12; Jn 11:44; 20:5,7 [f]Mt 26:12 **19:42** [g]ver 14,31 [h]ver 20,41 **20:1** [i]ver 18; Lk 8:2; Jn 19:25 [j]Mt 27:60,66 **20:2** [k]S Jn 13:23 [l]ver 13 **20:3** [m]Lk 24:12 **20:5** [n]ver 11 [o]S Jn 19:40 **20:7** [p]Jn 11:44 **20:8** [q]ver 4 **20:9** [r]Mt 22:29; Jn 2:22 [s]Lk 24:26, 46; Ac 2:24 **20:11** [t]ver 5 **20:12** [u]Mt 28:2, 3; Mk 16:5; Lk 24:4; Ac 1:10; S 5:19; 10:30 **20:13** [v]ver 15 [w]ver 2 **20:14** [x]Mk 16:9 [y]Lk 24:16; Jn 21:4 **20:15** [z]ver 13 **20:16** [a]S Jn 5:2 [b]S Mt 23:7 **20:17** [c]S Mt 28:10 [d]Jn 7:33 **20:18** [e]S ver 1 [f]Lk 24:10,22,23 **20:19** [g]S Jn 7:13 [h]S Jn 14:27 [i]ver 21,26; Lk 24:36-39

[d] *37* Zech. 12:10 [e] *39* Greek *a hundred litrai* (about 34 kilograms)

19:41 A NEW TOMB. The tomb had been hewn out of solid rock (Mk 15:46). It was probably large enough to walk into, but with a low entrance (20:11). After placing the body of Jesus in the tomb, Joseph rolled a big stone in front of its entrance (Mt 27:60).

20:9 HE HAD TO RISE. See Mt 28:6, note on the importance of Christ's resurrection, and Lk 24:6, note on the confirmation of Christ's resurrection.

20:16 JESUS APPEARS TO MARY. The first person to whom Jesus appears after his resurrection is Mary. She is not a particularly prominent person in the Gospels, yet Jesus appears first to her rather than to any of the outstanding leaders among the disciples. Throughout the ages, Jesus reveals his presence and love especially to those who are "least." God's special people are the unknown — those who, like Mary in her grief, maintain a steadfast love for their Lord.

20:17 DO NOT HOLD ON TO ME. This verse probably means, "Don't continue clinging to me; I am not yet going to ascend to my Father. You will still have opportunity to see me again." In the meantime he has a task for her.

THE REGENERATION OF THE DISCIPLES

***Jn 20:22** "And with that he breathed on them and said, 'Receive the Holy Spirit.' "*

The impartation of the Holy Spirit by Jesus to his disciples on resurrection day was not the baptism in the Spirit as experienced at Pentecost (Ac 1:5; 2:4). It was rather an infusing of the disciples for the first time with the regenerating presence of the Holy Spirit and with new life from the risen Christ.

(1) During Jesus' last discourse with his disciples before his trial and crucifixion, he promised them that they would receive the Holy Spirit as the One who would regenerate them: "he lives with you and will be in you"(Jn 14:17, see note). Jesus now fulfills that promise.

(2) That Jn 20:22 refers to regeneration can be inferred from the phrase, "he breathed on them." The Greek word for "breathed" (*emphusaō*) is the same verb used in the Septuagint (the Greek translation of the OT) at Ge 2:7, where God "breathed into his [Adam's] nostrils the breath of life, and the man became a living being." It is the same verb found in Eze 37:9, "Breathe into these slain, that they may live." John's use of this verb indicates that Jesus was giving the Spirit in order to bring forth life and a new creation. That is, just as God breathed into physical man the breath of life and he became a new creation (Ge 2:7), so Jesus now breathed on the disciples spiritually and they became a new creation (see article on REGENERATION, p. 178). Through his resurrection, Jesus became a "life-giving spirit" (1Co 15:45).

(3) The phrase "receive the Holy Spirit" establishes that the Spirit, *at that historical moment*, entered and began to live in the disciples. The verb form for "receive" is aorist imperative (Gk *labete*, from the word *lambanō*), denoting a single act of reception. The Holy Spirit was given to regenerate them, to make them new creatures in Christ (cf. 2Co 5:17). This "receiving" of life from the Spirit preceded both their receiving the authority of Jesus (Jn 20:23) and their baptism in the Holy Spirit on the day of Pentecost (Ac 2:4).

(4) Prior to this time, the disciples were technically true believers and followers of Jesus and were saved according to the old covenant provisions. Yet they were not regenerated in the full new covenant sense. Not until this point did the disciples enter into the new covenant provisions based on Jesus' death and resurrection (see Mt 26:28; Lk 22:20; 1Co 11:25; Eph 2:15–16; Heb 9:15–17; see article on REGENERATION, p. 178). It was also technically at this time and not at Pentecost that the church was born. The spiritual birth of the first disciples and the birth of the church are one and the same.

(5) This passage is crucial in understanding the Holy Spirit's ministry to God's people. These two statements are true: (a) the disciples received the Holy Spirit (i.e., were indwelt and regenerated by the Holy Spirit) before the day of Pentecost, and (b) the outpouring of the Spirit in Ac 2:4 was an experience occurring after their regeneration by the Spirit. Their baptism in the Spirit at Pentecost was, therefore, a second and distinct work of the Spirit in them.

(6) These two separate and distinct works of the Holy Spirit in the lives of Jesus' disciples are normative for all Christians. That is, all believers receive the Holy Spirit at the time of their regeneration, and afterwards must experience the baptism in the Spirit for power to be his witnesses (Ac 1:5,8; 2:4; see 2:39, note).

(7) There is no Scriptural foundation to suggest that Jesus' bestowal of the Holy Spirit in Jn 20:22 was simply symbolical prophecy of the coming of the Holy Spirit at Pentecost. The use of the aorist imperative for "receive" (see above) denotes reception at that moment and in that place. What occurred was a historical reality in space and time, and John records it as such.

he said this, he showed them his hands
and side.[j] The disciples were overjoyed[k]
when they saw the Lord.

The Disciples Receive the Holy Spirit

21Again Jesus said, "Peace be with
you![l] As the Father has sent me,[m] I am
sending you."[n] 22And with that he
breathed on them and said, "Receive the
Holy Spirit.[o] 23If you forgive anyone his
sins, they are forgiven; if you do not forgive them, they are not forgiven."[p]

Jesus Appears to Thomas

24Now Thomas[q] (called Didymus), one
of the Twelve, was not with the disciples
when Jesus came. 25So the other disciples
told him, "We have seen the Lord!"

But he said to them, "Unless I see the
nail marks in his hands and put my finger
where the nails were, and put my hand
into his side,[r] I will not believe it."[s]

26A week later his disciples were in the
house again, and Thomas was with them.
Though the doors were locked, Jesus
came and stood among them and said,
"Peace[t] be with you!"[u] 27Then he said to
Thomas, "Put your finger here; see my
hands. Reach out your hand and put it into
my side. Stop doubting and believe."[v]

28Thomas said to him, "My Lord and my
God!"

29Then Jesus told him, "Because you
have seen me, you have believed;[w]
blessed are those who have not seen and
yet have believed."[x]

30Jesus did many other miraculous
signs[y] in the presence of his disciples,
which are not recorded in this book.[z]
31But these are written that you may[f] believe[a] that Jesus is the Christ, the Son of
God,[b] and that by believing you may have
life in his name.[c]

Jesus and the Miraculous Catch of Fish

21 Afterward Jesus appeared again to
his disciples,[d] by the Sea of Tiberias.[g][e] It happened this way: 2Simon Peter,
Thomas[f] (called Didymus), Nathanael[g]
from Cana in Galilee,[h] the sons of Zebedee,[i] and two other disciples were together. 3"I'm going out to fish," Simon Peter
told them, and they said, "We'll go with
you." So they went out and got into the
boat, but that night they caught nothing.[j]
4Early in the morning, Jesus stood on
the shore, but the disciples did not realize
that it was Jesus.[k]

20:20 [j] Lk 24:39, 40; Jn 19:34 [k] Jn 16:20,22
20:21 [l] ver 19 [m] S Jn 3:17 [n] Mt 28:19; Jn 17:18
20:22 [o] Jn 7:39; Ac 2:38; 8:15-17; 19:2; Gal 3:2
20:23 [p] Mt 16:19; 18:18
20:24 [q] S Jn 11:16
20:25 [r] ver 20 [s] Mk 16:11
20:26 [t] S Jn 14:27 [u] ver 21
20:27 [v] ver 25; Lk 24:40
20:29 [w] S Jn 3:15 [x] 1Pe 1:8
20:30 [y] S Jn 2:11 [z] Jn 21:25
20:31 [a] S Jn 3:15; 19:35 [b] S Mt 4:3 [c] S Mt 25:46
21:1 [d] ver 14; Jn 20:19,26 [e] Jn 6:1
21:2 [f] S Jn 11:16 [g] Jn 1:45 [h] Jn 2:1 [i] S Mt 4:21
21:3 [j] Lk 5:5
21:4 [k] Lk 24:16; Jn 20:14

[f] *31* Some manuscripts *may continue to*
[g] *1* That is, Sea of Galilee

20:22 RECEIVE THE HOLY SPIRIT. For an extensive discussion of this important verse and how it relates to our regeneration and baptism in the Holy Spirit, see article on THE REGENERATION OF THE DISCIPLES, p. 212.

20:23 IF YOU FORGIVE ANYONE. See Mt 16:19, note.

20:28 MY LORD AND MY GOD. The Scriptures declare that Jesus is God. This is the foundation of the Christian faith and is of utmost importance for our salvation. Without Christ being divine, he could not have made atonement for the sins of the world. The deity of Jesus Christ is shown by the following:

(1) Divine names are given to him in Scripture: (a) God (20:28; Isa 9:6; Ro 9:5; Tit 2:13; Heb 1:8); (b) the Son of God (5:25; Mt 16:16–17; 8:29; 27:40,43; Mk 14:61–62; Lk 22:70); (c) the First and the Last (Rev 1:17; 2:8; 22:13); (d) the Alpha and the Omega (Rev 1:8; 22:13); (e) the Beginning and the End (Rev 22:13); (f) the Holy One (Hos 11:9; Ac 3:14); (g) the Lord (Lk 2:11; Ac 4:33; 9:17; 16:31); (h) Lord of all and Lord of glory (Ps 24:8–10; Ac 10:36; 1Co 2:8).

(2) Divine worship is given to Christ (5:23; 13:13; 20:28; Mt 14:33; Lk 5:8), and prayers are addressed to him (Ac 7:59; 1Co 1:2; 2Co 12:8–9).

(3) Divine offices are assigned to Christ: (a) creator of the universe (1:3; Col 1:16; Heb 1:8,10; Rev 3:14); (b) sustainer of all things (Col 1:17; Heb 1:3); (c) forgiver of sins (Mk 2:5,10; Lk 7:48–50); (d) bestower of resurrection life (5:28–29; 6:39–44); (e) judge of all people (5:21–23; Mt 25:31–46; Ac 17:31; 2Ti 4:1); (f) giver of salvation (5:24–26; 6:47; 10:28; 17:2).

(4) The NT sees Christ in OT statements about the Lord. Compare Ps 23:1 with Jn 10:11; Ps 102:24–27 with Heb 1:10–12; Isa 8:13–14 with 1Pe 2:7–8; Jer 17:10 with Rev 2:23; Eze 34:11–12 with Lk 19:10.

(5) The name of Jesus Christ is associated with that of God the Father (14:1,23; Mt 28:19; Ro 1:7; 2Co 13:14; Col 2:2; 1Th 3:11; Jas 1:1; Rev 5:13; 7:10).

(6) Christ's sinlessness and holiness testify to his divinity (Lk 1:35; 2Co 5:21; Heb 4:15).

(7) Christ was declared to be the Son of God by his resurrection (Ro 1:4).

These conclusive proofs of Christ's divinity mean that believers must act toward Christ in exactly the same manner as they act toward God the Father. They must believe in him, worship him, pray to him, serve him and love him (see also 1:1, note; Mk 1:11, note on the Trinity).

21:1 JESUS APPEARED AGAIN. See Mt 28:9, note on Christ's resurrection appearances.

21:3 I'M GOING OUT TO FISH. The disciples' plan to go fishing does not mean they were forsaking their commitment to Christ and their calling to preach the gospel. They knew that Jesus had risen from the grave, yet they did not know what to do next. They had not yet received the instruction to wait in Jerusalem until the Holy Spirit came on them in power (Ac 1:4–5). To go fishing was a necessity, for these men still had to provide for themselves and their families.

[5]He called out to them, "Friends, haven't you any fish?"

"No," they answered.

[6]He said, "Throw your net on the right side of the boat and you will find some." When they did, they were unable to haul the net in because of the large number of fish.[l]

[7]Then the disciple whom Jesus loved[m] said to Peter, "It is the Lord!" As soon as Simon Peter heard him say, "It is the Lord," he wrapped his outer garment around him (for he had taken it off) and jumped into the water. [8]The other disciples followed in the boat, towing the net full of fish, for they were not far from shore, about a hundred yards.[h] [9]When they landed, they saw a fire[n] of burning coals there with fish on it,[o] and some bread.

[10]Jesus said to them, "Bring some of the fish you have just caught."

[11]Simon Peter climbed aboard and dragged the net ashore. It was full of large fish, 153, but even with so many the net was not torn. [12]Jesus said to them, "Come and have breakfast." None of the disciples dared ask him, "Who are you?" They knew it was the Lord. [13]Jesus came, took the bread and gave it to them, and did the same with the fish.[p] [14]This was now the third time Jesus appeared to his disciples[q] after he was raised from the dead.

Jesus Reinstates Peter

[15]When they had finished eating, Jesus said to Simon Peter, "Simon son of John, do you truly love me more than these?"

"Yes, Lord," he said, "you know that I love you."[r]

Jesus said, "Feed my lambs."[s]

[16]Again Jesus said, "Simon son of John, do you truly love me?"

He answered, "Yes, Lord, you know that I love you."

Jesus said, "Take care of my sheep."[t]

[17]The third time he said to him, "Simon son of John, do you love me?"

Peter was hurt because Jesus asked him the third time, "Do you love me?"[u] He said, "Lord, you know all things;[v] you know that I love you."

Jesus said, "Feed my sheep.[w] [18]I tell you the truth, when you were younger you dressed yourself and went where you wanted; but when you are old you will stretch out your hands, and someone else will dress you and lead you where you do not want to go." [19]Jesus said this to indicate the kind of death[x] by which Peter would glorify God.[y] Then he said to him, "Follow me!"[z]

[20]Peter turned and saw that the disciple whom Jesus loved[a] was following them. (This was the one who had leaned back against Jesus at the supper and had said, "Lord, who is going to betray you?")[b] [21]When Peter saw him, he asked, "Lord, what about him?"

[22]Jesus answered, "If I want him to remain alive until I return,[c] what is that to you? You must follow me."[d] [23]Because of this, the rumor spread among the brothers[e] that this disciple would not die. But Jesus did not say that he would not die; he only said, "If I want him to remain alive until I return, what is that to you?"

21:6 [l]Lk 5:4-7 **21:7** [m]S Jn 13:23 **21:9** [n]Jn 18:18 [o]ver 10,13 **21:13** [p]ver 9 **21:14** [q]Jn 20:19, 26 **21:15** [r]Mt 26:33, 35; Jn 13:37 [s]Lk 12:32 **21:16** [t]2Sa 5:2; Eze 34:2; Mt 2:6; S Jn 10:11; Ac 20:28; 1Pe 5:2, 3 **21:17** [u]Jn 13:38 [v]Jn 16:30 [w]S ver 16 **21:19** [x]Jn 12:33; 18:32 [y]Jn 13:36; 2Pe 1:14 [z]S Mt 4:19 **21:20** [a]ver 7; S Jn 13:23 [b]Jn 13:25 **21:22** [c]S Mt 16:27 [d]ver 19; S Mt 4:19 **21:23** [e]S Ac 1:16

[h] *8* Greek *about two hundred cubits* (about 90 meters)

21:6 THROW YOUR NET ON THE RIGHT SIDE. It is crucial to receive guidance from the Lord in all our work. If we live without Christ's presence and guiding hand, then much of what we do becomes empty failure and wasted effort.

21:15 DO YOU TRULY LOVE ME. The most important question that Peter ever faced was whether he possessed a devoted love for his Lord. (1) Two Greek words for "love" are used here. The first, *agapaō*, means an intelligent and purposeful love, primarily of mind and will. The second, *phileō*, involves warm natural affection of the emotions, thus a more personal and feeling love. Through these two words, Jesus indicates that Peter's love must be not only of the will, but also of the heart, a love springing from both purpose and personal attachment. (2) Jesus' question to Peter is the great question for all believers. We must all have a personal heartfelt love for and devotion to Jesus (14:15; 16:27; Mt 10:37; Lk 7:47; 1Co 16:22; 2Co 5:14; Gal 5:6; Eph 6:24; Jas 1:12; 1Pe 1:8; Rev 2:4).

21:16 TAKE CARE OF MY SHEEP. Jesus' description of believers as lambs (v. 15) and sheep (v. 16) implies three things. (1) We need pastoral care. (2) We need to feed constantly on the Word. (3) Since sheep are prone to wander into danger, we need repeated guidance, protection and correction.

21:17 DO YOU LOVE ME? . . . FEED MY SHEEP. Jesus sees love as the basic qualification for Christian service. Other qualifications are needed (1Ti 3:1–13), but love for Christ and for others is indispensable (cf. 1Co 13:1–3).

21:18 YOU WILL STRETCH OUT YOUR HANDS. These words refer to the kind of death by which Peter would glorify God. Tradition records that Peter was crucified in Rome under Nero at about the same time that Paul was martyred (c. A.D. 67/68), and that at his own request he was crucified upside down because he considered himself unworthy to be crucified in the same manner as his Lord.

[24]This is the disciple who testifies to
these things[f] and who wrote them down.
We know that his testimony is true.[g]
[25]Jesus did many other things as well.[h]
If every one of them were written down, I suppose that even the whole world would not have room for the books that would be written.

21:24 [f]S Jn 15:27 [g]Jn 19:35
21:25 [h]Jn 20:30

THE MINISTRY OF JESUS

THE YEAR OF INAUGURATION

Event	Place	Matthew	Mark	Luke	John
Jesus baptized	Jordan River	3:13–17	1:9–11	3:21–23	1:29–39
Jesus tempted by Satan	Desert	4:1–11	1:12–13	4:1–13	
Jesus' first miracle	Cana				2:1–11
Jesus and Nicodemus	Judea				3:1–21
Jesus talks to a Samaritan woman	Samaria				4:5–42
Jesus heals an official's son	Cana				4:46–54
The people of Nazareth try to kill Jesus	Nazareth			4:16–31	

THE YEAR OF POPULARITY

Event	Place	Matthew	Mark	Luke	John
Jesus calls four fishermen	Sea of Galilee	4:18–22	1:16–20	5:1–11	
Jesus heals Peter's mother-in-law	Capernaum	8:14–17	1:29–34	4:38–41	
Jesus begins preaching in Galilee	Galilee	4:23–25	1:35–39	4:42–4	
Matthew decides to follow Jesus	Capernaum	9:9–13	2:13–17	5:27–32	
Jesus chooses twelve disciples	Galilee	10:2–4	3:13–19	6:12–15	
Jesus preaches the Sermon on the Mount	Galilee	5:1–7:29		6:20–49	
A sinful woman anoints Jesus	Capernaum			7:36–50	
Jesus travels again through Galilee	Galilee			8:1–3	
Jesus tells parables about the kingdom	Galilee	13:1–52	4:1–34	8:4–18	
Jesus quiets the storm	Sea of Galilee	8:23–27	4:35–41	8:22–25	
Jairus's daughter raised to life by Jesus	Capernaum	9:18–26	5:21–43	8:40–56	
Jesus sends out the twelve	Galilee	9:35—11:1	6:6–13	9:1–6	

THE YEAR OF OPPOSITION

Event	Place	Matthew	Mark	Luke	John
John the Baptist killed by Herod	Machaerus in Judea	14:1–12	6:14–29	9:7–9	
Jesus feeds the 5000	Near Bethsaida	14:13–21	6:30–44	9:10–17	6:1–14
Jesus walks on water	Sea of Galilee	14:22–23	6:45–52		6:16–21
Jesus feeds the 4000	Sea of Galilee	15:32–39	8:1–9		
Peter confesses Jesus as the Son of God	Caesarea Philippi	16:13–20	8:27–30	9:18–21	
Jesus predicts his death	Caesarea Philippi	16:21–26	8:31–37	9:22–25	
Jesus is transfigured	Mount Hermon	17:1–13	9:2–13	9:28–36	
Jesus pays his temple taxes	Capernaum	17:24–27			
Jesus attends the Feast of Tabernacles	Jerusalem				7:11–52
Jesus heals a man born blind	Jerusalem				9:1–41

THE MINISTRY OF JESUS

THE YEAR OF OPPOSITION (cont.)

Event	Place	Matthew	Mark	Luke	John
Jesus visits Mary and Martha	Bethany			10:38–42	
Jesus raises Lazarus from the dead	Bethany				11:1–44
Jesus begins his last trip to Jerusalem	Border road			17:11	
Jesus blesses the little children	Transjordan	19:13–15	10:13–16	18:15–17	
Jesus talks to the rich young man	Transjordan	19:16–30	10:17–31	18:18–30	
Jesus again predicts his death	Near the Jordan	20:17–19	10:32–34	18:31–34	
Jesus heals blind Bartimaeus	Jericho	20:29–34	10:46–52	18:35–43	
Jesus talks to Zacchaeus	Jericho			19:1–10	
Jesus visits Mary and Martha again	Bethany				11:55–12:1

THE LAST WEEK

Event	Place	Day of Week	Matthew	Mark	Luke	John
The triumphal entry	Jerusalem	Sunday	21:1–11	11:1–10	19:29–44	12:12–19
Jesus curses the fig tree	Jerusalem	Monday	21:18–19	11:12–14		
Jesus cleanses the temple	Jerusalem	Monday	21:12–13	11:15–18	19:45–48	
The authority of Jesus questioned	Jerusalem	Tuesday	21:23–27	11:27–33	20:1–8	
Jesus teaches in the temple	Jerusalem	Tuesday	21:28–23:29	12:1–44	20:9–21:4	
Jesus' feet anointed	Bethany	Tuesday	26:6–13	14:3–9		12:2–11
The plot against Jesus	Jerusalem	Wednesday	26:14–16	14:10–11	22:3–6	
The Last Supper	Jerusalem	Thursday	26:17–29	14:12–25	22:7–20	13:1–38
Jesus comforts his disciples	Jerusalem	Thursday				14:1–16:33
Jesus' high priestly prayer	Jerusalem	Thursday				17:1–26
Gethsemane	Jerusalem	Thursday	26:36–46	14:32–42	22:40–46	
Jesus' arrest and trial	Jerusalem	Friday	26:47–27:26	14:43–15:15	22:47–23:25	18:2–19:16
Jesus' crucifixion and death	Golgotha	Friday	27:27–56	15:16–41	23:26–49	19:17–30
The burial of Jesus	Garden tomb	Friday	27:57–66	15:42–47	23:50–56	19:31–42

RESURRECTION APPEARANCES

Event	Place	Day of week	Matthew	Mark	Luke	John	Acts	1 Corinthians
The empty tomb	Jerusalem	Easter Sunday	28:1–10	16:1–8	24:1–12	20:1–10		
To Mary Magdalene in the garden	Jerusalem	Easter Sunday		16:9–11		20:11–18		
To two people going to Emmaus	Road to Emmaus	Easter Sunday		16:12–13	24:13–32			
To Peter	Jerusalem	Easter Sunday			24:34			15:5
To the ten disciples in the upper room	Jerusalem	Easter Sunday		16:14	24:36–43	20:19–25		
To the eleven disciples in the upper room	Jerusalem	Following Sunday				20:26–31		15:5
To seven disciples fishing	Sea of Galilee	Some time later				21:1–25		
To the eleven disciples on a mountain	Galilee	Some time later	28:16–20	16:15–18				15:5
To more than five hundred	Unknown	Some time later						15:6
To James	Unknown	Some time later						15:7
To his disciples	Mount of Olives	Forty days after Easter			24:44–51		1:3–9	15:7
To Paul	Damascus	Several years later					9:1–19; 22:3–16; 26:9–18	9:1; 15:8

THE PARABLES OF JESUS

Parable	Matthew	Mark	Luke
Lamp under a bowl	5:14–15	4:21–22	8:16; 11:33
Wise and foolish builders	7:24–27		6:47–49
New cloth on an old garment	9:16	2:21	5:36
New wine in old wineskins	9:17	2:22	5:37–38
Sower and the soils	13:3–8, 18–23	4:3–8, 14–20	8:5–8, 11–15
Weeds	13:24–30, 36–43		
Mustard seed	13:31–32	4:30–32	13:18–19
Yeast	13:33		13:20–21
Hidden treasure	13:44		
Valuable pearl	13:45–46		
Net	13:47–50		

THE PARABLES OF JESUS (cont.)

Parable	Matthew	Mark	Luke
Owner of a house	13:52		
Lost sheep	18:12–14		15:4–7
Unmerciful servant	18:23–34		
Workers in the vineyard	20:1–16		
Two sons	21:28–32		
Tenants	21:33–44	12:1–11	20:9–18
Wedding banquet	22:2–14		
Fig tree	24:32–35	13:28–29	21:29–31
Faithful and wise servant	24:45–51	12:42–48	
Ten virgins	25:1–13		
Talents (minas)	25:14–30		19:12–27
Sheep and goats	25:31–46		
Growing seed		4:26–29	
Watchful servants		13:35–37	12:35–40
Moneylender			7:41–43
Good Samaritan			10:30–37
Friend in need			11:5–8
Rich fool			12:16–21
Unfruitful fig tree			13:6–9
Lowest seat at the feast			14:7–14
Great banquet			14:16–24
Cost of discipleship			14:28–33
Lost coin			15:8–10
Lost (prodigal) son			15:11–32
Shrewd manager			16:1–8
Rich man and Lazarus			16:19–31
Master and his servant			17:7–10
Persistent widow			18:2–8

THE MIRACLES OF JESUS

	Matthew	Mark	Luke	John
Healing Miracles				
Man with leprosy	8:2–4	1:40–42	5:12–13	
Roman centurion's servant	8:5–13		7:1–10	
Peter's mother-in-law	8:14–15	1:30–31	4:38–39	
Two men from Gadara	8:28–34	5:1–15	8:27–35	
Paralyzed man	9:2–7	2:3–12	5:18–25	
Woman with bleeding	9:20–22	5:25–29	8:43–48	

THE MIRACLES OF JESUS (cont.)

	Matthew	Mark	Luke	John
Healing Miracles				
Two blind men	9:27–31			
Mute, demon-possessed man	9:32–33			
Man with a shriveled hand	12:10–13	3:1–5	6:6–10	
Blind, mute, demon-possessed man	12:22		11:14	
Canaanite woman's daughter	15:21–28	7:24–30		
Boy with a demon	17:14–18	9:17–29	9:38–43	
Two blind men (including Bartimaeus)	20:29–34	10:46–52	18:35–43	
Deaf mute		7:31–37		
Possessed man in synagogue		1:23–26	4:33–35	
Blind man at Bethsaida		8:22–26		
Crippled woman			13:11–13	
Man with dropsy			14:1–4	
Ten men with leprosy			17:11–19	
The high priest's servant			22:50–51	
Official's son at Capernaum				4:46–54
Sick man at pool of Bethesda				5:1–9
Man born blind				9:1–7
Miracles showing power over nature				
Calming the storm	8:23–27	4:37–41	8:22–25	
Walking on water	14:25	6:48–51		6:19–21
Feeding of the 5000	14:15–21	6:35–44	9:12–17	6:5–13
Feeding of the 4000	15:32–38	8:1–9		
Coin in fish	17:24–27			
Fig tree withered	21:18–22	11:12–14, 20–25		
Large catch of fish			5:4–11	
Water turned into wine				2:1– 11
Another large catch of fish				21:1–11
Miracles of raising the dead				
Jairus's daughter	9:18–19, 23–25	5:22–24, 38–42	8:41–42, 49–56	
Widow's son at Nain			7:11–15	
Lazarus				11:1–44

MIRACLES OF THE APOSTLES

Miracle	Acts
Lame man cured (by Peter)	3:6–9
Death of Ananias and Sapphira	5:1–10
Saul's sight restored	9:17–18
Healing of Aeneas	9:33–35
Raising of Dorcas	9:36–41
Elymas blinded	13:8–11
Lame man cured (by Paul)	14:8–10
Demon cast out of a girl	16:16–18
Raising of Eutychus	20:9–10
Paul unharmed by viper	28:3–5
Healing of Publius's father	28:7–9

ACTS

Outline

Introduction (1:1–11)

I. The Outpouring of the Holy Spirit (1:12—2:41)
   A. Preparing for the Promise (1:12–26)
   B. The Day of Pentecost (2:1–41)

II. Early Days of the Church in Jerusalem (2:42—8:1a)
   A. Characteristics of the Apostolic Church After the Outpouring of the Spirit (2:42–47)
   B. A Remarkable Miracle and its Effects (3:1—4:31)
   C. The Continuing Experiment in Community Sharing (4:32—5:11)
   D. Further Healings and Resistance from the Religious Establishment (5:12–42)
   E. The Selection of Seven Deacons (6:1–7)
   F. Stephen: The First-known Christian Martyr (6:8—8:1a)

III. Persecution Leads to Expansion (8:1b—9:31)
   A. Christians Scattered Throughout Judea and Samaria (8:1b-4)
   B. Philip: The Ministry of an Evangelist (8:5–40)
   C. Saul of Tarsus: The Conversion of a Persecutor (9:1–31)

IV. Christianity Began Spreading to the Gentiles (9:32—12:25)
   A. Peter's Ministry at Lydda and Joppa (9:32–43)
   B. Peter's Mission to the Gentiles at Caesarea (10:1–48)
   C. Peter's Report to the Jerusalem Church and His Action Approved (11:1–18)
   D. Antioch: The First Gentile Church (11:19–30)
   E. Persecution Under Herod Agrippa I (12:1–23)
   F. Summary of the Church's Progress (12:24–25)

V. Paul's First Missionary Journey (13:1—14:28)
   A. Paul and Barnabas Commissioned by the Local Church at Antioch (13:1–3)
   B. The Territory Evangelized (13:4—14:28)

VI. The Jerusalem Council (15:1–35)

VII. Paul's Second Missionary Journey (15:36—18:22)
   A. Disagreement Between Paul and Barnabas (15:36–40)
   B. Old Territory Revisited (15:41—16:5)
   C. New Territory Evangelized (16:6—18:21)
   D. Return to Syrian Antioch (18:22)

VIII. Paul's Third Missionary Journey (18:23—21:16)
   A. En Route to Ephesus (18:23)
      Parenthesis: The Ministry of Apollos (18:24–28)
   B. A Lengthy Ministry at Ephesus (19:1–41)
   C. To Macedonia, Greece, and Back to Macedonia (20:1–5)
   D. Return Trip to Jerusalem (20:6—21:16)

IX. Paul's Arrest and Ministry During Imprisonment (21:17—28:31)
   A. In Jerusalem (21:17—23:35)
   B. In Caesarea (24:1—26:32)
   C. En Route to Rome (27:1—28:15)
   D. In Rome (28:16–31)

Author: Luke

Theme: The Triumphant Spread of the Gospel through the Power of the Holy Spirit

Date: c. A.D. 63

Background

The book of Acts, like the Gospel of Luke, is addressed to a man named "Theophilus" (1:1). Although the author is not identified by name in either book, the unanimous testimony of early Christianity and the corroborating internal evidence of the two books point to common authorship by Luke, "our dear friend . . . the doctor" (Col 4:14).

The Holy Spirit prompted Luke to write to Theophilus in order to fill a need in the Gentile church for a full account of the beginnings of Christianity—(1) the "former book" being his Gospel about Jesus' life, and (2) the latter book being his account in Acts about the outpouring of the Spirit at Jerusalem and the subsequent development of the early church. It is apparent that Luke was a skilled writer, a careful historian and an inspired theologian.

Acts selectively covers the first thirty years of the church's history. As a church historian, Luke traces the spread of the gospel from Jerusalem to Rome, mentioning no fewer than 32 countries, 54 cities, 9 Mediterranean islands, 95 different persons by name, and a variety of governmental officials and administrators by their precise titles. Archaeology continues to confirm Luke's amazing accuracy in all his details. As a theologian, Luke astutely describes the significance of various experiences and events in the church's early years.

In its first stages, NT Scripture comprised two collections: (1) the four Gospels and (2) the letters of Paul. Acts played an indispensable role as the connecting link between the two collections and rightly belongs in its present canonical order. Chs. 13–28 provide the historical background necessary for understanding more fully Paul's ministry and letters. Luke's "we" passages in Acts (16:1–17; 20:5—21:18; 27:1—28:16) reveal his personal participation in Paul's travels.

Purpose

Luke has at least two purposes in recounting the church's beginnings. (1) He shows that the gospel moved triumphantly from the narrow borders of Judaism into the Gentile world in spite of opposition and persecution. (2) He reveals the role of the Holy Spirit in the church's life and mission, emphasizing the baptism in the Spirit as God's provision for empowering the church to proclaim the gospel and to continue Jesus' ministry. Luke explicitly records three times that the baptism in the Spirit was accompanied by speaking in tongues (2:4ff; 10:45–46; 19:1–7). The context of these passages indicate that this was normative in early Christianity and is God's enduring pattern for the church.

Survey

Whereas Luke's Gospel records "all that Jesus began to do and to teach" (Ac 1:1), Acts describes what Jesus continued to do and teach after his ascension, by the power of the Holy Spirit working in and through his disciples and the early church. When Jesus ascended into heaven (1:9–11), his last instruction to his disciples was to wait in Jerusalem until they were baptized with the Holy Spirit (1:4–5). The key verse of Acts (1:8) contains a theological and geographical capsule summary of the book: Jesus promises the disciples they will receive power when the Holy Spirit comes on them—power to be his witnesses (1) "in Jerusalem" (chs. 1–7), (2) "in all Judea and Samaria" (chs. 8–12), and (3) "to the ends of the earth" (chs. 13–28).

Acts contains an intermingling of divine and human action. The entire church, not just the apostles, "preached the word wherever they went" (8:4). Deacons like Stephen and Philip (6:1–6) became mighty in the Holy Spirit and faith, performing "great wonders and miraculous signs" (6:8) and even shaking entire cities with the gospel (see 8:5–13). Godly people prayed fervently, saw angels, had visions, witnessed mighty signs and wonders, drove out demons, healed the sick and proclaimed the gospel with great boldness and authority. In spite of problems within the church, such as the Jewish-Gentile tension (ch. 15), and in spite of persistent persecution outside the church from religious and civil sources, the name of the Lord Jesus was magnified in word and deed from one city to the next.

Special Features

Nine major emphases characterize Acts: (1) The church: Acts reveals the church's source of power and the true nature of its mission, along with principles that should govern the church in every generation. (2) The Holy Spirit: the third person of the Trinity is mentioned specifically fifty times; the baptism in and ministry of the Spirit imparts power (1:8), boldness (4:31), holy fear of God (5:3,5,11), wisdom (6:3,10), guidance (16:6–10) and spiritual gifts (19:6). (3) Early church messages: Luke skillfully recounts inspired sermons by Peter, Stephen, Paul, James and others, providing insight into the early church not found elsewhere in the NT. (4) Prayer: the early Christians devoted themselves to regular and fervent prayer, sometimes lasting all night and producing great results. (5) Signs, wonders and miracles: these manifestations accompanied the proclamation of the gospel in the power of the Holy Spirit. (6) Persecution: proclaiming the gospel with power consistently stirred up religious and/or secular opposition and persecution. (7) Jew/Gentile sequence: throughout Acts the gospel goes first to the Jews and then to the Gentiles. (8) Women: special mention is made of women involved in the ongoing work of the church. (9) Triumph: no barriers (national, religious, cultural or racial) and no opposition or persecution could thwart the advance of the gospel.

Hermeneutical Principle

Believers ought to desire and expect, as the norm for today's church, all elements in the NT church's ministry and experience (except the writing of NT Scripture); these are attainable when the church moves in the full power of the Spirit. Nothing in Acts or the NT indicates that signs, wonders, miracles, spiritual gifts, or the apostolic standard for the church's life and ministry were to cease suddenly or permanently at the end of the apostolic age. Acts records what the church must be and do in any generation as it continues Jesus' ministry in the Pentecostal power of the Holy Spirit.

Reading Acts

In order to read the entire New Testament in one year, the book of Acts should be read in 46 days, according to the following schedule:
☐ 1 ☐ 2:1–36 ☐ 2:37–47 ☐ 3 ☐ 4:1–31 ☐ 4:32—5:11 ☐ 5:12–42 ☐ 6 ☐ 7:1–53 ☐ 7:54—8:8 ☐ 8:9–40 ☐ 9:1–31 ☐ 9:32–43 ☐ 10:1–23 ☐ 10:24–48 ☐ 11:1–18 ☐ 11:19–30 ☐ 12 ☐ 13:1–12 ☐ 13:13–52 ☐ 14 ☐ 15:1–21 ☐ 15:22–35 ☐ 15:36—16:15 ☐ 16:16–40 ☐ 17:1–15 ☐ 17:16–34 ☐ 18:1–23 ☐ 18:24—19:7 ☐ 19:8–41 ☐ 20:1–26 ☐ 20:27–38 ☐ 21:1–16 ☐ 21:17–36 ☐ 21:37—22:21 ☐ 22:22—23:11 ☐ 23:12–35 ☐ 24 ☐ 25:1–12 ☐ 25:13—26:1 ☐ 26:2–18 ☐ 26:19–32 ☐ 27:1–26 ☐ 27:27–44 ☐ 28:1–16 ☐ 28:17–31

NOTES

NOTES

COUNTRIES OF PEOPLE MENTIONED AT PENTECOST

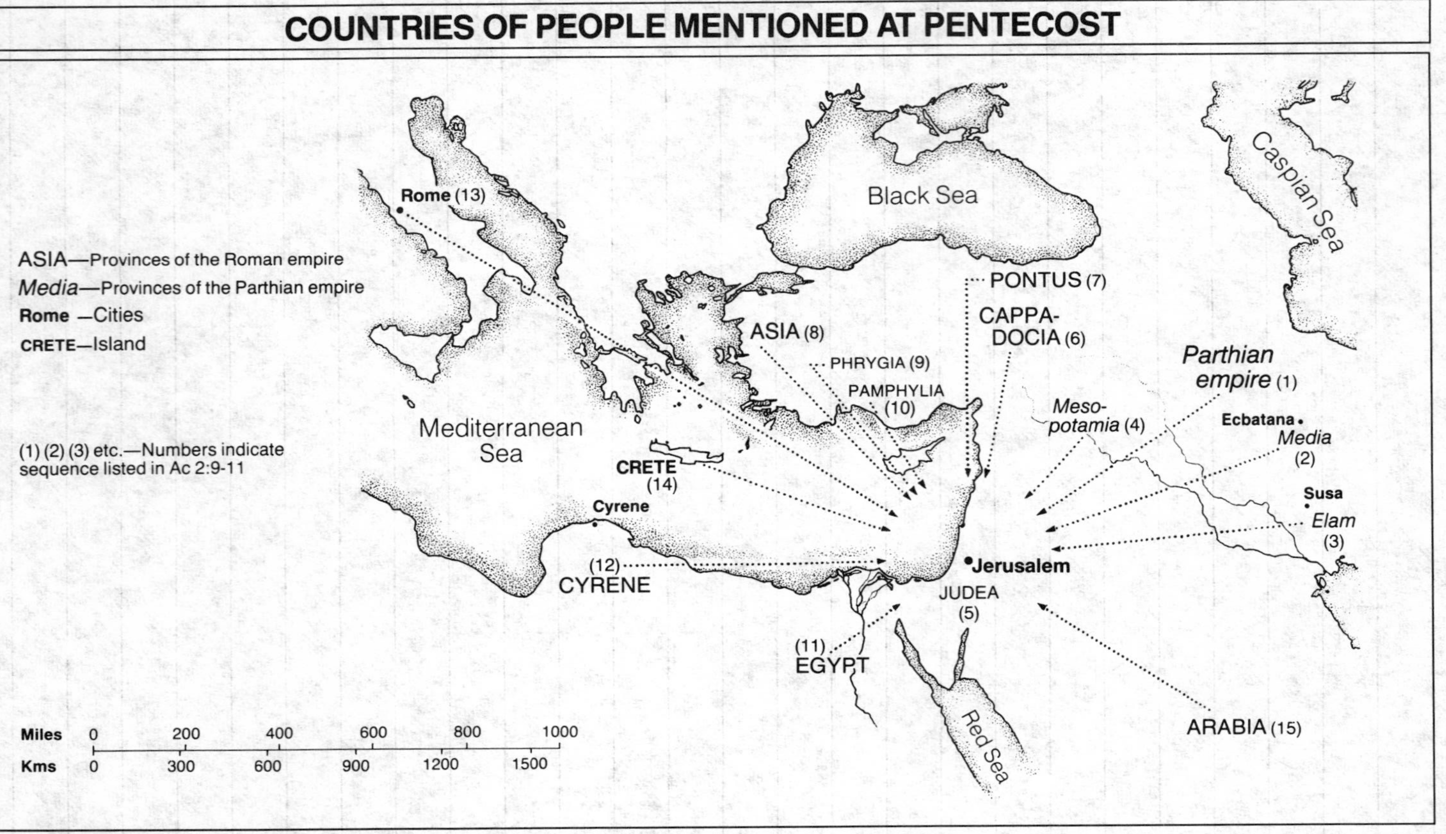

The Promised Baptism in the Spirit

1 In my former book,[a] Theophilus, I
wrote about all that Jesus began to do
and to teach[b] **2**until the day he was taken
up to heaven,[c] after giving instructions[d]
through the Holy Spirit to the apostles[e]
he had chosen.[f] **3**After his suffering, he
showed himself to these men and gave
many convincing proofs that he was alive.
He appeared to them[g] over a period of
forty days and spoke about the kingdom of
God.[h] **4**On one occasion, while he was eating with them, he gave them this command: "Do not leave Jerusalem, but wait[i]
for the gift my Father promised, which you
have heard me speak about.[j] **5**For John
baptized with[a] water,[k] but in a few days
you will be baptized with the Holy Spirit."[l] Ac 2:4-13
6So when they met together, they asked
him, "Lord, are you at this time going to
restore[m] the kingdom to Israel?"
7He said to them: "It is not for you to
know the times or dates the Father has
set by his own authority.[n] **8**But you will
receive power when the Holy Spirit comes

1:1 [a] Lk 1:1-4 [b] Lk 3:23 **1:2** [c] ver 9,11; S Mk 16:19 [d] Mt 28:19,20 [e] S Mk 6:30 [f] Jn 13:18; 15:16, 19 **1:3** [g] Mt 28:17; Lk 24:34,36; Jn 20:19,26; 21:1, 14; 1Co 15:5-7 [h] S Mt 3:2 **1:4** [i] Ps 27:14 [j] Lk 24:49; Jn 14:16; Ac 2:33 **1:5** [k] S Mk 1:4 [l] S Mk 1:8 **1:6** [m] Mt 17:11; Ac 3:21 **1:7** [n] Dt 29:29; Ps 102:13; Mt 24:36

[a] *5* Or *in*

1:1 MY FORMER BOOK. In Luke's Gospel we have the account of all Jesus began to do and to teach in the power of the Holy Spirit (Lk 4:1,18). In the book of Acts we have the continuing story of how Jesus' followers, in the same power of the Spirit, proclaimed the same gospel, worked the same kind of miracles and lived the same kind of life. The Holy Spirit reproducing the life and ministry of Jesus through the church is the theological keynote of Acts. The book could well be called "The Acts of the Holy Spirit." Observe the following concerning the Holy Spirit's inspired record in the book of Acts:

(1) All Scripture, including the historical narratives in Acts, has didactic (i.e., teaching) and theological significance. This is confirmed by two facts: (a) the Biblical declaration that "all Scripture is God-breathed and is useful for teaching, rebuking, correcting and training in righteousness" (2Ti 3:16); (b) Paul's statement that the OT historical narratives have a teaching and instructional purpose (1Co 10:11). He maintains that these stories are examples with practical and theological relevance for the believer (Ro 15:4). What is true for historical narrative in the OT is also true for Acts.

(2) Luke's inspired record of the history of the early church provides: (a) a definitive pattern of the Holy Spirit's activity to be followed during the entire church age, (b) data for developing a doctrine of the Holy Spirit and (c) revelation about how the Spirit's ministry must relate to the lives of believers in Christ. Note specifically two elements in this book that are theologically and practically normative: (i) the baptism in or filling with the Holy Spirit, God's promise for all believers (see 2:39, note; cf. 1:5,8; 2:4; 4:8,31; 8:15–17; 9:17; 10:44–46; 13:9,52; 15:8; 19:1–6); (ii) the Spirit's numerous activities that provided the church with the standards of righteousness, witness and power that God desires for his people in the last days (i.e., the church age).

1:3 SHOWED HIMSELF. See Mt 28:9, note on Christ's resurrection appearances.

1:4 GIFT MY FATHER PROMISED. The gift the Father promised (Joel 2:28–29; Mt 3:11) is the baptism in the Holy Spirit (see v. 5, note). The fulfillment of that promise is described as being "filled with the Holy Spirit" (2:4). Thus, "baptized in the Spirit" and "filled with the Spirit" are at times used interchangeably in Acts.

This baptism in the Holy Spirit should not be identified with receiving the Holy Spirit at regeneration (see article on REGENERATION, p. 178). These are two distinct works of the Spirit, often separated by a period of time (see article on THE REGENERATION OF THE DISCIPLES, p. 212).

1:5 WITH [IN] THE HOLY SPIRIT. The preposition "with" is the translation of the Greek word *en* and is often translated as "in." Many prefer the rendering, "you will be baptized in the Holy Spirit." Likewise, "baptized with water" may be translated "baptized in water." Jesus himself is the one who baptizes his believers in the Holy Spirit.

1:8 YOU WILL RECEIVE POWER. This is the key verse in the book of Acts. The primary purpose of the baptism in the Spirit is the receiving of power to witness for Christ so that the lost will be won over to him and taught to obey all that Christ commanded. The end result is that Christ may be known, loved, praised and made Lord of God's chosen people (cf. Mt 28:18–20; Lk 24:49; Jn 5:23; 15:26–27).

(1) "Power" (Gk *dunamis*) means more than strength or ability; it designates especially power in operation, in action. The baptism in the Holy Spirit will bring the personal power of the Holy Spirit into the believer's life (see article on BAPTISM IN THE HOLY SPIRIT, p. 228).

(2) Luke here does not relate the baptism in the Spirit to personal salvation and regeneration, but to the power within the believer to witness with great effect (see article on THE REGENERATION OF THE DISCIPLES, p. 212).

(3) The Holy Spirit's principal work in witnessing and proclamation concerns his coming upon believers for power and his testimony to Christ's saving work and resurrection (cf. 2:14–42). See next note for comments on how the Spirit witnesses and what that means in our personal lives.

1:8 YOU WILL BE MY WITNESSES. The baptism in the Holy Spirit not only imparts power to preach Jesus as Lord and Savior (see previous note), but also increases the effectiveness of that witness because of a strengthening and deepening relationship with the Father, Son and Holy Spirit that comes from being filled with the Spirit (cf. Jn 14:26; 15:26–27).

(1) The Holy Spirit discloses and makes more real to us the personal presence of Jesus (Jn 14:16–18). Any witness to an intimate fellowship with Jesus Christ himself will result in an ever-growing desire on our part to love, honor and please our Savior.

BAPTISM IN THE HOLY SPIRIT

***Ac 1:5** "For John baptized with water, but in a few days you will be baptized with the Holy Spirit."*

One of the cardinal doctrines of Scripture is the baptism in the Holy Spirit (see Ac 1:4, note on reading "baptism *in*" rather than "baptism with" the Holy Spirit). Concerning the baptism in the Holy Spirit, the Word of God teaches the following.

(1) The baptism in the Spirit is intended for all who profess faith in Christ, have been born again and have received the indwelling of the Spirit.

(2) One of Christ's key goals in his earthly mission was to baptize his followers in the Holy Spirit (Mt 3:11; Mk 1:8; Lk 3:16; Jn 1:33). He instructed his disciples not to begin witnessing until they were baptized in the Holy Spirit and "clothed with power from on high" (Lk 24:49; Ac 1:4–5,8). Jesus Christ himself did not enter his ministry until he had been "anointed . . . with the Holy Spirit and power" (Ac 10:38; cf. Lk 4:1,18).

(3) The baptism in the Holy Spirit is an operation of the Spirit distinct and separate from his work of regeneration. Just as the Spirit's sanctifying work is a distinct work complementing his regenerating work, so the baptism in the Spirit complements the regenerating and sanctifying work of the Spirit. On the day of Christ's resurrection he breathed on his disciples and said, "Receive the Holy Spirit" (Jn 20:22), indicating that regeneration and new life were being given to them (see article on THE REGENERATION OF THE DISCIPLES, p. 212). Then later he told them they must also be "clothed with power" by the Holy Spirit (Lk 24:49; cf. Ac 1:5,8). For the disciples it was clearly a post-regeneration experience (see Ac 11:17, note). One can be regenerated and indwelt by the Holy Spirit, but still not be baptized in the Holy Spirit (see Ac 19:6, note).

(4) To be baptized in the Spirit means to be filled with the Spirit (compare Ac 1:5; 2:4). However, this baptism occurred only at and after Pentecost. Concerning those filled with the Spirit before Pentecost (e.g., Lk 1:15,67), Luke does not use the term baptized in the Holy Spirit. This would occur only after Christ's ascension (Lk 24:49–51; Jn 16:7–14; Ac 1:4).

(5) The book of Acts presents speaking in tongues as an initial sign accompanying the baptism in the Holy Spirit (2:4; 10:45–46; 19:6). Baptism in the Holy Spirit is linked so closely with the external manifestation of speaking in tongues that this should be considered the norm when receiving that baptism (see article on SPEAKING IN TONGUES, p. 232).

(6) The baptism in the Holy Spirit will bring the personal boldness and power of the Spirit into the believer's life in order to accomplish mighty works in Christ's name and to make his or her witness and proclamation effective (cf. Ac 1:8; 2:14–41; 4:31; 6:8; Ro 15:18–19; 1Co 2:4). This power is not some impersonal force, but is a manifestation of the Holy Spirit by which Jesus and his glory and works are present with his people (Jn 14:16–18; 16:14; 1Co 12:7).

(7) Other results of a genuine baptism in the Holy Spirit are: (a) prophetic utterances and declarations of praise (Ac 2:4,17; 10:46; 1Co 14:2); (b) enhanced sensitivity to sin that grieves the Holy Spirit, a greater seeking after righteousness and a deeper awareness of God's judgment against ungodliness (see Jn 16:8, note; Ac 1:8, note); (c) a life that brings glory to Jesus Christ (Jn 16:13–14; Ac 4:33); (d) new visions (Ac 2:17); (e) a manifestation of the various gifts of the Spirit (1Co 12:4–10); (f) a greater desire to pray (Ac 2:41–42; 3:1; 4:23–31; 6:4; 10:9; Ro 8:26); (g) a deeper love and understanding of God's Word (Jn 16:13; Ac 2:42); and (h) an increasing awareness of God as one's Father (Ac 1:4; Ro 8:15; Gal 4:6).

(8) God's Word cites several conditions by which the baptism in the Holy Spirit is given. (a) We must accept by faith Jesus Christ as Lord and Savior and turn from sin and the world (Ac 2:38–40; 8:12–17). This involves surrendering our wills to God ("to those who obey him," Ac 5:32). We must turn from that which offends God before we can be "an instrument for noble purposes, made holy, useful to the Master" (2Ti 2:21). (b) We must desire to be filled. Christians should have a deep hunger for the baptism in the Spirit (Jn 7:37–39; cf. Isa 44:3; Mt 5:6; 6:33). (c) We often receive this baptism in answer to prayer (Lk 11:13; Ac 1:14; 2:1–4; 4:31; 8:15,17). (d) We should expect that God will baptize us in the Holy Spirit (Mk 11:24; Ac 1:4–5).

(9) The baptism in the Holy Spirit is sustained in the believer's life by prayer (Ac 4:31), witness (4:31,33), worship in the Spirit (Eph 5:18–19) and a sanctified life (see Eph 5:18, notes). However powerful the initial coming of the Holy Spirit on the believer may be, if this does not find expression in a life of prayer, witness and holiness, the experience will soon become a fading glory.

(10) The baptism in the Spirit occurs only once in a believer's life and points to the consecrating of the believer to God's work of witnessing in power and righteousness. The Bible teaches that there may be new fillings with the Holy Spirit after the believer has been baptized in the Spirit (see Ac 4:31, note; cf. 2:4; 4:8,31; 13:9; Eph 5:18). Thus, the baptism in the Spirit brings the believer into a relationship with the Spirit that is to be renewed (Ac 4:31) and maintained (Eph 5:18).

on you;[o] and you will be my witnesses[p]
in Jerusalem, and in all Judea and Samar-
Ac 2:32 ia,[q] and to the ends of the earth."[r]

Jesus Taken Up Into Heaven

9After he said this, he was taken up[s]
before their very eyes, and a cloud hid him
from their sight.
10They were looking intently up into
the sky as he was going, when suddenly
two men dressed in white[t] stood beside
them. 11"Men of Galilee,"[u] they said,
"why do you stand here looking into the
sky? This same Jesus, who has been taken
from you into heaven, will come back[v] in
the same way you have seen him go into
heaven."

Matthias Chosen to Replace Judas

12Then they returned to Jerusalem[w]
from the hill called the Mount of Olives,[x]
a Sabbath day's walk[b] from the city.
13When they arrived, they went upstairs
to the room[y] where they were staying.
Those present were Peter, John, James
and Andrew; Philip and Thomas, Bartholomew and Matthew; James son of Alphaeus and Simon the Zealot, and Judas son of
James.[z] 14They all joined together constantly in prayer,[a] along with the wom-
en[b] and Mary the mother of Jesus, and
with his brothers.[c]
15In those days Peter stood up among
the believers[c] (a group numbering about
a hundred and twenty) 16and said, "Brothers,[d] the Scripture had to be fulfilled[e]
which the Holy Spirit spoke long ago
through the mouth of David concerning
Judas,[f] who served as guide for those who
arrested Jesus— 17he was one of our
number[g] and shared in this ministry."[h]
18(With the reward[i] he got for his wickedness, Judas bought a field;[j] there he
fell headlong, his body burst open and all
his intestines spilled out. 19Everyone in
Jerusalem heard about this, so they called
that field in their language[k] Akeldama,
that is, Field of Blood.)
20"For," said Peter, "it is written in the
book of Psalms,

" 'May his place be deserted;
let there be no one to dwell in
it,'[d][l]

and,

" 'May another take his place of
leadership.'[e][m]

21Therefore it is necessary to choose one
of the men who have been with us the
whole time the Lord Jesus went in and out
among us, 22beginning from John's baptism[n] to the time when Jesus was taken
up from us. For one of these must become

1:8 [o]Ac 2:1-4 [p]S Lk 24:48 [q]Ac 8:1-25 [r]S Mt 28:19 **1:9** [s]ver 2; S Mk 16:19 **1:10** [t]S Jn 20:12 **1:11** [u]Ac 2:7 [v]S Mt 16:27 **1:12** [w]Lk 24:52 [x]S Mt 21:1 **1:13** [y]Ac 9:37; 20:8 [z]Mt 10:2-4; Mk 3:16-19; Lk 6:14-16 **1:14** [a]Ac 2:42; 4:24; 6:4; S Lk 18:1; S Ro 1:10 [b]Lk 23:49,55 [c]S Mt 12:46 **1:16** [d]Ac 6:3; 11:1,12,29; 14:2; 18:18,27; 21:7; S 22:5; S Ro 7:1 [e]ver 20; S Mt 1:22 [f]S Mt 10:4 **1:17** [g]Jn 6:70,71 [h]ver 25 **1:18** [i]Mt 26:14, 15 [j]Mt 27:3-10 **1:19** [k]S Jn 5:2 **1:20** [l]Ps 69:25 [m]Ps 109:8 **1:22** [n]S Mk 1:4

b *12* That is, about 3/4 mile (about 1,100 meters)
c *15* Greek *brothers*
d *20* Psalm 69:25
e *20* Psalm 109:8

(2) The Holy Spirit witnesses to "righteousness" (Jn 16:8,10) and "truth" (Jn 16:13), which "bring glory to" Christ (Jn 16:14), not only with words, but also in deeds. Thus, we who have received the witness of the Spirit to Christ's redemptive work will necessarily manifest Christlikeness, love, truth and righteousness in our lives (cf. 1Co 13).

(3) The baptism in the Holy Spirit gives power to witness for Christ and brings conviction of sin, righteousness and judgment on the lost (see Jn 16:8, note). The effects of such conviction will become evident both in those who sincerely proclaim the message and in those who receive it (2:39–40).

(4) The baptism in the Holy Spirit can be given only to those whose hearts are turned toward God in repentance from their wicked ways (2:38; 3:26). It is maintained by the same sincere commitment to Christ (see 5:32, note).

(5) The baptism in the Holy Spirit is a baptism into the Spirit who is holy (cf. "Spirit of holiness," Ro 1:4). Thus, if the Spirit is truly at work in us in all his fullness, we will live in greater conformity to Christ's holiness.

In light of these Scriptural truths, we who have been baptized in the Holy Spirit will have an intense desire to please Christ in whatever way we can; i.e., the fullness of the Spirit complements (i.e., completes, fills up) the saving and sanctifying work of the Holy Spirit in our lives. Those who claim the fullness of the Spirit, yet live a life contrary to the Spirit of holiness, are deceived and untruthful. Those who display spiritual gifts, miracles, spectacular signs or inspiring oratory, yet lack true faith, love and righteousness, are operating not by the Holy Spirit but by an unholy spirit not from God (Mt 7:21–23; cf. Mt 24:24; 2Co 11:13–15; see also article on TESTING FOR GENUINE BAPTISM IN THE SPIRIT, p. 254). For further comments on witnessing for Christ, see 13:31, note.

1:14 JOINED TOGETHER CONSTANTLY IN PRAYER. The experience of Pentecost always involves human responsibility. Those needing the Spirit's outpouring for power to do God's work should make themselves available to the Holy Spirit through commitment to God's will and through prayer (v. 4; 2:38; 9:11–17; cf. Isa 40:29–31; Lk 11:5–13; 24:49). Notice the parallels between the Spirit coming on Jesus and the Spirit coming on the disciples. (1) The Spirit descended on them after they had prayed (Lk 3:21–22; Ac 1:14; 2:4). (2) There were observable manifestations of the Spirit (Lk 3:22; Ac 2:2–4). (3) The ministries of both Jesus and the disciples began after the Spirit came on them (compare Mt 3:16 with 4:17; Lk 3:21–23 with 4:14–19; cf. Ac 2:14–47).

a witness[o] with us of his resurrection."
23So they proposed two men: Joseph
called Barsabbas (also known as Justus)
and Matthias. 24Then they prayed,[p]
"Lord, you know everyone's heart.[q] Show
us[r] which of these two you have chosen
25to take over this apostolic ministry,
which Judas left to go where he belongs."
26Then they cast lots, and the lot fell to
Matthias; so he was added to the eleven
apostles.[s]

The Holy Spirit Comes at Pentecost

2 When the day of Pentecost[t] came,
they were all together[u] in one place.
2Suddenly a sound like the blowing of a
violent wind came from heaven and filled
the whole house where they were sitting.[v]
3They saw what seemed to be tongues of
fire that separated and came to rest on
each of them. 4All of them were filled with
the Holy Spirit[w] and began to speak in
other tongues[f][x] as the Spirit enabled
them.
5Now there were staying in Jerusalem
God-fearing[y] Jews from every nation under heaven. 6When they heard this sound,
a crowd came together in bewilderment,
because each one heard them speaking in
his own language. 7Utterly amazed,[z] they
asked: "Are not all these men who are
speaking Galileans?[a] 8Then how is it that
each of us hears them in his own native
language? 9Parthians, Medes and Elamites; residents of Mesopotamia, Judea
and Cappadocia,[b] Pontus[c] and Asia,[d]
10Phrygia[e] and Pamphylia,[f] Egypt and
the parts of Libya near Cyrene;[g] visitors
from Rome 11(both Jews and converts to
Judaism); Cretans and Arabs—we hear
them declaring the wonders of God in our
own tongues!" 12Amazed and perplexed,
they asked one another, "What does this
mean?"
13Some, however, made fun of them
and said, "They have had too much
wine.[g]"[h] Ac 2:38-39

Peter Explains the Coming of the Spirit

14Then Peter stood up with the Eleven,
raised his voice and addressed the crowd:

1:22 [o] ver 8; S Lk 24:48
1:24 [p] Ac 6:6; 13:3; 14:23 [q] S Rev 2:23 [r] 1Sa 14:41
1:26 [s] Ac 2:14
2:1 [t] Lev 23:15, 16; Ac 20:16; 1Co 16:8 [u] Ac 1:14
2:2 [v] Ac 4:31
2:4 [w] S Lk 1:15 [x] S Mk 16:17
2:5 [y] Lk 2:25; Ac 8:2
2:7 [z] ver 12 [a] Ac 1:11
2:9 [b] 1Pe 1:1 [c] Ac 18:2; 1Pe 1:1 [d] Ac 16:6; 19:10; Ro 16:5; 1Co 16:19; 2Co 1:8; Rev 1:4
2:10 [e] Ac 16:6; 18:23 [f] Ac 13:13; 14:24; 15:38 [g] S Mt 27:32
2:13 [h] 1Co 14:23; Eph 5:18

[f] 4 Or *languages*; also in verse 11 [g] 13 Or *sweet wine*

2:1 PENTECOST. Pentecost was the second great festival of the Jewish year. It was a harvest festival when the firstfruits of the grain harvest were presented to God (cf. Lev 23:17). In like manner Pentecost symbolizes for the church the beginning of God's harvest for souls in the world.

2:2–3 A VIOLENT WIND . . . AND . . . TONGUES OF FIRE. These external manifestations demonstrated that God was present and active in a powerful way (cf. Ex 3:1–6; 1Ki 18:38–39). The "fire" may symbolize consecrating and separating believers to God for the work of bringing glory to Christ (Jn 16:13–14) and of witnessing for him (1:8). These two manifestations preceded the baptism in the Holy Spirit and were not repeated elsewhere in Acts.

2:4 FILLED WITH THE HOLY SPIRIT. What is the significance of the filling with the Holy Spirit at Pentecost? (1) It meant the beginning of the fulfillment of God's promise in Joel 2:28–29 to pour out his Spirit on all his people at the end times (cf. 1:4–5; Mt 3:11; Lk 24:49; Jn 1:33).

(2) Since the last days of this age had begun (v. 17; cf. Heb 1:2; 1Pe 1:20), everyone was now confronted with the decision to repent and believe in Christ (3:19; Mt 3:2; Lk 13:3; see Ac 2:17, notes).

(3) The disciples were "clothed with power from on high" (Lk 24:49; cf. Ac 1:8), enabling them to witness for Christ, to bring great conviction on the lost in relation to sin, righteousness and the judgment of God, and to turn them from sin to salvation in Christ (cf. 1:8, notes; 4:13,33; 6:8; Ro 15:19; see Jn 16:8, note).

(4) The Holy Spirit revealed his nature as a Spirit who longs and strives for the salvation of people of every nation. Those who received the baptism in the Holy Spirit were filled with the same longing for the salvation of the human race (vv. 38–40; 4:12,33; Ro 9:1–3; 10:1). Thus, Pentecost is the beginning of world missions (vv. 6–11,39; 1:8).

(5) The disciples became ministers of the Spirit. They not only preached Jesus crucified and resurrected, leading others to repentance and faith in Christ, but they also influenced converts to receive the "gift of the Holy Spirit" (vv. 38–39), whom they themselves had received at Pentecost. This leading others into the baptism in the Holy Spirit is the key to the apostolic work in the NT (see 8:17; 9:17–18; 10:44–46; 19:6).

(6) Through this baptism in the Spirit Christ's followers became successors to his earthly ministry. They continued to do and to teach, in the power of the Holy Spirit, the same things that Jesus "began both to do and to teach" (1:1; see Jn 14:12, note; see article on SIGNS OF BELIEVERS, p. 106).

2:4 BEGAN TO SPEAK IN OTHER TONGUES. For a discussion on the meaning of speaking in tongues at Pentecost and elsewhere in the NT church, and on the possibility of false tongues, see article on SPEAKING IN TONGUES, p. 232.

2:13 WINE. "Sweet wine" (Gk *gleukos*; see NIV footnote) normally refers to unfermented grape juice. Those mocking the disciples may have used this term rather than the common NT word for wine (*oinos*) because they believed that Jesus' disciples used only this type of wine. In this case, their mockery would have been spoken in sarcasm.

2:14–40 PETER'S PENTECOST SERMON. Peter's sermon at Pentecost, along with his message in 3:11–26, contains a pattern for the proclamation of the gospel.

SPEAKING IN TONGUES

***Ac 2:4** "All of them were filled with the Holy Spirit and began to speak in other tongues as the Spirit enabled them."*

Speaking in tongues, or glossalalia (from Gk *glōssais lalō*), was considered by NT Christians as a God-given sign accompanying the baptism in the Holy Spirit (see Ac 2:4; 10:45–47; 19:6). This Biblical pattern for the Spirit-filled life is still valid for us today.

TRUE SPEAKING IN TONGUES. (1) Tongues as a manifestation of the Spirit. Speaking in tongues is a supernatural manifestation of the Holy Spirit, i.e., a Spirit-inspired utterance whereby believers speak in a language (Gk *glōssa*) they have never learned (Ac 2:4; 1Co 14:14–15). It may be in existing spoken human languages (Ac 2:6) or in languages unknown on earth (cf. 1Co 13:1). It is not "ecstatic speech," as rendered in some translations, for the Bible never uses the term "ecstatic utterance" to refer to speaking in tongues.

(2) Tongues as a sign. Speaking in tongues is an inspired utterance whereby the believer's spirit and the Holy Spirit join in verbal praise and/or prophecy. God linked speaking in tongues with the baptism in the Spirit from the very beginning (Ac 2:4), so that the 120 believers at Pentecost, and believers thereafter, would have an experiential confirmation that they have indeed received the baptism in the Holy Spirit (cf. Ac 10:45–46). Thus this experience could be objectively validated as to place and time of reception. Throughout the history of the church, whenever tongues as a confirming sign has been denied or lost from view, the truth and experience of Pentecost has been distorted or ignored entirely.

(3) Tongues as a gift. Speaking in tongues is also described as a gift of the Holy Spirit to the believer (1Co 12:4–10). This gift has two main purposes: (a) Speaking in tongues accompanied by interpretation is used in public worship to communicate the content of the utterance to the congregation, so that all may enter into Spirit-directed worship, praise or prophecy (1Co 14:5–6,13–17). (b) Speaking in tongues is used by the believer to speak to God in his or her personal devotions and thus to build up one's spiritual life (1Co 14:4). It means speaking at the level of the spirit (14:2,14) for the purpose of praying (14:2,14–15,28), giving thanks (14:16–17) or singing (14:15; see 1Co 14, notes; see article on SPIRITUAL GIFTS FOR BELIEVERS, p. 350).

FALSE SPEAKING IN TONGUES. The mere occurrence of speaking in "other tongues," or any other supernatural manifestation, is not uncontestable evidence of the work and presence of the Spirit. Speaking in tongues can be counterfeited by human initiative or demonic activity. The Bible cautions us not to believe every spirit, but to examine whether our spiritual experiences really do come from God (see 1Jn 4:1, note).

(1) In order to be valid, speaking in tongues must be "as the Spirit enabled" (Ac 2:4). To follow the norm in the book of Acts, speaking in tongues must be the *spontaneous* result of the initial filling of the Holy Spirit. It is not a learned phenomenon, nor can it be taught by instructing believers to speak incoherent syllables.

(2) The Holy Spirit explicitly warns that in the last days there will be within the church hypocrisy (1Ti 4:1–2), signs and wonders from satanic powers (Mt 7:22–23; cf. 2Th 2:9), and deceitful workers disguising themselves as God's servants (2Co 11:13–15). We must heed these warnings about counterfeit spiritual manifestations and signs (Mt 7:22–23; 2Th 2:8–10).

(3) In order to discern whether our speaking in tongues is genuine, i.e., truly from the Holy Spirit, we must look for the Biblically defined results of the baptism in the Spirit (see article on TESTING FOR GENUINE BAPTISM IN THE SPIRIT, p. 254). If someone claiming to speak in tongues is not committed to Jesus Christ and the authority of Scripture, and is not attempting to obey the Word of God, whatever manifestations he or she may have are not from the Spirit (1Jn 3:6–10; 4:1–3; cf. Mt 24:11,24; Jn 8:31; Gal 1:9, note).

"Fellow Jews and all of you who live in
Jerusalem, let me explain this to you; listen carefully to what I say. 15These men
are not drunk, as you suppose. It's only
nine in the morning![i] 16No, this is what
was spoken by the prophet Joel:

17" 'In the last days, God says,
I will pour out my Spirit on all
people.[j]
Your sons and daughters will
prophesy,[k]
your young men will see visions,
your old men will dream dreams.
18Even on my servants, both men and
women,
I will pour out my Spirit in those
days,
and they will prophesy.[l]
19I will show wonders in the heaven
above
and signs on the earth below,[m]
blood and fire and billows of
smoke.
20The sun will be turned to darkness
and the moon to blood[n]
before the coming of the great and
glorious day of the Lord.
21And everyone who calls
on the name of the Lord[o] will be
saved.'[h][p]

22"Men of Israel, listen to this: Jesus of
Nazareth[q] was a man accredited by God
to you by miracles, wonders and signs,[r]
which God did among you through him,[s]

2:15 [i]1Th 5:7
2:17 [j]Nu 11:25; Isa 44:3; Eze 39:29; Jn 7:37-39; Ac 10:45 [k]S Ac 21:9
2:18 [l]Ac 21:9-12
2:19 [m]Lk 21:11
2:20 [n]S Mt 24:29
2:21 [o]Ge 4:26; 26:25; Ps 105:1; Ac 9:14; 1Co 1:2; 2Ti 2:22 [p]Joel 2:28-32; Ro 10:13
2:22 [q]S Mk 1:24 [r]S Jn 4:48 [s]S Jn 3:2

[h] *21* Joel 2:28-32

(1) Jesus is both Lord and Christ—crucified, resurrected and exalted (vv. 22–36; 3:13–15).

(2) Now at the right hand of his Father, Jesus Christ has received the authority to pour out the Holy Spirit on all believers (vv. 16–18,32–33; 3:19).

(3) Everyone must place his or her faith in Jesus as Lord, repent of sin and be baptized in connection with forgiveness of sins (vv. 36–38; 3:19).

(4) Believers must expect the promised gift of or baptism in the Holy Spirit after faith and repentance (vv. 38–39).

(5) Those who hear in faith must separate themselves from the world and be saved from this corrupt generation (v. 40; 3:26).

(6) Jesus Christ will return to restore God's kingdom completely (3:20–21).

2:16 SPOKEN BY THE PROPHET JOEL. The baptism in the Holy Spirit and the accompanying spiritual manifestations are a fulfillment of Joel 2:28–29. Joel in the eighth century B.C. had prophesied a great outpouring of the Holy Spirit to come on all the Lord's people.

2:17 THE LAST DAYS. (1) In the OT "the last days" were considered the time when the Lord would act in a mighty way to judge evil and bring salvation to his people (cf. Isa 2:2–21; 3:18—4:6; 10:20–23; Hos 1–2; Joel 1–3; Am 8:9–11; 9:9–12). (2) The NT reveals that "the last days" began with the first coming of Christ and the initial outpouring of the Spirit on God's people, and that the last days will end with the Lord's second coming (Mk 1:15; Lk 4:18–21; Heb 1:1–2). This specific time is characterized as the age of judgment against evil, authority over demons, salvation for the human race and the presence of the kingdom of God.

(a) These "last days" will be carried on by the power of the Spirit (Mt 12:28).

(b) "The last days" involve the invasion of God's power through Christ into the realm of Satan and sin. Yet the warfare has only begun; it is not yet consummated, for evil and satanic activity are still present in a mighty way (Eph 6:10–18). Only the second coming of Jesus will bring to an end the activity of evil forces and complete "the last days" (cf. 1Pe 1:3–5; Rev 19).

(c) "The last days" constitute a time of prophetic witness calling everyone to repent, believe in Christ and experience the outpouring of the Holy Spirit (1:8; 2:4,38–40; Joel 2:28–32). We must proclaim the saving work of Christ through the power of the Spirit, even as we anticipate the final day of wrath (Ro 2:5), i.e., "the great and glorious day of the Lord" (2:20b). We must live every day alertly, waiting for the day of redemption and the return of Christ for his people (Jn 14:3; 1Th 4:15–17).

(d) "The last days" inaugurate the kingdom of God, which now comes with all power (see Lk 11:20, note; see article on THE KINGDOM OF GOD, p. 28). We must experience the fullness of that power as we face spiritual warfare (2Co 10:3–5; Eph 6:11–12) and suffering because of righteousness (Mt 5:10–12; 1Pe 1:6–7).

2:17 SONS AND DAUGHTERS WILL PROPHESY. Peter associates the speaking in other tongues (vv. 4,11) with prophecy (vv. 17–18). Thus, speaking in other tongues is considered one form of prophesying. The essential meaning of prophecy is using one's voice for the service and glory of God under the direct initiation of the Holy Spirit. In the book of Acts: (1) the 120 "were filled with the Holy Spirit and began to speak in other tongues as the Spirit enabled them" (2:4); (2) the Holy Spirit came on Cornelius and his household, and Peter "heard them speaking in tongues and praising God" (10:44–47); and (3) the disciples at Ephesus, when "the Holy Spirit came on them, . . . spoke in tongues and prophesied" (19:6).

2:18 MY SERVANTS, BOTH MEN AND WOMEN. According to Joel's prophecy, applied by Peter, the baptism in the Holy Spirit is for those already in God's kingdom—i.e., believers, or God's servants, both men and women, who are saved and regenerated and who belong to God.

2:18 IN THOSE DAYS. Peter, quoting Joel, says that God will pour out his Spirit *in those days*. The outpouring of the Holy Spirit and the accompanying supernatural signs cannot be limited to just the one "day" of Pentecost. The power and blessing of the Holy Spirit is for every Christian to have and experience throughout the church age, i.e., the entire period of time between Christ's first and second coming (Rev 19–20; see Ac 2:39, note).

as you yourselves know. **23**This man was
handed over to you by God's set purpose
and foreknowledge;[t] and you, with the
help of wicked men,[i] put him to death by
nailing him to the cross.[u] **24**But God
raised him from the dead,[v] freeing him
from the agony of death, because it was
impossible for death to keep its hold on
him.[w] **25**David said about him:

"'I saw the Lord always before me.
Because he is at my right hand,
I will not be shaken.
26Therefore my heart is glad and my
tongue rejoices;
my body also will live in hope,
27because you will not abandon me to
the grave,
nor will you let your Holy One see
decay.[x]
28You have made known to me the
paths of life;
you will fill me with joy in your
presence.'[j][y]

29"Brothers,[z] I can tell you confidently
that the patriarch[a] David died and was
buried,[b] and his tomb is here[c] to this day.
30But he was a prophet and knew that God
had promised him on oath that he would
place one of his descendants on his
throne.[d] **31**Seeing what was ahead, he
spoke of the resurrection of the Christ,[k]
that he was not abandoned to the grave,
nor did his body see decay.[e] **32**God has
raised this Jesus to life,[f] and we are all
witnesses[g] of the fact. **33**Exalted[h] to the Ac 4:20
right hand of God,[i] he has received from
the Father[j] the promised Holy Spirit[k]
and has poured out[l] what you now see
and hear. **34**For David did not ascend to
heaven, and yet he said,

"'The Lord said to my Lord:
"Sit at my right hand
35until I make your enemies
a footstool for your feet."'[l][m]

36"Therefore let all Israel be assured of
this: God has made this Jesus, whom you
crucified, both Lord[n] and Christ."[o]

The Spirit Is for All Believers

37When the people heard this, they
were cut to the heart and said to Peter and
the other apostles, "Brothers, what shall
we do?"[p]
38Peter replied, "Repent and be baptized,[q] every one of you, in the name of
Jesus Christ for the forgiveness of your
sins.[r] And you will receive the gift of the
Holy Spirit.[s] **39**The promise is for you and
your children[t] and for all who are far off[u]
—for all whom the Lord our God will call." Ac 4:8
40With many other words he warned

2:23 [t]Isa 53:10; Ac 3:18; 4:28 [u]Mt 16:21; Lk 24:20; Ac 3:13 **2:24** [v]ver 32; Ac 13:30,33,34, 37; 17:31; Ro 6:4; 8:11; 10:9; 1Co 6:14; 15:15; Eph 1:20; Col 2:12; Heb 13:20; 1Pe 1:21 [w]Jn 20:9 **2:27** [x]ver 31; Ac 13:35 **2:28** [y]Ps 16:8-11 **2:29** [z]S Ac 22:5 [a]Ac 7:8,9 [b]Ac 13:36; 1Ki 2:10 [c]Ne 3:16 **2:30** [d]S Mt 1:1 **2:31** [e]Ps 16:10 **2:32** [f]S ver 24 [g]S Lk 24:48 **2:33** [h]S Php 2:9 [i]S Mk 16:19 [j]Ac 1:4 [k]Jn 7:39; 14:26; 15:26 [l]Ac 10:45 **2:35** [m]Ps 110:1; S Mt 22:44 **2:36** [n]S Mt 28:18 [o]S Lk 2:11 **2:37** [p]Lk 3:10,12, 14; Ac 16:30 **2:38** [q]ver 41; Ac 8:12,16,36,38; 9:18; 10:48; 16:15,33; 19:5; 22:16; Col 2:12 [r]Jer 36:3; Mk 1:4; S Lk 24:47; Ac 3:19 [s]S Jn 20:22 **2:39** [t]Isa 44:3; 65:23 [u]Isa 57:19; Ac 10:45; Eph 2:13

i *23* Or *of those not having the law* (that is, Gentiles) **j** *28* Psalm 16:8-11 **k** *31* Or *Messiah.* "The Christ" (Greek) and "the Messiah" (Hebrew) both mean "the Anointed One"; also in verse 36. **l** *35* Psalm 110:1

2:33 THE RIGHT HAND OF GOD. The pouring out of the Holy Spirit by Jesus proves that he is indeed the exalted Messiah, now sitting at the right hand of God and interceding for his representatives on earth (Heb 7:25). (1) From Jesus' baptism to the day of Pentecost the Spirit was on him as the Christ (i.e., the one anointed by the Spirit; cf. Lk 3:21–22; 4:1,14,18–19). Now at the right hand of God, he lives to pour out the same Spirit on those who believe in him. (2) In pouring out the Spirit, Jesus intends that the Spirit will mediate Jesus' presence to believers and empower them to continue to do all that he did while on earth.

2:38 REPENT AND BE BAPTIZED. Repentance, forgiveness of sins and baptism are the prior conditions for receiving the gift of the Holy Spirit. However, Peter's demand that his hearers be baptized in water before receiving the promise of the Father (cf. 1:4,8) must not be taken as an absolute requirement for the infilling with the Spirit, nor is baptism in the Spirit an automatic consequence of water baptism.

(1) In this situation, Peter required water baptism prior to receiving the promise because in the minds of his Jewish listeners, the rite of baptism was taken for granted as being involved in any conversion decision. Water baptism did not precede the baptism in the Spirit, however, in the instances recorded in 9:17–18 (the apostle Paul) and 10:44–48 (those in Cornelius's house).

(2) Each believer, after repenting of his or her sins and accepting Jesus Christ by faith, must "receive" (cf. Gal 3:14) a personal baptism in the Spirit. The gift of the Spirit in the book of Acts was consciously desired, sought and appropriated (1:4,14; 4:31; 8:14–17; 19:2–6); the only possible exception to the rule in the NT was the case of Cornelius (10:44–48). Consequently, the baptism in the Spirit should not be considered as a gift automatically provided to the believer in Christ.

2:39 FOR YOU AND YOUR CHILDREN AND FOR ALL. The promise of the baptism in the Holy Spirit was not just for those present on the day of Pentecost (v. 4), but for all who would believe in Christ throughout this age: "for you"—Peter's audience; "your children"—the next generation; "for all who are far off"—the third and subsequent generations. (1) The baptism in the Spirit with its accompanying power was not a once-for-all occurrence in the church's history. It did not cease with Pentecost (cf. v. 38; 8:15; 9:17; 10:44–46; 19:6), nor with the close of the apostolic age. (2) It is the birthright of every Christian to seek, expect and experience the same baptism in the Spirit that was promised and given to the NT Christians (1:4,8; Joel 2:28; Mt 3:11; Lk 24:49).

2:40 THIS CORRUPT GENERATION. No one can be saved who does not turn away from the corruption of present society (cf. Lk 9:41; 11:29; 17:25; Php

them; and he pleaded with them, "Save
yourselves from this corrupt generation."[v] **41**Those who accepted his message were baptized, and about three thousand were added to their number[w] that
day.

The Fellowship of the Believers

42They devoted themselves to the apostles' teaching[x] and to the fellowship, to
the breaking of bread[y] and to prayer.[z]
43Everyone was filled with awe, and many
wonders and miraculous signs were done
by the apostles.[a] **44**All the believers were
together and had everything in common.[b]
45Selling their possessions and goods,
they gave to anyone as he had need.[c]
46Every day they continued to meet together in the temple courts.[d] They broke
bread[e] in their homes and ate together
with glad and sincere hearts, **47**praising
God and enjoying the favor of all the people.[f] And the Lord added to their number[g] daily those who were being saved.

Peter Heals the Crippled Beggar

3 One day Peter and John[h] were going
up to the temple[i] at the time of
prayer—at three in the afternoon.[j] **2**Now
a man crippled from birth[k] was being carried to the temple gate[l] called Beautiful,
where he was put every day to beg[m] from
those going into the temple courts. **3**When
he saw Peter and John about to enter, he
asked them for money. **4**Peter looked
straight at him, as did John. Then Peter
said, "Look at us!" **5**So the man gave them
his attention, expecting to get something
from them.

6Then Peter said, "Silver or gold I do
not have, but what I have I give you. In the
name of Jesus Christ of Nazareth,[n] walk."
7Taking him by the right hand, he helped

2:40 [v]Dt 32:5; Php 2:15
2:41 [w]ver 47; Ac 4:4; 5:14; 6:1, 7; 9:31,35,42; 11:21,24; 14:1,21; 16:5; 17:12
2:42 [x]Mt 28:20 [y]S Mt 14:19 [z]S Ac 1:14
2:43 [a]Ac 5:12
2:44 [b]Ac 4:32
2:45 [c]Mt 19:21; Lk 12:33; 18:22; Ac 4:34,35; 6:1
2:46 [d]Lk 24:53; Ac 3:1; 5:21,42 [e]ver 42; S Mt 14:19
2:47 [f]S Ro 14:18 [g]S ver 41
3:1 [h]S Lk 22:8 [i]Ac 2:46 [j]Ps 55:17; Ac 10:30
3:2 [k]Ac 14:8 [l]Lk 16:20 [m]Jn 9:8
3:6 [n]ver 16; S Mk 1:24
3:8 [o]Isa 35:6; Ac 14:10
3:9 [p]Ac 4:16,21
3:10 [q]ver 2
3:11 [r]S Lk 22:8 [s]Jn 10:23; Ac 5:12
3:13 [t]Ex 3:6 [u]Ac 5:30; 7:32; 22:14 [v]Ac 2:23 [w]S Mt 27:2 [x]S Lk 23:4
3:14 [y]S Mk 1:24; Ac 4:27 [z]Ac 7:52 [a]Mk 15:11; Lk 23:18-25
3:15 [b]S Ac 2:24 [c]S Lk 24:48
3:16 [d]ver 6
3:17 [e]S Ac 22:5 [f]Lk 23:34 [g]Ac 13:27
3:18 [h]S Mt 1:22 [i]Ac 2:23 [j]S Lk 24:27 [k]Ac 17:2,3; 26:22, 23

him up, and instantly the man's feet and
ankles became strong. **8**He jumped to his
feet and began to walk. Then he went with
them into the temple courts, walking and
jumping,[o] and praising God. **9**When all
the people[p] saw him walking and praising
God, **10**they recognized him as the same
man who used to sit begging at the temple
gate called Beautiful,[q] and they were
filled with wonder and amazement at what Ac 5:15-
had happened to him. 16

Peter Speaks to the Onlookers

11While the beggar held on to Peter and
John,[r] all the people were astonished and
came running to them in the place called
Solomon's Colonnade.[s] **12**When Peter
saw this, he said to them: "Men of Israel,
why does this surprise you? Why do you
stare at us as if by our own power or godliness we had made this man walk? **13**The
God of Abraham, Isaac and Jacob,[t] the
God of our fathers,[u] has glorified his servant Jesus. You handed him over[v] to be
killed, and you disowned him before Pilate,[w] though he had decided to let him
go.[x] **14**You disowned the Holy[y] and Righteous One[z] and asked that a murderer be
released to you.[a] **15**You killed the author
of life, but God raised him from the dead.[b]
We are witnesses[c] of this. **16**By faith in
the name of Jesus,[d] this man whom you
see and know was made strong. It is
Jesus' name and the faith that comes
through him that has given this complete
healing to him, as you can all see. Ac 6:5

17"Now, brothers,[e] I know that you acted in ignorance,[f] as did your leaders.[g]
18But this is how God fulfilled[h] what he
had foretold[i] through all the prophets,[j]
saying that his Christ[m] would suffer.[k]
19Repent, then, and turn to God, so that

[m] *18* Or *Messiah*; also in verse 20

2:15). New Christians should be taught to break off from all evil companions, forsake the ungodly world, unite themselves to Christ and his people, and give themselves to God's work (2Co 6:14,17).

2:42 APOSTLES' TEACHING . . . FELLOWSHIP . . . BREAKING OF BREAD . . . PRAYER. See 12:5, note on the 15 characteristics of a NT church.

3:6 IN THE NAME OF JESUS . . . WALK. The healing of the crippled beggar was done by the power of Christ working through his apostles. Jesus said to his followers concerning those who would believe in him: "In my name . . . they will place their hands on sick people, and they will get well" (Mk 16:17–18). The church continued Jesus' healing ministry in obedience to his will. The miracle was accomplished through faith "in the name of Jesus Christ" and "gifts of healing" operating through Peter (see 1Co 12:1,9). Peter stated that he had no silver or gold, but would give the crippled beggar something much more valuable. Churches that possess a fair degree of material prosperity should ponder these words of Peter. Many churches today can no longer say "Silver and gold I do not have," nor do they seem capable of saying, "In the name of Jesus Christ of Nazareth, walk."

3:19 REPENT . . . AND TURN TO GOD. God has chosen to bless his people with the outpouring of the Holy Spirit only on the conditions of repentance, i.e., turning from sin and the unrighteous ways of their surrounding corrupt generation, and conversion, i.e., turning to God, listening to everything that Christ, the prophet, tells them (vv. 22–23), and always moving toward sincere obedience to Christ (cf. 2:38–41; 5:29–32).

3:19 TIMES OF REFRESHING. Throughout this

your sins may be wiped out,[l] that times
of refreshing may come from the Lord,
20and that he may send the Christ,[m] who
has been appointed for you—even Jesus.
21He must remain in heaven[n] until the
time comes for God to restore everything,[o] as he promised long ago through
his holy prophets.[p] **22**For Moses said,
'The Lord your God will raise up for you
a prophet like me from among your own
people; you must listen to everything he
tells you.[q] **23**Anyone who does not listen
to him will be completely cut off from
among his people.'[n][r]

24"Indeed, all the prophets[s] from Samuel on, as many as have spoken, have foretold these days. **25**And you are heirs[t] of
the prophets and of the covenant[u] God
made with your fathers. He said to Abraham, 'Through your offspring all peoples
on earth will be blessed.'[o][v] **26**When God
raised up[w] his servant, he sent him first[x]
to you to bless you by turning each of you
from your wicked ways."

Peter and John Before the Sanhedrin

4 The priests and the captain of the
temple guard[y] and the Sadducees[z]
came up to Peter and John while they were
speaking to the people. **2**They were greatly disturbed because the apostles were
teaching the people and proclaiming in
Jesus the resurrection of the dead.[a] **3**They
seized Peter and John, and because it was
evening, they put them in jail[b] until the
next day. **4**But many who heard the message believed, and the number of men
grew[c] to about five thousand.

5The next day the rulers,[d] elders and
teachers of the law met in Jerusalem. **6**Annas the high priest was there, and so were
Caiaphas,[e] John, Alexander and the other
men of the high priest's family. **7**They had
Peter and John brought before them and
began to question them: "By what power
or what name did you do this?"

8Then Peter, filled with the Holy Spirit,[f] said to them: "Rulers and elders of the
people![g] **9**If we are being called to ac- Ac 4:31
count today for an act of kindness shown
to a cripple[h] and are asked how he was
healed, **10**then know this, you and all the
people of Israel: It is by the name of Jesus Christ of Nazareth,[i] whom you crucified but whom God raised from the dead,[j]
that this man stands before you healed.
11He is

" 'the stone you builders rejected,
which has become the
capstone.'[p][q][k]

3:19 [l]Ps 51:1; Isa 43:25; 44:22; S Ac 2:38 **3:20** [m]S Lk 2:11 **3:21** [n]Ac 1:11 [o]Mt 17:11; Ac 1:6 [p]Lk 1:70 **3:22** [q]Dt 18:15, 18; Ac 7:37 **3:23** [r]Dt 18:19 **3:24** [s]S Lk 24:27 **3:25** [t]Ac 2:39 [u]Ro 9:4,5 [v]Ge 12:3; 22:18; 26:4; 28:14 **3:26** [w]ver 22; S Ac 2:24 [x]Ac 13:46; Ro 1:16 **4:1** [y]Lk 22:4 [z]Mt 3:7; 16:1,6; 22:23,34; Ac 5:17; 23:6-8

4:2 [a]Ac 17:18 **4:3** [b]Ac 5:18 **4:4** [c]S Ac 2:41 **4:5** [d]Lk 23:13 **4:6** [e]S Mt 26:3 **4:8** [f]S Lk 1:15 [g]ver 5; Lk 23:13 **4:9** [h]Ac 3:6 **4:10** [i]S Mk 1:24 [j]S Ac 2:24 **4:11** [k]Ps 118:22; Isa 28:16; Zec 10:4; Mt 21:42; Eph 2:20; 1Pe 2:7

[n] *23* Deut. 18:15,18,19 [o] *25* Gen. 22:18; 26:4
[p] *11* Or *cornerstone* [q] *11* Psalm 118:22

present age and until Christ's return, God will send "times of refreshing" (i.e., the outpouring of the Holy Spirit) to all who repent and are converted. Although perilous times will come toward the end of this age and a great falling away from the faith will occur (2Th 2:3; 2Ti 3:1), God still promises to send revival and times of refreshing on the faithful. Christ's presence, spiritual blessings, miracles and outpourings of the Spirit will come on the remnant who faithfully seek him and overcome the world, the sinful nature and Satan's dominion (cf. 26:18).

3:21 TIME COMES FOR GOD TO RESTORE EVERYTHING. Christ will return from heaven to put down evil and establish the kingdom of God on earth free from all sin. Ultimately all things prophesied in the OT to be restored (cf. Zec 12–14; Lk 1:32–33) will be restored. Christ will redeem or renovate all nature (Ro 8:18–23) and reign personally on the earth (see Rev 20–21). Note that not people on earth but Christ and the armies from heaven will bring in the triumph of God and his kingdom (Rev 19:11—20:9).

3:22 A PROPHET. Moses' prediction in Dt 18:18–19 that "the Lord your God will raise up for you a prophet like me" was a prophecy concerning Jesus Christ. In what way was Jesus like Moses? (1) Moses was anointed by the Spirit (Nu 11:17); the Spirit of the Lord was on Jesus to preach the gospel (Lk 4:18–19). (2) God used Moses to initiate the old covenant; Jesus brought in the new covenant. (3) Moses led Israel out of Egypt to Sinai and established the covenant relationship with God; Christ redeemed his people from sin and satanic bondage and established a new, living relationship with God whereby his people might enter the very presence of God. (4) Moses in the OT laws referred to the sacrifice of a lamb to bring redemption; Christ himself became the Lamb of God to give salvation to all who accept him. (5) Moses faithfully pointed to the law and the obligation of God's people to obey its commands in order to receive God's blessing; Christ pointed to himself and the Holy Spirit as God's way of fulfilling his will and receiving God's blessing and eternal life.

3:26 TURNING . . . FROM YOUR WICKED WAYS. Peter once again emphasizes that believing in Christ and receiving the baptism in the Holy Spirit are conditioned on turning from sin and being separated from evil (see 2:38,40, notes; 3:19, note; 8:21, note). In the original apostolic message, there was no promised blessing without holiness.

4:8 PETER, FILLED WITH THE HOLY SPIRIT. Peter received a fresh filling with the Holy Spirit that brought a sudden inspiration, wisdom and boldness by which to proclaim the truth of God. It is theologically significant that the filling with the Spirit was not a one-time experience, but a repetitive one. This episode is a fulfillment of Jesus' promise in Lk 12:11–12; other instances of renewed fillings can be found in Ac 7:55 and 13:9.

12Salvation is found in no one else, for
there is no other name under heaven given
to men by which we must be saved."[l]
13When they saw the courage of Peter
and John[m] and realized that they were unschooled, ordinary men,[n] they were astonished and they took note that these
men had been with Jesus.[o] **14**But since
they could see the man who had been
healed standing there with them, there
was nothing they could say. **15**So they ordered them to withdraw from the Sanhedrin[p] and then conferred together.
16"What are we going to do with these
men?"[q] they asked. "Everybody living in
Jerusalem knows they have done an outstanding miracle,[r] and we cannot deny it.
17But to stop this thing from spreading
any further among the people, we must
warn these men to speak no longer to anyone in this name."
18Then they called them in again and
commanded them not to speak or teach at
all in the name of Jesus.[s] **19**But Peter and
John replied, "Judge for yourselves whether it is right in God's sight to obey you
rather than God.[t] **20**For we cannot help
speaking[u] about what we have seen and
Ac 4:33 heard."[v]
21After further threats they let them go.
They could not decide how to punish
them, because all the people[w] were praising God[x] for what had happened. **22**For
the man who was miraculously healed
was over forty years old.

4:12 [l]S Mt 1:21; Jn 14:6; Ac 10:43; S Ro 11:14; 1Ti 2:5
4:13 [m]S Lk 22:8 [n]Mt 11:25 [o]Mk 3:14
4:15 [p]S Mt 5:22
4:16 [q]Jn 11:47 [r]Ac 3:6-10
4:18 [s]Am 7:13; Ac 5:40
4:19 [t]Ac 5:29
4:20 [u]Job 32:18; Jer 20:9; Am 3:8 [v]S Lk 24:48
4:21 [w]Ac 5:26 [x]S Mt 9:8

4:24 [y]S Ac 1:14 [z]Ne 9:6; Job 41:11; Isa 37:16
4:25 [a]Ac 1:16
4:26 [b]Ps 2:1,2; Da 9:25; Lk 4:18; Ac 10:38; Heb 1:9
4:27 [c]S Mt 14:1 [d]S Mt 27:2; Lk 23:12 [e]ver 30; Ac 3:13,14
4:28 [f]Ac 2:23
4:29 [g]ver 13,31; Ps 138:3; Ac 9:27; 13:46; 14:3; 28:31; Eph 6:19; Php 1:14
4:30 [h]S Jn 4:48 [i]ver 27

The Believers' Prayer

23On their release, Peter and John went
back to their own people and reported all
that the chief priests and elders had said
to them. **24**When they heard this, they
raised their voices together in prayer to
God.[y] "Sovereign Lord," they said, "you
made the heaven and the earth and the
sea, and everything in them.[z] **25**You
spoke by the Holy Spirit through the
mouth of your servant, our father David:[a]

" 'Why do the nations rage
and the peoples plot in vain?
26The kings of the earth take their
stand
and the rulers gather together
against the Lord
and against his Anointed One.[r]'[s][b]

27Indeed Herod[c] and Pontius Pilate[d] met
together with the Gentiles and the people[t] of Israel in this city to conspire
against your holy servant Jesus,[e] whom
you anointed. **28**They did what your power
and will had decided beforehand should
happen.[f] **29**Now, Lord, consider their
threats and enable your servants to speak
your word with great boldness.[g] **30**Stretch
out your hand to heal and perform miraculous signs and wonders[h] through the
name of your holy servant Jesus."[i]
31After they prayed, the place where

[r] *26* That is, Christ or Messiah [s] *26* Psalm 2:1,2 [t] *27* The Greek is plural.

4:12 SALVATION . . . IN NO ONE ELSE. The disciples were convinced that the greatest need of every individual was salvation from sin and the wrath of God, and they preached that this need could be met by no one other than the person of Jesus Christ. This reveals the exclusive nature of the gospel and the church's heavy responsibility of preaching the gospel to every person. If there were other ways of salvation, the church could be at ease. But according to Christ himself (Jn 14:6), there is no hope for anyone apart from salvation through Christ (cf. 10:43; 1Ti 2:5–6). This is the basis for the missionary imperative.

4:20 WE CANNOT HELP SPEAKING. The Holy Spirit created in the apostles an overwhelming desire to proclaim the gospel. Throughout the book of Acts the Spirit impelled believers to carry the gospel to others (1:8; 2:14–41; 3:12–26; 8:25,35; 9:15; 10:44–48; 13:1–4).

4:29 ENABLE YOUR SERVANTS TO SPEAK . . . WITH GREAT BOLDNESS. The disciples needed renewed courage to witness and speak for Christ. Throughout our Christian life, we too need to pray in order to overcome our fear of embarrassment, rejection, criticism or persecution. God's grace, through fillings of the Holy Spirit, will help us speak about Jesus with boldness (cf. Mt 10:32).

4:30 HEAL AND PERFORM MIRACULOUS SIGNS AND WONDERS. Preaching and miracles belong together (3:1–10; 4:8–22,29–33; 5:12–16; 6:7–8; 8:6ff; 15:12; 20:7ff). Miracles are accompanying signs by which Christ confirms the word of witnesses (14:3; cf. Mk 16:20). (1) "Miraculous signs" generally refer to deeds performed in order to certify the existence of a divine power, to give warning or to encourage faith. (2) "Wonders" refer to unusual events that cause the observer to marvel. Note that the church is *praying* that healings, miraculous signs and wonders will take place. The church today needs to pray earnestly that God will confirm the gospel with great power, miracles and abundant grace (v. 33).

4:31 THEY WERE ALL FILLED WITH THE HOLY SPIRIT. Several important truths stand out here. (1) The term "baptized with [or in] the Holy Spirit" (see 1:5, note) describes the consecrating work of the Holy Spirit in initiating the believer into divine power for witness. The terms "filled," "clothed" and "empowered" describe his actual equipping them for ministry (2:4; 4:8,31; 9:17; 13:9,52). As need arises, the "filling" may be repeated.

(2) The terms "pouring out the Spirit" (2:17–18; 10:45), "receiving the gift of the Holy Spirit" (2:38; 8:15), "coming of the Spirit on" (8:16; 10:44; 11:15;

they were meeting was shaken.[j] And they
were all filled with the Holy Spirit[k] and
Ac 6:3 spoke the word of God[l] boldly.[m]

The Believers Share Their Possessions

32All the believers were one in heart
and mind. No one claimed that any of his
possessions was his own, but they shared
everything they had.[n] **33**With great power
the apostles continued to testify[o] to the
resurrection[p] of the Lord Jesus, and much
Ac 5:32 grace[q] was upon them all. **34**There were
no needy persons among them. For from
time to time those who owned lands or
houses sold them,[r] brought the money
from the sales **35**and put it at the apostles'
feet,[s] and it was distributed to anyone as
he had need.[t]
36Joseph, a Levite from Cyprus, whom
the apostles called Barnabas[u] (which
means Son of Encouragement), **37**sold a
field he owned and brought the money and
put it at the apostles' feet.[v]

4:31 [j]Ac 2:2 [k]S Lk 1:15 [l]S Heb 4:12 [m]S ver 29
4:32 [n]Ac 2:44
4:33 [o]S Lk 24:48 [p]Ac 1:22 [q]S Ro 3:24
4:34 [r]Mt 19:21; Ac 2:45
4:35 [s]ver 37; Ac 5:2 [t]Ac 2:45; 6:1
4:36 [u]Ac 9:27; 11:22,30; 13:2; 1Co 9:6; Gal 2:1,9, 13
4:37 [v]ver 35; Ac 5:2

5:2 [w]Jos 7:11 [x]Ac 4:35,37
5:3 [y]S Mt 4:10 [z]Jn 13:2,27 [a]ver 9 [b]Dt 23:21
5:4 [c]Dt 23:22 [d]Lev 6:2
5:5 [e]ver 10; Ps 5:6 [f]ver 11
5:6 [g]Jn 19:40

Ananias and Sapphira

5 Now a man named Ananias, together
with his wife Sapphira, also sold a
piece of property. **2**With his wife's full
knowledge he kept back part of the money
for himself,[w] but brought the rest and put
it at the apostles' feet.[x]
3Then Peter said, "Ananias, how is it
that Satan[y] has so filled your heart[z] that
you have lied to the Holy Spirit[a] and have
kept for yourself some of the money you
received for the land?[b] **4**Didn't it belong
to you before it was sold? And after it was
sold, wasn't the money at your disposal?[c]
What made you think of doing such a
thing? You have not lied to men but to
God."[d]
5When Ananias heard this, he fell down
and died.[e] And great fear[f] seized all who
heard what had happened. **6**Then the
young men came forward, wrapped up his
body,[g] and carried him out and buried
him.
7About three hours later his wife came
in, not knowing what had happened. **8**Pe-

19:6) are different expressions for the occasion when believers are "filled with the Holy Spirit" (2:4; 4:31; 9:17).

(3) All the believers, including the apostles who had been previously filled (2:4), are freshly filled to meet the continuing opposition of the Jews (v. 29). Fresh fillings with the Holy Spirit are part of God's will and provision for all who have received the baptism in the Holy Spirit (cf. v. 8, note; 13:52). We should expect and seek those fillings.

(4) The Spirit here visits a whole congregation. Therefore, to fulfill God's will for the church, not only must individuals be filled with the Spirit (v. 8; 9:17; 13:9), but entire congregations (2:4; 4:31; 13:53) should experience repeated visitations of the Holy Spirit when special needs and challenges are present.

(5) God's moving upon the entire congregation with a renewed filling of the Holy Spirit results in boldness and power in witness, love for one another and abundant grace for all.

4:31 SPOKE THE WORD OF GOD BOLDLY. The inner power of the Spirit and the reality of God's presence brought about by the filling of the Spirit frees the believer from fear of others and greatly increases the courage to speak out for God.

4:33 WITH GREAT POWER. "Great power" is the distinguishing characteristic of apostolic preaching and witness (cf. 1:8) for three reasons: (1) Apostolic witness was based on God's Word (v. 29) and the conviction that it was given by the inspiration of the Holy Spirit (see article on THE INSPIRATION AND AUTHORITY OF SCRIPTURE, p. 474). (2) The disciples were conscious that they had been sent and commissioned by Jesus Christ himself, the resurrected Lord. (3) The Holy Spirit, through the disciples (v. 31), brought great conviction on those who heard the gospel concerning personal sin, Christ's righteousness and God's judgment (see Jn 16:8, note).

5:3 LIED TO THE HOLY SPIRIT. In order to gain glory and recognition, Ananias and Sapphira lied to the church about their giving. God considered this lie against the Holy Spirit a serious offense. The deaths of Ananias and Sapphira are intended to be standing examples of God's attitude toward any deceitful heart among those who profess to be born-again, Spirit-filled believers. Notice too that lying to the Holy Spirit is the same as lying to God (vv. 3–4; see Rev 22:15, note; see article on THE DOCTRINE OF THE HOLY SPIRIT, p. 240).

5:4 WHAT MADE YOU THINK OF DOING SUCH A THING? The root of the sin of Ananias and Sapphira was their love for money and the praise of others. This set them against the Holy Spirit (v. 9). Once the love of money and human praise takes possession of a person, his or her spirit becomes open to all kinds of satanic evil (1Ti 6:10). A person cannot love money and at the same time love and serve God (Mt 6:24; Jn 5:41–44).

5:5 ANANIAS . . . FELL DOWN AND DIED. God harshly struck down Ananias and Sapphira (vv. 5,10) in order to reveal his hatred of all deceit and dishonesty in the kingdom of God. One of the most abominable sins in the church is to deceive God's people about your relationship with Christ, your work for him and the extent of your ministry. To engage in this hypocrisy means using Christ's shed blood to glorify your own self before other people. This sin disregards the very purpose for which Christ suffered and died (Eph 1:4; Heb 13:12), indicating an absence of the fear of the Lord (vv. 5,11) and of respect and honor for the Holy Spirit (v. 3); it merits God's righteous judgment.

ter asked her, "Tell me, is this the price you and Ananias got for the land?"

"Yes," she said, "that is the price."[h]

9 Peter said to her, "How could you agree to test the Spirit of the Lord?[i] Look! The feet of the men who buried your husband are at the door, and they will carry you out also."

10 At that moment she fell down at his feet and died.[j] Then the young men came in and, finding her dead, carried her out and buried her beside her husband.[k] 11 Great fear[l] seized the whole church and all who heard about these events.

The Apostles Heal Many

12 The apostles performed many miraculous signs and wonders[m] among the people. And all the believers used to meet together[n] in Solomon's Colonnade.[o] 13 No one else dared join them, even though they were highly regarded by the people.[p] 14 Nevertheless, more and more men and women believed in the Lord and were added to their number.[q] 15 As a result, people brought the sick into the streets and laid them on beds and mats so that at least Peter's shadow might fall on some of them as he passed by.[r] 16 Crowds gathered also from the towns around Jerusalem, bringing their sick and those tormented by evil[u] spirits, and all of them were healed.[s]

Ac 8:6-7

The Apostles Persecuted

17 Then the high priest and all his associates, who were members of the party[t] of the Sadducees,[u] were filled with jealousy. 18 They arrested the apostles and put them in the public jail.[v] 19 But during the night an angel[w] of the Lord opened the doors of the jail[x] and brought them out.[y] 20 "Go, stand in the temple courts," he said, "and tell the people the full message of this new life."[z]

21 At daybreak they entered the temple courts, as they had been told, and began to teach the people.

When the high priest and his associates[a] arrived, they called together the Sanhedrin[b]—the full assembly of the elders of Israel—and sent to the jail for the apostles. 22 But on arriving at the jail, the officers did not find them there.[c] So they went back and reported, 23 "We found the jail securely locked, with the guards standing at the doors; but when we opened them, we found no one inside." 24 On hearing this report, the captain of the temple guard and the chief priests[d] were puzzled, wondering what would come of this.

25 Then someone came and said, "Look! The men you put in jail are standing in the temple courts teaching the people." 26 At that, the captain went with his officers and brought the apostles. They did not use force, because they feared that the people[e] would stone them.

27 Having brought the apostles, they made them appear before the Sanhedrin[f] to be questioned by the high priest. 28 "We gave you strict orders not to teach in this name,"[g] he said. "Yet you have filled Jerusalem with your teaching and are determined to make us guilty of this man's blood."[h]

29 Peter and the other apostles replied: "We must obey God rather than men![i] 30 The God of our fathers[j] raised Jesus from the dead[k]—whom you had killed by hanging him on a tree.[l] 31 God exalted him to his own right hand[m] as Prince and Savior[n] that he might give repentance and forgiveness of sins to Israel.[o] 32 We are witnesses of these things,[p] and so is the Holy Spirit,[q] whom God has given to those who obey him."

Ac 8:4

33 When they heard this, they were furi-

5:8 [h]ver 2
5:9 [i]ver 3
5:10 [j]ver 5 [k]ver 6
5:11 [l]ver 5; Ac 19:17
5:12 [m]S Jn 4:48; Ac 2:43 [n]Ac 4:32 [o]Jn 10:23; Ac 3:11
5:13 [p]Ac 2:47; 4:21
5:14 [q]S Ac 2:41
5:15 [r]Ac 19:12
5:16 [s]Mt 8:16; S Mk 16:17
5:17 [t]Ac 15:5 [u]S Ac 4:1
5:18 [v]Ac 4:3
5:19 [w]Ge 16:7; Ex 3:2; Mt 1:20; 2:13,19; 28:2; Lk 1:11; 2:9; S Jn 20:12; Ac 8:26; 10:3; 12:7,23; 27:23 [x]Ac 16:26 [y]Ps 34:7
5:20 [z]Jn 6:63,68
5:21 [a]Ac 4:5,6 [b]ver 27,34,41; S Mt 5:22
5:22 [c]Ac 12:18, 19
5:24 [d]Ac 4:1
5:26 [e]Ac 4:21
5:27 [f]S Mt 5:22
5:28 [g]Ac 4:18 [h]Mt 23:35; 27:25; Ac 2:23,36; 3:14, 15; 7:52
5:29 [i]Ex 1:17; Ac 4:19
5:30 [j]S Ac 3:13 [k]S Ac 2:24 [l]Ac 10:39; 13:29; Gal 3:13
5:31 [m]S Mk 16:19 [n]S Lk 2:11 [o]S Mt 1:21; Mk 1:4; Lk 24:47; Ac 2:38; 3:19; 10:43
5:32 [p]S Lk 24:48 [q]Jn 15:26

[u] 16 Greek *unclean*

5:11 GREAT FEAR SEIZED THE WHOLE CHURCH. God's judgment on the sin of Ananias and Sapphira caused an increase in humility, awe and fear. Without a proper fear of the holy God and his wrath against sin, God's people will soon return to the ungodly ways of the world, cease to experience the outpouring of the Spirit and God's miraculous presence, and be cut off from the flow of God's kingdom grace. The fear of the Lord is an essential element in the NT faith and in Biblical Christianity today.

5:16 ALL OF THEM WERE HEALED. The apostles did as their Lord had done: they healed those tormented with evil spirits (see Mk 1:34). This was a paramount sign that the kingdom of God had come among the people with great power (see article on POWER OVER SATAN AND DEMONS, p. 80). It is never wrong to pray that through the Holy Spirit we might do good and heal those oppressed by sickness and Satan (4:30).

5:29 OBEY GOD RATHER THAN MEN. The great question before every believer is not, "Is it expedient, safe, pleasurable or popular among other humans?" but, "What is right in the sight of God?" (cf. Gal 1:10).

5:32 HOLY SPIRIT ... TO THOSE WHO OBEY HIM. If there is no real obedience to Christ or a sincere seeking the righteousness of his kingdom (Mt 6:33; Ro 14:17), then any claim to possess the fullness of the Holy Spirit is invalid. Pentecost without the lordship of Christ is impossible (cf. 2:38–42), for

THE DOCTRINE OF THE HOLY SPIRIT

***Ac 5:3–4** "Then Peter said, 'Ananias, how is it that Satan has so filled your heart that you have lied to the Holy Spirit and have kept for yourself some of the money you received for the land? Didn't it belong to you before it was sold? And after it was sold, wasn't the money at your disposal? What made you think of doing such a thing? You have not lied to men but to God.'"*

It is essential that believers recognize the importance of the Holy Spirit in God's redemptive purpose. Many Christians have no idea what difference it would make if there were no Holy Spirit in this world. Without the Holy Spirit there would be no creation, no universe, no human race (Ge 1:2; Job 33:4). Without the Holy Spirit there would be no Bible (2Pe 1:21), no New Testament (Jn 14:26; 15:26–27; 1Co 2:10–14), no power to proclaim the gospel (Ac 1:8). Without the Holy Spirit there would be no faith, no new birth, no holiness, no Christians at all in the world. This article explores some of the basic teachings about the Holy Spirit.

THE PERSON OF THE HOLY SPIRIT. Throughout Scripture the Spirit is revealed as a person with an individuality all his own (2Co 3:17–18; Heb 9:14; 1Pe 1:2). He is a divine person like the Father and the Son. Thus we may never think of the Holy Spirit as a mere influence or power. He has personal characteristics, for he thinks (Ro 8:27), feels (Ro 15:30), wills (1Co 12:11), and has the capacity to love and to enjoy fellowship. He was sent by the Father to bring believers into the intimate presence and fellowship of Jesus (Jn 14:16–18,26; see article on JESUS AND THE HOLY SPIRIT, p. 136). In the light of these truths we should treat him as a person and regard him as the infinite living God within our hearts, worthy of our worship, love and surrender (see Mk 1:11, note on the Trinity).

THE WORK OF THE HOLY SPIRIT. (1) The revelation of the Holy Spirit in the OT. (a) The Spirit is the agent in creation. He is the co-creator of the universe (Ge 1:2; Ps 104:30), of humanity (Job 33:4) and of the animal world (Ps 104:25,30). (b) He is the divine agent in the communication of God's message to people. Holy men of God spoke as they were carried along by the Holy Spirit (2Sa 23:2; Isa 59:21; 2Pe 1:21). (c) He is the agent in service. His ministry in Israel involved the anointing or endowing of certain people to fill particular offices or perform certain tasks (Ge 41:38; Ex 35:31–34; Nu 11:17; 27:18; Jdg 6:34; 2Ki 2:15). (d) He is the agent in inward renewal, teaching God's people the way of faithfulness (Ne 9:20; Ps 143:10) and calling for repentance, obedience, righteousness and fellowship with God (Ps 51:10–12; Isa 11:2; 44:3; Eze 11:19; 37:14; Joel 2:28–29).

(2) The revelation of the Holy Spirit in the NT.

(a) The Holy Spirit is the agent of salvation, convicting us of guilt (Jn 16:7–8), revealing to us the truth about Jesus (Jn 14:16,26), giving us new birth (Jn 3:3–6) and incorporating us into the body of Christ (1Co 12:13). At conversion we receive the Spirit (Jn 3:3–6; 20:22) and become participants in the divine nature (2Pe 1:4; see article on THE REGENERATION OF THE DISCIPLES, p. 212).

(b) The Holy Spirit is the agent of sanctification. At conversion believers are indwelt by the Holy Spirit and come under his sanctifying influence (Ro 8:9; 1Co 6:19). Notice some of the things the Spirit does as he lives in us. He sanctifies us, i.e., cleanses, leads and motivates us into holy lives, delivering us from sin's bondage (Ro 8:2–4; Gal 5:16–17; 2Th 2:13). He tells us that we are children of God (Ro 8:16), helps us in our worship of God (Ac 10:46) and in our prayer lives, and intercedes for us as we cry out to God (Ro 8:26–27). He produces Christlike graces of character that glorify Christ (Gal 5:22–23; 1Pe 1:2). He is our divine teacher, guiding us into all truth (Jn 16:13; 14:26; 1Co 2:9–16), disclosing Jesus to us and guiding us into close fellowship and oneness with Jesus (Jn 14:16–18; 16:14). He continually imparts God's love to us (Ro 5:5) and gives us joy, comfort and help (Jn 14:16; 1Th 1:6).

(c) The Holy Spirit is the agent of service, empowering believers for service and witness. This work of the Holy Spirit is related to the baptism in the Spirit or the fullness of the Spirit (see article on BAPTISM IN THE HOLY SPIRIT, p. 228). When we are baptized in the Spirit, we receive power to witness for Christ and work effectively within the church and before the world (Ac 1:8). We receive the same divine anointing that descended on Christ (Jn 1:32–33) and on the disciples (Ac 2:4; see 1:5), enabling us to proclaim God's Word (Ac 1:8; 4:31) and work miracles (Ac 2:43; 3:2–8; 5:15; 6:8; 10:38). It is God's intended purpose that all Christians experience the baptism in the Holy Spirit throughout this age (Ac 2:39). In the area of service, the Holy Spirit gives spiritual gifts to individual members of the church to edify or strengthen the church (1Co 12–14). These gifts are a manifestation of the Spirit through individuals by which Christ's presence, love, truth and righteous standards are made real to the fellowship of believers for the common good (1Co 12:7–11).

(d) The Holy Spirit is the agent who incorporates believers into the one body of Christ (1Co 12:13), lives in the church (1Co 3:16), builds the church (Eph 2:22), inspires her worship (Php 3:3), directs her mission (Ac 13:2,4), appoints her workers (Ac 20:28), gives gifts to the church (1Co 12:1–11), anoints her preachers (Ac 2:4; 1Co 2:4), guards the gospel (2Ti 1:14) and promotes her righteousness (Jn 16:8; 1Co 3:16; 6:18–20).

(3) The various activities of the Spirit are complementary and not contradictory. At the same time, these facets of the Holy Spirit's work are interlocked and cannot be fully separated. We cannot experience (a) the fullness of new life in Christ, (b) righteousness as a way of living, (c) the power to witness for our Lord or (d) fellowship in his body without becoming involved in all four. For example, baptism in the Holy Spirit cannot be maintained independently of the Spirit's work of producing righteousness within us and leading us into the knowledge of and commitment to Biblical truth.

ous[r] and wanted to put them to death.
34But a Pharisee named Gamaliel,[s] a
teacher of the law,[t] who was honored by
all the people, stood up in the Sanhedrin
and ordered that the men be put outside
for a little while. 35Then he addressed
them: "Men of Israel, consider carefully
what you intend to do to these men.
36Some time ago Theudas appeared,
claiming to be somebody, and about four
hundred men rallied to him. He was killed,
all his followers were dispersed, and it all
came to nothing. 37After him, Judas the
Galilean appeared in the days of the census[u] and led a band of people in revolt. He
too was killed, and all his followers were
scattered. 38Therefore, in the present
case I advise you: Leave these men alone!
Let them go! For if their purpose or activity is of human origin, it will fail.[v] 39But
if it is from God, you will not be able to
stop these men; you will only find yourselves fighting against God."[w]

40His speech persuaded them. They
called the apostles in and had them
flogged.[x] Then they ordered them not
to speak in the name of Jesus, and let
them go.

41The apostles left the Sanhedrin, rejoicing[y] because they had been counted
worthy of suffering disgrace for the
Name.[z] 42Day after day, in the temple
courts[a] and from house to house, they
never stopped teaching and proclaiming
the good news[b] that Jesus is the Christ.[v][c]

5:33 [r]Ac 2:37; 7:54
5:34 [s]Ac 22:3 [t]Lk 2:46; 5:17
5:37 [u]Lk 2:1,2
5:38 [v]Mt 15:13
5:39 [w]2Ch 13:12; Pr 21:30; Isa 46:10; Ac 7:51; 11:17
5:40 [x]S Mt 10:17
5:41 [y]S Mt 5:12 [z]S Jn 15:21
5:42 [a]S Ac 2:46 [b]S Ac 13:32 [c]S Ac 9:22

The Choosing of the Seven

6 In those days when the number of disciples was increasing,[d] the Grecian
Jews[e] among them complained against
the Hebraic Jews because their widows[f]
were being overlooked in the daily distribution of food.[g] 2So the Twelve gathered
all the disciples[h] together and said, "It
would not be right for us to neglect the
ministry of the word of God[i] in order to
wait on tables. 3Brothers,[j] choose seven
men from among you who are known to be
full of the Spirit[k] and wisdom. We will
turn this responsibility over to them[l]
4and will give our attention to prayer[m] and
the ministry of the word."

Ac 7:55

5This proposal pleased the whole
group. They chose Stephen,[n] a man full of
faith and of the Holy Spirit;[o] also Philip,[p]
Procorus, Nicanor, Timon, Parmenas, and
Nicolas from Antioch, a convert to Judaism. 6They presented these men to the

Ac 14:9-10

6:1 [d]S Ac 2:41 [e]Ac 9:29 [f]Ac 9:39, 41; 1Ti 5:3 [g]Ac 4:35
6:2 [h]S Ac 11:26 [i]S Heb 4:12
6:3 [j]S Ac 1:16 [k]S Lk 1:15 [l]Ex 18:21; Ne 13:13
6:4 [m]S Ac 1:14
6:5 [n]ver 8; Ac 7:55-60; 11:19; 22:20 [o]S Lk 1:15 [p]Ac 8:5-40; 21:8

[v] 42 Or *Messiah*

---

the Spirit in all his power is given only to those living in "obedience that comes from faith" (Ro 1:5; see article on TESTING FOR GENUINE BAPTISM IN THE SPIRIT, p. 254).

6:3 FULL OF THE SPIRIT AND WISDOM. The apostles stipulated that the seven men had to give evidence of having continued faithfully under the influence of the Holy Spirit. Apparently the apostles assumed that not all believers continued to be full of the Spirit. In other words, those who fail to live faithfully by the Spirit (Gal 5:16–25) will cease to be full of the Spirit. Concerning the terms "full of the Holy Spirit" and "filled with the Holy Spirit," the following should be noted:

(1) The phrase "full of the Spirit" (cf. 6:5; 11:24) expresses a continuing character, quality or condition within believers that results from experiencing the Spirit's fullness and that enables them to minister in the power of the Holy Spirit and to speak under prophetic inspiration as the Spirit gives utterance.

(2) The term "filled with the Holy Spirit" is used in three ways: (a) to indicate the reception of the baptism in the Holy Spirit (1:5; 2:4; 9:17; 11:16); (b) to indicate the empowering of a believer or believers on a specific occasion to speak under the impulse of the Holy Spirit (4:8; 13:9; Lk 1:41–45,67–79); and (c) to indicate a general prophetic ministry under the inspiration or anointing of the Holy Spirit without specifying the duration of that ministry (4:31–33; 13:52; Lk 1:15).

(3) After the initial reception of the baptism in the Spirit, individuals who faithfully walk in the Spirit, putting to death the misdeeds of the body (Ro 8:13–14), may be described as "full of the Holy Spirit," i.e., maintaining the abiding fullness of the Holy Spirit (e.g., the seven men, especially Stephen, vv. 3,5; 7:55; or Barnabas, 11:24). Also, those who maintain the fullness of the Spirit may receive a fresh filling with the Spirit for a particular purpose or task, especially a divine enabling to speak under the impulse of the Holy Spirit.

6:4 GIVE OUR ATTENTION TO PRAYER. Baptism in the Holy Spirit alone is insufficient for effective Christian leadership. Church leaders must constantly devote themselves to prayer and to the preaching of the Word. The verb translated "give our attention to" (Gk *proskartereō*) denotes a steadfast and single-minded fidelity and a giving of much time to a certain course of action. The apostles felt that prayer and the ministry of the Word were the highest work of Christian leaders. Note the frequent references to prayer in Acts (see 1:14,24; 2:42; 4:24–31; 6:4,6; 9:40; 10:2,4,9,31; 11:5; 12:5; 13:3; 14:23; 16:25; 22:17; 28:8).

6:6 LAID THEIR HANDS ON THEM. In the NT the laying on of hands was used in five ways: (1) in connection with miracles of healing (28:8; Mt 9:18; Mk 5:23; 6:5); (2) in blessing others (Mt 19:13,15); (3) in connection with the baptism in the Spirit (8:17,19; 19:6); (4) in commissioning for a specific work (v. 6; 13:3); and (5) in imparting spiritual gifts by the elders (1Ti 4:14). As one of the means by which God mediates gifts and blessings to others, laying on of hands became a foundational doctrine in the early church

apostles, who prayed[q] and laid their hands on them.[r]

7So the word of God spread.[s] The number of disciples in Jerusalem increased rapidly,[t] and a large number of priests became obedient to the faith.

Stephen, Full of Grace and Power

Ac 11:27-28

8Now Stephen, a man full of God's grace and power, did great wonders and miraculous signs[u] among the people. **9**Opposition arose, however, from members of the Synagogue of the Freedmen (as it was called) — Jews of Cyrene[v] and Alexandria as well as the provinces of Cilicia[w] and Asia.[x] These men began to argue with Stephen, **10**but they could not stand up against his wisdom or the Spirit by whom he spoke.[y]

11Then they secretly[z] persuaded some men to say, "We have heard Stephen speak words of blasphemy against Moses and against God."[a]

Stephen Seized

12So they stirred up the people and the elders and the teachers of the law. They seized Stephen and brought him before the Sanhedrin.[b] **13**They produced false witnesses,[c] who testified, "This fellow never stops speaking against this holy place[d] and against the law. **14**For we have heard him say that this Jesus of Nazareth will destroy this place[e] and change the customs Moses handed down to us."[f]

15All who were sitting in the Sanhedrin[g] looked intently at Stephen, and they saw that his face was like the face of an angel.

Stephen's Speech to the Sanhedrin

7 Then the high priest asked him, "Are these charges true?"

2To this he replied: "Brothers and fathers,[h] listen to me! The God of glory[i] appeared to our father Abraham while he was still in Mesopotamia, before he lived in Haran.[j] **3**'Leave your country and your people,' God said, 'and go to the land I will show you.'[w][k]

4"So he left the land of the Chaldeans and settled in Haran. After the death of his father, God sent him to this land where you are now living.[l] **5**He gave him no inheritance here,[m] not even a foot of ground. But God promised him that he and his descendants after him would possess the land,[n] even though at that time Abraham had no child. **6**God spoke to him in this way: 'Your descendants will be strangers in a country not their own, and they will be enslaved and mistreated four hundred years.[o] **7**But I will punish the nation they serve as slaves,' God said, 'and afterward they will come out of that country and worship me in this place.'[x][p] **8**Then he gave Abraham the covenant of circumcision.[q] And Abraham became the father of Isaac and circumcised him eight days after his birth.[r] Later Isaac became the father of Jacob,[s] and Jacob became the father of the twelve patriarchs.[t]

9"Because the patriarchs were jealous of Joseph,[u] they sold him as a slave into Egypt.[v] But God was with him[w] **10**and rescued him from all his troubles. He gave Joseph wisdom and enabled him to gain the goodwill of Pharaoh king of Egypt; so he made him ruler over Egypt and all his palace.[x]

11"Then a famine struck all Egypt and Canaan, bringing great suffering, and our fathers could not find food.[y] **12**When Jacob heard that there was grain in Egypt,

w *3* Gen. 12:1 x *7* Gen. 15:13,14

6:6 [q]S Ac 1:24 [r]Nu 8:10; 27:18; Ac 9:17; 19:6; 28:8; 1Ti 4:14; S Mk 5:23 **6:7** [s]Ac 12:24; 19:20 [t]S Ac 2:41 **6:8** [u]S Jn 4:48 **6:9** [v]S Mt 27:32 [w]Ac 15:23,41; 22:3; 23:34 [x]S Ac 2:9 **6:10** [y]Lk 21:15 **6:11** [z]1Ki 21:10 [a]Mt 26:59-61 **6:12** [b]S Mt 5:22 **6:13** [c]Ex 23:1; Ps 27:12 [d]Mt 24:15; Ac 7:48; 21:28 **6:14** [e]S Jn 2:19 [f]Ac 15:1; 21:21; 26:3; 28:17 **6:15** [g]S Mt 5:22

7:2 [h]Ac 22:1 [i]Ps 29:3 [j]Ge 11:31; 15:7 **7:3** [k]Ge 12:1 **7:4** [l]Ge 12:5 **7:5** [m]Heb 11:13 [n]Ge 12:7; 17:8; 26:3 **7:6** [o]Ex 1:8-11; 12:40 **7:7** [p]Ge 15:13,14; Ex 3:12 **7:8** [q]Ge 17:9-14 [r]Ge 21:2-4 [s]Ge 25:26 [t]Ge 29:31-35; 30:5-13,17-24; 35:16-18,22-26 **7:9** [u]Ge 37:4,11 [v]Ge 37:28; Ps 105:17 [w]Ge 39:2,21,23; Hag 2:4 **7:10** [x]Ge 41:37-43; Ps 105:20-22 **7:11** [y]Ge 41:54

(Heb 6:2). It must not be disassociated from prayer, for prayer indicates that the gifts of grace, healing or baptism in the Holy Spirit are from God and not from the persons who are ministering.

Consecrating or ordaining the seven men here meant primarily two things. (1) It was a public witness by the church that these seven men had a history of perseverance in godliness and faithfulness to the Spirit's leading (cf. 1Ti 3:1–10). (2) It was an act consecrating the men to the work of God and a testimony of their willingness to accept the responsibility of God's call.

6:8 STEPHEN ... GOD'S GRACE AND POWER. The Holy Spirit empowered Stephen to perform "great wonders and miraculous signs among the people" and gave him great wisdom to preach the gospel in such a way that his opponents could not refute his arguments (v. 10; cf. Ex 4:15; Lk 21:15).

7:2–53 BROTHERS AND FATHERS, LISTEN. Stephen's speech before the Sanhedrin is a defense of the faith as preached by Christ and the apostles. He is the forerunner of all who defend the Biblical faith against those who oppose or distort its teaching, and he is the first to die for that reason. Jesus vindicates Stephen's action by standing in honor of him before his Father in heaven (v. 55, note). Stephen's love of the truth and his willingness to give his life to safeguard that truth contrast sharply with those who show little concern to "contend for the faith that was once for all entrusted to the saints" (Jude 3) and who, in the name of love, peace and tolerance, feel no need to oppose false teachers and distorters of the pure gospel for which Christ died (see Gal 1:9, note; see article on OVERSEERS AND THEIR DUTIES, p. 274).

he sent our fathers on their first visit.[z]
13On their second visit, Joseph told his
brothers who he was,[a] and Pharaoh
learned about Joseph's family.[b] **14**After
this, Joseph sent for his father Jacob and
his whole family,[c] seventy-five in all.[d]
15Then Jacob went down to Egypt, where
he and our fathers died.[e] **16**Their bodies
were brought back to Shechem and placed
in the tomb that Abraham had bought
from the sons of Hamor at Shechem for a
certain sum of money.[f]

17"As the time drew near for God to
fulfill his promise to Abraham, the number of our people in Egypt greatly increased.[g] **18**Then another king, who knew
nothing about Joseph, became ruler of
Egypt.[h] **19**He dealt treacherously with our
people and oppressed our forefathers by
forcing them to throw out their newborn
babies so that they would die.[i]

20"At that time Moses was born, and he
was no ordinary child.[y] For three months
he was cared for in his father's house.[j]
21When he was placed outside, Pharaoh's
daughter took him and brought him up as
her own son.[k] **22**Moses was educated in
all the wisdom of the Egyptians[l] and was
powerful in speech and action.

23"When Moses was forty years old, he
decided to visit his fellow Israelites. **24**He
saw one of them being mistreated by an
Egyptian, so he went to his defense and
avenged him by killing the Egyptian.
25Moses thought that his own people
would realize that God was using him to
rescue them, but they did not. **26**The next
day Moses came upon two Israelites who
were fighting. He tried to reconcile them
by saying, 'Men, you are brothers; why do
you want to hurt each other?'

27"But the man who was mistreating
the other pushed Moses aside and said,
'Who made you ruler and judge over us?[m]
28Do you want to kill me as you killed the
Egyptian yesterday?'[z] **29**When Moses
heard this, he fled to Midian, where he
settled as a foreigner and had two sons.[n]

30"After forty years had passed, an angel appeared to Moses in the flames of a
burning bush in the desert near Mount
Sinai. **31**When he saw this, he was amazed
at the sight. As he went over to look more
closely, he heard the Lord's voice:[o] **32**'I
am the God of your fathers,[p] the God of
Abraham, Isaac and Jacob.'[a] Moses trembled with fear and did not dare to look.[q]

33"Then the Lord said to him, 'Take off
your sandals; the place where you are
standing is holy ground.[r] **34**I have indeed
seen the oppression of my people in
Egypt. I have heard their groaning and
have come down to set them free. Now
come, I will send you back to Egypt.'[b][s]

35"This is the same Moses whom they
had rejected with the words, 'Who made
you ruler and judge?'[t] He was sent to be
their ruler and deliverer by God himself,
through the angel who appeared to him in
the bush. **36**He led them out of Egypt[u] and
did wonders and miraculous signs[v] in
Egypt, at the Red Sea[c][w] and for forty
years in the desert.[x]

37"This is that Moses who told the Israelites, 'God will send you a prophet like
me from your own people.'[d][y] **38**He was in
the assembly in the desert, with the angel[z] who spoke to him on Mount Sinai,
and with our fathers;[a] and he received
living words[b] to pass on to us.[c]

39"But our fathers refused to obey him.
Instead, they rejected him and in their
hearts turned back to Egypt.[d] **40**They told
Aaron, 'Make us gods who will go before
us. As for this fellow Moses who led us out
of Egypt—we don't know what has happened to him!'[e][e] **41**That was the time they
made an idol in the form of a calf. They
brought sacrifices to it and held a celebration in honor of what their hands had
made.[f] **42**But God turned away[g] and gave
them over to the worship of the heavenly

7:12 [z]Ge 42:1,2
7:13 [a]Ge 45:1-4 [b]Ge 45:16
7:14 [c]Ge 45:9,10 [d]Ge 46:26,27; Ex 1:5; Dt 10:22
7:15 [e]Ge 46:5-7; 49:33; Ex 1:6
7:16 [f]Ge 23:16-20; 33:18,19; 50:13; Jos 24:32
7:17 [g]Ex 1:7; Ps 105:24
7:18 [h]Ex 1:8
7:19 [i]Ex 1:10-22
7:20 [j]Ex 2:2; Heb 11:23
7:21 [k]Ex 2:3-10
7:22 [l]1Ki 4:30; Isa 19:11
7:27 [m]Ge 19:9; Nu 16:13
7:29 [n]Ex 2:11-15
7:31 [o]Ex 3:1-4
7:32 [p]S Ac 3:13 [q]Ex 3:6
7:33 [r]Ex 3:5; Jos 5:15
7:34 [s]Ex 3:7-10
7:35 [t]ver 27
7:36 [u]Ex 12:41; 33:1 [v]Ex 11:10; S Jn 4:48 [w]Ex 14:21 [x]Ex 15:25; 17:5,6
7:37 [y]Dt 18:15, 18; Ac 3:22
7:38 [z]ver 53 [a]Ex 19:17; Lev 27:34 [b]Dt 32:45-47; Heb 4:12 [c]Ro 3:2
7:39 [d]Nu 14:3,4
7:40 [e]Ex 32:1,23
7:41 [f]Ex 32:4-6; Ps 106:19,20; Rev 9:20
7:42 [g]Jos 24:20; Isa 63:10

[y] *20* Or *was fair in the sight of God*
[z] *28* Exodus 2:14 [a] *32* Exodus 3:6
[b] *34* Exodus 3:5,7,8,10 [c] *36* That is, Sea of Reeds [d] *37* Deut. 18:15 [e] *40* Exodus 32:1

7:38 THE ASSEMBLY IN THE DESERT. "The assembly in the desert" refers to Israel as the people of God. In Hebrew the word translated "church" is *qahal* and is rendered in the Septuagint (Greek translation of the OT) as *ekklēsia* (i.e., "assembly" or "church"). (1) Just as Moses led the church of the OT, Christ leads the church of the NT. The NT church, designated "Abraham's seed" (Gal 3:29; cf. Ro 4:11–18) and the "Israel of God" (Gal 6:16), stands in continuity with the church of the OT. (2) Like the OT church, the church of the NT is "in the desert," i.e., it is a pilgrim church, far from the promised land (Heb 11:6–16). For this reason we must never become too comfortable with life here on this earth.

7:42 GOD . . . GAVE THEM OVER. Stephen's words reflect a principle well established in Scripture and redemptive history. Those who persist in repudiating God are given over to the influence of evil, Satan and immorality (cf. Ro 1:24,28). Contrary to popular teaching, God does not continue to show love and forgiveness without any condition on our part. He forgives and communicates his love only to those who turn their hearts to him in sincere repentance and true obedience. For those who harden their hearts, resist

bodies.[h] This agrees with what is written
in the book of the prophets:

" 'Did you bring me sacrifices and
offerings
forty years in the desert, O house
of Israel?
43You have lifted up the shrine of
Molech
and the star of your god Rephan,
the idols you made to worship.
Therefore I will send you into
exile'[f][i] beyond Babylon.

44"Our forefathers had the tabernacle
of the Testimony[j] with them in the
desert. It had been made as God directed
Moses, according to the pattern he had
seen.[k] 45Having received the tabernacle,
our fathers under Joshua brought it with
them when they took the land from the
nations God drove out before them.[l] It
remained in the land until the time of David,[m] 46who enjoyed God's favor and
asked that he might provide a dwelling place for the God of Jacob.[g][n] 47But it
was Solomon who built the house for
him.[o]
48"However, the Most High[p] does not
live in houses made by men.[q] As the
prophet says:

49" 'Heaven is my throne,
and the earth is my footstool.[r]
What kind of house will you build for
me?
says the Lord.
Or where will my resting place be?
50Has not my hand made all these
things?'[h][s]

51"You stiff-necked people,[t] with uncircumcised hearts[u] and ears! You are
just like your fathers: You always resist
the Holy Spirit! 52Was there ever a prophet your fathers did not persecute?[v] They
even killed those who predicted the coming of the Righteous One. And now you
have betrayed and murdered him[w]—
53you who have received the law that was
put into effect through angels[x] but have
not obeyed it."

The Stoning of Stephen

54When they heard this, they were furious[y] and gnashed their teeth at him.
55But Stephen, full of the Holy Spirit,[z]
looked up to heaven and saw the glory of
God, and Jesus standing at the right hand

7:42 [h]Jer 19:13 **7:43** [i]Am 5:25-27 **7:44** [j]Ex 38:21; Nu 1:50; 17:7 [k]Ex 25:8,9,40 **7:45** [l]Jos 3:14-17; 18:1; 23:9; 24:18; Ps 44:2 [m]2Sa 7:2,6 **7:46** [n]2Sa 7:8-16; 1Ki 8:17; Ps 132:1-5 **7:47** [o]1Ki 6:1-38 **7:48** [p]S Mk 5:7 [q]1Ki 8:27; 2Ch 2:6 **7:49** [r]Mt 5:34,35 **7:50** [s]Isa 66:1,2 **7:51** [t]Ex 32:9; 33:3,5 [u]Lev 26:41; Dt 10:16; Jer 4:4; 9:26 **7:52** [v]S Mt 5:12 [w]Ac 3:14; 1Th 2:15 **7:53** [x]ver 38; Gal 3:19; Heb 2:2 **7:54** [y]Ac 5:33 **7:55** [z]S Lk 1:15

[f] *43* Amos 5:25-27 [g] *46* Some early manuscripts *the house of Jacob* [h] *50* Isaiah 66:1,2

the Spirit and refuse to accept God's salvation, there remains only his wrath (Ro 2:4–6,8).

7:44 ACCORDING TO THE PATTERN. God has always had a divine pattern to be followed by his people. (1) God had a pattern for Moses that served as the standard under the old covenant. (a) In Ex 12, God gave Moses specific instructions for the original Passover in Egypt, which became a pattern for all subsequent generations of Israelites to follow. (b) In Ex 20, God gave Moses the Ten Commandments as the pattern and moral standard for all subsequent generations. (c) In Ex 25, God instructed Moses to erect a tabernacle as a copy and shadow of heavenly things and the redemption that God planned to accomplish in the Lord Jesus Christ on earth. Moses carefully made the tabernacle and all its furnishings "exactly like the pattern" that God had fashioned in wisdom (Ex 25:9,40; cf. Heb 8:1–5).

(2) Just as surely as God had a pattern for the tabernacle under the old covenant, he has a pattern for his church under the new. The NT apostles did not arbitrarily decide how the church was to be fashioned. It was the Father and the Son, through what the Holy Spirit recorded in the Gospels, Acts, the letters and the letters to the seven churches (Rev 2–3), who established the apostolic pattern for the church.

(3) Tragically, after the apostolic age the church began to depart from divine revelation and modify God's heavenly pattern by accommodating itself culturally and organizationally according to human, earthly ideas. This has resulted in a proliferation of man-made patterns for the church.

(4) If the church of Jesus Christ is to experience again the full plan, power and presence of God, she must turn from her own ways and embrace the NT apostolic pattern as God's timeless standard for his church.

7:51 ALWAYS RESIST THE HOLY SPIRIT. The history of Israel is the story of a people who repeatedly refused to obey their God and his revealed Word. Instead of submitting to the restraints of his law, their hearts turned toward the ways and lifestyle of the ungodly nations around them. They killed the prophets who called them to repentance and who prophesied about the coming of Christ (vv. 52–53). This is what resisting the Holy Spirit means.

Likewise, the Israel of Christ under the new covenant must be aware of its tendency to live as did the Israel of God under the old. Christ's churches can turn from him and his Word and refuse to heed the voice of the Holy Spirit. When this happens, they too will incur judgment from God: the kingdom will be taken from them (see Ro 11:20–22; Rev 2–3).

7:55 SAW . . . JESUS STANDING. The Bible normally speaks of Jesus as seated at the right hand of God (2:34; Mk 14:62; Lk 22:69; Col 3:1). But here Jesus stood in order to welcome his first martyr to himself. Stephen had confessed Christ before fellow humans and defended the faith. Now Christ, in honor of his servant, confesses him before his heavenly Father. For all faithful believers near death, the Savior stands ready to receive you as your intercessor and advocate (cf. Mk 8:38; Lk 12:8; Ro 8:34; 1Jn 2:1).

Ac 8:14-17 of God.[a] 56"Look," he said, "I see heaven
open[b] and the Son of Man[c] standing at
the right hand of God."
57At this they covered their ears and,
yelling at the top of their voices, they all
rushed at him, 58dragged him out of the
city[d] and began to stone him.[e] Meanwhile,
the witnesses[f] laid their clothes[g]
at the feet of a young man named Saul.[h]
59While they were stoning him, Stephen
prayed, "Lord Jesus, receive my spirit."[i]
60Then he fell on his knees[j] and
cried out, "Lord, do not hold this sin
against them."[k] When he had said this, he
fell asleep.[l]

8 And Saul[m] was there, giving approval
to his death.

The Church Persecuted and Scattered

On that day a great persecution broke
out against the church at Jerusalem, and
all except the apostles were scattered[n]
throughout Judea and Samaria.[o] 2Godly
men buried Stephen and mourned deeply
for him. 3But Saul[p] began to destroy the
church.[q] Going from house to house, he
dragged off men and women and put them
in prison.

Philip in Samaria

4Those who had been scattered[r] Ac 8:26-40
preached the word wherever they went.[s]
5Philip[t] went down to a city in Samaria
and proclaimed the Christ[i] there. 6When
the crowds heard Philip and saw the miraculous
signs he did, they all paid close
attention to what he said. 7With shrieks,
evil[j] spirits came out of many,[u] and many Ac 19:11-12
paralytics and cripples were healed.[v] 8So
there was great joy in that city.

Simon the Sorcerer

9Now for some time a man named Simon
had practiced sorcery[w] in the city
and amazed all the people of Samaria. He
boasted that he was someone great,[x]
10and all the people, both high and low,
gave him their attention and exclaimed,
"This man is the divine power known as
the Great Power."[y] 11They followed him
because he had amazed them for a long
time with his magic. 12But when they be-

7:55 [a] S Mk 16:19 7:56 [b] S Mt 3:16 [c] S Mt 8:20 7:58 [d] Lk 4:29 [e] Lev 24:14,16 [f] Dt 17:7 [g] Ac 22:20 [h] Ac 8:1 7:59 [i] Ps 31:5; Lk 23:46 7:60 [j] Lk 22:41; Ac 9:40 [k] S Mt 5:44 [l] S Mt 9:24 8:1 [m] Ac 7:58 [n] ver 4; Ac 11:19 [o] Ac 9:31 8:3 [p] Ac 7:58 [q] Ac 9:1,13,21; 22:4,19; 26:10,11; 1Co 15:9; Gal 1:13,23; Php 3:6; 1Ti 1:13

8:4 [r] ver 1 [s] Ac 15:35 8:5 [t] Ac 6:5; 21:8 8:7 [u] S Mk 16:17 [v] S Mt 4:24 8:9 [w] Ac 13:6 [x] Ac 5:36 8:10 [y] Ac 14:11; 28:6

i 5 Or *Messiah* j 7 Greek *unclean*

8:1 A GREAT PERSECUTION. Saul seems to have been the leader (vv. 1–3; 9:1) of the church's first widespread persecution; it was intense and severe. Men and women were put in prison (v. 3) and beaten (22:19), and many were put to death (22:20; 26:10–11). Yet God used this persecution to start the great missionary work of the church (v. 4).

8:5–24 PHILIP WENT DOWN TO ... SAMARIA. Notice the sequence of events in this record of the outpouring of the Spirit on the Samaritan believers. (1) Philip preached the gospel of the kingdom and God confirmed the Word with miraculous signs (vv. 5–7).

(2) Many Samaritans received the Word of God (v. 14), believed in Jesus (v. 12), were healed and delivered from evil spirits (v. 7), and were baptized in water (vv. 12–13). Thus, they experienced salvation, the regenerative work of the Holy Spirit and the power of the kingdom of God (see v. 12, note).

(3) The Holy Spirit, however, "had not yet come upon any of them" after their conversion to Christ and their water baptism (v. 16).

(4) After some days following the Samaritans' conversion, Peter and John came to Samaria and prayed that the Samaritans might receive the Spirit (vv. 14–15). There was a definite interval between their conversion to Christ and their receiving the baptism in the Holy Spirit (vv. 16–17; cf. 2:4). The Samaritans' reception of the Spirit, in other words, follows the pattern of the disciples' experience at Pentecost (see articles on THE REGENERATION OF THE DISCIPLES, p. 212, and BAPTISM IN THE HOLY SPIRIT, p. 228).

(5) Some external manifestation must have accompanied receiving the Holy Spirit, undoubtedly speaking in other tongues and prophesying (see v. 18, note).

8:6 THE MIRACULOUS SIGNS HE DID. Christ's promise to use miraculous signs to confirm the preaching of the Word was not limited to the apostles (Mk 16:15–18; see article on SIGNS OF BELIEVERS, p. 106). He promises that the disciples' converts ("whoever believes") will perform signs in the name of Jesus, such as driving out demons (Mk 16:17) and healing the sick (Mk 16:18). This is exactly what Philip did.

8:12 THEY BELIEVED ... THE NAME OF JESUS CHRIST. The Samaritans fully met the conditions for salvation and were Christians before the Spirit came upon them. (1) They "believed" and were "baptized." Two facts make it clear that the faith of the Samaritans was genuine saving faith. (a) Both Philip (v. 12) and the apostles (v. 14) considered the Samaritans' faith to be valid. (b) The Samaritans publicly committed themselves to Christ by water baptism. Scripture affirms that "whoever believes and is baptized will be saved" (Mk 16:16). Thus, they were regenerated and indwelt by the Holy Spirit (Ro 8:9).

(2) Their receiving the Holy Spirit several days later (v. 17) was not for salvation. It was rather a receiving of the Spirit as the disciples did at Pentecost, i.e., to equip them with power for service and witness (1:8; 2:4). Luke uses the term "receive the Spirit" primarily in an empowering sense (1:8; 2:38; 8:17; 10:47; 19:2), not in the sense of new birth or regeneration (see articles on REGENERATION, p. 178, THE REGENERATION OF THE DISCIPLES, p. 212, and BAPTISM IN THE HOLY SPIRIT, p. 228).

(3) Some have taught that the faith of the Samaritans was not a saving and regenerating faith. Howev-

lieved Philip as he preached the good
news of the kingdom of God[z] and the
name of Jesus Christ, they were baptized,[a] both men and women. **13**Simon
himself believed and was baptized. And he
followed Philip everywhere, astonished by
the great signs and miracles[b] he saw.

Samaritans Receive the Spirit

14When the apostles in Jerusalem heard
that Samaria[c] had accepted the word of
God,[d] they sent Peter and John[e] to them.
15When they arrived, they prayed for them
that they might receive the Holy Spirit,[f]
16because the Holy Spirit had not yet
come upon any of them;[g] they had simply
been baptized into[k] the name of the Lord
Jesus.[h] **17**Then Peter and John placed
their hands on them,[i] and they received
Ac 9:17 the Holy Spirit.[j]

Peter Rebukes Simon

18When Simon saw that the Spirit was
given at the laying on of the apostles'
hands, he offered them money **19**and said,
"Give me also this ability so that everyone
on whom I lay my hands may receive the
Holy Spirit."

20Peter answered: "May your money
perish with you, because you thought you
could buy the gift of God with money![k]
21You have no part or share[l] in this ministry, because your heart is not right[m] before God. **22**Repent[n] of this wickedness
and pray to the Lord. Perhaps he will forgive you for having such a thought in your
heart. **23**For I see that you are full of bitterness and captive to sin."

24Then Simon answered, "Pray to the
Lord for me[o] so that nothing you have
said may happen to me."

25When they had testified and proclaimed the word of the Lord,[p] Peter and
John returned to Jerusalem, preaching the
gospel in many Samaritan villages.[q]

Philip and the Ethiopian

26Now an angel[r] of the Lord said to
Philip,[s] "Go south to the road—the
desert road—that goes down from Jerusalem to Gaza." **27**So he started out, and on

8:12 [z]S Mt 3:2 [a]S Ac 2:38
8:13 [b]ver 6; Ac 19:11
8:14 [c]ver 1 [d]S Heb 4:12 [e]S Lk 22:8
8:15 [f]S Jn 20:22
8:16 [g]S Ac 10:44; 19:2 [h]Mt 28:19; S Ac 2:38
8:17 [i]S Ac 6:6 [j]S Jn 20:22
8:20 [k]2Ki 5:16; Da 5:17; Mt 10:8; Ac 2:38
8:21 [l]Ne 2:20 [m]Ps 78:37
8:22 [n]Ac 2:38
8:24 [o]Ex 8:8; Nu 21:7; 1Ki 13:6; Jer 42:2
8:25 [p]S Ac 13:48 [q]ver 40
8:26 [r]S Ac 5:19 [s]Ac 6:5

[k] *16* Or *in*

er, it is unreasonable to believe that Philip, a man full of the Holy Spirit and wisdom (6:3–5), would baptize, heal and drive demons out of people whose faith he thought was not genuine.

8:16 HAD NOT YET COME UPON ANY OF THEM. The Spirit had not yet come upon any of them in the same way he descended on the believers on the day of Pentecost (2:4). He had not yet come upon them as the Father had promised (1:4) and as Christ had foretold when he said, "You will be baptized with the Holy Spirit" (1:5). Evidently they had not demonstrated the expected spiritual manifestations, especially divinely inspired utterances (see vv. 5–24, note; v. 18, note).

8:17 THEY RECEIVED THE HOLY SPIRIT. Through the laying on of hands, the Samaritans received the Holy Spirit in the same sense as the baptism in the Spirit that occurred at Pentecost (1:8; 2:4).

The Samaritans' "two-stage" experience—i.e., first believing, and then being filled with the Spirit—shows that the "two-stage" experience of the believers at Pentecost was not abnormal. The experiences of both Paul in 9:5–17 and the Ephesian disciples in 19:1–6 were the same as the Samaritans. They accepted Christ as Lord and afterwards were filled with the Spirit. There need not be a long time lapse, however, between saving faith and baptism in the Spirit, as demonstrated by the Gentiles at Caesarea (ch. 10).

8:18 WHEN SIMON SAW. The Spirit's coming upon the Samaritans was accompanied by observable external manifestations apparent even to Simon the sorcerer. It is reasonable to conclude that the observable manifestations were like those that occurred after the Spirit's coming upon the earliest disciples at Pentecost, i.e., speaking in other tongues (see 2:4; 10:45–46; 11:15, note; 19:6; see article on SPEAKING IN TONGUES, p. 232). This gave both the Samaritans and the apostles a verifiable sign that the Holy Spirit had come upon the new believers.

8:21 YOUR HEART IS NOT RIGHT. The baptism in the Holy Spirit throughout the book of Acts occurs only in the context of committed discipleship to Jesus Christ. (1) Simon, who sought the power and gift of the Holy Spirit as well as the authority to impart the gift (v. 19), was rejected by God because his heart was not right with God, and he was still wicked and "captive to sin" (vv. 22–23). The genuine gift of the Holy Spirit will be poured out only on those "who fear him and do what is right" (10:35, cf. 10:44–48; see also 5:32).

(2) Before and after the day of Pentecost, the followers of Christ were devoted to the risen Lord (1:2–14; 2:32) and engaged in continual prayer (1:14; 6:4). They lived lives of separation from sin and the world (2:38–40) and obeyed the apostles' teaching (2:42; 6:4). Repeated or new outpourings of the Spirit were given only to believers who had turned from their sins and wicked ways to lives of obedience to Christ (cf. 2:42; 3:1,19,22–26; 4:8,19–35; 5:29–32; 6:4; 8:14–21; 9:1–19; 10:34–47; 19:1–6; 24:16). Walking by the Spirit and being led by him are always conditions of being filled with the Spirit (see Gal 5:16–25; Eph 5:18).

(3) Any supernatural experience thought to be the baptism in the Spirit occurring in one who continues in the ways of the sinful nature is not from Christ (cf. 1Jn 4:1–6). It is rather a "counterfeit" baptism in the Spirit and may be accompanied by demonic gifts and powers (Mt 7:21–23; 2Th 2:7–10; see article on TESTING FOR GENUINE BAPTISM IN THE SPIRIT, p. 254).

his way he met an Ethiopian[1][t] eunuch,[u]
an important official in charge of all the
treasury of Candace, queen of the Ethiopi-
ans. This man had gone to Jerusalem to
worship,[v] 28 and on his way home was sitting in his chariot reading the book of Isaiah the prophet. 29 The Spirit told[w] Philip,
"Go to that chariot and stay near it."
30 Then Philip ran up to the chariot and
heard the man reading Isaiah the prophet.
"Do you understand what you are reading?" Philip asked.
31 "How can I," he said, "unless someone explains it to me?" So he invited Philip to come up and sit with him.
32 The eunuch was reading this passage
of Scripture:

"He was led like a sheep to the
slaughter,
and as a lamb before the shearer is
silent,
so he did not open his mouth.
33 In his humiliation he was deprived of
justice.
Who can speak of his descendants?
For his life was taken from the
earth."[m][x]

34 The eunuch asked Philip, "Tell me,
please, who is the prophet talking about,
himself or someone else?" 35 Then Philip
began[y] with that very passage of Scripture[z] and told him the good news[a] about
Jesus.
36 As they traveled along the road, they
came to some water and the eunuch said,
"Look, here is water. Why shouldn't I be
baptized?"[n][b] 38 And he gave orders to stop
the chariot. Then both Philip and the eunuch went down into the water and Philip
baptized him. 39 When they came up out of
the water, the Spirit of the Lord suddenly
took Philip away,[c] and the eunuch did not
see him again, but went on his way rejoicing. 40 Philip, however, appeared at Azotus and traveled about, preaching the gospel in all the towns[d] until he reached
Caesarea.[e]

Saul's Conversion

9:1–19pp — Ac 22:3–16; 26:9–18

9 Meanwhile, Saul was still breathing
out murderous threats against the
Lord's disciples.[f] He went to the high
priest 2 and asked him for letters to the
synagogues in Damascus,[g] so that if he
found any there who belonged to the
Way,[h] whether men or women, he might
take them as prisoners to Jerusalem. 3 As
he neared Damascus on his journey, suddenly a light from heaven flashed around
him.[i] 4 He fell to the ground and heard a
voice[j] say to him, "Saul, Saul, why do you
persecute me?"
5 "Who are you, Lord?" Saul asked.
"I am Jesus, whom you are persecuting," he replied. 6 "Now get up and go into
the city, and you will be told what you
must do."[k]
7 The men traveling with Saul stood
there speechless; they heard the sound[l]
but did not see anyone.[m] 8 Saul got up from
the ground, but when he opened his eyes
he could see nothing.[n] So they led him by
the hand into Damascus. 9 For three days
he was blind, and did not eat or drink anything.
10 In Damascus there was a disciple
named Ananias. The Lord called to him in
a vision,[o] "Ananias!"
"Yes, Lord," he answered.
11 The Lord told him, "Go to the house
of Judas on Straight Street and ask for a
man from Tarsus[p] named Saul, for he is
praying. 12 In a vision he has seen a man
named Ananias come and place his hands
on[q] him to restore his sight."
13 "Lord," Ananias answered, "I have

Ac 16:29-32

8:27 [t]Ps 68:31; 87:4; Zep 3:10 [u]Isa 56:3-5 [v]1Ki 8:41-43; Jn 12:20 **8:29** [w]Ac 10:19; 11:12; 13:2; 20:23; 21:11 **8:33** [x]Isa 53:7,8 **8:35** [y]Mt 5:2 [z]Lk 24:27; Ac 17:2; 18:28; 28:23 [a]S Ac 13:32 **8:36** [b]S Ac 2:38; 10:47 **8:39** [c]1Ki 18:12; 2Ki 2:16; Eze 3:12,14; 8:3; 11:1,24; 43:5; 2Co 12:2; 1Th 4:17; Rev 12:5

8:40 [d]ver 25 [e]Ac 10:1,24; 12:19; 21:8,16; 23:23,33; 25:1,4, 6,13 **9:1** [f]S Ac 8:3 **9:2** [g]Isa 17:1; Jer 49:23 [h]Ac 19:9,23; 22:4; 24:14,22 **9:3** [i]1Co 15:8 **9:4** [j]Isa 6:8 **9:6** [k]ver 16; Eze 3:22 **9:7** [l]Jn 12:29 [m]Da 10:7 **9:8** [n]ver 18 **9:10** [o]Ac 10:3,17, 19; 12:9; 16:9,10; 18:9 **9:11** [p]ver 30; Ac 11:25; 21:39; 22:3 **9:12** [q]S Mk 5:23

[1] *27* That is, from the upper Nile region
[m] *33* Isaiah 53:7,8 [n] *36* Some late manuscripts *baptized?" 37Philip said, "If you believe with all your heart, you may." The eunuch answered, "I believe that Jesus Christ is the Son of God."*

9:3–19 THE CONVERSION OF PAUL. Vv. 3–9 record Paul's conversion outside the city of Damascus (cf. 22:3–16; 26:9–18). That his conversion occurs here rather than later at the house of Judas (v. 11) is clear from the following: (1) Paul obeys Christ's instruction (v. 6; 22:10; 26:15–19), commits himself to be a "servant and . . . witness" of the gospel (26:16) and a missionary to the Gentiles (26:17–19), and gives himself to prayer (v. 11). (2) Paul is called "brother Saul" by Ananias (v. 17). Ananias already assumes Paul is a believer who has experienced the new birth (see Jn 3:3–6), is committed to Christ and to God's mission, and needs no more than to be baptized, have his sight restored and be filled with the Holy Spirit (vv. 17–18; see 9:17, note).

9:11 FOR HE IS PRAYING. After Paul encounters Jesus and accepts him as Lord and Messiah, he fasts and prays for guidance with an attitude of deep commitment to God. Saving faith and the consequent new birth will always result in believers seeking communion with their new Lord and Savior.

9:13 SAINTS. The believers in the NT are called "saints" (cf. 26:10; Ro 1:7; 1Co 1:2; Rev 13:7; 19:8). (1) The basic idea of the term "saint" (Gk *hagios*) is separation from sin and to God. Saints, in other words, are "God's separated ones" or "God's holy ones." This

heard many reports about this man and all
the harm he has done to your saints[r] in
Jerusalem.[s] **14**And he has come here with
authority from the chief priests[t] to arrest
all who call on your name."[u]
15But the Lord said to Ananias, "Go!
This man is my chosen instrument[v] to
carry my name before the Gentiles[w] and
their kings[x] and before the people of Israel. **16**I will show him how much he must
suffer for my name."[y]
17Then Ananias went to the house and
entered it. Placing his hands on[z] Saul, he
said, "Brother Saul, the Lord—Jesus, who
appeared to you on the road as you were
coming here—has sent me so that you
Ac 10:44-47 may see again and be filled with the Holy
Spirit."[a] **18**Immediately, something like
scales fell from Saul's eyes, and he could
see again. He got up and was baptized,[b]
19and after taking some food, he regained
his strength.

Saul in Damascus and Jerusalem

Saul spent several days with the disciples[c] in Damascus.[d] **20**At once he began
to preach in the synagogues[e] that Jesus
is the Son of God.[f] **21**All those who heard
him were astonished and asked, "Isn't he
the man who raised havoc in Jerusalem
among those who call on this name?[g] And
hasn't he come here to take them as prisoners to the chief priests?"[h] **22**Yet Saul
grew more and more powerful and baffled
the Jews living in Damascus by proving
that Jesus is the Christ.[o][i]
23After many days had gone by, the
Jews conspired to kill him,[j] **24**but Saul
learned of their plan.[k] Day and night they
kept close watch on the city gates in order
to kill him. **25**But his followers took him
by night and lowered him in a basket
through an opening in the wall.[l]
26When he came to Jerusalem,[m] he
tried to join the disciples, but they were all
afraid of him, not believing that he really
was a disciple. **27**But Barnabas[n] took him
and brought him to the apostles. He told
them how Saul on his journey had seen
the Lord and that the Lord had spoken to
him,[o] and how in Damascus he had
preached fearlessly in the name of Jesus.[p]
28So Saul stayed with them and moved
about freely in Jerusalem, speaking boldly
in the name of the Lord. **29**He talked and
debated with the Grecian Jews,[q] but they
tried to kill him.[r] **30**When the brothers[s]
learned of this, they took him down
to Caesarea[t] and sent him off to Tarsus.[u]
31Then the church throughout Judea,

9:13 [r]ver 32; Ac 26:10; Ro 1:7; 15:25,26,31; 16:2, 15; Eph 1:1; Php 1:1 [s]S Ac 8:3
9:14 [t]ver 2,21 [u]S Ac 2:21
9:15 [v]Ac 13:2; Ro 1:1; Gal 1:15; 1Ti 1:12 [w]Ro 11:13; 15:15, 16; Gal 1:16; 2:7, 8 [x]Ac 25:22,23; 26:1
9:16 [y]Ac 20:23; 21:11; 2Co 6:4-10; 11:23-27; 2Ti 1:8; 2:3,9
9:17 [z]S Ac 6:6 [a]S Lk 1:15
9:18 [b]S Ac 2:38
9:19 [c]S Ac 11:26 [d]Ac 26:20
9:20 [e]Ac 13:5,14; 14:1; 17:2,10,17; 18:4,19; 19:8 [f]S Mt 4:3
9:21 [g]S Ac 8:3 [h]ver 14
9:22 [i]S Lk 2:11; Ac 5:42; 17:3; 18:5,28
9:23 [j]S Ac 20:3
9:24 [k]Ac 20:3,19; 23:16,30
9:25 [l]1Sa 19:12; 2Co 11:32,33
9:26 [m]Ac 22:17; 26:20; Gal 1:17,18
9:27 [n]S Ac 4:36 [o]ver 3-6 [p]ver 20, 22
9:29 [q]Ac 6:1 [r]2Co 11:26
9:30 [s]S Ac 1:16 [t]S Ac 8:40 [u]S ver 11

[o] *22* Or *Messiah*

---

implies being led and sanctified by the Holy Spirit (Ro 8:14; 1Co 6:11; 2Th 2:13; 1Pe 1:2), and turning one's back on the world to follow Jesus (Jn 17:15–17). However, the term "saint" does not mean that the believer is already perfect or incapable of sin (cf. 1Jn 2:1). (2) Calling believers "saved sinners" is not a NT practice. As the common Biblical term for all believers, "saint" emphasizes (a) the Scriptural expectation that all believers conform to God's way of righteousness (Eph 5:3), and (b) the necessity that holiness be an internal reality for all who belong to Christ (1Co 1:30).

9:16 SUFFER FOR MY NAME. Paul's conversion and salvation meant not only a commission to preach the gospel but also a call to suffer for Christ. Paul is told from the beginning that he must undergo much suffering for the cause of Christ. In Christ's kingdom, suffering for his sake is a sign of God's highest favor (14:22; Mt 5:11–12; Ro 8:17; 2Ti 2:12) and the means to a fruitful ministry (Jn 12:24; 2Co 1:3–6); it results in abundant reward in heaven (Mt 5:12; 2Ti 2:12). Death must work in believers in order that God's life might flow from them to others (Ro 8:17–18, 36–37; 2Co 4:10–12). For additional passages on the sufferings of Paul, see 20:23; 2Co 4:8–18; 6:3–10; 11:23–27; Gal 6:17; 2Ti 1:11–12; see also 2Co 1:4, note; 11:23, note.

9:17 BROTHER SAUL. See note on vv. 3–19.

9:17 FILLED WITH THE HOLY SPIRIT. Three days after Paul's conversion he is filled with the Holy Spirit. Paul's experience parallels that of the disciples' at Pentecost (see article on BAPTISM IN THE HOLY SPIRIT, p. 228). First, he experiences the new birth and is saved (see vv. 3–19, note); then he is "filled with the Holy Spirit."

Although Luke does not specifically say that Paul spoke in tongues when he received the Pentecostal gift of the Holy Spirit, it is reasonable to assume that he did. (1) The NT norm indicates that one filled with the Spirit begins to speak in tongues (2:4; 10:45–46; 19:6; see 11:15, note). (2) Paul himself testifies that he frequently spoke in tongues: "I thank God that I speak in tongues more than all of you" (1Co 14:18).

9:18 HE . . . WAS BAPTIZED. Luke's primary concern is the actual baptism in the Spirit (v. 17), rather than whether Paul spoke in tongues. Seeking the Spirit's fullness should be centered on the Holy Spirit himself and not on any external manifestation. On the other hand, all believers who desire the fullness of the Holy Spirit should expect the spiritual manifestations of his coming (2:4,17).

9:31 THE FEAR OF THE LORD. Luke emphasizes the formula "to fear God," both in his Gospel (see Lk 1:50; 18:2; 23:40) and in Acts. It is the God-fearers (i.e., Gentile adherents to the Jewish faith) who form the starting point for the Gentile mission in ch. 10 (10:2,22,35; 13:16,26). The fear of the Lord produces trust and obedience, as well as the avoidance of evil (Job 28:28; Ps 111:10; Pr 1:7); this in turn results in the encouragement of the Holy Spirit.

Galilee and Samaria[v] enjoyed a time of peace. It was strengthened; and encouraged by the Holy Spirit, it grew in numbers,[w] living in the fear of the Lord.

Aeneas and Dorcas

32 As Peter traveled about the country, he went to visit the saints[x] in Lydda. 33 There he found a man named Aeneas, a paralytic who had been bedridden for eight years. 34 "Aeneas," Peter said to him, "Jesus Christ heals you.[y] Get up and take care of your mat." Immediately Aeneas got up. 35 All those who lived in Lydda and Sharon[z] saw him and turned to the Lord.[a]

36 In Joppa[b] there was a disciple named Tabitha (which, when translated, is Dorcas[p]), who was always doing good[c] and helping the poor. 37 About that time she became sick and died, and her body was washed and placed in an upstairs room.[d] 38 Lydda was near Joppa; so when the disciples[e] heard that Peter was in Lydda, they sent two men to him and urged him, "Please come at once!"

39 Peter went with them, and when he arrived he was taken upstairs to the room. All the widows[f] stood around him, crying and showing him the robes and other clothing that Dorcas had made while she was still with them.

40 Peter sent them all out of the room;[g] then he got down on his knees[h] and prayed. Turning toward the dead woman, he said, "Tabitha, get up."[i] She opened her eyes, and seeing Peter she sat up. 41 He took her by the hand and helped her to her feet. Then he called the believers and the widows and presented her to them alive. 42 This became known all over Joppa, and many people believed in the Lord.[j] 43 Peter stayed in Joppa for some time with a tanner named Simon.[k]

Cornelius Calls for Peter

10 At Caesarea[l] there was a man named Cornelius, a centurion in what was known as the Italian Regiment. 2 He and all his family were devout and God-fearing;[m] he gave generously to those in need and prayed to God regularly. 3 One day at about three in the afternoon[n] he had a vision.[o] He distinctly saw an angel[p] of God, who came to him and said, "Cornelius!"

4 Cornelius stared at him in fear. "What is it, Lord?" he asked.

The angel answered, "Your prayers and gifts to the poor have come up as a memorial offering[q] before God.[r] 5 Now send men to Joppa[s] to bring back a man named Simon who is called Peter. 6 He is staying with Simon the tanner,[t] whose house is by the sea."

7 When the angel who spoke to him had gone, Cornelius called two of his servants and a devout soldier who was one of his attendants. 8 He told them everything that had happened and sent them to Joppa.[u]

Peter's Vision

10:9–32Ref — Ac 11:5–14

9 About noon the following day as they were on their journey and approaching the

9:31 [v]Ac 8:1 [w]S Ac 2:41
9:32 [x]S ver 13
9:34 [y]Ac 3:6,16; 4:10
9:35 [z]1Ch 5:16; 27:29; SS 2:1; Isa 33:9; 35:2; 65:10 [a]S Ac 2:41
9:36 [b]Jos 19:46; 2Ch 2:16; Ezr 3:7; Jnh 1:3; Ac 10:5 [c]1Ti 2:10; Tit 3:8
9:37 [d]Ac 1:13; 20:8
9:38 [e]S Ac 11:26
9:39 [f]Ac 6:1; 1Ti 5:3
9:40 [g]Mt 9:25 [h]Lk 22:41; Ac 7:60 [i]S Lk 7:14
9:42 [j]S Ac 2:41
9:43 [k]Ac 10:6
10:1 [l]S Ac 8:40
10:2 [m]ver 22,35; Ac 13:16,26
10:3 [n]Ps 55:17; Ac 3:1 [o]S Ac 9:10 [p]S Ac 5:19
10:4 [q]Ps 20:3; S Mt 10:42; 26:13 [r]Rev 8:4
10:5 [s]S Ac 9:36
10:6 [t]Ac 9:43
10:8 [u]S Ac 9:36

p 36 Both *Tabitha* (Aramaic) and *Dorcas* (Greek) mean *gazelle*.

9:36 DORCAS . . . ALWAYS DOING GOOD. As God worked through Peter to heal (vv. 33–35) and to raise the dead (v. 40), he also worked through Dorcas with her deeds of kindness and love. Acts of love that help those in need are as much a manifestation of the Holy Spirit as are miracles, signs and wonders. Paul emphasized this truth in 1Co 13 (cf. 1Pe 4:10–11).

10:4 YOUR PRAYERS . . . A MEMORIAL OFFERING BEFORE GOD. God considers our prayers a sacrifice ascending to him, reminding him of our perseverance in calling on him in faith and devotion (see Ps 141:2; Heb 13:15–16).

10:9 PETER WENT UP ON THE ROOF TO PRAY. The Holy Spirit, the author of the Scriptures, has revealed that the NT Christians were a people devoted to much prayer. They understood that God's kingdom could not be manifested in its full power with only a few minutes of prayer a day (1:14; 2:42; 3:1; 6:4; Eph 6:18; Col 4:2). (1) The pious Jew prayed two or three times a day (cf. Ps 55:17; Da 6:10). It was the custom of Christ's followers, especially the apostles (6:4), to pray with the same devotion. Peter and John went up to the temple "at the time of prayer" (3:1), while Luke and Paul did the same (16:16). Peter prayed regularly at noon; God rewarded Cornelius for his faithfulness in keeping his hours of prayer (vv. 30ff).

(2) The Scriptures urge believers to continue faithfully in prayer (Ro 12:12), pray always (Lk 18:1), pray continually (1Th 5:17), pray everywhere (1Ti 2:8), pray on all occasions with all kinds of prayers (Eph 6:18), persevere in prayer (Col 4:2) and pray powerfully (Jas 5:16). These exhortations indicate there can be no real kingdom power in our battle against sin, Satan and the world, or victory in our attempt to win the lost, without much daily prayer.

(3) Would it not be pleasing to God in the light of the Lord's plea that his disciples watch and pray at least "one hour" (Mt 26:38–41), and in the light of the urgency of the end times in which we live, for every believer to commit at least one hour a day to prayer and the study of God's Word for the advancement of his kingdom on earth and all that this involves for us (Mt 6:10,33)?

(4) One hour of prayer might include the following:

city, Peter went up on the roof[v] to pray.
10He became hungry and wanted something to eat, and while the meal was being
prepared, he fell into a trance.[w] **11**He saw
heaven opened[x] and something like a
large sheet being let down to earth by its
four corners. **12**It contained all kinds of
four-footed animals, as well as reptiles of
the earth and birds of the air. **13**Then a
voice told him, "Get up, Peter. Kill and
eat."
14"Surely not, Lord!"[y] Peter replied. "I
have never eaten anything impure or unclean."[z]
15The voice spoke to him a second time,
"Do not call anything impure that God has
made clean."[a]
16This happened three times, and immediately the sheet was taken back to
heaven.
17While Peter was wondering about the
meaning of the vision,[b] the men sent by
Cornelius[c] found out where Simon's
house was and stopped at the gate.
18They called out, asking if Simon who
was known as Peter was staying there.
19While Peter was still thinking about
the vision,[d] the Spirit said[e] to him, "Simon, three[q] men are looking for you. **20**So
get up and go downstairs. Do not hesitate
to go with them, for I have sent them."[f]
21Peter went down and said to the men,
"I'm the one you're looking for. Why have
you come?"
22The men replied, "We have come from
Cornelius the centurion. He is a righteous
and God-fearing man,[g] who is respected
by all the Jewish people. A holy angel told
him to have you come to his house so that
he could hear what you have to say."[h]
23Then Peter invited the men into the
house to be his guests.

Peter at Cornelius' House

The next day Peter started out with
them, and some of the brothers[i] from Joppa went along.[j] **24**The following day he
arrived in Caesarea.[k] Cornelius was expecting them and had called together his
relatives and close friends. **25**As Peter entered the house, Cornelius met him and
fell at his feet in reverence. **26**But Peter
made him get up. "Stand up," he said, "I
am only a man myself."[l]
27Talking with him, Peter went inside
and found a large gathering of people.[m]
28He said to them: "You are well aware
that it is against our law for a Jew to associate with a Gentile or visit him.[n] But God
has shown me that I should not call any
man impure or unclean.[o] **29**So when I was
sent for, I came without raising any objec-
tion. May I ask why you sent for me?"
30Cornelius answered: "Four days ago I
was in my house praying at this hour, at
three in the afternoon. Suddenly a man in
shining clothes[p] stood before me **31**and
said, 'Cornelius, God has heard your
prayer and remembered your gifts to the
poor. **32**Send to Joppa for Simon who is
called Peter. He is a guest in the home of
Simon the tanner, who lives by the sea.'
33So I sent for you immediately, and it
was good of you to come. Now we are all
here in the presence of God to listen to
everything the Lord has commanded you
to tell us."
34Then Peter began to speak: "I now
realize how true it is that God does not
show favoritism[q] **35**but accepts men from
every nation who fear him and do what is
right.[r] **36**You know the message[s] God
sent to the people of Israel, telling the
good news[t] of peace[u] through Jesus
Christ, who is Lord of all.[v] **37**You know
what has happened throughout Judea, beginning in Galilee after the baptism that
John preached— **38**how God anointed[w]

10:9 [v] S Mt 24:17 **10:10** [w] Ac 22:17 **10:11** [x] S Mt 3:16 **10:14** [y] Ac 9:5 [z] Lev 11:4-8,13-20; 20:25; Dt 14:3-20; Eze 4:14 **10:15** [a] ver 28; Ge 9:3; Mt 15:11; Lk 11:41; Ac 11:9; Ro 14:14,17,20; 1Co 10:25; 1Ti 4:3,4; Tit 1:15 **10:17** [b] S Ac 9:10 [c] ver 7,8 **10:19** [d] S Ac 9:10 [e] S Ac 8:29 **10:20** [f] Ac 15:7-9 **10:22** [g] ver 2 [h] Ac 11:14

10:23 [i] S Ac 1:16 [j] ver 45; Ac 11:12 **10:24** [k] S Ac 8:40 **10:26** [l] Ac 14:15; Rev 19:10; 22:8,9 **10:27** [m] ver 24 **10:28** [n] Jn 4:9; 18:28; Ac 11:3 [o] S ver 14,15; Ac 15:8,9 **10:30** [p] S Jn 20:12 **10:34** [q] Dt 10:17; 2Ch 19:7; Job 34:19; Mk 12:14; Ro 2:11; Gal 2:6; Eph 6:9; Col 3:25; Jas 2:1; 1Pe 1:17 **10:35** [r] Ac 15:9 **10:36** [s] 1Jn 1:5 [t] S Ac 13:32 [u] S Lk 2:14 [v] S Mt 28:18 **10:38** [w] S Ac 4:26

[q] *19* One early manuscript *two*; other manuscripts do not have the number.

(a) praise, (b) singing to the Lord, (c) thanksgiving, (d) waiting on God, (e) reading the Word, (f) listening to the Holy Spirit, (g) praying the very words of Scripture, (h) confessing failings, (i) interceding for others, (j) petition for one's own needs and (k) praying in tongues.

10:19 THE SPIRIT SAID TO HIM. The Holy Spirit desires the salvation of all people (Mt 28:19; 2Pe 3:9). Since the apostles received the Spirit, they too wanted all people to be saved. Intellectually, however, they did not understand that salvation was no longer restricted to Israel, but was now for all nations (vv. 34–35). It was the Holy Spirit that brought the church to a broader vision. In Acts he is the power of the mission enterprise, directing the church into new areas of witness (8:29,39; 11:11–12; 13:2,4; 16:6; 19:21). The outpouring of the Spirit and the compulsion to mission always belong together (cf. 1:8). Even today, many believers desire the salvation of those in their own community, yet have not understood fully the Holy Spirit's purpose for world missions (see Mt 28:19, note; Lk 24:47, note).

10:34 GOD DOES NOT SHOW FAVORITISM. God has no favorite nation or race, nor does he favor any individual because of nationality, birth or position in life (cf. Jas 2:1). God favors and accepts those from every nation who turn from sin, believe in Christ, fear God and live righteously (v. 35; cf. Ro 2:6–11). All who continue in this manner of life will remain in God's love and favor (Jn 15:10).

Jesus of Nazareth with the Holy Spirit and
power, and how he went around doing
good and healing[x] all who were under the
power of the devil, because God was with
him.[y]
39"We are witnesses[z] of everything he
did in the country of the Jews and in Jerusalem. They killed him by hanging him on
a tree,[a] **40**but God raised him from the
dead[b] on the third day and caused him to
be seen. **41**He was not seen by all the people,[c] but by witnesses whom God had already chosen—by us who ate[d] and drank
with him after he rose from the dead. **42**He
commanded us to preach to the people[e]
and to testify that he is the one whom God
appointed as judge of the living and the
dead.[f] **43**All the prophets testify about
him[g] that everyone[h] who believes[i] in
him receives forgiveness of sins through
his name."[j]

Gentiles Receive the Spirit

44While Peter was still speaking these
words, the Holy Spirit came on[k] all who
heard the message. **45**The circumcised believers who had come with Peter[l] were
astonished that the gift of the Holy Spirit
had been poured out[m] even on the Gentiles.[n] **46**For they heard them speaking in
tongues[r][o] and praising God.
Then Peter said, **47**"Can anyone keep
these people from being baptized with wa-
Ac 11:15-17 ter?[p] They have received the Holy Spirit
just as we have."[q] **48**So he ordered that
they be baptized in the name of Jesus
Christ.[r] Then they asked Peter to stay
with them for a few days.

Peter Explains His Actions

11 The apostles and the brothers[s]
throughout Judea heard that the
Gentiles also had received the word of
God.[t] **2**So when Peter went up to Jerusalem, the circumcised believers[u] criticized
him **3**and said, "You went into the house
of uncircumcised men and ate with
them."[v]
4Peter began and explained everything
to them precisely as it had happened: **5**"I
was in the city of Joppa praying, and in a
trance I saw a vision.[w] I saw something
like a large sheet being let down from
heaven by its four corners, and it came
down to where I was. **6**I looked into it and
saw four-footed animals of the earth, wild
beasts, reptiles, and birds of the air.
7Then I heard a voice telling me, 'Get up,
Peter. Kill and eat.'
8"I replied, 'Surely not, Lord! Nothing
impure or unclean has ever entered my
mouth.'
9"The voice spoke from heaven a second time, 'Do not call anything impure
that God has made clean.'[x] **10**This happened three times, and then it was all
pulled up to heaven again.
11"Right then three men who had been
sent to me from Caesarea[y] stopped at the
house where I was staying. **12**The Spirit
told[z] me to have no hesitation about going with them.[a] These six brothers[b] also
went with me, and we entered the man's
house. **13**He told us how he had seen an
angel[c] appear in his house and say, 'Send
to Joppa for Simon who is called Peter.
14He will bring you a message[d] through
which you and all your household[e] will be
saved.'
15"As I began to speak, the Holy Spirit
came on[f] them as he had come on us at
the beginning.[g] **16**Then I remembered

10:38 x S Mt 4:23 y S Jn 3:2 **10:39** z ver 41; S Lk 24:48 a S Ac 5:30 **10:40** b S Ac 2:24 **10:41** c Jn 14:17, 22 d Lk 24:43; Jn 21:13; Ac 1:4 **10:42** e Mt 28:19, 20 f S Jn 5:22; Ac 17:31; Ro 14:9; 2Co 5:10; 2Ti 4:1; 1Pe 4:5 **10:43** g Isa 53:11; Ac 26:22 h Ac 15:9 i S Jn 3:15 j S Lk 24:27 **10:44** k Ac 8:15, 16; 11:15; 15:8; 19:6; S Lk 1:15 **10:45** l ver 23 m Ac 2:33,38 n Ac 11:18; 15:8 **10:46** o S Mk 16:17 **10:47** p Ac 8:36 q S Jn 20:22; Ac 11:17 **10:48** r S Ac 2:38 **11:1** s S Ac 1:16 t S Heb 4:12 **11:2** u Ac 10:45 **11:3** v Ac 10:25, 28; Gal 2:12 **11:5** w Ac 10:9-32; S 9:10 **11:9** x S Ac 10:15 **11:11** y S Ac 8:40 **11:12** z S Ac 8:29 a Ac 15:9; Ro 3:22 b ver 1,29; S Ac 1:16 **11:13** c S Ac 5:19 **11:14** d Ac 10:36 e Jn 4:53; Ac 16:15,31-34; 18:8; 1Co 1:11,16 **11:15** f S Ac 10:44 g Ac 2:4

r *46* Or *other languages*

10:38 HEALING ALL WHO WERE UNDER THE POWER OF THE DEVIL. See article on POWER OVER SATAN AND DEMONS, p. 80.

10:44 THE HOLY SPIRIT CAME ON ALL. The Gentile household of Cornelius listened and received the Word with saving faith (vv. 34–48; 11:14). (1) Because of their acceptance of Christ, God at once pours out the Holy Spirit on them as his witness that they have believed and received the regenerating life of Christ (cf. 11:17; 15:8–9).

(2) The coming of the Holy Spirit on Cornelius's household has the same purpose as the gift of the Spirit had for the disciples on the day of Pentecost (cf. 1:8; 2:4). This outpouring does not describe God's work of regeneration, but his coming on them for power. Note Peter's words later on, stressing the similarity of this experience with what happened on Pentecost (11:15,17).

(3) Obviously it is possible for one to be baptized in the Spirit immediately after exercising saving faith (see v. 46, note; cf. 11:17).

10:45 THE HOLY SPIRIT. For a discussion on the primary dimensions of the Holy Spirit's activity in the life of the believer, see article on THE DOCTRINE OF THE HOLY SPIRIT, p. 240.

10:46 HEARD THEM SPEAKING IN TONGUES. Peter and those with him considered speaking in tongues through the Spirit as the convincing sign of the baptism in the Holy Spirit. That is, just as God attested his actions at Pentecost by the sign of tongues (2:4), he causes the Gentiles in Cornelius's house to speak in tongues as a convincing sign to Peter and the other Jewish believers (see article on SPEAKING IN TONGUES, p. 232).

11:15 HOLY SPIRIT CAME ON THEM AS HE HAD COME ON US AT THE BEGINNING. The outpouring of the Holy Spirit at Pentecost (2:4) had set a pattern for the reception of the Spirit thereafter. The

what the Lord had said: 'John baptized
with[s] water,[h] but you will be baptized
with the Holy Spirit.'[i] **17**So if God gave
them the same gift[j] as he gave us,[k] who
believed in the Lord Jesus Christ, who was
Ac 13:9 I to think that I could oppose God?"

18When they heard this, they had no
further objections and praised God, saying, "So then, God has granted even the
Gentiles repentance unto life."[l]

The Church in Antioch

19Now those who had been scattered by
the persecution in connection with Stephen[m] traveled as far as Phoenicia, Cyprus and Antioch,[n] telling the message
only to Jews. **20**Some of them, however,
men from Cyprus[o] and Cyrene,[p] went to
Antioch[q] and began to speak to Greeks
also, telling them the good news[r] about
the Lord Jesus. **21**The Lord's hand was
with them,[s] and a great number of people
believed and turned to the Lord.[t]

22News of this reached the ears of the
church at Jerusalem, and they sent Barnabas[u] to Antioch. **23**When he arrived and
saw the evidence of the grace of God,[v] he
was glad and encouraged them all to remain true to the Lord with all their
hearts.[w] **24**He was a good man, full of the
Holy Spirit[x] and faith, and a great number
of people were brought to the Lord.[y]

25Then Barnabas went to Tarsus[z] to
look for Saul, **26**and when he found him,
he brought him to Antioch. So for a whole
year Barnabas and Saul met with the
church and taught great numbers of people. The disciples[a] were called Christians
first[b] at Antioch.

27During this time some prophets[c]
came down from Jerusalem to Antioch.
28One of them, named Agabus,[d] stood up
and through the Spirit predicted that a
severe famine would spread over the entire Roman world.[e] (This happened dur-
ing the reign of Claudius.)[f] **29**The disci- Ac 14:3
ples,[g] each according to his ability, decided to provide help[h] for the brothers[i]
living in Judea. **30**This they did, sending
their gift to the elders[j] by Barnabas[k] and
Saul.[l]

James Put to Death; Peter Imprisoned

12 It was about this time that King
Herod[m] arrested some who belonged to the church, intending to persecute them. **2**He had James, the brother of
John,[n] put to death with the sword.[o]
3When he saw that this pleased the

11:16 [h]S Mk 1:4 [i]S Mk 1:8 **11:17** [j]Ac 2:38 [k]Ac 10:45,47 **11:18** [l]Ro 10:12, 13; 2Co 7:10 **11:19** [m]Ac 8:1,4 [n]ver 26,27; Ac 13:1; 14:26; 18:22; Gal 2:11 **11:20** [o]Ac 4:36 [p]S Mt 27:32 [q]S ver 19 [r]S Ac 13:32 **11:21** [s]Lk 1:66 [t]S Ac 2:41 **11:22** [u]S Ac 4:36 **11:23** [v]Ac 13:43; 14:26; 15:40; 20:24 [w]Ac 14:22 **11:24** [x]S Lk 1:15 [y]S Ac 2:41 **11:25** [z]S Ac 9:11 **11:26** [a]ver 29; Ac 6:1,2; 9:19,26, 38; 13:52 [b]Ac 26:28; 1Pe 4:16 **11:27** [c]Ac 13:1; 15:32; 1Co 11:4; 12:28,29; 14:29, 32,37; S Eph 4:11 **11:28** [d]Ac 21:10 [e]S Mt 24:14 [f]Ac 18:2 **11:29** [g]S ver 26 [h]Ro 15:26; 2Co 8:1-4; 9:2 [i]ver 1,12; S Ac 1:16 **11:30** [j]Ac 14:23; 15:2,22; 20:17; 1Ti 5:17; Tit 1:5; Jas 5:14; 1Pe 5:1; 2Jn 1 [k]S Ac 4:36 [l]Ac 12:25 **12:1** [m]S Mt 14:1 **12:2** [n]S Mt 4:21 [o]Mk 10:39

[s] *16* Or *in*

baptism in the Spirit would be determined by the visible transformation of the individual, the infusion of joy, Spirit-inspired utterances and boldness in witness (2:4; 4:31; 8:15–19; 10:45–47; 19:6). Thus, when Peter pointed out to the apostles and brothers in Jerusalem that Cornelius's household had spoken in tongues when the Holy Spirit was poured out on them (cf. 10:45–46), they were convinced that God was granting salvation in Christ to the Gentiles (v. 18). Baptism in the Spirit should not be assumed today if such tangible manifestations as speaking in tongues are absent; nowhere in Acts is the baptism in the Holy Spirit considered an experience to be known by faith-perception alone (see 8:12,16, notes; 19:6, note; see articles on SPEAKING IN TONGUES, p. 232, and TESTING FOR GENUINE BAPTISM IN THE SPIRIT, p. 254).

11:17 US, WHO BELIEVED. The term "us, who believed" is a Greek aorist participle, normally describing action occurring before that of the main verb. Thus, a more literal translation would be "God gave them the same gift as he gave us also after believing." This agrees with the historical facts that the disciples had believed in Jesus and were regenerated by the Spirit before Pentecost (see article on THE REGENERATION OF THE DISCIPLES, p. 212).

11:18 WHEN THEY HEARD THIS. Peter's speech silenced all objections (vv. 4–18). God had baptized the Gentiles with the Holy Spirit (10:45), and accompanying this was the convincing evidence that they had spoken in other tongues (10:46). This was the only sign that was needed, and it was accepted without doubt.

11:23 REMAIN TRUE TO THE LORD. The NT disciples did not assume that those who received God's grace would automatically remain true to the Lord, for sin, the world and Satan's temptations could persuade a new believer to turn from the way of salvation in Christ. Barnabas gives us an example of how new converts ought to be treated: our main interest should be to help and encourage them to continue in faith, love and fellowship with Christ and his church (cf. 13:43; 14:22).

11:26 THE DISCIPLES WERE CALLED CHRISTIANS. The word "Christian" (Gk *christianos*) occurs only three times in the NT (11:26; 26:28; 1Pe 4:16). It originally was a term denoting a servant and follower of Christ. Today it has become a general term emptied of the original NT meaning. It should suggest the name of our Redeemer (Ro 3:24), the idea of our intimate relation to Christ (Ro 8:38–39), and the thought that we receive him as our Lord (Ro 5:1) and the source of eternal salvation (Heb 5:9). To claim the name "Christian" means that Christ and his Word revealed in Scripture have become our supreme authority and our only source of future hope (Col 1:5,27).

11:27 PROPHETS. The place of prophets in the church is recognized in the Pauline letters (see article on THE MINISTRY GIFTS OF THE CHURCH, p. 407).

TESTING FOR GENUINE BAPTISM IN THE SPIRIT

***Ac 10:44–45** "While Peter was still speaking these words, the Holy Spirit came on all who heard the message. The circumcised believers who had come with Peter were astonished that the gift of the Holy Spirit had been poured out even on the Gentiles."*

Scripture declares that believers must test and weigh all things alleging to be from the Holy Spirit (1Th 5:19–21; cf. 1Co 14:29). "Do not believe every spirit, but test the spirits to see whether they are from God" (1Jn 4:1). The following are Biblical principles by which to test whether a professed baptism in the Holy Spirit is from God.

(1) A genuine baptism in the Holy Spirit will cause us to love, magnify and glorify God the Father and the Lord Jesus Christ more than before (see Jn 16:13–14; Ac 2:11,36; 4:12; 7:55–56; 10:44–46). It is the Holy Spirit who causes love for God to grow in our hearts (Ro 5:5). Conversely, any assumed baptism in the Spirit that draws our prayers, worship and adoration toward anything or anyone other than God and the Lord Jesus is not from God.

(2) A genuine baptism in the Holy Spirit will increase the consciousness of our relationship with the heavenly Father (Ac 1:4; Ro 8:15–16), will lead to a greater awareness of Christ's presence in our daily lives (Jn 14:16–18,23; 15:26) and will increase the heartfelt cry of "*Abba*, Father" (Ro 8:15; Gal 4:6). Conversely, any assumed baptism in the Spirit that does not result in a greater fellowship with Christ and more intense communion with God as our Father is not from God.

(3) A genuine baptism in the Holy Spirit will cause a greater love for and appreciation of Scripture. The Spirit of truth (Jn 14:17), who inspired the Scriptures (2Ti 3:16; 2Pe 1:20–21), will deepen our love for the truth of God's Word (Jn 16:13; Ac 2:42; 3:22; 1Jn 4:6). Conversely, any assumed baptism in the Spirit that diminishes our hunger to read God's Word is not from God (cf. Jn 8:31; 15:4–7).

(4) A genuine baptism in the Holy Spirit will deepen our love and concern for other followers of Christ (Ac 2:42–47; 4:31–37). Christian fellowship and communion can take place only in the Spirit (2Co 13:14). Conversely, any assumed baptism in the Spirit that decreases our love for all who seek to sincerely follow Jesus Christ as Lord and Savior is not from God (compare Ro 5:5 with 1Jn 4:21).

(5) A genuine baptism in the Holy Spirit must be preceded by our turning from sin and faithfully obeying Christ (Ac 2:38; 8:15–24); it will be sustained only as long as we continue to be sanctified by the Spirit (Ac 2:40; 3:26; 5:29–32; 8:21; 26:18; Gal 5:16–25), to "put to death the misdeeds of the body" and to be "led by the Spirit of God" (Ro 8:13–14; cf. Gal 5:24–25). Conversely, any assumed baptism in the Spirit that rests on one who is not set free from sin and who lives according to the sinful nature cannot be ascribed to the Holy Spirit as its source (Ac 2:38–40; 8:18–23; Ro 6:22–23; 8:2–15); any power on that person is from another source, the deceptive activity of Satan (cf. Ps 5:4–5; 2Co 11:13–15; 2Th 2:9–10).

(6) A genuine baptism in the Holy Spirit will intensify our displeasure with the sinful enjoyments and godless pleasures of the world and will diminish the selfish pursuit of earthly riches and reputation (Ac 4:32–37; 8:14–24; 20:33; 1Jn 2:15–17). Conversely, any assumed baptism in the Spirit that increases one's acceptance of the world's ways and philosophies is not from God, for "we have not received the spirit of the world but the Spirit who is from God" (1Co 2:12).

(7) A genuine baptism in the Holy Spirit will give us a greater desire and power to witness concerning the saving work of the Lord Jesus Christ (cf. Lk 4:18; Ac 1:4–8; 2:1–4,37–42; 4:8–33; Ro 9:1–3; 10:1). Conversely, any assumed baptism in the Spirit that does not result in a more intense desire to see others enter into a saving relationship with Christ is not from God (see Ac 4:20, note).

(8) A genuine baptism in the Holy Spirit will cause us to be more receptive to the Spirit's operation within God's kingdom and his gifts within our personal lives, particularly the gift of speaking in tongues (Ac 2:4,16–18,43; 4:29–30; 5:12–16; 6:8; 8:5–7; 10:38,44–46; 1Co 12–14; Gal 3:5; see article on SPEAKING IN TONGUES, p. 232). Conversely, any assumed baptism in the Spirit that does not result in the manifestations of the Spirit in our lives is an obvious departure from the experience of NT believers and the norm presented in the book of Acts (Ac 2:4,18; 10:45–46; 19:6).

(9) A genuine baptism in the Holy Spirit will cause us to be more conscious of the work, guidance and presence of the Spirit in our daily lives. After receiving the fullness of the Spirit, NT believers were continually conscious of the Spirit's presence, power and guidance (Ac 2:4,16–18; 4:31; 6:5; 9:31; 10:19; 13:2,4,52; 15:28; 16:6–7; 20:23). Conversely, any assumed baptism in the Spirit that does not increase our awareness of the Spirit's presence, strengthen our desire to obey his leadings, and reinforce our goal to live before him in such a way as not to grieve him or put out his fire (Eph 4:30; 1Th 5:19) is not from God.

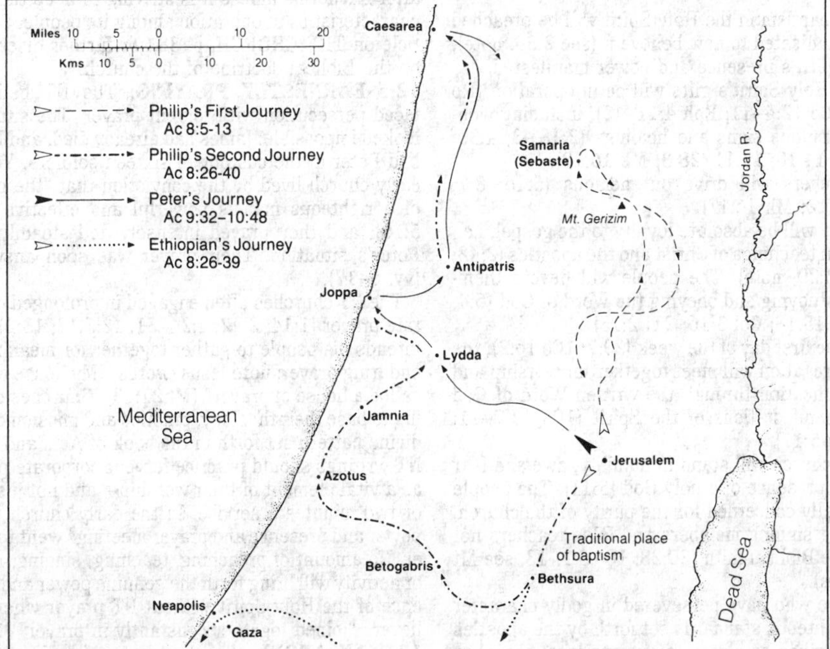

Jews,[p] he proceeded to seize Peter also.
This happened during the Feast of Unleavened Bread.[q] 4After arresting him, he put
him in prison, handing him over to be
guarded by four squads of four soldiers
each. Herod intended to bring him out for
public trial after the Passover.[r]
5So Peter was kept in prison, but the
church was earnestly praying to God for
him.[s]
6The night before Herod was to bring
him to trial, Peter was sleeping between
two soldiers, bound with two chains,[t] and
sentries stood guard at the entrance.
7Suddenly an angel[u] of the Lord appeared
and a light shone in the cell. He struck
Peter on the side and woke him up.
"Quick, get up!" he said, and the chains
fell off Peter's wrists.[v]
8Then the angel said to him, "Put on
your clothes and sandals." And Peter did
so. "Wrap your cloak around you and follow me," the angel told him. 9Peter followed him out of the prison, but he had no
idea that what the angel was doing was
really happening; he thought he was see-

12:3 [p] Ac 24:27; 25:9 [q] Ex 12:15; 23:15; Ac 20:6
12:4 [r] S Jn 11:55
12:5 [s] S Ac 1:14; Ro 15:30,31; Eph 6:18
12:6 [t] Ac 21:33
12:7 [u] S Ac 5:19 [v] Ps 107:14; Ac 16:26

12:2 JAMES ... PUT TO DEATH. God allowed James, the brother of John (cf. Mt 4:21), to die, yet he sent an angel to rescue Peter (vv. 3–17). That James should die while Peter lived for further ministry is the mysterious way of God with his people. James had the honor of being the first of the apostles to meet a martyr's death. He died as his Lord had done—for the cause of God (cf. Mk 10:36–39).

12:5 THE CHURCH. From the book of Acts as well as other passages in the NT, we gain insight into the norms or authoritative standards for a NT church. (1) First and foremost, a church will consist of people formed into local congregations and united by the Holy Spirit, diligently seeking a faithful personal relationship with God and Jesus Christ (13:2; 16:5; 20:7; Ro 16:3–4; 1Co 16:19; 2Co 11:28; Heb 11:6, note).

(2) Through its powerful witness, sinners will be saved, born again, baptized in water and added to the church; they will partake of the Lord's Supper and wait for Christ's return (2:41–42; 4:33; 5:14; 11:24; 1Co 11:26).

(3) The baptism in the Holy Spirit will be preached and communicated to new believers (see 2:39, note), and the Spirit's presence and power manifested.

(4) The Holy Spirit's gifts will be in operation (Ro 12:6–8; 1Co 12:4–11; Eph 4:11–12), including wonders, miraculous signs and healings (2:18,43; 4:30; 5:12; 6:8; 14:10; 19:11; 28:8; Mk 16:18).

(5) Believers will drive out demons (5:16; 8:7; 16:18; 19:12; Mk 16:17).

(6) There will be absolute loyalty to the gospel, i.e., the original teachings of Christ and the apostles (2:42; see Eph 2:20, note). The people will devote themselves to studying and obeying the Word of God (6:4; 18:11; Ro 15:18; Col 3:16; 2Ti 2:15).

(7) On the first day of the week (20:7; 1Co 16:2), the local congregation will meet together for worship and mutual edification through the written Word of God and the manifestations of the Spirit (1Co 12:7–11; 14:26; 1Ti 5:17).

(8) The church will stand in humility, awe and fear before the presence of a holy God (5:11). The people will be vitally concerned for the purity of the church, disciplining sinning members and false teachers not loyal to the Biblical faith (20:28; 1Co 5:1–13; see Mt 18:15, note).

(9) Those who have persevered in godly character and the righteous standards set forth by the apostles will be ordained as elders to oversee local churches and maintain their spiritual life (Mt 18:15, note; 1Co 5:1–5; 1Ti 3:1–7; Tit 1:5–9; see article on OVERSEERS AND THEIR DUTIES, p. 274).

(10) Likewise, the church will have deacons responsible for the temporal and material affairs of the church (see 1Ti 3:8, note).

(11) There will be observable love and fellowship in the Spirit among the members (2:42,44–46; see Jn 13:34, note), not only within the local congregation but also between other Bible-believing congregations (15:1–31; 2Co 8:1–8).

(12) The church will be a praying and fasting church (1:14; 6:4; 12:5; 13:2; Ro 12:12; Col 4:2; Eph 6:18).

(13) Believers will separate themselves from the prevailing world view and the spirit of their surrounding culture (2:40; Ro 12:2; 2Co 6:17; Gal 1:4; 1Jn 2:15–16).

(14) There will be suffering and affliction because of the world and its ways (4:1–3; 5:40; 9:16; 14:22).

(15) The church will actively help send missionaries to other lands (2:39; 13:2–4).

No local church has the right to call itself a church after NT norms unless it is striving to keep these 15 characteristics in operation among its people. See article on THE CHURCH, p. 38, for further discussion on the Biblical doctrine of the church.

12:5 EARNESTLY PRAYING. The NT believers faced persecution with fervent prayer. The situation looked impossible: James had already died, and Herod had Peter in the custody of sixteen soldiers. Yet the early church lived by the conviction that "the prayer of a righteous man is powerful and effective" (Jas 5:16), and they prayed intensely and steadily over Peter's situation. Their prayer was soon answered (vv. 6–17).

The NT churches often engaged in prolonged corporate prayer (1:14; 2:42; 4:24–31; 12:5,12; 13:2). God intends his people to gather together for meaningful, enduring prayer; note Jesus' words, "My house will be called a house of prayer" (Mt 21:13). Churches claiming to base their theology, practice and mission on the divine pattern set forth in the book of Acts and other NT writings should practice fervent corporate prayer as a vital element of their worship—and not just one or two minutes a service. In the early church God's power and presence and prayer meetings went together. No amount of preaching, teaching, singing, music or activity will bring forth the genuine power and presence of the Holy Spirit without NT prayer where believers "joined together constantly in prayer" (1:14).

12:7 AN ANGEL. Angels are "ministering spirits sent to serve those who will inherit salvation" (Heb 1:14; see 1:13, note).

ing a vision.[w] **10**They passed the first and
second guards and came to the iron gate
leading to the city. It opened for them by
itself,[x] and they went through it. When
they had walked the length of one street,
suddenly the angel left him.

11Then Peter came to himself[y] and
said, "Now I know without a doubt that
the Lord sent his angel and rescued me[z]
from Herod's clutches and from everything the Jewish people were anticipat-
ing."

12When this had dawned on him, he
went to the house of Mary the mother of
John, also called Mark,[a] where many people had gathered and were praying.[b]
13Peter knocked at the outer entrance,
and a servant girl named Rhoda came to
answer the door.[c] **14**When she recognized
Peter's voice, she was so overjoyed[d] she
ran back without opening it and exclaimed, "Peter is at the door!"

15"You're out of your mind," they told
her. When she kept insisting that it was
so, they said, "It must be his angel."[e]

16But Peter kept on knocking, and
when they opened the door and saw him,
they were astonished. **17**Peter motioned
with his hand[f] for them to be quiet and
described how the Lord had brought him
out of prison. "Tell James[g] and the brothers[h] about this," he said, and then he left
for another place.

18In the morning, there was no small
commotion among the soldiers as to what
had become of Peter. **19**After Herod had a
thorough search made for him and did not
find him, he cross-examined the guards
and ordered that they be executed.[i]

Herod's Death

Then Herod went from Judea to Caesarea[j] and stayed there a while. **20**He had
been quarreling with the people of Tyre
and Sidon;[k] they now joined together and
sought an audience with him. Having secured the support of Blastus, a trusted
personal servant of the king, they asked
for peace, because they depended on the
king's country for their food supply.[l]

21On the appointed day Herod, wearing
his royal robes, sat on his throne and delivered a public address to the people.
22They shouted, "This is the voice of a
god, not of a man." **23**Immediately, because Herod did not give praise to God, an
angel[m] of the Lord struck him down,[n] and
he was eaten by worms and died.

24But the word of God[o] continued to
increase and spread.[p]

25When Barnabas[q] and Saul had finished their mission,[r] they returned from[t]
Jerusalem, taking with them John, also
called Mark.[s]

Barnabas and Saul Sent Off

13 In the church at Antioch[t] there
were prophets[u] and teachers:[v]
Barnabas,[w] Simeon called Niger, Lucius
of Cyrene,[x] Manaen (who had been
brought up with Herod[y] the tetrarch) and
Saul. **2**While they were worshiping the
Lord and fasting, the Holy Spirit said,[z]
"Set apart for me Barnabas and Saul for
the work[a] to which I have called them."[b]
3So after they had fasted and prayed, they

12:9 [w]S Ac 9:10 **12:10** [x]Ac 5:19; 16:26 **12:11** [y]Lk 15:17 [z]Ps 34:7; Da 3:28; 6:22; 2Co 1:10; 2Pe 2:9 **12:12** [a]ver 25; Ac 13:5,13; 15:37, 39; Col 4:10; 2Ti 4:11; Phm 24; 1Pe 5:13 [b]ver 5 **12:13** [c]Jn 18:16, 17 **12:14** [d]Lk 24:41 **12:15** [e]S Mt 18:10 **12:17** [f]Ac 13:16; 19:33; 21:40 [g]S Ac 15:13 [h]S Ac 1:16 **12:19** [i]Ac 16:27 [j]S Ac 8:40 **12:20** [k]S Mt 11:21 [l]1Ki 5:9,11; Eze 27:17 **12:23** [m]S Ac 5:19 [n]1Sa 25:38; 2Sa 24:16,17; 2Ki 19:35 **12:24** [o]S Heb 4:12 [p]Ac 6:7; 19:20 **12:25** [q]S Ac 4:36 [r]Ac 11:30 [s]S ver 12 **13:1** [t]S Ac 11:19 [u]S Ac 11:27 [v]S Eph 4:11 [w]S Ac 4:36 [x]S Mt 27:32 [y]S Mt 14:1 **13:2** [z]S Ac 8:29 [a]Ac 14:26 [b]Ac 9:15; 22:21

[t] *25* Some manuscripts *to*

13:2 WORSHIPING ... AND FASTING. Spirit-filled Christians are especially sensitive to the communication of the Holy Spirit during prayer and fasting (see Mt 6:16, note). The communication from the Holy Spirit probably came through a prophetic utterance (cf. v. 1).

13:2 FOR THE WORK TO WHICH I HAVE CALLED THEM. Paul and Barnabas were called into missionary service and were commissioned by the church at Antioch. The nature of this work is described in 9:15; 13:5; 22:14–15,21; and 26:16–18. (1) Paul and Barnabas were called to preach the gospel, bringing men and women into a saving relationship with Christ. Scripture nowhere indicates that the NT missionaries were sent out into the world to do social or political work, i.e., to propagate the gospel and establish churches by embarking on all sorts of organized social or political activities for the benefit of the people of the Roman empire. Their goal was to bring people to Christ (16:31; 20:21), deliver them from Satan's power (26:18), cause the Holy Spirit to come on them (19:6) and establish them in churches. In these new Christians the Spirit came to live and reveal himself through love; he gave spiritual gifts (1Co 12–13) and transformed them from within so that their lives would bring glory to their living Savior.

(2) Missionaries of the gospel today ought to have the same paramount activity: to be ministers of and witnesses to the gospel, bringing others to Christ by delivering them from Satan's dominion (26:18), making them disciples, encouraging them to receive the Holy Spirit and his gifts (2:38; 8:17), and teaching them to obey all that Christ commanded (Mt 28:19–20). Accompanying this should be signs and wonders, the healing of the sick and deliverance for those oppressed by demons (2:43; 4:30; 8:7; 10:38; Mk 16:17–18). The supreme task of preaching the gospel, however, should also include personal acts of love and kindness to those in need (cf. Gal 2:10). In this way, all those called to bear witness to the gospel will model their ministry after Jesus (see Lk 9:2, note).

13:3 SENT THEM OFF. With this passage begins the great missionary movement "to the ends of the

placed their hands on them[c] and sent
them off.[d]

On Cyprus

4The two of them, sent on their way by
the Holy Spirit,[e] went down to Seleucia
and sailed from there to Cyprus.[f] **5**When
they arrived at Salamis, they proclaimed
the word of God[g] in the Jewish synagogues.[h] John[i] was with them as their
helper.

6They traveled through the whole island until they came to Paphos. There
they met a Jewish sorcerer[j] and false
prophet[k] named Bar-Jesus, **7**who was an
attendant of the proconsul,[l] Sergius Pau-
lus. The proconsul, an intelligent man,
sent for Barnabas and Saul because he
wanted to hear the word of God. **8**But Elymas the sorcerer[m] (for that is what his
name means) opposed them and tried to
turn the proconsul[n] from the faith.[o]
9Then Saul, who was also called Paul,
filled with the Holy Spirit,[p] looked
Ac 15:8 straight at Elymas and said, **10**"You are a
child of the devil[q] and an enemy of everything that is right! You are full of all kinds
of deceit and trickery. Will you never stop
perverting the right ways of the Lord?[r]
11Now the hand of the Lord is against
you.[s] You are going to be blind, and for a
time you will be unable to see the light of
the sun."[t]

13:3 [c]S Ac 6:6 [d]Ac 14:26
13:4 [e]ver 2,3 [f]Ac 4:36
13:5 [g]S Heb 4:12 [h]S Ac 9:20 [i]S Ac 12:12
13:6 [j]Ac 8:9 [k]S Mt 7:15
13:7 [l]ver 8,12; Ac 18:12; 19:38
13:8 [m]Ac 8:9 [n]S ver 7 [o]Isa 30:11; Ac 6:7
13:9 [p]S Lk 1:15
13:10 [q]Mt 13:38; Jn 8:44 [r]Hos 14:9
13:11 [s]Ex 9:3; 1Sa 5:6,7; Ps 32:4 [t]Ge 19:10,11; 2Ki 6:18

Immediately mist and darkness came
over him, and he groped about, seeking
someone to lead him by the hand. **12**When
the proconsul[u] saw what had happened,
he believed, for he was amazed at the
teaching about the Lord.

In Pisidian Antioch

13From Paphos,[v] Paul and his companions sailed to Perga in Pamphylia,[w] where
John[x] left them to return to Jerusalem.
14From Perga they went on to Pisidian
Antioch.[y] On the Sabbath[z] they entered
the synagogue[a] and sat down. **15**After the
reading from the Law[b] and the Prophets,
the synagogue rulers sent word to them,
saying, "Brothers, if you have a message
of encouragement for the people, please
speak."

16Standing up, Paul motioned with his
hand[c] and said: "Men of Israel and you
Gentiles who worship God, listen to me!
17The God of the people of Israel chose
our fathers; he made the people prosper
during their stay in Egypt, with mighty
power he led them out of that country,[d]
18he endured their conduct[u][e] for about
forty years in the desert,[f] **19**he overthrew
seven nations in Canaan[g] and gave their

13:12 [u]S ver 7
13:13 [v]ver 6 [w]S Ac 2:10 [x]S Ac 12:12
13:14 [y]Ac 14:19, 21 [z]ver 27,42,44; Ac 16:13; 18:4 [a]S Ac 9:20
13:15 [b]Ac 15:21
13:16 [c]S Ac 12:17
13:17 [d]Ex 6:6,7; Dt 7:6-8
13:18 [e]Dt 1:31 [f]Nu 14:33; Ps 95:10; Ac 7:36
13:19 [g]Dt 7:1

[u] *18* Some manuscripts *and cared for them*

---

earth" (1:8). The missionary principles described in ch. 13 are a model for all missionary-sending churches.

(1) Missionary activity is initiated by the Holy Spirit through spiritual leaders who are deeply devoted to the Lord and his kingdom, seeking him with prayer and fasting (v. 2).

(2) The church must be sensitive to the guidance and prophetic ministry and activity of the Holy Spirit (v. 2).

(3) Missionaries who go out must do so under the specific call and will of the Holy Spirit (v. 2b).

(4) By prayer and fasting, constantly seeking to be aligned with the Spirit's will (vv. 3–4), the church confirms that God has called certain individuals to missionary work. The goal is that the church send out only those whom the Spirit desires.

(5) Through the laying on of hands and the sending out of missionaries, the church indicates her commitment to the support and encouragement of those who go out. The responsibility of the sending church includes sending the missionaries on their way with love and in a manner worthy of God (3Jn 6), praying for them (13:3; Eph 6:18–19) and giving them financial support (Lk 10:7; 3Jn 6–8), including offerings of love for their needs (Php 4:10,14–18). Missionaries are considered an extension of the purpose, concern and mission of the sending church; the church thus becomes those who "work together for the truth" (3Jn 8; cf. Php 1:5).

(6) Those who go out as missionaries must be willing to risk their lives for the name of Jesus Christ (15:26).

13:8 THE SORCERER. The sorcerer was probably a Jewish astrologer. Astrologers taught that the destiny of the individual was determined by celestial bodies. They believed they could foretell the future by examining the position of the stars and planets. All sorcery or astrology stands in opposition to the gospel of Christ because it involves Satan and the demonic (v. 10).

13:9 SAUL . . . FILLED WITH THE HOLY SPIRIT. One may be baptized in the Spirit as was Paul (9:17), yet in times of special need receive fresh fillings with the Spirit. Such repeated fillings are necessary (1) in confronting opposition to the gospel (4:8–12), (2) in advancing the gospel (4:8,31) and (3) in directly challenging satanic activity (13:9,50–52). Repeated fillings with the Spirit should be the norm for all believers who are baptized in the Holy Spirit.

13:11 YOU ARE GOING TO BE BLIND. Miracles in the NT were not always healings; some, such as God's anger against Elymas (vv. 8–11) and Herod (12:20–23), involved judgment on ungodly individuals. God's anger against Ananias and Sapphira (5:1–11) is an example of a miraculous judgment against sin within the church.

land to his people[h] as their inheritance.[i]
20All this took about 450 years.
"After this, God gave them judges[j] until the time of Samuel the prophet.[k]
21Then the people asked for a king,[l] and
he gave them Saul[m] son of Kish, of the
tribe of Benjamin,[n] who ruled forty years.
22After removing Saul,[o] he made David
their king.[p] He testified concerning him:
'I have found David son of Jesse a man
after my own heart;[q] he will do everything
I want him to do.'[r]
23"From this man's descendants[s] God
has brought to Israel the Savior[t] Jesus,[u]
as he promised.[v] 24Before the coming of
Jesus, John preached repentance and baptism to all the people of Israel.[w] 25As John
was completing his work,[x] he said: 'Who
do you think I am? I am not that one.[y] No,
but he is coming after me, whose sandals
I am not worthy to untie.'[z]
26"Brothers,[a] children of Abraham,[b]
and you God-fearing Gentiles, it is to us
that this message of salvation[c] has been
sent. 27The people of Jerusalem and their
rulers did not recognize Jesus,[d] yet in
condemning him they fulfilled the words
of the prophets[e] that are read every Sabbath. 28Though they found no proper
ground for a death sentence, they asked
Pilate to have him executed.[f] 29When
they had carried out all that was written
about him,[g] they took him down from the
tree[h] and laid him in a tomb.[i] 30But God
raised him from the dead,[j] 31and for
many days he was seen by those who had
traveled with him from Galilee to Jerusalem.[k] They are now his witnesses[l] to our
people.
32"We tell you the good news:[m] What
God promised our fathers[n] 33he has fulfilled for us, their children, by raising up
Jesus.[o] As it is written in the second
Psalm:

" 'You are my Son;
today I have become your
Father.'[v][w][p]

34The fact that God raised him from the
dead, never to decay, is stated in these
words:

" 'I will give you the holy and sure
blessings promised to
David.'[x][q]

35So it is stated elsewhere:

" 'You will not let your Holy One see
decay.'[y][r]

36"For when David had served God's
purpose in his own generation, he fell
asleep;[s] he was buried with his fathers[t]
and his body decayed. 37But the one
whom God raised from the dead[u] did not
see decay.
38"Therefore, my brothers, I want you
to know that through Jesus the forgiveness of sins is proclaimed to you.[v]
39Through him everyone who believes[w] is
justified from everything you could not be
justified from by the law of Moses.[x]
40Take care that what the prophets have
said does not happen to you:

41" 'Look, you scoffers,
wonder and perish,
for I am going to do something in
your days
that you would never believe,
even if someone told you.'[z]"[y]

42As Paul and Barnabas were leaving
the synagogue,[z] the people invited them
to speak further about these things on the
next Sabbath. 43When the congregation

13:19 [h] Jos 19:51; Ac 7:45 [i] Ps 78:55
13:20 [j] Jdg 2:16 [k] 1Sa 3:19,20; Ac 3:24
13:21 [l] 1Sa 8:5,19 [m] 1Sa 10:1 [n] 1Sa 9:1,2
13:22 [o] 1Sa 15:23,26 [p] 1Sa 16:13; Ps 89:20 [q] 1Sa 13:14; Jer 3:15 [r] Isa 44:28
13:23 [s] S Mt 1:1 [t] S Lk 2:11 [u] Mt 1:21 [v] ver 32; 2Sa 7:11; 22:51; Jer 30:9
13:24 [w] S Mk 1:4
13:25 [x] Ac 20:24 [y] Jn 1:20 [z] Mt 3:11; Jn 1:27
13:26 [a] S Ac 22:5 [b] S Lk 3:8 [c] Ac 4:12; 28:28
13:27 [d] Ac 3:17 [e] S Lk 24:27; S Mt 1:22
13:28 [f] Mt 27:20-25; Ac 3:14
13:29 [g] S Mt 1:22; Lk 18:31 [h] S Ac 5:30 [i] Lk 23:53
13:30 [j] S Mt 16:21; 28:6; S Ac 2:24
13:31 [k] Mt 28:16 [l] S Lk 24:48
13:32 [m] Isa 40:9; 52:7; Ac 5:42; 8:35; 10:36; 14:7,15,21; 17:18 [n] Ac 26:6; Ro 1:2; 4:13; 9:4
13:33 [o] S Ac 2:24 [p] Ps 2:7; S Mt 3:17
13:34 [q] Isa 55:3
13:35 [r] Ps 16:10; Ac 2:27
13:36 [s] S Mt 9:24 [t] 2Sa 7:12; 1Ki 2:10; 2Ch 29:28; Ac 2:29
13:37 [u] S Ac 2:24
13:38 [v] S Lk 24:47; Ac 2:38
13:39 [w] S Jn 3:15 [x] S Ro 3:28
13:41 [y] Hab 1:5
13:42 [z] ver 14

[v] *33* Or *have begotten you* [w] *33* Psalm 2:7
[x] *34* Isaiah 55:3 [y] *35* Psalm 16:10
[z] *41* Hab. 1:5

13:31 HIS WITNESSES TO OUR PEOPLE. A witness (Gk *martus*) is "one who testifies by act or word to the truth." Christian witnesses are those who confirm and testify to the saving work of Jesus Christ by word, deed, life and, if necessary, even death. It involves seven principles:

(1) Christian witnessing is the obligation of all believers (1:8; Mt 4:19; 28:19–20).

(2) Christian witnesses must be missionary-minded, going to all the nations and bearing God's salvation to the ends of the earth (11:18; 13:2–4; 26:16–18; Mt 28:19–20; Lk 24:47).

(3) Christian witnesses speak primarily about the meaning of Christ's life, death, resurrection, saving power and promised Holy Spirit (2:32,38–39; 3:15; 10:39–41,43; 18:5; 26:16; 1Co 15:1–8).

(4) Christian witnesses must bring conviction concerning sin, righteousness and judgment (2:37–40; 7:51–54; 24:24–25; see Jn 16:8, note). Through such witness people are brought to saving faith (2:41; 4:33; 6:7; 11:21).

(5) Christian witnesses at times will suffer (7:57–60; 22:20; 2Co 11:23–29). The word "martyr" is derived from the Greek word for witness. Discipleship involves commitment, no matter what the cost.

(6) Christian witnessing must be accompanied by separation from the world (2:40), a life of righteousness (Ro 14:17), and an utter reliance on the Holy Spirit (4:29–33) that results in the manifestation of God's Spirit and power (1Co 2:4).

(7) Christian witnessing is prophetic (2:17), and empowered (1:8) and inspired by the Spirit (2:4; 4:8).

was dismissed, many of the Jews and devout converts to Judaism followed Paul
and Barnabas, who talked with them and
urged them to continue in the grace of
God.[a]
44On the next Sabbath almost the
whole city gathered to hear the word of
the Lord. 45When the Jews saw the
crowds, they were filled with jealousy and
talked abusively[b] against what Paul was
saying.[c]
46Then Paul and Barnabas answered
them boldly: "We had to speak the word
of God to you first.[d] Since you reject it and
do not consider yourselves worthy of eternal life, we now turn to the Gentiles.[e]
47For this is what the Lord has commanded us:

" 'I have made you[a] a light for the
Gentiles,[f]
that you[a] may bring salvation to
the ends of the earth.'[b]"[g]

48When the Gentiles heard this, they
were glad and honored the word of the
Lord;[h] and all who were appointed for
eternal life believed.
49The word of the Lord[i] spread
through the whole region. 50But the Jews
incited the God-fearing women of high
standing and the leading men of the city.
They stirred up persecution against Paul
and Barnabas, and expelled them from
their region.[j] 51So they shook the dust
from their feet[k] in protest against them
and went to Iconium.[l] 52And the disci-

13:43 [a]S Ac 11:23; 14:22; S Ro 3:24 **13:45** [b]Ac 18:6; 1Pe 4:4; Jude 10 [c]S 1Th 2:16 **13:46** [d]ver 26; Ac 3:26 [e]Mt 21:41; Ac 18:6; 22:21; 26:20; 28:28; Ro 11:11 **13:47** [f]S Lk 2:32 [g]Isa 49:6 **13:48** [h]ver 49; Ac 8:25; 15:35,36; 19:10,20 **13:49** [i]S ver 48 **13:50** [j]S 1Th 2:16 **13:51** [k]S Mt 10:14 [l]Ac 14:1,19,21; 16:2; 2Ti 3:11

[a] *47* The Greek is singular. [b] *47* Isaiah 49:6

13:48 APPOINTED FOR ETERNAL LIFE. Some have understood this verse as teaching arbitrary predestination. However, neither the context nor the word translated "appointed" (Gk *tetagmenoi*, from *tassō*) warrant this interpretation. (1) V. 46 explicitly emphasizes human responsibility in accepting or rejecting eternal life. The best rendering of *tetagmenoi*, therefore, is "were disposed": "and all who were disposed to eternal life believed." This rendering agrees completely with the affirmations of 1Ti 2:4; Tit 2:11; 2Pe 3:9 (see article on ELECTION AND PREDESTINATION, p. 402). (2) Furthermore, according to Paul, no person is unconditionally appointed for eternal life (see Ro 11:20–22).

13:52 FILLED . . . WITH THE HOLY SPIRIT. The Greek verb translated "filled" is in the imperfect tense, expressing continued action in past time. The disciples were being continually filled and empowered

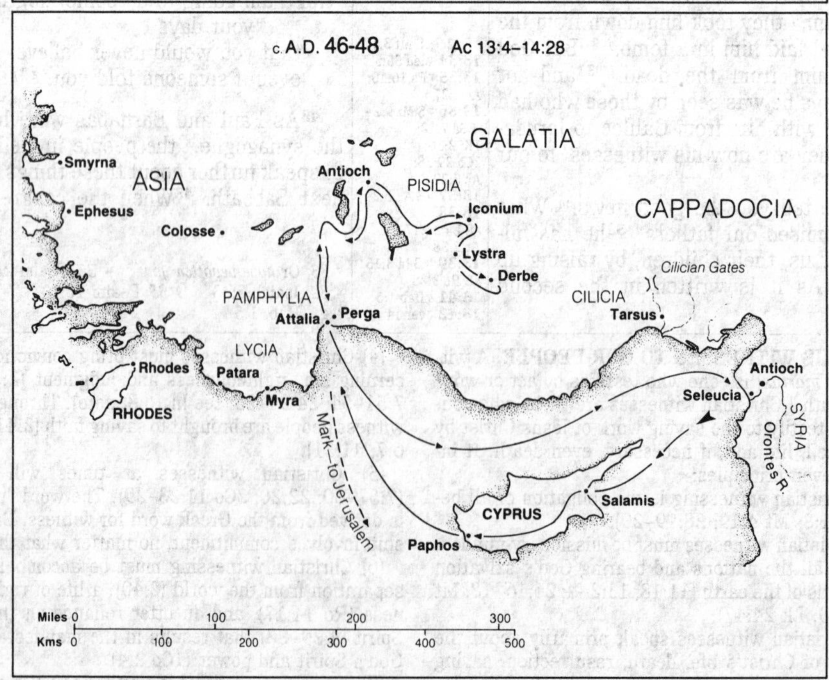

ples[m] were filled with joy and with the
Ro 5:15 Holy Spirit.[n]

In Iconium

14 At Iconium[o] Paul and Barnabas
went as usual into the Jewish synagogue.[p] There they spoke so effectively
that a great number[q] of Jews and Gentiles
believed. **2**But the Jews who refused to
believe stirred up the Gentiles and poi-
soned their minds against the brothers.[r]
3So Paul and Barnabas spent considerable time there, speaking boldly[s] for the
Lord, who confirmed the message of his
Ac 21:9-12 grace by enabling them to do miraculous
signs and wonders.[t] **4**The people of the
city were divided; some sided with the
Jews, others with the apostles.[u] **5**There
was a plot afoot among the Gentiles and
Jews,[v] together with their leaders, to mistreat them and stone them.[w] **6**But they
found out about it and fled[x] to the Lycaonian cities of Lystra and Derbe and to the
surrounding country, **7**where they continued to preach[y] the good news.[z]

In Lystra and Derbe

8In Lystra there sat a man crippled in
his feet, who was lame from birth[a] and
had never walked. **9**He listened to Paul as
he was speaking. Paul looked directly at
him, saw that he had faith to be healed[b]
10and called out, "Stand up on your
Ro 4:19-21 feet!"[c] At that, the man jumped up and
began to walk.[d]
11When the crowd saw what Paul had
done, they shouted in the Lycaonian language, "The gods have come down to us
in human form!"[e] **12**Barnabas they called
Zeus, and Paul they called Hermes because he was the chief speaker.[f] **13**The
priest of Zeus, whose temple was just outside the city, brought bulls and wreaths to
the city gates because he and the crowd
wanted to offer sacrifices to them.
14But when the apostles Barnabas and
Paul heard of this, they tore their clothes[g]
and rushed out into the crowd, shouting:
15"Men, why are you doing this? We too
are only men,[h] human like you. We are
bringing you good news,[i] telling you to
turn from these worthless things[j] to the
living God,[k] who made heaven and earth[l]
and sea and everything in them.[m] **16**In the
past, he let[n] all nations go their own
way.[o] **17**Yet he has not left himself without testimony:[p] He has shown kindness
by giving you rain from heaven and crops
in their seasons;[q] he provides you with
plenty of food and fills your hearts with
joy."[r] **18**Even with these words, they had
difficulty keeping the crowd from sacrificing to them.
19Then some Jews[s] came from Antioch
and Iconium[t] and won the crowd over.
They stoned Paul[u] and dragged him outside the city, thinking he was dead. **20**But
after the disciples[v] had gathered around
him, he got up and went back into the city.
The next day he and Barnabas left for
Derbe.

The Return to Antioch in Syria

21They preached the good news[w] in
that city and won a large number[x] of disciples. Then they returned to Lystra, Iconium[y] and Antioch, **22**strengthening the
disciples and encouraging them to remain

13:52 [m]S Ac 11:26 [n]S Lk 1:15
14:1 [o]S Ac 13:51 [p]S Ac 9:20 [q]S Ac 2:41
14:2 [r]S Ac 1:16
14:3 [s]S Ac 4:29 [t]S Jn 4:48
14:4 [u]Ac 17:4,5; 28:24
14:5 [v]S Ac 20:3 [w]ver 19
14:6 [x]Mt 10:23
14:7 [y]Ac 16:10 [z]ver 15,21; S Ac 13:32
14:8 [a]Ac 3:2
14:9 [b]Mt 9:28,29; 13:58
14:10 [c]Eze 2:1 [d]Ac 3:8
14:11 [e]Ac 8:10; 28:6
14:12 [f]Ex 7:1
14:14 [g]S Mk 14:63
14:15 [h]S Ac 10:26 [i]ver 7,21; S Ac 13:32 [j]1Sa 12:21; 1Th 1:9 [k]S Mt 16:16 [l]Ge 1:1 [m]Ps 146:6; Rev 14:7
14:16 [n]Ac 17:30 [o]Ps 81:12; Mic 4:5
14:17 [p]Ro 1:20 [q]Dt 11:14; Job 5:10; Ps 65:10 [r]Ps 4:7
14:19 [s]Ac 13:45 [t]S Ac 13:51 [u]2Co 11:25; 2Ti 3:11
14:20 [v]ver 22,28; S Ac 11:26
14:21 [w]S Ac 13:32 [x]S Ac 2:41 [y]S Ac 13:51

---

day by day. The Spirit's fullness is not merely a one-time initial experience, but a life of renewed fillings for God-given needs and tasks (cf. Eph 5:18).

14:3 MIRACULOUS SIGNS AND WONDERS. God intended that the preaching of the gospel be accompanied by miraculous signs to confirm the truth of the gospel (cf. Mk 16:20; see article on SIGNS OF BELIEVERS, p. 106). In this way the Lord worked with his people and bore witness to the truth of the message. Such confirmation of God's grace with signs and wonders is no less needed today as we face "terrible times in the last days" (1Ti 4:1; see 2Ti 3:1–13).

14:4 APOSTLES. Both Paul and Barnabas are called apostles. As a more general term, "apostle" was applied to the first Christian missionaries who were sent out by the church to preach the NT message (vv. 4,14). "Apostle" in a more specialized sense is applied only to those who received a direct commission by Christ to establish his original message and revelation (see Eph 2:20, note). Paul was an apostle in this special sense.

14:9 SAW THAT HE HAD FAITH. Discerning the faith of the crippled man most likely came through the Holy Spirit. Paul encouraged this man's faith by commanding him to stand up. Believers should pray for spiritual insight to recognize the faith of individuals needing God's grace and healing.

14:19 STONED PAUL. In NT times God did not always protect his servants from harm. This truth is inherent in the gospel and valid today as well: the kingdom of God advances at great cost to God's servants. Paul later described this incident of suffering by saying, "once I was stoned" (2Co 11:25; see Ac 9:16, note); he probably had this same episode in mind when he wrote to the Galatians, "I bear on my body the marks of Jesus" (Gal 6:17; see 2Co 11:23, note on Paul's suffering).

14:22 THROUGH MANY HARDSHIPS. Those who commit themselves to Christ's lordship and who will finally enter the kingdom of God must suffer "many hardships" along the way. Living in a hostile world, they must engage in spiritual warfare against sin and Satan's power (Eph 6:12; cf. Ro 8:17; 2Th 1:4–7; 2Ti 2:12). (1) Those who are faithful to Christ, his Word

true to the faith.[z] "We must go through
many hardships[a] to enter the kingdom of
God," they said. **23**Paul and Barnabas appointed elders[cb] for them in each church
and, with prayer and fasting,[c] committed
them to the Lord,[d] in whom they had put
their trust. **24**After going through Pisidia,
they came into Pamphylia,[e] **25**and when
they had preached the word in Perga, they
went down to Attalia.

26From Attalia they sailed back to Antioch,[f] where they had been committed to
the grace of God[g] for the work they had
now completed.[h] **27**On arriving there,
they gathered the church together and reported all that God had done through
them[i] and how he had opened the door[j]
of faith to the Gentiles. **28**And they stayed
there a long time with the disciples.[k]

The Council at Jerusalem

15 Some men[l] came down from Judea to Antioch and were teaching
the brothers:[m] "Unless you are circumcised,[n] according to the custom taught by
Moses,[o] you cannot be saved." **2**This
brought Paul and Barnabas into sharp dispute and debate with them. So Paul and
Barnabas were appointed, along with
some other believers, to go up to Jerusalem[p] to see the apostles and elders[q]
about this question. **3**The church sent
them on their way, and as they traveled
through Phoenicia[r] and Samaria, they
told how the Gentiles had been converted.[s] This news made all the brothers very
glad. **4**When they came to Jerusalem, they
were welcomed by the church and the
apostles and elders, to whom they reported everything God had done through
them.[t]

5Then some of the believers who belonged to the party[u] of the Pharisees[v]
stood up and said, "The Gentiles must be
circumcised and required to obey the law
of Moses."[w]

6The apostles and elders met to consider this question. **7**After much discussion,
Peter got up and addressed them: "Brothers, you know that some time ago God
made a choice among you that the Gentiles might hear from my lips the message
of the gospel and believe.[x] **8**God, who
knows the heart,[y] showed that he accepted them by giving the Holy Spirit to
them,[z] just as he did to us. **9**He made no Ac 19:1-7
distinction between us and them,[a] for he
purified their hearts by faith.[b] **10**Now
then, why do you try to test God[c] by putting on the necks of the disciples a yoke[d]
that neither we nor our fathers have been
able to bear? **11**No! We believe it is
through the grace[e] of our Lord Jesus that
we are saved, just as they are."

12The whole assembly became silent as
they listened to Barnabas and Paul telling
about the miraculous signs and wonders[f]
God had done among the Gentiles through
them.[g] **13**When they finished, James[h]
spoke up: "Brothers, listen to me. **14**Simon[d] has described to us how God at first

14:22 [z] Ac 11:23; 13:43 [a] Jn 16:33; 1Th 3:3; 2Ti 3:12 **14:23** [b] S Ac 11:30 [c] Ac 13:3 [d] Ac 20:32 **14:24** [e] S Ac 2:10 **14:26** [f] S Ac 11:19 [g] S Ac 11:23 [h] Ac 13:1,3 **14:27** [i] Ac 15:4, 12; 21:19 [j] 1Co 16:9; 2Co 2:12; Col 4:3; Rev 3:8 **14:28** [k] S Ac 11:26 **15:1** [l] ver 24; Gal 2:12 [m] S Ac 1:16 [n] ver 5; Gal 5:2,3 [o] S Ac 6:14 **15:2** [p] Gal 2:2 [q] S Ac 11:30 **15:3** [r] Ac 11:19 [s] Ac 14:27 **15:4** [t] ver 12; Ac 14:27; 21:19 **15:5** [u] Ac 5:17 [v] Mt 3:7 [w] ver 1 **15:7** [x] Ac 10:1-48 **15:8** [y] S Rev 2:23 [z] S Ac 10:44,47 **15:9** [a] Ac 10:28, 34; 11:12 [b] Ac 10:43 **15:10** [c] Ac 5:9 [d] S Mt 23:4; Gal 5:1 **15:11** [e] S Ro 3:24; Gal 2:16; Eph 2:5-8 **15:12** [f] S Jn 4:48 [g] ver 4; Ac 14:27; 21:19 **15:13** [h] Ac 12:17; 21:18; 1Co 15:7; Gal 1:19; 2:9,12

[c] *23* Or *Barnabas ordained elders*; or *Barnabas had elders elected* [d] *14* Greek *Simeon*, a variant of *Simon*; that is, Peter

and his righteous ways can expect trouble in this world (Jn 16:33). Only the lukewarm or compromising "believer" will find peace and comfort from the world (cf. Rev 3:14–17). (2) The present evil world and false believers will remain adversaries to the gospel of Christ until the Lord overthrows the world's evil system at his coming (Rev 19–20). Meanwhile the hope of believers is "stored up . . . in heaven" (Col 1:5) and will be "revealed in the last time" (1Pe 1:5). Their hope is not in this life nor in this world, but in the appearance of their Savior to take them to himself (Jn 14:1–3; 1Jn 3:2–3).

14:23 APPOINTED ELDERS. The appointing of elders (overseers or pastors) was done not only by seeking the Spirit's will through prayer and fasting, but also by examining the character, spiritual gifts, reputation and evidence of the Spirit's fruit in the men under consideration (1Ti 3:1–10). If they were found to be above reproach, they were appointed to serve (see article on MORAL QUALIFICATIONS FOR OVERSEERS, p. 458).

15:8 GOD, WHO KNOWS THE HEART. God's knowledge of the hearts of the Gentiles (i.e., Cornelius and his household) refers to his seeing saving faith within them. God testified to the genuineness of their faith (1) by cleansing their hearts with the inward work of regeneration by the Holy Spirit (v. 9), and (2) by baptizing them in the Spirit immediately afterwards, with the accompanying sign of speaking in tongues (10:44–46; 11:15–18).

15:11 THROUGH THE GRACE OF OUR LORD JESUS. The crucial question at the Jerusalem council was whether circumcision and obedience to the law of Moses were required for salvation. The delegates concluded that Gentiles were saved through the grace of the Lord Jesus, who forgave them and made them a new creation (see article on FAITH AND GRACE, p. 302). Grace comes to a person when he or she repents and believes in Christ as Lord and Savior (2:38–39). This response to God's grace enables him or her to receive power to become a child of God (Jn 1:12).

15:14 TAKING FROM THE GENTILES A PEOPLE. God's program for this age is to take from among all the nations a people, separated to him for his name. This body of Christ, gathered out of the present world system, prepares herself as the bride of Christ (Rev 19:7–8).

showed his concern by taking from the
Gentiles a people for himself.[i] 15The
words of the prophets are in agreement
with this, as it is written:

16" 'After this I will return
and rebuild David's fallen tent.
Its ruins I will rebuild,
and I will restore it,
17that the remnant of men may seek
the Lord,
and all the Gentiles who bear my
name,
says the Lord, who does these
things'[e][j]
18 that have been known for ages.[f][k]

19"It is my judgment, therefore, that we
should not make it difficult for the Gentiles who are turning to God. 20Instead we
should write to them, telling them to abstain from food polluted by idols,[l] from
sexual immorality,[m] from the meat of
strangled animals and from blood.[n] 21For
Moses has been preached in every city
from the earliest times and is read in the
synagogues on every Sabbath."[o]

The Council's Letter to Gentile Believers

22Then the apostles and elders,[p] with
the whole church, decided to choose some
of their own men and send them to Antioch[q] with Paul and Barnabas. They chose
Judas (called Barsabbas) and Silas,[r] two
men who were leaders among the brothers. 23With them they sent the following
letter:

The apostles and elders, your brothers,

To the Gentile believers in Antioch,[s] Syria[t] and Cilicia:[u]

Greetings.[v]

24We have heard that some went
out from us without our authoriza-
tion and disturbed you, troubling
your minds by what they said.[w] 25So
we all agreed to choose some men
and send them to you with our dear
friends Barnabas and Paul— 26men
who have risked their lives[x] for the
name of our Lord Jesus Christ.
27Therefore we are sending Judas
and Silas[y] to confirm by word of
mouth what we are writing. 28It
seemed good to the Holy Spirit[z] and
to us not to burden you with anything beyond the following requirements: 29You are to abstain from
food sacrificed to idols, from blood,
from the meat of strangled animals
and from sexual immorality.[a] You
will do well to avoid these things.

Farewell.

30The men were sent off and went down
to Antioch, where they gathered the
church together and delivered the letter.
31The people read it and were glad for its
encouraging message. 32Judas and Silas,[b] who themselves were prophets,[c]
said much to encourage and strengthen
the brothers. 33After spending some time
there, they were sent off by the brothers
with the blessing of peace[d] to return to
those who had sent them.[g] 35But Paul and
Barnabas remained in Antioch, where
they and many others taught and
preached[e] the word of the Lord.[f]

15:14 [i] 2Pe 1:1
15:17 [j] Am 9:11, 12
15:18 [k] Isa 45:21
15:20 [l] 1Co 8:7-13; 10:14-28; Rev 2:14,20 [m] 1Co 10:7,8; Rev 2:14,20 [n] ver 29; Ge 9:4; Lev 3:17; 7:26; 17:10-13; 19:26; Dt 12:16,23
15:21 [o] Ac 13:15; 2Co 3:14,15
15:22 [p] S Ac 11:30 [q] S Ac 11:19 [r] ver 27,32,40; Ac 16:19,25,29; 2Co 1:19; 1Th 1:1; 2Th 1:1; 1Pe 5:12
15:23 [s] ver 1; S Ac 11:19 [t] S Lk 2:2 [u] ver 41; S Ac 6:9 [v] Ac 23:25,26; Jas 1:1
15:24 [w] ver 1; Gal 1:7; 5:10
15:26 [x] Ac 9:23-25; 14:19; 1Co 15:30
15:27 [y] S ver 22
15:28 [z] Ac 5:32
15:29 [a] ver 20; Ac 21:25
15:32 [b] S ver 22 [c] S Ac 11:27
15:33 [d] 1Sa 1:17; Mk 5:34; Lk 7:50; Ac 16:36; 1Co 16:11
15:35 [e] Ac 8:4 [f] S Ac 13:48

[e] *17* Amos 9:11,12 [f] *17,18* Some manuscripts *things'— / [18]known to the Lord for ages is his work*
[g] *33* Some manuscripts *them, [34]but Silas decided to remain there*

15:16 DAVID'S FALLEN TENT. James indicates that Christ's redemptive mission includes both Jew and Gentile. "David's fallen tent" (see Am 9:11 in its context) refers to a remnant of Israel that survives God's judgment. (1) Amos's prophecy states the following: (a) God will judge sinful Israel, yet not totally. (b) He will destroy all the sinners in the house of Jacob (Am 9:10). (c) After the destruction of the ungodly Jews, God will "restore David's fallen tent" (Am 9:11). (2) The salvation of this purified Jewish remnant will result in the nations seeking the Lord (v. 17). Elsewhere Paul says the same thing when he refers to a blessing for the Gentiles that will come from the Jewish remnant's reconciliation to God (see Ro 11:11–15,25–26).

15:28 IT SEEMED GOOD TO THE HOLY SPIRIT. The Jerusalem council was directed by the Holy Spirit. Jesus promised that the Spirit would guide them into all truth (Jn 16:13). Decisions of the church must not be made by humans alone; they must seek the Spirit's guidance through prayer, fasting and commitment to God's Word until his will is clearly discerned (cf. 13:2–4). The church, if it is to be the church of Christ, must hear what the Spirit says to the churches (cf. Rev 2:7).

15:29 YOU ARE TO ABSTAIN FROM. The Holy Spirit (v. 28) suggested certain restrictions for Gentiles that would enable Jewish Christians to live in harmony with their Gentile brothers and sisters. The Gentiles would be expected to abstain from activities that were offensive to Jews. One measure of Christian maturity is the willingness to refrain from activities that some Christians think are right and others believe are wrong (see Paul's discussion in 1Co 8:1–11).

Disagreement Between Paul and Barnabas

36Some time later Paul said to Barnabas, "Let us go back and visit the brothers
in all the towns[g] where we preached the
word of the Lord[h] and see how they are
doing." **37**Barnabas wanted to take John,
also called Mark,[i] with them, **38**but Paul
did not think it wise to take him, because
he had deserted them[j] in Pamphylia and
had not continued with them in the work.
39They had such a sharp disagreement
that they parted company. Barnabas took
Mark and sailed for Cyprus, **40**but Paul
chose Silas[k] and left, commended by the
brothers to the grace of the Lord.[l] **41**He
went through Syria[m] and Cilicia,[n]
strengthening the churches.[o]

15:36 [g] Ac 13:4, 13,14,51; 14:1,6, 24,25 [h] S Ac 13:48 **15:37** [i] S Ac 12:12 **15:38** [j] Ac 13:13 **15:40** [k] S ver 22 [l] S Ac 11:23 **15:41** [m] ver 23; S Lk 2:2 [n] S Ac 6:9 [o] Ac 16:5

Timothy Joins Paul and Silas

16 He came to Derbe and then to Lystra,[p] where a disciple named Timothy[q] lived, whose mother was a Jewess
and a believer,[r] but whose father was a
Greek. **2**The brothers[s] at Lystra and Iconium[t] spoke well of him. **3**Paul wanted to
take him along on the journey, so he circumcised him because of the Jews who
lived in that area, for they all knew that
his father was a Greek.[u] **4**As they traveled
from town to town, they delivered the decisions reached by the apostles and elders[v] in Jerusalem[w] for the people to
obey.[x] **5**So the churches were strength-

16:1 [p] Ac 14:6 [q] Ac 17:14; 18:5; 19:22; 20:4; Ro 16:21; 1Co 4:17; 16:10; 2Co 1:1,19; Php 1:1; 2:19; Col 1:1; 1Th 1:1; 3:2,6; 2Th 1:1; 1Ti 1:2,18; 2Ti 1:2,5,6; Phm 1 [r] 2Ti 1:5 **16:2** [s] ver 40; S Ac 1:16 [t] S Ac 13:51

16:3 [u] Gal 2:3 **16:4** [v] S Ac 11:30 [w] Ac 15:2 [x] Ac 15:28,29

15:39 A SHARP DISAGREEMENT. At times disagreements will occur among believers who love the Lord and one another. When these cannot be resolved, it is best to agree to disagree and let God work his will in the lives of all concerned. Differences in opinions that lead to a separation, as in the case of Paul and Barnabas, must never be accompanied by bitterness and hostility. Both Paul and Barnabas continued their work for God with his blessing and grace.

16:5 THE CHURCHES WERE STRENGTHENED. For comments on the form that churches in the NT took, see note on 12:5.

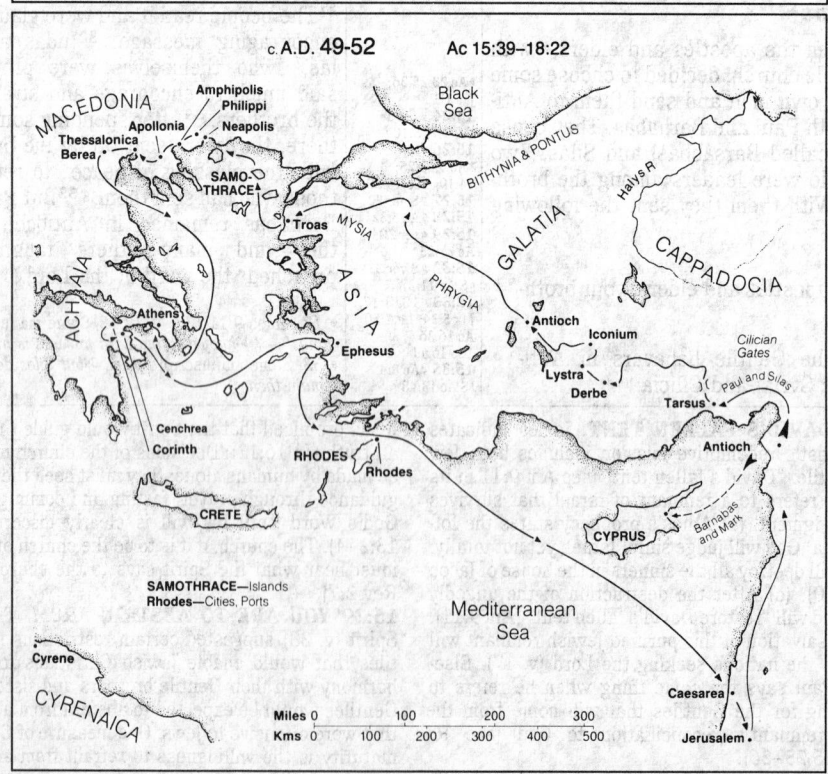

PAUL'S SECOND MISSIONARY JOURNEY

c. A.D. 49-52 Ac 15:39–18:22

MACEDONIA
Amphipolis
Philippi
Apollonia
Neapolis
Thessalonica
Berea
Black Sea
BITHYNIA & PONTUS
SAMOTHRACE
Troas
MYSIA
Halys R.
GALATIA
CAPPADOCIA
ACHAIA
ASIA
PHRYGIA
Athens
Antioch
Iconium
Ephesus
Cilician Gates
Lystra
Derbe
Paul and Silas
Tarsus
Cenchrea
Corinth
RHODES
Rhodes
Antioch
CRETE
CYPRUS
Barnabas and Mark
SAMOTHRACE—Islands
Rhodes—Cities, Ports
Mediterranean Sea
Cyrene
CYRENAICA
Caesarea
Jerusalem
Miles 0 100 200 300
Kms 0 100 200 300 400 500

ened[y] in the faith and grew daily in numbers.[z]

Paul's Vision of the Man of Macedonia

6Paul and his companions traveled throughout the region of Phrygia[a] and Galatia,[b] having been kept by the Holy Spirit from preaching the word in the province of Asia.[c] **7**When they came to the border of Mysia, they tried to enter Bithynia, but the Spirit of Jesus[d] would not allow them to. **8**So they passed by Mysia and went down to Troas.[e] **9**During the night Paul had a vision[f] of a man of Macedonia[g] standing and begging him, "Come over to Macedonia and help us." **10**After Paul had seen the vision, we[h] got ready at once to leave for Macedonia, concluding that God had called us to preach the gospel[i] to them.

Lydia's Conversion in Philippi

11From Troas[j] we put out to sea and sailed straight for Samothrace, and the next day on to Neapolis. **12**From there we traveled to Philippi,[k] a Roman colony and the leading city of that district of Macedonia.[l] And we stayed there several days.

13On the Sabbath[m] we went outside the city gate to the river, where we expected to find a place of prayer. We sat down and began to speak to the women who had gathered there. **14**One of those listening was a woman named Lydia, a dealer in purple cloth from the city of Thyatira,[n] who was a worshiper of God. The Lord opened her heart[o] to respond to Paul's message. **15**When she and the members of her household[p] were baptized,[q] she invited us to her home. "If you consider me a believer in the Lord," she said, "come and stay at my house." And she persuaded us.

Paul and Silas in Prison

16Once when we were going to the place of prayer,[r] we were met by a slave girl who had a spirit[s] by which she predicted the future. She earned a great deal of money for her owners by fortune-telling. **17**This girl followed Paul and the rest of us, shouting, "These men are servants of the Most High God,[t] who are telling you the way to be saved." **18**She kept this up for many days. Finally Paul became so troubled that he turned around and said to the spirit, "In the name of Jesus Christ I command you to come out of her!" At that moment the spirit left her.[u]

19When the owners of the slave girl realized that their hope of making money[v] was gone, they seized Paul and Silas[w] and dragged[x] them into the marketplace to face the authorities. **20**They brought them before the magistrates and said, "These men are Jews, and are throwing our city into an uproar[y] **21**by advocating customs unlawful for us Romans[z] to accept or practice."[a]

22The crowd joined in the attack against Paul and Silas, and the magistrates ordered them to be stripped and beaten.[b] **23**After they had been severely flogged, they were thrown into prison, and the jailer[c] was commanded to guard them carefully. **24**Upon receiving such orders, he put them in the inner cell and fastened their feet in the stocks.[d]

25About midnight[e] Paul and Silas[f] were praying and singing hymns[g] to God,

16:5 [y] Ac 9:31; 15:41 [z] S Ac 2:41
16:6 [a] Ac 2:10; 18:23 [b] Ac 18:23; Gal 1:2; 3:1 [c] S Ac 2:9
16:7 [d] Ro 8:9; Gal 4:6; Php 1:19; 1Pe 1:11
16:8 [e] ver 11; Ac 20:5; 2Co 2:12; 2Ti 4:13
16:9 [f] S Ac 9:10 [g] Ac 19:21,29; 20:1,3; Ro 15:26; 1Co 16:5; 1Th 1:7, 8
16:10 [h] ver 10-17; Ac 20:5-15; 21:1-18; 27:1-28:16 [i] Ac 14:7
16:11 [j] S ver 8
16:12 [k] Ac 20:6; Php 1:1; 1Th 2:2 [l] S ver 9
16:13 [m] S Ac 13:14
16:14 [n] Rev 1:11; 2:18,24 [o] Lk 24:45
16:15 [p] S Ac 11:14 [q] S Ac 2:38
16:16 [r] ver 13 [s] Dt 18:11; 1Sa 28:3,7
16:17 [t] S Mk 5:7
16:18 [u] S Mk 16:17
16:19 [v] ver 16; Ac 19:25,26 [w] S Ac 15:22 [x] Ac 8:3; 17:6; 21:30; Jas 2:6
16:20 [y] Ac 17:6
16:21 [z] ver 12 [a] Est 3:8
16:22 [b] 2Co 11:25; 1Th 2:2
16:23 [c] ver 27,36
16:24 [d] Job 13:27; 33:11; Jer 20:2,3; 29:26
16:25 [e] Ps 119:55,62 [f] S Ac 15:22 [g] S Eph 5:19

16:6 KEPT BY THE HOLY SPIRIT FROM PREACHING. Every initiative in evangelism and missionary activity, especially in the missionary journeys recorded in Acts, is the result of the leading of the Holy Spirit (1:8; 2:14–41; 4:8–12,31; 8:26–29,39–40; 10:19–20; 13:2; 16:6–10; 20:22). The guidance may have taken the form of a prophetic revelation, inward prompting, external circumstances or visions (vv. 6–9). Under the impulse of the Spirit believers moved forward to take the gospel to the unsaved. When checked by the Spirit from going in one direction, they would go in another, trusting in the Holy Spirit to either approve or disapprove of their traveling plans.

16:16 A SPIRIT BY WHICH SHE PREDICTED THE FUTURE. The slave girl's demonic utterances were regarded as a voice of a god; therefore, her services as a fortune-teller were much in demand. Through Paul, Christ showed his power over the world of evil (see article on POWER OVER SATAN AND DEMONS, p. 80).

16:23 SEVERELY FLOGGED. The Jewish law concerning whippings was "forty lashes minus one" (2Co 11:24). The Roman custom depended on the judge and could be terribly cruel. The beating was normally inflicted on the naked body.

16:25 PRAYING AND SINGING HYMNS. Paul and Silas had suffered the humiliation of imprisonment, their feet fastened in stocks and their backs lacerated. Yet in the middle of this suffering, they prayed and sang hymns of praise to God (cf. Mt 5:10–12). From their missionary experience we learn: (1) that the believer's joy is within, not conditioned by outward circumstances; persecution cannot destroy our peace and joy (Jas 1:2–4); (2) that Christ's enemies cannot destroy the believer's faith in and love for God (Ro 8:35–39); (3) that in the worst of circumstances God will provide sufficient grace for those who are in his will and suffer for his name's sake (Mt 5:10–12; 2Co 12:9–10); (4) that "the Spirit of glory and of God rests on" those who suffer for the name of Christ (1Pe 4:14).

and the other prisoners were listening to them. **26**Suddenly there was such a violent earthquake that the foundations of the prison were shaken.[h] At once all the prison doors flew open,[i] and everybody's chains came loose.[j] **27**The jailer woke up, and when he saw the prison doors open, he drew his sword and was about to kill himself because he thought the prisoners had escaped.[k] **28**But Paul shouted, "Don't harm yourself! We are all here!"

29The jailer called for lights, rushed in and fell trembling before Paul and Silas.[l] **30**He then brought them out and asked, "Sirs, what must I do to be saved?"[m]

31They replied, "Believe[n] in the Lord Jesus, and you will be saved[o]—you and your household."[p] **32**Then they spoke the word of the Lord to him and to all the others in his house. **33**At that hour of the night[q] the jailer took them and washed their wounds; then immediately he and all his family were baptized.[r] **34**The jailer brought them into his house and set a meal before them; he[s] was filled with joy because he had come to believe in God—he and his whole family.

(Ac 18:9-10)

35When it was daylight, the magistrates sent their officers to the jailer with the order: "Release those men." **36**The jailer[t] told Paul, "The magistrates have ordered that you and Silas be released. Now you can leave. Go in peace."[u]

37But Paul said to the officers: "They beat us publicly without a trial, even though we are Roman citizens,[v] and threw us into prison. And now do they want to get rid of us quietly? No! Let them come themselves and escort us out."

38The officers reported this to the magistrates, and when they heard that Paul and Silas were Roman citizens, they were alarmed.[w] **39**They came to appease them and escorted them from the prison, requesting them to leave the city.[x] **40**After Paul and Silas came out of the prison, they went to Lydia's house,[y] where they met with the brothers[z] and encouraged them. Then they left.

In Thessalonica

17 When they had passed through Amphipolis and Apollonia, they came to Thessalonica,[a] where there was a Jewish synagogue. **2**As his custom was, Paul went into the synagogue,[b] and on three Sabbath[c] days he reasoned with them from the Scriptures,[d] **3**explaining and proving that the Christ[h] had to suffer[e] and rise from the dead.[f] "This Jesus I am proclaiming to you is the Christ,[h]"[g] he said. **4**Some of the Jews were persuaded and joined Paul and Silas,[h] as did a large number of God-fearing Greeks and not a few prominent women.

5But the Jews were jealous; so they rounded up some bad characters from the marketplace, formed a mob and started a riot in the city.[i] They rushed to Jason's[j] house in search of Paul and Silas in order to bring them out to the crowd.[i] **6**But when they did not find them, they dragged[k] Jason and some other brothers[l] before the city officials, shouting: "These men who have caused trouble all over the world[m] have now come here,[n] **7**and Jason has welcomed them into his house. They are all defying Caesar's decrees, saying that there is another king, one called Jesus."[o] **8**When they heard this, the crowd and the city officials were thrown into turmoil. **9**Then they made Jason[p] and the others post bond and let them go.

In Berea

10As soon as it was night, the brothers sent Paul and Silas[q] away to Berea.[r] On arriving there, they went to the Jewish synagogue.[s] **11**Now the Bereans were of more noble character than the Thessalo-

16:26 [h] Ac 4:31 [i] Ac 5:19; 12:10 [j] Ac 12:7 **16:27** [k] Ac 12:19 **16:29** [l] S Ac 15:22 **16:30** [m] Ac 2:37 **16:31** [n] S Jn 3:15 [o] S Ro 11:14 [p] S Ac 11:14 **16:33** [q] ver 25 [r] S Ac 2:38 **16:34** [s] S Ac 11:14 **16:36** [t] ver 23,27 [u] S Ac 15:33 **16:37** [v] Ac 22:25-29 **16:38** [w] Ac 22:29 **16:39** [x] Mt 8:34; Lk 8:37 **16:40** [y] ver 14 [z] ver 2; S Ac 1:16 **17:1** [a] ver 11,13; Php 4:16; 1Th 1:1; 2Th 1:1; 2Ti 4:10 **17:2** [b] S Ac 9:20 [c] S Ac 13:14 [d] Ac 8:35; 18:28 **17:3** [e] Lk 24:26; Ac 3:18 [f] Lk 24:46; S Ac 2:24 [g] S Ac 9:22 **17:4** [h] S Ac 15:22 **17:5** [i] ver 13; S 1Th 2:16 [j] Ro 16:21 **17:6** [k] S Ac 16:19 [l] S Ac 1:16 [m] S Mt 24:14 [n] Ac 16:20 **17:7** [o] Lk 23:2; Jn 19:12 **17:9** [p] ver 5 **17:10** [q] S Ac 15:22 [r] ver 13; Ac 20:4 [s] S Ac 9:20

h *3* Or *Messiah* i *5* Or *the assembly of the people*

16:26 EVERYBODY'S CHAINS CAME LOOSE. Throughout the book of Acts, Luke emphasizes that nothing can stop the gospel of Christ carried by faithful believers. At Philippi God intervened, and Paul and Silas were delivered by an earthquake. This resulted in further progress for the gospel, notably, the salvation of the jailer and his household.

16:30 WHAT MUST I DO TO BE SAVED? This is the most important question one can ask. The apostles' response is, "Believe in the Lord Jesus" (v. 31). (1) To believe in the Lord Jesus is to focus our faith and commitment on the person of Christ. It means turning to him as a living person who is our Redeemer from sin, our Savior from damnation and the Lord of our lives. It means believing that he is the Son of God sent by the Father and that all he said is true and authoritative for our lives. It means believing that he forgives our sins, makes us his children, gives us the Holy Spirit, and is present with us always to help, guide, comfort and lead us to heaven.

(2) Saving faith is much more than believing truths about Christ. It causes us to draw near to him, remain in him, and commit our troubled lives to him with assurance that he, his Word and the Spirit will lead us through this life to the Father's eternal presence (see article on FAITH AND GRACE, p. 302).

17:11 EXAMINED THE SCRIPTURES EVERY DAY. The action of those in Berea is a model for all

nians,[t] for they received the message
with great eagerness and examined the
Scriptures[u] every day to see if what Paul
said was true.[v] 12Many of the Jews believed, as did also a number of prominent
Greek women and many Greek men.[w]
13When the Jews in Thessalonica
learned that Paul was preaching the word
of God at Berea,[x] they went there too,
agitating the crowds and stirring them up.
14The brothers[y] immediately sent Paul to
the coast, but Silas[z] and Timothy[a] stayed
at Berea. 15The men who escorted Paul
brought him to Athens[b] and then left with
instructions for Silas and Timothy to join
him as soon as possible.[c]

In Athens

16While Paul was waiting for them in
Athens, he was greatly distressed to see
that the city was full of idols. 17So he reasoned in the synagogue[d] with the Jews
and the God-fearing Greeks, as well as in
the marketplace day by day with those
who happened to be there. 18A group of
Epicurean and Stoic philosophers began
to dispute with him. Some of them asked,
"What is this babbler trying to say?" Others remarked, "He seems to be advocating
foreign gods." They said this because Paul
was preaching the good news[e] about
Jesus and the resurrection.[f] 19Then they
took him and brought him to a meeting of
the Areopagus,[g] where they said to him,
"May we know what this new teaching[h] is
that you are presenting? 20You are bringing some strange ideas to our ears, and we
want to know what they mean." 21(All the
Athenians[i] and the foreigners who lived
there spent their time doing nothing but
talking about and listening to the latest
ideas.)
22Paul then stood up in the meeting of
the Areopagus[j] and said: "Men of Athens! I see that in every way you are very
religious.[k] 23For as I walked around and
looked carefully at your objects of worship, I even found an altar with this inscription: TO AN UNKNOWN GOD. Now what you
worship as something unknown[l] I am going to proclaim to you.
24"The God who made the world and
everything in it[m] is the Lord of heaven and
earth[n] and does not live in temples built
by hands.[o] 25And he is not served by human hands, as if he needed anything, because he himself gives all men life and
breath and everything else.[p] 26From one
man he made every nation of men, that
they should inhabit the whole earth; and
he determined the times set for them and
the exact places where they should live.[q]
27God did this so that men would seek him
and perhaps reach out for him and find
him, though he is not far from each one of
us.[r] 28'For in him we live and move and
have our being.'[s] As some of your own
poets have said, 'We are his offspring.'
29"Therefore since we are God's offspring, we should not think that the divine
being is like gold or silver or stone—an
image made by man's design and skill.[t]
30In the past God overlooked[u] such ignorance,[v] but now he commands all people
everywhere to repent.[w] 31For he has set a
day when he will judge[x] the world with
justice[y] by the man he has appointed.[z]
He has given proof of this to all men by
raising him from the dead."[a]
32When they heard about the resurrection of the dead,[b] some of them sneered,
but others said, "We want to hear you
again on this subject." 33At that, Paul left
the Council. 34A few men became followers of Paul and believed. Among them was
Dionysius, a member of the Areopagus,[c]

17:11 [t]S ver 1 [u]Lk 16:29; Jn 5:39 [v]Dt 29:29 **17:12** [w]S Ac 2:41 **17:13** [x]S Heb 4:12 **17:14** [y]S Ac 9:30 [z]S Ac 15:22 [a]S Ac 16:1 **17:15** [b]ver 16,21, 22; Ac 18:1; 1Th 3:1 [c]Ac 18:5 **17:17** [d]S Ac 9:20 **17:18** [e]S Ac 13:32 [f]ver 31,32; Ac 4:2 **17:19** [g]ver 22 [h]Mk 1:27 **17:21** [i]S ver 15

17:22 [j]ver 19 [k]ver 16 **17:23** [l]Jn 4:22 **17:24** [m]Isa 42:5; Ac 14:15 [n]Dt 10:14; Isa 66:1,2; Mt 11:25 [o]1Ki 8:27; Ac 7:48 **17:25** [p]Ps 50:10-12; Isa 42:5 **17:26** [q]Dt 32:8; Job 12:23 **17:27** [r]Dt 4:7; Isa 55:6; Jer 23:23,24 **17:28** [s]Dt 30:20; Job 12:10; Da 5:23 **17:29** [t]Isa 40:18-20; Ro 1:23 **17:30** [u]Ac 14:16; Ro 3:25 [v]ver 23; 1Pe 1:14 [w]Lk 24:47; Tit 2:11,12 **17:31** [x]S Mt 10:15 [y]Ps 9:8; 96:13; 98:9 [z]S Ac 10:42 [a]S Ac 2:24 **17:32** [b]ver 18,31 **17:34** [c]ver 19,22

who listen to preachers and teachers expound the Scriptures. No interpretation or doctrine ought to be accepted passively. Rather, it must be examined carefully by personal study of the Scriptures. The word translated "examine" (Gk *anakrinō*) means "to sift up and down, make careful and exact research." Bible preaching should make Bible students out of the hearers. The truth of every doctrine should be examined according to the Word of God (see Eph 2:20, note).

17:16 HE WAS GREATLY DISTRESSED. At the sight of idolatry and moral corruption, Paul became indignant and grief-stricken; his spirit stirred over people who were lost and in need of salvation. Paul expressed the same attitude as Jesus did toward sin and its destructive work (see Jn 11:33, note). An attitude of holy anger toward sin and immorality should characterize all those who have the spirit of Christ. For the cause of Christ and the salvation of the lost, our spirits should rebel against sin denounced in Scripture, offensive to God and destructive to the human race (cf. 1Co 6:17).

17:30 COMMANDS ALL . . . TO REPENT. In times past, before full knowledge of God came through Jesus Christ, God overlooked much of human sin and ignorance of himself (cf. Ro 3:25). Now that his full and perfect revelation has come with Christ's appearing, all are commanded to repent and believe in Jesus as Lord and Savior. There are no exceptions, for God will not overlook anyone's sins. All must turn from sin or be condemned. Repentance, in other words, is essential for salvation (see Mt 3:2, note).

17:31 JUDGE THE WORLD WITH JUSTICE. For other Pauline references to the appointed day of judgment, see Ro 2:5,16; 1Co 1:8; Php 1:6,10; 1Th 5:2,4; 2Th 1:7–10; 2:2.

also a woman named Damaris, and a number of others.

In Corinth

18 After this, Paul left Athens[d] and went to Corinth.[e] **2**There he met a Jew named Aquila, a native of Pontus, who had recently come from Italy with his wife Priscilla,[f] because Claudius[g] had ordered all the Jews to leave Rome. Paul went to see them, **3**and because he was a tentmaker as they were, he stayed and worked with them.[h] **4**Every Sabbath[i] he reasoned in the synagogue,[j] trying to persuade Jews and Greeks.

5When Silas[k] and Timothy[l] came from Macedonia,[m] Paul devoted himself exclusively to preaching, testifying to the Jews that Jesus was the Christ.[j][n] **6**But when the Jews opposed Paul and became abusive,[o] he shook out his clothes in protest[p] and said to them, "Your blood be on your own heads![q] I am clear of my responsibility.[r] From now on I will go to the Gentiles."[s]

7Then Paul left the synagogue and went next door to the house of Titius Justus, a worshiper of God.[t] **8**Crispus,[u] the synagogue ruler,[v] and his entire household[w] believed in the Lord; and many of the Corinthians who heard him believed and were baptized.

9One night the Lord spoke to Paul in a vision:[x] "Do not be afraid;[y] keep on speaking, do not be silent. **10**For I am with you,[z] and no one is going to attack and harm you, because I have many people in this city." **11**So Paul stayed for a year and a half, teaching them the word of God.[a]

Ac 26:16-29

12While Gallio was proconsul[b] of Achaia,[c] the Jews made a united attack on Paul and brought him into court. **13**"This man," they charged, "is persuading the people to worship God in ways contrary to the law."

14Just as Paul was about to speak, Gallio said to the Jews, "If you Jews were making a complaint about some misdemeanor or serious crime, it would be reasonable for me to listen to you. **15**But since it involves questions about words and names and your own law[d]—settle the matter yourselves. I will not be a judge of such things." **16**So he had them ejected from the court. **17**Then they all turned on Sosthenes[e] the synagogue ruler[f] and beat him in front of the court. But Gallio showed no concern whatever.

Priscilla, Aquila and Apollos

18Paul stayed on in Corinth for some time. Then he left the brothers[g] and sailed for Syria,[h] accompanied by Priscilla and Aquila.[i] Before he sailed, he had his hair cut off at Cenchrea[j] because of a vow he had taken.[k] **19**They arrived at Ephesus,[l] where Paul left Priscilla and

18:1 [d]S Ac 17:15 [e]Ac 19:1; 1Co 1:2; 2Co 1:1,23; 2Ti 4:20 **18:2** [f]ver 19,26; Ro 16:3; 1Co 16:19; 2Ti 4:19 [g]Ac 11:28 **18:3** [h]Ac 20:34; 1Co 4:12; 1Th 2:9; 2Th 3:8 **18:4** [i]S Ac 13:14 [j]S Ac 9:20 **18:5** [k]S Ac 15:22 [l]S Ac 16:1 [m]S Ac 16:9; 17:14,15 [n]S Ac 9:22 **18:6** [o]S Ac 13:45 [p]S Mt 10:14 [q]2Sa 1:16; Eze 33:4 [r]Eze 3:17-19; Ac 20:26 [s]S Ac 13:46 **18:7** [t]Ac 16:14 **18:8** [u]1Co 1:14 [v]S Mk 5:22 [w]S Ac 11:14 **18:9** [x]S Ac 9:10 [y]S Mt 14:27 **18:10** [z]S Mt 28:20 **18:11** [a]S Heb 4:12 **18:12** [b]Ac 13:7, 8,12; 19:38 [c]ver 27; Ro 15:26; 1Co 16:15; 2Co 9:2; 1Th 1:7,8 **18:15** [d]Ac 23:29; 25:11,19 **18:17** [e]1Co 1:1 [f]ver 8 **18:18** [g]ver 27; S Ac 1:16 [h]S Lk 2:2 [i]S ver 2 [j]Ro 16:1 [k]Nu 6:2, 5,18; Ac 21:24 **18:19** [l]ver 21,24; Ac 19:1,17,26; 1Co 15:32; 16:8; Eph 1:1; 1Ti 1:3; Rev 1:11; 2:1

j 5 Or *Messiah;* also in verse 28

18:3 A TENTMAKER AS THEY WERE. Paul practiced a trade as well as preached the gospel; he was a tentmaker, earning his living in this way while traveling or staying in residence (20:34; 1Th 2:9; 2Th 3:8). From Paul's example it is clear that ministers who must work in order to help support themselves and their families are not engaged in a second-class ministry. A dual-vocational ministry has Biblical and apostolic precedence.

18:9 DO NOT BE AFRAID. This passage reveals the inner, human feelings of the apostle. Evidently opposition and hatred against Paul and the gospel were increasing, and Paul was becoming afraid and having doubts whether he should leave Corinth or become silent for a while (cf. 1Co 2:3). These same feelings will occur at times in the hearts of all God's faithful, as is evident even in such men as Elijah (1Ki 19:4) and Jeremiah (Jer 15:15). In such circumstances God will meet his saints and encourage their hearts. The promise of his presence (v. 10) is sufficient to deliver them from fear and to give the assurance and peace necessary to accomplish God's will for their lives (vv. 10–11).

18:10 FOR I AM WITH YOU. These words to Paul do not refer to Christ's general presence everywhere, i.e., his omnipresence (cf. 17:26–28; Ps 139; Jer 23:23–24; Am 9:2–4). Rather they refer to his special nearness to his faithful children. Christ's nearness means that he is personally here to communicate his will, love and fellowship to us. He is present to act in every situation of our lives to bless, help, protect and guide.

(1) We may learn something of the truth of "Christ with us" in the OT passages where God stated that he was with his faithful. When Moses was afraid to return to Egypt, God said: "I will be with you" (Ex 3:12). When Joshua assumed the leadership of Israel after Moses' death, God promised: "I will be with you; I will never leave you nor forsake you" (Jos 1:5). And God encouraged Israel with these words: "When you pass through the waters, I will be with you .... Do not be afraid, for I am with you" (Isa 43:2,5).

(2) In the NT Matthew states that the purpose of Jesus' coming to earth was to achieve the nearness of God to his people. His name is "Immanuel," meaning "God with us" (Mt 1:23). Again, at the end of his Gospel Matthew records Jesus' promise to his disciples: "And surely I am with you always" (Mt 28:20). Mark ends his Gospel with the words: "Then the disciples went out and preached everywhere, and the Lord worked with them" (Mk 16:20).

Aquila. He himself went into the synagogue and reasoned with the Jews.
20When they asked him to spend more
time with them, he declined. 21But as he
left, he promised, "I will come back if it is
God's will."[m] Then he set sail from Ephesus. 22When he landed at Caesarea,[n] he
went up and greeted the church and then
went down to Antioch.[o]

23After spending some time in Antioch,
Paul set out from there and traveled from
place to place throughout the region of
Galatia[p] and Phrygia,[q] strengthening all
the disciples.[r]

24Meanwhile a Jew named Apollos,[s] a
native of Alexandria, came to Ephesus.[t]
He was a learned man, with a thorough
knowledge of the Scriptures. 25He had
been instructed in the way of the Lord,
and he spoke with great fervor[k][u] and
taught about Jesus accurately, though he
knew only the baptism of John.[v] 26He began to speak boldly in the synagogue.
When Priscilla and Aquila[w] heard him,
they invited him to their home and explained to him the way of God more adequately.

27When Apollos wanted to go to Achaia,[x] the brothers[y] encouraged him and
wrote to the disciples there to welcome
him. On arriving, he was a great help to
those who by grace had believed. 28For he
vigorously refuted the Jews in public debate, proving from the Scriptures[z] that
Jesus was the Christ.[a]

Ephesian Disciples Receive the Spirit

19 While Apollos[b] was at Corinth,[c]
Paul took the road through the interior and arrived at Ephesus.[d] There he
found some disciples 2and asked them,

18:21 [m] Ro 1:10; 15:32; 1Co 4:19; Jas 4:15 **18:22** [n] S Ac 8:40 [o] S Ac 11:19 **18:23** [p] S Ac 16:6 [q] Ac 2:10; 16:6 [r] Ac 14:22; 15:32, 41 **18:24** [s] Ac 19:1; 1Co 1:12; 3:5,6, 22; 4:6; 16:12; Tit 3:13 [t] S ver 19 **18:25** [u] Ro 12:11 [v] S Mk 1:4 **18:26** [w] S ver 2 **18:27** [x] S ver 12 [y] ver 18; S Ac 1:16 **18:28** [z] Ac 8:35; 17:2 [a] ver 5; S Ac 9:22 **19:1** [b] S Ac 18:24 [c] S Ac 18:1 [d] S Ac 18:19

[k] 25 Or *with fervor in the Spirit*

18:23 STRENGTHENING ALL THE DISCIPLES. This begins Paul's third missionary journey (18:23—21:15). He leaves to visit the churches established on his first (chs. 13–14) and second (15:36—18:22) journeys. Paul never won converts and then forgot them; he was just as concerned with following up on new believers and strengthening them in the way of Christ. All new believers should be contacted immediately by established Christians, prayed with, instructed in the Christian way, and encouraged to meet with other believers for worship, prayer, the ministry of the Word and the manifestations of the Holy Spirit for the common good (2:42; Mt 28:19–20; 1Co 12:7–11; 14).

18:25 KNEW ONLY THE BAPTISM OF JOHN. At this time Apollos's understanding of the gospel was limited. He had accepted John's baptism and believed in Jesus as the crucified and resurrected Messiah. What he had not learned was that Jesus himself was now baptizing all believers in the Holy Spirit. The Ephesian disciples were in much the same situation (19:2,6).

19:1 EPHESUS . . . SOME DISCIPLES. Were these twelve disciples at Ephesus Christians or disciples of John the Baptist? Either is a possibility. (1) Some believe they were Christians. (a) Luke calls them "disciples," a word he commonly uses for Christians. Had Luke meant to indicate that they were disciples of only John the Baptist, not Christ, he most likely would have said so explicitly. (b) Paul speaks of them as already believing (v. 2). The verb "believe" is used about twenty times in Acts with no direct object. In every other case, the context indicates that believing in Christ for salvation is meant (see next note).

(2) Others maintain that the Ephesian disciples were disciples of John the Baptist who were still waiting for the Messiah. After they heard about Jesus from Paul, they believed in him as the predicted Christ and were born again by the Spirit (vv. 4–5).

(3) Whatever the case might be, it is clear that their being filled with the Holy Spirit came after their faith, their baptism and the laying on of hands (vv. 5–6).

19:2 DID YOU RECEIVE THE HOLY SPIRIT? Observe the following facts concerning Paul's question: (1) Paul's question strongly suggests that he regarded the Ephesian disciples as true converted Christians who had not yet been filled with the Holy Spirit.

(2) Paul's question here refers to the baptism in the Holy Spirit for power and ministry, the same as that which happened at Pentecost (cf. 1:8; 2:4). It cannot refer to the Spirit's indwelling presence in the believer, for Paul clearly knew that all believers have the Spirit living in them from the very moment of their belief, conversion and regeneration (Ro 8:9).

(3) The literal translation of Paul's question is, "Having believed, did you receive the Holy Spirit?" "Having believed" (Gk *pisteusantes*, from *pisteuō*) is an aorist participle, which normally indicates action prior to the action of the main verb (in this case, "receive"). Thus we may render this: "Did you receive the Holy Spirit after you believed?" This agrees fully with the context of the passage, for this is exactly what did happen to the Ephesian believers. (a) They had already believed in Christ before Paul met them (vv. 1–2). (b) They then listened to Paul and further believed all he told them about Christ and the Holy Spirit (v. 4). (c) Paul considered the Ephesians' belief in Christ to be genuine and adequate, for he baptized them in the name of the Lord Jesus (v. 5). (d) It was only then, after their belief and their water baptism, that Paul laid his hands on them and "the Holy Spirit came on them" (v. 6). Thus, there was an interval of time between their belief in Christ and the coming of the Spirit in all his power.

Paul's question here indicates that he thought it quite possible to "believe" in Christ without experiencing the baptism in the Holy Spirit. This passage is decisive in showing that one may be a Christian without possessing the fullness of the Holy Spirit (see article on BAPTISM IN THE HOLY SPIRIT, p. 228).

19:2 WE HAVE NOT EVEN HEARD. The response of the Ephesian believers does not mean they had

"Did you receive the Holy Spirit[e] when[l] you believed?"

They answered, "No, we have not even heard that there is a Holy Spirit."

3So Paul asked, "Then what baptism did you receive?"

"John's baptism," they replied.

4Paul said, "John's baptism[f] was a baptism of repentance. He told the people to believe in the one coming after him, that is, in Jesus."[g] **5**On hearing this, they were baptized into[m] the name of the Lord Jesus.[h] **6**When Paul placed his hands on them,[i] the Holy Spirit came on them,[j] and they spoke in tongues[n][k] and prophe-
Eph 5:18 sied. **7**There were about twelve men in all.

Paul in Ephesus

8Paul entered the synagogue[l] and spoke boldly there for three months, arguing persuasively about the kingdom of God.[m] **9**But some of them[n] became obstinate; they refused to believe and publicly maligned the Way.[o] So Paul left them. He took the disciples[p] with him and had discussions daily in the lecture hall of Tyrannus. **10**This went on for two years,[q] so that all the Jews and Greeks who lived in the province of Asia[r] heard the word of the Lord.[s]

11God did extraordinary miracles[t] through Paul, **12**so that even handkerchiefs and aprons that had touched him were taken to the sick, and their illnesses were cured[u] and the evil spirits left them. Ac 28:8-9

13Some Jews who went around driving out evil spirits[v] tried to invoke the name of the Lord Jesus over those who were demon-possessed. They would say, "In the name of Jesus,[w] whom Paul preaches, I command you to come out." **14**Seven sons of Sceva, a Jewish chief priest, were doing this. **15**⌞One day,⌟ the evil spirit answered them, "Jesus I know, and I know about Paul, but who are you?" **16**Then the man who had the evil spirit jumped on them and overpowered them all. He gave them such a beating that they ran out of the house naked and bleeding.

17When this became known to the Jews and Greeks living in Ephesus,[x] they were all seized with fear,[y] and the name of the Lord Jesus was held in high honor. **18**Many of those who believed now came and openly confessed their evil deeds. **19**A number who had practiced sorcery brought their scrolls together and burned them publicly. When they calculated the value of the scrolls, the total came to fifty thousand drachmas.[o] **20**In this way the word of the Lord[z] spread widely and grew in power.[a]

19:2 [e]S Jn 20:22 **19:4** [f]S Mk 1:4 [g]Jn 1:7 **19:5** [h]S Ac 2:38 **19:6** [i]S Ac 6:6 [j]S Ac 10:44 [k]S Mk 16:17 **19:8** [l]S Ac 9:20 [m]S Mt 3:2; Ac 28:23 **19:9** [n]Ac 14:4 [o]ver 23; S Ac 9:2 [p]ver 30; S Ac 11:26 **19:10** [q]Ac 20:31 [r]ver 22,26,27; S Ac 2:9 [s]S Ac 13:48 **19:11** [t]Ac 8:13 **19:12** [u]Ac 5:15 **19:13** [v]Mt 12:27 [w]Mk 9:38 **19:17** [x]S Ac 18:19 [y]Ac 5:5,11 **19:20** [z]S Ac 13:48 [a]Ac 6:7; 12:24

[l] *2* Or *after* [m] *5* Or *in* [n] *6* Or *other languages* [o] *19* A drachma was a silver coin worth about a day's wages.

---

never heard of the Holy Spirit. They certainly were acquainted with the OT teaching about the Spirit, and they most assuredly had heard John's message concerning the baptism in the Holy Spirit that the Christ was to bring (Lk 3:16). They had not yet heard that the Spirit was being poured out on believers (1:5,8).

19:5 THEY WERE BAPTIZED. Water baptism into "the name of the Lord Jesus" of these twelve people at Ephesus (v. 7) testifies that they had saving faith and were born again by the Spirit. This precedes their being filled with the Holy Spirit (v. 6).

19:6 THE HOLY SPIRIT CAME ON THEM. This event occurs some 25 years after the first Pentecost (2:4); yet, the pattern of these twelve people receiving the fullness of the Holy Spirit is consistent with the normal pattern already presented by Luke (see 8:5–24, note).

(1) They had believed in Jesus and were born again by the Spirit (see previous note).

(2) After they were baptized in water (v. 5), Paul laid his hands on them and they were baptized in the Holy Spirit.

(3) As the Holy Spirit came on them, they began speaking in tongues and prophesying. Luke never presents the outpouring of the Spirit as something one could only perceive by faith. Rather, he shows it to be a knowable and identifiable experience capable of being verified objectively; speaking in tongues was external and visible proof that the Holy Spirit had come on these followers of Jesus (see article on SPEAKING IN TONGUES, p. 232).

19:12 HANDKERCHIEFS AND APRONS. Paul's ministry at Ephesus was marked by extraordinary miracles of healing and deliverance from demons, accomplished directly or through handkerchiefs and aprons that had been in contact with his body (i.e., sweat cloths and aprons used in his leatherworking). Diseases disappeared and evil spirits left when the afflicted touched the cloth (cf. 5:15; Mk 5:27). Evangelists today who attempt to gain financial support by advertising handkerchiefs for healing are not acting according to Paul's motive and spirit, for Paul did not use these items to gain money. He simply multiplied the empowering that was on him through these tangible means, healing and delivering more people than he could personally touch with his hands.

19:19 PRACTICED SORCERY. The public burning of magical books shows that new believers were taught immediately to turn away from occult practices. Witchcraft, black magic, sorcery, spiritism and other occult practices are satanic activities completely incompatible with the Christian faith. One cannot be a true believer in Christ and at the same time deal with spirits or attempt to gain contact with the dead. God comdemns all such activity as detestable (Dt 18:9–13). Dabbling in the occult and spiritism will leave one open to powerful satanic influence and demonic possession.

21After all this had happened, Paul
decided to go to Jerusalem,[b] passing
through Macedonia[c] and Achaia.[d] "After
I have been there," he said, "I must visit
Rome also."[e] 22He sent two of his helpers,[f] Timothy[g] and Erastus,[h] to Macedonia, while he stayed in the province of
Asia[i] a little longer.

The Riot in Ephesus

23About that time there arose a great
disturbance about the Way.[j] 24A silversmith named Demetrius, who made silver
shrines of Artemis, brought in no little
business for the craftsmen. 25He called
them together, along with the workmen in
related trades, and said: "Men, you know
we receive a good income from this business.[k] 26And you see and hear how this
fellow Paul has convinced and led astray
large numbers of people here in Ephesus[l]
and in practically the whole province of
Asia.[m] He says that man-made gods are
no gods at all.[n] 27There is danger not only
that our trade will lose its good name, but
also that the temple of the great goddess
Artemis will be discredited, and the goddess herself, who is worshiped throughout the province of Asia and the world,
will be robbed of her divine majesty."

28When they heard this, they were furious and began shouting: "Great is Artemis
of the Ephesians!"[o] 29Soon the whole city
was in an uproar. The people seized Gaius[p] and Aristarchus,[q] Paul's traveling
companions from Macedonia,[r] and
rushed as one man into the theater.
30Paul wanted to appear before the crowd,
but the disciples[s] would not let him.
31Even some of the officials of the province, friends of Paul, sent him a message
begging him not to venture into the theater.

32The assembly was in confusion: Some
were shouting one thing, some another.[t]
Most of the people did not even know why
they were there. 33The Jews pushed Alexander to the front, and some of the crowd
shouted instructions to him. He motioned[u] for silence in order to make a defense before the people. 34But when they
realized he was a Jew, they all shouted in
unison for about two hours: "Great is Artemis of the Ephesians!"[v]

35The city clerk quieted the crowd and
said: "Men of Ephesus,[w] doesn't all the
world know that the city of Ephesus is the
guardian of the temple of the great Artemis and of her image, which fell from
heaven? 36Therefore, since these facts are
undeniable, you ought to be quiet and not
do anything rash. 37You have brought
these men here, though they have neither
robbed temples[x] nor blasphemed our goddess. 38If, then, Demetrius and his fellow
craftsmen[y] have a grievance against anybody, the courts are open and there are
proconsuls.[z] They can press charges. 39If
there is anything further you want to bring
up, it must be settled in a legal assembly.
40As it is, we are in danger of being
charged with rioting because of today's
events. In that case we would not be able
to account for this commotion, since there
is no reason for it." 41After he had said
this, he dismissed the assembly.

Through Macedonia and Greece

20 When the uproar had ended, Paul
sent for the disciples[a] and, after
encouraging them, said good-by and set
out for Macedonia.[b] 2He traveled through
that area, speaking many words of encouragement to the people, and finally arrived in Greece, 3where he stayed three
months. Because the Jews made a plot
against him[c] just as he was about to sail
for Syria,[d] he decided to go back through
Macedonia.[e] 4He was accompanied by So-
pater son of Pyrrhus from Berea, Aristarchus[f] and Secundus from Thessalonica,[g]
Gaius[h] from Derbe, Timothy[i] also, and
Tychicus[j] and Trophimus[k] from the province of Asia.[l] 5These men went on ahead
and waited for us[m] at Troas.[n] 6But we
sailed from Philippi[o] after the Feast of
Unleavened Bread, and five days later
joined the others at Troas,[p] where we
stayed seven days.

Eutychus Raised From the Dead at Troas

7On the first day of the week[q] we came
together to break bread.[r] Paul spoke to
the people and, because he intended to
leave the next day, kept on talking until
midnight. 8There were many lamps in the
upstairs room[s] where we were meeting.
9Seated in a window was a young man
named Eutychus, who was sinking into a
deep sleep as Paul talked on and on. When
he was sound asleep, he fell to the ground
from the third story and was picked up
dead. 10Paul went down, threw himself on
the young man[t] and put his arms around
him. "Don't be alarmed," he said. "He's
alive!"[u] 11Then he went upstairs again
and broke bread[v] and ate. After talking
until daylight, he left. 12The people took

19:21 [b] Ac 20:16, 22; 21:4,12,15; Ro 15:25 [c] S Ac 16:9 [d] S Ac 18:12 [e] Ro 15:24,28 **19:22** [f] Ac 13:5 [g] S Ac 16:1 [h] Ro 16:23; 2Ti 4:20 [i] ver 10, 26,27; S Ac 2:9 **19:23** [j] S Ac 9:2 **19:25** [k] Ac 16:16, 19,20 **19:26** [l] S Ac 18:19 [m] S Ac 2:9 [n] Dt 4:28; Ps 115:4; Isa 44:10-20; Jer 10:3-5; Ac 17:29; 1Co 8:4; Rev 9:20 **19:28** [o] S Ac 18:19 **19:29** [p] Ac 20:4; Ro 16:23; 1Co 1:14 [q] Ac 20:4; 27:2; Col 4:10; Phm 24 [r] S Ac 16:9 **19:30** [s] S Ac 11:26 **19:32** [t] Ac 21:34 **19:33** [u] S Ac 12:17 **19:34** [v] ver 28 **19:35** [w] S Ac 18:19

19:37 [x] Ro 2:22 **19:38** [y] ver 24 [z] Ac 13:7,8,12; 18:12 **20:1** [a] S Ac 11:26 [b] S Ac 16:9 **20:3** [c] ver 19; Ac 9:23,24; 14:5; 23:12,15,30; 25:3; 2Co 11:26; S 1Th 2:16 [d] S Lk 2:2 [e] S Ac 16:9 **20:4** [f] S Ac 19:29 [g] S Ac 17:1 [h] S Ac 19:29 [i] S Ac 16:1 [j] Eph 6:21; Col 4:7; Tit 3:12 [k] Ac 21:29; 2Ti 4:20 [l] S Ac 2:9 **20:5** [m] S Ac 16:10 [n] S Ac 16:8 **20:6** [o] S Ac 16:12 [p] S Ac 16:8 **20:7** [q] 1Co 16:2; Rev 1:10 [r] S Mt 14:19 **20:8** [s] Ac 1:13; 9:37 **20:10** [t] 1Ki 17:21; 2Ki 4:34 [u] Mt 9:23,24 **20:11** [v] ver 7; S Mt 14:19

the young man home alive and were greatly comforted.

Paul's Farewell to the Ephesian Elders

13We went on ahead to the ship and
sailed for Assos, where we were going to
take Paul aboard. He had made this arrangement because he was going there on
foot. 14When he met us at Assos, we took
him aboard and went on to Mitylene.
15The next day we set sail from there and
arrived off Kios. The day after that we
crossed over to Samos, and on the following day arrived at Miletus.[w] 16Paul had
decided to sail past Ephesus[x] to avoid
spending time in the province of Asia,[y] for
he was in a hurry to reach Jerusalem,[z] if
possible, by the day of Pentecost.[a]
17From Miletus,[b] Paul sent to Ephesus
for the elders[c] of the church. 18When they
arrived, he said to them: "You know how
I lived the whole time I was with you,[d]
from the first day I came into the province
of Asia.[e] 19I served the Lord with great
humility and with tears,[f] although I was
severely tested by the plots of the Jews.[g]
20You know that I have not hesitated to
preach anything[h] that would be helpful to
you but have taught you publicly and from
house to house. 21I have declared to both
Jews[i] and Greeks that they must turn to
God in repentance[j] and have faith in our
Lord Jesus.[k]
22"And now, compelled by the Spirit, I
am going to Jerusalem,[l] not knowing
what will happen to me there. 23I only
know that in every city the Holy Spirit
warns me[m] that prison and hardships are
facing me.[n] 24However, I consider my
life worth nothing to me,[o] if only I may
finish the race[p] and complete the task[q]
the Lord Jesus has given me[r]—the
task of testifying to the gospel of God's
grace.[s]
25"Now I know that none of you among
whom I have gone about preaching the
kingdom[t] will ever see me again.[u]
26Therefore, I declare to you today that I
am innocent of the blood of all men.[v]
27For I have not hesitated to proclaim to
you the whole will of God.[w] 28Keep watch
over yourselves and all the flock[x] of
which the Holy Spirit has made you overseers.[p][y] Be shepherds of the church of
God,[q][z] which he bought[a] with his own
blood.[b] 29I know that after I leave, savage

20:15 [w] ver 17; 2Ti 4:20
20:16 [x] S Ac 18:19 [y] S Ac 2:9 [z] S Ac 19:21 [a] S Ac 2:1
20:17 [b] ver 15 [c] S Ac 11:30
20:18 [d] Ac 18:19-21; 19:1-41 [e] S Ac 2:9
20:19 [f] Ps 6:6 [g] S ver 3
20:20 [h] ver 27; Ps 40:10; Jer 26:2; 42:4
20:21 [i] Ac 18:5 [j] S Ac 2:38 [k] Ac 24:24; 26:18; Eph 1:15; Col 2:5; Phm 5
20:22 [l] ver 16
20:23 [m] S Ac 8:29; 21:4 [n] S Ac 9:16
20:24 [o] Ac 21:13 [p] 2Ti 4:7 [q] 2Co 4:1 [r] Gal 1:1; Tit 1:3 [s] S Ac 11:23
20:25 [t] S Mt 4:23 [u] ver 38
20:26 [v] Eze 3:17-19; Ac 18:6
20:27 [w] S ver 20
20:28 [x] ver 29; S Jn 21:16 [y] S 1Ti 3:1 [z] S 1Co 10:32 [a] S 1Co 6:20 [b] S Ro 3:25

[p] 28 Traditionally *bishops* [q] 28 Many manuscripts *of the Lord*

20:19 WITH TEARS. Paul on several occasions mentions his serving the Lord with "tears" (v. 31; 2Co 2:4; Php 3:18). In this address to the Ephesian elders (vv. 17–38), he speaks of daily warning them with tears for a period of three years (v. 31). The tears were not the result of weakness; rather, Paul saw the lost condition of the human race, the evil of sin, the distortion of the gospel and the peril of rejecting the Lord as such grave realities that his preaching was often accompanied by tears (cf. Mk 9:24; Lk 19:41).

20:20 I HAVE NOT HESITATED TO PREACH ANYTHING. Paul preached whatever he believed was useful or needful for the salvation of his hearers. Ministers of the gospel must be faithful to declare the whole truth of God. They must not seek to satisfy the people's desires or gratify their tastes, nor should they seek to promote their own popularity. Even if they must speak words of rebuke, teach doctrines that challenge natural prejudices or preach Biblical standards that oppose the desires of the sinful nature, faithful preachers will deliver the whole truth for the sake of the flock (e.g., Gal 1:6–10; 2Ti 4:1–5).

20:22 COMPELLED BY THE SPIRIT. Paul knew that hardships and suffering awaited him (v. 23); yet he committed his way to God, not knowing whether it would mean life or death (see 21:4, note).

20:23 THE HOLY SPIRIT WARNS ME. The Holy Spirit's testimony that hardships and imprisonment awaited Paul was probably communicated through prophets in the churches.

20:24 I CONSIDER MY LIFE WORTH NOTHING. Paul's main concern was not preserving his own life; what counted most was that he might finish the ministry to which God had called him. Wherever it ended, even if in the sacrifice of his life, he would finish his course with joy and the prayer that "Christ will be exalted in my body, whether by life or by death" (Php 1:20). For Paul, life and service for Christ is represented as a race that one must run with absolute faithfulness to his or her Lord (cf. 13:25; 1Co 9:24; 2Ti 4:7; Heb 12:1).

20:26 I AM INNOCENT OF THE BLOOD OF ALL MEN. The word "blood" is used normally in the sense of bloodshed, i.e., the crime of causing someone's death (cf. 5:28; Mt 23:35; 27:25). (1) Here it means that if any should die spiritually and be lost forever, Paul would not be to blame. (2) If overseers do not want to be held responsible for the perishing of those under their ministry, they must declare to them the whole will of God.

20:28 KEEP WATCH OVER . . . ALL THE FLOCK. For a discussion of this classic passage on overseers in the church, see article on OVERSEERS AND THEIR DUTIES, p. 274.

20:29 SAVAGE WOLVES WILL COME IN. Influenced by ambition to build their own kingdoms or by the love of money, power or popularity (e.g., 1Ti 1:6–7; 2Ti 1:15; 4:3–4; 3Jn 9), imposters in the church will "distort" the original gospel as found in the NT (1) by repudiating or ignoring some of its fundamental truths; (2) by adding to it humanistic ideas, philosophies and psychologies; (3) by mixing its doctrines and practices with such things as "new age" teaching or the occult and spiritism; (4) and by tole-

wolves[c] will come in among you and will
not spare the flock.[d] 30Even from your
own number men will arise and distort the
truth in order to draw away disciples[e] after them. 31So be on your guard! Remember that for three years[f] I never stopped
warning each of you night and day with
tears.[g]

32"Now I commit you to God[h] and to the
word of his grace, which can build you up
and give you an inheritance[i] among all
those who are sanctified.[j] 33I have not
coveted anyone's silver or gold or clothing.[k] 34You yourselves know that these
hands of mine have supplied my own
needs and the needs of my companions.[l]
35In everything I did, I showed you that by
this kind of hard work we must help the
weak, remembering the words the Lord
Jesus himself said: 'It is more blessed to
give than to receive.' "

36When he had said this, he knelt down
with all of them and prayed.[m] 37They all
wept as they embraced him and kissed
him.[n] 38What grieved them most was his
statement that they would never see his
face again.[o] Then they accompanied him
to the ship.[p]

On to Jerusalem

21 After we[q] had torn ourselves away
from them, we put out to sea and
sailed straight to Cos. The next day we
went to Rhodes and from there to Patara.
2We found a ship crossing over to Phoenicia,[r] went on board and set sail. 3After
sighting Cyprus and passing to the south
of it, we sailed on to Syria.[s] We landed at
Tyre, where our ship was to unload its
cargo. 4Finding the disciples[t] there, we
stayed with them seven days. Through the
Spirit[u] they urged Paul not to go on to
Jerusalem. 5But when our time was up, we
left and continued on our way. All the disciples and their wives and children accompanied us out of the city, and there on the
beach we knelt to pray.[v] 6After saying
good-by to each other, we went aboard the
ship, and they returned home.

7We continued our voyage from Tyre[w]
and landed at Ptolemais, where we greeted the brothers[x] and stayed with them for
a day. 8Leaving the next day, we reached
Caesarea[y] and stayed at the house of
Philip[z] the evangelist,[a] one of the Seven.
9He had four unmarried daughters who
prophesied.[b]

10After we had been there a number of

20:29 [c]Eze 34:5; Mt 7:15 [d]ver 28
20:30 [e]S Ac 11:26
20:31 [f]Ac 19:10 [g]ver 19
20:32 [h]Ac 14:23 [i]S Eph 1:14; S Mt 25:34; Col 1:12; 3:24; Heb 9:15; 1Pe 1:4 [j]Ac 26:18
20:33 [k]1Sa 12:3; 1Co 9:12; 2Co 2:17; 7:2; 11:9; 12:14-17; 1Th 2:5
20:34 [l]S Ac 18:3
20:36 [m]Lk 22:41; Ac 9:40; 21:5
20:37 [n]S Lk 15:20
20:38 [o]ver 25 [p]Ac 21:5
21:1 [q]S Ac 16:10
21:2 [r]Ac 11:19
21:3 [s]S Lk 2:2
21:4 [t]S Ac 11:26 [u]ver 11; Ac 20:23
21:5 [v]Lk 22:41; Ac 9:40; 20:36
21:7 [w]Ac 12:20 [x]S Ac 1:16
21:8 [y]S Ac 8:40 [z]Ac 6:5; 8:5-40 [a]Eph 4:11; 2Ti 4:5
21:9 [b]Ex 15:20; Jdg 4:4; Ne 6:14; Lk 2:36; Ac 2:17; 1Co 11:5

---

rating immoral lifestyles contrary to God's righteous standards (see 1Ti 4:1; Rev 2–3). That such wolves did enter the flock and undermine apostolic doctrine and practice at Ephesus is evident from 1Ti 1:3–4,18–19; 4:1–3; 2Ti 1:15; 2:17–18; 3:1–8. The Pastoral Letters reveal that a general rejection of apostolic teaching was beginning to gain momentum throughout the province of Asia.

20:31 SO BE ON YOUR GUARD! Overseers of God's people must always be sensitive to and watch out for those within their congregations who are not earnestly committed to the original message of Christ and the apostles. They must be so united with the Holy Spirit that they are carefully and tearfully concerned for their people, never ceasing night and day to warn the flock about the danger facing them and ever pointing them to the only sure foundation—Christ and his Word.

20:33 I HAVE NOT COVETED ANYONE'S SILVER. Paul sets an example for all of God's ministers. He never desires wealth or seeks to get rich from his work in the gospel (cf. 2Co 12:14). Paul had great opportunity to amass wealth. He was an apostle with great influence over many believers and could perform miracles of healing; furthermore, the early Christians were disposed to give money and property to prominent church leaders for distribution to those in need (see 4:34–35,37). If Paul had taken advantage of his gifts and position, and the liberality of the believers, he could have lived an affluent lifestyle. This he did not do because of the guidance of the Holy Spirit and because of his love for the gospel (cf. 1Co 9:4–18; 2Co 11:7–12; 12:14–18; 1Th 2:5–6).

20:37 THEY ALL WEPT. This parting is a remarkable example of Christian fellowship and love. Paul had served the Ephesian elders with unselfish care and concern, sharing their joys and sorrows and ministering to them with tears and through testing (vv. 19,31). They were heartbroken and wept aloud at the thought of not seeing his face again (v. 38). The devoted love between Paul and these elders should characterize all who are co-laborers in the faith.

21:4 THROUGH THE SPIRIT THEY URGED PAUL NOT TO GO UP TO JERUSALEM. "Through the Spirit" means "on account of what the Spirit said." The Holy Spirit was not forbidding Paul to go to Jerusalem, for it was God's will that he go (see v. 14; 23:11). God, however, was giving Paul a warning that much suffering awaited him if he did go. Probably the Spirit had said the same thing at Tyre that he said at Caesarea (vv. 8–14). But Paul counted the cost and was willing even to die for the sake of the gospel (vv. 10–14).

21:10 A PROPHET NAMED AGABUS. Agabus, one of the prophets who foretold the famine of A.D. 46 (11:27–28), now predicts Paul's arrest and imprisonment. The closer Paul got to Jerusalem, the clearer and more definite were the revelations (v. 11). Agabus's prophecy did not say Paul should not go to Jerusalem, but what awaited him if he did go.

Note that in no recorded incident in the NT was the gift of prophecy ever used to give personal guidance to individuals in matters that could be decided according to Scriptural principles. Decisions related to morality, buying or selling, marriage, home and family must be made by applying and obeying the principles

OVERSEERS AND THEIR DUTIES

Ac 20:28 "Keep watch over yourselves and all the flock of which the Holy Spirit has made you overseers. Be shepherds of the church of God, which he bought with his own blood."

No church can function without designated leaders. Thus, as Ac 14:23 indicates, certain individuals were appointed to the office of elder or overseer by Spirit-filled believers who sought God's will through prayer and fasting, in accordance with the spiritual qualifications set down by the Holy Spirit in 1Ti 3:1–7 and Tit 1:5–9 (see article on MORAL QUALIFICATIONS FOR OVERSEERS, p. 458). Ultimately, therefore, it is the Spirit who makes someone an overseer of the church. Paul's speech to the Ephesian elders (Ac 20:18–35) is a classic passage giving Scriptural principles on how to function as an overseer within the visible church.

PROMOTING THE FAITH. (1) One of the major duties of overseers is to feed the sheep by teaching God's Word. They must always keep in mind that the flock given to them is no other than the people that God has purchased for himself with his Son's precious blood (cf. Ac 20:28; 1Co 6:20; 1Pe 1:19; 2:9; Rev 5:9). (2) In Ac 20:19–27, Paul describes how he served as a shepherd of the church in Ephesus; he has declared the whole will of God by faithfully warning and teaching the Ephesian Christians (20:27). Consequently he is able to say, "I am innocent of the blood of all men" (20:26; see note). Overseers today must likewise declare to their churches God's whole will. They must "preach the word . . . correct, rebuke and encourage—with great patience and careful instruction" (2Ti 4:2), and refuse to be preachers who seek to please people and say only what they want to hear (2Ti 4:3).

GUARDING THE FAITH. The true pastor must diligently protect the sheep from their enemies. Paul knows that in the church's future, Satan will raise up false teachers from within the church and infiltrate God's flock from the outside with imposters who adhere to unbiblical doctrine, worldly thought, and pagan and humanistic ideas; both will destroy the Biblical faith of God's people (see article on FALSE TEACHERS, p. 98). Paul calls them "savage wolves," meaning that they are strong, difficult to handle, ravenous and dangerous (see Ac 20:29, note; cf. Mt 10:16). Such individuals will draw people away from Christ's teachings and toward themselves and their distorted gospel. Paul's urgent plea (Ac 20:25–31) places a solemn obligation on all church leaders to guard the church and oppose all who would distort the fundamental revelation of NT faith.

(1) The true church consists of only those who by Christ's grace and the fellowship of the Holy Spirit are faithful to the Lord Jesus Christ and the Word of God (see article on THE INSPIRATION AND AUTHORITY OF SCRIPTURE, p. 474). Therefore, as a major aspect of guarding God's church, church leaders must discipline, correct in love (Eph 4:15) and firmly refute (2Ti 4:1–4; Tit 1:9–11) all within the church who "distort the truth" (Ac 20:30) by teaching things contrary to God's Word and apostolic witness.

(2) Church leaders, pastors of local congregations and administrative officials do well to remember that the Lord Jesus has made them responsible for the blood of all persons under their care (Ac 20:26–27; cf. Eze 3:20–21). If leaders fail to declare and perform God's whole purpose for the church (Ac 20:27), especially in the area of keeping watch over the flock (20:28), they will not be "innocent of the blood of all men" (20:26, see note; cf. Eze 34:1–10). Instead God will hold them guilty of the blood of all those who are lost because of the leaders' refusal to protect the flock from those who weaken and distort the Word (see also 2Ti 1:14, note; Rev 2:2, note).

(3) Exercising discipline with regard to theological, doctrinal and moral matters by and upon those who are responsible for the church's direction is especially important. Purity of doctrine and life and adherence to the inerrancy of Scripture must be carefully guarded in colleges, Bible schools, seminaries, publishing institutions and all organizational structures of the church (2Ti 1:13–14).

(4) The main issue here is one's attitude toward divinely inspired Scripture, which Paul calls the "word of his grace" (Ac 20:32). False teachers, pastors and leaders will attempt to weaken the authority of the Bible by their subversive teachings and unbiblical principles. By rejecting the full authority of God's Word, they deny that the Bible is true and trustworthy in all that it teaches (Ac 20:28–31; see Gal 1:6, note; 1Ti 4:1; 2Ti 3:8). These people, for the sake of the church, must be disciplined and removed from the fellowship (2Jn 9–11; see Gal 1:9, note).

(5) The church that fails to share the Holy Spirit's burning concern for church purity (Ac 20:18–35), refuses to maintain a firm stand for the truth, and refrains from disciplining those who undermine the authority of God's Word will soon cease to exist as a church according to NT norms (see Ac 12:5, note; see article on THE CHURCH, p. 38). It will become guilty of apostasy from the original revelation of Christ and the apostles, sliding further and further from the NT purpose, power and life.

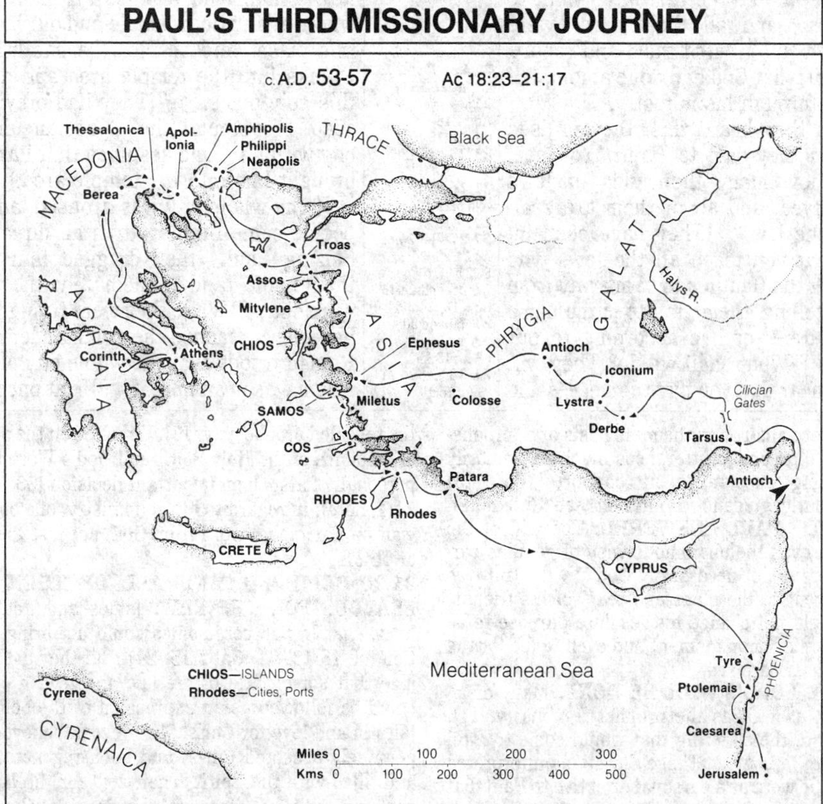

days, a prophet named Agabus[c] came down from Judea. **11**Coming over to us, he took Paul's belt, tied his own hands and feet with it and said, "The Holy Spirit says,[d] 'In this way the Jews of Jerusalem will bind[e] the owner of this belt and will hand him over to the Gentiles.' "[f]

12When we heard this, we and the people there pleaded with Paul not to go up
Ro 1:11 to Jerusalem. **13**Then Paul answered, "Why are you weeping and breaking my heart? I am ready not only to be bound, but also to die[g] in Jerusalem for the name of the Lord Jesus."[h] **14**When he would not be dissuaded, we gave up[i] and said, "The Lord's will be done."[j]

15After this, we got ready and went up to Jerusalem.[k] **16**Some of the disciples from Caesarea[l] accompanied us and brought us to the home of Mnason, where we were to stay. He was a man from Cyprus[m] and one of the early disciples.

Paul's Arrival at Jerusalem

17When we arrived at Jerusalem, the brothers[n] received us warmly.[o] **18**The next day Paul and the rest of us went to see James,[p] and all the elders[q] were present. **19**Paul greeted them and reported in detail what God had done among the Gentiles[r] through his ministry.[s]

20When they heard this, they praised God. Then they said to Paul: "You see, brother, how many thousands of Jews have believed, and all of them are zealous[t] for the law.[u] **21**They have been informed that you teach all the Jews who live among the Gentiles to turn away from Moses,[v] telling them not to circumcise their children[w] or live according to our customs.[x] **22**What shall we do? They will certainly hear that you have come, **23**so do what we tell you. There are four men with us who have made a vow.[y] **24**Take these men, join in their purification rites[z] and pay their expenses, so that they can have their heads shaved.[a] Then everybody will know there is no truth in these reports about you, but that you yourself are living in obedience to the law. **25**As for the Gentile believers, we have written to them our decision that they should abstain from food sacrificed to idols, from blood, from the meat of strangled animals and from sexual immorality."[b]

26The next day Paul took the men and purified himself along with them. Then he went to the temple to give notice of the date when the days of purification would end and the offering would be made for each of them.[c]

Paul Arrested

27When the seven days were nearly over, some Jews from the province of Asia saw Paul at the temple. They stirred up the whole crowd and seized him,[d] **28**shouting, "Men of Israel, help us! This is the man who teaches all men everywhere against our people and our law and this place. And besides, he has brought Greeks into the temple area and defiled this holy place."[e] **29**(They had previously seen Trophimus[f] the Ephesian[g] in the city with Paul and assumed that Paul had brought him into the temple area.)

30The whole city was aroused, and the people came running from all directions. Seizing Paul,[h] they dragged him[i] from the temple, and immediately the gates were shut. **31**While they were trying to kill him, news reached the commander of the Roman troops that the whole city of Jerusalem was in an uproar. **32**He at once took

21:10 [c]Ac 11:28 **21:11** [d]S Ac 8:29 [e]ver 33 [f]1Ki 22:11; Isa 20:2-4; Jer 13:1-11; Mt 20:19 **21:13** [g]Ac 20:24 [h]S Jn 15:21; S Ac 9:16 **21:14** [i]Ru 1:18 [j]S Mt 26:39 **21:15** [k]S Ac 19:21 **21:16** [l]S Ac 8:40 [m]ver 3,4 **21:17** [n]S Ac 9:30 [o]Ac 15:4 **21:18** [p]S Ac 15:13 [q]S Ac 11:30 **21:19** [r]Ac 14:27; 15:4,12 [s]Ac 1:17 **21:20** [t]Ac 22:3; Ro 10:2; Gal 1:14; Php 3:6 [u]Ac 15:1, 5 **21:21** [v]ver 28 [w]Ac 15:19-21; 1Co 7:18,19 [x]S Ac 6:14

21:23 [y]Nu 6:2,5, 18; Ac 18:18 **21:24** [z]ver 26; Ac 24:18 [a]Ac 18:18 **21:25** [b]Ac 15:20, 29 **21:26** [c]Nu 6:13-20; Ac 24:18 **21:27** [d]Jer 26:8; Ac 24:18; 26:21; S 1Th 2:16 **21:28** [e]Mt 24:15; Ac 6:13; 24:5,6 **21:29** [f]Ac 20:4; 2Ti 4:20 [g]S Ac 18:19 **21:30** [h]Ac 26:21 [i]S Ac 16:19

---

of God's Word and not on the mere basis of a "prophecy." The NT prophetic utterances involved primarily strengthening, encouragement, comfort (1Co 14:3) and, frequently, guidance in mission (see 16:6, note).

21:13 THEN PAUL ANSWERED. The will of the majority or even the unanimous wish of genuine caring believers is not necessarily God's will. Paul was not indifferent to the pleas and tears of his friends; still, he could not change his resolute purpose to be willing to suffer imprisonment and even to die for the name of the Lord Jesus.

21:14 THE LORD'S WILL BE DONE. Many disciples (v. 4), as well as the prophet Agabus (v. 11), prophesied of the suffering that would come to Paul if he went to Jerusalem. These Christians interpreted the prophetic word as a personal directive to Paul that he should not go to Jerusalem (vv. 4,12). Paul, although recognizing the truth of the revelation (v. 11), did not accept the disciples' sincere interpretation of the revealed prophecy (v. 13). He relied on the personal guidance of the Holy Spirit and God's Word to him personally for such an important decision (23:11; see 21:4, note). In regard to future ministry, one ought to wait on a personal word from God, not just the word of others.

21:20 BELIEVED, AND ALL OF THEM ARE ZEALOUS FOR THE LAW. James and Paul both knew that Jewish ceremonies could not bring salvation (cf. 15:13–21; Gal 2:15–21). But they did recognize that some parts of the law and Jewish custom could be followed as an expression of the believer's faith in and love for Christ. The Jewish believers had genuinely accepted Christ and been regenerated by and filled with the Spirit. Their zeal for the law and customs came not from an attitude of legalism, but from hearts dedicated to Christ and loyal to God's ways (see Mt 7:6).

some officers and soldiers and ran down
to the crowd. When the rioters saw the
commander and his soldiers, they stopped
beating Paul.[j]
33The commander came up and arrested him and ordered him to be bound[k] with
two[l] chains.[m] Then he asked who he was
and what he had done. 34Some in the
crowd shouted one thing and some another,[n] and since the commander could not
get at the truth because of the uproar, he
ordered that Paul be taken into the barracks.[o] 35When Paul reached the steps,[p]
the violence of the mob was so great he
had to be carried by the soldiers. 36The
crowd that followed kept shouting, "Away
with him!"[q]

Paul Speaks to the Crowd

22:3–16pp — Ac 9:1–22; 26:9–18

37As the soldiers were about to take
Paul into the barracks,[r] he asked the
commander, "May I say something to
you?"
"Do you speak Greek?" he replied.
38"Aren't you the Egyptian who started a
revolt and led four thousand terrorists out
into the desert[s] some time ago?"[t]
39Paul answered, "I am a Jew, from Tarsus[u] in Cilicia,[v] a citizen of no ordinary
city. Please let me speak to the people."
40Having received the commander's
permission, Paul stood on the steps and
motioned[w] to the crowd. When they were
all silent, he said to them in Aramaic[r]:[x]

22 1"Brothers and fathers,[y] listen
now to my defense."
2When they heard him speak to them in
Aramaic,[z] they became very quiet.
Then Paul said: 3"I am a Jew,[a] born in
Tarsus[b] of Cilicia,[c] but brought up in this
city. Under[d] Gamaliel[e] I was thoroughly
trained in the law of our fathers[f] and was
just as zealous[g] for God as any of you are
today. 4I persecuted[h] the followers of this
Way[i] to their death, arresting both men
and women and throwing them into prison,[j] 5as also the high priest and all the
Council[k] can testify. I even obtained letters from them to their brothers[l] in Damascus,[m] and went there to bring these
people as prisoners to Jerusalem to be
punished.
6"About noon as I came near Damascus, suddenly a bright light from heaven
flashed around me.[n] 7I fell to the ground
and heard a voice say to me, 'Saul! Saul!
Why do you persecute me?'
8" 'Who are you, Lord?' I asked.
" 'I am Jesus of Nazareth,[o] whom you
are persecuting,' he replied. 9My companions saw the light,[p] but they did not understand the voice[q] of him who was
speaking to me.
10" 'What shall I do, Lord?' I asked.
" 'Get up,' the Lord said, 'and go into
Damascus. There you will be told all that
you have been assigned to do.'[r] 11My
companions led me by the hand into Damascus, because the brilliance of the light
had blinded me.[s]
12"A man named Ananias came to see
me.[t] He was a devout observer of the law
and highly respected by all the Jews living
there.[u] 13He stood beside me and said,
'Brother Saul, receive your sight!' And at
that very moment I was able to see him.
14"Then he said: 'The God of our fathers[v] has chosen you to know his will
and to see[w] the Righteous One[x] and to
hear words from his mouth. 15You will be
his witness[y] to all men of what you have
seen[z] and heard. 16And now what are you

21:32 j Ac 23:27
21:33 k ver 11
l Ac 12:6
m Ac 20:23; 22:29; Eph 6:20; 2Ti 2:9
21:34 n Ac 19:32
o ver 37; Ac 22:24; 23:10,16,32
21:35 p ver 40
21:36 q Lk 23:18; Jn 19:15; Ac 22:22
21:37 r S ver 34
21:38 s Mt 24:26
t Ac 5:36
21:39 u S Ac 9:11
v S Ac 6:9
21:40
w S Ac 12:17
x S Jn 5:2
22:1 y Ac 7:2
22:2 z Ac 21:40; S Jn 5:2
22:3 a Ac 21:39
b S Ac 9:11
c S Ac 6:9
d Lk 10:39
e Ac 5:34
f Ac 26:5
g 1Ki 19:10; S Ac 21:20
22:4 h S Ac 8:3
i S Ac 9:2 j ver 19, 20
22:5 k Lk 22:66
l S Ac 1:16; 2:29; 13:26; 23:1; 28:17,21; S Ro 7:1; 9:3
m Ac 9:2
22:6 n Ac 9:3
22:8 o S Mk 1:24
22:9 p Ac 26:13
q Ac 9:7
22:10 r Ac 16:30
22:11 s Ac 9:8
22:12 t Ac 9:17
u Ac 10:22
22:14 v S Ac 3:13
w S 1Co 15:8
x Ac 7:52
22:15 y Ac 23:11; 26:16 z ver 14

r 40 Or possibly *Hebrew*; also in 22:2

22:16 BE BAPTIZED. Water baptism accompanied the proclamation of the gospel from the beginning of the church's mission (2:38,41). It was a rite of Christian initiation used in the NT to indicate that a person was committing himself or herself fully to Jesus Christ. By going into the baptismal water in the name of the Trinity (Mt 28:19) or of Christ (19:5), believers visibly demonstrated their faith before the Christian community.

(1) Water baptism "into Christ" (Gal 3:27) or "in the name of Jesus Christ" (2:38; cf. Mt 28:19) signifies that one now is the property of Christ and has a share in his life, his Spirit and his inheritance with God (Ro 8:14–17; Gal 3:26—4:7).

(2) Water baptism is a response to what Christ has done for the believer. To be valid, it must be preceded by repentance (2:38) and a personal faith in Christ (Col 2:12).

(3) Water baptism, when undertaken with a sincere heart of faith and commitment to Jesus as Lord and Savior, is a means of receiving grace from Christ (cf. 1Pe 3:21; see article on FAITH AND GRACE, p. 302).

(4) Water baptism is an outward sign and testimony of our receiving Christ as Lord and Savior and of the washing away of our sins (cf. 2:38; Tit 3:5; 1Pe 3:21).

(5) Water baptism portrays the union of the believer with Christ in his death, burial and resurrection (Ro 6:1–11; Col 2:11–12). This signifies an end (i.e., "death") to a life of sin (Ro 6:3–4,7,10,12; Col 3:3–14) and the beginning of a new life in Christ (Ro 6:4–5,11; Col 2:12–13). Therefore, water baptism involves a commitment to a lifelong practice of turning one's back on the world and all that is evil (Ro 6:6,11–13) and living a new life in the Spirit that reflects God's standards of righteousness (Col 2:1–17).

waiting for? Get up, be baptized[a] and
wash your sins away,[b] calling on his
name.'[c]
17"When I returned to Jerusalem[d] and
was praying at the temple, I fell into a
trance[e] 18and saw the Lord speaking.
'Quick!' he said to me. 'Leave Jerusalem
immediately, because they will not accept
your testimony about me.'
19" 'Lord,' I replied, 'these men know
that I went from one synagogue to another
to imprison[f] and beat[g] those who believe
in you. 20And when the blood of your martyr[s] Stephen was shed, I stood there giving my approval and guarding the clothes
of those who were killing him.'[h]
21"Then the Lord said to me, 'Go; I will
send you far away to the Gentiles.' "[i]

Paul the Roman Citizen

22The crowd listened to Paul until he
said this. Then they raised their voices
and shouted, "Rid the earth of him![j] He's
not fit to live!"[k]
23As they were shouting and throwing
off their cloaks[l] and flinging dust into the
air,[m] 24the commander ordered Paul to be
taken into the barracks.[n] He directed[o]
that he be flogged and questioned in order
to find out why the people were shouting
at him like this. 25As they stretched him
out to flog him, Paul said to the centurion
standing there, "Is it legal for you to flog
a Roman citizen who hasn't even been
found guilty?"[p]
26When the centurion heard this, he
went to the commander and reported it.
"What are you going to do?" he asked.
"This man is a Roman citizen."
27The commander went to Paul and
asked, "Tell me, are you a Roman citizen?"
"Yes, I am," he answered.
28Then the commander said, "I had to
pay a big price for my citizenship."
"But I was born a citizen," Paul replied.
29Those who were about to question
him[q] withdrew immediately. The commander himself was alarmed when he realized that he had put Paul, a Roman citizen,[r] in chains.[s]

Before the Sanhedrin

30The next day, since the commander
wanted to find out exactly why Paul was
being accused by the Jews,[t] he released
him[u] and ordered the chief priests and all
the Sanhedrin[v] to assemble. Then he
brought Paul and had him stand before
them.

23 Paul looked straight at the Sanhedrin[w] and said, "My brothers,[x] I
have fulfilled my duty to God in all good
conscience[y] to this day." 2At this the high
priest Ananias[z] ordered those standing
near Paul to strike him on the mouth.[a]
3Then Paul said to him, "God will strike
you, you whitewashed wall![b] You sit there
to judge me according to the law, yet you
yourself violate the law by commanding
that I be struck!"[c]
4Those who were standing near Paul
said, "You dare to insult God's high
priest?"
5Paul replied, "Brothers, I did not realize that he was the high priest; for it is
written: 'Do not speak evil about the ruler
of your people.'[t]"[d]
6Then Paul, knowing that some of them
were Sadducees[e] and the others Pharisees, called out in the Sanhedrin, "My
brothers,[f] I am a Pharisee,[g] the son of a
Pharisee. I stand on trial because of my
hope in the resurrection of the dead."[h]
7When he said this, a dispute broke out
between the Pharisees and the Sadducees, and the assembly was divided. 8(The
Sadducees say that there is no resurrec-

[s] *20* Or *witness* [t] *5* Exodus 22:28

22:16 [a] S Ac 2:38 [b] Lev 8:6; Ps 51:2; Eze 36:25; Jn 3:5; 1Co 6:11; Eph 5:26; Tit 3:5; Heb 10:22; 1Pe 3:21 [c] Ro 10:13 **22:17** [d] Ac 9:26 [e] Ac 10:10 **22:19** [f] ver 4; S Ac 8:3 [g] S Mt 10:17 **22:20** [h] Ac 7:57-60; 8:1 **22:21** [i] S Ac 9:15; S 13:46 **22:22** [j] Ac 21:36 [k] Ac 25:24 **22:23** [l] Ac 7:58 [m] 2Sa 16:13 **22:24** [n] S Ac 21:34 [o] ver 29 **22:25** [p] Ac 16:37 **22:29** [q] ver 24 [r] ver 24,25; Ac 16:38 [s] S Ac 21:33 **22:30** [t] Ac 23:28 [u] Ac 21:33 [v] S Mt 5:22 **23:1** [w] Ac 22:30 [x] S Ac 22:5 [y] Ac 24:16; 1Co 4:4; 2Co 1:12; 1Ti 1:5,19; 3:9; 2Ti 1:3; Heb 9:14; 10:22; 13:18; 1Pe 3:16,21 **23:2** [z] Ac 24:1 [a] Jn 18:22 **23:3** [b] Mt 23:27 [c] Lev 19:15; Dt 25:1,2; Jn 7:51 **23:5** [d] Ex 22:28 **23:6** [e] ver 7,8; S Ac 4:1 [f] S Ac 22:5 [g] Ac 26:5; Php 3:5 [h] Ac 24:15,21; 26:8

22:16 WASH YOUR SINS AWAY. Paul was converted and saved on the Damascus road (see 9:5, note). His baptism was his public testimony of forgiveness and commitment to forsake all sin and identify himself with the cause of Christ.

22:17 I FELL INTO A TRANCE. The term "trance" here denotes a state of mind where one's attention is primarily aware of the realm of the Spirit rather than that of the natural. At such times one is especially receptive to revelation from God. It means being brought by the Spirit into a deeper and more intense communion with God (see Peter's trance in 10:10 and 11:5; cf. 2Co 12:3–4).

23:1 IN ALL GOOD CONSCIENCE. The conscience is an inner awareness that witnesses to our personality concerning the rightness or wrongness of our actions. A "good conscience" gives the verdict that we have not offended God or his will. Paul's claim (probably referring to his public life before other humans) is sincere; note Php 3:6, where he states, "as for legalistic righteousness, faultless." Before his conversion he even believed he was doing God's will in persecuting believers (26:9).

Paul's commitment to God, his intense resolve to please him, and his "faultless" life even before his conversion to Christ shame and condemn professed believers who excuse their unfaithfulness to Christ by claiming that everyone sins and that it is impossible to live before God with a good conscience.

tion,[i] and that there are neither angels
nor spirits, but the Pharisees acknowledge them all.)
9There was a great uproar, and some of
the teachers of the law who were Pharisees[j] stood up and argued vigorously.
"We find nothing wrong with this man,"[k]
they said. "What if a spirit or an angel has
spoken to him?"[l] **10**The dispute became
so violent that the commander was afraid
Paul would be torn to pieces by them. He
ordered the troops to go down and take
him away from them by force and bring
him into the barracks.[m]
11The following night the Lord stood
near Paul and said, "Take courage![n] As
you have testified about me in Jerusalem,
so you must also testify in Rome."[o]

The Plot to Kill Paul

12The next morning the Jews formed a
conspiracy[p] and bound themselves with
an oath not to eat or drink until they had
killed Paul.[q] **13**More than forty men were
involved in this plot. **14**They went to the
chief priests and elders and said, "We
have taken a solemn oath not to eat anything until we have killed Paul.[r] **15**Now
then, you and the Sanhedrin[s] petition the
commander to bring him before you on the
pretext of wanting more accurate information about his case. We are ready to kill
him before he gets here."
16But when the son of Paul's sister
heard of this plot, he went into the barracks[t] and told Paul.
17Then Paul called one of the centurions and said, "Take this young man to the
commander; he has something to tell
him." **18**So he took him to the commander.
The centurion said, "Paul, the prisoner,[u] sent for me and asked me to bring
this young man to you because he has
something to tell you."
19The commander took the young man
by the hand, drew him aside and asked,
"What is it you want to tell me?"
20He said: "The Jews have agreed to
ask you to bring Paul before the Sanhedrin[v] tomorrow on the pretext of wanting
more accurate information about him.[w]
21Don't give in to them, because more
than forty[x] of them are waiting in ambush
for him. They have taken an oath not to
eat or drink until they have killed him.[y]
They are ready now, waiting for your consent to their request."
22The commander dismissed the young
man and cautioned him, "Don't tell anyone that you have reported this to me."

Paul Transferred to Caesarea

23Then he called two of his centurions
and ordered them, "Get ready a detachment of two hundred soldiers, seventy
horsemen and two hundred spearmen[u] to
go to Caesarea[z] at nine tonight.[a] **24**Provide mounts for Paul so that he may be
taken safely to Governor Felix."[b]
25He wrote a letter as follows:

26Claudius Lysias,

To His Excellency,[c] Governor Felix:
Greetings.[d]

27This man was seized by the
Jews and they were about to kill
him,[e] but I came with my troops and
rescued him,[f] for I had learned that
he is a Roman citizen.[g] **28**I wanted
to know why they were accusing
him, so I brought him to their Sanhedrin.[h] **29**I found that the accusation
had to do with questions about their
law,[i] but there was no charge
against him[j] that deserved death or
imprisonment. **30**When I was informed[k] of a plot[l] to be carried out
against the man, I sent him to you
at once. I also ordered his accusers[m]
to present to you their case against
him.

31So the soldiers, carrying out their orders, took Paul with them during the night
and brought him as far as Antipatris.
32The next day they let the cavalry[n] go on
with him, while they returned to the barracks.[o] **33**When the cavalry[p] arrived in
Caesarea,[q] they delivered the letter to the
governor[r] and handed Paul over to him.
34The governor read the letter and asked
what province he was from. Learning that
he was from Cilicia,[s] **35**he said, "I will
hear your case when your accusers[t] get

23:8 [i]Mt 22:23; 1Co 15:12
23:9 [j]Mk 2:16 [k]ver 29; Jer 26:16; S Lk 23:4; Ac 25:25; 26:31; 28:18 [l]Ac 22:7,17, 18
23:10 [m]S Ac 21:34
23:11 [n]S Mt 14:27 [o]Ac 19:21; 28:23
23:12 [p]S Ac 20:3 [q]ver 14,21,30; Ac 25:3
23:14 [r]ver 12
23:15 [s]ver 1; Ac 22:30
23:16 [t]ver 10; S Ac 21:34
23:18 [u]S Eph 3:1
23:20 [v]ver 1 [w]ver 14,15
23:21 [x]ver 13 [y]ver 12,14
23:23 [z]S Ac 8:40 [a]ver 33
23:24 [b]ver 26,33; Ac 24:1-3,10; 25:14
23:26 [c]Lk 1:3; Ac 24:3; 26:25 [d]Ac 15:23
23:27 [e]Ac 21:32 [f]Ac 21:33 [g]Ac 22:25-29
23:28 [h]Ac 22:30
23:29 [i]Ac 18:15; 25:19 [j]S ver 9
23:30 [k]ver 20,21 [l]S Ac 20:3 [m]ver 35; Ac 24:19; 25:16
23:32 [n]ver 23 [o]S Ac 21:34
23:33 [p]ver 23,24 [q]S Ac 8:40 [r]ver 26
23:34 [s]S Ac 6:9; 21:39
23:35 [t]ver 30; Ac 24:19; 25:16

[u] *23* The meaning of the Greek for this word is uncertain.

23:11 THE LORD STOOD NEAR PAUL. Paul is anxious and apprehensive about what will happen to him. It appears that he might be killed in Jerusalem and that his plans to carry the gospel to Rome and further west might never be realized. God appears to him at this critical time, encourages his heart and assures him that he will witness for God's cause in Rome. Scripture records that the Lord appeared to Paul three times in order to reassure him (18:9–10; 22:17–18; 23:11; see 18:10, note).

here." Then he ordered that Paul be kept
under guard[u] in Herod's palace.

The Trial Before Felix

24 Five days later the high priest Ananias[v] went down to Caesarea
with some of the elders and a lawyer
named Tertullus, and they brought their
charges[w] against Paul before the governor.[x] **2**When Paul was called in, Tertullus
presented his case before Felix: "We have
enjoyed a long period of peace under you,
and your foresight has brought about reforms in this nation. **3**Everywhere and in
every way, most excellent[y] Felix, we acknowledge this with profound gratitude.
4But in order not to weary you further, I
would request that you be kind enough to
hear us briefly.

5"We have found this man to be a trou-
blemaker, stirring up riots[z] among the
Jews[a] all over the world. He is a ringleader of the Nazarene[b] sect[c] **6**and even tried
to desecrate the temple;[d] so we seized
him. **8**By▼ examining him yourself you will
be able to learn the truth about all these
charges we are bringing against him."

9The Jews joined in the accusation,[e]
asserting that these things were true.

10When the governor[f] motioned for
him to speak, Paul replied: "I know that
for a number of years you have been a
judge over this nation; so I gladly make
my defense. **11**You can easily verify that
no more than twelve days[g] ago I went up
to Jerusalem to worship. **12**My accusers
did not find me arguing with anyone at the
temple,[h] or stirring up a crowd[i] in the
synagogues or anywhere else in the city.
13And they cannot prove to you the
charges they are now making against
me.[j] **14**However, I admit that I worship
the God of our fathers[k] as a follower of
the Way,[l] which they call a sect.[m] I believe everything that agrees with the Law
and that is written in the Prophets,[n]
15and I have the same hope in God as
these men, that there will be a resurrection[o] of both the righteous and the wicked.[p] **16**So I strive always to keep my conscience clear[q] before God and man.

17"After an absence of several years, I
came to Jerusalem to bring my people
gifts for the poor[r] and to present offerings. **18**I was ceremonially clean[s] when
they found me in the temple courts doing
this. There was no crowd with me, nor
was I involved in any disturbance.[t] **19**But
there are some Jews from the province of
Asia,[u] who ought to be here before you
and bring charges if they have anything
against me.[v] **20**Or these who are here
should state what crime they found in me
when I stood before the Sanhedrin—
21unless it was this one thing I shouted as
I stood in their presence: 'It is concerning
the resurrection of the dead that I am on
trial before you today.' "[w]

22Then Felix, who was well acquainted
with the Way,[x] adjourned the proceed-
ings. "When Lysias the commander
comes," he said, "I will decide your case."
23He ordered the centurion to keep Paul

23:35 [u]Ac 24:27 **24:1** [v]Ac 23:2 [w]Ac 23:30,35 [x]S Ac 23:24 **24:3** [y]Lk 1:3; Ac 23:26; 26:25 **24:5** [z]Ac 16:20; 17:6 [a]Ac 21:28 [b]S Mk 1:24 [c]ver 14; Ac 26:5; 28:22 **24:6** [d]Ac 21:28 **24:9** [e]S 1Th 2:16 **24:10** [f]S Ac 23:24 **24:11** [g]Ac 21:27; ver 1 **24:12** [h]Ac 25:8; 28:17 [i]ver 18
24:13 [j]Ac 25:7 **24:14** [k]S Ac 3:13 [l]S Ac 9:2 [m]S ver 5 [n]Ac 26:6,22; 28:23 **24:15** [o]Ac 23:6; 28:20 [p]S Mt 25:46 **24:16** [q]S Ac 23:1 **24:17** [r]Ac 11:29, 30; Ro 15:25-28, 31; 1Co 16:1-4,15; 2Co 8:1-4; Gal 2:10 **24:18** [s]Ac 21:26 [t]ver 12 **24:19** [u]S Ac 2:9 [v]Ac 23:30 **24:21** [w]Ac 23:6 **24:22** [x]S Ac 9:2

▼ *6-8* Some manuscripts *him and wanted to judge him according to our law. [7]But the commander, Lysias, came and with the use of much force snatched him from our hands [8]and ordered his accusers to come before you. By*

24:14 THE WAY. The salvation provided by Christ is called "the Way" (cf. 9:2; 16:17; 19:9,23; 24:14,22). The Greek word used here (*hodos*) denotes a path or road. The NT believer saw salvation in Christ not only as an experience to receive but also as a road to walk in faith and fellowship with Jesus. We must walk that road to the end in order to enter the final salvation of the age to come (see article on BIBLICAL WORDS FOR SALVATION, p. 292).

24:14 I BELIEVE EVERYTHING . . . WRITTEN. Paul's faith in the holy Scriptures as inerrant, infallible and trustworthy in all things lies in sharp contrast to many religious teachers of these last days who claim to believe only "some things" written in the Law and the Prophets (see article on THE INSPIRATION AND AUTHORITY OF SCRIPTURE, p. 474). Those who are of the spirit and mind of Christ (Mt 5:18) and of the apostles (2Ti 3:16; 1Pe 1:11) will believe and defend "everything" written in the Word of God. Those who are not of this mind will disagree with the words of the great apostle.

24:15 RESURRECTION OF BOTH THE RIGHTEOUS AND THE WICKED. The Bible teaches a resurrection of both the unrighteous and the righteous dead. The righteous will be resurrected to live forever in their redeemed bodies with the Lord (1Th 4:13–18), while the unrighteous will rise to be judged by God (for the two resurrections, see Da 12:2; Jn 5:28–29; Rev 20:12–15). The fact that both resurrections are mentioned in the same verse does not necessarily mean that both occur simultaneously (see Jn 5:29, note).

24:16 KEEP MY CONSCIENCE CLEAR. A clear conscience is listed in Scripture as one of our essential weapons for a successful spiritual life and ministry (2Co 1:12; 1Ti 1:19). (1) A good conscience involves an inner freedom of spirit that comes when we know that God is not offended by our thoughts and actions (see 23:1, note; Ps 32:1; 1Ti 1:5; 1Pe 3:16; 1Jn 3:21–22). (2) When a good conscience is corrupted, one's faith, prayer life, communion with God and life of good deeds are seriously damaged (Tit 1:15–16); if people reject a good conscience, that will lead to shipwreck of their faith (1Ti 1:19).

under guard[y] but to give him some freedom[z] and permit his friends to take care
of his needs.[a]
24Several days later Felix came with
his wife Drusilla, who was a Jewess. He
sent for Paul and listened to him as he
spoke about faith in Christ Jesus.[b] **25**As
Paul discoursed on righteousness, self-
control[c] and the judgment[d] to come, Felix was afraid[e] and said, "That's enough
for now! You may leave. When I find it
convenient, I will send for you." **26**At the
same time he was hoping that Paul would
offer him a bribe, so he sent for him frequently and talked with him.
27When two years had passed, Felix
was succeeded by Porcius Festus,[f] but
because Felix wanted to grant a favor to
the Jews,[g] he left Paul in prison.[h]

The Trial Before Festus

25 Three days after arriving in the
province, Festus[i] went up from
Caesarea[j] to Jerusalem, **2**where the chief
priests and Jewish leaders appeared before him and presented the charges
against Paul.[k] **3**They urgently requested
Festus, as a favor to them, to have Paul
transferred to Jerusalem, for they were
preparing an ambush to kill him along the
way.[l] **4**Festus answered, "Paul is being
held[m] at Caesarea,[n] and I myself am going there soon. **5**Let some of your leaders
come with me and press charges against
the man there, if he has done anything
wrong."
6After spending eight or ten days with
them, he went down to Caesarea, and the
next day he convened the court[o] and ordered that Paul be brought before him.[p]
7When Paul appeared, the Jews who had
come down from Jerusalem stood around
him, bringing many serious charges
against him,[q] which they could not
prove.[r]
8Then Paul made his defense: "I have
done nothing wrong against the law of the
Jews or against the temple[s] or against
Caesar."
9Festus, wishing to do the Jews a favor,[t] said to Paul, "Are you willing to go
up to Jerusalem and stand trial before me
there on these charges?"[u]
10Paul answered: "I am now standing
before Caesar's court, where I ought to be
tried. I have not done any wrong to the
Jews,[v] as you yourself know very well.
11If, however, I am guilty of doing anything deserving death, I do not refuse to
die. But if the charges brought against me
by these Jews are not true, no one has the
right to hand me over to them. I appeal to
Caesar!"[w]
12After Festus had conferred with his
council, he declared: "You have appealed
to Caesar. To Caesar you will go!"

Festus Consults King Agrippa

13A few days later King Agrippa and
Bernice arrived at Caesarea[x] to pay their
respects to Festus. **14**Since they were
spending many days there, Festus discussed Paul's case with the king. He said:
"There is a man here whom Felix left as
a prisoner.[y] **15**When I went to Jerusalem,
the chief priests and elders of the Jews
brought charges against him[z] and asked
that he be condemned.
16"I told them that it is not the Roman
custom to hand over any man before he
has faced his accusers and has had an
opportunity to defend himself against
their charges.[a] **17**When they came here
with me, I did not delay the case, but convened the court the next day and ordered
the man to be brought in.[b] **18**When his
accusers got up to speak, they did not
charge him with any of the crimes I had
expected. **19**Instead, they had some points
of dispute[c] with him about their own religion[d] and about a dead man named Jesus
who Paul claimed was alive. **20**I was at a

24:23 [y]Ac 23:35 [z]Ac 28:16 [a]Ac 23:16; 27:3
24:24 [b]S Ac 20:21
24:25 [c]Gal 5:23; 1Th 5:6; 1Pe 4:7; 5:8; 2Pe 1:6 [d]Ac 10:42 [e]Jer 36:16
24:27 [f]Ac 25:1,4,9,14 [g]Ac 12:3; 25:9 [h]Ac 23:35; 25:14
25:1 [i]S Ac 24:27 [j]S Ac 8:40
25:2 [k]ver 15; Ac 24:1
25:3 [l]S Ac 20:3
25:4 [m]Ac 24:23 [n]S Ac 8:40
25:6 [o]ver 17 [p]ver 10
25:7 [q]Mk 15:3; Lk 23:2,10; Ac 24:5,6 [r]Ac 24:13
25:8 [s]Ac 6:13; 24:12; 28:17
25:9 [t]Ac 24:27; 12:3 [u]ver 20
25:10 [v]ver 8
25:11 [w]ver 21, 25; Ac 26:32; 28:19
25:13 [x]S Ac 8:40
25:14 [y]Ac 24:27
25:15 [z]ver 2; Ac 24:1
25:16 [a]ver 4,5; Ac 23:30
25:17 [b]ver 6,10
25:19 [c]Ac 18:15; 23:29 [d]Ac 17:22

24:25 RIGHTEOUSNESS, SELF-CONTROL AND THE JUDGMENT TO COME. As Paul speaks before Felix about faith in Jesus Christ, preaching about "righteousness, self-control and the judgment to come," Felix becomes frightened. This corresponds to Jesus' words that when the Holy Spirit comes, he "will convict the world of guilt in regard to sin and righteousness and judgment" (Jn 16:8). The salvation of all people depends on the faithful proclamation of those solemn truths by which the Spirit produces conviction in the sinner (see Jn 16:8, note).

25:8 AGAINST THE LAW OF THE JEWS. Paul knows of no offense that he has committed against the Jews or the law. Paul indeed kept the moral law of the OT (cf. 21:24). He knew that the law's standards never change, any more than God himself does. To him, the law is holy, good and spiritual (Ro 7:12,14), expressing God's character and requirement for a righteous life (cf. Mt 5:18–19). Yet Paul did not keep the law as a set of codes or standards by which to make himself righteous. A righteous life requires the work of the Holy Spirit; only after we are regenerated through the grace of Christ can we successfully obey God's law as an expression of our desire to please God. We are never without God's law when we are under Christ's law (1Co 9:21; see Mt 5:17, note; Ro 3:21; 8:4).

loss how to investigate such matters; so I asked if he would be willing to go to Jerusalem and stand trial there on these charges.[e] **21**When Paul made his appeal to be held over for the Emperor's decision, I ordered him held until I could send him to Caesar."[f]

22Then Agrippa said to Festus, "I would like to hear this man myself."

He replied, "Tomorrow you will hear him."[g]

Paul Before Agrippa

26:12–18pp — Ac 9:3–8; 22:6–11

23The next day Agrippa and Bernice[h] came with great pomp and entered the audience room with the high ranking officers and the leading men of the city. At the command of Festus, Paul was brought in. **24**Festus said: "King Agrippa, and all who are present with us, you see this man! The whole Jewish community[i] has petitioned me about him in Jerusalem and here in Caesarea, shouting that he ought not to live any longer.[j] **25**I found he had done nothing deserving of death,[k] but because he made his appeal to the Emperor[l] I decided to send him to Rome. **26**But I have nothing definite to write to His Majesty about him. Therefore I have brought him before all of you, and especially before you, King Agrippa, so that as a result of this investigation I may have something to write. **27**For I think it is unreasonable to send on a prisoner without specifying the charges against him."

26 Then Agrippa said to Paul, "You have permission to speak for yourself."[m]

So Paul motioned with his hand[n] and began his defense: **2**"King Agrippa, I consider myself fortunate to stand before you[o] today as I make my defense against all the accusations of the Jews,[p] **3**and especially so because you are well acquainted with all the Jewish customs[q] and controversies.[r] Therefore, I beg you to listen to me patiently.

4"The Jews all know the way I have lived ever since I was a child,[s] from the beginning of my life in my own country, and also in Jerusalem. **5**They have known me for a long time[t] and can testify, if they are willing, that according to the strictest sect[u] of our religion, I lived as a Pharisee.[v] **6**And now it is because of my hope[w] in what God has promised our fathers[x] that I am on trial today. **7**This is the promise our twelve tribes[y] are hoping to see fulfilled as they earnestly serve God day and night.[z] O king, it is because of this hope that the Jews are accusing me.[a] **8**Why should any of you consider it incredible that God raises the dead?[b]

9"I too was convinced[c] that I ought to do all that was possible to oppose[d] the name of Jesus of Nazareth.[e] **10**And that is just what I did in Jerusalem. On the authority of the chief priests I put many of the saints[f] in prison,[g] and when they were put to death, I cast my vote against them.[h] **11**Many a time I went from one synagogue to another to have them punished,[i] and I tried to force them to blaspheme. In my obsession against them, I even went to foreign cities to persecute them.

12"On one of these journeys I was going to Damascus with the authority and commission of the chief priests. **13**About noon, O king, as I was on the road, I saw a light from heaven, brighter than the sun, blazing around me and my companions. **14**We all fell to the ground, and I heard a voice[j] saying to me in Aramaic,[w][k] 'Saul, Saul, why do you persecute me? It is hard for you to kick against the goads.'

15"Then I asked, 'Who are you, Lord?'

" 'I am Jesus, whom you are persecuting,' the Lord replied. **16**'Now get up and stand on your feet.[l] I have appeared to you to appoint you as a servant and as a witness of what you have seen of me and what I will show you.[m] **17**I will rescue you[n] from your own people and from the Gentiles.[o] I am sending you to them **18**to

25:20 [e]ver 9 **25:21** [f]ver 11,12 **25:22** [g]Ac 9:15 **25:23** [h]ver 13; Ac 26:30 **25:24** [i]ver 2,3,7 [j]Ac 22:22 **25:25** [k]S Ac 23:9 [l]S ver 11 **26:1** [m]Ac 9:15; 25:22 [n]S Ac 12:17 **26:2** [o]Ps 119:46 [p]Ac 24:1,5; 25:2, 7,11 **26:3** [q]ver 7; S Ac 6:14 [r]Ac 25:19

26:4 [s]Gal 1:13, 14; Php 3:5 **26:5** [t]Ac 22:3 [u]S Ac 24:5 [v]Ac 23:6; Php 3:5 **26:6** [w]Ac 23:6; 24:15; 28:20 [x]S Ac 13:32; Ro 15:8 **26:7** [y]Jas 1:1 [z]1Th 3:10; 1Ti 5:5 [a]ver 2 **26:8** [b]Ac 23:6 **26:9** [c]1Ti 1:13 [d]Jn 16:2 [e]S Jn 15:21 **26:10** [f]S Ac 9:13 [g]S Ac 8:3; 9:2,14, 21 [h]Ac 22:20 **26:11** [i]S Mt 10:17 **26:14** [j]Ac 9:7 [k]S Jn 5:2 **26:16** [l]Eze 2:1; Da 10:11 [m]Ac 22:14,15 **26:17** [n]Jer 1:8,19 [o]S Ac 9:15; S 13:46

w *14* Or *Hebrew*

26:18 PAUL'S DIVINE COMMISSION. This verse is a classic statement of what the Lord Jesus desires from the preaching of the gospel to the lost.

(1) "Open their eyes." The lost are blinded by Satan to the reality of their lost and perishing condition and to the truth of the gospel (2Co 4:4). Only preaching Jesus Christ in the power of the Holy Spirit will open their understanding (cf. 2Co 4:5; Eph 1:18).

(2) "Turn them from . . . the power of Satan to God." Satan is the ruler of the world, and all those without Christ are under his control and enslaved to his power. Satan's spirit works in all sinners, i.e., "in those who are disobedient" (Eph 2:2). The proclamation of the gospel in the power of the Spirit will rescue men and women from the power of Satan and bring them into the kingdom of Christ (see Col 1:13; 1Pe 2:9).

(3) "That they may receive forgiveness of sins." Forgiveness comes through faith in Christ that is based on his sacrificial death on the cross.

(4) "A place among those who are sanctified by faith in me." The one who is forgiven, delivered from the dominion of sin and Satan, and indwelt by and bap-

open their eyes[p] and turn them from darkness to light,[q] and from the power of Satan to God, so that they may receive forgiveness of sins[r] and a place among those
who are sanctified by faith in me.'[s]

19"So then, King Agrippa, I was not disobedient[t] to the vision from heaven.
20First to those in Damascus,[u] then to
those in Jerusalem[v] and in all Judea, and
to the Gentiles[w] also, I preached that they
should repent[x] and turn to God and prove
their repentance by their deeds.[y] 21That
is why the Jews seized me[z] in the temple
courts and tried to kill me.[a] 22But I have
had God's help to this very day, and so I
stand here and testify to small and great
alike. I am saying nothing beyond what
the prophets and Moses said would happen[b]— 23that the Christ[x] would suffer[c]
and, as the first to rise from the dead,[d]
would proclaim light to his own people
and to the Gentiles."[e]

24At this point Festus interrupted
Paul's defense. "You are out of your
mind,[f] Paul!" he shouted. "Your great
learning[g] is driving you insane."

25"I am not insane, most excellent[h]
Festus," Paul replied. "What I am saying
is true and reasonable. 26The king is familiar with these things,[i] and I can speak
freely to him. I am convinced that none of
this has escaped his notice, because it
was not done in a corner. 27King Agrippa,
do you believe the prophets? I know you
Eph 6:19 do."

28Then Agrippa said to Paul, "Do you
think that in such a short time you can
persuade me to be a Christian?"[j]

29Paul replied, "Short time or long—I
pray God that not only you but all who are
listening to me today may become what I
am, except for these chains."[k]

30The king rose, and with him the governor and Bernice[l] and those sitting with
them. 31They left the room, and while
talking with one another, they said, "This
man is not doing anything that deserves
death or imprisonment."[m]

32Agrippa said to Festus, "This man
could have been set free[n] if he had not
appealed to Caesar."[o]

26:18 [p]Isa 35:5 [q]Ps 18:28; Isa 42:7,16; Eph 5:8; Col 1:13; 1Pe 2:9 [r]Lk 24:47; Ac 2:38 [s]S Ac 20:21,32 **26:19** [t]Isa 50:5 **26:20** [u]Ac 9:19-25 [v]Ac 9:26-29; 22:17-20 [w]S Ac 9:15; S 13:46 [x]Ac 3:19 [y]Jer 18:11; 35:15; Mt 3:8; Lk 3:8 **26:21** [z]Ac 21:27, 30 [a]Ac 21:31 **26:22** [b]S Lk 24:27,44; Ac 10:43; 24:14 **26:23** [c]S Mt 16:21 [d]1Co 15:20,23; Col 1:18; Rev 1:5 [e]S Lk 2:32 **26:24** [f]S Jn 10:20; S 1Co 4:10 [g]Jn 7:15 **26:25** [h]S Ac 23:26 **26:26** [i]ver 3 **26:28** [j]Ac 11:26 **26:29** [k]S Ac 21:33 **26:30** [l]Ac 25:23 **26:31** [m]S Ac 23:9 **26:32** [n]Ac 28:18 [o]S Ac 25:11

27:1 [p]S Ac 16:10 [q]Ac 18:2; 25:12, 25 [r]Ac 10:1 **27:2** [s]S Ac 2:9 [t]S Ac 19:29 [u]S Ac 16:9 [v]S Ac 17:1 **27:3** [w]Mt 11:21 [x]ver 43 [y]Ac 24:23; 28:16 **27:4** [z]ver 7 **27:5** [a]S Ac 6:9 [b]S Ac 2:10 **27:6** [c]Ac 28:11 [d]ver 1; Ac 18:2; 25:12,25 **27:7** [e]ver 4 [f]ver 12,13,21; Tit 1:5 **27:9** [g]Lev 16:29-31; 23:27-29; Nu 29:7 **27:10** [h]ver 21 **27:12** [i]S ver 7

Paul Sails for Rome

27 When it was decided that we[p]
would sail for Italy,[q] Paul and
some other prisoners were handed over to
a centurion named Julius, who belonged to
the Imperial Regiment.[r] 2We boarded a
ship from Adramyttium about to sail for
ports along the coast of the province of
Asia,[s] and we put out to sea. Aristarchus,[t] a Macedonian[u] from Thessalonica,[v] was with us.

3The next day we landed at Sidon;[w] and
Julius, in kindness to Paul,[x] allowed him
to go to his friends so they might provide
for his needs.[y] 4From there we put out to
sea again and passed to the lee of Cyprus
because the winds were against us.[z]
5When we had sailed across the open sea
off the coast of Cilicia[a] and Pamphylia,[b]
we landed at Myra in Lycia. 6There the
centurion found an Alexandrian ship[c]
sailing for Italy[d] and put us on board. 7We
made slow headway for many days and
had difficulty arriving off Cnidus. When
the wind did not allow us to hold our
course,[e] we sailed to the lee of Crete,[f]
opposite Salmone. 8We moved along the
coast with difficulty and came to a place
called Fair Havens, near the town of Lasea.

9Much time had been lost, and sailing
had already become dangerous because
by now it was after the Fast.[y][g] So Paul
warned them, 10"Men, I can see that our
voyage is going to be disastrous and bring
great loss to ship and cargo, and to our
own lives also."[h] 11But the centurion, instead of listening to what Paul said, followed the advice of the pilot and of the
owner of the ship. 12Since the harbor was
unsuitable to winter in, the majority decided that we should sail on, hoping to
reach Phoenix and winter there. This was
a harbor in Crete,[i] facing both southwest
and northwest.

The Storm

13When a gentle south wind began to
blow, they thought they had obtained

x *23* Or *Messiah* y *9* That is, the Day of Atonement (Yom Kippur)

tized in the Holy Spirit is set apart from the world and now lives unto God in fellowship with all those saved by faith in Christ.

26:19 I WAS NOT DISOBEDIENT. Paul's conversion to Christ occurred on his journey to Damascus. From that moment on he recognized Jesus as Lord and Savior and dedicated his life to obeying him (cf. Ro 1:5).

26:20 PROVE THEIR REPENTANCE BY THEIR DEEDS. Paul did not preach, as some do, that salvation required "only trusting in Christ and his atoning death." The NT apostles declare that no individuals will be saved in Christ unless they "repent and turn to God and prove their repentance by their deeds" (see article on FAITH AND GRACE, p. 302).

what they wanted; so they weighed anchor and sailed along the shore of Crete. **14**Before very long, a wind of hurricane force,[j] called the "northeaster," swept down from the island. **15**The ship was caught by the storm and could not head into the wind; so we gave way to it and were driven along. **16**As we passed to the lee of a small island called Cauda, we were hardly able to make the lifeboat[k] secure. **17**When the men had hoisted it aboard, they passed ropes under the ship itself to hold it together. Fearing that they would run aground[l] on the sandbars of Syrtis, they lowered the sea anchor and let the ship be driven along. **18**We took such a violent battering from the storm that the next day they began to throw the cargo overboard.[m] **19**On the third day, they threw the ship's tackle overboard with their own hands. **20**When neither sun nor stars appeared for many days and the storm continued raging, we finally gave up all hope of being saved.

21After the men had gone a long time without food, Paul stood up before them and said: "Men, you should have taken my advice[n] not to sail from Crete;[o] then you would have spared yourselves this damage and loss. **22**But now I urge you to keep up your courage,[p] because not one of you will be lost; only the ship will be destroyed. **23**Last night an angel[q] of the God whose I am and whom I serve[r] stood beside me[s] **24**and said, 'Do not be afraid, Paul. You must stand trial before Caesar;[t] and God has graciously given you the lives of all who sail with you.'[u] **25**So keep up your courage,[v] men, for I have faith in God that it will happen just as he told me.[w] **26**Nevertheless, we must run aground[x] on some island."[y]

The Shipwreck

27On the fourteenth night we were still being driven across the Adriatic[z] Sea, when about midnight the sailors sensed they were approaching land. **28**They took soundings and found that the water was a hundred and twenty feet[a] deep. A short time later they took soundings again and found it was ninety feet[b] deep. **29**Fearing that we would be dashed against the rocks, they dropped four anchors from the stern and prayed for daylight. **30**In an attempt to escape from the ship, the sailors let the lifeboat[z] down into the sea, pretending they were going to lower some anchors from the bow. **31**Then Paul said to the centurion and the soldiers, "Unless these men stay with the ship, you cannot be saved."[a] **32**So the soldiers cut the ropes that held the lifeboat and let it fall away.

33Just before dawn Paul urged them all to eat. "For the last fourteen days," he said, "you have been in constant suspense and have gone without food—you haven't eaten anything. **34**Now I urge you to take some food. You need it to survive. Not one of you will lose a single hair from his head."[b] **35**After he said this, he took some bread and gave thanks to God in front of them all. Then he broke it[c] and began to eat. **36**They were all encouraged[d] and ate some food themselves. **37**Altogether there were 276 of us on board. **38**When they had eaten as much as they wanted, they lightened the ship by throwing the grain into the sea.[e]

39When daylight came, they did not recognize the land, but they saw a bay with a sandy beach,[f] where they decided to run the ship aground if they could. **40**Cutting loose the anchors,[g] they left them in the sea and at the same time untied the ropes that held the rudders. Then they hoisted the foresail to the wind and made for the

27:14 [j]Mk 4:37
27:16 [k]ver 30
27:17 [l]ver 26,39
27:18 [m]ver 19, 38; Jnh 1:5
27:21 [n]ver 10 [o]S ver 7
27:22 [p]ver 25,36
27:23 [q]S Ac 5:19 [r]Ro 1:9 [s]Ac 18:9; 23:11; 2Ti 4:17
27:24 [t]Ac 23:11 [u]ver 44
27:25 [v]ver 22,36 [w]Ro 4:20,21
27:26 [x]ver 17,39 [y]Ac 28:1
27:30 [z]ver 16
27:31 [a]ver 24
27:34 [b]S Mt 10:30
27:35 [c]S Mt 14:19
27:36 [d]ver 22,25
27:38 [e]ver 18; Jnh 1:5
27:39 [f]Ac 28:1
27:40 [g]ver 29

[z] *27* In ancient times the name referred to an area extending well south of Italy. [a] *28* Greek *twenty orguias* (about 37 meters) [b] *28* Greek *fifteen orguias* (about 27 meters)

27:24 DO NOT BE AFRAID, PAUL. As long as God has a place and purpose for one's life on earth and that person is seeking God and following the guidance of the Holy Spirit (cf. 23:11; 24:16), the Lord will protect him or her from death. The lives of the unsaved may also be spared because of God's influence and authority to save the righteous. All of God's faithful have the right to pray, "O Lord, I am yours; I serve you; be my protector" (cf. Ps 16:1–2).

27:25 KEEP UP YOUR COURAGE. Paul is a prisoner in the ship; nevertheless, he is a free man in Christ, living free from fear in God's presence, while those who sail with him are paralyzed with terror because of this danger at sea. In this life, only the sincere and faithful believer experiencing God's nearness can face life's dangers with courage and assurance in Christ.

27:31 UNLESS THESE MEN STAY WITH THE SHIP. Paul's statement here appears inconsistent with vv. 22,24. If God promises Paul that he will spare the lives of all those sailing with him (v. 24), and Paul reports the promise without qualification that "not one of you will be lost" (v. 22), how could the desertion of the sailors cause anyone's death among the passengers? The answer is in the Biblical truth that God's promises to his people are normally conditioned on their obedience to his will (see Ge 1:26–31 and 6:5–7; Ex 3:7–8 and Nu 14:28–34; 2Sa 7:12–16 and 1Ki 11:11–13; 12:16).

beach. 41But the ship struck a sandbar and ran aground. The bow stuck fast and would not move, and the stern was broken to pieces by the pounding of the surf.[h]

42The soldiers planned to kill the prisoners to prevent any of them from swimming away and escaping. 43But the centurion wanted to spare Paul's life[i] and kept them from carrying out their plan. He ordered those who could swim to jump overboard first and get to land. 44The rest were to get there on planks or on pieces of the ship. In this way everyone reached land in safety.[j]

Ashore on Malta

28 Once safely on shore, we[k] found out that the island[l] was called Malta. 2The islanders showed us unusual kindness. They built a fire and welcomed us all because it was raining and cold. 3Paul gathered a pile of brushwood and, as he put it on the fire, a viper, driven out by the heat, fastened itself on his hand. 4When the islanders saw the snake hanging from his hand,[m] they said to each other, "This man must be a murderer; for though he escaped from the sea, Justice has not allowed him to live."[n] 5But Paul shook the snake off into the fire and suffered no ill effects.[o] 6The people expected him to swell up or suddenly fall dead, but after waiting a long time and seeing nothing unusual happen to him, they changed their minds and said he was a god.[p]

7There was an estate nearby that belonged to Publius, the chief official of the island. He welcomed us to his home and for three days entertained us hospitably. 8His father was sick in bed, suffering from fever and dysentery. Paul went in to see him and, after prayer,[q] placed his hands on him[r] and healed him.[s] 9When this had happened, the rest of the sick on the island came and were cured. 10They honored us[t] in many ways and when we were ready to sail, they furnished us with the supplies we needed.

Jas 5:14-16

Arrival at Rome

11After three months we put out to sea in a ship that had wintered in the island. It was an Alexandrian ship[u] with the figurehead of the twin gods Castor and Pollux. 12We put in at Syracuse and stayed there three days. 13From there we set sail and arrived at Rhegium. The next day the south wind came up, and on the following day we reached Puteoli. 14There we found some brothers[v] who invited us to spend a week with them. And so we came to Rome. 15The brothers[w] there had heard that we were coming, and they traveled as far as the Forum of Appius and the Three Taverns to meet us. At the sight of these men Paul thanked God and was encouraged. 16When we got to Rome, Paul was allowed to live by himself, with a soldier to guard him.[x]

Paul Preaches at Rome Under Guard

17Three days later he called together the leaders of the Jews.[y] When they had assembled, Paul said to them: "My brothers,[z] although I have done nothing against our people[a] or against the customs of our ancestors,[b] I was arrested in Jerusalem and handed over to the Romans. 18They examined me[c] and wanted to release me,[d] because I was not guilty of any crime deserving death.[e] 19But when the Jews objected, I was compelled to appeal to Caesar[f]—not that I had any charge to bring against my own people. 20For this reason I have asked to see you and talk with you. It is because of the hope of Israel[g] that I am bound with this chain."[h]

21They replied, "We have not received any letters from Judea concerning you, and none of the brothers[i] who have come from there has reported or said anything bad about you. 22But we want to hear what your views are, for we know that people everywhere are talking against this sect."[j]

23They arranged to meet Paul on a certain day, and came in even larger numbers to the place where he was staying. From morning till evening he explained and declared to them the kingdom of God[k] and tried to convince them about Jesus[l] from

27:41 [h]2Co 11:25 **27:43** [i]ver 3 **27:44** [j]ver 22,31 **28:1** [k]S Ac 16:10 [l]Ac 27:26,39 **28:4** [m]Mk 16:18 [n]Lk 13:2,4 **28:5** [o]Lk 10:19 **28:6** [p]Ac 14:11 **28:8** [q]Jas 5:14,15 [r]S Ac 6:6 [s]Ac 9:40 **28:10** [t]Ps 15:4

28:11 [u]Ac 27:6 **28:14** [v]S Ac 1:16 **28:15** [w]S Ac 1:16 **28:16** [x]Ac 24:23; 27:3 **28:17** [y]Ac 25:2 [z]S Ac 22:5 [a]S Ac 25:8 [b]S Ac 6:14 **28:18** [c]Ac 22:24 [d]Ac 26:31,32 [e]S Ac 23:9 **28:19** [f]S Ac 25:11 **28:20** [g]Ac 26:6,7 [h]S Ac 21:33 **28:21** [i]S Ac 22:5 **28:22** [j]S Ac 24:5, 14 **28:23** [k]S Mt 3:2; Ac 19:8 [l]Ac 17:3

28:5 PAUL ... SUFFERED NO ILL EFFECTS. Paul's experience remarkably illustrates Jesus' promise in Mk 16:18 (see note on that verse).

28:16 WHEN WE GOT TO ROME. It had been Paul's desire to preach the gospel in Rome (Ro 15:22–29), and it was also God's will that he do so (23:11). Yet Paul arrived in Rome in chains and only after setbacks, storms, shipwreck and many trials. Though Paul remained faithful, God did not make his way easy and trouble free. Likewise, we may be in God's will and entirely faithful to him; nevertheless, he may direct us in unpleasant paths involving troubles. Yet we can know that "in all things God works for the good of those who love him" (Ro 8:28).

the Law of Moses and from the Prophets.[m] 24Some were convinced by what he
said, but others would not believe.[n]
25They disagreed among themselves and
began to leave after Paul had made this
final statement: "The Holy Spirit spoke
the truth to your forefathers when he
said[o] through Isaiah the prophet:

26" 'Go to this people and say,
"You will be ever hearing but never
understanding;
you will be ever seeing but never
perceiving."
27For this people's heart has become
calloused;[p]
they hardly hear with their ears,
and they have closed their eyes.
Otherwise they might see with their
eyes,
hear with their ears,
understand with their hearts
and turn, and I would heal them.'[c][q]

28"Therefore I want you to know that
God's salvation[r] has been sent to the
Gentiles,[s] and they will listen!"[d]
30For two whole years Paul stayed
there in his own rented house and welcomed all who came to see him. 31Boldly[t]
and without hindrance he preached the
kingdom of God[u] and taught about the
Lord Jesus Christ.

28:23 [m]S Ac 8:35 **28:24** [n]Ac 14:4; 17:4,5 **28:25** [o]S Heb 3:7 **28:27** [p]Ps 119:70 [q]Isa 6:9,10; S Mt 13:15 **28:28** [r]Lk 2:30 [s]S Ac 13:46 **28:31** [t]S Ac 4:29 [u]ver 23; S Mt 4:23

[c] *27* Isaiah 6:9,10 [d] *28* Some manuscripts *listen!" 29After he said this, the Jews left, arguing vigorously among themselves.*

28:30 FOR TWO WHOLE YEARS PAUL STAYED THERE. Luke's history of the early church is brought to an end here. What happened to Paul afterwards is generally thought to be the following. Paul remained in confinement for two years. He was able to receive visitors and preach the gospel to them. During this time he wrote the letters to the Ephesians, Philippians, Colossians and to Philemon. In approximately A.D. 63, Paul was acquitted and released. For the next few years he continued his missionary endeavors, perhaps going to Spain as he had planned (Ro 15:28). During this period he wrote 1 Timothy and Titus. Paul was again arrested, about A.D. 67, and was taken back to Rome. He wrote 2 Timothy during this second imprisonment at Rome. Paul's imprisonment ended with his martyrdom (tradition says by beheading) under the Roman emperor Nero.

28:31 PREACHED THE KINGDOM OF GOD. The book of Acts breaks off suddenly, with no formal conclusion to what God did through the Holy Spirit and the NT apostles. God intends that the acts of the Holy Spirit and the preaching of the gospel continue in the lives of Christ's people until the end of the age (2:17–21; Mt 28:18–20). Luke, under the inspiration of the Spirit, has revealed God's pattern of what the church should be and do. He has given us examples of the faithfulness of believers, the triumph of the gospel against the opposition of the enemy and the power of the Holy Spirit operating in the church and among people. This is God's pattern for present and future churches, and we must faithfully proclaim it and live it (2Ti 1:14). All churches must measure themselves by what the Spirit said and did among the earliest believers. If the power, righteousness, joy and faith found in our churches are not the same as what we read about in Acts, then we must ask God once more for a renewed faith in the resurrected Christ and for a fresh, new outpouring of his Spirit.

ROMANS

Outline

Introduction (1:1–17)

I. Humanity's Desperate Need of Righteousness (1:18—3:20)
   - A. The Gentile's Need (1:18–32)
   - B. The Jew's Need (2:1—3:8)
   - C. The Universal Need (3:9–20)

II. God's Glorious Provision of Righteousness (3:21—5:21)
   - A. Justification by Faith Summarized (3:21–31)
   - B. Justification by Faith Illustrated in Abraham (4:1–25)
   - C. The Blessings and Assurance Accompanying Justification (5:1–11)
   - D. Adam and Christ Contrasted (5:12–21)
     1. Adam/Sin/Condemnation/Death
     2. Christ/Grace/Justification/Life

III. The Outworking of Righteousness Through Faith (6:1—8:39)
   - A. Freedom From Slavery to Sin (6:1–23)
     1. Dying With Christ to Sin (6:1–14)
     2. Living With Christ as Servants of Righteousness (6:15–23)
   - B. Freedom From the Conflict Under the Law (7:1–25)
   - C. Freedom Through the Law of the Spirit of Life (8:1–39)

IV. Righteousness Through Faith as It Relates to Israel (9:1—11:36)
   - A. The Problem of Israel's Rejection (9:1—10:21)
   - B. The Triumph of God's Plan (11:1–36)

V. Practical Applications of Righteousness Through Faith (12:1—15:13)
   - A. The Believer and Consecration (12:1–2)
   - B. The Believer and Community (12:3–21)
   - C. The Believer and the State (13:1–7)
   - D. The Believer and the Law of Love (13:8—15:13)

Conclusion (15:14—16:27)

Author: Paul

Theme: The Righteousness of God Is Revealed

Date: c. A.D. 57

Background

Romans is Paul's longest, most theological and most influential letter. Probably for these reasons it is placed first among his thirteen NT books. Paul wrote Romans in connection with his apostolic mission to the Gentile world. Contrary to Roman Catholic tradition, the church in Rome was not founded by Peter or any other apostle. The Roman church may have been established by Paul's converts from Macedonia and Asia, as well as by Jews and proselytes converted on the day of Pentecost (Ac 2:10). Paul did not regard Rome as the specific territory of another apostle (Ro 15:20).

In the book of Romans Paul assures the believers at Rome that he has often planned to preach the gospel to them but so far has been hindered from coming (1:13–15; 15:22). He affirms his earnest desire to come to them, and he communicates his plans for coming soon (15:23–32).

At the time of writing, toward the end of his third missionary journey (cf. 15:25–26; Ac 20:2–3; 1Co 16:5–6), Paul was in Corinth as a guest in the home of Gaius (Ro 16:23; 1Co 1:14). As he penned Romans through his assistant Tertius (16:22), he was planning to return to Jerusalem for the day of Pentecost (Ac 20:16; probably spring A.D. 57 or 58) and to deliver personally a relief offering from the Gentile churches for the poverty-stricken saints in Jerusalem (15:25–27). Immediately afterwards, Paul hoped to go to Spain with the gospel, visiting the church in Rome on his way and receiving assistance from them as he headed further west (15:24,28).

Purpose

Paul wrote this letter to prepare the way for his anticipated ministry at Rome and his planned mission to Spain. His purpose was twofold. (1) Since the Romans apparently had received distorted rumors about Paul's message and theology (e.g., 3:8; 6:1–2,15), he felt it necessary to put into writing the gospel he had been preaching for twenty-five years. (2) He sought to correct certain problems in the church occurring because of wrong attitudes of Jews toward Gentiles (e.g., 2:1–29; 3:1,9) and Gentiles toward Jews (e.g., 11:11–36).

Survey

The theme of Romans is presented in 1:16–17, namely, that in the Lord Jesus a righteousness from God is revealed as the answer to his wrath against sin. Then Paul sets forth the gospel's foundational truths. First, he emphasizes that the problem of sin and humanity's need of righteousness are universal (1:18—3:20). Since both Jews and Gentiles are under sin and thus under God's wrath, no person can be justified before God apart from the gift of righteousness through faith in Jesus Christ (3:21—4:25).

Having been justified freely by grace through faith and having been given assurance of our salvation (ch. 5), God's gift of righteousness is demonstrated in our death with Christ to sin (ch. 6), our deliverance from the struggle of law-righteousness (ch. 7), and our adoption as God's children and our new life "through the Spirit," leading to glorification (ch. 8). God is working out his plan of redemption in spite of Israel's unbelief (chs. 9–11).

Finally, Paul declares that a transformed life in Christ results in the application of righteousness and love to all areas of behavior—social, civil and moral (chs. 12–14). Paul concludes Romans with an explanation of his personal plans (ch. 15) and a long list of personal greetings, a final admonition and a doxology (ch. 16).

Special Features

Seven major emphases characterize Romans. (1) Romans is Paul's most systematic letter, the theological letter *par excellence* in the NT. (2) Paul writes in a question and answer, or debating, style (e.g., 3:1,4–6,9,31). (3) Paul uses the OT extensively as Scriptural authority for his presentation of the true nature of the gospel. (4) Paul presents "a righteousness from God" as the core revelation of the gospel (1:16–17): God set things right in and through Jesus Christ. (5) Paul focuses on the twofold nature of sin, along with God's provision in Christ for each aspect: (a) sin as personal transgression (1:1—5:11), and the "sin" (Gk *hē hamartia*) principle, i.e., the inherent natural tendency to sin that lives within every person's heart since Adam's fall (5:12—8:39). (6) Ro 8 is the most extensive chapter in the Bible on the role of the Holy Spirit in the life of the believer. (7) Romans contains the Bible's most powerful discussion about the Jews' rejection of Christ (except for a remnant), and about God's plan for a full-circle redemption that ultimately comes back to Israel (chs. 9–11).

Reading Romans

In order to read the entire New Testament in one year, the book of Romans should be read in 21 days, according to the following schedule:
☐ 1:1–17 ☐ 1:18–32 ☐ 2 ☐ 3 ☐ 4 ☐ 5:1–11 ☐ 5:12–21 ☐ 6:1–14 ☐ 6:15—7:6 ☐ 7:7–25 ☐ 8:1–17 ☐ 8:18–39 ☐ 9:1–29 ☐ 9:30—10:21 ☐ 11:1–24 ☐ 11:25–36 ☐ 12:1–16 ☐ 12:17—13:14 ☐ 14:1—15:4 ☐ 15:5–33 ☐ 16

NOTES

1 Paul, a servant of Christ Jesus, called
to be an apostle[a] and set apart[b] for
the gospel of God[c]— **2**the gospel he
promised beforehand[d] through his prophets[e] in the Holy Scriptures[f] **3**regarding
his Son, who as to his human nature[g] was
a descendant of David,[h] **4**and who
through the Spirit[a] of holiness was declared with power to be the Son of God[b][i]
by his resurrection from the dead:[j] Jesus
Christ our Lord.[k] **5**Through him and for
his name's sake, we received grace[l] and
apostleship to call people from among all
the Gentiles[m] to the obedience that comes
from faith.[n] **6**And you also are among
those who are called to belong to Jesus
Christ.[o]

7To all in Rome who are loved by God[p]
and called to be saints:[q]

Grace and peace to you from God our
Father and from the Lord Jesus Christ.[r]

Paul's Longing to Visit Rome

8First, I thank my God through Jesus
Christ for all of you,[s] because your faith
is being reported all over the world.[t]
9God, whom I serve[u] with my whole heart
in preaching the gospel of his Son, is my
witness[v] how constantly I remember you
10in my prayers at all times;[w] and I pray
that now at last by God's will[x] the way
may be opened for me to come to you.[y]

1:1 [a]S 1Co 1:1 [b]S Ac 9:15 [c]Ro 15:16; S 2Co 2:12; 11:7; 1Th 2:8,9; 1Pe 4:17 **1:2** [d]S Ac 13:32; Tit 1:2 [e]Lk 1:70; Ro 3:21 [f]Gal 3:8 **1:3** [g]S Jn 1:14; Ro 9:5 [h]S Mt 1:1 **1:4** [i]S Mt 4:3 [j]S Ac 2:24 [k]1Co 1:2 **1:5** [l]1Ti 1:14 [m]S Ac 9:15 [n]Ac 6:7; Ro 16:26 **1:6** [o]Jude 1; Rev 17:14 **1:7** [p]Ro 8:39; 1Th 1:4 [q]S Ac 9:13 [r]1Co 1:3; Eph 1:2; 1Ti 1:2; Tit 1:4; 1Pe 1:2 **1:8** [s]1Co 1:4; Eph 1:16; 1Th 2:13; 2Th 1:3; 2Ti 1:3 [t]S Ro 10:18; 16:19 **1:9** [u]2Ti 1:3 [v]Job 16:19; Jer 42:5; 2Co 1:23; Gal 1:20; Php 1:8; 1Th 2:5,10 **1:10** [w]1Sa 12:23; S Lk 18:1; S Ac 1:14; Eph 1:16; Php 1:4; Col 1:9; 2Th 1:11; 2Ti 1:3; Phm 4 [x]S Ac 18:21 [y]ver 13; Ro 15:32

11I long to see you[z] so that I may impart to you some spiritual gift[a] to make
you strong— **12**that is, that you and I may
be mutually encouraged by each other's
faith. **13**I do not want you to be unaware,[b]
brothers,[c] that I planned many times to
come to you (but have been prevented
from doing so until now)[d] in order that I
might have a harvest among you, just as
I have had among the other Gentiles.

14I am obligated[e] both to Greeks and
non-Greeks, both to the wise and the foolish. **15**That is why I am so eager to preach
the gospel also to you who are at Rome.[f]

16I am not ashamed of the gospel,[g] because it is the power of God[h] for the salvation of everyone who believes:[i] first for
the Jew,[j] then for the Gentile.[k] **17**For in
the gospel a righteousness from God is
revealed,[l] a righteousness that is by
faith[m] from first to last,[c] just as it is written: "The righteous will live by faith."[d][n]

Ro 12:6-8

God's Wrath Against Mankind

18The wrath of God[o] is being revealed
from heaven against all the godlessness

1:11 [z]Ro 15:23 [a]1Co 1:7; 12:1-31 **1:13** [b]S Ro 11:25 [c]S Ro 7:1 [d]Ro 15:22,23 **1:14** [e]1Co 9:16 **1:15** [f]Ro 15:20 **1:16** [g]2Ti 1:8 [h]1Co 1:18 [i]S Jn 3:15 [j]Ac 3:26; 13:46 [k]S Ac 13:46; Ro 2:9,10 **1:17** [l]Ro 3:21; Php 3:9 [m]S Ro 9:30 [n]Hab 2:4; Gal 3:11; Heb 10:38 **1:18** [o]Jn 3:36; Ro 5:9; Eph 5:6; Col 3:6; 1Th 1:10; Rev 19:15

[a] 4 Or *who as to his spirit* [b] 4 Or *was appointed to be the Son of God with power* [c] 17 Or *is from faith to faith* [d] 17 Hab. 2:4

1:4 THE SPIRIT OF HOLINESS. The "Spirit of holiness" refers to the Holy Spirit, the third person in the divine Trinity. His holiness separates him distinctly from the spirit of humanity, sin and the world, and describes both his preeminent characteristic and his work (cf. Gal 5:16–24).

1:5 OBEDIENCE THAT COMES FROM FAITH. Note that Paul, both at the beginning of the letter to the Romans and at the end (16:26), defines faith in terms of "obedience." For Paul the nature of saving faith must be determined by its initial intention, namely, a joining of one's life to God through Jesus Christ in love, devotion, gratitude and obedience (see Jas 2:17, note; cf. Jn 15:10,14; Heb 5:8–9; see article on FAITH AND GRACE, p. 302).

1:7 CALLED TO BE SAINTS. Believers have been set apart (cf. v. 1) from sin and the world, brought near to God and consecrated for service (cf. Ex 19:6; Lev 21:15; 27:30). With this action of consecration, the Spirit renews the characters of believers in true holiness (see Ac 9:13, note; cf. Eph 4:23–24).

1:16 SALVATION. For a discussion of the meaning of the word "salvation," as well as two other words the Bible uses for salvation, see article on BIBLICAL WORDS FOR SALVATION, p. 292.

1:17 BY FAITH FROM FIRST TO LAST. The righteous person continues to live by faith, and in so doing, he or she continues to live a rich spiritual life (see 8:12–13; 14:13–23; Heb 10:38, note; see article on FAITH AND GRACE, p. 302).

1:18 THE WRATH OF GOD. The wrath (Gk *orgē*) of God is an expression of his righteousness and love. It is God's personal anger and unchanging reaction to all sin (Eze 7:8–9; Eph 5:6; Rev 19:15), provoked by the wicked behavior of individuals (Ex 4:14; Nu 12:1–9; 2Sa 6:6–7) and nations (Isa 10:5; 13:3; Jer 50:13; Eze 30:15) and by the unfaithfulness of God's people (Nu 25:3; 32:10–13; Dt 29:24–28).

(1) In the past God's anger and hatred toward sin was revealed in the flood (Ge 6–8), famine and plague (Eze 6:11ff), annihilation (Dt 29:22–23), scattering (La 4:16) and burning of the land (Isa 9:18–19).

(2) In the present God's anger is seen in his giving the wicked over to uncleanness and vile passions (see v. 24, note) and in bringing ruin and death to all who disobey God (1:18—3:20; 6:23; Eze 18:4; Eph 2:3).

(3) In the future the wrath of God will include great distress for the ungodly of this world (Mt 24:21; Rev 5–19) and a coming day of judgment for all people and nations (Eze 7:19; Da 8:19)—"a day of trouble and ruin, a day of darkness and gloom" (Zep 1:15), a day of reckoning for the unrighteous (2:5; Mt 3:7; Lk 3:17; Eph 5:6; Col 3:6; Rev 11:18; 14:8–10; 19:15). Ultimately God's wrath results in eternal punishment for the unrepentant (see Mt 10:28, note).

(4) God's wrath is not his final word to humans, for he has provided a way of escape. A person may repent of sin and turn in faith to Jesus Christ (5:8; Jn 3:36;

and wickedness of men who suppress the
truth by their wickedness, **19**since what
may be known about God is plain to them,
because God has made it plain to them.[p]
20For since the creation of the world
God's invisible qualities—his eternal
power and divine nature—have been
clearly seen, being understood from what
has been made,[q] so that men are without
excuse.[r]
21For although they knew God, they
neither glorified him as God nor gave
thanks to him, but their thinking became
futile and their foolish hearts were darkened.[s] **22**Although they claimed to be
wise, they became fools[t] **23**and exchanged the glory of the immortal God for
images[u] made to look like mortal man
and birds and animals and reptiles.
24Therefore God gave them over[v] in the
sinful desires of their hearts to sexual impurity for the degrading of their bodies
with one another.[w] **25**They exchanged the
truth of God for a lie,[x] and worshiped and
served created things[y] rather than the
Creator—who is forever praised.[z]
Amen.[a]
26Because of this, God gave them over[b]
to shameful lusts.[c] Even their women exchanged natural relations for unnatural
ones.[d] **27**In the same way the men also
abandoned natural relations with women
and were inflamed with lust for one another. Men committed indecent acts with other men, and received in themselves the
due penalty for their perversion.[e]
28Furthermore, since they did not think
it worthwhile to retain the knowledge of
God, he gave them over[f] to a depraved
mind, to do what ought not to be done.
29They have become filled with every kind
of wickedness, evil, greed and depravity.
They are full of envy, murder, strife, deceit and malice. They are gossips,[g]
30slanderers, God-haters, insolent, arrogant and boastful; they invent ways of doing evil; they disobey their parents;[h]
31they are senseless, faithless, heartless,[i] ruthless. **32**Although they know
God's righteous decree that those who do

1:19 [p]Ac 14:17
1:20 [q]Ps 19:1-6 [r]Ro 2:1
1:21 [s]Ge 8:21; Jer 2:5; 17:9; Eph 4:17,18
1:22 [t]1Co 1:20, 27; 3:18,19
1:23 [u]Dt 4:16,17; Ps 106:20; Jer 2:11; Ac 17:29
1:24 [v]ver 26,28; Ps 81:12; Eph 4:19 [w]1Pe 4:3
1:25 [x]Isa 44:20 [y]Jer 10:14; 13:25; 16:19,20 [z]Ro 9:5; 2Co 11:31 [a]S Ro 11:36
1:26 [b]ver 24,28 [c]Eph 4:19; 1Th 4:5 [d]Lev 18:22,23
1:27 [e]Lev 18:22; 20:13; 1Co 6:18
1:28 [f]ver 24,26
1:29 [g]2Co 12:20; 1Ti 5:13; Jas 3:2; 3Jn 10
1:30 [h]2Ti 3:2
1:31 [i]2Ti 3:3

1Th 1:10; 5:9; see article on BIBLICAL WORDS FOR SALVATION, p. 292).

(5) Believers united to Christ must participate in God's anger against sin, not in the sense of vengeance, but in a sincere love of righteousness and hatred of wickedness (see Heb 1:9, note). The NT recognizes a holy anger that hates what God hates, an anger evident above all in Jesus himself (Mk 3:5; Jn 2:12–17; Heb 1:9; see Lk 19:45, note), in Paul (Ac 17:16) and in righteous people (2Pe 2:7–8; Rev 2:6, note).

1:21 THEY NEITHER GLORIFIED HIM. Although vv. 21–28 primarily address the downward course of depravity among the unregenerate, they also contain principles indicating why one of the major sins of fallen Christian leaders is immorality (see next note).

(1) When leaders in the church become proud (v. 22), they seek honor for themselves (v. 21) and exalt themselves (the creature) rather than the Creator (v. 25). A door is then opened within their lives to sexual impurity and shameful lusts (vv. 24,26; see 2Pe 2:2,15, notes). If they do not turn and repent, they will ultimately be given over to a depraved mind (v. 28).

(2) Such people may continue in shameful lust and sin while justifying their actions as common human weakness, persuading themselves that they are still in fellowship with the Holy Spirit and in possession of salvation. They blind themselves to the warning of Scripture that "no immoral, impure or greedy person . . . has any inheritance in the kingdom of Christ" (Eph 5:5).

1:24 GOD GAVE THEM OVER. A primary sign of God's abandonment of any society or people is that they become obsessed with sexual immorality and perversion. (1) The term "God gave them over" means that God abandoned these persons to intensified lusts. The term "sinful desires" (Gk *epithumia*) denotes a passionate lust for forbidden sexual pleasure (cf. 2Co 12:21; Gal 5:19; Eph 5:3).

(2) The three stages of abandonment to impurity are: (a) God giving them over to sinful sexual pleasures that degrade the body (v. 24); (b) God giving them over to shameful homosexual or lesbian passions (vv. 26–27); after this, (c) God giving them over to a depraved mind, i.e., their minds justify their unrighteous actions and they become continually preoccupied with evil and the pleasures of sexual sin (v. 28). These three stages occur among all people who reject the truth of God's revelation and seek pleasure in ungodliness (v. 18; see v. 27, note).

(3) God has two purposes in abandoning the unrighteous to sin: (a) to allow sin and its consequences to accelerate as part of his judgment on them (2:2), and (b) to make them realize their need for salvation (2:4).

1:25 A LIE. The "lie" is the word of Satan, the father of lies (Jn 8:44): "you will be like God" (Ge 3:5). (1) To believe the lie is to reject "the truth of God" and participate in idolatry (Ge 3:5; Col 3:5; 2Th 2:11, note). (2) Humanity's propensity to believe the lie and worship self is the reason the Bible incessantly warns against pride. "In the pride of your heart you say, 'I am a god' " (Eze 28:2; cf. Pr 6:17; 8:13; 16:18; 1Ti 3:6; Jas 4:6; 1Jn 2:16).

1:27 MEN . . . WITH OTHER MEN. The apostle likely regarded the homosexual/lesbian abomination as the greatest evidence of human degeneracy resulting from immorality and God's abandonment (see Ge 19:4–5; Lev 18:22). Any nation that justifies homosexuality or lesbianism as an acceptable lifestyle is in its final stages of moral corruption (see v. 24, note). For other Scriptures about this horrible act see Ge 19:4–9; Lev 20:13; Dt 23:17; 1Ki 14:24; 15:12; 22:46; Isa 3:9; 1Co 6:9–10; 1Ti 1:10; 2Pe 2:6; Jude 7.

1:32 APPROVE OF THOSE WHO PRACTICE THEM. Paul's last word on human sinfulness is God's condemnation of a condition even more damning than

BIBLICAL WORDS FOR SALVATION

Ro 1:16 "I am not ashamed of the gospel, because it is the power of God for the salvation of everyone who believes: first for the Jew, then for the Gentile."

God freely offers us eternal life in Jesus Christ. But understanding the exact process by which that life becomes available to us is sometimes difficult. Therefore, God paints various pictures in the Bible to help us grasp the concept, each with its own unique emphasis. This article examines three of those pictures: Salvation, Redemption and Justification.

SALVATION. Salvation (Gk *sōtēria*) means "deliverance," "bringing safely through," "keeping from harm"; it is described in the Bible as "the way" or road that leads through life to eternal fellowship with God in heaven (Mt 7:14; Mk 12:14; Jn 14:6; Ac 16:17; 2Pe 2:2,21; cf. Ac 9:2; 22:4; Heb 10:20). This road of salvation must be walked to the very end. We can describe salvation as *one* way with *two* sides and *three* stages:

(1) The one way of salvation. Christ is the way to the Father (Jn 14:6; Ac 4:12). Salvation is provided for us by God's grace, which he gives in Christ Jesus (Ro 3:24), based on his death (3:25; 5:8), resurrection (5:10) and continued intercession for believers (Heb 7:25).

(2) The two sides of salvation. Salvation is received by grace through faith in Christ (Ro 3:22,24–25,28). That is, it comes as a result of God's grace (Jn 1:16) and the human response of faith (Ac 16:31; Ro 1:17; Eph 1:15; 2:8; see article on FAITH AND GRACE, p. 302).

(3) The three stages of salvation.

(a) The past stage of salvation includes the personal experience by which we as believers receive forgiveness of sins (Ac 10:43; Ro 4:6–8) and pass from spiritual death to spiritual life (1Jn 3:14; see article on REGENERATION, p. 178), from the power of sin to the power of the Lord (Ro 6:17–23), from Satan's dominion to God's dominion (Ac 26:18). It brings us into a new personal relationship with God (Jn 1:12) and rescues us from the penalty of sin (Ro 1:16; 6:23; 1Co 1:18).

(b) The present stage of salvation saves us from the practice and dominion of sin, filling us with the Holy Spirit. It includes: (i) the privilege of a person-to-person relationship with God as our Father and Jesus as our Lord and Savior (Mt 6:9; Jn 14:18–23; see Gal 4:6, note); (ii) the call to count ourselves dead to sin (Ro 6:1–14) and to submit to the leading of the Spirit (Ro 8:1–17) and God's Word (Jn 8:31; 14:21; 2Ti 3:15–16); (iii) the invitation to be filled with the Holy Spirit and the command to keep being filled (see Ac 2:33–39; Eph 5:18; see article on BAPTISM IN THE HOLY SPIRIT, p. 228); (iv) the demand to separate ourselves from sin (Ro 6:1–14) and the present corrupt generation (Ac 2:40; 2Co 6:17); and (v) the call to fight for God's kingdom against Satan and his demonic host (2Co 10:4–5; Eph 6:11,16; 1Pe 5:8).

(c) The future stage of salvation (Ro 13:11–12; 1Th 5:8–9; 1Pe 1:5) includes: (i) our deliverance from God's coming wrath (Ro 5:9; 1Co 3:15; 5:5; 1Th 1:10; 5:9); (ii) our sharing the divine glory (Ro 8:29; 1Co 15:49) and receiving a resurrected or transformed body (1Co 15:52); and (iii) our receiving rewards as faithful overcomers (see Rev 2:7, note). This future salvation is the goal toward which all Christians strive (1Co 9:24–27; Php 3:8–14). All present warnings, discipline and punishment have as their purpose that believers should not forfeit this future salvation (1Co 5:1–13; 9:24–27; Php 2:12,16; 2Pe 1:5–11; see Heb 12:1, note).

REDEMPTION. The root meaning of "redemption" (Gk *apolutrōsis*) is a ransom by the payment of a price. The expression denotes the means by which salvation is procured, namely, by the payment of a ransom. The doctrine of redemption can be summarized as follows:

(1) The state of sin out of which we must be redeemed: The NT represents humans as alienated from God (Ro 3:10–18), under the dominion of satanic powers (Ac 10:38; 26:18), slaves to sin (Ro 6:6; 7:14), and in need of deliverance from sin's guilt, punishment and power (Ac 26:18; Ro 1:18; 6:1–18,23; Eph 5:8; Col 1:13; 1Pe 2:9).

(2) The price paid to free us from this bondage: Christ secured the ransom by shedding his blood and giving his life (Mt 20:28; Mk 10:45; 1Co 6:20; Eph 1:7; Tit 2:14; Heb 9:12; 1Pe 1:18–19).

(3) The resultant state of the redeemed: Believers redeemed by Christ are now free from Satan's dominion and from the guilt and power of sin (Ac 26:18; Ro 6:7,12,14,18; Col 1:13). This freedom from sin, however, does not leave us free to do as we wish, for we become God's property. Freedom from sin makes us willing slaves of God (Ac 26:18; Ro 6:18,22; 1Co 6:19–20; 7:22–23).

JUSTIFICATION. The word "justify" (Gk *dikaioō*) means to be "righteous in God's sight" (Ro 2:13), to be "made righteous" (Ro 5:18–19), to "establish as right," or to "set or put right." It denotes being in a right relationship with God rather than receiving a mere legal, judicial declaration. God forgives repentant sinners, whom he had pronounced guilty through the law and condemned to eternal death, restores them to divine favor, and sets them in a right relationship (fellowship) with himself and his will. The apostle Paul reveals several truths about justification and how it is accomplished:

(1) Being put right with God is a gift (Ro 3:24; Eph 2:8). No one can put himself or herself right with God by keeping the law perfectly or by performing good works (Ro 4:2–6), "for all have sinned and fall short of the glory of God" (Ro 3:23).

(2) Being put right with God happens "through the redemption that came by Christ Jesus" (Ro 3:24). No one is justified who has not been redeemed by Christ from sin and its power.

(3) Being put right with God comes "by his grace" and is appropriated "through faith in Jesus Christ" as Lord and Savior (Ro 3:22–24; cf. 4:3–5; see article on FAITH AND GRACE, p. 302).

(4) Being put right with God is related to the forgiveness of our sins (Ro 4:7). Sinners are declared guilty (Ro 3:9–18,23) but are forgiven because of Christ's atoning death and resurrection (see Ro 3:25, note; 4:5, note; 4:25; 5:6–9).

(5) When we are put right with God through faith in Christ, we are crucified with Christ and Christ comes to live in us (Gal 2:16–21). Through this experience, we actually *become* righteous and begin living for God (2:19–21). This transforming work of Christ in us through the Spirit (cf. 2Th 2:13; 1Pe 1:2) cannot be separated from Christ's redemptive work for us. The work of Christ and the Spirit are interdependent.

such things deserve death,[j] they not only
continue to do these very things but also
approve[k] of those who practice them.

God's Righteous Judgment

2 You, therefore, have no excuse,[l] you
who pass judgment on someone else,
for at whatever point you judge the other,
you are condemning yourself, because you
who pass judgment do the same things.[m]
2Now we know that God's judgment
against those who do such things is based
on truth. **3**So when you, a mere man, pass
judgment on them and yet do the same
things, do you think you will escape God's
judgment? **4**Or do you show contempt for
the riches[n] of his kindness,[o] tolerance[p]
and patience,[q] not realizing that God's
kindness leads you toward repentance?[r]
5But because of your stubbornness and
your unrepentant heart, you are storing
up wrath against yourself for the day of
God's wrath[s], when his righteous judgment[t] will be revealed. **6**God "will give to
each person according to what he has
done."[e][u] **7**To those who by persistence in
doing good seek glory, honor[v] and immortality,[w] he will give eternal life.[x] **8**But for
those who are self-seeking and who reject
the truth and follow evil,[y] there will be
wrath and anger.[z] **9**There will be trouble
and distress for every human being who
does evil:[a] first for the Jew, then for the
Gentile;[b] **10**but glory, honor and peace for
everyone who does good: first for the Jew,
then for the Gentile.[c] **11**For God does not
show favoritism.[d]

12All who sin apart from the law will
also perish apart from the law, and all who
sin under the law[e] will be judged by the
law. **13**For it is not those who hear the law
who are righteous in God's sight, but it is

1:32 [j]S Ro 6:23 [k]Ps 50:18; Lk 11:48; Ac 8:1; 22:20 **2:1** [l]Ro 1:20 [m]2Sa 12:5-7; S Mt 7:1,2 **2:4** [n]Ro 9:23; 11:33; Eph 1:7,18; 2:7; 3:8,16; Col 2:2 [o]Ro 11:22 [p]Ro 3:25 [q]Ex 34:6; Ro 9:22; 1Ti 1:16; 1Pe 3:20; 2Pe 3:15 [r]2Pe 3:9 **2:5** [s]Ps 110:5; Rev 6:17 [t]Jude 6 **2:6** [u]Ps 62:12; S Mt 16:27 **2:7** [v]ver 10 [w]1Co 15:53,54; 2Ti 1:10 [x]S Mt 25:46 **2:8** [y]2Th 2:12 [z]Eze 22:31 **2:9** [a]Ps 32:10 [b]ver 10; Ro 1:16 **2:10** [c]ver 9; Ro 1:16 **2:11** [d]S Ac 10:34 **2:12** [e]Ro 3:19; 6:14; 1Co 9:20,21; Gal 4:21; 5:18; S Ro 7:4

e *6* Psalm 62:12; Prov. 24:12

the practice itself, i.e., supporting and encouraging evil by taking pleasure in the immoral actions of others. This is the ultimate in depravity—vicarious enjoyment of lust and evil. Sin becomes entertainment. (1) The word "approve" (Gk *suneudokeō*), meaning "agree with," "consent to" or "sympathize with," points to the casual enjoyment of the sins of others that prevails in human society.

(2) Today we know what great harm is produced by the portrayal of immorality that dominates the entertainment media; yet many approve of it and derive pleasure from it. Being entertained by watching other people sin and engage in ungodly actions, even while you yourself abstain, brings you under the same divine condemnation as those engaging in such evil practices. Sin is intensified in any society wherever it meets with no inhibition from the disapproval of others.

(3) Those (and especially those who profess faith in Christ) who use the immoral actions of others for entertainment and enjoyment are directly contributing to public opinion favorable to immorality and therefore to the corruption and eternal damnation of an indefinite number of other people. This sin is worthy of death and will be exposed and judged at the final day of judgment (2Th 2:12).

2:1 YOU . . . DO THE SAME THINGS. In ch. 1 Paul explained that the Gentiles were given over to sin. Now in ch. 2, he shows that the Jews practice the same things and also need salvation through Christ.

2:3 YET DO THE SAME THINGS. No one should attempt to direct others to do what is right while failing to correct his or her own evil conduct. Some churches attempt to persuade pagan society to follow Biblical law, while at the same time they are blind to the worldliness and immorality within their own membership (cf. Lk 6:42). Before the church seeks to influence the world to a better way of living, it must place its own life under the divine searchlight and reform itself accordingly.

2:7 GLORY, HONOR AND IMMORTALITY. In the very beginning of his treatise on salvation, Paul clarifies a fundamental truth concerning God's dealing with the entire human race: God punishes evildoers and rewards the righteous (see Jn 5:29, notes; Gal 6:7–8). (1) The righteous are those who have been justified by faith (1:16–17; 3:24) and persevere in doing what is right according to God's standard (vv. 7,10; cf. Mt 24:13; Col 1:23; Heb 3:14; Rev 2:10). They value highly the glory that comes from God (1:23; 2:7; 5:2; 8:18), and they seek eternal life (8:23; 1Co 15:51–57; 1Pe 1:4; Rev 21:1—22:5). (2) Those seeking immortality do so by grace through faith (3:24–25; Eph 1:4–7; 2:8–10; 2Ti 2:1; see Php 2:12–13, notes). The faithful enter into "glory, honor and immortality" by "persistence in doing good" (cf. Mt 24:12–13), through the enabling grace given to them by Christ (see Mt 7:21, note; see article on FAITH AND GRACE, p. 302). (3) Those who do evil are selfish, disobey the truth and take pleasure in unrighteousness. They receive anger and trouble (1:28–32; 2:8–9).

2:12–15 WILL ALSO PERISH. All who continue in sin, even though they have no knowledge of God's law, will perish because they have a measure of knowledge of right and wrong (vv. 14–15). God will not automatically save those who do not hear the gospel, nor will he give them a second chance after death. The eternal consequence facing those who have not had an adequate chance to understand the gospel should cause us to make an unfailing effort to take the gospel to every person in every nation (see Mt 4:19, note; 9:37, note).

2:13 THOSE WHO OBEY THE LAW . . . DECLARED RIGHTEOUS. Paul does not use the term "law" in the sense of a system of statutes that we may obey and earn our salvation without grace. "Law" here stands for God's will made known to the human race. Merely hearing God's Word avails nothing apart from faith, submission and obedience. There must be "obe-

those who obey[f] the law who will be declared righteous. 14(Indeed, when Gentiles, who do not have the law, do by nature things required by the law,[g] they are
a law for themselves, even though they do
not have the law, 15since they show that
the requirements of the law are written on
their hearts, their consciences also bearing witness, and their thoughts now accusing, now even defending them.) 16This
will take place on the day when God will
judge men's secrets[h] through Jesus
Christ,[i] as my gospel[j] declares.

The Jews and the Law

17Now you, if you call yourself a Jew; if
you rely on the law and brag about your
relationship to God;[k] 18if you know his
will and approve of what is superior because you are instructed by the law; 19if
you are convinced that you are a guide for
the blind, a light for those who are in the
dark, 20an instructor of the foolish, a
teacher of infants, because you have in the
law the embodiment of knowledge and
truth— 21you, then, who teach others, do
you not teach yourself? You who preach
against stealing, do you steal?[l] 22You
who say that people should not commit
adultery, do you commit adultery? You
who abhor idols, do you rob temples?[m]
23You who brag about the law,[n] do you
dishonor God by breaking the law? 24As it
is written: "God's name is blasphemed
among the Gentiles because of you."[f][o]

25Circumcision has value if you observe
the law,[p] but if you break the law, you
have become as though you had not been
circumcised.[q] 26If those who are not circumcised keep the law's requirements,[r]
will they not be regarded as though they
were circumcised?[s] 27The one who is not
circumcised physically and yet obeys the
law will condemn you[t] who, even though
you have the[g] written code and circumcision, are a lawbreaker.

28A man is not a Jew if he is only one
outwardly,[u] nor is circumcision merely
outward and physical.[v] 29No, a man is a
Jew if he is one inwardly; and circumcision
is circumcision of the heart,[w] by the Spirit,[x] not by the written code.[y] Such a
man's praise is not from men, but from
God.[z]

God's Faithfulness

3 What advantage, then, is there in being a Jew, or what value is there in
circumcision? 2Much in every way![a] First
of all, they have been entrusted with the
very words of God.[b]

3What if some did not have faith?[c] Will
their lack of faith nullify God's faithfulness?[d] 4Not at all! Let God be true,[e] and
every man a liar.[f] As it is written:

"So that you may be proved right
when you speak
and prevail when you judge."[h][g]

5But if our unrighteousness brings out
God's righteousness more clearly,[h] what
shall we say? That God is unjust in bringing his wrath on us? (I am using a human
argument.)[i] 6Certainly not! If that were
so, how could God judge the world?[j]
7Someone might argue, "If my falsehood
enhances God's truthfulness and so increases his glory,[k] why am I still condemned as a sinner?"[l] 8Why not say—as
we are being slanderously reported as
saying and as some claim that we say—
"Let us do evil that good may result"?[m]
Their condemnation is deserved.

No One Is Righteous

9What shall we conclude then? Are we
any better[i]?[n] Not at all! We have already
made the charge that Jews and Gentiles
alike are all under sin.[o] 10As it is written:

2:13 [f]Jas 1:22,23,25
2:14 [g]Ac 10:35
2:16 [h]Ecc 12:14; 1Co 4:5 [i]Ac 10:42 [j]Ro 16:25; 2Ti 2:8
2:17 [k]ver 23; Jer 8:8; Mic 3:11; Jn 5:45; Ro 9:4
2:21 [l]Mt 23:3,4
2:22 [m]Ac 19:37
2:23 [n]S ver 17
2:24 [o]Isa 52:5; Eze 36:22; 2Pe 2:2
2:25 [p]ver 13,27; Gal 5:3 [q]Jer 4:4; 9:25,26
2:26 [r]Ro 8:4 [s]S 1Co 7:19
2:27 [t]Mt 12:41,42
2:28 [u]Mt 3:9; Jn 8:39; Ro 9:6,7 [v]Gal 6:15
2:29 [w]Dt 30:6 [x]Php 3:3; Col 2:11 [y]Ro 7:6; 2Co 3:6 [z]Jn 5:44; 12:43; 1Co 4:5; 2Co 10:18; Gal 1:10; 1Th 2:4; 1Pe 3:4
3:2 [a]Ro 9:4,5 [b]Dt 4:8; Ps 147:19; Ac 7:38
3:3 [c]Ro 10:16; Heb 4:2 [d]2Ti 2:13
3:4 [e]Jn 3:33 [f]Ps 116:11 [g]Ps 51:4
3:5 [h]Ro 5:8 [i]Ro 6:19; Gal 3:15
3:6 [j]Ge 18:25; Ro 2:16
3:7 [k]ver 4 [l]Ro 9:19
3:8 [m]Ro 6:1
3:9 [n]ver 1 [o]ver 19,23; 1Ki 8:46; 2Ch 6:36; Ps 106:6; Ro 5:12; 11:32; Gal 3:22

f 24 Isaiah 52:5; Ezek. 36:22 g 27 Or *who, by means of a* h 4 Psalm 51:4 i 9 Or *worse*

dience that comes from faith" (1:5; cf. 16:26), expressing itself through love (Gal 5:6).

2:16 GOD WILL JUDGE MEN'S SECRETS. See article on THE JUDGMENT OF BELIEVERS, p. 368.

2:24 GOD'S NAME IS BLASPHEMED. The sins of the Jews gave occasion for the Gentiles to blaspheme God's name. Likewise today, the sins of permissive churches or professed believers enable the ungodly to blaspheme Christ's name.

2:29 CIRCUMCISION OF THE HEART, BY THE SPIRIT. This is God's work of grace in the hearts of believers whereby they participate in the divine nature and become capable of living a pure life separated from sin for God's glory (cf. Dt 10:16; Jer 4:4; 2Pe 1:4). Thus, holy living becomes the outward sign that we are under the new covenant.

3:9 ARE ALL UNDER SIN. In chs. 1–2, Paul has shown that all people, both Gentiles and Jews, are in bondage to sin. In 3:9–18 he explains why and teaches that all people possess a sinful nature that draws them toward sin and evil (see next note). The result is that all are guilty and stand under God's condemnation (v. 23). God's response to this tragic situation is to offer forgiveness, help, grace, righteousness and salvation to all through the redemption that is in Christ Jesus (vv. 21–26).

3:10–18 NO ONE RIGHTEOUS. These verses portray a correct understanding of human nature. All

"There is no one righteous, not even
one;
11 there is no one who understands,
no one who seeks God.
12All have turned away,
they have together become
worthless;
there is no one who does good,
not even one."[j][p]
13"Their throats are open graves;
their tongues practice deceit."[k][q]
"The poison of vipers is on their
lips."[l][r]
14 "Their mouths are full of cursing
and bitterness."[m][s]
15"Their feet are swift to shed blood;
16 ruin and misery mark their ways,
17and the way of peace they do not
know."[n][t]
18 "There is no fear of God before
their eyes."[o][u]

19Now we know that whatever the law
says,[v] it says to those who are under the
law,[w] so that every mouth may be silenced[x] and the whole world held accountable to God.[y] 20Therefore no one
will be declared righteous in his sight by
observing the law;[z] rather, through the
law we become conscious of sin.[a]

Righteousness Through Faith

21But now a righteousness from God,[b]
apart from law, has been made known, to
which the Law and the Prophets testify.[c]
22This righteousness from God[d] comes
through faith[e] in Jesus Christ[f] to all who
believe.[g] There is no difference,[h] 23for all
have sinned[i] and fall short of the glory of
God, 24and are justified[j] freely by his
grace[k] through the redemption[l] that
came by Christ Jesus. 25God presented

3:12 [p] Ps 14:1-3; 53:1-3; Ecc 7:20 **3:13** [q] Ps 5:9 [r] Ps 140:3 **3:14** [s] Ps 10:7 **3:17** [t] Isa 59:7,8 **3:18** [u] Ps 36:1 **3:19** [v] S Jn 10:34 [w] S Ro 2:12 [x] Ps 63:11; 107:42; Eze 16:63 [y] ver 9 **3:20** [z] Ac 13:39; Gal 2:16 [a] S Ro 4:15 **3:21** [b] Isa 46:13; Jer 23:6; Ro 1:17; 9:30 [c] Ac 10:43; Ro 1:2 **3:22** [d] Ro 1:17 [e] S Ro 9:30 [f] Gal 2:16; 3:22 [g] S Jn 3:15; Ro 4:11; 10:4 [h] Ro 10:12; Gal 3:28; Col 3:11 **3:23** [i] S ver 9 **3:24** [j] S Ro 4:25 [k] Jn 1:14,16,17; Ro 4:16; 5:21; 6:14; 11:5; 2Co 12:9; Eph 2:8; 4:7; Tit 2:11; Heb 4:16 [l] Ps 130:7; 1Co 1:30; Gal 4:5; Eph 1:7,14; Col 1:14; Heb 9:12

j *12* Psalms 14:1-3; 53:1-3; Eccles. 7:20
k *13* Psalm 5:9 **l** *13* Psalm 140:3
m *14* Psalm 10:7 **n** *17* Isaiah 59:7,8
o *18* Psalm 36:1

people in their natural state are sinners. Their entire being is adversely affected by sin and inclines toward conformity to the world (see article on THE CHRISTIAN'S RELATIONSHIP TO THE WORLD, p. 546), the devil (see Mt 4:10, note) and the sinful nature (see article on THE ACTS OF THE SINFUL NATURE AND THE FRUIT OF THE SPIRIT, p. 394). All are guilty of turning aside from the way of godliness to the way of selfishness.

3:18 NO FEAR OF GOD. Why does the deplorable condition of humanity continue? Because "there is no fear of God before their eyes." If there had been the fear of God, they would have sought reconciliation and peace. "Through the fear of the Lord a man avoids evil" (Pr 16:6; cf. Pr 3:7; 8:13; 9:10; see Ac 5:11, note).

3:21 A RIGHTEOUSNESS FROM GOD. This phrase refers to God's redemptive activity in the sphere of human sin by which he, in a just way (v. 26), puts us in a right relationship with himself and liberates us from the power of evil (note the OT, where the working of salvation and the manifestation of righteousness are essentially the same thing—see Ps 98:1–2; Isa 46:13; 51:5–8; 56:1; 62:1). (1) This revelation of God's righteousness in the gospel is not something that has ended. As the power of God for salvation that accompanies the believer, it is constantly fresh and relevant (see article on BIBLICAL WORDS FOR SALVATION, p. 292). (2) This righteousness from God comes to us through faith in Jesus Christ (v. 22).

3:22 FAITH. Faith in Jesus Christ as Lord and Savior is the only condition God requires for salvation. For a discussion of what saving faith is, see article on FAITH AND GRACE, p. 302.

3:24 JUSTIFIED FREELY BY HIS GRACE THROUGH THE REDEMPTION. This verse contains two of the most common words used by Paul to express salvation: "justified" and "redemption." For a discussion of these two concepts, see article on BIBLICAL WORDS FOR SALVATION, p. 292.

3:25 HIS BLOOD. The NT emphasizes several truths concerning Christ's death.

(1) It was a sacrifice, i.e., an offering of his blood, his life (cf. 1Co 5:7; Eph 5:2).

(2) It was vicarious, i.e., he died not for his own sake, but for the sake of others (5:8; 8:32; Mk 10:45; Eph 5:2).

(3) It was substitutionary, i.e., Christ suffered death as the penalty for our sin, as our substitute (6:23).

(4) It was propitiatory, i.e., Christ's death for sinners satisfied God's righteous nature and his moral order, thereby removing his wrath against the repentant sinner. God's integrity required that sin be punished and propitiation be made for our sake. Through propitiation by Christ's blood, God's holiness remained uncompromised and he was able to justly reveal his grace and love in salvation. It must be emphasized that God himself set forth Christ as a propitiation. God did not need to be persuaded to show mercy and love, for already "God was reconciling the world to himself in Christ" (2Co 5:19; cf. Jn 3:16; Ro 5:8; 8:3,32; 1Co 8:6; Eph 4:4–6).

(5) It was expiatory, i.e., a sacrifice to atone or make reparation for sin. As expiation, the sacrifice is directed toward annulling guilt. By Christ's death the guilt and power of sin that separated God and the believer were annulled.

(6) It was victorious, i.e., on the cross Christ fought against and was triumphant over the power of sin, of Satan and of his demonic host that held people captive. His death was the initial victory over the spiritual enemies of both God and humanity (8:3; Jn 12:31–32; Col 2:15). Thus, Christ's death is redemptive. By the ransom of his own life (1Pe 1:18–19), he liberated us from the enemies that hold the human race in bondage, i.e., sin (6:6), death (2Ti 1:10; 1Co 15:54–57) and Satan (Ac 10:38), making us free to serve God (6:18;

him as a sacrifice of atonement,[p][m]
through faith in his blood.[n] He did this to
demonstrate his justice, because in his
forbearance he had left the sins committed beforehand unpunished[o]— **26**he did it
to demonstrate his justice at the present
time, so as to be just and the one who
justifies those who have faith in Jesus.

27Where, then, is boasting?[p] It is excluded. On what principle? On that of observing the law? No, but on that of faith.
28For we maintain that a man is justified
by faith apart from observing the law.[q]
29Is God the God of Jews only? Is he not
the God of Gentiles too? Yes, of Gentiles
too,[r] **30**since there is only one God, who
will justify the circumcised by faith and
the uncircumcised through that same
faith.[s] **31**Do we, then, nullify the law by
this faith? Not at all! Rather, we uphold
the law.

Abraham Justified Apart From Works

4 What then shall we say[t] that Abraham, our forefather,[u] discovered in
this matter? **2**If, in fact, Abraham was justified by works, he had something to boast
about—but not before God.[v] **3**What does
the Scripture say? "Abraham believed
God, and it was credited to him as righteousness."[q][w]

4Now when a man works, his wages are
not credited to him as a gift,[x] but as an
obligation. **5**However, to the man who
does not work but trusts God who justifies
the wicked, his faith is credited as righteousness.[y] **6**David says the same thing
when he speaks of the blessedness of the
man to whom God credits righteousness
apart from works:

7"Blessed are they
  whose transgressions are forgiven,
  whose sins are covered.
8Blessed is the man
  whose sin the Lord will never count
    against him."[r][z]

9Is this blessedness only for the circumcised, or also for the uncircumcised?[a]
We have been saying that Abraham's faith
was credited to him as righteousness.[b]
10Under what circumstances was it credited? Was it after he was circumcised, or
before? It was not after, but before! **11**And
he received the sign of circumcision, a
seal of the righteousness that he had by
faith while he was still uncircumcised.[c]
So then, he is the father[d] of all who believe[e] but have not been circumcised, in
order that righteousness might be credited to them. **12**And he is also the father of

3:25 [m]Ex 25:17; Lev 16:10; Ps 65:3; Heb 2:17; 9:28; 1Jn 4:10 [n]Ac 20:28; Ro 5:9; Eph 1:7; Heb 9:12, 14; 13:12; 1Pe 1:19; Rev 1:5 [o]Ac 14:16; 17:30 **3:27** [p]Ro 2:17, 23; 4:2; 1Co 1:29-31; Eph 2:9 **3:28** [q]ver 20,21; Ac 13:39; Gal 2:16; 3:11; Eph 2:9; Jas 2:20, 24,26 **3:29** [r]Ac 10:34, 35; Ro 9:24; 10:12; 15:9; Gal 3:28 **3:30** [s]Ro 4:11,12; Gal 3:8 **4:1** [t]S Ro 8:31 [u]S Lk 3:8 **4:2** [v]1Co 1:31 **4:3** [w]ver 5,9,22; Ge 15:6; Gal 3:6; Jas 2:23

4:4 [x]Ro 11:6 **4:5** [y]ver 3,9,22; S Ro 9:30 **4:8** [z]Ps 32:1,2; 103:12; 2Co 5:19 **4:9** [a]Ro 3:30 [b]S ver 3 **4:11** [c]Ge 17:10, 11 [d]ver 16,17; S Lk 3:8 [e]S Ro 3:22

p *25* Or *as the one who would turn aside his wrath, taking away sin* q *3* Gen. 15:6; also in verse 22 r *8* Psalm 32:1,2

see article on BIBLICAL WORDS FOR SALVATION, p. 292).

All the above results of Christ's sacrificial death occur potentially for all people but only actually for individuals who through faith accept Jesus Christ and his death for them.

3:31 WE UPHOLD THE LAW. Salvation in Christ does not mean that the law has no value. In fact justification by faith upholds the law according to its right purpose and function. Through reconciliation with God and through the regenerating work of the Holy Spirit, the believer becomes capable of honoring and obeying God's moral law (see 8:2–4).

4:3 ABRAHAM BELIEVED GOD. Salvation by faith, not by deeds (i.e., keeping the law), is not an exclusively NT doctrine; it is also characteristic of the OT. Paul bypasses Moses and turns to Abraham as the example of faith. Abraham had faith in God, i.e., he maintained a loyal and devoted attachment to his God, believed in his promises (vv. 20–21; Ge 12:1–3; 15:5–6) and responded in obedience (Ge 12:1–4; 22:1–19; Heb 11:8–19; Jas 2:21–22).

4:5 FAITH IS CREDITED AS RIGHTEOUSNESS. Abraham's *faith* was credited as righteousness. The saving faith of the Christian is treated as equivalent to righteousness in regard to its effect.

(1) Paul speaks of "crediting as righteousness" or "crediting righteousness" six times in ch. 4, and in all cases Paul associates faith or belief with the crediting; it is the believer's "faith" that is credited as "righteousness" (vv. 3,5–6,9,11,22,24).

(2) The crediting of the believer's faith as righteousness, however, is not solely the result of faith or commitment to Christ; it is above all an act of divine grace and mercy (v. 16).

(3) When God sees the hearts of believers turn toward Christ in faith, he freely forgives their sins, credits their faith as righteousness and accepts them as his children (vv. 5–8; see article on BIBLICAL WORDS FOR SALVATION, p. 292). Along with this crediting of faith as righteousness, God also gives grace for sanctification (see v. 16; 5:2; Php 3:9; Tit 3:5–7).

(4) The faith that is credited as righteousness and brings forgiveness is faith in Christ and his atoning death (3:24–26). Absolutely nothing else but Christ's sacrificial death on the cross is the ground for reconciliation with God (see 5:10, note).

4:7 THEY WHOSE TRANSGRESSIONS ARE FORGIVEN. This quotation from Ps 32:1–2 shows that both David and Paul understood that one's faith credited as righteousness includes forgiveness of sin and reconciliation with God. It is a gift based on God's mercy, made possible through Christ's death on the cross (see v. 5, note; cf. 2Co 5:19,21).

4:12 FAITH THAT OUR FATHER ABRAHAM HAD. The faith of Abraham was a true faith that endured, believed, trusted, obeyed, grew strong and

the circumcised who not only are circumcised but who also walk in the footsteps
of the faith that our father Abraham had
before he was circumcised.
13It was not through law that Abraham
and his offspring received the promise[f]
that he would be heir of the world,[g] but
through the righteousness that comes by
faith.[h] **14**For if those who live by law are
heirs, faith has no value and the promise
is worthless,[i] **15**because law brings
wrath.[j] And where there is no law there
is no transgression.[k]

Abraham Justified by Faith

16Therefore, the promise comes by
faith, so that it may be by grace[l] and may
be guaranteed[m] to all Abraham's offspring
—not only to those who are of the law but
also to those who are of the faith of Abraham. He is the father of us all.[n] **17**As it is
written: "I have made you a father of many
nations."[s][o] He is our father in the sight
of God, in whom he believed—the God
who gives life[p] to the dead and calls[q]
things that are not[r] as though they were.
18Against all hope, Abraham in hope
believed and so became the father of many
nations,[s] just as it had been said to him,
"So shall your offspring be."[t][t] **19**Without
weakening in his faith, he faced the fact
that his body was as good as dead[u]—
since he was about a hundred years old[v]
—and that Sarah's womb was also dead.[w]
20Yet he did not waver through unbelief
regarding the promise of God, but was
strengthened[x] in his faith and gave glory
to God,[y] **21**being fully persuaded that God
had power to do what he had promised.[z] 1Co 13:2
22This is why "it was credited to him as
righteousness."[a] **23**The words "it was
credited to him" were written not for him
alone, **24**but also for us,[b] to whom God
will credit righteousness—for us who believe in him[c] who raised Jesus our Lord
from the dead.[d] **25**He was delivered over
to death for our sins[e] and was raised to
life for our justification.[f]

Peace and Joy

5 Therefore, since we have been justified[g] through faith,[h] we[u] have
peace[i] with God through our Lord Jesus
Christ,[j] **2**through whom we have gained
access[k] by faith into this grace in which
we now stand.[l] And we[u] rejoice in the
hope[m] of the glory of God. **3**Not only so,
but we[u] also rejoice in our sufferings,[n]

4:13 [f]S Ac 13:32; Gal 3:16,29 [g]Ge 17:4-6 [h]S Ro 9:30 **4:14** [i]Gal 3:18 **4:15** [j]Ro 7:7-25; 1Co 15:56; 2Co 3:7; Gal 3:10; S Ro 7:12 [k]Ro 3:20; 5:13; 7:7 **4:16** [l]S Ro 3:24 [m]Ro 15:8 [n]ver 11; S Lk 3:8; S Gal 3:16 **4:17** [o]Ge 17:5 [p]S Jn 5:21 [q]Isa 48:13 [r]1Co 1:28 **4:18** [s]ver 17 [t]Ge 15:5 **4:19** [u]Heb 11:11, 12 [v]Ge 17:17 [w]Ge 18:11 **4:20** [x]1Sa 30:6 [y]S Mt 9:8 **4:21** [z]Ge 18:14; S Mt 19:26 **4:22** [a]S ver 3 **4:24** [b]Ps 102:18; Hab 2:2; Ro 15:4; 1Co 9:10; 10:11; 2Ti 3:16,17 [c]Ro 10:9; 1Pe 1:21 [d]S Ac 2:24 **4:25** [e]Isa 53:5,6; Ro 5:6,8; 8:32; 2Co 5:21 [f]Isa 53:11; Ro 3:24; 5:1,9,16, 18; 8:30; 1Co 6:11; 2Co 5:15 **5:1** [g]S Ro 4:25 [h]S Ro 3:28 [i]S Lk 2:14 [j]ver 10

5:2 [k]Eph 2:18; 3:12 [l]1Co 15:1 [m]S Heb 3:6 **5:3** [n]S Mt 5:12

[s] *17* Gen. 17:5 [t] *18* Gen. 15:5 [u] *1,2,3* Or *let us*

---

gave glory to God (vv. 16–21). This is the type of faith that makes us children of God.

4:16 THE PROMISE COMES BY FAITH. Believers are saved through faith alone by grace. But two Biblical truths about the nature of saving faith should be noted. (1) While one is saved through faith alone, the faith that saves is not alone. James states "faith without deeds is dead" (Jas 2:14–26); Paul says it is "faith expressing itself through love" (Gal 5:6). Saving faith is a faith so vital that it cannot avoid the expressions of love for and obedience to the Savior and of service to others. Faith that merely trusts God to forgive our sins but does not include sincere repentance and an active commitment to Christ as Lord falls short of NT saving faith (see article on FAITH AND GRACE, p. 302).

(2) It is unbiblical to emphasize "faith" and ignore the broader picture of salvation. Salvation by faith includes not only being saved from condemnation but also being saved for fellowship with God, for holiness and for good works (Eph 2:10).

4:16 SO THAT IT MAY BE BY GRACE. If the salvation, justification and righteousness that God provides came by perfect obedience to the law, no one would be saved because no one has obeyed it perfectly. But since it comes through faith by grace, then *all* may be saved who turn to God. God mercifully forgives our sins and imparts divine grace (i.e., his Spirit and power) to regenerate our lives and make us God's children (see article on FAITH AND GRACE, p. 302).

4:22 CREDITED TO HIM AS RIGHTEOUSNESS. In Paul's illustration of justification in ch. 4, nowhere does he state that the righteousness of God or of Christ is actually credited or transferred to the believer. We must be careful not to describe justification by stating that it comes by Christ's OT law-keeping transferred to the believer. If it did come by a transferred keeping of the law, then it is not the same kind of faith as Abraham that is credited as righteousness (v. 12), and that in turn nullifies the promise (v. 14) and makes salvation a result of merit rather than of grace (v. 16). Paul emphatically declares justification and righteousness come "not through law" (v. 13), but by God'smercy, grace, love and forgiveness (vv. 6–9), and that Abraham's *faith* (i.e., his believing, his attachment to God, his strong confidence and unwavering assurance in God and his promises) is credited as righteousness, by the mercy and grace of God (vv. 16–22).

4:25 RAISED TO LIFE FOR OUR JUSTIFICATION. Justification does not exist without the life, presence and grace of Jesus Christ operating in our lives. Justification is not a single judicial act in the past, but a lifelong justification in fellowship with Jesus Christ our Lord.

5:1 THEREFORE, SINCE WE HAVE BEEN JUSTIFIED. Justification through faith brings the believer various results: peace with God, grace, hope, assurance, sufferings, the love of God, the Holy Spirit, salvation from wrath, reconciliation to God, salvation by the life and presence of Jesus, and joy in God (vv. 1–11).

because we know that suffering produces
perseverance;[o] **4**perseverance, character;
and character, hope. **5**And hope[p] does not
disappoint us, because God has poured
out his love[q] into our hearts by the Holy
Spirit,[r] whom he has given us.

6You see, at just the right time,[s] when
we were still powerless,[t] Christ died for
the ungodly.[u] **7**Very rarely will anyone die
for a righteous man, though for a good
man someone might possibly dare to die.
8But God demonstrates his own love for
us in this: While we were still sinners,
Christ died for us.[v]

9Since we have now been justified[w] by
his blood,[x] how much more shall we be
saved from God's wrath[y] through him!
10For if, when we were God's enemies,[z]
we were reconciled[a] to him through the
death of his Son, how much more, having
been reconciled, shall we be saved
through his life![b] **11**Not only is this so, but
we also rejoice in God through our Lord
Jesus Christ, through whom we have now
received reconciliation.[c]

Death Through Adam, Life Through Christ

12Therefore, just as sin entered the
world through one man,[d] and death
through sin,[e] and in this way death came
to all men, because all sinned[f]— **13**for
before the law was given, sin was in the
world. But sin is not taken into account
when there is no law.[g] **14**Nevertheless,
death reigned from the time of Adam to
the time of Moses, even over those who
did not sin by breaking a command, as did
Adam,[h] who was a pattern of the one to
come.[i]

15But the gift is not like the trespass.
For if the many died by the trespass of the

5:3 [o]S Heb 10:36 **5:5** [p]Php 1:20; S Heb 3:6; 1Jn 3:2,3 [q]ver 8; Jn 3:16; Ro 8:39 [r]Ac 2:33; 10:45; Tit 3:5,6 **5:6** [s]Mk 1:15; Gal 4:4; Eph 1:10 [t]ver 8,10 [u]Ro 4:25 **5:8** [v]Jn 3:16; 15:13; 1Pe 3:18; 1Jn 3:16; 4:10 **5:9** [w]S Ro 4:25 [x]S Ro 3:25 [y]S Ro 1:18 **5:10** [z]Ro 11:28; Col 1:21 [a]ver 11; Ro 11:15; 2Co 5:18,19; Col 1:20,22 [b]Ro 8:34; Heb 7:25 **5:11** [c]S ver 10 **5:12** [d]ver 15,16,17; Ge 3:1-7; 1Co 15:21,22 [e]ver 14,18; Ge 2:17; 3:19; S Ro 6:23 [f]S Ro 3:9 **5:13** [g]S Ro 4:15 **5:14** [h]Ge 3:11,12 [i]1Co 15:22,45

5:3 WE ALSO REJOICE IN OUR SUFFERINGS. Paul lists "sufferings" as one of the blessings of our salvation in Christ. (1) The word "sufferings" refers to all kinds of trials that may press in on us. This includes such things as the pressures of financial or physical need, trying circumstances, sorrow, sickness, persecution, mistreatment or loneliness.

(2) In the middle of these troubles God's grace enables us to seek his face more diligently and produces in us a persevering spirit and character that overcome the trials of life. Instead of driving us to despair, suffering produces perseverance (v. 3), perseverance produces proven character (v. 4), and proven character results in a mature hope that will not disappoint (v. 5).

(3) God's grace lets us look beyond our present problems to a fervent hope in God and a certain hope for the return of our Lord to establish righteousness and godliness in the new heaven and earth (1Th 4:13; Rev 19–22). In the meantime, God has poured out his love into our hearts by the Holy Spirit to comfort us in our trials and bring Christ's presence near (Jn 14:16–23).

5:5 GOD HAS POURED OUT HIS LOVE INTO OUR HEARTS. Christians experience the love of God (i.e., God's love for believers) in their hearts through the Holy Spirit, especially in times of trouble. The verb "poured out" is a present perfect tense in the indicative mood, expressing an existing condition from a prior action, i.e., the Spirit continues to flood our hearts with love. It is this ever-present experience of God's love that sustains us in sufferings (v. 3) and assures us that our hope for future glory is not illusory (vv. 4–5). Christ's return for us is sure (cf. 8:17; Ps 22:4–5; Jn 14:3; see article on THE RAPTURE, p. 440).

5:10 SAVED THROUGH HIS LIFE. The believer's salvation lies in Christ's blood and his resurrection life, whereby the believer is forgiven and reconciled to God. This is initial salvation (3:21–26; 4:5–9). The believer continues to be saved by a living faith and union with the living Christ (see article on BIBLICAL WORDS FOR SALVATION, p. 292). If God loved us enough to send his Son to die for us while we were enemies, how much more, now that we are his children, will he make every provision to save us from the wrath to come through our present faith in his Son (4:22–5:2; 5:9–10; 1Co 1:30; Php 2:12–16; Col 3:3–4; 1Th 1:10; 2Ti 2:12; Jas 1:12; see Rev 2:7, note).

5:12 SIN ENTERED THE WORLD THROUGH ONE MAN. In the fall of Adam, sin as an active principle or power gained entrance into the human race (vv. 17,19; Ge 3; 1Co 15:21–22). (1) Two results followed: (a) Sin and corruption entered into Adam's heart and life. (b) Adam transmitted sin into the life-stream of the human race, corrupting all people thereafter. All humans are now born into the world with an impulse toward sin and evil (v. 19; 1:21; 7:24; Ge 6:5,12; 8:21; Ps 14:1–3; Jer 17:9; Mk 7:21–22; 1Co 2:14; Gal 5:19–21; Eph 2:1–3; Col 1:21; 1Jn 5:19).

(2) Paul does not explain how Adam's sin is transmitted to his descendants. Nor does he say that all people were present in Adam and participated in his sin, and therefore inherit Adam's guilt. Nowhere does Paul say that Adam was the federal head of his descendants and that his sin was imputed to them. All are guilty before God because of their own personal sin, "because all sinned." The only doctrine that finds Biblical support is that men and women inherit a moral corruption and an impulse toward sin and evil (see 6:1, note).

(3) Death entered the world through sin, and now all people are subject to death, "because all sinned" (vv. 12,14; cf. 3:23; Ge 2:17; 3:19).

5:14 DEATH REIGNED FROM THE TIME OF ADAM TO THE TIME OF MOSES. The human race experienced death, not because they transgressed the spoken law of God with its death penalty as did Adam (vv. 13–14), but because they were in fact sinners by action as well by nature and transgressors of the law of conscience written in their hearts (2:14–15).

one man,[j] how much more did God's
grace and the gift that came by the grace
of the one man, Jesus Christ,[k] overflow to
Ro 8:6 the many! **16**Again, the gift of God is not
like the result of the one man's sin: The
judgment followed one sin and brought
condemnation, but the gift followed many
trespasses and brought justification.
17For if, by the trespass of the one man,
death[l] reigned through that one man,
how much more will those who receive
God's abundant provision of grace and of
the gift of righteousness reign in life[m]
through the one man, Jesus Christ.
18Consequently, just as the result of
one trespass was condemnation for all
men,[n] so also the result of one act of righteousness was justification[o] that brings
life[p] for all men. **19**For just as through the
disobedience of the one man[q] the many
were made sinners,[r] so also through the
obedience[s] of the one man the many will
be made righteous.
20The law was added so that the trespass might increase.[t] But where sin increased, grace increased all the more,[u]
21so that, just as sin reigned in death,[v] so
also grace[w] might reign through righteousness to bring eternal life[x] through
Jesus Christ our Lord.

Dead to Sin, Alive in Christ

6 What shall we say, then?[y] Shall we go
on sinning so that grace may in-
crease?[z] **2**By no means! We died to sin;[a]
how can we live in it any longer? **3**Or don't
you know that all of us who were baptized[b] into Christ Jesus were baptized into
his death? **4**We were therefore buried with
him through baptism into death[c] in order
that, just as Christ was raised from the

5:15 [j] ver 12,18,19 [k] Ac 15:11
5:17 [l] S ver 12 [m] Jn 10:10
5:18 [n] S ver 12 [o] S Ro 4:25 [p] Isa 53:11
5:19 [q] ver 12 [r] S Ro 3:9 [s] S Php 2:8
5:20 [t] Ro 3:20; 7:7,8; Gal 3:19 [u] Ro 6:1; 1Ti 1:13,14
5:21 [v] ver 12,14; S Ro 6:16 [w] S Ro 3:24 [x] S Mt 25:46
6:1 [y] S Ro 8:31 [z] ver 15; Ro 3:5,8
6:2 [a] S ver 6; ver 10,11; S ver 18; Ro 8:13; Col 3:3,5; 1Pe 2:24
6:3 [b] S Mt 28:19
6:4 [c] S ver 6

5:15 HOW MUCH MORE DID GOD'S GRACE. In vv. 12–21 Paul stresses the supreme adequacy of the redemption provided by Jesus Christ to undo the effects of the fall. This is the real point of the passage: Adam brought sin and death; Christ brought grace and life (v. 17).

5:18 JUSTIFICATION THAT BRINGS LIFE FOR ALL MEN. The condemnation for all people becomes actual for each person as he or she rejects God and his revelation written in their hearts or revealed in his written Word (cf. 2:12–16). The "justification that brings life" for all people is potential as well; it becomes actualized in individuals as they believe in Christ and receive grace, life and the gift of righteousness through Jesus Christ (v. 17).

5:21 GRACE. For a discussion of the meaning of the word "grace" in the Bible, see article on FAITH AND GRACE, p. 302.

6:1 SHALL WE GO ON SINNING? In ch. 6 Paul challenges the erroneous idea that believers may continue in sin and yet remain secure from condemnation because of God's grace through Christ. Paul answers this antinomian distortion of the doctrine of grace by emphasizing one fundamental truth: true believers are identified as being "in Christ" by virtue of their death to sin. They have been translated from sin's realm into another realm of life—with Christ (vv. 2–12). Since true believers have made a definitive separation from sin, they will not continue to live in sin. Conversely, if people keep living in sin, they are not true believers (cf. 1Jn 3:4–10). Throughout this chapter Paul emphasizes that individuals cannot be slaves to sin and slaves to Christ at the same time (vv. 11–13,16–18). If they offer themselves to sin, the result will be condemnation and eternal death (vv. 16,23).

6:1 SIN. (1) The NT uses several Greek words to describe sin in its various aspects. The most important are: (a) *Hamartia*, which means "transgression," "wrongdoing" or "sin against God" (Jn 9:41). (b) *Adikia*, which stands for "wrongdoing," "wickedness" or "injustice" (1:18; 1Jn 5:17). It can be described as a lack of love, since all wrongdoing stems from a failure to love (Mt 22:37–40; Lk 10:27–37). *Adikia* is also a personal power that can enslave and deceive (5:12; Heb 3:13). (c) *Anomia*, which denotes "wickedness," "lawlessness" and "defiance of God's law" (v. 19; 1Jn 3:4). (d) *Apistia*, which indicates "unbelief" or "unfaithfulness" (3:3; Heb 3:12).

(2) From these definitions we can conclude that the essence of sin is selfishness, i.e., a grasping of things or pleasures for ourselves, regardless of the welfare of others and the commandments of God. This leads to cruelty to others and to rebellion against God and his law. Ultimately sin becomes the refusal to be subject to God and his Word (1:18–25; 8:7). It is enmity against God (5:10; 8:7; Col 1:21) and disobedience to him (11:32; Eph 2:2; 5:6).

(3) Sin is also a moral corruption in humans that opposes all better human volitions. It causes us both to commit unrighteousness with delight and to take pleasure in the evil actions of others (1:21–32; cf. Ge 6:5). It is likewise a power that enslaves and corrupts (3:9; 6:12ff; 7:14; Gal. 3:22). Sin is rooted in human desire (Jas 1:14; 4:1–2; see 1Pe 2:11, note).

(4) Sin was brought into the human race through Adam (5:12), affects everyone (5:12), results in divine judgment (1:18), brings physical and spiritual death (v. 23; Ge 2:17), and can be eliminated as a power only by faith in Christ and his redemptive work (5:8–11; Gal 3:13; Eph 4:20–24; 1Jn 1:9; Rev 1:5).

6:2 DIED TO SIN. See v. 11, note.

6:4 BURIED WITH HIM THROUGH BAPTISM. Baptism for the Christian is a symbol of the believer's burial and resurrection with Christ, but it is more. When accompanied by true faith, baptism is part of our rejection of sin and our commitment to Christ, resulting in a continual flow of grace and divine life to us (see Ac 22:16, note on baptism). Baptism means identifying with Christ in his death and burial in order that we may live in union with his resurrected life (vv. 4–5). As surely as Christ rose from the dead, so surely we who exercise true saving faith in him will walk in newness of life (v. 5).

dead[d] through the glory of the Father, we
too may live a new life.[e]
5If we have been united with him like
this in his death, we will certainly also be
united with him in his resurrection.[f] **6**For
we know that our old self[g] was crucified
with him[h] so that the body of sin[i] might
be done away with,[v] that we should no
longer be slaves to sin[j]— **7**because anyone who has died has been freed from
sin.[k]
8Now if we died with Christ, we believe
that we will also live with him.[l] **9**For we
know that since Christ was raised from
the dead,[m] he cannot die again; death no
longer has mastery over him.[n] **10**The
death he died, he died to sin[o] once for
all;[p] but the life he lives, he lives to God.
11In the same way, count yourselves
dead to sin[q] but alive to God in Christ
Jesus. **12**Therefore do not let sin reign[r] in
your mortal body so that you obey its evil
desires. **13**Do not offer the parts of your

6:4 [d]S Ac 2:24 [e]Ro 7:6; S 2Co 5:17; Eph 4:22-24; Col 3:10
6:5 [f]ver 4,8; Ro 8:11; 2Co 4:10; Eph 2:6; Php 3:10, 11; Col 2:12; 3:1; 2Ti 2:11
6:6 [g]S Gal 5:24; Eph 4:22; Col 3:9 [h]S ver 2; ver 3-8; 2Co 4:10; Gal 2:20; 5:24; 6:14; Php 3:10; Col 2:12,20; 3:3 [i]Ro 7:24 [j]S ver 16
6:7 [k]S ver 18
6:8 [l]S ver 5
6:9 [m]ver 4; S Ac 2:24 [n]Rev 1:18
6:10 [o]S ver 2 [p]S Heb 7:27
6:11 [q]S ver 2
6:12 [r]ver 16
6:13 [s]ver 16,19; Ro 7:5 [t]Ro 12:1; 2Co 5:14,15; 1Pe 2:24
6:14 [u]S ver 16 [v]S Ro 2:12 [w]S Ro 3:24

body to sin, as instruments of wickedness,[s] but rather offer yourselves to God,
as those who have been brought from
death to life; and offer the parts of your
body to him as instruments of righteousness.[t] **14**For sin shall not be your master,[u] because you are not under law,[v] but
under grace.[w]

Slaves to Righteousness

15What then? Shall we sin because we
are not under law but under grace?[x] By no
means! **16**Don't you know that when you
offer yourselves to someone to obey him
as slaves, you are slaves to the one whom
you obey[y]—whether you are slaves to
sin,[z] which leads to death,[a] or to obedience, which leads to righteousness? **17**But

6:15 [x]ver 1,14 **6:16** [y]2Pe 2:19 [z]ver 6,12,14,17,20; Ge 4:7; Ps 51:5; 119:133; Jn 8:34; Ro 5:21; 7:14,23,25; 8:2; 2Pe 2:19 [a]S ver 23

[v] 6 Or *be rendered powerless*

6:6 OLD SELF . . . BODY OF SIN. Paul uses two terms here: (1) The "old self": this refers to the believer's unregenerate self, the person he or she once was, the life once lived in sin. This old self has been crucified (i.e., put to death) with Christ on the cross in order that the believer might receive a new life in Christ and become a new person (cf. Gal 2:20). (2) "Body of sin": this refers to the human body as controlled by sinful desires. Its slavery to sin has now been broken (cf. 2Co 5:17; Eph 4:22; Col 3:9–10). From this point on, believers must not allow their old mode of existence again to dominate their lives and bodies (2Co 5:17; Eph 4:22; Col 3:9–10).

6:7 FREED FROM SIN. See Jn 8:36, note.

6:10 HE DIED TO SIN. Although Christ was sinless, he suffered from and was humiliated by the power of sin for our sake (5:21; cf. 2Co 5:21). In his death, he died to sin's influence; in his resurrection, he triumphed over its power. Likewise, those who are united with him in his death are freed from sin's power (vv. 2,11) to walk in newness of life (vv. 4–5,10).

6:11 COUNT YOURSELVES DEAD TO SIN. The fundamental premise in ch. 6 is the believer's union with Christ in both his death and life. Therefore, if you are a true believer, you have died to sin—and you need to reckon with this fact. (1) You died to sin in God's sight. You are considered by God to have died with Christ on the cross and to have been raised up in his resurrection (vv. 5–10). (2) You died to sin when you were born again by the Spirit (see article on REGENERATION, p. 178). You have been given Christ's power to resist sin (vv. 14–18), to die to it daily by putting to death the misdeeds of the body (8:13), and to live a new life in obedience to God (vv. 5–14,18,22). (3) You died to sin in water baptism as you proclaimed your death to sin and committed yourself to reject sin and to live for Christ (vv. 3–5; see 6:4, note).

6:12 DO NOT LET SIN REIGN. Because sin has been dethroned, you must continually resist its effort to regain control. Since sin attempts to reign primarily through the desires of the body, these desires must be resisted by those with faith in Christ (see next note). We can do so by denying the evil desires of the body (v. 12), refusing to place any part of our body at the disposal of sin (v. 13), and presenting our bodies and our whole personalities as slaves to God and righteousness (vv. 13–19).

6:15 SHALL WE SIN? Some within the church in Paul's day thought that since grace pardons sin, the Christian does not need to be careful to resist sin. In answer to this, the apostle explains that every believer must continually reaffirm and implement his or her decision to resist sin and follow Christ (v. 19). (1) After accepting Christ, believers must continue to choose whom they will serve (v. 16). (a) They may return to sin, cease to oppose its dominion in their personal lives and become its slave once more, with death (spiritual and eternal) as the result (vv. 16,21,23); or (b) they may be freed from sin (v. 17) and may continue to present themselves as slaves of God and righteousness, with sanctification and eternal life as the result (vv. 19,22). (2) In the light of vv. 15–23, those not committed to Christ's lordship and not opposed to sin's dominion in their personal lives have no right to speak of Christ as their Savior: "No one can serve two masters" (Mt 6:24; see also Lk 6:46; 2Co 6:14—7:1; Jas 4:4; 1Jn 2:15–17).

6:16 SIN, WHICH LEADS TO DEATH. Paul solemnly warns believers who think they may securely sin because they are under grace. If believers give themselves to sin, they will in fact become slaves to sin (cf. Lk 16:13; Jn 8:34), resulting in "death" (cf. v. 23). "Death" here means "everlasting destruction and shut out from the presence of the Lord" (2Th 1:9), the opposite of "eternal life" (cf. v. 23).

6:17 OBEYED THE FORM OF TEACHING. In the early church new believers were committed to certain defined standards of teaching and conduct, based on apostolic principles and the believer's relation and commitment to Christ (cf. Mt 5–7; Ac 2:42). (1) These

FAITH AND GRACE

Ro 5:21 "So that, just as sin reigned in death, so also grace might reign through righteousness to bring eternal life through Jesus Christ our Lord."

Our salvation comes as a gift of God's *grace*, but it can only be appropriated by the human response of *faith*. To understand the process of salvation, we must understand these two words.

SAVING FAITH. Faith in Jesus Christ is the only condition God requires for salvation. Faith is not only a profession about Christ, but also an activity coming from the heart of the believer who seeks to follow Christ as Lord and Savior (cf. Mt 4:19; 16:24; Lk 9:23–25; Jn 10:4,27; 12:26; Rev 14:4). (1) The NT conception of faith includes four main elements:

(a) Faith means firmly believing and trusting in the crucified and risen Christ as our personal Lord and Savior (see Ro 1:17, note). It involves believing with all our hearts (Ro 6:17; Eph 6:6; Heb 10:22), yielding up our wills and committing our total selves to Jesus Christ as he is revealed in the NT.

(b) Faith involves repentance, i.e., in true sorrow turning from sin (Ac 17:30; 2Co 7:10) and turning to God through Christ. Saving faith is always a repentant faith (Ac 2:37–38; see Mt 3:2, note on repentance).

(c) Faith includes obedience to Jesus Christ and his Word as a way of life inspired by our faith, by our gratitude to God and by the regenerating work of the Spirit (Jn 3:3–6; 14:15,21–24; Heb 5:8–9). It is an "obedience that comes from faith" (Ro 1:5). Therefore, faith and obedience belong inseparably together (cf. Ro 16:26). Saving faith without the commitment to sanctification is illegitimate and impossible.

(d) Faith includes a heartfelt personal devotion and attachment to Jesus Christ that expresses itself in trust, love, gratitude and loyalty. Faith in an ultimate sense cannot properly be distinguished from love. It is a personal activity of sacrifice and self-giving directed toward Christ (cf. Mt 22:37; Jn 21:15–17; Ac 8:37; Ro 6:17; Gal 2:20; Eph 6:6; 1Pe 1:8).

(2) Faith in Jesus as Lord and Savior is both the act of a single moment and a continuing attitude that must grow and be strengthened (see Jn 1:12, note). Because we have faith in a definite person who died for us (Ro 4:25; 8:32; 1Th 5:9–10), our faith should become greater (Ro 4:20; 2Th 1:3; 1Pe 1:3–9). Trust and obedience develop into loyalty and devotion (Ro 14:8; 2Co 5:15); loyalty and devotion develop into an intense feeling of personal attachment to and love for the Lord Jesus Christ (Php 1:21; 3:8–10; see Jn 15:4, note; Gal 2:20, note). This faith in Christ brings us into a new relationship with God and exempts us from his wrath (Ro 1:18; 8:1); through that new relationship we become dead to sin (Ro 6:1–18) and indwelt by the Holy Spirit (Gal 3:5; 4:6).

GRACE. Grace is God's presence and love through Christ Jesus, given to believers by the Holy Spirit, imparting mercy, forgiveness, and the desire and power to do God's will (Jn 3:16; 1Co 15:10; Php 2:13; 1Ti 1:15–16). The whole movement of the Christian life from beginning to end is dependent on this grace.

(1) God gives a measure of grace as a gift (1Co 1:4) to unbelievers so that they may be able to believe in the Lord Jesus Christ (Eph 2:8–9; Tit 2:11; 3:4).

(2) God gives grace to believers to be "set free from sin" (Ro 6:20,22), "to will and to act according to his good purpose" (Php 2:13; cf. Tit 2:11–12; see Mt 7:21, note on obedience as a gift of God's grace), to pray (Zec 12:10), to grow in Christ (2Pe 3:18) and to witness for Christ (Ac 4:33; 11:23).

(3) God's grace must be diligently desired and sought (Heb 4:16). Some of the ways (i.e., means of grace) by which God's grace is received are: studying and obeying Scripture (Jn 15:1–11; 20:31; 2Ti 3:15); hearing the proclamation of the gospel (Lk 24:47; Ac 1:8; Ro 1:16; 1Co 1:17–18); praying (Heb 4:16; Jude 20); fasting (Mt 4:2; 6:16); worshiping Christ (Col 3:16); being continually filled with the Holy Spirit (Eph 5:18); and participating in the Lord's Supper (Ac 2:42; see Eph 2:9, note on how grace works).

(4) God's grace can be resisted (Heb 12:15), received in vain (2Co 6:1), put out (1Th 5:19), set aside (Gal 2:21) and abandoned by the believer (Gal 5:4).

thanks be to God[b] that, though you used to be slaves to sin,[c] you wholeheartedly obeyed the form of teaching[d] to which you were entrusted. **18**You have been set free from sin[e] and have become slaves to righteousness.[f]

19I put this in human terms[g] because you are weak in your natural selves. Just as you used to offer the parts of your body in slavery to impurity and to ever-increasing wickedness, so now offer them in slavery to righteousness[h] leading to holiness. **20**When you were slaves to sin,[i] you were free from the control of righteousness.[j] **21**What benefit did you reap at that time from the things you are now ashamed of? Those things result in death![k] **22**But now that you have been set free from sin[l] and have become slaves to God,[m] the benefit you reap leads to holiness, and the result is eternal life.[n] **23**For the wages of sin is death,[o] but the gift of God is eternal life[p] in[w] Christ Jesus our Lord.

Believers Die to the Law

7 Do you not know, brothers[q]—for I am speaking to men who know the law—that the law has authority over a man only as long as he lives? **2**For example, by law a married woman is bound to her husband as long as he is alive, but if her husband dies, she is released from the law of marriage.[r] **3**So then, if she marries another man while her husband is still alive, she is called an adulteress.[s] But if her husband dies, she is released from that law and is not an adulteress, even though she marries another man.

4So, my brothers, you also died to the law[t] through the body of Christ,[u] that you might belong to another,[v] to him who was raised from the dead, in order that we might bear fruit to God. **5**For when we were controlled by the sinful nature,[x][w] the sinful passions aroused by the law[x] were at work in our bodies,[y] so that we bore fruit for death.[z] **6**But now, by dying to what once bound us, we have been released from the law[a] so that we serve in the new way of the Spirit, and not in the old way of the written code.[b]

Struggling With Sin

7What shall we say, then?[c] Is the law sin? Certainly not![d] Indeed I would not have known what sin was except through the law.[e] For I would not have known what coveting really was if the law had not said, "Do not covet."[y][f] **8**But sin, seizing the opportunity afforded by the commandment,[g] produced in me every kind of covetous desire. For apart from law, sin is dead.[h] **9**Once I was alive apart from law; but when the commandment came, sin sprang to life and I died. **10**I found that the very commandment that was intended to bring life[i] actually brought death. **11**For sin, seizing the opportunity afforded by the commandment,[j] deceived me,[k] and

6:17 [b] Ro 1:8; S 2Co 2:14 [c] S ver 16 [d] 2Ti 1:13 **6:18** [e] S ver 2; ver 7,22; Ro 8:2; 1Pe 4:1; S ver 16 [f] S ver 22 **6:19** [g] Ro 3:5; Gal 3:15 [h] S ver 13; S ver 22 **6:20** [i] S ver 16 [j] ver 16 **6:21** [k] S ver 23 **6:22** [l] S ver 18 [m] ver 18,19; Ro 7:25; 1Co 7:22; Eph 6:6; 1Pe 2:16 [n] S Mt 25:46 **6:23** [o] ver 16,21; Ge 2:17; Pr 10:16; Eze 18:4; Ro 1:32; S 5:12; 7:5,13; 8:6,13; Gal 6:7,8; Jas 1:15 [p] S Mt 25:46 **7:1** [q] S Ac 1:16; S 22:5; Ro 1:13; 1Co 1:10; 5:11; 6:6; 14:20,26; Gal 3:15; 6:18 **7:2** [r] 1Co 7:39 **7:3** [s] S Lk 16:18
7:4 [t] ver 6; S Ro 6:6; 8:2; Gal 2:19; 3:23-25; 4:31; 5:1 [u] Col 1:22 [v] Gal 2:19,20 **7:5** [w] S Gal 5:24 [x] Ro 7:7-11 [y] Ro 6:13 [z] S Ro 6:23 **7:6** [a] S ver 4 [b] Ro 2:29; 2Co 3:6 **7:7** [c] S Ro 8:31 [d] S ver 12 [e] S Ro 4:15 [f] Ex 20:17; Dt 5:21 **7:8** [g] ver 11 [h] S Ro 4:15 **7:10** [i] Lev 18:5; Lk 10:26-28; S Ro 10:5; Gal 3:12
7:11 [j] ver 8 [k] Ge 3:13

[w] *23* Or *through* [x] *5* Or *the flesh*; also in verse 25 [y] *7* Exodus 20:17; Deut. 5:21

standards were most likely a summary of Christian doctrine and ethics to which converts subscribed when they accepted Christ as their new Master. It is the "sound doctrine" or "sound teaching" referred to in the Pastoral Letters (see 1Ti 1:10; 2Ti 1:13; 4:3; Tit 1:9; 2:1). (2) The supposition that Christianity has no pattern of teaching that regulates thought and practice, or that it is "legalism" to have rules of conduct, is alien to Paul's concept of the Christian faith. Christianity demands obedience from the heart to godly standards (see Mk 7:6, note on legalism).

7:4 DIED TO THE LAW. We no longer look to the OT law and sacrifices for salvation and acceptance from God (cf. Gal 3:23–25; 4:4–5). We have been separated from the old covenant of the law and united with Christ, and we now look to Christ for salvation. We must believe in Jesus (1Jn 5:13), receive his Spirit and grace (see article on FAITH AND GRACE, p. 302), and thereby receive forgiveness, be regenerated, and become able to "bear fruit to God" (6:22–23; 8:3–4; Mt 5:17, note; Eph 2:10; Gal 5:22–23; Col 1:5–6).

7:7–25 KNOWN WHAT SIN WAS EXCEPT THROUGH THE LAW. This section describes the pre-conversion experience of Paul or anyone else who attempts to please God without depending on his grace, mercy and strength (see 8:5; see article on FAITH AND GRACE, p. 302). (1) In vv. 7–12, Paul describes the stage of innocence until people reach an "age of accountability." They are "alive" (v. 9), i.e., without guilt and spiritual accountability, until they volitionally sin against God's law written externally or in their hearts (cf. 2:14–15; 7:7,9,11).

(2) In vv. 13–20, Paul depicts a state of slavery to sin because the law, when it becomes known, brings unconscious sin into consciousness and makes persons actual transgressors. Sin becomes their master, even though they try to resist it.

(3) In vv. 21–25, Paul discloses the utter despair that grips people as the knowledge and power of sin reduces them to wretchedness.

7:9–11 ONCE I WAS ALIVE. Paul's statements that "I was alive" and that "sin . . . put me to death" (v. 11) support the view that a child is innocent until he or she willfully sins against God's law from the heart (2:14–15; see previous note). The teaching that little infants come into the world guilty and worthy of eternal damnation is not found in Scripture.

through the commandment put me to
death. 12So then, the law is holy, and the
commandment is holy, righteous and
good.[l]
13Did that which is good, then, become
death to me? By no means! But in order
that sin might be recognized as sin, it produced death in me[m] through what was
good,[n] so that through the commandment
sin might become utterly sinful.
14We know that the law is spiritual; but
I am unspiritual,[o] sold[p] as a slave to
sin.[q] 15I do not understand what I do. For
what I want to do I do not do, but what I
hate I do.[r] 16And if I do what I do not
want to do, I agree that the law is good.[s]
17As it is, it is no longer I myself who do
it, but it is sin living in me.[t] 18I know that
nothing good lives in me, that is, in my
sinful nature.[z][u] For I have the desire to
do what is good, but I cannot carry it out.
19For what I do is not the good I want to
do; no, the evil I do not want to do—this
I keep on doing.[v] 20Now if I do what I do
not want to do, it is no longer I who do it,
but it is sin living in me that does it.[w]
21So I find this law at work:[x] When I
want to do good, evil is right there with
me. 22For in my inner being[y] I delight in
God's law;[z] 23but I see another law at
work in the members of my body, waging
war[a] against the law of my mind and making me a prisoner of the law of sin[b] at
work within my members. 24What a
wretched man I am! Who will rescue me
from this body of death?[c] 25Thanks be to
God—through Jesus Christ our Lord![d]
So then, I myself in my mind am a slave
to God's law,[e] but in the sinful nature a
slave to the law of sin.[f]

7:12 [l]ver 7,13,14, 16; Ro 8:4; Gal 3:21; 1Ti 1:8; S Ro 4:15 **7:13** [m]S Ro 6:23 [n]S ver 12 **7:14** [o]1Co 3:1 [p]1Ki 21:20,25; 2Ki 17:17 [q]S Ro 6:16 **7:15** [r]ver 19; Gal 5:17 **7:16** [s]S ver 12 **7:17** [t]ver 20 **7:18** [u]ver 25; S Gal 5:24 **7:19** [v]ver 15 **7:20** [w]ver 17 **7:21** [x]ver 23,25 **7:22** [y]Eph 3:16 [z]Ps 1:2; 40:8 **7:23** [a]Gal 5:17; Jas 4:1; 1Pe 2:11 [b]S Ro 6:16 **7:24** [c]Ro 6:6; 8:2 **7:25** [d]S 2Co 2:14 [e]S Ro 6:22 [f]S Ro 6:16 **8:1** [g]ver 34

Life Through the Spirit

8 Therefore, there is now no condemnation[g] for those who are in Christ

z 18 Or *my flesh*

7:12 THE LAW IS HOLY. See Mt 5:17, note; Gal 3:19, note.

7:14 THE LAW. Remember that Paul in ch. 7 is analyzing the state of an unregenerate person who is under OT law and accepts its truth, yet is conscious of his or her inability to live a life that pleases God (cf. v. 1). He is describing a conflict between a person who struggles on his or her own against the power of sin, demonstrating that we cannot attain justification, goodness and sanctification by our own attempts to resist sin and obey God's law. The conflict of the Christian, on the other hand, is quite different: it is the conflict of a person in union with Christ and the Holy Spirit against the power of sin (cf. Gal 5:16–18). In ch. 8 Paul describes the way to victory over sin through life in the Spirit.

7:14 I AM UNSPIRITUAL, SOLD AS A SLAVE TO SIN. More than any other words in ch. 7, these clearly point to a pre-conversion period under the law. This is so for the following reasons: (1) In ch. 7 Paul is demonstrating the insufficiency of the law to redeem us apart from grace, not the insufficiency of the gospel with grace (cf. Gal 3:24).

(2) In v. 5 Paul states that those who are "controlled by the sinful nature" (i.e., unspiritual, sensual) are bearing "fruit for death" (i.e., eternal death). And in 8:13 he maintains that "if you live according to the sinful nature, you will die" (cf. Gal 5:19–21). Thus the person referred to in ch. 7 is spiritually dead.

(3) The expression "sold as a slave to sin" means bondage to sin's power (cf. 1Ki 21:20,25; 2Ki 17:17). This cannot apply to a believer in Christ, since Christ, by the ransom of his blood (see Mt 20:28, note), has redeemed us from the power of sin and declares that sin no longer has dominion over us (6:14). Christ himself affirmed: "So if the Son sets you free, you will be free indeed" (Jn 8:36, note; cf. Ro 8:2). In fact, the name Jesus means "he will save his people from their sins" (Mt 1:21).

(4) Nor does the indwelling presence of the Holy Spirit (ch. 8) leave believers "sold as a slave to sin." Paul goes on to declare that "through Christ Jesus the law of the Spirit of life set me free from the law of sin" (8:2), and he includes himself with those "who do not live according to the sinful nature but according to the Spirit" (8:4), because "we have an obligation—but it is not to the sinful nature" (8:12).

7:15 WHAT I WANT TO DO I DO NOT DO. Those who attempt to obey God's commandments *without the saving grace of Christ* find themselves unable to accomplish the good intentions of their heart. They are not their own master; evil and sin rule within them. They are slaves to them (vv. 15–21) and are "prisoners of the law of sin" (v. 23). Only in Christ will God "provide a way out" of temptation, "so that you can stand up under it" (1Co 10:13).

7:22 I DELIGHT IN GOD'S LAW. Many under the OT law found that within the inward being (soul, reason) they delighted in God's law and commandments (cf. Ps 119; Isa 58:2). At the same time, however, as long as help was sought only from the law, sinful passions remained in control (v. 23). Likewise, there may be those in the church today who acknowledge the righteousness, purity and excellence of the gospel of Christ, yet because they have not experienced Christ's regenerating grace, find themselves in bondage to sin. As we attempt to live a life free from the bondage of sin and immorality, all our efforts will be useless if we are not truly born again, reconciled to God, redeemed from Satan's power and made new creatures in Christ, living a renewed life in the Spirit (Jn 3:3; Ro 8; 2Co 5:17).

7:24 WHAT A WRETCHED MAN I AM! The unregenerate person, after maintaining a losing conflict against sin, is at last taken prisoner (v. 23). Sin finally triumphs and the person is sold as a slave to sin (v. 14). His state is miserable; who can rescue him? The answer is "through Jesus Christ our Lord" (v. 25). It is he alone who will set us free "from the law of sin and death" (8:2).

Jesus,[a][h] **2**because through Christ Jesus[i]
the law of the Spirit of life[j] set me free[k]
from the law of sin[l] and death. **3**For what
the law was powerless[m] to do in that it
was weakened by the sinful nature,[b][n]
God did by sending his own Son in the
likeness of sinful man[o] to be a sin offering.[c][p] And so he condemned sin in sinful
man,[d] **4**in order that the righteous requirements[q] of the law might be fully met
in us, who do not live according to the
sinful nature but according to the Spirit.[r]
5Those who live according to the sinful
nature have their minds set on what that
nature desires;[s] but those who live in accordance with the Spirit have their minds
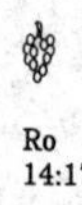
set on what the Spirit desires.[t] **6**The mind
of sinful man[e] is death,[u] but the mind
Ro 14:17 controlled by the Spirit is life[v] and peace;
7the sinful mind[f] is hostile to God.[w] It
does not submit to God's law, nor can it
do so. **8**Those controlled by the sinful nature[x] cannot please God.

8:1 [h]ver 39; S Ro 16:3 **8:2** [i]Ro 7:25 [j]1Co 15:45 [k]Jn 8:32,36; S Ro 6:18 [l]S Ro 6:16; S 7:4 **8:3** [m]Heb 7:18; 10:1-4 [n]Ro 7:18, 19; S Gal 5:24 [o]S Php 2:7 [p]Heb 2:14,17 **8:4** [q]Ro 2:26 [r]S Gal 5:16 **8:5** [s]Gal 5:19-21 [t]Gal 5:22-25 **8:6** [u]S Ro 6:23 [v]ver 13; Gal 6:8 **8:7** [w]Jas 4:4 **8:8** [x]S Gal 5:24

8:9 [y]S Gal 5:24 [z]ver 11; 1Co 6:19; 2Ti 1:14 [a]Jn 14:17; S Ac 16:7; 1Jn 4:13 **8:10** [b]ver 9; Ex 29:45; Jn 14:20,23; 2Co 13:5; Gal 2:20; Eph 3:17; Col 1:27; Rev 3:20

9You, however, are controlled not by
the sinful nature[y] but by the Spirit, if the
Spirit of God lives in you.[z] And if anyone
does not have the Spirit of Christ,[a] he
does not belong to Christ. **10**But if Christ
is in you,[b] your body is dead because of
sin, yet your spirit is alive because of righteousness. **11**And if the Spirit of him who
raised Jesus from the dead[c] is living in
you, he who raised Christ from the dead
will also give life to your mortal bodies[d]
through his Spirit, who lives in you.
12Therefore, brothers, we have an obligation—but it is not to the sinful nature,
to live according to it.[e] **13**For if you live

8:11 [c]S Ac 2:24 [d]Jn 5:21; S Ro 6:5 **8:12** [e]ver 4; S Gal 5:24

[a] *1* Some later manuscripts *Jesus, who do not live according to the sinful nature but according to the Spirit,* [b] *3* Or *the flesh*; also in verses 4, 5, 8, 9, 12 and 13 [c] *3* Or *man, for sin* [d] *3* Or *in the flesh* [e] *6* Or *mind set on the flesh* [f] *7* Or *the mind set on the flesh*

8:1 THOSE WHO ARE IN CHRIST JESUS. Paul has just shown that life without the grace of Christ is defeat, misery and bondage to sin. Now in ch. 8, Paul tells us that spiritual life, freedom from condemnation, victory over sin and fellowship with God come through union with Christ by the indwelling Holy Spirit. By receiving and following the Spirit, we are delivered from sin's power and are led onward to final glorification in Christ. This is the normal Christian life under the full provision of the gospel.

8:2 THE LAW OF THE SPIRIT. This "law of the Spirit of life" is the regulating and activating power and life of the Holy Spirit operating in the hearts of believers. The Holy Spirit comes into sinners and frees them from the power of sin (cf. 7:23). The law of the Spirit comes into full operation as believers commit themselves to obey the Spirit (vv. 4–5,13–14). They find a new power operating within, a power that allows them to overcome sin. "The law of sin and death" is the controlling power of sin, which places people in bondage (7:14) and reduces them to wretchedness (7:24).

8:4 THE LAW MIGHT BE FULLY MET IN US. The Holy Spirit working within believers allows them to live lives of righteousness, which is seen as the fulfillment of God's moral law. Thus, the operation of grace and obedience to God's law are not in conflict (cf. 2:13; 3:31; 6:15; 7:12,14). They both point to righteousness and holiness.

8:5–14 ACCORDING TO THE SINFUL NATURE . . . THE SPIRIT. Paul describes two classes of people: those who live according to the sinful nature and those who live according to the Spirit. (1) To live "according to the sinful nature" is to desire, take pleasure in, be occupied with and gratify the corrupt desires of sinful human nature. This includes not only sexual immorality, adultery, hatred, selfish ambition, outbursts of anger, and so forth (see Gal 5:19–21), but also obscenity, pornographic addiction, drug addiction, mental and emotional pleasure from sex scenes in plays, books, TV or movies, and the like (see article on THE ACTS OF THE SINFUL NATURE AND THE FRUIT OF THE SPIRIT, p. 394).

(2) To live "in accordance with the Spirit" is to seek and submit to the Holy Spirit's direction and enablement, and to concentrate one's attention on the things of God (see article on THE ACTS OF THE SINFUL NATURE AND THE FRUIT OF THE SPIRIT, p. 394).

(3) It is impossible to follow the sinful nature and the Spirit at the same time (vv. 7–8; Gal 5:17–18). If anyone fails to resist by the Spirit his or her sinful desires and instead lives according to the sinful nature (v. 13), he or she becomes God's enemy (v. 7; Jas 4:4) and can expect spiritual and eternal death (v. 13). Those who make the things of God their chief love and concern can expect eternal life and communion with God (vv. 10–11,15–16).

8:9 IF THE SPIRIT OF GOD LIVES IN YOU. All believers from the moment they accept Jesus Christ as Lord and Savior have the Holy Spirit living in them (cf. 1Co 3:16; 6:19–20; Eph 1:13–14; see article on THE DOCTRINE OF THE HOLY SPIRIT, p. 240).

8:10 YOUR BODY IS DEAD BECAUSE OF SIN. Because sin has invaded the physical aspect of our being, our bodies must die or be transformed (cf. 1Co 15:50–54; 1Th 4:13–17). Yet because Christ is in us, we now experience the life of the Spirit.

8:13 PUT TO DEATH THE MISDEEDS OF THE BODY. Paul emphasizes the necessity for continual warfare against all that would limit God's work in our lives (cf. 6:11–19), for sin is always striving to regain control over us. (1) This spiritual conflict, although directed against Satan and evil spiritual forces (Eph 6:12), is primarily against the passions and desires of the "sinful nature" (Gal 5:16–21; Jas 4:1; 1Pe 2:11). We as believers must continually decide whether we will surrender to sinful desires or to the demands of the divine nature in which we participate (Gal 5:16,18; 2Pe 1:4).

(2) The result of failing to put to death the misdeeds

according to the sinful nature, you will
die;[f] but if by the Spirit you put to death
the misdeeds of the body,[g] you will live,[h]
14because those who are led by the Spirit
of God[i] are sons of God.[j] 15For you did
not receive a spirit[k] that makes you a
slave again to fear,[l] but you received the
Spirit of sonship.[g] And by him we cry,
"Abba,[h] Father."[m] 16The Spirit himself
testifies with our spirit[n] that we are God's
children.[o] 17Now if we are children, then
we are heirs[p]—heirs of God and co-heirs
with Christ, if indeed we share in his sufferings[q] in order that we may also share
in his glory.[r]

Future Glory

18I consider that our present sufferings
are not worth comparing with the glory
that will be revealed in us.[s] 19The creation waits in eager expectation for the
sons of God[t] to be revealed. 20For the
creation was subjected to frustration, not
by its own choice, but by the will of the one
who subjected it,[u] in hope 21that[i] the creation itself will be liberated from its bondage to decay[v] and brought into the glorious freedom of the children of God.[w]

22We know that the whole creation has
been groaning[x] as in the pains of childbirth right up to the present time. 23Not

8:13 [f]S Ro 6:23 [g]S Ro 6:2 [h]ver 6; Gal 6:8 **8:14** [i]S Gal 5:18 [j]ver 19; Hos 1:10; Mal 3:17; Mt 5:9; S Jn 1:12; Gal 3:26; 4:5; Eph 1:5; Rev 21:7 **8:15** [k]S Jn 20:22 [l]S 2Ti 1:7 [m]Mk 14:36; Gal 4:5,6 **8:16** [n]2Co 1:22; Eph 1:13 [o]S ver 14; S Jn 1:12 **8:17** [p]S Ac 20:32; Gal 3:29; 4:7; Eph 3:6; Tit 3:7 [q]S 2Co 1:5 [r]2Ti 2:12; 1Pe 4:13 **8:18** [s]2Co 4:17; 1Pe 4:13; 5:1 **8:19** [t]S ver 14 **8:20** [u]Ge 3:17-19; 5:29 **8:21** [v]Ac 3:21; 2Pe 3:13; Rev 21:1 [w]S Jn 1:12 **8:22** [x]Jer 12:4

g *15* Or *adoption* h *15* Aramaic for *Father* i *20,21* Or *subjected it in hope. 21For*

of the body is spiritual death (vv. 6,13) and the loss of inheritance in God's kingdom (Gal 5:19–21). The words "you will die" mean that a Christian can pass from spiritual life back into spiritual death. Thus, the life of God that we receive at our new birth (Jn 3:3–6) can be extinguished in the soul of a believer who refuses to put to death by the Spirit the misdeeds of the body.

8:13–14 THOSE ... ARE SONS OF GOD. Paul gives the basis for the assurance of salvation here. If one is consistently putting to death the misdeeds of the body, then we are being led by the Spirit. Those led by the Spirit are God's children.

8:14 LED BY THE SPIRIT OF GOD. The Holy Spirit lives within the child of God in order to lead him or her to think, speak and act according to God's Word. (1) He leads primarily by promptings that (a) are inward urgings to do God's will and to put to death the misdeeds of the body (v. 13; Php 2:13; Tit 2:11–12); (b) are always in harmony with Scripture (1Co 2:12–13; cf. 2Pe 1:20–21); (c) are intended to give direction in life (Lk 4:1; Ac 10:19–20; 16:6–7); (d) are opposed to sinful desires (Gal 5:17–18; 1Pe 2:11); (e) are concerned with the guilt of sin, Christ's standard of righteousness and God's judgment against evil (Jn 16:8–11); (f) exhort believers to persevere in the faith and warn them concerning falling away from personal faith in Christ (v. 13; Heb 3:7–14); (g) become weaker the longer believers resist obeying the Spirit's prompting (1:28; Eph 4:17–19,30–31; 1Th 5:19); (h) result in spiritual death when rejected (vv. 6,13); (i) result in spiritual life and peace when obeyed (vv. 6,10–11,13; Gal 5:22–23).

(2) The Spirit's prompting comes by (a) reading God's Word (Jn 14:26; 15:7,26; 16:13; 2Ti 3:16–17); (b) praying fervently (v. 26; Ac 13:2–3); (c) listening to godly preaching and teaching (2Ti 4:1–2; Heb 13:7,17); (d) exercising the manifestations of the Spirit (see 1Co 12:7–10; 14:6); and (e) heeding the counsel of Christian parents and trustworthy spiritual leaders (Eph 6:1; Col 3:20).

8:16 THE SPIRIT HIMSELF TESTIFIES. The Holy Spirit imparts to us a confidence that through Christ and with Christ, we are now God's children (v. 15). He makes real the truth that Christ loved us, still loves us and lives for us in heaven as Mediator (cf. Heb 7:25). The Spirit also shows us that the Father loves us as his adopted children, no less than he loves his one and only Son (Jn 14:21,23; 17:23). Finally, the Spirit creates in us the love and confidence by which we cry to him, *"Abba,* Father" (v. 15).

8:17 IF ... WE SHARE IN HIS SUFFERINGS. Paul reminds us that a victorious life in the Spirit is no easy path. Jesus suffered, and we who follow him will also suffer. This suffering is considered a suffering with him (cf. 2Co 1:5; Php 3:10; Col 1:24; 2Ti 2:11–12), and it is the consequence of our relationship to God as children, our identification with Christ, our witness for him and our refusal to conform to the world (cf. 12:1–2).

8:18 OUR PRESENT SUFFERINGS. All the sufferings of this present age—sickness, pain, misery, disappointments, poverty, mistreatment, sorrow, persecution and trouble of any kind—must be considered insignificant when compared with the blessing, privileges and glory that will be given to the faithful believer in the age to come (cf. 2Co 4:17).

8:22 THE WHOLE CREATION HAS BEEN GROANING. In vv. 22–27 Paul speaks of a threefold groaning: of creation (v. 22), of believers (v. 23) and of the Holy Spirit (v. 26). The "creation" (i.e., animate and inanimate nature) has been subjected to suffering and physical catastrophies because of human sin (v. 20). Thus, God has purposed that nature itself will be redeemed and re-created. There will be a new heaven and a new earth, a restoration of all things according to God's will (cf. 2Co 5:17; Gal 6:15; Rev 21:1,5), when God's faithful children receive their full inheritance (vv. 14,23).

8:23 WE OURSELVES ... GROAN. Although believers possess the Spirit and his blessings, they still groan inwardly, desiring their full redemption. This groaning is for two reasons. (1) Believers, living in a sinful world that grieves them, still experience imperfection, pain and sorrow. The groaning expresses the deep sorrow felt at these circumstances (cf. 2Co 5:2–4). (2) They groan for complete redemption and the fullness of the Holy Spirit that will be given at the resurrection. They groan for the glory to be revealed and for the privileges of their full rights

only so, but we ourselves, who have the firstfruits of the Spirit,[y] groan[z] inwardly as we wait eagerly[a] for our adoption as sons, the redemption of our bodies.[b] 24For in this hope we were saved.[c] But hope that is seen is no hope at all.[d] Who hopes for what he already has? 25But if we hope for what we do not yet have, we wait for it patiently.[e]

26In the same way, the Spirit helps us in our weakness. We do not know what we ought to pray for, but the Spirit[f] himself intercedes for us[g] with groans that words cannot express. 27And he who searches our hearts[h] knows the mind of the Spirit, because the Spirit intercedes[i] for the saints in accordance with God's will.

More Than Conquerors

28And we know that in all things God works for the good[j] of those who love him,[j] who[k] have been called[k] according to his purpose.[l] 29For those God foreknew[m] he also predestined[n] to be conformed to the likeness of his Son,[o] that he might be the firstborn[p] among many brothers. 30And those he predestined,[q] he also called;[r] those he called, he also justified;[s] those he justified, he also glorified.[t]

31What, then, shall we say in response to this?[u] If God is for us,[v] who can be against us?[w] 32He who did not spare his own Son,[x] but gave him up for us all—how will he not also, along with him, graciously give us all things? 33Who will bring any charge[y] against those whom God has chosen? It is God who justifies. 34Who is he that condemns?[z] Christ Jesus, who died[a]—more than that, who was raised to life[b]—is at the right hand of God[c] and is also interceding for us.[d] 35Who shall separate us from the love of Christ?[e] Shall trouble or hardship or persecution or famine or nakedness or danger or sword?[f] 36As it is written:

8:23 [y]S 2Co 5:5 [z]2Co 5:2,4 [a]ver 19; Gal 5:5 [b]ver 11; Php 3:21 **8:24** [c]1Th 5:8; Tit 3:7 [d]S 2Co 4:18 **8:25** [e]Ps 37:7 **8:26** [f]ver 15,16 [g]Eph 6:18 **8:27** [h]S Rev 2:23 [i]S ver 34 **8:28** [j]Ge 50:20; Isa 38:17; Jer 29:11 [k]ver 30; Ro 11:29; 1Co 1:9; Gal 1:6,15; Eph 4:1,4; 1Th 2:12; 2Ti 1:9; Heb 9:15; 1Pe 2:9; 2Pe 1:10 [l]Eph 1:11; 3:11; Heb 6:17 **8:29** [m]Ro 11:2; 1Pe 1:2 [n]Eph 1:5, 11 [o]1Co 15:49; 2Co 3:18; Php 3:21; 1Jn 3:2 [p]S Col 1:18 **8:30** [q]Eph 1:5,11 [r]S ver 28 [s]S Ro 4:25 [t]Ro 9:23 **8:31** [u]Ro 4:1; 6:1; 7:7; 9:14,30 [v]Ex 3:12; Isa 41:10; Hag 1:13 [w]Ps 56:9; 118:6; Isa 8:10; Jer 20:11; Heb 13:6 **8:32** [x]Ge 22:13; Mal 3:17; Jn 3:16; Ro 5:8 **8:33** [y]Isa 50:8,9 **8:34** [z]ver 1 [a]Ro 5:6-8 [b]S Ac 2:24 [c]S Mk 16:19 [d]ver 27; Job 16:20; Isa 53:12; Heb 7:25; 9:24; 1Jn 2:1 **8:35** [e]ver 37-39 [f]1Co 4:11; 2Co 11:26,27

j *28* Some manuscripts *And we know that all things work together for good to those who love God*
k *28* Or *works together with those who love him to bring about what is good—with those who*

as children (cf. 2Co 5:4).

8:26 SPIRIT HIMSELF INTERCEDES FOR US WITH GROANS. Concerning the Holy Spirit's activity in helping the believer in prayer, three observations are important: (1) The child of God has two divine intercessors. Christ intercedes for the believer in heaven (v. 34; see Heb 7:25, note; 1Jn 2:1) and the Holy Spirit intercedes within the believer on earth. (2) "With groans" probably indicates that the Spirit intercedes with the groans uttered by the believer. These groanings occur in the believer's heart. (3) The spiritual desires and yearnings of believers find their source in the Holy Spirit, who dwells within our hearts. The Spirit himself sighs, groans and suffers within us, longing for the final day of redemption (vv. 23–25). He appeals to the Father on behalf of our needs "in accordance with God's will" (v. 27).

8:28 IN ALL THINGS GOD WORKS FOR THE GOOD. This passage greatly encourages God's children when we must endure suffering in this life. (1) God will bring good out of all affliction, trials, persecution and suffering; the good that God works is conforming us to the image of Christ and ultimately bringing about our glorification (v. 29). (2) This promise is limited to those who love God and have submitted to him through faith in Christ (cf. Ex 20:6; Dt 7:9; Ps 37:17; Isa 56:4–7; 1Co 2:9). (3) The "all things" do not include our sins and negligence (vv. 6,13; 6:16,21,23; Gal 6:8); no one can excuse sin by maintaining that God will work it out for good.

8:29 THOSE GOD FOREKNEW. "Foreknew" in this verse is equivalent to "foreloved" and is used in the sense of "to set loving regard on," "to choose to bestow love on from eternity" (cf. Ex 2:25; Ps 1:6; Hos 13:5; Mt 7:23; 1Co 8:3; Gal 4:9; 1Jn 3:1).

(1) Foreknowledge means that God purposed from eternity to love and redeem the human race through Christ (5:8; Jn 3:16). The recipient of God's foreknowledge or forelove is stated in the plural and refers to the church. That is, God's forelove is primarily of the corporate body of Christ (Eph 1:4; 2:4; 1Jn 4:19) and includes individuals only as they identify themselves with this corporate body through abiding faith in and union with Christ (Jn 15:1–6; see article on ELECTION AND PREDESTINATION, p. 402).

(2) The corporate body of Christ will attain to glorification (v. 30). Individual believers will fall short of such glorification if they separate themselves from that foreloved body and fail to maintain their faith in Christ (vv. 12–14,17; Col 1:21–23).

8:30 PREDESTINED. For an explanation of predestination, see article on ELECTION AND PREDESTINATION, p. 402.

8:34 IS ALSO INTERCEDING FOR US. See Heb 7:25, note on Christ's heavenly intercession for believers.

8:36 SHEEP TO BE SLAUGHTERED. The adversities listed by the apostle in vv. 35–36 have been the experience of God's people in all generations (Ac 14:22; 2Co 11:23–29; Heb 11:35–38). Believers should not think it strange if they experience trouble, persecution, hunger, poverty or danger. Trouble and calamity do not necessarily mean that God has deserted us, nor that he has stopped loving us (v. 35). On the contrary, our suffering as believers will open up the means by which we experience more of God's love and comfort (2Co 1:4–5). Paul assures us that in all these adversities we will overcome and be more than conquerors through Christ (vv. 37–39; cf. Mt 5:10–12; Php 1:29).

"For your sake we face death all day
long;
we are considered as sheep to be
slaughtered."[l][g]

37No, in all these things we are more than
conquerors[h] through him who loved us.[i]
38For I am convinced that neither death
nor life, neither angels nor demons,[m] neither the present nor the future,[j] nor any
powers,[k] **39**neither height nor depth, nor
anything else in all creation, will be able
to separate us from the love of God[l] that
is in Christ Jesus our Lord.[m]

God's Sovereign Choice

9 I speak the truth in Christ—I am not
lying,[n] my conscience confirms[o] it in
the Holy Spirit— **2**I have great sorrow and
unceasing anguish in my heart. **3**For I
could wish that I myself[p] were cursed[q]
and cut off from Christ for the sake of my
brothers,[r] those of my own race,[s] **4**the
people of Israel.[t] Theirs is the adoption
as sons;[u] theirs the divine glory,[v] the
covenants,[w] the receiving of the law,[x] the
temple worship[y] and the promises.[z]
5Theirs are the patriarchs,[a] and from
them is traced the human ancestry of
Christ,[b] who is God over all,[c] forever
praised![n][d] Amen.
6It is not as though God's word[e] had
failed. For not all who are descended from
Israel are Israel.[f] **7**Nor because they are
his descendants are they all Abraham's
children. On the contrary, "It is through
Isaac that your offspring will be reckoned."[o][g] **8**In other words, it is not the
natural children who are God's children,[h]
but it is the children of the promise who
are regarded as Abraham's offspring.[i]
9For this was how the promise was stated:
"At the appointed time I will return, and
Sarah will have a son."[p][j]
10Not only that, but Rebekah's children
had one and the same father, our father
Isaac.[k] **11**Yet, before the twins were born
or had done anything good or bad[l]—in
order that God's purpose[m] in election
might stand: **12**not by works but by him
who calls—she was told, "The older will
serve the younger."[q][n] **13**Just as it is written: "Jacob I loved, but Esau I hated."[r][o]
14What then shall we say?[p] Is God unjust? Not at all![q] **15**For he says to Moses,

"I will have mercy on whom I have
mercy,
and I will have compassion on
whom I have compassion."[s][r]

16It does not, therefore, depend on man's
desire or effort, but on God's mercy.[s]
17For the Scripture says to Pharaoh: "I
raised you up for this very purpose, that
I might display my power in you and that
my name might be proclaimed in all the
earth."[t][t] **18**Therefore God has mercy on

8:36 [g]Ps 44:22; 1Co 4:9; 15:30,31; 2Co 4:11; 6:9; 11:23 **8:37** [h]1Co 15:57 [i]Ro 5:8; Gal 2:20; Eph 5:2; Rev 1:5; 3:9 **8:38** [j]1Co 3:22 [k]Eph 1:21; Col 1:16; 1Pe 3:22 **8:39** [l]S Ro 5:8 [m]ver 1; S Ro 16:3 **9:1** [n]Ps 15:2; 2Co 11:10; Gal 1:20; 1Ti 2:7 [o]S Ro 1:9 **9:3** [p]Ex 32:32 [q]1Co 12:3; 16:22 [r]S Ac 22:5 [s]Ro 11:14 **9:4** [t]ver 6 [u]Ex 4:22; 6:7; Dt 7:6 [v]Heb 9:5 [w]Ge 17:2; Dt 4:13; Ac 3:25; Eph 2:12 [x]Ps 147:19 [y]Heb 9:1 [z]S Ac 13:32; S Gal 3:16 **9:5** [a]Ro 11:28 [b]Mt 1:1-16; Ro 1:3 [c]Jn 1:1; Col 2:9 [d]Ro 1:25; 2Co 11:31 **9:6** [e]S Heb 4:12 [f]Ro 2:28,29; Gal 6:16 **9:7** [g]Ge 21:12; Heb 11:18 **9:8** [h]S Ro 8:14 [i]S Gal 3:16 **9:9** [j]Ge 18:10,14 **9:10** [k]Ge 25:21 **9:11** [l]ver 16 [m]Ro 8:28 **9:12** [n]Ge 25:23 **9:13** [o]Mal 1:2,3 **9:14** [p]S Ro 8:31 [q]2Ch 19:7 **9:15** [r]Ex 33:19 **9:16** [s]Eph 2:8; Tit 3:5 **9:17** [t]Ex 9:16; 14:4; Ps 76:10

[l] *36* Psalm 44:22 [m] *38* Or *nor heavenly rulers* [n] *5* Or *Christ, who is over all. God be forever praised!* Or *Christ. God who is over all be forever praised!* [o] *7* Gen. 21:12 [p] *9* Gen. 18:10,14 [q] *12* Gen. 25:23 [r] *13* Mal. 1:2,3 [s] *15* Exodus 33:19 [t] *17* Exodus 9:16

8:39 THE LOVE OF GOD THAT IS IN CHRIST JESUS OUR LORD. If anyone fails in his or her spiritual life, it will neither be from a lack of divine grace and love (vv. 31–34), nor from external force or overwhelming adversity (vv. 35–39), but from their own neglect to remain in Christ Jesus (see Jn 15:6, note). Only "in Christ Jesus" is God's love revealed, and only in him do we experience it. Only as we remain in Christ Jesus as "our Lord" can we have the certainty that we will never be separated from God's love.

9:1 ISRAEL'S UNBELIEF. In chs. 9–11 Paul addresses the problem of Israel's past election (9:6–29), present rejection of the gospel (9:30—10:21), and future salvation (11:1–36). For an examination of his argument, see article on ISRAEL IN GOD'S PLAN OF SALVATION, p. 310.

9:2 I HAVE GREAT SORROW . . . IN MY HEART. Paul's ceaseless concern and sorrow over those without Christ (10:1; 11:14; 1Co 9:22) should be every Christian's attitude. This same attitude of grief and willingness to suffer for the salvation of others existed in Moses (Ex 32:32) and Jesus (Mt 23:37; Ro 3:24–25).

9:6 GOD'S WORD HAD FAILED. With this verse, Paul begins an extended discussion of God's dealings with the nation of Israel and the reason for their present unbelief (see article on ISRAEL IN GOD'S PLAN OF SALVATION, p. 310).

9:11 GOD'S PURPOSE. For comments on God's purpose fulfilled in Esau and Jacob, see article on ISRAEL IN GOD'S PLAN OF SALVATION, p. 310.

9:13 JACOB I LOVED, BUT ESAU I HATED. This verse does not mean that Jacob and his descendants were elected to eternal salvation while Esau and his descendants were elected to eternal damnation. Rather, it was an election of Jacob's descendants to be the channel of God's revelation and blessing to the world. Observe that according to chs. 9–11, the majority of Jacob's descendants failed to carry out their calling and thus were finally rejected by God (vv. 27,30–33; 10:3; 11:20). Furthermore, those who were not "loved" (i.e., the Gentiles) obeyed God through faith and became "sons of the living God" (vv. 25–26).

9:15 I WILL HAVE MERCY. This verse emphasizes the freedom of God's mercy. His overflowing active compassion cannot be earned or controlled by humans (v. 16). He has willed to have mercy on all (11:32).

9:18 ON WHOM HE WANTS TO HAVE MERCY. God intends to show mercy to those who repent and believe in Jesus as Lord and Savior, while he hardens

ISRAEL IN GOD'S PLAN OF SALVATION

Ro 9:6 "It is not as though God's word had failed. For not all who are descended from Israel are Israel."

INTRODUCTION. In Ro 9–11, Paul addresses the problem of Israel's past election, present rejection of the gospel and future salvation. These three chapters were written to answer the question Jewish believers were asking: how could God's promises to Abraham and the nation of Israel remain valid while the nation of Israel as a whole seems to have no part in the gospel? This article summarizes Paul's argument.

OVERVIEW. There are three elements to Paul's discussion of Israel in God's plan of salvation.

(1) The first (Ro 9:6–29) is an examination of Israel's past election. (a) In 9:6–13, Paul maintains that God's promise to Israel has not failed, for the promise never included any except the faithful in the nation. It was meant only for true Israel, those who were faithful to the promise (see Ge 12:1–3; 17:19). There is always an Israel within Israel who have received the promise. (b) In 9:14–29, Paul points out that God has the right to do as he pleases with individuals and nations. He has a right to reject Israel if they disobey and the right to show mercy to the Gentiles and offer them salvation if he chooses.

(2) The second major section (Ro 9:30—10:21) analyzes Israel's present rejection of the gospel. Their failure to respond to Christ is not due to an unconditional divine decree, but to their own unbelief and disobedience (see Ro 10:3, note).

(3) Finally, Paul explains (Ro 11) that the rejection of Israel is only partial and temporary. Israel will eventually accept God's salvation in Christ. There are several steps in his argument. (a) God has not rejected the true Israel, for he has remained faithful to the "remnant" that has remained faithful to him by accepting Christ (11:1–6). (b) God's present hardening of the majority of Israel has come because they refused to believe in Christ (11:7–10; cf. 9:31—10:21). (c) God has turned Israel's transgression (i.e., the crucifixion of Christ) into an opportunity to proclaim salvation to all the world (11:11–12,15). (d) During this present time of Israel's national unbelief, the salvation of individuals, both Jew and Gentile (cf. 10:12–13) depends on faith in Jesus Christ (11:13–24). (e) Belief in Jesus Christ by a portion of national Israel will take place in the future (11:25–29). (f) God's sincere purpose is to have mercy on all, both Jew and Gentile, and to include in his kingdom all people who believe in Christ (11:30–36; cf. 10:12–13; 11:20–24).

PERSPECTIVE. Several things stand out in these three chapters of the book of Romans.

(1) This discussion about Israel does not refer primarily to the eternal life and death of individuals after physical death. Rather, Paul is discussing God's dealing with nations and people historically, i.e., his right to use certain nations and people as he chooses. For example, the choice of the person Jacob over his brother Esau (Ro 9:11) was a choice for the purpose of founding and using the nations of Israel and Edom that came from them. It had nothing to do with their individual eternal destiny to salvation or condemnation. The point is that God has the right to call and place responsibility on those individuals and nations that he chooses.

(2) Paul expresses ceaseless concern for and intense sorrow over the Jewish nation (Ro 9:1–3). The very fact that Paul prays for his countrymen to be saved indicates that he did not believe the form of predestination theology that teaches that all people are foreordained either to heaven or hell before they are born. Rather, Paul's heartfelt desire and prayer is a reflection of God's desire for the Jewish people (cf. Ro 10:21; see Lk 19:41, note on Jesus weeping over Israel's rejection of God's way of salvation). The NT nowhere teaches that some people have been predestined to hell before they come into the world (see article on ELECTION AND PREDESTINATION, p. 402).

(3) The most significant element in this entire discussion is the issue of faith. The lost spiritual condition of the majority of Israel was not determined or fixed by an arbitrary decree of God, but came as a result of their own unwillingness to submit to God's plan of salvation through faith in Christ (Ro 9:33; 10:3; 11:20). Many Gentiles, however, accepted God's way of faith and attained the righteousness that is by faith. They obeyed God through faith and became "sons of the living God" (9:25–26). This underscores the importance of the obedience that comes through faith (1:5; 16:26) with respect to God's call and election.

(4) Hope is still offered to the nation of Israel if it ceases to continue in its unbelief (Ro 11:23). Similarly, the Gentile believers who now are a part of God's church are warned that they too face the same possibility of being cut off from salvation. Therefore, like the Israelites, they must be diligent to continue in the faith with fear (11:20–23). That warning is as valid today as it was when Paul wrote it.

whom he wants to have mercy, and he
hardens whom he wants to harden.[u]
19One of you will say to me:[v] "Then
why does God still blame us?[w] For who
resists his will?"[x] **20**But who are you, O
man, to talk back to God?[y] "Shall what is
formed say to him who formed it,[z] 'Why
did you make me like this?' "[u][a] **21**Does
not the potter have the right to make out
of the same lump of clay some pottery for
noble purposes and some for common
use?[b]
22What if God, choosing to show his
wrath and make his power known, bore
with great patience[c] the objects of his
wrath—prepared for destruction?[d]
23What if he did this to make the riches of
his glory[e] known to the objects of his mercy, whom he prepared in advance for glory[f]— **24**even us, whom he also called,[g]
not only from the Jews but also from the
Gentiles?[h] **25**As he says in Hosea:

> "I will call them 'my people' who are
> not my people;
> and I will call her 'my loved one'
> who is not my loved one,"[v][i]

26and,

> "It will happen that in the very place
> where it was said to them,
> 'You are not my people,'
> they will be called 'sons of the living
> God.' "[w][j]

27Isaiah cries out concerning Israel:

> "Though the number of the Israelites
> be like the sand by the sea,[k]
> only the remnant will be saved.[l]
> **28**For the Lord will carry out
> his sentence on earth with speed
> and finality."[x][m]

29It is just as Isaiah said previously:

> "Unless the Lord Almighty[n]
> had left us descendants,
> we would have become like Sodom,
> we would have been like
> Gomorrah."[y][o]

Israel's Unbelief

30What then shall we say?[p] That the
Gentiles, who did not pursue righteousness, have obtained it, a righteousness
that is by faith;[q] **31**but Israel, who pursued a law of righteousness,[r] has not attained it.[s] **32**Why not? Because they pursued it not by faith but as if it were by
works. They stumbled over the "stumbling stone."[t] **33**As it is written:

> "See, I lay in Zion a stone that
> causes men to stumble
> and a rock that makes them fall,
> and the one who trusts in him will
> never be put to shame."[z][u]

10 Brothers, my heart's desire[v] and
prayer to God for the Israelites is

9:18 [u]Ex 4:21; 7:3; 14:4,17; Dt 2:30; Jos 11:20; Ro 11:25
9:19 [v]Ro 11:19; 1Co 15:35; Jas 2:18 [w]Ro 3:7 [x]2Sa 16:10; 2Ch 20:6; Da 4:35
9:20 [y]Job 1:22; 9:12; 40:2 [z]Isa 64:8; Jer 18:6 [a]Isa 29:16; 45:9; 10:15
9:21 [b]2Ti 2:20
9:22 [c]S Ro 2:4 [d]Pr 16:4
9:23 [e]S Ro 2:4 [f]Ro 8:30
9:24 [g]S Ro 8:28 [h]S Ro 3:29
9:25 [i]Hos 2:23; 1Pe 2:10
9:26 [j]Hos 1:10; S Mt 16:16; S Ro 8:14
9:27 [k]Ge 22:17; Hos 1:10 [l]2Ki 19:4; Jer 44:14; 50:20; Joel 2:32; Ro 11:5
9:28 [m]Isa 10:22, 23
9:29 [n]Jas 5:4 [o]Isa 1:9; Ge 19:24-29; Dt 29:23; Isa 13:19; Jer 50:40
9:30 [p]S Ro 8:31 [q]Ro 1:17; 3:22; 4:5,13; 10:6; Gal 2:16; Php 3:9; Heb 11:7
9:31 [r]Dt 6:25; Isa 51:1; Ro 10:2, 3; 11:7 [s]Gal 5:4
9:32 [t]1Pe 2:8
9:33 [u]Isa 8:14; 28:16; Ro 10:11; 1Pe 2:6,8
10:1 [v]Ps 20:4

u *20* Isaiah 29:16; 45:9 v *25* Hosea 2:23
w *26* Hosea 1:10 x *28* Isaiah 10:22,23
y *29* Isaiah 1:9 z *33* Isaiah 8:14; 28:16

all those who refuse to repent and choose to continue in their sins and thereby reject salvation in Christ. This divine purpose does not change for any person or nation (cf. 2:4–11).

9:18 WHOM HE WANTS TO HARDEN. The hardening of Pharaoh's heart is at times attributed to God (Ex 4:21; 7:3,13; 9:12; 10:1; 11:10; 14:17) and at other times to Pharaoh himself (Ex 7:22–23; 8:15,32). Pharaoh, whose heart was already in opposition to God, received God's appropriate judgment. When he resisted God's will, God responded by hardening him even more (see Ex 7:3). Thus, God's hardening of Pharaoh's heart was not arbitrary; God acted according to his righteous principle of hardening all who reject him (cf. 1:21–32).

9:21 DOES NOT THE POTTER HAVE THE RIGHT? Paul argues for God's right to use certain people to accomplish his redemptive purpose without having to answer to anyone. (1) We must not interpret this to mean that God has no moral principles inherent in his own holy character as he deals with individuals and nations. God is governed in his nature not by the human will but by his love (Jn 3:16), mercy (Ps 25:6), and moral integrity and compassion (Ps 116:5). (2) Those who interpret vv. 6–29 to mean that God arbitrarily chooses some people for salvation and others for destruction have misconstrued the passage (see article on ELECTION AND PREDESTINATION, p. 402).

9:22–23 OBJECTS OF HIS WRATH . . . OBJECTS OF HIS MERCY. The phrase "objects of his wrath" refers to those being prepared for eternal destruction. People become objects of wrath by their own sinful acts and rebellion, as Paul stated earlier: "but because of your stubbornness and your unrepentant heart, you are storing up wrath" (2:5). However, objects of wrath may still repent, turn to God and receive his mercy. The phrase "objects of his mercy" refers to those, both Jew and Gentile, who believe and follow Jesus Christ (vv. 24–33).

9:32 THEY PURSUED IT NOT BY FAITH. The spiritual condition of the majority of Israel was due to their unwillingness to submit to God's plan of salvation through faith in Christ (v. 33). Many Gentiles, however, accepted God's way of salvation and attained the righteousness that is by faith (v. 30).

10:1 MY HEART'S DESIRE AND PRAYER TO GOD. For comments on how Paul's concern demonstrates that he did not adhere to the doctrine of individuals being predestined or foreordained to heaven or hell, see article on ISRAEL IN GOD'S PLAN OF SALVATION, p. 310.

that they may be saved. **2**For I can testify
about them that they are zealous[w] for
God, but their zeal is not based on knowledge. **3**Since they did not know the righteousness that comes from God and
sought to establish their own, they did not
submit to God's righteousness.[x] **4**Christ
is the end of the law[y] so that there may
be righteousness for everyone who believes.[z]

5Moses describes in this way the righteousness that is by the law: "The man
who does these things will live by
them."[a][a] **6**But the righteousness that is
by faith[b] says: "Do not say in your heart,
'Who will ascend into heaven?'[b]"[c] (that
is, to bring Christ down) **7**"or 'Who will
descend into the deep?'[c]"[d] (that is, to
bring Christ up from the dead).[e] **8**But
what does it say? "The word is near you;
it is in your mouth and in your heart,"[d][f]
that is, the word of faith we are proclaiming: **9**That if you confess[g] with your
mouth, "Jesus is Lord,"[h] and believe[i] in
your heart that God raised him from the
dead,[j] you will be saved.[k] **10**For it is with
your heart that you believe and are justified, and it is with your mouth that you
confess and are saved. **11**As the Scripture
says, "Anyone who trusts in him will never be put to shame."[e][l] **12**For there is no
difference between Jew and Gentile[m]—
the same Lord is Lord of all[n] and richly
blesses all who call on him, **13**for, "Everyone who calls on the name of the Lord[o]
will be saved."[f][p]

14How, then, can they call on the one
they have not believed in? And how can
they believe in the one of whom they have
not heard? And how can they hear without
someone preaching to them? **15**And how
can they preach unless they are sent? As
it is written, "How beautiful are the feet of
those who bring good news!"[g][q]

16But not all the Israelites accepted the
good news.[r] For Isaiah says, "Lord, who
has believed our message?"[h][s] **17**Consequently, faith comes from hearing the
message,[t] and the message is heard
through the word of Christ.[u] **18**But I ask:
Did they not hear? Of course they did:

> "Their voice has gone out into all the
> earth,
> their words to the ends of the
> world."[i][v]

19Again I ask: Did Israel not understand?
First, Moses says,

> "I will make you envious[w] by those
> who are not a nation;
> I will make you angry by a nation
> that has no understanding."[j][x]

20And Isaiah boldly says,

> "I was found by those who did not
> seek me;
> I revealed myself to those who did
> not ask for me."[k][y]

21But concerning Israel he says,

10:2 [w]S Ac 21:20 **10:3** [x]Ro 1:17; S 9:31 **10:4** [y]Gal 3:24; Ro 7:1-4 [z]S Ro 3:22 **10:5** [a]Lev 18:5; Dt 4:1; 6:24; Ne 9:29; Pr 19:16; Isa 55:3; Eze 20:11,13,21; S Ro 7:10 **10:6** [b]S Ro 9:30 [c]Dt 30:12 **10:7** [d]Dt 30:13 [e]S Ac 2:24 **10:8** [f]Dt 30:14 **10:9** [g]Mt 10:32 [h]S Jn 13:13 [i]S Jn 3:15 [j]S Ac 2:24 [k]S Ro 11:14 **10:11** [l]Isa 28:16; Ro 9:33 **10:12** [m]S Ro 3:22,29 [n]S Mt 28:18 **10:13** [o]S Ac 2:21 [p]Joel 2:32 **10:15** [q]Isa 52:7; Na 1:15 **10:16** [r]Heb 4:2 [s]Isa 53:1; Jn 12:38 **10:17** [t]Gal 3:2,5 [u]Col 3:16 **10:18** [v]Ps 19:4; S Mt 24:14; Ro 1:8; Col 1:6,23; 1Th 1:8 **10:19** [w]Ro 11:11,14 [x]Dt 32:21 **10:20** [y]Isa 65:1; Ro 9:30

[a] *5* Lev. 18:5 [b] *6* Deut. 30:12 [c] *7* Deut. 30:13
[d] *8* Deut. 30:14 [e] *11* Isaiah 28:16
[f] *13* Joel 2:32 [g] *15* Isaiah 52:7
[h] *16* Isaiah 53:1 [i] *18* Psalm 19:4
[j] *19* Deut. 32:21 [k] *20* Isaiah 65:1

10:3 THEY DID NOT SUBMIT. For comments on how ch. 10 fits into Paul's argument in chs. 9–11, see article on ISRAEL IN GOD'S PLAN OF SALVATION, p. 310.

10:9–10 CONFESS ... BELIEVE IN YOUR HEART. The essentials of salvation are summarized here. They center on belief in the lordship of Christ and his bodily resurrection. Faith must be in the heart, which includes the emotions, intellect and will, and it takes hold of the whole person. Faith must also involve committing oneself publicly to Jesus as Lord, both in word and deed (see article on FAITH AND GRACE, p. 302).

10:9 CONFESS ... 'JESUS IS LORD'. The earliest creed or confession of the NT church was not "Jesus is Savior," but "Jesus is Lord" (cf. Ac 8:16; 19:5; 1Co 12:3). Jesus Christ is specifically called Savior 16 times in the NT and Lord more than 450 times. (1) The current teaching in some evangelical circles that Jesus can be one's Savior without necessarily being one's Lord is found nowhere in the NT. No one can receive Jesus as Savior without receiving him as Lord. This is an essential ingredient in apostolic preaching (Ac 2:36–40).

(2) "Lord" (Gk *kyrios*) means having power, dominion, authority and the right to master. To confess "Jesus is Lord" is to declare him to be equal with God (v. 13; Jn 20:28; Ac 2:36; Heb 1:10) and worthy of power (Rev 5:12), worship (Php 2:10–11), trust (Jn 14:1; Heb 2:13), obedience (Heb 5:9) and prayer (Ac 7:59–60; 2Co 12:8).

(3) When NT Christians called Jesus "Lord," this was not just an outward profession but an inward sincere attitude of the heart (cf. 1Pe 3:15) by which they made Christ and his Word Lord over all of life (Lk 6:46–49; Jn 15:14). Jesus must be Lord of spiritual matters at home and in the church, as well as Lord in intellectual, financial, educational, recreational and vocational spheres, in fact, in *all* areas of life (12:1–2; 1Co 10:31).

10:9 GOD RAISED HIM FROM THE DEAD. Anyone denying Christ's bodily resurrection cannot legitimately claim to be a Christian. He or she is still an unbeliever, for the death and resurrection of Christ is the central event in salvation (1:4; 4:25; 5:10,17; 6:4–10; 8:11,34).

"All day long I have held out my
hands
to a disobedient and obstinate
people."[l][z]

A Remnant Chosen by Grace

11 I ask then: Did God reject his people? By no means![a] I am an Israelite myself, a descendant of Abraham,[b]
from the tribe of Benjamin.[c] **2**God did not
reject his people,[d] whom he foreknew.[e]
Don't you know what the Scripture says in
the passage about Elijah—how he appealed to God against Israel: **3**"Lord, they
have killed your prophets and torn down
your altars; I am the only one left, and
they are trying to kill me"[m]?[f] **4**And what
was God's answer to him? "I have reserved for myself seven thousand who
have not bowed the knee to Baal."[n][g] **5**So
too, at the present time there is a remnant[h] chosen by grace.[i] **6**And if by grace,
then it is no longer by works;[j] if it were,
grace would no longer be grace.[o]

7What then? What Israel sought so earnestly it did not obtain,[k] but the elect did.
The others were hardened,[l] **8**as it is written:

"God gave them a spirit of stupor,
eyes so that they could not see
and ears so that they could not
hear,[m]
to this very day."[p][n]

9And David says:

"May their table become a snare and
a trap,
a stumbling block and a retribution
for them.
10May their eyes be darkened so they
cannot see,[o]
and their backs be bent forever."[q][p]

Ingrafted Branches

11Again I ask: Did they stumble so as
to fall beyond recovery? Not at all![q] Rather, because of their transgression, salvation has come to the Gentiles[r] to make
Israel envious.[s] **12**But if their transgression means riches for the world, and their
loss means riches for the Gentiles,[t] how
much greater riches will their fullness
bring!

13I am talking to you Gentiles. Inas-
much as I am the apostle to the Gentiles,[u]
I make much of my ministry **14**in the hope
that I may somehow arouse my own people to envy[v] and save[w] some of them.
15For if their rejection is the reconciliation[x] of the world, what will their acceptance be but life from the dead?[y] **16**If the
part of the dough offered as firstfruits[z] is
holy, then the whole batch is holy; if the
root is holy, so are the branches.

17If some of the branches have been
broken off,[a] and you, though a wild olive
shoot, have been grafted in among the
others[b] and now share in the nourishing
sap from the olive root, **18**do not boast
over those branches. If you do, consider
this: You do not support the root, but the
root supports you.[c] **19**You will say then,
"Branches were broken off so that I could
be grafted in." **20**Granted. But they were

10:21 *z* Isa 65:2; Jer 35:17
11:1 *a* Lev 26:44; 1Sa 12:22; Ps 94:14; Jer 31:37; 33:24-26 *b* 2Co 11:22 *c* Php 3:5
11:2 *d* S ver 1 *e* S Ro 8:29
11:3 *f* 1Ki 19:10, 14
11:4 *g* 1Ki 19:18
11:5 *h* S Ro 9:27 *i* S Ro 3:24
11:6 *j* Ro 4:4
11:7 *k* Ro 9:31 *l* ver 25; S Ro 9:18
11:8 *m* S Mt 13:13-15 *n* Dt 29:4; Isa 29:10
11:10 *o* ver 8 *p* Ps 69:22,23
11:11 *q* ver 1 *r* S Ac 13:46 *s* ver 14; Ro 10:19
11:12 *t* ver 25
11:13 *u* S Ac 9:15
11:14 *v* ver 11; Ro 10:19; 1Co 10:33; 1Th 2:16 *w* S Mt 1:21; S Lk 2:11; S Jn 3:17; Ac 4:12; 16:31; 1Co 1:21; 1Ti 2:4; Tit 3:5
11:15 *x* S Ro 5:10 *y* Lk 15:24,32
11:16 *z* Lev 23:10,17; Nu 15:18-21
11:17 *a* Jer 11:16; Jn 15:2 *b* Ac 2:39; Eph 2:11-13
11:18 *c* Jn 4:22

l *21* Isaiah 65:2 **m** *3* 1 Kings 19:10,14
n *4* 1 Kings 19:18 **o** *6* Some manuscripts *by grace. But if by works, then it is no longer grace; if it were, work would no longer be work.*
p *8* Deut. 29:4; Isaiah 29:10
q *10* Psalm 69:22,23

11:1 DID GOD REJECT HIS PEOPLE? Paul now explains that God's rejection of Israel is only partial and temporary; Israel will eventually accept God's salvation in Christ. For comments on how ch. 11 fits into Paul's argument in chs. 9–11, see article on ISRAEL IN GOD'S PLAN OF SALVATION, p. 310.

11:5 CHOSEN BY GRACE. This phrase refers to God's gracious design in sending his Son into the world to save all who believe in him. Election proceeds from God's saving purpose "before the creation of the world" (Eph 1:4). Since the coming of the Savior and his death and resurrection, this choosing includes all who believe and obey Christ and the gospel. Thus, both God and humans are active in election. The goal of this choosing by grace is "to be holy and blameless" in God's sight (Eph 1:4; cf. Ro 3:22; 4:1–5,16; 11:11–24; 2Co 5:19–20; Eph 2:8–10; see article on ELECTION AND PREDESTINATION, p. 402).

11:7 THE OTHERS WERE HARDENED. See 9:18, note on the hardening of hearts.

11:11 SALVATION HAS COME TO THE GENTILES. Israel's transgression, i.e., their rejection and crucifixion of Jesus, has resulted in salvation coming to the whole world.

11:12 THEIR FULLNESS. The "fullness" of Israel may refer to a time when many in Israel will believe in Jesus Christ as God's divine Son and Messiah (see v. 15), bringing even greater blessing to the world.

11:14 AROUSE MY OWN PEOPLE TO ENVY. It should be the desire and prayer of all churches that God's power and blessing will rest on them to such a degree that some in Israel will be moved to jealousy and turn to the Lord. Christ's salvation and the privileges of his kingdom worked out in our lives will create in Israel a desire for the same blessings.

11:20 BECAUSE OF UNBELIEF. The key to Israel's destiny is not an arbitrary decree of God, but her own unbelief and rejection of God's grace in Christ (see article on ISRAEL IN GOD'S PLAN OF SALVATION, p. 310).

broken off because of unbelief, and you
stand by faith.[d] Do not be arrogant,[e] but
be afraid.[f] 21For if God did not spare the
natural branches, he will not spare you
either.

22Consider therefore the kindness[g] and
sternness of God: sternness to those who
fell, but kindness to you, provided that
you continue[h] in his kindness. Otherwise,
you also will be cut off.[i] 23And if they do
not persist in unbelief, they will be grafted
in, for God is able to graft them in again.[j]
24After all, if you were cut out of an olive
tree that is wild by nature, and contrary to
nature were grafted into a cultivated olive
tree,[k] how much more readily will these,
the natural branches, be grafted into their
own olive tree!

All Israel Will Be Saved

25I do not want you to be ignorant[l] of
this mystery,[m] brothers, so that you may
not be conceited:[n] Israel has experienced
a hardening[o] in part until the full number
of the Gentiles has come in.[p] 26And so all
Israel will be saved,[q] as it is written:

"The deliverer will come from Zion;
he will turn godlessness away from
Jacob.
27And this is[r] my covenant with them
when I take away their sins."[s] [r]

28As far as the gospel is concerned,
they are enemies[s] on your account; but as
far as election is concerned, they are
loved on account of the patriarchs,[t] 29for
God's gifts and his call[u] are irrevocable.[v]
30Just as you who were at one time disobedient[w] to God have now received mercy as
a result of their disobedience, 31so they
too have now become disobedient in order
that they too may now[t] receive mercy as
a result of God's mercy to you. 32For God
has bound all men over to disobedience[x]
so that he may have mercy on them all.

Doxology

33Oh, the depth of the riches[y] of the
wisdom and[u] knowledge of
God![z]
How unsearchable his judgments,
and his paths beyond tracing out![a]
34"Who has known the mind of the
Lord?
Or who has been his counselor?"[v] [b]
35"Who has ever given to God,
that God should repay him?"[w] [c]
36For from him and through him and to
him are all things.[d]
To him be the glory forever!
Amen.[e]

Living Sacrifices

12 Therefore, I urge you,[f] brothers,
in view of God's mercy, to offer

11:20 [d] 1Co 10:12; 2Co 1:24 [e] 1Ti 6:17 [f] 1Pe 1:17 **11:22** [g] Ro 2:4 [h] 1Co 15:2; Col 1:23; Heb 3:6 [i] Jn 15:2 **11:23** [j] 2Co 3:16 **11:24** [k] Jer 11:16 **11:25** [l] Ro 1:13; 1Co 10:1; 12:1; 2Co 1:8; 1Th 4:13 [m] S Ro 16:25 [n] Ro 12:16 [o] ver 7; S Ro 9:18 [p] Lk 21:24 **11:26** [q] Isa 45:17; Jer 31:34 **11:27** [r] Isa 59:20, 21; 27:9; Heb 8:10,12 **11:28** [s] Ro 5:10 [t] Dt 7:8; 10:15; Ro 9:5 **11:29** [u] S Ro 8:28 [v] S Heb 7:21 **11:30** [w] S Eph 2:2 **11:32** [x] S Ro 3:9 **11:33** [y] S Ro 2:4 [z] Ps 92:5; Eph 3:10; Col 2:3 [a] Job 5:9; 11:7; Ps 139:6; Ecc 8:17; Isa 40:28 **11:34** [b] Isa 40:13, 14; Job 15:8; 36:22; Jer 23:18; 1Co 2:16 **11:35** [c] Job 41:11; 35:7 **11:36** [d] 1Co 8:6; 11:12; Col 1:16; Heb 2:10 [e] Ro 16:27; Eph 3:21; 1Ti 1:17; 1Pe 5:11; Jude 25; Rev 5:13; 7:12 **12:1** [f] Eph 4:1; 1Pe 2:11

[r] *27* Or *will be* [s] *27* Isaiah 59:20,21; 27:9; Jer. 31:33,34 [t] *31* Some manuscripts do not have *now.* [u] *33* Or *riches and the wisdom and the* [v] *34* Isaiah 40:13 [w] *35* Job 41:11

11:22 YOU ALSO WILL BE CUT OFF. Paul directs a grave warning to all Gentile believers, i.e., to all Christian churches, denominations or fellowships. (1) The terrible possibility exists that God will "cut off" any individual, ministry, church or group of churches if they do not "continue in his kindness" and in the NT apostolic faith and standards of righteousness (v. 20).

(2) If God did not spare Israel, neither will he spare any particular church or fellowship (v. 21) if it rejects God's ways and conforms to the ways of this world (see 12:2, note). Therefore, all Christian churches are to "be afraid" (v. 20), keeping in mind both "the kindness and sternness of God" (v. 22) and making every effort to continue in the apostolic faith and practice of the NT. No Christian church or ministry may presume with confidence that it will never fall under God's judgment. With churches, as with individuals, "God does not show favoritism" (2:11; see also Rev 2–3, notes).

11:25 FULL NUMBER OF THE GENTILES. The "full number of the Gentiles" signifies the completion of God's purpose in calling out a people from among the Gentiles (Ac 15:14). It may also be related to a time when their wickedness is full, i.e., when sin in the world reaches a full level of rebellion against God (cf. Ge 15:16). At that time Christ will come to judge the world (Lk 21:24,27; cf. Ge 6:5–7,11–13; 18:20–33; 19:24–25; Lk 17:26–30).

11:26 ALL ISRAEL. The expression "all Israel" should be understood as the believers in Israel as a whole. (1) The number of Jews who believe in Christ will greatly increase during the dark days of the tribulation (Dt 4:30–31; Hos 5:14—6:3; Rev 7:1–8). The tribulation will end when Christ brings deliverance to the believers in Israel and destroys the remaining unbelieving Jews (Isa 10:20–23; Zec 13:8–9). All rebels (i.e., ungodly Jews) will be rooted out (Eze 20:34–38). (2) The believing remnant of Israel (i.e., the survivors at the end of the age) and the faithful in Israel of past generations constitute "all Israel" (cf. Eze 37:12–14).

11:29 GOD'S GIFTS AND HIS CALL. These words refer to the privileges of Israel mentioned in 9:4–5 and 11:26. The context clearly refers to Israel and God's purposes for her, and not to the spiritual gifts or ministerial calling associated with the Holy Spirit's work within the church (cf. 12:6–8; 1Co 12). The calling, placing and maintaining of someone in the office of pastor or overseer must be according to the personal character qualifications and spiritual history of the individual (see article on MORAL QUALIFICATIONS FOR OVERSEERS, p. 458).

12:1 YOUR BODIES AS LIVING SACRIFICES.

your bodies as living sacrifices,[g] holy and
pleasing to God—this is your spiritual[x]
act of worship. 2Do not conform[h] any
longer to the pattern of this world,[i] but be
transformed by the renewing of your
mind.[j] Then you will be able to test and
approve what God's will is[k]—his good,
pleasing[l] and perfect will.

3For by the grace given me[m] I say to
every one of you: Do not think of yourself
more highly than you ought, but rather
think of yourself with sober judgment, in
accordance with the measure of faith God
has given you. 4Just as each of us has one
body with many members, and these members do not all have the same function,[n]
5so in Christ we who are many form one
body,[o] and each member belongs to all
the others. 6We have different gifts,[p] according to the grace given us. If a man's
gift is prophesying,[q] let him use it in proportion to his[y] faith.[r] 7If it is serving, let
him serve; if it is teaching, let him teach;[s]
8if it is encouraging, let him encourage;[t]
if it is contributing to the needs of others,
let him give generously;[u] if it is leadership, let him govern diligently; if it is
showing mercy, let him do it cheerfully. Ro 15:19

Love

9Love must be sincere.[v] Hate what is
evil; cling to what is good.[w] 10Be devoted

12:1 [g]Ro 6:13, 16,19; 1Co 6:20; 1Pe 2:5 **12:2** [h]1Pe 1:14 [i]1Co 1:20; 2Co 10:2; 1Jn 2:15 [j]Eph 4:23 [k]S Eph 5:17 [l]S 1Ti 5:4 **12:3** [m]Ro 15:15; 1Co 15:10; Gal 2:9; Eph 3:7; 4:7; 1Pe 4:10,11 **12:4** [n]1Co 12:12-14; Eph 4:16 **12:5** [o]1Co 6:15; 10:17; 12:12,20, 27; Eph 2:16; 4:4, 25; 5:30; Col 3:15 **12:6** [p]1Co 7:7; 12:4,8-10 [q]S Eph 4:11 [r]1Pe 4:10,11 **12:7** [s]S Eph 4:11 **12:8** [t]Ac 11:23; 13:15; 15:32 [u]2Co 8:2; 9:5-13 **12:9** [v]2Co 6:6; 1Ti 1:5 [w]Ps 97:10; Am 5:15; 1Th 5:21,22

[x] *1* Or *reasonable* [y] *6* Or *in agreement with the*

Believers must possess a single-minded passion to please God in love, devotion, praise and holiness, and to offer their bodies for his service. (1) Our greatest desire should be to live lives of holiness and to be accepted by God. This requires separating ourselves from the world and drawing ever nearer to God (v. 2). We must live for God, worship him, obey him, take his side against sin and for righteousness, resist and hate evil, perform works of kindness for others, imitate Christ, follow him, serve him, live by the Spirit and be filled with the Spirit. (2) We must offer our bodies to God as dead to sin and as the temple of the Holy Spirit (see next note; cf. 1Co 6:15,19).

12:2 DO NOT CONFORM ... BUT BE TRANSFORMED. Paul implies several things here: (1) We must realize that the present world system is evil (Ac 2:40; Gal 1:4) and under Satan's rule (Jn 12:31; 1Jn 5:19; see article on THE CHRISTIAN'S RELATIONSHIP TO THE WORLD, p. 546).

(2) We must stand against the prevailing and popular forms of the spirit of this world, proclaiming instead the eternal truths and righteous standards of God's Word for Christ's sake (1Co 1:17–24).

(3) We must despise what is evil, love what is righteous (v. 9; 1Jn 2:15–17; see Heb 1:9, note) and refuse to yield to the various types of worldliness surrounding the church, such as greed, selfishness, expediency, humanistic thinking, political maneuvering for power, envy, hatred, revenge, impurity, filthy language, ungodly entertainment, tempting and immodest attire, immorality, drugs, alcohol and worldly companions.

(4) We must have our minds conformed to God's way of thinking (1Co 2:16; Php 2:5) by reading and meditating on his Word (Ps 119:11,148; Jn 8:31–32; 15:7). We must have our plans and ambitions determined by heavenly and eternal truths, not by this evil, temporal and transient age.

12:6 DIFFERENT GIFTS, ACCORDING TO THE GRACE. Paul lists what can be called the gifts of grace (Gk *charismata*). They are inward desires or dispositions as well as enablements or abilities (Php 2:13) given by the Holy Spirit to individuals in the congregation to build up God's people and express God's love to others (see 1Co 12:1, note; 14:12,26; 1Pe 4:10). Every believer has at least one such gift (1Co 12:11; 1Pe 4:10). However, one's primary gift does not exclude the exercise of any other of the gifts as need may arise. Paul's list of seven grace gifts should be taken as representative rather than exhaustive (see 1Co 12–14 for further explanation of spiritual gifts).

12:6 PROPHESYING. For comments on the gift of prophecy see articles on SPIRITUAL GIFTS FOR BELIEVERS, p. 350, and THE MINISTRY GIFTS OF THE CHURCH, p. 407.

12:7 SERVING . . . TEACHING. (1) "Serving" is the God-given desire, ability and power to give practical assistance to members and leaders of the church to help them fulfill their responsibilities to God (cf. Ac 6:2–3). (2) "Teaching" is the God-given desire, ability and power to examine and study God's Word, and to clarify, defend and proclaim its truth in such a way that others grow in grace and godliness (1Co 2:10–16; 1Ti 4:16; 6:3; 2Ti 4:1–2; see 2Ti 2:2, note; see articles on THE MINISTRY GIFTS OF THE CHURCH, p. 407, and BIBLE TRAINING FOR CHRISTIANS, p. 470).

12:8 ENCOURAGING ... CONTRIBUTING ... LEADERSHIP . . . SHOWING MERCY. (1) "Encouraging" is the God-given desire, ability and power to proclaim God's Word in such a way that it touches the heart, conscience and will of the hearers, stimulates faith, and produces a deeper commitment to Christ and a more thorough separation from the world (see Ac 11:23; 14:22; 15:30–32; 16:40; 1Co 14:3; 1Th 5:14–22; Heb 10:24–25).

(2) "Contributing" is the God-given desire, ability and power, because one has resources above life's basic needs, to give freely of one's personal possessions to the needs of God's work or people (2Co 8:1–8; Eph 4:28).

(3) "Leadership" is the God-given desire, ability and power to guide and oversee the various activities of the church for the spiritual good of all (Eph 4:11–12; 1Ti 3:1–7; Heb 13:7,17,24; see article on THE MINISTRY GIFTS OF THE CHURCH, p. 407).

(4) "Showing mercy" is the God-given desire, ability and power to help and comfort those in need or distress (cf. Eph 2:4).

12:9 HATE WHAT IS EVIL. See Heb 1:9, note.

to one another in brotherly love.[x] Honor
one another above yourselves.[y] **11**Never
be lacking in zeal, but keep your spiritual
fervor,[z] serving the Lord. **12**Be joyful in
hope,[a] patient in affliction,[b] faithful in
prayer.[c] **13**Share with God's people who
are in need.[d] Practice hospitality.[e]

14Bless those who persecute you;[f]
bless and do not curse. **15**Rejoice with
those who rejoice; mourn with those who
mourn.[g] **16**Live in harmony with one another.[h] Do not be proud, but be willing to
associate with people of low position.[z] Do
not be conceited.[i]

17Do not repay anyone evil for evil.[j] Be
careful to do what is right in the eyes of
everybody.[k] **18**If it is possible, as far as it
depends on you, live at peace with everyone.[l] **19**Do not take revenge,[m] my friends,
but leave room for God's wrath, for it is
written: "It is mine to avenge; I will repay,"[a][n] says the Lord. **20**On the contrary:

"If your enemy is hungry, feed him;
if he is thirsty, give him something
to drink.
In doing this, you will heap burning
coals on his head."[b][o]

21Do not be overcome by evil, but overcome evil with good.

Submission to the Authorities

13 Everyone must submit himself to
the governing authorities,[p] for
there is no authority except that which
God has established.[q] The authorities
that exist have been established by God.
2Consequently, he who rebels against the

12:10 [x]Ps 133:1; 1Th 4:9; Heb 13:1; 1Pe 1:22 [y]Php 2:3
12:11 [z]Ac 18:25
12:12 [a]Ro 5:2 [b]Heb 10:32,36 [c]S Lk 18:1
12:13 [d]S Ac 24:17 [e]2Ki 4:10; Job 31:32; 1Ti 3:2; 5:10; Heb 13:2; 1Pe 4:9
12:14 [f]S Mt 5:44
12:15 [g]Job 30:25
12:16 [h]S Ro 15:5 [i]ver 3; Ps 131:1; Isa 5:21; Jer 45:5; Ro 11:25
12:17 [j]ver 19; Pr 20:22; 24:29 [k]2Co 8:21
12:18 [l]S Mk 9:50; S Ro 14:19
12:19 [m]ver 17; Lev 19:18; Pr 20:22; 24:29 [n]Dt 32:35; Ge 50:19; 1Sa 26:10; Ps 94:1; Jer 51:36
12:20 [o]Pr 25:21,22; Ex 23:4; Mt 5:44; Lk 6:27
13:1 [p]Tit 3:1; 1Pe 2:13,14 [q]Da 2:21; 4:17; Jn 19:11
13:2 [r]Ex 16:8
13:3 [s]1Pe 2:14
13:4 [t]1Th 4:6
13:5 [u]Pr 24:21,22
13:6 [v]Mt 22:17
13:7 [w]Mt 17:25; 22:17,21; Lk 23:2
13:8 [x]ver 10; S Mt 5:43; Jn 13:34; Col 3:14
13:9 [y]Ex 20:13-15,17; Dt 5:17-19,21 [z]Mt 7:12 [a]Lev 19:18; S Mt 5:43

authority is rebelling against what God
has instituted,[r] and those who do so will
bring judgment on themselves. **3**For rulers hold no terror for those who do right,
but for those who do wrong. Do you want
to be free from fear of the one in authority? Then do what is right and he will commend you.[s] **4**For he is God's servant to do
you good. But if you do wrong, be afraid,
for he does not bear the sword for nothing.
He is God's servant, an agent of wrath to
bring punishment on the wrongdoer.[t]
5Therefore, it is necessary to submit to
the authorities, not only because of possible punishment but also because of conscience.[u]

6This is also why you pay taxes,[v] for
the authorities are God's servants, who
give their full time to governing. **7**Give everyone what you owe him: If you owe
taxes, pay taxes;[w] if revenue, then revenue; if respect, then respect; if honor,
then honor.

Responsibility Toward Others

8Let no debt remain outstanding, except the continuing debt to love one another, for he who loves his fellowman has
fulfilled the law.[x] **9**The commandments,
"Do not commit adultery," "Do not murder," "Do not steal," "Do not covet,"[c][y]
and whatever other commandment there
may be, are summed up[z] in this one rule:
"Love your neighbor as yourself."[d][a]

[z] *16* Or *willing to do menial work*
[a] *19* Deut. 32:35 [b] *20* Prov. 25:21,22
[c] *9* Exodus 20:13-15,17; Deut. 5:17-19,21
[d] *9* Lev. 19:18

12:10 BE DEVOTED TO ONE ANOTHER. All those devoted in faith to Jesus Christ must be devoted to one another as brothers and sisters in Christ (1Th 4:9–10), with a sincere, kind and tender affection. We must be concerned for our brothers' and sisters' welfare, needs and spiritual condition, sympathizing with them and helping them in their sorrows and troubles. We must honor one another, eagerly respecting the good qualities in other believers (see Jn 13:34–35, notes).

13:1 SUBMIT ... TO THE GOVERNING AUTHORITIES. God commands Christians to obey the state, for the state as an institution is ordained and established by God. God has instituted government because in this fallen world we need certain restraints to protect us from the chaos and lawlessness that is a natural result of sin. (1) The civil government, as does all of life, stands under God's law. (2) God has ordained the state to be an agent of justice, to restrain evil by punishing the wrongdoer and to protect the good in society (vv. 3–4; 1Pe 2:13–17). (3) Paul describes government as it should be. When it abandons its proper function, it is no longer from God nor operating according to his purpose. For example, when the state requires something contrary to God's Word, Christians must obey God rather than other humans (Ac 5:29; cf. Da 3:16–18; 6:6–10). (4) It is the duty of all believers to pray for those in authority (1Ti 2:1–2).

13:4 THE SWORD. The sword is frequently associated with death as an instrument of execution (Mt 26:52; Lk 21:24; Ac 12:2; 16:27; Heb 11:34; Rev 13:10). God has clearly commanded the execution of dangerous criminals who have committed vicious crimes (Ge 9:6; Nu 35:31,33).

13:8 LET NO DEBT REMAIN OUTSTANDING. Believers should have no unpaid debts. This does not mean that we are prohibited from borrowing from others in case of serious need (cf. Ex 22:25; Ps 37:26; Mt 5:42; Lk 6:35). But it does speak against both going into debt for unnecessary things and showing an attitude of indifference in repaying debts (cf. Ps 37:21). The only debt from which there is no release is love for one another.

10Love does no harm to its neighbor. Therefore love is the fulfillment of the law.[b]

11And do this, understanding the present time. The hour has come[c] for you to wake up from your slumber,[d] because our salvation is nearer now than when we first believed. 12The night is nearly over; the day is almost here.[e] So let us put aside the deeds of darkness[f] and put on the armor[g] of light. 13Let us behave decently, as in the daytime, not in orgies and drunkenness,[h] not in sexual immorality and debauchery, not in dissension and jealousy.[i] 14Rather, clothe yourselves with the Lord Jesus Christ,[j] and do not think about how to gratify the desires of the sinful nature.[e][k]

The Weak and the Strong

14 Accept him whose faith is weak,[l] without passing judgment on disputable matters. 2One man's faith allows him to eat everything, but another man, whose faith is weak, eats only vegetables.[m] 3The man who eats everything must not look down on[n] him who does not, and the man who does not eat everything must not condemn[o] the man who does, for God has accepted him. 4Who are you to judge someone else's servant?[p] To his own master he stands or falls. And he will stand, for the Lord is able to make him stand.

5One man considers one day more sacred than another;[q] another man considers every day alike. Each one should be fully convinced in his own mind. 6He who regards one day as special, does so to the Lord. He who eats meat, eats to the Lord, for he gives thanks to God;[r] and he who abstains, does so to the Lord and gives thanks to God. 7For none of us lives to himself alone[s] and none of us dies to himself alone. 8If we live, we live to the Lord; and if we die, we die to the Lord. So, whether we live or die, we belong to the Lord.[t]

9For this very reason, Christ died and returned to life[u] so that he might be the Lord of both the dead and the living.[v] 10You, then, why do you judge your brother? Or why do you look down on[w] your brother? For we will all stand before God's judgment seat.[x] 11It is written:

" 'As surely as I live,'[y] says the Lord,
'every knee will bow before me;
every tongue will confess to
God.' "[f][z]

12So then, each of us will give an account of himself to God.[a]

13Therefore let us stop passing judg-

13:10 [b]S ver 8; ver 9 **13:11** [c]1Co 7:29-31; 10:11; Jas 5:8; 1Pe 4:7; 1Jn 2:18; Rev 22:10 [d]Eph 5:14; 1Th 5:5,6 **13:12** [e]Heb 10:25; 1Jn 2:8 [f]Eph 5:11 [g]Eph 6:11,13; 1Th 5:8 **13:13** [h]S Eph 5:18 [i]Lk 21:34; Gal 5:20,21; Eph 5:18; 1Pe 4:3 **13:14** [j]Gal 3:27; Eph 4:24; Col 3:10,12 [k]S Gal 5:24 **14:1** [l]Ro 15:1; 1Co 8:9-12; 9:22 **14:2** [m]ver 14 **14:3** [n]ver 10; Lk 18:9 [o]ver 10, 13; Col 2:16 **14:4** [p]S Mt 7:1 **14:5** [q]Gal 4:10; Col 2:16 **14:6** [r]S Mt 14:19; 1Co 10:30,31; 1Ti 4:3,4 **14:7** [s]2Co 5:15; Gal 2:20 **14:8** [t]Php 1:20 **14:9** [u]Rev 1:18; 2:8 [v]S Ac 10:42; 2Co 5:15 **14:10** [w]ver 3; S Mt 7:1 [x]S 2Co 5:10 **14:11** [y]Isa 49:18 [z]Isa 45:23; Php 2:10,11 **14:12** [a]Mt 12:36; 1Pe 4:5

[e] *14* Or *the flesh* [f] *11* Isaiah 45:23

13:10 LOVE DOES NO HARM TO ITS NEIGHBOR. "Love" is fulfilled not only by positive commands (12:9–21; 1Co 13:4,6–7), but also by negative ones. All of the commandments mentioned here are negative in form (v. 9; cf. 1Co 13:4–6). (1) Love is positive; yet it is also negative in that it accounts for the human propensity toward sin, selfishness and cruelty. Eight of the Ten Commandments are negative because sin comes naturally, while goodness does not. The first evidence of Christian love is a turning from sin and all that brings harm and sorrow to others. (2) The idea that Christian ethics must be only positive is a fallacy based on the ideas of a society that seeks to free itself from prohibitions that curb the sinful nature's unrestrained desires (Gal 5:19–21).

13:12 THE NIGHT IS NEARLY OVER. Paul believed in the Lord's imminent return to transfer the faithful of his churches to heaven (see Jn 14:3, note; see article on THE RAPTURE, p. 440), an event that Paul believed could happen even in his generation. Christ warned that he would return at a time when the faithful were sure that he would not come (see Mt 24:42,44 notes). For this reason, God's children must always be spiritually ready and must "put aside the deeds of darkness" (see Lk 12:35, note).

13:14 CLOTHE YOURSELVES WITH THE LORD JESUS CHRIST. We must be so united and identified with Christ that we imitate his life as our pattern for living, adopt his principles, obey his commands and become like him. This calls for a complete rejection of immorality and the acts of the sinful nature (cf. Gal 5:19–21).

14:2 EAT EVERYTHING ... EATS ONLY VEGETABLES. A number of believers in Rome were divided over a disputable issue: some were committed to eating only vegetables, while others were eating vegetables and all other foods, including meat. Paul states that eating in and of itself is not a moral matter, but that one's personal attitude about what to eat could lead to unjustly condemning one another.

14:5 CONSIDERS ONE DAY MORE SACRED THAN ANOTHER. This probably refers to the special feast days of the OT ceremonial law. Some Christians apparently still regarded the holy days as having abiding usefulness, whereas many others were ignoring them. In his answer, Paul does not attempt to abrogate God's principle of setting aside one day in seven as a special day of rest and worship (see Mt 12:1, note). God himself set aside one day in seven to rest from daily work (Ge 2:2–3; cf. Ex 20:11; 31:17; Isa 58:13–14). In the NT the first day of the week is recognized as having a special significance because of Jesus' resurrection (Ac 20:7; 1Co 16:2; Rev 1:10).

14:13 STOP PASSING JUDGMENT. Though we must refrain from judging each other in trivial matters, believers should consider how to encourage each other to true Christlikeness and holiness when it concerns faith, doctrine and morals (Heb 10:24).

ment[b] on one another. Instead, make up
your mind not to put any stumbling block
or obstacle in your brother's way.[c] **14**As
one who is in the Lord Jesus, I am fully
convinced that no food[g] is unclean in itself.[d] But if anyone regards something as
unclean, then for him it is unclean.[e] **15**If
your brother is distressed because of what
you eat, you are no longer acting in love.[f]
Do not by your eating destroy your brother
for whom Christ died.[g] **16**Do not allow
what you consider good to be spoken of as
evil.[h] **17**For the kingdom of God is not a
matter of eating and drinking,[i] but of
Ro 15:30 righteousness, peace[j] and joy in the Holy
Spirit,[k] **18**because anyone who serves
Christ in this way is pleasing to God and
approved by men.[l]

19Let us therefore make every effort to
do what leads to peace[m] and to mutual
edification.[n] **20**Do not destroy the work of
God for the sake of food.[o] All food is
clean,[p] but it is wrong for a man to eat
anything that causes someone else to
stumble.[q] **21**It is better not to eat meat or
drink wine or to do anything else that will
cause your brother to fall.[r]

22So whatever you believe about these
things keep between yourself and God.
Blessed is the man who does not condemn[s] himself by what he approves.
23But the man who has doubts[t] is condemned if he eats, because his eating is
not from faith; and everything that does
not come from faith is sin.

15 We who are strong ought to bear
with the failings of the weak[u] and
not to please ourselves. **2**Each of us
should please his neighbor for his good,[v]
to build him up.[w] **3**For even Christ did not
please himself[x] but, as it is written: "The
insults of those who insult you have fallen

14:13 [b]ver 1; S Mt 7:1 [c]S 2Co 6:3 **14:14** [d]ver 20; S Ac 10:15 [e]1Co 8:7 **14:15** [f]Eph 5:2 [g]ver 20; 1Co 8:11 **14:16** [h]1Co 10:30 **14:17** [i]1Co 8:8 [j]Isa 32:17 [k]Ro 15:13; Gal 5:22 **14:18** [l]Lk 2:52; Ac 24:16; 2Co 8:21 **14:19** [m]Ps 34:14; Ro 12:18; 1Co 7:15; 2Ti 2:22; Heb 12:14 [n]Ro 15:2; 1Co 14:3-5,12,17, 26; 2Co 12:19; Eph 4:12,29 **14:20** [o]ver 15 [p]ver 14; S Ac 10:15 [q]ver 13; 1Co 8:9-12 **14:21** [r]S Mt 5:29 **14:22** [s]1Jn 3:21 **14:23** [t]ver 5 **15:1** [u]Ro 14:1; 1Th 5:14 **15:2** [v]S 1Co 10:24 [w]S Ro 14:19 **15:3** [x]2Co 8:9 [y]Ps 69:9 **15:4** [z]S Ro 4:23, 24 **15:5** [a]Ro 12:16; 1Co 1:10; 2Co 13:11; Eph 4:3; Php 2:2; Col 3:14; 1Pe 3:8 **15:6** [b]Ps 34:3 [c]Rev 1:6 **15:7** [d]Ro 14:1 **15:8** [e]Mt 15:24; Ac 3:25,26 [f]2Co 1:20 **15:9** [g]S Ro 3:29 [h]S Mt 9:8 [i]2Sa 22:50; Ps 18:49 **15:10** [j]Dt 32:43; Isa 66:10 **15:11** [k]Ps 117:1 **15:12** [l]S Rev 5:5

on me."[h][y] **4**For everything that was written in the past was written to teach us,[z]
so that through endurance and the encouragement of the Scriptures we might
have hope.

5May the God who gives endurance and
encouragement give you a spirit of unity[a]
among yourselves as you follow Christ
Jesus, **6**so that with one heart and mouth
you may glorify[b] the God and Father[c] of
our Lord Jesus Christ.

7Accept one another,[d] then, just as
Christ accepted you, in order to bring
praise to God. **8**For I tell you that Christ
has become a servant of the Jews[i][e] on
behalf of God's truth, to confirm the promises[f] made to the patriarchs **9**so that the
Gentiles[g] may glorify God[h] for his mercy,
as it is written:

> "Therefore I will praise you among
> the Gentiles;
> I will sing hymns to your name."[j][i]

10Again, it says,

> "Rejoice, O Gentiles, with his
> people."[k][j]

11And again,

> "Praise the Lord, all you Gentiles,
> and sing praises to him, all you
> peoples."[l][k]

12And again, Isaiah says,

> "The Root of Jesse[l] will spring up,
> one who will arise to rule over the
> nations;

[g] *14* Or *that nothing* [h] *3* Psalm 69:9
[i] *8* Greek *circumcision* [j] *9* 2 Samuel 22:50; Psalm 18:49 [k] *10* Deut. 32:43
[l] *11* Psalm 117:1

This involves sincerely evaluating (1Th 5:21; 1Jn 4:1), correcting and rebuking one another in love and humility (Lk 17:3), and, when necessary, exercising church discipline (cf. 1Co 5:12–13; 2Th 3:6,14; 1Ti 5:20–21; 2Ti 2:24–26; 4:2).

14:21 NOT TO . . . DRINK WINE. The Bible gave the NT Christian two major laws regarding wine (Gk *oinos*), which included both unfermented and fermented fruit of the vine (see article on WINE IN NEW TESTAMENT TIMES (1), p. 126): (1) the law of abstinence from wine when it is fermented and intoxicating (Pr 23:31; see 1Th 5:6, note; Tit 2:2, note); (2) the law of Christian love, which causes a person to abstain from what might lead others into harm (cf. 1Co 8:13; 10:27–32). Paul affirms that, in a pagan society (i.e., in a non-Jewish environment) where intoxicating beverages and drunkenness are prevalent, it is better to refuse to drink even the unfermented wines than to drink something that might cause another Christian to be led into sin. The use of nonintoxicating wines were technically safe for some believers, but they might influence weaker believers to drink fermented wine and thereby expose them to harm and drunkenness. Timothy carefully followed this law of Christian love (see 1Ti 5:23, note).

15:3 CHRIST DID NOT PLEASE HIMSELF. Disregarding the convictions of others in order to please ourselves destroys God's work (14:15,20); living sacrificially so as to help others will strengthen God's kingdom. Paul points to Christ's example, who did not live for his own interest but for the interests of others.

15:4 EVERYTHING THAT WAS WRITTEN IN THE PAST. The OT Scriptures are of utmost importance to the Christian's spiritual life. The wisdom and moral laws of God concerning every aspect of life, as well as his revelation concerning himself, salvation and Christ's coming, have permanent value (2Ti 3:16).

the Gentiles will hope in him."[m][m]

13 May the God of hope fill you with all
joy and peace[n] as you trust in him, so that
you may overflow with hope by the power
of the Holy Spirit.[o]

Paul the Minister to the Gentiles

14 I myself am convinced, my brothers,
that you yourselves are full of goodness,[p]
complete in knowledge[q] and competent to
instruct one another. 15 I have written you
quite boldly on some points, as if to remind you of them again, because of the
grace God gave me[r] 16 to be a minister of
Christ Jesus to the Gentiles[s] with the
priestly duty of proclaiming the gospel of
God,[t] so that the Gentiles might become
an offering[u] acceptable to God, sanctified
by the Holy Spirit.

17 Therefore I glory in Christ Jesus[v] in
my service to God.[w] 18 I will not venture to
speak of anything except what Christ has
accomplished through me in leading the
Gentiles[x] to obey God[y] by what I have
said and done— 19 by the power of signs
and miracles,[z] through the power of the
Spirit.[a] So from Jerusalem[b] all the way
around to Illyricum, I have fully pro-
1Co 1:7 claimed the gospel of Christ.[c] 20 It has always been my ambition to preach the gos-
pel[d] where Christ was not known, so that
I would not be building on someone else's
foundation.[e] 21 Rather, as it is written:

"Those who were not told about him
will see,
and those who have not heard will
understand."[n][f]

22 This is why I have often been hindered
from coming to you.[g]

Paul's Plan to Visit Rome

23 But now that there is no more place
for me to work in these regions, and since
I have been longing for many years to see
you,[h] 24 I plan to do so when I go to
Spain.[i] I hope to visit you while passing
through and to have you assist[j] me on my
journey there, after I have enjoyed your
company for a while. 25 Now, however, I
am on my way to Jerusalem[k] in the service[l] of the saints[m] there. 26 For Macedonia[n] and Achaia[o] were pleased to make a
contribution for the poor among the saints
in Jerusalem.[p] 27 They were pleased to do
it, and indeed they owe it to them. For if
the Gentiles have shared in the Jews' spiritual blessings, they owe it to the Jews to
share with them their material blessings.[q] 28 So after I have completed this
task and have made sure that they have
received this fruit, I will go to Spain[r] and
visit you on the way. 29 I know that when
I come to you,[s] I will come in the full
measure of the blessing of Christ.

30 I urge you, brothers, by our Lord
Jesus Christ and by the love of the Spirit,[t]
to join me in my struggle by praying to Gal 5:22-23
God for me.[u] 31 Pray that I may be rescued[v] from the unbelievers in Judea and
that my service[w] in Jerusalem may be acceptable to the saints[x] there, 32 so that by
God's will[y] I may come to you[z] with joy
and together with you be refreshed.[a]
33 The God of peace[b] be with you all.
Amen.

Personal Greetings

16 I commend[c] to you our sister
Phoebe, a servant[o] of the church
in Cenchrea.[d] 2 I ask you to receive her in
the Lord[e] in a way worthy of the saints[f]
and to give her any help she may need
from you, for she has been a great help to
many people, including me.

3 Greet Priscilla[p] and Aquila,[g] my fellow
workers[h] in Christ Jesus.[i] 4 They

15:12 [m] Isa 11:10; Mt 12:21
15:13 [n] Ro 14:17 [o] ver 19; 1Co 2:4; 4:20; 1Th 1:5
15:14 [p] Eph 5:9 [q] S 2Co 8:7; 2Pe 1:12
15:15 [r] S Ro 12:3
15:16 [s] S Ac 9:15 [t] ver 19; S Ro 1:1 [u] Isa 66:20
15:17 [v] Php 3:3 [w] Heb 2:17
15:18 [x] Ac 15:12; 21:19; Ro 1:5 [y] Ro 16:26
15:19 [z] S Jn 4:48; Ac 19:11 [a] S ver 13 [b] Ac 22:17-21 [c] S 2Co 2:12
15:20 [d] Ro 1:15 [e] 2Co 10:15,16
15:21 [f] Isa 52:15
15:22 [g] Ro 1:13
15:23 [h] Ac 19:21; Ro 1:10,11
15:24 [i] ver 28 [j] 1Co 16:6; Tit 3:13
15:25 [k] S Ac 19:21 [l] S Ac 24:17 [m] S Ac 9:13
15:26 [n] S Ac 16:9 [o] S Ac 18:12 [p] S Ac 24:17
15:27 [q] 1Co 9:11
15:28 [r] ver 24
15:29 [s] Ro 1:10, 11
15:30 [t] Gal 5:22; Col 1:8 [u] 2Co 1:11; Col 4:12
15:31 [v] 2Co 1:10; 2Th 3:2; 2Ti 3:11; 2Pe 2:9 [w] ver 25; S Ac 24:17 [x] S Ac 9:13
15:32 [y] S Ac 18:21 [z] Ro 1:10,13 [a] 1Co 16:18; Phm 7
15:33 [b] Ro 16:20; 2Co 13:11; Php 4:9; 1Th 5:23; 2Th 3:16; Heb 13:20
16:1 [c] S 2Co 3:1 [d] Ac 18:18
16:2 [e] Php 2:29 [f] S Ac 9:13
16:3 [g] S Ac 18:2 [h] S Php 2:25 [i] ver 7,9,10; Ro 8:1,39; 1Co 1:30; 2Co 5:17; Gal 1:22; 5:6; Eph 1:13

[m] *12* Isaiah 11:10 [n] *21* Isaiah 52:15 [o] *1* Or *deaconess* [p] *3* Greek *Prisca*, a variant of *Priscilla*

15:17 I GLORY. It is not wrong to speak excitedly and joyfully about what God is doing through us if it is done in a spirit of humility and thankfulness to God. Glorying should not be in mere numbers, but in a ministry that produces the obedience of faith in word and deed and that issues from a genuine work and manifestation of the Spirit in power (vv. 18–19).

15:20 WHERE CHRIST WAS NOT KNOWN. Paul's policy of ministry was missionary-centered. He chose to direct his labors in areas where the gospel had not been preached sufficiently, thereby enabling those who had not heard to have opportunity to accept Christ (v. 21).

15:29 FULL MEASURE OF THE BLESSING OF CHRIST. Paul's ministry was accompanied by the fullness of Christ's blessing, power, grace and presence. Whenever he ministered, this blessing would be imparted to other believers. We who serve the Lord and his churches should seek the same fullness in our ministries.

16:1 PHOEBE. Phoebe was probably the one who delivered this letter to the Romans. She was a servant (or woman deacon) in the church at Cenchrea who ministered to the poor, the sick and the needy, as well as assisted missionaries such as Paul. Paul's greetings to no less than eight women in this chapter indicate that women performed distinguished service in the churches.

risked their lives for me. Not only I
but all the churches of the Gentiles
are grateful to them.
5 Greet also the church that meets at
their house.[j]
Greet my dear friend Epenetus, who
was the first convert[k] to Christ in the
province of Asia.[l]
6 Greet Mary, who worked very hard for
you.
7 Greet Andronicus and Junias, my relatives[m] who have been in prison with
me.[n] They are outstanding among
the apostles, and they were in
Christ[o] before I was.
8 Greet Ampliatus, whom I love in the
Lord.
9 Greet Urbanus, our fellow worker in
Christ,[p] and my dear friend Stachys.
10 Greet Apelles, tested and approved in
Christ.[q]
Greet those who belong to the household[r] of Aristobulus.
11 Greet Herodion, my relative.[s]
Greet those in the household[t] of Narcis-
sus who are in the Lord.
12 Greet Tryphena and Tryphosa, those
women who work hard in the Lord.
Greet my dear friend Persis, another
woman who has worked very hard in
the Lord.
13 Greet Rufus,[u] chosen[v] in the Lord, and
his mother, who has been a mother to
me, too.

16:5 [j] 1Co 16:19; Col 4:15; Phm 2 [k] 1Co 16:15 [l] S Ac 2:9
16:7 [m] ver 11,21 [n] Col 4:10; Phm 23 [o] S ver 3
16:9 [p] S ver 3
16:10 [q] S ver 3 [r] S Ac 11:14
16:11 [s] ver 7,21 [t] S Ac 11:14
16:13 [u] Mk 15:21 [v] S 2Jn 1
16:15 [w] ver 2; S Ac 9:13 [x] ver 14
16:16 [y] 1Co 16:20; 2Co 13:12; 1Th 5:26; 1Pe 5:14
16:17 [z] Gal 1:8,9; 1Ti 1:3; 6:3 [a] Mt 18:15-17; 1Co 5:11; 2Th 3:6, 14; 2Ti 3:5; Tit 3:10; 2Jn 10
16:18 [b] Ro 14:18 [c] Php 3:19 [d] 2Sa 15:6; Ps 12:2; Isa 30:10; Col 2:4
16:19 [e] Ro 1:8 [f] S 1Co 14:20
16:20 [g] S Ro 15:33 [h] Ge 3:15 [i] S Mt 4:10 [j] 2Co 13:14; S Gal 6:18; 1Th 5:28; Rev 22:21
16:21 [k] S Ac 16:1 [l] Ac 13:1 [m] Ac 17:5 [n] ver 7,11
16:23 [o] S Ac 19:29

14 Greet Asyncritus, Phlegon, Hermes,
Patrobas, Hermas and the brothers
with them.
15 Greet Philologus, Julia, Nereus and his
sister, and Olympas and all the
saints[w] with them.[x]
16 Greet one another with a holy kiss.[y]
All the churches of Christ send greetings.

17 I urge you, brothers, to watch out for
those who cause divisions and put obstacles in your way that are contrary to the
teaching you have learned.[z] Keep away
from them.[a] 18 For such people are not
serving our Lord Christ,[b] but their own
appetites.[c] By smooth talk and flattery
they deceive[d] the minds of naive people.
19 Everyone has heard[e] about your obedience, so I am full of joy over you; but I
want you to be wise about what is good,
and innocent about what is evil.[f]
20 The God of peace[g] will soon crush[h]
Satan[i] under your feet.
The grace of our Lord Jesus be with
you.[j]
21 Timothy,[k] my fellow worker, sends
his greetings to you, as do Lucius,[l] Jason[m] and Sosipater, my relatives.[n]
22 I, Tertius, who wrote down this letter, greet you in the Lord.
23 Gaius,[o] whose hospitality I and the
whole church here enjoy, sends you his
greetings.

16:7 OUTSTANDING AMONG THE APOSTLES. Andronicus and Junias are called apostles. The word "apostles" here is used in the general sense to refer to traveling messengers or missionaries rather than in the special sense of the word "apostle" (1Co 9:1–2; 2Co 8:23; 12:2; Php 2:25; cf. Ac 14:4, note; see article on THE MINISTRY GIFTS OF THE CHURCH, p. 407).

16:17–18 WATCH OUT FOR THOSE. At the end of his letter, Paul gives a strong warning to the church in Rome to be alert to all those who do damage to the church by corrupting the "teaching" of Paul and the other apostles. They are to "watch out for" the proponents of false doctrine and "keep away from them" and their ministry. These may have been antinomians (i.e., against the law), who taught that because salvation is by grace, saving faith does not necessarily include obedience to Christ (cf. 6:1–2; 2Co 4:2; 11:3; Eph 4:14; Rev 2:4–5; see article on FALSE TEACHERS, p. 98). They believed that a person could live in sin and reject God's moral law, and yet possess eternal salvation. These false teachers were eloquent orators, speaking with comforting words and flattering speeches (cf. Jude 16), but in reality they were deceivers.

16:19 INNOCENT ABOUT WHAT IS EVIL. The word "innocent" (Gk *akeraios*) means "unmixed" or "pure," i.e., innocent like a child whose mind has not yet been exposed to evil or mixed with the values of the world (cf. 1Co 14:20). (1) This Biblical principle is in direct opposition to the idea advocated by some that children of Christians should be exposed to sin, immorality, ungodliness and the things of Satan in order to learn to confront temptation. Some suggest that children need not be guarded from ungodliness. However, according to Biblical revelation, this philosophy is not only against God's will, but is compatible with Satan's own desire that everyone be exposed to the knowledge of good and evil (Ge 3:5).

(2) Knowledge of evil, along with continual exposure to Satan's ways, will lead many from the path of faith and obedience. Lot found this out to his deep sorrow when he lost his entire family (Ge 13:12–13; 19:1–38). Scripture warns that "bad company corrupts good character" (1Co 15:33), and that "Jesus Christ . . . gave himself . . . to rescue us from the present evil age" (Gal 1:3–4). Those who advocate exposing innocent children to an ungodly environment and/or influence are in danger of violating Jesus' warning in Mt 18:6.

(3) Believers should do all in their power to keep their children from being exposed to sin's deceitfulness and the perverseness of this generation. To refuse to protect our children disregards the Holy Spirit's desire that they be innocent about what is evil.

Erastus,[p] who is the city's director of
public works, and our brother Quartus
send you their greetings.[q]

25Now to him who is able[q] to establish
you by my gospel[r] and the proclamation
of Jesus Christ, according to the revelation of the mystery[s] hidden for long ages
past, **26**but now revealed and made known
through the prophetic writings[t] by the
command of the eternal God, so that all
nations might believe and obey[u] him—
27to the only wise God be glory forever
through Jesus Christ! Amen.[v]

16:23 [p] Ac 19:22; 2Ti 4:20
16:25 [q] 2Co 9:8; Eph 3:20; Jude 24 [r] Ro 2:16; 2Ti 2:8 [s] Isa 48:6; Eph 1:9; 3:3-6,9; Col 1:26,27; 2:2; 1Ti 3:16
16:26 [t] Ro 1:2 [u] Ro 1:5
16:27 [v] S Ro 11:36

[q] 23 Some manuscripts *their greetings. 24May the grace of our Lord Jesus Christ be with all of you. Amen.*

THE GIFTS OF THE HOLY SPIRIT

A. The Ministry Gifts of the Church

Gift	Definition	General References	Specific examples
Apostle (Specific)	Those specifically commissioned by the resurrected Lord to establish the church and the original message of the gospel	Ac 4:33–37; 5:12,18–42; 6:6; 8:14,18; 9:27; 11:1; 15:1–6,22–23; 16:4; 1Co 9:5; 12:28–29; Gal 1:17; Eph 2:20; 4:11; Jude 17	12 apostles: Mt 10:2; Mk 3:14; Lk 6:13; Ac 1:15–26; Rev 21:14 Paul: Ro 1:1; 11:13; 1Co 1:1; 9:1–2; 15:9–10; 2Co 1:1; Gal 1:1; 1Ti 2:7 Peter: 1Pe 1:1; 2Pe 1:1
Apostle (General)	Any messenger commissioned as a missionary or for other special responsibilities	Ac 13:1–3; 1Co 12:28–29; Eph 4:11	Barnabas: Ac 14:4,14 Andronicus and Junias: Ro 16:7 Titus and others: 2Co 8:23 Epaphroditus: Php 2:25 James, Jesus' brother: Gal 1:19
Prophet	Those who spoke under the inspiration of the Holy Spirit, bringing a message from God to the church, and whose main motivation and concern were with the spiritual life and purity of the church	Ro 12:6; 1Co 12:10; 14:1–33; Eph 4:11; 1Th 5:20–21; 1Ti 1:18; 1Pe 4:11; 1Jn 4:1–3	Peter: Ac 2:14–40; 3:12–26; 4:8–12; 10:34–44 Paul: Ac 13:1,16–41 Barnabas: Ac 13:1 Simeon: Ac 13:1 Lucius: Ac 13:1 Manaen: Ac 13:1 Agabus: Ac 11:27–28; 21:10 Judas and Silas: Ac 15:32 John: Rev 1:1,3; 10:8–11; 11:18
Evangelist	Those gifted by God to proclaim the gospel to the unsaved	Eph 4:11	Philip: Ac 8:5–8,26–40; 21:8 Paul: Ac 26:16–18
Pastor (Elder or Overseer)	Those chosen and gifted to oversee the church and care for its spiritual needs	Ac 14:23; 15:1–6,22–23; 16:4; 20:17–38; Ro 12:8; Eph 4:11–12; Php 1:1; 1Ti 3:1–7; 5:17–20; Tit 1:5–9; Heb 13:17; 1Pe 5:1–5	Timothy: 1Ti 1:1–4; 4:12–16; 2Ti 1:1–6; 4:2,5 Titus: Tit 1:4–5 Peter: 1Pe 5:1 John: 1Jn 2:1,12–14 Gaius: 3Jn 1–7

Gift	Definition	General References	Specific examples
Teacher	Those gifted to clarify and explain God's Word in order to build up the church	Ro 12:7; Eph 4:11–12; Col 3:16; 1Ti 3:2; 5:17; 2Ti 2:2,24	Paul: Ac 15:35; 20:20; 28:31; Ro 12:19–21; 13:8–10; 1Co 4:17; 1Ti 1:5; 4:16; 2Ti 1:11 Barnabas: Ac 15:35 Apollos: Ac 18:25–28 Timothy: 1Co 4:17; 1Ti 1:3–5; 4:11–13; 6:2; 2Ti 4:2 Titus: Tit 2:1–3,9–10
Deacon	Those chosen and gifted to render practical assistance to members of the church	Ac 6:1–6; Ro 12:7; Php 1:1; 1Ti 3:8–13; 1Pe 4:11	Seven deacons: Ac 6:5 Phoebe: Ro 16:1–2
Helper	Those gifted for a variety of helpful deeds	1Co 12:28	Paul: Ac 20:35 Lydia: Ac 16:14–15 Gaius: 3Jn 5–8
Administrator	Those gifted to guide and oversee the various activities of the church	1Co 12:7; Eph 4:11–12; 1Ti 3:1–7; Heb 13:7–17,24	Peter: Ac 6:3–4; 11:1–18 Paul: Ac 20:17–35; 1Co 11:23–24; 14; 16:1–9
Encourager	Those gifted to motivate other Christians to a deeper faith and dedication to Christ, a fuller manifestation of the fruit of the Holy Spirit, and a more complete separation from the world	Ro 12:8; 1Co 14:3; 1Th 5:11,14–22; Heb 10:24–25	Barnabas: Ac 11:23–24; 14:22 Paul: Ac 14:22; 16:40; 20:1; Ro 8:26–39; 12:1–2; 2Co 6:14—7:1; Gal 5:16–26 Judas and Silas: Ac 15:32; 16:40 Timothy: 1Th 3:2; 2Ti 4:2 Titus: Tit 2:6,13 Peter: 1Pe 5:1–2 John: 1Jn 2:15–17; 3:1–3
Giver	Those gifted to give freely of their resources to the needs of God's people	Ac 2:44–45; 4:34–35; 11:29–30; 1Co 16:1–4; 2Co 8—9; Eph 4:28; 1Ti 6:17–19; Heb 13:16; 1Jn 3:16–18	Barnabas: Ac 4:36–37 Christians in Macedonia: Ro 15:26–27; 2Co 8:1–5 Christians in Achaia: Ro 15:26–27; 2Co 9:2
Comforter	Those gifted to give comfort by acts of mercy to people in distress	Ro 12:8; 2Co 1:3–7	Paul: 2Co 1:4 Hebrew Christians: Heb 10:34 Various Christians: Col 4:10–11 Dorcas: Ac 9:36–39

B. Manifestations of the Holy Spirit through Individual Believers

Gift	Definition	General References	Specific examples
Message of wisdom	An utterance from the Holy Spirit applying God's Word or wisdom to a specific situation	Ac 6:3; 1Co 12:8; 13:2,9,12	Stephen: Ac 6:10 James: Ac 15:13–21
Message of knowledge	An utterance from the Holy Spirit revealing knowledge about people, circumstances or Biblical truth	Ac 10:47–48; 13:2; 15:7–11; 1Co 12:8; 13:2,9,12; 14:25	Peter: Ac 5:9–10
Faith	Supernatural faith imparted by the Holy Spirit, enabling a Christian to believe God for the miraculous	Mt 21:21–22; Mk 9:23–24; 11:22–24; Lk 17:6; Ac 3:1–8; 6:5–8; 1Co 12:9; 13:2; Jas 5:14–15	A centurion: Mt 8:5–10 A sick woman: Mt 9:20–22 Two blind men: Mt 9:27–29 A Canaanite woman: Mt 15:22–28 A sinful woman: Lk 9:36–50 A leper: Lk 17:11–19
Healing	Restoring someone to physical health by divinely supernatural means	Mt 4:23–24; 8:16; 9:35; 10:1,8; Mk 1:32–34; 6:13; 16:18; Lk 4:40–41; 9:1–2; Jn 6:2; 14:12; Ac 4:30; 5:15–16; 19:11–12; 1Co 12:9,28,30	Jesus: see chart on THE MIRACLES OF JESUS, p. 219 Apostles: see chart on THE MIRACLES OF APOSTLES, p. 221
Miraculous powers	Divine supernatural power to alter the course of nature, including driving out demons	Mt 4:23–24; 8:16; 10:1,8; 13:54; Mk 1:32–33,39; 3:15; 6:13; 16:17; Lk 4:40–41; 9:1; 10:17; Jn 7:3; 10:25,32; 14:11; 15:24; Ac 2:22,43; 4:30; 5:15–16; 6:8; 8:6–7; 14:3; 15:12; 19:11–12; Ro 15:19; 1Co 12;10,29; 2Co 12:12; Gal 3:5	Jesus: see chart on THE MIRACLES OF JESUS, p. 220 Apostles: see chart on THE MIRACLES OF THE APOSTLES, p. 221
Prophecy	A special temporary ability to bring a word, warning, exhortation or revelation from God under the impulse of the Holy Spirit	Lk 12:12; Ac 2:17–18; 1Co 12:10; 13:9; 14:1–33; Eph 4:11; 1Th 5:20–21; 2Pe 1:20–21; 1Jn 4:1–3	Elizabeth: Lk 1:40–45 Mary: Lk 1:46–55 Zechariah: Lk 1:67–79 Peter: Ac 2:14–40; 4:8–12 Twelve men from Ephesus: Ac 19:6 Four daughters of Philip: Ac 21:9 Agabus: Ac 21:10–11
Distinguishing between spirits	Special ability to judge whether prophecies and utterances are from the Holy Spirit	1Co 12:10; 14:29	Peter: Ac 8:18–24 Paul: Ac 13:8–12; 16:16–18

Gift	Definition	General References	Specific examples
Speaking in tongues	Expressing oneself at the level of one's spirit under the direct influence of the Holy Spirit in a language he or she has not learned and does not know	1Co 12:10,28,30; 13:1; 14:1–40	Disciples: Ac 2:4–11 Cornelius and his family: Ac 10:44–45; 11:17 Ephesian believers: Ac 19:2–7 Paul: 1Co 14:6,15,18
Interpretation of tongues	Special ability to interpret what is spoken in tongues	1Co 12:10,30; 14:5,13,26–28	

1 CORINTHIANS

Outline

Introduction (1:1–9)

- I. Discussion of Problems About Which Paul Had Been Informed (1:10—6:20)
  - A. Divisions in the Church (1:10—4:21)
    - 1. Four Factions (1:10–17)
    - 2. Causes of the Divisions (1:18—4:5)
      - a. A Wrong Conception of Wisdom (1:18—3:4)
      - b. A Wrong Conception of Christian Ministry (3:5—4:5)
    - 3. An Appeal for Reconciliation (4:6–21)

    Principle: The church as the one body of Christ (cf. 12:12ff) should not be split into separate parts (1:10,13)
  - B. Moral Problems in the Church (5:1—6:20)
    - 1. A Problem of Incest and Church Discipline (5:1–13)
    - 2. The Problem of Secular Lawsuits Between Christians (6:1–11)
    - 3. The Problem of Sexual Immorality (6:12–20)

    Principle: You who are united with the Lord conduct yourself so as to bring honor to him (6:17,20)
- II. Answers to Questions About Which the Corinthians Had Written (7:1—16:9)
  - A. Questions Concerning Marriage (7:1–40)
    - 1. Marriage and Celibacy (7:1–9)
    - 2. Christian Obligations in Marriage (7:10–16)
    - 3. Principle of Contentment (7:17–24)
    - 4. Counsel to the Unmarried (7:25–38)
    - 5. Instruction About Remarriage (7:39–40)

    Principle: God gives some the gift of a husband or wife; others he gives the gift of remaining single for the sake of the kingdom (7:7,32)
  - B. Questions Concerning the Use of Christian Freedom (8:1—11:1)
    - 1. The Problem of Food Offered to Idols (8:1–13)
    - 2. Paul's Disciplined Use of Freedom (9:1–27)
    - 3. A Warning Against Presumptuous Overconfidence (10:1–13)
    - 4. The Incompatibility of Idol Feasts and the Lord's Table (10:14–23)
    - 5. Some General Principles and Practical Advice (10:24—11:1)

    Principle: Do everything to bring glory to God; do nothing that might make others stumble (10:31–32) or might disqualify you from the race (9:24–27)
  - C. Questions Concerning Public Worship (11:2—14:40)
    - 1. Women's Head Covering in Church (11:2–16)
    - 2. Behavior at the Lord's Supper (11:17–34)
    - 3. Spiritual Gifts (12:1—14:40)

    Principle: Let all things be done in a fitting and orderly way (14:40)
  - D. Questions Concerning the Resurrection (15:1–58)
    - 1. Q. How Can Some Say There Is No Resurrection of the Dead? (15:12)
      A. The Certainty of the Resurrection (15:1–34)
    - 2. Q. How Are the Dead Raised? With What Kind of Body Will They Come? (15:35)
      A. The Nature of the Resurrection Body (15:35–57)

3. Conclusion to the Question (15:58)
Principle: Christ's resurrection from the dead guarantees the resurrection of those who belong to Christ when he comes back (15:22–23)
E. Questions Concerning the Collection for God's People (16:1–9)
Final Instructions (16:10–24)

Author: Paul

Theme: Church Problems and Solutions

Date: A.D. 55/56

Background

Corinth, an ancient city of Greece, was in many ways the most prominent Greek metropolis of Paul's time. Like many of today's prosperous cities, Corinth was intellectually arrogant, materially affluent and morally corrupt. Sin of every kind flourished in this notoriously sensual city.

In conjunction with Priscilla and Aquila (16:19) and his own apostolic team (Ac 18:5), Paul founded the Corinthian church during his eighteen-month ministry at Corinth during his second missionary journey (Ac 18:1–17). The church was made up of some Jews but mostly of ex-pagan Gentiles. After Paul left Corinth, a variety of problems arose in the young church, requiring his apostolic authority and teaching by written correspondence and visits in person.

The first letter to the Corinthians was written during his three-year ministry at Ephesus (Ac 20:31) on his third missionary journey (Ac 18:23—21:15). Reports reached Paul at Ephesus about the problems at Corinth (1Co 1:11); afterwards a delegation from the Corinthian congregation (16:17) delivered a letter to Paul, requesting his instruction on a variety of issues (7:1; cf. 8:1; 12:1; 16:1). In response to the reports and the letter from Corinth, Paul wrote this letter.

Purpose

Paul had two primary reasons in mind as he penned this letter: (1) To correct the serious problems in the Corinthian church that had been reported to him. These were disorders that the Corinthians viewed lightly, but that Paul regarded as serious sin. (2) To provide counsel and instruction on a variety of questions about which the Corinthians had written. These included both issues of doctrine and personal and corporate conduct and purity.

Survey

This letter addresses the kinds of problems that churches experience when members remain "worldly" (3:1–3) and do not decisively separate themselves from the pagan society around them (2Co 6:17)—problems such as divisiveness (1:10–12; 11:17–22), tolerance of a sin like incest (5:1–13), sexual immorality in general (6:12–20), secular lawsuits between Christians (6:1–11), humanistic thinking about apostolic truth (ch. 15) and conflicts over "Christian freedom" (chs. 8; 10). Paul also instructs the Corinthians about matters related to celibacy and marriage (ch. 7), public worship, including the Lord's Supper (chs. 11—14), and the collection for the Jerusalem saints (16:1–4).

Among the most important contributions of 1 Corinthians is Paul's teaching on the manifestations and gifts of the Holy Spirit in the context of corporate worship (chs. 12—14). More than anywhere else in the NT, these chapters provide insight into the character and components of worship in the early church (cf. 14:26–33). Paul indicates that God's purpose for the church includes a wide variety of the Spirit's manifestations occurring through faithful believers (12:4–10) and individuals called to certain ministries (12:28–30)—a diversity within unity analogous to the many functions of a human body (12:12–27). In providing guidelines for the corporate function of spiritual gifts, Paul makes an essential distinction between individual and corporate edification (14:2–6,12,16–19,26), insisting that all public manifestations or gifts must flow out of love (ch. 13) and exist for the edification of the gathered believers (12:7; 14:4–6,26).

Special Features

Five major features characterize 1 Corinthians. (1) It is the most problem-centered letter in the NT. In addressing the various problems and issues at Corinth, Paul gives clear and enduring spiritual principles, each of which is applicable universally for the church (e.g. 1:10; 6:17,20; 7:7; 9:24–27; 10:31–32; 14:1–10; 15:22–23). (2) There is an overall emphasis on the oneness of the local church as the body of Christ, a focus that occurs in discussions about divisions, the Lord's Supper and spiritual gifts. (3) This letter contains the most extensive NT teaching on such important subjects as celibacy, and marriage and remarriage (ch. 7); the Lord's Supper (10:16–21; 11:17–34); tongues, prophecy and spiritual gifts in corporate gatherings (chs. 12; 14); agape love (ch. 13); and the resurrection of the body (ch. 15). (4) It provides invaluable wisdom for pastoral oversight in relation to church discipline (ch. 5). (5) It emphasizes the real possibility of falling away from the faith by those who persist in unrighteous behavior and do not hold firmly to Christ (6:9–10; 9:24–27; 10:5–12,20–21; 15:1–2).

Reading 1 Corinthians

In order to read the entire New Testament in one year, the book of 1 Corinthians should be read in 19 days, according to the following schedule:
☐ 1 ☐ 2 ☐ 3 ☐ 4 ☐ 5 ☐ 6 ☐ 7 ☐ 8 ☐ 9 ☐ 10:1–13 ☐ 10:14—11:1 ☐ 11:2–34 ☐ 12 ☐ 13 ☐ 14:1–25 ☐ 14:26–40 ☐ 15:1–34 ☐ 15:35–58 ☐ 16

NOTES

1

Paul, called to be an apostle[a] of Christ Jesus by the will of God,[b] and our brother Sosthenes,[c]

2To the church of God[d] in Corinth,[e] to those sanctified in Christ Jesus and called[f] to be holy, together with all those everywhere who call on the name[g] of our Lord Jesus Christ—their Lord and ours:

3Grace and peace to you from God our Father and the Lord Jesus Christ.[h]

Thanksgiving

4I always thank God for you[i] because of his grace given you in Christ Jesus. **5**For in him you have been enriched[j] in every way—in all your speaking and in all your knowledge[k]— **6**because our testimony[l] about Christ was confirmed in you.
1Co 12:1-31 **7**Therefore you do not lack any spiritual gift[m] as you eagerly wait for our Lord Jesus Christ to be revealed.[n] **8**He will keep you strong to the end, so that you will be blameless[o] on the day of our Lord Jesus Christ.[p] **9**God, who has called you[q] into fellowship with his Son Jesus Christ our Lord,[r] is faithful.[s]

Divisions in the Church

10I appeal to you, brothers,[t] in the name of our Lord Jesus Christ, that all of you agree with one another so that there may be no divisions among you[u] and that you may be perfectly united[v] in mind and thought. **11**My brothers, some from Chloe's household[w] have informed me that there are quarrels among you. **12**What I mean is this: One of you says, "I follow Paul";[x] another, "I follow Apollos";[y] another, "I follow Cephas[a]";[z] still another, "I follow Christ."

13Is Christ divided? Was Paul crucified for you? Were you baptized into[b] the name of Paul?[a] **14**I am thankful that I did not baptize any of you except Crispus[b] and Gaius,[c] **15**so no one can say that you were baptized into my name. **16**(Yes, I also baptized the household[d] of Stephanas;[e] beyond that, I don't remember if I baptized anyone else.) **17**For Christ did not send me to baptize,[f] but to preach the gospel—not with words of human wisdom,[g] lest the cross of Christ be emptied of its power.

Christ the Wisdom and Power of God

18For the message of the cross is foolishness[h] to those who are perishing,[i] but to us who are being saved[j] it is the power of God.[k] **19**For it is written:

1:1 [a]Ro 1:1; Eph 1:1; 2Ti 1:1 [b]S 2Co 1:1 [c]Ac 18:17 **1:2** [d]S 1Co 10:32 [e]S Ac 18:1 [f]Ro 1:7 [g]S Ac 2:21 **1:3** [h]S Ro 1:7 **1:4** [i]S Ro 1:8 **1:5** [j]2Co 9:11 [k]S 2Co 8:7 **1:6** [l]2Th 1:10; 1Ti 2:6; Rev 1:2 **1:7** [m]Ro 1:11; 1Co 12:1-31 [n]S Mt 16:27; S Lk 17:30; 1Th 1:10; S 2:19; Tit 2:13; Jas 5:7,8; 1Pe 1:13; 2Pe 3:12; S Rev 1:7 **1:8** [o]S 1Th 3:13 [p]Am 5:18; 1Co 5:5; Php 1:6, 10; 2:16; 1Th 5:2 **1:9** [q]S Ro 8:28 [r]1Jn 1:3 [s]Dt 7:9; Isa 49:7; 1Co 10:13; 1Th 5:24; 2Th 3:3; 2Ti 2:13; Heb 10:23; 11:11 **1:10** [t]S Ro 7:1 [u]1Co 11:18 [v]S Ro 15:5 **1:11** [w]S Ac 11:14 **1:12** [x]1Co 3:4,22 [y]S Ac 18:24 [z]Jn 1:42; 1Co 3:22; 9:5 **1:13** [a]S Mt 28:19 **1:14** [b]Ac 18:8 [c]S Ac 19:29 **1:16** [d]S Ac 11:14 [e]1Co 16:15 **1:17** [f]Jn 4:2; S Ac 2:38 [g]1Co 2:1,4,13 **1:18** [h]ver 21,23,25; 1Co 2:14 [i]2Co 2:15; 4:3; 2Th 2:10 [j]Ac 2:47 [k]ver 24; Ro 1:16

[a] *12* That is, Peter [b] *13* Or *in*; also in verse 15

1:2 CALLED TO BE HOLY. See Ac 9:13, note on the meaning of the term "saints."

1:7 YOU DO NOT LACK ANY SPIRITUAL GIFT. Paul commends the Corinthians because God in his grace (v. 4) has given them specific spiritual gifts. Such gifts are a valuable and indispensable accompaniment of the Holy Spirit's ministry in the church; without them believers fail to strengthen and help one another as God desires. Nowhere in this letter does Paul seek to eliminate these gifts. Rather he seeks to change the attitude of the Corinthians toward spiritual gifts so that they may use their gifts according to God's intention.

1:7 WAIT FOR OUR LORD JESUS CHRIST TO BE REVEALED. The early Christians lived in expectation of Christ's imminent return (see Mt 24:42, note; Jn 14:3, note). They fixed their faith firmly on the fact of the Lord's coming, living every day in anticipation of that great hope. Note that the Christian's hope is for the personal return of the Lord Jesus Christ, not for the general complex of events that comprises the last days (cf. 1Th 1:9–10; 4:13–17; Tit 2:13; Heb 9:28).

1:12 I FOLLOW PAUL ... APOLLOS ... CEPHAS. Division over leaders in the church was beginning to develop; some church members were becoming more attached to certain ministers of the gospel than to the gospel itself. Paul condemns this attitude, reminding them that neither he nor any other person was crucified for them. This same error is present today. Some believers become more attached to a pastor or evangelist than to Christ and his Word. This can cause them to betray Christian principles, and can even divide the church. We must always be careful to center our love and loyalty on God and his Word, not on any minister or person.

1:12 I FOLLOW CHRIST. The "Christ party" probably consisted of false teachers who were enemies of the apostle (4:18–19) and claimed to have a superior spirituality and "wisdom." They believed that their knowledge (8:1) brought freedom from the restraints of the law (6:12; 10:23) and from the demands of morality (5:2). They were attempting to win the church over to their own distorted gospel (2Co 11:4,20–21). It is against them and their converts at Corinth that Paul mainly contends.

1:17 CHRIST DID NOT SEND ME TO BAPTIZE. Paul is not minimizing Jesus' teaching concerning baptism (Mt 28:19). Rather, he makes it clear that he delegated the performing of baptism to his associates, as did Christ (Jn 4:1–2) and Peter (Ac 10:47–48). The apostle does not want to provide an opportunity for his converts to presume that they were "baptized into the name of Paul" (v. 13). Paul himself focused on preaching the gospel.

1:18 IT IS THE POWER OF GOD. The message of the cross not only involves wisdom and truth, but the active power of God coming down to save, heal, drive out demons and redeem from sin's power (see article on THE KINGDOM OF GOD, p. 28).

"I will destroy the wisdom of the
wise;
the intelligence of the intelligent I
will frustrate."[c][l]

20Where is the wise man?[m] Where is the
scholar? Where is the philosopher of this
age?[n] Has not God made foolish[o] the wisdom of the world? 21For since in the wisdom of God the world[p] through its wisdom did not know him, God was pleased
through the foolishness of what was
preached to save[q] those who believe.[r]
22Jews demand miraculous signs[s] and
Greeks look for wisdom, 23but we preach
Christ crucified:[t] a stumbling block[u] to
Jews and foolishness[v] to Gentiles, 24but
to those whom God has called,[w] both Jews
and Greeks, Christ the power of God[x] and
the wisdom of God.[y] 25For the foolishness[z] of God is wiser than man's wisdom,
and the weakness[a] of God is stronger
than man's strength.
26Brothers, think of what you were
when you were called.[b] Not many of you
were wise[c] by human standards; not
many were influential; not many were of
noble birth. 27But God chose[d] the foolish[e] things of the world to shame the
wise; God chose the weak things of the
world to shame the strong. 28He chose the
lowly things of this world and the despised things—and the things that are
not[f]—to nullify the things that are, 29so
that no one may boast before him.[g] 30It is
because of him that you are in Christ
Jesus,[h] who has become for us wisdom
from God—that is, our righteousness,[i]
holiness[j] and redemption.[k] 31Therefore,
as it is written: "Let him who boasts boast
in the Lord."[d][l]

2 When I came to you, brothers, I did
not come with eloquence or superior
wisdom[m] as I proclaimed to you the testimony about God.[e] 2For I resolved to know
nothing while I was with you except Jesus
Christ and him crucified.[n] 3I came to you[o]
in weakness[p] and fear, and with much
trembling.[q] 4My message and my preach-

1:19 [l]Isa 29:14
1:20 [m]Isa 19:11,12 [n]1Co 2:6,8; 3:18; 2Co 4:4; Gal 1:4 [o]ver 27; Job 12:17; Isa 44:25; Jer 8:9; Ro 1:22; 1Co 3:18,19
1:21 [p]ver 27,28; 1Co 6:2; 11:32 [q]S Ro 11:14 [r]S Ro 3:22
1:22 [s]S Mt 12:38; S Jn 2:11; S 4:48
1:23 [t]1Co 2:2; Gal 3:1 [u]S Lk 2:34 [v]S ver 18
1:24 [w]S Ro 8:28 [x]ver 18; Ro 1:16 [y]ver 30; S Col 2:3
1:25 [z]S ver 18 [a]2Co 13:4
1:26 [b]S Ro 8:28 [c]ver 20
1:27 [d]Jas 2:5 [e]ver 20; Ro 1:22; 1Co 3:18,19
1:28 [f]Ro 4:17
1:29 [g]Eph 2:9
1:30 [h]S Ro 16:3 [i]Jer 23:5,6; 33:16; 2Co 5:21; Php 3:9 [j]1Co 1:2 [k]S Ro 3:24
1:31 [l]Jer 9:23,24; Ps 34:2; 44:8; 2Co 10:17
2:1 [m]ver 4,13; 1Co 1:17
2:2 [n]Gal 6:14; 1Co 1:23 **2:3** [o]Ac 18:1-18 [p]1Co 4:10; 9:22; 2Co 11:29,30; 12:5,9,10; 13:9 [q]S 2Co 7:15

c *19* Isaiah 29:14 d *31* Jer. 9:24 e *1* Some manuscripts *as I proclaimed to you God's mystery*

1:20 THE WISDOM OF THE WORLD. The wisdom of the world is a wisdom that excludes God, emphasizes human self-sufficiency, makes humanity the highest authority and refuses to recognize God's revelation in Jesus Christ. (1) This wisdom God calls foolishness (3:19–20), for through it humans have failed to find the truth or come to know their Creator (v. 21). (2) The believer must develop a godly contempt for both human wisdom and a secular world view (see vv. 18–31; 2:1–16; Ac 17:18; Ro 1:20–32; Col 2:8, note; 2Th 2:10–12; 2Ti 3:1–9; 2Pe 2:1–3,7; Jude 4–19). The gospel and the message of the cross must never be accommodated to philosophy, science or any other so-called human wisdom (2:4–5; Gal 6:14).

1:21 THE FOOLISHNESS OF WHAT WAS PREACHED. It is not the method of preaching that is considered foolish, but the message of the lordship of the crucified and resurrected Christ.

1:27 GOD CHOSE THE FOOLISH THINGS. In vv. 25–29, Paul emphasizes that God's standards and values are different from those accepted by the world; God is now in the process of overthrowing the world's false standards and wisdom.

1:28 NULLIFY THE THINGS THAT ARE. Through Jesus' crucifixion and resurrection (vv. 18,23) and through choosing the lowly things of this world (vv. 26–27), God nullifies the esteemed things of this present age. God is now in the process of bringing humanistic philosophies, psychologies and all other worldly systems to an end.

1:30 CHRIST JESUS ... HAS BECOME FOR US WISDOM. It is through Christ, in Christ and with Christ that the believer receives wisdom from God and experiences righteousness (cf. Ro 4), sanctification (2Th 2:13–15) and redemption (Ro 3:24; Eph 4:30). As long as one is joined to Christ, Christ is the source of all these blessings (see Jn 15:1–6, notes on remaining in Christ).

2:1 I DID NOT COME WITH ... WISDOM. The content of Paul's preaching was not according to the latest human "wisdom," either in the world or the church. Instead he concentrated on the central truth of the gospel (redemption through Christ) and on the power of the Holy Spirit (see next note). He was well aware of his human limitations, his personal inadequacy, and his inner fear and trembling. Consequently, he relied not on himself but on his message and on the Spirit (v. 4). This resulted in a greater demonstration of the Spirit's work and power.

2:4 A DEMONSTRATION OF THE SPIRIT'S POWER. (1) As a demonstration of the Holy Spirit's power (1:18,24), Paul's preaching included (a) the Spirit's convicting people of sin, righteousness and judgment, and bearing witness to the saving power of the risen Christ (cf. chs. 5–6; see Jn 16:8, note; Ac 2:36–41); (b) the power to transform lives (1:26–27; cf. Ac 4:13); (c) the power to effect holiness in the believer (5:3–5); and (d) God's power manifested by signs and wonders (Ac 2:29–33; 4:29–30; 5:12; 14:3; 2Co 12:12).

(2) Several other NT passages emphasize that the preaching of the gospel was accompanied by a special power of the Holy Spirit: Mk 16:17–18; Lk 10:19; Ac 28:3–6; Ro 15:19; 1Co 4:20; 1Th 1:5; Heb 2:4.

(3) All ministers of the gospel should pray that through their ministry (a) persons will be saved (Ac 2:41; 11:21,24; 14:1), (b) new believers will be filled with the Holy Spirit (Ac 2:4; 4:31; 8:17; 19:6), (c) evil spirits will be driven out (Ac 5:16; 8:7; 16:18), (d) the sick will be healed (Ac 3:6; 4:29–30; 14:10), and (e) disciples will learn to obey Christ's righteous standards and teachings (Mt 28:18–20; Ac 11:23,26; see

ing were not with wise and persuasive
words,[r] but with a demonstration of the
Spirit's power,[s] **5**so that your faith might
not rest on men's wisdom, but on God's
power.[t]

Wisdom From the Spirit

6We do, however, speak a message of
wisdom among the mature,[u] but not the
wisdom of this age[v] or of the rulers of this
age, who are coming to nothing.[w] **7**No, we
speak of God's secret wisdom, a wisdom[x]
that has been hidden[y] and that God destined for our glory before time began.
8None of the rulers of this age[z] understood it, for if they had, they would not
have crucified the Lord of glory.[a] **9**However, as it is written:

"No eye has seen,
no ear has heard,
no mind has conceived
what God has prepared for those
who love him"[f][b]—

10but God has revealed[c] it to us by his
Spirit.[d]
The Spirit searches all things, even the
deep things of God. **11**For who among men
knows the thoughts of a man[e] except the
man's spirit[f] within him? In the same way
no one knows the thoughts of God except
the Spirit of God. **12**We have not received
the spirit[g] of the world[h] but the Spirit
who is from God, that we may understand
what God has freely given us. **13**This is
what we speak, not in words taught us by
human wisdom[i] but in words taught by
the Spirit, expressing spiritual truths in
spiritual words.[g] **14**The man without the
Spirit does not accept the things that
come from the Spirit of God,[j] for they are
foolishness[k] to him, and he cannot understand them, because they are spiritually
discerned. **15**The spiritual[l] man makes
judgments about all things, but he himself
is not subject to any man's judgment:

16"For who has known the mind of the
Lord
that he may instruct him?"[h][m]

But we have the mind of Christ.[n]

On Divisions in the Church

3 Brothers, I could not address you as
spiritual[o] but as worldly[p]—mere in-

2:4 [r]ver 1 [s]S Ro 15:13 **2:5** [t]2Co 4:7; 6:7 **2:6** [u]Eph 4:13; Php 3:15; Col 4:12; Heb 5:14; 6:1; Jas 1:4 [v]ver 8; S 1Co 1:20 [w]Ps 146:4 **2:7** [x]ver 1 [y]Ro 16:25 **2:8** [z]ver 6; S 1Co 1:20 [a]Ps 24:7; Ac 7:2; Jas 2:1 **2:9** [b]Isa 64:4; 65:17 **2:10** [c]S Mt 13:11; 2Co 12:1,7; Gal 1:12; 2:2; Eph 3:3,5 [d]Jn 14:26 **2:11** [e]Jer 17:9 [f]Pr 20:27 **2:12** [g]Ro 8:15 [h]1Co 1:20,27; Jas 2:5 **2:13** [i]ver 1,4; 1Co 1:17 **2:14** [j]Jn 14:17 [k]S 1Co 1:18 **2:15** [l]1Co 3:1; Gal 6:1 **2:16** [m]Isa 40:13; S Ro 11:34 [n]Jn 15:15 **3:1** [o]1Co 2:15 [p]Ro 7:14; 1Co 2:14

f *9* Isaiah 64:4 g *13* Or *Spirit, interpreting spiritual truths to spiritual men* h *16* Isaiah 40:13

article on SIGNS OF BELIEVERS, p. 106).

2:12 THAT WE MAY UNDERSTAND. The things that God has prepared for those who love him (v. 9) can be understood by believers through the Spirit's revelation and illumination (vv. 10–16). As believers read and study the Bible, the Spirit illuminates their understanding of the truth. The Spirit also gives to faithful believers a strong assurance of the divine origin of Scripture (Jn 16:13; Eph 1:17).

2:13 WORDS TAUGHT BY THE SPIRIT. Though Paul is writing about the divine origin of his preaching, vv. 9–13 suggest the steps by which the Holy Spirit also inspired the writing of Scripture.

Step 1: God desired to communicate his wisdom to humanity (vv. 7–9). This wisdom concerned our salvation, centering in Christ as the wisdom of God (cf. 1:30; 2:2,5).

Step 2: It is only through the Holy Spirit that God's truth and wisdom was revealed to humanity (v. 10). The Spirit knows fully the thoughts of God (v. 11).

Step 3: God's revelation was given to chosen believers through the indwelling presence of the Spirit (v. 12; cf. Ro 8:11,15).

Step 4: The writers of Scripture wrote with words taught by the Holy Spirit (v. 13); the Spirit directed the writers in the choice of the words they used (cf. Ex 24:4; Isa 51:16; Jer 1:9; 36:28,32; Eze 2:7; Mt 4:4). At the same time, the Spirit's guidance in the expression of divine truth was not mechanical; rather the Spirit used each writer's vocabulary and personal style.

Step 5: Divinely inspired Scripture is understood by spiritual believers as they examine its content through the illumination of the Holy Spirit (vv. 14–16).

Thus, both the thoughts and language of Scripture were inspired by the Spirit of God. Not a single writer uttered a false word or phrase. God's Word was protected from error and falsehood by the Holy Spirit (see article on THE INSPIRATION AND AUTHORITY OF SCRIPTURE, p. 474).

2:14 THE MAN WITHOUT THE SPIRIT. For comments on this verse, see article on THREE KINDS OF PEOPLE, p. 334.

2:16 WE HAVE THE MIND OF CHRIST. To have the mind of Christ means knowing his will and his redemptive plan and purpose (vv. 9–10). It means appraising and seeing things the way God sees them, valuing things the way he values them, loving what he loves and hating what he hates (v. 15; Heb 1:9). It means understanding God's holiness and sin's awfulness. Thus, receiving the Spirit and following the Spirit (v. 12) cause the believer's values and world view to become radically different from the ways and wisdom of this age (cf. Php 2:5–8).

3:1 NOT ADDRESS YOU AS SPIRITUAL. One of the Corinthian church's major problems was its attempt to experience God's blessings while refusing to separate itself from the world's evil ways (see article on THE CHRISTIAN'S RELATIONSHIP TO THE WORLD, p. 546). (1) The pastors and leaders of the Corinthian church were allowing professed converts to come into the congregations without forsaking their evil practices. The Corinthians were tolerating within their fellowship: selfish divisions (11:18), the world's philosophy (1:18–25; 3:19), jealousy and

fants[q] in Christ. 2I gave you milk, not solid food,[r] for you were not yet ready for
it.[s] Indeed, you are still not ready. 3You
are still worldly. For since there is jealousy and quarreling[t] among you, are you
not worldly? Are you not acting like mere
men? 4For when one says, "I follow Paul,"
and another, "I follow Apollos,"[u] are you
not mere men?

5What, after all, is Apollos?[v] And what
is Paul? Only servants,[w] through whom
you came to believe—as the Lord has assigned to each his task. 6I planted the
seed,[x] Apollos watered it, but God made
it grow. 7So neither he who plants nor he
who waters is anything, but only God, who
makes things grow. 8The man who plants
and the man who waters have one purpose, and each will be rewarded according
to his own labor.[y] 9For we are God's fellow workers;[z] you are God's field,[a] God's
building.[b]

10By the grace God has given me,[c] I
laid a foundation[d] as an expert builder,
and someone else is building on it. But
each one should be careful how he builds.
11For no one can lay any foundation other
than the one already laid, which is Jesus
Christ.[e] 12If any man builds on this foundation using gold, silver, costly stones,
wood, hay or straw, 13his work will be
shown for what it is,[f] because the Day[g]
will bring it to light. It will be revealed
with fire, and the fire will test the quality
of each man's work.[h] 14If what he has
built survives, he will receive his reward.[i]
15If it is burned up, he will suffer loss; he
himself will be saved, but only as one escaping through the flames.[j]

16Don't you know that you yourselves
are God's temple[k] and that God's Spirit
lives in you?[l] 17If anyone destroys God's

3:1 [q] 1Co 14:20 **3:2** [r] Heb 5:12-14; 1Pe 2:2 [s] Jn 16:12 **3:3** [t] Ro 13:13; 1Co 1:11; Gal 5:20 **3:4** [u] 1Co 1:12 **3:5** [v] S Ac 18:24 [w] 1Co 4:1; 2Co 6:4; Eph 3:7; Col 1:23, 25 **3:6** [x] Ac 18:4-11; 1Co 4:15; 9:1; 15:1 **3:8** [y] ver 14; Ps 18:20; 62:12; Mt 25:21; 1Co 9:17 **3:9** [z] Mk 16:20; 2Co 6:1; 1Th 3:2 [a] Isa 61:3 [b] Eph 2:20-22; 1Pe 2:5 **3:10** [c] S Ro 12:3 [d] Ro 15:20; S Eph 2:20 **3:11** [e] Isa 28:16; Eph 2:20 **3:13** [f] 1Co 4:5 [g] S 1Co 1:8; 2Th 1:7-10; 2Ti 1:12,18; 4:8 [h] Nu 31:22,23; Jer 23:28,29; Mal 3:3; S 2Th 1:7 **3:14** [i] S ver 8 **3:15** [j] Jude 23 **3:16** [k] 1Co 6:19; 2Co 6:16; Eph 2:21,22; Heb 3:6 [l] S Ro 8:9

quarreling (3:3), pride (3:21; 4:7), immorality (5:1), trivial lawsuits (6:1–8), attendance at idolatrous festivals (chs. 8; 10) and the rejection of apostolic teaching (14:36–37). Because the Corinthians failed to see the absolute necessity of apostolic truth, love and godly standards (6:9–10; 13), they abused the gifts of the Spirit (chs. 12; 14) and the "Lord's Supper" (11:20–34), and distorted the message of the gospel (1:18–31).

(2) Jesus himself warns that any church that tolerates within its fellowship the world's unrighteous practices or the distortion of Biblical truth (see Rev 2:20, note) will be rejected by him and lose its place in God's kingdom (cf. Rev 2:5,16; 3:15–16). The Spirit calls such a church to true repentance (5:2), to separation from the world (2Co 6:16–18), and to "perfecting holiness out of reverence for God" (2Co 7:1).

3:3 YOU ARE STILL WORLDLY. For comments on the difference between worldly and spiritual Christians, see article on THREE KINDS OF PEOPLE, p. 334.

3:15 HE WILL SUFFER LOSS. The Bible asserts that all the redeemed are free from God's judgment of condemnation (Jn 5:24; Ro 8:1; Heb 10:14–17). However, there is a future judgment for believers (1Jn 4:17) as to the degree of their faithfulness to God and the grace given to them during this life on earth (v. 10; 4:2–5; 2Co 5:10). In that judgment there is the possibility that a believer, although receiving salvation, may experience great loss (Gk *zēmioō*, meaning "to suffer loss or damage").

The careless believer is in danger of suffering loss or damage in the following ways: (1) a feeling of shame at Christ's coming (2Ti 2:15; 1Jn 2:28); (2) loss of his or her life's work for God (vv. 12–15); (3) loss of glory and honor before God (cf. Ro 2:7); (4) loss of opportunity for service and authority in heaven (Mt 25:14–30); (5) a low position in heaven (Mt 5:19; 19:30); (6) loss of rewards (cf. v. 14–15); and (7) repayment for the wrong done to others (Col 3:24–25). These passages should impress on us the necessity of complete dedication, including faithful, self-sacrificing service to our Lord (cf. Ro 12:1–2; Php 2:12; 4:3; see article on THE JUDGMENT OF BELIEVERS, p. 368).

3:15 BUT ONLY AS ONE ESCAPING THROUGH THE FLAMES. "Escaping through the flames" is probably an expression meaning "barely saved." God will evaluate the quality of life, influence, teaching and work in the church of each person, and especially here, of each minister. If his work is judged unworthy, he will lose his reward, yet he himself may be saved. Note that this passage does not teach a doctrine of purgatory; it addresses a judgment of works, not the cleansing of a person from mortal sins.

3:16 YOU YOURSELVES ARE GOD'S TEMPLE. The emphasis here is on the entire congregation of believers as God's temple and the dwelling place of the Spirit (cf. v. 9; 2Co 6:16; Eph 2:21). As the temple of God in the midst of a corrupt society, God's people in Corinth were not to participate in the evils prevalent in that society, but were to reject all forms of immorality. God's temple must be holy (v. 17) because God is holy (cf. 1Pe 1:14–16).

3:17 GOD WILL DESTROY HIM. Paul presents one of the strongest warnings in the NT to anyone responsible for building Christ's church. This passage has special relevance for all those in teaching/leadership positions. If anyone defiles or corrupts God's temple (i.e., a local congregation or a group of congregations), God himself will punish that individual with terrible ruin and eternal death. People corrupt and destroy Christ's church by: (1) engaging in immorality (5:1); (2) fostering lies, deceptions and selfish ambition (v. 3; Ac 5:1–11); (3) promoting false doctrine, rejecting apostolic revelation and showing indifference to Scriptural truth (1Ti 4:1; Jude 4); (4) accepting sin and worldliness within the congregation (5:1–2,5–7; Rev 3:17); (5) attempting to build the church by worldly wisdom or a distorted gospel (1:18—2:5; Php 1:15–16).

THREE KINDS OF PEOPLE

1Co 2:14–15 *"The man without the Spirit does not accept the things that come from the Spirit of God, for they are foolishness to him, and he cannot understand them, because they are spiritually discerned. The spiritual man makes judgments about all things, but he himself is not subject to any man's judgment."*

BASIC DIVISION. Scripture typically divides all humans into two classes.

(1) The natural, or unspiritual, man/woman (Gk *psuchikos*, 1Co 2:14) identifies the unregenerated person, i.e., one governed by mere natural instincts (2Pe 2:12). This kind of person does not have the Holy Spirit (Ro 8:9), is under Satan's dominion (Ac 26:18), and is enslaved to the body and its passions (Eph 2:3). He or she belongs to the world, is in sympathy with it (Jas 4:4) and rejects the things of the Spirit (1Co 2:14). The unspiritual person is not able to understand God and his ways, but instead relies on human reasoning or emotions.

(2) The spiritual man/woman (Gk *pneumatikos*, 1Co 2:15; 3:1) identifies the regenerated person, i.e., one who has the Holy Spirit. This person is spiritually minded, thinks the thoughts of God (1Co 2:11–13) and lives by the Spirit of God (Ro 8:4–17; Gal 5:16–26). Such an individual believes in Jesus Christ, strives to follow the leading of the indwelling Spirit, and resists sensual desires and sin's dominion (Ro 8:13–14).

How does one become a spiritual man/woman? When a person accepts by faith the salvation provided through Christ, he or she is regenerated; the Holy Spirit imparts to him or her a new nature by an infusion of divine life (2Pe 1:4; see article on REGENERATION, p. 178). He or she is born again (John 3:3,5,7), renewed (Ro 12:2), and made a new creation (2Co 5:17) and recipient of God's righteousness through faith in Christ (Php 3:9).

FURTHER DISTINCTION AMONG CHRISTIANS. Although born-again believers receive the new life of the Spirit, they retain the sinful nature with its evil inclinations (Gal 5:16–21). The sinful nature that remains in them cannot be made good; it must be put to death and overcome through the Spirit's power and grace (Ro 8:13). Believers overcome by denying themselves daily (Mt 16:24; Ro 8:12–13; Tit 2:12), removing every hindrance or sin (Heb 12:1), and resisting all sinful temptations (Ro 13:14; Gal 5:16; 1Pe 2:11). By the power of the Spirit believers themselves wage war against the sinful nature (Ro 8:13–14; Gal 5:16–18), crucify it (Gal 5:24) and put it to death daily (Col 3:5). By this process of self-denial and yielding to the Holy Spirit's sanctifying work, they will be set free from the power of their sinful nature and live as spiritual Christians (Ro 6:13; Gal 5:16).

Not all Christians make the required effort to fully overcome this sinful nature. In addressing the Corinthians, Paul notes (1Co 3:1,3) that some of them are behaving in a worldly or unspiritual (Gk *sarkikos*) manner; instead of consistently resisting the inclinations of their sinful nature, they often yielded to at least some of them. Although they were not living in persistent disobedience, they were in the process of compromising with the world, the sinful nature and the devil in some areas of their lives, while still wanting to remain a part of God's people (10:21; 2Co 6:14–18; 11:3; 13:5).

(1) The condition of worldly Christians. Although sin and rebellion were not the rule in their lives, nor had they entered into the serious immorality and unrighteousness that would separate them from God's kingdom (see 1Co 6:9–11; cf. Gal 5:21; Eph 5:5), these worldly Christians were behaving in such a way that they were no longer growing in grace, acting as if they were new converts who did not yet understand the full implication of salvation in Christ (1Co 3:1–2). Their worldliness was expressed in "jealousy and quarreling" (3:3). They were indifferent to and tolerant of immorality within the church (5:1–13; 6:13–20). They did not take God's Word or his apostle with utmost seriousness (4:18–19). They were going to law courts over trivial matters (6:8). Note that Paul considers the Corinthians who had entered into sexual immorality or other gross sins to be excluded altogether from salvation in Christ (1Co 5:1,9–11; 6:9–10).

(2) The perils of worldly Christians. These worldly Corinthian Christians were in danger of being led astray from sincere devotion to Christ (2Co 11:3) and being more and more conformed to the world (2Co 6:14–18). Because of this, they would be chastened and judged by the Lord, and if they continued to conform to the world, they would ultimately be excluded from God's kingdom (1Co 6:9–10; 11:31–32). In fact, spiritual death had already occurred for some of them who had committed flagrant sin leading to spiritual death (see 1Jn 3:15, note; 5:17, note; cf. Ro 8:13; 1Co 5:5; 2Co 12:21; 13:5).

(3) The warnings to worldly Christians. (a) Worldly Christians must know they are in danger of departing from the faith if they are unwilling to purify themselves from all that displeases God (Ro 6:14–16; 1Co 6:9–10; 2Co 11:3; Gal 6:7–9; Jas 1:12–16). (b) They must learn from the tragic example of the Israelites whom God destroyed because of sin (1Co 10:5–12). (c) They must understand that it is impossible to participate in the things of the Lord and the things of Satan at the same time (Mt 6:24; 1Co 10:21). (d) They must separate themselves completely from the world (2Co 6:14–18) and purify themselves "from everything that contaminates body and spirit, perfecting holiness out of reverence for God" (2Co 7:1).

temple, God will destroy him; for God's
temple is sacred, and you are that temple.
18Do not deceive yourselves. If any one
of you thinks he is wise[m] by the standards
of this age,[n] he should become a "fool" so
that he may become wise. 19For the wisdom of this world is foolishness[o] in God's
sight. As it is written: "He catches the
wise in their craftiness"[i];[p] 20and again,
"The Lord knows that the thoughts of the
wise are futile."[j][q] 21So then, no more
boasting about men![r] All things are
yours,[s] 22whether Paul or Apollos[t] or Cephas[k][u] or the world or life or death or the
present or the future[v]—all are yours,
23and you are of Christ,[w] and Christ is of
God.

Apostles of Christ

4 So then, men ought to regard us as
servants[x] of Christ and as those entrusted[y] with the secret things[z] of God.
2Now it is required that those who have
been given a trust must prove faithful. 3I
care very little if I am judged by you or by
any human court; indeed, I do not even
judge myself. 4My conscience[a] is clear,
but that does not make me innocent.[b] It
is the Lord who judges me.[c] 5Therefore
judge nothing[d] before the appointed time;
wait till the Lord comes.[e] He will bring to
light[f] what is hidden in darkness and will
expose the motives of men's hearts. At
that time each will receive his praise from
God.[g]
6Now, brothers, I have applied these
things to myself and Apollos for your benefit, so that you may learn from us the
meaning of the saying, "Do not go beyond
what is written."[h] Then you will not take
pride in one man over against another.[i]

3:18 [m] Isa 5:21; 1Co 8:2; Gal 6:3 [n] S 1Co 1:20
3:19 [o] ver 18; Ro 1:22; 1Co 1:20, 27 [p] Job 5:13
3:20 [q] Ps 94:11
3:21 [r] 1Co 4:6 [s] Ro 8:32
3:22 [t] ver 5,6 [u] S 1Co 1:12 [v] Ro 8:38
3:23 [w] 1Co 15:23; 2Co 10:7; Gal 3:29
4:1 [x] S 1Co 3:5 [y] 1Co 9:17; Tit 1:7 [z] S Ro 16:25
4:4 [a] S Ac 23:1 [b] Ro 2:13 [c] 2Co 10:18
4:5 [d] S Mt 7:1,2 [e] S 1Th 2:19 [f] Job 12:22; Ps 90:8; 1Co 3:13 [g] S Ro 2:29
4:6 [h] 1Co 1:19,31; 3:19,20 [i] 1Co 1:12; 3:4
4:7 [j] Jn 3:27; Ro 12:3,6
4:8 [k] Rev 3:17,18
4:9 [l] S Ro 8:36 [m] Ps 71:7; Heb 10:33
4:10 [n] S 1Co 1:18; Ac 17:18; 26:24 [o] 1Co 3:18; 2Co 11:19 [p] S 1Co 2:3
4:11 [q] Ro 8:35; 2Co 11:23-27
4:12 [r] S Ac 18:3 [s] Ro 12:14; 1Pe 3:9 [t] S Mt 5:44
4:13 [u] Jer 20:18; La 3:45
4:14 [v] 1Co 6:5; 15:34; 2Th 3:14 [w] S 1Th 2:11
4:15 [x] S ver 14 [y] 1Co 9:12,14,18, 23; 15:1
4:16 [z] 1Co 11:1; Php 3:17; 4:9; 1Th 1:6; 2Th 3:7,9
4:17 [a] 1Co 16:10 [b] S Ac 16:1 [c] S 1Ti 1:2 [d] S 1Co 7:17

7For who makes you different from anyone else? What do you have that you did
not receive?[j] And if you did receive it,
why do you boast as though you did not?
8Already you have all you want! Already you have become rich![k] You have
become kings—and that without us! How
I wish that you really had become kings so
that we might be kings with you! 9For it
seems to me that God has put us apostles
on display at the end of the procession,
like men condemned to die[l] in the arena.
We have been made a spectacle[m] to the
whole universe, to angels as well as to
men. 10We are fools for Christ,[n] but you
are so wise in Christ![o] We are weak, but
you are strong![p] You are honored, we are
dishonored! 11To this very hour we go
hungry and thirsty, we are in rags, we are
brutally treated, we are homeless.[q] 12We
work hard with our own hands.[r] When we
are cursed, we bless;[s] when we are persecuted,[t] we endure it; 13when we are slandered, we answer kindly. Up to this moment we have become the scum of the
earth, the refuse[u] of the world.
14I am not writing this to shame you,[v]
but to warn you, as my dear children.[w]
15Even though you have ten thousand
guardians in Christ, you do not have many
fathers, for in Christ Jesus I became your
father[x] through the gospel.[y] 16Therefore
I urge you to imitate me.[z] 17For this reason I am sending to you[a] Timothy,[b] my
son[c] whom I love, who is faithful in the
Lord. He will remind you of my way of life
in Christ Jesus, which agrees with what I
teach everywhere in every church.[d]

i *19* Job 5:13 j *20* Psalm 94:11 k *22* That is, Peter

4:5 EXPOSE THE MOTIVES OF MEN'S HEARTS. God will bring to light the secret acts of all persons and expose their true thoughts and motives, good as well as bad (Mt 6:3–4,6; 1Ti 5:24–25; see article on THE JUDGMENT OF BELIEVERS, p. 368). In other words, the inner lives of everyone will be revealed exactly as they were; nothing will be left hidden (Mk 4:22; Lk 12:2–3; Ro 2:16).

4:7 WHY DO YOU BOAST. The basis for Christian humility is to realize that the native endowments or spiritual gifts we possess are from God and thus provide no basis for superiority, status or pride. All that we have and all that we become are made possible by God and others. Consequently, there is no place for pride, but only gratefulness to God and others.

4:8 HAVE ALL YOU WANT ... HAVE BECOME RICH. Some at Corinth boasted of their wisdom, superior knowledge and spiritual gifts. Paul shows them that the true life of a faithful believer is the way of the cross and that suffering must precede glory (cf. Ro 8:17).

4:9–13 APOSTLES ... CONDEMNED TO DIE. Here Paul lists the trials endured by the apostles. The verb "put on display" suggests that God has appointed the apostles to a life of suffering, to be seen by the world, by angels and by the church. (1) Paul lacks (even at that present time) such things as food, drink and proper clothing. He is despised, roughly treated and homeless. He works hard night and day, and is cursed, persecuted, slandered, and considered the "scum of the earth, the refuse of the world" (cf. 2 Co 4:8–9; 6:4–5,8–10; 11:23–29; 12:10). (2) Although suffering was in one sense a special appointment of the apostolic ministry (cf. Ac 9:16), it is also the common lot of all believers who, united with Christ, are opposed to sin, immorality, Satan, worldly evils and injustice. Their suffering is seen as a fellowship of sharing in Christ's suffering (Ro 8:17; Php 1:29; 3:10; 1Th 3:3).

18Some of you have become arrogant,[e]
as if I were not coming to you.[f] **19**But I
will come to you very soon,[g] if the Lord
is willing,[h] and then I will find out not
only how these arrogant people are talking, but what power they have. **20**For the
kingdom of God is not a matter of[i] talk
but of power.[j] **21**What do you prefer?
Shall I come to you with a whip,[k] or in
love and with a gentle spirit?

Expel the Immoral Brother!

5 It is actually reported that there is
sexual immorality among you, and of
a kind that does not occur even among
pagans: A man has his father's wife.[l]
2And you are proud! Shouldn't you rather
have been filled with grief[m] and have put
out of your fellowship[n] the man who did
this? **3**Even though I am not physically
present, I am with you in spirit.[o] And I
have already passed judgment on the one
who did this, just as if I were present.
4When you are assembled in the name of
our Lord Jesus[p] and I am with you in spirit, and the power of our Lord Jesus is
present, **5**hand this man over[q] to Satan,[r]
so that the sinful nature[1] may be destroyed and his spirit saved on the day of
the Lord.[s]
6Your boasting is not good.[t] Don't you
know that a little yeast[u] works through
the whole batch of dough?[v] **7**Get rid of the
old yeast that you may be a new batch
without yeast—as you really are. For
Christ, our Passover lamb, has been sacri-

4:18 [e]Jer 43:2 [f]ver 21 **4:19** [g]1Co 16:5,6; 2Co 1:15,16 [h]S Ac 18:21 **4:20** [i]Ro 14:17 [j]S Ro 15:13 **4:21** [k]2Co 1:23; 2:1; 13:2,10 **5:1** [l]Lev 18:8; Dt 22:30; 27:20 **5:2** [m]2Co 7:7-11 [n]ver 13 **5:3** [o]Col 2:5; 1Th 2:17 **5:4** [p]2Th 3:6 **5:5** [q]1Ti 1:20 [r]S Mt 4:10 [s]S 1Co 1:8 **5:6** [t]Jas 4:16 [u]Mt 16:6,12 [v]Gal 5:9

[1] 5 Or *that his body*; or *that the flesh*

4:20 KINGDOM OF GOD . . . POWER. The "kingdom of God" reveals itself in power. Thus, members of that kingdom must have more than talk and message; they must manifest the power of the Spirit as well (2:4; Ac 1:8). In the NT this consisted of a power to convict people of sin, righteousness and judgment (Jn 16:8), to bring them into salvation (v. 15; Ac 26:16–18), to perform miracles (see 2:4, note; see article on THE KINGDOM OF GOD, p. 28) and to live a righteous life (Ro 14:17).

5:1 SEXUAL IMMORALITY AMONG YOU. Paul writes about a report of immorality in the Corinthian church and the refusal of the leaders to deal with the offender (vv. 1–8). He declares that the church, as a holy people, must not permit or tolerate immorality among its members. He gives three reasons why the church should discipline offending members:

(1) For the good of the offenders (v. 5). Excommunication might awaken them to the tragedy of their sin and their need for forgiveness and restoration.

(2) For the sake of the church's purity (vv. 6–8). Tolerating evil within a church will gradually lower the moral standard of all.

(3) For the good of the world (cf. v. 1). The church cannot win men and women to Christ if it is like the world (cf. Mt 5:13). For other NT passages on church discipline, see Mt 5:22; 18:15–17; 2Th 3:6; and Rev 2:19–23.

5:1 HAS HIS FATHER'S WIFE. The exact sin is not clear. Paul's reference to "his father's wife" probably means the offender was sexually involved with his stepmother. (1) Paul was dismayed and appalled that the church would tolerate such immorality. He sees this as much more serious than the actual sin of the individual.

(2) The permissiveness of the Corinthians speaks to our situation today. Many churches today are tolerant of and silent about immorality among their members, including adultery and all forms of sexual immorality. Premarital sexual intimacy, especially among church youth, is not only tolerated but at times justified on the pretense of love and commitment. More than a few leaders in the church fail to challenge in Christ's name the immoral dating habits of today's youth. Like the Corinthian leaders, they refuse to mourn over the defilement of God's people as the people become more and more like the society in which they live. In self-complacency these leaders permit sin because, so they claim, "we live in the modern day and must not be judgmental."

5:2 BEEN FILLED WITH GRIEF. Paul expresses what should be the normal reaction of a Spirit-filled church to the immorality found among its professing members. Those who embrace the Biblical view of God's holiness and his revulsion to sin will be moved to sorrow and regret (cf. Isa 6). They will remove wickedness from among them (vv. 2,4–5,7,13).

5:5 HAND THIS MAN OVER TO SATAN. To hand over to Satan means that the church must remove the immoral person from its fellowship and return him or her to Satan's domain. This will, in turn, expose him or her to the destructive influences of evil and the demonic (vv. 7,13). (1) This discipline has two purposes: (a) that the offender, by experiencing problems and physical suffering, may repent and ultimately be saved (cf. Lk 15:11–24); (b) that the church may "get rid of the old yeast" (v. 7; i.e., sinful influences), so that God's people may become a new bread of "sincerity and truth" (v. 8). (2) The same action can be taken by the church today in seeking the salvation of one who has forsaken the Christian life and returned to the world (cf. 1Ti 1:20).

5:6 A LITTLE YEAST WORKS THROUGH THE WHOLE BATCH. In the Bible, "yeast" (which produces fermentation) is a symbol of that which permeates the whole and corrupts truth, righteousness and spiritual life (Mk 8:15; Gal 5:7–9). Paul in this passage compares yeast with the process by which sin and wickedness slowly spread in a Christian community until many are corrupted by it. Any church that does not take radical action against sexual immorality among its members will find the influence of evil spreading throughout the fellowship and infecting many. Sin must be expelled rigorously, or in time the entire Christian fellowship will be corrupted and the Holy Spirit banished from the church (see Rev 2–3, notes).

ficed.[w] **8**Therefore let us keep the Festival, not with the old yeast, the yeast of
malice and wickedness, but with bread
without yeast,[x] the bread of sincerity and
truth.

9I have written you in my letter not to
associate[y] with sexually immoral people
— **10**not at all meaning the people of this
world[z] who are immoral, or the greedy
and swindlers, or idolaters. In that case
you would have to leave this world. **11**But
now I am writing you that you must not
associate with anyone who calls himself a
brother[a] but is sexually immoral or
greedy, an idolater[b] or a slanderer, a
drunkard or a swindler. With such a man
do not even eat.[c]

12What business is it of mine to judge
those outside[d] the church? Are you not to
judge those inside?[e] **13**God will judge
those outside. "Expel the wicked man
from among you."[m][f]

Lawsuits Among Believers

6 If any of you has a dispute with another, dare he take it before the ungodly
for judgment instead of before the
saints?[g] **2**Do you not know that the saints
will judge the world?[h] And if you are to
judge the world, are you not competent to
judge trivial cases? **3**Do you not know that
we will judge angels? How much more the
things of this life! **4**Therefore, if you have
disputes about such matters, appoint as
judges even men of little account in the
church![n] **5**I say this to shame you.[i] Is it
possible that there is nobody among you
wise enough to judge a dispute between
believers?[j] **6**But instead, one brother[k]
goes to law against another—and this in
front of unbelievers![l]

7The very fact that you have lawsuits
among you means you have been completely defeated already. Why not rather
be wronged? Why not rather be cheated?[m]
8Instead, you yourselves cheat and do
wrong, and you do this to your brothers.[n]

The Wicked Will Not Inherit the Kingdom

9Do you not know that the wicked will
not inherit the kingdom of God?[o] Do not
be deceived:[p] Neither the sexually immoral nor idolaters nor adulterers[q] nor male
prostitutes nor homosexual offenders[r]
10nor thieves nor the greedy nor drunkards nor slanderers nor swindlers[s] will
inherit the kingdom of God. **11**And that is
what some of you were.[t] But you were
washed,[u] you were sanctified,[v] you were

5:7 [w] Ex 12:3-6, 21; Mk 14:12; 1Pe 1:19
5:8 [x] Ex 12:14,15; Dt 16:3
5:9 [y] Eph 5:11; 2Th 3:6,14
5:10 [z] 1Co 10:27
5:11 [a] S Ro 7:1 [b] 1Co 10:7,14 [c] S Ro 16:17
5:12 [d] S Mk 4:11 [e] ver 3-5; 1Co 6:1-4
5:13 [f] Dt 13:5; 17:7; 19:19; 22:21,24; 24:7; Jdg 20:13
6:1 [g] Mt 18:17
6:2 [h] Mt 19:28; Lk 22:30; 1Co 5:12
6:5 [i] S 1Co 4:14 [j] Ac 1:15
6:6 [k] S Ro 7:1 [l] 2Co 6:14,15; 1Ti 5:8
6:7 [m] Mt 5:39,40
6:8 [n] 1Th 4:6
6:9 [o] S Mt 25:34 [p] Job 13:9; 1Co 15:33; Gal 6:7; Jas 1:16 [q] Lev 18:20; Dt 22:22 [r] Lev 18:22
6:10 [s] 1Ti 1:10; Rev 21:8; 22:15
6:11 [t] S Eph 2:2 [u] S Ac 22:16 [v] 1Co 1:2

[m] *13* Deut. 17:7; 19:19; 21:21; 22:21,24; 24:7
[n] *4* Or *matters, do you appoint as judges men of little account in the church?*

5:12 JUDGE THOSE INSIDE. Believers must not be involved in superficial or unjust criticism of another believer (cf. Mt 7:1–5). However, Paul here does indicate that the church must judge its members when serious sin, immorality or persistent ungodly conduct is involved. Such wicked actions demand judgment and discipline for the sake of the person involved, the purity of the church and the witness of Christ in the world (see v. 1, note).

6:1 BEFORE THE UNGODLY. When trivial disputes (v. 2) between Christians occur, they should be settled within the church and not in courts of law. The church must judge the right or wrong involved, render a verdict and exercise discipline if needed (see Mt 18:15, note). (1) This does not mean that a believer may not use courts in serious cases with unbelievers. Paul himself appealed to the judicial system more than once (see Ac 16:37–39; 25:10–12).

(2) Nor is Paul saying the church must allow its members to unlawfully abuse or mistreat the innocent, such as widows, children or the weak. Rather, Paul was speaking of issues where there was no clear right or wrong. Blatant sinful actions must not be tolerated, but handled according to Christ's instruction in Mt 18:15–17.

(3) Furthermore, in cases where a so-called "brother" has divorced or deserted his family and refuses to support his wife and children with alimony, a mother with the right motives and concern for her children may take recourse in the courts. Paul is not advocating that those who break the law be allowed to defraud and threaten the life or well-being of another. His statement in v. 8 indicates he is speaking of minor disputes where the wrong could be accepted and tolerated.

6:9 THE WICKED WILL NOT INHERIT THE KINGDOM. Some in Corinth were deceived into believing that even if they broke fellowship with Christ, denied him,and lived in immorality and injustice, their salvation and inheritance in God's kingdom were still secure. (1) However, Paul declares that spiritual death is the inevitable consequence of habitual sinning, even for the Christian (cf. Ro 8:13). No one can live for immoral gratification and still inherit the kingdom of God (cf. Ro 6:16; Jas 1:15; see 1Jn 2:4, note; 3:9, note). The apostle Paul repeats this cardinal teaching often (e.g., Gal 5:21 and Eph 5:5–6).

(2) Paul's warning is directed to the whole Christian community. We must not be deceived, for all who are "wicked will not inherit the kingdom of God." Salvation without the regenerating and sanctifying work of the Holy Spirit has no place in Paul's theology.

6:11 JUSTIFIED . . . BY THE SPIRIT. Justification involves not only the redeeming work of the Lord Jesus, but also the work of the Spirit of God in the believer's life (see article on BIBLICAL WORDS FOR SALVATION, p. 292).

justified[w] in the name of the Lord Jesus
Christ and by the Spirit of our God.

Sexual Immorality

12“Everything is permissible for me”—
but not everything is beneficial.[x] “Everything is permissible for me”—but I will
not be mastered by anything. **13**“Food for
the stomach and the stomach for food”—
but God will destroy them both.[y] The body
is not meant for sexual immorality, but for
the Lord,[z] and the Lord for the body. **14**By
his power God raised the Lord from the
dead,[a] and he will raise us also.[b] **15**Do
you not know that your bodies are members of Christ himself?[c] Shall I then take
the members of Christ and unite them
with a prostitute? Never! **16**Do you not
know that he who unites himself with a
prostitute is one with her in body? For it
is said, “The two will become one
flesh.”[o][d] **17**But he who unites himself with the Lord is one with him in
spirit.[e]

18Flee from sexual immorality.[f] All
other sins a man commits are outside his
body, but he who sins sexually sins
against his own body.[g] **19**Do you not know
that your body is a temple[h] of the Holy
Spirit, who is in you, whom you have received from God? You are not your own;[i]
20you were bought at a price.[j] Therefore
honor God with your body.[k]

6:11 [w] S Ro 4:25 **6:12** [x] 1Co 10:23 **6:13** [y] Col 2:22 [z] ver 15,19; Ro 12:1 **6:14** [a] S Ac 2:24 [b] S Ro 6:5; Eph 1:19,20; 1Th 4:16 **6:15** [c] S Ro 12:5 **6:16** [d] Ge 2:24; Mt 19:5; Eph 5:31 **6:17** [e] Jn 17:21-23; Ro 8:9-11; Gal 2:20 **6:18** [f] ver 9; 1Co 5:1; 2Co 12:21; Gal 5:19; Eph 5:3; 1Th 4:3,4; Heb 13:4 [g] Ro 6:12 **6:19** [h] Jn 2:21 [i] Ro 14:7,8 **6:20** [j] Ps 74:2; S Mt 20:28; Ac 20:28; 1Co 7:23; Rev 5:9; 14:4 [k] Php 1:20

7:1 [l] ver 8,26 **7:3** [m] Ex 21: 10; 1Pe 3:7 **7:5** [n] Ex 19:15; 1Sa 21:4,5 [o] S Mt 4:10 [p] 1Th 3:5 **7:6** [q] 2Co 8:8 **7:7** [r] ver 8; 1Co 9:5 [s] Mt 19:11,12; Ro 12:6; 1Co 12:4, 11 **7:8** [t] ver 1,26 **7:9** [u] 1Ti 5:14 **7:10** [v] Mal 2:14-16; S Lk 16:18

Marriage

7 Now for the matters you wrote about:
It is good for a man not to marry.[p][l]
2But since there is so much immorality,
each man should have his own wife, and
each woman her own husband. **3**The husband should fulfill his marital duty to his
wife,[m] and likewise the wife to her husband. **4**The wife’s body does not belong to
her alone but also to her husband. In the
same way, the husband’s body does not
belong to him alone but also to his wife.
5Do not deprive each other except by mutual consent and for a time,[n] so that you
may devote yourselves to prayer. Then
come together again so that Satan[o] will
not tempt you[p] because of your lack of
self-control. **6**I say this as a concession,
not as a command.[q] **7**I wish that all men
were as I am.[r] But each man has his own
gift from God; one has this gift, another
has that.[s]

8Now to the unmarried and the widows
I say: It is good for them to stay unmarried, as I am.[t] **9**But if they cannot control
themselves, they should marry,[u] for it is
better to marry than to burn with passion.

10To the married I give this command
(not I, but the Lord): A wife must not separate from her husband.[v] **11**But if she does,

[o] *16* Gen. 2:24 [p] *1* Or *“It is good for a man not to have sexual relations with a woman.”*

6:12 EVERYTHING IS PERMISSIBLE FOR ME. This statement is clearly a quotation of the theological position of Paul’s opponents. They thought they had the right to do anything they wished.

6:15 MEMBERS OF CHRIST. The apostle, warning against moral laxity, shows the terrible consequences of sexual immorality for the believer. When he joins his body to an immoral woman, it causes him to become one with her, to come under her domination (v. 16; cf. Ge 2:24), to desecrate what the cross has made holy (v. 15) and to sever himself from the kingdom of God (v. 9). In sexual immorality people virtually remove themselves from union with Christ by making their bodies members of immoral and ungodly persons.

6:18 FLEE FROM SEXUAL IMMORALITY. Sexual immorality is particularly abhorrent to God. More than any other sinful act, it desecrates the body, which is the temple of the Spirit (vv. 15–20). Therefore, Paul gives the admonition to flee from sexual immorality. The use of the present tense here indicates that the Christian must repeatedly flee sexual immorality (cf. Ge 39:12; see article on STANDARDS OF SEXUAL MORALITY, p. 509).

6:19 YOUR BODY IS A TEMPLE OF THE HOLY SPIRIT. As a Christian, your body is the personal dwelling place of the Holy Spirit (see also Ro 8:11, where the Spirit is God’s mark on you that you belong to him). Because the Spirit lives in you and you belong to God, your body must never be defiled by any impurity or evil, whether by immoral thoughts, desires, deeds, films, books or magazines. Rather, you must live in such a way as to honor and please God with your body (v. 20).

7:1 GOOD FOR A MAN NOT TO MARRY. The entire seventh chapter is Paul’s response to questions asked by the church in Corinth concerning marriage relationships. His instructions must be read in light of v. 26, “Because of the present crisis, I think that it is good.” A time of crisis and persecution was coming for the early Christians, and in this situation maintaining a marriage relationship would have been difficult.

7:3 THE HUSBAND SHOULD FULFILL. The commitment of marriage means that each partner relinquishes the exclusive right to his or her own body and gives the other a claim to it. That is, neither marriage partner may fail to submit to the normal sexual desires of the other. Such desires within marriage are natural and God-given, and to refuse to carry out one’s responsibility in fulfilling the other’s needs is to open up the marriage to Satan’s temptation of adultery (v. 5).

7:11 SHE MUST REMAIN UNMARRIED. In v. 10 Paul recognizes that God wants marriage to be permanent. He also acknowledges, however, that sometimes a marriage relationship may become so unbearable that separation from the partner is necessary. Paul, therefore, is not talking here about divorce permitted

she must remain unmarried or else be reconciled to her husband.[w] And a husband
must not divorce his wife.
12To the rest I say this (I, not the
Lord):[x] If any brother has a wife who is
not a believer and she is willing to live
with him, he must not divorce her. **13**And
if a woman has a husband who is not a
believer and he is willing to live with her,
she must not divorce him. **14**For the unbelieving husband has been sanctified
through his wife, and the unbelieving wife
has been sanctified through her believing
husband. Otherwise your children would
be unclean, but as it is, they are holy.[y]
15But if the unbeliever leaves, let him
do so. A believing man or woman is not
bound in such circumstances; God has
called us to live in peace.[z] **16**How do you
know, wife, whether you will save[a] your
husband?[b] Or, how do you know, husband, whether you will save your wife?
17Nevertheless, each one should retain
the place in life that the Lord assigned to
him and to which God has called him.[c]
This is the rule I lay down in all the
churches.[d] **18**Was a man already circumcised when he was called? He should not
become uncircumcised. Was a man uncircumcised when he was called? He should
not be circumcised.[e] **19**Circumcision is
nothing and uncircumcision is nothing.[f]
Keeping God's commands is what counts.
20Each one should remain in the situation
which he was in when God called him.[g]
21Were you a slave when you were called?
Don't let it trouble you—although if you
can gain your freedom, do so. **22**For he
who was a slave when he was called by
the Lord is the Lord's freedman;[h] similarly, he who was a free man when he was
called is Christ's slave.[i] **23**You were
bought at a price;[j] do not become slaves
of men. **24**Brothers, each man, as responsible to God, should remain in the situation God called him to.[k]
25Now about virgins: I have no command from the Lord,[l] but I give a judgment as one who by the Lord's mercy[m] is
trustworthy. **26**Because of the present crisis, I think that it is good for you to remain
as you are.[n] **27**Are you married? Do not
seek a divorce. Are you unmarried? Do not
look for a wife.[o] **28**But if you do marry,
you have not sinned;[p] and if a virgin marries, she has not sinned. But those who
marry will face many troubles in this life,
and I want to spare you this.
29What I mean, brothers, is that the
time is short.[q] From now on those who
have wives should live as if they had none;
30those who mourn, as if they did not;
those who are happy, as if they were not;
those who buy something, as if it were not
theirs to keep; **31**those who use the things
of the world, as if not engrossed in them.
For this world in its present form is passing away.[r]
32I would like you to be free from concern. An unmarried man is concerned
about the Lord's affairs[s]—how he can
please the Lord. **33**But a married man is

7:11 [w]ver 39; Ro 7:2,3
7:12 [x]ver 6,10; 2Co 11:17
7:14 [y]Mal 2:15
7:15 [z]S Ro 14:19; 1Co 14:33
7:16 [a]S Ro 11:14 [b]1Pe 3:1
7:17 [c]Ro 12:3 [d]1Co 4:17; 14:33; 2Co 8:18; 11:28
7:18 [e]Ac 15:1,2
7:19 [f]Ro 2:25-27; Gal 5:6; 6:15; Col 3:11
7:20 [g]ver 24
7:22 [h]Jn 8:32,36 [i]S Ro 6:22
7:23 [j]S 1Co 6:20
7:24 [k]ver 20
7:25 [l]ver 6; 2Co 8:8 [m]2Co 4:1; 1Ti 1:13,16
7:26 [n]ver 1,8
7:27 [o]ver 20,21
7:28 [p]ver 36
7:29 [q]ver 31; S Ro 13:11,12
7:31 [r]ver 29; S Heb 12:27
7:32 [s]1Ti 5:5

---

by God because of adultery (see Mt 19:9, note) or abandonment of a marriage partner (see v. 15, note). Rather, Paul is speaking of separation without legal divorce. He may be referring to situations where a marriage partner is acting in such a way as to endanger the physical or spiritual life of the spouse and children. In such conditions, it may be best that one of the partners leave the home and not remarry. It is inconceivable that Paul would advocate that a partner remain with a spouse who repeatedly brought physical harm and abuse on her and the children.

7:12 I SAY THIS (I, NOT THE LORD). Paul is not merely giving his own opinion here; rather he says that he does not have a saying of Jesus to confirm what he is about to write. However, he writes as one who has apostolic authority and is under divine inspiration (cf. vv. 25,40; 14:37).

7:14 HUSBAND . . . WIFE . . . CHILDREN. When a believer is involved in a marriage with an unbeliever, the marriage as well as the children born to that union are legitimate before God. Therefore, the believer should live with the unbeliever and not seek to divide the marriage or the home. Furthermore, because the husband or wife is a believer, he/she may have a special influence so that the spouse is led to accept Christ (cf. 1Pe 3:1–2).

7:15 IS NOT BOUND. In the event that an unbelieving partner abandons or divorces a believer, the marriage relation is dissolved and the believer is freed from his or her marital obligation. "Not bound in such circumstances" means that the believer is released from the marital contract. The word "bound" (Gk *douloō*) literally means "to enslave"; the faithful believer is no longer enslaved to his or her marriage vows. In this case, the abandoned believer is free to remarry, provided he or she marries a Christian (v. 39; see Mt 19:9, note on divorce).

7:19 KEEPING GOD'S COMMANDS. How can Paul, who emphasized so strongly salvation by faith (Ro 3–4), say that what really matters is "keeping God's commands"? Because salvation by faith must lead to obeying, loving and serving God. Anything less than such obedience falls short of NT saving faith (cf. Gal 5:6; 6:15).

7:31 THOSE WHO USE THE THINGS OF THE WORLD. We live in the period when all worldly things are hastening toward an end. For this reason life in this world should not be our utmost concern; we should direct our greatest attention toward our heavenly home (Heb 11:13–16).

concerned about the affairs of this world
—how he can please his wife— 34and his
interests are divided. An unmarried woman or virgin is concerned about the Lord's
affairs: Her aim is to be devoted to the
Lord in both body and spirit.[t] But a married woman is concerned about the affairs
of this world—how she can please her
husband. 35I am saying this for your own
good, not to restrict you, but that you may
live in a right way in undivided[u] devotion
to the Lord.

36If anyone thinks he is acting improp-
erly toward the virgin he is engaged to,
and if she is getting along in years and he
feels he ought to marry, he should do as
he wants. He is not sinning.[v] They should
get married. 37But the man who has settled the matter in his own mind, who is
under no compulsion but has control over
his own will, and who has made up his
mind not to marry the virgin—this man
also does the right thing. 38So then, he
who marries the virgin does right,[w] but he
who does not marry her does even better.[q]

39A woman is bound to her husband as
long as he lives.[x] But if her husband dies,
she is free to marry anyone she wishes,
but he must belong to the Lord.[y] 40In my
judgment,[z] she is happier if she stays as
she is—and I think that I too have the
Spirit of God.

Food Sacrificed to Idols

8 Now about food sacrificed to idols:[a]
We know that we all possess knowledge.[r][b] Knowledge puffs up, but love
builds up. 2The man who thinks he knows
something[c] does not yet know as he
ought to know.[d] 3But the man who loves
God is known by God.[e]

4So then, about eating food sacrificed to
idols:[f] We know that an idol is nothing at
all in the world[g] and that there is no God
but one.[h] 5For even if there are so-called
gods,[i] whether in heaven or on earth (as
indeed there are many "gods" and many
"lords"), 6yet for us there is but one God,[j]
the Father,[k] from whom all things came[l]
and for whom we live; and there is but one
Lord,[m] Jesus Christ, through whom all
things came[n] and through whom we live.

7But not everyone knows this.[o] Some
people are still so accustomed to idols
that when they eat such food they think of
it as having been sacrificed to an idol, and
since their conscience is weak,[p] it is defiled. 8But food does not bring us near to
God;[q] we are no worse if we do not eat,
and no better if we do.

9Be careful, however, that the exercise
of your freedom does not become a stumbling block[r] to the weak.[s] 10For if anyone
with a weak conscience sees you who

7:34 [t]Lk 2:37 **7:35** [u]Ps 86:11 **7:36** [v]ver 28 **7:38** [w]Heb 13:4 **7:39** [x]Ro 7:2,3 [y]2Co 6:14 **7:40** [z]ver 25 **8:1** [a]ver 4,7,10; Ac 15:20 [b]Ro 15:14
8:2 [c]1Co 3:18 [d]1Co 13:8,9,12; 1Ti 6:4 **8:3** [e]Jer 1:5; Ro 8:29; Gal 4:9 **8:4** [f]ver 1,7,10; Ex 34:15 [g]Ac 14:15; 1Co 10:19; Gal 4:8 [h]ver 6; Dt 6:4; Ps 86:10; Eph 4:6; 1Ti 2:5 **8:5** [i]2Th 2:4 **8:6** [j]S ver 4 [k]Mal 2:10 [l]S Ro 11:36 [m]Eph 4:5 [n]S Jn 1:3 **8:7** [o]ver 1 [p]Ro 14:14; 1Co 10:28 **8:8** [q]Ro 14:17 **8:9** [r]S 2Co 6:3; Gal 5:13 [s]Ro 14:1

[q] *36-38* Or *36If anyone thinks he is not treating his daughter properly, and if she is getting along in years, and he feels she ought to marry, he should do as he wants. He is not sinning. He should let her get married. 37But the man who has settled the matter in his own mind, who is under no compulsion but has control over his own will, and who has made up his mind to keep the virgin unmarried—this man also does the right thing. 38So then, he who gives his virgin in marriage does right, but he who does not give her in marriage does even better.* [r] *1* Or *"We all possess knowledge," as you say*

7:34 AN UNMARRIED WOMAN. Scripture maintains that the unmarried state is in no way inferior to the married. In fact, it is better in the most important way of all—the possibility of offering undistracted service to God. The unmarried man (vv. 32–33) or woman (v. 34) can concentrate on the things that belong to the Lord in a greater way than the married. To be "devoted to the Lord both in body and spirit" does not refer to ethical achievement, but to the possibility of a greater commitment to God unencumbered by family responsibilities, problems and concerns. The unmarried can devote themselves with all their gifts to the Lord, free from care, totally occupied with the Lord and his Word.

8:1 FOOD SACRIFICED TO IDOLS. In chs. 8–10 Paul deals with the question of the Corinthians about meat offered to idols and whether it is right to buy and eat this meat and to participate in festivals at idol temples (v. 10). (1) In treating this subject he reveals an important principle by which Christians of all ages should live. This principle applies to questionable activities that might tempt some believers to sin and lead them to spiritual ruin (v. 11). The Holy Spirit through Paul has directed Christians to always act with a love for other believers that may in fact require self-denial.

(2) Self-denial means limiting one's freedom and setting aside all questionable activities in order not to offend or weaken the sincere convictions of other Christians, which they believe to be based on Biblical principles. The opposite of self-denial is defending one's own right to engage in a questionable activity, one that may entice others to follow—to their own hurt (cf. Ro 14:1—15:3; Ac 15:29, note; 1Co 9:19, note).

8:2 DOES NOT YET KNOW. Those who base their right to do certain things on their "knowledge" and "mature understanding" show that in reality they do not know as they ought. Our knowledge in this life is always incomplete and imperfect. Thus, our actions must first be based on love for God and others. If love is our determining consideration, we will refuse to engage in or encourage any activity that might lead even one believer to stumble and head toward eternal ruin. Those who live by the rule of love are those who are "known by God" (v. 3). "The Lord knows those who are his" (2Ti 2:19).

have this knowledge eating in an idol's
temple, won't he be emboldened to eat
what has been sacrificed to idols?[t] **11**So
this weak brother, for whom Christ died,
is destroyed[u] by your knowledge. **12**When
you sin against your brothers[v] in this way
and wound their weak conscience, you sin
against Christ.[w] **13**Therefore, if what I eat
causes my brother to fall into sin, I will
never eat meat again, so that I will not
cause him to fall.[x]

The Rights of an Apostle

9 Am I not free?[y] Am I not an apostle?[z] Have I not seen Jesus our
Lord?[a] Are you not the result of my work
in the Lord?[b] **2**Even though I may not be
an apostle to others, surely I am to you!
For you are the seal[c] of my apostleship in
the Lord.

3This is my defense to those who sit in
judgment on me. **4**Don't we have the right
to food and drink?[d] **5**Don't we have the
right to take a believing wife[e] along with
us, as do the other apostles and the Lord's
brothers[f] and Cephas[s]?[g] **6**Or is it only I
and Barnabas[h] who must work for a living?

7Who serves as a soldier[i] at his own
expense? Who plants a vineyard[j] and
does not eat of its grapes? Who tends a
flock and does not drink of the milk? **8**Do
I say this merely from a human point of
view? Doesn't the Law say the same
thing? **9**For it is written in the Law of Moses: "Do not muzzle an ox while it is treading out the grain."[t][k] Is it about oxen that
God is concerned?[l] **10**Surely he says this
for us, doesn't he? Yes, this was written
for us,[m] because when the plowman plows
and the thresher threshes, they ought to
do so in the hope of sharing in the harvest.[n] **11**If we have sown spiritual seed
among you, is it too much if we reap a
material harvest from you?[o] **12**If others
have this right of support from you,
shouldn't we have it all the more?

But we did not use this right.[p] On the
contrary, we put up with anything rather
than hinder[q] the gospel of Christ. **13**Don't
you know that those who work in the temple get their food from the temple, and
those who serve at the altar share in what
is offered on the altar?[r] **14**In the same
way, the Lord has commanded that those
who preach the gospel should receive
their living from the gospel.[s]

15But I have not used any of these
rights.[t] And I am not writing this in the
hope that you will do such things for me.
I would rather die than have anyone deprive me of this boast.[u] **16**Yet when I
preach the gospel, I cannot boast, for I am
compelled to preach.[v] Woe to me if I do
not preach the gospel! **17**If I preach voluntarily, I have a reward;[w] if not voluntarily,
I am simply discharging the trust committed to me.[x] **18**What then is my reward?
Just this: that in preaching the gospel I
may offer it free of charge,[y] and so not
make use of my rights[z] in preaching it.

19Though I am free[a] and belong to no
man, I make myself a slave to everyone,[b]
to win as many as possible.[c] **20**To the
Jews I became like a Jew, to win the
Jews.[d] To those under the law I became
like one under the law (though I myself
am not under the law),[e] so as to win those
under the law. **21**To those not having the
law I became like one not having the law[f]
(though I am not free from God's law but
am under Christ's law),[g] so as to win
those not having the law. **22**To the weak
I became weak, to win the weak.[h] I have
become all things to all men[i] so that by

8:10 [t]ver 1,4,7 **8:11** [u]Ro 14:15,20 **8:12** [v]Mt 18:6 [w]Mt 25:40,45 **8:13** [x]S Mt 5:29 **9:1** [y]ver 19 [z]S 1Co 1:1; 2Co 12:12 [a]S 1Co 15:8 [b]1Co 3:6; 4:15 **9:2** [c]2Co 3:2,3 **9:4** [d]ver 14; S Ac 18:3 **9:5** [e]1Co 7:7,8 [f]S Mt 12:46 [g]S 1Co 1:12 **9:6** [h]S Ac 4:36 **9:7** [i]2Ti 2:3,4 [j]Dt 20:6; Pr 27:18; 1Co 3:6,8 **9:9** [k]Dt 25:4; 1Ti 5:18 [l]Dt 22:1-4; Pr 12:10 **9:10** [m]S Ro 4:23,24 [n]Pr 11:25; 2Ti 2:6

9:11 [o]ver 14; Ro 15:27; Gal 6:6 **9:12** [p]ver 15,18; S Ac 18:3 [q]2Co 6:3; 11:7-12 **9:13** [r]Lev 6:16,26; Dt 18:1 **9:14** [s]S 1Ti 5:18 **9:15** [t]ver 12,18; S Ac 18:3 [u]2Co 11:9,10 **9:16** [v]Ro 1:14; Ac 9:15; 26:16-18 **9:17** [w]1Co 3:8,14 [x]1Co 4:1; Gal 2:7; Col 1:25 **9:18** [y]2Co 11:7; 12:13 [z]ver 12,15 **9:19** [a]ver 1 [b]2Co 4:5; Gal 5:13 [c]Mt 18:15; 1Pe 3:1 **9:20** [d]Ac 16:3; 21:20-26; Ro 11:14 [e]S Ro 2:12 **9:21** [f]Ro 2:12,14 [g]Gal 6:2 **9:22** [h]S Ro 14:1; S 1Co 2:3 [i]1Co 10:33

[s] *5* That is, Peter [t] *9* Deut. 25:4

8:12 YOU SIN AGAINST CHRIST. Those who by their example lead another believer into sin and spiritual ruin (v. 11) sin not only against that person, but also against Christ himself. A great sin has been committed; the purpose for which Christ died is considered of little value in comparison to one's own self-centered desires (see Mt 18:7, note).

9:1 AM I NOT AN APOSTLE? Paul personally illustrates the principle set forth in 8:13 (see 8:1, note), that he is willing to set aside his own personal rights as an apostle in order not to hinder the gospel of Christ (v. 12; see 9:19, note).

9:14 RECEIVE THEIR LIVING FROM THE GOSPEL. Both the OT (Dt 25:4; cf. Lev 6:16,26; 7:6) and the NT (Mt 10:10; Lk 10:7) teach that those who are engaged in proclaiming God's Word should be supported by those who receive spiritual blessing from it (see Gal 6:6–10, note; 1Ti 5:18).

9:19 I MAKE MYSELF A SLAVE TO EVERYONE. Paul uses himself as an example of the principle of self-denial for the sake of others (see 8:1, note). He renounces his rights out of sympathetic consideration for the convictions of others (Ro 14:15–21), in order not to limit his ministry or hinder the gospel (v. 12). This does not mean that Paul compromises Christian principles or seeks to please others for the purpose of winning their esteem (Gal 1:8–10). What he affirms is that he is prepared to conform to the convictions of those whom he is trying to help, provided Christian principles are not violated. He understands that if he offends others by disregarding the conviction of their conscience, his ministry to them for Christ's sake could be seriously hindered (vv.12,19–23; see 8:1, note).

all possible means I might save some.[j]
23 I do all this for the sake of the gospel,
that I may share in its blessings.

24 Do you not know that in a race all the
runners run, but only one gets the prize?[k]
Run[l] in such a way as to get the prize.
25 Everyone who competes in the games
goes into strict training. They do it to get
a crown[m] that will not last; but we do it
to get a crown that will last forever.[n]
26 Therefore I do not run like a man running aimlessly;[o] I do not fight like a man
beating the air.[p] 27 No, I beat my body[q]
and make it my slave so that after I have
preached to others, I myself will not be
disqualified for the prize.[r]

Warnings From Israel's History

10 For I do not want you to be ignorant[s] of the fact, brothers, that
our forefathers were all under the cloud[t]
and that they all passed through the sea.[u]
2 They were all baptized into[v] Moses in
the cloud and in the sea. 3 They all ate the
same spiritual food[w] 4 and drank the same
spiritual drink; for they drank from the
spiritual rock[x] that accompanied them,
and that rock was Christ. 5 Nevertheless,
God was not pleased with most of them;
their bodies were scattered over the
desert.[y]

6 Now these things occurred as examples[u][z] to keep us from setting our hearts
on evil things as they did. 7 Do not be idolaters,[a] as some of them were; as it is written: "The people sat down to eat and drink
and got up to indulge in pagan revelry."[v][b]
8 We should not commit sexual immorality, as some of them did—and in one day
twenty-three thousand of them died.[c]
9 We should not test the Lord,[d] as some of
them did—and were killed by snakes.[e]
10 And do not grumble, as some of them
did[f]—and were killed[g] by the destroying
angel.[h]

11 These things happened to them as examples[i] and were written down as warnings for us,[j] on whom the fulfillment of
the ages has come.[k] 12 So, if you think you
are standing firm,[l] be careful that you
don't fall! 13 No temptation has seized you

9:22 [j] S Ro 11:14 **9:24** [k] Php 3:14; Col 2:18 [l] ver 25, 26; Gal 2:2; 5:7; Php 2:16; 2Ti 4:7; Heb 12:1 **9:25** [m] 2Ti 2:5 [n] 2Ti 4:8; Jas 1:12; 1Pe 5:4; Rev 2:10; 3:11 **9:26** [o] S ver 24 [p] 1Ti 6:12 **9:27** [q] Ro 8:13 [r] ver 24 **10:1** [s] S Ro 11:25 [t] Ex 13:21; Ps 105:39 [u] Ex 14:22,29; Ps 66:6 **10:2** [v] Ro 6:3 **10:3** [w] S Jn 6:31 **10:4** [x] Ex 17:6; Nu 20:11; Ps 78:15; 105:41 **10:5** [y] Nu 14:29; Heb 3:17; Jude 5 **10:6** [z] ver 11 **10:7** [a] ver 14 [b] Ex 32:4,6,19 **10:8** [c] Nu 25:1-9 **10:9** [d] Ex 17:2; Ps 78:18; 95:9; 106:14 [e] Nu 21:5,6 **10:10** [f] Nu 16:41; 17:5,10 [g] Nu 16:49 [h] Ex 12:23; 1Ch 21:15; Heb 11:28 **10:11** [i] ver 6 [j] S Ro 4:24 [k] S Ro 13:11 **10:12** [l] Ro 11:20; 2Co 1:24

[u] *6* Or *types*; also in verse 11 [v] *7* Exodus 32:6

9:24 THE PRIZE. The "prize," the "crown that will last forever" (v. 25), refers to the victory of eternal salvation, the precious goal of the Christian life (cf. 1:8; 4:5; 6:2,9–10; 15:12–19). This goal can only be achieved by giving up some of our rights for the sake of others (8:7–13) and by renouncing those things that would take us out of the race altogether (10:5–22).

9:24 RUN IN SUCH A WAY AS TO GET THE PRIZE. Paul illustrates the principle that if we fail to exercise self-control, self-denial and love in our relationships with others, we ourselves will be rejected by God (see next note).

9:27 I MYSELF WILL NOT BE DISQUALIFIED. "Be disqualified" (Gk *adokimos*) conveys the idea of "failing the test" or "being rejected." Paul uses this same term in 2Co 13:5, where he states that Christ does not live in any who "fail the test" (Gk *adokimoi*). Paul is not referring merely to the loss of a ministerial reward. What he recognizes is the possibility that he may fail to get the prize (i.e., the inheritance) of final salvation (vv. 24–25) if he should stop living a holy life, exercising self-control and enduring hardships for Christ (vv. 25–27).

10:1 I DO NOT WANT YOU TO BE IGNORANT. The fact that one may be redeemed, partake of divine grace, and yet later be rejected by God because of evil conduct (see 9:27, note) is now verified by examples from Israel's experience (vv. 1–12).

10:5 BODIES WERE SCATTERED OVER THE DESERT. The Israelites had experienced God's grace in the exodus. They had been delivered from bondage (v. 1), baptized (v. 2) and divinely sustained in the desert, experiencing close fellowship with Christ (vv. 3–4). Yet in spite of these spiritual blessings, they failed to please God, and were destroyed by him in the desert. They forfeited their election, and thus failed to reach the promised land (cf. Nu 14:30). Paul's point is this: just as God did not tolerate Israel's idolatry, sin and immorality, so he will not tolerate the sin of believers under the new covenant.

10:6 THESE THINGS OCCURRED AS EXAMPLES. God's terrible judgment on the disobedient Israelites serves as an example and a warning for those under the new covenant not to desire evil things. Paul warns the Corinthians that if they repeat Israel's unfaithfulness (vv. 7–10), they too will receive God's judgment and fail to enter the promised heavenly country.

10:11 WRITTEN DOWN AS WARNINGS. The history of God's judgment of his people was written down in Scripture to provide those in the NT with ample warnings against sinning and falling from grace (v. 12).

10:12 BE CAREFUL THAT YOU DON'T FALL! The Israelites, as God's elect, thought they could safely dabble in sin, idolatry and immorality; yet they met with condemnation. So also those Corinthians who believe they can securely live in worldly gratification must realize that condemnation also awaits them.

10:13 GOD IS FAITHFUL. Professing believers may not justify sinning with excuses that they are simply human and thus imperfect, or that in this life all born-again believers continue sinning in word, thought and deed (cf. Ro 6:1). At the same time, Paul assures the Corinthians that no true believer need fall from God's grace.

(1) The Holy Spirit explicitly affirms that God provides his children with adequate grace to overcome every temptation and thus to resist sinning (cf. Rev

except what is common to man. And God
is faithful;[m] he will not let you be tempted beyond what you can bear.[n] But when
you are tempted, he will also provide a
way out so that you can stand up under it.

Idol Feasts and the Lord's Supper

14Therefore, my dear friends,[o] flee
from idolatry.[p] **15**I speak to sensible people; judge for yourselves what I say. **16**Is
not the cup of thanksgiving for which we
give thanks a participation in the blood of
Christ? And is not the bread that we
break[q] a participation in the body of
Christ?[r] **17**Because there is one loaf, we,
who are many, are one body,[s] for we all
partake of the one loaf.
18Consider the people of Israel: Do not
those who eat the sacrifices[t] participate
in the altar? **19**Do I mean then that a sacrifice offered to an idol is anything, or that
an idol is anything?[u] **20**No, but the sacrifices of pagans are offered to demons,[v]
not to God, and I do not want you to be
participants with demons. **21**You cannot
drink the cup of the Lord and the cup of
demons too; you cannot have a part in
both the Lord's table and the table of demons.[w] **22**Are we trying to arouse the
Lord's jealousy?[x] Are we stronger than
he?[y]

The Believer's Freedom

23"Everything is permissible"—but not
everything is beneficial.[z] "Everything is
permissible"—but not everything is constructive. **24**Nobody should seek his own
good, but the good of others.[a]
25Eat anything sold in the meat market
without raising questions of conscience,[b]
26for, "The earth is the Lord's, and everything in it."[w][c]
27If some unbeliever invites you to a
meal and you want to go, eat whatever is
put before you[d] without raising questions
of conscience. **28**But if anyone says to you,
"This has been offered in sacrifice," then
do not eat it, both for the sake of the man
who told you and for conscience' sake[x][e]
— **29**the other man's conscience, I mean,
not yours. For why should my freedom[f]
be judged by another's conscience? **30**If I
take part in the meal with thankfulness,
why am I denounced because of something I thank God for?[g]
31So whether you eat or drink or what-

10:13 [m] S 1Co 1:9 [n] 2Pe 2:9
10:14 [o] Heb 6:9; 1Pe 2:11; 1Jn 2:7; Jude 3 [p] ver 7; 1Jn 5:21
10:16 [q] S Mt 14:19 [r] Mt 26:26-28; 1Co 11:23-25
10:17 [s] S Ro 12:5
10:18 [t] Lev 7:6, 14,15
10:19 [u] S 1Co 8:4
10:20 [v] Lev 17:7; Dt 32:17; Ps 106:37; Rev 9:20
10:21 [w] 2Co 6:15, 16
10:22 [x] Dt 32:16, 21; 1Ki 14:22; Ps 78:58; Jer 44:8 [y] Ecc 6:10; Isa 45:9
10:23 [z] 1Co 6:12
10:24 [a] ver 33; S Ro 15:1,2; 1Co 13:5; Php 2:4, 21
10:25 [b] S Ac 10:15; 1Co 8:7
10:26 [c] Ps 24:1; Ex 9:29; 19:5; Job 41:11; Ps 50:12; 1Ti 4:4
10:27 [d] Lk 10:7
10:28 [e] 1Co 8:7, 10-12
10:29 [f] 1Co 9:1, 19
10:30 [g] S Ro 14:6

[w] *26* Psalm 24:1 [x] *28* Some manuscripts *conscience' sake, for "the earth is the Lord's and everything in it"*

2:7,17,26). God's faithfulness expresses itself in two ways: (a) he will not allow us to be tempted above that which we can bear, and (b) he will with each temptation provide a way by which we can endure the temptation and overcome sin (cf. 2Th 3:3).

(2) God's grace (Eph 2:8–10; Tit 2:11–14), the blood of Jesus Christ (Eph 2:13; 1Pe 2:24), the Word of God (Eph 6:17; 2Ti 3:16–17), the Spirit's indwelling power (Tit 3:5–6; 1Pe 1:5) and Christ's heavenly intercession bring sufficient power for the believer's warfare against sin and the spiritual forces of wickedness (Eph 6:10–18; Heb 7:25).

(3) If Christians yield to sin, it is not because Christ's provision of grace is inadequate, but because believers fail to resist their own sinful desires by the power of the Spirit (Ro 8:13–14; Gal 5:16,24; Jas 1:13–15). God's "divine power has given us everything we need for life and godliness" (2Pe 1:3), and through the salvation provided by Christ we can "live a life worthy of the Lord and may please him in every way: bearing fruit in every good work, . . . being strengthened with all power according to his glorious might so that you may have great endurance and patience" (Col 1:10–11; see Mt 4:1, note on how to conquer temptation). We can bear every temptation and find a way out if we sincerely desire to and if we depend on God's power and faithfulness.

10:16 THE CUP OF THANKSGIVING. The cup we take at the Lord's Supper typifies Christ's death and his sacrificial suffering for sinful men and women. "Participation in the blood of Christ" refers to the believer sharing in the salvation provided by Christ's death (cf. 11:25). Scripture does not teach that the bread and the fruit of the vine actually become Christ's body and blood (see 11:24–25, note on the Lord's Supper).

10:20 OFFERED TO DEMONS. Idolatry involves the worship of demons (cf. Dt 32:17; Ps 106:35–38) and is associated with greed or covetousness (see Col 3:5, note). Therefore, demonic powers stand behind love for worldly possessions, honor or position.

10:21 THE CUP OF THE LORD AND THE CUP OF DEMONS. As participating in the Lord's Supper is a sharing in Christ's redemption, so participating in idolatrous feasts is a sharing with demons (v. 20). The error of some at Corinth was failing to distinguish between righteousness and unrighteousness, between that which is holy and that which is defiled, between that which is of Christ and that which is of the devil. They did not understand God's holy jealousy (v. 22; cf. Ex 20:5; Dt 4:24; Jos 24:19) and the seriousness of compromising with the world. Christ himself spoke of this fatal error: "No one can serve two masters" (Mt 6:24).

10:31 DO IT ALL FOR THE GLORY OF GOD. The main object of the believer's life is to please God and promote his glory. Thus what cannot be done for God's glory (i.e., in honor and thanksgiving to him as our Lord, Creator and Redeemer) should not be done at all. We honor him by obedience, thankfulness, reliance, prayer, faith and loyalty. This rule ("do it all for the glory of God") must be a primary direction of our lives, a guide for our conduct and a test of our actions.

ever you do, do it all for the glory of God.[h]
32Do not cause anyone to stumble,[i]
whether Jews, Greeks or the church of
God[j]— 33even as I try to please everybody in every way.[k] For I am not seeking
my own good but the good of many,[l] so
11 that they may be saved.[m] 1Follow
my example,[n] as I follow the example of Christ.[o]

Propriety in Worship

2I praise you[p] for remembering me in
everything[q] and for holding to the teachings,[y] just as I passed them on to you.[r]
3Now I want you to realize that the head
of every man is Christ,[s] and the head of
the woman is man,[t] and the head of
Christ is God.[u] 4Every man who prays or
prophesies[v] with his head covered dishonors his head. 5And every woman who
prays or prophesies[w] with her head uncovered dishonors her head—it is just as
though her head were shaved.[x] 6If a woman does not cover her head, she should
have her hair cut off; and if it is a disgrace
for a woman to have her hair cut or shaved
off, she should cover her head. 7A man

10:31 [h]Zec 14:21; Col 3:17; 1Pe 4:11 **10:32** [i]S Mt 5:29; Ac 24:16; S 2Co 6:3 [j]Ac 20:28; 1Co 1:2; 11:16,22; 15:9; 1Ti 3:5,15 **10:33** [k]Ro 15:2; 1Co 9:22 [l]S ver 24 [m]S Ro 11:14 **11:1** [n]S 1Co 4:16 [o]Ro 15:3; 1Pe 2:21 **11:2** [p]ver 17,22 [q]1Co 4:17 [r]ver 23; 1Co 15:2,3; 2Th 2:15; 3:6 **11:3** [s]S Eph 1:22 [t]Ge 3:16; Eph 5:23 [u]1Co 3:23 **11:4** [v]S Ac 11:27 **11:5** [w]S Ac 21:9 [x]Dt 21:12

[y] 2 Or *traditions*

11:1 FOLLOW THE EXAMPLE OF CHRIST. The believer, like Paul, is called to follow Christ's example and become a Christlike person (cf. Ro 13:14; Gal 3:27). What is Christlikeness?

(1) Christlikeness is, first and foremost, love for God and for others (Mt 22:37–39; Lk 10:27). The believer's love for God motivates and directs his or her love for others (1Jn 4:20–21), just as Christ's love for God was always first and his love for others subordinate to and based on that love for the Father (cf. Mt 22:37–39; Jn 17:23–24).

(2) Christ's love for his Father was revealed in his concern for God's glory (Mt 6:9; Jn 12:28; 17:4), for his will (Mt 26:42; Jn 4:34; Heb 10:7–12), for his Word (Mt 26:54; Jn 8:28; 17:14,17) and for the nearness of his presence (Lk 5:16; Jn 17:21). We see this love in his faithfulness to God (Heb 3:2) and his willingness to carry out God's will by sacrificing his life for our redemption (Mt 26:42; Jn 3:16–17; Heb 10:4–9). Christ's love for his Father is further revealed in his love for righteousness and hatred of sin (see Heb 1:9, note).

(3) Christ's love for humans was seen in his compassion (Mt 9:36; 14:14; 15:32; 20:34; cf. Lk 15:11–24), kindness (Mt 8:3,16–17; 9:22), tears (Jn 11:35), humility (Mt 11:29), good deeds (Ac 10:38), gentleness (Mt 11:29), forgiveness (Lk 23:34), patience (Lk 13:34) and mercy (Mt 15:22–28; Jude 21). He also demonstrated love when he rebuked sin (Mt 16:23; Mk 9:19; 10:13–14), expressed anger at those who were cruel, heartless or insensitive to the suffering and needs of others (see Mk 3:5, note), warned us of hell (Mt 5:29–30; Lk 12:5) and offered himself as a sacrifice (Mt 26:38; Jn 10:11,17–18; 13:1).

11:2 TEACHINGS. "Teachings" were instructions relating to doctrine, moral standards and codes of conduct that Paul delivered to the churches by Christ's authority. Note that the instruction of ch. 11 outlines God's will for his people in such matters as outward dress, modesty, appearance and proper conduct. To teach that God is concerned only with inner attitudes and not with "externals" departs from God's clear revelation in Scripture. To dress properly and modestly is a Biblical principle of lasting validity (see 1Ti 2:9, note).

11:3 HEAD OF EVERY MAN. Paul is concerned about the proper relationship between men and women, and he seeks to uphold that relationship as ordained by God. (1) He maintains that in Christ a perfect spiritual equality exists among men and women as heirs of God's grace, yet it is an equality involving order and subordination with respect to authority (see Gal 3:28, note). As God is the head of Christ, Christ is the head of man, and man the head of woman. The word "head" seems to express both authority and divine order (cf. 3:23; 11:8,10; 15:28; Jdg 10:18; Eph 1:21–22; 5:23–24; Col 1:18; 2:10).

(2) Paul bases the husband's headship not on cultural considerations but on God's creative activity and purpose in creating the woman to help the man (vv. 8–9; Ge 2:18; see 1Ti 2:13, note).

(3) Subordination is not demeaning to one's person, for it does not imply suppression or oppression. Rather it states that the husband must recognize the worth God places on the woman and that his responsibility involves protecting and leading her in such a way as to fulfill God's will for her in the home and the church.

(4) Just as Christ is not inferior or second-class because the Father is his head, so the woman is not a second-class person because man is her head. Furthermore, in God's kingdom leadership never implies being "greater." Servanthood and obedience are the keys to greatness in the kingdom (Mt 20:25–28; Php 2:5–9). Paul's treatment of the relationship of men and women should be studied in conjunction with his treatment of the wife's and husband's responsibilities in marriage (see Eph 5:21–23, notes).

11:6 SHE SHOULD COVER HER HEAD. The woman covered her head in Paul's day in order to show modesty and subordination to her husband and to demonstrate her dignity. The veil meant that she was to be respected and honored as a woman. Without a veil she had no dignity; men did not respect women without veils because they were in effect flaunting themselves publicly and shamefully. Thus, the veil served as a sign of the value and glory of womanhood as God created her.

The principle behind the wearing of veils is still needed today. A Christian woman should dress in a modest and careful way, with honorable and dignified attire that allows her to go anywhere with security and profound respect. When dressing modestly and properly for the glory of God, a woman enhances her own God-given place of dignity and worth.

ought not to cover his head,[z] since he is
the image[y] and glory of God; but the woman is the glory of man. 8For man did not
come from woman, but woman from
man;[z] 9neither was man created for woman, but woman for man.[a] 10For this reason, and because of the angels, the woman ought to have a sign of authority on her
head.

11In the Lord, however, woman is not
independent of man, nor is man independent of woman. 12For as woman came
from man, so also man is born of woman.
But everything comes from God.[b] 13Judge
for yourselves: Is it proper for a woman to
pray to God with her head uncovered?
14Does not the very nature of things teach
you that if a man has long hair, it is a
disgrace to him, 15but that if a woman has
long hair, it is her glory? For long hair is
given to her as a covering. 16If anyone
wants to be contentious about this, we
have no other practice—nor do the
churches of God.[c]

11:7 [y]Ge 1:26; 5:1; 9:6; Jas 3:9
11:8 [z]Ge 2:21-23; 1Ti 2:13
11:9 [a]Ge 2:18
11:12 [b]S Ro 11:36
11:16 [c]S 1Co 7:17; S 10:32

The Lord's Supper

11:23–25pp — Mt 26:26–28; Mk 14:22–24; Lk 22:17–20

17In the following directives I have no
praise for you,[d] for your meetings do more
harm than good. 18In the first place, I hear
that when you come together as a church,
there are divisions[e] among you, and to
some extent I believe it. 19No doubt there
have to be differences among you to show
which of you have God's approval.[f]
20When you come together, it is not the
Lord's Supper you eat, 21for as you eat,
each of you goes ahead without waiting
for anybody else.[g] One remains hungry,

11:17 [d]ver 2,22
11:18 [e]1Co 1:10-12; 3:3
11:19 [f]1Jn 2:19
11:21 [g]2Pe 2:13; Jude 12

[z] 4-7 Or *4Every man who prays or prophesies with long hair dishonors his head. 5And every woman who prays or prophesies with no covering of hair, on her head dishonors her head—she is just like one of the "shorn women." 6If a woman has no covering, let her be for now with short hair, but since it is a disgrace for a woman to have her hair shorn or shaved, she should grow it again. 7A man ought not to have long hair*

11:10 SIGN OF AUTHORITY ON HER HEAD. Once again Paul emphasizes that a woman should be veiled in public, i.e., have a symbol of "authority" on her head (see vv. 3,6, notes). The phrase "because of the angels" may refer to the fact that angels are concerned with proper order and are shocked at conduct that is not in tune with God's will (cf. 4:9).

11:14 IF A MAN HAS LONG HAIR. God desires that the physical differences between men and women be observed. (1) Paul uses hair as an example, stating that the length of the hair of men and women should be such as to distinguish between one and the other. A woman's hair should be long in comparison to the man's, symbolizing her acceptance of the dignity and worth of her womanhood as God created her (see v. 6, note). A man's hair, in contrast to the woman's, should be short.

(2) In NT times, long hair was disgraceful and shunned by Jewish men as well as by those of first-century Corinth. Pictures portraying Jesus as having long hair are based wholly on the imagination of the artists from the Middle Ages, not on Biblical or historical evidence (thousands of paintings and sculptures from NT times prove this). The apostle would not have written, "if a man has long hair, it is a disgrace to him," if Christ had worn his hair long as did women. Therefore, Paul's statement is in conflict, not with Jesus' custom, but with the invention of artists (cf. Ex 20:4).

11:20 THE LORD'S SUPPER. The Lord's Supper is described in four passages: Mt 26:26–29; Mk 14:22–25; Lk 22:15–20; 1Co 11:23–25. Its significance relates to the past, the present and the future.

(1) The past significance. (a) It is a remembrance (Gk *anamnēsis*; vv. 24–26; Lk 22:19) of Christ's death for the believer's redemption from sin and condemnation. Through the Lord's Supper we are once again confronted with the saving death of Christ and its redemptive significance for our lives. Christ's death is our ultimate motivation against falling into sin and for abstaining from all appearance of evil (1Th 5:22). (b) It is a thanksgiving (Gk *eucharistia*) for the blessings and salvation of God made available by Christ's sacrifice on the cross (v. 24; Mt 26:27; Mk 14:23; Lk 22:19).

(2) The present significance. (a) The Lord's Supper is a fellowship (Gk *koinōnia*) with Christ and a participation in the benefits of his sacrificial death, as well as a fellowship with the other members of the body of Christ (10:16–17). In this supper with the risen Lord, he as the host becomes present in a special way (cf. Mt 18:20; Lk 24:35). (b) It is a recognition and proclamation of the new covenant (Gk *kainē diathēkē*) by which believers reaffirm the lordship of Christ and our commitment to do his will, to remain loyal, to resist sin and to identify ourselves with his mission (v. 25; Mt 26:28; Mk 14:24; Lk 22:20; see article on THE OLD COVENANT AND THE NEW COVENANT, p. 500).

(3) The future significance. (a) The Lord's Supper is a foretaste of the future kingdom of God and the future Messianic banquet when all believers will be with the Lord (Mt 8:11; 22:1–14; Mk 14:25; Lk 13:29; 22:17–18,30). (b) It looks forward to Christ's imminent return for his people (v. 26) and dramatizes the prayer, "Your kingdom come" (Mt 6:10; cf. Rev 22:20).

At the Lord's Supper all the above significances are made meaningful only if we come before the Lord in true faith, sincere prayer and with commitment to God's Word and will.

11:21 ANOTHER GETS DRUNK. "One remains hungry, another gets drunk" can be translated, "One remains hungry, another is filled to the full." This is a preferred translation for the following reasons. (1) The word "drunk" (Gk *methuō*) carries two meanings. It can refer (a) to being drunk or (b) to being filled or satisfied without reference to intoxication (see Jn

another gets drunk. 22Don't you have
homes to eat and drink in? Or do you despise the church of God[h] and humiliate
those who have nothing?[i] What shall I
say to you? Shall I praise you[j] for this?
Certainly not!

23For I received from the Lord[k] what I
also passed on to you:[l] The Lord Jesus,
on the night he was betrayed, took bread,
24and when he had given thanks, he broke
it and said, "This is my body,[m] which is for
you; do this in remembrance of me." 25In
the same way, after supper he took the
cup, saying, "This cup is the new covenant[n] in my blood;[o] do this, whenever
you drink it, in remembrance of me." 26For
whenever you eat this bread and drink
this cup, you proclaim the Lord's death
until he comes.[p]

27Therefore, whoever eats the bread or
drinks the cup of the Lord in an unworthy
manner will be guilty of sinning against
the body and blood of the Lord.[q] 28A man
ought to examine himself[r] before he eats
of the bread and drinks of the cup. 29For
anyone who eats and drinks without recognizing the body of the Lord eats and
drinks judgment on himself. 30That is why
many among you are weak and sick, and
a number of you have fallen asleep.[s]
31But if we judged ourselves, we would
not come under judgment.[t] 32When we
are judged by the Lord, we are being disciplined[u] so that we will not be condemned
with the world.[v]

33So then, my brothers, when you come
together to eat, wait for each other. 34If
anyone is hungry,[w] he should eat at
home,[x] so that when you meet together it
may not result in judgment.

And when I come[y] I will give further
directions.

Spiritual Gifts

12 Now about spiritual gifts,[z] brothers, I do not want you to be igno-

11:22 [h] S 1Co 10:32 [i] Jas 2:6 [j] ver 2,17
11:23 [k] Gal 1:12 [l] S ver 2
11:24 [m] 1Co 10:16
11:25 [n] S Lk 22:20 [o] 1Co 10:16
11:26 [p] S 1Co 1:7
11:27 [q] Heb 10:29
11:28 [r] 2Co 13:5
11:30 [s] S Mt 9:24
11:31 [t] Ps 32:5; 1Jn 1:9
11:32 [u] Ps 94:12; 118:18; Pr 3:11, 12; Heb 12:7-10; Rev 3:19 [v] Jn 15:18,19
11:34 [w] ver 21 [x] ver 22 [y] S 1Co 4:19
12:1 [z] Ro 1:11; 1Co 1:7; 14:1,37

2:10, note on the use of this word in relation to the wedding at Cana).

(2) The context of this verse clearly relates to the meal in general. When the Corinthians gathered together for their fellowship meals before eating the Lord's Supper (cf. 2Pe 2:13; Jude 12), some gathered in small groups and ate their meals separately (vv. 18–19). The poor who could not contribute to the meal were ignored and left hungry. Paul was not referring to an issue of intoxication here; if he had been, he surely would have severely condemned it as he did elsewhere in the letter (cf. 6:10). He regarded drunkenness not merely as an issue of disregard for others, but also a condition so serious that it excludes one from God's kingdom (6:10; Gal 5:21).

11:24–25 MY BODY . . . MY BLOOD. These words refer to Christ's body given in death and his blood shed sacrificially on the cross. When Christ said of the bread, "This is my body," he meant that it represented his body. The "cup" represented the blood of Christ shed for ratification of the "new covenant." To eat the bread and drink the cup means to proclaim and accept the benefits of Christ's sacrificial death (v. 26).

11:27 EATS . . . DRINKS . . . UNWORTHY MANNER. To eat in an unworthy manner is to participate at the Lord's table with an indifferent, self-centered and irreverent spirit, without any intention or desire of departing from known sins and of accepting the covenant of grace with all its promises and obligations. Those who participate in such an unworthy manner sin terribly against the Lord. They are guilty of recrucifying Christ and immediately come under special judgment and retribution (vv. 29–32). To "be guilty of sinning against the body and blood of the Lord" means being held responsible for his death.

11:32 BEING DISCIPLINED. The purpose of the Lord's judgment (cf. v. 30) is that we might not be condemned eternally with the world. This merciful purpose avails for all who repent and judge themselves rightly (v. 31).

12:1 ABOUT SPIRITUAL GIFTS. In chs. 12–14 Paul deals with the gifts of the Holy Spirit given to the body of Christ. These gifts were an indispensable part of the early church's life and ministry. God intends that these gifts continue in operation until Christ returns (see 1:7, note). His purposes for the spiritual gifts are as follows:

(1) To manifest the grace, power and love of the Spirit among his people in their public gatherings, homes, families and individual lives (vv. 4–7; 14:25; Ro 15:18–19; Eph 4:8);

(2) To help make the preaching of the gospel effective by giving supernatural confirmation to the message (Mk 16:15–20; Ac 14:8–18; 16:16–18; 19:11–20; 28:1–10);

(3) To meet human needs and to strengthen and build up spiritually both the church (vv. 7,14–30; 14:3,12,26) and individual believers (14:4), i.e., to perfect believers in "love, which comes from a pure heart and a good conscience and a sincere faith" (1Ti 1:5; cf. 1Co 13);

(4) To wage effective spiritual war against Satan and the forces of evil (Isa 61:1; Ac 8:5–7; 26:18; Eph 6:11–12). Passages dealing with spiritual gifts include Ro 12:3–8; 1Co 1:7; 12–14; Eph 4:4–16; 1Pe 4:10–11.

12:1–6 SPIRITUAL GIFTS. The terms that the Bible uses for spiritual gifts specify their nature. (1) "Spiritual gifts" (Gk *pneumatika*, derived from *pneuma*, "Spirit") refers to supernatural manifestations that come as gifts from the Holy Spirit operating through believers for the common good (vv. 1,7; 14:1).

(2) "Gifts" or "grace gifts" (Gk *charismata*, derived from *charis*, "grace") indicates that spiritual gifts involve both an inward motivation and the power to perform ministry (i.e., actualized enablement), received from the Spirit; such gifts strengthen spiritually the body of Christ and those in need of spiritual help (v. 4; see Ro 12:6, note; Eph 4:11; 1Pe 4:10; see article on THE MINISTRY GIFTS OF THE

rant.[a] **2**You know that when you were pagans,[b] somehow or other you were influenced and led astray to mute idols.[c]
3Therefore I tell you that no one who is
speaking by the Spirit of God says, "Jesus
be cursed,"[d] and no one can say, "Jesus is
Lord,"[e] except by the Holy Spirit.[f]

4There are different kinds of gifts, but
the same Spirit.[g] **5**There are different
kinds of service, but the same Lord.
6There are different kinds of working, but
the same God[h] works all of them in all
men.[i]

7Now to each one the manifestation of
the Spirit is given for the common good.[j]
8To one there is given through the Spirit
the message of wisdom,[k] to another the
message of knowledge[l] by means of the
same Spirit, **9**to another faith[m] by the
same Spirit, to another gifts of healing[n]
by that one Spirit, **10**to another miraculous powers,[o] to another prophecy,[p] to
another distinguishing between spirits,[q]
to another speaking in different kinds of
tongues,[a][r] and to still another the interpretation of tongues.[a] **11**All these are the
work of one and the same Spirit,[s] and he
gives them to each one, just as he determines.

One Body, Many Parts

12The body is a unit, though it is made
up of many parts; and though all its parts
are many, they form one body.[t] So it is
with Christ.[u] **13**For we were all baptized[v]
by[b] one Spirit[w] into one body—whether
Jews or Greeks, slave or free[x]—and we
were all given the one Spirit to drink.[y]

14Now the body is not made up of one
part but of many.[z] **15**If the foot should
say, "Because I am not a hand, I do not
belong to the body," it would not for that
reason cease to be part of the body. **16**And
if the ear should say, "Because I am not
an eye, I do not belong to the body," it
would not for that reason cease to be part
of the body. **17**If the whole body were an
eye, where would the sense of hearing be?
If the whole body were an ear, where
would the sense of smell be? **18**But in fact
God has arranged[a] the parts in the body,
every one of them, just as he wanted them
to be.[b] **19**If they were all one part, where
would the body be? **20**As it is, there are
many parts, but one body.[c]

21The eye cannot say to the hand, "I
don't need you!" And the head cannot say
to the feet, "I don't need you!" **22**On the
contrary, those parts of the body that
seem to be weaker are indispensable,
23and the parts that we think are less honorable we treat with special honor. And
the parts that are unpresentable are treated with special modesty, **24**while our pre-
sentable parts need no special treatment.
But God has combined the members of the
body and has given greater honor to the
parts that lacked it, **25**so that there should

12:1 [a]S Ro 11:25
12:2 [b]S Eph 2:2
[c]Ps 115:5; Jer 10:5; Hab 2:18,19
12:3 [d]Ro 9:3; 1Co 16:22
[e]S Jn 13:13
[f]1Jn 4:2,3
12:4 [g]ver 8-11; Ro 12:4-8; Eph 4:11; Heb 2:4
12:6 [h]Eph 4:6
[i]S Php 2:13
12:7 [j]1Co 14:12; Eph 4:12
12:8 [k]1Co 2:6
[l]S 2Co 8:7
12:9 [m]Mt 17:19, 20; 1Co 13:2
[n]ver 28,30; Mt 10:1
12:10 [o]ver 28-30; Gal 3:5
[p]S Eph 4:11
[q]1Jn 4:1
[r]S Mk 16:17
12:11 [s]S ver 4
12:12 [t]S Ro 12:5
[u]ver 27
12:13 [v]S Mk 1:8
[w]Eph 2:18
[x]Gal 3:28; Col 3:11
[y]Jn 7:37-39
12:14 [z]ver 12,20
12:18 [a]ver 28
[b]ver 11
12:20 [c]ver 12,14; S Ro 12:5

[a] *10* Or *languages*; also in verse 28 [b] *13* Or *with*; or *in*

CHURCH, p. 407).

(3) "Service" or "ministries" (Gk *diakoniai*, derived from *diakonia*, "service") emphasizes that there are different ways of service and that certain gifts involve receiving the ability and power to help others (vv. 4–5,27–31; Eph 4:7,11–13). Paul indicates that the ministry aspect of the gifts reflect the "servant" ministry of the Lord Jesus. Thus the operation of the gifts are defined in terms of Christ's presence and operation among us (cf. v. 3; 1:4).

(4) "Working" or "effects" (Gk *energēmata*, from *energēs*, "active, energetic") signifies that spiritual gifts are direct operations of the power of God the Father and produce certain results (vv. 6,10).

(5) "The manifestation of the Spirit" (Gk *phanerōsis*, from *phaneros*, "manifest") emphasizes that spiritual gifts are direct manifestations of the working and presence of the Holy Spirit in the congregation (vv. 7–11).

12:3 JESUS IS LORD. Paul begins the discussion on spiritual gifts with the truth that the gifts and manifestations of the Holy Spirit will exalt Jesus as Lord of the church. The ultimate criterion of the Spirit's activity is an ever-growing expression of the person, presence, power, love and righteousness of the Lord Jesus Christ. In the manifestation of spiritual gifts Christ himself ministers by the Spirit through his people to his people (see vv. 12–27; Mt 25:40).

12:7 MANIFESTATION OF THE SPIRIT. For comments on spiritual gifts as manifestations of the Spirit, as well as a description of the various gifts listed here, see article on SPIRITUAL GIFTS FOR BELIEVERS, p. 350.

12:12 SO IT IS WITH CHRIST. See v. 1, note on spiritual gifts and the body of Christ.

12:13 WE WERE ALL BAPTIZED BY ONE SPIRIT. The baptism "by one Spirit" refers neither to water baptism nor to Christ's baptism of the believer in the Holy Spirit, such as occurred on the day of Pentecost (see Mk 1:8; Ac 2:4, note). Rather, it refers to the Spirit's baptizing believers into Christ's body, uniting them in the body and making them spiritually one with other believers. It is a spiritual transformation (i.e., regeneration) that occurs at conversion and puts the believer "in Christ" (see article on REGENERATION, p. 178).

12:25 PARTS SHOULD HAVE EQUAL CONCERN FOR EACH OTHER. Spiritual gifts should not be the basis for honoring a person or considering one believer as more important than another (vv. 22–24). Rather each person is placed in Christ's body according to God's will (v. 18), and all members are important for

be no division in the body, but that its
parts should have equal concern for each
other. **26**If one part suffers, every part suffers with it; if one part is honored, every
part rejoices with it.
27Now you are the body of Christ,[d] and
each one of you is a part of it.[e] **28**And in
the church[f] God has appointed first of all
apostles,[g] second prophets,[h] third teachers, then workers of miracles, also those
having gifts of healing,[i] those able to help
others, those with gifts of administration,[j] and those speaking in different
kinds of tongues.[k] **29**Are all apostles? Are
all prophets? Are all teachers? Do all
work miracles? **30**Do all have gifts of healing? Do all speak in tongues[c]?[l] Do all
1Co 14:1-40 interpret? **31**But eagerly desire[d][m] the
greater gifts.

Love

And now I will show you the most excellent way.
13 If I speak in the tongues[e][n] of men
and of angels, but have not love, I
am only a resounding gong or a clanging
cymbal. **2**If I have the gift of prophecy[o]
and can fathom all mysteries[p] and all
knowledge,[q] and if I have a faith[r] that
can move mountains,[s] but have not love,
I am nothing. **3**If I give all I possess to the 1Th 3:7
poor[t] and surrender my body to the
flames,[f][u] but have not love, I gain nothing.
4Love is patient,[v] love is kind. It does
not envy, it does not boast, it is not
proud.[w] **5**It is not rude, it is not self-seeking,[x] it is not easily angered,[y] it keeps no
record of wrongs.[z] **6**Love does not delight
in evil[a] but rejoices with the truth.[b] **7**It
always protects, always trusts, always
hopes, always perseveres.[c]
8Love never fails. But where there are
prophecies,[d] they will cease; where there

12:27 [d] Eph 1:23; 4:12; Col 1:18,24 [e] S Ro 12:5 **12:28** [f] S 1Co 10:32 [g] S Eph 4:11 [h] S Eph 4:11 [i] ver 9 [j] Ro 12:6-8 [k] ver 10; S Mk 16:17 **12:30** [l] ver 10 **12:31** [m] 1Co 14:1, 39 **13:1** [n] ver 8; S Mk 16:17 **13:2** [o] ver 8; S Eph 4:11; S Ac 11:27 [p] 1Co 14:2 [q] S 2Co 8:7 [r] 1Co 12:9 [s] Mt 17:20; 21:21 **13:3** [t] Lk 19:8; S Ac 2:45 [u] Da 3:28 **13:4** [v] 1Th 5:14 [w] 1Co 5:2 **13:5** [x] S 1Co 10:24 [y] S Mt 5:22 [z] Job 14:16,17; Pr 10:12; 17:9; 1Pe 4:8 **13:6** [a] 2Th 2:12 [b] 2Jn 4; 3Jn 3,4 **13:7** [c] ver 8,13 **13:8** [d] ver 2

c *30* Or *other languages* d *31* Or *But you are eagerly desiring* e *1* Or *languages* f *3* Some early manuscripts *body that I may boast*

the spiritual well-being and proper functioning of the body. Spiritual gifts must be used, not in pride or for personal exaltation, but with the sincere desire to help others and with a heart that genuinely cares for each other (see ch. 13).

12:28 IN THE CHURCH GOD HAS APPOINTED. Paul gives here a partial list of the ministry gifts (see Ro 12:6–8 and Eph 4:11–13 for other lists of ministry gifts). See article on THE MINISTRY GIFTS OF THE CHURCH, p. 407, for the definition of apostles, prophets, evangelists, pastors and teachers; see also Jn 6:2, note, for definition of "miracles"; Ro 12:7–8, for notes on the gift of "helping others" ("showing mercy") and the gift of "administration" ("leadership").

12:30 DO ALL SPEAK IN TONGUES? Paul's rhetorical question here implies a negative answer. The context in ch. 12 shows that Paul is referring to the use of the gift of tongues and its companion gift of interpretation in public worship services. He is not attempting to limit the use of tongues in prayer and praise privately addressed to God (cf. 14:5). Most believers baptized in the Holy Spirit find it easy to pray in tongues as they yield themselves to the Spirit. On the day of Pentecost (Ac 2:4), at Caesarea (Ac 10:44–46) and at Ephesus (Ac 19:2–6), all who were filled with the Spirit spoke in tongues as a sign that they had received the fullness of the Spirit (see article on SPEAKING IN TONGUES, p. 232).

13:1 BUT HAVE NOT LOVE. Ch. 13 is a continuation of Paul's discussion on the question of spiritual gifts. Here he emphasizes that to possess spiritual gifts without having love amounts to nothing (vv. 1–3). The "most excellent way" (12:31) is the exercise of spiritual gifts in love (vv. 4–8). As the only context in which spiritual gifts can fulfill God's will, love must be the governing principle of all spiritual manifestations. Paul therefore exhorts the Corinthians to "follow the way of love and eagerly desire spiritual gifts" (14:1). They must earnestly desire the things of the Spirit because they sincerely want to help, comfort and bless others in this life.

13:2 I AM NOTHING. Those whose lives are filled with "religious activities" are not necessarily approved by God; in fact, they may not be believers at all. For example, those who speak in tongues, prophesy, have knowledge or achieve great works of faith, yet at the same time lack Christlike love and righteousness, are "nothing" in God's sight. In God's judgment their spirituality and profession of faith are empty (v. 1), and they have no real place in his kingdom (cf. 6:9–10). They are not only lacking in the Spirit's fullness, but are also empty of his indwelling presence. The spiritual manifestations through them are not from God but from another spirit, i.e., an evil spirit (see Ac 8:21, note; 1Jn 4:1, note; see article on TESTING FOR GENUINE BAPTISM IN THE SPIRIT, p. 254). What is essential to true Christian faith is love expressed through an ethic that does no harm to others and perseveres in loyalty to Christ and his Word (see also v. 13, note).

13:4–7 LOVE IS PATIENT. This section describes love as an activity and a behavior, not just as an inner feeling or motivation. The various aspects of love included here characterize God the Father, Son and Holy Spirit. Every believer must seek to grow in this kind of love.

13:8 TONGUES, THEY WILL BE STILLED. Spiritual gifts such as prophecy, tongues and knowledge will cease at the end of this age. That time is described as "when perfection comes" (v. 10)—i.e., at the end of history, when the believer's knowledge and character become perfect in eternity after Christ's second coming (v. 12; 1:7). Until then, we need the Holy Spirit and his gifts in our churches. There is no indication here or elsewhere in Scripture

SPIRITUAL GIFTS FOR BELIEVERS

***1Co 12:7** "Now to each one the manifestation of the Spirit is given for the common good."*

GENERAL PERSPECTIVE. The Holy Spirit is manifested through a variety of spiritual gifts given to believers (1Co 12:7). These manifestations of the Spirit are intended for the upbuilding and sanctification of the church (1Co 12:7; see 14:26, note). These spiritual gifts are not the same as the gifts and ministries mentioned in Ro 12:6–8 and Eph 4:11, whereby a believer receives the power and ability to minister in a more permanent manner in the church. The list in 1Co 12:8–10 is not necessarily exhaustive, and the gifts may occur in various combinations.

(1) The manifestations of the Spirit are given according to the Spirit's will (1Co 12:11) when need arises and according to the believer's eager desire (12:31; 14:1).

(2) Some gifts may be manifested through an individual on a regular basis, and a believer may have more than one gift to minister to particular needs. The believer ought to desire "gifts," not just one gift (1Co 12:31; 14:1).

(3) It is unscriptural and unwise to assume that because someone exercises a spectacular gift, that person is more spiritual than one who has less spectacular gifts. Furthermore, possessing a gift does not mean that God approves of all a person does or teaches. Spiritual gifts must not be confused with the fruit of the Spirit, which relates more directly to Christian character and sanctification (Gal 5:22–23).

(4) The Spirit's manifestation through gifts may be counterfeited by Satan or false workers disguising themselves as servants of Christ (Mt 7:21–23; 24:11,24; 2Co 11:13–15; 2Th 2:8–10). The believer must not believe every spiritual manifestation, but ought to "test the spirits to see whether they are from God, because many false prophets have gone out into the world" (1Jn 4:1; cf. 1Th 5:20–21; see article on TESTING FOR GENUINE BAPTISM IN THE SPIRIT, p. 254).

INDIVIDUAL GIFTS. In 1Co 12:8–10, Paul lists a variety of gifts that the Holy Spirit gives to believers. Though he does not define their characteristics here, we can glean from other passages of Scripture what they might be.

(1) *Message of wisdom*. This is a wise utterance spoken through the operation of the Holy Spirit. It applies the revelation of God's Word or the Holy Spirit's wisdom to a specific situation or problem (Ac 6:10; 15:13–22). It is not, however, the same as having the wisdom of God for daily living. This is obtained by diligent study and meditation on God's ways and Word, and by prayer (Jas 1:5–6).

(2) *Message of knowledge*. This is an utterance inspired by the Holy Spirit that reveals knowledge about people, circumstances or Biblical truth. It is often connected closely with prophecy (Ac 5:1–10; 10:47–48; 15:7–11; 1Co 14:24–25).

(3) *Faith*. This is not saving faith, but a special supernatural faith imparted by the Holy Spirit that enables the Christian to believe God for the extraordinary and miraculous. It is a faith that moves mountains (1Co 13:2) and is often found in combination with other manifestations such as healings and miracles (see Mt 17:20, note on true faith; Mk 11:22–24; Lk 17:6). It also may refer to a special gift by which one inspires faith in members of the congregation.

(4) *Gifts of healing*. These gifts are given to the church to restore physical health by supernatural means (Mt 4:23–25; 10:1; Ac 3:6–8; 4:30). The plural ("gifts") indicates healing of various illnesses and suggests that every act of healing is a special gift of God. Although gifts of healing are not given to every member of the body in a special way (cf. 1Co 12:11,30), all members may pray for the sick. When faith is present, the sick will be healed (see article on DIVINE HEALING, p. 20.) Healing may also come as a result of obedience to the instructions of Jas 5:14–16 (see Jas 5:15, notes).

(5) *Miraculous powers*. These are deeds of supernatural power that alter the normal course of nature. They include divine acts in which God's kingdom is manifested against Satan and evil spirits (see Jn 6:2, note; see article on THE KINGDOM OF GOD, p. 28).

(6) *Prophecy*. We must distinguish between prophecy as a temporary manifestation of the Spirit (1Co 12:10) and prophecy as a ministry gift of the church (Eph 4:11). As a ministry gift, prophecy is given only to some believers, who must then function as prophets within the church (see article on THE MINISTRY GIFTS OF THE CHURCH, p. 407). As a spiritual manifestation, prophecy is potentially available to every Spirit-filled Christian (Ac 2:17–18).

Concerning prophecy as a spiritual manifestation: (a) Prophecy is a special gift that enables a believer to bring a word or revelation directly from God under the impulse of the Holy Spirit (1Co 14:24–25,29–31). It is not the delivery of a previously prepared sermon. (b) In both the OT and the NT, prophecy is not primarily foretelling the future, but proclaiming God's will and exhorting and encouraging God's people to righteousness, faithfulness and endurance (14:3). (c) The message may expose the condition of a person's heart (14:25) or offer strengthening, encouragement, comfort, warning and judgment (14:3,25–26,31). (d) The church may not receive such prophecy as an infallible message, for many false prophets will enter the church (1Jn 4:1). Therefore, all prophecy must be tested for genuineness and truth (1Co 14:29,32; 1Th 5:20–21) by asking whether it conforms to God's Word (1Jn 4:1), whether it promotes godly living (1Ti 6:3), and whether it is uttered by one who is sincerely living under Christ's lordship (1Co 12:3). (e) Prophecy operates under God's will and not the will of humans. The NT never indicates that the church actively sought revelation or direction from those claiming to be prophets. Prophecy was given to the church only when God initiated the message (1Co 12:11; 2Pe 1:21).

(7) *Distinguishing between spirits*. This gift is a special Spirit-given ability to properly discern and judge prophecies and to distinguish whether or not an utterance is from the Holy Spirit (see 1Co 14:29, note; 1Jn 4:1). Toward the end of the age when false teachers (see Mt 24:5, notes) and distortion of Biblical Christianity will greatly increase (see 1Ti 4:1, note), this gift will be extremely important for the church.

(8) *Speaking in different kinds of tongues*. Concerning "tongues" (Gk *glōssa*, meaning language) as a supernatural manifestation of the Spirit, the following must be pointed out:

(a) Tongues may be an existing spoken language (Ac 2:4–6) or a language unknown on earth, e.g., "tongues . . . of angels" (1Co 13:1; see ch. 14, notes; see article on SPEAKING IN TONGUES, p. 232). Such speech has not been learned and is often unintelligible both to the speaker (14:14) and to the hearers (14:16).

(b) Speaking in tongues involves the human spirit and the Spirit of God intermingling so that the believer communicates directly to God (i.e., in prayer, praise, blessing or thanksgiving), giving expression or utterance at the level of one's spirit rather than the mind (1Co 14:2,14) and praying for oneself or others under the direct influence of the Holy Spirit apart from the activity of the mind (cf. 1Co 14:2,4,15,28; Jude 20).

(c) Tongues in the congregation must be accompanied by a Spirit-given interpretation that communicates the content and meaning of the utterance to the community of believers (1Co 14:3,27–28). It may contain a revelation, knowledge, prophecy or teaching for the assembly (cf. 1Co 14:6).

(d) Speaking in tongues within the congregation must be regulated. The speaker may never be "in ecstasy" or "out of control" (1Co 14:27–28; see article on SPEAKING IN TONGUES, p. 232).

(9) *Interpretation of tongues*. This is the Spirit-given ability to understand and communicate the meaning of an utterance spoken in tongues. When interpreted for the congregation, tongues function either as a directive to worship and prayer or as prophecy. The body of believers can then participate in this Spirit-inspired revelation. Interpreted tongues can thus be a means of edification as the whole congregation responds to the utterance (cf. 14:6,13). The gift may be given to the one who speaks in tongues or to someone else. Those who speak in tongues should pray also for the gift of interpretation (1Co 14:13).

are tongues,[e] they will be stilled; where
there is knowledge, it will pass away. 9For
we know in part[f] and we prophesy in part,
10but when perfection comes,[g] the imperfect disappears. 11When I was a child, I
talked like a child, I thought like a child,
I reasoned like a child. When I became a
man, I put childish ways[h] behind me.
12Now we see but a poor reflection as in
a mirror;[i] then we shall see face to face.[j]
Now I know in part; then I shall know
fully, even as I am fully known.[k]

13And now these three remain: faith,
hope and love.[l] But the greatest of these
is love.[m]

13:8 [e]ver 1 **13:9** [f]ver 12; S 1Co 8:2 **13:10** [g]Php 3:12 **13:11** [h]Ps 131:2 **13:12** [i]Job 26:14; 36:26 [j]Ge 32:30; Job 19:26; 1Jn 3:2 [k]1Co 8:3; Gal 4:9 **13:13** [l]Ro 5:2-5; Gal 5:5,6; Eph 4:2-5; Col 1:4, 5; 1Th 1:3; 5:8; Heb 6:10-12 [m]Mt 22:37-40; 1Co 16:14; Gal 5:6; 1Jn 4:7-12,16

14:1 [n]1Co 16:14 [o]ver 39; 1Co 12:31 [p]S 1Co 12:1 [q]ver 39; S Eph 4:11

Gifts of Prophecy and Tongues

14 Follow the way of love[n] and eagerly desire[o] spiritual gifts,[p] especially the gift of prophecy.[q] 2For anyone
who speaks in a tongue[g][r] does not speak
to men but to God. Indeed, no one understands him;[s] he utters mysteries[t] with
his spirit.[h] 3But everyone who prophesies
speaks to men for their strengthening,[u]
encouragement[v] and comfort. 4He who

14:2 [r]S Mk 16:17 [s]ver 6-11,16 [t]1Co 13:2 **14:3** [u]ver 4,5,12, 17,26; S Ro 14:19 [v]ver 31

[g] 2 Or *another language*; also in verses 4, 13, 14, 19, 26 and 27 [h] 2 Or *by the Spirit*

that the manifestation of the Spirit through his gifts would cease at the end of the apostolic age.

13:13 THE GREATEST ... IS LOVE. It is clear from this chapter that God exalts Christlike character more than ministry, faith or the possession of spiritual gifts. (1) God values and emphasizes character that acts in love, patience (v. 4), kindness (v. 4), unselfishness (v. 5), hatred for evil and love for the truth (v. 6), honesty (v. 6) and endurance in righteousness (v. 7) much more than faith to move mountains or to perform great achievements in the church (vv. 1–2,8,13).

(2) The greatest in God's kingdom will be those who are great in inward godliness and love for God, not necessarily those who are greatest in outward accomplishments (see Lk 22:24–30, note). God's love poured out within the believer's heart through the Holy Spirit is always greater than faith, hope or anything else (Ro 5:5).

14:1 DESIRE SPIRITUAL GIFTS. Believers who possess genuine love for others in the body of Christ must desire spiritual gifts in order to be able to help, comfort, encourage and strengthen those in need (cf. 12:17). They may not wait passively for God to give the gifts of the Spirit (12:7–10). Instead, they must earnestly desire, seek and pray for those gifts, especially those that serve to exhort, comfort and strengthen (vv. 3,13,19,26).

14:2 SPEAKS IN A TONGUE. The Corinthians had overestimated the importance of the gift of tongues in public worship (see article on SPIRITUAL GIFTS FOR BELIEVERS, p. 350) and were emphasizing it at the expense of the other gifts. Furthermore, they were exercising this gift without interpretation. Paul seeks to correct this abuse by pointing out the unprofitableness of tongues without interpretation in public services. An outline of this chapter is as follows:

(1) Prophecy edifies the church more than uninterpreted tongues (vv. 1–4).

(2) Prophecy and tongues with interpretation are equally important to the church (v. 5).

(3) Speaking in tongues in public worship services without interpretation is of no benefit to others (vv. 6–12).

(4) Those who speak or pray in tongues in the church should seek to edify the church by praying for the gift of interpretation (v. 13).

(5) In Paul's personal life speaking in tongues to God is an important means of worship and spiritual growth (vv. 14–19).

(6) Prophecy is more useful than uninterpreted tongues because prophecy brings conviction of sin and the knowledge of God's presence (vv. 20–25).

(7) Speaking in tongues and prophesying must be regulated so that order is maintained in the church (vv. 26–40).

14:2 DOES NOT SPEAK TO MEN BUT TO GOD. There are basically two ways to understand this verse. (1) Some believe that this verse indicates that the principal use of tongues, whether in the church or in private, is a speaking directed primarily to God and not to humans. When tongues are directed to God, the speaker communes with God by the Holy Spirit in the form of prayer, praise, singing, blessing and thanksgiving. What is spoken are "mysteries," i.e., things not understandable to the speaker or hearers (cf. vv. 2,13–17). Interpretation of the utterance (vv. 5,13) in tongues allows the congregation to enter into this manifestation of the Spirit-directed worship and thus to say "Amen" (v. 16) to the Spirit-inspired prayer or praise (v. 16; see also v. 6, note).

(2) On the other hand Paul's statement may mean that only God understands a tongue unless it is interpreted (v. 5). The implication would be that tongues, when interpreted, are directed to humans. This view is supported by Paul's statement that the reason why tongue-speaking is not spoken to humans is because "no one understands" it (see v. 6, note).

14:3 PROPHESIES ... STRENGTHENING. The gift of prophecy in the church is motivated by the Holy Spirit, not primarily to foretell the future, but to strengthen the believer's faith, spiritual life and moral resolve to remain faithful to Christ and his teachings. Prophecy is not, however, preaching a prepared sermon, but giving a spontaneous word under the impulse of the Spirit for the edification of the individual or the congregation (see article on SPIRITUAL GIFTS FOR BELIEVERS, p. 350).

14:4 EDIFIES HIMSELF. Tongues without interpretation edifies (i.e., builds up one's faith and spiritual life; see v. 26, note) the speaker because it puts him or her in direct communion with God by the Spirit (cf. Eph 3:16; Jude 20), bypassing the mind. Paul states that he prays and communes with God in this way as well as with the mind (vv. 14–15).

speaks in a tongue[w] edifies[x] himself, but
he who prophesies[y] edifies the church. 5I
would like every one of you to speak in
tongues,[i] but I would rather have you
prophesy.[z] He who prophesies is greater
than one who speaks in tongues,[i] unless
he interprets, so that the church may be
edified.[a]

6Now, brothers, if I come to you and
speak in tongues, what good will I be to
you, unless I bring you some revelation[b]
or knowledge[c] or prophecy or word of instruction?[d] 7Even in the case of lifeless
things that make sounds, such as the flute
or harp, how will anyone know what tune
is being played unless there is a distinction in the notes? 8Again, if the trumpet
does not sound a clear call, who will get
ready for battle?[e] 9So it is with you. Unless you speak intelligible words with
your tongue, how will anyone know what
you are saying? You will just be speaking
into the air. 10Undoubtedly there are all
sorts of languages in the world, yet none
of them is without meaning. 11If then I do
not grasp the meaning of what someone is
saying, I am a foreigner to the speaker,
and he is a foreigner to me.[f] 12So it is
with you. Since you are eager to have spiritual gifts,[g] try to excel in gifts that build
up[h] the church.

13For this reason anyone who speaks in
a tongue should pray that he may interpret what he says.[i] 14For if I pray in a
tongue, my spirit prays,[j] but my mind is
unfruitful. 15So what shall I do? I will pray
with my spirit,[k] but I will also pray with
my mind; I will sing[l] with my spirit, but
I will also sing with my mind. 16If you are
praising God with your spirit, how can one
who finds himself among those who do not
understand[j] say "Amen"[m] to your thanksgiving,[n] since he does not know what you
are saying? 17You may be giving thanks
well enough, but the other man is not edified.[o]

18I thank God that I speak in tongues
more than all of you. 19But in the church
I would rather speak five intelligible
words to instruct others than ten thousand words in a tongue.[p]

20Brothers, stop thinking like children.[q] In regard to evil be infants,[r] but in
your thinking be adults. 21In the Law[s] it
is written:

14:4 [w]S Mk 16:17 [x]S ver 3 [y]S 1Co 13:2 **14:5** [z]Nu 11:29 [a]S ver 3 **14:6** [b]ver 26; Eph 1:17 [c]S 2Co 8:7 [d]Ro 6:17 **14:8** [e]Nu 10:9; Jer 4:19 **14:11** [f]Ge 11:7 **14:12** [g]S 1Co 12:1 [h]S ver 3 **14:13** [i]ver 5 **14:14** [j]ver 2 **14:15** [k]ver 2,14 [l]S Eph 5:19 **14:16** [m]Dt 27:15-26; 1Ch 16:36; Ne 8:6; Ps 106:48; Rev 5:14; 7:12 [n]S Mt 14:19; 1Co 11:24 **14:17** [o]S ver 3 **14:19** [p]ver 6 **14:20** [q]1Co 3:11; Eph 4:14; Heb 5:12,13; 1Pe 2:2 [r]Jer 4:22; Mt 10:16; Ro 16:19 **14:21** [s]ver 34; S Jn 10:34

i *5* Or *other languages*; also in verses 6, 18, 22, 23 and 39 **j** *16* Or *among the inquirers*

14:5 I WOULD LIKE EVERY ONE OF YOU TO SPEAK IN TONGUES. Paul's wish here refers to tongue-speaking in private devotion to God. Clearly such tongues have value for the individual Christian's personal worship and prayer (vv. 2,4). Paul adds that authentic tongues accompanied with interpretation in the assembly bring edification to the church, just as prophecy does. Tongues without interpretation does nothing for the church (vv. 7–9).

14:6 SPEAK IN TONGUES, WHAT GOOD WILL I BE TO YOU, UNLESS. Speaking in tongues can at times be directed toward the Christian community. Paul describes the hypothetical situation of coming to the Corinthians and speaking in tongues in the worship service. Such speaking would be of no benefit to them "unless" he brings some revelation or word of instruction. The construction of this verse suggests that his speaking in tongues, when interpreted, would consist of a message containing revelation, knowledge, prophecy or instruction to the congregation. This interpretation finds support in v. 8, where Paul gives the analogy of a trumpet that brings a message and warns to prepare for battle. In other words, speaking in tongues with interpretation can bring a message to God's people, such as a message to prepare for spiritual warfare with Satan, sin and the world's ungodly elements, or it can challenge us to be ready for Christ's imminent return.

14:8 TRUMPET . . . READY FOR BATTLE. Those who speak in tongues should produce sounds easy to be identified (v. 7). Like trumpets, they must convey a clear message. Thus, those speaking in a tongue must pray that they may interpret what they say for the edification of others (v. 12).

14:15 PRAY WITH MY SPIRIT . . . PRAY WITH MY MIND. Paul refers to his own experience, to his own private use of tongues. "I pray with my spirit" means to pray in tongues with one's own spirit under the impulse of the Holy Spirit. The believer's spirit prays as the Holy Spirit gives the utterance (cf. 12:7,11; Ac 2:4). Paul is speaking here of the private use of tongues directed to God. Paul used tongues not only for praying, but also for singing, praising and giving thanks to God (vv. 14–16). To "pray with my mind" means to pray and praise with one's own mind in a learned language, also under the impulse of the Spirit.

14:18 I SPEAK IN TONGUES. Paul considered the gift of tongues an important part of his spiritual life, which was frequently given to praying, singing, praising and giving thanks in tongues. He speaks with reverence and gratitude for this manifestation of the Spirit. Some have interpreted this verse to mean that Paul spoke more learned languages than the Corinthians. However, this interpretation is incorrect, for the word "more" (Gk *mallon*) is not an adjective modifying the noun "tongues," but a comparative adverb, modifying the verb "speak." Thus, Paul did not say "I speak in more languages," but rather, "I speak in tongues more (i.e., more often) than all of you."

14:19 BUT IN THE CHURCH. In the church Paul preferred to utter a few words that people could understand than to speak ten thousand words in tongues without an interpretation. Vv. 18–19 imply that Paul spoke in tongues more in private devotions than in public worship.

"Through men of strange tongues
and through the lips of foreigners
I will speak to this people,
but even then they will not listen to
me,"[k][t]
says the Lord.

22Tongues, then, are a sign, not for believers but for unbelievers; prophecy,[u]
however, is for believers, not for unbelievers. 23So if the whole church comes together and everyone speaks in tongues,
and some who do not understand[1] or
some unbelievers come in, will they not
say that you are out of your mind?[v] 24But
if an unbeliever or someone who does not
understand[m] comes in while everybody is
prophesying, he will be convinced by all
that he is a sinner and will be judged by
all, 25and the secrets[w] of his heart will be
laid bare. So he will fall down and worship
God, exclaiming, "God is really among
you!"[x]

14:21 [t]Dt 28:49; Isa 28:11,12 **14:22** [u]ver 1 **14:23** [v]Ac 2:13 **14:25** [w]Ro 2:16 [x]Isa 45:14; Zec 8:23

14:26 [y]S Ro 7:1 [z]1Co 12:7-10 [a]S Eph 5:19 [b]ver 6 [c]ver 2 [d]1Co 12:10 [e]S Ro 14:19 **14:29** [f]ver 32,37; S 1Co 13:2 [g]1Co 12:10

Orderly Worship

26What then shall we say, brothers?[y]
When you come together, everyone[z] has
a hymn,[a] or a word of instruction,[b] a revelation, a tongue[c] or an interpretation.[d]
All of these must be done for the strengthening[e] of the church. 27If anyone speaks
in a tongue, two—or at the most three—
should speak, one at a time, and someone
must interpret. 28If there is no interpreter, the speaker should keep quiet in the
church and speak to himself and God.

29Two or three prophets[f] should
speak, and the others should weigh carefully what is said.[g] 30And if a revelation
comes to someone who is sitting down,
the first speaker should stop. 31For you
can all prophesy in turn so that everyone
may be instructed and encouraged. 32The
spirits of prophets are subject to the con-

k *21* Isaiah 28:11,12 l *23* Or *some inquirers* m *24* Or *or some inquirer*

14:22 TONGUES, THEN, ARE A SIGN. Tongues within the congregation become a negative sign to unbelievers in that they signify that the unbeliever is separated from God and cannot understand what is occurring (vv. 21,23). Prophecy, however, is a sign to believers, for they recognize that it is a supernatural work of the Holy Spirit and a proof that God is at work in the church (vv. 24–25). Tongues also may be a sign to believers indicating that the Spirit is being poured out (cf. Ac 10:44–46; 11:15–17) and manifested among God's people (cf. 12:7,10).

14:24 UNBELIEVER . . . JUDGED BY ALL. One of the surest signs that the Holy Spirit is present and at work in any congregation is his conviction of sin, righteousness and judgment (see Jn 16:8, note). (1) Through the manifestation of the Spirit among God's people, sin will be exposed, repentance called for, and sinners convicted. Where there is no exposing of unrighteousness, no conviction of sin or no plea for repentance, the Holy Spirit is clearly not at work according to the Biblical pattern. (2) The exposing of sin within a person's heart (v. 25) does not require a special gift of revelation or "mind reading." The word of prophecy and its moral truth when proclaimed under the impulse of the Spirit is sufficient to convict the sinner's heart (Heb 4:12).

14:26 ALL OF THESE . . . FOR THE STRENGTHENING. The principal purpose of all spiritual gifts is to strengthen the church and the individual (vv. 3–4,12,17,26). "Strengthening" (Gk *oikodomeō*) means to promote spiritual life, maturity and godly character in believers. It is a work of the Holy Spirit through spiritual gifts by which believers are increasingly spiritually transformed in order that they may not be conformed to this world (Ro 12:2–8), but may be built up in sanctification, love for God, concern for others, purity of heart, a good conscience and a sincere faith (see ch. 13; Ro 8:13; 14:1–4,26; Gal 5:16–26; Eph 2:19–22; 4:11–16; Col 3:16; 1Th 5:11; Jude 20; see 1Ti 1:5, note).

14:27 SOMEONE MUST INTERPRET. In the use of spiritual gifts there must be order and balance. The Biblical guidelines for speaking in tongues within the church are: (1) In any one meeting there must not be more than two or three who speak, pray or praise in tongues, and this must be done with interpretation (vv. 27–28). (2) Speaking in tongues must be done by one person at a time (v. 27). (3) All speaking in tongues must be judged by the church as to its authenticity (vv. 29,32). (4) If there is no interpreter present, a believer may speak in tongues privately in prayer to God (v. 28).

14:29 THE OTHERS SHOULD WEIGH CAREFULLY. All prophecy must be evaluated as to what is said. This shows that NT prophecy was less than infallible and might need to be corrected. (1) At times prophecy and speaking in tongues might not be a word from God (cf. 1Jn 4:1). Even evil spirits, through the presence of false teachers or prophets, can work in the congregation. Prophesying, speaking in tongues or possessing any supernatural gift is no guarantee that one is a true prophet or a true believer (see article on FALSE TEACHERS, p. 98), for spiritual gifts may be counterfeited by Satan (Mt 24:24; 2Th 2:9–12; Rev 13:13–14).

(2) If the church has not set up proper and orderly ways (cf. v. 40) to judge prophecies, it has failed to follow Biblical guidelines. Note too that prophecy was not considered an irresistible impulse of the Spirit, for only one prophet could speak at a time (vv. 30–32).

(3) What should be the church's attitude toward prophetic messages? (a) All prophecy must be tested according to the standard of Biblical truth (cf. Dt 13:1–3). Believers should look for its fulfillment (cf. Dt 18:22), preparing themselves for the possibility that the prophecy may or may not be fulfilled. (b) If the word of prophecy is an exhortation, the congregation needs to ask, "What must we do to obey the will of the Spirit?"

14:31 YOU CAN ALL PROPHESY IN TURN. The

trol of prophets.[h] **33**For God is not a God
of disorder[i] but of peace.[j]
As in all the congregations[k] of the
saints,[l] **34**women should remain silent in
the churches. They are not allowed to
speak,[m] but must be in submission,[n] as
the Law[o] says. **35**If they want to inquire
about something, they should ask their
own husbands at home; for it is disgraceful for a woman to speak in the church.
36Did the word of God[p] originate with
you? Or are you the only people it has
reached? **37**If anybody thinks he is a
prophet[q] or spiritually gifted,[r] let him acknowledge that what I am writing to you
is the Lord's command.[s] **38**If he ignores
this, he himself will be ignored.[n]
39Therefore, my brothers, be eager[t] to
prophesy,[u] and do not forbid speaking in
tongues. **40**But everything should be done
Gal 3:5 in a fitting and orderly[v] way.

The Resurrection of Christ

15 Now, brothers, I want to remind
you of the gospel[w] I preached to
you,[x] which you received and on which
you have taken your stand. **2**By this gospel you are saved,[y] if you hold firmly[z] to
the word I preached to you. Otherwise,
you have believed in vain.
3For what I received[a] I passed on to
you[b] as of first importance[o]: that Christ
died for our sins[c] according to the Scriptures,[d] **4**that he was buried,[e] that he was
raised[f] on the third day[g] according to the
Scriptures,[h] **5**and that he appeared to Peter,[p][i] and then to the Twelve.[j] **6**After
that, he appeared to more than five hundred of the brothers at the same time,
most of whom are still living, though some
have fallen asleep.[k] **7**Then he appeared to
James,[l] then to all the apostles,[m] **8**and
last of all he appeared to me also,[n] as to
one abnormally born.
9For I am the least of the apostles[o] and
do not even deserve to be called an apostle, because I persecuted[p] the church of
God.[q] **10**But by the grace[r] of God I am
what I am, and his grace to me[s] was not

14:32 [h] 1Jn 4:1 **14:33** [i] ver 40 [j] S Ro 15:33 [k] S 1Co 7:17; S 10:32 [l] S Ac 9:13 **14:34** [m] 1Co 11:5, 13 [n] S Eph 5:22; 1Ti 2:11,12 [o] ver 21; Ge 3:16 **14:36** [p] S Heb 4:12 **14:37** [q] S Ac 11:27; 1Co 13:2; 2Co 10:7 [r] 1Co 2:15; S 12:1 [s] 1Jn 4:6 **14:39** [t] ver 1; 1Co 12:31 [u] ver 1; S Eph 4:11 **14:40** [v] ver 33; Col 2:5 **15:1** [w] Isa 40:9; Ro 2:16 [x] S 1Co 3:6; S Gal 1:8 **15:2** [y] Ro 1:16 [z] S Ro 11:22 **15:3** [a] Gal 1:12 [b] S 1Co 11:2 [c] Isa 53:5; Jn 1:29; S Gal 1:4; 1Pe 2:24 [d] S Mt 26:24; S Lk 24:27; S 24:44; Ac 17:2; 26:22,23 **15:4** [e] Mt 27:59, 60 [f] S Ac 2:24 [g] S Mt 16:21 [h] Jn 2:21,22; Ac 2:25,30,31

15:5 [i] Lk 24:34 [j] Mk 16:14; Lk 24:36-43 **15:6** [k] ver 18,20; S Mt 9:24 **15:7** [l] S Ac 15:13 [m] Lk 24:33,36,37; Ac 1:3,4 **15:8** [n] Ac 9:3-6,17; 1Co 9:1; Gal 1:16 **15:9** [o] 2Co 12:11; Eph 3:8; 1Ti 1:15 [p] S Ac 8:3 [q] S 1Co 10:32 **15:10** [r] S Ro 3:24 [s] S Ro 12:3

n 38 Some manuscripts *If he is ignorant of this, let him be ignorant* **o** 3 Or *you at the first*
p 5 Greek *Cephas*

distinction between prophecy as a spiritual gift and prophecy as part of Scripture must be clearly maintained, even though in both cases a message is received from God. (1) The writers of Scripture received their message by direct inspiration of the Holy Spirit and communicated it without error. The result was an infallible message (see article on THE INSPIRATION AND AUTHORITY OF SCRIPTURE, p. 474).

(2) However, prophecy as described in chs. 12 and 14 may not be assigned the same authority or infallibility as the inspired Word of God (2Ti 3:16). Although coming from the impulse of the Spirit, this kind of prophecy must never be considered inerrant. Its message is always subject to human mixture and error. This is why prophecy today may never be equated with Scripture. Furthermore, present-day prophecy may not be accepted by the local church until other believers judge the utterance's content in order to determine its validity (see v. 29, note; 12:10). The primary basis for judging is the written Word of God: does it conform to apostolic teaching? God's written Word must always stand in judgment over all experiences and utterances.

14:34 WOMEN SHOULD REMAIN SILENT. This verse may be interpreted by v. 35 in the sense of forbidding women to interrupt the service by asking questions that could be asked at home. In 11:5 Paul assumes that women pray and prophesy in public assemblies (cf. the "everyone" of 14:23–24,31).

14:39 PROPHESY, AND DO NOT FORBID ... TONGUES. This double injunction concludes Paul's discussion of prophecy and tongues. If the Corinthians refuse to recognize that his instructions are "the Lord's commands," then they prove they are neither prophets nor the people of the Spirit (vv. 37–38). Churches today that claim to follow God's Word, yet forbid speaking in tongues and do not earnestly desire that their people prophesy, should ask themselves how vv. 37–38 might apply to them.

15:2 IF YOU HOLD FIRMLY TO THE WORD I PREACHED. Believers are not those who merely have faith in Jesus Christ. Rather believers are those who have faith in Christ as he is revealed in the full message of the gospel (vv. 1–4). Their faith in Christ is always bound to God's Word and the doctrine of the apostles (vv. 1,3; 11:2,23; Ro 6:17; Gal 1:12). For this reason, believers can be described as people who submit to the Christ of the Bible as Lord and Savior and who live under the Word of God. They submit without reservation to its authority, hold firmly to its teaching, trust its promises, heed its warnings and follow its commands. They are a people captive to God's Word, using Scripture to test all human ideas and accepting nothing that is contrary to the Bible.

15:8 AND LAST OF ALL. Paul's statement "last of all" must be taken absolutely. Paul was the last of the apostles defined in the sense of receiving a special commission through a personal meeting with the risen Lord in order to join in forming the original and fundamental testimony of Christ (cf. Ac 9:3–8; 22:6–11; 26:12–18). The NT apostles were the beginning and the foundation stones of the church (see Eph 2:20, note; cf. Mt 16:18; Rev 21:14). Therefore this NT apostolic office is unique and unrepeatable. As direct witnesses and messengers of the risen Lord, they built the foundation of the church of Jesus Christ, a foundation that can never be added to or altered. Thus, these apostles can have no successors.

without effect. No, I worked harder than
all of them[t]—yet not I, but the grace of
God that was with me.[u] **11**Whether, then,
it was I or they,[v] this is what we preach,
and this is what you believed.

The Resurrection of the Dead

12But if it is preached that Christ has
been raised from the dead,[w] how can some
of you say that there is no resurrection[x]
of the dead?[y] **13**If there is no resurrection
of the dead, then not even Christ has been
raised. **14**And if Christ has not been
raised,[z] our preaching is useless and so
is your faith. **15**More than that, we are
then found to be false witnesses about
God, for we have testified about God that
he raised Christ from the dead.[a] But he
did not raise him if in fact the dead are not
raised. **16**For if the dead are not raised,
then Christ has not been raised either.
17And if Christ has not been raised, your
faith is futile; you are still in your sins.[b]
18Then those also who have fallen
asleep[c] in Christ are lost. **19**If only for this
life we have hope in Christ, we are to be
pitied more than all men.[d]

20But Christ has indeed been raised
from the dead,[e] the firstfruits[f] of those
who have fallen asleep.[g] **21**For since
death came through a man,[h] the resurrection of the dead[i] comes also through a
man. **22**For as in Adam all die, so in Christ
all will be made alive.[j] **23**But each in his
own turn: Christ, the firstfruits;[k] then,
when he comes,[l] those who belong to
him.[m] **24**Then the end will come, when he
hands over the kingdom[n] to God the Father after he has destroyed all dominion,
authority and power.[o] **25**For he must
reign[p] until he has put all his enemies
under his feet.[q] **26**The last enemy to be
destroyed is death.[r] **27**For he "has put
everything under his feet."[q][s] Now when it
says that "everything" has been put under
him, it is clear that this does not include
God himself, who put everything under
Christ.[t] **28**When he has done this, then
the Son himself will be made subject to
him who put everything under him,[u] so
that God may be all in all.[v]

29Now if there is no resurrection, what
will those do who are baptized for the
dead? If the dead are not raised at all, why
are people baptized for them? **30**And as for
us, why do we endanger ourselves every
hour?[w] **31**I die every day[x]—I mean that,
brothers—just as surely as I glory over
you in Christ Jesus our Lord. **32**If I fought
wild beasts[y] in Ephesus[z] for merely human reasons, what have I gained? If the
dead are not raised,

"Let us eat and drink,
for tomorrow we die."[r][a]

33Do not be misled:[b] "Bad company corrupts good character."[c] **34**Come back to
your senses as you ought, and stop sinning; for there are some who are ignorant
of God[d]—I say this to your shame.[e]

The Resurrection Body

35But someone may ask,[f] "How are the
dead raised? With what kind of body will
they come?"[g] **36**How foolish![h] What you
sow does not come to life unless it dies.[i]
37When you sow, you do not plant the
body that will be, but just a seed, perhaps
of wheat or of something else. **38**But God
gives it a body as he has determined, and
to each kind of seed he gives its own
body.[j] **39**All flesh is not the same: Men
have one kind of flesh, animals have another, birds another and fish another.
40There are also heavenly bodies and
there are earthly bodies; but the splendor
of the heavenly bodies is one kind, and the
splendor of the earthly bodies is another.
41The sun has one kind of splendor,[k] the
moon another and the stars another;[l] and
star differs from star in splendor.

42So will it be[m] with the resurrection of
the dead.[n] The body that is sown is perishable, it is raised imperishable;[o] **43**it is
sown in dishonor, it is raised in glory;[p] it
is sown in weakness, it is raised in power;

q *27* Psalm 8:6 r *32* Isaiah 22:13

15:10 [t]2Co 11:23; Col 1:29 [u]S Php 2:13
15:11 [v]Gal 2:6
15:12 [w]ver 4 [x]S Jn 11:24 [y]Ac 17:32; 23:8; 2Ti 2:18
15:14 [z]1Th 4:14
15:15 [a]S Ac 2:24
15:17 [b]S Ro 4:25
15:18 [c]ver 6,20; S Mt 9:24
15:19 [d]S 1Co 4:9
15:20 [e]1Pe 1:3 [f]ver 23; S Ac 26:23 [g]ver 6, 18; S Mt 9:24
15:21 [h]S Ro 5:12 [i]ver 12
15:22 [j]Ro 5:14-18; S 1Co 6:14
15:23 [k]ver 20 [l]ver 52; S 1Th 2:19 [m]S 1Co 3:23
15:24 [n]Da 2:44; 7:14,27; 2Pe 1:11 [o]Ro 8:38
15:25 [p]Isa 9:7; 52:7 [q]ver 27; S Mt 22:44
15:26 [r]2Ti 1:10; Rev 20:14; 21:4
15:27 [s]ver 25; Ps 8:6; S Mt 22:44 [t]S Mt 28:18
15:28 [u]Php 3:21 [v]1Co 3:23
15:30 [w]2Co 11:26
15:31 [x]S Ro 8:36
15:32 [y]2Co 1:8 [z]S Ac 18:19 [a]Isa 22:13; Lk 12:19
15:33 [b]S 1Co 6:9 [c]Pr 22:24,25
15:34 [d]S Gal 4:8 [e]S 1Co 4:14
15:35 [f]Ro 9:19 [g]Eze 37:3
15:36 [h]Lk 11:40; 12:20 [i]Jn 12:24
15:38 [j]Ge 1:11
15:41 [k]Ps 19:4-6 [l]Ps 8:1,3
15:42 [m]Da 12:3; Mt 13:43 [n]ver 12 [o]ver 50,53,54
15:43 [p]Php 3:21; Col 3:4

15:17 IF CHRIST HAS NOT BEEN RAISED. Some were denying Christ's bodily resurrection (v. 12). In response, Paul states that if Christ has not been raised, then there is no deliverance from sin. Clearly those who deny the objective reality of the resurrection of Christ are denying the Christian faith altogether. They are false witnesses who speak against God and his Word. Their faith is worthless; they are not, therefore, authentic Christians.

15:29 BAPTIZED FOR THE DEAD. These words (meaning "baptized because of the dead") may refer to those who became Christians and were baptized because they wanted to be reunited with their departed Christian friends or family members in the life to come. Doing so would be useless "if the dead are not raised" at all (vv. 16–17).

15:35–54 HOW ARE THE DEAD RAISED? Paul begins here a discussion of the doctrine of what the resurrection of the dead involves. For comments on these verses, see article on THE RESURRECTION OF THE BODY, p. 357.

THE RESURRECTION OF THE BODY

1Co 15:35 "But someone may ask, 'How are the dead raised? With what kind of body will they come?' "

The resurrection of the body is an essential doctrine in Scripture. It refers to God's raising of a body from the dead and reuniting it with the person's soul and spirit, from which it was separated during the intermediate state.

(1) The Bible reveals at least three reasons why the resurrection of the body is necessary. (a) The body is essential to the total human personality; humans are incomplete without a body. Thus, the redemption Christ offers applies to the whole person, including the body (Ro 8:18–25). (b) The body is the temple of the Holy Spirit (1Co 6:19); it will become once more a temple of the Spirit at the resurrection. (c) To undo the result of sin at all levels, humanity's final enemy (death of the body) must be conquered through the resurrection (1Co 15:26).

(2) Both the OT (compare Ge 22:1–14 with Heb 11:17–19; Ps 16:10 with Ac 2:24ff; cf. Job 19:25–27; Isa 26:19; Da 12:2; Hos 13:14) and the NT (Lk 14:13–14; 20:35–36; Jn 5:21,28–29; 6:39–40,44,54; 1Co 15:22–23; Php 3:11; 1Th 4:14–16; Rev 20:4–6,13) teach the future bodily resurrection.

(3) Our bodily resurrection is guaranteed by the fact of Christ's resurrection (see Mt 28:6, note; Ac 17:31; 1Co 15:12,20–23).

(4) In general terms, the believer's resurrected body will be like the Lord's own resurrected body (Ro 8:29; 1Co 15:20,42–44,49; Php 3:20–21; 1Jn 3:2). More specifically, the resurrected body will be: (a) a body possessing continuity and identity with the body of this life and therefore recognizable (Lk 16:19–31); (b) a body changed into a heavenly body adapted for the new heaven and new earth (1Co 15:42–44,47–48; Rev 21:1); (c) an imperishable body, free from decay and death (1Co 15:42); (d) a glorified body, like Christ's (1Co 15:43; Php 3:20–21); (e) a powerful body not subject to disease or weakness (1Co 15:43); (f) a spiritual (i.e., not natural, but supernatural) body, not bound by the laws of nature (Lk 24:31; Jn 20:19; 1Co 15:44); (g) a body capable of eating and drinking (Lk 14:15; 22:14–18,30; 24:43).

(5) When believers receive their new bodies, they put on immortality (1Co 15:53). Scripture indicates at least three purposes for this: (a) so that believers may become all that God intended for humans at creation (cf. 1Co 2:9); (b) so that believers may come to know God in the full way he wants them to know him (Jn 17:3); (c) so that God may express his love to his children as he desires (Jn 3:16; Eph 2:7; 1Jn 4:8–16).

(6) The faithful who are still alive at Christ's return for his followers will experience the same bodily transformation as those who have died in Christ prior to the day of resurrection (1Co 15:51–53). They will be given new bodies identical to the bodies given to those raised from the dead at that time. They will never experience physical death (see article on THE RAPTURE, p. 440).

(7) Jesus speaks of a resurrection of life for the believer and a resurrection of judgment for the wicked (Jn 5:28–29).

44it is sown a natural body, it is raised a
spiritual body.[q]
If there is a natural body, there is also
a spiritual body. **45**So it is written: "The
first man Adam became a living being"[s];[r]
the last Adam,[s] a life-giving spirit.[t]
46The spiritual did not come first, but the
natural, and after that the spiritual.[u]
47The first man was of the dust of the
earth,[v] the second man from heaven.[w]
48As was the earthly man, so are those
who are of the earth; and as is the man
from heaven, so also are those who are
of heaven.[x] **49**And just as we have borne
the likeness of the earthly man,[y] so shall
we[t] bear the likeness of the man from
heaven.[z]
50I declare to you, brothers, that flesh
and blood[a] cannot inherit the kingdom of
God,[b] nor does the perishable inherit the
imperishable.[c] **51**Listen, I tell you a mystery:[d] We will not all sleep,[e] but we will
all be changed[f]— **52**in a flash, in the
twinkling of an eye, at the last trumpet.
For the trumpet will sound,[g] the dead[h]
will be raised imperishable, and we will be
changed. **53**For the perishable[i] must
clothe itself with the imperishable,[j] and
the mortal with immortality. **54**When the
perishable has been clothed with the imperishable, and the mortal with immortality, then the saying that is written will
come true: "Death has been swallowed up
in victory."[u][k]

55"Where, O death, is your victory?
Where, O death, is your sting?"[v][l]

56The sting of death is sin,[m] and the power of sin is the law.[n] **57**But thanks be to
God![o] He gives us the victory through our
Lord Jesus Christ.[p]
58Therefore, my dear brothers, stand
firm. Let nothing move you. Always give
yourselves fully to the work of the Lord,[q]
because you know that your labor in the
Lord is not in vain.[r]

15:44 [q]ver 50
15:45 [r]Ge 2:7 [s]Ro 5:14 [t]Jn 5:21; 6:57,58; Ro 8:2
15:46 [u]ver 44
15:47 [v]Ge 2:7; 3:19; Ps 90:3 [w]Jn 3:13,31
15:48 [x]Php 3:20, 21
15:49 [y]Ge 5:3 [z]S Ro 8:29
15:50 [a]Eph 6:12; Heb 2:14 [b]S Mt 25:34 [c]ver 42,53,54
15:51 [d]1Co 13:2; 14:2 [e]S Mt 9:24 [f]2Co 5:4; Php 3:21
15:52 [g]S Mt 24:31 [h]Jn 5:25
15:53 [i]ver 42,50, 54 [j]2Co 5:2,4
15:54 [k]Isa 25:8; Heb 2:14; Rev 20:14
15:55 [l]Hos 13:14
15:56 [m]S Ro 5:12 [n]S Ro 4:15
15:57 [o]S 2Co 2:14 [p]Ro 8:37; Heb 2:14,15
15:58 [q]1Co 16:10 [r]Isa 65:23

16:1 [s]S Ac 24:17 [t]S Ac 9:13 [u]S Ac 16:6
16:2 [v]Ac 20:7 [w]2Co 9:4,5
16:3 [x]2Co 3:1; 8:18,19
16:5 [y]S 1Co 4:19 [z]S Ac 16:9
16:6 [a]Ro 15:24; Tit 3:13
16:7 [b]S Ac 18:21
16:8 [c]S Ac 18:19 [d]S Ac 2:1
16:9 [e]S Ac 14:27
16:10 [f]S Ac 16:1 [g]1Co 15:58
16:11 [h]1Ti 4:12 [i]2Co 1:16; 3Jn 6 [j]S Ac 15:33
16:12 [k]S Ac 18:24
16:13 [l]1Co 1:8; 2Co 1:21; Gal 5:1; Php 1:27; 1Th 3:8; S Tit 1:9 [m]S Eph 6:10
16:14 [n]1Co 14:1

The Collection for God's People

16 Now about the collection[s] for
God's people:[t] Do what I told the
Galatian[u] churches to do. **2**On the first
day of every week,[v] each one of you
should set aside a sum of money in keeping with his income, saving it up, so that
when I come no collections will have to be
made.[w] **3**Then, when I arrive, I will give
letters of introduction to the men you approve[x] and send them with your gift to
Jerusalem. **4**If it seems advisable for me to
go also, they will accompany me.

Personal Requests

5After I go through Macedonia, I will
come to you[y]—for I will be going through
Macedonia.[z] **6**Perhaps I will stay with you
awhile, or even spend the winter, so that
you can help me on my journey,[a] wherever I go. **7**I do not want to see you now
and make only a passing visit; I hope to
spend some time with you, if the Lord permits.[b] **8**But I will stay on at Ephesus[c]
until Pentecost,[d] **9**because a great door
for effective work has opened to me,[e] and
there are many who oppose me.
10If Timothy[f] comes, see to it that he
has nothing to fear while he is with you,
for he is carrying on the work of the
Lord,[g] just as I am. **11**No one, then,
should refuse to accept him.[h] Send him on
his way[i] in peace[j] so that he may return
to me. I am expecting him along with the
brothers.
12Now about our brother Apollos:[k] I
strongly urged him to go to you with the
brothers. He was quite unwilling to go
now, but he will go when he has the opportunity.
13Be on your guard; stand firm[l] in the
faith; be men of courage; be strong.[m] **14**Do
everything in love.[n]

[s] *45* Gen. 2:7 [t] *49* Some early manuscripts *so let us* [u] *54* Isaiah 25:8 [v] *55* Hosea 13:14

15:51 A MYSTERY. The mystery Paul declares is the truth that when Jesus returns from heaven for his church, those believers who are alive will have their bodies immediately transformed and made imperishable and immortal (see Jn 14:3, note; see article on THE RAPTURE, p. 440).

15:51 WE WILL NOT ALL SLEEP. Paul's use of "we" indicates he held to the NT perspective that Christ could come for the faithful of his churches in Paul's own generation. Although Christ did not return in Paul's lifetime, Paul did not err in believing as he did, for he knew that Christ could come at any time. All who look for Christ to return during their lifetime share the NT viewpoint. The words of Jesus and the entire NT urge every believer to believe it is the last hour and to live in the hope that Christ might return in his or her lifetime (cf. 1:7–8; Ro 13:12; Php 3:20; 1Th 1:10; 4:15–17; Tit 2:13; Jas 5:8–9; 1Jn 2:18,28; Rev 22:7,12,20; see Mt 24:42,44, notes; Lk 12:35, note). Thus, those who do not look for him in their lifetime are not living according to the apostolic pattern.

15:52 WE WILL BE CHANGED. See article on THE RESURRECTION OF THE BODY, p. 357.

16:1 NOW ABOUT THE COLLECTION. In ch. 16 Paul gives direction for the collection for the poor believers at Jerusalem, describes his future plans and speaks about his fellow workers in the Lord.

15You know that the household of
Stephanas[o] were the first converts[p] in
Achaia,[q] and they have devoted themselves to the service[r] of the saints.[s] I
urge you, brothers, **16**to submit[t] to such
as these and to everyone who joins in the
work, and labors at it. **17**I was glad when
Stephanas, Fortunatus and Achaicus arrived, because they have supplied what
was lacking from you.[u] **18**For they refreshed[v] my spirit and yours also. Such
men deserve recognition.[w]

Final Greetings

19The churches in the province of Asia[x]
send you greetings. Aquila and Priscilla[w][y] greet you warmly in the Lord, and so
does the church that meets at their
house.[z] **20**All the brothers here send you
greetings. Greet one another with a holy
kiss.[a]

21I, Paul, write this greeting in my own
hand.[b]

22If anyone does not love the Lord[c]—a
curse[d] be on him. Come, O Lord[x]![e]

23The grace of the Lord Jesus be with
you.[f]

24My love to all of you in Christ Jesus.
Amen.[y]

16:15 [o] 1Co 1:16 [p] Ro 16:5 [q] S Ac 18:12 [r] S Ac 24:17 [s] S Ac 9:13 **16:16** [t] 1Th 5:12; Heb 13:17 **16:17** [u] 2Co 11:9; Php 2:30 **16:18** [v] Ro 15:32; Phm 7 [w] Php 2:29 **16:19** [x] S Ac 2:9 [y] S Ac 18:2 [z] S Ro 16:5 **16:20** [a] S Ro 16:16 **16:21** [b] Gal 6:11; Col 4:18; 2Th 3:17; Phm 19 **16:22** [c] Eph 6:24 [d] Ro 9:3 [e] Rev 22:20 **16:23** [f] S Ro 16:20

w *19* Greek *Prisca,* a variant of *Priscilla*
x *22* In Aramaic the expression *Come, O Lord* is *Marana tha.*
y *24* Some manuscripts do not have *Amen.*

16:22 A CURSE. Paul ends this letter by reminding all professing believers that to claim to be believers, yet not to love the Lord, is to be accursed or doomed. To "not love the Lord" means to fail to have a heartfelt love for him, to disobey him (Jn 14:21) and to distort the apostolic gospel of NT revelation (see Gal 1:9, note). To be accursed means being excluded from the true spiritual church on earth and finally from the heavenly kingdom of the age to come. Paul wants his readers to understand that the ultimate test of Christian discipleship is a personal, heartfelt loyalty to the Lord Jesus Christ (cf. Ro 10:9).

16:22 COME, O LORD! The Aramaic expression *marana tha* was probably used as a prayer or greeting among Christians. The early church was constantly praying that Christ might return soon. Christians are those who long for his appearing (see 2Ti 4:8) and express this longing in word and deed (1Th 1:10; Rev 22:20).

2 CORINTHIANS

Outline

Introduction (1:1–11)

- I. Paul's Defense for the Sake of the Loyal Majority (1:12—7:16)
  - A. Denial That He Has Been Fickle (1:12–22)
  - B. Explanation of His Change in Travel Plans (1:23—2:17)
  - C. Clarification Concerning the Character of His Ministry (3:1—6:10)
    1. It Is in the Service of a New Covenant (3:1–18)
    2. It Is in Openness and Truth (4:1–6)
    3. It Is in Personal Suffering (4:7—5:10)
    4. It Is in Compassionate Dedication (5:11—6:10)
  - D. Personal Appeal to and Affectionate Regard for the Corinthians (6:11—7:16)
- II. The Collection for Needy Christians in Jerusalem (8:1—9:15)
  - A. The Grace of Christian Generosity (8:1–15)
  - B. Titus to Head Up Arrangements for the Collection (8:16–24)
  - C. An Appeal for a Ready Response (9:1–5)
  - D. An Appeal for a Generous Response (9:6–15)
- III. Paul's Reply to the Rebellious Minority (10:1—13:10)
  - A. An Answer to Charges of Cowardice and Weakness (10:1–18)
  - B. A Reluctant Self-defense of His Apostleship (11:1—12:18)
    1. Apology for Boastful Tone (11:1–15)
    2. Affirms He Is Not Inferior to the Judaizers (11:16—12:10)
    3. Legitimate Claims to Apostleship (12:11–18)
  - C. An Upcoming Third Visit Mentioned as a Warning (12:19—13:10)
    1. Apprehensiveness Concerning the Corinthians (12:19–21)
    2. Determination to Be Firm (13:1–10)

Conclusion (13:11–14)

Author: Paul

Theme: Glory Through Suffering

Date: A.D. 55/56

Background

Paul wrote this letter to the church at Corinth and to believers throughout Achaia (1:1), identifying himself twice by name (1:1; 10:1). Having founded the Corinthian church during his second missionary journey, Paul and the Corinthians had frequent contacts thereafter because of problems in the church (see Introduction to 1 Corinthians).

The sequence of these contacts and the setting for writing 2 Corinthians are as follows. (1) After some initial contacts and correspondence between Paul and the church (e.g., 1Co 1:11; 5:9; 7:1), Paul wrote 1 Corinthians from Ephesus (spring A.D. 55 or 56). (2) Next, Paul made a trip across the Aegean Sea to Corinth to deal with further problems in the church. This visit between 1 and 2 Corinthians (cf. 13:1–2) was a painful one for Paul and the congregation (2:1–2). (3) After this painful visit, reports reached Paul at Ephesus that antagonists were still attacking him and his apostolic authority at Corinth, in hopes of persuading a portion of the church to reject Paul. (4) In response to this report, Paul wrote 2 Corinthians from Macedonia (fall A.D. 55 or 56).

(5) Shortly thereafter Paul traveled to Corinth again (13:1), where he remained for about three months (cf. Ac 20:1–3a), and from there he wrote Romans.

Purpose

Paul wrote this letter to address three categories of people at Corinth. (1) First, he wrote to encourage the majority at Corinth who remained faithful to him as their spiritual father. (2) He wrote to challenge and expose the false apostles who continued to speak against him personally, hoping to undermine his authority and apostleship and to distort his message. (3) He also wrote to reprimand the minority in the church who were being influenced by Paul's opponents and who were resisting his authority and correction. Paul reaffirmed his integrity and apostolic authority, clarified his motives and warned them against further rebellion. 2 Corinthians served to prepare the church as a whole for his impending visit.

Survey

2 Corinthians has three main divisions. (1) In the first (chs. 1–7), Paul begins by thanking God for his comfort in the midst of suffering for the gospel, commends the Corinthians for disciplining a serious offender and defends his integrity in changing his travel plans. In 3:1—6:10 Paul shares the most extensive insight in the NT on the true character of Christian ministry. He stresses the importance of separation from the world (6:11—7:1) and expresses joy in learning from Titus of the repentance of many in the Corinthian church who had previously rebelled against his authority (ch. 7).

(2) In chs. 8 and 9, Paul exhorts the Corinthians to match the wholehearted Christian generosity of the Macedonians in contributing to the offering he was raising for the distressed Christians at Jerusalem.

(3) The letter's tone changes in chs. 10–13. Here Paul defends his apostleship by setting forth his calling, qualifications and sufferings as a true apostle. By this Paul hopes the Corinthians will discern the false apostles among them and thereby be spared further discipline when he arrives again in person. Paul concludes 2 Corinthians with the only trinitarian benediction in the NT (13:14).

Special Features

Four major features characterize this letter. (1) It is the most autobiographical of all Paul's letters. His many personal references are made with transparent humility, apology and even embarrassment, but out of necessity because of the situation at Corinth. (2) It surpasses all other Pauline letters in revealing the intensity and depth of Paul's love and concern for his spiritual children. (3) It contains the NT's most developed theology about Christian suffering (1:3–11; 4:7–18; 6:3–10; 11:23–30; 12:1–10) and about Christian giving (chs. 8–9). (4) Key terms, such as weakness, grief, tears, danger, distress, suffering, comfort, boasting, truth, ministry and glory, underscore the unique character of this letter.

Reading 2 Corinthians

In order to read the entire New Testament in one year, the book of 2 Corinthians should be read in 12 days, according to the following schedule:
☐ 1:1—2:4 ☐ 2:5—3:6 ☐ 3:7—4:18 ☐ 5:1—6:2 ☐ 6:3—7:1 ☐ 7:2–16 ☐ 8–9 ☐ 10 ☐ 11:1–15 ☐ 11:16–33 ☐ 12 ☐ 13

NOTES

1 Paul, an apostle[a] of Christ Jesus by
the will of God,[b] and Timothy[c] our
brother,

To the church of God[d] in Corinth,[e] together with all the saints throughout
Achaia:[f]

2Grace and peace to you from God our
Father and the Lord Jesus Christ.[g]

The God of All Comfort

3Praise be to the God and Father of our
Lord Jesus Christ,[h] the Father of compassion and the God of all comfort, **4**who comforts us[i] in all our troubles, so that we
can comfort those in any trouble with the
comfort we ourselves have received from
God. **5**For just as the sufferings of Christ
flow over into our lives,[j] so also through
Christ our comfort overflows. **6**If we are
distressed, it is for your comfort and salvation;[k] if we are comforted, it is for your
comfort, which produces in you patient
endurance of the same sufferings we suffer. **7**And our hope for you is firm, because
we know that just as you share in our
sufferings,[l] so also you share in our comfort.

8We do not want you to be unin-
formed,[m] brothers, about the hardships
we suffered[n] in the province of Asia.[o] We
were under great pressure, far beyond our
ability to endure, so that we despaired
even of life. **9**Indeed, in our hearts we felt
the sentence of death. But this happened
that we might not rely on ourselves but on
God,[p] who raises the dead.[q] **10**He has delivered us from such a deadly peril,[r] and
he will deliver us. On him we have set our
hope[s] that he will continue to deliver us,
11as you help us by your prayers.[t] Then
many will give thanks[u] on our[a] behalf for
the gracious favor granted us in answer to
the prayers of many.

Paul's Change of Plans

12Now this is our boast: Our conscience[v] testifies that we have conducted
ourselves in the world, and especially in
our relations with you, in the holiness[w]
and sincerity[x] that are from God. We have
done so not according to worldly wisdom[y]
but according to God's grace. **13**For we do
not write you anything you cannot read or
understand. And I hope that, **14**as you
have understood us in part, you will come
to understand fully that you can boast of
us just as we will boast of you in the day
of the Lord Jesus.[z]

15Because I was confident of this, I
planned to visit you[a] first so that you
might benefit twice.[b] **16**I planned to visit
you on my way[c] to Macedonia[d] and to
come back to you from Macedonia, and
then to have you send me on my way[e] to
Judea.[f] **17**When I planned this, did I do it
lightly? Or do I make my plans in a worldly manner[g] so that in the same breath I
say, "Yes, yes" and "No, no"?

18But as surely as God is faithful,[h] our

1:1 [a]S 1Co 1:1 [b]1Co 1:1; Eph 1:1; Col 1:1; 2Ti 1:1 [c]S Ac 16:1 [d]S 1Co 10:32 [e]S Ac 18:1 [f]S Ac 18:12
1:2 [g]S Ro 1:7
1:3 [h]Eph 1:3; 1Pe 1:3
1:4 [i]Isa 49:13; 51:12; 66:13; 2Co 7:6,7,13
1:5 [j]Ro 8:17; 2Co 4:10; Gal 6:17; Php 3:10; Col 1:24; 1Pe 4:13
1:6 [k]2Co 4:15
1:7 [l]S ver 5
1:8 [m]S Ro 11:25 [n]1Co 15:32 [o]S Ac 2:9
1:9 [p]Jer 17:5,7 [q]S Jn 5:21
1:10 [r]S Ro 15:31 [s]1Ti 4:10
1:11 [t]Ro 15:30; Php 1:19 [u]2Co 4:15; 9:11
1:12 [v]S Ac 23:1 [w]1Th 2:10 [x]2Co 2:17 [y]1Co 1:17; 2:1,4, 13
1:14 [z]S 1Co 1:8
1:15 [a]S 1Co 4:19 [b]Ro 1:11,13; 15:29
1:16 [c]1Co 16:5-7 [d]S Ac 16:9 [e]1Co 16:11; 3Jn 6 [f]Ac 19:21
1:17 [g]2Co 10:2,3; 11:18
1:18 [h]S 1Co 1:9

[a] *11* Many manuscripts *your*

1:4 COMFORTS US IN ALL OUR TROUBLES. The word "comfort" (Gk *paraklēsis*) means to stand beside a person, encouraging and helping him or her in a time of trouble. God supremely fulfills this role, for he sends to his children the Holy Spirit to comfort them (see Jn 14:16, note). Paul has learned in his many troubles that no suffering, however severe, can separate believers from the care and compassion of their heavenly Father (Ro 8:35–39). God occasionally permits troubles in our lives in order that we, having experienced his comfort, may comfort others in their troubles.

1:5 SUFFERINGS . . . COMFORT. Throughout this letter, Paul emphasizes that the Christian life includes both suffering (a sharing or partnership with Christ in suffering) and the comfort of Christ. That is, in this age Christ suffers with and for his people because of the tragedy of sin (cf. Mt 25:42–45; Ro 8:22–26). Our suffering is not necessarily a suffering because of disobedience, but is often a suffering at the hands of Satan, the world and false believers as we share in the cause of Christ.

1:8–10 WE DESPAIRED EVEN OF LIFE. A faithful believer, living in obedient fellowship with Christ and loved by him, may yet undergo experiences that involve danger, fear and despair, and may encounter circumstances that weigh one down beyond the human power of endurance. (1) When severe troubles occur in our lives, we need not feel that God has forsaken us or has stopped loving us. Rather, we must remind ourselves that these very things happened to God's faithful servants of NT times. (2) God allows these desperate trials so that Christ might come near and, as we look to him in faith, give us the grace to bring us to victory (2:14; 12:7–10; 13:4).

1:11 AS YOU HELP US BY YOUR PRAYERS. An indisputable Biblical principle is that our prayers for others will release God's power and activity in others' lives. Because of this, we should be encouraged to intercede for those in need (cf. Ro 1:9; Eph 1:16; Php 1:3; Col 1:3; 1Th 1:2).

1:12 THIS IS OUR BOAST. Paul's basis for rejoicing and boasting was the sincerity and integrity of his behavior. He had determined that for his entire Christian life he would remain faithful to his Lord, refuse to conform to the world that crucified his Savior, and persevere in holiness until God called him home (Ro 12:1–2). In the eternal age to come, our greatest joy will be the consciousness that we have lived our lives in "holiness and sincerity" for Christ our Savior.

message to you is not “Yes” and “No.”
19For the Son of God,[i] Jesus Christ, who
was preached among you by me and Silas[b][j] and Timothy,[k] was not “Yes” and
“No,” but in him it has always[l] been
“Yes.” **20**For no matter how many promises[m] God has made, they are “Yes” in
Christ. And so through him the “Amen”[n]
is spoken by us to the glory of God.[o]
21Now it is God who makes both us and
you stand firm[p] in Christ. He anointed[q]
us, **22**set his seal[r] of ownership on us, and
put his Spirit in our hearts as a deposit,
guaranteeing what is to come.[s]
23I call God as my witness[t] that it was
in order to spare you[u] that I did not return
to Corinth. **24**Not that we lord it over[v]
your faith, but we work with you for your
joy, because it is by faith you stand firm.[w]

2 **1**So I made up my mind that I would
not make another painful visit to
you.[x] **2**For if I grieve you,[y] who is left to
make me glad but you whom I have
grieved? **3**I wrote as I did[z] so that when
I came I should not be distressed[a] by
those who ought to make me rejoice. I had
confidence[b] in all of you, that you would
all share my joy. **4**For I wrote you[c] out of
great distress and anguish of heart and
with many tears, not to grieve you but to
let you know the depth of my love for you.

1:19 [i] S Mt 4:3 [j] S Ac 15:22 [k] S Ac 16:1 [l] Heb 13:8
1:20 [m] Ro 15:8 [n] S 1Co 14:16 [o] Ro 15:9
1:21 [p] S 1Co 16:13 [q] 1Jn 2:20,27
1:22 [r] Ge 38:18; Eze 9:4; Hag 2:23 [s] S 2Co 5:5
1:23 [t] S Ro 1:9 [u] 1Co 4:21; 2Co 2:1,3; 13:2,10
1:24 [v] 1Pe 5:3 [w] Ro 11:20; 1Co 15:1
2:1 [x] S 2Co 1:23
2:2 [y] 2Co 7:8
2:3 [z] ver 4,9; 2Co 7:8,12 [a] 2Co 12:21 [b] 2Co 7:16; 8:22; Gal 5:10; 2Th 3:4; Phm 21
2:4 [c] ver 3,9; 2Co 7:8,12
2:5 [d] 1Co 5:1,2
2:6 [e] 1Co 5:4,5; 2Co 7:11
2:7 [f] Gal 6:1; Eph 4:32; Col 3:13
2:9 [g] ver 3,4; 2Co 7:8,12 [h] 2Co 7:15; 10:6
2:11 [i] S Mt 4:10 [j] Lk 22:31; 2Co 4:4; 1Pe 5:8,9
2:12 [k] S Ac 16:8 [l] S Ro 1:1; 2Co 4:3,4; 8:18; 9:13; 1Th 3:2 [m] S Ac 14:27
2:13 [n] 2Co 7:5 [o] 2Co 7:6,13; 8:6,

Forgiveness for the Sinner

5If anyone has caused grief,[d] he has
not so much grieved me as he has grieved
all of you, to some extent—not to put it
too severely. **6**The punishment[e] inflicted
on him by the majority is sufficient for
him. **7**Now instead, you ought to forgive
and comfort him,[f] so that he will not be
overwhelmed by excessive sorrow. **8**I urge
you, therefore, to reaffirm your love for
him. **9**The reason I wrote you[g] was to see
if you would stand the test and be obedient in everything.[h] **10**If you forgive anyone, I also forgive him. And what I have
forgiven—if there was anything to forgive
—I have forgiven in the sight of Christ for
your sake, **11**in order that Satan[i] might
not outwit us. For we are not unaware of
his schemes.[j]

Ministers of the New Covenant

12Now when I went to Troas[k] to preach
the gospel of Christ[l] and found that the
Lord had opened a door[m] for me, **13**I still
had no peace of mind,[n] because I did not
find my brother Titus[o] there. So I said

16,23; 12:18; Gal 2:1,3; Tit 1:4

[b] *19* Greek *Silvanus*, a variant of *Silas*

1:20 AMEN. The concluding “Amen” of the Christian’s prayer and proclamation expresses confidence in God’s love and faithfulness and the certainty of his promises. It is the voice of faith, reaffirming and identifying with the truth of Christ’s unshakable gospel. In Rev 3:14 the Lord Jesus is called the “Amen.”

1:22 SPIRIT IN OUR HEARTS AS A DEPOSIT. Paul outlines four aspects of God’s work in believers through the Spirit. (1) The Holy Spirit establishes believers and helps them persevere in their life of faith (see 1Pe 1:5, note).

(2) The Spirit anoints believers in order to give them power to witness (see Ac 1:8, notes), to perform the works of Christ (Isa 61:1; Mt 10:19–20; Jn 14:12; Ac 10:38) and to know the truth (1Jn 2:20).

(3) The Spirit is the official seal of God’s ownership, marking believers as his own property and producing godly character within their human personalities (cf. 3:18; Gal 5:22; Eph 1:13).

(4) The Spirit is an indwelling “deposit,” i.e., a guarantee and a first installment to believers that a greater life with Christ will come in the future (5:5; Ro 8:23; see Eph 1:13–14, note).

2:4 OUT OF GREAT DISTRESS AND ANGUISH OF HEART. One of the essential qualifications of the Christian minister is a loving and sensitive heart, one that breaks into tears when it sees God’s people drifting from the path of righteousness into sin and error (cf. Ps 126:5–6; Mk 9:24, note; see Lk 19:41, note; Jn 11:35, note; Ac 20:19, note).

2:6 THE PUNISHMENT . . . IS SUFFICIENT. From this passage we gain insight into the NT pattern of discipline toward a member of the church who commits a serious offense (e.g., immorality, adultery, etc.; see 1Co 5). (1) In order to defend the integrity of Christ’s church (cf. 1Co 5:1–2), the church must punish the offender with a punishment sufficient to produce spiritual reformation, yet not so harsh as to deny hope of divine mercy and reentry into the fellowship (v. 7). Note that forgiveness and love were not given unconditionally to the offender.

(2) After sufficient punishment, if the offender is repentant and sorrowful, he or she must be forgiven and comforted in a spirit of love (vv. 7–8).

(3) The offender’s punishment and restoration must be done in a spirit of gentleness (Gal 6:1), sorrow, earnestness, indignation, fear of God and his Word, zeal for God’s reputation, and readiness to see justice done by bringing the guilty to accountability (see 7:11; cf. 1Co 5:5,13).

Many churches today have abandoned NT church discipline. They advocate tolerance of sin, call for unconditional forgiveness, offer cheap grace and refuse to hear what the Spirit says to the churches (see Rev 2–3). As a result, sin is taken lightly and the fear of God is absent from their churches (see Mt 18:15, note on church discipline).

2:11 SATAN MIGHT NOT OUTWIT US. One of our key defenses against Satan’s attack is awareness of the enemy’s continual effort to gain an advantage over us and lead us away from devotion to Christ (see Eph 6:11, note).

good-by to them and went on to Macedonia.[p]
14But thanks be to God,[q] who always
leads us in triumphal procession in Christ
and through us spreads everywhere the
fragrance[r] of the knowledge[s] of him.
15For we are to God the aroma[t] of Christ
among those who are being saved and
those who are perishing.[u] **16**To the one we
are the smell of death;[v] to the other, the
fragrance of life. And who is equal to such
a task?[w] **17**Unlike so many, we do not peddle the word of God for profit.[x] On the
contrary, in Christ we speak before God
with sincerity,[y] like men sent from God.[z]

3 Are we beginning to commend ourselves[a] again? Or do we need, like
some people, letters of recommendation[b]
to you or from you? **2**You yourselves are
our letter, written on our hearts, known
and read by everybody.[c] **3**You show that
you are a letter from Christ, the result of
our ministry, written not with ink but with
the Spirit of the living God,[d] not on tablets of stone[e] but on tablets of human
hearts.[f]
4Such confidence[g] as this is ours
through Christ before God. **5**Not that we
are competent in ourselves[h] to claim anything for ourselves, but our competence
comes from God.[i] **6**He has made us competent as ministers of a new covenant[j]—
not of the letter[k] but of the Spirit; for the
letter kills, but the Spirit gives life.[l]

2:13 [p]S Ac 16:9
2:14 [q]Ro 6:17; 7:25; 1Co 15:57; 2Co 9:15 [r]Eze 20:41; Eph 5:2; Php 4:18 [s]S 2Co 8:7
2:15 [t]S ver 14; Ge 8:21; Ex 29:18; Nu 15:3 [u]S 1Co 1:18
2:16 [v]S Lk 2:34; Jn 3:36 [w]2Co 3:5, 6
2:17 [x]S Ac 20:33; 2Co 4:2; 1Th 2:5 [y]1Co 5:8 [z]2Co 1:12; 12:19
3:1 [a]Ro 16:1; 2Co 5:12; 10:12, 18; 12:11 [b]Ac 18:27; Ro 16:1; 1Co 16:3
3:2 [c]1Co 9:2
3:3 [d]S Mt 16:16 [e]ver 7; Ex 24:12; 31:18; 32:15,16 [f]Pr 3:3; 7:3; Jer 31:33; Eze 36:26
3:4 [g]S Eph 3:12
3:5 [h]2Co 2:16 [i]1Co 15:10
3:6 [j]S Lk 22:20 [k]Ro 2:29; 7:6 [l]Jn 6:63
3:7 [m]ver 9; S Ro 4:15 [n]ver 13; Ex 34:29-35; Isa 42:21
3:9 [o]ver 7; Dt 27:26 [p]Ro 1:17; 3:21,22
3:12 [q]Ro 5:4,5; 8:24,25 [r]S Ac 4:29
3:13 [s]ver 7; Ex 34:33
3:14 [t]Ro 11:7,8; 2Co 4:4 [u]Ac 13:15; 15:21

The Glory of the New Covenant

7Now if the ministry that brought
death,[m] which was engraved in letters on
stone, came with glory, so that the Israelites could not look steadily at the face of
Moses because of its glory,[n] fading
though it was, **8**will not the ministry of the
Spirit be even more glorious? **9**If the ministry that condemns men[o] is glorious,
how much more glorious is the ministry
that brings righteousness![p] **10**For what
was glorious has no glory now in comparison with the surpassing glory. **11**And if
what was fading away came with glory,
how much greater is the glory of that
which lasts!
12Therefore, since we have such a
hope,[q] we are very bold.[r] **13**We are not
like Moses, who would put a veil over his
face[s] to keep the Israelites from gazing at
it while the radiance was fading away.
14But their minds were made dull,[t] for to
this day the same veil remains when the
old covenant[u] is read.[v] It has not been
removed, because only in Christ is it taken
away. **15**Even to this day when Moses is
read, a veil covers their hearts. **16**But
whenever anyone turns to the Lord,[w] the
veil is taken away.[x] **17**Now the Lord is the
Spirit,[y] and where the Spirit of the Lord
is, there is freedom.[z] **18**And we, who with

[v]ver 6 **3:16** [w]Ro 11:23 [x]Ex 34:34; Isa 25:7 **3:17** [y]Isa 61:1, 2; Gal 4:6,7 [z]S Jn 8:32

2:14 TRIUMPHAL PROCESSION IN CHRIST. Paul describes believers as being displayed by God to the world as a triumph and trophy of Christ's redeeming grace. Through this triumphal procession, the knowledge of Christ and the redeemed lives of believers are manifested as a sweet aroma before God and humans. To God it is pleasing; to humans it results in life or death (vv. 15–16).

2:17 PEDDLE THE WORD OF GOD. Paul here describes preachers who were watering down the demands of the gospel to gain money, acceptance and success (cf. 11:4,12–15). They were talented and persuasive, yet secretly insincere. They were greedy for money and prominence (cf. Jn 10:12–13; Php 1:15,17; 1Pe 5:2; 2Pe 2:1–3,14–16).

3:3 WRITTEN ... ON TABLETS OF HUMAN HEARTS. Under the new covenant established by Christ's blood (Mt 26:28), the Holy Spirit writes the law of God, not on tablets of stone as at Sinai (Ex 31:18), but on "tablets of human hearts" (see article on THE OLD COVENANT AND THE NEW COVENANT, p. 500). Believers have God's law in their hearts, and through the power of the Spirit they are able to obey it (cf. Jer 31:33; Eze 11:19). This internal law consists of love for God and other people (cf. Mt 22:34–40; Ro 13:8–10).

3:6 THE LETTER KILLS. It is not the law or written Word of God itself that destroys. Rather, it is the demands of the law without the Spirit's life and power that brings condemnation (vv. 7,9; cf. Jer 31:33; Ro 3:31; see article on FAITH AND GRACE, p. 302). Through salvation in Christ the Spirit gives to the believer spiritual life and power in order to fulfill God's will. With the Holy Spirit the letter no longer kills.

3:8 THE MINISTRY OF THE SPIRIT. Paul calls the new covenant "the ministry of the Spirit." Through faith in Christ one receives the Holy Spirit, is born again (see article on REGENERATION, p. 178) and is promised the baptism in the Spirit (Ac 1:8; 2:4). All the redemptive benefits in Christ come by way of the Spirit. It is he who mediates Christ's presence and all his blessings (v. 9; see article on THE DOCTRINE OF THE HOLY SPIRIT, p. 240).

3:17 THE SPIRIT ... THERE IS FREEDOM. The freedom that comes through Christ (Gal 5:1) is, first and foremost, liberation from the condemnation and slavery of sin (vv. 7–9; Ro 6:6,14; 8:2; Eph 4:22–24; Col 3:9–10) and the whole dominion of Satan (Ac 26:18; Col 1:13; 1Pe 5:8). (1) True liberation begins with the believer's union with Christ (Ac 4:12; Eph 1:7) and his or her receiving the Holy Spirit (see article on REGENERATION, p. 178). Liberation from spiritual bondage is maintained through the Spirit's continued indwelling and through obedience to his direction (Ro 8:1ff; Gal 5:18; cf. Jn 15:1–11).

unveiled faces all reflect[c][a] the Lord's glory,[b] are being transformed into his likeness[c] with ever-increasing glory, which
comes from the Lord, who is the Spirit.

Treasures in Jars of Clay

4 Therefore, since through God's mercy[d] we have this ministry, we do not
lose heart.[e] **2**Rather, we have renounced
secret and shameful ways;[f] we do not use
deception, nor do we distort the word of
God.[g] On the contrary, by setting forth
the truth plainly we commend ourselves
to every man's conscience[h] in the sight of
God. **3**And even if our gospel[i] is veiled,[j]
it is veiled to those who are perishing.[k]
4The god[l] of this age[m] has blinded[n] the
minds of unbelievers, so that they cannot
see the light of the gospel of the glory of
Christ,[o] who is the image of God.[p] **5**For
we do not preach ourselves,[q] but Jesus
Christ as Lord,[r] and ourselves as your
servants[s] for Jesus' sake. **6**For God, who
said, "Let light shine out of darkness,"[d][t]
made his light shine in our hearts[u] to give
us the light of the knowledge of the glory
of God in the face of Christ.[v]

7But we have this treasure in jars of
clay[w] to show that this all-surpassing
power is from God[x] and not from us. **8**We
are hard pressed on every side,[y] but not
crushed; perplexed,[z] but not in despair;
9persecuted,[a] but not abandoned;[b]
struck down, but not destroyed.[c] **10**We
always carry around in our body the death
of Jesus,[d] so that the life of Jesus may
also be revealed in our body.[e] **11**For we
who are alive are always being given over
to death for Jesus' sake,[f] so that his life
may be revealed in our mortal body. **12**So
then, death is at work in us, but life is at
work in you.[g]

13It is written: "I believed; therefore I
have spoken."[e][h] With that same spirit of
faith[i] we also believe and therefore
speak, **14**because we know that the one
who raised the Lord Jesus from the dead[j]
will also raise us with Jesus[k] and present
us with you in his presence.[l] **15**All this is
for your benefit, so that the grace that is
reaching more and more people may
cause thanksgiving[m] to overflow to the
glory of God.

16Therefore we do not lose heart.[n]
Though outwardly we are wasting away,

3:18 [a]1Co 13:12 [b]Jn 17:22,24; 2Co 4:4,6 [c]S Ro 8:29 **4:1** [d]1Co 7:25; 1Ti 1:13,16 [e]ver 16; Ps 18:45; Isa 40:31 **4:2** [f]Ro 6:21; S 1Co 4:5 [g]2Co 2:17; S Heb 4:12 [h]2Co 5:11 **4:3** [i]S 2Co 2:12 [j]2Co 3:14 [k]S 1Co 1:18 **4:4** [l]S Jn 12:31 [m]S 1Co 1:20 [n]2Co 3:14 [o]ver 6 [p]S Jn 14:9 **4:5** [q]1Co 1:13 [r]1Co 1:23 [s]1Co 9:19 **4:6** [t]Ge 1:3; Ps 18:28 [u]2Pe 1:19 [v]ver 4 **4:7** [w]Job 4:19; Isa 64:8; 2Ti 2:20 [x]Jdg 7:2; 1Co 2:5; 2Co 6:7 **4:8** [y]2Co 7:5 [z]Gal 4:20 **4:9** [a]Jn 15:20; Ro 8:35 [b]Heb 13:5 [c]Ps 37:24; Pr 24:16 **4:10** [d]S Ro 6:6; S 2Co 1:5 [e]S Ro 6:5 **4:11** [f]Ro 8:36 **4:12** [g]2Co 13:9 **4:13** [h]Ps 116:10 [i]1Co 12:9 **4:14** [j]S Ac 2:24 [k]1Th 4:14 [l]Eph 5:27; Col 1:22; Jude 24 **4:15** [m]2Co 1:11; 9:11 **4:16** [n]ver 1; Ps 18:45

c *18* Or *contemplate* d *6* Gen. 1:3
e *13* Psalm 116:10

(2) Freedom provided by Christ is not a freedom for believers to do what they want (1Co 10:23–24) but to do what they should (Ro 6:18–23). Spiritual freedom must never be used as a cover-up for evil or as a justification for conflict (Jas 4:1–2; 1Pe 2:16–23). Christian liberation frees believers for service to God (1Th 1:9) and other people (1Co 9:19) in the way of righteousness (Ro 6:18ff). We are now Christ's slaves (Ro 1:1; 1Co 7:22; Php 1:1), living to God by grace (Ro 5:21; 6:10–13).

3:18 REFLECT THE LORD'S GLORY. As we experience Christ's nearness, love, righteousness and power through prayer and the Holy Spirit, it results in our being transformed into his likeness (4:6; cf. Col 1:15; Heb 1:3). In this age the transformation is progressive and partial. But when Christ returns, we will see him face to face, and our transformation will be complete (1Jn 3:2; Rev 22:4).

4:4 GOD OF THIS AGE. The "god of this age" refers to Satan (cf. Jn 12:31; 14:30; 16:11; Eph 2:2; 1Jn 5:19), who holds power over much of the activity of this present age. His rule is, however, temporary and conditional. He continues only by God's permissive will until the end of history (Rev 19:11—20:10). Those who do not submit themselves to Jesus Christ remain under Satan's sway. He blinds their eyes to the truth and glory of the gospel in order that they might not be saved. The solution to this fatal situation is to bind his activity through intercession and to preach the gospel in the power of the Spirit (Ac 1:8) in order that people may hear, understand and choose to believe or disbelieve (vv. 5–6; see Mt 4:10, note on Satan).

4:7 THIS TREASURE IN JARS OF CLAY. Christians are "jars of clay" who at times experience sadness, tears, troubles, perplexities, weakness and fears (cf. 1:4,8–9; 7:5). Yet because of the heavenly "treasure" within them, they are not defeated. Christianity is not the removal of weakness, nor is it merely the manifestation of divine power. Rather, it is the manifestation of divine power through human weakness (12:9). This means (1) that in every affliction we may be more than conquerors by God's power and love (Ro 8:37), and (2) that our weakness, troubles and suffering open us up to Christ's abundant grace and allow his life to be revealed in our bodies (vv. 8–11; cf. 12:7–10).

4:8 HARD PRESSED . . . BUT NOT CRUSHED. If you experience Christ's presence and power in your life, absolutely no trouble, sickness or tragedy will cause your spiritual defeat. When outward circumstances become unbearable and your human resources are exhausted, God's resources are given to expand your faith, hope and strength. Under no circumstances will God forsake his faithful children (Ro 8:35–39; Heb 13:5).

4:11–12 GIVEN OVER TO DEATH. To minister life to another person, we must share Christ's sufferings and experience the working of death in our own lives (v. 12). Self-denial, trouble, disappointment and suffering for Christ's sake will allow our lives to minister grace to others (cf. 11:23–29; Ro 8:36–37; Php 1:29; 1Pe 4:14). Jesus taught this same great principle of brokenness in Jn 12:24–25.

yet inwardly[o] we are being renewed[p] day
by day. 17For our light and momentary
troubles are achieving for us an eternal
glory that far outweighs them all.[q] 18So
we fix our eyes not on what is seen, but
on what is unseen.[r] For what is seen is
temporary, but what is unseen is eternal.

Our Heavenly Dwelling

5 Now we know that if the earthly[s]
tent[t] we live in is destroyed, we have
a building from God, an eternal house in
heaven, not built by human hands. 2Mean-
while we groan,[u] longing to be clothed
with our heavenly dwelling,[v] 3because
when we are clothed, we will not be found
naked. 4For while we are in this tent, we
groan[w] and are burdened, because we do
not wish to be unclothed but to be clothed
with our heavenly dwelling,[x] so that what
is mortal may be swallowed up by life.
5Now it is God who has made us for this
very purpose and has given us the Spirit
as a deposit, guaranteeing what is to
come.[y]
6Therefore we are always confident and
know that as long as we are at home in the
body we are away from the Lord. 7We live
by faith, not by sight.[z] 8We are confident,
I say, and would prefer to be away from
the body and at home with the Lord.[a] 9So
we make it our goal to please him,[b]
whether we are at home in the body or
away from it. 10For we must all appear
before the judgment seat of Christ, that
each one may receive what is due him[c] for
the things done while in the body, whether
good or bad.

The Ministry of Reconciliation

11Since, then, we know what it is to fear
the Lord,[d] we try to persuade men. What
we are is plain to God, and I hope it is also
plain to your conscience.[e] 12We are not
trying to commend ourselves to you
again,[f] but are giving you an opportunity
to take pride in us,[g] so that you can answer those who take pride in what is seen
rather than in what is in the heart. 13If we
are out of our mind,[h] it is for the sake of
God; if we are in our right mind, it is for
you. 14For Christ's love compels us, because we are convinced that one died for
all, and therefore all died.[i] 15And he died
for all, that those who live should no longer live for themselves[j] but for him who
died for them[k] and was raised again.
16So from now on we regard no one

4:16 [o]Ro 7:22 [p]Ps 103:5; Isa 40:31; Col 3:10
4:17 [q]Ps 30:5; Ro 8:18; 1Pe 1:6,7
4:18 [r]2Co 5:7; Ro 8:24; Heb 11:1
5:1 [s]1Co 15:47 [t]Isa 38:12; 2Pe 1:13,14
5:2 [u]ver 4; Ro 8:23 [v]ver 4; 1Co 15:53,54
5:4 [w]ver 2; Ro 8:23 [x]ver 2; 1Co 15:53,54
5:5 [y]Ro 8:23; 2Co 1:22; Eph 1:13,14
5:7 [z]1Co 13:12; S 2Co 4:18
5:8 [a]S Jn 12:26
5:9 [b]Ro 14:18; Eph 5:10; Col 1:10; 1Th 4:1
5:10 [c]S Mt 16:27; Ac 10:42; Ro 2:16; 14:10; Eph 6:8
5:11 [d]Job 23:15; Heb 10:31; 12:29; Jude 23 [e]2Co 4:2
5:12 [f]S 2Co 3:1 [g]2Co 1:14
5:13 [h]2Co 11:1, 16,17; 12:11
5:14 [i]Ro 6:6,7; Gal 2:20; Col 3:3
5:15 [j]Ro 14:7-9 [k]Ro 4:25

4:16 OUTWARDLY . . . INWARDLY. "Outwardly" refers to the physical body, subject to decay and moving toward death because of mortality and the troubles of life (v. 17). "Inwardly" refers to the human spirit that has the spiritual life of Christ. Although our bodies age and decay, we experience ongoing renewal through the constant impartation of Christ's life and power; his influence enables our minds, emotions and wills to be conformed to his likeness and eternal purpose.

4:17 MOMENTARY TROUBLE . . . ETERNAL GLORY. The hardships endured in the lives of those who remain faithful to Christ are light in comparison to the abundance of glory we have through Christ. This glory is already present in part, but will be fully experienced in the future (cf. Ro 8:18). When we reach our heavenly inheritance, we will say that the severest tribulations were nothing compared with the glory of the eternal state. Therefore, we must not lose hope or give up our faith as we face our problems.

5:1 IF THE EARTHLY TENT. Paul uses the conditional clause, "if the earthly tent we live in is destroyed," because he knows that Christ could return soon, in which case he would not experience death; rather, his body would be immediately transformed (see article on THE RAPTURE, p. 440). This same double possibility (death or transformation) exists for believers today. Christ has stated we do not know the day or the hour of his return (Mt 24:36,42,44); since this event is imminent, we have a powerful motivation for holy living (see Mt 24:42, notes; 1Jn 3:2–3).

5:1 EARTHLY TENT . . . A BUILDING. (1) The term "earthly tent" refers either to the believer's earthly body or to the believer's earthly life. (2) The "building from God, an eternal house in heaven, not built by human hands" likely refers either to a temporary body prepared for believers in heaven while they await their resurrection body, or to the environment of the heavenly existence.

Some have used this difficult passage to teach that after death and while awaiting resurrection, believers exist as disembodied spirits, vague shadows or naked souls without form. However, note that both Moses and Elijah on the Mount of Transfiguration appeared clothed with a heavenly body, even though they were awaiting their resurrection bodies (see article on THE RESURRECTION OF THE BODY, p. 357). Furthermore, in Rev 6:9–11 souls in heaven wear white robes and are described as being visible; they are not naked souls.

5:8 AT HOME WITH THE LORD. This verse and others (e.g., Lk 23:42–43; Php 1:23) clearly teach that there is no lapse of time between death and the life to come. The believer's death brings him or her immediately into Christ's presence (1Co 13:12). Thus, "to die is gain" (Php 1:21). This does not mean that Christ is not present with believers now, for the Holy Spirit's work is to mediate Christ's presence to the believer (see article on THE DOCTRINE OF THE HOLY SPIRIT, p. 240). But it does indicate that we are now with the Lord by faith and not by sight (Heb 11:1).

5:10 THE JUDGMENT SEAT OF CHRIST. For comments on what happens to believers on the day of judgment, see article on THE JUDGMENT OF BELIEVERS, p. 368.

THE JUDGMENT OF BELIEVERS

2Co 5:10 "For we must all appear before the judgment seat of Christ, that each one may receive what is due him for the things done while in the body, whether good or bad."

The Bible teaches that believers will someday have to give an account at "the judgment seat of Christ." Concerning the judgment of believers, the following facts should be kept in mind:

(1) All Christians will be subject to judgment; there will be no exceptions (Ro 14:12; 1Co 3:12–15; 2Co 5:10).

(2) This judgment will occur when Christ returns for his church (see Jn 14:3, note; 1Th 4:14–17).

(3) The judge is Christ (Jn 5:22; 2Ti 4:8).

(4) The Bible speaks of the believer's judgment as something solemn and serious, especially since it includes the possibility of damage or "loss" (1Co 3:15; 2Jn 8), of being ashamed before him "at his coming" (1Jn 2:28) and of burning up one's whole life's work (1Co 3:13–15). The believer's judgment, however, will not involve a declaration of condemnation by God.

(5) Everything will be made manifest. The word "appear" (Gk *phaneroō*, 2Co 5:10) means "to be revealed openly or publicly." God will examine and openly reveal, in its true reality, (a) our secret acts (Mk 4:22; Ro 2:16), (b) our character (Ro 2:5–11), (c) our words (Mt 12:36–37), (d) our good deeds (Eph 6:8), (e) our attitudes (Mt 5:22), (f) our motives (1Co 4:5), (g) our lack of love (Col 3:18—4:1), and (h) our work and ministry (1Co 3:13).

(6) In sum, believers will have to give an account of their faithfulness or unfaithfulness to God (Mt 25:21,23; 1Co 4:2–5) and of their deeds in light of the grace, opportunity and understanding made available to them (Lk 12:48; Jn 5:24; Ro 8:1).

(7) The believer's bad deeds, when repented of, are forgiven with respect to eternal punishment (Ro 8:1), but they are still taken into account when being judged for repayment: "Anyone who does wrong will be repaid for his wrong" (Col 3:25; cf. Ecc 12:14; 1Co 3:15; 2Co 5:10). The believer's good deeds and love are remembered by God and rewarded (Heb 6:10): "The Lord will reward everyone for whatever good he does" (Eph 6:8).

(8) The specific results of the believer's judgment will be varied. There will be either the gain or loss of joy (1Jn 2:28), divine approval (Mt 25:21), tasks and authority (Mt 25:14–30), position (Mt 5:19; 19:30), rewards (1Co 3:12–14; Php 3:14; 2Ti 4:8) and honor (Ro 2:10; cf. 1Pe 1:7).

(9) The impending judgment of Christians should perfect in them the fear of the Lord (2Co 5:11; Php 2:12; 1Pe 1:17) and cause them to be clear minded and self-controlled, to watch and pray (1Pe 4:5,7), to live holy and godly lives (2Pe 3:11), and to show mercy and kindness to all (Mt 5:7; cf. 2Ti 1:16–18).

from a worldly[l] point of view. Though we
once regarded Christ in this way, we do so
no longer. 17 Therefore, if anyone is in
Christ,[m] he is a new creation;[n] the old has
gone, the new has come![o] 18 All this is
from God,[p] who reconciled us to himself
through Christ[q] and gave us the ministry
of reconciliation: 19 that God was reconciling the world to himself in Christ, not
counting men's sins against them.[r] And
he has committed to us the message of
reconciliation. 20 We are therefore Christ's
ambassadors,[s] as though God were making his appeal through us.[t] We implore
you on Christ's behalf: Be reconciled
to God.[u] 21 God made him who had no
sin[v] to be sin[f] for us, so that in him we
might become the righteousness of
God.[w]

6

As God's fellow workers[x] we urge
you not to receive God's grace in
vain.[y] 2 For he says,

"In the time of my favor I heard you,
and in the day of salvation I helped
you."[g][z]

I tell you, now is the time of God's favor,
now is the day of salvation.

Paul's Hardships

3 We put no stumbling block in anyone's
path,[a] so that our ministry will not be
discredited. 4 Rather, as servants of God
we commend ourselves in every way: in
great endurance; in troubles, hardships
and distresses; 5 in beatings, imprisonments[b] and riots; in hard work, sleepless
nights and hunger;[c] 6 in purity, understanding, patience and kindness; in the
Holy Spirit[d] and in sincere love;[e] 7 in
truthful speech[f] and in the power of
God;[g] with weapons of righteousness[h] in
the right hand and in the left; 8 through
glory and dishonor,[i] bad report[j] and
good report; genuine, yet regarded as impostors;[k] 9 known, yet regarded as unknown; dying,[l] and yet we live on;[m] beat-
en, and yet not killed; 10 sorrowful, yet al-

5:16 [l] 2Co 10:4; 11:18 **5:17** [m] S Ro 16:3 [n] S Jn 1:13; S Ro 6:4; Gal 6:15 [o] Isa 65:17; Rev 21:4,5 **5:18** [p] S Ro 11:36 [q] S Ro 5:10 **5:19** [r] S Ro 4:8 **5:20** [s] 2Co 6:1; Eph 6:20 [t] ver 18 [u] Isa 27:5 **5:21** [v] Heb 4:15; 7:26; 1Pe 2:22,24; 1Jn 3:5 [w] S Ro 1:17; S 1Co 1:30 **6:1** [x] S 1Co 3:9; 2Co 5:20 [y] 1Co 15:2 **6:2** [z] Isa 49:8; Ps 69:13; Isa 55:6 **6:3** [a] S Mt 5:29; Ro 14:13,20; 1Co 8:9,13; 9:12; 10:32 **6:5** [b] Ac 16:23; 2Co 11:23-25 [c] 1Co 4:11 **6:6** [d] 1Co 2:4; 1Th 1:5 [e] Ro 12:9; 1Ti 1:5 **6:7** [f] 2Co 4:2 [g] 2Co 4:7 [h] Ro 13:12; 2Co 10:4; Eph 6:10-18 **6:8** [i] 1Co 4:10 [j] 1Co 4:13 [k] Mt 27:63 **6:9** [l] S Ro 8:36 [m] 2Co 1:8-10; 4:10,11

[f] *21* Or *be a sin offering* [g] *2* Isaiah 49:8

5:17 HE IS A NEW CREATION. Through the creative command of God (4:6), those who accept Jesus Christ by faith are made a new creation that belongs to God's totally new world in which the Spirit rules (Ro 8:14; Gal 5:25; Eph 2:10). The believer becomes a new person (Gal 6:15; Eph 2:10,15; 4:24; Col 3:10) renewed after God's image (4:16; 1Co 15:49; Eph 4:24; Col 3:10), sharing his glory (3:18) with a renewed knowledge (Col 3:10) and understanding (Ro 12:2), and living a life of holiness (Eph 4:24).

5:18 RECONCILED US TO HIMSELF. Reconciliation (Gk *katallagē*) is one aspect of Christ's work of redemption—the restoration of the sinner to fellowship with God. (1) The sin and rebellion of the human race has resulted in hostility toward and alienation from God (Eph 2:3; Col 1:21). This rebellion elicits God's wrath and judgment (Ro 1:18,24–32; 1Co 15:25–26; Eph 5:6).

(2) Through Christ's atoning death, God has removed the barrier of sin and opened a way for the sinner to return to God (v. 19; Ro 3:25; 5:10; Eph 2:15–16).

(3) Reconciliation becomes effective for each person through his or her personal repentance and faith in Christ (Mt 3:2; Ro 3:22).

(4) The church has been given the ministry of reconciliation, calling all people to be reconciled to God (v. 20; see Ro 3:25, note).

5:21 MADE HIM WHO HAD NO SIN TO BE SIN. Scripture nowhere states that Christ actually became a "sinner," for he remained the spotless Lamb of God. But Christ did take our sin upon himself, and God the Father made him the object of his judgment when Christ became an offering for our sins on the cross (Isa 53:10). In taking our punishment, Jesus made it possible for God to justly forgive sinners (Isa 53:5; Ro 3:24–26).

5:21 WE MIGHT BECOME THE RIGHTEOUSNESS OF GOD. (1) Righteousness here does not refer to a legal righteousness, but to the experiential righteousness of the children of God as a new creation, i.e., to their character and moral state founded on and flowing from their faith in Christ (Php 3:9; see Ro 3:21, note; 4:22, note). The whole context of the passage (vv. 14–21) is concerned with believers living for Christ (v. 15), being controlled by "Christ's love" (v. 14), becoming a "new creation" (v. 17), and fulfilling the ministry of reconciliation as representatives of God and his righteousness in the world (vv. 18–20; see 1Co 1:30, note on Jesus Christ as the righteousness of the believer).

(2) God's righteousness is manifested and experienced by the believer in this world by remaining in Christ. Only to the extent that we live in union and fellowship with Christ do we become the righteousness of God (see Jn 15:4–5; Gal 2:20, note; 1Jn 1:9).

6:1 NOT TO RECEIVE GOD'S GRACE IN VAIN. Paul unquestionably believed that a believer could receive God's grace and experience salvation (v. 2), and afterwards, through spiritual carelessness or deliberate sin, abandon the faith and life of the gospel and again be lost. All people must be urged to be reconciled to God and to receive his grace (5:20). Those who receive God's grace must be urged not to receive it in vain (cf. vv. 14–18).

6:4 IN TROUBLES . . . DISTRESSES. See 11:23, note on Paul's suffering.

6:10 POOR. It is not contradictory to the gospel for a truly dedicated Christian to be financially poor. Paul affirms he possessed little of this world's goods, yet as God's servant he made others spiritually rich (cf. 8:9; Ac 3:1ff; Eph 3:8).

ways rejoicing;[n] poor, yet making many
rich;[o] having nothing,[p] and yet possessing everything.[q]
11 We have spoken freely to you, Corinthians, and opened wide our hearts to
you.[r] 12 We are not withholding our affection from you, but you are withholding
yours from us. 13 As a fair exchange—I
speak as to my children[s]—open wide
your hearts[t] also.

Do Not Be Yoked With Unbelievers

14 Do not be yoked together[u] with unbelievers.[v] For what do righteousness and
wickedness have in common? Or what fellowship can light have with darkness?[w]
15 What harmony is there between Christ
and Belial[h]?[x] What does a believer[y] have
in common with an unbeliever?[z] 16 What
agreement is there between the temple of
God and idols?[a] For we are the temple[b]
of the living God.[c] As God has said: "I will
live with them and walk among them, and
I will be their God, and they will be my
people."[i][d]

17 "Therefore come out from them[e]
and be separate,
says the Lord.
Touch no unclean thing,
and I will receive you."[j][f]

18 "I will be a Father to you,
and you will be my sons and
daughters,[g]
says the Lord Almighty."[k][h]

7 Since we have these promises,[i] dear
friends,[j] let us purify ourselves from
everything that contaminates body and
spirit, perfecting holiness[k] out of reverence for God.

Paul's Joy

2 Make room for us in your hearts.[l] We
have wronged no one, we have corrupted
no one, we have exploited no one. 3 I do not
say this to condemn you; I have said before that you have such a place in our
hearts[m] that we would live or die with you.
4 I have great confidence in you; I take
great pride in you.[n] I am greatly encouraged;[o] in all our troubles my joy knows no
bounds.[p]

5 For when we came into Macedonia,[q]
this body of ours had no rest, but we were
harassed at every turn[r]—conflicts on the
outside, fears within.[s] 6 But God, who

6:10 [n] S Mt 5:12; 2Co 7:4; Php 2:17; 4:4; Col 1:24; 1Th 1:6 [o] 2Co 8:9 [p] Ac 3:6 [q] Ro 8:32; 1Co 3:21
6:11 [r] 2Co 7:3
6:13 [s] S 1Th 2:11 [t] 2Co 7:2
6:14 [u] Ge 24:3; Dt 22:10; 1Co 5:9, 10 [v] 1Co 6:6 [w] Eph 5:7,11; 1Jn 1:6
6:15 [x] 1Co 10:21 [y] Ac 5:14 [z] 1Co 6:6
6:16 [a] 1Co 10:21 [b] S 1Co 3:16 [c] S Mt 16:16 [d] Lev 26:12; Jer 32:38; Eze 37:27; Rev 21:3
6:17 [e] Rev 18:4 [f] Isa 52:11; Eze 20:34,41
6:18 [g] Ex 4:22; 2Sa 7:14; 1Ch 17:13; Isa 43:6; S Ro 8:14 [h] 2Sa 7:8
7:1 [i] 2Co 6:17,18 [j] S 1Co 10:14 [k] 1Th 4:7; 1Pe 1:15,16
7:2 [l] 2Co 6:12,13
7:3 [m] 2Co 6:11, 12; Php 1:7
7:4 [n] ver 14; 2Co 8:24 [o] ver 13 [p] S 2Co 6:10
7:5 [q] 2Co 2:13; S Ac 16:9 [r] 2Co 4:8 [s] Dt 32:25

h *15* Greek *Beliar,* a variant of *Belial*
i *16* Lev. 26:12; Jer. 32:38; Ezek. 37:27
j *17* Isaiah 52:11; Ezek. 20:34,41
k *18* 2 Samuel 7:14; 7:8

6:14 YOKED TOGETHER WITH UNBELIEVERS. In God's eyes people ultimately are divided into two categories: those who are in Christ and those who are not (vv. 14–16; see article on THREE KINDS OF PEOPLE, p. 334). Therefore, believers must not be in voluntary partnership or in intimate association with unbelievers, for such relationships can corrupt their relationship with Christ. This includes partnership in business, secret orders (lodges), dating, marriage and close friendships. A Christian's association with unbelievers should be only such as is necessary for social or economic existence, or to show unbelievers the way of salvation (see article on SPIRITUAL SEPARATION FOR BELIEVERS, p. 371).

6:16 THE TEMPLE OF GOD AND IDOLS. Paul presents a strong argument that a born-again believer, as the temple of God and the Holy Spirit (Jn 14:23; 1Co 6:19), cannot be indwelt by a demon. (1) Idols both in the OT and NT represented demons (Dt 32:17; 1Co 10:20–21). Therefore, the worst form of desecration in the OT was to erect idols in God's own temple (2Ki 21:7,11–14). Likewise, we must never desecrate our bodies as the Spirit's dwelling place by allowing demons access (cf. v. 15, where "Belial" refers to Satan; see also Lk 10:19, note; 2Ti 2:25–26; 1Jn 4:4; 5:18).

(2) Although an evil spirit cannot live alongside the Holy Spirit within the true believer, there may be circumstances in which an evil spirit lives in an individual who is actively in the process of conversion, but has not yet been fully regenerated by the Spirit (see article on REGENERATION, p. 178). Conversion may at times require the driving out of demons from a person who sincerely desires to follow Christ, yet is undergoing problems with certain sins. Until the demonic power or stronghold is broken, that person cannot experience a full salvation and so become "the temple of the living God" (cf. Mt 12:28–29).

6:17 AND BE SEPARATE. See article on SPIRITUAL SEPARATION FOR BELIEVERS, p. 371.

7:1 SINCE WE HAVE THESE PROMISES. Paul makes it unmistakably clear that one cannot claim God's gracious promises listed in 6:16–18 without a life of separation and holiness (see article on SPIRITUAL SEPARATION FOR BELIEVERS, p. 371). This explains why some have lost their Christian joy (Jn 15:11), divine protection (Jn 17:12,14–15), answer to prayers (Jn 15:7,16) and the sense of God's fatherly presence (Jn 14:21,23). To compromise with the world is to lose God's presence and promises.

7:1 LET US PURIFY OURSELVES. Believers must make a clean break with every form of ungodly compromise and continually resist the sinful desires of the body. We must put to death our sinful deeds, hate them more and more, and run away from them (vv. 9–11; Ro 8:12–13; Gal 5:16).

7:5 HARASSED . . . FEARS. Once again Paul's words and experiences remind us that outward problems and inward fears can be the experience of truly dedicated, born-again believers.

7:6 COMFORTS THE DOWNCAST. As a God of mercy and comfort (1:3), it is God's nature to comfort

SPIRITUAL SEPARATION FOR BELIEVERS

***2Co 6:17–18** "Therefore come out from them and be separate, says the Lord. Touch no unclean thing, and I will receive you. I will be a Father to you, and you will be my sons and daughters, says the Lord Almighty."*

The concept of separation from evil is fundamental to God's relationship with his people. According to the Bible, separation involves two dimensions—one negative and the other positive: (a) separating yourself morally and spiritually from sin and from everything that is contrary to Jesus Christ, righteousness and God's Word; (b) drawing near to God in a close and intimate fellowship through dedication, worship and service. Separation in this twofold sense results in a relationship where God is our heavenly Father who lives with us and is our God, and we in turn are his sons and daughters (2Co 6:16–18).

(1) In the OT separation was an ongoing requirement for God's people (Ex 23:24; Lev 20:22–26; Isa 52:11; Jer 51:45). They were expected to be holy, different and separated from all other peoples in order to belong to God as his very own.

(2) In the NT God commanded separation of the believer (a) from the corrupt world system and from unholy compromise (Jn 17:15–16; 2Ti 3:1–5; Jas 1:27; 4:4; see article on THE CHRISTIAN'S RELATIONSHIP TO THE WORLD, p. 546), (b) from those in the church who sin and refuse to repent (Mt 18:15–17; 1Co 5:9–11; 2Th 3:6–15), and (c) from false teachers, churches or cults who teach theological error and deny Biblical truths (see Mt 7:15; Ro 16:17; Gal 1:9, note; Tit 3:9–11; 2Pe 2:17–22; 1Jn 4:1; 2Jn 10–11; Jude 12–13).

(3) Our attitude in separation must be one of (a) hatred toward sin, unrighteousness and the corrupt world system (Ro 12:9; Heb 1:9; 1Jn 2:15), (b) opposition to false doctrine (Gal 1:9), (c) genuine love for those from whom we must separate (Jn 3:16; 1Co 5:5; Gal 6:1; cf. Ro 9:1–3; 2Co 2:1–8; 11:28–29; Jude 22), and (d) fear of God as we perfect holiness (2Co 7:1).

(4) The purpose of separation is that we as God's people might (a) persevere in salvation (1Ti 4:16; Rev 2:14–17), faith (1Ti 1:19; 6:10,20–21) and holiness (Jn 17:14–21; 2Co 7:1); (b) live wholly for God as our Lord and Father (Mt 22:37; 2Co 6:16–18); and (c) convince the unbelieving world of the truth and blessings of the gospel (Jn 17:21; Php 2:15).

(5) If we separate ourselves properly, God himself rewards us by drawing near with his protection, blessing and fatherly care. He promises to be everything that a good Father should be. He will be our counselor and guide; he will love and cherish us as his own children (2Co 6:16–18).

(6) The refusal of believers to separate themselves from evil will inevitably result in the loss of fellowship with God (2Co 6:16), of acceptance by the Father (6:17) and of our rights as children (6:18; cf. Ro 8:15–16).

comforts the downcast,[t] comforted us by
the coming of Titus,[u] **7**and not only by his
coming but also by the comfort you had
given him. He told us about your longing
for me, your deep sorrow, your ardent concern for me, so that my joy was greater
than ever.

8Even if I caused you sorrow by my letter,[v] I do not regret it. Though I did regret
it—I see that my letter hurt you, but only
for a little while— **9**yet now I am happy,
not because you were made sorry, but because your sorrow led you to repentance.
For you became sorrowful as God intended and so were not harmed in any way by
us. **10**Godly sorrow brings repentance that
leads to salvation[w] and leaves no regret,
but worldly sorrow brings death. **11**See
what this godly sorrow has produced in
you: what earnestness, what eagerness to
clear yourselves, what indignation, what
alarm, what longing, what concern,[x] what
readiness to see justice done. At every
point you have proved yourselves to be
innocent in this matter. **12**So even though
I wrote to you,[y] it was not on account of
the one who did the wrong[z] or of the injured party, but rather that before God you
could see for yourselves how devoted to
us you are. **13**By all this we are encouraged.

In addition to our own encouragement,
we were especially delighted to see how
happy Titus[a] was, because his spirit has
been refreshed by all of you. **14**I had boasted to him about you,[b] and you have not
embarrassed me. But just as everything
we said to you was true, so our boasting
about you to Titus[c] has proved to be true
as well. **15**And his affection for you is all
the greater when he remembers that you
were all obedient,[d] receiving him with
fear and trembling.[e] **16**I am glad I can
have complete confidence in you.[f]

Generosity Encouraged

8 And now, brothers, we want you to
know about the grace that God has
given the Macedonian[g] churches. **2**Out of
the most severe trial, their overflowing joy
and their extreme poverty welled up in
rich generosity.[h] **3**For I testify that they
gave as much as they were able,[i] and
even beyond their ability. Entirely on their
own, **4**they urgently pleaded with us for
the privilege of sharing[j] in this service[k]
to the saints.[l] **5**And they did not do as we
expected, but they gave themselves first
to the Lord and then to us in keeping with
God's will. **6**So we urged[m] Titus,[n] since he
had earlier made a beginning, to bring
also to completion[o] this act of grace on
your part. **7**But just as you excel in everything[p]—in faith, in speech, in knowledge,[q] in complete earnestness and in
your love for us[1]—see that you also excel
in this grace of giving.

8I am not commanding you,[r] but I want
to test the sincerity of your love by comparing it with the earnestness of others.
9For you know the grace[s] of our Lord
Jesus Christ,[t] that though he was rich,

7:6 [t]2Co 1:3,4 [u]ver 13; S 2Co 2:13
7:8 [v]2Co 2:2,4
7:10 [w]Ac 11:18
7:11 [x]ver 7
7:12 [y]ver 8; 2Co 2:3,9 [z]1Co 5:1,2
7:13 [a]ver 6; S 2Co 2:13
7:14 [b]ver 4 [c]ver 6
7:15 [d]2Co 2:9; 10:6 [e]Ps 55:5; 1Co 2:3; Php 2:12
7:16 [f]S 2Co 2:3
8:1 [g]S Ac 16:9
8:2 [h]Ex 36:5; 2Co 9:11
8:3 [i]1Co 16:2
8:4 [j]ver 1 [k]S Ac 24:17 [l]S Ac 9:13
8:6 [m]ver 17; 2Co 12:18 [n]ver 16,23; S 2Co 2:13 [o]ver 10,11
8:7 [p]2Co 9:8 [q]Ro 15:14; 1Co 1:5; 12:8; 13:1,2; 14:6
8:8 [r]1Co 7:6
8:9 [s]S Ro 3:24 [t]2Co 13:14

[1] 7 Some manuscripts *in our love for you*

those who are depressed and downcast. In fact, the more we are afflicted, the greater will be the comfort and nearness of Christ in our life. Note that it was through the agency of Titus that God comforted Paul. We should always be sensitive to the Holy Spirit's leading us to comfort a person in need.

7:10 GODLY SORROW . . . WORLDLY SORROW. Paul identifies two kinds of sorrow here. (1) There is a genuine sorrow for sin that leads to repentance, i.e., a change of heart that causes us to turn from sin to God. This type of repentance leads to salvation. For Paul, repentance from sin and faith in Christ are human responsibilities in salvation (see Mt 3:2, note). (2) In contrast, the unrepentant often become sorry only for the consequences of their sin; such sorrow results in eternal death and judgment (Mt 13:42,50; 25:30; Ro 6:23).

8:1—9:15 THE MACEDONIAN CHURCHES. These two chapters deal with instruction about the offering for the poor believers in Jerusalem. Paul's words contain the most complete teaching about Christian giving found in the NT. The principles given here are a guide for believers and churches for all time (see next note).

8:2 RICH GENEROSITY. These two chapters reveal important principles and promises of Christian giving: (1) We belong to God; what we have is held as a trust for our Lord (v. 5). (2) We must make the basic decision in our hearts to serve God and not money (v. 5; Mt 6:24). (3) We give in order to help those in need (v. 14; 9:12; Pr 19:17; Gal 2:10), to advance God's kingdom (1Co 9:14; Php 4:15–18), to store up treasures in heaven (Mt 6:20; Lk 6:32–35) and to learn to fear the Lord (Dt 14:22–23). (4) Giving should be in proportion to our income (vv. 3,12; 1Co 16:2). (5) Giving is seen as a proof of our love (v. 24) and should be done sacrificially (v. 3) and voluntarily (9:7). (6) By giving to God we sow not only money but also faith, time and service, thus reaping greater faith and blessing (v. 5; 9:6,10–12). (7) When God supplies an abundance it is so that we may multiply our good works (9:8; Eph 4:28). (8) Giving increases our dedication to God (Mt 6:21) and activates the work of God in our financial affairs (Lk 6:38).

8:9 HE BECAME POOR. Sacrificial giving was an essential part of Christ's nature and character. By his becoming poor, we now partake of his eternal riches. God wants the same attitude among believers as evi-

yet for your sakes he became poor,[u] so
that you through his poverty might become rich.[v]
10And here is my advice[w] about what is
best for you in this matter: Last year you
were the first not only to give but also to
have the desire to do so.[x] 11Now finish the
work, so that your eager willingness[y] to
do it may be matched by your completion
of it, according to your means. 12For if the
willingness is there, the gift is acceptable
according to what one has,[z] not according
to what he does not have.
13Our desire is not that others might be
relieved while you are hard pressed, but
that there might be equality. 14At the
present time your plenty will supply what
they need,[a] so that in turn their plenty
will supply what you need. Then there will
be equality, 15as it is written: "He who
gathered much did not have too much, and
he who gathered little did not have too
little."[m][b]

Titus Sent to Corinth

16I thank God,[c] who put into the heart[d]
of Titus[e] the same concern I have for you.
17For Titus not only welcomed our appeal,
but he is coming to you with much enthusiasm and on his own initiative.[f] 18And
we are sending along with him the brother[g] who is praised by all the churches[h]
for his service to the gospel.[i] 19What is
more, he was chosen by the churches to
accompany us[j] as we carry the offering,
which we administer in order to honor the
Lord himself and to show our eagerness to
help.[k] 20We want to avoid any criticism of
the way we administer this liberal gift.
21For we are taking pains to do what is
right, not only in the eyes of the Lord but
also in the eyes of men.[l]
22In addition, we are sending with them
our brother who has often proved to us in
many ways that he is zealous, and now
even more so because of his great confidence in you. 23As for Titus,[m] he is my
partner[n] and fellow worker[o] among you;
as for our brothers,[p] they are representatives of the churches and an honor to
Christ. 24Therefore show these men the
proof of your love and the reason for our
pride in you,[q] so that the churches can
see it.

9 There is no need[r] for me to write to
you about this service[s] to the
saints.[t] 2For I know your eagerness to
help,[u] and I have been boasting[v] about it
to the Macedonians, telling them that
since last year[w] you in Achaia[x] were
ready to give; and your enthusiasm has
stirred most of them to action. 3But I am
sending the brothers[y] in order that our
boasting about you in this matter should
not prove hollow, but that you may be
ready, as I said you would be.[z] 4For if any
Macedonians[a] come with me and find you
unprepared, we—not to say anything
about you—would be ashamed of having
been so confident. 5So I thought it necessary to urge the brothers[b] to visit you in
advance and finish the arrangements for
the generous gift you had promised. Then
it will be ready as a generous gift,[c] not as
one grudgingly given.[d]

Sowing Generously

6Remember this: Whoever sows sparingly will also reap sparingly, and whoever sows generously will also reap generously.[e] 7Each man should give what he
has decided in his heart to give,[f] not reluctantly or under compulsion,[g] for God
loves a cheerful giver.[h] 8And God is able[i]
to make all grace abound to you, so that
in all things at all times, having all that
you need,[j] you will abound in every good
work. 9As it is written:

> "He has scattered abroad his gifts[k] to
> the poor;
> his righteousness endures
> forever."[n][l]

10Now he who supplies seed to the sower
and bread for food[m] will also supply and
increase your store of seed and will en-

[m] *15* Exodus 16:18 [n] *9* Psalm 112:9

8:9 [u] Mt 20:28; Php 2:6-8 [v] 2Co 6:10 **8:10** [w] 1Co 7:25, 40 [x] 1Co 16:2,3; 2Co 9:2 **8:11** [y] ver 12,19; Ex 25:2; 2Co 9:2 **8:12** [z] Mk 12:43, 44; 2Co 9:7 **8:14** [a] Ac 4:34; 2Co 9:12 **8:15** [b] Ex 16:18 **8:16** [c] S 2Co 2:14 [d] Rev 17:17 [e] S 2Co 2:13 **8:17** [f] ver 6 **8:18** [g] 2Co 12:18 [h] S 1Co 7:17 [i] S 2Co 2:12 **8:19** [j] Ac 14:23; 1Co 16:3,4 [k] ver 11,12 **8:21** [l] Ro 12:17; S 14:18; S Tit 2:14 **8:23** [m] S 2Co 2:13 [n] Phm 17 [o] S Php 2:25 [p] ver 18,22 **8:24** [q] 2Co 7:4,14; 9:2 **9:1** [r] 1Th 4:9 [s] S Ac 24:17 [t] S Ac 9:13 **9:2** [u] 2Co 8:11,12, 19 [v] 2Co 7:4,14; 8:24 [w] 2Co 8:10 [x] S Ac 18:12 **9:3** [y] 2Co 8:23 [z] 1Co 16:2 **9:4** [a] Ro 15:26 **9:5** [b] ver 3 [c] Php 4:17 [d] 2Co 12:17,18 **9:6** [e] Pr 11:24,25; 22:9; Gal 6:7,9 **9:7** [f] Ex 25:2; 2Co 8:12 [g] Dt 15:10 [h] Ro 12:8 **9:8** [i] Eph 3:20 [j] Php 4:19 **9:9** [k] Mal 3:10 [l] Ps 112:9 **9:10** [m] Isa 55:10

dence of his grace working within us. All the gifts of grace and salvation, the kingdom of heaven, and even disgrace for the sake of Christ are the everlasting riches we have received in exchange for the rags of sin (Lk 12:15; Eph 1:3; Php 4:11–13,18–19; Heb 11:26; Rev 3:17).

9:6 WILL ALSO REAP SPARINGLY. Christians can give either generously or sparingly; God will reward them accordingly (see Mt 7:1–2). To Paul, giving is not a loss, but a form of saving; it results in substantial benefits for those who give (see 8:2, note; 9:11, note). He is not speaking primarily of the quantity given, but of the quality of our hearts' desires and motives. The poor widow gave little, but God considered it much because of the proportion she gave and her complete dedication (see Lk 21:1–4, note; cf. Pr 11:24–25; 19:17; Mt 10:41–42; Lk 6:38).

9:8 GRACE ABOUND TO YOU. Believers who give what they can to help those in need will find that God's grace provides a sufficiency for their own needs, and even more, that they abound in every good work (cf. Eph 4:28).

large the harvest of your righteousness.[n]
11You will be made rich[o] in every way so
that you can be generous[p] on every occasion, and through us your generosity will
result in thanksgiving to God.[q]
12This service that you perform is not
only supplying the needs[r] of God's people
but is also overflowing in many expressions of thanks to God.[s] **13**Because of the
service[t] by which you have proved yourselves, men will praise God[u] for the obedience that accompanies your confession[v]
of the gospel of Christ,[w] and for your generosity[x] in sharing with them and with
everyone else. **14**And in their prayers for
you their hearts will go out to you, because of the surpassing grace God has
given you. **15**Thanks be to God[y] for his
indescribable gift![z]

9:10 [n]Hos 10:12
9:11 [o]1Co 1:5
[p]ver 5 [q]2Co 1:11; 4:15
9:12 [r]2Co 8:14
[s]S 2Co 1:11
9:13 [t]S 2Co 8:4
[u]S Mt 9:8
[v]S Heb 3:1
[w]S 2Co 2:12
[x]ver 5
9:15 [y]S 2Co 2:14
[z]Ro 5:15,16

10:1 [a]Mt 11:29
[b]Gal 5:2; Eph 3:1
10:2 [c]S 1Co 4:21
[d]Ro 12:2
10:3 [e]ver 2
10:4 [f]S 2Co 6:7
[g]1Co 2:5 [h]ver 8; Jer 1:10; 23:29; 2Co 13:10
10:5 [i]Isa 2:11,12; 1Co 1:19
[j]2Co 9:13

Paul's Defense of His Ministry

10 By the meekness and gentleness[a]
of Christ, I appeal to you—I,
Paul,[b] who am "timid" when face to face
with you, but "bold" when away! **2**I beg
you that when I come I may not have to
be as bold[c] as I expect to be toward some
people who think that we live by the standards of this world.[d] **3**For though we live
in the world, we do not wage war as the
world does.[e] **4**The weapons we fight
with[f] are not the weapons of the world.
On the contrary, they have divine power[g]
to demolish strongholds.[h] **5**We demolish
arguments and every pretension that sets
itself up against the knowledge of God,[i]
and we take captive every thought to
make it obedient[j] to Christ. **6**And we will
be ready to punish every act of disobedi-

9:11 MADE RICH IN EVERY WAY. In order for generosity to be outwardly expressed, the heart must be made rich in sincere love and compassion for others. Giving of ourselves and our possessions results in (1) supplying the needs of poorer brothers and sisters, (2) praise and thanksgiving to God (v. 12) and (3) reciprocal love from those who receive our help (v. 14).

10:1 I APPEAL TO YOU—I, PAUL. The majority of Corinthian believers had accepted Paul's authority and submitted to his teachings and apostleship (7:8–16). Yet there was a minority, led by false ministers undermining the gospel and doing Satan's work (11:13), who continued to resist him and to slander his person and character. In chs. 10–13 Paul addresses these false believers.

10:4 WEAPONS WE FIGHT WITH. Our warfare is against spiritual forces of evil (Eph 6:12). Therefore, worldly weapons such as human ingenuity, talents, wealth, organizational skills, eloquence, propaganda, charisma and personality are in themselves inadequate to pull down Satan's strongholds. The only weapons adequate to destroy the fortresses of Satan, unrighteousness and false teaching are those God gives.

(1) These weapons are powerful because they are spiritual and come from God. Elsewhere Paul lists some of these weapons—commitment to truth, righteous living, gospel proclamation, faith, love, hope of salvation, the Word of God, and persevering prayer (Eph 6:11–19; 1Th 5:8). By using these weapons against the enemy, the church will emerge victorious. God's presence and kingdom will be powerfully revealed in order to save sinners, drive out demons, sanctify believers, baptize in the Holy Spirit and heal the sick (see article on SIGNS OF BELIEVERS, p. 106).

(2) The church today is often tempted to meet the world's challenge through the world's weapons, i.e., through humanistic wisdom, philosophy, psychology, exciting attractions, entertainment-based church performances, etc. These often serve as a substitute for the basic NT practices of intense prayer, meditation on God's Word, and proclamation of the gospel in power. Worldly weapons cannot bring about a Holy Spirit revival, for such weapons cannot possibly destroy sin's strongholds, deliver us from Satan's power or overthrow the evil passions running rampant in the world today. If we use the world's weapons, we will only secularize the church and separate it from the weapons of faith, righteousness and the power of the Spirit. Tragically, the church itself will then be overshadowed by the power of darkness and its families thrown down and taken captive by the world's forces.

10:5 TAKE CAPTIVE EVERY THOUGHT. Christian warfare involves bringing all our thoughts into alignment with Christ's will; failure to do so will lead to immorality and spiritual death (Ro 6:16,23; 8:13). Use the following four steps to bring your thought life under Christ's lordship. (1) Be aware that God knows every thought and that nothing is hidden from him (Ps 94:11; 139:2,4,23–24). We will have to give account to God for our thoughts as well as for our words and deeds (5:10; Ecc 12:14; Mt 12:35–37; Ro 14:12).

(2) Be aware that the mind is a battleground. Some thoughts originate with us, while others come directly from the enemy. To take captive every thought requires warfare against both our sinful nature and satanic forces (Eph 6:12–13; cf. Mt 4:3–11). Steadfastly resist and reject evil and unwholesome thoughts in the name of the Lord Jesus Christ (Php 4:8). Remember that we as believers overcome our adversary by the blood of the Lamb, by the word of our testimony, and by persistently saying "No!" to the devil, temptation and sin (Tit 2:11–12; Jas 4:7; Rev 12:11; cf. Mt 4:3–11).

(3) Be resolute in focusing your mind on Christ and heavenly things rather than on earthly things (Php 3:19; Col 3:2), for the mind controlled by the Spirit is life and peace (Ro 8:6–7). Fill your mind with God's Word (Ps 1:1–3; 19:7–14; 119) and with those things that are noble, excellent and praiseworthy (Php 4:8).

(4) Always be careful what your eyes see and your ears hear. Resolutely refuse (a) to let your eyes be an instrument for lust (Job 31:1; 1Jn 2:16), or (b) to set any worthless or evil thing before your eyes, whether in books, magazines, pictures, television programs, or in real life (Ps 101:3; Isa 33:14–15; Ro 13:14).

ence, once your obedience is complete.[k]
7You are looking only on the surface of
things.[o][l] If anyone is confident that he
belongs to Christ,[m] he should consider
again that we belong to Christ just as
much as he.[n] 8For even if I boast somewhat freely about the authority the Lord
gave us[o] for building you up rather than
pulling you down,[p] I will not be ashamed
of it. 9I do not want to seem to be trying
to frighten you with my letters. 10For
some say, "His letters are weighty and
forceful, but in person he is unim-
pressive[q] and his speaking amounts to
nothing."[r] 11Such people should realize
that what we are in our letters when we
are absent, we will be in our actions when
we are present.
12We do not dare to classify or compare
ourselves with some who commend themselves.[s] When they measure themselves
by themselves and compare themselves
with themselves, they are not wise. 13We,
however, will not boast beyond proper limits, but will confine our boasting to the
field God has assigned to us,[t] a field that
reaches even to you. 14We are not going
too far in our boasting, as would be the
case if we had not come to you, for we did
get as far as you[u] with the gospel of
Christ.[v] 15Neither do we go beyond our
limits[w] by boasting of work done by others.[p][x] Our hope is that, as your faith continues to grow,[y] our area of activity
among you will greatly expand, 16so that
we can preach the gospel[z] in the regions
beyond you.[a] For we do not want to boast
about work already done in another man's
territory. 17But, "Let him who boasts
boast in the Lord."[q][b] 18For it is not the
one who commends himself[c] who is approved, but the one whom the Lord commends.[d]

10:6 [k]2Co 2:9; 7:15
10:7 [l]S Jn 7:24; 2Co 5:12 [m]1Co 1:12; S 3:23; 14:37 [n]2Co 11:23
10:8 [o]ver 13,15 [p]ver 4; Jer 1:10; 2Co 13:10
10:10 [q]ver 1; 1Co 2:3; Gal 4:13, 14 [r]1Co 1:17; 2Co 11:6
10:12 [s]ver 18; S 2Co 3:1
10:13 [t]ver 15,16; S Ro 12:3
10:14 [u]S 1Co 3:6 [v]S 2Co 2:12
10:15 [w]ver 13 [x]Ro 15:20 [y]2Th 1:3
10:16 [z]S Ro 1:1; S 2Co 2:12 [a]S Ac 19:21
10:17 [b]Jer 9:24; Ps 34:2; 44:8; 1Co 1:31
10:18 [c]ver 12 [d]S Ro 2:29
11:1 [e]ver 4,19, 20; Mt 17:17 [f]ver 16,17,21; 2Co 5:13
11:2 [g]Hos 2:19; Eph 5:26,27 [h]S 2Co 4:14
11:3 [i]Ge 3:1-6, 13; 1Ti 2:14; Rev 12:9
11:4 [j]1Co 3:11 [k]Ro 8:15 [l]Gal 1:6-9 [m]S ver 1
11:5 [n]2Co 12:11; Gal 2:6
11:6 [o]S 1Co 1:17 [p]S 2Co 8:7; Eph 3:4
11:7 [q]2Co 12:13 [r]S Ro 1:1 [s]1Co 9:18
11:8 [t]Php 4:15, 18
11:9 [u]Php 4:15, 18 [v]2Co 12:13,14, 16
11:10 [w]S Ro 9:1

Paul and the False Apostles

11 I hope you will put up with[e] a little
of my foolishness;[f] but you are already doing that. 2I am jealous for you
with a godly jealousy. I promised you to
one husband,[g] to Christ, so that I might
present you[h] as a pure virgin to him. 3But
I am afraid that just as Eve was deceived
by the serpent's cunning,[i] your minds
may somehow be led astray from your sincere and pure devotion to Christ. 4For if
someone comes to you and preaches a
Jesus other than the Jesus we preached,[j]
or if you receive a different spirit[k] from
the one you received, or a different gospel[l] from the one you accepted, you put
up with it[m] easily enough. 5But I do not
think I am in the least inferior to those
"super-apostles."[n] 6I may not be a trained
speaker,[o] but I do have knowledge.[p] We
have made this perfectly clear to you in
every way.
7Was it a sin[q] for me to lower myself in
order to elevate you by preaching the gospel of God[r] to you free of charge?[s] 8I
robbed other churches by receiving support from them[t] so as to serve you. 9And
when I was with you and needed something, I was not a burden to anyone, for
the brothers who came from Macedonia
supplied what I needed.[u] I have kept myself from being a burden to you[v] in any
way, and will continue to do so. 10As surely as the truth of Christ is in me,[w] nobody

[o] 7 Or *Look at the obvious facts* [p] 13-15 Or *13We, however, will not boast about things that cannot be measured, but we will boast according to the standard of measurement that the God of measure has assigned us—a measurement that relates even to you. 14 . . . . 15Neither do we boast about things that cannot be measured in regard to the work done by others.* [q] 17 Jer. 9:24

10:12 MEASURE THEMSELVES BY THEMSELVES. To compare ourselves with contemporary standards and the lives of believers around us shows that we are yet without proper understanding of God's will. The standard by which we must measure ourselves is revealed by Christ and the apostles in the NT.

11:3 YOUR MINDS . . . LED ASTRAY. Some at Corinth were in grave danger of being deceived by false preachers and accepting a distorted gospel (v. 4). By accepting the teachings of these "deceitful workmen" (v. 13), they were being led astray from wholehearted devotion to Christ. In the churches today there are those who appear as ministers of righteousness, yet whose teachings contradict God's Word and lead their followers to spiritual disaster (see next two notes; Mt 23:13, note). We must be on our guard against them (see articles on FALSE TEACHERS, p. 98, and OVERSEERS AND THEIR DUTIES, p. 274).

11:4 PREACHES . . . A DIFFERENT GOSPEL. False teachers may state that Biblical revelation is true, but at the same time allege that they possess extrabiblical revelations or knowledge equal in authority to Scripture and valid for the church as a whole. Such false teaching usually draws the Christian faith into a syncretism with other religions or philosophies. This results in the following errors: (1) The supposed new revelation is put on the same level of authority as the original apostolic Biblical revelation in Christ. (2) Scripture becomes less important and Christ takes second place to "saints" or to founders of a movement or church. (3) The false teachers claim to have deeper or exclusive understanding of so-called "hidden revelations" in Scripture.

in the regions of Achaia[x] will stop this
boasting[y] of mine. **11**Why? Because I do
not love you? God knows[z] I do![a] **12**And I
will keep on doing what I am doing in
order to cut the ground from under those
who want an opportunity to be considered
equal with us in the things they boast
about.

13For such men are false apostles,[b] deceitful[c] workmen, masquerading as apostles of Christ.[d] **14**And no wonder, for Satan[e] himself masquerades as an angel of
light. **15**It is not surprising, then, if his
servants masquerade as servants of righteousness. Their end will be what their
actions deserve.[f]

Paul Boasts About His Sufferings

16I repeat: Let no one take me for a
fool.[g] But if you do, then receive me just
as you would a fool, so that I may do a
little boasting. **17**In this self-confident
boasting I am not talking as the Lord
would,[h] but as a fool.[i] **18**Since many are
boasting in the way the world does,[j] I too
will boast.[k] **19**You gladly put up with[l]
fools since you are so wise![m] **20**In fact, you
even put up with[n] anyone who enslaves
you[o] or exploits you or takes advantage
of you or pushes himself forward or slaps
you in the face. **21**To my shame I admit
that we were too weak[p] for that!

What anyone else dares to boast about
—I am speaking as a fool—I also dare to
boast about.[q] **22**Are they Hebrews? So am
I.[r] Are they Israelites? So am I.[s] Are they
Abraham's descendants? So am I.[t] **23**Are

11:10 [x]S Ac 18:12 [y]1Co 9:15 **11:11** [z]ver 31; S Ro 1:9 [a]2Co 12:15 **11:13** [b]S Mt 7:15 [c]Tit 1:10 [d]Rev 2:2 **11:14** [e]S Mt 4:10 **11:15** [f]S Mt 16:27; Php 3:19 **11:16** [g]ver 1 **11:17** [h]1Co 7:12, 25 [i]ver 21 **11:18** [j]2Co 5:16; 10:4 [k]ver 21; Php 3:3,4 **11:19** [l]S ver 1 [m]1Co 4:10 **11:20** [n]S ver 1 [o]Gal 2:4; 4:9; 5:1 **11:21** [p]2Co 10:1, 10 [q]ver 17,18; Php 3:4 **11:22** [r]Php 3:5 [s]Ro 9:4; 11:1 [t]S Lk 3:8; Ro 11:1

11:13 DECEITFUL WORKMEN, MASQUERADING AS APOSTLES. The great deceiver Satan (v. 3; Jn 8:44) uses evil people as his agents, transforming them into "false apostles, deceitful workmen." (1) The Bible speaks of these deceitful leaders as people who, energized by Satan, (a) appear to accomplish great things for God (v. 15; Rev 13:2), (b) preach attractive gospel messages (v. 4; see 1Ti 4:1, note), and (c) appear to be righteous but in reality reject godliness and deny its power (2Ti 3:5).

(2) These people disguise themselves as "apostles of Christ" and "servants of righteousness" (v. 15). Thus, they imitate genuine ministers of Christ, putting into their message every available "form of godliness" (2Ti 3:5). They may be sincerely caring and loving, and they may preach forgiveness, peace, fulfillment, love and many other helpful things—but they live under Satan's influence. Their gospel is one of human reason and not a true interpretation of God's revelation found in Scripture (cf. Gal 1:6–7; 1Pe 2:1–3). Their message deviates from NT apostolic doctrine (see 1Jn 4:1, note).

(3) All believers must beware of these misleading ministers and leaders (vv. 3–4; Mt 7:15; 16:6) and not be deceived by their charisma, eloquent oration, education, miracles, numerical success or popular message.

(4) All religious leaders must be judged according to their attitude and loyalty to the blood redemption of Jesus Christ and to the gospel as presented by Christ and the NT writers (see Gal 1:9, note; see article on FALSE TEACHERS, p. 98).

11:23 PAUL'S SUFFERINGS. The Holy Spirit, through Paul's words, reveals the anguish and suffering of someone fully committed to Christ, his Word and the cause for which Christ died. Paul was in fellowship with God's feelings and in sympathy with the heart and pathos of Christ. Here are twenty ways Paul shared Christ's sufferings:

(1) "many hardships" encountered in serving God (Ac 14:22);

(2) great distress at the overwhelming sin in society (Ac 17:16);

(3) serving the Lord with "many tears" (2:4);

(4) warning the church "night and day with tears" for three years because of the destruction brought about by the distortion of the gospel through teachers not faithful to Biblical apostolic faith (Ac 20:31; see article on OVERSEERS AND THEIR DUTIES, p. 274);

(5) grief in departing from beloved believers (Ac 20:17–38), and his broken heart at their sorrow (21:13);

(6) "great sorrow and unceasing anguish" in his heart because of the refusal of his "brothers" to accept the gospel of Christ (Ro 9:2–3; 10:1);

(7) many trials and troubles that came to him in his work for Christ (4:8–12; 11:23–29; 1Co 4:11–13);

(8) grief over sin tolerated in the church (2:1–3; 12:21; 1Co 5:1–2; 6:8–10);

(9) "great distress and anguish of heart" as he wrote to those who were forsaking Christ and the true gospel (2:4);

(10) his groaning with the desire to be with Christ and free from the sin and concern of this world (5:1–4; cf. Php 1:23);

(11) his being "harassed at every turn" because of his commitment to the church's moral and doctrinal purity (7:5; 11:3–4);

(12) his daily "concern for all the churches" (11:28);

(13) his inward burning for Christians led into sin (11:29);

(14) his having to declare eternal condemnation for those who preached a gospel other than that of the revealed NT faith (Gal 1:6–9);

(15) his experience of "pains of childbirth" for those fallen from grace (Gal 4:19; 5:4);

(16) his "tears" over enemies of Christ's cross (Php 3:18);

(17) his "distress" in wondering whether some might fall from the faith (1Th 3:5–8);

(18) persecution because of his passion for righteousness and godliness (2Ti 3:12);

(19) sorrow at the defections of Asian believers (2Ti 1:15); and

(20) his anguished plea to Timothy to guard the true faith in light of the coming apostasy (1Ti 4:1; 6:20; 2Ti 1:14).

they servants of Christ?[u] (I am out of my mind to talk like this.) I am more. I have worked much harder,[v] been in prison more frequently,[w] been flogged more severely,[x] and been exposed to death again and again.[y] **24**Five times I received from the Jews the forty lashes[z] minus one. **25**Three times I was beaten with rods,[a] once I was stoned,[b] three times I was shipwrecked,[c] I spent a night and a day in the open sea, **26**I have been constantly on the move. I have been in danger from rivers, in danger from bandits, in danger from my own countrymen,[d] in danger from Gentiles; in danger in the city,[e] in danger in the country, in danger at sea; and in danger from false brothers.[f] **27**I have labored and toiled[g] and have often gone without sleep; I have known hunger and thirst and have often gone without food;[h] I have been cold and naked. **28**Besides everything else, I face daily the pressure of my concern for all the churches.[i] **29**Who is weak, and I do not feel weak?[j] Who is led into sin,[k] and I do not inwardly burn?

30If I must boast, I will boast[l] of the things that show my weakness.[m] **31**The God and Father of the Lord Jesus, who is to be praised forever,[n] knows[o] that I am not lying. **32**In Damascus the governor under King Aretas had the city of the Damascenes guarded in order to arrest me.[p] **33**But I was lowered in a basket from a window in the wall and slipped through his hands.[q]

11:23 [u]S 1Co 3:5 [v]S 1Co 15:10 [w]Ac 16:23; 2Co 6:4,5 [x]Ac 16:23; 2Co 6:4,5 [y]S Ro 8:36 **11:24** [z]Dt 25:3 **11:25** [a]Ac 16:22 [b]Ac 14:19 [c]Ac 27:1-44 **11:26** [d]S Ac 20:3 [e]Ac 21:31 [f]Gal 2:4 **11:27** [g]S Ac 18:3; Col 1:29 [h]1Co 4:11,12; 2Co 6:5 **11:28** [i]S 1Co 7:17 **11:29** [j]S Ro 14:1; S 1Co 2:3 [k]S Mt 5:29 **11:30** [l]ver 16; Gal 6:14; 2Co 12:5,9 [m]S 1Co 2:3 **11:31** [n]Ro 1:25; 9:5 [o]ver 11; S Ro 1:9 **11:32** [p]Ac 9:24 **11:33** [q]Ac 9:25

12:1 [r]ver 5,9; 2Co 11:16,30 [s]ver 7; S 1Co 2:10 **12:2** [t]S Ro 16:3 [u]ver 4; S Ac 8:39 [v]Eph 4:10 [w]2Co 11:11 **12:4** [x]ver 2 [y]Lk 23:43; Rev 2:7 **12:5** [z]ver 9,10; S 1Co 2:3 **12:6** [a]2Co 10:8 [b]ver 11; 2Co 11:16 **12:7** [c]ver 1; S 1Co 2:10 [d]Nu 33:55 [e]S Mt 4:10 **12:8** [f]Mt 26:39, 44 **12:9** [g]S Ro 3:24

Paul's Vision and His Thorn

12 I must go on boasting.[r] Although there is nothing to be gained, I will go on to visions and revelations[s] from the Lord. **2**I know a man in Christ[t] who fourteen years ago was caught up[u] to the third heaven.[v] Whether it was in the body or out of the body I do not know—God knows.[w] **3**And I know that this man—whether in the body or apart from the body I do not know, but God knows— **4**was caught up[x] to paradise.[y] He heard inexpressible things, things that man is not permitted to tell. **5**I will boast about a man like that, but I will not boast about myself, except about my weaknesses.[z] **6**Even if I should choose to boast,[a] I would not be a fool,[b] because I would be speaking the truth. But I refrain, so no one will think more of me than is warranted by what I do or say.

7To keep me from becoming conceited because of these surpassingly great revelations,[c] there was given me a thorn in my flesh,[d] a messenger of Satan,[e] to torment me. **8**Three times I pleaded with the Lord to take it away from me.[f] **9**But he said to me, "My grace[g] is sufficient for you, for my power[h] is made perfect in weakness.[i]"[j] Therefore I will boast all the more gladly about my weaknesses, so that Christ's power may rest on me. **10**That is why, for Christ's sake, I delight[k] in weaknesses, in insults, in hardships,[l] in perse-

[h]S Php 4:13 [i]S 1Co 2:3 [j]1Ki 19:12 **12:10** [k]S Mt 5:12 [l]2Co 6:4

12:2 A MAN IN CHRIST. Paul refers to himself as "a man in Christ" who was taken up to heaven to receive revelations, probably concerning Christ's gospel and the unspeakable glories of heaven reserved for believers (v. 7; cf. Ro 8:18; 2Ti 4:8). This great privilege and revelation given to Paul strengthened him, enabling him to endure the long and severe sufferings during his apostolic ministry.

12:2 THIRD HEAVEN. Scripture indicates that there are three heavens. (1) The first heaven is the atmosphere that surrounds the earth (Hos 2:18; Da 7:13). (2) The second heaven is that of the stars (Ge 1:14–18). (3) The third heaven, also called paradise (vv. 3–4; Lk 23:43; Rev 2:7), is God's abode and the home of all departed believers (5:8; Php 1:23). Its location is not revealed.

12:7 A THORN IN MY FLESH. The word "thorn" communicates the idea of pain, trouble, sufferings, humiliation or physical infirmities, but not temptation to sin (cf. Gal 4:13–14). (1) Paul's thorn remains undefined, so that all those with a "thorn" can readily apply the spiritual lesson of this passage to themselves. (2) Paul's thorn is attributed to demonic activity or origin, permitted yet limited by God (cf. Job 2:1ff). (3) At the same time, Paul's thorn was given to keep him from becoming proud over revelations that he had received. (4) Paul's thorn kept him dependent in greater measure on divine grace (v. 9, note; Heb 12:10).

12:8 THREE TIMES I PLEADED. Many times when God answers a sincere prayer with a refusal, something much better is given (see next note; Eph 3:20).

12:9 MY GRACE IS SUFFICIENT FOR YOU. Grace is God's presence, favor and power. It is a force, a heavenly strength given those who call on God. This grace will rest on faithful believers who accept their weaknesses and difficulties for the gospel's sake (Php 4:13; see article on FAITH AND GRACE, p. 302). (1) The greater our weakness and trials for Christ, the more grace God will give to accomplish his will. What he gives is always sufficient for us to live our daily lives, to work for him, and to endure our suffering and "thorns" in the flesh (cf. 1Co 10:13). As long as we draw near to Christ, Christ will give us his heavenly strength. (2) We should boast and see eternal value in our weaknesses, for they cause Christ's power to rest on us and live within us as we walk through life toward our heavenly home.

cutions,[m] in difficulties. For when I am
weak, then I am strong.[n]

Paul's Concern for the Corinthians

11I have made a fool of myself,[o] but you
drove me to it. I ought to have been commended by you, for I am not in the least
inferior to the "super-apostles,"[p] even
though I am nothing.[q] **12**The things that
mark an apostle—signs, wonders and
miracles[r]—were done among you with
great perseverance. **13**How were you inferior to the other churches, except that I
was never a burden to you?[s] Forgive me
this wrong![t]

14Now I am ready to visit you for the
third time,[u] and I will not be a burden to
you, because what I want is not your possessions but you. After all, children
should not have to save up for their parents,[v] but parents for their children.[w]
15So I will very gladly spend for you everything I have and expend myself as well.[x]
If I love you more,[y] will you love me less?
16Be that as it may, I have not been a
burden to you.[z] Yet, crafty fellow that I
am, I caught you by trickery! **17**Did I exploit you through any of the men I sent
you? **18**I urged[a] Titus[b] to go to you and
I sent our brother[c] with him. Titus did not
exploit you, did he? Did we not act in the
same spirit and follow the same course?

19Have you been thinking all along that
we have been defending ourselves to you?
We have been speaking in the sight of
God[d] as those in Christ; and everything
we do, dear friends,[e] is for your strengthening.[f] **20**For I am afraid that when I
come[g] I may not find you as I want you
to be, and you may not find me as you
want me to be.[h] I fear that there may be
quarreling,[i] jealousy, outbursts of anger,
factions,[j] slander,[k] gossip,[l] arrogance[m]
and disorder.[n] **21**I am afraid that when I
come again my God will humble me before
you, and I will be grieved[o] over many who
have sinned earlier[p] and have not repented of the impurity, sexual sin and debauchery[q] in which they have indulged.

Final Warnings

13 This will be my third visit to you.[r]
"Every matter must be established
by the testimony of two or three witnesses."[r][s] **2**I already gave you a warning
when I was with you the second time. I
now repeat it while absent:[t] On my return
I will not spare[u] those who sinned earlier[v] or any of the others, **3**since you are
demanding proof that Christ is speaking
through me.[w] He is not weak in dealing
with you, but is powerful among you. **4**For
to be sure, he was crucified in weakness,[x]
yet he lives by God's power.[y] Likewise,
we are weak[z] in him, yet by God's power
we will live with him[a] to serve you.

5Examine yourselves[b] to see whether
you are in the faith; test yourselves.[c] Do
you not realize that Christ Jesus is in you[d]
—unless, of course, you fail the test?
6And I trust that you will discover that we
have not failed the test. **7**Now we pray to
God that you will not do anything wrong.
Not that people will see that we have
stood the test but that you will do what is
right even though we may seem to have
failed. **8**For we cannot do anything against
the truth, but only for the truth. **9**We are

r *1* Deut. 19:15

12:10 m 2Th 1:4 n 2Co 13:4
12:11 o 2Co 11:1 p 2Co 11:5 q 1Co 15:9,10
12:12 r S Jn 4:48
12:13 s ver 14; 1Co 9:12,18 t 2Co 11:7
12:14 u 2Co 13:1 v 1Co 4:14,15 w Pr 19:14
12:15 x Php 2:17; 1Th 2:8 y 2Co 11:11
12:16 z 2Co 11:9
12:18 a 2Co 8:6, 16 b S 2Co 2:13 c 2Co 8:18
12:19 d Ro 9:1 e S 1Co 10:14 f S Ro 14:19; 2Co 10:8
12:20 g 2Co 2:1-4 h 1Co 4:21 i 1Co 1:11; 3:3 j Gal 5:20 k Ro 1:30 l S Ro 1:29 m 1Co 4:18 n 1Co 14:33
12:21 o 2Co 2:1,4 p 2Co 13:2 q S 1Co 6:18
13:1 r 2Co 12:14 s Dt 19:15; S Mt 18:16
13:2 t ver 10 u 2Co 1:23 v 2Co 12:21
13:3 w Mt 10:20; 1Co 5:4
13:4 x 1Co 1:25; Php 2:7,8; 1Pe 3:18 y Ro 1:4; 6:4; 1Co 6:14 z ver 9; S 1Co 2:3 a S Ro 6:5
13:5 b 1Co 11:28 c La 3:40; Jn 6:6 d S Ro 8:10

12:15 SPEND . . . AND EXPEND MYSELF AS WELL. Paul's spirit of dedicated love for those he is trying to help is an example for all pastors, teachers and missionaries. It reveals a committed love (cf. 6:11–13; 7:1–4) like that of a father for his children. It is a love ready to be spent to the utmost for the sake of the other, a love that does not think of itself but shows genuine concern for those under its care. Paul seeks nothing in return but the response of their hearts turned toward Christ. Every faithful minister of the gospel should have this type of love.

12:20 SLANDER, GOSSIP. The Bible condemns sins of speech that harm other people as grave offenses against the Christian law of love. Any kind of disparaging speech that defames the character of another person must be resisted. The discussion or exposing of another's misdeeds should be done only with a sincere motive to help that person or to protect others and God's kingdom (Ro 1:29; Eph 4:31; 2Ti 4:10,14–15; 1Pe 2:1).

12:21 I WILL BE GRIEVED OVER MANY WHO HAVE SINNED. Christian ministers must mourn over those in the church who refuse to repent of and forsake their sin, for they are spiritually dead. The tragic message for them is Paul's word to the Corinthians (1Co 6:9), the Galatians (Gal 5:21) and the Ephesians (Eph 5:5–6), a word pronouncing exclusion from God's kingdom.

13:2 I WILL NOT SPARE. A minister's love for his people (see 12:15, note) demands sternness as well as affection. There comes a time when patience runs its course, and when, for the good of the church, offenders should no longer be spared. A holy righteousness, not indulgence, is required.

13:5 EXAMINE . . . WHETHER YOU ARE IN THE FAITH. No knowledge is as important to believers as the certainty that they have eternal life (cf. 1Jn 5:13; see Jn 17:3, note). All professing Christians should examine themselves to determine that their salvation is a present reality (see article on ASSURANCE OF SALVATION, p. 552).

glad whenever we are weak[e] but you are
strong;[f] and our prayer is for your perfection.[g] **10**This is why I write these things
when I am absent, that when I come I may
not have to be harsh[h] in my use of authority—the authority the Lord gave me for
building you up, not for tearing you
down.[i]

Final Greetings

11Finally, brothers,[j] good-by. Aim for
perfection, listen to my appeal, be of one
mind, live in peace.[k] And the God of love[l]
and peace[m] will be with you.
12Greet one another with a holy kiss.[n]
13All the saints send their greetings.[o]
14May the grace of the Lord Jesus
Christ,[p] and the love of God,[q] and the
fellowship of the Holy Spirit[r] be with you
all.

13:9 [e]S 1Co 2:3 [f]2Co 4:12 [g]ver 11; Eph 4:13
13:10 [h]S 2Co 1:23 [i]2Co 10:8
13:11 [j]1Th 4:1; 2Th 3:1 [k]S Mk 9:50 [l]1Jn 4:16 [m]S Ro 15:33; Eph 6:23
13:12 [n]S Ro 16:16
13:13 [o]Php 4:22
13:14 [p]S Ro 16:20; 2Co 8:9 [q]Ro 5:5; Jude 21 [r]Php 2:1

13:14 GRACE . . . LOVE . . . FELLOWSHIP. Paul's benediction witnesses to the NT church's belief in the Trinity. Paul prays that the Corinthians may continually experience (1) the grace of Christ, i.e., his nearness, power, mercy and comfort; (2) the fatherly love of God with all his blessings; and (3) a deepening fellowship with the Holy Spirit. If this threefold reality is our abiding blessing, then our everlasting salvation will be assured.

A. The Holy Spirit in Relation to Creation and Revelation

Task	References
1. Active in creation	Ge 1:2; Job 33:4
2. Imparts life to God's creatures	Ge 2:7; Job 33:4; Ps 104:30
3. Inspired the prophets and apostles	Nu 11:29; Isa 59:21; Mic 3:8; Zec. 7:12; 2Ti 3:16; 2Pe 1:21
4. Speaks through the Word	2Sa 23:1–2; Ac 1:16–20; Eph 6:17; Heb 3:7–11; 9:8; 10:15

B. The Holy Spirit in Relation to Jesus Christ

Task	References
1. Jesus was conceived in Mary by the Spirit	Mt 1:18,20–23; Lk 1:34–35
2. Was filled with the Spirit	Mt 3:16–17; Mk 1:12–13; Lk 3:21–22; Lk 4:1
3. Preached in the Spirit	Isa 11:2–4; 61:1–2; Lk 4:16–27
4. Performed miracles by the power of the Spirit	Isa 61:1; Mt 12:28; Lk 11:20; Ac 10:38
5. Will baptize believers in the Holy Spirit	Mt 3:11; Mk 1:8; Lk 3:16; Jn 1:33; Ac 1:4–5; 11:16
6. Promises the Holy Spirit as the Counselor	Jn 14:16–18,25–26; 15:26–27; 16:7–15
7. Promises the ministry of the Holy Spirit to flow to believers	Jn 7:37–39
8. Is revealed to believers by the Spirit	Jn 16:13–15
9. Offered himself on the cross through the Spirit	Heb 9:14
10. Was raised from the dead by the Spirit	Ro 1:3–4; 8:11
11. Received the Spirit from the Father	Jn 16:5–14; Ac 2:33
12. Poured out the Spirit upon believers	Ac 2:33,38–39
13. Is glorified by the Spirit	Jn 16:13–14
14. Spirit prays for his return	Rev 22:17

C. The Holy Spirit in Relation to the Church

Task	References
1. Dwells in the church as his temple	1Co 3:16; Eph 2:22; cf. Hag 2:5
2. Is poured out like rain upon the church	Ac 1:5; 2:1–4,16–21; cf. Isa 32:15; 44:3; Hos 6:3; Joel 2:23–32
3. Speaks to the church	Rev 2:7,11,17,27; 3:6,13,22
4. Creates fellowship in the church	2Co 13:14; Php 2:1
5. Unites the church	1Co 12:13; Eph 4:4
6. Gives gifts to the church	Ro 12:6–8; Eph 4:11; see chart on THE GIFTS OF THE HOLY SPIRIT
7. Strengthens the church through supernatural manifestations	Ac 4:30–33; 1Co 12:7–13; 14:1–33
8. Appoints leaders for the church	Ac 20:28; Eph 4:11; see chart on THE GIFTS OF THE HOLY SPIRIT

C. The Holy Spirit in Relation to the Church (cont.)

Task	References
9. Works through Spirit-filled people	Ac 6:3,5,8; 8:6–12; 15:28,32; cf. Nu 27:18; Jdg 6:34; 1Sa 16:13; Zec 4:6
10. Empowers preachers	1Co 2:4
11. Commissions people of God	Ac 13:2–4
12. Directs the missionary enterprise	Ac 8:29,39; 16:6–7; 20:23
13. Guards the church against error	2Ti 1:14
14. Warns the church of apostasy	1Ti 4:1; cf. Ne 9:30
15. Equips the church for spiritual warfare	Eph 6:10–18
16. Glorifies Christ	Jn 16:13–15
17. Promotes righteousness	Ro 14:17; Eph 2:21–22; 3:16–21; 1Th 4:7–8

D. The Holy Spirit in Relation to Individual Believers

Task	References
1. Lives in every believer	Ro 8:11; 1Co 6:15–20; 2Co 3:3; Eph 1:13; Heb 6:4; 1Jn 3:24; 4:13
2. Convicts us of sin	Jn 16:7–11; Ac 2:37
3. Regenerates us	Jn 3:5–6; 14:17; 20:22; Ro 8:9; 2Co 3:6; Tit 3:5
4. Imparts God's love to us	Ro 5:5
5. Makes us realize God is our Father	Ro 8:14–16; Gal 4:6
6. Enables us to say "Jesus is Lord"	1Co 12:3
7. Reveals Christ to us	Jn 15:26; 16:14–15; 1Co 2:10–11
8. Reveals God's truth to us	Ne 9:20; Jn 14:16–17,26; 16:13–14; 1Co 2:9–16
9. Enables us to distinguish truth from error	1Jn 4:1–3
10. Incorporates us into the church	1Co 12:13
11. Is given to all who ask	Lk 11:13
12. Baptizes us into the body of Christ	1Co 12:13
13. Is the One into whom we are baptized by Christ	Mt 3:11; Mk 1:8; Lk 3:16; Jn 1:33; Ac 1:4–5; 11:16
14. Fills us	Lk 1:15,41,67; Ac 2:4; 4:8,31; 6:3–5; 7:55; 11:24; 13:9,52; Eph 5:18; cf. Ex 31:3; Jdg 14:19; 1Sa 10:10
15. Gives us power and boldness to witness	Lk 1:15–17; 24:47–49; Ac 1:8; 4:31; 6:9–10; 19:6; Ro 9:1–3
16. Gives us special gifts	Mk 16:17–18; 1Co 1:7; 12:7–11; 1Pe 4:10–11; see chart on THE GIFTS OF THE HOLY SPIRIT
17. Gives visions and prophecy	Joel 2:28–29; Ac 2:17–18; 10:9–22; 1Co 14:1–5,21–25
18. Develops his fruit in us	Ro 14:17; 1Co 13; Gal 5:22–23; 1Th 1:6

D. The Holy Spirit in Relation to Individual Believers (cont.)

Task	References
19. Enables us to live a holy life	Ps 51:10–12; 143:10; Eze 11:19–20; 37:26; Ro 8:4–10; 15:16; Gal 5:16–18,25; Php 2:12–13; 2Th 2:13; 1Pe 1:2
20. Frees us from the power of sin	Ro 8:2; Eph 3:16
21. Enables us to fight Satan with the Word	Eph 6:17
22. Enables us to speak in difficult moments	Mt 10:17–20; Mk 13:11; Lk 12:11–12
23. Gives us comfort and encouragement	Jn 14:17–18,26–27; Ac 9:31
24. Helps us to pray	Ac 4:23–24; Ro 8:26; Eph 6:18; Jude 20
25. Enables us to worship	Jn 4:23–24; Ac 10:46; Eph 5:18–19; Php 3:3
26. Is grieved by our sin	Ge 6:3; Eph 4:30; cf. Mt 12:31–32
27. Is our pledge of final redemption	2Co 1:22; 5:5; Eph 1:13–14
28. Makes us yearn for Christ's return	Ro 8:23; Rev 22:20
29. Gives life to our mortal bodies	Ro 8:11

E. The Holy Spirit in Relation to Sinners

Task	References
1. Convicts of sin, righteousness and judgment	Jn 16:7–11
2. Commissions believers to proclaim the gospel to sinners	Ac 1:8; 2:17,21; 4:31; 11:12–18; 13:1–4
3. Reveals the saving truth of the gospel	Lk 4:18–19; Jn 15:26–27; Ac 4:8; 11:15,18; 14:3; 1Co 2:4,12; 1Th 1:5

GALATIANS

Outline

Introduction (1:1–10)
- A. Greetings (1:1–5)
- B. Astonishment at Their Lapse From the Gospel of Grace (1:6–10)

I. Paul Defends the Authority of His Gospel and Calling (Personal) (1:11—2:21)
- A. It Was Revealed to Him by Christ (1:11–24)
- B. It Was Recognized and Ratified by James, Peter and John (2:1–10)
- C. It Was Vindicated in Conflict With Peter (2:11–21)

II. Paul Defends the Message of His Gospel (Doctrinal) (3:1—4:31)
- A. Receiving the Spirit and New Life Is by Faith Rather Than by Works (3:1–14)
- B. Salvation Is Through Promise Rather Than Through Law (3:15–24)
- C. Those Who Trust in Christ Are Children Rather Than Slaves (3:25—4:7)
- D. An Appeal for the Galatians to Reconsider Their Action (4:8–20)
- E. Those Who Trust in the Law Are Slaves Rather Than Children (4:21–31)

III. Paul Defends the Freedom of His Gospel (Practical) (5:1—6:10)
- A. Christian Freedom Relates to Salvation by Grace (5:1–12)
  1. Preserve Christian Freedom (5:1)
  2. The Consequence of Submitting to Circumcision in the Law (5:2–12)
- B. Christian Freedom Must Not Become an Excuse for Indulging the Sinful Nature (5:13–26)
  1. The Command of Love (5:13–15)
  2. Live by the Spirit, Not by the Sinful Nature (5:16–26)
- C. Christian Freedom Must Be Expressed Through the Law of Christ (6:1–10)
  1. Carry Each Other's Burdens (6:1–5)
  2. Assist Ministers of the Word (6:6)
  3. Do Not Become Weary in Doing Good (6:7–10)

Conclusion (6:11–18)

Author: Paul

Theme: Salvation by Grace Through Faith

Date: c. A.D. 49

Background

Paul wrote this letter (1:1; 5:2; 6:11) "to the churches in Galatia" (1:2). Some believe the Galatians were the Gauls in northern Galatia. It is far more likely that Paul wrote this letter to cities in the southern region of the province of Galatia (Pisidian Antioch, Iconium, Lystra, Derbe) where he and Barnabas evangelized and established churches during their first missionary journey (Ac 13–14). The most satisfactory date for writing is shortly after Paul returned to his sending church in Antioch of Syria and just prior to the Jerusalem council (Ac 15).

The main issue in Galatians is the same one debated and resolved at Jerusalem (c. A.D. 49; cf. Ac 15). The main issue involves a twofold question: Is faith in Jesus Christ as Lord and Savior the only prerequisite for salvation? (2) Or is obedience to certain OT Jewish practices and laws required in order to gain salvation in Christ? It appears that Paul wrote Galatians before the law controversy was formally debated at Jerusalem and the official church position was pronounced. This would mean that Galatians was the first letter that Paul wrote.

Purpose

Paul learned that certain Jewish teachers were unsettling his new converts in Galatia by imposing on them circumcision and the yoke of the Mosaic law as necessary requirements for salvation and inclusion in the church. On hearing this, Paul wrote (1) to deny emphatically that legal requirements such as circumcision under the old covenant have anything to do with the operation of God's grace in Christ for salvation under the new covenant; and (2) to reaffirm clearly that we receive the Holy Spirit and are imparted spiritual life through faith in the Lord Jesus Christ, and not through attachment to OT law.

Survey

From the contents of this letter, it appears that Paul's Jewish opponents in Galatia were attacking him personally in order to undermine his influence in the churches. Paul's opponents charged that (1) he was not among the original apostles and therefore was without authentic authority (cf. 1:1,7,12; 2:8–9); (2) his message departed from the gospel preached at Jerusalem (cf. 1:9; 2:2–10); and (3) his message of grace would result in lawless living (cf. 5:1,13,16,19–21).

Paul responded directly to all three charges. (1) He vigorously defended his own authority as an apostle of Jesus Christ, authority received directly from God and endorsed by James, Peter and John (chs. 1–2). (2) He passionately defended the gospel of salvation as being by grace through faith in Christ (chs. 3–4). (3) Finally, Paul earnestly maintained that the true gospel of Christ involves a freedom from the slavery of Jewish legalism on the one hand, and a freedom from sin and the acts of the sinful nature on the other. True Christian freedom involves living by the Spirit and fulfilling the law of Christ (chs. 5–6).

Galatians contains a character sketch of the Jewish believers who opposed Paul in Galatia, Antioch and Jerusalem (Ac 15:1–2,5), and throughout most of the places in which he ministered. Paul characterized them as disturbers, perverters (1:7), hinderers (5:7), and individuals seeking to make a good impression outwardly and to avoid persecution because of the offense of Christ's cross (6:12). Indirectly Paul described them as people-pleasers (1:10), false brothers (2:4), the circumcision group (2:12) and manipulators (3:1).

Special Features

Four unique features characterize this letter. (1) It is the most vigorous NT defense of the essential nature of the gospel. Its tone is sharp, intense and urgent, as Paul deals with erring opponents (e.g., 1:8–9; 5:12) and rebukes the Galatians for their gullibility (1:6; 3:1; 4:19–20). (2) It is second only to 2 Corinthians in containing autobiographical references. (3) This is Paul's only letter explicitly addressed to a plurality of churches (see, however, Introduction to Ephesians). (4) It contains a list of the fruit of the Spirit (5:22–23) and the most extensive NT catalogue of the acts of the sinful nature (5:19–21).

Reading Galatians

In order to read the entire New Testament in one year, the book of Galatians should be read in 8 days, according to the following schedule:
☐ 1 ☐ 2 ☐ 3:1–14 ☐ 3:15–25 ☐ 3:26—4:20 ☐ 4:21—5:15 ☐ 5:16–26 ☐ 6

NOTES

1 Paul, an apostle[a]—sent not from
men nor by man,[b] but by Jesus
Christ[c] and God the Father,[d] who raised
him from the dead[e]— **2**and all the brothers with me,[f]

To the churches in Galatia:[g]

3Grace and peace to you from God our
Father and the Lord Jesus Christ,[h] **4**who
gave himself for our sins[i] to rescue us
from the present evil age,[j] according to
the will of our God and Father,[k] **5**to whom
be glory for ever and ever. Amen.[l]

No Other Gospel

6I am astonished that you are so quickly deserting the one who called[m] you by
the grace of Christ and are turning to a
different gospel[n]— **7**which is really no
gospel at all. Evidently some people are
throwing you into confusion[o] and are trying to pervert[p] the gospel of Christ. **8**But
even if we or an angel from heaven should
preach a gospel other than the one we
preached to you,[q] let him be eternally
condemned![r] **9**As we have already said,
so now I say again: If anybody is preaching to you a gospel other than what you
accepted,[s] let him be eternally condemned!

10Am I now trying to win the approval

1:1 [a]S 1Co 1:1 [b]ver 11,12 [c]ver 15,16; S Ac 9:15; 20:24 [d]ver 15,16; S Ac 9:15; 20:24 [e]S Ac 2:24 **1:2** [f]Php 4:21 [g]S Ac 16:6 **1:3** [h]S Ro 1:7 **1:4** [i]S Mt 20:28; S Ro 4:25; S 1Co 15:3; Gal 2:20 [j]S 1Co 1:20 [k]S Php 4:20 **1:5** [l]S Ro 11:36 **1:6** [m]ver 15; S Ro 8:28 [n]2Co 11:4 **1:7** [o]Ac 15:24; Gal 5:10 [p]Jer 23:16,36 **1:8** [q]ver 11,16; 1Co 15:1; 2Co 11:4; Gal 2:2 [r]Ro 9:3 **1:9** [s]Ro 16:17

1:4 RESCUE US FROM THE PRESENT EVIL AGE. This verse is probably an early confession of faith that was well known throughout the NT churches. It connects Christ's death with the forgiveness of sins and deliverance from "the present evil age." Essential to Christ's saving purpose is the deliverance of believers from the evil that dominates this world's societies. The first gospel message preached after the Pentecostal outpouring of the Holy Spirit contained the words: "Save yourselves from this corrupt generation" (Ac 2:40). Believers must live for God and refuse to be governed by the prevailing values, wisdom, opinions, corrupt desires and selfish pleasures of the people of the world (cf. Ro 12:2, note; Tit 2:14; see article on THE CHRISTIAN'S RELATIONSHIP TO THE WORLD, p. 546).

1:6 A DIFFERENT GOSPEL. False teachers had come to the Galatians, trying to persuade them to reject Paul's teaching and accept "a different gospel." Their gospel taught that salvation involved not only believing in Christ, but also being incorporated into the Jewish faith by being circumcised (5:2), observing the law (3:5) and keeping Jewish holy days (4:10). (1) The Bible clearly affirms that there is only one gospel, "the gospel of Christ" (v. 7). It has come to us through the "revelation from Jesus Christ" (v. 12) and the inspiration of the Holy Spirit (see article on THE INSPIRATION AND AUTHORITY OF SCRIPTURE, p. 474). This gospel is defined and revealed in the Bible, the Word of God. (2) Any teachings, doctrines or ideas originating from persons, churches or traditions and not expressed or implied in God's Word may not be included in the gospel of Christ (v. 11). To mix them with the original content of the gospel is to "pervert the gospel of Christ" (v. 7).

1:9 LET HIM BE ETERNALLY CONDEMNED! The words "eternally condemned" (Gk *anathema*) mean that one lies under God's curse, is doomed to destruction, and will receive God's wrath and damnation. (1) The apostle Paul reveals the Holy Spirit's inspired attitude of judgment and indignation toward those who try to distort the original gospel of Christ (v. 7) and change the truth of apostolic witness. This same attitude was evident in Jesus Christ (see Mt 23:13, note), Peter (2Pe 2), John (2Jn 7–11) and Jude (Jude 3–4,12–19), and will be found in the heart of every follower of Christ who loves Christ's gospel as revealed in God's Word and who believes that it is the indispensable Good News of salvation for a world lost in sin (Ro 10:14–15).

(2) Condemned are all those who preach a gospel contrary to the message Paul preached, as revealed to him by Christ (vv. 11–12; see v. 6, note). Anyone adding to or taking away from the original and fundamental gospel of Christ and the apostles stands under God's curse; "God will take away from him his share in the tree of life" (Rev 22:18–19).

(3) God commands believers to defend the faith (Jude 3, note), to correct in love (2Ti 2:25–26), and to separate themselves from teachers, ministers and others in the church who deny fundamental Bible truths taught by Jesus and the apostles (vv. 8–9; Ro 16:17–18; 2Co 6:17). These truths include:

(a) The deity of Christ and his virgin birth (Mt 1:23; see Jn 20:28, note);

(b) The full inspiration and authority of God's Word in all it teaches (see article on THE INSPIRATION AND AUTHORITY OF SCRIPTURE, p. 474);

(c) The historicity of the fall of Adam (Ro 5:12–19);

(d) The inherent corruption of human nature (Ge 6:5; 8:21; Ro 1:21–32; 3:10–18; 7:14,21);

(e) Humanity's lostness without Christ (see Ac 4:12, note; Ro 1:16–32; 10:13–15);

(f) Salvation by grace through faith in Christ as Lord and Savior, accomplished by his death and blood atonement (Ro 3:24–25; 5:10; see article on FAITH AND GRACE, p. 302);

(g) Christ's bodily resurrection (see Mt 28:6, note; 1Co 15:3–4);

(h) The historical reality of miracles in both the OT and NT (1Co 10:1);

(i) The reality of Satan and demons as spiritual beings (Mt 4:1; 8:28; 2Co 4:4; Eph 2:2; 6:11–18; 1Pe 5:8);

(j) The Biblical teaching about hell (see Mt 10:28, note);

(k) Christ's literal return to earth (Jn 14:3, note; Ac 1:11; 1Co 1:7, note; Rev 19:11, note).

(4) Similar passages containing warnings against false teachers are found in Ro 16:17; 2Pe 2:17–22; 2Jn 9–11; Jude 12–13; see 2Co 11:13, note; see article on FALSE TEACHERS, p. 98.

1:10 OR AM I TRYING TO PLEASE MEN? One cannot be a genuine minister of the gospel and try to

of men, or of God? Or am I trying to please men?[t] If I were still trying to please men, I would not be a servant of Christ.

Paul Called by God

11I want you to know, brothers,[u] that the gospel I preached[v] is not something that man made up. **12**I did not receive it from any man,[w] nor was I taught it; rather, I received it by revelation[x] from Jesus Christ.[y]

13For you have heard of my previous way of life in Judaism,[z] how intensely I persecuted the church of God[a] and tried to destroy it.[b] **14**I was advancing in Judaism beyond many Jews of my own age and was extremely zealous[c] for the traditions of my fathers.[d] **15**But when God, who set me apart from birth[a][e] and called me[f] by his grace, was pleased **16**to reveal his Son in me so that I might preach him among the Gentiles,[g] I did not consult any man,[h] **17**nor did I go up to Jerusalem to see those who were apostles before I was, but I went immediately into Arabia and later returned to Damascus.[i]

18Then after three years,[j] I went up to Jerusalem[k] to get acquainted with Peter[b] and stayed with him fifteen days. **19**I saw none of the other apostles—only James,[l] the Lord's brother. **20**I assure you before God[m] that what I am writing you is no lie.[n] **21**Later I went to Syria[o] and Cilicia.[p] **22**I was personally unknown to the churches of Judea[q] that are in Christ.[r] **23**They only heard the report: "The man who formerly persecuted us is now preaching the faith[s] he once tried to destroy."[t] **24**And they praised God[u] because of me.

Paul Accepted by the Apostles

2 Fourteen years later I went up again to Jerusalem,[v] this time with Barnabas.[w] I took Titus[x] along also. **2**I went in response to a revelation[y] and set before them the gospel that I preach among the Gentiles.[z] But I did this privately to those who seemed to be leaders, for fear that I was running or had run my race[a] in vain. **3**Yet not even Titus,[b] who was with me, was compelled to be circumcised, even though he was a Greek.[c] **4**⌊This matter arose⌋ because some false brothers[d] had infiltrated our ranks to spy on[e] the freedom[f] we have in Christ Jesus and to make us slaves. **5**We did not give in to them for a moment, so that the truth of the gospel[g] might remain with you.

6As for those who seemed to be important[h]—whatever they were makes no difference to me; God does not judge by external appearance[i]—those men added nothing to my message.[j] **7**On the contrary, they saw that I had been entrusted with the task[k] of preaching the gospel to the Gentiles,[c][l] just as Peter[m] had been to the Jews.[d] **8**For God, who was at work in the ministry of Peter as an apostle[n] to the Jews, was also at work in my ministry as an apostle[o] to the Gentiles. **9**James,[p] Peter[e][q] and John, those reputed to be pil-

1:10 [t]S Ro 2:29
1:11 [u]1Co 15:1 [v]S ver 8
1:12 [w]ver 1 [x]ver 16; S 1Co 2:10 [y]1Co 11:23; 15:3
1:13 [z]Ac 26:4,5 [a]S 1Co 10:32 [b]S Ac 8:3
1:14 [c]S Ac 21:20 [d]Mt 15:2
1:15 [e]Isa 49:1,5; Jer 1:5 [f]S Ac 9:15; S Ro 8:28
1:16 [g]S Ac 9:15; Gal 2:9 [h]Mt 16:17
1:17 [i]Ac 9:2, 19-22
1:18 [j]Ac 9:22,23 [k]Ac 9:26,27
1:19 [l]Mt 13:55; S Ac 15:13
1:20 [m]S Ro 1:9 [n]S Ro 9:1
1:21 [o]S Lk 2:2 [p]S Ac 6:9
1:22 [q]1Th 2:14 [r]S Ro 16:3
1:23 [s]Ac 6:7 [t]S Ac 8:3
1:24 [u]S Mt 9:8
2:1 [v]Ac 15:2 [w]S Ac 4:36 [x]S 2Co 2:13
2:2 [y]S 1Co 2:10 [z]Ac 15:4,12 [a]S 1Co 9:24
2:3 [b]ver 1; S 2Co 2:13 [c]Ac 16:3; 1Co 9:21
2:4 [d]S Ac 1:16; 2Co 11:26 [e]Jude 4 [f]Gal 5:1,13
2:5 [g]ver 14
2:6 [h]ver 2 [i]S Ac 10:34; S Rev 2:23 [j]1Co 15:11
2:7 [k]1Th 2:4; 1Ti 1:11 [l]S Ac 9:15 [m]ver 9, 11,14
2:8 [n]Ac 1:25 [o]S 1Co 1:1
2:9 [p]S Ac 15:13 [q]ver 7,11,14

[a] *15* Or *from my mother's womb* [b] *18* Greek *Cephas* [c] *7* Greek *uncircumcised* [d] *7* Greek *circumcised*; also in verses 8 and 9 [e] *9* Greek *Cephas*; also in verses 11 and 14

please people by compromising the truths of the gospel (cf. 1Co 4:3–6). Paul regarded it his duty to speak "not trying to please men but God, who tests our hearts" (1Th 2:4, note). All followers of the gospel of Christ must make it their aim to please God, even if it means displeasing some people (cf. Ac 5:29; Eph 6:6; Col 3:22).

1:15 GOD, WHO SET ME APART. Although Paul was primarily referring to his apostolic ministry, there is a sense in which each believer has been set apart by grace so that God may reveal his Son in him or her. We have been separated from sin and the present evil age (see v. 4, note), that we might live in fellowship with God and witness to Jesus Christ before the world. To be set apart means to be with God, for God and near God—living in faith and obedience for his glory and the revealing of his Son (see article on SPIRITUAL SEPARATION FOR BELIEVERS, p. 371).

2:5 NOT GIVE IN TO THEM FOR A MOMENT. Paul was tolerant of and patient toward many things (cf. 1Co 13:4–7), but unyielding when it came to the "truth of the gospel." The revelation that he received from Christ (1:12) is the one and only gospel that possesses the power for the salvation of all who believe (Ro 1:16). Paul understood that this gospel may never be compromised for the sake of peace, unity or current opinion. Both the glory of Jesus Christ and the salvation of the lost were at stake. Today if we relinquish any part of the gospel according to NT revelation, we begin to tear down the only message that saves us from eternal destruction (cf. Mt 18:6).

2:6 GOD DOES NOT JUDGE BY EXTERNAL APPEARANCE. God does not show favoritism to any person because of his or her heritage, reputation, position or accomplishment (cf. Lev 19:15; Dt 10:17; Job 34:19; Ac 10:34; Eph 6:9). (1) God sees and evaluates the heart, i.e., the inner person, and his favor rests on those whose hearts are sincerely turned toward him in love, faith and purity (cf. 1Sa 16:7; Mt 23:28; Lk 16:15; Jn 7:24; 2Co 10:7; see 1Co 13:1, note). (2) Thus God does not prefer the love, fellowship and prayers of the educated more than the uneducated, the rich more than the poor, or the powerful more than the weak; God's eternal principle is that he "accepts men from every nation who fear him and do what is right" (Ac 10:35).

lars,[r] gave me and Barnabas[s] the right
hand of fellowship when they recognized
the grace given to me.[t] They agreed that
we should go to the Gentiles,[u] and they to
the Jews. **10**All they asked was that we
should continue to remember the poor,[v]
the very thing I was eager to do.

Paul Opposes Peter

11When Peter[w] came to Antioch,[x] I opposed him to his face, because he was
clearly in the wrong. **12**Before certain men
came from James,[y] he used to eat with the
Gentiles.[z] But when they arrived, he began to draw back and separate himself
from the Gentiles because he was afraid of
those who belonged to the circumcision
group.[a] **13**The other Jews joined him in his
hypocrisy, so that by their hypocrisy even
Barnabas[b] was led astray.

14When I saw that they were not acting
in line with the truth of the gospel,[c] I said
to Peter[d] in front of them all, "You are a
Jew, yet you live like a Gentile and not like
a Jew.[e] How is it, then, that you force
Gentiles to follow Jewish customs?[f]

15"We who are Jews by birth[g] and not
'Gentile sinners'[h] **16**know that a man is
not justified by observing the law,[i] but by
faith in Jesus Christ.[j] So we, too, have put
our faith in Christ Jesus that we may be
justified by faith in Christ and not by observing the law, because by observing the
law no one will be justified.[k]

17"If, while we seek to be justified in
Christ, it becomes evident that we ourselves are sinners,[l] does that mean that
Christ promotes sin? Absolutely not![m] **18**If
I rebuild what I destroyed, I prove that I
am a lawbreaker. **19**For through the law I
died to the law[n] so that I might live for
God.[o] **20**I have been crucified with
Christ[p] and I no longer live, but Christ
lives in me.[q] The life I live in the body, I
live by faith in the Son of God,[r] who loved
me[s] and gave himself for me.[t] **21**I do not
set aside the grace of God, for if righteous-

2:9 [r] 1Ti 3:15; Rev 3:12 [s] ver 1; S Ac 4:36 [t] S Ro 12:3 [u] S Ac 9:15
2:10 [v] S Ac 24:17
2:11 [w] ver 7,9,14 [x] S Ac 11:19
2:12 [y] S Ac 15:13 [z] Ac 11:3 [a] Ac 10:45; 11:2
2:13 [b] ver 1; S Ac 4:36
2:14 [c] ver 5 [d] ver 7,9,11 [e] Ac 10:28 [f] ver 12
2:15 [g] Php 3:4,5 [h] 1Sa 15:18; Lk 24:7
2:16 [i] S Ro 3:28 [j] S Ro 9:30 [k] S Ro 3:28; S 4:25
2:17 [l] ver 15 [m] Gal 3:21
2:19 [n] S Ro 7:4 [o] Ro 6:10,11,14; 2Co 5:15
2:20 [p] S Ro 6:6 [q] S Ro 8:10; 1Pe 4:2 [r] S Mt 4:3 [s] S Ro 8:37 [t] S Gal 1:4

2:10 REMEMBER THE POOR. A repeated theme in Scripture is the special importance of helping the poor (Ex 23:10–11; Dt 15:7–11; Jer 22:16; Am 2:6–7; Mt 6:2–4; Jn 13:29). There will always be those around us who need help. The poor, especially "those who belong to the family of believers" (6:10), require both our material assistance and our prayers.

2:11 I OPPOSED HIM TO HIS FACE. Any minister or spiritual leader who is guilty of error and hypocrisy (v. 13) must be opposed and rebuked (cf. 1Ti 5:20). This must be applied without respect of persons; even a prominent person like the apostle Peter, who was used mightily by God, needed corrective rebuke (vv. 11–17; cf. 1Ti 5:20–21). Scripture indicates that Peter recognized his error and accepted Paul's rebuke in a humble and repentant manner. He later refers to Paul as "our dear brother Paul" (2Pe 3:15).

2:12 AFRAID OF ... CIRCUMCISION GROUP. Those "who belonged to the circumcision group" were Jewish Christians, especially in the Jerusalem church, who believed that the OT sign of circumcision was necessary for all new covenant believers. They also taught that Jewish believers should not eat with any uncircumcised Gentile believers who did not follow Jewish customs and dietary restrictions. Peter, although knowing that God accepted Gentile believers without partiality (Ac 10:34–35), denied his own conviction out of fear of criticism and the possible loss of authority in the Jerusalem church. His separation from table fellowship with Gentile believers encouraged the error that there were two bodies of Christ—Jewish and Gentile.

2:16 JUSTIFIED BY ... FAITH. Paul deals here with the question of how sinners can be justified, i.e., forgiven of their sins, accepted by God and put in a right relationship with him. This will happen not by "observing the law," but by a living faith in Christ Jesus (see article on BIBLICAL WORDS FOR SALVATION, p. 292).

2:19 I DIED TO THE LAW. See Ro 7:4, note on the meaning of dying to the law; Mt 5:17, note on the believer's relation to the law.

2:20 I HAVE BEEN CRUCIFIED WITH CHRIST. Paul describes his relationship to Christ in terms of a profound personal attachment to and reliance on his Lord. Those who have faith in Christ live their lives in intimate union with their Lord, both in his death and resurrection. (1) All believers have been crucified with Christ on the cross. They have died to the law as a means of salvation and now live through Christ for God (v. 19). Because of salvation in Christ, sin no longer has control over them (see Ro 6:11, note; cf. Ro 6:4,8,14; Gal 5:24; 6:14; Col 2:12,20).

(2)We who have been crucified with Christ now live with him in his resurrection life. Christ and his strength live within us, becoming the source of all of life and the center of all our thoughts, words and deeds (Jn 15:1–6; Eph 3:17). It is through the Holy Spirit that Christ's risen life is continually communicated to us (Jn 16:13–14; Ro 8:10–11).

(3) Our sharing in Christ's death and resurrection is appropriated through faith, i.e., the confident belief, love, devotion and loyalty we have in the Son of God, who loved us and gave himself for us (cf. Jn 3:16; see article on FAITH AND GRACE, p. 302). This living by faith can be seen as living by the Spirit (3:3; 5:25; cf. Ro 8:9–11).

2:21 RIGHTEOUSNESS. Paul's understanding of justification (vv. 16–17) and righteousness includes more than a mere legal declaration by God. The righteousness that comes through faith involves a moral change (v. 19), the grace of God (v. 21) and a relationship with Christ whereby we share his resurrected life (v. 20). This is confirmed in 3:21, where Paul makes it clear that the righteousness that comes through faith in Christ imparts life, a life that is seen as receiving the Spirit (3:2–3,14; see article on BIBLICAL WORDS FOR SALVATION, p. 292).

ness could be gained through the law,[u] Christ died for nothing!"[f]

Faith or Observance of the Law

3 You foolish[v] Galatians![w] Who has bewitched you?[x] Before your very eyes Jesus Christ was clearly portrayed as crucified.[y] 2I would like to learn just one thing from you: Did you receive the Spirit[z] by observing the law,[a] or by believing what you heard?[b] 3Are you so foolish? After beginning with the Spirit, are you now trying to attain your goal by human effort? 4Have you suffered so much for nothing—if it really was for nothing? 5Does God give you his Spirit and work miracles[c] among you because you observe the law, or because you believe what
Eph 4:7-12 you heard?[d]

6Consider Abraham: "He believed God, and it was credited to him as righteousness."[g][e] 7Understand, then, that those who believe[f] are children of Abraham.[g] 8The Scripture foresaw that God would justify the Gentiles by faith, and announced the gospel in advance to Abraham: "All nations will be blessed through you."[h][h] 9So those who have faith[i] are blessed along with Abraham, the man of faith.[j]

10All who rely on observing the law[k] are under a curse,[l] for it is written: "Cursed is everyone who does not continue to do everything written in the Book of the Law."[i][m] 11Clearly no one is justified before God by the law,[n] because, "The righteous will live by faith."[j][o] 12The law is not based on faith; on the contrary, "The man who does these things will live by them."[k][p] 13Christ redeemed us from the curse of the law[q] by becoming a curse for us, for it is written: "Cursed is everyone who is hung on a tree."[l][r] 14He redeemed us in order that the blessing given to Abraham might come to the Gentiles through Christ Jesus,[s] so that by faith we might receive the promise of the Spirit.[t]

The Law and the Promise

15Brothers,[u] let me take an example from everyday life. Just as no one can set aside or add to a human covenant that has been duly established, so it is in this case. 16The promises were spoken to Abraham and to his seed.[v] The Scripture does not say "and to seeds," meaning many people, but "and to your seed,"[m][w] meaning one person, who is Christ. 17What I mean is this: The law, introduced 430 years[x] later, does not set aside the covenant previously established by God and thus do away with the promise. 18For if the inheritance depends on the law, then it no long-

f *21* Some interpreters end the quotation after verse 14. g *6* Gen. 15:6 h *8* Gen. 12:3; 18:18; 22:18 i *10* Deut. 27:26 j *11* Hab. 2:4 k *12* Lev. 18:5 l *13* Deut. 21:23 m *16* Gen. 12:7; 13:15; 24:7

2:21 u Gal 3:21
3:1 v Lk 24:25 w S Ac 16:6 x Gal 5:7 y 1Co 1:23
3:2 z S Jn 20:22 a ver 5,10; Gal 2:16 b Ro 10:17; Heb 4:2
3:5 c 1Co 12:10 d ver 2,10; Gal 2:16
3:6 e Ge 15:6; S Ro 4:3
3:7 f ver 9 g S Lk 3:8
3:8 h Ge 12:3; 18:18; 22:18; 26:4; Ac 3:25
3:9 i ver 7; Ro 4:16 j Ro 4:18-22
3:10 k ver 2,5; Gal 2:16 l ver 13; S Ro 4:15 m Dt 27:26; Jer 11:3
3:11 n S Ro 3:28 o Hab 2:4; S Ro 9:30; Heb 10:38
3:12 p Lev 18:5; S Ro 10:5
3:13 q Gal 4:5 r Dt 21:23; S Ac 5:30
3:14 s Ro 4:9,16 t ver 2; Joel 2:28; S Jn 20:22; S Ac 2:33
3:15 u S Ro 7:1
3:16 v Ge 17:19; Ps 132:11; Mic 7:20; Lk 1:55; Ro 4:13,16; 9:4,8; Gal 3:29; 4:28 w Ge 12:7; 13:15; 17:7,8,10; 24:7
3:17 x Ge 15:13, 14; Ex 12:40; Ac 7:6

3:2 DID YOU RECEIVE THE SPIRIT BY . . . BELIEVING? Paul demonstrates the superiority of salvation by grace through faith in Christ over the attempt to gain salvation through obedience to the law. Through faith in Christ we receive the Holy Spirit and all his blessings, including the gift of eternal life (vv. 2–3,5,14,21; 4:6). However, the person who relies on the law to gain salvation does not receive the Spirit and life, for mere law cannot impart life (v. 21).

3:5 HIS SPIRIT. Paul's references to the Spirit (vv. 2,5,14; 4:6) include both the baptism in the Spirit and the Spirit's subsequent special operations (cf. Ac 1:4–5; 2:4; 8:14–17; 10:44–47; 11:16–17; 19:1–6; 1Co 12:4–11). This is indicated by (1) the use of the term "miracles" (Gk *dunamis*), which implies that the apostle is thinking of the charismatic manifestations of the Spirit and his coming with "power" (Gk *dunamis*) at Pentecost (Ac 1:8; cf. 2:1–4); (2) the use of the present participles ("give" and "work"), which indicate the continuous manifestation of the Spirit's gifts; (3) the use of the expression "the promise of the Spirit" (v. 14), which is nearly identical to Peter's words in Ac 2:33 (cf. Lk 24:49; Ac 1:4); and (4) the affirmation in 4:6 that adoption as God's children occurred prior to and is the basis for sending the Spirit into the believer's heart.

3:5 HIS SPIRIT . . . WORK MIRACLES. The ongoing work of the Spirit in the Galatian churches involved miracles. For Paul, receiving the Holy Spirit was not just an invisible inward work, but an experience that revealed itself in divine power among believers. The gifts of the Spirit were a determinative norm for the Spirit's presence and authority (cf. 1Co 12–14). Conversion and the baptism in the Holy Spirit should continually result in the working of miracles and the other manifestations of the Spirit.

3:6 IT WAS CREDITED TO HIM AS RIGHTEOUSNESS. See Ro 4:5,22, notes.

3:11 THE RIGHTEOUS WILL LIVE BY FAITH. Paul quotes Hab 2:4 to illustrate justification by faith (cf. Ro 1:17). Habakkuk emphasizes that one who is justified by faith possesses actual inward righteousness, for he contrasts the righteous person with the unrighteous person whose "desires are not upright" (Hab 2:4). Thus, Paul believed justification involved an actual inner righteousness through the indwelling Holy Spirit (see article on BIBLICAL WORDS FOR SALVATION, p. 292).

3:14 BLESSING GIVEN TO ABRAHAM. The content of God's promise to Abraham (v. 8) is defined as "the promise of the Spirit" (cf. Lk 24:49; Ac 1:4–5). To receive the Spirit is to have righteousness, life and all the other spiritual blessings (see v. 5, note; 4:6, note).

er depends on a promise;[y] but God in his
grace gave it to Abraham through a promise.
19What, then, was the purpose of the
law? It was added because of transgressions[z] until the Seed[a] to whom the promise referred had come. The law was put
into effect through angels[b] by a mediator.[c] **20**A mediator,[d] however, does not
represent just one party; but God is one.
21Is the law, therefore, opposed to the
promises of God? Absolutely not![e] For if
a law had been given that could impart
life, then righteousness would certainly
have come by the law.[f] **22**But the Scripture declares that the whole world is a
prisoner of sin,[g] so that what was promised, being given through faith in Jesus
Christ, might be given to those who believe.
23Before this faith came, we were held
prisoners[h] by the law, locked up until
faith should be revealed.[i] **24**So the law
was put in charge to lead us to Christ[n][j]
that we might be justified by faith.[k]
25Now that faith has come, we are no longer under the supervision of the law.[l]

3:18 [y]Ro 4:14
3:19 [z]Ro 5:20
[a]ver 16 [b]Dt 33:2; Ac 7:53
[c]Ex 20:19; Dt 5:5
3:20 [d]1Ti 2:5; Heb 8:6; 9:15; 12:24
3:21 [e]Gal 2:17; S Ro 7:12
[f]Gal 2:21
3:22 [g]Ro 3:9-19; 11:32
3:23 [h]Ro 11:32
[i]ver 25
3:24 [j]ver 19; Ro 10:4; S 4:15
[k]Gal 2:16
3:25 [l]S Ro 7:4
3:26 [m]S Ro 8:14
3:27 [n]S Mt 28:19
[o]S Ro 13:14
3:28 [p]1Co 12:13; Col 3:11 [q]Ge 1:27; 5:2; Joel 2:29
[r]Jn 10:16; 17:11; Eph 2:14,15
3:29 [s]S 1Co 3:23
[t]ver 16; S Lk 3:8
[u]S Ro 8:17
[v]ver 16
4:3 [w]ver 8,9,24, 25; Gal 2:4
[x]Col 2:8,20
4:4 [y]Mk 1:15; Ro 5:6; Eph 1:10
[z]S Jn 3:17
[a]S Jn 1:14
[b]Lk 2:27
4:5 [c]S Ro 3:24
[d]Jn 1:12

Sons of God

26You are all sons of God[m] through
faith in Christ Jesus, **27**for all of you who
were baptized into Christ[n] have clothed
yourselves with Christ.[o] **28**There is neither Jew nor Greek, slave nor free,[p] male
nor female,[q] for you are all one in Christ
Jesus.[r] **29**If you belong to Christ,[s] then
you are Abraham's seed,[t] and heirs[u] according to the promise.[v]

4 What I am saying is that as long as
the heir is a child, he is no different
from a slave, although he owns the whole
estate. **2**He is subject to guardians and
trustees until the time set by his father.
3So also, when we were children, we were
in slavery[w] under the basic principles of
the world.[x] **4**But when the time had fully
come,[y] God sent his Son,[z] born of a woman,[a] born under law,[b] **5**to redeem[c] those
under law, that we might receive the full
rights[d] of sons.[e] **6**Because you are sons,
God sent the Spirit of his Son[f] into our

[e]S Ro 8:14 **4:6** [f]S Ac 16:7

[n] *24* Or *charge until Christ came*

3:19 WHAT, THEN, WAS THE PURPOSE OF THE LAW? The word for "law" (Gk *nomos*; Heb *torah*) means "teaching" or "direction." The law can refer to the Ten Commandments, the Pentateuch or any commandment in the OT; Paul's use of law here would include the sacrificial system of the Mosaic covenant. Concerning the law Paul states several things: (1) It was given by God "because of transgressions," i.e., in order to show sin as the violation of God's will and to awaken humanity's sense of need for God's mercy, grace and salvation in Christ (v. 24; cf. Ro 5:20; 8:2).

(2) Although the OT law was holy, good and righteous (Ro 7:12), it was inadequate in that it could not impart spiritual life or moral strength (v. 21; Ro 8:3; Heb 7:18–19).

(3) The law acted as a temporary tutor for God's people until salvation through faith in Christ came (vv. 22–26). As such, the law revealed God's will for his people's behavior (Ex 19:4–6; 20:1–17; 21:1 — 24:8), provided for blood sacrifices to cover the people's sins (see Lev 1:5; 16:33) and pointed to Christ's atoning death (Heb 9:14; 10:12–14).

(4) The law was given "to lead us to Christ that we might be justified by faith" (v. 24). But now that Christ has come, the supervisory function of the law has ended (v. 25). Therefore we no longer seek salvation through the old covenant provisions, including obedience to its laws and the sacrificial system. Salvation now comes according to new covenant provisions, especially Jesus' atoning death and glorious resurrection, and the subsequent privilege of belonging to Christ (vv. 27–29; see Mt 5:17, note on the Christian's relation to law).

3:28 MALE NOR FEMALE. Paul removes all ethnic, racial, national, social and sexual distinctions with regard to one's spiritual relationship with Jesus Christ. All in Christ are equal heirs of "the gracious gift of life" (1Pe 3:7), the promised Spirit (v. 14; 4:6) and renewal in God's image (Col 3:10–11). On the other hand, within the context of spiritual equality men remain men and women remain women (Ge 1:27). Their God-assigned roles in marriage and society remain unchanged (1Pe 3:1–4; see Eph 5:22–23, notes; 1Ti 2:13,15, notes).

4:2 TRUSTEES UNTIL THE TIME SET BY HIS FATHER. Paul's statement here, although primarily used to illustrate the situation of a believer under the OT covenant, indicates that godly parents normally oversaw the instruction of their children (see Dt 6:7). Such supervision would have been done through education in the home or by placing the children under godly teachers. Scripture clearly teaches that parents should do all they can to ensure that their children receive a holy and Christlike education and are guarded from the world's ungodly philosophies and unbiblical principles (see Lk 1:17, note; see article on PARENTS AND CHILDREN, p. 432).

4:6 THE SPIRIT WHO CALLS OUT, *"ABBA*, FATHER." One of the Holy Spirit's tasks is to create in God's children a feeling of filial love that causes them to know God as their Father. (1) The term *"Abba"* is Aramaic, meaning "Father." It was the word Jesus used when referring to the heavenly Father. The combining of the Aramaic term *"Abba"* with the Greek term for father (*patēr*) expresses the depth of intimacy, deep emotion, earnestness, warmth and confidence by which the Spirit causes us to cry out to God (cf. Mk 14:36; Ro 8:15,26–27). Two sure signs of the Spirit's work within us are the spontaneous cry to God as "Father" and the spontaneous obedience to Jesus

hearts,[g] the Spirit who calls out, *"Abba,*[o]
Father."[h] 7So you are no longer a slave,
but a son; and since you are a son, God
has made you also an heir.[i]

Paul's Concern for the Galatians

8Formerly, when you did not know
God,[j] you were slaves[k] to those who by
nature are not gods.[l] 9But now that you
know God—or rather are known by God[m]
—how is it that you are turning back to
those weak and miserable principles? Do
you wish to be enslaved[n] by them all over
again?[o] 10You are observing special days
and months and seasons and years![p] 11I
fear for you, that somehow I have wasted
my efforts on you.[q]

12I plead with you, brothers,[r] become
like me, for I became like you. You have
done me no wrong. 13As you know, it was
because of an illness[s] that I first
preached the gospel to you. 14Even
though my illness was a trial to you, you
did not treat me with contempt or scorn.
Instead, you welcomed me as if I were an
angel of God, as if I were Christ Jesus
himself.[t] 15What has happened to all your
joy? I can testify that, if you could have
done so, you would have torn out your
eyes and given them to me. 16Have I now
become your enemy by telling you the
truth?[u]

17Those people are zealous to win you
over, but for no good. What they want is
to alienate you ⌊from us⌋, so that you may
be zealous for them.[v] 18It is fine to be
zealous, provided the purpose is good, and
to be so always and not just when I am
with you.[w] 19My dear children,[x] for whom
I am again in the pains of childbirth until
Christ is formed in you,[y] 20how I wish I
could be with you now and change my
tone, because I am perplexed about you!

Hagar and Sarah

21Tell me, you who want to be under the
law,[z] are you not aware of what the law
says? 22For it is written that Abraham had
two sons, one by the slave woman[a] and
the other by the free woman.[b] 23His son
by the slave woman was born in the ordinary way;[c] but his son by the free woman
was born as the result of a promise.[d]

24These things may be taken figuratively, for the women represent two covenants. One covenant is from Mount Sinai
and bears children who are to be slaves:
This is Hagar. 25Now Hagar stands for
Mount Sinai in Arabia and corresponds to
the present city of Jerusalem, because she
is in slavery with her children. 26But the
Jerusalem that is above[e] is free, and she
is our mother. 27For it is written:

> "Be glad, O barren woman,
> who bears no children;
> break forth and cry aloud,
> you who have no labor pains;
> because more are the children of the
> desolate woman
> than of her who has a husband."[p][f]

28Now you, brothers, like Isaac, are
children of promise.[g] 29At that time the
son born in the ordinary way[h] persecuted
the son born by the power of the Spirit.[i]
It is the same now. 30But what does the
Scripture say? "Get rid of the slave woman
and her son, for the slave woman's son
will never share in the inheritance with
the free woman's son."[q][j] 31Therefore,

4:6 [g] Ro 5:5 [h] Ro 8:15,16 **4:7** [i] S Ro 8:17 **4:8** [j] Ro 1:28; 1Co 1:21; 15:34; 1Th 4:5; 2Th 1:8 [k] S ver 3 [l] 2Ch 13:9; Isa 37:19; Jer 2:11; 5:7; 16:20; 1Co 8:4,5 **4:9** [m] 1Co 8:3 [n] S ver 3 [o] Col 2:20 **4:10** [p] Ro 14:5; Col 2:16 **4:11** [q] 1Th 3:5 **4:12** [r] S Ro 7:1; Gal 6:18 **4:13** [s] 1Co 2:3 **4:14** [t] Mt 10:40 **4:16** [u] Am 5:10 **4:17** [v] Gal 2:4,12 **4:18** [w] ver 13,14 **4:19** [x] S 1Th 2:11 [y] Ro 8:29; Eph 4:13

4:21 [z] S Ro 2:12 **4:22** [a] Ge 16:15 [b] Ge 21:2 **4:23** [c] ver 28,29; Ro 9:7,8 [d] Ge 17:16-21; 18:10-14; 21:1; Heb 11:11 **4:26** [e] Heb 12:22; Rev 3:12; 21:2,10 **4:27** [f] Isa 54:1 **4:28** [g] ver 23; S Gal 3:16 **4:29** [h] ver 23 [i] Ge 21:9 **4:30** [j] Ge 21:10

[o] *6* Aramaic for *Father* [p] *27* Isaiah 54:1
[q] *30* Gen. 21:10

---

as "Lord" (see 1Co 12:3, note).

(2) Paul may have in mind primarily the baptism in the Holy Spirit and his continual filling (cf. Ac 1:5; 2:4; Eph 5:18), since God makes our relationship to him as children the cause for sending the Spirit. That is, because we are already "sons" through faith in Christ, God pours forth the Spirit into our hearts. The receiving of "the full rights of sons" (v. 5) precedes the sending of the Spirit of God's Son (see 3:5, notes).

4:13 AN ILLNESS. This illness may have been eye trouble (v. 15), malaria, Paul's thorn in the flesh (2Co 12:7) or a physical disability due to stoning. Whatever it was, it seems to have involved some kind of physical problem. Faithful believers who do the Lord's will and are active in Christian service are not immune from times of ill health, bodily pain or weakness.

4:19 THE PAINS OF CHILDBIRTH. "The pains of childbirth" (Gk *ōdinō*) pictures the heartache, pain and yearning by which Paul desires the salvation of those Galatians who have become alienated from Christ and have "fallen away from grace" (5:4). He represents them as needing a second spiritual birth and himself as a mother suffering once more with birth pangs in order that Christ might be formed in them.

4:22 ABRAHAM HAD TWO SONS. Paul uses an illustration to show the difference between the old and new covenants. Hagar represents the old covenant established at Mount Sinai (v. 25); her children now live under this covenant and are "born in the ordinary way" (v. 23), i.e., they do not have the Holy Spirit. Sarah, Abraham's other wife, represents the new covenant; her children, i.e., believers in Christ, possess the Spirit and are true children of God who are "born by the power of the Spirit" (v. 29; see article on THE OLD COVENANT AND THE NEW COVENANT, p. 500).

brothers, we are not children of the slave
woman,[k] but of the free woman.[l]

Freedom in Christ

5 It is for freedom that Christ has set us
free.[m] Stand firm,[n] then, and do not
let yourselves be burdened again by a
yoke of slavery.[o]
2Mark my words! I, Paul, tell you that
if you let yourselves be circumcised,[p]
Christ will be of no value to you at all.
3Again I declare to every man who lets
himself be circumcised that he is obligated to obey the whole law.[q] **4**You who are
trying to be justified by law[r] have been
alienated from Christ; you have fallen
away from grace.[s] **5**But by faith we eagerly await through the Spirit the righteousness for which we hope.[t] **6**For in Christ
Jesus[u] neither circumcision nor uncircumcision has any value.[v] The only thing
that counts is faith expressing itself
through love.[w]
7You were running a good race.[x] Who
cut in on you[y] and kept you from obeying
the truth? **8**That kind of persuasion does
not come from the one who calls you.[z] **9**"A
little yeast works through the whole batch
of dough."[a] **10**I am confident[b] in the Lord
that you will take no other view.[c] The one
who is throwing you into confusion[d] will
pay the penalty, whoever he may be.
11Brothers, if I am still preaching circumcision, why am I still being persecuted?[e]
In that case the offense[f] of the cross has
been abolished. **12**As for those agitators,[g]
I wish they would go the whole way and
emasculate themselves!
13You, my brothers, were called to be
free.[h] But do not use your freedom to indulge the sinful nature[r];[i] rather, serve
one another[j] in love. **14**The entire law is
summed up in a single command: "Love
your neighbor as yourself."[s][k] **15**If you
keep on biting and devouring each other,
watch out or you will be destroyed by each
other.

Life by the Spirit

16So I say, live by the Spirit,[l] and you
will not gratify the desires of the sinful
nature.[m] **17**For the sinful nature desires
what is contrary to the Spirit, and the
Spirit what is contrary to the sinful nature.[n] They are in conflict with each other, so that you do not do what you want.[o]
18But if you are led by the Spirit,[p] you are
not under law.[q]
19The acts of the sinful nature are obvious: sexual immorality,[r] impurity and debauchery; **20**idolatry and witchcraft; ha-

[r] *13* Or *the flesh*; also in verses 16, 17, 19 and 24
[s] *14* Lev. 19:18

4:31 [k]S Ro 7:4 [l]ver 22
5:1 [m]ver 13; Jn 8:32; Gal 2:4; S Ro 7:4 [n]S 1Co 16:13 [o]S Mt 23:4; Gal 2:4
5:2 [p]ver 3,6,11, 12; Ac 15:1
5:3 [q]Ro 2:25; Gal 3:10; Jas 2:10
5:4 [r]S Ro 3:28 [s]Heb 12:15; 2Pe 3:17
5:5 [t]Ro 8:23,24
5:6 [u]S Ro 16:3 [v]S 1Co 7:19 [w]1Th 1:3; Jas 2:22
5:7 [x]S 1Co 9:24 [y]Gal 3:1
5:8 [z]S Ro 8:28
5:9 [a]1Co 5:6
5:10 [b]S 2Co 2:3 [c]Php 3:15 [d]ver 12; Gal 1:7
5:11 [e]Gal 4:29; 6:12 [f]S Lk 2:34
5:12 [g]ver 10
5:13 [h]S ver 1 [i]S ver 24; 1Co 8:9; 1Pe 2:16 [j]1Co 9:19; 2Co 4:5; Eph 5:21
5:14 [k]Lev 19:18; S Mt 5:43; Gal 6:2
5:16 [l]ver 18,25; Ro 8:2,4-6,9,14; S 2Co 5:17 [m]S ver 24
5:17 [n]Ro 8:5-8 [o]Ro 7:15-23
5:18 [p]S ver 16 [q]S Ro 2:12; 1Ti 1:9
5:19 [r]S 1Co 6:18

5:4 FALLEN AWAY FROM GRACE. Some Galatians had transferred their faith in Christ to faith in legalistic observances of the law (1:6–7; 5:3). Paul states that they have fallen away from grace. To fall away from grace is to be alienated from Christ (cf. Jn 15:4–6) and to abandon the principle of God's grace that brings life and salvation. It is to have one's association with Christ nullified and to no longer remain "in Christ" (see Jn 15:6, note; 2Pe 2:15,20–22; see article on FAITH AND GRACE, p. 302).

5:6 FAITH EXPRESSING ITSELF THROUGH LOVE. The Bible maintains that a person is saved through faith (2:15–16; Ro 3:22; Eph 2:8–9). (1) In this passage Paul defines the exact nature of that faith. Saving faith is a living faith in a living Savior, a faith so vital that it cannot avoid expression in love-motivated deeds. (2) Faith that does not sincerely love and obey Christ (cf. 1Jn 2:3; 5:3), show a real concern for the work of God's kingdom (cf. Mt 12:28), and actively resist sin and the world (vv. 16–17) does not qualify as saving faith (cf. Jas 2:14–16; see article on FAITH AND GRACE, p. 302).

5:7 KEPT YOU FROM OBEYING THE TRUTH. False teaching either takes the form of denying the cardinal truths of the Christian faith (see 1:9, note), or it states that something else besides what is found in the NT is required for a believer to be a complete Christian (cf. 1:6; 2:16; 5:2,6). (1) All Christian teaching must undergo the test of apostolic truth, i.e., does the teaching conform to the original message of Christ and the apostles found in the NT? (cf. 1:11–12; 2:1–2,7–9; see Eph 2:20, note). We must ask: Does a teaching contain less than the apostolic message? Does it add something unbiblical to the truth while acknowledging the apostolic message? (2) We must never test teaching solely by feelings, experience, results, miracles or by what other people are saying. The NT is the ultimate standard for truth. (3) We must beware of any teaching that says God's Word is no longer sufficient and that the church needs modern scholarship, science, philosophy, psychology or new revelations in order to reach maturity in Christ.

5:13 CALLED TO BE FREE. See 2Co 3:17, note on Christian freedom.

5:17 THE SPIRIT . . . THE SINFUL NATURE. The spiritual conflict within believers involves the whole person; the struggle is whether they will surrender to the sinful nature's inclinations and again submit to sin's control, or whether they will yield to the Spirit's demands and continue under Christ's dominion (v. 16; Ro 8:4–14). The battlefield is within Christians themselves, and the conflict must continue throughout their earthly lives if they are to eventually reign with Christ (Ro 7:7–25; 2Ti 2:12; Rev 12:11; see Eph 6:11, note).

5:19 ACTS OF THE SINFUL NATURE. For comments on the individual acts, see article on THE ACTS OF THE SINFUL NATURE AND THE FRUIT OF THE SPIRIT, p. 394.

tred, discord, jealousy, fits of rage, selfish
ambition, dissensions, factions **21**and
envy; drunkenness, orgies, and the like.[s]
I warn you, as I did before, that those who
live like this will not inherit the kingdom
of God.[t]

22But the fruit[u] of the Spirit is love,[v]
joy, peace,[w] patience, kindness, goodness, faithfulness, **23**gentleness and self-
control.[x] Against such things there is no
Col 1:6-8 law.[y] **24**Those who belong to Christ Jesus
have crucified the sinful nature[z] with its
passions and desires.[a] **25**Since we live by
the Spirit,[b] let us keep in step with the
Spirit. **26**Let us not become conceited,[c]
provoking and envying each other.

Doing Good to All

6 Brothers, if someone is caught in a
sin, you who are spiritual[d] should restore[e] him gently. But watch yourself, or
you also may be tempted. **2**Carry each other's burdens, and in this way you will fulfill the law of Christ.[f] **3**If anyone thinks
he is something[g] when he is nothing, he
deceives himself.[h] **4**Each one should test
his own actions. Then he can take pride in
himself,[i] without comparing himself to
somebody else,[j] **5**for each one should carry his own load.[k]

6Anyone who receives instruction in
the word must share all good things with
his instructor.[l]

7Do not be deceived:[m] God cannot be
mocked. A man reaps what he sows.[n]
8The one who sows to please his sinful
nature,[o] from that nature[t] will reap destruction;[p] the one who sows to please
the Spirit, from the Spirit will reap eternal
life.[q] **9**Let us not become weary in doing
good,[r] for at the proper time we will reap
a harvest if we do not give up.[s] **10**Therefore, as we have opportunity, let us do
good[t] to all people, especially to those
who belong to the family[u] of believers.

Not Circumcision but a New Creation

11See what large letters I use as I write
to you with my own hand![v]

12Those who want to make a good impression outwardly[w] are trying to compel
you to be circumcised.[x] The only reason
they do this is to avoid being persecuted[y]
for the cross of Christ. **13**Not even those
who are circumcised obey the law,[z] yet
they want you to be circumcised that they
may boast about your flesh.[a] **14**May I never boast except in the cross of our Lord

5:21 [s]Mt 15:19; Ro 13:13 [t]S Mt 25:34 **5:22** [u]Mt 7:16-20; Eph 5:9 [v]Col 3:12-15 [w]Mal 2:6 **5:23** [x]S Ac 24:25 [y]ver 18 **5:24** [z]ver 13, 16-21; S Ro 6:6; 7:5,18; 8:3-5,8,9, 12,13; 13:14; Gal 6:8; Col 2:11 [a]ver 16,17 **5:25** [b]S ver 16 **5:26** [c]Php 2:3 **6:1** [d]1Co 2:15; 3:1 [e]S Mt 18:15; S 2Co 2:7 **6:2** [f]1Co 9:21; Jas 2:8 **6:3** [g]Ro 12:3; 1Co 8:2 [h]1Co 3:18 **6:4** [i]2Co 13:5 [j]2Co 10:12 **6:5** [k]ver 2; Jer 31:30 **6:6** [l]1Co 9:11,14; 1Ti 5:17,18 **6:7** [m]S 1Co 6:9 [n]Pr 22:8; Jer 34:17; Hos 10:12,13; 2Co 9:6 **6:8** [o]S Gal 5:24 [p]Job 4:8; Hos 8:7; S Ro 6:23 [q]Jas 3:18 **6:9** [r]1Co 15:58; 2Co 4:1 [s]Job 42:12; Ps 126:5; Heb 12:3; Rev 2:10 **6:10** [t]Pr 3:27; S Tit 2:14

[u]Eph 2:19; 1Pe 4:17 **6:11** [v]S 1Co 16:21 **6:12** [w]Mt 23:25,26 [x]Ac 15:1 [y]Gal 5:11 **6:13** [z]Ro 2:25 [a]Php 3:3

t *8* Or *his flesh, from the flesh*

5:21 NOT INHERIT THE KINGDOM OF GOD. Although Paul maintains that it is impossible to inherit the kingdom of God by observing the law (2:16; 5:4), he does teach it is possible to shut oneself out of the kingdom by engaging in evil practices (see 1Co 6:9, note; Mt 25:41–46; Eph 5:7–11).

5:22–23 THE FRUIT OF THE SPIRIT. For comments on the various aspects of the fruit of the Spirit, see article on THE ACTS OF THE SINFUL NATURE AND THE FRUIT OF THE SPIRIT, p. 394.

6:1 RESTORE HIM GENTLY. The word "restore" (Gk *katartizō*) is used in the NT for mending fishing nets (Mt 4:21) or for perfecting human character (2Co 13:11). Thus, to restore a person means to lead him or her back to true repentance and to a full commitment to Jesus Christ and his ways. This may involve disciplinary action (see Mt 13:30, note), undertaken "gently."

(1) Paul is not thinking of the serious sins that bring public disgrace to the congregation (cf. 1Co 5:5). Such sins may require temporary expulsion from the fellowship before restoration is granted (1Co 5:11).

(2) The restoration that Paul mentions here does not refer to restoration to leadership positions or teaching roles within the church. Qualifications and standards for those desiring to serve in ministerial positions involve more than a person's present spiritual condition. They require a history of persevering faithfulness to God's principles for righteousness in order that they may set an example for believers (1Ti 4:12; see article on MORAL QUALIFICATIONS FOR OVERSEERS, p. 458).

6:2 CARRY EACH OTHER'S BURDENS. To carry each other's burdens includes helping needy people in times of sickness, sorrow and financial stress. Paul may have in mind the support of missionaries and teachers (see v. 6, note; cf. Ro 15:1; 1Co 9:14). To carry another's burden is a divine quality (Ps 55:22; 1Pe 5:7).

6:6–10 SHARE ALL GOOD THINGS. It is the duty of all who are taught God's Word to help provide material support for those who instruct (1Co 9:14; 1Ti 5:18). Those who are worthy of support include faithful pastors, workers, teachers, evangelists or missionaries (1Co 9:14; 3Jn 6–8). To refuse to give support, if means are available, is to sow selfishness and reap destruction (vv. 7–9). To give to those who minister in the Word is a part of doing good to those who belong to the family of believers (v. 10); "at the proper time we will reap" (v. 9) both reward (Mt 10:41–42) and eternal life (v. 8).

6:7 GOD CANNOT BE MOCKED. Those who claim to be born-again, Spirit-filled followers of Christ (v. 3), while at the same time consciously sowing to please the sinful nature (5:19–21), are guilty of mocking and despising God. Let there be no deception: such persons will not reap "eternal life" but "destruction" (v. 8) and "death" (Ro 6:20–23).

6:14 THE WORLD HAS BEEN CRUCIFIED TO ME. The cross of Christ, representing the horrible

THE ACTS OF THE SINFUL NATURE AND THE FRUIT OF THE SPIRIT

Gal 5:22–23 "But the fruit of the Spirit is love, joy, peace, patience, kindness, goodness, faithfulness, gentleness and self-control. Against such things there is no law."

No passage in the Bible draws a clearer contrast between the lifestyle of the Spirit-filled believer and that of the person controlled by the sinful human nature than Gal 5:16–26. Paul not only discusses general lifestyle differences by emphasizing that the Spirit and the sinful nature are at war with each other, but he also includes a specific list of both the acts of the sinful nature and the fruit of the Spirit.

THE ACTS OF THE SINFUL NATURE. "Sinful nature" (Gk *sarx*) pictures the human nature with its corrupt desires. The sinful nature remains within Christians after their conversion and is their deadly enemy (Ro 8:6–8,13; Gal 5:17,21). Those who practice the acts of the sinful nature cannot inherit God's kingdom (Gal 5:21). Therefore, this sinful nature must be resisted and put to death in a continual warfare that the believer wages through the power of the Holy Spirit (Ro 8:4–14; see Gal 5:17, note). The acts of the sinful nature (Gal 5:19–21) include:

(1) "Sexual immorality" (Gk *porneia*), i.e., immoral sexual conduct and intercourse; it includes taking pleasure in pornographic pictures, films or writings (cf. Ex 20:14; Mt 5:31–32; 19:9; Ac 15:20,29; 21:25; 1Co 5:1);

(2) "Impurity" (Gk *akatharsia*), i.e., sexual sins, evil deeds and vices, including thoughts and desires of the heart (Eph 5:3; Col 3:5);

(3) "Debauchery" (Gk *aselgeia*), i.e., sensuality; following one's passions and desires to the point of having no shame or public decency (2Co 12:21);

(4) "Idolatry" (Gk *eidōlolatria*), i.e., worship of spirits, persons or graven images; trust in any person, institution or thing as having equal or greater authority than God and his Word (Col 3:5);

(5) "Witchcraft" (Gk *pharmakeia*), i.e., sorcery, spiritism, black magic, worship of demons and use of drugs to produce "spiritual" experiences (Ex 7:11,22; 8:18; Rev 9:21; 18:23);

(6) "Hatred" (Gk *echthra*), i.e., intense, hostile intentions and acts; extreme dislike or enmity;

(7) "Discord" (Gk *eris*), i.e., quarreling, antagonism; a struggle for superiority (Ro 1:29; 1Co 1:11; 3:3);

(8) "Jealousy" (Gk *zēlos*), i.e., resentfulness, envy of another's success (Ro 13:13; 1Co 3:3);

(9) "Fits of rage" (Gk *thumos*), i.e., explosive anger that flames into violent words or deeds (Col 3:8);

(10) "Selfish ambition" (Gk *eritheia*), i.e., seeking of power (2Co 12:20; Php 1:16–17);

(11) "Dissensions" (Gk *dichostasia*), i.e., introducing divisive teachings not supported by God's Word (Ro 16:17);

(12) "Factions" (Gk *hairesis*), i.e., division within the congregation into selfish groups or cliques that destroy the unity of the church (1Co 11:19);

(13) "Envy" (Gk *phthonos*), i.e., resentful dislike of another person who has something that one desires;

(14) "Drunkenness" (Gk *methē*), i.e., impairing one's mental or physical control by alcoholic drink;

(15) "Orgies" (Gk *kōmos*), i.e., excessive feasting and revelry; a party spirit involving alcohol, drugs, sex, or the like.

Paul's final comment on the acts of the sinful nature is stern and forceful: any so-called Christians who engage in these types of activities shut themselves out of the kingdom of God, i.e., they do not possess eternal salvation (Gal 5:21; see 1Co 6:9, note).

THE FRUIT OF THE SPIRIT. Contrasted to the acts of the sinful nature is a single-minded lifestyle called "the fruit of the Spirit." This is produced in God's children as they allow the Spirit to so direct and influence their lives that they destroy sin's power, especially the acts of the sinful nature, and walk in fellowship with God (see Ro 8:5–14, note; 8:14, note; cf. 2Co 6:6; Eph 4:2–3; 5:9; Col 3:12–15; 2Pe 1:4–9). The fruit of the Spirit includes:

(1) "Love" (Gk *agapē*), i.e., a caring for and seeking the highest good of another person without motive of personal gain (Ro 5:5; 1Co 13; Eph 5:2; Col 3:14);

(2) "Joy" (Gk *chara*), i.e., the feeling of gladness based on the love, grace, blessings, promises and nearness of God that belong to those who believe in Christ (Ps 119:16; 2Co 6:10; 12:9; Php 1:4; 1Pe 1:8);

(3) "Peace" (Gk *eirēnē*), i.e., the quietness of heart and mind based on the knowledge that all is well between the believer and his or her heavenly Father (Ro 15:33; Php 4:7; 1Th 5:23; Heb 13:20);

(4) "Patience" (Gk *makrothumia*), i.e., endurance, long-suffering; being slow to anger or despair (Eph 4:2; 2Ti 3:10; Heb 12:1);

(5) "Kindness" (Gk *chrēstotēs*), i.e., not wanting to hurt anyone or cause them pain (Eph 4:32; Col 3:12; 1Pe 2:3);

(6) "Goodness" (Gk *agathōsunē*), i.e., zeal for truth and righteousness and a hatred of evil; it can be expressed in acts of kindness (Lk 7:37–50) or in rebuking and correcting evil (Mt 21:12–13);

(7) "Faithfulness" (Gk *pistis*), i.e., firm and unswerving loyalty to a person to whom one is united by promise, commitment, trustworthiness and honesty (Mt 23:23; Ro 3:3; 1Ti 6:12; 2Ti 2:2; 4:7; Tit 2:10);

(8) "Gentleness" (Gk *prautēs*), i.e., restraint coupled with strength and courage; it describes a person who can be angry when anger is needed and humbly submissive when submission is needed (2Ti 2:25; 1Pe 3:15; for gentleness in Jesus, compare Mt 11:29 with Mt 23 and Mk 3:5; in Paul, compare 2Co 10:1 with 10:4–6 and Gal 1:9; in Moses, compare Nu 12:3 with Ex 32:19–20);

(9) "Self-control" (Gk *egkrateia*), i.e., mastering one's own desires and passions, including faithfulness to one's marriage vows; also purity (1Co 7:9; 9:25; Tit 1:8; 2:5).

Paul's final comment on the fruit of the Spirit indicates that there are no restrictions to the lifestyle indicated here. Christians can—in fact, must—practice these virtues over and over again; they will never discover a law prohibiting them from living according to these principles.

Jesus Christ,[b] through which[u] the world
has been crucified to me, and I to the
world.[c] 15Neither circumcision nor uncircumcision means anything;[d] what counts
is a new creation.[e] 16Peace and mercy to
all who follow this rule, even to the Israel
of God.

17Finally, let no one cause me trouble,
for I bear on my body the marks[f] of Jesus.
18The grace of our Lord Jesus Christ[g]
be with your spirit,[h] brothers. Amen.

6:14 [b] 1Co 2:2 [c] S Ro 6:2,6 **6:15** [d] S 1Co 7:19 [e] S 2Co 5:17 **6:17** [f] Isa 44:5; S 2Co 1:5; 11:23 **6:18** [g] S Ro 16:20 [h] Php 4:23; 2Ti 4:22; Phm 25

[u] *14* Or *whom*

death that the Savior suffered for our eternal salvation, is now the barrier by which the world is fenced off from us and us from the world. "The world" means everything that is opposed to God, his kingdom and his righteousness (cf. 4:3; 1Co 2:12; 3:19; 1Jn 2:15–17). (1) For those who make the cross their life and their boast, the world with all its accepted standards, values, opinions, honors and lifestyles is no longer cherished or loved. (2) For us to be "crucified with Christ" (2:20) includes our being crucified to the world. There is no sharing in the salvation and glory of Christ's cross without turning our backs on all the earthly pleasures that draw our hearts away from Christ and his nearness.

6:16 ISRAEL OF GOD. This term refers to all God's people under the new covenant, i.e., both believing Jews and believing Gentiles. All who through "the cross of our Lord Jesus Christ" are crucified to the world (v. 14) and become a "new creation" (v. 15) constitute the true "Israel of God" (cf. Ro 2:28–29; 9:7–8; Eph 2:14–22; Php 3:3; 1Pe 2:9).

EPHESIANS

Outline

Christian Greetings (1:1–2)
- I. The Christian's Redemption (1:3—3:19)
  - A. Thanksgiving for God's Glorious Plan (1:3–14)
    Prayer: For the Believer's Spiritual Enlightenment (1:15–23)
  - B. Results of Redemption (2:1—3:19)
    1. Releases Us From Sin and Death to New Life in Christ (2:1–10)
    2. Reconciles Us to Others Who Are Being Saved (2:11–15)
    3. Unites Us in Christ in One Household (2:16–22)
    4. Reveals God's Wisdom Through the Church (3:1–13)
    Prayer: For the Believer's Spiritual Fulfillment (3:14–19)
- II. The Christian's New Life (4:1—5:21)
  - A. In Harmony With God's Purpose for the Church (4:1–16)
  - B. A New Life of Purity (4:17—5:7)
  - C. Living as Children of Light (5:8–14)
  - D. Careful and Spirit-filled (5:15–21)
- III. The Christian's Close Relationships (5:22—6:9)
  - A. Wives and Husbands (5:22–23)
  - B. Children and Parents (6:1–4)
  - C. Slaves and Masters (6:5–9)
- IV. The Christian's Warfare (6:10–20)
  - A. Our Ally—God (6:10–11a)
  - B. Our Enemy—Satan and His Forces (6:11b-12)
  - C. Our Equipment—Full Armor of God (6:13–20)

Conclusion (6:21–24)

Author: Paul

Theme: Christ and the Church

Date of Writing: C. A.D. 62

Background

Ephesians is one of the mountain peaks of Biblical revelation and has a unique place among Paul's letters. Rather than being hammered out on the anvil of doctrinal controversy or pastoral problems as many of Paul's other letters were, Ephesians conveys the impression of a rich overflow of revelation growing out of Paul's personal prayer life. Paul wrote this letter while a prisoner on behalf of Christ (3:1; 4:1; 6:20), most likely at Rome. Ephesians has numerous affinities with Colossians and probably was penned shortly after Colossians. Both letters may have been carried simultaneously to their destination by a co-worker of Paul named Tychicus (6:21; cf. Col 4:7).

It is commonly believed that Paul wrote Ephesians with a wider readership in mind than just the church in Ephesus—perhaps intending it to serve as a circular letter for churches throughout the province of Asia. Originally each church in Asia Minor may have inserted its own name in 1:1, testifying to the relevance of its profound message for all true churches of Jesus Christ. Many think Ephesians is the so-called letter to the Laodiceans, mentioned by Paul in Col 4:16.

Purpose

Paul's immediate purpose for writing Ephesians is implied in 1:15–17. He prayerfully longs for his readers to advance in faith, love, wisdom and revelation of the Father of glory. He earnestly desires that they live lives worthy of the Lord Jesus Christ (e.g., 4:1–3; 5:1–2). Paul, therefore, seeks to strengthen their faith and spiritual foundations by revealing the fullness of God's eternal purpose of redemption "in Christ" (1:3–14; 3:10–12) for the church (1:22–23; 2:11–22; 3:21; 4:11–16; 5:25–27) and for each individual (1:15–21; 2:1–10; 3:16–20; 4:1–3,17–32; 5:1—6:20).

Survey

In the simplest possible terms there are two basic themes in the NT: (1) how we are redeemed by God, and (2) how we as the redeemed must live. Chs. 1–3 of Ephesians address largely the former theme, while chs. 4–6 focus on the latter.

(1) Chs. 1–3 are introduced by an opening paragraph that is one of the most profound passages in the Bible (1:3–14). This magnificent hymn of redemption offers praise for the Father's election, predestination and adoption of us as his children (1:3–6), for the Son redeeming us through his blood (1:7–12), and for the Spirit as our seal and first installment of our inheritance (1:13–14). In these chapters Paul stresses that in redemption by grace through faith God is reconciling us to himself (2:1–10) and to others who are being saved (2:11–15), and is uniting us in Christ in one body, the church (2:16–22). The goal of redemption is "to bring all things in heaven and on earth together under one head, even Christ" (1:10).

(2) Chs. 4–6 consist largely of practical instructions for the church about the demands that redemption in Christ makes on our lives individually and corporately. Among the 35 directives given in Ephesians on how the redeemed ought to live, three broad categories are emphasized. (1) Believers are called to a new life of purity and separation from the world. They are called to "be holy and blameless in his sight" (1:4), "become a holy temple" (2:21), "live a life worthy of [their] calling" (4:1), "become mature" (4:13), live "in true righteousness and holiness" (4:24), "live a life of love" (5:2; cf. 3:17–19), and be holy "through the word" (5:26) in order that Christ may have a "church, without stain or wrinkle . . . holy and blameless" (5:27). (2) Believers are called to a new way of life in family and vocational relationships (5:22—6:9). These relationships are to be governed by principles that mark believers as distinctly different from the secular society in which they live. (3) Finally, believers are called to stand firm against all the devil's schemes and against the formidable "spiritual forces of evil in the heavenly realms" (6:10–20).

Special Features

Four major features characterize this letter. (1) The unfolding of great theological truth in chs. 1–3 is interrupted by two of the most powerful apostolic prayers of the NT: one asks for wisdom and revelation in a knowledge of God (1:15–23); the other focuses on knowing the love, power and glory of God (3:14–21). (2) "In Christ," a weighty Pauline expression (160 times in Paul's letters), is especially prominent in Ephesians (c. 36 times). "Every spiritual blessing" and every practical issue of life relate to being "in Christ." (3) God's eternal purpose and goal for the church is emphasized in Ephesians. (4) There is a multifaceted emphasis on the role of the Holy Spirit in the Christian life (1:13–14,17; 2:18; 3:5,16,20; 4:3–4,30; 5:18; 6:17–18).

Reading Ephesians

In order to read the entire New Testament in one year, the book of Ephesians should be read in 9 days, according to the following schedule:
☐ 1:1–14 ☐ 1:15—2:10 ☐ 2:11–22 ☐ 3 ☐ 4:1–16 ☐ 4:17—5:2 ☐ 5:3–21 ☐ 5:22—6:9 ☐ 6:10–24

NOTES

1 Paul, an apostle[a] of Christ Jesus by
the will of God,[b]

To the saints[c] in Ephesus,[a][d] the faithful[b][e] in Christ Jesus:

2 Grace and peace to you from God our
Father and the Lord Jesus Christ.[f]

Spiritual Blessings in Christ

3 Praise be to the God and Father of our
Lord Jesus Christ,[g] who has blessed us in
the heavenly realms[h] with every spiritual
blessing in Christ. 4 For he chose us[i] in
him before the creation of the world[j] to be
holy and blameless[k] in his sight. In love[l]
5 he[c] predestined[m] us to be adopted as his
sons[n] through Jesus Christ, in accordance
with his pleasure[o] and will— 6 to the
praise of his glorious grace,[p] which he
has freely given us in the One he loves.[q]
7 In him we have redemption[r] through his
blood,[s] the forgiveness of sins, in accordance with the riches[t] of God's grace
8 that he lavished on us with all wisdom
and understanding. 9 And he[d] made
known to us the mystery[u] of his will according to his good pleasure, which he
purposed[v] in Christ, 10 to be put into effect
when the times will have reached their
fulfillment[w]—to bring all things in heav-
en and on earth together under one head,
even Christ.[x]

11 In him we were also chosen,[e] having
been predestined[y] according to the plan
of him who works out everything in conformity with the purpose[z] of his will, 12 in
order that we, who were the first to hope
in Christ, might be for the praise of his
glory.[a] 13 And you also were included in
Christ[b] when you heard the word of
truth,[c] the gospel of your salvation. Having believed, you were marked in him with
a seal,[d] the promised Holy Spirit,[e] 14 who
is a deposit guaranteeing our inheritance[f] until the redemption[g] of those
who are God's possession—to the praise
of his glory.[h]

Thanksgiving and Prayer

15 For this reason, ever since I heard
about your faith in the Lord Jesus[i] and
your love for all the saints,[j] 16 I have not

1:1 aS 1Co 1:1 bS 2Co 1:1 cS Ac 9:13 dS Ac 18:19 eCol 1:2
1:2 fS Ro 1:7
1:3 g2Co 1:3; 1Pe 1:3 hver 20; Eph 2:6; 3:10; 6:12
1:4 i2Th 2:13 jS Mt 25:34 kLev 11:44; 20:7; 2Sa 22:24; Ps 15:2; Eph 5:27; Col 1:22 lEph 4:2,15,16
1:5 mver 11; Ro 8:29,30 nS Ro 8:14,15 oLk 12:32; 1Co 1:21; Col 1:19
1:6 pver 12,14 qMt 3:17
1:7 rver 14; S Ro 3:24 sS Ro 3:25 tS Ro 2:4
1:9 uS Ro 16:25 vS ver 11
1:10 wMk 1:15; Ro 5:6; Gal 4:4 xCol 1:20
1:11 yver 5; Ro 8:29,30 zver 9; Ro 8:28; Eph 3:11; Heb 6:17
1:12 aver 6,14
1:13 bS Ro 16:3 cEph 4:21; Col 1:5 dEph 4:30 eJn 14:16,17
1:14 fS Ac 20:32; S 2Co 5:5 gver 7; S Ro 3:24 hver 6,12 **1:15** iS Ac 20:21 jS Col 1:4

a *1* Some early manuscripts do not have *in Ephesus.* **b** *1* Or *believers who are* **c** *4,5* Or *sight in love.* 5*He* **d** *8,9* Or *us. With all wisdom and understanding,* 9*he* **e** *11* Or *were made heirs*

1:1 IN CHRIST JESUS. Every "faithful" believer has life only "in Christ Jesus." (1) The terms "in Christ Jesus," "in the Lord," "in him," etc., occur 160 times in Paul's writings (36 times in Ephesians). "In Christ" means that the believer now lives and acts in the sphere of Christ Jesus. Union with Christ is the redeemed Christian's new environment. "In Christ" believers have conscious communion with their Lord, and in this relationship their very lives are seen as the life of Christ living in them (see Gal 2:20, note). This personal fellowship with Christ is the most important thing in Christian experience. Union with Christ comes as a gift of God through faith.

(2) The Bible contrasts our new life "in Christ" with our old unregenerated life "in Adam." Whereas the old life is characterized by disobedience, sin, condemnation and death, our new life "in Christ" is characterized by salvation, life in the Spirit, abundant grace, righteousness and eternal life (see Ro 5:12–21; 6; 8; 14:17–19; 1Co 15:21–22,45–49; Php 2:1–5; 4:6–9; see article on FAITH AND GRACE, p. 302).

1:4 CHOSE. See article on ELECTION AND PREDESTINATION, p. 402.

1:5 PREDESTINED. See article on ELECTION AND PREDESTINATION, p. 402.

1:5 ADOPTED. See 1Jn 3:1, note.

1:13 SEAL . . . HOLY SPIRIT. As a seal, the Holy Spirit is given to believers as God's mark of ownership. By bestowing the Spirit, God marks us as his own (see 2Co 1:22). Therefore, we have the evidence that we are God's adopted children and that our redemption is real when the Holy Spirit is present in our lives (v. 5). We can know that we really belong to God when the Spirit regenerates and renews us (Jn 1:12–13; 3:3–6), delivers us from the power of sin (Ro 8:1–17; Gal 5:16–25), gives us a consciousness of God as our Father (v. 5; Ro 8:15; Gal 4:6) and fills us with power to witness for him (Ac 1:8; 2:4).

1:13 HOLY SPIRIT. The Holy Spirit and his place in the believer's redemption is a central emphasis in the book of Ephesians. The Holy Spirit (1) is the mark or seal of God's ownership (v. 13); (2) is the first installment of the believer's inheritance (v. 14); (3) is the Spirit of wisdom and revelation (v. 17); (4) helps the believer when he or she draws near to God (2:18); (5) builds the body of believers into a holy temple (2:21–22); (6) reveals the mystery of Christ (3:4–5); (7) strengthens the believer with power in the inner being (3:16); (8) motivates unity in the Christian faith in full Christlikeness (4:3,13–14); (9) grieves at sin in the life of the believer (4:30); (10) desires to repeatedly fill and empower the believer (5:18); and (11) helps in prayer and spiritual warfare (6:18).

1:13–14 HOLY SPIRIT . . . A DEPOSIT. The Holy Spirit is a "deposit," i.e., a first installment or down payment, guaranteeing our inheritance. In this age the Holy Spirit is given to believers as a down payment of what we are going to have in greater fullness in the future. His presence and work in our lives is a pledge of our future inheritance (cf. Ro 8:23; 2Co 1:22; 5:5).

1:16–20 IN MY PRAYERS. Paul's prayer for the Ephesians reflects God's highest desire for every believer in Christ. He prays that the Spirit might work in them in greater measure (cf. 3:16). The reason for this increased measure of the Spirit's impartation is that believers may receive more wisdom, revelation

stopped giving thanks for you,[k] remembering you in my prayers.[l] **17**I keep asking that the God of our Lord Jesus Christ,
the glorious Father,[m] may give you the
Spirit[f] of wisdom[n] and revelation, so that
you may know him better. **18**I pray also
that the eyes of your heart may be enlightened[o] in order that you may know the
hope to which he has called[p] you, the
riches[q] of his glorious inheritance[r] in the
saints,[s] **19**and his incomparably great
power for us who believe. That power[t] is
like the working of his mighty strength,[u]
20which he exerted in Christ when he
raised him from the dead[v] and seated him
at his right hand[w] in the heavenly
realms,[x] **21**far above all rule and authority, power and dominion,[y] and every title[z]
that can be given, not only in the present
age but also in the one to come.[a] **22**And
God placed all things under his feet[b] and
appointed him to be head[c] over everything for the church, **23**which is his body,[d]
the fullness of him[e] who fills everything
in every way.[f]

Made Alive in Christ

2 As for you, you were dead in your
transgressions and sins,[g] **2**in which
you used to live[h] when you followed the
ways of this world[i] and of the ruler of the
kingdom of the air,[j] the spirit who is now
at work in those who are disobedient.[k]
3All of us also lived among them at one
time,[l] gratifying the cravings of our sinful
nature[g][m] and following its desires and
thoughts. Like the rest, we were by nature
objects of wrath. **4**But because of his great
love for us,[n] God, who is rich in mercy,
5made us alive with Christ even when we
were dead in transgressions[o]—it is by
grace you have been saved.[p] **6**And God
raised us up with Christ[q] and seated us
with him[r] in the heavenly realms[s] in
Christ Jesus, **7**in order that in the coming
ages he might show the incomparable
riches of his grace,[t] expressed in his
kindness[u] to us in Christ Jesus. **8**For it is
by grace[v] you have been saved,[w] through
faith[x]—and this not from yourselves, it is
the gift of God— **9**not by works,[y] so that
no one can boast.[z] **10**For we are God's

1:16 [k]S Ro 1:8 [l]S Ro 1:10 **1:17** [m]Jn 20:17; Ro 15:6; Rev 1:6 [n]Ex 28:3; Isa 11:2; Php 1:9; Col 1:9 **1:18** [o]Job 42:5; 2Co 4:6; Heb 6:4 [p]S Ro 8:28 [q]ver 7; S Ro 2:4 [r]ver 11 [s]Col 1:12 **1:19** [t]Eph 3:7; Col 1:29 [u]Isa 40:26; Eph 6:10 **1:20** [v]S Ac 2:24 [w]S Mk 16:19 [x]S ver 3 **1:21** [y]Eph 3:10; Col 1:16 [z]Php 2:9, 10 [a]S Mt 12:32 **1:22** [b]S Mt 22:44; S 28:18 [c]1Co 11:3; Eph 4:15; 5:23; Col 1:18; 2:19 **1:23** [d]S 1Co 12:27 [e]S Jn 1:16; Eph 3:19 [f]Eph 4:10 **2:1** [g]ver 5; Col 2:13 **2:2** [h]ver 3,11-13; Ro 11:30; 1Co 6:11; 5:8; Col 3:7; Tit 3:3; 1Pe 4:3 [i]Ro 12:2 [j]S Jn 12:31 [k]Eph 5:6 **2:3** [l]S ver 2 [m]S Gal 5:24

2:4 [n]S Jn 3:16 **2:5** [o]ver 1; Ps 103:12 [p]ver 8; Jn 5:24; S Ac 15:11 **2:6** [q]S Ro 6:5 [r]Eph 1:20 [s]S Eph 1:3 **2:7** [t]S Ro 2:4 [u]Tit 3:4 **2:8** [v]S Ro 3:24 [w]ver 5 [x]S Ro 9:30 **2:9** [y]Dt 9:5; Ro 4:2; 2Ti 1:9; Tit 3:5 [z]1Co 1:29

[f] *17* Or *a spirit* [g] *3* Or *our flesh*

and knowledge concerning God's redemptive purposes for present and future salvation (vv. 17–18), and experience a more abundant "power" of the Holy Spirit in their lives (vv. 19–20).

1:19 HIS . . . POWER. In order for believers to advance in grace, achieve victory over Satan and sin, witness effectively for Christ and gain final salvation, they must have God's power moving toward them (cf. 1Pe 1:5). This power is an activity, manifestation and strength of the Holy Spirit working within faithful believers. It is the same power and Spirit that raised Christ from the dead and seated him at God's right hand (v. 20; Ro 8:11–16,26–27; Gal 5:22–25).

2:2 THOSE . . . DISOBEDIENT. Vv. 1–4 reveal a major reason why Christians should have great compassion and mercy for those still living in transgressions and sins. (1) All who are without Christ are controlled by "the ruler of the kingdom of the air," i.e., Satan (v. 2). Their minds are blinded by Satan to the truth of God (v. 2; 2Co 4:3–4). They are enslaved to sin and the cravings of the sinful nature (v. 3; Lk 4:18). (2) Because of the spiritual condition of unregenerate people, they cannot understand or accept the truth apart from God's grace (vv. 5,8; 1Co 1:18; Tit 2:11–14). (3) Christians must see everyone from the Biblical perspective. Those involved in immorality and pride are to be pitied because of their slavery to sin and Satan (vv. 1–3; cf. Jn 3:16). (4) Those who are without Christ are still responsible for their sins, for God gives every human being a measure of light and grace by which to seek God and escape sin's bondage through faith in Christ (Jn 1:9; Ro 1:18–32; 2:1–16).

2:8 BY GRACE . . . THROUGH FAITH. See article on FAITH AND GRACE, p. 302.

2:9 NOT BY WORKS. One cannot be saved by works, good deeds of love or strenuous efforts to keep God's commandments. One must be saved by the grace of God. The reasons for this are the following: (1) All the unsaved are spiritually dead (v. 1), under Satan's dominion (v. 2), enslaved to sin (v. 3) and under God's condemnation (v. 3).

(2) In order to be saved one must receive God's provision of salvation (vv. 4–5), be forgiven of sin (Ro 4:7–8), be made spiritually alive (Col 1:13), be delivered from the power of Satan and sin (Col 1:13), be made a new creation (v. 10; 2Co 5:17) and receive the Holy Spirit (Jn 7:37–39; 20:22). No amount of self-effort can accomplish the above.

(3) What brings salvation is God's grace through faith (vv. 5,8). God's gift of grace includes the following: (a) First comes the call to repentance and faith (Ac 2:38). With this call comes the work of the Holy Spirit within a person, giving him or her the power and ability to respond to God. (b) Those who respond in faith and repentance and accept Christ as Lord and Savior receive additional grace to be regenerated or born again by the Spirit (see article on REGENERATION, p. 178) and to be filled with the Spirit (Ac 1:8; 2:38; Eph 5:18). (c) Those who become new creatures in Christ receive continuing grace to live the Christian life, resist sin and serve God (Ro 8:13–14; 2Co 9:8). Believers strive to live for God by his grace that works within them (1Co 15:10). God's grace operates within committed believers both to will and to act according to God's good purpose (Php 2:12–13). From beginning to end, salvation is by the grace of God (see

ELECTION AND PREDESTINATION

Eph 1:4–5 "For he chose us in him before the creation of the world to be holy and blameless in his sight. In love he predestined us to be adopted as his sons through Jesus Christ, in accordance with his pleasure and will."

ELECTION. God's choice of those who believe in Christ is an important doctrine to the apostle Paul (see Ro 8:29–33; 9:6–26; 11:5,7,28; Col 3:12; 1Th 1:4; 2Th 2:13; Tit 1:1). Election (Gk *eklegō*) refers to God's choice in Christ of a people in order that they should be holy and blameless in his sight (cf. 2Th 2:13). Paul sees this election as expressing God's love as God receives as his own all who receive his Son, Jesus (Jn 1:12). The doctrine of election involves the following truths:

(1) Election is Christocentric, i.e., election of humans occurs only in union with Jesus Christ. "He chose us in him" (Eph 1:4; see 1:1, note). Jesus himself is first of all the elect of God. Concerning Jesus, God states, "Here is my servant whom I have chosen" (Mt 12:18; cf. Isa 42:1,6; 1Pe 2:4). Christ, as the elect, is the foundation of our election. Only in union with Christ do we become members of the elect (Eph 1:4,6–7,9–10,12–13). No one is elect apart from union with Christ through faith.

(2) Election is "in him . . . through his blood" (Eph 1:7). God purposed before creation (1:4) to form a people through Christ's redemptive death on the cross. Thus election is grounded in Christ's sacrificial death to save us from our sins (Ac 20:28; Ro 3:24–26).

(3) Election in Christ is primarily corporate, i.e., an election of a people (Eph 1:4–5,7,9). The elect are called "the body of Christ" (4:12), "my church" (Mt 16:18), "a people belonging to God" (1Pe 2:9) and the "bride" of Christ (Rev 19:7). Therefore, election is corporate and embraces individual persons only as they identify and associate themselves with the body of Christ, the true church (Eph 1:22–23; see Robert Shank, *Elect in the Son*, [Minneapolis: Bethany House Publishers], pp. 45–55).

(4) The election to salvation and holiness of the body of Christ is always certain. But the certainty of election for individuals remains conditional on their personal living faith in Jesus Christ and perseverance in union with him. Paul demonstrates this as follows. (a) God's eternal purpose for the church is that we should "be holy and blameless in his sight" (Eph 1:4). This refers both to forgiveness of sins (1:7) and to the church's sanctification and holiness. God's elect people are being led by the Holy Spirit toward sanctification and holiness (see Ro 8:14; Gal 5:16–25). The apostle repeatedly emphasizes this paramount purpose of God (see Eph 2:10; 3:14–19; 4:1–3,13–24; 5:1–18). (b) Fulfillment of this purpose for the corporate church is certain: Christ will "present her to himself as a radiant church . . . holy and blameless" (Eph 5:27). (c) Fulfillment of this purpose for individuals in the church is conditional. Christ will present us "holy and blameless in his sight" (Eph 1:4) only if we continue in the faith. Paul states this clearly: Christ will "present you holy in his sight without blemish . . . if you continue in your faith, established and firm, not moved from the hope held out in the gospel" (Col 1:22–23).

(5) Election to salvation in Christ is offered to all (Jn 3:16–17; 1Ti 2:4–6; Tit 2:11; Heb 2:9) and becomes actual for particular persons contingent on their repentance and faith as they accept God's gift of salvation in Christ (Eph 2:8; 3:17; cf. Ac 20:21; Ro 1:16; 4:16). At the point of faith, the believer is incorporated into Christ's elect body (the church) by the Holy Spirit (1Co 12:13), thereby becoming one of the elect. Thus, both God and humans have a decision in election (see Ro 8:29, note; 2Pe 1:1–11).

PREDESTINATION. Predestination (Gk *proorizō*) means "to decide beforehand" and applies to God's purposes comprehended in election. Election is God's choice "in Christ" of a people (the true church) for himself. Predestination comprehends what will happen to God's people (all genuine believers in Christ).

(1) God predestines his elect to be: (a) called (Ro 8:30); (b) justified (Ro 3:24; 8:30); (c) glorified (Ro 8:30); (d) conformed to the likeness of his Son (Ro 8:29); (e) holy and blameless (Eph 1:4); (f) adopted as God's children (1:5); (g) redeemed (1:7); (h) recipients of an inheritance (1:14); (i) for the praise of his glory (Eph 1:12; 1Pe 2:9); (j) recipients of the Holy Spirit (Eph 1:13; Gal 3:14); and (k) created to do good works (Eph 2:10).

(2) Predestination, like election, refers to the corporate body of Christ (i.e., the true spiritual church), and comprehends individuals only in association with that body through a living faith in Jesus Christ (Eph 1:5,7,13; cf. Ac 2:38–41; 16:31).

SUMMARY. Concerning election and predestination, we might use the analogy of a great ship on its way to heaven. The ship (the church) is chosen by God to be his very own vessel. Christ is the Captain and Pilot of this ship. All who desire to be a part of this elect ship and its Captain can do so through a living faith in Christ, by which they come on board the ship. As long as they are on the ship, in company with the ship's Captain, they are among the elect. If they choose to abandon the ship and Captain, they cease to be part of the elect. Election is always only in union with the Captain and his ship. Predestination tells us about the ship's destination and what God has prepared for those remaining on it. God invites everyone to come aboard the elect ship through faith in Jesus Christ.

workmanship,[a] created[b] in Christ Jesus
to do good works,[c] which God prepared in
advance for us to do.

One in Christ

11Therefore, remember that formerly[d]
you who are Gentiles by birth and called
"uncircumcised" by those who call themselves "the circumcision" (that done in the
body by the hands of men)[e]— **12**remember that at that time you were separate
from Christ, excluded from citizenship in
Israel and foreigners[f] to the covenants of
the promise,[g] without hope[h] and without
God in the world. **13**But now in Christ
Jesus you who once[i] were far away have
been brought near[j] through the blood of
Christ.[k]
14For he himself is our peace,[l] who has
made the two one[m] and has destroyed the
barrier, the dividing wall of hostility, **15**by
abolishing in his flesh[n] the law with its
commandments and regulations.[o] His
purpose was to create in himself one[p]
new man out of the two, thus making
peace, **16**and in this one body to reconcile
both of them to God through the cross,[q]
by which he put to death their hostility.
17He came and preached peace[r] to you
who were far away and peace to those
who were near.[s] **18**For through him we
both have access[t] to the Father[u] by one
Spirit.[v]
19Consequently, you are no longer foreigners and aliens,[w] but fellow citizens[x]
with God's people and members of God's
household,[y] **20**built[z] on the foundation[a]
of the apostles and prophets,[b] with Christ
Jesus himself[c] as the chief cornerstone.[d]
21In him the whole building is joined together and rises to become a holy temple[e]
in the Lord. **22**And in him you too are being built together to become a dwelling in
which God lives by his Spirit.[f]

Paul the Preacher to the Gentiles

3 For this reason I, Paul, the prisoner[g]
of Christ Jesus for the sake of you
Gentiles—
2Surely you have heard about the administration of God's grace that was given
to me[h] for you, **3**that is, the mystery[i]
made known to me by revelation,[j] as I
have already written briefly. **4**In reading
this, then, you will be able to understand
my insight[k] into the mystery of Christ,
5which was not made known to men in
other generations as it has now been revealed by the Spirit to God's holy apostles
and prophets.[l] **6**This mystery is that
through the gospel the Gentiles are heirs[m]

2:10 [a]Isa 29:23; 43:7; 60:21 [b]Eph 4:24 [c]S Tit 2:14 **2:11** [d]S ver 2 [e]Col 2:11 **2:12** [f]Isa 14:1; 65:1 [g]Gal 3:17 [h]1Th 4:13 **2:13** [i]S ver 2 [j]ver 17 [k]Col 1:20 **2:14** [l]ver 15; S Jn 14:27 [m]1Co 12:13; Eph 3:6 **2:15** [n]Col 1:21,22 [o]Col 2:14 [p]Gal 3:28 **2:16** [q]2Co 5:18; Col 1:20,22 **2:17** [r]S Lk 2:14 [s]ver 13; Ps 148:14; Isa 57:19 **2:18** [t]Eph 3:12 [u]Col 1:12 [v]1Co 12:13; Eph 4:4 **2:19** [w]ver 12 [x]Php 3:20 [y]Gal 6:10 **2:20** [z]1Co 3:9 [a]Mt 16:18; 1Co 3:10; Rev 21:14 [b]S Eph 4:11 [c]1Co 3:11 [d]S Ac 4:11; 1Pe 2:4-8 **2:21** [e]1Co 3:16, 17 **2:22** [f]1Co 3:16 **3:1** [g]Ac 23:18; Eph 4:1; 2Ti 1:8; Phm 1,9 **3:2** [h]Col 1:25 **3:3** [i]S Ro 16:25 [j]S 1Co 2:10

3:4 [k]2Co 11:6 **3:5** [l]Ro 16:26; S Eph 4:11 **3:6** [m]S Ro 8:17

---

article on FAITH AND GRACE, p. 302).

2:18 ACCESS TO THE FATHER. Access to God the Father is through Jesus Christ by the Holy Spirit. "Access" means that we who have faith in Christ have the freedom and right to approach our heavenly Father with confidence that we will be accepted, loved and welcomed. (1) This access is gained through Christ—his shed blood on the cross (v. 13; Ro 5:1–2) and his heavenly intercession for all who come to him (Heb 7:25; cf. 4:14–16). (2) Access to God requires the Holy Spirit's help. The Spirit's indwelling power makes it possible to pray and call on God according to his will and purpose (Jn 14:16–17; 16:13–14; Ro 8:15–16,26–27).

2:20 FOUNDATION ... APOSTLES. The church can only be a true church if it is founded on the Christ-inspired infallible revelation to the first apostles. (1) The NT apostles were the original messengers, witnesses and authorized representatives of the crucified and risen Lord. They were the foundation stones of the church, and their message is preserved in the writings of the NT as the original, fundamental testimony to the gospel of Christ, valid for all times.

(2) All believers and churches are dependent on the words, message and faith of the first apostles as historically recorded in Acts and in the apostles' inspired writings. Their authority is retained in the NT, and later generations of the church have the task of obeying the apostolic revelation and of witnessing to its truth. The gospel given to the NT apostles through the Holy Spirit is the enduring source of life, truth and direction for the church.

(3) All believers and churches are true believers and true churches only so long as they do the following: (a) They must agree with and sincerely strive to follow the apostles' original teaching and revelation concerning the gospel as found in the NT (Ac 2:42). To reject the apostles' teachings is to reject the Lord himself (Jn 16:13–15; 1Co 14:36–38; Gal 1:9–11). (b) They must continue the apostolic mission by communicating anew the apostolic message to the world and the church through faithful proclamation and teaching in the power of the Spirit (Ac 1:8; 2Ti 1:8–14; Tit 1:7–9). (c) They must not only believe the apostolic message but also defend and guard it against all distortion or alteration. The apostles' original revelation as found in the NT can never be replaced or nullified by later revelation, testimony or prophecy (Ac 20:27–31; 1Ti 6:20).

3:4 MYSTERY OF CHRIST. Paul speaks of the "mystery of Christ," hidden for ages past in God (v. 9) and now made known by revelation (v. 3) through the Spirit to the apostles and prophets (v. 5). The mystery is God's purpose to "bring all things in heaven and on earth together under one head, even Christ" (1:10), and to include people of all nations in the promise of life and salvation (v. 6; Ro 16:25–26; 2Ti 1:1). From the Jews and the Gentile nations God created "in Christ Jesus" (v. 6) a new people for himself (1:4–6; 2:16; 4:4,16; Mt 16:18; Col 1:24–28; 1Pe 2:9–10).

together with Israel, members together of
one body,[n] and sharers together in the
promise in Christ Jesus.[o]
7I became a servant of this gospel[p] by
the gift of God's grace given me[q] through
the working of his power.[r] **8**Although I
am less than the least of all God's people,[s] this grace was given me: to preach
to the Gentiles[t] the unsearchable riches
of Christ,[u] **9**and to make plain to everyone
the administration of this mystery,[v]
which for ages past was kept hidden in
God, who created all things. **10**His intent
was that now, through the church, the
manifold wisdom of God[w] should be made
known[x] to the rulers and authorities[y] in
the heavenly realms,[z] **11**according to his
eternal purpose[a] which he accomplished
in Christ Jesus our Lord. **12**In him and
through faith in him we may approach
God[b] with freedom and confidence.[c] **13**I
ask you, therefore, not to be discouraged
because of my sufferings for you, which
are your glory.

A Prayer for the Ephesians

14For this reason I kneel[d] before the
Father, **15**from whom his whole family[h] in
heaven and on earth derives its name. **16**I
pray that out of his glorious riches[e] he
may strengthen you with power[f] through
his Spirit in your inner being,[g] **17**so that
Christ may dwell in your hearts[h] through
faith. And I pray that you, being rooted[i]
and established in love, **18**may have power, together with all the saints,[j] to grasp
how wide and long and high and deep[k] is
the love of Christ, **19**and to know this love
that surpasses knowledge[l]—that you
may be filled[m] to the measure of all the
fullness of God.[n]
20Now to him who is able[o] to do immeasurably more than all we ask[p] or imagine,
according to his power[q] that is at work
within us, **21**to him be glory in the church
and in Christ Jesus throughout all generations, for ever and ever! Amen.[r]

Unity in the Body of Christ

4 As a prisoner[s] for the Lord, then, I
urge you to live a life worthy[t] of the
calling[u] you have received. **2**Be completely humble and gentle; be patient, bearing
with one another[v] in love.[w] **3**Make every
effort to keep the unity[x] of the Spirit
through the bond of peace.[y] **4**There is
one body[z] and one Spirit[a]— just as you
were called to one hope when you were
called[b]— **5**one Lord,[c] one faith, one bap-

3:6 [n]Eph 2:15,16 [o]Eze 47:22 **3:7** [p]S 1Co 3:5 [q]S Ro 12:3 [r]Eph 1:19; Col 1:29 **3:8** [s]S 1Co 15:9 [t]S Ac 9:15 [u]S Ro 2:4 **3:9** [v]S Ro 16:25 **3:10** [w]S Ro 11:33; 1Co 2:7 [x]1Pe 1:12 [y]Eph 1:21; 6:12; Col 2:10,15 [z]S Eph 1:3 **3:11** [a]S Eph 1:11 **3:12** [b]Eph 2:18 [c]2Co 3:4; Heb 3:14; 4:16; 10:19,35; 1Jn 2:28; 3:21; 4:17 **3:14** [d]Php 2:10 **3:16** [e]ver 8; S Ro 2:4 [f]S Php 4:13 [g]Ro 7:22 **3:17** [h]S Ro 8:10 [i]Col 2:7 **3:18** [j]Eph 1:15 [k]Job 11:8,9; Ps 103:11 **3:19** [l]Php 4:7 [m]Col 2:10 [n]Eph 1:23 **3:20** [o]Ro 16:25; 2Co 9:8 [p]1Ki 3:13 [q]ver 7 **3:21** [r]S Ro 11:36 **4:1** [s]S Eph 3:1 [t]Php 1:27; Col 1:10; 1Th 2:12 [u]S Ro 8:28 **4:2** [v]Col 3:12,13 [w]ver 15,16; Eph 1:4 **4:3** [x]S Ro 15:5 [y]Col 3:15 **4:4** [z]S Ro 12:5 [a]1Co 12:13; Eph 2:18 [b]S Ro 8:28 **4:5** [c]1Co 8:6

h *15* Or *whom all fatherhood*

3:7 GOD'S GRACE. The grace of God, given to each believer to accomplish God's will, is an energizing strength that flows from the risen Christ and operates through the Holy Spirit indwelling the believer (1:19; 4:7; Ac 6:8; 11:23; 14:26; 1Co 15:10; 2Co 12:9; Php 2:13; Col 1:29; Tit 2:11–13; see article on FAITH AND GRACE, p. 302).

3:10 RULERS AND AUTHORITIES. There are two possible interpretations of this verse. (1) The "rulers and authorities in the heavenly realms" may refer to good angels (cf. Col 1:16). They see God's astonishing wisdom as he demonstrates that wisdom through the church (1Pe 1:10–12). (2) The "rulers and authorities in the heavenly realms" may refer to the ruling powers of darkness in the spiritual realm (cf. 6:12; Da 10:13,20–21) to whom God's "eternal purpose" (v. 11) is being made known through the church's intercession and through spiritual warfare (cf. 6:12–18; Da 9:2–23; 10:12–13; 2Co 10:4–5).

3:16–19 STRENGTHEN ... INNER BEING. To have the "inner being" strengthened by the Spirit is to have our feelings, thoughts and purposes placed more and more under his influence and direction so that the Spirit can manifest his power through us in greater measure. The purpose of this strengthening is fourfold: (1) that Christ may establish his presence in our hearts (vv. 16–17; cf. Ro 8:9–10); (2) that we may be grounded in sincere love for God, Christ and others; (3) that we may comprehend with our minds and experience in our lives Christ's love for us (vv. 18–19); (4) that we may be filled with "all the fullness of God" (v. 19), i.e., that God's presence may so fill us that we reflect from our innermost being the character and stature that belong to the Lord Jesus Christ (cf. 4:13,15,22–24).

3:20 IMMEASURABLY MORE. God will do for us not only more than we ask and desire in prayer, but also even more than our imagination can perceive. This promise is conditioned and dependent on the degree of the Holy Spirit's presence, power and grace operating in our lives (1:19; 3:16–19; Isa 65:24; Jn 15:7; Php 2:13).

4:3 KEEP THE UNITY. "The unity of the Spirit" cannot be created by any human being. It already exists for those who have believed the truth and received Christ as the apostle proclaimed in chs. 1–3. The Ephesians are now to keep that unity, not through human efforts or organizations, but by living "a life worthy of the calling [they] have received" (v. 1). Spiritual unity is maintained by being loyal to the truth and by keeping in step with the Spirit (vv. 1–3,14–15; Gal 5:22–26). It cannot be attained "by human effort" (Gal 3:3).

4:5 ONE LORD. Essential to Christian faith and unity is the confession that there is only "one Lord." (1) That there is only "one Lord" means that Jesus Christ's work of redemption is perfect and sufficient, and no other redeemer or mediator is needed to give the believer complete salvation (1Ti 2:5–6; Heb 9:15).

tism; **6**one God and Father of all,[d] who is
over all and through all and in all.[e]
7But to each one of us[f] grace[g] has
been given[h] as Christ apportioned it.
8This is why it[i] says:

"When he ascended on high,
he led captives[i] in his train
and gave gifts to men."[j][j]

9(What does "he ascended" mean except
that he also descended to the lower, earthly regions[k]? **10**He who descended is the
very one who ascended[k] higher than all
the heavens, in order to fill the whole universe.)[l] **11**It was he who gave[m] some to
be apostles,[n] some to be prophets,[o] some
to be evangelists,[p] and some to be pastors
and teachers,[q] **12**to prepare God's people
for works of service, so that the body of
1Ti 4:14 Christ[r] may be built up[s] **13**until we all
reach unity[t] in the faith and in the knowledge of the Son of God[u] and become mature,[v] attaining to the whole measure of
the fullness of Christ.[w]
14Then we will no longer be infants,[x]
tossed back and forth by the waves,[y] and
blown here and there by every wind of
teaching and by the cunning and craftiness of men in their deceitful scheming.[z]
15Instead, speaking the truth in love,[a] we
will in all things grow up into him who is
the Head,[b] that is, Christ. **16**From him the
whole body, joined and held together by
every supporting ligament, grows[c] and
builds itself up[d] in love,[e] as each part
does its work.

Living as Children of Light

17So I tell you this, and insist on it in
the Lord, that you must no longer[f] live as
the Gentiles do, in the futility of their
thinking.[g] **18**They are darkened in their
understanding[h] and separated from the
life of God[i] because of the ignorance that
is in them due to the hardening of their
hearts.[j] **19**Having lost all sensitivity,[k]
they have given themselves over[l] to sensuality[m] so as to indulge in every kind of
impurity, with a continual lust for more.
20You, however, did not come to know
Christ that way. **21**Surely you heard of him
and were taught in him in accordance with
the truth that is in Jesus. **22**You were
taught, with regard to your former way of
life, to put off[n] your old self,[o] which is
being corrupted by its deceitful desires;[p]
23to be made new in the attitude of your
minds;[q] **24**and to put on[r] the new self,[s]
created to be like God in true righteousness and holiness.[t]

4:6 [d]Dt 6:4; Zec 14:9 [e]S Ro 11:36 **4:7** [f]1Co 12:7,11 [g]S Ro 3:24 [h]S Ro 12:3 **4:8** [i]Col 2:15 [j]Ps 68:18 **4:10** [k]Pr 30:1-4 [l]Eph 1:23 **4:11** [m]ver 8 [n]1Co 12:28; Eph 2:20; 3:5; 2Pe 3:2; Jude 17 [o]S Ac 11:27; Ro 12:6; 1Co 12:10,28; 13:2,8; 14:1,39; Eph 2:20; 3:5; 2Pe 3:2 [p]Ac 21:8; 2Ti 4:5 [q]Ac 13:1; Ro 2:21; 12:7; 1Co 12:28; 14:26; 1Ti 1:7; Jas 3:1 **4:12** [r]S 1Co 12:27 [s]S Ro 14:19 **4:13** [t]ver 3,5 [u]S Php 3:8 [v]S 1Co 2:6; Col 1:28 [w]Jn 1:16; Eph 1:23; 3:19 **4:14** [x]S 1Co 14:20 [y]Isa 57:20; Jas 1:6 [z]Eph 6:11 **4:15** [a]ver 2,16; Eph 1:4 [b]S Eph 1:22 **4:16** [c]Col 2:19 [d]1Co 12:7 [e]ver 2, 15; Eph 1:4 **4:17** [f]Eph 2:2 [g]Ro 1:21 **4:18** [h]Dt 29:4; Ro 1:21 [i]Eph 2:12 [j]2Co 3:14 **4:19** [k]1Ti 4:2 [l]Ro 1:24 [m]Col 3:5; 1Pe 4:3 **4:22** [n]ver 25,31; Col 3:5,8,9; Jas 1:21; 1Pe 2:1 [o]S Ro 6:6 [p]Jer 17:9; Heb 3:13 **4:23** [q]Ro 12:2; Col 3:10 **4:24** [r]S Ro 13:14 [s]S Ro 6:4 [t]Eph 2:10

i *8* Or *God* **j** *8* Psalm 68:18 **k** *9* Or *the depths of the earth*

The believer is to draw near to God through Christ alone (Heb 7:25).

(2) "One Lord" also means that to profess equal or greater allegiance to any authority (secular or religious) other than God revealed in Christ and the inspired Word is the same as withdrawing oneself from Christ's lordship and thus from the life that is in him alone. There can be no lordship of Christ or "unity of the Spirit" (v. 3) apart from the affirmation that the Lord Jesus is the ultimate authority for the believer and that Christ's authority is communicated in God's written Word.

4:11 IT WAS HE WHO GAVE. See article on THE MINISTRY GIFTS OF THE CHURCH, p. 407.

4:13 UNITY IN THE FAITH. In ch. 4 Paul teaches that the "unity of the Spirit" (v. 3) and the "unity in the faith" are maintained and perfected by: (1) accepting only the faith and message of the NT apostles, prophets, evangelists, pastors and teachers (vv. 11–12); (2) growing in grace, advancing toward spiritual maturity and growing up in all aspects into Christ (v. 15), and being filled with all the fullness of Christ and God (v. 13; cf. 3:19); (3) no longer being children who accept "every wind of teaching" but who instead have a knowledge of the truth by which to reject false teachers (vv. 14–15); (4) holding and speaking the revealed truth of Scripture in love (v. 15); and (5) living in "true righteousness and holiness" (v. 24; cf. vv. 17–32).

4:14 NO LONGER BE INFANTS. In vv. 13–15 Paul defines spiritually "mature" persons who possess the fullness of Christ. (1) To be spiritually mature means not being infants who are unstable, easily deceived by the false doctrines of others and susceptible to crafty showmanship. People remain infants if their understanding of and commitment to Biblical truth are inadequate (vv. 14–15). (2) To be spiritually mature involves "speaking the truth in love" (v. 15). The truth of the gospel as presented in the NT is to be held in love, presented in love and contended for in a spirit of love. The love is first directed to "Christ" (v. 15), and then to the church (v. 16) and to one another (v. 32; cf. 1Co 16:14).

4:15 TRUTH IN LOVE. Maintaining the unity in the faith (v. 13) must be based on an active love that seeks to resolve problems and reconcile differences by mutual loyalty and obedience to Christ and his Word. This means that holding and speaking NT truth in love has priority over loyalty to Christian institutions, tradition, individual people or the visible church. Any attempt to maintain fellowship or unity must never invalidate God's Word or be based on the compromise of Biblical truth (v. 14). Faithfulness to Scripture may involve separation from a part of the visible church that has become unfaithful to Christ and apostolic doctrine (see 2:20, note). Subsequently the Holy Spirit will initiate the formation of a new visible church loyal to Christ and the original NT truth.

THE MINISTRY GIFTS OF THE CHURCH

***Eph 4:11** "It was he who gave some to be apostles, some to be prophets, some to be evangelists, and some to be pastors and teachers."*

THE GIVER. Eph 4:11 lists the ministry gifts (i.e., gifted spiritual leaders) that Christ gave to the church. Paul states that Christ gave these ministry gifts (1) for preparing God's people for works of service (4:12) and (2) for the spiritual growth and development of the body of Christ as God intended (4:13–16; see article on SPIRITUAL GIFTS FOR BELIEVERS, p. 350).

APOSTLES. The title "apostle" is applied to certain leaders in the NT. The verb *apostellō* means to send someone on a special mission as a messenger and personal representative of the one who sends him. The title is used of Christ (Heb 3:1), the twelve disciples (Mt 10:2), Paul (Ro 1:1; 2Co 1:1; Gal 1:1) and others (Ac 14:4,14; Ro 16:7; Gal 1:19; 2:8–9; 1Th 2:6–7).

(1) The term "apostle" was used in the NT in a general sense for a commissioned representative of a church, such as the first Christian missionaries. Therefore, in the NT "apostle" referred to any messenger appointed and sent as a missionary or for some other special responsibility (see Ac 14:4,14; Ro 16:7; 2Co 8:23; Php 2:25). They were men who manifested extraordinary spiritual leadership, were anointed with power to confront directly the powers of darkness and to confirm the gospel with miracles, and were dedicated to establishing churches according to apostolic truth and purity. These itinerant servants risked their lives for the name of the Lord Jesus Christ and the advancement of the gospel (Ac 11:21–26; 13:50; 14:19–22; 15:25–26). They were Spirit-filled men of faith and prayer (see Ac 11:23–25; 13:2–5,46–52; 14:1–7,14,21–23).

(2) Apostles in this general sense remain essential to God's purpose in the church. If churches cease to send out Spirit-filled persons, then the spread of the gospel into all the world will be hindered. On the other hand, as long as the church produces and sends such people, it will fulfill its missionary task and remain faithful to the Lord's Great Commission (Mt 28:18–20).

(3) The term "apostle" is also used in a special sense, referring to those who saw Jesus after his resurrection and were personally commissioned by the resurrected Lord to preach the gospel and establish the church (e.g., the twelve disciples and Paul). They possessed a unique authority within the church that related to divine revelation and the original gospel message that can no longer exist in anyone today (see Eph 2:20, note). Thus, the office of apostle in this specialized sense is unique and unrepeatable. The original apostles can have no successors (see 1Co 15:8, note).

(4) A primary task of the NT apostles was to establish churches and to ensure that they were founded on, or restored to, sincere devotion to Christ and the NT faith (cf. Jn 21:15–17; 1Co 12:28; 2Co 11:2–3; Eph 4:11–12; Php 1:17). This task involved two main burdens: (a) an urgent God-given desire to maintain the church's purity and its separation from sin and the world (1Co 5:1–5; 2Co 6:14–18; Jas 2:14–26; 1Pe 2:11; 4:1–5; 1Jn 2:1,15–17; 3:3–10) and (b) a continuing burden to proclaim the NT gospel and to defend it against heresy, new theological trends and false teachers (Ro 16:17; 1Co 11:2; 2Co 11:3–4,14, notes; Gal 1:9, note; 2Pe 2:1–3; 1Jn 4:1–6; 2Jn 7–11; Jude 3–4,12–13; see article on OVERSEERS AND THEIR DUTIES, p. 274).

(5) Although the first apostles who laid the church's foundation have no successors, the church today is still dependent on their words, message and faith. The church must obey and remain faithful to their original writings. To reject the inspired revelation of the apostles is to cease being a church according to the Biblical pattern and to reject the Lord himself (Jn 16:13–15; 1Co 14:36–38; Gal 1:9–11). On the other hand, to believe the apostolic message, obey it and guard it against all distortion is to remain true to the Holy Spirit (Ac 20:28; 2Ti 1:14) and to guarantee God's continued life, blessing and presence within the church (see Eph 2:20, note).

PROPHETS. Prophets were believers who spoke under the direct impulse of the Holy Spirit in the name of God and whose main concern was the spiritual life and purity of the church. Under the new covenant they were raised up and empowered by the Holy Spirit to bring a message from God to his people (Ac 2:17; 4:8; 21:4).

(1) OT prophets are foundational for understanding the prophetic ministry in the early church. Their primary task was to speak a word of God by the Spirit in order to encourage God's people to remain faithful to their covenant relationship. They also, at times, predicted the future as the Spirit revealed it to them. Christ and the apostles serve as examples of the OT ideal (Ac 3:22–23; 13:1–2).

(2) Prophets functioned within the NT church in the following ways: (a) They were Spirit-filled proclaimers and interpreters of the Word of God, called by God to warn, exhort, comfort and edify (Ac 2:14–36; 3:12–26; 1Co 12:10; 14:3). (b) They were to exercise the gift of prophecy (see article on SPIRITUAL GIFTS FOR BELIEVERS, p. 350). (c) They were at times seers (cf. 1Ch 29:29) who foretold the future (Ac 11:28; 21:10–11). (d) Like the OT prophets, the NT prophets were called to expose sin, proclaim righteousness, warn of judgment to come, and combat worldliness and lukewarmness among God's people (Lk 1:14–17). Because of their message of righteousness, prophets and their ministry can expect rejection by many in the churches during times of lukewarmness and apostasy.

(3) The prophet's character, burden, desire and ability include: (a) a zeal for church purity (Jn 17:15–17; 1Co 6:9–11; Gal 5:22–25); (b) a deep sensitivity to evil and the capacity to identify, define and hate unrighteousness (Ro 12:9; Heb 1:9); (c) a keen understanding of the danger of false teachings (Mt 7:15; 24:11,24; Gal 1:9; 2Co 11:12–15); (d) an inherent dependence on God's Word to validate the prophet's message (Lk 4:17–19; 1Co 15:3–4; 2Ti 3:16; 1Pe 4:11); (e) a concern for the spiritual success of God's kingdom and a sharing in the feelings of God (Mt 21:11–13; 23:37; Lk 13:34; Jn 2:14–17; Ac 20:27–31).

(4) The prophets' messages are not to be regarded as infallible. Their messages are subject to the evaluation of the church, other prophets and God's Word. The congregation is required to discern and test whether their witness is from God (1Co 14:29–33; 1Jn 4:1).

(5) Prophets continue to be essential to God's purpose for the church. A church that rejects God's prophets will be a declining church, drifting toward worldliness and the compromise of Biblical truth (1Co 14:3; cf. Mt 23:31–38; Lk 11:49; Ac 7:51–52). If prophets are not allowed to bring words of rebuke and warning, words prompted by the Spirit, words exposing sin and unrighteousness (Jn 16:8–11), then the church will become a place where the voice of the Spirit can no longer be heard. Ecclesiastical politics and worldly power will replace the Spirit (2Ti 3:1–9; 4:3–5; 2Pe 2:1–3,12–22). On the other hand, if the church, with its leaders, hears the voice of the prophets, it will be moved to renewed life and fellowship with Christ, sin will be forsaken, and the Spirit's presence will be evident among the faithful (1Co 14:3; 1Th 5:19–21; Rev 3:20–22).

EVANGELISTS. In the NT, evangelists were men of God who were gifted and commissioned by God to proclaim the gospel (i.e., good news) of salvation to the unsaved and to help establish a new work in a city. When proclaimed it always carries with it the offer and power of salvation.

(1) The ministry of Philip "the evangelist" (Ac 21:8) gives a clear picture of the work of an evangelist according to the NT pattern. (a) Philip preached the gospel of Christ (Ac 8:4–5,35). (b) Many were saved and baptized with water (Ac 8:6,12). Signs, miracles, healings and deliverance from evil spirits accompanied his preaching (Ac 8:6–7,13). (d) He was concerned that new converts be filled with the Holy Spirit (Ac 8:12–17; cf. 2:38; 19:1–6).

(2) The evangelist is essential to God's purpose for the church. The church that fails to encourage and support the ministry of the evangelist will cease to gain converts as God desires. It will become a static church, devoid of growth and missionary outreach. The church that values the spiritual gift of the evangelist and maintains an earnest love and care for the lost will proclaim the message of salvation with convicting and saving power (Ac 2:14–41).

PASTORS. Pastors are those who oversee and care for the spiritual needs of a local congregation. They are also called "elders" (Ac 20:17; Tit 1:5) and "overseers" (1Ti 3:1; Tit 1:7).

(1) The task of pastors is to proclaim sound doctrine, refute heresy (Tit 1:9–11), teach God's Word and exercise leadership in the local church (1Th 5:12; 1Ti 3:1–5); be an example of purity and sound doctrine (Tit 2:7–8); and see to it that all believers remain in divine grace (Heb 12:15; 13:17; 1Pe 5:2). Their task is described in Ac 20:28–31 as safeguarding apostolic truth and God's flock by watching out for false doctrine and false teachers within the church (see article on OVERSEERS AND THEIR DUTIES, p. 274). Pastors function as shepherds, of which Jesus as the good Shepherd is a model (Jn 10:11–16; 1Pe 2:25; 5:2–4).

(2) The NT pattern shows a plurality of pastors directing the spiritual life of a local church (Ac 20:28; Php 1:1). Pastors were chosen, not through politics or power plays, but through the Spirit's wisdom given to the body as it examined the candidate's spiritual qualifications (see article on MORAL QUALIFICATIONS FOR OVERSEERS, p. 458).

(3) Pastors are essential to God's purpose for his church. The church that fails to select godly and faithful pastors will cease to be governed according to the mind of the Spirit (see 1Ti 3:1–7). It will be a church left open to the destructive forces of Satan and the world (see Ac 20:28–31). The preaching of the Word will be distorted and the standards of the gospel lost (2Ti 1:13–14). Members and families of the church will not be cared for according to God's purpose (1Ti 4:6,12–16; 6:20–21). Many will turn away from the truth and turn aside to myths (2Ti 4:4). On the other hand, if godly pastors are appointed, believers will be nourished on the words of faith and sound doctrine and disciplined for the purpose of godliness (1Ti 4:6–7). The church will be taught to persevere in the teaching of Christ and the apostles and thus ensure salvation for itself and those who hear (1Ti 4:16; 2Ti 2:2).

TEACHERS. Teachers are those who have a special, God-given gift to clarify, expound and proclaim God's Word in order to build up the body of Christ (Eph 4:12).

(1) The special task of teachers is to guard, by the help of the Holy Spirit, the gospel entrusted to them (2Ti 1:11–14). They are faithfully to point the church to Biblical revelation and to the original message of Christ and the apostles, and to persevere in this task.

(2) The principal purpose of Biblical teaching is to preserve truth and to produce holiness by leading Christ's body into an uncompromising commitment to the godly lifestyle set forth in God's Word. Scripture states that the goal of Christian instruction is "love, which comes from a pure heart and a good conscience and a sincere faith" (1Ti 1:5). Thus, the evidence of Christian learning is not just in what one knows, but how one lives—i.e., the manifestation of love, purity, faith and godliness.

(3) Teachers are essential to God's purpose for his church. The church that rejects or refuses to hear those teachers and theologians who remain faithful to Scriptural revelation will stop being concerned about the genuineness of the Biblical message and the correct interpretation of the original teaching of Christ and the apostles. The church in which such teachers and theologians remain silent will not continue steadfast in the truth. New winds of doctrine will be uncritically accepted, and religious experience and human ideas, rather than revealed truth, will be the ultimate guide to the church's doctrine, standards and practices. On the other hand, the church that listens to godly teachers and theologians will have its teachings and practices measured by the original and fundamental testimony of the gospel, its false ideas exposed and the purity of Christ's original message handed down to its children. God's inspired Word will become the test of all teaching, and the church will be ever reminded that the Spirit's inspired Word is ultimate truth and authority, and as such, stands over the churches and their institutions.

25Therefore each of you must put off
falsehood and speak truthfully[u] to his
neighbor, for we are all members of one
body.[v] **26**"In your anger do not sin"[l]:[w] Do
not let the sun go down while you are still
angry, **27**and do not give the devil a foothold.[x] **28**He who has been stealing must
steal no longer, but must work,[y] doing
something useful with his own hands,[z]
that he may have something to share with
those in need.[a]

29Do not let any unwholesome talk
come out of your mouths,[b] but only what
is helpful for building others up[c] according to their needs, that it may benefit
those who listen. **30**And do not grieve the
Holy Spirit of God,[d] with whom you were
sealed[e] for the day of redemption.[f] **31**Get
rid of[g] all bitterness, rage and anger,
brawling and slander, along with every
form of malice.[h] **32**Be kind and compassionate to one another,[i] forgiving each
other, just as in Christ God forgave you.[j]

5 Be imitators of God,[k] therefore, as
dearly loved children[l] **2**and live a life
of love, just as Christ loved us[m] and gave
himself up for us[n] as a fragrant offering
and sacrifice to God.[o]

3But among you there must not be even
a hint of sexual immorality,[p] or of any
kind of impurity, or of greed,[q] because
these are improper for God's holy people.
4Nor should there be obscenity, foolish
talk[r] or coarse joking, which are out of
place, but rather thanksgiving.[s] **5**For of
this you can be sure: No immoral, impure
or greedy person — such a man is an idolater[t] — has any inheritance[u] in the kingdom of Christ and of God.[m][v] **6**Let no one
deceive you[w] with empty words, for because of such things God's wrath[x] comes
on those who are disobedient.[y] **7**Therefore do not be partners with them.

8For you were once[z] darkness, but now
you are light in the Lord. Live as children
of light[a] **9**(for the fruit[b] of the light consists in all goodness,[c] righteousness and
truth) **10**and find out what pleases the
Lord.[d] **11**Have nothing to do with the
fruitless deeds of darkness,[e] but rather
expose them. **12**For it is shameful even to
mention what the disobedient do in secret.
13But everything exposed by the light[f]
becomes visible, **14**for it is light that
makes everything visible. This is why it is
said:

"Wake up, O sleeper,[g]
rise from the dead,[h]
and Christ will shine on you."[i]

15Be very careful, then, how you live[j]
— not as unwise but as wise, **16**making
the most of every opportunity,[k] because
the days are evil.[l] **17**Therefore do not be
foolish, but understand what the Lord's
will is.[m] **18**Do not get drunk on wine,[n]

4:25 [u] Ps 15:2; Lev 19:11; Zec 8:16; Col 3:9 [v] S Ro 12:5 **4:26** [w] Ps 4:4; S Mt 5:22 **4:27** [x] 2Co 2:10, 11 **4:28** [y] Ac 20:35 [z] 1Th 4:11 [a] Gal 6:10 **4:29** [b] Mt 12:36; Eph 5:4; Col 3:8 [c] S Ro 14:19 **4:30** [d] Isa 63:10; 1Th 5:19 [e] 2Co 1:22; 5:5; Eph 1:13 [f] Ro 8:23 **4:31** [g] S ver 22 [h] Col 3:8; 1Pe 2:1 **4:32** [i] 1Pe 3:8 [j] Mt 6:14,15; Col 3:12,13 **5:1** [k] Mt 5:48; Lk 6:36 [l] S Jn 1:12 **5:2** [m] S Jn 13:34 [n] ver 25; S Gal 1:4; 2:20 [o] Heb 7:27 **5:3** [p] S 1Co 6:18 [q] Col 3:5 **5:4** [r] Eph 4:29 [s] S ver 20 **5:5** [t] Col 3:5 [u] S Ac 20:32 [v] S Mt 25:34 **5:6** [w] S Mk 13:5 [x] S Ro 1:18 [y] Eph 2:2 **5:8** [z] S Eph 2:2 [a] Jn 8:12; S Lk 16:8; S Ac 26:18 **5:9** [b] Mt 7:16-20; Gal 5:22 [c] Ro 15:14 **5:10** [d] S 1Ti 5:4 **5:11** [e] Ro 13:12; 2Co 6:14 **5:13** [f] Jn 3:20,21 **5:14** [g] Ro 13:11 [h] Isa 26:19; Jn 5:25 [i] Isa 60:1; Mal 4:2

5:15 [j] ver 2 **5:16** [k] Col 4:5 [l] Eph 6:13 **5:17** [m] Ro 12:2; Col 1:9; 1Th 4:3 **5:18** [n] Lev 10:9; Pr 20:1; Isa 28:7; Ro 13:13

[l] 26 Psalm 4:4 [m] 5 Or *kingdom of the Christ and God*

4:30 GRIEVE . . . HOLY SPIRIT. The Holy Spirit, who lives within the believer (Ro 8:9; 1Co 6:19), is a Person who can experience intense grief or sorrow as Jesus himself did when he wept over Jerusalem or grieved on other occasions (Mt 23:37; Mk 3:5; Lk 19:41; Jn 11:35). (1) Believers cause the Holy Spirit grief or pain when they ignore his presence, voice or leading (Ro 8:5–17; Gal 5:16–25; 6:7–9). (2) Grieving the Spirit leads to resisting the Holy Spirit (Ac 7:51); this, in turn, leads to putting out the Spirit's fire (1Th 5:19), and finally to insulting the Spirit of grace (Heb 10:29). This last activity may be identified with blasphemy against the Spirit, for which there is no forgiveness (see Mt 12:31, note).

5:5 BE SURE. The apostle Paul, as well as the Ephesians, knew with unqualified certainty that all individuals (whether within or outside of the church) who were immoral, impure or greedy (i.e., loved things more than God) were excluded from Christ's kingdom. This was taught with strong conviction by the apostles and the NT church (see 1Co 6:9, note; Gal 5:21, note). People who committed such sins gave clear evidence of not being saved, of being devoid of the life of God and of being separated from eternal life (see Jn 8:42, note; 1Jn 3:15, note).

5:6 DECEIVE. Paul knew that some teachers would tell the Ephesians they need not fear God's wrath against their immorality. Thus he admonishes, "Let no one deceive you." It is apparent here that one may be deceived into believing that some immoral and impure persons do have an inheritance in the kingdom of Christ (see article on FALSE TEACHERS, p. 98).

5:11 DEEDS OF DARKNESS. Those whose allegiance belongs to Christ cannot be neutral or silent with respect to the "deeds of darkness" and immorality (vv. 3–6). They must be ever ready to expose, rebuke and speak against wickedness in all forms. To cry out sincerely against unrighteousness is to hate sin (Heb 1:9), to stand beside God against evil (Ps 94:16) and to remain faithful to Christ, who also exposed deeds of evil (Jn 7:7; 15:18–20; cf. Lk 22:28).

5:18 WINE. The fullness of the Holy Spirit is contingent on the response of believers to the grace given them to attain and maintain sanctification. That is, a person cannot be "drunk on wine" and at the same time "filled with the Spirit." Paul warns all believers about the acts of the sinful nature — that those who practice such things "will not inherit the kingdom of God" (Gal 5:19–21; cf. Eph 5:3–7). Furthermore, those who "live like this" (Gal 5:21) will have no part in the abiding presence and fullness of the Holy Spirit. In other words, to lack "the fruit of the Spirit" (Gal

End which leads to debauchery. Instead, be
filled with the Spirit.[o] **19**Speak to one another with psalms, hymns and spiritual
songs.[p] Sing and make music in your
heart to the Lord, **20**always giving
thanks[q] to God the Father for everything,
in the name of our Lord Jesus Christ.

21Submit to one another[r] out of reverence for Christ.

Wives and Husbands

5:22–6:9pp — Col 3:18–4:1

22Wives, submit to your husbands[s] as
to the Lord.[t] **23**For the husband is the
head of the wife as Christ is the head of
the church,[u] his body, of which he is the
Savior. **24**Now as the church submits to
Christ, so also wives should submit to
their husbands[v] in everything.

25Husbands, love your wives,[w] just as
Christ loved the church and gave himself
up for her[x] **26**to make her holy,[y] cleansing[n] her by the washing[z] with water
through the word, **27**and to present her to
himself[a] as a radiant church, without
stain or wrinkle or any other blemish, but
holy and blameless.[b] **28**In this same way,
husbands ought to love their wives[c] as
their own bodies. He who loves his wife
loves himself. **29**After all, no one ever hated his own body, but he feeds and cares
for it, just as Christ does the church—
30for we are members of his body.[d] **31**"For
this reason a man will leave his father and
mother and be united to his wife, and the
two will become one flesh."[o][e] **32**This is a
profound mystery—but I am talking
about Christ and the church. **33**However,
each one of you also must love his wife[f]
as he loves himself, and the wife must
respect her husband.

Children and Parents

6 Children, obey your parents in the
Lord, for this is right.[g] **2**"Honor your

5:18 [o]S Lk 1:15
5:19 [p]Ps 27:6; 95:2; Ac 16:25; 1Co 14:15,26; Col 3:16
5:20 [q]ver 4; Job 1:21; Ps 34:1; Col 3:17; Heb 13:15
5:21 [r]Gal 5:13; 1Pe 5:5
5:22 [s]Ge 3:16; 1Co 14:34; Col 3:18; 1Ti 2:12; Tit 2:5; 1Pe 3:1,5,6 [t]Eph 6:5
5:23 [u]S Eph 1:22
5:24 [v]S ver 22
5:25 [w]ver 28,33; Col 3:19 [x]S ver 2
5:26 [y]Jn 17:19; Heb 2:11; 10:10, 14; 13:12 [z]S Ac 22:16
5:27 [a]S 2Co 4:14 [b]Eph 1:4
5:28 [c]ver 25
5:30 [d]S Ro 12:5; S 1Co 12:27
5:31 [e]Ge 2:24; Mt 19:5; 1Co 6:16
5:33 [f]ver 25
6:1 [g]Pr 6:20; Col 3:20

[n] *26* Or *having cleansed* [o] *31* Gen. 2:24

5:22–23) is to lose the fullness of the Spirit (see Ac 8:21, note).

5:18 FILLED WITH THE SPIRIT. "Be filled" (present passive imperative) carries the meaning in Greek of "repeatedly being filled." God's children must experience constant renewal (3:14–19; 4:22–24; Ro 12:2) by repeatedly being filled with the Holy Spirit. (1) Christians are to be baptized in the Holy Spirit after conversion (see Ac 1:5; 2:4), yet they are to be filled with the Spirit repeatedly for worship, service and witness (see Ac 4:31–33, note). (2) Believers experience repeated fillings with the Spirit by maintaining a living faith in Jesus Christ (Gal 3:5), being filled with God's Word (Col 3:16), praying, giving thanks and singing to the Lord (vv. 19–20; 1Co 14:15), serving others (v. 21) and doing what the Holy Spirit desires (4:30; Ro 8:1–14; Gal 5:16ff; 1Th 5:19). (3) Several results of being filled with the Spirit are noted here: (a) speaking with joy to God in psalms, hymns and spiritual songs (v. 19), (b) giving thanks (v. 20) and (c) submitting to one another (v. 21).

5:19 SING . . . TO THE LORD. All our spiritual songs, both in the church and in private, should be first and foremost directed to God as prayers of praise or petition (cf. Ps 40:3; 77:6). (1) Songs of praise or any spiritual song can be a manifestation of the Holy Spirit (v. 18ff; 1Co 14:14ff). (2) Singing spiritual songs is a means of edification, teaching, giving thanks and praying (Col 3:16). (3) Christian singing is an expression of joy (v. 19). (4) The goal of singing hymns or spiritual songs is not entertainment or individual aggrandizement, but worship and praise of God (Ro 15:9–11; Rev 5:9–10).

5:21 SUBMIT TO ONE ANOTHER. Mutual submission in Christ is a general spiritual principle. This principle is to be applied first of all to the Christian family. Submission, humility, gentleness, patience and tolerance must be characteristic of each member. The wife must submit (i.e., yield in love) to the husband's responsibility of leadership in the family (see next note). The husband must submit to the needs of the wife in an attitude of love and self-giving (see v. 23, note). Children must submit to the authority of the parents in obedience (see 6:1, note). And parents must submit to the needs of their children and bring them up in the instruction of the Lord (see 6:4, note).

5:22 WIVES, SUBMIT. The wife is given the God-appointed task of helping and submitting to her husband (vv. 22–24). Her duty to her husband includes love (Tit 2:4), respect (v. 33; 1Pe 3:1–2), assistance (Ge 2:18), purity (Tit 2:5; 1Pe 3:2), submissiveness (v. 22; 1Pe 3:5), development of a gentle and quiet spirit (1Pe 3:4), and being a good mother (Tit 2:4) and homemaker (1Ti 2:15; 5:14; Tit 2:5). A wife's submissiveness to her husband is seen by God as an actual part of her obedience to Jesus, "as to the Lord" (see also Gal 3:28, note; 1Ti 2:13,15, notes; Tit 2:4, note).

5:23 HUSBAND . . . HEAD. God has established the family as the basic unit in society. Every family must have a leader. Therefore, God has assigned to the husband the responsibility of being the head of the wife and family (vv. 23–33; 6:4). His headship must be exercised in love, gentleness and consideration for his wife and family (vv. 25–30; 6:4). The husband's God-given responsibility as "head of the wife" includes: (1) provision for the family's spiritual and domestic needs (vv. 23–24; Ge 3:16–19; 1Ti 5:8); (2) love, protection and interest in her welfare in the same way that Christ loves the church (vv. 25–33); (3) honor, understanding, appreciation and thoughtfulness (Col 3:19; 1Pe 3:7); (4) absolute faithfulness to the marriage relationship (v. 31; Mt 5:27–28).

6:1 CHILDREN, OBEY. Normally children of believers must remain under parental guidance until they become part of another family unit through marriage. (1) Small children must be taught to obey and honor their parents by being brought up in the training and instruction of the Lord (Pr 13:24; 22:6; see next note).

father and mother"—which is the first
commandment with a promise— **3**"that it
may go well with you and that you may
enjoy long life on the earth."[p][h]

4Fathers, do not exasperate your children;[i] instead, bring them up in the training and instruction of the Lord.[j]

Slaves and Masters

5Slaves, obey your earthly masters with
respect[k] and fear, and with sincerity of
heart,[l] just as you would obey Christ.[m]
6Obey them not only to win their favor
when their eye is on you, but like slaves
of Christ,[n] doing the will of God from your
heart. **7**Serve wholeheartedly, as if you
were serving the Lord, not men,[o] **8**because you know that the Lord will reward
everyone for whatever good he does,[p]
whether he is slave or free.

9And masters, treat your slaves in the
same way. Do not threaten them, since
you know that he who is both their Master
and yours[q] is in heaven, and there is no
favoritism[r] with him.

6:3 [h]Ex 20:12; Dt 5:16
6:4 [i]Col 3:21 [j]Ge 18:19; Dt 6:7; Pr 13:24; 22:6
6:5 [k]1Ti 6:1; Tit 2:9; 1Pe 2:18 [l]Col 3:22 [m]Eph 5:22
6:6 [n]S Ro 6:22
6:7 [o]Col 3:23
6:8 [p]S Mt 16:27; Col 3:24
6:9 [q]Job 31:13,14 [r]S Ac 10:34
6:10 [s]2Sa 10:12; Ps 27:14; Hag 2:4; 1Co 16:13; 2Ti 2:1 [t]Eph 1:19
6:11 [u]ver 13; Ro 13:12; 1Th 5:8
6:12 [v]1Co 15:50; Heb 2:14 [w]Eph 1:21; 3:10 [x]Ro 8:38 [y]S Eph 1:3
6:13 [z]ver 11; S 2Co 6:7
6:14 [a]Isa 11:5 [b]Ps 132:9; Isa 59:17; 1Th 5:8
6:15 [c]Isa 52:7; Ro 10:15
6:16 [d]1Jn 5:4 [e]S Mt 5:37
6:17 [f]Isa 59:17

The Armor of God

10Finally, be strong in the Lord[s] and in
his mighty power.[t] **11**Put on the full armor of God[u] so that you can take your
stand against the devil's schemes. **12**For
our struggle is not against flesh and
blood,[v] but against the rulers, against the
authorities,[w] against the powers[x] of this
dark world and against the spiritual
forces of evil in the heavenly realms.[y]
13Therefore put on the full armor of God,[z]
so that when the day of evil comes, you
may be able to stand your ground, and
after you have done everything, to stand.
14Stand firm then, with the belt of truth
buckled around your waist,[a] with the
breastplate of righteousness in place,[b]
15and with your feet fitted with the readiness that comes from the gospel of
peace.[c] **16**In addition to all this, take up
the shield of faith,[d] with which you can
extinguish all the flaming arrows of the
evil one.[e] **17**Take the helmet of salvation[f]

p *3* Deut. 5:16

(2) Older children, even after marriage, must show respect for the counsel of their parents (v. 2) and honor them in old age through care and financial support if needed (Mt 15:1–6). (3) Children who honor their parents will be blessed by God, here on earth and in eternity (v. 3).

6:4 FATHERS, . . . YOUR CHILDREN. For an extended discussion of the parents' role in bringing up their children, see article on PARENTS AND CHILDREN, p. 432.

6:11 ARMOR OF GOD. Christians are engaged in a spiritual conflict with evil. This spiritual conflict is described as a warfare of faith (2Co 10:4; 1Ti 1:18–19; 6:12) that continues until they enter the life to come (2Ti 4:7–8; see Gal 5:17, note). (1) The believer's victory has been secured by Christ himself through Christ's death on the cross. Jesus waged a triumphant battle against Satan, disarmed the evil powers and authorities (Col 2:15; cf. Mt 12:29; Lk 10:18; Jn 12:31), led captives in his train (4:8) and redeemed the believer from Satan's power (1:7; Ac 26:18; Ro 3:24; Col 1:13–14).

(2) At the present time Christians are involved in a spiritual warfare that they wage by the power of the Holy Spirit (Ro 8:13): (a) against the sinful desires within themselves (1Pe 2:11; see Gal 5:17, note), (b) against the ungodly pleasures of the world and temptations of every sort (Mt 13:22; Gal 1:4; Jas 1:14–15; 1Jn 2:16), and (c) against Satan and his forces (see next note). Believers are called on to separate themselves from the present world system (see article on SPIRITUAL SEPARATION FOR BELIEVERS, p. 371), hating its evil (Heb 1:9; see article on THE CHRISTIAN'S RELATIONSHIP TO THE WORLD, p. 546), overcoming and dying to its temptations (Gal 6:14; 1Jn 5:4), and condemning openly its sin (Jn 7:7).

(3) Christian soldiers must wage war against all evil, not in their own power (2Co 10:3) but with spiritual weapons (vv. 10–18; cf. 2Co 10:4–5).

(4) In their warfare of faith Christians are called on to endure hardships like good soldiers of Christ (2Ti 2:3), suffer for the gospel (Mt 5:10–12; Ro 8:17; 2Co 11:23; 2Ti 1:8), fight the good fight of the faith (1Ti 6:12; 2Ti 4:7), wage war (2Co 10:3), persevere (v. 18), conquer (Ro 8:37), be victorious (1Co 15:57), triumph (2Co 2:14), defend the gospel (Php 1:16), contend for the faith (Php 1:27; Jude 3), not be frightened by opponents (Php 1:28), put on the full armor of God, stand firm (v. 14), destroy Satan's strongholds (2Co 10:4), take captive every thought (2Co 10:5) and become powerful in battle (Heb 11:34).

6:12 FORCES OF EVIL. Christians face a spiritual conflict with Satan and a host of evil spirits (see Mt 4:10, note on Satan; see article on POWER OVER SATAN AND DEMONS, p. 80). (1) These powers of darkness are the spiritual forces of evil (Jn 12:31; 14:30; 16:11; 2Co 4:4; 1Jn 5:19) who energize the ungodly (2:2), oppose God's will (Ge 3:1–7; Da 10:12–13; Mt 13:38–39) and frequently attack the believers of this age (1Pe 5:8). (2) They constitute a great multitude (Rev 12:4,7) and are organized into a highly systematized empire of evil with rank and order (2:2; Jn 14:30).

6:17 THE SWORD OF THE SPIRIT. The "sword of the Spirit" is the believer's offensive weapon to be used in the war against evil's power. Satan will make every effort to undermine or destroy the Christian's confidence in that sword, "which is the word of God." The church must defend the inspired Scriptures against allegations that Scripture is not God's Word in everything it teaches. To abandon the attitude of Christ and the apostles toward God's inspired Word is to destroy its power to rebuke or correct, to redeem, to heal, to drive out demons and to overcome all evil.

and the sword of the Spirit,[g] which is the
word of God.[h] 18And pray in the Spirit[i] on
all occasions[j] with all kinds of prayers
and requests.[k] With this in mind, be alert
and always keep on praying[l] for all the
saints.

19Pray also for me,[m] that whenever I
open my mouth, words may be given me
1Th so that I will fearlessly[n] make known the
1:5 mystery[o] of the gospel, 20for which I am
an ambassador[p] in chains.[q] Pray that I
may declare it fearlessly, as I should.

6:17 [g] Isa 49:2 [h] S Heb 4:12
6:18 [i] Ro 8:26,27 [j] S Lk 18:1 [k] Mt 26:41; Php 1:4; 4:6 [l] S Ac 1:14; Col 1:3
6:19 [m] S 1Th 5:25 [n] S Ac 4:29 [o] S Ro 16:25
6:20 [p] 2Co 5:20 [q] S Ac 21:33
6:21 [r] S Ac 20:4
6:22 [s] Col 4:7-9 [t] Col 2:2; 4:8
6:23 [u] Gal 6:16; 2Th 3:16; 1Pe 5:14

Final Greetings

21Tychicus,[r] the dear brother and
faithful servant in the Lord, will tell you
everything, so that you also may know
how I am and what I am doing. 22I am
sending him to you for this very purpose,
that you may know how we are,[s] and that
he may encourage you.[t]

23Peace[u] to the brothers, and love with
faith from God the Father and the Lord
Jesus Christ. 24Grace to all who love our
Lord Jesus Christ with an undying love.

To deny Scripture's absolute trustworthiness in all it teaches is to deliver ourselves into Satan's hand (cf. 2Pe 1:21, note; Mt 4:1–11; see article on THE INSPIRATION AND AUTHORITY OF SCRIPTURE, p. 474).

6:18 PRAY IN THE SPIRIT. The Christian's warfare against Satan's spiritual forces calls for an intensity in prayer, i.e., praying "in the Spirit," "on all occasions," "with all kinds of prayers," "for all the saints," "and always keep on praying." Prayer is not to be seen just as another weapon, but as part of the actual conflict itself, where the victory is won for ourselves and others by working together with God himself. To fail to pray diligently, with all kinds of prayer in all situations, is to surrender to the enemy (Lk 18:1; Ro 12:12; Php 4:6; Col 4:2; 1Th 5:17).

PHILIPPIANS

Outline

Introduction (1:1–11)
- A. Christian Greetings (1:1–2)
- B. Thanksgiving and Prayer for the Philippians (1:3–11)

I. Paul's Present Circumstances (1:12–26)
- A. The Gospel Has Advanced Because of His Imprisonment (1:12–14)
- B. In Every Way Christ is Proclaimed (1:15–18)
- C. His Readiness for Life or Death (1:19–26)

II. Matters of Concern to the Church (1:27—4:9)
- A. Paul's Exhortation to the Philippians (1:27—2:18)
  1. To Steadfastness (1:27–30)
  2. To Unity (2:1–2)
  3. To Humility and Servanthood (2:3–11)
  4. To Obedience and Blameless Conduct (2:12–18)
- B. Paul's Messengers to the Church (2:19–30)
  1. Timothy (2:19–24)
  2. Epaphroditus (2:25–30)
- C. Paul's Warning Concerning Erroneous Teaching (3:1–21)
  1. The False Circumcision Versus the True (3:1–16)
  2. The Earthly-minded Versus the Spiritual (3:17–21)
- D. Paul's Concluding Counsel (4:1–9)
  1. Stability and Harmony (4:1–3)
  2. Joy and Gentleness (4:4–5)
  3. Freedom from Anxiety (4:6–7)
  4. Control of the Mind and the Will (4:8–9)

Conclusion (4:10–23)
- A. Grateful Acknowledgment of Gifts Received (4:10–20)
- B. Final Greetings and Benediction (4:21–23)

Author: Paul

Theme: Joy in Living for Christ

Date: c. A.D. 62/63

Background

The city of Philippi in eastern Macedonia, ten miles inland from the Aegean Sea, was named after King Philip II of Macedon, father of Alexander the Great. In Paul's day, it was an honored Roman city and military post.

The church in Philippi was founded by Paul and his team of co-laborers (Silas, Timothy, Luke) on his second missionary journey in response to a God-given vision at Troas (Ac 16:9–40). A strong bond of friendship developed between the apostle and the Philippian church. Several times the church sent Paul financial help (2Co 11:9; Php 4:15–16) and contributed generously to his offering for the distressed Christians in Jerusalem (cf. 2Co 8—9). It appears that Paul visited the church twice on his third missionary journey (Ac 20:1,3,6).

Purpose

From prison (1:7,13–14), most likely in Rome (Ac 28:16–31), Paul wrote this letter to the Philippian believers to thank them for their recent generous gift carried to him by Epaphroditus (4:14–19) and to update them on his present circumstances. In addition, he wrote to assure the congregation of the triumph of God's purpose in his imprisonment (1:12–30), to reassure the church that their messenger (Epaphroditus) had fulfilled his charge faithfully and was not returning to them prematurely (2:25–30), and to encourage them to press on to know the Lord in unity, humility, fellowship and peace.

Survey

Unlike many of Paul's letters, Philippians was not written primarily because of church problems or conflicts. Its basic tone is one of cordial affection and appreciation for the congregation. From salutation (1:1) to benediction (4:23), the letter focuses on Christ Jesus as the purpose for living and the believer's hope for eternal life.

Within this letter, Paul does address three minor problems at Philippi: (1) their *discouragement* over his prolonged imprisonment (1:12–26); (2) small seeds of *disunity* between two women in the church (4:2; cf. 2:2–4); and (3) the ever-present threat among the churches of *disloyalty* because of Judaizers and the earthly-minded (ch. 3). In connection with these three potential problems, we have Paul's richest teaching about (1) joy in the midst of all life's circumstances (e.g., 1:4,12; 2:17–18; 4:4,11–13), (2) Christian humility and service (2:1–16), and (3) the surpassing value of knowing Christ (ch. 3).

Special Features

Five major features characterize this letter. (1) It is highly personal and affectionate, reflecting Paul's close relationship to the Philippian believers. (2) It is highly Christocentric, reflecting Paul's close relationship with Christ (e.g. 1:21; 3:7–14). (3) It contains one of the most profound Christological statements in the Bible (2:5–11). (4) It is preeminently the NT "letter of joy." (5) It presents an especially vigorous standard of the Christian life, including living in humility and as a servant (2:1–8), pressing earnestly toward the goal (3:13–14), rejoicing in the Lord always (4:4), experiencing freedom from anxiety (4:6), being content in all circumstances (4:11) and doing all things through Christ's enabling grace (4:13).

Reading Philippians

In order to read the entire New Testament in one year, the book of Philippians should be read in 5 days, according to the following schedule:
☐ 1 ☐ 2:1–18 ☐ 2:19—3:11 ☐ 3:12—4:3 ☐ 4:4–23

NOTES

1 Paul and Timothy,[a] servants of
Christ Jesus,

To all the saints[b] in Christ Jesus at Philippi,[c] together with the overseers[a][d] and
deacons:[e]

2Grace and peace to you from God our
Father and the Lord Jesus Christ.[f]

Thanksgiving and Prayer

3I thank my God every time I remember
you.[g] **4**In all my prayers for all of you, I
always pray[h] with joy **5**because of your
partnership[i] in the gospel from the first
day[j] until now, **6**being confident of this,
that he who began a good work in you will
carry it on to completion[k] until the day of
Christ Jesus.[l]

7It is right[m] for me to feel this way
about all of you, since I have you in my
heart;[n] for whether I am in chains[o] or
defending[p] and confirming the gospel, all
of you share in God's grace with me. **8**God
can testify[q] how I long for all of you with
the affection of Christ Jesus.

9And this is my prayer: that your love[r]
may abound more and more in knowledge
and depth of insight,[s] **10**so that you may
be able to discern what is best and may be
pure and blameless until the day of
Christ,[t] **11**filled with the fruit of righteousness[u] that comes through Jesus
Christ—to the glory and praise of God.

Paul's Chains Advance the Gospel

12Now I want you to know, brothers,
that what has happened to me has really
served to advance the gospel. **13**As a result, it has become clear throughout the
whole palace guard[b] and to everyone else
that I am in chains[v] for Christ. **14**Because
of my chains,[w] most of the brothers in the
Lord have been encouraged to speak the
word of God more courageously and fearlessly.[x]

15It is true that some preach Christ out
of envy and rivalry, but others out of goodwill. **16**The latter do so in love, knowing
that I am put here for the defense of the
gospel.[y] **17**The former preach Christ out
of selfish ambition,[z] not sincerely, sup-

1:1 [a]S Ac 16:1; 2Co 1:1 [b]S Ac 9:13 [c]S Ac 16:12 [d]S 1Ti 3:1 [e]1Ti 3:8
1:2 [f]S Ro 1:7
1:3 [g]S Ro 1:8
1:4 [h]S Ro 1:10
1:5 [i]Ac 2:42; Php 4:15 [j]Ac 16:12-40
1:6 [k]Ps 138:8 [l]ver 10; S 1Co 1:8
1:7 [m]2Pe 1:13 [n]2Co 7:3 [o]ver 13, 14,17; S Ac 21:33 [p]ver 16
1:8 [q]S Ro 1:9
1:9 [r]1Th 3:12 [s]S Eph 1:17
1:10 [t]ver 6; S 1Co 1:8
1:11 [u]S Jas 3:18
1:13 [v]ver 7,14, 17; S Ac 21:33
1:14 [w]ver 7,13, 17; S Ac 21:33 [x]S Ac 4:29
1:16 [y]ver 7,12
1:17 [z]Php 2:3

[a] *1* Traditionally *bishops* [b] *13* Or *whole palace*

1:4 JOY. Joy is an integral part of our salvation in Christ. It is an inner peace and delight in God the Father, Son and Holy Spirit, and in the blessing that flows from our relationship with them (cf. 2Co 13:14). Scriptural teaching about joy includes the following: (1) Joy is associated with the salvation God provides in Christ (1Pe 1:3–6; cf. Ps 5:11; 9:2; Isa 35:10) and with God's Word (Jer 15:16; cf. Ps 119:14).

(2) Joy flows from God as one aspect of the Spirit's fruit (Ps 16:11; Ro 15:13; Gal 5:22). It does not come automatically, but is experienced only as we maintain an abiding relationship with Christ (Jn 15:1–11). Our joy becomes greater when the Spirit mediates a deep sense of God's presence and nearness in our lives (cf. Jn 14:15–21; see 16:14, note). Jesus taught that the fullness of joy is inseparably connected to our remaining in his Word, loving others, obeying his commands (Jn 15:7,10–11) and being separated from the world (Jn 17:13–17).

(3) Joy as a delight in God's nearness and his redemptive gifts cannot be destroyed by pain, suffering, weakness or difficult circumstances (Mt 5:12; Ac 16:23–25; 2Co 12:9).

1:6 BEING CONFIDENT OF THIS. Paul's confidence in the Philippians is based not only on God's good work in them, but also on their zeal and sacrifice for the faith (vv. 5,7; 4:15–18). God's faithfulness always avails for faithful believers, but his faithfulness can do nothing for those who resist his grace (see 2:13, note; 2Ti 2:13, note).

1:9 LOVE MAY ABOUND ... IN KNOWLEDGE. Love, if it is to be Christian, must be based on Biblical revelation and knowledge. (1) In the NT "knowledge" (Gk *epignōsis*) is not merely head knowledge, but is a spiritual knowing in the heart. It refers to God's revelation as experientially known and involves a personal relationship with God rather than intellectually knowing facts about God (vv. 10–11; Eph 3:16–19; see article on BIBLE TRAINING FOR CHRISTIANS, p. 470).

(2) Thus, to know God's Word (cf. Ro 7:1) or to know God's will (Ac 22:14; Ro 2:18) implies a knowledge that expresses itself in fellowship, obedience, life and nearness to God (Jn 17:3; 1Jn 4:8). Knowing theological truth (1Ti 6:3; Tit 1:9; see Gal 1:9, note) has as its goal love for God and freedom from sin (Ro 6:6; see article on BIBLE TRAINING FOR CHRISTIANS, p. 470). "Depth of insight" means that the believer, through love and knowledge, discerns what is good and evil.

1:10 PURE AND BLAMELESS. "Pure" means "without any mixture of evil"; "blameless" means "not causing offense" to God or another person. Such holiness must be the ultimate aim of all believers in the light of Christ's imminent return. Only by an abounding love poured out within our hearts by the Holy Spirit (Ro 5:5; cf. Tit 3:5–6) and a full commitment to God's Word will we be "pure and blameless until the day of Christ."

1:16 THE DEFENSE OF THE GOSPEL. God gave Paul the important task of defending the content of the gospel as defined in Scripture. Likewise, all believers are called to defend Biblical truth and to resist those who would distort the faith (v. 27; see Gal 1:9, note; Jude 3, note; see article on THE MINISTRY GIFTS OF THE CHURCH, p. 407). Paul's words seem foreign to those ministers today who feel no need to "contend for the faith that was once for all entrusted to the saints" (Jude 3).

posing that they can stir up trouble for me
while I am in chains.[c][a] **18**But what does
it matter? The important thing is that in
every way, whether from false motives or
true, Christ is preached. And because of
this I rejoice.

Yes, and I will continue to rejoice, **19**for
I know that through your prayers[b] and
the help given by the Spirit of Jesus
Christ,[c] what has happened to me will
turn out for my deliverance.[d][d] **20**I eagerly
expect[e] and hope that I will in no way be
ashamed, but will have sufficient courage[f] so that now as always Christ will be
exalted in my body,[g] whether by life or by
death.[h] **21**For to me, to live is Christ[i] and
to die is gain. **22**If I am to go on living in
the body, this will mean fruitful labor for
me. Yet what shall I choose? I do not
know! **23**I am torn between the two: I desire to depart[j] and be with Christ,[k] which
is better by far; **24**but it is more necessary
for you that I remain in the body. **25**Convinced of this, I know that I will remain,
and I will continue with all of you for your
progress and joy in the faith, **26**so that
through my being with you again your joy
in Christ Jesus will overflow on account
of me.

1:17 [a]ver 7,13, 14; S Ac 21:33
1:19 [b]2Co 1:11 [c]S Ac 16:7 [d]Phm 22
1:20 [e]Ro 8:19 [f]ver 14 [g]1Co 6:20 [h]Ro 14:8
1:21 [i]Gal 2:20
1:23 [j]2Ti 4:6 [k]S Jn 12:26

The Privilege of Suffering

27Whatever happens, conduct yourselves in a manner worthy[l] of the gospel
of Christ. Then, whether I come and see
you or only hear about you in my absence,
I will know that you stand firm[m] in one
spirit, contending[n] as one man for the
faith of the gospel **28**without being frightened in any way by those who oppose you.
This is a sign to them that they will be
destroyed, but that you will be saved—
and that by God. **29**For it has been granted
to you[o] on behalf of Christ not only to
believe on him, but also to suffer[p] for him,
30since you are going through the same
struggle[q] you saw[r] I had, and now hear[s]
that I still have.

Imitating Christ's Humility

2 If you have any encouragement from
being united with Christ, if any comfort from his love, if any fellowship with
the Spirit,[t] if any tenderness and compassion,[u] **2**then make my joy complete[v] by
being like-minded,[w] having the same love,
being one[x] in spirit and purpose. **3**Do

1:27 [l]S Eph 4:1 [m]S 1Co 16:13 [n]Jude 3
1:29 [o]Mt 5:11, 12; Ac 5:41 [p]S Ac 14:22
1:30 [q]1Th 2:2; Heb 10:32 [r]Ac 16:19-40 [s]ver 13
2:1 [t]2Co 13:14 [u]Col 3:12
2:2 [v]S Jn 3:29 [w]Php 4:2 [x]S Ro 15:5

c *16,17* Some late manuscripts have verses 16 and 17 in reverse order. d *19* Or *salvation*

1:19 THE SPIRIT OF JESUS CHRIST. The Holy Spirit, who dwells in the believer, is called the "Spirit of Jesus Christ" (cf. Ac 16:7; Ro 8:9; Gal 4:6) because it is Christ who imparts the Spirit to the believer at conversion (see article on THE REGENERATION OF THE DISCIPLES, p. 212) and subsequently baptizes the believer in the Spirit (see Ac 1:8, note; see article on BAPTISM IN THE HOLY SPIRIT, p. 228). This Spirit is the same Spirit who anointed Jesus to bring redemption to the world (see Lk 4:18; see article on JESUS AND THE HOLY SPIRIT, p. 136).

1:21 TO DIE IS GAIN. True believers, living in the center of God's will, need not fear death. They know God has a purpose for their living and that death, when it comes, is simply the end of their earthly mission and the beginning of a greater life with Christ (vv. 20–25; see Ro 8:28, note). The following are some Scripturally revealed truths concerning the deaths of believers:

(1) For Christians, death is not the end of life, but a new beginning. It need not be feared (1Co 15:55–57), but must be seen as the point of transition to a fuller life. Death is a release from the troubles of this world (2Co 4:17) and from the earthly body into heavenly life and glory (2Co 5:1–5). Paul speaks of physical death as sleep (1Co 15:6,18,20; 1Th 4:13–15), implying that death is rest from earthly labor and suffering (cf. Rev 14:13). It is a doorway into God's presence (v. 23).

(2) Scripture speaks of death in comforting terms. The death of the saints is "precious in the sight of the LORD" (Ps 116:15), being carried by the angels "to Abraham's side" (Lk 16:22), being with Jesus in "paradise" (Lk 23:43), going to the Father's house, where there are "many rooms" (Jn 14:2), a blessed "departure" (2Ti 4:6) in order to "be with Christ" (v. 23) and "at home with the Lord" (2Co 5:8), a "gain" (v. 21) "which is better by far" (v. 23), and a falling "asleep in Christ" (1Co 15:18; cf. Jn 11:11; 1Th 4:13).

(3) Concerning the time between death and bodily resurrection, Scripture teaches the following: (a) At the time of death believers are brought into Christ's presence (v. 23; 2Co 5:8). (b) They are fully conscious (Lk 16:19ff), experiencing joy at the kindness and love shown to them (cf. Eph 2:7). (c) Heaven is like a home, i.e., a place of rest and security (Rev 6:11) and a place of community and fellowship with other believers (see Jn 14:2, note). (d) Activities in heaven will include worship and singing (Ps 87; Rev 14:2–3; 15:2), assigned tasks (Lk 19:17), and eating and drinking (Lk 14:15; 22:14–18; Rev 22:2). (e) While awaiting the bodily resurrection, believers are not invisible disembodied spirits. At death they are clothed with a temporary heavenly form (Lk 9:30–32; 2Co 5:1–4). (f) In heaven believers will maintain their personal identities (Mt 8:11; Lk 9:30–32). (g) They will continue to be concerned about God's purposes on earth (Rev 6:9–11).

1:27 STAND FIRM IN ONE SPIRIT. The true essence of the unity of the Spirit consists of living in a worthy manner (cf. Eph 4:1–3), standing firm in one spirit and purpose (cf. Eph 4:3), striving side by side like warriors for the defense of the gospel according to apostolic revelation (v. 16; cf. Eph 4:13–15) and defending gospel truth against those who are "enemies of the cross of Christ" (3:18, note).

nothing out of selfish ambition or vain
conceit,[y] but in humility consider others
better than yourselves.[z] 4Each of you
should look not only to your own interests, but also to the interests of others.[a]
5Your attitude should be the same as
that of Christ Jesus:[b]

6Who, being in very nature[e] God,[c]
did not consider equality with God[d]
something to be grasped,
7but made himself nothing,[e]
taking the very nature[f] of a
servant,[f]
being made in human likeness.[g]
8And being found in appearance as a
man,
he humbled himself
and became obedient to death[h]—
even death on a cross![i]
9Therefore God exalted him[j] to the
highest place
and gave him the name that is
above every name,[k]
10that at the name of Jesus every knee
should bow,[l]
in heaven and on earth and under
the earth,[m]
11and every tongue confess that Jesus
Christ is Lord,[n]
to the glory of God the Father.

2:3 [y] Gal 5:26 [z] Ro 12:10; 1Pe 5:5
2:4 [a] S 1Co 10:24
2:5 [b] S Mt 11:29
2:6 [c] Jn 1:1; S 14:9 [d] Jn 5:18
2:7 [e] 2Co 8:9 [f] S Mt 20:28 [g] S Jn 1:14; Ro 8:3; Heb 2:17
2:8 [h] S Mt 26:39; Jn 10:18; Ro 5:19; Heb 5:8 [i] S 1Co 1:23
2:9 [j] Isa 52:13; 53:12; Da 7:14; Ac 2:33; Heb 2:9 [k] Eph 1:20,21
2:10 [l] Ps 95:6; Isa 45:23; Ro 14:11 [m] Mt 28:18; Eph 1:10; Col 1:20
2:11 [n] S Jn 13:13

Shining as Stars

12Therefore, my dear friends, as you

[e] 6 Or *in the form of* [f] 7 Or *the form*

2:3 IN HUMILITY. Due to fallen humanity's innate self-centeredness the world does not highly regard humility. Yet the Bible's God-centered view of humanity and salvation places the utmost importance on humility. (1) To be humble means we will be conscious of our weaknesses and quick to give credit to God and others for what we accomplish (Jn 3:27; 5:19; 14:10; Jas 4:6).

(2) We must be humble because we are lowly creatures (Ge 18:27) who are sinful apart from Christ (Lk 18:9–14) and can boast in nothing (Ro 7:18; Gal 6:3) except in the Lord (2Co 10:17). We are dependent on God for our worth and fruitfulness and can accomplish nothing of lasting good without God's help and the help of others (Ps 8:4–5; Jn 15:1–16).

(3) God lives with those who walk humbly (Isa 57:15; Mic 6:8). God gives more grace to the humble, but opposes the proud (Jas 4:6; 1Pe 5:5). His most zealous children serve "the Lord with great humility" (Ac 20:19).

(4) As believers we must live in humility toward others, considering them more important than ourselves (cf. Ro 12:3).

(5) The opposite of humility is pride, an exaggerated feeling of self-importance and self-esteem in a person who believes in his or her own merit, superiority and accomplishments. The inevitable tendency of human nature and the world is toward pride, not humility (1Jn 2:16; cf. Isa 14:13–14; Eze 28:17; 1Ti 6:17).

2:5 YOUR ATTITUDE SHOULD BE THE SAME. Paul emphasizes how Jesus left incomparable glory in heaven and took the humiliating position of a servant, becoming obedient to death to benefit others (vv. 5–8). Christ's humility of heart and mind must be found in his followers, who are called to live sacrificially and unselfishly, caring about others and doing good to them.

2:6 BEING IN VERY NATURE GOD. Jesus Christ has always been God by nature, equal with the Father before, during and after his time on earth (see Jn 1:1; 8:58; 17:24; 20:28, note; Col 1:15,17; see Mk 1:11, note; Jn 20:28, note). That Christ "did not consider equality with God something to be grasped" means he let go of his privileges and glory in heaven in order that we on earth might be saved.

2:7 MADE HIMSELF NOTHING. The Greek literally says he "emptied himself," i.e., laid aside his heavenly glory (Jn 17:4), position (Jn 5:30; Heb 5:8), riches (2Co 8:9), rights (Lk 22:27; Mt 20:28) and the use of his divine attributes (Jn 5:19; 8:28; 14:10). This "emptying himself" meant not only a voluntary restraint on his divine capacities and privileges, but also an acceptance of suffering, misunderstanding, ill-treatment, hatred and a cursed death on the cross.

2:7 NATURE OF A SERVANT . . . HUMAN LIKENESS. For passages in the Bible dealing with Christ taking the nature of a servant, see Mk 13:32; Lk 2:40–52; Ro 8:3; 2Co 8:9; Heb 2:7,14. Although he remained fully divine, Christ took on a human nature with its temptations, humiliations and weaknesses, yet was without sin (vv. 7–8; Heb 4:15).

2:12 WORK OUT YOUR SALVATION. As believers saved by grace, we must work out our salvation to the end. If we fail to do this, we will lose the salvation given us. (1) We do not work out our salvation by mere human effort, but by means of God's grace and the Spirit's power given to us (see article on FAITH AND GRACE, p. 302).

(2) In order to work out our salvation we must resist sin and follow the desires of the Holy Spirit within us. This involves a sustained effort to use every God-appointed means for defeating evil and revealing Christ's life. Thus, working out our salvation focuses on the importance of sanctification (see Gal 5:17, note; see article on THE ACTS OF THE SINFUL NATURE AND THE FRUIT OF THE SPIRIT, p. 394).

(3) We work out our salvation by ever drawing near to Christ (see Heb 7:25, note) and receiving his power to will and to act according to God's good pleasure (see v. 13, note). Thus we are "God's fellow workers" (1Co 3:9) in bringing our salvation to completion in heaven.

(4) Working out our salvation is so vital that it must be performed "with fear and trembling" (see next note).

2:12 FEAR AND TREMBLING. In the salvation accomplished through Christ, Paul finds room for "fear and trembling." All of God's children should possess a holy fear that trembles at God's Word (Isa 66:2) and causes them to turn away from all evil (Pr 3:7; 8:13). The fear (Gk *phobos*) of the Lord is not, as is often defined, merely "reverential trust," but includes an

have always obeyed—not only in my presence, but now much more in my absence
—continue to work out your salvation
with fear and trembling,[o] **13**for it is God
who works in you[p] to will and to act according to his good purpose.[q]

14Do everything without complaining[r]
or arguing, **15**so that you may become
blameless[s] and pure, children of God[t]
without fault in a crooked and depraved
generation,[u] in which you shine like stars
in the universe **16**as you hold out[g] the
word of life—in order that I may boast on
the day of Christ[v] that I did not run[w] or
labor for nothing.[x] **17**But even if I am being poured out like a drink offering[y] on
the sacrifice[z] and service coming from
your faith, I am glad and rejoice with all
of you.[a] **18**So you too should be glad and
rejoice with me.

Timothy and Epaphroditus

19I hope in the Lord Jesus to send Timothy[b] to you soon,[c] that I also may be
cheered when I receive news about you.
20I have no one else like him,[d] who takes
a genuine interest in your welfare. **21**For
everyone looks out for his own interests,[e]
not those of Jesus Christ. **22**But you know
that Timothy has proved himself, because
as a son with his father[f] he has served
with me in the work of the gospel. **23**I
hope, therefore, to send him as soon as I
see how things go with me.[g] **24**And I am
confident[h] in the Lord that I myself will
come soon.

25But I think it is necessary to send
back to you Epaphroditus, my brother, fellow worker[i] and fellow soldier,[j] who is
also your messenger, whom you sent to
take care of my needs.[k] **26**For he longs for
all of you[l] and is distressed because you
heard he was ill. **27**Indeed he was ill, and
almost died. But God had mercy on him,
and not on him only but also on me, to
spare me sorrow upon sorrow. **28**Therefore I am all the more eager to send him,[m]
so that when you see him again you may
be glad and I may have less anxiety.
29Welcome him in the Lord with great joy,
and honor men like him,[n] **30**because he
almost died for the work of Christ, risking
his life to make up for the help you could
not give me.[o]

No Confidence in the Flesh

3 Finally, my brothers, rejoice in the
Lord! It is no trouble for me to write
the same things to you again,[p] and it is a
safeguard for you.

2Watch out for those dogs,[q] those men

2:12 [o]S 2Co 7:15 **2:13** [p]Ezr 1:5; 1Co 12:6; 15:10; Gal 2:8; Heb 13:21 [q]Eph 1:5 **2:14** [r]1Co 10:10; 1Pe 4:9 **2:15** [s]S 1Th 3:13 [t]Mt 5:45,48; Eph 5:1 [u]Ac 2:40 **2:16** [v]S 1Co 1:8 [w]S 1Co 9:24 [x]1Th 2:19 **2:17** [y]2Co 12:15; 2Ti 4:6 [z]Ro 15:16 [a]S 2Co 6:10 **2:19** [b]S Ac 16:1 [c]ver 23 **2:20** [d]1Co 16:10 **2:21** [e]S 1Co 10:24 **2:22** [f]1Co 4:17; 1Ti 1:2

2:23 [g]ver 19 **2:24** [h]Php 1:25 **2:25** [i]Ro 16:3,9, 21; 2Co 8:23; Php 4:3; Col 4:11; Phm 1 [j]Phm 2 [k]Php 4:18 **2:26** [l]Php 1:8 **2:28** [m]ver 25 **2:29** [n]1Co 16:18; 1Ti 5:17 **2:30** [o]1Co 16:17 **3:1** [p]Php 2:18 **3:2** [q]Ps 22:16,20; Rev 22:15

[g] 16 Or *hold on to*

---

awe of God's power, holiness and righteous retribution, and a dread of sinning against him and facing the consequences (cf. Ex 3:6; Ps 119:120; Lk 12:4–5). It is not a destructive fear, but a controlling and redeeming fear that leads to God's nearness and blessing, to moral purity, and to life and salvation (cf. Ps 5:7; 85:9; Pr 14:27; 16:6).

2:13 GOD WHO WORKS IN YOU. God's grace is at work in his children to produce in them both the desire and power to do his will (see article on FAITH AND GRACE, p. 302). However, God's work is not one of compulsion or irresistible grace. The work of grace within us (1:6; 1Th 5:24; 2Ti 4:18; Tit 3:5–7) is always dependent on our faithfulness and cooperation (vv. 12,14–16).

2:15 CROOKED AND DEPRAVED GENERATION. Jesus and the apostles emphasized that the world we live in is an "unbelieving and perverse generation" (Mt 17:17; cf. 12:39; Ac 2:40). The people of the world hold wrong views, have warped values, follow immoral ways of life and reject the norms of God's Word. God's children must separate themselves from the world and be blameless, pure and without fault in order to proclaim Christ's glorious redemption to the lost world (cf. 1Jn 2:15).

2:17 POURED OUT LIKE A DRINK OFFERING. Paul's love and concern for the Philippians was such that he was willing to give his life for them as if it were an offering to God. (1) Paul would not regret but rather rejoice in being the victim of sacrifice, if only it would deepen their faith in and love for Christ (cf. 2Ti 4:6). (2) If Paul had such sacrificial love for his spiritual children, what sacrifice and suffering should we be willing to undergo for the faith of our own children? If, in order to make our children as complete as possible in the Lord, it became necessary for us to pour out our lives, and even our blood, as an offering to the Lord, then we ought to be prepared to make such a sacrifice (see article on PARENTS AND CHILDREN, p. 432, outlining fifteen steps parents should take to lead their children to godly living).

2:19 TIMOTHY. Timothy was a good example of what a minister and missionary of God should be. He was an eager and obedient student of God's Word (2Ti 3:15), a worthy servant of Christ (1Th 3:2), a man of good reputation (Ac 16:2), beloved and faithful (1Co 4:17), genuinely concerned for others (v. 20), dependable (2Ti 4:9,21), and devoted to Paul and the gospel (v. 22; Ro 16:21).

2:21 FOR EVERYONE LOOKS OUT FOR HIS OWN INTERESTS. There are ministers who preach, teach, pastor or write, not out of genuine concern for the furtherance of the gospel, but for their own interests, glory, prestige and selfish ambition. Rather than seeking to please the Lord Jesus, they seek instead to please people and gain their favor (vv. 20–21; 1:15; 2Ti 4:10,16). Such ministers are not true servants of the Lord.

3:2 DOGS . . . MEN WHO DO EVIL . . . MUTILATORS. Paul's greatest trial was the grief he experi-

who do evil, those mutilators of the flesh.
3For it is we who are the circumcision,[r]
we who worship by the Spirit of God, who
glory in Christ Jesus,[s] and who put no
confidence in the flesh— **4**though I myself
have reasons for such confidence.[t]
If anyone else thinks he has reasons to
put confidence in the flesh, I have more:
5circumcised[u] on the eighth day, of the
people of Israel,[v] of the tribe of Benjamin,[w] a Hebrew of Hebrews; in regard to
the law, a Pharisee;[x] **6**as for zeal,[y] persecuting the church;[z] as for legalistic righteousness,[a] faultless.

Paul's Desire to Gain Christ

7But whatever was to my profit I now
consider loss[b] for the sake of Christ.
8What is more, I consider everything a
loss compared to the surpassing greatness of knowing[c] Christ Jesus my Lord,
for whose sake I have lost all things. I
consider them rubbish, that I may gain
Christ[d] **9**and be found in him, not having
a righteousness of my own that comes
from the law,[e] but that which is through
faith in Christ—the righteousness[f] that
comes from God and is by faith.[g] **10**I want
to know[h] Christ and the power of his resurrection and the fellowship of sharing in
his sufferings,[i] becoming like him in his
death,[j] **11**and so, somehow, to attain to
the resurrection[k] from the dead.

Pressing on Toward the Goal

12Not that I have already obtained all
this, or have already been made perfect,[l]
but I press on to take hold[m] of that for
which Christ Jesus took hold of me.[n]
13Brothers, I do not consider myself yet to
have taken hold of it. But one thing I do:
Forgetting what is behind[o] and straining
toward what is ahead, **14**I press on[p] toward the goal to win the prize[q] for which

3:3 [r] Ro 2:28,29; Gal 6:15; Col 2:11 [s] Ro 15:17; Gal 6:14
3:4 [t] 2Co 11:21
3:5 [u] S Lk 1:59 [v] 2Co 11:22 [w] Ro 11:1 [x] Ac 23:6
3:6 [y] S Ac 21:20 [z] S Ac 8:3 [a] ver 9; Ro 10:5
3:7 [b] Mt 13:44; Lk 14:33
3:8 [c] ver 10; Jer 9:23,24; Jn 17:3; Eph 4:13; S 2Pe 1:2
[d] Ps 73:25
3:9 [e] ver 6; Ro 10:5 [f] Jer 33:16 [g] S Ro 9:30
3:10 [h] S ver 8 [i] S 2Co 1:5 [j] S Ro 6:3-5
3:11 [k] S Jn 11:24; S Ro 6:5; Rev 20:5,6
3:12 [l] 1Co 13:10 [m] 1Ti 6:12 [n] Ac 9:5,6
3:13 [o] Lk 9:62 **3:14** [p] Heb 6:1 [q] 1Co 9:24

---

enced because of those who distorted the gospel of Christ. His love for Christ, the church and redemptive truth was so strong that it drove him to oppose fervently those who perverted pure doctrine, describing them as "dogs" and "men who do evil" (see 1:17, note; Gal 1:9, note; cf. Mt 23). "Mutilators of the flesh" is Paul's expression for the rite of circumcision as taught by the Judaizers, who claimed that the OT sign of circumcision was necessary for salvation. Paul states that true circumcision is the Spirit's work in the heart of a person when sin and evil are cut away (v. 3; Ro 2:25–29; Col 2:11).

3:8–11 THAT I MAY GAIN CHRIST. These verses show the apostle's heart and the essence of Christianity. Paul's greatest longing was to know Christ and to experience his personal fellowship and nearness in a more intimate way. His pursuit involved the following:

(1) To know Christ personally as well as to know his ways, nature and character as revealed in God's Word. True knowledge of Christ involves listening to his Word, following his Spirit, responding to his dealings in faith, truth and obedience, and identifying with his concerns and purposes.

(2) To be found in Christ (v. 9), i.e., to have a union and fellowship with Christ that produces a righteousness experienced only as a gift from God (1:10–11; 1Co 1:30, note; see article on BIBLICAL WORDS FOR SALVATION, p. 292).

(3) To know the power of his resurrection (v. 10), i.e., to experience renewal of life, deliverance from sin (Ro 6:4; Eph 2:5–6), and the Spirit's power to bring about effective witness, healing, miracles and finally one's own resurrection from the dead (v. 11; Eph 1:18–20).

(4) To share in Christ's sufferings by self-denial, crucifixion of the old self, and suffering for the sake of Christ and his cause (cf. 1:29; Ac 9:16; Ro 6:5–6; 1Co 15:31; 2Co 4:10; Gal 2:20; Col 1:24; 1Pe 4:13).

3:9 THE RIGHTEOUSNESS THAT COMES FROM GOD. The righteousness of believers consists first of all in being forgiven, justified and accepted by God through faith (see Ro 4:5, note).

(1) However, our righteousness is more than this. God's Word states that our righteousness is Christ Jesus himself, living within our hearts (cf. 1:20–21; Ro 8:10; 1Co 1:30; Gal 2:20; Eph 3:17; Col 3:4); in Jer 23:5–6 the Messiah is referred to as the "righteous Branch" and "The LORD Our Righteousness." Thus the righteousness we have is not of ourselves but of Jesus, in whom we put our faith (1Co 1:30, note; Gal 2:20, note). Through this indwelling, we become in him "the righteousness of God" (see 2Co 5:21, note).

(2) The ground for our salvation and our only hope of righteousness is the sacrificial death and shed blood of Christ (Ro 3:24; 4:25; 5:9; 8:3–4; 1Co 15:3; Gal 1:4; 2:20; Eph 1:7; Heb 9:14; 1Pe 1:18–19; 1Jn 4:10) and his resurrection life within our hearts (Ro 4:25; 5:9–10; 8:10–11; Gal 2:20; Col 3:1–3; see Ro 4:22, note).

3:13 BUT ONE THING I DO. Paul sees himself as a runner in a race (cf. Heb 12:1, note), exerting all his strength and pressing on with intense concentration in order not to fall short of the goal that Christ has set for his life—Paul's perfect oneness with Christ (vv. 8–10), his final salvation and his resurrection from the dead (v. 11). (1) This was the motive of Paul's life. He had received a glimpse of the glory of heaven (2Co 12:4) and had resolved that his whole life, by God's grace, would be centered around his determination to press on and someday get to heaven and see Christ face to face (cf. 2Ti 4:8; Rev 2:10; 22:4).

(2) Such determination is necessary for all of us. Throughout our lives all kinds of distractions and temptations, such as life's worries, riches and evil desires, threaten to choke off our commitment to the Lord (cf. Mk 4:19; Lk 8:14). What is needed is a "forgetting what is behind," i.e., the corrupt world and our old life of sin (cf. Ge 19:17,26; Lk 17:32), and a "straining" for final salvation in Christ.

God has called[r] me heavenward in Christ
Jesus.
15All of us who are mature[s] should
take such a view of things.[t] And if on
some point you think differently, that too
God will make clear to you.[u] **16**Only let us
live up to what we have already attained.
17Join with others in following my example,[v] brothers, and take note of those
who live according to the pattern we gave
you.[w] **18**For, as I have often told you before and now say again even with tears,[x]
many live as enemies of the cross of
Christ.[y] **19**Their destiny[z] is destruction,
their god is their stomach,[a] and their glory is in their shame.[b] Their mind is on
earthly things.[c] **20**But our citizenship[d] is
in heaven.[e] And we eagerly await a Savior
from there, the Lord Jesus Christ,[f] **21**who,
by the power[g] that enables him to bring
everything under his control, will transform our lowly bodies[h] so that they will be
like his glorious body.[i]

4 Therefore, my brothers, you whom I
love and long for,[j] my joy and crown,
that is how you should stand firm[k] in the
Lord, dear friends!

Exhortations

2I plead with Euodia and I plead with
Syntyche to agree with each other[l] in the
Lord. **3**Yes, and I ask you, loyal yokefel-
low,**[h]** help these women who have contended at my side in the cause of the gospel, along with Clement and the rest of my
fellow workers,[m] whose names are in the
book of life.[n]
4Rejoice in the Lord always. I will say
it again: Rejoice![o] **5**Let your gentleness
be evident to all. The Lord is near.[p] **6**Do
not be anxious about anything,[q] but in
everything, by prayer and petition, with
thanksgiving, present your requests to
God.[r] **7**And the peace of God,[s] which
transcends all understanding,[t] will guard
your hearts and your minds in Christ
Jesus.
8Finally, brothers, whatever is true,
whatever is noble, whatever is right,

3:14 [r]S Ro 8:28
3:15 [s]S 1Co 2:6
[t]Gal 5:10
[u]Eph 1:17; 1Th 4:9
3:17 [v]S 1Co 4:16
[w]S 1Ti 4:12
3:18 [x]Ac 20:31
[y]Gal 6:12
3:19 [z]Ps 73:17
[a]Ro 16:18
[b]Ro 6:21; Jude 13
[c]Ro 8:5,6; Col 3:2
3:20 [d]Eph 2:19
[e]Col 3:1; Heb 12:22
[f]S 1Co 1:7
3:21 [g]Eph 1:19
[h]1Co 15:43-53
[i]Ro 8:29; Col 3:4
4:1 [j]Php 1:8
[k]S 1Co 16:13
4:2 [l]Php 2:2
4:3 [m]S Php 2:25
[n]S Rev 20:12
4:4 [o]Ps 85:6; 97:12; Hab 3:18; S Mt 5:12; Ro 12:12; Php 3:1
4:5 [p]Ps 119:151; 145:18; Heb 10:37; Jas 5:8,9
4:6 [q]Mt 6:25-34
[r]Eph 6:18; 1Ti 2:1
4:7 [s]Isa 26:3; S Jn 14:27
[t]Eph 3:19

h *3* Or *loyal Syzygus*

3:18 ENEMIES OF THE CROSS OF CHRIST. These enemies can best be understood as professed believers who were corrupting the gospel by immoral lives and false teachings. One key to Paul's greatness was that he was a man of intense feeling whose heart was stirred to the core when the gospel was distorted or when those whom he served were in danger (see v. 2, note; Gal 1:9, note; see article OVERSEERS AND THEIR DUTIES, p. 274).

3:20 OUR CITIZENSHIP IS IN HEAVEN. Christians are no longer citizens of this world; they have become strangers and aliens on the earth (Ro 8:22–24; Gal 4:26; Heb 11:13; 12:22–23; 13:14; 1Pe 1:17; 2:11). (1) In regard to our life's walk, values and direction, heaven is now our fatherland. We have been born from above (Jn 3:3), our names are written on heaven's register (4:3), our lives are guided by heavenly standards, and our rights and inheritance are reserved in heaven.

(2) It is to heaven that our prayers ascend (cf. 2Ch 6:21; 30:27) and our hope is directed. Many of our friends and family members are already there, and we will be there soon. Jesus is there also, preparing a place for us, and he has promised to return and take us to himself (see Jn 14:2–3, notes; cf. Jn 3:3; 14:1–4; Ro 8:17; Eph 2:6; Col 3:1–3; Heb 6:19–20; 12:22–24; 1Pe 1:4–5; Rev 7:9–17). For these reasons we long for a better country, i.e., a heavenly one. Therefore, God is not ashamed to be called our God, and he has prepared for us an eternal city (Heb 11:16).

4:4 REJOICE IN THE LORD ALWAYS. The believer must rejoice and gain strength by recalling the Lord's grace, nearness and promises (see 1:4, note).

4:5 THE LORD IS NEAR. We must believe the Lord may come at any time. The NT depicts Christ's return as imminent (see Lk 12:35–40, note); therefore, we must be ready, working and watching at all times (Mt 24:36; 25:1–13; Ro 13:12–14).

4:6 DO NOT BE ANXIOUS ABOUT ANYTHING. The one essential cure for worry is prayer, for the following reasons: (1) Through prayer we renew our trust in the Lord's faithfulness by casting all our anxieties and problems on him who cares for us (Mt 6:25–34; 1Pe 5:7). (2) God's peace comes to guard our hearts and minds as a result of our communion with Christ Jesus (vv. 6–7; Isa 26:3; Col 3:15). (3) God strengthens us to do all the things he desires of us (v. 13; 3:20, note; Eph 3:16). (4) We receive mercy, grace and help in time of need (Heb 4:16). (5) We are assured that in all things God works for our good (see v. 11, note; Ro 8:28, note).

4:7 PEACE OF GOD . . . WILL GUARD YOUR HEARTS. When we call on God from hearts that remain in Christ and his Word (Jn 15:7), then God's peace will flood our troubled souls. (1) This peace is an inner tranquility mediated by the Holy Spirit (Ro 8:15–16). It involves a firm conviction that Jesus is near and that God's love will be active in our lives for good (Ro 8:28,32; cf. Isa 26:3). (2) When we lay our troubles before God in prayer, this peace will stand guard at the door of our hearts and minds, preventing the cares and heartaches of life from upsetting our lives and undermining our hope in Christ (v. 6; Isa 26:3–4,12; 37:1–7; Ro 8:35–39; 1Pe 5:7). (3) If fear and anxiety return, prayer, petition and thanksgiving will once again place us under the peace of God that guards our hearts. Once more we will feel safe and rejoice in the Lord (v. 4).

4:8 WHATEVER IS PURE. To experience God's peace and freedom from anxiety, believers must fix their minds on those things that are true, noble, right, pure, etc. If you do these things, says Paul, "the God of peace will be with you " (v. 9). The consequence of fixing our minds on the unholy things of the world is

whatever is pure, whatever is lovely, whatever is admirable—if anything is excellent or praiseworthy—think about such things. **9**Whatever you have learned or received or heard from me, or seen in me—put it into practice.[u] And the God of peace[v] will be with you.

Thanks for Their Gifts

10I rejoice greatly in the Lord that at last you have renewed your concern for me.[w] Indeed, you have been concerned, but you had no opportunity to show it. **11**I am not saying this because I am in need, for I have learned to be content[x] whatever the circumstances. **12**I know what it is to be in need, and I know what it is to have plenty. I have learned the secret of being content in any and every situation, whether well fed or hungry,[y] whether living in plenty or in want.[z] **13**I can do everything through him who gives me strength.[a]

14Yet it was good of you to share[b] in my troubles. **15**Moreover, as you Philippians know, in the early days[c] of your acquaintance with the gospel, when I set out from Macedonia,[d] not one church shared with me in the matter of giving and receiving, except you only;[e] **16**for even when I was in Thessalonica,[f] you sent me aid again and again when I was in need.[g] **17**Not that I am looking for a gift, but I am looking for what may be credited to your account.[h] **18**I have received full payment and even more; I am amply supplied, now that I have received from Epaphroditus[i] the gifts you sent. They are a fragrant[j] offering, an acceptable sacrifice, pleasing to God. **19**And my God will meet all your needs[k] according to his glorious riches[l] in Christ Jesus.

20To our God and Father[m] be glory for ever and ever. Amen.[n]

Final Greetings

21Greet all the saints in Christ Jesus. The brothers who are with me[o] send greetings. **22**All the saints[p] send you greetings, especially those who belong to Caesar's household.

23The grace of the Lord Jesus Christ[q] be with your spirit.[r] Amen.[i]

4:9 [u] S 1Co 4:16 [v] S Ro 15:33
4:10 [w] 2Co 11:9
4:11 [x] 1Ti 6:6,8; Heb 13:5
4:12 [y] S 1Co 4:11 [z] 2Co 11:9
4:13 [a] 2Co 12:9; Eph 3:16; Col 1:11; 1Ti 1:12; 2Ti 4:17
4:14 [b] Php 1:7
4:15 [c] Php 1:5 [d] S Ac 16:9 [e] 2Co 11:8,9
4:16 [f] S Ac 17:1 [g] 1Th 2:9
4:17 [h] 1Co 9:11, 12
4:18 [i] Php 2:25 [j] S 2Co 2:14
4:19 [k] Ps 23:1; 2Co 9:8 [l] S Ro 2:4
4:20 [m] Gal 1:4; 1Th 1:3; 3:11,13 [n] S Ro 11:36
4:21 [o] Gal 1:2
4:22 [p] S Ac 9:13
4:23 [q] S Ro 16:20 [r] S Gal 6:18

i *23* Some manuscripts do not have *Amen.*

that the joy, nearness and peace of God are lost and our hearts are no longer guarded.

4:11 I HAVE LEARNED TO BE CONTENT. The key to contentment is realizing that God has given you in your present circumstances everything you need to remain victorious in Christ (1Co 15:57; 2Co 2:14; 1Jn 5:4). The ability to live triumphantly above changing circumstances comes from Christ's power flowing in and through you (v. 13; see 1Ti 6:8, note). This ability does not come naturally, however; it must be learned through dependence on Christ.

4:13 I CAN DO EVERYTHING THROUGH HIM. Christ's power and grace rest on believers to enable them do all that he has asked them to do (see article on FAITH AND GRACE, p. 302).

4:16 YOU SENT ME AID AGAIN AND AGAIN. The Philippian church was a missionary church that ministered to Paul's needs during his travels (vv. 15–17; 1:4–5). Missionary support is honored and accepted by God as "a fragrant offering, an acceptable sacrifice, pleasing to God" (v. 18). Thus, what we give to the support of a faithful missionary is regarded as an offering brought to God. What is done for one of the least of our brothers or sisters is done for the Lord himself (Mt 25:40).

4:19 WILL MEET ALL YOUR NEEDS. Paul emphasizes the loving care of God the Father for his children. He will meet all your needs (material and spiritual) as you present them to him. He will meet them "in Christ Jesus." Only in union with Christ and in his fellowship can we experience God's provision. Among the many Scriptural promises that give hope and encouragement to God's people concerning his care and help are: Ge 28:15; 50:20; Ex 33:14; Dt 2:7; 32:7–14; 33:27; Jos 1:9; 1Sa 7:12; 1Ki 17:6,16; 2Ch 20:17; Ps 18:35; 23; 121; Isa 25:4; 32:2; 40:11; 41:10; 43:1–2; 46:3–4; Joel 2:21–27; Mal 3:10; Mt 6:25–34; 14:20; 23:37; Lk 6:38; 12:7; 22:35; Jn 10:27–28; 17:11; Ro 8:28,31–39; 2Ti 1:12; 4:18; 1Pe 5:7.

COLOSSIANS

Outline

Introduction (1:1–12)
- A. Christian Greetings (1:1–2)
- B. Thanksgiving for Their Faith, Love and Hope (1:3–8)
- C. Prayer for Their Spiritual Advancement (1:9–12)

I. Powerful Doctrine (1:13—2:23)
- A. The Absolute Preeminence of Christ (1:13–23)
  1. As Vicarious Redeemer (1:14; cf. 1:20,22)
  2. As Lord of Creation (1:15–17)
  3. As Head of the Church (1:18)
  4. As Reconciler of All Things (1:19–20)
  5. As Reconciler of the Colossians to God (1:21–23)
- B. Paul's Ministry of God's Mystery in Christ (1:24—2:7)
  1. Filling Up the Afflictions of Christ (1:24–25)
  2. Perfecting Believers in Christ (1:26—2:7)
- C. Warnings Against Erroneous Teaching (2:8–23)
  1. Problem: Teaching Not According to Christ (2:8)
     Solution: Made Complete in Christ (2:9–15)
  2. Problem: Religious Practices Not According to Christ (2:16–23)
     Solution: Crucified With Christ (2:20)

II. Practical Instructions (3:1—4:6)
- A. Concerning Personal Conduct (3:1–17)
  1. When Christ Is Our Life (3:1–4)
  2. Laying Aside the Old Life of Sin (3:5–9)
  3. Putting on the New Self in Christ (3:10–17)
- B. Concerning Domestic Relations (3:18—4:1)
  1. Wives and Husbands (3:18–19)
  2. Children and Parents (3:20–21)
  3. Slaves and Masters (3:22—4:1)
- C. Concerning Spiritual Influence (4:2–6)
  1. A Life Devoted to Prayer (4:2–4)
  2. Wise Conduct Toward Outsiders (4:5)
  3. Speech Seasoned with Grace (4:6)

Conclusion (4:7–18)

Author: Paul

Theme: Supremacy of Christ

Date: c. A.D. 62

Background

The city of Colosse was located near Laodicea (cf. 4:16) in southwest Asia Minor, about 100 miles directly east of Ephesus. The Colossian church appears to have been founded as a result of Paul's exceptional three-year ministry at Ephesus (Ac 20:31), the effects of which were so powerful and far-reaching that "all the Jews and Greeks who lived in the province of Asia heard the word of the Lord" (Ac 19:10). Although Paul may never have visited Colosse in person (2:1), he had maintained contact with the church through Epaphras, one of his converts and associates from Colosse (1:7; 4:12).

The occasion for this letter was the appearance of false teaching that threatened the spiritual future of the Colossian church (2:8). When Epaphras, a leader in the Colossian church and perhaps its founder, traveled to visit Paul and to inform him about the situation at Colosse (1:8; 4:12), Paul responded by writing this letter. He was a prisoner at the time (4:3,10,18), most likely at Rome (Ac 28:16–31) awaiting his appeal before Caesar (Ac 25:11–12). Paul's co-worker, Tychicus, delivered the letter in person to Colosse on Paul's behalf (4:7).

The exact nature of the Colossian heresy is not described explicitly in the letter, for the original readers knew it well. From Paul's statements made in opposition to the false teachings, however, it is apparent that the heresy undermining and replacing the centrality of Jesus Christ was a strange mixture of Christian teaching, certain extrabiblical Jewish traditions and pagan philosophy (similar to the mixture of cults today).

Purpose

Paul wrote (1) to combat the dangerous false teaching at Colosse that was supplanting Christ's centrality and supremacy in creation, revelation, redemption and the church; and (2) to stress the true nature of new life in Christ and its demands on the believer.

Survey

After greeting the church and expressing gratitude for their faith, love and hope, and for their continued progress as believers, Paul focuses on two key issues: correct doctrine (1:13—2:23) and practical exhortations (3:1—4:6).

Theologically, Paul emphasizes the true character and glory of the Lord Jesus Christ. He is the image of the invisible God (1:15), the fullness of deity in bodily form (2:9), the Creator of all things (1:16–17), the head of the church (1:18) and the all-sufficient source of our salvation (1:14,20–22). Whereas Christ is completely adequate, the Colossian heresy is utterly inadequate—hollow, deceitful and humanistic (2:8); superficially spiritual and arrogant (2:18); and without power against the sinful desires of the body (2:23).

In his practical exhortations, Paul appeals for a life grounded in the complete sufficiency of Christ as the only way to progress in Christian living. The reality of the indwelling Christ (1:27) must be evident in Christian behavior (3:1–17), domestic relationships (3:18—4:1) and spiritual discipline (4:2–6).

Special Features

Three major features characterize this letter. (1) More than any other NT book, Colossians focuses on the twofold truth of Christ's preeminence and the believer's completeness in him. (2) It strongly affirms Christ's full deity (2:9) and contains one of the most exalted passages in the NT about his glory (1:15–23). (3) It is sometimes regarded as a "twin letter" with Ephesians, because the two have certain resemblances in content and were written about the same time.

Reading Colossians

In order to read the entire New Testament in one year, the book of Colossians should be read in 5 days, according to the following schedule:
☐ 1:1–23 ☐ 1:24—2:5 ☐ 2:6–23 ☐ 3:1—4:1 ☐ 4:2–18

NOTES

1 Paul, an apostle[a] of Christ Jesus by the will of God,[b] and Timothy[c] our brother,

2 To the holy and faithful[a] brothers in Christ at Colosse:

Grace[d] and peace to you from God our Father.[b][e]

Thanksgiving and Prayer

3 We always thank God,[f] the Father of our Lord Jesus Christ, when we pray for you, **4** because we have heard of your faith in Christ Jesus and of the love[g] you have for all the saints[h]— **5** the faith and love that spring from the hope[i] that is stored up for you in heaven[j] and that you have already heard about in the word of truth,[k] the gospel **6** that has come to you. All over the world[l] this gospel is bearing fruit[m] and growing, just as it has been doing among you since the day you heard it and understood God's grace in all its truth. **7** You learned it from Epaphras,[n] our dear fellow servant, who is a faithful minister[o] of Christ on our[c] behalf, **8** and who also told us of your love in the Spirit.[p]

1Th 1:6

9 For this reason, since the day we heard about you,[q] we have not stopped praying for you[r] and asking God to fill you with the knowledge of his will[s] through all spiritual wisdom and understanding.[t] **10** And we pray this in order that you may live a life worthy[u] of the Lord and may please him[v] in every way: bearing fruit in every good work, growing in the knowledge of God,[w] **11** being strengthened with all power[x] according to his glorious might so that you may have great endurance and patience,[y] and joyfully **12** giving thanks to the Father,[z] who has qualified you[d] to share in the inheritance[a] of the saints in the kingdom of light.[b] **13** For he has rescued us from the dominion of darkness[c] and brought us into the kingdom[d] of the Son he loves,[e] **14** in whom we have redemption,[e][f] the forgiveness of sins.[g]

The Supremacy of Christ

15 He is the image[h] of the invisible

1:1 *a* S 1Co 1:1 *b* S 2Co 1:1 *c* S Ac 16:1 **1:2** *d* Col 4:18 *e* S Ro 1:7 **1:3** *f* S Ro 1:8 **1:4** *g* Gal 5:6 *h* S Ac 9:13; Eph 1:15; Phm 5 **1:5** *i* ver 23; 1Th 5:8; Tit 1:2 *j* 1Pe 1:4 *k* S 2Ti 2:15 **1:6** *l* ver 23; S Ro 10:18 *m* Jn 15:16 **1:7** *n* Col 4:12; Phm 23 *o* Col 4:7 **1:8** *p* Ro 15:30 **1:9** *q* ver 4; Eph 1:15 *r* S Ro 1:10 *s* S Eph 5:17 *t* S Eph 1:17 **1:10** *u* S Eph 4:1 *v* S 2Co 5:9 *w* ver 6 **1:11** *x* S Php 4:13 *y* Eph 4:2 **1:12** *z* Eph 5:20 *a* S Ac 20:32 *b* S Ac 26:18 **1:13** *c* S Ac 26:18 *d* 2Pe 1:11 *e* Mt 3:17 **1:14** *f* S Ro 3:24 *g* Eph 1:7 **1:15** *h* S Jn 14:9

a 2 Or *believing* **b** 2 Some manuscripts *Father and the Lord Jesus Christ* **c** 7 Some manuscripts *your* **d** 12 Some manuscripts *us* **e** 14 A few late manuscripts *redemption through his blood*

1:2 FAITHFUL BROTHERS ... AT COLOSSE. Paul wrote to the Colossians because the church there was being infiltrated by false teachers who taught that commitment to Jesus Christ and adherence to apostolic doctrine were inadequate for full redemption. This false teaching mixed human "philosophy" and "tradition" with the gospel (2:8) and called for the worship of angels as intermediaries between God and humans (2:18). The false teachers demanded observance to certain Jewish religious requirements (2:16,21–23) and justified their error by claiming revelation through visions (2:18). (1) The underlying philosophy behind these errors appears today in the teaching that Jesus Christ and the original gospel of the NT are not adequate to meet our spiritual needs (see 2Pe 1:3, note).

(2) Paul refutes this heresy by showing that Christ is not only our personal Savior, but the head of the church and Lord of the universe and creation. Therefore, Jesus Christ and his power in our lives, not human philosophy or wisdom, redeems us and saves us eternally; intermediaries are unnecessary, and we must approach him directly.

(3) Being a believer means believing in Christ and his gospel, trusting him, loving him and living in his presence. We must not add anything to the gospel or promote modern, humanistic wisdom or philosophy.

1:9 KNOWLEDGE OF HIS WILL. The knowledge of God's will results from praying and remaining in his Word and in fellowship with him. Only this kind of knowledge results in spiritual wisdom and understanding and transforms our hearts and lives (vv. 9–11; see Php 1:9, note).

1:9–12 WE HAVE NOT STOPPED PRAYING FOR YOU. This is one of Paul's four great NT apostolic prayers, spoken under the inspiration of the Spirit (the other three are Eph 1:16–19; 3:14–19; Php 1:9–11). From these prayers we learn how to pray for others, such as our children, friends, fellow believers, missionaries, pastors, etc. We must pray that they may (1) understand God's will, (2) gain spiritual wisdom, (3) live holy lives pleasing to the Lord, (4) bear fruit for Christ, (5) be strengthened spiritually by the Holy Spirit, (6) persevere in faith and righteousness, (7) give thanks to the Father, (8) continue in the hope of heaven, (9) experience Christ's nearness, (10) know Christ's love, (11) be filled with God's fullness, (12) show love and kindness to others, (13) discern evil, (14) be sincere and blameless, and (15) eagerly await the Lord's return.

1:11 STRENGTHENED ... ACCORDING TO HIS GLORIOUS MIGHT. In order to live in a manner worthy of the Lord (v. 10), we must be strengthened by his power. This impartation of power is an ongoing experience of receiving from God his own life. Nothing else can enable us to overcome sin, Satan and the world (cf. Php 4:13; see article on FAITH AND GRACE, p. 302).

1:13 FROM THE DOMINION OF DARKNESS. Central to redemption is deliverance from the dominion and power of darkness, i.e., from Satan (Mt 4:8–11; Lk 22:52–53; Eph 2:2; 6:12). We are now in Christ's kingdom and under his rule (Ro 6:17–22; see Ac 26:18, note).

1:15 THE FIRSTBORN OVER ALL CREATION. This phrase does not mean Christ was a created being. Rather, "firstborn" has the OT meaning often given the word: "first in position," "heir" or "supreme" (e.g., Ex 4:22; Jer 31:9; note Ps 89:27, where "firstborn" is used of David's rulership, although he was not a first-

God,[i] the firstborn[j] over all creation.
16For by him all things were created:[k]
things in heaven and on earth, visible and
invisible, whether thrones or powers or
rulers or authorities;[l] all things were created by him and for him.[m] 17He is before
all things,[n] and in him all things hold together. 18And he is the head[o] of the body,
the church;[p] he is the beginning and the
firstborn[q] from among the dead,[r] so that
in everything he might have the supremacy. 19For God was pleased[s] to have all his
fullness[t] dwell in him, 20and through him
to reconcile[u] to himself all things, whether things on earth or things in heaven,[v] by
making peace[w] through his blood,[x] shed
on the cross.

21Once you were alienated from God
and were enemies[y] in your minds[z] because of[f] your evil behavior. 22But now he
has reconciled[a] you by Christ's physical
body[b] through death to present you[c] holy
in his sight, without blemish and free from
accusation[d]— 23if you continue[e] in your
faith, established[f] and firm, not moved
from the hope[g] held out in the gospel.
This is the gospel that you heard and that
has been proclaimed to every creature under heaven,[h] and of which I, Paul, have
become a servant.[i]

Paul's Labor for the Church

24Now I rejoice[j] in what was suffered
for you, and I fill up in my flesh what is
still lacking in regard to Christ's afflictions,[k] for the sake of his body, which is
the church.[l] 25I have become its servant[m]
by the commission God gave me[n] to
present to you the word of God[o] in its
fullness— 26the mystery[p] that has been
kept hidden for ages and generations, but
is now disclosed to the saints. 27To them
God has chosen to make known[q] among
the Gentiles the glorious riches[r] of this
mystery, which is Christ in you,[s] the hope
of glory.

28We proclaim him, admonishing[t] and
teaching everyone with all wisdom,[u] so
that we may present everyone perfect[v] in
Christ. 29To this end I labor,[w] struggling[x]
with all his energy, which so powerfully
works in me.[y]

2 I want you to know how much I am
struggling[z] for you and for those at
Laodicea,[a] and for all who have not met
me personally. 2My purpose is that they
may be encouraged in heart[b] and united
in love, so that they may have the full
riches of complete understanding, in order that they may know the mystery[c] of
God, namely, Christ, 3in whom are hidden
all the treasures of wisdom and knowledge.[d] 4I tell you this so that no one may
deceive you by fine-sounding arguments.[e]

1:15 [i]S Jn 1:18; 1Ti 1:17; Heb 11:27 [j]S ver 18 **1:16** [k]S Jn 1:3 [l]Eph 1:20,21 [m]S Ro 11:36 **1:17** [n]S Jn 1:2 **1:18** [o]S Eph 1:22 [p]ver 24; S 1Co 12:27 [q]ver 15; Ps 89:27; Ro 8:29; Heb 1:6 [r]Ac 26:23; Rev 1:5 **1:19** [s]S Eph 1:5 [t]S Jn 1:16 **1:20** [u]S Ro 5:10 [v]Eph 1:10 [w]S Lk 2:14 [x]Eph 2:13 **1:21** [y]Ro 5:10 [z]Eph 2:3 **1:22** [a]ver 20; S Ro 5:10 [b]Ro 7:4 [c]S 2Co 4:14 [d]Eph 1:4; 5:27 **1:23** [e]S Ro 11:22 [f]Eph 3:17 [g]ver 5 [h]ver 6; S Ro 10:18 [i]ver 25; S 1Co 3:5 **1:24** [j]S 2Co 6:10 [k]S 2Co 1:5 [l]S 1Co 12:27 **1:25** [m]ver 23; S 1Co 3:5 [n]Eph 3:2 [o]S Heb 4:12 **1:26** [p]S Ro 16:25 **1:27** [q]S Mt 13:11 [r]S Ro 2:4 [s]S Ro 8:10 **1:28** [t]Col 3:16 [u]1Co 2:6,7 [v]Mt 5:48; Eph 5:27 **1:29** [w]1Co 15:10; 2Co 11:23 [x]Col 2:1 [y]Eph 1:19; 3:7 **2:1** [z]Col 1:29; 4:12 [a]Col 4:13,15,16; Rev 1:11; 3:14 **2:2** [b]Eph 6:22; Col 4:8 [c]S Ro 16:25 **2:3** [d]Isa 11:2; Jer 23:5; Ro 11:33; 1Co 1:24,30 **2:4** [e]S Ro 16:18

[f] 21 Or *minds, as shown by*

born son). Christ is heir and ruler of all creation as the eternal Son (cf. v. 18; Heb 1:1–2).

1:16 BY HIM ALL THINGS WERE CREATED. Paul affirms the creative activity of Christ. (1) All things, both material and spiritual, owe their existence to Christ's work as the active agent in creation (Jn 1:3; Heb 1:2). (2) All things hold together and are sustained in him (v. 17; Heb 1:3).

1:18 FIRSTBORN FROM AMONG THE DEAD. Jesus Christ was the first to rise from the dead with a spiritual and immortal body (1Co 15:20). On his resurrection day Jesus became head of the church. The NT church began on the day of Jesus' resurrection when the disciples received the Holy Spirit (see article on THE REGENERATION OF THE DISCIPLES, p. 212). The fact that Christ is the "firstborn from among the dead" implies the subsequent resurrection of all those for whom he died.

1:19 ALL HIS FULLNESS DWELL IN HIM. Paul states the deity of Christ in the plainest of terms. The full and complete Godhead with all its powers and nature resides with Christ (2:9; cf. Heb 1:8).

1:20 RECONCILE TO HIMSELF ALL THINGS. Humanity and everything in the universe are brought in unity and harmony under Christ (cf. vv. 16–18). It does not mean, however, that all people are reconciled irrespective of their wills. The person who rejects Christ's offer of reconciliation remains God's enemy (Ro 2:4–10).

1:23 IF YOU CONTINUE IN YOUR FAITH. Notice the human responsibility and activity that Paul states are essential for Christians to appear finally before Christ "holy in his sight, without blemish and free from accusation" (v. 22). We must (1) "continue in [our] faith," i.e., maintain a persevering faith in Jesus as Lord and Savior (see article on FAITH AND GRACE, p. 302); (2) be "established and firm" in the teaching of Jesus and the apostles; and (3) be "not moved from the hope held out in the gospel," i.e., we must not return to our former state of hopelessness with its soul-destroying vices (3:5–11; see Heb 10:38, note).

1:24 SUFFERED FOR YOU. Paul sees Christ still suffering, not for our redemption, but in fellowship with his people as they carry the gospel to the lost (cf. Ac 9:4). Paul rejoices because he is allowed to share in Christ's sufferings (Php 3:10; cf. 2Co 1:4–5, notes; 4:7, note; 11:23, note on Paul's sufferings).

1:27 CHRIST IN YOU, THE HOPE OF GLORY. Christ's living in us is our assurance of future glory and eternal life. Only his indwelling and our continual intimate communion with him can dispel any doubt about obtaining heaven. To have him is to have life (cf. Ro 8:11; Eph 1:13–14; 1Jn 5:11–12).

5For though I am absent from you in body,
I am present with you in spirit[f] and delight to see how orderly[g] you are and how
firm[h] your faith in Christ[i] is.

Freedom From Human Regulations Through Life With Christ

6So then, just as you received Christ
Jesus as Lord,[j] continue to live in him,
7rooted[k] and built up in him, strengthened in the faith as you were taught,[l] and
overflowing with thankfulness.
8See to it that no one takes you captive
through hollow and deceptive philosophy,[m] which depends on human tradition
and the basic principles of this world[n]
rather than on Christ.
9For in Christ all the fullness[o] of the
Deity lives in bodily form, 10and you have
been given fullness in Christ, who is the
head[p] over every power and authority.[q]
11In him you were also circumcised,[r] in
the putting off of the sinful nature,[g][s] not
with a circumcision done by the hands of
men but with the circumcision done by
Christ, 12having been buried with him in
baptism[t] and raised with him[u] through
your faith in the power of God, who raised
him from the dead.[v]
13When you were dead in your sins[w]
and in the uncircumcision of your sinful
nature,[h] God made you[i] alive[x] with
Christ. He forgave us all our sins,[y] 14hav-
ing canceled the written code, with its regulations,[z] that was against us and that
stood opposed to us; he took it away, nailing it to the cross.[a] 15And having disarmed the powers and authorities,[b] he
made a public spectacle of them, triumphing over them[c] by the cross.[j]
16Therefore do not let anyone judge

2:5 [f]1Co 5:4; 1Th 2:17 [g]1Co 14:40 [h]1Pe 5:9 [i]S Ac 20:21 2:6 [j]S Jn 13:13; Col 1:10 2:7 [k]Eph 3:17 [l]Eph 4:21 2:8 [m]1Ti 6:20 [n]ver 20; Gal 4:3 2:9 [o]S Jn 1:16 2:10 [p]S Eph 1:22 [q]S Mt 28:18 2:11 [r]Ro 2:29; Php 3:3 [s]S Gal 5:24 2:12 [t]S Mt 28:19 [u]S Ro 6:5 [v]S Ac 2:24 2:13 [w]Eph 2:1,5 [x]Eph 2:5 [y]Eph 4:32 2:14 [z]Eph 2:15 [a]1Pe 2:24 2:15 [b]ver 10; Eph 6:12 [c]Mt 12:29; Lk 10:18; Jn 12:31

g *11* Or *the flesh* h *13* Or *your flesh*
i *13* Some manuscripts *us* j *15* Or *them in him*

2:8 DECEPTIVE PHILOSOPHY ... RATHER THAN ON CHRIST. Paul warns us to be on guard against all philosophies, religions and traditions that emphasize humans functioning independently from God and his written revelation. Today one of the greatest philosophical threats to Biblically based Christianity is "secular humanism." This has become the underlying philosophy and accepted religion in most of secular education, government and society in general, and is the established viewpoint of most of the news and entertainment media throughout the world.

(1) What does the philosophy of humanism teach? (a) It teaches that humanity, the universe and all that exists consist only of matter and energy shaped into their present form by impersonal chance. (b) It teaches that humans have not been created by a personal God, but are the product of a chance process of evolution. (c) It rejects belief in a personal, infinite God and denies that the Bible is God's inspired revelation to the human race. (d) It asserts that knowledge does not exist apart from human discovery and that human reason determines the appropriate ethics of society, thus making human beings the ultimate authority. (e) It seeks to modify or improve human behavior through education, economic redistribution, modern psychology or human wisdom. (f) It teaches that moral standards are not absolute but relative, determined by what makes people happy, brings them pleasure, or seems good for society according to the goals set by its leaders; Biblical values and morality are rejected. (g) It considers human self-fulfillment, satisfaction and pleasure to be the highest good in life. (h) It maintains that people should learn to cope with death and the difficulties in life without belief in or dependence on God.

(2) The philosophy of humanism began with Satan and is an expression of Satan's lie that humans can be like God (Ge 3:5). Scripture identifies humanists as those who have "exchanged the truth of God for a lie, and worshiped and served created things rather than the Creator. . . ." (Ro 1:25).

(3) All Christian leaders, pastors and parents must do their utmost to protect their sons and daughters from humanistic indoctrination by exposing its error and instilling in them a godly contempt for its destructive influence (Ro 1:20–32; 2Co 10:4–5; 2Ti 3:1–10; Jude 4–20; see 1Co 1:20, note; 2Pe 2:19, note).

2:11 CIRCUMCISION DONE BY CHRIST. In the OT circumcision was the sign that the individual Israelite stood in a covenant relationship with God (Ge 17:9–14). It symbolized a cutting away or separation from sin and all that was unholy in the world. The believer under the NT covenant has undergone a spiritual circumcision, namely, the "putting off of the sinful nature." This is a spiritual act whereby Christ cuts away our old unregenerate nature of rebellion against God and imparts to us the spiritual or resurrection life of Christ (vv. 12–13); it is a circumcision of the heart (Dt 10:16; 30:6; Jer 4:4; 9:26; Ro 2:29).

2:14 WRITTEN CODE, WITH ITS REGULATIONS. This refers to the Law of Moses, i.e., to commandments that pointed to right conduct but could not give life and the power to obey God (Gal 3:21). The old covenant as a way to salvation has been nailed to the cross (i.e., abolished), and God established a better covenant through Christ and by his Spirit (2Co 3:6–9; Heb 8:6–13; 10:16–17,29; 12:24; see article on THE OLD COVENANT AND THE NEW COVENANT, p. 500).

2:15 DISARMED THE POWERS AND AUTHORITIES. Christ triumphed over all the demonic forces and satanic powers of the world through his death on the cross (cf. Eph 6:12). He stripped them of their power to hold men and women captive to evil's dominion against their will (cf. 1:13; Mt 12:29; Lk 10:18; 11:20–22; Heb 2:14). The child of God shares in this triumph. We not only gain victory over the world and temptation (1Jn 4:4), but we also possess the power to wage war against the spiritual forces of evil (see Eph 6:12, note; see article on SIGNS OF BELIEVERS, p. 106).

2:16 EAT ... DRINK ... SABBATH DAY. "What

you[d] by what you eat or drink,[e] or with regard to a religious festival,[f] a New Moon celebration[g] or a Sabbath day.[h] 17These are a shadow of the things that were to come;[i] the reality, however, is found in Christ. 18Do not let anyone who delights in false humility[j] and the worship of angels disqualify you for the prize.[k] Such a person goes into great detail about what he has seen, and his unspiritual mind puffs him up with idle notions. 19He has lost connection with the Head,[l] from whom the whole body,[m] supported and held together by its ligaments and sinews, grows as God causes it to grow.[n]

20Since you died with Christ[o] to the basic principles of this world,[p] why, as though you still belonged to it, do you submit to its rules:[q] 21"Do not handle! Do not taste! Do not touch!"? 22These are all destined to perish[r] with use, because they are based on human commands and teachings.[s] 23Such regulations indeed have an appearance of wisdom, with their self-imposed worship, their false humility[t] and their harsh treatment of the body, but they lack any value in restraining sensual indulgence.

Rules for Holy Living

3 Since, then, you have been raised with Christ,[u] set your hearts on things above, where Christ is seated at the right hand of God.[v] 2Set your minds on things above, not on earthly things.[w] 3For you died,[x] and your life is now hidden with Christ in God. 4When Christ, who is your[k] life,[y] appears,[z] then you also will appear with him in glory.[a]

5Put to death,[b] therefore, whatever belongs to your earthly nature:[c] sexual immorality,[d] impurity, lust, evil desires and greed,[e] which is idolatry.[f] 6Because of these, the wrath of God[g] is coming.[l] 7You used to walk in these ways, in the life you once lived.[h] 8But now you must rid yourselves[i] of all such things as these: anger, rage, malice, slander,[j] and filthy language from your lips.[k] 9Do not lie to each other,[l] since you have taken off your old self[m] with its practices 10and have put on the new self,[n] which is being renewed[o] in knowledge in the image of its Creator.[p] 11Here there is no Greek or Jew,[q] circumcised or uncircumcised,[r] barbarian, Scythian, slave or free,[s] but Christ is all,[t] and is in all.

12Therefore, as God's chosen people, holy and dearly loved, clothe yourselves[u] with compassion, kindness, humility,[v] gentleness and patience.[w] 13Bear with each other[x] and forgive whatever griev-

2:16 [d]Ro 14:3,4 [e]Mk 7:19; Ro 14:17 [f]Lev 23:2; Ro 14:5 [g]1Ch 23:31 [h]Mk 2:27,28; Gal 4:10 **2:17** [i]Heb 8:5; 10:1 **2:18** [j]ver 23 [k]1Co 9:24; Php 3:14 **2:19** [l]S Eph 1:22 [m]S 1Co 12:27 [n]Eph 4:16 **2:20** [o]S Ro 6:6 [p]ver 8; Gal 4:3,9 [q]ver 14,16 **2:22** [r]1Co 6:13 [s]Isa 29:13; Mt 15:9; Tit 1:14 **2:23** [t]ver 18 **3:1** [u]S Ro 6:5 [v]S Mk 16:19 **3:2** [w]Php 3:19,20 **3:3** [x]S Ro 6:2; 2Co 5:14 **3:4** [y]Gal 2:20 [z]1Co 1:7 [a]1Pe 1:13; 1Jn 3:2 **3:5** [b]S Ro 6:2; S Eph 4:22 [c]S Gal 5:24 [d]S 1Co 6:18 [e]Eph 5:3 [f]Gal 5:19-21; Eph 5:5 **3:6** [g]S Ro 1:18 **3:7** [h]S Eph 2:2 **3:8** [i]S Eph 4:22 [j]Eph 4:31 [k]Eph 4:29 **3:9** [l]S Eph 4:22, 25 [m]S Ro 6:6 **3:10** [n]S Ro 6:4; S 13:14 [o]Ro 12:2; S 2Co 4:16; Eph 4:23 [p]Eph 2:10 **3:11** [q]Ro 10:12; 1Co 12:13 [r]S 1Co 7:19 [s]Gal 3:28 [t]Eph 1:23 **3:12** [u]ver 10 [v]Php 2:3 [w]2Co 6:6; Gal 5:22,23; Eph 4:2 **3:13** [x]Eph 4:2

k *4* Some manuscripts *our* **l** *6* Some early manuscripts *coming on those who are disobedient*

you eat or drink" probably refers to Jewish ascetic dietary rules urged on the Colossians as necessary for salvation (cf. v. 17). "A religious festival, a New Moon celebration or a Sabbath day" probably refers to certain required holy days of the Jewish calendar. Paul teaches that a Christian is freed from legal and ceremonial obligations of this kind (Gal 4:4–11; 5:1; see Mt 12:1, note on the Sabbath; Mk 7:6, note on legalism).

2:18 WORSHIP OF ANGELS. False teachers were saying that angels should be called on and worshiped as mediators in order for people to make contact with God. To Paul, calling on angels would be displacing Jesus Christ as the supreme and sufficient Head of the church (v. 19); consequently, he warns against this. Today the belief that Jesus Christ is not the only intermediary between God and humans is promoted in the practice of worshiping and praying to dead saints, who act as patrons and mediators. This practice robs Christ of his supremacy and centrality in God's redemptive plan. Worship and prayer to anyone other than God the Father, the Son and the Holy Spirit are unbiblical and must be rejected (see 1:2, note).

3:2 SET YOUR MINDS ON THINGS ABOVE. Because our lives are with Christ in heaven (v. 3), we must set our minds on and let our attitudes be determined by things above. We must value, judge and consider everything from an eternal and heavenly perspective. Our goals and pursuits should be to seek spiritual things (vv. 1–4), resist sin (vv. 5–11) and put on Christ's character (vv. 12–17). Spiritual graces, power, experiences and blessings are all with Christ in heaven. He bestows those things on all who sincerely ask, diligently seek and persistently knock (Lk 11:1–13; 1Co 12:11; Eph 1:3; 4:7–8).

3:4 CHRIST, WHO IS YOUR LIFE. Although right doctrine (2Ti 1:13–14) and holy lives (3:5–17; Jn 14:15,21) are an essential part of redemption in Christ, it is fellowship with and love for Christ as a person that must always be kept central (cf. Ro 3:22). Notice the emphasis on the believer's personal communion with Christ in this letter (1:27; 2:6–7,10,20; 3:1,3–4).

3:5 GREED, WHICH IS IDOLATRY. What is idolatry? (1) It is allowing things to become the focus of a person's desires, values and dependence, displacing reliance on and faith in God himself (cf. Ex 20:3–6; Dt 7:25–26; Isa 40:18–23). For this reason greed is called idolatry. (2) Idolatry can involve professing allegiance to God and his Word while at the same time giving equal or greater allegiance to persons, institutions, traditions or authorities on earth. Nothing may be placed higher than one's faithful relationship to God and his Word as revealed in the Bible (Ro 1:22–23; Eph 5:5).

ances you may have against one another.
Forgive as the Lord forgave you.[y] 14And
over all these virtues put on love,[z] which
binds them all together in perfect unity.[a]
15Let the peace of Christ[b] rule in your
hearts, since as members of one body[c]
you were called to peace.[d] And be thankful. 16Let the word of Christ[e] dwell in you
richly as you teach and admonish one another with all wisdom,[f] and as you sing
psalms,[g] hymns and spiritual songs with
gratitude in your hearts to God.[h] 17And
whatever you do,[i] whether in word or
deed, do it all in the name of the Lord
Jesus, giving thanks[j] to God the Father
through him.

Rules for Christian Households

3:18–4:1pp — Eph 5:22–6:9

18Wives, submit to your husbands,[k] as
is fitting in the Lord.
19Husbands, love your wives and do not
be harsh with them.
20Children, obey your parents in everything, for this pleases the Lord.
21Fathers, do not embitter your children, or they will become discouraged.
22Slaves, obey your earthly masters in
everything; and do it, not only when their
eye is on you and to win their favor, but
with sincerity of heart and reverence for
the Lord. 23Whatever you do, work at it
with all your heart, as working for the
Lord, not for men, 24since you know that
you will receive an inheritance[l] from the
Lord as a reward.[m] It is the Lord Christ
you are serving. 25Anyone who does
wrong will be repaid for his wrong, and
there is no favoritism.[n]

4 Masters, provide your slaves with
what is right and fair,[o] because you
know that you also have a Master in
heaven.

Further Instructions

2Devote yourselves to prayer,[p] being

3:13 [y]Eph 4:32
3:14 [z]1Co 13:1-13
[a]S Ro 15:5
3:15 [b]S Jn 14:27
[c]S Ro 12:5
[d]S Ro 14:19
3:16 [e]Ro 10:17
[f]Col 1:28 [g]Ps 47:7
[h]S Eph 5:19
3:17 [i]1Co 10:31
[j]S Eph 5:20
3:18 [k]S Eph 5:22
3:24 [l]S Ac 20:32
[m]S Mt 16:27
3:25 [n]S Ac 10:34
4:1 [o]Lev 25:43,53
4:2 [p]S Lk 18:1

3:16 WORD OF CHRIST DWELL IN YOU. The word of Christ (i.e., Scripture) must be continually read, studied, meditated on and prayed over until it richly dwells in us. When this is our experience, our thoughts, words, deeds and motivations will be influenced and controlled by Christ (Ps 119:11; Jn 15:7; see 1Co 15:2, note). Psalms, hymns and spiritual songs should be used to teach the Word and admonish believers to live lives of obedience to Christ (see Eph 5:19, note on spiritual singing).

3:17 WHATEVER YOU DO, WHETHER IN WORD OR DEED. The Bible presents general principles that permit Spirit-led believers to determine the rightness or wrongness of actions not expressly mentioned in God's Word. In everything that we say, do, think or enjoy, we must ask the following questions: (1) Can it be done to God's glory (1Co 10:31)? (2) Can it be done "in the name of the Lord Jesus," asking his blessing on the activity (see Jn 14:13, note)? (3) Can it be done while sincerely giving thanks to God? (4) Is it a Christlike action (1Jn 2:6)? (5) Will it weaken the sincere convictions of other Christians (see 1Co 8:1, note)? (6) Will it weaken my desire for spiritual things, God's Word and prayer (Lk 8:14; see Mt 5:6, note)? (7) Will it weaken or hinder my witness for Christ (Mt 5:13–16)?

3:18–19 WIVES, SUBMIT TO YOUR HUSBANDS. See Eph 5:21–23, notes; 1Ti 2:13–15, notes on the responsibility of wives and husbands in the family relationship.

3:20 CHILDREN, OBEY YOUR PARENTS. See Eph 6:1, note on the responsibility of children in the family relationship.

3:21 FATHERS, DO NOT EMBITTER YOUR CHILDREN. For a discussion of this passage, including fifteen steps on how parents can lead their children to Christ, see article on PARENTS AND CHILDREN, p. 432.

3:22 SLAVES, OBEY YOUR EARTHLY MASTERS. Paul instructs slaves how to live in a Christian way within their tragic situation. He never indicates that the slave-master relationship is ordained by God or should be perpetuated. Rather he sows the seeds for its abolition in Phm 10,12,14–17,21, and in the meantime seeks to regulate it to the benefit of both masters and slaves (Eph 6:5–9; 1Ti 6:1–2; Tit 2:9–10; cf. 1Pe 2:18–19).

3:23 AS WORKING FOR THE LORD. Paul exhorts Christians to regard all labor as a service rendered to the Lord. We must work as though Christ were our employer, knowing that all work performed "for the Lord" will someday be rewarded (v. 24; cf. Eph 6:6–8).

3:25 ANYONE WHO DOES WRONG. Within family, church and employment relationships (vv. 12–25), Paul is concerned about the demonstration of love, justice and fairness to one another. If taken seriously, these verses would eliminate much of the unloving and unjust treatment of others within our homes and churches. Specifically, we learn that: (1) Mistreatment of others by Christians is a serious matter affecting our future glory in heaven (cf. 2Co 5:10). (a) Those who treat others in love and goodness will receive reward from the Lord (v. 24; Eph 6:8). (b) Anyone who mistreats and does wrong to another believer "will be repaid for his wrong." The guilty will carry that wrong to judgment and bear the consequences without partiality (Dt 10:17; 2Ch 19:7; Ac 10:34; Ro 2:11).

(2) The principle of future accountability to God should help motivate our love, kindness and mercy toward all human beings. Let all believers keep in mind that God will hold his children responsible for the way they have treated one another (Gal 6:7; see Mt 22:37,39 notes; Jn 13:34, note; see article on THE JUDGMENT OF BELIEVERS, p. 368).

4:2 DEVOTE YOURSELVES TO PRAYER, BEING WATCHFUL. "Devote yourselves" (Gk *proskartereō*) means "continue steadfast" or "persevere," implying strong persistence and fervor, a holding fast to prayer. "Being watchful" (Gk *grēgoreō*) means "being spiritually awake or alert." (1) In order to devote ourselves

watchful and thankful. **3**And pray for us,
too, that God may open a door[q] for our
message, so that we may proclaim the
mystery[r] of Christ, for which I am in
chains.[s] **4**Pray that I may proclaim it
clearly, as I should. **5**Be wise[t] in the way
you act toward outsiders;[u] make the most
of every opportunity.[v] **6**Let your conversation be always full of grace,[w] seasoned
with salt,[x] so that you may know how to
answer everyone.[y]

Final Greetings

7Tychicus[z] will tell you all the news
about me. He is a dear brother, a faithful
minister and fellow servant[a] in the Lord.
8I am sending him to you for the express
purpose that you may know about our[m]
circumstances and that he may encourage
your hearts.[b] **9**He is coming with Onesimus,[c] our faithful and dear brother, who
is one of you.[d] They will tell you everything that is happening here.
10My fellow prisoner Aristarchus[e]
sends you his greetings, as does Mark,[f]
the cousin of Barnabas.[g] (You have received instructions about him; if he comes
to you, welcome him.) **11**Jesus, who is
called Justus, also sends greetings. These
are the only Jews among my fellow workers[h] for the kingdom of God, and they
have proved a comfort to me. **12**Epaphras,[i] who is one of you[j] and a servant
of Christ Jesus, sends greetings. He is always wrestling in prayer for you,[k] that
you may stand firm in all the will of God,
mature[l] and fully assured. **13**I vouch for
him that he is working hard for you and for
those at Laodicea[m] and Hierapolis. **14**Our
dear friend Luke,[n] the doctor, and Demas[o] send greetings. **15**Give my greetings
to the brothers at Laodicea,[p] and to Nym-
pha and the church in her house.[q]
16After this letter has been read to you,
see that it is also read[r] in the church of
the Laodiceans and that you in turn read
the letter from Laodicea.
17Tell Archippus:[s] "See to it that you
complete the work you have received in
the Lord."[t]
18I, Paul, write this greeting in my own
hand.[u] Remember[v] my chains.[w] Grace be
with you.[x]

4:3 [q] S Ac 14:27 [r] S Ro 16:25 [s] S Ac 21:33 **4:5** [t] Eph 5:15 [u] S Mk 4:11 [v] Eph 5:16 **4:6** [w] Eph 4:29 [x] Mk 9:50 [y] 1Pe 3:15 **4:7** [z] S Ac 20:4 [a] Eph 6:21,22; Col 1:7 **4:8** [b] Eph 6:21,22; Col 2:2 **4:9** [c] Phm 10 [d] ver 12 **4:10** [e] S Ac 19:29 [f] S Ac 12:12 [g] S Ac 4:36 **4:11** [h] S Php 2:25 **4:12** [i] Col 1:7; Phm 23 [j] ver 9 [k] S Ro 15:30 [l] S 1Co 2:6 **4:13** [m] S Col 2:1 **4:14** [n] 2Ti 4:11; Phm 24 [o] 2Ti 4:10; Phm 24 **4:15** [p] S Col 2:1 [q] S Ro 16:5 **4:16** [r] 2Th 3:14; S 1Ti 4:13 **4:17** [s] Phm 2 [t] 2Ti 4:5 **4:18** [u] S 1Co 16:21 [v] Heb 13:3 [w] S Ac 21:33 [x] 1Ti 6:21; 2Ti 4:22; Tit 3:15; Heb 13:25

m *8* Some manuscripts *that he may know about your*

---

intensely to prayer, we must be alert to the many things that would detour us from this purpose. Satan and the weakness of our human nature will try to cause us to neglect prayer itself or to become distracted while praying. We must discipline ourselves to achieve the prayer required for Christian victory. (2) This was an essential practice of those in the NT church who were baptized in the Spirit: "They devoted themselves . . . to prayer" (Ac 2:42). This devotion to prayer must be undergirded by thanksgiving to Christ for what he has done for us.

4:3 GOD MAY OPEN A DOOR. Paul was confident that God was working by opening and shutting doors in order to direct his life and ministry. The fruitfulness of our lives and our witness depends both on his providence and on his direct intervention. We should pray for God to open doors for us and to indicate where we ought to work (cf. Ac 16:6–10).

4:6 CONVERSATION ... FULL OF GRACE ... SALT. A believer's speech must be pleasant, winsome, kind and gracious. It must be language that results from the operation of God's grace in our hearts and speaks the truth in love (Eph 4:15). "Seasoned with salt" may mean conversation that is appropriate, and marked by purity and not corruption (cf. Eph 4:29). Graceful speech, however, does not rule out fervent and stern words, when necessary, to oppose those false believers who are enemies of the cross (see Mt 23; Ac 15:1–2; Gal 1:9).

4:12 ALWAYS WRESTLING IN PRAYER. "Wrestling" (Gk *agōnizō*, from which we derive the English word "agonize") denotes an intense desire, an agonizing or a striving in prayer. Faithful NT believers not only were devoted to prayer (v. 2), but *agonized* with strong pleadings. The needs of our families, churches and the world are no less significant today. We must pray fervently, knowing that in our wrestling Christ's energy is working powerfully in us (cf. 1:29) and his purpose being realized on behalf of others.

4:16 AFTER THIS LETTER HAS BEEN READ. Paul's letters were read out loud to the congregation when they assembled for worship. The Colossian Christians, after receiving this letter, would most likely make a copy of it to keep for themselves and then send the letter on to the nearby Laodiceans. The "letter from Laodicea" was probably the letter we call Ephesians (see Introduction to Ephesians).

4:18 REMEMBER MY CHAINS. During Paul's first Roman imprisonment he wrote Colossians, Philemon, Ephesians and Philippians. In spite of being unjustly confined to prison for four or more years, note how these letters are filled with "thankfulness" (1:3,12; 2:7; 3:15; 4:2), "grace" (Eph 1:2,6–7; 2:5; 3:2; 4:7; 6:24), "joy" (Php 1:4,18; 2:2; 3:1; 4:1,4) and "love" (Phm 5,7,9).

PARENTS AND CHILDREN

***Col 3:21** "Fathers, do not embitter your children, or they will become discouraged."*

It is the solemn obligation of parents (Gk *patēr*; plural, *pateres*, can mean "fathers" or "father and mother") to give their children the instruction and correction that belong to a Christian upbringing. Parents should be examples of Christian life and conduct, caring more for their children's salvation than for their jobs, professions, ministry in the church or social standing (cf. Ps 127:3).

(1) According to Paul's word in Eph 6:4 and Col 3:21, as well as God's instruction in many OT passages (see Dt 4:9–10; 6:7; Ps 78:3–7; Pr 1:8; 6:20), it is the responsibility of parents to give their children the upbringing that prepares them for lives pleasing to God. It is the family, not the church or church school, that is primarily responsible for the Biblical and spiritual training of the children. Church and church school only assist parental training.

(2) The very core of Christian nurture is this: The heart of the father must be turned to the heart of the child in order to bring the heart of the child to the heart of the Savior (see Lk 1:17, note).

(3) In bringing up their children, parents should show no favoritism, encourage as well as correct, punish only intentional wrongdoing, and dedicate their lives in love to their children with hearts of compassion, kindness, humility, gentleness and patience (Col 3:12–14,21).

(4) Here are fifteen steps that you as parents should take to lead your children to lives of godliness in Christ:

(a) Dedicate your children to God at the beginning of their lives (1Sa 1:28; Lk 2:22).

(b) Teach your children to fear the Lord and turn away from evil, to love righteousness and to hate sin. Instill in them an awareness of God's attitude and judgment toward sin (see Heb 1:9, note).

(c) Teach your children to obey you through Biblical discipline (Dt 8:5; Pr 3:11–12; 13:24; 23:13–14; 29:15,17; Heb 12:7).

(d) Protect your children from ungodly influences by being aware of Satan's attempts to destroy them spiritually through attraction to the world or through immoral companions (Pr 13:20; 28:7; 1Jn 2:15–17).

(e) Make your children aware that God is always observing and evaluating what they do, think and say (Ps 139:1–12).

(f) Bring your children early in life to personal faith, repentance and water baptism in Christ (Mt 19:14).

(g) Establish your children in a spiritual church where God's Word is proclaimed, his righteous standards honored and the Holy Spirit manifested. Teach them the motto, "I am a friend to all who fear you" (Ps 119:63; see Ac 12:5, note).

(h) Encourage your children to remain separated from the world and to witness and work for God (2Co 6:14—7:1; Jas 4:4). Teach them that they are strangers and aliens on this earth (Heb 11:13–16), that their real home and citizenship is in heaven with Christ (Php 3:20; Col 3:1–3).

(i) Instruct your children in the importance of the baptism in the Holy Spirit (Ac 1:4–5,8; 2:4,39).

(j) Teach your children that God loves them and has a specific purpose for their lives (Lk 1:13–17; Ro 8:30; 1Pe 1:3–9).

(k) Instruct your children daily in God's Word, both in conversation and family devotions (Dt 4:9; 6:5–7; 1Ti 4:6; 2Ti 3:15).

(l) Through example and exhortation, encourage your children to live lives devoted to prayer (Ac 6:4; Ro 12:12; Eph 6:18; Jas 5:16).

(m) Prepare your children to suffer and endure persecution because of righteousness (Mt 5:10–12). They must know that "everyone who wants to live a godly life in Christ Jesus will be persecuted" (2Ti 3:12).

(n) Lift your children up to God by constant and earnest intercession (Eph 6:18; Jas 5:16–18; see Jn 17:1, note on Jesus' prayer for his disciples as a model of parents' prayers for their children).

(o) Have such love and concern for your children that you would be willing to pour out your life as if it were a sacrifice to the Lord, in order to deepen their faith and make their lives what they should be in the Lord (see Php 2:17, note).

1 THESSALONIANS

Outline

Christian Greetings (1:1)
- I. Paul's Personal Gratitude for the Thessalonians (1:2—3:13)
  - A. Rejoices About Their New Life in Christ (1:2–10)
    - 1. Their Faith, Love and Hope (1:2–3)
    - 2. Their Genuine Conversion (1:4–6)
    - 3. Their Good Example to Others (1:7–10)
  - B. Reminiscences About His Role in Their Lives (2:1—3:8)
    - 1. Reviews His Labors (2:1–12)
    - 2. Recalls Their Response (2:13–16)
    - 3. Retains His Interest (2:17—3:8)
  - C. Prays for an Opportunity to Return, and for Their Spiritual Advancement and Establishment in Holiness (3:9–13)
- II. Paul's Practical Instruction to the Thessalonians (4:1—5:22)
  - A. Concerning Sexual Purity (4:1–8)
  - B. Concerning Brotherly Love (4:9–10)
  - C. Concerning Honest Labor (4:11–12)
  - D. Concerning the Coming of Christ (4:13—5:11)
    - 1. The State of the Dead in Christ (4:13–18)
    - 2. The Readiness of Those Living in Christ (5:1–11)
  - E. Concerning Esteem for Spiritual Leaders (5:12–13)
  - F. Concerning Christian Living (5:14–18)
  - G. Concerning Spiritual Discernment (5:19–22)

Conclusion (5:23–28)
- A. Prayer for Their Sanctification and Preservation (5:23–24)
- B. Final Requests and Benediction (5:25–28)

Author: Paul

Theme: The Return of Christ

Date of Writing: c. A.D. 51

Background

Thessalonica, located slightly less than a hundred miles southwest of Philippi, was the capital, foremost city and harbor of the Roman province of Macedonia. Among the city's population of 200,000 was a strong Jewish community. When Paul founded the Thessalonian church on his second missionary journey, his fruitful ministry there was prematurely terminated because of intense Jewish hostility (Ac 17:1–9).

Forced to leave Thessalonica, Paul went to Berea where another brief but successful ministry was cut short by persecution stirred up by hostile Jews who followed him from Thessalonica (Ac 17:10–13). Paul then traveled to Athens (Ac 17:15–34), where Timothy joined him afterwards. Paul sent Timothy back to Thessalonica to check on the infant church (3:1–5) while Paul went on to Corinth (Ac 18:1–17). Upon completing the assignment, Timothy traveled to Corinth with a report for Paul about the Thessalonian church (3:6–8). In response to Timothy's report, Paul wrote this letter to the Thessalonians, perhaps three to six months after founding the church.

Purpose

Because Paul was forced by persecution to leave Thessalonica abruptly, his young converts received only minimal instruction about the Christian life. When Paul learned from Timothy about their present circumstances, he wrote this letter (1) to express his joy in their steadfast faith and perseverance in the midst of persecution, (2) to instruct them further in holiness and godly living, and (3) to clarify certain beliefs, especially concerning the status of believers who die before Christ's return.

Survey

After greeting the church (1:1), Paul joyfully commends the Thessalonians for their enduring zeal and faith in the face of great adversity (1:2–10; 2:13–16). Paul responds to criticism by reminding the church of the purity of his motives (2:1–6), the sincerity of his affection and concern for the flock (2:7–8,17–20; 3:1–10), and the integrity of his conduct among them (2:9–12).

Paul emphasizes the necessity and importance of holiness and power in the Christian life. The believer must be holy (3:13; 4:1–8; 5:23–24), and the gospel must be accompanied by the power and manifestation of the Holy Spirit (1:5). Paul admonishes the Thessalonians not to put out the Spirit's fire by despising his manifestations, especially prophecy (5:19–20).

A prominent theme is Christ's return to deliver his people from God's wrath on the earth (1:10; 4:13–18; 5:1–11). Apparently some Thessalonian believers had died already, raising concern about their participation in the final salvation to be revealed at the Lord's coming. Accordingly, Paul explains God's plan for departed saints when Christ returns for his church (4:13–18) and exhorts the living about the importance of being ready when Christ comes (5:1–11). Paul concludes by praying for the sanctification and preservation of the Thessalonians (5:23–24).

Special Features

Four major features characterize this letter. (1) It is among the very first books written in the NT. (2) It contains key passages about God raising the deceased saints when Christ returns to catch up his church (4:13–18) and about "the day of the Lord" (5:1–11). (3) All five chapters contain some reference to Christ's return and its significance for believers (1:10; 2:19; 3:13; 4:13–18; 5:1–11,23). (4) It provides unique insight (a) into the life of a zealous but immature church in the early 50s, and (b) into the quality of Paul's ministry as a pioneer of the gospel.

Reading 1 Thessalonians

In order to read the entire New Testament in one year, the book of 1 Thessalonians should be read in 4 days, according to the following schedule:

☐ 1:1–2:16 ☐ 2:17–3:13 ☐ 4 ☐ 5

NOTES

1

Paul, Silas[a][a] and Timothy,[b]

To the church of the Thessalonians[c]
in God the Father and the Lord Jesus
Christ:

Grace and peace to you.[b][d]

Thanksgiving for the Thessalonians' Faith

2We always thank God for all of you,[e]
mentioning you in our prayers.[f] **3**We continually remember before our God and Father[g] your work produced by faith,[h] your
labor prompted by love,[i] and your endurance inspired by hope[j] in our Lord Jesus
Christ.

4For we know, brothers loved by God,[k]
that he has chosen you, **5**because our gospel[l] came to you not simply with words,
but also with power,[m] with the Holy Spirit
2Ti 1:8 and with deep conviction. You know[n] how
we lived among you for your sake. **6**You
became imitators of us[o] and of the Lord;
in spite of severe suffering,[p] you welcomed the message with the joy[q] given by
Heb 12:11 the Holy Spirit.[r] **7**And so you became a
model[s] to all the believers in Macedonia[t]
and Achaia.[u] **8**The Lord's message[v] rang
out from you not only in Macedonia and
Achaia—your faith in God has become
known everywhere.[w] Therefore we do not
need to say anything about it, **9**for they
themselves report what kind of reception
you gave us. They tell how you turned[x] to
God from idols[y] to serve the living and
true God,[z] **10**and to wait for his Son from
heaven,[a] whom he raised from the dead[b]
—Jesus, who rescues us from the coming
wrath.[c]

Paul's Ministry in Thessalonica

2

You know, brothers, that our visit to
you[d] was not a failure.[e] **2**We had previously suffered[f] and been insulted in
Philippi,[g] as you know, but with the help
of our God we dared to tell you his gospel
in spite of strong opposition.[h] **3**For the
appeal we make does not spring from error or impure motives,[i] nor are we trying
to trick you.[j] **4**On the contrary, we speak
as men approved by God to be entrusted

1:1 [a]S Ac 15:22 [b]S Ac 16:1; 2Th 1:1 [c]S Ac 17:1 [d]S Ro 1:7 **1:2** [e]S Ro 1:8; Eph 5:20 [f]S Ro 1:10 **1:3** [g]S Php 4:20 [h]Gal 5:6; 2Th 1:11; Jas 2:14-26 [i]1Th 3:6; 2Th 1:3; S 1Co 13:13 [j]Ro 8:25 **1:4** [k]Col 3:12; 2Th 2:13 **1:5** [l]S 2Co 2:12; 2Th 2:14 [m]Ro 1:16; S Ro 15:13 [n]1Th 2:10 **1:6** [o]S 1Co 4:16 [p]Ac 17:5-10 [q]S 2Co 6:10 [r]Ac 13:52 **1:7** [s]S 1Ti 4:12 [t]S Ac 16:9 [u]S Ac 18:12 **1:8** [v]2Th 3:1 [w]Ro 1:8 **1:9** [x]Ac 14:15 [y]1Co 12:2; Gal 4:8 [z]S Mt 16:16 **1:10** [a]S 1Co 1:7 [b]S Ac 2:24 [c]S Ro 1:18 **2:1** [d]1Th 1:5,9 [e]2Th 1:10 **2:2** [f]Ac 14:19; 16:22; Php 1:30 [g]S Ac 16:12 [h]Ac 17:1-9 **2:3** [i]2Co 2:17 [j]2Co 4:2

[a] *1* Greek *Silvanus*, a variant of *Silas* [b] *1* Some early manuscripts *you from God our Father and the Lord Jesus Christ*

1:4 HE HAS CHOSEN YOU. Paul's description of those who belong to the elect is found in vv. 6–10. They are those who imitate Christ, endure suffering with the joy given by the Holy Spirit, and model faith and righteousness. They have turned from sin, now serve God, and are waiting for God's Son to return from heaven. The doctrine some hold that people who profess Christ as Savior will be saved regardless of how they live (e.g., whether or not they repent, accept Christ as Lord, persevere in the faith or possess the fruit of the Spirit) is not found anywhere in God's Word and is a flagrant corruption of the original doctrine of salvation preached by Christ and the apostles (see articles on ELECTION AND PREDESTINATION, p. 402, and FAITH AND GRACE, p. 302).

1:5 WITH POWER, WITH THE HOLY SPIRIT. The apostolic preaching of the gospel consisted of four essential elements: (1) The apostles proclaimed the gospel of God (2:8) and Christ (3:2) to others.

(2) They preached God's Word in the power of the Holy Spirit (Mt 3:11; Ac 1:5–8; 2:4). This power resulted in conviction of sin, deliverance from satanic bondage, and the performing of miracles and healings (see Ac 4:30, note; 1Co 2:4, note).

(3) The message was proclaimed "with deep conviction." Because of their faith in Christ, and through the work of the Spirit in them, they possessed in their hearts a full assurance of the truth and power of the message (cf. Ro 1:16).

(4) Those who believed the message obeyed God's Word and lived it out in their lives; they were models of holiness and righteousness.

Without these four elements accompanying the proclamation of the gospel, Christ's full redemption will not be experienced in the churches.

1:10 TO WAIT FOR HIS SON FROM HEAVEN. The great hope of the Thessalonian believers was Christ's return and his delivering them from "the coming wrath." (1) A true NT conversion to Christ involves (a) turning from sin and (b) turning to God to wait for his Son to return (v. 9). Waiting for Christ implies a sustained expectation of Christ's return and a readiness for that time.

(2) "The coming wrath" refers to the future judgment that occurs during the tribulation period. However, believers need not fear, for God is sending Jesus back to deliver us from that time of wrath. Clearly Christ's return for his faithful precedes this coming wrath (see Rev 3:10, note; see article on THE GREAT TRIBULATION, p. 52).

(3) This is the first reference in 1 Thessalonians to Christ's return, when he comes to catch up his saints and take them to his Father's house (see Jn 14:3, note); the other passages are 2:19; 3:13; 4:17, 5:1–11,23.

2:1 OUR VISIT TO YOU. In ch. 2 Paul vindicates his conduct while he was with the Thessalonians. Paul had been slandered by his opponents and accused of insincerity in his preaching of the gospel.

2:4 WE SPEAK . . . NOT TRYING TO PLEASE MEN. Every preacher of the gospel faces the temptation to please other people, i.e., seek acceptance, approval and glory from others (v. 6) by preaching only what will not offend. (1) Yielding to this temptation may take the form of tolerating sin and lukewarmness in the congregation (cf. Rev 2:20; 3:15–16). It may also involve the use of flattering speech in order to gain financial offerings, numerical gain, political of-

with the gospel.[k] We are not trying to
please men[l] but God, who tests our
hearts.[m] **5**You know we never used flattery, nor did we put on a mask to cover up
greed[n]—God is our witness.[o] **6**We were
not looking for praise from men,[p] not
from you or anyone else.
As apostles[q] of Christ we could have
been a burden to you,[r] **7**but we were gentle among you, like a mother caring for her
little children.[s] **8**We loved you so much
that we were delighted to share with you
not only the gospel of God[t] but our lives
as well,[u] because you had become so dear
to us. **9**Surely you remember, brothers,
our toil and hardship; we worked[v] night
and day in order not to be a burden to
anyone[w] while we preached the gospel of
God to you.
10You are witnesses,[x] and so is God,[y]
of how holy,[z] righteous and blameless we
were among you who believed. **11**For you
know that we dealt with each of you as a
father deals with his own children,[a] **12**encouraging, comforting and urging you to
live lives worthy[b] of God, who calls[c] you
into his kingdom and glory.
13And we also thank God continually[d]
because, when you received the word of
God,[e] which you heard from us, you accepted it not as the word of men, but as
it actually is, the word of God, which is at
work in you who believe. **14**For you, brothers, became imitators[f] of God's churches
in Judea,[g] which are in Christ Jesus: You
suffered from your own countrymen[h] the
same things those churches suffered from
the Jews, **15**who killed the Lord Jesus[i]
and the prophets[j] and also drove us out.
They displease God and are hostile to all
men **16**in their effort to keep us from
speaking to the Gentiles[k] so that they
may be saved. In this way they always
heap up their sins to the limit.[l] The wrath
of God has come upon them at last.[c]

Paul's Longing to See the Thessalonians

17But, brothers, when we were torn
away from you for a short time (in person,
not in thought),[m] out of our intense longing we made every effort to see you.[n]
18For we wanted to come to you—certainly I, Paul, did, again and again—but Sa-

2:4 [k] Gal 2:7; 1Ti 1:11 [l] S Ro 2:29 [m] S Rev 2:23
2:5 [n] S Ac 20:33 [o] ver 10; S Ro 1:9
2:6 [p] Jn 5:41,44 [q] 1Co 9:1,2 [r] 2Co 11:7-11
2:7 [s] S ver 11
2:8 [t] S Ro 1:1 [u] 2Co 12:15; 1Jn 3:16
2:9 [v] S Ac 18:3 [w] S 2Co 11:9; 2Th 3:8
2:10 [x] 1Th 1:5 [y] ver 5; S Ro 1:9 [z] 2Co 1:12
2:11 [a] ver 7; 1Co 4:14; Gal 4:19; S 1Ti 1:2; Phm 10; S 1Jn 2:1
2:12 [b] S Eph 4:1 [c] S Ro 8:28
2:13 [d] 1Th 1:2; S Ro 1:8 [e] S Heb 4:12
2:14 [f] 1Th 1:6 [g] Gal 1:22 [h] Ac 17:5; 2Th 1:4
2:15 [i] Lk 24:20; Ac 2:23 [j] S Mt 5:12
2:16 [k] Ac 13:45, 50; 17:5; S 20:3; 21:27; 24:9 [l] Mt 23:32
2:17 [m] 1Co 5:3; Col 2:5 [n] 1Th 3:10

c *16* Or *them fully*

fice or praise from others (vv. 4–6). (2) If this occurs, irreparable damage is done to the righteousness and integrity of Christ's church. For this reason it is essential that our motive in preaching should always be to seek God's approval and not other people's (1Co 4:5; Gal 1:9–10; see Lk 1:17, note; 2Ti 4:3–4, note).

2:7 LIKE A MOTHER CARING FOR HER LITTLE CHILDREN. Paul and his helpers offer an example of the spiritual attitude that all missionaries, evangelists and pastors should have as they preach the gospel. (1) As missionaries, they had a mother's gentle and caring attitude; under great sacrifice, they made a special effort to nurture, protect and meet the spiritual needs of the new converts.

(2) Their gentleness implies they did not act like important or superior persons.

(3) The missionaries possessed such a yearning and love for the Thessalonians that they were willing to share their very lives with the people (v. 8).

(4) They devoted long hours, even to the point of weariness, in order to bring them the gospel (v. 9).

(5) They lived holy and blameless lives before the people, encouraging and urging them as any father would (vv. 10–12).

2:10 HOW HOLY, RIGHTEOUS AND BLAMELESS WE WERE. Paul does not accept the erroneous view of "sinning Christianity," which says that the salvation provided by Christ and his atoning blood is not adequate to save us from sin's bondage and power. This unbiblical doctrine maintains that all Christians must expect to sin against God daily in word, thought and deed throughout their earthly lives. Contrary to the above doctrine, (1) Paul affirms, with regard to his own conduct among the Thessalonians, that he was "holy, righteous and blameless." (2) Paul called both the church and God himself as witnesses that God's sufficient grace through Christ had enabled him, as he affirmed elsewhere, to purify himself "from everything that contaminates body and spirit, perfecting holiness out of reverence for God" (2Co 7:1; cf. 2Co 1:12; 2:17; 6:3–10; 1Th 1:5; 2Ti 1:3).

2:16 THE WRATH OF GOD HAS COME UPON THEM. Paul denounces the Jews who oppose the gospel (vv. 14–16) and speaks of God's wrath already being upon them. This wrath includes both God's turning the already hardened Jews of Israel over to blindness and futile thinking (cf. Ro 1:21), and the future outpouring of his wrath foretold by Christ (Mt 21:43; 23:38; 24:15–28; Lk 21:5–24; 23:27–31).

2:18 BUT SATAN STOPPED US. Paul's missionary endeavors had at times been frustrated by Satan. Scriptural truths concerning Satan's opposition to faithful believers include the following: (1) Satan is permitted by God to war against believers and hinder them from doing what they sincerely desire to do for Christ (Eph 6:11–12; cf. Da 10:13,20–21; Zec 3:1; Mt 4:1–10).

(2) Satan's power is, however, subject to God's overruling (Job 1:9–12; 2:6); God can overrule for good (2Co 12:7–9).

(3) Satan's opposition can be overcome by the prayers of saints, by the blood of the Lamb, by the word of our testimony and by our committed love for God (cf. Rev 12:11); therefore, Satan's opposition need not be permanent (cf. 3:11). To this end, we must pray daily for deliverance from his schemes and power (see 3:5, note; Mt 4:10, note on Satan; 6:13; Eph 6:12, note).

tan[o] stopped us.[p] **19**For what is our hope,
our joy, or the crown[q] in which we will
glory[r] in the presence of our Lord Jesus
when he comes?[s] Is it not you? **20**Indeed,
you are our glory[t] and joy.

3 So when we could stand it no longer,[u]
we thought it best to be left by ourselves in Athens.[v] **2**We sent Timothy,[w]
who is our brother and God's fellow worker[d][x] in spreading the gospel of Christ,[y] to
strengthen and encourage you in your
faith, **3**so that no one would be unsettled
by these trials.[z] You know quite well that
we were destined for them.[a] **4**In fact,
when we were with you, we kept telling
you that we would be persecuted. And it
turned out that way, as you well know.[b]
5For this reason, when I could stand it no
longer,[c] I sent to find out about your
faith.[d] I was afraid that in some way the
tempter[e] might have tempted you and our
efforts might have been useless.[f]

Timothy's Encouraging Report

6But Timothy[g] has just now come to us
from you[h] and has brought good news
about your faith and love.[i] He has told us
that you always have pleasant memories
of us and that you long to see us, just as
we also long to see you.[j] **7**Therefore,
brothers, in all our distress and persecu-
2Th 1:3 tion we were encouraged about you because of your faith. **8**For now we really
live, since you are standing firm[k] in the
Lord. **9**How can we thank God enough for
you[l] in return for all the joy we have in
the presence of our God because of you?[m]
10Night and day we pray[n] most earnestly
that we may see you again[o] and supply
what is lacking in your faith.

Paul's Prayer for the Church

11Now may our God and Father[p] himself and our Lord Jesus clear the way for
us to come to you. **12**May the Lord make
your love increase and overflow for each
other[q] and for everyone else, just as ours
does for you. **13**May he strengthen your
hearts so that you will be blameless[r] and
holy in the presence of our God and Father[s] when our Lord Jesus comes[t] with
all his holy ones.[u]

Living to Please God

4 Finally, brothers,[v] we instructed you
how to live[w] in order to please God,[x]
as in fact you are living. Now we ask you
and urge you in the Lord Jesus to do this
more and more. **2**For you know what instructions we gave you by the authority of
the Lord Jesus.
3It is God's will[y] that you should be
sanctified: that you should avoid sexual
immorality;[z] **4**that each of you should

2:18 [o]S Mt 4:10 [p]Ro 1:13; 15:22 **2:19** [q]Isa 62:3; Php 4:1 [r]2Co 1:14 [s]S Mt 16:27; S Lk 17:30; S 1Co 1:7; 4:5; 1Th 3:13; 2Th 1:8-10; 1Pe 1:7; 1Jn 2:28; S Rev 1:7 **2:20** [t]2Co 1:14 **3:1** [u]ver 5 [v]S Ac 17:15 **3:2** [w]S Ac 16:1 [x]S 1Co 3:9 [y]S 2Co 2:12 **3:3** [z]Mk 4:17; Jn 16:33; Ro 5:3; 2Co 1:4; 4:17; 2Ti 3:12 [a]S Ac 9:16; 14:22 **3:4** [b]1Th 2:14 **3:5** [c]ver 1 [d]ver 2 [e]Mt 4:3 [f]Gal 2:2; Php 2:16 **3:6** [g]S Ac 16:1 [h]Ac 18:5 [i]1Th 1:3 [j]1Th 2:17,18 **3:8** [k]S 1Co 16:13 **3:9** [l]1Th 1:2 [m]1Th 2:19,20 **3:10** [n]2Ti 1:3 [o]1Th 2:17 **3:11** [p]ver 13; S Php 4:20 **3:12** [q]Php 1:9; 1Th 4:9,10; 2Th 1:3 **3:13** [r]Ps 15:2; 1Co 1:8; Php 2:15; 1Th 5:23; 1Ti 6:14; 2Pe 3:14 [s]ver 11; S Php 4:20 [t]S 1Th 2:19 [u]Mt 25:31; 2Th 1:7 **4:1** [v]2Co 13:11; 2Th 3:1 [w]S Eph 4:1 [x]S 2Co 5:9

4:3 [y]S Eph 5:17 [z]S 1Co 6:18

[d] *2* Some manuscripts *brother and fellow worker;* other manuscripts *brother and God's servant*

3:3 TRIALS. The followers of Christ must not regard trouble and persecution as alien to the Christian life. (1) True believers who refuse to conform to the prevailing characteristics of their world will "be persecuted" (v. 4; cf. Ac 14:22; Ro 8:18; 2Ti 3:12). (2) These trials must not be identified with the outpouring of God's wrath on the ungodly at the end of time (5:9; Mt 24:21; 2Th 1:6; Rev 3:10, note).

3:5 THE TEMPTER MIGHT HAVE TEMPTED YOU. This is the second time Paul has referred to Satan's activity in this letter (cf. 2:18). Paul firmly believed in Satan and the realm of evil spirits (Eph 2:2; 2Th 2:9), as did Jesus Christ (Mt 13:39; Mk 3:14–15; 4:15; Lk 4:1–13,33–41). Today many no longer believe in a personal Satan; he is seldom mentioned, exposed or confronted directly in or by the church. The devil has tempted us to believe that he is no longer a real enemy who takes people captive, and that we need no longer drive out evil spirits as Jesus and the early NT believers did. Many churches feel no need to challenge Satan directly with the power of Christ's kingdom (see Mt 4:10, note on Satan; see article on POWER OVER SATAN AND DEMONS, p. 80).

3:13 BLAMELESS AND HOLY . . . WHEN OUR LORD JESUS COMES. Paul often prayed with Christ's return in mind (cf. Php 1:10). He considered it a tragedy if at the Lord's return some within the church were caught living in sin or lukewarmness. Jesus emphasized this same concern (Mt 24:42–51; 25:1–13). In light of Christ's return, the Biblical standard is to be "blameless and holy." We must be wholeheartedly committed to the Lord and separated from all that offends him. The phrase "with all his holy ones" refers to departed saints who are already with the Lord in heaven (see article on THE RAPTURE, p. 440).

4:3 IT IS GOD'S WILL. Although they lived in a society where sexual immorality was commonplace and acceptable, the apostles did not compromise God's holiness and truth. They would not lower their standards to accommodate the ideas or trends of their society. Whenever they found low standards in some of the churches (cf. Rev 2:14–15,20), they rebuked and sought to correct them. In the light of today's prevalent low morals, apostolic-type leaders are still needed to call the church to God's standards of righteousness.

4:3–7 AVOID SEXUAL IMMORALITY. God imposes on all believers high standards of purity and sanctification with regard to sexual matters. For a discussion of what these standards are, see article on STANDARDS OF SEXUAL MORALITY, p. 509.

learn to control his own body[e][a] in a way
that is holy and honorable, **5**not in passionate lust[b] like the heathen,[c] who do
not know God;[d] **6**and that in this matter
no one should wrong his brother or take
advantage of him.[e] The Lord will punish
men[f] for all such sins,[g] as we have already told you and warned you. **7**For God
did not call us to be impure, but to live a
holy life.[h] **8**Therefore, he who rejects this
instruction does not reject man but God,
who gives you his Holy Spirit.[i]

9Now about brotherly love[j] we do not
need to write to you,[k] for you yourselves
have been taught by God[l] to love each
other.[m] **10**And in fact, you do love all the
brothers throughout Macedonia.[n] Yet we
urge you, brothers, to do so more and
more.[o]

11Make it your ambition to lead a quiet
life, to mind your own business and to
work with your hands,[p] just as we told
you, **12**so that your daily life may win the
respect of outsiders[q] and so that you will
not be dependent on anybody.

The Coming of the Lord

13Brothers, we do not want you to be
ignorant[r] about those who fall asleep,[s] or
to grieve like the rest of men, who have no
hope.[t] **14**We believe that Jesus died and
rose again[u] and so we believe that God
will bring with Jesus those who have fall-
en asleep in him.[v] **15**According to the
Lord's own word, we tell you that we who
are still alive, who are left till the coming
of the Lord,[w] will certainly not precede
those who have fallen asleep.[x] **16**For the
Lord himself will come down from heav-
en,[y] with a loud command, with the voice
of the archangel[z] and with the trumpet
call of God,[a] and the dead in Christ will
rise first.[b] **17**After that, we who are still
alive and are left[c] will be caught up together with them in the clouds[d] to meet
the Lord in the air. And so we will be with
the Lord[e] forever. **18**Therefore encourage
each other[f] with these words.

5 Now, brothers, about times and
dates[g] we do not need to write to
you,[h] **2**for you know very well that the day

4:4 [a]1Co 7:2,9 **4:5** [b]Ro 1:26 [c]Eph 4:17 [d]S Gal 4:8 **4:6** [e]Lev 25:17; 1Co 6:8 [f]Dt 32:35; Ps 94:1; Ro 2:5-11; 12:19; Heb 10:30,31 [g]Heb 13:4 **4:7** [h]Lev 11:44; 1Pe 1:15 **4:8** [i]Eze 36:27; Ro 5:5; 2Co 1:22; Gal 4:6; 1Jn 3:24 **4:9** [j]S Ro 12:10 [k]1Th 5:1 [l]S Jn 6:45 [m]S Jn 13:34 **4:10** [n]S Ac 16:9 [o]S 1Th 3:12 **4:11** [p]Eph 4:28; 2Th 3:10-12 **4:12** [q]S Mk 4:11 **4:13** [r]S Ro 11:25 [s]S Mt 9:24 [t]Eph 2:12 **4:14** [u]Ro 14:9; 1Co 15:3,4; 2Co 5:15 [v]1Co 15:18 **4:15** [w]S 1Co 1:7 [x]1Co 15:52 **4:16** [y]S Mt 16:27 [z]Jude 9 [a]S Mt 24:31 [b]1Co 15:23; 2Th 2:1; Rev 14:13 **4:17** [c]1Co 15:52 [d]Ac 1:9; S Ac 8:39; S Rev 1:7; 11:12 [e]S Jn 12:26 **4:18** [f]1Th 5:11 **5:1** [g]Ac 1:7 [h]1Th 4:9

[e] 4 Or *learn to live with his own wife*; or *learn to acquire a wife*

4:6 WRONG HIS BROTHER. Sexual immorality wrongs another person, whether a believer or not. To wrong (Gk *pleonokteō*) means "to go beyond what is right," "to transgress," "to overreach." All sexual activity or play outside of marriage is an act of terrible injustice against another individual. Adultery violates the rights of another married person. Sexual looseness before marriage defiles and robs another person of the holiness and chastity that God desires for him or her. It destroys the purity and virginity that must be brought into a marriage.

4:8 DOES NOT REJECT MAN BUT GOD. Those who reject the instructions of the apostle on sanctification and purity are rejecting God. (1) To disregard Paul's admonition is to stand squarely against the Holy Spirit, and the purity that the Spirit desires. God will judge and punish church members who disregard moral purity for the satisfaction of their own lusts (v. 6; cf. Heb 13:4).

(2) All those in the world and within the visible church who reject the truth and have "delighted in wickedness" (see 2Th 2:12, note) will be abandoned by Christ when faithful believers are caught up "to meet the Lord in the air" (v. 17; see article on THE RAPTURE, p. 440). They will suffer destruction (5:3), wrath (5:9), punishment (2Th 1:8) and condemnation (2Th 1:9; 2:12) at the final coming of Christ from heaven in blazing fire to punish all who "do not obey the gospel of our Lord Jesus" (2Th 1:7–8).

4:13 ABOUT THOSE WHO FALL ASLEEP. This phrase refers to believers who had died and whose souls were in heaven; it does not mean that the dead are unconscious in a sort of soul-sleep (cf. Php 1:21, note). The Thessalonians did not understand how the resurrection of Christians who had already died related to the catching up of living Christians at Christ's coming (see Jn 14:3, note). They apparently thought that those who died before Christ returns for the church (vv. 16–17) would not be resurrected until a much later time. Paul tells them that the dead in Christ will rise at the same time the Lord returns for the faithful of his churches (see article on THE RAPTURE, p. 440).

4:14–18 THE COMING OF THE LORD. The event described by Paul in these verses is often referred to as "the rapture of the church." For a discussion of this future event, see article on THE RAPTURE, p. 440.

4:18 ENCOURAGE EACH OTHER. Paul inspires hope in the Thessalonians, not by telling them to prepare for martyrdom during the period of "the day of the Lord" (5:2–10), i.e., the tribulation (Rev 6–19), but by informing them of the rapture (see vv. 14–17; Jn 14:3, note; 1Co 15:51–58; see article on THE RAPTURE, p. 440). Knowing this doctrine, they will be able to encourage each other.

5:1 TIMES AND DATES. Having spoken about Christ's return to catch up his followers from the earth (4:13–18), Paul now turns to the subject of God's final judgment on all those who reject salvation in Christ in the final days, that terrible time called "the day of the Lord" (v. 2). The believers' rapture (4:17) must be simultaneous with the beginning of "the day of the Lord" in order for Christ's return to be imminent and unexpected, as Christ himself taught (see Mt 24:42,44, notes).

5:2 THE DAY OF THE LORD. The "day of the Lord" normally refers not to a 24-hour day but to an extended period of time when God's enemies are overthrown

THE RAPTURE

***1Th 4:16–17** "For the Lord himself will come down from heaven with a loud command, with the voice of the archangel and with the trumpet call of God, and the dead in Christ will rise first. After that we who are still alive and are left will be caught up together with them in the clouds to meet the Lord in the air. And so we will be with the Lord forever."*

The word "rapture" is derived from the Latin word *raptu*, which means "caught away or caught up." This Latin word is equivalent to the Greek *harpazō*, translated as "caught up" in 1Th 4:17. This event, described here and in 1Co 15, refers to the catching up of the church from the earth to meet the Lord in the air. It involves only the faithful of Christ's churches.

(1) Just prior to the rapture, as Christ is descending from heaven for his church, the resurrection of the "dead in Christ" will occur (1Th 4:16). This is not the same resurrection described in Rev 20:4, for the latter is an event occurring after Christ returns to earth, destroys the wicked and binds Satan (Rev 19:11—20:3). The resurrection in Rev 20:4 relates to the martyred dead of the tribulation and possibly to OT saints (see Rev 20:6, note).

(2) At the same time as the dead in Christ rise, living believers will be transfigured; their bodies will be clothed with immortality (1Co 15:51,53). This will happen in a very short time, "in the twinkling of an eye" (1Co 15:52).

(3) Both the resurrected believers and the transfigured believers will be caught up together to meet Christ in the air, that is, in the atmosphere between earth and heaven.

(4) They will be visibly united with Christ (1Th 4:16–17), taken to his Father's house in heaven (see Jn 14:2–3, notes) and united with loved ones who have died (1Th 4:13–18).

(5) They will be removed from all distress (2Co 5:2,4; Php 3:21), from all persecution and oppression (see Rev 3:10, note), from the entire realm of sin and from death (1Co 15:51–56); the rapture delivers them from "the coming wrath" (1Th 1:10, note; 5:9), i.e., from the great tribulation.

(6) The hope that our Savior will soon return to take us out of the world to "be with the Lord forever" (1Th 4:17) is the blessed hope of all the redeemed (Tit 2:13). It is a major source of comfort for suffering believers (1Th 4:17–18; 5:10).

(7) Paul uses "we" in 1Th 4:17 because he knows the Lord's return could have happened in his own lifetime, and he communicates this same anticipation to the Thessalonians. The Bible insists on a continual waiting with eagerness for the return of our Lord. Believers today must be ever watchful and hopeful for Christ's return to take them to himself (cf. Ro 13:11; 1Co 7:29; 10:11; 15:51–52; Php 4:5).

(8) The portion of the professing church that fails to abstain from evil and is unfaithful to Christ will be left behind (see Mt 25:1, note; Lk 12:45, note). They will remain as part of the apostate church (see Rev 17:1, note; see article on THE AGE OF THE ANTICHRIST, p. 447), subject to God's wrath.

(9) Following the rapture is the day of the Lord, the day that brings distress and wrath to the ungodly (1Th 5:2–10; see 5:2, note). That will be followed by the second stage of Christ's coming, when he comes to destroy the ungodly and to reign on earth (see Mt 24:42,44 notes).

of the Lord[i] will come like a thief in the
night.[j] **3**While people are saying, "Peace
and safety,"[k] destruction will come on
them suddenly,[l] as labor pains on a pregnant woman, and they will not escape.[m]
4But you, brothers, are not in darkness[n] so that this day should surprise you
like a thief.[o] **5**You are all sons of the
light[p] and sons of the day. We do not belong to the night or to the darkness. **6**So
then, let us not be like others, who are
asleep,[q] but let us be alert[r] and self-controlled.[s] **7**For those who sleep, sleep at
night, and those who get drunk, get drunk
at night.[t] **8**But since we belong to the
day,[u] let us be self-controlled, putting on
faith and love as a breastplate,[v] and the
hope of salvation[w] as a helmet.[x] **9**For God
did not appoint us to suffer wrath[y] but to
receive salvation through our Lord Jesus
Christ.[z] **10**He died for us so that, whether
we are awake or asleep, we may live together with him.[a] **11**Therefore encourage
one another[b] and build each other up,[c]
just as in fact you are doing.

5:2 [i]S 1Co 1:8 [j]S Lk 12:39 **5:3** [k]Jer 4:10; 6:14; Eze 13:10 [l]Job 15:21; Ps 35:8; 55:15; Isa 29:5; 47:9,11 [m]2Th 1:9 **5:4** [n]S Ac 26:18; 1Jn 2:8 [o]ver 2 **5:5** [p]S Lk 16:8 **5:6** [q]Ro 13:11 [r]S Mt 25:13 [s]S Ac 24:25 **5:7** [t]Ac 2:15; Ro 13:13; 2Pe 2:13 **5:8** [u]ver 5 [v]S Eph 6:14 [w]Ro 8:24 [x]Isa 59:17; Eph 6:17 **5:9** [y]1Th 1:10 [z]2Th 2:13,14 **5:10** [a]Ro 14:9; 2Co 5:15 **5:11** [b]1Th 4:18 [c]Eph 4:29 **5:12** [d]Ro 16:6, 12; 1Co 15:10

Final Instructions

12Now we ask you, brothers, to respect
those who work hard[d] among you, who
are over you in the Lord[e] and who admonish you. **13**Hold them in the highest regard
in love because of their work. Live in
peace with each other.[f] **14**And we urge
you, brothers, warn those who are idle,[g]
encourage the timid, help the weak,[h] be
patient with everyone. **15**Make sure that
nobody pays back wrong for wrong,[i] but

[e]1Ti 5:17; Heb 13:17 **5:13** [f]S Mk 9:50 **5:14** [g]2Th 3:6,7,11 [h]Ro 14:1; 1Co 8:7-12 **5:15** [i]Ro 12:17; 1Pe 3:9

(Isa 2:12–21; 13:9–16; 34:1–4; Jer 46:10; Joel 1:15 – 2:11,28; 3:9,12–17; Am 5:18–20; Zec 14:1–3), followed by Christ's earthly reign (Zep 3:14–17; Rev 20:4–7). (1) This "day" begins when direct divine judgment falls upon the world toward the end of this age (v. 3). The tribulation period is included within the day of the Lord (Rev 6–19; see 6:1, note). This wrath of God culminates with Christ's coming to destroy all the wicked (Joel 3:14; see Rev 16:16, note; 19:11–21).

(2) The day of the Lord apparently begins at a time when people are hoping for peace and safety (v. 3).

(3) The "day" will not overtake faithful believers like a thief, for they are appointed to receive salvation, not wrath, and they are alert and self-controlled, living in faith, love and righteousness (vv. 4–9).

(4) Believers are delivered from this "coming wrath" (1:10, note) through the Lord Jesus Christ (v. 9) when he comes to catch up the faithful of his churches and take them to heaven (cf. 4:17; see Jn 14:3, note; Rev. 3:10, note; see article on THE RAPTURE, p. 440).

(5) The day of the Lord will end after the millennial kingdom (Rev 20:4–10) at the creation of the new heaven and new earth (cf. 2Pe 3:13; Rev 21:1).

5:2 LIKE A THIEF IN THE NIGHT. This metaphor means that the time when the day of the Lord begins is uncertain and unexpected. There is no way one can date it (see Mt 24:42–44, notes on the Lord's teaching on the unexpected time of his coming for the church).

5:3 PEACE AND SAFETY. It is the unbeliever who will be saying, "Peace and safety." This could mean that the world will be expecting and hoping for peace. The day of the Lord and its worldwide distress will come on them suddenly, destroying any hope for peace and security.

5:4 YOU, BROTHERS, ARE NOT IN DARKNESS. Believers do not live in sin and rebellion. They belong to the day that precedes the night and will not experience God's appointed night of wrath (vv. 8–9; see article on THE RAPTURE, p. 440).

5:6 LET US BE ALERT. "Be alert" (Gk *grēgoreō*) means to "stay awake and keep watch." The context (vv. 4–9) indicates that Paul is not exhorting his readers to "be alert" for the "day of the Lord" (v. 2), but rather to be spiritually prepared in order to escape the wrath of that day (cf. 2:11–12; Lk 21:34–36). (1) If we wish to escape God's wrath (v. 3), we must remain spiritually awake and morally alert, and continue in faith, love and the hope of salvation (vv. 8–9; see Lk 21:36, note; Eph 6:11, note). (2) Since the faithful will be protected from God's wrath (see v. 2, note; see article on THE RAPTURE, p. 440), they must not fear the day of the Lord, but must "wait for his Son from heaven . . . Jesus, who rescues us from the coming wrath" (1:10).

5:6 SELF-CONTROLLED. The word "self-controlled" (Gk *nēphō*) had two meanings in NT times. (1) The literal meaning, as given by various Greek lexicons, is "a state of abstinence from wine," "to drink no wine," "to abstain from wine," "to be completely unaffected by wine" or "to be sober." It carries a figurative or metaphorical meaning of alertness, self-restraint or self-control, i.e., to be alert spiritually and self-controlled, just as someone who does not drink alcoholic wine.

(2) The context here supports the view that Paul had the literal meaning in mind. The words "let us be alert and self-controlled" are contrasted with the words of the following verse, "those who get drunk, get drunk at night" (v. 7). Thus, Paul's contrast of *nēphō* with physical drunkenness would indicate that he was including the literal meaning of "abstinence from wine." Compare Jesus' statement about those who eat and drink with drunkards and are thus caught unaware by his return (Mt 24:48–51).

5:9 NOT APPOINT US TO SUFFER WRATH. One reason why the hope of Christ's return is such a comfort to believers (4:17–18) is that he delivers us from God's terrible wrath, i.e., the judgments of the day of the Lord (v. 2–3; cf. Rev 6:16–17; 11:18; 14:10,19; 15:1,7; 16:1,19; 19:15).

5:10 LIVE TOGETHER WITH HIM. Paul identifies our hope of salvation and our deliverance from the day of God's wrath with Christ's sacrificial death and his return to take us to live together with him.

always try to be kind to each other[j] and
to everyone else.

16Be joyful always;[k] 17pray continually;[l] 18give thanks in all circumstances,[m]
for this is God's will for you in Christ
Jesus.

19Do not put out the Spirit's fire;[n] 20do
not treat prophecies[o] with contempt.
21Test everything.[p] Hold on to the good.[q]
22Avoid every kind of evil.

23May God himself, the God of peace,[r]
sanctify you through and through. May
your whole spirit, soul[s] and body be kept
blameless[t] at the coming of our Lord
Jesus Christ.[u] 24The one who calls[v] you
is faithful[w] and he will do it.[x]

25Brothers, pray for us.[y] 26Greet all the
brothers with a holy kiss.[z] 27I charge you
before the Lord to have this letter read to
all the brothers.[a]

28The grace of our Lord Jesus Christ be
with you.[b]

5:15 [j] Eph 4:32 **5:16** [k] Php 4:4 **5:17** [l] S Lk 18:1 **5:18** [m] S Eph 5:20 **5:19** [n] Eph 4:30 **5:20** [o] 1Co 14:1-40 **5:21** [p] 1Co 14:29; 1Jn 4:1 [q] Ro 12:9 **5:23** [r] S Ro 15:33 [s] Heb 4:12 [t] S 1Th 3:13 [u] S 1Th 2:19 **5:24** [v] S Ro 8:28 [w] S 1Co 1:9 [x] Nu 23:19; Php 1:6 **5:25** [y] Eph 6:19; Col 4:3; 2Th 3:1; Heb 13:18 **5:26** [z] S Ro 16:16 **5:27** [a] 2Th 3:14; S 1Ti 4:13 **5:28** [b] S Ro 16:20

5:17 PRAY CONTINUALLY. To pray is to abide in the presence of the Father, continually crying out for his grace and blessing. "Continually" does not mean to be constantly uttering formal prayers. Rather, it implies recurrent prayer of all kinds and on all occasions throughout the day (Lk 18:1; Ro 12:12; Eph 6:18; Col 4:2).

5:19–20 DO NOT PUT OUT THE SPIRIT'S FIRE. (1) Paul equates putting out the Spirit's fire with the depreciation and rejection of the Holy Spirit's supernatural manifestations such as prophesying. To repress or reject the right and orderly use of prophecy or other spiritual gifts will result in the loss of any manifestation of the Spirit among believers (1Co 12:7–10,28–30). The Spirit's ministry is described in Jn 14:26; 15:26–27; 16:13–14; Ac 1:8; 13:2; Ro 8:4,11,16,26; 1Co 2:9–14; 12:1–11; Gal 5:22–25.

(2) These two verses clearly indicate that churches other than the one in Corinth experienced spiritual gifts in public worship. Note carefully that although prophetic utterances were not to be treated with contempt, they also were not to be accepted until they had been examined carefully (v. 21; see 1Co 14:29, note).

5:23 SANCTIFY YOU THROUGH AND THROUGH. Paul's final prayer for the Thessalonian believers is that they be sanctified. For a discussion of what the Bible means by sanctification, see article on SANCTIFICATION, p. 526.

2 THESSALONIANS

Outline

Christian Greetings (1:1–2)
- I. Paul Encourages the Thessalonians in Persecution (1:3–12)
  - A. His Gratitude for Their Spiritual Growth (1:3)
  - B. His Praise to Other Churches for Their Endurance (1:4)
  - C. His Assurance Concerning the Final Outcome (1:5–10)
  - D. His Prayers for Them (1:11–12)
- II. Paul Corrects the Thessalonians in Profession (2:1–17)
  - A. The Day of the Lord Has Not Come (2:1–2)
  - B. The Man of Lawlessness Will First Be Revealed (2:3–12)
  - C. Stand Firm in the Assurance of Truth and Grace (2:13–17)
- III. Paul Admonishes the Thessalonians in Practice (3:1–15)
  - A. To Pray for Him (3:1–2)
  - B. To Remain Steadfast in the Lord (3:3–5)
  - C. To Keep Aloof From the Unruly and to Live a Disciplined Life (3:6–15)

Final Greeting and Benediction (3:16–18)

Author: Paul

Theme: The Return of Christ

Date of Writing: c. A.D. 51 or 52

Background

When this letter was written, the situation in the Thessalonian church was much the same as when Paul wrote his first letter (see Introduction to 1 Thessalonians). It is likely, therefore, that this letter was written only a few months after 1 Thessalonians while Paul was still working in Corinth with Silas and Timothy (1:1; cf. Ac 18:5). Apparently when Paul was informed about the reception of his first letter and about new developments in the Thessalonian church, he was prompted to write this second letter.

Purpose

Paul's purpose is similar to that of 1 Thessalonians: (1) to encourage his young, persecuted converts; (2) to exhort them to live disciplined lives and to work for a living; and (3) to correct some erroneous beliefs about end-time events related to "the day of the Lord" (2:2).

Survey

Whereas the tone of Paul's relationship to the Thessalonians in his first letter is that of a tender nurse caring for little ones (1Th 2:7), in this letter it is more that of a father disciplining some unruly children and correcting their course (3:7–12; cf. 1Th 2:11). He does commend them for their steadfast faith and again encourages them to remain faithful through the persecution they are encountering (1:3–7).

The main section of the letter deals with the eschatological day of the Lord (2:1–12; cf. 1:6–10). It appears from 2:2 that some at Thessalonica were claiming, either by a "prophecy" (a revelation), a "report" (verbal message) or a "letter" (supposedly from Paul), that the time of great tribulation and the day of the Lord had begun. Paul corrects this misunderstanding by stating that three significant events will signal that the day of the Lord has arrived (2:2): (1) a major apostasy and rebellion will occur (2:3), (2) God's appointed restraint against evil will be lifted (2:6–7), and (3) "the man of lawlessness" will be revealed (2:3–4,8–12). Paul rebukes those in the church who are using the expectation of Christ's imminent return as an excuse for not working daily. He exhorts all believers to live diligent and disciplined lives (3:6–12).

Special Features

Three major features characterize this letter. (1) It contains one of the NT's most developed passages about unrestrained lawlessness and deception at the end of history (2:3–12). (2) God's righteous judgment that will accompany Christ's second coming is described here in apocalyptic terms, similar to the book of Revelation (1:6–10; 2:8). (3) It uses terms for the eschatological antichrist not found elsewhere in the Bible (2:3,8).

Reading 2 Thessalonians

In order to read the entire New Testament in one year, the book of 2 Thessalonians should be read in 3 days, according to the following schedule:
☐ 1 ☐ 2 ☐ 3

NOTES

1 Paul, Silas[a][a] and Timothy,[b]
To the church of the Thessalonians[c]
in God our Father and the Lord Jesus
Christ:

2Grace and peace to you from God the
Father and the Lord Jesus Christ.[d]

Thanksgiving and Prayer

3We ought always to thank God for
you,[e] brothers, and rightly so, because
your faith is growing more and more, and
the love every one of you has for each
Heb 11:29-35 other is increasing.[f] **4**Therefore, among
God's churches we boast[g] about your perseverance and faith[h] in all the persecutions and trials you are enduring.[i]

5All this is evidence[j] that God's judgment is right, and as a result you will be
counted worthy[k] of the kingdom of God,
for which you are suffering. **6**God is just:[l]
He will pay back trouble to those who
trouble you[m] **7**and give relief to you who
are troubled, and to us as well. This will
happen when the Lord Jesus is revealed
from heaven[n] in blazing fire[o] with his
powerful angels.[p] **8**He will punish[q] those
who do not know God[r] and do not obey
the gospel of our Lord Jesus.[s] **9**They will
be punished with everlasting destruction[t]
and shut out from the presence of the
Lord[u] and from the majesty of his power[v]
10on the day[w] he comes to be glorified[x] in
his holy people and to be marveled at
among all those who have believed. This
includes you, because you believed our
testimony to you.[y]

11With this in mind, we constantly pray
for you,[z] that our God may count you worthy[a] of his calling,[b] and that by his power
he may fulfill every good purpose[c] of
yours and every act prompted by your
faith.[d] **12**We pray this so that the name of
our Lord Jesus may be glorified in you,[e]
and you in him, according to the grace of
our God and the Lord Jesus Christ.[b]

Concerning the Lord's Coming

2 Concerning the coming of our Lord
Jesus Christ[f] and our being gathered
to him,[g] we ask you, brothers, **2**not to
become easily unsettled or alarmed by
some prophecy, report or letter[h] supposed to have come from us, saying that
the day of the Lord[i] has already come.[j]
3Don't let anyone deceive you[k] in any
way, for ⌊that day will not come⌋ until the

1:1 [a]S Ac 15:22 [b]S Ac 16:1; 1Th 1:1 [c]S Ac 17:1 **1:2** [d]S Ro 1:7 **1:3** [e]S Ro 1:8; Eph 5:20 [f]S 1Th 3:12 **1:4** [g]2Co 7:14 [h]1Th 1:3 [i]1Th 1:6; 2:14; S 3:3 **1:5** [j]Php 1:28 [k]Lk 20:35 **1:6** [l]Lk 18:7,8 [m]Ro 12:19; Col 3:25; S Rev 6:10 **1:7** [n]S Lk 17:30 [o]Heb 10:27; S 12:29; 2Pe 3:7; S Rev 1:14 [p]Jude 14 **1:8** [q]Ps 79:6; Isa 66:15; Jer 10:25 [r]S Gal 4:8 [s]Ro 2:8; S 2Co 2:12 **1:9** [t]Php 3:19; 1Th 5:3; 2Pe 3:7 [u]2Ki 17:18 [v]Isa 2:10,19; 2Th 2:8 **1:10** [w]1Co 3:13 [x]Jn 17:10 [y]1Co 1:6 **1:11** [z]S Ro 1:10 [a]ver 5 [b]S Ro 8:28 [c]Ro 15:14 [d]1Th 1:3 **1:12** [e]Isa 24:15; Php 2:9-11 **2:1** [f]S 1Th 2:19 [g]Mk 13:27; 1Th 4:15-17 **2:2** [h]ver 15; 2Th 3:17 [i]S 1Co 1:8 [j]2Ti 2:18 **2:3** [k]S Mk 13:5

[a] *1* Greek *Silvanus,* a variant of *Silas* [b] *12* Or *God and Lord, Jesus Christ*

1:5 GOD'S JUDGMENT IS RIGHT. The Thessalonians were persevering in faith amid persecution and trials (v. 4). Their attitude was "evidence" of God's righteous judgment, meaning that God judged the Thessalonians to be worthy of his grace and the kingdom for which they were suffering. Their unjust suffering was also a sign that the persecutors opposed God's own people and would thus experience God's justice and retribution (vv. 5–9).

1:7 GIVE RELIEF TO YOU. Although God will begin to pay back the wicked (v. 6) at the beginning of the tribulation (Rev 6; see article on THE GREAT TRIBULATION, p. 52), complete retribution (vv. 6–9) will occur only at the end of the age when the Lord Jesus returns to earth in final judgment (vv. 7–10; Rev 19:11–21). Similarly, partial relief will come to God's people when he removes them from earth to be with him always (see article on THE RAPTURE, p. 440), but full relief will occur only when the Lord Jesus returns to earth with his saints to judge evil and govern the human race. Full relief means seeing Christ "glorified in you, and you in him" at the final day (v. 12). This is the total victory, when righteousness reigns, sin is defeated and Christ's faithful followers are vindicated (Rev 6:9–11; 19:14–15).

1:9 EVERLASTING DESTRUCTION. This is the clearest statement in Paul's letters concerning the eternal future punishment of the wicked (see Mt 10:28, note on hell).

1:10 HE COMES TO BE GLORIFIED. This passage is not speaking of the time when believers will be taken from earth to meet Christ in the air (Jn 14:2–3; 1Th 4:17). Rather, it speaks of the revelation of Jesus Christ in power and great glory to destroy the present world system and inaugurate his thousand-year reign on earth (Rev 19:11—20:4).

2:1 THE COMING OF OUR LORD JESUS CHRIST. In his first letter to the Thessalonians, Paul assured all true believers that they would be caught up to meet the Lord in the air, and thus would be with their Lord forever (1Th 4:13–18). This event would deliver them from God's coming wrath (1Th 1:10; 5:9–10). Now, however, false teachers were teaching that the day of the Lord had already begun and that God's final wrath was being poured out on the earth (see next note).

2:2 EASILY UNSETTLED OR ALARMED. The Thessalonians were alarmed because of what the false teachers were saying about the day of the Lord (see previous note). He tells them not to worry, for the day of God's wrath has not yet arrived. Two things will signal its arrival: (1) There must come a specific "rebellion," and (2) the "man of lawlessness" will be revealed (v. 3). Paul goes on to state that these two events will not be fulfilled until the one who holds it back "is taken out of the way" (v. 7).

Paul's words "by some prophecy, report or letter" may indicate that the false teaching was being passed on through tongues and interpretation or through prophecy (see 1Co 14:29, note on judging tongues and prophecy).

2:3 THAT DAY WILL NOT COME UNTIL. Paul explains the events that will signal the beginning of the

rebellion[l] occurs and the man of lawlessness[c] is revealed,[m] the man doomed to
destruction. **4**He will oppose and will exalt
himself over everything that is called
God[n] or is worshiped, so that he sets himself up in God's temple, proclaiming himself to be God.[o]

The Man of Lawlessness

5Don't you remember that when I was
with you I used to tell you these things?[p]
6And now you know what is holding him
back,[q] so that he may be revealed at the
proper time. **7**For the secret power of lawlessness is already at work; but the one
who now holds it back[r] will continue to do
so till he is taken out of the way. **8**And
then the lawless one will be revealed,[s]
whom the Lord Jesus will overthrow with
the breath of his mouth[t] and destroy by
the splendor of his coming.[u] **9**The coming
of the lawless one will be in accordance
with the work of Satan[v] displayed in all
kinds of counterfeit miracles, signs and
wonders,[w] **10**and in every sort of evil that
deceives those who are perishing.[x] They
perish because they refused to love the
truth and so be saved.[y] **11**For this reason

2:3 [l] Mt 24:10-12 [m] ver 8; Da 7:25; 8:25; 11:36; Rev 13:5,6 **2:4** [n] 1Co 8:5 [o] Isa 14:13,14; Eze 28:2 **2:5** [p] 1Th 3:4 **2:6** [q] ver 7 **2:7** [r] ver 6 **2:8** [s] S ver 3 [t] Isa 11:4; Rev 2:16; 19:15 [u] S Lk 17:30 **2:9** [v] S Mt 4:10 [w] Mt 24:24; Rev 13:13; S Jn 4:48 **2:10** [x] S 1Co 1:18 [y] Pr 4:6; Jn 3:17-19

[c] *3* Some manuscripts *sin*

day of the Lord and discusses the destruction of the man of lawlessness and the unrighteous at the end of the age. The sequence of events is as follows: (1) Throughout the entire church age, a "secret power of lawlessness" (v. 7) is at work, reminding us that the end is coming; evil will become progressively unrestrained as history draws to a close. (2) As that power becomes stronger, apostasy in the church will reach major proportions (v. 3; cf. Mt 24:12; 2Ti 4:3–4). (3) The restrainer (i.e., "the one who now holds it back") of the "secret power" is then taken out of the way (vv. 6–7). (4) Next, the man of lawlessness is revealed (vv. 3–4,7,9–10). (5) The apostasy reaches its climax in total rebellion against God and his Word; God sends a deluding influence on those who did not love the truth (vv. 9–11). (6) Sometime afterward the man of lawlessness is destroyed along with all who delighted in wickedness (v. 12); this occurs at Christ's coming after the tribulation, i.e., at the end of the age (v. 8; Rev 19:20–21).

2:3 REBELLION OCCURS AND THE MAN OF LAWLESSNESS IS REVEALED. For a discussion of the "rebellion" and "the man of lawlessness," see article on THE AGE OF THE ANTICHRIST, p. 447.

2:6 WHAT IS HOLDING HIM BACK. Something or someone is holding back the man of lawlessness. When the one who holds him back is taken out of the way, then the day of the Lord will begin (v. 7; see article on THE AGE OF THE ANTICHRIST, p. 447, for a discussion of the restrainer).

2:7 SECRET POWER OF LAWLESSNESS IS ALREADY AT WORK. The "secret power of lawlessness" is a behind-the-scenes activity of evil powers throughout the course of human history, preparing the way for the rebellion and the man of lawlessness. (1) It is an insidious process that entraps unbelievers and prepares many within the church to turn from true faith and to accept the lie embodied in the apostate church. It involves a spirit or movement against true Biblical faith and divine law; it seeks freedom from moral restraint and it takes pleasure in sin (vv. 10–12; see v. 12, note). (2) Though this spirit existed already in Paul's day, it will be especially prevalent in the world and in Christianity toward the end of the age (see Mt 24:11, note; 2Ti 4:3–4, note; see article on THE AGE OF THE ANTICHRIST, p. 447).

2:8 WHOM THE LORD JESUS WILL OVERTHROW. After Satan and the man of lawlessness have done their work of deceit and evil (vv. 9–10), they will be overthrown by Christ's coming to earth at the end of the tribulation (see Rev 19:20, note).

2:9 IN ALL KINDS OF COUNTERFEIT MIRACLES, SIGNS AND WONDERS. For a discussion of the activities of the lawless one, see article on THE AGE OF THE ANTICHRIST, p. 447.

2:10 LOVE THE TRUTH. From the very beginning of creation the central issue in humanity's relationship with God has been either our disregard of the Word and the truth of God or our love for them. This is also a pivotal issue in the last days of this age. Salvation will be experienced only by those who through faith in Christ fervently and sincerely "love the truth," who believe with unwavering conviction what God has said, and who reject all new revelation or teaching that conflicts with that truth (see Mt 24:5,11, notes; see article on THE GREAT TRIBULATION, p. 52).

2:11 SENDS THEM A POWERFUL DELUSION. After the removal of the restrainer (see article on THE AGE OF THE ANTICHRIST, p. 447) and the revelation of the lawless one, there will be no more opportunity for salvation for a particular group of people: (1) This group consists of all those inside or outside the church who, after adequately hearing the truth of God's Word, have willingly and intentionally refused to love that truth and have chosen instead to delight in the wickedness of the world (see vv. 10,12, notes).

(2) God will send those individuals a powerful delusion so that they may never again have an opportunity to believe the truth they refused to love (v. 12). They are forever doomed to believe "the lie" (i.e., the claims of the lawless one).

(3) God's purpose in sending the "powerful delusion" is that they "will be condemned" (v. 12). Therefore, for those who have heard and understood God's Word, yet have not loved its truth but have chosen instead the pleasure of sin, "no sacrifice for sins is left, but only a fearful expectation of judgment" (Heb 10:26–27; see article on PERSONAL APOSTASY, p. 492).

(4) Salvation during the days of the tribulation will be offered only to those who never had an adequate opportunity to receive the knowledge of the truth or to hear and understand the gospel (cf. Rev 7:14; 11:3; 14:6–7). Those who proclaim the gospel during those days may include the 144,000 from the tribes of Israel (see Rev 7:4, note), the two witnesses (see Rev 11:3, note) and the angels (see Rev 14:6, note).

THE AGE OF THE ANTICHRIST

***2Th 2:3–4** "Don't let anyone deceive you in any way, for that day will not come until the rebellion occurs and the man of lawlessness is revealed, the man doomed to destruction. He will oppose and will exalt himself over everything that is called God or is worshiped, so that he sets himself up in God's temple, proclaiming himself to be God."*

According to the Bible, the antichrist (cf. 1Jn 2:18) is coming, the one who engineers Satan's final onslaught against Christ and the saints just before Christ establishes his kingdom on earth. Paul's terms for the antichrist are "the man of lawlessness" and "the man doomed to destruction" (2Th 2:3). Other terms used in the Bible are the "beast coming out of the sea" (Rev 13:1–10), "a scarlet beast" (Rev 17:3) and "the beast" (Rev 17:8,16; 19:19–20; 20:10).

SIGNS OF THE ANTICHRIST'S COMING. Unlike the rapture (see article on THE RAPTURE, p. 440), the coming of the antichrist will not be without warning. Several signs point to his coming and his appearance. At least three events must occur before he appears on earth: (1) the "secret power of lawlessness," already at work in the world, must intensify (2Th 2:7); (2) the "rebellion" must come (2:3); (3) "the one who now holds it back" must be removed (2:7).

(1) The "secret power of lawlessness," that behind-the-scenes activity of evil powers evident throughout the world (see 2Th 2:7, note), will increase until it reaches its climax in the complete ridicule of and disregard for any standards and commands held sacred in the Bible. Because of a prevailing spirit of lawlessness, the love of many will grow cold (Mt 24:10–12; Lk 18:8). Yet a faithful remnant will remain loyal to the apostolic faith as revealed in the NT (Mt 24:13; 25:10; Lk 18:7; see Rev 2:7, note). Through these faithful people, the church will remain a warrior church, wielding the sword of the Spirit (see Eph 6:11, note).

(2) The "rebellion" (Gk *apostasia*), literally meaning "departure," "falling away" or "abandonment," will occur. In the last days, many within the professing church will depart from Biblical truth.

(a) Both Jesus and Paul paint a dismal picture of the condition of much of the visible church—morally, spiritually and doctrinally—as the present age closes (cf. Mt 24:5,10–13,24; 1Ti 4:1; 2Ti 4:3–4). Paul in particular stresses that the churches will be invaded by godless elements in the last days.

(b) This "rebellion" within the church will have two dimensions. (i) *Theological apostasy* is the departure from and rejection of a part or all of the original teachings of Christ and the apostles (1Ti 4:1; 2Ti 4:3). False leaders will offer "salvation" and cheap grace and ignore Christ's demand for repentance, separation from immorality, and loyalty to God and his standards (2Pe 2:1–3,12–19). False gospels centering on human desires and goals of self-interest will become popular (see 2Ti 4:3–4, note). (ii) *Moral apostasy* is the severing of one's saving relationship with Christ and returning to sin and immorality. Apostates may proclaim right doctrine and NT teaching, yet abandon God's moral standards (Isa 29:13; Mt 23:25–28; see article on PERSONAL APOSTASY, p. 492). Many churches will tolerate almost anything for the sake of numbers, money, success and honor (see 1Ti 4:1, note). The gospel of the cross with its call to suffer (Php 1:29), to radically renounce sin (Ro 8:13), to sacrifice for God's kingdom and to deny oneself will become rare (Mt 24:12; 2Ti 3:1–5; 4:3).

(c) Both the history of the church and the predicted apostasy of the last days warn all believers not to take for granted a continual progress of God's kingdom through all ages until the end. At some point in time in the history of the church, rebellion against God and his Word will reach astounding proportions. The day of the Lord will bring God's wrath on those who reject his truth (1Th 5:2–9).

(d) The ultimate triumph of God's kingdom and his righteousness in the world, therefore, depends not on the gradual increase of the professing church's success, but on the final intervention of God when he breaks into the world with righteous judgment (Rev 19–22; see 2Th 2:7–8; 1Ti 4:1, note; 2Pe 3:10–13; and the book of Jude).

(3) A decisive event must occur before the "man of lawlessness" can be revealed and the day of the Lord can begin (2Th 2:2–3), namely, the taking "out of the way" of someone (2:7) or something that "holds back" the secret power of lawlessness and the man of lawlessness (2:3–6). When the restrainer is taken out of the way, the day of the Lord can begin (2:6–7).

(a) "The one who now holds it back" may best be understood as referring to the Holy Spirit, who alone has the power to hold back evil, the man of lawlessness, and Satan (2Th 2:9). The restrainer is referred to by both the masculine article ("the one who now holds it back," 2:7) and by the neuter article ("what is holding him back," 2:6). Likewise, the word for "Spirit" in the Greek can be referred to by a masculine or neuter pronoun (see Ge 6:3; Jn 16:8, note; Ro 8:13; see Gal 5:17 on the Spirit's work of restraining sin).

(b) At the beginning of the final seven years of tribulation, the Holy Spirit will be "taken out of the way." This does not mean he is taken out of the world, but only that his restraining influence against lawlessness and the antichrist's entrance will cease. All restraints against sin will be removed and the satanically inspired rebellion will begin. However, the Spirit will still remain on earth during the tribulation to convict people of their sins, convert them to Christ and empower them (Rev 7:9,14; 11:1–11; 14:6–7).

(c) The Holy Spirit's being taken out of the way enables the man of lawlessness to come on the scene (2Th 2:3–4). God will send a deluding influence on all those who refused to love the truth (see 2:11, note); they will accept the claims of the man of lawlessness, and human society will degenerate to a depth of depravity never before seen.

(d) The Holy Spirit's sin-restraining ministry is carried on largely through the church, which is the temple of the Holy Spirit (1Co 3:16; 6:19). Therefore, many interpreters believe the Spirit's removal is a strong indication that the rapture of the faithful will occur at the same time (1Th 4:17); i.e., Christ's return to gather his churches to himself and to deliver them from the coming wrath (1Th 1:10) will occur before the beginning of the day of the Lord and the revelation of the man of lawlessness (see article on THE RAPTURE, p. 440).

(e) Some scholars believe that the restrainer of 2Th 2:6 (neuter gender) refers to the Holy Spirit and his restraining ministry, while in 2:7 the "one who now holds it back" (masculine gender) refers to the believers who are gathered together to Christ and taken out of the way, i.e., caught up to meet Christ in the air to be with the Lord (1Th 4:17).

THE ANTICHRIST'S ACTIVITIES. As the day of the Lord begins, the "man of lawlessness" is revealed. He will be a world ruler who will make a covenant with Israel seven years before the end of the age (see Da 9:27). (1) His true identification will be confirmed three and one-half years later as he becomes the world ruler and sets up in the Jewish temple the abomination that causes desolation (Da 9:27; 2Th 2:4,8–9; see article on THE GREAT TRIB-

ULATION, p. 52). (2) The antichrist will declare himself to be God and will severely persecute those who remain loyal to Christ (Rev 11:6–7; 13:7,15–18). He will demand worship, evidently from a great temple that he uses as the center of his pronouncements (cf. Da 7:8,25; 8:4; 11:31,36). Humans have sought this divine status since the beginning of creation (see 2Th 2:8, note; Rev 13:8,12, notes; see article on THE GREAT TRIBULATION, p. 52). (3) The "man of lawlessness" will demonstrate through Satan's power great signs, wonders and miracles in order to propagate error (2Th 2:9). "Counterfeit miracles" refers to genuine supernatural miracles that deceive people into accepting a lie. (a) It is possible these demonstrations of the supernatural will be seen on television around the world. Millions will be impressed, deceived and persuaded by this apparent charismatic leader because they have no deep commitment to or love for the truth of God's Word (2:9–12). (b) The words of both Paul (2Th 2:9) and Jesus (Mt 24:24) should caution believers against assuming that everything miraculous comes from God. Apparent manifestations of the Spirit (1Co 12:7–10) and alleged experiences from God or the Spirit must be tested by the person's loyalty to Christ and Scripture.

THE DEFEAT OF THE ANTICHRIST. At the end of the tribulation, Satan will gather many nations at Armageddon under the direction of the antichrist and make war against God and his people in a battle that will involve the entire world (see Rev 16:16, note). When that time comes, Christ will return and supernaturally intervene to destroy the antichrist, his armies and all who disobey the gospel (see 19:15–21, notes). Thereupon Christ will bind Satan and establish his kingdom on earth (20:1–6).

God sends them[z] a powerful delusion[a] so that they will believe the lie[b] 12and so that all will be condemned who have not believed the truth but have delighted in wickedness.[c]

Stand Firm

13But we ought always to thank God for you,[d] brothers loved by the Lord, because from the beginning God chose you[d][e] to be saved[f] through the sanctifying work of the Spirit[g] and through belief in the truth. 14He called you[h] to this through our gospel,[i] that you might share in the glory of our Lord Jesus Christ. 15So then, brothers, stand firm[j] and hold to the teachings[e] we passed on to you,[k] whether by word of mouth or by letter.

16May our Lord Jesus Christ himself and God our Father,[l] who loved us[m] and by his grace gave us eternal encouragement and good hope, 17encourage[n] your hearts and strengthen[o] you in every good deed and word.

Request for Prayer

3 Finally, brothers,[p] pray for us[q] that the message of the Lord[r] may spread rapidly and be honored, just as it was with you.[s] 2And pray that we may be delivered from wicked and evil men,[t] for not everyone has faith. 3But the Lord is faithful,[u] and he will strengthen and protect you from the evil one.[v] 4We have confidence[w] in the Lord that you are doing and will continue to do the things we command. 5May the Lord direct your hearts[x] into God's love and Christ's perseverance.

Warning Against Idleness

6In the name of the Lord Jesus Christ,[y] we command you, brothers, to keep away from[z] every brother who is idle[a] and does not live according to the teaching[f] you received from us.[b] 7For you yourselves know how you ought to follow our example.[c] We were not idle when we were with you, 8nor did we eat anyone's food without paying for it. On the contrary, we worked[d] night and day, laboring and toiling so that we would not be a burden to any of you. 9We did this, not because we do not have the right to such help,[e] but in order to make ourselves a model for you to follow.[f] 10For even when we were with you,[g] we gave you this rule: "If a man will not work,[h] he shall not eat."

11We hear that some among you are idle. They are not busy; they are busybodies.[i] 12Such people we command and urge in the Lord Jesus Christ[j] to settle down and earn the bread they eat.[k] 13And as for you, brothers, never tire of doing what is right.[l]

14If anyone does not obey our instruction in this letter, take special note of him.

2:11 [z]Ro 1:28 [a]Mt 24:5; S Mk 13:5 [b]Ro 1:25
2:12 [c]Ro 1:32; 2:8
2:13 [d]S Ro 1:8 [e]Eph 1:4 [f]1Th 5:9 [g]1Pe 1:2
2:14 [h]S Ro 8:28; S 11:29 [i]1Th 1:5
2:15 [j]S 1Co 16:13 [k]S 1Co 11:2
2:16 [l]S Php 4:20 [m]S Jn 3:16
2:17 [n]1Th 3:2 [o]2Th 3:3
3:1 [p]1Th 4:1 [q]S 1Th 5:25 [r]1Th 1:8 [s]1Th 2:13
3:2 [t]S Ro 15:31
3:3 [u]S 1Co 1:9 [v]S Mt 5:37
3:4 [w]S 2Co 2:3
3:5 [x]1Ch 29:18
3:6 [y]1Co 5:4 [z]ver 14; S Ro 16:17 [a]ver 7, 11 [b]S 1Co 11:2
3:7 [c]ver 9; S 1Co 4:16
3:8 [d]S Ac 18:3; Eph 4:28
3:9 [e]1Co 9:4-14 [f]ver 7; S 1Co 4:16
3:10 [g]1Th 3:4 [h]1Th 4:11
3:11 [i]ver 6,7; 1Ti 5:13
3:12 [j]1Th 4:1 [k]1Th 4:11; Eph 4:28
3:13 [l]Gal 6:9

d *13* Some manuscripts *because God chose you as his firstfruits* **e** *15* Or *traditions* **f** *6* Or *tradition*

2:12 DELIGHTED IN WICKEDNESS. Delighting in wickedness while refusing to love the truth (v. 10) will be the deciding factor in God's judgment in the last days. (1) Those destined to experience God's wrath will be those who did not love the truth and therefore participated in, and entertained themselves with, evil and immorality (see 2Ti 3:1, note). They will be abandoned to divine justice, demonic deception and the power of darkness (see Lk 23:35, note; Ro 1:32, note; 1Ti 4:1, note).

(2) Those experiencing condemnation during the "day of the Lord" (see v. 2, note) will include not only unbelievers, but also those guilty of apostasy from the true faith. They chose to enjoy sin instead of enjoying God and refused to take a stand against the immorality of the last days (see vv. 3,7, notes; 2Ti 4:3–4, note).

3:1 PRAY FOR US. Paul was able to accomplish what he did for Christ partly because of the prayers of God's people. Therefore he often sought the prayers of those to whom he ministered, aware that God's will for his life and ministry would not be fully realized without the intercession of fellow believers (cf. Ro 15:30–32; 2Co 1:11; Php 1:19; Col 4:2; 1Th 5:25). This spiritual principle of God's kingdom is valid today. We need the prayers of other believers and they need our prayers. With faithful intercession in the churches, God's desires will be accomplished, Satan's purposes frustrated (v. 3) and the Spirit's full power revealed (Ac 4:24–33).

3:3 PROTECT YOU FROM THE EVIL ONE. When believers earnestly pray, they can be assured that God will protect them from Satan. God will strengthen them to face any temptation that may assail them (1Co 10:13; Heb 2:18) and will protect them from the powerful forces of the demonic (see Eph 6:12, note).

3:6 WHO IS IDLE. Those who were idle were people who were loafing and unwilling to work. They were taking advantage of the church's generosity (cf. 1Th 4:9–10) and receiving support from brothers who made a living by ordinary occupations (vv. 6–15). (1) Paul says that such people must be disciplined by keeping away from them and not associating with them (vv. 6,14). (2) Although Paul advocates that help must be given to those in real need, he nowhere teaches that believers ought to give food or money to able-bodied people who refuse to work steadily for a living (cf. v. 10).

3:12 SETTLE DOWN AND EARN. Christians must not be loafers, but must work hard in order to provide for themselves and their families and to have enough to help others in need (1Co 16:1; 2Co 8:1–15; Eph 4:28).

Do not associate with him,[m] in order that
he may feel ashamed.[n] **15**Yet do not regard him as an enemy, but warn him as a
brother.[o]

Final Greetings

16Now may the Lord of peace[p] himself
give you peace at all times and in every
way. The Lord be with all of you.[q]

17I, Paul, write this greeting in my own
hand,[r] which is the distinguishing mark
in all my letters. This is how I write.

18The grace of our Lord Jesus Christ be
with you all.[s]

3:14 [m] ver 6; S Ro 16:17
[n] S 1Co 4:14
3:15 [o] Gal 6:1; 1Th 5:14; Phm 16
3:16 [p] S Ro 15:33
[q] Ru 2:4
3:17
[r] S 1Co 16:21
3:18 [s] S Ro 16:20

1 TIMOTHY

Outline

Introduction (1:1–20)
- I. Directions Concerning the Church's Ministry (2:1—4:5)
  - A. The Prominence of Prayer (2:1–8)
  - B. The Appropriate Conduct of Women (2:9–15)
  - C. Qualifications for Overseers (Elders) (3:1–7)
    - 1. Personal
      - a. Above Reproach (3:2)
      - b. Temperate (3:2)
      - c. Self-controlled (3:2)
      - d. Respectable (3:2)
      - e. Hospitable (3:2)
      - f. Able to Teach (3:2)
      - g. Not Given to Drunkenness (3:3)
      - h. Not Violent (3:3)
      - i. Gentle (3:3)
      - j. Not Quarrelsome (3:3)
      - k. Not a Lover of Money (3:3)
      - l. Not a Recent Convert (3:6)
      - m. Good Reputation With Outsiders (3:7)
    - 2. Family
      - a. Husband of One Wife (3:2)
      - b. Manages His Own Family Well (3:4–5)
      - c. Has Obedient and Respectful Children (3:4)
  - D. Qualifications for Deacons (3:8–13)
    - 1. Personal
      - a. Worthy of Respect (3:8)
      - b. Sincere (3:8)
      - c. Not Indulging in Much Wine (3:8)
      - d. Not Pursuing Dishonest Gain (3:8)
      - e. Holds to the Faith With a Clear Conscience (3:9)
      - f. Tested and Above Reproach (3:10)
    - 2. Family
      - a. Husband of One Wife (3:12)
      - b. A Godly and Trustworthy Wife (3:11)
      - c. Manages His Children and Household Well (3:12)
  - E. Reasons the Church Must Require High Qualifications for Its Leaders (3:14—4:5)
- II. Directions Concerning Timothy's Ministry (4:6—6:19)
  - A. His Personal Life (4:6–16)
  - B. His Relationship to Persons in the Church (5:1—6:19)
    - 1. Older and Younger Men (5:1)
    - 2. Older and Younger Women (5:2)
    - 3. Widows (5:3–16)
    - 4. Elders and Prospective Elders (5:17–25)
    - 5. Servants (6:1–2)
    - 6. False Teachers (6:3–10)
      Parenthesis: Exhortation to Timothy Himself (6:11–16)
    - 7. The Rich (6:17–19)

Conclusion (6:20–21)

Author: Paul

Theme: Sound Doctrine and Godliness

Date of Writing: c. A.D. 65

Background

1 and 2 Timothy and Titus—commonly referred to as "The Pastoral Letters"—are letters from Paul (1Ti 1:1; 2Ti 1:1; Tit 1:1) to Timothy (at Ephesus) and Titus (at Crete) concerning pastoral care of the churches. Some critics have questioned Paul's authorship of these letters, but the early church emphatically placed them among Paul's authentic letters. Although differences in style and vocabulary do exist in the Pastoral Letters when compared with Paul's other letters, these differences may be adequately and convincingly accounted for within the context of Paul's advanced years and his personal concerns for the ministries of Timothy and Titus.

Paul wrote 1 Timothy after the events recorded at the end of Acts. Paul's first Roman imprisonment (Ac 28) apparently ended in his freedom (2Ti 4:16–17). Afterwards, according to Clement of Rome (c. A.D. 96) and the Muratorian Canon (c. A.D. 190), Paul went from Rome westward to Spain and fulfilled a long-desired ministry there (cf. Ro 15:23–24,28). Based on data in the Pastoral Letters, Paul then returned to the Aegean Sea region (especially Crete, Macedonia and Greece) for further ministry. During this time (c. A.D. 64–65), Paul commissioned Timothy as his apostolic representative to minister in Ephesus, and Titus to do the same at Crete. From Macedonia Paul wrote his first letter to Timothy, and a short time later he wrote to Titus. Afterwards, Paul again became a prisoner in Rome, during which time he wrote a second letter to Timothy, shortly before his martyrdom in A.D. 67/68 (see 2Ti 4:6–8; see also Introduction to 2 Timothy).

Purpose

Paul had a threefold purpose in writing 1 Timothy: (1) to exhort Timothy himself about his ministry and personal life; (2) to urge Timothy to defend the purity of the gospel and its holy standards from corruption by false teachers; and (3) to give Timothy instructions concerning various church matters and problems at Ephesus.

Survey

One of Paul's chief concerns communicated to his younger assistant is that Timothy earnestly contend for the faith and refute the false teachings that were diluting the saving power of the gospel (1:3–7; 4:1–8; 6:3–5,20–21). Paul also instructs Timothy about the spiritual and character qualifications for church leadership and provides a composite picture of the kind of persons who are permitted to become spiritual leaders of the churches (see the detailed list of qualifications in the above outline).

Among other things, Paul instructs Timothy how to relate to various groups within the church, such as women (2:9–15; 5:2), widows (5:3–16), older and younger men (5:1), elders (5:17–25), slaves (6:1–2), false teachers (6:3–10) and the rich (6:17–19). Paul gives Timothy five clear instructions to fulfill (1:18–20; 3:14–16; 4:11–16; 5:21–25; 6:20–21). In this letter Paul conveys affection for Timothy as his convert and son in the faith and sets forth a high standard of godliness for Timothy's life and the life of the church.

Special Features

Four major features characterize this letter. (1) Addressed directly to Timothy as Paul's representative to the church at Ephesus, the letter is very personal and written with deep emotion and feeling. (2) Along with 2 Timothy, it stresses more than any other NT letter the pastoral responsibility to keep the gospel pure and free from false teachings that would weaken its saving power. (3) It emphasizes the supreme value of the gospel, the demonic influence behind its corruption, the church's holy calling and the high qualifications God requires for its leaders. (4) It provides the most specific direction in the NT about how a pastor is to relate properly to both sexes and to all age and social groups in the church.

Reading 1 Timothy

In order to read the entire New Testament in one year, the book of 1 Timothy should be read in 6 days, according to the following schedule:
☐ 1 ☐ 2 ☐ 3 ☐ 4 ☐ 5 ☐ 6

NOTES

1 Paul, an apostle of Christ Jesus by the command of God[a] our Savior[b] and of Christ Jesus our hope,[c]

2To Timothy[d] my true son[e] in the faith:

Grace, mercy and peace from God the Father and Christ Jesus our Lord.[f]

Warning Against False Teachers

3As I urged you when I went into Macedonia,[g] stay there in Ephesus[h] so that you may command certain men not to teach false doctrines[i] any longer **4**nor to devote themselves to myths[j] and endless genealogies.[k] These promote controversies[l] rather than God's work—which is by faith. **5**The goal of this command is love, which comes from a pure heart[m] and a good conscience[n] and a sincere faith.[o] **6**Some have wandered away from these and turned to meaningless talk. **7**They want to be teachers[p] of the law, but they do not know what they are talking about or what they so confidently affirm.[q]

8We know that the law is good[r] if one uses it properly. **9**We also know that law[a] is made not for the righteous[s] but for lawbreakers and rebels,[t] the ungodly and sinful, the unholy and irreligious; for those who kill their fathers or mothers, for murderers, **10**for adulterers and perverts, for slave traders and liars and perjurers—and for whatever else is contrary to the sound doctrine[u] **11**that conforms to the glorious gospel of the blessed God, which he entrusted to me.[v]

The Lord's Grace to Paul

12I thank Christ Jesus our Lord, who has given me strength,[w] that he considered me faithful, appointing me to his service.[x] **13**Even though I was once a blasphemer and a persecutor[y] and a violent man, I was shown mercy[z] because I acted in ignorance and unbelief.[a] **14**The grace of our Lord was poured out on me abundantly,[b] along with the faith and love that are in Christ Jesus.[c]

15Here is a trustworthy saying[d] that deserves full acceptance: Christ Jesus came into the world to save sinners[e]—of whom I am the worst. **16**But for that very reason I was shown mercy[f] so that in me, the worst of sinners, Christ Jesus might display his unlimited patience[g] as an example for those who would believe[h] on him and receive eternal life.[i] **17**Now to the King[j] eternal, immortal,[k] invisible,[l] the only God,[m] be honor and glory for ever and ever. Amen.[n]

Charge to Timothy

18Timothy, my son,[o] I give you this instruction in keeping with the prophecies once made about you,[p] so that by following them you may fight the good fight,[q] **19**holding on to faith and a good con-

1:1 [a]S 2Co 1:1; Tit 1:3 [b]S Lk 1:47 [c]Col 1:27
1:2 [d]S Ac 16:1 [e]ver 18; 1Co 4:17; S 1Th 2:11; 2Ti 1:2; Tit 1:4 [f]S Ro 1:7
1:3 [g]S Ac 16:9 [h]S Ac 18:19 [i]Gal 1:6,7; 1Ti 6:3
1:4 [j]1Ti 4:7; 2Ti 4:4; Tit 1:14 [k]Tit 3:9 [l]S 2Ti 2:14
1:5 [m]2Ti 2:22 [n]S Ac 23:1; 1Ti 4:2 [o]Gal 5:6; 2Ti 1:5
1:7 [p]S Eph 4:11 [q]Job 38:2
1:8 [r]Ro 7:12
1:9 [s]Gal 5:23 [t]Gal 3:19
1:10 [u]1Ti 6:3; 2Ti 1:13; 4:3; Tit 1:9; 2:1
1:11 [v]Gal 2:7; 1Th 2:4; Tit 1:3
1:12 [w]S Php 4:13 [x]S Ac 9:15
1:13 [y]S Ac 8:3 [z]ver 16 [a]Ac 26:9
1:14 [b]2Co 4:15 [c]2Ti 1:13; S 1Th 1:3
1:15 [d]1Ti 3:1; 4:9; 2Ti 2:11; Tit 3:8 [e]Mk 2:17; S Jn 3:17
1:16 [f]ver 13 [g]S Ro 2:4 [h]S Jn 3:15 [i]S Mt 25:46
1:17 [j]Rev 15:3 [k]1Ti 6:16 [l]S Col 1:15 [m]Jude 25 [n]S Ro 11:36
1:18 [o]S ver 2 [p]1Ti 4:14 [q]1Ti 6:12; 2Ti 2:3; 4:7

[a] 9 Or *that the law*

1:3 NOT TO TEACH FALSE DOCTRINES. Seven years before Paul wrote this letter he warned the Ephesian elders that false teachers would try to distort the true message of Christ (see Ac 20:29, note). Now that this was happening, Paul exhorted Timothy to confront them boldly. This young pastor must not compromise with the false teachings that were corrupting both the law and the gospel. He must faithfully fight a good fight against them (v. 18) by proclaiming the original faith as taught by Christ and the apostles (2Ti 1:13–14).

1:5 THE GOAL OF THIS COMMAND. The supreme goal of all instruction from God's Word is not Bible knowledge in itself, but an inward moral transformation that expresses itself in love, purity of heart, a clear conscience, and faith without hypocrisy (see Ac 24:16, note on a good conscience; see article on BIBLE TRAINING FOR CHRISTIANS, p. 470). Concerning this truth two important facts must be kept in mind. (1) The Biblical concept of teaching and learning is not primarily to impart knowledge or to prepare oneself academically. It is to produce holiness and a righteous lifestyle, conforming to God's ways (cf. 2Ti 1:13). (2) The teacher of God's Word must be someone whose life illustrates perseverance in truth, faith and holiness (3:1–13).

1:8 THE LAW IS GOOD. See Mt 5:17, note on the law and the Christian; cf. Ro 7:12.

1:13 A BLASPHEMER AND A PERSECUTOR. Before his conversion, Paul was a violent persecutor of believers (cf. Ac 8:3; 9:1–2,4–5; 22:4–5; 26:9–11; Gal 1:13). His terrible crimes against God's people were sufficient reason for ranking himself as the worst of sinners (vv. 14–15; cf. 1Co 15:9; Eph 3:8). Yet, because he sincerely believed he was serving God (Ac 23:1; 26:9), he was shown mercy and great patience, and was given the opportunity to repent and accept Christ as Lord (Ac 9:1–19). God's mercy toward Paul should encourage us to present the gospel to sinners, confident that God's power and grace can redeem and change their lives.

1:18 IN KEEPING WITH THE PROPHECIES. Evidently prophecies had been made regarding God's will for Timothy's ministry in the church (see 1Co 14:29, note; see article on SPIRITUAL GIFTS FOR BELIEVERS, p. 350). Paul exhorts Timothy to remain faithful to that revealed will for his life. As a pastor and overseer of the church, he must remain loyal to the true apostolic faith and fight against the false doctrines creeping into the church.

1:19 SO HAVE SHIPWRECKED THEIR FAITH. Paul warns Timothy several times of the terrible pos-

science.[r] Some have rejected these and
so have shipwrecked their faith.[s]
20Among them are Hymenaeus[t] and Alexander,[u] whom I have handed over to
Satan[v] to be taught not to blaspheme.

Instructions on Worship

2 I urge, then, first of all, that requests,
prayers,[w] intercession and thanksgiving be made for everyone— **2**for kings and
all those in authority,[x] that we may live
peaceful and quiet lives in all godliness[y]
and holiness. **3**This is good, and pleases[z]
God our Savior,[a] **4**who wants[b] all men[c]
to be saved[d] and to come to a knowledge
of the truth.[e] **5**For there is one God[f] and
one mediator[g] between God and men, the
man Christ Jesus,[h] **6**who gave himself as
a ransom[i] for all men—the testimony[j]
given in its proper time.[k] **7**And for this
purpose I was appointed a herald and an
apostle—I am telling the truth, I am not
lying[l]—and a teacher[m] of the true faith
to the Gentiles.[n]
8I want men everywhere to lift up holy
hands[o] in prayer, without anger or disputing.
9I also want women to dress modestly,
with decency and propriety, not with
braided hair or gold or pearls or expensive
clothes,[p] **10**but with good deeds,[q] appropriate for women who profess to worship
God.
11A woman should learn in quietness
and full submission.[r] **12**I do not permit a
woman to teach or to have authority over
a man; she must be silent.[s] **13**For Adam

1:19 [r] ver 5; S Ac 23:1 [s] 1Ti 6:21; 2Ti 2:18 **1:20** [t] 2Ti 2:17 [u] 2Ti 4:14 [v] 1Co 5:5 **2:1** [w] Eph 6:18 **2:2** [x] Ezr 6:10; Ro 13:1 [y] 1Ti 3:16; 4:7,8; 6:3,5,6,11; 2Ti 3:5; Tit 1:1 **2:3** [z] S 1Ti 5:4 [a] S Lk 1:47 **2:4** [b] Eze 18:23, 32; 33:11 [c] 1Ti 4:10; Tit 2:11; 2Pe 3:9 [d] S Jn 3:17; S Ro 11:14 [e] 2Ti 2:25; Tit 1:1; Heb 10:26 **2:5** [f] Dt 6:4; Ro 3:29,30; 10:12 [g] S Gal 3:20 [h] Ro 1:3 **2:6** [i] S Mt 20:28 [j] S 1Co 1:6 [k] 1Ti 6:15; Tit 1:3 **2:7** [l] S Ro 9:1 [m] 2Ti 1:11 [n] S Ac 9:15 **2:8** [o] Ps 24:4; 63:4; 134:2; 141:2; Lk 24:50 **2:9** [p] 1Pe 3:3 **2:10** [q] Pr 31:13 **2:11** [r] 1Pe 3:3,4 **2:12** [s] S Eph 5:22

sibility of apostasy (4:1; 5:11–15; 6:9–10; see article on PERSONAL APOSTASY, p. 492).

1:20 HAVE HANDED OVER TO SATAN. Paul's action probably means that these two men were excommunicated from the church. Salvation and union with the body of Christ (the church) protect us from Satan's power. To be expelled from the church, on the other hand, exposes one's life to destructive, satanic attacks (cf. Job 2:6–7; 1Co 5:5; Rev 2:22). Church discipline serves to bring the individual back to repentance, true faith and salvation in Christ (see 1Co 5:5, note).

2:4 WHO WANTS ALL MEN TO BE SAVED. The Bible reveals two aspects of God's will for mankind with regard to salvation: his perfect will and his permissive will (see Mt 7:21; Lk 7:30; 13:34; Jn 7:17; Ac 7:51). (1) God's perfect will sincerely desires "all men to be saved"; he doesn't want anyone to perish, "but everyone to come to repentance" (2Pe 3:9). This aspect of God's will reflects what he desires, not necessarily what he permits.

(2) God's permissive will reflects what he allows or permits, but not necessarily what he desires. That many people remain lost is only in accordance with this aspect of God's will, not his perfect will. If some choose to remain unsaved, God will permit it, for he does not coerce those who refuse to accept his Son's salvation. Therefore, much that happens in the world is contrary to God's perfect will (e.g., sin, lust, violence, hatred and impenitence), yet is within his permissive will.

(3) These two aspects of God's will also function in the category of personal tragedy and sorrow. Many personal sufferings and troubles are permitted by God, but are not necessarily his intention or ultimate will for that person. Because of rebellion, sin or carelessness in individuals, trouble and sorrow may occur without God desiring it. Personal suffering may at times be the result of the divine principle of reaping what we sow (Gal 6:7).

2:5 ONE MEDIATOR . . . CHRIST JESUS. We must draw near to God only through Christ Jesus (Heb 7:25), relying on his sacrificial death to cover our sins and praying in faith for strength and mercy to help us with all of our needs (Heb 4:14–16). We must not allow any other created being to take Christ's place by praying to him or her (see Heb 8:6; 9:15; 12:24).

2:6 A RANSOM FOR ALL. See Mt 20:28, note.

2:8 MEN EVERYWHERE TO LIFT UP HOLY HANDS. In the NT church's public worship, it was apparently customary for worshipers to offer prayers aloud (see Ac 4:24–31; cf. Ezr 3:12–13). To be acceptable, prayer had to be offered by those who were living holy and righteous lives, i.e., with "holy hands."

2:9 WOMEN TO DRESS MODESTLY, WITH DECENCY. It is God's will that Christian women dress modestly and discreetly. (1) The word "decency" (Gk *aidos*) implies a certain shame in exposing the body. It involves a refusal to dress in such a way as to draw attention to the body and to pass the boundaries of proper reserve. The source of modesty is in a person's heart or inner character. In other words, modesty is the outward manifestation of an inward purity.

(2) Dressing immodestly, which may excite impure desires in others, is as wrong as the immoral desire it provokes. No activity or condition justifies the wearing of immodest attire that would expose the body in such a way as to stimulate lust in someone else (cf. Gal 5:13; Eph 4:27; Tit 2:11–12; see Mt 5:28, note).

(3) It is a sad commentary on any church when the Biblical standard for modest dress is ignored and the world's customs are passively adopted. In a day of sexual permissiveness, the church should act and dress differently from a corrupt society that throws aside and ridicules the Spirit's desire for modesty, purity and godly restraint (cf. Ro 12:1–2).

2:9 BRAIDED HAIR OR GOLD. This possibly means the braiding of hair with gold or other articles of luxury.

2:13 ADAM WAS FORMED FIRST. Paul's argument for man's responsibility as head and spiritual leader in the home and church (see Eph 5:23, note; see article on PARENTS AND CHILDREN, p. 432) has two bases. (1) It is based on God's purpose in creation. God created man first, thus revealing God's intention that man was to direct and give leadership

was formed first, then Eve.[t] 14And Adam
was not the one deceived; it was the woman who was deceived and became a sinner.[u] 15But women[b] will be saved[c]
through childbearing—if they continue in
faith, love[v] and holiness with propriety.

Overseers and Deacons

3 Here is a trustworthy saying:[w] If anyone sets his heart on being an overseer,[d][x] he desires a noble task. 2Now the
overseer must be above reproach,[y] the
husband of but one wife,[z] temperate,[a]
self-controlled, respectable, hospitable,[b]
able to teach,[c] 3not given to drunkenness,[d] not violent but gentle, not quarrelsome,[e] not a lover of money.[f] 4He must
manage his own family well and see that
his children obey him with proper respect.[g] 5(If anyone does not know how to
manage his own family, how can he take
care of God's church?)[h] 6He must not be
a recent convert, or he may become conceited[i] and fall under the same judgment[j] as the devil. 7He must also have a
good reputation with outsiders,[k] so that
he will not fall into disgrace and into the
devil's trap.[l]

8Deacons,[m] likewise, are to be men
worthy of respect, sincere, not indulging

2:13 [t]Ge 2:7,22; 1Co 11:8 **2:14** [u]Ge 3:1-6, 13; 2Co 11:3 **2:15** [v]1Ti 1:14 **3:1** [w]S 1Ti 1:15 [x]Ac 20:28; Php 1:1; Tit 1:7 **3:2** [y]Tit 1:6-8 [z]ver 12 [a]ver 11; Tit 2:2 [b]S Ro 12:13 [c]2Ti 2:24 **3:3** [d]Tit 1:7 [e]2Ti 2:24 [f]Lk 16:14; 1Ti 6:10; 2Ti 3:2; Heb 13:5; 1Pe 5:2 **3:4** [g]ver 12; Tit 1:6 **3:5** [h]S 1Co 10:32 **3:6** [i]1Ti 6:4; 2Ti 3:4 [j]S 2Pe 2:4 **3:7** [k]S Mk 4:11 [l]2Ti 2:26 **3:8** [m]Php 1:1

b *15* Greek *she* **c** *15* Or *restored*
d *1* Traditionally *bishop*; also in verse 2

to the woman and family. The woman, created after man, was designed to be his companion and helper in fulfilling God's desire for their lives (Ge 2:18; 1Co 11:8–9; 14:34). (2) It is also based on the disastrous consequences when man and woman abandoned their God-given roles in the Garden of Eden. Eve, by acting independently of her husband as head, ate the forbidden fruit. Adam, by neglecting his responsibility of leadership under God, consented to Eve's disobedience. As a result he too fell and brought sin and death into the human race (v. 14; Ge 3:6,12; Ro 5:12).

2:15 WOMEN WILL BE SAVED THROUGH CHILDBEARING. Paul says that women in general will be saved by faith in God and by accepting the sphere of activity assigned to them by their Creator. (1) Woman's highest position and true dignity is in the home as a godly wife and mother. No greater joy, inner delight, blessing or honor can come to her than when, as a Christian wife and mother, she bears children (5:14), loves them (Tit 2:4), brings them up to live Christlike lives for God's glory (cf. 2Ti 1:5; 3:14–15; see article on PARENTS AND CHILDREN, p. 432), and continues ever faithful to her Savior (v. 15b).

(2) The honor and dignity of childbearing must not be depreciated by the Christian. It was the childbearing of Mary that became the channel of salvation to the world (Ge 3:15; Mt 1:18–25).

(3) Those societies, cultures and churches that compromise or reject God's purpose for women and thereby depreciate the Christian family, home and motherhood will increasingly experience disintegration in their marriages, families and societies (see 2Ti 3:3, note).

(4) Paul's address to Christian women is not intended to demean women who are not married or who are unable to have children. The faith, love and sanctity of such women can be as great as those with a family (see 1Co 7:34, note).

3:1–7 IF ANYONE SETS HIS HEART ON BEING AN OVERSEER. For comments on the important qualifications for being an overseer or pastor, see article on MORAL QUALIFICATIONS FOR OVERSEERS, p. 458.

3:2 MUST BE ABOVE REPROACH. The prospective overseer *must* be "above reproach" (Gk *anepilēmptos*, literally meaning "not to be laid hold of"). This has to do with proven observable conduct that is blameless in marital life, family life, social life and business life. No overseer should have a justifiable charge of immorality or misdoing alleged against him. Rather, he must have a blameless reputation with those inside and outside the church (see v. 7, note), because he has not marred his Christian life with serious sin or immorality by habit or incident. He therefore can set an example for all to follow (see 4:12, note).

3:3 NOT GIVEN TO DRUNKENNESS. This phrase (Gk *mē paroinon*, from *mē*, meaning "not," and *paroinos*, a compound meaning "at, by, near, next to or with wine") is literally translated "not by, near or with wine," "not being beside wine." The Bible here requires that no overseer may "sit beside wine" or "be with wine." In other words, he should not drink intoxicating wine, be tempted or enticed by it, or "eat and drink with drunkards" (Mt 24:49).

(1) Total abstinence from fermented wine was the standard for kings and judges in the OT (Pr 31:4–7). It was also the standard for all who sought the highest level of consecration to God (Lev 10:8–11; Nu 6:1–5; Jdg 13:4–7; 1Sa 1:14–15; Jer 35:2–6; see Pr 23:31, where it ultimately becomes God's standard for all his people).

(2) Those who rule in Christ's church certainly should not have a lower standard. Furthermore, all believers in the church are called priests and kings (1Pe 2:9; Rev 1:6) and as such should live by God's highest standard (Jn 2:3, note; Eph 5:18, note; 1Th 5:6, note; Tit 2:2, note; see articles on WINE IN NEW TESTAMENT TIMES (1) and (2), p. 126 and p. 174).

3:4 MANAGE HIS OWN FAMILY WELL. A key qualification for the candidate desiring the office of overseer is faithfulness in marriage and family relationships. For more on this, see MORAL QUALIFICATIONS FOR OVERSEERS, p. 458.

3:7 HE MUST ALSO HAVE A GOOD REPUTATION. The overseer or prospective overseer must "have a good reputation" with two groups: (a) insiders, i.e., church members (vv. 1–6), and (b) outsiders, i.e., those outside of the church (v. 7). He must have a past and an ongoing reputation of a righteous lifestyle that accords with the gospel of Christ.

MORAL QUALIFICATIONS FOR OVERSEERS

***1Ti 3:1–2** "Here is a trustworthy saying: If anyone sets his heart on being an overseer, he desires a noble task. Now the overseer must be above reproach, the husband of but one wife, temperate, self-controlled, respectable, hospitable, able to teach."*

If a man wants to be an "overseer" (Gk *episkopos*, i.e., one who has pastoral oversight; a pastor), he desires an important work (1Ti 3:1). However, such people must have that desire confirmed by God's Word (3:1–10; 4:12) and the church (3:10), for God has established for the church certain specific qualifications. Any professed call of God to do the work of a pastor must be tested by the members of the church according to the Biblical standards of 1Ti 3:1–13; 4:12; Tit 1:5–9 (see article on THE MINISTRY GIFTS OF THE CHURCH, p. 407). The church must not endorse any person for ministerial work based solely on his desire, education, burden, or alleged vision or call. The church today has no right to diminish the requirements that God has set forth by the Holy Spirit. They stand as absolutes and must be followed for the sake of God's name, his kingdom and the credibility of the high office of overseer.

(1) The standards listed for overseers are primarily moral and spiritual. The proven character of those who seek leadership in the church is more important than personality, preaching gifts, administrative abilities or academic accomplishments. The focal point of the qualifications falls on behavior that has persevered in godly wisdom, right choices and personal holiness. The spiritual history of the person who desires the office of overseer has to "first be tested" (cf. 1Ti 3:10). Thus, the Holy Spirit sets forth the high standard that the candidate must be a believer who has steadfastly adhered to Jesus Christ and his principles of righteousness, and who can therefore serve as a role model of faithfulness, truth, honesty and purity. In other words, his character must reflect Christ's teaching in Mt 25:21, that being "faithful with a few things" leads to a position of being "in charge of many things."

(2) Above all, Christian leaders must "set an example for the believers" (1Ti 4:12; cf. 1Pe 5:3), i.e., their Christian life and steadfast faith can be set before the congregation as preeminently worthy of imitation. (a) Overseers must demonstrate the highest example of perseverance in godliness, faithfulness, purity in the face of temptation, and loyalty to and love for Christ and the gospel (1Ti 4:12,15). (b) God's people must learn Christian ethics and true godliness not only from the Word of God but also from the example of pastors who live according to apostolic standards. Pastors whose quality of life is an illustration of the faith are absolutely essential in God's plan for Christian leadership. To throw aside the principle of having godly leadership that has set an unblemished pattern for those of the church to follow is to ignore Scripture's clear teaching. Pastors must be people whose faithfulness to Christ can be set forth as a pattern or example (cf. 1Co 11:1; Php 3:17; 1Th 1:6; 2Th 3:7,9; 2Ti 1:13).

(3) The Holy Spirit regards the believer's leadership in home, marriage and family relationships as of the highest importance (1Ti 3:2,4–5; Tit 1:6). The overseer must be an example to the family of God *especially* in his faithfulness to his wife and children. After all, if he has failed in this realm, "how can he take care of God's church?" (1Ti 3:5). He must be "the husband of but one wife" (1Ti 3:2). The phrase defends the position that a candidate for the office of an overseer should be a believer who has remained morally faithful to his wife. The literal translation of the Greek (*mias gunaikos*, an attributive genitive) is "a one-woman man," i.e., the faithful husband of his wife. This means that the candidate must be a person who gives evidence of being faithful in this all-important area. Persevering moral faithfulness to one's wife and family is required for anyone desiring to be a leader and an example in the church.

(4) Consequently, persons within the church who become guilty of serious sin or moral transgressions have disqualified themselves from the office of pastor and from any position of high leadership in the local church (cf. 1Ti 3:8–12). Such people may be abundantly pardoned by God's grace, but they have lost the capacity to serve as models of unfailing perseverance in faith, love, purity and sound doctrine (4:11–16; Tit 1:9).

(5) Futhermore, 1Ti 3:2,7 sets forth the principle that an overseer who throws aside his loyalty to God and his Word, and his fidelity to wife and family must be removed from the office of an overseer. He cannot thereafter be regarded as "above reproach" (3:2). Concerning one among God's people who commits adultery, God's Word states that "his shame will never be wiped away" (Pr 6:33).

(6) This does not mean that God or the church will not forgive. God will indeed forgive any sin listed in 1Ti 3:1–13 if there is godly sorrow and repentance for that sin. Let it be clear that such a person may be mercifully forgiven and restored in his relationship to God and the church. However, what the Holy Spirit is stating is that there are some sins so grave that the disgrace and shame (i.e., reproach) of that sin will remain with an individual even after forgiveness (cf. 2Sa 12:9–14).

(7) But what about King David? His continuation as Israel's king in spite of his sins of adultery and murder (2Sa 11:1–21; 12:9–15) is sometimes viewed as Biblical justification for one's continuance as an overseer even though he has violated the above-mentioned standards. This comparison, however, is faulty on several counts. (a) The office of the king of Israel under the old covenant and that of spiritual overseer of the church of Jesus Christ under the new covenant are two entirely different things. God allowed not only David but also many kings who were exceptionally wicked to remain as kings of Israel. Leadership of the NT church that was purchased with the blood of Jesus Christ requires much higher spiritual standards. (b) According to God's revelation and requirements in the NT, David would not have qualified for the office of an overseer in a NT church. He had multiple wives, was guilty of marital unfaithfulness, failed miserably to manage his own household, and was a murderer and a violent man of bloodshed. Note too that because of his sin, David remained under God's punishment for the rest of his life (2Sa 12:9–12).

(8) Today's churches must not turn from the righteous requirements for an overseer set forth by God in the original revelation of the apostles. Instead the church must require from its leaders the highest standard of holiness, perseverance in faithfulness to God and his Word, and godly living. They are to be earnestly prayed for, encouraged and supported, while they "set an example for the believers in speech, in life, in love, in faith and in purity" (1Ti 4:12).

in much wine,[n] and not pursuing dishonest gain. 9They must keep hold of the deep
truths of the faith with a clear conscience.[o] 10They must first be tested;[p]
and then if there is nothing against them,
let them serve as deacons.
11In the same way, their wives[e] are to
be women worthy of respect, not malicious talkers[q] but temperate[r] and trustworthy in everything.
12A deacon must be the husband of but
one wife[s] and must manage his children
and his household well.[t] 13Those who
have served well gain an excellent standing and great assurance in their faith in
Christ Jesus.
14Although I hope to come to you soon,
I am writing you these instructions so
that, 15if I am delayed, you will know how
people ought to conduct themselves in
God's household, which is the church[u] of
the living God,[v] the pillar and foundation
of the truth. 16Beyond all question, the
mystery[w] of godliness[x] is great:

He[f] appeared in a body,[g][y]
  was vindicated by the Spirit,
was seen by angels,
  was preached among the nations,[z]
was believed on in the world,
  was taken up in glory.[a]

3:8 [n] 1Ti 5:23; Tit 1:7; 2:3 3:9 [o] S Ac 23:1 3:10 [p] 1Ti 5:22 3:11 [q] 2Ti 3:3; Tit 2:3 [r] ver 2 3:12 [s] ver 2 [t] ver 4 3:15 [u] ver 5; S 1Co 10:32 [v] S Mt 16:16 3:16 [w] S Ro 16:25 [x] S 1Ti 2:2 [y] S Jn 1:14 [z] Ps 9:11; Col 1:23 [a] S Mk 16:19 4:1 [b] Jn 16:13; S Ac 8:29; 1Co 2:10 [c] 2Ti 3:1; 2Pe 3:3 [d] S Mk 13:5

Instructions to Timothy

4 The Spirit[b] clearly says that in later
times[c] some will abandon the faith
and follow deceiving spirits[d] and things

[e] *11* Or *way, deaconesses* [f] *16* Some manuscripts *God* [g] *16* Or *in the flesh*

3:8 DEACONS. Deacon (Gk *diakonos*) means "servant." One of their functions in the NT church is suggested in Ac 6:1–6. They were to assist pastors by administrating the temporal and material affairs of the church so that pastors might give themselves to prayer and the ministry of the Word (Ac 6:2). The spiritual qualifications for deacons are essentially the same as for pastors (compare vv. 1–7 with vv. 8–13; see Ac 6:3).

3:8 NOT INDULGING IN MUCH WINE. Concerning this qualification, the following should be noted (see also v. 3, note). (1) It is morally unthinkable that the apostle was approving the moderate use of all the kinds of wine available in his day. Many wines were mixed and dangerous (cf. Pr 23:29–35).

(2) Some interpret Paul as saying that deacons must not be habitual drunkards, thereby implicitly condoning moderate alcoholic drinking. However, Paul states that drunkenness is such a terrible sin that it excludes one from God's kingdom (1Co 6:10). It is absurd, therefore, that Paul would actually require, as one of his high standards for deacons (cf. v. 2), that the deacon not be a habitual drunkard (i.e., someone who is unsaved). Paul must have a different meaning in mind for "wine" than intoxicating wine.

(3) Rather than condoning moderate alcoholic drinking, Paul was most likely warning against the excessive desire and use, within a pagan society, of legitimate unfermented types of wines (see article on WINE IN NEW TESTAMENT TIMES (1), p. 126). Addiction even to nonintoxicating wine was a vice prevalent in pagan societies, and corresponded to gluttony (see Pliny, *Natural History*, 14.28.139). Paul was emphasizing self-control in all areas of life, even in something good; note Pr 25:27, which states that "it is not good to eat too much honey."

(4) The apostle Paul was not alone in this kind of admonition. Rabbinic literature contains warnings about the excessive use of the sweet unfermented juice of the grape. This literature states concerning *tirosh*, a grape drink that included "all kinds of sweet juices and must, and does not include fermented wine" (Tosef., Ned. IV.3), that "if drunk in moderation it gives leadership; ... if drunk in excess it leads to poverty" (Yoma 76b). "One that drinks it habitually is certain to become poor" (*The Jewish Encyclopedia*, 12.533; see article on WINE IN NEW TESTAMENT TIMES (1), p. 126).

3:15 CHURCH ... PILLAR AND FOUNDATION OF THE TRUTH. The church must be the foundation of the truth of the gospel. It upholds and preserves the truth revealed by Christ and the apostles by receiving and obeying it (Mt 13:23), hiding it in the heart (Ps 119:11), proclaiming it as the word of life (Php 2:16), defending it (Php 1:16) and demonstrating its power in the Holy Spirit (Mk 16:15–20; Ac 1:8; 4:29–33; 6:8).

4:1 SOME WILL ABANDON THE FAITH. The Holy Spirit has explicitly revealed that in later times there will be a falling away both from a personal faith in Jesus Christ (see article on PERSONAL APOSTASY, p. 492) and from Scriptural truth (cf. 2Th 2:3; Jude 3–4). (1) There will appear within the church ministers who are highly gifted and mightily anointed by God. Some will accomplish great things for God and preach gospel truth effectively, but they will depart from the faith and gradually turn to seducing spirits and false doctrines. Because of their former anointing and zeal for God, they will mislead many (see article on THE GREAT TRIBULATION, p. 52).

(2) Many believers will fall away from the faith because they will fail to love the truth (2Th 2:10) and resist the sinful trends of the last days (cf. Mt 24:5,10–12; see 2Ti 3:2–3, notes). Thus, the distorted gospel of compromising ministers and educators will find little resistance in many churches (4:1; 2Ti 3:5; 4:3; see 2Co 11:13, note).

(3) The popularity of unbiblical teaching will be primarily the result of Satan's directing his demonic hosts in a more intensified opposition to God's work. Christ's second coming will be preceded by a greater intensity of satanism, spiritism, the occult, demon-possession and demonic deception in the world and in the church (Eph 6:11–12; see articles on POWER OVER SATAN AND DEMONS, p. 80, and THE AGE OF THE ANTICHRIST, p. 447).

(4) The believer's protection against such deception involves utter loyalty to God and his inspired Word,

taught by demons. **2**Such teachings come through hypocritical liars, whose consciences have been seared as with a hot iron.[e] **3**They forbid people to marry[f] and order them to abstain from certain foods,[g] which God created[h] to be received with thanksgiving[i] by those who believe and who know the truth. **4**For everything God created is good,[j] and nothing is to be rejected[k] if it is received with thanksgiving, **5**because it is consecrated by the word of God[l] and prayer.

6If you point these things out to the brothers, you will be a good minister of Christ Jesus, brought up in the truths of the faith[m] and of the good teaching that you have followed.[n] **7**Have nothing to do with godless myths and old wives' tales;[o] rather, train yourself to be godly.[p] **8**For physical training is of some value, but godliness has value for all things,[q] holding promise for both the present life[r] and the life to come.[s]

9This is a trustworthy saying[t] that deserves full acceptance **10**(and for this we labor and strive), that we have put our hope in the living God,[u] who is the Savior of all men,[v] and especially of those who believe.

11Command and teach these things.[w] **12**Don't let anyone look down on you[x] because you are young, but set an example[y] for the believers in speech, in life, in love, in faith[z] and in purity. **13**Until I come,[a] devote yourself to the public reading of Scripture,[b] to preaching and to teaching. **14**Do not neglect your gift, which was given you through a prophetic message[c] when the body of elders[d] laid their hands on you.[e] 2Ti 1:6

15Be diligent in these matters; give yourself wholly to them, so that everyone may see your progress. **16**Watch your life and doctrine closely. Persevere in them, because if you do, you will save[f] both yourself and your hearers.

Advice About Widows, Elders and Slaves

5 Do not rebuke an older man[g] harshly,[h] but exhort him as if he were your father. Treat younger men[i] as brothers, **2**older women as mothers, and younger women as sisters, with absolute purity.

3Give proper recognition to those widows who are really in need.[j] **4**But if a widow has children or grandchildren, these should learn first of all to put their religion into practice by caring for their own family and so repaying their parents and grandparents,[k] for this is pleasing to God.[l] **5**The widow who is really in need[m] and left all alone puts her hope in God[n] and continues night and day to pray[o] and to ask God for help. **6**But the widow who lives for pleasure is dead even while she lives.[p] **7**Give the people these instructions,[q] too, so that no one may be open to blame. **8**If anyone does not provide for his relatives, and especially for his immediate family, he has denied[r] the faith and is worse than an unbeliever.

4:2 [e] Eph 4:19 **4:3** [f] Heb 13:4 [g] Col 2:16 [h] Ge 1:29; 9:3 [i] ver 4; Ro 14:6; 1Co 10:30 **4:4** [j] Ge 1:10,12, 18,21,25,31; Mk 7:18,19; Ro 14:14-18 [k] S Ac 10:15 **4:5** [l] S Heb 4:12 **4:6** [m] 1Ti 1:10 [n] 2Ti 3:15 **4:7** [o] 1Ti 1:4; 2Ti 2:16 [p] S 1Ti 2:2 **4:8** [q] 1Ti 6:6 [r] Ps 37:9,11; Pr 22:4; Mt 6:33; Mk 10:29,30 [s] Mk 10:29,30 **4:9** [t] S 1Ti 1:15 **4:10** [u] S Mt 16:16 [v] S Lk 1:47; S 2:11 **4:11** [w] 1Ti 5:7; 6:2 **4:12** [x] S 2Ti 1:7; Tit 2:15 [y] Php 3:17; 1Th 1:7; 2Th 3:9; Tit 2:7; 1Pe 5:3 [z] 1Ti 1:14 **4:13** [a] 1Ti 3:14 [b] Lk 4:16; Ac 13:14-16; Col 4:16; 1Th 5:27 **4:14** [c] 1Ti 1:18 [d] S Ac 11:30 [e] S Ac 6:6; 2Ti 1:6 **4:16** [f] S Ro 11:14 **5:1** [g] Tit 2:2 [h] Lev 19:32 [i] Tit 2:6 **5:3** [j] ver 5,16 **5:4** [k] ver 8; Eph 6:1,2 [l] Ro 12:2; Eph 5:10; 1Ti 2:3 **5:5** [m] ver 3,16 [n] 1Co 7:34; 1Pe 3:5 [o] Lk 2:37; S Ro 1:10 **5:6** [p] S Lk 15:24 **5:7** [q] 1Ti 4:11; 6:2 **5:8** [r] 2Pe 2:1; Jude 4

---

and the knowledge that persons of great charisma and anointing can be deceived and then deceive others with their mixture of truth and error. This awareness must be accompanied by a true desire within the believer's heart to do God's will (Jn 7:17) and to walk in righteousness and the fear of God (Ps 25:4–5,12–15).

(5) Faithful believers must not think that because apostasy is prevalent within Christianity during the last days that authentic revival cannot occur or evangelism according to the NT pattern cannot be successful. God has promised that during the "last days" he will save all who call on his name and separate themselves from this corrupt generation (Ac 2:16–21,33,38–40; 3:19), and he will pour out his Spirit on them.

4:12 SET AN EXAMPLE. This is one of the most important qualifications for a church leader. The Greek word translated "example" is *tupos*, meaning "model," "image," "ideal" or "pattern." A pastor, above all else, must be a model of faithfulness, purity and perseverance in godly living. The office of overseer may be occupied only by those of whom the church can say, "This leader has lived a godly life worthy of emulation." For more on this, see MORAL QUALIFICATIONS FOR OVERSEERS, p. 458.

4:16 IF YOU DO, YOU WILL SAVE BOTH YOURSELF AND YOUR HEARERS. Living a holy life (v. 12), remaining sensitive to the Spirit's operation and gifts (v. 14), teaching sound doctrine (vv. 13,15–16), guarding the faith (6:20; 2Ti 1:13–14; see article on OVERSEERS AND THEIR DUTIES, p. 274) and watching over one's spiritual life (v. 16) are more than a ministerial obligation for Timothy. These things are essential for his own salvation (present and future: see article on BIBLICAL WORDS FOR SALVATION, p. 292) and for those to whom he ministers (cf. 2Ti 3:13–15).

5:5 THE WIDOW . . . NIGHT AND DAY TO PRAY. Widows who have given themselves to the supreme work of prayer should receive recognition and help (if need be) from the church (v. 3). One is reminded of the widow Anna, who "never left the temple but worshiped night and day, fasting and praying" (Lk 2:37). Early Christianity called such a widow "the intercessor of the church," "the keeper of the door" and "the altar of God."

9No widow may be put on the list of
widows unless she is over sixty, has been
faithful to her husband,[h] **10**and is well
known for her good deeds,[s] such as bringing up children, showing hospitality,[t]
washing the feet[u] of the saints, helping
those in trouble[v] and devoting herself to
all kinds of good deeds.
11As for younger widows, do not put
them on such a list. For when their sensual desires overcome their dedication to
Christ, they want to marry. **12**Thus they
bring judgment on themselves, because
they have broken their first pledge. **13**Besides, they get into the habit of being idle
and going about from house to house. And
not only do they become idlers, but also
gossips[w] and busybodies,[x] saying things
they ought not to. **14**So I counsel younger
widows to marry,[y] to have children, to
manage their homes and to give the enemy no opportunity for slander.[z] **15**Some
have in fact already turned away to follow
Satan.[a]
16If any woman who is a believer has
widows in her family, she should help

5:10 [s]Ac 9:36; 1Ti 6:18; 1Pe 2:12 [t]S Ro 12:13 [u]S Lk 7:44 [v]ver 16
5:13 [w]S Ro 1:29 [x]2Th 3:11
5:14 [y]1Co 7:9 [z]1Ti 6:1
5:15 [a]S Mt 4:10
5:16 [b]ver 3-5
5:17 [c]S Ac 11:30 [d]Php 2:29; 1Th 5:12
5:18 [e]Dt 25:4; 1Co 9:7-9 [f]Lk 10:7; Lev 19:13; Dt 24:14,15; Mt 10:10; 1Co 9:14
5:19 [g]S Ac 11:30 [h]S Mt 18:16
5:20 [i]2Ti 4:2; Tit 1:13; 2:15 [j]Dt 13:11
5:21 [k]1Ti 6:13; 2Ti 4:1
5:22 [l]S Ac 6:6 [m]Eph 5:11 [n]Ps 18:26

them and not let the church be burdened
with them, so that the church can help
those widows who are really in need.[b]
17The elders[c] who direct the affairs of
the church well are worthy of double hon-
or,[d] especially those whose work is
preaching and teaching. **18**For the Scripture says, "Do not muzzle the ox while it
is treading out the grain,"[i][e] and "The
worker deserves his wages."[j][f] **19**Do not
entertain an accusation against an elder[g]
unless it is brought by two or three witnesses.[h] **20**Those who sin are to be rebuked[i] publicly, so that the others may
take warning.[j]
21I charge you, in the sight of God and
Christ Jesus[k] and the elect angels, to
keep these instructions without partiality,
and to do nothing out of favoritism.
22Do not be hasty in the laying on of
hands,[l] and do not share in the sins of
others.[m] Keep yourself pure.[n]
23Stop drinking only water, and use a

h *9* Or *has had but one husband* **i** *18* Deut. 25:4
j *18* Luke 10:7

5:9 MAY BE PUT ON THE LIST. The church in Ephesus apparently had an official list of widows who were entitled to material support from the church. The church gave such assistance because in NT times there was no government help or pensions for widows who had no family or children to help them. The widows were required to demonstrate certain spiritual qualifications (vv. 9–10), including perseverance in good works (v. 10) and prayer (v. 5).

5:17–19 ELDERS WHO DIRECT THE AFFAIRS OF THE CHURCH WELL. These verses concern the proper honor of elders (i.e., overseers) who rule well in the local church and watch over the souls of believers (see article on OVERSEERS AND THEIR DUTIES, p. 274). Those who sincerely work hard at preaching and teaching (cf. 1Co 15:10; 1Th 5:12–13) must receive double honor. This refers to (1) helping them with financial support (cf. 1Co 9:7–14) and (2) submitting to them with regard to matters of Christian conduct (Heb 13:7; 1Pe 5:5).

5:20 REBUKED PUBLICLY. God's Word gives principles and guidelines with regard to the discipline of elders or pastors (vv. 20–22). Because godly leaders are essential to the church, the following actions must be taken when a pastor or church worker sins and that sin is confirmed (v. 19). (1) Elders must not cover up or remain silent about the sins of other elders. The offending elder must "be rebuked" and disciplined. His sin must be exposed "publicly," in order that the rest of the elders may "take warning" and have a godly fear of sinning. (2) Paul warns that the above discipline must be carried out without partiality or favoritism because all will one day stand in the presence of God, Jesus Christ and the elect angels (v. 21).

5:22 DO NOT BE HASTY IN THE LAYING ON OF HANDS. Regarding the ordination of an elder (cf. 4:14; Ac 6:6), Paul maintains several things: (1) No one is to be ordained to this position hastily. That is, proper caution and Scriptural guidelines must be obeyed and followed (see Tit 1:5, note; see article on MORAL QUALIFICATIONS FOR OVERSEERS, p. 458). (2) Ordaining a man as an elder is a public declaration to the church that the person's life has met God's standard of perseverance in godliness as found in 3:1–7. In other words, those to be ordained to a position of leadership must have a history of faithfulness to the Lord during the time of their Christian profession. (3) For a church to ordain or appoint anyone to a position of leadership within the church hastily, i.e., in disregard to God's guidelines, causes it to "share in" that person's sins. Paul's admonition to "keep yourself pure" means to refuse to become involved in the choosing or ordaining of anyone unworthy for the office of pastor.

5:23 USE A LITTLE WINE. (1) This text clearly implies that Timothy did not normally drink any of the types of wine used by the Jews of NT times (see article on WINE IN NEW TESTAMENT TIMES (1), p. 126). If it had been Timothy's habit to drink wine, Paul would not have had to advise him to use a little wine for medicinal purposes (see 3:3, note).

(2) Timothy had developed stomach trouble, probably due to the alkali in the water at Ephesus. Paul therefore recommends that Timothy use a little wine with that water to neutralize the harmful effect of the alkali. Wine used for the stomach, according to ancient Greek writings on medicine, was often unintoxicating. Athenaeus states, "Let him take sweet wine, either mixed with water or warmed, especially that kind called *protropos* [juice coming from the grapes before they are pressed], as being good for the stomach, for sweet wine [*oinos*] does not make the head

little wine[o] because of your stomach and
your frequent illnesses.
24The sins of some men are obvious,
reaching the place of judgment ahead of
them; the sins of others trail behind them.
25In the same way, good deeds are obvious, and even those that are not cannot be
hidden.

6 All who are under the yoke of slavery
should consider their masters worthy
of full respect,[p] so that God's name and
our teaching may not be slandered.[q]
2Those who have believing masters are
not to show less respect for them because
they are brothers.[r] Instead, they are to
serve them even better, because those
who benefit from their service are believers, and dear to them. These are the
things you are to teach and urge on
them.[s]

Love of Money

3If anyone teaches false doctrines[t] and
does not agree to the sound instruction[u]
of our Lord Jesus Christ and to godly
teaching, **4**he is conceited[v] and understands nothing. He has an unhealthy interest in controversies and quarrels about
words[w] that result in envy, strife, malicious talk, evil suspicions **5**and constant
friction between men of corrupt mind, who
have been robbed of the truth[x] and who
think that godliness is a means to financial gain.
6But godliness with contentment[y] is
great gain.[z] **7**For we brought nothing into
the world, and we can take nothing out of
it.[a] **8**But if we have food and clothing, we
will be content with that.[b] **9**People who
want to get rich[c] fall into temptation and
a trap[d] and into many foolish and harmful
desires that plunge men into ruin and destruction. **10**For the love of money[e] is a
root of all kinds of evil. Some people, eager for money, have wandered from the
faith[f] and pierced themselves with many
griefs.[g]

Paul's Charge to Timothy

11But you, man of God,[h] flee from all
this, and pursue righteousness, godliness,[i] faith, love,[j] endurance and gentleness. **12**Fight the good fight[k] of the faith.
Take hold of[l] the eternal life[m] to which
you were called when you made your good
confession[n] in the presence of many witnesses. **13**In the sight of God, who gives
life to everything, and of Christ Jesus, who
while testifying before Pontius Pilate[o]
made the good confession,[p] I charge you[q]
14to keep this command without spot or
blame[r] until the appearing of our Lord
Jesus Christ,[s] **15**which God will bring
about in his own time[t]—God, the
blessed[u] and only Ruler,[v] the King of
kings and Lord of lords,[w] **16**who alone is
immortal[x] and who lives in unapproachable light,[y] whom no one has seen or can

5:23 [o]1Ti 3:8
6:1 [p]S Eph 6:5 [q]1Ti 5:14; Tit 2:5, 8
6:2 [r]Phm 16 [s]1Ti 4:11
6:3 [t]1Ti 1:3 [u]S 1Ti 1:10
6:4 [v]1Ti 3:6; 2Ti 3:4 [w]S 2Ti 2:14
6:5 [x]2Ti 3:8; Tit 1:15
6:6 [y]Php 4:11; Heb 13:5 [z]1Ti 4:8
6:7 [a]Job 1:21; Ps 49:17; Ecc 5:15
6:8 [b]Pr 30:8; Heb 13:5
6:9 [c]Pr 15:27; 28:20 [d]1Ti 3:7
6:10 [e]S 1Ti 3:3 [f]ver 21; Jas 5:19 [g]Jos 7:21
6:11 [h]2Ti 3:17 [i]ver 3,5,6; S 1Ti 2:2 [j]1Ti 1:14; 2Ti 2:22; 3:10
6:12 [k]1Co 9:25, 26; S 1Ti 1:18 [l]ver 19; Php 3:12 [m]S Mt 25:46 [n]S Heb 3:1
6:13 [o]Jn 18:33-37 [p]ver 12 [q]1Ti 5:21; 2Ti 4:1
6:14 [r]S 1Th 3:13 [s]S 1Co 1:7; 2Ti 1:10; 4:1,8
6:15 [t]1Ti 2:6; Tit 1:3 [u]1Ti 1:11 [v]1Ti 1:17 [w]Dt 10:17; Ps 136:3; Da 2:47; Rev 1:5; 17:14; 19:16
6:16 [x]1Ti 1:17 [y]Ps 104:2; 1Jn 1:7

heavy" (Athenaeus, *Banquet*, 2.24; see also Pliny, *Natural History* 14.18).

(3) Timothy, out of respect for the apostle Paul, would use a "little wine" when needed, and *only* for medicinal purposes. He would use it as an exception to his rule of abstinence. To quote the advice of Paul to Timothy in order to justify the drinking of intoxicating wine for personal gratification is to distort the intent of this passage.

6:1 UNDER THE YOKE OF SLAVERY. See Col 3:22, note.

6:3 GODLY TEACHING. Any message that does not come from the Lord Jesus and does not carry with it a fervent call for godliness and holiness is a different gospel than that presented in the NT.

6:5 MEN OF CORRUPT MIND. Paul returns to the discussion of false teachers (cf. ch. 1), informing Timothy what his judgment on such people must be. Modern indifference to extrabiblical doctrine is unapostolic and ignores the clear admonitions in this and other NT letters (cf. Gal 1:9).

6:6 GODLINESS ... IS GREAT GAIN. The false teachers at Ephesus outwardly practiced "godliness" in order to gain an abundance of riches. They were driven by an underlying motivation of greed and taught that their wealth was a sign of God's approval on their teachings.

6:8 WE WILL BE CONTENT WITH THAT. Believers should be content with the basics of food, clothing and shelter. If special financial needs arise, we must look to God to provide (Ps 50:15), while we continue to work (2Th 3:7–8), help those in need (2Co 8:2–3) and serve God with generous giving (2Co 8:3; 9:6–7). We must not want to get rich (vv. 9–11).

6:9 RICH FALL INTO TEMPTATION. See article on RICHES AND POVERTY, p. 152.

6:12 FIGHT THE GOOD FIGHT OF THE FAITH. The word "fight" is from the Greek word meaning "agonize." Paul sees the Christian life as a fight, an intense struggle that requires persevering in loyalty to Christ and contending with adversaries of the gospel. All of us are called to defend the gospel in whatever occupation God has placed us (see Eph 6:11–12, notes).

6:14 UNTIL THE APPEARING. Paul's admonition to Timothy clearly reveals that he believes that Christ's appearing could occur within his lifetime. The NT apostles repeatedly encouraged believers in their generation to expect and hope for the Lord's return in their lifetimes (Php 3:20; 1Th 1:9–10; Tit 2:13; Heb 9:28). Loving the Lord and longing for his return and immediate presence must be a basic motivation in our lives (see Rev 21:1—22:15).

6:16 WHO ALONE IS IMMORTAL. This term expresses God's transcendence. God is different and independent from his creation—whether humans, an-see.[z] To him be honor and might forever. Amen.[a]

17Command those who are rich[b] in this present world not to be arrogant nor to put their hope in wealth,[c] which is so uncertain, but to put their hope in God,[d] who richly provides us with everything for our enjoyment.[e] 18Command them to do good, to be rich in good deeds,[f] and to be generous and willing to share.[g] 19In this way they will lay up treasure for themselves[h] as a firm foundation for the coming age, so that they may take hold of[i] the life that is truly life.

20Timothy, guard what has been entrusted[j] to your care. Turn away from godless chatter[k] and the opposing ideas of what is falsely called knowledge, 21which some have professed and in so doing have wandered from the faith.[l]

Grace be with you.[m]

6:16 [z] S Jn 1:18 [a] S Ro 11:36 **6:17** [b] ver 9 [c] Ps 62:10; Jer 49:4; Lk 12:20, 21 [d] 1Ti 4:10 [e] Ac 14:17 **6:18** [f] S 1Ti 5:10 [g] Ro 12:8,13; Eph 4:28 **6:19** [h] S Mt 6:20 [i] ver 12; Php 3:12 **6:20** [j] 2Ti 1:12,14 [k] 2Ti 2:16 **6:21** [l] ver 10; 2Ti 2:18 [m] S Col 4:18

gels, spirits, or physical or material things (Ex 24:9–18; Isa 6:1–3; 40:12–26; 55:8–9; Eze 1). (1) God must not be placed on the same level with humans or any other beings he has created. His being and existence are in a totally different realm. He dwells in perfect and pure existence, far above his creation. He is not part of his creation nor is his creation a part of him. Furthermore, believers are not God and will never be "gods." We will always be limited and dependent beings, even in the age to come.

(2) Although a radical division exists between God and all creation, God is also present and active throughout the world. He lives and manifests himself in his people who repent of their sins and live by faith in Christ (Ex 33:17–23; Isa 57:15; see Mt 10:31, note; Ro 8:28, note; Gal 2:20, note).

6:20 GUARD WHAT HAS BEEN ENTRUSTED. For the fourth time, Paul charges Timothy to guard the faith that has been entrusted to him (1:18–19; 4:6–11; 6:13–16; 6:20). The Greek literally means "keep the deposit" and refers to the sacred obligation of keeping safe a treasured possession committed to one's care. The gospel of Christ has been committed to us by the Holy Spirit (2Ti 1:14; 3:16). We must proclaim the pure and full gospel in the Pentecostal power of the Spirit (Ac 2:4), ever ready to defend the precious truths when they are attacked, distorted or denied.

2 TIMOTHY

Outline

Introduction (1:1–4)
- I. Paul's Charge to Timothy (1:5–18)
  - A. Fan Into Flame the Gift of God (1:5–7)
  - B. Be Willing to Suffer for the Gospel (1:8–10)
  - C. Paul's Example (1:11–12)
  - D. Keep and Guard the Truth (1:13–14)
  - E. Disloyal and Loyal Friends of Paul in Rome (1:15–18)
- II. Requirements for a Faithful Minister (2:1–26)
  - A. Be Strong in Grace (2:1)
  - B. Entrust the Message to Reliable Men (2:2)
  - C. Endure Hardship (2:3–7)
    1. Like a Good Soldier (2:3–4)
    2. Like a Disciplined Athlete (2:5)
    3. Like a Hardworking Farmer (2:6–7)
  - D. Die With and Suffer for Jesus Christ (2:8–13)
  - E. Avoid Foolish Arguments and Defend the Gospel in an Irreproachable Manner (2:14–26)
- III. The Approaching Final Upsurge of Evil (3:1–9)
- IV. Endurance in the Truth (3:10–17)
  - A. As Learned From Paul (3:10–14)
  - B. As Learned From the Scriptures (3:15–17)
- V. Preach the Word (4:1–5)
- VI. Paul's Testimony and Instructions (4:6–18)
  - A. Paul's Farewell Testimony (4:6–8)
  - B. Personal Instruction to Timothy (4:9–13)
  - C. A Word of Caution (4:14–15)
  - D. The Assurance of God's Faithfulness (4:16–18)

Conclusion (4:19–22)

Author: Paul

Theme: Steadfast Endurance

Date of Writing: c. A.D. 67

Background

This is Paul's last letter. At the time of writing, the emperor Nero was attempting to stop the spread of the Christian faith in Rome by severely persecuting believers; Paul was again the emperor's prisoner in Rome (1:16). He was suffering deprivation as a common criminal (2:9), deserted by most of his friends (1:15), and aware that his ministry was over and his death near (4:6–8,18; see Introduction to 1 Timothy for a fuller discussion of authorship and background).

Paul writes to Timothy as a "dear son" (1:2) and faithful co-worker (cf. Ro 16:21). His closeness to and reliance on Timothy is seen in naming him a co-sender of six letters, in Timothy's presence with Paul during his first imprisonment (Php 1:1; Col 1:1; Phm 1) and in Paul's two personal letters to him. As Paul faces the imminent prospect of execution, he twice requests Timothy to join him in Rome again (4:9,21). Timothy was still at Ephesus (1:18; 4:19) when Paul wrote him this second letter.

Purpose

Knowing that Timothy was timid and facing hardship, and realizing the prospect of severe persecution from outside the church and false teachers from within, Paul exhorts Timothy to guard the gospel, preach the Word, endure hardship and fulfill his charge.

Survey

In ch. 1 Paul assures Timothy of his continuing love and prayers and urges him to remain uncompromisingly faithful to the gospel, to diligently guard the truth and to follow Paul's example.

In ch. 2 Paul charges his spiritual son to preserve the faith by passing on its truths to reliable men who will teach it to others also (2:2). He admonishes the young pastor to endure hardship like a good soldier (2:3), to serve God diligently and handle the word of truth accurately (2:15), to separate himself from those who depart from apostolic truth (2:18–21), to keep himself pure (2:22) and to labor patiently as a teacher (2:23–26).

In the next chapter Paul informs Timothy that evil and apostasy will increase (3:1–9), but that he must be unwaveringly faithful to his heritage and to the Scriptures (3:10–17).

In the final chapter Paul charges Timothy to preach the Word and discharge all the duties of his ministry (4:1–5). He concludes by updating Timothy on his present circumstances as he faces the end, urging Timothy to come soon (4:6–22).

Special Features

Five major features characterize this letter. (1) It contains Paul's last recorded words before his execution by Nero in Rome almost 35 years after his Damascus road conversion to Christ. (2) It contains one of the clearest statements in the Bible about the divine inspiration and purpose of Scripture (3:16–17): Paul emphasizes that Scripture must be accurately interpreted by ministers of the Word (2:15) and urges the commitment of God's Word to reliable men who can then teach others (2:2). (3) Terse exhortations occur throughout the letter; e.g., "fan into flame the gift of God" (1:6), "do not be ashamed" (1:8), suffer for the gospel (1:8), "keep . . . the pattern of sound teaching" (1:13), "guard the good deposit" (1:14), "be strong in the grace" (2:1), pass on the message (2:2), "endure hardship" (2:3), be diligent in the Word (2:15), "avoid" (2:16), "flee . . . pursue" (2:22), beware of approaching apostasy (3:1–9), "continue" in the truth (3:14), "preach the Word" (4:2), "do the work of an evangelist" (4:5) and "discharge all the duties of your ministry" (4:5). (4) The recurring themes of its many exhortations are to hold fast to the faith (Jesus Christ and the original apostolic gospel), guard it from distortion and corruption, oppose false teachers, and preach the true gospel with unswerving perseverance. (5) Paul's farewell testimony is a moving example of courage and hope in the face of certain martyrdom (4:6–8).

Reading 2 Timothy

In order to read the entire New Testament in one year, the book of 2 Timothy should be read in 4 days, according to the following schedule:
□ 1 □ 2 □ 3 □ 4

NOTES

1 Paul, an apostle[a] of Christ Jesus by
the will of God,[b] according to the
promise of life that is in Christ Jesus,[c]

2To Timothy,[d] my dear son:[e]

Grace, mercy and peace from God the
Father and Christ Jesus our Lord.[f]

Encouragement to Be Faithful

3I thank God,[g] whom I serve, as my
forefathers did, with a clear conscience,[h]
as night and day I constantly remember
you in my prayers.[i] **4**Recalling your
tears,[j] I long to see you,[k] so that I may
be filled with joy. **5**I have been reminded
of your sincere faith,[l] which first lived in
your grandmother Lois and in your mother
Eunice[m] and, I am persuaded, now lives in
you also. **6**For this reason I remind you to
fan into flame the gift of God, which is in
Heb 2:4 you through the laying on of my hands.[n]
7For God did not give us a spirit of timidity,[o]
but a spirit of power,[p] of love and of
self-discipline.

8So do not be ashamed[q] to testify about
our Lord, or ashamed of me his prisoner.[r]
But join with me in suffering for the gospel,[s]
by the power of God, **9**who has
saved[t] us and called[u] us to a holy life—
not because of anything we have done[v]
but because of his own purpose and grace.
This grace was given us in Christ Jesus
before the beginning of time, **10**but it has
now been revealed[w] through the appearing
of our Savior, Christ Jesus,[x] who has
destroyed death[y] and has brought life and
immortality to light through the gospel.
11And of this gospel[z] I was appointed[a] a
herald and an apostle and a teacher.[b]
12That is why I am suffering as I am. Yet
I am not ashamed,[c] because I know whom
I have believed, and am convinced that he
is able to guard[d] what I have entrusted to
him for that day.[e] 1Pe 3:15

13What you heard from me,[f] keep[g] as
the pattern[h] of sound teaching,[i] with
faith and love in Christ Jesus.[j] **14**Guard[k]
the good deposit that was entrusted to
you—guard it with the help of the Holy
Spirit who lives in us.[l]

15You know that everyone in the prov-

1:1 [a]S 1Co 1:1 [b]S 2Co 1:1 [c]Eph 3:6; Tit 1:2; 1Ti 6:19 **1:2** [d]S Ac 16:1 [e]S 1Ti 1:2 [f]S Ro 1:7 **1:3** [g]S Ro 1:8 [h]S Ac 23:1 [i]S Ro 1:10 **1:4** [j]Ac 20:37 [k]2Ti 4:9 **1:5** [l]1Ti 1:5 [m]Ac 16:1; 2Ti 3:15 **1:6** [n]S Ac 6:6; 1Ti 4:14 **1:7** [o]Jer 42:11; Ro 8:15; 1Co 16:10,11; 1Ti 4:12; Heb 2:15 [p]Isa 11:2 **1:8** [q]ver 12,16; Mk 8:38 [r]S Eph 3:1 [s]2Ti 2:3,9; 4:5 **1:9** [t]S Ro 11:14 [u]S Ro 8:28 [v]S Eph 2:9 **1:10** [w]Eph 1:9 [x]S 1Ti 6:14 [y]1Co 15:26,54 **1:11** [z]ver 8 [a]S Ac 9:15 [b]1Ti 2:7 **1:12** [c]ver 8,16; Mk 8:38 [d]ver 14; 1Ti 6:20 [e]ver 18; S 1Co 1:8; 2Ti 4:8 **1:13** [f]2Ti 2:2 [g]S Tit 1:9 [h]Ro 6:17 [i]S 1Ti 1:10 [j]S 1Th 1:3; 1Ti 1:14 **1:14** [k]ver 12 [l]S Ro 8:9

1:4 I LONG TO SEE YOU. Paul is now a prisoner in Rome awaiting death, forsaken by many of his friends (v. 15; 4:16), and longing to see Timothy once more. He begs his co-worker to remain faithful to the truth of the gospel and to hurry to come to him during his last days on earth (4:21).

1:6 FAN INTO FLAME THE GIFT OF GOD. The "gift" (Gk *charisma*) given to Timothy is compared to a fire (cf. 1Th 5:19) that he must fan into flame. The gift was probably a special gift and power from the Holy Spirit to fulfill his ministry. Note that the gifts and power bestowed on us by the Spirit do not automatically remain strong and vital. They must be fueled by God's grace through our prayer, faith, obedience and diligence.

1:12 TO GUARD WHAT I HAVE ENTRUSTED. Paul does not define what he has entrusted to God. It may refer to his apostolic work, teaching, or even his life.

1:13 KEEP AS THE PATTERN OF SOUND TEACHING. The "sound teaching" is the original and fundamental revelation of Christ and the apostles, the doctrines taught to Timothy by Paul. Timothy must hold these truths fast in faith in and love for Jesus Christ, and never depart from them or compromise them even if it means suffering, rejection and disgrace. Today it is popular in some churches to emphasize that experience, not doctrine, is the most important thing. This is firmly contradicted in Paul's Pastoral Letters (cf. 4:3; 1Ti 1:10; 6:3; Tit 1:9,13; 2:1–2,8).

1:14 GUARD IT WITH THE HELP OF THE HOLY SPIRIT. Pastoral leaders must guard and defend the gospel committed to them even in a day when many depart from the NT faith (3:13–15; 4:2–5; 1Ti 4:1). (1) They must defend it against attack, and challenge the church if it is tempted to lay aside the truth. This duty is essential to ensure salvation for themselves and for those under their charge (see 3:14–15; 1Ti 4:16, note; see article on OVERSEERS AND THEIR DUTIES, p. 274). (2) Guarding the deposit of faith must be done with the help of the Holy Spirit. It is he who inspired the infallible truths of Scripture (see 3:16; 2Pe 1:21) and it is he who is the great guide and defender of the truth (Jn 16:13). Defending the ancient faith once for all entrusted to the saints (Jude 3) means standing faithfully alongside the Spirit (Jn 14:17; 15:26–27; 16:13).

1:15 EVERYONE . . . HAS DESERTED ME. This is one of the saddest times in Paul's life. He is in prison in Rome with no hope of freedom. He is undergoing persecution for the sake of the gospel that he loved and for which he was soon to give his life (4:6–7). He is also experiencing such a staggering defection from him and his gospel in the east that he states, "everyone in the province of Asia has deserted me."

(1) Yet even through this terrible trial, Paul maintains his faith in God. He is assured that Christ will guard the true gospel and his ministry (v. 12), that there will always be people like Timothy who will guard and proclaim it (v. 14; 2:2), and that at his death the Lord will bring him safely to his heavenly kingdom (4:6,8,18).

(2) Paul's sorrowful plight will be the experience of many of the faithful in the last days. Those loyal to the NT gospel will suffer similar grief as they see many abandon the true Biblical faith (Mt 24:10; see 1Ti 4:1, note) and as they find their ministry rejected by those who want to be in harmony with the prevailing spirit of this evil age (see 4:3–4, note). As Paul painfully discovered, many will desert the true child

ince of Asia[m] has deserted me,[n] including
Phygelus and Hermogenes.
16 May the Lord show mercy to the
household of Onesiphorus,[o] because he
often refreshed me and was not ashamed[p]
of my chains.[q] 17 On the contrary, when he
was in Rome, he searched hard for me
until he found me. 18 May the Lord grant
that he will find mercy from the Lord on
that day![r] You know very well in how
many ways he helped me[s] in Ephesus.[t]

2 You then, my son,[u] be strong[v] in the
grace that is in Christ Jesus. 2 And the
things you have heard me say[w] in the
presence of many witnesses[x] entrust to
reliable men who will also be qualified to
teach others. 3 Endure hardship with us[y]
like a good soldier[z] of Christ Jesus. 4 No
one serving as a soldier gets involved in
civilian affairs—he wants to please his
commanding officer. 5 Similarly, if anyone
competes as an athlete, he does not receive the victor's crown[a] unless he competes according to the rules. 6 The hard-
working farmer should be the first to receive a share of the crops.[b] 7 Reflect on
what I am saying, for the Lord will give
you insight into all this.
8 Remember Jesus Christ, raised from
the dead,[c] descended from David.[d] This
is my gospel,[e] 9 for which I am suffering[f]
even to the point of being chained[g] like a
criminal. But God's word[h] is not chained.
10 Therefore I endure everything[i] for the
sake of the elect,[j] that they too may obtain the salvation[k] that is in Christ Jesus,
with eternal glory.[l]
11 Here is a trustworthy saying:[m]

If we died with him,
we will also live with him;[n]
12 if we endure,
we will also reign with him.[o]
If we disown him,
he will also disown us;[p]
13 if we are faithless,
he will remain faithful,[q]
for he cannot disown himself.

A Workman Approved by God

14 Keep reminding them of these things.
Warn them before God against quarreling
about words;[r] it is of no value, and only
ruins those who listen. 15 Do your best to
present yourself to God as one approved,
a workman who does not need to be
ashamed and who correctly handles the
word of truth.[s] 16 Avoid godless chatter,[t]
because those who indulge in it will become more and more ungodly. 17 Their
teaching will spread like gangrene.
Among them are Hymenaeus[u] and Phile-
tus, 18 who have wandered away from the
truth. They say that the resurrection has
already taken place,[v] and they destroy
the faith of some.[w] 19 Nevertheless, God's
solid foundation stands firm,[x] sealed with
this inscription: "The Lord knows those
who are his,"[a][y] and, "Everyone who confesses the name of the Lord[z] must turn
away from wickedness."
20 In a large house there are articles not
only of gold and silver, but also of wood
and clay; some are for noble purposes and
some for ignoble.[a] 21 If a man cleanses

1:15 m S Ac 2:9 n 2Ti 4:10,11,16 **1:16** o 2Ti 4:19 p ver 8,12; Mk 8:38 q S Ac 21:33 **1:18** r S ver 12 s Heb 6:10 t S Ac 18:19 **2:1** u S 1Ti 1:2 v S Eph 6:10 **2:2** w 2Ti 1:13 x 1Ti 6:12 **2:3** y ver 9; 2Ti 1:8; 4:5 z S 1Ti 1:18 **2:5** a S 1Co 9:25 **2:6** b 1Co 9:10 **2:8** c S Ac 2:24 d S Mt 1:1 e Ro 2:16; 16:25 **2:9** f S Ac 9:16 g S Ac 21:33 h S Heb 4:12 **2:10** i Col 1:24 j Tit 1:1 k 2Co 1:6 l 2Co 4:17; 1Pe 5:10 **2:11** m S 1Ti 1:15 n Ro 6:2-11 **2:12** o Ro 8:17; 1Pe 4:13 p Mt 10:33 **2:13** q Ro 3:3; S 1Co 1:9 **2:14** r ver 23; 1Ti 1:4; 6:4; Tit 3:9 **2:15** s Eph 1:13; Col 1:5; Jas 1:18 **2:16** t Tit 3:9; 1Ti 6:20 **2:17** u 1Ti 1:20 **2:18** v 2Th 2:2 w 1Ti 1:19; 6:21 **2:19** x Isa 28:16 y Ex 33:12; Nu 16:5; Jn 10:14; 1Co 8:3; Gal 4:9 z 1Co 1:2 **2:20** a Ro 9:21

a *19* Num. 16:5 (see Septuagint)

---

of God who remains loyal to the NT gospel.

2:2 ENTRUST TO RELIABLE MEN. For comments on the church's responsibility in instructing Christians in the faith, see article on BIBLE TRAINING FOR CHRISTIANS, p. 470.

2:3 ENDURE HARDSHIP. Ministers of the gospel who remain loyal to Christ and the gospel will be called on to endure hardship (cf. 1:8; 2:9; 2Co 11:23–29). Like soldiers, they must be willing to undergo difficulties and suffering and to wage spiritual warfare in wholehearted devotion to their Lord (Eph 6:10–18); like athletes, they must be willing to sacrifice and live lives of strict discipline (v. 5); like farmers, they must be committed to hard work and long hours (v. 6).

2:12 IF WE ENDURE. Those who "endure" (Gk *hupomenō*) and remain steadfast in the faith to the end will live (cf. v. 11; Mt 10:22; 24:13) and reign with Christ (4:18; Rev 20:4). Christ will disown on the day of judgment those who do not endure and who disown him either in word or deed (cf. Mt 10:33; 25:1–12; see article on PERSONAL APOSTASY, p. 492).

2:13 HE WILL REMAIN FAITHFUL. Christ will most certainly carry out both his promises to us (cf. Mt 10:32) and his warnings (cf. Mt 10:33). Divine faithfulness is a comfort for those who remain loyal (1Th 5:24; 2Th 3:3; Heb 10:23) and a solemn warning for those who depart from the faith. God must remain faithful to his Word (2Sa 7:28; Jer 10:10; Tit 1:2; Rev 3:7).

2:19 FOUNDATION STANDS FIRM. Despite the fact that many may stray from the truth (Mt 24:11) and false teachers may make inroads into the church (vv. 14–18), God's purpose for his faithful followers cannot be thwarted. "God's solid foundation," i.e., the true church, cannot be destroyed. On this foundation two truths are inscribed, referring to those who belong to Christ's church. (1) God unerringly knows those who remain true to his original gospel and those who compromise its truths (cf. Ge 18:19; Ex 33:12,17; Nu 16:5; 1Co 8:1–3), and (2) those who really belong to God turn away from wickedness and false teaching (cf. 1Ti 6:3–5,11).

2:21 CLEANSES HIMSELF. In God's external or visible church on earth there are many "articles." There are articles "for noble purposes," i.e., faithful

BIBLE TRAINING FOR CHRISTIANS

***2Ti 2:2** "And the things you have heard me say in the presence of many witnesses, entrust to reliable men who will also be qualified to teach others."*

The church has the responsibility to safeguard the true and original apostolic doctrine found in Scripture and commit it to others without compromise or corruption. This implies the necessity of Biblical instruction within the church.

(1) The Bible gives the following reasons for Biblical or theological training, whether in home, church or school:

(a) to entrust the gospel of Christ to faithful believers in order that they may know (2Ti 3:15), guard (2Ti 1:14, note), and teach the true Biblical faith (1Ti 4:6,11; 2Ti 2:2) and righteous standards (see Ro 6:17, note; 1Ti 6:3);

(b) to show students the vital necessity to "contend for the faith that was once for all entrusted to the saints" (Jude 3, note), and to give them the means by which to defend it against all false theologies (see Ac 20:31, note; Gal 1:9, note; 1Ti 4:1, note; 6:3–4; Tit 1:9; see article on FALSE TEACHERS, p. 98);

(c) to lead students into continual growth in character through "godly teaching" (1Ti 6:3; cf. Jos 1:8; Ps 1:2–3; 119:97–100; Mt 28:20; Jn 17:14–18; 1Th 4:1; 1Ti 1:5, note; 4:7,16; 2Ti 3:16);

(d) to equip students to strengthen and bring to maturity other believers, so that together they may reflect Christ's image in the home, the local church and the body of Christ (Eph 4:11–16);

(e) to bring students to a deeper understanding and experience of God's kingdom on earth and its conflict against Satan's power (Eph 6:10–18; see article on THE KINGDOM OF GOD, p. 28);

(f) to motivate students, through the eternal truths of the gospel, to be wholeheartedly committed to evangelizing the lost and preaching the gospel to all nations in the power of the Holy Spirit (Mt 28:18–20; Mk 16:15–20);

(g) to deepen students' experience of Christ's love, personal fellowship and gift of the Spirit (Jn 17:3,21,26; Eph 3:18–19) by urging them to follow the leading of the indwelling Holy Spirit (Ro 8:14), by bringing them into the baptism in the Holy Spirit (cf. Ac 2:4; see article on BAPTISM IN THE HOLY SPIRIT, p. 228), and by teaching them to pray (Mt 6:9, note), fast (Mt 6:16, note) and worship, as they long for the glorious appearing of Jesus Christ with the spiritual intensity of NT saints (2Ti 4:8; Tit 2:13).

(2) It is obvious from these purposes of Biblical training that instruction must be done only by those who are fervently loyal to Scripture as God's fully inspired Word (2Ti 1:13–14; see article on THE INSPIRATION AND AUTHORITY OF SCRIPTURE, p. 474) and to the Holy Spirit and his ministry of truth, righteousness and power (1:14).

(3) Note that true Biblical training emphasizes true righteousness (i.e., knowing, being *and* doing) rather than mere apprehension of Biblical facts or truths. The great doctrines revealed in Scripture are redemptive truths, not academic ones. As issues involving life or death, they demand a personal response and decision from both teacher and student (Jas 2:17; see Php 1:9, note).

himself from the latter, he will be an instrument for noble purposes, made holy,
useful to the Master and prepared to do
any good work.[b]

22Flee the evil desires of youth, and
pursue righteousness, faith, love[c] and
peace, along with those who call on the
Lord[d] out of a pure heart.[e] **23**Don't have
anything to do with foolish and stupid arguments, because you know they produce
quarrels.[f] **24**And the Lord's servant must
not quarrel; instead, he must be kind to
everyone, able to teach, not resentful.[g]
25Those who oppose him he must gently
instruct, in the hope that God will grant
them repentance leading them to a knowledge of the truth,[h] **26**and that they will
come to their senses and escape from the
trap of the devil,[i] who has taken them
captive to do his will.

2:21 [b]2Co 9:8; Eph 2:10; 2Ti 3:17 **2:22** [c]1Ti 1:14; 6:11 [d]S Ac 2:21 [e]1Ti 1:5 **2:23** [f]S ver 14 **2:24** [g]1Ti 3:2,3 **2:25** [h]S 1Ti 2:4 **2:26** [i]1Ti 3:7

3:1 [j]1Ti 4:1; 2Pe 3:3 **3:2** [k]S 1Ti 3:3 [l]Ro 1:30 [m]2Pe 2:10-12 [n]Ro 1:30 **3:4** [o]Ps 25:3 [p]1Ti 3:6; 6:4 **3:5** [q]S 1Ti 2:2 [r]S Ro 16:17 **3:6** [s]Jude 4 **3:7** [t]S 1Ti 2:4 **3:8** [u]Ex 7:11 [v]Ac 13:8

Godlessness in the Last Days

3 But mark this: There will be terrible
times in the last days.[j] **2**People will
be lovers of themselves, lovers of money,[k]
boastful, proud,[l] abusive,[m] disobedient to
their parents,[n] ungrateful, unholy, **3**without love, unforgiving, slanderous, without
self-control, brutal, not lovers of the good,
4treacherous,[o] rash, conceited,[p] lovers of
pleasure rather than lovers of God—
5having a form of godliness[q] but denying
its power. Have nothing to do with them.[r]
6They are the kind who worm their
ways[s] into homes and gain control over
weak-willed women, who are loaded down
with sins and are swayed by all kinds of
evil desires, **7**always learning but never
able to acknowledge the truth.[t] **8**Just as
Jannes and Jambres opposed Moses,[u] so
also these men oppose[v] the truth—men

---

believers who separate from evil and hold firmly to the true gospel according to Biblical revelation, and articles for "ignoble" purposes, i.e., false believers who stray from the truth (vv. 14–19). Those among the faithful who desire to be useful to the Master must keep themselves separate from all religions and professed believers advocating doctrines contrary to Scripture (v. 19). Any contact with those who teach unbiblical doctrine may be made only for the purpose of correction in love, in order that they might repent and turn to the truth (v. 25).

3:1 TERRIBLE TIMES IN THE LAST DAYS. The last days include the entire Christian era. Yet Paul prophesies through the Holy Spirit (cf. 1Ti 4:1) that things will become worse as the end approaches (cf. 2Pe 3:3; 1Jn 2:18; Jude 17–18). (1) The last days will be marked by ever-increasing wickedness in the world, a collapse of moral standards, and the multiplying of false believers and churches within God's kingdom (Mt 24:11–12; see 1Ti 4:1, note; see article on THE AGE OF THE ANTICHRIST, p. 447). These times will be especially grievous and trying for God's true servants.

(2) Paul issues this warning in order to fortify those ministers and their churches who remain loyal to Christ and his revelation. The full blessing of salvation in Christ and the mighty outpouring of the Holy Spirit will still be available for those who remain true to NT faith and practice. The church in apostasy only means greater grace and power for those who hold fast to the original faith entrusted to the saints (Ac 4:33; Ro 5:20; Jude 3).

3:2 LOVERS OF THEMSELVES. Paul gives a list of sins that all have their root in self-love (vv. 2–4). Today some teach that a lack of love for oneself is the root of sin. Apostolic revelation teaches the opposite.

3:3 WITHOUT LOVE. In the last days believers must be prepared to face an overwhelming deluge of ungodliness. (1) The apostle prophesies that Satan will bring great destruction on the family. Children will be "disobedient to their parents" (v. 2), and men and women will be "without love" (Gk *astorgoi*). This can be translated "without family affection" and refers to a lack of the feelings of natural tenderness and love, as demonstrated by a mother who rejects her children or kills her baby, a father who abandons his family, or children who neglect to care for their aging parents (see Lk 1:17, note).

(2) Men and women will become lovers of money and pleasure and will pursue their own selfish desires (v. 2). Parenthood, with its demands for sacrificial love and nurture, will no longer be considered a worthy or dignified task (vv. 2–4). Loving parents will be replaced more and more by those who are selfish and brutal and who abandon their children (cf. Ps 113:9; 127:3–5; Pr 17:6; Tit 2:4–5; see 2Ti 4:3–4, note).

(3) If Christian parents are to save their families in the difficult times of the last days, they must shield them against the corrupt values of the society in which they live (Jn 21:15–17; Ac 20:28–30), separate them from the world's ways and refuse to let the ungodly influence their children (Ac 2:40; Ro 12:1–2; see article on SPIRITUAL SEPARATION FOR BELIEVERS, p. 371). They must accept God's plan for the family (see Eph 5:21–25, notes; see article on PARENTS AND CHILDREN, p. 432) and not live as the ungodly do (Lev 18:3–5; Eph 4:17). They and their families must indeed become strangers and aliens on earth (Heb 11:13–16).

3:5 HAVING A FORM OF GODLINESS. Paul refers to those who profess to be Christians and appear to be religious, but who do not manifest God's power that can save them from sin, selfishness and immorality. Such people tolerate immorality within their churches and teach that a person may practice the sins listed in vv. 2–4 and yet inherit salvation and God's kingdom (cf. vv. 5–9; 4:3–4; 2Pe 2:12–19; see 1Co 6:9, note).

3:8 OPPOSE THE TRUTH. False teachers in the church can often be identified by their opposition or indifference to the essential truths of the gospel (see 1Ti 4:1, note).

of depraved minds,[w] who, as far as the
faith is concerned, are rejected. **9**But they
will not get very far because, as in the
case of those men,[x] their folly will be
clear to everyone.

Paul's Charge to Timothy

10You, however, know all about my
teaching,[y] my way of life, my purpose,
faith, patience, love, endurance, **11**persecutions, sufferings—what kinds of things
happened to me in Antioch,[z] Iconium[a]
and Lystra,[b] the persecutions I endured.[c]
Yet the Lord rescued[d] me from all of
them.[e] **12**In fact, everyone who wants to
live a godly life in Christ Jesus will be
persecuted,[f] **13**while evil men and impostors will go from bad to worse,[g] deceiving
and being deceived.[h] **14**But as for you,
continue in what you have learned and
have become convinced of, because you
know those from whom you learned it,[i]
15and how from infancy[j] you have known
the holy Scriptures,[k] which are able to
make you wise[l] for salvation through
faith in Christ Jesus. **16**All Scripture is
God-breathed[m] and is useful for teaching,[n] rebuking, correcting and training in
righteousness,[o] **17**so that the man of
God[p] may be thoroughly equipped for every good work.[q]

4 In the presence of God and of Christ
Jesus, who will judge the living and
the dead,[r] and in view of his appearing[s]
and his kingdom, I give you this charge:[t]
2Preach[u] the Word;[v] be prepared in season and out of season; correct, rebuke[w]
and encourage[x]—with great patience and
careful instruction. **3**For the time will
come when men will not put up with sound
doctrine.[y] Instead, to suit their own desires, they will gather around them a
great number of teachers to say what their
itching ears want to hear.[z] **4**They will
turn their ears away from the truth and
turn aside to myths.[a] **5**But you, keep your
head in all situations, endure hardship,[b]
do the work of an evangelist,[c] discharge
all the duties of your ministry.

6For I am already being poured out like
a drink offering,[d] and the time has come

3:8 [w]1Ti 6:5
3:9 [x]Ex 7:12; 8:18; 9:11
3:10 [y]1Ti 4:6
3:11 [z]Ac 13:14, 50 [a]S Ac 13:51 [b]Ac 14:6 [c]2Co 11:23-27 [d]S Ro 15:31 [e]Ps 34:19
3:12 [f]Jn 15:20; S Ac 14:22
3:13 [g]2Ti 2:16 [h]S Mk 13:5
3:14 [i]2Ti 1:13
3:15 [j]2Ti 1:5 [k]Jn 5:39 [l]Dt 4:6; Ps 119:98,99
3:16 [m]2Pe 1:20, 21 [n]S Ro 4:23,24 [o]Dt 29:29
3:17 [p]1Ti 6:11 [q]2Ti 2:21
4:1 [r]S Ac 10:42 [s]ver 8; S 1Ti 6:14 [t]1Ti 5:21; 6:13
4:2 [u]1Ti 4:13 [v]Gal 6:6 [w]1Ti 5:20; Tit 1:13; 2:15 [x]Tit 2:15
4:3 [y]S 1Ti 1:10 [z]Isa 30:10
4:4 [a]S 1Ti 1:4
4:5 [b]2Ti 1:8; 2:3, 9 [c]Ac 21:8; Eph 4:11
4:6 [d]Nu 15:1-12; 28:7,24; Php 2:17

3:12 LIVE A GODLY LIFE . . . BE PERSECUTED. Persecution in one form or another is inevitable for those who want to live a godly life in Christ Jesus (Mt 5:10–12; 10:22; Ac 14:22; Php 1:29; 1Pe 4:12). Loyalty to Christ, his truth and his righteous standards involves a constant determination not to compromise our faith or give in to the deluge of voices calling us to conform to the world and to lay aside Scriptural truth. Because of their godly standards, the faithful will be deprived of privilege and will be ridiculed; they will experience grief at seeing godliness rejected by the majority. We should all ask ourselves: have I suffered persecution because of my commitment to live in a godly manner? Or is my lack of suffering a sign that I have not stood firmly for the righteousness for which Christ died?

3:16–17 ALL SCRIPTURE IS GOD-BREATHED. A discussion of the inspiration and authority of Scripture can be found in the article THE INSPIRATION AND AUTHORITY OF SCRIPTURE, p. 474.

4:3–4 WILL NOT PUT UP WITH SOUND DOCTRINE. Throughout the history of the church some have always refused to love sound doctrine; yet as the end draws near, the situation will grow worse (cf. 3:1–5; 1Ti 4:1). (1) "Men will not put up with sound doctrine" (v. 3). Many will profess to be Christians, gather at churches, appear to revere God, but will not tolerate the original NT apostolic faith or the Biblical demand to separate from unrighteousness (3:5; cf. Ro 1:16; see article on SPIRITUAL SEPARATION FOR BELIEVERS, p. 371).

(2) "They will turn their ears away from the truth" (v. 4). Sound Biblical preaching from a man of God will no longer be tolerated by many within the churches. Those who turn from the truth will want preaching that demands less than the true gospel (cf. 2:18; 3:7–8; 1Ti 6:5; Tit 1:14). They will not accept God's Word when it speaks of repentance, sin, damnation, and the necessity of holiness and separation from the world (cf. 3:15–17; Jer 5:31; Eze 33:32).

(3) "They will gather around them a great number of teachers to say what their itching ears want to hear" (v. 3). These professing believers will not seek pastors according to the standards of God's Word (cf. 1:13–14; 1Ti 3:1–10) but will seek those who conform to their own self-seeking and worldly desires. They will choose preachers with gifts of oratory, the ability to entertain, and messages that reassure them that they can remain a Christian while living according to the sinful nature (cf. Ro 8:4–13; 2Pe 2).

(4) The Holy Spirit warns all who remain faithful to God and submit to his Word to expect persecution and suffering because of righteousness (3:10–12; Mt 5:10–12). Furthermore, they must separate from people, churches and institutions who deny God's power in salvation and who preach a compromising gospel (3:5; see Gal 1:9, note; 1Ti 4:1–2; 2Pe 2:1; Jude 3; Rev 2:24). We must ever be loyal to the NT gospel and to God's faithful ministers who proclaim it. Doing this, we can be assured of intimate fellowship with Christ (Rev 3:20–22) and times of refreshing from the Lord (Ac 3:19–20).

4:4 THE TRUTH. God's written Word must be our ultimate guide to truth and practice. (1) We must use God's Word, given by the Holy Spirit, as our full and sufficient guide by which to judge what we believe and do. (2) The tendency within some churches to base doctrine, practice or new truth on subjective experiences, miracles, success, man-centered goals or man-made theories without solid Scriptural authentication will be one of Satan's chief means of deception in the apostasy of the last days (see Mt 24:5,11, notes; 2Th 2:11, note; see article on THE GREAT TRIBULATION, p. 52).

for my departure.[e] 7I have fought the
good fight,[f] I have finished the race,[g] I
have kept the faith. 8Now there is in store
for me[h] the crown of righteousness,[i]
which the Lord, the righteous Judge, will
award to me on that day[j]—and not only
to me, but also to all who have longed for
his appearing.[k]

Personal Remarks

9Do your best to come to me quickly,[l]
10for Demas,[m] because he loved this
world,[n] has deserted me and has gone to
Thessalonica.[o] Crescens has gone to Galatia,[p] and Titus[q] to Dalmatia. 11Only
Luke[r] is with me.[s] Get Mark[t] and bring
him with you, because he is helpful to me
in my ministry. 12I sent Tychicus[u] to Ephesus.[v] 13When you come, bring the cloak
that I left with Carpus at Troas,[w] and my
scrolls, especially the parchments.

14Alexander[x] the metalworker did me
a great deal of harm. The Lord will repay
him for what he has done.[y] 15You too
should be on your guard against him, because he strongly opposed our message.

16At my first defense, no one came to
my support, but everyone deserted me.
May it not be held against them.[z] 17But
the Lord stood at my side[a] and gave me
strength,[b] so that through me the message might be fully proclaimed and all the
Gentiles might hear it.[c] And I was delivered from the lion's mouth.[d] 18The Lord
will rescue me from every evil attack[e] and
will bring me safely to his heavenly kingdom.[f] To him be glory for ever and ever.
Amen.[g]

Final Greetings

19Greet Priscilla[b] and Aquila[h] and the
household of Onesiphorus.[i] 20Erastus[j]
stayed in Corinth, and I left Trophimus[k]
sick in Miletus.[l] 21Do your best to get
here before winter.[m] Eubulus greets you,
and so do Pudens, Linus, Claudia and all
the brothers.

22The Lord be with your spirit.[n] Grace
be with you.[o]

4:6 [e] Php 1:23
4:7 [f] S 1Ti 1:18 [g] S 1Co 9:24; Ac 20:24
4:8 [h] Col 1:5; 1Pe 1:4 [i] S 1Co 9:25 [j] S 2Ti 1:12 [k] S 1Ti 6:14
4:9 [l] ver 21; Tit 3:12
4:10 [m] Col 4:14; Phm 24 [n] 1Jn 2:15 [o] S Ac 17:1 [p] S Ac 16:6 [q] S 2Co 2:13
4:11 [r] Col 4:14; Phm 24 [s] 2Ti 1:15 [t] S Ac 12:12
4:12 [u] S Ac 20:4 [v] S Ac 18:19
4:13 [w] S Ac 16:8
4:14 [x] Ac 19:33; 1Ti 1:20 [y] Ps 28:4; 109:20; Ro 2:6; 12:19
4:16 [z] Ac 7:60
4:17 [a] Ac 23:11 [b] S Php 4:13 [c] S Ac 9:15 [d] 1Sa 17:37; Ps 22:21; Da 6:22; 1Co 15:32
4:18 [e] Ps 121:7; 2Pe 2:9 [f] ver 1 [g] S Ro 11:36
4:19 [h] S Ac 18:2 [i] 2Ti 1:16
4:20 [j] Ac 19:22 [k] Ac 20:4; 21:29 [l] Ac 20:15,17
4:21 [m] ver 9; Tit 3:12
4:22 [n] S Gal 6:18 [o] S Col 4:18

b 19 Greek *Prisca*, a variant of *Priscilla*

4:7 FOUGHT THE GOOD FIGHT. In reviewing his life for God, Paul knows death is imminent (v. 6) and describes his Christian life in the following terms. (1) He considers the Christian life as a "good fight," the only fight worth fighting. He fought against Satan (Eph 6:12), Jewish and pagan vices (3:1–5; Ro 1:21–32; Gal 5:19–21), Judaism (Ac 14:19; 20:19; Gal 5:1–6), antinomianism and immorality in the church (3:5; 4:3; Ro 6; 1Co 5:1; 6:9–10; 2Co 12:20–21), false teachers (vv. 3–5; Ac 20:28–31; Ro 16:17–18), the distortion of the gospel (Gal 1:6–12), worldliness (Ro 12:2) and sin (Ro 6; 8:13; 1Co 9:24–27). (2) He has finished his race amid trials and temptations and has remained faithful to his Lord and Savior throughout his life (cf. 2:12; Heb 10:23; 11; 12:1–2). (3) He has kept the faith in times of severe testing, great discouragement and much trouble, both when forsaken by friends and opposed by false teachers. He never compromised the original truth of the gospel (1:13–14; 2:2; 3:14–16; 1Ti 6:12).

4:8 CROWN OF RIGHTEOUSNESS. Because Paul remained faithful to his Lord and the gospel entrusted to him, the Spirit witnessed to him that God's loving approval and the "crown of righteousness" was awaiting him in heaven. God has reserved in heaven rewards for all who keep the faith in righteousness (cf. Mt 19:27–29; 2Co 5:10).

4:8 ALL WHO HAVE LONGED FOR HIS APPEARING. The NT Christians possessed an intense longing for the Lord's return to take them from earth to be with him forever (see 1Th 4:13–18; cf. Php 3:20–21; Tit 2:13; see article on THE RAPTURE, p. 440). A distinctive mark of God's people is that they do not feel at home in this world and are looking forward to their heavenly home (Heb 11:13–16).

4:17 THE LORD STOOD AT MY SIDE. Because of the severe persecution against Christians in Rome, no one dared identify himself or herself with the faithful and outspoken apostle (v. 16). Paul was deeply disappointed and felt deserted. But in such times he experienced the Lord's special nearness as he stood by him and strengthened him (cf. Ac 23:11; 27:23; Ro 4:20; 2Co 1:3–5; Eph 6:10; Php 4:13).

4:22 GRACE BE WITH YOU. These are the last words of Paul recorded in Scripture, written while awaiting martyrdom in a Roman prison. From the world's perspective, Paul's life was about to end in tragic failure. (1) For thirty years he had given up everything for Christ; he had gained little but persecution and hatred from his own countrymen. His preaching had resulted in the establishment of a good number of churches, yet many of these churches were falling away from loyalty to him and from the apostolic faith (1:15). And now in prison, with all his loyal friends gone except for Luke (vv. 11,16), he awaits death. These circumstances point to apparent failure with regard to his Gentile mission. Yet, the battle-scarred apostle of the cross shows no regrets as he lays down his life for his Lord.

(2) Now, 2,000 years later, Paul's influence surpasses that of all God's servants in the kingdom. His writings are a crucial part of Scripture and have led countless numbers to faith in Christ. Let no one who has remained faithful to Jesus Christ, though he or she seems to have accomplished little for God, think that death terminates the results. God takes our faithful efforts and multiplies them far beyond what we would have imagined or ever hoped for. Even our apparent failure may be seed whose harvest will be reaped bountifully by others (Jn 4:37–38).

THE INSPIRATION AND AUTHORITY OF SCRIPTURE

2Ti 3:16–17 "All Scripture is God-breathed and is useful for teaching, rebuking, correcting and training in righteousness, so that the man of God may be thoroughly equipped for every good work."

"Scripture" as used in 2Ti 3:16 refers primarily to the OT writings (3:15). There is indication, however, that at about the time Paul wrote 2 Timothy some NT writings were already viewed as inspired and authoritative Scripture (1Ti 5:18, which quotes Lk 10:7; 2Pe 3:15–16). For us today, Scripture refers to the authoritative writings of both the OT and NT, i.e., "the Bible." They are God's original message to humanity and the only infallible witness to God's saving activity for all people.

(1) Paul affirms that all Scripture is "God-breathed" (Gk *theopneustos*, from two Greek words: *theos*, meaning "God," and *pneō*, meaning "to breathe). Scripture is the very life and Word of God. Down to the very words of the original manuscripts, the Bible is without error, absolutely true, trustworthy and infallible. This is true not only when it speaks of salvation, ethical values and morality, but it is also without error on all subjects about which it speaks, including history and the cosmos (cf. 2Pe 1:20–21; note also the attitude of the psalmist toward Scripture in Ps 119).

(2) Jesus Christ himself taught that Scripture is God's inspired Word to even the smallest detail (Mt 5:18). He also affirmed that all he said he received from the Father and is true (Jn 5:19,30–31; 7:16; 8:26). He further spoke of revelation yet to come (i.e., the truth revealed in the NT) from the Holy Spirit through the apostles (Jn 16:13; cf. 14:16–17; 15:26–27).

(3) To deny the full inspiration of holy Scripture, therefore, is to set aside the fundamental witness of Jesus Christ (Mt 5:18; 15:3–6; Lk 16:7; 24:25–27,44–45; Jn 10:35), the Holy Spirit (Jn 15:26; 16:13; 1Co 2:12–13; 1Ti 4:1) and the apostles (2Ti 3:16; 2Pe 1:20–21). Furthermore, to limit or disregard its inerrancy is to impair its divine authority.

(4) In his work of inspiration by his Spirit, God, while not violating the personality of the writers, moved on them in such a way that they wrote without error (2Ti 3:16; 2Pe 1:20–21; see 1Co 2:12–13, notes).

(5) The inspired Word of God is the expression of God's wisdom and character and is therefore able to give wisdom and spiritual life through faith in Christ (Mt 4:4; Jn 6:63; 2Ti 3:15; 1Pe 2:2).

(6) The Bible is God's infallible, true witness to his saving activity for humanity in Christ Jesus. For this reason Scripture is incomparable, forever finished and uniquely binding. No human words or declarations of religious institutions are equal to its authority.

(7) All doctrines, commentaries, interpretations, explanations and traditions must be judged and legitimized by the words and message in Scripture.

(8) God's Word must be received, believed and obeyed as the final authority in all things pertaining to life and godliness (Mt 5:17–19; Jn 14:21; 15:10; 2Ti 3:15–16). It must be used in the church as the final authority in all matters for teaching, rebuking, correcting and training in righteous living (2Ti 3:16–17). One cannot submit to Christ's lordship without submitting to God and his Word as the ultimate authority (Jn 8:31–32,37).

(9) The Bible can only be understood when we are in a right relation to the Holy Spirit. It is he who opens our minds to understand its meaning and gives us the inward witness of its authority (see 1Co 2:12, note; see article on THREE KINDS OF PEOPLE, p. 334).

(10) We must use God's inspired Word to conquer the power of sin, Satan and the world in our lives (Mt 4:4; Eph 6:12,17; Jas 1:21).

(11) Scripture must be loved, treasured and guarded by all church members who see it as God's only truth for a lost and dying world. We must safeguard its doctrines by faithfully adhering to its teaching, proclaiming its saving message, entrusting it to reliable people, and defending it against all who would distort or destroy its eternal truths (see Php 1:16; 2Ti 1:13–14, notes; 2:2; Jude 3).

(12) Finally, we should note that inerrant inspiration applies only to the original writing of the Biblical books. Thus, whenever one finds in Scripture something that appears to be in error, rather than assuming that the writer made a mistake, one should remember that three possibilities exist with regard to any apparent problem: (a) the existing copies of the original manuscript may not be totally accurate; (b) the present-day translation of the Hebrew or Greek Biblical text may be faulty; or (c) one's understanding or interpretation of the Biblical text may be inadequate or incorrect.

TITUS

Outline

Introduction (1:1–4)

I. Instruction About Appointing Elders (1:5–9)
   A. Appoint Elders in Every Town (1:5)
   B. Various Qualifications for Elders (1:6–9)
      1. Personal
         a. Blameless (1:6)
         b. A Trustworthy Steward (1:7)
         c. Not Overbearing (1:7)
         d. Not Quick-tempered (1:7)
         e. Not Given to Drunkenness (1:7)
         f. Not Violent (1:7)
         g. Not Pursuing Dishonest Gain (1:7)
         h. Hospitable (1:8)
         i. Loves What Is Good (1:8)
         j. Self-controlled (1:8)
         k. Upright (1:8)
         l. Devout/Holy (1:8)
         m. Holding Firmly to the Trustworthy Message (1:9)
         n. Able to Encourage From the Word (1:9)
         o. Able to Refute Those Who Oppose the Word (1:9)
      2. Family
         a. Husband of One Wife (1:6)
         b. Has Believing Children (1:6)
         c. His Children Are Not Wild or Disobedient (1:6)

II. Instruction Concerning False Teachers (1:10–16)
   A. Their Character (1:10)
   B. Their Conduct (1:11–12)
   C. Their Correction (1:13–16)

III. Instruction Concerning Various Groups in the Churches (2:1–15)
   A. The Scope of the Instruction (2:1–10)
   B. The Foundation for the Instruction (2:11–14)
   C. The Responsibility of Titus (2:15)

IV. Exhortations Concerning Good Works (3:1–11)
   A. Our Conduct Toward Others (3:1–2)
   B. God's Mercy Toward Us (3:3–7)
   C. Discerning What Is Profitable and Unprofitable (3:8–11)

Conclusion (3:12–15)

Author: Paul

Theme: Sound Doctrine and Good Works

Date of Writing: c. A.D. 65/66

Background

Like 1 and 2 Timothy, Titus is a personal letter from Paul to one of his younger assistants. It is called a "Pastoral Letter" because it deals with matters relating to church order and ministry. Titus, a Gentile convert (Gal 2:3), became a close companion of Paul in the apostolic ministry. Although not mentioned by name in Acts (perhaps because he was Luke's brother), Titus's closeness to the apostle Paul is indicated by (1) the thirteen references to Titus in Paul's letters,

(2) his being one of Paul's converts and sons (1:4) in the ministry (like Timothy) and a trustworthy co-worker (2Co 8:23), (3) his serving as Paul's representative on at least one important mission to Corinth during Paul's third missionary journey (2Co 2:12–13; 7:6–15; 8:6,16–24), and (4) his working as a co-laborer with Paul at Crete (1:5).

Paul and Titus worked together briefly on the island of Crete (southwest of Asia Minor in the Mediterranean Sea) between Paul's first and second Roman imprisonments (see Introduction to 1 Timothy). Paul commissioned Titus to continue working with the Cretans (1:5) while he traveled on to Macedonia (cf. 1Ti 1:3). Sometime thereafter Paul wrote this letter to Titus, instructing him to complete the task that the two of them had begun. It is probable that Paul sent the letter with Zenas and Apollos who were traveling through Crete (3:13).

In this letter Paul conveys his plans to send either Artemas or Tychicus soon to replace Titus, at which time Titus was to join Paul at Nicopolis (Greece), where the apostle planned to remain during the winter (3:12). We know that this did occur, since Paul later reassigned Titus to Dalmatia (modern Yugoslavia) (2Ti 4:10).

Purpose

Paul wrote primarily to instruct Titus in his task of (1) setting in order what Paul had left unfinished in the churches of Crete, including the appointment of elders (1:5); (2) helping the churches grow in faith, in knowledge of the truth and in godly living (1:1); (3) silencing false teachers (1:11); and (4) coming to Paul after Titus is relieved by Artemas or Tychicus (3:12).

Survey

Paul discusses four main issues in this letter. (1) He instructs Titus about the character and spiritual qualifications necessary for all those who are to be selected as elders (or overseers) in the church. Elders must be godly men of proven character who have succeeded as leaders in their own homes (1:5–9). (2) Paul directs Titus to teach sound doctrine and to rebuke and silence false teachers (1:10—2:1). In the course of the letter, Paul gives two succinct summaries of sound doctrine (2:11–14; 3:4–7). (3) Paul delineates for Titus (cf. 1Ti 5:1—6:2) the proper role of older men (2:1–2), older women (2:3–4), young women (2:4–5), young men (2:6–8) and slaves (2:9–10). (4) Finally, Paul emphasizes that good works and a righteous life are the necessary fruit of genuine faith (1:16; 2:7,14; 3:1,8,14; cf. Jas 2:14–26).

Special Features

Three major features characterize this letter. (1) It contains two short classic summaries of the true nature of salvation in Christ Jesus (2:11–14; 3:4–7). (2) It emphasizes that the church and its ministry must be built on strong spiritual, theological and ethical foundations. (3) It contains one of two NT lists enumerating the required qualifications for leadership in the church's ministry (1:5–9; cf. 1Ti 3:1–13).

Reading Titus

In order to read the entire New Testament in one year, the book of Titus should be read in 2 days, according to the following schedule:
☐ 1–2 ☐ 3

NOTES

1 Paul, a servant of God[a] and an apostle[b] of Jesus Christ for the faith of
God's elect and the knowledge of the
truth[c] that leads to godliness[d]— **2**a faith
and knowledge resting on the hope of
eternal life,[e] which God, who does not
lie,[f] promised before the beginning of
time,[g] **3**and at his appointed season[h] he
brought his word to light[i] through the
preaching entrusted to me[j] by the command of God[k] our Savior,[l]

4To Titus,[m] my true son[n] in our common faith:

Grace and peace from God the Father
and Christ Jesus our Savior.[o]

Titus' Task on Crete

1:6–8Ref — 1Ti 3:2–4

5The reason I left you in Crete[p] was
that you might straighten out what was
left unfinished and appoint[a] elders[q] in every town, as I directed you. **6**An elder
must be blameless,[r] the husband of but
one wife, a man whose children believe
and are not open to the charge of being
wild and disobedient. **7**Since an overseer[b][s] is entrusted with God's work,[t] he
must be blameless—not overbearing, not
quick-tempered, not given to drunkenness, not violent, not pursuing dishonest
gain.[u] **8**Rather he must be hospitable,[v]
one who loves what is good,[w] who is self-
controlled,[x] upright, holy and disciplined.
9He must hold firmly[y] to the trustworthy
message as it has been taught, so that he
can encourage others by sound doctrine[z]
and refute those who oppose it.

10For there are many rebellious people,
mere talkers[a] and deceivers, especially
those of the circumcision group.[b] **11**They
must be silenced, because they are ruining whole households[c] by teaching things
they ought not to teach—and that for the
sake of dishonest gain. **12**Even one of
their own prophets[d] has said, "Cretans[e]
are always liars, evil brutes, lazy gluttons." **13**This testimony is true. Therefore,
rebuke[f] them sharply, so that they will be
sound in the faith[g] **14**and will pay no attention to Jewish myths[h] or to the commands[i] of those who reject the truth.[j]
15To the pure, all things are pure,[k] but to
those who are corrupted and do not be-

1:1 [a]Ro 1:1; Jas 1:1 [b]S 1Co 1:1 [c]S 1Ti 2:4 [d]S 1Ti 2:2
1:2 [e]Tit 3:7; 2Ti 1:1 [f]Nu 23:19; Heb 6:18 [g]2Ti 1:9
1:3 [h]1Ti 2:6; 6:15 [i]2Ti 1:10 [j]S 1Ti 1:11 [k]S 2Co 1:1; 1Ti 1:1 [l]S Lk 1:47
1:4 [m]S 2Co 2:13 [n]S 1Ti 1:2 [o]S Ro 1:7
1:5 [p]Ac 27:7 [q]S Ac 11:30
1:6 [r]S 1Th 3:13; 1Ti 3:2
1:7 [s]S 1Ti 3:1 [t]1Co 4:1 [u]S 1Ti 3:3,8
1:8 [v]S Ro 12:13 [w]2Ti 3:3 [x]Tit 2:2, 5,6,12
1:9 [y]S 1Co 16:13; 1Ti 1:19; 2Ti 1:13; 3:14 [z]S 1Ti 1:10
1:10 [a]1Ti 1:6 [b]Ac 10:45; 11:2
1:11 [c]1Ti 5:13
1:12 [d]Ac 17:28 [e]Ac 2:11
1:13 [f]S 1Ti 5:20 [g]Tit 2:2
1:14 [h]S 1Ti 1:4 [i]S Col 2:22 [j]2Ti 4:4
1:15 [k]Ps 18:26; Mt 15:10,11; Mk 7:14-19; Ac 10:9-16,28; Col 2:20-22

[a] 5 Or *ordain* [b] 7 Traditionally *bishop*

1:1 TRUTH THAT LEADS TO GODLINESS. Those who say they proclaim the true gospel must be ready to have their message judged by whether it produces godliness in the lives of those who accept it. No church or denomination has the right to claim that its message or doctrine agrees with the "sound doctrine" of the apostles (v. 9; 2Ti 1:11–14; 2:2; 3:10–12) and "the sound instruction of our Lord Jesus Christ" (1Ti 6:3) if that message or doctrine does not lead its adherents to lives of godliness (v. 16, note; 1Ti 6:3; Heb 1:9; see 1Co 13:1, note).

1:2 GOD, WHO DOES NOT LIE. See Heb 6:18, note.

1:5 APPOINT ELDERS . . . AS I DIRECTED YOU. All pastoral ministries must refer back to and be based on the message of Jesus Christ as proclaimed by the apostles; i.e., they must be founded on the apostolic standard of vv. 5–9 and 1Ti 3:1–7. Such ministry is valid only as long as it holds firmly to the trustworthy Word in accordance with the teaching, the ministry and the writings of the NT (v. 9; Ac 14:23; see Eph 2:20, note).

1:6 BLAMELESS, THE HUSBAND OF BUT ONE WIFE. See article on MORAL QUALIFICATIONS FOR OVERSEERS, p. 458.

1:7 OVERSEER. The terms "elder" (Gk *presbuteros*, v. 6) and "overseer" (Gk *episkopos*, v. 7) are interchangeable and refer to the same church office. The former points to the spiritual maturity and dignity required for the office; the latter refers to the task of overseeing the church as a steward of God's house.

1:7 HE MUST BE BLAMELESS. God insists on the highest moral standards for overseers in the church. If leaders are not above reproach, then the church will depart from righteousness because of the lack of godly role models. For more on this, see article on MORAL QUALIFICATIONS FOR OVERSEERS, p. 458.

1:9 HOLD FIRMLY TO THE TRUSTWORTHY MESSAGE. Elders must not only meet the moral and spiritual standards listed in vv. 6–8, but they must also hold firmly to the original apostolic testimony about the saving work of Jesus Christ, love it, know it and give their lives for it. This is essential for two reasons. (1) They must be able to teach, encourage and exhort from God's Word in order to lead the hearts and minds of God's people to wholehearted devotion to Christ, truth and righteousness (cf. 2Ti 4:2). (2) They must be able to correct those who teach things contrary to Scripture in order to lead them to the truth (2Ti 2:24–26). If correction is refused, then they must convince other believers of the error of those teachings (see articles on THE MINISTRY GIFTS OF THE CHURCH, p. 407, and OVERSEERS AND THEIR DUTIES, p. 274).

1:15 ALL THINGS ARE PURE. Paul is probably speaking about the ritual purity of Jewish food laws (cf. Mt 15:10–11; Mk 7:15; 1Ti 4:3–5). Some teachers were obsessed with the distinction between pure and impure food, teaching that proper observance in these things was essential for true righteousness. They ignored true moral character, inward purity and outward righteousness (v. 16). Paul emphasizes that if a person's moral condition is pure, then distinction between pure and impure foods has no moral meaning for him or her. Paul is not referring to things or actions that are morally wrong, but only to ceremonial purity.

lieve, nothing is pure.[l] In fact, both their
minds and consciences are corrupted.[m]
16They claim to know God, but by their
actions they deny him.[n] They are detestable, disobedient and unfit for doing anything good.[o]

What Must Be Taught to Various Groups

2 You must teach what is in accord with
sound doctrine.[p] 2Teach the older
men[q] to be temperate,[r] worthy of respect, self-controlled,[s] and sound in
faith,[t] in love and in endurance.
3Likewise, teach the older women to be
reverent in the way they live, not to be
slanderers[u] or addicted to much wine,[v]
but to teach what is good. 4Then they can
train the younger women[w] to love their
husbands and children, 5to be self-controlled[x] and pure, to be busy at home,[y] to
be kind, and to be subject to their husbands,[z] so that no one will malign the
word of God.[a]
6Similarly, encourage the young men[b]
to be self-controlled.[c] 7In everything set
them an example[d] by doing what is
good.[e] In your teaching show integrity,
seriousness 8and soundness of speech
that cannot be condemned, so that those
who oppose you may be ashamed because
they have nothing bad to say about us.[f]
9Teach slaves to be subject to their
masters in everything,[g] to try to please
them, not to talk back to them, 10and not
to steal from them, but to show that they
can be fully trusted, so that in every way
they will make the teaching about God our
Savior[h] attractive.[i]
11For the grace[j] of God that brings sal-

1:15 [l] Ro 14:14, 23 [m] 1Ti 6:5
1:16 [n] Jer 5:2; 12:2; 1Jn 2:4 [o] Hos 8:2,3
2:1 [p] S 1Ti 1:10
2:2 [q] 1Ti 5:1 [r] 1Ti 3:2 [s] ver 5,6, 12; Tit 1:8 [t] Tit 1:13
2:3 [u] 1Ti 3:11 [v] 1Ti 3:8
2:4 [w] 1Ti 5:2
2:5 [x] ver 2,6,12; Tit 1:8 [y] 1Ti 5:14 [z] S Eph 5:22 [a] 1Ti 6:1; S Heb 4:12
2:6 [b] 1Ti 5:1 [c] ver 2,5,12; Tit 1:8
2:7 [d] S 1Ti 4:12 [e] S ver 14
2:8 [f] S 1Pe 2:12
2:9 [g] S Eph 6:5
2:10 [h] S Lk 1:47 [i] Mt 5:16
2:11 [j] S Ro 3:24

1:16 THEY CLAIM . . . THEY DENY HIM. One of the greatest abominations in God's eyes is to profess faith in Christ and the hope of eternal life (v. 2), while at the same time to live in disobedience to him and his Word (cf. Lk 6:46; Jn 14:12; 15:10–14; 1Jn 2:4).

2:2 OLDER MEN TO BE TEMPERATE. The clear intent of this text is that older men must be an example to all believers of offering themselves to God as living sacrifices without the use of intoxicating wine (see 1Ti 3:2,11, where this word is used in reference to pastors and women). This is supported by the following facts:

(1) "Temperate" (Gk *nēphalios*) is defined in NT Greek lexicons with the primary meaning of abstaining from wine. Consider the following definitions: "The word originally connotes abstinence from alcohol" (Reinecher and Rogers); "one who does not drink wine" (*Greek Dictionary of Byzantius*, Athens, 1839); "not with wine, wineless" (Liddell and Scott); "free from all infusion of wine" (Moulton-Milligan); "holding no wine" (Kittel and Friedrich); "not mixed with wine" (Abbott-Smith); "literally, of a state of abstinence from wine" (Brown, *Dictionary of New Testament Theology*, Vol. 1). Brown adds: "*Nēphalios* occurs only in the Pastoral Letters and denotes the abstinence style of life required of bishops (1Ti 3:2), women (1Ti 3:11) and elders (Tit 2:2)." R. Laird Harris states that "it is used regularly in the classical authors meaning free from all wine" (*The Bible Today*, p. 139).

(2) Jewish writers, contemporaries of Paul and Peter, confirm the common use of the primary definition. Josephus states in reference to Jewish priests that "they are in all respects pure and abstinent (*nēphalioi*), being forbidden to drink wine while they wear the priestly robe" (*Antiquities*, 3.12.2). Philo states that the regenerate soul "abstains (*nēphein*) continually and during the whole of its life" (*Drunkedness*, 37).

(3) In the light of the foregoing, it cannot be reasonably supposed that Paul used this term without knowledge of its principal meaning (cf. 1Th 5:6, note).

2:4–5 WOMEN TO LOVE THEIR HUSBANDS AND CHILDREN. God has a distinct purpose for the woman in relation to family, home and motherhood. (1) God's desire for a wife and mother is that her attention and devotion be focused on her family. The home, husband and children must be the center of a Christian mother's world; this is her divinely appointed way of honoring the Word of God (cf. Dt 6:7; Pr 31:27; 1Ti 5:14).

(2) The woman's specific God-given tasks as they relate to the family include: (a) caring for the children God has entrusted to her (v. 4; 1Ti 5:14) as a service for the Lord (Ps 127:3; Mt 18:5; Lk 9:48); (b) being a helper and faithful companion to her husband (vv. 4–5; cf. Ge 2:18); (c) helping the father train the children in godly character and practical life skills (Dt 6:7; Pr 1:8–9; Col 3:20; 1Ti 5:10; see article on PARENTS AND CHILDREN, p. 432); (d) providing hospitality (Isa 58:6–8; Lk 14:12–14; 1Ti 5:10); (e) using her skill to provide for the needs of the home (Pr 31:13,15–16,18–19,22,24); (f) caring in her home for elderly parents (1Ti 5:8; Jas 1:27).

(3) Mothers who desire to fulfill God's plan for their lives and their families, but because of economic necessity must seek employment away from the children, should commit their circumstances to the Lord while praying to God to make a way for her to fulfill her God-given place and function in the home with her children (Pr 3:5–6; 1Ti 5:3; see also Eph 5:21–23, notes).

2:7 SET THEM AN EXAMPLE. See article on MORAL QUALIFICATIONS FOR OVERSEERS, p. 458.

2:11 THE GRACE OF GOD. Vv. 11–14 describe the character and purpose of God's saving grace. According to Paul, saving grace (1) instructs believers to decisively reject the ungodly passions, pleasures and values of the present age and regard them as abominable (v. 12; cf. Ro 1:18–32; 2Ti 2:22; 1Jn 2:15–17), and (2) commands and empowers believers to live "upright and godly lives," while waiting expectantly for the blessed hope and appearing of Christ Jesus (v. 13; Gal 5:5; Col 1:5; 2Ti 4:8; see article on FAITH AND GRACE, p. 302).

vation has appeared[k] to all men.[l] **12**It teaches us to say "No" to ungodliness and worldly passions,[m] and to live self-controlled,[n] upright and godly lives[o] in this present age, **13**while we wait for the blessed hope—the glorious appearing[p] of our great God and Savior, Jesus Christ,[q] **14**who gave himself for us[r] to redeem us from all wickedness[s] and to purify[t] for himself a people that are his very own,[u] eager to do what is good.[v]

15These, then, are the things you should teach. Encourage and rebuke with all authority. Do not let anyone despise you.

Doing What Is Good

3 Remind the people to be subject to rulers and authorities,[w] to be obedient, to be ready to do whatever is good,[x] **2**to slander no one,[y] to be peaceable and considerate, and to show true humility toward all men.

3At one time[z] we too were foolish, disobedient, deceived and enslaved by all kinds of passions and pleasures. We lived in malice and envy, being hated and hating one another. **4**But when the kindness[a] and love of God our Savior[b] appeared,[c] **5**he saved us,[d] not because of righteous things we had done,[e] but because of his mercy.[f] He saved us through the washing[g] of rebirth and renewal[h] by the Holy Spirit, **6**whom he poured out on us[i] generously through Jesus Christ our Savior, **7**so that, having been justified by his grace,[j] we might become heirs[k] having the hope[l] of eternal life.[m] **8**This is a trustworthy saying.[n] And I want you to stress these things, so that those who have trusted in God may be careful to devote themselves to doing what is good.[o] These things are excellent and profitable for everyone.

9But avoid[p] foolish controversies and genealogies and arguments and quarrels[q] about the law,[r] because these are unprofitable and useless.[s] **10**Warn a divisive person once, and then warn him a second time. After that, have nothing to do with him.[t] **11**You may be sure that such a man is warped and sinful; he is self-condemned.

12As soon as I send Artemas or Tychicus[u] to you, do your best to come to me at Nicopolis, because I have decided to winter there.[v] **13**Do everything you can to help Zenas the lawyer and Apollos[w] on their way and see that they have everything they need. **14**Our people must learn to devote themselves to doing what is good,[x] in order that they may provide for daily necessities and not live unproductive lives.

15Everyone with me sends you greetings. Greet those who love us in the faith.[y]

Grace be with you all.

2:11 [k]2Ti 1:10 [l]S 1Ti 2:4
2:12 [m]Tit 3:3 [n]ver 2,5,6; Tit 1:8 [o]2Ti 3:12
2:13 [p]S 1Co 1:7; S 1Ti 6:14 [q]2Pe 1:1
2:14 [r]S Mt 20:28 [s]S Mt 1:21 [t]Heb 1:3; 1Jn 1:7 [u]Ex 19:5; Dt 4:20; 14:2; Ps 135:4; Mal 3:17; 1Pe 2:9 [v]ver 7; Pr 16:7; Mt 5:16; 2Co 8:21; Eph 2:10; Tit 3:1, 8,14; 1Pe 2:12,15; 3:13
3:1 [w]Ro 13:1; 1Pe 2:13,14 [x]S 2Ti 2:21; S Tit 2:14
3:2 [y]Eph 4:31
3:3 [z]S Eph 2:2
3:4 [a]Eph 2:7 [b]S Lk 1:47 [c]Tit 2:11
3:5 [d]S Ro 11:14 [e]S Eph 2:9 [f]1Pe 1:3 [g]S Ac 22:16 [h]Ro 12:2
3:6 [i]S Ro 5:5
3:7 [j]S Ro 3:24 [k]S Ro 8:17 [l]Ro 8:24 [m]S Mt 25:46; Tit 1:2
3:8 [n]S 1Ti 1:15 [o]S Tit 2:14
3:9 [p]2Ti 2:16 [q]S 2Ti 2:14 [r]Tit 1:10-16 [s]2Ti 2:14
3:10 [t]S Ro 16:17
3:12 [u]S Ac 20:4 [v]2Ti 4:9,21
3:13 [w]S Ac 18:24
3:14 [x]S Tit 2:14
3:15 [y]1Ti 1:2

2:13 THE BLESSED HOPE. The "blessed hope" for which every Christian should long is "the glorious appearing of our great God and Savior, Jesus Christ" and our union with him for eternity (see Jn 14:3, note; see article on THE RAPTURE, p. 440). This hope is capable of being realized at any time (cf. Mt 24:42; Lk 12:36–40; Jas 5:7–9). Thus, Christians should never surrender their prayerful hope that perhaps today the trumpet will sound and the Lord will return.

2:14 GAVE HIMSELF FOR US. Christ shed his blood on the cross (1Pe 1:18–19) in order (1) to redeem us from all wickedness and the desire to defy God's law and holy standards (cf. 1Jn 3:4), and (2) to make us a holy people, separated from sin and the world to be God's very own special possession. Those struggling with sin and Satan's power should know that if Christ died for their redemption, how much more will he now give adequate grace to live victoriously over the power of sin and evil (Ro 5:9–11).

3:1 SUBJECT TO RULERS. Since it is important for the ongoing witness and furtherance of the gospel, believers must be obedient to civil and governmental authorities, obey civil law, be good citizens and act as respectful neighbors (cf. Mt 17:24–27; 22:15–22; Ro 13:1–7; 1Pe 2:13–17). The only exception occurs when governmental law conflicts with Biblical teaching (cf. Ac 5:29).

3:5 WASHING OF REBIRTH. This refers to the new birth of believers, symbolically pictured in Christian baptism (see article on REGENERATION, p. 178). "Renewal by the Holy Spirit" points to the constant imparting of divine life to believers as they surrender their lives to God (cf. Ro 12:2).

3:6 POURED OUT ON US GENEROUSLY. Paul's reference to the Holy Spirit's work points back to the outpouring of the Spirit on the day of Pentecost and afterward (cf. Ac 2:33; 11:15). God supplies an abundant and adequate supply of his grace and power as a result of the new birth and the Spirit's work in us.

3:10 DIVISIVE PERSON . . . HAVE NOTHING TO DO WITH HIM. Divisive persons here are false teachers who teach opinions and doctrines that have no Biblical basis. After a second admonition proves ineffective in dealing with such persons, they must be rejected, i.e., expelled from church membership. Those who reject Biblical truth and substitute their own ideas and opinions are "warped and sinful" (v. 11).

3:14 DOING WHAT IS GOOD. Paul emphasizes that "doing what is good" is the result of the believer's conversion and life in the Holy Spirit (vv. 4–8). Believers must "set an example by doing what is good" (2:7), and must be "eager to do what is good" (2:14), "ready to do whatever is good" (v. 1) and "careful to devote themselves to doing what is good" (v. 8).

PHILEMON

Outline

Christian Greetings (1–3)

- I. Appreciation for Philemon (4–7)
  - A. An Object of Thankful Prayer (4–6)
  - B. An Occasion of Great Joy (7)
- II. Appeal for Onesimus (8–21)
  - A. An Entreaty Rather Than a Command (8–11)
  - B. Motives for Sending Onesimus Back (12–16)
  - C. A Substitutionary Appeal (17–19)
  - D. A Positive Response Expected From Philemon (20–21)

Closing Matters (22–25)

- A. Hopes to Make a Visit Soon (22)
- B. Greetings From Paul's Companions (23–24)
- C. Benediction (25)

Author: Paul

Theme: Reconciliation

Date of Writing: C. A.D. 62

Background

Paul wrote this "prison letter" (vv. 1,9) as a personal letter to a man named Philemon, most likely during Paul's first imprisonment at Rome (Ac 28:16–31). The identical names mentioned in Philemon (vv. 1–2,10,23–24) and Colossians (Col 4:9–10,12,14,17) indicate that Philemon lived at Colosse, and that both letters were written and delivered at the same time.

Philemon was a slaveowner (v. 16) and church member at Colosse (compare vv. 1–2 with Col 4:17), perhaps a convert of Paul (v. 19). Onesimus was Philemon's slave who had run away to Rome; there he came into contact with Paul, who led him to Christ. A strong bond of friendship developed between the two of them (vv. 9–13). Paul now reluctantly sends Onesimus back to Philemon, accompanied by Paul's co-worker Tychicus and this letter (cf. Col 4:7–9).

Purpose

Paul wrote Philemon to deal with the specific problem of his runaway slave Onesimus. According to Roman law, a runaway slave could be punished by death. Paul intercedes on Onesimus's behalf with Philemon and petitions him to graciously receive Onesimus back as a fellow believer and as Paul's companion, with the same love with which he would receive Paul himself.

Survey

Paul's appeal to Philemon goes as follows: (1) He entreats Philemon as a Christian brother (vv. 8–9,20–21) to receive Onesimus back, not as a slave but as a brother in Christ (vv. 15–16). (2) In a wordplay Paul observes that Onesimus (whose name means "useful") was formerly "useless," but now is "useful" to both Paul and Philemon (vv. 10–12). (3) Paul wishes Onesimus could remain with him in Rome, but sends him back instead to his lawful master (vv. 13–14). (4) Paul offers himself as a substitute for Onesimus's debt and reminds Philemon of his indebtedness to

Paul (vv. 17–19). The letter concludes with greetings from some of Paul's co-workers in Rome (vv. 23–24) and with a benediction (v. 25).

Special Features

Three major features characterize this letter. (1) This is the shortest of all Paul's letters. (2) More than any other NT portion, it illustrates how Paul and the early church dealt with the problem of Roman slavery. Rather than attacking it directly or stirring up armed rebellion, Paul set forth Christian principles that removed the harshness of Roman slavery and eventually led to its banishment altogether within Christianity. (3) It provides unique insight into Paul's inner life, for he identifies himself with a slave so closely that he calls Onesimus "my very heart" (v. 12).

Reading Philemon

In order to read the entire New Testament in one year, the book of Philemon should be read in 1 day: ☐ Philemon

NOTES

1Paul, a prisoner[a] of Christ Jesus, and
Timothy[b] our brother,[c]

To Philemon our dear friend and fellow
worker,[d] **2**to Apphia our sister, to Archippus[e] our fellow soldier[f] and to the church
that meets in your home:[g]

3Grace to you and peace from God our
Father and the Lord Jesus Christ.[h]

Thanksgiving and Prayer

4I always thank my God[i] as I remember you in my prayers,[j] **5**because I hear
about your faith in the Lord Jesus[k] and
your love for all the saints.[l] **6**I pray that
you may be active in sharing your faith, so
that you will have a full understanding of
every good thing we have in Christ. **7**Your
love has given me great joy and encouragement,[m] because you, brother, have refreshed[n] the hearts of the saints.

Paul's Plea for Onesimus

8Therefore, although in Christ I could
be bold and order you to do what you
ought to do, **9**yet I appeal to you[o] on the
basis of love. I then, as Paul—an old man
and now also a prisoner[p] of Christ Jesus
— **10**I appeal to you for my son[q] Onesimus,[a][r] who became my son while I was
in chains.[s] **11**Formerly he was useless to
you, but now he has become useful both
to you and to me.
12I am sending him—who is my very
heart—back to you. **13**I would have liked
to keep him with me so that he could take
your place in helping me while I am in
chains[t] for the gospel. **14**But I did not
want to do anything without your consent,
so that any favor you do will be spontaneous and not forced.[u] **15**Perhaps the reason he was separated from you for a little
while was that you might have him back
for good— **16**no longer as a slave,[v] but
better than a slave, as a dear brother.[w] He
is very dear to me but even dearer to you,
both as a man and as a brother in the Lord.
17So if you consider me a partner,[x] welcome him as you would welcome me. **18**If
he has done you any wrong or owes you
anything, charge it to me.[y] **19**I, Paul, am
writing this with my own hand.[z] I will pay
it back—not to mention that you owe me
your very self. **20**I do wish, brother, that
I may have some benefit from you in the
Lord; refresh[a] my heart in Christ. **21**Confident[b] of your obedience, I write to you,
knowing that you will do even more than
I ask.
22And one thing more: Prepare a guest
room for me, because I hope to be[c] restored to you in answer to your prayers.[d]

23Epaphras,[e] my fellow prisoner[f] in
Christ Jesus, sends you greetings. **24**And
so do Mark,[g] Aristarchus,[h] Demas[i] and
Luke, my fellow workers.[j]
25The grace of the Lord Jesus Christ be
with your spirit.[k]

1:1 [a]ver 9,23; S Eph 3:1 [b]S Ac 16:1 [c]2Co 1:1 [d]S Php 2:25 **1:2** [e]Col 4:17 [f]Php 2:25 [g]S Ro 16:5 **1:3** [h]S Ro 1:7 **1:4** [i]S Ro 1:8 [j]S Ro 1:10 **1:5** [k]S Ac 20:21 [l]S Col 1:4; 1Th 3:6 **1:7** [m]2Co 7:4,13 [n]ver 20; Ro 15:32; 1Co 16:18 **1:9** [o]1Co 1:10 [p]ver 1,23; S Eph 3:1 **1:10** [q]S 1Th 2:11 [r]Col 4:9 [s]S Ac 21:33 **1:13** [t]ver 10; S Ac 21:33 **1:14** [u]2Co 9:7; 1Pe 5:2 **1:16** [v]1Co 7:22 [w]Mt 23:8; S Ac 1:16; 1Ti 6:2 **1:17** [x]2Co 8:23 **1:18** [y]Ge 43:9 **1:19** [z]S 1Co 16:21 **1:20** [a]ver 7; 1Co 16:18 **1:21** [b]S 2Co 2:3 **1:22** [c]Php 1:25; 2:24; Heb 13:19 [d]2Co 1:11; Php 1:19 **1:23** [e]Col 1:7 [f]ver 1; Ro 16:7; Col 4:10 **1:24** [g]S Ac 12:12 [h]S Ac 19:29 [i]Col 4:14; 2Ti 4:10 [j]ver 1 **1:25** [k]S Gal 6:18

[a] *10 Onesimus* means *useful.*

1 A PRISONER OF CHRIST JESUS. Paul wrote this letter to Philemon during Paul's two-year imprisonment in Rome (vv. 1,9; cf. Ac 28:30).

2 THE CHURCH THAT MEETS IN YOUR HOME. Philemon evidently made his home available as a place of worship for the believers in Colosse. House churches were common in NT times (cf. Ro 16:5; 1Co 16:19; Col 4:15). It is not until the third century that separate church buildings are mentioned.

10 ONESIMUS. Onesimus, a slave belonging to Philemon, had run away, possibly taking with him some of his master's goods (vv. 15–16,18–19). Somehow he reached Rome, came into contact with Paul and was converted to Christ under Paul's ministry. Paul now writes this letter, asking Philemon to take Onesimus back with kindness, love and forgiveness.

12 SENDING HIM . . . BACK TO YOU. The NT did not advocate a direct movement to free the slaves, even Christian slaves. To have initiated such an effort in the socio-political conditions of NT times would have destroyed the church and the cause of Christ. Instead of direct confrontation, guidelines were laid down for both the Christian slave and master that would undermine slavery from within and eventually bring about its abolition (vv. 10,12,14–17,21; see v. 16, note).

14 SPONTANEOUS AND NOT FORCED. Onesimus should be set free if he so desires. The ethics and love demanded in the gospel of Christ all point to this fact. Yet, Paul does not state it directly. He wanted Philemon and all masters to do it voluntarily.

16 AS A DEAR BROTHER. Slavery cannot exist among believers who have seen the truth of Christian brotherhood. Onesimus must no longer be treated as a slave, but as a fellow believer and dear brother, one who in God's sight is equal with the apostle Paul and with Philemon (see Col 3:22, note).

HEBREWS

Outline

I. The Argument: Christ and the Christian Faith Are Superior to Judaism (1:1—10:18)
  A. In Revelation (1:1—4:13)
    Jesus Christ Is the Full and Final Revelation of God to Humanity
    1. Superior to the Prophets (1:1–3)
    2. Superior to the Angels (1:4—2:18)
       Exhortation: Danger of Neglect (2:1–4)
    3. Superior to Moses (3:1–6)
       Exhortation: Danger of Unbelief (3:7–19)
    4. Superior to Joshua (4:1–13)
  B. In Meditation (4:14—10:18)
    As Our Great High Priest, Jesus Far Surpasses the Levitical Priesthood
    1. Superior in His Qualifications (4:14—7:25)
       Exhortation: Danger of Immaturity and Encouragement to Press On (5:11—6:20)
    2. Superior in His Character (7:26–28)
    3. Superior in His Ministry (8:1—10:18)
       a. Located in a Better Sanctuary (8:1–5)
       b. Based on a Better Covenant (8:6–13)
       c. Performed Through a Better Service (9:1–22)
       d. Fulfilled by a Better Sacrifice (9:23—10:18)

II. The Application: Exhortation to Steadfastness (10:19—13:17)
  A. In the Realm of Salvation (10:19–38)
  B. In the Realm of Faith (10:39—11:40)
    1. The Nature of Faith (10:39—11:3)
    2. Examples of Faith From the Old Testament (11:4–38)
    3. The Vindication of Faith: Completed in Christ (11:39–40)
  C. In the Realm of Endurance (12:1–13)
  D. In the Realm of Holiness (12:14—13:17)
    1. The Priority of Holiness (12:14–29)
    2. The Practice of Holiness (13:1–17)

Conclusion (13:18–25)

Author: Undesignated

Theme: The Better Covenant

Date: A.D. 67–69 (uncertain)

Background

The destination of this letter is uncertain, though Rome is a likely possibility. The book's title in the oldest Greek manuscripts is simply "To the Hebrews." However, its content reveals that the letter was written to Jewish Christians. The author's use of the Septuagint (Greek translation of the OT) when quoting from the OT indicates that the readers were probably Greek-speaking Jews outside of Palestine. The phrase "those from Italy send you their greetings" (13:24) most likely means that the author was writing to Rome and was including greetings from Italian believers living away from their homeland. The recipients may have consisted of house churches within the larger church community at Rome, some of whom were on the verge of forsaking their faith in Jesus and turning back to their former Jewish faith because of persecution and discouragement.

The author of Hebrews is not identified in its original title nor in the book, though he was well known to his readers (13:18–24). For some reason, his identity was lost by the end of the first century. Subsequently in early church tradition (second to fourth centuries) many different opinions were expressed about who may have written Hebrews. The opinion that Paul wrote Hebrews did not prevail until the fifth century.

Many conservative Bible scholars today believe Paul's authorship is unlikely, since the author's polished and Alexandrian writing style, reliance on the Septuagint, manner of introducing OT quotations, method of argument and teaching, structure of the argumentation and exclusion of personal identification are all distinctly different from that of Paul. Moreover, while Paul always appeals to his firsthand revelation from Christ (cf. Gal 1:11–12), this writer places himself among the second-generation Christians to whom the gospel was confirmed by eyewitnesses of Jesus' ministry (2:3). Among the men mentioned by name in the NT, Luke's description of Apollos in Ac 18:24–28 most perfectly fits the profile of the author of Hebrews.

Regardless of who wrote Hebrews, this much is certain: the author wrote with the apostolic fullness of the Spirit and with apostolic insight, revelation and authority. The absence of any reference in Hebrews to the destruction of the Jerusalem temple and its Levitical worship strongly suggests the author wrote before A.D. 70.

Purpose

Hebrews was written primarily to Jewish Christians who were undergoing persecution and discouragement. The writer strives to strengthen their faith in Christ by carefully explaining the superiority and finality of God's revelation and redemption in Jesus Christ. He shows that God's redemptive provisions under the old covenant have been fulfilled and made obsolete by Jesus' coming and the establishment of the new covenant through his atoning death. The writer challenges his readers (1) to hold on to their confession of Christ until the end, (2) to go on to spiritual maturity and (3) not to turn back to condemnation by abandoning faith in Jesus Christ.

Survey

Hebrews is more like a sermon than a letter. The author describes his work as a "word of exhortation" (13:22). It has three major divisions. (1) First, Jesus as the powerful Son of God (1:1–3) is declared to be God's full revelation to humanity—greater than the prophets (1:1–3), angels (1:4—2:18), Moses (3:1–6) and Joshua (4:1–11). A solemn warning occurs in this division about the consequences of spiritually drifting from the faith or hardening one's heart in unbelief (2:1–3; 3:7—4:2). (2) The second division presents Jesus as the high priest whose qualifications (4:14—5:10; 6:19—7:25), character (7:26–28) and ministry (8:1—10:18) are perfect and everlasting. A solemn warning is given about remaining spiritually immature or even "falling away" after becoming partakers of Christ (5:11—6:12). (3) The final division (10:19—13:17) strongly exhorts believers to persevere in salvation, faith, suffering and holiness.

Special Features

Eight major features characterize this letter. (1) It is unique among NT letters in its format: "it begins like a treatise, proceeds like a sermon, and concludes like a letter" (Origen). (2) It is the NT's most polished book, approaching classical Greek style more nearly than any other NT writer (except perhaps for Luke in Lk 1:1–4). (3) It is the only NT writing that develops the concept of Jesus' high priestly ministry. (4) Its Christology is richly varied, with more than twenty names and titles for Christ being used. (5) Its key word is "better" (13 times). Jesus is better than the angels and all OT mediators. He offers a better rest, covenant, hope, priesthood, sacrifice/blood atonement, and better promises. (6) It contains the foremost chapter in the Bible on faith (ch. 11). (7) It is saturated with OT references and allusions that provide a rich insight into early Christian interpretation of OT history and worship, particularly in the realm of typology. (8) It warns about the dangers of spiritual apostasy more than any other NT writing.

Reading Hebrews

In order to read the entire New Testament in one year, the book of Hebrews should be read in 17 days, according to the following schedule:
☐ 1 ☐ 2 ☐ 3 ☐ 4:1–13 ☐ 4:14–5:10 ☐ 5:11–6:20 ☐ 7 ☐ 8 ☐ 9:1–10 ☐ 9:11–28 ☐ 10:1–18 ☐ 10:19–39 ☐ 11:1–16 ☐ 11:17–40 ☐ 12:1–13 ☐ 12:14–29 ☐ 13

NOTES

The Son Superior to Angels

1 In the past God spoke[a] to our forefathers through the prophets[b] at many
times and in various ways,[c] 2 but in these
last days[d] he has spoken to us by his
Son,[e] whom he appointed heir[f] of all
things, and through whom[g] he made the
universe.[h] 3 The Son is the radiance of
God's glory[i] and the exact representation
of his being,[j] sustaining all things[k] by his
powerful word. After he had provided purification for sins,[l] he sat down at the
right hand of the Majesty in heaven.[m] 4 So
he became as much superior to the angels
as the name he has inherited is superior
to theirs.[n]
5 For to which of the angels did God ever
say,

"You are my Son;
today I have become your
Father[a]"[b]?[o]

Or again,

"I will be his Father,
and he will be my Son"[c]?[p]

6 And again, when God brings his firstborn[q] into the world,[r] he says,

"Let all God's angels worship him."[d][s]

7 In speaking of the angels he says,

"He makes his angels winds,
his servants flames of fire."[e][t]

8 But about the Son he says,

"Your throne, O God, will last for ever
and ever,[u]
and righteousness will be the
scepter of your kingdom.
9 You have loved righteousness and
hated wickedness;
therefore God, your God, has set
you above your companions[v]
by anointing you with the oil[w] of
joy."[f][x]

10 He also says,

"In the beginning, O Lord, you laid
the foundations of the earth,
and the heavens are the work of
your hands.[y]
11 They will perish, but you remain;
they will all wear out like a
garment.[z]
12 You will roll them up like a robe;
like a garment they will be
changed.
But you remain the same,[a]
and your years will never end."[g][b]

13 To which of the angels did God ever say,

1:1 [a] Jn 9:29; Heb 2:2,3; 4:8; 12:25 [b] Lk 1:70; Ac 2:30 [c] Nu 12:6, 8
1:2 [d] Dt 4:30; Heb 9:26; 1Pe 1:20 [e] ver 5; S Mt 3:17; Heb 3:6; 5:8; 7:28 [f] Ps 2:8; Mt 11:27; S 28:18 [g] S Jn 1:3 [h] Heb 11:3
1:3 [i] Jn 1:14 [j] S Jn 14:9 [k] Col 1:17 [l] Tit 2:14; Heb 7:27; 9:11-14 [m] S Mk 16:19
1:4 [n] Eph 1:21; Php 2:9,10; Heb 8:6
1:5 [o] Ps 2:7; S Mt 3:17 [p] 2Sa 7:14
1:6 [q] Jn 3:16; S Col 1:18 [r] Heb 10:5 [s] Dt 32:43 (LXX and DSS) Ps 97:7
1:7 [t] Ps 104:4
1:8 [u] S Lk 1:33
1:9 [v] Php 2:9 [w] Isa 61:1,3 [x] Ps 45:6,7
1:10 [y] Ps 8:6; Zec 12:1
1:11 [z] Isa 34:4; 51:6; S Heb 12:27
1:12 [a] Heb 13:8 [b] Ps 102:25-27

[a] 5 Or *have begotten you* [b] 5 Psalm 2:7
[c] 5 2 Samuel 7:14; 1 Chron. 17:13
[d] 6 Deut. 32:43 (see Dead Sea Scrolls and Septuagint) [e] 7 Psalm 104:4
[f] 9 Psalm 45:6,7 [g] 12 Psalm 102:25-27

1:1–2 SPOKEN TO US BY HIS SON. These verses establish a major theme of this letter: in the past God used the prophets as his foremost instrument of revelation, but now he has spoken or revealed himself to us by his Son Jesus Christ, who is supreme over all things. God's Word through his Son is final; it fulfills and transcends all previous words by God. Absolutely nothing, neither prophets (v. 1) nor angels (v. 4), has greater authority than Christ. He is the only way to eternal salvation and the only mediator between God and humans. The author confirms Christ's supremacy by listing seven great revelations about Christ (vv. 2–3).

1:3 SAT DOWN AT THE RIGHT HAND. After Christ provided the forgiveness of our sins by his death on the cross, he took his place of authority at God's right hand. Christ's redeeming activity in heaven involves his ministry as divine mediator (8:6; 13:15; 1Jn 2:1–2), high priest (2:17–18; 4:14–16; 8:1–3), intercessor (7:25) and baptizer in the Spirit (Ac 2:33).

1:4 SUPERIOR TO THE ANGELS. Just as Jesus is superior to the prophets because he is the Son, so he is superior to angels because he is the Son (vv. 4–14). Angels had played an important part in the giving of the OT covenant (Dt 33:2; Ac 7:53; Gal 3:19). The author, writing to Jewish believers, establishes Christ's superiority to the angels by quoting from the OT.

1:5 TODAY I HAVE BECOME YOUR FATHER. See Jn 1:14, note.

1:8 ABOUT THE SON ... O GOD. The author is pointing out the deity of Christ (see Jn 1:1, note).

1:9 LOVED RIGHTEOUSNESS AND HATED WICKEDNESS. It is not enough for God's children to love righteousness; they must also hate evil. We see this clearly in Christ's devotion to righteousness (Isa 11:5) and his hatred of wickedness in his life, ministry and death (see Jn 3:19, note; 11:33, note). (1) Christ's faithfulness to his Father while on earth, as demonstrated by his love of righteousness and hatred of wickedness, is the basis for God's anointing of his Son. In the same way, our anointing will come only as we identify with our Master's attitude toward righteousness and evil (Ps 45:7).

(2) Our love of righteousness and hatred of evil will increase by two means: (a) by growing in heartfelt love and compassion for those whose lives are being destroyed by sin, and (b) by experiencing more and more oneness with our God and Savior, who "loved righteousness and hated wickedness" (see Pr 8:13; Ps 94:16; 97:10; Am 5:15; Ro 12:9; 1Jn 2:15; Rev 2:6).

1:13 THE ANGELS. "Angels" (Heb *malak*; Gk *angelos*, meaning "messenger") are described as God's messengers and servants, created before the earth began (Job 38:4–7). (1) The Bible speaks of good and

"Sit at my right hand[c]
until I make your enemies
a footstool[d] for your feet"[h]?[e]

14Are not all angels ministering spirits[f]
sent to serve those who will inherit[g] salvation?[h]

Warning Against Drifting Away

2 We must pay more careful attention,
therefore, to what we have heard, so
that we do not drift away.[i] 2For if the
message spoken[j] by angels[k] was binding, and every violation and disobedience
received its just punishment,[l] 3how shall
we escape if we ignore such a great salvation?[m] This salvation, which was first announced by the Lord,[n] was confirmed to
us by those who heard him.[o] 4God also
testified to it by signs, wonders and various miracles,[p] and gifts of the Holy Spirit[q] distributed according to his will.[r]

1Pe 4:10-11

1:13 [c]ver 3; S Mk 16:19 [d]Jos 10:24; Heb 10:13 [e]Ps 110:1; S Mt 22:44 1:14 [f]Ps 91:11; 103:20; Da 7:10 [g]Mt 25:34; Mk 10:17; S Ac 20:32 [h]S Ro 11:14; Heb 2:3; 5:9; 9:28 2:1 [i]S Ro 11:22 2:2 [j]S Heb 1:1 [k]Dt 33:2; Ac 7:53; Gal 3:19 [l]Heb 10:28 2:3 [m]Heb 10:29; 12:25 [n]Heb 1:2 [o]S Lk 1:2 2:4 [p]Mk 16:20; S Jn 4:48 [q]S 1Co 12:4 [r]S Eph 1:5

2:6 [s]Heb 4:4 [t]Job 7:17; Ps 144:3 2:8 [u]Ps 8:4-6; S Mt 22:44

Jesus Made Like His Brothers

5It is not to angels that he has subjected the world to come, about which we are
speaking. 6But there is a place where
someone[s] has testified:

"What is man that you are mindful of
him,
the son of man that you care for
him?[t]
7You made him a little[i] lower than the
angels;
you crowned him with glory and
honor
8 and put everything under his
feet."[j][u]

In putting everything under him, God left
nothing that is not subject to him. Yet at
present we do not see everything subject
to him. 9But we see Jesus, who was made

[h] *13* Psalm 110:1 [i] *7* Or *him for a little while*; also in verse 9 [j] *8* Psalm 8:4-6

evil angels. All angels were created good and holy, but with a freedom of choice. At Satan's rebellion (see Mt 4:10, note) many remained faithful to God, yet some did not. They turned from God's fellowship and grace, forfeiting eternal life. Many identify the demons of the NT with these fallen angels (Mt 25:41; Rev 12:7; see Jude 6, note; see article on POWER OVER SATAN AND DEMONS, p. 80).

(2) Good angels are spirit beings comprising a vast host (1Ki 22:19; Ps 68:17; 148:2; Da 7:9–10). They praise God (Rev 5:11,18–20), do his will (Ps 103:20), see his face (Mt 18:10), are subject to Christ (1Pe 3:22), are superior to humans (2:6–7) and inhabit heavenly spheres (Mk 13:32; Gal 1:8). They seem to have different ranks and functions (1Th 4:16; Jude 9), do not marry (Mt 22:30), are immortal (Lk 20:34–36) and must not be worshiped (Col 2:18; Rev 19:9–10).

(3) Their activity on earth is primarily related to their part in Christ's redemptive mission (see Mt 1:20–24; 2:13; 28:2; Lk 1–2; Ac 1:10; Rev 14:6–7). They rejoice over one sinner who repents (Lk 15:10), care for God's people (v. 14; Da 3:25; 6:22; Mt 18:10), give direction (Ac 8:26; 10:1–6), appear in dreams (Mt 1:20), can appear in human form (usually as young men, cf. 13:2), protect saints who fear God and hate evil (Ps 34:7; 91:11; Ac 12:7–10), bring answers to prayer (Da 9:21–23; Ac 10:4), strengthen people in trials (Mt 4:11; Lk 22:43), wage war against the demonic (Rev 12:7–9), carry the saved to heaven (Lk 16:22) and observe the church on earth (1Co 11:10; Eph 3:10; 1Ti 5:21).

(4) During the end-time events, the war between Michael with the holy angels and Satan with his demonic host will intensify (Rev 12:7–9). The holy angels will come with Christ when he returns (Mt 24:30–31) and will be present at the judgment of the entire human race (Lk 12:8–9).

(5) In the OT the title "angel of the LORD" is believed by many theologians to be God himself or more probably an appearing of the pre-incarnate Christ (cf. Ge 16:7; 31:11–13; 32:24–30; Ex 3:2–6; Jdg 13:2–3).

2:1–3 SO THAT WE DO NOT DRIFT AWAY. One reason the writer of Hebrews emphasizes the superiority of God's Son and his revelation is to stress to those who have experienced salvation that they must take with intense seriousness the original witness and doctrine of Christ and the apostles. Therefore, we must pay close attention to God's Word, our relation to Christ and the leading of the Holy Spirit (Gal 5:16–25). (1) Neglect, carelessness or apathy is fatal. A believer who, because of negligence, allows the truth and teachings of the gospel to slip, is in great danger of being swept along downstream past a fixed landing place and of failing to gain security.

(2) Like the recipients of this letter, all Christians are tempted to become indifferent to God's Word. Because of carelessness and indifference, we may easily begin to pay less attention to God's warnings (v. 2), stop persevering in our struggle against sin (12:4; 1Pe 2:11), and slowly drift away from God's Son, Jesus Christ (vv. 1–3; 6:4–8; 10:31–32; see Ro 8:13, note).

2:4 GOD ALSO TESTIFIED TO IT. The Holy Spirit through the writer of Hebrews reaffirms that God confirmed and supported the gospel message with signs, wonders, miracles and gifts of the Spirit (Ac 2:22). After his resurrection Christ promised that miraculous confirmation of the gospel message would accompany all who believe (see article on SIGNS OF BELIEVERS, p. 106). God desires that the believer's witness be more than simply words (Mk 16:20; Jn 10:25; Ac 2:22,43; 1Co 2:4–5; Gal 3:5; 1Th 1:5; 1Pe 1:12; see Ac 4:30, note).

2:8 WE DO NOT SEE EVERYTHING SUBJECT. In this fallen world dominated by Satan, all is not yet in subjection to Christ. Yet Jesus is already crowned with glory and honor in heaven (v. 9); all the evil powers in the world are doomed to defeat and judgment.

2:9 TASTE DEATH FOR EVERYONE. Christ experienced the humiliation and suffering of death for all

a little lower than the angels, now
crowned with glory and honor[v] because
he suffered death,[w] so that by the grace of
God he might taste death for everyone.[x]
10In bringing many sons to glory, it was
fitting that God, for whom and through
whom everything exists,[y] should make
the author of their salvation perfect
through suffering.[z] **11**Both the one who
makes men holy[a] and those who are made
holy[b] are of the same family. So Jesus is
not ashamed to call them brothers.[c] **12**He
says,

"I will declare your name to my
brothers;
in the presence of the congregation
I will sing your praises."[k][d]

13And again,

"I will put my trust in him,"[l][e]

And again he says,

"Here am I, and the children God has
given me."[m][f]

14Since the children have flesh and
blood,[g] he too shared in their humanity[h]
so that by his death he might destroy[i]
him who holds the power of death—that
is, the devil[j]— **15**and free those who all
their lives were held in slavery by their
fear[k] of death. **16**For surely it is not angels he helps, but Abraham's descendants.[l] **17**For this reason he had to be
made like his brothers[m] in every way, in
order that he might become a merciful[n]
and faithful high priest[o] in service to
God,[p] and that he might make atonement
for[n] the sins of the people.[q] **18**Because he
himself suffered when he was tempted,
he is able to help those who are being
tempted.[r]

Jesus Greater Than Moses

3 Therefore, holy brothers,[s] who share
in the heavenly calling,[t] fix your
thoughts on Jesus, the apostle and high
priest[u] whom we confess.[v] **2**He was faithful to the one who appointed him, just as
Moses was faithful in all God's house.[w]
3Jesus has been found worthy of greater
honor than Moses,[x] just as the builder of
a house has greater honor than the house

2:9 [v]ver 7; Ac 3:13; S Php 2:9 [w]Php 2:7-9 [x]2Co 5:15
2:10 [y]S Ro 11:36 [z]Lk 24:26; Heb 5:8,9; 7:28
2:11 [a]Heb 13:12 [b]S Eph 5:26 [c]S Mt 28:10
2:12 [d]Ps 22:22; 68:26
2:13 [e]Isa 8:17 [f]Isa 8:18; Jn 10:29
2:14 [g]1Co 15:50; Eph 6:12 [h]S Jn 1:14 [i]Ge 3:15; 1Co 15:54-57; 2Ti 1:10 [j]1Jn 3:8
2:15 [k]S 2Ti 1:7
2:16 [l]S Lk 3:8
2:17 [m]ver 14; S Php 2:7 [n]Heb 5:2 [o]Heb 3:1; 4:14,15; 5:5,10; 7:26,28; 8:1,3; 9:11 [p]Heb 5:1 [q]S Ro 3:25
2:18 [r]Heb 4:15
3:1 [s]Heb 2:11 [t]S Ro 8:28 [u]S Heb 2:17 [v]1Ti 6:12; Heb 4:14; 10:23; 2Co 9:13
3:2 [w]ver 5; Nu 12:7
3:3 [x]Dt 34:12

k *12* Psalm 22:22 l *13* Isaiah 8:17
m *13* Isaiah 8:18 n *17* Or *and that he might turn aside God's wrath, taking away*

people. His death was not, as some claim, a "limited atonement." Since he bore the punishment of the sins of all humanity, his death avails for all who accept him (see Ro 3:25, note).

2:10 PERFECT THROUGH SUFFERING. This does not mean that Christ needed to be made morally and spiritually perfect. What was perfected was his role as author or leader—one who goes before to make a way for others to follow. He could only be the perfect Savior of all those who believe if he first endured suffering and death as a human. His obedience and death qualified him to be the perfect representative of fallen humanity and to bear the penalty of sin on their behalf.

2:11 THE ONE WHO MAKES MEN HOLY. "The one who makes men holy" is Christ (cf. 10:10,14,29; 13:12) and "those who are made holy" are those who have been redeemed from sin's guilt and power and set apart as God's people. Christ's consecration of himself to die for us provides the way for our sanctification (see article on SANCTIFICATION, p. 526).

2:14 SHARED IN THEIR HUMANITY. Because those whom Jesus came to redeem are flesh and blood (i.e., human), Jesus also had to take on human nature. For only as a true human being could he qualify to redeem the human race from Satan's power. Christ died to destroy Satan's power over those who believe (cf. 1Jn 3:8) and to deliver them from the fear of death (Rev 1:18) by promising eternal life with God (Jn 17:3; Rev 21–22).

2:17 MERCIFUL AND FAITHFUL HIGH PRIEST. Christ became one with humanity in order to become a high priest and so to represent believers before God. (1) In this ministry, the Son's death makes atonement by removing God's wrath against us because of our sins (cf. Ro 1:18; 5:10). As a result we can now approach God in confidence. (2) The Son mercifully sympathizes with us when we are tempted and comes to our aid because he, as a human, has experienced suffering, trials and temptations, yet did not sin (cf. 4:14–15; 2Co 6:2).

2:18 HE IS ABLE TO HELP. When we are tempted to be disloyal to God and give in to sin, we must pray to Christ, who triumphed over temptation and now, as our high priest, promises to give us the strength and grace to resist sin. Our responsibility is to draw near to him in time of trouble; his responsibility is to give help in every time of need (see 4:16, note).

3:1 HOLY BROTHERS. This letter was probably written to a group of Jewish Christians who, after their conversion to Christ, had been exposed to persecution and discouragement (10:32–39). That the readers were true born-again Christians is apparent from the following: (1) 2:1–4, which speaks of the danger of their drifting away from salvation; (2) 3:1, where the readers are called "holy brothers, who share in the heavenly calling"; (3) 3:6, where they are called God's house. For further evidence that the readers were saved by Christ, see 3:12–19; 4:14–16; 6:9–12,18–20; 10:19–25,32–36; 12:1–29; 13:1–6,10–14,20–21.

3:1 APOSTLE AND HIGH PRIEST. Under the old covenant Moses (vv. 2–5) was the apostle (i.e., one sent by God with his authority) and Aaron (5:1–5) the high priest of God's people. Now under the new covenant, these two offices are combined in the person of Jesus.

itself. **4**For every house is built by someone, but God is the builder of everything.[y]
5Moses was faithful as a servant[z] in all
God's house,[a] testifying to what would be
said in the future. **6**But Christ is faithful
as a son[b] over God's house. And we are
his house,[c] if we hold on[d] to our courage
and the hope[e] of which we boast.

Warning Against Unbelief

7So, as the Holy Spirit says:[f]

"Today, if you hear his voice,
8 do not harden your hearts[g]
as you did in the rebellion,
during the time of testing in the desert,
9where your fathers tested and tried me
and for forty years saw what I did.[h]
10That is why I was angry with that generation,
and I said, 'Their hearts are always going astray,
and they have not known my ways.'
11So I declared on oath in my anger,[i]
'They shall never enter my rest.'"[j][o][k]

12See to it, brothers, that none of you
has a sinful, unbelieving heart that turns
away from the living God.[l] **13**But encourage one another daily,[m] as long as it is
called Today, so that none of you may be
hardened by sin's deceitfulness.[n] **14**We
have come to share in Christ if we hold
firmly[o] till the end the confidence[p] we
had at first. **15**As has just been said:

"Today, if you hear his voice,
do not harden your hearts
as you did in the rebellion."[p][q]

16Who were they who heard and rebelled? Were they not all those Moses led
out of Egypt?[r] **17**And with whom was he
angry for forty years? Was it not with
those who sinned, whose bodies fell in the
desert?[s] **18**And to whom did God swear
that they would never enter his rest[t] if

3:4 [y]Ge 1:1
3:5 [z]Ex 14:31 [a]ver 2; Nu 12:7
3:6 [b]S Heb 1:2 [c]S 1Co 3:16; 1Ti 3:15 [d]ver 14; S Ro 11:22; Heb 4:14 [e]Ro 5:2; Heb 6:11,18,19; 7:19; 11:1
3:7 [f]Ac 28:25; Heb 9:8; 10:15
3:8 [g]ver 15; Heb 4:7
3:9 [h]Nu 14:33; Dt 1:3; Ac 7:36
3:11 [i]Dt 1:34,35 [j]Heb 4:3,5 [k]Ps 95:7-11
3:12 [l]S Mt 16:16
3:13 [m]Heb 10:24,25 [n]Jer 17:9; Eph 4:22
3:14 [o]ver 6 [p]S Eph 3:12
3:15 [q]ver 7,8; Ps 95:7,8; Heb 4:7
3:16 [r]Nu 14:2
3:17 [s]Nu 14:29; Ps 106:26; 1Co 10:5
3:18 [t]Nu 14:20-23; Dt 1:34,35

o *11* Psalm 95:7-11 p *15* Psalm 95:7,8

3:6 IF WE HOLD ON TO OUR COURAGE AND THE HOPE. The conditional statements in the book of Hebrews deserve special attention (see 2:3; 3:6,14; 10:26), for they warn that salvation is conditional. (1) The security of believers is maintained only as they cooperate with God's grace by persevering in faith and holiness to the end of their earthly existence. This truth was emphasized by Christ (Jn 8:31; Rev 2:7,11,17,25–26; 3:5,11–12,21) and is a repeated admonition in the letter to the Hebrews (2:1; 3:6,14; 4:16; 7:25; 10:34–38; 12:1–4,14). (2) The reassurance of salvation for church members who willfully sin, so prevalent in some circles today, finds no place in the NT (Rev 3:14–16; see Lk 12:42–48, note; Jn 15:6, note).

3:7 THE HOLY SPIRIT SAYS. Along with other NT writers, the writer of Hebrews regards Scripture in the ultimate and truest sense as the words of the Holy Spirit rather than the mere words of humans (cf. 9:8; 10:15; 2Ti 3:16; 2Pe 1:21; see article on THE INSPIRATION AND AUTHORITY OF SCRIPTURE, p. 474). When we read the Bible, we should not think that we are reading merely the opinions of Matthew, Paul, Peter, John, etc., but the very words of the Holy Spirit revealing God's will for the church and for our lives.

3:7–11 TODAY, IF YOU HEAR HIS VOICE. Quoting Ps 95:7–11, the writer refers to Israel's disobedience in the desert after their exodus from Egypt as a warning for believers under the new covenant. Because of the Israelites' failure to resist sin and remain loyal to God, they were barred from entering into the promised land. Likewise, believers must realize that they too may fail to enter God's rest in heaven if they disobey and allow their hearts to grow hard.

3:8 DO NOT HARDEN YOUR HEARTS. The Holy Spirit speaks to us concerning sin, righteousness and judgment (Jn 16:8–11; Ro 8:11–14; Gal 5:16–25). If we ignore his voice, our hearts will increasingly grow hard and unyielding until they are no longer sensitive to God's Word or the desires of the Spirit (v. 7). Commitment to truth and to righteous living will no longer be a priority, but we will more and more seek pleasure in the ways of the world rather than God's ways (v. 10). The Holy Spirit warns us that God will not go on pleading with us indefinitely if we harden our hearts in rebellion (vv. 7–11; Ge 6:3). There is a point of no return (vv. 10–11; 6:6; 10:26).

3:12 TURNS AWAY FROM THE LIVING GOD. At regular intervals throughout this letter, the author warns his readers about the danger of falling away from the faith. For more on this subject, see article on PERSONAL APOSTASY, p. 492.

3:13 ENCOURAGE ONE ANOTHER DAILY. Many ministers fail to "encourage" or admonish believers to continue in the faith. Such ministers do not preach the urgent warnings of the apostles (Col 1:21–23; 1Ti 4:1,16; Jas 5:19–20; 2Pe 1:8–11; 1Jn 2:23–25), the writer of Hebrews (2:3; 3:6–19) or Jesus himself (Mt 24:11–13; Jn 15:1–6).

3:18 THEY WOULD NEVER ENTER HIS REST. The possibility of the believer missing God's promised rest is illustrated by the Israelites who failed to enter the promised land after Moses had led them out of Egypt. The writer points out two things: (1) The Israelites had experienced God's redemptive power (v. 16), seen God's mighty works (v. 9), and yet were disobedient because they would not believe God's promises or heed his warnings (vv. 18–19). Therefore, they were destroyed in the desert (v. 17) and failed to enter the promised land. (2) The Israelites' initial experiences with God did not guarantee their safe arrival in Canaan. By failing to persevere, they threw aside their only source of security: the grace, mercy

PERSONAL APOSTASY

***Heb 3:12** "See to it, brothers, that none of you has a sinful, unbelieving heart that turns away from the living God."*

Apostasy (Gk *apostasia*) appears twice in the NT as a noun (Ac 21:21; 2Th 2:3) and here in Heb 3:12 as a verb (Gk *aphistēmi*, translated "turn away"). The Greek term is defined as a falling away, defection, rebellion, abandonment, withdrawal or turning from what one has formerly turned to.

(1) To apostatize means to sever one's saving relationship with Christ or to withdraw from vital union with and true faith in him (see article on FAITH AND GRACE, p. 302). Thus, individual apostasy is possible only for those who have first experienced salvation, regeneration and renewal through the Holy Spirit (cf. Lk 8:13; Heb 6:4–5); it is not a mere denial of NT doctrine by the unsaved within the visible church. Apostasy may involve two separate, though related, aspects: (a) theological apostasy, i.e., a rejection of all or some of the original teachings of Christ and the apostles (1Ti 4:1; 2Ti 4:3), and (b) moral apostasy, i.e., the former believer ceases to remain in Christ and instead becomes enslaved again to sin and immorality (Isa 29:13; Mt 23:25–28; Ro 6:15–23; 8:6–13).

(2) The Bible issues urgent warnings about apostasy, designed both to alert us to the deadly danger of abandoning our union with Christ and to motivate us to persevere in faith and obedience. The divine purpose of these warning passages must not be weakened by the view that states, "the warnings are real, but the possibility of actual apostasy is not." Rather, we must see these warnings as speaking to the reality of our probationary period, and we should regard them with alarm if we want to attain final salvation. A few of the many NT warning passages are: Mt 24:4–5,11–13; Jn 15:1–6; Ac 11:21–23; 14:21–22; 1Co 15:1–2; Col 1:21–23; 1Ti 4:1,16; 6:10–12; 2Ti 4:2–5; Heb 2:1–3; 3:6–8,12–14; 6:4–6; Jas 5:19–20; 2Pe 1:8–11; 1Jn 2:23–25.

(3) Examples of actual apostasy can be found in Isa 1:2–4; Jer 2:1–9; Ac 1:25; Gal 5:4; 1Ti 1:18–20; 2Pe 2:1,15,20–22; Jude 4,11–13; see article on THE AGE OF THE ANTICHRIST, p. 447, for comments on apostasy predicted to occur within the professing church in the last days of this age.

(4) The steps that lead to apostasy are as follows:

(a) Believers, through unbelief, fail to take the truths, exhortations, warnings, promises and teachings of God's Word with utmost seriousness (Mk 1:15; Lk 8:13; Jn 5:44,47; 8:46).

(b) As the realities of the world become greater than the realities of God's heavenly kingdom, believers gradually cease to draw near to God through Christ (Heb 4:16; 7:19,25; 11:6).

(c) Through the deceitfulness of sin, they become increasingly tolerant of sin in their own lives (1Co 6:9–10; Eph 5:5; Heb 3:13). They no longer love righteousness and hate wickedness (see Heb 1:9, note).

(d) Through hardness of heart (Heb 3:8,13) and rejecting God's way (3:10), they ignore the repeated voice and rebuke of the Holy Spirit (Eph 4:30; 1Th 5:19–22).

(e) The Holy Spirit is grieved (Eph 4:30; cf. Heb 3:7–8), and his fire put out (1Th 5:19) and his temple violated (1Co 3:16). He eventually departs from the former believers (Jdg 16:20; Ps 51:11; Ro 8:13; 1Co 3:16–17; Heb 3:14).

(5) If apostasy continues on its course unchecked, individuals may eventually reach the point when no second beginning is possible. (a) Those who once had a saving experience with Christ but deliberately and continually harden their hearts to the Spirit's voice (Heb 3:7–19), continue to sin willfully (Heb 10:26), and refuse to repent and return to God may reach a point of no return where repentance and salvation is no longer possible (Heb 6:4–6). There is a limit to God's patience (see 1Sa 2:25; 3:14; Mt 12:31–32; 2Th 2:9–11; Heb 10:26–29,31; 1Jn 5:16). (b) This point of no return cannot be defined in advance. Therefore, the only safeguard against the danger of ultimate apostasy is found in the admonition: "Today, if you hear his voice, do not harden your hearts" (Heb 3:7–8,15; 4:7).

(6) It must be emphasized that while apostasy is a danger for all who drift from the faith (Heb 2:1–3) and fall away from God (6:6), it is not made complete without constant and willful sinning against the voice of the Holy Spirit (see Mt 12:31, note on sin against the Holy Spirit).

(7) Those who by unbelieving hearts depart from God (Heb 3:12) may think they are Christians but their indifference to the demands of Christ and the Spirit and the warnings of Scripture points otherwise. Because of this possibility of self-deception, Paul urges all those claiming salvation to "examine yourselves to see whether you are in the faith; test yourselves" (2Co 13:5, note).

(8) Those who genuinely become concerned about their spiritual condition and find in their hearts the desire to return to God in repentance have sure evidence they have not committed unpardonable apostasy. Scripture clearly affirms that God does not want anyone to perish (2Pe 3:9; cf. Isa 1:18–19; 55:6–7) and declares that God will receive all who were once under saving grace if they repent and return to him (compare Gal 5:4 with 4:19; 1Co 5:1–5 with 2Co 2:5–11; see also Lk 15:11–24; Ro 11:20–23; Jas 5:19–20; Rev 3:14–20; note the example of Peter, Mt 16:16; 26:74–75; Jn 21:15–22).

not to those who disobeyed[q]?[u] 19So we
see that they were not able to enter, because of their unbelief.[v]

A Sabbath-Rest for the People of God

4 Therefore, since the promise of entering his rest still stands, let us be careful that none of you be found to have fallen
short of it.[w] 2For we also have had the
gospel preached to us, just as they did;
but the message they heard was of no value to them, because those who heard did
not combine it with faith.[r][x] 3Now we who
have believed enter that rest, just as God
has said,

> "So I declared on oath in my anger,
> 'They shall never enter my
> rest.' "[s][y]

And yet his work has been finished since
the creation of the world. 4For somewhere
he has spoken about the seventh day in
these words: "And on the seventh day God
rested from all his work."[t][z] 5And again in
the passage above he says, "They shall
never enter my rest."[a]
6It still remains that some will enter
that rest, and those who formerly had the
gospel preached to them did not go in,
because of their disobedience.[b] 7There-
fore God again set a certain day, calling it
Today, when a long time later he spoke
through David, as was said before:

> "Today, if you hear his voice,
> do not harden your hearts."[u][c]

8For if Joshua had given them rest,[d] God
would not have spoken[e] later about another day. 9There remains, then, a Sabbath-rest for the people of God; 10for anyone who enters God's rest also rests from
his own work,[f] just as God did from his.[g]
11Let us, therefore, make every effort to
enter that rest, so that no one will fall by
following their example of disobedience.[h]
12For the word of God[i] is living[j] and
active.[k] Sharper than any double-edged
sword,[l] it penetrates even to dividing
soul and spirit, joints and marrow; it
judges the thoughts and attitudes of the
heart.[m] 13Nothing in all creation is hidden
from God's sight.[n] Everything is uncovered and laid bare before the eyes of him
to whom we must give account.

Jesus the Great High Priest

14Therefore, since we have a great high
priest[o] who has gone through the heavens,[v][p] Jesus the Son of God,[q] let us hold
firmly to the faith we profess.[r] 15For we
do not have a high priest[s] who is unable
to sympathize with our weaknesses, but
we have one who has been tempted in every way, just as we are[t]—yet was without sin.[u] 16Let us then approach[v] the

3:18 [u]Heb 4:6 **3:19** [v]Ps 78:22; 106:24; Jn 3:36 **4:1** [w]Heb 12:15 **4:2** [x]1Th 2:13 **4:3** [y]Ps 95:11; Dt 1:34,35; Heb 3:11 **4:4** [z]Ge 2:2,3; Ex 20:11 **4:5** [a]Ps 95:11; S ver 3 **4:6** [b]ver 11; Heb 3:18 **4:7** [c]Ps 95:7,8; Heb 3:7,8,15 **4:8** [d]Jos 22:4 [e]S Heb 1:1 **4:10** [f]Lev 23:3; Rev 14:13 [g]ver 4 **4:11** [h]ver 6; Heb 3:18 **4:12** [i]S Mk 4:14; Lk 5:1; 11:28; Jn 10:35; Ac 12:24; 1Th 2:13; 2Ti 2:9; 1Pe 1:23; 1Jn 2:14; Rev 1:2, 9 [j]Ac 7:38; 1Pe 1:23 [k]Isa 55:11; Jer 23:29; 1Th 2:13 [l]Eph 6:17; S Rev 1:16 [m]1Co 14:24,25 **4:13** [n]Ps 33:13-15; Pr 5:21; Jer 16:17; 23:24; Da 2:22 **4:14** [o]S Heb 2:17 [p]Heb 6:20; 8:1; 9:24 [q]S Mt 4:3 [r]S Heb 3:1 **4:15** [s]S Heb 2:17 [t]Heb 2:18 [u]S 2Co 5:21 **4:16** [v]S Heb 7:19

[q] *18* Or *disbelieved* [r] *2* Many manuscripts *because they did not share in the faith of those who obeyed* [s] *3* Psalm 95:11; also in verse 5 [t] *4* Gen. 2:2 [u] *7* Psalm 95:7,8 [v] *14* Or *gone into heaven*

---

and presence of "the living God" (v. 12).

4:1 HIS REST . . . HAVE FALLEN SHORT OF IT. Ceasing to persevere in faith and in obedience to Jesus results in the failure to reach the eternal promised rest of heaven (cf. 11:16; 12:22–24). (1) The phrase "let us be careful" is spoken in the light of this terrible possibility and of God's judgment. (2) Perseverance in faith requires that we continue to draw near to God through Christ with sincere determination (v. 16; 7:25).

4:3 ENTER THAT REST. Only we who have believed the saving message of Christ enter God's spiritual rest. Christ takes our burdens and sins and gives us the "rest" of his forgiveness, salvation and Spirit (Mt 11:28). However, in this life our rest is only partial, for we are pilgrims plodding through a harsh world. One by one, as we die in the Lord, we enter his perfect rest in heaven (see next note).

4:9 REMAINS, THEN, A SABBATH-REST. God's promised rest is not only earthly, but heavenly as well (vv. 7–8; cf. 13:14). For believers, there remains an eternal rest in heaven (Jn 14:1–3; cf. Heb 11:10,16). Entering this final rest means ceasing from the labors, sufferings and persecutions common to our lives on this earth (cf. Rev 14:13), participating in God's own rest, and experiencing unending joy, delight, love and fellowship with God and other redeemed saints. It will be a seventh day without end (Rev 21–22).

4:11 MAKE EVERY EFFORT TO ENTER. In light of the glorious blessing of the eternal state and the terrible fate of those who fail to enter it, believers must diligently strive to arrive at the heavenly home of God's people. This requires pressing on toward the heavenly goal (Php 3:13–14) and clinging to the Word (v. 12) in devotion to prayer (v. 16).

4:12 THE WORD OF GOD. The Word of God determines who will enter into God's rest. It is a sharp sword that cuts into our innermost being in order to discern whether our thoughts and motives are spiritual or unspiritual. It has two edges, either cutting to save our lives or judging us to eternal death (cf. Jn 6:63; 12:48). Therefore, our response to God's Word should be to draw near to Jesus as our high priest (vv. 14–16).

4:14 WE HAVE A GREAT HIGH PRIEST. See 8:1, note on Jesus' ministry as high priest.

4:16 APPROACH THE THRONE OF GRACE WITH CONFIDENCE. Because Christ sympathizes with our weaknesses (v. 15), we can confidently approach the heavenly throne, knowing that our prayers and petitions are welcomed and desired by our heavenly Father (cf. 10:19–20). It is called the "throne of

throne of grace with confidence,[w] so that
we may receive mercy and find grace to
help us in our time of need.

5 Every high priest is selected from
among men and is appointed to represent them in matters related to God,[x] to
offer gifts and sacrifices[y] for sins.[z] **2**He
is able to deal gently with those who are
ignorant and are going astray,[a] since he
himself is subject to weakness.[b] **3**This is
why he has to offer sacrifices for his own
sins, as well as for the sins of the people.[c]

4No one takes this honor upon himself;
he must be called by God, just as Aaron
was.[d] **5**So Christ also did not take upon
himself the glory[e] of becoming a high
priest.[f] But God said[g] to him,

"You are my Son;
today I have become your
Father.[w]"[x][h]

6And he says in another place,

"You are a priest forever,
in the order of Melchizedek."[i][y][j]

7During the days of Jesus' life on earth,
he offered up prayers and petitions[k] with
loud cries and tears[l] to the one who could
save him from death, and he was heard[m]
because of his reverent submission.[n] **8**Although he was a son,[o] he learned obedience from what he suffered[p] **9**and, once
made perfect,[q] he became the source of
eternal salvation for all who obey him
10and was designated by God to be high
priest[r] in the order of Melchizedek.[s]

Warning Against Immaturity

6:4–6Ref — Heb 10:26–31

11We have much to say about this, but
it is hard to explain because you are slow
to learn. **12**In fact, though by this time you
ought to be teachers, you need someone to
teach you the elementary truths[t] of God's
word all over again. You need milk, not
solid food![u] **13**Anyone who lives on milk,
being still an infant,[v] is not acquainted
with the teaching about righteousness.
14But solid food is for the mature,[w] who
by constant use have trained themselves
to distinguish good from evil.[x]

6 Therefore let us leave[y] the elementary teachings[z] about Christ and go on
to maturity, not laying again the foundation of repentance from acts that lead to
death,[z][a] and of faith in God, **2**instruction
about baptisms,[b] the laying on of hands,[c]
the resurrection of the dead,[d] and eternal

w 5 Or *have begotten you* x 5 Psalm 2:7
y 6 Psalm 110:4 z 1 Or *from useless rituals*

4:16 [w]S Eph 3:12
5:1 [x]Heb 2:17
[y]Heb 8:3; 9:9
[z]Heb 7:27
5:2 [a]Isa 29:24; Heb 2:18; 4:15
[b]Heb 7:28
5:3 [c]Lev 9:7; 16:6; Heb 7:27; 9:7
5:4 [d]Ex 28:1; Nu 14:40; 18:7
5:5 [e]Jn 8:54
[f]S Heb 2:17
[g]S Heb 1:1
[h]Ps 2:7; S Mt 3:17
5:6 [i]ver 10; Ge 14:18; Heb 6:20; 7:1-22
[j]Ps 110:4; Heb 7:17,21
5:7 [k]Lk 22:41-44
[l]Mt 27:46,50; Lk 23:46
[m]Ps 22:24
[n]Mk 14:36
5:8 [o]S Heb 1:2
[p]S Php 2:8
5:9 [q]S Heb 2:10
5:10 [r]ver 5; S Heb 2:17
[s]S ver 6
5:12 [t]Heb 6:1
[u]1Co 3:2; 1Pe 2:2
5:13 [v]S 1Co 14:20
5:14 [w]S 1Co 2:6
[x]Isa 7:15
6:1 [y]Php 3:12-14
[z]Heb 5:12
[a]Heb 9:14
6:2 [b]Jn 3:25
[c]S Ac 6:6
[d]S Ac 2:24; Ac 17:18,32

grace" because from it flow God's love, help, mercy, forgiveness, spiritual power, outpouring of the Holy Spirit, spiritual gifts, the fruit of the Spirit, and all that we need under any circumstances. One of the greatest blessings of salvation is that Christ is now our high priest, opening a way to his personal presence whereby we can always seek the help we need.

5:1 EVERY HIGH PRIEST. Two qualifications are necessary for a valid priesthood: (1) The priest must be sympathetic, gentle and patient with those who go astray through ignorance, unintentional sin or weakness (v. 2; 4:15; cf. Lev 4; Nu 15:27–29). (2) He must be appointed by God (vv. 4–6). Christ qualified in both ways.

5:6 THE ORDER OF MELCHIZEDEK. Melchizedek is a mysterious OT figure who appears in Ge 14 as God's priest of Salem (perhaps Jerusalem, 7:1; Ge 14:18; Ps 110:1–4) before the time of the Levitical priesthood. Christ's priesthood is of the same kind as Melchizedek (see 7:1–3, notes).

5:7 LOUD CRIES AND TEARS. This passage probably refers to the intensity of Jesus' prayer in the Garden of Gethsemane. Jesus' prayer was "heard" not in the sense that God removed all that was involved in death, but in the sense that he received God's aid to undergo his appointed suffering. There will be times when we too face trials and our fervent prayers seem to go unanswered. In such times, we must remember that Jesus was tested in the same way and that God will give us sufficient grace to undergo what he allows for our lives (see Mt 26:39, note).

5:8 HE LEARNED OBEDIENCE. Christ learned by experience the suffering and cost that often result from faithful obedience to God in a corrupt world (cf. 12:2; Isa 50:4–6; Php 2:8). He became a perfect Savior and high priest because his suffering and death were accomplished without sin. Therefore, he was qualified in every way (vv. 1–6) to bring us eternal salvation (v. 9; see 2:10, note).

5:9 SALVATION FOR ALL WHO OBEY HIM. The eternal salvation gained by Jesus' suffering (v. 8) is made available only to those who are obedient to him through faith. The faith that saves is an obedient faith (Jn 8:31; Ro 1:5; 16:26; Jas 2:17–26).

5:12 MILK, NOT SOLID FOOD. See article on THREE KINDS OF PEOPLE, p. 334.

5:14 DISTINGUISH GOOD FROM EVIL. Those who are weak and immature in the faith lack spiritual sensitivity and discernment with regard to what is good and what is evil in this life, and what honors God and what dishonors God. Mature believers, on the other hand, have trained their senses to carefully distinguish between good and evil through the continual practice of righteousness and obedience. Having learned to love righteousness and hate wickedness (see 1:9, note), having renewed their minds according to principles of righteousness (Ro 12:1–2), and being enabled by the Holy Spirit to see things from God's point of view, they are able to receive the solid food of God's Word and grow toward the full stature of Christ (cf. Eph 4:13).

judgment. 3And God permitting,[e] we will
do so.

Warning Against Falling Away

4It is impossible for those who have
once been enlightened,[f] who have tasted
the heavenly gift,[g] who have shared in the
Holy Spirit,[h] 5who have tasted the goodness[i] of the word of God[j] and the powers
of the coming age, 6if they fall away, to be
brought back to repentance,[k] because[a] to
their loss they are crucifying the Son of
God[l] all over again and subjecting him to
public disgrace.
7Land that drinks in the rain often falling on it and that produces a crop useful
to those for whom it is farmed receives the
blessing of God. 8But land that produces
thorns and thistles is worthless and is in
danger of being cursed.[m] In the end it will
be burned.
9Even though we speak like this, dear
friends,[n] we are confident of better things
in your case—things that accompany salvation. 10God is not unjust; he will not
forget your work and the love you have
shown him as you have helped his people
and continue to help them.[o] 11We want
each of you to show this same diligence to
the very end, in order to make your hope[p]
sure. 12We do not want you to become
lazy, but to imitate[q] those who through
faith and patience[r] inherit what has been
promised.[s]

The Certainty of God's Promise

13When God made his promise to Abraham, since there was no one greater for
him to swear by, he swore by himself,[t]
14saying, "I will surely bless you and give
you many descendants."[b][u] 15And so after
waiting patiently, Abraham received what
was promised.[v]
16Men swear by someone greater than
themselves, and the oath confirms what is
said and puts an end to all argument.[w]
17Because God wanted to make the unchanging[x] nature of his purpose very
clear to the heirs of what was promised,[y]
he confirmed it with an oath. 18God did
this so that, by two unchangeable things
in which it is impossible for God to lie,[z]
we who have fled to take hold of the hope[a]
offered to us may be greatly encouraged.
19We have this hope as an anchor for the
soul, firm and secure. It enters the inner
sanctuary behind the curtain,[b] 20where
Jesus, who went before us, has entered on
our behalf.[c] He has become a high priest[d]
forever, in the order of Melchizedek.[e]

Melchizedek the Priest

7 This Melchizedek was king of Salem[f]
and priest of God Most High.[g] He met
Abraham returning from the defeat of the
kings and blessed him,[h] 2and Abraham
gave him a tenth of everything. First, his
name means "king of righteousness";
then also, "king of Salem" means "king of
peace." 3Without father or mother, without genealogy,[i] without beginning of

6:3 [e] Ac 18:21
6:4 [f] Heb 10:32 [g] Eph 2:8 [h] Gal 3:2
6:5 [i] Ps 34:8 [j] S Heb 4:12
6:6 [k] 2Pe 2:21; 1Jn 5:16 [l] S Mt 4:3
6:8 [m] Ge 3:17,18; Isa 5:6; 27:4
6:9 [n] S 1Co 10:14
6:10 [o] S Mt 10:40,42; 1Th 1:3
6:11 [p] S Heb 3:6
6:12 [q] Heb 13:7 [r] 2Th 1:4; Jas 1:3; Rev 13:10; 14:12 [s] Heb 10:36
6:13 [t] Ge 22:16; Lk 1:73
6:14 [u] Ge 22:17
6:15 [v] Ge 21:5
6:16 [w] Ex 22:11
6:17 [x] ver 18; Ps 110:4 [y] Ro 4:16; Heb 11:9
6:18 [z] Nu 23:19; Tit 1:2 [a] S Heb 3:6
6:19 [b] Lev 16:2; Heb 9:2,3,7
6:20 [c] S Heb 4:14 [d] S Heb 2:17 [e] S Heb 5:6
7:1 [f] Ps 76:2 [g] S Mk 5:7 [h] ver 6; Ge 14:18-20
7:3 [i] ver 6

[a] 6 Or *repentance while* [b] 14 Gen. 22:17

6:4–6 IT IS IMPOSSIBLE ... TO BE BROUGHT BACK TO REPENTANCE. Here the author of Hebrews discusses the consequences of apostasy (falling away from the faith). For more on this, see article on PERSONAL APOSTASY, p. 492.

6:6 IF THEY FALL AWAY. This phrase (Gk *parapesontas*, from *parapiptō*) is an aorist participle and should be rendered in the past tense—literally, "having fallen away." The word "if" does not appear in any Greek text. The writer of Hebrews presents "falling away" as a real possibility.

6:9–20 BETTER THINGS IN YOUR CASE. The writer is confident that his readers have not entered into the apostasy described in vv. 4–8. He assures them that for those who remain loyal to Christ in faith and love (vv. 10–12), their hope of eternal salvation is certain and unchangeable, because God cannot lie and his promises remain steadfast (vv. 13–20).

6:18 IMPOSSIBLE FOR GOD TO LIE. Because God cannot lie, his promises to Abraham are true (v. 14). God's truthfulness applies not only to his word to Abraham, but also to his Word in all Scripture. That is, because Scripture is the inspired Word of God, it is completely true and trustworthy. The truth of God's Word is inherent in the very words and sentences of Scripture. Its authors were guided by the Holy Spirit to write the original manuscripts in such a way that the transmission of God's message to humanity was communicated without error (see article on THE INSPIRATION AND AUTHORITY OF SCRIPTURE, p. 474).

7:1 MELCHIZEDEK. Melchizedek, a contemporary of Abraham, was a Canaanite king of Salem and a priest of God (Ge 14:18). Abraham paid tithes to him and was blessed by him (vv. 2–7). The author of Hebrews considered him a type of Jesus Christ, who was both priest and king (v. 3). Christ's priesthood is "in the order of Melchizedek" (6:20), meaning that Christ is both before and greater than Abraham, Levi and the Levitical priests.

7:3 WITHOUT FATHER OR MOTHER. This does not mean that Melchizedek literally had no parents or family or that he was an angel. It simply means that Scripture does not record his genealogy and says nothing about his beginning and end. Therefore, he serves as a type of the eternal Christ, whose priesthood will never end (vv. 24–25).

days or end of life, like the Son of God[j]
he remains a priest forever.
4 Just think how great he was: Even the
patriarch[k] Abraham gave him a tenth of
the plunder![l] 5 Now the law requires the
descendants of Levi who become priests
to collect a tenth from the people[m]—that
is, their brothers—even though their
brothers are descended from Abraham.
6 This man, however, did not trace his descent from Levi, yet he collected a tenth
from Abraham and blessed[n] him who had
the promises.[o] 7 And without doubt the
lesser person is blessed by the greater.
8 In the one case, the tenth is collected by
men who die; but in the other case, by him
who is declared to be living.[p] 9 One might
even say that Levi, who collects the tenth,
paid the tenth through Abraham, 10 because when Melchizedek met Abraham,
Levi was still in the body of his ancestor.

Jesus Like Melchizedek

11 If perfection could have been attained
through the Levitical priesthood (for on
the basis of it the law was given to the
people),[q] why was there still need for another priest to come[r]—one in the order of
Melchizedek,[s] not in the order of Aaron?
12 For when there is a change of the priesthood, there must also be a change of the
law. 13 He of whom these things are said
belonged to a different tribe,[t] and no one
from that tribe has ever served at the altar.[u] 14 For it is clear that our Lord descended from Judah,[v] and in regard to
that tribe Moses said nothing about
priests. 15 And what we have said is even
more clear if another priest like Melchizedek appears, 16 one who has become a
priest not on the basis of a regulation as
to his ancestry but on the basis of the
power of an indestructible life. 17 For it is
declared:

"You are a priest forever,
in the order of Melchizedek."[c][w]

18 The former regulation is set aside because it was weak and useless[x] 19 (for the
law made nothing perfect),[y] and a better
hope[z] is introduced, by which we draw
near to God.[a]
20 And it was not without an oath! Others became priests without any oath,
21 but he became a priest with an oath
when God said to him:

"The Lord has sworn
and will not change his mind:[b]
'You are a priest forever.' "[c][c]

22 Because of this oath, Jesus has become
the guarantee of a better covenant.[d]

Jesus Our Intercessor

23 Now there have been many of those
priests, since death prevented them from
continuing in office; 24 but because Jesus
lives forever, he has a permanent priesthood.[e] 25 Therefore he is able to save[f]

7:3 [j]S Mt 4:3 **7:4** [k]Ac 2:29 [l]Ge 14:20 **7:5** [m]Nu 18:21,26 **7:6** [n]Ge 14:19,20 [o]Ro 4:13 **7:8** [p]Heb 5:6; 6:20 **7:11** [q]ver 18,19; Heb 8:7 [r]Heb 10:1 [s]ver 17; S Heb 5:6 **7:13** [t]ver 11 [u]ver 14
7:14 [v]Isa 11:1; Mt 1:3; 2:6; Lk 3:33; Rev 5:5 **7:17** [w]Ps 110:4; ver 21; S Heb 5:6 **7:18** [x]Ro 8:3 **7:19** [y]ver 11; Ro 3:20; 7:7,8; Gal 3:21; Heb 9:9; 10:1 [z]S Heb 3:6 [a]ver 25; Heb 4:16; 10:1,22; Jas 4:8 **7:21** [b]Nu 23:19; 1Sa 15:29; Mal 3:6; Ro 11:29 [c]Ps 110:4; S Heb 5:6 **7:22** [d]S Lk 22:20 **7:24** [e]ver 28 **7:25** [f]S Ro 11:14

[c] *17,21* Psalm 110:4

7:11 IF PERFECTION COULD HAVE BEEN ATTAINED. Because the Levitical priesthood was imperfect (cf. 10:4) and administered by sinful humans (vv. 27–28), it was replaced by the perfect priest, the Son of God. Christ is a perfect priest because he is wholly righteous, had to die only once as a sacrifice for our sins, serves as our eternal priest before God in heaven, and lives forever (vv. 24–28). Therefore, he is able to save completely and forever all who come to God through him (see v. 25, note).

7:19 THE LAW MADE NOTHING PERFECT. The OT law was imperfect because it could not impart divine life or the power to fulfill its demands, nor did it offer complete and perfect access to God (v. 25; see Gal 3:19, note).

7:25 ALWAYS LIVES TO INTERCEDE. Christ lives in heaven in his Father's presence (8:1), interceding for each and every one of his followers according to the Father's will (cf. Ro 8:33–34; 1Ti 2:5; 1Jn 2:1). (1) Through Christ's ministry of intercession, we experience God's love and presence and find mercy and grace to help in any kind of need (4:16), temptation (Lk 22:32), weakness (4:15; 5:2), sin (1Jn 1:9; 2:1) and trial (Ro 8:31–39).

(2) Christ's high-priestly prayer for his people (Jn 17), as well as his desire to pour out the Spirit on all believers (Ac 2:33), help us understand the content of Christ's intercessory ministry (see Jn 17:1, note).

(3) Through Christ's intercession, the one who comes (i.e., continually comes, for the Greek participle is in the present tense, emphasizing continual activity) to God may receive grace to be saved completely. Christ's intercession as our high priest is essential to our salvation. Without that and without his grace, mercy and help mediated to us through that intercession, we would fall away from God, once again be enslaved to sin and Satan's dominion, and incur just condemnation. Our only hope is to come to God through Christ in faith (see 1Pe 1:5, note).

(4) Note that Christ does not remain an advocate and intercessor for those who refuse to confess and forsake sin and who depart from fellowship with God (cf. 1Jn 1:5–7,9; 3:10). His intercession to "save completely" is only for "those who come to God through him" (cf. 4:16). There is no safety and security for those who deliberately sin and refuse to seek God (10:21–31; see 3:6, note; see article on PERSONAL APOSTASY, p. 492).

(5) Since Christ is our only mediator and intercessor in heaven, any attempt to treat angels or dead saints as mediators and to offer prayers to the Father through them is both futile and unbiblical (see Col 1:2,

completely[d] those who come to God[g]
through him, because he always lives to
intercede for them.[h]
26Such a high priest[i] meets our need—
one who is holy, blameless, pure, set apart
from sinners,[j] exalted above the heavens.[k] **27**Unlike the other high priests, he
does not need to offer sacrifices[l] day after day, first for his own sins,[m] and then
for the sins of the people. He sacrificed for
their sins once for all[n] when he offered
himself.[o] **28**For the law appoints as high
priests men who are weak;[p] but the oath,
which came after the law, appointed the
Son,[q] who has been made perfect[r] forever.

The High Priest of a New Covenant

8 The point of what we are saying is
this: We do have such a high priest,[s]
who sat down at the right hand of the
throne of the Majesty in heaven,[t] **2**and
who serves in the sanctuary, the true tabernacle[u] set up by the Lord, not by man.
3Every high priest[v] is appointed to offer both gifts and sacrifices,[w] and so it
was necessary for this one also to have
something to offer.[x] **4**If he were on earth,
he would not be a priest, for there are
already men who offer the gifts prescribed
by the law.[y] **5**They serve at a sanctuary
that is a copy[z] and shadow[a] of what is in
heaven. This is why Moses was warned[b]
when he was about to build the tabernacle: "See to it that you make everything
according to the pattern shown you on the
mountain."[e][c] **6**But the ministry Jesus has
received is as superior to theirs as the
covenant[d] of which he is mediator[e] is superior to the old one, and it is founded on
better promises.
7For if there had been nothing wrong
with that first covenant, no place would
have been sought for another.[f] **8**But God
found fault with the people and said[f]:

"The time is coming, declares the
Lord,
when I will make a new covenant[g]
with the house of Israel
and with the house of Judah.
9It will not be like the covenant
I made with their forefathers[h]
when I took them by the hand
to lead them out of Egypt,
because they did not remain faithful
to my covenant,
and I turned away from them,
declares the Lord.
10This is the covenant[i] I will make
with the house of Israel
after that time, declares the Lord.
I will put my laws in their minds
and write them on their hearts.[j]
I will be their God,
and they will be my people.[k]
11No longer will a man teach his
neighbor,
or a man his brother, saying, 'Know
the Lord,'
because they will all know me,[l]
from the least of them to the
greatest.
12For I will forgive their wickedness
and will remember their sins no
more."[m][g][n]

13By calling this covenant "new,"[o] he
has made the first one obsolete;[p] and
what is obsolete and aging will soon disappear.

7:25 [g]S ver 19 [h]S Ro 8:34
7:26 [i]S Heb 2:17 [j]S 2Co 5:21 [k]S Heb 4:14
7:27 [l]Heb 5:1 [m]S Heb 5:3 [n]Ro 6:10; Heb 9:12,26,28; 10:10; 1Pe 3:18 [o]Eph 5:2; Heb 9:14,28
7:28 [p]Heb 5:2 [q]S Heb 1:2 [r]S Heb 2:10
8:1 [s]S Heb 2:17 [t]S Mk 16:19; S Heb 4:14
8:2 [u]Heb 9:11,24
8:3 [v]S Heb 2:17 [w]Heb 5:1; 9:9 [x]Heb 9:14
8:4 [y]Heb 5:1; 9:9
8:5 [z]Heb 9:23 [a]Col 2:17; Heb 10:1 [b]Heb 11:7; 12:25 [c]Ex 25:40
8:6 [d]ver 8,13; S Lk 22:20 [e]S Gal 3:20
8:7 [f]Heb 7:11,18; 10:1
8:8 [g]ver 6,13; S Lk 22:20
8:9 [h]Ex 19:5,6; 20:1-17
8:10 [i]Ro 11:27 [j]2Co 3:3; Heb 10:16 [k]Eze 11:20; Zec 8:8
8:11 [l]Isa 54:13; S Jn 6:45
8:12 [m]Heb 10:17 [n]Jer 31:31-34
8:13 [o]ver 6,8; S Lk 22:20 [p]2Co 5:17

[d] *25* Or *forever* [e] *5* Exodus 25:40 [f] *8* Some manuscripts may be translated *fault and said to the people.* [g] *12* Jer. 31:31-34

note; 2:18, note).

8:1 WE DO HAVE SUCH A HIGH PRIEST. After Christ took upon himself the punishment for our sins by giving his life as a sacrifice, he entered heaven, where he serves in God's presence on behalf of us who believe. Jesus' ministry as high priest (cf. 2:17) embraces six areas: (1) Jesus was both the priest and the sacrifice itself. He offered himself for all people as a perfect sacrifice for sin by shedding his blood and dying in the sinner's place (2:17–18; 4:15; 7:26–28; Mk 10:45; 1Co 15:3; 1Pe 1:18–19; 2:22–24; 3:18).

(2) Jesus mediates the new and better covenant in order that all "who are called may receive the promised eternal inheritance" (9:15–22; see article on THE OLD COVENANT AND THE NEW COVENANT, p. 500), and with confidence may have continual access to God (4:16; 6:19–20; 7:25; 10:19–22; see Jn 17:1, note on Jesus' high-priestly prayer).

(3) He is in heaven in God's presence to give God's grace to us who believe (4:14–16). By this grace mediated to us by him, Christ regenerates us (Jn 3:3) and pours out the Holy Spirit on us (Ac 1:4; 2:4,33).

(4) Jesus acts as a mediator between God and all who have broken God's law and seek forgiveness and reconciliation (1Jn 2:1–2).

(5) Jesus holds his priesthood permanently, sympathizing with believers' temptations and aiding them in their needs (2:18; 4:15–16).

(6) Jesus lives forever to intercede continually in heaven for all those who in faith "come to God through him" (7:25). He will eventually bring the believer's salvation to final fulfillment (7:25, note; 9:28, note).

8:6–13 COVENANT . . . IS SUPERIOR. A significant theme of chs. 8–10 is the contrast between the old covenant that was centered around the Law of Moses and the new covenant that was instituted by Jesus Christ. See article on THE OLD COVENANT AND THE NEW COVENANT, p. 500.

Worship in the Earthly Tabernacle

9 Now the first covenant had regulations for worship and also an earthly sanctuary.[q] **2**A tabernacle[r] was set up. In its first room were the lampstand,[s] the table[t] and the consecrated bread;[u] this was called the Holy Place.[v] **3**Behind the second curtain was a room called the Most Holy Place,[w] **4**which had the golden altar of incense[x] and the gold-covered ark of the covenant.[y] This ark contained the gold jar of manna,[z] Aaron's staff that had budded,[a] and the stone tablets of the covenant.[b] **5**Above the ark were the cherubim of the Glory,[c] overshadowing the atonement cover.[h][d] But we cannot discuss these things in detail now.

6When everything had been arranged like this, the priests entered regularly[e] into the outer room to carry on their ministry. **7**But only the high priest entered[f] the inner room,[g] and that only once a year,[h] and never without blood,[i] which he offered for himself[j] and for the sins the people had committed in ignorance.[k] **8**The Holy Spirit was showing[l] by this that the way[m] into the Most Holy Place had not yet been disclosed as long as the first tabernacle was still standing. **9**This is an illustration[n] for the present time, indicating that the gifts and sacrifices being offered[o] were not able to clear the conscience[p] of the worshiper. **10**They are only a matter of food[q] and drink[r] and various ceremonial washings[s]—external regulations[t] applying until the time of the new order.

The Blood of Christ

11When Christ came as high priest[u] of the good things that are already here,[i][v] he went through the greater and more perfect tabernacle[w] that is not man-made,[x] that is to say, not a part of this creation. **12**He did not enter by means of the blood of goats and calves;[y] but he entered the Most Holy Place[z] once for all[a] by his own blood,[b] having obtained eternal redemption. **13**The blood of goats and bulls[c] and the ashes of a heifer[d] sprinkled on those who are ceremonially unclean sanctify them so that they are outwardly clean. **14**How much more, then, will the blood of Christ, who through the eternal Spirit[e] offered himself[f] unblemished to God, cleanse our consciences[g] from acts that

9:1 [q]Ex 25:8 **9:2** [r]Ex 25:8,9 [s]Ex 25:31-39 [t]Ex 25:23-29 [u]Ex 25:30; Lev 24:5-8 [v]Ex 26:33,34 **9:3** [w]Ex 26:31-33 **9:4** [x]Ex 30:1-5 [y]Ex 25:10-22 [z]Ex 16:32,33 [a]Nu 17:10 [b]Ex 31:18; 32:15 **9:5** [c]Ex 25:17-19 [d]Ex 25:20-22; 26:34 **9:6** [e]Nu 28:3 **9:7** [f]Lev 16:11-19 [g]ver 2,3 [h]Lev 16:34 [i]Lev 16:11,14 [j]Lev 16:11; Heb 5:2,3 [k]Heb 5:2,3 **9:8** [l]S Heb 3:7 [m]Jn 14:6; Heb 10:19,20 **9:9** [n]Heb 10:1 [o]Heb 5:1; 8:3 [p]S Heb 7:19 **9:10** [q]Lev 11:2-23 [r]Nu 6:3; Col 2:16 [s]Lev 11:25,28,40 [t]Heb 7:16 **9:11** [u]S Heb 2:17 [v]Heb 10:1 [w]ver 24; Heb 8:2 [x]S Jn 2:19 **9:12** [y]ver 19; Lev 16:6,15; Heb 10:4 [z]ver 24 [a]ver 26,28; S Heb 7:27 [b]ver 14; S Ro 3:25 **9:13** [c]Heb 10:4 [d]Nu 19:9,17,18 **9:14** [e]1Pe 3:18 [f]S Eph 5:2 [g]Ps 51:2; 65:3; Jer 33:8; Zec 13:1; S Tit 2:14; Heb 10:2,22

h *5* Traditionally *the mercy seat* i *11* Some early manuscripts *are to come*

9:1–7 THE FIRST COVENANT. In his discussion on how the new covenant is so much superior to the old (or first) covenant, the writer to the Hebrews analyzes the major features of worship and sacrifice in Israel's religion. See article on THE OLD COVENANT AND THE NEW COVENANT, p. 500.

9:4 ARK OF THE COVENANT. The ark of the covenant was a sacred box or chest containing a jar of manna (a reminder of God's provision), Aaron's staff (a reminder of God's mighty acts), and the two stone tablets on which were written the Ten Commandments (a reminder of the law's importance as God's standard of holiness for his people). The lid of the ark was a golden plate called the atonement cover, or mercy seat, which declared God's redeeming mercy through shed blood (see next note).

9:5 THE ATONEMENT COVER. On the Day of Atonement, both the bull's blood that made atonement for the high priest and his family and the goat's blood that served as a sin offering for the nation were sprinkled on the atonement cover before God (Lev 16:2,14). The earthly atonement cover is a figure or type of the heavenly throne of grace, which believers approach because of Christ's blood in order to receive grace and help (4:16).

9:7 THE INNER ROOM. The inner sanctuary, called the Most Holy Place, symbolized God's presence. The high priest was strictly forbidden to enter the Most Holy Place more than once a year. The Holy Spirit was teaching that under the old covenant, unimpeded access to God's presence was not yet possible because intimate communion with him could exist only when a person's inward conscience had been cleansed perfectly (vv. 8–9). This cleansing was provided for when Christ died as an eternal sacrifice for sin.

9:14 THE BLOOD OF CHRIST. The blood of Jesus Christ is central to the NT concept of redemption (1Co 10:16; 11:27; Eph 2:13; 1Pe 1:2; Rev 7:14; 12:11). On the cross Christ shed his innocent blood in order to remove our sins and to reconcile us with God (5:8; Ro 5:19; Php 2:8; cf. Lev 16).

By his blood Christ accomplished the following: (1) His blood forgives the sins of all who repent and believe (Mt 26:28). (2) His blood ransoms all believers from the power of Satan and evil powers (Ac 20:28; Eph 1:7; 1Pe 1:18–19; Rev 5:9; 12:11). (3) His blood justifies all who believe in him (Ro 3:24–25). (4) His blood cleanses believers' consciences that they might serve God without guilt in full assurance (9:14; 10:22; 13:18). (5) His blood sanctifies God's people (13:12; 1Jn 1:7–10). (6) His blood opens the way for believers to come directly before God through Christ in order to find grace, mercy, help and salvation (7:25; 10:19; Eph 2:13,18). (7) His blood is a guarantee of all the promises of the new covenant (10:29; 13:20; Mt 26:28; 1Co 11:25). (8) The saving, reconciling and purifying power of Christ's blood is continually appropriated to believers as they come to God through Christ (7:25; 10:22; 1Jn 1:7).

THE OLD COVENANT AND THE NEW COVENANT

***Heb 8:6** "But the ministry Jesus has received is as superior to theirs as the covenant of which he is mediator is superior to the old one, and it is founded on better promises."*

Heb 8–10 describes numerous aspects of the old covenant, such as the worship, regulations and sacrificial ritual in the tabernacle; it discusses the various rooms and furniture of this OT worship center. The author's purpose is twofold: (1) to contrast the high priest's service in the earthly sanctuary under the old covenant with Christ's ministry as high priest in the heavenly sanctuary under the new covenant; (2) to show how these various aspects in the old covenant foreshadow or serve as a type of the ministry of Christ, the one who inaugurated the new covenant. This article summarizes the relationship between these two covenants.

(1) Under the old covenant, salvation and a right relationship with God came through a faith expressed by obedience to his law and its sacrificial system. Sacrifices in the OT had three main purposes: (a) They taught God's people the gravity of sin. Sin separated sinners from a holy God, and they could be reconciled to God and find forgiveness only through the shedding of blood (Ex 12:3–14; Lev 16; 17:11; Heb 9:22). (b) They provided a way for Israel to come to God through faith, obedience and love (cf. Heb 4:16; 7:25; 10:1). (c) They pointed forward to or foreshadowed (Heb 8:5; 10:1) Christ's perfect sacrifice for the sins of the human race (cf. Jn 1:29; 1Pe 1:18–19; see Ex 12:3–14; Lev 16; see Gal 3:19, note).

(2) Jeremiah prophesied that at some time in the future God would make a new covenant, a better one, with his people (Jer 31:31–34; cf. Heb 8:8–12). It is a better covenant than the old (cf. Ro 7) because it completely forgives the sins of the repentant (Heb 8:12), makes them children of God (Ro 8:15–16), gives them a new heart and nature so that they can spontaneously love and obey God (Heb 8:10; cf. Eze 11:19–20), brings them into an intimate personal relationship with Jesus Christ and the Father (Heb 8:11), and provides a greater experience in the Holy Spirit (Joel 2:28; Ac 1:5–8; 2:16–17,33,38–39; Ro 8:14–15,26).

(3) Jesus is the one who instituted the new covenant or new testament (both ideas are present in the Greek word *diathēkē*), and his heavenly ministry is far superior to the ministry of OT earthly priests. The new covenant is an agreement, promise, last will and testament, and a statement of intention to bestow divine grace and blessing on those who respond to God in obedient faith. Specifically, it is a covenant of promise for those who through faith accept Christ as God's Son, receive his promises, and commit themselves personally to him and to the obligations of the new covenant.

(a) Jesus Christ's position as mediator of the new covenant (Heb 8:6; 9:15; 12:24) is based on his sacrificial death (Mt 26:28; Mk 14:24; Heb 9:14–15; 10:29; 12:24). The promises and obligations of this new covenant are embodied in the entire NT. Its purpose is (i) to save from guilt and condemnation all those who believe in Christ and commit their lives to the truths and obligations of his covenant (Heb 9:16–17; cf. Mk 14:24; 1Co 11:25), and (ii) to form them into a people who are God's very own (Heb 8:10; cf. Eze 11:19–20; 1Pe 2:9).

(b) Jesus' sacrifice is a better one than the sacrifices of the old covenant because it was a voluntary and obedient sacrifice of a righteous person (Jesus Christ) rather than the involuntary sacrifice of an animal. Jesus' sacrifice and fulfillment of God's will were perfect and thus opened the way for complete forgiveness, reconciliation and sanctification (Heb 10:10,15–17).

(c) The new covenant can be called the new covenant of the Spirit, for it is the Holy Spirit who ministers life and power to those who accept God's covenant (2Co 3:1–6; see Jn 17:3, note; see articles on BIBLICAL WORDS FOR SALVATION, p. 292, and FAITH AND GRACE, p. 302).

(4) All who participate in the new covenant through Jesus Christ receive its blessings and salvation only as they persevere in faith and obedience (see Heb 3:6, note). The faithless are excluded from its blessings (see 3:18, note; see article on PERSONAL APOSTASY, p. 492).

(5) With the coming of the new covenant through Christ, the old covenant became obsolete (Heb 8:13). In doing so, however, the new covenant does not render the entire body of OT Scripture obsolete, but only the Mosaic covenant whereby salvation was gained by obedience to the law and its sacrificial system. The OT is not obsolete; much of its revelation points toward Christ and, as God's inspired Word, is useful for teaching, rebuking, correcting and training in righteousness (see article on THE INSPIRATION AND AUTHORITY OF SCRIPTURE, p. 474).

lead to death,[j][h] so that we may serve the
living God![i]
15For this reason Christ is the mediator[j] of a new covenant,[k] that those who
are called[l] may receive the promised[m]
eternal inheritance[n]—now that he has
died as a ransom to set them free from the
sins committed under the first covenant.[o]
16In the case of a will,[k] it is necessary
to prove the death of the one who made it,
17because a will is in force only when
somebody has died; it never takes effect
while the one who made it is living. 18This
is why even the first covenant was not put
into effect without blood.[p] 19When Moses
had proclaimed[q] every commandment of
the law to all the people, he took the blood
of calves,[r] together with water, scarlet
wool and branches of hyssop, and sprinkled the scroll and all the people.[s] 20He
said, "This is the blood of the covenant,
which God has commanded you to
keep."[l][t] 21In the same way, he sprinkled
with the blood both the tabernacle and
everything used in its ceremonies. 22In
fact, the law requires that nearly everything be cleansed with blood,[u] and without the shedding of blood there is no forgiveness.[v]
23It was necessary, then, for the copies[w] of the heavenly things to be purified
with these sacrifices, but the heavenly
things themselves with better sacrifices
than these. 24For Christ did not enter a
man-made sanctuary that was only a copy
of the true one;[x] he entered heaven itself,[y] now to appear for us in God's presence.[z] 25Nor did he enter heaven to offer
himself again and again, the way the high
priest enters the Most Holy Place[a] every
year with blood that is not his own.[b]
26Then Christ would have had to suffer
many times since the creation of the
world.[c] But now he has appeared[d] once
for all[e] at the end of the ages to do away
with sin by the sacrifice of himself.[f]
27Just as man is destined to die once,[g]
and after that to face judgment,[h] 28so
Christ was sacrificed once[i] to take away
the sins of many people; and he will appear a second time,[j] not to bear sin,[k] but
to bring salvation[l] to those who are waiting for him.[m]

Christ's Sacrifice Once for All

10 The law is only a shadow[n] of the
good things[o] that are coming—
not the realities themselves.[p] For this
reason it can never, by the same sacrifices
repeated endlessly year after year, make
perfect[q] those who draw near to worship.[r] 2If it could, would they not have
stopped being offered? For the worshipers
would have been cleansed once for all,
and would no longer have felt guilty for
their sins.[s] 3But those sacrifices are an
annual reminder of sins,[t] 4because it is
impossible for the blood of bulls and
goats[u] to take away sins.[v]
5Therefore, when Christ came into the
world,[w] he said:

"Sacrifice and offering you did not
desire,
but a body you prepared for me;[x]
6with burnt offerings and sin offerings
you were not pleased.
7Then I said, 'Here I am—it is written
about me in the scroll[y]—
I have come to do your will,
O God.' "[m][z]

8First he said, "Sacrifices and offerings,
burnt offerings and sin offerings you did
not desire, nor were you pleased with

9:14 [h]Heb 6:1 [i]S Mt 16:16 9:15 [j]S Gal 3:20 [k]S Lk 22:20 [l]S Ro 8:28; S 11:29 [m]Heb 6:15; 10:36 [n]S Ac 20:32 [o]Heb 7:22 9:18 [p]Ex 24:6-8 9:19 [q]Heb 1:1 [r]ver 12 [s]Ex 24:6-8 9:20 [t]Ex 24:8; S Mt 26:28 9:22 [u]Ex 29:21; Lev 8:15 [v]Lev 17:11 9:23 [w]Heb 8:5 9:24 [x]Heb 8:2 [y]ver 12; S Heb 4:14 [z]S Ro 8:34 9:25 [a]Heb 10:19 [b]ver 7,8 9:26 [c]Heb 4:3 [d]1Jn 3:5 [e]ver 12,28; S Heb 7:27 [f]ver 12 9:27 [g]Ge 3:19 [h]2Co 5:10 9:28 [i]ver 12,26; S Heb 7:27 [j]S Mt 16:27 [k]1Pe 2:24 [l]Heb 5:9 [m]S 1Co 1:7 10:1 [n]Col 2:17; Heb 8:5 [o]Heb 9:11 [p]Heb 9:23 [q]ver 4, 11; S Heb 7:19 [r]S Heb 7:19 10:2 [s]Heb 9:9 10:3 [t]Lev 16:34; Heb 9:7 10:4 [u]Heb 9:12, 13 [v]ver 1,11 10:5 [w]Heb 1:6 [x]Heb 2:14; 1Pe 2:24 10:7 [y]Ezr 6:2; Jer 36:2 [z]Ps 40:6-8; S Mt 26:39

j *14* Or *from useless rituals* k *16* Same Greek word as *covenant*; also in verse 17
l *20* Exodus 24:8 m *7* Psalm 40:6-8 (see Septuagint)

9:15 MEDIATOR OF A NEW COVENANT. For comments on Jesus' function as mediator of a new covenant, see article on THE OLD COVENANT AND THE NEW COVENANT, p. 500.

9:28 WILL APPEAR A SECOND TIME. Under the old covenant, the Israelites watched intensely for the reappearance of their high priest after he had gone into the sanctuary to make atonement. Likewise believers, knowing that their high priest has entered the heavenly sanctuary as their advocate, wait with earnest hope for his reappearing to bring a complete salvation (see Jn 14:3, note; 2Ti 4:8; see article on THE RAPTURE, p. 440).

10:1 THE SAME SACRIFICES REPEATED ENDLESSLY. For comments on the purposes of OT sacrifices, see article on THE OLD COVENANT AND THE NEW COVENANT, p. 500.

10:4 THE BLOOD OF BULLS. The blood of animals was only a temporary provision or atonement for the sins of the people; ultimately, a human was needed to serve as a substitute for humanity. Thus Christ came to earth and was born as a human so that he might offer himself in our place (2:9,14, notes). Furthermore, only a human who was free from sin could take our punishment for sin (2:14–18; 4:15) and thus adequately and perfectly satisfy the demands of God's holiness (cf. Ro 3:25–26).

10:5–10 SACRIFICE AND OFFERING. Ps 40:6–8 is cited to prove that the voluntary and obedient sacrifice of Jesus Christ is better than the involuntary animal sacrifices in the OT; see article on THE OLD COVENANT AND THE NEW COVENANT, p. 500.

them"[a] (although the law required them
to be made). 9Then he said, "Here I am, I
have come to do your will."[b] He sets aside
the first to establish the second. 10And by
that will, we have been made holy[c]
through the sacrifice of the body[d] of Jesus
Christ once for all.[e]
11Day after day every priest stands and
performs his religious duties; again and
again he offers the same sacrifices,[f]
which can never take away sins.[g] 12But
when this priest had offered for all time
one sacrifice for sins,[h] he sat down at the
right hand of God.[i] 13Since that time he
waits for his enemies to be made his footstool,[j] 14because by one sacrifice he has
made perfect[k] forever those who are being made holy.[l]
15The Holy Spirit also testifies[m] to us
about this. First he says:

16"This is the covenant I will make
with them
after that time, says the Lord.
I will put my laws in their hearts,
and I will write them on their
minds."[n][n]

17Then he adds:

"Their sins and lawless acts
I will remember no more."[o][o]

18And where these have been forgiven,
there is no longer any sacrifice for sin.

A Call to Persevere

19Therefore, brothers, since we have
confidence[p] to enter the Most Holy
Place[q] by the blood of Jesus, 20by a new
and living way[r] opened for us through the
curtain,[s] that is, his body, 21and since we
have a great priest[t] over the house of
God,[u] 22let us draw near to God[v] with a
sincere heart in full assurance of faith,[w]
having our hearts sprinkled to cleanse us
from a guilty conscience[x] and having our
bodies washed with pure water.[y] 23Let us
hold unswervingly to the hope[z] we profess,[a] for he who promised is faithful.[b]
24And let us consider how we may spur
one another on toward love and good
deeds.[c] 25Let us not give up meeting together,[d] as some are in the habit of doing,
but let us encourage one another[e]—and
all the more as you see the Day approaching.[f]
26If we deliberately keep on sinning[g]
after we have received the knowledge of
the truth,[h] no sacrifice for sins is left,
27but only a fearful expectation of judgment and of raging fire[i] that will consume
the enemies of God. 28Anyone who rejected the law of Moses died without mercy on
the testimony of two or three witnesses.[j]
29How much more severely do you think
a man deserves to be punished who has
trampled the Son of God[k] under foot,[l]
who has treated as an unholy thing the
blood of the covenant[m] that sanctified
him,[n] and who has insulted the Spirit[o] of
grace?[p] 30For we know him who said, "It

10:8 [a]ver 5,6; S Mk 12:33 **10:9** [b]ver 7 **10:10** [c]ver 14; S Eph 5:26 [d]Heb 2:14; 1Pe 2:24 [e]S Heb 7:27 **10:11** [f]Heb 5:1 [g]ver 1,4 **10:12** [h]Heb 5:1 [i]S Mk 16:19 **10:13** [j]Jos 10:24; Heb 1:13 **10:14** [k]ver 1 [l]ver 10; S Eph 5:26 **10:15** [m]S Heb 3:7 **10:16** [n]Jer 31:33; Heb 8:10 **10:17** [o]Jer 31:34; Heb 8:12 **10:19** [p]S Eph 3:12 [q]Lev 16:2; Eph 2:18; Heb 9:8, 12,25 **10:20** [r]Heb 9:8 [s]Heb 6:19; 9:3 **10:21** [t]S Heb 2:17 [u]S Heb 3:6 **10:22** [v]ver 1; S Heb 7:19 [w]Eph 3:12 [x]Eze 36:25; Heb 9:14; 12:24; 1Pe 1:2 [y]S Ac 22:16 **10:23** [z]S Heb 3:6 [a]S Heb 3:1 [b]S 1Co 1:9 **10:24** [c]S Tit 2:14 **10:25** [d]Ac 2:42 [e]Heb 3:13 [f]S 1Co 3:13 **10:26** [g]Ex 21:14; Nu 15:30; Heb 5:2; 6:4-8; 2Pe 2:20 [h]S 1Ti 2:4 **10:27** [i]Isa 26:11; 2Th 1:7; Heb 9:27; 12:29 **10:28** [j]Dt 17:6,7; S Mt 18:16; Heb 2:2 **10:29** [k]S Mt 4:3 [l]Heb 6:6 [m]S Mt 26:28 [n]1Co 6:11; Rev 1:5 [o]Eph 4:30; Heb 6:4 [p]Heb 2:3; 12:25

[n] *16* Jer. 31:33 [o] *17* Jer. 31:34

10:14 MADE PERFECT FOREVER THOSE WHO ARE BEING MADE HOLY. The one offering of Christ on the cross and its benefit (i.e., perfect salvation) are eternally efficacious. Perfect salvation in Christ is imparted to all who are being made holy as they draw near to God through Christ (v. 22; 7:25). Note that the Greek word "made holy" here and in v. 10 is a present participle, emphasizing continuous action in the present.

10:19 SINCE WE HAVE. In contrast to the limited access to God that the Israelites had, Christ, by giving his life as a perfect sacrifice, has opened a way into God's very presence and the throne of grace. Therefore, we as believers may in gratefulness constantly draw near to God in prayer.

10:22 LET US DRAW NEAR. Faith and drawing near to God through Jesus Christ are inseparable. (1) Faith is defined as sincerely coming to God and believing in his goodness (11:6). By coming to God through Christ, one finds mercy, grace, help (v. 1; 4:16; 7:19), salvation (7:25), sanctification (v. 14) and cleansing (v. 22). (2) Clearly this implies that where there is no drawing near to God in prayer and fellowship with Christ, there is no saving faith (cf. v. 38). Jesus himself equates faith with earnest prayer to God (Lk 18:8).

10:25 AS YOU SEE THE DAY APPROACHING. The day of Christ's return for his faithful is approaching (see article on THE RAPTURE, p. 440). As it does, we will face many spiritual trials and persecutions, and much doctrinal deception. We must meet together regularly in order to encourage one another to hold firmly to Christ and the apostolic faith of the new covenant.

10:26 IF WE DELIBERATELY KEEP ON SINNING. The author of Hebrews here speaks of the falling away from Christ about which he warned his readers in 6:4–8 (see article on PERSONAL APOSTASY, p. 492).

10:29 TRAMPLED THE SON OF GOD. To keep on sinning deliberately after we have received the knowledge of the truth (v. 26) is (1) to be guilty of trampling underfoot Jesus Christ, treating him with contempt, and despising his life and death; (2) to count the blood of Christ as unworthy of our loyalty; and (3) to insult and rebel against the Holy Spirit, who brings God's grace to our hearts (see article on PERSONAL APOSTASY, p. 492).

is mine to avenge; I will repay,"[p][q] and
again, "The Lord will judge his people."[q][r]
31It is a dreadful thing[s] to fall into the
hands[t] of the living God.[u]
32Remember those earlier days after
you had received the light,[v] when you
stood your ground in a great contest in the
face of suffering.[w] 33Sometimes you were
publicly exposed to insult and persecution;[x] at other times you stood side by
side with those who were so treated.[y]
34You sympathized with those in prison[z]
and joyfully accepted the confiscation of
your property, because you knew that you
yourselves had better and lasting possessions.[a]
35So do not throw away your confidence;[b] it will be richly rewarded. 36You
need to persevere[c] so that when you have
done the will of God, you will receive what
he has promised.[d] 37For in just a very
little while,

"He who is coming[e] will come and
will not delay.[f]
38 But my righteous one[r] will live by
faith.[g]
And if he shrinks back,
I will not be pleased with him."[s][h]

39But we are not of those who shrink back
and are destroyed, but of those who believe and are saved.

By Faith

11 Now faith is being sure of what we
hope for[i] and certain of what we
do not see.[j] 2This is what the ancients
were commended for.[k]
3By faith we understand that the universe was formed at God's command,[l] so
that what is seen was not made out of
what was visible.

The Faith of the Patriarchs

4By faith Abel offered God a better sacrifice than Cain did. By faith he was commended[m] as a righteous man, when God
spoke well of his offerings.[n] And by faith
he still speaks, even though he is dead.[o]
5By faith Enoch was taken from this
life, so that he did not experience death;
he could not be found, because God had
taken him away.[p] For before he was tak-
en, he was commended as one who
pleased God. 6And without faith it is impossible to please God, because anyone
who comes to him[q] must believe that he
exists and that he rewards those who earnestly seek him.
7By faith Noah, when warned about
things not yet seen,[r] in holy fear built an
ark[s] to save his family.[t] By his faith he
condemned the world and became heir of
the righteousness that comes by faith.[u]

The Faith of Abraham and Family

8By faith Abraham, when called to go to
a place he would later receive as his inheritance,[v] obeyed and went,[w] even though

10:30 [q] Dt 32:35; Ro 12:19 [r] Dt 32:36; Ps 135:14 **10:31** [s] S 2Co 5:11 [t] Isa 19:16 [u] S Mt 16:16 **10:32** [v] Heb 6:4 [w] Php 1:29,30 **10:33** [x] 1Co 4:9 [y] Php 4:14; 1Th 2:14 **10:34** [z] Heb 13:3 [a] Heb 11:16; 1Pe 1:4,5 **10:35** [b] S Eph 3:12 **10:36** [c] Ro 5:3; Heb 12:1; Jas 1:3, 4,12; 5:11; 2Pe 1:6 [d] Heb 6:15; 9:15 **10:37** [e] Mt 11:3 [f] Rev 22:20 **10:38** [g] Ro 1:17; Gal 3:11 [h] Hab 2:3, 4 **11:1** [i] S Heb 3:6 [j] S 2Co 4:18 **11:2** [k] ver 4,39 **11:3** [l] Ge 1; Jn 1:3; Heb 1:2; 2Pe 3:5 **11:4** [m] ver 2,39 [n] Ge 4:4; 1Jn 3:12 [o] Heb 12:24 **11:5** [p] Ge 5:21-24 **11:6** [q] Heb 7:19 **11:7** [r] S ver 1 [s] Ge 6:13-22 [t] 1Pe 3:20 [u] Ge 6:9; Eze 14:14,20; S Ro 9:30 **11:8** [v] Ge 12:7 [w] Ge 12:1-4; Ac 7:2-4

[p] *30* Deut. 32:35 [q] *30* Deut. 32:36; Psalm 135:14 [r] *38* One early manuscript *But the righteous* [s] *38* Hab. 2:3,4

10:38 MY RIGHTEOUS ONE WILL LIVE BY FAITH. This fundamental principle, affirmed four times in Scripture (Hab 2:4; Ro 1:17; Gal 3:11; Heb 10:38), governs our relationship to God and our participation in the salvation provided through Jesus Christ. (1) This cardinal truth affirms that the righteous will possess eternal life by faithfully drawing near to God with a sincere believing heart (see v. 22, note). (2) For anyone who shrinks back from Christ and deliberately keeps on sinning, God "will not be pleased with him" and he will incur eternal damnation.

11:1 NOW FAITH IS. Ch. 11 demonstrates the nature of the only kind of faith acceptable before God, a faith triumphant in the worst of situations. It is a faith that believes in spiritual realities (v. 1), leads to righteousness (v. 4), seeks God (v. 6), believes in his goodness (v. 6), has confidence in his Word (vv. 7,11), obeys his commands (v. 8), regulates life on his promises (vv. 13,39), rejects the spirit of this present evil age (v. 13), seeks a heavenly home (vv. 14–16; cf. 13:13–14), perseveres in testing (vv. 17–19), blesses the next generation (v. 21), refuses sin's pleasures (v. 25), endures persecution (v. 27), performs mighty acts of righteousness (vv. 33–35), suffers for God (vv. 25,35–38), and does not return to "the country they had left," i.e., the world (vv. 15–16; see article on FAITH AND GRACE, p. 302).

11:3 UNIVERSE WAS FORMED AT GOD'S COMMAND. The faith by which we understand that God created the world is faith in the divinely inspired revelation found in Ge 1 and other passages (cf. Ps 33:6,9; Isa 55:11).

11:4 A BETTER SACRIFICE. God accepted Abel's sacrifice because Abel was righteous, devoted and obedient (cf. Pr 15:8; Mt 23:35; 1Jn 3:12).

11:6 BELIEVE THAT HE EXISTS. This verse describes the convictions that are a part of saving faith. (1) We must believe in the existence of a personal, infinite, holy God who cares for us. (2) We must believe that God will reward us when we earnestly seek him, knowing that our greatest reward is the joy and presence of God himself. He is our shield and our very great reward (Ge 15:1; cf. Dt 4:29; Mt 7:7–8, note; Jn 14:21, note). (2) We must diligently seek God and earnestly desire his presence and his grace.

11:8 BY FAITH ABRAHAM ... OBEYED. Faith and obedience are inseparable, just as unbelief and disobedience are inseparable (3:18–19; see Jn 3:36, note).

he did not know where he was going. **9**By faith he made his home in the promised land[x] like a stranger in a foreign country; he lived in tents,[y] as did Isaac and Jacob, who were heirs with him of the same promise.[z] **10**For he was looking forward to the city[a] with foundations,[b] whose architect and builder is God.[c]

11By faith Abraham, even though he was past age—and Sarah herself was barren[d]—was enabled to become a father[e] because he[t] considered him faithful[f] who had made the promise. **12**And so from this one man, and he as good as dead,[g] came descendants as numerous as the stars in the sky and as countless as the sand on the seashore.[h]

13All these people were still living by faith when they died. They did not receive the things promised;[i] they only saw them and welcomed them from a distance.[j] And they admitted that they were aliens and strangers on earth.[k] **14**People who say such things show that they are looking for a country of their own. **15**If they had been thinking of the country they had left, they would have had opportunity to return.[l] **16**Instead, they were longing for a better country—a heavenly one.[m] Therefore God is not ashamed[n] to be called their God,[o] for he has prepared a city[p] for them.

17By faith Abraham, when God tested him, offered Isaac as a sacrifice.[q] He who had received the promises was about to sacrifice his one and only son, **18**even though God had said to him, "It is through Isaac that your offspring[u] will be reckoned."[v][r] **19**Abraham reasoned that God could raise the dead,[s] and figuratively speaking, he did receive Isaac back from death.

11:9 [x]Ac 7:5 [y]Ge 12:8; 18:1,9 [z]Heb 6:17
11:10 [a]Heb 12:22; 13:14 [b]Rev 21:2,14 [c]ver 16
11:11 [d]Ge 17:17-19; 18:11-14 [e]Ge 21:2 [f]S 1Co 1:9
11:12 [g]Ro 4:19 [h]Ge 22:17
11:13 [i]ver 39 [j]S Mt 13:17 [k]Ge 23:4; Lev 25:23; Php 3:20; 1Pe 1:17; 2:11
11:15 [l]Ge 24:6-8
11:16 [m]2Ti 4:18 [n]Mk 8:38 [o]Ge 26:24; 28:13; Ex 3:6,15 [p]ver 10; Heb 13:14
11:17 [q]Ge 22:1-10; Jas 2:21
11:18 [r]Ge 21:12; Ro 9:7
11:19 [s]Ro 4:21; S Jn 5:21
11:20 [t]Ge 27:27-29,39,40
11:21 [u]Ge 48:1,8-22
11:22 [v]Ge 50:24,25; Ex 13:19; Jos 24:32
11:23 [w]Ex 2:2 [x]Ex 1:16,22
11:24 [y]Ex 2:10,11
11:25 [z]ver 37
11:26 [a]Heb 13:13 [b]Lk 14:33 [c]Heb 10:35
11:27 [d]Ex 12:50,51
11:28 [e]1Co 10:10 [f]Ex 12:21-23
11:29 [g]Ex 14:21-31

20By faith Isaac blessed Jacob and Esau in regard to their future.[t]

21By faith Jacob, when he was dying, blessed each of Joseph's sons,[u] and worshiped as he leaned on the top of his staff.

22By faith Joseph, when his end was near, spoke about the exodus of the Israelites from Egypt and gave instructions about his bones.[v]

The Faith of Moses

23By faith Moses' parents hid him for three months after he was born,[w] because they saw he was no ordinary child, and they were not afraid of the king's edict.[x]

24By faith Moses, when he had grown up, refused to be known as the son of Pharaoh's daughter.[y] **25**He chose to be mistreated[z] along with the people of God rather than to enjoy the pleasures of sin for a short time. **26**He regarded disgrace[a] for the sake of Christ[b] as of greater value than the treasures of Egypt, because he was looking ahead to his reward.[c] **27**By faith he left Egypt,[d] not fearing the king's anger; he persevered because he saw him who is invisible. **28**By faith he kept the Passover and the sprinkling of blood, so that the destroyer[e] of the firstborn would not touch the firstborn of Israel.[f]

The Faith of the Israelites and Rahab

29By faith the people passed through the Red Sea[w] as on dry land; but when the Egyptians tried to do so, they were drowned.[g]

[t] *11* Or *By faith even Sarah, who was past age, was enabled to bear children because she* [u] *18* Greek *seed* [v] *18* Gen. 21:12 [w] *29* That is, Sea of Reeds

11:10 LOOKING FORWARD TO THE CITY. Abraham knew that the earthly land of promise was not the end of his pilgrimage. Rather, it pointed beyond to the heavenly city that God had prepared for his faithful servants. Abraham serves as an example for all God's people; we must realize that we are only traveling through this world on our way to our true home in heaven. In this life we must not seek ultimate security in or be fascinated with this present world (vv. 14,16; 13:14). We must see ourselves as strangers and exiles on the earth. This is not our homeland, but foreign territory; the end of our pilgrimage will be "a better country" (v. 16), "the heavenly Jerusalem" (12:22) and the "city that is to come" (13:14).

11:13 DID NOT RECEIVE THE THINGS PROMISED. These OT saints died with the faith that God had something better in store for them. In their lifetime they did not see the final promised blessing of the redeemed. Their basic hope was for eternal life with God in a heavenly homeland, and they fixed their eyes on their citizenship in the new heaven and the new earth (vv. 13–16; cf. Isa 65:17; 66:22; Php 3:20; Rev 21:1). Believers today must also persevere in faith and trust in God, even when they do not see all of God's promises fulfilled in their lives. The faith that God approves of is a faith that is able to surrender God's promises back to him for their fulfillment according to his will.

11:16 GOD IS NOT ASHAMED. Those who honor God by living as "aliens and strangers" (1Pe 2:11) and by desiring a better country God will honor by calling himself their God. He will not be ashamed to acknowledge them as his very own children (cf. Ex 3:6).

11:25 ENJOY THE PLEASURES OF SIN. Every believer faces the recurring choice either of enjoying the passing pleasures of sin or of suffering as he or she continues in obedience to God's will (see Gal 5:17, note).

30By faith the walls of Jericho fell, after
the people had marched around them for
seven days.[h]
31By faith the prostitute Rahab, because she welcomed the spies, was not
killed with those who were disobedient.[x][i]

The Faith of the Judges and Prophets

32And what more shall I say? I do not
have time to tell about Gideon,[j] Barak,[k]
Samson,[l] Jephthah,[m] David,[n] Samuel[o]
and the prophets, 33who through faith
conquered kingdoms,[p] administered justice, and gained what was promised; who
shut the mouths of lions,[q] 34quenched the
fury of the flames,[r] and escaped the edge
of the sword;[s] whose weakness was
turned to strength;[t] and who became
powerful in battle and routed foreign armies.[u] 35Women received back their
dead, raised to life again.[v] Others were
tortured and refused to be released, so
End that they might gain a better resurrection.
36Some faced jeers and flogging,[w] while
still others were chained and put in prison.[x] 37They were stoned[y];[y] they were
sawed in two; they were put to death by
the sword.[z] They went about in sheepskins and goatskins,[a] destitute, persecuted and mistreated— 38the world was not
worthy of them. They wandered in deserts
and mountains, and in caves[b] and holes in
the ground.
39These were all commended[c] for their
faith, yet none of them received what had
been promised.[d] 40God had planned
something better for us so that only together with us[e] would they be made perfect.[f]

God Disciplines His Sons

12 Therefore, since we are surrounded by such a great cloud of witnesses, let us throw off everything that
hinders and the sin that so easily entangles, and let us run[g] with perseverance[h]
the race marked out for us. 2Let us fix our
eyes on Jesus,[i] the author[j] and perfecter
of our faith, who for the joy set before him
endured the cross,[k] scorning its shame,[l]
and sat down at the right hand of the
throne of God.[m] 3Consider him who endured such opposition from sinful men, so
that you will not grow weary[n] and lose
heart.
4In your struggle against sin, you have

11:30 [h]Jos 6:12-20 **11:31** [i]Jos 2:1, 9-14; 6:22-25; Jas 2:25 **11:32** [j]Jdg 6-8 [k]Jdg 4-5 [l]Jdg 13-16 [m]Jdg 11-12 [n]1Sa 16:1,13 [o]1Sa 1:20 **11:33** [p]2Sa 8:1-3 [q]Da 6:22 **11:34** [r]Da 3:19-27 [s]Ex 18:4 [t]2Ki 20:7 [u]Jdg 15:8 **11:35** [v]1Ki 17:22,23; 2Ki 4:36,37 **11:36** [w]Jer 20:2; 37:15 [x]Ge 39:20 **11:37** [y]2Ch 24:21 [z]1Ki 19:10; Jer 26:23 [a]2Ki 1:8 **11:38** [b]1Ki 18:4; 19:9 **11:39** [c]ver 2,4 [d]ver 13; Heb 10:36 **11:40** [e]Rev 6:11 [f]S Heb 2:10 **12:1** [g]S 1Co 9:24 [h]S Heb 10:36 **12:2** [i]Ps 25:15 [j]Heb 2:10 [k]Php 2:8,9; Heb 2:9 [l]Heb 13:13 [m]S Mk 16:19 **12:3** [n]Gal 6:9; Rev 2:3

[x] 31 Or *unbelieving* [y] 37 Some early manuscripts *stoned; they were put to the test;*

11:35 OTHERS WERE TORTURED. God permitted some of his faithful children to experience great suffering and trouble. Though they enjoyed divine companionship, God did not deliver all of them from suffering and death (vv. 35–39). (1) Notice that through faith some "escaped the edge of the sword" (v. 34) and some "were put to death by the sword" (v. 37). Through faith one was delivered and another died (cf. 1Ki 19:10; Jer 26:23; Ac 12:2). Sincere faith will not only lead believers to do great things for God (vv. 33–35), but will also at times bring them into suffering, persecution, hardship and destitution (vv. 35–39; cf. Ps 44:22; Ro 8:36).

(2) Faithfulness to God does not guarantee comfort or deliverance from persecution in this world. But it does assure us of God's grace, help and strength in times of persecution, trials or suffering (cf. 12:2; Jer 20:1,7–8; 37:13–15; 38:5; 2Co 6:9).

11:38 THEY WANDERED IN DESERTS AND MOUNTAINS. God's faithful saints refused to conform to the world's low standards or to enjoy its immoral pleasures, and in return they received scorn and affliction from the world. Because they rejected the world, they were rejected by the world. Even though blessings were promised for the faithful in the OT (Dt 29:9; Jos 1:8), they had to endure persecution and destitution (vv. 35–39). In the NT the faithful are taught to expect adversity (see 2Ti 3:12, note), be identified with the cross (see Mt 10:38, note; Gal 2:20, note) and follow the "man of sorrows" (Isa 53:3; cf. Heb 12:2).

11:40 SO THAT ONLY TOGETHER WITH US. All the OT saints died without receiving the full blessings and promises of God. But at Christ's death and resurrection, he procured perfect salvation for them, and they will receive their full inheritance with us in the new heaven and earth (Rev 20–22).

12:1 THE RACE MARKED OUT FOR US. This race is the lifelong test of faith in this world (10:23,38; 11; 12:25; 13:13). (1) The race must be run with "perseverance" (Gk *hupomonē*), i.e., with patience and endurance (cf. 10:36; Php 3:12–14). The way of victory is the same as that of the saints in ch. 11—pressing on to the finish (cf. 6:11–12; 12:1–4; Lk 21:19; 1Co 9:24–25; Php 3:11–14; Rev 3:21). (2) The race must be run by throwing off the sins that impede or slow us down and by fixing our eyes, lives and hearts on Jesus and the example of persevering obedience he set on earth (vv. 1–4). (3) The race must be run with an awareness that the greatest danger confronting us is the temptation to yield to sin (vv. 1,4), to return to "the country [we] had left" (11:15; Jas 1:12), and to once again become citizens of the world (11:13; Jas 4:4; 1Jn 2:15; see Heb 11:10, note).

12:2 FIX OUR EYES ON JESUS. In our race of faith we look to Jesus as (1) our example of trust in God (2:13), of commitment to his will (10:7–10; Mk 14:36), of prayer (5:7; Mk 1:35; Jn 17), of overcoming temptation and suffering (2:10; 4:15), of endurance in loyalty to the Father (vv. 2–3), and of seeking the joy of completing the work to which God has called us (v. 2; cf. Lk 15:6,24,32; Jn 15:11); (2) our source of strength, love, grace, mercy and help (4:16; 7:25; 10:22; Rev 3:21).

not yet resisted to the point of shedding your blood.[o] **5**And you have forgotten that word of encouragement that addresses you as sons:

"My son, do not make light of the
Lord's discipline,
and do not lose heart[p] when he
rebukes you,
6because the Lord disciplines those he
loves,[q]
and he punishes everyone he
accepts as a son."[z r]

7Endure hardship as discipline; God is treating you as sons.[s] For what son is not disciplined by his father? **8**If you are not disciplined (and everyone undergoes discipline),[t] then you are illegitimate children and not true sons. **9**Moreover, we have all had human fathers who disciplined us and we respected them for it. How much more should we submit to the Father of our spirits[u] and live![v] **10**Our fathers disciplined us for a little while as they thought best; but God disciplines us for our good, that we may share in his holiness.[w] **11**No discipline seems pleasant at the time, but painful. Later on, however, it produces a harvest of righteousness and peace[x] for those who have been trained by it. Jas 3:17-18

12Therefore, strengthen your feeble arms and weak knees.[y] **13**"Make level paths for your feet,"[a z] so that the lame may not be disabled, but rather healed.[a]

Warning Against Refusing God

14Make every effort to live in peace with all men[b] and to be holy;[c] without holiness no one will see the Lord.[d] **15**See to it that no one misses the grace of God[e] and that no bitter root[f] grows up to cause trouble and defile many. **16**See that no one is sexually immoral,[g] or is godless like Esau, who for a single meal sold his inheritance rights as the oldest son.[h] **17**Afterward, as you know, when he wanted to inherit this blessing, he was rejected. He could bring about no change of mind, though he sought the blessing with tears.[i]

18You have not come to a mountain that

12:4 [o]Heb 10:32-34; 13:13
12:5 [p]ver 3
12:6 [q]Ps 94:12; 119:75; Rev 3:19 [r]Pr 3:11,12
12:7 [s]Dt 8:5; 2Sa 7:14; Pr 13:24
12:8 [t]1Pe 5:9
12:9 [u]Nu 16:22; 27:16; Rev 22:6 [v]Isa 38:16
12:10 [w]S 2Pe 1:4
12:11 [x]Isa 32:17; Jas 3:17,18
12:12 [y]Isa 35:3
12:13 [z]Pr 4:26 [a]Gal 6:1
12:14 [b]S Ro 14:19 [c]Ro 6:22 [d]S Mt 5:8
12:15 [e]Gal 5:4; Heb 3:12; 4:1 [f]Dt 29:18
12:16 [g]S 1Co 6:18 [h]Ge 25:29-34
12:17 [i]Ge 27:30-40

[z] *6* Prov. 3:11,12 [a] *13* Prov. 4:26

12:5 THE LORD'S DISCIPLINE. Note several facts about God's discipline of believers and the hardships and troubles he allows us to suffer. (1) They are a sign that we are God's children (vv. 7–8).

(2) They are an assurance of God's love and concern for us (v. 6).

(3) The Lord's discipline has two purposes: (a) that we might not be finally condemned with the world (1Co 11:31–32), and (b) that we might share God's holiness and continue to live sanctified lives without which we will never see the Lord (vv. 10–11,14).

(4) There are two possible consequences of the Lord's discipline. (a) We may endure the hardships God leads us through, submit to God's will and continue to remain faithful (vv. 5–6). By doing this we will continue to live as God's spiritual children (vv. 7–9) and share his holiness (v. 10); it will yield the harvest of righteousness (v. 11). (b) We may "make light of" the discipline of our Father (v. 5), rebel against God because of suffering and hardship, and thereby fall away from God (v. 25; 3:12–14).

(5) Under God's will, trouble may come (a) as a result of our spiritual warfare with Satan (Eph 6:11–18), (b) as a test to strengthen our faith (1Pe 1:6–7) and our works (Mt 7:24–27; 1Co 3:13–15), or (c) as a preparation for us to comfort others (2Co 1:3–5) and to manifest the life of Christ (2Co 4:8–10,12,16).

(6) In all kinds of adversity we must seek God, examine our lives (2Ch 26:5; Ps 3:4; 9:12; 34:17) and forsake all that is contrary to his holiness (vv. 10,14; Ps 66:18).

12:14 MAKE EVERY EFFORT . . . TO BE HOLY. To be holy is to be separated from sin and set apart for God; it is to be close to God, to be like him, and to seek his presence, righteousness and fellowship with all our hearts. Above all things, holiness is God's priority for his followers (Eph 4:21–24). (1) Holiness was God's purpose for his people when he planned their salvation in Christ (Eph 1:4).

(2) Holiness was Christ's purpose for his people when he came to this earth (Mt 1:21; 1Co 1:2,30).

(3) Holiness was Christ's purpose for his people when he gave himself for them on the cross (Eph 5:25–27).

(4) Holiness is God's purpose in making us a new creation and in giving us the Holy Spirit (Ro 8:2–15; Gal 5:16–25; Eph 2:10).

(5) Without holiness no one can be useful to God (2Ti 2:20–21).

(6) Without holiness there is no nearness to or fellowship with God (Ps 15:1–2).

(7) Without holiness no one will see the Lord (v. 14; Mt 5:8).

12:15 BITTER ROOT. A "bitter root" refers to a spirit and attitude characterized by intense animosity and resentment. Here it may refer to an attitude of bitter resentment toward God's discipline instead of humble submission to his will for our lives. Bitterness can also be directed toward persons in the church. It results in defiling the person who is bitter, i.e., making him or her unfit to approach God in prayer. Bitterness in the community of believers can spread and defile many, destroying the holiness without which "no one will see the Lord" (v. 14).

12:18–25 MOUNTAIN THAT CAN BE TOUCHED. The awesome circumstances of the giving of the law (cf. Ex 19:10–25; Dt 4:11–12; 5:22–26) and the features of the gospel are contrasted. The consequences of turning away from the gospel are far more dreadful

can be touched and that is burning with
fire; to darkness, gloom and storm;[j] **19**to
a trumpet blast[k] or to such a voice speaking words[l] that those who heard it
begged that no further word be spoken to
them,[m] **20**because they could not bear
what was commanded: "If even an animal
touches the mountain, it must be
stoned."[b][n] **21**The sight was so terrifying
that Moses said, "I am trembling with
fear."[c][o]

22But you have come to Mount Zion,[p]
to the heavenly Jerusalem,[q] the city[r] of
the living God.[s] You have come to thousands upon thousands of angels in joyful
assembly, **23**to the church of the firstborn,[t] whose names are written in heav-
en.[u] You have come to God, the judge of
all men,[v] to the spirits of righteous men
made perfect,[w] **24**to Jesus the mediator[x]
of a new covenant, and to the sprinkled
blood[y] that speaks a better word than the
blood of Abel.[z]

25See to it that you do not refuse[a] him
who speaks.[b] If they did not escape when
they refused him who warned[c] them on
earth, how much less will we, if we turn
away from him who warns us from heav-
en?[d] **26**At that time his voice shook the
earth,[e] but now he has promised, "Once
more I will shake not only the earth but
also the heavens."[d][f] **27**The words "once
more" indicate the removing of what can
be shaken[g]—that is, created things—so
that what cannot be shaken may remain.

28Therefore, since we are receiving a
kingdom that cannot be shaken,[h] let us be
thankful, and so worship God acceptably
with reverence and awe,[i] **29**for our "God
is a consuming fire."[e][j]

12:18 [j]Ex 19:12-22; 20:18; Dt 4:11 **12:19** [k]Ex 20:18 [l]Dt 4:12 [m]Ex 20:19; Dt 5:5,25; 18:16 **12:20** [n]Ex 19:12,13 **12:21** [o]Dt 9:19 **12:22** [p]Isa 24:23; 60:14; Rev 14:1 [q]S Gal 4:26 [r]Heb 11:10; 13:14 [s]S Mt 16:16 **12:23** [t]Ex 4:22 [u]S Rev 20:12 [v]Ge 18:25; Ps 94:2 [w]Php 3:12 **12:24** [x]S Gal 3:20 [y]Heb 9:19; 10:22; 1Pe 1:2 [z]Ge 4:10; Heb 11:4 **12:25** [a]Heb 3:12 [b]S Heb 1:1 [c]Heb 8:5; 11:7 [d]Dt 18:19; Heb 2:2,3; 10:29 **12:26** [e]Ex 19:18 [f]Hag 2:6 **12:27** [g]Isa 34:4; 54:10; 1Co 7:31; Heb 1:11,12; 2Pe 3:10; 1Jn 2:17 **12:28** [h]Ps 15:5; Da 2:44 [i]Mal 2:5; 4:2; Heb 13:15 **12:29** [j]Ex 24:17; Dt 4:24; 9:3; Ps 97:3; Isa 33:14; S 2Th 1:7 **13:1** [k]S Ro 12:10 **13:2** [l]Job 31:32; Mt 25:35; S Ro 12:13 [m]Ge 18:1-33; 19:1-3 **13:3** [n]Mt 25:36; Col 4:18; Heb 10:34 **13:4** [o]Mal 2:15; 1Co 7:38; 1Ti 4:3 [p]Dt 22:22;

Concluding Exhortations

13 Keep on loving each other as
brothers.[k] **2**Do not forget to entertain strangers,[l] for by so doing some people have entertained angels without
knowing it.[m] **3**Remember those in prison[n]
as if you were their fellow prisoners, and
those who are mistreated as if you yourselves were suffering.

4Marriage should be honored by all,[o]
and the marriage bed kept pure, for God
will judge the adulterer and all the sexually immoral.[p] **5**Keep your lives free from
the love of money[q] and be content with
what you have,[r] because God has said,

"Never will I leave you;
never will I forsake you."[f][s]

6So we say with confidence,

"The Lord is my helper; I will not be
afraid.
What can man do to me?"[g][t]

7Remember your leaders,[u] who spoke
the word of God[v] to you. Consider the outcome of their way of life and imitate[w] their
faith. **8**Jesus Christ is the same yesterday
and today and forever.[x]

9Do not be carried away by all kinds of

1Co 6:9; Rev 22:15 **13:5** [q]S 1Ti 3:3 [r]Php 4:11; 1Ti 6:6,8 [s]Dt 31:6,8; Jos 1:5 **13:6** [t]Ps 118:6,7 **13:7** [u]ver 17,24; 1Co 16:16 [v]S Heb 4:12 [w]Heb 6:12 **13:8** [x]Ps 102:27; Heb 1:12

[b] *20* Exodus 19:12,13 [c] *21* Deut. 9:19 [d] *26* Haggai 2:6 [e] *29* Deut. 4:24 [f] *5* Deut. 31:6 [g] *6* Psalm 118:6,7

than were the consequences of rejecting the law.

12:26–29 SHOOK THE EARTH. God will one day bring down the present world order and shake to pieces the whole material universe. The present form of the world is not eternal; it will be destroyed by fire and replaced by a new heaven and earth (Rev 20:11; 21:1; cf. 2Pe 3:10–13). The only thing that will survive in its present form will be God's kingdom and those who belong to it (v. 28).

13:1 LOVING EACH OTHER AS BROTHERS. In the NT church believers thought of and addressed each other as brothers and sisters in Christ (cf. 1Th 4:9–10; 1Pe 1:22; 2Pe 1:7). Christian brotherhood comes from our mutual relationship with the Father and his only Son (1:2). As we participate in the grace of Christ, we are all made sons and daughters with him and fellow heirs of the Father's blessings (1:2; Jn 1:12–13; Ro 8:14–17; Eph 1:5–7). Because of this brotherhood, we are taught by the Father to love each other (1Th 4:9; 1Jn 4:11; see Jn 13:34–35, notes).

13:4 MARRIAGE SHOULD BE HONORED. God has high standards for his people in marriage and sexuality. For a discussion of this important issue, see article on STANDARDS OF SEXUAL MORALITY, p. 509.

13:5 FREE FROM THE LOVE OF MONEY. Notice that this exhortation follows the warning against immorality (v. 4). Greed and immorality are closely connected in the NT (1Co 5:11; 6:9–10; Eph 5:3; Col 3:5). All too often the love of abundance and luxury and the constant desire for wealth open up a person to sexual sins (see 1Ti 6:6–10).

13:6 THE LORD IS MY HELPER. No matter how limited our earthly possessions may be or how trying our circumstances, we never need fear that God will desert or forsake us (cf. Jos 1:5). Scripture declares that the heavenly Father cares for us. Thus, we can say with the author of Hebrews, who echoes the psalmist, "The Lord is my helper; I will not be afraid." This can be affirmed with confidence in times of distress, trials or trouble (see Mt 6:30,33 notes).

13:8 JESUS CHRIST IS THE SAME. The truth that Jesus Christ does not change provides a sure anchor for our faith. It means that present-day believers must not be content until they experience the same salvation, communion with God, baptism in the Holy Spirit

STANDARDS OF SEXUAL MORALITY

***Heb 13:4** "Marriage should be honored by all, and the marriage bed kept pure, for God will judge the adulterer and all the sexually immoral."*

Above all, believers must be morally and sexually pure (2Co 11:2; Tit 2:5; 1Pe 3:2). The word "pure" (Gk *hagnos* or *amiantos*) means to be free from all taint of that which is lewd. It suggests refraining from all acts and thoughts that incite desire not in accordance with one's virginity or one's marriage vows. It stresses restraint and avoidance of all sexual actions and excitements that would defile one's purity before God. It includes controlling one's own body "in a way that is holy and honorable" (1Th 4:4), and not in "passionate lust" (4:5). This Scriptural instruction is for both those who are single and those who are married. With regard to the Biblical teaching concerning sexual morality, note the following:

(1) Sexual intimacy is reserved for the marriage relationship and is approved and blessed by God only in that state. Through marriage the husband and wife become one flesh according to God's will. The physical and emotional pleasures resulting from a faithful marriage relationship are ordained by God and held in honor by him.

(2) Adultery, sexual immorality, homosexuality, sensuality, impurity and degrading passions are considered grave sins in God's sight, since they are a transgression of the law of love and a defiling of the marriage relationship. Such sins are severely condemned in Scripture and place one outside God's kingdom (Ro 1:24–32; 1Co 6:9–10; Gal 5:19–21).

(3) Sexual immorality and impurity include not only forbidden intercourse or consummated acts, but also involve any act of sexual gratification with another person other than one's marriage partner, achieved by uncovering or exploring the nakedness of that person. The contemporary teaching that says sexual intimacy among "committed" unmarried youth and adults is acceptable as long as it stops short of full sexual union is a teaching contrary to God's holiness and the Biblical standard of purity. God explicitly prohibits having any kind of "sexual relations with" (literally, "uncovering the nakedness of") anyone who is not a lawful wife or husband (Lev 18:6–30; 20:11,17,19–21).

(4) The believer must exercise self-control with reference to all sexual matters before marriage. To justify premarital intimacy in the name of Christ merely on the ground of a real or a felt commitment to another flagrantly compromises God's holy standards with the world's impure ways and, in effect, justifies immorality. After marriage, sexual intimacy must be confined to one's marriage partner. The Bible names self-control as one aspect of the Spirit's fruit, the positive and pure behavior that is in contrast to immoral sexual play, gratification, adultery and impurity. One's faith commitment to God's will with regard to purity will open the way to receiving this gift of self-control through the Spirit (Gal 5:22–24).

(5) Biblical terms used for sexual immorality, describing the breadth of its evil, are as follows: (a) Sexual immorality (Gk *porneia*) describes a wide variety of sexual activities before or outside of marriage; it is not limited to consummated sexual acts. Any intimate sexual activity or play outside the marriage relationship, including the touching of the intimate parts of the body or seeing another person's nakedness, is included in this term and is clearly a transgression of God's moral standards for his people (see Lev 18:6–30; 20:11–12,17,19–21; 1Co 6:18; 1Th 4:3). (b) Debauchery, or sensuality, (Gk *aselgeia*) denotes the absence of clear moral principles, especially disregard of sexual self-control that maintains pure behavior (see 1Ti 2:9, note on modesty). It includes the inclination toward indulging in or arousing sinful lust, and thus is a participation in Biblically unjustifiable conduct (Gal 5:19; Eph 4:19; 1Pe 4:3; 2Pe 2:2,18). (c) Exploiting, or taking advantage of someone, (Gk *pleonekteō*) means to deprive another of the moral purity that God desires for that person in order to satisfy one's own self-centered desires. To arouse in another person sexual desires that cannot be righteously fulfilled is to exploit or take advantage of that person (1Th 4:6; cf. Eph 4:19). (d) Lust (Gk *epithumia*) is having an immoral desire that one would fulfill if the opportunity arose (Eph 4:19,22; 1Pe 4:3; 2Pe 2:18; see Mt 5:28, note).

strange teachings.[y] It is good for our
hearts to be strengthened[z] by grace, not
by ceremonial foods,[a] which are of no value to those who eat them.[b] 10We have an
altar from which those who minister at the
tabernacle[c] have no right to eat.[d]

11The high priest carries the blood of
animals into the Most Holy Place as a sin
offering,[e] but the bodies are burned outside the camp.[f] 12And so Jesus also suffered outside the city gate[g] to make the
people holy[h] through his own blood.[i]
13Let us, then, go to him[j] outside the
camp, bearing the disgrace he bore.[k]
14For here we do not have an enduring
city,[l] but we are looking for the city that
is to come.[m]

15Through Jesus, therefore, let us continually offer to God a sacrifice[n] of praise
—the fruit of lips[o] that confess his name.
16And do not forget to do good and to
share with others,[p] for with such sacrifices[q] God is pleased.

17Obey your leaders[r] and submit to
their authority. They keep watch over
you[s] as men who must give an account.
Obey them so that their work will be a joy,
not a burden, for that would be of no advantage to you.

13:9 [y]Eph 4:14 [z]Col 2:7 [a]Col 2:16 [b]Heb 9:10
13:10 [c]Heb 8:5 [d]1Co 9:13; 10:18
13:11 [e]Lev 16:15 [f]Ex 29:14; Lev 4:12,21; 9:11; 16:27
13:12 [g]Jn 19:17 [h]S Eph 5:26 [i]S Ro 3:25
13:13 [j]Lk 9:23 [k]Heb 11:26
13:14 [l]Heb 12:27 [m]Php 3:20; Heb 11:10,27; 12:22
13:15 [n]1Pe 2:5 [o]Isa 57:19; Hos 14:2
13:16 [p]Ro 12:13 [q]Php 4:18
13:17 [r]ver 7,24 [s]Isa 62:6; Ac 20:28
13:18 [t]S 1Th 5:25 [u]S Ac 23:1
13:19 [v]Phm 22
13:20 [w]S Ro 15:33 [x]Ge 9:16; 17:7,13,19; Isa 55:3; 61:8; Eze 37:26; S Mt 26:28 [y]S Ac 2:24 [z]S Jn 10:11
13:21 [a]2Co 9:8 [b]S Php 2:13 [c]1Jn 3:22 [d]S Ro 11:36
13:22 [e]1Pe 5:12

18Pray for us.[t] We are sure that we
have a clear conscience[u] and desire to
live honorably in every way. 19I particularly urge you to pray so that I may be restored to you soon.[v]

20May the God of peace,[w] who through
the blood of the eternal covenant[x]
brought back from the dead[y] our Lord
Jesus, that great Shepherd of the sheep,[z]
21equip you with everything good for doing his will,[a] and may he work in us[b]
what is pleasing to him,[c] through Jesus
Christ, to whom be glory for ever and ever.
Amen.[d]

22Brothers, I urge you to bear with my
word of exhortation, for I have written you
only a short letter.[e]

23I want you to know that our brother
Timothy[f] has been released. If he arrives
soon, I will come with him to see you.

24Greet all your leaders[g] and all God's
people. Those from Italy[h] send you their
greetings.

25Grace be with you all.[i]

13:23 [f]S Ac 16:1 **13:24** [g]ver 7,17 [h]Ac 18:2 **13:25** [i]S Col 4:18

and kingdom power that the NT believers experienced in their service to God through Christ Jesus (see article on THE KINGDOM OF GOD, p. 28).

13:12 MAKE THE PEOPLE HOLY. Jesus suffered outside the city gate of Jerusalem in order that we might be made holy, i.e., separated from the old sinful life and dedicated to God's service (see article on SPIRITUAL SEPARATION FOR BELIEVERS, p. 371).

13:13 LET US, THEN, GO TO HIM. To be a follower of Christ involves going "outside the camp." For these Jewish Christians the camp represented Judaism. For us it represents the world with all its sinful pleasures, ungodly values and temporal goals. We must bear the disgrace Christ bore in order to follow him, sympathize with him, be his friend, identify with him, and announce to the world our commitment to his standards and purposes. In going outside the gate we find ourselves strangers and aliens on the earth (v. 14; 11:13). Yet we are not without a city, for we seek a city that is to come, a city with foundations, "whose architect and builder is God" (11:10,14,16; 13:14).

13:17 OBEY THEM. Obedience and faithfulness to Christian leaders, pastors and teachers must be based on a higher loyalty to God. The believer's loyalty on a descending scale is as follows: (1) first, to God in a person-to-person relationship (see Mt 22:37, note), including faithfulness to the truth and principles of his Word (see article on THE INSPIRATION AND AUTHORITY OF SCRIPTURE, p. 474); (2) second, to the visible church as it remains faithful to God and his written Word (Jn 15:12; Gal 6:10); (3) third, to human leaders within the church, as long as they remain faithful and loyal to God, to his Word and to his purpose for the church.

JAMES

Outline

Christian Greetings (1:1)

- I. Facing Trials and Benefiting From Them (1:2–18)
  - A. Accept Them as a Means of Growth (1:2–4)
  - B. Pray for Wisdom in Coping With Them (1:5–8)
  - C. Rejoice in Their Leveling Action (1:9–12)
  - D. Recognize the Difference Between Trials and Temptations (1:13–18)
- II. Hearing the Word and Doing It (1:19–27)
- III. Being Impartial and Showing It (2:1–13)
- IV. Professing Faith and Proving It (2:14–26)
- V. Recognizing Pitfalls and Avoiding Them (3:1—5:6)
  - A. The Unruly Tongue (3:1–12)
  - B. Unspiritual Wisdom (3:13–18)
  - C. Sinful Behavior (4:1–10)
  - D. Speaking Against a Brother (4:11–12)
  - E. Presumptuous Living (4:13–17)
  - F. Selfish Wealth (5:1–6)
- VI. Christian Virtues and Living (5:7–20)
  - A. Patience and Endurance (5:7–11)
  - B. Simple Honesty (5:12)
  - C. Prevailing Prayers for the Sick (5:13–18)
  - D. Reclaiming the Wandering (5:19–20)

Author: James

Theme: Faith That Works

Date: A.D. 45–49

Background

James is classified as a "general letter" because it was originally addressed to a wider audience than a local church. The salutation, "to the twelve tribes scattered among the nations" (1:1), along with other references (2:19,21), indicate that the letter was written initially to Jewish Christians living outside Palestine. It is possible that the recipients of the letter were among the first converts in Jerusalem who, after Stephen's martyrdom, were scattered by persecution (Ac 8:1) as far as Phoenicia, Cyprus, Antioch and beyond (Ac 11:19). This would explain (1) the letter's opening emphasis on joyfully enduring trials that test faith and require perseverance (1:2–12), (2) James's personal knowledge of the "scattered" believers, and (3) the authoritative tone of the letter. As leader of the Jerusalem church, James was writing to his scattered sheep.

The author's prominence is indicated by the way he identifies himself simply as "James" (1:1). James, the half-brother of Jesus and the leader of the Jerusalem church, is generally regarded as the author. His speech at the Jerusalem council (Ac 15:13–21) as well as descriptions of him elsewhere in the NT (e.g., Ac 12:17; 21:18; Gal 1:19; 2:9,12; 1Co 15:7) correspond perfectly with what is known about the author of this letter. James most likely wrote his letter during the 40s. This early date for writing is indicated by several factors, such as the fact that James uses the

Greek term *synagōgē* to refer to the Christians' place of meeting (2:2). According to the Jewish historian Josephus, James, the Lord's brother, was martyred at Jerusalem in A.D. 62.

Purpose

James wrote (1) to encourage Jewish believers who were suffering various trials that were testing their faith, (2) to correct erroneous ideas about the nature of saving faith, and (3) to exhort and instruct the readers about the practical outworkings of their faith in righteous living and good deeds.

Survey

This letter covers a wide variety of topics related to living a genuine Christian life. James urges believers to joyfully endure and benefit from their trials (1:2–11); to resist temptations (1:12–18); to be doers of the Word, not just hearers (1:19–27); and to demonstrate an active faith, not an empty profession (2:14–26). He solemnly warns about the sinfulness of an unruly tongue (3:1–12; 4:11–12), worldly wisdom (3:13–16), sinful behavior (4:1–10), presumptuous living (4:13–17) and self-centered wealth (5:1–6). James concludes with an emphasis on patience, prayer and reclaiming the wandering (5:7–20).

Throughout its five chapters, the relationship between true faith and godly living is emphasized. Genuine faith is a tested faith (1:2–16), is an active faith (1:19–27), loves one's neighbor as oneself (2:1–12), manifests itself in good deeds (2:14–26), keeps a tight rein on the tongue (3:1–12), seeks God's wisdom (3:13–18), submits to God as the righteous judge (4:1–12), trusts God in daily living (4:13–17), is not self-centered or self-indulgent (5:1–6), is patient in suffering (5:7–12) and is diligent in prayer (5:13–20).

Special Features

Seven major features characterize this letter (1) It is most likely the first book written in the NT. (2) Although it contains only two references to Christ by name, there are more reminiscences of Jesus' teaching in this letter, including at least fifteen allusions to the Sermon on the Mount, than in all the other NT letters combined. (3) More than half of its 108 verses are imperatives or commands. (4) In many ways it is the Proverbs of the NT, for (a) it is full of godly wisdom and practical instructions for living a genuine Christian life, and (b) it is written in terse style, with crisp commands and vivid analogies. (5) James is an astute observer of the operations of nature and of fallen human nature. He often draws lessons from the former to expose the latter (e.g., 3:1–12). (6) It emphasizes more than any other NT book the necessary relation between faith and deeds (esp. 2:14–26). (7) James is sometimes called the Amos of the NT, because he vigorously addresses issues of social injustice and inequality.

Reading James

In order to read the entire New Testament in one year, the book of James should be read in 4 days, according to the following schedule:
☐ 1 ☐ 2:1—3:13 ☐ 3:14—4:12 ☐ 4:13—5:20

NOTES

1 James,[a] a servant of God[b] and of the
Lord Jesus Christ,

To the twelve tribes[c] scattered[d]
among the nations:

Greetings.[e]

Trials and Temptations

2Consider it pure joy, my brothers,
whenever you face trials of many kinds,[f]
3because you know that the testing of
your faith[g] develops perseverance.[h]
4Perseverance must finish its work so
that you may be mature[i] and complete,
not lacking anything. 5If any of you lacks
wisdom, he should ask God,[j] who gives
generously to all without finding fault,
and it will be given to him.[k] 6But when he
asks, he must believe and not doubt,[l] because he who doubts is like a wave of the
sea, blown and tossed by the wind. 7That
man should not think he will receive anything from the Lord; 8he is a double-minded man,[m] unstable[n] in all he does.

9The brother in humble circumstances
ought to take pride in his high position.[o]
10But the one who is rich should take
pride in his low position, because he will
pass away like a wild flower.[p] 11For the
sun rises with scorching heat[q] and withers[r] the plant; its blossom falls and its
beauty is destroyed.[s] In the same way,
the rich man will fade away even while he
goes about his business.

12Blessed is the man who perseveres
under trial,[t] because when he has stood
the test, he will receive the crown of life[u]
that God has promised to those who love
him.[v]

13When tempted, no one should say,
"God is tempting me." For God cannot be
tempted by evil, nor does he tempt anyone; 14but each one is tempted when, by
his own[w] evil desire, he is dragged away
and enticed. 15Then, after desire has conceived, it gives birth to sin;[x] and sin,
when it is full-grown, gives birth to
death.[y]

16Don't be deceived,[z] my dear brothers.[a] 17Every good and perfect gift is from
above,[b] coming down from the Father of
the heavenly lights,[c] who does not
change[d] like shifting shadows. 18He
chose to give us birth[e] through the word
of truth,[f] that we might be a kind of firstfruits[g] of all he created.

Listening and Doing

19My dear brothers,[h] take note of this:
Everyone should be quick to listen, slow
to speak[i] and slow to become angry, 20for
man's anger[j] does not bring about the
righteous life that God desires. 21There-
fore, get rid of[k] all moral filth and the evil
that is so prevalent and humbly accept the

1:1 [a]S Ac 15:13 [b]Ro 1:1; Tit 1:1 [c]Ac 26:7 [d]Dt 32:26; Jn 7:35; 1Pe 1:1 [e]Ac 15:23 **1:2** [f]ver 12; S Mt 5:12; Heb 10:34; 12:11 **1:3** [g]1Pe 1:7 [h]S Heb 10:36 **1:4** [i]S 1Co 2:6 **1:5** [j]1Ki 3:9,10; Pr 2:3-6 [k]Ps 51:6; Da 1:17; 2:21; S Mt 7:7 **1:6** [l]S Mt 21:21; Mk 11:24 **1:8** [m]Ps 119:113; Jas 4:8 [n]2Pe 2:14; 3:16 **1:9** [o]S Mt 23:12 **1:10** [p]Job 14:2; Ps 103:15,16; Isa 40:6,7; 1Co 7:31; 1Pe 1:24 **1:11** [q]Mt 20:12 [r]Ps 102:4,11 [s]Isa 40:6-8

1:12 [t]ver 2; Ge 22:1; Jas 5:11; 1Pe 3:14 [u]S 1Co 9:25 [v]Ex 20:6; 1Co 2:9; 8:3; Jas 2:5 **1:14** [w]Pr 19:3 **1:15** [x]Ge 3:6; Job 15:35; Ps 7:14; Isa 59:4 [y]S Ro 6:23 **1:16** [z]S 1Co 6:9 [a]ver 19; Jas 2:5 **1:17** [b]Ps 85:12; Jn 3:27; Jas 3:15, 17 [c]Ge 1:16; Ps 136:7; Da 2:22; 1Jn 1:5 [d]Nu 23:19; Ps 102:27; Mal 3:6

1:18 [e]S Jn 1:13 [f]S 2Ti 2:15 [g]Jer 2:3; Rev 14:4 **1:19** [h]ver 16; Jas 2:5 [i]Pr 10:19; Jas 3:3-12 **1:20** [j]S Mt 5:22 **1:21** [k]S Eph 4:22

1:2 TRIALS. The word "trials" (Gk *peirasmos*) refers to persecution and troubles from the world or Satan. (1) The believer must meet these trials with joy (cf. Mt 5:11–12; Ro 5:3; 1Pe 1:6), for testing will develop persevering faith, proven character and mature hope (cf. Ro 5:3–5). Our faith can only reach full maturity when faced with difficulties and opposition (vv. 3–4). (2) James calls these trials a "testing of your faith." Trials are sometimes brought into believers' lives so that God can test the sincerity of their faith. Scripture nowhere teaches that troubles in life are always an indication that God is displeased with us. They can be a sign that he recognizes our firm commitment to him (cf. Job 1–2).

1:4 YOU MAY BE MATURE. "Mature" (Gk *teleios*) reflects the Biblical idea of maturity, defined as a right relationship with God that bears fruit in a sincere endeavor to love him with all one's heart in undivided devotion, obedience and blamelessness (Dt 6:5; 18:13; Mt 22:37; see 1Th 2:10, note; see article on SANCTIFICATION, p. 526).

1:5 IF ANY OF YOU LACKS WISDOM. Wisdom means the spiritual capacity to see and evaluate life and conduct from God's point of view. It involves making right choices and doing right things according to both God's will revealed in his Word and the leading of the Spirit (Ro 8:4–17). We can receive wisdom by coming to God and asking for it in faith (vv. 6–8; cf. Pr 2:6; 1Co 1:30).

1:9–10 THE BROTHER IN HUMBLE CIRCUMSTANCES . . . THE ONE WHO IS RICH. See article on RICHES AND POVERTY, p. 152.

1:13 TEMPTED. No person who sins can evade guilt by throwing the blame on God. God may test us in order to strengthen our faith, but never with the intent of leading us to sin. God's nature demonstrates that he cannot be a source of temptation to sin.

1:14 BY HIS OWN EVIL DESIRE. Temptation essentially comes from our own inward desires or inclinations (cf. Mt 15:19). If evil desire is not resisted and purged by the Holy Spirit, it leads to sin and then to spiritual death (v. 15; Ro 6:23; 7:5,10,13).

1:21 GET RID OF ALL MORAL FILTH. The Word of God, either preached or written, cannot effectively take hold of a person's life if he or she is not separated from moral filth and evil. (1) God commands believers to set aside all the ungodly filth that permeates a corrupt society and seeks to influence them and their families. This filth defiles people's souls and blights their lives (cf. Eph 4:22,25,31; Col 3:8; 1Pe 2:1).

(2) Scripture tells us what is improper for God's holy people. Accordingly, we must not engage in any kind of impurity or obscenity (Eph 5:3–4). We must be aware that allowing *any kind* of moral filth into our lives or homes, including filthy language or obscenity through videos or television, grieves the Spirit and

word planted in you,[l] which can save you.
22Do not merely listen to the word, and
so deceive yourselves. Do what it says.[m]
23Anyone who listens to the word but does
not do what it says is like a man who looks
at his face in a mirror **24**and, after looking
at himself, goes away and immediately
forgets what he looks like. **25**But the man
who looks intently into the perfect law
that gives freedom,[n] and continues to do
this, not forgetting what he has heard, but
doing it—he will be blessed in what he
does.[o]
26If anyone considers himself religious
and yet does not keep a tight rein on his
tongue,[p] he deceives himself and his religion is worthless. **27**Religion that God our
Father accepts as pure and faultless is
this: to look after[q] orphans and widows[r]
in their distress and to keep oneself from
being polluted by the world.[s]

Favoritism Forbidden

2 My brothers, as believers in our glorious[t] Lord Jesus Christ, don't show
favoritism.[u] **2**Suppose a man comes into
your meeting wearing a gold ring and fine
clothes, and a poor man in shabby clothes
also comes in. **3**If you show special attention to the man wearing fine clothes and
say, "Here's a good seat for you," but say
to the poor man, "You stand there" or "Sit
on the floor by my feet," **4**have you not
discriminated among yourselves and become judges[v] with evil thoughts?
5Listen, my dear brothers:[w] Has not
God chosen those who are poor in the eyes
of the world[x] to be rich in faith[y] and to
inherit the kingdom[z] he promised those
who love him?[a] **6**But you have insulted
the poor.[b] Is it not the rich who are exploiting you? Are they not the ones who
are dragging you into court?[c] **7**Are they
not the ones who are slandering the noble
name of him to whom you belong?
8If you really keep the royal law found
in Scripture, "Love your neighbor as yourself,"[a][d] you are doing right. **9**But if you
show favoritism,[e] you sin and are convict-

1:21 [l] Eph 1:13 **1:22** [m] S Mt 7:21; Jas 2:14-20 **1:25** [n] Ps 19:7; Jn 8:32; Gal 2:4; Jas 2:12 [o] S Jn 13:17 **1:26** [p] Ps 34:13; 39:1; 141:3; Jas 3:2-12; 1Pe 3:10 **1:27** [q] Mt 25:36 [r] Dt 14:29; Job 31:16,17,21; Ps 146:9; Isa 1:17,23 [s] Ro 12:2; Jas 4:4; 2Pe 1:4; 2:20 **2:1** [t] Ac 7:2; 1Co 2:8 [u] ver 9; Dt 1:17; Lev 19:15; Pr 24:23; S Ac 10:34 **2:4** [v] S Jn 7:24 **2:5** [w] Jas 1:16,19 [x] Job 34:19; 1Co 1:26-28 [y] Lk 12:21; Rev 2:9 [z] S Mt 25:34 [a] S Jas 1:12 **2:6** [b] 1Co 11:22 [c] Ac 8:3; 16:19 **2:8** [d] Lev 19:18; S Mt 5:43 **2:9** [e] ver 1

[a] *8* Lev. 19:18

violates God's holy standards for his people. God's Word warns us, "Let no one deceive you with empty words, for because of such things God's wrath comes .... Therefore do not be partners with them" (Eph 5:6–7).

(3) We as believers must take righteousness and holiness seriously. Our houses must be swept clean and filled with God's Word and the holiness of Christ (Mt 12:43–45).

1:21 WORD PLANTED IN YOU. Christians begin their new life in Christ by being born again "through the word of truth" (v. 18; see article on REGENERATION, p. 178). New life in Christ demands that we get rid of all moral filth that offends the Holy Spirit (see previous note), and that we be steadfast in accepting God's Word into our hearts. The term "planted" (Gk *emphutos*) implies that the Word must become a part of our very nature. The implanted Word brings us to our final salvation (cf. Mt 13:3–23; Ro 1:16; 1Co 15:2; Eph 1:13; see Jn 6:54, note).

1:25 LAW THAT GIVES FREEDOM. This law (cf. 2:12) is the will of God internalized in our hearts by the indwelling Holy Spirit (cf. Eze 11:19–20). Through faith in Christ we receive not only mercy and forgiveness (2:12–13), but also the power and freedom to obey God's law (Ro 3:31; see 8:4, note). It is called the "law that gives freedom" because the believer desires to do God's will: "I will walk about in freedom, for I have sought out your precepts" (Ps 119:45). It must never be viewed as a freedom to violate Christ's commands, but rather as the freedom and power to obey them.

1:27 RELIGION ... PURE AND FAULTLESS. James gives two principles that define the content of true Christianity. (1) Genuine love for those in need. In NT days, orphans and widows had few ways to support themselves; they often had no guardian or helper. Believers were expected to show them the same care and love that God shows toward the fatherless and widows (see Dt 10:18; Ps 68:5; 146:9; Mt 6:32). Today among our brothers and sisters in Christ are those who need loving care. We should seek to alleviate their distress and thereby show them that God cares for them (see Lk 7:13, note; cf. Gal 6:10).

(2) Keeping ourselves holy before God. James says that love for others must be accompanied by a love for God expressed in separation from the world's sinful ways. Love for others must be accompanied by holiness before God or it is not Christian love.

2:1 FAVORITISM. To show favoritism is to give special attention to people because of their wealth, clothing or position. To do so is wrong for several reasons. (1) It displeases God, who does not look at the outward appearance but at the heart (1Sa 16:7). (2) It is not motivated by genuine love for all (v. 8). The admiration of social status is a sin against the law of love. (3) It makes us "judges with evil thoughts" (v. 4); instead of honoring "our glorious Lord" and accepting persons on the basis of their faith in Christ, we unjustly favor the rich or influential from an evil motive for the advantage we might receive.

2:5 HAS NOT GOD CHOSEN THOSE WHO ARE POOR. The poor are special and precious to God (cf. Isa 61:1; Lk 4:18; 6:20; 7:22). Often it is the poor in this world who are the richest in faith and spiritual gifts and who, in their need, cry out most intensely to God in sincere hunger for his presence, mercy and help (Lk 6:20–21). The economically depressed around the world learn that they cannot put their trust in material possessions. Therefore, they respond more readily to Jesus' invitation to "come to me, all you who are weary and burdened, and I will give you rest" (Mt 11:28; see article on RICHES AND POVERTY, p. 152).

ed by the law as lawbreakers.[f] **10**For whoever keeps the whole law and yet stumbles[g] at just one point is guilty of breaking all of it.[h] **11**For he who said, "Do not commit adultery,"[b][i] also said, "Do not murder."[c][j] If you do not commit adultery but do commit murder, you have become a lawbreaker.

12Speak and act as those who are going to be judged[k] by the law that gives freedom,[l] **13**because judgment without mercy will be shown to anyone who has not been merciful.[m] Mercy triumphs over judgment!

Faith and Deeds

14What good is it, my brothers, if a man claims to have faith but has no deeds?[n] Can such faith save him? **15**Suppose a brother or sister is without clothes and daily food.[o] **16**If one of you says to him, "Go, I wish you well; keep warm and well fed," but does nothing about his physical needs, what good is it?[p] **17**In the same way, faith by itself, if it is not accompanied by action, is dead.[q]

18But someone will say, "You have faith; I have deeds."

Show me your faith without deeds,[r] and I will show you my faith[s] by what I do.[t] **19**You believe that there is one God.[u] Good! Even the demons believe that[v]—and shudder.

20You foolish man, do you want evidence that faith without deeds is useless[d]?[w] **21**Was not our ancestor Abraham considered righteous for what he did when he offered his son Isaac on the altar?[x] **22**You see that his faith and his actions were working together,[y] and his faith was made complete by what he did.[z] **23**And the scripture was fulfilled that says, "Abraham believed God, and it was credited to him as righteousness,"[e][a] and he was called God's friend.[b] **24**You see that

2:9 [f]Dt 1:17
2:10 [g]Jas 3:2 [h]Mt 5:19; Gal 3:10; 5:3
2:11 [i]Ex 20:14; Dt 5:18 [j]Ex 20:13; Dt 5:17
2:12 [k]S Mt 16:27 [l]S Jas 1:25
2:13 [m]Mt 5:7; 9:13; 12:7; 18:32-35; Lk 6:37
2:14 [n]Mt 7:26; Jas 1:22-25
2:15 [o]Mt 25:35, 36
2:16 [p]Lk 3:11; 1Jn 3:17,18
2:17 [q]ver 20,26; Gal 5:6
2:18 [r]Ro 3:28 [s]Heb 11 [t]Mt 7:16, 17; Jas 3:13
2:19 [u]Dt 6:4; Mk 12:29; 1Co 8:4-6 [v]Mt 8:29; Lk 4:34
2:20 [w]ver 17,26
2:21 [x]Ge 22:9,12
2:22 [y]Heb 11:17 [z]1Th 1:3
2:23 [a]Ge 15:6; S Ro 4:3 [b]2Ch 20:7; Isa 41:8

[b] *11* Exodus 20:14; Deut. 5:18 [c] *11* Exodus 20:13; Deut. 5:17 [d] *20* Some early manuscripts *dead* [e] *23* Gen. 15:6

2:12 SPEAK AND ACT. We must speak and act from the perspective of those who will be judged by God and the "law that gives freedom," i.e., the law and love of God poured into our hearts by God's Spirit. God will condemn all showing of favoritism, for it transgresses the law of love (see v. 1, note; see article on THE JUDGMENT OF BELIEVERS, p. 368).

2:14 FAITH BUT HAS NO DEEDS. Vv. 14–26 treat the ever-present problem of those in the church who profess to have saving faith in the Lord Jesus Christ, yet at the same time show no evidence of sincere devotion to him and his Word. (1) Saving faith is always a living faith that does not stop with mere confession of Christ as Savior, but also prompts obedience to him as Lord. Thus, obedience is an essential aspect of faith. Only those who obey can believe, and only those who believe can obey (see v. 24, note; Ro 1:5, note on "obedience that comes from faith"; see article on FAITH AND GRACE, p. 302).

(2) Note that there is no contradiction between Paul and James with regard to the matter of saving faith. Normally Paul emphasizes faith as the means by which we accept Christ as Savior (Ro 3:22). James calls attention to the fact that true faith must be an active and enduring faith that shapes our very existence.

2:17 NOT ACCOMPANIED BY ACTION, IS DEAD. (1) True saving faith is so vital that it cannot help but express itself in godly action and devotion to Jesus Christ. Deeds without faith are dead deeds. Faith without deeds is dead faith. True faith always manifests itself in obedience to God and compassionate deeds done for needy people (see v. 22, note; Ro 1:5, note; see article on FAITH AND GRACE, p. 302).

(2) James is directing his teaching against those in the church who professed faith in Christ and his blood atonement and believed that such profession was all that was necessary for salvation. They believed that a personal, obedient relationship with Christ as Lord was not essential. James says that such faith is dead and will produce neither salvation nor anything good (vv. 14–16,20–24). The only kind of faith that saves is "faith expressing itself through love" (Gal 5:6).

(3) On the other hand, we must not think that we maintain a living faith solely by our own effort. The grace of God, the indwelling Holy Spirit and the intercession of Christ (see Heb 7:25, note) work in our lives to enable us to respond to God 'by faith from first to last" (Ro 1:17). If we ever stop being receptive to God's grace and the leading of the Spirit, then our faith will die.

2:21 CONSIDERED RIGHTEOUS FOR WHAT HE DID. Abraham's righteousness came not from "observing the law" (Ro 3:28), but through faith and actions working together in love. His willingness to sacrifice Isaac was an expression of his faith in and commitment to God (see Ge 15:6; 22:1). James uses the example of Abraham to demolish the belief that faith can exist without commitment to and love for God. The apostle Paul uses the example of Abraham's faith to destroy the view that salvation rests on the merit of one's own deeds rather than on God's grace (Ro 4:3; Gal 3:6).

2:22 FAITH AND HIS ACTIONS WERE WORKING TOGETHER. James is not saying that faith *and* actions save us. This separates faith from deeds. James contends instead for faith at work. Thus, faith and deeds can never be separated; the latter flows naturally from the former (see Gal 5:6, note).

2:24 JUSTIFIED BY WHAT HE DOES. The Greek word *ergōn*, here translated "what he does," is used by James with a different meaning than the same word used by Paul in Eph 2:9, there translated "works." (1) For James, "what he does" refers to the obligations to God and fellow humans that are commanded in Scripture and that proceed from a sincere faith, a pure

a person is justified by what he does and
not by faith alone.
25In the same way, was not even Rahab
the prostitute considered righteous for
what she did when she gave lodging to the
spies and sent them off in a different direction?[c] 26As the body without the spirit
is dead, so faith without deeds is dead.[d]

Taming the Tongue

3 Not many of you should presume to be
teachers,[e] my brothers, because you
know that we who teach will be judged[f]
more strictly.[g] 2We all stumble[h] in many
ways. If anyone is never at fault in what
he says,[i] he is a perfect man,[j] able to
keep his whole body in check.[k]
3When we put bits into the mouths of
horses to make them obey us, we can turn
the whole animal.[l] 4Or take ships as an
example. Although they are so large and
are driven by strong winds, they are
steered by a very small rudder wherever
the pilot wants to go. 5Likewise the
tongue is a small part of the body, but it
makes great boasts.[m] Consider what a
great forest is set on fire by a small spark.
6The tongue also is a fire,[n] a world of evil
among the parts of the body. It corrupts
the whole person,[o] sets the whole course
of his life on fire, and is itself set on fire
by hell.[p]
7All kinds of animals, birds, reptiles
and creatures of the sea are being tamed
and have been tamed by man, 8but no man
can tame the tongue. It is a restless evil,
full of deadly poison.[q]
9With the tongue we praise our Lord
and Father, and with it we curse men, who
have been made in God's likeness.[r] 10Out
of the same mouth come praise and cursing. My brothers, this should not be.
11Can both fresh water and salt[f] water
flow from the same spring? 12My brothers, can a fig tree bear olives, or a grapevine bear figs?[s] Neither can a salt spring
produce fresh water.

Two Kinds of Wisdom

13Who is wise and understanding
among you? Let him show it[t] by his good
life, by deeds[u] done in the humility that
comes from wisdom. 14But if you harbor
bitter envy and selfish ambition[v] in your
hearts, do not boast about it or deny the
truth.[w] 15Such "wisdom" does not come
down from heaven[x] but is earthly, unspiritual, of the devil.[y] 16For where you have
envy and selfish ambition,[z] there you find
disorder and every evil practice.
17But the wisdom that comes from
heaven[a] is first of all pure; then peace-
loving,[b] considerate, submissive, full of
mercy[c] and good fruit, impartial and sincere.[d] 18Peacemakers[e] who sow in peace
raise a harvest of righteousness.[f]

End

Submit Yourselves to God

4 What causes fights and quarrels[g]
among you? Don't they come from
your desires that battle[h] within you? 2You
want something but don't get it. You kill[i]
and covet, but you cannot have what you
want. You quarrel and fight. You do not

[f] 11 Greek *bitter* (see also verse 14)

2:25 [c]S Heb 11:31 **2:26** [d]ver 17,20 **3:1** [e]S Eph 4:11 [f]S Mt 7:1 [g]Ro 2:21 **3:2** [h]1Ki 8:46; Ro 3:9-20; Jas 2:10; 1Jn 1:8 [i]Ps 39:1; Pr 10:19; 1Pe 3:10 [j]S Mt 12:37 [k]Jas 1:26 **3:3** [l]Ps 32:9 **3:5** [m]Ps 12:3,4; 73:8,9 **3:6** [n]Pr 16:27 [o]Mt 15:11,18,19 [p]S Mt 5:22 **3:8** [q]Ps 140:3; Ro 3:13 **3:9** [r]Ge 1:26,27; 1Co 11:7 **3:12** [s]Mt 7:16 **3:13** [t]Jas 2:18 [u]S 1Pe 2:12 **3:14** [v]ver 16; 2Co 12:20 [w]Jas 5:19 **3:15** [x]ver 17; Jas 1:17 [y]1Ti 4:1 **3:16** [z]ver 14; Gal 5:20,21 **3:17** [a]1Co 2:6; Jas 1:17 [b]Heb 12:11 [c]Lk 6:36 [d]Ro 12:9 **3:18** [e]Mt 5:9; S Ro 14:19 [f]Pr 11:18; Isa 32:17; Hos 10:12; Php 1:11 **4:1** [g]Tit 3:9 [h]S Ro 7:23 **4:2** [i]Mt 5:21,22; Jas 5:6; 1Jn 3:15

heart, the grace of God and the desire to please Christ. (2) For Paul, "works" refers to a desire to gain favor and salvation through obeying the law by one's own effort rather than through repentance and faith in Christ. (3) Note that both Paul and James state emphatically that true saving faith will inevitably produce deeds of love (1:27; 2:8; Gal 5:6; 1Co 13; cf. Jn 14:15).

3:1 TEACHERS. This includes pastors, church leaders, missionaries, preachers of the Word or anyone who gives instruction to a congregation. The teacher must understand that no one has a more solemn responsibility than those who teach the Word of God. In the future judgment, Christian teachers will be judged more strictly than other believers.

3:6 THE TONGUE ALSO IS A FIRE. James emphasizes our inclination to sin in our speaking. Sins of speech include harsh and unkind words, lying, exaggeration, teaching false doctrine, slander, gossiping, boasting, etc. Mature believers keep their tongues under control by the guidance of the Holy Spirit, taking "captive every thought to make it obedient to Christ" (2Co 10:5). Because of the tendency to sin with the tongue, James exhorts every person to "be quick to listen, slow to speak and slow to become angry" (1:19).

3:14 SELFISH AMBITION. "Selfish ambition" refers to the vice that prompts us to promote our own interests. Selfish ambition in the church is (1) "earthly," i.e., it defiles that which is holy and of the Spirit; (2) "unspiritual," i.e., without the Holy Spirit; and (3) "of the devil," i.e., it is inspired by demons (see 1Ti 4:1, note).

4:1 WHAT CAUSES FIGHTS AND QUARRELS AMONG YOU? The major source of quarrels and conflicts in the church centers in a desire for recognition, honor, power, pleasure, money and superiority. The satisfaction of selfish desires becomes more important than righteousness and God's will (cf. Mk 4:19; Lk 8:14; Gal 5:16–20). When this happens, self-centered conflicts are created in the fellowship. Those responsible show themselves to be without the Spirit and outside of God's kingdom (Gal 5:19–21; Jude 16–19).

4:2 YOU KILL. This phrase may be used figuratively in the sense of hate (cf. Mt 5:21–22).

have, because you do not ask God. 3When
you ask, you do not receive,[j] because you
ask with wrong motives,[k] that you may
spend what you get on your pleasures.
4You adulterous[l] people, don't you
know that friendship with the world[m] is
hatred toward God?[n] Anyone who
chooses to be a friend of the world becomes an enemy of God.[o] 5Or do you think
Scripture says without reason that the
spirit he caused to live in us[p] envies intensely?[g] 6But he gives us more grace.
That is why Scripture says:

"God opposes the proud
but gives grace to the humble."[h][q]

7Submit yourselves, then, to God. Resist the devil,[r] and he will flee from you.
8Come near to God and he will come near
to you.[s] Wash your hands,[t] you sinners,
and purify your hearts,[u] you double-minded.[v] 9Grieve, mourn and wail. Change
your laughter to mourning and your joy to
gloom.[w] 10Humble yourselves before the
Lord, and he will lift you up.[x]
11Brothers, do not slander one another.[y] Anyone who speaks against his
brother or judges him[z] speaks against the
law[a] and judges it. When you judge the
law, you are not keeping it,[b] but sitting in
judgment on it. 12There is only one Lawgiver and Judge,[c] the one who is able to
save and destroy.[d] But you—who are you
to judge your neighbor?[e]

Boasting About Tomorrow

13Now listen,[f] you who say, "Today or
tomorrow we will go to this or that city,
spend a year there, carry on business and
make money."[g] 14Why, you do not even
know what will happen tomorrow. What is
your life? You are a mist that appears for
a little while and then vanishes.[h] 15In-
stead, you ought to say, "If it is the Lord's
will,[i] we will live and do this or that."
16As it is, you boast and brag. All such
boasting is evil.[j] 17Anyone, then, who

4:3 [j]Ps 18:41; S Mt 7:7 [k]Ps 66:18; 1Jn 3:22; 5:14 **4:4** [l]Isa 54:5; Jer 3:20; Hos 2:2-5; 3:1; 9:1 [m]S Jas 1:27 [n]Ro 8:7; 1Jn 2:15 [o]Jn 15:19 **4:5** [p]1Co 6:19 **4:6** [q]Pr 3:34; S Mt 23:12 **4:7** [r]Eph 4:27; 6:11; 1Pe 5:6-9 **4:8** [s]Ps 73:28; Zec 1:3; Mal 3:7; Heb 7:19 [t]Isa 1:16 [u]Ps 24:4; Jer 4:14 [v]Ps 119:113; Jas 1:8 **4:9** [w]Lk 6:25 **4:10** [x]ver 6; Job 5:11; 1Pe 5:6 **4:11** [y]Ro 1:30; 2Co 12:20; 1Pe 2:1 [z]S Mt 7:1 [a]Jas 2:8 [b]Jas 1:22 **4:12** [c]Isa 33:22; S Jas 5:9 [d]Mt 10:28 [e]S Mt 7:1 **4:13** [f]Jas 5:1 [g]Pr 27:1; Lk 12:18-20 **4:14** [h]Job 7:7; Ps 39:5; 102:3; 144:4; Isa 2:22 **4:15** [i]S Ac 18:21 **4:16** [j]1Co 5:6

g *5* Or *that God jealously longs for the spirit that he made to live in us*; or *that the Spirit he caused to live in us longs jealously* h *6* Prov. 3:34

4:3 WHEN YOU ASK, YOU DO NOT RECEIVE. God refuses to answer the prayers of those who are selfishly ambitious, love pleasure, and desire honor, power or riches (see v. 1, note). All of us should take note, for God will not listen to our prayers if we have hearts filled with selfish desires. Scripture tells us God hears only the prayers of the righteous (Ps 34:13–15; 66:18–19), of those who call on him in truth (145:18), of the genuinely repentant and humble (Lk 18:14), and of those who ask according to his will (1Jn 5:14).

4:4 FRIENDSHIP WITH THE WORLD IS HATRED TOWARD GOD. "Friendship with the world" is spiritual adultery, i.e., unfaithfulness to God and our pledge of commitment to him (1Jn 2:15–17; cf. Isa 54:5; Jer 3:20). It involves embracing the world's sin, values and evil pleasures (see article on THE CHRISTIAN'S RELATIONSHIP TO THE WORLD, p. 546). God will not accept such friendship (Mt 6:24), for he is a jealous God (Ex 20:5; Dt 5:9).

One example of such friendship is participation in secret orders (e.g., lodge membership) that demand unscriptural religious oaths and yoking together with unbelievers, both of which are forbidden in God's Word (Mt 5:33–37; 2Co 6:14). Believers cannot belong to such groups without compromising Christian doctrine (2Pe 3:16), godly standards, separation from the world (2Co 6:17–18), and loyalty to Christ (Mt 6:24).

4:5 THE SPIRIT . . . ENVIES INTENSELY. The construction of this verse in the Greek is unclear. It may mean that the human spirit naturally hates God and neighbor and desires the sinful pleasures of the world (v. 4). Yet this can be changed by God's grace, which comes to all who humbly accept salvation in Christ (v. 6).

4:6 GOD OPPOSES THE PROUD. It should be impressed on our hearts and minds how much God hates pride. Pride causes God to turn from our prayers and withhold his presence and grace. To be exalted in our own minds or to seek the honor and esteem of others in order to satisfy our pride is to shut out God's help. But for those who humbly submit to God and draw near to him, he gives abundant grace, mercy and help in every situation of life (see Php 2:3, note; Heb 4:16; 7:25).

4:8 COME NEAR TO GOD. God promises to come near to all who turn from sin, purify their hearts and call on him in true repentance. God's nearness will bring his presence, grace, blessings and love.

4:11 DO NOT SLANDER ONE ANOTHER. By neglecting to learn all the facts about a situation, by failing to speak to an accused person about a problem, and by slandering him or her, we set aside God's law of love.

4:15 IF IT IS THE LORD'S WILL. In making goals and plans for the future, believers must always consider God and his will. We must not act like the rich fool (Lk 12:16–21); rather we must recognize that true happiness and useful living are completely dependent on God. The principle by which we live must be, "If it is the Lord's will." If our prayer is truly, "May your will be done" (Mt 26:42), then we have the assurance that our present and future is in the protective care of our heavenly Father (cf. Ac 18:21; 1Co 4:19; 16:7; Heb 6:3).

4:16 BOASTING. For those who set goals and succeed in meeting them, the temptation is to boast. Boasting is based on the false assumption that whatever we accomplished, we did by ourselves and not with the help of God and others. The NT urges us to boast in our weaknesses and our dependence on God (2Co 11:30; 12:5,9).

knows the good he ought to do and
doesn't do it, sins.[k]

Warning to Rich Oppressors

5 Now listen,[l] you rich people,[m] weep
and wail[n] because of the misery that
is coming upon you. 2Your wealth has rotted, and moths have eaten your clothes.[o]
3Your gold and silver are corroded. Their
corrosion will testify against you and eat
your flesh like fire. You have hoarded
wealth in the last days.[p] 4Look! The
wages you failed to pay the workmen[q]
who mowed your fields are crying out
against you. The cries[r] of the harvesters
have reached the ears of the Lord Almighty.[s] 5You have lived on earth in luxury and self-indulgence. You have fattened
yourselves[t] in the day of slaughter.[i][u]
6You have condemned and murdered[v] innocent men,[w] who were not opposing you.

Patience in Suffering

7Be patient, then, brothers, until the
Lord's coming.[x] See how the farmer waits
for the land to yield its valuable crop and
how patient he is[y] for the autumn and
spring rains.[z] 8You too, be patient and
stand firm, because the Lord's coming[a] is
near.[b] 9Don't grumble against each other,
brothers,[c] or you will be judged. The
Judge[d] is standing at the door![e]
10Brothers, as an example of patience
in the face of suffering, take the prophets[f] who spoke in the name of the Lord.
11As you know, we consider blessed[g]
those who have persevered. You have
heard of Job's perseverance[h] and have
seen what the Lord finally brought
about.[i] The Lord is full of compassion
and mercy.[j]
12Above all, my brothers, do not swear
—not by heaven or by earth or by anything else. Let your "Yes" be yes, and your
"No," no, or you will be condemned.[k]

The Prayer of Faith

13Is any one of you in trouble? He
should pray.[l] Is anyone happy? Let him
sing songs of praise.[m] 14Is any one of you
sick? He should call the elders[n] of the
church to pray over him and anoint him
with oil[o] in the name of the Lord. 15And

4:17 [k]Lk 12:47; Jn 9:41
5:1 [l]Jas 4:13 [m]Lk 6:24; 1Ti 6:9; Jas 2:2-6 [n]Isa 13:6; Eze 30:2
5:2 [o]Job 13:28; Ps 39:11; Isa 50:9; Mt 6:19, 20
5:3 [p]ver 7,8
5:4 [q]Lev 19:13; Jer 22:13; Mal 3:5 [r]Dt 24:15 [s]Ro 9:29
5:5 [t]Eze 16:49; Am 6:1; Lk 16:19 [u]Jer 12:3; 25:34
5:6 [v]Jas 4:2 [w]Heb 10:38
5:7 [x]S 1Co 1:7 [y]Gal 6:9 [z]Dt 11:14; Jer 5:24; Joel 2:23
5:8 [a]S 1Co 1:7 [b]S Ro 13:11
5:9 [c]Jas 4:11 [d]Ps 94:2; 1Co 4:5; Jas 4:12; 1Pe 4:5 [e]Mt 24:33
5:10 [f]S Mt 5:12
5:11 [g]Mt 5:10 [h]Job 1:21,22; 2:10; S Heb 10:36 [i]Job 42:10,12-17 [j]Ex 34:6; Nu 14:18; Ps 103:8
5:12 [k]Mt 5:34-37
5:13 [l]Ps 50:15 [m]Col 3:16
5:14 [n]S Ac 11:30 [o]Ps 23:5; Isa 1:6; Mk 6:13; 16:18; Lk 10:34

i 5 Or *yourselves as in a day of feasting*

5:1 YOU RICH PEOPLE, WEEP AND WAIL. The Bible does not teach that all rich people are ungodly. Nevertheless, what James is describing is characteristic of many people with wealth (vv. 1–6; 2:1–3). The exceptions are the rich people who are not possessed by their wealth and use it instead to advance the gospel and to help those in need (see article on RICHES AND POVERTY, p. 152).

5:7 BE PATIENT . . . UNTIL THE LORD'S COMING. James speaks of Christ's return as drawing near (v. 8). Christ will come as judge to punish the wicked and to reward the righteous and deliver them from wrongs they have suffered (v. 9). Patience is the virtue of enduring injustice, suffering, trouble and mistreatment, while committing our lives to God in the faith that he will make all things right at his coming (Dt 32:35; Ro 12:12; Heb 10:30; 12:1–2).

5:9 STANDING AT THE DOOR. The motive for patience and perseverance in the faith is the imminent coming of the Lord (v. 8). He is "standing at the door." The door may not open until tomorrow, or next week, or next year, but it could open at any time.

5:11 JOB'S PERSEVERANCE. The word "perseverance" (Gk *hupomonē*) indicates endurance in whatever trials we may face without losing our faith in God. It is born of a faith that triumphs to the end in the midst of sufferings (Job 13:15). The outcome of the Lord's dealings with Job reveals that in all Job's troubles, God cared deeply about him and mercifully sustained him. James wants us to know that God is concerned about all his people and that, in their suffering, he will sustain them in love and mercy.

5:13 IS ANY ONE OF YOU IN TROUBLE . . . HAPPY? When you are experiencing trouble, poverty or distress, Scripture invites you to seek strength from God through prayer. Draw near to your mediator, Jesus Christ. He will represent you before God, make intercession for you (Heb 7:25), and give mercy and grace to help in time of need (Heb 4:16). Take seriously God's Word: "Cast all your anxiety on him because he cares for you" (1Pe 5:7). If we are happy in the Lord, we must sing songs of praise to him (cf. Ps 33:2–3; 81:1–2; 92:1–3; 98:4–6; 144:9; 149:1–5; 150).

5:15 MAKE THE SICK PERSON WELL. James is speaking of physical sickness. We may deal with illness by asking for the prayers of the elders or leaders of the church. (1) It is the duty of pastors and leaders of the church to pray for the sick and to anoint them with oil. The oil probably represents the healing power of the Holy Spirit; it was used as an aid to faith (cf. Mk 6:13).

(2) It is prayer that James emphasizes as most important. Effective prayer must be offered in faith if the sick are to be healed. The Lord will give faith according to his will (see Mt 17:20, note; see article on DIVINE HEALING, p. 20).

(3) People may not always be healed; nevertheless, the church must continue to seek the kingdom's healing power in compassion for the sick and to the glory of Christ (see article on DIVINE HEALING, p. 20).

5:15 IF HE HAS SINNED. James recognizes that sickness may be due to sin (v. 16). Therefore, whenever sickness occurs, one should examine himself or herself before the Lord in prayer to determine if the sickness is due to personal sin. The word "if" makes it clear that sickness is not always the result of personal sin (see article on DIVINE HEALING, p. 20).

the prayer offered in faith[p] will make the
sick person well; the Lord will raise him
up. If he has sinned, he will be forgiven.
16Therefore confess your sins[q] to each
other and pray for each other so that you
1Pe 2:24 may be healed.[r] The prayer of a righteous
man is powerful and effective.[s]
17Elijah was a man just like us.[t] He
prayed earnestly that it would not rain,
and it did not rain on the land for three
and a half years.[u] **18**Again he prayed, and
the heavens gave rain, and the earth produced its crops.[v]
19My brothers, if one of you should
wander from the truth[w] and someone
should bring him back,[x] **20**remember this:
Whoever turns a sinner from the error of
his way will save[y] him from death and
cover over a multitude of sins.[z]

5:15 [p]Jas 1:6 **5:16** [q]Mt 3:6; Ac 19:18 [r]Heb 12:13; 1Pe 2:24 [s]S Mt 7:7; S Jn 9:31 **5:17** [t]Ac 14:15 [u]1Ki 17:1; Lk 4:25 **5:18** [v]1Ki 18:41-45 **5:19** [w]Jas 3:14 [x]S Mt 18:15 **5:20** [y]S Ro 11:14 [z]1Pe 4:8

5:16 CONFESS . . . PRAY . . . BE HEALED. This verse gives us an important reason why healing is often lacking in the Christian community. Sin must be confessed to others, and fervent prayer for one another be made to God. Sin in the church hinders the prayers of believers and blocks God's healing power from being manifested in the congregation.

5:16 PRAYER OF A RIGHTEOUS MAN IS POWERFUL. The prayers of the righteous (1) bring them near to God (Heb 7:25); (2) open the way to a Spirit-filled life (Lk 11:13; Ac 1:14); (3) bring them power for ministry (Ac 1:8; 4:31,33) and Christian devotion (Eph 1:19); (4) build them up spiritually (Jude 20); (5) give them insight into Christ's provision for them (Eph 1:18–19); (6) help them overcome Satan (Da 10:12–13; Eph 6:12,18); (7) clarify God's will for them (Ps 32:6–8; Pr 3:5–6; Mk 1:35–39); (8) enable them to receive spiritual gifts (1Co 14:1); (9) bring them into fellowship with God (Mt 6:9; Jn 7:37; 14:16,18,21); (10) bring them grace, mercy and peace (Php 4:6–7; Heb 4:16); (11) bring the lost to Christ (v. 20; Gal 4:19); (12) bring them the wisdom, revelation and knowledge of Christ (Eph 1:17); (13) bring them healing (v. 15); (14) bring them deliverance from trouble (Ps 34:4–7; Php 1:19); (15) glorify God with praise and thanksgiving (Ps 100:4); (16) make Christ's presence real to them (Jn 14:21; Rev 3:20); and (17) ensure them of their final salvation and of Christ's intercession for them (Heb 7:25).

5:18 HE PRAYED, AND THE HEAVENS GAVE RAIN. Elijah was a man who had faith that his prayers to God would accomplish much, even to the point of God's intervention in the course of nature. He believed that prayer by a righteous person does change things (vv. 13–16; Ps 34:6; Isa 38:1–5; Mt 17:21; 26:41,53; Mk 11:24; 2Th 3:1).

(1) We must be careful not to accept any teaching that undermines our faith in the power of prayer to bring about God's intervention in our lives. One such teaching is the concept of "fate," the pagan notion that everything we do and everything that happens to us is fixed unchangeably in advance, long before it occurs. Belief in fate is contrary to Scripture and causes one to assume that both good and bad are absolutely determined and unalterable, and that nothing is really changed by fervent, believing prayer.

(2) Scripture teaches that God deals with his children, not through absolute determinism, but by divine providence, whereby he interacts with and responds to the prayers of the righteous. Our prayers and faith in God do cause many good things to happen that would otherwise not occur (Ex 32:9–14).

5:19–20 IF ONE OF YOU SHOULD WANDER. Believers should do everything possible to turn back to God those who stray from the truth (e.g., Gal 4:19; 6:1; 2Ti 2:18,25–26; Jude 22–23). The salvation of a wandering brother or sister should always be a high priority in the Christian community. If the backslider returns to Christ, the one who converts him or her will have saved the sinner "from death," i.e., spiritual death and eternal separation from God (cf. Ro 6:23; Gal 6:8; Rev 20:14).

1 PETER

Outline

Christian Greetings (1:1–2)
- I. The Believer's Relationship to God (1:3—2:10)
  - A. Salvation Through Faith (1:3–12)
  - B. Holiness Through Obedience (1:13—2:10)
- II. The Believer's Relationship to Others (2:11—3:12)
  - A. Public Responsibilities (2:11–17)
  - B. Domestic Responsibilities (2:18—3:7)
    - 1. Slaves' Responsibility to Their Masters (2:18–25)
    - 2. Wives' Responsibility to Their Husbands (3:1–6)
    - 3. Husbands' Responsibility to Their Wives (3:7)
  - C. Summary of Principles Governing the Believer's Relationship to Others (3:8–12)
- III. The Believer's Relationship to Suffering (3:13—5:11)
  - A. Endurance in the Face of Suffering (3:13—4:11)
    - 1. Because of the Blessing of Suffering Unjustly (3:13–17)
    - 2. Because of the Powerful Example of Christ (3:18—4:6)
    - 3. Because of the Urgency of the End Time (4:7–11)
  - B. Rejoicing in the Face of Suffering (4:12–19)
    - 1. Because It Tests the Reality of Our Faith (4:12)
    - 2. Because It Is a Sharing in Christ's Sufferings (4:13a,14–16)
    - 3. Because It Prepares Us for the Glory of His Coming (4:13b,17–19)
  - C. Exhortations in the Face of Suffering (5:1–11)
    - 1. To Elders—Shepherd the Flock (5:1–4)
    - 2. To Younger Men (5:5–11)

Conclusion (5:12–14)

Author: Peter

Theme: Suffering for Christ

Date: A.D. 60–63

Background

This is the first of two NT letters written by the apostle Peter (1:1; 2Pe 1:1). Peter testifies that he wrote his first letter with the assistance of Silas (Gk *Silvanus*) as his scribe (5:12). Silas's fluent Greek and writing style are reflected here, while possibly Peter's own less polished Greek appears in his second letter. The tone and content of 1 Peter is consistent with what we know about Simon Peter. His years of close fellowship with the Lord Jesus underlie his recalling of Jesus' death (1:11,19; 2:21–24; 3:18; 5:1) and resurrection (1:3,21; 3:21); indirectly he seems to refer even to Jesus' post-resurrection appearance to him in Galilee (2:25; 5:2a; cf. Jn 21:15–23). In addition, many similarities occur between this letter and Peter's sermons recorded in Acts.

Peter addresses this letter to "strangers . . . scattered" throughout the Roman provinces of Asia Minor (1:1). Some of these may have been converts who had responded to Peter's message on the day of Pentecost and had returned to their respective cities with their newfound faith (cf. Ac 2:9–10). These believers are called "aliens and strangers" (2:11) to remind them that their

Christian pilgrimage is in a world that is hostile to Jesus Christ and from which they can expect persecution. Peter probably wrote this letter in response to reports from believers in Asia Minor of growing opposition (4:12–16) that did not yet have official governmental sanction (2:12–17).

Peter wrote from "Babylon" (5:13). This may be understood literally as the country of Babylon in Mesopotamia or as a figurative expression for Rome, the supreme center of organized godlessness in the first century. Although Peter may once have visited the large colony of orthodox Jews in Babylon, we can more readily account for Peter, Silas (5:12) and Mark (5:13) being together at Rome (Col 4:10; cf. Papias's comments about Peter and Mark at Rome) in the early 60s rather than at literal Babylon. Peter wrote most likely from Rome between A.D. 60–63, surely before the terrible bloodbath of Nero in Rome began (A.D. 64).

Purpose

Peter wrote this letter of joyful hope to provide believers with a divine and eternal perspective on their earthly lives and to give practical guidance to those who were beginning to experience a fiery trial of suffering as Christians in a pagan environment. Peter was concerned that believers should not provoke governmental structures unnecessarily and that they should follow Jesus' example in suffering innocently, righteously and nobly.

Survey

1 Peter begins by reminding believers (1) that they have a glorious calling and heavenly inheritance in Jesus Christ (1:2–5); (2) that their faith and love in this life will be subjected to testing and refining and will result in praise, glory and honor at the Lord's appearing (1:6–9); (3) that this great salvation was foreseen by the OT prophets (1:10–12); and (4) that believers must live holy lives, clearly different from the unregenerate world around them (1:13–21). Believers, chosen and sanctified (1:2), are growing infants who need the pure milk of the Word (2:1–3), living stones who are being built into a spiritual house (2:4–10), and aliens who are passing through a foreign land (2:11–12); they must live honorably and humbly in their relations with all people during their journey (2:13—3:12).

The preeminent message of 1 Peter concerns submission and suffering righteously for Christ's sake and according to his own example (2:18–24; 3:9—5:11). Peter assures believers that for righteous suffering they will obtain God's favor and reward. In the context of this teaching concerning suffering for Christ, Peter stresses the interrelated themes of salvation, hope, love, joy, faith, holiness, humility, fear of God, obedience and submission.

Special Features

Five major features characterize this letter. (1) Along with Hebrews and Revelation, its message revolves around believers who are facing the prospect of severe persecution because of their identity with Jesus Christ. (2) More than any other NT letter, it provides instruction on how to respond as a Christian to unjust persecution and suffering (3:9—5:11). (3) Peter stresses the truth that believers are aliens and strangers on earth (1:1; 2:11). (4) Many OT titles for God's people are applied to NT believers (e.g., 2:5,9–10). (5) It contains one of the most difficult NT passages to interpret: when, where and how Jesus "went and preached to the spirits in prison who disobeyed . . . in the days of Noah" (3:19–20).

Reading 1 Peter

In order to read the entire New Testament in one year, the book of 1 Peter should be read in 5 days, according to the following schedule:
☐ 1:1–21 ☐ 1:22—2:25 ☐ 3 ☐ 4 ☐ 5

NOTES

1 Peter, an apostle of Jesus Christ,[a]
To God's elect,[b] strangers in the
world,[c] scattered[d] throughout Pontus,[e]
Galatia,[f] Cappadocia, Asia and Bithynia,[g] **2**who have been chosen according to
the foreknowledge[h] of God the Father,
through the sanctifying work of the Spirit,[i] for obedience[j] to Jesus Christ and
sprinkling by his blood:[k]

Grace and peace be yours in abundance.[l]

Praise to God for a Living Hope

3Praise be to the God and Father of our
Lord Jesus Christ![m] In his great mercy[n]
he has given us new birth[o] into a living
hope[p] through the resurrection of Jesus
Christ from the dead,[q] **4**and into an inheritance[r] that can never perish, spoil or
fade[s]—kept in heaven for you,[t] **5**who
through faith are shielded by God's power[u] until the coming of the salvation[v] that
is ready to be revealed[w] in the last time.
6In this you greatly rejoice,[x] though now
for a little while[y] you may have had to
suffer grief in all kinds of trials.[z] **7**These
have come so that your faith—of greater
worth than gold, which perishes even
though refined by fire[a]—may be proved
genuine[b] and may result in praise, glory
and honor[c] when Jesus Christ is revealed.[d] **8**Though you have not seen him,
you love him; and even though you do not
see him now, you believe in him[e] and are
filled with an inexpressible and glorious
joy, **9**for you are receiving the goal of your
faith, the salvation of your souls.[f]
10Concerning this salvation, the prophets, who spoke[g] of the grace that was to
come to you,[h] searched intently and with
the greatest care,[i] **11**trying to find out the
time and circumstances to which the Spirit of Christ[j] in them was pointing when he
predicted[k] the sufferings of Christ and the
glories that would follow. **12**It was revealed to them that they were not serving
themselves but you,[l] when they spoke of

1:1 [a]2Pe 1:1 [b]Mt 24:22 [c]S Heb 11:13 [d]S Jas 1:1 [e]Ac 2:9; 18:2 [f]S Ac 16:6 [g]Ac 16:7 **1:2** [h]Ro 8:29 [i]2Th 2:13 [j]ver 14, 22 [k]Heb 10:22; 12:24 [l]S Ro 1:7 **1:3** [m]2Co 1:3; Eph 1:3 [n]Tit 3:5 [o]ver 23; S Jn 1:13 [p]ver 13,21; S Heb 3:6 [q]1Co 15:20; 1Pe 3:21 **1:4** [r]S Ac 20:32; S Ro 8:17 [s]1Pe 5:4 [t]Col 1:5; 2Ti 4:8 **1:5** [u]1Sa 2:9; Jn 10:28 [v]S Ro 11:14 [w]S Ro 8:18 **1:6** [x]Ro 5:2 [y]1Pe 5:10 [z]Jas 1:2; 1Pe 4:12 **1:7** [a]Job 23:10; Ps 66:10; Pr 17:3; Isa 48:10 [b]Jas 1:3 [c]2Co 4:17 [d]ver 13; S 1Th 2:19; 1Pe 4:13 **1:8** [e]Jn 20:29 **1:9** [f]Ro 6:22 **1:10** [g]S Mt 26:24 [h]ver 13 [i]S Mt 13:17 **1:11** [j]S Ac 16:7; 2Pe 1:21 [k]S Mt 26:24 **1:12** [l]S Ro 4:24

1:2 THE FOREKNOWLEDGE OF GOD. Divine foreknowledge must be understood as God's eternal love and intention for his people, the church (see Ro 8:29, note). The "chosen" are the company of true believers, chosen in harmony with God's determination to redeem the church by the blood of Jesus Christ through the Spirit's sanctifying work (see article on ELECTION AND PREDESTINATION, p. 402). All believers must participate in their election by being eager to make their calling and election sure (see 2Pe 1:5,10, notes).

1:2 SANCTIFYING WORK OF THE SPIRIT. For a discussion of the Christian's life of sanctification, see article on SANCTIFICATION, p. 526.

1:3 GIVEN US NEW BIRTH. See article on REGENERATION, p. 178.

1:5 THROUGH FAITH ARE SHIELDED BY GOD'S POWER. This verse presents four truths concerning the security of believers, a particularly relevant message for Peter's audience since many of them were experiencing intense persecution. (1) Believers are "shielded by God's power" against all the forces of evil that would destroy their lives and salvation in Christ (2Ti 4:18; Jude 1,24; cf. Ro 8:31–39).

(2) The essential condition required for God's protection is "faith" (see article on FAITH AND GRACE, p. 302). God's shielding us by his grace does not work arbitrarily, for only "through faith" are believers protected by God's power, just as only "through faith" are believers saved (Eph 2:8). Thus, a living faith in Christ as Lord and Savior is our present responsibility in maintaining God's continued protection (v. 9; Jn 15:4,6; Col 1:23; 2Ti 3:14–15; 4:7; Rev 3:8,10).

(3) The ultimate goal of God's protection through the believer's faith is "salvation." Here salvation refers to the future dimension of salvation (cf. Ro 1:16), i.e., the obtaining of an inheritance in heaven (v. 4) and "the salvation of your souls" (v. 9).

1:7 YOUR FAITH ... PROVED GENUINE. The theme of suffering is emphasized throughout this letter (2:19–23; 3:14–17; 4:1–6,12–19; 5:10). We must rejoice in our trials (v. 6), because remaining faithful to Christ in the midst of them will purify our faith and result in praise, glory and honor both to us and to the Lord Jesus at his coming. The Lord considers our perseverance through trials and our faith in Christ precious to him throughout eternity.

1:8 HAVE NOT SEEN HIM, YOU LOVE. God considers the faith of believers today as greater than the faith of those who saw and heard Jesus personally, even after his resurrection. Believers now, although they have never seen him, love him and believe in him. According to Jesus, there is a special blessing for "those who have not seen and yet have believed" (Jn 20:29). As we live by faith we are given joy as God's gift to us (Ps 16:11; Jn 16:24; Ro 15:13; Gal 5:22).

1:11 SPIRIT OF CHRIST IN THEM. Our faith is based not only on the Word of God in the NT but also on God's Word in the OT. The Holy Spirit through the prophets predicted Christ's sufferings and the glories to follow (Ge 49:10; Ps 22; Isa 52:13—53:12; Da 2:44; Zec 9:9–10; 13:7; cf. Lk 24:26–27; see 2Pe 1:21, note). The Spirit is called "the Spirit of Christ" because he spoke about Christ through the prophets and he was sent from Christ (vv. 11–12; cf. Jn 16:7; 20:22; Ac 2:33).

1:12 PREACHED ... BY THE HOLY SPIRIT. The same Spirit who inspired the OT prophets (v. 11) has inspired the truth of the gospel; thus, the message originates from God, not from humans. On the day of Pentecost, the same Spirit who inspired the truth of the gospel began to give power to all believers to proclaim the message (Ac 1:8; 2:4).

the things that have now been told you by
those who have preached the gospel to
you[m] by the Holy Spirit sent from heav-
en.[n] Even angels long to look into these
things.

Be Holy

13Therefore, prepare your minds for action; be self-controlled;[o] set your hope[p]
fully on the grace to be given you[q] when
Jesus Christ is revealed.[r] **14**As obedient[s]
children, do not conform[t] to the evil desires you had when you lived in ignorance.[u] **15**But just as he who called you is
holy, so be holy in all you do;[v] **16**for it is
written: "Be holy, because I am holy."[a][w]
17Since you call on a Father[x] who
judges each man's work[y] impartially,[z]
live your lives as strangers[a] here in reverent fear.[b] **18**For you know that it was not
with perishable things such as silver or
gold that you were redeemed[c] from the
empty way of life[d] handed down to you
from your forefathers, **19**but with the precious blood[e] of Christ, a lamb[f] without
blemish or defect.[g] **20**He was chosen before the creation of the world,[h] but was
revealed in these last times[i] for your
sake. **21**Through him you believe in God,[j]
who raised him from the dead[k] and glorified him,[l] and so your faith and hope[m] are
in God.
22Now that you have purified[n] yourselves by obeying[o] the truth so that you
have sincere love for your brothers, love
one another deeply,[p] from the heart.[b]
23For you have been born again,[q] not of
perishable seed, but of imperishable,[r]
through the living and enduring word of
God.[s] **24**For,

"All men are like grass,
and all their glory is like the
flowers of the field;
the grass withers and the flowers fall,
25 but the word of the Lord stands
forever."[c][t]

And this is the word that was preached to
you.

2 Therefore, rid yourselves[u] of all malice and all deceit, hypocrisy, envy,
and slander[v] of every kind. **2**Like newborn babies, crave pure spiritual milk,[w] so
that by it you may grow up[x] in your salvation, **3**now that you have tasted that the
Lord is good.[y]

The Living Stone and a Chosen People

4As you come to him, the living Stone[z]
—rejected by men but chosen by God[a]
and precious to him— **5**you also, like liv-

1:12 [m]ver 25 [n]S Lk 24:49 **1:13** [o]S Ac 24:25 [p]ver 3,21; S Heb 3:6 [q]ver 10 [r]ver 7; S 1Co 1:7 **1:14** [s]ver 2,22 [t]Ro 12:2 [u]Eph 4:18 **1:15** [v]Isa 35:8; 1Th 4:7; 1Jn 3:3 **1:16** [w]Lev 11:44, 45; 19:2; 20:7 **1:17** [x]S Mt 6:9 [y]S Mt 16:27 [z]S Ac 10:34 [a]S Heb 11:13 [b]Heb 12:28 **1:18** [c]S Mt 20:28; S 1Co 6:20 [d]Gal 4:3 **1:19** [e]S Ro 3:25 [f]S Jn 1:29 [g]Ex 12:5 **1:20** [h]Eph 1:4; S Mt 25:34 [i]Heb 9:26 **1:21** [j]Ro 4:24; 10:9 [k]S Ac 2:24 [l]Php 2:7-9; Heb 2:9 [m]ver 3, 13; S Heb 3:6 **1:22** [n]Jas 4:8 [o]ver 2,14 [p]S Jn 13:34; S Ro 12:10 **1:23** [q]ver 3; S Jn 1:13 [r]Jn 1:13 [s]S Heb 4:12 **1:25** [t]Isa 40:6-8; S Jas 1:10,11 **2:1** [u]S Eph 4:22 [v]S Jas 4:11 **2:2** [w]1Co 3:2; Heb 5:12,13 [x]Eph 4:15,16 **2:3** [y]Ps 34:8; Heb 6:5 **2:4** [z]ver 7 [a]Isa 42:1

[a] *16* Lev. 11:44,45; 19:2; 20:7 [b] *22* Some early manuscripts *from a pure heart* [c] *25* Isaiah 40:6-8

1:14 DO NOT CONFORM. See Ro 12:2, note.
1:16 BE HOLY. God is holy, and what is true of God must be true of his people. Holiness carries the thought of being separated from the ungodly ways of the world and set apart for love, for service and for worship of God. Holiness is the goal and purpose of our election in Christ (Eph 1:4); it means being like God and being dedicated to him, while living to please him (Ro 12:1; Eph 1:4; 2:10; 1Jn 3:2–3; see Heb 12:14, note). It is accomplished by the Spirit of God, who cleanses our souls from sin, renews us in the image of Christ, and enables us by an infusion of grace to obey God according to his Word (Gal 5:16,22–23,25; Col 3:10; Tit 3:5; 2Pe 1:9). For more on holiness as a way of life, see article on SANCTIFICATION, p. 526.
1:17 WHO JUDGES. See article on THE JUDGMENT OF BELIEVERS, p. 368.
1:17 LIVE . . . IN REVERENT FEAR. See Ac 5:11, note; 9:31, note; Ro 3:19, note; Php 2:12, note.
1:18 REDEEMED. See article on BIBLICAL WORDS FOR SALVATION, p. 292.
1:19 THE PRECIOUS BLOOD OF CHRIST. Scripture plainly sets forth Christ's sacrificial death as that which procures the believer's redemption, i.e., release from bondage to sin (cf. Eph 1:7; see Heb 9:14, note).
1:22 LOVE ONE ANOTHER DEEPLY. See Jn 13:34–35, notes; Ro 12:10, note.
1:25 THE WORD OF THE LORD STANDS FOREVER. Peter's quotation of Isa 40:6–8 indicates that, like the earth itself, all human glory and attainments (such as culture, science and philosophy) come and go (cf. Ps 90:5–10; Jas 4:13–17). But God's Word abides forever. All human endeavors and the prevailing spirit of the world must be constantly judged by the Bible, rather than the Bible being judged by them. Those who bend God's Word to conform to the intellectual trends and diluted standards of their generation betray the "living and enduring word of God" (v. 23).
2:2 CRAVE PURE SPIRITUAL MILK. As born-again children of God (1Co 6:19; Gal 4:6), we should long for the pure milk of God's Word (1:23–25). A sure sign of our spiritual growth is a deep desire to feed on the living and enduring Word of God. Thus, we must be alert to a loss of hunger and thirst for God's Word, a yearning that we can destroy through wrong attitudes (v. 1) and through being "choked by life's worries, riches and pleasures" (Lk 8:14; see Mt 5:6, note; 1Co 15:2, note).
2:5 A HOLY PRIESTHOOD. In the OT the priesthood was restricted to a qualified minority. Their distinctive activity was to offer sacrifices to God on behalf of his people and to communicate directly with God (Ex 19:6; 28:1; 2Ch 29:11). Now through Jesus Christ, every Christian has been made a priest before God (Rev 1:6; 5:10; 20:6). The priesthood of all

SANCTIFICATION

***1Pe 1:2** "Who have been chosen according to the foreknowledge of God the Father, through the sanctifying work of the Spirit, for obedience to Jesus Christ and sprinkling by his blood: Grace and peace be yours in abundance."*

Sanctification (Gk *hagiasmos*) means to make holy, to consecrate, to separate from the world, and to be set apart from sin so that we may have intimate fellowship with God and serve him gladly (see article on SPIRITUAL SEPARATION FOR BELIEVERS, p. 371).

(1) In addition to the word "sanctify" (cf. 1Th 5:23), the Scriptural standard of sanctification is expressed in such terms as "love the Lord your God with all your heart . . . soul . . . mind" (Mt 22:37), "blameless and holy" (1Th 3:13), "perfecting holiness" (2Co 7:1), "love, which comes from a pure heart and a good conscience and a sincere faith" (1Ti 1:5), "pure and blameless" (Php 1:10), "set free from sin" (Ro 6:18), "died to sin" (Ro 6:2), "in slavery to righteousness leading to holiness" (Ro 6:19), "obey his commands" (1Jn 3:22), and "overcomes the world" (1Jn 5:4). Such terms describe the operation of the Holy Spirit through salvation in Christ by which he delivers us from sin's bondage and power (Ro 6:1–11), separates us from the sinful practices of this present world, renews our nature according to the image of Christ, produces in us the fruit of the Spirit, and enables us to live holy and victorious lives of dedication to God (Jn 17:15–19,23; Ro 6:5,13,16,19; 12:1; Gal 5:16,22–23; see 2Co 5:17, note).

(2) These terms do not imply an absolute perfection, but an ethical righteousness of unblemished character demonstrated in purity, obedience and blamelessness (Php 2:14–15; Col 1:22; 1Th 2:10; cf. Lk 1:6). Christians, by the grace of God given to them, have died with Christ and are set free from sin's power and dominion (Ro 6:18); therefore, they need not and ought not sin, but can find adequate victory in their Savior, Jesus Christ. Through the Holy Spirit we are able not to sin (1Jn 2:1; 3:6), even though we never come to the place where we are free from temptation and the possibility of sin.

(3) Sanctification is not optional for believers in Christ. Scripture teaches that "without holiness no one will see the Lord" (Heb 12:14).

(4) God's children achieve sanctification by faith (Ac 26:18), by union with Christ in his death and resurrection (Jn 15:4–10; Ro 6:1–11; 1Co 1:30), by the blood of Christ (1Jn 1:7–9), by the Word (Jn 17:17), and by the regenerating and sanctifying work of the Holy Spirit in their hearts (Jer 31:31–34; Ro 8:13; 1Co 6:11; Php 2:12–13; 2Th 2:13).

(5) Sanctification is both a work of God and a work of his people (Php 2:12–13). In order to accomplish God's will in sanctification, believers must participate in the Spirit's sanctifying work by ceasing to do evil (Ro 6:1–2), purifying themselves "from everything that contaminates body and spirit" (2Co 7:1; cf. Ro 6:12; Gal 5:16–25), and keeping themselves from being polluted by the world (Jas 1:27; cf. Ro 6:13,19; 8:13; 12:1–2; 13:14; Eph 4:31; 5:18; Col 3:5,10; Heb 6:1; Jas 4:8).

(6) True sanctification requires that believers maintain intimate communion with Christ (see Jn 15:4, note), engage in fellowship with believers (Eph 4:15–16), devote themselves to prayer (Mt 6:5–13; Col 4:2) obey God's Word (Jn 17:17), be sensitive to God's presence and care (Mt 6:25–34), love righteousness and hate wickedness (Heb 1:9), put sin to death (Ro 6), submit to God's discipline (Heb 12:5–11), continue to obey, and be filled with the Holy Spirit (Ro 8:14; Eph 5:18).

(7) In the NT, sanctification is not pictured as a slow process of forsaking sin little by little. Rather, it is presented as a definitive act by which the believer by grace is set free from Satan's bondage and makes a clear break with sin in order to live for God (Ro 6:18; 2Co 5:17; Eph 2:4–6; Col 3:1–3). At the same time, however, sanctification is described as a lifelong process by which we continue to put to death the misdeeds of the body (Ro 8:1–17), are progressively transformed into Christ's likeness (2Co 3:18), grow in grace (2Pe 3:18), and exercise a greater love for God and others (Mt 22:37–39; 1Jn 4:7–8,11,20–21).

(8) Sanctification can involve a definite crisis experience after initial salvation. Believers may receive a clear revelation of God's holiness as well as a consciousness that God is calling them to separate themselves in a greater way from sin and the world and to walk closer to God (2Co 6:16–18). Through this awareness, believers present themselves to God as living sacrifices and receive from the Holy Spirit grace, purity, power and victory to live holy lives pleasing to God (Ro 6:19–22; 12:1–2).

ing stones, are being built[b] into a spiritual
house[c] to be a holy priesthood,[d] offering
spiritual sacrifices acceptable to God
through Jesus Christ.[e] **6**For in Scripture it
says:

"See, I lay a stone in Zion,
a chosen and precious
cornerstone,[f]
and the one who trusts in him
will never be put to shame."[d][g]

7Now to you who believe, this stone is
precious. But to those who do not believe,[h]

"The stone the builders rejected[i]
has become the capstone,[e]"[f][j]

8and,

"A stone that causes men to stumble
and a rock that makes them
fall."[g][k]

They stumble because they disobey the
message—which is also what they were
destined for.[l]

9But you are a chosen people,[m] a royal
priesthood,[n] a holy nation,[o] a people belonging to God,[p] that you may declare the
praises of him who called you out of darkness into his wonderful light.[q] **10**Once you
were not a people, but now you are the
people of God;[r] once you had not received
mercy, but now you have received mercy.
11Dear friends,[s] I urge you, as aliens
and strangers in the world,[t] to abstain

2:5 [b]Pr 9:1; 1Co 3:9; Eph 2:20-22 [c]1Ti 3:15 [d]ver 9; Ex 19:6; Isa 61:6; Rev 1:6; 5:10; 20:6 [e]Php 4:18; Heb 13:15
2:6 [f]Eph 2:20 [g]Isa 28:16; Ro 9:32,33; 10:11
2:7 [h]2Co 2:16 [i]ver 4 [j]Ps 118:22; S Ac 4:11
2:8 [k]Isa 8:14; S Lk 2:34 [l]Ro 9:22
2:9 [m]Dt 10:15; 1Sa 12:22 [n]ver 5 [o]Ex 19:6; Dt 7:6; Isa 62:12 [p]S Tit 2:14 [q]S Ac 26:18
2:10 [r]Hos 1:9,10; 2:23; Ro 9:25,26
2:11 [s]S 1Co 10:14 [t]S Heb 11:13 [u]Ro 13:14; Gal 5:16 [v]Jas 4:1
2:12 [w]Php 2:15; Tit 2:8; S Tit 2:14; 1Pe 3:16 [x]S Mt 9:8
2:13 [y]Ro 13:1; Tit 3:1
2:14 [z]Ro 13:4 [a]Ro 13:3
2:15 [b]1Pe 3:17; 4:19 [c]S ver 12
2:16 [d]S Jn 8:32 [e]Gal 5:13 [f]S Ro 6:22
2:17 [g]S Ro 12:10 [h]Pr 24:21; Ro 13:7
2:18 [i]S Eph 6:5 [j]Jas 3:17
2:19 [k]1Pe 3:14, 17
2:20 [l]1Pe 3:17
2:21 [m]S Ac 14:22; Php 1:29; 1Pe 3:9

from sinful desires,[u] which war against
your soul.[v] **12**Live such good lives among
the pagans that, though they accuse you
of doing wrong, they may see your good
deeds[w] and glorify God[x] on the day he
visits us.

Submission to Rulers and Masters

13Submit yourselves for the Lord's
sake to every authority[y] instituted among
men: whether to the king, as the supreme
authority, **14**or to governors, who are sent
by him to punish those who do wrong[z]
and to commend those who do right.[a]
15For it is God's will[b] that by doing good
you should silence the ignorant talk of
foolish men.[c] **16**Live as free men,[d] but do
not use your freedom as a cover-up for
evil;[e] live as servants of God.[f] **17**Show
proper respect to everyone: Love the
brotherhood of believers,[g] fear God, hon-
or the king.[h]

18Slaves, submit yourselves to your
masters with all respect,[i] not only to
those who are good and considerate,[j] but
also to those who are harsh. **19**For it is
commendable if a man bears up under the
pain of unjust suffering because he is conscious of God.[k] **20**But how is it to your
credit if you receive a beating for doing
wrong and endure it? But if you suffer for
doing good and you endure it, this is commendable before God.[l] **21**To this[m] you

d *6* Isaiah 28:16 e *7* Or *cornerstone*
f *7* Psalm 118:22 g *8* Isaiah 8:14

---

believers means the following: (1) All believers have direct access to God through Christ (3:18; Jn 14:6; Ac 4:12; Eph 2:18).

(2) All believers are under obligation to live holy lives (vv. 5,9; 1:14–17).

(3) All believers must offer up "spiritual sacrifices" to God, including: (a) living in obedience to God and nonconformity to the world (Ro 12:1–2); (b) praying to and praising God (Ps 50:14; Heb 13:15); (c) serving with whole hearts and willing minds (1Ch 28:9; Eph 5:1–2; Php 2:17); (d) performing good deeds (Heb 13:16); (e) giving of our material possessions (Ro 12:13; Php 4:18); and (f) presenting our bodies to God as instruments of righteousness (Ro 6:13,19).

(4) All believers must intercede and pray for one another and for all people (Col 4:12; 1Ti 2:1; Rev 8:3).

(5) All believers must declare the Word and pray for its success (v. 9; 3:15; Ac 4:31; 1Co 14:26; 2Th 3:1; Heb 13:15).

(6) All believers may administer baptism and the Lord's Supper (Mt 28:19; Lk 22:19).

2:9 A HOLY NATION. Believers are set apart from the world in order to belong completely to God (cf. Ac 20:28; Tit 2:14) and to proclaim the gospel of salvation to his glory and praise (cf. Ex 19:6; Isa 43:20–21).

2:11 ALIENS AND STRANGERS. Our new position as God's own possession sets us apart from the people of this world to become aliens in this world. We now live in a country to which we do not belong, and our true citizenship is with Christ in heaven (cf. Php 3:20; Heb 11:9–16). Because we are foreigners on this earth, we must abstain from the world's evil pleasures, which seek to destroy our souls (see article on THE ACTS OF THE SINFUL NATURE AND THE FRUIT OF THE SPIRIT, p. 394).

2:13 SUBMIT . . . TO EVERY AUTHORITY. See Ro 13:1, note.

2:21 CHRIST SUFFERED . . . FOLLOW IN HIS STEPS. The highest glory and privilege of any believer is to suffer for Christ and the gospel. In suffering, believers follow the example of Christ and the apostles (Isa 53; Mt 16:21; 20:28; Ac 9:16, note; Heb 5:8). (1) Christians must be willing to suffer (4:1; 2Co 11:23), i.e., to share in the sufferings of Christ (4:13; 2Co 1:5; Php 3:10), and expect suffering to be a part of their ministry (1Co 11:1; 2Co 4:10–12).

(2) Suffering for Christ is called suffering "according to God's will" (4:19), for his "name" (Ac 9:16), "for the gospel" (2Ti 1:8), "for what is right" (3:14) and for "the kingdom of God" (2Th 1:5).

(3) Suffering for Christ is a way to arrive at spiritual

were called,[n] because Christ suffered for
you,[o] leaving you an example,[p] that you
should follow in his steps.

22 "He committed no sin,[q]
and no deceit was found in his
mouth."[h][r]

23 When they hurled their insults at him,[s]
he did not retaliate; when he suffered, he
made no threats.[t] Instead, he entrusted
himself[u] to him who judges justly.[v] 24 He
himself bore our sins[w] in his body on the
tree,[x] so that we might die to sins[y] and
live for righteousness; by his wounds you
End have been healed.[z] 25 For you were like
sheep going astray,[a] but now you have
returned to the Shepherd[b] and Overseer
of your souls.[c]

Wives and Husbands

3 Wives, in the same way be submissive[d] to your husbands[e] so that, if
any of them do not believe the word, they
may be won over[f] without words by the
behavior of their wives, 2 when they see
the purity and reverence of your lives.
3 Your beauty should not come from outward adornment, such as braided hair and
the wearing of gold jewelry and fine
clothes.[g] 4 Instead, it should be that of
your inner self,[h] the unfading beauty of a
gentle and quiet spirit, which is of great
worth in God's sight.[i] 5 For this is the way
the holy women of the past who put their
hope in God[j] used to make themselves
beautiful.[k] They were submissive to their
own husbands, 6 like Sarah, who obeyed
Abraham and called him her master.[l] You
are her daughters if you do what is right
and do not give way to fear.

7 Husbands,[m] in the same way be considerate as you live with your wives, and
treat them with respect as the weaker
partner and as heirs with you of the gracious gift of life, so that nothing will hinder your prayers.

Christian Conduct

8 Finally, all of you, live in harmony with
one another;[n] be sympathetic, love as
brothers,[o] be compassionate and humble.[p] 9 Do not repay evil with evil[q] or insult with insult,[r] but with blessing,[s] be-

2:21 [n]S Ro 8:28 [o]1Pe 3:18; 4:1,13 [p]S Mt 11:29; 16:24
2:22 [q]S 2Co 5:21 [r]Isa 53:9
2:23 [s]Heb 12:3; 1Pe 3:9 [t]Isa 53:7 [u]Lk 23:46 [v]Ps 9:4
2:24 [w]Isa 53:4, 11; Heb 9:28 [x]S Ac 5:30 [y]S Ro 6:2 [z]Dt 32:39; Ps 103:3; Isa 53:5; Heb 12:13; Jas 5:16
2:25 [a]Isa 53:6 [b]S Jn 10:11 [c]Job 10:12
3:1 [d]1Pe 2:18 [e]S Eph 5:22 [f]1Co 7:16; 9:19
3:3 [g]Isa 3:18-23; 1Ti 2:9
3:4 [h]Ro 7:22; Eph 3:16 [i]S Ro 2:29
3:5 [j]1Ti 5:5 [k]Est 2:15
3:6 [l]Ge 18:12
3:7 [m]Eph 5:25-33; Col 3:19
3:8 [n]S Ro 15:5 [o]S Ro 12:10 [p]Eph 4:2; 1Pe 5:5
3:9 [q]Ro 12:17; 1Th 5:15 [r]1Pe 2:23 [s]S Mt 5:44

h *22* Isaiah 53:9

maturity (Heb 2:10), to obtain God's blessing (4:14) and to minister life to others (2Co 4:10–12). Sharing in Christ's suffering is a prerequisite for being glorified with Christ (Ro 8:17) and attaining eternal glory (Ro 8:18). In this sense it may be regarded as a precious gift from God (v. 19; Php 1:29).

(4) In living for Christ and the gospel, suffering should not be sought, but believers must be willing to undergo it out of devotion to Christ.

2:24 BORE OUR SINS. Christ bore our sins on the cross (cf. Isa 53:4,11–12), becoming our substitute by taking on himself the penalty for our sins (Jn 1:29; Heb 9:28; 10:10). The purpose of this substitutionary death was that we might be totally separated from sin's guilt, power and influence. By his death Christ removed our guilt and the punishment for our sins, opening a way whereby we might justly return to God (Ro 3:24–26) and receive grace to live righteously before him (Ro 6:2–3; 2Co 5:15; Gal 2:20). Peter uses the word "healed" in relation to salvation with all its benefits (cf. Isa 53:5; Mt 8:16–17).

3:1 HUSBANDS . . . MAY BE WON OVER. Peter instructs a wife how to act in order to bring her unsaved husband to Christ. (1) She must be submissive to her husband and recognize his leadership in the family (see Eph 5:22, note). (2) She must conduct herself in a pure and reverent manner, with a gentle and quiet spirit (vv. 2–4; see 1Ti 2:13,15, notes). (3) She must attempt to win her husband more by her behavior than by her words.

3:3–4 BEAUTY . . . OF YOUR INNER SELF. Gaudy or expensive adornment is contrary to the spirit of modesty that God desires for the Christian wife (see 1Ti 2:9, note). (1) What God highly values in a Christian wife is a gentle and quiet disposition (cf. Mt 11:29; 21:5) that seeks to honor him by giving herself to help her husband and family achieve God's will for their lives. (a) The adjective "gentle" describes an unassuming disposition that expresses itself in gracious submissiveness and a concern for others (cf. Mt 5:5; 2Co 10:1; Gal 5:23). (b) The adjective "quiet" refers to a disposition that is not boisterous and does not create disturbances. In other words, God declares that true beauty is a matter of character and not a matter of decoration.

(2) Christian wives must remain loyal to Christ and his Word in a world governed by materialism, manipulative fashions, self-assertion, obsession with sex, and contempt for the values of home and family.

3:7 HUSBANDS. Peter mentions three things that husbands must be concerned about with regard to their wives. (1) Husbands must be considerate and understanding, living with their wives in love and in harmony with God's Word (Eph 5:25–33; Col 3:19).

(2) They must treat them with respect as equal heirs of God's grace and salvation. Wives must be honored, provided for and protected according to their needs. "Weaker" probably refers to the woman's physical strength. A husband must praise and highly treasure his wife as she strives to love and help him according to God's will (vv. 1–6; see Eph 5:23, note).

(3) They must avoid any unjust and improper treatment of their wives. Peter indicates that a husband who fails to live with his wife in an understanding way and to give her honor as a fellow child of God will damage his relation with God by creating a barrier between his prayers and God (cf. Col 3:19).

cause to this[t] you were called[u] so that you may inherit a blessing.[v] **10**For,

"Whoever would love life
and see good days
must keep his tongue from evil
and his lips from deceitful speech.
11He must turn from evil and do good;
he must seek peace and pursue it.
12For the eyes of the Lord are on the righteous
and his ears are attentive to their prayer,
but the face of the Lord is against those who do evil."[i][w]

Suffering for Doing Good

13Who is going to harm you if you are eager to do good?[x] **14**But even if you should suffer for what is right, you are blessed.[y] "Do not fear what they fear[j]; do not be frightened."[k][z] **15**But in your hearts set apart Christ as Lord. Always be prepared to give an answer[a] to everyone who asks you to give the reason for the hope[b]
1Jn 1:2 that you have. But do this with gentleness and respect, **16**keeping a clear conscience,[c] so that those who speak maliciously against your good behavior in Christ may be ashamed of their slander.[d] **17**It is better, if it is God's will,[e] to suffer for doing good[f] than for doing evil. **18**For Christ died for sins[g] once for all,[h] the righteous for the unrighteous, to bring you to God.[i] He was put to death in the body[j] but made alive by the Spirit,[k] **19**through whom[l] also he went and preached to the spirits in prison[l] **20**who disobeyed long ago when God waited patiently[m] in the days of Noah while the ark was being built.[n] In it only a few people, eight in all,[o] were saved[p] through water, **21**and this water symbolizes baptism that now saves you[q] also—not the removal of dirt from the body but the pledge[m] of a good conscience[r] toward God. It saves you by the resurrection of Jesus Christ,[s] **22**who has gone into heaven[t] and is at God's right hand[u]—with angels, authorities and powers in submission to him.[v]

Living for God

4 Therefore, since Christ suffered in his body,[w] arm yourselves also with the same attitude, because he who has suffered in his body is done with sin.[x] **2**As a result, he does not live the rest of his earthly life for evil human desires,[y] but rather for the will of God. **3**For you have spent enough time in the past[z] doing what pagans choose to do—living in debauchery, lust, drunkenness, orgies, carousing and detestable idolatry.[a] **4**They

3:9 [t]S 1Pe 2:21 [u]S Ro 8:28 [v]Heb 6:14
3:12 [w]Ps 34:12-16
3:13 [x]S Tit 2:14
3:14 [y]ver 17; 1Pe 2:19,20; 4:15,16 [z]Isa 8:12,13
3:15 [a]Col 4:6 [b]S Heb 3:6
3:16 [c]ver 21; S Ac 23:1 [d]1Pe 2:12,15
3:17 [e]1Pe 2:15; 4:19 [f]1Pe 2:20; 4:15,16
3:18 [g]1Pe 2:21; 4:1,13 [h]S Heb 7:27 [i]S Ro 5:2 [j]Col 1:22; 1Pe 4:1 [k]1Pe 4:6
3:19 [l]1Pe 4:6
3:20 [m]S Ro 2:4 [n]Ge 6:3,5,13,14 [o]Ge 8:18 [p]Heb 11:7
3:21 [q]S Ac 22:16 [r]ver 16; S Ac 23:1 [s]1Pe 1:3
3:22 [t]S Heb 4:14 [u]S Mk 16:19 [v]S Mt 28:18; S Ro 8:38
4:1 [w]S 1Pe 2:21 [x]S Ro 6:18
4:2 [y]Ro 6:2; 1Pe 1:14
4:3 [z]S Eph 2:2 [a]S Ro 13:13

[i] 12 Psalm 34:12-16 [j] 14 Or *not fear their threats* [k] 14 Isaiah 8:12 [l] 18,19 Or *alive in the spirit, 19through which* [m] 21 Or *response*

3:10 LOVE LIFE AND SEE GOOD DAYS. Peter quotes Ps 34:12–16 to emphasize that those who turn away from evil in both word and deed and pursue peace (Mt 5:37; Jas 5:12) will experience (1) lives full of God's blessing and favor, (2) God's close presence with his help and grace (v. 12), and (3) God's answer to their prayers (cf. Jas 5:16; 1Jn 3:21–22).

3:15 IN YOUR HEARTS SET APART CHRIST AS LORD. Peter calls for an inner reverence for and commitment to Christ as Lord that is always ready to speak for him and to explain the gospel to others (cf. Isa 8:13). Thus, we must know God's Word and truth in order to rightly witness for Christ and lead others to him (cf. Jn 4:4–26).

3:19 PREACHED TO THE SPIRITS. Vv. 18–20 have long been difficult for interpreters. (1) One view is that Christ, after his death and resurrection (v. 18), went to imprisoned angels who had sinned in Noah's day (v. 20; cf. 2Pe 2:4–5) and proclaimed to them his victory over death and Satan (v. 22). Another interpretation is that Christ by the Holy Spirit proclaimed through the mouth of Noah (cf. 2Pe 2:5) a message of warning to Noah's disobedient generation, who are now in Hades awaiting final judgment. This interpretation fits best with the context, which speaks of the disobedient and unsaved people of Noah's day. It would be in harmony with Peter's statement that the Spirit of Christ spoke in times past through the prophets (2Pe 1:20–21). (2) Neither this passage nor 4:6 teaches that unregenerate sinners will have a second chance to accept salvation after death. After death comes judgment (see Heb 9:27) and one's fixed destiny in eternity (Lk 16:26).

3:21 BAPTISM THAT NOW SAVES YOU ALSO. Water baptism saves us in the sense that it is an obedient expression of our repentance, our faith in Christ and our commitment to come out of the world. It is our confession and pledge that we belong to Christ and have died and risen with him (Ac 2:38–39; Ro 6:3–5; 10:9–10; Gal 3:27; Col 2:12). Note the comparison with the flood (v. 20): just as Noah's obedience to God's instructions regarding the flood was a testimony to his faith that preceded the flood, so going through the waters of baptism is a testimony to our faith that brought salvation through Christ before we were baptized.

4:1 HE WHO HAS SUFFERED. Those who willingly suffer for Christ's cause find it easier to resist sin and to follow God's will. They have united themselves with Christ and shared his cross. As a result the pull of sin is made insignificant and God's will paramount (v. 2). This spiritual principle will work in the lives of all believers. Obeying God even when it means suffering, ridicule or rejection will strengthen us morally and spiritually, and we will receive from God a greater grace (v. 14).

think it strange that you do not plunge
with them into the same flood of dissipation, and they heap abuse on you.[b] **5**But
they will have to give account to him who
is ready to judge the living and the dead.[c]
6For this is the reason the gospel was
preached even to those who are now
dead,[d] so that they might be judged
according to men in regard to the body,
but live according to God in regard to the
spirit.

7The end of all things is near.[e] Therefore be clear minded and self-controlled[f]
so that you can pray. **8**Above all, love each
other deeply,[g] because love covers over a
multitude of sins.[h] **9**Offer hospitality[i] to
one another without grumbling.[j] **10**Each
one should use whatever gift he has received to serve others,[k] faithfully[l] administering God's grace in its various
forms. **11**If anyone speaks, he should do it
as one speaking the very words of God.[m]
If anyone serves, he should do it with the
strength God provides,[n] so that in all
things God may be praised[o] through Jesus
Christ. To him be the glory and the power
End for ever and ever. Amen.[p]

Suffering for Being a Christian

12Dear friends, do not be surprised at
the painful trial you are suffering,[q] as
though something strange were happen-
ing to you. **13**But rejoice[r] that you participate in the sufferings of Christ,[s] so that
you may be overjoyed when his glory is
revealed.[t] **14**If you are insulted because
of the name of Christ,[u] you are blessed,[v]
for the Spirit of glory and of God rests on
you. **15**If you suffer, it should not be as a
murderer or thief or any other kind of
criminal, or even as a meddler. **16**However, if you suffer as a Christian, do not be
ashamed, but praise God that you bear
that name.[w] **17**For it is time for judgment
to begin with the family of God;[x] and if it
begins with us, what will the outcome be
for those who do not obey the gospel of
God?[y] **18**And,

> "If it is hard for the righteous to be
> saved,
> what will become of the ungodly
> and the sinner?"[n][z]

19So then, those who suffer according
to God's will[a] should commit themselves
to their faithful Creator and continue to do
good.

4:4 [b] 1Pe 3:16
4:5 [c] S Ac 10:42
4:6 [d] 1Pe 3:19
4:7 [e] S Ro 13:11 [f] S Ac 24:25
4:8 [g] S 1Pe 1:22 [h] Pr 10:12; Jas 5:20
4:9 [i] S Ro 12:13 [j] Php 2:14
4:10 [k] Ro 12:6,7 [l] 1Co 4:2
4:11 [m] 1Th 2:4 [n] Eph 6:10 [o] 1Co 10:31 [p] S Ro 11:36
4:12 [q] 1Pe 1:6,7
4:13 [r] S Mt 5:12 [s] S 2Co 1:5 [t] Ro 8:17; 1Pe 1:7; 5:1
4:14 [u] S Jn 15:21 [v] Mt 5:11
4:16 [w] Ac 5:41
4:17 [x] Jer 25:29; Eze 9:6; Am 3:2; 1Ti 3:15 [y] 2Th 1:8
4:18 [z] Pr 11:31; Lk 23:31
4:19 [a] 1Pe 2:15; 3:17

[n] *18* Prov. 11:31

4:6 THOSE WHO ARE NOW DEAD. This term is best understood as referring to those to whom the gospel was preached while they were still living on earth, but who are now dead. They heard the gospel and believed, and although they have died (i.e., "judged according to men in regard to the body"), they now live with God. The verse could be paraphrased to read, "the gospel was preached to those who believed and later died, that they might have eternal life with God."

4:7 END OF ALL THINGS IS NEAR. We should view our lives in light of Christ's imminent coming and the end of the world (cf. Heb 10:25; Jas 5:8–9; 1Jn 2:18). To Peter, this calls for the following commitments: (1) to pray to God fervently and daily (see Ac 10:9, note; 12:5, note; Col 4:2,12, notes); (2) to love one another deeply, from the heart (v. 8; cf. 1:22; Mt 22:37–39; 1Th 4:9–10; 2Pe 1:7); (3) to be hospitable and kind to those in need (v. 9); (4) to serve other believers through the use of spiritual gifts given by the Spirit (v. 10; see article on SPIRITUAL GIFTS FOR BELIEVERS, p. 350); (5) to witness for Christ and serve God in the power of the Spirit (v. 11; Ac 1:5–8); (6) to praise God (v. 11); and (7) to remain loyal to Christ in trials (vv. 12–19).

4:12 THE PAINFUL TRIAL. The NT emphasizes that trials are the inevitable experience of faithful believers in an ungodly world controlled by Satan and opposed to the gospel. Those who are committed to Jesus Christ with a devoted and loyal faith, who live by the Spirit and who love the truth of the gospel will experience trouble and sorrow. In fact, suffering because of righteousness is an evidence of the genuineness of your devotion to Christ (cf. Mt 5:10–12; Ac 14:22; Ro 8:17–18; 2Ti 2:12). For this reason problems in your life may be a sign that you are pleasing God and are faithful to him. They frequently accompany your warfare of faith against sin, the ungodly world and Satan (1:6–9; Eph 6:12). Through painful trials God allows you to share in his suffering and forms within you the quality of character he desires (Ro 5:3–5; 2Co 1:3–7; Jas 1:2–4). Yet when you suffer and remain faithful to Christ, you will be considered blessed, for "the Spirit of glory and of God rests on you" (v. 14, note; see 2:21, note).

4:13 REJOICE THAT YOU PARTICIPATE IN. It is a principle within God's kingdom that suffering for Christ's cause will increase the depth of the believer's joy in the Lord (see Mt 5:10–12; Ac 5:41; 16:25; Ro 5:3; Col 1:24; Heb 10:34; see next note). Therefore, those involved in little or no suffering for the Lord are not to be envied.

4:14 THE SPIRIT OF GLORY AND OF GOD. Those who suffer because of their loyalty to Christ are blessed (cf. v. 13; 3:14; Mt 5:11–12), for the Holy Spirit will rest on them in a special way. Their lives will be full of the presence of the Spirit to work in them, bless them, help them and provide them with a foretaste of heaven's glory (cf. Isa 11:2; Jn 1:29–34; 16:15; Ac 6:15).

4:17 JUDGMENT TO BEGIN WITH THE FAMILY OF GOD. See article on THE JUDGMENT OF BELIEVERS, p. 368.

To Elders and Young Men

5 To the elders among you, I appeal as
a fellow elder,[b] a witness[c] of Christ's
sufferings and one who also will share in
the glory to be revealed:[d] 2Be shepherds
of God's flock[e] that is under your care,
serving as overseers—not because you
must, but because you are willing, as God
wants you to be;[f] not greedy for money,[g]
but eager to serve; 3not lording it over[h]
those entrusted to you, but being examples[i] to the flock. 4And when the Chief
Shepherd[j] appears, you will receive the
crown of glory[k] that will never fade
away.[l]

5Young men, in the same way be submissive[m] to those who are older. All of
you, clothe yourselves with humility[n] toward one another, because,

> "God opposes the proud
> but gives grace to the humble."[o][o]

6Humble yourselves, therefore, under
God's mighty hand, that he may lift you up
in due time.[p] 7Cast all your anxiety on
him[q] because he cares for you.[r]

8Be self-controlled[s] and alert. Your enemy the devil prowls around[t] like a roaring lion[u] looking for someone to devour.
9Resist him,[v] standing firm in the faith,[w]
because you know that your brothers
throughout the world are undergoing the
same kind of sufferings.[x]

10And the God of all grace, who called
you[y] to his eternal glory[z] in Christ, after
you have suffered a little while,[a] will himself restore you and make you strong,[b]
firm and steadfast. 11To him be the power
for ever and ever. Amen.[c]

Final Greetings

12With the help of Silas,[p][d] whom I regard as a faithful brother, I have written
to you briefly,[e] encouraging you and testifying that this is the true grace of God.
Stand fast in it.[f]

13She who is in Babylon, chosen together with you, sends you her greetings, and
so does my son Mark.[g] 14Greet one another with a kiss of love.[h]

Peace[i] to all of you who are in Christ.

5:1 [b]S Ac 11:30 [c]S Lk 24:48 [d]1Pe 1:5,7; 4:13; Rev 1:9 **5:2** [e]S Jn 21:16 [f]2Co 9:7; Phm 14 [g]S 1Ti 3:3 **5:3** [h]Eze 34:4; Mt 20:25-28 [i]S 1Ti 4:12 **5:4** [j]S Jn 10:11 [k]S 1Co 9:25 [l]1Pe 1:4 **5:5** [m]Eph 5:21 [n]1Pe 3:8 [o]Pr 3:34; S Mt 23:12 **5:6** [p]Job 5:11; Jas 4:10 **5:7** [q]Ps 37:5; Mt 6:25 [r]Ps 55:22; Heb 13:5 **5:8** [s]S Ac 24:25 [t]Job 1:7 [u]2Ti 4:17 **5:9** [v]S Jas 4:7 [w]Col 2:5 [x]S Ac 14:22 **5:10** [y]S Ro 8:28 [z]2Co 4:17; 2Ti 2:10 [a]1Pe 1:6 [b]Ps 18:32; 2Th 2:17 **5:11** [c]S Ro 11:36 **5:12** [d]S Ac 15:22 [e]Heb 13:22 [f]S 1Co 16:13 **5:13** [g]S Ac 12:12 **5:14** [h]S Ro 16:16 [i]S Eph 6:23

[o] *5* Prov. 3:34 [p] *12* Greek *Silvanus*, a variant of *Silas*

5:2 BE SHEPHERDS OF GOD'S FLOCK. Elders (overseers or pastors) have the responsibility of caring for believers, discipling them, feeding them with the Word and protecting them (see articles on THE MINISTRY GIFTS OF THE CHURCH, p. 407, and OVERSEERS AND THEIR DUTIES, p. 274).

5:2 NOT GREEDY FOR MONEY. Pastors and church leaders must beware of two dangerous sins: (1) The desire for money (see 1Ti 3:3,8; Tit 1:7). The NT standard for those who oversee God's work is to receive adequate support from the church (Lk 10:7; 1Co 9:14; 1Ti 5:17) and to be content with basic and necessary provisions for themselves and their families. No minister ought to make himself rich from God's work. Those who fall victim to this desire open themselves up to sins of greed, compromise and theft. For the sake of money, they compromise God's Word, righteous standards and kingdom principles.

(2) The desire for power. Those greedy for power will dominate those whom they are to serve by excessively using their authority. Instead, the pastor must lead the church by being an example to the flock in devotion to Christ, humble service, perseverance in righteousness, steadfastness in prayer, and love for the Word.

5:5 CLOTHE YOURSELVES WITH HUMILITY. Humility must be the mark of all God's people. It means an absence of pride, a consciousness of one's weaknesses, and the disposition to ascribe to God and others the credit for what one is achieving or has accomplished (cf. Mt 11:29; Php 2:3–4; Col 3:12). The word "clothe" (Gk *egkomboomai*) means to attach a piece of clothing to oneself. In NT times slaves fastened a white piece of cloth or apron over their clothing so that others would know that they were slaves. Peter exhorts us to tie the cloth of humility on ourselves in order (1) to be identified as believers in Christ as we act humbly toward others, and (2) to receive God's grace and help (vv. 5–7). Peter may have had in mind Jesus' action of tying on a towel and washing the disciples' feet (Jn 13:4–5).

5:7 HE CARES FOR YOU. God's care for the troubles of every one of his children is a truth emphasized throughout his Word (see Ps 27:10; 37:5; 40:17; 55:22; Mt 6:25–30; 10:29–31; 11:30; Php 4:6, note). All your fears, anxieties and concerns must be decisively cast on God (cf. Ps 55:22; Lk 12:11–12).

5:8 YOUR ENEMY THE DEVIL. When humanity fell into sin, Satan became the ruler of the world (Jn 12:31; 14:30; 16:11). He dominates the whole world (1Jn 5:19), patrols this earth, and is commander of a host of evil spirits through whom he enslaves and keeps captive those without Christ (Eph 2:2; see article on POWER OVER SATAN AND DEMONS, p. 80). Only believers have been delivered from his power (see article on THE KINGDOM OF GOD, p. 28). Yet, as a roaring lion, he remains a threat to believers (Ps 22:13; Eze 22:25) and seeks to destroy them, especially through experiences of suffering (vv. 8–10). He will spiritually destroy anyone who abandons God's protection. Through our faith in Christ's blood (Rev 12:11), our spiritual warfare by the Spirit (Eph 6:11–18) and our prayers to God (Mt 6:13), we are fully equipped to defeat Satan's schemes (Eph 6:11), to resist him and to stand firm in the faith (v. 9). "The one who is in you is greater than the one who is in the world" (1Jn 4:4).

2 PETER

Outline

Christian Greetings (1:1–2)

- I. The Commendation of True Knowledge (1:2b-21)
  - A. The Transforming Power of a True Knowledge of God (1:2b-4)
  - B. The Progressive Character of Christian Growth (1:5–11)
  - C. The Apostle's Attestation of the Word of Truth (1:12–21)
    - 1. His Motive (1:12–15)
    - 2. His Method (1:16–21)
      - a. Eyewitness of the Prophetic Word (1:16–19)
      - b. Inspiration of Prophetic Scripture (1:20–21)
- II. The Condemnation of False Teachers (2:1–22)
  - A. What to Expect From False Teachers (2:1–3)
  - B. What They May Expect From God (2:4–10a)
  - C. Some Characteristics of False Teachers (2:10b-19)
  - D. The Dangers of Relapse From the Truth (2:20–22)
- III. The Certainty of the Lord's Coming (3:1–18a)
  - A. Denial of His Coming (3:1–7)
  - B. Assurance of His Coming (3:8–10)
  - C. Living for His Coming (3:11–18a)

Benediction (3:18b)

Author: Peter

Theme: Faithful Truth Versus False Teachers

Date: c. A.D. 66–68

Background

In the salutation, Simon Peter identifies himself as author of this letter; he later remarks that this is his second letter to the readers (3:1), indicating that he is writing the same believers in Asia Minor who had received his first letter (1Pe 1:1). Since Peter, like Paul, was put to death by an edict of the wicked Nero (who himself died in June, A.D. 68), it is most likely that Peter wrote this letter between A.D. 66–68, shortly before his martyrdom in Rome (1:13–15).

Some scholars in ancient and modern times, ignoring certain remarkable similarities between 1 and 2 Peter and stressing instead the differences between them, have assumed that Peter was not the author of this letter. However, the differences in content, vocabulary, emphases and literary style between the two letters can be accounted for adequately by the different circumstances of both Peter and his readers in the two letters. (1) The original circumstances of the recipients had changed from serious persecution inflicted by their surrounding society to serious assault from within by false teachers that threatened the churches' foundations of truth and righteousness. (2) Peter's circumstances were also different. Whereas he had the skilled assistance of Silas when writing his first letter (1Pe 5:12), it appears that Silas was not available when writing this one. Peter may have used his own rough Galilean Greek or relied on a less capable scribe than Silas.

Purpose

Peter wrote (1) to exhort believers to diligently pursue godliness and a true knowledge of Christ, and (2) to expose and repudiate the insidious activity of false prophets and teachers among the churches in Asia Minor who were undermining apostolic truth. Peter summarizes his purpose in 3:17–18, where he exhorts true believers (1) to be on their guard so that they may not "be carried away by the error of lawless men" (3:17), and (2) to "grow in the grace and the knowledge of our Lord and Savior Jesus Christ" (3:18).

Survey

This short letter earnestly instructs believers to take hold of life and godliness through a true knowledge of Christ. The first chapter emphasizes the importance of Christian growth. Having begun by faith, the believer must diligently pursue moral excellence, knowledge, self-control, perseverance, godliness, brotherly kindness and selfless love, resulting in a mature faith and true knowledge of the Lord Jesus (1:3–11).

The next chapter solemnly warns about false prophets and teachers who were arising among the churches. Peter denounces them as lawless men (2:1,3; 3:17) who indulge the corrupt desires of the sinful nature (2:2,7,10,13–14,18–19), who are greedy (2:3,14–15), arrogant (2:18) and self-willed (2:10), and who despise authority (2:10–12). Peter seeks to protect true believers against those destructive heresies (2:1) by exposing their evil motives and conduct.

In ch. 3, Peter refutes the skepticism of these teachers about the Lord's coming (3:3–4). As Noah's generation mistakenly scoffed at the idea of the judgment of a great flood from God, these scoffers are equally blind concerning the promises of Christ's return. But with the same decisive action as the judgment of the flood (3:5–6), Christ will return and dissolve the present earth by fire (3:7–12) and create a righteous new order (3:13). In view of this, believers must live holy and godly lives in this present age (3:11,14).

Special Features

Four major features characterize this letter. (1) This letter contains one of the strongest statements in the Bible about the inspiration, reliability and authority of Scripture (1:19–21). (2) Ch. 2 and Jude's letter are remarkably similar in their denunciation of false teachers. Perhaps Jude, facing at a later date the same problem of false teachers, utilized portions of Peter's inspired teaching to make the same point (see Introduction to Jude). (3) Ch. 3 is one of the great NT chapters on the second coming of Christ. (4) Peter indirectly refers to Paul's writings as Scripture by mentioning them in relation to "the other Scriptures" (3:15–16).

Reading 2 Peter

In order to read the entire New Testament in one year, the book of 2 Peter should be read in 3 days, according to the following schedule:
□ 1 □ 2 □ 3

NOTES

1 Simon Peter, a servant[a] and apostle of Jesus Christ,[b]

To those who through the righteousness[c] of our God and Savior Jesus Christ[d] have received a faith as precious as ours:

2Grace and peace be yours in abundance[e] through the knowledge of God and of Jesus our Lord.[f]

Making One's Calling and Election Sure

3His divine power[g] has given us everything we need for life and godliness through our knowledge of him[h] who called us[i] by his own glory and goodness. **4**Through these he has given us his very great and precious promises,[j] so that through them you may participate in the divine nature[k] and escape the corruption in the world caused by evil desires.[l]

5For this very reason, make every effort to add to your faith goodness; and to goodness, knowledge;[m] **6**and to knowledge, self-control;[n] and to self-control, perseverance;[o] and to perseverance, godliness;[p] **7**and to godliness, brotherly kindness; and to brotherly kindness, love.[q] **8**For if you possess these qualities in increasing measure, they will keep you from being ineffective and unproductive[r] in your knowledge of our Lord Jesus Christ.[s] **9**But if anyone does not have them, he is nearsighted and blind,[t] and has forgotten that he has been cleansed from his past sins.[u]

10Therefore, my brothers, be all the more eager to make your calling[v] and election sure. For if you do these things, you will never fall,[w] **11**and you will receive a rich welcome into the eternal kingdom[x] of our Lord and Savior Jesus Christ.[y]

Eyewitnesses of Christ's Majesty

12So I will always remind you of these things,[z] even though you know them and are firmly established in the truth[a] you now have. **13**I think it is right to refresh your memory[b] as long as I live in the tent of this body,[c] **14**because I know that I will soon put it aside,[d] as our Lord Jesus Christ has made clear to me.[e] **15**And I will make every effort to see that after my departure[f] you will always be able to remember these things.

16We did not follow cleverly invented stories when we told you about the power and coming of our Lord Jesus Christ,[g] but we were eyewitnesses of his majesty.[h] **17**For he received honor and glory from God the Father when the voice came to him from the Majestic Glory, saying, "This is my Son, whom I love; with him I am well pleased."[a][i] **18**We ourselves heard this voice that came from heaven when we were with him on the sacred mountain.[j]

1:1 [a]Ro 1:1 [b]1Pe 1:1 [c]Ro 3:21-26 [d]Tit 2:13 **1:2** [e]S Ro 1:7 [f]ver 3,8; 2Pe 2:20; 3:18; S Php 3:8 **1:3** [g]1Pe 1:5 [h]S ver 2 [i]S Ro 8:28 **1:4** [j]2Co 7:1 [k]Eph 4:24; Heb 12:10; 1Jn 3:2 [l]Jas 1:27; 2Pe 2:18-20 **1:5** [m]S ver 2; Col 2:3 **1:6** [n]S Ac 24:25 [o]S Heb 10:36 [p]ver 3 **1:7** [q]S Ro 12:10; 1Th 3:12 **1:8** [r]Jn 15:2; Col 1:10; Tit 3:14 [s]S ver 2 **1:9** [t]1Jn 2:11 [u]Eph 5:26; S Mt 1:21 **1:10** [v]S Ro 8:28 [w]Ps 15:5; 2Pe 3:17; Jude 24 **1:11** [x]Ps 145:13; 2Ti 4:18 [y]2Pe 2:20; 3:18 **1:12** [z]Php 3:1; 1Jn 2:21; Jude 5 [a]2Jn 2 **1:13** [b]2Pe 3:1 [c]Isa 38:12; 2Co 5:1,4 **1:14** [d]2Ti 4:6 [e]Jn 13:36; 21:18, 19 **1:15** [f]Lk 9:31 **1:16** [g]Mk 13:26; 14:62 [h]Mt 17:1-8 **1:17** [i]S Mt 3:17 **1:18** [j]Mt 17:6

[a] *17* Matt. 17:5; Mark 9:7; Luke 9:35

1:3 EVERYTHING WE NEED FOR LIFE AND GODLINESS. The love of our heavenly Father, salvation through Jesus Christ, Christ's intercession for us in heaven, the indwelling of and baptism in the Holy Spirit, the communion of the saints and God's inspired Word are sufficient to meet all that believers need for life and godliness (Mt 11:28–30; Heb 4:16; 7:25; 9:14).

(1) No additional human wisdom, technique or theory is needed to complete the sufficiency of God's Word that reveals our perfect salvation in Christ. The words of Jesus, the NT apostolic faith and God's grace were adequate in the early days of the church to meet the needs of the lost, and they are just as adequate today. Absolutely nothing can offer more height, depth, strength and help than what Jesus himself proclaimed and provided and what the apostles testified to in Biblical revelation. Jesus Christ alone is "the way and the truth and the life" (Jn 14:6).

(2) If the gospel we hold is found wanting in these days, it is because our gospel is something less than the gospel of Christ and the apostles.

1:4 PARTICIPATE IN THE DIVINE NATURE. Our participation in God's very nature is another description of the new birth by which we receive God's life (see article on REGENERATION, p. 178). We share God's nature in order to conform to God and his holiness (cf. 1Co 6:19; Eph 4:24).

1:5 ADD TO YOUR FAITH. Peter lists the virtues a Christian must develop in order to be spiritually victorious and fruitful before God (v. 8). The phrase "make every effort" demonstrates that believers must be actively involved in their Christian growth (cf. Php 2:12–13). Those who become Christians must immediately strive to add to their faith these seven qualities (vv. 5–8). Note that godly characteristics do not automatically grow without our diligent effort to cultivate them (see article on THE ACTS OF THE SINFUL NATURE AND THE FRUIT OF THE SPIRIT, p. 394).

1:10 MAKE YOUR CALLING AND ELECTION SURE. Our faith and salvation must not be taken for granted. We will continue faithful to the end only if we make every effort by God's grace to add to our faith the spiritual qualities listed in vv. 5–9 (see article on ELECTION AND PREDESTINATION, p. 402).

1:11 RICH WELCOME INTO THE ETERNAL KINGDOM. Some believers, because of negligence, will barely make it into the kingdom (1Co 3:15), while others who remain steadfast in holiness will be welcomed richly with honor (Mt 25:21; Ac 7:55–56; 2Ti 4:7–8,18).

Prophecy of Scripture

[19]And we have the word of the prophets
made more certain,[k] and you will do well
to pay attention to it, as to a light[l] shining
in a dark place, until the day dawns[m] and
the morning star[n] rises in your hearts.[o]
[20]Above all, you must understand[p] that
no prophecy of Scripture came about by
the prophet's own interpretation. [21]For
prophecy never had its origin in the will of
man, but men spoke from God[q] as they
were carried along by the Holy Spirit.[r]

False Teachers and Their Destruction

2 But there were also false prophets[s]
among the people, just as there will
be false teachers among you.[t] They will
secretly introduce destructive heresies,
even denying the sovereign Lord[u] who
bought them[v] — bringing swift destruction on themselves. [2]Many will follow
their shameful ways[w] and will bring the
way of truth into disrepute. [3]In their
greed[x] these teachers will exploit you[y]
with stories they have made up. Their condemnation has long been hanging over
them, and their destruction has not been
sleeping.

[4]For if God did not spare angels when
they sinned,[z] but sent them to hell,[b] putting them into gloomy dungeons[c] to be

1:19 [k]1Pe 1:10, 11 [l]Ps 119:105 [m]Lk 1:78 [n]Rev 22:16 [o]2Co 4:6 **1:20** [p]2Pe 3:3 **1:21** [q]2Ti 3:16 [r]2Sa 23:2; Ac 1:16; 3:18; 1Pe 1:11 **2:1** [s]Dt 13:1-3; Jer 6:13; S Mt 7:15 [t]1Ti 4:1 [u]Jude 4 [v]S 1Co 6:20 **2:2** [w]Jude 4 **2:3** [x]ver 14 [y]2Co 2:17; 1Th 2:5 **2:4** [z]Ge 6:1-4

b *4* Greek *Tartarus* **c** *4* Some manuscripts *into chains of darkness*

1:19 WORD OF THE PROPHETS MADE MORE CERTAIN. Peter contrasts humanistic ideas with God's Word (v. 16). He goes on to attest to the divine origin of Scripture and affirms that all prophecy originated from God, not from humans (cf. v. 16). This assures us that God's message is infallible (incapable of mistakes or errors) and inerrant (free from error, falsehood or deceit). Infallibility and inerrancy cannot be separated, for the inerrancy of Scripture is the result of the infallibility of God's own Word. Scripture in its entirety is true and reliable in all its teaching (2Sa 23:2; Jer 1:7–9; 1Co 14:37; see article on THE INSPIRATION AND AUTHORITY OF SCRIPTURE, p. 474).

1:20 NO PROPHECY OF SCRIPTURE. No prophecy in Scripture came about by the writer's own ideas or reasoning, but it came from the Holy Spirit.

1:21 MEN SPOKE FROM GOD . . . BY THE HOLY SPIRIT. Peter affirms the divine origin and authority of prophecy in Scripture. All believers must likewise maintain a strong uncompromising view of holy Scripture as inspired and authoritative. There are several reasons for this. (1) It is the only way to be true to what Jesus Christ, the apostles and the Bible itself teach about Scripture (see Ps 119; Jn 5:47, note; see article on THE INSPIRATION AND AUTHORITY OF SCRIPTURE, p. 474).

(2) Without a strong view of holy Scripture, the church has no true and sure foundation for its faith, no certainty of salvation, no moral absolutes, no message to preach without doubt, no sure expectancy for the baptism in the Holy Spirit and the working of miracles, and no hope for Christ's imminent return.

(3) Without a strong view of holy Scripture, Bible-believing Christians have no absolute and objective truth based on the authority of God himself by which to judge and reject this world's ever-changing values, human philosophies and the culture's ungodly practices (Ps 119:160).

(4) Without a strong view of holy Scripture, Christians will not be ready to withstand the extreme difficulties of the last days (see 1Th 2:1–12; 1Ti 4:1, note; 2Ti 3:1, note).

(5) Without a strong view of holy Scripture, the full authority and teaching of the Bible are weakened; the Bible will subsequently be replaced by subjective religious experience or by independent and critical reasoning (2:1–3).

2:1 THERE WILL BE FALSE TEACHERS AMONG YOU. The Holy Spirit repeatedly warns that there will be many false teachers within the churches. The warnings concerning teachers and leaders who introduce destructive heresies among God's people began with Jesus (see Mt 24:11, note; 24:24–25) and were continued by the Spirit through Paul (see 2Th 2:7, note; 1Ti 4:1, note; 2Ti 3:1–5), Peter (vv. 1–22), John (1Jn 2:18; 4:1; 2Jn 7–11); Jude (Jude 3–4,12,18) and Christ's letters to the seven churches (see Rev 2:2,6, notes).

2:1 DENYING THE SOVEREIGN LORD WHO BOUGHT THEM. According to Peter, the false teachers within the church who were "denying [Gk *arneomai*, meaning to disown or renounce] the sovereign Lord" had left the straight way, wandered off (v. 15) and become "springs without water" (v. 17). At one time they had escaped the wickedness of the world through Jesus Christ, but now were again entangled in sin (v. 20).

2:2 WAY OF TRUTH INTO DISREPUTE. Many professed believers will follow these false preachers and their "shameful" (i.e., sexually immoral) ways. Because of the sinful lifestyles of the leaders and their followers, God and his gospel will be put to shame (see 2Ti 4:3–4, note).

2:3 IN THEIR GREED . . . STORIES THEY HAVE MADE UP. The false teachers will commercialize the gospel, being experts in greed and in getting money from believers to enhance their ministries and affluent lifestyles. (1) Believers must be aware that one of the chief methods of false ministers is to use "stories they have made up," i.e., to tell impressive, but false, stories, or to give exaggerated statistics in order to inspire God's people to give money. They glorify themselves and enhance their ministries with these fabricated stories (cf. 2Co 2:17). Thus, the unwary and sincere child of God becomes an object of exploitation. (2) Because these ministers defile God's truth and people with greed and deceit, they are assigned to condemnation and destruction.

2:4 ANGELS . . . SENT THEM TO HELL. This probably refers to the angels who rebelled with Satan against God (Eze 28:15), becoming the wicked spirits

held for judgment;[a] **5**if he did not spare
the ancient world[b] when he brought the
flood on its ungodly people,[c] but protected Noah, a preacher of righteousness, and
seven others;[d] **6**if he condemned the cities of Sodom and Gomorrah by burning
them to ashes,[e] and made them an example[f] of what is going to happen to the
ungodly;[g] **7**and if he rescued Lot,[h] a righteous man, who was distressed by the
filthy lives of lawless men[i] **8**(for that righteous man,[j] living among them day after
day, was tormented in his righteous soul
by the lawless deeds he saw and heard)—
9if this is so, then the Lord knows how to
rescue godly men from trials[k] and to hold
the unrighteous for the day of judgment,[l]
while continuing their punishment.[d]
10This is especially true of those who follow the corrupt desire[m] of the sinful nature[e] and despise authority.

Bold and arrogant, these men are not
afraid to slander celestial beings;[n] **11**yet
even angels, although they are stronger
and more powerful, do not bring slanderous accusations against such beings in
the presence of the Lord.[o] **12**But these
men blaspheme in matters they do not understand. They are like brute beasts, creatures of instinct, born only to be caught
and destroyed, and like beasts they too
will perish.[p]

2:4 [a]1Ti 3:6; Jude 6; Rev 20:1,2
2:5 [b]2Pe 3:6
[c]Ge 6:5-8:19
[d]Heb 11:7; 1Pe 3:20
2:6 [e]Ge 19:24,25
[f]Nu 26:10; Jude 7
[g]Mt 10:15; 11:23, 24; Ro 9:29
2:7 [h]Ge 19:16
[i]2Pe 3:17
2:8 [j]Heb 11:4
2:9 [k]Ps 37:33; S Ro 15:31; Rev 3:10
[l]S Mt 10:15
2:10 [m]2Pe 3:3; Jude 16,18
[n]Jude 8
2:11 [o]Jude 9
2:12 [p]Ps 49:12; Jude 10
2:13 [q]S Ro 13:13; 1Th 5:7
[r]1Co 11:20,21; Jude 12
2:14 [s]ver 18
[t]Jas 1:8; 2Pe 3:16
[u]ver 3 [v]Eph 2:3
2:15 [w]Nu 22:4-20; 31:16; Dt 23:4; Jude 11; Rev 2:14
2:16 [x]Nu 22:21-30
2:17 [y]Jude 12
[z]Jude 13
2:18 [a]Jude 16
[b]ver 20; 2Pe 1:4
2:19 [c]S Ro 6:16

13They will be paid back with harm for
the harm they have done. Their idea of
pleasure is to carouse in broad daylight.[q]
They are blots and blemishes, reveling in
their pleasures while they feast with
you.[f][r] **14**With eyes full of adultery, they
never stop sinning; they seduce[s] the unstable;[t] they are experts in greed[u]—an
accursed brood![v] **15**They have left the
straight way and wandered off to follow
the way of Balaam[w] son of Beor, who
loved the wages of wickedness. **16**But he
was rebuked for his wrongdoing by a donkey—a beast without speech—who
spoke with a man's voice and restrained
the prophet's madness.[x]

17These men are springs without water[y] and mists driven by a storm. Blackest
darkness is reserved for them.[z] **18**For
they mouth empty, boastful words[a] and,
by appealing to the lustful desires of sinful human nature, they entice people who
are just escaping[b] from those who live in
error. **19**They promise them freedom,
while they themselves are slaves of depravity—for a man is a slave to whatever
has mastered him.[c] **20**If they have escaped the corruption of the world by

[d] *9* Or *unrighteous for punishment until the day of judgment* [e] *10* Or *the flesh* [f] *13* Some manuscripts *in their love feasts*

---

spoken of in the NT. Why some of the wicked spirits are in dungeons and some are free to work with Satan on earth is not explained in Scripture (cf. Jude 6; see article on POWER OVER SATAN AND DEMONS, p. 80).

2:8 TORMENTED IN HIS RIGHTEOUS SOUL. An essential characteristic of truly righteous people is that they love righteousness and hate wickedness (see Heb 1:9, note). Their souls are distressed and tormented (vv. 7–8) by the sin, immorality and ungodliness in the world (e.g., Eze 9:4; Jn 2:13–16; Ac 17:16).

2:9 RESCUE GODLY MEN. Lot's response to the evil and immorality around him (v. 8) became a test that determined both his own deliverance and his destiny in eternity. (1) God rescued Lot because he rejected evil and was repulsed at the "filthy lives of lawless men" (v. 7; see previous note).

(2) When Christ returns to receive his people (see Jn 14:3, note) and to pour out his wrath on the ungodly (3:10–12), he will gather to himself those in the visible church who, because of their faith in and love for him,. are, like Lot, tormented by sensual conduct, filthy living and blatant sin within society (see article on THE RAPTURE, p. 440).

(3) We can be sure that God knows how to deliver his faithful believers from immoral and corrupt people in every generation (cf. Mt 6:13; 2Ti 4:18; Rev 3:10).

2:10 DESPISE AUTHORITY . . . CELESTIAL BEINGS. Peter speaks of unrighteous and immoral people who, like the homosexuals of Sodom (v. 8; cf. Ge 19:4–11), despise all manner of authority that restrains evil, including Christ and his Word.

2:15 WAY OF BALAAM. This refers to a love for personal honor and material gain at the expense of God's people (cf. Nu 31:16; Rev 2:14). Peter emphasizes that sexual immorality, love of honor and greed for money characterize false teachers and preachers.

2:16 SPOKE WITH A MAN'S VOICE. Peter clearly believes in the miracles recorded in the OT. Today self-appointed critics within the church arrogantly scoff at the miracles recorded in God's Word and regard those who believe in them as being unenlightened or naive. Genuine children of God, however, believe in God and accept all the Bible's miracles. They also believe that God performs miracles today in response to the prayers and faith of his people (see Jn 6:2, note).

2:19 THEY PROMISE THEM FREEDOM. The spirit of lawlessness that promises freedom from godly restraint will be especially prevalent in society and in the church in the last days before Christ comes again (see 1Ti 4:1, note; 2Ti 3:1, note). God's moral absolutes will be considered outdated and mere legalistic restraint to one's personal autonomy, self-fulfillment and happiness. As people set themselves up as the ultimate authority, they become slaves of depravity (see Ro 1:24,27, notes).

2:20 ESCAPED . . . ARE AGAIN ENTANGLED.

knowing[d] our Lord and Savior Jesus
Christ[e] and are again entangled in it and
overcome, they are worse off at the end
than they were at the beginning.[f] **21**It
would have been better for them not to
have known the way of righteousness,
than to have known it and then to turn
their backs on the sacred command that
was passed on to them.[g] **22**Of them the
proverbs are true: "A dog returns to its
vomit,"[g][h] and, "A sow that is washed
goes back to her wallowing in the mud."

The Day of the Lord

3 Dear friends,[i] this is now my second
letter to you. I have written both of
them as reminders[j] to stimulate you to
wholesome thinking. **2**I want you to recall
the words spoken in the past by the holy
prophets[k] and the command given by our
Lord and Savior through your apostles.[l]

3First of all, you must understand that
in the last days[m] scoffers will come, scoff-
ing and following their own evil desires.[n]
4They will say, "Where is this 'coming' he
promised?[o] Ever since our fathers died,
everything goes on as it has since the beginning of creation."[p] **5**But they deliberately forget that long ago by God's word[q]
the heavens existed and the earth was
formed out of water and by water.[r] **6**By
these waters also the world of that time[s]
was deluged and destroyed.[t] **7**By the
same word the present heavens and earth
are reserved for fire,[u] being kept for the
day of judgment[v] and destruction of ungodly men.

8But do not forget this one thing, dear
friends: With the Lord a day is like a thousand years, and a thousand years are like
a day.[w] **9**The Lord is not slow in keeping
his promise,[x] as some understand slow-
ness. He is patient[y] with you, not wanting
anyone to perish, but everyone to come to
repentance.[z]

10But the day of the Lord will come like
a thief.[a] The heavens will disappear with
a roar;[b] the elements will be destroyed by
fire,[c] and the earth and everything in it
will be laid bare.[h][d]

11Since everything will be destroyed in
this way, what kind of people ought you to
be? You ought to live holy and godly lives
12as you look forward[e] to the day of God
and speed its coming.[i][f] That day will
bring about the destruction of the heavens
by fire, and the elements will melt in the
heat.[g] **13**But in keeping with his promise
we are looking forward to a new heaven
and a new earth,[h] the home of righteousness.

14So then, dear friends, since you are
looking forward to this, make every effort
to be found spotless, blameless[i] and at

2:20 [d]S 2Pe 1:2 [e]2Pe 1:11; 3:18 [f]Mt 12:45 **2:21** [g]Eze 18:24; Heb 6:4-6; 10:26, 27 **2:22** [h]Pr 26:11 **3:1** [i]S 1Co 10:14 [j]2Pe 1:13 **3:2** [k]Lk 1:70; Ac 3:21 [l]S Eph 4:11 **3:3** [m]1Ti 4:1; 2Ti 3:1 [n]2Pe 2:10; Jude 18 **3:4** [o]Isa 5:19; Eze 12:22; Mt 24:48; S Lk 17:30 [p]Mk 10:6 **3:5** [q]Ge 1:6,9; Heb 11:3 [r]Ps 24:2 **3:6** [s]2Pe 2:5 [t]Ge 7:21,22 **3:7** [u]ver 10,12; S 2Th 1:7 [v]S Mt 10:15 **3:8** [w]Ps 90:4 **3:9** [x]Hab 2:3; Heb 10:37 [y]S Ro 2:4 [z]S 1Ti 2:4; Rev 2:21 **3:10** [a]S Lk 12:39 [b]Isa 34:4 [c]ver 7, 12; S 2Th 1:7 [d]Mt 24:35; S Heb 12:27; Rev 21:1 **3:12** [e]S 1Co 1:7 [f]Ps 50:3 [g]ver 10 **3:13** [h]Isa 65:17; 66:22; Rev 21:1 **3:14** [i]S 1Th 3:13

[g] 22 Prov. 26:11 [h] 10 Some manuscripts *be burned up* [i] 12 Or *as you wait eagerly for the day of God to come*

Vv. 20–22 obviously mean that some of the false teachers were once redeemed from sin's power, and then forfeited salvation (cf. vv. 1,15).

3:4 WHERE IS THIS 'COMING' HE PROMISED? In the last days, the period between Christ's first and second coming, false teachers will deny that Christ will return to destroy the ungodly and the world (cf. Rev 19:11–21).

3:7 RESERVED FOR FIRE. Because sin has contaminated the heavens and earth, God has determined to completely destroy them by fire (vv. 7,10,12). This day will come as surely as the flood did in Noah's time. God's intervention to purify the earth by fire signifies that he will not allow sin to go unpunished forever.

3:8 A DAY IS LIKE A THOUSAND YEARS. God views time from the perspective of eternity (cf. Ps 90:4). "A thousand years" looks different to God than to humans. He can accomplish in one day what we might expect would take a thousand years, or he can take a thousand years to accomplish what we would like to see done in a day.

3:9 NOT WANTING ANYONE TO PERISH. The delay of Christ's return is related to the preaching of the gospel of the kingdom to the whole world (Mt 24:14). God wants everyone to hear the gospel and does not desire anyone to perish eternally (1Ti 2:4). This does not mean that all will be saved, for if a person rejects God's grace and salvation, then he or she remains lost.

3:10 THE DAY OF THE LORD. The day of the Lord refers to the events that begin with Christ's return to catch up the faithful of his churches to meet him in the air (see article on THE RAPTURE, p. 440) and culminates with the destruction of the present heaven and earth and the creation of the new heaven and the new earth (Rev 21–22; see 1Th 5:2, note on the day of the Lord). The beginning of the day of the Lord is unknown and will be marked by an unexpected suddenness (see Mt 24:42,44, notes).

3:11 HOLY AND GODLY LIVES. Because God will soon destroy the world and judge the unrighteous, we must not become attached to this world's system or things within it. Our values, goals and purposes in life must be centered around God and the hope of a new heaven and a new earth (v. 13; see articles on SPIRITUAL SEPARATION FOR BELIEVERS, p. 371, and SANCTIFICATION, p. 526).

3:12 SPEED ITS COMING. The church can help shorten the time before Christ's return by (1) committing themselves to evangelism and missionary work throughout the whole world (v. 9; Mt 24:14), and (2) eagerly desiring his return by praying, "Come, Lord Jesus" (Rev 22:20; cf. Mt 6:10).

3:13 LOOKING FORWARD TO A NEW HEAVEN. See Heb 11:10, note.

peace with him. 15Bear in mind that our
Lord's patience[j] means salvation,[k] just
as our dear brother Paul also wrote you
with the wisdom that God gave him.[l]
16He writes the same way in all his letters, speaking in them of these matters.
His letters contain some things that are
hard to understand, which ignorant and
unstable[m] people distort,[n] as they do the
other Scriptures,[o] to their own destruction.

17Therefore, dear friends, since you already know this, be on your guard[p] so
that you may not be carried away by the
error[q] of lawless men[r] and fall from your
secure position.[s] 18But grow in the
grace[t] and knowledge[u] of our Lord and
Savior Jesus Christ.[v] To him be glory both
now and forever! Amen.[w]

3:15 [j]S Ro 2:4 [k]ver 9 [l]Eph 3:3 **3:16** [m]Jas 1:8; 2Pe 2:14 [n]Ps 56:5; Jer 23:36 [o]ver 2 **3:17** [p]1Co 10:12 [q]2Pe 2:18 [r]2Pe 2:7 [s]Rev 2:5 **3:18** [t]S Ro 3:24 [u]S 2Pe 1:2 [v]2Pe 1:11; 2:20 [w]S Ro 11:36

3:16 HIS LETTERS ... OTHER SCRIPTURES. Peter speaks of Paul's letters as being on the same level as the other inspired and authoritative Scriptures, i.e., the OT. When we talk of "Scripture" today, we mean the writings of both the OT and NT, God's original message to humanity and his witness to his saving activity in Jesus Christ (see article on THE INSPIRATION AND AUTHORITY OF SCRIPTURE, p. 474).

1 JOHN

Outline

Introduction (1:1–4)
- I. Fellowship With God (1:5—2:28)
  - A. The Principles of Fellowship With God (1:5—2:2)
    1. "No Darkness" in God (1:5)
    2. No Fellowship in the Darkness (1:6)
    3. Fellowship in the Light (1:7)
    4. Fellowship in the Cleansing of Sin (1:8—2:2)
  - B. The Manifestations of Fellowship With God (2:3–28)
    1. Obedience (2:3–5)
    2. Christlikeness (2:6)
    3. Love (2:7–11)
    4. Separation From the World (2:12–17)
    5. Loyalty to the Truth (2:18–28)
- II. Children of God (2:29—3:24)
  - A. Characteristics of God's Children (2:29—3:18)
  - B. Confidence of God's Children (3:19–24)
- III. Spirit of Truth (4:1–6)
  - A. Recognizing the Spirit of Error (4:1,3,5)
  - B. Affirming the Spirit of Truth (4:2,4,6)
- IV. Love of God (4:7—5:3)
  - A. Divine Origin of Love (4:7–10)
  - B. Proper Response to God's Love (4:11–13,19–21)
  - C. Abiding in God's Love (4:14–16)
  - D. Perfection of Love (4:17–18)
  - E. Obedience of Love (5:1–3)
- V. Assurances From God (5:4–20)
  - A. About Overcoming the World (5:4–5)
  - B. About the Trustworthiness of the Gospel (5:6–10)
  - C. About Eternal Life in His Son (5:11–13)
  - D. About Answers to Prayer (5:14–17)
  - E. About Three Great Certainties (5:18–20)

Conclusion (5:21)

Author: John

Theme: Truth and Righteousness

Date: A.D. 85–95

Background

Five NT books are associated with the name John: a Gospel, three letters, and the book of Revelation. Although John does not identify himself by name in this letter, second-century witnesses (e.g., Papias, Irenaeus, Tertullian, Clement of Alexandria) affirm that it was written by the apostle John, one of Jesus' original twelve disciples. Strong similarities in style, vocabulary and themes between 1 John and the Gospel of John substantiate the reliable testimony of ancient

Christianity that both books were written by the apostle John (see Introduction to John's Gospel).

The recipients of this letter are undesignated. There are no greetings or mention of persons, places or events in the letter. The most likely explanation for this uncommon format is that John wrote from his residence at Ephesus to a number of churches in the province of Asia over which he had apostolic responsibility (cf. Rev 1:11). Since the congregations shared a common problem and similar needs, John wrote this as a circular letter and dispatched it by a personal emissary along with his verbal greetings.

The foremost background issue in this letter is the problem of false teaching about salvation in Christ and its operation in the believer. Certain people, formerly associated with the readers, had left the congregations (2:19), but the results of their false teaching were still distorting the gospel as to how they might "know" that they had eternal life. Doctrinally, their heresy denied that Jesus is the Christ (2:22; cf. 5:1) or that Christ came in the flesh (4:2–3); ethically, they taught that obeying Christ's commands (2:3–4; 5:3) and living holy lives separated from sin (3:7–12) and the world (2:15–17) were not necessary for saving faith (cf. 1:6; 5:4–5).

Purpose

John's purpose in writing this letter was twofold: (1) to expose and repudiate the doctrinal and ethical errors of the false teachers, and (2) to exhort his spiritual children to pursue a life of holy fellowship with God in truth and righteousness, in the full joy (1:4) and assurance (5:13) of eternal life, through an obedient faith in Jesus as the Son of God (4:15; 5:3–5,12), and by the abiding presence of the Holy Spirit (2:20; 4:4,13). Some believe that it was also intended as a letter accompanying the Gospel of John.

Survey

Belief and behavior are inseparably woven together in this letter. The false teachers, whom John calls "antichrists" (2:18–22), were departing from the apostolic teaching about Christ and righteous living. Like 2 Peter and Jude, 1 John vigorously repudiates and condemns the false teachers (e.g., 2:18–19,22–23,26; 4:1,3,5) with their destructive beliefs and behavior.

On the positive side, 1 John sets forth the characteristics of true fellowship with God (e.g., 1:3—2:2) and reveals five specific tests by which believers may know with assurance that they have eternal life: (1) the test of apostolic truth about Christ (1:1–3; 2:21–23; 4:2–3,15; 5:1,5,10,20); (2) the test of an obedient faith that keeps Christ's commands (2:3–11; 5:3–4); (3) the test of holy living, i.e., turning from sin to fellowship with God (1:6–9; 2:3–6,15–17,29; 3:1–10; 5:2–3); (4) the test of love for God and other believers (2:9–11; 3:10–11,14,16–18; 4:7–12,18–21); and (5) the test of the Spirit's witness (2:20,27; 4:13; 5:7–12). John concludes that people may know with confidence that they have eternal life (5:13) when the fruit of these five areas is evident in their lives.

Special Features

Five major features characterize this letter. (1) It defines the Christian life by using contrasting terms and by seeming to allow no middle ground between light and darkness, truth and lies, righteousness and sin, love and hate, loving God and loving the world, children of God and children of the devil, etc. (2) Significantly, it is the only NT writing to speak of Jesus as our advocate [Gk *paraklētos*] with the Father when we sin as sincere believers (2:1–2; cf. Jn 14:16–17,26; 15:26; 16:7–8). (3) Its message is grounded almost entirely in the apostolic witness rather than in prior OT revelation; references to OT Scripture are noticeably absent. (4) Since it presents Christology in connection with refuting a particular kind of heresy, it focuses on the incarnation and blood (i.e., the cross) of Jesus without making specific mention of his resurrection. (5) Its style is simple and repetitive as John discusses certain terms such as "light," "truth," "believe," "remain;" "know," "love," "righteousness," "witness," "born of God" and "eternal life."

Reading 1 John

In order to read the entire New Testament in one year, the book of 1 John should be read in 5 days, according to the following schedule:
☐ 1:1—2:14 ☐ 2:15—3:10 ☐ 3:11–24 ☐ 4 ☐ 5

NOTES

The Word of Life

1 That which was from the beginning,[a]
which we have heard, which we have
seen with our eyes,[b] which we have
looked at and our hands have touched[c]—
this we proclaim concerning the Word of
life. **2**The life appeared;[d] we have seen it
and testify to it,[e] and we proclaim to you
Rev 1:9 the eternal life,[f] which was with the Father and has appeared to us. **3**We proclaim
to you what we have seen and heard,[g] so
that you also may have fellowship with us.
And our fellowship is with the Father and
with his Son, Jesus Christ.[h] **4**We write
this[i] to make our[a] joy complete.[j]

Walking in the Light

5This is the message we have heard[k]
from him and declare to you: God is
light;[l] in him there is no darkness at all.
6If we claim to have fellowship with him
yet walk in the darkness,[m] we lie and do
not live by the truth.[n] **7**But if we walk in
the light,[o] as he is in the light, we have
fellowship with one another, and the blood
of Jesus, his Son, purifies us from all[b]
sin.[p]
8If we claim to be without sin,[q] we deceive ourselves and the truth is not in us.[r]
9If we confess our sins, he is faithful and
just and will forgive us our sins[s] and purify us from all unrighteousness.[t] **10**If we
claim we have not sinned,[u] we make him
out to be a liar[v] and his word has no place
in our lives.[w]

2 My dear children,[x] I write this to you
so that you will not sin. But if anybody
does sin, we have one who speaks to the
Father in our defense[y]—Jesus Christ,
the Righteous One. **2**He is the atoning

1:1 [a]S Jn 1:2 [b]S Lk 24:48; Jn 1:14; 19:35; Ac 4:20; 2Pe 1:16; 1Jn 4:14 [c]Jn 20:27 **1:2** [d]Jn 1:1-4; 11:25; 14:6; 1Ti 3:16; 1Pe 1:20; 1Jn 3:5, 8 [e]S Jn 15:27 [f]S Mt 25:46 **1:3** [g]S ver 1 [h]1Co 1:9 **1:4** [i]1Jn 2:1 [j]S Jn 3:29 **1:5** [k]1Jn 3:11 [l]1Ti 6:16 **1:6** [m]Jn 3:19-21; 8:12; 2Co 6:14; Eph 5:8; 1Jn 2:11 [n]Jn 3:19-21; 1Jn 2:4; 4:20 **1:7** [o]Isa 2:5 [p]Heb 9:14; Rev 1:5; 7:14 **1:8** [q]Pr 20:9; Jer 2:35; Ro 3:9-19; Jas 3:2 [r]Jn 8:44; 1Jn 2:4 **1:9** [s]Ps 32:5; 51:2; Pr 28:13 [t]ver 7; Mic 7:18-20; Heb 10:22 **1:10** [u]ver 8 [v]1Jn 5:10 [w]Jn 5:38; 1Jn 2:14 **2:1** [x]ver 12,13,28; 1Jn 3:7,18; 4:4; 5:21; S 1Th 2:11 [y]S Ro 8:34; 1Ti 2:5

[a] 4 Some manuscripts *your* [b] 7 Or *every*

1:2 ETERNAL LIFE. John defines eternal life in terms of Christ. It can be found only through faith in and fellowship with Jesus Christ (vv. 2,6–7; 2:22–25; 5:20).

1:3 FELLOWSHIP WITH US. "Fellowship" (Gk *koinōnia*) literally means "having in common" and involves sharing and participation. Christians have fellowship because they have a common faith (Tit 1:4; Jude 3), common grace of God in Christ (1Co 1:9; Php 1:7), common indwelling of the Spirit (Jn 20:22; Ro 8:9,11), common gifts of the Spirit (Ro 15:27) and a common enemy (2:15–18; 1Pe 5:8). There can be no true fellowship with those who reject the teaching of NT faith (2Jn 7–11; see Gal 1:9, note).

1:6 FELLOWSHIP WITH HIM. To "walk in the darkness" means to live in sin and immoral pleasure. Such people do not "have fellowship with him," i.e., they are not born of God (cf. 3:7–9; Jn 3:19; 2Co 6:14). Those who have fellowship with God experience his grace and live lives of holiness in his presence (v. 7; 2:4; 3:10).

1:7 WALK IN THE LIGHT. This means to believe God's truth as revealed in his Word and to make a sincere and sustained effort by his grace to follow it in word and deed. "The blood of Jesus, his Son, purifies us from all sin" refers to the ongoing work of sanctification within the believer and the continual cleansing through Christ's blood for our inadvertent sins. John is probably not thinking here of deliberate sin against God, since he speaks of walking in the light. This continual purifying allows us to have intimate fellowship with God (see article on SANCTIFICATION, p. 526).

1:8 IF WE CLAIM TO BE WITHOUT SIN. John uses the noun ("sin") rather than the verb to emphasize sin as a principle in human nature. (1) John is probably arguing against those who affirm that sin does not exist as a principle or power in human nature, or those who say their evil actions are not really sin. This heresy is with us today in those who deny the fact of sin and interpret evil in terms of deterministic, psychological or social causes (see Ro 6:1, note; 7:9–11, note). (2) Believers must be aware that the sinful nature is a constant threat in their lives and that they must ever be putting to death its misdeeds through the Holy Spirit who lives within (Ro 8:13; Gal 5:16–25).

1:9 CONFESS OUR SINS. We must admit our sins and seek forgiveness and purifying from God. The two results are (1) forgiveness and reconciliation with God, and (2) the purifying from (i.e., removal of) guilt and the destruction of sin's power in order to live lives of holiness (Ps 32:1–5; Pr 28:13; Jer 31:34; Lk 15:18; Ro 6:2–14).

1:10 CLAIM WE HAVE NOT SINNED. If we claim that we have never sinned and therefore do not need the saving efficacy of Christ's death, we are making God a liar (cf. Ro 3:23).

2:1 SO THAT YOU WILL NOT SIN. John believed that born-again Christians are still capable of some kinds of sin. However, he does not teach that the Christian *must* sin; instead he exhorts his readers to live without sin (cf. Ro 6:15, note; 1Th 2:10, note). For those who do fall into sin, the remedy is to confess and forsake that sin (see 1:9, note). The assurance of forgiveness lies in the blood of Jesus Christ (v. 2; 1:7) and his heavenly ministry as "one who speaks to the Father in our defense" (Gk *paraklētos*). Jesus intercedes before God on our behalf on the basis of his atoning death, our repentance and our faith in him (cf. Ro 8:34; Heb 7:25, note; see also 1Jn 3:15, note).

2:2 ATONING SACRIFICE. As our "atoning sacrifice," Jesus took on himself the punishment for our sins and satisfied God's righteous judgment against sin. Forgiveness is now offered to everyone throughout the world and is received by those who turn to Christ in repentance and faith (4:9,14; Jn 1:29; 3:16; 5:24; see article on BIBLICAL WORDS FOR SALVATION, p. 292).

sacrifice for our sins,[z] and not only for
ours but also for[c] the sins of the whole
world.[a]

3We know[b] that we have come to know
him[c] if we obey his commands.[d] 4The
man who says, "I know him,"[e] but does
not do what he commands is a liar, and the
truth is not in him.[f] 5But if anyone obeys
his word,[g] God's love[d] is truly made complete in him.[h] This is how we know[i] we
are in him: 6Whoever claims to live in him
must walk as Jesus did.[j]

7Dear friends,[k] I am not writing you a
new command but an old one, which you
have had since the beginning.[l] This old
command is the message you have heard.
8Yet I am writing you a new command;[m]
its truth is seen in him and you, because
the darkness is passing[n] and the true
light[o] is already shining.[p]

9Anyone who claims to be in the light
but hates his brother[q] is still in the darkness.[r] 10Whoever loves his brother lives
in the light,[s] and there is nothing in him[e]
to make him stumble.[t] 11But whoever
hates his brother[u] is in the darkness and
walks around in the darkness;[v] he does
not know where he is going, because the
darkness has blinded him.[w]

12I write to you, dear children,[x]
because your sins have been
forgiven on account of his
name.[y]
13I write to you, fathers,
because you have known him who
is from the beginning.[z]
I write to you, young men,
because you have overcome[a] the
evil one.[b]
I write to you, dear children,[c]
because you have known the
Father.
14I write to you, fathers,
because you have known him who
is from the beginning.[d]
I write to you, young men,
because you are strong,[e]
and the word of God[f] lives in
you,[g]
and you have overcome the evil
one.[h]

Do Not Love the World

15Do not love the world or anything in
the world.[i] If anyone loves the world, the
love of the Father is not in him.[j] 16For
everything in the world—the cravings of
sinful man,[k] the lust of his eyes[l] and the
boasting of what he has and does—comes
not from the Father but from the world.
17The world and its desires pass away,[m]
but the man who does the will of God[n]
lives forever.

Warning Against Antichrists

18Dear children, this is the last hour;[o]
and as you have heard that the antichrist
is coming,[p] even now many antichrists
have come.[q] This is how we know it is the
last hour. 19They went out from us,[r] but
they did not really belong to us. For if they
had belonged to us, they would have remained with us; but their going showed
that none of them belonged to us.[s]

20But you have an anointing[t] from the
Holy One,[u] and all of you know the
truth.[f][v] 21I do not write to you because

2:2 [z] Ro 3:25; 1Jn 4:10 [a] S Mt 1:21; S Jn 3:17
2:3 [b] ver 5; 1Jn 3:24; 4:13; 5:2 [c] S ver 4 [d] S Jn 14:15
2:4 [e] ver 3; Tit 1:16; 1Jn 3:6; 4:7,8 [f] 1Jn 1:6,8
2:5 [g] S Jn 14:15 [h] 1Jn 4:12 [i] S ver 3
2:6 [j] S Mt 11:29
2:7 [k] S 1Co 10:14 [l] ver 24; 1Jn 3:11, 23; 4:21; 2Jn 5,6
2:8 [m] S Jn 13:34 [n] Ro 13:12; Heb 10:25 [o] Jn 1:9 [p] Eph 5:8; 1Th 5:5
2:9 [q] ver 11; Lev 19:17; 1Jn 3:10,15,16; 4:20,21 [r] 1Jn 1:5
2:10 [s] 1Jn 3:14 [t] ver 11; Ps 119:165
2:11 [u] S ver 9 [v] S 1Jn 1:6 [w] Jn 11:9; 12:35
2:12 [x] S ver 1 [y] S 1Jn 3:23
2:13 [z] S Jn 1:1 [a] S Jn 16:33 [b] ver 14; S Mt 5:37 [c] S ver 1
2:14 [d] S Jn 1:1 [e] Eph 6:10 [f] S Heb 4:12 [g] Jn 5:38; 1Jn 1:10 [h] S ver 13
2:15 [i] Ro 12:2 [j] Jas 4:4
2:16 [k] Ge 3:6; Ro 13:14; Eph 2:3 [l] Pr 27:20
2:17 [m] S Heb 12:27 [n] Mt 12:50
2:18 [o] S Ro 13:11 [p] ver 22; 1Jn 4:3; 2Jn 7 [q] 1Jn 4:1
2:19 [r] Ac 20:30 [s] 1Co 11:19
2:20 [t] ver 27; 2Co 1:21 [u] S Mk 1:24 [v] Jer 31:34; Mt 13:11; Jn 14:26

[c] *2* Or *He is the one who turns aside God's wrath, taking away our sins, and not only ours but also*
[d] *5* Or *word, love for God* [e] *10* Or *it*
[f] *20* Some manuscripts *and you know all things*

2:4 DOES NOT DO WHAT HE COMMANDS. John was contending against a misunderstanding of the doctrine of grace and salvation. He opposed antinomian teachers, who taught that forsaking a sinful life was optional for the believer. (1) They declared that one can legitimately claim to "know" God in a saving relationship and at the same time be indifferent to God's will and his commands, and disobey them (see Jn 17:3, note). (2) Those who make such a claim, John states, are liars and do not have God's truth in them. The attempt to be justified through faith in Christ without a commitment to follow Christ is doomed to failure.

2:10 WHOEVER LOVES HIS BROTHER. See Jn 13:34–35, notes.

2:15–16 THE WORLD. See article on THE CHRISTIAN'S RELATIONSHIP TO THE WORLD, p. 546.

2:18 MANY ANTICHRISTS. An antichrist or false Christ will come toward the end of the age to rule the world and to lead a great rebellion against Christ and the NT faith (see Rev 13:1,8,18, notes; 19:20; 20:10; see article on THE AGE OF THE ANTICHRIST, p. 447). Yet John says that "many antichrists" have already entered into the church. These are professed believers who love the world and its sinful pleasures and distort the gospel and its message of the cross, thus placing themselves against Christ and his righteousness.

2:19 THEY WENT OUT FROM US. When the antichrists departed from fellowship with true believers, they were not in a saving relationship with Christ. This allows for two possibilities: (1) They were never true believers to begin with, or (2) they had once been in a saving relationship with Christ but afterward abandoned their faith in Christ (see article on PERSONAL APOSTASY, p. 492).

2:20 AN ANOINTING. Believers receive an anointing from Christ, namely, the Holy Spirit (cf. 2Co 1:21–22). Through the Spirit we "know the truth" (see v. 27, note).

you do not know the truth, but because
you do know it[w] and because no lie comes
from the truth. 22 Who is the liar? It is the
man who denies that Jesus is the Christ.
Such a man is the antichrist—he denies
the Father and the Son.[x] 23 No one who
denies the Son has the Father; whoever
acknowledges the Son has the Father
also.[y]

24 See that what you have heard from
the beginning[z] remains in you. If it does,
you also will remain in the Son and in the
Father.[a] 25 And this is what he promised
us—even eternal life.[b]

26 I am writing these things to you about
those who are trying to lead you astray.[c]
27 As for you, the anointing[d] you received
from him remains in you, and you do not
need anyone to teach you. But as his
anointing teaches you about all things[e]
and as that anointing is real, not counterfeit—just as it has taught you, remain in
him.[f]

Children of God

28 And now, dear children,[g] continue in
him, so that when he appears[h] we may be
confident[i] and unashamed before him at
his coming.[j]

29 If you know that he is righteous,[k] you
know that everyone who does what is
right has been born of him.[l]

2:21 [w] 2Pe 1:12; Jude 5
2:22 [x] 1Jn 4:3; 2Jn 7
2:23 [y] Jn 8:19; 14:7; 1Jn 4:15; 5:1; 2Jn 9
2:24 [z] S ver 7 [a] Jn 14:23; 15:4; 1Jn 1:3; 2Jn 9
2:25 [b] S Mt 25:46
2:26 [c] 1Jn 3:7
2:27 [d] ver 20 [e] 1Co 2:12 [f] Jn 15:4
2:28 [g] S ver 1 [h] Col 3:4; 1Jn 3:2 [i] S Eph 3:12 [j] S 1Th 2:19
2:29 [k] 1Jn 3:7 [l] S Jn 1:13
3:1 [m] S Jn 3:16 [n] ver 2,10; S Jn 1:12 [o] Jn 15:21; 16:3
3:2 [p] S 1Co 10:14 [q] ver 1,10; S Jn 1:12 [r] Col 3:4; 1Jn 2:28 [s] Ro 8:29; 2Pe 1:4 [t] Ps 17:15; Jn 17:24; 2Co 3:18
3:3 [u] 2Co 7:1; 2Pe 3:13,14 [v] Ps 18:26
3:4 [w] 1Jn 5:17
3:5 [x] ver 8; S Jn 3:17 [y] S 2Co 5:21
3:6 [z] ver 9; 1Jn 5:18 [a] 3Jn 11 [b] S 1Jn 2:4
3:7 [c] S 1Jn 2:1 [d] 1Jn 2:26 [e] 1Jn 2:29
3:8 [f] ver 10; Jn 8:44 [g] S Mt 4:3 [h] Heb 2:14
3:9 [i] S Jn 1:13 [j] ver 6; Ps 119:3; 1Jn 5:18 [k] 1Pe 1:23

3 How great is the love[m] the Father has
lavished on us, that we should be
called children of God![n] And that is what
we are! The reason the world does not
know us is that it did not know him.[o]
2 Dear friends,[p] now we are children of
God,[q] and what we will be has not yet
been made known. But we know that
when he appears,[g][r] we shall be like
him,[s] for we shall see him as he is.[t] 3 Everyone who has this hope in him purifies
himself,[u] just as he is pure.[v]

4 Everyone who sins breaks the law; in
fact, sin is lawlessness.[w] 5 But you know
that he appeared so that he might take
away our sins.[x] And in him is no sin.[y] 6 No
one who lives in him keeps on sinning.[z]
No one who continues to sin has either
seen him[a] or known him.[b]

7 Dear children,[c] do not let anyone lead
you astray.[d] He who does what is right is
righteous, just as he is righteous.[e] 8 He
who does what is sinful is of the devil,[f]
because the devil has been sinning from
the beginning. The reason the Son of
God[g] appeared was to destroy the devil's
work.[h] 9 No one who is born of God[i] will
continue to sin,[j] because God's seed[k] re-

g 2 Or *when it is made known*

2:24 HEARD FROM THE BEGINNING. Believers will remain in Christ and experience salvation only as long as they remain in the original teaching of Christ and the apostles (see Eph 2:20, note). This suggests two things: (1) To abandon the original gospel of NT faith is spiritually fatal and separates one from Jesus Christ (cf. Gal 1:6–8; 5:1–4). Believers must be Biblical in their theology in the sense of always adhering to the teachings of the NT. (2) It is dangerous to run after new teachings or teachers who preach new things not found in the Christian faith (cf. Jude 3). For this reason, it is important to study and hold firmly to God's Word; our very souls and our eternal destiny depend on it.

2:27 HIS ANOINTING TEACHES YOU. All children of God are given the "anointing" (i.e., the Holy Spirit) to help lead them into truth (Jn 14:26; 16:13). As believers remain in Christ and read the Word of God, the Spirit helps them understand its redemptive truths. (1) All believers may study and know God's truth and learn from each other through mutual teaching and exhorting (Mt 28:20; Eph 3:18; Col 3:16). (2) Thus, believers have two safeguards against doctrinal error—Biblical revelation (cf. v. 24) and the Holy Spirit. (3) Believers do not need those who teach extrabiblical doctrine. This is the meaning of John's words, "you do not need anyone to teach you."

3:1 CHILDREN OF GOD. The truth that God is our heavenly Father and we are his children is one of the greatest revelations in the NT. (1) Being a child of God is the highest privilege of our salvation (Jn 1:12; Gal 4:7). (2) Being a child of God is the basis for our faith and trust in God (Mt 6:25–34) and our hope of glory for the future. As God's children, we are heirs of God and co-heirs with Christ (Ro 8:16–17; Gal 4:7). (3) God wants us to be increasingly made aware through the Holy Spirit, the "Spirit of sonship" (Ro 8:15), that we are his children. The Spirit produces the cry "*Abba,* Father" in our hearts (see Gal 4:6, note) and gives us the desire to be "led by the Spirit" (Ro 8:14). (4) Being a child of God is the basis for our discipline by the Father (Heb 12:6–7,11) and the reason we live to please God (v. 9; 4:17–19). God's ultimate goal in making us his children is to save us forever (Jn 3:16) and to conform us to the likeness of his Son (Ro 8:29).

3:6 LIVES IN HIM. The words "lives in him" and "born of God" (v. 9) are equivalent expressions. Only those who continue to live in God continue to be born of God (see Jn 15:4, note; see article on REGENERATION, p. 178).

3:6 SEEN HIM OR KNOWN HIM. The verbs "seen" and "known" are in the perfect tense (the Greek perfect tense refers to action that occurred in the past with its results continuing to the present moment). Therefore, John says that no one who is living in sin has seen (and continues to see) him, nor has he known (and continues to know) him. Thus, this can be applied either to those who have never had real faith in Christ or to apostates who knew God in the past but have not continued knowing him in the present.

THE CHRISTIAN'S RELATIONSHIP TO THE WORLD

1Jn 2:15–16 "Do not love the world or anything in the world. If anyone loves the world, the love of the Father is not in him. For everything in the world—the cravings of sinful man, the lust of his eyes and the boasting of what he has and does—comes not from the Father but from the world."

The term "world" (Gk *kosmos*) often refers to the vast system of this age that Satan promotes and that exists independent of God. It consists not only in the obviously evil, immoral and sinful pleasures of the world, but also refers to the spirit of rebellion against or indifference to God and his revelation that exists within all human enterprises not under Christ's lordship. In this age Satan uses the world's ideas, morality, philosophies, psychology, desires, governments, culture, education, science, art, medicine, music, economic systems, entertainment, mass media, religions, sports, agriculture, etc., to oppose God, his people, his Word and his righteous standards (Mt 16:26; 1Co 2:12; 3:19; Tit 2:12; 1Jn 2:15–16). For example, Satan will use the medical profession to promote the killing of unborn babies, agriculture to produce life-destroying drugs such as alcohol and narcotics, educational systems to promote ungodly and humanistic philosophy, and the entertainment media to destroy godly standards. Believers must be aware that behind all human enterprises there is a spirit or power that moves against God and his Word, some to a lesser degree, some to a greater degree. Finally, the "world" also includes all man-made religious systems and all unbiblical, worldly or lukewarm "Christian" organizations and churches.

(1) Satan (see Mt 4:10, note on Satan) is the god of the present world system (see Jn 12:31, note; 14:30; 16:11; 2Co 4:4; 1Jn 5:19). Along with a host of subordinate evil spirits, he controls it (Da 10:13; Lk 4:5–7; Eph 6:12–13; see article on POWER OVER SATAN AND DEMONS, p. 80).

(2) Satan has organized the world into political, cultural, economic and religious systems that are innately hostile toward God and his people (Jn 7:7; 15:18; Jas 4:4; 1Jn 2:16,18) and that refuse to submit to his truth, which exposes its evil (Jn 7:7).

(3) The world and the true church are two distinct groups of people. The world is under Satan's dominion (see Jn 12:31, note); the church belongs exclusively to God (Eph 5:23–24; Rev 21:2; see article on THREE KINDS OF PEOPLE, p. 334). Thus, believers must separate themselves from the world (see article on SPIRITUAL SEPARATION FOR BELIEVERS, p. 371).

(4) In the world believers are aliens and strangers (Heb 11:13; 1Pe 2:11). (a) They must come out of the world (Jn 15:19), not be conformed to the world (see Ro 12:2, note), not love the world (1Jn 2:15), overcome the world (1Jn 5:4), hate the world's evil (see Heb 1:9, note), die to the world (Gal 6:14) and be delivered from the world (Col 1:13–14). (b) Loving the world (cf. 1Jn 2:15) defiles our fellowship with God and leads to spiritual destruction. It is impossible to love the world and the Father at the same time (Mt 6:24; Lk 16:13; see Jas 4:4, note). To love the world means to be in intimate fellowship with and devoted to its values, interest, ways and pleasures; it means taking pleasure in or enjoying what is offensive and opposed to God (see Lk 23:35, note). Note, of course, that the terms "world" and "earth" are not synonymous; God does not forbid a love for the created earth, i.e., nature, mountains, forests, etc.

(5) According to 1Jn 2:16, three aspects of the sinful world create open hostility to God: (a) "The cravings of sinful man": this includes impure desires and running after sinful pleasures and sensual gratification (1Co 6:18; Php 3:19; Jas 1:14). (b) "The lust of his eyes": this refers to coveting or lusting after things that are attractive to the eye but forbidden by God, including the desire to watch that which gives sinful pleasure (Ex 20:17; Ro 7:7). In the present modern age this includes the desire to entertain oneself by viewing pornography, violence, ungodliness and immorality on stage and on television, or in movies or magazines (Ge 3:6; Jos 7:21; 2Sa 11:2; Mt 5:28). (c) "The boasting of what he has and does": this means the spirit of arrogance and self-sufficient independence that does not recognize God as Lord or his Word as final authority. It is the spirit that seeks to exalt, glorify and promote oneself as the center of life (Jas 4:16).

(6) Believers must not have close fellowship with those who participate in the world's evil system (see Mt 9:11, note; 2Co 6:14, note), must condemn openly their sin (Jn 7:7; Eph 5:11, note), must be light and salt to them (Mt 5:13–14), must love them (Jn 3:16) and must attempt to win them to Christ (Mk 16:15; Jude 22–23).

(7) From the world the true Christian will experience trouble (Jn 16:2–3), hatred (Jn 15:19), persecution (Mt 5:10–12) and suffering (Ro 8:22–23; 1Pe 2:19–21). Using the lures of the world, Satan makes an unceasing effort to destroy the life of God in the Christian (2Co 11:3; 1Pe 5:8).

(8) The world system is temporary and will be destroyed by God (Da 2:34–35,44; 1Co 7:31; 2Th 1:7–10; 2Pe 3:10, note; Rev 18:2). Even now it is passing away (1Jn 2:17).

mains in him; he cannot go on sinning,
because he has been born of God. 10This
is how we know who the children of God[l]
are and who the children of the devil[m] are:
Anyone who does not do what is right is
not a child of God; nor is anyone who does
not love[n] his brother.[o]

Love One Another

11This is the message you heard[p] from
the beginning:[q] We should love one another.[r] 12Do not be like Cain, who belonged to the evil one[s] and murdered his
brother.[t] And why did he murder him?
Because his own actions were evil and his
brother's were righteous.[u] 13Do not be
surprised, my brothers, if the world hates
you.[v] 14We know that we have passed
from death to life,[w] because we love our
brothers. Anyone who does not love remains in death.[x] 15Anyone who hates his
brother[y] is a murderer,[z] and you know
that no murderer has eternal life in him.[a]
16This is how we know what love is:
Jesus Christ laid down his life for us.[b] And
we ought to lay down our lives for our
brothers.[c] 17If anyone has material possessions and sees his brother in need but
has no pity on him,[d] how can the love of
God be in him?[e] 18Dear children,[f] let us
not love with words or tongue but with
actions and in truth.[g] 19This then is how
we know that we belong to the truth, and
how we set our hearts at rest in his presence 20whenever our hearts condemn us.
For God is greater than our hearts, and he
knows everything.

3:10 [l] ver 1,2; S Jn 1:12 [m] ver 8 [n] 1Jn 4:8 [o] S 1Jn 2:9 **3:11** [p] 1Jn 1:5 [q] S 1Jn 2:7 [r] Jn 13:34,35; 15:12; 1Jn 4:7,11, 21; 2Jn 5 **3:12** [s] S Mt 5:37 [t] Ge 4:8 [u] Ps 38:20; Pr 29:10 **3:13** [v] Jn 15:18, 19; 17:14 **3:14** [w] Jn 5:24 [x] S 1Jn 2:9 **3:15** [y] S 1Jn 2:9 [z] Mt 5:21,22; Jn 8:44 [a] Gal 5:20, 21; Rev 21:8 **3:16** [b] Jn 10:11 [c] Jn 15:13; Php 2:17; 1Th 2:8 **3:17** [d] Dt 15:7,8; Jas 2:15,16 [e] 1Jn 4:20 **3:18** [f] S 1Jn 2:1 [g] Eze 33:31; Ro 12:9

3:9 HE CANNOT GO ON SINNING. The verb "to sin" (Gk *hamartanō*) is a present active infinitive, implying continued action. John emphasizes that those truly born of God cannot make sin their way of life, because God's life cannot exist in those who practice sin (cf. 1:5–7; 2:3–11,15–17,24–29; 3:6–24; 4:7–8, 20).

(1) The new birth produces spiritual life that results in an ever-present relationship with God. In this letter, every time John speaks of the new birth of the believer, he uses the Greek perfect tense to emphasize the continued and sustained relationship that the new birth began (2:29; 3:9; 4:7; 5:1,4,18; see article on REGENERATION, p. 178).

(2) For people to have God's life in them (i.e., be born of God) and to go on sinning is a spiritual impossibility. Believers may occasionally lapse from God's high standard, but they will not continue in sin (vv. 6,10).

(3) That which keeps the faithful from sinning is "God's seed" in them, i.e., God's very life, Spirit and nature living in them (5:11–12; Jn 1:1; 15:4; 2Pe 1:4).

(4) By faith (5:4), the indwelling Christ, the Spirit's power and the written Word (see 1Th 2:10, note), all believers can live moment by moment free from offense and sin.

3:10 CHILDREN OF GOD . . . CHILDREN OF THE DEVIL. This is the heart and conclusion of John's teaching in 2:28—3:10. He has warned his readers not to be deceived about the nature of salvation (v. 7). Consequently, the believer must reject any theology or teaching that alleges that one can be out of fellowship with God (1:3), continue to sin, do the works of the devil (v. 8), love the world (2:15), do harm to others (vv. 14–18), and yet be a child of God who is saved and destined for heaven.

Contrary to this false teaching, John clearly believed that anyone who continues in sin (see v. 9, note) "is of the devil" (v. 8) and "is not a child of God." If those who habitually practice sin claim to possess eternal life and be God's children, they are deceived and are liars (cf. 2:4). Furthermore, what characterizes true children of God is a love for God shown by keeping his commands (5:2) and demonstrating genuine concern for the spiritual and physical needs of other believers (vv. 16–17).

3:15 NO MURDERER HAS ETERNAL LIFE. The Bible generally distinguishes between different kinds of sins: unintentional sins (Lev 4:2,13,22; 5:4–6), less serious sins (Mt 5:19), deliberate sins (5:16–17) and sins bringing spiritual death (5:16). John emphasizes that there are certain sins that true born-again believers will not commit because of the eternal life of Christ abiding in them (cf. 2:11,15–16; 3:6–8,10,14–15; 4:20; 5:2; 2Jn 9). These sins, because of their gravity and their origin in the very center of one's spirit, indicate an intense rebellion against God, a severing from Christ, a falling from grace and a separation from the vital life of salvation (Gal 5:4).

(1) Examples of sins that give conclusive evidence that one is still in bondage to wickedness or has fallen from grace and eternal life are apostasy (2:19; 4:6; Heb 10:26–31), murder (v. 15; 2:11), sexual impurity or immorality (Ro 1:21–27; 1Co 5; Eph 5:5; Rev 21:8), abandonment of one's family (1Ti 5:8), leading others into sin (Mt 18:6–10), and cruelty (Mt 24:48–51). These abominable sins reveal utter rejection of honor toward God and loving care for others (cf. 2:9–10; 3:6–10; 1Co 6:9–11; Gal 5:19–21; 1Th 4:5; 2Ti 3:1–5; Heb 3:7–19). Thus, anyone who says, "I have fellowship with Jesus Christ, am indwelt by the Spirit, and am in a saving relationship with him," yet participates in the above-mentioned sins, is deceiving himself or herself and "is a liar, and the truth is not in him" (2:4; cf. 1:6; 3:7–8).

(2) Believers must keep in mind, however, that all sin, even the less serious ones, can lead to a weakening of spiritual life, to a rejection of the Holy Spirit's leading, and thus, to spiritual death (Ro 6:15–23; 8:5–13).

3:17 HIS BROTHER IN NEED. Love is expressed by sincerely helping persons in need, i.e., by sharing our earthly possessions with them (cf. Jas 2:14–17). To refuse to give of our food, clothing or money to help others in real need is to close our hearts to them (cf. Dt 15:7–11). This also includes giving our money to help bring the gospel to those who have not heard (4:9–10).

21Dear friends,[h] if our hearts do not
condemn us, we have confidence before
God[i] **22**and receive from him anything we
ask,[j] because we obey his commands[k]
and do what pleases him.[l] **23**And this is
his command: to believe[m] in the name of
his Son, Jesus Christ,[n] and to love one
another as he commanded us.[o] **24**Those
who obey his commands[p] live in him,[q]
and he in them. And this is how we know
that he lives in us: We know it by the
Spirit he gave us.[r]

Test the Spirits

4 Dear friends,[s] do not believe every
spirit,[t] but test the spirits to see
whether they are from God, because many
false prophets have gone out into the
world.[u] **2**This is how you can recognize
the Spirit of God: Every spirit that acknowledges that Jesus Christ has come in
the flesh[v] is from God,[w] **3**but every spirit
that does not acknowledge Jesus is not
from God. This is the spirit of the antichrist,[x] which you have heard is coming
and even now is already in the world.[y]
4You, dear children,[z] are from God and
have overcome them,[a] because the one
who is in you[b] is greater than the one who
is in the world.[c] **5**They are from the
world[d] and therefore speak from the
viewpoint of the world, and the world listens to them. **6**We are from God, and whoever knows God listens to us; but whoever
is not from God does not listen to us.[e]
This is how we recognize the Spirit[h] of
truth[f] and the spirit of falsehood.[g]

God's Love and Ours

7Dear friends, let us love one another,[h]
for love comes from God. Everyone who
loves has been born of God[i] and knows
God.[j] **8**Whoever does not love does not
know God, because God is love.[k] **9**This is
how God showed his love among us: He
sent his one and only Son[i][l] into the world

3:21 [h]S 1Co 10:14 [i]S Eph 3:12; 1Jn 5:14 **3:22** [j]S Mt 7:7 [k]S Jn 14:15 [l]Jn 8:29; Heb 13:21 **3:23** [m]Jn 6:29 [n]S Lk 24:47; Jn 1:12; 3:18; 20:31; 1Co 6:11; 1Jn 5:13 [o]S Jn 13:34 **3:24** [p]1Jn 2:3 [q]1Jn 2:6; 4:15 [r]1Th 4:8; 1Jn 4:13 **4:1** [s]S 1Co 10:14 [t]Jer 29:8; 1Co 12:10; 2Th 2:2 [u]S Mt 7:15; 1Jn 2:18 **4:2** [v]S Jn 1:14; 1Jn 2:23 [w]1Co 12:3 **4:3** [x]1Jn 2:22; 2Jn 7 [y]1Jn 2:18 **4:4** [z]S 1Jn 2:1 [a]S Jn 16:33 [b]Ro 8:31 [c]2Ki 6:16; S Jn 12:31 **4:5** [d]Jn 15:19; 17:14,16 **4:6** [e]Jn 8:47 [f]S Jn 14:17 [g]S Mk 13:5 **4:7** [h]S 1Jn 3:11 [i]S Jn 1:13 [j]S 1Jn 2:4 **4:8** [k]ver 7,16 **4:9** [l]Jn 1:18

h *6* Or *spirit* **i** *9* Or *his only begotten Son*

3:22 BECAUSE WE OBEY HIS COMMANDS. Why are some prayers answered and others not? John declares that an effective prayer life is related to our devotion to God. Obeying, loving and pleasing God (Jn 8:29; 2Co 5:9; Eph 5:10; Heb 13:21) are indispensable conditions in order to receive what we ask for in prayer (cf. Ps 50:14–15; Pr 15:29; Isa 59:1–2; Mt 6:15; Mk 11:25; Jas 5:16).

4:1 TEST THE SPIRITS. The reason for testing every spirit (i.e., a person moved or inspired by a spirit) is that "many false prophets" will enter the church. This will be especially true as tolerance for unbiblical doctrine increases toward the end of the age (see Mt 24:11, note; 1Ti 4:1, note; 2Ti 4:3–4, note; 2Pe 2:1–2). Christians are commanded to test all professed Christian teachers, writers, preachers and prophets, and in fact any individual who claims his or her work or message comes from the Holy Spirit. Believers may never assume that a ministry or spiritual experience is from God merely because one claims it is. Furthermore, no teaching or doctrine may be accepted as true solely on the basis of success, miracles or apparent anointing (Mt 7:22; 1Co 14:29; 2Th 2:8–10; 2Jn 7; Rev 13:4; 16:14; 19:20).

(1) All teaching must be tested against the revelation of God's truth in Scripture (see Gal 1:9, note).

(2) It is the spirit of the teaching that must be tested. Does the teaching bear the same kind of spirit and emphasis as NT apostolic teaching? Beware of any teaching that a person claims to have received from the Holy Spirit or an angel that cannot be supported by sound Biblical exegesis.

(3) Teachers' lives must be tested as to their relation to the ungodly world (see v. 5; see article on THE CHRISTIAN'S RELATIONSHIP TO THE WORLD, p. 546) and to Christ's lordship (vv. 2,6; Ro 10:9, note; see article on TESTING FOR GENUINE BAPTISM IN THE SPIRIT, p. 254).

4:2 JESUS CHRIST HAS COME IN THE FLESH. Theological liberalism and religious cults betray themselves as "antichrist" (v. 3) when they deny the full deity of Jesus Christ (see Jn 1:1, note), his virgin birth (see Mt 1:23, note), or his redemptive death and resurrection for our salvation (vv. 9–10; 2:2; see article on BIBLICAL WORDS FOR SALVATION, p. 292). Every departure from Biblical revelation about Christ opens itself up to demonic "spirits" of deception (v. 1) because it sets aside the authority and complete trustworthiness of God's Word (see 2Pe 1:3, note; see article on THE INSPIRATION AND AUTHORITY OF SCRIPTURE, p. 474).

4:4 THE ONE WHO IS IN YOU IS GREATER. Scripture emphasizes that the Holy Spirit lives in the believer (1Co 6:19). Through the Spirit, we can overcome the evil in the world, including sin, Satan, trials, temptations, sorrow, persecution and false teaching, and we can victoriously achieve God's will for our lives.

4:7 LET US LOVE ONE ANOTHER. Although love is an aspect of the Spirit's fruit (Gal 5:22–23) and an evidence of the new birth (2:29; 3:9–10; 5:1), it is also something that we are responsible to develop. For this reason John exhorts us to love others, to be concerned about them and to seek their welfare. John is not talking about a feeling of goodwill, but a decision and disposition to help people in their needs (3:16–18; cf. Lk 6:31). John urges us to demonstrate love for three reasons: (1) Love is the very nature of God (vv. 7–9), which he showed by giving his own Son for us (vv. 9–10). We share his nature because we are born of him (v. 7). (2) Because God loved us, we who have experienced his love, forgiveness and help are obligated to help others, even at great personal cost. (3) If we love one another, God continues to live in us and his love is made complete in us (v. 12).

that we might live through him.[m] **10**This is
love: not that we loved God, but that he
loved us[n] and sent his Son as an atoning
sacrifice for[j] our sins.[o] **11**Dear friends,[p]
since God so loved us,[q] we also ought to
love one another.[r] **12**No one has ever seen
God;[s] but if we love one another, God
lives in us and his love is made complete
in us.[t]

13We know[u] that we live in him and he
in us, because he has given us of his Spirit.[v] **14**And we have seen and testify[w] that
the Father has sent his Son to be the Savior of the world.[x] **15**If anyone acknowledges that Jesus is the Son of God,[y] God
lives in him and he in God.[z] **16**And so
we know and rely on the love God has
for us.

God is love.[a] Whoever lives in love lives
in God, and God in him.[b] **17**In this way,
love is made complete[c] among us so that
we will have confidence[d] on the day of
judgment,[e] because in this world we are
like him. **18**There is no fear in love. But
perfect love drives out fear,[f] because fear
has to do with punishment. The one who
fears is not made perfect in love.

19We love because he first loved us.[g]
20If anyone says, "I love God," yet hates
his brother,[h] he is a liar.[i] For anyone who
does not love his brother, whom he has
seen,[j] cannot love God, whom he has not
seen.[k] **21**And he has given us this command:[l] Whoever loves God must also love
his brother.[m]

Faith in the Son of God

5 Everyone who believes[n] that Jesus is
the Christ[o] is born of God,[p] and everyone who loves the father loves his child
as well.[q] **2**This is how we know[r] that we
love the children of God:[s] by loving God
and carrying out his commands. **3**This is
love for God: to obey his commands.[t] And
his commands are not burdensome,[u] **4**for
everyone born of God[v] overcomes[w] the
world. This is the victory that has overcome the world, even our faith. **5**Who is it
that overcomes the world? Only he who
believes that Jesus is the Son of God.[x]

6This is the one who came by water and
blood[y]—Jesus Christ. He did not come by
water only, but by water and blood. And
it is the Spirit who testifies, because the
Spirit is the truth.[z] **7**For there are three[a]
that testify: **8**the[k] Spirit, the water and
the blood; and the three are in agreement.
9We accept man's testimony,[b] but God's
testimony is greater because it is the testimony of God,[c] which he has given about
his Son. **10**Anyone who believes in the Son
of God has this testimony in his heart.[d]
Anyone who does not believe God has
made him out to be a liar,[e] because he has
not believed the testimony God has given
about his Son. **11**And this is the testimony:
God has given us eternal life,[f] and this
life is in his Son.[g] **12**He who has the Son
has life; he who does not have the Son of
God does not have life.[h]

The Certainties of Faith

13I write these things to you who be-

4:9 [m]Jn 3:16,17; 1Jn 5:11
4:10 [n]Ro 5:8,10 [o]S Ro 3:25
4:11 [p]S 1Co 10:14 [q]S Jn 3:16 [r]Jn 15:12; S 1Jn 3:11
4:12 [s]S Jn 1:18 [t]ver 17; 1Jn 2:5
4:13 [u]S 1Jn 2:3 [v]1Jn 3:24
4:14 [w]S Jn 15:27 [x]S Lk 2:11; S Jn 3:17
4:15 [y]S 1Jn 2:23; 5:5 [z]1Jn 3:24
4:16 [a]ver 8 [b]ver 12,13; 1Jn 3:24
4:17 [c]ver 12; 1Jn 2:5 [d]S Eph 3:12 [e]S Mt 10:15
4:18 [f]Ro 8:15
4:19 [g]ver 10
4:20 [h]S 1Jn 2:9 [i]S 1Jn 1:6; 2:4 [j]1Jn 3:17 [k]ver 12; S Jn 1:18
4:21 [l]1Jn 2:7 [m]S Mt 5:43; S 1Jn 2:9
5:1 [n]S Jn 3:15 [o]1Jn 2:22; 4:2,15 [p]S Jn 1:13; S 1Jn 2:23 [q]Jn 8:42
5:2 [r]S 1Jn 2:3 [s]1Jn 3:14
5:3 [t]S Jn 14:15 [u]Mt 11:30; 23:4
5:4 [v]S Jn 1:13 [w]S Jn 16:33
5:5 [x]ver 1; S 1Jn 2:23
5:6 [y]Jn 19:34 [z]S Jn 14:17
5:7 [a]S Mt 18:16
5:9 [b]Jn 5:34 [c]Mt 3:16,17; Jn 5:32,37; 8:17,18
5:10 [d]Ro 8:16; Gal 4:6 [e]Jn 3:33; 1Jn 1:10
5:11 [f]S Mt 25:46 [g]S Jn 1:4
5:12 [h]Jn 3:15,16,36

j *10* Or *as the one who would turn aside his wrath, taking away* k *7,8* Late manuscripts of the Vulgate *testify in heaven: the Father, the Word and the Holy Spirit, and these three are one. 8And there are three that testify on earth: the* (not found in any Greek manuscript before the sixteenth century)

4:17 CONFIDENCE ON THE DAY OF JUDGMENT. If we remain in Christ, have fellowship with the Father (1:3), strive to obey his commands (2:3), remain separate from the world (2:15–17), remain in the truth (2:24) and love others (vv. 7–12), then we can have confidence that we will not be condemned on the day of judgment (v. 18; see article on ASSURANCE OF SALVATION, p. 552).

5:1 BELIEVES . . . LOVES. Genuine faith will express itself in gratitude to and love for the Father and Jesus Christ his Son. Faith and love are inseparable, for when we are born of God, the Holy Spirit pours the love of God into our hearts (Ro 5:5).

5:2 THIS IS HOW WE KNOW. Love for others is genuine Christian love only if it is accompanied by love for God and obedience to his commands (cf. 2:3; 3:23; Jn 15:10; see Mt 22:37, note; Jn 14:21, note).

5:4 OVERCOME THE WORLD, EVEN OUR FAITH. The faith that overcomes the world is a faith that sees eternal realities, experiences God's power and loves Christ to such an extent that the world's sinful pleasures, secular values, ungodly ways and selfish materialism not only lose their attraction for us, but also are looked on with disgust, aversion and grief (see Rev 2:7, note).

5:6 BY WATER AND BLOOD. This phrase probably refers to Jesus' baptism at the beginning of his ministry and to his death on the cross. John may have written this because some were teaching that the divine Christ did not experience death. He maintains that Jesus Christ died as the God-man and is thereby fully able to make atonement for our sins. The Spirit also bears witness to this truth (vv. 7–8).

5:12 HE WHO HAS THE SON HAS LIFE. All people should hear the gospel because eternal life is in God's Son and cannot be received or possessed in any other way. He is the only "way . . . and the life" (Jn 14:6). Eternal life is Christ's life in us. We have it as we maintain a vital faith relationship with him (Jn 15:4; see Jn 17:3, note; Col 3:4).

5:13 THAT YOU MAY KNOW THAT YOU HAVE ETERNAL LIFE. John declares his purpose in writ-

lieve in the name of the Son of God[i] so
that you may know that you have eternal
life.[j] **14**This is the confidence[k] we have in
approaching God: that if we ask anything
according to his will, he hears us.[l] **15**And
if we know that he hears us—whatever
we ask—we know[m] that we have what we
asked of him.[n]

16If anyone sees his brother commit a
sin that does not lead to death, he should
pray and God will give him life.[o] I refer to
those whose sin does not lead to death.
There is a sin that leads to death.[p] I am
not saying that he should pray about
that.[q] **17**All wrongdoing is sin,[r] and there
is sin that does not lead to death.[s]

18We know that anyone born of God[t]
does not continue to sin; the one who was
born of God keeps him safe, and the evil
one[u] cannot harm him.[v] **19**We know that
we are children of God,[w] and that the
whole world is under the control of the
evil one.[x] **20**We know also that the Son of
God has come[y] and has given us understanding,[z] so that we may know him who
is true.[a] And we are in him who is true—
even in his Son Jesus Christ. He is the true
God and eternal life.[b]

21Dear children,[c] keep yourselves from
idols.[d]

5:13 [i]S 1Jn 3:23 [j]ver 11; S Mt 25:46 **5:14** [k]S Eph 3:12; 1Jn 3:21 [l]S Mt 7:7 **5:15** [m]ver 18,19, 20 [n]1Ki 3:12 **5:16** [o]Jas 5:15 [p]Ex 23:21; Heb 6:4-6; 10:26 [q]Jer 7:16; 14:11 **5:17** [r]1Jn 3:4 [s]ver 16; 1Jn 2:1 **5:18** [t]S Jn 1:13 [u]S Mt 5:37 [v]Jn 14:30 **5:19** [w]1Jn 4:6 [x]Jn 12:31; 14:30; 17:15 **5:20** [y]ver 5 [z]Lk 24:45 [a]Jn 17:3 [b]ver 11; S Mt 25:46 **5:21** [c]S 1Jn 2:1 [d]1Co 10:14; 1Th 1:9

ing this letter: to provide God's people with the Biblical standard for assurance of salvation. For a discussion of this, see article on ASSURANCE OF SALVATION, p. 552.

5:14 ASK ANYTHING ACCORDING TO HIS WILL. In our prayers we must submit to God and pray that his will may be done in our lives (Jn 14:13). We know God's will in many instances because it is revealed in Scripture. At other times it becomes clear only as we earnestly seek his will. Once we know his will about any given issue, then we can ask in confidence and faith. When we do this, we know that he hears us and that his purposes for us will be accomplished (see 3:22, note).

5:16 HE SHOULD PRAY AND GOD WILL GIVE HIM LIFE. John refers to a type of prayer according to God's will that we can have confidence that he will answer (cf. vv. 14–15), i.e., prayer for spiritually weak believers who need the prayers of God's people to minister life and grace to them. The conditions guiding such a prayer are the following: (1) The person needing prayer must be a brother or sister, i.e., a believer who has committed sin unintentionally or inadvertently, and whose sin did not involve a deliberate rebellion against God's will (see next note). Thus, they have not committed sin to the point of spiritual death (cf. Ro 8:13); they still have spiritual life, but are weak spiritually. They are repentant and desire to be free from all that displeases God, yet need help in conquering the power of Satan and sin.

(2) For such people the church must pray that God will give them "life." "Life" here means a restoration of spiritual strength and God's grace (see article on FAITH AND GRACE, p. 302), which is being threatened by the sin (cf. Ro 8:6; 2Co 3:6; 1Pe 3:7). God promises to answer that prayer.

(3) For former believers who have committed a sin "that leads to death" (i.e., spiritual death), the church cannot pray with assurance that God will give more grace and life. This type of sin involves willful transgression that comes from a deliberate refusal to obey him (see article on THE ACTS OF THE SINFUL NATURE AND THE FRUIT OF THE SPIRIT, p. 394). Such persons, having died spiritually, can only be given life if they repent and turn to God (see Ro 8:13, note). We must pray that God will so direct the circumstances of their lives that they may have an adequate opportunity to accept once more God's salvation in Christ.

5:17 SIN THAT DOES NOT LEAD TO DEATH. John distinguishes between two types of sins: (1) Less serious sins that occur unconsciously or inadvertently and do not immediately lead to spiritual death; and (2) sins so terrible that they indicate a purposeful rebellion against God and his Word, resulting from or leading to spiritual death and separation from the life of God (see 3:15, note; see Ro 8:13; Gal 5:4, note; cf. Nu 15:31).

5:19 WHOLE WORLD IS UNDER THE CONTROL. We will never adequately understand the NT unless we recognize its underlying conviction that Satan is the god of this world. He is the evil one and his power controls the present evil age (cf. Lk 13:16; 2Co 4:4; Gal 1:4; Eph 6:12; Heb 2:14; see Mt 4:10, note; see article on THE KINGDOM OF GOD, p. 28).

(1) Scripture does not teach that God is now in direct control of the ungodly world that involves sinful people, evil, cruelty, injustice, etc. In no way does God desire or cause all the suffering in the world, nor is everything that happens his perfect will (see Mt 23:37; Lk 13:34; 19:41–44). The Bible indicates that at this present time the world is not under God's dominion, but is in rebellion against his rule and is enslaved to Satan. Because of this condition Christ came to die (Jn 3:16) and to reconcile the world to God (2Co 5:18–19). We should never use the statement "God is in control" in order to free ourselves from the responsibility of battling sin, evil or spiritual lukewarmness.

(2) However, there is a sense in which God *is* in control of the ungodly world. God is sovereign, and thus all things happen under his permissive will and oversight, or at times through his direct involvement according to his purpose. Nevertheless, at this time in history God has limited his supreme power and rule over the world. Yet this self-limitation is only temporary, for at the time determined by his wisdom he will destroy Satan and all evil (Rev 19–20). Only then will "the kingdom of the world . . . become the kingdom of our Lord and of his Christ, and he will reign for ever and ever" (Rev 11:15).

ASSURANCE OF SALVATION

***1Jn 5:13** "I write these things to you who believe in the name of the Son of God so that you may know that you have eternal life."*

Every Christian desires to have assurance of salvation, i.e., the certainty that when Christ returns or when death comes, he or she will go to be with the Lord Jesus in heaven (Php 1:23). John's purpose in writing his first letter is that God's people may have that assurance (1Jn 5:13). Note that nowhere in the letter does John state that a past experience of conversion constitutes an assurance or guarantee of salvation. To assume we possess eternal life based solely on a past experience or on a faith that is no longer vital is a grave error. This letter sets out nine ways for us to know that we are in a saving relationship with Jesus Christ.

(1) We have assurance of eternal life if we believe "in the name of the Son of God" (1Jn 5:13; cf. 4:15; 5:1,5). There is no eternal life or assurance of salvation without an earnest faith in Jesus Christ that confesses him as God's Son, sent to be our Lord and Savior (see article on FAITH AND GRACE, p. 302).

(2) We have assurance of eternal life if we are honoring Christ as Lord of our lives and are sincerely trying to obey his commands. "We know that we have come to know him if we obey his commands. The man who says, 'I know him,' but does not do what he commands is a liar, and the truth is not in him. But if anyone obeys his word, God's love is truly made complete in him. This is how we know we are in him" (1Jn 2:3–5; cf. 3:24; 5:2; Jn 8:31,51; 14:21–24; 15:9–14; Heb 5:9).

(3) We have assurance of eternal life if we love the Father and the Son rather than the world, and if we overcome the influence of the world. "Do not love the world or anything in the world. If anyone loves the world, the love of the Father is not in him. For everything in the world—the cravings of sinful man, the lust of his eyes and the boasting of what he has and does—comes not from the Father but from the world" (1Jn 2:15–16; cf. 4:4–6; 5:4; see article on THE CHRISTIAN'S RELATIONSHIP TO THE WORLD, p. 546).

(4) We have assurance of eternal life if we habitually and persistently practice righteousness rather than sin. "If you know that he is righteous, you know that everyone who does what is right has been born of him" (1Jn 2:29). On the other hand, "He who does what is sinful is of the devil" (3:7–10; see 3:9, note).

(5) We have assurance of eternal life if we love our brothers and sisters. "We know that we have passed from death to life, because we love our brothers . . . . This then is how we know that we belong to the truth, and how we set our hearts at rest in his presence" (1Jn 3:14,19; cf. 2:9–11; 3:23; 4:8,11–12,16,20; 5:1; Jn 13:34–35).

(6) We have assurance of eternal life if we are conscious of the Holy Spirit dwelling within us. "And this is how we know that he [Jesus Christ] lives in us: We know it by the Spirit he gave us" (1Jn 3:24). Again, "We know that we live in him and he is us, because he has given us of his Spirit" (4:13).

(7) We have assurance of eternal life if we are striving to follow Jesus' example and live as he lived. "Whoever claims to live in him must walk as Jesus did" (1Jn 2:6; cf. Jn 8:12; 13:15).

(8) We have assurance of eternal life if we believe, accept and remain in the "Word of life," i.e., the living Christ (1Jn 1:1), and in the original message of Christ and the NT apostles. "See that what you have heard from the beginning remains in you. If it does, you also will remain in the Son and in the Father" (2:24; cf. 1:1–5; 4:6).

(9) We have assurance of eternal life if we have an earnest longing and an unbending hope for Christ's return to receive us to himself. "Dear friends, now we are children of God, and what we will be has not yet been made known. But we know that when he appears, we shall be like him, for we shall see him as he is. Everyone who has this hope in him purifies himself, just as he is pure" (1Jn 3:2–3; cf. Jn 14:1–3).

2 JOHN

Outline

Christian Greetings (1–3)
  A. To the Chosen Lady and Her Children (1)
  B. On Behalf of the Truth (2–3)
I. Commendation and Commandment (4–6)
  A. Past Loyalty to Truth Commended (4)
  B. Love and Obedience Commanded (5–6)
II. Counsel and Warning (7–11)
  A. Recognize False Teachers (7)
  B. Beware of Being Influenced by Them (8–9)
  C. Refuse Them the Use of Your Home (10–11)
Conclusion (12–13)

Author: John

Theme: Walking in Truth

Date: A.D. 85–95

Background

The author identifies himself as "the elder" (v. 1). This was probably a title of honor widely ascribed to the apostle John during the last two decades of the first century because of his advanced age and his venerated position of authority as the only surviving original apostle.

John addresses this letter to "the chosen lady and her children" (v. 1). Some interpret "the chosen lady" figuratively as a local church, "her children" as the members, and her "chosen sister" (v. 13) as a sister congregation. Others interpret the addressee literally as a prominent Christian widow of John's acquaintance in one of the nearby church communities in Asia Minor over which he had spiritual authority. Her family (v. 1) and her sister's children (v. 13) are persons of prominence among the churches in that region. As with John's other letters, 2 John was probably written from Ephesus in the late 80s or early 90s.

Purpose

John wrote this letter to caution "the chosen lady" about extending hospitality, greetings or support to traveling ministers (teachers, evangelists and prophets) who departed from the apostolic truth and propagated false teaching, lest she help spread their error and thereby share their guilt. It repudiates the same false teaching that is denounced in 1 John.

Survey

This letter underscores a warning also found in 1 John about the danger of false teachers who deny the incarnation of Jesus Christ and depart from the apostolic message (vv. 7–8). John commends "the chosen lady" and her children for "walking in the truth" (v. 4). True love involves obeying Christ's commands and loving each other (v. 6). Christian love must discern between truth and error and not provide an open door to false teachers (vv. 7–9). To cordially receive false teachers is to participate in their error (vv. 10–11). The letter is brief because John plans soon to visit the lady "face to face" (v. 12).

Special Features

Three major features characterize this letter. (1) It is the shortest book in the NT. (2) It is strikingly similar to 1 and 3 John in its message, vocabulary and simple writing style. (3) It provides an important balance to the message of 3 John by advising caution concerning the indiscriminate support of ministers not belonging to one's own congregation. It urges careful discernment in the light of the teachings of Christ and the apostles before supporting such ministers.

Reading 2 John

In order to read the entire New Testament in one year, the book of 2 John should be read in 1 day: □ 2 John

NOTES

1 The elder,[a]

To the chosen[b] lady and her children,
whom I love in the truth[c]—and not I only,
but also all who know the truth[d]— 2 because of the truth,[e] which lives in us[f] and
will be with us forever:

3 Grace, mercy and peace from God the
Father and from Jesus Christ,[g] the Father's Son, will be with us in truth and
love.

4 It has given me great joy to find some
of your children walking in the truth,[h]
just as the Father commanded us. 5 And
now, dear lady, I am not writing you a new
command but one we have had from the
beginning.[i] I ask that we love one another. 6 And this is love:[j] that we walk in
obedience to his commands.[k] As you have
heard from the beginning,[l] his command
is that you walk in love.

7 Many deceivers, who do not acknowledge Jesus Christ[m] as coming in the
flesh,[n] have gone out into the world.[o]
Any such person is the deceiver and the
antichrist.[p] 8 Watch out that you do not
lose what you have worked for, but that
you may be rewarded fully.[q] 9 Anyone who
runs ahead and does not continue in the
teaching of Christ[r] does not have God;
whoever continues in the teaching has
both the Father and the Son.[s] 10 If anyone
comes to you and does not bring this
teaching, do not take him into your house
or welcome him.[t] 11 Anyone who welcomes him shares[u] in his wicked work.

12 I have much to write to you, but I do
not want to use paper and ink. Instead, I
hope to visit you and talk with you face to
face,[v] so that our joy may be complete.[w]

13 The children of your chosen[x] sister
send their greetings.

1:1 [a]S Ac 11:30; 3Jn 1 [b]ver 13; Ro 16:13; 1Pe 5:13 [c]ver 3 [d]Jn 8:32; 1Ti 2:4 **1:2** [e]2Pe 1:12 [f]Jn 14:17; 1Jn 1:8 **1:3** [g]S Ro 1:7 **1:4** [h]3Jn 3,4 **1:5** [i]S 1Jn 2:7 **1:6** [j]1Jn 2:5 [k]S Jn 14:15 [l]S 1Jn 2:7 **1:7** [m]1Jn 2:22; 4:2,3 [n]S Jn 1:14 [o]1Jn 4:1 [p]S 1Jn 2:18 **1:8** [q]S Mt 10:42; Mk 10:29,30; 1Co 3:8; Heb 10:35,36; 11:26 **1:9** [r]Jn 8:31 [s]S 1Jn 2:23 **1:10** [t]S Ro 16:17 **1:11** [u]1Ti 5:22 **1:12** [v]3Jn 13,14 [w]S Jn 3:29 **1:13** [x]ver 1

1 CHOSEN LADY. Some take this to mean John's letter was addressed to a godly woman named *Kyria* (Greek, meaning "lady") and her family. However, the term "chosen lady and her children" is most likely a figurative way of saying "the church and its members" (cf. 1Pe 5:13).

1 I LOVE IN THE TRUTH. John loves and cares for others in a way consistent with NT revelation about Christ. It is possible to love others, yet not be committed to the truth of God's Word. Such persons place love, acceptance, friendship and unity above the truth and commands of God (vv. 5–6). On the other hand, it is also possible for a person in the church to promote Biblical truth and defend its doctrines, yet not show love and concern for others. What God requires is that we demonstrate both love for his truth and love for others. We must speak the truth in love (Eph 4:15; cf. 1Co 13:6).

3 GRACE, MERCY AND PEACE. The conditions for receiving God's grace, mercy and peace are to guard the truth (vv. 7–11) and to love others (vv. 5–6). To fail to do either will cause the church to lose God's blessings.

5 LOVE ONE ANOTHER. See Jn 13:34–35, notes.

6 HIS COMMANDS. See Jn 14:21, note.

7 MANY DECEIVERS. John warns that many deceivers and false teachers are perverting God's Word and attempting to persuade Christians to accept their views. Their false teaching concerns the person of Jesus Christ. They deny that Jesus Christ was the eternal Son of God, born of the virgin (Mt 1:18; Lk 1:27), whose blood provides forgiveness for the sins of all who believe (1Jn 2:2; 4:9–10) and who is "the true God and eternal life" (1Jn 5:20).

9 DOES NOT CONTINUE IN THE TEACHING OF CHRIST. Those who reject the original revelation of Christ and the apostles do not have God. Although they may claim to know God (1Jn 2:4), they are deceived if they do not continue in the teaching of Christ; those who forsake Christ's doctrine forsake Christ. All theology that does not hold to the truth and righteousness revealed in the NT is not Christian theology and must be rejected (see Eph 2:20, note).

10 DO NOT . . . WELCOME HIM. The believer's love for and faithfulness to Christ and the Word of God must lead him or her to reject and count as an enemy of Christ's gospel any professed believer (minister or layperson) who is not committed to the "teaching of Christ" and the apostles (v. 9). Those who distort and oppose the NT faith must not be received into the fellowship of believers. (1) God warns true believers to guard against accepting false teaching (v. 8). They must be aware that "many deceivers . . . have gone out into the world" (v. 7).

(2) Believers must consider all supposed Christian teachers who do not continue in the teaching of Christ as teachers who do not have God (v. 9) and who are condemned by God (see Gal 1:9, note).

(3) God commands believers not to give encouragement or financial support to, or to remain under, the ministry of such teachers. To do so is to join them in opposing God and his Word and to come under the same condemnation as the compromising teachers (v. 11).

(4) These authoritative words of John, inspired by the Holy Spirit, are an offense to many in the church today. They feel John's admonition lacks a loving attitude or a spirit of unity. However, John's instruction will seem wrong only to those who have little concern for Christ's glory, for the authority of God's Word and for people whose eternal souls are destroyed by throwing aside God's truth.

3 JOHN

Outline

Christian Greetings (1)
- I. Commendation of Gaius (2–8)
  - A. For His Spiritual Health (2)
  - B. For His Walking in the Truth (3–4)
  - C. For His Hospitality to Traveling Brothers (5–8)
- II. Counsel to Gaius (9–12)
  - A. Concerning the Bad Example of Diotrephes (9–11)
  - B. Concerning the Good Example of Demetrius (12)

Conclusion (13–14)

Author: John

Theme: Acting Faithfully

Date: A.D. 85–95

Background

John, the beloved apostle, again identifies himself by the title of "the elder" (v. 1; see Introduction to 2 John). This personal letter is addressed to a loyal believer named Gaius (v. 1), probably in one of the church communities in Asia Minor. As with John's other letters, 3 John was most likely written from Ephesus in the late 80s or early 90s.

Toward the end of the first century, itinerant ministers who traveled from city to city were commonly supported by believers who received them into their homes and helped them on their way (vv. 5–8; cf. 2Jn 10). Gaius was one of many faithful Christians who graciously hosted and supported trustworthy traveling ministers (vv. 1–8). However, a leader named Diotrephes arrogantly resisted John's authority and refused to receive traveling brothers whom John had sent.

Purpose

John wrote to commend Gaius for his faithful hospitality and support of trustworthy traveling ministers, to indirectly warn the rebellious leader Diotrephes and to prepare the way for his own personal visit.

Survey

Three men are mentioned by name in 3 John. (1) Gaius is warmly commended for his godly walk in the truth (vv. 3–4) and his exemplary hospitality to traveling brothers (vv. 5–8). (2) Diotrephes, a dictatorial leader, is denounced for his pride ("loves to be first," v. 9) and its manifestations: rejecting a previous letter from John (v. 9), slandering John, refusing to receive John's messengers and threatening to excommunicate those who do (v. 10). (3) Demetrius, perhaps the bearer of this letter or a pastor in a nearby community, is commended as a man of good reputation and loyalty to the truth (v. 12).

Special Features

Two major features characterize this letter. (1) Though brief, it provides insight into several important facets of early church history toward the end of the first century. (2) There are remarkable similarities between 3 and 2 John. Nevertheless, the two letters differ in one important aspect: 3 John commends hospitality and support for trustworthy traveling ministers, while 2 John urges that hospitality and support not be given to untrustworthy ministers, so that believers might not be found promoting error or evil deeds.

Reading 3 John

In order to read the entire New Testament in one year, the book of 3 John should be read in 1 day: □ 3 John

NOTES

1The elder,[a]

To my dear friend Gaius, whom I love
in the truth.

2Dear friend, I pray that you may enjoy
good health and that all may go well with
you, even as your soul is getting along
well. **3**It gave me great joy to have some
brothers[b] come and tell about your faithfulness to the truth and how you continue
to walk in the truth.[c] **4**I have no greater
joy than to hear that my children[d] are
walking in the truth.[e]
5Dear friend, you are faithful in what
you are doing for the brothers,[f] even
though they are strangers to you.[g] **6**They
have told the church about your love. You
will do well to send them on their way[h] in
a manner worthy[i] of God. **7**It was for the
sake of the Name[j] that they went out,
receiving no help from the pagans.[k] **8**We
ought therefore to show hospitality to
such men so that we may work together
for the truth.
9I wrote to the church, but Diotrephes,
who loves to be first, will have nothing to
do with us. **10**So if I come,[l] I will call
attention to what he is doing, gossiping
maliciously about us. Not satisfied with
that, he refuses to welcome the brothers.[m]

1:1 [a]S Ac 11:30; 2Jn 1 **1:3** [b]ver 5,10; S Ac 1:16 [c]2Jn 4 **1:4** [d]S 1Jn 2:1 [e]ver 3 **1:5** [f]S ver 3 [g]Ro 12:13; Heb 13:2 **1:6** [h]1Co 16:11; 2Co 1:16 [i]S Eph 4:1 **1:7** [j]S Jn 15:21 [k]Ac 20:33,35 **1:10** [l]ver 14; 2Jn 12 [m]ver 5

2 ALL MAY GO WELL. It is normally God's will that believers be healthy and that our lives be accompanied by his blessings. He wants all to go well with us, i.e., that our work, plans, purposes, ministry, families, etc., go according to God's will and direction. Thus, God's blessings through redemption in Christ are intended to meet both physical and spiritual needs.

Concerning prosperity, both physical and spiritual, Scripture teaches the following: (1) The word here translated "all may go well" (Gk *euodoō*) literally means "to have a good journey, to be led along a good road." According to that meaning, John's primary prayer was that as believers walk the road of salvation, they may continue in God's will and his truth and enjoy his blessing (cf. vv. 3–4).

(2) It is God's will that we earn enough to provide shelter, food and clothing for ourselves and our families, and have enough to help others and to further Christ's cause (Php 4:15–19). We know that God is able to give us enough for our needs (2Co 9:8–12) and that he promises to supply us "according to his glorious riches in Christ Jesus" (Php 4:19).

(3) Although we may pray that God will supply all our needs materially, we must recognize the Bible's teaching that God may allow his children to experience times of need. (a) We may be in want or experience need in order to be encouraged to trust him more and to develop our faith, spiritual endurance and ministry (Ro 8:35–39; 2Co 4:7–12; 6:4–10; 12:7–10; 1Pe 1:6–7). (b) We may undergo severe distress when our testimony about and service to Christ (Lk 6:20–23; Heb 10:32–34; 1Pe 2:19–21; Rev 2:9–10) bring persecution and oppression from the world. (c) We may experience poverty due to national or natural circumstances, such as war, famine, drought, or poor economic or social conditions (Ac 11:28–30; 2Co 8:2, 12–14).

(4) God's presence, help and blessing in our physical lives is related to the prosperity of our spiritual lives. We must seek God's will (Mt 6:10; 26:39; Heb 10:7–9), obey the Holy Spirit (Ro 8:14), remain separated from the world (Ro 12:1–2; 2Co 6:16–18), love God's Word (Jas 1:21; 1Pe 2:2), seek his help in prayer (Mt 6:11; Heb 4:16), work hard (2Th 3:6–12), trust him to supply our needs (Mt 6:25–34; 1Pe 5:7), and live by the principle of seeking first the kingdom of God and his righteousness (Mt 6:33; see Mt 6:11, note; Lk 11:3, note; Col 4:12, note; see article on DIVINE HEALING, p. 20).

(5) Although our souls may be getting along well, we will not automatically be exempt from difficulties in other areas of our lives. Adversity, troubles and needs must be faced by prayer and trust in God.

5 YOU ARE FAITHFUL. John praises Gaius for one particular aspect of his walking in the truth (vv. 3–4), namely, that he has been faithful in helping traveling missionaries (vv. 5–8). He has supplied them with lodging, food, money and whatever other help they needed for their journey (cf. Tit 3:13). His commitment to Christ's missionary cause was so impressive that missionaries had specifically mentioned it to John (v. 6). Gaius's action toward these preachers of the gospel came from his love for them, for the gospel and for those without Christ.

7 FOR THE SAKE OF THE NAME. Vv. 5–8 refer to traveling messengers of the gospel of Christ. It is a duty and privilege of God's people to contribute to missionary needs and work. (1) Receiving, sending and supporting missionaries must be done in a manner worthy of God (v. 6; 1Co 9:14; Php 4:10–18). They must not be treated like beggars, but must be received as the Lord (Mt 10:40) and as his servants carrying the gospel to all the world (see Mt 28:19, note).

(2) The sending of missionaries in the early church consisted of providing for their journey and supplying them with food and with money to pay expenses and live adequately (see Gal 6:6–10, note; Php 4:16, note; Tit 3:13). By supporting missionaries God's people worked together in spreading the truth (v. 8).

7 RECEIVING NO HELP FROM THE PAGANS. Missionaries who leave their homes and go to other places to proclaim the name of the Lord Jesus Christ should refuse help from the unbelievers they are trying to win to Christ. To accept help from an unbeliever might hinder the gospel and expose the missionary to charges of preaching for financial gain (cf. 1Co 9:12). Therefore, missionaries should receive help from individual believers and from the church (Lk 10:7; 1Co 9:14; 1Ti 5:18). In contributing to the missionary work of our church, we must remember the words of Christ, "Anyone who receives a prophet because he is a prophet will receive a prophet's reward, and anyone who receives a righteous man because he is a righteous man will receive a righteous man's reward" (Mt 10:41, note).

He also stops those who want to do so and
puts them out of the church.[n]

11Dear friend, do not imitate what is
evil but what is good.[o] Anyone who does
what is good is from God.[p] Anyone who
does what is evil has not seen God.[q] **12**Demetrius
is well spoken of by everyone[r]—
and even by the truth itself. We also speak
well of him, and you know that our testimony
is true.[s]

13I have much to write you, but I do not
want to do so with pen and ink. **14**I hope
to see you soon, and we will talk face to
face.[t]

Peace to you.[u] The friends here send
their greetings. Greet the friends there by
name.[v]

1:10 [n] Jn 9:22 **1:11** [o] Ps 34:14; 37:27 [p] 1Jn 2:29 [q] 1Jn 3:6,9,10 **1:12** [r] 1Ti 3:7 [s] Jn 19:35; 21:24 **1:14** [t] 2Jn 12 [u] S Ro 1:7; S Eph 6:23 [v] Jn 10:3

JUDE

Outline

Christian Greetings (1–2)

I. An Explanation for Writing the Letter (3–4)
II. Exposing the False Teachers (5–16)
  A. Their Doom Illustrated From the Past (5–7)
    1. The Experience of Israel (5)
    2. The Experience of Unbelieving Rebellious Angels (6)
    3. The Experience of Sodom and Gomorrah (7)
  B. Their Description in the Present (8–16)
    1. Abusive Speech (8–10)
    2. Unholy Character (11)
    3. Guilty Conduct (12–16)
III. Exhorting the True Believers (17–23)
  A. Remember the Predictions of the Apostles (17–19)
  B. Keep Yourselves in God's Love (20–21)
  C. Help Others in Mercy, Mixed With Fear (22–23)

Doxology (24–25)

Author: Jude

Theme: Contending for the Faith

Date: A.D. 70–80

Background

Jude identifies himself simply as the "brother of James" (v. 1). The only brothers in the NT by the names of Jude (Judas) and James are the half-brothers of Jesus (Mt 13:55; Mk 6:3). Perhaps Jude mentioned James because his brother's prominence as leader of the Jerusalem church would serve to clarify his own identity and authority.

This brief but hard-hitting letter was written against false teachers who were blatantly antinomian (i.e., they taught that salvation by grace allowed them to sin without condemnation) and who were contemptuously denying the original apostolic revelation about the person and nature of Jesus Christ (v. 4). Thus they were dividing the churches on what to believe (vv. 19a,22) and how to behave (vv. 4,8,16). Jude describes these unprincipled men as "ungodly" (v. 15) and as those who "do not have the Spirit" (v. 19).

The probable relationship between Jude and 2Pe 2:1—3:4 has a bearing on when Jude was written. Most likely Jude was familiar with 2 Peter (vv. 17–18) and therefore wrote after Peter, i.e., sometime between A.D. 70–80. The recipients are not identified specifically, but may have been the same as those addressed in 2 Peter (see Introduction to 2 Peter).

Purpose

Jude wrote this letter (1) to urgently warn believers about the serious threat of false teachers and their subversive influence within the churches, and (2) to forcefully challenge all true believers to rise up and "contend for the faith that was once for all entrusted to the saints" (v. 3).

Survey

After his greetings (vv. 1–2), Jude reveals that his original intention was to write about the nature of salvation (v. 3a). However, he was constrained instead to write this letter because of the apostate teachers who were perverting God's grace and in so doing were undermining truth and righteousness in the churches (v. 4). Jude indicts them as sexually impure (vv. 4,8,16,18), compromising like Cain (v. 11), greedy like Balaam (v. 11), rebellious like Korah (v. 11), arrogant (vv. 8,16), deceptive (vv. 4a,12), sensual (v. 19) and divisive (v. 19). He declares the certainty of God's judgment on all who commit such sins and illustrates the same by six OT examples (vv. 5–11). A twelvefold description of their lives reveals their ripeness for God's wrath (vv. 12–16). Believers are exhorted to guard themselves and to have compassion mixed with fear for those who are wavering (vv. 20–23). Jude concludes with a crescendo of inspiration in his benediction (vv. 24–25).

Special Features

Four major features characterize this letter. (1) It contains the NT's most direct and vigorous denunciation of false teachers. It underscores for all generations the seriousness of the threat that false teaching always poses to genuine faith and holy living. (2) It demonstrates a fondness for illustrating in series of threes—e.g., three OT examples of judgment (vv. 5–7), a threefold description of the false teachers (v. 8) and three OT examples of unholy men (v. 11). (3) Under the full influence of the Holy Spirit, Jude freely refers to written sources: (a) OT Scriptures (vv. 5–7,11), (b) Jewish traditions (vv. 9,14–15) and (c) 2 Peter, quoting directly from 3:3, which he acknowledges as being from the apostles (vv. 17–18). (4) It contains the most majestic NT benediction.

Reading Jude

In order to read the entire New Testament in one year, the book of Jude should be read in 1 day:
☐ Jude

NOTES

1Jude,[a] a servant of Jesus Christ[b] and
a brother of James,

To those who have been called,[c] who
are loved by God the Father and kept by[a]
Jesus Christ:[d]

2Mercy, peace[e] and love be yours in
abundance.[f]

Contend for the Faith

3Dear friends,[g] although I was very eager to write to you about the salvation we
share,[h] I felt I had to write and urge you
to contend[i] for the faith[j] that was once
for all entrusted to the saints.[k] **4**For certain men whose condemnation was writ-
ten about[b] long ago have secretly slipped
in among you.[l] They are godless men,
who change the grace of our God into a
license for immorality and deny Jesus
Christ our only Sovereign and Lord.[m]

The Doom of False Teachers

5Though you already know all this,[n] I
want to remind you[o] that the Lord[c] delivered his people out of Egypt, but later destroyed those who did not believe.[p] **6**And
the angels who did not keep their positions of authority but abandoned their
own home—these he has kept in darkness, bound with everlasting chains for
judgment on the great Day.[q] **7**In a similar
way, Sodom and Gomorrah[r] and the surrounding towns[s] gave themselves up to
sexual immorality and perversion. They
serve as an example of those who suffer
the punishment of eternal fire.[t]

8In the very same way, these dreamers
pollute their own bodies, reject authority
and slander celestial beings.[u] **9**But even
the archangel[v] Michael,[w] when he was
disputing with the devil about the body of
Moses,[x] did not dare to bring a slanderous accusation against him, but said, "The
Lord rebuke you!"[y] **10**Yet these men
speak abusively against whatever they do
not understand; and what things they do
understand by instinct, like unreasoning
animals—these are the very things that
destroy them.[z]

11Woe to them! They have taken the
way of Cain;[a] they have rushed for profit
into Balaam's error;[b] they have been destroyed in Korah's rebellion.[c]

12These men are blemishes at your love

1:1 [a]Mt 13:55; Jn 14:22; Ac 1:13 [b]Ro 1:1 [c]Ro 1:6,7 [d]Jn 17:12
1:2 [e]Gal 6:16; 1Ti 1:2 [f]S Ro 1:7
1:3 [g]S 1Co 10:14 [h]Tit 1:4 [i]1Ti 6:12 [j]ver 20; Ac 6:7 [k]S Ac 9:13
1:4 [l]Gal 2:4 [m]Tit 1:16; 2Pe 2:1; 1Jn 2:22
1:5 [n]S 1Jn 2:20 [o]2Pe 1:12,13; 3:1, 2 [p]Nu 14:29; Dt 1:32; 2:15; Ps 106:26; 1Co 10:1-5; Heb 3:16,17
1:6 [q]S 2Pe 2:4,9
1:7 [r]S Mt 10:15 [s]Dt 29:23 [t]S Mt 25:41; 2Pe 3:7
1:8 [u]2Pe 2:10
1:9 [v]1Th 4:16 [w]Da 10:13,21; 12:1; Rev 12:7 [x]Dt 34:6 [y]Zec 3:2
1:10 [z]2Pe 2:12
1:11 [a]Ge 4:3-8; Heb 11:4; 1Jn 3:12 [b]S 2Pe 2:15 [c]Nu 16:1-3,31-35

a *1* Or *for*; or *in* **b** *4* Or *men who were marked out for condemnation* **c** *5* Some early manuscripts *Jesus*

2 MERCY . . . IN ABUNDANCE. The word "be . . . in abundance" (Gk *plēthunō*) literally means "be multiplied." As we draw near to God, his mercy, peace and love can be doubled, tripled or even quadrupled to us.

3 THE FAITH . . . ENTRUSTED TO THE SAINTS. Those faithful to Christ are placed under the solemn obligation to "contend for the faith" that God delivered to the apostles and saints (Php 1:27; cf. 1Ti 1:18; 6:12). (1) "The faith" consists of the gospel proclaimed by Christ and the apostles. It is the fixed and unalterable truth, given by the Holy Spirit and embodied in the NT. However, "the faith" is more than objective truth. It is also a way of life to be lived in love and purity (Col 1:9–11; 1Ti 1:5). It is a kingdom that comes in power to baptize all believers in the Holy Spirit (see articles on THE KINGDOM OF GOD, p. 28, and BAPTISM IN THE HOLY SPIRIT, p. 228), that they may proclaim the gospel to all nations (Mk 16:15–17; see 1Th 1:5, note) with signs and miracles and gifts of the Spirit (see Ac 2:22; 14:3; Ro 15:19; Heb 2:4, note; see article on SIGNS OF BELIEVERS, p. 106).

(2) The word "contend" (Gk *epagonizomai*) describes the battle that the faithful believer must fight in the defense of the faith. It means literally to "struggle," "suffer," "be under great stress" or "fight a fight." We must exert ourselves to the utmost in the defense of God's Word and the NT faith, even though it may be costly and agonizing. We must deny ourselves and, if need be, accept martyrdom for the sake of the gospel (cf. 2Ti 4:7).

(3) Contending for the faith means (a) taking a direct stand against those within the visible church who deny the Bible's authority or distort the ancient faith as presented by Christ and the apostles, and (b) proclaiming it as redemptive truth to all people (see Jn 5:47, note; see article on THE INSPIRATION AND AUTHORITY OF SCRIPTURE, p. 474). Those whose allegiance is to Christ and the full NT faith must never allow its message to be weakened by compromising its authority, distorting its truth, or explaining away its power and promises.

4 GRACE OF OUR GOD INTO A LICENSE FOR IMMORALITY. Jude denounces certain persons who teach that salvation by grace allows professed believers to indulge in serious sin and yet not be condemned by God. They may have taught that God will freely forgive those who continually engage in sexual lust, or that those who presently live in moral filth are eternally secure if they have trusted in Christ at some time in the past (cf. Ro 5:20; 6:1). They preached pardon for sin but not the imperative of holiness.

6 THE ANGELS. Jude refers to angels who did not remain in their initial position of authority, but who rebelled against God, broke his law, and are now in prison awaiting judgment. However, not all fallen angels are locked up, for Satan and many demons are on the earth right now (see 2 Pe 2:4, note).

8 REJECT AUTHORITY. See 2Pe 2:10, note.

9 MICHAEL . . . DISPUTING WITH THE DEVIL. If the greatest archangel Michael refused to slander Satan but relied on God's power, how much more should we as humans refrain from bringing slanderous accusations against all things, including evil spirits (see 2Pe 2:11).

12 TWICE DEAD. The apostate teachers among

feasts,[d] eating with you without the
slightest qualm—shepherds who feed
only themselves.[e] They are clouds without rain,[f] blown along by the wind;[g] autumn trees, without fruit and uprooted[h]
—twice dead. **13**They are wild waves of
the sea,[i] foaming up their shame;[j] wandering stars, for whom blackest darkness
has been reserved forever.[k]
14Enoch,[l] the seventh from Adam,
prophesied about these men: "See, the
Lord is coming[m] with thousands upon
thousands of his holy ones[n] **15**to judge[o]
everyone, and to convict all the ungodly of
all the ungodly acts they have done in the
ungodly way, and of all the harsh words
ungodly sinners have spoken against
him."[p] **16**These men are grumblers[q] and
faultfinders; they follow their own evil desires;[r] they boast[s] about themselves and
flatter others for their own advantage.

A Call to Persevere

17But, dear friends, remember what the
apostles[t] of our Lord Jesus Christ foretold.[u] **18**They said to you, "In the last
times[v] there will be scoffers who will follow their own ungodly desires."[w] **19**These
are the men who divide you, who follow
mere natural instincts and do not have the
Spirit.[x]
20But you, dear friends, build yourselves up[y] in your most holy faith[z] and
pray in the Holy Spirit.[a] **21**Keep yourselves in God's love as you wait[b] for the
mercy of our Lord Jesus Christ to bring
you to eternal life.[c]
22Be merciful to those who doubt;
23snatch others from the fire and save
them;[d] to others show mercy, mixed with
fear—hating even the clothing stained by
corrupted flesh.[e]

Doxology

24To him who is able[f] to keep you from
falling and to present you before his glorious presence[g] without fault[h] and with
great joy— **25**to the only God[i] our Savior
be glory, majesty, power and authority,
through Jesus Christ our Lord, before all
ages, now and forevermore![j] Amen.[k]

1:12 [d] 2Pe 2:13; 1Co 11:20-22 [e] Eze 34:2,8,10 [f] Pr 25:14; 2Pe 2:17 [g] Eph 4:14 [h] Mt 15:13 **1:13** [i] Isa 57:20 [j] Php 3:19 [k] 2Pe 2:17 **1:14** [l] Ge 5:18, 21-24 [m] S Mt 16:27 [n] Dt 33:2; Da 7:10; Zec 14:5; Heb 12:22 **1:15** [o] 2Pe 2:6-9 [p] 1Ti 1:9 **1:16** [q] 1Co 10:10 [r] ver 18; 2Pe 2:10 [s] 2Pe 2:18 **1:17** [t] S Eph 4:11 [u] Heb 2:3; 2Pe 3:2 **1:18** [v] 1Ti 4:1; 2Ti 3:1; 2Pe 3:3

[w] ver 16; 2Pe 2:1; 3:3 **1:19** [x] 1Co 2:14, 15 **1:20** [y] Col 2:7; 1Th 5:11 [z] ver 3 [a] Eph 6:18 **1:21** [b] Tit 2:13; Heb 9:28; 2Pe 3:12 [c] S Mt 25:46 **1:23** [d] Am 4:11; Zec 3:2-5; 1Co 3:15 [e] Rev 3:4

1:24 [f] S Ro 16:25 [g] S 2Co 4:14 [h] Col 1:22 **1:25** [i] Jn 5:44; 1Ti 1:17 [j] Heb 13:8 [k] S Ro 11:36

Jude's readers are "twice dead" (literally, "twice having died"). The false teachers were once believers in Christ who had "crossed over from death to life" (Jn 5:24) but had sometime afterward severed their union with Christ and gone out of life back into death (cf. Eph 2:1; see Ro 8:13, note). The previous verse gives the reason for their spiritual death.

14 ENOCH . . . PROPHESIED. Jude may be quoting from the book of Enoch, written prior to 110 B.C., or simply from Jewish tradition. Jude's use of this passage confirms only the truth of Enoch's prophecy; it does not mean that he endorses the entire book of Enoch.

18 IN THE LAST TIMES. See 1Ti 4:1, note; 2Ti 3:1, note.

20 BUILD YOURSELVES UP. Believers must defend and propagate the faith and resist false teaching in four ways. (1) By building ourselves up in our most holy faith. The holy faith is the NT revelation handed down by Christ and the apostles (v. 3). This requires study of God's Word and a determined effort to know the truth and teachings of Scripture (cf. Ac 2:42; 20:27; 2Ti 2:15; Heb 5:12).

(2) By praying in the Spirit. We must pray by the enabling power of the Holy Spirit, i.e., by looking to the Spirit to inspire, guide, energize, sustain and help us to do battle in our praying (see Ro 8:26, note; cf. Gal 4:6; Eph 6:18). Praying in the Spirit includes both praying with one's mind and praying with one's spirit (see 1Co 14:15, note).

(3) By remaining in the sphere of God's love for us. This involves faithful obedience to God and his Word (Jn 15:9–10).

(4) By longing and waiting for our Lord's return and the eternal glory that will accompany his return (see Jn 14:2, note).

THE LAST DAYS OF HISTORY

Event	Description	References
Last Days of Preparation	Increase of false prophets and religious compromise within the church	Mt 24:4–5,10–11,24; Lk 18:8; 2Th 2:3; 1Ti 4:1; 2Ti 3:1,13; 4:3–4; 2Pe 2:1–3; 3:3–4
	Increase of crime and disregard of God's law	Mt 24:12,37–39; Lk 17:26–30; 18:8; 1Ti 4:1; 2Ti 3:1–8
	Increase of wars, famines and earthquakes	Mt 24:6–8; Mk 13:7–8; Lk 21:9
	Decrease in love and family affection	Mt 10:21; 24:12; Mk 13:12; 2Ti 3:1–3
	More severe persecution of God's people	Mt 10:22–23; 24:9–10; Mk 13:13; Jn 15:19–20; 16:33; Ac 14:22; Ro 5:3
	Those who stand firm will be saved	Mt 24:13; Mk 13:13
	Gospel will be preached to the whole world	Mt 24:14; Mk 13:10
	The Spirit will be poured out on God's people	Ac 2:17–21,38–39

Event	Description	References
The Rapture	Believers must be prepared and wait constantly for this imminent event	Mt 24:42,44; 25:1–13; Mk 13:33–37; Lk 12:35; 21:19,34–36; Ro 13:11; Php 4:5; 1Th 1:10; 4:16–18; 5:6–11; 2Ti 4:8; Tit 2:13
	Christ will come unexpectedly, since the time cannot be calculated	Mt 24:36,42,44; 25:5–7,13; Mk 13:32–37; Lk 12:35–46
	Christ will come to catch up believers living on earth at this time	Lk 21:36; Jn 14:3; 1Th 1:10; 4:15–17; 2Th 2:1; Rev 3:10–11
	Believers will be delivered from the coming wrath	Lk 21:36; 1Th 1:10; 5:2–9; Rev 3:10–11
	Believers living at this time will receive transformed bodies	Ro 8:23; 1Co 15:51–54; 1Th 4:16–17
	Believers who died before this event will rise and be caught up with Christ	1Co 15:50–55; 1Th 4:16–17
	All raptured saints will be judged by Christ	Jn 5:22; Ro 14:12; 1Co 3:12–15; 2Co 5:10; 2Ti 4:8
	Believers will be judged according to their deeds	Ecc 12:14; Mt 5:22; 12:36–37; Mk 4:22; Ro 2:5–11,16; 1Co 4:5; 2Co 5:10; Eph 6:8; Col 3:23–25
	Faithful believers will receive rewards	Mt 5:11–12; 25:14–23; Lk 19:12–19; 22:28–30; Gal 6:8–10; 1Co 3:12–14; 9:25–27; 13:3; Eph 6:8; 2Ti 4:8; Heb 6:10; 1Pe 5:4; Rev 2:7,11,17,26–28; 3:4–5,12,21
	Less faithful believers will not be condemned, but will receive little or no reward	Ecc 12:14; Mt 5:19; 1Co 2:13–15; 2Co 5:10; Col 3:25; 1Jn 2:28

Event	Description	References
The Tribulation	The faithful in Christ's churches will be kept from this time of trial	Lk 21:36; Jn 14:1–3; 2Co 5:2,4; Php 3:20–21; 1Th 1:10; 4:16–18; 5:8–10; Rev 3:10
	Will begin after the restrainer is taken out of the way	2Th 2:6–8
	Will begin after the secret power of lawlessness intensifies	2Th 2:7–8
	Will begin after a great rebellion against the faith occurs	2Th 2:3
	The antichrist (the man of lawlessness) will appear	Da 9:26–27; 2Th 2:3–10; Rev 13:1–18; 16:2; 17:9–18; 19:19–20
	Will begin with the opening of the seven seals	Rev 6:1
	A time of worldwide distress	Mt 24:21–22; Rev 6—19
	Will last for seven years	Da 9:27
	False prophets will perform great signs and wonders	Mt 24:24; 2Th 2:8–10; Rev 13:13; 16:14; 19:20
	The gospel will be preached by angels and possibly Jews	Rev 7:1–4; 11:3–6; 14:6–7
	People will be saved during these days	Dt 4:30–31; Rev 7:9–17; 14:6–7; 11:13
	Many Jews will turn to Christ	Ro 11:25–26; Rev 7:1–8
	Those who had opportunity to believe in Jesus before the rapture will have no further opportunity to repent	Mt 25:1–12; Lk 12:45–46; 2Th 2:10–12
	Will be a time of persecution for all who are faithful to Jesus	Da 12:10; Mt 24:15–21; Rev 6:9–11; 7:9–17; 9:3–5; 12:12,17; 13:7,15–17; 14:6,13; 17:6; 18:24; 20:4

Event	Description	References
The Great Tribulation	Last three and one-half years of "The Tribulation"	Da 9:27; Rev 11:1–2; 12:6; 13:5–7
	Will begin with the abomination that causes desolation standing in the holy place (the temple)	Da 9:27; 12:11; Mt 24:15; Mk 13:14; 2Th 2:4; Rev 13:14–15
	Demonic activity will increase greatly	Rev 9:3–11,14–19; 16:12–14
	Sorcery and witchcraft will increase greatly	1Ti 4:1; Rev 9:21; 18:23; 22:15
	Cosmic events related to sun, moon and stars will occur	Isa 13:9–11; Mt 24:29; Mk 13:24–25; Lk 21:25; Rev 6:12–14; 8:10,12; 9:2
	Religious deceit will be widespread	Mt 24:24; Mk 13:6,21–22; 2Th 2:9–11
	Time of terrible suffering for Jews	Jer 30:5–7; Rev 11:2; 12:12–17
	The world's worst and most intense time of worldwide distress	Da 12:1; Mt 24:21; Mk 13:15–19; Rev 6:9–17; 9:1—9:21; 16:1–21
	God will extend his wrath on the ungodly	Isa 13:6–13; Jer 30:4–11; Da 12:1; Zec 14:1–4; Rev 3:10; 6:17; 9:1–6,18–21; 14:9–11; 19:15
	The apostate church will be destroyed	Rev 17:16–17
	Two witnesses who preached the gospel and were killed will be resurrected	Rev 11:11–12
	End of great tribulation can be known by definite signs	Mt 24:15–29,32–33; Mk 13:28–29; Lk 21:28
	Will end with the battle of Armageddon and God's full wrath on the ungodly	Jer 25:29–38; Eze 39:17–20; Joel 3:2,9–17; Zep 3:8; Zec 14:2–5; Rev 14:9–11,14–20; 16:12–21; 19:17–18
	Christ will triumph over the antichrist and his armies	Mt 24:30–31; 2Pe 3:10–13; Rev 19:11–21

Event	Description	References
The Antichrist	Ruler during the tribulation who controls the entire world	Da 7:2–7,24–27; 8:4; 11:36; Rev 13:1–18; 17:11–17
	An incredibly wicked person, a "man of lawlessness" and sin	Da 9:27; 2Th 2:3; Rev 13:12
	Described as a beast	Rev 13:1–18; 17:3,8,16; 19:19–20; 20:10
	Will set up an image of himself in the temple and will demand worship	Da 7:8,25; 11:31,36; Mt 24:15; Mk 13:14; 2Th 2:3–4; Rev 13:4,8,12,14–15; 14:9; 16:2

Event	Description	References
The Antichrist (cont.)	Will exercise miracles through the power of Satan	Mt 24:24; 2Th 2:9–10; Rev 13:3,12–14; 16:14; 17:8
	Will have ability to deceive the nations	1Th 2:9–10; 1Jn 2:18; Rev 20:3
	Will be assisted by the false prophet (the beast of the earth)	Rev 13:11–17; 16:13; 19:20; 20:10
	Will kill the two witnesses who proclaimed the gospel	Rev 11:7–10
	Will attempt to kill all who do not have the mark of the beast	Rev 6:9; 13:15–17; 14:12–13
	Will eventually destroy the religious system with which he was aligned	Rev 17:16–17
	Will be defeated by Christ when Christ returns to earth to establish his kingdom	2Th 2:8; Rev 16:16; 19:15–21

Event	Description	References
Christ's glorious appearing from heaven to judge and to wage war	Christ will return with believers and his angels	2Th 1:7–10; Jude 14–15; Rev 19:14
	Christ will gather the tribulation saints	Mt 24:31; 25:31–40,46; Mk 13:27; Rev 20:4
	Unbelievers will be unprepared for this event	Mt 24:38–39,43
	Christ will separate peoples on earth	Mt 13:40–41,47–50; 25:31–46
	Nations will be enraged at this event	Rev 11:18
	Saints will rejoice at this event	Rev 19:1–8
	Christ will judge and destroy the ungodly, including the antichrist and Satan	Isa 13:6–12; Eze 20:34–38; Mt 13:41–50; 24:30; 25:41–46; Lk 19:11–27; 1Th 5:1–11; 2Th 2:7–10,12; Rev 6:16–17; 11:18; 17:14; 18:1–24; 19:11—20:3
	Tribulation saints will receive rewards	Mt 5:11–12; 1Co 3:12–14; 9:25–27; Gal 6:9–10; 2Ti 4:8; Rev 20:4
	Tribulation saints will share in Christ's glory and kingdom	Mt 25:31–40; Ro 8:29; 2Th 2:13–14; Rev 20:4

Event	Description	References
The Millennium	Satan will be bound	Rev 20:2–3
	Tribulation saints (and possibly OT saints) will rise from the dead	Rev 20:4
	The church and all martyred tribulation saints will reign with Christ	Rev 2:26–27; 3:21; 5:9–10; 11:15–18; 20:4–6
	Christ will reign on earth over the tribulation saints alive at his coming	Isa 9:6–7; Mic 4:1–8; Da 2:44; Zec 14:6–9; Rev 5:10; 11:15–18; 20:4–6
	Time span of reign will be a thousand years	Rev 20:4–7
	God's children will have rest	2Th 1:7
	Nature will be restored to its original order and perfection	Ps 96:11–13; 98:7–9; Isa 14:7–8; 35:1–2,6–7; 51:3; 55:12–13; Eze 34:25; Ro 8:18–23
	Satan will be released for a brief time at the end of the Millennium	Rev 20:7
	Will end with Christ turning over the kingdom to the Father	1Co 15:24

Event	Description	References
The Final Judgment	Final battle of Gog and Magog	Rev 20:7–9
	All the wicked will be raised from the dead to face judgment	Isa 26:19–21; Da 12:2; Jn 5:28–29; Rev 20:12–15
	The great white throne judgment	Rev 20:11–15
	All God's enemies will be put into the lake of fire	2Th 2:9; Rev 20:10,12–15; 21:8

Event	Description	References
The New Heaven and New Earth	God will destroy the present earth	Ps 102:25–26; Isa 34:4; 51:6; Hag 2:6; Heb 12:26–28; 2Pe 3:7,10,12
	God will create a new heaven and a new earth	Isa 51:6; 65:17; 66:22; Ro 8:19–21; 2Pe 3:10–13; Rev 21:1—22:6
	God will wipe away all effects of sin	2Pe 3:13; Rev 21:4; 22:3,15
	New earth will become the headquarters of God	Rev 21:1–3

REVELATION

Outline

The Prologue (1:1–8)

- I. The Exalted Lord and His Churches (1:9—3:22)
  - A. Vision of the Exalted Lord Among the Lampstands (1:9–20)
  - B. His Messages to the Seven Churches (2:1—3:22)
- II. The Worthy Lamb and His Role in the Outcome of History (4:1—11:19)
  - A. Vision of the Majestic Court of Heaven (4:1—5:14)
    - 1. The Creator-God on His Throne in Awesome Holiness (4:1–11)
    - 2. The Sealed Scroll and the Worthy Lamb (5:1–14)
  - B. Vision of the Lamb in Relation to the Seven Seals and Seven Trumpets (6:1—11:19)
    - 1. Opening the First Six Seals (6:1–17)
      FIRST INTERLUDE: The Two Multitudes (7:1–17)
    - 2. Opening the Seventh Seal: Seven Angels with Seven Trumpets (8:1–6)
    - 3. The First Six Trumpets (8:7—9:21)
      SECOND INTERLUDE: The Little Scroll (10:1–11)
      The Two Witnesses (11:1–14)
    - 4. The Seventh Trumpet (11:15–19)
- III. The Lord God and His Christ in the Great Conflict With Satan (12:1—22:5)
  - A. Perspective of the Conflict (12:1—15:8)
    - 1. From the Viewpoint of the Earth's Enemies (12:1—13:18)
      - a. The Dragon (12:1–17)
      - b. The Sea Beast (13:1–10)
      - c. The Earth Beast (13:11–18)
    - 2. From the Viewpoint of Heaven (14:1–20)
      THIRD INTERLUDE: Seven Angels With Seven Plagues (15:1–8)
  - B. Final Progression of the Conflict (16:1—19:10)
    - 1. The Seven Bowls of God's Wrath (16:1–21)
    - 2. Judgment of the Great Prostitute (17:1–18)
    - 3. The Fall of Babylon the Great (18:1–24)
    - 4. Rejoicing in Heaven (19:1–10)
  - C. Climax of the Conflict (19:11—20:10)
    - 1. The Return and Triumph of Christ (19:11–18)
    - 2. The Defeat of the Beast and His Allies (19:19–21)
    - 3. Binding, Releasing and Finally Defeating Satan (20:1–10)
  - D. Aftermath of the Conflict (20:11—22:5)
    - 1. Great White Throne Judgment (20:11–15)
    - 2. The Doom of the Unrighteous (20:14–15; 21:8)
    - 3. New Heaven and New Earth (21:1—22:5)

The Epilogue (22:6–21)

Author: John

Theme: Conflict and Consummation

Date: c. A.D. 90–96

Background

Revelation is the last NT book and the most unusual. It is at once an apocalypse (1:1–2,20), a prophecy (1:3; 22:7,10,18–19) and a composite of seven letters (1:4,11; 2:1—3:22). ("Apocalypse" is derived from the Greek word *apocalypsis*, translated "revelation" in 1:1.) The book is an apocalypse with regard to the nature of its content, a prophecy with respect to its message and a letter in relation to its addressees.

Five important facts about the book's background are revealed in ch. 1. (1) It is "the revelation of Jesus Christ" (1:1). (2) This revelation was communicated supernaturally to the author through the exalted Christ, angels and visions (1:1,10–18). (3) The communication was to God's servant John (1:1,4,9; 22:8). (4) John received the visions and apocalyptic message while exiled on the island of Patmos (50 miles southwest of Ephesus) because of God's Word and John's own testimony (1:9). (5) The original recipients were seven churches in the province of Asia (1:4,11).

Historical and internal evidence point to John the apostle as the author. Irenaeus verifies that Polycarp (Irenaeus knew Polycarp, and Polycarp knew the apostle John) spoke about John writing Revelation near the end of Domitian's reign as Roman emperor (A.D. 81–96).

The book's content reflects the historical circumstances of Domitian's reign when he demanded that all his subjects address him as "Lord and God." The emperor's decree undoubtedly created a confrontation between those willing to worship the emperor and faithful Christians who confessed that only Jesus was "Lord and God." Thus the book was written at a time when believers were undergoing a measure of serious persecution because of the word of their testimony, a situation that obviously forms the background to Revelation itself (1:19; 2:10,13; 6:9–11; 7:14–17; 11:7; 12:11,17; 17:6; 18:24; 19:2; 20:4).

Purpose

The purpose of the book is threefold. (1) The letters to the seven churches reveal that serious deviation from the NT apostolic standard of truth and righteousness was occurring among many churches in Asia. John writes on Christ's behalf to rebuke their compromise and sin, and to call them to repent and return to their first love. (2) In view of persecution resulting from Domitian's self-deification, Revelation was given to the churches to strengthen their faith, resolve and loyalty to Jesus Christ, and to inspire them to be overcomers and remain faithful even unto death. (3) Finally, it was written to provide believers of all generations with God's perspective on their fierce conflict with Satan's combined forces by revealing the future outcome of history. It particularly discloses the events during the last seven years preceding Christ's second coming— that God will prevail and vindicate the saints by pouring out his wrath on Satan's kingdom; this will be followed by the second coming of Christ.

Survey

The prophetic message of this book is communicated through dramatic apocalyptic images and symbolism, depicting the consummation of the whole Biblical message of redemption. It features Christ's role as the worthy Lamb who was slain (ch. 5) and the wrathful Lamb who is coming to judge the world and purge it of evil (chs. 6–19). The other major symbolic images in the book are the dragon (Satan), the sea beast (the antichrist), the earth beast (the false prophet) and Babylon the Great (the center of satanic deception and world power).

After the prologue (1:1–8), there are three main sections in the book. In the first section (1:9—3:22), John has an awesome vision of the exalted Christ in the midst of the lampstands (churches) who commissions John to write letters to seven churches in Asia Minor (1:11,19). Each letter (2:1—3:22) includes a symbolic description of the exalted Lord from the opening vision, an evaluation of the church, words of commendation or rebuke or both, words of warning to five churches, an exhortation to hear and repent, and a promise to all overcomers. Emphasis on the number seven in this section indicates that the letters represent a collective fullness of what the exalted Lord says to the church in every city and generation.

The book's second main section (4:1—11:19) contains visions of things in heaven and on earth concerning the Lamb and his role in the outcome of history. It begins with a vision of the majestic heavenly court where God sits enthroned in holiness and unapproachable light (ch. 4). Ch. 5 focuses on a sealed scroll of destiny in God's right hand and on the Lamb, who alone is worthy to break its seals and disclose its contents. The opening of the first six seals (ch. 6) continues the vision begun in chs. 4–5, except now the scene shifts to events on earth. The first five seals unveil God's judgments in the last days that lead up to the end. The sixth seal announces God's coming wrath. The book's "First Interlude" occurs in ch. 7, describing the sealing of the 144,000 on the threshold of the great tribulation (7:1–8) and the reward of the saints in heaven after the great tribulation (7:9–17). Chs. 8–9 reveal the opening of the seventh seal, unveiling another series of judgments, i.e., the seven trumpets. A "Second Interlude" occurs between the sixth and seventh trumpets, involving John and a little scroll (10:1–11), and two mighty prophetic witnesses in the great city (11:1–14). Finally, the seventh trumpet (11:15–19) serves as a preview of the consummation (v. 15) and a prelude to the final scenes of God's unfolding mystery (chs. 12–22).

The third main section (12:1—22:5) provides a detailed picture of the great end-time conflict between God and his adversary, Satan. Chs. 12–13 reveal that the saints on earth must face a terrible conspiracy and triad of evil, consisting of (1) the dragon (ch. 12), (2) the sea beast (13:1–10) and (3) the earth beast (13:11–18). Chs. 14–15 contain visions to reassure the tribulation saints that justice will prevail as God is about to pour out his final wrath on the civilization of the antichrist. A full disclosure of God's wrath then occurs in the series of seven bowl judgments (ch. 16), the judgment of the great prostitute (ch. 17), and the fall of Babylon the Great (ch. 18). At this point, great rejoicing bursts forth in heaven, and the marriage supper of the Lamb and his bride is announced (19:1–10).

However, the grand finale is yet to occur. John then sees heaven opened and Christ riding forth on the white horse as the King of kings and Lord of lords to defeat the beast and all his allies (19:11–21). Satan's final defeat is preceded by his being bound for a thousand years (20:1–6), during which Christ reigns with the saints (20:4) and after which Satan is released for a short time (20:7–9) and then thrown into "the lake of fire" forever (20:10). The apocalyptic prophecy concludes with the great white throne judgment scene (20:11–15), the just doom of the wicked (20:14–15; 21:8), and the new heaven and new earth as the destiny of the saints (21:1—22:5). The book ends with warnings about heeding its message and entering into eternal life (22:6–21).

Special Features

Eight major features characterize this book. (1) Revelation is the only NT book classified as prophecy and apocalyptic. (2) As an apocalyptic book, its message is conveyed in symbols that represent realities about future times and events while preserving a certain enigma or mystery. (3) Numbers are used prolifically, including 2; 3; 3 and 1/2; 4; 5; 6; 7; 10; 12; 24; 42; 144; 666; 1,000; 1,260; 7,000; 12,000; 144,000; 100,000,000; and 200,000,000. The book especially features the number seven, which occurs no less than 54 times and symbolizes perfect completeness or fullness. (4) Visions are prominent, with the scenes often shifting in locale from earth to heaven and back to earth. (5) Angels are prominently associated with the visions and the heavenly decrees. (6) It is a polemical book that (a) exposes the demonic character of any earthly ruler's claim to deity, and (b) reveals Jesus Christ as the exalted Lord and the ruler of the kings of the earth (1:5; 19:16). (7) It is a dramatic book that makes the truth of its message as vivid and forceful as possible. (8) It breathes the spirit of OT prophecy without any formal OT quotations.

Interpretation

This is the most difficult NT book to interpret. Although the original readers probably understood its message without excessive perplexity, in subsequent centuries varying opinions about the book have resulted in four major schools of interpretation. (1) The *preterist* interpretation views the book and its prophecies as having been fulfilled in the original historical setting of the Roman empire, except for chs. 19–22—which await future fulfillment. (2) The *historicist* interpretation views Revelation as a prophetic forecast of the entire sweep of church history from John's day to the end of the age. (3) The *idealist* interpretation regards the book's symbolism as conveying certain timeless spiritual principles about good and evil in history generally, without reference to actual historical events. (4) The *futurist* interpretation approaches chs. 4–22 as prophecy concerning events in history that will occur only at the end of this age. This study Bible interprets Revelation primarily from the futurist perspective.

Reading Revelation

In order to read the entire New Testament in one year, the book of Revelation should be read in 24 days, according to the following schedule:
☐ 1 ☐ 2:1–17 ☐ 2:18–3:6 ☐ 3:7–22 ☐ 4 ☐ 5 ☐ 6 ☐ 7 ☐ 8 ☐ 9 ☐ 10 ☐ 11 ☐ 12 ☐ 13:1–10 ☐ 13:11–14:20 ☐ 15 ☐ 16 ☐ 17 ☐ 18 ☐ 19:1–10 ☐ 19:11–21 ☐ 20 ☐ 21 ☐ 22

NOTES

Prologue

1 The revelation of Jesus Christ, which
God gave[a] him to show his servants
what must soon take place.[b] He made it
known by sending his angel[c] to his servant John,[d] **2**who testifies to everything
he saw—that is, the word of God[e] and the
testimony of Jesus Christ.[f] **3**Blessed is
the one who reads the words of this prophecy, and blessed are those who hear it and
take to heart what is written in it,[g] because the time is near.[h]

Greetings and Doxology

4John,

To the seven churches[i] in the province of Asia:

Grace and peace to you[j] from him who is, and who was, and who is to come,[k] and from the seven spirits[a][l] before his throne,
5and from Jesus Christ, who is the faithful witness,[m] the firstborn from the dead,[n] and the ruler of the kings of the earth.[o]

To him who loves us[p] and has freed us from our sins by his blood,[q]
6and has made us to be a kingdom and priests[r] to serve his God and Father[s]—to him be glory and power for ever and ever! Amen.[t]

7Look, he is coming with the clouds,[u]
and every eye will see him,
even those who pierced him;[v]
and all the peoples of the earth will mourn[w] because of him.
So shall it be! Amen.

8"I am the Alpha and the Omega,"[x]
says the Lord God, "who is, and who was,
and who is to come,[y] the Almighty."[z]

One Like a Son of Man

9I, John,[a] your brother and companion
in the suffering[b] and kingdom[c] and patient endurance[d] that are ours in Jesus,
was on the island of Patmos because of
the word of God[e] and the testimony of
Jesus.[f] **10**On the Lord's Day[g] I was in the Rev 11:3
Spirit,[h] and I heard behind me a loud
voice like a trumpet,[i] **11**which said:
"Write on a scroll what you see[j] and send
it to the seven churches:[k] to Ephesus,[l]
Smyrna,[m] Pergamum,[n] Thyatira,[o] Sardis,[p] Philadelphia[q] and Laodicea."[r]
12I turned around to see the voice that
was speaking to me. And when I turned I
saw seven golden lampstands,[s] **13**and

1:1 [a]Jn 12:49; 17:8 [b]ver 19; Da 2:28,29; Rev 22:6 [c]Rev 22:16 [d]ver 4, 9; Rev 22:8
1:2 [e]ver 9; S Heb 4:12 [f]ver 9; 1Co 1:6; Rev 6:9; 12:17; 19:10
1:3 [g]Lk 11:28; Rev 22:7 [h]S Ro 13:11
1:4 [i]ver 11,20 [j]S Ro 1:7 [k]ver 8; Rev 4:8; 11:17; 16:5 [l]Isa 11:2; Rev 3:1; 4:5; 5:6
1:5 [m]Isa 55:4; Jn 18:37; Rev 3:14 [n]Ps 89:27; Col 1:18 [o]S 1Ti 6:15 [p]S Ro 8:37 [q]S Ro 3:25
1:6 [r]S 1Pe 2:5; Rev 5:10; 20:6 [s]Ro 15:6 [t]S Ro 11:36
1:7 [u]Da 7:13; S Mt 16:27; 24:30; 26:64; S Lk 17:30; S 1Co 1:7; S 1Th 2:19; 4:16, 17 [v]Jn 19:34,37 [w]Zec 12:10; Mt 24:30
1:8 [x]S ver 17; Rev 21:6; 22:13 [y]S ver 4 [z]Rev 4:8; 15:3; 19:6
1:9 [a]ver 1 [b]S Ac 14:22; 2Co 1:7; Php 4:14 [c]ver 6 [d]2Ti 2:12 [e]ver 2; S Heb 4:12 [f]S ver 2
1:10 [g]Ac 20:7 [h]Rev 4:2; 17:3; 21:10 [i]Ex 20:18; Rev 4:1
1:11 [j]ver 19 [k]ver 4,20 [l]S Ac 18:19 [m]Rev 2:8 [n]Rev 2:12 [o]Ac 16:14; Rev 2:18,24 [p]Rev 3:1 [q]Rev 3:7 [r]S Col 2:1; Rev 3:14
1:12 [s]ver 20; Ex 25:31-40; Zec 4:2; Rev 2:1

[a] 4 Or *the sevenfold Spirit*

1:1 REVELATION OF JESUS CHRIST. This book is a revelation from Jesus Christ about himself. This is extremely important, for (1) it reveals Jesus' evaluation of his churches 60 to 65 years after his resurrection and ascension, and (2) it discloses future events concerning the tribulation, God's triumph over evil, Christ's return to reign on earth and the blessedness of God's eternal kingdom.

1:3 BLESSED IS THE ONE WHO READS. This is the first of seven "beatitudes" or blessings found in Revelation, given to those who read, hear and obey the things written in the book. The other six blessings are found in 14:13; 16:15; 19:9; 20:6; 22:7; 22:14 (cf. Lk 11:28). That believers must keep the commands of Revelation indicates that this is a practical book with moral instructions and not merely a prophecy about the future. We should read the book not only to understand God's future program for the world and his people, but also to learn and apply great spiritual principles. Above all it should draw us nearer to Jesus Christ in faith, hope and love.

1:4 TO THE SEVEN CHURCHES. Revelation is addressed to seven churches in Asia (located in what is now part of western Turkey). Each particular church was comprised of various congregations. These churches were probably selected because they represented the totality of churches of that day, for the word "seven" stands for a complete whole. What was said to them is meant for the whole church. In other words, the "seven churches" represent all the churches throughout this church age. The "seven spirits" may represent the perfection and ministry of the Holy Spirit to the church (cf. 4:5; 5:6; Isa 11:2–3).

1:7 HE IS COMING. The primary purpose of the book of Revelation is to describe the triumph of God's kingdom when Christ returns to establish his kingdom on earth; the end-time events surrounding that coming are also set forth (cf. Da 7:13; Mt 24:29–30). It presents an eschatology of victory for the faithful, teaching that history will end in the judgment of Satan's system in this world (chs. 17–18) and in the eternal reign of Christ and his people (20:4; 21:1—22:5).

1:8 THE ALPHA AND THE OMEGA. Alpha is the first letter of the Greek alphabet and Omega is the last letter. God is eternal, and from creation to consummation he is Lord over all. To him belong the final victory over evil and the rulership over all things (cf. 22:13).

1:9 ISLAND OF PATMOS. Patmos is a small island in the Aegean Sea, about 50 miles southwest of Ephesus. John was a prisoner there because he faithfully proclaimed the gospel and remained loyal to Christ and his Word.

1:10 IN THE SPIRIT. This expression refers to a special intensity of spiritual awareness and receptivity to the communication of the Holy Spirit by which visions may be received (cf. Ac 10:10).

1:12 SEVEN GOLDEN LAMPSTANDS. These stands hold oil lamps, not candles; they represent the seven churches mentioned in v. 11 (cf. v. 20).

among the lampstands[t] was someone
"like a son of man,"[b][u] dressed in a robe
reaching down to his feet[v] and with a
golden sash around his chest.[w] **14**His
head and hair were white like wool, as
white as snow, and his eyes were like
blazing fire.[x] **15**His feet were like bronze
glowing in a furnace,[y] and his voice was
like the sound of rushing waters.[z] **16**In
his right hand he held seven stars,[a] and
out of his mouth came a sharp double-
edged sword.[b] His face was like the sun[c]
shining in all its brilliance.

17When I saw him, I fell at his feet[d] as
though dead. Then he placed his right
hand on me[e] and said: "Do not be afraid.[f]
I am the First and the Last.[g] **18**I am the
Living One; I was dead,[h] and behold I am
alive for ever and ever![i] And I hold the
keys of death and Hades.[j]

19"Write, therefore, what you have
seen,[k] what is now and what will take
place later. **20**The mystery of the seven
stars that you saw in my right hand[l] and
of the seven golden lampstands[m] is this:
The seven stars are the angels[c] of the
seven churches,[n] and the seven lampstands are the seven churches.[o]

To the Church in Ephesus

2 "To the angel[d] of the church in Ephesus[p] write:

These are the words of him who
holds the seven stars in his right
hand[q] and walks among the seven
golden lampstands:[r] **2**I know your
deeds,[s] your hard work and your
perseverance. I know that you cannot tolerate wicked men, that you
have tested[t] those who claim to be
apostles but are not, and have found
them false.[u] **3**You have persevered
and have endured hardships for
my name,[v] and have not grown
weary.

4Yet I hold this against you: You
have forsaken your first love.[w] **5**Remember the height from which you
have fallen! Repent[x] and do the
things you did at first. If you do not
repent, I will come to you and remove your lampstand[y] from its
place. **6**But you have this in your favor: You hate the practices of the
Nicolaitans,[z] which I also hate.

7He who has an ear, let him hear[a]
what the Spirit says to the churches.
To him who overcomes,[b] I will give

1:13 [t] Rev 2:1 [u] Eze 1:26; Da 7:13; 10:16; Rev 14:14 [v] Isa 6:1 [w] Da 10:5; Rev 15:6 **1:14** [x] Da 7:9; 10:6; Rev 2:18; 19:12 **1:15** [y] Eze 1:7; Da 10:6; Rev 2:18 [z] Eze 43:2; Rev 14:2; 19:6 **1:16** [a] ver 20; Rev 2:1; 3:1 [b] Isa 1:20; 49:2; Heb 4:12; Rev 2:12,16; 19:15,21 [c] Jdg 5:31; Mt 17:2 **1:17** [d] Eze 1:28; Da 8:17,18 [e] Da 8:18 [f] S Mt 14:27 [g] Isa 41:4; 44:6; 48:12; Rev 2:8; 22:13 **1:18** [h] Ro 6:9; Rev 2:8 [i] Dt 32:40; Da 4:34; 12:7; Rev 4:9,10; 10:6; 15:7 [j] Rev 9:1; 20:1 **1:19** [k] ver 11; Hab 2:2 **1:20** [l] S ver 16 [m] S ver 12 [n] ver 4, 11 [o] Mt 5:14,15 **2:1** [p] S Ac 18:19 [q] Rev 1:16 [r] Rev 1:12,13 **2:2** [s] ver 19; Rev 3:1,8,15 [t] 1Jn 4:1 [u] 2Co 11:13 **2:3** [v] S Jn 15:21

2:4 [w] Jer 2:2; Mt 24:12 **2:5** [x] ver 16,22; Rev 3:3,19 [y] Rev 1:20 **2:6** [z] ver 15 **2:7** [a] S Mt 11:15; ver 11,17,29; Rev 3:6,13,22; 13:9 [b] S Jn 16:33

[b] *13* Daniel 7:13 [c] *20* Or *messengers* [d] *1* Or *messenger*; also in verses 8, 12 and 18

1:13 A SON OF MAN. This term refers to the exalted Christ, a term also used by the OT prophet Daniel (Da 7:13; 10:5,16). In this vision, Christ is described as king, priest and judge of his churches (vv. 13–16).

1:16 SEVEN STARS. The seven stars represent either angels who are assigned, each to a church, to assist it in its spiritual warfare (see v. 20; cf. Mt 18:10), or the pastors of these churches. The "double-edged sword" represents the Word of God, which either cuts away sin from the churches and brings God's grace, or in judgment cuts a church away from God's kingdom (3:14–22).

1:19 WHAT YOU HAVE SEEN, WHAT IS NOW AND WHAT WILL TAKE PLACE. Here we have an outline of the book of Revelation: (1) the things John saw (ch. 1); (2) the things that are now (chs. 2–3); (3) the things that will take place in the future (i.e., events preceding and following Christ's coming to earth, chs. 4–22).

1:20 THE SEVEN CHURCHES. See article on CHRIST'S MESSAGE TO THE SEVEN CHURCHES, p. 576.

2:2 WHO CLAIM TO BE APOSTLES. One of the major concerns Christ expresses in his final message to the seven churches was that they not fall away by tolerating false teachers, prophets or apostles who were distorting his Word or weakening its power and authority. (1) Christ instructs the churches to test all who claim spiritual authority. (2) Note Christ's condemnation of the churches in Pergamum (vv. 14–16) and Thyatira (v. 20) for accepting rather than withstanding those disloyal to the truth and the standards of God's Word (see article on OVERSEERS AND THEIR DUTIES, p. 274).

2:4 FORSAKEN YOUR FIRST LOVE. This refers to the Ephesians' first deep love for and devotion to Christ and his Word (Jn 14:15,21; 15:10). (1) This warning teaches us that knowing correct doctrine, obeying some of the commands, and worshiping in the church are not enough (Mt 5:17). The church must have above all a heartfelt love for Jesus Christ and all his Word (2Co 11:3; cf. Dt 10:12). (2) Sincere love for Christ results in single-hearted devotion to him, purity of life and a love of the truth (2Co 11:3; see Mt 22:37,39, notes; Jn 21:15, note).

2:5 REMOVE YOUR LAMPSTAND. Christ will reject any congregation or church and remove it from his kingdom if it does not repent of its declining love for and obedience to the Lord Jesus Christ.

2:6 YOU HATE THE PRACTICES OF THE NICOLAITANS, WHICH I ALSO HATE. The Nicolaitans (cf. v. 15) probably affirmed, as did the teaching of Balaam (see v. 14, note), that sexual immorality did not affect one's salvation in Christ. The NT clearly states the contrary; such persons will not inherit God's kingdom (1Co 6:9–10). God hates the heresy that teaches we can be saved and at the same time live immoral lives. To hate what God hates is an essential characteristic of those loyal to Christ (Ps 139:21; Pr 8:13; see Jn 3:19, note).

the right to eat from the tree of
life,[c] which is in the paradise[d] of
God.

To the Church in Smyrna

8"To the angel of the church in Smyrna[e]
write:

These are the words of him who is
the First and the Last,[f] who died
and came to life again.[g] 9I know
your afflictions and your poverty—
yet you are rich![h] I know the slander of those who say they are Jews
and are not,[i] but are a synagogue of
Satan.[j] 10Do not be afraid of what
you are about to suffer. I tell you,
the devil will put some of you in prison to test you,[k] and you will suffer
persecution for ten days.[l] Be faithful,[m] even to the point of death, and
I will give you the crown of life.[n]
11He who has an ear, let him
hear[o] what the Spirit says to the
churches. He who overcomes will
not be hurt at all by the second
death.[p]

To the Church in Pergamum

12"To the angel of the church in Pergamum[q] write:

These are the words of him
who has the sharp, double-edged
sword.[r] 13I know where you live—
where Satan has his throne. Yet you
remain true to my name. You did not
renounce your faith in me,[s] even in
the days of Antipas, my faithful witness,[t] who was put to death in your
city—where Satan lives.[u]
14Nevertheless, I have a few
things against you:[v] You have people there who hold to the teaching of
Balaam,[w] who taught Balak to entice the Israelites to sin by eating
food sacrificed to idols[x] and by committing sexual immorality.[y] 15Like-
wise you also have those who hold
to the teaching of the Nicolaitans.[z]
16Repent[a] therefore! Otherwise, I
will soon come to you and will fight
against them with the sword of my
mouth.[b]
17He who has an ear, let him

2:7 [c]Ge 2:9; 3:22-24; Rev 22:2,14,19 [d]Lk 23:43
2:8 [e]Rev 1:11 [f]S Rev 1:17 [g]Rev 1:18
2:9 [h]2Co 6:10; Jas 2:5 [i]Rev 3:9 [j]ver 13,24; S Mt 4:10
2:10 [k]Rev 3:10 [l]Da 1:12,14 [m]ver 13; Rev 17:14 [n]S Mt 10:22; S 1Co 9:25
2:11 [o]S ver 7 [p]Rev 20:6,14; 21:8
2:12 [q]Rev 1:11 [r]ver 16; S Rev 1:16
2:13 [s]Rev 14:12 [t]Rev 1:5; 11:3 [u]ver 9,24; S Mt 4:10
2:14 [v]ver 20 [w]S 2Pe 2:15 [x]S Ac 15:20 [y]1Co 6:13
2:15 [z]ver 6
2:16 [a]S ver 5 [b]2Th 2:8; S Rev 1:16

2:7 TO HIM WHO OVERCOMES. An overcomer (Gk *nikōn*) is one who, by God's grace received through faith in Christ, has experienced the new birth and remains constant in victory over sin, the world and Satan. (1) Surrounded by great opposition and rebellion, overcomers refuse to conform to the world and to any ungodliness within the visible church (v. 24). They hear and respond to what the Spirit says to the churches, remain faithful to Christ to the very end (v. 26) and accept only God's standard revealed in his holy Word (3:8).

(2) Overcomers in God's churches, and only the overcomers, will eat of the tree of life, will not be hurt by the second death (v. 11), will receive hidden manna and be given a new name in heaven (v. 17), will be given authority over the nations (v. 26), will not have their names removed from the book of life but will be honored by Christ before his Father and the angels (3:5), will remain with God in his temple and will bear the name of God, Christ and the new Jerusalem (3:12), will sit with Christ on his throne (3:21), and will be forever God's children (21:7).

(3) The secret of victory for overcomers is Christ's atoning death, their own faithful testimony about Jesus, and their perseverance in love for Christ even to death (12:11; cf. 1Jn 5:4). Note that we either overcome sin, the world and Satan, or we are overcome by them and are ultimately thrown into the lake of fire (v. 11; 3:5; 20:15; 21:8). There is no intermediate group.

2:9 POVERTY. Poverty (Gk *ptōcheia*) means "having nothing at all." The poverty of the Christians at Smyrna was extensive; they were economically destitute, yet Jesus says they were spiritually rich. Note the contrast to the Laodicean church, which had great material wealth, yet was considered spiritually "wretched, pitiful, poor" (3:17; cf. Mt 6:20; 2Co 6:10; Jas 2:5).

2:11 THE SECOND DEATH. This refers to eternal punishment, the lake of fire (cf. 20:6,14; 21:8), which only the faithful overcomer will escape (see v. 7, note).

2:13 WHERE SATAN HAS HIS THRONE. This may mean a place where the influence of Satan and evil was in great prominence, for Pergamum was a center of imperial worship.

2:14 THE TEACHING OF BALAAM. Balaam was a false prophet who sold his services to a heathen king and advised him to tempt Israel to compromise their faith by idolatry and immorality (Nu 22:5,7; 25:1–2; 31:16; see 2Pe 2:15, note). The teaching of Balaam therefore refers to corrupt teachers and preachers who were leading people into fatal compromise with immorality, worldliness and false ideologies, all for the sake of personal advancement or monetary gain. The church at Pergamum evidently had teachers who taught that saving faith and a lifestyle of immorality were compatible.

2:16 FIGHT AGAINST THEM. Jesus opposes any within his churches who promote a tolerant attitude toward sin (v. 15; see v. 6, note; 1Co 5:2, note; Gal 5:21, note); he promises to wage war against immoral professing believers if they do not repent.

2:17 HEAR WHAT THE SPIRIT SAYS. We must heed the warnings of the Holy Spirit today. He continues to speak the same words Christ spoke to the seven churches of Asia, commanding us to overcome sin in the world and not to tolerate immorality. If we fail to overcome in this important area, we lose God's presence and the Spirit's power and become enemies

CHRIST'S MESSAGE TO THE SEVEN CHURCHES

***Rev 1:19–20** "Write, therefore, what you have seen, what is now and what will take place later. The mystery of the seven stars that you saw in my right hand and of the seven golden lampstands is this: The seven stars are the angels of the seven churches, and the seven lampstands are the seven churches."*

Christ's messages to seven local churches existing in western Asia Minor (see Rev 1:4, note) are intended for the exhortation, warning and edification of believers and churches throughout this entire age (cf. 2:7,11,17,29; 3:6,13,22). The value of these messages for churches today includes: (1) a revelation of what Jesus Christ himself loves and values in his churches as well as what he hates and condemns; (2) a clear statement from Christ regarding (a) the consequences of disobedience and spiritual neglect and (b) the rewards for spiritual vigilance and faithfulness to Christ; (3) a standard by which any church or individual may judge their true spiritual state before God; (4) an example of the methods of Satan's attack on the church or the individual Christian. This article examines each of these aspects by using a question and answer format.

(1) What does Christ praise? Christ praises a church for not tolerating wicked persons (Rev 2:2); for testing the life, doctrine and claims of Christian leaders (2:2); for persevering in faith, love, witness, service and suffering for Christ (2:3,10,13,19,26); for hating what God hates (2:6); for overcoming sin, Satan and the ungodly world (2:7,11,17,26; 3:5,12,21); for refusing to conform to immorality in the world and worldliness in the church (2:24; 3:4); and for keeping God's Word (3:8,10).

(2) How does Christ reward churches that persevere and remain loyal to him and his Word? He rewards such churches (a) by delivering them from the time of trial that will come upon the whole world (Rev 3:10); (b) by giving them his love, presence and intimate fellowship (3:20); and (c) by blessing them with eternal life with God (Rev 2:11,17,26; 3:5,12; 21:7).

(3) What does Christ condemn? Christ condemns a church for diminishing an intimate personal devotion to himself and God (Rev 2:4); for departing from Biblical faith; for tolerating immoral church leaders, teachers or laypersons (2:14–15,20); for becoming spiritually dead (3:1) or lukewarm (3:15–16); and for substituting outward success and affluence (3:17) for real spirituality, i.e., purity, righteousness and spiritual wisdom (3:18).

(4) How does Christ punish churches that decline spiritually and tolerate immorality? He punishes such churches (a) by removing them from their place in God's kingdom (Rev 2:5; 3:16); (b) by causing them to lose God's presence, the genuine power of the Spirit, the true Biblical message of salvation and the protection of their members from Satan's destruction (Rev 2:5,16,22–23; 3:4,16; see Mt 13, notes concerning the good and the evil within the kingdom of heaven during this age); and (c) by placing their leaders under God's judgment (Rev 2:20–23).

(5) What does Christ's message reveal about the natural trend of churches toward spiritual stagnation, decline and apostasy? (a) The seven letters suggest that it is the inherent tendency of churches to err, to accept false teaching, and to adapt to the evil, anti-God elements of the world (see Gal 5:17, note). (b) In addition, we see that churches are often affected by apostate, wicked and unfaithful people (Rev 2:2,14–15,20). For this reason a church's present spiritual state can never be taken as a valid test of God's will or as an ultimate justification for determining truth and sound doctrine. The gospel, i.e., the original message of Christ and the apostles, is the ultimate authority by which to measure truth and falsehood.

(6) How can churches avoid spiritual decline and the accompanying judgment by Christ? These letters reveal several ways. (a) First and foremost, all churches must be willing to "hear what the Spirit says to the churches" (Rev 2:5–7,16–17,21). The Word of Jesus Christ must always be the church's guide (1:1–5), for his Word, as revealed to the NT apostles through the Holy Spirit, is the guide by which churches must examine their beliefs and activities and renew their spiritual lives (2:7,11,17,29). (b) Churches must continually examine their spiritual condition before God and, if necessary, correct their degree of toleration of worldliness and immorality among their members (2:4,14–15,20; 3:1–2,14–17). (c) Spiritual decline can be halted in any church or group only if there is sincere repentance and a diligent return to the original love, truth, purity and power of Jesus Christ's Biblical revelation (2:5–7,16–17; 3:1–3,15–22).

THE SEVEN CHURCHES OF REVELATION

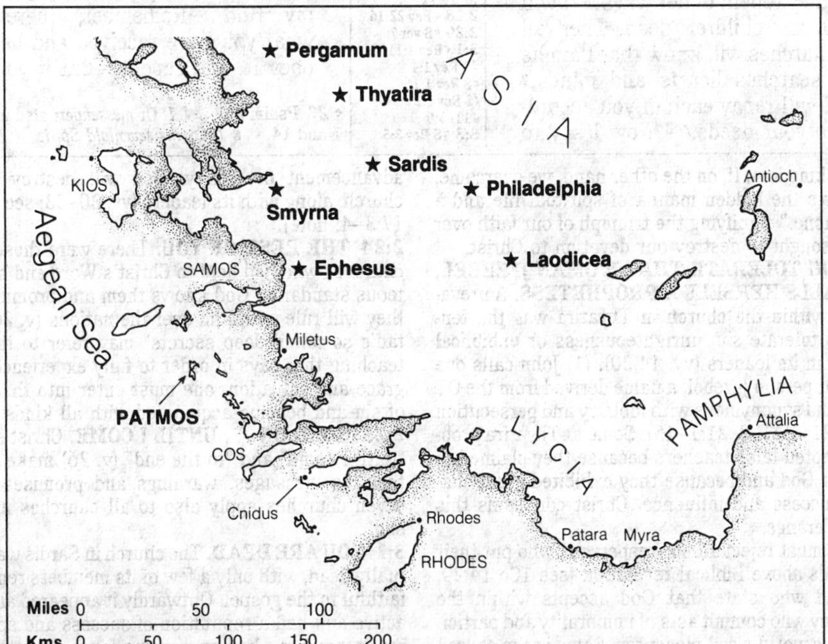

hear[c] what the Spirit says to the
churches. To him who overcomes,[d]
I will give some of the hidden manna.[e] I will also give him a white
stone with a new name[f] written on
it, known only to him who receives
it.[g]

To the Church in Thyatira

18"To the angel of the church in Thyatira[h]
write:

These are the words of the Son of
God,[i] whose eyes are like blazing
fire and whose feet are like burnished bronze.[j] 19I know your
deeds,[k] your love and faith, your
service and perseverance, and that
you are now doing more than you did
at first.

20Nevertheless, I have this
against you: You tolerate that woman Jezebel,[l] who calls herself a
prophetess. By her teaching she
misleads my servants into sexual
immorality and the eating of food
sacrificed to idols.[m] 21I have given
her time[n] to repent of her immorality, but she is unwilling.[o] 22So I will
cast her on a bed of suffering, and I
will make those who commit adultery[p] with her suffer intensely, unless they repent of her ways. 23I will
strike her children dead. Then all
the churches will know that I am he
who searches hearts and minds,[q]
and I will repay each of you according to your deeds.[r] 24Now I say to
the rest of you in Thyatira, to you
who do not hold to her teaching and
have not learned Satan's so-called
deep secrets (I will not impose any
other burden on you):[s] 25Only hold
on to what you have[t] until I come.[u]

26To him who overcomes[v] and
does my will to the end,[w] I will give
authority over the nations[x]—

27'He will rule them with an iron
scepter;[y]
he will dash them to pieces
like pottery'[e][z]—

just as I have received authority
from my Father. 28I will also give
him the morning star.[a] 29He who
has an ear, let him hear[b] what the
Spirit says to the churches.

To the Church in Sardis

3 "To the angel[f] of the church in Sardis[c] write:

These are the words of him who
holds the seven spirits[g][d] of God and
the seven stars.[e] I know your
deeds;[f] you have a reputation of being alive, but you are dead.[g] 2Wake
up! Strengthen what remains and is
about to die, for I have not found
your deeds complete in the sight of
my God. 3Remember, therefore,
what you have received and heard;
obey it, and repent.[h] But if you do

2:17 [c]S ver 7 [d]S Jn 16:33 [e]Jn 6:49,50 [f]Isa 56:5; 62:2; 65:15 [g]Rev 19:12 **2:18** [h]ver 24; Ac 16:14; Rev 1:11 [i]S Mt 4:3 [j]S Rev 1:14,15 **2:19** [k]S ver 2 **2:20** [l]1Ki 16:31; 21:25; 2Ki 9:7 [m]ver 14; S Ac 15:20 **2:21** [n]Ro 2:4; 2Pe 3:9 [o]Ro 2:5; Rev 9:20; 16:9,11 **2:22** [p]Rev 17:2; 18:9 **2:23** [q]1Sa 16:7; 1Ki 8:39; Ps 139:1,2,23; Pr 21:2; Jer 17:10; Lk 16:15; Ro 8:27; 1Th 2:4 [r]S Mt 16:27 **2:24** [s]Ac 15:28 **2:25** [t]Rev 3:11 [u]S Mt 16:27 **2:26** [v]S Jn 16:33 [w]Mt 10:22 [x]Ps 2:8; Rev 3:21 **2:27** [y]Rev 12:5; 19:15 [z]Ps 2:9; Isa 30:14; Jer 19:11 **2:28** [a]Rev 22:16 **2:29** [b]S ver 7 **3:1** [c]Rev 1:11 [d]S Rev 1:4 [e]S Rev 1:16 [f]S Rev 2:2 [g]1Ti 5:6 **3:3** [h]S Rev 2:5

e *27* Psalm 2:9 f *1* Or *messenger*; also in verses 7 and 14 g *1* Or *the sevenfold Spirit*

---

of God's kingdom. If, on the other hand, we overcome, we receive the hidden manna of spiritual life and a "white stone," signifying the triumph of our faith over all that sought to destroy our devotion to Christ.

2:20 YOU TOLERATE THAT WOMAN JEZEBEL, WHO CALLS HERSELF A PROPHETESS. A prevalent sin within the church in Thyatira was the tendency to tolerate sin, unrighteousness or unbiblical teaching in its leaders (vv. 14,20). (1) John calls one particular person Jezebel, a name derived from the OT Jezebel and synonymous with idolatry and persecution (1Ki 16:21; 19:1–3; 21:1–15). Some at Thyatira probably accepted false teachers because they claimed to speak for God and because they exhibited great charisma, success and influence. Christ condemns this sin of tolerance.

(2) We must reject all spokespersons who put their own words above Biblical revelation (see 1Co 14:29, note) and who state that God accepts within the church any who commit acts of immorality and participate in the world's evil pleasures. Some in the church will often tolerate such false teaching because of indifference, personal friendships or fear of confrontation, or because of a desire for peace, harmony, personal advancement or money. God will destroy such a church, along with its leaders (vv. 20–23; see also Lk 17:3–4, note).

2:24 THE REST OF YOU. There were those in the churches who had held to Christ's Word and his righteous standards. God knows them and promises that they will rule with him over the nations (v. 26). "Satan's so-called deep secrets" may refer to the false teaching that says in order to fully experience God's grace and salvation, one must enter into the depths of sin and become acquainted with all kinds of evil.

2:25 HOLD ON . . . UNTIL I COME. Christ's words "until I come" and "to the end" (v. 26) make it clear that his messages, warnings and promises to the seven churches apply also to all churches until the end.

3:1 YOU ARE DEAD. The church in Sardis was spiritually dead, with only a few of its members remaining faithful to the gospel. Outwardly it appeared alive and active and had a reputation of success and spirituality. It may have had an exciting form of worship, but not the true power and righteousness of the Holy Spirit. But Jesus saw the inner lives and hearts of the people.

not wake up, I will come like a
thief,[i] and you will not know at
what time[j] I will come to you.
4Yet you have a few people in Sardis who have not soiled their
clothes.[k] They will walk with me,
dressed in white,[l] for they are worthy. 5He who overcomes[m] will, like
them, be dressed in white.[n] I will
never blot out his name from the
book of life,[o] but will acknowledge
his name before my Father[p] and his
angels. 6He who has an ear, let him
hear[q] what the Spirit says to the
churches.

To the Church in Philadelphia

7"To the angel of the church in Philadelphia[r] write:

These are the words of him who is
holy[s] and true,[t] who holds the key
of David.[u] What he opens no one can
shut, and what he shuts no one can
open. 8I know your deeds.[v] See, I
have placed before you an open
door[w] that no one can shut. I know
that you have little strength, yet you
have kept my word and have not denied my name.[x] 9I will make those
who are of the synagogue of Satan,[y]
who claim to be Jews though they
are not,[z] but are liars — I will make
them come and fall down at your
feet[a] and acknowledge that I have
loved you.[b] 10Since you have kept
my command to endure patiently, I
will also keep you[c] from the hour of
trial that is going to come upon the
whole world[d] to test[e] those who
live on the earth.[f]
11I am coming soon.[g] Hold on to
what you have,[h] so that no one will
take your crown.[i] 12Him who overcomes[j] I will make a pillar[k] in the
temple of my God. Never again will
he leave it. I will write on him the

3:3 [i]S Lk 12:39 [j]Lk 12:39 **3:4** [k]Jude 23 [l]ver 5,18; Rev 4:4; 6:11; 7:9,13,14; 19:14 **3:5** [m]S Jn 16:33 [n]S ver 4 [o]S Rev 20:12 [p]Mt 10:32 **3:6** [q]S Rev 2:7 **3:7** [r]Rev 1:11 [s]S Mk 1:24 [t]1Jn 5:20; Rev 6:10; 19:11 [u]Isa 22:22; Mt 16:19
3:8 [v]S Rev 2:2 [w]S Ac 14:27 [x]Rev 2:13 **3:9** [y]Rev 2:9 [z]Rev 2:9 [a]Isa 49:23 [b]Isa 43:4; S Ro 8:37 **3:10** [c]2Pe 2:9 [d]S Mt 24:14 [e]Rev 2:10 [f]Rev 6:10; 8:13; 11:10; 13:8,14; 17:8 **3:11** [g]S Mt 16:27 [h]Rev 2:25 [i]S 1Co 9:25 **3:12** [j]S Jn 16:33 [k]Gal 2:9

3:4 A FEW PEOPLE IN SARDIS. Throughout church history, there have always been a few (i.e., a remnant) who have not "soiled their clothes" and who have sought to return to the simplicity and purity of devotion to Christ that the apostles and many others in the NT knew (2Co 11:3).

3:5 BLOT OUT HIS NAME. Clearly any person who experiences the new birth, but later refuses to persevere in faith and to overcome, will have his or her name taken out of the book of life (see 2:7, note). To have one's name blotted out of the book of life is to lose eternal life itself (2:7,10–11) and to be condemned to the lake of fire in the end (20:15). This is what the Spirit says to the churches (v. 6; 13:8; 17:8; 20:12; 21:27; cf. Ex 32:32).

3:7 PHILADELPHIA. Philadelphia was a faithful church that kept Christ's Word and did not deny him. They had endured opposition from the world and resisted conforming to the evil trends of other churches, yet had persevered in loyalty to Christ and the truth of the NT gospel (vv. 7–10). Because of their persevering faithfulness, God promises to deliver them from the hour of trial (see next note).

3:10 THE HOUR OF TRIAL. Christ's promise to keep the faithful in Philadelphia from the hour of trial is identical to Paul's promise to the Thessalonians that they would be rescued from the "coming wrath" (1Th 1:10); it extends to all of God's faithful throughout the ages (vv. 13,22). This hour includes the divinely appointed time of trial, wrath and distress that will come on "the whole world" in the last years of this age, just prior to the establishment of Christ's kingdom on earth (5:10; 6–19; 20:4). Concerning this time, the Bible reveals the following truths.

(1) This time of trial involves God's wrath on the ungodly (chs. 6–18; Dt 4:26–31; Isa 13:6–13; 17:4–11; Jer 30:4–11; Eze 20:33–38; Da 9:27; 12:1; Zec 14:1–4; Mt 24:9–31; see 1Th 5:2, note; see article on THE GREAT TRIBULATION, p. 52).

(2) Also included in this time of trial, however, is Satan's wrath on the godly, i.e., on those accepting Christ during this terrible time. For them there will be hunger, thirst, exposure to elements (7:16), and great suffering and tears (7:9–17; Da 12:10; Mt 24:15–21). They will experience indirectly the natural catastrophes of war, famine and death. They will be persecuted, tortured, and many will suffer martyrdom (6:11; 13:7; 14:13). They will undergo the ravages of Satan and demonic forces (9:3–5; 12:12), evil and violence from wicked people, and persecution by the antichrist (6:9; 12:17; 13:15–17). They will suffer loss of home and will need to flee in fear (Mt 24:15–20). It will be an especially disastrous time for those with families and children (Mt 24:19), so terrible that the tribulation saints who die are counted blessed, for they rest from their labor and are free from persecution (14:13).

(3) For those who are overcomers before that day arrives (see 2:7, note; Lk 21:36, note), God will keep them from that hour of trial, most likely through the rapture, i.e., the catching up of the faithful to meet Christ in the air before God pours out his wrath (see Jn 14:3, note; see article on THE RAPTURE, p. 440). This deliverance is a reward for those who persevere in keeping God's Word in true faith.

(4) Present-day believers who hope to escape all these things that are going to come on the world will do so only by faithfulness to Christ and his Word and by constant vigilance in prayer (see Lk 21:36, note), so that they will not be deceived (see Mt 24:5, note).

3:11 I AM COMING SOON. The close connection of this verse with v. 10 indicates (1) that Christ's coming to take up his church from the earth will be the means of their deliverance (cf. 1Th 1:10; 4:14–18), and (2) that rescue from the hour of trial and tribulation will come only to those faithful of the churches who hold on to Christ and his Word (v. 8).

name of my God[l] and the name of
the city of my God,[m] the new Jerusalem,[n] which is coming down out of
heaven from my God; and I will also
write on him my new name. 13He
who has an ear, let him hear[o] what
the Spirit says to the churches.

To the Church in Laodicea

14"To the angel of the church in Laodicea[p] write:

These are the words of the Amen,
the faithful and true witness,[q] the
ruler of God's creation.[r] 15I know
your deeds,[s] that you are neither
cold nor hot.[t] I wish you were either
one or the other! 16So, because you
are lukewarm—neither hot nor cold
—I am about to spit you out of my
mouth. 17You say, 'I am rich; I have
acquired wealth and do not need a
thing.'[u] But you do not realize that
you are wretched, pitiful, poor, blind
and naked.[v] 18I counsel you to buy
from me gold refined in the fire,[w] so
you can become rich; and white
clothes[x] to wear, so you can cover
your shameful nakedness;[y] and
salve to put on your eyes, so you can
see.

19Those whom I love I rebuke and
discipline.[z] So be earnest, and repent.[a] 20Here I am! I stand at the
door[b] and knock. If anyone hears
my voice and opens the door,[c] I will
come in[d] and eat with him, and he
with me.

21To him who overcomes,[e] I will
give the right to sit with me on my
throne,[f] just as I overcame[g] and
sat down with my Father on his
throne. 22He who has an ear, let him
hear[h] what the Spirit says to the
churches."

The Throne in Heaven

4 After this I looked, and there before
me was a door standing open[i] in
heaven. And the voice I had first heard
speaking to me like a trumpet[j] said,
"Come up here,[k] and I will show you what
must take place after this."[l] 2At once I
was in the Spirit,[m] and there before me
was a throne in heaven[n] with someone
sitting on it. 3And the one who sat there
had the appearance of jasper[o] and carne-
lian.[p] A rainbow,[q] resembling an emer-
ald,[r] encircled the throne. 4Surround-

3:12 [l]Rev 14:1; 22:4 [m]Eze 48:35 [n]Gal 4:26; Rev 21:2,10
3:13 [o]S Rev 2:7
3:14 [p]S Col 2:1; Rev 1:11 [q]Jn 18:37; Rev 1:5 [r]Pr 8:22; Jn 1:3; Col 1:16,18
3:15 [s]S Rev 2:2 [t]Ro 12:11
3:17 [u]Hos 12:8; 1Co 4:8 [v]Pr 13:7
3:18 [w]S 1Pe 1:7 [x]S ver 4 [y]Rev 16:15
3:19 [z]Dt 8:5; Pr 3:12; 1Co 11:32; Heb 12:5,6 [a]S Rev 2:5
3:20 [b]Mt 24:33; Jas 5:9 [c]Lk 12:36 [d]S Ro 8:10
3:21 [e]S Jn 16:33 [f]S Mt 19:28 [g]Rev 5:5
3:22 [h]S Rev 2:7
4:1 [i]S Mt 3:16 [j]Rev 1:10 [k]Rev 11:12 [l]Rev 1:19; 22:6
4:2 [m]S Rev 1:10 [n]ver 9,10; 1Ki 22:19; Isa 6:1; Eze 1:26-28; Da 7:9; Rev 20:11
4:3 [o]Rev 21:11 [p]Rev 21:20 [q]Eze 1:28; Rev 10:1 [r]Rev 21:19

3:15–16 NEITHER COLD NOR HOT . . . LUKEWARM . This describes the spiritual condition of the church in Laodicea. (1) A lukewarm church is one that compromises with the world and resembles its surrounding society; it professes Christianity, yet in reality is spiritually wretched and pitiful (vv. 17–18). (2) Christ severely warns the church about his judgment against spiritual lukewarmness (vv. 15–17). (3) Christ sincerely invites the church to repent and be restored to a place of faith, righteousness, revelation and fellowship (vv. 18–19). (4) In the midst of a lukewarm church age, Christ's promises to overcoming churches remain valid. He will come to them in blessing and in the power of the Spirit (vv. 20–22), opening a door that no one can shut, so that they may glorify his name and proclaim the everlasting gospel (v. 8).

3:20 IF ANYONE HEARS MY VOICE. In its self-sufficient prosperity and worldliness (vv. 15–18), the church in Laodicea had excluded the Lord Jesus Christ from its congregations. Christ's invitation, spoken from outside the door, is a request for fellowship with any individual who will repent of and overcome the spiritual lukewarmness of the church (v. 21).

3:22 THE SPIRIT . . . THE CHURCHES. The distinction between the churches and the Holy Spirit must be continually affirmed. Churches are subordinate to the Spirit of God and to his inspired Word (2Ti 3:15–16; 1Pe 1:24–25; 2Pe 1:20–21). This distinction between the Spirit and the churches can be expressed by the following Biblical truths. (1) The Spirit is not the possession of the churches or any human institution. He is the Spirit of God and of Christ, not the Spirit of the churches (v. 1). The Spirit remains free to come and leave according to God's righteous standards (Jn 1:33; 4:24; 7:39; 14:17).

(2) The Holy Spirit represents Christ's present lordship over the churches. The Spirit and his Word are the ultimate authority. Churches must constantly judge their beliefs and actions by the Spirit. They must never trust in, obey and listen to themselves alone. The Spirit and the inspired Word are greater than the churches of history.

(3) The Holy Spirit will remain with any church only as long as it remains faithful to Christ and his Word and hears what the Spirit says to the churches (2:5,16,22–23; 3:3,15–16).

4:1 AFTER THIS. Many Bible expositors believe that at this point in Revelation, Christ has already taken the faithful overcomers of his churches out of the world. Thus, the catching up of the true church (see Jn 14:3, note; see article on THE RAPTURE, p. 440) precedes the tribulation period (chs. 6–18). This is believed for the following reasons: (1) Beginning with 4:1, the terms "church" or "churches" disappear until 22:16. (2) The bride of Christ (i.e., the church) appears in ch. 19 already with Christ in heaven before he returns to earth to judge the wicked and to reign in the millennial kingdom (see 20:4, note). (3) The promise given to the Philadelphia church to keep it from the hour of worldwide trial pertains to all believers who stand true to Christ before the tribulation (see 3:10, note).

4:4 TWENTY-FOUR ELDERS. Who are these el-

ing the throne were twenty-four other
thrones, and seated on them were twenty-
four elders.[s] They were dressed in white[t]
and had crowns of gold on their heads.
5From the throne came flashes of lightning, rumblings and peals of thunder.[u]
Before the throne, seven lamps[v] were
blazing. These are the seven spirits[h][w] of
God. **6**Also before the throne there was
what looked like a sea of glass,[x] clear as
crystal.

In the center, around the throne, were
four living creatures,[y] and they were covered with eyes, in front and in back.[z] **7**The
first living creature was like a lion, the
second was like an ox, the third had a face
like a man, the fourth was like a flying
eagle.[a] **8**Each of the four living creatures[b] had six wings[c] and was covered
with eyes all around,[d] even under his
wings. Day and night[e] they never stop
saying:

"Holy, holy, holy
is the Lord God Almighty,[f]
who was, and is, and is to come."[g]

9Whenever the living creatures give glory,
honor and thanks to him who sits on the
throne[h] and who lives for ever and ever,[i]
10the twenty-four elders[j] fall down before
him[k] who sits on the throne,[l] and worship him who lives for ever and ever. They
lay their crowns before the throne and
say:

11"You are worthy, our Lord and God,
to receive glory and honor and
power,[m]
for you created all things,
and by your will they were created
and have their being."[n]

The Scroll and the Lamb

5 Then I saw in the right hand of him
who sat on the throne[o] a scroll with
writing on both sides[p] and sealed[q] with
seven seals. **2**And I saw a mighty angel[r]
proclaiming in a loud voice, "Who is worthy to break the seals and open the
scroll?" **3**But no one in heaven or on earth
or under the earth could open the scroll or
even look inside it. **4**I wept and wept because no one was found who was worthy
to open the scroll or look inside. **5**Then
one of the elders said to me, "Do not weep!
See, the Lion[s] of the tribe of Judah,[t] the
Root of David,[u] has triumphed. He is able
to open the scroll and its seven seals."

6Then I saw a Lamb,[v] looking as if it
had been slain, standing in the center of
the throne, encircled by the four living
creatures[w] and the elders.[x] He had seven
horns and seven eyes,[y] which are the sev-
en spirits[h][z] of God sent out into all the
earth. **7**He came and took the scroll from

4:4 [s] ver 10; Rev 5:6,8,14; 11:16; 19:4 [t] S Rev 3:4,5
4:5 [u] Ex 19:16; Rev 8:5; 11:19; 16:18 [v] Zec 4:2 [w] S Rev 1:4
4:6 [x] Rev 15:2 [y] ver 8,9; Eze 1:5; Rev 5:6; 6:1; 7:11; 14:3; 15:7; 19:4 [z] Eze 1:18; 10:12
4:7 [a] Eze 1:10; 10:14
4:8 [b] S ver 6 [c] Isa 6:2 [d] Eze 1:18 [e] Rev 14:11 [f] Isa 6:3; S Rev 1:8 [g] S Rev 1:4
4:9 [h] ver 2; Ps 47:8; S Rev 5:1 [i] S Rev 1:18
4:10 [j] S ver 4 [k] Dt 33:3; Rev 5:8, 14; 7:11; 11:16 [l] S ver 2
4:11 [m] Rev 1:6; 5:12 [n] Ac 14:15; Rev 10:6
5:1 [o] ver 7,13; Rev 4:2,9; 6:16 [p] Eze 2:9,10 [q] Isa 29:11; Da 12:4
5:2 [r] Rev 10:1
5:5 [s] Ge 49:9 [t] S Heb 7:14 [u] Isa 11:1,10; Ro 15:12; Rev 22:16
5:6 [v] ver 8,9,12, 13; S Jn 1:29 [w] S Rev 4:6 [x] S Rev 4:4 [y] Zec 4:10 [z] S Rev 1:4

[h] *5,6* Or *the sevenfold Spirit*

ders? Some believe they represent the entire church in heaven (see Jn 14:3, note; 2Ti 4:8; 1Pe 5:4). Others believe they may be ruling angels; note, however, that angels stand around the elders (7:11; cf. 5:8–10). Still others believe they represent Israel and the church joined in worship to God and the Lamb, i.e., the combining of 12 (Israel) and 12 (the church) equals 24 (God's people of both ages).

4:5 SEVEN SPIRITS OF GOD. The seven spirits of God represent the presence of the Holy Spirit at God's throne. The language may come from the sevenfold expression of the Spirit in Isa 11:2. The Holy Spirit is like a burning fire filled with judgment against sin and with God's purity (cf. Isa 4:4; Jn 16:8).

4:6 FOUR LIVING CREATURES. These four creatures probably represent the entire living creation (v. 7). All of God's living creatures will bring glory and honor to him in heaven and be redeemed from the curse of sin (vv. 8–11).

4:8 HOLY, HOLY, HOLY. The entire creation emphasizes and praises God's holiness. To be holy means to be separated from sin, unrighteousness and evil, and to be dedicated to righteousness, goodness, justice and purity. Holiness is an eternal attribute of God; his holiness will never change (cf. Isa 6).

5:1 A SCROLL. This scroll is of utmost importance, for it contains the revelation of what God has determined for the future course of the world and humanity. It describes how the world will be judged and portrays the final triumph of God and his people over all evil. When each seal is opened, a portion of the book's content is revealed in a vision (ch. 6; cf. Eze 2:9–10).

5:4 I WEPT AND WEPT. John weeps because he knows that if a worthy person is not found to open the book, God's purpose of judgment and blessing for the world will remain unfulfilled.

5:5 THE LION OF THE TRIBE OF JUDAH. Christ is pictured as a Lion, indicating he will rule all the earth. He is from the tribe of Judah and the family of David. These titles of Jesus as the conquering Messiah (Ge 49:9–10) and eternal king accord with the promises made to David (Isa 11:1,10).

5:6 AS IF IT HAD BEEN SLAIN. Christ, appearing as a Lamb that bears the marks of having been slain, represents his giving of himself on the cross for the sins of the human race. It signifies that Christ's worthiness, power, authority and victory come from his sacrificial death (vv. 9–14). "Lamb" is Revelation's foremost symbol for Christ (e.g., vv. 6–7; 12:11; 15:3; 17:14; 21:22; 22:1,3). Christ's judgment is on those who rejected his sacrifice as the Lamb of God (6:16–17). The "seven horns" represent the power and strength of a ruler (1Ki 22:11; Da 7:24); for "seven spirits," see 4:5, note.

the right hand of him who sat on the
throne.[a] 8And when he had taken it, the
four living creatures[b] and the twenty-four
elders[c] fell down before the Lamb. Each
one had a harp[d] and they were holding
golden bowls full of incense, which are the
prayers[e] of the saints. 9And they sang a
new song:[f]

"You are worthy[g] to take the scroll
and to open its seals,
because you were slain,
and with your blood[h] you
purchased[i] men for God
from every tribe and language and
people and nation.[j]
10You have made them to be a kingdom
and priests[k] to serve our God,
and they will reign on the earth."[l]

11Then I looked and heard the voice of
many angels, numbering thousands upon
thousands, and ten thousand times ten
thousand.[m] They encircled the throne and
the living creatures[n] and the elders.[o]
12In a loud voice they sang:

"Worthy is the Lamb,[p] who was
slain,[q]
to receive power and wealth and
wisdom and strength
and honor and glory and praise!"[r]

13Then I heard every creature in heav-
en and on earth and under the earth[s] and
on the sea, and all that is in them, singing:

"To him who sits on the throne[t] and
to the Lamb[u]
be praise and honor and glory and
power,
for ever and ever!"[v]

14The four living creatures[w] said,
"Amen,"[x] and the elders[y] fell down and
worshiped.[z]

The Seals

6 I watched as the Lamb[a] opened the
first of the seven seals.[b] Then I heard
one of the four living creatures[c] say in a
voice like thunder,[d] "Come!" 2I looked,
and there before me was a white horse![e]
Its rider held a bow, and he was given a
crown,[f] and he rode out as a conqueror
bent on conquest.[g]
3When the Lamb opened the second
seal, I heard the second living creature[h]
say, "Come!" 4Then another horse came
out, a fiery red one.[i] Its rider was given
power to take peace from the earth[j] and
to make men slay each other. To him was
given a large sword.
5When the Lamb opened the third seal,
I heard the third living creature[k] say,

5:7 [a]S ver 1 **5:8** [b]S Rev 4:6 [c]S Rev 4:4 [d]Rev 14:2; 15:2 [e]Ps 141:2; Rev 8:3,4 **5:9** [f]Ps 40:3; 98:1; 149:1; Isa 42:10; Rev 14:3,4 [g]Rev 4:11 [h]Heb 9:12 [i]S 1Co 6:20 [j]S Rev 13:7 **5:10** [k]S 1Pe 2:5 [l]Rev 3:21; 20:4 **5:11** [m]Da 7:10; Heb 12:22; Jude 14 [n]S Rev 4:6 [o]S Rev 4:4 **5:12** [p]ver 13 [q]ver 9 [r]Rev 1:6; 4:11 **5:13** [s]ver 3; Php 2:10 [t]S ver 1, 7 [u]ver 6; Rev 6:16; 7:10 [v]1Ch 29:11; Mal 1:6; 2:2; S Ro 11:36 **5:14** [w]S Rev 4:6 [x]Rev 4:9 [y]S Rev 4:4 [z]Rev 4:10 **6:1** [a]S Rev 5:6 [b]Rev 5:1 [c]S Rev 4:6,7 [d]Rev 14:2; 19:6 **6:2** [e]Zec 1:8; 6:3; Rev 19:11 [f]Zec 6:11; Rev 14:14; 19:12 [g]Ps 45:4 **6:3** [h]Rev 4:7 **6:4** [i]Zec 1:8; 6:2 [j]Mt 10:34 **6:5** [k]Rev 4:7

5:8 THE PRAYERS OF SAINTS. This refers to the intercession of the saints for the coming of the kingdom when they will reign on earth (vv. 9–10). Their prayer is, "Your kingdom come, your will be done on earth as it is in heaven" (Mt 6:10; see 6:6, note; 2Pe 3:12, note; cf. Ps 141:2).

6:1 THE LAMB OPENED. Jesus Christ himself (i.e., the Lamb) opens all the seals, which disclose God's devastating judgments on the world (vv. 1,3,5,7,9,12). The judgments are divine in origin, for they have been given into Christ's hands (5:1,7; cf. Jn 5:22). Throughout the book of Revelation, the plague judgments are called God's wrath (vv. 16–17; 11:18; 14:10,19; 15:1,7; 16:1,19; 19:15).

6:1 THE FIRST OF THE SEVEN SEALS. Some interpreters understand the opening of the first seal as the beginning of the seven-year tribulation, that future time of unprecedented suffering and judgment leading up to Christ's second coming (see Da 9:27; cf. Jer 30:7; Da 12:1; Rev 6:17; 7:14; see article on THE GREAT TRIBULATION, p. 52). Others believe the seals describe the final three and one-half years of the seven-year tribulation, often called the great tribulation. Still others see them as the beginning of God's judgment toward the end of the age. God's judgments are revealed in successive series. The first series is the seven seals (ch. 6); the second, the seven trumpet judgments (chs. 8–9; 11:15–19); and the third, the "seven bowls of God's wrath" (ch. 16; see 8:1, note).

6:2 A WHITE HORSE. Four horsemen come out as the first four seals are opened (cf. Zec 1:8–17; 6:1–8), representing God's judgment on the corrupt and evil world system and the ungodly. The rider of the white horse is thought by many Bible interpreters to be the antichrist (1Jn 2:18), the future world ruler who is to begin his activity at the beginning of the last seven years (see article on THE AGE OF THE ANTICHRIST, p. 447). He is allowed by God to deceive all who oppose Christ. His initial conquest will be accomplished without open warfare, for peace is taken from the earth beginning with the second horseman (v. 4; cf. Da 9:26–27; 1Th 5:3). On the other hand, all the other horsemen are personifications, so the rider on the white horse may simply represent conquest or a strong spirit of antichrist let loose in the end time.

6:4 HORSE . . . FIERY RED ONE. The red horse and its rider represent war and violent death, which God will allow in bringing his wrath on the world (cf. Zec 1:8; 6:2). The tribulation will be a time of violence, murder and war.

6:5 A BLACK HORSE. The black horse and its rider symbolize great famine (cf. Jer 4:26–28; La 4:8–9; 5:10). Basic necessities of life will be scarce and prices extremely high; hunger will spread throughout the world. The oil and wine refer to the olive tree and grapevine, which are not hurt as much by drought as the grain. Though famines have occurred throughout the church age (Mt 24:7), this passage is dealing with a specific famine during the tribulation.

"Come!" I looked, and there before me was
a black horse![l] Its rider was holding a
pair of scales in his hand. **6**Then I heard
what sounded like a voice among the four
living creatures,[m] saying, "A quart[i] of
wheat for a day's wages,[j] and three
quarts of barley for a day's wages,[j][n] and
do not damage[o] the oil and the wine!"
7When the Lamb opened the fourth
seal, I heard the voice of the fourth living
creature[p] say, "Come!" **8**I looked, and
there before me was a pale horse![q] Its
rider was named Death, and Hades[r] was
following close behind him. They were
given power over a fourth of the earth to
kill by sword, famine and plague, and by
the wild beasts of the earth.[s]
9When he opened the fifth seal, I saw
under[t] the altar[u] the souls of those who
had been slain[v] because of the word of
God[w] and the testimony they had maintained.
10They called out in a loud voice,
"How long,[x] Sovereign Lord,[y] holy and
true,[z] until you judge the inhabitants of
the earth[a] and avenge our blood?"[b]
11Then each of them was given a white
robe,[c] and they were told to wait a little
longer, until the number of their fellow
servants and brothers who were to be
killed as they had been was completed.[d]

6:5 [l] Zec 6:2
6:6 [m] S Rev 4:6,7
[n] Eze 4:16
[o] Rev 7:1,3; 9:4
6:7 [p] Rev 4:7
6:8 [q] Zec 6:3
[r] Hos 13:14; Rev 1:18; 20:13, 14 [s] Jer 15:2,3; 24:10; Eze 5:12, 17
6:9 [t] Ex 29:12; Lev 4:7
[u] Rev 14:18; 16:7
[v] Rev 20:4
[w] Ro 1:2; S Heb 4:12
6:10 [x] Ps 119:84; Zec 1:12
[y] Lk 2:29; 2Pe 2:1
[z] S Rev 3:7
[a] S Rev 3:10
[b] Dt 32:43; 2Ki 9:7; Ps 79:10; Rev 16:6; 18:20; 19:2
6:11 [c] S Rev 3:4
[d] Heb 11:40
6:12 [e] Ps 97:4; Isa 29:6; Eze 38:19; Rev 8:5; 11:13; 16:18 [f] S Mt 24:29
[g] Isa 50:3
6:13 [h] S Mt 24:29; Rev 8:10; 9:1
[i] Isa 34:4
6:14 [j] S 2Pe 3:10; Rev 20:11; 21:1
[k] Ps 46:2; Isa 54:10; Jer 4:24; Eze 38:20; Na 1:5; Rev 16:20; 21:1

12I watched as he opened the sixth seal.
There was a great earthquake.[e] The sun
turned black[f] like sackcloth[g] made of
goat hair, the whole moon turned blood
red, **13**and the stars in the sky fell to
earth,[h] as late figs drop from a fig tree[i]
when shaken by a strong wind. **14**The sky
receded like a scroll, rolling up,[j] and every
mountain and island was removed
from its place.[k]
15Then the kings of the earth, the
princes, the generals, the rich, the mighty,
and every slave and every free man[l] hid
in caves and among the rocks of the mountains.[m]
16They called to the mountains
and the rocks, "Fall on us[n] and hide us
from the face of him who sits on the
throne[o] and from the wrath of the Lamb!
17For the great day[p] of their wrath has
come, and who can stand?"[q]

144,000 Sealed

7 After this I saw four angels standing
at the four corners[r] of the earth,

6:15 [l] Rev 19:18 [m] Isa 2:10,19,21 **6:16** [n] Hos 10:8; Lk 23:30 [o] S Rev 5:1 **6:17** [p] Joel 1:15; 2:1,2,11,31; Zep 1:14,15; Rev 16:14 [q] Ps 76:7; Na 1:6; Mal 3:2 **7:1** [r] Isa 11:12

i 6 Greek *a choinix* (probably about a liter)
j 6 Greek *a denarius*

6:8 A PALE HORSE. The pale horse and its rider named Death symbolize a terrible intensification of war, famine, death, plagues, disease and evil beasts. This judgment will be so terrible that one-fourth of the human race will be killed.

6:9 SLAIN BECAUSE OF THE WORD OF GOD. When the fifth seal is opened, John sees what is happening in heaven. Those "slain because of the word of God" are those who are martyred for their faith in Christ and the truth of his Word. (1) They are told to have patience, for many more will yet die for their faith (cf. 7:13–14; 13:15; 18:24; 20:4). (2) The period of tribulation will be a terrible time of persecution for those who accept the gospel and remain faithful to God and his Word (see 3:10, note; 7:9, note; 14:6, note). Perhaps all the martyrs of past ages are included among those under the altar.

6:10 JUDGE . . . AND AVENGE OUR BLOOD. Those in heaven pray that the wicked who have rejected God and killed his followers will receive divine justice. There are times when God leads his people to pray for justice to prevail, for evil to be destroyed, for righteousness to be established on earth, and for Christ to be exalted above all those who oppose him. The prayer is not for personal vengeance, for it comes out of a concern for God, righteousness and the suffering of his people.

6:11 BROTHERS WHO WERE TO BE KILLED. Some people will be given the opportunity to be saved during the tribulation, namely, those on earth who had never adequately heard or understood the gospel. But those who heard the gospel before the rapture of the church and yet continued to live in sin will be given no further opportunity for salvation after the church is taken out of the world (see article on THE RAPTURE, p. 440). God will send them a powerful delusion, that they may never believe again (see 2Th 2:10–12, notes).

6:12 GREAT EARTHQUAKE. The catastrophic judgments of God portrayed here involve a physical shaking of the world, cosmic upheaval, and great darkness and terror for earth's inhabitants (vv. 15–17; cf. Isa 34:4; Joel 2:30–31; Hag 2:6; Mt 24:29). This is not the end of the tribulation. There is yet a seventh seal (ch. 8).

6:16 FALL ON US. The ungodly who are left behind after believers are caught up from the earth to meet the Lord in the air (1Th 4:17) will experience intense fear and despair as they attempt to run and hide.

6:16 THE WRATH OF THE LAMB. The Lamb's wrath portrayed in chs. 6–19 should alert all readers to see the extent that God hates sin, immorality and impenitent wickedness. It is identical with the wrath of God (cf. 15:7; see Ro 1:18, note; Heb 1:9, note). The faithful of Christ's churches are not appointed to suffer God's wrath (1Th 5:9), for Jesus has promised to rescue them from the coming wrath (see 3:10, note; 1Th 1:10, note; see article on THE RAPTURE, p. 440).

7:1 I SAW FOUR ANGELS. Ch. 7 is an interlude between the sixth and seventh seals, revealing those who became faithful to Christ during the great tribulation. Those who take their stand for God (6:17) are both Jew (vv. 3–8) and non-Jew (vv. 9–10,13–15).

holding back the four winds[s] of the earth
to prevent[t] any wind from blowing on the
land or on the sea or on any tree. 2Then
I saw another angel coming up from the
east, having the seal[u] of the living God.[v]
He called out in a loud voice to the four
angels who had been given power to harm
the land and the sea:[w] 3"Do not harm[x] the
land or the sea or the trees until we put
a seal on the foreheads[y] of the servants
of our God." 4Then I heard the number[z]
of those who were sealed: 144,000[a] from
all the tribes of Israel.

5From the tribe of Judah 12,000 were
sealed,
from the tribe of Reuben 12,000,
from the tribe of Gad 12,000,
6from the tribe of Asher 12,000,
from the tribe of Naphtali 12,000,
from the tribe of Manasseh 12,000,
7from the tribe of Simeon 12,000,
from the tribe of Levi 12,000,
from the tribe of Issachar 12,000,
8from the tribe of Zebulun 12,000,
from the tribe of Joseph 12,000,
from the tribe of Benjamin 12,000.

The Great Multitude in White Robes

9After this I looked and there before me
was a great multitude that no one could
count, from every nation, tribe, people and
language,[b] standing before the throne[c]
and in front of the Lamb. They were wearing white robes[d] and were holding palm
branches in their hands. 10And they cried
out in a loud voice:

"Salvation belongs to our God,[e]
who sits on the throne,[f]
and to the Lamb."

11All the angels were standing around the
throne and around the elders[g] and the
four living creatures.[h] They fell down on
their faces[i] before the throne and worshiped God, 12saying:

"Amen!
Praise and glory
and wisdom and thanks and honor
and power and strength
be to our God for ever and ever.
Amen!"[j]

13Then one of the elders asked me,
"These in white robes[k]—who are they,
and where did they come from?"
14I answered, "Sir, you know."
And he said, "These are they who have
come out of the great tribulation; they
have washed their robes[l] and made them
white in the blood of the Lamb.[m] 15There-
fore,

"they are before the throne of God[n]
and serve him[o] day and night in
his temple;[p]
and he who sits on the throne[q] will
spread his tent over them.[r]
16Never again will they hunger;
never again will they thirst.[s]
The sun will not beat upon them,
nor any scorching heat.[t]
17For the Lamb at the center of the
throne will be their shepherd;[u]

7:1 [s]Jer 49:36; Eze 37:9; Da 7:2; Zec 6:5; Mt 24:31 [t]S Rev 6:6 **7:2** [u]Rev 9:4 [v]S Mt 16:16 [w]ver 1 **7:3** [x]S Rev 6:6 [y]Eze 9:4; Rev 9:4; 14:1; 22:4 **7:4** [z]Rev 9:16 [a]Rev 14:1,3 **7:9** [b]S Rev 13:7 [c]ver 15 [d]S Rev 3:4 **7:10** [e]Ps 3:8; Rev 12:10; 19:1 [f]S Rev 5:1 **7:11** [g]S Rev 4:4 [h]S Rev 4:6 [i]S Rev 4:10 **7:12** [j]S Ro 11:36; Rev 5:12-14 **7:13** [k]S Rev 3:4 **7:14** [l]Rev 22:14 [m]Heb 9:14; 1Jn 1:7; Rev 12:11 **7:15** [n]ver 9 [o]Rev 22:3 [p]Rev 11:19 [q]S Rev 5:1 [r]Isa 4:5,6; Rev 21:3 **7:16** [s]Jn 6:35 [t]Isa 49:10 **7:17** [u]S Jn 10:11

They accept the everlasting gospel proclaimed by angels (14:6).

7:2 SEAL OF THE LIVING GOD. The seal was a tool or ring that stamped an owner's mark of identification on something. God's seal on a person identifies that person as belonging to God and under his care (cf. Eph 1:13).

7:4 144,000 FROM ALL THE TRIBES OF ISRAEL. The 144,000 are described as servants of God (v. 3) from the tribes of Israel (vv. 4–8). God will put a seal or mark on their foreheads to indicate consecration and ownership (cf. 9:4; Eze 9:1–6; 2Ti 2:19). (1) They may be the first converts of a great gospel harvest of souls gathered from every nation, tribe, people and language during the tribulation (v. 9).

(2) Some Bible interpreters believe these new believers from the tribes of Israel will be commissioned and empowered by the Spirit to preach the gospel during the tribulation days.

(3) Their being sealed by God does not mean they are protected from physical death or from martyrdom resulting from Satan's persecution (v. 14). However, they are protected from God's direct judgment and from demonic affliction (9:4).

7:9 A GREAT MULTITUDE. John describes a scene in heaven of a great multitude of people from all nations who come to salvation through faith in Christ. They will be with God (v. 15), free from pain and sorrow (vv. 16–17; see 6:9, note). Many believe that this multitude saved by the "blood of the Lamb" are tribulation saints, because John states that they "have come out of the great tribulation" (v. 14). Those who accept Christ are special objects of persecution from Satan and evil people (cf. 12:9–17).

7:14 THE GREAT TRIBULATION. The great tribulation is a time of divine judgment on an ungodly world that has rejected Christ, but it is also a time of satanic wrath and persecution against those who receive Christ and his Word during the tribulation (12:12). During this period, many saints will suffer terribly as objects of the wrath of Satan and the ungodly (vv. 9–17; 6:9–11; 20:4; cf. 14:13). So intense is the conflict between righteousness and wickedness that it can only be called a "great tribulation." This phrase in the Greek literally reads "the tribulation, the great"; in the Greek language repeating the article "the" makes a statement emphatic.

7:17 GOD WILL WIPE AWAY EVERY TEAR. This promise may refer to the removal of any memory that might cause us suffering, regret or remorse. In heaven

he will lead them to springs of
living water.[v]
And God will wipe away every tear
from their eyes."[w]

The Seventh Seal and the Golden Censer

8 When he opened the seventh seal,[x]
there was silence in heaven for about
half an hour.
2And I saw the seven angels[y] who
stand before God, and to them were given
seven trumpets.[z]
3Another angel,[a] who had a golden
censer, came and stood at the altar. He
was given much incense to offer, with the
prayers of all the saints,[b] on the golden
altar[c] before the throne. **4**The smoke of
the incense, together with the prayers of
the saints, went up before God[d] from the
angel's hand. **5**Then the angel took the
censer, filled it with fire from the altar,[e]
and hurled it on the earth; and there came
peals of thunder,[f] rumblings, flashes of
lightning and an earthquake.[g]

The First Four Trumpets

6Then the seven angels who had the
seven trumpets[h] prepared to sound them.
7The first angel[i] sounded his trumpet,
and there came hail and fire[j] mixed with
blood, and it was hurled down upon the
earth. A third[k] of the earth was burned
up, a third of the trees were burned up,
and all the green grass was burned up.[l]
8The second angel sounded his trumpet, and something like a huge mountain,[m] all ablaze, was thrown into the sea.
A third[n] of the sea turned into blood,[o] **9**a
third[p] of the living creatures in the sea
died, and a third of the ships were destroyed.
10The third angel sounded his trumpet,
and a great star, blazing like a torch, fell
from the sky[q] on a third of the rivers and
on the springs of water[r]— **11**the name of
the star is Wormwood.[k] A third[s] of the
waters turned bitter, and many people
died from the waters that had become bitter.[t]
12The fourth angel sounded his trumpet, and a third of the sun was struck, a
third of the moon, and a third of the stars,
so that a third[u] of them turned dark.[v] A
third of the day was without light, and
also a third of the night.[w]
13As I watched, I heard an eagle that
was flying in midair[x] call out in a loud
voice: "Woe! Woe! Woe[y] to the inhabitants of the earth,[z] because of the trumpet blasts about to be sounded by the other three angels!"

The Fifth and Sixth Trumpets

9 The fifth angel sounded his trumpet,
and I saw a star that had fallen from
the sky to the earth.[a] The star was given

7:17 [v]S Jn 4:10 [w]Isa 25:8; 35:10; 51:11; 65:19; Rev 21:4 **8:1** [x]Rev 6:1 **8:2** [y]ver 6-13; Rev 9:1,13; 11:15 [z]S Mt 24:31 **8:3** [a]Rev 7:2 [b]Rev 5:8 [c]ver 5; Ex 30:1-6; Heb 9:4; Rev 9:13 **8:4** [d]Ps 141:2 **8:5** [e]Lev 16:12,13 [f]S Rev 4:5 [g]S Rev 6:12 **8:6** [h]S ver 2 **8:7** [i]S ver 2 [j]Eze 38:22 [k]ver 7-12; Rev 9:15,18; 12:4 [l]Rev 9:4 **8:8** [m]Jer 51:25 [n]S ver 7 [o]Rev 16:3 **8:9** [p]S ver 7 **8:10** [q]Isa 14:12; Rev 6:13; 9:1 [r]Rev 14:7; 16:4 **8:11** [s]S ver 7 [t]Jer 9:15; 23:15 **8:12** [u]S ver 7 [v]Ex 10:21-23; Rev 6:12,13 [w]Eze 32:7 **8:13** [x]Rev 14:6; 19:17 [y]Rev 9:12; 11:14; 12:12 [z]S Rev 3:10 **9:1** [a]Rev 8:10

k *11* That is, Bitterness

nothing that involves deprivation, suffering or sorrow remains (v. 16).

8:1 THE SEVENTH SEAL. The opening of the seventh seal initiates the seven trumpets of judgment; thus, the trumpet judgments are the seventh seal. The trumpet judgments are partial judgments (chs. 8–9; 11:15–19), while the judgments of the seven bowls (ch. 16) are more severe. The seventh trumpet judgment will announce the seven bowls of judgment (11:15; 16:1–21). The silence in heaven is due to the horror of the coming judgments against sin.

8:3 PRAYERS OF ALL THE SAINTS. The repeated mentioning of the prayers of the saints (5:8; 8:3–4) indicates that the intercessory prayers of believers are extremely important in the destruction of evil and the establishment of righteousness on the earth (see 5:8, note). (1) John mentions the prayers of *all* the saints. Thus, the prayers of tribulation saints on earth are joined by the intercession of all the saints in heaven (cf. 6:9–11). The saints in heaven are vitally concerned about the events on earth. (2) Note that God in some sense stores up our prayers. Although the Lord may not answer all our prayers immediately, he does not throw them aside, but keeps them for the proper time of fulfillment.

8:7 HAIL AND FIRE MIXED WITH BLOOD. The first four trumpet judgments begin. (1) One-third of the earth's vegetation is destroyed by fire and hail; one-third of the sea and rivers is polluted; the heavens, sun, moon and stars are darkened for a third part of both day and night (vv. 7–13). (2) The judgments affect humans also, for many are killed (v. 11). The judgment is limited to one-third of the world, because the purpose of the judgment is partially to warn people and bring them to repentance (9:20–21).

8:8 HUGE MOUNTAIN, ALL ABLAZE. This may be a great burning meteor, which falls into the sea and kills one-third of the sea creatures and destroys many ships.

8:11 WORMWOOD. "Wormwood" is a bitter plant, representing God's judgment and human sorrow (see Dt 29:18; Pr 5:4; Jer 9:15; Am 5:7).

8:13 AN EAGLE THAT WAS FLYING. The eagle's threefold cry of woe is to warn that the next three trumpet judgments will be much more intense and devastating than those that preceded. The fifth and sixth judgments will involve horrible demonic forces (ch. 9).

9:1 THE STAR . . . THE ABYSS. The star falling from the sky is probably an angel who carries out God's judgment; it is referred to as "he" in v. 2. The Abyss is the place of imprisonment for demons (cf. 11:7; 17:8; 20:1,3; Lk 8:31; 2Pe 2:4; Jude 6). The beast, who is the antichrist, comes out of the Abyss

the key[b] to the shaft of the Abyss.[c]
2When he opened the Abyss, smoke rose
from it like the smoke from a gigantic furnace.[d] The sun and sky were darkened[e]
by the smoke from the Abyss.[f] **3**And out
of the smoke locusts[g] came down upon
the earth and were given power like that
of scorpions[h] of the earth. **4**They were
told not to harm[i] the grass of the earth
or any plant or tree,[j] but only those people who did not have the seal of God on
their foreheads.[k] **5**They were not given
power to kill them, but only to torture
them for five months.[l] And the agony
they suffered was like that of the sting of
a scorpion[m] when it strikes a man. **6**During those days men will seek death, but
will not find it; they will long to die, but
death will elude them.[n]

7The locusts looked like horses prepared for battle.[o] On their heads they
wore something like crowns of gold, and
their faces resembled human faces.[p]
8Their hair was like women's hair, and
their teeth were like lions' teeth.[q] **9**They
had breastplates like breastplates of iron,
and the sound of their wings was like the
thundering of many horses and chariots
rushing into battle.[r] **10**They had tails and
stings like scorpions, and in their tails
they had power to torment people for five
months.[s] **11**They had as king over them
the angel of the Abyss,[t] whose name in

9:1 [b]Rev 1:18 [c]ver 2,11; S Lk 8:31
9:2 [d]Ge 19:28; Ex 19:18 [e]Joel 2:2,10 [f]ver 1,11; S Lk 8:31
9:3 [g]Ex 10:12-15 [h]ver 5,10
9:4 [i]S Rev 6:6 [j]Rev 8:7 [k]S Rev 7:2,3
9:5 [l]ver 10 [m]ver 3
9:6 [n]Job 3:21; 7:15; Jer 8:3; Rev 6:16
9:7 [o]Joel 2:4 [p]Da 7:8
9:8 [q]Joel 1:6
9:9 [r]Joel 2:5
9:10 [s]ver 3,5,19
9:11 [t]ver 1,2; S Lk 8:31 [u]Rev 16:16 [v]Job 26:6; 28:22; 31:12; Ps 88:11
9:12 [w]S Rev 8:13
9:13 [x]Ex 30:1-3 [y]Rev 8:3
9:14 [z]Rev 7:1 [a]Ge 15:18; Dt 1:7; Jos 1:4; Isa 11:15; Rev 16:12
9:15 [b]Rev 20:7 [c]S Rev 8:7 [d]ver 18
9:16 [e]Rev 5:11; 7:4
9:17 [f]Rev 11:5 [g]ver 18; Ps 11:6; Isa 30:33; Eze 38:22; Rev 14:10; 19:20; 20:10; 21:8
9:18 [h]S Rev 8:7 [i]ver 15 [j]S ver 17

Hebrew[u] is Abaddon,[v] and in Greek,
Apollyon.[1]

12The first woe is past; two other woes
are yet to come.[w]

13The sixth angel sounded his trumpet,
and I heard a voice coming from the
horns[m][x] of the golden altar that is before
God.[y] **14**It said to the sixth angel who had
the trumpet, "Release the four angels[z]
who are bound at the great river Euphrates."[a] **15**And the four angels who had been
kept ready for this very hour and day and
month and year were released[b] to kill a
third[c] of mankind.[d] **16**The number of the
mounted troops was two hundred million.
I heard their number.[e]

17The horses and riders I saw in my
vision looked like this: Their breastplates
were fiery red, dark blue, and yellow as
sulfur. The heads of the horses resembled
the heads of lions, and out of their
mouths[f] came fire, smoke and sulfur.[g]
18A third[h] of mankind was killed[i] by the
three plagues of fire, smoke and sulfur[j]
that came out of their mouths. **19**The power of the horses was in their mouths and
in their tails; for their tails were like
snakes, having heads with which they inflict injury.

20The rest of mankind that were not

[1] *11 Abaddon* and *Apollyon* mean *Destroyer.*
[m] *13* That is, projections

(11:7), and Satan will be imprisoned there for one thousand years (20:3).

9:3 LOCUSTS CAME DOWN. These locusts represent an increased number of demons and demonic activity released on the earth toward the end of history (see previous note; see Mt 25:41, note on fallen angels). They have the power of scorpions to cause pain and misery (v. 10). Their assault is directed against the wicked on the earth for a time period of five months (vv. 5,10), though they are not permitted to torment believers (v. 4).

9:6 SEEK DEATH, BUT WILL NOT FIND IT. The pain inflicted by the demonic locusts will be so severe that people will want to die, but will not be able to. This judgment reveals (1) that evil and impenitence will most certainly receive divine retribution (see Ro 1:18, note), and (2) that when people oppose God and his truth and seek evil, they become the prey of the demonic. Evil forces will possess their very nature, soul and life (see 1Ti 4:1, note; see article on POWER OVER SATAN AND DEMONS, p. 80).

9:7 THE LOCUSTS LOOKED LIKE HORSES. The appearance and sound of the demons will be terrifying (vv. 7–9). Their "breastplates" (v. 9) may indicate that man-made weapons cannot destroy them.

9:11 AS KING OVER THEM. The leading angel of the demonic locusts is called "Abaddon," or "Apollyon," which means Destroyer, or Destruction (cf. Job 26:6; Pr 15:11).

9:14 RELEASE THE FOUR ANGELS. The sixth angel releases four angels; these must be evil angels or demons, since holy angels are not bound. They are let loose to kill one-third of the world's population (v. 15). They are released from the river Euphrates, because in OT history the Euphrates area symbolized a military invasion by which God brings judgment (cf. Isa 8:5–8; 10:5–7).

9:16 TWO HUNDRED MILLION. Bible interpreters differ widely as to the meaning of the two hundred million mounted troops. (1) Some say they represent demonlike evil spirits from the Abyss under the leadership of the four angels (v. 14; see v. 3, note). (2) Others see the mounted troops as representing many armies gathered for battle.

9:18 FIRE, SMOKE AND SULFUR. What John saw is a reminder of God's judgment on Sodom and Gomorrah (Ge 19:24,28; cf. Jude 7). These words are God's warning that those who indulge in the sinful ways of Sodom will most surely experience Sodom's judgment (Ge 19:14).

9:20 STILL DID NOT REPENT. Even God's judgment does not bring people to repentance. This demonstrates the depth of human depravity and its love for sinful pleasure (cf. Jer 17:9). The most prominent sins of the last days and the tribulation period are (vv. 20–21): (1) the worship of demons and participation in spiritism, the occult and magic (Dt 32:17; 1Co 10:20); (2) murder and violence; (3) magic arts (Gk

killed by these plagues still did not repent[k] of the work of their hands;[l] they
did not stop worshiping demons,[m] and
idols of gold, silver, bronze, stone and
wood—idols that cannot see or hear or
walk.[n] 21 Nor did they repent[o] of their
murders, their magic arts,[p] their sexual
immorality[q] or their thefts.

The Angel and the Little Scroll

10 Then I saw another mighty angel[r]
coming down from heaven.[s] He
was robed in a cloud, with a rainbow[t]
above his head; his face was like the sun,[u]
and his legs were like fiery pillars.[v] 2 He
was holding a little scroll,[w] which lay
open in his hand. He planted his right foot
on the sea and his left foot on the land,[x]
3 and he gave a loud shout like the roar of
a lion.[y] When he shouted, the voices of
the seven thunders[z] spoke. 4 And when
the seven thunders spoke, I was about to
write;[a] but I heard a voice from heaven[b]
say, "Seal up what the seven thunders
have said and do not write it down."[c]
5 Then the angel I had seen standing on
the sea and on the land[d] raised his right
hand to heaven.[e] 6 And he swore[f] by him
who lives for ever and ever,[g] who created
the heavens and all that is in them, the
earth and all that is in it, and the sea and
all that is in it,[h] and said, "There will be
no more delay![i] 7 But in the days when the
seventh angel is about to sound his trumpet,[j] the mystery[k] of God will be accomplished, just as he announced to his servants the prophets."[l]
8 Then the voice that I had heard from
heaven[m] spoke to me once more: "Go,
take the scroll[n] that lies open in the hand
of the angel who is standing on the sea
and on the land."
9 So I went to the angel and asked him
to give me the little scroll. He said to me,
"Take it and eat it. It will turn your stomach sour, but in your mouth it will be as
sweet as honey."[o] 10 I took the little scroll
from the angel's hand and ate it. It tasted
as sweet as honey in my mouth,[p] but
when I had eaten it, my stomach turned
sour. 11 Then I was told, "You must prophesy[q] again about many peoples, nations,
languages and kings."[r]

The Two Witnesses

11 I was given a reed like a measuring rod[s] and was told, "Go and
measure the temple of God and the altar,
and count the worshipers there. 2 But exclude the outer court;[t] do not measure it,

9:20 [k] S Rev 2:21 [l] Dt 4:28; 31:29; Jer 1:16; Mic 5:13; Ac 7:41 [m] S 1Co 10:20 [n] Ps 115:4-7; 135:15-17; Da 5:23 **9:21** [o] S Rev 2:21 [p] Isa 47:9,12; Rev 18:23 [q] Rev 17:2,5 **10:1** [r] Rev 5:2 [s] Rev 18:1; 20:1 [t] Eze 1:28; Rev 4:3 [u] Mt 17:2; Rev 1:16 [v] Rev 1:15 **10:2** [w] ver 8-10; Rev 5:1 [x] ver 5,8 **10:3** [y] Hos 11:10 [z] Rev 4:5 **10:4** [a] Rev 1:11, 19 [b] ver 8 [c] Da 8:26; 12:4,9; Rev 22:10 **10:5** [d] ver 1,2 [e] Dt 32:40; Da 12:7 **10:6** [f] Ge 14:22; Ex 6:8; Nu 14:30 [g] S Rev 1:18 [h] Ps 115:15; 146:6; Rev 4:11; 14:7 [i] Rev 16:17 **10:7** [j] S Mt 24:31 [k] S Ro 16:25 [l] Am 3:7 **10:8** [m] ver 4 [n] ver 2 **10:9** [o] Jer 15:16; Eze 2:8-3:3 **10:10** [p] S ver 9 **10:11** [q] Eze 37:4, 9 [r] Da 3:4; S Rev 13:7

11:1 [s] Eze 40:3; Rev 21:15 **11:2** [t] Eze 40:17,20

---

pharmekeia), which involves drugs, occult worship and witchcraft (18:23; 21:8; 22:15; Gal 5:20; see next note); (4) sexual immorality, lust and pornography; (5) thefts and lawlessness (cf. Ro 1:24,28–31).

9:21 THEIR MAGIC ARTS. Magic arts will be greatly revived in the last days before and during the tribulation period (18:23; 21:8; 22:15; 1Ti 4:1). Magic arts is associated with the occult, which includes contact with the dead, supernatural powers, paranormal energies or demonic forces in order to gain power to manipulate or influence things or people. The use of drugs may be involved with magic arts.

10:1 ANOTHER MIGHTY ANGEL. Ch. 10 reveals the vision of the angel with the little scroll. It is an interlude between the sixth trumpet (blown in 9:13) and the seventh trumpet (blown in 11:15).

10:2 A LITTLE SCROLL. The angel planting his right foot on the sea and his left foot on the land signifies that this little scroll contains a message affecting the destiny of the whole world.

10:3 SEVEN THUNDERS. These signify certain aspects of God's coming wrath and judgment (cf. 8:5; 11:19; 16:18), though John is forbidden to disclose the message of the seven peals of thunder (v. 4). This indicates that during the tribulation period, judgments not revealed in the seals, trumpets and bowls will occur. Therefore, no one knows in advance everything that will happen. Thus we should not be dogmatic about the sequence of events in the book of Revelation.

10:7 MYSTERY OF GOD. Within the period following the sound of the seventh trumpet (11:15), all the prophecies that God revealed to his prophets about the final days will come to pass. This concerns the fulfillment of God's purpose in Christ's return to earth and the establishment of his kingdom (11:15).

10:9 TAKE IT AND EAT IT. The "little scroll," tasting as sweet as honey but turning sour in John's stomach, refers to the scroll's mixture of blessing and curse. God's word is sweet, both to hear and to obey for his servants (Ps 19:9–10), but it also pronounces the judgment on sin and evil that unbelievers must face (cf. Lk 19:41–44; cf. Jer 15:16; 20:8–9; Eze 3:1–3; Am 5:10).

11:1 MEASURE THE TEMPLE. Ch. 11 continues an interlude (begun in ch. 10) that discusses Israel and the temple and gives an appraisal of her spiritual life. The events recorded here occur in the city where the "Lord was crucified," i.e., Jerusalem (v. 8). Israel is basically still in unbelief during this part of the tribulation. The "temple of God" may imply the existence of a temple in Jerusalem at this time; it will be desecrated by the antichrist (see 13:14–15; Da 9:27; 12:11; 2Th 2:4; see article on THE GREAT TRIBULATION, p. 52). The measuring of the temple signifies God's measuring of the spiritual condition of the Jewish people (cf. Eze 40; Zec 2).

11:2 TRAMPLE ON THE HOLY CITY. During the tribulation, Israel and the "holy city" will be oppressed by the Gentiles and suffer greatly for 42 months (see Lk 21:24, note). Israel will be severely judged because of her rejection of Christ and her im-

because it has been given to the Gentiles.[u] They will trample on the holy city[v]
for 42 months.[w] ³And I will give power to
my two witnesses,[x] and they will prophesy for 1,260 days,[y] clothed in sackcloth."[z] ⁴These are the two olive trees[a]
and the two lampstands that stand before
the Lord of the earth.[b] ⁵If anyone tries to
harm them, fire comes from their mouths
and devours their enemies.[c] This is how
anyone who wants to harm them must
die.[d] ⁶These men have power to shut up
the sky[e] so that it will not rain during the
time they are prophesying;[f] and they
have power to turn the waters into blood[g]
and to strike the earth with every kind of
plague as often as they want.

⁷Now when they have finished their testimony, the beast[h] that comes up from the
Abyss[i] will attack them,[j] and overpower
and kill them. ⁸Their bodies will lie in the
street of the great city,[k] which is figuratively called Sodom[l] and Egypt, where
also their Lord was crucified.[m] ⁹For three
and a half days men from every people,
tribe, language and nation[n] will gaze on
their bodies and refuse them burial.[o]
¹⁰The inhabitants of the earth[p] will gloat
over them and will celebrate by sending
each other gifts,[q] because these two
prophets had tormented those who live on
the earth.

¹¹But after the three and a half days[r]
a breath of life from God entered them,[s]
and they stood on their feet, and terror
struck those who saw them. ¹²Then they
heard a loud voice from heaven saying to
them, "Come up here."[t] And they went up
to heaven in a cloud,[u] while their enemies
looked on.

¹³At that very hour there was a severe
earthquake[v] and a tenth of the city collapsed. Seven thousand people were
killed in the earthquake, and the survivors were terrified and gave glory[w] to the
God of heaven.[x]

¹⁴The second woe has passed; the third
woe is coming soon.[y]

The Seventh Trumpet

¹⁵The seventh angel sounded his trumpet,[z] and there were loud voices[a] in heav-
en, which said:

"The kingdom of the world has
become the kingdom of our
Lord and of his Christ,[b]
and he will reign for ever and
ever."[c]

¹⁶And the twenty-four elders,[d] who were
seated on their thrones before God, fell on
their faces[e] and worshiped God, ¹⁷saying:

"We give thanks[f] to you, Lord God
Almighty,[g]
the One who is and who was,[h]
because you have taken your great
power
and have begun to reign.[i]
¹⁸The nations were angry;[j]
and your wrath has come.

11:2 [u] Lk 21:24 [v] S Rev 21:2 [w] ver 3; Da 7:25; 12:7; Rev 12:6,14; 13:5 **11:3** [x] Rev 1:5; 2:13 [y] S ver 2 [z] Ge 37:34; 2Sa 3:31; Ne 9:1; Jnh 3:5 **11:4** [a] Ps 52:8; Jer 11:16; Zec 4:3, 11 [b] Zec 4:14 **11:5** [c] 2Sa 22:9; 2Ki 1:10; Jer 5:14; Rev 9:17,18 [d] Nu 16:29,35 **11:6** [e] S Lk 4:25 [f] ver 3 [g] Ex 7:17, 19; Rev 8:8 **11:7** [h] Rev 13:1-4 [i] S Lk 8:31 [j] Da 7:21; Rev 13:7 **11:8** [k] Rev 16:19 [l] Isa 1:9; Jer 23:14; Eze 16:46 [m] Heb 13:12 **11:9** [n] S Rev 13:7 [o] Ps 79:2,3 **11:10** [p] S Rev 3:10 [q] Ne 8:10,12; Est 9:19,22 **11:11** [r] ver 9 [s] Eze 37:5,9,10,14 **11:12** [t] Rev 4:1 [u] 2Ki 2:11; Ac 1:9 **11:13** [v] S Rev 6:12 [w] Rev 14:7; 16:9; 19:7 [x] Rev 16:11 **11:14** [y] S Rev 8:13 **11:15** [z] S Mt 24:31 [a] Rev 16:17; 19:1 [b] Rev 12:10 [c] Ps 145:13; Da 2:44; 7:14,27; Mic 4:7; Zec 14:9; Lk 1:33 **11:16** [d] S Rev 4:4 [e] S Rev 4:10 **11:17** [f] Ps 30:12 [g] S Rev 1:8 [h] S Rev 1:4 [i] Rev 19:6 **11:18** [j] Ps 2:1

morality like that of Sodom (vv. 8,13). The "42 months" probably refers to the final three and one-half years of the tribulation (see Da 9:27; cf. 7:25; 12:7).

11:3 MY TWO WITNESSES. God will send two witnesses to preach the gospel and prophesy about the future; they will possess great supernatural power (vv. 5–6) and perform their ministry in the power of the Spirit. They will be a great threat to the antichrist and the entire wicked world for a period of 1,260 days and counteract the signs and wonders of the prophets of the antichrist (13:13–14). The two witnesses have the power of both Moses and Elijah.

11:4 OLIVE TREES . . . LAMPSTANDS. By using this language John says that the two witnesses will be empowered by the Holy Spirit in order to reveal the light or truth of God (see Zec 4:2–14).

11:7 THE BEAST . . . KILL THEM. The two witnesses are killed because they brought the truth of the gospel and faithfully cried out against the sins of the people. Jerusalem is called "Sodom" because of its immorality and "Egypt" because of its worldliness (v. 8). The beast is the antichrist (cf. 13:1; 14:9,11; 15:2; 16:2; 17:3,13; 19:20; 20:10) or the "man of lawlessness" (2Th 2:3–10). Note that the two witnesses could not be killed until they finished their work. This is true of all of God's servants who remain faithful to him.

11:11 TERROR STRUCK THOSE WHO SAW THEM. Because of the resurrection of the two witnesses (vv. 11–12) and God's judgment (v. 13), a remnant in Jerusalem will receive the message of the two witnesses and give glory to God (v. 13).

11:15 THE SEVENTH ANGEL SOUNDED. The sounding of the seventh trumpet brings an announcement that the world has become the kingdom of Christ, and he will reign forever (see 20:4, note; Eze 21:26–27; Da 2:44; 4:3; 6:26; Zec 14:9). In other words, the seventh trumpet involves events extending to Christ's return, including therefore the judgments of the seven bowls (beginning in ch. 16). The sound of the seventh trumpet is followed by a parenthetical passage that reveals some events related to the tribulation period (12:1—15:4).

11:16 TWENTY-FOUR ELDERS. The twenty-four elders prophesy what will happen at Christ's coming. The nations will be enraged (v. 18), the dead will be judged (v. 18), and God will destroy those who destroy the earth, i.e., those who are evil (cf. 19:20–21).

The time has come for judging the
dead,[k]
and for rewarding your servants the
prophets[l]
and your saints and those who
reverence your name,
both small and great[m]—
and for destroying those who destroy
the earth."

19Then God's temple[n] in heaven was
opened, and within his temple was seen
the ark of his covenant.[o] And there came
flashes of lightning, rumblings, peals of
thunder,[p] an earthquake and a great hail-
storm.[q]

The Woman and the Dragon

12 A great and wondrous sign[r] appeared in heaven:[s] a woman
clothed with the sun, with the moon under
her feet and a crown of twelve stars[t] on
her head. **2**She was pregnant and cried out
in pain[u] as she was about to give birth.
3Then another sign appeared in heav-
en:[v] an enormous red dragon[w] with sev-
en heads[x] and ten horns[y] and seven
crowns[z] on his heads. **4**His tail swept a
third[a] of the stars out of the sky and flung
them to the earth.[b] The dragon stood in
front of the woman who was about to give
birth, so that he might devour her child[c]
the moment it was born. **5**She gave birth
to a son, a male child, who will rule all the
nations with an iron scepter.[d] And her
child was snatched up[e] to God and to his
throne. **6**The woman fled into the desert
to a place prepared for her by God, where
she might be taken care of for 1,260
days.[f]

7And there was war in heaven. Michael[g] and his angels fought against the
dragon,[h] and the dragon and his angels[i]
fought back. **8**But he was not strong
enough, and they lost their place in heav-
en. **9**The great dragon was hurled down—
that ancient serpent[j] called the devil,[k]
or Satan,[l] who leads the whole world
astray.[m] He was hurled to the earth,[n] and
his angels with him.

10Then I heard a loud voice in heaven[o]
say:

"Now have come the salvation[p] and
the power and the kingdom of
our God,
and the authority of his Christ.
For the accuser of our brothers,[q]
who accuses them before our God
day and night,
has been hurled down.
11They overcame[r] him

11:18 [k]Rev 20:12 [l]Rev 10:7 [m]S Rev 19:5
11:19 [n]Rev 15:5,8 [o]Ex 25:10-22; 2Ch 5:7; Heb 9:4 [p]S Rev 4:5 [q]Rev 16:21
12:1 [r]ver 3 [s]Rev 11:19 [t]Ge 37:9
12:2 [u]Isa 26:17; Gal 4:19
12:3 [v]ver 1; Rev 15:1 [w]ver 9,13,16,17; Rev 13:1 [x]Rev 13:1; 17:3,7,9 [y]Da 7:7,20; Rev 13:1; 17:3,7,12,16 [z]Rev 19:12
12:4 [a]S Rev 8:7 [b]Da 8:10 [c]Mt 2:16
12:5 [d]Ps 2:9; Rev 2:27; 19:15 [e]S Ac 8:39
12:6 [f]S Rev 11:2
12:7 [g]S Jude 9 [h]ver 3 [i]Mt 25:41
12:9 [j]ver 15; Ge 3:1-7 [k]Mt 25:41; Rev 20:2 [l]S Mt 4:10 [m]Rev 20:3,8,10 [n]Lk 10:18; Jn 12:31
12:10 [o]Rev 11:15 [p]Rev 7:10 [q]Job 1:9-11; Zec 3:1; 1Pe 5:8
12:11 [r]S Jn 16:33; Rev 15:2

12:1 WONDROUS SIGN APPEARED. Ch. 12 presents four great conflicts between God and Satan: (1) Satan's conflict with Christ and his work of redemption (vv. 1–5), (2) Satan's conflict with the faithful of Israel (vv. 6,13–16), (3) Satan's conflict with heaven (vv. 7–9) and (4) Satan's conflict with believers (vv. 10–11,17).

12:1 A WOMAN. This woman refers to the faithful of Israel through whom the Messiah (i.e., the Christ child, vv. 2,4–5) came into the world (cf. Ro 9:5). This is indicated not only by the birth of the child, but also by the reference to the sun and the moon (see Ge 37:9–11) and the twelve stars, which would naturally refer to the twelve tribes of Israel.

12:3 AN ENORMOUS RED DRAGON. This dragon is Satan (see v. 9). The seven heads, horns and crowns may represent his great power.

12:4 A THIRD OF THE STARS. This may refer to Satan's original fall from heaven and the angels who fell with him (2Pe 2:4; Jude 6), or to the great power that Satan has in the universe over those who oppose his power. Satan attempts to destroy the Christ child.

12:5 A MALE CHILD. The male child is Jesus Christ (19:15) and the snatching up of the child refers to his ascension into heaven after his resurrection (Lk 24:51; Ac 1:9–11).

12:6 THE WOMAN FLED. Here the woman refers to the persecuted faithful ones of Israel during the last half of the tribulation (cf. the 1,260 days, exactly half of the length of the tribulation period). (1) During the tribulation, the faithful of Israel are God-fearing Jews who oppose the religion of the antichrist. Sincerely searching the Scriptures, they accept the truth about Jesus Christ as the Messiah (Dt 4:30–31; Zec 13:8–9). They receive divine help during the last three and a half years of the tribulation, and Satan will not be allowed to overcome them completely (see vv. 13–16). (2) Those from Israel who accept the religion of the antichrist and reject the Scriptural truth of the Messiah will be judged and destroyed in the days of the great tribulation (see Isa 10:21–23; Eze 11:17–21; 20:34–38; Zec 13:8–9).

12:7–9 WAR IN HEAVEN. The tribulation will involve not only great spiritual conflict on earth, but also war in heaven. Satan and his angels will put forth a supreme effort to defeat God and his angels in heaven. (1) Satan is defeated, hurled down to earth (cf. Lk 10:18) and allowed no further access to heaven. (2) Heaven rejoices (vv. 10–12), for Satan is no longer a spiritual force in heavenly places (see Eph 6:12, note). At the same time it causes "woe" to those on earth (vv. 12–13). This fall of Satan may begin the great tribulation.

12:10 ACCUSER OF OUR BROTHERS. Satan accuses believers before God of serving God for personal advantage (cf. Job 1:6–11; Zec 3:1).

12:11 THEY OVERCAME HIM. Faithful believers on earth overcome Satan by being freed from his power by the blood of the Lamb, by determining to speak for Christ and by showing a willingness to serve Christ at any cost.

by the blood of the Lamb[s]
and by the word of their
testimony;[t]
they did not love their lives so
much
as to shrink from death.[u]
12Therefore rejoice, you heavens[v]
and you who dwell in them!
But woe[w] to the earth and the sea,[x]
because the devil has gone down to
you!
He is filled with fury,
because he knows that his time is
short."

13When the dragon[y] saw that he had
been hurled to the earth, he pursued the
woman who had given birth to the male
child.[z] **14**The woman was given the two
wings of a great eagle,[a] so that she might
fly to the place prepared for her in the
desert, where she would be taken care of
for a time, times and half a time,[b] out of
the serpent's reach. **15**Then from his
mouth the serpent[c] spewed water like a
river, to overtake the woman and sweep
her away with the torrent. **16**But the earth
helped the woman by opening its mouth
and swallowing the river that the dragon
had spewed out of his mouth. **17**Then the
dragon was enraged at the woman and
went off to make war[d] against the rest of
her offspring[e]—those who obey God's
commandments[f] and hold to the testimo-
13 ny of Jesus.[g] **1**And the dragon[n]
stood on the shore of the sea.

The Beast out of the Sea

And I saw a beast coming out of the
sea.[h] He had ten horns and seven heads,[i]
with ten crowns on his horns, and on each
head a blasphemous name.[j] **2**The beast I
saw resembled a leopard,[k] but had feet
like those of a bear[l] and a mouth like that
of a lion.[m] The dragon gave the beast his
power and his throne and great authority.[n] **3**One of the heads of the beast seemed
to have had a fatal wound, but the fatal
wound had been healed.[o] The whole
world was astonished[p] and followed the
beast. **4**Men worshiped the dragon because he had given authority to the beast,
and they also worshiped the beast and
asked, "Who is like[q] the beast? Who can
make war against him?"
5The beast was given a mouth to utter
proud words and blasphemies[r] and to
exercise his authority for forty-two
months.[s] **6**He opened his mouth to blaspheme God, and to slander his name and
his dwelling place and those who live in
heaven.[t] **7**He was given power to make
war[u] against the saints and to conquer
them. And he was given authority over
every tribe, people, language and nation.[v]
8All inhabitants of the earth[w] will worship

12:11 [s]S Rev 7:14 [t]Rev 6:9 [u]Lk 14:26; Rev 2:10
12:12 [v]Ps 96:11; Isa 44:23; 49:13; Rev 18:20 [w]S Rev 8:13 [x]Rev 10:6
12:13 [y]ver 3 [z]ver 5
12:14 [a]Ex 19:4 [b]S Rev 11:2
12:15 [c]ver 9
12:17 [d]Rev 11:7; 13:7 [e]Ge 3:15 [f]S Jn 14:15
[g]S Rev 1:2
13:1 [h]Da 7:1-6; Rev 15:2; 16:13 [i]S Rev 12:3 [j]Da 11:36; Rev 17:3
13:2 [k]Da 7:6 [l]Da 7:5 [m]Da 7:4 [n]Rev 2:13; 16:10
13:3 [o]ver 12,14 [p]Rev 17:8
13:4 [q]Ex 15:11
13:5 [r]Da 7:8,11, 20,25; 11:36; 2Th 2:4 [s]S Rev 11:2
13:6 [t]Rev 12:12
13:7 [u]Da 7:21; Rev 11:7 [v]Rev 5:9; 7:9; 10:11; 17:15
13:8 [w]ver 12,14; S Rev 3:10

[n] *1* Some late manuscripts *And I*

12:12 DEVIL ... FILLED WITH FURY. Satan, knowing he is doomed and will shortly be defeated, has power only on the earth. The short time refers to the tribulation period. His great fury results in widespread suffering for the saints (v. 11).

12:13 PURSUED THE WOMAN. Satan attempts to destroy the woman (see v. 6, note). Those from Israel who accept Christ will be hunted and persecuted by Satan and the followers of the antichrist (cf. Mt 24:15–21). God will give supernatural protection for the saints of Israel during this time (vv. 14–16).

12:17 DRAGON ... WENT OFF TO MAKE WAR. Satan, confined to earth, knows he has only a short time to persecute the woman (see v. 6, note) and the rest of her offspring. "The woman" may refer to the faithful of Israel in Judea and "the rest of her offspring" to believing Jews elsewhere in the world.

13:1 A BEAST COMING OUT OF THE SEA. Ch. 13 describes the conflict between the antichrist and God and his people during the tribulation. The beast coming out of the sea is history's final great world government, consisting of ten kingdoms under the control of the antichrist (see Da 2:40–44; 7:7,24–27; see Rev 17:12, note). The sea represents many nations (cf. 17:15). Satan gives his power to this government and uses it against God and his people (v. 2). See 17:8–11 for the angel's explanation of the beast.

13:2 BEAST ... LEOPARD. The beast here, the same beast of v. 1, represents not only the end-time Gentile world kingdom, but also the king of that kingdom. The beast is a person, as cruel as a beast, who will gain the political and religious power of the world at that time (see 17:13; Da 7:4–6; 8:25; 9:27). He is called the "man of lawlessness" in 2Th 2:3–4 and the "antichrist" in 1Jn 2:18 ("anti" means "instead of"; thus the antichrist may claim he is the real Christ, the true Messiah, Mt 24:24–25; 2Th 2:3–4). He will make a covenant with the nation of Israel (Da 9:27).

13:3 A FATAL WOUND. It appears to the whole world that the antichrist has suffered a fatal wound, but is brought back to life again by Satan's supernatural power (vv. 2,14; cf. 2Th 2:9; see Rev 17:8, note). Evidently God will permit Satan to try to duplicate Christ's power. This may be Satan's chief means of deceiving the human race (cf. 2Th 2:9–10).

13:7 MAKE WAR AGAINST THE SAINTS. During the tribulation, people will have to choose whether to follow the easy and popular way of the new religion or to believe in Christ and remain faithful. (1) Those who remain faithful to God and his Word will be persecuted and possibly killed (see 6:9, note; 7:9, note). (2) Satan will "conquer them," not in the sense that their faith is destroyed, but in the martyrdom of many (6:9–11). For "forty-two months" the antichrist will make war against the saints (v. 5).

13:8 ALL ... WILL WORSHIP THE BEAST. The

the beast—all whose names have not
been written in the book of life[x] belonging
to the Lamb[y] that was slain from the creation of the world.[oz]
9He who has an ear, let him hear.[a]

10If anyone is to go into captivity,
into captivity he will go.
If anyone is to be killed[p] with the
sword,
with the sword he will be killed.[b]

This calls for patient endurance and faithfulness[c] on the part of the saints.[d]

The Beast out of the Earth

11Then I saw another beast, coming out
of the earth.[e] He had two horns like a
lamb, but he spoke like a dragon.[f] **12**He
exercised all the authority[g] of the first
beast on his behalf,[h] and made the earth
and its inhabitants worship the first
beast,[i] whose fatal wound had been
healed.[j] **13**And he performed great and
miraculous signs,[k] even causing fire to
come down from heaven[l] to earth in full
view of men. **14**Because of the signs[m] he
was given power to do on behalf of the
first beast, he deceived[n] the inhabitants
of the earth.[o] He ordered them to set up
an image in honor of the beast who was
wounded by the sword and yet lived.[p]
15He was given power to give breath to
the image of the first beast, so that it
could speak and cause all who refused to
worship[q] the image to be killed.[r] **16**He
also forced everyone, small and great,[s]
rich and poor, free and slave, to receive a
mark on his right hand or on his forehead,[t] **17**so that no one could buy or sell
unless he had the mark,[u] which is the
name of the beast or the number of his
name.[v]
18This calls for wisdom.[w] If anyone has
insight, let him calculate the number of
the beast, for it is man's number.[x] His
number is 666.

The Lamb and the 144,000

14 Then I looked, and there before me
was the Lamb,[y] standing on
Mount Zion,[z] and with him 144,000[a] who
had his name and his Father's name[b]
written on their foreheads.[c] **2**And I heard

13:8 [x]S Rev 20:12 [y]S Jn 1:29 [z]S Mt 25:34 **13:9** [a]S Rev 2:7 **13:10** [b]Jer 15:2; 43:11 [c]S Heb 6:12 [d]Rev 14:12 **13:11** [e]ver 1,2 [f]Rev 16:13 **13:12** [g]ver 4 [h]ver 14; Rev 19:20 [i]ver 15; Rev 14:9,11; 16:2; 19:20; 20:4 [j]ver 3 **13:13** [k]S Mt 24:24 [l]1Ki 18:38; 2Ki 1:10; Lk 9:54; Rev 20:9 **13:14** [m]2Th 2:9, 10 [n]Rev 12:9 [o]S Rev 3:10 [p]ver 3,12 **13:15** [q]S ver 12 [r]Da 3:3-6 **13:16** [s]S Rev 19:5 [t]Rev 7:3; 14:9; 20:4 **13:17** [u]Rev 14:9 [v]ver 18; Rev 14:11; 15:2 **13:18** [w]Rev 17:9 [x]Rev 15:2; 21:17 **14:1** [y]S Rev 5:6 [z]Ps 2:6; Heb 12:22 [a]ver 3; Rev 7:4 [b]Rev 3:12; 22:4 [c]S Rev 7:3

[o] *8* Or *written from the creation of the world in the book of life belonging to the Lamb that was slain*
[p] *10* Some manuscripts *anyone kills*

---

antichrist declares himself to be deity and possesses supernatural power of the demonic world (2Th 2:4,9). Accordingly, he will be worshiped (vv. 4,8,12; 14:9; 16:2). The religion of the antichrist, in other words, teaches the doctrine of the divinity of humanity (cf. Ge 3:5). Instead of the truth that in Christ God became flesh (Jn 1:14), he speaks the lie that in himself humanity has and can become God (2Th 2:4). New Age teaching today emphasizes this doctrine of the antichrist and may be preparing the masses for its ultimate acceptance.

13:8 LAMB THAT WAS SLAIN FROM THE CREATION. Christ's redemptive death for the salvation of humanity was decreed from the very beginning of the creation of the world (see 17:8, note; Ge 3:15; 1Pe 1:18–20).

13:11 ANOTHER BEAST. This other beast will assist the first beast (see v. 2, note), directing the world to worship the antichrist (v. 12) and misleading humanity by working great miracles (vv. 13–14; cf. Dt 13:1–3; 2Th 2:9–12). He is also referred to as "the false prophet" (19:20; 20:10). An image of the antichrist will probably be placed in God's temple (Da 9:27; Mt 24:15; 2Th 2:4). His "two horns like a lamb" signify his attempt to deceive by portraying himself as a loving, gentle and caring person. In reality, however, his character is not like that of a lamb but of a dragon (cf. Mt 7:15).

13:12 WORSHIP THE FIRST BEAST. The second beast will promote an ecumenical false church that will worship the antichrist. He will bring this about largely by performing great signs and wonders (vv. 13–14). His ministry will in some ways counterfeit the supernatural ministry of the Holy Spirit (cf. 2Th 2:9–10).

13:15 REFUSED TO WORSHIP THE IMAGE TO BE KILLED. A decree will be given to kill all who refuse to worship the world ruler and his images. In other words, many who resist the antichrist and remain faithful to Jesus will pay with their lives (see 6:9, note; 14:12–13; 17:9–17).

13:16 A MARK. The antichrist will seek to gain total economic control of the world. All people must worship him and receive a mark on their hands or foreheads in order to buy or sell (vv. 16–17), identifying the followers of the world religion promoted by the antichrist. Those who refuse to take the mark will be hunted down in order to be killed (v. 15).

13:18 HIS NUMBER IS 666. Although the antichrist is called "the beast" throughout Revelation, his number is 666. Many commentators believe that six is the number for humanity in Scripture and three is the number for God. Therefore, the three sixes could very well refer to a man who makes himself god. Like the Roman emperors and many both before and after them, he believes he is a god (see v. 8, note; 2Th 2:4).

14:1 WITH HIM 144,000. Chs. 14 and 15 introduce the judgments of chs. 16–18, showing the reward awaiting those who persevere in their faith in Jesus (v. 12; 15:2–4). Ch. 14 begins by describing the scene of 144,000 outstanding believers appearing in heaven close to the Lamb. The 144,000 symbolically represent the most consecrated and faithful of God's people of all time, who enjoy a special position and favor in heaven (see next note). Thus the number 144,000 does not mean they are limited to that number. Any believer may be among this group by consecrated and devoted faith, love and service.

a sound from heaven like the roar of rushing waters[d] and like a loud peal of thunder.[e] The sound I heard was like that of
harpists playing their harps.[f] **3**And they
sang a new song[g] before the throne and
before the four living creatures[h] and the
elders.[i] No one could learn the song except the 144,000[j] who had been redeemed from the earth. **4**These are those
who did not defile themselves with wom-
en, for they kept themselves pure.[k] They
follow the Lamb wherever he goes.[l] They
were purchased from among men[m] and offered as firstfruits[n] to God and the Lamb.
5No lie was found in their mouths;[o] they
are blameless.[p]

The Three Angels

6Then I saw another angel flying in
midair,[q] and he had the eternal gospel to
proclaim to those who live on the earth[r]
—to every nation, tribe, language and
people.[s] **7**He said in a loud voice, "Fear
God[t] and give him glory,[u] because the
hour of his judgment has come. Worship
him who made[v] the heavens, the earth,
the sea and the springs of water."[w]

8A second angel followed and said,
"Fallen! Fallen is Babylon the Great,[x]
which made all the nations drink the maddening wine of her adulteries."[y]

9A third angel followed them and said
in a loud voice: "If anyone worships the
beast[z] and his image[a] and receives his
mark on the forehead[b] or on the hand,
10he, too, will drink of the wine of God's
fury,[c] which has been poured full
strength into the cup of his wrath.[d] He
will be tormented with burning sulfur[e] in
the presence of the holy angels and of the
Lamb. **11**And the smoke of their torment
rises for ever and ever.[f] There is no rest
day or night[g] for those who worship the
beast and his image,[h] or for anyone who
receives the mark of his name."[i] **12**This
calls for patient endurance[j] on the part of
the saints[k] who obey God's commandments[l] and remain faithful to Jesus.

13Then I heard a voice from heaven say,
"Write: Blessed are the dead who die in
the Lord[m] from now on."

"Yes," says the Spirit,[n] "they will rest
from their labor, for their deeds will follow
them."

The Harvest of the Earth

14I looked, and there before me was a
white cloud,[o] and seated on the cloud was
one "like a son of man"[q][p] with a crown[q]
of gold on his head and a sharp sickle in
his hand. **15**Then another angel came out
of the temple[r] and called in a loud voice
to him who was sitting on the cloud, "Take
your sickle[s] and reap, because the time to
reap has come, for the harvest[t] of the
earth is ripe." **16**So he who was seated on

14:2 [d]S Rev 1:15 [e]Rev 6:1 [f]Rev 5:8; 15:2
14:3 [g]S Rev 5:9 [h]S Rev 4:6 [i]S Rev 4:4 [j]ver 1
14:4 [k]2Co 11:2; Rev 3:4 [l]Rev 7:17 [m]Rev 5:9 [n]Jer 2:3; Jas 1:18
14:5 [o]Ps 32:2; Zep 3:13; Jn 1:47; 1Pe 2:22 [p]Eph 5:27
14:6 [q]Rev 8:13; 19:17 [r]S Rev 3:10 [s]S Rev 13:7
14:7 [t]Ps 34:9; Rev 15:4 [u]S Rev 11:13 [v]S Rev 10:6 [w]Rev 8:10; 16:4
14:8 [x]Isa 21:9; Jer 51:8; Rev 16:19; 17:5; 18:2,10 [y]Rev 17:2,4; 18:3, 9
14:9 [z]S Rev 13:12 [a]Rev 13:14 [b]S Rev 13:16
14:10 [c]Isa 51:17; Jer 25:15 [d]Jer 51:7; Rev 18:6 [e]S Rev 9:17
14:11 [f]Isa 34:10; Rev 19:3 [g]Rev 4:8 [h]ver 9; S Rev 13:12 [i]Rev 13:17
14:12 [j]S Heb 6:12 [k]Rev 13:10 [l]S Jn 14:15
14:13 [m]1Co 15:18; 1Th 4:16 [n]Rev 2:7; 22:17
14:14 [o]Mt 17:5 [p]Da 7:13; S Rev 1:13 [q]S Rev 6:2
14:15 [r]ver 17; Rev 11:19 [s]ver 18; Joel 3:13; Mk 4:29 [t]Jer 51:33

q *14* Daniel 7:13

14:4 DID NOT DEFILE THEMSELVES WITH WOMEN. This phrase is best understood in a spiritual sense. The 144,000 overcomers remained pure by refusing to conform to the pagan world system (see article on THE CHRISTIAN'S RELATIONSHIP TO THE WORLD, p. 546) or to become a part of the apostate church of the last days (see 17:1, notes). Note the character of those who will be close to Christ in heaven. (1) They are separated from the world and the apostate church (see article on SPIRITUAL SEPARATION FOR BELIEVERS, p. 371). (2) They follow Christ (cf. Mk 8:34; Jn 14:21, note). (3) They give themselves to God and Christ (v. 4). (4) They do not speak lies (v. 5; cf. 21:27—22:15). (5) They are morally blameless (see article on SANCTIFICATION, p. 526).

14:6 THE ETERNAL GOSPEL TO PROCLAIM. During the last half of the tribulation the gospel of Jesus will be proclaimed by an angel (or angels) to the entire world in clarity, power and warning. It is a call to fear God, give him glory, and worship him rather than the antichrist (vv. 7,9).

14:8 FALLEN IS BABYLON. Babylon represents the political, religious and commercial system of the whole world in the time of the end (see 17:1, note), and its fall is foretold here (see chs. 17–18 for more details).

14:9 IF ANYONE WORSHIPS THE BEAST. Those who worship the beast and receive his mark (see 13:16, note) will seal their doom, suffer severe divine judgments and be tormented for ever and ever (vv. 9–11; 9:4,13–21; 16:2; see Mt 10:28, note). The warning is directed to unbelievers (v. 6) and to saints who will be tempted to deny their faith in the face of the great danger of martyrdom (vv. 12–13).

14:12 WHO OBEY GOD'S COMMANDMENTS. The fate of the followers of the beast is awful (vv. 9–11). Therefore, the saints must continue to "obey God's commandments and remain faithful to Jesus." For their allegiance to Christ they will probably die (see next note).

14:13 BLESSED . . . DIE IN THE LORD. Those dying for their faith in Christ during the tribulation are especially blessed. They are released from persecution, torture and suffering and are taken to be with Christ.

14:14–16 LIKE A SON OF MAN. One like a son of man (i.e., Christ) is pictured as ready to wield the sickle of judgment on a world ripe with wickedness (vv. 14–20). Vv. 14–16 are a prediction or preview of the events of 16:12–16 and 19:11–20.

the cloud swung his sickle over the earth,
and the earth was harvested.
17Another angel came out of the temple
in heaven, and he too had a sharp sickle.[u]
18Still another angel, who had charge of
the fire, came from the altar[v] and called
in a loud voice to him who had the sharp
sickle, "Take your sharp sickle[w] and gather the clusters of grapes from the earth's
vine, because its grapes are ripe." 19The
angel swung his sickle on the earth, gathered its grapes and threw them into the
great winepress of God's wrath.[x] 20They
were trampled in the winepress[y] outside
the city,[z] and blood[a] flowed out of the
press, rising as high as the horses' bridles
for a distance of 1,600 stadia.[r]

Seven Angels With Seven Plagues

15 I saw in heaven another great and
marvelous sign:[b] seven angels[c]
with the seven last plagues[d]—last, because with them God's wrath is completed. 2And I saw what looked like a sea of
glass[e] mixed with fire and, standing beside the sea, those who had been victorious[f] over the beast[g] and his image[h] and
over the number of his name.[i] They held
harps[j] given them by God 3and sang the
song of Moses[k] the servant of God[l] and
the song of the Lamb:[m]

"Great and marvelous are your
deeds,[n]
Lord God Almighty.[o]
Just and true are your ways,[p]
King of the ages.
4Who will not fear you, O Lord,[q]
and bring glory to your name?[r]
For you alone are holy.
All nations will come
and worship before you,[s]
for your righteous acts[t] have been
revealed."

5After this I looked and in heaven the
temple,[u] that is, the tabernacle of the
Testimony,[v] was opened.[w] 6Out of the
temple[x] came the seven angels with the
seven plagues.[y] They were dressed in
clean, shining linen[z] and wore golden
sashes around their chests.[a] 7Then one of
the four living creatures[b] gave to the sev-
en angels[c] seven golden bowls filled with
the wrath of God, who lives for ever and
ever.[d] 8And the temple was filled with
smoke[e] from the glory of God and from
his power, and no one could enter the temple[f] until the seven plagues of the seven
angels were completed.

The Seven Bowls of God's Wrath

16 Then I heard a loud voice from the
temple[g] saying to the seven angels,[h] "Go, pour out the seven bowls of
God's wrath on the earth."[i]
2The first angel went and poured out
his bowl on the land,[j] and ugly and painful sores[k] broke out on the people who
had the mark of the beast and worshiped
his image.[l]
3The second angel poured out his bowl
on the sea, and it turned into blood like

14:17 [u]S ver 15 **14:18** [v]Rev 6:9; 8:5; 16:7 [w]S ver 15 **14:19** [x]Rev 19:15 **14:20** [y]ver 19; Isa 63:3; Joel 3:13; Rev 19:15 [z]Heb 13:12; Rev 11:8 [a]Ge 49:11; Dt 32:14 **15:1** [b]Rev 12:1,3 [c]ver 6-8; Rev 16:1; 17:1; 21:9 [d]Lev 26:21; Rev 9:20 **15:2** [e]Rev 4:6 [f]Rev 12:11 [g]Rev 13:1 [h]Rev 13:14 [i]Rev 13:17 [j]Rev 5:8; 14:2 **15:3** [k]Ex 15:1 [l]Jos 1:1 [m]S Rev 5:9 [n]Ps 111:2 [o]S Rev 1:8 [p]Ps 145:17 **15:4** [q]Jer 10:7 [r]Ps 86:9 [s]Isa 66:23 [t]Rev 19:8 **15:5** [u]Rev 11:19 [v]Ex 38:21; Nu 1:50 [w]S Mt 3:16 **15:6** [x]Rev 14:15 [y]S ver 1 [z]Eze 9:2; Da 10:5 [a]Rev 1:13 **15:7** [b]S Rev 4:6 [c]S ver 1 [d]S Rev 1:18 **15:8** [e]Isa 6:4 [f]Ex 40:34,35; 1Ki 8:10,11; 2Ch 5:13,14 **16:1** [g]Rev 11:19 [h]S Rev 15:1 [i]ver 2-21; Ps 79:6; Zep 3:8 **16:2** [j]Rev 8:7 [k]ver 11; Ex 9:9-11; Dt 28:35 [l]Rev 13:15-17; 14:9

[r] *20* That is, about 180 miles (about 300 kilometers)

14:19 THE GREAT WINEPRESS. In Biblical days grapes were put in a trough and trampled by foot to remove the wine (i.e., the juice of the grape). The treading of grapes was used in the OT as a figure for the execution of divine wrath on the ungodly (Isa 63:3; cf. Rev 19:15). At Christ's return after the tribulation, all unbelievers in the world will be gathered and judged in the Valley of Jehoshaphat (Ps 110:6; Joel 3:2,12–14; see Mt 25:32, note) and then killed (see Mt 13:40; Lk 17:37, note; cf. Ps 97:3–5; Pr 2:22; Isa 63:1–6; 66:15–17; Jer 25:30–33; Rev 19:15).

14:20 BLOOD FLOWED OUT. A great slaughter occurs in the last days of the tribulation. This refers to the battle of Armageddon (Zec 14:1–4; see Rev 16:16, note; 19:17–19).

15:1 SEVEN LAST PLAGUES. These plagues contain God's final judgments on the earth during the tribulation. They are called judgments of the "seven golden bowls" (v. 7), and they begin in ch. 16. The seven bowls of judgment may be the unfolding of the seventh trumpet judgment (see 11:15, note).

15:2 VICTORIOUS OVER THE BEAST. Standing on a crystal surface (cf. 4:6) are those who did not abandon their faith in Christ when persecuted, threatened or killed by the antichrist (cf. 13:7–11).

15:5 THE TABERNACLE OF THE TESTIMONY. John saw a temple in heaven like the tabernacle in the OT that contained the Ten Commandments (Ex 32:15; 40:34–35; Nu 17:7). This signifies that the judgments are the result of God's opposition to sin and of human rejection of his law and Word.

15:7 FILLED WITH THE WRATH OF GOD. This will be the last of the divine judgments on a wicked world before Christ's reign. The fact that no one can enter the temple until the plagues are completed means that no one can intercede to stop the judgment (v. 8). God has declared the end; his judgment will be complete and without mercy.

16:1 GOD'S WRATH. Pouring out the seven bowls of God's wrath now begins, at a point just before Christ returns to earth. A great world war will occur toward the end of these judgments (v. 14; see v. 16, note; Da 11:36–45), judgments more intense and severe than the preceding ones.

16:3 IT TURNED INTO BLOOD. The sea becomes so corrupt that every living creature in it dies and its

that of a dead man, and every living thing
in the sea died.[m]
4 The third angel poured out his bowl on
the rivers and springs of water,[n] and they
became blood.[o] 5 Then I heard the angel in
charge of the waters say:

"You are just in these judgments,[p]
you who are and who were,[q] the
Holy One,[r]
because you have so judged;[s]
6 for they have shed the blood of your
saints and prophets,[t]
and you have given them blood to
drink[u] as they deserve."

7 And I heard the altar[v] respond:

"Yes, Lord God Almighty,[w]
true and just are your judgments."[x]

8 The fourth angel[y] poured out his bowl
on the sun,[z] and the sun was given power
to scorch people with fire.[a] 9 They were
seared by the intense heat and they
cursed the name of God,[b] who had control
over these plagues, but they refused to
repent[c] and glorify him.[d]
10 The fifth angel poured out his bowl on
the throne of the beast,[e] and his kingdom
was plunged into darkness.[f] Men gnawed
their tongues in agony 11 and cursed[g] the
God of heaven[h] because of their pains and
their sores,[i] but they refused to repent of
what they had done.[j]
12 The sixth angel poured out his bowl
on the great river Euphrates,[k] and its water was dried up to prepare the way[l] for
the kings from the East.[m] 13 Then I saw
three evil[s] spirits[n] that looked like
frogs;[o] they came out of the mouth of the
dragon,[p] out of the mouth of the beast[q]
and out of the mouth of the false prophet.[r] 14 They are spirits of demons[s] performing miraculous signs,[t] and they go
out to the kings of the whole world,[u] to
gather them for the battle[v] on the great
day[w] of God Almighty.
15 "Behold, I come like a thief![x] Blessed
is he who stays awake[y] and keeps his
clothes with him, so that he may not go
naked and be shamefully exposed."[z]
16 Then they gathered the kings togeth-

16:3 [m] Ex 7:17-21; Rev 8:8,9; Rev 11:6
16:4 [n] Rev 8:10 [o] Ex 7:17-21
16:5 [p] Rev 15:3 [q] S Rev 1:4 [r] Rev 15:4 [s] Rev 6:10
16:6 [t] Lk 11:49-51 [u] Isa 49:26; Rev 17:6; 18:24
16:7 [v] Rev 6:9; 14:18 [w] S Rev 1:8 [x] Rev 15:3; 19:2
16:8 [y] Rev 8:12 [z] Rev 6:12 [a] Rev 14:18
16:9 [b] ver 11,21 [c] S Rev 2:21 [d] S Rev 11:13
16:10 [e] Rev 13:2 [f] Ex 10:21-23; Isa 8:22; Rev 8:12; 9:2
16:11 [g] ver 9,21 [h] Rev 11:13 [i] ver 2 [j] S Rev 2:21
16:12 [k] S Rev 9:14 [l] Isa 11:15,16 [m] Isa 41:2; 46:11
16:13 [n] Rev 18:2 [o] Ex 8:6 [p] S Rev 12:3 [q] S Rev 13:1 [r] Rev 19:20; 20:10
16:14 [s] 1Ti 4:1 [t] S Mt 24:24 [u] S Mt 24:14 [v] Rev 17:14; 19:19; 20:8 [w] S Rev 6:17
16:15 [x] S Lk 12:39 [y] Lk 12:37 [z] Rev 3:18

[s] *13* Greek *unclean*

polluted color looks like blood (Ex 7:20–25). This also happens with the rivers and springs (v. 4).

16:7 JUST ARE YOUR JUDGMENTS. Those who question God's righteousness in his judgments do not understand sin's terrible evil or God's intense hatred of it. A holy and just God must of necessity oppose and punish evil (see Jn 3:19, note; Heb 1:9, note; cf. Ps 119:137).

16:9 INTENSE HEAT. A great heat wave will spread across the earth and become so unbearable that people will blaspheme God (cf. Mal 4:1). Their hearts will be so hardened that they will refuse to repent (see v. 11, note). Compare this with the condition of those in heaven, of whom it is said, "the sun will not beat upon them, nor any scorching heat" (7:16).

16:10 THE THRONE OF THE BEAST. The fifth bowl begins to throw the world dominion of the antichrist into confusion. This special judgment centers on his headquarters and followers.

16:11 REFUSED TO REPENT. Even in the middle of God's terrible judgment, men and women will choose to live in sin and to persist in their rebellion against righteousness. Repentance is the only act that will stop God's judgments (cf. 2:21; 9:21; 16:9), but that act they refuse to do.

16:12 KINGS FROM THE EAST. These are nations from the Orient that will participate in a great conflict, driven by satanic power to the war of Armageddon (see v. 16, note; 19:17–21). The sixth angel prepares the way for the final war of the age by a drying up of the river Euphrates, allowing armies from the east to approach the vicinity of Israel (Isa 11:15).

16:13 FROGS. These unclean spirits are demons who can work miracles and thus deceive the nations in order to support evil, sin and the antichrist. The "dragon" must be identified with Satan (12:9), and the "beast" with the antichrist (see ch. 13).

16:14 SPIRITS OF DEMONS PERFORMING MIRACULOUS SIGNS. During the tribulation rulers of the nations will be demonized. Deceived by Satan through miracles, they will enter into an insane scheme plunging the entire world into a great holocaust (see article on THE GREAT TRIBULATION, p. 52, and THE AGE OF THE ANTICHRIST, p. 447).

16:16 ARMAGEDDON. Armageddon (Gk *harmagedōn*), located in north-central Palestine, means "the mountain of Megiddo"; it will be the center of "the battle on the great day of God Almighty" (v. 14). This war will occur toward the end of the tribulation and conclude when Christ returns to destroy the wicked (see 14:19, note), to deliver his people and to inaugurate his Messianic kingdom. Note the following concerning this event. (1) The prophets of the OT prophesied the event (Dt 32:43; Jer 25:31; Joel 3:2,9–17; Zep 3:8; Zec 14:2–5).

(2) Satan and demons will gather together many nations under the direction of the antichrist in order to make war against God, his armies and his people, and to destroy Jerusalem (vv. 13–14,16; 17:14; 19:14,19; see also Eze 38–39, Zec 14:2). Although the focal point will be in the land of Israel, the event of Armageddon will involve the whole world (Jer 25:29–38).

(3) Christ will return and supernaturally intervene to destroy the antichrist and his armies (19:19–21; Zec 14:1–5) and all who disobey the gospel (Ps 110:5;

er[a] to the place that in Hebrew[b] is called
Armageddon.[c]
17The seventh angel poured out his
bowl into the air,[d] and out of the temple[e]
came a loud voice[f] from the throne, saying, "It is done!"[g] **18**Then there came
flashes of lightning, rumblings, peals of
thunder[h] and a severe earthquake.[i] No
earthquake like it has ever occurred since
man has been on earth,[j] so tremendous
was the quake. **19**The great city[k] split into
three parts, and the cities of the nations
collapsed. God remembered[l] Babylon the
Great[m] and gave her the cup filled with
the wine of the fury of his wrath.[n] **20**Every
island fled away and the mountains could
not be found.[o] **21**From the sky huge hailstones[p] of about a hundred pounds each
fell upon men. And they cursed God[q] on
account of the plague of hail,[r] because
the plague was so terrible.

The Woman on the Beast

17 One of the seven angels[s] who had
the seven bowls[t] came and said to
me, "Come, I will show you the punishment[u] of the great prostitute,[v] who sits
on many waters.[w] **2**With her the kings of
the earth committed adultery and the inhabitants of the earth were intoxicated
with the wine of her adulteries."[x]
3Then the angel carried me away in the
Spirit[y] into a desert.[z] There I saw a woman sitting on a scarlet[a] beast that was
covered with blasphemous names[b] and
had seven heads and ten horns.[c] **4**The
woman was dressed in purple and scarlet,
and was glittering with gold, precious
stones and pearls.[d] She held a golden
cup[e] in her hand, filled with abominable
things and the filth of her adulteries.[f]
5This title was written on her forehead:

MYSTERY[g]
BABYLON THE GREAT[h]
THE MOTHER OF PROSTITUTES[i]
AND OF THE ABOMINATIONS OF THE EARTH.

16:16 [a] ver 14 [b] Rev 9:11 [c] Jdg 5:19; 2Ki 23:29,30; Zec 12:11 **16:17** [d] Eph 2:2 [e] Rev 14:15 [f] Rev 11:15 [g] Rev 21:6 **16:18** [h] S Rev 4:5 [i] S Rev 6:12 [j] Da 12:1; Mt 24:21 **16:19** [k] S Rev 17:18 [l] Rev 18:5 [m] S Rev 14:8 [n] Rev 14:10 **16:20** [o] S Rev 6:14 **16:21** [p] Eze 13:13; 38:22; Rev 8:7; 11:19 [q] ver 9,11 [r] Ex 9:23-25 **17:1** [s] S Rev 15:1 [t] Rev 15:7 [u] Rev 16:19 [v] ver 5,15,16; Isa 23:17; Rev 19:2 [w] Jer 51:13 **17:2** [x] S Rev 14:8 **17:3** [y] S Rev 1:10 [z] Rev 12:6,14 [a] Rev 18:12,16 [b] Rev 13:1 [c] S Rev 12:3 **17:4** [d] Eze 28:13; Rev 18:16 [e] Jer 51:7; Rev 18:6 [f] ver 2; S Rev 14:8 **17:5** [g] ver 7 [h] S Rev 14:8 [i] ver 1,2

Isa 66:15–16; 2Th 1:7–10). God will also send destruction and earthquakes on the whole world at this time (vv. 18–19; Jer 25:29–33).

16:19 BABYLON THE GREAT. See next note.

17:1 SAID TO ME. Chs. 17–18 portray the fall of Babylon the Great. (1) Babylon (v. 5) is the symbol for the whole world system dominated by Satan and manifesting wickedness politically, religiously and commercially. (2) Babylon will be completely destroyed during the last three and a half years of this age. Religious Babylon (i.e., the prostitute) will be destroyed by the antichrist (vv. 16–17), while political Babylon will be destroyed by Christ at his coming (19:11–21).

17:1 THE GREAT PROSTITUTE. This represents religious Babylon and encompasses all false religions, including apostate Christianity. In the Bible prostitution and adultery, when used figuratively, normally denote religious apostasy and unfaithfulness to God (Isa 1:21; Jer 3:9; Eze 16:14–18,32; Jas 4:4), and signify a people who profess to serve God while actually worshiping and serving other gods. Note the sharp contrast between the great prostitute and the bride of the Lamb (see 19:7–8). The prostitute is subject to Satan; the bride is subject to Christ. Satan clothes the one (v. 4); God clothes the other (19:8). Eternal death is the portion of the prostitute; eternal glory the lot of the bride.

Concerning this false religion, (1) the prostitute will reject the gospel of Christ and the apostles, the power of godliness and the basic doctrines of Christianity (Mt 24:24; 2Ti 3:5; 4:3).

(2) She will enter into partnership with the powers and philosophy of "Babylon," i.e., the world system with its immorality (v. 2; 3:16). Religious and political power will be combined to take spiritual control over the nations (v. 18).

(3) Her leaders will persecute Christ's true followers (v. 6). She will be a melting pot for many faiths and creeds, and doctrine will not be of primary importance. Her chief concern will be fellowship and unity with her religious system, values and goals. She will become a "home for demons and a haunt for every evil spirit" (18:2; Isa 47:12–13).

(4) All true believers are commanded to come out of her or they will be condemned with her (18:4).

(5) God will cause the antichrist to destroy her (see v. 16, note).

17:2 INHABITANTS OF THE EARTH. The true kinship of the great prostitute (see previous note) is not with Christ but with the world. (1) Hypocrites and false prophets achieve worldly success as a result of her doctrine, for she encourages worldly people to join her. The false religious system allows her members to profess to be of God, yet at the same time to commit adultery. (2) Compromise with political power and toleration of unrighteousness are her trademarks. As a prostitute the apostate church sells her favor to the world at every opportunity (18:3).

17:3 A SCARLET BEAST. This beast is the world government or political Babylon, which supports the apostate spiritual power. For comments on the "seven heads," see v. 10, note; on the "ten horns," see v. 12, note.

17:4 A GOLDEN CUP. This cup, "filled with abominable things" but beautiful on the outside, reveals the spiritual condition of the apostate church of the last days (cf. Mt 23:27–28). The church that holds the golden cup will offer people both God and worldly satisfaction, i.e., a perverted Christianity that assures its members they can enjoy immorality and still be accepted by God.

17:5 BABYLON THE GREAT. The origin of the name "Babylon" is from "Babel," which symbolizes false religion, sorcery, astrology and rebellion against God (Ge 10:8–10; 11:4; Isa 47:13).

6 I saw that the woman was drunk with the
blood of the saints,[j] the blood of those
who bore testimony to Jesus.

When I saw her, I was greatly astonished. 7 Then the angel said to me: "Why
are you astonished? I will explain to you
the mystery[k] of the woman and of the
beast she rides, which has the seven
heads and ten horns.[l] 8 The beast, which
you saw, once was, now is not, and will
come up out of the Abyss[m] and go to his
destruction.[n] The inhabitants of the
earth[o] whose names have not been written in the book of life[p] from the creation
of the world will be astonished[q] when
they see the beast, because he once was,
now is not, and yet will come.

9 "This calls for a mind with wisdom.[r]
The seven heads[s] are seven hills on
which the woman sits. 10 They are also
seven kings. Five have fallen, one is, the
other has not yet come; but when he does
come, he must remain for a little while.
11 The beast who once was, and now is
not,[t] is an eighth king. He belongs to the
seven and is going to his destruction.

12 "The ten horns[u] you saw are ten
kings who have not yet received a kingdom, but who for one hour[v] will receive
authority as kings along with the beast.
13 They have one purpose and will give
their power and authority to the beast.[w]
14 They will make war[x] against the Lamb,
but the Lamb will overcome[y] them because he is Lord of lords and King of
kings[z] — and with him will be his called,
chosen[a] and faithful followers."

15 Then the angel said to me, "The waters[b] you saw, where the prostitute sits,
are peoples, multitudes, nations and languages.[c] 16 The beast and the ten horns[d]
you saw will hate the prostitute.[e] They
will bring her to ruin[f] and leave her naked;[g] they will eat her flesh[h] and burn
her with fire.[i] 17 For God has put it into
their hearts[j] to accomplish his purpose
by agreeing to give the beast their power
to rule,[k] until God's words are fulfilled.[l]
18 The woman you saw is the great city[m]
that rules over the kings of the earth."

The Fall of Babylon

18 After this I saw another angel[n]
coming down from heaven.[o] He
had great authority, and the earth was illuminated by his splendor.[p] 2 With a
mighty voice he shouted:

"Fallen! Fallen is Babylon the Great![q]

17:6 [j] Rev 16:6; 18:24 **17:7** [k] ver 5 [l] ver 3; S Rev 12:3 **17:8** [m] S Lk 8:31 [n] Rev 13:10 [o] S Rev 3:10 [p] S Rev 20:12 [q] Rev 13:3 **17:9** [r] Rev 13:18 [s] ver 3 **17:11** [t] ver 8 **17:12** [u] S Rev 12:3 [v] Rev 18:10,17,19 **17:13** [w] ver 17 **17:14** [x] S Rev 16:14 [y] S Jn 16:33 [z] S 1Ti 6:15 [a] Mt 22:14 **17:15** [b] ver 1; Isa 8:7; Jer 47:2 [c] S Rev 13:7 **17:16** [d] S Rev 12:3 [e] ver 1 [f] Rev 18:17, 19 [g] Eze 16:37,39 [h] Rev 19:18 [i] Rev 18:8 **17:17** [j] 2Co 8:16 [k] ver 13 [l] Jer 39:16; Rev 10:7 **17:18** [m] Rev 16:19; 18:10,18,19,21 **18:1** [n] Rev 17:1 [o] Rev 10:1; 20:1 [p] Eze 43:2 **18:2** [q] S Rev 14:8

17:6 THE BLOOD OF THE SAINTS. The false religion in league with the world system will persecute everyone truly devoted to Christ and the Biblical faith.

17:8 WRITTEN IN THE BOOK OF LIFE FROM THE CREATION OF THE WORLD. These words cannot be used to prove a predetermined individual election to salvation or damnation, for according to John, a person's name may be erased from the book of life by disloyalty and a failure to overcome (3:5; see 13:8, note; cf. Ps 69:28).

17:8 BEAST ... ONCE WAS ... NOW IS NOT, AND YET WILL COME. Some interpret this verse to mean the antichrist is a person who once lived in history, but is now dead, and in the future will come up out of the Abyss, remain on earth for a period and then finally be destroyed (cf. vv. 8–11; 19:20). Others relate it to John's statement in 13:3 (see note).

17:10 SEVEN KINGS. Some believe the seven kings represent seven secular kingdoms of the world (the five fallen kingdoms are most likely Egypt, Assyria, Babylonia, Medo-Persia and Greece). John informs his readers that the Roman empire is part of this sequence (i.e., the one that "is"). The one yet to come refers to the feet of iron and clay on the image pictured in Da 2. This kingdom represents the nationalistic states that have followed the fall of the Roman empire, up to and including the present time. The next kingdom, the eighth (v. 11), will be that of the antichrist.

17:11 AN EIGHTH KING. The beast, i.e., the antichrist (ch. 13), will be the head of the final world empire. He "belongs to the seven" (see previous note), but is also "an eighth." This may mean that he belongs to the same ungodly world system as did the first seven, yet he is not a part of them (see v. 8, note). The antichrist will be destroyed at the end of the tribulation.

17:12 TEN HORNS ... TEN KINGS. These kings are ten nations that will have great political power and support the future world ruler (v. 13). They make up a world confederacy of nations that will oppose Christ and the true Biblical faith (cf. Da 7:23–25).

17:14 MAKE WAR AGAINST THE LAMB. Christ will overthrow the antichrist and those who align themselves with him at the final battle (see 16:14,16, notes).

17:15 WATERS. The prostitute sitting on the waters indicates that there will be one ecumenical, universal, apostate religious system in the first part of the tribulation. This will be replaced by the religion of the antichrist when he gains great political power (Mt 24:15; 2Th 2:3–4).

17:16 WILL HATE THE PROSTITUTE. Sometime during the antichrist's rule, the prostitute (see v. 1, note) will be hated by the antichrist and his supporters, and they will utterly destroy her and her institutions. This is God's judgment against the world religious system that rejected God's truth in Christ. This may occur at the midpoint of the seven-year tribulation, when the beast professes to be god and demands that all worship him (13:8,15; cf. Da 9:27; 11:36–38; see article on THE GREAT TRIBULATION, p. 52, and THE AGE OF THE ANTICHRIST, p. 447).

18:2 FALLEN IS BABLYON THE GREAT! In ch. 18, Babylon the Great is portrayed primarily in its commercial and political aspect. (1) Some believe

She has become a home for demons
and a haunt for every evil[t] spirit,[r]
a haunt for every unclean and
detestable bird.[s]
3For all the nations have drunk
the maddening wine of her
adulteries.[t]
The kings of the earth committed
adultery with her,[u]
and the merchants of the earth
grew rich[v] from her excessive
luxuries."[w]

4Then I heard another voice from heaven say:

"Come out of her, my people,[x]
so that you will not share in her
sins,
so that you will not receive any of
her plagues;[y]
5for her sins are piled up to heaven,[z]
and God has remembered[a] her
crimes.
6Give back to her as she has given;
pay her back[b] double[c] for what
she has done.
Mix her a double portion from her
own cup.[d]
7Give her as much torture and grief
as the glory and luxury she gave
herself.[e]
In her heart she boasts,
'I sit as queen; I am not a widow,
and I will never mourn.'[f]
8Therefore in one day[g] her plagues
will overtake her:
death, mourning and famine.
She will be consumed by fire,[h]
for mighty is the Lord God who
judges her.

9"When the kings of the earth who committed adultery with her[i] and shared her
luxury[j] see the smoke of her burning,[k]
they will weep and mourn over her.[l]
10Terrified at her torment, they will stand
far off[m] and cry:

" 'Woe! Woe, O great city,[n]
O Babylon, city of power!
In one hour[o] your doom has come!'

11"The merchants[p] of the earth will
weep and mourn[q] over her because no one
buys their cargoes any more[r]— 12cargoes of gold, silver, precious stones and
pearls; fine linen, purple, silk and scarlet
cloth; every sort of citron wood, and articles of every kind made of ivory, costly
wood, bronze, iron and marble;[s] 13cargoes of cinnamon and spice, of incense,
myrrh and frankincense, of wine and olive
oil, of fine flour and wheat; cattle and
sheep; horses and carriages; and bodies
and souls of men.[t]
14"They will say, 'The fruit you longed
for is gone from you. All your riches and
splendor have vanished, never to be recovered.' 15The merchants who sold these
things and gained their wealth from her[u]
will stand far off,[v] terrified at her torment. They will weep and mourn[w] 16and
cry out:

" 'Woe! Woe, O great city,[x]
dressed in fine linen, purple and
scarlet,
and glittering with gold, precious
stones and pearls![y]
17In one hour[z] such great wealth has
been brought to ruin!'[a]

"Every sea captain, and all who travel
by ship, the sailors, and all who earn their
living from the sea,[b] will stand far off.[c]
18When they see the smoke of her burn-

18:2 [r]Rev 16:13 [s]Isa 13:21,22; 34:11,13-15; Jer 50:39; 51:37; Zep 2:14,15 **18:3** [t]S Rev 14:8 [u]Rev 17:2 [v]ver 11,15,23; Eze 27:9-25 [w]ver 7,9 **18:4** [x]Isa 48:20; Jer 50:8; 51:6,9, 45; 2Co 6:17 [y]Ge 19:15 **18:5** [z]2Ch 28:9; Ezr 9:6; Jer 51:9 [a]Rev 16:19 **18:6** [b]Ps 137:8; Jer 50:15,29 [c]Isa 40:2 [d]Rev 14:10; 16:19; 17:4 **18:7** [e]Eze 28:2-8 [f]Ps 10:6; Isa 47:7, 8; Zep 2:15 **18:8** [g]ver 10; Isa 9:14; 47:9; Jer 50:31,32 [h]Rev 17:16 **18:9** [i]ver 3; Rev 14:8; 17:2,4 [j]ver 3,7 [k]ver 18; Rev 14:11; 19:3 [l]Jer 51:8; Eze 26:17,18 **18:10** [m]ver 15,17 [n]ver 16,19 [o]ver 17; Rev 17:12 **18:11** [p]Eze 27:27 [q]ver 15,19; Eze 27:31 [r]S ver 3 **18:12** [s]Eze 27:12-22; Rev 17:4 **18:13** [t]Eze 27:13; 1Ti 1:10 **18:15** [u]S ver 3 [v]ver 10,17 [w]ver 11,19; Eze 27:31 **18:16** [x]ver 10,19 [y]Rev 17:4 **18:17** [z]ver 10; Rev 17:12 [a]Rev 17:16 [b]Eze 27:28-30 [c]ver 10,15

t 2 Greek *unclean*

Babylon here represents a literal city or nation that embodies the ungodly aspects of the city described in the chapter. (2) Others believe it represents the whole ungodly world system brought under the antichrist's rule. Here her commercial system is destroyed; in ch. 19 her political system is judged by God at the end of the tribulation (cf. 19:17–21; Isa 13:1–11).

18:4 COME OUT OF HER, MY PEOPLE. This is God's prophetic call to the last generation of believers to come out of Babylon the Great (v. 2), because those among God's people who remain in the ungodly system will inevitably "share in her sins" and therefore "receive . . . her plagues." The call to be separate from the world and false religious institutions has been an essential aspect of salvation throughout redemptive history (cf. Isa 52:11; Jer 51:45; 1Co 11:32; see article on SPIRITUAL SEPARATION FOR BELIEVERS, p. 371).

18:7 GLORY AND LUXURY SHE GAVE HERSELF. The suffering and misery to fall on commercial Babylon will be in proportion to the self-glorifying and luxurious lifestyle she lived. The rich, powerful and unscrupulous enterprisers who rejected God and piled up wealth to the injury of others will be stripped of their wealth in one day (v. 8; cf. Jas 5:1–6).

18:9 KINGS . . . WEEP AND MOURN OVER HER. All those whose main concern was money, luxury and gratification of pleasure will weep and mourn, for the god of their life is destroyed. They can no longer profit in merchandise, since their great riches are gone (cf. Jas 5:1–9). God clearly indicates here his hatred for businesses and governments founded on greed and oppressive power. He stands against individuals who seek riches, status and pleasure instead of the humble values of Jesus Christ. Those who live in selfish luxury and pleasure will be brought down by God's wrath.

ing,[d] they will exclaim, 'Was there ever a
city like this great city[e]?'[f] 19They will
throw dust on their heads,[g] and with
weeping and mourning[h] cry out:

" 'Woe! Woe, O great city,[i]
where all who had ships on the sea
became rich through her wealth!
In one hour she has been brought to
ruin![j]
20Rejoice over her, O heaven![k]
Rejoice, saints and apostles and
prophets!
God has judged her for the way she
treated you.' "[l]

21Then a mighty angel[m] picked up a
boulder the size of a large millstone and
threw it into the sea,[n] and said:

"With such violence
the great city[o] of Babylon will be
thrown down,
never to be found again.
22The music of harpists and musicians,
flute players and trumpeters,
will never be heard in you again.[p]
No workman of any trade
will ever be found in you again.
The sound of a millstone
will never be heard in you again.[q]
23The light of a lamp
will never shine in you again.
The voice of bridegroom and bride
will never be heard in you again.[r]
Your merchants were the world's
great men.[s]
By your magic spell[t] all the
nations were led astray.
24In her was found the blood of
prophets and of the saints,[u]
and of all who have been killed on
the earth."[v]

18:18 [d]ver 9; Rev 19:3 [e]S Rev 17:18 [f]Eze 27:32; Rev 13:4 **18:19** [g]Jos 7:6; La 2:10; Eze 27:30 [h]ver 11, 15; Eze 27:31 [i]ver 10,16; Rev 17:18 [j]Rev 17:16 **18:20** [k]Jer 51:48; S Rev 12:12 [l]Rev 19:2 **18:21** [m]Rev 5:2; 10:1 [n]Jer 51:63 [o]S Rev 17:18 **18:22** [p]Isa 24:8; Eze 26:13 [q]Jer 25:10 **18:23** [r]Jer 7:34; 16:9; 25:10 [s]ver 3; Isa 23:8 [t]Na 3:4 **18:24** [u]Rev 16:6; 17:6 [v]Jer 51:49; Mt 23:35

Hallelujah!

19 After this I heard what sounded
like the roar of a great multitude[w]
in heaven shouting:

"Hallelujah![x]
Salvation[y] and glory and power[z]
belong to our God,
2 for true and just are his
judgments.[a]
He has condemned the great
prostitute[b]
who corrupted the earth by her
adulteries.
He has avenged on her the blood of
his servants."[c]

3And again they shouted:

"Hallelujah![d]
The smoke from her goes up for ever
and ever."[e]

4The twenty-four elders[f] and the four
living creatures[g] fell down[h] and worshiped God, who was seated on the
throne. And they cried:

"Amen, Hallelujah!"[i]

5Then a voice came from the throne,
saying:

"Praise our God,
all you his servants,[j]
you who fear him,
both small and great!"[k]

6Then I heard what sounded like a
great multitude,[l] like the roar of rushing
waters[m] and like loud peals of thunder,
shouting:

"Hallelujah![n]
For our Lord God Almighty[o]
reigns.[p]
7Let us rejoice and be glad

19:1 [w]ver 6; Rev 11:15 [x]ver 3, 4,6 [y]Rev 7:10; 12:10 [z]Rev 4:11; 7:12 **19:2** [a]Rev 16:7 [b]S Rev 17:1 [c]S Rev 6:10 **19:3** [d]ver 1,4,6 [e]Isa 34:10; Rev 14:11 **19:4** [f]S Rev 4:4 [g]S Rev 4:6 [h]S Rev 4:10 [i]ver 1,3,6 **19:5** [j]Ps 134:1 [k]ver 18; Ps 115:13; Rev 11:18; 13:16; 20:12 **19:6** [l]ver 1; Rev 11:15 [m]S Rev 1:15 [n]ver 1,3,4 [o]S Rev 1:8 [p]Rev 11:15

18:20 REJOICE OVER HER. All the godly in heaven and earth rejoice at God's righteous judgment on the great satanic system of evil with all its wicked manifestations, sinful pleasures, self-centered luxury, humanistic government and godless commerce. The exuberant celebration of the saints in heaven, described in 19:1–10, is proportionate to their present grief at evil's triumph in this world. The mark of God's true children is their distress at the immoral conduct around them. They will be tormented day after day by the lawless deeds they see and about which they hear (2Pe 2:7–8).

18:21 NEVER TO BE FOUND AGAIN. An angel declares the final fall of political Babylon. The antichrist and his ungodly world system will be totally destroyed at "the battle on the great day of God Almighty," when Christ returns to earth (16:14; see 14:8; 16:14,16, notes; 19:11–21; cf. the record of Babylon's fall in Da 5).

19:1 AFTER THIS. Ch. 19 deals with the end of the tribulation and Christ's glorious second coming to earth to destroy the ungodly and reign with his people.

19:1 HALLELUJAH! This is the first of four times the word "Hallelujah" occurs in the NT (see vv. 1,3–4,6). It is derived from two Hebrew words: *halal*, meaning "praise," and *jah*, meaning "Yahweh" or "LORD"; thus, it means "Praise the Lord!" The people in heaven praise the Lord because God has judged the world and avenged those who suffered at its hand, and because Jesus Christ is returning to earth to reign (vv. 6,11; 20:4). This is heaven's "Hallelujah Chorus."

19:7 HIS BRIDE HAS MADE HERSELF READY. The chronology of ch. 19 places the bride (i.e., the church, 2Co 11:2) already in heaven before Christ's coming to earth. Many interpreters believe this indicates the church has already been caught up to heav-

and give him glory![q]
For the wedding of the Lamb[r] has
come,
and his bride[s] has made herself
ready.
8Fine linen,[t] bright and clean,
was given her to wear."
(Fine linen stands for the righteous acts[u]
of the saints.)

9Then the angel said to me,[v] "Write:[w]
'Blessed are those who are invited to the
wedding supper of the Lamb!' "[x] And he
added, "These are the true words of
God."[y]
10At this I fell at his feet to worship
him.[z] But he said to me, "Do not do it! I
am a fellow servant with you and with
your brothers who hold to the testimony
of Jesus. Worship God![a] For the testimony
of Jesus[b] is the spirit of prophecy."

The Rider on the White Horse

11I saw heaven standing open[c] and
there before me was a white horse, whose
rider[d] is called Faithful and True.[e] With
justice he judges and makes war.[f] **12**His
eyes are like blazing fire,[g] and on his head
are many crowns.[h] He has a name written
on him[i] that no one knows but he him-

19:7 [q]S Rev 11:13 [r]ver 9; Mt 22:2; 25:10; Eph 5:32 [s]Rev 21:2,9; 22:17 **19:8** [t]ver 14; Rev 15:6 [u]Isa 61:10; Eze 44:17; Zec 3:4; Rev 15:4 **19:9** [v]ver 10 [w]Rev 1:19 [x]Lk 14:15 [y]Rev 21:5; 22:6 **19:10** [z]Rev 22:8 [a]Ac 10:25,26; Rev 22:9 [b]S Rev 1:2 **19:11** [c]S Mt 3:16 [d]ver 19,21; Rev 6:2 [e]Rev 3:14 [f]Ex 15:3; Ps 96:13; Isa 11:4 **19:12** [g]S Rev 1:14 [h]Rev 6:2; 12:3 [i]ver 16 [j]S Rev 2:17 **19:13** [k]Isa 63:2,3 [l]Jn 1:1 **19:14** [m]ver 8 [n]S Rev 3:4 **19:15** [o]ver 21; S Rev 1:16 [p]Isa 11:4; 2Th 2:8 [q]Ps 2:9; Rev 2:27; 12:5 [r]S Rev 14:20 **19:16** [s]ver 12 [t]S 1Ti 6:15 **19:17** [u]ver 21 [v]Rev 8:13; 14:6 [w]Jer 12:9; Eze 39:17 [x]Isa 34:6;

self.[j] **13**He is dressed in a robe dipped in
blood,[k] and his name is the Word of God.[l]
14The armies of heaven were following
him, riding on white horses and dressed in
fine linen,[m] white[n] and clean. **15**Out of his
mouth comes a sharp sword[o] with which
to strike down[p] the nations. "He will rule
them with an iron scepter."[u][q] He treads
the winepress[r] of the fury of the wrath of
God Almighty. **16**On his robe and on his
thigh he has this name written:[s]

KING OF KINGS AND LORD OF LORDS.[t]

17And I saw an angel standing in the
sun, who cried in a loud voice to all the
birds[u] flying in midair,[v] "Come,[w] gather
together for the great supper of God,[x]
18so that you may eat the flesh of kings,
generals, and mighty men, of horses and
their riders, and the flesh of all people,[y]
free and slave,[z] small and great."[a]
19Then I saw the beast[b] and the kings
of the earth[c] and their armies gathered
together to make war against the rider on
the horse[d] and his army. **20**But the beast
was captured, and with him the false

Jer 46:10 **19:18** [y]Eze 39:18-20 [z]Rev 6:15 [a]S ver 5 **19:19** [b]S Rev 13:1 [c]Rev 16:14,16 [d]ver 11,21

[u] *15* Psalm 2:9

en before Christ's coming pictured in vv. 11–21 (see article on THE RAPTURE, p. 440). Two reasons are given: (1) The bride is entirely dressed and ready in heaven for the "wedding of the Lamb"; thus, the church must already be raptured and in heaven. (2) The bride who is already in heaven is fully clothed in "the righteous acts of the saints" (v. 8). For the righteous acts of the saints to be complete, they must be in heaven and delivered from all impurity.

19:10 OF JESUS IS THE SPIRIT OF PROPHECY. Ultimately, all prophecy is related to Jesus and his redemptive work and exalts him.

19:11 I SAW HEAVEN STANDING OPEN. This verse sets forth the beginning of Christ's second coming to earth as King of kings and Lord of lords (v. 16). He comes from heaven as the Warrior-Messiah (cf. 2Th 1:7–8) to establish truth and justice (Ps 96:13), to judge the nations and to wage war against evil (cf. Jn 5:30). This is the event for which the faithful of all generations have waited.

19:14 ARMIES. The armies who return with Christ include all the saints who are already in heaven (cf. 17:14). Their white clothing confirms this.

19:15 STRIKE DOWN THE NATIONS. When Christ returns to earth, he will punish the wicked nations. To "rule them with an iron scepter" means to destroy them (cf. Ps 2:9). "He treads the winepress" indicates the awfulness of his judgment (cf. Isa 64:1–2; Zec 14:3–4; Mt 24:29–30; cf. Rev 14:19, note).

19:15 FURY OF THE WRATH OF GOD ALMIGHTY. This is a stern reminder that God hates sin. The sentimental view that Christ tolerates sin and immorality because of his love finds no place in Christ's own revelation of himself in this book (see next note).

19:17 THE GREAT SUPPER OF GOD. This supper refers to the battle of Armageddon (see 16:16, note). (1) The destruction of God's enemies will be so great that it will require a multitude of birds to clean up the battlefield. It is called the "great supper of God," for God will provide food for the birds of prey. (2) The scene is one of judgment against this world's terrible cruelty and evil. Other prophecies that in all probability refer to this coming event are 14:14–20; 16:13–16; 17:14; Jer 51:27–36; Eze 39:17–20; Joel 3:9–15; Zep 3:8; Zec 14:2–5.

19:19 TO MAKE WAR. In preparation for the war, God through demonic agency will gather the nations together in the vicinity of Armageddon (see 16:16, note; Jer 25:32–33; Joel 3:2; Zep 3:8; Zec 14:2–3). (1) The war will end swiftly with the destruction of the antichrist and all the ungodly (vv. 19–21). (2) God's judgment not only includes the gathered armies but extends to the entire world (Jer 25:29–33).

19:20 FALSE PROPHET . . . THE MIRACULOUS SIGNS. John again describes the false prophet by one outstanding characteristic: he deceived many by performing miraculous signs (cf. 13:13–15; cf. 2Th 2:9–10). The conclusion is obvious: in the last days those who seek to persevere in faithfulness to Christ and his commandments (cf. 14:12) must not base their evaluation of truth solely on success or miracles. The Lord himself solemnly warns: "For false Christs

prophet[e] who had performed the miraculous signs[f] on his behalf.[g] With these
signs he had deluded[h] those who had received the mark of the beast[i] and worshiped his image.[j] The two of them were
thrown alive into the fiery lake[k] of burning sulfur.[l] **21**The rest of them were killed
with the sword[m] that came out of the
mouth of the rider on the horse,[n] and all
the birds[o] gorged themselves on their
flesh.

The Thousand Years

20 And I saw an angel coming down
out of heaven,[p] having the key[q] to
the Abyss[r] and holding in his hand a
great chain. **2**He seized the dragon, that
ancient serpent, who is the devil, or Satan,[s] and bound him for a thousand
years.[t] **3**He threw him into the Abyss,[u]
and locked and sealed[v] it over him, to
keep him from deceiving the nations[w]
anymore until the thousand years were
ended. After that, he must be set free for
a short time.

4I saw thrones[x] on which were seated
those who had been given authority to
judge.[y] And I saw the souls of those who
had been beheaded[z] because of their testimony for Jesus[a] and because of the word
of God.[b] They had not worshiped the
beast[c] or his image and had not received
his mark on their foreheads or their
hands.[d] They came to life and reigned[e]
with Christ a thousand years. **5**(The rest
of the dead did not come to life until the
thousand years were ended.) This is the

19:20 [e] Rev 16:13 [f] S Mt 24:24 [g] Rev 13:12 [h] Rev 13:14 [i] Rev 13:16 [j] Rev 13:15 [k] Da 7:11; Rev 20:10,14,15; 21:8 [l] S Rev 9:17
19:21 [m] ver 15; S Rev 1:16 [n] ver 11,19 [o] ver 17
20:1 [p] Rev 10:1; 18:1 [q] Rev 1:18 [r] S Lk 8:31
20:2 [s] S Mt 4:10 [t] Isa 24:22; S 2Pe 2:4
20:3 [u] ver 1 [v] Da 6:17; Mt 27:66 [w] ver 8, 10; Rev 12:9
20:4 [x] Da 7:9 [y] Mt 19:28; Rev 3:21 [z] Rev 6:9 [a] S Rev 1:2 [b] S Heb 4:12 [c] S Rev 13:12 [d] S Rev 13:16 [e] ver 6; Rev 22:5

and false prophets will appear and perform great signs and miracles to deceive even the elect—if that were possible" (Mt 24:24; see article on THE GREAT TRIBULATION, p. 52).

19:21 THE REST OF THEM WERE KILLED. God destroys the wicked throughout the whole earth (see Jer 25:29–33). Therefore no unsaved or unrighteous person will enter God's thousand-year kingdom (20:4). During the tribulation, the gospel was adequately presented by angels from the skies to everyone living on earth. Those who rejected the truth were given "a powerful delusion so that they will believe the lie and so that all will be condemned who have not believed the truth" (2Th 2:11–12). Note that the unrighteous "will not inherit the kingdom of God" (1Co 6:9–11; cf. Gal 5:21). They will be separated from the righteous after Christ returns in glory and will be assigned to eternal punishment (Mt 25:31–46).

20:2 DRAGON ... BOUND HIM FOR A THOUSAND YEARS. After Christ's return and the events of ch. 19, Satan will be bound and imprisoned for a thousand years, in order that he may not deceive the nations. This implies a complete cessation of his influence during this time. After the thousand years, he will be released for a short time in order to deceive those who rebel against God's rule (vv. 3,7–9). Satan's most characteristic work is to deceive (see Ge 3:13; Mt 24:24; 2Th 2:9–10).

20:3 KEEP HIM FROM DECEIVING THE NATIONS ANYMORE. The nations that will exist during Christ's reign on earth are formed from those believers who are alive at the end of the tribulation (see 19:21, note; 20:4, note). Although at times the term "nations" is used specifically of the ungodly, John also uses it to represent the saved (21:24; 22:2).

20:4 THRONES ON WHICH WERE SEATED. Those who sit on the thrones are probably the overcomers from all churches of all time (cf. 2:7, note), possibly including the OT saints (see Eze 37:11–14; Eph 2:14–22; 3:6; Heb 11:39–40). Those who came to life after Christ's return are said to be the faithful who died during the tribulation (6:9; 12:17). John does not mention the resurrection of the church saints who have died, for this occurred when Christ removed his church from earth and took it to heaven (i.e., the rapture; see Jn 14:3, note; 1Co 15:51, note; see article on THE RAPTURE, p. 440).

20:4 REIGNED WITH CHRIST A THOUSAND YEARS. This thousand-year reign of Christ is sometimes called "the millennium," meaning "a thousand years" (*mille* is a Latin word meaning "thousand," and *annus* a Latin word meaning "year"). The characteristics of this reign are the following:

(1) It was predicted in the OT (Isa 9:6; 65:19–25; Da 7:13–14; Mic 4:1–8; Zec 14:1–9; cf. Rev 2:25–28).

(2) Satan will be bound (see vv. 2,3, notes).

(3) Christ's reign will be shared by the faithful of his churches (2:26–27; 3:21; 5:10; 20:4), and possibly also by the resurrected OT saints (see Eze 37:11–14; Eph 2:14–22; 3:6; Heb 11:39–40) and martyred tribulation saints (see previous note).

(4) The people ruled by Christ will consist of those on earth who were faithful to Christ during the tribulation and who survived until the Lord's coming and those born during the millennium (14:12; 18:4; Isa 65:20–23; see Mt 25:1, note).

(5) No unsaved persons will enter the kingdom (see 19:21, note).

(6) Those reigning with Christ stand far above all the nations, for they will minister to and rule both Israel and the other nations (v. 6; 3:21; 5:10; Mt 19:28).

(7) There will be peace, safety, prosperity and righteousness throughout the earth (Isa 2:2–4; Mic 4:4; Zec 9:10).

(8) Nature will be restored to its original order, perfection and beauty (Ps 96:11–13; 98:7–9; Isa 14:7–8; 35:1–2,6–7; 51:3; 55:12–13; 65:25; Eze 34:25; Ro 8:18–23).

(9) The nations during this reign are obliged to continue in faith in Christ and obedience to his rule. However, some will choose the way of rebellion and disobedience and will be punished (vv. 7–10).

(10) At the end of the thousand years, the kingdom will be handed over by Jesus to the Father (1Co 15:24); then will begin the final and everlasting kingdom of God and the Lamb (21:1—22:5).

first resurrection.[f] **6**Blessed[g] and holy
are those who have part in the first resurrection. The second death[h] has no power
over them, but they will be priests[i] of God
and of Christ and will reign with him[j] for
a thousand years.

Satan's Doom

7When the thousand years are over,[k]
Satan will be released from his prison
8and will go out to deceive the nations[l] in
the four corners of the earth[m]—Gog and
Magog[n]—to gather them for battle.[o] In
number they are like the sand on the seashore.[p] **9**They marched across the
breadth of the earth and surrounded[q] the
camp of God's people, the city he loves.[r]
But fire came down from heaven[s] and devoured them. **10**And the devil, who deceived them,[t] was thrown into the lake of
burning sulfur,[u] where the beast[v] and the
false prophet[w] had been thrown. They will
be tormented day and night for ever and
ever.[x]

The Dead Are Judged

11Then I saw a great white throne[y] and
him who was seated on it. Earth and sky
fled from his presence,[z] and there was no
place for them. **12**And I saw the dead,
great and small,[a] standing before the
throne, and books were opened.[b] Another
book was opened, which is the book of
life.[c] The dead were judged[d] according to
what they had done[e] as recorded in the
books. **13**The sea gave up the dead that
were in it, and death and Hades[f] gave up
the dead[g] that were in them, and each
person was judged according to what he
had done.[h] **14**Then death[i] and Hades[j]
were thrown into the lake of fire.[k] The
lake of fire is the second death.[l] **15**If anyone's name was not found written in the
book of life,[m] he was thrown into the lake
of fire.

The New Jerusalem

21 Then I saw a new heaven and a
new earth,[n] for the first heaven
and the first earth had passed away,[o] and
there was no longer any sea. **2**I saw the

20:5 [f]ver 6; Lk 14:14; Php 3:11; 1Th 4:16 **20:6** [g]Rev 14:13 [h]S Rev 2:11 [i]S 1Pe 2:5 [j]ver 4; Rev 22:5 **20:7** [k]ver 2 **20:8** [l]ver 3,10; Rev 12:9 [m]Isa 11:12; Eze 7:2; Rev 7:1 [n]Eze 38:2; 39:1 [o]S Rev 16:14 [p]Eze 38:9,15; Heb 11:12 **20:9** [q]Eze 38:9,16 [r]Ps 87:2 [s]Eze 38:22; 39:6; S Rev 13:13 **20:10** [t]ver 3,8; Rev 12:9; 19:20 [u]S Rev 9:17 [v]Rev 16:13 [w]Rev 16:13 [x]Rev 14:10,11 **20:11** [y]S Rev 4:2 [z]S Rev 6:14 **20:12** [a]S Rev 19:5 [b]Da 7:10 [c]ver 15; Ex 32:32; Dt 29:20; Da 12:1; Mal 3:16; Lk 10:20; Rev 3:5; 21:27 [d]Rev 11:18 [e]Jer 17:10; S Mt 16:27 **20:13** [f]Rev 1:18; 6:8 [g]Isa 26:19 [h]S Mt 16:27 **20:14** [i]1Co 15:26 [j]ver 13 [k]S Rev 19:20 [l]S Rev 2:11 **20:15** [m]S ver 12 **21:1** [n]S 2Pe 3:13 [o]S Rev 6:14

20:6 THE FIRST RESURRECTION. This term includes the resurrection of Christ and all God's people, in contrast to the resurrection of the wicked at the end of the millennium (vv. 12–13; Isa 26:19–21; Da 12:2,13; Mt 27:52–53; Jn 11:25–26; 14:19; 1Co 15:20,52; see article on THE RAPTURE, p. 440).

20:7 SATAN WILL BE RELEASED. At the close of Christ's reign, Satan will be released. (1) Satan himself, deceived in believing he can yet defeat God, will be allowed to deceive those who desire to rebel against Christ's rule and will gather a multitude of such rebels together. (2) "Gog and Magog" (v. 8; derived from Eze 38–39) represent all the nations of the world and their spirit of rebellion against God and righteousness.

20:8 DECEIVE THE NATIONS. This is the last rebellion against God in history. Many of those born during the millennium evidently choose to reject Christ's visible lordship and choose instead Satan and his lie. God's judgment is total destruction (v. 9).

20:10 THE DEVIL . . . THE LAKE OF BURNING SULFUR. Satan's power will not last forever, for God will throw him into the lake of burning sulfur (see Isa 14:9–17). There he will not rule, but will be tormented day and night forever.

20:11–13 GREAT WHITE THRONE. The judgment described here is called the "Great White Throne Judgment" and includes the lost of all ages. Some believe that those saved during Christ's thousand-year reign on earth will be included in this judgment.

20:11 EARTH AND SKY FLED. This may refer to the destruction of the universe and the creation of a new heaven and earth (21:1; cf. Isa 51:6; 2Pe 3:7,10–12).

20:14 THE LAKE OF FIRE. The Bible portrays a terrible picture of the final destiny of the lost. (1) It speaks of "trouble and distress" (Ro 2:9), "weeping and gnashing of teeth" (Mt 22:13; 25:30), "everlasting destruction" (2Th 1:9), and a "fiery furnace" (Mt 13:42,50). It speaks of "gloomy dungeons" (2Pe 2:4), "eternal punishment" (Mt 25:46), a "hell, where the fire never goes out" (Mk 9:43), a "fiery lake of burning sulfur" (19:20), and "the smoke of their torment rises for ever and ever. There is no rest day or night" (14:11). Indeed, "It is a dreadful thing to fall into the hands of the living God" (Heb 10:31); "It would be better for him if he had not been born" (Mt 26:24; see also Mt 10:28, note).

(2) The believers of the NT church were keenly aware of the fate of those who lived in sin. It was for this reason they preached with tears (see Mk 9:24; Ac 20:19, note) and defended God's infallible Word and saving gospel against all distortion and false doctrine (see Php 1:17, note; 2Ti 1:14, note; see article on OVERSEERS AND THEIR DUTIES, p. 274).

(3) The solemn fact of eternal punishment for the wicked is the greatest motivation for carrying the gospel to all the world and doing everything possible to persuade people to repent and receive Christ before it is too late (see Jn 3:16, note).

20:15 BOOK OF LIFE. See 3:5, note.

21:1 A NEW HEAVEN AND A NEW EARTH. The final goal and expectation of the NT faith is a new, transformed and redeemed world where Christ lives with his people and righteousness dwells in holy perfection (cf. Ps 102:25–26; Isa 65:17; 66:22; Ro 8:19–22; Heb 1:12; 12:27; 2Pe 3:13). To erase all traces of sin, there will be a destruction of the earth, stars and galaxies. Heaven and earth will be shaken (Hag 2:6; Heb 12:26–28) and will vanish like smoke

Holy City,[p] the new Jerusalem, coming
down out of heaven from God,[q] prepared
as a bride[r] beautifully dressed for her
husband. 3And I heard a loud voice from
the throne saying, "Now the dwelling of
God is with men, and he will live with
them.[s] They will be his people, and God
himself will be with them and be their
God.[t] 4He will wipe every tear from their
eyes.[u] There will be no more death[v] or
mourning or crying or pain,[w] for the old
order of things has passed away."[x]
5He who was seated on the throne[y]
said, "I am making everything new!"[z]
Then he said, "Write this down, for these
words are trustworthy and true."[a]
6He said to me: "It is done.[b] I am the
Alpha and the Omega,[c] the Beginning and
the End. To him who is thirsty I will give
to drink without cost[d] from the spring of
the water of life.[e] 7He who overcomes[f]
will inherit all this, and I will be his God
and he will be my son.[g] 8But the cowardly, the unbelieving, the vile, the murderers, the sexually immoral, those who practice magic arts, the idolaters and all liars[h]
—their place will be in the fiery lake of
burning sulfur.[i] This is the second
death."[j]

21:2 [p] ver 10; Ne 11:18; Isa 52:1; Rev 11:2; 22:19 [q] ver 10; Heb 11:10; 12:22; Rev 3:12 [r] S Rev 19:7 **21:3** [s] Ex 25:8; 2Ch 6:18; Eze 48:35; Zec 2:10 [t] S 2Co 6:16 **21:4** [u] S Rev 7:17 [v] Isa 25:8; 1Co 15:26; Rev 20:14 [w] Isa 35:10; 65:19 [x] S 2Co 5:17 **21:5** [y] Rev 4:9; 20:11 [z] ver 4 [a] Rev 19:9; 22:6 **21:6** [b] Rev 16:17 [c] Rev 1:8; 22:13 [d] Isa 55:1 [e] S Jn 4:10 **21:7** [f] S Jn 16:33 [g] ver 3; 2Sa 7:14; 2Co 6:16; S Ro 8:14 **21:8** [h] ver 27; Ps 5:6; 1Co 6:9; Heb 12:14; Rev 22:15 [i] S Rev 9:17 [j] S Rev 2:11

21:9 [k] S Rev 15:1,6,7 [l] S Rev 19:7 **21:10** [m] Eze 40:2; Rev 17:3 [n] S Rev 1:10 [o] S ver 2 **21:11** [p] ver 23; Isa 60:1,2;

9One of the seven angels who had the
seven bowls full of the seven last
plagues[k] came and said to me, "Come, I
will show you the bride,[l] the wife of the
Lamb." 10And he carried me away[m] in the
Spirit[n] to a mountain great and high, and
showed me the Holy City, Jerusalem, coming down out of heaven from God.[o] 11It
shone with the glory of God,[p] and its brilliance was like that of a very precious jewel, like a jasper,[q] clear as crystal.[r] 12It
had a great, high wall with twelve gates,[s]
and with twelve angels at the gates. On
the gates were written the names of the
twelve tribes of Israel.[t] 13There were
three gates on the east, three on the
north, three on the south and three on the
west. 14The wall of the city had twelve
foundations,[u] and on them were the
names of the twelve apostles[v] of the
Lamb.
15The angel who talked with me had a
measuring rod[w] of gold to measure the
city, its gates[x] and its walls. 16The city
was laid out like a square, as long as it

Eze 43:2; Rev 15:8; 22:5 [q] ver 18,19; Rev 4:3 [r] Rev 4:6 **21:12** [s] ver 15,21,25; Rev 22:14 [t] Eze 48:30-34 **21:14** [u] S Eph 2:20; Heb 11:10 [v] Ac 1:26; Eph 2:20 **21:15** [w] Eze 40:3; Rev 11:1 [x] S ver 12

(Isa 51:6); the stars will be dissolved (Isa 34:4) and the elements destroyed (2Pe 3:7,10,12). The renewed earth will become the dwelling place of both humans and God (vv. 2–3,10; 22:3–5). All the redeemed will possess bodies like Christ's resurrection body, ones that are real, visible and tangible, but incorruptible and immortal (Ro 8:23; 1Co 15:51–56).

21:2 NEW JERUSALEM. The new Jerusalem already exists in heaven (Gal 4:26); it will soon come to earth as the city of God for which Abraham and all of God's faithful waited, and of which God is architect and builder (Php 3:20; Heb 11:10,13,16). The new earth will become God's headquarters, and he will remain with his people forever (cf. Lev 26:11–12; Jer 31:33; Eze 37:27; Zec 8:8).

21:4 WIPE EVERY TEAR FROM THEIR EYES. The effects of sin, such as sorrow, pain, unhappiness and death (7:16–17; Ge 3; Isa 35:10; 65:19; Ro 5:12), are gone forever, for the evil things of the first heaven and earth have completely passed away. Believers, although remembering all things worth remembering, will evidently not remember that which would cause them sorrow (Isa 65:17).

21:7 HE WHO OVERCOMES. God himself declares who will inherit the blessings of the new heaven and the new earth—those who faithfully persevere as Christ's overcomers (see 2:7, note). Those who do not overcome sin and ungodliness will be thrown into the fiery lake (see next note).

21:8 BUT THE COWARDLY, THE UNBELIEVING. God mentions several classes of people whose place will be in the fiery lake of burning sulfur. (1) The "cowardly" are those who fear the disapproval and threat of people more than they value loyalty to Christ and the truth of his Word. Their personal safety and status among others mean more than faithfulness. Among "the cowardly" are the compromisers among God's people who give up the fight and do not conquer (cf. Mk 8:35; 1Th 2:4, note; 2Ti 2:12–13, notes).

(2) The "unbelieving" include former believers in Christ who were overcome by various sins, such as those listed here. To profess Christ and then practice such evil is an abomination to God.

(3) Many churches today proclaim that it is possible for a person to be simultaneously a true child of God and an immoral person, liar, adulterer, homosexual or murderer. Such people contradict God's clear words here (cf. 1Co 6:9–10; Gal 5:19–21; Eph 5:5–7).

21:9 THE BRIDE, THE WIFE OF THE LAMB. This metaphor for the new city means that God's people live within it. John uses symbolic language to describe the Holy City, whose glory cannot be totally comprehended by human understanding, (see 21:9—22:5).

21:12–14 TWELVE GATES. The wall of the city suggests the security that the saved have in the new city. The twelve gates represent Israel (v. 12) and the twelve foundations represent the church (v. 14). This emphasizes the unity of God's people of OT and NT times.

21:16 LAID OUT LIKE A SQUARE. The size of the city indicates that it will have sufficient space for the believers of all ages. "1,200 stadia" is approximately 1,400 miles. The city is portrayed as a square. In the OT the Most Holy Place where God met his people was a perfect square. The entire city will be filled with

was wide. He measured the city with the
rod and found it to be 12,000 stadia[v] in
length, and as wide and high as it is long.
17He measured its wall and it was 144
cubits[w] thick,[x] by man's[y] measurement,
which the angel was using. 18The wall
was made of jasper,[z] and the city of pure
gold, as pure as glass.[a] 19The foundations of the city walls were decorated with
every kind of precious stone.[b] The first
foundation was jasper,[c] the second sap-
phire, the third chalcedony, the fourth em-
erald, 20the fifth sardonyx, the sixth car-
nelian,[d] the seventh chrysolite, the eighth
beryl, the ninth topaz, the tenth chryso-
prase, the eleventh jacinth, and the
twelfth amethyst.[y] 21The twelve gates[e]
were twelve pearls,[f] each gate made of a
single pearl. The great street of the city
was of pure gold, like transparent glass.[g]
22I did not see a temple[h] in the city,
because the Lord God Almighty[i] and the
Lamb[j] are its temple. 23The city does not
need the sun or the moon to shine on it,
for the glory of God[k] gives it light,[l] and
the Lamb[m] is its lamp. 24The nations will
walk by its light, and the kings of the
earth will bring their splendor into it.[n]
25On no day will its gates[o] ever be shut,[p]
for there will be no night there.[q] 26The
glory and honor of the nations will be
brought into it.[r] 27Nothing impure will
ever enter it, nor will anyone who does
what is shameful or deceitful,[s] but only
those whose names are written in the
Lamb's book of life.[t]

The River of Life

22 Then the angel showed me the river[u] of the water of life,[v] as clear
as crystal,[w] flowing[x] from the throne of
God and of the Lamb 2down the middle of
the great street of the city. On each side
of the river stood the tree of life,[y] bearing
twelve crops of fruit, yielding its fruit every month. And the leaves of the tree are
for the healing of the nations.[z] 3No longer
will there be any curse.[a] The throne of
God and of the Lamb will be in the city,
and his servants will serve him.[b] 4They
will see his face,[c] and his name will be on
their foreheads.[d] 5There will be no more
night.[e] They will not need the light of a
lamp or the light of the sun, for the Lord
God will give them light.[f] And they will
reign for ever and ever.[g]
6The angel said to me,[h] "These words
are trustworthy and true.[i] The Lord, the
God of the spirits of the prophets,[j] sent
his angel[k] to show his servants the things
that must soon take place."

Jesus Is Coming

7"Behold, I am coming soon![l] Blessed[m]
is he who keeps the words of the prophecy
in this book."[n]
8I, John, am the one who heard and saw
these things.[o] And when I had heard and
seen them, I fell down to worship at the
feet[p] of the angel who had been showing
them to me. 9But he said to me, "Do not
do it! I am a fellow servant with you and
with your brothers the prophets and of all
who keep the words of this book.[q] Worship God!"[r]
10Then he told me, "Do not seal up[s] the
words of the prophecy of this book,[t] be-

21:17 [y]Rev 13:18 **21:18** [z]S ver 11 [a]ver 21 **21:19** [b]Ex 28:17-20; Isa 54:11,12; Eze 28:13 [c]S ver 11 **21:20** [d]Rev 4:3 **21:21** [e]S ver 12 [f]Isa 54:12 [g]ver 18 **21:22** [h]Jn 4:21,23 [i]S Rev 1:8 [j]S Rev 5:6 **21:23** [k]S ver 11 [l]Isa 24:23; 60:19,20; Rev 22:5 [m]S Rev 5:6 **21:24** [n]ver 26; Isa 60:3,5 **21:25** [o]S ver 12 [p]Isa 60:11 [q]Zec 14:7; Rev 22:5 **21:26** [r]ver 24 **21:27** [s]Isa 52:1; Joel 3:17; Rev 22:14,15 [t]S Rev 20:12 **22:1** [u]Ps 36:8; 46:4 [v]ver 17; S Jn 4:10 [w]Rev 4:6 [x]Eze 47:1; Zec 14:8 **22:2** [y]S Rev 2:7 [z]Eze 47:12 **22:3** [a]Zec 14:11 [b]Rev 7:15 **22:4** [c]S Mt 5:8 [d]S Rev 7:3 **22:5** [e]Rev 21:25; Zec 14:7 [f]Isa 60:19,20; Rev 21:23 [g]Da 7:27; Rev 20:4 **22:6** [h]Rev 1:1 [i]Rev 21:5 [j]1Co 14:32; Heb 12:9 [k]ver 16; Rev 1:1 **22:7** [l]ver 12,20; S Mt 16:27 [m]Rev 1:3; 16:15 [n]ver 10,18,19 **22:8** [o]S Rev 1:1 [p]Rev 19:10 **22:9** [q]ver 10,18,19 [r]Rev 19:10 **22:10** [s]Da 8:26; Rev 10:4 [t]ver 7,18,19

[v] *16* That is, about 1,400 miles (about 2,200 kilometers) [w] *17* That is, about 200 feet (about 65 meters) [x] *17* Or *high* [y] *20* The precise identification of some of these precious stones is uncertain.

God's glory and holiness.

21:22 LORD . . . LAMB ARE ITS TEMPLE. God's presence and nearness will permeate the entire city, not just a temple.

21:24–26 THE NATIONS WILL WALK. The new Jerusalem does not include the whole new earth, for the city has gates through which the righteous may enter and leave. The new Jerusalem may be the capital of the new earth.

21:25 NO NIGHT THERE. This refers only to the Holy City, for John does not say there is no night on the new earth. Some believe that there will be night outside the city, for God has promised that day and night will never pass away (Ge 8:22; Ps 104:5; 148:3–6; Isa 66:22–23; Jer 33:20–21,25).

22:1 RIVER OF THE WATER OF LIFE. This could be a literal river symbolizing the Holy Spirit and the life, blessing and spiritual power that he gives (cf. 7:17; 21:6; 22:17; Isa 44:3; Jn 7:37–39).

22:2 THE TREE OF LIFE. This tree refers to the eternal life given to all who populate the new city (Ge 2:9; 3:22). The healing leaves picture the absence of anything that brings physical or spiritual harm (cf. Eze 47:12); note that even in our new bodies we will be dependent on the Lord for life, strength and health.

22:4 THEY WILL SEE HIS FACE. This is the final goal of redemptive history: God living among his faithful people on an earth purged from all evil. On this new earth the saints will see and live with Jesus, the Lamb of God, who through love redeemed them by his death on the cross. Their greatest happiness will be: "Blessed are the pure in heart, for they will see God" (Ex 33:20,23; Isa 33:17; Mt 5:8; Jn 14:9; 1Jn 3:2).

22:7 I AM COMING SOON! See 1Co 15:51, note on the NT time perspective related to Christ's return (see also Ro 13:12, note).

22:10 DO NOT SEAL UP THE WORDS. The mes-

cause the time is near.[u] 11Let him who
does wrong continue to do wrong; let him
who is vile continue to be vile; let him who
does right continue to do right; and let
him who is holy continue to be holy."[v]

12"Behold, I am coming soon![w] My reward is with me,[x] and I will give to everyone according to what he has done.[y] 13I
am the Alpha and the Omega,[z] the First
and the Last,[a] the Beginning and the
End.[b]
14"Blessed are those who wash their
robes,[c] that they may have the right to
the tree of life[d] and may go through the
gates[e] into the city.[f] 15Outside[g] are the
dogs,[h] those who practice magic arts, the
sexually immoral, the murderers, the idolaters and everyone who loves and practices falsehood.
16"I, Jesus,[i] have sent my angel[j] to
give you[z] this testimony for the
churches.[k] I am the Root[l] and the Offspring of David,[m] and the bright Morning
Star."[n]

17The Spirit[o] and the bride[p] say,
"Come!" And let him who hears say,
"Come!" Whoever is thirsty, let him come;
and whoever wishes, let him take the free
gift of the water of life.[q]

18I warn everyone who hears the words
of the prophecy of this book:[r] If anyone
adds anything to them,[s] God will add to
him the plagues described in this book.[t]
19And if anyone takes words away[u] from
this book of prophecy,[v] God will take
away from him his share in the tree of
life[w] and in the holy city, which are described in this book.
20He who testifies to these things[x]
says, "Yes, I am coming soon."[y]
Amen. Come, Lord Jesus.[z]
21The grace of the Lord Jesus be with
God's people.[a] Amen.

22:10 [u] S Ro 13:11 **22:11** [v] Eze 3:27; Da 12:10 **22:12** [w] ver 7,20; S Mt 16:27 [x] Isa 40:10; 62:11 [y] S Mt 16:27 **22:13** [z] Rev 1:8 [a] S Rev 1:17 [b] Rev 21:6 **22:14** [c] Rev 7:14 [d] S Rev 2:7 [e] S Rev 21:12 [f] S Rev 21:27 **22:15** [g] Dt 23:18; 1Co 6:9,10; Gal 5:19-21; Col 3:5,6; Rev 21:8 [h] Php 3:2 **22:16** [i] Rev 1:1 [j] ver 6 [k] Rev 1:4 [l] S Rev 5:5 [m] S Mt 1:1 [n] 2Pe 1:19; Rev 2:28

22:17 [o] Rev 2:7; 14:13 [p] S Rev 19:7 [q] S Jn 4:10 **22:18** [r] ver 7,10, 19 [s] Dt 4:2; 12:32; Pr 30:6 [t] Rev 15:6-16:21 **22:19** [u] Dt 4:2; 12:32; Pr 30:6 [v] ver 7,10,18 [w] S Rev 2:7

22:20 [x] Rev 1:2 [y] ver 7,12; S Mt 16:27 [z] 1Co 16:22 **22:21** [a] S Ro 16:20

[z] *16* The Greek is plural.

---

sage and prophecy of the book must be proclaimed to all believers and all churches (cf. Da 12:4).

22:11 CONTINUE TO DO WRONG. This may mean that those who reject John's prophecy will continue in their sins. Believers, however, must persevere in righteousness and holiness until Christ's return.

22:12 ACCORDING TO WHAT HE HAS DONE. See 1Co 3:15, note; see article on THE JUDGMENT OF BELIEVERS, p. 368.

22:15 EVERYONE WHO LOVES AND PRACTICES FALSEHOOD. Notice how the Bible's last two chapters focus on the issue of lying. Those who practice falsehood are mentioned three times: (1) All liars "will be in the fiery lake of burning sulfur" (21:8); (2) those who do what is "deceitful" will not enter God's eternal city (21:27); (3) those who love and practice falsehood will be outside God's eternal kingdom. Lying is the last sin condemned in the Bible, possibly because it was a lie that brought the fall of the human race (Ge 3:1–5; cf. Jn 8:44). These solemn words should be a warning for all in the churches who believe that God tolerates lying and deceit.

22:17 THE SPIRIT AND THE BRIDE SAY, COME! The last mention of the Holy Spirit in the Bible shows him inspiring the bride (i.e., the church) to invite all who want salvation to come to Christ. The church is now empowered by the Spirit to accomplish the evangelism of the world (Ac 1:5–8; 2:4).

22:19 GOD WILL TAKE AWAY. John ends this revelation of Jesus Christ by warning about the terrible possibility of losing one's share in the tree of life and the Holy City. We may not have a careless attitude toward this book or any part of God's holy Scripture. Such an attitude is manifested if we choose to believe only certain parts of God's revelation and reject other parts that we do not like, or if we teach our own ideas as if they were part of God's Word itself (v. 18). As at the beginning of the human pilgrimage on earth, failure to take God's Word with absolute seriousness is a matter of life and death (see Ge 3:3–4).

22:20 COME, LORD JESUS. The Bible ends with Jesus' promise that he is coming soon, to which John responds, "Come, Lord Jesus." This longing is shared by all true Christians. (1) This prayer is a confession that until he comes, our redemption remains incomplete, evil and sin are not yet overthrown, and this world is not yet renewed.

(2) We have every reason to believe that the day is fast approaching when he who is called "the Word of God" (19:13) and "the bright Morning Star" (v. 16) will come down from heaven to take his faithful away from the earth to his Father's house (Jn 14:1–3; 1Th 4:16–18), after which he will triumphantly return in glory to reign forever as "KING OF KINGS AND LORD OF LORDS" (19:16). This is our unfailing hope and joyful expectation (2Pe 1:19).

Table of Weights and Measures

BIBLICAL UNIT		APPROXIMATE AMERICAN EQUIVALENT	APPROXIMATE METRIC EQUIVALENT
		WEIGHTS	
talent	*(60 minas)*	75 pounds	34 kilograms
mina	*(50 shekels)*	1 1/4 pounds	0.6 kilogram
shekel	*(2 bekas)*	2/5 ounce	11.5 grams
pim	*(2/3 shekel)*	1/3 ounce	7.6 grams
beka	*(10 gerahs)*	1/5 ounce	5.5 grams
gerah		1/50 ounce	0.6 gram
		LENGTH	
cubit		18 inches	0.5 meter
span		9 inches	23 centimeters
handbreadth		3 inches	8 centimeters
		CAPACITY	
		Dry Measure	
cor [homer]	*(10 ephahs)*	6 bushels	220 liters
lethek	*(5 ephahs)*	3 bushels	110 liters
ephah	*(10 omers)*	3/5 bushel	22 liters
seah	*(1/3 ephah)*	7 quarts	7.3 liters
omer	*(1/10 ephah)*	2 quarts	2 liters
cab	*(1/18 ephah)*	1 quart	1 liter
		Liquid Measure	
bath	*(1 ephah)*	6 gallons	22 liters
hin	*(1/6 bath)*	4 quarts	4 liters
log	*(1/72 bath)*	1/3 quart	0.3 liter

The figures of the table are calculated on the basis of a shekel equaling 11.5 grams, a cubit equaling 18 inches and an ephah equaling 22 liters. The quart referred to is either a dry quart (slightly larger than a liter) or a liquid quart (slightly smaller than a liter), whichever is applicable. The ton referred to in the footnotes is the American ton of 2,000 pounds.

This table is based upon the best available information, but it is not intended to be mathematically precise; like the measurement equivalents in the footnotes, it merely gives approximate amounts and distances. Weights and measures differed somewhat at various times and places in the ancient world. There is uncertainty particularly about the ephah and the bath; further discoveries may give more light on these units of capacity.

SUBJECT INDEX

This subject index will enable you to locate where various topics are discussed in the study notes and articles. Page numbers are given in boldface type.

READING PLAN

Reading the New Testament in One Year

The reading schedules at the end of each introduction are reprinted here in a plan for reading the entire New Testament in one year.

JANUARY		FEBRUARY		MARCH		APRIL	
1	Matt 1	**1**	Matt 22:15–46	**1**	Acts 11:1–18	**1**	Mark 1:1–20
2	Matt 2	**2**	Matt 23	**2**	Acts 11:19–30	**2**	Mark 1:21–45
3	Matt 3	**3**	Matt 24:1–35	**3**	Acts 12	**3**	Mark 2:1–22
4	Matt 4	**4**	Matt 24:36–51	**4**	Acts 13:1–12	**4**	Mark 2:23–3:12
5	Matt 5:1–20	**5**	Matt 25:1–30	**5**	Acts 13:13–52	**5**	Mark 3:13–35
6	Matt 5:21–48	**6**	Matt 25:31–46	**6**	Acts 14	**6**	Mark 4:1–20
7	Matt 6:1–18	**7**	Matt 26:1–30	**7**	Acts 15:1–21	**7**	Mark 4:21–41
8	Matt 6:19–7:6	**8**	Matt 26:31–56	**8**	Acts 15:22–35	**8**	Mark 5:1–20
9	Matt 7:7–29	**9**	Matt 26:57–75	**9**	Acts 15:36–16:15	**9**	Mark 5:21–43
10	Matt 8:1–27	**10**	Matt 27:1–26	**10**	Acts 16:16–40	**10**	Mark 6:1–29
11	Matt 8:28–9:17	**11**	Matt 27:27–44	**11**	Acts 17:1–15	**11**	Mark 6:30–56
12	Matt 9:18–38	**12**	Matt 27:45–66	**12**	Acts 17:16–34	**12**	Mark 7:1–23
13	Matt 10:1–23	**13**	Matt 28	**13**	Acts 18:1–23	**13**	Mark 7:24–8:13
14	Matt 10:24–42	**14**	Acts 1	**14**	Acts 18:24–19:7	**14**	Mark 8:14–26
15	Matt 11:1–30	**15**	Acts 2:1–21	**15**	Acts 19:8–41	**15**	Mark 8:27–9:13
16	Matt 12:1–21	**16**	Acts 2:22–47	**16**	Acts 20:1–16	**16**	Mark 9:14–32
17	Matt 12:22–50	**17**	Acts 3	**17**	Acts 20:17–38	**17**	Mark 9:33–50
18	Matt 13:1–23	**18**	Acts 4:1–31	**18**	Acts 21:1–16	**18**	Mark 10:1–31
19	Matt 13:24–43	**19**	Acts 4:32–5:11	**19**	Acts 21:17–36	**19**	Mark 10:32–52
20	Matt 13:44–14:12	**20**	Acts 5:12–42	**20**	Acts 21:37–22:21	**20**	Mark 11:1–26
21	Matt 14:13–36	**21**	Acts 6	**21**	Acts 22:22–23:11	**21**	Mark 11:27–12:17
22	Matt 15:1–28	**22**	Acts 7:1–53	**22**	Acts 23:12–35	**22**	Mark 12:18–44
23	Matt 15:29–16:12	**23**	Acts 7:54–8:8	**23**	Acts 24	**23**	Mark 13
24	Matt 16:13–17:13	**24**	Acts 8:9–40	**24**	Acts 25:1–12	**24**	Mark 14:1–26
25	Matt 17:14–18:14	**25**	Acts 9:1–31	**25**	Acts 25:13–26:1	**25**	Mark 14:27–52
26	Matt 18:15–35	**26**	Acts 9:32–43	**26**	Acts 26:2–18	**26**	Mark 14:53–72
27	Matt 19:1–15	**27**	Acts 10:1–23	**27**	Acts 26:19–32	**27**	Mark 15:1–20
28	Matt 19:16–20:16	**28**	Acts 10:24–48	**28**	Acts 27:1–26	**28**	Mark 15:21–47
29	Matt 20:17–34	**29**	Heb 13	**29**	Acts 27:27–44	**29**	Mark 16
30	Matt 21:1–32			**30**	Acts 28:1–16	**30**	Jude
31	Matt 21:33–22:14			**31**	Acts 28:17–31		

MAY
1 1 Pet 1:1–21
2 1 Pet 1:22–2:25
3 1 Pet 3
4 1 Pet 4
5 1 Pet 5
6 2 Pet 1
7 2 Pet 2
8 2 Pet 3
9 Jas 1
10 Jas 2–3:13
11 Jas 3:14–4:12
12 Jas 4:13–5:20
13 Luke 1:1–25
14 Luke 1:26–56
15 Luke 1:57–80
16 Luke 2:1–20
17 Luke 2:21–52
18 Luke 3
19 Luke 4:1–13
20 Luke 4:14–44
21 Luke 5:1–16
22 Luke 5:17–39
23 Luke 6:1–16
24 Luke 6:17–49
25 Luke 7:1–35
26 Luke 7:36–50
27 Luke 8:1–21
28 Luke 8:22–39
29 Luke 8:40–56
30 Luke 9:1–17
31 Luke 9:18–36

JUNE
1 Luke 9:37–62
2 Luke 10:1–24
3 Luke 10:25–42
4 Luke 11:1–13
5 Luke 11:14–36
6 Luke 11:37–54
7 Luke 12:1–21
8 Luke 12:22–48
9 Luke 12:49–59
10 Luke 13:1–21
11 Luke 13:22–35
12 Luke 14:1–24
13 Luke 14:25–15:10
14 Luke 15:11–32
15 Luke 16
16 Luke 17:1–19
17 Luke 17:20–18:14
18 Luke 18:15–43
19 Luke 19:1–27
20 Luke 19:28–48
21 Luke 20:1–19
22 Luke 20:20–21:4
23 Luke 21:5–38
24 Luke 22:1–38
25 Luke 22:39–65
26 Luke 22:66–23:25
27 Luke 23:26–49
28 Luke 23:50–24:12
29 Luke 24:13–35
30 Luke 24:36–53

JULY
1 1 Thess 1–2:16
2 1 Thess 2:17–3:13
3 1 Thess 4
4 1 Thess 5
5 2 Thess 1
6 2 Thess 2
7 2 Thess 3
8 1 Cor 1
9 1 Cor 2
10 1 Cor 3
11 1 Cor 4
12 1 Cor 5
13 1 Cor 6
14 1 Cor 7
15 1 Cor 8
16 1 Cor 9
17 1 Cor 10:1–13
18 1 Cor 10:14–11:1
19 1 Cor 11:2–34
20 1 Cor 12
21 1 Cor 13
22 1 Cor 14
23 1 Cor 15:1–34
24 1 Cor 15:35–58
25 1 Cor 16
26 2 Cor 1–2:4
27 2 Cor 2:5–3:6
28 2 Cor 3:7–4:18
29 2 Cor 5:1–6:2
30 2 Cor 6:3–7:1
31 2 Cor 7:2–16

AUGUST
1 2 Cor 8–9
2 2 Cor 10
3 2 Cor 11:1–15
4 2 Cor 11:16–33
5 2 Cor 12
6 2 Cor 13
7 Rom 1:1–17
8 Rom 1:18–32
9 Rom 2
10 Rom 3
11 Rom 4
12 Rom 5:1–11
13 Rom 5:12–21
14 Rom 6:1–14
15 Rom 6:15–7:6
16 Rom 7:7–25
17 Rom 8:1–17
18 Rom 8:18–39
19 Rom 9:1–29
20 Rom 9:30–10:21
21 Rom 11:1–24
22 Rom 11:25–36
23 Rom 12:1–16
24 Rom 12:17–13:14
25 Rom 14–15:4
26 Rom 15:5–13
27 Rom 15:14–33
28 Rom 16
29 Gal 1
30 Gal 2
31 Gal 3:1–14

SEPTEMBER
1 Gal 3:15–25
2 Gal 3:26–4:20
3 Gal 4:21–5:15
4 Gal 5:16–26
5 Gal 6
6 Eph 1:1–14
7 Eph 1:15–2:10
8 Eph 2:11–22
9 Eph 3
10 Eph 4:1–16
11 Eph 4:17–5:2
12 Eph 5:3–21
13 Eph 5:22–6:9
14 Eph 6:10–24
15 Php 1
16 Php 2:1–18
17 Php 2:19–3:11
18 Php 3:12–4:3
19 Php 4:4–23
20 Col 1:1–23
21 Col 1:24–2:5
22 Col 2:6–23
23 Col 3:1–4:1
24 Col 4:2–18
25 Philemon
26 Heb 1
27 Heb 2
28 Heb 3
29 Heb 4:1–13
30 Heb 4:14–5:10

OCTOBER
1 Heb 5:11–6:20
2 Heb 7
3 Heb 8
4 Heb 9:1–10
5 Heb 9:11–28
6 Heb 10:1–18
7 Heb 10:19–39
8 Heb 11:1–16
9 Heb 11:17–40
10 Heb 12:1–13
11 Heb 12:14–29
12 Heb 13
13 Titus 1–2
14 Titus 3
15 1 Tim 1
16 1 Tim 2
17 1 Tim 3
18 1 Tim 4
19 1 Tim 5
20 1 Tim 6
21 2 Tim 1
22 2 Tim 2
23 2 Tim 3
24 2 Tim 4
25 John 1:1–18
26 John 1:19–51
27 John 2
28 John 3:1–21
29 John 3:22–36
30 John 4:1–26
31 John 4:27–54

NOVEMBER
1 John 5:1–30
2 John 5:31–47
3 John 6:1–24
4 John 6:25–59
5 John 6:60–71
6 John 7:1–24
7 John 7:25–8:11
8 John 8:12–30
9 John 8:31–47
10 John 8:48–59
11 John 9
12 John 10:1–21
13 John 10:22–42
14 John 11:1–16
15 John 11:17–57
16 John 12:1–19
17 John 12:20–50
18 John 13:1–30
19 John 13:31–14:14
20 John 14:15–31
21 John 15:1–17
22 John 15:18–16:16
23 John 16:17–33
24 John 17
25 John 18:1–27
26 John 18:28–19:16
27 John 19:17–42
28 John 20:1–18
29 John 20:19–31
30 John 21

DECEMBER
1 1 John 1–2:14
2 1 John 2:15–3:10
3 1 John 3:11–24
4 1 John 4
5 1 John 5
6 2 John
7 3 John
8 Rev 1
9 Rev 2:1–17
10 Rev 2:18–3:6
11 Rev 3:7–22
12 Rev 4
13 Rev 5
14 Rev 6
15 Rev 7
16 Rev 8
17 Rev 9
18 Rev 10
19 Rev 11
20 Rev 12
21 Rev 13:1–10
22 Rev 13:11–14:20
23 Rev 15
24 Rev 16
25 Rev 17
26 Rev 18
27 Rev 19:1–10
28 Rev 19:11–21
29 Rev 20
30 Rev 21
31 Rev 22

CONCORDANCE

Concordance

Word or block entries marked with an asterisk (*) list every verse in the Bible in which the word appears. Words in parentheses after an entry remind the reader to check other forms of that word in locating a passage.

AARON

Genealogy of (Ex 6:16-20; Jos 21:4, 10; 1Ch 6: 3-15).

Priesthood of (Ex 28:1; Nu 17; Heb 5:1-4; 7), garments (Ex 28; 39), consecration (Ex 29), ordination (Lev 8).

Spokesman for Moses (Ex 4:14-16, 27-31; 7: 1-2). Supported Moses' hands in battle (Ex 17: 8-13). Built golden calf (Ex 32; Dt 9:20). Talked against Moses (Nu 12). Priesthood opposed (Nu 16); staff budded (Nu 17). Forbidden to enter land (Nu 20:1-12). Death (Nu 20:22-29; 33:38-39).

ABADDON*

Rev 9:11 whose name in Hebrew is *A*,

ABANDON (ABANDONED)

Dt 4:31 he will not *a* or destroy you
1Ki 6:13 and will not *a* my people Israel."
Ne 9:19 compassion you did not *a* them
9:31 an end to them or *a* them,
Ps 16:10 you will not *a* me to the grave,
Ac 2:27 you will not *a* me to the grave,
1Ti 4: 1 in later times some will *a* the faith

ABANDONED (ABANDON)

Ge 24:27 who has not *a* his kindness
2Co 4: 9 persecuted, but not *a*; struck down,

ABBA*

Mk 14:36 "*A*, Father," he said, "everything is
Ro 8:15 And by him we cry, "*A*, Father."
Gal 4: 6 the Spirit who calls out, "*A*, Father

ABEDNEGO

Deported to Babylon with Daniel (Da 1:1-6). Name changed from Azariah (Da 1:7). Refused defilement by food (Da 1:8-20). Refused idol worship (Da 3:1-12); saved from furnace (Da 3:13-30).

ABEL

Second son of Adam (Ge 4:2). Offered proper sacrifice (Ge 4:4; Heb 11:4). Murdered by Cain (Ge 4:8; Mt 23:35; Lk 11:51; 1Jn 3:12).

ABHOR (ABHORS)

Lev 26:30 of your idols, and I will *a* you.
Dt 7:26 Utterly *a* and detest it,
Ps 26: 5 I *a* the assembly of evildoers
119:163 I hate and *a* falsehood
139: 21 and *a* those who rise up against you
Am 6: 8 "I *a* the pride of Jacob
Ro 2:22 You who *a* idols, do you rob

ABHORS (ABHOR)

Pr 11: 1 The LORD *a* dishonest scales,

ABIATHAR

High priest in days of Saul and David (1Sa 22; 2Sa 15; 1Ki 1-2; Mk 2:26). Escaped Saul's slaughter of priests (1Sa 22:18-23). Supported David in Absalom's revolt (2Sa 15:24-29). Supported Adonijah (1Ki 1:7-42); deposed by Solomon (1Ki 2:22-35; cf. 1Sa 2:31-35).

ABIGAIL

1. Sister of David (1Ch 2:16-17).

2. Wife of Nabal (1Sa 25:30); pled for his life with David (1Sa 25:14-35). Became David's wife after Nabal's death (1Sa 25:36-42); bore him Kileab (2Sa 3:3) also known as Daniel (1Ch 3:1).

ABIHU

Son of Aaron (Ex 6:23; 24:1, 9); killed for offering unauthorized fire (Lev 10; Nu 3:2-4; 1Ch 24: 1-2).

ABIJAH

1. Second son of Samuel (1Ch 6:28); a corrupt judge (1Sa 8:1-5).

2. An Aaronic priest (1Ch 24:10; Lk 1:5).

3. Son of Jeroboam I of Israel; died as prophesied by Ahijah (1Ki 14:1-18).

4. Son of Rehoboam; king of Judah who fought Jeroboam I attempting to reunite the kingdom (1Ki 14:31-15:8; 2Ch 12:16-14:1; Mt 1:7).

ABILITY (ABLE)

Ex 35:34 tribe of Dan, the *a* to teach others.
Dt 8:18 for it is he who gives you the *a*
Ezr 2:69 According to their *a* they gave
Mt 25:15 one talent, each according to his *a*.
Ac 11:29 disciples, each according to his *a*,
2Co 1: 8 far beyond our *a* to endure,
8: 3 were able, and even beyond their *a*.

ABIMELECH

1. King of Gerar who took Abraham's wife Sarah, believing her to be his sister (Ge 20). Later made a covenant with Abraham (Ge 21:22-33).

2. King of Gerar who took Isaac's wife Rebekah, believing her to be his sister (Ge 26:1-11). Later made a covenant with Isaac (Ge 26:12-31).

3. Son of Gideon (Jdg 8:31). Attempted to make himself king (Jdg 9).

ABISHAG*

Shunammite virgin; attendant of David in his old age (1Ki 1:1-15; 2:17-22).

ABISHAI

Son of Zeruiah, David's sister (1Sa 26:6; 1Ch 2: 16). One of David's chief warriors (1Ch 11:15-21): against Edom (1Ch 18:12-13), Ammon (2Sa 10), Absalom (2Sa 18), Sheba (2Sa 20). Wanted to kill Saul (1Sa 26), killed Abner (2Sa 2:18-27; 3:22-39), wanted to kill Shimei (2Sa 16:5-13; 19:16-23).

ABLE (ABILITY ENABLE ENABLED ENABLES ENABLING)

Nu 14:16 'The LORD was not *a*
1Ch 29:14 that we should be *a* to give
2Ch 2: 6 who is *a* to build a temple for him,
Eze 7:19 and gold will not be *a* to save them
Da 3:17 the God we serve is *a* to save us
4:37 walk in pride he is *a* to humble.
Mt 9:28 "Do you believe that I am *a*
Lk 13:24 will try to enter and will not be *a* to
14:30 to build and was not *a* to finish.'
21:15 none of your adversaries will be *a*
21:36 and that you may be *a* to stand
Ac 5:39 you will not be *a* to stop these men;
Ro 8:39 will be *a* to separate us
14: 4 for the Lord is *a* to make him stand
16:25 to him who is *a* to establish you
2Co 9: 8 God is *a* to make all grace abound
Eph 3:20 him who is *a* to do immeasurably
6:13 you may be *a* to stand your ground,
1Ti 3: 2 respectable, hospitable, *a* to teach,
2Ti 1:12 and am convinced that he is *a*
2:24 kind to everyone, *a* to teach,
3:15 which are *a* to make you wise
Heb 2:18 he is *a* to help those who are being
7:25 he is *a* to save completely
Jas 3: 2 *a* to keep his whole body in check.
Jude :24 To him who is *a* to keep you
Rev 5: 5 He is *a* to open the scroll

ABNER

Cousin of Saul and commander of his army (1Sa 14:50; 17:55-57; 26). Made Ish-Bosheth king after Saul (2Sa 2:8-10), but later defected to David (2Sa 3:6-21). Killed Asahel (2Sa 2:18-32), for which he was killed by Joab and Abishai (2Sa 3:22-39).

ABOLISH (ABOLISHED ABOLISHING)

Hos 2:18 I will *a* from the land,
Mt 5:17 that I have come to *a* the Law

ABOLISHED (ABOLISH)

Gal 5:11 the offense of the cross has been *a*.

ABOLISHING* (ABOLISH)

Eph 2:15 by *a* in his flesh the law

ABOMINATION*

Da 11:31 set up the *a* that causes desolation.
12:11 *a* that causes desolation is set up,
Mt 24:15 the holy place 'the *a* that causes
Mk 13:14 you see 'the *a* that causes

ABOUND (ABOUNDING)

2Co 9: 8 able to make all grace *a* to you,
9: 8 you will *a* in every good work.
Php 1: 9 that your love may *a* more

ABOUNDING (ABOUND)

Ex 34: 6 slow to anger, *a* in love
Nu 14:18 *a* in love and forgiving sin
Ne 9:17 slow to anger and *a* in love.
Ps 86: 5 *a* in love to all who call to you.
86:15 slow to anger, *a* in love
103: 8 slow to anger, *a* in love.
Joel 2:13 slow to anger and *a* in love,
Jnh 4: 2 slow to anger and *a* in love,

ABRAHAM

Abram, son of Terah (Ge 11:26-27), husband of Sarah (Ge 11:29).

Covenant relation with the LORD (Ge 12:1-3; 13: 14-17; 15; 17; 22:15-18; Ex 2:24; Ne 9:8; Ps 105; Mic 7:20; Lk 1:68-75; Ro 4; Heb 6:13-15).

Called from Ur, via Haran, to Canaan (Ge 12:1; Ac 7:2-4; Heb 11:8-10). Moved to Egypt, nearly lost Sarah to Pharoah (Ge 12:10-20). Divided the land with Lot; settled in Hebron (Ge 13). Saved Lot from four kings (Ge 14:1-16); blessed by Melchizedek (Ge 14:17-20; Heb 7:1-20). Declared righteous by faith (Ge 15:6; Ro 4:3; Gal 3:6-9). Fathered Ishmael by Hagar (Ge 16).

Name changed from Abram (Ge 17:5; Ne 9:7). Circumcised (Ge 17; Ro 4:9-12). Entertained three visitors (Ge 18); promised a son by Sarah (Ge 18: 9-15; 17:16). Questioned destruction of Sodom and Gomorrah (Ge 18:16-33). Moved to Gerar; nearly lost Sarah to Abimelech (Ge 20). Fathered Isaac by Sarah (Ge 21:1-7; Ac 7:8; Heb 11:11-12); sent away Hagar and Ishmael (Ge 21:8-21; Gal 4:22-30). Covenant with Abimelech (Ge 21:22-32). Tested by offering Isaac (Ge 22; Heb 11:17-19; Jas 2: 21-24). Sarah died; bought field of Ephron for burial (Ge 23). Secured wife for Isaac (Ge 24). Fathered children by Keturah (Ge 25:1-6; 1Ch 1:32-33). Death (Ge 25:7-11).

Called servant of God (Ge 26:24), friend of God (2Ch 20:7; Isa 41:8; Jas 2:23), prophet (Ge 20:7), father of Israel (Ex 3:15; Isa 51:2; Mt 3:9; Jn 8: 39-58).

ABSALOM

Son of David by Maacah (2Sa 3:3; 1Ch 3:2). Killed Amnon for rape of his sister Tamar; banished by David (2Sa 13). Returned to Jerusalem; received by David (2Sa 14). Rebelled against David; siezed kingdom (2Sa 15-17). Killed (2Sa 18).

ABSENT

Col 2: 5 though I am *a* from you in body,

ABSOLUTE*

1Ti 5: 2 women as sisters, with *a* purity.

ABSTAIN (ABSTAINS)

Ex 19:15 *A* from sexual relations."
Nu 6: 3 he must *a* from wine and other
Ac 15:20 them to *a* from food polluted
1Pe 2:11 to *a* from sinful desires,

ABSTAINS* (ABSTAIN)

Ro 14: 6 thanks to God; and he who *a*,

ABUNDANCE (ABUNDANT)

Ge 41:29 Seven years of great *a* are coming
Job 36:31 and provides food in *a*.
Ps 66:12 but you brought us to a place of *a*.
Ecc 5:12 but the *a* of a rich man
Isa 66:11 and delight in her overflowing *a*."
Jer 2:22 and use an *a* of soap,
Mt 13:12 given more, and he will have an *a*.
25:29 given more, and he will have an *a*.
Lk 12:15 consist in the *a* of his possessions."
1Pe 1: 2 Grace and peace be yours in *a*.
2Pe 1: 2 yours in *a* through the knowledge
Jude : 2 peace and love be yours in *a*.

ABUNDANT (ABUNDANCE)

Dt 28:11 will grant you *a* prosperity—
32: 2 like *a* rain on tender plants.
Job 36:28 and *a* showers fall on mankind.
Ps 68: 9 You gave *a* showers, O God;
78:15 gave them water as *a* as the seas;
132: 15 I will bless her with *a* provisions;
145: 7 will celebrate your *a* goodness
Pr 12:11 works his land will have *a* food,
28:19 works his land will have *a* food,
Jer 33: 9 and will tremble at the *a* prosperity
Ro 5:17 who receive God's *a* provision

ABUSIVE

2Ti 3: 2 *a*, disobedient to their parents,

ABYSS*

Lk 8:31 not to order them to go into the *A*.
Rev 9: 1 the key to the shaft of the *A*.
9: 2 When he opened the *A*, smoke rose
9: 2 darkened by the smoke from the *A*.
9:11 king over them the angel of the *A*,
11: 7 up from the *A* will attack them,

Rev 17: 8 and will come up out of the *A*
20: 1 having the key to the *A*
20: 3 He threw him into the *A*,

ACCEPT (ACCEPTABLE ACCEPTANCE ACCEPTED ACCEPTS)
Ex 23: 8 "Do not *a* a bribe,
Dt 16:19 Do not *a* a bribe, for a bribe blinds
Job 42: 8 and I will *a* his prayer and not deal
Pr 10: 8 The wise in heart *a* commands,
19:20 Listen to advice and *a* instruction,
Ro 15: 7 *A* one another, then, just
Jas 1:21 humbly *a* the word planted in you,

ACCEPTABLE (ACCEPT)
Pr 21: 3 is more *a* to the LORD

ACCEPTANCE* (ACCEPT)
Ro 11:15 what will their *a* be but life
1Ti 1:15 saying that deserves full *a*:
4: 9 saying that deserves full *a*

ACCEPTED (ACCEPT)
Ge 4: 7 will you not be *a*? But if you do not
Job 42: 9 and the LORD *a* Job's prayer.
Lk 4:24 "no prophet is *a* in his hometown.
Gal 1: 9 you a gospel other than what you *a*,

ACCEPTS (ACCEPT)
Ps 6: 9 the LORD *a* my prayer.
Jn 13:20 whoever *a* anyone I send *a* me;
13:20 whoever *a* me *a* the one who sent

ACCESS
Ro 5: 2 through whom we have gained *a*
Eph 2:18 For through him we both have *a*

ACCOMPANIED (ACCOMPANY)
1Co 10: 4 from the spiritual rock that *a* them,
Jas 2:17 if it is not *a* by action, is dead.

ACCOMPANIES (ACCOMPANY)
2Co 9:13 obedience that *a* your confession

ACCOMPANY (ACCOMPANIED ACCOMPANIES)
Dt 28: 2 *a* you if you obey the LORD your
Mk 16:17 these signs will *a* those who believe
Heb 6: 9 your case—things that *a* salvation.

ACCOMPLISH
Ecc 2: 2 And what does pleasure *a*?"
Isa 44:28 and will *a* all that I please;
55:11 but will *a* what I desire

ACCORD
Nu 24:13 not do anything of my own *a*,
Jn 10:18 but I lay it down of my own *a*.
12:49 For I did not speak of my own *a*,

ACCOUNT (ACCOUNTABLE)
Ge 2: 4 This is the *a* of the heavens
5: 1 This is the written *a* of Adam's line
6: 9 This is the *a* of Noah.
10: 1 This is the *a* of Shem, Ham
11:10 This is the *a* of Shem.
11:27 This is the *a* of Terah.
25:12 This is the *a* of Abraham's son
25:19 This is the *a* of Abraham's son
36: 1 This is the *a* of Esau (that is, Edom
36: 9 This is the *a* of Esau the father
37: 2 This is the *a* of Jacob.
Mt 12:36 to give *a* on the day of judgment
Lk 16: 2 Give an *a* of your management,
Ro 14:12 each of us will give an *a* of himself
Heb 4:13 of him to whom we must give *a*.

ACCOUNTABLE* (ACCOUNT)
Eze 3:18 and I will hold you *a* for his blood.
3:20 and I will hold you *a* for his blood.
33: 6 but I will hold the watchman *a*
33: 8 and I will hold you *a* for his blood.
34:10 and will hold them *a* for my flock.
Da 6: 2 The satraps were made *a* to them
Jnh 1:14 Do not hold us *a* for killing
Ro 3:19 and the whole world held *a* to God.

ACCURATE
Dt 25:15 You must have *a* and honest
Pr 11: 1 but *a* weights are his delight.

ACCURSED (CURSE)
2Pe 2:14 experts in greed—an *a* brood!

ACCUSATION (ACCUSE)
1Ti 5:19 Do not entertain an *a*

ACCUSATIONS (ACCUSE)
2Pe 2:11 do not bring slanderous *a*

ACCUSE (ACCUSATION ACCUSATIONS ACCUSER ACCUSES ACCUSING)
Pr 3:30 Do not *a* a man for no reason—
Lk 3:14 and don't *a* people falsely—

ACCUSER (ACCUSE)
Jn 5:45 Your *a* is Moses, on whom your
Rev 12:10 For the *a* of our brothers,

ACCUSES (ACCUSE)
Job 40: 2 Let him who *a* God answer him!"
Rev 12:10 who *a* them before our God day

ACCUSING (ACCUSE)
Ro 2:15 and their thoughts now *a*,

ACHAN*
Sin at Jericho caused defeat at Ai; stoned (Jos 7; 22:20; 1Ch 2:7).

ACHE*
Pr 14:13 Even in laughter the heart may *a*,

ACHIEVE
Isa 55:11 *a* the purpose for which I sent it.

ACHISH
King of Gath before whom David feigned insanity (1Sa 21:10-15). Later "ally" of David (2Sa 27-29).

ACKNOWLEDGE (ACKNOWLEDGED ACKNOWLEDGES)
Pr 3: 6 in all your ways *a* him,
Jer 3:13 Only *a* your guilt—
Hos 6: 3 let us press on to *a* him.
Mt 10:32 *a* him before my Father in heaven.
Lk 12: 8 *a* him before the angels of God.
1Jn 4: 3 spirit that does not *a* Jesus is not

ACKNOWLEDGED (ACKNOWLEDGE)
Lk 7:29 *a* that God's way was right,

ACKNOWLEDGES* (ACKNOWLEDGE)
Ps 91:14 for he *a* my name.
Mt 10:32 "Whoever *a* me before men,
Lk 12: 8 whoever *a* me before men,
1Jn 2:23 whoever *a* the Son has the Father
4: 2 Every spirit that *a* that Jesus Christ
4:15 If anyone *a* that Jesus is the Son

ACQUIRES (ACQUIRING)
Pr 18:15 of the discerning *a* knowledge;

ACQUIRING* (ACQUIRES)
Pr 1: 3 for *a* a disciplined and prudent life,

ACQUIT (ACQUITTING)
Ex 23: 7 to death, for I will not *a* the guilty.

ACQUITTING* (ACQUIT)
Dt 25: 1 *a* the innocent and condemning
Pr 17:15 *A* the guilty and condemning

ACT (ACTION ACTIONS ACTIVE ACTIVITY ACTS)
Ps 119:126 It is time for you to *a*, O LORD;

ACTION (ACT)
2Co 9: 2 has stirred most of them to *a*.
Jas 2:17 if it is not accompanied by *a*,
1Pe 1:13 minds for *a*; be self-controlled;

ACTIONS (ACT)
Mt 11:19 wisdom is proved right by her *a*."
Gal 6: 4 Each one should test his own *a*.
Tit 1:16 but by their *a* they deny him.

ACTIVE* (ACT)
Phm : 6 I pray that you may be *a*
Heb 4:12 For the word of God is living and *a*

ACTIVITY (ACT)
Ecc 3: 1 a season for every *a* under heaven:
3:17 for there will be a time for every *a*,

ACTS (ACT)
1Ch 16: 9 tell of all his wonderful *a*.
Ps 71:16 proclaim your mighty *a*,
71:24 tell of your righteous *a*
105: 2 tell of all his wonderful *a*.
106: 2 Who can proclaim the mighty *a*
145: 4 they will tell of your mighty *a*.
145: 12 all men may know of your mighty *a*
150: 2 Praise him for his *a* of power;
Isa 64: 6 all our righteous *a* are like filthy
Mt 6: 1 not to do your '*a* of righteousness'

ADAM
1. First man (Ge 1:26-2:25; Ro 5:14; 1Ti 2:13). Sin of (Ge 3; Hos 6:7; Ro 5:12-21). Children of (Ge 4:1-5:5). Death of (Ge 5:5; Ro 5:12-21; 1Co 15:22).
2. City (Jos 3:16).

ADD (ADDED)
Dt 4: 2 Do not *a* to what I command you
12:32 do not *a* to it or take away from it.
Pr 1: 5 let the wise listen and *a*
9: 9 he will *a* to his learning.
30: 6 Do not *a* to his words,
Mt 6:27 by worrying can *a* a single hour
Lk 12:25 by worrying can *a* a single hour
Rev 22:18 God will *a* to him the plagues

ADDED (ADD)
Ecc 3:14 nothing can be *a* to it and nothing
Ac 2:47 Lord *a* to their number daily those
Ro 5:20 The law was *a* so that the trespass
Gal 3:19 It was *a* because of transgressions

ADDICTED*
Tit 2: 3 to be slanderers or *a* to much wine,

ADMINISTRATION*
1Co 12:28 with gifts of *a*, and those speaking
Eph 3: 2 Surely you have heard about the *a*
3: 9 to everyone the *a* of this mystery,

ADMIRABLE*
Php 4: 8 whatever is lovely, whatever is *a*—

ADMIT
Hos 5:15 until they *a* their guilt.

ADMONISH* (ADMONISHING)
Col 3:16 and *a* one another with all wisdom,
1Th 5:12 you in the Lord and who *a* you.

ADMONISHING* (ADMONISH)
Col 1:28 *a* and teaching everyone

ADONIJAH
1. Son of David by Haggith (2Sa 3:4; 1Ch 3:2). Attempted to be king after David; killed by Solomon's order (1Ki 1-2).
2. Levite; teacher of the Law (2Ch 17:8).

ADOPTED (ADOPTION)
Eph 1: 5 In love he predestined us to be *a*

ADOPTION* (ADOPTED)
Ro 8:23 as we wait eagerly for our *a* as sons,
9: 4 Theirs is the *a* as sons; theirs

ADORE*
SS 1: 4 How right they are to *a* you!

ADORNMENT* (ADORNS)
1Pe 3: 3 should not come from outward *a*,

ADORNS* (ADORNMENT)
Ps 93: 5 holiness *a* your house
Isa 61:10 as a bride *a* herself with her jewels.
61:10 bridegroom *a* his head like a priest,

ADULTERER (ADULTERY)
Lev 20:10 both the *a* and the adulteress must
Heb 13: 4 for God will judge the *a*

ADULTERERS (ADULTERY)
1Co 6: 9 idolaters nor *a* nor male prostitutes
1Ti 1:10 for murderers, for *a* and perverts,

ADULTERESS (ADULTERY)
Hos 3: 1 she is loved by another and is an *a*.

ADULTERIES (ADULTERY)
Jer 3: 8 sent her away because of all her *a*.

ADULTEROUS (ADULTERY)
Mk 8:38 in this *a* and sinful generation,
Jas 4: 4 You *a* people, don't you know that

ADULTERY (ADULTERER ADULTERERS ADULTERESS ADULTERIES ADULTEROUS)
Ex 20:14 "You shall not commit *a*.
Dt 5:18 "You shall not commit *a*.
Mt 5:27 that it was said, 'Do not commit *a*.'
5:28 lustfully has already committed *a*
5:32 the divorced woman commits *a*.
15:19 murder, *a*, sexual immorality, theft
19: 9 marries another woman commits *a*
19:18 do not commit *a*, do not steal,
Mk 7:21 theft, murder, *a*, greed, malice,
10:11 marries another woman commits *a*
10:12 another man, she commits *a*."
10:19 do not commit *a*, do not steal,
Lk 16:18 a divorced woman commits *a*.
16:18 marries another woman commits *a*
18:20 'Do not commit *a*, do not murder,
Jn 8: 4 woman was caught in the act of *a*.
Rev 18: 3 of the earth committed *a* with her,

ADULTS*
1Co 14:20 but in your thinking be *a.*

ADVANCE (ADVANCED)
Ps 18:29 With your help I can *a*
Php 1:12 has really served to *a* the gospel.

ADVANCED (ADVANCE)
Job 32: 7 *a* years should teach wisdom.'

ADVANTAGE
Ex 22:22 "Do not take *a* of a widow
Dt 24:14 Do not take *a* of a hired man who is
Ro 3: 1 What *a,* then, is there
2Co 11:20 or exploits you or takes *a* of you
1Th 4: 6 should wrong his brother or take *a*

ADVERSITY*
Pr 17:17 and a brother is born for *a.*
Isa 30:20 the Lord gives you the bread of *a*

ADVICE (ADVISERS)
1Ki 12: 8 rejected the *a* the elders
12:14 he followed the *a* of the young men
2Ch 10: 8 rejected the *a* the elders
Pr 12: 5 but the *a* of the wicked is deceitful.
12:15 but a wise man listens to *a.*
19:20 Listen to *a* and accept instruction,
20:18 Make plans by seeking *a;*

ADVISERS (ADVICE)
Pr 11:14 but many *a* make victory sure.

ADVOCATE*
Job 16:19 my *a* is on high.

AFFLICTED (AFFLICTION)
Job 2: 7 and *a* Job with painful sores
36: 6 but gives the *a* their rights.
Ps 9:12 he does not ignore the cry of the *a.*
9:18 nor the hope of the *a* ever perish.
119: 67 Before I was *a* I went astray,
119: 71 It was good for me to be *a*
119: 75 and in faithfulness you have *a* me.
Isa 49:13 will have compassion on his *a* ones.
53: 4 smitten by him, and *a.*
53: 7 He was oppressed and *a,*
Na 1:12 Although I have *a* you, ⌞O Judah,⌟

AFFLICTION (AFFLICTED AFFLICTIONS)
Dt 16: 3 bread of *a,* because you left Egypt
Ps 107: 41 he lifted the needy out of their *a*
Isa 30:20 of adversity and the water of *a,*
48:10 in the furnace of *a.*
La 3:33 For he does not willingly bring *a*
Ro 12:12 patient in *a,* faithful in prayer.

AFFLICTIONS (AFFLICTION)
Col 1:24 lacking in regard to Christ's *a,*

AFRAID (FEAR)
Ge 3:10 and I was *a* because I was naked;
26:24 Do not be *a,* for I am with you;
Ex 2:14 Then Moses was *a* and thought,
3: 6 because he was *a* to look at God.
Dt 1:21 Do not be *a;* do not be discouraged
1:29 "Do not be terrified; do not be *a*
20: 1 do not be *a* of them,
20: 3 Do not be fainthearted or *a;*
2Ki 25:24 "Do not be *a* of the Babylonian
1Ch 13:12 David was *a* of God that day
Ps 27: 1 of whom shall I be *a?*
56: 3 When I am *a,* / I will trust in you.
56: 4 in God I trust; I will not be *a.*
Pr 3:24 lie down, you will not be *a;*
Isa 10:24 do not be *a* of the Assyrians,
12: 2 I will trust and not be *a.*
44: 8 Do not tremble, do not be *a.*
Jer 1: 8 Do not be *a* of them, for I am
Mt 8:26 You of little faith, why are you so *a*
10:28 be *a* of the One who can destroy
10:31 So don't be *a;* you are worth more
Mk 5:36 "Don't be *a;* just believe."
Lk 9:34 and they were *a* as they entered
Jn 14:27 hearts be troubled and do not be *a.*
Ac 27:24 beside me and said, 'Do not be *a,*
Ro 11:20 Do not be arrogant, but be *a.*
Heb 13: 6 Lord is my helper; I will not be *a.*

AGAG (AGAGITE)
King of Amalekites not killed by Saul (1Sa 15).

AGAGITE (AGAG)
Est 8: 3 to the evil plan of Haman the *A,*

AGED (AGES)
Job 12:12 Is not wisdom found among the *a?*
Pr 17: 6 children are a crown to the *a,*

AGES (AGED)
Ro 16:25 the mystery hidden for long *a* past,
Eph 2: 7 that in the coming *a* he might show
3: 9 which for *a* past was kept hidden
Col 1:26 that has been kept hidden for *a*
Rev 15: 3 King of the *a.*

AGONY
Lk 16:24 because I am in *a* in this fire.'
Rev 16:10 Men gnawed their tongues in *a*

AGREE (AGREEMENT AGREES)
Mt 18:19 on earth *a* about anything you ask
Ro 7:16 want to do, I *a* that the law is good.
Php 4: 2 with Syntyche to *a* with each other

AGREEMENT (AGREE)
2Co 6:16 What *a* is there between the temple

AGREES* (AGREE)
Ac 7:42 This *a* with what is written
24:14 I believe everything that *a*
1Co 4:17 which *a* with what I teach

AGRIPPA*
Descendant of Herod; king before whom Paul pled his case in Caesarea (Ac 25:13-26:32).

AHAB
1. Son of Omri; king of Israel (1Ki 16:28-22:40), husband of Jezebel (1Ki 16:31). Promoted Baal worship (1Ki 16:31-33); opposed by Elijah (1Ki 17: 1; 18; 21), a prophet (1Ki 20:35-43), Micaiah (1Ki 22:1-28). Defeated Ben-Hadad (1Ki 20). Killed for failing to kill Ben-Hadad and for murder of Naboth (1Ki 20:35-21:40).
2. A false prophet (Jer 29:21-22).

AHAZ
1. Son of Jotham; king of Judah, (2Ki 16; 2Ch 28). Idolatry of (2Ki 16:3-4, 10-18; 2Ch 28:1-4, 22-25). Defeated by Aram and Israel (2Ki 16:5-6; 2Ch 28:5-15). Sought help from Assyria rather than the LORD (2Ki 16:7-9; 2Ch 28:16-21; Isa 7).
2. Benjamite, descendant of Saul (1Ch 8:35-36).

AHAZIAH
1. Son of Ahab; king of Israel (1Ki 22:51-2Ki 1: 18; 2Ch 20:35-37). Made an unsuccessful alliance with Jehoshaphat of Judah (2Ch 20:35-37). Died for seeking Baal rather than the LORD (2Ki 1).
2. Son of Jehoram; king of Judah (2Ki 8:25-29; 9:14-29), also called Jehoahaz (2Ch 21:17-22:9; 25:23). Killed by Jehu while visiting Joram (2Ki 9: 14-29; 2Ch 22:1-9).

AHIJAH
1Sa 14:18 Saul said to *A,* "Bring the ark
1Ki 14: 2 *A* the prophet is there—the one

AHIMELECH
1. Priest who helped David in his flight from Saul (1Sa 21-22).
2. One of David's warriors (1Sa 26:6).

AHITHOPHEL
One of David's counselors who sided with Absalom (2Sa 15:12, 31-37; 1Ch 27:33-34); committed suicide when his advice was ignored (2Sa 16:15-17:23).

AI
Jos 7: 4 they were routed by the men of *A,*
8:28 So Joshua burned *A* and made it

AID
Isa 38:14 troubled; O Lord, come to my *a!*"
Php 4:16 you sent me *a* again and again

AIM
1Co 7:34 Her *a* is to be devoted to the Lord
2Co 13:11 *A* for perfection, listen

AIR
Mt 8:20 and birds of the *a* have nests,
Lk 9:58 and birds of the *a* have nests,
1Co 9:26 not fight like a man beating the *a.*
14: 9 You will just be speaking into the *a*
Eph 2: 2 of the ruler of the kingdom of the *a,*
1Th 4:17 clouds to meet the Lord in the *a.*

ALABASTER*
Mt 26: 7 came to him with an *a* jar
Mk 14: 3 a woman came with an *a* jar
Lk 7:37 she brought an *a* jar of perfume,

ALARM (ALARMED)
2Co 7:11 indignation, what *a,* what longing,

ALARMED (ALARM)
Mk 13: 7 and rumors of wars, do not be *a.*
2Th 2: 2 not to become easily unsettled or *a*

ALERT*
Jos 8: 4 All of you be on the *a.*
Ps 17:11 with eyes *a,* to throw me
Isa 21: 7 let him be *a,* / fully *a.*"
Mk 13:33 Be *a!* You do not know
Eph 6:18 be *a* and always keep on praying
1Th 5: 6 but let us be *a* and self-controlled.
1Pe 5: 8 Be self-controlled and *a.*

ALIEN (ALIENATED ALIENS)
Ex 22:21 "Do not mistreat an *a*
Lev 24:22 are to have the same law for the *a*
Ps 146: 9 The LORD watches over the *a*

ALIENATED (ALIEN)
Gal 5: 4 by law have been *a* from Christ;
Col 1:21 Once you were *a* from God

ALIENS (ALIEN)
Ex 23: 9 know how it feels to be *a,*
1Pe 2:11 as *a* and strangers in the world,

ALIVE (LIVE)
1Sa 2: 6 LORD brings death and makes *a;*
Lk 24:23 vision of angels, who said he was *a.*
Ac 1: 3 convincing proofs that he was *a.*
Ro 6:11 but *a* to God in Christ Jesus.
1Co 15:22 so in Christ all will be made *a.*
Eph 2: 5 made us *a* with Christ

ALMIGHTY (MIGHT)
Ge 17: 1 "I am God *A;* walk before me
Ex 6: 3 to Isaac and to Jacob as God *A,*
Ru 1:20 the *A* has made my life very bitter.
Job 11: 7 Can you probe the limits of the *A?*
33: 4 the breath of the *A* gives me life.
Ps 89: 8 O LORD God *A,* who is like you?
91: 1 will rest in the shadow of the *A.*
Isa 6: 3 "Holy, holy, holy is the LORD *A;*
45:13 says the LORD *A.*"
47: 4 the LORD *A* is his name—
48: 2 the LORD *A* is his name:
51:15 the LORD *A* is his name.
54: 5 the LORD *A* is his name—
Am 5:14 the LORD God *A* will be with you,
5:15 the LORD God *A* will have mercy
Rev 4: 8 holy is the Lord God *A,* who was,
19: 6 For our Lord God *A* reigns.

ALPHA*
Rev 1: 8 "I am the *A* and the Omega,"
21: 6 I am the *A* and the Omega,
22:13 I am the *A* and the Omega,

ALTAR
Ge 8:20 Then Noah built an *a* to the LORD
12: 7 So he built an *a* there to the LORD
13:18 where he built an *a* to the LORD.
22: 9 Abraham built an *a* there
22: 9 his son Isaac and laid him on the *a,*
26:25 Isaac built an *a* there and called
35: 1 and build an *a* there to God,
Ex 17:15 Moses built an *a* and called it
27: 1 "Build an *a* of acacia wood,
30: 1 "Make an *a* of acacia wood
37:25 They made the *a* of incense out
Dt 27: 5 an *a* to the LORD your God, an *a*
Jos 8:30 on Mount Ebal an *a* to the LORD,
22:10 built an imposing *a* there
Jdg 6:24 So Gideon built an *a* to the LORD
21: 4 the next day the people built an *a*
1Sa 7:17 he built an *a* there to the LORD.
14:35 Then Saul built an *a* to the LORD;
2Sa 24:25 David built an *a* to the LORD
1Ki 12:33 sacrifices on the *a* he had built
13: 2 "O *a, a!* This is what the LORD
16:32 He set up an *a* for Baal
18:30 and he repaired the *a* of the LORD
2Ki 16:11 So Uriah the priest built an *a*
1Ch 21:26 David built an *a* to the LORD
2Ch 4: 1 made a bronze *a* twenty cubits
4:19 the golden *a;* the tables
15: 8 He repaired the *a* of the LORD
32:12 'You must worship before one *a*
33:16 he restored the *a* of the LORD
Ezr 3: 2 to build the *a* of the God of Israel
Isa 6: 6 taken with tongs from the *a.*
Eze 40:47 the *a* was in front of the temple.
Mt 5:23 if you are offering your gift at the *a*
Ac 17:23 found an *a* with this inscription:
Heb 13:10 We have an *a* from which those
Rev 6: 9 I saw under the *a* the souls

ALTER*
Ps 89:34 or *a* what my lips have uttered.

ALWAYS
Dt 15:11 There will *a* be poor people
Ps 16: 8 I have set the LORD *a* before me.
51: 3 and my sin is *a* before me.

Pr 23: 7 who is *a* thinking about the cost.
Mt 26:11 The poor you will *a* have with you,
28:20 And surely I am with you *a*,
Mk 14: 7 The poor you will *a* have with you,
Jn 12: 8 You will *a* have the poor
1Co 13: 7 *a* protects, *a* trusts, *a* hopes, *a*
Php 4: 4 Rejoice in the Lord *a*.
1Pe 3:15 *A* be prepared to give an answer

AMALEKITES
Ex 17: 8 *A* came and attacked the Israelites
1Sa 15: 2 'I will punish the *A*

AMASA
Nephew of David (1Ch 2:17). Commander of Absalom's forces (2Sa 17:24-27). Returned to David (2Sa 19:13). Killed by Joab (2Sa 20:4-13).

AMASSES*
Pr 28: 8 *a* it for another, who will be kind

AMAZED
Mt 7:28 the crowds were *a* at his teaching,
Mk 6: 6 And he was *a* at their lack of faith.
10:24 The disciples were *a* at his words.
Ac 2: 7 Utterly *a*, they asked: "Are not all
13:12 for he was *a* at the teaching about

AMAZIAH
1. Son of Joash; king of Judah (2Ki 14; 2Ch 25). Defeated Edom (2Ki 14:7; 2Ch 25:5-13); defeated by Israel for worshiping Edom's gods (2Ki 14:8-14; 2Ch 25:14-24).
2. Idolatrous priest who opposed Amos (Am 7:10-17).

AMBASSADOR* (AMBASSADORS)
Eph 6:20 for which I am an *a* in chains.

AMBASSADORS (AMBASSADOR)
2Co 5:20 We are therefore Christ's *a*,

AMBITION*
Ro 15:20 It has always been my *a*
Gal 5:20 fits of rage, selfish *a*, dissensions,
Php 1:17 preach Christ out of selfish *a*,
2: 3 Do nothing out of selfish *a*
1Th 4:11 Make it your *a* to lead a quiet life,
Jas 3:14 and selfish *a* in your hearts,
3:16 where you have envy and selfish *a*,

AMENDS
Pr 14: 9 Fools mock at making *a* for sin,

AMNON
Firstborn of David (2Sa 3:2; 1Ch 3:1). Killed by Absalom for raping his sister Tamar (2Sa 13).

AMON
1. Son of Manasseh; king of Judah (2Ki 21:18-26; 1Ch 3:14; 2Ch 33:21-25).
2. Ruler of Samaria under Ahab (1Ki 22:26; 2Ch 18:25).

AMOS
1. Prophet from Tekoa (Am 1:1; 7:10-17).
2. Ancestor of Jesus (Lk 3:25).

ANAK (ANAKITES)
Nu 13:28 even saw descendants of *A* there.

ANAKITES (ANAK)
Dt 1:28 We even saw the *A* there.'"
2:10 and numerous, and as tall as the *A*.
9: 2 "Who can stand up against the *A*?"

ANANIAS
1. Husband of Sapphira; died for lying to God (Ac 5:1-11).
2. Disciple who baptized Saul (Ac 9:10-19).
3. High priest at Paul's arrest (Ac 22:30-24:1).

ANCESTORS (ANCESTRY)
1Ki 19: 4 I am no better than my *a*."

ANCESTRY (ANCESTORS)
Ro 9: 5 from them is traced the human *a*

ANCHOR
Heb 6:19 We have this hope as an *a*

ANCIENT
Da 7: 9 and the *A* of Days took his seat.
7:13 He approached the *A* of Days
7:22 until the *A* of Days came

ANDREW*
Apostle; brother of Simon Peter (Mt 4:18; 10:2; Mk 1:16-18, 29; 3:18; 13:3; Lk 6:14; Jn 1:35-44; 6:8-9; 12:22; Ac 1:13).

ANGEL (ANGELS ARCHANGEL)
Ge 16: 7 The *a* of the LORD found Hagar
22:11 But the *a* of the LORD called out
Ex 23:20 I am sending an *a* ahead of you
Nu 22:23 When the donkey saw the *a*
Jdg 2: 1 The *a* of the LORD went up
6:22 Gideon realized that it was the *a*
13:15 Manoah said to the *a* of the LORD
2Sa 24:16 The *a* of the LORD was then
1Ki 19: 7 The *a* of the LORD came back
2Ki 19:35 That night the *a* of the LORD went
Ps 34: 7 The *a* of the LORD encamps
Hos 12: 4 He struggled with the *a*
Mt 2:13 an *a* of the Lord appeared
28: 2 for an *a* of the Lord came
Lk 1:26 God sent the *a* Gabriel
2: 9 An *a* of the Lord appeared to them,
22:43 An *a* from heaven appeared to him
Ac 6:15 his face was like the face of an *a*.
12: 7 Suddenly an *a* of the Lord
2Co 11:14 Satan himself masquerades as an *a*
Gal 1: 8 or an *a* from heaven should preach

ANGELS (ANGEL)
Ps 91:11 command his *a* concerning you
Mt 4: 6 command his *a* concerning you,
13:39 of the age, and the harvesters are *a*.
13:49 The *a* will come and separate
18:10 For I tell you that their *a*
25:41 prepared for the devil and his *a*.
Lk 4:10 command his *a* concerning you
20:36 for they are like the *a*.
1Co 6: 3 you not know that we will judge *a*?
13: 1 in the tongues of men and of *a*,
Col 2:18 and the worship of *a* disqualify you
Heb 1: 4 as much superior to the *a*
1: 6 "Let all God's *a* worship him."
1: 7 "He makes his *a* winds,
1:14 Are not all *a* ministering spirits
2: 7 made him a little lower than the *a*;
2: 9 was made a little lower than the *a*,
13: 2 some people have entertained *a*
1Pe 1:12 Even *a* long to look
2Pe 2: 4 For if God did not spare *a*
Jude : 6 *a* who did not keep their positions

ANGER (ANGERED ANGRY)
Ex 15: 7 You unleashed your burning *a*;
22:24 My *a* will be aroused, and I will kill
32:10 alone so that my *a* may burn
32:11 "why should your *a* burn
32:12 Turn from your fierce *a*; relent
32:19 his *a* burned and he threw
34: 6 slow to *a*, abounding in love
Lev 26:28 then in my *a* I will be hostile
Nu 14:18 slow to *a*, abounding in love
25:11 has turned my *a* away
32:10 LORD's *a* was aroused that day
32:13 The LORD's *a* burned
Dt 9:19 I feared the *a* and wrath
29:28 In furious *a* and in great wrath
Jdg 14:19 Burning with *a*, he went up
2Sa 12: 5 David burned with *a*
2Ki 22:13 Great is the LORD's *a* that burns
Ne 9:17 slow to *a* and abounding in love.
Ps 30: 5 For his *a* lasts only a moment,
78:38 Time after time he restrained his *a*
86:15 slow to *a*, abounding in love
90: 7 We are consumed by your *a*
103: 8 slow to *a*, abounding in love.
Pr 15: 1 but a harsh word stirs up *a*.
29:11 A fool gives full vent to his *a*,
30:33 so stirring up *a* produces strife."
Jnh 4: 2 slow to *a* and abounding in love,
Eph 4:26 "In your *a* do not sin": Do not let
Jas 1:20 for man's *a* does not bring about

ANGERED (ANGER)
Pr 22:24 do not associate with one easily *a*,
1Co 13: 5 it is not easily *a*, it keeps no record

ANGRY (ANGER)
Ps 2:12 Kiss the Son, lest he be *a*
95:10 For forty years I was *a*
Pr 29:22 An *a* man stirs up dissension,
Mt 5:22 But I tell you that anyone who is *a*
Jas 1:19 slow to speak and slow to become *a*

ANGUISH
Ps 118: 5 In my *a* I cried to the LORD,
Jer 4:19 Oh, my *a*, my *a*!
Zep 1:15 a day of distress and *a*,
Lk 21:25 nations will be in *a* and perplexity
22:44 in *a*, he prayed more earnestly,
Ro 9: 2 and unceasing *a* in my heart.

ANIMALS
Ge 1:24 wild *a*, each according to its kind."
7:16 The *a* going in were male
Dt 14: 4 These are the *a* you may eat: the ox
Job 12: 7 ask the *a*, and they will teach you,
Isa 43:20 The wild *a* honor me,

ANNOUNCE (ANNOUNCED)
Mt 6: 2 give to the needy, do not *a* it

ANNOUNCED (ANNOUNCE)
Isa 48: 5 before they happened I *a* them
Gal 3: 8 and *a* the gospel in advance

ANNOYANCE*
Pr 12:16 A fool shows his *a* at once,

ANNUAL*
Ex 30:10 This *a* atonement must be made
Jdg 21:19 there is the *a* festival of the LORD
1Sa 1:21 family to offer the *a* sacrifice
2:19 husband to offer the *a* sacrifice.
20: 6 an *a* sacrifice is being made there
2Ch 8:13 New Moons and the three *a* feasts
Heb 10: 3 those sacrifices are an *a* reminder

ANOINT (ANOINTED ANOINTING)
Ex 30:26 use it to *a* the Tent of Meeting,
30:30 "*A* Aaron and his sons
1Sa 9:16 *A* him leader over my people Israel
15: 1 to *a* you king over his people Israel;
2Ki 9: 3 what the LORD says: I *a* you king
Ps 23: 5 You *a* my head with oil;
Da 9:24 prophecy and to *a* the most holy.
Jas 5:14 and *a* him with oil in the name

ANOINTED (ANOINT)
1Ch 16:22 "Do not touch my *a* ones;
Ps 105: 15 "Do not touch my *a* ones;
Isa 61: 1 because the LORD has *a* me
Da 9:26 the *A* One will be cut off
Lk 4:18 because he has *a* me
Ac 10:38 how God *a* Jesus of Nazareth

ANOINTING (ANOINT)
Lev 8:12 some of the *a* oil on Aaron's head
1Ch 29:22 *a* him before the LORD to be ruler
Ps 45: 7 by *a* you with the oil of joy.
Heb 1: 9 by *a* you with the oil of joy."
1Jn 2:20 you have an *a* from the Holy One,
2:27 about all things and as that *a* is real,

ANT* (ANTS)
Pr 6: 6 Go to the *a*, you sluggard;

ANTICHRIST* (ANTICHRISTS)
1Jn 2:18 have heard that the *a* is coming,
2:22 a man is the *a*— he denies
4: 3 of the *a*, which you have heard is
2Jn : 7 person is the deceiver and the *a*.

ANTICHRISTS* (ANTICHRIST)
1Jn 2:18 even now many *a* have come.

ANTIOCH
Ac 11:26 were called Christians first at *A*.

ANTS* (ANT)
Pr 30:25 *A* are creatures of little strength,

ANXIETIES* (ANXIOUS)
Lk 21:34 drunkenness and the *a* of life,

ANXIETY (ANXIOUS)
1Pe 5: 7 Cast all your *a* on him

ANXIOUS (ANXIETIES ANXIETY)
Pr 12:25 An *a* heart weighs a man down,
Php 4: 6 Do not be *a* about anything,

APOLLOS*
Christian from Alexandria, learned in the Scriptures; instructed by Aquila and Priscilla (Ac 18:24-28). Ministered at Corinth (Ac 19:1; 1Co 1:12; 3; Tit 3:13).

APOLLYON*
Rev 9:11 is Abaddon, and in Greek, *A*.

APOSTLE (APOSTLES APOSTLES')
Ro 11:13 as I am the *a* to the Gentiles,
1Co 9: 1 Am I not an *a*? Have I not seen
2Co 12:12 The things that mark an *a*— signs,
Gal 2: 8 of Peter as an *a* to the Jews,
1Ti 2: 7 was appointed a herald and an *a*—
2Ti 1:11 I was appointed a herald and an *a*
Heb 3: 1 *a* and high priest whom we confess.

APOSTLES (APOSTLE)
See also Andrew, Bartholomew, James, John, Judas, Matthew, Matthias, Nathanael, Paul, Peter, Philip, Simon, Thaddaeus, Thomas.
Mk 3:14 twelve—designating them *a*—
Lk 11:49 'I will send them prophets and *a*,
Ac 1:26 so he was added to the eleven *a*.

Ac 2:43 signs were done by the *a.*
1Co 12:28 God has appointed first of all *a,*
15: 9 For I am the least of the *a*
2Co 11:13 masquerading as *a* of Christ.
Eph 2:20 built on the foundation of the *a*
4:11 It was he who gave some to be *a,*
Rev 21:14 names of the twelve *a* of the Lamb.

APOSTLES' (APOSTLE)
Ac 5: 2 the rest and put it at the *a'* feet.
8:18 at the laying on of the *a'* hands,

APPEAL
Ac 25:11 I *a* to Caesar!" After Festus had
Phm : 9 yet I *a* to you on the basis of love.

APPEAR (APPEARANCE APPEARANCES APPEARED APPEARING APPEARS)
Ge 1: 9 to one place, and let dry ground *a.*"
Lev 16: 2 I *a* in the cloud over the atonement
Mt 24:30 of the Son of Man will *a* in the sky,
Mk 13:22 false prophets will *a* and perform
Lk 19:11 of God was going to *a* at once.
2Co 5:10 we must all *a* before the judgment
Col 3: 4 also will *a* with him in glory.
Heb 9:24 now to *a* for us in God's presence.
9:28 and he will *a* a second time,

APPEARANCE (APPEAR)
1Sa 16: 7 Man looks at the outward *a,*
Isa 52:14 his *a* was so disfigured beyond that
53: 2 in his *a* that we should desire him.
Gal 2: 6 God does not judge by external *a*—

APPEARANCES* (APPEAR)
Jn 7:24 Stop judging by mere *a,*

APPEARED (APPEAR)
Nu 14:10 glory of the LORD *a* at the Tent
Mt 1:20 an angel of the Lord *a* to him
Lk 2: 9 An angel of the Lord *a* to them,
1Co 15: 5 and that he *a* to Peter,
Heb 9:26 now he has *a* once for all at the end

APPEARING (APPEAR)
1Ti 6:14 until the *a* of our Lord Jesus Christ,
2Ti 1:10 through the *a* of our Savior,
4: 8 to all who have longed for his *a.*
Tit 2:13 the glorious *a* of our great God

APPEARS (APPEAR)
Mal 3: 2 Who can stand when he *a?*
Col 3: 4 When Christ, who is your life, *a,*
1Pe 5: 4 And when the Chief Shepherd *a,*
1Jn 3: 2 But we know that when he *a,*

APPETITE
Pr 16:26 The laborer's *a* works for him;
Ecc 6: 7 yet his *a* is never satisfied.
Jer 50:19 his *a* will be satisfied

APPLES
Pr 25:11 is like *a* of gold in settings of silver.

APPLY (APPLYING)
Pr 22:17 *a* your heart to what I teach,
23:12 *A* your heart to instruction

APPLYING (APPLY)
Pr 2: 2 and *a* your heart to understanding,

APPOINT (APPOINTED)
Ps 61: 7 *a* your love and faithfulness
1Th 5: 9 For God did not *a* us
Tit 1: 5 and *a* elders in every town,

APPOINTED (APPOINT)
Dt 1:15 *a* them to have authority over you
Pr 8:23 I was *a* from eternity,
Da 11:27 an end will still come at the *a* time.
Hab 2: 3 For the revelation awaits an *a* time;
Jn 15:16 Chose you and *a* you to go
Ro 9: 9 "At the *a* time I will return,

APPROACH (APPROACHING)
Ex 24: 2 but Moses alone is to *a* the LORD;
Eph 3:12 in him we may *a* God with freedom
Heb 4:16 Let us then *a* the throne of grace

APPROACHING (APPROACH)
Heb 10:25 all the more as you see the Day *a.*
1Jn 5:14 is the confidence we have in *a* God:

APPROPRIATE
1Ti 2:10 *a* for women who profess

APPROVAL (APPROVE)
Jdg 18: 6 Your journey has the LORD's *a.*"
Jn 6:27 the Father has placed his seal of *a.*"
1Co 11:19 to show which of you have God's *a*
Gal 1:10 trying to win the *a* of men,

APPROVE (APPROVAL APPROVED APPROVES)
Ro 2:18 if you know his will and *a*
12: 2 and *a* what God's will is—

APPROVED* (APPROVE)
Ro 14:18 pleasing to God and *a* by men.
16:10 Greet Apelles, tested and *a*
2Co 10:18 who commends himself who is *a,*
1Th 2: 4 as men *a* by God to be entrusted
2Ti 2:15 to present yourself to God as one *a,*

APPROVES* (APPROVE)
Ro 14:22 not condemn himself by what he *a.*

APT*
Pr 15:23 A man finds joy in giving an *a* reply

AQUILA*
Husband of Priscilla; co-worker with Paul, instructor of Apollos (Ac 18; Ro 16:3; 1Co 16:19; 2Ti 4:19).

ARABIA
Gal 1:17 but I went immediately into *A*
4:25 Hagar stands for Mount Sinai in *A*

ARARAT
Ge 8: 4 came to rest on the mountains of *A.*

ARAUNAH
2Sa 24:16 threshing floor of *A* the Jebusite.

ARBITER* (ARBITRATE)
Lk 12:14 who appointed me a judge or an *a*

ARBITRATE* (ARBITER)
Job 9:33 If only there were someone to *a*

ARCHANGEL* (ANGEL)
1Th 4:16 with the voice of the *a*
Jude : 9 *a* Michael, when he was disputing

ARCHER
Pr 26:10 Like an *a* who wounds at random

ARCHIPPUS*
Col 4:17 Tell *A:* "See to it that you complete
Phm : 2 to *A* our fellow soldier

ARCHITECT*
Heb 11:10 whose *a* and builder is God.

AREOPAGUS*
Ac 17:19 brought him to a meeting of the *A,*
17:22 up in the meeting of the *A*
17:34 of the *A,* also a woman named

ARGUE (ARGUMENT ARGUMENTS)
Job 13: 3 and to *a* my case with God.
13: 8 Will you *a* the case for God?
Pr 25: 9 If you *a* your case with a neighbor,

ARGUMENT (ARGUE)
Heb 6:16 is said and puts an end to all *a.*

ARGUMENTS (ARGUE)
Isa 41:21 "Set forth your *a,*" says Jacob's
Col 2: 4 you by fine-sounding *a.*
2Ti 2:23 to do with foolish and stupid *a,*
Tit 3: 9 and *a* and quarrels about the law,

ARK
Ge 6:14 So make yourself an *a*
Ex 25:21 and put in the *a* the Testimony,
Dt 10: 5 put the tablets in the *a* I had made,
1Sa 4:11 The *a* of God was captured,
7: 2 that the *a* remained at Kiriath
2Sa 6:17 They brought the *a* of the LORD
1Ki 8: 9 There was nothing in the *a*
1Ch 13: 9 out his hand to steady the *a,*
2Ch 35: 3 "Put the sacred *a* in the temple that
Heb 9: 4 This *a* contained the gold jar
11: 7 in holy fear built an *a*
Rev 11:19 within his temple was seen the *a*

ARM (ARMY)
Nu 11:23 "Is the LORD's *a* too short?
Dt 4:34 hand and an outstretched *a,*
7:19 mighty hand and outstretched *a,*
Ps 44: 3 it was your right hand, your *a,*
98: 1 his right hand and his holy *a*
Jer 27: 5 outstretched *a* I made the earth
1Pe 4: 1 *a* yourselves also with the same

ARMAGEDDON*
Rev 16:16 that in Hebrew is called *A.*

ARMIES (ARMY)
1Sa 17:26 Philistine that he should defy the *a*
Rev 19:14 *a* of heaven were following him,

ARMOR (ARMY)
1Ki 20:11 on his *a* should not boast like one
Jer 46: 4 put on your *a!*
Ro 13:12 deeds of darkness and put on the *a*
Eph 6:11 Put on the full *a* of God
6:13 Therefore put on the full *a* of God,

ARMS (ARMY)
Dt 33:27 underneath are the everlasting *a.*
Ps 18:32 It is God who *a* me with strength
Pr 31:17 her *a* are strong for her tasks.
31:20 She opens her *a* to the poor
Isa 40:11 He gathers the lambs in his *a*
Mk 10:16 And he took the children in his *a,*
Heb 12:12 strengthen your feeble *a*

ARMY (ARM ARMIES ARMOR ARMS)
Ps 33:16 No king is saved by the size of his *a*
Joel 2: 2 a large and mighty *a* comes,
2: 5 like a mighty *a* drawn up for battle.
2:11 thunders at the head of his *a;*
Rev 19:19 the rider on the horse and his *a.*

AROMA
Ge 8:21 The LORD smelled the pleasing *a*
Ex 29:18 a pleasing *a,* an offering made
Lev 3:16 made by fire, a pleasing *a.*
2Co 2:15 For we are to God the *a* of Christ

AROUSE (AROUSED)
Ro 11:14 I may somehow *a* my own people

AROUSED (AROUSE)
Ps 78:58 they *a* his jealousy with their idols.

ARRANGED
1Co 12:18 But in fact God has *a* the parts

ARRAYED*
Ps 110: 3 *A* in holy majesty,
Isa 61:10 and *a* me in a robe of righteousness

ARREST
Mt 10:19 But when they *a* you, do not worry

ARROGANCE (ARROGANT)
1Sa 2: 3 or let your mouth speak such *a,*
Pr 8:13 I hate pride and *a,*
Mk 7:22 lewdness, envy, slander, *a* and folly
2Co 12:20 slander, gossip, *a* and disorder.

ARROGANT (ARROGANCE)
Ps 5: 5 The *a* cannot stand
119: 78 May the *a* be put to shame
Pr 17: 7 *A* lips are unsuited to a fool—
21:24 *a* man—"Mocker" is his name;
Ro 1:30 God-haters, insolent, *a*
11:20 Do not be *a,* but be afraid.
1Ti 6:17 in this present world not to be *a*

ARROW (ARROWS)
Ps 91: 5 nor the *a* that flies by day,
Pr 25:18 Like a club or a sword or a sharp *a*

ARROWS (ARROW)
Ps 64: 3 and aim their words like deadly *a.*
64: 7 But God will shoot them with *a;*
127: 4 Like *a* in the hands of a warrior
Pr 26:18 firebrands or deadly *a*
Eph 6:16 you can extinguish all the flaming *a*

ARTAXERXES
King of Persia; allowed rebuilding of temple under Ezra (Ezr 4; 7), and of walls of Jerusalem under his cupbearer Nehemiah (Ne 2; 5:14; 13:6).

ARTEMIS
Ac 19:28 "Great is *A* of the Ephesians!"

ASA
King of Judah (1Ki 15:8-24; 1Ch 3:10; 2Ch 14-16). Godly reformer (2Ch 15); in later years defeated Israel with help of Aram, not the LORD (1Ki 15:16-22; 2Ch 16).

ASAHEL
1. Nephew of David, one of his warriors (2Sa 23:24; 1Ch 2:16; 11:26; 27:7). Killed by Abner (2Sa 2); avenged by Joab (2Sa 3:22-39).
2. Levite; teacher (2Ch 17:8).

ASAPH
1. Recorder to Hezekiah (2Ki 18:18, 37; Isa 36:3, 22).
2. Levitical musician (1Ch 6:39; 15:17-19; 16:4-7, 37). Sons of (1Ch 25; 2Ch 5:12; 20:14; 29:13; 35:15; Ezr 2:41; 3:10; Ne 7:44; 11:17; 12:27-47). Psalms of (2Ch 29:30; Ps 50; 73-83).

ASCEND* (ASCENDED ASCENDING)
Dt 30:12 "Who will *a* into heaven to get it
Ps 24: 3 Who may *a* the hill of the LORD?
Isa 14:13 "I will *a* to heaven;
14:14 I will *a* above the tops of the clouds
Jn 6:62 of Man *a* to where he was before!
Ac 2:34 For David did not *a* to heaven,
Ro 10: 6 'Who will *a* into heaven?' " (that is,

ASCENDED (ASCEND)
Ps 68:18 When you *a* on high,
Eph 4: 8 "When he *a* on high,

ASCENDING (ASCEND)
Ge 28:12 and the angels of God were *a*
Jn 1:51 and the angels of God *a*

ASCRIBE*
1Ch 16:28 *A* to the LORD, O families
16:28 *a* to the LORD glory and strength,
16:29 *a* to the LORD the glory due his
Job 36: 3 I will *a* justice to my Maker.
Ps 29: 1 *A* to the LORD, O mighty ones,
29: 1 *a* to the LORD glory and strength.
29: 2 *A* to the LORD the glory due his
96: 7 *A* to the LORD, O families
96: 7 *a* to the LORD glory and strength.
96: 8 *A* to the LORD the glory due his

ASHAMED (SHAME)
Mk 8:38 If anyone is *a* of me and my words
Lk 9:26 If anyone is *a* of me and my words,
Ro 1:16 I am not *a* of the gospel,
2Ti 1: 8 So do not be *a* to testify about our
2:15 who does not need to be *a*

ASHER
Son of Jacob by Zilpah (Ge 30:13; 35:26; 46:17; Ex 1:4; 1Ch 2:2). Tribe of blessed (Ge 49:20; Dt 33:24-25), numbered (Nu 1:40-41; 26:44-47), allotted land (Jos 10:24-31; Eze 48:2), failed to fully possess (Jdg 1:31-32), failed to support Deborah (Jdg 5:17), supported Gideon (Jdg 6:35; 7:23) and David (1Ch 12:36), 12,000 from (Rev 7:6).

ASHERAH (ASHERAHS)
Ex 34:13 and cut down their *A* poles.
1Ki 18:19 the four hundred prophets of *A*,

ASHERAHS* (ASHERAH)
Jdg 3: 7 and served the Baals and the *A*.

ASHES
Job 42: 6 and repent in dust and *a*."
Mt 11:21 ago in sackcloth and *a*.

ASHTORETHS
Jdg 2:13 and served Baal and the *A*.
1Sa 7: 4 put away their Baals and *A*,

ASLEEP (SLEEP)
1Co 15:18 who have fallen *a* in Christ are lost.
1Th 4:13 be ignorant about those who fall *a*,

ASSEMBLY
Ps 1: 5 nor sinners in the *a* of the righteous
35:18 I will give you thanks in the great *a*
82: 1 God presides in the great *a*;
149: 1 his praise in the *a* of the saints.

ASSIGNED
1Ki 7:14 and did all the work *a* to him.
Mk 13:34 with his *a* task, and tells the one
1Co 3: 5 as the Lord has *a* to each his task.
7:17 place in life that the Lord *a* to him
2Co 10:13 to the field God has *a* to us,

ASSOCIATE
Pr 22:24 do not *a* with one easily angered,
Jn 4: 9 (For Jews do not *a* with Samaritans
Ac 10:28 law for a Jew to *a* with a Gentile
Ro 12:16 but be willing to *a* with people
1Co 5: 9 to *a* with sexually immoral people
5:11 am writing you that you must not *a*
2Th 3:14 Do not *a* with him,

ASSURANCE (ASSURED)
Heb 10:22 with a sincere heart in full *a* of faith

ASSURED (ASSURANCE)
Col 4:12 the will of God, mature and fully *a*.

ASTRAY
Ps 119: 67 Before I was afflicted I went *a*,
Pr 10:17 ignores correction leads others *a*.
20: 1 whoever is led *a* by them is not
Isa 53: 6 We all, like sheep, have gone *a*,
Jer 50: 6 their shepherds have led them *a*
Jn 16: 1 you so that you will not go *a*.
1Pe 2:25 For you were like sheep going *a*,
1Jn 3: 7 do not let anyone lead you *a*.

ASTROLOGERS
Isa 47:13 Let your *a* come forward,
Da 2: 2 *a* to tell him what he had dreamed.

ATE (EAT)
Ge 3: 6 wisdom, she took some and *a* it.
27:25 Jacob brought it to him and he *a*;
2Sa 9:11 Mephibosheth *a* at David's table
Ps 78:25 Men *a* the bread of angels;
Jer 15:16 When your words came, I *a* them;
Eze 3: 3 So I *a* it, and it tasted as sweet
Mt 14:20 They all *a* and were satisfied,
15:37 They all *a* and were satisfied.
Mk 6:42 They all *a* and were satisfied,
Lk 9:17 They all *a* and were satisfied,

ATHALIAH
Granddaughter of Omri; wife of Jehoram and mother of Ahaziah; encouraged their evil ways (2Ki 8:18, 27; 2Ch 22:2). At death of Ahaziah she made herself queen, killing all his sons but Joash (2Ki 11:1-3; 2Ch 22:10-12); killed six years later when Joash was revealed (2Ki 11:4-16; 2Ch 23:1-15).

ATHLETE*
2Ti 2: 5 if anyone competes as an *a*,

ATONE* (ATONEMENT)
Ex 30:15 to the LORD to *a* for your lives.
2Ch 29:24 for a sin offering to *a* for all Israel,
Da 9:24 an end to sin, to *a* for wickedness,

ATONED* (ATONEMENT)
Dt 21: 8 And the bloodshed will be *a* for.
1Sa 3:14 guilt of Eli's house will never be *a*
Pr 16: 6 faithfulness sin is *a* for;
Isa 6: 7 guilt is taken away and your sin *a*
22:14 your dying day this sin will not be *a*
27: 9 then, will Jacob's guilt be *a* for,

ATONEMENT (ATONE ATONED)
Ex 25:17 "Make an *a* cover of pure gold—
30:10 Once a year Aaron shall make *a*
Lev 17:11 it is the blood that makes *a*
23:27 this seventh month is the Day of *A*.
Nu 25:13 and made *a* for the Israelites."
Ro 3:25 presented him as a sacrifice of *a*,
Heb 2:17 that he might make *a* for the sins

ATTACK
Ps 109: 3 they *a* me without cause.

ATTAINED
Php 3:16 up to what we have already *a*.
Heb 7:11 If perfection could have been *a*

ATTENTION (ATTENTIVE)
Pr 4: 1 pay *a* and gain understanding.
4:20 My son, pay *a* to what I say;
5: 1 My son, pay *a* to my wisdom,
7:24 pay *a* to what I say.
22:17 Pay *a* and listen to the sayings
Ecc 7:21 Do not pay *a* to every word people
Isa 42:20 many things, but have paid no *a*;
Tit 1:14 and will pay no *a* to Jewish myths
Heb 2: 1 We must pay more careful *a*,

ATTENTIVE (ATTENTION)
Ne 1:11 let your ear be *a* to the prayer
1Pe 3:12 and his ears are *a* to their prayer,

ATTITUDE (ATTITUDES)
Eph 4:23 new in the *a* of your minds;
Php 2: 5 Your *a* should be the same
1Pe 4: 1 yourselves also with the same *a*,

ATTITUDES (ATTITUDE)
Heb 4:12 it judges the thoughts and *a*

ATTRACTIVE
Tit 2:10 teaching about God our Savior *a*.

AUDIENCE
Pr 29:26 Many seek an *a* with a ruler,

AUTHORITIES (AUTHORITY)
Ro 13: 1 *a* that exist have been established
13: 5 it is necessary to submit to the *a*,
13: 6 for the *a* are God's servants,
Eph 3:10 and *a* in the heavenly realms,
6:12 but against the rulers, against the *a*,
Col 1:16 thrones or powers or rulers or *a*;
2:15 having disarmed the powers and *a*,
Tit 3: 1 people to be subject to rulers and *a*,
1Pe 3:22 *a* and powers in submission to him.

AUTHORITY (AUTHORITIES)
Mt 7:29 because he taught as one who had *a*
9: 6 the Son of Man has *a* on earth
28:18 "All *a* in heaven and on earth has
Mk 1:22 he taught them as one who had *a*,
2:10 the Son of Man has *a* on earth
Lk 4:32 because his message had *a*.
5:24 the Son of Man has *a* on earth
Jn 10:18 *a* to lay it down and *a*
Ac 1: 7 the Father has set by his own *a*.
Ro 7: 1 that the law has *a* over a man only
13: 1 for there is no *a* except that which
13: 2 rebels against the *a* is rebelling
1Co 11:10 to have a sign of *a* on her head.
15:24 he has destroyed all dominion, *a*
1Ti 2: 2 for kings and all those in *a*,
2:12 to teach or to have *a* over a man;
Tit 2:15 Encourage and rebuke with all *a*.
Heb 13:17 your leaders and submit to their *a*.

AUTUMN*
Dt 11:14 both *a* and spring rains,
Ps 84: 6 the *a* rains also cover it with pools.
Jer 5:24 who gives *a* and spring rains
Joel 2:23 both *a* and spring rains, as before.
Jas 5: 7 and how patient he is for the *a*
Jude :12 blown along by the wind; *a* trees,

AVENGE (VENGEANCE)
Lev 26:25 sword upon you to *a* the breaking
Dt 32:35 It is mine to *a*; I will repay.
32:43 for he will *a* the blood
Ro 12:19 "It is mine to *a*; I will repay,"
Heb 10:30 "It is mine to *a*; I will repay,"
Rev 6:10 of the earth and *a* our blood?"

AVENGER (VENGEANCE)
Nu 35:27 the *a* of blood may kill the accused
Jos 20: 3 find protection from the *a* of blood.
Ps 8: 2 to silence the foe and the *a*.

AVENGES (VENGEANCE)
Ps 94: 1 O LORD, the God who *a*,

AVENGING (VENGEANCE)
1Sa 25:26 and from *a* yourself with your own
Na 1: 2 The LORD is a jealous and *a* God;

AVOID (AVOIDS)
Pr 4:15 *A* it, do not travel on it;
20: 3 It is to a man's honor to *a* strife,
20:19 so *a* a man who talks too much.
Ecc 7:18 who fears God will *a* all extremes.
1Th 4: 3 you should *a* sexual immorality;
5:22 *A* every kind of evil.
2Ti 2:16 *A* godless chatter, because those
Tit 3: 9 But *a* foolish controversies

AVOIDS* (AVOID)
Pr 16: 6 of the LORD a man *a* evil.
16:17 The highway of the upright *a* evil;

AWAITS (WAIT)
Pr 15:10 Stern discipline *a* him who leaves
28:22 and is unaware that poverty *a* him.

AWAKE (WAKE)
Ps 17:15 when I *a*, I will be satisfied
Pr 6:22 when you *a*, they will speak to you.

AWARD*
2Ti 4: 8 will *a* to me on that day—

AWARE
Ex 34:29 he was not *a* that his face was
Mt 24:50 and at an hour he is not *a* of.
Lk 12:46 and at an hour he is not *a* of.

AWE* (AWESOME OVERAWED)
1Sa 12:18 So all the people stood in *a*
1Ki 3:28 they held the king in *a*,
Job 25: 2 "Dominion and *a* belong to God;
Ps 119:120 I stand in *a* of your laws.
Ecc 5: 7 Therefore stand in *a* of God.
Isa 29:23 will stand in *a* of the God of Israel.
Jer 2:19 and have no *a* of me,"
33: 9 they will be in *a* and will tremble
Hab 3: 2 I stand in *a* of your deeds,
Mal 2: 5 and stood in *a* of my name.
Mt 9: 8 they were filled with *a*;
Lk 1:65 The neighbors were all filled with *a*
5:26 They were filled with *a* and said,
7:16 They were all filled with *a*
Ac 2:43 Everyone was filled with *a*,
Heb 12:28 acceptably with reverence and *a*,

AWESOME* (AWE)
Ge 28:17 and said, "How *a* is this place!
Ex 15:11 *a* in glory,
34:10 among will see how *a* is the work
Dt 4:34 or by great and *a* deeds,
7:21 is among you, is a great and *a* God.
10:17 the great God, mighty and *a*,
10:21 and *a* wonders you saw
28:58 revere this glorious and *a* name—
34:12 performed the *a* deeds that Moses

Jdg 13: 6 like an angel of God, very *a*.
2Sa 7:23 *a* wonders by driving out nations
1Ch 17:21 *a* wonders by driving out nations
Ne 1: 5 of heaven, the great and *a* God,
4:14 and *a*, and fight for your brothers,
9:32 the great, mighty and *a* God,
Job 10:16 again display your *a* power
37:22 God comes in *a* majesty.
Ps 45: 4 let your right hand display *a* deeds.
47: 2 How *a* is the LORD Most High,
65: 5 us with *a* deeds of righteousness,
66: 3 to God, "How *a* are your deeds!
66: 5 how *a* his works in man's behalf!
68:35 You are *a*, O God,
89: 7 he is more *a* than all who surround
99: 3 praise your great and *a* name—
106: 22 and *a* deeds by the Red Sea.
111: 9 holy and *a* is his name.
145: 6 of the power of your *a* works,
Isa 64: 3 when you did *a* things that we did
Eze 1:18 Their rims were high and *a*,
1:22 expanse, sparkling like ice, and *a*.
Da 2:31 dazzling statue, *a* in appearance.
9: 4 "O Lord, the great and *a* God,
Zep 2:11 The LORD will be *a* to them

AX
Mt 3:10 The *a* is already at the root
Lk 3: 9 The *a* is already at the root

BAAL
Jdg 6:25 Tear down your father's altar to *B*
1Ki 16:32 *B* in the temple of *B* that he built
18:25 Elijah said to the prophets of *B*,
19:18 knees have not bowed down to *B*
2Ki 10:28 Jehu destroyed *B* worship in Israel.
Jer 19: 5 places of *B* to burn their sons
Ro 11: 4 have not bowed the knee to *B*."

BAASHA
King of Israel (1Ki 15:16-16:7; 2Ch 16:1-6).

BABBLER* (BABBLING)
Ac 17:18 "What is this *b* trying to say?"

BABBLING* (BABBLER)
Mt 6: 7 do not keep on *b* like pagans,

BABIES* (BABY)
Ge 25:22 The *b* jostled each other within her
Ex 2: 6 "This is one of the Hebrew *b*,"
Lk 18:15 also bringing *b* to Jesus
Ac 7:19 them to throw out their newborn *b*
1Pe 2: 2 Like newborn *b*, crave pure

BABY* (BABIES BABY'S)
Ex 2: 6 She opened it and saw the *b*.
2: 7 women to nurse the *b* for you?"
2: 9 So the woman took the *b*
2: 9 "Take this *b* and nurse him for me,
1Ki 3:17 I had a *b* while she was there
3:18 was born, this woman also had a *b*.
3:26 give her the living *b*! Don't kill him
3:27 Give the living *b* to the first woman
Isa 49:15 "Can a mother forget the *b*
Lk 1:41 the *b* leaped in her womb,
1:44 the *b* in my womb leaped for joy.
1:57 time for Elizabeth to have her *b*,
2: 6 the time came for the *b* to be born,
2:12 You will find a *b* wrapped in strips
2:16 the *b*, who was lying in the manger.
Jn 16:21 but when her *b* is born she forgets

BABY'S* (BABY)
Ex 2: 8 the girl went and got the *b* mother.

BABYLON
Ps 137: 1 By the rivers of *B* we sat and wept
Jer 29:10 seventy years are completed for *B*,
51:37 *B* will be a heap of ruins,
Rev 14: 8 "Fallen! Fallen is *B* the Great,
17: 5 MYSTERY *B* THE GREAT

BACKS
2Pe 2:21 and then to turn their *b*

BACKSLIDING* (BACKSLIDINGS)
Jer 2:19 your *b* will rebuke you.
3:22 I will cure you of *b*."
14: 7 For our *b* is great;
15: 6 "You keep on *b*.
Eze 37:23 them from all their sinful *b*,

BACKSLIDINGS* (BACKSLIDING)
Jer 5: 6 and their *b* many.

BALAAM
Prophet who attempted to curse Israel (Nu 22-24; Dt 23:4-5; 2Pe 2:15; Jude 11). Killed in Israel's vengeance on Midianites (Nu 31:8; Jos 13:22).

BALAK
Moabite king who hired Balaam to curse Israel (Nu 22-24; Jos 24:9).

BALDHEAD
2Ki 2:23 "Go on up, you *b*!" they said.

BALM
Jer 8:22 Is there no *b* in Gilead?

BANISH (BANISHED)
Jer 25:10 I will *b* from them the sounds of joy

BANISHED (BANISH)
Dt 30: 4 Even if you have been *b*

BANNER
Ex 17:15 and called it The LORD is my *B*.
SS 2: 4 and his *b* over me is love.
Isa 11:10 the Root of Jesse will stand as a *b*

BANQUET
SS 2: 4 He has taken me to the *b* hall,
Lk 14:13 when you give a *b*, invite the poor,

BAPTISM* (BAPTIZE)
Mt 21:25 John's *b*—where did it come from?
Mk 1: 4 and preaching a *b* of repentance
10:38 baptized with the *b* I am baptized
10:39 baptized with the *b* I am baptized
11:30 John's *b*—was it from heaven,
Lk 3: 3 preaching a *b* of repentance
12:50 But I have a *b* to undergo,
20: 4 John's *b*—was it from heaven,
Ac 1:22 beginning from John's *b*
10:37 after the *b* that John preached—
13:24 and *b* to all the people of Israel.
18:25 though he knew only the *b* of John.
19: 3 did you receive?" "John's *b*,"
19: 3 "Then what *b* did you receive?"
19: 4 "John's *b* was a *b* of repentance.
Ro 6: 4 with him through *b* into death
Eph 4: 5 one Lord, one faith, one *b*;
Col 2:12 having been buried with him in *b*
1Pe 3:21 this water symbolizes *b* that now

BAPTISMS* (BAPTIZE)
Heb 6: 2 instruction about *b*, the laying

BAPTIZE* (BAPTISM BAPTISMS BAPTIZED BAPTIZING)
Mt 3:11 He will *b* you with the Holy Spirit
3:11 "I *b* you with water for repentance.
Mk 1: 8 I *b* you with water, but he will
1: 8 he will *b* you with the Holy Spirit."
Lk 3:16 He will *b* you with the Holy Spirit
3:16 John answered them all, "I *b* you
Jn 1:25 "Why then do you *b*
1:26 nor the Prophet?" "I *b* with water,"
1:33 and remain is he who will *b*
1:33 me to *b* with water told me,
1Co 1:14 I am thankful that I did not *b* any
1:17 For Christ did not send me to *b*,

BAPTIZED* (BAPTIZE)
Mt 3: 6 they were *b* by him in the Jordan
3:13 to the Jordan to be *b* by John.
3:14 saying, "I need to be *b* by you,
3:16 as Jesus was *b*, he went up out
Mk 1: 5 they were *b* by him in the Jordan
1: 9 and was *b* by John in the Jordan.
10:38 or be *b* with the baptism I am
10:38 with the baptism I am *b* with?"
10:39 and be *b* with the baptism I am
10:39 with the baptism I am *b* with,
16:16 believes and is *b* will be saved,
Lk 3: 7 to the crowds coming out to be *b*
3:12 Tax collectors also came to be *b*.
3:21 were being *b*, Jesus was *b* too.
7:29 because they had been *b* by John.
7:30 they had not been *b* by John.)
Jn 3:22 spent some time with them, and *b*.
3:23 were constantly coming to be *b*.
4: 2 in fact it was not Jesus who *b*,
Ac 1: 5 For John *b* with water,
1: 5 but in a few days you will be *b*
2:38 Repent and be *b*, every one of you,
2:41 who accepted his message were *b*,
8:12 they were *b*, both men and women.
8:13 Simon himself believed and was *b*.
8:16 they had simply been *b*
8:36 Why shouldn't I be *b*?"
8:38 into the water and Philip *b* him.
9:18 was *b*, and after taking some food,
10:47 people from being *b* with water?
10:48 So he ordered that they be *b*
11:16 what the Lord had said, 'John *b*
11:16 you will be *b* with the Holy Spirit.'
16:15 members of her household were *b*,
16:33 he and all his family were *b*.
Ac 18: 8 heard him believed and were *b*.
19: 5 they were *b* into the name
22:16 be *b* and wash your sins away,
Ro 6: 3 *b* into Christ Jesus were *b*
1Co 1:13 Were you *b* into the name of Paul?
1:15 so no one can say that you were *b*
1:16 I also *b* the household of Stephanas
1:16 I don't remember if I *b* anyone else
10: 2 They were all *b* into Moses
12:13 For we were all *b* by one Spirit
15:29 what will those do who are *b*
15:29 why are people *b* for them?
Gal 3:27 all of you who were *b*

BAPTIZING* (BAPTIZE)
Mt 3: 7 coming to where he was *b*,
28:19 *b* them in the name of the Father
Mk 1: 4 *b* in the desert region
Jn 1:28 of the Jordan, where John was *b*.
1:31 but the reason I came *b*
3:23 also was *b* at Aenon near Salim,
3:26 he is *b*, and everyone is going
4: 1 and *b* more disciples than John,
10:40 to the place where John had been *b*

BAR-JESUS*
Ac 13: 6 and false prophet named *B*,

BARABBAS
Mt 27:26 Then he released *B* to them.

BARAK*
Judge who fought with Deborah against Canaanites (Jdg 4-5; 1Sa 12:11; Heb 11:32).

BARBARIAN*
Col 3:11 circumcised or uncircumcised, *b*,

BARBS*
Nu 33:55 allow to remain will become *b*

BARE
Hos 2: 3 as *b* as on the day she was born;
Heb 4:13 and laid *b* before the eyes of him

BARNABAS*
Disciple, originally Joseph (Ac 4:36), prophet (Ac 13:1), apostle (Ac 14:14). Brought Paul to apostles (Ac 9:27), Antioch (Ac 11:22-29; Gal 2:1-13), on the first missionary journey (Ac 13-14). Together at Jerusalem Council, they separated over John Mark (Ac 15). Later co-workers (1Co 9:6; Col 4:10).

BARREN
Ge 11:30 Sarai was *b*; she had no children.
29:31 her womb, but Rachel was *b*.
Ps 113: 9 He settles the *b* woman
Isa 54: 1 "Sing, O *b* woman,
Lk 1: 7 children, because Elizabeth was *b*;
Gal 4:27 "Be glad, O *b* woman,
Heb 11:11 and Sarah herself was *b*—

BARTHOLOMEW*
Apostle (Mt 10:3; Mk 3:18; Lk 6:14; Ac 1:13). Possibly also known as Nathanael (Jn 1:45-49; 21:2).

BARUCH
Jeremiah's secretary (Jer 32:12-16; 36; 43:1-6; 45:1-2).

BARZILLAI
1. Gileadite who aided David during Absalom's revolt (2Sa 17:27; 19:31-39).
2. Son-in-law of 1. (Ezr 2:61; Ne 7:63).

BASHAN
Jos 22: 7 Moses had given land in *B*,
Ps 22:12 strong bulls of *B* encircle me.

BASIN
Ex 30:18 "Make a bronze *b*,

BASKET
Ex 2: 3 she got a papyrus *b* for him
Ac 9:25 him in a *b* through an opening
2Co 11:33 I was lowered in a *b* from a window

BATCH*
Ro 11:16 then the whole *b* is holy;
1Co 5: 6 through the whole *b* of dough?
5: 7 old yeast that you may be a new *b*
Gal 5: 9 through the whole *b* of dough."

BATH (BATHING)
Jn 13:10 person who has had a *b* needs only

BATHING (BATH)
2Sa 11: 2 From the roof he saw a woman *b*.

BATHSHEBA*
Wife of Uriah who committed adultery with and became wife of David (2Sa 11), mother of Solomon (2Sa 12:24; 1Ki 1-2; 1Ch 3:5).

BATTLE (BATTLES)
1Sa 17:47 for the b is the LORD's,
2Ch 20:15 For the b is not yours, but God's.
Ps 24: 8 the LORD mighty in b.
Ecc 9:11 or the b to the strong,
Isa 31: 4 down to do b on Mount Zion
Eze 13: 5 in the b on the day of the LORD.
Rev 16:14 them for the b on the great day
20: 8 and Magog—to gather them for b.

BATTLES* (BATTLE)
1Sa 8:20 to go out before us and fight our b."
18:17 and fight the b of the LORD."
25:28 because he fights the LORD's b.
2Ch 32: 8 God to help us and to fight our b."

BEAR (BEARING BEARS BIRTH BIRTHRIGHT BORE BORN CHILDBEARING CHILDBIRTH FIRSTBORN NEWBORN REBIRTH)
Ge 4:13 punishment is more than I can b.
Ps 38: 4 like a burden too heavy to b.
Isa 11: 7 The cow will feed with the b,
53:11 and he will b their iniquities.
Da 7: 5 beast, which looked like a b.
Mt 7:18 A good tree cannot b bad fruit,
Jn 15: 2 branch that does b fruit he prunes
15: 8 glory, that you b much fruit,
15:16 appointed you to go and b fruit—
Ro 7: 4 in order that we might b fruit
15: 1 ought to b with the failings
1Co 10:13 tempted beyond what you can b.
Col 3:13 B with each other and forgive

BEARD
Lev 19:27 or clip off the edges of your b.
Isa 50: 6 to those who pulled out my b;

BEARING (BEAR)
Eph 4: 2 b with one another in love.
Col 1:10 b fruit in every good work,
Heb 13:13 outside the camp, b the disgrace he

BEARS (BEAR)
1Ki 8:43 house I have built b your Name.
Ps 68:19 who daily b our burdens.

BEAST (BEASTS)
Rev 13:18 him calculate the number of the b,
16: 2 people who had the mark of the b
19:20 who had received the mark of the b

BEASTS (BEAST)
Da 7: 3 Four great b, each different
1Co 15:32 If I fought wild b in Ephesus

BEAT (BEATEN BEATING BEATINGS)
Isa 2: 4 They will b their swords
Joel 3:10 B your plowshares into swords
Mic 4: 3 They will b their swords
1Co 9:27 I b my body and make it my slave

BEATEN (BEAT)
Lk 12:47 do what his master wants will be b
12:48 deserving punishment will be b
2Co 11:25 Three times I was b with rods,

BEATING (BEAT)
1Co 9:26 I do not fight like a man b the air.
1Pe 2:20 if you receive a b for doing wrong

BEATINGS (BEAT)
Pr 19:29 and b for the backs of fools.

BEAUTIFUL* (BEAUTY)
Ge 6: 2 that the daughters of men were b,
12:11 "I know what a b woman you are.
12:14 saw that she was a very b woman.
24:16 The girl was very b, a virgin;
26: 7 of Rebekah, because she is b."
29:17 Rachel was lovely in form, and b.
49:21 that bears b fawns.
Nu 24: 5 "How b are your tents, O Jacob,
Dt 21:11 among the captives a b woman
Jos 7:21 saw in the plunder a b robe
1Sa 25: 3 was an intelligent and b woman,
2Sa 11: 2 The woman was very b,
13: 1 the b sister of Absalom son
14:27 and she became a b woman.
1Ki 1: 3 throughout Israel for a b girl
1: 4 The girl was very b; she took care
Est 2: 2 for b young virgins for the king.
2: 3 realm to bring all these b girls
Job 38:31 "Can you bind the b Pleiades?
42:15 land were there found women as b
Ps 48: 2 It is b in its loftiness,
Pr 11:22 is a b woman who shows no
24: 4 filled with rare and b treasures.
Ecc 3:11 He has made everything b
SS 1: 8 *Lover* If you do not know, most b
1:10 Your cheeks are b with earrings,
1:15 Oh, how b!
1:15 *Lover* How b you are, my darling!
2:10 my b one, and come with me.
2:13 my b one, come with me."
4: 1 How b you are, my darling!
4: 1 Oh, how b!
4: 7 All b you are, my darling;
5: 9 most b of women?
6: 1 most b of women?
6: 4 *Lover* You are b, my darling,
7: 1 How b your sandaled feet,
7: 6 How b you are and how pleasing,
Isa 4: 2 of the LORD will be b
28: 5 a b wreath
52: 7 How b on the mountains
Jer 3:19 the most b inheritance
6: 2 so b and delicate.
11:16 with fruit b in form.
46:20 "Egypt is a b heifer,
Eze 7:20 They were proud of their b jewelry
16: 7 and became the most b of jewels.
16:12 and a b crown on your head.
16:13 You became very b and rose
20: 6 and honey, the most b of all lands.
20:15 and honey, most b of all lands—
23:42 and b crowns on their heads.
27:24 traded with you b garments,
31: 3 with b branches overshadowing
31: 9 I made it b
33:32 who sings love songs with a b voice
Da 4:12 Its leaves were b, its fruit abundant
4:21 with b leaves and abundant fruit,
8: 9 to the east and toward the B Land.
11:16 will establish himself in the B Land
11:41 He will also invade the B Land.
11:45 the seas at the b holy mountain.
Zec 9:17 How attractive and b they will be!
Mt 23:27 which look b on the outside
26:10 She has done a b thing to me.
Mk 14: 6 She has done a b thing to me.
Lk 21: 5 temple was adorned with b stones
Ac 3: 2 carried to the temple gate called B,
3:10 at the temple gate called B,
Ro 10:15 "How b are the feet
1Pe 3: 5 in God used to make themselves b.

BEAUTY* (BEAUTIFUL)
Est 1:11 order to display her b to the people
2: 3 let b treatments be given to them.
2: 9 her with her b treatments
2:12 months of b treatments prescribed
Ps 27: 4 to gaze upon the b of the LORD
37:20 LORD's enemies will be like the b
45:11 The king is enthralled by your b;
50: 2 From Zion, perfect in b,
Pr 6:25 lust in your heart after her b
31:30 is deceptive, and b is fleeting;
Isa 3:24 instead of b, branding.
28: 1 to the fading flower, his glorious b,
28: 4 That fading flower, his glorious b,
33:17 Your eyes will see the king in his b
53: 2 He had no b or majesty
61: 3 to bestow on them a crown of b
La 2:15 the perfection of b,
Eze 16:14 had given you made your b perfect,
16:14 the nations on account of your b,
16:15 passed by and your b became his.
16:15 " 'But you trusted in your b
16:25 lofty shrines and degraded your b,
27: 3 "I am perfect in b."
27: 4 your builders brought your b
27:11 they brought your b to perfection.
28: 7 draw their swords against your b
28:12 full of wisdom and perfect in b.
28:17 proud on account of your b,
31: 7 It was majestic in b,
31: 8 could match its b.
Jas 1:11 blossom falls and its b is destroyed.
1Pe 3: 3 Your b should not come
3: 4 the unfading b of a gentle

BED (SICKBED)
Isa 28:20 The b is too short to stretch out on,
Lk 11: 7 and my children are with me in b.
17:34 night two people will be in one b;
Heb 13: 4 and the marriage b kept pure,

BEELZEBUB*
Mt 10:25 of the house has been called B,
12:24 "It is only by B, the prince
12:27 And if I drive out demons by B,
Mk 3:22 possessed by B! By the prince
Lk 11:15 "By B, the prince of demons,
11:18 claim that I drive out demons by B.
11:19 Now if I drive out demons by B,

BEER
Pr 20: 1 Wine is a mocker and b a brawler;

BEERSHEBA
Ge 21:14 and wandered in the desert of B.
Jdg 20: 1 all the Israelites from Dan to B
1Sa 3:20 to B recognized that Samuel was
2Sa 3:10 and Judah from Dan to B."
17:11 Let all Israel, from Dan to B—
24: 2 the tribes of Israel from Dan to B
24:15 of the people from Dan to B died.
1Ki 4:25 from Dan to B, lived in safety,
1Ch 21: 2 count the Israelites from B to Dan.
2Ch 30: 5 throughout Israel, from B to Dan,

BEFALLS*
Pr 12:21 No harm b the righteous,

BEGGING
Ps 37:25 or their children b bread.
Ac 16: 9 of Macedonia standing and b him,

BEGINNING
Ge 1: 1 In the b God created the heavens
Ps 102: 25 In the b you laid the foundations
111: 10 of the LORD is the b of wisdom;
Pr 1: 7 of the LORD is the b of knowledge
9:10 of the LORD is the b of wisdom,
Ecc 3:11 fathom what God has done from b
Isa 40:21 Has it not been told you from the b
46:10 I make known the end from the b,
Mt 24: 8 All these are the b of birth pains.
Lk 1: 3 investigated everything from the b,
Jn 1: 1 In the b was the Word,
1Jn 1: 1 That which was from the b,
Rev 21: 6 and the Omega, the B and the End.
22:13 and the Last, the B and the End.

BEHAVE (BEHAVIOR)
Ro 13:13 Let us b decently, as in the daytime

BEHAVIOR (BEHAVE)
1Pe 3: 1 without words by the b of their wives,
3:16 maliciously against your good b

BEHEMOTH*
Job 40:15 "Look at the b,

BELIEVE (BELIEVED BELIEVER BELIEVERS BELIEVES BELIEVING)
Ex 4: 1 "What if they do not b me
1Ki 10: 7 I did not b these things until I came
2Ch 9: 6 But I did not b what they said
Ps 78:32 of his wonders, they did not b.
Hab 1: 5 that you would not b,
Mt 18: 6 one of these little ones who b in me
21:22 If you b, you will receive whatever
27:42 from the cross, and we will b in him
Mk 1:15 Repent and b the good news!"
5:36 ruler, "Don't be afraid; just b."
9:24 "I do b; help me overcome my
9:42 one of these little ones who b in me
11:24 b that you have received it,
15:32 the cross, that we may see and b."
16:16 but whoever does not b will be
16:17 signs will accompany those who b:
Lk 8:12 so that they may not b and be saved.
8:13 They b for a while, but in the time
8:50 just b, and she will be healed."
22:67 you will not b me,
24:25 to b all that the prophets have
Jn 1: 7 that through him all men might b.
3:18 does not b stands condemned
4:42 "We no longer b just
5:38 for you do not b the one he sent.
5:46 believed Moses, you would b me,
6:29 to b in the one he has sent."
6:69 We b and know that you are
7: 5 his own brothers did not b in him.
8:24 if you do not b that I am the one I
9:35 "Do you b in the Son of Man?"
9:36 "Tell me so that I may b in him."
9:38 "Lord, I b," and he worshiped him.
10:26 you do not b because you are not
10:37 Do not b me unless I do what my
10:38 you do not b me, b the miracles,
11:27 "I b that you are the Christ,
12:37 they still would not b in him.
12:39 For this reason they could not b,
12:44 in me, he does not b in me only,
13:19 does happen you will b that I am
14:10 Don't you b that I am in the Father
14:11 B me when I say that I am
14:11 or at least b on the evidence
16:30 This makes us b that you came
16:31 "You b at last!" Jesus answered.
17:21 that the world may b that you have

Jn 19:35 he testifies so that you also may *b*.
20:27 Stop doubting and *b*."
20:31 written that you may *b* that Jesus is
Ac 16:31 They replied, "*B* in the Lord Jesus,
19: 4 the people to *b* in the one coming
24:14 I *b* everything that agrees
26:27 Agrippa, do you *b* the prophets?
Ro 3:22 faith in Jesus Christ to all who *b*.
4:11 he is the father of all who *b*
10: 9 *b* in your heart that God raised him
10:10 For it is with your heart that you *b*
10:14 And how can they *b* in the one
16:26 so that all nations might *b*
1Co 1:21 preached to save those who *b*.
Gal 3:22 might be given to those who *b*.
Php 1:29 of Christ not only to *b* on him,
1Th 4:14 We *b* that Jesus died and rose again
2Th 2:11 delusion so that they will *b* the lie
1Ti 4:10 and especially of those who *b*.
Tit 1: 6 a man whose children *b*
Heb 11: 6 comes to him must *b* that he exists
Jas 1: 6 But when he asks, he must *b*
2:19 Even the demons *b* that—
2:19 You *b* that there is one God.
1Pe 2: 7 to you who *b*, this stone is precious
1Jn 3:23 to *b* in the name of his Son,
4: 1 Dear friends, do not *b* every spirit,
5:13 things to you who *b* in the name

BELIEVED (BELIEVE)

Ge 15: 6 Abram *b* the LORD, and he
Ex 4:31 signs before the people, and they *b*.
Isa 53: 1 Who has *b* our message
Jnh 3: 5 The Ninevites *b* God.
Lk 1:45 is she who has *b* that what the Lord
Jn 1:12 to those who *b* in his name,
2:22 Then they *b* the Scripture
3:18 because he has not *b* in the name
5:46 If you *b* Moses, you would believe
7:39 whom those who *b*
11:40 "Did I not tell you that if you *b*,
12:38 "Lord, who has *b* our message
20: 8 He saw and *b*.
20:29 who have not seen and yet have *b*."
Ac 13:48 were appointed for eternal life *b*.
19: 2 the Holy Spirit when you *b*?"
Ro 4: 3 Scripture say? "Abraham *b* God,
10:14 call on the one they have not *b* in?
10:16 "Lord, who has *b* our message?"
1Co 15: 2 Otherwise, you have *b* in vain.
Gal 3: 6 Consider Abraham: "He *b* God,
2Th 2:12 who have not *b* the truth
1Ti 3:16 was *b* on in the world,
2Ti 1:12 because I know whom I have *b*,
Jas 2:23 that says, "Abraham *b* God,

BELIEVER* (BELIEVE)

1Ki 18: 3 (Obadiah was a devout *b*
Ac 16: 1 whose mother was a Jewess and a *b*
16:15 "If you consider me a *b* in the Lord
1Co 7:12 brother has a wife who is not a *b*
7:13 has a husband who is not a *b*
2Co 6:15 What does a *b* have in common
1Ti 5:16 any woman who is a *b* has widows

BELIEVERS* (BELIEVE)

Jn 4:41 of his words many more became *b*.
Ac 1:15 among the *b* (a group numbering
2:44 All the *b* were together
4:32 All the *b* were one in heart
5:12 And all the *b* used to meet together
9:41 he called the *b* and the widows
10:45 The circumcised *b* who had come
11: 2 the circumcised *b* criticized him
15: 2 along with some other *b*,
15: 5 Then some of the *b* who belonged
15:23 To the Gentile *b* in Antioch,
21:25 for the Gentile *b*, we have written
1Co 6: 5 to judge a dispute between *b*?
14:22 is for *b*, not for unbelievers.
14:22 not for *b* but for unbelievers;
Gal 6:10 who belong to the family of *b*.
1Th 1: 7 a model to all the *b* in Macedonia
1Ti 4:12 set an example for the *b* in speech,
6: 2 benefit from their service are *b*,
Jas 2: 1 *b* in our glorious Lord Jesus Christ,
1Pe 2:17 Love the brotherhood of *b*,

BELIEVES* (BELIEVE)

Pr 14:15 A simple man *b* anything,
Mk 9:23 is possible for him who *b*."
11:23 *b* that what he says will happen,
16:16 Whoever *b* and is baptized will be
Jn 3:15 that everyone who *b*
3:16 that whoever *b* in him shall not
3:18 Whoever *b* in him is not
3:36 Whoever *b* in the Son has eternal
5:24 *b* him who sent me has eternal life
6:35 and he who *b* in me will never be

Jn 6:40 and *b* in him shall have eternal life,
6:47 he who *b* has everlasting life.
7:38 Whoever *b* in me, as the Scripture
11:25 He who *b* in me will live, even
11:26 and *b* in me will never die.
12:44 Jesus cried out, "When a man *b*
12:46 so that no one who *b*
Ac 10:43 about him that everyone who *b*
13:39 him everyone who *b* is justified
Ro 1:16 for the salvation of everyone who *b*
10: 4 righteousness for everyone who *b*.
1Jn 5: 1 Everyone who *b* that Jesus is
5: 5 Only he who *b* that Jesus is the Son
5:10 Anyone who *b* in the Son

BELIEVING* (BELIEVE)

Jn 20:31 and that by *b* you may have life
Ac 9:26 not *b* that he really was a disciple.
1Co 7:14 sanctified through her *b* husband.
7:15 A *b* man or woman is not bound
9: 5 right to take a *b* wife along with us,
Gal 3: 2 or by *b* what you heard? Are you
1Ti 6: 2 Those who have *b* masters are not

BELLY

Ge 3:14 You will crawl on your *b*
Da 2:32 its *b* and thighs of bronze,
Mt 12:40 three nights in the *b* of a huge fish,

BELONG (BELONGING BELONGS)

Ge 40: 8 "Do not interpretations *b* to God?
Lev 25:55 for the Israelites *b* to me
Dt 10:14 LORD your God *b* the heavens,
29:29 The secret things *b*
Job 12:13 "To God *b* wisdom and power;
12:16 To him *b* strength and victory;
25: 2 "Dominion and awe *b* to God;
Ps 47: 9 for the kings of the earth *b* to God;
95: 4 and the mountain peaks *b* to him.
115: 16 The highest heavens *b*
Jer 5:10 for these people do not *b*
Jn 8:44 You *b* to your father, the devil,
15:19 As it is, you do not *b* to the world,
Ro 1: 6 called to *b* to Jesus Christ.
7: 4 that you might *b* to another,
8: 9 of Christ, he does not *b* to Christ.
14: 8 we live or die, we *b* to the Lord.
1Co 7:39 but he must *b* to the Lord.
15:23 when he comes, those who *b*
Gal 3:29 If you *b* to Christ, then you are
5:24 Those who *b* to Christ Jesus have
1Th 5: 5 We do not *b* to the night
5: 8 But since we *b* to the day, let us be
1Jn 3:19 then is how we know that we *b*

BELONGING (BELONG)

1Pe 2: 9 a holy nation, a people *b* to God,

BELONGS (BELONG)

Lev 27:30 *b* to the LORD; it is holy
Dt 1:17 of any man, for judgment *b* to God.
Job 41:11 Everything under heaven *b* to me.
Ps 22:28 for dominion *b* to the LORD
89:18 Indeed, our shield *b* to the LORD,
111: 10 To him *b* eternal praise.
Eze 18: 4 For every living soul *b* to me,
Jn 8:47 He who *b* to God hears what God
Ro 12: 5 each member *b* to all the others.
Rev 7:10 "Salvation *b* to our God,

BELOVED* (LOVE)

Dt 33:12 "Let the *b* of the LORD rest secure
SS 5: 9 How is your *b* better than others,
5: 9 *Friends* How is your *b* better
Jer 11:15 "What is my *b* doing in my temple

BELSHAZZAR

King of Babylon in days of Daniel (Da 5).

BELT

Ex 12:11 with your cloak tucked into your *b*,
1Ki 18:46 and, tucking his cloak into his *b*,
2Ki 4:29 "Tuck your cloak into your *b*,
9: 1 "Tuck your cloak into your *b*,
Isa 11: 5 Righteousness will be his *b*
Eph 6:14 with the *b* of truth buckled

BENEFICIAL* (BENEFIT)

1Co 6:12 for me"—but not everything is *b*.
10:23 but not everything is *b*.

BENEFIT (BENEFICIAL BENEFITS)

Job 22: 2 "Can a man be of *b* to God?
Isa 38:17 Surely it was for my *b*
Ro 6:22 the *b* you reap leads to holiness,
2Co 4:15 All this is for your *b*,

BENEFITS (BENEFIT)

Ps 103: 2 and forget not all his *b*.
Jn 4:38 you have reaped the *b* of their labor

BENJAMIN

Twelfth son of Jacob by Rachel (Ge 35:16-24; 46:19-21; 1Ch 2:2). Jacob refused to send him to Egypt, but relented (Ge 42-45). Tribe of blessed (Ge 49:27; Dt 33:12), numbered (Nu 1:37; 26:41), allotted land (Jos 18:11-28; Eze 48:23), failed to fully possess (Jdg 1:21), nearly obliterated (Jdg 20-21), sided with Ish-Bosheth (2Sa 2), but turned to David (1Ch 12:2, 29). 12,000 from (Rev 7:8).

BEREANS*

Ac 17:11 the *B* were of more noble character

BESTOWING* (BESTOWS)

Pr 8:21 *b* wealth on those who love me

BESTOWS (BESTOWING)

Ps 84:11 the LORD *b* favor and honor;

BETHANY

Mk 11: 1 and *B* at the Mount of Olives,

BETHEL

Ge 28:19 He called that place *B*,

BETHLEHEM

Ru 1:19 went on until they came to *B*.
1Sa 16: 1 I am sending you to Jesse of *B*.
2Sa 23:15 from the well near the gate of *B*!"
Mic 5: 2 "But you, *B* Ephrathah,
Mt 2: 1 After Jesus was born in *B* in Judea,
2: 6 " 'But you, *B*, in the land of Judah,

BETHPHAGE

Mt 21: 1 came to *B* on the Mount of Olives,

BETHSAIDA

Jn 12:21 who was from *B* in Galilee,

BETRAY (BETRAYED BETRAYS)

Ps 89:33 nor will I ever *b* my faithfulness.
Pr 25: 9 do not *b* another man's confidence,
Mt 10:21 "Brother will *b* brother to death,
26:21 the truth, one of you will *b* me."

BETRAYED (BETRAY)

Mt 27: 4 "for I have *b* innocent blood."

BETRAYS (BETRAY)

Pr 11:13 A gossip *b* a confidence,
20:19 A gossip *b* a confidence;

BEULAH*

Isa 62: 4 and your land *B*;

BEWITCHED*

Gal 3: 1 foolish Galatians! Who has *b* you?

BEZALEL

Judahite craftsman in charge of building the tabernacle (Ex 31:1-11; 35:30-39:31).

BIDDING*

Ps 103: 20 you mighty ones who do his *b*,
148: 8 stormy winds that do his *b*,

BILDAD

One of Job's friends (Job 8; 18; 25).

BILHAH

Servant of Rachel, mother of Jacob's sons Dan and Naphtali (Ge 30:1-7; 35:25; 46:23-25).

BIND (BINDS BOUND)

Dt 6: 8 and *b* them on your foreheads.
Pr 3: 3 *b* them around your neck,
6:21 *B* them upon your heart forever;
7: 3 *B* them on your fingers;
Isa 61: 1 me to *b* up the brokenhearted,
Mt 16:19 whatever you *b* on earth will be

BINDS (BIND)

Ps 147: 3 and *b* up their wounds.
Isa 30:26 when the LORD *b* up the bruises

BIRD (BIRDS)

Pr 27: 8 Like a *b* that strays from its nest
Ecc 10:20 a *b* of the air may carry your words,

BIRDS (BIRD)

Mt 8:20 and *b* of the air have nests,
Lk 9:58 and *b* of the air have nests,

BIRTH (BEAR)

Ps 51: 5 Surely I was sinful at *b*,
58: 3 Even from *b* the wicked go astray;
Isa 26:18 but we gave *b* to wind.
Mt 1:18 This is how the *b* of Jesus Christ
24: 8 these are the beginning of *b* pains.
Jn 3: 6 Flesh gives *b* to flesh, but the Spirit
1Pe 1: 3 great mercy he has given us new *b*

BIRTHRIGHT (BEAR)
Ge 25:34 So Esau despised his *b.*

BITTEN
Nu 21: 8 anyone who is *b* can look at it

BITTER (BITTERNESS EMBITTER)
Ex 12: 8 along with *b* herbs, and bread made
Pr 27: 7 what is *b* tastes sweet.

BITTERNESS (BITTER)
Pr 14:10 Each heart knows its own *b,*
17:25 and *b* to the one who bore him.
Ro 3:14 full of cursing and *b."*
Eph 4:31 Get rid of all *b,* rage and anger,

BLACK
Zec 6: 6 The one with the *b* horses is going
Rev 6: 5 and there before me was a *b* horse!

BLAMELESS* (BLAMELESSLY)
Ge 6: 9 *b* among the people of his time,
17: 1 walk before me and be *b.*
Dt 18:13 You must be *b* before the LORD
2Sa 22:24 I have been *b* before him
22:26 to the *b* you show yourself *b,*
Job 1: 1 This man was *b* and upright;
1: 8 one on earth like him; he is *b*
2: 3 one on earth like him; he is *b*
4: 6 and your *b* ways your hope?
8:20 God does not reject a *b* man
9:20 if I were *b,* it would pronounce me
9:21 "Although I am *b,*
9:22 'He destroys both the *b*
12: 4 though righteous and *b!*
22: 3 gain if your ways were *b?*
31: 6 and he will know that I am *b*—
Ps 15: 2 He whose walk is *b*
18:23 I have been *b* before him
18:25 to the *b* you show yourself *b,*
19:13 Then will I be *b,*
26: 1 for I have led a *b* life;
26:11 But I lead a *b* life;
37:18 The days of the *b* are known
37:37 Consider the *b,* observe the upright
84:11 from those whose walk is *b.*
101: 2 I will be careful to lead a *b* life—
101: 2 house with *b* heart.
101: 6 he whose walk is *b*
119: 1 Blessed are they whose ways are *b,*
119: 80 May my heart be *b*
Pr 2: 7 a shield to those whose walk is *b,*
2:21 and the *b* will remain in it;
11: 5 of the *b* makes a straight way
11:20 in those whose ways are *b.*
19: 1 Better a poor man whose walk is *b*
20: 7 The righteous man leads a *b* life;
28: 6 Better a poor man whose walk is *b*
28:10 *b* will receive a good inheritance.
28:18 He whose walk is *b* is kept safe,
Eze 28:15 You were *b* in your ways
1Co 1: 8 so that you will be *b* on the day
Eph 1: 4 world to be holy and *b* in his sight.
5:27 any other blemish, but holy and *b.*
Php 1:10 and *b* until the day of Christ,
2:15 so that you may become *b* and pure
1Th 2:10 and *b* we were among you who
3:13 hearts so that you will be *b*
5:23 and body be kept *b* at the coming
Tit 1: 6 An elder must be *b,* the husband of
1: 7 he must be *b*— not overbearing,
Heb 7:26 *b,* pure, set apart from sinners,
2Pe 3:14 effort to be found spotless, *b*
Rev 14: 5 found in their mouths; they are *b.*

BLAMELESSLY* (BLAMELESS)
Lk 1: 6 commandments and regulations *b.*

BLASPHEME* (BLASPHEMED BLASPHEMER BLASPHEMES BLASPHEMIES BLASPHEMING BLASPHEMOUS BLASPHEMY)
Ex 22:28 "Do not *b* God or curse the ruler
Ac 26:11 and I tried to force them to *b.*
1Ti 1:20 over to Satan to be taught not to *b.*
2Pe 2:12 these men *b* in matters they do not
Rev 13: 6 He opened his mouth to *b* God,

BLASPHEMED* (BLASPHEME)
Lev 24:11 of the Israelite woman *b* the Name
2Ki 19: 6 of the king of Assyria have *b* me.
19:22 Who is it you have insulted and *b?*
Isa 37: 6 of the king of Assyria have *b* me.
37:23 Who is it you have insulted and *b?*
52: 5 my name is constantly *b.*
Eze 20:27 your fathers *b* me by forsaking me:
Ac 19:37 robbed temples nor *b* our goddess.
Ro 2:24 name is *b* among the Gentiles

BLASPHEMER* (BLASPHEME)
Lev 24:14 "Take the *b* outside the camp.
24:23 they took the *b* outside the camp
1Ti 1:13 I was once a *b* and a persecutor

BLASPHEMES* (BLASPHEME)
Lev 24:16 anyone who *b* the name
24:16 native-born, when he *b* the Name,
Nu 15:30 native-born or alien, *b* the LORD,
Mk 3:29 whoever *b* against the Holy Spirit
Lk 12:10 but anyone who *b* against the Holy

BLASPHEMIES* (BLASPHEME)
Ne 9:18 or when they committed awful *b.*
9:26 to you; they committed awful *b.*
Mk 3:28 and *b* of men will be forgiven them.
Rev 13: 5 and *b* and to exercise his authority

BLASPHEMING* (BLASPHEME)
Mt 9: 3 "This fellow is *b!"* Knowing their
Mk 2: 7 He's *b!* Who can forgive sins

BLASPHEMOUS* (BLASPHEME)
Rev 13: 1 and on each head a *b* name.
17: 3 that was covered with *b* names

BLASPHEMY* (BLASPHEME)
Mt 12:31 and *b* will be forgiven men,
12:31 the *b* against the Spirit will not be
26:65 Look, now you have heard the *b.*
26:65 "He has spoken *b!* Why do we
Mk 14:64 "You have heard the *b.*
Lk 5:21 "Who is this fellow who speaks *b?*
Jn 10:33 replied the Jews, "but for *b,*
10:36 Why then do you accuse me of *b*
Ac 6:11 words of *b* against Moses

BLAST*
Ex 15: 8 By the *b* of your nostrils
19:13 horn sounds a long *b* may they go
19:16 and a very loud trumpet *b.*
Nu 10: 5 When a trumpet *b* is sounded,
10: 6 At the sounding of a second *b,*
10: 6 The *b* will be the signal
10: 9 sound a *b* on the trumpets.
Jos 6: 5 you hear them sound a long *b*
6:16 the priests sounded the trumpet *b,*
2Sa 22:16 at the *b* of breath from his nostrils.
Job 4: 9 at the *b* of his anger they perish.
39:25 At the *b* of the trumpet he snorts,
Ps 18:15 the *b* of breath from your nostrils.
98: 6 and the *b* of the ram's horn—
147: 17 Who can withstand his icy *b?*
Isa 27: 8 with his fierce *b* he drives her out,
Eze 22:20 a furnace to melt it with a fiery *b,*
Am 2: 2 tumult amid war cries and the *b*
Heb 12:19 to a trumpet *b* or to such a voice

BLEATING*
1Sa 15:14 "What then is this *b* of sheep

BLEMISH (BLEMISHES)
Lev 22:21 be without defect or *b*
Eph 5:27 or wrinkle or any other *b,*
Col 1:22 without *b* and free from accusation
1Pe 1:19 a lamb without *b* or defect.

BLEMISHES* (BLEMISH)
2Pe 2:13 and *b,* reveling in their pleasures
Jude :12 These men are *b* at your love feasts

BLESS (BLESSED BLESSES BLESSING BLESSINGS)
Ge 12: 3 I will *b* those who *b* you,
32:26 not let you go unless you *b* me."
Dt 7:13 He will love you and *b* you
33:11 *B* all his skills, O LORD,
Ps 72:15 and *b* him all day long.
Ro 12:14 Bless those who persecute you; *b*

BLESSED (BLESS)
Ge 1:22 God *b* them and said, "Be fruitful
2: 3 And God *b* the seventh day
22:18 nations on earth will be *b,*
Nu 24: 9 "May those who bless you be *b*
1Ch 17:27 have *b* it, and it will be *b* forever."
Ps 1: 1 *B* is the man
2:12 *B* are all who take refuge in him.
32: 2 *B* is the man
33:12 *B* is the nation whose God is
40: 4 *B* is the man
41: 1 *B* is he who has regard for the weak
84: 5 *B* are those whose strength is
89:15 *B* are those who have learned
94:12 *B* is the man you discipline,
106: 3 *B* are they who maintain justice,
112: 1 *B* is the man who fears the LORD,
118: 26 *B* is he who comes in the name
119: 1 *B* are they whose ways are
119: 2 *B* are they who keep his statutes
Ps 127: 5 *B* is the man
Pr 3:13 *B* is the man who finds wisdom,
8:34 *B* is the man who listens to me,
28:20 A faithful man will be richly *b,*
29:18 but *b* is he who keeps the law.
31:28 Her children arise and call her *b;*
Isa 30:18 *B* are all who wait for him!
Mal 3:12 Then all the nations will call you *b,*
3:15 But now we call the arrogant *b.*
Mt 5: 3 saying: "*B* are the poor in spirit,
5: 4 *B* are those who mourn,
5: 5 *B* are the meek,
5: 6 *B* are those who hunger
5: 7 *B* are the merciful,
5: 8 *B* are the pure in heart,
5: 9 *B* are the peacemakers,
5:10 *B* are those who are persecuted
5:11 "*B* are you when people insult you,
Lk 1:48 on all generations will call me *b,*
Jn 12:13 "*B* is he who comes in the name
Ac 20:35 'It is more *b* to give than to receive
Tit 2:13 while we wait for the *b* hope—
Jas 1:12 *B* is the man who perseveres
Rev 1: 3 *B* is the one who reads the words
22: 7 *B* is he who keeps the words
22:14 "*B* are those who wash their robes,

BLESSES (BLESS)
Ps 29:11 the LORD *b* his people with peace.
Ro 10:12 and richly *b* all who call on him,

BLESSING (BLESS)
Ge 27: 4 so that I may give you my *b*
Dt 23: 5 turned the curse into a *b* for you,
33: 1 This is the *b* that Moses the man
Pr 10:22 The *b* of the LORD brings wealth,
Eze 34:26 there will be showers of *b.*

BLESSINGS (BLESS)
Dt 11:29 proclaim on Mount Gerizim the *b,*
Jos 8:34 all the words of the law—the *b*
Pr 10: 6 *B* crown the head of the righteous,
Ro 15:27 shared in the Jews' spiritual *b,*

BLIND (BLINDED)
Mt 15:14 a *b* man leads a *b* man, both will fall
23:16 "Woe to you, *b* guides! You say,
Mk 10:46 a *b* man, Bartimaeus (that is,
Lk 6:39 "Can a *b* man lead a *b* man?
Jn 9:25 I was *b* but now I see!"

BLINDED (BLIND)
Jn 12:40 elsewhere: "He has *b* their eyes
2Co 4: 4 The god of this age has *b* the minds

BLOOD (BLOODSHED BLOODTHIRSTY)
Ge 4:10 Your brother's *b* cries out to me
9: 6 "Whoever sheds the *b* of man,
Ex 12:13 and when I see the *b,* I will pass
24: 8 "This is the *b* of the covenant that
Lev 16:15 and take its *b* behind the curtain
17:11 For the life of a creature is in the *b,*
Dt 12:23 eat the *b,* because the *b* is the life,
Ps 72:14 for precious is their *b* in his sight.
Pr 6:17 hands that shed innocent *b,*
Isa 1:11 pleasure in the *b* of bulls and lambs
Mt 26:28 This is my *b* of the covenant,
27:24 "I am innocent of this man's *b,"*
Mk 14:24 "This is my *b* of the covenant,
Lk 22:44 drops of *b* falling to the ground.
Jn 6:53 of the Son of Man and drink his *b,*
Ac 15:20 of strangled animals and from *b.*
20:26 innocent of the *b* of all men.
Ro 3:25 of atonement, through faith in his *b*
5: 9 have now been justified by his *b,*
1Co 11:25 cup is the new covenant in my *b;*
Eph 1: 7 we have redemption through his *b,*
2:13 near through the *b* of Christ.
Col 1:20 by making peace through his *b,*
Heb 9: 7 once a year, and never without *b,*
9:12 once for all by his own *b,*
9:20 "This is the *b* of the covenant,
9:22 of *b* there is no forgiveness.
12:24 word than the *b* of Abel.
1Pe 1:19 but with the precious *b* of Christ,
1Jn 1: 7 and the *b* of Jesus, his Son,
Rev 1: 5 has freed us from our sins by his *b,*
5: 9 with your *b* you purchased men
7:14 white in the *b* of the Lamb.
12:11 him by the *b* of the Lamb
19:13 He is dressed in a robe dipped in *b,*

BLOODSHED (BLOOD)
Jer 48:10 on him who keeps his sword from *b*
Eze 35: 6 did not hate *b, b* will pursue you.
Hab 2:12 to him who builds a city with *b*

BLOODTHIRSTY* (BLOOD)
Ps 5: 6 *b* and deceitful men
26: 9 my life with *b* men,

Ps 55:23 *b* and deceitful men
59: 2 and save me from *b* men.
139: 19 Away from me, you *b* men!
Pr 29:10 *B* men hate a man of integrity

BLOSSOM
Isa 35: 1 the wilderness will rejoice and *b*.

BLOT (BLOTS)
Ex 32:32 then *b* me out of the book you have
Ps 51: 1 *b* out my transgressions.
Rev 3: 5 I will never *b* out his name

BLOTS (BLOT)
Isa 43:25 "I, even I, am he who *b* out

BLOWN
Eph 4:14 and *b* here and there by every wind
Jas 1: 6 doubts is like a wave of the sea, *b*
Jude :12 without rain, *b* along by the wind;

BLUSH
Jer 6:15 they do not even know how to *b*.

BOAST (BOASTS)
1Ki 20:11 armor should not *b* like one who
Ps 34: 2 My soul will *b* in the LORD;
44: 8 In God we make our *b* all day long,
Pr 27: 1 Do not *b* about tomorrow,
Jer 9:23 or the rich man *b* of his riches,
1Co 1:31 Let him who boasts *b* in the Lord."
2Co 10:17 Let him who boasts *b* in the Lord."
11:30 I do not inwardly burn? If I must *b*,
Gal 6:14 May I never *b* except in the cross
Eph 2: 9 not by works, so that no one can *b*.

BOASTS (BOAST)
Jer 9:24 but let him who *b* boast about this:

BOAZ
Wealthy Bethlehemite who showed favor to Ruth (Ru 2), married her (Ru 4). Ancestor of David (Ru 4:18-22; 1Ch 2:12-15), Jesus (Mt 1:5-16; Lk 3:23-32).

BODIES (BODY)
Isa 26:19 their *b* will rise.
Ro 12: 1 to offer your *b* as living sacrifices,
1Co 6:15 not know that your *b* are members
Eph 5:28 to love their wives as their own *b*.

BODILY (BODY)
Col 2: 9 of the Deity lives in *b* form,

BODY (BODIES BODILY EMBODIMENT)
Zec 13: 6 What are these wounds on your *b*?'
Mt 10:28 afraid of those who kill the *b*
26:26 saying, "Take and eat; this is my *b*
26:41 spirit is willing, but the *b* is weak."
Mk 14:22 saying, "Take it; this is my *b*."
Lk 22:19 saying, "This is my *b* given for you;
Jn 13:10 wash his feet; his whole *b* is clean.
Ro 6:13 Do not offer the parts of your *b*
12: 4 us has one *b* with many members,
1Co 6:19 not know that your *b* is a temple
6:20 Therefore honor God with your *b*.
11:24 "This is my *b*, which is for you;
12:12 The *b* is a unit, though it is made up
12:13 baptized by one Spirit into one *b*—
15:44 a natural *b*, it is raised a spiritual *b*.
Eph 1:23 which is his *b*, the fullness
4:25 for we are all members of one *b*.
5:30 for we are members of his *b*.
Php 1:20 Christ will be exalted in my *b*,
Col 1:24 sake of his *b*, which is the church.

BOLD (BOLDNESS)
Ps 138: 3 you made me *b* and stouthearted.
Pr 21:29 A wicked man puts up a *b* front,
28: 1 but the righteous are as *b* as a lion.

BOLDNESS* (BOLD)
Lk 11: 8 of the man's *b* he will get up
Ac 4:29 to speak your word with great *b*.

BONDAGE
Ezr 9: 9 God has not deserted us in our *b*.

BONES
Ge 2:23 "This is now bone of my *b*
Ps 22:14 and all my *b* are out of joint.
22:17 I can count all my *b*;
Eze 37: 1 middle of a valley; it was full of *b*.
Jn 19:36 "Not one of his *b* will be broken,"

BOOK (BOOKS)
Ex 32:33 against me I will blot out of my *b*.
Jos 1: 8 Do not let this *B* of the Law depart
2Ki 22: 8 "I have found the *B* of the Law
2Ch 34:15 "I have found the *B* of the Law
Ne 8: 8 They read from the *B* of the Law
Ps 69:28 May they be blotted out of the *b*
Da 12: 1 name is found written in the *b*—
Jn 20:30 which are not recorded in this *b*.
Php 4: 3 whose names are in the *b* of life.
Rev 3: 5 never blot out his name from the *b*
20:12 *b* was opened, which is the *b*
20:15 was not found written in the *b*
21:27 written in the Lamb's *b* of life.
22:18 him the plagues described in this *b*.

BOOKS* (BOOK)
Ecc 12:12 Of making many *b* there is no end,
Da 7:10 and the *b* were opened.
Jn 21:25 for the *b* that would be written.
Rev 20:12 the throne, and *b* were opened.
20:12 they had done as recorded in the *b*.

BORE (BEAR)
Isa 53:12 For he *b* the sin of many,
1Pe 2:24 He himself *b* our sins in his body

BORN (BEAR)
Ecc 3: 2 a time to be *b* and a time to die,
Isa 9: 6 For to us a child is *b*,
66: 8 Can a country be *b* in a day
Lk 2:11 of David a Savior has been *b* to you
Jn 3: 3 see the kingdom of God unless he is *b* again.
3: 4 How can a man be *b* when he is old
3: 5 unless he is *b* of water
3: 7 at my saying, 'You must be *b* again
3: 8 it is with everyone *b* of the Spirit."
1Pe 1:23 For you have been *b* again,
1Jn 3: 9 because he has been *b* of God.
4: 7 Everyone who loves has been *b*
5: 1 believes that Jesus is the Christ is *b*
5: 4 for everyone *b* of God overcomes
5:18 We know that anyone *b*

BORROWER
Pr 22: 7 and the *b* is servant to the lender.

BOTHER (BOTHERING)
Lk 11: 7 one inside answers, 'Don't *b* me.

BOTHERING (BOTHER)
Lk 18: 5 yet because this widow keeps *b* me,

BOUGHT (BUY)
Ac 20:28 which he *b* with his own blood.
1Co 6:20 You are not your own; you were *b*
7:23 You were *b* at a price; do not
2Pe 2: 1 the sovereign Lord who *b* them—

BOUND (BIND)
Is 56: 3 Let no foreigner who has *b* himself
Mt 16:19 bind on earth will be *b* in heaven,
18:18 bind on earth will be *b* in heaven,
Ro 7: 2 by law a married woman is *b*
1Co 7:39 A woman is *b* to her husband
Jude : 6 *b* with everlasting chains
Rev 20: 2 and *b* him for a thousand years.

BOUNDARY (BOUNDS)
Nu 34: 3 your southern *b* will start
Pr 23:10 Do not move an ancient *b* stone
Hos 5:10 who move *b* stones.

BOUNDS (BOUNDARY)
2Co 7: 4 all our troubles my joy knows no *b*.

BOUNTY*
Ge 49:26 than the *b* of the age-old hills.
Dt 28:12 heavens, the storehouse of his *b*,
1Ki 10:13 he had given her out of his royal *b*.
Ps 65:11 You crown the year with your *b*,
68:10 from your *b*, O God, you provided
Jer 31:12 rejoice in the *b* of the LORD—
31:14 my people will be filled with my *b*

BOW (BOWED BOWS)
Dt 5: 9 You shall not *b* down to them
1Ki 22:34 But someone drew his *b* at random
Ps 5: 7 in reverence will I *b* down
44: 6 I do not trust in my *b*,
95: 6 Come, let us *b* down in worship,
138: 2 I will *b* down toward your holy
Isa 44:19 Shall I *b* down to a block of wood?"
45:23 Before me every knee will *b*;
Ro 14:11 'every knee will *b* before me;
Php 2:10 name of Jesus every knee should *b*,

BOWED (BOW)
Ps 145: 14 and lifts up all who are *b* down.
146: 8 the LORD lifts up those who are *b*

BOWS (BOW)
Isa 44:15 he makes an idol and *b* down to it.
44:17 he *b* down to it and worships.

BOY (BOY'S BOYS)
Ge 21:17 God heard the *b* crying,
22:12 not lay a hand on the *b*
Jdg 13: 5 *b* is to be a Nazirite,
1Sa 2:11 *b* ministered before the LORD.
3: 8 the LORD was calling the *b*.
Isa 7:16 before the *b* knows enough
Mt 17:18 demon, and it came out of the *b*
Lk 2:43 the *b* Jesus stayed behind

BOY'S (BOY)
1Ki 17:22 the *b* life returned to him
2Ki 4:34 the *b* body grew warm

BOYS (BOY)
Ge 25:24 twin *b* in her womb
Ex 1:18 they let the *b* live.

BRACE*
Job 38: 3 *B* yourself like a man;
40: 7 out of the storm: "*B* yourself like
Na 2: 1 *b* yourselves,

BRAG*
Am 4: 5 and *b* about your freewill offerings
Ro 2:17 *b* about your relationship to God;
2:23 temples? You who *b* about the law,
Jas 4:16 As it is, you boast and *b*.

BRAIDED
1Ti 2: 9 not with *b* hair or gold or pearls
1Pe 3: 3 as *b* hair and the wearing

BRANCH (BRANCHES)
Isa 4: 2 In that day the *B* of the LORD will
Jer 23: 5 up to David a righteous *B*,
33:15 I will make a righteous *B* sprout
Zec 3: 8 going to bring my servant, the *B*.
6:12 is the man whose name is the *B*,
Jn 15: 2 while every *b* that does bear fruit
15: 4 No *b* can bear fruit by itself;

BRANCHES (BRANCH)
Jn 15: 5 "I am the vine; you are the *b*.
Ro 11:21 if God did not spare the natural *b*,

BRAVE
2Sa 2: 7 Now then, be strong and *b*,
13:28 you this order? Be strong and *b*."

BREACH (BREAK)
Ps 106: 23 stood in the *b* before him

BREACHING (BREAK)
Pr 17:14 Starting a quarrel is like *b* a dam;

BREAD
Ex 12: 8 and *b* made without yeast.
23:15 the Feast of Unleavened *B*;
25:30 Put the *b* of the Presence
Dt 8: 3 that man does not live on *b* alone
Ps 78:25 Men ate the *b* of angels;
Pr 30: 8 but give me only my daily *b*.
Ecc 11: 1 Cast your *b* upon the waters,
Isa 55: 2 Why spend money on what is not *b*
Mt 4: 3 tell these stones to become *b*."
4: 4 'Man does not live on *b* alone,
6:11 Give us today our daily *b*.
26:26 Jesus took *b*, gave thanks
Mk 14:22 Jesus took *b*, gave thanks
Lk 4: 3 tell this stone to become *b*."
4: 4 'Man does not live on *b* alone.'"
9:13 "We have only five loaves of *b*
11: 3 Give us each day our daily *b*.
22:19 And he took *b*, gave thanks
Jn 6:33 For the *b* of God is he who comes
6:35 Jesus declared, "I am the *b* of life.
6:41 "I am the *b* that came
6:48 I am the *b* of life.
6:51 I am the living *b* that came
6:51 This *b* is my flesh, which I will give
21:13 took the *b* and gave it to them,
1Co 10:16 And is not the *b* that we break
11:23 took *b*, and when he had given
11:26 For whenever you eat this *b*

BREAK (BREACH BREACHING BREAKERS BREAKING BREAKS BROKE BROKEN BROKENNESS)
Nu 30: 2 he must not *b* his word
Jdg 2: 1 'I will never *b* my covenant
Pr 25:15 and a gentle tongue can *b* a bone.
Isa 42: 3 A bruised reed he will not *b*,
Mal 2:15 and do not *b* faith with the wife
Mt 12:20 A bruised reed he will not *b*,
Ac 20: 7 week we came together to *b* bread.
1Co 10:16 the bread that we *b* a participation
Rev 5: 2 "Who is worthy to *b* the seals

BREAKERS* (BREAK)
Ps 42: 7 all your waves and *b*
93: 4 mightier than the *b* of the sea—
Jnh 2: 3 all your waves and *b*

BREAKING (BREAK)
Jos 9:20 fall on us for *b* the oath we swore
Eze 16:59 oath by *b* the covenant.
17:18 the oath by *b* the covenant.
Ac 2:42 to the *b* of bread and to prayer.
Jas 2:10 at just one point is guilty of *b* all

BREAKS (BREAK)
Jer 23:29 "and like a hammer that *b* a rock
1Jn 3: 4 Everyone who sins *b* the law;

BREASTPIECE (BREASTPLATE)
Ex 28:15 Fashion a *b* for making decisions—

BREASTPLATE* (BREASTPIECE)
Isa 59:17 He put on righteousness as his *b*,
Eph 6:14 with the *b* of righteousness in place
1Th 5: 8 putting on faith and love as a *b*,

BREASTS
La 4: 3 Even jackals offer their *b*

BREATH (BREATHED GOD-BREATHED)
Ge 2: 7 into his nostrils the *b* of life,

BREATHED (BREATH)
Ge 2: 7 *b* into his nostrils the breath of life,
Mk 15:37 With a loud cry, Jesus *b* his last.
Jn 20:22 And with that he *b* on them

BREEDS*
Pr 13:10 Pride only *b* quarrels,

BRIBE
Ex 23: 8 "Do not accept a *b*,
Dt 16:19 for a *b* blinds the eyes of the wise
27:25 "Cursed is the man who accepts a *b*
Pr 6:35 will refuse the *b*, however great it

BRIDE
Isa 62: 5 as a bridegroom rejoices over his *b*,
Rev 19: 7 and his *b* has made herself ready.
21: 2 as a *b* beautifully dressed
21: 9 I will show you the *b*, the wife
22:17 The Spirit and the *b* say, "Come!"

BRIDEGROOM
Ps 19: 5 which is like a *b* coming forth
Mt 25: 1 and went out to meet the *b*.
25: 5 The *b* was a long time in coming,

BRIGHTENS* (BRIGHTNESS)
Pr 16:15 When a king's face *b*, it means life;
Ecc 8: 1 Wisdom *b* a man's face

BRIGHTER (BRIGHTNESS)
Pr 4:18 shining ever *b* till the full light

BRIGHTNESS* (BRIGHTENS BRIGHTER)
2Sa 22:13 Out of the *b* of his presence
23: 4 like the *b* after rain
Ps 18:12 of the *b* of his presence clouds
Isa 59: 9 for *b*, but we walk in deep shadows.
60: 3 and kings to the *b* of your dawn.
60:19 will the *b* of the moon shine on you
Da 12: 3 who are wise will shine like the *b*
Am 5:20 pitch-dark, without a ray of *b?*

BRILLIANCE* (BRILLIANT)
Ac 22:11 the *b* of the light had blinded me.
Rev 1:16 was like the sun shining in all its *b*.
21:11 its *b* was like that of a very precious

BRILLIANT* (BRILLIANCE)
Ecc 9:11 or wealth to the *b*
Eze 1: 4 and surrounded by *b* light.
1:27 and *b* light surrounded him.

BRINK*
Pr 5:14 I have come to the *b* of utter ruin

BRITTLE
Da 2:42 will be partly strong and partly *b*.

BROAD
Mt 7:13 and *b* is the road that leads

BROKE (BREAK)
Mt 26:26 took bread, gave thanks and *b* it,
Mk 14:22 took bread, gave thanks and *b* it,
Ac 2:46 They *b* bread in their homes
20:11 he went upstairs again and *b* bread
1Co 11:24 when he had given thanks, he *b* it

BROKEN (BREAK)
Ps 34:20 not one of them will be *b*.
51:17 The sacrifices of God are a *b* spirit;
Ecc 4:12 of three strands is not quickly *b*.
Lk 20:18 on that stone will be *b* to pieces,
Jn 7:23 the law of Moses may not be *b*,
10:35 and the Scripture cannot be *b*—
19:36 "Not one of his bones will be *b*,"
Ro 11:20 they were *b* off because of unbelief,

BROKENHEARTED* (HEART)
Ps 34:18 The LORD is close to the *b*
109: 16 and the needy and the *b*.
147: 3 He heals the *b*
Isa 61: 1 He has sent me to bind up the *b*,

BROKENNESS* (BREAK)
Isa 65:14 and wail in *b* of spirit.

BRONZE
Ex 27: 2 and overlay the altar with *b*.
30:18 "Make a *b* basin, with its *b* stand,
Nu 21: 9 So Moses made a *b* snake
Da 2:32 and thighs of *b*, its legs of iron,
10: 6 legs like the gleam of burnished *b*,
Rev 1:15 His feet were like *b* glowing
2:18 whose feet are like burnished *b*.

BROTHER (BROTHER'S BROTHERHOOD BROTHERLY BROTHERS)
Pr 17:17 and a *b* is born for adversity.
18:24 a friend who sticks closer than a *b*.
27:10 neighbor nearby than a *b* far away.
Mt 5:24 and be reconciled to your *b*;
18:15 "If your *b* sins against you,
Mk 3:35 Whoever does God's will is my *b*
Lk 17: 3 "If your *b* sins, rebuke him,
Ro 14:15 not by your eating destroy your *b*
14:21 anything else that will cause your *b*
1Co 8:13 if what I eat causes my *b* to fall
2Th 3: 6 away from every *b* who is idle
3:15 as an enemy, but warn him as a *b*.
Phm :16 but better than a slave, as a dear *b*.
Jas 2:15 Suppose a *b* or sister is
4:11 Anyone who speaks against his *b*
1Jn 2: 9 hates his *b* is still in the darkness.
2:10 Whoever loves his *b* lives
2:11 But whoever hates his *b* is
3:10 is anyone who does not love his *b*.
3:15 who hates his *b* is a murderer,
3:17 material possessions and sees his *b*
4:20 For anyone who does not love his *b*
4:20 yet hates his *b*, he is a liar.
4:21 loves God must also love his *b*.
5:16 If anyone sees his *b* commit a sin

BROTHER'S (BROTHER)
Ge 4: 9 "Am I my *b* keeper?" The LORD
Mt 7: 5 remove the speck from your *b* eye.
Ro 14:13 or obstacle in your *b* way.

BROTHERHOOD (BROTHER)
1Pe 2:17 Love the *b* of believers, fear God,

BROTHERLY* (BROTHER)
Ro 12:10 devoted to one another in *b* love.
1Th 4: 9 Now about *b* love we do not need
2Pe 1: 7 and to godliness, *b* kindness;
1: 7 kindness; and to *b* kindness,

BROTHERS (BROTHER)
Jos 1:14 You are to help your *b*
Ps 133: 1 is when *b* live together in unity!
Pr 6:19 who stirs up dissension among *b*.
Mt 12:49 "Here are my mother and my *b*.
19:29 everyone who has left houses or *b*
25:40 one of the least of these *b* of mine,
Mk 3:33 "Who are my mother and my *b?*"
10:29 or *b* or sisters or mother or father
Lk 21:16 will be betrayed even by parents, *b*,
22:32 turned back, strengthen your *b*."
Jn 7: 5 his own *b* did not believe in him.
Ac 15:32 to encourage and strengthen the *b*.
Ro 9: 3 off from Christ for the sake of my *b*
1Co 8:12 sin against your *b* in this way
2Co 11:26 and in danger from false *b*.
Gal 2: 4 some false *b* had infiltrated our
1Th 4:10 you do love all the *b*
5:26 Greet all the *b* with a holy kiss.
1Ti 6: 2 for them because they are *b*.
Heb 2:11 Jesus is not ashamed to call them *b*.
2:17 to be made like his *b* in every way,
13: 1 Keep on loving each other as *b*.
1Pe 1:22 you have sincere love for your *b*,
3: 8 be sympathetic, love as *b*,
1Jn 3:14 death to life, because we love our *b*.
3:16 to lay down our lives for our *b*.
3Jn :10 he refuses to welcome the *b*.
Rev 12:10 For the accuser of our *b*,

BROW
Ge 3:19 By the sweat of your *b*

BRUISED (BRUISES)
Isa 42: 3 A *b* reed he will not break,
Mt 12:20 A *b* reed he will not break,

BRUISES (BRUISED)
Isa 30:26 when the LORD binds up the *b*

BRUTAL (BRUTE)
2Ti 3: 3 slanderous, without self-control, *b*,

BRUTE* (BRUTAL)
Ps 73:22 I was a *b* beast before you.
2Pe 2:12 They are like *b* beasts, creatures

BUBBLING*
Pr 18: 4 the fountain of wisdom is a *b* brook
Isa 35: 7 the thirsty ground *b* springs.

BUCKET*
Isa 40:15 the nations are like a drop in a *b*;

BUCKLED* (BUCKLER)
Eph 6:14 belt of truth *b* around your waist,

BUCKLER* (BUCKLED)
Ps 35: 2 Take up shield and *b*;

BUD (BUDDED)
Isa 27: 6 Israel will *b* and blossom

BUDDED (BUD)
Heb 9: 4 Aaron's staff that had *b*,

BUILD (BUILDER BUILDERS BUILDING BUILDS BUILT REBUILD REBUILT)
2Sa 7: 5 Are you the one to *b* me a house
1Ki 6: 1 he began to *b* the temple
Ecc 3: 3 a time to tear down and a time to *b*,
Mt 16:18 and on this rock I will *b* my church,
Ac 20:32 which can *b* you up and give you
Ro 15: 2 neighbor for his good, to *b* him up.
1Co 14:12 excel in gifts that *b* up the church.
1Th 5:11 one another and *b* each other up,
Jude :20 *b* yourselves up in your most holy

BUILDER* (BUILD)
1Co 3:10 I laid a foundation as an expert *b*,
Heb 3: 3 the *b* of a house has greater honor
3: 4 but God is the *b* of everything.
11:10 whose architect and *b* is God.

BUILDERS (BUILD)
Ps 118: 22 The stone the *b* rejected
Mt 21:42 " 'The stone the *b* rejected
Mk 12:10 " 'The stone the *b* rejected
Lk 20:17 " 'The stone the *b* rejected
Ac 4:11 " 'the stone you *b* rejected,
1Pe 2: 7 "The stone the *b* rejected

BUILDING (BUILD)
Ezr 3: 8 to supervise the *b* of the house
Ne 4:17 of Judah who were *b* the wall.
Ro 15:20 so that I would not be *b*
1Co 3: 9 you are God's field, God's *b*.
2Co 5: 1 we have a *b* from God, an eternal
10: 8 us for *b* you up rather
13:10 the Lord gave me for *b* you up,
Eph 2:21 him the whole *b* is joined together
4:29 helpful for *b* others up according

BUILDS (BUILD)
Ps 127: 1 Unless the LORD *b* the house,
Pr 14: 1 The wise woman *b* her house,
1Co 3:10 one should be careful how he *b*.
3:12 If any man *b* on this foundation
8: 1 Knowledge puffs up, but love *b* up.
Eph 4:16 grows and *b* itself up in love,

BUILT (BUILD)
1Ki 6:14 So Solomon *b* the temple
Mt 7:24 is like a wise man who *b* his house
Lk 6:49 is like a man who *b* a house
Ac 17:24 does not live in temples *b* by hands.
1Co 3:14 If what he has *b* survives, he will
2Co 5: 1 in heaven, not *b* by human hands.
Eph 2:20 *b* on the foundation of the apostles
4:12 the body of Christ may be *b* up
Col 2: 7 live in him, rooted and *b* up in him,
1Pe 2: 5 are being *b* into a spiritual house

BULL (BULLS)
Lev 4: 3 bring to the LORD a young *b*

BULLS (BULL)
1Ki 7:25 The Sea stood on twelve *b*,
Heb 10: 4 it is impossible for the blood of *b*

BURDEN (BURDENED BURDENS BURDENSOME)
Ps 38: 4 like a *b* too heavy to bear.
Ecc 1:13 What a heavy *b* God has laid

Mt 11:30 my yoke is easy and my *b* is light."
Ac 15:28 to us not to *b* you with anything
2Co 11: 9 from being a *b* to you in any way,
12:14 and I will not be a *b* to you,
1Th 2: 9 day in order not to be a *b* to anyone
2Th 3: 8 so that we would not be a *b* to any
Heb 13:17 not a *b*, for that would be

BURDENED* (BURDEN)
Isa 43:23 have not *b* you with grain offerings
43:24 But you have *b* me with your sins
Mic 6: 3 How have I *b* you? Answer me.
Mt 11:28 all you who are weary and *b*,
2Co 5: 4 are in this tent, we groan and are *b*,
Gal 5: 1 do not let yourselves be *b* again
1Ti 5:16 not let the church be *b* with them,

BURDENS (BURDEN)
Ps 68:19 who daily bears our *b*.
Lk 11:46 down with *b* they can hardly carry,
Gal 6: 2 Carry each other's *b*,

BURDENSOME (BURDEN)
1Jn 5: 3 And his commands are not *b*,

BURIED (BURY)
Ru 1:17 die I will die, and there I will be *b*.
Ro 6: 4 *b* with him through baptism
1Co 15: 4 that he was *b*, that he was raised
Col 2:12 having been *b* with him in baptism

BURN (BURNING BURNT)
Dt 7: 5 and *b* their idols in the fire.
Ps 79: 5 long will your jealousy *b* like fire?
1Co 7: 9 to marry than to *b* with passion.

BURNING (BURN)
Ex 27:20 so that the lamps may be kept *b*.
Lev 6: 9 the fire must be kept *b* on the altar.
Ps 18:28 You, O LORD, keep my lamp *b*;
Pr 25:22 you will heap *b* coals on his head,
Ro 12:20 you will heap *b* coals on his head."
Rev 19:20 alive into the fiery lake of *b* sulfur.

BURNISHED*
1Ki 7:45 of the LORD were of *b* bronze.
Eze 1: 7 and gleamed like *b* bronze.
Da 10: 6 and legs like the gleam of *b* bronze,
Rev 2:18 and whose feet are like *b* bronze.

BURNT (BURN)
Ge 8:20 he sacrificed *b* offerings on it.
22: 2 as a *b* offering on one
Ex 10:25 and *b* offerings to present
18:12 brought a *b* offering and other
40: 6 Place the altar of *b* offering in front
Lev 1: 3 " 'If the offering is a *b* offering
Jos 8:31 offered to the LORD *b* offerings
Jdg 6:26 offer the second bull as a *b* offering
13:16 But if you prepare a *b* offering,
1Ki 3: 4 offered a thousand *b* offerings
9:25 year Solomon sacrificed *b* offerings
10: 5 and the *b* offerings he made
Ezr 3: 2 Israel to sacrifice *b* offerings on it,
Eze 43:18 for sacrificing *b* offerings

BURST
Ps 98: 4 *b* into jubilant song with music;
Isa 44:23 *B* into song, you mountains,
49:13 *b* into song, O mountains!
52: 9 *B* into songs of joy together,
54: 1 *b* into song, shout for joy,
55:12 will *b* into song before you,

BURY (BURIED)
Mt 8:22 and let the dead *b* their own dead."
Lk 9:60 "Let the dead *b* their own dead,

BUSH
Ex 3: 2 the *b* was on fire it did not burn up.
Mk 12:26 the account of the *b*, how God said
Lk 20:37 But in the account of the *b*,
Ac 7:35 who appeared to him in the *b*.

BUSINESS
Ecc 4: 8 a miserable *b!*
Da 8:27 and went about the king's *b*.
1Co 5:12 What *b* is it of mine to judge those
1Th 4:11 to mind your own *b* and to work
Jas 1:11 even while he goes about his *b*.

BUSY*
1Ki 18:27 Perhaps he is deep in thought, or *b*,
20:40 While your servant was *b* here
Isa 32: 6 his mind is *b* with evil:
Hag 1: 9 of you is *b* with his own house.
2Th 3:11 They are not *b*; they are
Tit 2: 5 to be *b* at home, to be kind,

BUSYBODIES*
2Th 3:11 They are not busy; they are *b*.
1Ti 5:13 *b*, saying things they ought not to.

BUY (BOUGHT BUYS)
Pr 23:23 *B* the truth and do not sell it;
Isa 55: 1 Come, *b* wine and milk
Rev 13:17 so that no one could *b* or sell

BUYS (BUY)
Pr 31:16 She considers a field and *b* it;

BYWORD (WORD)
1Ki 9: 7 Israel will then become a *b*
Ps 44:14 You have made us a *b*
Joel 2:17 a *b* among the nations.

CAESAR
Mt 22:21 "Give to *C* what is Caesar's,

CAIN
Firstborn of Adam (Ge 4:1), murdered brother Abel (Ge 4:1-16; 1Jn 3:12).

CAKE
Hos 7: 8 Ephraim is a flat *c* not turned over.

CALEB
Judahite who spied out Canaan (Nu 13:6); allowed to enter land because of faith (Nu 13:30-14:38; Dt 1:36). Possessed Hebron (Jos 14:6-15:19).

CALF
Ex 32: 4 into an idol cast in the shape of a *c*,
Pr 15:17 than a fattened *c* with hatred.
Lk 15:23 Bring the fattened *c* and kill it.
Ac 7:41 made an idol in the form of a *c*.

CALL (CALLED CALLING CALLS)
1Ki 18:24 I will *c* on the name of the LORD.
2Ki 5:11 *c* on the name of the LORD his
1Ch 16: 8 to the LORD, *c* on his name;
Ps 105: 1 to the LORD, *c* on his name;
116: 13 and *c* on the name of the LORD.
116: 17 and *c* on the name of the LORD.
145: 18 near to all who *c* on him,
Pr 31:28 children arise and *c* her blessed;
Isa 5:20 Woe to those who *c* evil good
12: 4 to the LORD, *c* on his name;
55: 6 *c* on him while he is near.
65:24 Before they *c* I will answer;
Jer 33: 3 '*C* to me and I will answer you
Zep 3: 9 that all of them may *c* on the name
Zec 13: 9 They will *c* on my name
Mt 9:13 come to *c* the righteous,
Mk 2:17 I have not come to *c* the righteous,
Lk 5:32 I have not come to *c* the righteous,
Ac 2:39 all whom the Lord our God will *c*."
9:14 to arrest all who *c* on your name."
9:21 among those who *c* on this name?
Ro 10:12 and richly blesses all who *c* on him,
11:29 gifts and his *c* are irrevocable.
1Co 1: 2 with all those everywhere who *c*
1Th 4: 7 For God did not *c* us to be impure,
2Ti 2:22 along with those who *c*

CALLED (CALL)
Ge 2:23 she shall be *c* 'woman,'
5: 2 he blessed them and *c* them "man
12: 8 and *c* on the name of the LORD.
21:33 and there he *c* upon the name
26:25 and *c* on the name of the LORD.
1Sa 3: 5 and said, "Here I am; you *c* me."
2Ch 7:14 if my people, who are *c*
Ps 34: 6 This poor man *c*, and the LORD
116: 4 Then I *c* on the name of the LORD
Isa 56: 7 for my house will be *c*
La 3:55 I *c* on your name, O LORD,
Hos 11: 1 and out of Egypt I *c* my son.
Mt 1:16 was born Jesus, who is *c* Christ.
2:15 "Out of Egypt I *c* my son."
21:13 " 'My house will be *c* a house
Mk 11:17 " 'My house will be *c*
Lk 1:32 will be *c* the Son of the Most High.
1:35 to be born will be *c* the Son of God.
Ro 1: 1 *c* to be an apostle and set apart
1: 6 among those who are *c* to belong
1: 7 loved by God and *c* to be saints:
8:28 who have been *c* according
8:30 And those he predestined, he also *c*
1Co 1: 1 *c* to be an apostle of Christ Jesus
1: 2 in Christ Jesus and *c* to be holy,
1:24 but to those whom God has *c*,
1:26 of what you were when you were *c*.
7:15 God has *c* us to live in peace.
7:17 and to which God has *c* him.
Gal 1: 6 deserting the one who *c* you
1:15 from birth and *c* me by his grace,
5:13 You, my brothers, were *c* to be free
Eph 1:18 the hope to which he has *c* you,
4: 4 as you were *c* to one hope
Col 3:15 of one body you were *c* to peace.
2Th 2:14 He *c* you to this through our gospel
1Ti 6:12 life to which you were *c*
2Ti 1: 9 who has saved us and *c* us
Heb 9:15 that those who are *c* may receive
1Pe 1:15 But just as he who *c* you is holy,
2: 9 of him who *c* you out of darkness
3: 9 to this you were *c* so that you may
5:10 who *c* you to his eternal glory
2Pe 1: 3 of him who *c* us by his own glory
Jude : 1 To those who have been *c*,

CALLING (CALL)
Isa 40: 3 A voice of one *c*:
Mt 3: 3 "A voice of one *c* in the desert,
Mk 1: 3 "a voice of one *c* in the desert,
10:49 Cheer up! On your feet! He's *c* you
Lk 3: 4 "A voice of one *c* in the desert,
Jn 1:23 I am the voice of one *c* in the desert
Ac 22:16 wash your sins away, *c* on his name
Eph 4: 1 worthy of the *c* you have received.
2Th 1:11 may count you worthy of his *c*,
2Pe 1:10 all the more eager to make your *c*

CALLOUS* (CALLOUSED)
Ps 17:10 They close up their *c* hearts,
73: 7 From their *c* hearts comes iniquity;
119: 70 Their hearts are *c* and unfeeling,

CALLOUSED* (CALLOUS)
Isa 6:10 Make the heart of this people *c*;
Mt 13:15 this people's heart has become *c*;
Ac 28:27 this people's heart has become *c*;

CALLS (CALL)
Ps 147: 4 and *c* them each by name.
Isa 40:26 and *c* them each by name.
Joel 2:32 And everyone who *c*
Mt 22:43 speaking by the Spirit, *c* him 'Lord
Jn 10: 3 He *c* his own sheep by name
Ac 2:21 And everyone who *c*
Ro 10:13 "Everyone who *c* on the name
1Th 2:12 who *c* you into his kingdom
5:24 The one who *c* you is faithful

CALM (CALMS)
Ps 107: 30 They were glad when it grew *c*,
Isa 7: 4 keep *c* and don't be afraid.
Eze 16:42 I will be *c* and no longer angry.

CALMS* (CALM)
Pr 15:18 but a patient man *c* a quarrel.

CAMEL
Mt 19:24 it is easier for a *c* to go
23:24 strain out a gnat but swallow a *c*.
Mk 10:25 It is easier for a *c* to go
Lk 18:25 it is easier for a *c* to go

CAMP (ENCAMPS)
Heb 13:13 outside the *c*, bearing the disgrace

CANAAN (CANAANITE CANAANITES)
Ge 10:15 *C* was the father of Sidon his
Lev 14:34 "When you enter the land of *C*,
25:38 of Egypt to give you the land of *C*
Nu 13: 2 men to explore the land of *C*,
33:51 'When you cross the Jordan into *C*,
Jdg 4: 2 a king of *C*, who reigned in Hazor.
1Ch 16:18 "To you I will give the land of *C*
Ps 105: 11 "To you I will give the land of *C*
Ac 13:19 he overthrew seven nations in *C*

CANAANITE (CANAAN)
Ge 10:18 Later the *C* clans scattered
28: 1 "Do not marry a *C* woman.
Jos 5: 1 all the *C* kings along the seacoast
Jdg 1:32 lived among the *C* inhabitants

CANAANITES (CANAAN)
Ex 33: 2 before you and drive out the *C*,

CANCEL (CANCELED)
Dt 15: 1 seven years you must *c* debts.

CANCELED (CANCEL)
Mt 18:27 pity on him, *c* the debt
Lk 7:42 so he *c* the debts of both.
Col 2:14 having *c* the written code,

CANDLESTICKS see LAMPSTANDS

CANOPY*
2Sa 22:12 He made darkness his *c*
2Ki 16:18 away the Sabbath *c* that had been
Ps 18:11 made darkness his covering, his *c*
Isa 4: 5 over all the glory will be a *c*.
40:22 stretches out the heavens like a *c*,
Jer 43:10 he will spread his royal *c*

CAPERNAUM
Mt 4:13 Nazareth, he went and lived in *C*,

Jn 6:59 teaching in the synagogue in *C.*

CAPITAL
Dt 21:22 guilty of a *c* offense is put to death

CAPSTONE* (STONE)
Ps 118: 22 has become the *c;*
Zec 4: 7 he will bring out the *c* to shouts
Mt 21:42 has become the *c;*
Mk 12:10 has become the *c;*
Lk 20:17 has become the *c'?*
Ac 4:11 which has become the *c.'*
1Pe 2: 7 has become the *c,"*

CAPTIVATE* (CAPTIVE)
Pr 6:25 or let her *c* you with her eyes,

CAPTIVATED* (CAPTIVE)
Pr 5:19 may you ever be *c* by her love.
5:20 Why be *c,* my son, by an adulteress

CAPTIVE (CAPTIVATE CAPTIVATED CAPTIVES CAPTIVITY CAPTURED)
Ac 8:23 full of bitterness and *c* to sin."
2Co 10: 5 and we take *c* every thought
Col 2: 8 See to it that no one takes you *c*
2Ti 2:26 who has taken them *c* to do his will.

CAPTIVES (CAPTIVE)
Ps 68:18 you led *c* in your train;
Isa 61: 1 to proclaim freedom for the *c*
Eph 4: 8 he led *c* in his train

CAPTIVITY (CAPTIVE)
Dt 28:41 because they will go into *c.*
2Ki 25:21 So Judah went into *c,* away
Jer 30: 3 Israel and Judah back from *c*
52:27 So Judah went into *c,* away
Eze 29:14 I will bring them back from *c*

CAPTURED (CAPTIVE)
1Sa 4:11 The ark of God was *c,*
2Sa 5: 7 David *c* the fortress of Zion,
2Ki 17: 6 the king of Assyria *c* Samaria

CARCASS
Jdg 14: 9 taken the honey from the lion's *c.*
Mt 24:28 there is a *c,* there the vultures

CARE (CAREFUL CARES CARING)
Ps 8: 4 the son of man that you *c* for him?
65: 9 You *c* for the land and water it;
144: 3 what is man that you *c* for him,
Pr 29: 7 The righteous *c* about justice
Mk 5:26 deal under the *c* of many doctors
Lk 10:34 him to an inn and took *c* of him.
18: 4 I don't fear God or *c* about men,
Jn 21:16 Jesus said, "Take *c* of my sheep."
1Ti 3: 5 how can he take *c* of God's church
6:20 what has been entrusted to your *c.*
Heb 2: 6 the son of man that you *c* for him?
1Pe 5: 2 of God's flock that is under your *c,*

CAREFUL* (CARE)
Ge 31:24 "Be *c* not to say anything to Jacob,
31:29 'Be *c* not to say anything to Jacob,
Ex 19:12 'Be *c* that you do not go up
23:13 "Be *c* to do everything I have said
34:12 Be *c* not to make a treaty
34:15 "Be *c* not to make a treaty
Lev 18: 4 and be *c* to follow my decrees.
25:18 " 'Follow my decrees and be *c*
26: 3 and are *c* to obey my commands,
Dt 2: 4 afraid of you, but be very *c.*
4: 9 before you today? Only be *c,*
4:23 Be *c* not to forget the covenant
5:32 So be *c* to do what the LORD your
6: 3 be *c* to obey so that it may go well
6:12 be *c* that you do not forget
6:25 And if we are *c* to obey all this law
7:12 attention to these laws and are *c*
8: 1 Be *c* to follow every command I am
8:11 Be *c* that you do not forget
11:16 Be *c,* or you will be enticed
12: 1 and laws you must be *c* to follow
12:13 Be *c* not to sacrifice your burnt
12:19 Be *c* not to neglect the Levites
12:28 Be *c* to obey all these regulations I
12:30 be *c* not to be ensnared
15: 5 are *c* to follow all these commands
15: 9 Be *c* not to harbor this wicked
17:10 Be *c* to do everything they direct
24: 8 cases of leprous diseases be very *c*
Jos 1: 7 Be *c* to obey all the law my servant
1: 8 so that you may be *c*
22: 5 But be very *c* to keep
23: 6 be *c* to obey all that is written
23:11 be very *c* to love the LORD your
1Ki 8:25 if only your sons are *c* in all they do
2Ki 10:31 Yet Jehu was not *c* to keep the law
17:37 You must always be *c*
21: 8 if only they will be *c*
1Ch 22:13 if you are *c* to observe the decrees
28: 8 Be *c* to follow all the commands
2Ch 6:16 if only your sons are *c* in all they do
33: 8 if only they will be *c*
Ezr 4:22 Be *c* not to neglect this matter.
Job 36:18 Be *c* that no one entices you
Ps 101: 2 I will be *c* to lead a blameless life—
Pr 13:24 he who loves him is *c*
27:23 give *c* attention to your herds;
Isa 7: 4 Be *c,* keep calm and don't be afraid.
Jer 17:21 Be *c* not to carry a load
17:24 But if you are *c* to obey me,
22: 4 For if you are *c* to carry out these
Eze 11:20 will follow my decrees and be *c*
18:19 has been *c* to keep all my decrees,
20:19 follow my decrees and be *c*
20:21 they were not *c* to keep my laws—
36:27 you to follow my decrees and be *c*
37:24 and be *c* to keep my decrees.
Mic 7: 5 be *c* of your words.
Hag 1: 5 "Give *c* thought to your ways.
1: 7 "Give *c* thought to your ways.
2:15 give *c* thought to this from this day
2:18 Give *c* thought: Is there yet any
2:18 give *c* thought to the day
Mt 2: 8 and make a *c* search for the child.
6: 1 "Be *c* not to do your 'acts
16: 6 "Be *c,"* Jesus said to them.
Mk 8:15 "Be *c,"* Jesus warned them.
Lk 21:34 Be *c,* or your hearts will be weighed
Ro 12:17 Be *c* to do what is right in the eyes
1Co 3:10 each one should be *c* how he builds
8: 9 Be *c,* however, that the exercise
10:12 standing firm, be *c* that you don't
Eph 5:15 Be very *c,* then, how you live—
2Ti 4: 2 great patience and *c* instruction.
Tit 3: 8 may be *c* to devote themselves
Heb 2: 1 We must pay more *c* attention,
4: 1 let us be *c* that none

CARELESS*
Mt 12:36 for every *c* word they have spoken.

CARES* (CARE)
Dt 11:12 It is a land the LORD your God *c*
Job 39:16 she *c* not that her labor was in vain,
Ps 55:22 Cast your *c* on the LORD
142: 4 no one *c* for my life.
Pr 12:10 A righteous man *c* for the needs
Ecc 5: 3 when there are many *c,*
Jer 12:11 because there is no one who *c.*
30:17 Zion for whom no one *c.'*
Na 1: 7 He *c* for those who trust in him,
Jn 10:13 and *c* nothing for the sheep.
Eph 5:29 but he feeds and *c* for it, just
1Pe 5: 7 on him because he *c* for you.

CARING* (CARE)
1Th 2: 7 like a mother *c* for her little
1Ti 5: 4 practice by *c* for their own family

CARPENTER (CARPENTER'S)
Mk 6: 3 does miracles! Isn't this the *c?*

CARPENTER'S* (CARPENTER)
Mt 13:55 "Isn't this the *c* son? Isn't his

CARRIED (CARRY)
Ex 19: 4 and how I *c* you on eagles' wings
Dt 1:31 how the LORD your God *c* you,
Isa 53: 4 and *c* our sorrows,
63: 9 he lifted them up and *c* them
Mt 8:17 and *c* our diseases."
Heb 13: 9 Do not be *c* away by all kinds
2Pe 1:21 as they were *c* along by the Holy
3:17 so that you may not be *c* away

CARRIES (CARRY)
Dt 32:11 and *c* them on its pinions.
Isa 40:11 and *c* them close to his heart;

CARRY (CARRIED CARRIES CARRYING)
Lev 16:22 goat will *c* on itself all their sins
26:15 and fail to *c* out all my commands
Isa 46: 4 I have made you and I will *c* you;
Lk 14:27 anyone who does not *c* his cross
Gal 6: 2 *C* each other's burdens,
6: 5 for each one should *c* his own load.

CARRYING (CARRY)
Jn 19:17 *C* his own cross, he went out
1Jn 5: 2 loving God and *c* out his

CARVED (CARVES)
Nu 33:52 Destroy all their *c* images
Mic 5:13 I will destroy your *c* images

CARVES* (CARVED)
Dt 27:15 "Cursed is the man who *c* an image

CASE
Pr 18:17 to present his *c* seems right,
22:23 for the LORD will take up their *c*
23:11 he will take up their *c* against you.

CAST (CASTING)
Ex 34:17 "Do not make *c* idols.
Lev 16: 8 He is to *c* lots for the two goats—
Ps 22:18 and *c* lots for my clothing.
55:22 *C* your cares on the LORD
Pr 16:33 The lot is *c* into the lap,
Ecc 11: 1 *C* your bread upon the waters,
Jn 19:24 and *c* lots for my clothing."
1Pe 5: 7 *C* all your anxiety on him

CASTING (CAST)
Pr 18:18 *C* the lot settles disputes
Mt 27:35 divided up his clothes by *c* lots.

CATCH (CATCHES CAUGHT)
Lk 5: 4 and let down the nets for a *c."*
5:10 from now on you will *c* men."

CATCHES (CATCH)
Job 5:13 He *c* the wise in their craftiness,
1Co 3:19 "He *c* the wise in their craftiness";

CATTLE
Ps 50:10 and the *c* on a thousand hills.

CAUGHT (CATCH)
Ge 22:13 there in a thicket he saw a ram *c*
2Co 12: 2 who fourteen years ago was *c* up
1Th 4:17 and are left will be *c* up together with them

CAUSE (CAUSES)
Pr 24:28 against your neighbor without *c,*
Ecc 8: 3 Do not stand up for a bad *c,*
Mt 18: 7 of the things that *c* people to sin!
Ro 14:21 else that will *c* your brother
1Co 10:32 Do not *c* anyone to stumble,

CAUSES (CAUSE)
Ps 7:16 The trouble he *c* recoils on himself;
Isa 8:14 a stone that *c* men to stumble
Mt 5:29 If your right eye *c* you to sin,
5:30 And if your right hand *c* you to sin,
18: 6 if anyone *c* one of these little ones
18: 8 or your foot *c* you to sin,
Ro 14:20 to eat anything that *c* someone else
1Co 8:13 if what I eat *c* my brother to fall
1Pe 2: 8 "A stone that *c* men to stumble

CAUTIOUS*
Pr 12:26 A righteous man is *c* in friendship,

CEASE
Ps 46: 9 He makes wars *c* to the ends

CELEBRATE*
Ex 10: 9 we are to *c* a festival to the LORD
12:14 generations to come you shall *c* it
12:17 *C* this day as a lasting ordinance
12:17 "*C* the Feast of Unleavened Bread,
12:47 community of Israel must *c* it.
12:48 to *c* the LORD's Passover must
23:14 are to *c* a festival to me.
23:15 "*C* the Feast of Unleavened Bread;
23:16 "*C* the Feast of Harvest
23:16 "*C* the Feast of Ingathering
34:18 "*C* the Feast of Unleavened Bread.
34:22 "*C* the Feast of Weeks
Lev 23:39 *c* the festival to the LORD
23:41 *C* this as a festival to the LORD
23:41 for the generations to come; *c* it
Nu 9: 2 "Have the Israelites *c* the Passover
9: 3 *C* it at the appointed time,
9: 4 told the Israelites to *c* the Passover,
9: 6 of them could not *c* the Passover
9:10 they may still *c* the LORD's
9:11 are to *c* it on the fourteenth day
9:12 When they *c* the Passover,
9:13 on a journey fails to *c* the Passover,
9:14 to *c* the LORD's Passover must do
29:12 *C* a festival to the LORD
Dt 16: 1 *c* the Passover of the LORD your
16:10 Then *c* the Feast of Weeks
16:13 *C* the Feast of Tabernacles
16:15 For seven days *c* the Feast
Jdg 16:23 to Dagon their god and to *c,*
2Sa 6:21 the LORD's people Israel—I will *c*
2Ki 23:21 "*C* the Passover to the LORD your
2Ch 30: 1 and *c* the Passover to the LORD,
30: 2 decided to *c* the Passover
30: 3 able to *c* it at the regular time
30: 5 and *c* the Passover to the LORD,

2Ch 30:13 in Jerusalem to *c* the Feast
30:23 to *c* the festival seven more days;
Ne 8:12 of food and to *c* with great joy,
12:27 to *c* joyfully the dedication
Est 9:21 to have them *c* annually
Ps 145: 7 They will *c* your abundant
Isa 30:29 as on the night you *c* a holy festival
Na 1:15 *C* your festivals, O Judah,
Zec 14:16 and to *c* the Feast of Tabernacles.
14:18 up to *c* the Feast of Tabernacles.
14:19 up to *c* the Feast of Tabernacles.
Mt 26:18 I am going to *c* the Passover
Lk 15:23 Let's have a feast and *c.*
15:24 So they began to *c.*
15:29 goat so I could *c* with my friends.
15:32 But we had to *c* and be glad,
Rev 11:10 will *c* by sending each other gifts,

CELESTIAL*
2Pe 2:10 afraid to slander *c* beings;
Jude : 8 authority and slander *c* beings.

CENSER (CENSERS)
Lev 16:12 is to take a *c* full of burning coals
Rev 8: 3 Another angel, who had a golden *c,*

CENSERS (CENSER)
Nu 16: 6 Take *c* and tomorrow put fire

CENTURION
Mt 8: 5 had entered Capernaum, a *c* came
27:54 When the *c* and those
Mk 15:39 And when the *c,* who stood there
Lk 7: 3 The *c* heard of Jesus and sent some
23:47 The *c,* seeing what had happened,
Ac 10: 1 a *c* in what was known
27: 1 handed over to a *c* named Julius,

CEPHAS* (PETER)
Jn 1:42 You will be called *C*" (which,
1Co 1:12 another, "I follow *C*"; still another,
3:22 Paul or Apollos or *C* or the world
9: 5 and the Lord's brothers and *C?*

CEREMONIAL* (CEREMONY)
Lev 14: 2 at the time of his *c* cleansing,
15:13 off seven days for his *c* cleansing;
Mk 7: 3 they give their hands a *c* washing,
Jn 2: 6 used by the Jews for *c* washing,
3:25 Jew over the matter of *c* washing.
11:55 to Jerusalem for their *c* cleansing
18:28 to avoid *c* uncleanness the Jews did
Heb 9:10 drink and various *c* washings—
13: 9 not by *c* foods, which are

CEREMONIALLY* (CEREMONY)
Lev 4:12 outside the camp to a place *c* clean,
5: 2 touches anything *c* unclean—
6:11 the camp to a place that is *c* clean.
7:19 anyone *c* clean may eat it.
7:19 touches anything *c* unclean must
10:14 Eat them in a *c* clean place;
11: 4 not have a split hoof; it is *c* unclean
12: 2 birth to a son will be *c* unclean
12: 7 and then she will be *c* clean
13: 3 he shall pronounce him *c* unclean.
14: 8 with water; then he will be *c* clean.
15:28 and after that she will be *c* clean.
15:33 lies with a woman who is *c* unclean.
17:15 he will be *c* unclean till evening.
21: 1 must not make himself *c* unclean
22: 3 of your descendants is *c* unclean
27:11 he vowed is a *c* unclean animal—
Nu 5: 2 who is *c* unclean because of a dead
6: 7 must not make himself *c* unclean
8: 6 Israelites and make them *c* clean.
9: 6 they were *c* unclean on account
9:13 But if a man who is *c* clean
18:11 household who is *c* clean may eat
18:13 household who is *c* clean may eat
19: 7 but he will be *c* unclean till evening
19: 9 and put them in a *c* clean place
19:18 Then a man who is *c* clean is
Dt 12:15 Both the *c* unclean and the clean
12:22 Both the *c* unclean and the clean
14: 7 they are *c* unclean for you.
15:22 Both the *c* unclean and the clean
1Sa 20:26 to David to make him *c* unclean—
2Ch 13:11 the bread on the *c* clean table
30:17 for all those who were not *c* clean
Ezr 6:20 themselves and were all *c* clean.
Ne 12:30 Levites had purified themselves *c,*
Isa 66:20 of the LORD in *c* clean vessels.
Eze 22:10 period, when they are *c* unclean.
Ac 24:18 I was *c* clean when they found me
Heb 9:13 those who are *c* unclean sanctify

CEREMONY* (CEREMONIAL CEREMONIALLY)
Ge 50:11 Egyptians are holding a solemn *c*
Ex 12:25 as he promised, observe this *c.*
12:26 'What does this *c* mean to you?'
13: 5 are to observe this *c* in this month:

CERTAIN (CERTAINTY)
2Pe 1:19 word of the prophets made more *c,*

CERTAINTY* (CERTAIN)
Lk 1: 4 so that you may know the *c*
Jn 17: 8 They knew with *c* that I came

CERTIFICATE* (CERTIFIED)
Dt 24: 1 and he writes her a *c* of divorce,
24: 3 and writes her a *c* of divorce,
Isa 50: 1 "Where is your mother's *c*
Jer 3: 8 I gave faithless Israel her *c*
Mt 5:31 divorces his wife must give her a *c*
19: 7 that a man give his wife a *c*
Mk 10: 4 a man to write a *c* of divorce

CERTIFIED* (CERTIFICATE)
Jn 3:33 has accepted it has *c* that God is

CHAFF
Ps 1: 4 They are like *c*
35: 5 May they be like *c* before the wind,
Da 2:35 became like *c* on a threshing floor
Mt 3:12 up the *c* with unquenchable fire."

CHAINED (CHAINS)
2Ti 2: 9 But God's word is not *c.*

CHAINS (CHAINED)
Eph 6:20 for which I am an ambassador in *c.*
Col 4:18 Remember my *c.*
2Ti 1:16 and was not ashamed of my *c.*
Jude : 6 with everlasting *c* for judgment

CHAMPION
Ps 19: 5 like a *c* rejoicing to run his course.

CHANCE
Ecc 9:11 but time and *c* happen to them all.

CHANGE (CHANGED)
1Sa 15:29 of Israel does not lie or *c* his mind;
Ps 110: 4 and will not *c* his mind:
Jer 7: 5 If you really *c* your ways
Mal 3: 6 "I the LORD do not *c.*
Mt 18: 3 unless you *c* and become like little
Heb 7:21 and will not *c* his mind:
Jas 1:17 who does not *c* like shifting

CHANGED (CHANGE)
1Sa 10: 6 you will be *c* into a different person
Hos 11: 8 My heart is *c* within me;
1Co 15:51 but we will all be *c*— in a flash,

CHARACTER*
Ru 3:11 that you are a woman of noble *c.*
Pr 12: 4 of noble *c* is her husband's crown,
31:10 A wife of noble *c* who can find?
Ac 17:11 noble *c* than the Thessalonians,
Ro 5: 4 perseverance, *c;* and *c,* hope.
1Co 15:33 "Bad company corrupts good *c.*"

CHARGE (CHARGES)
Job 34:13 him in *c* of the whole world?
Ro 8:33 Who will bring any *c*
1Co 9:18 the gospel I may offer it free of *c,*
2Co 11: 7 the gospel of God to you free of *c?*
2Ti 4: 1 I give you this *c:* Preach the Word;
Phm :18 or owes you anything, *c* it to me.

CHARGES (CHARGE)
Isa 50: 8 Who then will bring *c* against me?

CHARIOT (CHARIOTS)
2Ki 2:11 suddenly a *c* of fire and horses
Ps 104: 3 He makes the clouds his *c*
Ac 8:28 sitting in his *c* reading the book

CHARIOTS (CHARIOT)
2Ki 6:17 and *c* of fire all around Elisha.
Ps 20: 7 Some trust in *c* and some in horses,
68:17 The *c* of God are tens of thousands

CHARM* (CHARMING)
Pr 17: 8 bribe is a *c* to the one who gives it;
31:30 *C* is deceptive, and beauty is

CHARMING* (CHARM)
Pr 26:25 his speech is *c,* do not believe
SS 1:16 Oh, how *c!*

CHASE (CHASES)
Lev 26: 8 Five of you will *c* a hundred,

CHASES* (CHASE)
Pr 12:11 he who *c* fantasies lacks judgment.
28:19 one who *c* fantasies will have his

CHASM*
Lk 16:26 and you a great *c* has been fixed,

CHATTER* (CHATTERING)
1Ti 6:20 Turn away from godless *c*
2Ti 2:16 Avoid godless *c,* because those

CHATTERING* (CHATTER)
Pr 10: 8 but a *c* fool comes to ruin.
10:10 and a *c* fool comes to ruin.

CHEAT* (CHEATED CHEATING CHEATS)
Mal 1:14 "Cursed is the *c* who has
1Co 6: 8 you yourselves *c* and do wrong,

CHEATED* (CHEAT)
Ge 31: 7 yet your father has *c* me
1Sa 12: 3 Whom have I *c?* Whom have I
12: 4 "You have not *c* or oppressed us,"
Lk 19: 8 if I have *c* anybody out of anything,
1Co 6: 7 Why not rather be *c?* Instead,

CHEATING* (CHEAT)
Am 8: 5 and *c* with dishonest scales,

CHEATS* (CHEAT)
Lev 6: 2 or if he *c* him, or if he finds lost

CHEEK (CHEEKS)
Mt 5:39 someone strikes you on the right *c,*
Lk 6:29 If someone strikes you on one *c,*

CHEEKS (CHEEK)
Isa 50: 6 my *c* to those who pulled out my

CHEERFUL* (CHEERS)
Pr 15:13 A happy heart makes the face *c,*
15:15 but the *c* heart has a continual feast
15:30 A *c* look brings joy to the heart,
17:22 A *c* heart is good medicine,
2Co 9: 7 for God loves a *c* giver.

CHEERS (CHEERFUL)
Pr 12:25 but a kind word *c* him up.

CHEMOSH
2Ki 23:13 for *C* the vile god of Moab,

CHERISH (CHERISHED CHERISHES)
Ps 17:14 You still the hunger of those you *c;*

CHERISHED (CHERISH)
Ps 66:18 If I had *c* sin in my heart,

CHERISHES* (CHERISH)
Pr 19: 8 he who *c* understanding prospers.

CHERUB (CHERUBIM)
Ex 25:19 Make one *c* on one end
Eze 28:14 You were anointed as a guardian *c,*

CHERUBIM (CHERUB)
Ge 3:24 side of the Garden of Eden *c*
1Sa 4: 4 who is enthroned between the *c.*
2Sa 6: 2 enthroned between the *c* that are
22:11 He mounted the *c* and flew;
1Ki 6:23 a pair of *c* of olive wood,
2Ki 19:15 of Israel, enthroned between the *c,*
1Ch 13: 6 who is enthroned between the *c*—
Ps 18:10 He mounted the *c* and flew;
80: 1 who sit enthroned between the *c,*
99: 1 he sits enthroned between the *c,*
Isa 37:16 of Israel, enthroned between the *c,*
Eze 10: 1 was over the heads of the *c.*

CHEST
Ex 25:10 "Have them make a *c*
2Ki 12: 9 Jehoiada the priest took a *c*
Da 2:32 its *c* and arms of silver, its belly
Rev 1:13 with a golden sash around his *c.*

CHEWS
Lev 11: 3 divided and that *c* the cud.

CHIEF
1Pe 5: 4 And when the *C* Shepherd appears,

CHILD (CHILDISH CHILDREN CHILDREN'S GRANDCHILDREN)
Pr 20:11 Even a *c* is known by his actions,
22: 6 Train a *c* in the way he should go,
22:15 Folly is bound up in the heart of a *c*
23:13 not withhold discipline from a *c;*
29:15 *c* left to himself disgraces his mother.
Isa 7:14 The virgin will be with *c*
9: 6 For to us a *c* is born,
11: 6 and a little *c* will lead them.
66:13 As a mother comforts her *c,*

Mt 1:23 "The virgin will be with c
18: 2 He called a little c and had him
Lk 1:42 and blessed is the c you will bear!
1:80 And the c grew and became strong
1Co 13:11 When I was a c, I talked like a c,
1Jn 5: 1 who loves the father loves his c

CHILDBEARING (BEAR)
Ge 3:16 greatly increase your pains in c;

CHILDBIRTH (BEAR)
Gal 4:19 the pains of c until Christ is formed

CHILDISH* (CHILD)
1Co 13:11 When I became a man, I put c ways

CHILDREN (CHILD)
Ex 20: 5 punishing the c for the sin
Dt 4: 9 Teach them to your c
6: 7 Impress them on your c.
11:19 them to your c, talking about them
14: 1 You are the c of the LORD your
24:16 nor c put to death for their fathers;
30:19 so that you and your c may live
32:46 so that you may command your c
Job 1: 5 "Perhaps my c have sinned
Ps 8: 2 From the lips of c and infants
78: 5 forefathers to teach their c,
Pr 17: 6 Children's c are a crown
20: 7 blessed are his c after him.
31:28 Her c arise and call her blessed;
Joel 1: 3 Tell it to your c,
Mal 4: 6 the hearts of the fathers to their c,
Mt 7:11 how to give good gifts to your c,
11:25 and revealed them to little c.
18: 3 you change and become like little c
19:14 "Let the little c come to me,
21:16 " 'From the lips of c and infants
Mk 9:37 one of these little c in my name
10:14 "Let the little c come to me,
10:16 And he took the c in his arms,
13:12 C will rebel against their parents
Lk 10:21 and revealed them to little c.
18:16 "Let the little c come to me,
Jn 1:12 the right to become c of God—
Ac 2:39 The promise is for you and your c
Ro 8:16 with our spirit that we are God's c.
1Co 14:20 Brothers, stop thinking like c.
2Co 12:14 parents, but parents for their c.
Eph 6: 1 C, obey your parents in the Lord,
6: 4 do not exasperate your c; instead,
Col 3:20 C, obey your parents in everything,
3:21 Fathers, do not embitter your c,
1Ti 3: 4 and see that his c obey him
3:12 and must manage his c and his
5:10 bringing up c, showing hospitality,
Heb 2:13 and the c God has given me."
1Jn 3: 1 that we should be called c of God!

CHILDREN'S (CHILD)
Isa 54:13 and great will be your c peace.

CHOKE
Mk 4:19 come in and c the word,

CHOOSE (CHOOSES CHOSE CHOSEN)
Dt 30:19 Now c life, so that you
Jos 24:15 then c for yourselves this day
Pr 8:10 C my instruction instead of silver,
16:16 to c understanding rather
Jn 15:16 You did not c me, but I chose you

CHOOSES (CHOOSE)
Mt 11:27 to whom the Son c to reveal him.
Lk 10:22 to whom the Son c to reveal him."
Jn 7:17 If anyone c to do God's will,

CHOSE (CHOOSE)
Ge 13:11 So Lot c for himself the whole plain
Ps 33:12 the people he c for his inheritance.
Jn 15:16 but I c you and appointed you to go
1Co 1:27 But God c the foolish things
Eph 1: 4 he c us in him before the creation
2Th 2:13 from the beginning God c you

CHOSEN (CHOOSE)
Isa 41: 8 Jacob, whom I have c,
Mt 22:14 For many are invited, but few are c
Lk 10:42 Mary has c what is better,
23:35 the Christ of God, the C One."
Jn 15:19 but I have c you out of the world.
1Pe 1:20 He was c before the creation
2: 9 But you are a c people, a royal

CHRIST (CHRIST'S CHRISTIAN CHRISTIANS CHRISTS)
Mt 1:16 was born Jesus, who is called C.
16:16 Peter answered, "You are the C,
22:42 "What do you think about the C?
Mk 1: 1 of the gospel about Jesus C,
Mk 8:29 Peter answered, "You are the C."
14:61 "Are you the C, the Son
Lk 9:20 Peter answered, "The C of God."
Jn 1:41 found the Messiah" (that is, the C).
20:31 you may believe that Jesus is the C,
Ac 2:36 you crucified, both Lord and C."
5:42 the good news that Jesus is the C.
9:22 by proving that Jesus is the C.
9:34 said to him, "Jesus C heals you.
17: 3 proving that the C had to suffer
18:28 the Scriptures that Jesus was the C.
26:23 that the C would suffer and,
Ro 1: 4 from the dead: Jesus C our Lord.
3:22 comes through faith in Jesus C
5: 1 God through our Lord Jesus C,
5: 6 we were still powerless, C died
5: 8 While we were still sinners, C died
5:11 in God through our Lord Jesus C,
5:17 life through the one man, Jesus C.
6: 4 as C was raised from the dead
6: 9 that since C was raised
6:23 life in C Jesus our Lord.
7: 4 to the law through the body of C,
8: 1 for those who are in C Jesus,
8: 9 Spirit of C, he does not belong to C.
8:17 heirs of God and co-heirs with C,
8:34 Who is he that condemns? C Jesus,
8:35 us from the love of C?
9: 5 is traced the human ancestry of C,
10: 4 C is the end of the law
12: 5 so in C we who are many form one
13:14 yourselves with the Lord Jesus C,
14: 9 C died and returned to life
15: 3 For even C did not please himself
15: 5 yourselves as you follow C Jesus,
15: 7 then, just as C accepted you,
16:18 people are not serving our Lord C,
1Co 1: 2 to those sanctified in C Jesus
1: 7 for our Lord Jesus C to be revealed.
1:13 Is C divided? Was Paul crucified
1:17 For C did not send me to baptize,
1:23 but we preach C crucified:
1:30 of him that you are in C Jesus,
2: 2 except Jesus C and him crucified.
3:11 one already laid, which is Jesus C.
5: 7 For C, our Passover lamb,
6:15 bodies are members of C himself?
8: 6 and there is but one Lord, Jesus C,
8:12 conscience, you sin against C.
10: 4 them, and that rock was C.
11: 1 as I follow the example of C.
11: 3 the head of every man is C,
12:27 Now you are the body of C,
15: 3 that C died for our sins according
15:14 And if C has not been raised,
15:22 so in C all will be made alive.
15:57 victory through our Lord Jesus C.
2Co 1: 5 as the sufferings of C flow
2:14 us in triumphal procession in C
3: 3 show that you are a letter from C,
3:14 because only in C is it taken away.
4: 4 light of the gospel of the glory of C,
4: 5 not preach ourselves, but Jesus C
4: 6 of the glory of God in the face of C.
5:10 before the judgment seat of C,
5:17 Therefore, if anyone is in C,
6:15 What harmony is there between C
10: 1 the meekness and gentleness of C,
11: 2 you to one husband, to C,
Gal 1: 7 are trying to pervert the gospel of C
2: 4 on the freedom we have in C Jesus
2:16 but by faith in Jesus C.
2:17 does that mean that C promotes sin
2:20 I have been crucified with C
2:21 C died for nothing!" You foolish
3:13 C redeemed us from the curse
3:16 meaning one person, who is C.
3:26 of God through faith in C Jesus,
4:19 of childbirth until C is formed
5: 1 for freedom that C has set us free.
5: 4 by law have been alienated from C;
5:24 to C Jesus have crucified the sinful
6:14 in the cross of our Lord Jesus C,
Eph 1: 3 with every spiritual blessing in C.
1:10 together under one head, even C.
1:20 which he exerted in C
2: 5 made us alive with C
2:10 created in C Jesus
2:12 time you were separate from C,
2:20 with C Jesus himself as the chief
3: 8 the unsearchable riches of C,
3:17 so that C may dwell in your hearts
4: 7 has been given as C apportioned it.
4:13 measure of the fullness of C.
4:15 into him who is the Head, that is, C
4:32 just as in C God forgave you.
5: 2 as C loved us and gave himself up
5:21 out of reverence for C.
5:23 as C is the head of the church,
Eph 5:25 just as C loved the church
Php 1:18 motives or true, C is preached.
1:21 to live is C and to die is gain.
1:23 I desire to depart and be with C,
1:27 worthy of the gospel of C.
1:29 on behalf of C not only to believe
2: 5 be the same as that of C Jesus:
3: 7 now consider loss for the sake of C.
3:10 I want to know C and the power
3:18 as enemies of the cross of C.
4:19 to his glorious riches in C Jesus.
Col 1: 4 heard of your faith in C Jesus
1:27 which is C in you, the hope of glory
1:28 may present everyone perfect in C.
2: 2 the mystery of God, namely, C,
2: 6 as you received C Jesus as Lord,
2: 9 For in C all the fullness
2:13 God made you alive with C.
2:17 the reality, however, is found in C.
3: 1 then, you have been raised with C,
3: 3 and your life is now hidden with C
3:15 Let the peace of C rule
1Th 5: 9 through our Lord Jesus C.
2Th 2: 1 the coming of our Lord Jesus C
2:14 in the glory of our Lord Jesus C.
1Ti 1:12 I thank C Jesus our Lord, who has
1:15 C Jesus came into the world
1:16 C Jesus might display his unlimited
2: 5 the man C Jesus, who gave himself
2Ti 1: 9 us in C Jesus before the beginning
1:10 appearing of our Savior, C Jesus,
2: 1 in the grace that is in C Jesus.
2: 3 us like a good soldier of C Jesus.
2: 8 Remember Jesus C, raised
2:10 the salvation that is in C Jesus,
3:12 life in C Jesus will be persecuted,
3:15 salvation through faith in C Jesus.
4: 1 presence of God and of C Jesus,
Tit 2:13 our great God and Savior, Jesus C,
Heb 3: 6 But C is faithful as a son
3:14 to share in C if we hold firmly
5: 5 So C also did not take
6: 1 the elementary teachings about C
9:11 When C came as high priest
9:14 more, then, will the blood of C,
9:15 For this reason C is the mediator
9:24 For C did not enter a man-made
9:26 Then C would have had
9:28 so C was sacrificed once
10:10 of the body of Jesus C once for all.
13: 8 Jesus C is the same yesterday
1Pe 1: 2 for obedience to Jesus C
1: 3 of Jesus C from the dead,
1:11 he predicted the sufferings of C
1:19 but with the precious blood of C,
2:21 because C suffered for you,
3:15 in your hearts set apart C as Lord.
3:18 For C died for sins once for all,
3:21 you by the resurrection of Jesus C,
4:13 participate in the sufferings of C,
4:14 insulted because of the name of C,
2Pe 1: 1 and Savior Jesus C have received
1:16 and coming of our Lord Jesus C,
1Jn 2: 1 Jesus C, the Righteous One.
2:22 man who denies that Jesus is the C.
3:16 Jesus C laid down his life for us.
3:23 in the name of his Son, Jesus C,
4: 2 that Jesus C has come
5: 1 believes that Jesus is the C is born
5:20 even in his Son Jesus C.
2Jn : 9 teaching of C does not have God;
Jude : 4 deny Jesus C our only Sovereign
Rev 1: 1 The revelation of Jesus C,
1: 5 from Jesus C, who is the faithful
11:15 kingdom of our Lord and of his C,
20: 4 reigned with C a thousand years.
20: 6 they will be priests of God and of C

CHRIST'S (CHRIST)
1Co 9:21 from God's law but am under C law
2Co 5:14 For C love compels us,
5:20 We are therefore C ambassadors,
12: 9 so that C power may rest on me.
Col 1:22 by C physical body through death

CHRISTIAN* (CHRIST)
Ac 26:28 you can persuade me to be a C?"
1Pe 4:16 as a C, do not be ashamed,

CHRISTIANS* (CHRIST)
Ac 11:26 The disciples were called C first

CHRISTS* (CHRIST)
Mt 24:24 For false C and false prophets will
Mk 13:22 For false C and false prophets will

CHURCH
Mt 16:18 and on this rock I will build my c,
18:17 if he refuses to listen even to the c,

Ac 20:28 Be shepherds of the *c* of God,
1Co 5:12 of mine to judge those outside the *c*
14: 4 but he who prophesies edifies the *c.*
14:12 to excel in gifts that build up the *c.*
14:26 done for the strengthening of the *c.*
15: 9 because I persecuted the *c* of God.
Gal 1:13 how intensely I persecuted the *c*
Eph 5:23 as Christ is the head of the *c,*
Col 1:18 he is the head of the body, the *c;*
1:24 the sake of his body, which is the *c.*

CHURNING
Pr 30:33 For as *c* the milk produces butter,

CIRCLE
Isa 40:22 enthroned above the *c* of the earth,

CIRCUMCISE (CIRCUMCISED CIRCUMCISION)
Dt 10:16 *C* your hearts, therefore,

CIRCUMCISED (CIRCUMCISE)
Ge 17:10 Every male among you shall be *c.*
17:12 who is eight days old must be *c,*
Jos 5: 3 and *c* the Israelites at Gibeath
Gal 5: 2 that if you let yourselves be *c,*

CIRCUMCISION (CIRCUMCISE)
Ro 2:25 *C* has value if you observe the law,
2:29 and *c* is *c* of the heart, by the Spirit,
1Co 7:19 *C* is nothing and uncircumcision is

CIRCUMSTANCES
Php 4:11 to be content whatever the *c.*
1Th 5:18 continually; give thanks in all *c,*

CITIES (CITY)
Lk 19:17 small matter, take charge of ten *c.'*
19:19 'You take charge of five *c.'*

CITIZENS (CITIZENSHIP)
Eph 2:19 but fellow *c* with God's people

CITIZENSHIP* (CITIZENS)
Ac 22:28 "I had to pay a big price for my *c.*"
Eph 2:12 excluded from *c* in Israel
Php 3:20 But our *c* is in heaven.

CITY (CITIES)
Mt 5:14 A *c* on a hill cannot be hidden.
Ac 18:10 I have many people in this *c.*"
Heb 13:14 here we do not have an enduring *c,*
Rev 21: 2 saw the Holy *C,* the new

CIVILIAN*
2Ti 2: 4 a soldier gets involved in *c* affairs—

CLAIM (CLAIMS RECLAIM)
Pr 25: 6 do not *c* a place among great men;
1Jn 1: 6 If we *c* to have fellowship
1: 8 If we *c* to be without sin, we
1:10 If we *c* we have not sinned,

CLAIMS (CLAIM)
Jas 2:14 if a man *c* to have faith
1Jn 2: 6 Whoever *c* to live in him must walk
2: 9 Anyone who *c* to be in the light

CLANGING*
1Co 13: 1 a resounding gong or a *c* cymbal.

CLAP* (CLAPPED CLAPS)
Job 21: 5 *c* your hand over your mouth.
Ps 47: 1 *C* your hands, all you nations;
98: 8 Let the rivers *c* their hands,
Pr 30:32 *c* your hand over your mouth!
Isa 55:12 will *c* their hands.
La 2:15 *c* their hands at you;

CLAPPED* (CLAP)
2Ki 11:12 and the people *c* their hands
Eze 25: 6 Because you have *c* your hands

CLAPS* (CLAP)
Job 27:23 It *c* its hands in derision
34:37 scornfully he *c* his hands among us
Na 3:19 *c* his hands at your fall,

CLASSIFY*
2Co 10:12 dare to *c* or compare ourselves

CLAUDIUS
Ac 11:28 happened during the reign of *C.)*
18: 2 because *C* had ordered all the Jews

CLAY
Isa 45: 9 Does the *c* say to the potter,
64: 8 We are the *c,* you are the potter;
Jer 18: 6 "Like *c* in the hand of the potter,
La 4: 2 are now considered as pots of *c,*
Da 2:33 partly of iron and partly of baked *c.*
Ro 9:21 of the same lump of *c* some pottery

2Co 4: 7 we have this treasure in jars of *c*
2Ti 2:20 and *c;* some are for noble purposes

CLEAN (CLEANNESS CLEANSE CLEANSED CLEANSES CLEANSING)
Ge 7: 2 seven of every kind of *c* animal,
Lev 4:12 the camp to a place ceremonially *c,*
16:30 you will be *c* from all your sins.
Ps 24: 4 He who has *c* hands and a pure
51: 7 with hyssop, and I will be *c;*
Pr 20: 9 I am *c* and without sin"?
Eze 36:25 I will sprinkle *c* water on you,
Mt 8: 2 are willing, you can make me *c.*"
12:44 the house unoccupied, swept *c*
23:25 You *c* the outside of the cup
Mk 7:19 Jesus declared all foods "*c.*")
Jn 13:10 to wash his feet; his whole body is *c*
15: 3 are already *c* because of the word
Ac 10:15 impure that God has made *c.*"
Ro 14:20 All food is *c,* but it is wrong

CLEANNESS (CLEAN)
2Sa 22:25 according to my *c* in his sight.

CLEANSE (CLEAN)
Ps 51: 2 and *c* me from my sin.
51: 7 *C* me with hyssop, and I will be
Pr 20:30 Blows and wounds *c* away evil,
Heb 9:14 *c* our consciences from acts that
10:22 having our hearts sprinkled to *c* us

CLEANSED (CLEAN)
Heb 9:22 requires that nearly everything be *c*
2Pe 1: 9 has forgotten that he has been *c*

CLEANSES* (CLEAN)
2Ti 2:21 If a man *c* himself from the latter,

CLEANSING (CLEAN)
Eph 5:26 *c* her by the washing with water

CLEFT*
Ex 33:22 I will put you in a *c* in the rock

CLEVER
Isa 5:21 and *c* in their own sight.

CLING
Ro 12: 9 Hate what is evil; *c* to what is good.

CLINGS
Ps 63: 8 My soul *c* to you;

CLOAK
Ex 12:11 with your *c* tucked into your belt,
2Ki 4:29 "Tuck your *c* into your belt,
9: 1 "Tuck your *c* into your belt,
Mt 5:40 let him have your *c* as well.

CLOSE (CLOSER CLOSES)
2Ki 11: 8 Stay *c* to the king wherever he goes
2Ch 23: 7 Stay *c* to the king wherever he goes
Ps 34:18 LORD is *c* to the brokenhearted
148: 14 of Israel, the people *c* to his heart.
Isa 40:11 and carries them *c* to his heart;
Jer 30:21 himself to be *c* to me?'

CLOSER (CLOSE)
Ex 3: 5 "Do not come any *c,*" God said.
Pr 18:24 there is a friend who sticks *c*

CLOSES (CLOSE)
Pr 28:27 he who *c* his eyes to them receives

CLOTHE (CLOTHED CLOTHES CLOTHING)
Ps 45: 3 *c* yourself with splendor
Isa 52: 1 *c* yourself with strength.
Ro 13:14 *c* yourselves with the Lord Jesus
Col 3:12 *c* yourselves with compassion,
1Pe 5: 5 *c* yourselves with humility

CLOTHED (CLOTHE)
Ps 30:11 removed my sackcloth and *c* me
104: 1 you are *c* with splendor
Pr 31:22 she is *c* in fine linen and purple.
31:25 She is *c* with strength and dignity;
Isa 61:10 For he has *c* me with garments
Lk 24:49 until you have been *c* with power
Gal 3:27 into Christ have *c* yourselves

CLOTHES (CLOTHE)
Dt 8: 4 Your *c* did not wear out
Mt 6:25 the body more important than *c?*
6:28 "And why do you worry about *c?*
27:35 they divided up his *c* by casting lots
Jn 11:44 Take off the grave *c* and let him go

CLOTHING (CLOTHE)
Dt 22: 5 A woman must not wear men's *c,*
Job 29:14 I put on righteousness as my *c;*
Ps 22:18 and cast lots for my *c.*

Mt 7:15 They come to you in sheep's *c,*
1Ti 6: 8 But if we have food and *c,*

CLOUD (CLOUDS)
Ex 13:21 them in a pillar of *c* to guide them
1Ki 18:44 *c* as small as a man's hand is rising
Pr 16:15 his favor is like a rain *c* in spring.
Isa 19: 1 See, the LORD rides on a swift *c*
Lk 21:27 of Man coming in a *c* with power
Heb 12: 1 by such a great *c* of witnesses,
Rev 14:14 seated on the *c* was one "like a son

CLOUDS (CLOUD)
Dt 33:26 and on the *c* in his majesty.
Ps 68: 4 extol him who rides on the *c*—
104: 3 He makes the *c* his chariot
Pr 25:14 Like *c* and wind without rain
Da 7:13 coming with the *c* of heaven.
Mt 24:30 of Man coming on the *c* of the sky,
26:64 and coming on the *c* of heaven."
Mk 13:26 coming in *c* with great power
1Th 4:17 with them in the *c* to meet the Lord
Rev 1: 7 Look, he is coming with the *c,*

CLUB
Pr 25:18 Like a *c* or a sword or a sharp arrow

CO-HEIRS* (INHERIT)
Ro 8:17 heirs of God and *c* with Christ,

COALS
Pr 25:22 you will heap burning *c* on his head
Ro 12:20 you will heap burning *c* on his head

COARSE*
Eph 5: 4 or *c* joking, which are out of place,

CODE*
Ro 2:27 even though you have the written *c*
2:29 by the Spirit, not by the written *c.*
7: 6 not in the old way of the written *c.*
Col 2:14 having canceled the written *c,*

COINS
Mt 26:15 out for him thirty silver *c.*
Lk 15: 8 suppose a woman has ten silver *c*

COLD
Pr 25:25 Like *c* water to a weary soul
Mt 10:42 if anyone gives even a cup of *c* water
24:12 the love of most will grow *c,*

COLLECTION
1Co 16: 1 Now about the *c* for God's people:

COLT
Zec 9: 9 on a *c,* the foal of a donkey.
Mt 21: 5 on a *c,* the foal of a donkey.'"

COMB
Ps 19:10 than honey from the *c.*

COMFORT* (COMFORTED COMFORTER COMFORTERS COMFORTING COMFORTS)
Ge 5:29 "He will *c* us in the labor
37:35 and daughters came to *c* him,
Ru 2:13 "You have given me *c*
1Ch 7:22 and his relatives came to *c* him.
Job 2:11 sympathize with him and *c* him.
7:13 When I think my bed will *c* me
16: 5 *c* from my lips would bring you
36:16 to the *c* of your table laden
Ps 23: 4 rod and your staff, they *c* me.
71:21 and *c* me once again.
119: 50 My *c* in my suffering is this:
119: 52 and I find *c* in them.
119: 76 May your unfailing love be my *c,*
119: 82 I say, "When will you *c* me?"
Isa 40: 1 *C, c* my people,
51: 3 The LORD will surely *c* Zion
51:19 who can *c* you?—
57:18 I will guide him and restore *c*
61: 2 to *c* all who mourn,
66:13 so will I *c* you;
Jer 16: 7 food to *c* those who mourn
31:13 I will give them *c* and joy instead
La 1: 2 there is none to *c* her.
1: 9 there was none to *c* her.
1:16 No one is near to *c* me,
1:17 but there is no one to *c* her.
1:21 but there is no one to *c* me.
2:13 that I may *c* you,
Eze 16:54 all you have done in giving them *c.*
Na 3: 7 Where can I find anyone to *c* you?"
Zec 1:17 and the LORD will again *c* Zion
10: 2 they give *c* in vain.
Lk 6:24 you have already received your *c.*
Jn 11:19 and Mary to *c* them in the loss
1Co 14: 3 encouragement and *c.*
2Co 1: 3 of compassion and the God of all *c,*
1: 4 so that we can *c* those

2Co 1: 4 with the *c* we ourselves have
1: 5 through Christ our *c* overflows.
1: 6 if we are comforted, it is for your *c*,
1: 6 it is for your *c* and salvation;
1: 7 so also you share in our *c*.
2: 7 you ought to forgive and *c* him,
7: 7 also by the *c* you had given him.
Php 2: 1 if any *c* from his love,
Col 4:11 and they have proved a *c* to me.

COMFORTED* (COMFORT)
Ge 24:67 Isaac was *c* after his mother's death
37:35 comfort him, but he refused to be *c*.
2Sa 12:24 Then David *c* his wife Bathsheba,
Job 42:11 They *c* and consoled him
Ps 77: 2 and my soul refused to be *c*.
86:17 have helped me and *c* me.
Isa 12: 1 and you have *c* me.
52: 9 for the LORD has *c* his people,
54:11 lashed by storms and not *c*,
66:13 and you will be *c* over Jerusalem."
Jer 31:15 and refusing to be *c*,
Mt 2:18 and refusing to be *c*,
5: 4 for they will be *c*.
Lk 16:25 but now he is *c* here and you are
Ac 20:12 man home alive and were greatly *c*.
2Co 1: 6 if we are *c*, it is for your comfort,
7: 6 *c* us by the coming of Titus,

COMFORTER* (COMFORT)
Ecc 4: 1 and they have no *c*;
4: 1 and they have no *c*.
Jer 8:18 O my *C* in sorrow,

COMFORTERS* (COMFORT)
Job 16: 2 miserable *c* are you all!
Ps 69:20 for *c*, but I found none.

COMFORTING* (COMFORT)
Isa 66:11 satisfied at her *c* breasts;
Zec 1:13 *c* words to the angel who talked
Jn 11:31 *c* her, noticed how quickly she got
1Th 2:12 *c* and urging you to live lives

COMFORTS* (COMFORT)
Job 29:25 I was like one who *c* mourners.
Isa 49:13 For the LORD *c* his people
51:12 "I, even I, am he who *c* you.
66:13 As a mother *c* her child,
2Co 1: 4 who *c* us in all our troubles,
7: 6 But God, who *c* the downcast,

COMMAND (COMMANDED COMMANDING COMMANDMENT COMMANDMENTS COMMANDS)
Ex 7: 2 You are to say everything I *c* you,
Nu 14:41 are you disobeying the LORD's *c*?
24:13 to go beyond the *c* of the LORD—
Dt 4: 2 Do not add to what I *c* you
8: 1 to follow every *c* I am giving you
12:32 See that you do all I *c* you;
15:11 I *c* you to be openhanded
30:16 For I *c* you today to love
32:46 so that you may *c* your children
Ps 91:11 For he will *c* his angels concerning
Pr 13:13 but he who respects a *c* is rewarded
Ecc 8: 2 Obey the king's *c*, I say,
Jer 1: 7 you to and say whatever I *c* you.
1:17 and say to them whatever I *c* you.
7:23 Walk in all the ways I *c* you,
11: 4 Obey me and do everything I *c* you
26: 2 Tell them everything I *c* you;
Joel 2:11 mighty are those who obey his *c*.
Mt 4: 6 He will *c* his angels concerning you
15: 3 why do you break the *c* of God
Lk 4:10 " 'He will *c* his angels concerning
Jn 14:15 love me, you will obey what I *c*.
15:12 My *c* is this: Love each other
15:14 friends if you do what I *c*.
15:17 This is my *c*: Love each other.
1Co 14:37 writing to you is the Lord's *c*.
Gal 5:14 law is summed up in a single *c*:
1Ti 1: 5 goal of this *c* is love, which comes
6:14 to you keep this *c* without spot
6:17 *C* those who are rich
Heb 11: 3 universe was formed at God's *c*,
2Pe 2:21 on the sacred *c* that was passed
3: 2 and the *c* given by our Lord
1Jn 2: 7 I am not writing you a new *c*
3:23 this is his *c*: to believe in the name
4:21 And he has given us this *c*:
2Jn : 6 his *c* is that you walk in love.

COMMANDED (COMMAND)
Ge 2:16 And the LORD God *c* the man,
7: 5 Noah did all that the LORD *c* him.
50:12 Jacob's sons did as he had *c* them:
Ex 7: 6 did just as the LORD *c* them.
19: 7 all the words the LORD had *c* him
Dt 4: 5 laws as the LORD my God *c* me,
6:24 The LORD *c* us to obey all these
Jos 1: 9 Have I not *c* you? Be strong
1:16 Whatever you have *c* us we will do,
2Sa 5:25 So David did as the LORD *c* him,
2Ki 17:13 the entire Law that I *c* your fathers
21: 8 careful to do everything I *c* them
2Ch 33: 8 do everything I *c* them concerning
Ps 33: 9 he *c*, and it stood firm.
78: 5 which he *c* our forefathers
148: 5 for he *c* and they were created.
Mt 28:20 to obey everything I have *c* you.
1Co 9:14 Lord has *c* that those who preach
1Jn 3:23 and to love one another as he *c* us.
2Jn : 4 in the truth, just as the Father *c* us.

COMMANDING (COMMAND)
2Ti 2: 4 he wants to please his *c* officer.

COMMANDMENT* (COMMAND)
Jos 22: 5 But be very careful to keep the *c*
Mt 22:36 which is the greatest *c* in the Law?"
22:38 This is the first and greatest *c*.
Mk 12:31 There is no *c* greater than these."
Lk 23:56 the Sabbath in obedience to the *c*.
Jn 13:34 "A new *c* I give you: Love one
Ro 7: 8 the opportunity afforded by the *c*,
7: 9 when the *c* came, sin sprang to life
7:10 that the very *c* that was intended
7:11 and through the *c* put me to death.
7:11 the opportunity afforded by the *c*,
7:12 and the *c* is holy, righteous
7:13 through the *c* sin might become
13: 9 and whatever other *c* there may be,
Eph 6: 2 which is the first *c* with a promise
Heb 9:19 Moses had proclaimed every *c*

COMMANDMENTS* (COMMAND)
Ex 20: 6 who love me and keep my *c*.
34:28 of the covenant—the Ten *C*.
Dt 4:13 to you his covenant, the Ten *C*,
5:10 who love me and keep my *c*.
5:22 These are the *c* the LORD
6: 6 These *c* that I give you today are
9:10 were all the *c* the LORD
10: 4 The Ten *C* he had proclaimed
Ecc 12:13 Fear God and keep his *c*,
Mt 5:19 one of the least of these *c*
19:17 If you want to enter life, obey the *c*
22:40 the Prophets hang on these two *c*."
Mk 10:19 You know the *c*: 'Do not murder,
12:28 "Of all the *c*, which is the most
Lk 1: 6 observing all the Lord's *c*
18:20 You know the *c*: 'Do not commit
Ro 13: 9 The *c*, "Do not commit adultery,"
Eph 2:15 in his flesh the law with its *c*
Rev 12:17 those who obey God's *c*
14:12 part of the saints who obey God's *c*

COMMANDS (COMMAND)
Ex 24:12 and *c* I have written for their
25:22 give you all my *c* for the Israelites.
34:32 gave them all the *c* the LORD had
Lev 22:31 "Keep my *c* and follow them.
Nu 15:39 and so you will remember all the *c*
Dt 7: 9 those who love him and keep his *c*.
7:11 Therefore, take care to follow the *c*
11: 1 decrees, his laws and his *c* always.
11:27 the blessing if you obey the *c*
28: 1 carefully follow all his *c* I give you
30:10 LORD your God and keep his *c*
Jos 22: 5 to walk in all his ways, to obey his *c*
1Ki 2: 3 and keep his decrees and *c*,
8:58 in all his ways and to keep the *c*,
8:61 to live by his decrees and obey his *c*
1Ch 28: 7 unswerving in carrying out my *c*
29:19 devotion to keep your *c*,
2Ch 31:21 in obedience to the law and the *c*,
Ne 1: 5 those who love him and obey his *c*,
Ps 78: 7 but would keep his *c*.
112: 1 who finds great delight in his *c*.
119: 10 do not let me stray from your *c*.
119: 32 I run in the path of your *c*,
119: 35 Direct me in the path of your *c*,
119: 47 for I delight in your *c*
119: 48 I lift up my hands to your *c*,
119: 73 me understanding to learn your *c*.
119: 86 All your *c* are trustworthy;
119: 96 but your *c* are boundless.
119: 98 Your *c* make me wiser
119:115 that I may keep the *c* of my God!
119:127 Because I love your *c*
119:131 longing for your *c*.
119:143 but your *c* are my delight.
119:151 and all your *c* are true.
119:172 for all your *c* are righteous.
119:176 for I have not forgotten your *c*.
Pr 2: 1 and store up my *c* within you,
3: 1 but keep my *c* in your heart,
6:23 For these *c* are a lamp,
10: 8 The wise in heart accept *c*,
Isa 48:18 you had paid attention to my *c*,
Da 9: 4 all who love him and obey his *c*,
Mt 5:19 teaches these *c* will be called great
Mk 7: 8 You have let go of the *c* of God
7: 9 way of setting aside the *c* of God
Jn 14:21 Whoever has my *c* and obeys them,
15:10 If you obey my *c*, you will remain
Ac 17:30 but now he *c* all people everywhere
1Co 7:19 Keeping God's *c* is what counts.
1Jn 2: 3 come to know him if we obey his *c*.
2: 4 but does not do what he *c* is a liar,
3:22 we obey his *c* and do what pleases
3:24 Those who obey his *c* live in him,
5: 2 loving God and carrying out his *c*.
5: 3 And his *c* are not burdensome,
5: 3 This is love for God: to obey his *c*.
2Jn : 6 that we walk in obedience to his *c*.

COMMEMORATE
Ex 12:14 "This is a day you are to *c*;

COMMEND* (COMMENDABLE COMMENDED COMMENDS)
Ps 145: 4 One generation will *c* your works
Ecc 8:15 So I *c* the enjoyment of life,
Ro 13: 3 do what is right and he will *c* you.
16: 1 I *c* to you our sister Phoebe,
2Co 3: 1 beginning to *c* ourselves again?
4: 2 the truth plainly we *c* ourselves
5:12 trying to *c* ourselves to you again,
6: 4 as servants of God we *c* ourselves
10:12 with some who *c* themselves.
1Pe 2:14 and to *c* those who do right.

COMMENDABLE* (COMMEND)
1Pe 2:19 For it is *c* if a man bears up
2:20 you endure it, this is *c* before God.

COMMENDED* (COMMEND)
Ne 11: 2 The people *c* all the men who
Job 29:11 and those who saw me *c* me,
Lk 16: 8 master *c* the dishonest manager
Ac 15:40 *c* by the brothers to the grace
2Co 12:11 I ought to have been *c* by you,
Heb 11: 2 This is what the ancients were *c* for
11: 4 By faith he was *c* as a righteous
11: 5 he was *c* as one who pleased God.
11:39 These were all *c* for their faith,

COMMENDS* (COMMEND)
Pr 15: 2 of the wise *c* knowledge,
2Co 10:18 but the one whom the Lord *c*.
10:18 not the one who *c* himself who is

COMMIT (COMMITS COMMITTED)
Ex 20:14 "You shall not *c* adultery.
Dt 5:18 "You shall not *c* adultery.
1Sa 7: 3 and *c* yourselves to the LORD
Ps 31: 5 Into your hands I *c* my spirit;
37: 5 *C* your way to the LORD;
Pr 16: 3 *C* to the LORD whatever you do,
Mt 5:27 that it was said, 'Do not *c* adultery.'
5:32 causes her to *c* adultery,
19:18 do not *c* adultery, do not steal,
Mk 10:19 do not *c* adultery, do not steal,
Lk 18:20 'Do not *c* adultery, do not murder,
23:46 into your hands I *c* my spirit."
Ac 20:32 I *c* you to God and to the word
Ro 2:22 do you *c* adultery? You who abhor
2:22 that people should not *c* adultery,
13: 9 "Do not *c* adultery,"
1Co 10: 8 We should not *c* sexual immorality,
Jas 2:11 do not *c* adultery but do *c* murder,
1Pe 4:19 to God's will should *c* themselves
Rev 2:22 I will make those who *c* adultery

COMMITS (COMMIT)
Pr 6:32 man who *c* adultery lacks
29:22 a hot-tempered one *c* many sins.
Ecc 8:12 a wicked man *c* a hundred crimes
Eze 18:12 He *c* robbery.
18:14 who sees all the sins his father *c*,
18:24 from his righteousness and *c* sin
18:26 from his righteousness and *c* sin,
22:11 you one man *c* a detestable offense
Mt 5:32 the divorced woman *c* adultery.
19: 9 marries another woman *c* adultery
Mk 10:11 marries another woman *c* adultery
10:12 another man, she *c* adultery."
Lk 16:18 a divorced woman *c* adultery.
16:18 marries another woman *c* adultery,

COMMITTED (COMMIT)
Nu 5: 7 and must confess the sin he has *c*.
1Ki 8:61 But your hearts must be fully *c*
15:14 Asa's heart was fully *c*
2Ch 16: 9 those whose hearts are fully *c*
Mt 5:28 lustfully has already *c* adultery
11:27 "All things have been *c* to me

Lk 10:22 "All things have been *c* to me
Ac 14:23 *c* them to the Lord,
14:26 where they had been *c* to the grace
1Co 9:17 I am simply discharging the trust *c*
2Co 5:19 And he has *c* to us the message
1Pe 2:22 "He *c* no sin,
Rev 17: 2 the kings of the earth *c* adultery
18: 3 of the earth *c* adultery with her,
18: 9 kings of the earth who *c* adultery

COMMON
Ge 11: 1 had one language and a *c* speech.
Lev 10:10 between the holy and the *c*,
Pr 22: 2 Rich and poor have this in *c*:
29:13 the oppressor have this in *c*:
Ac 2:44 together and had everything in *c*.
1Co 10:13 has seized you except what is *c*
2Co 6:14 and wickedness have in *c*?

COMPANION (COMPANIONS)
Ps 55:13 my *c*, my close friend,
55:20 My *c* attacks his friends;
Pr 13:20 but a *c* of fools suffers harm.
28: 7 a *c* of gluttons disgraces his father.
29: 3 *c* of prostitutes squanders his
Rev 1: 9 your brother and *c* in the suffering

COMPANIONS (COMPANION)
Ps 45: 7 your God, has set you above your *c*
Pr 18:24 A man of many *c* may come to ruin
Heb 1: 9 your God, has set you above your *c*

COMPANY
Ps 14: 5 present in the *c* of the righteous.
Pr 21:16 comes to rest in the *c* of the dead.
24: 1 do not desire their *c*;
Jer 15:17 I never sat in the *c* of revelers,
1Co 15:33 "Bad *c* corrupts good character."

COMPARE* (COMPARED COMPARING COMPARISON)
Job 28:17 Neither gold nor crystal can *c*
28:19 The topaz of Cush cannot *c* with it;
39:13 but they cannot *c* with the pinions
Ps 86: 8 no deeds can *c* with yours.
89: 6 skies above can *c* with the LORD?
Pr 3:15 nothing you desire can *c* with her.
8:11 nothing you desire can *c* with her.
Isa 40:18 To whom, then, will you *c* God?
40:18 What image will you *c* him to?
40:25 "To whom will you *c* me?
46: 5 "To whom will you *c* me
La 2:13 With what can I *c* you,
Eze 31: 8 *c* with its branches—
Da 1:13 Then *c* our appearance with that
Mt 11:16 "To what can I *c* this generation?
Lk 7:31 I *c* the people of this generation?
13:18 What shall I *c* it to? It is like
13:20 What shall I *c* the kingdom of God
2Co 10:12 and *c* themselves with themselves,
10:12 or *c* ourselves with some who

COMPARED* (COMPARE)
Jdg 8: 2 What have I accomplished *c* to you
8: 3 What was I able to do *c* to you?"
Isa 46: 5 you liken me that we may be *c*?
Eze 31: 2 Who can be *c* with you in majesty?
31:18 the trees of Eden can be *c* with you
Php 3: 8 I consider everything a loss *c*

COMPARING* (COMPARE)
Ro 8:18 present sufferings are not worth *c*
2Co 8: 8 the sincerity of your love by *c* it
Gal 6: 4 without *c* himself to somebody else

COMPARISON* (COMPARE)
2Co 3:10 now in *c* with the surpassing glory.

COMPASSION* (COMPASSIONATE COMPASSIONS)
Ex 33:19 I will have *c* on whom I will have *c*.
Dt 13:17 he will show you mercy, have *c*
28:54 man among you will have no *c*
30: 3 restore your fortunes and have *c*
32:36 and have *c* on his servants
Jdg 2:18 for the LORD had *c* on them
1Ki 3:26 son was alive was filled with *c*
2Ki 13:23 and had *c* and showed concern
2Ch 30: 9 and your children will be shown *c*
Ne 9:19 of your great *c* you did not
9:27 and in your great *c* you gave them
9:28 in your *c* you delivered them time
Ps 51: 1 according to your great *c*
77: 9 Has he in anger withheld his *c*?"
90:13 Have *c* on your servants.
102: 13 You will arise and have *c* on Zion,
103: 4 and crowns you with love and *c*.
103: 13 As a father has *c* on his children,
103: 13 so the LORD has *c*
116: 5 our God is full of *c*.
Ps 119: 77 Let your *c* come to me that I may
119:156 Your *c* is great, O LORD;
135: 14 and have *c* on his servants.
145: 9 he has *c* on all he has made.
Isa 13:18 will they look with *c* on children.
14: 1 The LORD will have *c* on Jacob;
27:11 so their Maker has no *c* on them,
30:18 he rises to show you *c*.
49:10 He who has *c* on them will guide
49:13 and will have *c* on his afflicted ones
49:15 and have no *c* on the child she has
51: 3 and will look with *c* on all her ruins
54: 7 with deep *c* I will bring you back.
54: 8 I will have *c* on you,"
54:10 says the LORD, who has *c* on you.
60:10 in favor I will show you *c*.
63: 7 to his *c* and many kindnesses.
63:15 and *c* are withheld from us.
Jer 12:15 I will again have *c* and will bring
13:14 *c* to keep me from destroying them
15: 6 I can no longer show *c*.
21: 7 show them no mercy or pity or *c*.'
30:18 and have *c* on his dwellings;
31:20 I have great *c* for him,"
33:26 restore their fortunes and have *c*
42:12 I will show you *c* so that he will
42:12 so that he will have *c* on you
La 3:32 he brings grief, he will show *c*,
Eze 9: 5 without showing pity or *c*.
16: 5 or had *c* enough to do any
39:25 and will have *c* on all the people
Hos 2:19 in love and *c*.
11: 8 all my *c* is aroused.
13:14 "I will have no *c*,
14: 3 for in you the fatherless find *c*."
Am 1:11 stifling all *c*,
Jnh 3: 9 with *c* turn from his fierce anger
3:10 he had *c* and did not bring
Mic 7:19 You will again have *c* on us;
Zec 7: 9 show mercy and *c* to one another.
10: 6 because I have *c* on them.
Mal 3:17 as in *c* a man spares his son who
Mt 9:36 When he saw the crowds, he had *c*
14:14 he had *c* on them and healed their
15:32 "I have *c* for these people;
20:34 Jesus had *c* on them and touched
Mk 1:41 with *c*, Jesus reached out his hand
6:34 and saw a large crowd, he had *c*
8: 2 "I have *c* for these people;
Lk 15:20 and was filled with *c* for him;
Ro 9:15 and I will have *c* on whom I have *c*
2Co 1: 3 the Father of *c* and the God
Php 2: 1 and *c*, then make my joy complete
Col 3:12 clothe yourselves with *c*, kindness,
Jas 5:11 The Lord is full of *c* and mercy.

COMPASSIONATE* (COMPASSION)
Ex 22:27 out to me, I will hear, for I am *c*.
34: 6 the LORD, the *c* and gracious God
2Ch 30: 9 LORD your God is gracious and *c*.
Ne 9:17 gracious and *c*, slow to anger
Ps 86:15 O Lord, are a *c* and gracious God,
103: 8 The LORD is *c* and gracious,
111: 4 the LORD is gracious and *c*.
112: 4 the gracious and *c* and righteous
145: 8 The LORD is gracious and *c*,
La 4:10 With their own hands *c* women
Joel 2:13 for he is gracious and *c*,
Jnh 4: 2 that you are a gracious and *c* God,
Eph 4:32 Be kind and *c* to one another,
1Pe 3: 8 love as brothers, be *c* and humble.

COMPASSIONS* (COMPASSION)
La 3:22 for his *c* never fail.

COMPELLED (COMPULSION)
Ac 20:22 "And now, *c* by the Spirit,
1Co 9:16 I cannot boast, for I am *c* to preach.

COMPELS (COMPULSION)
Job 32:18 and the spirit within me *c* me;
2Co 5:14 For Christ's love *c* us, because we

COMPETENCE* (COMPETENT)
2Co 3: 5 but our *c* comes from God.

COMPETENT* (COMPETENCE)
Ro 15:14 and *c* to instruct one another.
1Co 6: 2 are you not *c* to judge trivial cases?
2Co 3: 5 Not that we are *c* in ourselves to claim
3: 6 He has made us *c* as ministers

COMPETES*
1Co 9:25 Everyone who *c* in the games goes
2Ti 2: 5 Similarly, if anyone *c* as an athlete,
2: 5 unless he *c* according to the rules.

COMPLACENCY* (COMPLACENT)
Pr 1:32 and the *c* of fools will destroy them
Eze 30: 9 ships to frighten Cush out of her *c*.

COMPLACENT* (COMPLACENCY)
Isa 32: 9 You women who are so *c*,
32:11 Tremble, you *c* women;
Am 6: 1 Woe to you who are *c* in Zion,
Zep 1:12 and punish those who are *c*,

COMPLAINING*
Php 2:14 Do everything without *c* or arguing

COMPLETE
Dt 16:15 your hands, and your joy will be *c*.
Jn 3:29 That joy is mine, and it is now *c*.
15:11 and that your joy may be *c*.
16:24 will receive, and your joy will be *c*.
17:23 May they be brought to *c* unity
Ac 20:24 *c* the task the Lord Jesus has given
Php 2: 2 then make my joy *c*
Col 4:17 to it that you *c* the work you have
Jas 1: 4 so that you may be mature and *c*,
2:22 his faith was made *c* by what he did
1Jn 1: 4 We write this to make our joy *c*.
2: 5 God's love is truly made *c* in him.
4:12 and his love is made *c* in us.
4:17 love is made *c* among us
2Jn :12 to face, so that our joy may be *c*.

COMPLIMENTS*
Pr 23: 8 and will have wasted your *c*.

COMPREHEND* (COMPREHENDED)
Job 28:13 Man does not *c* its worth;
Ecc 8:17 No one can *c* what goes
8:17 he knows, he cannot really *c* it.

COMPREHENDED* (COMPREHEND)
Job 38:18 Have you *c* the vast expanses

COMPULSION (COMPELLED COMPELS)
2Co 9: 7 not reluctantly or under *c*,

CONCEAL (CONCEALED CONCEALS)
Ps 40:10 I do not *c* your love and your truth
Pr 25: 2 It is the glory of God to *c* a matter;

CONCEALED (CONCEAL)
Jer 16:17 nor is their sin *c* from my eyes.
Mt 10:26 There is nothing *c* that will not be
Mk 4:22 and whatever is *c* is meant
Lk 8:17 nothing *c* that will not be known
12: 2 There is nothing *c* that will not be

CONCEALS* (CONCEAL)
Pr 10:18 He who *c* his hatred has lying lips,
28:13 He who *c* his sins does not prosper,

CONCEIT* (CONCEITED CONCEITS)
Isa 16: 6 her overweening pride and *c*,
Jer 48:29 her overweening pride and *c*,
Php 2: 3 out of selfish ambition or vain *c*,

CONCEITED* (CONCEIT)
1Sa 17:28 I know how *c* you are and how
Ro 11:25 brothers, so that you may not be *c*:
12:16 Do not be *c*.
2Co 12: 7 To keep me from becoming *c*
Gal 5:26 Let us not become *c*, provoking
1Ti 3: 6 or he may become *c* and fall
6: 4 he is *c* and understands nothing.
2Ti 3: 4 of the good, treacherous, rash, *c*,

CONCEITS* (CONCEIT)
Ps 73: 7 evil *c* of their minds know no

CONCEIVED (CONCEIVES)
Ps 51: 5 from the time my mother *c* me.
Mt 1:20 what is *c* in her is from the Holy
1Co 2: 9 no mind has *c*
Jas 1:15 after desire has *c*, it gives birth

CONCEIVES* (CONCEIVED)
Ps 7:14 *c* trouble gives birth

CONCERN* (CONCERNED)
Ge 39: 6 he did not *c* himself with anything
39: 8 "my master does not *c* himself
1Sa 23:21 "The LORD bless you for your *c*
2Ki 13:23 and had compassion and showed *c*
Job 9:21 I have no *c* for myself;
19: 4 my error remains my *c* alone.
Ps 131: 1 I do not *c* myself with great matters
Pr 29: 7 but the wicked have no such *c*.
Eze 36:21 I had *c* for my holy name, which
Ac 15:14 God at first showed his *c* by taking
18:17 But Gallio showed no *c* whatever.
1Co 7:32 I would like you to be free from *c*.
12:25 that its parts should have equal *c*
2Co 7: 7 your deep sorrow, your ardent *c*
7:11 what alarm, what longing, what *c*,
8:16 of Titus the same *c* I have for you.
11:28 of my *c* for all the churches.
Php 4:10 at last you have renewed your *c*

CONCERNED (CONCERN)
Ex 2:25 Israelites and was *c* about them.
Ps 142: 4 no one is *c* for me.
Jnh 4:10 "You have been *c* about this vine,
4:11 Should I not be *c* about that great
1Co 7:32 An unmarried man is *c* about
9: 9 Is it about oxen that God is *c?*
Php 4:10 you have been *c,* but you had no

CONCESSION*
1Co 7: 6 I say this as a *c,* not as a command.

CONDEMN* (CONDEMNATION CONDEMNED CONDEMNING CONDEMNS)
Job 9:20 innocent, my mouth would *c* me;
10: 2 I will say to God: Do not *c* me,
34:17 Will you *c* the just and mighty One
34:29 if he remains silent, who can *c* him?
40: 8 Would you *c* me to justify yourself?
Ps 94:21 and *c* the innocent to death.
109: 7 and may his prayers *c* him.
109: 31 from those who *c* him.
Isa 50: 9 Who is he that will *c* me?
Mt 12:41 with this generation and *c* it;
12:42 with this generation and *c* it;
20:18 They will *c* him to death
Mk 10:33 They will *c* him to death
Lk 6:37 Do not *c,* and you will not be
11:31 men of this generation and *c* them;
11:32 with this generation and *c* it;
Jn 3:17 Son into the world to *c* the world,
7:51 "Does our law *c* anyone
8:11 "Then neither do I *c* you,"
12:48 very word which I spoke will *c* him
Ro 2:27 yet obeys the law will *c* you who,
14: 3 everything must not *c* the man who
14:22 is the man who does not *c* himself
2Co 7: 3 this to *c* you; I have said
1Jn 3:20 presence whenever our hearts *c* us.
3:21 if our hearts do not *c* us,

CONDEMNATION* (CONDEMN)
Jer 42:18 of *c* and reproach; you will never
44:12 and horror, of *c* and reproach.
Ro 3: 8 may result"? Their *c* is deserved.
5:16 followed one sin and brought *c,*
5:18 of one trespass was *c* for all men,
8: 1 there is now no *c* for those who are
2Pe 2: 3 Their *c* has long been hanging
Jude : 4 certain men whose *c* was written

CONDEMNED* (CONDEMN)
Dt 13:17 of those *c* things shall be found
Job 32: 3 to refute Job, and yet had *c* him.
Ps 34:21 the foes of the righteous will be *c.*
34:22 will be *c* who takes refuge in him.
37:33 let them be *c* when brought to trial.
79:11 preserve those *c* to die.
102: 20 and release those *c* to death."
Mt 12: 7 you would not have *c* the innocent.
12:37 and by your words you will be *c."*
23:33 How will you escape being *c* to hell
27: 3 betrayed him, saw that Jesus was *c,*
Mk 14:64 They all *c* him as worthy of death.
16:16 whoever does not believe will be *c.*
Lk 6:37 condemn, and you will not be *c.*
Jn 3:18 Whoever believes in him is not *c,*
3:18 does not believe stands *c* already
5:24 has eternal life and will not be *c;*
5:29 who have done evil will rise to be *c.*
8:10 Has no one *c* you?" "No one, sir,"
16:11 prince of this world now stands *c.*
Ac 25:15 against him and asked that he be *c.*
Ro 3: 7 why am I still *c* as a sinner?"
8: 3 And so he *c* sin in sinful man,
14:23 But the man who has doubts is *c*
1Co 4: 9 like men *c* to die in the arena.
11:32 disciplined so that we will not be *c*
Gal 1: 8 let him be eternally *c!* As we have
1: 9 let him be eternally *c!* Am I now
2Th 2:12 that all will be *c* who have not
Tit 2: 8 of speech that cannot be *c,*
Heb 11: 7 By his faith he *c* the world
Jas 5: 6 You have *c* and murdered innocent
5:12 and your "No," no, or you will be *c*
2Pe 2: 6 if he *c* the cities of Sodom
Rev 19: 2 He has *c* the great prostitute

CONDEMNING* (CONDEMN)
Dt 25: 1 the innocent and *c* the guilty.
1Ki 8:32 *c* the guilty and bringing
Pr 17:15 the guilty and *c* the innocent—
Ac 13:27 yet in *c* him they fulfilled the words
Ro 2: 1 judge the other, you are *c* yourself,

CONDEMNS* (CONDEMN)
Job 15: 6 Your own mouth *c* you, not mine;
Pr 12: 2 but the LORD *c* a crafty man.
Ro 8:34 Who is he that *c?* Christ Jesus,
2Co 3: 9 the ministry that *c* men is glorious,

CONDITION
Pr 27:23 Be sure you know the *c*

CONDUCT (CONDUCTED CONDUCTS)
Pr 10:23 A fool finds pleasure in evil *c,*
20:11 by whether his *c* is pure and right.
21: 8 but the *c* of the innocent is upright.
Ecc 6: 8 how to *c* himself before others?
Jer 4:18 "Your own *c* and actions
17:10 to reward a man according to his *c,*
Eze 7: 3 I will judge you according to your *c*
Php 1:27 *c* yourselves in a manner worthy
1Ti 3:15 to *c* themselves in God's household

CONDUCTED* (CONDUCT)
2Co 1:12 testifies that we have *c* ourselves

CONDUCTS* (CONDUCT)
Ps 112: 5 who *c* his affairs with justice.

CONFESS* (CONFESSED CONFESSES CONFESSING CONFESSION)
Lev 5: 5 he must *c* in what way he has
16:21 and *c* over it all the wickedness
26:40 " 'But if they will *c* their sins
Nu 5: 7 must *c* the sin he has committed.
1Ki 8:33 back to you and *c* your name,
8:35 toward this place and *c* your name
2Ch 6:24 they turn back and *c* your name,
6:26 toward this place and *c* your name
Ne 1: 6 I *c* the sins we Israelites, including
Ps 32: 5 I said, "I will *c*
38:18 I *c* my iniquity;
Jn 1:20 fail to *c,* but confessed freely,
12:42 they would not *c* their faith
Ro 10: 9 That if you *c* with your mouth,
10:10 it is with your mouth that you *c*
14:11 every tongue will *c* to God.' "
Php 2:11 every tongue *c* that Jesus Christ is
Heb 3: 1 and high priest whom we *c.*
13:15 the fruit of lips that *c* his name.
Jas 5:16 Therefore *c* your sins to each other
1Jn 1: 9 If we *c* our sins, he is faithful

CONFESSED* (CONFESS)
1Sa 7: 6 day they fasted and there they *c,*
Ne 9: 2 in their places and *c* their sins
Da 9: 4 to the LORD my God and *c:*
Jn 1:20 but *c* freely, "I am not the Christ."
Ac 19:18 and openly *c* their evil deeds.

CONFESSES* (CONFESS)
Pr 28:13 whoever *c* and renounces them
2Ti 2:19 and, "Everyone who *c* the name

CONFESSING* (CONFESS)
Ezr 10: 1 While Ezra was praying and *c,*
Da 9:20 *c* my sin and the sin
Mt 3: 6 *C* their sins, they were baptized
Mk 1: 5 *C* their sins, they were baptized

CONFESSION* (CONFESS)
Ezr 10:11 Now make *c* to the LORD,
Ne 9: 3 and spent another quarter in *c*
2Co 9:13 obedience that accompanies your *c*
1Ti 6:12 called when you made your good *c*
6:13 Pontius Pilate made the good *c,*

CONFIDENCE* (CONFIDENT)
Jdg 9:26 and its citizens put their *c* in him.
2Ki 18:19 On what are you basing this *c*
2Ch 32: 8 And the people gained *c*
32:10 On what are you basing your *c,*
Job 4: 6 Should not your piety be your *c*
Ps 71: 5 my *c* since my youth.
Pr 3:26 for the LORD will be your *c*
3:32 but takes the upright into his *c.*
11:13 A gossip betrays a *c,*
20:19 A gossip betrays a *c;*
25: 9 do not betray another man's *c,*
31:11 Her husband has full *c* in her
Isa 32:17 will be quietness and *c* forever.
36: 4 On what are you basing this *c*
Jer 17: 7 whose *c* is in him.
49:31 which lives in *c,"*
Eze 29:16 a source of *c* for the people of Israel
Mic 7: 5 put no *c* in a friend.
2Co 2: 3 I had *c* in all of you, that you would
3: 4 Such *c* as this is ours
7: 4 I have great *c* in you; I take great
7:16 I am glad I can have complete *c*
8:22 so because of his great *c* in you.
Eph 3:12 God with freedom and *c.*
Php 3: 3 and who put no *c* in the flesh—
3: 4 I myself have reasons for such *c.*
3: 4 reasons to put *c* in the flesh,
2Th 3: 4 We have *c* in the Lord that you are
Heb 3:14 till the end the *c* we had at first.
Heb 4:16 the throne of grace with *c,*
10:19 since we have *c* to enter the Most
10:35 So do not throw away your *c;*
13: 6 So we say with *c,*
1Jn 3:21 we have *c* before God and receive
4:17 us so that we will have *c* on the day
5:14 This is the *c* we have

CONFIDENT* (CONFIDENCE)
Job 6:20 because they had been *c;*
Ps 27: 3 even then will I be *c.*
27:13 I am still *c* of this:
Lk 18: 9 To some who were *c*
2Co 1:15 Because I was *c* of this, I planned
5: 6 Therefore we are always *c*
5: 8 We are *c,* I say, and would prefer
9: 4 ashamed of having been so *c.*
10: 7 If anyone is *c* that he belongs
Gal 5:10 I am *c* in the Lord that you will
Php 1: 6 day until now, being *c* of this,
2:24 I am *c* in the Lord that I myself will
Phm :21 *C* of your obedience, I write to you,
Heb 6: 9 we are *c* of better things
1Jn 2:28 that when he appears we may be *c*

CONFIDES*
Ps 25:14 The LORD *c* in those who fear him

CONFORM* (CONFORMED CONFORMITY CONFORMS)
Ro 12: 2 Do not *c* any longer to the pattern
1Pe 1:14 do not *c* to the evil desires you had

CONFORMED* (CONFORM)
Eze 5: 7 *c* to the standards of the nations
11:12 but have *c* to the standards
Ro 8:29 predestined to be *c* to the likeness

CONFORMITY* (CONFORM)
Eph 1:11 in *c* with the purpose of his will,

CONFORMS* (CONFORM)
1Ti 1:11 to the sound doctrine that *c*

CONQUEROR* (CONQUERORS)
Mic 1:15 I will bring a *c* against you
Rev 6: 2 he rode out as a *c* bent on conquest.

CONQUERORS (CONQUEROR)
Ro 8:37 than *c* through him who loved us.

CONSCIENCE* (CONSCIENCE-STRICKEN CONSCIENCES CONSCIENTIOUS)
Ge 20: 5 I have done this with a clear *c*
20: 6 I know you did this with a clear *c,*
1Sa 25:31 have on his *c* the staggering burden
Job 27: 6 my *c* will not reproach me as long
Ac 23: 1 to God in all good *c* to this day."
24:16 to keep my *c* clear before God
Ro 9: 1 my *c* confirms it in the Holy Spirit
13: 5 punishment but also because of *c.*
1Co 4: 4 My *c* is clear, but that does not
8: 7 since their *c* is weak, it is defiled.
8:10 with a weak *c* sees you who have
8:12 in this way and wound their weak *c*
10:25 without raising questions of *c,*
10:27 you without raising questions of *c.*
10:28 man who told you and for *c'* sake—
10:29 freedom be judged by another's *c?*
10:29 the other man's *c,* I mean,
2Co 1:12 Our *c* testifies that we have
4: 2 to every man's *c* in the sight of God
5:11 and I hope it is also plain to your *c.*
1Ti 1: 5 and a good *c* and a sincere faith.
1:19 holding on to faith and a good *c.*
3: 9 truths of the faith with a clear *c.*
2Ti 1: 3 as my forefathers did, with a clear *c*
Heb 9: 9 able to clear the *c* of the worshiper.
10:22 to cleanse us from a guilty *c*
13:18 We are sure that we have a clear *c*
1Pe 3:16 and respect, keeping a clear *c,*
3:21 the pledge of a good *c* toward God.

CONSCIENCE-STRICKEN* (CONSCIENCE)
1Sa 24: 5 David was *c* for having cut
2Sa 24:10 David was *c* after he had counted

CONSCIENCES* (CONSCIENCE)
Ro 2:15 their *c* also bearing witness,
1Ti 4: 2 whose *c* have been seared
Tit 1:15 their minds and *c* are corrupted.
Heb 9:14 cleanse our *c* from acts that lead

CONSCIENTIOUS* (CONSCIENCE)
2Ch 29:34 for the Levites had been more *c*

CONSCIOUS*
Ro 3:20 through the law we become *c* of sin
1Pe 2:19 of unjust suffering because he is *c*

CONSECRATE (CONSECRATED)
Ex 13: 2 "*C* to me every firstborn male.
40: 9 *c* it and all its furnishings,
Lev 20: 7 " '*C* yourselves and be holy,
25:10 *C* the fiftieth year and proclaim
1Ch 15:12 fellow Levites are to *c* yourselves

CONSECRATED (CONSECRATE)
Ex 29:43 and the place will be *c* by my glory.
Lev 8:30 So he *c* Aaron and his garments
2Ch 7:16 *c* this temple so that my Name may
Lk 2:23 is to be *c* to the Lord"),
1Ti 4: 5 because it is *c* by the word of God

CONSENT
1Co 7: 5 except by mutual *c* and for a time,

CONSIDER (CONSIDERATE CONSIDERED CONSIDERS)
1Sa 12:24 *c* what great things he has done
16: 7 "Do not *c* his appearance
2Ch 19: 6 "*C* carefully what you do,
Job 37:14 stop and *c* God's wonders.
Ps 8: 3 When I *c* your heavens,
77:12 and *c* all your mighty deeds.
107: 43 and *c* the great love of the LORD.
143: 5 and *c* what your hands have done.
Pr 6: 6 *c* its ways and be wise!
20:25 and only later to *c* his vows.
Ecc 7:13 *C* what God has done:
Lk 12:24 *C* the ravens: They do not sow
12:27 about the rest? "*C* how the lilies
Php 2: 3 but in humility *c* others better
3: 8 I *c* everything a loss compared
Heb 10:24 And let us *c* how we may spur one
Jas 1: 2 *C* it pure joy, my brothers,

CONSIDERATE* (CONSIDER)
Tit 3: 2 to be peaceable and *c*,
Jas 3:17 then peace-loving, *c*, submissive,
1Pe 2:18 only to those who are good and *c*,
3: 7 in the same way be *c* as you live

CONSIDERED (CONSIDER)
Job 1: 8 "Have you *c* my servant Job?
2: 3 "Have you *c* my servant Job?
Ps 44:22 we are *c* as sheep to be slaughtered.
Isa 53: 4 yet we *c* him stricken by God,
Ro 8:36 we are *c* as sheep to be slaughtered

CONSIDERS (CONSIDER)
Pr 31:16 She *c* a field and buys it;
Ro 14: 5 One man *c* one day more sacred
Jas 1:26 If anyone *c* himself religious

CONSIST (CONSISTS)
Lk 12:15 a man's life does not *c*

CONSISTS (CONSIST)
Eph 5: 9 fruit of the light *c* in all goodness,

CONSOLATION
Ps 94:19 your *c* brought joy to my soul.

CONSPIRE
Ps 2: 1 Why do the nations *c*

CONSTANT
Dt 28:66 You will live in *c* suspense,
Pr 19:13 wife is like a *c* dripping.
27:15 a *c* dripping on a rainy day;
Ac 27:33 "you have been in *c* suspense
Heb 5:14 by *c* use have trained themselves

CONSTRUCTIVE*
1Co 10:23 but not everything is *c*.

CONSULT
Pr 15:12 he will not *c* the wise.
Gal 1:16 I did not *c* any man, nor did I go up

CONSUME (CONSUMES CONSUMING)
Jn 2:17 "Zeal for your house will *c* me."

CONSUMES (CONSUME)
Ps 69: 9 for zeal for your house *c* me,

CONSUMING (CONSUME)
Dt 4:24 For the LORD your God is a *c* fire,
Heb 12:29 and awe, for our "God is a *c* fire."

CONTAIN* (CONTAINED CONTAINS)
1Ki 8:27 the highest heaven, cannot *c* you.
2Ch 2: 6 the highest heavens, cannot *c* him?
6:18 the highest heavens, cannot *c* you.
Ecc 8: 8 power over the wind to *c* it;
2Pe 3:16 His letters *c* some things that are

CONTAINED (CONTAIN)
Heb 9: 4 This ark *c* the gold jar of manna,

CONTAINS (CONTAIN)
Pr 15: 6 of the righteous *c* great treasure,

CONTAMINATES*
2Co 7: 1 from everything that *c* body

CONTEMPT
Pr 14:31 He who oppresses the poor shows *c*
17: 5 He who mocks the poor shows *c*
18: 3 When wickedness comes, so does *c*
Da 12: 2 others to shame and everlasting *c*.
Mal 1: 6 O priests, who show *c* for my name.
Ro 2: 4 Or do you show *c* for the riches
Gal 4:14 you did not treat me with *c*
1Th 5:20 do not treat prophecies with *c*.

CONTEND (CONTENDED CONTENDING CONTENTIOUS)
Ge 6: 3 "My Spirit will not *c*
Ps 35: 1 *C*, O LORD, with those who
Isa 49:25 I will *c* with those who *c* with you,
Jude : 3 you to *c* for the faith that was once

CONTENDED (CONTEND)
Php 4: 3 help these women who have *c*

CONTENDING* (CONTEND)
Php 1:27 *c* as one man for the faith

CONTENT* (CONTENTMENT)
Jos 7: 7 If only we had been *c* to stay
Pr 13:25 The righteous eat to their hearts' *c*,
19:23 one rests *c*, untouched by trouble.
Ecc 4: 8 yet his eyes were not *c*
Lk 3:14 don't accuse people falsely—be *c*
Php 4:11 to be *c* whatever the circumstances
4:12 I have learned the secret of being *c*
1Ti 6: 8 and clothing, we will be *c* with that.
Heb 13: 5 and be *c* with what you have,

CONTENTIOUS* (CONTEND)
1Co 11:16 If anyone wants to be *c* about this,

CONTENTMENT* (CONTENT)
Job 36:11 and their years in *c*.
SS 8:10 like one bringing *c*.
1Ti 6: 6 But godliness with *c* is great gain.

CONTEST*
Heb 10:32 in a great *c* in the face of suffering.

CONTINUAL (CONTINUE)
Pr 15:15 but the cheerful heart has a *c* feast.
Eph 4:19 of impurity, with a *c* lust for more.

CONTINUE (CONTINUAL CONTINUES CONTINUING)
1Ki 8:23 servants who *c* wholeheartedly
2Ch 6:14 servants who *c* wholeheartedly
Ps 36:10 *C* your love to those who know you
Ac 13:43 urged them to *c* in the grace of God
Ro 11:22 provided that you *c* in his kindness.
Gal 3:10 Cursed is everyone who does not *c*
Php 2:12 *c* to work out your salvation
Col 1:23 if you *c* in your faith, established
2: 6 received Christ Jesus as Lord, *c*
1Ti 2:15 if they *c* in faith, love and holiness
2Ti 3:14 *c* in what you have learned
1Jn 2:28 And now, dear children, *c* in him,
3: 9 born of God will *c* to sin,
5:18 born of God does not *c* to sin;
2Jn : 9 and does not *c* in the teaching
Rev 22:11 and let him who is holy *c* to be holy
22:11 let him who does right *c* to do right;

CONTINUES (CONTINUE)
Ps 100: 5 *c* through all generations.
119: 90 Your faithfulness *c*
2Co 10:15 Our hope is that, as your faith *c*
1Jn 3: 6 No one who *c* to sin has

CONTINUING (CONTINUE)
Ro 13: 8 the *c* debt to love one another,

CONTRIBUTION (CONTRIBUTIONS)
Ro 15:26 pleased to make a *c* for the poor

CONTRIBUTIONS (CONTRIBUTION)
2Ch 24:10 all the people brought their *c* gladly
31:12 they faithfully brought in the *c*,

CONTRITE*
Ps 51:17 a broken and *c* heart,
Isa 57:15 also with him who is *c* and lowly
57:15 and to revive the heart of the *c*.
66: 2 he who is humble and *c* in spirit,

CONTROL (CONTROLLED CONTROLS SELF-CONTROL SELF-CONTROLLED)
Pr 29:11 a wise man keeps himself under *c*.
1Co 7: 9 But if they cannot *c* themselves,
1Co 7:37 but has *c* over his own will,
1Th 4: 4 you should learn to *c* his own body

CONTROLLED (CONTROL)
Ps 32: 9 but must be *c* by bit and bridle
Ro 8: 6 but the mind *c* by the Spirit is life
8: 8 Those *c* by the sinful nature cannot

CONTROLS* (CONTROL)
Job 37:15 you know how God *c* the clouds
Pr 16:32 a man who *c* his temper

CONTROVERSIES*
Ac 26: 3 with all the Jewish customs and *c*.
1Ti 1: 4 These promote *c* rather
6: 4 He has an unhealthy interest in *c*
Tit 3: 9 But avoid foolish *c* and genealogies

CONVERSATION
Col 4: 6 Let your *c* be always full of grace,

CONVERT
1Ti 3: 6 He must not be a recent *c*,

CONVICT (CONVICTION)
Pr 24:25 with those who *c* the guilty,
Jn 16: 8 he will *c* the world of guilt in regard
Jude :15 and to *c* all the ungodly

CONVICTION* (CONVICT)
1Th 1: 5 the Holy Spirit and with deep *c*.

CONVINCE* (CONVINCED CONVINCING)
Ac 28:23 and tried to *c* them about Jesus

CONVINCED* (CONVINCE)
Ge 45:28 "I'm *c*! My son Joseph is still alive.
Lk 16:31 will not be *c* even if someone rises
Ac 19:26 and hear how this fellow Paul has *c*
26: 9 "I too was *c* that I ought
26:26 I am *c* that none of this has escaped
28:24 Some were *c* by what he said,
Ro 2:19 if you are *c* that you are a guide
8:38 For I am *c* that neither death
14: 5 Each one should be fully *c*
14:14 I am fully *c* that no food is unclean
15:14 I myself am *c*, my brothers,
1Co 14:24 he will be *c* by all that he is a sinner
2Co 5:14 we are *c* that one died for all,
Php 1:25 *C* of this, I know that I will remain,
2Ti 1:12 and am *c* that he is able
3:14 have learned and have become *c*

CONVINCING* (CONVINCE)
Ac 1: 3 and gave many *c* proofs that he was

COOLNESS*
Pr 25:13 Like the *c* of snow at harvest time

COPIES (COPY)
Heb 9:23 for the *c* of the heavenly things

COPY (COPIES)
Dt 17:18 for himself on a scroll a *c* of this law
Heb 8: 5 They serve at a sanctuary that is a *c*
9:24 sanctuary that was only a *c*

CORBAN*
Mk 7:11 received from me is *C*' (that is,

CORD (CORDS)
Jos 2:18 you have tied this scarlet *c*
Ecc 4:12 *c* of three strands is not quickly

CORDS (CORD)
Pr 5:22 the *c* of his sin hold him fast.
Isa 54: 2 lengthen your *c*,
Hos 11: 4 them with *c* of human kindness,

CORINTH
Ac 18: 1 Paul left Athens and went to *C*.
1Co 1: 2 To the church of God in *C*,
2Co 1: 1 To the church of God in *C*,

CORNELIUS*
Roman to whom Peter preached; first Gentile Christian (Ac 10).

CORNER (CORNERS)
Ru 3: 9 "Spread the *c* of your garment
Pr 21: 9 Better to live on a *c* of the roof
25:24 Better to live on a *c* of the roof
Ac 26:26 because it was not done in a *c*.

CORNERS (CORNER)
Mt 6: 5 on the street *c* to be seen by men.
22: 9 Go to the street *c* and invite

CORNERSTONE* (STONE)
Job 38: 6 or who laid its *c*—
Isa 28:16 a precious *c* for a sure foundation;
Jer 51:26 rock will be taken from you for a *c*,

Zec 10: 4 From Judah will come the c,
Eph 2:20 Christ Jesus himself as the chief c.
1Pe 2: 6 a chosen and precious c,

CORRECT* (CORRECTED CORRECTING CORRECTION CORRECTIONS CORRECTS)
Job 6:26 Do you mean to c what I say,
40: 2 contends with the Almighty c him?
Jer 10:24 C me, LORD, but only with justice
2Ti 4: 2 c, rebuke and encourage—

CORRECTED* (CORRECT)
Pr 29:19 A servant cannot be c

CORRECTING* (CORRECT)
2Ti 3:16 c and training in righteousness,

CORRECTION* (CORRECT)
Lev 26:23 things you do not accept my c
Job 36:10 He makes them listen to c
Pr 5:12 How my heart spurned c!
10:17 whoever ignores c leads others
12: 1 but he who hates c is stupid.
13:18 but whoever heeds c is honored.
15: 5 whoever heeds c shows prudence.
15:10 he who hates c will die.
15:12 A mocker resents c;
15:32 whoever heeds c gains
29:15 The rod of c imparts wisdom,
Jer 2:30 they did not respond to c.
5: 3 crushed them, but they refused c.
7:28 LORD its God or responded to c.
Zep 3: 2 she accepts no c.
3: 7 you will fear me / and accept c!'

CORRECTIONS* (CORRECT)
Pr 6:23 and the c of discipline

CORRECTS* (CORRECT)
Job 5:17 "Blessed is the man whom God c;
Pr 9: 7 Whoever c a mocker invites insult;

CORRUPT (CORRUPTED CORRUPTION CORRUPTS)
Ge 6:11 Now the earth was c in God's sight
Ps 14: 1 They are c, their deeds are vile;
14: 3 they have together become c;
Pr 4:24 keep c talk far from your lips.
6:12 who goes about with a c mouth,
19:28 A c witness mocks at justice,

CORRUPTED (CORRUPT)
2Co 7: 2 wronged no one, we have c no one,
Tit 1:15 but to those who are c and do not

CORRUPTION (CORRUPT)
2Pe 1: 4 escape the c in the world caused
2:20 If they have escaped the c

CORRUPTS* (CORRUPT)
Ecc 7: 7 and a bribe c the heart.
1Co 15:33 "Bad company c good character."
Jas 3: 6 It c the whole person, sets

COST (COSTS)
Nu 16:38 sinned at the c of their lives.
Pr 4: 7 Though it c all you have, get
7:23 little knowing it will c him his life.
Isa 55: 1 milk without money and without c.
Lk 14:28 and estimate the c to see
Rev 21: 6 to drink without c from the spring

COSTS (COST)
Pr 6:31 it c him all the wealth of his house.

COUNCIL
Ps 89: 7 In the c of the holy ones God is
107: 32 and praise him in the c of the elders

COUNSEL (COUNSELOR COUNSELS)
1Ki 22: 5 "First seek the c of the LORD."
2Ch 18: 4 "First seek the c of the LORD."
Job 38: 2 "Who is this that darkens my c
42: 3 'Who is this that obscures my c
Ps 1: 1 walk in the c of the wicked
73:24 You guide me with your c,
107: 11 despised the c of the Most High.
Pr 8:14 C and sound judgment are mine;
15:22 Plans fail for lack of c,
27: 9 from his earnest c.
Isa 28:29 wonderful in c and magnificent
1Ti 5:14 So I c younger widows to marry,
Rev 3:18 I c you to buy from me gold refined

COUNSELOR (COUNSEL)
Isa 9: 6 Wonderful C, Mighty God,
Jn 14:16 he will give you another C to be
14:26 But the C, the Holy Spirit,
15:26 "When the C comes, whom I will
16: 7 the C will not come to you;
Ro 11:34 Or who has been his c?"

COUNSELS (COUNSEL)
Ps 16: 7 I will praise the LORD, who c me;

COUNT (COUNTED COUNTING COUNTS)
Ps 22:17 I can c all my bones;
Ro 4: 8 whose sin the Lord will never c
6:11 c yourselves dead to sin
2Th 1:11 that our God may c you worthy

COUNTED (COUNT)
Ac 5:41 because they had been c worthy
2Th 1: 5 and as a result you will be c worthy

COUNTERFEIT*
2Th 2: 9 displayed in all kinds of c miracles,
1Jn 2:27 not c— just as it has taught you,

COUNTING (COUNT)
2Co 5:19 not c men's sins against them.

COUNTRY
Pr 28: 2 When a c is rebellious, it has many
29: 4 By justice a king gives a c stability,
Isa 66: 8 Can a c be born in a day
Lk 15:13 off for a distant c and there
Jn 4:44 prophet has no honor in his own c.)
2Co 11:26 in danger in the c, in danger at sea;
Heb 11:14 looking for a c of their own.

COUNTRYMEN
2Co 11:26 danger from my own c, in danger

COUNTS (COUNT)
Jn 6:63 The Spirit gives life; the flesh c
1Co 7:19 God's commands is what c.
Gal 5: 6 only thing that c is faith expressing

COURAGE* (COURAGEOUS)
Jos 2:11 everyone's c failed because of you,
5: 1 and they no longer had the c
2Sa 4: 1 he lost c, and all Israel became
7:27 So your servant has found c
1Ch 17:25 So your servant has found c to pray
2Ch 15: 8 son of Oded the prophet, he took c.
19:11 Act with c, and may the LORD be
Ezr 7:28 I took c and gathered leading men
10: 4 We will support you, so take c
Ps 107: 26 in their peril their c melted away.
Eze 22:14 Will your c endure or your hands
Da 11:25 and c against the king of the South.
Mt 14:27 said to them: "Take c!
Mk 6:50 spoke to them and said, "Take c!
Ac 4:13 When they saw the c of Peter
23:11 "Take c! As you have testified
27:22 now I urge you to keep up your c,
27:25 So keep up your c, men,
1Co 16:13 stand firm in the faith; be men of c;
Php 1:20 will have sufficient c so that now
Heb 3: 6 if we hold on to our c and the hope

COURAGEOUS* (COURAGE)
Dt 31: 6 Be strong and c.
31: 7 of all Israel, "Be strong and c,
31:23 son of Nun: "Be strong and c,
Jos 1: 6 and c, because you will lead these
1: 7 Be strong and very c.
1: 9 commanded you? Be strong and c.
1:18 Only be strong and c!"
10:25 Be strong and c.
1Ch 22:13 Be strong and c.
28:20 "Be strong and c, and do the work.
2Ch 26:17 priest with eighty other c priests
32: 7 with these words: "Be strong and c.

COURSE
Ps 19: 5 a champion rejoicing to run his c.
Pr 2: 8 for he guards the c of the just
15:21 of understanding keeps a straight c.
16: 9 In his heart a man plans his c,
17:23 to pervert the c of justice.
Jas 3: 6 sets the whole c of his life on fire,

COURT (COURTS)
Pr 22:22 and do not crush the needy in c,
25: 8 do not bring hastily to c,
Mt 5:25 adversary who is taking you to c.
1Co 4: 3 judged by you or by any human c;

COURTS (COURT)
Ps 84:10 Better is one day in your c
100: 4 and his c with praise;
Am 5:15 maintain justice in the c.
Zec 8:16 and sound judgment in your c;

COURTYARD
Ex 27: 9 "Make a c for the tabernacle.

COUSIN
Col 4:10 as does Mark, the c of Barnabas.

COVENANT (COVENANTS)
Ge 9: 9 "I now establish my c with you
17: 2 I will confirm my c between me
Ex 19: 5 if you obey me fully and keep my c,
24: 7 Then he took the Book of the C
Dt 4:13 declared to you his c, the Ten
29: 1 in addition to the c he had made
Jdg 2: 1 'I will never break my c with you,
1Sa 23:18 of them made a c before the LORD
1Ki 8:21 in which is the c of the LORD that
8:23 you who keep your c of love
2Ki 23: 2 the words of the Book of the C,
1Ch 16:15 He remembers his c forever,
2Ch 6:14 you who keep your c of love
34:30 the words of the Book of the C,
Ne 1: 5 who keeps his c of love
Job 31: 1 "I made a c with my eyes
Ps 105: 8 He remembers his c forever,
Pr 2:17 ignored the c she made before God
Isa 42: 6 you to be a c for the people
61: 8 make an everlasting c with them.
Jer 11: 2 "Listen to the terms of this c
31:31 "when I will make a new c
31:32 It will not be like the c
31:33 "This is the c I will make
Eze 37:26 I will make a c of peace with them;
Da 9:27 He will confirm a c with many
Hos 6: 7 Like Adam, they have broken the c
Mal 2:14 the wife of your marriage c.
3: 1 of the c, whom you desire,
Mt 26:28 blood of the c, which is poured out
Mk 14:24 "This is my blood of the c,
Lk 22:20 "This cup is the new c in my blood,
1Co 11:25 "This cup is the new c in my blood;
2Co 3: 6 as ministers of a new c—
Gal 4:24 One c is from Mount Sinai
Heb 8: 6 as the c of which he is mediator is
8: 8 when I will make a new c
9:15 Christ is the mediator of a new c,
12:24 to Jesus the mediator of a new c,

COVENANTS (COVENANT)
Ro 9: 4 theirs the divine glory, the c,
Gal 4:24 for the women represent two c.

COVER (COVER-UP COVERED COVERING COVERINGS COVERS)
Ex 25:17 "Make an atonement c of pure gold
25:21 Place the c on top of the ark
33:22 and c you with my hand
Lev 16: 2 in the cloud over the atonement c.
Ps 32: 5 and did not c up my iniquity.
91: 4 He will c you with his feathers,
Hos 10: 8 say to the mountains, "C us!"
Lk 23:30 and to the hills, "C us!" '
1Co 11: 6 If a woman does not c her head,
11: 6 shaved off, she should c her head.
11: 7 A man ought not to c his head,
Jas 5:20 and c over a multitude of sins.

COVER-UP* (COVER)
1Pe 2:16 but do not use your freedom as a c

COVERED (COVER)
Ps 32: 1 whose sins are c.
85: 2 and c all their sins.
Isa 6: 2 With two wings they c their faces,
51:16 c you with the shadow of my hand
Ro 4: 7 whose sins are c.
1Co 11: 4 with his head c dishonors his head.

COVERING (COVER)
1Co 11:15 For long hair is given to her as a c.

COVERINGS (COVER)
Ge 3: 7 and made c for themselves.
Pr 31:22 She makes c for her bed;

COVERS (COVER)
Pr 10:12 but love c over all wrongs.
17: 9 He who c over an offense promotes
2Co 3:15 Moses is read, a veil c their hearts.
1Pe 4: 8 love c over a multitude of sins.

COVET* (COVETED COVETING COVETOUS)
Ex 20:17 You shall not c your neighbor's
20:17 "You shall not c your neighbor's
34:24 and no one will c your land
Dt 5:21 "You shall not c your neighbor's
7:25 Do not c the silver and gold
Mic 2: 2 They c fields and seize them,
Ro 7: 7 if the law had not said, "Do not c."
13: 9 "Do not steal," "Do not c,"
Jas 4: 2 c, but you cannot have what you

COVETED* (COVET)
Jos 7:21 weighing fifty shekels, I c them
Ac 20:33 I have not c anyone's silver or gold

COVETING
Ro 7: 7 what *c* really was if the law

COVETOUS* (COVET)
Ro 7: 8 in me every kind of *c* desire.

COWARDLY*
Rev 21: 8 But the *c*, the unbelieving, the vile,

COWS
Ge 41: 2 of the river there came up seven *c*,
Ex 25: 5 skins dyed red and hides of sea *c*;
Nu 4: 6 are to cover this with hides of sea *c*,
1Sa 6: 7 Hitch the *c* to the cart,

CRAFTINESS* (CRAFTY)
Job 5:13 He catches the wise in their *c*,
1Co 3:19 "He catches the wise in their *c*";
Eph 4:14 and *c* of men in their deceitful

CRAFTSMAN
Pr 8:30 Then I was the *c* at his side.

CRAFTY* (CRAFTINESS)
Ge 3: 1 the serpent was more *c* than any
1Sa 23:22 They tell me he is very *c*.
Job 5:12 He thwarts the plans of the *c*,
15: 5 you adopt the tongue of the *c*.
Pr 7:10 like a prostitute and with *c* intent.
12: 2 but the LORD condemns a *c* man.
14:17 and a *c* man is hated.
2Co 12:16 *c* fellow that I am, I caught you

CRAVE* (CRAVED CRAVES CRAVING CRAVINGS)
Nu 11: 4 with them began to *c* other food,
Dt 12:20 you *c* meat and say, "I would like
Pr 23: 3 Do not *c* his delicacies,
23: 6 do not *c* his delicacies;
31: 4 not for rulers to *c* beer,
Mic 7: 1 none of the early figs that I *c*.
1Pe 2: 2 newborn babies, *c* pure spiritual

CRAVED* (CRAVE)
Nu 11:34 the people who had *c* other food.
Ps 78:18 by demanding the food they *c*.
78:29 for he had given them what they *c*.
78:30 turned from the food they *c*,

CRAVES* (CRAVE)
Pr 13: 4 The sluggard *c* and gets nothing,
21:10 The wicked man *c* evil;
21:26 All day long he *c* for more,

CRAVING* (CRAVE)
Job 20:20 he will have no respite from his *c*;
Ps 106: 14 In the desert they gave in to their *c*;
Pr 10: 3 but he thwarts the *c* of the wicked.
13: 2 the unfaithful have a *c* for violence.
21:25 The sluggard's *c* will be the death
Jer 2:24 sniffing the wind in her *c*—

CRAVINGS* (CRAVE)
Ps 10: 3 He boasts of the *c* of his heart;
Eph 2: 3 gratifying the *c* of our sinful nature
1Jn 2:16 in the world—the *c* of sinful man,

CRAWL
Ge 3:14 You will *c* on your belly

CREATE* (CREATED CREATES CREATING CREATION CREATOR)
Ps 51:10 *C* in me a pure heart, O God,
Isa 4: 5 Then the LORD will *c* over all
45: 7 I bring prosperity and *c* disaster;
45: 7 I form the light and *c* darkness,
45:18 he did not *c* it to be empty,
65:17 "Behold, I will *c* / new heavens
65:18 for I will *c* Jerusalem to be a delight
65:18 forever in what I will *c*,
Jer 31:22 The LORD will *c* a new thing
Mal 2:10 one Father? Did not one God *c* us?
Eph 2:15 His purpose was to *c*

CREATED* (CREATE)
Ge 1: 1 In the beginning God *c* the heavens
1:21 God *c* the great creatures of the sea
1:27 So God *c* man in his own image,
1:27 in the image of God he *c* him;
1:27 male and female he *c* them.
2: 4 and the earth when they were *c*.
5: 1 When God *c* man, he made him
5: 2 He *c* them male and female
5: 2 when they were *c*, he called them
6: 7 whom I have *c*, from the face
Dt 4:32 from the day God *c* man
Ps 89:12 You *c* the north and the south;
89:47 what futility you have *c* all men!
102: 18 a people not yet *c* may praise
104: 30 you send your Spirit, / they are *c*,
139: 13 For you *c* my inmost being;
148: 5 for he commanded and they were *c*
Isa 40:26 Who *c* all these?
41:20 that the Holy One of Israel has *c* it.
42: 5 he who *c* the heavens and stretched
43: 1 he who *c* you, O Jacob,
43: 7 whom I *c* for my glory,
45: 8 I, the LORD, have *c* it.
45:12 and *c* mankind upon it.
45:18 he who *c* the heavens,
48: 7 They are *c* now, and not long ago;
54:16 And it is I who have *c* the destroyer
54:16 "See, it is I who *c* the blacksmith
57:16 the breath of man that I have *c*.
Eze 21:30 In the place where you were *c*,
28:13 the day you were *c* they were
28:15 ways from the day you were *c*
Mk 13:19 when God *c* the world, until now—
Ro 1:25 and served *c* things rather
1Co 11: 9 neither was man *c* for woman,
Eph 2:10 *c* in Christ Jesus to do good works,
3: 9 hidden in God, who *c* all things.
4:24 *c* to be like God in true
Col 1:16 For by him all things were *c*:
1:16 all things were *c* by him
1Ti 4: 3 which God *c* to be received
4: 4 For everything God *c* is good,
Heb 12:27 *c* things—so that what cannot be
Jas 1:18 a kind of firstfruits of all he *c*.
Rev 4:11 and by your will they were *c*
4:11 for you *c* all things,
10: 6 who *c* the heavens and all that is

CREATES* (CREATE)
Am 4:13 *c* the wind,

CREATING* (CREATE)
Ge 2: 3 the work of *c* that he had done.
Isa 57:19 *c* praise on the lips of the mourners

CREATION* (CREATE)
Hab 2:18 he who makes it trusts in his own *c*;
Mt 13:35 hidden since the *c* of the world."
25:34 for you since the *c* of the world.
Mk 10: 6 of *c* God 'made them male
16:15 and preach the good news to all *c*.
Jn 17:24 me before the *c* of the world.
Ro 1:20 For since the *c* of the world God's
8:19 The *c* waits in eager expectation
8:20 For the *c* was subjected
8:21 in hope that the *c* itself will be
8:22 that the whole *c* has been groaning
8:39 depth, nor anything else in all *c*,
2Co 5:17 he is a new *c*; the old has gone,
Gal 6:15 anything; what counts is a new *c*.
Eph 1: 4 us in him before the *c* of the world
Col 1:15 God, the firstborn over all *c*.
Heb 4: 3 finished since the *c* of the world.
4:13 Nothing in all *c* is hidden
9:11 that is to say, not a part of this *c*.
9:26 times since the *c* of the world.
1Pe 1:20 chosen before the *c* of the world,
2Pe 3: 4 as it has since the beginning of *c*."
Rev 3:14 true witness, the ruler of God's *c*.
13: 8 slain from the *c* of the world.
17: 8 life from the *c* of the world will be

CREATOR* (CREATE)
Ge 14:19 *C* of heaven and earth.
14:22 God Most High, *C* of heaven
Dt 32: 6 Is he not your Father, your *C*,
Ecc 12: 1 Remember your *C*
Isa 27:11 and their *C* shows them no favor.
40:28 the *C* of the ends of the earth.
43:15 Israel's *C*, your King."
Mt 19: 4 the beginning the *C* 'made them
Ro 1:25 created things rather than the *C*—
Col 3:10 in knowledge in the image of its *C*.
1Pe 4:19 themselves to their faithful *C*

CREATURE (CREATURES)
Lev 17:11 For the life of a *c* is in the blood,
17:14 the life of every *c* is its blood.
Ps 136: 25 and who gives food to every *c*.
Eze 1:15 beside each *c* with its four faces.
Rev 4: 7 The first living *c* was like a lion,

CREATURES (CREATURE)
Ge 6:19 bring into the ark two of all living *c*,
8:21 again will I destroy all living *c*,
Ps 104: 24 the earth is full of your *c*.
Eze 1: 5 was what looked like four living *c*.

CREDIT (CREDITED CREDITOR CREDITS)
Lk 6:33 what *c* is that to you? Even
Ro 4:24 to whom God will *c* righteousness
1Pe 2:20 it to your *c* if you receive a beating

CREDITED (CREDIT)
Ge 15: 6 and he *c* it to him as righteousness.
Ps 106: 31 This was *c* to him as righteousness
Eze 18:20 of the righteous man will be *c*
Ro 4: 3 and it was *c* to him as righteousness
4: 4 his wages are not *c* to him as a gift,
4: 5 his faith is *c* as righteousness.
4: 9 saying that Abraham's faith was *c*
4:23 The words "it was *c*
Gal 3: 6 and it was *c* to him as righteousness
Php 4:17 for what may be *c* to your account.
Jas 2:23 and it was *c* to him as righteousness

CREDITOR (CREDIT)
Dt 15: 2 Every *c* shall cancel the loan he has

CREDITS (CREDIT)
Ro 4: 6 whom God *c* righteousness apart

CRETANS (CRETE)
Tit 1:12 "*C* are always liars, evil brutes,

CRETE (CRETANS)
Ac 27:12 harbor in *C*, facing both southwest

CRIED (CRY)
Ex 2:23 groaned in their slavery and *c* out,
14:10 They were terrified and *c* out
Nu 20:16 but when we *c* out to the LORD,
Jos 24: 7 But they *c* to the LORD for help,
Jdg 3: 9 But when they *c* out to the LORD,
3:15 Again the Israelites *c* out
4: 3 they *c* to the LORD for help.
6: 6 the Israelites that they *c* out
10:12 Maonites oppressed you and you *c*
1Sa 7: 9 He *c* out to the LORD
12: 8 they *c* to the LORD for help,
12:10 They *c* out to the LORD and said,
Ps 18: 6 I *c* to my God for help.

CRIMINALS
Lk 23:32 both *c*, were also led out with him

CRIMSON
Isa 1:18 though they are red as *c*,
63: 1 with his garments stained *c*?

CRIPPLED
2Sa 9: 3 of Jonathan; he is *c* in both feet."
Mk 9:45 better for you to enter life *c*

CRISIS*
1Co 7:26 of the present *c*, I think that it is

CRITICISM*
2Co 8:20 We want to avoid any *c*

CROOKED*
Dt 32: 5 but a warped and *c* generation.
2Sa 22:27 to the *c* you show yourself shrewd.
Ps 18:26 to the *c* you show yourself shrewd.
125: 5 But those who turn to *c* ways
Pr 2:15 whose paths are *c*
5: 6 her paths are *c*, but she knows it
8: 8 none of them is *c* or perverse.
10: 9 he who takes *c* paths will be found
Ecc 7:13 what he has made *c*?
Isa 59: 8 have turned them into *c* roads;
La 3: 9 he has made my paths *c*.
Lk 3: 5 The *c* roads shall become straight,
Php 2:15 children of God without fault in a *c*

CROP (CROPS)
Mt 13: 8 where it produced a *c*— a hundred,
21:41 share of the *c* at harvest time."

CROPS (CROP)
Pr 3: 9 with the firstfruits of all your *c*;
10: 5 He who gathers *c* in summer is
28: 3 like a driving rain that leaves no *c*.
2Ti 2: 6 the first to receive a share of the *c*.

CROSS (CROSSED CROSSING)
Dt 4:21 swore that I would not *c* the Jordan
12:10 But you will *c* the Jordan
Mt 10:38 and anyone who does not take his *c*
16:24 and take up his *c* and follow me.
Mk 8:34 and take up his *c* and follow me.
Lk 9:23 take up his *c* daily and follow me.
14:27 anyone who does not carry his *c*
Jn 19:17 Carrying his own *c*, he went out
Ac 2:23 to death by nailing him to the *c*.
1Co 1:17 lest the *c* of Christ be emptied
1:18 the message of the *c* is foolishness
Gal 5:11 offense of the *c* has been abolished.
6:12 persecuted for the *c* of Christ.
6:14 in the *c* of our Lord Jesus Christ,
Eph 2:16 both of them to God through the *c*,
Php 2: 8 even death on a *c*!
3:18 as enemies of the *c* of Christ.
Col 1:20 through his blood, shed on the *c*.
2:14 he took it away, nailing it to the *c*.
2:15 triumphing over them by the *c*.

Heb 12: 2 set before him endured the *c*,

CROSSED (CROSS)
Jos 4: 7 When it *c* the Jordan, the waters
Jn 5:24 he has *c* over from death to life.

CROSSING (CROSS)
Ge 48:14 he was the younger, and *c* his arms,

CROSSROADS (ROAD)
Jer 6:16 "Stand at the *c* and look;

CROUCHING
Ge 4: 7 sin is *c* at your door; it desires

CROWD (CROWDS)
Ex 23: 2 Do not follow the *c* in doing wrong.

CROWDS (CROWD)
Mt 9:36 he saw the *c*, he had compassion

CROWED (CROWS)
Mt 26:74 the man!" Immediately a rooster *c*.

CROWN (CROWNED CROWNS)
Pr 4: 9 present you with a *c* of splendor."
10: 6 Blessings *c* the head
12: 4 noble character is her husband's *c*,
16:31 Gray hair is a *c* of splendor;
17: 6 Children's children are a *c*
Isa 35:10 everlasting joy will *c* their heads.
51:11 everlasting joy will *c* their heads.
61: 3 to bestow on them a *c* of beauty
62: 3 You will be a *c* of splendor
Eze 16:12 and a beautiful *c* on your head.
Zec 9:16 like jewels in a *c*.
Mt 27:29 and then twisted together a *c* of thorns
Mk 15:17 then twisted together a *c* of thorns
Jn 19: 2 The soldiers twisted together a *c*
19: 5 When Jesus came out wearing the *c*
1Co 9:25 it to get a *c* that will last forever.
9:25 it to get a *c* that will not last;
Php 4: 1 and long for, my joy and *c*,
1Th 2:19 or the *c* in which we will glory
2Ti 2: 5 he does not receive the victor's *c*
4: 8 store for me the *c* of righteousness,
Jas 1:12 he will receive the *c*
1Pe 5: 4 you will receive the *c*
Rev 2:10 and I will give you the *c* of life.
3:11 so that no one will take your *c*.
14:14 a son of man" with a *c* of gold

CROWNED* (CROWN)
Ps 8: 5 and *c* him with glory and honor.
Pr 14:18 the prudent are *c* with knowledge.
SS 3:11 crown with which his mother *c* him
Heb 2: 7 you *c* him with glory and honor
2: 9 now *c* with glory and honor

CROWNS (CROWN)
Ps 103: 4 and *c* me with love and compassion
149: 4 he *c* the humble with salvation.
Pr 11:26 blessing *c* him who is willing to sell.
Rev 4: 4 and had *c* of gold on their heads.
4:10 They lay their *c* before the throne
12: 3 ten horns and seven *c* on his heads.
19:12 and on his head are many *c*.

CROWS (CROWED)
Mt 26:34 this very night, before the rooster *c*

CRUCIFIED* (CRUCIFY)
Mt 20:19 to be mocked and flogged and *c*.
26: 2 of Man will be handed over to be *c*
27:26 and handed him over to be *c*.
27:35 When they had *c* him, they divided
27:38 Two robbers were *c* with him,
27:44 same way the robbers who were *c*
28: 5 looking for Jesus, who was *c*.
Mk 15:15 and handed him over to be *c*.
15:24 And they *c* him.
15:25 the third hour when they *c* him.
15:27 They *c* two robbers with him,
15:32 Those *c* with him also heaped
16: 6 for Jesus the Nazarene, who was *c*.
Lk 23:23 insistently demanded that he be *c*,
23:33 *c* him, along with the criminals—
24: 7 be *c* and on the third day be raised
24:20 sentenced to death, and they *c* him;
Jn 19:16 him over to them to be *c*.
19:18 Here they *c* him, and with him two
19:20 for the place where Jesus was *c* was
19:23 When the soldiers *c* Jesus,
19:32 of the first man who had been *c*
19:41 At the place where Jesus was *c*,
Ac 2:36 whom you *c*, both Lord and Christ
4:10 whom you *c* but whom God raised
Ro 6: 6 For we know that our old self was *c*
1Co 1:13 Is Christ divided? Was Paul *c*
1:23 but we preach Christ *c*: a stumbling
2: 2 except Jesus Christ and him *c*.
2: 8 they would not have *c* the Lord
2Co 13: 4 to be sure, he was *c* in weakness,
Gal 2:20 I have been *c* with Christ
3: 1 Christ was clearly portrayed as *c*.
5:24 Christ Jesus have *c* the sinful
6:14 which the world has been *c*
Rev 11: 8 where also their Lord was *c*.

CRUCIFY* (CRUCIFIED CRUCIFYING)
Mt 23:34 Some of them you will kill and *c*;
27:22 They all answered, "*C* him!" "Why
27:23 they shouted all the louder, "*C* him
27:31 Then they led him away to *c* him.
Mk 15:13 "*C* him!" they shouted.
15:14 they shouted all the louder, "*C* him
15:20 Then they led him out to *c* him.
Lk 23:21 they kept shouting, "*C* him! *C* him
Jn 19: 6 they shouted, "*C*! *C*!"
19: 6 "You take him and *c* him.
19:10 either to free you or to *c* you?"
19:15 Crucify him!" "Shall I *c* your king
19:15 away! Take him away! *C* him!"

CRUCIFYING* (CRUCIFY)
Heb 6: 6 to their loss they are *c* the Son

CRUSH (CRUSHED)
Ge 3:15 he will *c* your head,
Isa 53:10 it was the LORD's will to *c* him
Ro 16:20 The God of peace will soon *c* Satan

CRUSHED (CRUSH)
Ps 34:18 and saves those who are *c* in spirit.
Pr 17:22 but a *c* spirit dries up the bones.
18:14 but a *c* spirit who can bear?
Isa 53: 5 he was *c* for our iniquities;
2Co 4: 8 not *c*; perplexed, but not in despair;

CRY (CRIED)
Ex 2:23 *c* for help because of their slavery
Ps 5: 2 Listen to my *c* for help,
34:15 and his ears are attentive to their *c*;
40: 1 he turned to me and heard my *c*.
130: 1 Out of the depths I *c* to you,
Pr 21:13 to the *c* of the poor,
La 2:18 *c* out to the Lord.
Hab 2:11 The stones of the wall will *c* out,
Lk 19:40 keep quiet, the stones will *c* out."

CUNNING
2Co 11: 3 deceived by the serpent's *c*,
Eph 4:14 and by the *c* and craftiness of men

CUP
Ps 23: 5 my *c* overflows.
Isa 51:22 from that *c*, the goblet of my wrath,
51:22 the *c* that made you stagger;
Mt 10:42 if anyone gives even a *c* of cold water
20:22 "Can you drink the *c* I am going
23:25 You clean the outside of the *c*
23:26 First clean the inside of the *c*
26:27 Then he took the *c*, gave thanks
26:39 may this *c* be taken from me.
26:42 possible for this *c* to be taken away
Mk 9:41 anyone who gives you a *c* of water
10:38 "Can you drink the *c* I drink
10:39 "You will drink the *c* I drink
14:23 Then he took the *c*, gave thanks
14:36 Take this *c* from me.
Lk 11:39 Pharisees clean the outside of the *c*
22:17 After taking the *c*, he gave thanks
22:20 after the supper he took the *c*,
22:20 "This *c* is the new covenant
22:42 if you are willing, take this *c*
Jn 18:11 I not drink the *c* the Father has
1Co 10:16 Is not the *c* of thanksgiving
10:21 the *c* of the Lord and the *c*
11:25 after supper he took the *c*, saying,
11:25 "This *c* is the new covenant

CUPBEARER
Ge 40: 1 the *c* and the baker of the king
Ne 1:11 I was *c* to the king.

CURE (CURED)
Jer 17: 9 and beyond *c*.
30:15 your pain that has no *c*?
Hos 5:13 But he is not able to *c* you,
Lk 9: 1 out all demons and to *c* diseases,

CURED (CURE)
Mt 11: 5 those who have leprosy are *c*,
Lk 6:18 troubled by evil spirits were *c*,

CURSE (ACCURSED CURSED CURSES CURSING)
Ge 4:11 Now you are under a *c*
8:21 "Never again will I *c* the ground
12: 3 and whoever curses you I will *c*;
Dt 11:26 before you today a blessing and a *c*
Dt 11:28 the *c* if you disobey the commands
21:23 hung on a tree is under God's *c*.
23: 5 turned the *c* into a blessing for you,
Job 1:11 he will surely *c* you to your face."
2: 5 he will surely *c* you to your face."
2: 9 *C* God and die!" He replied,
Ps 109: 28 They may *c*, but you will bless;
Pr 3:33 The LORD's *c* is on the house
24:24 peoples will *c* him and nations
Mal 2: 2 and I will *c* your blessings.
Lk 6:28 bless those who *c* you, pray
Ro 12:14 persecute you; bless and do not *c*.
Gal 3:10 on observing the law are under a *c*,
3:13 of the law by becoming a *c* for us,
Jas 3: 9 with it we *c* men, who have been
Rev 22: 3 No longer will there be any *c*.

CURSED (CURSE)
Ge 3:17 "*C* is the ground because of you;
Dt 27:15 "*C* is the man who carves an image
27:16 "*C* is the man who dishonors his
27:17 "*C* is the man who moves his
27:18 "*C* is the man who leads the blind
27:19 *C* is the man who withholds justice
27:20 "*C* is the man who sleeps
27:21 "*C* is the man who has sexual
27:22 "*C* is the man who sleeps
27:23 "*C* is the man who sleeps
27:24 "*C* is the man who kills his
27:25 "*C* is the man who accepts a bribe
27:26 "*C* is the man who does not uphold
Jer 17: 5 "*C* is the one who trusts in man,
Mal 1:14 "*C* is the cheat who has
Ro 9: 3 I could wish that I myself were *c*
1Co 4:12 When we are *c*, we bless;
12: 3 "Jesus be *c*," and no one can say,
Gal 3:10 "*C* is everyone who does not
3:13 *C* is everyone who is hung on a tree

CURSES (CURSE)
Ex 21:17 "Anyone who *c* his father
Lev 20: 9 " 'If anyone *c* his father or mother,
Nu 5:23 is to write these *c* on a scroll
Jos 8:34 the blessings and the *c*—just
Pr 20:20 If a man *c* his father or mother,
28:27 to them receives many *c*.
Mt 15: 4 and 'Anyone who *c* his father
Mk 7:10 and, 'Anyone who *c* his father

CURSING (CURSE)
Ps 109: 18 He wore *c* as his garment;
Ro 3:14 "Their mouths are full of *c*
Jas 3:10 the same mouth come praise and *c*.

CURTAIN
Ex 26:31 "Make a *c* of blue, purple
26:33 The *c* will separate the Holy Place
Mt 27:51 At that moment the *c*
Mk 15:38 The *c* of the temple was torn in two
Lk 23:45 the *c* of the temple was torn in two.
Heb 6:19 the inner sanctuary behind the *c*,
9: 3 Behind the second *c* was a room
10:20 opened for us through the *c*,

CUSTOM
Job 1: 5 This was Job's regular *c*.
Mk 10: 1 and as was his *c*, he taught them.
Lk 4:16 into the synagogue, as was his *c*.
Ac 17: 2 As his *c* was, Paul went

CUT
Lev 19:27 " 'Do not *c* the hair at the sides
21: 5 of their beards or *c* their bodies.
1Ki 3:25 "*C* the living child in two
Isa 51: 1 to the rock from which you were *c*
53: 8 For he was *c* off from the land
Da 2:45 of the rock *c* out of a mountain,
9:26 the Anointed One will be *c* off
Mt 3:10 not produce good fruit will be *c*
24:22 If those days had not been *c* short,
1Co 11: 6 for a woman to have her hair *c*

CYMBAL* (CYMBALS)
1Co 13: 1 a resounding gong or a clanging *c*.

CYMBALS (CYMBAL)
1Ch 15:16 instruments: lyres, harps and *c*.
2Ch 5:12 dressed in fine linen and playing *c*,
Ps 150: 5 praise him with resounding *c*.

CYRUS
Persian king who allowed exiles to return (2Ch 36:22-Ezr 1:8), to rebuild temple (Ezr 5:13-6:14), as appointed by the LORD (Isa 44:28-45:13).

DAGON
Jdg 16:23 offer a great sacrifice to *D* their god
1Sa 5: 2 Dagon's temple and set it beside *D*.

DAMASCUS
Ac 9: 3 As he neared *D* on his journey,

DAN
1. Son of Jacob by Bilhah (Ge 30:4-6; 35:25; 46:23). Tribe of blessed (Ge 49:16-17; Dt 33:22), numbered (Nu 1:39; 26:43), allotted land (Jos 19:40-48; Eze 48:1), failed to fully possess (Jdg 1:34-35), failed to support Deborah (Jdg 5:17), possessed Laish/Dan (Jdg 18).
2. Northernmost city in Israel (Ge 14:14; Jdg 18; 20:1).

DANCE (DANCED DANCING)
Ecc 3: 4 a time to mourn and a time to *d*,
Mt 11:17 and you did not *d*;

DANCED (DANCE)
2Sa 6:14 *d* before the LORD
Mk 6:22 of Herodias came in and *d*,

DANCING (DANCE)
Ps 30:11 You turned my wailing into *d*;
149: 3 Let them praise his name with *d*

DANGER
Pr 22: 3 A prudent man sees *d*
27:12 The prudent see *d* and take refuge,
Mt 5:22 will be in *d* of the fire of hell.
Ro 8:35 famine or nakedness or *d* or sword?
2Co 11:26 I have been in *d* from rivers,

DANIEL
1. Hebrew exile to Babylon, name changed to Belteshazzar (Da 1:6-7). Refused to eat unclean food (Da 1:8-21). Interpreted Nebuchadnezzar's dreams (Da 2; 4), writing on the wall (Da 5). Thrown into lion's den (Da 6). Visions of (Da 7-12).
2. Son of David (1Ch 3:1).

DARIUS
1. King of Persia (Ezr 4:5), allowed rebuilding of temple (Ezr 5-6).
2. Mede who conquered Babylon (Da 5:31).

DARK (DARKENED DARKENS DARKNESS)
Job 34:22 There is no *d* place, no deep
Ps 18: 9 *d* clouds were under his feet.
Pr 31:15 She gets up while it is still *d*;
SS 1: 6 Do not stare at me because I am *d*,
Jn 12:35 in the *d* does not know where he is
Ro 2:19 a light for those who are in the *d*,
2Pe 1:19 as to a light shining in a *d* place,

DARKENED (DARK)
Joel 2:10 the sun and moon are *d*,
Mt 24:29 " 'the sun will be *d*,
Ro 1:21 and their foolish hearts were *d*.
Eph 4:18 They are *d* in their understanding

DARKENS (DARK)
Job 38: 2 "Who is this that *d* my counsel

DARKNESS (DARK)
Ge 1: 2 *d* was over the surface of the deep,
1: 4 he separated the light from the *d*.
Ex 10:22 and total *d* covered all Egypt
20:21 approached the thick *d* where God
2Sa 22:29 the LORD turns my *d* into light.
Ps 18:28 my God turns my *d* into light.
91: 6 the pestilence that stalks in the *d*,
112: 4 Even in *d* light dawns
139: 12 even the *d* will not be dark to you;
Pr 4:19 the way of the wicked is like deep *d*
Isa 5:20 and light for *d*,
42:16 I will turn the *d* into light
45: 7 I form the light and create *d*,
58:10 then your light will rise in the *d*,
61: 1 and release from *d*,
Joel 2:31 The sun will be turned to *d*
Mt 4:16 the people living in *d*
6:23 how great is that *d*! "No one can
Lk 11:34 are bad, your body also is full of *d*.
23:44 and *d* came over the whole land
Jn 1: 5 The light shines in the *d*,
3:19 but men loved *d* instead of light
Ac 2:20 The sun will be turned to *d*
2Co 4: 6 who said, "Let light shine out of *d*
6:14 fellowship can light have with *d*?
Eph 5: 8 For you were once *d*, but now you
5:11 to do with the fruitless deeds of *d*,
1Pe 2: 9 out of *d* into his wonderful light.
2Pe 2:17 Blackest *d* is reserved for them.
1Jn 1: 5 in him there is no *d* at all.
2: 9 but hates his brother is still in the *d*.
Jude :6 in *d*, bound with everlasting chains
:13 for whom blackest *d* has been

DASH
Ps 2: 9 you will *d* them to pieces like

DAUGHTER (DAUGHTERS)
Ex 1:10 she took him to Pharaoh's *d*
Jdg 11:48 to commemorate the *d* of Jephthah
Est 2: 7 Mordecai had taken her as his own *d*
Ps 9:14 praises in the gates of the *D* of Zion
137: 8 O *D* of Babylon, doomed
Isa 62:11 "Say to the *D* of Zion,
Zec 9: 9 Shout, *D* of Jerusalem!
Mk 5:34 "*D*, your faith has healed you.
7:29 the demon has left your *d*.

DAUGHTERS (DAUGHTER)
Ge 6: 2 the *d* of men were beautiful,
19:36 Lot's *d* became pregnant
Nu 36:10 Zelophehad's *d* did as the LORD
Joel 2:28 sons and *d* will prophesy,

DAVID
Son of Jesse (Ru 4:17-22; 1Ch 2:13-15), ancestor of Jesus (Mt 1:1-17; Lk 3:31). Wives and children (1Sa 18; 25:39-44; 2Sa 3:2-5; 5:13-16; 11:27; 1Ch 3:1-9).
Anointed king by Samuel (1Sa 16:1-13). Musician to Saul (1Sa 16:14-23; 18:10). Killed Goliath (1Sa 17). Relation with Jonathan (1Sa 18:1-4; 19-20; 23:16-18; 2Sa 1). Disfavor of Saul (1Sa 18:6-23:29). Spared Saul's life (1Sa 24; 26). Among Philistines (1Sa 21:10-14; 27-30). Lament for Saul and Jonathan (2Sa 1).
Anointed king of Judah (2Sa 2:1-11). Conflict with house of Saul (2Sa 2-4). Anointed king of Israel (2Sa 5:1-4; 1Ch 11:1-3). Conquered Jerusalem (2Sa 5:6-10; 1Ch 11:4-9). Brought ark to Jerusalem (2Sa 6; 1Ch 13; 15-16). The LORD promised eternal dynasty (2Sa 7; 1Ch 17; Ps 132). Showed kindness to Mephibosheth (2Sa 9). Adultery with Bathsheba, murder of Uriah (2Sa 11-12). Son Amnon raped daughter Tamar; killed by Absalom (2Sa 13). Absalom's revolt (2Sa 14-17); death (2Sa 18). Sheba's revolt (2Sa 20). Victories: Philistines (2Sa 5:17-25; 1Ch 14:8-17; 2Sa 21:15-22; 1Ch 20:4-8), Ammonites (2Sa 10; 1Ch 19), various (2Sa 8; 1Ch 18). Mighty men (2Sa 23:8-39; 1Ch 11-12). Punished for numbering army (2Sa 24; 1Ch 21). Appointed Solomon king (1Ki 1:28-2:9). Prepared for building of temple (1Ch 22-29). Last words (2Sa 23:1-7). Death (1Ki 2:10-12; 1Ch 29:28).
Psalmist (Mt 22:43-45), musician (Am 6:5), prophet (2Sa 23:2-7; Ac 1:16; 2:30).
Psalms of: 2 (Ac 4:25), 3-32, 34-41, 51-65, 68-70, 86, 95 (Heb 4:7), 101, 103, 108-110, 122, 124, 131, 133, 138-145.

DAWN (DAWNED DAWNS)
Ps 37: 6 your righteousness shine like the *d*,
Pr 4:18 is like the first gleam of *d*,
Isa 14:12 O morning star, son of the *d*!
Am 4:13 he who turns *d* to darkness,
5: 8 who turns blackness into *d*

DAWNED (DAWN)
Isa 9: 2 a light has *d*.
Mt 4:16 a light has *d*."

DAWNS* (DAWN)
Ps 65: 8 where morning *d* and evening
112: 4 in darkness light *d* for the upright,
Hos 10:15 When that day *d*,
2Pe 1:19 until the day *d* and the morning

DAY (DAYS)
Ge 1: 5 God called the light "*d*,"
1: 5 and there was morning—the first *d*
1: 8 there was morning—the second *d*.
1:13 there was morning—the third *d*.
1:19 there was morning—the fourth *d*.
1:23 there was morning—the fifth *d*.
1:31 there was morning—the sixth *d*.
2: 2 so on the seventh *d* he rested
8:22 *d* and night
Ex 16:30 the people rested on the seventh *d*.
20: 8 "Remember the Sabbath *d*
Lev 16:30 on this *d* atonement will be made
23:28 because it is the *D* of Atonement,
Nu 14:14 before them in a pillar of cloud by *d*
Jos 1: 8 meditate on it *d* and night,
2Ki 7: 9 This is a *d* of good news
25:30 *D* by *d* the king gave Jehoiachin
1Ch 16:23 proclaim his salvation *d* after *d*.
Ne 8:18 *D* after *d*, from the first *d*
Ps 84:10 Better is one *d* in your courts
96: 2 proclaim his salvation *d* after *d*.
118: 24 This is the *d* the LORD has made;
Pr 27: 1 not know what a *d* may bring forth.
Isa 13: 9 a cruel *d*, with wrath and fierce
Jer 46:10 But that *d* belongs to the Lord,
50:31 "for your *d* has come,
Eze 30: 2 "Alas for that *d*!"
Joel 1:15 "Alas for that *d*!
2:31 and dreadful *d* of the LORD.
Am 3:14 On the *d* I punish Israel for her sins
5:20 Will not the *d* of the LORD be
Ob :15 "The *d* of the LORD is near
Zep 1:14 The great *d* of the LORD is near—
Zec 2:11 joined with the LORD in that *d*
14: 1 A *d* of the LORD is coming
14: 7 It will be a unique *d*,
Mal 4: 5 dreadful *d* of the LORD comes.
Mt 24:38 up to the *d* Noah entered the ark;
Lk 11: 3 Give us each *d* our daily bread.
17:24 in his *d* will be like the lightning,
Ac 5:42 *D* after *d*, in the temple courts
17:11 examined the Scriptures every *d*
17:17 as in the marketplace *d* by *d*
Ro 14: 5 man considers every *d* alike.
1Co 5: 5 his spirit saved on the *d* of the Lord
2Co 4:16 we are being renewed *d* by *d*.
11:25 I spent a night and a *d*
1Th 5: 2 for you know very well that the *d*
5: 4 so that this *d* should surprise you
2Th 2: 2 saying that the *d* of the Lord has
Heb 7:27 need to offer sacrifices *d* after *d*,
2Pe 3: 8 With the Lord a *d* is like
3:10 *d* of the Lord will come like a thief.
Rev 6:17 For the great *d* of their wrath has
16:14 on the great *d* of God Almighty.

DAYS (DAY)
Dt 17:19 he is to read it all the *d* of his life
32: 7 Remember the *d* of old;
Ps 23: 6 all the *d* of my life,
34:12 and desires to see many good *d*,
39: 5 have made my *d* a mere
90:10 The length of our *d* is seventy years
90:12 Teach us to number our *d* aright,
103: 15 As for man, his *d* are like grass,
128: 5 all the *d* of your life;
Pr 31:12 all the *d* of her life.
Ecc 9: 9 all the *d* of this meaningless life
12: 1 Creator in the *d* of your youth,
Isa 38:20 all the *d* of our lives
Da 7: 9 and the Ancient of *D* took his seat.
7:13 He approached the Ancient of *D*
7:22 until the Ancient of *D* came
Hos 3: 5 and to his blessings in the last *d*.
Joel 2:29 I will pour out my Spirit in those *d*.
Mic 4: 1 In the last *d*
Lk 19:43 The *d* will come upon you
Ac 2:17 by the prophet Joel: " 'In the last *d*,
2Ti 3: 1 will be terrible times in the last *d*.
Heb 1: 2 in these last *d* he has spoken to us
2Pe 3: 3 that in the last *d* scoffers will come,

DAZZLING*
Da 2:31 *d* statue, awesome in appearance.
Mk 9: 3 His clothes became *d* white,

DEACON* (DEACONS)
1Ti 3:12 A *d* must be the husband of

DEACONS* (DEACON)
Php 1: 1 together with the overseers and *d*:
1Ti 3: 8 *D*, likewise, are to be men worthy
3:10 against them, let them serve as *d*.

DEAD (DIE)
Lev 17:15 who eats anything found *d*
Dt 18:11 or spiritist or who consults the *d*.
Isa 8:19 Why consult the *d* on behalf
Mt 8:22 and let the *d* bury their own *d*."
28: 7 'He has risen from the *d*
Lk 15:24 For this son of mine was *d*
24:46 rise from the *d* on the third day,
Ro 6:11 count yourselves *d* to sin
1Co 15:29 do who are baptized for the *d*?
Eph 2: 1 you were *d* in your transgressions
1Th 4:16 and the *d* in Christ will rise first.
Jas 2:17 is not accompanied by action, is *d*.
2:26 so faith without deeds is *d*.
Rev 14:13 Blessed are the *d* who die
20:12 And I saw the *d*, great and small,

DEADENED* (DIE)
Jn 12:40 and *d* their hearts,

DEAR* (DEARER)
2Sa 1:26 you were very *d* to me.
Ps 102: 14 For her stones are *d*
Jer 31:20 Is not Ephraim my *d* son,
Jn 2: 4 "*D* woman, why do you involve me
19:26 he said to his mother, "*D* woman,
Ac 15:25 to you with our *d* friends Barnabas
Ro 16: 5 Greet my *d* friend Epenetus,
16: 9 in Christ, and my *d* friend Stachys.
16:12 Greet my *d* friend Persis, another
1Co 4:14 but to warn you, as my *d* children.
10:14 my *d* friends, flee from idolatry.
15:58 Therefore, my *d* brothers,
2Co 7: 1 we have these promises, *d* friends,

2Co 12:19 and everything we do, *d* friends,
Gal 4:19 My *d* children, for whom I am
Eph 6:21 the *d* brother and faithful servant
Php 2:12 my *d* friends, as you have always
4: 1 firm in the Lord, *d* friends!
Col 1: 7 Epaphras, our *d* fellow servant,
4: 7 He is a *d* brother, a faithful
4: 9 our faithful and *d* brother,
4:14 Our *d* friend Luke, the doctor,
1Th 2: 8 because you had become so *d* to us.
1Ti 6: 2 their service are believers, and *d*
2Ti 1: 2 To Timothy, my *d* son: Grace,
Phm : 1 To Philemon our *d* friend
:16 He is very *d* to me but
:16 better than a slave, as a *d* brother.
Heb 6: 9 we speak like this, *d* friends,
Jas 1:16 Don't be deceived, my *d* brothers.
1:19 My *d* brothers, take note of this:
2: 5 thoughts? Listen, my *d* brothers:
1Pe 2:11 *D* friends, I urge you, as aliens
4:12 *D* friends, do not be surprised
2Pe 3: 1 *D* friends, this is now my second
3: 8 not forget this one thing, *d* friends:
3:14 *d* friends, since you are looking
3:15 just as our *d* brother Paul
3:17 *d* friends, since you already know
1Jn 2: 1 My *d* children, I write this to you
2: 7 *D* friends, I am not writing you
2:12 I write to you, *d* children,
2:13 I write to you, *d* children,
2:18 *D* children, this is the last hour;
2:28 *d* children, continue in him,
3: 2 *D* friends, now we are children
3: 7 *D* children, do not let anyone lead
3:18 love of God be in him? *D* children,
3:21 *D* friends, if our hearts do not
4: 1 *D* friends, do not believe every
4: 4 *d* children, are from God
4: 7 *D* friends, let us love one another,
4:11 *D* friends, since God so loved us,
5:21 *D* children, keep yourselves
2Jn : 5 *d* lady, I am not writing you a new
3Jn : 1 The elder, To my *d* friend Gaius,
: 2 *D* friend, I pray that you may enjoy
: 5 *D* friend, you are faithful
:11 *D* friend, do not imitate what is evil
Jude : 3 *D* friends, although I was very
:17 But, *d* friends, remember what
:20 *d* friends, build yourselves up

DEARER* (DEAR)
Phm :16 dear to me but even *d* to you,

DEATH (DIE)
Ex 21:12 kills him shall surely be put to *d.*
Nu 35:16 the murderer shall be put to *d.*
Dt 30:19 set before you life and *d,*
Ru 1:17 if anything but *d* separates you
2Ki 4:40 O man of God, there is *d* in the pot
Job 26: 6 *D* is naked before God;
Ps 23: 4 the valley of the shadow of *d,*
44:22 for your sake we face *d* all day long
89:48 What man can live and not see *d,*
116: 15 is the *d* of his saints.
Pr 8:36 all who hate me love *d.*"
11:19 he who pursues evil goes to his *d.*
14:12 but in the end it leads to *d.*
15:11 *D* and Destruction lie open
16:25 but in the end it leads to *d.*
18:21 tongue has the power of life and *d,*
19:18 do not be a willing party to his *d.*
23:14 and save his soul from *d.*
Ecc 7: 2 for *d* is the destiny of every man;
Isa 25: 8 he will swallow up *d* forever.
53:12 he poured out his life unto *d,*
Eze 18:23 pleasure in the *d* of the wicked?
18:32 pleasure in the *d* of anyone,
33:11 pleasure in the *d* of the wicked,
Hos 13:14 Where, O *d,* are your plagues?
Jn 5:24 he has crossed over from *d* to life.
Ro 4:25 delivered over to *d* for our sins
5:12 and in this way *d* came to all men,
5:14 *d* reigned from the time of Adam
6: 3 Jesus were baptized into his *d?*
6:23 For the wages of sin is *d,*
7:24 me from this body of *d?*
8:13 put to *d* the misdeeds of the body,
8:36 your sake we face *d* all day long;
1Co 15:21 For since *d* came through a man,
15:26 The last enemy to be destroyed is *d*
15:55 Where, O *d,* is your sting?"
2Ti 1:10 who has destroyed *d* and has
Heb 2:14 him who holds the power of *d*—
1Jn 5:16 There is a sin that leads to *d.*
Rev 1:18 And I hold the keys of *d* and Hades
2:11 hurt at all by the second *d.*
20: 6 The second *d* has no power
20:14 The lake of fire is the second *d.*
20:14 Then *d* and Hades were thrown

Rev 21: 4 There will be no more *d*
21: 8 This is the second *d.*"

DEBAUCHERY*
Ro 13:13 not in sexual immorality and *d,*
2Co 12:21 and *d* in which they have indulged.
Gal 5:19 impurity and *d;* idolatry
Eph 5:18 drunk on wine, which leads to *d.*
1Pe 4: 3 living in *d,* lust, drunkenness,

DEBORAH*
1. Prophetess who led Israel to victory over Canaanites (Jdg 4-5).
2. Rebekah's nurse (Ge 35:8).

DEBT* (DEBTOR DEBTORS DEBTS)
Dt 15: 3 must cancel any *d* your brother
24: 6 the upper one—as security for a *d,*
1Sa 22: 2 or in *d* or discontented gathered
Job 24: 9 of the poor is seized for a *d.*
Mt 18:25 that he had be sold to repay the *d.*
18:27 canceled the *d* and let him go.
18:30 into prison until he could pay the *d.*
18:32 'I canceled all that *d* of yours
Lk 7:43 who had the bigger *d* canceled."
Ro 13: 8 Let no *d* remain outstanding,
13: 8 continuing *d* to love one another,

DEBTOR* (DEBT)
Isa 24: 2 for *d* as for creditor.

DEBTORS* (DEBT)
Hab 2: 7 Will not your *d* suddenly arise?
Mt 6:12 as we also have forgiven our *d.*
Lk 16: 5 called in each one of his master's *d.*

DEBTS* (DEBT)
Dt 15: 1 seven years you must cancel *d.*
15: 2 time for canceling *d* has been
15: 9 the year for canceling *d,* is near,"
31:10 in the year for canceling *d,*
2Ki 4: 7 "Go, sell the oil and pay your *d.*
Ne 10:31 the land and will cancel all *d.*
Pr 22:26 or puts up security for *d;*
Mt 6:12 Forgive us our *d,*
Lk 7:42 so he canceled the *d* of both.

DECAY*
Ps 16:10 will you let your Holy One see *d.*
49: 9 and not see *d.*
49:14 their forms will *d* in the grave,
Pr 12: 4 a disgraceful wife is like *d*
Isa 5:24 so their roots will *d*
Hab 3:16 *d* crept into my bones,
Ac 2:27 will you let your Holy One see *d.*
2:31 to the grave, nor did his body see *d.*
13:34 never to *d,* is stated in these words:
13:35 will not let your Holy One see *d.*'
13:37 raised from the dead did not see *d.*
Ro 8:21 liberated from its bondage to *d*

DECEIT (DECEIVE)
Ps 5: 9 with their tongue they speak *d.*
Isa 53: 9 nor was any *d* in his mouth.
Da 8:25 He will cause *d* to prosper,
Zep 3:13 nor will *d* be found in their mouths.
Mk 7:22 greed, malice, *d,* lewdness, envy,
Ac 13:10 You are full of all kinds of *d*
Ro 1:29 murder, strife, *d* and malice.
3:13 their tongues practice *d.*"
1Pe 2: 1 yourselves of all malice and all *d,*
2:22 and no *d* was found in his mouth."

DECEITFUL (DECEIVE)
Jer 17: 9 The heart is *d* above all things
Hos 10: 2 Their heart is *d,*
2Co 11:13 men are false apostles, *d* workmen,
Eph 4:14 of men in their *d* scheming.
4:22 is being corrupted by its *d* desires;
1Pe 3:10 and his lips from *d* speech.
Rev 21:27 who does what is shameful or *d,*

DECEITFULNESS* (DECEIVE)
Ps 119:118 for their *d* is in vain.
Mt 13:22 and the *d* of wealth choke it,
Mk 4:19 the *d* of wealth and the desires
Heb 3:13 of you may be hardened by sin's *d.*

DECEIVE (DECEIT DECEITFUL DECEITFULNESS DECEIVED DECEIVER DECEIVERS DECEIVES DECEIVING DECEPTION DECEPTIVE)
Lev 19:11 " 'Do not *d* one another.
Pr 14: 5 A truthful witness does not *d,*
24:28 or use your lips to *d.*
Jer 37: 9 Do not *d* yourselves, thinking,
Zec 13: 4 garment of hair in order to *d.*
Mt 24: 5 'I am the Christ,' and will *d* many.
24:11 will appear and *d* many people.
24:24 and miracles to *d* even the elect—

Mk 13: 6 'I am he,' and will *d* many.
13:22 and miracles to *d* the elect—
Ro 16:18 and flattery they *d* the minds
1Co 3:18 Do not *d* yourselves.
Eph 5: 6 Let no one *d* you with empty words
Col 2: 4 this so that no one may *d* you
2Th 2: 3 Don't let anyone *d* you in any way,
Jas 1:22 to the word, and so *d* yourselves.
1Jn 1: 8 we *d* ourselves and the truth is not
Rev 20: 8 and will go out to *d* the nations

DECEIVED (DECEIVE)
Ge 3:13 "The serpent *d* me, and I ate."
Lk 21: 8 "Watch out that you are not *d.*
1Co 6: 9 the kingdom of God? Do not be *d:*
2Co 11: 3 Eve was *d* by the serpent's cunning
Gal 6: 7 Do not be *d:* God cannot be
1Ti 2:14 And Adam was not the one *d;*
2Ti 3:13 to worse, deceiving and being *d.*
Tit 3: 3 *d* and enslaved by all kinds
Jas 1:16 Don't be *d,* my dear brothers.
Rev 13:14 he *d* the inhabitants of the earth.
20:10 And the devil, who *d* them,

DECEIVER (DECEIVE)
Mt 27:63 while he was still alive that *d* said,
2Jn : 7 Any such person is the *d*

DECEIVERS* (DECEIVE)
Ps 49: 5 when wicked *d* surround me—
Tit 1:10 and *d,* especially those
2Jn : 7 Many *d,* who do not acknowledge

DECEIVES (DECEIVE)
Pr 26:19 is a man who *d* his neighbor
Mt 24: 4 "Watch out that no one *d* you.
Mk 13: 5 "Watch out that no one *d* you.
Gal 6: 3 when he is nothing, he *d* himself.
2Th 2:10 sort of evil that *d* those who are
Jas 1:26 he *d* himself and his religion is

DECEIVING* (DECEIVE)
Lev 6: 2 by *d* his neighbor about something
1Ti 4: 1 follow *d* spirits and things taught
2Ti 3:13 go from bad to worse, *d*
Rev 20: 3 him from *d* the nations anymore

DECENCY* (DECENTLY)
1Ti 2: 9 women to dress modestly, with *d*

DECENTLY* (DECENCY)
Ro 13:13 Let us behave *d,* as in the daytime,

DECEPTION (DECEIVE)
Pr 14: 8 but the folly of fools is *d.*
26:26 His malice may be concealed by *d,*
Mt 27:64 This last *d* will be worse
2Co 4: 2 we do not use *d,* nor do we distort

DECEPTIVE (DECEIVE)
Pr 11:18 The wicked man earns *d* wages,
31:30 Charm is *d,* and beauty is fleeting;
Jer 7: 4 Do not trust in *d* words and say,
Col 2: 8 through hollow and *d* philosophy,

DECIDED (DECISION)
2Co 9: 7 man should give what he has *d*

DECISION (DECIDED)
Ex 28:29 heart on the breastpiece of *d*
Joel 3:14 multitudes in the valley of *d!*

DECLARE (DECLARED DECLARING)
1Ch 16:24 *D* his glory among the nations,
Ps 19: 1 The heavens *d* the glory of God;
96: 3 *D* his glory among the nations,
Isa 42: 9 and new things I *d;*

DECLARED (DECLARE)
Mk 7:19 Jesus *d* all foods "clean.")
Ro 2:13 the law who will be *d* righteous.
3:20 no one will be *d* righteous

DECLARING (DECLARE)
Ps 71: 8 *d* your splendor all day long.
Ac 2:11 we hear them *d* the wonders

DECREE (DECREED DECREES)
Ex 15:25 There the LORD made a *d*
1Ch 16:17 He confirmed it to Jacob as a *d,*
Ps 2: 7 I will proclaim the *d* of the LORD:
7: 6 Awake, my God; *d* justice.
81: 4 this is a *d* for Israel,
148: 6 he gave a *d* that will never pass
Da 4:24 and this is the *d* the Most High has
Lk 2: 1 Augustus issued a *d* that a census
Ro 1:32 know God's righteous *d* that those

DECREED (DECREE)
Ps 78: 5 He *d* statutes for Jacob
Jer 40: 2 LORD your God *d* this disaster

La 3:37 happen if the Lord has not *d* it?
Da 9:24 "Seventy 'sevens' are *d*
9:26 and desolations have been *d.*
Lk 22:22 Son of Man will go as it has been *d,*

DECREES (DECREE)
Ge 26: 5 my commands, my *d* and my laws
Ex 15:26 to his commands and keep all his *d,*
18:16 inform them of God's *d* and laws."
18:20 Teach them the *d* and laws,
Lev 10:11 Israelites all the *d* the LORD has
18: 4 and be careful to follow my *d.*
18: 5 Keep my *d* and laws,
18:26 you must keep my *d* and my laws.
Ps 119: 12 teach me your *d.*
119: 16 I delight in your *d;*
119: 48 and I meditate on your *d.*
119:112 My heart is set on keeping your *d*

DEDICATE (DEDICATED DEDICATION)
Nu 6:12 He must *d* himself to the LORD
Pr 20:25 for a man to *d* something rashly

DEDICATED (DEDICATE)
Lev 21:12 he has been *d* by the anointing oil
Nu 6: 9 thus defiling the hair he has *d,*
6:18 shave off the hair that he *d.*
18: 6 *d* to the LORD to do the work
1Ki 8:63 and all the Israelites *d* the temple
2Ch 29:31 "You have now *d* yourselves
Ne 3: 1 They *d* it and set its doors in place,

DEDICATION (DEDICATE)
Nu 6:19 shaved off the hair of his *d,*
Jn 10:22 came the Feast of *D* at Jerusalem.
1Ti 5:11 sensual desires overcome their *d*

DEED (DEEDS)
Jer 32:10 and sealed the *d,* had it witnessed,
32:16 After I had given the *d* of purchase
Col 3:17 you do, whether in word or *d,*
2Th 2:17 and strengthen you in every good *d*

DEEDS (DEED)
Dt 3:24 or on earth who can do the *d*
4:34 or by great and awesome *d,*
34:12 the awesome *d* that Moses
1Sa 2: 3 and by him *d* are weighed.
1Ch 16:24 his marvelous *d* among all peoples.
Job 34:25 Because he takes note of their *d,*
Ps 26: 7 and telling of all your wonderful *d.*
45: 4 right hand display awesome *d.*
65: 5 with awesome *d* of righteousness,
66: 3 "How awesome are your *d!*
71:17 day I declare your marvelous *d.*
72:18 who alone does marvelous *d.*
73:28 I will tell of all your *d.*
75: 1 men tell of your wonderful *d.*
77:11 I will remember the *d* of the LORD
77:12 and consider all your mighty *d.*
78: 4 the praiseworthy *d* of the LORD,
78: 7 and would not forget his *d*
86: 8 no *d* can compare with yours.
86:10 you are great and do marvelous *d;*
88:12 or your righteous *d* in the land
90:16 May your *d* be shown
92: 4 For you make me glad by your *d,*
96: 3 his marvelous *d* among all peoples.
107: 8 and his wonderful *d* for men,
107: 15 and his wonderful *d* for men,
107: 21 and his wonderful *d* for men.
107: 24 his wonderful *d* in the deep.
107: 31 and his wonderful *d* for men.
111: 3 Glorious and majestic are his *d,*
145: 6 and I will proclaim your great *d.*
Jer 32:19 purposes and mighty are your *d.*
Hab 3: 2 I stand in awe of your *d,* O LORD.
Mt 5:16 that they may see your good *d*
Lk 1:51 He has performed mighty *d*
23:41 we are getting what our *d* deserve.
Ac 26:20 prove their repentance by their *d.*
1Ti 6:18 rich in good *d,* and to be generous
Heb 10:24 on toward love and good *d.*
Jas 2:14 claims to have faith but has no *d?*
2:18 Show me your faith without *d,*
2:20 faith without *d* is useless?
2:26 so faith without *d* is dead.
1Pe 2:12 they may see your good *d*
Rev 2:19 I know your *d,* your love and faith,
2:23 each of you according to your *d.*
3: 1 I know your *d;* you have
3: 2 I have not found your *d* complete
3: 8 I know your *d.*
3:15 I know your *d,* that you are neither
14:13 for their *d* will follow them."
15: 3 "Great and marvelous are your *d,*

DEEP (DEPTH DEPTHS)
Ge 1: 2 was over the surface of the *d,*
8: 2 Now the springs of the *d*

Ps 42: 7 *D* calls to *d*
Lk 5: 4 to Simon, "Put out into *d* water,
1Co 2:10 all things, even the *d* things
1Ti 3: 9 hold of the *d* truths of the faith

DEER
Ps 42: 1 As the *d* pants for streams of water,

DEFAMED*
Isa 48:11 How can I let myself be *d?*

DEFEATED
1Co 6: 7 have been completely *d* already.

DEFEND (DEFENDED DEFENDER DEFENDING DEFENDS DEFENSE)
Ps 72: 4 He will *d* the afflicted
74:22 Rise up, O God, and *d* your cause;
82: 2 "How long will you *d* the unjust
82: 3 *D* the cause of the weak
119:154 *D* my cause and redeem me;
Pr 31: 9 *d* the rights of the poor and needy
Isa 1:17 *D* the cause of the fatherless,
1:23 They do not *d* the cause
Jer 5:28 they do not *d* the rights of the poor.
50:34 He will vigorously *d* their cause

DEFENDED (DEFEND)
Jer 22:16 He *d* the cause of the poor

DEFENDER (DEFEND)
Ex 22: 2 the *d* is not guilty of bloodshed;
Ps 68: 5 to the fatherless, a *d* of widows,
Pr 23:11 for their *D* is strong;

DEFENDING (DEFEND)
Ps 10:18 *d* the fatherless and the oppressed,
Ro 2:15 now accusing, now even *d* them.)
Php 1: 7 or *d* and confirming the gospel,

DEFENDS* (DEFEND)
Dt 10:18 He *d* the cause of the fatherless
33: 7 With his own hands he *d* his cause.
Isa 51:22 your God, who *d* his people:

DEFENSE (DEFEND)
Ps 35:23 Awake, and rise to my *d!*
Php 1:16 here for the *d* of the gospel.
1Jn 2: 1 speaks to the Father in our *d*—

DEFERRED*
Pr 13:12 Hope *d* makes the heart sick,

DEFIED
1Sa 17:45 armies of Israel, whom you have *d.*
1Ki 13:26 the man of God who *d* the word

DEFILE (DEFILED)
Da 1: 8 Daniel resolved not to *d* himself
Rev 14: 4 are those who did not *d* themselves

DEFILED (DEFILE)
Isa 24: 5 The earth is *d* by its people;

DEFRAUD
Lev 19:13 Do not *d* your neighbor or rob him.
Mk 10:19 do not *d,* honor your father

DEITY*
Col 2: 9 of the *D* lives in bodily form,

DELAY
Ecc 5: 4 vow to God, do not *d* in fulfilling it.
Isa 48: 9 my own name's sake I *d* my wrath;
Heb 10:37 is coming will come and will not *d.*
Rev 10: 6 and said, "There will be no more *d!*

DELICACIES
Ps 141: 4 let me not eat of their *d.*
Pr 23: 3 Do not crave his *d,*
23: 6 do not crave his *d;*

DELICIOUS*
Pr 9:17 food eaten in secret is *d!"*

DELIGHT* (DELIGHTED DELIGHTFUL DELIGHTING DELIGHTS)
Lev 26:31 and I will take no *d* in the pleasing
Dt 30: 9 The LORD will again *d* in you
1Sa 2: 1 for I *d* in your deliverance.
15:22 "Does the LORD *d*
Ne 1:11 the prayer of your servants who *d*
Job 22:26 Surely then you will find *d*
27:10 Will he find *d* in the Almighty?
Ps 1: 2 But his *d* is in the law of the LORD
16: 3 in whom is all my *d.*
35: 9 and *d* in his salvation.
35:27 those who *d* in my vindication
37: 4 *D* yourself in the LORD
43: 4 to God, my joy and my *d.*
51:16 You do not *d* in sacrifice,
51:19 whole burnt offerings to *d* you;

Ps 62: 4 they take *d* in lies.
68:30 Scatter the nations who *d* in war.
111: 2 by all who *d* in them.
112: 1 who finds great *d* in his commands.
119: 16 I *d* in your decrees;
119: 24 Your statutes are my *d;*
119: 35 for there I find *d.*
119: 47 for I *d* in your commands
119: 70 but I *d* in your law.
119: 77 for your law is my *d.*
119: 92 If your law had not been my *d,*
119:143 but your commands are my *d.*
119:174 and your law is my *d.*
147: 10 nor his *d* in the legs of a man;
149: 4 For the LORD takes *d*
Pr 1:22 How long will mockers *d*
2:14 who *d* in doing wrong
8:30 I was filled with *d* day after day,
11: 1 but accurate weights are his *d.*
29:17 he will bring *d* to your soul.
Ecc 2:10 My heart took *d* in all my work,
SS 1: 4 We rejoice and *d* in you;
2: 3 I *d* to sit in his shade,
Isa 5: 7 are the garden of his *d.*
11: 3 he will *d* in the fear of the LORD.
13:17 and have no *d* in gold.
32:14 the *d* of donkeys, a pasture
42: 1 my chosen one in whom I *d;*
55: 2 and your soul will *d* in the richest
58:13 if you call the Sabbath a *d*
61:10 I *d* greatly in the LORD;
62: 4 for the LORD will take *d* in you,
65:18 for I will create Jerusalem to be a *d*
65:19 and take *d* in my people;
66: 3 their souls *d* in their abominations;
66:11 *d* in her overflowing abundance."
Jer 9:24 for in these I *d,"*
15:16 they were my joy and my heart's *d,*
31:20 the child in whom I *d?*
49:25 the town in which I *d?*
Eze 24:16 away from you the *d* of your eyes.
24:21 in which you take pride, the *d*
24:25 and glory, the *d* of their eyes,
Hos 7: 3 *d* the king with their wickedness,
Mic 1:16 for the children in whom you *d;*
7:18 but *d* to show mercy.
Zep 3:17 He will take great *d* in you,
Mt 12:18 the one I love, in whom I *d;*
Mk 12:37 large crowd listened to him with *d.*
Lk 1:14 He will be a joy and *d* to you,
Ro 7:22 in my inner being I *d* in God's law;
1Co 13: 6 Love does not *d* in evil
2Co 12:10 for Christ's sake, I *d* in weaknesses,
Col 2: 5 and *d* to see how orderly you are

DELIGHTED (DELIGHT)
2Sa 22:20 he rescued me because he *d* in me.
1Ki 10: 9 who has *d* in you and placed you
2Ch 9: 8 who has *d* in you and placed you
Ps 18:19 he rescued me because he *d* in me.
Lk 13:17 but the people were *d* with all

DELIGHTFUL* (DELIGHT)
Ps 16: 6 surely I have a *d* inheritance.
SS 1: 2 for your love is more *d* than wine.
4:10 How *d* is your love, my sister,
Mal 3:12 for yours will be a *d* land,"

DELIGHTING* (DELIGHT)
Pr 8:31 and *d* in mankind.

DELIGHTS (DELIGHT)
Est 6: 6 for the man the king *d* to honor?"
Ps 22: 8 since he *d* in him."
35:27 who *d* in the well-being
36: 8 from your river of *d.*
37:23 if the LORD *d* in a man's way
147: 11 the LORD *d* in those who fear him,
Pr 3:12 as a father the son he *d* in.
10:23 of understanding *d* in wisdom.
11:20 he *d* in those whose ways are
12:22 but he *d* in men who are truthful.
14:35 A king *d* in a wise servant,
18: 2 but *d* in airing his own opinions.
23:24 he who has a wise son *d* in him.
Col 2:18 Do not let anyone who *d*

DELILAH*
Woman who betrayed Samson (Jdg 16:4-22).

DELIVER (DELIVERANCE DELIVERED DELIVERER DELIVERS)
Dt 32:39 and no one can *d* out of my hand.
Ps 22: 8 Let him *d* him,
72:12 For he will *d* the needy who cry out
79: 9 *d* us and forgive our sins
109: 21 of the goodness of your love, *d* me.
119:170 *d* me according to your promise.
Mt 6:13 but *d* us from the evil one.'

2Co 1:10 hope that he will continue to *d* us,

DELIVERANCE (DELIVER)
1Sa 2: 1 for I delight in your *d.*
Ps 3: 8 From the LORD comes *d.*
32: 7 and surround me with songs of *d.*
33:17 A horse is a vain hope for *d;*
Ob :17 But on Mount Zion will be *d;*

DELIVERED (DELIVER)
Ps 34: 4 he *d* me from all my fears.
107: 6 and he *d* them from their distress.
116: 8 have *d* my soul from death,
Da 12: 1 written in the book—will be *d.*
Ro 4:25 He was *d* over to death for our sins

DELIVERER* (DELIVER)
Jdg 3: 9 for them a *d,* Othniel son of Kenaz,
3:15 and he gave them a *d*— Ehud,
2Sa 22: 2 is my rock, my fortress and my *d;*
2Ki 13: 5 The LORD provided a *d* for Israel,
Ps 18: 2 is my rock, my fortress and my *d;*
40:17 You are my help and my *d;*
70: 5 You are my help and my *d;*
140: 7 O Sovereign LORD, my strong *d,*
144: 2 my stronghold and my *d,*
Ac 7:35 sent to be their ruler and *d*
Ro 11:26 "The *d* will come from Zion;

DELIVERS (DELIVER)
Ps 34:17 he *d* them from all their troubles.
34:19 but the LORD *d* him from them all
37:40 The LORD helps them and *d* them
37:40 he *d* them from the wicked

DELUSION*
2Th 2:11 God sends them a powerful *d*

DEMAND (DEMANDED)
Lk 6:30 belongs to you, do not *d* it back.

DEMANDED (DEMAND)
Lk 12:20 This very night your life will be *d*
12:48 been given much, much will be *d;*

DEMETRIUS
Ac 19:24 A silversmith named *D,* who made

DEMON* (DEMONS)
Mt 9:33 And when the *d* was driven out,
11:18 and they say, 'He has a *d.'*
17:18 Jesus rebuked the *d,* and it came
Mk 7:26 to drive the *d* out of her daughter.
7:29 the *d* has left your daughter."
7:30 lying on the bed, and the *d* gone.
Lk 4:33 there was a man possessed by a *d,*
4:35 Then the *d* threw the man
7:33 wine, and you say, 'He has a *d.'*
8:29 driven by the *d* into solitary places.
9:42 the *d* threw him to the ground
11:14 When the *d* left, the man who had
11:14 was driving out a *d* that was mute.
Jn 8:49 "I am not possessed by a *d,"*
10:21 Can a *d* open the eyes of the blind
10:21 sayings of a man possessed by a *d.*

DEMON-POSSESSED* (DEMON-POSSESSION)
Mt 4:24 those suffering severe pain, the *d,*
8:16 many who were *d* were brought
8:28 two *d* men coming
8:33 what had happened to the *d* men.
9:32 man who was *d* and could not talk
12:22 they brought him a *d* man who was
Mk 1:32 brought to Jesus all the sick and *d.*
5:16 what had happened to the *d* man—
5:18 the man who had been *d* begged
Lk 8:27 met by a *d* man from the town.
8:36 the people how the *d* man had been
Jn 7:20 "You are *d,"* the crowd answered.
8:48 that you are a Samaritan and *d?"*
8:52 "Now we know that you are *d!*
10:20 Many of them said, "He is *d*
Ac 19:13 Jesus over those who were *d.*

DEMON-POSSESSION* (DEMON-POSSESSED)
Mt 15:22 is suffering terribly from *d."*

DEMONS* (DEMON)
Dt 32:17 to *d,* which are not God—
Ps 106: 37 and their daughters to *d.*
Mt 7:22 and in your name drive out *d*
8:31 *d* begged Jesus, "If you drive us
9:34 prince of *d* that he drives out *d."*
10: 8 who have leprosy, drive out *d.*
12:24 of *d,* that this fellow drives out
12:24 that this fellow drives out *d."*
12:27 And if I drive out *d* by Beelzebub,
12:28 if I drive out *d* by the Spirit of God,
Mk 1:34 He also drove out many *d,*
1:34 but he would not let the *d* speak
1:39 their synagogues and driving out *d.*
3:15 to have authority to drive out *d.*
3:22 the prince of *d* he is driving out *d."*
5:12 The *d* begged Jesus, "Send us
5:15 possessed by the legion of *d,*
6:13 They drove out many *d*
9:38 "we saw a man driving out *d*
16: 9 out of whom he had driven seven *d*
16:17 In my name they will drive out *d;*
Lk 4:41 *d* came out of many people,
8: 2 from whom seven *d* had come out;
8:30 because many *d* had gone into him.
8:32 The *d* begged Jesus to let them go
8:33 When the *d* came out of the man,
8:35 from whom the *d* had gone out,
8:38 from whom the *d* had gone out
9: 1 and authority to drive out all *d*
9:49 "we saw a man driving out *d*
10:17 the *d* submit to us in your name."
11:15 the prince of *d,* he is driving out *d."*
11:18 you claim that I drive out *d*
11:19 Now if I drive out *d* by Beelzebub,
11:20 if I drive out *d* by the finger of God,
13:32 'I will drive out *d* and heal people
Ro 8:38 neither angels nor *d,* neither
1Co 10:20 of pagans are offered to *d,*
10:20 you to be participants with *d.*
10:21 of the Lord and the cup of *d* too;
10:21 the Lord's table and the table of *d.*
1Ti 4: 1 spirits and things taught by *d.*
Jas 2:19 Good! Even the *d* believe that—
Rev 9:20 they did not stop worshiping *d,*
16:14 of *d* performing miraculous signs,
18: 2 She has become a home for *d*

DEMONSTRATE* (DEMONSTRATES DEMONSTRATION)
Ro 3:25 He did this to *d* his justice,
3:26 he did it to *d* his justice

DEMONSTRATES* (DEMONSTRATE)
Ro 5: 8 God *d* his own love for us in this:

DEMONSTRATION* (DEMONSTRATE)
1Co 2: 4 but with a *d* of the Spirit's power,

DEN
Da 6:16 and threw him into the lions' *d.*
Mt 21:13 you are making it a *'d* of robbers.' "
Mk 11:17 you have made it 'a *d* of robbers.' "
Lk 19:46 but you have made it 'a *d* of robbers

DENARII* (DENARIUS)
Mt 18:28 who owed him a hundred *d.*
Lk 7:41 One owed him five hundred *d,*

DENARIUS (DENARII)
Mt 20: 2 agreed to pay them a *d* for the day
Mk 12:15 Bring me a *d* and let me look at it."

DENIED (DENY)
Mt 26:70 But he *d* it before them all.
Mk 14:68 But he *d* it.
Lk 22:57 But he *d* it.
Jn 18:25 He *d* it, saying, "I am not."
1Ti 5: 8 he has *d* the faith and is worse
Rev 3: 8 my word and have not *d* my name.

DENIES (DENY)
1Jn 2:22 It is the man who *d* that Jesus is
2:23 No one who *d* the Son has

DENY (DENIED DENIES DENYING)
Ex 23: 6 "Do not *d* justice to your poor
Job 27: 5 till I die, I will not *d* my integrity.
Isa 5:23 but *d* justice to the innocent.
La 3:35 to *d* a man his rights
Am 2: 7 and *d* justice to the oppressed.
Mt 16:24 he must *d* himself and take up his
Mk 8:34 he must *d* himself and take up his
Lk 9:23 he must *d* himself and take up his
22:34 you will *d* three times that you
Ac 4:16 miracle, and we cannot *d* it.
Tit 1:16 but by their actions they *d* him.
Jas 3:14 do not boast about it or *d* the truth.
Jude : 4 *d* Jesus Christ our only Sovereign

DENYING* (DENY)
Eze 22:29 mistreat the alien, *d* them justice.
2Ti 3: 5 a form of godliness but *d* its power.
2Pe 2: 1 *d* the sovereign Lord who bought

DEPART (DEPARTED DEPARTS DEPARTURE)
Ge 49:10 The scepter will not *d* from Judah,
Job 1:21 and naked I will *d.*
Mt 25:41 *'D* from me, you who are cursed,
Php 1:23 I desire to *d* and be with Christ,

DEPARTED (DEPART)
1Sa 4:21 "The glory has *d* from Israel"—
Ps 119: 102 I have not *d* from your laws,

DEPARTS (DEPART)
Ecc 5:15 and as he comes, so he *d.*

DEPARTURE (DEPART)
Lk 9:31 spoke about his *d,* which he was
2Ti 4: 6 and the time has come for my *d.*
2Pe 1:15 after my *d* you will always be able

DEPEND
Ps 62: 7 My salvation and my honor *d*

DEPOSES*
Da 2:21 he sets up kings and *d* them.

DEPOSIT
Mt 25:27 money on *d* with the bankers,
Lk 19:23 didn't you put my money on *d,*
2Co 1:22 put his Spirit in our hearts as a *d,*
5: 5 and has given us the Spirit as a *d,*
Eph 1:14 who is a *d* guaranteeing our
2Ti 1:14 Guard the good *d* that was

DEPRAVED* (DEPRAVITY)
Eze 16:47 ways you soon became more *d*
23:11 and prostitution she was more *d*
Ro 1:28 he gave them over to a *d* mind,
Php 2:15 fault in a crooked and *d* generation,
2Ti 3: 8 oppose the truth—men of *d* minds,

DEPRAVITY* (DEPRAVED)
Ro 1:29 of wickedness, evil, greed and *d.*
2Pe 2:19 they themselves are slaves of *d*—

DEPRIVE
Dt 24:17 Do not *d* the alien or the fatherless
Pr 18: 5 or to *d* the innocent of justice.
31: 5 *d* all the oppressed of their rights.
Isa 10: 2 to *d* the poor of their rights
29:21 with false testimony *d* the innocent
La 3:36 to *d* a man of justice—
1Co 7: 5 Do not *d* each other
9:15 die than have anyone *d* me

DEPTH (DEEP)
Ro 8:39 any powers, neither height nor *d,*
11:33 the *d* of the riches of the wisdom

DEPTHS (DEEP)
Ps 130: 1 Out of the *d* I cry to you, O LORD;

DERIDES*
Pr 11:12 who lacks judgment *d* his neighbor,

DERIVES*
Eph 3:15 in heaven and on earth *d* its name.

DESCEND (DESCENDED DESCENDING)
Ro 10: 7 "or 'Who will *d* into the deep?' "

DESCENDED (DESCEND)
Eph 4: 9 except that he also *d* to the lower,
Heb 7:14 For it is clear that our Lord *d*

DESCENDING (DESCEND)
Ge 28:12 of God were ascending and *d* on it.
Mt 3:16 the Spirit of God *d* like a dove
Mk 1:10 and the Spirit *d* on him like a dove.
Jn 1:51 and *d* on the Son of Man."

DESECRATING*
Ne 13:17 you are doing—*d* the Sabbath day?
13:18 against Israel by *d* the Sabbath."
Isa 56: 2 who keeps the Sabbath without *d* it
56: 6 who keep the Sabbath without *d* it
Eze 44: 7 *d* my temple while you offered me

DESERT
Nu 32:13 wander in the *d* forty years,
Dt 8:16 He gave you manna to eat in the *d,*
29: 5 years that I led you through the *d,*
Ne 9:19 you did not abandon them in the *d.*
Ps 78:19 "Can God spread a table in the *d?*
78:52 led them like sheep through the *d.*
Pr 21:19 Better to live in a *d*
Isa 32: 2 like streams of water in the *d*
32:15 and the *d* becomes a fertile field,
35: 6 and streams in the *d.*
43:20 because I provide water in the *d*
Mk 1: 3 "a voice of one calling in the *d,*
1:13 and he was in the *d* forty days,
Rev 12: 6 fled into the *d* to a place prepared

DESERTED (DESERTS)
Ezr 9: 9 our God has not *d* us
Mt 26:56 all the disciples *d* him and fled.
2Ti 1:15 in the province of Asia has *d* me,

DESERTING (DESERTS)
Gal 1: 6 are so quickly *d* the one who called

DESERTS (DESERTED DESERTING)
Zec 11:17 who *d* the flock!

DESERVE* (DESERVED DESERVES)
Ge 40:15 to *d* being put in a dungeon."
Lev 26:21 times over, as your sins *d.*
Jdg 20:10 it can give them what they *d*
1Sa 26:16 you and your men *d* to die,
1Ki 2:26 You *d* to die, but I will not put you
Ps 28: 4 bring back upon them what they *d.*
94: 2 pay back to the proud what they *d.*
103: 10 he does not treat us as our sins *d*
Pr 3:27 from those who *d* it,
Ecc 8:14 men who get what the righteous *d,*
8:14 men who get what the wicked *d,*
Isa 66: 6 repaying his enemies all they *d.*
Jer 14:16 out on them the calamity they *d.*
17:10 according to what his deeds *d.*"
21:14 I will punish you as your deeds *d,*
32:19 to his conduct and as his deeds *d.*
49:12 "If those who do not *d*
La 3:64 Pay them back what they *d,*
Eze 16:59 I will deal with you as you *d,*
Zec 1: 6 to us what our ways and practices *d*
Mt 8: 8 I do not *d* to have you come
22: 8 those I invited did not *d* to come.
Lk 7: 6 for I do not *d* to have you come
23:15 he has done nothing to *d* death.
23:41 for we are getting what our deeds *d*
Ro 1:32 those who do such things *d* death,
1Co 15: 9 even *d* to be called an apostle,
16:18 Such men *d* recognition.
2Co 11:15 end will be what their actions *d.*
Rev 16: 6 blood to drink as they *d.*"

DESERVED* (DESERVE)
2Sa 19:28 descendants *d* nothing
Ezr 9:13 less than our sins have *d*
Job 33:27 but I did not get what I *d.*
Ac 23:29 charge against him that *d* death
Ro 3: 8 Their condemnation is *d.*

DESERVES* (DESERVE)
Nu 35:31 the life of a murderer, who *d* to die.
Dt 25: 2 If the guilty man *d* to be beaten,
25: 2 the number of lashes his crime *d,*
Jdg 9:16 and if you have treated him as he *d*
2Sa 12: 5 the man who did this *d* to die!
Job 34:11 upon him what his conduct *d.*
Jer 51: 6 he will pay her what she *d.*
Lk 7: 4 "This man *d* to have you do this,
10: 7 for the worker *d* his wages.
Ac 26:31 is not doing anything that *d* death
1Ti 1:15 saying that *d* full acceptance:
4: 9 saying that *d* full acceptance
5:18 and "The worker *d* his wages."
Heb 10:29 severely do you think a man *d*

DESIGNATED
Lk 6:13 also *d* apostles: Simon (whom he
Heb 5:10 and was *d* by God to be high priest

DESIRABLE* (DESIRE)
Ge 3: 6 and also *d* for gaining wisdom,
Pr 22: 1 A good name is more *d*
Jer 3:19 and give you a *d* land,

DESIRE* (DESIRABLE DESIRED DESIRES)
Ge 3:16 Your *d* will be for your husband,
Dt 5:21 You shall not set your *d*
1Sa 9:20 to whom is all the *d* of Israel turned
2Sa 19:38 anything you *d* from me I will do
23: 5 and grant me my every *d?*
1Ch 29:18 keep this *d* in the hearts
2Ch 1:11 "Since this is your heart's *d*
9: 8 and his *d* to uphold them forever,
Job 13: 3 But I *d* to speak to the Almighty
21:14 We have no *d* to know your ways.
Ps 10:17 O LORD, the *d* of the afflicted;
20: 4 May he give you the *d*
21: 2 You have granted him the *d*
27:12 me over to the *d* of my foes,
40: 6 Sacrifice and offering you did not *d*
40: 8 I *d* to do your will, O my God;
40:14 may all who *d* my ruin
41: 2 him to the *d* of his foes.
51: 6 Surely you *d* truth
70: 2 may all who *d* my ruin
73:25 earth has nothing I *d* besides you
Pr 3:15 nothing you *d* can compare
8:11 and nothing you *d* can compare
10:24 what the righteous *d* will be
11:23 The *d* of the righteous ends only
12:12 The wicked *d* the plunder
17:16 since he has no *d* to get wisdom?
24: 1 do not *d* their company;
Ecc 12: 5 and *d* no longer is stirred.
SS 6:12 my *d* set me among the royal
7:10 and his *d* is for me.
Isa 26: 8 are the *d* of our hearts.
53: 2 appearance that we should *d* him.
55:11 but will accomplish what I *d*
Eze 24:25 delight of their eyes, their heart's *d,*
Hos 6: 6 For I *d* mercy, not sacrifice,
Mic 7: 3 the powerful dictate what they *d*—
Mal 3: 1 whom you *d,* will come," says
Mt 9:13 learn what this means: 'I *d* mercy,
12: 7 what these words mean, 'I *d* mercy,
Jn 8:44 want to carry out your father's *d.*
Ro 7: 8 in me every kind of covetous *d.*
7:18 For I have the *d* to do what is good,
9:16 depend on man's *d* or effort,
10: 1 my heart's *d* and prayer to God
1Co 12:31 But eagerly *d* the greater gifts.
14: 1 and eagerly *d* spiritual gifts,
2Co 8:10 but also to have the *d* to do so.
8:13 Our *d* is not that others might be
Php 1:23 I *d* to depart and be with Christ,
Heb 10: 5 Sacrifice and offering you did not *d*
10: 8 and sin offerings you did not *d,*
13:18 *d* to live honorably in every way.
Jas 1:14 by his own evil *d,* he is dragged
1:15 Then, after *d* has conceived,
2Pe 2:10 of those who follow the corrupt *d*

DESIRED (DESIRE)
Hag 2: 7 and the *d* of all nations will come,
Lk 22:15 "I have eagerly *d* to eat this

DESIRES* (DESIRE)
Ge 4: 7 at your door; it *d* to have you,
41:16 will give Pharaoh the answer he *d.*"
2Sa 3:21 rule over all that your heart *d.*"
1Ki 11:37 rule over all that your heart *d;*
Job 17:11 and so are the *d* of my heart.
31:16 "If I have denied the *d* of the poor
Ps 34:12 and *d* to see many good days,
37: 4 he will give you the *d* of your heart.
103: 5 who satisfies your *d* with good things,
140: 8 do not grant the wicked their *d,*
145: 16 satisfy the *d* of every living thing.
145: 19 He fulfills the *d* of those who fear
Pr 11: 6 the unfaithful are trapped by evil *d.*
13: 4 *d* of the diligent are fully satisfied.
19:22 What a man *d* is unfailing love;
Ecc 6: 2 so that he lacks nothing his heart *d,*
SS 2: 7 or awaken love / until it so *d.*
3: 5 or awaken love / until it so *d.*
8: 4 or awaken love / until it so *d.*
Hab 2: 4 his *d* are not upright—
Mk 4:19 and the *d* for other things come in
Ro 1:24 over in the sinful *d* of their hearts
6:12 body so that you obey its evil *d.*
8: 5 set on what that nature *d;*
8: 5 set on what the Spirit *d.*
13:14 to gratify the *d* of the sinful nature.
Gal 5:16 and you will not gratify the *d*
5:17 the sinful nature *d* what is contrary
5:24 nature with its passions and *d.*
Eph 2: 3 and following its *d* and thoughts.
4:22 being corrupted by its deceitful *d;*
Col 3: 5 impurity, lust, evil *d* and greed,
1Ti 3: 1 an overseer, he *d* a noble task.
5:11 their sensual *d* overcome their
6: 9 and harmful *d* that plunge men
2Ti 2:22 Flee the evil *d* of youth,
3: 6 are swayed by all kinds of evil *d,*
4: 3 Instead, to suit their own *d,*
Jas 1:20 about the righteous life that God *d.*
4: 1 from your *d* that battle within you?
1Pe 1:14 conform to the evil *d* you had
2:11 to abstain from sinful *d,* which war
4: 2 of his earthly life for evil human *d,*
2Pe 1: 4 in the world caused by evil *d.*
2:18 to the lustful *d* of sinful human
3: 3 and following their own evil *d.*
1Jn 2:17 The world and its *d* pass away,
Jude :16 they follow their own evil *d;*
:18 will follow their own ungodly *d.*"

DESOLATE (DESOLATION)
Isa 54: 1 are the children of the *d* woman
Gal 4:27 are the children of the *d* woman

DESOLATION (DESOLATE)
Da 11:31 up the abomination that causes *d.*
12:11 abomination that causes *d* is set up,
Mt 24:15 'the abomination that causes *d,*'

DESPAIR (DESPAIRED)
Isa 61: 3 instead of a spirit of *d.*
2Co 4: 8 perplexed, but not in *d;* persecuted,

DESPAIRED* (DESPAIR)
2Co 1: 8 ability to endure, so that we *d*

DESPERATE*
2Sa 12:18 He may do something *d.*"
Ps 60: 3 have shown your people *d* times;
79: 8 for we are in *d* need.
142: 6 for I am in *d* need;

DESPISE (DESPISED DESPISES)
2Sa 12: 9 Why did you *d* the word
Job 5:17 so do not *d* the discipline
36: 5 God is mighty, but does not *d* men;
42: 6 Therefore I *d* myself
Ps 51:17 O God, you will not *d.*
102: 17 he will not *d* their plea.
Pr 1: 7 but fools *d* wisdom and discipline.
3:11 do not *d* the LORD's discipline
6:30 Men do not *d* a thief if he steals
23:22 do not *d* your mother
Jer 14:21 of your name do not *d* us;
Am 5:10 and *d* him who tells the truth.
5:21 "I hate, I *d* your religious feasts;
Mt 6:24 devoted to the one and *d* the other.
Lk 16:13 devoted to the one and *d* the other.
1Co 11:22 Or do you *d* the church of God
Tit 2:15 Do not let anyone *d* you.
2Pe 2:10 of the sinful nature and *d* authority.

DESPISED (DESPISE)
Ge 25:34 So Esau *d* his birthright.
Ps 22: 6 by men and *d* by the people.
Pr 12: 8 but men with warped minds are *d.*
Isa 53: 3 He was *d* and rejected by men,
53: 3 he was *d,* and we esteemed him not
1Co 1:28 of this world and the *d* things—

DESPISES (DESPISE)
Pr 14:21 He who *d* his neighbor sins,
15:20 but a foolish man *d* his mother.
15:32 who ignores discipline *d* himself,
Zec 4:10 "Who *d* the day of small things?

DESTINED (DESTINY)
Lk 2:34 "This child is *d* to cause the falling
1Co 2: 7 and that God *d* for our glory
Col 2:22 These are all *d* to perish with use,
1Th 3: 3 know quite well that we were *d*
Heb 9:27 Just as man is *d* to die once,
1Pe 2: 8 which is also what they were *d* for.

DESTINY* (DESTINED PREDESTINED)
Job 8:13 Such is the *d* of all who forget God;
Ps 73:17 then I understood their final *d.*
Ecc 7: 2 for death is the *d* of every man;
9: 2 share a common *d*— the righteous
9: 3 the sun: The same *d* overtakes all.
Isa 65:11 and fill bowls of mixed wine for *D,*
Php 3:19 Their *d* is destruction, their god is

DESTITUTE
Ps 102: 17 to the prayer of the *d;*
Pr 31: 8 for the rights of all who are *d.*
Heb 11:37 *d,* persecuted and mistreated—

DESTROY (DESTROYED DESTROYING DESTROYS DESTRUCTION DESTRUCTIVE)
Ge 6:17 floodwaters on the earth to *d* all life
9:11 will there be a flood to *d* the earth."
Pr 1:32 complacency of fools will *d* them;
Mt 10:28 of the One who can *d* both soul
Mk 14:58 'I will *d* this man-made temple
Lk 4:34 to *d* us? I know who you are—
Jn 10:10 only to steal and kill and *d;*
Ac 8: 3 But Saul began to *d* the church.
Rev 11:18 destroying those who *d* the earth."

DESTROYED (DESTROY)
Dt 8:19 you today that you will surely be *d.*
Job 19:26 And after my skin has been *d,*
Pr 6:15 he will suddenly be *d*—
11: 3 the unfaithful are *d*
21:28 listens to him will be *d* forever.
29: 1 will suddenly be *d*—
Isa 55:13 which will not be *d.*"
Da 2:44 up a kingdom that will never be *d,*
6:26 his kingdom will not be *d,*
1Co 5: 5 so that the sinful nature may be *d*
8:11 for whom Christ died, is *d*
15:24 Father after he has *d* all dominion,
15:26 The last enemy to be *d* is death.
2Co 4: 9 abandoned; struck down, but not *d.*
5: 1 if the earthly tent we live in is *d,*
Gal 5:15 or you will be *d* by each other.
Eph 2:14 the two one and has *d* the barrier,
2Ti 1:10 who has *d* death and has brought
Heb 10:39 of those who shrink back and are *d,*
2Pe 2:12 born only to be caught and *d,*
3:10 the elements will be *d* by fire,
3:11 Since everything will be *d*
Jude : 5 later *d* those who did not believe.
:11 have been *d* in Korah's rebellion.

DESTROYING (DESTROY)
Jer 23: 1 “Woe to the shepherds who are *d*

DESTROYS (DESTROY)
Pr 6:32 whoever does so *d* himself.
11: 9 mouth the godless *d* his neighbor,
18: 9 is brother to one who *d.*
28:24 he is partner to him who *d.*
Ecc 9:18 but one sinner *d* much good.
1Co 3:17 If anyone *d* God's temple,

DESTRUCTION (DESTROY)
Nu 32:15 and you will be the cause of their *d*
Pr 16:18 Pride goes before *d,*
17:19 he who builds a high gate invites *d.*
24:22 for those two will send sudden *d*
Hos 13:14 Where, O grave, is your *d?*
Mt 7:13 broad is the road that leads to *d,*
Lk 6:49 it collapsed and its *d* was complete
Jn 17:12 except the one doomed to *d*
Ro 9:22 of his wrath—prepared for *d?*
Gal 6: 8 from that nature will reap *d;*
Php 3:19 Their destiny is *d,* their god is their
1Th 5: 3 *d* will come on them suddenly,
2Th 1: 9 punished with everlasting *d*
2: 3 is revealed, the man doomed to *d.*
1Ti 6: 9 that plunge men into ruin and *d.*
2Pe 2: 1 bringing swift *d* on themselves.
2: 3 and their *d* has not been sleeping.
3: 7 of judgment and *d* of ungodly men.
3:12 That day will bring about the *d*
3:16 other Scriptures, to their own *d.*
Rev 17: 8 out of the Abyss and go to his *d.*
17:11 to the seven and is going to his *d.*

DESTRUCTIVE (DESTROY)
2Pe 2: 1 will secretly introduce *d* heresies,

DETERMINED (DETERMINES)
Job 14: 5 Man's days are *d;*
Isa 14:26 This is the plan *d* for the whole
Da 11:36 for what has been *d* must take place
Ac 17:26 and he *d* the times set for them

DETERMINES* (DETERMINED)
Ps 147: 4 He *d* the number of the stars
Pr 16: 9 but the LORD *d* his steps.
1Co 12:11 them to each one, just as he *d.*

DETEST (DETESTABLE DETESTED DETESTS)
Lev 11:10 in the water—you are to *d.*
Pr 8: 7 for my lips *d* wickedness.
13:19 but fools *d* turning from evil.
16:12 Kings *d* wrongdoing,
24: 9 and men *d* a mocker.
29:27 The righteous *d* the dishonest;
29:27 the wicked *d* the upright.

DETESTABLE (DETEST)
Pr 6:16 seven that are *d* to him:
21:27 The sacrifice of the wicked is *d*—
28: 9 even his prayers are *d.*
Isa 1:13 Your incense is *d* to me.
41:24 he who chooses you is *d.*
44:19 Shall I make a *d* thing
Jer 44: 4 ‘Do not do this *d* thing that I hate!’
Eze 8:13 doing things that are even more *d.*”
Lk 16:15 among men is *d* in God's sight.
Tit 1:16 They are *d,* disobedient
1Pe 4: 3 orgies, carousing and *d* idolatry.

DETESTED* (DETEST)
Zec 11: 8 The flock *d* me, and I grew weary

DETESTS* (DETEST)
Dt 22: 5 LORD your God *d* anyone who
23:18 the LORD your God *d* them both.
25:16 LORD your God *d* anyone who
Pr 3:32 for the LORD *d* a perverse man
11:20 The LORD *d* men
12:22 The LORD *d* lying lips,
15: 8 The LORD *d* the sacrifice
15: 9 The LORD *d* the way
15:26 The LORD *d* the thoughts
16: 5 The LORD *d* all the proud of heart
17:15 the LORD *d* them both.
20:10 the LORD *d* them both.
20:23 The LORD *d* differing weights,

DEVIATE*
2Ch 8:15 They did not *d* from the king's

DEVICES*
Ps 81:12 to follow their own *d.*

DEVIL* (DEVIL'S)
Mt 4: 1 the desert to be tempted by the *d.*
4: 5 the *d* took him to the holy city
4: 8 *d* took him to a very high mountain
4:11 the *d* left him, and angels came
13:39 the enemy who sows them is the *d.*
25:41 the eternal fire prepared for the *d*
Lk 4: 2 forty days he was tempted by the *d.*
4: 3 *d* said to him, “If you are the Son
4: 5 The *d* led him up to a high place
4: 9 The *d* led him to Jerusalem
4:13 When the *d* had finished all this
8:12 then the *d* comes and takes away
Jn 6:70 of you is a *d!*” (He meant Judas,
8:44 You belong to your father, the *d,*
13: 2 the *d* had already prompted Judas
Ac 10:38 were under the power of the *d,*
13:10 “You are a child of the *d*
Eph 4:27 and do not give the *d* a foothold.
1Ti 3: 6 under the same judgment as the *d.*
2Ti 2:26 and escape from the trap of the *d,*
Heb 2:14 the *d*— and free those who all their
Jas 3:15 but is earthly, unspiritual, of the *d.*
4: 7 Resist the *d,* and he will flee
1Pe 5: 8 Your enemy the *d* prowls
1Jn 3: 8 because the *d* has been sinning
3: 8 who does what is sinful is of the *d,*
3:10 and who the children of the *d* are:
Jude : 9 with the *d* about the body of Moses
Rev 2:10 the *d* will put some of you in prison
12: 9 that ancient serpent called the *d*
12:12 the *d* has gone down to you!
20: 2 that ancient serpent, who is the *d,*
20:10 And the *d,* who deceived them,

DEVIL'S* (DEVIL)
Eph 6:11 stand against the *d* schemes.
1Ti 3: 7 into disgrace and into the *d* trap.
1Jn 3: 8 was to destroy the *d* work.

DEVIOUS*
Pr 2:15 and who are *d* in their ways.
14: 2 he whose ways are *d* despises him.
21: 8 The way of the guilty is *d,*

DEVOTE* (DEVOTED DEVOTING DEVOTION DEVOUT)
1Ch 22:19 Now *d* your heart and soul
2Ch 31: 4 Levites so they could *d* themselves
Job 11:13 “Yet if you *d* your heart to him
Jer 30:21 for who is he who will *d* himself
Mic 4:13 You will *d* their ill-gotten gains
1Co 7: 5 so that you may *d* yourselves
Col 4: 2 *D* yourselves to prayer, being
1Ti 1: 4 nor to *d* themselves to myths
4:13 *d* yourself to the public reading
Tit 3: 8 may be careful to *d* themselves
3:14 people must learn to *d* themselves

DEVOTED (DEVOTE)
1Ki 11: 4 and his heart was not fully *d*
Ezr 7:10 For Ezra had *d* himself to the study
Ps 86: 2 Guard my life, for I am *d* to you.
Mt 6:24 or he will be *d* to the one
Mk 7:11 from me is Corban' (that is, a gift *d*
Ac 2:42 They *d* themselves
18: 5 Paul *d* himself exclusively
Ro 12:10 Be *d* to one another
1Co 7:34 Her aim is to be *d* to the Lord
16:15 and they have *d* themselves
2Co 7:12 for yourselves how *d* to us you are.

DEVOTING* (DEVOTE)
1Ti 5:10 *d* herself to all kinds of good deeds.

DEVOTION* (DEVOTE)
2Ki 20: 3 and with wholehearted *d* and have
1Ch 28: 9 and serve him with wholehearted *d*
29: 3 in my *d* to the temple
29:19 son Solomon the wholehearted *d*
2Ch 32:32 and his acts of *d* are written
35:26 of Josiah's reign and his acts of *d,*
Job 6:14 despairing man should have the *d*
15: 4 and hinder *d* to God.
Isa 38: 3 and with wholehearted *d* and have
Jer 2: 2 “ ‘I remember the *d* of your youth,
Eze 33:31 With their mouths they express *d,*
1Co 7:35 way in undivided *d* to the Lord.
2Co 11: 3 from your sincere and pure *d*

DEVOUR (DEVOURED DEVOURING DEVOURS)
2Sa 2:26 “Must the sword *d* forever?
Mk 12:40 They *d* widows' houses
1Pe 5: 8 lion looking for someone to *d.*

DEVOURED (DEVOUR)
Jer 30:16 But all who devour you will be *d;*

DEVOURING (DEVOUR)
Gal 5:15 keep on biting and *d* each other,

DEVOURS (DEVOUR)
2Sa 11:25 the sword *d* one as well as another.
Pr 21:20 but a foolish man *d* all he has.

DEVOUT* (DEVOTE)
1Ki 18: 3 (Obadiah was a *d* believer
Isa 57: 1 *d* men are taken away,
Lk 2:25 Simeon, who was righteous and *d.*
Ac 10: 2 his family were *d* and God-fearing;
10: 7 a *d* soldier who was one of his attendants
13:43 and *d* converts to Judaism followed
22:12 He was a *d* observer of the law

DEW
Jdg 6:37 If there is *d* only on the fleece

DICTATED
Jer 36: 4 and while Jeremiah *d* all the words

DIE (DEAD DEADENED DEATH DIED DIES DYING)
Ge 2:17 when you eat of it you will surely *d*
3: 3 you must not touch it, or you will *d*
3: 4 will not surely *d,*” the serpent said
Ex 11: 5 Every firstborn son in Egypt will *d,*
Ru 1:17 Where you *d* I will *d,* and there I
2Ki 14: 6 each is to *d* for his own sins.”
Job 2: 9 Curse God and *d!*” He replied,
Pr 5:23 He will *d* for lack of discipline,
10:21 but fools *d* for lack of judgment.
15:10 he who hates correction will *d.*
23:13 with the rod, he will not *d.*
Ecc 3: 2 a time to be born and a time to *d,*
Isa 22:13 “for tomorrow we *d!*”
66:24 their worm will not *d,* nor will their
Jer 31:30 everyone will *d* for his own sin;
Eze 3:18 that wicked man will *d* for his sin,
3:19 he will *d* for his sin; but you will
3:20 block before him, he will *d.*
18: 4 soul who sins is the one who will *d.*
18:20 soul who sins is the one who will *d.*
18:31 Why will you *d,* O house of Israel?
33: 8 ‘O wicked man, you will surely *d,*’
Mt 26:52 “for all who draw the sword will *d*
Mk 9:48 “ ‘their worm does not *d,*
Jn 8:21 and you will *d* in your sin.
11:26 and believes in me will never *d.*
Ro 5: 7 Very rarely will anyone *d*
14: 8 and if we *d,* we *d* to the Lord.
1Co 15:22 in Adam all *d,* so in Christ all will
15:31 I *d* every day—I mean that,
15:32 for tomorrow we *d.*”
Php 1:21 to live is Christ and to *d* is gain.
Heb 9:27 Just as man is destined to *d* once,
1Pe 2:24 so that we might *d* to sins
Rev 14:13 Blessed are the dead who *d*

DIED (DIE)
1Ki 16:18 So he *d,* because of the sins he had
1Ch 1:51 Hadad also *d.*
10:13 Saul *d* because he was unfaithful
Lk 16:22 “The time came when the beggar *d*
Ro 5: 6 we were still powerless, Christ *d*
5: 8 we were still sinners, Christ *d*
6: 2 By no means! We *d* to sin;
6: 7 anyone who has *d* has been freed
6: 8 if we *d* with Christ, we believe that
6:10 The death he *d,* he *d* to sin once
14: 9 Christ *d* and returned to life
14:15 brother for whom Christ *d.*
1Co 8:11 for whom Christ *d,* is destroyed
15: 3 that Christ *d* for our sins according
2Co 5:14 *d* for all, and therefore all *d.*
5:15 he *d* for all, that those who live
Col 2:20 Since you *d* with Christ
3: 3 For you *d,* and your life is now
1Th 4:14 We believe that Jesus *d*
5:10 He *d* for us so that, whether we are
2Ti 2:11 If we *d* with him,
Heb 9:15 now that he has *d* as a ransom
9:17 in force only when somebody has *d*
1Pe 3:18 For Christ *d* for sins once for all,
Rev 2: 8 who *d* and came to life again.

DIES (DIE)
Job 14:14 If a man *d,* will he live again?
Pr 11: 7 a wicked man *d,* his hope perishes;
26:20 without gossip a quarrel *d* down.
Jn 11:25 in me will live, even though he *d;*
12:24 But if it *d,* it produces many seeds.
Ro 7: 2 but if her husband *d,* she is released
14: 7 and none of us *d* to himself alone.
1Co 7:39 But if her husband *d,* she is free
15:36 does not come to life unless it *d.*

DIFFERENCE* (DIFFERENT)
2Sa 19:35 Can I tell the *d* between what is
2Ch 12: 8 so that they may learn the *d*
Eze 22:26 they teach that there is no *d*
44:23 are to teach my people the *d*
Ro 3:22 There is no *d,* for all have sinned

Ro 10:12 For there is no *d* between Jew
Gal 2: 6 whatever they were makes no *d*

DIFFERENCES* (DIFFERENT)
1Co 11:19 to be *d* among you to show which

DIFFERENT* (DIFFERENCE DIFFERENCES DIFFERING DIFFERS)
Lev 19:19 " 'Do not mate *d* kinds of animals.
Nu 14:24 my servant Caleb has a *d* spirit
1Sa 10: 6 you will be changed into a *d* person
Est 1: 7 each one *d* from the other,
3: 8 whose customs are *d* from those
Da 7: 3 Four great beasts, each *d*
7: 7 It was *d* from all the former beasts,
7:19 which was *d* from all the others
7:23 It will be *d* from all the other
7:24 them another king will arise, *d*
11:29 but this time the outcome will be *d*
Mk 16:12 Jesus appeared in a *d* form
Ro 12: 6 We have *d* gifts, according
1Co 4: 7 For who makes you *d*
12: 4 There are *d* kinds of gifts,
12: 5 There are *d* kinds of service,
12: 6 There are *d* kinds of working,
12:10 speaking in *d* kinds of tongues,
12:28 and those speaking in *d* kinds
2Co 11: 4 or a *d* gospel from the one you
11: 4 or if you receive a *d* spirit
Gal 1: 6 and are turning to a *d* gospel—
4: 1 he is no *d* from a slave,
Heb 7:13 are said belonged to a *d* tribe,
Jas 2:25 and sent them off in a *d* direction?

DIFFERING* (DIFFERENT)
Dt 25:13 Do not have two *d* weights
25:14 Do not have two *d* measures
Pr 20:10 Differing weights and *d* measures
20:10 *D* weights and differing measures
20:23 The LORD detests *d* weights,

DIFFERS* (DIFFERENT)
1Co 15:41 and star *d* from star in splendor.

DIFFICULT (DIFFICULTIES)
Ex 18:22 but have them bring every *d* case
Dt 30:11 commanding you today is not too *d*
2Ki 2:10 "You have asked a *d* thing,"
Eze 3: 5 of obscure speech and *d* language,
Ac 15:19 that we should not make it *d*

DIFFICULTIES* (DIFFICULT)
Dt 31:17 and *d* will come upon them,
31:21 when many disasters and *d* come
2Co 12:10 in hardships, in persecutions, in *d*.

DIGNITY
Pr 31:25 She is clothed with strength and *d*;

DIGS
Pr 26:27 If a man *d* a pit, he will fall into it;

DILIGENCE (DILIGENT)
Ezr 5: 8 The work is being carried on with *d*
Heb 6:11 to show this same *d* to the very end

DILIGENT (DILIGENCE)
Pr 10: 4 but *d* hands bring wealth.
12:24 *D* hands will rule,
12:27 the *d* man prizes his possessions.
13: 4 of the *d* are fully satisfied.
21: 5 The plans of the *d* lead to profit
1Ti 4:15 Be *d* in these matters; give yourself

DINAH*
Only daughter of Jacob, by Leah (Ge 30:21; 46:15). Raped by Shechem; avenged by Simeon and Levi (Ge 34).

DINE
Pr 23: 1 When you sit to *d* with a ruler,

DIOTREPHES*
3Jn : 9 but *D*, who loves to be first,

DIRECT (DIRECTED DIRECTIVES DIRECTS)
Ge 18:19 so that he will *d* his children
Dt 17:10 to do everything they *d* you to do.
Ps 119: 35 *D* me in the path of your
119:133 *D* my footsteps according
Jer 10:23 it is not for man to *d* his steps.
2Th 3: 5 May the Lord *d* your hearts
1Ti 5:17 The elders who *d* the affairs

DIRECTED (DIRECT)
Ge 24:51 master's son, as the LORD has *d*."
Nu 16:40 as the LORD *d* him through Moses
Dt 2: 1 Sea, as the LORD had *d* me.
6: 1 laws the LORD your God *d* me
Jos 11: 9 did to them as the LORD had *d*:
11:23 just as the LORD had *d* Moses,
Pr 20:24 A man's steps are *d* by the LORD.
Jer 13: 2 as the LORD *d*, and put it
Ac 7:44 It had been made as God *d* Moses,
Tit 1: 5 elders in every town, as I *d* you.

DIRECTIVES* (DIRECT)
1Co 11:17 In the following *d* I have no praise

DIRECTS (DIRECT)
Ps 42: 8 By day the LORD *d* his love,
Isa 48:17 who *d* you in the way you should

DIRGE*
Mt 11:17 we sang a *d*,
Lk 7:32 we sang a *d*,

DISABLED*
Jn 5: 3 number of *d* people used to lie—
Heb 12:13 so that the lame may not be *d*,

DISAGREEMENT*
Ac 15:39 had such a sharp *d* that they parted

DISAPPEAR (DISAPPEARED DISAPPEARS)
Mt 5:18 will by any means *d* from the Law
Lk 16:17 earth to *d* than for the least stroke
Heb 8:13 is obsolete and aging will soon *d*.
2Pe 3:10 The heavens will *d* with a roar;

DISAPPEARED (DISAPPEAR)
1Ki 20:40 busy here and there, the man *d*."

DISAPPEARS (DISAPPEAR)
1Co 13:10 perfection comes, the imperfect *d*.

DISAPPOINT* (DISAPPOINTED)
Ro 5: 5 And hope does not *d* us,

DISAPPOINTED (DISAPPOINT)
Ps 22: 5 in you they trusted and were not *d*.

DISAPPROVE*
Pr 24:18 or the LORD will see and *d*

DISARMED*
Col 2:15 And having *d* the powers

DISASTER
Ex 32:12 and do not bring *d* on your people.
Ps 57: 1 wings until the *d* has passed.
Pr 1:26 I in turn will laugh at your *d*;
3:25 Have no fear of sudden *d*
6:15 Therefore *d* will overtake him
16: 4 even the wicked for a day of *d*.
17: 5 over *d* will not go unpunished.
27:10 house when *d* strikes you—
Isa 45: 7 I bring prosperity and create *d*;
Jer 17:17 you are my refuge in the day of *d*.
Eze 7: 5 An unheard-of *d* is coming.

DISCERN (DISCERNED DISCERNING DISCERNMENT)
Ps 19:12 Who can *d* his errors?
139: 3 You *d* my going out and my lying
Php 1:10 you may be able to *d* what is best

DISCERNED (DISCERN)
1Co 2:14 because they are spiritually *d*.

DISCERNING (DISCERN)
1Ki 3: 9 So give your servant a *d* heart
3:12 I will give you a wise and *d* heart,
Pr 1: 5 and let the *d* get guidance—
8: 9 To the *d* all of them are right;
10:13 on the lips of the *d*,
14: 6 knowledge comes easily to the *d*.
14:33 in the heart of the *d*
15:14 The *d* heart seeks knowledge,
16:21 The wise in heart are called *d*,
17:24 A *d* man keeps wisdom in view,
17:28 and *d* if he holds his tongue.
18:15 heart of the *d* acquires knowledge;
19:25 rebuke a *d* man, and he will gain
28: 7 He who keeps the law is a *d* son,

DISCERNMENT (DISCERN)
Ps 119:125 I am your servant; give me *d*
Pr 3:21 preserve sound judgment and *d*,
17:10 A rebuke impresses a man of *d*
28:11 a poor man who has *d* sees

DISCHARGED* (DISCHARGING)
Ecc 8: 8 As no one is *d* in time of war,

DISCHARGING* (DISCHARGED)
1Co 9:17 I am simply *d* the trust committed

DISCIPLE (DISCIPLES DISCIPLES')
Mt 10:42 these little ones because he is my *d*,
Lk 14:26 his own life—he cannot be my *d*.
14:27 and follow me cannot be my *d*.
14:33 everything he has cannot be my *d*.
Jn 13:23 of them, the *d* whom Jesus loved,
19:26 and the *d* whom he loved standing
21: 7 Then the *d* whom Jesus loved said
21:20 saw that the *d* whom Jesus loved

DISCIPLES (DISCIPLE)
Mt 10: 1 He called his twelve *d* to him
26:56 Then all the *d* deserted him
28:19 Therefore go and make *d*
Mk 3: 7 withdrew with his *d* to the lake,
16:20 Then the *d* went out and preached
Lk 6:13 he called his *d* to him and chose
Jn 2:11 and his *d* put their faith in him.
6:66 many of his *d* turned back
8:31 to my teaching, you are really my *d*
12:16 At first his *d* did not understand all
13:35 men will know that you are my *d*
15: 8 showing yourselves to be my *d*.
20:20 The *d* were overjoyed
Ac 6: 1 the number of *d* was increasing,
11:26 The *d* were called Christians first
14:22 strengthening the *d*
18:23 Phrygia, strengthening all the *d*.

DISCIPLES' (DISCIPLE)
Jn 13: 5 and began to wash his *d* feet,

DISCIPLINE* (DISCIPLINED DISCIPLINES SELF-DISCIPLINE)
Dt 4:36 made you hear his voice to *d* you.
11: 2 and experienced the *d*
21:18 listen to them when they *d* him,
Job 5:17 so do not despise the *d*
Ps 6: 1 or *d* me in your wrath.
38: 1 or *d* me in your wrath.
39:11 You rebuke and *d* men for their sin;
94:12 Blessed is the man you *d*, O LORD
Pr 1: 2 for attaining wisdom and *d*;
1: 7 but fools despise wisdom and *d*.
3:11 do not despise the LORD's *d*
5:12 You will say, "How I hated *d*!
5:23 He will die for lack of *d*,
6:23 and the corrections of *d*
10:17 He who heeds *d* shows the way
12: 1 Whoever loves *d* loves knowledge,
13:18 He who ignores *d* comes to poverty
13:24 who loves him is careful to *d* him.
15: 5 A fool spurns his father's *d*,
15:10 Stern *d* awaits him who leaves
15:32 He who ignores *d* despises himself,
19:18 *D* your son, for in that there is hope
22:15 the rod of *d* will drive it far
23:13 Do not withhold *d* from a child;
23:23 get wisdom, *d* and understanding.
29:17 *D* your son, and he will give you
Jer 17:23 would not listen or respond to *d*.
30:11 I will *d* you but only with justice;
32:33 would not listen or respond to *d*.
46:28 I will *d* you but only with justice;
Hos 5: 2 I will *d* all of them.
Heb 12: 5 do not make light of the Lord's *d*,
12: 7 as *d*; God is treating you
12: 8 (and everyone undergoes *d*),
12:11 No *d* seems pleasant at the time,
Rev 3:19 Those whom I love I rebuke and *d*.

DISCIPLINED* (DISCIPLINE)
Pr 1: 3 for acquiring a *d* and prudent life,
Isa 26:16 when you *d* them,
Jer 31:18 and I have been *d*.
31:18 'You *d* me like an unruly calf,
1Co 11:32 we are being *d* so that we will not
Tit 1: 8 upright, holy and *d*.
Heb 12: 7 For what son is not *d* by his father?
12: 8 you are not *d* (and everyone
12: 9 all had human fathers who *d* us
12:10 Our fathers *d* us for a little while

DISCIPLINES* (DISCIPLINE)
Dt 8: 5 so the LORD your God *d* you.
8: 5 your heart that as a man *d* his son,
Ps 94:10 Does he who *d* nations not punish?
Pr 3:12 the LORD *d* those he loves,
Heb 12: 6 because the Lord *d* those he loves,
12:10 but God *d* us for our good,

DISCLOSED
Lk 8:17 is nothing hidden that will not be *d*,
Col 1:26 and generations, but is now *d*
Heb 9: 8 Holy Place had not yet been *d*

DISCORD
Gal 5:20 idolatry and witchcraft; hatred, *d*,

DISCOURAGED* (DISCOURAGEMENT)
Nu 32: 9 they *d* the Israelites
Dt 1:21 Do not be afraid; do not be *d*."
31: 8 Do not be afraid; do not be *d*."
Jos 1: 9 Do not be terrified; do not be *d*,
8: 1 "Do not be afraid; do not be *d*.

Jos 10:25 "Do not be afraid; do not be *d.*
1Ch 22:13 Do not be afraid or *d.*
28:20 or *d,* for the LORD God,
2Ch 20:15 or *d* because of this vast army.
20:17 Do not be afraid; do not be *d.*
32: 7 or *d* because of the king of Assyria
Job 4: 5 to you, and you are *d;*
Isa 42: 4 he will not falter or be *d*
Eph 3:13 to be *d* because of my sufferings
Col 3:21 children, or they will become *d.*

DISCOURAGEMENT* (DISCOURAGED)
Ex 6: 9 of their *d* and cruel bondage.

DISCOVERED
2Ki 23:24 book that Hilkiah the priest had *d*

DISCREDIT* (DISCREDITED)
Ne 6:13 would give me a bad name to *d* me.
Job 40: 8 "Would you *d* my justice?

DISCREDITED (DISCREDIT)
2Co 6: 3 so that our ministry will not be *d.*

DISCRETION*
1Ch 22:12 May the LORD give you *d*
Pr 1: 4 knowledge and *d* to the young—
2:11 *D* will protect you,
5: 2 that you may maintain *d*
8:12 I possess knowledge and *d.*
11:22 a beautiful woman who shows no *d.*

DISCRIMINATED*
Jas 2: 4 have you not *d* among yourselves

DISEASE (DISEASES)
Mt 4:23 and healing every *d* and sickness
9:35 and healing every *d* and sickness.
10: 1 and to heal every *d* and sickness.

DISEASES (DISEASE)
Ps 103: 3 and heals all my *d;*
Mt 8:17 and carried our *d."*
Mk 3:10 those with *d* were pushing forward
Lk 9: 1 drive out all demons and to cure *d,*

DISFIGURE* (DISFIGURED)
Mt 6:16 for they *d* their faces

DISFIGURED (DISFIGURE)
Isa 52:14 his appearance was so *d*

DISGRACE (DISGRACEFUL DISGRACES)
Ps 44:15 My *d* is before me all day long,
52: 1 you who are a *d* in the eyes of God?
74:21 not let the oppressed retreat in *d;*
Pr 6:33 Blows and *d* are his lot,
11: 2 When pride comes, then comes *d,*
14:34 but sin is a *d* to any people.
19:26 is a son who brings shame and *d.*
Mt 1:19 want to expose her to public *d,*
Ac 5:41 of suffering *d* for the Name.
1Co 11: 6 and if it is a *d* for a woman
11:14 it is a *d* to him, but that
1Ti 3: 7 so that he will not fall into *d*
Heb 6: 6 and subjecting him to public *d.*
11:26 He regarded *d* for the sake
13:13 the camp, bearing the *d* he bore.

DISGRACEFUL (DISGRACE)
Pr 10: 5 during harvest is a *d* son.
12: 4 a *d* wife is like decay in his bones.
17: 2 wise servant will rule over a *d* son,
1Co 14:35 for it is *d* for a woman to speak

DISGRACES (DISGRACE)
Pr 28: 7 of gluttons *d* his father.
29:15 but a child left to himself *d* his mother

DISGUISES*
Pr 26:24 A malicious man *d* himself

DISH
Pr 19:24 sluggard buries his hand in the *d;*
Mt 23:25 the outside of the cup and *d,*

DISHONEST*
Ex 18:21 trustworthy men who hate *d* gain
Lev 19:35 " 'Do not use *d* standards
1Sa 8: 3 They turned aside after *d* gain
Pr 11: 1 The LORD abhors *d* scales,
13:11 *D* money dwindles away,
20:23 and *d* scales do not please him.
29:27 The righteous detest the *d;*
Jer 22:17 are set only on *d* gain,
Eze 28:18 By your many sins and *d* trade
Hos 12: 7 The merchant uses *d* scales;
Am 8: 5 and cheating with *d* scales,
Mic 6:11 Shall I acquit a man with *d* scales,
Lk 16: 8 master commended the *d* manager
16:10 whoever is *d* with very little will
Lk 16:10 with very little will also be *d*
1Ti 3: 8 wine, and not pursuing *d* gain.
Tit 1: 7 not violent, not pursuing *d* gain.
1:11 and that for the sake of *d* gain.

DISHONOR* (DISHONORED DISHONORS)
Lev 18: 7 " 'Do not *d* your father
18: 8 wife; that would *d* your father.
18:10 daughter; that would *d* you.
18:14 " 'Do not *d* your father's brother
18:16 that would *d* your brother.
20:19 for that would *d* a close relative;
Dt 22:30 he must not *d* his father's bed.
Pr 30: 9 and so *d* the name of my God.
Jer 14:21 do not *d* your glorious throne.
20:11 their *d* will never be forgotten.
La 2: 2 princes down to the ground in *d.*
Eze 22:10 are those who *d* their fathers' bed;
Jn 8:49 I honor my Father and you *d* me.
Ro 2:23 do you *d* God by breaking the law?
1Co 15:43 it is sown in *d,* it is raised in glory;
2Co 6: 8 through glory and *d,* bad report

DISHONORED* (DISHONOR)
Lev 20:11 father's wife, he has *d* his father.
20:17 He has *d* his sister and will be held
20:20 with his aunt, he has *d* his uncle.
20:21 of impurity; he has *d* his brother.
Dt 21:14 as a slave, since you have *d* her.
Ezr 4:14 proper for us to see the king *d,*
1Co 4:10 You are honored, we are *d!*

DISHONORS* (DISHONOR)
Dt 27:16 Cursed is the man who *d* his father
27:20 for he *d* his father's bed."
Job 20: 3 I hear a rebuke that *d* me,
Mic 7: 6 For a son *d* his father,
1Co 11: 4 with his head covered *d* his head.
11: 5 her head uncovered *d* her head—

DISILLUSIONMENT*
Ps 7:14 conceives trouble gives birth to *d.*

DISMAYED
Isa 28:16 the one who trusts will never be *d.*
41:10 do not be *d,* for I am your God.

DISOBEDIENCE* (DISOBEY)
Jos 22:22 in rebellion or *d* to the LORD,
Jer 43: 7 So they entered Egypt in *d*
Ro 5:19 as through the *d* of the one man
11:30 mercy as a result of their *d,*
11:32 to *d* so that he may have mercy
2Co 10: 6 ready to punish every act of *d,*
Heb 2: 2 and *d* received its just punishment,
4: 6 go in, because of their *d.*
4:11 fall by following their example of *d.*

DISOBEDIENT* (DISOBEY)
Ne 9:26 "But they were *d* and rebelled
Lk 1:17 and the *d* to the wisdom
Ac 26:19 I was not *d* to the vision
Ro 10:21 hands to a *d* and obstinate people."
11:30 as you who were at one time *d*
11:31 so they too have now become *d*
Eph 2: 2 now at work in those who are *d.*
5: 6 comes on those who are *d.*
5:12 to mention what the *d* do in secret.
2Ti 3: 2 proud, abusive, *d* to their parents,
Tit 1: 6 to the charge of being wild and *d.*
1:16 *d* and unfit for doing anything
3: 3 At one time we too were foolish, *d,*
Heb 11:31 killed with those who were *d.*

DISOBEY* (DISOBEDIENCE DISOBEDIENT DISOBEYED DISOBEYING DISOBEYS)
Dt 11:28 the curse if you *d* the commands
2Ch 24:20 'Why do you *d* the LORD's
Est 3: 3 Why do you *d* the king's command
Jer 42:13 and so *d* the LORD your God,
Ro 1:30 they *d* their parents; they are
1Pe 2: 8 because they *d* the message—

DISOBEYED* (DISOBEY)
Nu 14:22 and in the desert but who *d* me
27:14 both of you *d* my command
Jdg 2: 2 Yet you have *d* me.
Ne 9:29 arrogant and *d* your commands.
Isa 24: 5 they have *d* the laws,
Jer 43: 4 and all the people *d* the LORD's
Lk 15:29 for you and never *d* your orders.
Heb 3:18 rest if not to those who *d?*
1Pe 3:20 the spirits in prison who *d* long ago

DISOBEYING* (DISOBEY)
Nu 14:41 "Why are you *d* the LORD's

DISOBEYS* (DISOBEY)
Eze 33:12 man will not save him when he *d,*

DISORDER
1Co 14:33 For God is not a God of *d*
2Co 12:20 slander, gossip, arrogance and *d.*
Jas 3:16 there you find *d* and every evil

DISOWN (DISOWNS)
Pr 30: 9 I may have too much and *d* you
Mt 10:33 I will *d* him before my Father
26:35 to die with you, I will never *d* you."
2Ti 2:12 If we *d* him,

DISOWNS (DISOWN)
Lk 12: 9 he who *d* me before men will be

DISPENSATION see ADMINISTRATION, TRUST

DISPLACES
Pr 30:23 a maidservant who *d* her mistress.

DISPLAY (DISPLAYED DISPLAYS)
Ps 45: 4 your right hand *d* awesome deeds.
Eze 39:21 I will *d* my glory among the nations
Ro 9:17 that I might *d* my power in you
1Co 4: 9 on *d* at the end of the procession,
1Ti 1:16 Christ Jesus might *d* his unlimited

DISPLAYED (DISPLAY)
Jn 9: 3 work of God might be *d* in his life.
2Th 2: 9 the work of Satan *d* in all kinds

DISPLAYS (DISPLAY)
Isa 44:23 he *d* his glory in Israel.

DISPLEASE (DISPLEASED)
1Th 2:15 They *d* God and are hostile

DISPLEASED (DISPLEASE)
2Sa 11:27 David had done *d* the LORD.

DISPUTABLE* (DISPUTE)
Ro 14: 1 passing judgment on *d* matters.

DISPUTE (DISPUTABLE DISPUTES DISPUTING)
Pr 17:14 before a *d* breaks out.
1Co 6: 1 If any of you has a *d* with another,

DISPUTES (DISPUTE)
Pr 18:18 Casting the lot settles *d*

DISPUTING (DISPUTE)
1Ti 2: 8 in prayer, without anger or *d.*

DISQUALIFIED*
1Co 9:27 I myself will not be *d* for the prize.

DISREPUTE*
2Pe 2: 2 will bring the way of truth into *d.*

DISSENSION* (DISSENSIONS)
Pr 6:14 he always stirs up *d.*
6:19 and a man who stirs up *d*
10:12 Hatred stirs up *d,*
15:18 A hot-tempered man stirs up *d,*
16:28 A perverse man stirs up *d,*
28:25 A greedy man stirs up *d,*
29:22 An angry man stirs up *d,*
Ro 13:13 debauchery, not in *d* and jealousy.

DISSENSIONS* (DISSENSION)
Gal 5:20 selfish ambition, *d,* factions

DISSIPATION*
Lk 21:34 will be weighed down with *d,*
1Pe 4: 4 with them into the same flood of *d,*

DISTINCTION
Ac 15: 9 He made no *d* between us

DISTINGUISH (DISTINGUISHING)
1Ki 3: 9 and to *d* between right and wrong.
Heb 5:14 themselves to *d* good from evil.

DISTINGUISHING
1Co 12:10 the *d* between spirits,

DISTORT
Ac 20:30 and *d* the truth in order
2Co 4: 2 nor do we *d* the word of God.
2Pe 3:16 ignorant and unstable people *d,*

DISTRACTED*
Lk 10:40 But Martha was *d* by all

DISTRESS (DISTRESSED)
2Ch 15: 4 in their *d* they turned to the LORD
Ps 18: 6 In my *d* I called to the LORD;
81: 7 In your *d* you called and I rescued
120: 1 I call on the LORD in my *d,*
Jnh 2: 2 "In my *d* I called to the LORD,
Mt 24:21 For then there will be great *d,*

Jas 1:27 after orphans and widows in their *d*

DISTRESSED (DISTRESS)
Lk 12:50 how *d* I am until it is completed!
Ro 14:15 If your brother is *d*

DIVIDE (DIVIDED DIVIDING DIVISION DIVISIONS DIVISIVE)
Ps 22:18 They *d* my garments among them

DIVIDED (DIVIDE)
Mt 12:25 household *d* against itself will not
Lk 23:34 they *d* up his clothes by casting lots
1Co 1:13 Is Christ *d?* Was Paul crucified

DIVIDING (DIVIDE)
Eph 2:14 destroyed the barrier, the *d* wall
Heb 4:12 it penetrates even to *d* soul

DIVINATION
Lev 19:26 " 'Do not practice *d* or sorcery.

DIVINE
Ro 1:20 his eternal power and *d* nature—
2Co 10: 4 they have *d* power
2Pe 1: 4 you may participate in the *d* nature

DIVISION (DIVIDE)
Lk 12:51 on earth? No, I tell you, but *d.*
1Co 12:25 so that there should be no *d*

DIVISIONS (DIVIDE)
Ro 16:17 to watch out for those who cause *d*
1Co 1:10 another so that there may be no *d*
11:18 there are *d* among you,

DIVISIVE* (DIVIDE)
Tit 3:10 Warn a *d* person once,

DIVORCE* (DIVORCED DIVORCES)
Dt 22:19 he must not *d* her as long as he lives
22:29 He can never *d* her as long
24: 1 and he writes her a certificate of *d,*
24: 3 and writes her a certificate of *d,*
Isa 50: 1 is your mother's certificate of *d*
Jer 3: 8 faithless Israel her certificate of *d*
Mal 2:16 "I hate *d,*" says the LORD God
Mt 1:19 he had in mind to *d* her quietly.
5:31 must give her a certificate of *d.*'
19: 3 for a man to *d* his wife for any
19: 7 man give his wife a certificate of *d*
19: 8 permitted you to *d* your wives
Mk 10: 2 Is it lawful for a man to *d* his wife?"
10: 4 a man to write a certificate of *d*
1Co 7:11 And a husband must not *d* his wife.
7:12 to live with him, he must not *d* her.
7:13 to live with her, she must not *d* him
7:27 Are you married? Do not seek a *d.*

DIVORCED* (DIVORCE)
Lev 21: 7 or *d* from their husbands,
21:14 not marry a widow, a *d* woman,
22:13 daughter becomes a widow or is *d,*
Nu 30: 9 or *d* woman will be binding on her.
Dt 24: 4 then her first husband, who *d* her,
1Ch 8: 8 after he had *d* his wives Hushim
Eze 44:22 not marry widows or *d* women;
Mt 5:32 marries the *d* woman commits adultery.
Lk 16:18 who marries a *d* woman commits

DIVORCES* (DIVORCE)
Jer 3: 1 "If a man *d* his wife
Mt 5:31 'Anyone who *d* his wife must give
5:32 tell you that anyone who *d* his wife,
19: 9 tell you that anyone who *d* his wife,
Mk 10:11 "Anyone who *d* his wife
10:12 And if she *d* her husband
Lk 16:18 "Anyone who *d* his wife

DOCTOR
Mt 9:12 "It is not the healthy who need a *d,*

DOCTRINE* (DOCTRINES)
1Ti 1:10 to the sound *d* that conforms
4:16 Watch your life and *d* closely.
2Ti 4: 3 men will not put up with sound *d.*
Tit 1: 9 can encourage others by sound *d*
2: 1 is in accord with sound *d.*

DOCTRINES* (DOCTRINE)
1Ti 1: 3 not to teach false *d* any longer
6: 3 If anyone teaches false *d*

DOEG*
Edomite; Saul's head shepherd; responsible for murder of priests at Nob (1Sa 21:7; 22:6-23; Ps 52).

DOG (DOGS)
Pr 26:11 As a *d* returns to its vomit,
Ecc 9: 4 a live *d* is better off than a dead lion
2Pe 2:22 "A *d* returns to its vomit," and,

DOGS (DOG)
Mt 7: 6 "Do not give *d* what is sacred;
15:26 bread and toss it to their *d.*"

DOMINION
Job 25: 2 "*D* and awe belong to God;
Ps 22:28 for *d* belongs to the LORD

DONKEY
Nu 22:30 *d* said to Balaam, "Am I not your
Zec 9: 9 gentle and riding on a *d,*
Mt 21: 5 gentle and riding on a *d,*
2Pe 2:16 for his wrongdoing by a *d*—

DOOR (DOORS)
Job 31:32 for my *d* was always open
Ps 141: 3 keep watch over the *d* of my lips.
Mt 6: 6 close the *d* and pray to your Father
7: 7 and the *d* will be opened to you.
Ac 14:27 how he had opened the *d* of faith
1Co 16: 9 a great *d* for effective work has
2Co 2:12 found that the Lord had opened a *d*
Rev 3:20 I stand at the *d* and knock.

DOORFRAMES
Dt 6: 9 Write them on the *d* of your houses

DOORKEEPER
Ps 84:10 I would rather be a *d* in the house

DOORS (DOOR)
Ps 24: 7 be lifted up, you ancient *d,*

DORCAS
Ac 9:36 is *D),* who was always doing good

DOUBLE
2Ki 2: 9 "Let me inherit a *d* portion
1Ti 5:17 church well are worthy of *d* honor,

DOUBLE-EDGED (EDGE)
Heb 4:12 Sharper than any *d* sword,
Rev 1:16 of his mouth came a sharp *d* sword.
2:12 of him who has the sharp, *d* sword.

DOUBLE-MINDED* (MIND)
Ps 119:113 I hate *d* men,
Jas 1: 8 he is a *d* man, unstable
4: 8 and purify your hearts, you *d.*

DOUBT (DOUBTING DOUBTS)
Mt 14:31 he said, "why did you *d?*"
21:21 if you have faith and do not *d,*
Mk 11:23 and does not *d* in his heart
Jas 1: 6 he must believe and not *d,*
Jude :22 Be merciful to those who *d;*

DOUBTING* (DOUBT)
Jn 20:27 Stop *d* and believe."

DOUBTS* (DOUBT)
Lk 24:38 and why do *d* rise in your minds?
Ro 14:23 the man who has *d* is condemned
Jas 1: 6 he who *d* is like a wave of the sea,

DOVE (DOVES)
Ge 8: 8 Then he sent out a *d* to see
Mt 3:16 Spirit of God descending like a *d*

DOVES (DOVE)
Lev 12: 8 is to bring two *d* or two young
Mt 10:16 as snakes and as innocent as *d.*
Lk 2:24 "a pair of *d* or two young pigeons."

DOWNCAST
Ps 42: 5 Why are you *d,* O my soul?
2Co 7: 6 But God, who comforts the *d,*

DOWNFALL
Hos 14: 1 Your sins have been your *d!*

DRAGON
Rev 12: 7 and his angels fought against the *d,*
13: 2 The *d* gave the beast his power
20: 2 He seized the *d,* that ancient

DRAW (DRAWING DRAWS)
Mt 26:52 "for all who *d* the sword will die
Jn 12:32 up from the earth, will *d* all men
Heb 10:22 let us *d* near to God

DRAWING (DRAW)
Lk 21:28 because your redemption is *d* near

DRAWS (DRAW)
Jn 6:44 the Father who sent me *d* him,

DREAD (DREADFUL)
Ps 53: 5 they were, overwhelmed with *d,*

DREADFUL (DREAD)
Mt 24:19 How *d* it will be in those days
Heb 10:31 It is a *d* thing to fall into the hands

DREAM
Joel 2:28 your old men will *d* dreams,
Ac 2:17 your old men will *d* dreams.

DRESS
1Ti 2: 9 I also want women to *d* modestly,

DRIFT*
Heb 2: 1 so that we do not *d* away.

DRINK (DRINKING DRINKS DRUNK DRUNKARD DRUNKARD'S DRUNKARDS DRUNKENNESS)
Ex 29:40 of a hin of wine as a *d* offering.
Nu 6: 3 He must not *d* grape juice
Jdg 7: 5 from those who kneel down to *d.*"
2Sa 23:15 that someone would get me a *d*
Pr 5:15 *D* water from your own cistern,
Mt 20:22 "Can you *d* the cup I am going to *d*
26:27 saying, "*D* from it, all of you.
Mk 16:18 and when they *d* deadly poison,
Lk 12:19 Take life easy; eat, *d* and be merry
Jn 7:37 let him come to me and *d.*
18:11 Shall I not *d* the cup the Father has
1Co 10: 4 and drank the same spiritual *d;*
12:13 were all given the one Spirit to *d.*
Php 2:17 being poured out like a *d* offering
2Ti 4: 6 being poured out like a *d* offering,
Rev 14:10 too, will *d* of the wine of God's fury
21: 6 to *d* without cost from the spring

DRINKING (DRINK)
Ro 14:17 God is not a matter of eating and *d,*

DRINKS (DRINK)
Isa 5:22 and champions at mixing *d,*
Jn 4:13 "Everyone who *d* this water will be
6:54 and *d* my blood has eternal life,
1Co 11:27 or *d* the cup of the Lord

DRIPPING
Pr 19:13 wife is like a constant *d.*
27:15 a constant *d* on a rainy day;

DRIVE (DRIVES)
Ex 23:30 Little by little I will *d* them out
Nu 33:52 *d* out all the inhabitants of the land
Jos 13:13 Israelites did not *d* out the people
23:13 will no longer *d* out these nations
Pr 22:10 *D* out the mocker, and out goes
Mt 10: 1 authority to *d* out evil spirits
Jn 6:37 comes to me I will never *d* away.

DRIVES (DRIVE)
Mt 12:26 If Satan *d* out Satan, he is divided
1Jn 4:18 But perfect love *d* out fear,

DROP (DROPS)
Pr 17:14 so *d* the matter before a dispute
Isa 40:15 Surely the nations are like a *d*

DROPS (DROP)
Lk 22:44 his sweat was like *d* of blood falling

DROSS
Ps 119:119 of the earth you discard like *d;*
Pr 25: 4 Remove the *d* from the silver,

DROUGHT
Jer 17: 8 It has no worries in a year of *d*

DROWNED
Ex 15: 4 are *d* in the Red Sea.
Mt 18: 6 and to be *d* in the depths of the sea.
Heb 11:29 tried to do so, they were *d.*

DROWSINESS*
Pr 23:21 and *d* clothes them in rags.

DRUNK (DRINK)
1Sa 1:13 Eli thought she was *d* and said
Ac 2:15 men are not *d,* as you suppose.
Eph 5:18 Do not get *d* on wine, which leads

DRUNKARD (DRINK)
Mt 11:19 and a *d,* a friend of tax collectors
1Co 5:11 or a slanderer, a *d* or a swindler.

DRUNKARD'S* (DRINK)
Pr 26: 9 Like a thornbush in a *d* hand

DRUNKARDS (DRINK)
Pr 23:21 for *d* and gluttons become poor,
1Co 6:10 nor the greedy nor *d* nor slanderers

DRUNKENNESS (DRINK)
Lk 21:34 weighed down with dissipation, *d*

Ro 13:13 and *d,* not in sexual immorality
Gal 5:21 factions and envy; *d,* orgies,
1Ti 3: 3 not given to *d,* not violent
1Pe 4: 3 living in debauchery, lust, *d,* orgies,

DRY
Ge 1: 9 place, and let *d* ground appear."
Ex 14:16 go through the sea on *d* ground.
Jos 3:17 the crossing on *d* ground.
Isa 53: 2 and like a root out of *d* ground.
Eze 37: 4 '*D* bones, hear the word

DULL
Isa 6:10 make their ears *d*
2Co 3:14 But their minds were made *d,*

DUST
Ge 2: 7 man from the *d* of the ground
3:19 for *d* you are
Job 42: 6 and repent in *d* and ashes."
Ps 22:15 you lay me in the *d* of death.
103: 14 he remembers that we are *d.*
Ecc 3:20 all come from *d,* and to *d* all return.
Mt 10:14 shake the *d* off your feet
1Co 15:47 was of the *d* of the earth,

DUTIES (DUTY)
2Ti 4: 5 discharge all the *d* of your ministry

DUTY (DUTIES)
Ecc 12:13 for this is the whole *d* of man.
Ac 23: 1 I have fulfilled my *d* to God
1Co 7: 3 husband should fulfill his marital *d*

DWELL (DWELLING DWELLINGS DWELLS DWELT)
Ex 25: 8 for me, and I will *d* among them.
2Sa 7: 5 the one to build me a house to *d* in?
1Ki 8:27 "But will God really *d* on earth?
Ps 23: 6 I will *d* in the house of the LORD
37: 3 *d* in the land and enjoy safe pasture
61: 4 I long to *d* in your tent forever
Pr 8:12 wisdom, *d* together with prudence;
Isa 33:14 of us can *d* with the consuming fire
43:18 do not *d* on the past.
Jn 5:38 nor does his word *d* in you,
Eph 3:17 so that Christ may *d* in your hearts
Col 1:19 to have all his fullness *d* in him,
3:16 the word of Christ *d* in you richly

DWELLING (DWELL)
Lev 26:11 I will put my *d* place among you,
Dt 26:15 from heaven, your holy *d* place,
Ps 90: 1 Lord, you have been our *d* place
2Co 5: 2 to be clothed with our heavenly *d,*
Eph 2:22 to become a *d* in which God lives

DWELLINGS (DWELL)
Lk 16: 9 will be welcomed into eternal *d.*

DWELLS (DWELL)
Ps 46: 4 holy place where the Most High *d.*
91: 1 He who *d* in the shelter

DWELT (DWELL)
Dt 33:16 of him who *d* in the burning bush.

DYING (DIE)
Ro 7: 6 by *d* to what once bound us,
2Co 6: 9 yet regarded as unknown; *d,*

EAGER
Pr 31:13 and works with *e* hands.
Ro 8:19 The creation waits in *e* expectation
1Co 14:12 Since you are *e* to have spiritual
14:39 my brothers, be *e* to prophesy,
Tit 2:14 a people that are his very own, *e*
1Pe 5: 2 greedy for money, but *e* to serve;

EAGLE (EAGLE'S EAGLES)
Dt 32:11 like an *e* that stirs up its nest
Eze 1:10 each also had the face of an *e.*
Rev 4: 7 the fourth was like a flying *e.*
12:14 given the two wings of a great *e,*

EAGLE'S (EAGLE)
Ps 103: 5 your youth is renewed like the *e.*

EAGLES (EAGLE)
Isa 40:31 They will soar on wings like *e;*

EAR (EARS)
Ex 21: 6 and pierce his *e* with an awl.
Ps 5: 1 Give *e* to my words, O LORD,
Pr 2: 2 turning your *e* to wisdom
1Co 2: 9 no *e* has heard,
12:16 if the *e* should say, "Because I am
Rev 2: 7 He who has an *e,* let him hear what

EARN (EARNED EARNINGS)
2Th 3:12 down and *e* the bread they eat.

EARNED (EARN)
Pr 31:31 Give her the reward she has *e,*

EARNESTNESS
2Co 7:11 what *e,* what eagerness
8: 7 in complete *e* and in your love

EARNINGS (EARN)
Pr 31:16 out of her *e* she plants a vineyard.

EARRING (EARRINGS)
Pr 25:12 Like an *e* of gold or an ornament

EARRINGS (EARRING)
Ex 32: 2 Take off the gold *e* that your wives,

EARS (EAR)
Job 42: 5 My *e* had heard of you
Ps 34:15 and his *e* are attentive to their cry;
Pr 21:13 If a man shuts his *e* to the cry
26:17 Like one who seizes a dog by the *e*
Isa 6:10 hear with their *e,*
Mt 11:15 He who has *e,* let him hear.
2Ti 4: 3 to say what their itching *e* want
1Pe 3:12 his *e* are attentive to their prayer,

EARTH (EARTH'S EARTHLY)
Ge 1: 1 God created the heavens and the *e.*
1: 2 Now the *e* was formless and empty,
7:24 The waters flooded the *e*
14:19 Creator of heaven and *e.*
1Ki 8:27 "But will God really dwell on *e?*
Job 26: 7 he suspends the *e* over nothing.
Ps 24: 1 *e* is the LORD's, and everything
46: 6 he lifts his voice, the *e* melts.
90: 2 or you brought forth the *e*
97: 5 before the Lord of all the *e.*
102: 25 you laid the foundations of the *e,*
108: 5 and let your glory be over all the *e.*
Pr 8:26 before he made the *e* or its fields
Isa 6: 3 the whole *e* is full of his glory."
24:20 The *e* reels like a drunkard,
37:16 You have made heaven and *e.*
40:22 enthroned above the circle of the *e,*
51: 6 the *e* will wear out like a garment
54: 5 he is called the God of all the *e.*
55: 9 the heavens are higher than the *e,*
65:17 new heavens and a new *e.*
66: 1 and the *e* is my footstool.
Jer 10:10 When he is angry, the *e* trembles;
23:24 "Do not I fill heaven and *e?"*
33:25 and the fixed laws of heaven and *e,*
Hab 2:20 let all the *e* be silent before him."
Mt 5: 5 for they will inherit the *e.*
5:35 or by the *e,* for it is his footstool;
6:10 done on *e* as it is in heaven.
16:19 bind on *e* will be bound
24:35 Heaven and *e* will pass away,
28:18 and on *e* has been given to me.
Lk 2:14 on *e* peace to men
Jn 12:32 when I am lifted up from the *e,*
Ac 4:24 "you made the heaven and the *e*
7:49 and the *e* is my footstool.
1Co 10:26 The *e* is the Lord's, and everything
Eph 3:15 in heaven and on *e* derives its name
Php 2:10 in heaven and on *e* and under the *e,*
Heb 1:10 you laid the foundations of the *e,*
2Pe 3:13 to a new heaven and a new *e,*
Rev 8: 7 A third of the *e* was burned up,
12:12 But woe to the *e* and the sea,
20:11 *E* and sky fled from his presence,
21: 1 I saw a new heaven and a new *e,*
21: 1 and the first *e* had passed away,

EARTH'S (EARTH)
Job 38: 4 when I laid the *e* foundation?

EARTHENWARE
Pr 26:23 Like a coating of glaze over *e*

EARTHLY (EARTH)
Eph 4: 9 descended to the lower, *e* regions?
Php 3:19 Their mind is on *e* things.
Col 3: 2 on things above, not on *e* things.
3: 5 whatever belongs to your *e* nature:

EARTHQUAKE (EARTHQUAKES)
Eze 38:19 at that time there shall be a great *e*
Mt 28: 2 There was a violent *e,* for an angel
Rev 6:12 There was a great *e.*

EARTHQUAKES (EARTHQUAKE)
Mt 24: 7 There will be famines and *e*

EASE
Pr 1:33 and be at *e,* without fear of harm."

EASIER (EASY)
Lk 16:17 It is *e* for heaven and earth
18:25 it is *e* for a camel to go

EAST
Ge 2: 8 God had planted a garden in the *e,*
Ps 103: 12 as far as the *e* is from the west,
Eze 43: 2 God of Israel coming from the *e.*
Mt 2: 1 Magi from the *e* came to Jerusalem
2: 2 We saw his star in the *e*

EASY (EASIER)
Mt 11:30 For my yoke is *e* and my burden is

EAT (ATE EATEN EATER EATING EATS)
Ge 2:16 "You are free to *e* from any tree
2:17 but you must not *e* from the tree
3:19 you will *e* your food
Ex 12:11 *E* it in haste; it is the LORD's
Lev 11: 2 these are the ones you may *e:*
17:12 "None of you may *e* blood,
Dt 8:16 He gave you manna to *e*
14: 4 These are the animals you may *e:*
Jdg 14:14 "Out of the eater, something to *e;*
2Sa 9: 7 and you will always *e* at my table."
Pr 31:27 and does not *e* the bread of idleness
Isa 55: 1 come, buy and *e!*
65:25 and the lion will *e* straw like the ox,
Eze 3: 1 *e* what is before you, *e* this scroll;
Mt 14:16 You give them something to *e."*
15: 2 wash their hands before they *e!"*
26:26 "Take and *e;* this is my body."
Mk 14:14 where I may *e* the Passover
Lk 10: 8 and are welcomed, *e* what is set
12:19 Take life easy; *e,* drink
12:22 what you will *e;* or about your body
Jn 4:32 to *e* that you know nothing about."
6:31 bread from heaven to *e.'"*
6:52 can this man give us his flesh to *e?"*
Ac 10:13 Kill and *e."*
Ro 14: 2 faith allows him to *e* everything,
14:15 is distressed because of what you *e,*
14:20 to *e* anything that causes someone
14:21 It is better not to *e* meat
1Co 5:11 With such a man do not even *e.*
8:13 if what I *e* causes my brother to fall
10:25 *E* anything sold in the meat market
10:27 *e* whatever is put before you
10:31 So whether you *e* or drink
11:26 For whenever you *e* this bread
2Th 3:10 man will not work, he shall not *e."*
Rev 2: 7 the right to *e* from the tree of life,
3:20 I will come in and *e* with him,

EATEN (EAT)
Ge 3:11 Have you *e* from the tree that I
Ac 10:14 "I have never *e* anything impure
Rev 10:10 when I had *e* it, my stomach turned

EATER (EAT)
Isa 55:10 for the sower and bread for the *e,*

EATING (EAT)
Ex 34:28 and forty nights without *e* bread
Ro 14:15 not by your *e* destroy your brother
14:17 kingdom of God is not a matter of *e*
14:23 because his *e* is not from faith;
1Co 8: 4 about *e* food sacrificed to idols:
8:10 you who have this knowledge *e*
Jude :12 *e* with you without the slightest

EATS (EAT)
1Sa 14:24 "Cursed be any man who *e* food
Lk 15: 2 "This man welcomes sinners and *e*
Jn 6:51 If anyone *e* of this bread, he will live
6:54 Whoever *e* my flesh and drinks my
Ro 14: 2 faith is weak, *e* only vegetables.
14: 3 man who *e* everything must not
14: 6 He who *e* meat, *e* to the Lord,
14:23 has doubts is condemned if he *e,*
1Co 11:27 whoever *e* the bread or drinks

EBAL
Dt 11:29 and on Mount *E* the curses.
Jos 8:30 Joshua built on Mount *E* an altar

EBENEZER
1Sa 7:12 He named it *E,* saying, "Thus far

EDEN
Ge 2: 8 in *E;* and there he put the man
Eze 28:13 You were in *E,*

EDGE (DOUBLE-EDGED)
Mt 9:20 and touched the *e* of his cloak.

EDICT
Heb 11:23 they were not afraid of the king's *e.*

EDIFICATION (EDIFIED EDIFIES)
Ro 14:19 leads to peace and to mutual *e.*

EDIFIED* (EDIFICATION)
1Co 14: 5 so that the church may be *e.*
14:17 but the other man is not *e.*

EDIFIES* (EDIFICATION)
1Co 14: 4 but he who prophesies *e* the church
14: 4 speaks in a tongue *e* himself,

EDOM
Ge 36: 1 the account of Esau (that is, *E).*
36: 8 *E)* settled in the hill country of Seir
Isa 63: 1 Who is this coming from *E,*
Ob : 1 Sovereign LORD says about *E*—

EDUCATED*
Ac 7:22 Moses was *e* in all the wisdom

EFFECT* (EFFECTIVE)
Job 41:26 sword that reaches him has no *e,*
Isa 32:17 *e* of righteousness will be quietness
Ac 7:53 put into *e* through angels
1Co 15:10 his grace to me was not without *e.*
Gal 3:19 put into *e* through angels
Eph 1:10 put into *e* when the times will have
Heb 9:17 it never takes *e* while the one who
9:18 put into *e* without blood.

EFFECTIVE* (EFFECT)
1Co 16: 9 a great door for *e* work has opened
Jas 5:16 a righteous man is powerful and *e.*

EFFORT*
Ecc 2:19 into which I have poured my *e*
Da 6:14 and made every *e* until sundown
Lk 13:24 "Make every *e* to enter
Jn 5:44 yet make no *e* to obtain the praise
Ro 9:16 depend on man's desire or *e,*
14:19 make every *e* to do what leads
Gal 3: 3 to attain your goal by human *e?*
Eph 4: 3 Make every *e* to keep the unity
1Th 2:16 to all men in their *e* to keep us
2:17 intense longing we made every *e*
Heb 4:11 make every *e* to enter that rest,
12:14 Make every *e* to live in peace
2Pe 1: 5 make every *e* to add
1:15 And I will make every *e* to see that
3:14 make every *e* to be found spotless,

EGG
Lk 11:12 for an *e,* will give him a scorpion?

EGLON
1. Fat king of Moab killed by Ehud (Jdg 3:12-30).
2. City in Canaan (Jos 10).

EGYPT (EGYPTIANS)
Ge 12:10 went down to *E* to live there
37:28 Ishmaelites, who took him to *E.*
42: 3 went down to buy grain from *E.*
45:20 the best of all *E* will be yours.' "
46: 6 and all his offspring went to *E.*
47:27 Now the Israelites settled in *E*
Ex 3:11 and bring the Israelites out of *E?"*
12:40 lived in *E* was 430 years.
12:41 all the LORD's divisions left *E.*
32: 1 Moses who brought us up out of *E,*
Nu 11:18 We were better off in *E!"*
14: 4 choose a leader and go back to *E."*
24: 8 "God brought them out of *E;*
Dt 6:21 "We were slaves of Pharaoh in *E,*
1Ki 4:30 greater than all the wisdom of *E.*
10:28 horses were imported from *E*
11:40 but Jeroboam fled to *E,*
14:25 king of *E* attacked Jerusalem.
2Ch 35:20 Neco king of *E* went up to fight
36: 3 The king of *E* dethroned him
Isa 19:23 a highway from *E* to Assyria.
Hos 11: 1 and out of *E* I called my son.
Mt 2:15 "Out of *E* I called my son."
Heb 11:27 By faith he left *E,* not fearing
Rev 11: 8 is figuratively called Sodom and *E,*

EGYPTIANS (EGYPT)
Nu 14:13 "Then the *E* will hear about it!

EHUD
Left-handed judge who delivered Israel from Moabite king, Eglon (Jdg 3:12-30).

EKRON
1Sa 5:10 So they sent the ark of God to *E.*

ELAH
Son of Baasha; king of Israel (1Ki 16:6-14).

ELATION
Pr 28:12 righteous triumph, there is great *e;*

ELDER* (ELDERLY ELDERS)
Isa 3: 2 the soothsayer and *e,*
1Ti 5:19 an accusation against an *e*
Tit 1: 6 *e* must be blameless, the husband
1Pe 5: 1 among you, I appeal as a fellow *e,*
2Jn : 1 The *e,* To the chosen lady
3Jn : 1 The *e,* To my dear friend Gaius,

ELDERLY* (ELDER)
Lev 19:32 show respect for the *e*

ELDERS (ELDER)
1Ki 12: 8 rejected the advice the *e* gave him
Mt 15: 2 break the tradition of the *e?*
Mk 7: 3 holding to the tradition of the *e.*
7: 5 to the tradition of the *e* instead
Ac 11:30 gift to the *e* by Barnabas
14:23 and Barnabas appointed *e* for them
15: 2 the apostles and *e* about this
15: 4 the church and the apostles and *e,*
15: 6 and *e* met to consider this question.
15:22 and *e,* with the whole church,
15:23 The apostles and *e,* your brothers,
16: 4 and *e* in Jerusalem for the people
20:17 to Ephesus for the *e* of the church.
21:18 and all the *e* were present.
23:14 They went to the chief priests and *e*
24: 1 to Caesarea with some of the *e*
1Ti 4:14 when the body of *e* laid their hands
5:17 The *e* who direct the affairs
Tit 1: 5 and appoint *e* in every town,
Jas 5:14 He should call the *e* of the church
1Pe 5: 1 To the *e* among you, I appeal
Rev 4: 4 seated on them were twenty-four *e.*
4:10 the twenty-four *e* fall

ELEAZAR
Third son of Aaron (Ex 6:23-25). Succeeded Aaron as high priest (Nu 20:26; Dt 10:6). Allotted land to tribes (Jos 14:1). Death (Jos 24:33).

ELECT* (ELECTION)
Mt 24:22 the sake of the *e* those days will be
24:24 miracles to deceive even the *e*—
24:31 and they will gather his *e*
Mk 13:20 sake of the *e,* whom he has chosen,
13:22 and miracles to deceive the *e*—
13:27 gather his *e* from the four winds,
Ro 11: 7 it did not obtain, but the *e* did.
1Ti 5:21 and Christ Jesus and the *e* angels,
2Ti 2:10 everything for the sake of the *e,*
Tit 1: 1 Christ for the faith of God's *e*
1Pe 1: 1 To God's *e,* strangers in the world,

ELECTION* (ELECT)
Ro 9:11 God's purpose in *e* might stand:
11:28 but as far as *e* is concerned,
2Pe 1:10 to make your calling and *e* sure.

ELEMENTARY* (ELEMENTS)
Heb 5:12 someone to teach you the *e* truths
6: 1 us leave the *e* teachings about

ELEMENTS* (ELEMENTARY)
2Pe 3:10 the *e* will be destroyed by fire,
3:12 and the *e* will melt in the heat.

ELEVATE*
2Co 11: 7 to *e* you by preaching the gospel

ELI
High priest in youth of Samuel (1Sa 1-4). Blessed Hannah (1Sa 1:12-18); raised Samuel (1Sa 2:11-26). Prophesied against because of wicked sons (1Sa 2:27-36). Death of Eli and sons (1Sa 4:11-22).

ELIHU
One of Job's friends (Job 32-37).

ELIJAH
Prophet; predicted famine in Israel (1Ki 17:1; Jas 5:17). Fed by ravens (1Ki 17:2-6). Raised Sidonian widow's son (1Ki 17:7-24). Defeated prophets of Baal at Carmel (1Ki 18:16-46). Ran from Jezebel (1Ki 19:1-9). Prophesied death of Azariah (2Ki 1). Succeeded by Elishah (1Ki 19:19-21; 2Ki 2:1-18). Taken to heaven in whirlwind (2Ki 2:11-12).
Return prophesied (Mal 4:5-6); equated with John the Baptist (Mt 17:9-13; Mk 9:9-13; Lk 1:17). Appeared with Moses in transfiguration of Jesus (Mt 17:1-8; Mk 9:1-8).

ELIMELECH
Ru 1: 3 Now *E,* Naomi's husband, died,

ELIPHAZ
1. Firstborn of Esau (Ge 36).
2. One of Job's friends (Job 4-5; 15; 22).

ELISHA
Prophet; successor of Elijah (1Ki 19:16-21); inherited his cloak (2Ki 2:1-18). Purified bad water (2Ki 2:19-22). Cursed young men (2Ki 2:23-25). Aided Israel's defeat of Moab (2Ki 3). Provided widow with oil (2Ki 4:1-7). Raised Shunammite woman's son (2Ki 4:8-37). Purified food (2Ki 4:38-41). Fed 100 men (2Ki 4:42-44). Healed Naaman's leprosy (2Ki 5). Made axhead float (2Ki 6:1-7). Captured Arameans (2Ki 6:8-23). Political adviser to Israel (2Ki 6:24-8:6; 9:1-3; 13:14-19), Damascus (2Ki 8:7-15). Death (2Ki 13:20).

ELIZABETH*
Mother of John the Baptist, relative of Mary (Lk 1:5-58).

ELKANAH
Husband of Hannah, father of Samuel (1Sa 1-2).

ELOI*
Mt 27:46 *"E, E, lama sabachthani?"*—
Mk 15:34 *"E, E, lama sabachthani?"*—

ELOQUENCE* (ELOQUENT)
1Co 2: 1 come with *e* or superior wisdom

ELOQUENT* (ELOQUENCE)
Ex 4:10 "O Lord, I have never been *e,*

ELYMAS
Ac 13: 8 *E* the sorcerer (for that is what his

EMBEDDED*
Ecc 12:11 sayings like firmly *e* nails—

EMBERS
Pr 26:21 As charcoal to *e* and as wood to fire

EMBITTER* (BITTER)
Col 3:21 Fathers, do not *e* your children,

EMBODIMENT* (BODY)
Ro 2:20 have in the law the *e* of knowledge

EMPTIED (EMPTY)
1Co 1:17 the cross of Christ be *e* of its power.

EMPTY (EMPTIED)
Ge 1: 2 Now the earth was formless and *e,*
Job 26: 7 the northern skies over *e* space;
Isa 45:18 he did not create it to be *e,*
55:11 It will not return to me *e,*
Jer 4:23 and it was formless and *e;*
Lk 1:53 but has sent the rich away *e.*
Eph 5: 6 no one deceive you with *e* words,
1Pe 1:18 from the *e* way of life handed
2Pe 2:18 For they mouth *e,* boastful words

ENABLE (ABLE)
Lk 1:74 to *e* us to serve him without fear
Ac 4:29 *e* your servants to speak your word

ENABLED* (ABLE)
Lev 26:13 *e* you to walk with heads held high.
Ru 4:13 And the LORD *e* her to conceive,
Jn 6:65 unless the Father has *e* him."
Ac 2: 4 other tongues as the Spirit *e* them.
7:10 and *e* him to gain the goodwill
Heb 11:11 was *e* to become a father

ENABLES (ABLE)
Php 3:21 by the power that *e* him

ENABLING* (ABLE)
Ac 14: 3 the message of his grace by *e* them

ENCAMPS* (CAMP)
Ps 34: 7 The angel of the LORD *e*

ENCOURAGE* (ENCOURAGED ENCOURAGEMENT ENCOURAGES ENCOURAGING)
Dt 1:38 *E* him, because he will lead Israel
3:28 and *e* and strengthen him,
2Sa 11:25 Say this to *e* Joab."
19: 7 Now go out and *e* your men.
Job 16: 5 But my mouth would *e* you;
Ps 10:17 you *e* them, and you listen
64: 5 They *e* each other in evil plans,
Isa 1:17 *e* the oppressed.
Jer 29: 8 to the dreams you *e* them to have.
Ac 15:32 to *e* and strengthen the brothers.
Ro 12: 8 if it is encouraging, let him *e;*
Eph 6:22 how we are, and that he may *e* you.
Col 4: 8 and that he may *e* your hearts.
1Th 3: 2 to strengthen and *e* you
4:18 Therefore *e* each other
5:11 Therefore *e* one another
5:14 those who are idle, *e* the timid,
2Th 2:17 *e* your hearts and strengthen you

2Ti 4: 2 rebuke and *e*—with great patience
Tit 1: 9 so that he can *e* others
2: 6 *e* the young men to be
2:15 *E* and rebuke with all authority.
Heb 3:13 But *e* one another daily, as long
10:25 but let us *e* one another—

ENCOURAGED* (ENCOURAGE)

Jdg 7:11 you will be *e* to attack the camp."
20:22 But the men of Israel *e* one another
2Ch 22: 3 for his mother *e* him
32: 6 and *e* them with these words:
35: 2 and *e* them in the service
Eze 13:22 you *e* the wicked not to turn
Ac 9:31 It was strengthened; and *e*
11:23 and *e* them all to remain true
16:40 met with the brothers and *e* them.
18:27 the brothers *e* him and wrote
27:36 They were all *e* and ate some food
28:15 men Paul thanked God and was *e*.
Ro 1:12 and I may be mutually *e*
1Co 14:31 everyone may be instructed and *e*.
2Co 7: 4 I am greatly *e*; in all our troubles
7:13 By all this we are *e*.
Php 1:14 brothers in the Lord have been *e*
Col 2: 2 My purpose is that they may be *e*
1Th 3: 7 persecution we were *e* about you
Heb 6:18 offered to us may be greatly *e*.

ENCOURAGEMENT* (ENCOURAGE)

Ac 4:36 Barnabas (which means Son of *E*),
13:15 a message of *e* for the people,
20: 2 speaking many words of *e*
Ro 15: 4 *e* of the Scriptures we might have
15: 5 and *e* give you a spirit of unity
1Co 14: 3 to men for their strengthening, *e*
2Co 7:13 to our own *e*, we were especially
Php 2: 1 If you have any *e* from being united
2Th 2:16 and by his grace gave us eternal *e*
Phm : 7 love has given me great joy and *e*,
Heb 12: 5 word of *e* that addresses you

ENCOURAGES* (ENCOURAGE)

Isa 41: 7 The craftsman *e* the goldsmith,

ENCOURAGING* (ENCOURAGE)

Ac 14:22 *e* them to remain true to the faith.
15:31 and were glad for its *e* message.
20: 1 for the disciples and, after *e* them,
Ro 12: 8 if it is *e*, let him encourage;
1Th 2:12 *e*, comforting and urging you
1Pe 5:12 *e* you and testifying that this is

ENCROACH

Pr 23:10 or *e* on the fields of the fatherless,

END (ENDS)

Ps 119: 33 then I will keep them to the *e*.
119:112 to the very *e*.
Pr 1:19 Such is the *e* of all who go
5: 4 but in the *e* she is bitter as gall,
5:11 At the *e* of your life you will groan,
14:12 but in the *e* it leads to death.
14:13 and joy may *e* in grief.
16:25 but in the *e* it leads to death.
19:20 and in the *e* you will be wise.
20:21 will not be blessed at the *e*.
23:32 In the *e* it bites like a snake
25: 8 for what will you do in the *e*
28:23 in the *e* gain more favor
29:21 he will bring grief in the *e*.
Ecc 3:11 done from beginning to *e*.
7: 8 The *e* of a matter is better
12:12 making many books there is no *e*,
Eze 7: 2 The *e*! The *e* has come
Mt 10:22 firm to the *e* will be saved.
24:13 firm to the *e* will be saved.
24:14 nations, and then the *e* will come.
Lk 21: 9 but the *e* will not come right away
Ro 10: 4 Christ is the *e* of the law
1Co 15:24 the *e* will come, when he hands
Rev 21: 6 Omega, the Beginning and the *E*.
22:13 the Last, the Beginning and the *E*.

ENDS (END)

Ps 19: 4 their words to the *e* of the world.
Pr 20:17 he *e* up with a mouth full of gravel.
Isa 49: 6 salvation to the *e* of the earth."
62:11 proclamation to the *e* of the earth:
Ac 13:47 salvation to the *e* of the earth.'"
Ro 10:18 their words to the *e* of the world."

ENDURANCE* (ENDURE)

Ro 15: 4 through *e* and the encouragement
15: 5 May the God who gives *e*
2Co 1: 6 which produces in you patient *e*
6: 4 in great *e*; in troubles, hardships
Col 1:11 might so that you may have great *e*
1Th 1: 3 and your *e* inspired by hope
1Ti 6:11 faith, love, *e* and gentleness.
2Ti 3:10 patience, love, *e*, persecutions,
Tit 2: 2 and sound in faith, in love and in *e*.
Rev 1: 9 and patient *e* that are ours in Jesus,
13:10 This calls for patient *e*
14:12 This calls for patient *e* on the part

ENDURE (ENDURANCE ENDURED ENDURES ENDURING)

Ps 72:17 May his name *e* forever;
Pr 12:19 Truthful lips *e* forever,
27:24 for riches do not *e* forever,
Ecc 3:14 everything God does will *e* forever;
Da 2:44 to an end, but it will itself *e* forever.
Mal 3: 2 who can *e* the day of his coming?
1Co 4:12 when we are persecuted, we *e* it;
2Co 1: 8 far beyond our ability to *e*,
2Ti 2: 3 *E* hardship with us like a good
2:10 Therefore I *e* everything
2:12 if we *e*, / we will also reign
4: 5 head in all situations, *e* hardship,
Heb 12: 7 *E* hardship as discipline; God is
1Pe 2:20 a beating for doing wrong and *e* it?
2:20 suffer for doing good and you *e* it,
Rev 3:10 kept my command to *e* patiently,

ENDURED* (ENDURE)

Ps 123: 3 for we have *e* much contempt.
123: 4 We have *e* much ridicule
132: 1 and all the hardships he *e*.
Ac 13:18 and *e* their conduct forty years
2Ti 3:11 and Lystra, the persecutions I *e*.
Heb 12: 2 set before him *e* the cross,
12: 3 him who *e* such opposition
Rev 2: 3 and have *e* hardships for my name,

ENDURES (ENDURE)

Ps 102: 12 renown *e* through all generations.
112: 9 his righteousness *e* forever;
136: 1 *His love e forever.*
Da 9:15 made for yourself a name that *e*
2Co 9: 9 his righteousness *e* forever."

ENDURING (ENDURE)

2Th 1: 4 persecutions and trials you are *e*.
1Pe 1:23 through the living and *e* word

ENEMIES (ENEMY)

Ps 23: 5 in the presence of my *e*.
110: 1 hand until I make your *e*
Pr 16: 7 his *e* live at peace with him.
Isa 59:18 wrath to his *e*
Mic 7: 6 a man's *e* are the members
Mt 5:44 Love your *e* and pray
10:36 a man's *e* will be the members
Lk 6:27 Love your *e*, do good
6:35 But love your *e*, do good to them,
20:43 hand until I make your *e*
Ro 5:10 For if, when we were God's *e*,
1Co 15:25 reign until he has put all his *e*
Php 3:18 many live as *e* of the cross of Christ
Heb 1:13 hand until I make your *e*
10:13 for his *e* to be made his footstool,

ENEMY (ENEMIES ENMITY)

Pr 24:17 Do not gloat when your *e* falls;
25:21 If your *e* is hungry, give him food
27: 6 but an *e* multiplies kisses.
29:24 of a thief is his own *e*;
Lk 10:19 to overcome all the power of the *e*;
Ro 12:20 "If your *e* is hungry, feed him;
1Co 15:26 The last *e* to be destroyed is death.
1Ti 5:14 and to give the *e* no opportunity
1Pe 5: 8 Your *e* the devil prowls

ENERGY*

Col 1:29 struggling with all his *e*, which

ENGRAVED

Isa 49:16 I have *e* you on the palms
2Co 3: 7 which was *e* in letters on stone,

ENHANCES*

Ro 3: 7 my falsehood *e* God's truthfulness

ENJOY (JOY)

Dt 6: 2 and so that you may *e* long life.
Ps 37: 3 dwell in the land and *e* safe pasture.
Pr 28:16 ill-gotten gain will *e* a long life.
Ecc 3:22 better for a man than to *e* his work,
Eph 6: 3 and that you may *e* long life
Heb 11:25 rather than to *e* the pleasures of sin
3Jn : 2 I pray that you may *e* good health

ENJOYMENT (JOY)

Ecc 4: 8 and why am I depriving myself of *e*
1Ti 6:17 us with everything for our *e*.

ENLARGE (ENLARGES)

2Co 9:10 *e* the harvest of your righteousness.

ENLARGES (ENLARGE)

Dt 33:20 Blessed is he who *e* Gad's domain!

ENLIGHTENED* (LIGHT)

Eph 1:18 that the eyes of your heart may be *e*
Heb 6: 4 for those who have once been *e*,

ENMITY* (ENEMY)

Ge 3:15 And I will put *e*

ENOCH

1. Son of Cain (Ge 4:17-18).
2. Descendant of Seth; walked with God and taken by him (Ge 5:18-24; Heb 11:5). Prophet (Jude 14).

ENSLAVED (SLAVE)

Gal 4: 9 Do you wish to be *e* by them all
Tit 3: 3 and *e* by all kinds of passions

ENSNARE (SNARE)

Pr 5:22 of a wicked man *e* him;
Ecc 7:26 but the sinner she will *e*.

ENSNARED* (SNARE)

Dt 7:25 for yourselves, or you will be *e* by it
12:30 be careful not to be *e*
Ps 9:16 the wicked are *e* by the work
Pr 6: 2 *e* by the words of your mouth,
22:25 and get yourself *e*.

ENTANGLED (ENTANGLES)

2Pe 2:20 and are again *e* in it and overcome,

ENTANGLES* (ENTANGLED)

Heb 12: 1 and the sin that so easily *e*,

ENTER (ENTERED ENTERING ENTERS ENTRANCE)

Ps 95:11 "They shall never *e* my rest."
100: 4 *E* his gates with thanksgiving
Pr 2:10 For wisdom will *e* your heart,
Mt 5:20 will certainly not *e* the kingdom
7:13 "*E* through the narrow gate.
7:21 Lord,' will *e* the kingdom of heaven
18: 3 you will never *e* the kingdom
18: 8 It is better for you to *e* life maimed
19:17 to *e* life, obey the commandments
19:23 man to *e* the kingdom of heaven.
Mk 9:43 It is better for you to *e* life maimed
9:45 It is better for you to *e* life crippled
9:47 for you to *e* the kingdom of God
10:15 like a little child will never *e* it."
10:23 is for the rich to *e* the kingdom
Lk 13:24 will try to *e* and will not be able to.
13:24 "Make every effort to *e*
18:17 like a little child will never *e* it."
18:24 is for the rich to *e* the kingdom
Jn 3: 5 no one can *e* the kingdom of God.
Heb 3:11 'They shall never *e* my rest.'"
4:11 make every effort to *e* that rest,

ENTERED (ENTER)

Ps 73:17 me till I *e* the sanctuary of God;
Eze 4:14 meat has ever *e* my mouth."
Ac 11: 8 or unclean has ever *e* my mouth.'
Ro 5:12 as sin *e* the world through one man,
Heb 9:12 but he *e* the Most Holy Place once

ENTERING (ENTER)

Mt 21:31 the prostitutes are *e* the kingdom
Lk 11:52 have hindered those who were *e*."
Heb 4: 1 the promise of *e* his rest still stands,

ENTERS (ENTER)

Mk 7:18 you see that nothing that *e* a man
Jn 10: 2 The man who *e* by the gate is

ENTERTAIN* (ENTERTAINED ENTERTAINMENT)

Jdg 16:25 "Bring out Samson to *e* us."
Mt 9: 4 "Why do you *e* evil thoughts
1Ti 5:19 Do not *e* an accusation
Heb 13: 2 Do not forget to *e* strangers,

ENTERTAINED* (ENTERTAIN)

Ac 28: 7 and for three days *e* us hospitably.
Heb 13: 2 so doing some people have *e* angels

ENTERTAINMENT* (ENTERTAIN)

Da 6:18 without any *e* being brought to him

ENTHRALLED*

Ps 45:11 The king is *e* by your beauty;

ENTHRONED* (THRONE)

1Sa 4: 4 who is *e* between the cherubim.
2Sa 6: 2 who is *e* between the cherubim that
2Ki 19:15 of Israel, *e* between the cherubim,
1Ch 13: 6 who is *e* between the cherubim—
Ps 2: 4 The One *e* in heaven laughs;

Ps 9:11 to the LORD, *e* in Zion;
22: 3 Yet you are *e* as the Holy One;
29:10 The LORD sits *e* over the flood;
29:10 the LORD is *e* as King forever.
55:19 God, who is *e* forever,
61: 7 May he be *e* in God's presence
80: 1 who sit *e* between the cherubim,
99: 1 he sits *e* between the cherubim,
102: 12 But you, O LORD, sit *e* forever;
113: 5 the One who sits *e* on high,
132: 14 here I will sit *e*, for I have desired it
Isa 14:13 I will sit *e* on the mount
37:16 of Israel, *e* between the cherubim,
40:22 He sits *e* above the circle
52: 2 rise up, sit *e*, O Jerusalem.

ENTHRONES* (THRONE)
Job 36: 7 he *e* them with kings

ENTHUSIASM*
2Co 8:17 he is coming to you with much *e*
9: 2 and your *e* has stirred most of them

ENTICE* (ENTICED ENTICES)
Pr 1:10 My son, if sinners *e* you,
2Pe 2:18 they *e* people who are just escaping
Rev 2:14 who taught Balak to *e* the Israelites

ENTICED* (ENTICE)
Dt 4:19 do not be *e* into bowing
11:16 or you will be *e* to turn away
2Ki 17:21 Jeroboam *e* Israel away
Job 31: 9 If my heart has been *e* by a woman,
31:27 so that my heart was secretly *e*
Jas 1:14 desire, he is dragged away and *e*.

ENTICES* (ENTICE)
Dt 13: 6 your closest friend secretly *e* you,
Job 36:18 Be careful that no one *e* you
Pr 16:29 A violent man *e* his neighbor

ENTIRE
Gal 5:14 The *e* law is summed up

ENTRANCE (ENTER)
Mt 27:60 stone in front of the *e* to the tomb
Mk 15:46 a stone against the *e* of the tomb.
16: 3 away from the *e* of the tomb?"
Jn 11:38 cave with a stone laid across the *e*.
20: 1 had been removed from the *e*.

ENTRUST (TRUST)
Jn 2:24 Jesus would not *e* himself to them,
2Ti 2: 2 the presence of many witnesses *e*

ENTRUSTED (TRUST)
Jer 13:20 Where is the flock that was *e* to you
Jn 5:22 but has *e* all judgment to the Son,
Ro 3: 2 they have been *e* with the very
6:17 of teaching to which you were *e*.
1Co 4: 1 as those *e* with the secret things
1Th 2: 4 by God to be *e* with the gospel.
1Ti 1:11 of the blessed God, which he *e*
6:20 guard what has been *e* to your care.
2Ti 1:12 able to guard what I have *e* to him
1:14 Guard the good deposit that was *e*
Tit 1: 3 light through the preaching *e* to me
1: 7 Since an overseer is *e*
1Pe 2:23 he *e* himself to him who judges
5: 3 not lording it over those *e* to you,
Jude : 3 once for all *e* to the saints.

ENVIES
Jas 4: 5 spirit he caused to live in us *e*

ENVIOUS (ENVY)
Dt 32:21 I will make them *e*
Pr 24:19 or be *e* of the wicked,
Ro 10:19 "I will make you *e*

ENVOY
Pr 13:17 but a trustworthy *e* brings healing.

ENVY (ENVIOUS ENVYING)
Pr 3:31 Do not *e* a violent man
14:30 but *e* rots the bones.
23:17 Do not let your heart *e* sinners,
24: 1 Do not *e* wicked men,
Mk 7:22 malice, deceit, lewdness, *e*, slander
Ro 1:29 They are full of *e*, murder, strife,
11:14 arouse my own people to *e*
1Co 13: 4 It does not *e*, it does not boast,
Gal 5:21 factions and *e*; drunkenness, orgies
Php 1:15 that some preach Christ out of *e*
1Ti 6: 4 and quarrels about words that result in *e*,
Tit 3: 3 lived in malice and *e*, being hated
Jas 3:14 But if you harbor bitter *e*
3:16 where you have *e* and selfish
1Pe 2: 1 *e*, and slander of every kind.

ENVYING* (ENVY)
Gal 5:26 provoking and *e* each other.

EPHAH
Eze 45:11 The *e* and the bath are

EPHESUS
Ac 18:19 at *E*, where Paul left Priscilla
19: 1 the interior and arrived at *E*.
Eph 1: 1 To the saints in *E*, the faithful
Rev 2: 1 the angel of the church in *E* write:

EPHRAIM
1. Second son of Joseph (Ge 41:52; 46:20). Blessed as firstborn by Jacob (Ge 48). Tribe of numbered (Nu 1:33; 26:37), blessed (Dt 33:17), allotted land (Jos 16:4-9; Eze 48:5), failed to fully possess (Jos 16:10; Jdg 1:29).
2. Synonymous with Northern Kingdom (Isa 7: 17; Hos 5).

EQUAL (EQUALITY EQUITY)
Dt 33:25 and your strength will *e* your days.
1Sa 9: 2 without *e* among the Israelites—
Isa 40:25 who is my *e*?" says the Holy One.
46: 5 you compare me or count me *e*?
Da 1:19 and he found none *e* to Daniel,
Jn 5:18 making himself *e* with God.
1Co 12:25 that its parts should have *e* concern
2Co 2:16 And who is *e* to such a task?

EQUALITY* (EQUAL)
2Co 8:13 pressed, but that there might be *e*.
8:14 Then there will be *e*, as it is written:
Php 2: 6 did not consider *e*

EQUIP* (EQUIPPED)
Heb 13:21 *e* you with everything good

EQUIPPED (EQUIP)
2Ti 3:17 man of God may be thoroughly *e*

EQUITY* (EQUAL)
Ps 96:10 he will judge the peoples with *e*.
98: 9 and the peoples with *e*.
99: 4 you have established *e*;

ERODES*
Job 14:18 "But as a mountain *e* and crumbles

ERROR (ERRORS)
Jas 5:20 Whoever turns a sinner from the *e*
2Pe 2:18 escaping from those who live in *e*.

ERRORS* (ERROR)
Ps 19:12 Who can discern his *e*?
Ecc 10: 4 calmness can lay great *e* to rest.

ESAU
Firstborn of Isaac, twin of Jacob (Ge 25:21-26). Also called Edom (Ge 25:30). Sold Jacob his birthright (Ge 25:29-34); lost blessing (Gen 27). Married Hittites (Ge 26:34), Ishmaelites (Ge 28:6-9). Reconciled to Jacob (Gen 33). Genealogy (Ge 36). The LORD chose Jacob over Esau (Mal 1:2-3), but gave Esau land (Dt 2:2-12). Descendants eventually obliterated (Ob 1-21; Jer 49:7-22).

ESCAPE (ESCAPED ESCAPES ESCAPING)
Ps 68:20 from the Sovereign LORD comes *e*
Pr 11: 9 through knowledge the righteous *e*.
Ro 2: 3 think you will *e* God's judgment?
1Th 5: 3 woman, and they will not *e*.
2Ti 2:26 and *e* from the trap of the devil,
Heb 2: 3 how shall we *e* if we ignore such
12:25 If they did not *e* when they refused
2Pe 1: 4 and *e* the corruption in the world

ESCAPED (ESCAPE)
2Pe 2:20 If they have *e* the corruption

ESCAPES (ESCAPE)
Pr 12:13 but a righteous man *e* trouble.

ESCAPING (ESCAPE)
1Co 3:15 only as one *e* through the flames.
2Pe 2:18 they entice people who are just *e*

ESTABLISH (ESTABLISHED ESTABLISHES)
Ge 6:18 But I will *e* my covenant with you,
17:21 But my covenant I will *e* with Isaac
2Sa 7:11 the LORD himself will *e* a house
1Ki 9: 5 I will *e* your royal throne
1Ch 28: 7 I will *e* his kingdom forever
Ps 90:17 *e* the work of our hands for us—
Isa 26:12 LORD, you *e* peace for us;
Ro 10: 3 God and sought to *e* their own,
16:25 able to *e* you by my gospel
Heb 10: 9 sets aside the first to *e* the second.

ESTABLISHED (ESTABLISH)
Ge 9:17 the sign of the covenant I have *e*
Ex 6: 4 also *e* my covenant with them
Pr 16:12 a throne is *e* through righteousness.

ESTABLISHES (ESTABLISH)
Job 25: 2 he *e* order in the heights of heaven.
Isa 42: 4 till he *e* justice on earth.

ESTATE
Ps 136: 23 who remembered us in our low *e*

ESTEEMED
Pr 22: 1 to be *e* is better than silver or gold.
Isa 53: 3 he was despised, and we *e* him not.

ESTHER
Jewess, originally named Hadassah, who lived in Persia; cousin of Mordecai (Est 2:7). Chosen queen of Xerxes (Est 2:8-18). Persuaded by Mordecai to foil Haman's plan to exterminate the Jews (Est 3-4). Revealed Haman's plans to Xerxes, resulting in Haman's death (Est 7), the Jews' preservation (Est 8-9), Mordecai's exaltation (Est 8:15; 9:4; 10). Decreed celebration of Purim (Est 9:18-32).

ETERNAL* (ETERNALLY ETERNITY)
Ge 21:33 the name of the LORD, the *E* God.
Dt 33:27 The *e* God is your refuge,
1Ki 10: 9 of the LORD's *e* love for Israel,
Ps 16:11 with *e* pleasures at your right hand.
21: 6 you have granted him *e* blessings
111: 10 To him belongs *e* praise.
119: 89 Your word, O LORD, is *e*;
119:160 all your righteous laws are *e*.
Ecc 12: 5 Then man goes to his *e* home
Isa 26: 4 LORD, the LORD, is the Rock *e*.
47: 7 the *e* queen!'
Jer 10:10 he is the living God, the *e* King.
Da 4: 3 His kingdom is an *e* kingdom;
4:34 His dominion is an *e* dominion;
Hab 3: 6 His ways are *e*.
Mt 18: 8 two feet and be thrown into *e* fire.
19:16 good thing must I do to get *e* life?"
19:29 as much and will inherit *e* life.
25:41 into the *e* fire prepared for the devil
25:46 but the righteous to *e* life."
25:46 they will go away to *e* punishment,
Mk 3:29 be forgiven; he is guilty of an *e* sin."
10:17 "what must I do to inherit *e* life?"
10:30 and in the age to come, *e* life.
Lk 10:25 "what must I do to inherit *e* life?"
16: 9 will be welcomed into *e* dwellings.
18:18 what must I do to inherit *e* life?"
18:30 and, in the age to come, *e* life."
Jn 3:15 believes in him may have *e* life.
3:16 him shall not perish but have *e* life.
3:36 believes in the Son has *e* life,
4:14 spring of water welling up to *e* life."
4:36 now he harvests the crop for *e* life,
5:24 believes him who sent me has *e* life
5:39 that by them you possess *e* life.
6:27 but for food that endures to *e* life,
6:40 believes in him shall have *e* life,
6:54 and drinks my blood has *e* life,
6:68 You have the words of *e* life.
10:28 I give them *e* life, and they shall
12:25 in this world will keep it for *e* life.
12:50 that his command leads to *e* life.
17: 2 all people that he might give *e* life
17: 3 this is *e* life: that they may know
Ac 13:46 yourselves worthy of *e* life,
13:48 were appointed for *e* life believed.
Ro 1:20 his *e* power and divine nature—
2: 7 and immortality, he will give *e* life.
5:21 righteousness to bring *e* life
6:22 to holiness, and the result is *e* life.
6:23 but the gift of God is *e* life
16:26 by the command of the *e* God,
2Co 4:17 for us an *e* glory that far outweighs
4:18 temporary, but what is unseen is *e*.
5: 1 from God, an *e* house in heaven,
Gal 6: 8 from the Spirit will reap *e* life.
Eph 3:11 to his *e* purpose which he
2Th 2:16 his grace gave us *e* encouragement
1Ti 1:16 believe on him and receive *e* life.
1:17 Now to the King *e*, immortal,
6:12 Take hold of the *e* life
2Ti 2:10 is in Christ Jesus, with *e* glory.
Tit 1: 2 resting on the hope of *e* life,
3: 7 heirs having the hope of *e* life.
Heb 5: 9 he became the source of *e* salvation
6: 2 of the dead, and *e* judgment.
9:12 having obtained *e* redemption.
9:14 through the *e* Spirit offered himself
9:15 the promised *e* inheritance—
13:20 of the *e* covenant brought back
1Pe 5:10 you to his *e* glory in Christ,

2Pe 1:11 into the *e* kingdom of our Lord
1Jn 1: 2 and we proclaim to you the *e* life,
2:25 what he promised us—even *e* life.
3:15 know that no murderer has *e* life
5:11 God has given us *e* life,
5:13 you may know that you have *e* life.
5:20 He is the true God and *e* life.
Jude : 7 who suffer the punishment of *e* fire.
:21 Christ to bring you to *e* life.
Rev 14: 6 and he had the *e* gospel to proclaim

ETERNALLY* (ETERNAL)
Gal 1: 8 let him be *e* condemned! As we
1: 9 let him be *e* condemned! Am I now

ETERNITY* (ETERNAL)
Ps 93: 2 you are from all *e*.
Pr 8:23 I was appointed from *e*,
Ecc 3:11 also set *e* in the hearts of men;

ETHIOPIAN*
Jer 13:23 Can the *E* change his skin
Ac 8:27 and on his way he met an *E* eunuch

EUNUCH (EUNUCHS)
Ac 8:27 on his way he met an Ethiopian *e*,

EUNUCHS (EUNUCH)
Isa 56: 4 "To the *e* who keep my Sabbaths,
Mt 19:12 For some are *e* because they were

EUTYCHUS*
Ac 20: 9 was a young man named *E*,

EVANGELIST* (EVANGELISTS)
Ac 21: 8 stayed at the house of Philip the *e*,
2Ti 4: 5 hardship, do the work of an *e*,

EVANGELISTS* (EVANGELIST)
Eph 4:11 some to be prophets, some to be *e*,

EVE*
Ge 3:20 Adam named his wife *E*,
4: 1 Adam lay with his wife *E*,
2Co 11: 3 as *E* was deceived by the serpent's
1Ti 2:13 For Adam was formed first, then *E*

EVEN-TEMPERED* (TEMPER)
Pr 17:27 and a man of understanding is *e*.

EVENING
Ge 1: 5 there was *e*, and there was morning

EVER (EVERLASTING FOREVER FOREVERMORE)
Ex 15:18 LORD will reign for *e* and *e*."
Dt 8:19 If you *e* forget the LORD your
1Ki 3:12 anyone like you, nor will there *e* be.
Job 4: 7 were the upright *e* destroyed?
Ps 5:11 let them *e* sing for joy.
10:16 The LORD is King for *e* and *e*;
21: 4 length of days, for *e* and *e*.
25: 3 will *e* be put to shame,
25:15 My eyes are *e* on the LORD,
26: 3 for your love is *e* before me,
45: 6 O God, will last for *e* and *e*;
45:17 nations will praise you for *e* and *e*.
48:14 For this God is our God for *e* and *e*;
52: 8 God's unfailing love for *e* and *e*.
61: 8 will I *e* sing praise to your name
71: 6 I will *e* praise you.
84: 4 they are *e* praising you.
89:33 nor will I *e* betray my faithfulness.
111: 8 They are steadfast for *e* and *e*,
119: 44 your law, for *e* and *e*.
119: 98 for they are *e* with me.
132: 12 sit on your throne for *e* and *e*."
145: 1 I will praise your name for *e* and *e*.
145: 2 and extol your name for *e* and *e*.
145: 21 his holy name for *e* and *e*.
Pr 4:18 shining *e* brighter till the full light
5:19 may you *e* be captivated
Isa 66: 8 Who has *e* heard of such a thing?
66: 8 Who has *e* seen such things?
Jer 7: 7 I gave your forefathers for *e* and *e*.
25: 5 and your fathers for *e* and *e*.
31:36 the descendants of Israel *e* cease
Da 2:20 be to the name of God for *e* and *e*;
7:18 it forever—yes, for *e* and *e*.'
12: 3 like the stars for *e* and *e*.
Mic 4: 5 our God for *e* and *e*.
Mt 13:14 you will be *e* seeing but never
13:14 " 'You will be *e* hearing
Mk 4:12 *e* hearing but never understanding;
Jn 1:18 No one has *e* seen God,
Gal 1: 5 to whom be glory for *e* and *e*.
Eph 3:21 all generations, for *e* and *e*!
Php 4:20 and Father be glory for *e* and *e*.
1Ti 1:17 be honor and glory for *e* and *e*.
2Ti 4:18 To him be glory for *e* and *e*.
Heb 1: 8 O God, will last for *e* and *e*,
13:21 to whom be glory for *e* and *e*.
1Pe 4:11 the glory and the power for *e* and *e*.
5:11 To him be the power for *e* and *e*.
1Jn 4:12 No one has *e* seen God;
Rev 1: 6 him be glory and power for *e* and *e*!
1:18 and behold I am alive for *e* and *e*!
21:27 Nothing impure will *e* enter it,
22: 5 And they will reign for *e* and *e*.

EVER-INCREASING* (INCREASE)
Ro 6:19 to impurity and to *e* wickedness,
2Co 3:18 into his likeness with *e* glory,

EVERLASTING* (EVER)
Ge 9:16 and remember the *e* covenant
17: 7 an *e* covenant between me and you
17: 8 I will give as an *e* possession to you
17:13 in your flesh is to be an *e* covenant.
17:19 an *e* covenant for his descendants
48: 4 *e* possession to your descendants
Nu 18:19 It is an *e* covenant of salt
Dt 33:15 and the fruitfulness of the *e* hills;
33:27 and underneath are the *e* arms.
2Sa 23: 5 made with me an *e* covenant,
1Ch 16:17 to Israel as an *e* covenant:
16:36 from *e* to *e*.
29:10 from *e* to *e*.
Ezr 9:12 to your children as an *e* inheritance
Ne 9: 5 your God, who is from *e* to *e*."
Ps 41:13 from *e* to *e*.
52: 5 God will bring you down to *e* ruin:
74: 3 toward these *e* ruins,
78:66 he put them to *e* shame.
90: 2 from *e* to *e* you are God.
103: 17 But from *e* to *e*
105: 10 to Israel as an *e* covenant:
106: 48 from *e* to *e*.
119:142 Your righteousness is *e*
139: 24 and lead me in the way *e*.
145: 13 Your kingdom is an *e* kingdom,
Isa 9: 6 *E* Father, Prince of Peace.
24: 5 and broken the *e* covenant.
30: 8 it may be an *e* witness.
33:14 Who of us can dwell with *e* burning
35:10 *e* joy will crown their heads.
40:28 The LORD is the *e* God,
45:17 the LORD with an *e* salvation;
45:17 to ages *e*.
51:11 *e* joy will crown their heads.
54: 8 but with *e* kindness
55: 3 I will make an *e* covenant with you,
55:13 for an *e* sign,
56: 5 I will give them an *e* name
60:15 I will make you the *e* pride
60:19 for the LORD will be your *e* light,
60:20 the LORD will be your *e* light,
61: 7 and *e* joy will be theirs.
61: 8 and make an *e* covenant with them.
63:12 to gain for himself *e* renown,
Jer 5:22 an *e* barrier it cannot cross.
23:40 I will bring upon you *e* disgrace—
23:40 *e* shame that will not be forgotten."
25: 9 of horror and scorn, and an *e* ruin.
31: 3 "I have loved you with an *e* love;
32:40 I will make an *e* covenant
50: 5 the LORD in an *e* covenant
Eze 16:60 and I will establish an *e* covenant
37:26 with them; it will be an *e* covenant.
Da 7:14 dominion is an *e* dominion that will
7:27 His kingdom will be an *e* kingdom,
9:24 to bring in *e* righteousness,
12: 2 others to shame and *e* contempt.
12: 2 some to *e* life, others to shame
Mic 6: 2 you *e* foundations of the earth.
Hab 1:12 O LORD, are you not from *e*?
Jn 6:47 the truth, he who believes has *e* life.
2Th 1: 9 punished with *e* destruction
Jude : 6 bound with *e* chains for judgment

EVER-PRESENT*
Ps 46: 1 an *e* help in trouble

EVIDENCE (EVIDENT)
Jn 14:11 on the *e* of the miracles themselves.
Ac 11:23 and saw the *e* of the grace of God,
2Th 1: 5 All this is *e* that God's judgment is
Jas 2:20 do you want *e* that faith

EVIDENT (EVIDENCE)
Php 4: 5 Let your gentleness be *e* to all.

EVIL (EVILDOER EVILDOERS EVILS)
Ge 2: 9 of the knowledge of good and *e*.
3: 5 be like God, knowing good and *e*."
6: 5 of his heart was only *e* all the time.
Ex 32:22 how prone these people are to *e*.
Jdg 2:11 Then the Israelites did *e* in the eyes
3: 7 The Israelites did *e* in the eyes
3:12 Once again the Israelites did *e*
Jdg 4: 1 the Israelites once again did *e*
6: 1 Again the Israelites did *e*
10: 6 Again the Israelites did *e*
13: 1 Again the Israelites did *e*
1Ki 11: 6 So Solomon did *e* in the eyes
16:25 But Omri did *e* in the eyes
2Ki 15:24 Pekahiah did *e* in the eyes
Job 1: 1 he feared God and shunned *e*.
1: 8 a man who fears God and shuns *e*."
34:10 Far be it from God to do *e*,
36:21 Beware of turning to *e*,
Ps 5: 4 not a God who takes pleasure in *e*;
23: 4 I will fear no *e*,
34:13 keep your tongue from *e*
34:14 Turn from *e* and do good;
34:16 is against those who do *e*,
37: 1 Do not fret because of *e* men
37: 8 do not fret—it leads only to *e*.
37:27 Turn from *e* and do good;
49: 5 fear when *e* days come,
51: 4 and done what is *e* in your sight,
97:10 those who love the LORD hate *e*,
101: 4 I will have nothing to do with *e*.
141: 4 not my heart be drawn to what is *e*,
Pr 4:27 keep your foot from *e*.
8:13 To fear the LORD is to hate *e*;
10:23 A fool finds pleasure in *e* conduct,
11:19 he who pursues *e* goes to his death.
11:27 *e* comes to him who searches for it.
14:16 man fears the LORD and shuns *e*,
17:13 If a man pays back *e* for good,
20:30 Blows and wounds cleanse away *e*,
24:19 Do not fret because of *e* men
24:20 for the *e* man has no future hope,
26:23 are fervent lips with an *e* heart.
28: 5 *E* men do not understand justice,
29: 6 An *e* man is snared by his own sin,
Ecc 12:14 whether it is good or *e*.
Isa 5:20 Woe to those who call *e* good
13:11 I will punish the world for its *e*,
55: 7 and the *e* man his thoughts.
Jer 4:14 wash the *e* from your heart
18: 8 nation I warned repents of its *e*,
18:11 So turn from your *e* ways,
Eze 33:11 Turn! Turn from your *e* ways!
33:13 he will die for the *e* he has done.
33:15 and does no *e*, he will surely live;
Am 5:13 for the times are *e*.
Hab 1:13 Your eyes are too pure to look on *e*;
Zec 8:17 do not plot *e* against your neighbor,
Mt 5:45 He causes his sun to rise on the *e*
6:13 but deliver us from the *e* one.'
7:11 If you, then, though you are *e*,
12:34 you who are *e* say anything good?
12:35 and the *e* man brings *e* things out
12:35 out of the *e* stored up in him.
12:43 "When an *e* spirit comes out
15:19 out of the heart come *e* thoughts,
Mk 7:21 come *e* thoughts, sexual
Lk 6:45 and the *e* man brings *e* things out
11:13 If you then, though you are *e*,
Jn 3:19 of light because their deeds were *e*.
3:20 Everyone who does *e* hates
17:15 you protect them from the *e* one.
Ro 1:30 they invent ways of doing *e*;
2: 8 who reject the truth and follow *e*,
2: 9 for every human being who does *e*:
3: 8 "Let us do *e* that good may result"?
6:12 body so that you obey its *e* desires.
7:19 no, the *e* I do not want to do—
7:21 to do good, *e* is right there with me.
12: 9 Hate what is *e*; cling
12:17 Do not repay anyone *e* for *e*.
12:21 Do not be overcome by *e*,
14:16 good to be spoken of as *e*.
16:19 and innocent about what is *e*.
1Co 13: 6 Love does not delight in *e*
14:20 In regard to *e* be infants,
Eph 5:16 because the days are *e*.
6:12 forces of *e* in the heavenly realms.
6:16 all the flaming arrows of the *e* one.
Col 3: 5 impurity, lust, *e* desires and greed,
1Th 5:22 Avoid every kind of *e*.
2Th 3: 3 and protect you from the *e* one.
1Ti 6:10 of money is a root of all kinds of *e*.
2Ti 2:22 Flee the *e* desires of youth,
3: 6 are swayed by all kinds of *e* desires,
3:13 while *e* men and impostors will go
Heb 5:14 to distinguish good from *e*.
Jas 1:13 For God cannot be tempted by *e*,
1:21 and the *e* that is so prevalent,
3: 6 a world of *e* among the parts
3: 8 It is a restless *e*, full
1Pe 2:16 your freedom as a cover-up for *e*;
3: 9 Do not repay *e* with *e* or insult
3:10 must keep his tongue from *e*
3:17 for doing good than for doing *e*.
1Jn 2:13 you have overcome the *e* one.
2:14 and you have overcome the *e* one.

1Jn 3:12 who belonged to the *e* one
5:18 and the *e* one cannot harm him.
5:19 is under the control of the *e* one.
3Jn :11 do not imitate what is *e*

EVILDOER* (EVIL)
2Sa 3:39 the LORD repay the *e* according
Ps 101: 8 I will cut off every *e*
Mal 4: 1 and every *e* will be stubble,

EVILDOERS* (EVIL)
1Sa 24:13 saying goes, 'From *e* come evil
Job 8:20 or strengthen the hands of *e*.
34: 8 He keeps company with *e*;
34:22 where *e* can hide.
Ps 14: 4 Will *e* never learn—
14: 6 You *e* frustrate the plans
26: 5 I abhor the assembly of *e*
36:12 See how the *e* lie fallen—
53: 4 Will the *e* never learn—
59: 2 Deliver me from *e*
64: 2 from that noisy crowd of *e*.
92: 7 and all *e* flourish,
92: 9 all *e* will be scattered.
94: 4 all the *e* are full of boasting.
94:16 will take a stand for me against *e*?
119:115 Away from me, you *e*,
125: 5 the LORD will banish with the *e*.
141: 4 deeds with men who are *e*;
141: 5 ever against the deeds of *e*;
141: 9 from the traps set by *e*.
Pr 21:15 but terror to *e*.
Isa 1: 4 a brood of *e*,
31: 2 against those who help *e*.
Jer 23:14 They strengthen the hands of *e*,
Hos 10: 9 the *e* in Gibeah?
Mal 3:15 Certainly the *e* prosper, and
Mt 7:23 you *e*!' "Therefore everyone who
Lk 13:27 Away from me, all you *e*!'
18:11 *e*, adulterers—or even like this tax

EVILS* (EVIL)
Mk 7:23 All these *e* come from inside

EWE
2Sa 12: 3 one little *e* lamb he had bought.

EXACT*
Ge 43:21 the *e* weight—in the mouth
Est 4: 7 including the *e* amount
Mt 2: 7 from them the *e* time the star had
Jn 4:53 realized that this was the *e* time
Ac 17:26 the *e* places where they should live.
Heb 1: 3 the *e* representation of his being,

EXALT* (EXALTED EXALTS)
Ex 15: 2 my father's God, and I will *e* him.
Jos 3: 7 begin to *e* you in the eyes
1Sa 2:10 and *e* the horn of his anointed."
1Ch 25: 5 the promises of God to *e* him.
29:12 power to *e* and give strength to all.
Job 19: 5 If indeed you would *e* yourselves
Ps 30: 1 I will *e* you, O LORD,
34: 3 let us *e* his name together.
35:26 may all who *e* themselves over me
37:34 He will *e* you to inherit the land;
38:16 *e* themselves over me
75: 6 or from the desert can *e* a man.
89:17 and by your favor you *e* our horn.
99: 5 *E* the LORD our God
99: 9 *E* the LORD our God
107: 32 Let them *e* him in the assembly
118: 28 you are my God, and I will *e* you.
145: 1 I will *e* you, my God the King;
Pr 4: 8 Esteem her, and she will *e* you;
25: 6 Do not *e* yourself in the king's
Isa 24:15 *e* the name of the LORD, the God
25: 1 I will *e* you and praise your name,
Eze 29:15 and will never again *e* itself
Da 4:37 *e* and glorify the King of heaven,
11:36 He will *e* and magnify himself
11:37 but will *e* himself above them all.
Hos 11: 7 he will by no means *e* them.
2Th 2: 4 will *e* himself over everything that is

EXALTED* (EXALT)
Ex 15: 1 for he is highly *e*.
15:21 for he is highly *e*.
Nu 24: 7 their kingdom will be *e*.
Jos 4:14 That day the LORD *e* Joshua
2Sa 5:12 and had *e* his kingdom for the sake
22:47 *E* be God, the Rock, my Savior!
22:49 You *e* me above my foes;
23: 1 of the man *e* by the Most High,
1Ch 14: 2 that his kingdom had been highly *e*
17:17 as though I were the most *e* of men,
29:11 you are *e* as head over all.
29:25 The LORD highly *e* Solomon
Ne 9: 5 and may it be *e* above all blessing
Job 24:24 For a little while they are *e*,
36:22 "God is *e* in his power.
37:23 beyond our reach and *e* in power;
Ps 18:46 *E* be God my Savior!
18:48 You *e* me above my foes;
21:13 Be *e*, O LORD, in your strength;
27: 6 Then my head will be *e*
35:27 they always say, "The LORD be *e*,
40:16 "The LORD be *e*!"
46:10 I will be *e* among the nations,
46:10 I will be *e* in the earth."
47: 9 he is greatly *e*.
57: 5 Be *e*, O God, above the heavens;
57:11 Be *e*, O God, above the heavens;
70: 4 "Let God be *e*!"
89:13 hand is strong, your right hand *e*.
89:19 I have *e* a young man
89:24 through my name his horn will be *e*
89:27 the most *e* of the kings of the earth.
89:42 You have *e* the right hand
92: 8 But you, O LORD, are *e* forever.
92:10 You have *e* my horn like that
97: 9 you are *e* far above all gods.
99: 2 he is *e* over all the nations.
108: 5 Be *e*, O God, above the heavens,
113: 4 The LORD is *e* over all the nations
138: 2 for you have *e* above all things
148: 13 for his name alone is *e*;
Pr 11:11 of the upright a city is *e*,
30:32 have played the fool and *e* yourself,
Isa 2:11 the LORD alone will be *e*
2:12 for all that is *e*
2:17 the LORD alone will be *e*
5:16 the LORD Almighty will be *e*
6: 1 *e*, and the train of his robe filled
12: 4 and proclaim that his name is *e*.
24: 4 the *e* of the earth languish.
33: 5 The LORD is *e*, for he dwells
33:10 "Now will I be *e*;
52:13 be raised and lifted up and highly *e*.
Jer 17:12 A glorious throne, *e*
La 2:17 he has *e* the horn of your foes.
Eze 21:26 The lowly will be *e* and the *e* will be
Hos 13: 1 he was *e* in Israel.
Mic 6: 6 and bow down before the *e* God?
Mt 23:12 whoever humbles himself will be *e*.
Lk 14:11 he who humbles himself will be *e*."
18:14 he who humbles himself will be *e*."
Ac 2:33 *E* to the right hand of God,
5:31 God *e* him to his own right hand
Php 1:20 always Christ will be *e* in my body,
2: 9 Therefore God *e* him
Heb 7:26 from sinners, *e* above the heavens.

EXALTS* (EXALT)
1Sa 2: 7 he humbles and he *e*.
Job 36: 7 and *e* them forever.
Ps 75: 7 He brings one down, he *e* another.
Pr 14:34 Righteousness *e* a nation,
Mt 23:12 For whoever *e* himself will be
Lk 14:11 For everyone who *e* himself will be
18:14 For everyone who *e* himself will be

EXAMINE (EXAMINED EXAMINES)
Ps 11: 4 his eyes *e* them.
17: 3 you probe my heart and *e* me
26: 2 *e* my heart and my mind;
Jer 17:10 and *e* the mind,
20:12 Almighty, you who *e* the righteous
La 3:40 Let us *e* our ways and test them,
1Co 11:28 A man ought to *e* himself
2Co 13: 5 *E* yourselves to see whether you

EXAMINED (EXAMINE)
Job 13: 9 Would it turn out well if he *e* you?
Ac 17:11 *e* the Scriptures every day to see

EXAMINES (EXAMINE)
Ps 11: 5 The LORD *e* the righteous,
Pr 5:21 and he *e* all his paths.

EXAMPLE* (EXAMPLES)
2Ki 14: 3 In everything he followed the *e*
Ecc 9:13 also saw under the sun this *e*
Eze 14: 8 and make him an *e* and a byword.
Jn 13:15 have set you an *e* that you should
Ro 7: 2 as long as he lives? For *e*,
1Co 11: 1 Follow my *e*, as I follow
11: 1 as I follow the *e* of Christ.
Gal 3:15 let me take an *e* from everyday life.
Php 3:17 Join with others in following my *e*,
2Th 3: 7 how you ought to follow our *e*.
1Ti 1:16 as an *e* for those who would believe
4:12 set an *e* for the believers in speech,
Tit 2: 7 In everything set them an *e*
Heb 4:11 fall by following their *e*
Jas 3: 4 Or take ships as an *e*.
5:10 as an *e* of patience in the face
1Pe 2:21 leaving you an *e*, that you should
2Pe 2: 6 made them an *e* of what is going
Jude : 7 as an *e* of those who suffer

EXAMPLES* (EXAMPLE)
1Co 10: 6 Now these things occurred as *e*
10:11 as *e* and were written down
1Pe 5: 3 to you, but being *e* to the flock.

EXASPERATE*
Eph 6: 4 Fathers, do not *e* your children;

EXCEL* (EXCELLENT)
Ge 49: 4 as the waters, you will no longer *e*,
1Co 14:12 to *e* in gifts that build up the church
2Co 8: 7 But just as you *e* in everything—
8: 7 also *e* in this grace of giving.

EXCELLENT (EXCEL)
1Co 12:31 now I will show you the most *e* way
Php 4: 8 if anything is *e* or praiseworthy—
1Ti 3:13 have served well gain an *e* standing
Tit 3: 8 These things are *e* and profitable

EXCESSIVE
Eze 18: 8 or take *e* interest.
2Co 2: 7 not be overwhelmed by *e* sorrow.

EXCHANGE (EXCHANGED)
Mt 16:26 Or what can a man give in *e*
Mk 8:37 Or what can a man give in *e*
2Co 6:13 As a fair *e*— I speak

EXCHANGED (EXCHANGE)
Ps 106: 20 They *e* their Glory
Jer 2:11 But my people have *e* their Glory
Hos 4: 7 they *e* their Glory
Ro 1:23 *e* the glory of the immortal God
1:25 They *e* the truth of God for a lie,
1:26 their women *e* natural relations

EXCLAIM
Ps 35:10 My whole being will *e*,

EXCUSE* (EXCUSES)
Ps 25: 3 who are treacherous without *e*.
Lk 14:18 Please *e* me.'
14:19 Please *e* me.'
Jn 15:22 they have no *e* for their sin.
Ro 1:20 so that men are without *e*.
2: 1 You, therefore, have no *e*,

EXCUSES* (EXCUSE)
Lk 14:18 "But they all alike began to make *e*.

EXERTED*
Eph 1:20 which he *e* in Christ

EXHORT*
1Ti 5: 1 but *e* him as if he were your father.

EXILE
2Ki 17:23 taken from their homeland into *e*
25:11 into *e* the people who remained

EXISTED* (EXISTS)
2Pe 3: 5 ago by God's word the heavens *e*

EXISTS (EXISTED)
Heb 2:10 and through whom everything *e*,
11: 6 to him must believe that he *e*

EXPANSE
Ge 1: 7 So God made the *e* and separated
1: 8 God called the *e* "sky."

EXPECT (EXPECTATION EXPECTED EXPECTING)
Mt 24:44 at an hour when you do not *e* him.
Lk 12:40 at an hour when you do not *e* him."
Php 1:20 I eagerly *e* and hope that I will

EXPECTATION (EXPECT)
Ro 8:19 waits in eager *e* for the sons
Heb 10:27 but only a fearful *e* of judgment

EXPECTED (EXPECT)
Pr 11: 7 all he *e* from his power comes
Hag 1: 9 "You *e* much, but see, it turned out

EXPECTING (EXPECT)
Lk 6:35 and lend to them without *e*

EXPEL* (EXPELLED)
1Co 5:13 *E* the wicked man from among you

EXPELLED (EXPEL)
Eze 28:16 and I *e* you, O guardian cherub,

EXPENSE (EXPENSIVE)
1Co 9: 7 Who serves as a soldier at his own *e*

EXPENSIVE* (EXPENSE)
Mt 26: 7 jar of very *e* perfume,

Mk 14: 3 jar of very *e* perfume,
Lk 7:25 those who wear *e* clothes
Jn 12: 3 a pint of pure nard, an *e* perfume;
1Ti 2: 9 or gold or pearls or *e* clothes,

EXPERT
1Co 3:10 I laid a foundation as an *e* builder,

EXPLAINING (EXPLAINS)
Ac 17: 3 *e* and proving that the Christ had

EXPLAINS* (EXPLAINING)
Ac 8:31 he said, "unless someone *e* it to me

EXPLOIT* (EXPLOITED EXPLOITING EXPLOITS)
Pr 22:22 Do not *e* the poor because they are
Isa 58: 3 and *e* all your workers.
2Co 12:17 Did I *e* you through any
12:18 Titus did not *e* you, did he?
2Pe 2: 3 greed these teachers will *e* you

EXPLOITED* (EXPLOIT)
2Co 7: 2 no one, we have *e* no one.

EXPLOITING* (EXPLOIT)
Jas 2: 6 Is it not the rich who are *e* you?

EXPLOITS (EXPLOIT)
2Co 11:20 or *e* you or takes advantage of you

EXPLORE
Nu 13: 2 "Send some men to *e* the land

EXPOSE (EXPOSED)
1Co 4: 5 will *e* the motives of men's hearts.
Eph 5:11 of darkness, but rather *e* them.

EXPOSED (EXPOSE)
Jn 3:20 for fear that his deeds will be *e*.
Eph 5:13 everything *e* by the light becomes

EXPRESS (EXPRESSING)
Ro 8:26 us with groans that words cannot *e*.

EXPRESSING* (EXPRESS)
1Co 2:13 *e* spiritual truths in spiritual words.
Gal 5: 6 thing that counts is faith *e* itself

EXTENDS (EXTENT)
Pr 31:20 and *e* her hands to the needy.
Lk 1:50 His mercy *e* to those who fear him,

EXTENT (EXTENDS)
Jn 13: 1 he now showed them the full *e*

EXTERNAL
Gal 2: 6 judge by *e* appearance—

EXTINGUISH (EXTINGUISHED)
Eph 6:16 which you can *e* all the flaming

EXTINGUISHED (EXTINGUISH)
2Sa 21:17 the lamp of Israel will not be *e*."

EXTOL*
Job 36:24 Remember to *e* his work,
Ps 34: 1 I will *e* the LORD at all times;
68: 4 *e* him who rides on the clouds—
95: 2 and *e* him with music and song.
109: 30 mouth I will greatly *e* the LORD;
111: 1 I will *e* the LORD with all my heart
115: 18 it is we who *e* the LORD,
117: 1 *e* him, all you peoples.
145: 2 and *e* your name for ever and ever.
145: 10 your saints will *e* you.
147: 12 *E* the LORD, O Jerusalem;

EXTORT*
Lk 3:14 "Don't *e* money and don't accuse

EXTRAORDINARY*
Ac 19:11 God did *e* miracles through Paul,

EXTREME (EXTREMES)
2Co 8: 2 and their *e* poverty welled up

EXTREMES* (EXTREME)
Ecc 7:18 who fears God will avoid all *e*.

EXULT
Ps 89:16 they *e* in your righteousness.
Isa 45:25 will be found righteous and will *e*.

EYE (EYES)
Ge 3: 6 good for food and pleasing to the *e*,
Ex 21:24 you are to take life for life, *e* for *e*,
Dt 19:21 life for life, *e* for *e*, tooth for tooth,
Ps 94: 9 Does he who formed the *e* not see?
Mt 5:29 If your right *e* causes you to sin,
5:38 '*E* for *e*, and tooth for tooth.'
6:22 "The *e* is the lamp of the body.
Mt 7: 3 of sawdust in your brother's *e*
1Co 2: 9 "No *e* has seen,
12:16 I am not an *e*, I do not belong
15:52 of an *e*, at the last trumpet.
Eph 6: 6 favor when their *e* is on you,
Col 3:22 not only when their *e* is on you
Rev 1: 7 and every *e* will see him,

EYES (EYE)
Nu 15:39 the lusts of your own hearts and *e*.
33:55 remain will become barbs in your *e*
Dt 11:12 the *e* of the LORD your God are
12:25 right in the *e* of the LORD.
16:19 for a bribe blinds the *e* of the wise
Jos 23:13 on your backs and thorns in your *e*,
1Sa 15:17 you were once small in your own *e*,
1Ki 10: 7 I came and saw with my own *e*.
2Ki 9:30 heard about it, she painted her *e*,
2Ch 16: 9 For the *e* of the LORD range
Job 31: 1 "I made a covenant with my *e*
36: 7 He does not take his *e*
Ps 25:15 My *e* are ever on the LORD,
36: 1 God before his *e*.
101: 6 My *e* will be on the faithful
118: 23 and it is marvelous in our *e*.
119: 18 Open my *e* that I may see
119: 37 my *e* away from worthless things;
121: 1 I lift up my *e* to the hills—
123: 1 I lift up my *e* to you,
139: 16 your *e* saw my unformed body.
141: 8 But my *e* are fixed on you,
Pr 3: 7 Do not be wise in your own *e*;
4:25 Let your *e* look straight ahead,
15: 3 The *e* of the LORD are everywhere
17:24 a fool's *e* wander to the ends
Isa 6: 5 and my *e* have seen the King,
33:17 Your *e* will see the king
42: 7 to open *e* that are blind,
Jer 24: 6 My *e* will watch over them
Hab 1:13 Your *e* are too pure to look on evil;
Mt 6:22 If your *e* are good, your whole
21:42 and it is marvelous in our *e*'?
Lk 16:15 ones who justify yourselves in the *e*
24:31 Then their *e* were opened
Jn 4:35 open your *e* and look at the fields!
Ac 1: 9 he was taken up before their very *e*,
2Co 4:18 So we fix our *e* not on what is seen,
8:21 not only in the *e* of the Lord but
Eph 1:18 also that the *e* of your heart may be
Heb 12: 2 Let us fix our *e* on Jesus, the author
Jas 2: 5 poor in the *e* of the world to be rich
1Pe 3:12 For the *e* of the Lord are
Rev 7:17 wipe away every tear from their *e*."
21: 4 He will wipe every tear from their *e*

EYEWITNESSES* (WITNESS)
Lk 1: 2 by those who from the first were *e*
2Pe 1:16 but we were *e* of his majesty.

EZEKIEL*
Priest called to be prophet to the exiles (Eze 1-3). Symbolically acted out destruction of Jerusalem (Eze 4-5; 12; 24).

EZRA*
Priest and teacher of the Law who led a return of exiles to Israel to reestablish temple and worship (Ezr 7-8). Corrected intermarriage of priests (Ezr 9-10). Read Law at celebration of Feast of Tabernacles (Ne 8). Participated in dedication of Jerusalem's walls (Ne 12).

FACE (FACES)
Ge 32:30 "It is because I saw God *f* to *f*,
Ex 3: 6 Moses hid his *f*, because he was
33:11 would speak to Moses *f* to *f*,
33:20 But," he said, "you cannot see my *f*
34:29 was not aware that his *f* was radiant
Nu 6:25 the LORD make his *f* shine
12: 8 With him I speak *f* to *f*,
14:14 O LORD, have been seen *f* to *f*,
Dt 5: 4 The LORD spoke to you *f* to *f* out
31:17 I will hide my *f* from them,
34:10 whom the LORD knew *f* to *f*,
Jdg 6:22 the angel of the LORD *f* to *f*!"
2Ki 14: 8 challenge: "Come, meet me *f* to *f*."
1Ch 16:11 seek his *f* always.
2Ch 7:14 and seek my *f* and turn
25:17 of Israel: "Come, meet me *f* to *f*."
Ezr 9: 6 and disgraced to lift up my *f* to you,
Ps 4: 6 Let the light of your *f* shine upon us
27: 8 Your *f*, LORD, I will seek.
31:16 Let your *f* shine on your servant;
44: 3 and the light of your *f*,
44:22 Yet for your sake we *f* death all day
51: 9 Hide your *f* from my sins
67: 1 and make his *f* shine upon us; *Selah*
80: 3 make your *f* shine upon us,
105: 4 seek his *f* always.
Ps 119:135 Make your *f* shine
SS 2:14 and your *f* is lovely.
Isa 50: 7 Therefore have I set my *f* like flint,
50: 8 Let us *f* each other!
54: 8 I hid my *f* from you for a moment,
Jer 32: 4 and will speak with him *f* to *f*
34: 3 and he will speak with you *f* to *f*.
Eze 1:10 Each of the four had the *f* of a man,
20:35 *f* to *f*, I will execute judgment
Mt 17: 2 His *f* shone like the sun,
18:10 angels in heaven always see the *f*
Lk 9:29 the appearance of his *f* changed,
Ro 8:36 "For your sake we *f* death all day
1Co 13:12 mirror; then we shall see *f* to *f*
2Co 3: 7 could not look steadily at the *f*
4: 6 the glory of God in the *f* of Christ.
10: 1 who am "timid" when *f* to *f*
1Pe 3:12 but the *f* of the Lord is
2Jn :12 to visit you and talk with you *f* to *f*,
3Jn :14 see you soon, and we will talk *f* to *f*.
Rev 1:16 His *f* was like the sun shining
22: 4 They will see his *f*, and his name

FACES (FACE)
2Co 3:18 who with unveiled *f* all reflect

FACTIONS
2Co 12:20 outbursts of anger, *f*, slander,
Gal 5:20 selfish ambition, dissensions, *f*

FADE (FADING)
Jas 1:11 the rich man will *f* away
1Pe 5: 4 of glory that will never *f* away.

FADING (FADE)
2Co 3: 7 *f* though it was, will not
3:11 if what was *f* away came with glory,
3:13 at it while the radiance was *f* away.

FAIL (FAILED FAILING FAILINGS FAILS FAILURE)
Lev 26:15 and *f* to carry out all my commands
1Ki 2: 4 you will never *f* to have a man
1Ch 28:20 He will not *f* you or forsake you
2Ch 34:33 they did not *f* to follow the LORD,
Ps 89:28 my covenant with him will never *f*.
Pr 15:22 Plans *f* for lack of counsel,
Isa 51: 6 my righteousness will never *f*.
La 3:22 for his compassions never *f*.
Lk 22:32 Simon, that your faith may not *f*.
2Co 13: 5 unless, of course, you *f* the test?

FAILED (FAIL)
Jos 23:14 has been fulfilled; not one has *f*.
1Ki 8:56 Not one word has *f*
Ps 77: 8 Has his promise *f* for all time?
Ro 9: 6 as though God's word had *f*.
2Co 13: 6 discover that we have not *f* the test.

FAILING (FAIL)
1Sa 12:23 sin against the LORD by *f* to pray

FAILINGS (FAIL)
Ro 15: 1 ought to bear with the *f* of the weak

FAILS (FAIL)
Jer 14: 6 their eyesight *f*
Joel 1:10 the oil *f*.
1Co 13: 8 Love never *f*.

FAILURE* (FAIL)
1Th 2: 1 that our visit to you was not a *f*.

FAINT
Isa 40:31 they will walk and not be *f*.

FAINTHEARTED* (HEART)
Dt 20: 3 Do not be *f* or afraid; do not be
20: 8 shall add, "Is any man afraid or *f*?

FAIR (FAIRNESS)
Pr 1: 3 doing what is right and just and *f*;
Col 4: 1 slaves with what is right and *f*,

FAIRNESS* (FAIR)
Pr 29:14 If a king judges the poor with *f*,

FAITH* (FAITHFUL FAITHFULLY FAITHFULNESS FAITHLESS)
Ex 21: 8 because he has broken *f* with her.
Dt 32:51 both of you broke *f* with me
Jos 22:16 'How could you break *f*
Jdg 9:16 and in good *f* when you made
9:19 and in good *f* toward Jerub-Baal
1Sa 14:33 "You have broken *f*," he said.
2Ch 20:20 Have *f* in the LORD your God
20:20 have *f* in his prophets and you will
Isa 7: 9 If you do not stand firm in your *f*,
26: 2 the nation that keeps *f*.
Hab 2: 4 but the righteous will live by his *f*—
Mal 2:10 by breaking *f* with one another?

Mal 2:11 one another? Judah has broken *f*.
2:14 because you have broken *f* with her
2:15 and do not break *f* with the wife
2:16 in your spirit, and do not break *f*.
Mt 6:30 O you of little *f*? So do not worry,
8:10 anyone in Israel with such great *f*.
8:26 He replied, "You of little *f*,
9: 2 When Jesus saw their *f*, he said
9:22 he said, "your *f* has healed you."
9:29 According to your *f* will it be done
13:58 there because of their lack of *f*.
14:31 of little *f*," he said, "why did you
15:28 "Woman, you have great *f*!
16: 8 Jesus asked, "You of little *f*,
17:20 if you have *f* as small as a mustard
17:20 "Because you have so little *f*.
21:21 if you have *f* and do not doubt,
24:10 many will turn away from the *f*
Mk 2: 5 When Jesus saw their *f*, he said
4:40 still have no *f*?" They were
5:34 "Daughter, your *f* has healed you.
6: 6 he was amazed at their lack of *f*.
10:52 said Jesus, "your *f* has healed you."
11:22 "Have *f* in God," Jesus answered.
16:14 he rebuked them for their lack of *f*
Lk 5:20 When Jesus saw their *f*, he said,
7: 9 I have not found such great *f*
7:50 the woman, "Your *f* has saved you;
8:25 "Where is your *f*?" he asked his
8:48 "Daughter, your *f* has healed you.
12:28 will he clothe you, O you of little *f*!
17: 5 "Increase our *f*!" He replied,
17: 6 "If you have *f* as small
17:19 your *f* has made you well."
18: 8 will he find *f* on the earth?"
18:42 your sight; your *f* has healed you."
22:32 Simon, that your *f* may not fail.
Jn 2:11 and his disciples put their *f* in him.
7:31 in the crowd put their *f* in him.
8:30 he spoke, many put their *f* in him.
11:45 had seen what Jesus did, put their *f*
12:11 to Jesus and putting their *f* in him.
12:42 they would not confess their *f*
14:12 anyone who has *f* in me will do
Ac 3:16 By *f* in the name of Jesus, this man
3:16 *f* that comes through him that has
6: 5 full of *f* and of the Holy Spirit;
6: 7 of priests became obedient to the *f*.
11:24 full of the Holy Spirit and *f*,
13: 8 to turn the proconsul from the *f*.
14: 9 saw that he had *f* to be healed
14:22 them to remain true to the *f*.
14:27 the door of *f* to the Gentiles.
15: 9 for he purified their hearts by *f*.
16: 5 were strengthened in the *f*
20:21 and have *f* in our Lord Jesus.
24:24 as he spoke about *f* in Christ Jesus.
26:18 those who are sanctified by *f*
27:25 for I have *f* in God that it will
Ro 1: 5 to the obedience that comes from *f*.
1: 8 because your *f* is being reported all
1:12 encouraged by each other's *f*.
1:17 is by *f* from first to last,
1:17 "The righteous will live by *f*."
3: 3 What if some did not have *f*?
3: 3 lack of *f* nullify God's faithfulness?
3:22 comes through *f* in Jesus Christ
3:25 a sacrifice of atonement, through *f*
3:26 one who justifies those who have *f*
3:27 the law? No, but on that of *f*.
3:28 by *f* apart from observing the law.
3:30 through that same *f*.
3:30 will justify the circumcised by *f*
3:31 nullify the law by this *f*? Not at all!
4: 5 his *f* is credited as righteousness.
4: 9 that Abraham's *f* was credited
4:11 had by *f* while he was still
4:12 of the *f* that our father Abraham
4:13 the righteousness that comes by *f*.
4:14 *f* has no value and the promise is
4:16 Therefore, the promise comes by *f*,
4:16 are of the *f* of Abraham.
4:19 Without weakening in his *f*,
4:20 but was strengthened in his *f*
5: 1 we have been justified through *f*,
5: 2 access by *f* into this grace
9:30 a righteousness that is by *f*;
9:32 Because they pursued it not by *f*
10: 6 the righteousness that is by *f* says:
10: 8 the word of *f* we are proclaiming:
10:17 *f* comes from hearing the message,
11:20 of unbelief, and you stand by *f*.
12: 3 measure of *f* God has given you.
12: 6 let him use it in proportion to his *f*.
14: 1 Accept him whose *f* is weak,
14: 2 One man's *f* allows him
14: 2 but another man, whose *f* is weak,
14:23 because his eating is not from *f*;
14:23 that does not come from *f* is sin.
1Co 2: 5 so that your *f* might not rest
12: 9 to another *f* by the same Spirit,
13: 2 and if I have a *f* that can move
13:13 And now these three remain: *f*,
15:14 is useless and so is your *f*.
15:17 has not been raised, your *f* is futile;
16:13 stand firm in the *f*; be men
2Co 1:24 Not that we lord it over your *f*,
1:24 because it is by *f* you stand firm.
4:13 With that same spirit of *f* we
5: 7 We live by *f*, not by sight.
8: 7 in *f*, in speech, in knowledge,
10:15 as your *f* continues to grow,
13: 5 to see whether you are in the *f*;
Gal 1:23 now preaching the *f* he once tried
2:16 Jesus that we may be justified by *f*
2:16 but by *f* in Jesus Christ.
2:16 have put our *f* in Christ Jesus that
2:20 I live by *f* in the Son of God,
3: 8 would justify the Gentiles by *f*,
3: 9 So those who have *f* are blessed
3: 9 along with Abraham, the man of *f*.
3:11 "The righteous will live by *f*."
3:12 based on *f*; on the contrary,
3:14 by *f* we might receive the promise
3:22 being given through *f*
3:23 Before this *f* came, we were held
3:23 up until *f* should be revealed.
3:24 that we might be justified by *f*.
3:25 that *f* has come, we are no longer
3:26 of God through *f* in Christ Jesus,
5: 5 But by *f* we eagerly await
5: 6 that counts is *f* expressing itself
Eph 1:15 ever since I heard about your *f*
2: 8 through *f*—and this not
3:12 through *f* in him we may approach
3:17 dwell in your hearts through *f*.
4: 5 one Lord, one *f*, one baptism;
4:13 up until we all reach unity in the *f*
6:16 to all this, take up the shield of *f*,
6:23 love with *f* from God the Father
Php 1:25 for your progress and joy in the *f*,
1:27 as one man for the *f* of the gospel
2:17 and service coming from your *f*,
3: 9 comes from God and is by *f*.
3: 9 that which is through *f* in Christ—
Col 1: 4 heard of your *f* in Christ Jesus
1: 5 the *f* and love that spring
1:23 continue in your *f*, established
2: 5 and how firm your *f* in Christ is.
2: 7 in the *f* as you were taught,
2:12 him through your *f* in the power
1Th 1: 3 Father your work produced by *f*,
1: 8 your *f* in God has become known
3: 2 and encourage you in your *f*,
3: 5 I sent to find out about your *f*.
3: 6 brought good news about your *f*
3: 7 about you because of your *f*.
3:10 supply what is lacking in your *f*.
5: 8 on *f* and love as a breastplate,
2Th 1: 3 because your *f* is growing more
1: 4 and *f* in all the persecutions
1:11 and every act prompted by your *f*.
3: 2 evil men, for not everyone has *f*.
1Ti 1: 2 To Timothy my true son in the *f*:
1: 4 than God's work—which is by *f*.
1: 5 a good conscience and a sincere *f*.
1:14 along with the *f* and love that are
1:19 and so have shipwrecked their *f*.
1:19 on to *f* and a good conscience.
2: 7 of the true *f* to the Gentiles.
2:15 if they continue in *f*, love
3: 9 of the *f* with a clear conscience.
3:13 assurance in their *f* in Christ Jesus.
4: 1 later times some will abandon the *f*
4: 6 brought up in the truths of the *f*
4:12 in life, in love, in *f* and in purity.
5: 8 he has denied the *f* and is worse
6:10 have wandered from the *f*
6:11 pursue righteousness, godliness, *f*,
6:12 Fight the good fight of the *f*.
6:21 so doing have wandered from the *f*.
2Ti 1: 5 been reminded of your sincere *f*,
1:13 with *f* and love in Christ Jesus.
2:18 and they destroy the *f* of some.
2:22 and pursue righteousness, *f*,
3: 8 as far as the *f* is concerned,
3:10 my purpose, *f*, patience, love,
3:15 wise for salvation through *f*
4: 7 finished the race, I have kept the *f*.
Tit 1: 1 Christ for the *f* of God's elect
1: 2 a *f* and knowledge resting
1: 4 my true son in our common *f*:
1:13 so that they will be sound in the *f*
2: 2 self-controlled, and sound in *f*,
3:15 Greet those who love us in the *f*.
Phm : 5 because I hear about your *f*
: 6 may be active in sharing your *f*,
Heb 4: 2 heard did not combine it with *f*.
Heb 4:14 firmly to the *f* we profess.
6: 1 and of *f* in God, instruction about
6:12 but to imitate those who through *f*
10:22 heart in full assurance of *f*,
10:38 But my righteous one will live by *f*.
11: 1 *f* is being sure of what we hope for
11: 3 By *f* we understand that
11: 4 And by *f* he still speaks, even
11: 4 By *f* Abel offered God a better
11: 4 By *f* he was commended
11: 5 By *f* Enoch was taken from this life
11: 6 And without *f* it is impossible
11: 7 By his *f* he condemned the world
11: 7 By *f* Noah, when warned about
11: 7 the righteousness that comes by *f*.
11: 8 By *f* Abraham, when called to go
11: 9 By *f* he made his home
11:11 By *f* Abraham, even though he was
11:13 living by *f* when they died.
11:17 By *f* Abraham, when God tested
11:20 By *f* Isaac blessed Jacob
11:21 By *f* Jacob, when he was dying,
11:22 By *f* Joseph, when his end was near
11:23 By *f* Moses' parents hid him
11:24 By *f* Moses, when he had grown up
11:27 By *f* he left Egypt, not fearing
11:28 By *f* he kept the Passover
11:29 By *f* the people passed
11:30 By *f* the walls of Jericho fell,
11:31 By *f* the prostitute Rahab,
11:33 through *f* conquered kingdoms,
11:39 were all commended for their *f*,
12: 2 the author and perfecter of our *f*,
13: 7 way of life and imitate their *f*.
Jas 1: 3 of your *f* develops perseverance.
2: 5 the eyes of the world to be rich in *f*
2:14 has no deeds? Can such *f* save him?
2:14 if a man claims to have *f*
2:17 In the same way, *f* by itself,
2:18 I will show you my *f* by what I do.
2:18 Show me your *f* without deeds,
2:18 "You have *f*; I have deeds."
2:20 do you want evidence that *f*
2:22 You see that his *f* and his actions
2:22 and his *f* was made complete
2:24 by what he does and not by *f* alone.
2:26 so *f* without deeds is dead.
5:15 in *f* will make the sick person well;
1Pe 1: 5 who through *f* are shielded
1: 7 These have come so that your *f*—
1: 9 you are receiving the goal of your *f*,
1:21 and so your *f* and hope are in God.
5: 9 Resist him, standing firm in the *f*,
2Pe 1: 1 Jesus Christ have received a *f*
1: 5 effort to add to your *f* goodness;
1Jn 5: 4 overcome the world, even our *f*.
Jude : 3 to contend for the *f* that was once
:20 up in your most holy *f*
Rev 2:13 You did not renounce your *f* in me,
2:19 your love and *f*, your service

FAITHFUL* (FAITH)

Nu 12: 7 he is *f* in all my house.
Dt 7: 9 your God is God; he is the *f* God,
32: 4 A *f* God who does no wrong,
1Sa 2:35 I will raise up for myself a *f* priest,
2Sa 20:19 We are the peaceful and *f* in Israel.
22:26 "To the *f* you show yourself *f*,
1Ki 3: 6 because he was *f* to you
2Ch 31:18 were *f* in consecrating themselves.
31:20 and *f* before the LORD his God.
Ne 9: 8 You found his heart *f* to you,
Ps 12: 1 the *f* have vanished
18:25 To the *f* you show yourself *f*,
25:10 of the LORD are loving and *f*
31:23 The LORD preserves the *f*,
33: 4 he is *f* in all he does.
37:28 and will not forsake his *f* ones.
78: 8 whose spirits were not *f* to him.
78:37 they were not *f* to his covenant.
89:19 to your *f* people you said:
89:24 My *f* love will be with him,
89:37 the *f* witness in the sky."
97:10 for he guards the lives of his *f* ones
101: 6 My eyes will be on the *f* in the land,
111: 7 The works of his hands are *f*
145: 13 The LORD is *f* to all his promises
146: 6 the LORD, who remains *f* forever.
Pr 2: 8 and protects the way of his *f* ones.
20: 6 but a *f* man who can find?
28:20 A *f* man will be richly blessed,
31:26 and *f* instruction is on her tongue.
Isa 1:21 See how the *f* city has become
1:26 the *F* City."
49: 7 because of the LORD, who is *f*,
55: 3 my *f* love promised to David.
Jer 42: 5 *f* witness against us if we do not act
Eze 43:11 so that they may be *f* to its design
48:11 who were *f* in serving me

Hos 11:12 even against the *f* Holy One.
Zec 8: 8 I will be *f* and righteous to them
Mt 24:45 Who then is the *f* and wise servant,
25:21 'Well done, good and *f* servant!
25:21 You have been *f* with a few things;
25:23 You have been *f* with a few things;
25:23 'Well done, good and *f* servant!
Lk 12:42 then is the *f* and wise manager,
Ro 12:12 patient in affliction, *f* in prayer.
1Co 1: 9 his Son Jesus Christ our Lord, is *f*.
4: 2 been given a trust must prove *f*.
4:17 my son whom I love, who is *f*
10:13 And God is *f*; he will not let you be
2Co 1:18 no"? But as surely as God is *f*,
Eph 1: 1 in Ephesus, the *f* in Christ Jesus:
6:21 the dear brother and *f* servant
Col 1: 2 and *f* brothers in Christ at Colosse:
1: 7 who is a *f* minister of Christ
4: 7 a *f* minister and fellow servant
4: 9 He is coming with Onesimus, our *f*
1Th 5:24 The one who calls you is *f*
2Th 3: 3 the Lord is *f*, and he will strengthen
1Ti 1:12 he considered me *f*, appointing me
5: 9 has been *f* to her husband,
2Ti 2:13 he will remain *f*,
Heb 2:17 and *f* high priest in service to God,
3: 2 He was *f* to the one who appointed
3: 2 as Moses was *f* in all God's house.
3: 5 Moses was *f* as a servant
3: 6 But Christ is *f* as a son
8: 9 because they did not remain *f*,
10:23 for he who promised is *f*.
11:11 he considered him *f* who had made
1Pe 4:19 themselves to their *f* Creator
5:12 whom I regard as a *f* brother,
1Jn 1: 9 he is *f* and just and will forgive us
3Jn : 5 you are *f* in what you are doing
Rev 1: 5 who is the *f* witness, the firstborn
2:10 Be *f*, even to the point of death,
2:13 the days of Antipas, my *f* witness,
3:14 the words of the Amen, the *f*
14:12 commandments and remain *f*
17:14 his called, chosen and *f* followers."
19:11 whose rider is called *F* and True.

FAITHFULLY* (FAITH)
Dt 11:13 if you *f* obey the commands I am
Jos 2:14 *f* when the LORD gives us the land
1Sa 12:24 and serve him *f* with all your heart;
1Ki 2: 4 and if they walk *f* before me
2Ki 20: 3 how I have walked before you *f*
22: 7 because they are acting *f*."
2Ch 19: 9 must serve *f* and wholeheartedly
31:12 they *f* brought in the contributions,
31:15 and Shecaniah assisted him *f*
32: 1 all that Hezekiah had so *f* done,
34:12 The men did the work *f*.
Ne 9:33 you have acted *f*, while we did
13:14 so *f* done for the house of my God
Isa 38: 3 how I have walked before you *f*
Jer 23:28 one who has my word speak it *f*.
Eze 18: 9 and *f* keeps my laws.
44:15 and who *f* carried out the duties
1Pe 4:10 *f* administering God's grace

FAITHFULNESS* (FAITH)
Ge 24:27 not abandoned his kindness and *f*
24:49 if you will show kindness and *f*
32:10 and *f* you have shown your servant.
47:29 you will show me kindness and *f*.
Ex 34: 6 *f*, maintaining love to thousands,
Jos 24:14 the LORD and serve him with all *f*.
1Sa 26:23 man for his righteousness and *f*.
2Sa 2: 6 now show you kindness and *f*,
15:20 May kindness and *f* be with you."
Ps 30: 9 Will it proclaim your *f*?
36: 5 your *f* to the skies.
40:10 I speak of your *f* and salvation.
54: 5 in your *f* destroy them.
57: 3 God sends his love and his *f*.
57:10 your *f* reaches to the skies.
61: 7 appoint your love and *f*
71:22 the harp for your *f*, O my God;
85:10 Love and *f* meet together;
85:11 *F* springs forth from the earth,
86:15 to anger, abounding in love and *f*.
88:11 your *f* in Destruction?
89: 1 mouth I will make your *f* known
89: 2 that you established your *f*
89: 5 your *f* too, in the assembly
89: 8 and your *f* surrounds you.
89:14 love and *f* go before you.
89:33 nor will I ever betray my *f*.
89:49 which in your *f* you swore to David
91: 4 his *f* will be your shield
92: 2 and your *f* at night,
98: 3 and his *f* to the house of Israel;
100: 5 *f* continues through all
108: 4 your *f* reaches to the skies.
Ps 111: 8 done in *f* and uprightness.
115: 1 because of your love and *f*.
117: 2 the *f* of the LORD endures forever.
119: 75 and in *f* you have afflicted me.
119: 90 *f* continues through all
138: 2 name for your love and your *f*,
143: 1 in your *f* and righteousness
Pr 3: 3 Let love and *f* never leave you;
14:22 plan what is good find love and *f*.
16: 6 Through love and *f* sin is atoned for
20:28 Love and *f* keep a king safe;
Isa 11: 5 and *f* the sash around his waist.
16: 5 in *f* a man will sit on it—
25: 1 for in perfect *f*
38:18 cannot hope for your *f*.
38:19 about your *f*.
42: 3 In *f* he will bring forth justice;
61: 8 In my *f* I will reward them
La 3:23 great is your *f*.
Hos 2:20 I will betroth you in *f*,
4: 1 "There is no *f*, no love,
Mt 23:23 of the law—justice, mercy and *f*.
Ro 3: 3 lack of faith nullify God's *f*?
Gal 5:22 patience, kindness, goodness, *f*,
3Jn : 3 and tell about your *f* to the truth
Rev 13:10 and *f* on the part of the saints.

FAITHLESS* (FAITH)
Ps 78:57 fathers they were disloyal and *f*,
101: 3 The deeds of *f* men I hate;
119:158 I look on the *f* with loathing,
Pr 14:14 The *f* will be fully repaid
Jer 3: 6 you seen what *f* Israel has done?
3: 8 I gave *f* Israel her certificate
3:11 "*F* Israel is more righteous
3:12 *f* Israel,' declares the LORD,
3:14 *f* people," declares the LORD,
3:22 "Return, *f* people;
12: 1 Why do all the *f* live at ease?
Ro 1:31 they are senseless, *f*, heartless,
2Ti 2:13 if we are *f*,

FALL (FALLEN FALLING FALLS)
Ps 37:24 though he stumble, he will not *f*,
55:22 he will never let the righteous *f*.
69: 9 of those who insult you *f* on me.
145: 14 The LORD upholds all those who *f*
Pr 11:28 Whoever trusts in his riches will *f*,
Isa 40: 7 The grass withers and the flowers *f*,
Mt 7:25 yet it did not *f*, because it had its
Lk 10:18 "I saw Satan *f* like lightning
11:17 a house divided against itself will *f*.
23:30 say to the mountains, "*F* on us!"
Ro 3:23 and *f* short of the glory of God,
Heb 6: 6 if they *f* away, to be brought back

FALLEN (FALL)
2Sa 1:19 How the mighty have *f*!
Isa 14:12 How you have *f* from heaven,
1Co 11:30 and a number of you have *f* asleep.
15: 6 though some have *f* asleep.
15:18 who have *f* asleep in Christ are lost.
15:20 of those who have *f* asleep.
Gal 5: 4 you have *f* away from grace.
1Th 4:15 precede those who have *f* asleep.

FALLING (FALL)
Jude :24 able to keep you from *f*

FALLS (FALL)
Pr 11:14 For lack of guidance a nation *f*,
24:17 Do not gloat when your enemy *f*;
28:14 he who hardens his heart *f*
Mt 13:21 of the word, he quickly *f* away.
21:44 He who *f* on this stone will be
Jn 12:24 a kernel of wheat *f* to the ground
Ro 14: 4 To his own master he stands or *f*.

FALSE (FALSEHOOD FALSELY)
Ex 20:16 "You shall not give *f* testimony
23: 1 "Do not spread *f* reports.
23: 7 Have nothing to do with a *f* charge
Dt 5:20 "You shall not give *f* testimony
Pr 12:17 but a *f* witness tells lies.
13: 5 The righteous hate what is *f*,
14: 5 but a *f* witness pours out lies.
14:25 but a *f* witness is deceitful.
19: 5 A *f* witness will not go unpunished,
19: 9 A *f* witness will not go unpunished,
21:28 A *f* witness will perish,
25:18 is the man who gives *f* testimony
Isa 44:25 who foils the signs of *f* prophets
Jer 23:16 they fill you with *f* hopes.
Mt 7:15 "Watch out for *f* prophets.
15:19 theft, *f* testimony, slander.
19:18 not steal, do not give *f* testimony,
24:11 and many *f* prophets will appear
24:24 For *f* Christs and *f* prophets will
Mk 10:19 do not give *f* testimony, do not
13:22 For *f* Christs and *f* prophets will
Lk 6:26 their fathers treated the *f* prophets.
18:20 not steal, do not give *f* testimony,
Jn 1:47 in whom there is nothing *f*."
1Co 15:15 found to be *f* witnesses about God,
2Co 11:13 For such men are *f* apostles,
11:26 and in danger from *f* brothers.
Gal 2: 4 some *f* brothers had infiltrated our
Php 1:18 whether from *f* motives or true,
Col 2:18 anyone who delights in *f* humility
2:23 their *f* humility and their harsh
1Ti 1: 3 not to teach *f* doctrines any longer
6: 3 If anyone teaches *f* doctrines
2Pe 2: 1 also *f* prophets among the people,
2: 1 there will be *f* teachers among you.
1Jn 4: 1 many *f* prophets have gone out
Rev 16:13 out of the mouth of the *f* prophet.
19:20 with him the *f* prophet who had
20:10 and the *f* prophet had been thrown.

FALSEHOOD* (FALSE)
Job 21:34 left of your answers but *f*!"
31: 5 "If I have walked in *f*
Ps 52: 3 *f* rather than speaking the truth.
119:163 I hate and abhor *f*
Pr 30: 8 Keep *f* and lies far from me;
Isa 28:15 and *f* our hiding place."
Ro 3: 7 "If my *f* enhances God's
Eph 4:25 each of you must put off *f*
1Jn 4: 6 Spirit of truth and the spirit of *f*.
Rev 22:15 everyone who loves and practices *f*

FALSELY (FALSE)
Lev 19:12 " 'Do not swear *f* by my name
Mt 5:11 *f* say all kinds of evil against you
Lk 3:14 and don't accuse people *f*—
1Ti 6:20 ideas of what is *f* called knowledge,

FALTER*
Pr 24:10 If you *f* in times of trouble,
Isa 42: 4 he will not *f* or be discouraged

FAME
Jos 9: 9 of the *f* of the LORD your God.
Isa 66:19 islands that have not heard of my *f*
Hab 3: 2 LORD, I have heard of your *f*;

FAMILIES (FAMILY)
Ps 68: 6 God sets the lonely in *f*,

FAMILY (FAMILIES)
Pr 15:27 greedy man brings trouble to his *f*,
31:15 she provides food for her *f*
Mk 5:19 to your *f* and tell them how much
Lk 9:61 go back and say good-by to my *f*."
12:52 in one *f* divided against each other,
Ac 10: 2 He and all his *f* were devout
16:33 and all his *f* were baptized.
16:34 he and his whole *f*.
1Ti 3: 4 He must manage his own *f* well
3: 5 how to manage his own *f*,
5: 4 practice by caring for their own *f*
5: 8 and especially for his immediate *f*,

FAMINE
Ge 12:10 Now there was a *f* in the land,
26: 1 Now there was a *f* in the land—
41:30 seven years of *f* will follow them.
Ru 1: 1 the judges ruled, there was a *f*
1Ki 18: 2 Now the *f* was severe in Samaria,
Am 8:11 but a *f* of hearing the words
Ro 8:35 or persecution or *f* or nakedness

FAN*
2Ti 1: 6 you to *f* into flame the gift of God,

FANTASIES*
Ps 73:20 you will despise them as *f*.
Pr 12:11 but he who chases *f* lacks judgment
28:19 one who chases *f* will have his fill

FAST (FASTING)
Dt 10:20 Hold *f* to him and take your oaths
11:22 in all his ways and to hold *f* to him
13: 4 serve him and hold *f* to him.
30:20 to his voice, and hold *f* to him.
Jos 22: 5 to hold *f* to him and to serve him
23: 8 to hold *f* to the LORD your God,
2Ki 18: 6 He held *f* to the LORD
Ps 119: 31 I hold *f* to your statutes, O LORD;
139: 10 your right hand will hold me *f*.
Mt 6:16 "When you *f*, do not look somber
1Pe 5:12 Stand *f* in it.

FASTING (FAST)
Ps 35:13 and humbled myself with *f*.
Ac 13: 2 were worshiping the Lord and *f*,
14:23 and *f*, committed them to the Lord

FATHER (FATHER'S FATHERED FATHERLESS FATHERS FOREFATHERS)

Ge 2:24 this reason a man will leave his *f*
17: 4 You will be the *f* of many nations.
Ex 20:12 "Honor your *f* and your mother,
21:15 "Anyone who attacks his *f*
21:17 "Anyone who curses his *f*
Lev 18: 7 " 'Do not dishonor your *f*
19: 3 you must respect his mother and *f*,
20: 9 " 'If anyone curses his *f* or mother,
Dt 1:31 carried you, as a *f* carries his son,
5:16 "Honor your *f* and your mother,
21:18 son who does not obey his *f*
32: 6 Is he not your *F*, your Creator,
2Sa 7:14 I will be his *f*, and he will be my son
1Ch 17:13 I will be his *f*, and he will be my son
22:10 will be my son, and I will be his *f*.
28: 6 to be my son, and I will be his *f*.
Job 38:28 Does the rain have a *f*?
Ps 2: 7 today I have become your *F*.
27:10 Though my *f* and mother forsake
68: 5 A *f* to the fatherless, a defender
89:26 to me, 'You are my *F*,
103: 13 As a *f* has compassion
Pr 3:12 as a *f* the son he delights in.
10: 1 A wise son brings joy to his *f*,
17:21 there is no joy for the *f* of a fool.
17:25 A foolish son brings grief to his *f*
23:22 Listen to your *f*, who gave you life,
23:24 *f* of a righteous man has great joy;
28: 7 of gluttons disgraces his *f*.
28:24 He who robs his *f* or mother
29: 3 loves wisdom brings joy to his *f*,
Isa 9: 6 Everlasting *F*, Prince of Peace.
45:10 Woe to him who says to his *f*,
63:16 But you are our *F*,
Jer 2:27 They say to wood, 'You are my *f*,'
3:19 I thought you would call me '*F*'
31: 9 because I am Israel's *f*,
Eze 18:19 the son not share the guilt of his *f*?'
Mic 7: 6 For a son dishonors his *f*,
Mal 1: 6 If I am a *f*, where is the honor due
2:10 we not all one *F*? Did not one God
Mt 3: 9 'We have Abraham as our *f*.'
5:16 and praise your *F* in heaven.
6: 9 " 'Our *F* in heaven,
6:26 yet your heavenly *F* feeds them.
10:37 "Anyone who loves his *f*
11:27 no one knows the *F* except the Son
15: 4 'Honor your *f* and mother'
18:10 the face of my *F* in heaven.
19: 5 this reason a man will leave his *f*
19:19 honor your *f* and mother,'
19:29 or brothers or sisters or *f* or mother
23: 9 And do not call anyone on earth '*f*,'
Mk 7:10 'Honor your *f* and your mother,' and,
Lk 9:59 "Lord, first let me go and bury my *f*
12:53 *f* against son and son against *f*,
14:26 and does not hate his *f* and mother,
18:20 honor your *f* and mother.' "
23:34 Jesus said, "*F*, forgive them,
Jn 3:35 The *F* loves the Son and has placed
4:21 you will worship the *F* neither
5:17 "My *F* is always at his work
5:18 he was even calling God his own *F*,
5:20 For the *F* loves the Son
6:44 the *F* who sent me draws him,
6:46 No one has seen the *F*
8:19 "You do not know me or my *F*,"
8:28 speak just what the *F* has taught me
8:41 The only *F* we have is God himself
8:42 God were your *F*, you would love
8:44 You belong to your *f*, the devil,
10:17 reason my *F* loves me is that I lay
10:30 I and the *F* are one."
10:38 and understand that the *F* is in me,
14: 6 No one comes to the *F*
14: 9 who has seen me has seen the *F*.
14:28 for the *F* is greater than I.
15: 9 "As the *F* has loved me,
15:23 He who hates me hates my *F*
20:17 'I am returning to my *F* and your *F*,
Ac 13:33 today I have become your *F*.'
Ro 4:11 he is the *f* of all who believe
4:16 He is the *f* of us all.
8:15 And by him we cry, "*Abba, F.*"
1Co 4:15 for in Christ Jesus I became your *f*
2Co 6:18 "I will be a *F* to you,
Eph 5:31 this reason a man will leave his *f*
6: 2 "Honor your *f* and mother"—
Php 2:11 to the glory of God the *F*.
Heb 1: 5 today I have become your *F*"?
12: 7 what son is not disciplined by his *f*?
1Jn 1: 3 And our fellowship is with the *F*
2:15 the love of the *F* is not in him.
2:22 he denies the *F* and the Son.

FATHER'S (FATHER)

Pr 13: 1 A wise son heeds his *f* instruction,
15: 5 A fool spurns his *f* discipline,
19:13 A foolish son is his *f* ruin,
Mt 16:27 going to come in his *F* glory
Lk 2:49 had to be in my *F* house?"
Jn 2:16 How dare you turn my *F* house
10:29 can snatch them out of my *F* hand.
14: 2 In my *F* house are many rooms;
15: 8 to my *F* glory, that you bear much

FATHERED (FATHER)

Dt 32:18 You deserted the Rock, who *f* you;

FATHERLESS (FATHER)

Dt 10:18 He defends the cause of the *f*
14:29 the *f* and the widows who live
24:17 Do not deprive the alien or the *f*
24:19 Leave it for the alien, the *f*
26:12 the alien, the *f* and the widow,
Ps 68: 5 A father to the *f*, a defender
82: 3 Defend the cause of the weak and *f*
Pr 23:10 or encroach on the fields of the *f*,

FATHERS (FATHER)

Ex 20: 5 for the sin of the *f* to the third
Jer 31:29 'The *f* have eaten sour grapes,
Mal 4: 6 the hearts of the children to their *f*;
Lk 1:17 the hearts of the *f* to their children
11:11 "Which of you *f*, if your son asks
Jn 4:20 Our *f* worshiped on this mountain,
1Co 4:15 you do not have many *f*,
Eph 6: 4 *F*, do not exasperate your children;
Col 3:21 *F*, do not embitter your children,
Heb 12: 9 all had human *f* who disciplined us

FATHOM* (FATHOMED)

Job 11: 7 "Can you *f* the mysteries of God?
Ps 145: 3 his greatness no one can *f*.
Ecc 3:11 yet they cannot *f* what God has
Isa 40:28 and his understanding no one can *f*
1Co 13: 2 and can *f* all mysteries and all

FATHOMED* (FATHOM)

Job 5: 9 performs wonders that cannot be *f*,
9:10 performs wonders that cannot be *f*,

FATTENED

Pr 15:17 than a *f* calf with hatred.
Lk 15:23 Bring the *f* calf and kill it.

FAULT (FAULTS)

1Sa 29: 3 I have found no *f* in him."
Mt 18:15 and show him his *f*, just
Php 2:15 of God without *f* in a crooked
Jas 1: 5 generously to all without finding *f*,
Jude :24 his glorious presence without *f*

FAULTFINDERS*

Jude :16 These men are grumblers and *f*;

FAULTLESS*

Pr 8: 9 they are *f* to those who have
Php 3: 6 as for legalistic righteousness, *f*.
Jas 1:27 Father accepts as pure and *f* is this:

FAULTS* (FAULT)

Job 10: 6 that you must search out my *f*
Ps 19:12 Forgive my hidden *f*.

FAVOR (FAVORITISM)

Ge 4: 4 The LORD looked with *f* on Abel
6: 8 But Noah found *f* in the eyes
Ex 33:12 and you have found *f* with me.'
34: 9 if I have found *f* in your eyes,"
Lev 26: 9 " 'I will look on you with *f*
Nu 11:15 if I have found *f* in your eyes—
Jdg 6:17 "If now I have found *f* in your eyes,
1Sa 2:26 in *f* with the LORD and with men.
2Sa 2: 6 and I too will show you the same *f*
2Ki 13: 4 Jehoahaz sought the LORD's *f*,
2Ch 33:12 In his distress he sought the *f*
Est 7: 3 "If I have found *f* with you, O king,
Ps 90:17 May the *f* of the Lord our God rest
Pr 8:35 and receives *f* from the LORD.
18:22 and receives *f* from the LORD.
19: 6 Many curry *f* with a ruler,
Isa 61: 2 proclaim the year of the LORD's *f*
Zec 11: 7 called one *F* and the other Union,
Lk 1:30 Mary, you have found *f* with God.
2:14 to men on whom his *f* rests."
2:52 and in *f* with God and men.
4:19 to proclaim the year of the Lord's *f*
2Co 6: 2 now is the time of God's *f*,

FAVORITISM* (FAVOR)

Ex 23: 3 and do not show *f* to a poor man
Lev 19:15 to the poor or *f* to the great,
Ac 10:34 true it is that God does not show *f*
Ro 2:11 For God does not show *f*.
Eph 6: 9 and there is no *f* with him.
Col 3:25 for his wrong, and there is no *f*.
1Ti 5:21 and to do nothing out of *f*.
Jas 2: 1 Lord Jesus Christ, don't show *f*.
2: 9 But if you show *f*, you sin

FEAR (AFRAID FEARED FEARS FRIGHTENED GOD-FEARING)

Dt 6:13 *F* the LORD your God, serve him
10:12 but to *f* the LORD your God,
31:12 and learn to *f* the LORD your God
31:13 and learn to *f* the LORD your God
Jos 4:24 you might always *f* the LORD
24:14 "Now *f* the LORD and serve him
1Sa 12:14 If you *f* the LORD and serve
12:24 But be sure to *f* the LORD
2Sa 23: 3 when he rules in the *f* of God,
2Ch 19: 7 let the *f* of the LORD be upon you.
26: 5 who instructed him in the *f* of God.
Job 1: 9 "Does Job *f* God for nothing?"
Ps 2:11 Serve the LORD with *f*
19: 9 The *f* of the LORD is pure,
23: 4 I will *f* no evil,
27: 1 whom shall I *f*?
33: 8 Let all the earth *f* the LORD;
34: 7 around those who *f* him,
34: 9 *F* the LORD, you his saints,
46: 2 Therefore we will not *f*,
86:11 that I may *f* your name.
90:11 great as the *f* that is due you.
91: 5 You will not *f* the terror of night,
111: 10 *f* of the LORD is the beginning
118: 4 Let those who *f* the LORD say:
128: 1 Blessed are all who *f* the LORD,
145: 19 of those who *f* him;
147: 11 delights in those who *f* him,
Pr 1: 7 *f* of the LORD is the beginning
1:33 and be at ease, without *f* of harm."
8:13 To *f* the LORD is to hate evil;
9:10 *f* of the LORD is the beginning
10:27 The *f* of the LORD adds length
14:27 The *f* of the LORD is a fountain
15:33 *f* of the LORD teaches a man
16: 6 through the *f* of the LORD a man
19:23 The *f* of the LORD leads to life:
22: 4 Humility and the *f* of the LORD
29:25 *F* of man will prove to be a snare,
31:21 she has no *f* for her household;
Ecc 12:13 *F* God and keep his
Isa 11: 3 delight in the *f* of the LORD.
33: 6 the *f* of the LORD is the key
35: 4 "Be strong, do not *f*;
41:10 So do not *f*, for I am with you;
41:13 and says to you, Do not *f*;
43: 1 "*F* not, for I have redeemed you;
51: 7 Do not *f* the reproach of men
54:14 you will have nothing to *f*.
Jer 17: 8 It does not *f* when heat comes;
Lk 12: 5 I will show you whom you should *f*:
2Co 5:11 we know what it is to *f* the Lord,
Php 2:12 to work out your salvation with *f*
1Jn 4:18 But perfect love drives out *f*,
Jude :23 to others show mercy, mixed with *f*
Rev 14: 7 "*F* God and give him glory,

FEARED (FEAR)

Job 1: 1 he *f* God and shunned evil.
Ps 76: 7 You alone are to be *f*.
Mal 3:16 those who *f* the LORD talked

FEARS (FEAR)

Job 1: 8 a man who *f* God and shuns evil."
2: 3 a man who *f* God and shuns evil.
Ps 34: 4 he delivered me from all my *f*.
112: 1 is the man who *f* the LORD,
Pr 14:16 A wise man *f* the LORD
14:26 He who *f* the LORD has a secure
31:30 a woman who *f* the LORD is
2Co 7: 5 conflicts on the outside, *f* within.
1Jn 4:18 The one who *f* is not made perfect

FEAST (FEASTING FEASTS)

Pr 15:15 the cheerful heart has a continual *f*.
2Pe 2:13 pleasures while they *f* with you.

FEASTING (FEAST)

Pr 17: 1 than a house full of *f*, with strife.

FEASTS (FEAST)

Am 5:21 "I hate, I despise your religious *f*;
Jude :12 men are blemishes at your love *f*,

FEATHERS

Ps 91: 4 He will cover you with his *f*,

FEEBLE

Job 4: 3 you have strengthened *f* hands.
Isa 35: 3 Strengthen the *f* hands,
Heb 12:12 strengthen your *f* arms

FEED (FEEDS)
Jn 21:15 Jesus said, "*F* my lambs."
21:17 Jesus said, "*F* my sheep.
Ro 12:20 "If your enemy is hungry, *f* him;
Jude :12 shepherds who *f* only themselves.

FEEDS (FEED)
Pr 15:14 but the mouth of a fool *f* on folly.
Mt 6:26 yet your heavenly Father *f* them.
Jn 6:57 so the one who *f* on me will live

FEEL
Jdg 16:26 me where I can *f* the pillars that
Ps 115: 7 they have hands, but cannot *f*,

FEET (FOOT)
Ru 3: 8 discovered a woman lying at his *f*.
Ps 8: 6 you put everything under his *f*:
22:16 have pierced my hands and my *f*.
40: 2 he set my *f* on a rock
56:13 and my *f* from stumbling,
66: 9 and kept our *f* from slipping.
73: 2 as for me, my *f* had almost slipped;
110: 1 a footstool for your *f*."
119:105 Your word is a lamp to my *f*
Pr 4:26 Make level paths for your *f*
Isa 52: 7 are the *f* of those who bring good
Da 2:33 its *f* partly of iron and partly
Na 1:15 the *f* of one who brings good news,
Mt 10:14 shake the dust off your *f*
22:44 enemies under your *f*." '
Lk 1:79 to guide our *f* into the path of peace
20:43 a footstool for your *f*." '
24:39 Look at my hands and my *f*.
Jn 13: 5 and began to wash his disciples' *f*,
13:14 also should wash one another's *f*.
Ro 3:15 "Their *f* are swift to shed blood;
10:15 "How beautiful are the *f*
16:20 will soon crush Satan under your *f*.
1Co 12:21 And the head cannot say to the *f*,
15:25 has put all his enemies under his *f*.
Eph 1:22 God placed all things under his *f*
1Ti 5:10 washing the *f* of the saints,
Heb 1:13 a footstool for your *f*"?
2: 8 and put everything under his *f*."
12:13 "Make level paths for your *f*,"
Rev 1:15 His *f* were like bronze glowing

FELIX
Governor before whom Paul was tried (Ac 23:23-24:27).

FELLOWSHIP
Ex 20:24 burnt offerings and *f* offerings,
Lev 3: 1 If someone's offering is a *f* offering,
1Co 1: 9 who has called you into *f*
5: 2 out of your *f* the man who did this?
2Co 6:14 what *f* can light have with darkness
13:14 and the *f* of the Holy Spirit be
Gal 2: 9 and Barnabas the right hand of *f*
Php 2: 1 if any *f* with the Spirit,
3:10 the *f* of sharing in his sufferings,
1Jn 1: 3 And our *f* is with the Father
1: 3 so that you also may have *f* with us.
1: 6 claim to have *f* with him yet walk
1: 7 we have *f* with one another,

FEMALE
Ge 1:27 male and *f* he created them.
5: 2 He created them male and *f*
Mt 19: 4 Creator 'made them male and *f*,'
Mk 10: 6 God 'made them male and *f*.'
Gal 3:28 *f*, for you are all one in Christ Jesus

FEROCIOUS
Mt 7:15 but inwardly they are *f* wolves.

FERTILE (FERTILIZE)
Isa 32:15 and the desert becomes a *f* field,
Jer 2: 7 I brought you into a *f* land

FERTILIZE* (FERTILE)
Lk 13: 8 and I'll dig around it and *f* it.

FERVOR*
Ac 18:25 and he spoke with great *f*
Ro 12:11 but keep your spiritual *f*, serving

FESTIVAL
1Co 5: 8 Therefore let us keep the *F*,
Col 2:16 or with regard to a religious *f*,

FESTUS
Successor of Felix; sent Paul to Caesar (Ac 25-26).

FEVER
Job 30:30 my body burns with *f*.
Mt 8:14 mother-in-law lying in bed with a *f*.
Lk 4:38 was suffering from a high *f*,
Jn 4:52 "The *f* left him yesterday
Ac 28: 8 suffering from *f* and dysentery.

FIELD (FIELDS)
Ge 4: 8 Abel, "Let's go out to the *f*."
Lev 19: 9 reap to the very edges of your *f*
19:19 Do not plant your *f* with two kinds
Pr 31:16 She considers a *f* and buys it;
Isa 40: 6 glory is like the flowers of the *f*.
Mt 6:28 See how the lilies of the *f* grow.
6:30 how God clothes the grass of the *f*,
13:38 *f* is the world, and the good seed
13:44 is like treasure hidden in a *f*.
Lk 14:18 I have just bought a *f*, and I must go
1Co 3: 9 you are God's *f*, God's building.
1Pe 1:24 glory is like the flowers of the *f*;

FIELDS (FIELD)
Ru 2: 2 go to the *f* and pick up the leftover
Lk 2: 8 were shepherds living out in the *f*
Jn 4:35 open your eyes and look at the *f*!

FIG (FIGS SYCAMORE-FIG)
Ge 3: 7 so they sewed *f* leaves together
Jdg 9:10 "Next, the trees said to the *f* tree,
1Ki 4:25 man under his own vine and *f* tree.
Pr 27:18 He who tends a *f* tree will eat its
Mic 4: 4 and under his own *f* tree,
Zec 3:10 to sit under his vine and *f* tree,'
Mt 21:19 Seeing a *f* tree by the road,
Lk 13: 6 "A man had a *f* tree, planted
Jas 3:12 brothers, can a *f* tree bear olives,
Rev 6:13 drop from a *f* tree when shaken

FIGHT (FIGHTING FIGHTS FOUGHT)
Ex 14:14 The LORD will *f* for you; you need
Dt 1:30 going before you, will *f* for you,
3:22 the LORD your God himself will *f*
Ne 4:20 Our God will *f* for us!"
Ps 35: 1 *f* against those who *f* against me.
Jn 18:36 my servants would *f*
1Co 9:26 I do not *f* like a man beating the air.
2Co 10: 4 The weapons we *f*
1Ti 1:18 them you may *f* the good *f*,
6:12 Fight the good *f* of the faith.
2Ti 4: 7 fought the good *f*, I have finished

FIGHTING (FIGHT)
Jos 10:14 Surely the LORD was *f* for Israel!

FIGHTS (FIGHT)
Jos 23:10 the LORD your God *f* for you,
1Sa 25:28 because he *f* the LORD's battles.
Jas 4: 1 What causes *f* and quarrels

FIGS (FIG)
Lk 6:44 People do not pick *f*
Jas 3:12 grapevine bear *f*? Neither can a salt

FILL (FILLED FILLING FILLS FULL FULLNESS FULLY)
Ge 1:28 and increase in number; *f* the earth
Ps 16:11 you will *f* me with joy
81:10 wide your mouth and I will *f* it.
Pr 28:19 who chases fantasies will have his *f*
Hag 2: 7 and I will *f* this house with glory,'
Jn 6:26 you ate the loaves and had your *f*.
Ac 2:28 you will *f* me with joy
Ro 15:13 the God of hope *f* you with all joy

FILLED (FILL)
Ex 31: 3 I have *f* him with the Spirit of God,
35:31 he has *f* him with the Spirit of God,
Dt 34: 9 son of Nun was *f* with the spirit
1Ki 8:10 the cloud *f* the temple
8:11 glory of the LORD *f* his temple.
2Ch 5:14 of the LORD *f* the temple of God.
7: 1 the glory of the LORD *f* the temple
Ps 72:19 may the whole earth be *f*
119: 64 The earth is *f* with your love,
Isa 6: 4 and the temple was *f* with smoke.
Eze 10: 3 and a cloud *f* the inner court.
10: 4 The cloud *f* the temple,
43: 5 the glory of the LORD *f* the temple
Hab 2:14 For the earth will be *f*
3: 3 and his praise *f* the earth.
Mt 5: 6 for they will be *f*.
Lk 1:15 and he will be *f* with the Holy Spirit
1:41 and Elizabeth was *f* with the Holy
1:67 His father Zechariah was *f*
2:40 and became strong; he was *f*
Jn 12: 3 the house was *f* with the fragrance
Ac 2: 2 *f* the whole house where they were
2: 4 All of them were *f*
4: 8 Then Peter, *f* with the Holy Spirit,
4:31 they were all *f* with the Holy Spirit
9:17 and be *f* with the Holy Spirit."
13: 9 called Paul, *f* with the Holy Spirit,
Eph 5:18 Instead, be *f* with the Spirit.
Php 1:11 *f* with the fruit of righteousness
Rev 15: 8 And the temple was *f* with smoke

FILLING (FILL)
Eze 44: 4 the glory of the LORD *f* the temple

FILLS (FILL)
Nu 14:21 of the LORD *f* the whole earth,
Ps 107: 9 and *f* the hungry with good things.
Eph 1:23 fullness of him who *f* everything

FILTH (FILTHY)
Isa 4: 4 The Lord will wash away the *f*
Jas 1:21 rid of all moral *f* and the evil that is

FILTHY (FILTH)
Isa 64: 6 all our righteous acts are like *f* rags;
Col 3: 8 and *f* language from your lips.
2Pe 2: 7 by the *f* lives of lawless men

FINAL (FINALITY)
Ps 73:17 then I understood their *f* destiny.

FINALITY* (FINAL)
Ro 9:28 on earth with speed and *f*."

FINANCIAL*
1Ti 6: 5 that godliness is a means to *f* gain.

FIND (FINDS FOUND)
Nu 32:23 be sure that your sin will *f* you out.
Dt 4:29 you will *f* him if you look for him
1Sa 23:16 and helped him *f* strength in God.
Job 23: 3 If only I knew where to *f* him;
Ps 36: 7 *f* refuge in the shadow
62: 5 *F* rest, O my soul, in God alone;
91: 4 under his wings you will *f* refuge;
Pr 8:17 and those who seek me *f* me.
14:22 those who plan what is good *f* love
20: 6 but a faithful man who can *f*?
24:14 if you *f* it, there is a future hope
31:10 A wife of noble character who can *f*
Jer 6:16 and you will *f* rest for your souls.
29:13 and *f* me when you seek me
Mt 7: 7 seek and you will *f*; knock
11:29 and you will *f* rest for your souls.
16:25 loses his life for me will *f* it.
22: 9 invite to the banquet anyone you *f*.'
Lk 11: 9 seek and you will *f*; knock
18: 8 will he *f* faith on the earth?"
Jn 10: 9 come in and go out, and *f* pasture.

FINDS (FIND)
Ps 62: 1 My soul *f* rest in God alone;
112: 1 who *f* great delight
119:162 like one who *f* great spoil.
Pr 3:13 Blessed is the man who *f* wisdom,
8:35 For whoever *f* me *f* life
11:27 He who seeks good *f* good will,
18:22 He who *f* a wife *f* what is good
Mt 7: 8 he who seeks *f*; and to him who
10:39 Whoever *f* his life will lose it,
Lk 11:10 he who seeks *f*; and to him who
12:37 whose master *f* them watching
12:43 servant whom the master *f* doing
15: 4 go after the lost sheep until he *f* it?
15: 8 and search carefully until she *f* it?

FINE-SOUNDING* (SOUND)
Col 2: 4 may deceive you by *f* arguments.

FINGER
Ex 8:19 to Pharaoh, "This is the *f* of God."
31:18 of stone inscribed by the *f* of God.
Dt 9:10 two stone tablets inscribed by the *f*
Lk 11:20 But if I drive out demons by the *f*
16:24 to dip the tip of his *f* in water
Jn 8: 6 to write on the ground with his *f*.
20:25 and put my *f* where the nails were,

FINISH (FINISHED)
Jn 4:34 him who sent me and to *f* his work.
5:36 that the Father has given me to *f*,
Ac 20:24 if only I may *f* the race
2Co 8:11 Now *f* the work, so that your eager
Jas 1: 4 Perseverance must *f* its work

FINISHED (FINISH)
Ge 2: 2 seventh day God had *f* the work he
Jn 19:30 the drink, Jesus said, "It is *f*."
2Ti 4: 7 I have *f* the race, I have kept

FIRE
Ex 3: 2 in flames of *f* from within a bush.
13:21 in a pillar of *f* to give them light,
Lev 6:12 *f* on the altar must be kept burning;
9:24 *F* came out from the presence
1Ki 18:38 Then the *f* of the LORD fell
2Ki 2:11 suddenly a chariot of *f*
Isa 5:24 as tongues of *f* lick up straw
30:27 and his tongue is a consuming *f*.
Jer 23:29 my word like *f*," declares

Da 3:25 four men walking around in the *f*,
Zec 3: 2 stick snatched from the *f*?"
Mal 3: 2 For he will be like a refiner's *f*
Mt 3:11 you with the Holy Spirit and with *f*.
3:12 the chaff with unquenchable *f*."
5:22 will be in danger of the *f* of hell.
18: 8 and be thrown into eternal *f*.
25:41 into the eternal *f* prepared
Mk 9:43 where the *f* never goes out.
9:48 and the *f* is not quenched.'
9:49 Everyone will be salted with *f*.
Lk 3:16 you with the Holy Spirit and with *f*.
12:49 I have come to bring *f* on the earth,
Ac 2: 3 to be tongues of *f* that separated
1Co 3:13 It will be revealed with *f*,
1Th 5:19 Do not put out the Spirit's *f*;
Heb 12:29 for our "God is a consuming *f*."
Jas 3: 5 set on *f* by a small spark.
3: 6 also is a *f*, a world of evil
2Pe 3:10 the elements will be destroyed by *f*,
Jude : 7 suffer the punishment of eternal *f*.
:23 snatch others from the *f*
Rev 1:14 and his eyes were like blazing *f*.
20:14 The lake of *f* is the second death.

FIRM*
Ex 14:13 Stand *f* and you will see
15: 8 surging waters stood *f* like a wall;
Jos 3:17 the covenant of the LORD stood *f*
2Ch 20:17 stand *f* and see the deliverance
Ezr 9: 8 giving us a *f* place in his sanctuary,
Job 11:15 you will stand *f* and without fear.
36: 5 he is mighty, and *f* in his purpose.
41:23 they are *f* and immovable.
Ps 20: 8 but we rise up and stand *f*.
30: 7 you made my mountain stand *f*;
33: 9 he commanded, and it stood *f*.
33:11 of the LORD stand *f* forever,
37:23 he makes his steps *f*;
40: 2 and gave me a *f* place to stand.
75: 3 it is I who hold its pillars *f*.
78:13 made the water stand *f* like a wall.
89: 2 that your love stands *f* forever,
89: 4 and make your throne *f*
93: 5 Your statutes stand *f*;
119: 89 it stands *f* in the heavens.
Pr 4:26 and take only ways that are *f*.
10:25 but the righteous stand *f* forever.
12: 7 the house of the righteous stands *f*.
Isa 7: 9 If you do not stand *f* in your faith,
22:17 about to take *f* hold of you
22:23 drive him like a peg into a *f* place;
22:25 into the *f* place will give way;
Eze 13: 5 so that it will stand *f* in the battle
Zec 8:23 nations will take *f* hold of one Jew
Mt 10:22 he who stands *f* to the end will be
24:13 he who stands *f* to the end will be
Mk 13:13 he who stands *f* to the end will be
Lk 21:19 By standing *f* you will gain life.
1Co 10:12 So, if you think you are standing *f*,
15:58 my dear brothers, stand *f*.
16:13 on your guard; stand *f* in the faith;
2Co 1: 7 for you is *f*, because we know that
1:21 who makes both us and you stand *f*
1:24 because it is by faith you stand *f*.
Gal 5: 1 Stand *f*, then, and do not let
Eph 6:14 Stand *f* then, with the belt
Php 1:27 I will know that you stand *f*
4: 1 that is how you should stand *f*
Col 1:23 in your faith, established and *f*,
2: 5 and how *f* your faith in Christ is.
4:12 that you may stand *f* in all the will
1Th 3: 8 since you are standing *f* in the Lord
2Th 2:15 stand *f* and hold to the teachings
1Ti 6:19 a *f* foundation for the coming age,
2Ti 2:19 God's solid foundation stands *f*,
Heb 6:19 an anchor for the soul, *f* and secure
Jas 5: 8 You too, be patient and stand *f*,
1Pe 5: 9 Resist him, standing *f* in the faith,
5:10 make you strong, *f* and steadfast.

FIRST
Ge 1: 5 and there was morning—the *f* day.
13: 4 and where he had *f* built an altar.
Ex 34:19 *f* offspring of every womb belongs
1Ki 22: 5 "*F* seek the counsel of the LORD."
Pr 18:17 *f* to present his case seems right,
Isa 44: 6 I am the *f* and I am the last;
48:12 I am the *f* and I am the last.
Mt 5:24 *F* go and be reconciled
6:33 But seek *f* his kingdom
7: 5 *f* take the plank out
19:30 But many who are *f* will be last,
20:16 last will be *f*, and the *f* will be last."
20:27 wants to be *f* must be your slave—
22:38 This is the *f* and greatest
23:26 *F* clean the inside of the cup
Mk 9:35 to be *f*, he must be the very last,
10:31 are *f* will be last, and the last *f*."
10:44 wants to be *f* must be slave
13:10 And the gospel must *f* be preached
Lk 13:30 will be *f*, and *f* who will be last."
Jn 8: 7 let him be the *f* to throw a stone
Ac 11:26 disciples were called Christians *f*
Ro 1:16 *f* for the Jew, then for the Gentile.
1:17 is by faith from *f* to last,
2: 9 *f* for the Jew, then for the Gentile;
2:10 *f* for the Jew, then for the Gentile.
1Co 12:28 in the church God has appointed *f*
15:45 "The *f* man Adam became a living
2Co 8: 5 they gave themselves *f* to the Lord
Eph 6: 2 which is the *f* commandment
1Th 4:16 and the dead in Christ will rise *f*.
1Ti 2:13 For Adam was formed *f*, then Eve.
Heb 10: 9 He sets aside the *f*
Jas 3:17 comes from heaven is *f* of all pure;
1Jn 4:19 We love because he *f* loved us.
3Jn : 9 but Diotrephes, who loves to be *f*,
Rev 1:17 I am the *F* and the Last.
2: 4 You have forsaken your *f* love.
22:13 and the Omega, the *F* and the Last,

FIRSTBORN (BEAR)
Ex 11: 5 Every *f* son in Egypt will die,
34:20 Redeem all your *f* sons.
Ps 89:27 I will also appoint him my *f*,
Lk 2: 7 and she gave birth to her *f*, a son.
Ro 8:29 that he might be the *f*
Col 1:15 image of the invisible God, the *f*
1:18 and the *f* from among the dead,
Heb 1: 6 when God brings his *f*
12:23 of the *f*, whose names are written
Rev 1: 5 who is the faithful witness, the *f*

FIRSTFRUITS
Ex 23:16 the Feast of Harvest with the *f*
23:19 "Bring the best of the *f* of your soil
Ro 8:23 who have the *f* of the Spirit,
1Co 15:23 Christ, the *f*; then, when he comes,
Rev 14: 4 offered as *f* to God and the Lamb.

FISH (FISHERS)
Ge 1:26 let them rule over the *f* of the sea
Jnh 1:17 But the LORD provided a great *f*
Mt 7:10 asks for a *f*, will give him a snake?
12:40 three nights in the belly of a huge *f*,
14:17 loaves of bread and two *f*,"
Mk 6:38 they said, "Five—and two *f*."
Lk 5: 6 of *f* that their nets began to break.
9:13 loaves of bread and two *f*—
Jn 6: 9 small barley loaves and two small *f*,
21: 5 haven't you any *f*?" "No,"
21:11 It was full of large *f*, 153, but

FISHERMEN
Mk 1:16 a net into the lake, for they were *f*.

FISHERS (FISH)
Mt 4:19 "and I will make you *f* of men."
Mk 1:17 "and I will make you *f* of men."

FISHHOOK*
Job 41: 1 pull in the leviathan with a *f*

FISTS
Mt 26:67 and struck him with their *f*.

FIT (FITTING)
Jdg 17: 6 no king; everyone did as he saw *f*.
21:25 no king; everyone did as he saw *f*.

FITTING* (FIT)
Ps 33: 1 it is *f* for the upright to praise him.
147: 1 how pleasant and *f* to praise him!
Pr 10:32 of the righteous know what is *f*,
19:10 It is not *f* for a fool to live in luxury
26: 1 honor is not *f* for a fool.
1Co 14:40 everything should be done in a *f*
Col 3:18 to your husbands, as is *f* in the Lord
Heb 2:10 sons to glory, it was *f* that God,

FIX* (FIXED)
Dt 11:18 *F* these words of mine
Job 14: 3 Do you *f* your eye on such a one?
Pr 4:25 *f* your gaze directly before you.
Isa 46: 8 "Remember this, *f* it in mind,
Am 9: 4 I will *f* my eyes upon them
2Co 4:18 we *f* our eyes not on what is seen,
Heb 3: 1 heavenly calling, *f* your thoughts
12: 2 Let us *f* our eyes on Jesus,

FIXED* (FIX)
2Ki 8:11 stared at him with a *f* gaze
Job 38:10 when I *f* limits for it
Ps 141: 8 my eyes are *f* on you, O Sovereign
Pr 8:28 *f* securely the fountains of the deep
Jer 33:25 and night and the *f* laws of heaven
Lk 16:26 and you a great chasm has been *f*,

FLAME (FLAMES FLAMING)
2Ti 1: 6 you to fan into *f* the gift of God,

FLAMES (FLAME)
1Co 3:15 only as one escaping through the *f*.
13: 3 and surrender my body to the *f*,

FLAMING (FLAME)
Eph 6:16 you can extinguish all the *f* arrows

FLANK
Eze 34:21 Because you shove with *f*

FLASH
1Co 15:52 in a *f*, in the twinkling of an eye,

FLATTER* (FLATTERING FLATTERS FLATTERY)
Job 32:21 nor will I *f* any man;
Ps 78:36 But then they would *f* him
Jude :16 *f* others for their own advantage.

FLATTERING* (FLATTER)
Ps 12: 2 their *f* lips speak with deception.
12: 3 May the LORD cut off all *f* lips
Pr 26:28 and a *f* mouth works ruin.
28:23 than he who has a *f* tongue.
Eze 12:24 or *f* divinations among the people

FLATTERS* (FLATTER)
Ps 36: 2 For in his own eyes he *f* himself
Pr 29: 5 Whoever *f* his neighbor

FLATTERY* (FLATTER)
Job 32:22 for if I were skilled in *f*,
Da 11:32 With *f* he will corrupt those who
Ro 16:18 and *f* they deceive the minds
1Th 2: 5 You know we never used *f*,

FLAWLESS*
2Sa 22:31 the word of the LORD is *f*.
Job 11: 4 You say to God, 'My beliefs are *f*
Ps 12: 6 And the words of the LORD are *f*,
18:30 the word of the LORD is *f*.
Pr 30: 5 "Every word of God is *f*;
SS 5: 2 my dove, my *f* one.

FLEE (FLEES)
Ps 139: 7 Where can I *f* from your presence?
1Co 6:18 *F* from sexual immorality.
10:14 my dear friends, *f* from idolatry.
1Ti 6:11 But you, man of God, *f* from all this
2Ti 2:22 *F* the evil desires of youth,
Jas 4: 7 Resist the devil, and he will *f*

FLEECE
Jdg 6:37 I will place a wool *f*

FLEES (FLEE)
Pr 28: 1 The wicked man *f* though no one

FLEETING*
Job 14: 2 like a *f* shadow, he does not endure
Ps 39: 4 let me know how *f* is my life.
89:47 Remember how *f* is my life.
144: 4 his days are like a *f* shadow.
Pr 21: 6 is a *f* vapor and a deadly snare.
31:30 Charm is deceptive, and beauty is *f*

FLESH
Ge 2:23 and *f* of my *f*;
2:24 and they will become one *f*.
2Ch 32: 8 With him is only the arm of *f*,
Job 19:26 yet in my *f* I will see God;
Eze 11:19 of stone and give them a heart of *f*.
36:26 of stone and give you a heart of *f*.
Mt 19: 5 and the two will become one *f*'?
Mk 10: 8 and the two will become one *f*.'
Jn 1:14 The Word became *f* and made his
6:51 This bread is my *f*, which I will give
1Co 6:16 "The two will become one *f*."
15:39 All *f* is not the same: Men have one
Eph 5:31 and the two will become one *f*."
6:12 For our struggle is not against *f*
Php 3: 2 do evil, those mutilators of the *f*.
1Jn 4: 2 come in the *f* is from God,
Jude :23 the clothing stained by corrupted *f*.

FLIGHT
Dt 32:30 or two put ten thousand to *f*,

FLINT
Isa 50: 7 Therefore have I set my face like *f*,
Zec 7:12 They made their hearts as hard as *f*

FLIRTING*
Isa 3:16 *f* with their eyes,

FLOCK (FLOCKS)
Ps 77:20 You led your people like a *f*
78:52 he brought his people out like a *f*;

Ps 95: 7 the *f* under his care.
Isa 40:11 He tends his *f* like a shepherd:
Jer 10:21 and all their *f* is scattered.
23: 2 "Because you have scattered my *f*
31:10 watch over his *f* like a shepherd.'
Eze 34: 2 not shepherds take care of the *f*?
Zec 11:17 who deserts the *f*!
Mt 26:31 the sheep of the *f* will be scattered.'
Lk 12:32 little *f*, for your Father has been
Jn 10:16 shall be one *f* and one shepherd.
Ac 20:28 all the *f* of which the Holy Spirit
1Co 9: 7 Who tends a *f* and does not drink
1Pe 5: 2 Be shepherds of God's *f* that is
5: 3 but being examples to the *f*.

FLOCKS (FLOCK)
Lk 2: 8 keeping watch over their *f* at night.

FLOG (FLOGGED FLOGGING)
Pr 19:25 *F* a mocker, and the simple will
Ac 22:25 to *f* a Roman citizen who hasn't

FLOGGED (FLOG)
Jn 19: 1 Pilate took Jesus and had him *f*.
Ac 5:40 the apostles in and had them *f*.
16:23 After they had been severely *f*,
2Co 11:23 frequently, been *f* more severely,

FLOGGING (FLOG)
Heb 11:36 *f*, while still others were chained

FLOOD (FLOODGATES)
Ge 7: 7 ark to escape the waters of the *f*.
Mal 2:13 You *f* the LORD's altar with tears.
Mt 24:38 For in the days before the *f*,
2Pe 2: 5 world when he brought the *f*

FLOODGATES (FLOOD)
Ge 7:11 the *f* of the heavens were opened.
Mal 3:10 see if I will not throw open the *f*

FLOOR
Jas 2: 3 or "Sit on the *f* by my feet,"

FLOUR
Lev 2: 1 his offering is to be of fine *f*.
Nu 7:13 filled with fine *f* mixed with oil
28: 9 of an ephah of fine *f* mixed with oil.

FLOURISH (FLOURISHES FLOURISHING)
Ps 72: 7 In his days the righteous will *f*;
92: 7 and all evildoers *f*,
92:12 The righteous will *f* like a palm tree
Pr 14:11 but the tent of the upright will *f*.

FLOURISHES (FLOURISH)
Pr 12:12 but the root of the righteous *f*.

FLOURISHING (FLOURISH)
Ps 52: 8 *f* in the house of God;

FLOW (FLOWING)
Nu 13:27 and it does *f* with milk and honey!
Jn 7:38 streams of living water will *f*

FLOWER (FLOWERS)
Job 14: 2 up like a *f* and withers away;
Ps 103: 15 he flourishes like a *f* of the field;
Jas 1:10 he will pass away like a wild *f*.

FLOWERS (FLOWER)
Isa 40: 6 and all their glory is like the *f*
40: 7 The grass withers and the *f* fall,
1Pe 1:24 and all their glory is like the *f*

FLOWING (FLOW)
Ex 3: 8 a land *f* with milk and honey—
33: 3 Go up to the land *f* with milk
Nu 16:14 us into a land *f* with milk
Jos 5: 6 a land *f* with milk and honey.
Ps 107: 33 *f* springs into thirsty ground,
107: 35 the parched ground into *f* springs;
Jer 32:22 a land *f* with milk and honey.
Eze 20: 6 a land *f* with milk and honey,
Rev 22: 1 *f* from the throne of God

FLUTE
Ps 150: 4 praise him with the strings and *f*,
Mt 11:17 " 'We played the *f* for you,
1Co 14: 7 that make sounds, such as the *f*

FOAL*
Zec 9: 9 on a colt, the *f* of a donkey.
Mt 21: 5 on a colt, the *f* of a donkey.' "

FOILS*
Ps 33:10 The LORD *f* the plans
Isa 44:25 who *f* the signs of false prophets

FOLDING* (FOLDS)
Pr 6:10 a little *f* of the hands to rest—
24:33 a little *f* of the hands to rest—

FOLDS (FOLDING)
Ecc 4: 5 The fool *f* his hands

FOLLOW (FOLLOWED FOLLOWING FOLLOWS)
Ex 23: 2 Do not *f* the crowd in doing wrong.
Lev 18: 4 and be careful to *f* my decrees.
Dt 5: 1 Learn them and be sure to *f* them.
17:19 *f* carefully all the words of this law
1Ki 11: 6 he did not *f* the LORD completely,
2Ch 34:33 they did not fail to *f* the LORD,
Ps 23: 6 Surely goodness and love will *f* me
119:166 and I *f* your commands.
Mt 4:19 *f* me," Jesus said, "and I will make
8:19 I will *f* you wherever you go."
8:22 But Jesus told him, "*F* me,
16:24 and take up his cross and *f* me.
19:27 "We have left everything to *f* you!
Lk 9:23 take up his cross daily and *f* me.
9:61 Still another said, "I will *f* you,
Jn 10: 4 his sheep *f* him because they know
10: 5 But they will never *f* a stranger;
10:27 I know them, and they *f* me.
12:26 Whoever serves me must *f* me;
21:19 Then he said to him, "*F* me!"
1Co 1:12 One of you says, "I *f* Paul";
11: 1 *F* my example, as I follow
14: 1 *F* the way of love and eagerly
2Th 3: 9 ourselves a model for you to *f*.
1Pe 2:21 that you should *f* in his steps.
Rev 14: 4 They *f* the Lamb wherever he goes.

FOLLOWED (FOLLOW)
Nu 32:11 they have not *f* me wholeheartedly,
Dt 1:36 he *f* the LORD wholeheartedly."
Jos 14:14 he *f* the LORD, the God of Israel,
2Ch 10:14 he *f* the advice of the young men
Mt 4:20 once they left their nets and *f* him.
9: 9 and Matthew got up and *f* him.
26:58 But Peter *f* him at a distance,
Lk 18:43 he received his sight and *f* Jesus,

FOLLOWING (FOLLOW)
Ps 119: 14 I rejoice in *f* your statutes
Php 3:17 Join with others in *f* my example,
1Ti 1:18 by *f* them you may fight the good

FOLLOWS (FOLLOW)
Jn 8:12 Whoever *f* me will never walk

FOLLY (FOOL)
Pr 14:29 a quick-tempered man displays *f*.
19: 3 A man's own *f* ruins his life,
Ecc 10: 1 so a little *f* outweighs wisdom
Mk 7:22 envy, slander, arrogance and *f*.
2Ti 3: 9 their *f* will be clear to everyone.

FOOD (FOODS)
Ge 1:30 I give every green plant for *f*."
Pr 12: 9 to be somebody and have no *f*.
12:11 his land will have abundant *f*,
20:13 you will have *f* to spare.
20:17 *F* gained by fraud tastes sweet
21:20 of the wise are stores of choice *f*
22: 9 for he shares his *f* with the poor.
23: 3 for that *f* is deceptive.
23: 6 Do not eat the *f* of a stingy man,
25:21 If your enemy is hungry, give him *f*
31:14 bringing her *f* from afar.
31:15 she provides *f* for her family
Isa 58: 7 not to share your *f* with the hungry
Eze 18: 7 but gives his *f* to the hungry
Da 1: 8 to defile himself with the royal *f*
Mt 3: 4 His *f* was locusts and wild honey.
6:25 Is not life more important than *f*,
Jn 4:32 "I have *f* to eat that you know
4:34 have brought him *f*?" "My *f*,"
6:27 Do not work for *f* that spoils,
6:55 my flesh is real *f* and my blood is
Ac 15:20 to abstain from *f* polluted by idols,
Ro 14:14 fully convinced that no *f* is unclean
1Co 8: 1 Now about *f* sacrificed to idols:
8: 8 But *f* does not bring us near to God
2Co 11:27 and have often gone without *f*;
1Ti 6: 8 But if we have *f* and clothing,
Heb 5:14 But solid *f* is for the mature,
Jas 2:15 sister is without clothes and daily *f*.

FOODS (FOOD)
Mk 7:19 Jesus declared all *f* "clean.")

FOOL (FOLLY FOOL'S FOOLISH FOOLISHNESS FOOLS)
1Sa 25:25 his name is *F*, and folly goes
Ps 14: 1 The *f* says in his heart,
Pr 10:10 and a chattering *f* comes to ruin.
10:18 and whoever spreads slander is a *f*.
12:15 The way of a *f* seems right to him,
12:16 A *f* shows his annoyance at once,
14:16 but a *f* is hotheaded and reckless.
15: 5 A *f* spurns his father's discipline,
17:12 than a *f* in his folly.
17:16 use is money in the hand of a *f*,
17:21 To have a *f* for a son brings grief;
17:28 Even a *f* is thought wise
18: 2 A *f* finds no pleasure
20: 3 but every *f* is quick to quarrel.
23: 9 Do not speak to a *f*,
24: 7 Wisdom is too high for a *f*;
26: 4 Do not answer a *f* according
26: 5 Answer a *f* according to his folly,
26: 7 is a proverb in the mouth of a *f*.
26:11 so a *f* repeats his folly.
26:12 for a *f* than for him.
27:22 Though you grind a *f* in a mortar,
28:26 He who trusts in himself is a *f*,
29:11 A *f* gives full vent to his anger,
29:20 for a *f* than for him.
Mt 5:22 But anyone who says, 'You *f*!'
Lk 12:20 "But God said to him, 'You *f*!
1Co 3:18 he should become a "*f*"
2Co 11:21 I am speaking as a *f*— I

FOOL'S (FOOL)
Pr 14: 3 A *f* talk brings a rod to his back,
18: 7 A *f* mouth is his undoing,

FOOLISH (FOOL)
Pr 10: 1 but a *f* son grief to his mother.
14: 1 her own hands the *f* one tears hers
15:20 but a *f* man despises his mother.
17:25 A *f* son brings grief to his father
19:13 A *f* son is his father's ruin,
Mt 7:26 practice is like a *f* man who built
25: 2 of them were *f* and five were wise.
Lk 11:40 You *f* people! Did not the one who
24:25 He said to them, "How *f* you are,
1Co 1:20 Has not God made *f* the wisdom
1:27 God chose the *f* things of the world
Gal 3: 1 died for nothing!" You *f* Galatians!
Eph 5: 4 should there be obscenity, *f* talk
5:17 Therefore do not be *f*,
Tit 3: 9 But avoid *f* controversies

FOOLISHNESS (FOOL)
1Co 1:18 of the cross is *f* to those who are
1:21 through the *f* of what was preached
1:23 block to Jews and *f* to Gentiles,
1:25 For the *f* of God is wiser
2:14 for they are *f* to him, and he cannot
3:19 of this world is *f* in God's sight.

FOOLS (FOOL)
Pr 1: 7 but *f* despise wisdom and discipline
3:35 but *f* he holds up to shame.
12:23 but the heart of *f* blurts out folly.
13:19 but *f* detest turning from evil.
13:20 but a companion of *f* suffers harm.
14: 9 *F* mock at making amends for sin,
14:24 but the folly of *f* yields folly.
Ecc 7: 5 than to listen to the song of *f*.
7: 6 so is the laughter of *f*.
10: 6 *F* are put in many high positions,
Mt 23:17 You blind *f*! Which is greater:
Ro 1:22 they became *f* and exchanged
1Co 4:10 We are *f* for Christ, but you are

FOOT (FEET FOOTHOLD)
Jos 1: 3 every place where you set your *f*,
Ps 121: 3 He will not let your *f* slip—
Pr 3:23 and your *f* will not stumble;
4:27 keep your *f* from evil.
25:17 Seldom set *f* in your neighbor's
Isa 1: 6 From the sole of your *f* to the top
Mt 18: 8 or your *f* causes you to sin,
Lk 4:11 so that you will not strike your *f*
1Co 12:15 If the *f* should say, "Because I am
Rev 10: 2 He planted his right *f* on the sea

FOOTHOLD* (FOOT)
Ps 69: 2 where there is no *f*.
73: 2 I had nearly lost my *f*.
Eph 4:27 and do not give the devil a *f*.

FOOTSTEPS (STEP)
Ps 119: 133 Direct my *f* according

FOOTSTOOL
Ps 99: 5 and worship at his *f*;
110: 1 a *f* for your feet."
Isa 66: 1 and the earth is my *f*.
Mt 5:35 for it is his *f*; or by Jerusalem,
Ac 7:49 and the earth is my *f*.
Heb 1:13 a *f* for your feet"?
10:13 for his enemies to be made his *f*,

FORBEARANCE*
Ro 3:25 because in his *f* he had left the sins

FORBID
1Co 14:39 and do not *f* speaking in tongues.
1Ti 4: 3 They *f* people to marry

FORCE (FORCED FORCEFUL FORCES FORCING)
Jn 6:15 to come and make him king by *f*,
Ac 26:11 and I tried to *f* them to blaspheme.
Gal 2:14 that you *f* Gentiles

FORCED (FORCE)
Mt 27:32 and they *f* him to carry the cross.
Phm :14 do will be spontaneous and not *f*.

FORCEFUL* (FORCE)
Mt 11:12 forcefully advancing, and *f* men lay
2Co 10:10 "His letters are weighty and *f*,

FORCES (FORCE)
Mt 5:41 If someone *f* you to go one mile,
Eph 6:12 and against the spiritual *f* of evil

FORCING (FORCE)
Lk 16:16 and everyone is *f* his way into it.

FOREFATHERS (FATHER)
Heb 1: 1 spoke to our *f* through the prophets
1Pe 1:18 handed down to you from your *f*,

FOREHEAD (FOREHEADS)
Ex 13: 9 a reminder on your *f* that the law
13:16 on your *f* that the LORD brought
1Sa 17:49 and struck the Philistine on the *f*.
Rev 13:16 a mark on his right hand or on his *f*,

FOREHEADS (FOREHEAD)
Dt 6: 8 hands and bind them on your *f*.
Rev 9: 4 not have the seal of God on their *f*.
14: 1 his Father's name written on their *f*

FOREIGN (FOREIGNER FOREIGNERS)
Ge 35: 2 "Get rid of the *f* gods you have
2Ch 14: 3 He removed the *f* altars
33:15 He got rid of the *f* gods
Isa 28:11 with *f* lips and strange tongues

FOREIGNER (FOREIGN)
Lk 17:18 give praise to God except this *f*?"
1Co 14:11 I am a *f* to the speaker,

FOREIGNERS (FOREIGN)
Eph 2:12 *f* to the covenants of the promise,
2:19 you are no longer *f* and aliens,

FOREKNEW* (KNOW)
Ro 8:29 For those God *f* he
11: 2 not reject his people, whom he *f*.

FOREKNOWLEDGE* (KNOW)
Ac 2:23 to you by God's set purpose and *f*;
1Pe 1: 2 to the *f* of God the Father,

FORESAW*
Gal 3: 8 Scripture *f* that God would justify

FOREST
Jas 3: 5 Consider what a great *f* is set

FOREVER (EVER)
Ge 3:22 the tree of life and eat, and live *f*."
6: 3 Spirit will not contend with man *f*,
Ex 3:15 This is my name *f*, the name
2Sa 7:26 so that your name will be great *f*.
1Ki 2:33 may there be the LORD's peace *f*."
9: 3 by putting my Name there *f*.
1Ch 16:15 He remembers his covenant *f*,
16:34 his love endures *f*.
16:41 "for his love endures *f*."
17:24 and that your name will be great *f*.
2Ch 5:13 his love endures *f*."
20:21 for his love endures *f*."
Ps 9: 7 The LORD reigns *f*;
23: 6 dwell in the house of the LORD *f*.
28: 9 be their shepherd and carry them *f*.
29:10 the LORD is enthroned as King *f*.
33:11 the plans of the LORD stand firm *f*,
37:28 They will be protected *f*,
44: 8 and we will praise your name *f*.
61: 4 I long to dwell in your tent *f*
72:19 Praise be to his glorious name *f*;
73:26 and my portion *f*.
77: 8 Has his unfailing love vanished *f*?
79:13 will praise you *f*;
81:15 and their punishment would last *f*.
86:12 I will glorify your name *f*.
89: 1 of the LORD's great love *f*;
92: 8 But you, O LORD, are exalted *f*.
100: 5 is good and his love endures *f*;
102: 12 But you, O LORD, sit enthroned *f*;
104: 31 of the LORD endure *f*;
107: 1 his love endures *f*.
Ps 110: 4 "You are a priest *f*,
111: 3 and his righteousness endures *f*.
112: 6 man will be remembered *f*.
117: 2 of the LORD endures *f*.
118: 1 his love endures *f*.
119: 111 Your statutes are my heritage *f*;
119: 152 that you established them to last *f*.
136: 1 *His love endures f.*
146: 6 the LORD, who remains faithful *f*.
Pr 10:25 but the righteous stand firm *f*.
27:24 for riches do not endure *f*,
Isa 25: 8 he will swallow up death *f*.
26: 4 Trust in the LORD *f*,
32:17 will be quietness and confidence *f*.
40: 8 but the word of our God stands *f*."
51: 6 But my salvation will last *f*,
51: 8 But my righteousness will last *f*,
57:15 he who lives *f*, whose name is holy:
59:21 from this time on and *f*,"
Jer 33:11 his love endures *f*."
Eze 37:26 put my sanctuary among them *f*.
Da 2:44 to an end, but it will itself endure *f*.
3: 9 live *f*! You have issued a decree,
Jn 6:51 eats of this bread, he will live *f*.
14:16 Counselor to be with you *f*—
Ro 9: 5 who is God over all, *f* praised!
16:27 to the only wise God be glory *f*
1Co 9:25 it to get a crown that will last *f*.
1Th 4:17 And so we will be with the Lord *f*.
Heb 5: 6 "You are a priest *f*,
7:17 "You are a priest *f*,
7:24 Jesus lives *f*, he has a permanent
13: 8 same yesterday and today and *f*.
1Pe 1:25 but the word of the Lord stands *f*."
1Jn 2:17 who does the will of God lives *f*.
2Jn : 2 lives in us and will be with us *f*:

FOREVERMORE (EVER)
Ps 113: 2 both now and *f*.

FORFEIT
Mk 8:36 the whole world, yet *f* his soul?
Lk 9:25 and yet lose or *f* his very self?

FORGAVE (FORGIVE)
Ps 32: 5 and you *f*
65: 3 you *f* our transgressions
78:38 you *f* their iniquities
Eph 4:32 just as in Christ God *f* you.
Col 2:13 He *f* us all our sins, having
3:13 Forgive as the Lord *f* you.

FORGET (FORGETS FORGETTING FORGOT FORGOTTEN)
Dt 4:23 Be careful not to *f* the covenant
6:12 that you do not *f* the LORD,
2Ki 17:38 Do not *f* the covenant I have made
Ps 9:17 all the nations that *f* God.
10:12 Do not *f* the helpless.
50:22 "Consider this, you who *f* God,
78: 7 and would not *f* his deeds
103: 2 and *f* not all his benefits.
119: 93 I will never *f* your precepts,
137: 5 may my right hand *f* its skill.
Pr 3: 1 My son, do not *f* my teaching,
4: 5 do not *f* my words or swerve
Isa 49:15 "Can a mother *f* the baby
51:13 that you *f* the LORD your Maker,
Jer 2:32 Does a maiden *f* her jewelry,
23:39 I will surely *f* you and cast you out
Heb 6:10 he will not *f* your work
13: 2 Do not *f* to entertain strangers,
13:16 And do not *f* to do good
2Pe 3: 8 But do not *f* this one thing,

FORGETS (FORGET)
Jn 16:21 her baby is born she *f* the anguish
Jas 1:24 immediately *f* what he looks like.

FORGETTING* (FORGET)
Php 3:13 *F* what is behind and straining
Jas 1:25 to do this, not *f* what he has heard,

FORGIVE* (FORGAVE FORGIVENESS FORGIVES FORGIVING)
Ge 50:17 I ask you to *f* your brothers the sins
50:17 please *f* the sins of the servants
Ex 10:17 Now *f* my sin once more
23:21 he will not *f* your rebellion,
32:32 But now, please *f* their sin—
34: 9 *f* our wickedness and our sin,
Nu 14:19 with your great love, *f* the sin
Dt 29:20 will never be willing to *f* him;
Jos 24:19 He will not *f* your rebellion
1Sa 15:25 *f* my sin and come back with me,
25:28 Please *f* your servant's offense,
1Ki 8:30 place, and when you hear, *f*.
8:34 and *f* the sin of your people Israel
8:36 and *f* the sin of your servants,
8:39 *F* and act; deal with each man
1Ki 8:50 *f* all the offenses they have
8:50 *f* your people, who have sinned
2Ki 5:18 But may the LORD *f* your servant
5:18 may the LORD *f* your servant
24: 4 and the LORD was not willing to *f*.
2Ch 6:21 place; and when you hear, *f*.
6:25 and *f* the sin of your people Israel
6:27 and *f* the sin of your servants,
6:30 *F*, and deal with each man
6:39 *f* your people, who have sinned
7:14 will *f* their sin and will heal their
Job 7:21 and *f* my sins?
Ps 19:12 *F* my hidden faults.
25:11 *f* my iniquity, though it is great.
79: 9 deliver us and *f* our sins
Isa 2: 9 do not *f* them.
Jer 5: 1 I will *f* this city.
5: 7 "Why should I *f* you?
18:23 Do not *f* their crimes
31:34 "For I will *f* their wickedness
33: 8 and will *f* all their sins of rebellion
36: 3 then I will *f* their wickedness
50:20 for I will *f* the remnant I spare.
Da 9:19 O Lord, listen! O Lord, *f*! O Lord,
Hos 1: 6 that I should at all *f* them.
14: 2 "*F* all our sins
Am 7: 2 *f*! How can Jacob survive?
Mt 6:12 *F* us our debts,
6:14 For if you *f* men when they sin
6:14 heavenly Father will also *f* you.
6:15 But if you do not *f* men their sins,
6:15 your Father will not *f* your sins.
9: 6 authority on earth to *f* sins..
18:21 many times shall I *f* my brother
18:35 you *f* your brother from your heart
Mk 2: 7 Who can *f* sins but God alone?"
2:10 authority on earth to *f* sins
11:25 anything against anyone, *f* him,
11:25 in heaven may *f* you your sins."
Lk 5:21 Who can *f* sins but God alone?"
5:24 authority on earth to *f* sins..
6:37 *F*, and you will be forgiven.
11: 4 *F* us our sins,
11: 4 *f* everyone who sins against us.
17: 3 rebuke him, and if he repents, *f* him
17: 4 and says, 'I repent,' *f* him."
23:34 Jesus said, "Father, *f* them,
Jn 20:23 If you *f* anyone his sins, they are
20:23 if you do not *f* them, they are not
Ac 8:22 Perhaps he will *f* you
2Co 2: 7 you ought to *f* and comfort him,
2:10 If you *f* anyone, I also *f* him.
2:10 if there was anything to *f*—
12:13 a burden to you? *F* me this wrong!
Col 3:13 and *f* whatever grievances you may
3:13 *F* as the Lord forgave you.
Heb 8:12 For I will *f* their wickedness
1Jn 1: 9 and just and will *f* us our sins

FORGIVENESS* (FORGIVE)
Ps 130: 4 But with you there is *f*;
Mt 26:28 out for many for the *f* of sins.
Mk 1: 4 of repentance for the *f* of sins.
Lk 1:77 salvation through the *f* of their sins,
3: 3 of repentance for the *f* of sins.
24:47 and *f* of sins will be preached
Ac 5:31 that he might give repentance and *f*
10:43 believes in him receives *f* of sins
13:38 that through Jesus the *f*
26:18 so that they may receive *f* of sins
Eph 1: 7 through his blood, the *f* of sins,
Col 1:14 in whom we have redemption, the *f*
Heb 9:22 the shedding of blood there is no *f*.

FORGIVES* (FORGIVE)
Ps 103: 3 He *f* all my sins
Mic 7:18 pardons sin and *f* the transgression
Lk 7:49 "Who is this who even *f* sins?"

FORGIVING* (FORGIVE)
Ex 34: 7 and *f* wickedness, rebellion and sin.
Nu 14:18 abounding in love and *f* sin
Ne 9:17 But you are a *f* God, gracious
Ps 86: 5 You are *f* and good, O Lord,
99: 8 you were to Israel a *f* God,
Da 9: 9 The Lord our God is merciful and *f*
Eph 4:32 to one another, *f* each other,

FORGOT (FORGET)
Dt 32:18 you *f* the God who gave you birth.
Ps 78:11 They *f* what he had done,
106: 13 But they soon *f* what he had done

FORGOTTEN (FORGET)
Job 11: 6 God has even *f* some of your sin.
Ps 44:20 If we had *f* the name of our God
Isa 17:10 You have *f* God your Savior;
Hos 8:14 Israel has *f* his Maker
Lk 12: 6 Yet not one of them is *f* by God.

2Pe 1: 9 and has *f* that he has been cleansed

FORM (FORMED)

Isa 52:14 *f* marred beyond human likeness—
2Ti 3: 5 having a *f* of godliness

FORMED (FORM)

Ge 2: 7 —the LORD God *f* the man
2:19 Now the LORD God had *f* out
Ps 103: 14 for he knows how we are *f*,
Ecc 11: 5 or how the body is *f* in a mother's
Isa 29:16 Shall what is *f* say to him who *f* it,
45:18 but *f* it to be inhabited—
49: 5 he who *f* me in the womb
Jer 1: 5 "Before I *f* you in the womb I knew
Ro 9:20 "Shall what is *f* say to him who *f* it,
Gal 4:19 of childbirth until Christ is *f* in you,
1Ti 2:13 For Adam was *f* first, then Eve.
Heb 11: 3 understand that the universe was *f*
2Pe 3: 5 and the earth was *f* out of water

FORMLESS*

Ge 1: 2 Now the earth was *f* and empty,
Jer 4:23 and it was *f* and empty;

FORSAKE (FORSAKEN)

Dt 31: 6 he will never leave you nor *f* you."
Jos 1: 5 I will never leave you nor *f* you.
24:16 "Far be it from us to *f* the LORD
2Ch 15: 2 but if you *f* him, he will *f* you.
Ps 27:10 Though my father and mother *f* me
94:14 he will never *f* his inheritance.
Isa 55: 7 Let the wicked *f* his way
Heb 13: 5 never will I *f* you."

FORSAKEN (FORSAKE)

Ps 22: 1 my God, why have you *f* me?
37:25 I have never seen the righteous *f*
Mt 27:46 my God, why have you *f* me?"
Rev 2: 4 You have *f* your first love.

FORTRESS

2Sa 22: 2 "The LORD is my rock, my *f*
Ps 18: 2 The LORD is my rock, my *f*
31: 2 a strong *f* to save me.
59:16 for you are my *f*,
71: 3 for you are my rock and my *f*.
Pr 14:26 who fears the LORD has a secure *f*,

FORTUNE-TELLING*

Ac 16:16 deal of money for her owners by *f*.

FORTY

Ge 7: 4 on the earth for *f* days and *f* nights,
18:29 "What if only *f* are found there?"
Ex 16:35 The Israelites ate manna *f* years,
24:18 on the mountain *f* days and *f* nights
Nu 14:34 For *f* years—one year for each
Jos 14: 7 I was *f* years old when Moses
1Sa 4:18 He had led Israel *f* years.
2Sa 5: 4 king, and he reigned *f* years.
1Ki 19: 8 he traveled *f* days and *f* nights
2Ki 12: 1 and he reigned in Jerusalem *f* years
2Ch 9:30 in Jerusalem over all Israel *f* years.
Eze 29:12 her cities will lie desolate *f* years
Jnh 3: 4 "*F* more days and Nineveh will be
Mt 4: 2 After fasting *f* days and *f* nights,

FOUGHT (FIGHT)

1Co 15:32 If I *f* wild beasts in Ephesus
2Ti 4: 7 I have *f* the good fight, I have

FOUND (FIND)

2Ki 22: 8 "I have *f* the Book of the Law
1Ch 28: 9 If you seek him, he will be *f* by you;
2Ch 15:15 sought God eagerly, and he was *f*
Isa 55: 6 Seek the LORD while he may be *f*;
65: 1 I was *f* by those who did not seek
Da 5:27 on the scales and *f* wanting.
Mt 1:18 she was *f* to be with child
Lk 15: 6 with me; I have *f* my lost sheep.'
15: 9 with me; I have *f* my lost coin.'
15:24 is alive again; he was lost and is *f*.'
Ac 4:12 Salvation is *f* in no one else,
Ro 10:20 "I was *f* by those who did not seek
Jas 2: 8 If you really keep the royal law *f*
Rev 5: 4 no one was *f* who was worthy

FOUNDATION (FOUNDATIONS FOUNDED)

Isa 28:16 a precious cornerstone for a sure *f*;
Mt 7:25 because it had its *f* on the rock.
Lk 14:29 For if he lays the *f* and is not able
Ro 15:20 building on someone else's *f*.
1Co 3:10 I laid a *f* as an expert builder,
3:11 For no one can lay any *f* other
Eph 2:20 built on the *f* of the apostles
1Ti 3:15 the pillar and *f* of the truth.
2Ti 2:19 God's solid *f* stands firm,
Heb 6: 1 not laying again the *f* of repentance

FOUNDATIONS (FOUNDATION)

Ps 102: 25 In the beginning you laid the *f*
Heb 1:10 O Lord, you laid the *f* of the earth,

FOUNDED (FOUNDATION)

Jer 10:12 he *f* the world by his wisdom
Heb 8: 6 and it is *f* on better promises.

FOUNTAIN

Ps 36: 9 For with you is the *f* of life;
Pr 14:27 The fear of the LORD is a *f* of life,
18: 4 the *f* of wisdom is a bubbling brook.
Zec 13: 1 "On that day a *f* will be opened

FOX (FOXES)

Lk 13:32 He replied, "Go tell that *f*,

FOXES (FOX)

SS 2:15 the little *f*
Mt 8:20 "*F* have holes and birds

FRAGRANCE (FRAGRANT)

Ex 30:38 it to enjoy its *f* must be cut
Jn 12: 3 filled with the *f* of the perfume.
2Co 2:14 us spreads everywhere the *f*
2:16 of death; to the other, the *f* of life.

FRAGRANT (FRAGRANCE)

Eph 5: 2 as a *f* offering and sacrifice to God.
Php 4:18 They are a *f* offering, an acceptable

FREE (FREED FREEDOM FREELY)

Ge 2:16 "You are *f* to eat from any tree
Ps 118: 5 and he answered by setting me *f*.
119: 32 for you have set my heart *f*.
146: 7 The LORD sets prisoners *f*,
Pr 6: 3 then do this, my son, to *f* yourself,
Jn 8:32 and the truth will set you *f*."
8:36 if the Son sets you *f*, you will be *f*
Ro 6:18 You have been set *f* from sin
8: 2 of life set me *f* from the law of sin
1Co 12:13 whether Jews or Greeks, slave or *f*
Gal 3:28 slave nor *f*, male nor female,
5: 1 for freedom that Christ has set us *f*.
1Pe 2:16 *f* men, but do not use your freedom

FREED (FREE)

Ps 116: 16 you have *f* me from my chains.
Ro 6: 7 anyone who has died has been *f*
Rev 1: 5 has *f* us from our sins by his blood,

FREEDOM (FREE)

Ps 119: 45 I will walk about in *f*,
Isa 61: 1 to proclaim *f* for the captives
Lk 4:18 me to proclaim *f* for the prisoners
Ro 8:21 into the glorious *f* of the children
1Co 7:21 although if you can gain your *f*,
2Co 3:17 the Spirit of the Lord is, there is *f*.
Gal 2: 4 ranks to spy on the *f* we have
5:13 But do not use your *f* to indulge
Jas 1:25 into the perfect law that gives *f*,
1Pe 2:16 but do not use your *f* as a cover-up

FREELY (FREE)

Isa 55: 7 and to our God, for he will *f* pardon
Mt 10: 8 Freely you have received, *f* give.
Ro 3:24 and are justified *f* by his grace
Eph 1: 6 which he has *f* given us

FRESH

Jas 3:11 Can both *f* water and salt water

FRET*

Ps 37: 1 Do not *f* because of evil men
37: 7 do not *f* when men succeed
37: 8 do not *f*—it leads only to evil.
Pr 24:19 Do not *f* because of evil men

FRICTION

1Ti 6: 5 and constant *f* between men

FRIEND (FRIENDS FRIENDSHIP)

Ex 33:11 as a man speaks with his *f*.
2Ch 20: 7 descendants of Abraham your *f*?
Pr 17:17 A *f* loves at all times,
18:24 there is a *f* who sticks closer
27: 6 Wounds from a *f* can be trusted
27:10 Do not forsake your *f* and the *f*
Isa 41: 8 you descendants of Abraham my *f*,
Mt 11:19 a *f* of tax collectors and "sinners."'
Lk 11: 8 him the bread because he is his *f*,
Jn 19:12 "If you let this man go, you are no *f*
Jas 2:23 and he was called God's *f*.
4: 4 Anyone who chooses to be a *f*

FRIENDS (FRIEND)

Pr 16:28 and a gossip separates close *f*.
17: 9 the matter separates close *f*.
Zec 13: 6 given at the house of my *f*.'
Jn 15:13 that he lay down his life for his *f*.
15:14 You are my *f* if you do what I

FRIENDSHIP (FRIEND)

Jas 4: 4 don't you know that *f*

FRIGHTENED (FEAR)

Php 1:28 gospel without being *f* in any way
1Pe 3:14 fear what they fear; do not be *f*."

FROGS

Ex 8: 2 plague your whole country with *f*.
Rev 16:13 three evil spirits that looked like *f*;

FRUIT (FRUITFUL)

Jdg 9:11 'Should I give up my *f*, so good
Ps 1: 3 which yields its *f* in season
Pr 11:30 The *f* of the righteous is a tree
12:14 From the *f* of his lips a man is filled
27:18 He who tends a fig tree will eat its *f*
Isa 11: 1 from his roots a Branch will bear *f*.
27: 6 and fill all the world with *f*.
32:17 The *f* of righteousness will be peace
Jer 17: 8 and never fails to bear *f*."
Hos 10:12 reap the *f* of unfailing love,
14: 2 that we may offer the *f* of our lips.
Am 8: 1 showed me: a basket of ripe *f*.
Mt 3: 8 Produce *f* in keeping
3:10 does not produce good *f* will be cut
7:16 By their *f* you will recognize them.
7:17 good *f*, but a bad tree bears bad *f*.
7:20 by their *f* you will recognize them.
12:33 a tree good and its *f* will be good,
Lk 3: 9 does not produce good *f* will be cut
6:43 nor does a bad tree bear good *f*.
13: 6 and he went to look for *f* on it,
Jn 15: 2 branch in me that bears no *f*,
15:16 and bear *f*—*f* that will last.
Ro 7: 4 in order that we might bear *f*
Gal 5:22 But the *f* of the Spirit is love, joy,
Php 1:11 with the *f* of righteousness that
Col 1:10 bearing *f* in every good work,
Heb 13:15 the *f* of lips that confess his name.
Jas 3:17 and good *f*, impartial and sincere.
Jude :12 autumn trees, without *f*
Rev 22: 2 of *f*, yielding its *f* every month.

FRUITFUL (FRUIT)

Ge 1:22 "Be *f* and increase in number
9: 1 "Be *f* and increase in number
35:11 be *f* and increase in number.
Ex 1: 7 the Israelites were *f* and multiplied
Ps 128: 3 Your wife will be like a *f* vine
Jn 15: 2 prunes so that it will be even more *f*.
Php 1:22 this will mean *f* labor for me.

FRUITLESS*

Eph 5:11 to do with the *f* deeds of darkness,

FRUSTRATION

Ro 8:20 For the creation was subjected to *f*,

FUEL

Isa 44:19 "Half of it I used for *f*;

FULFILL (FULFILLED FULFILLMENT FULFILLS)

Nu 23:19 Does he promise and not *f*?
Ps 61: 8 and *f* my vows day after day.
116: 14 I will *f* my vows to the LORD
138: 8 The LORD will *f* his purpose,
Ecc 5: 5 than to make a vow and not *f* it.
Isa 46:11 far-off land, a man to *f* my purpose.
Jer 33:14 'when I will *f* the gracious promise
Mt 1:22 place to *f* what the Lord had said
3:15 us to do this to *f* all righteousness."
4:14 *f* what was said
5:17 come to abolish them but to *f* them.
8:17 This was to *f* what was spoken
12:17 This was to *f* what was spoken
21: 4 place to *f* what was spoken
Jn 12:38 This was to *f* the word
13:18 But this is to *f* the scripture:
15:25 But this is to *f* what is written
1Co 7: 3 husband should *f* his marital duty

FULFILLED (FULFILL)

Jos 21:45 of Israel failed; every one was *f*.
23:14 Every promise has been *f*;
Pr 13:12 but a longing *f* is a tree of life.
13:19 A longing *f* is sweet to the soul,
Mt 2:15 so was *f* what the Lord had said
2:17 the prophet Jeremiah was *f*:
2:23 So was *f* what was said
13:14 In them is *f* the prophecy of Isaiah:
13:35 So was *f* what was spoken
26:54 would the Scriptures be *f* that say it
26:56 of the prophets might be *f*."
27: 9 by Jeremiah the prophet was *f*:
Mk 13: 4 that they are all about to be *f*?"
14:49 But the Scriptures must be *f*."
Lk 4:21 "Today this scripture is *f*
18:31 about the Son of Man will be *f*.

Lk 24:44 Everything must be *f* that is
Jn 18: 9 words he had spoken would be *f*:
19:24 the Scripture might be *f* which said,
19:28 and so that the Scripture would be *f*
19:36 so that the Scripture would be *f*:
Ac 1:16 to be *f* which the Holy Spirit spoke
Ro 13: 8 loves his fellowman has *f* the law.
Jas 2:23 And the scripture was *f* that says,

FULFILLMENT (FULFILL)
Ro 13:10 Therefore love is the *f* of the law.

FULFILLS (FULFILL)
Ps 57: 2 to God, who *f* ⌊his purpose⌋ for me.
145: 19 He *f* the desires of those who fear

FULL (FILL)
2Ch 24:10 them into the chest until it was *f*.
Ps 127: 5 whose quiver is *f* of them.
Pr 27: 7 He who is *f* loathes honey,
31:11 Her husband has *f* confidence
Isa 6: 3 the whole earth is *f* of his glory."
11: 9 for the earth will be *f*
Lk 4: 1 Jesus, *f* of the Holy Spirit,
Jn 10:10 may have life, and have it to the *f*.
Ac 6: 3 known to be *f* of the Spirit
6: 5 a man *f* of faith and of the Holy
7:55 But Stephen, *f* of the Holy Spirit,
11:24 *f* of the Holy Spirit and faith,

FULL-GROWN* (GROW)
Jas 1:15 when it is *f*, gives birth to death.

FULLNESS* (FILL)
Dt 33:16 gifts of the earth and its *f*
Jn 1:16 From the *f* of his grace we have all
Ro 11:12 greater riches will their *f* bring!
Eph 1:23 the *f* of him who fills everything
3:19 to the measure of all the *f* of God.
4:13 to the whole measure of the *f*
Col 1:19 to have all his *f* dwell in him,
1:25 to you the word of God in its *f*—
2: 9 in Christ all the *f* of the Deity lives
2:10 and you have been given *f* in Christ

FULLY (FILL)
1Ki 8:61 your hearts must be *f* committed
2Ch 16: 9 whose hearts are *f* committed
Ps 119: 4 that are to be *f* obeyed.
119:138 they are *f* trustworthy.
Pr 13: 4 of the diligent are *f* satisfied.
Lk 6:40 everyone who is *f* trained will be
Ro 4:21 being *f* persuaded that God had
14: 5 Each one should be *f* convinced
1Co 13:12 shall know *f*, even as I am *f* known.
15:58 Always give yourselves *f*
2Ti 4:17 the message might be *f* proclaimed

FURIOUS (FURY)
Dt 29:28 In *f* anger and in great wrath
Jer 32:37 where I banish them in my *f* anger

FURNACE
Isa 48:10 in the *f* of affliction.
Da 3: 6 be thrown into a blazing *f*."
Mt 13:42 will throw them into the fiery *f*,

FURY (FURIOUS)
Isa 14: 6 and in *f* subdued nations
Jer 21: 5 and a mighty arm in anger and *f*
Rev 14:10 will drink of the wine of God's *f*,
16:19 with the wine of the *f* of his wrath.
19:15 the winepress of the *f* of the wrath

FUTILE (FUTILITY)
Mal 3:14 You have said, 'It is *f* to serve God.
1Co 3:20 that the thoughts of the wise are *f*."

FUTILITY (FUTILE)
Eph 4:17 in the *f* of their thinking.

FUTURE
Ps 37:37 there is a *f* for the man of peace.
Pr 23:18 There is surely a *f* hope for you,
Ecc 7:14 anything about his *f*.
8: 7 Since no man knows the *f*,
Jer 29:11 plans to give you hope and a *f*.
31:17 So there is hope for your *f*,"
Ro 8:38 neither the present nor the *f*,
1Co 3:22 life or death or the present or the *f*

GABRIEL*
Angel who interpreted Daniel's visions (Da 8: 16-26; 9:20-27); announced births of John (Lk 1: 11-20), Jesus (Lk 1:26-38).

GAD
1. Son of Jacob by Zilpah (Ge 30:9-11; 35:26; 1Ch 2:2). Tribe of blessed (Ge 49:19; Dt 33:20-21), numbered (Nu 1:25; 26:18), allotted land east of the Jordan (Nu 32; 34:14; Jos 18:7; 22), west (Eze 48:27-28), 12,000 from (Rev 7:5).
2. Prophet; seer of David (1Sa 22:5; 2Sa 24: 11-19; 1Ch 29:29).

GAIN (GAINED GAINS)
Ex 14:17 And I will *g* glory through Pharaoh
Ps 60:12 With God we will *g* the victory,
Pr 4: 1 pay attention and *g* understanding.
8: 5 You who are simple, *g* prudence;
28:16 he who hates ill-gotten *g* will enjoy
28:23 in the end *g* more favor
Isa 63:12 to *g* for himself everlasting renown
Da 2: 8 that you are trying to *g* time,
Mk 8:36 it for a man to *g* the whole world,
Lk 9:25 it for a man to *g* the whole world,
21:19 standing firm you will *g* life.
1Co 13: 3 but have not love, I *g* nothing.
Php 1:21 to live is Christ and to die is *g*.
3: 8 that I may *g* Christ and be found
1Ti 3:13 have served well *g* an excellent
6: 5 godliness is a means to financial *g*.
6: 6 with contentment is great *g*.

GAINED (GAIN)
Jer 32:20 have *g* the renown that is still yours
Ro 5: 2 through whom we have *g* access

GAINS (GAIN)
Pr 3:13 the man who *g* understanding,
11:16 A kindhearted woman *g* respect,
15:32 heeds correction *g* understanding.
29:23 but a man of lowly spirit *g* honor.
Mt 16:26 for a man if he *g* the whole world,

GALILEE
Isa 9: 1 but in the future he will honor *G*
Mt 4:15 *G* of the Gentiles—
26:32 I will go ahead of you into *G*."
28:10 Go and tell my brothers to go to *G*;

GALL
Mt 27:34 mixed with *g*; but after tasting it,

GALLIO
Ac 18:12 While *G* was proconsul of Achaia,

GALLOWS
Est 7:10 Haman on the *g* he had prepared

GAMALIEL
Ac 5:34 But a Pharisee named *G*, a teacher

GAMES
1Co 9:25 in the *g* goes into strict training.

GAP
Eze 22:30 stand before me in the *g* on behalf

GAPE*
Ps 35:21 They *g* at me and say, "Aha! Aha!

GARDEN (GARDENER)
Ge 2: 8 the LORD God had planted a *g*
2:15 put him in the *G* of Eden to work it
SS 4:12 You are a *g* locked up, my sister,
Isa 58:11 You will be like a well-watered *g*,
Jer 31:12 They will be like a well-watered *g*,
Eze 28:13 the *g* of God;
31: 9 Eden in the *g* of God.

GARDENER (GARDEN)
Jn 15: 1 true vine, and my Father is the *g*.

GARLAND*
Pr 1: 9 They will be a *g* to grace your head
4: 9 She will set a *g* of grace

GARMENT (GARMENTS)
Ps 102: 26 they will all wear out like a *g*.
Isa 50: 9 They will all wear out like a *g*;
51: 6 the earth will wear out like a *g*
61: 3 and a *g* of praise
Mt 9:16 of unshrunk cloth on an old *g*,
Jn 19:23 This *g* was seamless, woven
Heb 1:11 they will all wear out like a *g*.

GARMENTS (GARMENT)
Ge 3:21 The LORD God made *g* of skin
Ex 28: 2 Make sacred *g* for your brother
Lev 16:23 and take off the linen *g* he put
16:24 holy place and put on his regular *g*.
Isa 61:10 me with *g* of salvation
63: 1 with his *g* stained crimson?
Joel 2:13 and not your *g*.
Zec 3: 4 and I will put rich *g* on you."
Jn 19:24 "They divided my *g* among them

GATE (GATES)
Ps 118: 20 This is the *g* of the LORD
Pr 31:23 husband is respected at the city *g*,
31:31 works bring her praise at the city *g*.
Mt 7:13 For wide is the *g* and broad is
7:13 "Enter through the narrow *g*.
Jn 10: 1 not enter the sheep pen by the *g*,
10: 2 enters by the *g* is the shepherd
10: 7 "I tell you the truth, I am the *g*
10: 9 I am the *g*; whoever enters
Heb 13:12 also suffered outside the city *g*
Rev 21:21 each *g* made of a single pearl.

GATES (GATE)
Ps 24: 7 Lift up your heads, O you *g*;
24: 9 Lift up your heads, O you *g*;
100: 4 Enter his *g* with thanksgiving
118: 19 Open for me the *g* of righteousness
Isa 60:11 Your *g* will always stand open,
60:18 and your *g* Praise.
62:10 Pass through, pass through the *g*!
Mt 16:18 the *g* of Hades will not overcome it
Rev 21:12 On the *g* were written the names
21:21 The twelve *g* were twelve pearls,
21:25 On no day will its *g* ever be shut,
22:14 may go through the *g* into the city.

GATH
1Sa 17:23 the Philistine champion from *G*,
2Sa 1:20 "Tell it not in *G*,
Mic 1:10 Tell it not in *G*;

GATHER (GATHERED GATHERS)
Ps 106: 47 and *g* us from the nations,
Isa 11:12 and *g* the exiles of Israel;
Jer 3:17 and all nations will *g* in Jerusalem
23: 3 "I myself will *g* the remnant
31:10 who scattered Israel will *g* them
Zep 2: 1 *G* together, *g* together,
3:20 At that time I will *g* you;
Zec 14: 2 I will *g* all the nations to Jerusalem
Mt 12:30 he who does not *g* with me scatters
13:30 then *g* the wheat and bring it
23:37 longed to *g* your children together,
24:31 and they will *g* his elect
25:26 *g* where I have not scattered seed?
Mk 13:27 and *g* his elect from the four winds,
Lk 3:17 and to *g* the wheat into his barn,
11:23 and he who does not *g* with me,
13:34 longed to *g* your children together,

GATHERED (GATHER)
Ex 16:18 and he who *g* little did not have too
Pr 30: 4 Who has *g* up the wind
Mt 25:32 All the nations will be *g* before him
2Co 8:15 and he who *g* little did not have too
2Th 2: 1 Lord Jesus Christ and our being *g*
Rev 16:16 Then they *g* the kings together

GATHERS (GATHER)
Ps 147: 2 he *g* the exiles of Israel.
Pr 10: 5 He who *g* crops in summer is a wise
Isa 40:11 He *g* the lambs in his arms
Mt 23:37 a hen *g* her chicks under her wings,

GAVE (GIVE)
Ge 2:20 man *g* names to all the livestock,
3: 6 She also *g* some to her husband,
14:20 Abram *g* him a tenth of everything.
28: 4 the land God *g* to Abraham."
35:12 The land I *g* to Abraham
39:23 *g* him success in whatever he did.
47:11 *g* them property in the best part
Ex 4:11 to him, "Who *g* man his mouth?
31:18 he *g* him the two tablets
Dt 2:12 did in the land the LORD *g* them
2:36 The LORD our God *g* us all
3:12 I *g* the Reubenites and the Gadites
3:13 I *g* to the half tribe of Manasseh.
3:15 And I *g* Gilead to Makir.
3:16 Gadites I *g* the territory extending
8:16 He *g* you manna to eat in the desert
26: 9 us to this place and *g* us this land,
32: 8 the Most High *g* the nations their
Jos 11:23 and he *g* it as an inheritance
13:14 tribe of Levi he *g* no inheritance,
14:13 *g* him Hebron as his inheritance.
21:44 The LORD *g* them rest
24:13 I *g* you a land on which you did not
1Sa 27: 6 So on that day Achish *g* him Ziklag
2Sa 12: 8 I *g* you the house of Israel
1Ki 4:29 God *g* Solomon wisdom
5:12 The LORD *g* Solomon wisdom,
Ezr 2:69 According to their ability they *g*
Ne 9:15 In their hunger you *g* them bread
9:20 You *g* your good Spirit
9:22 You *g* them kingdoms and nations,
9:27 compassion you *g* them deliverers,
Job 1:21 LORD *g* and the LORD has taken
42:10 prosperous again and *g* him twice
Ps 69:21 and *g* me vinegar for my thirst.
135: 12 he *g* their land as an inheritance,
Ecc 12: 7 the spirit returns to God who *g* it.
Eze 3: 2 and he *g* me the scroll to eat.

Mt 1:25 And he *g* him the name Jesus.
25:35 and you *g* me something to drink,
25:42 and you *g* me nothing to drink,
26:26 Jesus took bread, *g* thanks
27:50 in a loud voice, he *g* up his spirit.
Mk 6: 7 *g* them authority over evil spirits.
Jn 1:12 he *g* the right to become children
3:16 so loved the world that he *g* his one
17: 4 by completing the work you *g* me
17: 6 you *g* them to me and they have
19:30 bowed his head and *g* up his spirit.
Ac 1: 3 *g* many convincing proofs that he
2:45 they *g* to anyone as he had need.
11:17 *g* them the same gift as he *g* us,
Ro 1:24 Therefore God *g* them
1:26 God *g* them over to shameful lusts.
1:28 he *g* them over to a depraved mind,
8:32 not spare his own Son, but *g* him up
2Co 5:18 *g* us the ministry of reconciliation:
8: 3 For I testify that they *g* as much
8: 5 they *g* themselves first to the Lord
Gal 1: 4 who *g* himself for our sins
2:20 who loved me and *g* himself for me
Eph 4: 8 and *g* gifts to men."
5: 2 as Christ loved us and *g* himself up
5:25 and *g* himself up for her
2Th 2:16 and by his grace *g* us eternal
1Ti 2: 6 who *g* himself as a ransom
Tit 2:14 who *g* himself for us to redeem us
1Jn 3:24 We know it by the Spirit he *g* us.

GAZE

Ps 27: 4 to *g* upon the beauty of the LORD
Pr 4:25 fix your *g* directly before you.

GEDALIAH

Governor of Judah appointed by Nebuchadnezzar (2Ki 25:22-26; Jer 39-41).

GEHAZI*

Servant of Elisha (2Ki 4:12-5:27; 8:4-5).

GENEALOGIES

1Ti 1: 4 themselves to myths and endless *g*.
Tit 3: 9 avoid foolish controversies and *g*

GENERATION (GENERATIONS)

Ex 3:15 am to be remembered from *g* to *g*.
Nu 32:13 until the whole *g* of those who had
Dt 1:35 of this evil *g* shall see the good land
Jdg 2:10 After that whole *g* had been
Ps 24: 6 Such is the *g* of those who seek him
48:13 tell of them to the next *g*.
71:18 I declare your power to the next *g*,
78: 4 we will tell the next *g*
102: 18 Let this be written for a future *g*,
112: 2 the *g* of the upright will be blessed
145: 4 One *g* will commend your works
La 5:19 your throne endures from *g* to *g*.
Da 4: 3 his dominion endures from *g* to *g*.
4:34 his kingdom endures from *g* to *g*.
Joel 1: 3 and their children to the next *g*.
Mt 12:39 adulterous *g* asks for a miraculous
17:17 "O unbelieving and perverse *g*,"
23:36 all this will come upon this *g*.
24:34 this *g* will certainly not pass away
Mk 9:19 "O unbelieving *g*," Jesus replied,
13:30 this *g* will certainly not pass away
Lk 1:50 who fear him, from *g* to *g*.
11:29 Jesus said, "This is a wicked *g*.
11:30 will the Son of Man be to this *g*.
11:50 Therefore this *g* will be held
21:32 this *g* will certainly not pass away
Ac 2:40 Save yourselves from this corrupt *g*
Php 2:15 fault in a crooked and depraved *g*,

GENERATIONS (GENERATION)

Ge 9:12 a covenant for all *g* to come:
17: 7 after you for the *g* to come,
17: 9 after you for the *g* to come.
Ex 20: 6 a thousand *g* of those
31:13 and you for the *g* to come,
Dt 7: 9 covenant of love to a thousand *g*
32: 7 consider the *g* long past.
1Ch 16:15 he commanded, for a thousand *g*,
Job 8: 8 "Ask the former *g*
Ps 22:30 future *g* will be told about the Lord
33:11 of his heart through all *g*.
45:17 your memory through all *g*;
89: 1 faithfulness known through all *g*.
90: 1 throughout all *g*.
100: 5 continues through all *g*.
102: 12 your renown endures through all *g*.
105: 8 he commanded, for a thousand *g*,
119: 90 continues through all *g*;
135: 13 renown, O LORD, through all *g*.
145: 13 dominion endures through all *g*.
146: 10 your God, O Zion, for all *g*.
Pr 27:24 and a crown is not secure for all *g*.
Isa 41: 4 forth the *g* from the beginning?
Isa 51: 8 my salvation through all *g*."
Lk 1:48 now on all *g* will call me blessed,
Eph 3: 5 not made known to men in other *g*
3:21 in Christ Jesus throughout all *g*,
Col 1:26 been kept hidden for ages and *g*,

GENEROSITY* (GENEROUS)

2Co 8: 2 poverty welled up in rich *g*.
9:11 and through us your *g* will result
9:13 and for your *g* in sharing with them

GENEROUS* (GENEROSITY)

Ps 37:26 They are always *g* and lend freely;
112: 5 Good will come to him who is *g*
Pr 11:25 A *g* man will prosper;
22: 9 A *g* man will himself be blessed,
Mt 20:15 Or are you envious because I am *g*
2Co 9: 5 Then it will be ready as a *g* gift,
9: 5 for the *g* gift you had promised.
9:11 way so that you can be *g*
1Ti 6:18 and to be *g* and willing to share.

GENTILE (GENTILES)

Ac 21:25 As for the *G* believers, we have
Ro 1:16 first for the Jew, then for the *G*.
2: 9 first for the Jew, then for the *G*;
2:10 first for the Jew, then for the *G*.
10:12 difference between Jew and *G*—

GENTILES (GENTILE)

Isa 42: 6 and a light for the *G*,
49: 6 also make you a light for the *G*,
49:22 "See, I will beckon to the *G*,
Lk 2:32 a light for revelation to the *G*
21:24 on by the *G* until the times
Ac 9:15 to carry my name before the *G*
10:45 been poured out even on the *G*.
11:18 granted even the *G* repentance unto
13:16 and you *G* who worship God,
13:46 of eternal life, we now turn to the *G*
13:47 I have made you a light for the *G*,
14:27 opened the door of faith to the *G*.
15:14 by taking from the *G* a people
18: 6 From now on I will go to the *G*."
22:21 I will send you far away to the *G*.'"
26:20 and in all Judea, and to the *G* also,
28:28 salvation has been sent to the *G*,
Ro 2:14 when *G*, who do not have the law,
3: 9 and *G* alike are all under sin.
3:29 Is he not the God of *G* too? Yes,
9:24 from the Jews but also from the *G*?
11:11 to the *G* to make Israel envious.
11:12 their loss means riches for the *G*,
11:13 as I am the apostle to the *G*,
15: 9 I will praise you among the *G*;
15: 9 so that the *G* may glorify God
1Co 1:23 block to Jews and foolishness to *G*,
Gal 1:16 I might preach him among the *G*,
2: 2 gospel that I preach among the *G*.
2: 8 my ministry as an apostle to the *G*.
2: 9 agreed that we should go to the *G*,
3: 8 that God would justify the *G*
3:14 to the *G* through Christ Jesus,
Eph 3: 6 the gospel the *G* are heirs together
3: 8 to the *G* the unsearchable riches
Col 1:27 among the *G* the glorious riches
1Ti 2: 7 a teacher of the true faith to the *G*.
2Ti 4:17 and all the *G* might hear it.

GENTLE* (GENTLENESS)

Dt 28:54 Even the most *g* and sensitive man
28:56 The most *g* and sensitive woman
28:56 and *g* that she would not venture
2Sa 18: 5 Be *g* with the young man Absalom
1Ki 19:12 And after the fire came a *g* whisper
Job 41: 3 Will he speak to you with *g* words?
Pr 15: 1 A *g* answer turns away wrath,
25:15 and a *g* tongue can break a bone.
Jer 11:19 I had been like a *g* lamb led
Zec 9: 9 *g* and riding on a donkey,
Mt 11:29 for I am *g* and humble in heart,
21: 5 *g* and riding on a donkey,
Ac 27:13 When a *g* south wind began
1Co 4:21 or in love and with a *g* spirit?
Eph 4: 2 Be completely humble and *g*;
1Th 2: 7 but we were *g* among you,
1Ti 3: 3 not violent but *g*, not quarrelsome,
1Pe 3: 4 the unfading beauty of a *g*

GENTLENESS* (GENTLE)

2Co 10: 1 By the meekness and *g* of Christ,
Gal 5:23 faithfulness, *g* and self-control.
Php 4: 5 Let your *g* be evident to all.
Col 3:12 kindness, humility, *g* and patience.
1Ti 6:11 faith, love, endurance and *g*.
1Pe 3:15 But do this with *g* and respect,

GENUINE*

2Co 6: 8 *g*, yet regarded as impostors;
Php 2:20 who takes a *g* interest
1Pe 1: 7 may be proved *g* and may result

GERIZIM

Dt 27:12 on Mount *G* to bless the people:

GERSHOM

Ex 2:22 and Moses named him *G*, saying,

GETHSEMANE*

Mt 26:36 disciples to a place called *G*,
Mk 14:32 They went to a place called *G*,

GHOST see also SPIRIT

Lk 24:39 a *g* does not have flesh and bones,

GIBEON

Jos 10:12 "O sun, stand still over *G*,

GIDEON*

Judge, also called Jerub-Baal; freed Israel from Midianites (Jdg 6-8; Heb 11:32). Given sign of fleece (Jdg 8:36-40).

GIFT (GIFTED GIFTS)

Pr 18:16 A *g* opens the way for the giver
21:14 A *g* given in secret soothes anger,
Ecc 3:13 in all his toil—this is the *g* of God.
Mt 5:23 if you are offering your *g*
Jn 4:10 "If you knew the *g* of God
Ac 1: 4 wait for the *g* my Father promised,
2:38 And you will receive the *g*
11:17 So if God gave them the same *g*
Ro 6:23 but the *g* of God is eternal life
12: 6 If a man's *g* is prophesying,
1Co 7: 7 each man has his own *g* from God;
2Co 8:12 the *g* is acceptable according
9:15 be to God for his indescribable *g*!
Eph 2: 8 it is the *g* of God—not by works,
1Ti 4:14 not neglect your *g*, which was
2Ti 1: 6 you to fan into flame the *g* of God,
Heb 6: 4 who have tasted the heavenly *g*,
Jas 1:17 and perfect *g* is from above,
1Pe 3: 7 with you of the gracious *g* of life,
4:10 should use whatever *g* he has
Rev 22:17 let him take the free *g* of the water

GIFTED* (GIFT)

1Co 14:37 he is a prophet or spiritually *g*,

GIFTS (GIFT)

Ps 76:11 bring *g* to the One to be feared.
112: 9 He has scattered abroad his *g*
Pr 25:14 of *g* he does not give.
Mt 2:11 and presented him with *g* of gold
7:11 Father in heaven give good *g*
7:11 to give good *g* to your children,
Lk 11:13 to give good *g* to your children,
Ac 10: 4 and *g* to the poor have come up
Ro 11:29 for God's *g* and his call are
12: 6 We have different *g*, according
1Co 12: 1 Now about spiritual *g*, brothers,
12: 4 There are different kinds of *g*,
12:28 those with *g* of administration,
12:30 all work miracles? Do all have *g*
12:31 But eagerly desire the greater *g*.
14: 1 and eagerly desire spiritual *g*,
14:12 eager to have spiritual *g*,
14:12 excel in *g* that build up the church.
2Co 9: 9 "He has scattered abroad his *g*
Eph 4: 8 and gave *g* to men."
Heb 2: 4 and *g* of the Holy Spirit distributed
9: 9 indicating that the *g* and sacrifices

GILEAD

1Ch 27:21 the half-tribe of Manasseh in *G*:
Jer 8:22 Is there no balm in *G*?
46:11 "Go up to *G* and get balm,

GILGAL

Jos 5: 9 So the place has been called *G*

GIRD*

Ps 45: 3 *G* your sword upon your side,

GIRL

Ge 24:16 *g* was very beautiful, a virgin;
2Ki 5: 2 a young *g* from Israel.
Mk 5:41 Little *g*, I say to you, get up!

GIVE (GAVE GIVEN GIVER GIVES GIVING LIFE-GIVING)

Ge 28: 4 you and your descendants the blessing *g* to Abraham
28:22 that you *g* me I will *g* you a tenth."
Ex 20:16 "You shall not *g* false testimony
30:15 The rich are not to *g* more
Nu 6:26 and *g* you peace."'
Dt 5:20 "You shall not *g* false testimony
15:10 *G* generously to him and do
15:14 *G* to him as the LORD your God
1Sa 1:11 then I will *g* him to the LORD

1Sa 1:28 So now I *g* him to the LORD.
2Ch 15: 7 be strong and do not *g* up,
Pr 21:26 but the righteous *g* without sparing
23:26 My son, *g* me your heart
25:21 if he is thirsty, *g* him water to drink
30: 8 but *g* me only my daily bread.
31:31 *G* her the reward she has earned,
Ecc 3: 6 a time to search and a time to *g* up,
Isa 42: 8 I will not *g* my glory to another
Eze 36:26 I will *g* you a new heart
Mt 6:11 *G* us today our daily bread.
7:11 know how to *g* good gifts
10: 8 Freely you have received, freely *g*.
16:19 I will *g* you the keys
22:21 "*G* to Caesar what is Caesar's,
Mk 8:37 Or what can a man *g* in exchange
10:19 not steal, do not *g* false testimony,
Lk 6:38 *G*, and it will be given to you.
11: 3 *G* us each day our daily bread.
11:13 Father in heaven *g* the Holy Spirit
14:33 who does not *g* up everything he
Jn 10:28 I *g* them eternal life, and they shall
13:34 "A new commandment I *g* you:
14:16 he will *g* you another Counselor
14:27 I do not *g* to you as the world gives.
14:27 leave with you; my peace I *g* you.
17: 2 people that he might *g* eternal life
Ac 20:35 blessed to *g* than to receive.' "
Ro 2: 7 immortality, he will *g* eternal life.
8:32 with him, graciously *g* us all things
12: 8 let him *g* generously;
13: 7 *G* everyone what you owe him:
14:12 each of us will *g* an account
2Co 9: 7 Each man should *g* what he has
Gal 2: 5 We did not *g* in to them
6: 9 reap a harvest if we do not *g* up.
Heb 10:25 Let us not *g* up meeting together,
Rev 14: 7 "Fear God and *g* him glory,

GIVEN (GIVE)
Nu 8:16 are to be *g* wholly to me.
Dt 26:11 things the LORD your God has *g*
Job 3:23 Why is life *g* to a man
Ps 115: 16 but the earth he has *g* to man.
Isa 9: 6 to us a son is *g*,
Mt 6:33 and all these things will be *g* to you
7: 7 "Ask and it will be *g* to you;
13:12 Whoever has will be *g* more,
22:30 people will neither marry nor be *g*
25:29 everyone who has will be *g* more,
Lk 6:38 Give, and it will be *g* to you.
8:10 kingdom of God has been *g* to you,
11: 9 Ask and it will be *g* to you;
22:19 saying, "This is my body *g* for you;
Jn 3:27 man can receive only what is *g* him
15: 7 you wish, and it will be *g* you.
17:24 I want those you have *g* me to be
17:24 the glory you have *g* me
18:11 the cup the Father has *g* me?"
Ac 5:32 whom God has *g* to those who
20:24 the task the Lord Jesus has *g* me—
Ro 5: 5 the Holy Spirit, whom he has *g* us.
1Co 4: 2 those who have been *g* a trust must
11:24 and when he had *g* thanks,
12:13 we were all *g* the one Spirit to drink
2Co 5: 5 and has *g* us the Spirit as a deposit,
Eph 1: 6 which he has freely *g* us
4: 7 to each one of us grace has been *g*
1Ti 4:14 was *g* you through a prophetic
1Jn 4:13 because he has *g* us of his Spirit.

GIVER* (GIVE)
Pr 18:16 A gift opens the way for the *g*
2Co 9: 7 for God loves a cheerful *g*.

GIVES (GIVE)
Job 35:10 who *g* songs in the night,
Ps 119: 130 The unfolding of your words *g* light;
Pr 3:34 but *g* grace to the humble.
11:24 One man *g* freely, yet gains
14:30 A heart at peace *g* life to the body,
15:30 good news *g* health to the bones.
19: 6 of a man who *g* gifts.
25:26 is a righteous man who *g* way
28:27 He who *g* to the poor will lack
29: 4 justice a king *g* a country stability,
Isa 40:29 He *g* strength to the weary
Hab 2:15 "Woe to him who *g* drink
Mt 10:42 if anyone *g* even a cup of cold water
Jn 5:21 even so the Son *g* life to whom he is
6:63 The Spirit *g* life; the flesh counts
1Co 15:57 He *g* us the victory
2Co 3: 6 the letter kills, but the Spirit *g* life.
1Th 4: 8 who *g* you his Holy Spirit.
Jas 1:25 into the perfect law that *g* freedom,
4: 6 but *g* grace to the humble."
1Pe 5: 5 but *g* grace to the humble."

GIVING (GIVE)
Ne 8: 8 *g* the meaning so that the people
Est 9:19 a day for *g* presents to each other.
Ps 19: 8 *g* joy to the heart.
Pr 15:23 A man finds joy in *g* an apt reply—
Mt 6: 4 so that your *g* may be in secret.
24:38 marrying and *g* in marriage,
Ac 15: 8 them by *g* the Holy Spirit to them,
2Co 8: 7 also excel in this grace of *g*.
Php 4:15 shared with me in the matter of *g*

GLAD* (GLADDENS GLADNESS)
Ex 4:14 his heart will be *g* when he sees you
Jos 22:33 They were *g* to hear the report
Jdg 8:25 "We'll be *g* to give them."
18:20 household?" Then the priest was *g*.
1Sa 19: 5 and you saw it and were *g*.
2Sa 1:20 daughters of the Philistines be *g*,
1Ki 8:66 *g* in heart for all the good things
1Ch 16:31 heavens rejoice, let the earth be *g*;
2Ch 7:10 and *g* in heart for the good things
Ps 5:11 let all who take refuge in you be *g*;
9: 2 I will be *g* and rejoice in you;
14: 7 let Jacob rejoice and Israel be *g*!
16: 9 Therefore my heart is *g*
21: 6 made him *g* with the joy
31: 7 I will be *g* and rejoice in your love,
32:11 Rejoice in the LORD and be *g*,
40:16 rejoice and be *g* in you;
45: 8 music of the strings makes you *g*.
46: 4 whose streams make *g* the city
48:11 the villages of Judah are *g*
53: 6 let Jacob rejoice and Israel be *g*!
58:10 The righteous will be *g*
67: 4 May the nations be *g* and sing
68: 3 But may the righteous be *g*
69:32 The poor will see and be *g*—
70: 4 rejoice and be *g* in you;
90:14 for joy and be *g* all our days.
90:15 Make us *g* for as many days
92: 4 For you make me *g* by your deeds,
96:11 heavens rejoice, let the earth be *g*;
97: 1 LORD reigns, let the earth be *g*;
97: 8 and the villages of Judah are *g*
105: 38 Egypt was *g* when they left,
107: 30 They were *g* when it grew calm,
118: 24 let us rejoice and be *g* in it.
149: 2 of Zion be *g* in their King.
Pr 23:15 then my heart will be *g*;
23:25 May your father and mother be *g*;
29: 6 a righteous one can sing and be *g*.
Ecc 8:15 sun than to eat and drink and be *g*.
Isa 25: 9 let us rejoice and be *g*
35: 1 and the parched land will be *g*;
65:18 But be *g* and rejoice forever
66:10 with Jerusalem and be *g* for her,
Jer 20:15 who made him very *g*, saying,
31:13 Then maidens will dance and be *g*,
41:13 were with him, they were *g*.
50:11 "Because you rejoice and are *g*,
La 4:21 be *g*, O Daughter of Edom,
Joel 2:21 be *g* and rejoice.
2:23 Be *g*, O people of Zion,
Hab 1:15 and so he rejoices and is *g*.
Zep 3:14 Be *g* and rejoice with all your heart
Zec 2:10 and be *g*, O Daughter of Zion.
8:19 will become joyful and *g* occasions
10: 7 their hearts will be *g* as with wine.
Mt 5:12 be *g*, because great is your reward
Lk 15:32 But we had to celebrate and be *g*,
Jn 4:36 and the reaper may be *g* together.
8:56 my day; he saw it and was *g*."
11:15 for your sake I am *g* I was not there
14:28 you would be *g* that I am going
Ac 2:26 Therefore my heart is *g*
2:46 together with *g* and sincere hearts,
11:23 he was *g* and encouraged them all
13:48 they were *g* and honored the word
15: 3 news made all the brothers very *g*.
15:31 were *g* for its encouraging message.
1Co 16:17 was *g* when Stephanas, Fortunatus
2Co 2: 2 who is left to make me *g*
7:16 I am *g* I can have complete
13: 9 We are *g* whenever we are weak
Gal 4:27 "Be *g*, O barren woman,
Php 2:17 I am *g* and rejoice with all of you.
2:18 So you too should be *g* and rejoice
2:28 you see him again you may be *g*
Rev 19: 7 Let us rejoice and be *g*

GLADDENS* (GLAD)
Ps 104: 15 wine that *g* the heart of man,

GLADNESS* (GLAD)
2Ch 29:30 So they sang praises with *g*
Est 8:16 a time of happiness and joy, *g*
8:17 there was joy and *g*
Job 3:22 who are filled with *g*
Ps 35:27 shout for joy and *g*;
45:15 They are led in with joy and *g*;
51: 8 Let me hear joy and *g*;
65:12 the hills are clothed with *g*.
100: 2 Worship the LORD with *g*;
Ecc 5:20 God keeps him occupied with *g*
9: 7 Go, eat your food with *g*,
Isa 16:10 *g* are taken away from the orchards
35:10 *G* and joy will overtake them,
51: 3 Joy and *g* will be found in her,
51:11 *G* and joy will overtake them,
61: 3 the oil of *g* / instead of mourning,
Jer 7:34 and *g* and to the voices of bride
16: 9 and *g* and to the voices of bride
25:10 from them the sounds of joy and *g*,
31:13 I will turn their mourning into *g*;
33:11 once more the sounds of joy and *g*,
48:33 Joy and *g* are gone
Joel 1:16 joy and *g*

GLAZE*
Pr 26:23 of *g* over earthenware

GLEAM*
Pr 4:18 of the righteous is like the first *g*
Da 10: 6 legs like the *g* of burnished bronze,

GLOAT (GLOATS)
Pr 24:17 Do not *g* when your enemy falls;

GLOATS* (GLOAT)
Pr 17: 5 whoever *g* over disaster will not go

GLORIES* (GLORY)
1Pe 1:11 and the *g* that would follow.

GLORIFIED* (GLORY)
Isa 66: 5 'Let the LORD be *g*,
Eze 39:13 day I am *g* will be a memorable day
Da 4:34 and *g* him who lives forever.
Jn 7:39 since Jesus had not yet been *g*.
11: 4 glory so that God's Son may be *g*
12:16 after Jesus was *g* did they realize
12:23 come for the Son of Man to be *g*.
12:28 "I have *g* it, and will glorify it again
13:31 Son of Man *g* and God is *g* in him.
13:32 If God is *g* in him, God will glorify
Ac 3:13 our fathers, has *g* his servant Jesus.
Ro 1:21 they neither *g* him as God
8:30 those he justified, he also *g*.
2Th 1:10 comes to be *g* in his holy people
1:12 of our Lord Jesus may be *g* in you,
1Pe 1:21 him from the dead and *g* him,

GLORIFIES* (GLORY)
Lk 1:46 My soul *g* the Lord
Jn 8:54 as your God, is the one who *g* me.

GLORIFY* (GLORY)
Ps 34: 3 *G* the LORD with me;
63: 3 my lips will *g* you.
69:30 and *g* him with thanksgiving.
86:12 I will *g* your name forever.
Isa 60:13 and I will *g* the place of my feet.
Da 4:37 and exalt and *g* the King of heaven,
Jn 8:54 Jesus replied, "If I *g* myself,
12:28 glorified it, and will *g* it again."
12:28 *g* your name!" Then a voice came
13:32 God will *g* the Son in himself,
13:32 in himself, and will *g* him at once.
17: 1 *G* your Son, that your Son may
17: 1 your Son, that your Son may *g* you.
17: 5 *g* me in your presence
21:19 death by which Peter would *g* God.
Ro 15: 6 and mouth you may *g* the God
15: 9 so that the Gentiles may *g* God
1Pe 2:12 and *g* God on the day he visits us.
Rev 16: 9 they refused to repent and *g* him.

GLORIFYING* (GLORY)
Lk 2:20 *g* and praising God

GLORIOUS* (GLORY)
Dt 28:58 not revere this *g* and awesome
33:29 and your *g* sword.
1Ch 29:13 and praise your *g* name.
Ne 9: 5 "Blessed be your *g* name,
Ps 16: 3 they are the *g* ones
45:13 All *g* is the princess
66: 2 make his praise *g*.
72:19 Praise be to his *g* name forever;
87: 3 *G* things are said of you,
111: 3 *G* and majestic are his deeds,
145: 5 of the *g* splendor of your majesty,
145: 12 the *g* splendor of your kingdom.
Isa 3: 8 defying his *g* presence.
4: 2 the LORD will be beautiful and *g*,
11:10 and his place of rest will be *g*.
12: 5 for he has done *g* things;
28: 1 to the fading flower, his *g* beauty,
28: 4 That fading flower, his *g* beauty,

Isa 28: 5 will be a *g* crown,
42:21 to make his law great and *g*.
60: 7 and I will adorn my *g* temple.
63:12 who sent his *g* arm of power
63:14 to make for yourself a *g* name.
63:15 from your lofty throne, holy and *g*.
64:11 *g* temple, where our fathers praised
Jer 13:18 for your *g* crowns
14:21 do not dishonor your *g* throne.
17:12 A *g* throne, exalted
48:17 how broken the *g* staff!'
Mt 19:28 the Son of Man sits on his *g* throne,
Lk 9:31 appeared in *g* splendor, talking
Ac 2:20 of the great and *g* day of the Lord.
Ro 8:21 and brought into the *g* freedom
2Co 3: 8 of the Spirit be even more *g?*
3: 9 how much more *g* is the ministry
3: 9 ministry that condemns men is *g*,
3:10 For what was *g* has no glory now
Eph 1: 6 to the praise of his *g* grace,
1:17 *g* Father, may give you the Spirit
1:18 the riches of his *g* inheritance
3:16 of his *g* riches he may strengthen
Php 3:21 so that they will be like his *g* body.
4:19 to his *g* riches in Christ Jesus.
Col 1:11 all power according to his *g* might
1:27 among the Gentiles the *g* riches
1Ti 1:11 to the *g* gospel of the blessed God,
Tit 2:13 the *g* appearing of our great God
Jas 2: 1 believers in our *g* Lord Jesus Christ
1Pe 1: 8 with an inexpressible and *g* joy,
Jude :24 before his *g* presence without fault

GLORIOUSLY* (GLORY)
Isa 24:23 and before its elders, *g*.

GLORY (GLORIES GLORIFIED GLORIFIES GLORIFY GLORIFYING GLORIOUS GLORIOUSLY)
Ex 14: 4 But I will gain *g* for myself
14:17 And I will gain *g* through Pharaoh
15:11 awesome in *g*,
16:10 and there was the *g* of the LORD
24:16 and the *g* of the LORD settled
33:18 Moses said, "Now show me your *g*
40:34 and the *g* of the LORD filled
Nu 14:21 the *g* of the LORD fills the whole
Dt 5:24 LORD our God has shown us his *g*
Jos 7:19 "My son, give *g* to the LORD,
1Sa 4:21 "The *g* has departed from Israel"—
1Ch 16:10 *G* in his holy name;
16:24 Declare his *g* among the nations,
16:28 ascribe to the LORD *g*
29:11 and the *g* and the majesty
Ps 8: 1 You have set your *g*
8: 5 and crowned him with *g* and honor
19: 1 The heavens declare the *g* of God;
24: 7 that the King of *g* may come in.
26: 8 the place where your *g* dwells.
29: 1 ascribe to the LORD *g*
29: 9 And in his temple all cry, "*G!*"
57: 5 let your *g* be over all the earth.
66: 2 Sing the *g* of his name;
72:19 the whole earth be filled with his *g*.
96: 3 Declare his *g* among the nations,
102: 15 of the earth will revere your *g*.
108: 5 and let your *g* be over all the earth.
149: 9 This is the *g* of all his saints.
Pr 19:11 it is to his *g* to overlook an offense.
25: 2 It is the *g* of God to conceal
Isa 4: 5 over all the *g* will be a canopy.
6: 3 the whole earth is full of his *g*."
24:16 "*G* to the Righteous One."
26:15 You have gained *g* for yourself;
35: 2 they will see the *g* of the LORD,
40: 5 the *g* of the LORD will be revealed
42: 8 I will not give my *g* to another
42:12 Let them give *g* to the LORD
43: 7 whom I created for my *g*,
44:23 he displays his *g* in Israel.
48:11 I will not yield my *g* to another.
66:18 and they will come and see my *g*.
66:19 They will proclaim my *g*
Eze 1:28 the likeness of the *g* of the LORD.
10: 4 the radiance of the *g* of the LORD.
43: 2 and the land was radiant with his *g*.
44: 4 and saw the *g* of the LORD filling
Hab 2:14 knowledge of the *g* of the LORD,
3: 3 His *g* covered the heavens
Zec 2: 5 'and I will be its *g* within.'
Mt 16:27 in his Father's *g* with his angels,
24:30 of the sky, with power and great *g*.
25:31 sit on his throne in heavenly *g*.
25:31 the Son of Man comes in his *g*,
Mk 8:38 in his Father's *g* with the holy
13:26 in clouds with great power and *g*.
Lk 2: 9 and the *g* of the Lord shone
2:14 saying, "*G* to God in the highest,
9:26 and in the *g* of the Father
Lk 9:26 of him when he comes in his *g*
9:32 they saw his *g* and the two men
19:38 in heaven and *g* in the highest!"
21:27 in a cloud with power and great *g*.
24:26 these things and then enter his *g?*"
Jn 1:14 We have seen his *g*, the *g* of the One
2:11 He thus revealed his *g*,
8:50 I am not seeking *g* for myself;
8:54 myself, my *g* means nothing.
11: 4 for God's *g* so that God's Son may
11:40 you would see the *g* of God?"
12:41 he saw Jesus' *g* and spoke about
14:13 so that the Son may bring *g*
15: 8 is to my Father's *g*, that you bear
16:14 He will bring *g* to me by taking
17: 4 I have brought you *g* on earth
17: 5 presence with the *g* I had with you
17:10 *g* has come to me through them.
17:22 given them the *g* that you gave
17:24 to see my *g*, the *g* you have given
Ac 7: 2 The God of *g* appeared
7:55 up to heaven and saw the *g* of God,
Ro 1:23 exchanged the *g* of the immortal
2: 7 by persistence in doing good seek *g*
2:10 then for the Gentile; but *g*,
3: 7 truthfulness and so increases his *g*,
3:23 and fall short of the *g* of God,
4:20 in his faith and gave *g* to God,
8:17 that we may also share in his *g*.
8:18 with the *g* that will be revealed
9: 4 theirs the divine *g*, the covenants,
9:23 riches of his *g* known to the objects
9:23 whom he prepared in advance for *g*
11:36 To him be the *g* forever! Amen.
15:17 Therefore I *g* in Christ Jesus
16:27 to the only wise God be *g* forever
1Co 2: 7 for our *g* before time began.
10:31 whatever you do, do it all for the *g*
11: 7 but the woman is the *g* of man.
11: 7 since he is the image and *g* of God;
11:15 it is her *g?* For long hair is given
15:43 it is raised in *g*; it is sown
2Co 1:20 spoken by us to the *g* of God.
3: 7 in letters on stone, came with *g*,
3: 7 the face of Moses because of its *g*,
3:10 comparison with the surpassing *g*.
3:10 what was glorious has no *g* now
3:11 how much greater is the *g*
3:11 what was fading away came with *g*,
3:18 faces all reflect the Lord's *g*,
3:18 likeness with ever-increasing *g*,
4: 4 of the gospel of the *g* of Christ,
4: 6 of the knowledge of the *g* of God
4:15 to overflow to the *g* of God.
4:17 us an eternal *g* that far outweighs
Gal 1: 5 to whom be *g* for ever and ever.
Eph 1:12 might be for the praise of his *g*.
1:14 to the praise of his *g*.
3:13 for you, which are your *g*.
3:21 to him be *g* in the church
Php 1:11 to the *g* and praise of God.
2:11 to the *g* of God the Father.
3: 3 of God, who *g* in Christ Jesus,
4:20 and Father be *g* for ever and ever.
Col 1:27 Christ in you, the hope of *g*.
3: 4 also will appear with him in *g*.
1Th 2:12 you into his kingdom and *g*.
2:19 in which we will *g* in the presence
2:20 Indeed, you are our *g* and joy.
2Th 2:14 in the *g* of our Lord Jesus Christ.
1Ti 1:17 be honor and *g* for ever and ever.
3:16 was taken up in *g*.
2Ti 2:10 is in Christ Jesus, with eternal *g*.
4:18 To him be *g* for ever and ever.
Heb 1: 3 The Son is the radiance of God's *g*
2: 7 you crowned him with *g* and honor
2: 9 now crowned with *g* and honor
2:10 In bringing many sons to *g*,
5: 5 take upon himself the *g*
9: 5 the ark were the cherubim of the *G*,
13:21 to whom be *g* for ever and ever.
1Pe 1: 7 *g* and honor when Jesus Christ is
1:24 and all their *g* is like the flowers
4:11 To him be the *g* and the power
4:13 overjoyed when his *g* is revealed.
4:14 for the Spirit of *g* and of God rests
5: 1 will share in the *g* to be revealed:
5: 4 of *g* that will never fade away.
5:10 you to his eternal *g* in Christ,
2Pe 1: 3 of him who called us by his own *g*
1:17 and *g* from God the Father
1:17 came to him from the Majestic *G*,
3:18 To him be *g* both now and forever!
Jude :25 to the only God our Savior be *g*,
Rev 1: 6 to him be *g* and power for ever
4: 9 the living creatures give *g*,
4:11 to receive *g* and honor and power,
5:12 and honor and *g* and praise!"
5:13 and honor and *g* and power,
Rev 7:12 Praise and *g*
11:13 and gave *g* to the God of heaven.
14: 7 "Fear God and give him *g*,
15: 4 and bring *g* to your name?
15: 8 with smoke from the *g* of God
19: 1 *g* and power belong to our God,
19: 7 and give him *g!*
21:11 It shone with the *g* of God,
21:23 for the *g* of God gives it light,
21:26 *g* and honor of the nations will be

GLOWING
Eze 8: 2 was as bright as *g* metal.
Rev 1:15 His feet were like bronze *g*

GLUTTONS* (GLUTTONY)
Pr 23:21 for drunkards and *g* become poor,
28: 7 of *g* disgraces his father.
Tit 1:12 always liars, evil brutes, lazy *g*."

GLUTTONY* (GLUTTONS)
Pr 23: 2 throat if you are given to *g*.

GNASHING
Mt 8:12 where there will be weeping and *g*

GNAT* (GNATS)
Mt 23:24 You strain out a *g* but swallow

GNATS (GNAT)
Ex 8:16 of Egypt the dust will become *g*."

GOADS
Ecc 12:11 The words of the wise are like *g*,
Ac 26:14 hard for you to kick against the *g*.'

GOAL*
Lk 13:32 on the third day I will reach my *g*.'
2Co 5: 9 So we make it our *g* to please him,
Gal 3: 3 to attain your *g* by human effort?
Php 3:14 on toward the *g* to win the prize
1Ti 1: 5 The *g* of this command is love,
1Pe 1: 9 for you are receiving the *g*

GOAT (GOATS SCAPEGOAT)
Ge 15: 9 "Bring me a heifer, a *g* and a ram,
30:32 and every spotted or speckled *g*.
37:31 slaughtered a *g* and dipped
Ex 26: 7 Make curtains of *g* hair for the tent
Lev 16: 9 shall bring the *g* whose lot falls
Nu 7:16 one male *g* for a sin offering;
Isa 11: 6 the leopard will lie down with the *g*
Da 8: 5 suddenly a *g* with a prominent

GOATS (GOAT)
Nu 7:17 five male *g* and five male lambs
Mt 25:32 separates the sheep from the *g*.
Heb 10: 4 of bulls and *g* to take away sins.

GOD (GOD'S GODLINESS GODLY GODS)
Ge 1: 1 In the beginning *G* created
1: 2 and the Spirit of *G* was hovering
1: 3 And *G* said, "Let there be light,"
1: 7 So *G* made the expanse
1: 9 And *G* said, "Let the water
1:11 Then *G* said, "Let the land produce
1:20 And *G* said, "Let the water teem
1:21 So *G* created the great creatures
1:25 *G* made the wild animals according
1:26 Then *G* said, "Let us make man
1:27 So *G* created man in his own image
1:31 *G* saw all that he had made,
2: 3 And *G* blessed the seventh day
2: 7 And the LORD *G* formed the man
2: 8 the LORD *G* had planted a garden
2:18 The LORD *G* said, "It is not good
2:22 Then the LORD *G* made a woman
3: 1 to the woman, "Did *G* really say,
3: 5 you will be like *G*, knowing good
3: 8 from the LORD *G* among the trees
3: 9 But the LORD *G* called to the man
3:21 The LORD *G* made garments
3:22 LORD *G* said, "The man has now
3:23 So the LORD *G* banished him
5: 1 When *G* created man, he made him
5:22 Enoch walked with *G* 300 years
5:24 because *G* took him away.
6: 2 sons of *G* saw that the daughters
6: 9 of his time, and he walked with *G*.
6:12 *G* saw how corrupt the earth had
8: 1 But *G* remembered Noah
9: 1 Then *G* blessed Noah and his sons,
9: 6 for in the image of *G*
9:16 everlasting covenant between *G*
14:18 He was priest of *G* Most High,
14:19 Blessed be Abram by *G* Most High,
16:13 "You are the *G* who sees me,"
17: 1 "I am *G* Almighty; walk before me
17: 7 to be your *G* and the *G*
21: 4 him, as *G* commanded him.

Ge 21: 6 "G has brought me laughter,
21:20 G was with the boy as he grew up.
21:22 G is with you in everything you do.
21:33 name of the LORD, the Eternal G.
22: 1 Some time later G tested Abraham.
22: 8 "G himself will provide the lamb
22:12 Now I know that you fear G,
25:11 Abraham's death, G blessed his
28:12 and the angels of G were ascending
28:17 other than the house of G;
31:42 But G has seen my hardship
31:50 remember that G is a witness
32: 1 and the angels of G met him.
32:28 because you have struggled with G
32:30 "It is because I saw G face to face,
33:11 for G has been gracious to me
35: 1 and build an altar there to G,
35: 5 and the terror of G fell
35:10 G said to him, "Your name is Jacob
35:11 G said to him, "I am G Almighty;
41:51 G has made me forget all my
41:52 G has made me fruitful in the land
50:20 but G intended it for good
50:24 But G will surely come to your aid
Ex 2:24 G heard their groaning
3: 5 "Do not come any closer," G said.
3: 6 because he was afraid to look at G.
3:12 And G said, "I will be with you.
3:14 what shall I tell them?" G said
4:27 he met Moses at the mountain of G
6: 7 own people, and I will be your G.
8:10 is no one like the LORD our G.
10:16 sinned against the LORD your G
13:18 So G led the people
15: 2 He is my G, and I will praise him,
16:12 that I am the LORD your G.' "
17: 9 with the staff of G in my hands."
18: 5 camped near the mountain of G.
19: 3 Then Moses went up to G,
20: 1 And G spoke all these words:
20: 2 the LORD your G, who brought
20: 5 the LORD your G, am a jealous G,
20: 7 the name of the LORD your G,
20:10 a Sabbath to the LORD your G.
20:12 the LORD your G is giving you.
20:19 But do not have G speak to us
20:20 the fear of G will be with you
22:20 "Whoever sacrifices to any g other
22:28 "Do not blaspheme G
23:19 to the house of the LORD your G.
31:18 inscribed by the finger of G.
34: 6 the compassionate and gracious G,
34:14 name is Jealous, is a jealous G.
Lev 2:13 salt of the covenant of your G out
11:44 the LORD your G; consecrate
18:21 not profane the name of your G.
19: 2 the LORD your G, am holy.
20: 7 because I am the LORD your G.
21: 6 They must be holy to their G
22:33 out of Egypt to be your G.
26:12 walk among you and be your G,
Nu 15:40 and will be consecrated to your G.
22:18 the command of the LORD my G.
22:38 I must speak only what G puts
23:19 G is not a man, that he should lie,
25:13 zealous for the honor of his G
Dt 1:17 for judgment belongs to G.
1:21 the LORD your G has given you
1:30 The LORD your G, who is going
3:22 LORD your G himself will fight
3:24 For what g is there in heaven
4:24 is a consuming fire, a jealous G.
4:29 there you seek the LORD your G,
4:31 the LORD your G is a merciful G;
4:39 heart this day that the LORD is G
5: 9 the LORD your G, am a jealous G,
5:11 the name of the LORD your G,
5:12 the LORD your G has commanded
5:14 a Sabbath to the LORD your G.
5:15 the LORD your G brought you out
5:16 the LORD your G has commanded
5:16 the LORD your G is giving you.
5:24 LORD our G has shown us his
5:26 of the living G speaking out of fire,
6: 2 them may fear the LORD your G
6: 4 LORD our G, the LORD is one.
6: 5 Love the LORD your G
6:13 the LORD your G, serve him only
6:16 Do not test the LORD your G
7: 6 holy to the LORD your G.
7: 9 your G is G; he is the faithful G,
7:12 the LORD your G will keep his
7:19 LORD your G will do the same
7:21 is a great and awesome G.
8: 5 the LORD your G disciplines you.
8:11 do not forget the LORD your G,
8:18 But remember the LORD your G,
9:10 inscribed by the finger of G.
10:12 but to fear the LORD your G,

Dt 10:14 the LORD your G belong
10:17 For the LORD your G is G of gods
10:21 He is your praise; he is your G,
11: 1 Love the LORD your G
11:13 to love the LORD your G
12:12 rejoice before the LORD your G,
12:28 in the eyes of the LORD your G.
13: 3 The LORD your G is testing you
13: 4 the LORD your G you must
15: 6 the LORD your G will bless you
15:19 the LORD your G every firstborn
16:11 rejoice before the LORD your G
16:17 the LORD your G has blessed you.
18:13 before the LORD your G.
18:15 The LORD your G will raise up
19: 9 to love the LORD your G
22: 5 the LORD your G detests anyone
23: 5 the LORD your G loves you.
23:14 the LORD your G moves about
23:21 a vow to the LORD your G,
25:16 the LORD your G detests anyone
26: 5 declare before the LORD your G:
29:13 that he may be your G
29:29 belong to the LORD our G,
30: 2 return to the LORD your G
30: 4 the LORD your G will gather you
30: 6 The LORD your G will circumcise
30:16 today to love the LORD your G,
30:20 you may love the LORD your G,
31: 6 for the LORD your G goes
32: 3 Oh, praise the greatness of our G!
32: 4 A faithful G who does no wrong,
33:27 The eternal G is your refuge,
Jos 1: 9 for the LORD your G will be
14: 8 the LORD my G wholeheartedly.
14: 9 the LORD my G wholeheartedly.'
14:14 the G of Israel, wholeheartedly.
22: 5 to love the LORD your G,
22:22 The Mighty One, G, the LORD!
22:34 Between Us that the LORD is G.
23: 8 to hold fast to the LORD your G,
23:11 careful to love the LORD your G.
23:14 the LORD your G gave you has
23:15 of the LORD your G has come true
24:19 He is a holy G; he is a jealous G.
24:23 to the LORD, the G of Israel."
Jdg 5: 3 to the LORD, the G of Israel.
16:28 O G, please strengthen me just
Ru 1:16 be my people and your G my G.
2:12 by the LORD, the G of Israel,
1Sa 2: 2 there is no Rock like our G.
2: 3 for the LORD is a G who knows,
2:25 another man, G may mediate
10:26 men whose hearts G had touched.
12:12 the LORD your G was your king.
16:15 spirit from G is tormenting you.
17:26 defy the armies of the living G?"
17:36 defied the armies of the living G.
17:45 the G of the armies of Israel,
17:46 world will know that there is a G
23:16 and helped him find strength in G.
28:15 and G has turned away from me.
30: 6 strength in the LORD his G.
2Sa 7:22 and there is no G but you,
7:23 on earth that G went out to redeem
14:14 But G does not take away life;
21:14 G answered prayer in behalf
22: 3 my G is my rock, in whom I take
22:31 "As for G, his way is perfect;
22:32 And who is the Rock except our G
22:33 It is G who arms me with strength
22:47 Exalted be G, the Rock, my Savior!
1Ki 2: 3 what the LORD your G requires:
4:29 G gave Solomon wisdom
5: 5 for the Name of the LORD my G,
8:23 there is no G like you in heaven
8:27 "But will G really dwell on earth?
8:60 may know that the LORD is G
8:61 committed to the LORD our G,
10:24 to hear the wisdom G had put
15:30 he provoked the LORD, the G
18:21 If the LORD is G, follow him;
18:36 it be known today that you are G
18:37 are G, and that you are turning
20:28 a g of the hills and not a g
2Ki 5:15 "Now I know that there is no G
18: 5 in the LORD, the G of Israel.
19:15 G of Israel, enthroned
19:19 Now, O LORD our G, deliver us
1Ch 12:18 for your G will help you."
13: 2 if it is the will of the LORD our G,
16:35 Cry out, "Save us, O G our Savior;
17:20 and there is no G but you,
17:24 the G over Israel, is Israel's G!'
21: 8 said to G, "I have sinned greatly
22: 1 house of the LORD G is to be here,
22:19 soul to seeking the LORD your G.
28: 2 for the footstool of our G,
28: 9 acknowledge the G of your father,

1Ch 28:20 for the LORD G, my G, is with you
29: 1 not for man but for the LORD G.
29: 2 provided for the temple of my G—
29: 3 of my G I now give my personal
29:10 G of our father Israel,
29:13 Now, our G, we give you thanks,
29:16 O LORD our G, as for all this
29:17 my G, that you test the heart
29:18 G of our fathers Abraham,
2Ch 2: 4 for the Name of the LORD my G
5:14 of the LORD filled the temple of G
6: 4 be to the LORD, the G of Israel,
6:14 there is no G like you in heaven
6:18 "But will G really dwell on earth
10:15 for this turn of events was from G,
13:12 G is with us; he is our leader.
15: 3 was without the true G,
15:12 the G of their fathers,
15:15 They sought G eagerly,
18:13 I can tell him only what my G says
19: 3 have set your heart on seeking G."
19: 7 with the LORD our G there is no
20: 6 are you not the G who is in heaven?
20:20 Have faith in the LORD your G
25: 8 for G has the power to help
26: 5 sought the LORD, G gave him
30: 9 for the LORD your G is gracious
30:19 who sets his heart on seeking G—
31:21 he sought his G and worked
32:31 G left him to test him
33:12 the favor of the LORD his G
34:33 fail to follow the LORD, the G
Ezr 6:21 to seek the LORD, the G of Israel.
7:18 accordance with the will of your G.
7:23 Whatever the G of heaven has
8:22 "The gracious hand of our G is
8:31 The hand of our G was on us,
9: 6 "O my G, I am too ashamed
9: 9 our G has not deserted us
9:13 our G, you have punished us less
9:15 G of Israel, you are righteous!
Ne 1: 5 the great and awesome G,
5: 9 fear of our G to avoid the reproach
5:15 for G I did not act like that.
7: 2 feared G more than most men do.
8: 8 from the Book of the Law of G,
8:18 from the Book of the Law of G.
9: 5 and praise the LORD your G,
9:17 But you are a forgiving G,
9:31 you are a gracious and merciful G.
9:32 the great, mighty and awesome G,
10:29 oath to follow the Law of G given
10:39 not neglect the house of our G."
12:43 G had given them great joy.
13:11 Why is the house of G neglected?"
13:26 He was loved by his G,
13:31 Remember me with favor, O my G.
Job 1: 1 he feared G and shunned evil.
1:22 by charging G with wrongdoing.
2:10 Shall we accept good from G,
4:17 a mortal be more righteous than G?
5:17 is the man whom G corrects;
8: 3 Does G pervert justice?
8:20 "Surely G does not reject
9: 2 a mortal be righteous before G?
11: 7 Can you fathom the mysteries of G
12:13 "To G belong wisdom and power;
16: 7 Surely, O G, you have worn me out
19:26 yet in my flesh I will see G;
21:19 'G stores up a man's punishment
21:22 Can anyone teach knowledge to G,
22:12 "Is not G in the heights of heaven?
22:13 Yet you say, 'What does G know?
22:21 "Submit to G and be at peace
25: 2 "Dominion and awe belong to G;
25: 4 can a man be righteous before G?
26: 6 Death is naked before G;
30:20 O G, but you do not answer;
31: 6 let G weigh me in honest scales
31:14 do when G confronts me?
32:13 let G refute him, not man.'
33: 6 I am just like you before G;
33:14 For G does speak—now one way,
33:26 He prays to G and finds favor
34:10 Far be it from G to do evil,
34:12 is unthinkable that G would do
34:23 G has no need to examine men
34:33 Should G then reward you
36: 5 "G is mighty, but does not despise
36:26 is G— beyond our understanding!
37:22 G comes in awesome majesty.
Ps 5: 4 You are not a G who takes pleasure
7:11 G is a righteous judge,
10:14 O G, do see trouble and grief;
14: 5 for G is present in the company
18: 2 my G is my rock, in whom I take
18:28 my G turns my darkness into light.
18:30 As for G, his way is perfect;
18:31 And who is the Rock except our G

Ps 18:32 It is G who arms me with strength
18:46 Exalted be G my Savior!
19: 1 The heavens declare the glory of G;
22: 1 G, my G, why have you forsaken
22:10 womb you have been my G.
27: 9 O G my Savior.
29: 3 the G of glory thunders,
31: 5 redeem me, O LORD, the G
31:14 I say, "You are my G."
33:12 the nation whose G is the LORD,
35:24 righteousness, O LORD my G;
37:31 The law of his G is in his heart;
40: 3 a hymn of praise to our G.
40: 8 I desire to do your will, O my G;
42: 1 so my soul pants for you, O G.
42: 2 thirsts for G, for the living G.
42: 5 Put your hope in G,
42: 8 a prayer to the G of my life.
42:11 Put your hope in G,
43: 4 to G, my joy and my delight.
44: 8 In G we make our boast all day
45: 6 O G, will last for ever and ever;
45: 7 therefore G, your G, has set you
46: 1 G is our refuge and strength,
46: 5 G will help her at break of day.
46:10 "Be still, and know that I am G;
47: 1 shout to G with cries of joy.
47: 6 Sing praises to G, sing praises;
47: 7 For G is the King of all the earth;
48: 9 Within your temple, O G,
49: 7 or give to G a ransom for him—
50: 2 G shines forth.
50: 3 Our G comes and will not be silent;
51: 1 Have mercy on me, O G,
51:10 Create in me a pure heart, O G,
51:17 O G, you will not despise.
53: 2 any who seek G.
54: 4 Surely G is my help;
55:19 G, who is enthroned forever,
56: 4 In G, whose word I praise,
56:10 In G, whose word I praise,
56:13 that I may walk before G
57: 3 G sends his love and his
57: 7 My heart is steadfast, O G,
59:17 are my fortress, my loving G.
62: 1 My soul finds rest in G alone;
62: 7 my honor depend on G;
62: 8 for G is our refuge.
62:11 One thing G has spoken,
63: 1 O G, you are my G,
65: 5 O G our Savior,
66: 1 Shout with joy to G, all the earth!
66: 3 Say to G, "How awesome are your
66: 5 Come and see what G has done,
66:16 listen, all you who fear G;
66:20 Praise be to G,
68: 4 Sing to G, sing praise to his name,
68: 6 G sets the lonely in families,
68:20 Our G is a G who saves;
68:24 has come into view, O G,
68:35 You are awesome, O G,
69: 5 You know my folly, O G;
70: 1 Hasten, O G, to save me;
70: 4 "Let G be exalted!"
70: 5 come quickly to me, O G.
71:17 my youth, O G, you have taught
71:18 do not forsake me, O G,
71:19 reaches to the skies, O G,
71:22 harp for your faithfulness, O my G;
73:17 me till I entered the sanctuary of G;
73:26 but G is the strength of my heart
76:11 Make vows to the LORD your G
77:13 What g is so great as our God?
77:14 You are the G who performs
78:19 Can G spread a table in the desert?
79: 9 Help us, O G our Savior,
81: 1 Sing for joy to G our strength;
82: 1 G presides in the great assembly;
84: 2 out for the living G.
84:10 a doorkeeper in the house of my G
84:11 For the LORD G is a sun
86:12 O Lord my G, with all my heart;
86:15 a compassionate and gracious G,
87: 3 O city of G: Selah
89: 7 of the holy ones G is greatly feared;
90: 2 to everlasting you are G.
91: 2 my G, in whom I trust."
94:22 my G the rock in whom I take
95: 7 for he is our G
99: 8 you were to Israel a forgiving G,
99: 9 Exalt the LORD our G
100: 3 Know that the LORD is G.
108: 1 My heart is steadfast, O G;
113: 5 Who is like the LORD our G,
115: 3 Our G is in heaven;
116: 5 our G is full of compassion.
123: 2 look to the LORD our G,
136: 2 Give thanks to the G of gods.
136: 26 Give thanks to the G of heaven.

Ps 139: 17 to me are your thoughts, O G!
139: 23 Search me, O G, and know my
143: 10 for you are my G;
144: 2 He is my loving G and my fortress,
147: 1 is to sing praises to our G,
Pr 3: 4 in the sight of G and man.
14:31 to the needy honors G.
25: 2 of G to conceal a matter;
30: 5 "Every word of G is flawless;
Ecc 2:26 G gives wisdom, knowledge
3:11 cannot fathom what G has done
3:13 in all his toil—this is the gift of G.
3:14 G does it so that men will revere him.
5: 4 When you make a vow to G,
5:19 in his work—this is a gift of G.
8:12 who are reverent before G.
11: 5 cannot understand the work of G,
12: 7 the spirit returns to G who gave it.
12:13 Fear G and keep his
Isa 5:16 the holy G will show himself holy
9: 6 Wonderful Counselor, Mighty G,
12: 2 Surely G is my salvation;
25: 9 "Surely this is our G;
28:11 G will speak to this people,
29:23 will stand in awe of the G of Israel.
30:18 For the LORD is a G of justice.
35: 4 your G will come,
37:16 you alone are G over all
40: 1 says your G.
40: 3 a highway for our G.
40: 8 the word of our G stands forever."
40:18 then, will you compare G?
40:28 The LORD is the everlasting G,
41:10 not be dismayed, for I am your G.
41:13 For I am the LORD, your G,
43:10 Before me no g was formed,
44: 6 apart from me there is no G.
44:15 he also fashions a g and worships it;
45:18 he is G;
48:17 "I am the LORD your G,
52: 7 "Your G reigns!"
52:12 G of Israel will be your rear guard.
55: 7 to our G, for he will freely pardon.
57:21 says my G, "for the wicked."
59: 2 you from your G;
60:19 and your G will be your glory.
61: 2 and the day of vengeance of our G,
61:10 my soul rejoices in my G.
62: 5 so will your G rejoice over you.
Jer 7:23 I will be your G and you will be my
10:10 But the LORD is the true G;
10:12 But G made the earth by his power;
23:23 "Am I only a G nearby,"
23:36 distort the words of the living G,
31:33 I will be their G,
32:27 "I am the LORD, the G
42: 6 for we will obey the LORD our G."
51:10 what the LORD our G has done.'
51:56 For the LORD is a G of retribution
Eze 28:13 the garden of G;
34:31 and I am your G, declares
Da 2:28 there is a G in heaven who reveals
3:17 the G we serve is able to save us
3:29 for no other g can save in this way
6:16 "May your G, whom you serve
9: 4 O Lord, the great and awesome G,
10:12 to humble yourself before your G,
11:36 things against the G of gods.
Hos 1: 9 my people, and I am not your G.
1:10 will be called 'sons of the living G.'
4: 6 you have ignored the law of your G
6: 6 acknowledgment of G rather
9: 8 The prophet, along with my G,
12: 6 and wait for your G always.
Joel 2:13 Return to the LORD your G,
2:23 rejoice in the LORD your G,
Am 4:12 prepare to meet your G, O Israel."
4:13 the LORD G Almighty is his name
Jnh 1: 6 Get up and call on your g!
4: 2 a gracious and compassionate G,
Mic 6: 8 and to walk humbly with your G.
7: 7 I wait for G my Savior;
7:18 Who is a G like you,
Na 1: 2 LORD is a jealous and avenging G;
Hab 3:18 I will be joyful in G my Savior.
Zep 3:17 The LORD your G is with you,
Zec 14: 5 Then the LORD my G will come,
Mal 2:10 Father? Did not one G create us?
2:16 says the LORD G of Israel,
3: 8 Will a man rob G? Yet you rob me.
Mt 1:23 which means, "G with us."
4: 4 comes from the mouth of G.'"
4: 7 'Do not put the Lord your G
4:10 'Worship the Lord your G,
5: 8 for they will see G.
6:24 You cannot serve both G
19: 6 Therefore what G has joined
19:26 but with G all things are possible."
22:21 and to G what is God's."

Mt 22:32 He is not the G of the dead
22:37 "'Love the Lord your G
27:46 which means, "My G, my G,
Mk 2: 7 Who can forgive sins but G alone?"
7:13 Thus you nullify the word of G
10: 6 of creation G 'made them male
10: 9 Therefore what G has joined
10:18 "No one is good—except G alone.
10:27 all things are possible with G."
11:22 "Have faith in G," Jesus answered.
12:17 and to G what is God's."
12:29 the Lord our G, the Lord is one.
12:30 Love the Lord your G
15:34 which means, "My G, my G,
16:19 and he sat at the right hand of G.
Lk 1:30 Mary, you have found favor with G
1:37 For nothing is impossible with G."
1:47 my spirit rejoices in G my Savior,
2:14 "Glory to G in the highest,
2:52 and in favor with G and men.
4: 8 'Worship the Lord your G
5:21 Who can forgive sins but G alone?"
8:39 tell how much G has done for you."
10: 9 'The kingdom of G is near you.'
10:27 "'Love the Lord your G
13:18 "What is the kingdom of G like?
18:19 "No one is good—except G alone.
18:27 with men is possible with G."
20:25 and to G what is God's."
20:38 He is not the G of the dead,
22:69 at the right hand of the mighty G."
Jn 1: 1 was with G, and the Word was G.
1:18 ever seen G, but G the One and Only,
1:29 Lamb of G, who takes away the sin
3:16 "For G so loved the world that he
3:34 the one whom G has sent speaks
4:24 G is spirit, and his worshipers must
5:44 praise that comes from the only G?
6:29 answered, "The work of G is this:
7:17 my teaching comes from G or
8:42 to them, "If G were your Father,
8:47 belongs to G hears what G says.
11:40 you would see the glory of G?"
13: 3 from G and was returning to G;
13:31 of Man glorified and G is glorified
14: 1 Trust in G; trust also in me.
17: 3 the only true G, and Jesus Christ,
20:17 your Father, to my G and your G
20:28 "My Lord and my G!"
20:31 the Son of G, and that
Ac 2:11 wonders of G in our own tongues!"
2:24 But G raised him from the dead,
2:33 Exalted to the right hand of G,
2:36 G has made this Jesus, whom you
3:15 but G raised him from the dead.
3:19 Repent, then, and turn to G,
4:31 and spoke the word of G boldly.
5: 4 You have not lied to men but to G
5:29 "We must obey G rather than men!
5:31 G exalted him to his own right
5:32 whom G has given
7:55 to heaven and saw the glory of G,
8:21 your heart is not right before G.
11: 9 anything impure that G has made
12:24 But the word of G continued
13:32 What G promised our fathers he
15:10 to test G by putting on the necks
17:23 TO AN UNKNOWN G.
17:30 In the past G overlooked such
20:27 to you the whole will of G.
20:32 "Now I commit you to G
24:16 keep my conscience clear before G
Ro 1:16 the power of G for the salvation
1:17 a righteousness from G is revealed,
1:18 The wrath of G is being revealed
1:24 Therefore G gave them
1:26 G gave them over to shameful lusts
2:11 For G does not show favoritism.
2:16 when G will judge men's secrets
3: 4 Let G be true, and every man a liar.
3:19 world held accountable to G.
3:23 and fall short of the glory of G,
3:29 Is G the G of Jews only? Is he not
4: 3 say? "Abraham believed G,
4: 6 to whom G credits righteousness
4:17 the G who gives life to the dead
4:24 to whom G will credit
5: 1 we have peace with G
5: 5 because G has poured out his love
5: 8 G demonstrates his own love for us
6:22 and have become slaves to G,
6:23 but the gift of G is eternal life
8: 7 the sinful mind is hostile to G.
8:17 heirs of G and co-heirs with Christ,
8:28 in all things G works for the good
9:14 What then shall we say? Is G unjust
9:18 Therefore G has mercy
10: 9 in your heart that G raised him
11: 2 G did not reject his people,

Ro 11:22 the kindness and sternness of *G:*
11:32 For *G* has bound all men
13: 1 exist have been established by *G.*
14:12 give an account of himself to *G.*
16:20 *G* of peace will soon crush Satan
1Co 1:18 are being saved it is the power of *G.*
1:20 Has not *G* made foolish
1:25 For the foolishness of *G* is wiser
1:27 But *G* chose the foolish things
2: 9 what *G* has prepared
2:11 of *G* except the Spirit of *G.*
3: 6 watered it, but *G* made it grow.
3:17 God's temple, *G* will destroy
6:20 Therefore honor *G* with your body.
7: 7 each man has his own gift from *G;*
7:15 *G* has called us to live in peace.
7:20 was in when *G* called him.
7:24 each man, as responsible to *G,*
8: 3 man who loves *G* is known by *G.*
8: 8 food does not bring us near to *G;*
10:13 *G* is faithful; he will not let you be
10:31 do it all for the glory of *G.*
12:24 But *G* has combined the members
14:33 For *G* is not a *G* of disorder
15:24 over the kingdom to *G* the Father
15:28 so that *G* may be all in all.
15:34 are some who are ignorant of *G*—
15:57 be to *G!* He gives us the victory
2Co 1: 9 rely on ourselves but on *G,*
2:14 be to *G,* who always leads us
2:15 For we are to *G* the aroma of Christ
2:17 we do not peddle the word of *G*
3: 5 but our competence comes from *G.*
4: 2 nor do we distort the word of *G.*
4: 7 this all-surpassing power is from *G*
5: 5 Now it is *G* who has made us
5:19 that *G* was reconciling the world
5:20 though *G* were making his appeal
5:21 *G* made him who had no sin
6:16 we are the temple of the living *G.*
9: 7 for *G* loves a cheerful giver.
9: 8 *G* is able to make all grace abound
10:13 to the field *G* has assigned to us,
Gal 2: 6 *G* does not judge by external
3: 5 Does *G* give you his Spirit
3: 6 Abraham: "He believed *G,*
3:11 justified before *G* by the law,
3:26 You are all sons of *G* through faith
6: 7 not be deceived: *G* cannot be
Eph 1:22 *G* placed all things under his feet
2: 8 it is the gift of *G*— not by works,
2:10 which *G* prepared in advance for us
2:22 in which *G* lives by his Spirit.
4: 6 one baptism; one *G* and Father
4:24 to be like *G* in true righteousness
5: 1 Be imitators of *G,* therefore,
6: 6 doing the will of *G* from your heart.
Php 2: 6 Who, being in very nature *G,*
2: 9 Therefore *G* exalted him
2:13 for it is *G* who works in you to will
4: 7 peace of *G,* which transcends all
4:19 And my *G* will meet all your needs
Col 1:19 For *G* was pleased
2:13 *G* made you alive with Christ.
1Th 2: 4 trying to please men but *G,*
2:13 but as it actually is, the word of *G,*
3: 9 How can we thank *G* enough
4: 7 For *G* did not call us to be impure,
4: 9 taught by *G* to love each other.
5: 9 For *G* did not appoint us
1Ti 2: 5 one mediator between *G* and men,
4: 4 For everything *G* created is good,
5: 4 for this is pleasing to *G.*
2Ti 1: 6 you to fan into flame the gift of *G,*
Tit 1: 2 which *G,* who does not lie,
2:13 glorious appearing of our great *G*
Heb 1: 1 In the past *G* spoke
3: 4 but *G* is the builder of everything.
4: 4 "And on the seventh day *G* rested
4:12 For the word of *G* is living
6:10 *G* is not unjust; he will not forget
6:18 in which it is impossible for *G* to lie
7:19 by which we draw near to *G.*
7:25 come to *G* through him,
10:22 draw near to *G* with a sincere heart
10:31 to fall into the hands of the living *G*
11: 5 commended as one who pleased *G.*
11: 6 faith it is impossible to please *G,*
12: 7 as discipline; *G* is treating you
12:10 but *G* disciplines us for our good,
12:29 for our "*G* is a consuming fire."
13:15 offer to *G* a sacrifice of praise—
Jas 1:12 crown of life that *G* has promised
1:13 For *G* cannot be tempted by evil,
1:27 Religion that *G* our Father accepts
2:19 You believe that there is one *G.*
2:23 "Abraham believed *G,*
4: 4 the world becomes an enemy of *G.*
4: 6 "*G* opposes the proud

Jas 4: 8 Come near to *G* and he will come
1Pe 1:23 the living and enduring word of *G.*
2:20 this is commendable before *G.*
3:18 the unrighteous, to bring you to *G.*
4:11 it with the strength *G* provides,
5: 5 because, "*G* opposes the proud
2Pe 1:21 but men spoke from *G*
2: 4 For if *G* did not spare angels
1Jn 1: 5 *G* is light; in him there is no
2:17 the will of *G* lives forever.
3: 1 we should be called children of *G!*
3: 9 born of *G* will continue to sin,
3:10 we know who the children of *G* are
3:20 For *G* is greater than our hearts,
4: 7 for love comes from *G.*
4: 8 not know *G,* because *G* is love.
4: 9 This is how *G* showed his love
4:11 Dear friends, since *G* so loved us,
4:12 No one has ever seen *G;*
4:15 *G* lives in him and he in *G.*
4:16 *G* is love.
4:20 "I love *G,*" yet hates his brother,
4:21 Whoever loves *G* must
5: 2 that we love the children of *G:*
5: 3 love for *G:* to obey his commands.
5: 4 born of *G* overcomes the world.
5:10 does not believe *G* has made him
5:14 have in approaching *G:*
5:18 born of *G* does not continue to sin;
Rev 4: 8 holy is the Lord *G* Almighty,
7:12 be to our *G* for ever and ever.
7:17 *G* will wipe away every tear
11:16 fell on their faces and worshiped *G,*
15: 3 Lord *G* Almighty.
17:17 For *G* has put it into their hearts
19: 6 For our Lord *G* Almighty reigns.
21: 3 Now the dwelling of *G* is with men,
21:23 for the glory of *G* gives it light,

GOD-BREATHED* (BREATH)
2Ti 3:16 All Scripture is *G* and is useful

GOD-FEARING* (FEAR)
Ecc 8:12 that it will go better with *G* men,
Ac 2: 5 staying in Jerusalem *G* Jews
10: 2 all his family were devout and *G;*
10:22 He is a righteous and *G* man,
13:26 of Abraham, and you *G* Gentiles,
13:50 But the Jews incited the *G* women
17: 4 as did a large number of *G* Greeks
17:17 with the Jews and the *G* Greeks,

GOD-HATERS* (HATE)
Ro 1:30 They are gossips, slanderers, *G,*

GOD'S (GOD)
2Ch 20:15 For the battle is not yours, but *G.*
Job 37:14 stop and consider *G* wonders.
Ps 52: 8 I trust in *G* unfailing love
69:30 I will praise *G* name in song
Mk 3:35 Whoever does *G* will is my brother
Jn 7:17 If anyone chooses to do *G* will,
10:36 'I am *G* Son'? Do not believe me
Ro 2: 3 think you will escape *G* judgment?
2: 4 not realizing that *G* kindness leads
3: 3 lack of faith nullify *G* faithfulness?
7:22 in my inner being I delight in *G* law
9:16 or effort, but on *G* mercy.
11:29 for *G* gifts and his call are
12: 2 and approve what *G* will is—
12:13 Share with *G* people who are
13: 6 for the authorities are *G* servants,
1Co 7:19 Keeping *G* commands is what
2Co 6: 2 now is the time of *G* favor,
Eph 1: 7 riches of *G* grace that he lavished
1Th 4: 3 It is *G* will that you should be
sanctified;
5:18 for this is *G* will for you
1Ti 6: 1 so that *G* name and our teaching
2Ti 2:19 *G* solid foundation stands firm,
Tit 1: 7 overseer is entrusted with *G* work,
Heb 1: 3 The Son is the radiance of *G* glory
9:24 now to appear for us in *G* presence.
11: 3 was formed at *G* command,
1Pe 2:15 For it is *G* will that
3: 4 which is of great worth in *G* sight.
1Jn 2: 5 *G* love is truly made complete

GODLESS
Job 20: 5 the joy of the *g* lasts but a moment.
1Ti 6:20 Turn away from *g* chatter

GODLINESS (GOD)
1Ti 2: 2 and quiet lives in all *g* and holiness.
4: 8 but *g* has value for all things,
6: 5 and who think that *g* is a means
6: 6 *g* with contentment is great gain.
6:11 and pursue righteousness, *g,* faith,
2Pe 1: 6 and to perseverance, *g;*

GODLY (GOD)
Ps 4: 3 that the LORD has set apart the *g*
2Co 7:10 *G* sorrow brings repentance that
11: 2 jealous for you with a *g* jealousy.
2Ti 3:12 everyone who wants to live a *g* life
2Pe 3:11 You ought to live holy and *g* lives

GODS (GOD)
Ex 20: 3 "You shall have no other *g*
Dt 5: 7 "You shall have no other *g*
1Ch 16:26 For all the *g* of the nations are idols
Ps 82: 6 "I said, 'You are "*g*";
Jn 10:34 have said you are *g*'? If he called
Ac 19:26 He says that man-made *g* are no *g*

GOG
Eze 38:18 When *G* attacks the land of Israel,
Rev 20: 8 *G* and Magog—to gather them

GOLD
1Ki 20: 3 'Your silver and *g* are mine,
Job 22:25 then the Almighty will be your *g,*
23:10 tested me, I will come forth as *g.*
28:15 cannot be bought with the finest *g,*
31:24 "If I have put my trust in *g*
Ps 19:10 They are more precious than *g,*
119:127 more than *g,* more than pure *g,*
Pr 3:14 and yields better returns than *g.*
22: 1 esteemed is better than silver or *g.*
Hag 2: 8 The silver is mine and the *g* is mine
Mt 2:11 and presented him with gifts of *g*
Rev 3:18 to buy from me *g* refined in the fire,

GOLGOTHA*
Mt 27:33 to a place called *G* (which means
Mk 15:22 to the place called *G* (which means
Jn 19:17 (which in Aramaic is called *G).*

GOLIATH
Philistine giant killed by David (1Sa 17; 21:9).

GOMORRAH
Ge 19:24 sulfur on Sodom and *G*—
Mt 10:15 and *G* on the day of judgment
2Pe 2: 6 and *G* by burning them to ashes,
Jude : 7 *G* and the surrounding towns gave

GOOD
Ge 1: 4 God saw that the light was *g,*
1:10 And God saw that it was *g.*
1:12 And God saw that it was *g.*
1:18 And God saw that it was *g.*
1:21 And God saw that it was *g.*
1:25 And God saw that it was *g.*
1:31 he had made, and it was very *g.*
2: 9 and the tree of the knowledge of *g*
2: 9 pleasing to the eye and *g* for food.
2:18 "It is not *g* for the man to be alone.
3:22 become like one of us, knowing *g*
50:20 but God intended it for *g*
2Ch 7: 3 "He is *g;* / his love endures
31:20 doing what was *g* and right
Job 2:10 Shall we accept *g* from God,
Ps 14: 1 there is no one who does *g.*
34: 8 Taste and see that the LORD is *g;*
34:14 Turn from evil and do *g;*
37: 3 Trust in the LORD and do *g;*
37:27 Turn from evil and do *g;*
52: 9 for your name is *g.*
53: 3 there is no one who does *g,*
84:11 no *g* thing does he withhold
86: 5 You are forgiving and *g,* O Lord
100: 5 For the LORD is *g* and his love
103: 5 satisfies your desires with *g* things,
112: 5 *G* will come to him who is
119: 68 You are *g,* and what you do is *g;*
133: 1 How *g* and pleasant it is
145: 9 The LORD is *g* to all;
147: 1 How *g* it is to sing praises
Pr 3: 4 you will win favor and a *g* name
3:27 Do not withhold *g*
11:27 He who seeks *g* finds *g* will,
13:22 A *g* man leaves an inheritance
14:22 those who plan what is *g* find love
15: 3 on the wicked and the *g.*
15:23 and how *g* is a timely word!
15:30 *g* news gives health to the bones.
17:22 A cheerful heart is *g* medicine,
18:22 He who finds a wife finds what is *g*
19: 2 It is not *g* to have zeal
22: 1 A *g* name is more desirable
31:12 She brings him *g,* not harm,
Ecc 12:14 whether it is *g* or evil.
Isa 5:20 Woe to those who call evil *g*
40: 9 You who bring *g* tidings
52: 7 the feet of those who bring *g* news,
61: 1 me to preach *g* news to the poor.
Jer 6:16 ask where the *g* way is,
13:23 Neither can you do *g*

Jer 32:39 the *g* of their children after them.
Eze 34:14 I will tend them in a *g* pasture,
Mic 6: 8 has showed you, O man, what is *g*.
Na 1:15 the feet of one who brings *g* news,
Mt 5:45 sun to rise on the evil and the *g*,
7:11 Father in heaven give *g* gifts
7:17 Likewise every *g* tree bears *g* fruit,
7:18 A *g* tree cannot bear bad fruit,
12:35 The *g* man brings *g* things out
13: 8 Still other seed fell on *g* soil,
13:24 is like a man who sowed *g* seed
13:48 and collected the *g* fish in baskets,
19:17 "There is only One who is *g*.
22:10 both *g* and bad, and the wedding
25:21 'Well done, *g* and faithful servant!
Mk 1:15 Repent and believe the *g* news!"
3: 4 lawful on the Sabbath: to do *g*
4: 8 Still other seed fell on *g* soil.
8:36 What *g* is it for a man
10:18 "No one is *g*— except God alone.
16:15 preach the *g* news to all creation.
Lk 2:10 I bring you *g* news
3: 9 does not produce *g* fruit will be
6:27 do *g* to those who hate you,
6:43 nor does a bad tree bear *g* fruit.
6:45 The *g* man brings *g* things out
8: 8 Still other seed fell on *g* soil.
9:25 What *g* is it for a man
14:34 "Salt is *g*, but if it loses its saltiness,
18:19 "No one is *g*— except God alone.
19:17 " 'Well done, my *g* servant!'
Jn 10:11 "I am the *g* shepherd.
Ro 3:12 there is no one who does *g*,
7:12 is holy, righteous and *g*.
7:16 want to do, I agree that the law is *g*.
7:18 I have the desire to do what is *g*,
8:28 for the *g* of those who love him,
10:15 feet of those who bring *g* news!"
12: 2 his *g*, pleasing and perfect will.
12: 9 Hate what is evil; cling to what is *g*.
13: 4 For he is God's servant to do you *g*
16:19 you to be wise about what is *g*,
1Co 7: 1 It is *g* for a man not to marry.
10:24 should seek his own *g*, but the *g*
15:33 Bad company corrupts *g* character
2Co 9: 8 you will abound in every *g* work.
Gal 4:18 provided the purpose is *g*,
6: 9 us not become weary in doing *g*,
6:10 as we have opportunity, let us do *g*
Eph 2:10 in Christ Jesus to do *g* works,
6: 8 everyone for whatever *g* he does,
Php 1: 6 that he who began a *g* work
Col 1:10 bearing fruit in every *g* work,
1Th 5:21 Hold on to the *g*.
1Ti 3: 7 have a *g* reputation with outsiders,
4: 4 For everything God created is *g*,
6:12 Fight the *g* fight of the faith.
6:18 them to do *g*, to be rich in *g* deeds,
2Ti 3:17 equipped for every *g* work.
4: 7 I have fought the *g* fight, I have
Tit 1: 8 loves what is *g*, who is
2: 7 an example by doing what is *g*.
2:14 his very own, eager to do what is *g*.
Heb 5:14 to distinguish *g* from evil.
10:24 on toward love and *g* deeds.
12:10 but God disciplines us for our *g*,
13:16 do not forget to do *g* and to share
Jas 4:17 who knows the *g* he ought to do
1Pe 2: 3 you have tasted that the Lord is *g*.
2:12 Live such *g* lives among the pagans
2:18 not only to those who are *g*
3:17 to suffer for doing *g*

GOODS
Ecc 5:11 As *g* increase,

GORGE
Pr 23:20 or *g* themselves on meat,

GOSHEN
Ge 45:10 You shall live in the region of *G*
Ex 8:22 differently with the land of *G*,

GOSPEL
Ro 1:16 I am not ashamed of the *g*,
15:16 duty of proclaiming the *g* of God,
15:20 to preach the *g* where Christ was
1Co 1:17 to preach the *g*— not with words
9:12 rather than hinder the *g* of Christ.
9:14 who preach the *g* should receive
9:16 Woe to me if I do not preach the *g*!
15: 1 you of the *g* I preached to you,
15: 2 By this *g* you are saved,
2Co 4: 4 light of the *g* of the glory of Christ,
9:13 your confession of the *g*
Gal 1: 7 a different *g*— which is really no *g*
Eph 6:15 comes from the *g* of peace.
Php 1:27 in a manner worthy of the *g*
Col 1:23 This is the *g* that you heard
1Th 2: 4 by God to be entrusted with the *g*.
2Th 1: 8 do not obey the *g* of our Lord Jesus
2Ti 1:10 immortality to light through the *g*.
Rev 14: 6 he had the eternal *g* to proclaim

GOSSIP*
Pr 11:13 A *g* betrays a confidence,
16:28 and a *g* separates close friends.
18: 8 of a *g* are like choice morsels;
20:19 A *g* betrays a confidence;
26:20 without *g* a quarrel dies down.
26:22 of a *g* are like choice morsels;
2Co 12:20 slander, *g*, arrogance and disorder.

GOVERN (GOVERNMENT)
Ge 1:16 the greater light to *g* the day
Job 34:17 Can he who hates justice *g*?
Ro 12: 8 it is leadership, let him *g* diligently;

GOVERNMENT (GOVERN)
Isa 9: 6 and the *g* will be on his shoulders.

GRACE* (GRACIOUS)
Ps 45: 2 lips have been anointed with *g*,
Pr 1: 9 will be a garland to *g* your head
3:22 an ornament to *g* your neck.
3:34 but gives *g* to the humble.
4: 9 She will set a garland of *g*
Isa 26:10 Though *g* is shown to the wicked,
Jnh 2: 8 forfeit the *g* that could be theirs.
Zec 12:10 of Jerusalem a spirit of *g*
Lk 2:40 and the *g* of God was upon him.
Jn 1:14 who came from the Father, full of *g*
1:16 of his *g* we have all received one
1:17 *g* and truth came through Jesus
Ac 4:33 and much *g* was upon them all.
6: 8 a man full of God's *g* and power,
11:23 saw the evidence of the *g* of God,
13:43 them to continue in the *g* of God.
14: 3 message of his *g* by enabling them
14:26 they had been committed to the *g*
15:11 We believe it is through the *g*
15:40 by the brothers to the *g* of the Lord
18:27 to those who by *g* had believed.
20:24 testifying to the gospel of God's *g*.
20:32 to God and to the word of his *g*,
Ro 1: 5 we received *g* and apostleship
1: 7 *G* and peace to you
3:24 and are justified freely by his *g*
4:16 be by *g* and may be guaranteed
5: 2 access by faith into this *g*
5:15 came by the *g* of the one man,
5:15 how much more did God's *g*
5:17 God's abundant provision of *g*
5:20 where sin increased, *g* increased all
5:21 also *g* might reign
6: 1 on sinning so that *g* may increase?
6:14 you are not under law, but under *g*.
6:15 we are not under law but under *g*?
11: 5 there is a remnant chosen by *g*.
11: 6 if by *g*, then it is no longer by works
11: 6 if it were, *g* would no longer be *g*.
12: 3 For by the *g* given me I say
12: 6 according to the *g* given us.
15:15 because of the *g* God gave me
16:20 The *g* of our Lord Jesus be
1Co 1: 3 *G* and peace to you
1: 4 of his *g* given you in Christ Jesus.
3:10 By the *g* God has given me,
15:10 But by the *g* of God I am what I am
15:10 but the *g* of God that was with me.
15:10 his *g* to me was not without effect.
16:23 The *g* of the Lord Jesus be with you
2Co 1: 2 *G* and peace to you
1:12 wisdom but according to God's *g*.
4:15 so that the *g* that is reaching more
6: 1 not to receive God's *g* in vain.
8: 1 to know about the *g* that God has
8: 6 also to completion this act of *g*
8: 7 also excel in this *g* of giving.
8: 9 For you know the *g*
9: 8 able to make all *g* abound to you,
9:14 of the surpassing *g* God has given
12: 9 "My *g* is sufficient for you,
13:14 May the *g* of the Lord Jesus Christ,
Gal 1: 3 *G* and peace to you
1: 6 the one who called you by the *g*
1:15 from birth and called me by his *g*,
2: 9 when they recognized the *g* given
2:21 I do not set aside the *g* of God,
3:18 God in his *g* gave it to Abraham
5: 4 you have fallen away from *g*.
6:18 The *g* of our Lord Jesus Christ be
Eph 1: 2 *G* and peace to you
1: 6 to the praise of his glorious *g*,
1: 7 riches of God's *g* that he lavished
2: 5 it is by *g* you have been saved.
2: 7 the incomparable riches of his *g*,
2: 8 For it is by *g* you have been saved,
3: 2 of God's *g* that was given to me
3: 7 by the gift of God's *g* given me
3: 8 God's people, this *g* was given me:
4: 7 to each one of us *g* has been given
6:24 *G* to all who love our Lord Jesus
Php 1: 2 *G* and peace to you
1: 7 all of you share in God's *g* with me.
4:23 The *g* of the Lord Jesus Christ be
Col 1: 2 *G* and peace to you
1: 6 understood God's *g* in all its truth.
4: 6 conversation be always full of *g*,
4:18 *G* be with you.
1Th 1: 1 and the Lord Jesus Christ: *G*
5:28 The *g* of our Lord Jesus Christ be
2Th 1: 2 *G* and peace to you
1:12 according to the *g* of our God
2:16 and by his *g* gave us eternal
3:18 The *g* of our Lord Jesus Christ be
1Ti 1: 2 my true son in the faith: *G*,
1:14 The *g* of our Lord was poured out
6:21 *G* be with you.
2Ti 1: 2 To Timothy, my dear son: *G*,
1: 9 This *g* was given us in Christ Jesus
1: 9 because of his own purpose and *g*.
2: 1 be strong in the *g* that is
4:22 *G* be with you.
Tit 1: 4 *G* and peace from God the Father
2:11 For the *g* of God that brings
3: 7 having been justified by his *g*,
3:15 *G* be with you all.
Phm : 3 *G* to you and peace
:25 The *g* of the Lord Jesus Christ be
Heb 2: 9 that by the *g* of God he might taste
4:16 find *g* to help us in our time of need
4:16 the throne of *g* with confidence,
10:29 and who has insulted the Spirit of *g*
12:15 See to it that no one misses the *g*
13: 9 hearts to be strengthened by *g*,
13:25 *G* be with you all.
Jas 4: 6 but gives *g* to the humble."
4: 6 But he gives us more *g*. That is why
1Pe 1: 2 *G* and peace be yours in abundance
1:10 who spoke of the *g* that was
1:13 fully on the *g* to be given you
4:10 faithfully administering God's *g*
5: 5 but gives *g* to the humble."
5:10 the God of all *g*, who called you
5:12 and testifying that this is the true *g*
2Pe 1: 2 *G* and peace be yours in abundance
3:18 But grow in the *g* and knowledge
2Jn : 3 and will be with us forever: *G*,
Jude : 4 who change the *g* of our God
Rev 1: 4 *G* and peace to you
22:21 The *g* of the Lord Jesus be

GRACIOUS (GRACE)
Ex 34: 6 the compassionate and *g* God,
Nu 6:25 and be *g* to you;
Ne 9:17 But you are a forgiving God, *g*
Ps 67: 1 May God be *g* to us and bless us
Pr 22:11 a pure heart and whose speech is *g*
Isa 30:18 Yet the LORD longs to be *g* to you

GRAIN
Lev 2: 1 When someone brings a *g* offering
Lk 17:35 women will be grinding *g* together;
1Co 9: 9 ox while it is treading out the *g*."

GRANDCHILDREN (CHILD)
1Ti 5: 4 But if a widow has children or *g*,

GRANDMOTHER (MOTHER)
2Ti 1: 5 which first lived in your *g* Lois

GRANT (GRANTED)
Ps 20: 5 May the LORD *g* all your requests
51:12 *g* me a willing spirit, to sustain me.

GRANTED (GRANT)
Pr 10:24 what the righteous desire will be *g*.
Mt 15:28 great faith! Your request is *g*."
Php 1:29 For it has been *g* to you on behalf

GRAPES
Nu 13:23 branch bearing a single cluster of *g*.
Jer 31:29 'The fathers have eaten sour *g*,
Eze 18: 2 " 'The fathers eat sour *g*,
Mt 7:16 Do people pick *g* from thornbushes
Rev 14:18 and gather the clusters of *g*

GRASPED
Php 2: 6 with God something to be *g*,

GRASS
Ps 103: 15 As for man, his days are like *g*,
Isa 40: 6 "All men are like *g*,
Mt 6:30 If that is how God clothes the *g*
1Pe 1:24 "All men are like *g*,

GRASSHOPPERS
Nu 13:33 We seemed like *g* in our own eyes,

GRATIFY* (GRATITUDE)
Ro 13:14 think about how to *g* the desires
Gal 5:16 and you will not *g* the desires

GRATITUDE (GRATIFY)
Col 3:16 and spiritual songs with *g*

GRAVE (GRAVES)
Nu 19:16 who touches a human bone or a *g*,
Dt 34: 6 day no one knows where his *g* is.
Ps 5: 9 Their throat is an open *g*;
49:15 will redeem my life from the *g*;
Pr 7:27 Her house is a highway to the *g*,
Hos 13:14 Where, O *g*, is your destruction?
Jn 11:44 "Take off the *g* clothes
Ac 2:27 you will not abandon me to the *g*,

GRAVES (GRAVE)
Eze 37:12 I am going to open your *g*
Jn 5:28 are in their *g* will hear his voice
Ro 3:13 "Their throats are open *g*;

GRAY
Pr 16:31 *G* hair is a crown of splendor;
20:29 *g* hair the splendor of the old.

GREAT (GREATER GREATEST GREATNESS)
Ge 12: 2 I will make your name *g*,
12: 2 "I will make you into a *g* nation
Ex 32:11 out of Egypt with *g* power
Nu 14:19 In accordance with your *g* love,
Dt 4:32 so *g* as this ever happened,
10:17 the *g* God, mighty and awesome,
29:28 in *g* wrath the LORD uprooted
Jos 7: 9 do for your own *g* name?"
Jdg 16: 5 you the secret of his *g* strength
2Sa 7:22 "How *g* you are, O Sovereign
22:36 you stoop down to make me *g*.
24:14 for his mercy is *g*; but do not let me
1Ch 17:19 made known all these *g* promises.
Ps 18:35 you stoop down to make me *g*.
19:11 in keeping them there is *g* reward.
47: 2 the *g* King over all the earth!
57:10 For *g* is your love, reaching
68:11 and *g* was the company
89: 1 of the LORD's *g* love forever;
103: 11 so *g* is his love for those who fear
107: 43 consider the *g* love of the LORD.
108: 4 For *g* is your love, higher
117: 2 For *g* is his love toward us,
119:165 *G* peace have they who love your
145: 3 *G* is the LORD and most worthy
Pr 22: 1 is more desirable than *g* riches;
23:24 of a righteous man has *g* joy;
Isa 42:21 to make his law *g* and glorious.
Jer 27: 5 With my *g* power and outstretched
32:19 *g* are your purposes and mighty are
La 3:23 *g* is your faithfulness.
Da 9: 4 "O Lord, the *g* and awesome God,
Joel 2:11 The day of the LORD is *g*;
2:20 Surely he has done *g* things.
Zep 1:14 "The *g* day of the LORD is near—
Mal 1:11 My name will be *g*
4: 5 the prophet Elijah before that *g*
Mt 20:26 whoever wants to become *g*
Mk 10:43 whoever wants to become *g*
Lk 6:23 because *g* is your reward in heaven.
6:35 Then your reward will be *g*,
21:27 in a cloud with power and *g* glory.
Eph 1:19 and his incomparably *g* power
2: 4 But because of his *g* love for us,
1Ti 6: 6 with contentment is *g* gain.
Tit 2:13 glorious appearing of our *g* God
Heb 2: 3 if we ignore such a *g* salvation?
1Jn 3: 1 How *g* is the love the Father has
Rev 6:17 For the *g* day of their wrath has
20:11 Then I saw a *g* white throne

GREATER (GREAT)
Mt 11:11 there has not risen anyone *g*
12: 6 I tell you that one *g*
12:41 and now one *g* than Jonah is here.
12:42 now one *g* than Solomon is here.
Mk 12:31 There is no commandment *g*
Jn 1:50 You shall see *g* things than that."
3:30 He must become *g*; I must become
14:12 He will do even *g* things than these
15:13 *G* love has no one than this,
1Co 12:31 But eagerly desire the *g* gifts.
2Co 3:11 how much *g* is the glory
Heb 3: 3 the builder of a house has *g* honor
3: 3 worthy of *g* honor than Moses,
7: 7 lesser person is blessed by the *g*.
11:26 as of *g* value than the treasures
1Jn 3:20 For God is *g* than our hearts,
4: 4 is in you is *g* than the one who is

GREATEST (GREAT)
Mt 22:38 is the first and *g* commandment.
23:11 *g* among you will be your servant.
Lk 9:48 least among you all—he is the *g*."
1Co 13:13 But the *g* of these is love.

GREATNESS* (GREAT)
Ex 15: 7 In the *g* of your majesty
Dt 3:24 to show to your servant your *g*
32: 3 Oh, praise the *g* of our God!
1Ch 29:11 O LORD, is the *g* and the power
2Ch 9: 6 half the *g* of your wisdom was told
Est 10: 2 account of the *g* of Mordecai
Ps 145: 3 his *g* no one can fathom.
150: 2 praise him for his surpassing *g*.
Isa 63: 1 forward in the *g* of his strength?
Eze 38:23 I will show my *g* and my holiness,
Da 4:22 your *g* has grown until it reaches
5:18 and *g* and glory and splendor.
7:27 and *g* of the kingdoms
Mic 5: 4 will live securely, for then his *g*
Lk 9:43 And they were all amazed at the *g*
Php 3: 8 compared to the surpassing *g*

GREED (GREEDY)
Lk 12:15 on your guard against all kinds of *g*
Ro 1:29 kind of wickedness, evil, *g*
Eph 5: 3 or of any kind of impurity, or of *g*,
Col 3: 5 evil desires and *g*, which is idolatry
2Pe 2:14 experts in *g*— an accursed brood!

GREEDY (GREED)
Pr 15:27 A *g* man brings trouble
1Co 6:10 nor thieves nor the *g* nor drunkards
Eph 5: 5 No immoral, impure or *g* person—
1Pe 5: 2 not *g* for money, but eager to serve;

GREEK (GREEKS)
Gal 3:28 There is neither Jew nor *G*,
Col 3:11 Here there is no *G* or Jew,

GREEKS (GREEK)
1Co 1:22 miraculous signs and *G* look

GREEN
Ps 23: 2 makes me lie down in *g* pastures,

GREW (GROW)
Lk 1:80 And the child *g* and became strong
2:52 And Jesus *g* in wisdom and stature,
Ac 9:31 by the Holy Spirit, it *g* in numbers,
16: 5 in the faith and *g* daily in numbers.

GRIEF (GRIEFS GRIEVANCES GRIEVE GRIEVED)
Ps 10:14 O God, do see trouble and *g*;
Pr 10: 1 but a foolish son *g* to his mother.
14:13 and joy may end in *g*.
17:21 To have a fool for a son brings *g*;
Ecc 1:18 the more knowledge, the more *g*.
La 3:32 Though he brings *g*, he will show
Jn 16:20 but your *g* will turn to joy.
1Pe 1: 6 had to suffer *g* in all kinds of trials.

GRIEFS* (GRIEF)
1Ti 6:10 pierced themselves with many *g*.

GRIEVANCES* (GRIEF)
Col 3:13 forgive whatever *g* you may have

GRIEVE (GRIEF)
Eph 4:30 do not *g* the Holy Spirit of God,
1Th 4:13 or to *g* like the rest of men,

GRIEVED (GRIEF)
Isa 63:10 and *g* his Holy Spirit.

GRINDING
Lk 17:35 women will be *g* grain together;

GROAN (GROANING GROANS)
Ro 8:23 *g* inwardly as we wait eagerly
2Co 5: 4 For while we are in this tent, we *g*

GROANING (GROAN)
Ex 2:24 God heard their *g* and he
Eze 21: 7 'Why are you *g*?' you shall say,
Ro 8:22 that the whole creation has been *g*

GROANS (GROAN)
Ro 8:26 with *g* that words cannot express.

GROUND
Ge 1:10 God called the dry *g* "land,"
3:17 "Cursed is the *g* because of you;
4:10 blood cries out to me from the *g*.
Ex 3: 5 where you are standing is holy *g*."
15:19 walked through the sea on dry *g*.
Isa 53: 2 and like a root out of dry *g*.
Mt 10:29 fall to the *g* apart from the will
25:25 and hid your talent in the *g*.
Jn 8: 6 to write on the *g* with his finger.
Eph 6:13 you may be able to stand your *g*,

GROW (FULL-GROWN GREW GROWING GROWS)
Pr 13:11 by little makes it *g*.
20:13 not love sleep or you will *g* poor;
Isa 40:31 they will run and not *g* weary,
Mt 6:28 See how the lilies of the field *g*.
1Co 3: 6 watered it, but God made it *g*.
2Pe 3:18 But *g* in the grace and knowledge

GROWING (GROW)
Col 1: 6 this gospel is bearing fruit and *g*,
1:10 *g* in the knowledge of God,
2Th 1: 3 your faith is *g* more and more,

GROWS (GROW)
Eph 4:16 *g* and builds itself up in love,
Col 2:19 *g* as God causes it to grow.

GRUMBLE (GRUMBLED GRUMBLERS GRUMBLING)
1Co 10:10 And do not *g*, as some of them did
Jas 5: 9 Don't *g* against each other,

GRUMBLED (GRUMBLE)
Ex 15:24 So the people *g* against Moses,
Nu 14:29 and who has *g* against me.

GRUMBLERS* (GRUMBLE)
Jude :16 These men are *g* and faultfinders;

GRUMBLING (GRUMBLE)
Jn 6:43 "Stop *g* among yourselves,"
1Pe 4: 9 to one another without *g*.

GUARANTEE (GUARANTEEING)
Heb 7:22 Jesus has become the *g*

GUARANTEEING* (GUARANTEE)
2Co 1:22 as a deposit, *g* what is to come.
5: 5 as a deposit, *g* what is to come.
Eph 1:14 who is a deposit *g* our inheritance

GUARD (GUARDS)
1Sa 2: 9 He will *g* the feet of his saints,
Ps 141: 3 Set a *g* over my mouth, O LORD;
Pr 2:11 and understanding will *g* you.
4:13 *g* it well, for it is your life.
4:23 Above all else, *g* your heart,
7: 2 *g* my teachings as the apple
Isa 52:12 the God of Israel will be your rear *g*
Mk 13:33 Be on *g*! Be alert! You do not know
Lk 12: 1 "Be on your *g* against the yeast
12:15 Be on your *g* against all kinds
Ac 20:31 So be on your *g*! Remember that
1Co 16:13 Be on your *g*; stand firm in the faith
Php 4: 7 will *g* your hearts and your minds
1Ti 6:20 *g* what has been entrusted
2Ti 1:14 *G* the good deposit that was

GUARDS (GUARD)
Pr 13: 3 He who *g* his lips *g* his life,
19:16 who obeys instructions *g* his life,
21:23 He who *g* his mouth and his tongue
22: 5 he who *g* his soul stays far

GUIDANCE (GUIDE)
Pr 1: 5 and let the discerning get *g*—
11:14 For lack of *g* a nation falls,
24: 6 for waging war you need *g*,

GUIDE (GUIDANCE GUIDED GUIDES)
Ex 13:21 of cloud to *g* them on their way
15:13 In your strength you will *g* them
Ne 9:19 cease to *g* them on their path,
Ps 25: 5 *g* me in your truth and teach me,
43: 3 let them *g* me;
48:14 he will be our *g* even to the end.
67: 4 and *g* the nations of the earth.
73:24 You *g* me with your counsel,
139: 10 even there your hand will *g* me,
Pr 4:11 I *g* you in the way of wisdom
6:22 When you walk, they will *g* you;
Isa 58:11 The LORD will *g* you always;
Jn 16:13 comes, he will *g* you into all truth.

GUIDED (GUIDE)
Ps 107: 30 he *g* them to their desired haven.

GUIDES (GUIDE)
Ps 23: 3 He *g* me in paths of righteousness
25: 9 He *g* the humble in what is right
Pr 11: 3 The integrity of the upright *g* them,
16:23 A wise man's heart *g* his mouth,
Mt 23:16 "Woe to you, blind *g*! You say,
23:24 You blind *g*! You strain out a gnat

GUILT (GUILTY)
Lev 5:15 It is a *g* offering.
Ps 32: 5 the *g* of my sin.
38: 4 My *g* has overwhelmed me
Isa 6: 7 your *g* is taken away and your sin
Jer 2:22 the stain of your *g* is still before me
Eze 18:19 'Why does the son not share the *g*

GUILTY (GUILT)
Ex 34: 7 does not leave the *g* unpunished;
Mk 3:29 Spirit will never be forgiven; he is *g*
Jn 8:46 Can any of you prove me *g* of sin?
1Co 11:27 in an unworthy manner will be *g*
Heb 10: 2 and would no longer have felt *g*
10:22 to cleanse us from a *g* conscience
Jas 2:10 at just one point is *g* of breaking all

HABAKKUK*
Prophet to Judah (Hab 1:1; 3:1).

HABIT
1Ti 5:13 they get into the *h* of being idle
Heb 10:25 as some are in the *h* of doing,

HADAD
Edomite adversary of Solomon (1Ki 11:14-25).

HADES*
Mt 16:18 the gates of *H* will not overcome it.
Rev 1:18 And I hold the keys of death and *H*
6: 8 *H* was following close behind him.
20:13 and *H* gave up the dead that were
20:14 *H* were thrown into the lake of fire.

HAGAR
Servant of Sarah, wife of Abraham, mother of Ishmael (Ge 16:1-6; 25:12). Driven away by Sarah while pregnant (Ge 16:5-16); after birth of Isaac (Ge 21:9-21; Gal 4:21-31).

HAGGAI*
Post-exilic prophet who encouraged rebuilding of the temple (Ezr 5:1; 6:14; Hag 1-2).

HAIL
Ex 9:19 the *h* will fall on every man
Rev 8: 7 and there came *h* and fire mixed

HAIR (HAIRS HAIRY)
Lev 19:27 " 'Do not cut the *h* at the sides
Nu 6: 5 he must let the *h* of his head grow
Pr 16:31 Gray *h* is a crown of splendor;
20:29 gray *h* the splendor of the old.
Lk 7:44 and wiped them with her *h*.
21:18 But not a *h* of your head will perish
Jn 11: 2 and wiped his feet with her *h*.
12: 3 and wiped his feet with her *h*.
1Co 11: 6 for a woman to have her *h* cut
11: 6 she should have her *h* cut off;
11:14 that if a man has long *h*,
11:15 For long *h* is given to her
11:15 but that if a woman has long *h*,
1Ti 2: 9 not with braided *h* or gold or pearls
1Pe 3: 3 as braided *h* and the wearing
Rev 1:14 and *h* were white like wool,

HAIRS (HAIR)
Mt 10:30 even the very *h* of your head are all
Lk 12: 7 the very *h* of your head are all

HAIRY (HAIR)
Ge 27:11 "But my brother Esau is a *h* man,

HALF
Ex 30:13 This *h* shekel is an offering
Jos 8:33 *H* of the people stood in front
1Ki 3:25 give *h* to one and *h* to the other."
10: 7 Indeed, not even *h* was told me;
Est 5: 3 Even up to *h* the kingdom,
Da 7:25 him for a time, times and *h* a time.
Mk 6:23 up to *h* my kingdom."

HALF-TRIBE (TRIBE)
Nu 32:33 and the *h* of Manasseh son

HALLELUJAH*
Rev 19: 1, 3, 4, 6.

HALLOWED* (HOLY)
Mt 6: 9 *h* be your name,
Lk 11: 2 *h* be your name,

HALT
Job 38:11 here is where your proud waves *h*'?

HALTER*
Pr 26: 3 for the horse, a *h* for the donkey,

HAM
Son of Noah (Ge 5:32; 1Ch 1:4), father of Canaan (Ge 9:18; 10:6-20; 1Ch 1:8-16). Saw Noah's nakedness (Ge 9:20-27).

HAMAN
Agagite nobleman honored by Xerxes (Est 3:1-2). Plotted to exterminate the Jews because of Mordecai (Est 3:3-15). Forced to honor Mordecai (Est 5-6). Plot exposed by Esther (Est 5:1-8; 7:1-8). Hanged (Est 7:9-10).

HAMPERED*
Pr 4:12 you walk, your steps will not be *h*;

HAND (HANDED HANDFUL HANDS OPENHANDED)
Ge 24: 2 "Put your *h* under my thigh.
47:29 put your *h* under my thigh
Ex 13: 3 out of it with a mighty *h*.
15: 6 Your right *h*, O LORD,
33:22 and cover you with my *h*
Dt 12: 7 in everything you have put your *h*
1Ki 8:42 and your mighty *h* and your
13: 4 But the *h* he stretched out
1Ch 29:14 you only what comes from your *h*.
29:16 it comes from your *h*, and all
2Ch 6:15 with your *h* you have fulfilled it—
Ne 4:17 materials did their work with one *h*
Job 40: 4 I put my *h* over my mouth.
Ps 16: 8 Because he is at my right *h*,
32: 4 your *h* was heavy upon me;
37:24 the LORD upholds him with his *h*.
44: 3 it was your right *h*, your arm,
45: 9 at your right *h* is the royal bride
63: 8 your right *h* upholds me.
75: 8 In the *h* of the LORD is a cup
91: 7 ten thousand at your right *h*,
98: 1 his right *h* and his holy arm
109: 31 at the right *h* of the needy one,
110: 1 "Sit at my right *h*
137: 5 may my right *h* forget its skill.
139: 10 even there your *h* will guide me,
145: 16 You open your *h*
Pr 27:16 or grasping oil with the *h*.
Ecc 5:15 that he can carry in his *h*.
9:10 Whatever your *h* finds to do,
Isa 11: 8 the young child put his *h*
40:12 the waters in the hollow of his *h*,
41:13 who takes hold of your right *h*
44: 5 still another will write on his *h*,
48:13 My own *h* laid the foundations
64: 8 we are all the work of your *h*.
La 3: 3 he has turned his *h* against me
Da 10:10 *h* touched me and set me trembling
Jnh 4:11 people who cannot tell their right *h*
Hab 3: 4 rays flashed from his *h*,
Mt 5:30 if your right *h* causes you to sin,
6: 3 know what your right *h* is doing,
12:10 a man with a shriveled *h* was there.
18: 8 If your *h* or your foot causes you
22:44 "Sit at my right *h*
26:64 at the right *h* of the Mighty One
Mk 3: 1 a man with a shriveled *h* was there.
9:43 If your *h* causes you to sin, cut it off
12:36 "Sit at my right *h*
16:19 and he sat at the right *h* of God.
Lk 6: 6 there whose right *h* was shriveled.
20:42 "Sit at my right *h*
22:69 at the right *h* of the mighty God."
Jn 10:28 one can snatch them out of my *h*.
20:27 Reach out your *h* and put it
Ac 7:55 Jesus standing at the right *h* of God
1Co 12:15 I am not a *h*, I do not belong
Heb 1:13 "Sit at my right *h*
Rev 13:16 to receive a mark on his right *h*

HANDED (HAND)
Da 7:25 The saints will be *h* over to him
1Ti 1:20 whom I have *h* over to Satan

HANDFUL (HAND)
Ecc 4: 6 Better one *h* with tranquillity

HANDLE (HANDLES)
Col 2:21 "Do not *h*! Do not taste! Do not

HANDLES (HANDLE)
2Ti 2:15 who correctly *h* the word of truth.

HANDS (HAND)
Ge 27:22 but the *h* are the *h* of Esau."
Ex 17:11 As long as Moses held up his *h*,
29:10 his sons shall lay their *h* on its head
Dt 6: 8 Tie them as symbols on your *h*
Jdg 7: 6 lapped with their *h* to their mouths.
2Ki 11:12 and the people clapped their *h*
2Ch 6: 4 who with his *h* has fulfilled what he
Ps 22:16 they have pierced my *h*
24: 4 He who has clean *h* and a pure
31: 5 Into your *h* I commit my spirit;
31:15 My times are in your *h*;
47: 1 Clap your *h*, all you nations;
63: 4 and in your name I will lift up my *h*
Pr 10: 4 Lazy *h* make a man poor,
21:25 because his *h* refuse to work.
31:13 and works with eager *h*.
31:20 and extends her *h* to the needy.
Ecc 10:18 if his *h* are idle, the house leaks.
Isa 35: 3 Strengthen the feeble *h*,
49:16 you on the palms of my *h*;
55:12 will clap their *h*.
65: 2 All day long I have held out my *h*
La 3:41 Let us lift up our hearts and our *h*
Lk 23:46 into your *h* I commit my spirit."
Ac 6: 6 who prayed and laid their *h*
8:18 at the laying on of the apostles' *h*,
13: 3 they placed their *h* on them
19: 6 When Paul placed his *h* on them,
28: 8 placed his *h* on him and healed him
1Th 4:11 and to work with your *h*,
1Ti 2: 8 to lift up holy *h* in prayer,
4:14 body of elders laid their *h* on you.
5:22 hasty in the laying on of *h*,
2Ti 1: 6 you through the laying on of my *h*.
Heb 6: 2 the laying on of *h*, the resurrection

HANDSOME*
Ge 39: 6 Now Joseph was well-built and *h*,
1Sa 16:12 a fine appearance and *h* features.
17:42 ruddy and *h*, and he despised him.
2Sa 14:25 praised for his *h* appearance
1Ki 1: 6 also very *h* and was born next
SS 1:16 *Beloved* How *h* you are, my lover!
Eze 23: 6 all of them *h* young men,
23:12 horsemen, all *h* young men.
23:23 with them, *h* young men,
Da 1: 4 without any physical defect, *h*,
Zec 11:13 the *h* price at which they priced me

HANG (HANGED HANGING HUNG)
Mt 22:40 and the Prophets *h* on these two

HANGED (HANG)
Mt 27: 5 Then he went away and *h* himself.

HANGING (HANG)
Ac 10:39 They killed him by *h* him on a tree,

HANNAH*
Wife of Elkanah, mother of Samuel (1Sa 1). Prayer at dedication of Samuel (1Sa 2:1-10). Blessed (1Sa 2:18-21).

HAPPIER (HAPPY)
Mt 18:13 he is *h* about that one sheep
1Co 7:40 she is *h* if she stays as she is—

HAPPINESS* (HAPPY)
Dt 24: 5 bring *h* to the wife he has married.
Est 8:16 For the Jews it was a time of *h*
Job 7: 7 my eyes will never see *h* again.
Ecc 2:26 gives wisdom, knowledge and *h*,
Mt 25:21 Come and share your master's *h*!'
25:23 Come and share your master's *h*!'

HAPPY* (HAPPIER HAPPINESS)
Ge 30:13 The women will call me *h*."
30:13 Then Leah said, "How *h* I am!
1Ki 4:20 they drank and they were *h*.
10: 8 How *h* your men must be!
10: 8 men must be! How *h* your officials,
2Ch 9: 7 How *h* your men must be!
9: 7 men must be! How *h* your officials,
Est 5: 9 Haman went out that day *h*
5:14 the king to the dinner and be *h*."
Ps 10: 6 I'll always be *h* and never have
68: 3 may they be *h* and joyful.
113: 9 as a *h* mother of children.
137: 8 *h* is he who repays you
Pr 15:13 A *h* heart makes the face cheerful,
Ecc 3:12 better for men than to be *h*
5:19 to accept his lot and be *h*
7:14 When times are good, be *h*;
11: 9 Be *h*, young man, while you are
Jnh 4: 6 Jonah was very *h* about the vine.
Zec 8:19 and glad occasions and *h* festivals
1Co 7:30 those who are *h*, as if they were not
2Co 7: 9 yet now I am *h*, not because you
7:13 delighted to see how *h* Titus was,
Jas 5:13 Is anyone *h*? Let him sing songs

HARD (HARDEN HARDENED HARDENING HARDENS HARDER HARDSHIP HARDSHIPS)
Ge 18:14 Is anything too *h* for the LORD?
1Ki 10: 1 came to test him with *h* questions.
Pr 14:23 All *h* work brings a profit,
Jer 32:17 Nothing is too *h* for you.
Zec 7:12 They made their hearts as *h* as flint
Mt 19:23 it is *h* for a rich man
Mk 10: 5 your hearts were *h* that Moses
Jn 6:60 disciples said, "This is a *h* teaching.

Ac 20:35 of *h* work we must help the weak,
26:14 It is *h* for you to kick
Ro 16:12 woman who has worked very *h*
1Co 4:12 We work *h* with our own hands.
2Co 6: 5 imprisonments and riots; in *h* work
1Th 5:12 to respect those who work *h*
Rev 2: 2 your *h* work and your

HARDEN (HARD)
Ex 4:21 I will *h* his heart so that he will not
Ps 95: 8 do not *h* your hearts as you did
Ro 9:18 he hardens whom he wants to *h*.
Heb 3: 8 do not *h* your hearts

HARDENED (HARD)
Ex 10:20 But the LORD *h* Pharaoh's heart,

HARDENING* (HARD)
Ro 11:25 Israel has experienced a *h* in part
Eph 4:18 in them due to the *h* of their hearts.

HARDENS* (HARD)
Pr 28:14 he who *h* his heart falls into trouble
Ro 9:18 and he *h* whom he wants to harden.

HARDER (HARD)
1Co 15:10 No, I worked *h* than all of them—
2Co 11:23 I have worked much *h*, been

HARDHEARTED* (HEART)
Dt 15: 7 do not be *h* or tightfisted

HARDSHIP (HARD)
Ro 8:35 Shall trouble or *h* or persecution
2Ti 2: 3 Endure *h* with us like a good
4: 5 endure *h*, do the work
Heb 12: 7 Endure *h* as discipline; God is

HARDSHIPS (HARD)
Ac 14:22 go through many *h* to enter
2Co 6: 4 in troubles, *h* and distresses;
12:10 in insults, in *h*, in persecutions,
Rev 2: 3 and have endured *h* for my name,

HARM (HARMS)
1Ch 16:22 do my prophets no *h*."
Ps 105: 15 do my prophets no *h*."
121: 6 the sun will not *h* you by day,
Pr 3:29 not plot *h* against your neighbor,
12:21 No *h* befalls the righteous,
31:12 She brings him good, not *h*,
Jer 10: 5 they can do no *h*
29:11 to prosper you and not to *h* you,
Ro 13:10 Love does no *h* to its neighbor.
1Co 11:17 for your meetings do more *h*
1Jn 5:18 the evil one cannot *h* him.

HARMONY*
Zec 6:13 there will be *h* between the two.'
Ro 12:16 Live in *h* with one another.
2Co 6:15 What *h* is there between Christ
1Pe 3: 8 live in *h* with one another;

HARMS* (HARM)
Pr 8:36 whoever fails to find me *h* himself;

HARP (HARPS)
Ge 4:21 the father of all who play the *h*
1Sa 16:23 David would take his *h* and play.
Ps 33: 2 Praise the LORD with the *h*;
98: 5 with the *h* and the sound of singing
150: 3 praise him with the *h* and lyre,
Rev 5: 8 Each one had a *h* and they were

HARPS (HARP)
Ps 137: 2 we hung our *h*,

HARSH
Pr 15: 1 but a *h* word stirs up anger.
Col 2:23 and their *h* treatment of the body,
3:19 and do not be *h* with them.
1Pe 2:18 but also to those who are *h*.
Jude :15 of all the *h* words ungodly sinners

HARVEST (HARVESTERS)
Ge 8:22 seedtime and *h*,
Ex 23:16 the Feast of *H* with the firstfruits
Dt 16:15 God will bless you in all your *h*
Pr 10: 5 during *h* is a disgraceful son.
Jer 8:20 "The *h* is past,
Joel 3:13 for the *h* is ripe.
Mt 9:37 *h* is plentiful but the workers are
Lk 10: 2 He told them, "The *h* is plentiful,
Jn 4:35 at the fields! They are ripe for *h*.
1Co 9:11 if we reap a material *h* from you?
2Co 9:10 the *h* of your righteousness.
Gal 6: 9 at the proper time we will reap a *h*
Heb 12:11 it produces a *h* of righteousness
Jas 3:18 in peace raise a *h* of righteousness.
Rev 14:15 for the *h* of the earth is ripe."

HARVESTERS (HARVEST)
Ru 2: 3 to glean in the fields behind the *h*.

HASTE (HASTEN HASTY)
Ex 12:11 it in *h*; it is the LORD's Passover.
Pr 21: 5 as surely as *h* leads to poverty.
29:20 Do you see a man who speaks in *h*?

HASTEN (HASTE)
Ps 70: 1 *H*, O God, to save me;
119: 60 I will *h* and not delay

HASTY* (HASTE)
Pr 19: 2 nor to be *h* and miss the way.
Ecc 5: 2 do not be *h* in your heart
1Ti 5:22 Do not be *h* in the laying

HATE (GOD-HATERS HATED HATES HATING HATRED)
Lev 19:17 " 'Do not *h* your brother
Ps 5: 5 you *h* all who do wrong.
36: 2 too much to detect or *h* his sin.
45: 7 righteousness and *h* wickedness.
97:10 those who love the LORD *h* evil,
119:104 therefore I *h* every wrong path.
119:163 I *h* and abhor falsehood
139: 21 Do I not *h* those who *h* you,
Pr 8:13 To fear the LORD is to *h* evil;
9: 8 rebuke a mocker or he will *h* you;
13: 5 The righteous *h* what is false,
25:17 too much of you, and he will *h* you.
29:10 Bloodthirsty men *h* a man
Ecc 3: 8 a time to love and a time to *h*,
Isa 61: 8 I *h* robbery and iniquity.
Eze 35: 6 Since you did not *h* bloodshed,
Am 5:15 *H* evil, love good;
Mal 2:16 "I *h* divorce," says the LORD God
Mt 5:43 your neighbor and *h* your enemy.'
10:22 All men will *h* you because of me,
Lk 6:22 Blessed are you when men *h* you,
6:27 do good to those who *h* you,
14:26 does not *h* his father and mother,
Ro 12: 9 *H* what is evil; cling to what is good

HATED (HATE)
Mal 1: 3 loved Jacob, but Esau I have *h*,
Jn 15:18 keep in mind that it *h* me first.
Ro 9:13 "Jacob I loved, but Esau I *h*."
Eph 5:29 no one ever *h* his own body,
Heb 1: 9 righteousness and *h* wickedness;

HATES (HATE)
Pr 6:16 There are six things the LORD *h*,
13:24 He who spares the rod *h* his son,
15:27 but he who *h* bribes will live.
26:28 A lying tongue *h* those it hurts,
Jn 3:20 Everyone who does evil *h* the light,
12:25 while the man who *h* his life
1Jn 2: 9 *h* his brother is still in the darkness.
4:20 "I love God," yet *h* his brother,

HATING (HATE)
Jude :23 *h* even the clothing stained

HATRED (HATE)
Pr 10:12 *H* stirs up dissension,
15:17 than a fattened calf with *h*.
Jas 4: 4 with the world is *h* toward God?

HAUGHTY
Pr 6:17 detestable to him: / *h* eyes,
16:18 a *h* spirit before a fall.

HAVEN
Ps 107: 30 he guided them to their desired *h*.

HAY
1Co 3:12 costly stones, wood, *h* or straw,

HEAD (HEADS HOTHEADED)
Ge 3:15 he will crush your *h*,
Nu 6: 5 no razor may be used on his *h*.
Jdg 16:17 If my *h* were shaved, my strength
1Sa 9: 2 a *h* taller than any of the others.
2Sa 18: 9 Absalom's *h* got caught in the tree.
Ps 23: 5 You anoint my *h* with oil;
133: 2 is like precious oil poured on the *h*,
Pr 10: 6 Blessings crown the *h*
25:22 will heap burning coals on his *h*,
Isa 59:17 and the helmet of salvation on his *h*
Eze 33: 4 his blood will be on his own *h*.
Mt 8:20 of Man has no place to lay his *h*."
Jn 19: 2 crown of thorns and put it on his *h*.
Ro 12:20 will heap burning coals on his *h*."
1Co 11: 3 and the *h* of Christ is God.
11: 5 her *h* uncovered dishonors her *h*—
12:21 And the *h* cannot say to the feet,
Eph 1:22 him to be *h* over everything
5:23 For the husband is the *h* of the wife
Col 1:18 And he is the *h* of the body,
2Ti 4: 5 keep your *h* in all situations,
Rev 14:14 with a crown of gold on his *h*
19:12 and on his *h* are many crowns.

HEADS (HEAD)
Lev 26:13 you to walk with *h* held high.
Ps 22: 7 they hurl insults, shaking their *h*:
24: 7 Lift up your *h*, O you gates;
Isa 35:10 everlasting joy will crown their *h*.
51:11 everlasting joy will crown their *h*.
Mt 27:39 shaking their *h* and saying,
Lk 21:28 stand up and lift up your *h*,
Ac 18: 6 "Your blood be on your own *h*!
Rev 4: 4 and had crowns of gold on their *h*.

HEAL* (HEALED HEALING HEALS)
Nu 12:13 please *h* her!" The LORD replied
Dt 32:39 I have wounded and I will *h*,
2Ki 20: 5 and seen your tears; I will *h* you.
20: 8 the sign that the LORD will *h* me
2Ch 7:14 their sin and will *h* their land.
Job 5:18 he injures, but his hands also *h*.
Ps 6: 2 *h* me, for my bones are in agony.
41: 4 *h* me, for I have sinned against you
Ecc 3: 3 a time to kill and a time to *h*,
Isa 19:22 he will strike them and *h* them.
19:22 respond to their pleas and *h* them.
57:18 seen his ways, but I will *h* him;
57:19 "And I will *h* them."
Jer 17:14 *H* me, O LORD, and I will be
30:17 and *h* your wounds,'
33: 6 I will *h* my people and will let them
La 2:13 Who can *h* you?
Hos 5:13 not able to *h* your sores.
6: 1 but he will *h* us;
7: 1 whenever I would *h* Israel,
14: 4 "I will *h* their waywardness
Na 3:19 Nothing can *h* your wound;
Zec 11:16 or seek the young, or *h* the injured,
Mt 8: 7 said to him, "I will go and *h* him."
10: 1 to *h* every disease and sickness.
10: 8 *H* the sick, raise the dead,
12:10 "Is it lawful to *h* on the Sabbath?"
13:15 and turn, and I would *h* them.'
17:16 but they could not *h* him."
Mk 3: 2 if he would *h* him on the Sabbath.
6: 5 on a few sick people and *h* them.
Lk 4:23 to me: 'Physician, *h* yourself!
5:17 present for him to *h* the sick.
6: 7 to see if he would *h* on the Sabbath.
7: 3 him to come and *h* his servant.
8:43 years, but no one could *h* her.
9: 2 kingdom of God and to *h* the sick.
10: 9 *H* the sick who are there
13:32 and *h* people today and tomorrow,
14: 3 "Is it lawful to *h* on the Sabbath
Jn 4:47 begged him to come and *h* his son,
12:40 nor turn—and I would *h* them."
Ac 4:30 Stretch out your hand to *h*
28:27 and turn, and I would *h* them.'

HEALED* (HEAL)
Ge 20:17 to God, and God *h* Abimelech,
Ex 21:19 and see that he is completely *h*.
Lev 13:37 hair has grown in it, the itch is *h*.
14: 3 If the person has been *h*
Jos 5: 8 were in camp until they were *h*.
1Sa 6: 3 you will be *h*, and you will know
2Ki 2:21 LORD says: 'I have *h* this water.
2Ch 30:20 heard Hezekiah and *h* the people.
Ps 30: 2 and you *h* me.
107: 20 He sent forth his word and *h* them;
Isa 6:10 and turn and be *h*."
53: 5 and by his wounds we are *h*.
Jer 14:19 us so that we cannot be *h*?
17:14 Heal me, O LORD, and I will be *h*;
51: 8 perhaps she can be *h*.
51: 9 but she cannot be *h*;
51: 9 " 'We would have *h* Babylon,
Eze 34: 4 the weak or *h* the sick
Hos 11: 3 it was I who *h* them.
Mt 4:24 and the paralyzed, and he *h* them.
8: 8 the word, and my servant will be *h*.
8:13 his servant was *h* at that very hour.
8:16 with a word and *h* all the sick.
9:21 If I only touch his cloak, I will be *h*
9:22 he said, "your faith has *h* you."
9:22 woman was *h* from that moment.
12:15 him, and he *h* all their sick,
12:22 Jesus *h* him, so that he could both
14:14 on them and *h* their sick.
14:36 and all who touched him were *h*.
15:28 And her daughter was *h*
15:30 laid them at his feet; and he *h* them
17:18 and he was *h* from that moment.
19: 2 followed him, and he *h* them there.
21:14 to him at the temple, and he *h* them
Mk 1:34 and Jesus *h* many who had various
3:10 For he had *h* many, so that those

Mk 5:23 hands on her so that she will be *h*
5:28 If I just touch his clothes, I will be *h*
5:34 "Daughter, your faith has *h* you.
6:13 people with oil and *h* them.
6:56 and all who touched him were *h*.
10:52 said Jesus, "your faith has *h* you."
Lk 4:40 hands on each one, he *h* them.
5:15 and to be *h* of their sicknesses.
6:18 and to be *h* of their diseases.
7: 7 the word, and my servant will be *h*.
8:47 and how she had been instantly *h*.
8:48 "Daughter, your faith has *h* you.
8:50 just believe, and she will be *h*."
9:11 and *h* those who needed healing.
9:42 *h* the boy and gave him back
13:14 Jesus had *h* on the Sabbath,
13:14 So come and be *h* on those days,
14: 4 he *h* him and sent him away.
17:15 when he saw he was *h*, came back,
18:42 your sight; your faith has *h* you."
22:51 touched the man's ear and *h* him.
Jn 5:10 said to the man who had been *h*,
5:13 man who was *h* had no idea who it
Ac 4: 9 and are asked how he was *h*,
4:10 stands before you *h*.
4:14 who had been *h* standing there
4:22 man who was miraculously *h* was
5:16 evil spirits, and all of them were *h*.
8: 7 paralytics and cripples were *h*.
14: 9 saw that he had faith to be *h*
28: 8 placed his hands on him and *h* him.
Heb 12:13 may not be disabled, but rather *h*.
Jas 5:16 for each other so that you may be *h*
1Pe 2:24 by his wounds you have been *h*.
Rev 13: 3 but the fatal wound had been *h*.
13:12 whose fatal wound had been *h*.

HEALING* (HEAL)

2Ch 28:15 food and drink, and *h* balm.
Pr 12:18 but the tongue of the wise brings *h*.
13:17 but a trustworthy envoy brings *h*.
15: 4 The tongue that brings *h* is a tree
16:24 sweet to the soul and *h* to the bones
Isa 58: 8 and your *h* will quickly appear;
Jer 8:15 for a time of *h*
8:22 Why then is there no *h*
14:19 for a time of *h*
30:12 your injury beyond *h*.
30:13 no *h* for you.
33: 6 I will bring health and *h* to it;
46:11 there is no *h* for you.
Eze 30:21 It has not been bound up for *h*
47:12 for food and their leaves for *h*."
Mal 4: 2 rise with *h* in its wings.
Mt 4:23 and *h* every disease and sickness
9:35 and *h* every disease and sickness.
Lk 6:19 coming from him and *h* them all.
9: 6 gospel and *h* people everywhere.
9:11 and healed those who needed *h*.
Jn 7:23 angry with me for *h* the whole man
Ac 3:16 him that has given this complete *h*
10:38 *h* all who were under the power
1Co 12: 9 to another gifts of *h*
12:28 also those having gifts of *h*,
12:30 Do all have gifts of *h*? Do all speak
Rev 22: 2 are for the *h* of the nations.

HEALS* (HEAL)

Ex 15:26 for I am the LORD, who *h* you."
Lev 13:18 a boil on his skin and it *h*,
Ps 103: 3 and *h* all your diseases;
147: 3 He *h* the brokenhearted
Isa 30:26 and *h* the wounds he inflicted.
Ac 9:34 said to him, "Jesus Christ *h* you.

HEALTH* (HEALTHIER HEALTHY)

1Sa 25: 6 And good *h* to all that is yours!
25: 6 Good *h* to you and your household
Ps 38: 3 of your wrath there is no *h*
38: 7 there is no *h* in my body.
Pr 3: 8 This will bring *h* to your body
4:22 and *h* to a man's whole body.
15:30 and good news gives *h* to the bones
Isa 38:16 You restored me to *h*
Jer 30:17 But I will restore you to *h*
33: 6 I will bring *h* and healing to it;
3Jn : 2 I pray that you may enjoy good *h*

HEALTHIER* (HEALTH)

Da 1:15 end of the ten days they looked *h*

HEALTHY* (HEALTH)

Ge 41: 5 Seven heads of grain, *h* and good,
41: 7 of grain swallowed up the seven *h*,
Ps 73: 4 their bodies are *h* and strong.
Zec 11:16 or heal the injured, or feed the *h*,
Mt 9:12 "It is not the *h* who need a doctor,
Mk 2:17 "It is not the *h* who need a doctor,
Lk 5:31 "It is not the *h* who need a doctor,

HEAP

Pr 25:22 you will *h* burning coals
Ro 12:20 you will *h* burning coals

HEAR (HEARD HEARING HEARS)

Ex 15:14 The nations will *h* and tremble;
22:27 I will *h*, for I am compassionate.
Nu 14:13 Then the Egyptians will *h* about it!
Dt 1:16 *H* the disputes between your
4:36 heaven he made you *h* his voice
6: 4 *H*, O Israel: The LORD our God,
19:20 The rest of the people will *h* of this
31:13 must *h* it and learn
Jos 7: 9 of the country will *h* about this
1Ki 8:30 *H* the supplication of your servant
2Ki 19:16 O LORD, and *h*; open your eyes,
2Ch 7:14 then will I *h* from heaven
Job 31:35 ("Oh, that I had someone to *h* me!
Ps 94: 9 he who implanted the ear not *h*?
95: 7 Today, if you *h* his voice,
Ecc 7:21 or you may *h* your servant cursing
Isa 21: 3 I am staggered by what I *h*,
29:18 that day the deaf will *h* the words
30:21 your ears will *h* a voice behind you,
51: 7 *H* me, you who know what is right,
59: 1 nor his ear too dull to *h*.
65:24 while they are still speaking I will *h*
Jer 5:21 who have ears but do not *h*:
Eze 33: 7 so *h* the word I speak and give
37: 4 'Dry bones, *h* the word
Mt 11: 5 the deaf *h*, the dead are raised,
11:15 He who has ears, let him *h*.
13:17 and to *h* what you *h* but did not *h* it
Mk 12:29 answered Jesus, "is this: '*H*,
Lk 7:22 the deaf *h*, the dead are raised,
Jn 8:47 reason you do not *h* is that you do
Ac 13: 7 he wanted to *h* the word of God.
13:44 gathered to *h* the word of the Lord.
17:32 "We want to *h* you again
Ro 2:13 is not those who *h* the law who are
10:14 they *h* without someone preaching
2Ti 4: 3 what their itching ears want to *h*.
Heb 3: 7 "Today, if you *h* his voice,
Rev 1: 3 and blessed are those who *h* it

HEARD (HEAR)

Ex 2:24 God *h* their groaning and he
Dt 4:32 has anything like it ever been *h* of?
2Sa 7:22 as we have *h* with our own ears.
Job 42: 5 My ears had *h* of you
Isa 40:21 Have you not *h*?
40:28 Have you not *h*?
66: 8 Who has ever *h* of such a thing?
Jer 18:13 Who has ever *h* anything like this?
Da 10:12 your words were *h*, and I have
12: 8 I *h*, but I did not understand.
Hab 3:16 I *h* and my heart pounded,
Mt 5:21 "You have *h* that it was said
5:27 "You have *h* that it was said,
5:33 you have *h* that it was said
5:38 "You have *h* that it was said,
5:43 "You have *h* that it was said,
Lk 12: 3 in the dark will be *h* in the daylight,
Jn 8:26 and what I have *h* from him I tell
Ac 2: 6 because each one *h* them speaking
1Co 2: 9 no ear has *h*,
2Co 12: 4 He *h* inexpressible things,
1Th 2:13 word of God, which you *h* from us,
2Ti 1:13 What you *h* from me, keep
Jas 1:25 not forgetting what he has *h*,
Rev 22: 8 am the one who *h* and saw these

HEARING (HEAR)

Isa 6: 9 Be ever *h*, but never understanding
Mt 13:14 will be ever *h* but never
Mk 4:12 ever *h* but never understanding;
Ac 28:26 will be ever *h* but never
Ro 10:17 faith comes from *h* the message,
1Co 12:17 where would the sense of *h* be?

HEARS (HEAR)

Jn 5:24 whoever *h* my word and believes
1Jn 5:14 according to his will, he *h* us.
Rev 3:20 If anyone *h* my voice and opens

HEART (BROKENHEARTED FAINT-HEARTED HARDHEARTED HEART'S HEARTACHE HEARTS KINDHEARTED SIMPLEHEARTED STOUTHEARTED WHOLEHEARTED WHOLEHEARTEDLY)

Ge 6: 5 of his *h* was only evil all the time.
Ex 4:21 But I will harden his *h*
25: 2 each man whose *h* prompts him
35:21 and whose *h* moved him came
Lev 19:17 Do not hate your brother in your *h*.
Dt 4: 9 or let them slip from your *h* as long
4:29 if you look for him with all your *h*
6: 5 LORD your God with all your *h*
10:12 LORD your God with all your *h*
11:13 and to serve him with all your *h*
13: 3 you love him with all your *h*
15:10 and do so without a grudging *h*;
26:16 observe them with all your *h*
29:18 you today whose *h* turns away
30: 2 and obey him with all your *h*
30: 6 you may love him with all your *h*
30:10 LORD your God with all your *h*
Jos 22: 5 and to serve him with all your *h*
23:14 You know with all your *h*
1Sa 10: 9 God changed Saul's *h*,
12:20 serve the LORD with all your *h*.
12:24 serve him faithfully with all your *h*;
13:14 sought out a man after his own *h*
14: 7 I am with you *h* and soul."
16: 7 but the LORD looks at the *h*."
17:32 "Let no one lose *h* on account
1Ki 2: 4 faithfully before me with all their *h*
3: 9 So give your servant a discerning *h*
3:12 give you a wise and discerning *h*,
8:48 back to you with all their *h*
9: 3 and my *h* will always be there.
9: 4 walk before me in integrity of *h*
10:24 the wisdom God had put in his *h*.
11: 4 and his *h* was not fully devoted
14: 8 and followed me with all his *h*,
15:14 Asa's *h* was fully committed
2Ki 22:19 Because your *h* was responsive
23: 3 with all his *h* and all his soul,
1Ch 28: 9 for the LORD searches every *h*
2Ch 6:38 back to you with all their *h*
7:16 and my *h* will always be there.
15:12 of their fathers, with all their *h*
15:17 Asa's *h* was fully committed
17: 6 His *h* was devoted to the ways
22: 9 sought the LORD with all his *h*."
34:31 with all his *h* and all his soul,
36:13 stiff-necked and hardened his *h*
Ezr 1: 5 everyone whose *h* God had moved
Ne 4: 6 the people worked with all their *h*.
Job 19:27 How my *h* yearns within me!
22:22 and lay up his words in your *h*.
37: 1 "At this my *h* pounds
Ps 9: 1 you, O LORD, with all my *h*;
14: 1 The fool says in his *h*,
16: 9 Therefore my *h* is glad
19:14 and the meditation of my *h*
20: 4 he give you the desire of your *h*
24: 4 who has clean hands and a pure *h*,
26: 2 examine my *h* and my mind;
37: 4 will give you the desires of your *h*.
37:31 The law of his God is in his *h*;
44:21 since he knows the secrets of the *h*
45: 1 My *h* is stirred by a noble theme
51:10 Create in me a pure *h*, O God,
51:17 a broken and contrite *h*,
53: 1 The fool says in his *h*,
66:18 If I had cherished sin in my *h*,
73: 1 to those who are pure in *h*.
73:26 My flesh and my *h* may fail,
86:11 give me an undivided *h*,
90:12 that we may gain a *h* of wisdom.
97:11 and joy on the upright in *h*.
108: 1 My *h* is steadfast, O God;
109: 22 and my *h* is wounded within me.
111: 1 I will extol the LORD with all my *h*
112: 7 his *h* is steadfast, trusting
112: 8 His *h* is secure, he will have no fear
119: 2 and seek him with all their *h*.
119: 10 I seek you with all my *h*;
119: 11 I have hidden your word in my *h*
119: 30 I have set my *h* on your laws.
119: 32 for you have set my *h* free.
119: 34 and obey it with all my *h*.
119: 36 Turn my *h* toward your statutes
119: 58 sought your face with all my *h*;
119: 69 I keep your precepts with all my *h*.
119:111 they are the joy of my *h*.
119:112 My *h* is set on keeping your
119:145 I call with all my *h*; answer me,
125: 4 to those who are upright in *h*.
138: 1 you, O LORD, with all my *h*;
139: 23 Search me, O God, and know my *h*
Pr 2: 2 applying your *h* to understanding,
3: 1 but keep my commands in your *h*,
3: 3 write them on the tablet of your *h*.
3: 5 Trust in the LORD with all your *h*
4: 4 hold of my words with all your *h*;
4:21 keep them within your *h*;
4:23 Above all else, guard your *h*,
6:21 Bind them upon your *h* forever;
7: 3 write them on the tablet of your *h*.
10: 8 The wise in *h* accept commands,
13:12 Hope deferred makes the *h* sick,
14:13 Even in laughter the *h* may ache,
14:30 A *h* at peace gives life to the body,
15:13 A happy *h* makes the face cheerful,
15:15 the cheerful *h* has a continual feast.
15:28 *h* of the righteous weighs its

Pr 15:30 A cheerful look brings joy to the *h,*
16:23 A wise man's *h* guides his mouth,
17:22 A cheerful *h* is good medicine,
20: 9 can say, "I have kept my *h* pure;
22:11 He who loves a pure *h*
22:17 apply your *h* to what I teach,
22:18 when you keep them in your *h*
23:15 My son, if your *h* is wise,
23:19 and keep your *h* on the right path.
23:26 My son, give me your *h*
24:17 stumbles, do not let your *h* rejoice,
27:19 so a man's *h* reflects the man.
Ecc 5: 2 do not be hasty in your *h*
8: 5 wise *h* will know the proper time
11:10 banish anxiety from your *h*
SS 3: 1 I looked for the one my *h* loves;
4: 9 You have stolen my *h,* my sister,
5: 2 *Beloved* I slept but my *h* was awake
5: 4 my *h* began to pound for him.
8: 6 Place me like a seal over your *h,*
Isa 6:10 Make the *h* of this people calloused
40:11 and carries them close to his *h;*
57:15 and to revive the *h* of the contrite.
66:14 you see this, your *h* will rejoice
Jer 3:15 give you shepherds after my own *h,*
4:14 wash the evil from your *h*
9:26 of Israel is uncircumcised in *h."*
17: 9 The *h* is deceitful above all things
20: 9 is in my *h* like a fire,
24: 7 I will give them a *h* to know me,
29:13 when you seek me with all your *h.*
32:39 I will give them singleness of *h*
32:41 them in this land with all my *h*
51:46 Do not lose *h* or be afraid
Eze 11:19 I will give them an undivided *h*
18:31 and get a new *h* and a new spirit.
36:26 I will give you a new *h*
44: 7 foreigners uncircumcised in *h*
Da 7: 4 and the *h* of a man was given to it.
Joel 2:12 "return to me with all your *h,*
2:13 Rend your *h*
Zep 3:14 Be glad and rejoice with all your *h,*
Mt 5: 8 Blessed are the pure in *h,*
5:28 adultery with her in his *h.*
6:21 treasure is, there your *h* will be
11:29 for I am gentle and humble in *h,*
12:34 of the *h* the mouth speaks.
13:15 For this people's *h* has become
15:18 out of the mouth come from the *h,*
15:19 For out of the *h* come evil thoughts
18:35 forgive your brother from your *h."*
22:37 the Lord your God with all your *h*
Mk 11:23 and does not doubt in his *h*
12:30 the Lord your God with all your *h*
12:33 To love him with all your *h,*
Lk 2:19 and pondered them in her *h.*
2:51 treasured all these things in her *h.*
6:45 out of the good stored up in his *h,*
6:45 overflow of his *h* his mouth speaks.
8:15 for those with a noble and good *h,*
10:27 the Lord your God with all your *h*
12:34 treasure is, there your *h* will be
Jn 12:27 "Now my *h* is troubled,
Ac 1:24 "Lord, you know everyone's *h.*
2:37 they were cut to the *h*
4:32 All the believers were one in *h*
8:21 your *h* is not right before God.
15: 8 who knows the *h,* showed that he
16:14 The Lord opened her *h* to respond
28:27 For this people's *h* has become
Ro 1: 9 with my whole *h* in preaching
2:29 is circumcision of the *h,*
10: 9 in your *h* that God raised him
10:10 is with your *h* that you believe
15: 6 with one *h* and mouth you may
1Co 14:25 the secrets of his *h* will be laid bare.
2Co 2: 4 anguish of *h* and with many tears,
4: 1 this ministry, we do not lose *h.*
4:16 Therefore we do not lose *h.*
9: 7 give what he has decided in his *h*
Eph 1:18 eyes of your *h* may be enlightened
5:19 make music in your *h* to the Lord,
6: 5 and with sincerity of *h,* just
6: 6 doing the will of God from your *h.*
Php 1: 7 since I have you in my *h;* for
Col 2: 2 is that they may be encouraged in *h*
3:22 but with sincerity of *h*
3:23 work at it with all your *h,*
1Ti 1: 5 which comes from a pure *h*
3: 1 If anyone sets his *h*
2Ti 2:22 call on the Lord out of a pure *h.*
Phm :12 who is my very *h*— back to you.
:20 in the Lord; refresh my *h* in Christ.
Heb 4:12 the thoughts and attitudes of the *h.*
1Pe 1:22 one another deeply, from the *h.*

HEART'S* (HEART)

2Ch 1:11 "Since this is your *h* desire
Jer 15:16 they were my joy and my *h* delight,
Eze 24:25 delight of their eyes, their *h* desire,
Ro 10: 1 my *h* desire and prayer to God

HEARTACHE* (HEART)

Pr 15:13 but *h* crushes the spirit.

HEARTLESS*

La 4: 3 but my people have become *h*
Ro 1:31 they are senseless, faithless, *h,*

HEARTS (HEART)

Lev 26:41 their uncircumcised *h* are humbled
Dt 6: 6 are to be upon your *h.*
10:16 Circumcise your *h,* therefore,
11:18 Fix these words of mine in your *h*
30: 6 your God will circumcise your *h*
Jos 11:20 himself who hardened their *h*
24:23 and yield your *h* to the LORD,
1Sa 7: 3 to the LORD with all your *h,*
10:26 valiant men whose *h* God had
2Sa 15: 6 and so he stole the *h* of the men
1Ki 8:39 for you alone know the *h* of all men
8:61 your *h* must be fully committed
18:37 are turning their *h* back again."
1Ch 29:18 and keep their *h* loyal to you.
2Ch 6:30 (for you alone know the *h* of men),
11:16 tribe of Israel who set their *h*
29:31 all whose *h* were willing brought
Ps 7: 9 who searches minds and *h,*
33:21 In him our *h* rejoice,
62: 8 pour out your *h* to him,
95: 8 do not harden your *h* as you did
Ecc 3:11 also set eternity in the *h* of men;
Isa 26: 8 are the desire of our *h.*
29:13 but their *h* are far from me.
35: 4 say to those with fearful *h,*
51: 7 people who have my law in your *h:*
63:17 harden our *h* so we do not revere
65:14 out of the joy of their *h,*
Jer 4: 4 circumcise your *h,*
12: 2 but far from their *h.*
17: 1 on the tablets of their *h*
31:33 and write it on their *h.*
Mal 4: 6 He will turn the *h* of the fathers
Mt 15: 8 but their *h* are far from me.
Mk 6:52 the loaves; their *h* were hardened.
7: 6 but their *h* are far from me.
7:21 out of men's *h,* come evil thoughts,
Lk 1:17 to turn the *h* of the fathers
16:15 of men, but God knows your *h.*
24:32 "Were not our *h* burning within us
Jn 5:42 not have the love of God in your *h.*
14: 1 "Do not let your *h* be troubled.
14:27 Do not let your *h* be troubled
Ac 7:51 with uncircumcised *h* and ears!
11:23 true to the Lord with all their *h.*
15: 9 for he purified their *h* by faith.
28:27 understand with their *h*
Ro 1:21 and their foolish *h* were darkened.
2:15 of the law are written on their *h,*
5: 5 love into our *h* by the Holy Spirit,
8:27 who searches our *h* knows
1Co 4: 5 will expose the motives of men's *h.*
2Co 1:22 put his Spirit in our *h* as a deposit,
3: 2 written on our *h,* known
3: 3 but on tablets of human *h.*
4: 6 shine in our *h* to give us the light
6:11 and opened wide our *h* to you.
6:13 to my children—open wide your *h*
7: 2 Make room for us in your *h.*
Gal 4: 6 the Spirit of his Son into our *h,*
Eph 3:17 dwell in your *h* through faith.
Php 4: 7 will guard your *h* and your minds
Col 3: 1 set your *h* on things above,
3:15 the peace of Christ rule in your *h,*
3:16 with gratitude in your *h* to God.
1Th 2: 4 men but God, who tests our *h.*
3:13 May he strengthen your *h*
2Th 2:17 encourage your *h* and strengthen
Phm : 7 have refreshed the *h* of the saints.
Heb 3: 8 do not harden your *h*
8:10 and write them on their *h.*
10:16 I will put my laws in their *h,*
10:22 having our *h* sprinkled
Jas 4: 8 purify your *h,* you double-minded.
2Pe 1:19 the morning star rises in your *h.*
1Jn 3:20 For God is greater than our *h,*

HEAT

Ps 19: 6 nothing is hidden from its *h.*
2Pe 3:12 and the elements will melt in the *h.*

HEAVEN (HEAVENLY HEAVENS HEAVENWARD)

Ge 14:19 Creator of *h* and earth.
28:12 with its top reaching to *h,*
Ex 16: 4 rain down bread from *h* for you.
20:22 that I have spoken to you from *h:*
Dt 26:15 from *h,* your holy dwelling place,
30:12 "Who will ascend into *h* to get it
1Ki 8:27 the highest *h,* cannot contain you.
8:30 Hear from *h,* your dwelling place,
22:19 the host of *h* standing around him
2Ki 2: 1 up to *h* in a whirlwind,
19:15 You have made *h* and earth.
2Ch 7:14 then will I hear from *h*
Isa 14:12 How you have fallen from *h,*
66: 1 "*H* is my throne,
Da 7:13 coming with the clouds of *h.*
Mt 3: 2 for the kingdom of *h* is near."
3:16 At that moment *h* was opened,
4:17 for the kingdom of *h* is near."
5:12 because great is your reward in *h,*
5:19 great in the kingdom of *h.*
6: 9 " 'Our Father in *h,*
6:10 done on earth as it is in *h.*
6:20 up for yourselves treasures in *h,*
7:21 Lord,' will enter the kingdom of *h,*
16:19 bind on earth will be bound in *h,*
18: 3 will never enter the kingdom of *h.*
18:18 bind on earth will be bound in *h,*
19:14 the kingdom of *h* belongs to such
19:21 and you will have treasure in *h.*
19:23 man to enter the kingdom of *h.*
23:13 the kingdom of *h* in men's faces.
24:35 *H* and earth will pass away,
26:64 and coming on the clouds of *h."*
28:18 "All authority in *h*
Mk 1:10 he saw *h* being torn open
10:21 and you will have treasure in *h.*
13:31 *H* and earth will pass away,
14:62 and coming on the clouds of *h."*
16:19 he was taken up into *h*
Lk 3:21 *h* was opened and the Holy Spirit
10:18 saw Satan fall like lightning from *h.*
10:20 that your names are written in *h."*
12:33 in *h* that will not be exhausted,
15: 7 in *h* over one sinner who repents
18:22 and you will have treasure in *h.*
21:33 *H* and earth will pass away,
24:51 left them and was taken up into *h.*
Jn 3:13 No one has ever gone into *h*
6:38 down from *h* not to do my will
12:28 Then a voice came from *h,*
Ac 1:11 has been taken from you into *h,*
7:49 the prophet says: " '*H* is my
7:55 looked up to *h* and saw the glory
9: 3 a light from *h* flashed around him.
26:19 disobedient to the vision from *h.*
Ro 10: 6 'Who will ascend into *h?*' " (that is,
1Co 15:47 the earth, the second man from *h.*
2Co 5: 1 an eternal house in *h,* not built
12: 2 ago was caught up to the third *h.*
Eph 1:10 to bring all things in *h*
Php 2:10 *h* and on earth and under the earth,
3:20 But our citizenship is in *h.*
Col 1:16 things in *h* and on earth, visible
4: 1 that you also have a Master in *h.*
1Th 1:10 and to wait for his Son from *h,*
4:16 himself will come down from *h,*
Heb 1: 3 hand of the Majesty in *h.*
8: 5 and shadow of what is in *h.*
9:24 he entered *h* itself, now to appear
12:23 whose names are written in *h.*
1Pe 1: 4 spoil or fade—kept in *h* for you,
3:22 who has gone into *h* and is
2Pe 3:13 we are looking forward to a new *h*
Rev 5:13 Then I heard every creature in *h*
11:19 God's temple in *h* was opened,
12: 7 And there was war in *h.*
15: 5 this I looked and in *h* the temple,
19: 1 of a great multitude in *h* shouting:
19:11 I saw *h* standing open and there
21: 1 Then I saw a new *h* and a new earth
21:10 coming down out of *h* from God.

HEAVENLY (HEAVEN)

Ps 8: 5 him a little lower than the *h* beings
2Co 5: 2 to be clothed with our *h* dwelling,
Eph 1: 3 in the *h* realms with every spiritual
1:20 at his right hand in the *h* realms,
2Ti 4:18 bring me safely to his *h* kingdom.
Heb 12:22 to the *h* Jerusalem, the city

HEAVENS (HEAVEN)

Ge 1: 1 In the beginning God created the *h*
11: 4 with a tower that reaches to the *h,*
Dt 33:26 who rides on the *h* to help you
1Ki 8:27 The *h,* even the highest heaven,
2Ch 2: 6 since the *h,* even the highest
Ezr 9: 6 and our guilt has reached to the *h.*
Ne 9: 6 You made the *h,* even the highest
Job 11: 8 They are higher than the *h*—
38:33 Do you know the laws of the *h?*
Ps 8: 3 When I consider your *h,*
19: 1 The *h* declare the glory of God;
33: 6 of the LORD were the *h* made,
57: 5 Be exalted, O God, above the *h;*

Ps 102: 25 the *h* are the work of your hands.
103: 11 as high as the *h* are above the earth,
108: 4 is your love, higher than the *h*;
115: 16 The highest *h* belong to the LORD
119: 89 it stands firm in the *h*.
135: 6 in the *h* and on the earth,
139: 8 If I go up to the *h*, you are there;
148: 1 Praise the LORD from the *h*,
Isa 40:26 Lift your eyes and look to the *h*:
45: 8 "You *h* above, rain
51: 6 Lift up your eyes to the *h*,
55: 9 "As the *h* are higher than the earth,
65:17 new *h* and a new earth.
Jer 31:37 if the *h* above can be measured
32:17 you have made the *h* and the earth
Eze 1: 1 *h* were opened and I saw visions
Da 12: 3 shine like the brightness of the *h*,
Joel 2:30 I will show wonders in the *h*
Mt 24:31 from one end of the *h* to the other.
Mk 13:27 of the earth to the ends of the *h*.
Eph 4:10 who ascended higher than all the *h*,
Heb 4:14 priest who has gone through the *h*,
7:26 from sinners, exalted above the *h*.
2Pe 3: 5 ago by God's word the *h* existed
3:10 The *h* will disappear with a roar;

HEAVENWARD (HEAVEN)
Php 3:14 for which God has called me *h*

HEAVIER (HEAVY)
Pr 27: 3 provocation by a fool is *h* than both

HEAVY (HEAVIER)
1Ki 12: 4 and the *h* yoke he put on us,
Ecc 1:13 What a *h* burden God has laid
Isa 47: 6 you laid a very *h* yoke.
Mt 23: 4 They tie up *h* loads and put them

HEBREW (HEBREWS)
Ge 14:13 and reported this to Abram the *H*.
2Ki 18:26 speak to us in *H* in the hearing
Php 3: 5 tribe of Benjamin, a *H* of Hebrews;

HEBREWS (HEBREW)
Ex 9: 1 of the *H*, says: "Let my people go,
2Co 11:22 Are they *H*? So am I.

HEBRON
Ge 13:18 near the great trees of Mamre at *H*,
23: 2 died at Kiriath Arba (that is, *H*)
Jos 14:13 and gave him *H* as his inheritance.
20: 7 *H*) in the hill country of Judah.
21:13 the priest they gave *H* (a city
2Sa 2:11 king in *H* over the house

HEDGE
Job 1:10 "Have you not put a *h* around him

HEED (HEEDS)
Ecc 7: 5 It is better to *h* a wise man's rebuke

HEEDS (HEED)
Pr 13: 1 wise son *h* his father's instruction,
13:18 whoever *h* correction is honored.
15: 5 whoever *h* correction shows
15:32 whoever *h* correction gains

HEEL
Ge 3:15 and you will strike his *h*."

HEIR (INHERIT)
Gal 4: 7 God has made you also an *h*.
Heb 1: 2 whom he appointed *h* of all things,

HEIRS (INHERIT)
Ro 8:17 then we are *h*— *h* of God
Gal 3:29 and *h* according to the promise.
Eph 3: 6 gospel the Gentiles are *h* together
1Pe 3: 7 as *h* with you of the gracious gift

HELD (HOLD)
Ex 17:11 As long as Moses *h* up his hands,
Dt 4: 4 but all of you who *h* fast
2Ki 18: 6 He *h* fast to the LORD
SS 3: 4 I *h* him and would not let him go
Isa 65: 2 All day long I have *h* out my hands
Ro 10:21 day long I have *h* out my hands
Col 2:19 and *h* together by its ligaments

HELL*
Mt 5:22 will be in danger of the fire of *h*.
5:29 body to be thrown into *h*.
5:30 for your whole body to go into *h*.
10:28 destroy both soul and body in *h*.
18: 9 and be thrown into the fire of *h*.
23:15 as much a son of *h* as you are.
23:33 you escape being condemned to *h*?
Mk 9:43 than with two hands to go into *h*,
9:45 have two feet and be thrown into *h*.
9:47 two eyes and be thrown into *h*,
Lk 12: 5 has power to throw you into *h*.
Lk 16:23 In *h*, where he was in torment,
Jas 3: 6 and is itself set on fire by *h*.
2Pe 2: 4 but sent them to *h*, putting them

HELMET
Isa 59:17 and the *h* of salvation on his head;
Eph 6:17 Take the *h* of salvation
1Th 5: 8 and the hope of salvation as a *h*.

HELP (HELPED HELPER HELPFUL HELPING HELPLESS HELPS)
Ex 23: 5 leave it there; be sure you *h* him
Lev 25:35 *h* him as you would an alien
Dt 33:26 who rides on the heavens to *h* you
2Ch 16:12 even in his illness he did not seek *h*
Ps 18: 6 I cried to my God for *h*.
30: 2 my God, I called to you for *h*
33:20 he is our *h* and our shield.
46: 1 an ever-present *h* in trouble.
72:12 the afflicted who have no one to *h*.
79: 9 *H* us, O God our Savior,
108: 12 for the *h* of man is worthless.
115: 9 he is their *h* and shield.
121: 1 where does my *h* come from?
Ecc 4:10 his friend can *h* him up.
Isa 41:10 I will strengthen you and *h* you;
Jnh 2: 2 depths of the grave I called for *h*,
Mk 9:24 *h* me overcome my unbelief!"
Lk 11:46 will not lift one finger to *h* them.
Ac 16: 9 Come over to Macedonia and *h* us
18:27 he was a great *h* to those who
20:35 of hard work we must *h* the weak,
26:22 I have had God's *h* to this very day,
1Co 12:28 those able to *h* others, those
2Co 9: 2 For I know your eagerness to *h*,
1Ti 5:16 she should *h* them and not let

HELPED (HELP)
1Sa 7:12 "Thus far has the LORD *h* us."

HELPER (HELP)
Ge 2:18 I will make a *h* suitable for him."
Ps 10:14 you are the *h* of the fatherless.
Heb 13: 6 Lord is my *h*; I will not be afraid.

HELPFUL (HELP)
Eph 4:29 only what is *h* for building others

HELPING (HELP)
Ac 9:36 always doing good and *h* the poor.
1Ti 5:10 *h* those in trouble and devoting

HELPLESS (HELP)
Ps 10:12 Do not forget the *h*.
Mt 9:36 because they were harassed and *h*,

HELPS (HELP)
Ro 8:26 the Spirit *h* us in our weakness.

HEN
Mt 23:37 as a *h* gathers her chicks
Lk 13:34 as a *h* gathers her chicks

HERALD
1Ti 2: 7 for this purpose I was appointed a *h*
2Ti 1:11 of this gospel I was appointed a *h*

HERBS
Ex 12: 8 with bitter *h*, and bread made

HERITAGE (INHERIT)
Ps 61: 5 you have given me the *h*
119: 111 Your statutes are my *h* forever;
127: 3 Sons are a *h* from the LORD,

HEROD
1. King of Judea who tried to kill Jesus (Mt 2; Lk 1:5).
2. Son of 1. Tetrarch of Galilee who arrested and beheaded John the Baptist (Mt 14:1-12; Mk 6:14-29; Lk 3:1, 19-20; 9:7-9); tried Jesus (Lk 23:6-15).
3. Grandson of 1. King of Judea who killed James (Ac 12:2); arrested Peter (Ac 12:3-19). Death (Ac 12:19-23).

HERODIAS
Wife of Herod the Tetrarch who persuaded her daughter to ask for John the Baptist's head (Mt 14:1-12; Mk 6:14-29).

HEWN
Isa 51: 1 the quarry from which you were *h*;

HEZEKIAH
King of Judah. Restored the temple and worship (2Ch 29-31). Sought the LORD for help against Assyria (2Ki 18-19; 2Ch 32:1-23; Isa 36-37). Illness healed (2Ki 20:1-11; 2Ch 32:24-26; Isa 38). Judged for showing Babylonians his treasures (2Ki 20:12-21; 2Ch 32:31; Isa 39).

HID (HIDE)
Ge 3: 8 and they *h* from the LORD God
Ex 2: 2 she *h* him for three months.
Jos 6:17 because she *h* the spies we sent.
1Ki 18:13 I *h* a hundred of the LORD's
2Ch 22:11 she *h* the child from Athaliah
Isa 54: 8 I *h* my face from you for a moment,
Mt 13:44 When a man found it, he *h* it again,
25:25 and *h* your talent in the ground.
Heb 11:23 By faith Moses' parents *h* him

HIDDEN (HIDE)
1Sa 10:22 has *h* himself among the baggage."
Job 28:11 and brings *h* things to light.
Ps 19:12 Forgive my *h* faults.
78: 2 I will utter *h* things, things from of old—
119: 11 I have *h* your word in my heart
Pr 2: 4 and search for it as for *h* treasure,
27: 5 rebuke than *h* love.
Isa 59: 2 your sins have *h* his face from you,
Da 2:22 He reveals deep and *h* things;
Mt 5:14 A city on a hill cannot be *h*.
10:26 or *h* that will not be made known.
11:25 because you have *h* these things
13:35 I will utter things *h*
13:44 of heaven is like treasure *h*
Mk 4:22 For whatever is *h* is meant
Ro 16:25 of the mystery *h* for long ages past,
1Co 2: 7 a wisdom that has been *h*
Eph 3: 9 for ages past was kept *h* in God,
Col 1:26 the mystery that has been kept *h*
2: 3 in whom are *h* all the treasures
3: 3 and your life is now *h* with Christ

HIDE (HID HIDDEN HIDING)
Dt 31:17 I will *h* my face from them,
Ps 17: 8 *h* me in the shadow of your wings
27: 5 he will *h* me in the shelter
143: 9 for I *h* myself in you.
Isa 53: 3 one from whom men *h* their faces

HIDING (HIDE)
Ps 32: 7 You are my *h* place;
Pr 28:12 to power, men go into *h*.

HIGH
Ge 14:18 He was priest of God Most *H*,
14:22 God Most *H*, Creator of heaven
Ps 21: 7 the unfailing love of the Most *H*
82: 6 you are all sons of the Most *H*.'
Isa 14:14 I will make myself like the Most *H*
Da 4:17 know that the Most *H* is sovereign
Mk 5: 7 Jesus, Son of the Most *H* God?
Heb 7: 1 and priest of God Most *H*.

HIGHWAY
Isa 40: 3 a *h* for our God.

HILL (HILLS)
Ps 24: 3 ascend the *h* of the LORD?
Isa 40: 4 every mountain and *h* made low;
Mt 5:14 A city on a *h* cannot be hidden.
Lk 3: 5 every mountain and *h* made low.

HILLS (HILL)
1Ki 20:23 "Their gods are gods of the *h*.
Ps 50:10 and the cattle on a thousand *h*.
121: 1 I lift up my eyes to the *h*—
Hos 10: 8 and to the *h*, "Fall on us!"
Lk 23:30 and to the *h*, "Cover us!"'
Rev 17: 9 The seven heads are seven *h*

HINDER (HINDERED HINDERS)
1Sa 14: 6 Nothing can *h* the LORD
Mt 19:14 come to me, and do not *h* them,
1Co 9:12 anything rather than *h* the gospel
1Pe 3: 7 so that nothing will *h* your prayers.

HINDERED (HINDER)
Lk 11:52 and you have *h* those who were

HINDERS (HINDER)
Heb 12: 1 let us throw off everything that *h*

HINT*
Eph 5: 3 even a *h* of sexual immorality,

HIP
Ge 32:32 socket of Jacob's *h* was touched

HIRAM
King of Tyre; helped David build his palace (2Sa 5:11-12; 1Ch 14:1); helped Solomon build the temple (1Ki 5; 2Ch 2) and his navy (1Ki 9:10-27; 2Ch 8).

HIRED
Lk 15:15 and *h* himself out to a citizen
Jn 10:12 *h* hand is not the shepherd who

HOARDED (HOARDS)
Ecc 5:13 wealth h to the harm of its owner,
Jas 5: 3 You have h wealth in the last days.

HOARDS (HOARDED)
Pr 11:26 People curse the man who h grain,

HOLD (HELD HOLDS)
Ex 20: 7 LORD will not h anyone guiltless
Lev 19:13 " 'Do not h back the wages
Dt 5:11 LORD will not h anyone guiltless
11:22 in all his ways and to h fast to him
13: 4 serve him and h fast to him.
30:20 listen to his voice, and h fast to him
Jos 22: 5 to h fast to him and to serve him
2Ki 4:16 "you will h a son in your arms."
Ps 18:16 from on high and took h of me;
73:23 you h me by my right hand.
Pr 4: 4 "Lay h of my words
Isa 41:13 who takes h of your right hand
54: 2 do not h back;
Eze 3:18 and I will h you accountable
3:20 and I will h you accountable
33: 6 I will h the watchman accountable
Zec 8:23 nations will take firm h of one Jew
Mk 11:25 if you h anything against anyone,
Jn 20:17 Jesus said, "Do not h on to me,
Php 2:16 as you h out the word of life—
3:12 but I press on to take h of that
Col 1:17 and in him all things h together.
1Th 5:21 H on to the good.
1Ti 6:12 Take h of the eternal life
Heb 10:23 Let us h unswervingly

HOLDS (HOLD)
Pr 10:19 but he who h his tongue is wise.
17:28 and discerning if he h his tongue.

HOLES
Hag 1: 6 to put them in a purse with h in it."
Mt 8:20 "Foxes have h and birds

HOLINESS* (HOLY)
Ex 15:11 majestic in h,
Dt 32:51 because you did not uphold my h
1Ch 16:29 the LORD in the splendor of his h.
2Ch 20:21 him for the splendor of his h
Ps 29: 2 in the splendor of his h.
89:35 Once for all, I have sworn by my h
93: 5 h adorns your house
96: 9 in the splendor of his h;
Isa 29:23 they will acknowledge the h
35: 8 it will be called the Way of H.
Eze 36:23 I will show the h of my great name,
38:23 I will show my greatness and my h,
Am 4: 2 LORD has sworn by his h:
Lk 1:75 fear in h and righteousness
Ro 1: 4 the Spirit of h was declared
6:19 to righteousness leading to h.
6:22 the benefit you reap leads to h,
1Co 1:30 our righteousness, h
2Co 1:12 in the h and sincerity that are
7: 1 perfecting h out of reverence
Eph 4:24 God in true righteousness and h.
1Ti 2: 2 quiet lives in all godliness and h.
2:15 love and h with propriety.
Heb 12:10 that we may share in his h.
12:14 without h no one will see the Lord.

HOLY (HALLOWED HOLINESS)
Ge 2: 3 the seventh day and made it h,
Ex 3: 5 you are standing is h ground."
16:23 a h Sabbath to the LORD.
19: 6 kingdom of priests and a h nation.'
20: 8 the Sabbath day by keeping it h.
26:33 Place from the Most H Place.
26:33 curtain will separate the H Place
28:36 seal: H TO THE LORD.
29:37 Then the altar will be most h,
30:10 It is most h to the LORD."
30:29 them so they will be most h,
31:13 I am the LORD, who makes you h.
40: 9 all its furnishings, and it will be h.
Lev 10: 3 I will show myself h;
10:10 must distinguish between the h
10:13 in a h place, because it is your share
11:44 and be h, because I am h.
11:45 therefore be h, because I am h.
19: 2 'Be h because I, the LORD your
19: 8 he has desecrated what is h
19:24 the fourth year all its fruit will be h,
20: 3 and profaned my h name.
20: 7 " 'Consecrate yourselves and be h,
20: 8 I am the LORD, who makes you h.
20:26 You are to be h to me because I,
21: 6 They must be h to their God
21: 8 Consider them h, because I
22: 9 am the LORD, who makes them h.
22:32 Do not profane my h name.
Lev 25:12 For it is a jubilee and is to be h
27: 9 given to the LORD becomes h.
Nu 4:15 they must not touch the h things
6: 5 He must be h until the period
20:12 as h in the sight of the Israelites,
20:13 and where he showed himself h.
Dt 5:12 the Sabbath day by keeping it h,
23:14 Your camp must be h,
26:15 from heaven, your h dwelling place
33: 2 He came with myriads of h ones
Jos 5:15 place where you are standing is h."
24:19 He is a h God; he is a jealous God.
1Sa 2: 2 "There is no one h like the LORD;
6:20 of the LORD, this h God?
21: 5 even on missions that are not h.
2Ki 4: 9 often comes our way is a h man
1Ch 16:10 Glory in his h name;
16:35 may give thanks to your h name,
29: 3 I have provided for this h temple:
2Ch 30:27 heaven, his h dwelling place.
Ezr 9: 2 and have mingled the h race
Ne 11: 1 the h city, while the remaining nine
Job 6:10 not denied the words of the H One.
Ps 2: 6 King on Zion, my h hill."
11: 4 The LORD is in his h temple;
16:10 will you let your H One see decay.
22: 3 you are enthroned as the H One;
24: 3 Who may stand in his h place?
30: 4 praise his h name.
77:13 Your ways, O God, are h.
78:54 to the border of his h land,
99: 3 he is h.
99: 5 he is h.
99: 9 for the LORD our God is h.
105: 3 Glory in his h name;
111: 9 h and awesome is his name.
Pr 9:10 of the H One is understanding.
Isa 5:16 the h God will show himself h
6: 3 H, h, h is the LORD Almighty;
8:13 is the one you are to regard as h,
29:23 they will keep my name h;
40:25 who is my equal?" says the H One.
43: 3 the H One of Israel, your Savior;
54: 5 H One of Israel is your Redeemer;
57:15 who lives forever, whose name is h:
58:13 and the LORD's h day honorable,
Jer 17:22 but keep the Sabbath day h,
Eze 20:41 I will show myself h among you
22:26 to my law and profane my h things;
28:22 and show myself h within her.
28:25 I will show myself h among them
36:20 nations they profaned my h name,
38:16 when I show myself h through you
44:23 the difference between the h
Da 9:24 prophecy and to anoint the most h.
Hab 2:20 But the LORD is in his h temple;
Zec 14: 5 and all the h ones with him.
14:20 On that day H TO THE LORD
Mt 24:15 in the h place 'the abomination
Mk 1:24 the H One of God!" "Be quiet!"
Lk 1:35 the h one to be born will be called
1:49 h is his name.
4:34 the H One of God!" "Be quiet!"
Jn 6:69 and know that you are the H One
Ac 2:27 will you let your H One see decay.
13:35 will not let your H One see decay.'
Ro 1: 2 prophets in the H Scriptures
7:12 and the commandment is h,
11:16 if the root is h, so are the branches.
12: 1 as living sacrifices, h and pleasing
1Co 1: 2 in Christ Jesus and called to be h,
7:14 be unclean, but as it is, they are h.
Eph 1: 4 the creation of the world to be h
2:21 and rises to become a h temple
3: 5 by the Spirit to God's h apostles
5: 3 improper for God's h people.
5:26 up for her to make her h,
Col 1:22 death to present you h in his sight,
1Th 2:10 and so is God, of how h,
3:13 and h in the presence of our God
3:13 comes with all his h ones.
4: 7 us to be impure, but to live a h life.
2Th 1:10 to be glorified in his h people
1Ti 2: 8 to lift up h hands in prayer,
2Ti 1: 9 saved us and called us to a h life—
2:21 for noble purposes, made h,
3:15 you have known the h Scriptures,
Tit 1: 8 upright, h and disciplined.
Heb 2:11 Both the one who makes men h
7:26 one who is h, blameless, pure,
10:10 we have been made h
10:14 those who are being made h.
10:19 to enter the Most H Place
12:14 in peace with all men and to be h;
13:12 gate to make the people h
1Pe 1:15 But just as he who called you is h,
1:16 is written: "Be h, because I am h."
2: 5 house to be a h priesthood,
2: 9 a royal priesthood, a h nation,
1Pe 3: 5 For this is the way the h women
2Pe 3:11 You ought to live h and godly lives
Jude :14 upon thousands of his h ones
Rev 3: 7 are the words of him who is h
4: 8 "H, h, h is the Lord God
15: 4 For you alone are h.
20: 6 and h are those who have part
22:11 let him who is h continue to be h."

HOME (HOMES)
Dt 6: 7 Talk about them when you sit at h
11:19 about them when you sit at h
20: 5 Let him go h, or he may die
24: 5 is to be free to stay at h
Ru 1:11 "Return h, my daughters.
2Sa 7:10 them so that they can have a h
1Ch 16:43 and David returned h to bless his
Ps 84: 3 Even the sparrow has found a h,
113: 9 settles the barren woman in her h
Pr 3:33 but he blesses the h of the righteous
27: 8 is a man who strays from his h.
Ecc 12: 5 Then man goes to his eternal h
Eze 36: 8 for they will soon come h.
Mic 2: 2 They defraud a man of his h,
Mt 1:24 and took Mary h as his wife.
Mk 10:29 "no one who has left h or brothers
Lk 10:38 named Martha opened her h
Jn 14:23 to him and make our h with him.
19:27 this disciple took her into his h.
Ac 16:15 baptized, she invited us to her h.
Tit 2: 5 to be busy at h, to be kind,

HOMELESS*
1Co 4:11 we are brutally treated, we are h.

HOMES (HOME)
Ne 4:14 daughters, your wives and your h."
Isa 32:18 in secure h,
Mk 10:30 as much in this present age (h,
1Ti 5:14 to manage their h and to give

HOMETOWN
Mt 13:57 "Only in his h
Lk 4:24 "no prophet is accepted in his h.

HOMOSEXUAL*
1Co 6: 9 male prostitutes nor h offenders

HONEST (HONESTY)
Lev 19:36 Use h scales and h weights,
Dt 25:15 and h weights and measures,
Job 31: 6 let God weigh me in h scales
Pr 12:17 truthful witness gives h testimony,

HONESTY (HONEST)
2Ki 12:15 they acted with complete h.

HONEY (HONEYCOMB)
Ex 3: 8 a land flowing with milk and h—
Jdg 14: 8 a swarm of bees and some h,
1Sa 14:26 they saw the h oozing out,
Ps 19:10 than h from the comb.
119:103 sweeter than h to my mouth!
Pr 25:16 If you find h, eat just enough—
SS 4:11 milk and h are under your tongue.
Isa 7:15 and h when he knows enough
Eze 3: 3 it tasted as sweet as h in my mouth.
Mt 3: 4 His food was locusts and wild h.
Rev 10: 9 mouth it will be as sweet as h."

HONEYCOMB (HONEY)
SS 4:11 Your lips drop sweetness as the h,
5: 1 I have eaten my h and my honey;

HONOR (HONORABLE HONORABLY HONORED HONORS)
Ex 20:12 "H your father and your mother,
Nu 20:12 trust in me enough to h me
25:13 he was zealous for the h of his God
Dt 5:16 "H your father and your mother,
Jdg 4: 9 going about this, the h will not be
1Sa 2: 8 and has them inherit a throne of h.
2:30 Those who h me I will h,
1Ch 29:12 Wealth and h come from you;
2Ch 1:11 or h, nor for the death
18: 1 had great wealth and h,
Est 6: 6 for the man the king delights to h
Ps 8: 5 and crowned him with glory and h.
45:11 h him, for he is your lord.
84:11 the LORD bestows favor and h;
Pr 3: 9 H the LORD with your wealth,
3:35 The wise inherit h,
15:33 and humility comes before h.
18:12 but humility comes before h.
20: 3 It is to a man's h to avoid strife,
25:27 is it honorable to seek one's own h.
Isa 29:13 and h me with their lips,
Jer 33: 9 and h before all nations
Mt 13:57 own house is a prophet without h."
15: 4 'H your father and mother'

Mt 15: 8 These people *h* me with their lips,
19:19 *h* your father and mother,'
23: 6 they love the place of *h* at banquets
Mk 6: 4 own house is a prophet without *h*."
Lk 14: 8 do not take the place of *h*,
Jn 5:23 that all may *h* the Son just
7:18 does so to gain *h* for himself,
12:26 My Father will *h* the one who
Ro 12:10 *H* one another above yourselves.
1Co 6:20 Therefore *h* God with your body.
Eph 6: 2 "*H* your father and mother"—
1Ti 5:17 well are worthy of double *h*,
Heb 2: 7 you crowned him with glory and *h*
Rev 4: 9 *h* and thanks to him who sits

HONORABLE (HONOR)
1Th 4: 4 body in a way that is holy and *h*,

HONORABLY (HONOR)
Heb 13:18 and desire to live *h* in every way.

HONORED (HONOR)
Ps 12: 8 when what is vile is *h* among men.
Pr 13:18 but whoever heeds correction is *h*.
Da 4:34 I *h* and glorified him who lives
1Co 12:26 if one part is *h*, every part rejoices
Heb 13: 4 Marriage should be *h* by all,

HONORS (HONOR)
Ps 15: 4 but *h* those who fear the LORD,
Pr 14:31 to the needy *h* God.

HOOF
Ex 10:26 not a *h* is to be left behind.

HOOKS
Isa 2: 4 and their spears into pruning *h*.
Joel 3:10 and your pruning *h* into spears.
Mic 4: 3 and their spears into pruning *h*.

HOPE (HOPES)
Job 13:15 Though he slay me, yet will I *h*
Ps 25: 3 No one whose *h* is in you
33:17 A horse is a vain *h* for deliverance;
33:18 on those whose *h* is
42: 5 Put your *h* in God,
62: 5 my *h* comes from him.
119: 74 for I have put my *h* in your word.
130: 5 and in his word I put my *h*.
130: 7 O Israel, put your *h* in the LORD,
146: 5 whose *h* is in the LORD his God,
147: 11 who put their *h* in his unfailing love
Pr 13:12 *H* deferred makes the heart sick,
23:18 There is surely a future *h* for you,
Isa 40:31 but those who *h* in the LORD
Jer 29:11 plans to give you *h* and a future.
La 3:21 and therefore I have *h*:
Zec 9:12 to your fortress, O prisoners of *h*;
Ro 5: 4 character; and character, *h*.
8:20 in *h* that the creation itself will be
8:24 But *h* that is seen is no *h* at all.
8:25 if we *h* for what we do not yet have,
12:12 Be joyful in *h*, patient in affliction,
15: 4 of the Scriptures we might have *h*.
15:13 May the God of *h* fill you
1Co 13:13 now these three remain: faith, *h*
15:19 for this life we have *h* in Christ,
Eph 2:12 without *h* and without God
Col 1:27 Christ in you, the *h* of glory.
1Th 1: 3 and your endurance inspired by *h*
5: 8 and the *h* of salvation as a helmet.
1Ti 4:10 that we have put our *h*
6:17 but to put their *h* in God,
Tit 1: 2 resting on the *h* of eternal life,
2:13 while we wait for the blessed *h*—
Heb 6:19 We have this *h* as an anchor
10:23 unswervingly to the *h* we profess,
11: 1 faith is being sure of what we *h* for
1Jn 3: 3 Everyone who has this *h*

HOPES (HOPE)
1Co 13: 7 always *h*, always perseveres.

HORN (HORNS)
Ex 19:13 when the ram's *h* sounds a long
27: 2 Make a *h* at each of the four
Da 7: 8 This *h* had eyes like the eyes

HORNS (HORN)
Da 7:24 ten *h* are ten kings who will come
Rev 5: 6 He had seven *h* and seven eyes,
12: 3 and ten *h* and seven crowns
13: 1 He had ten *h* and seven heads,
17: 3 and had seven heads and ten *h*.

HORRIBLE (HORROR)
Jer 5:30 "A *h* and shocking thing

HORROR (HORRIBLE)
Jer 2:12 and shudder with great *h*,"

HORSE
Ps 147: 10 not in the strength of the *h*,
Pr 26: 3 A whip for the *h*, a halter
Zec 1: 8 before me was a man riding a red *h*
Rev 6: 2 and there before me was a white *h*!
6: 4 Come!" Then another *h* came out,
6: 5 and there before me was a black *h*!
6: 8 and there before me was a pale *h*!
19:11 and there before me was a white *h*,

HOSANNA
Mt 21: 9 "*H* in the highest!"
Mk 11: 9 "*H*!"
Jn 12:13 "*H*!"

HOSEA
Prophet whose wife and family pictured the unfaithfulness of Israel (Hos 1-3).

HOSHEA (JOSHUA)
1. Original name of Joshua (Nu 13:16).
2. Last king of Israel (2Ki 15:30; 17:1-6).

HOSPITABLE* (HOSPITALITY)
1Ti 3: 2 self-controlled, respectable, *h*,
Tit 1: 8 Rather he must be *h*, one who loves

HOSPITABLY* (HOSPITALITY)
Ac 28: 7 and for three days entertained us *h*.

HOSPITALITY* (HOSPITABLE HOSPITABLY)
Ro 12:13 Practice *h*.
16:23 whose *h* I and the whole church
1Ti 5:10 as bringing up children, showing *h*,
1Pe 4: 9 Offer *h* to one another
3Jn : 8 therefore to show *h* to such men

HOSTILE (HOSTILITY)
Ro 8: 7 the sinful mind is *h* to God.

HOSTILITY (HOSTILE)
Eph 2:14 wall of *h*, by abolishing
2:16 by which he put to death their *h*.

HOT
1Ti 4: 2 have been seared as with a *h* iron.
Rev 3:15 that you are neither cold nor *h*.

HOT-TEMPERED (TEMPER)
Pr 15:18 A *h* man stirs up dissension,
19:19 A *h* man must pay the penalty;
22:24 Do not make friends with a *h* man,
29:22 and a *h* one commits many sins.

HOTHEADED (HEAD)
Pr 14:16 but a fool is *h* and reckless.

HOUR
Ecc 9:12 knows when his *h* will come:
Mt 6:27 you by worrying can add a single *h*
Lk 12:40 the Son of Man will come at an *h*
Jn 12:23 The *h* has come for the Son of Man
12:27 for this very reason I came to this *h*

HOUSE (HOUSEHOLD HOUSEHOLDS HOUSES STOREHOUSE)
Ex 12:22 the door of his *h* until morning.
20:17 shall not covet your neighbor's *h*.
Nu 12: 7 he is faithful in all my *h*.
Dt 5:21 desire on your neighbor's *h*
2Sa 7:11 LORD himself will establish a *h*
1Ch 17:23 and his *h* be established forever.
Ne 10:39 "We will not neglect the *h*
Ps 23: 6 I will dwell in the *h* of the LORD
27: 4 dwell in the *h* of the LORD
69: 9 for zeal for your *h* consumes me,
84:10 a doorkeeper in the *h* of my God
122: 1 "Let us go to the *h* of the LORD."
127: 1 Unless the LORD builds the *h*,
Pr 7:27 Her *h* is a highway to the grave,
21: 9 than share a *h* with a quarrelsome
Isa 56: 7 a *h* of prayer for all nations."
Jer 7:11 Has this *h*, which bears my Name,
18: 2 "Go down to the potter's *h*,
Eze 33: 7 made you a watchman for the *h*
Joel 3:18 will flow out of the LORD's *h*
Zec 13: 6 given at the *h* of my friends.'
Mt 7:24 is like a wise man who built his *h*
10:11 and stay at his *h* until you leave.
12:29 can anyone enter a strong man's *h*
21:13 My *h* will be called a *h* of prayer,'
Mk 3:25 If a *h* is divided against itself,
11:17 " 'My *h* will be called
Lk 6:48 He is like a man building a *h*,
10: 7 Do not move around from *h* to *h*.
11:17 a *h* divided against itself will fall.
11:24 'I will return to the *h* I left.'
15: 8 sweep the *h* and search carefully
19: 9 Today salvation has come to this *h*,
Jn 2:16 How dare you turn my Father's *h*
2:17 "Zeal for your *h* will consume me."
12: 3 the *h* was filled with the fragrance
14: 2 In my Father's *h* are many rooms;
Ac 20:20 you publicly and from *h* to *h*.
Ro 16: 5 the church that meets at their *h*.
Heb 3: 3 the builder of a *h* has greater honor
1Pe 2: 5 built into a spiritual *h* to be a holy

HOUSEHOLD (HOUSE)
Ex 12: 3 lamb for his family, one for each *h*.
Jos 24:15 my *h*, we will serve the LORD."
Pr 31:21 it snows, she has no fear for her *h*;
31:27 over the affairs of her *h*
Mic 7: 6 are the members of his own *h*.
Mt 10:36 will be the members of his own *h*.'
12:25 or *h* divided against itself will not
Ac 16:31 you will be saved—you and your *h*
Eph 2:19 people and members of God's *h*,
1Ti 3:12 manage his children and his *h* well.
3:15 to conduct themselves in God's *h*,

HOUSEHOLDS (HOUSE)
Tit 1:11 because they are ruining whole *h*

HOUSES (HOUSE)
Ex 12:27 passed over the *h* of the Israelites
Mt 19:29 everyone who has left *h* or brothers

HOVERING* (HOVERS)
Ge 1: 2 of God was *h* over the waters.
Isa 31: 5 Like birds *h* overhead,

HOVERS* (HOVERING)
Dt 32:11 and *h* over its young,

HULDAH*
Prophetess inquired by Hilkiah for Josiah (2Ki 22; 2Ch 34:14-28).

HUMAN (HUMANITY)
Lev 24:17 If anyone takes the life of a *h* being,
Isa 52:14 his form marred beyond *h* likeness
Jn 8:15 You judge by *h* standards;
Ro 1: 3 as to his *h* nature was a descendant
9: 5 from them is traced the *h* ancestry
1Co 1:17 not with words of *h* wisdom,
1:26 of you were wise by *h* standards;
2:13 not in words taught us by *h* wisdom
2Co 3: 3 of stone but on tablets of *h* hearts.
Gal 3: 3 to attain your goal by *h* effort?
2Pe 2:18 lustful desires of sinful *h* nature,

HUMANITY* (HUMAN)
Heb 2:14 he too shared in their *h* so that

HUMBLE (HUMBLED HUMBLES HUMILIATE HUMILIATED HUMILITY)
Nu 12: 3 (Now Moses was a very *h* man,
2Ch 7:14 will *h* themselves and pray
Ps 18:27 You save the *h*
25: 9 He guides the *h* in what is right
149: 4 he crowns the *h* with salvation.
Pr 3:34 but gives grace to the *h*.
Isa 66: 2 he who is *h* and contrite in spirit,
Mt 11:29 for I am gentle and *h* in heart,
Eph 4: 2 Be completely *h* and gentle;
Jas 4: 6 but gives grace to the *h*."
4:10 *H* yourselves before the Lord,
1Pe 5: 5 but gives grace to the *h*."
5: 6 *H* yourselves,

HUMBLED (HUMBLE)
Mt 23:12 whoever exalts himself will be *h*,
Lk 14:11 who exalts himself will be *h*,
Php 2: 8 he *h* himself

HUMBLES* (HUMBLE)
1Sa 2: 7 he *h* and he exalts.
Isa 26: 5 He *h* those who dwell on high,
Mt 18: 4 whoever *h* himself like this child is
23:12 whoever *h* himself will be exalted.
Lk 14:11 he who *h* himself will be exalted."
18:14 he who *h* himself will be exalted."

HUMILIATE* (HUMBLE)
Pr 25: 7 than for him to *h* you
1Co 11:22 and *h* those who have nothing?

HUMILIATED (HUMBLE)
Jer 31:19 I was ashamed and *h*
Lk 14: 9 *h*, you will have to take the least

HUMILITY* (HUMBLE)
Ps 45: 4 of truth, *h* and righteousness;
Pr 11: 2 but with *h* comes wisdom.
15:33 and *h* comes before honor.
18:12 but *h* comes before honor.
22: 4 *H* and the fear of the LORD
Zep 2: 3 Seek righteousness, seek *h*;
Ac 20:19 I served the Lord with great *h*

Php 2: 3 but in *h* consider others better
Col 2:18 let anyone who delights in false *h*
2:23 their false *h* and their harsh
3:12 *h*, gentleness and patience.
Tit 3: 2 and to show true *h* toward all men.
Jas 3:13 in the *h* that comes from wisdom.
1Pe 5: 5 clothe yourselves with *h*

HUNG (HANG)
Dt 21:23 anyone who is *h* on a tree is
Mt 18: 6 him to have a large millstone *h*
Lk 19:48 all the people *h* on his words.
Gal 3:13 "Cursed is everyone who is *h*

HUNGER (HUNGRY)
Ne 9:15 In their *h* you gave them bread
Pr 6:30 to satisfy his *h* when he is starving.
Mt 5: 6 Blessed are those who *h*
Lk 6:21 Blessed are you who *h* now,
2Co 6: 5 sleepless nights and *h*; in purity,
11:27 I have known *h* and thirst
Rev 7:16 Never again will they *h*;

HUNGRY (HUNGER)
Job 24:10 carry the sheaves, but still go *h*.
Ps 107: 9 and fills the *h* with good things.
146: 7 and gives food to the *h*.
Pr 19:15 and the shiftless man goes *h*.
25:21 If your enemy is *h*, give him food
27: 7 to the *h* even what is bitter tastes
Isa 58: 7 not to share your food with the *h*
58:10 spend yourselves in behalf of the *h*
Eze 18: 7 but gives his food to the *h*
18:16 but gives his food to the *h*
Mt 15:32 I do not want to send them away *h*,
25:35 For I was *h* and you gave me
25:42 For I was *h* and you gave me
Lk 1:53 He has filled the *h* with good things
Jn 6:35 comes to me will never go *h*,
Ro 12:20 "If your enemy is *h*, feed him;
1Co 4:11 To this very hour we go *h*
Php 4:12 whether well fed or *h*,

HUR
Ex 17:12 Aaron and *H* held his hands up—

HURL
Mic 7:19 *h* all our iniquities into the depths

HURT (HURTS)
Ecc 8: 9 it over others to his own *h*.
Mk 16:18 deadly poison, it will not *h* them
Rev 2:11 He who overcomes will not be *h*

HURTS* (HURT)
Ps 15: 4 even when it *h*,
Pr 26:28 A lying tongue hates those it *h*,

HUSBAND (HUSBAND'S HUSBANDS)
Pr 31:11 Her *h* has full confidence in her
31:23 Her *h* is respected at the city gate,
31:28 her *h* also, and he praises her:
Isa 54: 5 For your Maker is your *h*—
Jer 3:14 the LORD, "for I am your *h*.
3:20 like a woman unfaithful to her *h*,
Jn 4:17 "I have no *h*," she replied.
Ro 7: 2 a married woman is bound to her *h*
1Co 7: 2 and each woman her own *h*.
7: 3 The *h* should fulfill his marital duty
7:10 wife must not separate from her *h*.
7:11 And a *h* must not divorce his wife.
7:13 And if a woman has a *h* who is not
7:14 For the unbelieving *h* has been
7:39 A woman is bound to her *h* as long
7:39 But if her *h* dies, she is free
2Co 11: 2 I promised you to one *h*, to Christ,
Gal 4:27 woman than of her who has a *h*."
Eph 5:23 For the *h* is the head of the wife
5:33 and the wife must respect her *h*.
1Ti 3: 2 the *h* of but one wife, temperate,
3:12 A deacon must be the *h* of
5: 9 has been faithful to her *h*,
Tit 1: 6 An elder must be blameless, the *h*

HUSBANDMAN see GARDENER

HUSBAND'S (HUSBAND)
Dt 25: 5 Her *h* brother shall take her
Pr 12: 4 of noble character is her *h* crown,
1Co 7: 4 the *h* body does not belong

HUSBANDS (HUSBAND)
Eph 5:22 submit to your *h* as to the Lord.
5:25 *H*, love your wives, just
5:28 *h* ought to love their wives
Col 3:18 submit to your *h*, as is fitting
3:19 *H*, love your wives and do not be
Tit 2: 4 the younger women to love their *h*
2: 5 and to be subject to their *h*,
1Pe 3: 1 same way be submissive to your *h*
3: 7 *H*, in the same way be considerate

HUSHAI
Wise man of David who frustrated Ahithophel's advice and foiled Absalom's revolt (2Sa 15:32-37; 16:15-17:16; 1Ch 27:33).

HYMN* (HYMNS)
Ps 40: 3 a *h* of praise to our God.
Mt 26:30 they had sung a *h*, they went out
Mk 14:26 they had sung a *h*, they went out
1Co 14:26 everyone has a *h*, or a word

HYMNS* (HYMN)
Ac 16:25 Silas were praying and singing *h*
Ro 15: 9 I will sing *h* to your name."
Eph 5:19 to one another with psalms, *h*
Col 3:16 *h* and spiritual songs with gratitude

HYPOCRISY* (HYPOCRITE HYPOCRITES HYPOCRITICAL)
Mt 23:28 but on the inside you are full of *h*
Mk 12:15 we?" But Jesus knew their *h*.
Lk 12: 1 yeast of the Pharisees, which is *h*.
Gal 2:13 The other Jews joined him in his *h*,
2:13 by their *h* even Barnabas was led
1Pe 2: 1 *h*, envy, and slander of every kind.

HYPOCRITE* (HYPOCRISY)
Mt 7: 5 You *h*, first take the plank out
Lk 6:42 You *h*, first take the plank out

HYPOCRITES* (HYPOCRISY)
Ps 26: 4 nor do I consort with *h*;
Mt 6: 2 as the *h* do in the synagogues
6: 5 when you pray, do not be like the *h*
6:16 do not look somber as the *h* do,
15: 7 You *h*! Isaiah was right
22:18 their evil intent, said, "You *h*,
23:13 of the law and Pharisees, you *h*!
23:15 of the law and Pharisees, you *h*!
23:23 of the law and Pharisees, you *h*!
23:25 of the law and Pharisees, you *h*!
23:27 you *h*! You are like whitewashed
23:29 of the law and Pharisees, you *h*!
24:51 and assign him a place with the *h*,
Mk 7: 6 when he prophesied about you *h*;
Lk 12:56 *H*! You know how
13:15 The Lord answered him, "You *h*!

HYPOCRITICAL* (HYPOCRISY)
1Ti 4: 2 teachings come through *h* liars,

HYSSOP
Ex 12:22 Take a bunch of *h*, dip it
Ps 51: 7 with *h*, and I will be clean;
Jn 19:29 the sponge on a stalk of the *h* plant,

ICHABOD
1Sa 4:21 She named the boy *I*, saying,

IDLE* (IDLENESS IDLERS)
Dt 32:47 They are not just *i* words for you—
Job 11: 3 Will your *i* talk reduce men
Ecc 10:18 if his hands are *i*, the house leaks.
11: 6 at evening let not your hands be *i*,
Isa 58:13 as you please or speaking *i* words,
Col 2:18 mind puffs him up with *i* notions.
1Th 5:14 those who are *i*, encourage
2Th 3: 6 away from every brother who is *i*
3: 7 We were not *i* when we were
3:11 We hear that some among you are *i*
1Ti 5:13 they get into the habit of being *i*

IDLENESS* (IDLE)
Pr 31:27 and does not eat the bread of *i*.

IDLERS* (IDLE)
1Ti 5:13 And not only do they become *i*,

IDOL (IDOLATER IDOLATERS IDOLATRY IDOLS)
Ex 20: 4 make for yourself an *i* in the form
32: 4 made it into an *i* cast in the shape
Isa 40:19 As for an *i*, a craftsman casts it,
41: 7 He nails down the *i*
44:15 he makes an *i* and bows down to it.
44:17 From the rest he makes a god, his *i*;
Hab 2:18 "Of what value is an *i*,
1Co 8: 4 We know that an *i* is nothing at all

IDOLATER* (IDOL)
1Co 5:11 an *i* or a slanderer, a drunkard
Eph 5: 5 greedy person—such a man is an *i*

IDOLATERS (IDOL)
1Co 5:10 or the greedy and swindlers, or *i*.
6: 9 Neither the sexually immoral nor *i*

IDOLATRY (IDOL)
1Sa 15:23 and arrogance like the evil of *i*.
1Co 10:14 my dear friends, flee from *i*.
Gal 5:20 and debauchery; *i* and witchcraft;
Col 3: 5 evil desires and greed, which is *i*.
1Pe 4: 3 orgies, carousing and detestable *i*.

IDOLS (IDOL)
Dt 32:16 angered him with their detestable *i*.
Ps 78:58 aroused his jealousy with their *i*.
Isa 44: 9 All who make *i* are nothing,
Eze 23:39 sacrificed their children to their *i*,
Ac 15:20 to abstain from food polluted by *i*,
21:25 abstain from food sacrificed to *i*,
1Co 8: 1 Now about food sacrificed to *i*:
1Jn 5:21 children, keep yourselves from *i*.
Rev 2:14 to sin by eating food sacrificed to *i*

IGNORANT (IGNORE)
1Co 15:34 for there are some who are *i* of God
Heb 5: 2 to deal gently with those who are *i*
1Pe 2:15 good you should silence the *i* talk
2Pe 3:16 which *i* and unstable people distort

IGNORE (IGNORANT IGNORED IGNORES)
Dt 22: 1 do not *i* it but be sure
Ps 9:12 he does not *i* the cry of the afflicted
Heb 2: 3 if we *i* such a great salvation?

IGNORED (IGNORE)
Hos 4: 6 you have *i* the law of your God,
1Co 14:38 he ignores this, he himself will be *i*.

IGNORES* (IGNORE)
Pr 10:17 whoever *i* correction leads others
13:18 He who *i* discipline comes
15:32 He who *i* discipline despises
1Co 14:38 If he *i* this, he himself will be

ILL (ILLNESS)
Mt 4:24 brought to him all who were *i*

ILL-GOTTEN
Pr 1:19 the end of all who go after *i* gain;
10: 2 *I* treasures are of no value,

ILL-TEMPERED* (TEMPER)
Pr 21:19 than with a quarrelsome and *i* wife.

ILLEGITIMATE
Heb 12: 8 then you are *i* children

ILLNESS (ILL)
2Ki 8: 9 'Will I recover from this *i*?'"
2Ch 16:12 even in his *i* he did not seek help
Ps 41: 3 and restore him from his bed of *i*.
Isa 38: 9 king of Judah after his *i*

ILLUMINATED*
Rev 18: 1 and the earth was *i* by his splendor.

IMAGE (IMAGES)
Ge 1:26 "Let us make man in our *i*,
1:27 So God created man in his own *i*,
9: 6 for in the *i* of God
Dt 27:15 "Cursed is the man who carves an *i*
Isa 40:18 What *i* will you compare him to?
Da 3: 1 King Nebuchadnezzar made an *i*
1Co 11: 7 since he is the *i* and glory of God;
2Co 4: 4 glory of Christ, who is the *i* of God.
Col 1:15 He is the *i* of the invisible God,
3:10 in knowledge in the *i* of its Creator.
Rev 13:14 them to set up an *i* in honor

IMAGES (IMAGE)
Ps 97: 7 All who worship *i* are put to shame,
Jer 10:14 His *i* are a fraud;
Ro 1:23 of the immortal God for *i* made

IMAGINATION (IMAGINE)
Eze 13: 2 who prophesy out of their own *i*:

IMAGINE (IMAGINATION)
Eph 3:20 more than all we ask or *i*,

IMITATE (IMITATORS)
1Co 4:16 Therefore I urge you to *i* me.
Heb 6:12 but to *i* those who through faith
13: 7 of their way of life and *i* their faith.
3Jn :11 do not *i* what is evil but what is

IMITATORS* (IMITATE)
Eph 5: 1 Be *i* of God, therefore,
1Th 1: 6 You became *i* of us and of the Lord
2:14 became *i* of God's churches

IMMANUEL*
Isa 7:14 birth to a son, and will call him *I*.
8: 8 O *I*!"
Mt 1:23 and they will call him *I*"—

IMMORAL* (IMMORALITY)
Pr 6:24 keeping you from the *i* woman,
1Co 5: 9 to associate with sexually *i* people
5:10 the people of this world who are *i*,
5:11 but is sexually *i* or greedy,

1Co 6: 9 Neither the sexually *i* nor idolaters
Eph 5: 5 No *i*, impure or greedy person—
Heb 12:16 See that no one is sexually *i*,
13: 4 the adulterer and all the sexually *i*.
Rev 21: 8 the murderers, the sexually *i*,
22:15 the sexually *i*, the murderers,

IMMORALITY* (IMMORAL)
Nu 25: 1 in sexual *i* with Moabite women,
Jer 3: 9 Because Israel's *i* mattered so little
Mt 15:19 murder, adultery, sexual *i*, theft,
Mk 7:21 sexual *i*, theft, murder, adultery,
Ac 15:20 from sexual *i*, from the meat
15:29 animals and from sexual *i*.
21:25 animals and from sexual *i*."
Ro 13:13 not in sexual *i* and debauchery,
1Co 5: 1 reported that there is sexual *i*
6:13 The body is not meant for sexual *i*,
6:18 Flee from sexual *i*.
7: 2 But since there is so much *i*,
10: 8 We should not commit sexual *i*,
Gal 5:19 sexual *i*, impurity and debauchery;
Eph 5: 3 must not be even a hint of sexual *i*,
Col 3: 5 sexual *i*, impurity, lust, evil desires
1Th 4: 3 that you should avoid sexual *i*;
Jude : 4 grace of our God into a license for *i*
: 7 gave themselves up to sexual *i*
Rev 2:14 and by committing sexual *i*.
2:20 misleads my servants into sexual *i*
2:21 given her time to repent of her *i*,
9:21 their sexual *i* or their thefts.

IMMORTAL* (IMMORTALITY)
Ro 1:23 glory of the *i* God for images made
1Ti 1:17 Now to the King eternal, *i*,
6:16 who alone is *i* and who lives

IMMORTALITY* (IMMORTAL)
Pr 12:28 along that path is *i*.
Ro 2: 7 honor and *i*, he will give eternal life
1Co 15:53 and the mortal with *i*.
15:54 with *i*, then the saying that is
2Ti 1:10 and *i* to light through the gospel.

IMPARTIAL*
Jas 3:17 and good fruit, *i* and sincere.

IMPARTS*
Pr 29:15 The rod of correction *i* wisdom,

IMPERFECT*
1Co 13:10 perfection comes, the *i* disappears.

IMPERISHABLE
1Co 15:42 it is raised *i*; it is sown in dishonor,
15:50 nor does the perishable inherit the *i*
1Pe 1:23 not of perishable seed, but of *i*,

IMPLANTED*
Ps 94: 9 Does he who *i* the ear not hear?

IMPLORE*
Mal 1: 9 "Now *i* God to be gracious to us.
2Co 5:20 We *i* you on Christ's behalf:

IMPORTANCE* (IMPORTANT)
1Co 15: 3 passed on to you as of first *i*:

IMPORTANT (IMPORTANCE)
Mt 6:25 Is not life more *i* than food,
23:23 have neglected the more *i* matters
Mk 12:29 "The most *i* one," answered Jesus,
12:33 as yourself is more *i* than all burnt
Php 1:18 The *i* thing is that in every way,

IMPOSSIBLE
Mt 17:20 Nothing will be *i* for you."
19:26 "With man this is *i*,
Mk 10:27 "With man this is *i*, but not
Lk 1:37 For nothing is *i* with God."
18:27 "What is *i* with men is possible
Ac 2:24 it was *i* for death to keep its hold
Heb 6: 4 It is *i* for those who have once been
6:18 things in which it is *i* for God to lie,
10: 4 because it is *i* for the blood of bulls
11: 6 without faith it is *i* to please God,

IMPOSTORS
2Ti 3:13 and *i* will go from bad to worse,

IMPRESS* (IMPRESSES)
Dt 6: 7 *I* them on your children.

IMPRESSES* (IMPRESS)
Pr 17:10 A rebuke *i* a man of discernment

IMPROPER*
Eph 5: 3 these are *i* for God's holy people.

IMPURE (IMPURITY)
Ac 10:15 not call anything *i* that God has
Eph 5: 5 No immoral, *i* or greedy person—
1Th 2: 3 spring from error or *i* motives,
4: 7 For God did not call us to be *i*,
Rev 21:27 Nothing *i* will ever enter it,

IMPURITY (IMPURE)
Ro 1:24 hearts to sexual *i* for the degrading
Gal 5:19 sexual immorality, *i*
Eph 4:19 as to indulge in every kind of *i*,
5: 3 or of any kind of *i*, or of greed,
Col 3: 5 *i*, lust, evil desires and greed,

INCENSE
Ex 30: 1 altar of acacia wood for burning *i*.
40: 5 Place the gold altar of *i* in front
Ps 141: 2 my prayer be set before you like *i*;
Mt 2:11 him with gifts of gold and of *i*
Heb 9: 4 which had the golden altar of *i*
Rev 5: 8 were holding golden bowls full of *i*,
8: 4 The smoke of the *i*, together

INCLINATION (INCLINES)
Ge 6: 5 and that every *i* of the thoughts

INCLINES* (INCLINATION)
Ecc 10: 2 The heart of the wise *i* to the right,

INCOME
Ecc 5:10 wealth is never satisfied with his *i*.
1Co 16: 2 sum of money in keeping with his *i*,

INCOMPARABLE*
Eph 2: 7 ages he might show the *i* riches

INCREASE (EVER-INCREASING INCREASED INCREASES INCREASING)
Ge 1:22 "Be fruitful and *i* in number
3:16 "I will greatly *i* your pains
8:17 be fruitful and *i* in number upon it
Ps 62:10 though your riches *i*,
Pr 22:16 oppresses the poor to *i* his wealth
Isa 9: 7 Of the *i* of his government
Mt 24:12 Because of the *i* of wickedness,
Lk 17: 5 said to the Lord, "*I* our faith!"
Ac 12:24 But the word of God continued to *i*
Ro 5:20 added so that the trespass might *i*.
1Th 3:12 May the Lord make your love *i*

INCREASED (INCREASE)
Ac 6: 7 of disciples in Jerusalem *i* rapidly,
Ro 5:20 But where sin *i*, grace *i* all the more

INCREASES (INCREASE)
Pr 24: 5 and a man of knowledge *i* strength;

INCREASING (INCREASE)
Ac 6: 1 when the number of disciples was *i*,
2Th 1: 3 one of you has for each other is *i*.
2Pe 1: 8 these qualities in *i* measure,

INCREDIBLE*
Ac 26: 8 of you consider it *i* that God raises

INDECENT
Ro 1:27 Men committed *i* acts

INDEPENDENT*
1Co 11:11 however, woman is not *i* of man,
11:11 of man, nor is man *i* of woman.

INDESCRIBABLE*
2Co 9:15 Thanks be to God for his *i* gift!

INDESTRUCTIBLE*
Heb 7:16 on the basis of the power of an *i* life

INDIGNANT
Mk 10:14 When Jesus saw this, he was *i*.

INDISPENSABLE*
1Co 12:22 seem to be weaker are *i*,

INEFFECTIVE*
2Pe 1: 8 they will keep you from being *i*

INEXPRESSIBLE*
2Co 12: 4 He heard *i* things, things that man
1Pe 1: 8 are filled with an *i* and glorious joy,

INFANCY* (INFANTS)
2Ti 3:15 from *i* you have known the holy

INFANTS (INFANCY)
Ps 8: 2 From the lips of children and *i*
Mt 21:16 " 'From the lips of children and *i*
1Co 3: 1 but as worldly—mere *i* in Christ.
14:20 In regard to evil be *i*,
Eph 4:14 Then we will no longer be *i*,

INFIRMITIES*
Isa 53: 4 Surely he took up our *i*
Mt 8:17 "He took up our *i*

INFLAMED
Ro 1:27 were *i* with lust for one another.

INFLUENTIAL*
1Co 1:26 not many were *i*; not many were

INHABITANTS (INHABITED)
Nu 33:55 " 'But if you do not drive out the *i*
Rev 8:13 Woe! Woe to the *i* of the earth,

INHABITED (INHABITANTS)
Isa 45:18 but formed it to be *i*—

INHERIT (CO-HEIRS HEIR HEIRS HERITAGE INHERITANCE)
Dt 1:38 because he will lead Israel to *i* it.
Jos 1: 6 people to *i* the land I swore
Ps 37:11 But the meek will *i* the land
37:29 the righteous will *i* the land
Zec 2:12 The LORD will *i* Judah
Mt 5: 5 for they will *i* the earth.
19:29 as much and will *i* eternal life.
Mk 10:17 "what must I do to *i* eternal life?"
Lk 10:25 "what must I do to *i* eternal life?"
18:18 what must I do to *i* eternal life?"
1Co 6: 9 the wicked will not *i* the kingdom
15:50 blood cannot *i* the kingdom of God
Rev 21: 7 He who overcomes will *i* all this,

INHERITANCE (INHERIT)
Lev 20:24 I will give it to you as an *i*,
Dt 4:20 to be the people of his *i*,
10: 9 the LORD is their *i*, as the LORD
Jos 14: 3 two-and-a-half tribes their *i* east
Ps 16: 6 surely I have a delightful *i*.
33:12 the people he chose for his *i*.
136: 21 and gave their land as an *i*,
Pr 13:22 A good man leaves an *i*
Mt 25:34 blessed by my Father; take your *i*,
Eph 1:14 who is a deposit guaranteeing our *i*
5: 5 has any *i* in the kingdom of Christ
Col 1:12 you to share in the *i* of the saints
3:24 you know that you will receive an *i*
Heb 9:15 receive the promised eternal *i*—
1Pe 1: 4 and into an *i* that can never perish,

INIQUITIES (INIQUITY)
Ps 78:38 he forgave their *i*
103: 10 or repay us according to our *i*.
Isa 53: 5 he was crushed for our *i*;
53:11 and he will bear their *i*.
59: 2 But your *i* have separated
Mic 7:19 and hurl all our *i* into the depths

INIQUITY (INIQUITIES)
Ps 25:11 forgive my *i*, though it is great.
32: 5 and did not cover up my *i*.
51: 2 Wash away all my *i*
51: 9 and blot out all my *i*.
Isa 53: 6 the *i* of us all.

INJURED
Eze 34:16 will bind up the *i* and strengthen
Zec 11:16 or heal the *i*, or feed the healthy,

INJUSTICE
2Ch 19: 7 the LORD our God there is no *i*

INK
2Co 3: 3 not with *i* but with the Spirit

INN*
Lk 2: 7 there was no room for them in the *i*
10:34 took him to an *i* and took care

INNOCENT
Ex 23: 7 do not put an *i* or honest person
Dt 25: 1 acquitting the *i* and condemning
Pr 6:17 hands that shed *i* blood,
17:26 It is not good to punish an *i* man,
Mt 10:16 shrewd as snakes and as *i* as doves.
27: 4 "for I have betrayed *i* blood."
27:24 I am *i* of this man's blood," he said.
Ac 20:26 declare to you today that I am *i*
Ro 16:19 what is good, and *i* about what is
1Co 4: 4 but that does not make me *i*.

INQUIRE
Isa 8:19 should not a people *i* of their God?

INSCRIPTION
Mt 22:20 And whose *i*?" "Caesar's,"
2Ti 2:19 with this *i*: "The Lord knows those

INSIGHT
1Ki 4:29 Solomon wisdom and very great *i*,
Ps 119: 99 I have more *i* than all my teachers,
Pr 5: 1 listen well to my words of *i*,
21:30 There is no wisdom, no *i*, no plan
Php 1: 9 more in knowledge and depth of *i*,
2Ti 2: 7 for the Lord will give you *i*

INSOLENT
Ro 1:30 God-haters, *i*, arrogant

INSPIRED*
Hos 9: 7 the *i* man a maniac.
1Th 1: 3 and your endurance *i* by hope

INSTALLED
Ps 2: 6 "I have *i* my King

INSTINCT* (INSTINCTS)
2Pe 2:12 are like brute beasts, creatures of *i*,
Jude :10 things they do understand by *i*,

INSTINCTS* (INSTINCT)
Jude :19 who follow mere natural *i*

INSTITUTED
Ro 13: 2 rebelling against what God has *i*,
1Pe 2:13 to every authority *i* among men:

INSTRUCT (INSTRUCTED INSTRUCTION INSTRUCTIONS INSTRUCTOR)
Ps 32: 8 I will *i* you and teach you
105: 22 to *i* his princes as he pleased
Pr 9: 9 *I* a wise man and he will be wiser
Ro 15:14 and competent to *i* one another.
1Co 2:16 that he may *i* him?"
14:19 to *i* others than ten thousand words
2Ti 2:25 who oppose him he must gently *i*,

INSTRUCTED (INSTRUCT)
2Ch 26: 5 who *i* him in the fear of God.
Pr 21:11 a wise man is *i*, he gets knowledge.
Isa 50: 4 LORD has given me an *i* tongue,
Mt 13:52 who has been *i* about the kingdom
1Co 14:31 in turn so that everyone may be *i*

INSTRUCTION (INSTRUCT)
Pr 1: 8 Listen, my son, to your father's *i*
4: 1 Listen, my sons, to a father's *i*;
4:13 Hold on to *i*, do not let it go;
8:10 Choose my *i* instead of silver,
8:33 Listen to my *i* and be wise;
13: 1 A wise son heeds his father's *i*,
13:13 He who scorns *i* will pay for it,
16:20 Whoever gives heed to *i* prospers,
16:21 and pleasant words promote *i*.
19:20 Listen to advice and accept *i*,
23:12 Apply your heart to *i*
1Co 14: 6 or prophecy or word of *i*?
14:26 or a word of *i*, a revelation,
Eph 6: 4 up in the training and *i* of the Lord.
1Th 4: 8 he who rejects this *i* does not reject
2Th 3:14 If anyone does not obey our *i*
1Ti 1:18 I give you this *i* in keeping
6: 3 to the sound *i* of our Lord Jesus
2Ti 4: 2 with great patience and careful *i*.

INSTRUCTIONS (INSTRUCT)
1Ti 3:14 I am writing you these *i* so that,

INSTRUCTOR (INSTRUCT)
Gal 6: 6 share all good things with his *i*.

INSTRUMENT* (INSTRUMENTS)
Eze 33:32 beautiful voice and plays an *i* well,
Ac 9:15 This man is my chosen *i*
2Ti 2:21 he will be an *i* for noble purposes,

INSTRUMENTS (INSTRUMENT)
Ro 6:13 as *i* of wickedness, but rather offer

INSULT (INSULTED INSULTS)
Pr 9: 7 corrects a mocker invites *i*;
12:16 but a prudent man overlooks an *i*.
Mt 5:11 Blessed are you when people *i* you,
Lk 6:22 when they exclude you and *i* you
1Pe 3: 9 evil with evil or *i* with *i*,

INSULTED (INSULT)
Heb 10:29 and who has *i* the Spirit of grace?
Jas 2: 6 love him? But you have *i* the poor.
1Pe 4:14 If you are *i* because of the name

INSULTS (INSULT)
Ps 22: 7 they hurl *i*, shaking their heads:
69: 9 the *i* of those who insult you fall
Pr 22:10 quarrels and *i* are ended.
Mk 15:29 passed by hurled *i* at him,
Jn 9:28 Then they hurled *i* at him and said,
Ro 15: 3 "The *i* of those who insult you have
2Co 12:10 in *i*, in hardships, in persecutions,
1Pe 2:23 When they hurled their *i* at him,

INTEGRITY*
Dt 9: 5 or your *i* that you are going
1Ki 9: 4 if you walk before me in *i* of heart
1Ch 29:17 the heart and are pleased with *i*.
Ne 7: 2 because he was a man of *i*
Job 2: 3 And he still maintains his *i*,
2: 9 "Are you still holding on to your *i*?
6:29 reconsider, for my *i* is at stake.
27: 5 till I die, I will not deny my *i*.
Ps 7: 8 according to my *i*, O Most High.
25:21 May *i* and uprightness protect me,
41:12 In my *i* you uphold me
78:72 David shepherded them with *i*
Pr 10: 9 The man of *i* walks securely,
11: 3 The *i* of the upright guides them,
13: 6 Righteousness guards the man of *i*,
17:26 or to flog officials for their *i*.
29:10 Bloodthirsty men hate a man of *i*
Isa 45:23 my mouth has uttered in all *i*
59: 4 no one pleads his case with *i*.
Mt 22:16 "we know you are a man of *i*
Mk 12:14 we know you are a man of *i*.
Tit 2: 7 your teaching show *i*, seriousness

INTELLIGENCE (INTELLIGENT)
Isa 29:14 the *i* of the intelligent will vanish."
1Co 1:19 *i* of the intelligent I will frustrate."

INTELLIGENT (INTELLIGENCE)
Isa 29:14 the intelligence of the *i* will vanish

INTELLIGIBLE
1Co 14:19 I would rather speak five *i* words

INTENDED
Ge 50:20 place of God? You *i* to harm me,

INTENSE
1Th 2:17 out of our *i* longing we made every
Rev 16: 9 They were seared by the *i* heat

INTERCEDE (INTERCEDES INTERCEDING INTERCESSION INTERCESSOR)
Heb 7:25 he always lives to *i* for them.

INTERCEDES* (INTERCEDE)
Ro 8:26 but the Spirit himself *i* for us
8:27 because the Spirit *i* for the saints

INTERCEDING* (INTERCEDE)
Ro 8:34 hand of God and is also *i* for us.

INTERCESSION* (INTERCEDE)
Isa 53:12 and made *i* for the transgressors.
1Ti 2: 1 *i* and thanksgiving be made

INTERCESSOR* (INTERCEDE)
Job 16:20 My *i* is my friend

INTEREST (INTERESTS)
Lev 25:36 Do not take *i* of any kind from him,
Dt 23:20 You may charge a foreigner *i*,
Mt 25:27 would have received it back with *i*.
Php 2:20 who takes a genuine *i*

INTERESTS (INTEREST)
1Co 7:34 his wife—and his *i* are divided.
Php 2: 4 only to your own *i*, but also to the *i*
2:21 everyone looks out for his own *i*,

INTERFERE*
Ezr 6: 7 Do not *i* with the work

INTERMARRY (MARRY)
Dt 7: 3 Do not *i* with them.
Ezr 9:14 and *i* with the peoples who commit

INTERPRET (INTERPRETATION INTERPRETER INTERPRETS)
Ge 41:15 "I had a dream, and no one can *i* it.
Mt 16: 3 you cannot *i* the signs of the times.
1Co 12:30 Do all *i*? But eagerly desire
14:13 pray that he may *i* what he says.
14:27 one at a time, and someone must *i*.

INTERPRETATION (INTERPRET)
1Co 12:10 and to still another the *i* of tongues.
14:26 a revelation, a tongue or an *i*.
2Pe 1:20 about by the prophet's own *i*.

INTERPRETER (INTERPRET)
1Co 14:28 If there is no *i*, the speaker should

INTERPRETS (INTERPRET)
1Co 14: 5 he *i*, so that the church may be

INVADED
2Ki 17: 5 king of Assyria *i* the entire land,
24: 1 king of Babylon *i* the land,

INVENT* (INVENTED)
Ro 1:30 boastful; they *i* ways of doing evil;

INVENTED* (INVENT)
2Pe 1:16 We did not follow cleverly *i* stories

INVESTIGATED
Lk 1: 3 I myself have carefully *i* everything

INVISIBLE*
Ro 1:20 of the world God's *i* qualities—
Col 1:15 He is the image of the *i* God,
1:16 and on earth, visible and *i*,
1Ti 1:17 immortal, *i*, the only God,
Heb 11:27 because he saw him who is *i*.

INVITE (INVITED INVITES)
Mt 22: 9 *i* to the banquet anyone you find.'
25:38 did we see you a stranger and *i* you
Lk 14:12 do not *i* your friends, your brothers
14:13 you give a banquet, *i* the poor,

INVITED (INVITE)
Zep 1: 7 he has consecrated those he has *i*.
Mt 22:14 For many are *i*, but few are chosen
25:35 I was a stranger and you *i* me in,
Lk 14:10 But when you are *i*, take the lowest
Rev 19: 9 'Blessed are those who are *i*

INVITES (INVITE)
Pr 18: 6 and his mouth *i* a beating.
1Co 10:27 If some unbeliever *i* you to a meal

INVOLVED
2Ti 2: 4 a soldier gets *i* in civilian affairs—

IRON
2Ki 6: 6 threw it there, and made the *i* float.
Ps 2: 9 will rule them with an *i* scepter;
Pr 27:17 As *i* sharpens *i*,
Da 2:33 and thighs of bronze, its legs of *i*,
1Ti 4: 2 have been seared as with a hot *i*.
Rev 2:27 He will rule them with an *i* scepter;
12: 5 all the nations with an *i* scepter.
19:15 He will rule them with an *i* scepter

IRRELIGIOUS*
1Ti 1: 9 and sinful, the unholy and *i*;

IRREVOCABLE*
Ro 11:29 for God's gifts and his call are *i*.

ISAAC

Son of Abraham by Sarah (Ge 17:19; 21:1-7; 1Ch 1:28). Abrahamic covenant perpetuated through (Ge 17:21; 26:2-5). Offered up by Abraham (Ge 22; Heb 11:17-19). Rebekah taken as wife (Ge 24). Inherited Abraham's estate (Ge 25:5). Fathered Esau and Jacob (Ge 25:19-26; 1Ch 1:34). Nearly lost Rebekah to Abimelech (Ge 26:1-11). Covenant with Abimelech (Ge 26:12-31). Tricked into blessing Jacob (Ge 27). Death (Ge 35:27-29). Father of Israel (Ex 3:6; Dt 29:13; Ro 9:10).

ISAIAH

Prophet to Judah (Isa 1:1). Called by the LORD (Isa 6). Announced judgment to Ahaz (Isa 7), deliverance from Assyria to Hezekiah (2Ki 19; Isa 36-37), deliverance from death to Hezekiah (2Ki 20:1-11; Isa 38). Chronicler of Judah's history (2Ch 26:22; 32:32).

ISH-BOSHETH*

Son of Saul who attempted to succeed him as king (2Sa 2:8-4:12; 1Ch 8:33).

ISHMAEL

Son of Abraham by Hagar (Ge 16; 1Ch 1:28). Blessed, but not son of covenant (Ge 17:18-21; Gal 4:21-31). Sent away by Sarah (Ge 21:8-21). Children (Ge 25:12-18; 1Ch 1:29-31). Death (Ge 25:17).

ISLAND
Rev 1: 9 was on the *i* of Patmos
16:20 Every *i* fled away

ISRAEL (ISRAEL'S ISRAELITE ISRAELITES)

1. Name given to Jacob (see JACOB).

2. Corporate name of Jacob's descendants; often specifically Northern Kingdom.

Ex 28:11 Engrave the names of the sons of *I*
28:29 of the sons of *I* over his heart
Nu 24:17 a scepter will rise out of *I*.
Dt 6: 4 Hear, O *I*: The LORD our God,
10:12 O *I*, what does the LORD your
Jos 4:22 *I* crossed the Jordan on dry ground
Jdg 17: 6 In those days *I* had no king;
Ru 2:12 of *I*, under whose wings you have
1Sa 3:20 *I* from Dan to Beersheba
4:21 "The glory has departed from *I*"—
14:23 So the LORD rescued *I* that day,
15:26 has rejected you as king over *I*!"
17:46 will know that there is a God in *I*.
18:16 But all *I* and Judah loved David,
2Sa 5: 2 'You will shepherd my people *I*,
5: 3 they anointed David king over *I*.
14:25 In all *I* there was not a man

1Ki 1:35 I have appointed him ruler over *I*
10: 9 of the LORD's eternal love for *I*,
18:17 "Is that you, you troubler of *I*?"
19:18 Yet I reserve seven thousand in *I*—
2Ki 5: 8 know that there is a prophet in *I*."
1Ch 17:22 made your people *I* your very own
21: 1 incited David to take a census of *I*.
29:25 Solomon in the sight of all *I*
2Ch 9: 8 of the love of your God for *I*
Ps 73: 1 Surely God is good to *I*,
81: 8 if you would but listen to me, O *I*!
98: 3 his faithfulness to the house of *I*;
99: 8 you were to *I* a forgiving God,
Isa 11:12 and gather the exiles of *I*;
27: 6 *I* will bud and blossom
44:21 O *I*, I will not forget you.
46:13 my splendor to *I*.
Jer 2: 3 *I* was holy to the LORD,
23: 6 and *I* will live in safety.
31: 2 I will come to give rest to *I*."
31:10 'He who scattered *I* will gather
31:31 covenant with the house of *I*
33:17 sit on the throne of the house of *I*,
Eze 3:17 you a watchman for the house of *I*;
33: 7 you a watchman for the house of *I*;
34: 2 prophesy against the shepherds of *I*
37:28 that I the LORD make *I* holy,
39:23 of *I* went into exile for their sin,
Da 9:20 my sin and the sin of my people *I*
Hos 11: 1 "When *I* was a child, I loved him,
Am 4:12 prepare to meet your God, O *I*."
7:11 and *I* will surely go into exile,
8: 2 "The time is ripe for my people *I*;
9:14 I will bring back my exiled people *I*
Mic 5: 2 one who will be ruler over *I*,
Zep 3:13 The remnant of *I* will do no wrong;
Zec 11:14 brotherhood between Judah and *I*.
Mal 1: 5 even beyond the borders of *I*!'
Mt 2: 6 be the shepherd of my people *I*.'"
10: 6 Go rather to the lost sheep of *I*.
15:24 only to the lost sheep of *I*."
Mk 12:29 'Hear, O *I*, the Lord our God,
Lk 22:30 judging the twelve tribes of *I*.
Ac 1: 6 going to restore the kingdom to *I*?"
9:15 and before the people of *I*.
Ro 9: 4 of my own race, the people of *I*.
9: 6 all who are descended from *I* are *I*.
9:31 but *I*, who pursued a law
11: 7 What *I* sought so earnestly it did
11:26 And so all *I* will be saved,
Gal 6:16 who follow this rule, even to the *I*
Eph 2:12 excluded from citizenship in *I*
3: 6 Gentiles are heirs together with *I*,
Heb 8: 8 covenant with the house of *I*
Rev 7: 4 144,000 from all the tribes of *I*.
21:12 the names of the twelve tribes of *I*.

ISRAEL'S (ISRAEL)
Jdg 10:16 he could bear *I* misery no longer.
2Sa 23: 1 *I* singer of songs:
Isa 44: 6 *I* King and Redeemer, the LORD
Jer 3: 9 Because *I* immorality mattered
31: 9 because I am *I* father,
Jn 3:10 "You are *I* teacher," said Jesus,

ISRAELITE (ISRAEL)
Ex 16: 1 The whole *I* community set out
35:29 All the *I* men and women who
Nu 8:16 offspring from every *I* woman.
20: 1 the whole *I* community arrived
20:22 The whole *I* community set out
Jn 1:47 "Here is a true *I*, in whom there is
Ro 11: 1 I am an *I* myself, a descendant

ISRAELITES (ISRAEL)
Ex 1: 7 the *I* were fruitful and multiplied
2:23 The *I* groaned in their slavery
3: 9 the cry of the *I* has reached me,
12:35 The *I* did as Moses instructed
12:37 The *I* journeyed from Rameses
14:22 and the *I* went through the sea
16:12 I have heard the grumbling of the *I*.
16:35 The *I* ate manna forty years,
24:17 To the *I* the glory of the LORD
28:30 decisions for the *I* over his heart
29:45 Then I will dwell among the *I*
31:16 The *I* are to observe the Sabbath,
33: 5 "Tell the *I*, 'You are a stiff-necked
39:42 The *I* had done all the work just
Lev 22:32 be acknowledged as holy by the *I*.
25:46 rule over your fellow *I* ruthlessly.
25:55 for the *I* belong to me as servants.
Nu 2:32 These are the *I*, counted according
6:23 'This is how you are to bless the *I*.
9: 2 "Have the *I* celebrate the Passover
9:17 the *I* set out; wherever the cloud
10:12 Then the *I* set out from the Desert
14: 2 All the *I* grumbled against Moses
20:12 as holy in the sight of the *I*,
Nu 21: 6 they bit the people and many *I* died
26:65 had told those *I* they would surely
27:12 and see the land I have given the *I*.
33: 3 The *I* set out from Rameses
35:10 "Speak to the *I* and say to them:
Dt 33: 1 on the *I* before his death.
Jos 1: 2 about to give to them—to the *I*.
5: 6 The *I* had moved about
7: 1 the *I* acted unfaithfully in regard
8:32 There in the presence of the *I*,
18: 1 of the *I* gathered at Shiloh
21: 3 the *I* gave the Levites the following
22: 9 of Manasseh left the *I* at Shiloh
Jdg 2:11 Then the *I* did evil in the eyes
3:12 Once again the *I* did evil
4: 1 the *I* once again did evil in the eyes
6: 1 Again the *I* did evil in the eyes
10: 6 Again the *I* did evil in the eyes
13: 1 Again the *I* did evil in the eyes
1Sa 17: 2 Saul and the *I* assembled
1Ki 8:63 and all the *I* dedicated the temple
9:22 did not make slaves of any of the *I*;
12: 1 for all the *I* had gone there
12:17 But as for the *I* who were living
2Ki 17:24 towns of Samaria to replace the *I*.
1Ch 9: 2 in their own towns were some *I*,
10: 1 fought against Israel; the *I* fled
11: 4 and all the *I* marched to Jerusalem,
2Ch 7: 6 and all the *I* were standing.
Ne 1: 6 the sins we *I*, including myself
Jer 16:14 who brought the *I* up out of Egypt,'
Hos 1:10 "Yet the *I* will be like the sand
3: 1 Love her as the LORD loves the *I*,
Am 4: 5 boast about them, you *I*,
Mic 5: 3 return to join the *I*.
Ro 9:27 the number of the *I* be like the sand
10: 1 for the *I* is that they may be saved.
10:16 But not all the *I* accepted the good
2Co 11:22 Are they *I*? So am I.

ISSACHAR
Son of Jacob by Leah (Ge 30:18; 35:23; 1Ch 2:1). Tribe of blessed (Ge 49:14-15; Dt 33:18-19), numbered (Nu 1:29; 26:25), allotted land (Jos 19:17-23; Eze 48:25), assisted Deborah (Jdg 5:15), 12,000 from (Rev 7:7).

ISSUING*
Da 9:25 From the *i* of the decree to restore

ITALY
Ac 27: 1 decided that we would sail for *I*,
Heb 13:24 from *I* send you their greetings.

ITCHING*
2Ti 4: 3 to say what their *i* ears want to hear

ITHAMAR
Son of Aaron (Ex 6:23; 1Ch 6:3). Duties at tabernacle (Ex 38:21; Nu 4:21-33; 7:8).

ITTAI
2Sa 15:19 The king said to *I* the Gittite,

IVORY
1Ki 10:22 silver and *i*, and apes and baboons.
22:39 the palace he built and inlaid with *i*

JABBOK
Ge 32:22 and crossed the ford of the *J*.
Dt 3:16 and out to the *J* River,

JABESH
1Sa 11: 1 And all the men of *J* said to him,
31:12 wall of Beth Shan and went to *J*,
1Ch 10:12 and his sons and brought them to *J*.

JABESH GILEAD
Jdg 21: 8 that no one from *J* had come to
2Sa 2: 4 the men of *J* who had buried Saul,
1Ch 10:11 the inhabitants of *J* heard

JACOB
Second son of Isaac, twin of Esau (Ge 26:21-26; 1Ch 1:34). Bought Esau's birthright (Ge 26:29-34); tricked Isaac into blessing him (Ge 27:1-37). Fled to Haran (Ge 28:1-5). Abrahamic covenant perpetuated through (Ge 28:13-15; Mal 1:2). Vision at Bethel (Ge 28:10-22). Served Laban for Rachel and Leah (Ge 29:1-30). Children (Ge 29:31-30:24; 35:16-26; 1Ch 2-9). Flocks increased (Ge 30:25-43). Returned to Canaan (Ge 31). Wrestled with God; name changed to Israel (Ge 32:22-32). Reconciled to Esau (Ge 33). Returned to Bethel (Ge 35:1-15). Favored Joseph (Ge 37:3). Sent sons to Egypt during famine (Ge 42-43). Settled in Egypt (Ge 46). Blessed Ephraim and Manasseh (Ge 48). Blessed sons (Ge 49:1-28; Heb 11:21). Death (Ge 49:29-33). Burial (Ge 50:1-14).

JAEL*
Woman who killed Canaanite general, Sisera (Jdg 4:17-22; 5:24-27).

JAIR
Judge from Gilead (Jdg 10:3-5).

JAIRUS*
Synagogue ruler whose daughter Jesus raised (Mk 5:22-43; Lk 8:41-56).

JAMES
1. Apostle; brother of John (Mt 4:21-22; 10:2; Mk 3:17; Lk 5:1-10). At transfiguration (Mt 17:1-13; Mk 9:1-13; Lk 9:28-36). Killed by Herod (Ac 12:2).
2. Apostle; son of Alphaeus (Mt 10:3; Mk 3:18; Lk 6:15).
3. Brother of Jesus (Mt 13:55; Mk 6:3; Lk 24:10; Gal 1:19) and Judas (Jude 1). With believers before Pentecost (Ac 1:13). Leader of church at Jerusalem (Ac 12:17; 15; 21:18; Gal 2:9, 12). Author of epistle (Jas 1:1).

JAPHETH
Son of Noah (Ge 5:32; 1Ch 1:4-5). Blessed (Ge 9:18-28). Sons of (Ge 10:2-5).

JAR (JARS)
Ge 24:14 let down your *j* that I may have
1Ki 17:14 'The *j* of flour will not be used up
Jer 19: 1 "Go and buy a clay *j* from a potter.
Lk 8:16 hides it in a *j* or puts it under a bed.

JARS (JAR)
Jn 2: 6 Nearby stood six stone water *j*,
2Co 4: 7 we have this treasure in *j* of clay

JASPER
Ex 28:20 row a chrysolite, an onyx and a *j*.
Eze 28:13 chrysolite, onyx and *j*,
Rev 4: 3 sat there had the appearance of *j*
21:19 The first foundation was *j*,

JAVELIN
1Sa 17:45 me with sword and spear and *j*,

JAWBONE
Jdg 15:15 Finding a fresh *j* of a donkey,

JEALOUS (JEALOUSY)
Ex 20: 5 the LORD your God, am a *j* God,
34:14 whose name is Jealous, is a *j* God.
Dt 4:24 God is a consuming fire, a *j* God.
6:15 is a *j* God and his anger will burn
32:21 They made me *j* by what is no god
Jos 24:19 He is a holy God; he is a *j* God.
Eze 16:38 of my wrath and *j* anger.
16:42 my *j* anger will turn away from you
23:25 I will direct my *j* anger against you,
36: 6 in my *j* wrath because you have
Joel 2:18 the LORD will be *j* for his land
Na 1: 2 LORD is a *j* and avenging God;
Zep 3: 8 consumed by the fire of my *j* anger.
Zec 1:14 I am very *j* for Jerusalem and Zion,
8: 2 "I am very *j* for Zion; I am burning
2Co 11: 2 I am *j* for you with a godly jealousy

JEALOUSY (JEALOUS)
Ps 79: 5 How long will your *j* burn like fire?
Pr 6:34 for *j* arouses a husband's fury,
27: 4 but who can stand before *j*?
SS 8: 6 its *j* unyielding as the grave.
Zep 1:18 In the fire of his *j*
Zec 8: 2 I am burning with *j* for her."
Ro 13:13 debauchery, not in dissension and *j*
1Co 3: 3 For since there is *j* and quarreling
10:22 trying to arouse the Lord's *j*?
2Co 11: 2 I am jealous for you with a godly *j*.
12:20 *j*, outbursts of anger, factions,
Gal 5:20 hatred, discord, *j*, fits of rage,

JEERS*
Heb 11:36 Some faced *j* and flogging,

JEHOAHAZ
1. Son of Jehu; king of Israel (2Ki 13:1-9).
2. Son of Josiah; king of Judah (2Ki 23:31-34; 2Ch 36:1-4).

JEHOASH
1. See JOASH.
2. Son of Jehoahaz; king of Israel. Defeat of Aram prophesied by Elisha (2Ki 13:10-25). Defeated Amaziah in Jerusalem (2Ki 14:1-16; 2Ch 25:17-24).

JEHOIACHIN
Son of Jehoiakim; king of Judah exiled by Nebuchadnezzar (2Ki 24:8-17; 2Ch 36:8-10; Jer 22:24-30; 24:1). Raised from prisoner status (2Ki 25:

JEHOIACHIN
Son of Jehoiakim; king of Judah exiled by Nebuchadnezzar (2Ki 24:8-17; 2Ch 36:8-10; Jer 22:24-30; 24:1). Raised from prisoner status (2Ki 25:27-30; Jer 52:31-34).

JEHOIADA

Priest who sheltered Joash from Athaliah (2Ki 11-12; 2Ch 22:11-24:16).

JEHOIAKIM

Son of Josiah; made king of Judah by Pharaoh Neco (2Ki 23:34-24:6; 2Ch 36:4-8; Jer 22:18-23). Burned scroll of Jeremiah's prophecies (Jer 36).

JEHORAM

1. Son of Jehoshaphat; king of Judah (2Ki 8: 16-24). Prophesied against by Elijah; killed by the LORD (2Ch 21).

2. See JORAM.

JEHOSHAPHAT

Son of Asa; king of Judah. Strengthened his kingdom (2Ch 17). Joined with Ahab against Aram (2Ki 22; 2Ch 18). Established judges (2Ch 19). Joined with Joram against Moab (2Ki 3; 2Ch 20).

JEHU

1. Prophet against Baasha (2Ki 16:1-7).

2. King of Israel. Anointed by Elijah to obliterate house of Ahab (1Ki 19:16-17); anointed by servant of Elisha (2Ki 9:1-13). Killed Joram and Ahaziah (2Ki 9:14-29; 2Ch 22:7-9), Jezebel (2Ki 9:30-37), relatives of Ahab (2Ki 10:1-17), ministers of Baal (2Ki 10:18-29). Death (2Ki 10:30-36).

JEPHTHAH

Judge from Gilead who delivered Israel from Ammon (Jdg 10:6-12:7). Made rash vow concerning his daughter (Jdg 11:30-40).

JEREMIAH

Prophet to Judah (Jer 1:1-3). Called by the LORD (Jer 1). Put in stocks (Jer 20:1-3). Threatened for prophesying (Jer 11:18-23; 26). Opposed by Hananiah (Jer 28). Scroll burned (Jer 36). Imprisoned (Jer 37). Thrown into cistern (Jer 38). Forced to Egypt with those fleeing Babylonians (Jer 43).

JERICHO

Nu 22: 1 along the Jordan across from *J*.
Jos 3:16 the people crossed over opposite *J*.
5:10 camped at Gilgal on the plains of *J*,
Lk 10:30 going down from Jerusalem to *J*,
Heb 11:30 By faith the walls of *J* fell,

JEROBOAM

1. Official of Solomon; rebelled to become first king of Israel (1Ki 11:26-40; 12:1-20; 2Ch 10). Idolatry (1Ki 12:25-33); judgment for (1Ki 13-14; 2Ch 13).

2. Son of Jehoash; king of Israel (1Ki 14:23-29).

JERUSALEM

Jos 10: 1 of *J* heard that Joshua had taken Ai
15: 8 of the Jebusite city (that is, *J*).
Jdg 1: 8 The men of Judah attacked *J* also
1Sa 17:54 head and brought it to *J*,
2Sa 5: 5 and in *J* he reigned over all Israel
5: 6 and his men marched to *J*
9:13 And Mephibosheth lived in *J*,
11: 1 But David remained in *J*.
15:29 took the ark of God back to *J*
24:16 stretched out his hand to destroy *J*,
1Ki 3: 1 the LORD, and the wall around *J*.
9:15 the wall of *J*, and Hazor, Megiddo
9:19 whatever he desired to build in *J*,
10:26 cities and also with him in *J*.
10:27 as common in *J* as stones,
11: 7 of *J*, Solomon built a high place
11:13 my servant and for the sake of *J*,
11:36 always have a lamp before me in *J*,
11:42 Solomon reigned in *J*
12:27 at the temple of the LORD in *J*,
14:21 and he reigned seventeen years in *J*
14:25 Shishak king of Egypt attacked *J*.
15: 2 and he reigned in *J* three years.
15:10 and he reigned in *J* forty-one years.
22:42 he reigned in *J* twenty-five years.
2Ki 8:17 and he reigned in *J* eight years.
8:26 and he reigned in *J* one year.
12: 1 and he reigned in *J* forty years.
12:17 Then he turned to attack *J*.
14: 2 he reigned in *J* twenty-nine years.
14:13 Then Jehoash went to *J*
15: 2 and he reigned in *J* fifty-two years.
15:33 and he reigned in *J* sixteen years.
16: 2 and he reigned in *J* sixteen years.
16: 5 Israel marched up to fight against *J*
18: 2 he reigned in *J* twenty-nine years.
18:17 Lachish to King Hezekiah at *J*.
19:31 For out of *J* will come a remnant,
21: 1 and he reigned in *J* fifty-five years.
21:12 going to bring such disaster on *J*
21:19 and he reigned in *J* two years.
22: 1 he reigned in *J* thirty-one years.
23:27 and I will reject *J*, the city I chose,
23:31 and he reigned in *J* three months.
23:36 and he reigned in *J* eleven years.
24: 8 and he reigned in *J* three months.
24:10 king of Babylon advanced on *J*
24:14 He carried into exile all *J*:
24:18 and he reigned in *J* eleven years.
24:20 anger that all this happened to *J*
25: 1 king of Babylon marched against *J*
25: 9 royal palace and all the houses of *J*.
1Ch 11: 4 and all the Israelites marched to *J*,
21:16 sword in his hand extended over *J*.
2Ch 1: 4 he had pitched a tent for it in *J*.
3: 1 the LORD in *J* on Mount Moriah,
6: 6 now I have chosen *J* for my Name
9: 1 she came to *J* to test him
20:15 and all who live in Judah and *J*!
20:27 and *J* returned joyfully to *J*,
29: 8 LORD has fallen on Judah and *J*;
36:19 and broke down the wall of *J*;
Ezr 1: 2 a temple for him at *J* in Judah.
2: 1 to Babylon (they returned to *J*
3: 1 people assembled as one man in *J*.
4:12 up to us from you have gone to *J*
4:24 of God in *J* came to a standstill
6:12 or to destroy this temple in *J*.
7: 8 Ezra arrived in *J* in the fifth month
9: 9 a wall of protection in Judah and *J*.
10: 7 for all the exiles to assemble in *J*.
Ne 1: 2 the exile, and also about *J*.
1: 3 The wall of *J* is broken down,
2:11 to *J*, and after staying there three
2:17 Come, let us rebuild the wall of *J*,
2:20 you have no share in *J* or any claim
3: 8 They restored *J* as far as the Broad
4: 8 fight against *J* and stir up trouble
11: 1 leaders of the people settled in *J*,
12:27 At the dedication of the wall of *J*,
12:43 in *J* could be heard far away.
Ps 51:18 build up the walls of *J*.
79: 1 they have reduced *J* to rubble.
122: 2 in your gates, O *J*.
122: 3 *J* is built like a city
122: 6 Pray for the peace of *J*:
125: 2 As the mountains surround *J*,
128: 5 may you see the prosperity of *J*,
137: 5 If I forget you, O *J*,
147: 2 The LORD builds up *J*;
147: 12 Extol the LORD, O *J*;
SS 6: 4 lovely as *J*,
Isa 1: 1 and *J* that Isaiah son of Amoz saw
2: 1 saw concerning Judah and *J*:
3: 1 is about to take from *J* and Judah
3: 8 *J* staggers,
4: 3 recorded among the living in *J*.
8:14 And for the people of *J* he will be
27:13 LORD on the holy mountain in *J*.
31: 5 the LORD Almighty will shield *J*;
33:20 your eyes will see *J*,
40: 2 Speak tenderly to *J*,
40: 9 You who bring good tidings to *J*,
52: 1 O *J*, the holy city.
52: 2 rise up, sit enthroned, O *J*.
62: 6 on your walls, O *J*;
62: 7 give him no rest till he establishes *J*
65:18 for I will create *J* to be a delight
Jer 2: 2 and proclaim in the hearing of *J*:
3:17 time they will call *J* The Throne
4: 5 and proclaim in *J* and say:
4:14 O *J*, wash the evil from your heart
5: 1 "Go up and down the streets of *J*,
6: 6 and build siege ramps against *J*.
8: 5 Why does *J* always turn away?
9:11 "I will make *J* a heap of ruins,
13:27 Woe to you, O *J*!
23:14 And among the prophets of *J*
24: 1 into exile from *J* to Babylon
26:18 *J* will become a heap of rubble,
32: 2 of Babylon was then besieging *J*,
33:10 the streets of *J* that are deserted,
39: 1 This is how *J* was taken: In
51:50 and think on *J*."
52:14 broke down all the walls around *J*.
La 1: 7 *J* remembers all the treasures
Eze 14:21 send against *J* my four dreadful
16: 2 confront *J* with her detestable
Da 6:10 the windows opened toward *J*.
9: 2 of *J* would last seventy years.
9:12 done like what has been done to *J*.
9:25 and rebuild *J* until the Anointed
Joel 3: 1 restore the fortunes of Judah and *J*,
3:16 and thunder from *J*;
3:17 *J* will be holy;
Am 2: 5 will consume the fortresses of *J*."
Ob :11 and cast lots for *J*,
Mic 1: 5 Is it not *J*?
4: 2 the word of the LORD from *J*.
Zep 3:16 On that day they will say to *J*,
Zec 1:14 'I am very jealous for *J* and Zion,
1:17 comfort Zion and choose *J*.'"
2: 2 He answered me, "To measure *J*,
2: 4 '*J* will be a city without walls
8: 3 I will return to Zion and dwell in *J*.
8: 8 I will bring them back to live in *J*;
8:15 determined to do good again to *J*
8:22 powerful nations will come to *J*
9: 9 Shout, Daughter of *J*!
9:10 and the war-horses from *J*,
12: 3 I will make *J* an immovable rock
12:10 the inhabitants of *J* a spirit of grace
14: 2 the nations to *J* to fight against it;
14: 8 living water will flow out from *J*,
14:16 that have attacked *J* will go up
Mt 16:21 to his disciples that he must go to *J*
20:18 said to them, "We are going up to *J*
21:10 When Jesus entered *J*, the whole
23:37 "O *J*, *J*, you who kill the prophets
Mk 10:33 "We are going up to *J*," he said,
Lk 2:22 Mary took him to *J* to present him
2:41 Every year his parents went to *J*
2:43 the boy Jesus stayed behind in *J*,
4: 9 The devil led him to *J*
9:31 about to bring to fulfillment at *J*.
9:51 Jesus resolutely set out for *J*,
13:34 die outside *J*! "O *J*, *J*,
18:31 told them, "We are going up to *J*,
19:41 As he approached *J* and saw
21:20 "When you see *J* being surrounded
21:24 *J* will be trampled
24:47 name to all nations, beginning at *J*.
Jn 4:20 where we must worship is in *J*."
Ac 1: 4 this command: "Do not leave *J*,
1: 8 and you will be my witnesses in *J*,
6: 7 of disciples in *J* increased rapidly,
20:22 by the Spirit, I am going to *J*,
23:11 As you have testified about me in *J*
Ro 15:19 So from *J* all the way
Gal 4:25 corresponds to the present city of *J*
4:26 But the *J* that is above is free,
Heb 12:22 to the heavenly *J*, the city
Rev 3:12 the new *J*, which is coming
21: 2 I saw the Holy City, the new *J*,
21:10 and showed me the Holy City, *J*,

JESSE

Father of David (Ru 4:17-22; 1Sa 16; 1Ch 2: 12-17).

JESUS

LIFE: Genealogy (Mt 1:1-17; Lk 3:21-37). Birth announced (Mt 1:18-25; Lk 1:26-45). Birth (Mt 2: 1-12; Lk 2:1-40). Escape to Egypt (Mt 2:13-23). As a boy in the temple (Lk 2:41-52). Baptism (Mt 3: 13-17; Mk 1:9-11; Lk 3:21-22; Jn 1:32-34). Temptation (Mt 4:1-11; Mk 1:12-13; Lk 4:1-13). Ministry in Galilee (Mt 4:12-18:35; Mk 1:14-9:50; Lk 4: 14-13:9; Jn 1:35-2:11; 4; 6), Transfiguration (Mt 17:1-8; Mk 9:2-8; Lk 9:28-36), on the way to Jerusalem (Mt 19-20; Mk 10; Lk 13:10-19:27), in Jerusalem (Mt 21-25; Mk 11-13; Lk 19:28-21:38; Jn 2: 12-3:36; 5; 7-12). Last supper (Mt 26:17-35; Mk 14:12-31; Lk 22:1-38; Jn 13-17). Arrest and trial (Mt 26:36-27:31; Mk 14:43-15:20; Lk 22:39-23:25; Jn 18:1-19:16). Crucifixion (Mt 27:32-66; Mk 15: 21-47; Lk 23:26-55; Jn 19:28-42). Resurrection and appearances (Mt 28; Mk 16; Lk 24; Jn 20-21; Ac 1:1-11; 7:56; 9:3-6; 1Co 15:1-8; Rev 1:1-20).

MIRACLES. Healings: official's son (Jn 4:43-54), demoniac in Capernaum (Mk 1:23-26; Lk 4: 33-35), Peter's mother-in-law (Mt 8:14-17; Mk 1: 29-31; Lk 4:38-39), leper (Mt 8:2-4; Mk 1:40-45; Lk 5:12-16), paralytic (Mt 9:1-8; Mk 2:1-12; Lk 5: 17-26), cripple (Jn 5:1-9), shriveled hand (Mt 12: 10-13; Mk 3:1-5; Lk 6:6-11), centurion's servant (Mt 8:5-13; Lk 7:1-10), widow's son raised (Lk 7: 11-17), demoniac (Mt 12:22-23; Lk 11:14), Gadarene demoniacs (Mt 8:28-34; Mk 5:1-20; Lk 8: 26-39), woman's bleeding and Jairus' daughter (Mt 9:18-26; Mk 5:21-43; Lk 8:40-56), blind man (Mt 9: 27-31), mute man (Mt 9:32-33), Canaanite woman's daughter (Mt 15:21-28; Mk 7:24-30), deaf man (Mk 7:31-37), blind man (Mk 8:22-26), demoniac boy (Mt 17:14-18; Mk 9:14-29; Lk 9:37-43), ten lepers (Lk 17:11-19), man born blind (Jn 9:1-7), Lazarus raised (Jn 11), crippled woman (Lk 13: 11-17), man with dropsy (Lk 14:1-6), two blind men (Mt 20:29-34; Mk 10:46-52; Lk 18:35-43), Malchus' ear (Lk 22:50-51). Other Miracles: water to wine (Jn 2:1-11), catch of fish (Lk 5:1-11), storm stilled (Mt 8:23-27; Mk 4:37-41; Lk 8:22-25), 5,000 fed (Mt 14:15-21; Mk 6:35-44; Lk 9:10-17; Jn 6:1-14), walking on water (Mt 14:25-33; Mk 6: 48-52; Jn 6:15-21), 4,000 fed (Mt 15:32-39; Mk 8: 1-9), money from fish (Mt 17:24-27), fig tree cursed (Mt 21:18-22; Mk 11:12-14), catch of fish (Jn 21: 1-14).

MAJOR TEACHING: Sermon on the Mount (Mt 5-7; Lk 6:17-49), to Nicodemus (Jn 3), to Samaritan woman (Jn 4), Bread of Life (Jn 6:22-59), at Feast of Tabernacles (Jn 7-8), woes to Pharisees (Mt 23; Lk 11:37-54), Good Shepherd (Jn 10:1-18), Olivet Discourse (Mt 24-25; Mk 13; Lk 21:5-36), Upper Room Discourse (Jn 13-16).

PARABLES: Sower (Mt 13:3-23; Mk 4:3-25; Lk 8:5-18), seed's growth (Mk 4:26-29), wheat and weeds (Mt 13:24-30, 36-43), mustard seed (Mt 13:31-32; Mk 4:30-32), yeast (Mt 13:33; Lk 13:20-21), hidden treasure (Mt 13:44), valuable pearl (Mt 13:45-46), net (Mt 13:47-51), house owner (Mt 13:52), good Samaritan (Lk 10:25-37), unmerciful servant (Mt 18:15-35), lost sheep (Mt 18:10-14; Lk 15:4-7), lost coin (Lk 15:8-10), prodigal son (Lk 15:11-32), dishonest manager (Lk 16:1-13), rich man and Lazarus (Lk 16:19-31), persistent widow (Lk 18:1-8), Pharisee and tax collector (Lk 18:9-14), payment of workers (Mt 20:1-16), tenants and the vineyard (Mt 21:28-46; Mt 12:1-12; Lk 20:9-19), wedding banquet (Mt 22:1-14), faithful servant (Mt 24:45-51), ten virgins (Mt 25:1-13), talents (Mt 25:1-30; Lk 19:12-27).

DISCIPLES see APOSTLES. Call of (Jn 1:35-51; Mt 4:18-22; 9:9; Mk 1:16-20; 2:13-14; Lk 5:1-11, 27-28). Named Apostles (Mk 3:13-19; Lk 6:12-16). Twelve sent out (Mt 10; Mk 6:7-11; Lk 9:1-5). Seventy sent out (Lk 10:1-24). Defection of (Jn 6:60-71; Mt 26:56; Mk 14:50-52). Final commission (Mt 28:16-20; Jn 21:15-23; Ac 1:3-8).

Ac 2:32 God has raised this *J* to life,
9: 5 "I am *J*, whom you are persecuting
9:34 said to him, "*J* Christ heals you.
15:11 of our Lord *J* that we are saved,
16:31 "Believe in the Lord *J*,
20:24 the task the Lord *J* has given me—
Ro 3:24 redemption that came by Christ *J*.
5:17 life through the one man, *J* Christ.
8: 1 for those who are in Christ *J*,
1Co 1: 7 for our Lord *J* Christ to be revealed
2: 2 except *J* Christ and him crucified.
6:11 in the name of the Lord *J* Christ
8: 6 and there is but one Lord, *J* Christ,
12: 3 and no one can say, "*J* is Lord,"
2Co 4: 5 not preach ourselves, but *J* Christ
13: 5 Do you not realize that Christ *J* is
Gal 2:16 but by faith in *J* Christ.
3:28 for you are all one in Christ *J*.
5: 6 in Christ *J* neither circumcision
6:17 bear on my body the marks of *J*.
Eph 1: 5 as his sons through *J* Christ,
2:10 created in Christ *J*
2:20 with Christ *J* himself as the chief
Php 1: 6 until the day of Christ *J*.
2: 5 be the same as that of Christ *J*:
2:10 name of *J* every knee should bow,
Col 3:17 do it all in the name of the Lord *J*,
1Th 1:10 whom he raised from the dead—*J*,
4:14 We believe that *J* died
5:23 at the coming of our Lord *J* Christ.
2Th 1: 7 when the Lord *J* is revealed
2: 1 the coming of our Lord *J* Christ
1Ti 1:15 Christ *J* came into the world
2Ti 1:10 appearing of our Savior, Christ *J*,
2: 3 us like a good soldier of Christ *J*.
3:12 life in Christ *J* will be persecuted,
Tit 2:13 our great God and Savior, *J* Christ,
Heb 2: 9 But we see *J*, who was made a little
2:11 So *J* is not ashamed to call them
3: 1 fix your thoughts on *J*, the apostle
3: 3 *J* has been found worthy
4:14 through the heavens, *J* the Son
6:20 where *J*, who went before us,
7:22 *J* has become the guarantee
7:24 but because *J* lives forever,
8: 6 But the ministry *J* has received is
12: 2 Let us fix our eyes on *J*, the author
12:24 to *J* the mediator of a new
1Pe 1: 3 the resurrection of *J* Christ
2Pe 1:16 and coming of our Lord *J* Christ,
1Jn 1: 7 and the blood of *J*, his Son,
2: 1 *J* Christ, the Righteous One.
2: 6 to live in him must walk as *J* did.
4:15 anyone acknowledges that *J* is
Rev 1: 1 The revelation of *J* Christ,
22:16 *J*, have sent my angel
22:20 Come, Lord *J*.

JETHRO

Father-in-law and adviser of Moses (Ex 3:1; 18). Also known as Reuel (Ex 2:18).

JEW (JEWS JEWS' JUDAISM)

Est 2: 5 of Susa a *J* of the tribe of Benjamin,
Zec 8:23 of one *J* by the hem of his robe
Ac 21:39 "I am a *J*, from Tarsus in Cilicia,
Ro 1:16 first for the *J*, then for the Gentile.
2:28 A man is not a *J* if he is only one
10:12 there is no difference between *J*
1Co 9:20 To the Jews I became like a *J*,
Gal 2:14 "You are a *J*, yet you live like
3:28 There is neither *J* nor Greek,
Col 3:11 Here there is no Greek or *J*,

JEWEL (JEWELRY JEWELS)

Pr 20:15 that speak knowledge are a rare *j*.
SS 4: 9 with one *j* of your necklace.
Rev 21:11 that of a very precious *j*,

JEWELRY (JEWEL)

Ex 35:22 and brought gold *j* of all kinds:
Jer 2:32 Does a maiden forget her *j*,
Eze 16:11 you with *j*: I put bracelets
1Pe 3: 3 wearing of gold *j* and fine clothes.

JEWELS (JEWEL)

Isa 54:12 your gates of sparkling *j*,
61:10 as a bride adorns herself with her *j*.
Zec 9:16 like *j* in a crown.

JEWS (JEW)

Ne 4: 1 He ridiculed the *J*,
Est 3:13 kill and annihilate all the *J*—
4:14 and deliverance for the *J* will arise
Mt 2: 2 who has been born king of the *J*?
27:11 "Are you the king of the *J*?" "Yes,
Jn 4: 9 (For *J* do not associate
4:22 for salvation is from the *J*.
19: 3 saying, "Hail, king of the *J*!"
Ac 20:21 I have declared to both *J*
Ro 3:29 Is God the God of *J* only?
9:24 not only from the *J* but
15:27 they owe it to the *J* to share
1Co 1:22 *J* demand miraculous signs
9:20 To the *J* I became like a Jew,
12:13 whether *J* or Greeks, slave or free
Gal 2: 8 of Peter as an apostle to the *J*,
Rev 2: 9 slander of those who say they are *J*
3: 9 claim to be *J* though they are not,

JEWS' (JEW)

Ro 15:27 shared in the *J* spiritual blessings,

JEZEBEL

Sidonian wife of Ahab (1Ki 16:31). Promoted Baal worship (1Ki 16:32-33). Killed prophets of the LORD (1Ki 18:4, 13). Opposed Elijah (1Ki 19:1-2). Had Naboth killed (1Ki 21). Death prophesied (1Ki 21:17-24). Killed by Jehu (2Ki 9:30-37).

JEZREEL

2Ki 9:36 at *J* dogs will devour Jezebel's flesh
10: 7 and sent them to Jehu in *J*.
Hos 1: 4 house of Jehu for the massacre at *J*,

JOAB

Nephew of David (1Ch 2:16). Commander of his army (2Sa 8:16). Victorious over Ammon (2Sa 10; 1Ch 19), Rabbah (2Sa 11; 1Ch 20), Jerusalem (1Ch 11:6), Absalom (2Sa 18), Sheba (2Sa 20). Killed Abner (2Sa 3:22-39), Amasa (2Sa 20:1-13). Numbered David's army (2Sa 24; 1Ch 21). Sided with Adonijah (1Ki 1:17, 19). Killed by Benaiah (1Ki 2:5-6, 28-35).

JOASH

Son of Ahaziah; king of Judah. Sheltered from Athaliah by Jehoiada (2Ki 11; 2Ch 22:10-23:21). Repaired temple (2Ki 12; 2Ch 24).

JOB

Wealthy man from Uz; feared God (Job 1:1-5). Righteousness tested by disaster (Job 1:6-22), personal affliction (Job 2). Maintained innocence in debate with three friends (Job 3-31), Elihu (Job 32-37). Rebuked by the LORD (Job 38-41). Vindicated and restored to greater stature by the LORD (Job 42). Example of righteousness (Eze 14:14, 20).

JOCHEBED*

Mother of Moses and Aaron (Ex 6:20; Nu 26:59).

JOEL

Prophet (Joel 1:1; Ac 2:16).

JOHN

1. Son of Zechariah and Elizabeth (Lk 1). Called the Baptist (Mt 3:1-12; Mk 1:2-8). Witness to Jesus (Mt 3:11-12; Mk 1:7-8; Lk 3:15-18; Jn 1:6-35; 3:27-30; 5:33-36). Doubts about Jesus (Mt 11:2-6; Lk 7:18-23). Arrest (Mt 4:12; Mk 1:14). Execution (Mt 14:1-12; Mk 6:14-29; Lk 9:7-9). Ministry compared to Elijah (Mt 11:7-19; Mk 9:11-13; Lk 7:24-35).

2. Apostle; brother of James (Mt 4:21-22; 10:2; Mk 3:17; Lk 5:1-10). At transfiguration (Mt 17:1-13; Mk 9:1-13; Lk 9:28-36). Desire to be greatest (Mk 10:35-45). Leader of church at Jerusalem (Ac 4:1-3; Gal 2:9). Elder who wrote epistles (2Jn 1; 3Jn 1). Prophet who wrote Revelation (Rev 1:1; 22:8).

3. Cousin of Barnabas, co-worker with Paul, (Ac 12:12-13:13; 15:37), see MARK.

JOIN (JOINED JOINS)

Ne 10:29 all these now *j* their brothers
Pr 23:20 Do not *j* those who drink too much
24:21 and do not *j* with the rebellious,
Jer 3:18 of Judah will *j* the house of Israel,
Eze 37:17 *J* them together into one stick
Da 11:34 who are not sincere will *j* them.
Ro 15:30 to *j* me in my struggle by praying
2Ti 1: 8 *j* with me in suffering for the gospel

JOINED (JOIN)

Zec 2:11 "Many nations will be *j*
Mt 19: 6 Therefore what God has *j* together,
Mk 10: 9 Therefore what God has *j* together,
Ac 1:14 They all *j* together constantly
Eph 2:21 him the whole building is *j* together
4:16 *j* and held together

JOINS (JOIN)

1Co 16:16 and to everyone who *j* in the work,

JOINT (JOINTS)

Ps 22:14 and all my bones are out of *j*.

JOINTS (JOINT)

Heb 4:12 even to dividing soul and spirit, *j*

JOKING*

Ge 19:14 his sons-in-law thought he was *j*.
Pr 26:19 and says, "I was only *j*!"
Eph 5: 4 or coarse *j*, which are out of place,

JONAH

Prophet in days of Jeroboam II (2Ki 14:25). Called to Nineveh; fled to Tarshish (Jnh 1:1-3). Cause of storm; thrown into sea (Jnh 1:4-16). Swallowed by fish (Jnh 1:17). Prayer (Jnh 2). Preached to Nineveh (Jnh 3). Attitude reproved by the LORD (Jnh 4). Sign of (Mt 12:39-41; Lk 11:29-32).

JONATHAN

Son of Saul (1Sa 13:16; 1Ch 8:33). Valiant warrior (1Sa 13-14). Relation to David (1Sa 18:1-4; 19-20; 23:16-18). Killed at Gilboa (1Sa 31). Mourned by David (2Sa 1).

JOPPA

Ezr 3: 7 logs by sea from Lebanon to *J*,
Jnh 1: 3 to *J*, where he found a ship bound
Ac 9:43 Peter stayed in *J* for some time

JORAM

1. Son of Ahab; king of Israel. Fought with Jehoshaphat against Moab (2Ki 3). Killed with Ahaziah by Jehu (2Ki 8:25-29; 9:14-26; 2Ch 22:5-9).

2. See JEHORAM.

JORDAN

Ge 13:10 plain of the *J* was well watered,
Nu 22: 1 and camped along the *J*
34:12 boundary will go down along the *J*
Dt 3:27 you are not going to cross this *J*.
Jos 1: 2 get ready to cross the *J* River
3:11 go into the *J* ahead of you.
3:17 ground in the middle of the *J*,
4:22 Israel crossed the *J* on dry ground.'
2Ki 2: 7 and Elisha had stopped at the *J*.
2:13 and stood on the bank of the *J*.
5:10 wash yourself seven times in the *J*,
6: 4 They went to the *J* and began
Ps 114: 3 the *J* turned back;
Isa 9: 1 along the *J*— The people walking
Jer 12: 5 manage in the thickets by the *J*?
Mt 3: 6 baptized by him in the *J* River.
4:15 the way to the sea, along the *J*,
Mk 1: 9 and was baptized by John in the *J*.

JOSEPH

1. Son of Jacob by Rachel (Ge 30:24; 1Ch 2:2). Favored by Jacob, hated by brothers (Ge 37:3-4). Dreams (Ge 37:5-11). Sold by brothers (Ge 37:12-36). Served Potiphar; imprisoned by false accusation (Ge 39). Interpreted dreams of Pharaoh's servants (Ge 40), of Pharaoh (Ge 41:4-40). Made greatest in Egypt (Ge 41:41-57). Sold grain to brothers (Ge 42-45). Brought Jacob and sons to Egypt (Ge 46-47). Sons Ephraim and Manasseh blessed (Ge 48). Blessed (Ge 49:22-26; Dt 33:13-17). Death (Ge 50:22-26; Ex 13:19; Heb 11:22). 12,000 from (Rev 7:8).

2. Husband of Mary, mother of Jesus (Mt 1:16-24; 2:13-19; Lk 1:27; 2; Jn 1:45).

3. Disciple from Arimathea, who gave his tomb for Jesus' burial (Mt 27:57-61; Mk 15:43-47; Lk 24:50-52).

4. Original name of Barnabas (Ac 4:36).

JOSHUA (HOSHEA)

1. Son of Nun; name changed from Hoshea (Nu 13:8, 16; 1Ch 7:27). Fought Amalekites under Moses (Ex 17:9-14). Servant of Moses on Sinai (Ex 24:13; 32:17). Spied Canaan (Nu 13). With Caleb, allowed to enter land (Nu 14:6, 30). Succeeded Moses (Dt 1:38; 31:1-8; 34:9).

Charged Israel to conquer Canaan (Jos 1). Crossed Jordan (Jos 3-4). Circumcised sons of wilderness wanderings (Jos 5). Conquered Jericho (Jos 6), Ai (Jos 7-8), five kings at Gibeon (Jos 10:1-28), southern Canaan (Jos 10:29-43), northern Canaan (Jos 11-12). Defeated at Ai (Jos 7). Deceived by Gibeonites (Jos 9). Renewed covenant (Jos 8:30-35; 24:1-27). Divided land among tribes (Jos 13-22). Last words (Jos 23). Death (Jos 24:28-31).

2. High priest during rebuilding of temple (Hag 1-2; Zec 3:1-9; 6:11).

JOSIAH

Son of Amon; king of Judah (2Ki 21:26; 1Ch 3:14). Prophesied (1Ki 13:2). Book of Law discovered during his reign (2Ki 22; 2Ch 34:14-31). Reforms (2Ki 23:1-25; 2Ch 34:1-13; 35:1-19). Killed by Pharaoh Neco (2Ki 23:29-30; 2Ch 35:20-27).

JOTHAM

1. Son of Gideon (Jdg 9).
2. Son of Azariah (Uzziah); king of Judah (2Ki 15:32-38; 2Ch 26:21-27:9).

JOURNEY

Dt 1:33 who went ahead of you on your *j*,
1:7 over your *j* through this vast desert
Jdg 18:6 Your *j* has the LORD's approval."
Ezr 8:21 and ask him for a safe *j* for us
Job 16:22 before I go on the *j* of no return.
Isa 35:8 The unclean will not *j* on it;
Mt 25:14 it will be like a man going on a *j*,
Ro 15:24 to have you assist me on my *j* there

JOY* (ENJOY ENJOYMENT JOYFUL JOYOUS OVERJOYED REJOICE REJOICES REJOICING)

Ge 31:27 so I could send you away with *j*
Lev 9:24 shouted for *j* and fell facedown.
Dt 16:15 and your *j* will be complete.
Jdg 9:19 may Abimelech be your *j*,
1Ch 12:40 and sheep, for there was *j* in Israel.
16:27 strength and *j* in his dwelling place.
16:33 sing for *j* before the LORD,
29:17 with *j* how willingly your people
29:22 drank with great *j* in the presence
2Ch 30:26 There was great *j* in Jerusalem,
Ezr 3:12 while many others shouted for *j*.
3:13 of the shouts of *j* from the sound
6:16 of the house of God with *j*.
6:22 with *j* by changing the attitude
6:22 *j* the Feast of Unleavened Bread,
Ne 8:10 for the *j* of the LORD is your
8:12 and to celebrate with great *j*,
8:17 And their *j* was very great.
12:43 God had given them great *j*.
Est 8:16 a time of happiness and *j*,
8:17 there was *j* and gladness
9:17 and made it a day of feasting and *j*.
9:18 and made it a day of feasting and *j*.
9:19 as a day of *j* and feasting,
9:22 and *j* and giving presents of food
9:22 their sorrow was turned into *j*
Job 3:7 may no shout of *j* be heard in it.
6:10 my *j* in unrelenting pain—
8:21 and your lips with shouts of *j*.
9:25 they fly away without a glimpse of *j*
10:20 from me so I can have a moment's *j*
20:5 the *j* of the godless lasts
33:26 he sees God's face and shouts for *j*;
38:7 and all the angels shouted for *j*?
Ps 4:7 have filled my heart with greater *j*
5:11 let them ever sing for *j*.
16:11 me with *j* in your presence,
19:8 giving *j* to the heart.
20:5 We will shout for *j*
21:1 How great is his *j* in the victories
21:6 with the *j* of your presence.
27:6 will I sacrifice with shouts of *j*;
28:7 My heart leaps for *j*
30:11 sackcloth and clothed me with *j*,
33:3 play skillfully, and shout for *j*.
35:27 shout for *j* and gladness;
42:4 with shouts of *j* and thanksgiving
43:4 to God, my *j* and my delight.
45:7 by anointing you with the oil of *j*.
45:15 They are led in with *j* and gladness;
47:1 shout to God with cries of *j*.
47:5 God has ascended amid shouts of *j*,
48:2 the *j* of the whole earth.
51:8 Let me hear *j* and gladness;
51:12 to me the *j* of your salvation
65:8 you call forth songs of *j*.
Ps 65:13 they shout for *j* and sing.
66:1 Shout with *j* to God, all the earth!
67:4 the nations be glad and sing for *j*,
71:23 My lips will shout for *j*
81:1 Sing for *j* to God our strength;
86:4 Bring *j* to your servant,
89:12 Hermon sing for *j* at your name.
90:14 for *j* and be glad all our days.
92:4 I sing for *j* at the works
94:19 your consolation brought *j*
95:1 let us sing for *j* to the LORD;
96:12 the trees of the forest will sing for *j*;
97:11 and *j* on the upright in heart.
98:4 for *j* to the LORD, all the earth,
98:6 shout for *j* before the LORD,
98:8 the mountains sing together for *j*;
100:1 for *j* to the LORD, all the earth.
105:43 his chosen ones with shouts of *j*;
106:5 share in the *j* of your nation
107:22 and tell of his works with songs of *j*
118:15 Shouts of *j* and victory
119:111 they are the *j* of my heart.
126:2 our tongues with songs of *j*.
126:3 and we are filled with *j*.
126:5 will reap with songs of *j*.
126:6 will return with songs of *j*,
132:9 may your saints sing for *j*."
132:16 and her saints will ever sing for *j*.
137:3 tormentors demanded songs of *j*;
137:6 my highest *j*.
149:5 and sing for *j* on their beds.
Pr 10:1 A wise son brings *j* to his father,
10:28 The prospect of the righteous is *j*,
11:10 wicked perish, there are shouts of *j*.
12:20 but *j* for those who promote peace.
14:10 and no one else can share its *j*.
14:13 and *j* may end in grief.
15:20 A wise son brings *j* to his father,
15:23 A man finds *j* in giving an apt reply
15:30 A cheerful look brings *j*
17:21 there is no *j* for the father of a fool.
21:15 it brings *j* to the righteous
23:24 of a righteous man has great *j*;
27:9 incense bring *j* to the heart,
27:11 my son, and bring *j* to my heart;
29:3 A man who loves wisdom brings *j*
Ecc 8:15 Then *j* will accompany him
11:9 let your heart give you *j* in the days
Isa 9:3 and increased their *j*;
12:3 With *j* you will draw water
12:6 Shout aloud and sing for *j*,
16:9 shouts of *j* over your ripened fruit
16:10 *J* and gladness are taken away
22:13 But see, there is *j* and revelry,
24:11 all *j* turns to gloom,
24:14 raise their voices, they shout for *j*;
26:19 wake up and shout for *j*.
35:2 will rejoice greatly and shout for *j*.
35:6 the mute tongue shout for *j*.
35:10 Gladness and *j* will overtake them,
35:10 everlasting *j* will crown their heads
42:11 Let the people of Sela sing for *j*;
44:23 Sing for *j*, O heavens,
48:20 Announce this with shouts of *j*
49:13 Shout for *j*, O heavens;
51:3 *J* and gladness will be found in her,
51:11 Gladness and *j* will overtake them,
51:11 everlasting *j* will crown their heads
52:8 together they shout for *j*.
52:9 Burst into songs of *j* together,
54:1 burst into song, shout for *j*,
55:12 You will go out in *j*
56:7 give them *j* in my house of prayer.
58:14 then you will find your *j*
60:5 heart will throb and swell with *j*;
60:15 and the *j* of all generations.
61:7 and everlasting *j* will be theirs.
65:14 out of the *j* of their hearts,
65:18 and its people a *j*.
66:5 that we may see your *j*!'
Jer 7:34 will bring an end to the sounds of *j*
15:16 they were my *j* and my heart's
16:9 will bring an end to the sounds of *j*
25:10 banish from them the sounds of *j*
31:7 "Sing with *j* for Jacob;
31:12 shout for *j* on the heights of Zion;
31:13 give them comfort and *j* instead
33:9 this city will bring me renown, *j*,
33:11 be heard once more the sounds of *j*
48:33 *J* and gladness are gone
48:33 no one treads them with shouts of *j*
48:33 they are not shouts of *j*.
51:48 will shout for *j* over Babylon,
La 2:15 the *j* of the whole earth?"
5:15 *J* is gone from our hearts;
Eze 7:7 not *j*, upon the mountains.
24:25 their *j* and glory, the delight
Joel 1:12 Surely the *j* of mankind
1:16 *j* and gladness
Mt 13:20 and at once receives it with *j*.
13:44 in his *j* went and sold all he had
28:8 afraid yet filled with *j*,
Mk 4:16 and at once receive it with *j*.
Lk 1:14 He will be a *j* and delight to you,
1:44 the baby in my womb leaped for *j*.
1:58 great mercy, and they shared her *j*.
2:10 news of great *j* that will be
6:23 "Rejoice in that day and leap for *j*,
8:13 the word with *j* when they hear it,
10:17 The seventy-two returned with *j*
10:21 full of *j* through the Holy Spirit,
24:41 still did not believe it because of *j*
24:52 returned to Jerusalem with great *j*.
Jn 3:29 That *j* is mine, and it is now
3:29 full of *j* when he hears
15:11 and that your *j* may be complete.
15:11 this so that my *j* may be in you
16:20 but your grief will turn to *j*.
16:21 because of her *j* that a child is born
16:22 and no one will take away your *j*.
16:24 and your *j* will be complete.
17:13 measure of my *j* within them.
Ac 2:28 with *j* in your presence.'
8:8 So there was great *j* in that city.
13:52 And the disciples were filled with *j*
14:17 and fills your hearts with *j*."
16:34 he was filled with *j* because he had come
Ro 14:17 peace and *j* in the Holy Spirit,
15:13 the God of hope fill you with all *j*
15:32 will I may come to you with *j*
16:19 so I am full of *j* over you;
2Co 1:24 but we work with you for your *j*,
2:3 that you would all share my *j*.
7:4 our troubles my *j* knows no
7:7 so that my *j* was greater than ever.
8:2 their overflowing *j* and their
Gal 4:15 What has happened to all your *j*?
5:22 *j*, peace, patience, kindness,
Php 1:4 I always pray with *j*
1:25 for your progress and *j* in the faith,
1:26 being with you again your *j*
2:2 then make my *j* complete
2:29 him in the Lord with great *j*,
4:1 and long for, my *j* and crown,
1Th 1:6 with the *j* given by the Holy Spirit.
2:19 For what is our hope, our *j*,
2:20 Indeed, you are our glory and *j*.
3:9 you in return for all the *j* we have
2Ti 1:4 so that I may be filled with *j*.
Phm :7 Your love has given me great *j*
Heb 1:9 by anointing you with the oil of *j*."
12:2 for the *j* set before him endured
13:17 them so that their work will be a *j*,
Jas 1:2 Consider it pure *j*, my brothers,
4:9 to mourning and your *j* to gloom.
1Pe 1:8 with an inexpressible and glorious *j*
1Jn 1:4 this to make our *j* complete.
2Jn :4 It has given me great *j* to find some
:12 so that our *j* may be complete.
3Jn :3 It gave me great *j* to have some
:4 I have no greater *j*
Jude :24 without fault and with great *j*—

JOYFUL* (JOY)

Dt 16:14 Be *j* at your Feast—you, your sons
1Sa 18:6 with *j* songs and with tambourines
1Ki 8:66 *j* and glad in heart
1Ch 15:16 as singers to sing *j* songs,
2Ch 7:10 *j* and glad in heart
Ps 68:3 may they be happy and *j*.
100:2 come before him with *j* songs.
Ecc 9:7 and drink your wine with a *j* heart,
Isa 24:8 the *j* harp is silent.
Jer 31:4 and go out to dance with the *j*.
Hab 3:18 I will be *j* in God my Savior.
Zec 8:19 and tenth months will become *j*
10:7 Their children will see it and be *j*;
Ro 12:12 Be *j* in hope, patient in affliction,
1Th 5:16 Be *j* always; pray continually;
Heb 12:22 thousands of angels in *j* assembly,

JOYOUS* (JOY)

Est 8:15 the city of Susa held a *j* celebration.

JUBILANT

Ps 96:12 let the fields be *j*, and everything
98:4 burst into *j* song with music;

JUBILEE

Lev 25:11 The fiftieth year shall be a *j* for you;

JUDAH (JUDEA)

1. Son of Jacob by Leah (Ge 29:35; 35:23; 1Ch 2:1). Did not want to kill Joseph (Ge 37:26-27). Among Canaanites, fathered Perez by Tamar (Ge 38). Tribe of blessed as ruling tribe (Ge 49:8-12; Dt 33:7), numbered (Nu 1:27; 26:22), allotted land

(Jos 15; Eze 48:7), failed to fully possess (Jos 15: 63; Jdg 1:1-20).
2. Name used for people and land of Southern Kingdom.
Ru 1: 7 take them back to the land of J.
2Sa 2: 4 king over the house of J.
Isa 1: 1 The vision concerning J
3: 8 J is falling;
Jer 13:19 All J will be carried into exile,
30: 3 bring my people Israel and J back
Hos 1: 7 I will show love to the house of J;
Zec 10: 4 From J will come the cornerstone,
Mt 2: 6 least among the rulers of J;
Heb 7:14 that our Lord descended from J,
8: 8 and with the house of J.
Rev 5: 5 of the tribe of J, the Root of David,

JUDAISM (JEW)
Ac 13:43 devout converts to J followed Paul
Gal 1:13 of my previous way of life in J,
1:14 advancing in J beyond many Jews

JUDAS
1. Apostle; son of James (Lk 6:16; Jn 14:22; Ac 1:13). Probably also called Thaddaeus (Mt 10:3; Mk 3:18).
2. Brother of James and Jesus (Mt 13:55; Mk 6: 3), also called Jude (Jude 1).
3. Christian prophet (Ac 15:22-32).
4. Apostle, also called Iscariot, who betrayed Jesus (Mt 10:4; 26:14-56; Mk 3:19; 14:10-50; Lk 6: 16; 22:3-53; Jn 6:71; 12:4; 13:2-30; 18:2-11). Suicide of (Mt 27:3-5; Ac 1:16-25).

JUDEA (JUDAH)
Mt 2: 1 born in Bethlehem in J,
24:16 are in J flee to the mountains.
Lk 3: 1 Pontius Pilate was governor of J,
Ac 1: 8 and in all J and Samaria,
9:31 Then the church throughout J,
1Th 2:14 imitators of God's churches in J,

JUDGE (JUDGED JUDGES JUDGING JUDGMENT JUDGMENTS)
Ge 16: 5 May the LORD j between you
18:25 Will not the J of all the earth do
Lev 19:15 but j your neighbor fairly.
Dt 1:16 between your brothers and j fairly,
17:12 man who shows contempt for the j
32:36 The LORD will j his people
Jdg 2:18 Whenever the LORD raised up a j
1Sa 2:10 the LORD will j the ends
3:13 that I would j his family forever
7:15 j over Israel all the days of his life.
24:12 May the LORD j between you
1Ki 8:32 J between your servants,
1Ch 16:33 for he comes to j the earth.
2Ch 6:23 J between your servants, repaying
19: 7 J carefully, for with the LORD our
Job 9:15 plead with my J for mercy.
Ps 7: 8 J me, O LORD, according
7: 8 let the LORD j the peoples.
7:11 God is a righteous j,
9: 8 He will j the world in righteousness
50: 6 for God himself is j.
51: 4 and justified when you j.
75: 2 it is I who j uprightly.
76: 9 when you, O God, rose up to j,
82: 8 Rise up, O God, j the earth,
94: 2 Rise up, O J of the earth;
96:10 he will j the peoples with equity.
96:13 He will j the world in righteousness
98: 9 He will j the world in righteousness
110: 6 He will j the nations, heaping up
Pr 31: 9 Speak up and j fairly;
Isa 2: 4 He will j between the nations
3:13 he rises to j the people.
11: 3 He will not j by what he sees
33:22 For the LORD is our j,
Jer 11:20 Almighty, you who j righteously
Eze 7: 3 I will j you according
7:27 by their own standards I will j them
18:30 O house of Israel, I will j you,
20:36 so I will j you, declares
22: 2 "Son of man, will you j her?
34:17 I will j between one sheep
Joel 3:12 sit to j all the nations on every side.
Mic 3:11 Her leaders j for a bribe,
4: 3 He will j between many peoples
Mt 7: 1 Do not j, or you too will be judged.
Lk 6:37 "Do not j, and you will not be
18: 2 there was a j who neither feared
Jn 5:27 And he has given him authority to j
5:30 By myself I can do nothing; I j only
8:16 But if I do j, my decisions are right,
12:47 For I did not come to j the world,
12:48 There is a j for the one who rejects
Ac 10:42 as j of the living and the dead.
17:31 a day when he will j the world
Ro 2:16 day when God will j men's secrets
3: 6 how could God j the world?
14:10 then, why do you j your brother?
1Co 4: 3 indeed, I do not even j myself.
4: 5 Therefore j nothing
6: 2 And if you are to j the world,
6: 2 that the saints will j the world?
Gal 2: 6 not j by external appearance—
Col 2:16 Therefore do not let anyone j you
2Ti 4: 1 who will j the living and the dead,
4: 8 which the Lord, the righteous J,
Heb 10:30 "The Lord will j his people."
12:23 come to God, the j of all men,
13: 4 for God will j the adulterer
Jas 4:12 There is only one Lawgiver and J,
4:12 who are you to j your neighbor?
1Pe 4: 5 to him who is ready to j the living
Rev 20: 4 who had been given authority to j.

JUDGED (JUDGE)
Mt 7: 1 "Do not judge, or you too will be j.
1Co 4: 3 I care very little if I am j by you
10:29 For why should my freedom be j
11:31 But if we j ourselves, we would not
14:24 all that he is a sinner and will be j
Jas 3: 1 who teach will be j more strictly.
Rev 20:12 The dead were j according

JUDGES (JUDGE)
Jdg 2:16 Then the LORD raised up j,
Job 9:24 he blindfolds its j.
Ps 58:11 there is a God who j the earth."
75: 7 But it is God who j:
Pr 29:14 If a king j the poor with fairness,
Jn 5:22 Moreover, the Father j no one,
1Co 4: 4 It is the Lord who j me.
Heb 4:12 it j the thoughts and attitudes
1Pe 1:17 on a Father who j each man's work
2:23 himself to him who j justly.
Rev 19:11 With justice he j and makes war.

JUDGING (JUDGE)
Ps 9: 4 on your throne, j righteously.
Pr 24:23 To show partiality in j is not good:
Isa 16: 5 one who in j seeks justice
Mt 19:28 j the twelve tribes of Israel.
Jn 7:24 Stop j by mere appearances,

JUDGMENT (JUDGE)
Nu 33: 4 for the LORD had brought j
Dt 1:17 of any man, for j belongs to God.
32:41 and my hand grasps it in j,
1Sa 25:33 May you be blessed for your good j
Ps 1: 5 the wicked will not stand in the j,
9: 7 he has established his throne for j.
76: 8 From heaven you pronounced j,
82: 1 he gives j among the "gods":
119: 66 Teach me knowledge and good j,
143: 2 Do not bring your servant into j,
Pr 3:21 preserve sound j and discernment,
6:32 man who commits adultery lacks j;
8:14 Counsel and sound j are mine;
10:21 but fools die for lack of j.
11:12 man who lacks j derides his
12:11 but he who chases fantasies lacks j.
17:18 A man lacking in j strikes hands
18: 1 he defies all sound j.
28:16 A tyrannical ruler lacks j,
Ecc 12:14 God will bring every deed into j,
Isa 3:14 The LORD enters into j
28: 6 justice to him who sits in j,
53: 8 By oppression and j he was taken
66:16 the LORD will execute j
Jer 2:35 But I will pass j on you
25:31 he will bring j on all mankind
51:18 when their j comes, they will
Eze 11:10 and I will execute j on you
Da 7:22 pronounced j in favor of the saints
Am 7: 4 Sovereign LORD was calling for j
Zec 8:16 and sound j in your courts;
Mal 3: 5 "So I will come near to you for j.
Mt 5:21 who murders will be subject to j.'
5:22 with his brother will be subject to j.
10:15 on the day of j than for that town.
11:24 on the day of j than for you."
12:36 have to give account on the day of j
12:41 up at the j with this generation
Jn 5:22 but has entrusted all j to the Son,
5:30 as I hear, and my j is just,
7:24 appearances, and make a right j."
8:26 "I have much to say in j of you.
9:39 "For j I have come into this world,
12:31 Now is the time for j on this world;
16: 8 to sin and righteousness and j:
16:11 in regard to j, because the prince
Ac 24:25 self-control and the j to come,
Ro 2: 1 you who pass j on someone else,
2: 2 Now we know that God's j
5:16 The j followed one sin
Ro 12: 3 rather think of yourself with sober j
14:10 stand before God's j seat.
14:13 Therefore let us stop passing j
1Co 7:40 In my j, she is happier if she stays
11:29 body of the Lord eats and drinks j
2Co 5:10 appear before the j seat of Christ,
2Th 1: 5 is evidence that God's j is right,
1Ti 3: 6 fall under the same j as the devil.
5:12 Thus they bring j on themselves,
Heb 6: 2 of the dead, and eternal j.
9:27 to die once, and after that to face j,
10:27 but only a fearful expectation of j
Jas 2:13 j without mercy will be shown
4:11 are not keeping it, but sitting in j
1Pe 4:17 For it is time for j to begin
2Pe 2: 9 the unrighteous for the day of j,
3: 7 being kept for the day of j
1Jn 4:17 have confidence on the day of j,
Jude : 6 bound with everlasting chains for j
Rev 14: 7 because the hour of his j has come.

JUDGMENTS (JUDGE)
Jer 1:16 I will pronounce my j on my people
Da 9:11 and sworn j written in the Law
Hos 6: 5 my j flashed like lightning
Ro 11:33 How unsearchable his j,
1Co 2:15 spiritual man makes j about all
Rev 16: 7 true and just are your j."

JUG
1Sa 26:12 and water j near Saul's head,
1Ki 17:12 of flour in a jar and a little oil in a j.

JUST* (JUSTICE JUSTIFICATION JUSTIFIED JUSTIFIES JUSTIFY JUSTIFYING JUSTLY)
Ge 18:19 LORD by doing what is right and j,
Dt 2:12 j as Israel did in the land
6: 3 j as the LORD, the God
27: 3 and honey, j as the LORD,
30: 9 j as he delighted in your fathers,
32: 4 and all his ways are j.
32: 4 upright and j is he.
32:47 They are not j idle words for you—
32:50 j as your brother Aaron died
2Sa 8:15 doing what was j and right
1Ch 18:14 doing what was j and right
2Ch 12: 6 and said, "The LORD is j."
Ne 9:13 and laws that are j and right,
9:33 you have been j; you have acted
Job 34:17 Will you condemn the j
35: 2 Elihu said: "Do you think this is j?
Ps 37:28 For the LORD loves the j
37:30 and his tongue speaks what is j.
99: 4 what is j and right.
111: 7 of his hands are faithful and j;
119:121 I have done what is righteous and j;
Pr 1: 3 doing what is right and j and fair;
2: 8 for he guards the course of the j
2: 9 will understand what is right and j
8: 8 All the words of my mouth are j;
8:15 and rulers make laws that are j;
12: 5 The plans of the righteous are j,
21: 3 To do what is right and j
Isa 32: 7 even when the plea of the needy is j
58: 2 They ask me for j decisions
Jer 4: 2 if in a truthful, j and righteous way
22: 3 what the LORD says: Do what is j
22:15 He did what was right and j,
23: 5 do what is j and right in the land.
33:15 he will do what is j and right
Eze 18: 5 who does what is j and right.
18:19 Since the son has done what is j
18:21 and does what is j and right,
18:25 'The way of the Lord is not j.'
18:27 and does what is j and right,
18:29 'The way of the Lord is not j.'
33:14 and does what is j and right—
33:16 He has done what is j and right;
33:17 But it is their way that is not j.
33:17 'The way of the Lord is not j.'
33:19 and does what is j and right,
33:20 'The way of the Lord is not j.'
45: 9 and oppression and do what is j
Da 4:37 does is right and all his ways are j.
Jn 5:30 as I hear, and my judgment is j,
Ro 3:26 as to be j and the one who justifies
2Th 1: 6 God is j: He will pay back trouble
Heb 2: 2 received its j punishment,
1Jn 1: 9 and j and will forgive us our sins
Rev 15: 3 J and true are your ways,
16: 5 "You are j in these judgments,
16: 7 true and j are your judgments."
19: 2 for true and j are his judgments.

JUSTICE* (JUST)
Ge 49:16 "Dan will provide j for his people
Ex 23: 2 do not pervert j by siding
23: 6 "Do not deny j to your poor people
Lev 19:15 " 'Do not pervert j; do not show

Dt 16:19 Do not pervert *j* or show partiality.
16:20 Follow *j* and *j* alone,
24:17 the alien or the fatherless of *j*,
27:19 Cursed is the man who withholds *j*
1Sa 8: 3 accepted bribes and perverted *j*.
2Sa 15: 4 and I would see that he gets *j*."
15: 6 came to the king asking for *j*,
1Ki 3:11 for discernment in administering *j*,
3:28 wisdom from God to administer *j*.
7: 7 the Hall of *J*, where he was to judge
10: 9 to maintain *j* and righteousness."
2Ch 9: 8 to maintain *j* and righteousness."
Ezr 7:25 and judges to administer *j*
Est 1:13 experts in matters of law and *j*,
Job 8: 3 Does God pervert *j*?
9:19 matter of *j*, who will summon him?
19: 7 though I call for help, there is no *j*.
27: 2 as God lives, who has denied me *j*,
29:14 *j* was my robe and my turban.
31:13 "If I have denied *j*
34: 5 but God denies me *j*.
34:12 that the Almighty would pervert *j*.
34:17 Can he who hates *j* govern?
36: 3 I will ascribe *j* to my Maker.
36:17 *j* have taken hold of you.
37:23 in his *j* and great righteousness,
40: 8 "Would you discredit my *j*?
Ps 7: 6 Awake, my God; decree *j*.
9: 8 he will govern the peoples with *j*.
9:16 The LORD is known by his *j*;
11: 7 he loves *j*;
33: 5 LORD loves righteousness and *j*;
36: 6 your *j* like the great deep.
37: 6 *j* of your cause like the noonday
45: 6 a scepter of *j* will be the scepter
72: 1 Endow the king with your *j*, O God
72: 2 your afflicted ones with *j*.
89:14 *j* are the foundation of your throne;
97: 2 *j* are the foundation of his throne.
99: 4 The King is mighty, he loves *j*—
101: 1 I will sing of your love and *j*;
103: 6 and *j* for all the oppressed.
106: 3 Blessed are they who maintain *j*,
112: 5 who conducts his affairs with *j*.
140: 12 I know that the LORD secures *j*
Pr 8:20 along the paths of *j*,
16:10 and his mouth should not betray *j*.
17:23 to pervert the course of *j*.
18: 5 or to deprive the innocent of *j*.
19:28 A corrupt witness mocks at *j*,
21:15 When *j* is done, it brings joy
28: 5 Evil men do not understand *j*,
29: 4 By *j* a king gives a country stability
29: 7 The righteous care about *j*
29:26 from the LORD that man gets *j*.
Ecc 3:16 place of *j*—wickedness was there.
5: 8 poor oppressed in a district, and *j*
Isa 1:17 Seek *j*,
1:21 She once was full of *j*;
1:27 Zion will be redeemed with *j*,
5: 7 he looked for *j*, but saw bloodshed;
5:16 Almighty will be exalted by his *j*,
5:23 but deny *j* to the innocent.
9: 7 it with *j* and righteousness
10: 2 and withhold *j* from the oppressed of
11: 4 with *j* he will give decisions
16: 5 one who in judging seeks *j*
28: 6 He will be a spirit of *j*
28:17 I will make *j* the measuring line
29:21 deprive the innocent of *j*.
30:18 For the LORD is a God of *j*.
32: 1 and rulers will rule with *j*.
32:16 *J* will dwell in the desert
33: 5 with *j* and righteousness.
42: 1 and he will bring *j* to the nations.
42: 3 In faithfulness he will bring forth *j*;
42: 4 till he establishes *j* on earth.
51: 4 my *j* will become a light
51: 5 my arm will bring *j* to the nations.
56: 1 "Maintain *j*
59: 4 No one calls for *j*;
59: 8 there is no *j* in their paths.
59: 9 So *j* is far from us,
59:11 We look for *j*, but find none;
59:14 So *j* is driven back,
59:15 that there was no *j*.
61: 8 "For I, the LORD, love *j*;
Jer 9:24 *j* and righteousness on earth,
10:24 Correct me, LORD, but only with *j*
12: 1 speak with you about your *j*:
21:12 " 'Administer *j* every morning;
30:11 I will discipline you but only with *j*;
46:28 I will discipline you but only with *j*;
La 3:36 to deprive a man of *j*—
Eze 22:29 mistreat the alien, denying them *j*.
34:16 I will shepherd the flock with *j*.
Hos 2:19 you in righteousness and *j*,
12: 6 maintain love and *j*,
Am 2: 7 and deny *j* to the oppressed.
Am 5: 7 You who turn *j* into bitterness
5:12 and you deprive the poor of *j*
5:15 maintain *j* in the courts.
5:24 But let *j* roll on like a river,
6:12 But you have turned *j* into poison
Mic 3: 1 Should you not know *j*,
3: 8 and with *j* and might,
3: 9 who despise *j*
Hab 1: 4 and *j* never prevails.
1: 4 so that *j* is perverted.
Zep 3: 5 by morning he dispenses his *j*,
Zec 7: 9 'Administer true *j*; show mercy
Mal 2:17 or "Where is the God of *j*?"
3: 5 and deprive aliens of *j*,
Mt 12:18 he will proclaim *j* to the nations.
12:20 till he leads *j* to victory.
23:23 important matters of the law—*j*,
Lk 11:42 you neglect *j* and the love of God.
18: 3 'Grant me *j* against my adversary.'
18: 5 I will see that she gets *j*,
18: 7 And will not God bring about *j*
18: 8 he will see that they get *j*,
Ac 8:33 humiliation he was deprived of *j*.
17:31 with *j* by the man he has appointed.
28: 4 *J* has not allowed him to live."
Ro 3:25 He did this to demonstrate his *j*,
3:26 it to demonstrate his *j*
2Co 7:11 what readiness to see *j* done.
Heb 11:33 administered *j*, and gained what
Rev 19:11 With *j* he judges and makes war.

JUSTIFICATION* (JUST)
Eze 16:52 for you have furnished some *j*
Ro 4:25 and was raised to life for our *j*.
5:16 many trespasses and brought *j*.
5:18 of righteousness was *j* that brings

JUSTIFIED* (JUST)
Ps 51: 4 and *j* when you judge.
Lk 18:14 rather than the other, went home *j*
Ac 13:39 from everything you could not be *j*
13:39 him everyone who believes is *j*
Ro 3:24 and are *j* freely by his grace
3:28 For we maintain that a man is *j*
4: 2 If, in fact, Abraham was *j* by works,
5: 1 since we have been *j* through faith,
5: 9 Since we have now been *j*
8:30 those he called, he also *j*; those he *j*,
10:10 heart that you believe and are *j*,
1Co 6:11 you were *j* in the name
Gal 2:16 in Christ Jesus that we may be *j*
2:16 observing the law no one will be *j*.
2:16 sinners' know that a man is not *j*
2:17 "If, while we seek to be *j* in Christ,
3:11 Clearly no one is *j* before God
3:24 to Christ that we might be *j* by faith
5: 4 to be *j* by law have been alienated
Tit 3: 7 so that, having been *j* by his grace,
Jas 2:24 You see that a person is *j*

JUSTIFIES* (JUST)
Ro 3:26 one who *j* those who have faith
4: 5 but trusts God who *j* the wicked,
8:33 God has chosen? It is God who *j*.

JUSTIFY* (JUST)
Est 7: 4 such distress would *j* disturbing
Job 40: 8 you condemn me to *j* yourself?
Isa 53:11 my righteous servant will *j* many,
Lk 10:29 But he wanted to *j* himself,
16:15 "You are the ones who *j* yourselves
Ro 3:30 who will *j* the circumcised by faith
Gal 3: 8 that God would *j* the Gentiles

JUSTIFYING* (JUST)
Job 32: 2 angry with Job for *j* himself rather

JUSTLY* (JUST)
Ps 58: 1 Do you rulers indeed speak *j*?
67: 4 for you rule the peoples *j*
Jer 7: 5 and deal with each other *j*,
Mic 6: 8 To act *j* and to love mercy
Lk 23:41 We are punished *j*,
1Pe 2:23 himself to him who judges *j*.

KADESH
Nu 20: 1 of Zin, and they stayed at *K*.
Dt 1:46 And so you stayed in *K* many days

KADESH BARNEA
Nu 32: 8 I sent them from *K* to look over

KEBAR
Eze 1: 1 among the exiles by the *K* River,

KEDORLAOMER
Ge 14:17 Abram returned from defeating *K*

KEEP (KEEPER KEEPING KEEPS KEPT)
Ge 31:49 "May the LORD *k* watch
Ex 15:26 his commands and *k* all his
20: 6 and *k* my commandments.
Lev 15:31 You must *k* the Israelites separate
Nu 6:24 and *k* you;
Dt 4: 2 but *k* the commands of the LORD
6:17 Be sure to *k* the commands
7: 9 who love him and *k* his commands.
7:12 your God will *k* his covenant
11: 1 your God and *k* his requirements,
13: 4 *K* his commands and obey him;
30:10 your God and *k* his commands
30:16 and to *k* his commands, decrees
Jos 22: 5 careful to *k* the commandment
1Ki 8:58 and to *k* the commands,
2Ki 17:19 Judah did not *k* the commands
23: 3 the LORD and *k* his commands,
1Ch 29:18 and *k* their hearts loyal to you.
2Ch 6:14 you who *k* your covenant of love
34:31 the LORD and *k* his commands,
Job 14:16 but not *k* track of my sin.
Ps 18:28 You, O LORD, *k* my lamp burning
19:13 *K* your servant also from willful
78:10 they did not *k* God's covenant
119: 2 Blessed are they who *k* his statutes
119: 9 can a young man *k* his way pure?
121: 7 The LORD will *k* you
141: 3 *k* watch over the door of my lips.
Pr 4:21 *k* them within your heart;
4:24 *k* corrupt talk far from your lips.
30: 8 *K* falsehood and lies far from me;
Ecc 3: 6 a time to *k* and a time
12:13 and *k* his commandments,
Isa 26: 3 You will *k* in perfect peace
42: 6 I will *k* you and will make you
58:13 "If you *k* your feet
Jer 16:11 forsook me and did not *k* my law.
Eze 20:19 and be careful to *k* my laws.
Mt 10:10 for the worker is worth his *k*.
Lk 12:35 and *k* your lamps burning,
17:33 tries to *k* his life will lose it,
Jn 10:24 How long will you *k* us in suspense
12:25 in this world will *k* it for eternal life
Ac 2:24 for death to *k* its hold on him.
18: 9 "Do not be afraid; *k* on speaking,
Ro 7:19 want to do—this I *k* on doing.
12:11 but *k* your spiritual fervor,
14:22 you believe about these things *k*
16:17 *K* away from them.
1Co 1: 8 He will *k* you strong to the end,
2Co 12: 7 To *k* me from becoming conceited
Gal 5:25 let us *k* in step with the Spirit.
Eph 4: 3 Make every effort to *k* the unity
2Th 3: 6 to *k* away from every brother who
1Ti 5:22 *K* yourself pure.
2Ti 4: 5 *k* your head in all situations,
Heb 9:20 God has commanded you to *k*."
13: 5 *K* your lives free from the love
Jas 1:26 and yet does not *k* a tight rein
2: 8 If you really *k* the royal law found
3: 2 able to *k* his whole body in check.
2Pe 1: 8 will *k* you from being ineffective
Jude :21 *K* yourselves in God's love
:24 able to *k* you from falling
Rev 3:10 also *k* you from the hour
22: 9 of all who *k* the words of this book.

KEEPER (KEEP)
Ge 4: 9 I my brother's *k*?" The LORD

KEEPING (KEEP)
Ex 20: 8 the Sabbath day by *k* it holy.
Dt 5:12 the Sabbath day by *k* it holy,
13:18 *k* all his commands that I am
Ps 19:11 in *k* them there is great reward.
119:112 My heart is set on *k* your decrees
Pr 15: 3 *k* watch on the wicked
Mt 3: 8 Produce fruit in *k* with repentance.
Lk 2: 8 *k* watch over their flocks at night.
1Co 7:19 *K* God's commands is what counts.
2Co 8: 5 and then to us in *k* with God's will.
Jas 4:11 you are not *k* it, but sitting
1Pe 3:16 and respect, *k* a clear conscience,
2Pe 3: 9 Lord is not slow in *k* his promise,

KEEPS (KEEP)
Ne 1: 5 who *k* his covenant of love
Ps 15: 4 who *k* his oath
Pr 12:23 A prudent man *k* his knowledge
15:21 of understanding *k* a straight
17:28 a fool is thought wise if he *k* silent,
29:11 a wise man *k* himself under control
Isa 56: 2 who *k* the Sabbath
Da 9: 4 who *k* his covenant of love
Am 5:13 Therefore the prudent man *k* quiet
Jn 7:19 Yet not one of you *k* the law.
8:51 if anyone *k* my word, he will never
1Co 13: 5 is not easily angered, it *k* no record

Jas 2:10 For whoever *k* the whole law
Rev 22: 7 Blessed is he who *k* the words

KEILAH
1Sa 23:13 that David had escaped from *K,*

KEPT (KEEP)
Ex 12:42 Because the LORD *k* vigil that
Dt 7: 8 and *k* the oath he swore
2Ki 18: 6 he *k* the commands the LORD had
Ne 9: 8 You have *k* your promise
Ps 130: 3 If you, O LORD, *k* a record of sins,
Isa 38:17 In your love you *k* me
Mt 19:20 these I have *k,* "the young man
2Co 11: 9 I have *k* myself from being
2Ti 4: 7 finished the race, I have *k* the faith.
1Pe 1: 4 spoil or fade—*k* in heaven for you,

KERNEL
Mk 4:28 then the full *k* in the head.
Jn 12:24 a *k* of wheat falls to the ground

KEY (KEYS)
Isa 33: 6 the fear of the LORD is the *k*
Rev 20: 1 having the *k* to the Abyss

KEYS* (KEY)
Mt 16:19 I will give you the *k* of the kingdom
Rev 1:18 And I hold the *k* of death

KICK*
Ac 26:14 for you to *k* against the goads.'

KILL (KILLED KILLS)
Ecc 3: 3 a time to *k* and a time to heal,
Mt 10:28 *k* the body but cannot *k* the soul.
17:23 They will *k* him, and on the third
Mk 9:31 will *k* him, and after three days
10:34 spit on him, flog him and *k* him.

KILLED (KILL)
Ge 4: 8 his brother Abel and *k* him.
Ex 2:12 he *k* the Egyptian and hid him
13:15 the LORD *k* every firstborn
Nu 35:11 who has *k* someone accidentally
1Sa 17:50 down the Philistine and *k* him.
Ne 9:26 They *k* your prophets, who had
Hos 6: 5 I *k* you with the words
Lk 11:48 they *k* the prophets, and you build
Ac 3:15 You *k* the author of life,

KILLS (KILL)
Ex 21:12 *k* him shall surely be put to death.
Lev 24:21 but whoever *k* a man must be put
2Co 3: 6 for the letter *k,* but the Spirit gives

KIND (KINDNESS KINDNESSES KINDS)
Ge 1:24 animals, each according to its *k.*"
2Ch 10: 7 "If you will be *k* to these people
Pr 11:17 A *k* man benefits himself,
12:25 but a *k* word cheers him up.
14:21 blessed is he who is *k* to the needy.
14:31 whoever is *k* to the needy honors
19:17 He who is *k* to the poor lends
Da 4:27 by being *k* to the oppressed.
Lk 6:35 because he is *k* to the ungrateful
1Co 13: 4 Love is patient, love is *k.*
15:35 With what *k* of body will they
Eph 4:32 Be *k* and compassionate
1Th 5:15 but always try to be *k* to each other
2Ti 2:24 instead, he must be *k* to everyone,
Tit 2: 5 to be busy at home, to be *k,*

KINDHEARTED* (HEART)
Pr 11:16 A *k* woman gains respect,

KINDNESS (KIND)
Ge 24:12 and show *k* to my master Abraham
32:10 I am unworthy of all the *k*
39:21 he showed him *k* and granted him
Jdg 8:35 failed to show *k* to the family
Ru 2:20 has not stopped showing his *k*
2Sa 9: 3 to whom I can show God's *k?*"
22:51 he shows unfailing *k*
Ps 18:50 he shows unfailing *k*
141: 5 righteous man strike me—it is a *k;*
Isa 54: 8 but with everlasting *k*
Jer 9:24 I am the LORD, who exercises *k,*
Hos 11: 4 I led them with cords of human *k,*
Ac 14:17 He has shown *k* by giving you rain
Ro 11:22 Consider therefore the *k*
2Co 6: 6 understanding, patience and *k;*
Gal 5:22 peace, patience, *k,* goodness,
Eph 2: 7 expressed in his *k* to us
Col 3:12 yourselves with compassion, *k,*
Tit 3: 4 But when the *k* and love
2Pe 1: 7 brotherly *k;* and to brotherly *k,*

KINDNESSES* (KIND)
Ps 106: 7 did not remember your many *k,*
Isa 63: 7 I will tell of the *k* of the LORD,
Isa 63: 7 to his compassion and many *k.*

KINDS (KIND)
Ge 1:12 bearing seed according to their *k*
1Co 12: 4 There are different *k* of gifts,
1Ti 6:10 of money is a root of all *k* of evil.
1Pe 1: 6 had to suffer grief in all *k* of trials.

KING (KING'S KINGDOM KINGDOMS KINGS)

1. Kings of Judah and Israel: see Saul, David, Solomon.

2. Kings of Judah: see Rehoboam, Abijah, Asa, Jehoshaphat, Jehoram, Ahaziah, Athaliah (Queen), Joash, Amaziah, Azariah (Uzziah), Jotham, Ahaz, Hezekiah, Manasseh, Amon, Josiah, Jehoahaz, Jehoiakim, Jehoiachin, Zedekiah.

3. Kings of Israel: see Jeroboam I, Nadab, Baasha, Elah, Zimri, Tibni, Omri, Ahab, Ahaziah, Joram, Jehu, Jehoahaz, Jehoash, Jeroboam II, Zechariah, Shallum, Menahem, Pekah, Pekahiah, Hoshea.

Ex 1: 8 a new *k,* who did not know about
Dt 17:14 "Let us set a *k* over us like all
Jdg 17: 6 In those days Israel had no *k;*
1Sa 8: 5 now appoint a *k* to lead us,
11:15 as *k* in the presence of the LORD.
12:12 the LORD your God was your *k.*
2Sa 2: 4 and there they anointed David *k*
1Ki 1:30 Solomon your son shall be *k*
Ps 2: 6 "I have installed my *K*
24: 7 that the *K* of glory may come in.
44: 4 You are my *K* and my God,
47: 7 For God is the *K* of all the earth;
Isa 32: 1 See, a *k* will reign in righteousness
Jer 30: 9 and David their *k,*
Hos 3: 5 their God and David their *k.*
Mic 2:13 *k* will pass through before them,
Zec 9: 9 See, your *k* comes to you,
Mt 2: 2 is the one who has been born *k*
27:11 "Are you the *k* of the Jews?" "Yes,
Lk 19:38 "Blessed is the *k* who comes
23: 3 "Are you the *k* of the Jews?" "Yes,
23:38 THE *K* OF THE JEWS.
Jn 1:49 of God; you are the *K* of Israel."
12:13 "Blessed is the *K* of Israel!"
Ac 17: 7 saying that there is another *k,*
1Ti 1:17 Now to the *K* eternal, immortal,
6:15 the *K* of kings and Lord of lords,
Heb 7: 1 This Melchizedek was *k* of Salem
1Pe 2:13 to the *k,* as the supreme authority,
2:17 of believers, fear God, honor the *k.*
Rev 15: 3 *K* of the ages.
17:14 he is Lord of lords and *K* of kings—
19:16 *K* OF KINGS AND LORD

KING'S (KING)
Pr 21: 1 The *k* heart is in the hand
Ecc 8: 3 in a hurry to leave the *k* presence.

KINGDOM (KING)
Ex 19: 6 you will be for me a *k* of priests
Dt 17:18 When he takes the throne of his *k,*
2Sa 7:12 body, and I will establish his *k.*
1Ki 11:31 to tear the *k* out of Solomon's hand
1Ch 17:11 own sons, and I will establish his *k.*
29:11 Yours, O LORD, is the *k;*
Ps 45: 6 justice will be the scepter of your *k.*
103: 19 and his *k* rules over all.
145: 11 They will tell of the glory of your *k*
Eze 29:14 There they will be a lowly *k.*
Da 2:39 "After you, another *k* will rise,
4: 3 His *k* is an eternal *k;*
7:27 His *k* will be an everlasting *k,*
Ob :21 And the *k* will be the LORD's.
Mt 3: 2 Repent, for the *k* of heaven is near
4:17 Repent, for the *k* of heaven is near
4:23 preaching the good news of the *k,*
5: 3 for theirs is the *k* of heaven.
5:10 for theirs is the *k* of heaven.
5:19 great in the *k* of heaven.
5:19 least in the *k* of heaven,
5:20 you will certainly not enter the *k*
6:10 your *k* come,
6:33 But seek first his *k* and his
7:21 Lord,' will enter the *k* of heaven,
8:11 Isaac and Jacob in the *k* of heaven.
8:12 the subjects of the *k* will be thrown
9:35 preaching the good news of the *k*
10: 7 preach this message: 'The *k*
11:11 least in the *k* of heaven is greater
11:12 the *k* of heaven has been forcefully
12:25 "Every *k* divided against itself will
12:26 How then can his *k* stand?
12:28 then the *k* of God has come
13:11 knowledge of the secrets of the *k*
13:19 hears the message about the *k*
13:24 "The *k* of heaven is like a man who
13:31 *k* of heaven is like a mustard seed,
13:33 "The *k* of heaven is like yeast that
Mt 13:38 stands for the sons of the *k.*
13:41 of his *k* everything that causes sin
13:43 the sun in the *k* of their Father.
13:44 *k* of heaven is like treasure hidden
13:45 the *k* of heaven is like a merchant
13:47 *k* of heaven is like a net that was let
13:52 has been instructed about the *k*
16:19 the keys of the *k* of heaven;
16:28 the Son of Man coming in his *k.*"
18: 1 the greatest in the *k* of heaven?"
18: 3 you will never enter the *k*
18: 4 the greatest in the *k* of heaven.
18:23 the *k* of heaven is like a king who
19:12 because of the *k* of heaven.
19:14 for the *k* of heaven belongs to such
19:23 man to enter the *k* of heaven.
19:24 for a rich man to enter the *k* of God
20: 1 "For the *k* of heaven is like
20:21 the other at your left in your *k.*"
21:31 the prostitutes are entering the *k*
21:43 "Therefore I tell you that the *k*
22: 2 "The *k* of heaven is like a king who
23:13 You shut the *k* of heaven
24: 7 rise against nation, and *k* against *k.*
24:14 gospel of the *k* will be preached
25: 1 "At that time the *k*
25:34 the *k* prepared for you
26:29 anew with you in my Father's *k.*"
Mk 1:15 "The *k* of God is near.
3:24 If a *k* is divided against itself,
3:24 against itself, that *k* cannot stand.
4:11 "The secret of the *k*
4:26 "This is what the *k* of God is like.
4:30 "What shall we say the *k*
6:23 I will give you, up to half my *k.*"
9: 1 before they see the *k* of God come
9:47 better for you to enter the *k* of God
10:14 for the *k* of God belongs to such
10:15 anyone who will not receive the *k*
10:23 for the rich to enter the *k* of God!"
10:24 how hard it is to enter the *k* of God
10:25 for a rich man to enter the *k* of God
11:10 "Blessed is the coming *k*
12:34 "You are not far from the *k* of God
13: 8 rise against nation, and *k* against *k.*
14:25 day when I drink it anew in the *k*
15:43 who was himself waiting for the *k*
Lk 1:33 Jacob forever; his *k* will never
4:43 of the *k* of God to the other towns
6:20 for yours is the *k* of God.
7:28 in the *k* of God is greater than he."
8: 1 proclaiming the good news of the *k*
8:10 knowledge of the secrets of the *k*
9: 2 out to preach the *k* of God
9:11 spoke to them about the *k* of God,
9:27 before they see the *k* of God."
9:60 you go and proclaim the *k* of God
9:62 fit for service in the *k* of God."
10: 9 'The *k* of God is near you.'
10:11 sure of this: The *k* of God is near.'
11: 2 your *k* come.
11:17 "Any *k* divided against itself will
11:18 himself, how can his *k* stand?
11:20 then the *k* of God has come to you.
12:31 seek his *k,* and these things will be
12:32 has been pleased to give you the *k.*
13:18 "What is the *k* of God like?
13:20 What shall I compare the *k* of God
13:28 all the prophets in the *k* of God,
13:29 places at the feast in the *k* of God.
14:15 eat at the feast in the *k* of God."
16:16 the good news of the *k*
17:20 when the *k* of God would come,
17:20 *k* of God does not come with careful
17:21 because the *k* of God is within you
18:16 for the *k* of God belongs to such
18:17 anyone who will not receive the *k*
18:24 for the rich to enter the *k* of God!
18:25 for a rich man to enter the *k* of God
18:29 for the sake of the *k* of God will fail
19:11 and the people thought that the *k*
21:10 rise against nation, and *k* against *k.*
21:31 you know that the *k* of God is near.
22:16 until it finds fulfillment in the *k*
22:18 the vine until the *k* of God comes."
22:29 And I confer on you a *k,* just
22:30 and drink at my table in my *k*
23:42 me when you come into your *k.*"
23:51 he was waiting for the *k* of God.
Jn 3: 3 no one can see the *k* of God.
3: 5 no one can enter the *k* of God.
18:36 now my *k* is from another place."
18:36 "My *k* is not of this world.
Ac 1: 3 and spoke about the *k* of God.
1: 6 going to restore the *k* to Israel?"
8:12 he preached the good news of the *k*
14:22 hardships to enter the *k* of God,"
19: 8 arguing persuasively about the *k*
20:25 about preaching the *k* will ever see

Ac 28:23 and declared to them the *k* of God
28:31 hindrance he preached the *k*
Ro 14:17 For the *k* of God is not a matter
1Co 4:20 For the *k* of God is not a matter
6: 9 the wicked will not inherit the *k*
6:10 swindlers will inherit the *k* of God.
15:24 hands over the *k* to God the Father
15:50 blood cannot inherit the *k* of God,
Gal 5:21 live like this will not inherit the *k*
Eph 2: 2 and of the ruler of the *k* of the air,
5: 5 has any inheritance in the *k*
Col 1:12 of the saints in the *k* of light.
1:13 and brought us into the *k*
4:11 among my fellow workers for the *k*
1Th 2:12 who calls you into his *k* and glory.
2Th 1: 5 will be counted worthy of the *k*
2Ti 4: 1 in view of his appearing and his *k*,
4:18 bring me safely to his heavenly *k*.
Heb 1: 8 will be the scepter of your *k*.
12:28 we are receiving a *k* that cannot be
Jas 2: 5 to inherit the *k* he promised those
2Pe 1:11 into the eternal *k* of our Lord
Rev 1: 6 has made us to be a *k* and priests
1: 9 companion in the suffering and *k*
5:10 You have made them to be a *k*
11:15 of the world has become the *k*
11:15 "The *k* of the world has become
12:10 the power and the *k* of our God,
16:10 his *k* was plunged into darkness.
17:12 who have not yet received a *k*,

KINGDOMS (KING)
2Ki 19:15 God over all the *k* of the earth.
19:19 so that all *k* on earth may know
2Ch 20: 6 rule over all the *k* of the nations.
Ps 68:32 Sing to God, O *k* of the earth,
Isa 37:16 God over all the *k* of the earth.
37:20 so that all *k* on earth may know
Eze 29:15 It will be the lowliest of *k*
37:22 or be divided into two *k*.
Da 4:17 Most High is sovereign over the *k*
7:17 great beasts are four *k* that will rise
Zep 3: 8 to gather the *k*

KINGS (KING)
Ps 2: 2 The *k* of the earth take their stand
47: 9 for the *k* of the earth belong to God
68:29 *k* will bring you gifts.
72:11 All *k* will bow down to him
110: 5 he will crush *k* on the day
149: 8 to bind their *k* with fetters,
Pr 16:12 *K* detest wrongdoing,
Isa 24:21 and the *k* on the earth below.
52:15 and *k* will shut their mouths
60:11 their *k* led in triumphal procession.
Da 2:21 he sets up *k* and deposes them.
7:24 ten horns are ten *k* who will come
Lk 21:12 and you will be brought before *k*
1Co 4: 8 You have become *k*—
1Ti 2: 2 for *k* and all those in authority,
6:15 the King of *k* and Lord of lords,
Rev 1: 5 and the ruler of the *k* of the earth.
17:14 he is Lord of lords and King of *k*—
19:16 KING OF *K* AND LORD

KINSMAN-REDEEMER (REDEEM)
Ru 3: 9 over me, since you are a *k*."
4:14 day has not left you without a *k*.

KISS (KISSED KISSES)
Ps 2:12 *K* the Son, lest he be angry
Pr 24:26 is like a *k* on the lips.
SS 1: 2 *Beloved* Let him *k* me
8: 1 I would *k* you,
Lk 22:48 the Son of Man with a *k*?"
Ro 16:16 Greet one another with a holy *k*.
1Co 16:20 Greet one another with a holy *k*.
2Co 13:12 Greet one another with a holy *k*.
1Th 5:26 Greet all the brothers with a holy *k*
1Pe 5:14 Greet one another with a *k* of love.

KISSED (KISS)
Mk 14:45 Judas said, "Rabbi!" and *k* him.
Lk 7:38 *k* them and poured perfume

KISSES* (KISS)
Pr 27: 6 but an enemy multiplies *k*.
SS 1: 2 with the *k* of his mouth—

KNEE (KNEES)
Isa 45:23 Before me every *k* will bow;
Ro 14:11 'every *k* will bow before me;
Php 2:10 name of Jesus every *k* should bow,

KNEEL (KNELT)
Est 3: 2 But Mordecai would not *k* down
Ps 95: 6 let us *k* before the LORD our
Eph 3:14 For this reason I *k*

KNEES (KNEE)
1Ki 19:18 all whose *k* have not bowed
Isa 35: 3 steady the *k* that give way;
Da 6:10 times a day he got down on his *k*
Lk 5: 8 he fell at Jesus' *k* and said,
Heb 12:12 your feeble arms and weak *k*.

KNELT* (KNEEL)
1Ki 1:16 Bathsheba bowed low and *k*
2Ch 6:13 and then *k* down before the whole
7: 3 they *k* on the pavement
29:29 everyone present with him *k* down
Est 3: 2 officials at the king's gate *k* down
Mt 8: 2 and *k* before him and said,
9:18 a ruler came and *k* before him
15:25 The woman came and *k* before him
17:14 a man approached Jesus and *k*
27:29 *k* in front of him and mocked him.
Lk 22:41 *k* down and prayed, "Father,
Ac 20:36 he *k* down with all of them
21: 5 there on the beach we *k* to pray.

KNEW (KNOW)
2Ch 33:13 Manasseh *k* that the LORD is God
Job 23: 3 If only I *k* where to find him;
Pr 24:12 "But we *k* nothing about this,"
Jer 1: 5 you in the womb I *k* you,
Jnh 4: 2 I *k* that you are a gracious
Mt 7:23 tell them plainly, 'I never *k* you.
12:25 Jesus *k* their thoughts
Jn 2:24 himself to them, for he *k* all men.
14: 7 If you really *k* me, you would know

KNIFE
Ge 22:10 and took the *k* to slay his son.
Pr 23: 2 and put a *k* to your throat

KNOCK* (KNOCKS)
Mt 7: 7 *k* and the door will be opened
Lk 11: 9 *k* and the door will be opened
Rev 3:20 I am! I stand at the door and *k*.

KNOCKS (KNOCK)
Mt 7: 8 and to him who *k*, the door will be

KNOW (FOREKNEW FOREKNOWLEDGE KNEW KNOWING KNOWLEDGE KNOWN KNOWS)
Ge 22:12 Now I *k* that you fear God,
Ex 6: 7 you will *k* that I am the LORD
14: 4 and the Egyptians will *k* that I am
33:13 teach me your ways so I may *k* you
Dt 7: 9 *K* therefore that the LORD your
18:21 "How can we *k* when a message
Jos 4:24 of the earth might *k* that the hand
23:14 You *k* with all your heart
1Sa 17:46 the whole world will *k* that there is
1Ki 8:39 heart (for you alone *k* the hearts
Job 11: 6 *K* this: God has even forgotten
19:25 I *k* that my Redeemer lives,
42: 3 things too wonderful for me to *k*.
Ps 9:10 Those who *k* your name will trust
46:10 "Be still, and *k* that I am God;
100: 3 *K* that the LORD is God.
139: 1 and you *k* me.
139: 23 Search me, O God, and *k* my heart;
145: 12 so that all men may *k*
Pr 27: 1 for you do not *k* what a day may
30: 4 Tell me if you *k*!
Ecc 8: 5 wise heart will *k* the proper time
Isa 29:15 "Who sees us? Who will *k*?"
40:21 Do you not *k*?
Jer 6:15 they do not even *k* how to blush.
22:16 Is that not what it means to *k* me?"
24: 7 I will give them a heart to *k* me,
31:34 his brother, saying, '*K* the LORD,'
33: 3 unsearchable things you do not *k*.'
Eze 2: 5 they will *k* that a prophet has been
6:10 they will *k* that I am the LORD;
Da 11:32 people who *k* their God will firmly
Mt 6: 3 let your left hand *k* what your right
7:11 *k* how to give good gifts
9: 6 But so that you may *k* that the Son
22:29 you do not *k* the Scriptures
24:42 you do not *k* on what day your
26:74 "I don't *k* the man!" Immediately
Mk 12:24 you do not *k* the Scriptures
Lk 1: 4 so that you may *k* the certainty
11:13 *k* how to give good gifts
12:48 But the one who does not *k*
13:25 'I don't *k* you or where you come
21:31 you *k* that the kingdom of God is
23:34 for they do not *k* what they are
Jn 1:26 among you stands one you do not *k*
3:11 we speak of what we *k*,
4:22 we worship what we do *k*,
4:42 and we *k* that this man really is
6:69 and *k* that you are the Holy One
7:28 You do not *k* him, but I *k* him
Jn 8:14 for I *k* where I came from
8:19 "You do not *k* me or my Father,"
8:32 Then you will *k* the truth,
8:55 Though you do not *k* him, I *k* him.
9:25 One thing I do *k*.
10: 4 him because they *k* his voice.
10:14 I *k* my sheep and my sheep *k* me—
10:27 I *k* them, and they follow me.
12:35 the dark does not *k* where he is
13:17 Now that you *k* these things,
13:35 all men will *k* that you are my
14:17 you *k* him, for he lives with you
15:21 for they do not *k* the One who sent
16:30 we can see that you *k* all things
17: 3 that they may *k* you, the only true
17:23 to let the world *k* that you sent me
21:15 he said, "you *k* that I love you."
21:24 We *k* that his testimony is true.
Ac 1: 7 "It is not for you to *k* the times
1:24 "Lord, you *k* everyone's heart.
Ro 3:17 and the way of peace they do not *k*
6: 3 Or don't you *k* that all
6: 6 For we *k* that our old self was
6:16 Don't you *k* that when you offer
7:14 We *k* that the law is spiritual;
7:18 I *k* that nothing good lives in me,
8:22 We *k* that the whole creation has
8:26 We do not *k* what we ought to pray
8:28 we *k* that in all things God works
1Co 1:21 through its wisdom did not *k* him,
2: 2 For I resolved to *k* nothing
3:16 Don't you *k* that you yourselves
5: 6 Don't you *k* that a little yeast
6: 2 Do you not *k* that the saints will
6:15 Do you not *k* that your bodies are
6:16 Do you not *k* that he who unites
6:19 Do you not *k* that your body is
7:16 How do you *k*, wife, whether you
8: 2 does not yet *k* as he ought to *k*.
9:13 Don't you *k* that those who work
9:24 Do you not *k* that
13: 9 For we *k* in part and we prophesy
13:12 Now I *k* in part; then I shall *k* fully,
15:58 because you *k* that your labor
2Co 5: 1 we *k* that if the earthly tent we live
5:11 we *k* what it is to fear the Lord,
8: 9 For you *k* the grace
Gal 1:11 you to *k*, brothers, that the gospel I
2:16 not 'Gentile sinners' *k* that a man
Eph 1:17 so that you may *k* him better.
1:18 in order that you may *k* the hope
6: 8 you *k* that the Lord will reward
6: 9 since you *k* that he who is both
Php 3:10 I want to *k* Christ and the power
4:12 I *k* what it is to be in need,
Col 2: 2 order that they may *k* the mystery
4: 1 because you *k* that you
4: 6 so that you may *k* how
1Th 3: 3 You *k* quite well that we were
5: 2 for you *k* very well that the day
2Th 1: 8 punish those who do not *k* God
1Ti 1: 7 they do not *k* what they are talking
3: 5 (If anyone does not *k* how
3:15 you will *k* how people ought
2Ti 1:12 because I *k* whom I have believed,
2:23 you *k* they produce quarrels.
3:14 you *k* those from whom you
Heb 8:11 because they will all *k* me,
11: 8 he did not *k* where he was going.
Jas 1: 3 because you *k* that the testing
3: 1 you *k* that we who teach will be
4: 4 don't you *k* that friendship
4:14 *k* what will happen tomorrow.
1Pe 1:18 For you *k* that it was not
2Pe 1:12 even though you *k* them
1Jn 2: 3 We *k* that we have come
2: 4 The man who says, "I *k* him,"
2: 5 This is how we *k* we are in him:
2:11 he does not *k* where he is going,
2:20 and all of you *k* the truth.
2:29 you *k* that everyone who does
3: 1 not *k* us is that it did not *k* him.
3: 2 But we *k* that when he appears,
3:10 This is how we *k* who the children
3:14 We *k* that we have passed
3:16 This is how we *k* what love is:
3:19 then is how we *k* that we belong
3:24 We *k* it by the Spirit he gave us.
4: 8 does not love does not *k* God,
4:13 We *k* that we live in him
4:16 so we *k* and rely on the love God
5: 2 This is how we *k* that we love
5:13 so that you may *k* that you have
5:15 And if we *k* that he hears us—
5:18 We *k* that anyone born
5:20 We *k* also that the Son
Rev 2: 2 I *k* your deeds, your hard work
2: 9 I *k* your afflictions and your
2:19 I *k* your deeds, your love and faith,

Rev 3: 3 you will not *k* at what time I will
3:15 I *k* your deeds, that you are neither

KNOWING (KNOW)

Ge 3: 5 and you will be like God, *k* good
3:22 now become like one of us, *k* good
Jn 19:28 *k* that all was now completed,
Php 3: 8 of *k* Christ Jesus my Lord,
Phm :21 *k* that you will do even more
Heb 13: 2 entertained angels without *k* it.

KNOWLEDGE (KNOW)

Ge 2: 9 the tree of the *k* of good and evil.
2:17 eat from the tree of the *k* of good
2Ch 1:10 and *k*, that I may lead this people,
Job 21:22 "Can anyone teach *k* to God,
38: 2 counsel with words without *k*?
42: 3 obscures my counsel without *k*?'
Ps 19: 2 night after night they display *k*.
73:11 Does the Most High have *k*?"
94:10 Does he who teaches man lack *k*?
119: 66 Teach me *k* and good judgment,
139: 6 Such *k* is too wonderful for me,
Pr 1: 4 *k* and discretion to the young—
1: 7 of the LORD is the beginning of *k*,
2: 5 and find the *k* of God.
2: 6 from his mouth come *k*
2:10 and *k* will be pleasant to your soul.
3:20 by his *k* the deeps were divided,
8:10 *k* rather than choice gold,
8:12 I possess *k* and discretion.
9:10 *k* of the Holy One is understanding
10:14 Wise men store up *k*,
12: 1 Whoever loves discipline loves *k*,
12:23 A prudent man keeps his *k*
13:16 Every prudent man acts out of *k*,
14: 6 *k* comes easily to the discerning.
15: 7 The lips of the wise spread *k*;
15:14 The discerning heart seeks *k*,
17:27 A man of *k* uses words
18:15 heart of the discerning acquires *k*;
19: 2 to have zeal without *k*,
19:25 discerning man, and he will gain *k*.
20:15 lips that speak *k* are a rare jewel.
23:12 and your ears to words of *k*.
24: 4 through *k* its rooms are filled
Ecc 7:12 but the advantage of *k* is this:
Isa 11: 2 the Spirit of *k* and of the fear
11: 9 full of the *k* of the LORD
40:14 Who was it that taught him *k*
Jer 3:15 who will lead you with *k*
Hos 4: 6 are destroyed from lack of *k*.
Hab 2:14 filled with the *k* of the glory
Mal 2: 7 lips of a priest ought to preserve *k*,
Mt 13:11 The *k* of the secrets of the kingdom
Lk 8:10 The *k* of the secrets of the kingdom
11:52 you have taken away the key to *k*.
Ac 18:24 with a thorough *k* of the Scriptures
Ro 1:28 worthwhile to retain the *k* of God,
10: 2 but their zeal is not based on *k*.
11:33 riches of the wisdom and *k* of God!
1Co 8: 1 *K* puffs up, but love builds up.
8:11 Christ died, is destroyed by your *k*.
12: 8 to another the message of *k*
13: 2 can fathom all mysteries and all *k*,
13: 8 where there is *k*, it will pass away.
2Co 2:14 everywhere the fragrance of the *k*
4: 6 light of the *k* of the glory of God
8: 7 in *k*, in complete earnestness
11: 6 a trained speaker, but I do have *k*.
Eph 3:19 to know this love that surpasses *k*
4:13 and in the *k* of the Son of God
Php 1: 9 and more in *k* and depth of insight,
Col 1: 9 God to fill you with the *k* of his will
1:10 every good work, growing in the *k*
2: 3 all the treasures of wisdom and *k*.
3:10 which is being renewed in *k*
1Ti 2: 4 and to come to a *k* of the truth.
6:20 ideas of what is falsely called *k*,
Tit 1: 1 and the *k* of the truth that leads
Heb 10:26 after we have received the *k*
2Pe 1: 5 and to goodness, *k*; and to *k*,
3:18 grow in the grace and *k* of our Lord

KNOWN (KNOW)

Ex 6: 3 the LORD I did not make myself *k*
Ps 16:11 You have made *k* to me the path
89: 1 I will make your faithfulness *k*
98: 2 LORD has made his salvation *k*
105: 1 make *k* among the nations what he
119:168 for all my ways are *k* to you.
Pr 20:11 Even a child is *k* by his actions,
Isa 12: 4 make *k* among the nations what he
46:10 *k* the end from the beginning,
61: 9 Their descendants will be *k*
Eze 38:23 I will make myself *k* in the sight
39: 7 " 'I will make *k* my holy name
Mt 10:26 or hidden that will not be made *k*.
24:43 of the house had *k* at what time
Lk 19:42 had only *k* on this day what would
Jn 15:15 from my Father I have made *k*
16:14 from what is mine and making it *k*
17:26 I have made you *k* to them,
Ac 2:28 You have made *k* to me the paths
Ro 1:19 since what may be *k* about God is
3:21 apart from law, has been made *k*,
9:22 his wrath and make his power *k*,
11:34 "Who has *k* the mind of the Lord?
15:20 the gospel where Christ was not *k*,
16:26 and made *k* through the prophetic
1Co 2:16 "For who has *k* the mind
8: 3 But the man who loves God is *k*
13:12 know fully, even as I am fully *k*.
2Co 3: 2 written on our hearts, *k*
Gal 4: 9 or rather are *k* by God—
Eph 3: 5 which was not made *k* to men
6:19 will fearlessly make *k* the mystery
2Ti 3:15 infancy you have *k* the holy
2Pe 2:21 than to have *k* it and then

KNOWS (KNOW)

1Sa 2: 3 for the LORD is a God who *k*,
Est 4:14 And who *k* but that you have come
Job 23:10 But he *k* the way that I take;
Ps 44:21 since he *k* the secrets of the heart?
94:11 The LORD *k* the thoughts of man;
103: 14 for he *k* how we are formed,
Ecc 8: 7 Since no man *k* the future,
8:17 Even if a wise man claims he *k*,
9:12 no man *k* when his hour will come:
Isa 29:16 "He *k* nothing"?
Jer 9:24 that he understands and *k* me,
Mt 6: 8 for your Father *k* what you need
11:27 No one *k* the Son
24:36 "No one *k* about that day or hour,
Lk 12:47 "That servant who *k* his master's
16:15 of men, but God *k* your hearts.
Ac 15: 8 who *k* the heart, showed that he
Ro 8:27 who searches our hearts *k* the mind
1Co 2:11 who among men *k* the thoughts
8: 2 who thinks he *k* something does
2Ti 2:19 The Lord *k* those who are his," and
Jas 4:17 who *k* the good he ought to do
1Jn 4: 6 and whoever *k* God listens to us;
4: 7 born of God and *k* God.

KOHATHITE (KOHATHITES)

Nu 3:29 The *K* clans were to camp

KOHATHITES (KOHATHITE)

Nu 3:28 The *K* were responsible
4:15 *K* are to carry those things that are

KORAH

Levite who led rebellion against Moses and Aaron (Nu 16; Jude 11).

KORAZIN

Mt 11:21 "Woe to you, *K*! Woe to you,

LABAN

Brother of Rebekah (Ge 24:29), father of Rachel and Leah (Ge 29:16). Received Abraham's servant (Ge 24:29-51). Provided daughters as wives for Jacob in exchange for Jacob's service (Ge 29:1-30). Provided flocks for Jacob's service (Ge 30:25-43). After Jacob's departure, pursued and covenanted with him (Ge 31).

LABOR (LABORING)

Ex 1:11 to oppress them with forced *l*,
20: 9 Six days you shall *l* and do all your
Dt 5:13 Six days you shall *l* and do all your
Ps 127: 1 its builders *l* in vain.
128: 2 You will eat the fruit of your *l*;
Pr 12:24 but laziness ends in slave *l*.
Isa 54: 1 you who were never in *l*;
55: 2 and your *l* on what does not satisfy
Mt 6:28 They do not *l* or spin.
Jn 4:38 have reaped the benefits of their *l*."
1Co 3: 8 rewarded according to his own *l*.
15:58 because you know that your *l*
Gal 4:27 you who have no *l* pains;
Php 2:16 day of Christ that I did not run or *l*
Rev 14:13 "they will rest from their *l*,

LABORING* (LABOR)

2Th 3: 8 *l* and toiling so that we would not

LACK (LACKED LACKING LACKS)

Ps 34: 9 for those who fear him *l* nothing.
Pr 5:23 He will die for *l* of discipline,
10:21 but fools die for *l* of judgment.
11:14 For *l* of guidance a nation falls,
15:22 Plans fail for *l* of counsel,
28:27 to the poor will *l* nothing,
Mk 6: 6 he was amazed at their *l* of faith.
16:14 he rebuked them for their *l* of faith
Ro 3: 3 Will their *l* of faith nullify God's
1Co 1: 7 you do not *l* any spiritual gift
7: 5 because of your *l* of self-control.
Col 2:23 *l* any value in restraining sensual

LACKED (LACK)

Dt 2: 7 and you have not *l* anything.
Ne 9:21 them in the desert; they *l* nothing,
1Co 12:24 honor to the parts that *l* it,

LACKING (LACK)

Pr 17:18 A man *l* in judgment strikes hands
Ro 12:11 Never be *l* in zeal, but keep your
Jas 1: 4 and complete, not *l* anything.

LACKS (LACK)

Pr 6:32 who commits adultery *l* judgment;
11:12 man who *l* judgment derides his
12:11 he who chases fantasies *l* judgment
15:21 delights a man who *l* judgment,
24:30 of the man who *l* judgment;
25:28 is a man who *l* self-control.
28:16 A tyrannical ruler *l* judgment,
31:11 and *l* nothing of value.
Eze 34: 8 because my flock *l* a shepherd
Jas 1: 5 any of you *l* wisdom, he should ask

LAID (LAY)

Isa 53: 6 and the LORD has *l* on him
Mk 6:29 took his body and *l* it in a tomb.
Lk 6:48 and *l* the foundation on rock.
Ac 6: 6 and *l* their hands on them.
1Co 3:11 other than the one already *l*,
1Ti 4:14 body of elders *l* their hands on you.
1Jn 3:16 Jesus Christ *l* down his life for us.

LAKE

Mt 8:24 a furious storm came up on the *l*,
14:25 out to them, walking on the *l*.
Mk 4: 1 into a boat and sat in it out on the *l*,
Lk 8:33 down the steep bank into the *l*
Jn 6:25 him on the other side of the *l*,
Rev 19:20 into the fiery *l* of burning sulfur.
20:14 The *l* of fire is the second death.

LAMB (LAMB'S LAMBS)

Ge 22: 8 "God himself will provide the *l*
Ex 12:21 and slaughter the Passover *l*.
Nu 9:11 are to eat the *l*, together
2Sa 12: 4 he took the ewe *l* that belonged
Isa 11: 6 The wolf will live with the *l*,
53: 7 he was led like a *l* to the slaughter,
Mk 14:12 to sacrifice the Passover *l*,
Jn 1:29 *L* of God, who takes away the sin
Ac 8:32 as a *l* before the shearer is silent,
1Co 5: 7 our Passover *l*, has been sacrificed.
1Pe 1:19 a *l* without blemish or defect.
Rev 5: 6 Then I saw a *L*, looking
5:12 "Worthy is the *L*, who was slain,
7:14 white in the blood of the *L*.
14: 4 They follow the *L* wherever he
15: 3 of God and the song of the *L*:
17:14 but the *L* will overcome them
19: 9 to the wedding supper of the *L*!'"
21:23 gives it light, and the *L* is its lamp.

LAMB'S (LAMB)

Rev 21:27 written in the *L* book of life.

LAMBS (LAMB)

Lk 10: 3 I am sending you out like *l*
Jn 21:15 Jesus said, "Feed my *l*."

LAME

Isa 33:23 even the *l* will carry off plunder.
35: 6 Then will the *l* leap like a deer,
Mt 11: 5 The blind receive sight, the *l* walk,
15:31 the *l* walking and the blind seeing.
Lk 14:21 the crippled, the blind and the *l*.'

LAMENT

2Sa 1:17 took up this *l* concerning Saul
Eze 19: 1 Take up a *l* concerning the princes

LAMP (LAMPS LAMPSTAND LAMPSTANDS)

2Sa 22:29 You are my *l*, O LORD;
Ps 18:28 You, O LORD, keep my *l* burning;
119:105 Your word is a *l* to my feet
132: 17 and set up a *l* for my anointed one.
Pr 6:23 For these commands are a *l*,
20:27 *l* of the LORD searches the spirit
31:18 and her *l* does not go out at night.
Mt 6:22 "The eye is the *l* of the body.
Lk 8:16 "No one lights a *l* and hides it
Rev 21:23 gives it light, and the Lamb is its *l*.
22: 5 They will not need the light of a *l*

LAMPS (LAMP)

Mt 25: 1 be like ten virgins who took their *l*
Lk 12:35 for service and keep your *l* burning,

Rev 4: 5 the throne, seven *l* were blazing.

LAMPSTAND (LAMP)
Ex 25:31 "Make a *l* of pure gold
Zec 4: 2 "I see a solid gold *l* with a bowl
4:11 on the right and the left of the *l*?"
Heb 9: 2 In its first room were the *l*,
Rev 2: 5 and remove your *l* from its place.

LAMPSTANDS (LAMP)
2Ch 4: 7 He made ten gold *l* according
Rev 1:12 when I turned I saw seven golden *l*,
1:20 and of the seven golden *l* is this:

LAND (LANDS)
Ge 1:10 God called the dry ground "*l*,"
1:11 "Let the *l* produce vegetation:
1:24 "Let the *l* produce living creatures
12: 1 and go to the *l* I will show you.
12: 7 To your offspring I will give this *l*."
13:15 All the *l* that you see I will give
15:18 "To your descendants I give this *l*,
50:24 out of this *l* to the *l* he promised
Ex 3: 8 a *l* flowing with milk and honey—
6: 8 to the *l* I swore with uplifted hand
33: 3 Go up to the *l* flowing with milk
Lev 25:23 *l* must not be sold permanently,
Nu 14: 8 us into that *l*, a *l* flowing with milk
35:33 Do not pollute the *l* where you are.
Dt 1: 8 See, I have given you this *l*.
8: 7 God is bringing you into a good *l*—
11:10 The *l* you are entering to take
28:21 you from the *l* you are entering
29:19 will bring disaster on the watered *l*
34: 1 LORD showed him the whole *l*—
Jos 13: 2 "This is the *l* that remains:
14: 4 Levites received no share of the *l*
14: 9 *l* on which your feet have walked
2Sa 21:14 answered prayer in behalf of the *l*.
2Ki 17: 5 of Assyria invaded the entire *l*,
24: 1 king of Babylon invaded the *l*,
25:21 into captivity, away from her *l*.
2Ch 7:14 their sin and will heal their *l*.
7:20 then I will uproot Israel from my *l*,
36:21 The *l* enjoyed its sabbath rests;
Ezr 9:11 entering to possess is a *l* polluted
Ne 9:36 in the *l* you gave our forefathers
Ps 37:11 But the meek will inherit the *l*
37:29 the righteous will inherit the *l*
136: 21 and gave their *l* as an inheritance,
142: 5 my portion in the *l* of the living."
Pr 2:21 For the upright will live in the *l*,
12:11 who works his *l* will have abundant
Isa 6:13 though a tenth remains in the *l*,
53: 8 cut off from the *l* of the living;
Jer 2: 7 But you came and defiled my *l*
Eze 36:24 and bring you back into your own *l*.

LANDS (LAND)
Ps 111: 6 giving them the *l* of other nations.
Eze 20: 6 honey, the most beautiful of all *l*.
Zec 10: 9 in distant *l* they will remember me.

LANGUAGE (LANGUAGES)
Ge 11: 1 Now the whole world had one *l*
11: 9 there the LORD confused the *l*
Ps 19: 3 There is no speech or *l*
Jn 8:44 When he lies, he speaks his native *l*
Ac 2: 6 heard them speaking in his own *l*.
Col 3: 8 slander, and filthy *l* from your lips.
Rev 5: 9 from every tribe and *l* and people
7: 9 every nation, tribe, people and *l*,
14: 6 to every nation, tribe, *l* and people.

LANGUAGES (LANGUAGE)
Zec 8:23 "In those days ten men from all *l*

LAODICEA
Rev 3:14 the angel of the church in *L* write:

LAP
Jdg 7: 5 "Separate those who *l* the water

LASHES
Pr 17:10 more than a hundred *l* a fool.
2Co 11:24 from the Jews the forty *l* minus one

LAST (LASTING LASTS LATTER)
Ex 14:24 During the *l* watch of the night
2Sa 23: 1 These are the *l* words of David:
Isa 2: 2 and Jerusalem: In the *l* days
41: 4 and with the *l*— I am he."
44: 6 I am the first and I am the *l*;
48:12 I am the first and I am the *l*.
Hos 3: 5 and to his blessings in the *l* days.
Mic 4: 1 In the *l* days
Mt 19:30 But many who are first will be *l*,
20: 8 beginning with the *l* ones hired
21:37 *L* of all, he sent his son to them.
Mk 9:35 must be the very *l*, and the servant
Mk 10:31 are first will be *l*, and the *l* first."
15:37 a loud cry, Jesus breathed his *l*.
Jn 6:40 and I will raise him up at the *l* day."
15:16 and bear fruit—fruit that will *l*.
Ac 2:17 " 'In the *l* days, God says,
Ro 1:17 is by faith from first to *l*,
1Co 15:26 *l* enemy to be destroyed is death.
15:52 of an eye, at the *l* trumpet.
2Ti 3: 1 will be terrible times in the *l* days.
2Pe 3: 3 in the *l* days scoffers will come,
Jude :18 "In the *l* times there will be
Rev 1:17 I am the First and the *L*.
22:13 the First and the *L*, the Beginning

LASTING (LAST)
Ex 12:14 to the LORD—a *l* ordinance.
Lev 24: 8 of the Israelites, as a *l* covenant.
Nu 25:13 have a covenant of a *l* priesthood,
Heb 10:34 had better and *l* possessions.

LASTS (LAST)
Ps 30: 5 For his anger *l* only a moment,
2Co 3:11 greater is the glory of that which *l*!

LATTER (LAST)
Job 42:12 The LORD blessed the *l* part
Mt 23:23 You should have practiced the *l*,
Php 1:16 *l* do so in love, knowing that I am

LAUGH (LAUGHED LAUGHS LAUGHTER)
Ps 59: 8 But you, O LORD, *l* at them;
Pr 31:25 she can *l* at the days to come.
Ecc 3: 4 a time to weep and a time to *l*,
Lk 6:21 for you will *l*.
6:25 Woe to you who *l* now,

LAUGHED (LAUGH)
Ge 17:17 Abraham fell facedown; he *l*
18:12 So Sarah *l* to herself as she thought,

LAUGHS (LAUGH)
Ps 2: 4 The One enthroned in heaven *l*;
37:13 but the Lord *l* at the wicked,

LAUGHTER (LAUGH)
Ge 21: 6 Sarah said, "God has brought me *l*,
Ps 126: 2 Our mouths were filled with *l*,
Pr 14:13 Even in *l* the heart may ache,
Jas 4: 9 Change your *l* to mourning

LAVISHED
Eph 1: 8 of God's grace that he *l* on us
1Jn 3: 1 great is the love the Father has *l*

LAW (LAWFUL LAWGIVER LAWS)
Lev 24:22 are to have the same *l* for the alien
Nu 6:13 " 'Now this is the *l* for the Nazirite
Dt 1: 5 Moses began to expound this *l*,
6:25 to obey all this *l* before the LORD
27:26 of this *l* by carrying them out."
31:11 you shall read this *l* before them
31:26 "Take this Book of the *L*
Jos 1: 7 to obey all the *l* my servant Moses
1: 8 of the *L* depart from your mouth;
22: 5 and the *l* that Moses the servant
2Ki 22: 8 of the *L* in the temple of the LORD
2Ch 6:16 walk before me according to my *l*,
17: 9 the Book of the *L* of the LORD;
34:14 of the *L* of the LORD that had
Ezr 7: 6 versed in the *L* of Moses,
Ne 8: 2 Ezra the priest brought the *L*
8: 8 from the Book of the *L* of God,
Ps 1: 2 and on his *l* he meditates day
19: 7 The *l* of the LORD is perfect,
37:31 The *l* of his God is in his heart;
40: 8 your *l* is within my heart."
119: 18 wonderful things in your *l*.
119: 70 but I delight in your *l*.
119: 72 *l* from your mouth is more precious
119: 77 for your *l* is my delight.
119: 97 Oh, how I love your *l*!
119:163 but I love your *l*.
119:165 peace have they who love your *l*,
Pr 28: 9 If anyone turns a deaf ear to the *l*,
29:18 but blessed is he who keeps the *l*.
Isa 2: 3 The *l* will go out from Zion,
8:20 To the *l* and to the testimony!
42:21 to make his *l* great and glorious.
Jer 2: 8 deal with the *l* did not know me;
8: 8 for we have the *l* of the LORD,"
31:33 "I will put my *l* in their minds
Mic 4: 2 The *l* will go out from Zion,
Hab 1: 7 they are a *l* to themselves
Zec 7:12 as flint and would not listen to the *l*
Mt 5:17 that I have come to abolish the *L*
7:12 sums up the *L* and the Prophets.
22:36 greatest commandment in the *L*?"
22:40 All the *L* and the Prophets hang
23:23 more important matters of the *l*—
Lk 11:52 "Woe to you experts in the *l*,
Lk 16:17 stroke of a pen to drop out of the *L*.
24:44 me in the *L* of Moses,
Jn 1:17 For the *l* was given through Moses;
Ac 13:39 justified from by the *l* of Moses.
Ro 2:12 All who sin apart from the *l* will
2:15 of the *l* are written on their hearts,
2:20 you have in the *l* the embodiment
2:25 value if you observe the *l*,
3:19 we know that whatever the *l* says,
3:20 in his sight by observing the *l*;
3:21 apart from *l*, has been made known
3:28 by faith apart from observing the *l*.
3:31 Not at all! Rather, we uphold the *l*.
4:13 It was not through *l* that Abraham
4:15 worthless, because *l* brings wrath.
4:16 not only to those who are of the *l*
5:13 for before the *l* was given,
5:20 *l* was added so that the trespass
6:14 because you are not under *l*,
6:15 we are not under *l* but under grace?
7: 1 that the *l* has authority
7: 4 also died to the *l* through the body
7: 5 aroused by the *l* were at work
7: 6 released from the *l* so that we serve
7: 7 then? Is the *l* sin? Certainly not!
7: 8 For apart from *l*, sin is dead.
7:12 *l* is holy, and the commandment is
7:14 We know that the *l* is spiritual;
7:22 my inner being I delight in God's *l*;
7:25 in my mind am a slave to God's *l*,
8: 2 because through Christ Jesus the *l*
8: 3 For what the *l* was powerless to do
8: 4 of the *l* might be fully met in us,
8: 7 It does not submit to God's *l*,
9: 4 covenants, the receiving of the *l*,
9:31 who pursued a *l* of righteousness,
10: 4 Christ is the end of the *l*
13: 8 his fellowman has fulfilled the *l*.
13:10 love is the fulfillment of the *l*.
1Co 6: 6 goes to *l* against another—
9: 9 For it is written in the *L* of Moses:
9:20 the *l* I became like one under the *l*
9:21 I became like one not having the *l*
15:56 and the power of sin is the *l*.
Gal 2:16 justified by observing the *l*,
2:19 For through the *l* I died to the *l*
3: 2 the Spirit by observing the *l*,
3: 5 you because you observe the *l*,
3:10 on observing the *l* are under a curse
3:11 justified before God by the *l*,
3:13 curse of the *l* by becoming a curse
3:17 The *l*, introduced 430 years later,
3:19 then, was the purpose of the *l*?
3:21 Is the *l*, therefore, opposed
3:23 we were held prisoners by the *l*,
3:24 So the *l* was put in charge to lead us
4:21 you who want to be under the *l*,
5: 3 obligated to obey the whole *l*.
5: 4 justified by *l* have been alienated
5:14 The entire *l* is summed up
5:18 by the Spirit, you are not under *l*.
6: 2 and in this way you will fulfill the *l*
Eph 2:15 flesh the *l* with its commandments
Php 3: 9 of my own that comes from the *l*,
1Ti 1: 8 We know that the *l* is good
Heb 7:12 there must also be a change of the *l*.
7:19 (for the *l* made nothing perfect),
10: 1 The *l* is only a shadow
Jas 1:25 intently into the perfect *l* that gives
2: 8 If you really keep the royal *l* found
2:10 For whoever keeps the whole *l*
4:11 or judges him speaks against the *l*
1Jn 3: 4 Everyone who sins breaks the *l*;

LAWFUL (LAW)
Mt 12:12 Therefore it is *l* to do good

LAWGIVER* (LAW)
Isa 33:22 the LORD is our *l*,
Jas 4:12 There is only one *L* and Judge,

LAWLESS (LAWLESSNESS)
2Th 2: 8 And then the *l* one will be revealed
Heb 10:17 "Their sins and *l* acts

LAWLESSNESS* (LAWLESS)
2Th 2: 3 and the man of *l* is revealed,
2: 7 power of *l* is already at work;
1Jn 3: 4 sins breaks the law; in fact, sin is *l*.

LAWS (LAW)
Ex 21: 1 "These are the *l* you are to set
Lev 25:18 and be careful to obey my *l*,
Dt 4: 1 and *l* I am about to teach you.
30:16 decrees and *l*; then you will live
Ps 119: 30 I have set my heart on your *l*.
119: 43 for I have put my hope in your *l*.
119:120 I stand in awe of your *l*.
119:164 for your righteous *l*.

Ps 119:175 and may your *l* sustain me.
Eze 36:27 and be careful to keep my *l.*
Heb 8:10 I will put my *l* in their minds
10:16 I will put my *l* in their hearts,

LAWSUITS
Hos 10: 4 therefore *l* spring up
1Co 6: 7 The very fact that you have *l*

LAY (LAID LAYING LAYS)
Ex 29:10 and his sons shall *l* their hands
Lev 1: 4 He is to *l* his hand on the head
4:15 the community are to *l* their hands
Nu 8:10 the Israelites are to *l* their hands
27:18 whom is the spirit, and *l* your hand
1Sa 26: 9 Who can *l* a hand on the LORD's
Job 1:12 on the man himself do not *l* a finger
22:22 and *l* up his words in your heart.
Ecc 10: 4 calmness can *l* great errors to rest.
Isa 28:16 "See, I *l* a stone in Zion,
Mt 8:20 of Man has no place to *l* his head."
28: 6 Come and see the place where he *l.*
Mk 6: 5 *l* his hands on a few sick people
Lk 9:58 of Man has no place to *l* his head."
Jn 10:15 and I *l* down my life for the sheep.
10:18 but I *l* it down of my own accord.
15:13 that he *l* down his life
Ac 8:19 on whom I *l* my hands may receive
Ro 9:33 I *l* in Zion a stone that causes men
1Co 3:11 no one can *l* any foundation other
1Pe 2: 6 "See, I *l* a stone in Zion,
1Jn 3:16 And we ought to *l* down our lives
Rev 4:10 They *l* their crowns

LAYING (LAY)
Lk 4:40 and *l* his hands on each one,
Ac 8:18 at the *l* on of the apostles' hands,
1Ti 5:22 Do not be hasty in the *l* on of hands
2Ti 1: 6 is in you through the *l*
Heb 6: 1 not *l* again the foundation
6: 2 instruction about baptisms, the *l*

LAYS (LAY)
Jn 10:11 The good shepherd *l* down his life

LAZARUS
1. Poor man in Jesus' parable (Lk 16:19-31).
2. Brother of Mary and Martha whom Jesus raised from the dead (Jn 11:1-12:19).

LAZINESS* (LAZY)
Pr 12:24 but *l* ends in slave labor.
19:15 *L* brings on deep sleep,

LAZY* (LAZINESS)
Ex 5: 8 They are *l;* that is why they are
5:17 Pharaoh said, "*L,* that's what you
5:17 "Lazy, that's what you are—*l!*
Pr 10: 4 *L* hands make a man poor,
12:27 The *l* man does not roast his game,
26:15 he is too *l* to bring it back
Ecc 10:18 If a man is *l,* the rafters sag;
Mt 25:26 replied, 'You wicked, *l* servant!
Tit 1:12 liars, evil brutes, *l* gluttons."
Heb 6:12 We do not want you to become *l,*

LEAD (LEADER LEADERS LEADERSHIP LEADS LED)
Ex 15:13 "In your unfailing love you will *l*
Nu 14: 8 with us, he will *l* us into that land,
Dt 31: 2 and I am no longer able to *l* you.
Jos 1: 6 because you will *l* these people
1Sa 8: 5 now appoint a king to *l* us,
2Ch 1:10 knowledge, that I may *l* this people
Ps 27:11 *l* me in a straight path
61: 2 *l* me to the rock that is higher
139: 24 and *l* me in the way everlasting.
143: 10 *l* me on level ground.
Pr 4:11 and *l* you along straight paths.
Ecc 5: 6 Do not let your mouth *l* you
Isa 11: 6 and a little child will *l* them.
49:10 and *l* them beside springs of water.
Da 12: 3 those who *l* many to righteousness,
Mt 6:13 And *l* us not into temptation,
Lk 11: 4 And *l* us not into temptation.' "
Gal 3:24 So the law was put in charge to *l* us
1Th 4:11 it your ambition to *l* a quiet life,
1Jn 3: 7 do not let anyone *l* you astray.
Rev 7:17 he will *l* them to springs

LEADER (LEAD)
1Sa 7: 6 Samuel was *l* of Israel at Mizpah.
10: 1 Has not the LORD anointed you *l*
12: 2 I have been your *l* from my youth
13:14 and appointed him *l* of his people,

LEADERS (LEAD)
Heb 13: 7 Remember your *l,* who spoke
13:17 Obey your *l* and submit

LEADERSHIP* (LEAD)
Nu 33: 1 by divisions under the *l* of Moses
Ps 109: 8 may another take his place of *l.*
Ac 1:20 " 'May another take his place of *l.*'
Ro 12: 8 if it is *l,* let him govern diligently;

LEADS (LEAD)
Dt 27:18 is the man who *l* the blind astray
Ps 23: 2 he *l* me beside quiet waters,
37: 8 do not fret—it *l* only to evil.
68: 6 he *l* forth the prisoners
Pr 2:18 For her house *l* down to death
10:17 ignores correction *l* others astray.
14:23 but mere talk *l* only to poverty.
16:25 but in the end it *l* to death.
19:23 The fear of the LORD *l* to life:
20: 7 righteous man *l* a blameless life;
21: 5 as surely as haste *l* to poverty.
Isa 40:11 he gently *l* those that have young.
Mt 7:13 and broad is the road that *l*
12:20 till he *l* justice to victory.
15:14 If a blind man *l* a blind man,
Jn 10: 3 sheep by name and *l* them out.
Ro 6:16 which *l* to death, or to obedience,
6:22 the benefit you reap *l* to holiness,
14:19 effort to do what *l* to peace
2Co 2:14 always *l* us in triumphal procession
7:10 sorrow brings repentance that *l*
Tit 1: 1 of the truth that *l* to godliness—

LEAH
Wife of Jacob (Ge 29:16-30); bore six sons and one daughter (Ge 29:31-30:21; 34:1; 35:23).

LEAN (LEANED)
Pr 3: 5 *l* not on your own understanding;

LEANED (LEAN)
Ge 47:31 as he *l* on the top of his staff.
Jn 21:20 (This was the one who had *l* back
Heb 11:21 as he *l* on the top of his staff.

LEAP (LEAPED LEAPS)
Isa 35: 6 Then will the lame *l* like a deer,
Mal 4: 2 *l* like calves released from the stall.
Lk 6:23 "Rejoice in that day and *l* for joy,

LEAPED (LEAP)
Lk 1:41 heard Mary's greeting, the baby *l*

LEAPS (LEAP)
Ps 28: 7 My heart *l* for joy

LEARN (LEARNED LEARNING LEARNS)
Dt 4:10 so that they may *l* to revere me
5: 1 *L* them and be sure to follow them.
31:12 and *l* to fear the LORD your God
Ps 119: 7 as I *l* your righteous laws.
Isa 1:17 *l* to do right!
26: 9 of the world *l* righteousness.
Mt 11:29 yoke upon you and *l* from me,
Jn 14:31 world must *l* that I love the Father
1Th 4: 4 that each of you should *l*
1Ti 2:11 A woman should *l* in quietness
5: 4 these should *l* first of all

LEARNED (LEARN)
Ps 119:152 Long ago I *l* from your statutes
Mt 11:25 things from the wise and *l,*
Php 4: 9 Whatever you have *l* or received
4:11 for I have *l* to be content whatever
2Ti 3:14 continue in what you have *l*
Heb 5: 8 he *l* obedience from what he

LEARNING (LEARN)
Pr 1: 5 let the wise listen and add to their *l,*
9: 9 man and he will add to his *l.*
Isa 44:25 who overthrows the *l* of the wise
Jn 7:15 "How did this man get such *l*
2Ti 3: 7 always *l* but never able

LEARNS (LEARN)
Jn 6:45 and *l* from him comes to me.

LEATHER
2Ki 1: 8 and with a *l* belt around his waist."
Mt 3: 4 and he had a *l* belt around his waist

LEAVES
Ge 3: 7 so they sewed fig *l* together
Eze 47:12 for food and their *l* for healing."
Rev 22: 2 the *l* of the tree are for the healing

LEBANON
Dt 11:24 from the desert to *L,*
1Ki 4:33 from the cedar of *L*

LED (LEAD)
Ex 3: 1 and he *l* the flock to the far side
Dt 8: 2 the LORD your God *l* you all
1Ki 11: 3 and his wives *l* him astray.
2Ch 26:16 his pride *l* to his downfall.
Ne 13:26 he was *l* into sin by foreign women.
Ps 68:18 you *l* captives in your train;
78:52 he *l* them like sheep
Pr 7:21 persuasive words she *l* him astray;
20: 1 whoever is *l* astray
Isa 53: 7 he was *l* like a lamb to the slaughter
Jer 11:19 I had been like a gentle lamb *l*
Am 2:10 and I *l* you forty years in the desert
Mt 4: 1 Then Jesus was *l* by the Spirit
27:31 they *l* him away to crucify him.
Lk 4: 1 was *l* by the Spirit in the desert,
Ac 8:32 "He was *l* like a sheep
Ro 8:14 those who are *l* by the Spirit
2Co 7: 9 your sorrow *l* you to repentance.
Gal 5:18 But if you are *l* by the Spirit,
Eph 4: 8 he *l* captives in his train

LEEKS*
Nu 11: 5 melons, *l,* onions and garlic.

LEFT
Dt 28:14 or to the *l,* following other gods
Jos 1: 7 turn from it to the right or to the *l,*
23: 6 aside to the right or to the *l.*
2Ki 22: 2 aside to the right or to the *l.*
Pr 4:27 Do not swerve to the right or the *l;*
Isa 30:21 turn to the right or to the *l,*
Mt 6: 3 do not let your *l* hand know what
25:33 on his right and the goats on his *l.*

LEGALISTIC*
Php 3: 6 as for *l* righteousness, faultless.

LEGION
Mk 5: 9 "My name is *L,*" he replied,

LEND (LENDER LENDS MONEYLENDER)
Lev 25:37 You must not *l* him money
Dt 15: 8 freely *l* him whatever he needs.
Ps 37:26 are always generous and *l* freely;
Eze 18: 8 He does not *l* at usury
Lk 6:34 if you *l* to those from whom you

LENDER (LEND)
Pr 22: 7 and the borrower is servant to the *l.*
Isa 24: 2 for borrower as for *l,*

LENDS (LEND)
Ps 15: 5 who *l* his money without usury
112: 5 to him who is generous and *l* freely,
Pr 19:17 to the poor *l* to the LORD,

LENGTH (LONG)
Ps 90:10 The *l* of our days is seventy years—
Pr 10:27 The fear of the LORD adds *l* to life

LENGTHY* (LONG)
Mk 12:40 and for a show make *l* prayers.
Lk 20:47 and for a show make *l* prayers.

LEOPARD
Isa 11: 6 the *l* will lie down with the goat,
Da 7: 6 beast, one that looked like a *l.*
Rev 13: 2 The beast I saw resembled a *l,*

LEPROSY (LEPROUS)
Nu 12:10 toward her and saw that she had *l;*
2Ki 5: 1 was a valiant soldier, but he had *l.*
7: 3 men with *l* at the entrance
2Ch 26:21 King Uzziah had *l*
Mt 11: 5 those who have *l* are cured,
Lk 17:12 ten men who had *l* met him.

LEPROUS (LEPROSY)
Ex 4: 6 and when he took it out, it was *l,*

LETTER (LETTERS)
Mt 5:18 not the smallest *l,* not the least
2Co 3: 2 You yourselves are our *l,* written
3: 6 for the *l* kills, but the Spirit gives
2Th 3:14 not obey our instruction in this *l,*

LETTERS (LETTER)
2Co 3: 7 which was engraved in *l* on stone,
10:10 "His *l* are weighty and forceful,
2Pe 3:16 His *l* contain some things that are

LEVEL
Ps 143: 10 lead me on *l* ground.
Pr 4:26 Make *l* paths for your feet
Isa 26: 7 The path of the righteous is *l;*
40: 4 the rough ground shall become *l,*
Jer 31: 9 on a *l* path where they will not
Heb 12:13 "Make *l* paths for your feet,"

LEVI (LEVITE LEVITES LEVITICAL)
1. Son of Jacob by Leah (Ge 29:34; 46:11; 1Ch 2:1). With Simeon avenged rape of Dinah (Ge 34). Tribe of blessed (Ge 49:5-7; Dt 33:8-11), chosen as priests (Nu 3-4), numbered (Nu 3:39; 26:62), allot-

ted cities, but not land (Nu 18; 35; Dt 10:9; Jos 13: 14; 21), land (Eze 48:8-22), 12,000 from (Rev 7:7).
2. See MATTHEW.

LEVIATHAN

Job 41: 1 pull in the *l* with a fishhook
Ps 74:14 you who crushed the heads of *L*
Isa 27: 1 *L* the gliding serpent,

LEVITE (LEVI)

Dt 26:12 you shall give it to the *L*, the alien,
Jdg 19: 1 a *L* who lived in a remote area

LEVITES (LEVI)

Nu 1:53 The *L* are to be responsible
3:12 "I have taken the *L*
8: 6 "Take the *L* from among the other
18:21 I give to the *L* all the tithes in Israel
35: 7 must give the *L* forty-eight towns,
2Ch 31: 2 assigned the priests and *L*
Mal 3: 3 he will purify the *L* and refine them

LEVITICAL (LEVI)

Heb 7:11 attained through the *L* priesthood

LEWDNESS

Mk 7:22 malice, deceit, *l*, envy, slander,

LIAR* (LIE)

Dt 19:18 and if the witness proves to be a *l*,
Job 34: 6 I am considered a *l*;
Pr 17: 4 *l* pays attention to a malicious
19:22 better to be poor than a *l*.
30: 6 will rebuke you and prove you a *l*.
Mic 2:11 If a *l* and deceiver comes and says,
Jn 8:44 for he is a *l* and the father of lies.
8:55 I did not, I would be a *l* like you,
Ro 3: 4 Let God be true, and every man a *l*.
1Jn 1:10 we make him out to be a *l*
2: 4 not do what he commands is a *l*,
2:22 Who is the *l*? It is the man who
4:20 yet hates his brother, he is a *l*.
5:10 God has made him out to be a *l*,

LIARS* (LIE)

Ps 63:11 the mouths of *l* will be silenced.
116: 11 "All men are *l*."
Isa 57: 4 the offspring of *l*?
Mic 6:12 her people are *l*
1Ti 1:10 for slave traders and *l* and perjurers
4: 2 come through hypocritical *l*,
Tit 1:12 "Cretans are always *l*, evil brutes,
Rev 3: 9 though they are not, but are *l*—
21: 8 magic arts, the idolaters and all *l*—

LIBERATED*

Ro 8:21 that the creation itself will be *l*

LICENSE

Jude : 4 of our God into a *l* for immorality

LICK

Ps 72: 9 and his enemies will *l* the dust.
Isa 49:23 they will *l* the dust at your feet.
Mic 7:17 They will *l* dust like a snake,

LIE (LIAR LIARS LIED LIES LYING)

Lev 18:22 " 'Do not *l* with a man
19:11 " 'Do not *l*.
Nu 23:19 God is not a man, that he should *l*,
Dt 6: 7 when you *l* down and when you get
25: 2 the judge shall make him *l* down
1Sa 15:29 the Glory of Israel does not *l*
Ps 4: 8 I will *l* down and sleep in peace,
23: 2 me *l* down in green pastures,
89:35 and I will not *l* to David—
Pr 3:24 when you *l* down, you will not be
Isa 11: 6 leopard will *l* down with the goat,
28:15 for we have made a *l* our refuge
Jer 9: 5 They have taught their tongues to *l*
23:14 They commit adultery and live a *l*.
Eze 13: 6 are false and their divinations a *l*.
34:14 they will *l* down in good grazing
Ro 1:25 exchanged the truth of God for a *l*,
Col 3: 9 Do not *l* to each other,
2Th 2:11 so that they will believe the *l*
Tit 1: 2 which God, who does not *l*,
Heb 6:18 which it is impossible for God to *l*,
1Jn 2:21 because no *l* comes from the truth.
Rev 14: 5 No *l* was found in their mouths;

LIED (LIE)

Ac 5: 4 You have not *l* to men but to God."

LIES (LIE)

Lev 6: 3 finds lost property and *l* about it,
Ps 5: 6 You destroy those who tell *l*;
10: 7 His mouth is full of curses and *l*
12: 2 Everyone *l* to his neighbor;
34:13 and your lips from speaking *l*.
58: 3 they are wayward and speak *l*.
Ps 144: 8 whose mouths are full of *l*,
Pr 6:19 a false witness who pours out *l*
12:17 but a false witness tells *l*.
19: 5 he who pours out *l* will not go free.
19: 9 and he who pours out *l* will perish.
29:12 If a ruler listens to *l*,
30: 8 Keep falsehood and *l* far from me;
Isa 59: 3 Your lips have spoken *l*,
Jer 5:31 The prophets prophesy *l*,
9: 3 like a bow, to shoot *l*;
14:14 "The prophets are prophesying *l*
Hos 11:12 Ephraim has surrounded me with *l*,
Jn 8:44 for he is a liar and the father of *l*.

LIFE (LIVE)

Ge 1:30 everything that has the breath of *l*
2: 7 into his nostrils the breath of *l*,
2: 9 of the garden were the tree of *l*
6:17 to destroy all *l* under the heavens,
9: 5 for the *l* of his fellow man.
9:11 Never again will all *l* be cut
Ex 21: 6 Then he will be his servant for *l*.
21:23 you are to take *l* for *l*, eye for eye,
23:26 I will give you a full *l* span.
Lev 17:14 the *l* of every creature is its blood.
24:17 " 'If anyone takes the *l*
24:18 must make restitution—*l* for *l*.
Nu 35:31 a ransom for the *l* of a murderer,
Dt 4:42 one of these cities and save his *l*.
12:23 because the blood is the *l*,
19:21 Show no pity: *l* for *l*, eye for eye,
30:15 I set before you today *l*
30:19 Now choose *l*, so that you
30:20 For the LORD is your *l*,
32:39 I put to death and I bring to *l*,
32:47 words for you—they are your *l*.
1Sa 19: 5 He took his *l* in his hands
Job 2: 6 hands; but you must spare his *l*."
33: 4 of the Almighty gives me *l*.
33:30 that the light of *l* may shine on him.
Ps 16:11 known to me the path of *l*;
17:14 this world whose reward is in this *l*.
23: 6 all the days of my *l*,
27: 1 LORD is the stronghold of my *l*—
34:12 Whoever of you loves *l*
36: 9 For with you is the fountain of *l*;
39: 4 let me know how fleeting is my *l*.
41: 2 will protect him and preserve his *l*;
49: 7 No man can redeem the *l*
49: 8 the ransom for a *l* is costly,
63: 3 Because your love is better than *l*,
69:28 they be blotted out of the book of *l*
91:16 With long *l* will I satisfy him
104: 33 I will sing to the LORD all my *l*;
119: 25 preserve my *l* according to your word
Pr 1: 3 a disciplined and prudent *l*,
3: 2 will prolong your *l* many years
3:18 of *l* to those who embrace her;
4:23 for it is the wellspring of *l*.
6:23 are the way to *l*,
6:26 adulteress preys upon your very *l*.
7:23 little knowing it will cost him his *l*.
8:35 For whoever finds me finds *l*
10:11 of the righteous is a fountain of *l*,
10:27 of the LORD adds length to *l*,
11:30 of the righteous is a tree of *l*,
13: 3 He who guards his lips guards his *l*,
13:12 but a longing fulfilled is a tree of *l*.
13:14 of the wise is a fountain of *l*,
14:27 of the LORD is a fountain of *l*,
15: 4 that brings healing is a tree of *l*,
16:22 Understanding is a fountain of *l*
19: 3 A man's own folly ruins his *l*,
19:23 The fear of the LORD leads to *l*:
21:21 finds *l*, prosperity and honor.
Isa 53:10 LORD makes his *l* a guilt offering,
53:11 he will see the light of *l*
53:12 he poured out his *l* unto death,
Jer 10:23 that a man's *l* is not his own;
La 3:58 you redeemed my *l*.
Eze 18:27 and right, he will save his *l*.
37: 5 enter you, and you will come to *l*.
Da 12: 2 some to everlasting *l*, others
Jnh 2: 6 you brought my *l* up from the pit,
Mal 2: 5 a covenant of *l* and peace,
Mt 6:25 Is not *l* more important than food,
7:14 and narrow the road that leads to *l*,
10:39 Whoever finds his *l* will lose it,
16:21 and on the third day be raised to *l*.
16:25 wants to save his *l* will lose it,
18: 8 better for you to enter *l* maimed
19:16 thing must I do to get eternal *l*?"
19:29 as much and will inherit eternal *l*.
20:28 to give his *l* as a ransom for many."
25:46 but the righteous to eternal *l*."
Mk 8:35 but whoever loses his *l* for me
9:43 better for you to enter *l* maimed
10:17 "what must I do to inherit eternal *l*
10:30 and in the age to come, eternal *l*.
Mk 10:45 to give his *l* as a ransom for many."
Lk 6: 9 to save *l* or to destroy it?"
9:22 and on the third day be raised to *l*."
9:24 wants to save his *l* will lose it,
12:15 a man's *l* does not consist
12:22 do not worry about your *l*,
12:25 can add a single hour to his *l*?
14:26 even his own *l*— he cannot be my
17:33 tries to keep his *l* will lose it,
21:19 standing firm you will gain *l*.
Jn 1: 4 In him was *l*, and that *l* was
3:15 believes in him may have eternal *l*.
3:36 believes in the Son has eternal *l*,
4:14 of water welling up to eternal *l*."
5:21 raises the dead and gives them *l*,
5:24 him who sent me has eternal *l*
5:26 For as the Father has *l* in himself,
5:39 that by them you possess eternal *l*.
5:40 refuse to come to me to have *l*.
6:27 for food that endures to eternal *l*,
6:33 down from heaven and gives *l*
6:35 Jesus declared, "I am the bread of *l*
6:40 believes in him shall have eternal *l*,
6:47 he who believes has everlasting *l*.
6:48 I am the bread of *l*.
6:51 give for the *l* of the world."
6:53 and drink his blood, you have no *l*
6:63 The Spirit gives *l*; the flesh counts
6:68 You have the words of eternal *l*.
8:12 but will have the light of *l*."
10:10 I have come that they may have *l*,
10:15 and I lay down my *l* for the sheep.
10:17 loves me is that I lay down my *l*—
10:28 I give them eternal *l*, and they shall
11:25 "I am the resurrection and the *l*.
12:25 The man who loves his *l* will lose it,
12:50 his command leads to eternal *l*.
13:37 I will lay down my *l* for you."
14: 6 am the way and the truth and the *l*.
15:13 lay down his *l* for his friends.
17: 2 people that he might give eternal *l*
17: 3 Now this is eternal *l*: that they may
20:31 that by believing you may have *l*
Ac 2:32 God has raised this Jesus to *l*,
3:15 You killed the author of *l*,
11:18 the Gentiles repentance unto *l*."
13:48 appointed for eternal *l* believed.
Ro 2: 7 immortality, he will give eternal *l*.
4:25 was raised to *l* for our justification.
5:10 shall we be saved through his *l*!
5:18 was justification that brings *l*
5:21 righteousness to bring eternal *l*
6: 4 the Father, we too may live a new *l*.
6:13 have been brought from death to *l*;
6:22 holiness, and the result is eternal *l*.
6:23 but the gift of God is eternal *l*
8: 6 mind controlled by the Spirit is *l*
8:11 also give *l* to your mortal bodies
8:38 convinced that neither death nor *l*,
1Co 15:19 If only for this *l* we have hope
15:36 What you sow does not come to *l*
2Co 2:16 to the other, the fragrance of *l*.
3: 6 letter kills, but the Spirit gives *l*.
4:10 so that the *l* of Jesus may
5: 4 is mortal may be swallowed up by *l*.
Gal 2:20 The *l* I live in the body, I live
3:21 had been given that could impart *l*,
6: 8 from the Spirit will reap eternal *l*.
Eph 4: 1 I urge you to live a *l* worthy
Php 2:16 as you hold out the word of *l*—
4: 3 whose names are in the book of *l*.
Col 1:10 order that you may live a *l* worthy
3: 3 your *l* is now hidden with Christ
1Th 4:12 so that your daily *l* may win
1Ti 1:16 on him and receive eternal *l*.
4: 8 for both the present *l* and the *l*
4:12 in *l*, in love, in faith and in purity.
4:16 Watch your *l* and doctrine closely.
6:12 Take hold of the eternal *l*
6:19 hold of the *l* that is truly *l*.
2Ti 1: 9 saved us and called us to a holy *l*—
1:10 destroyed death and has brought *l*
3:12 to live a godly *l* in Christ Jesus will
Tit 1: 2 resting on the hope of eternal *l*,
3: 7 heirs having the hope of eternal *l*.
Heb 7:16 of the power of an indestructible *l*.
Jas 1:12 crown of *l* that God has promised
3:13 Let him show it by his good *l*,
1Pe 3: 7 with you of the gracious gift of *l*,
3:10 "Whoever would love *l*
4: 2 rest of his earthly *l* for evil human
2Pe 1: 3 given us everything we need for *l*
1Jn 1: 1 proclaim concerning the Word of *l*.
2:25 he promised us—even eternal *l*.
3:14 we have passed from death to *l*,
3:16 Jesus Christ laid down his *l* for us.
5:11 has given us eternal *l*, and this *l* is
5:20 He is the true God and eternal *l*.
Jude :21 Christ to bring you to eternal *l*.

Rev 2: 7 the right to eat from the tree of *l*,
2: 8 who died and came to *l* again.
2:10 and I will give you the crown of *l*.
3: 5 name from the book of *l*,
13: 8 written in the book of *l* belonging
17: 8 in the book of *l* from the creation
20:12 was opened, which is the book of *l*.
20:15 not found written in the book of *l*,
21: 6 from the spring of the water of *l*.
21:27 written in the Lamb's book of *l*.
22: 1 me the river of the water of *l*,
22: 2 side of the river stood the tree of *l*,
22:14 may have the right to the tree of *l*
22:17 take the free gift of the water of *l*.
22:19 from him his share in the tree of *l*

LIFE-GIVING (GIVE)
Pr 15:31 He who listens to a *l* rebuke
1Co 15:45 being"; the last Adam, a *l* spirit.

LIFETIME (LIVE)
Ps 30: 5 but his favor lasts a *l*;
Lk 16:25 in your *l* you received your good

LIFT (LIFTED LIFTING LIFTS)
Ps 3: 3 you bestow glory on me and *l*
28: 2 as I *l* up my hands
63: 4 in your name I will *l* up my hands.
91:12 they will *l* you up in their hands,
121: 1 I *l* up my eyes to the hills—
123: 1 I *l* up my eyes to you,
134: 2 *L* up your hands in the sanctuary
143: 8 for to you I *l* up my soul.
Isa 40: 9 *l* up your voice with a shout,
La 2:19 *L* up your hands to him
3:41 Let us *l* up our hearts and our
Mt 4: 6 they will *l* you up in their hands,
Lk 21:28 stand up and *l* up your heads,
1Ti 2: 8 everywhere to *l* up holy hands
Jas 4:10 the Lord, and he will *l* you up.
1Pe 5: 6 that he may *l* you up in due time.

LIFTED (LIFT)
Ne 8: 6 and all the people *l* their hands
Ps 24: 7 be *l* up, you ancient doors,
40: 2 He *l* me out of the slimy pit,
41: 9 has *l* up his heel against me.
Isa 52:13 *l* up and highly exalted.
63: 9 he *l* them up and carried them
Jn 3:14 Moses *l* up the snake in the desert,
8:28 "When you have *l* up the Son
12:32 when I am *l* up from the earth,
12:34 'The Son of Man must be *l* up'?
13:18 shares my bread has *l* up his heel

LIFTING (LIFT)
Ps 141: 2 may the *l* up of my hands be like

LIFTS (LIFT)
Ps 113: 7 and *l* the needy from the ash heap;

LIGAMENT* (LIGAMENTS)
Eph 4:16 held together by every supporting *l*

LIGAMENTS* (LIGAMENT)
Col 2:19 held together by its *l* and sinews,

LIGHT (ENLIGHTENED LIGHTS)
Ge 1: 3 "Let there be *l*," and there was *l*.
Ex 13:21 in a pillar of fire to give them *l*,
25:37 it so that they *l* the space in front
2Sa 22:29 LORD turns my darkness into *l*.
Job 38:19 "What is the way to the abode of *l*?
Ps 4: 6 Let the *l* of your face shine upon us
18:28 my God turns my darkness into *l*.
19: 8 giving *l* to the eyes.
27: 1 LORD is my *l* and my salvation—
36: 9 in your *l* we see *l*.
56:13 God in the *l* of life.
76: 4 You are resplendent with *l*,
89:15 who walk in the *l* of your presence,
104: 2 He wraps himself in *l*
119:105 and a *l* for my path.
119:130 The unfolding of your words gives *l*;
139: 12 for darkness is as *l* to you.
Pr 4:18 till the full *l* of day.
Isa 2: 5 let us walk in the *l* of the LORD.
9: 2 have seen a great *l*;
42: 6 and a *l* for the Gentiles,
45: 7 I form the *l* and create darkness,
49: 6 also make you a *l* for the Gentiles,
53:11 he will see the *l* of life
60: 1 "Arise, shine, for your *l* has come,
60:19 LORD will be your everlasting *l*,
Eze 1:27 and brilliant *l* surrounded him.
Mic 7: 8 the LORD will be my *l*.
Mt 4:16 have seen a great *l*;
5:14 "You are the *l* of the world.
5:15 it gives *l* to everyone in the house.
5:16 let your *l* shine before men,
Mt 6:22 your whole body will be full of *l*.
11:30 yoke is easy and my burden is *l*."
17: 2 his clothes became as white as the *l*
24:29 and the moon will not give its *l*;
Mk 13:24 and the moon will not give its *l*;
Lk 2:32 a *l* for revelation to the Gentiles
8:16 those who come in can see the *l*.
11:33 those who come in may see the *l*.
Jn 1: 4 and that life was the *l* of men.
1: 5 The *l* shines in the darkness,
1: 7 witness to testify concerning that *l*,
1: 9 The true *l* that gives *l*
3:19 but men loved darkness instead of *l*
3:20 Everyone who does evil hates the *l*,
8:12 he said, "I am the *l* of the world.
9: 5 in the world, I am the *l* of the world
12:35 Walk while you have the *l*,
12:46 I have come into the world as a *l*,
Ac 13:47 " 'I have made you a *l*
Ro 13:12 darkness and put on the armor of *l*.
2Co 4: 6 made his *l* shine in our hearts
6:14 Or what fellowship can *l* have
11:14 masquerades as an angel of *l*.
Eph 5: 8 but now you are *l* in the Lord.
1Th 5: 5 You are all sons of the *l*
1Ti 6:16 and who lives in unapproachable *l*,
1Pe 2: 9 of darkness into his wonderful *l*.
2Pe 1:19 as to a *l* shining in a dark place,
1Jn 1: 5 God is *l*; in him there is no
1: 7 But if we walk in the *l*,
2: 9 Anyone who claims to be in the *l*
Rev 21:23 for the glory of God gives it *l*,
22: 5 for the Lord God will give them *l*.

LIGHTNING
Ex 9:23 and *l* flashed down to the ground.
20:18 and *l* and heard the trumpet
Ps 18:12 with hailstones and bolts of *l*.
Eze 1:13 it was bright, and *l* flashed out of it.
Da 10: 6 his face like *l*, his eyes like flaming
Mt 24:27 For as the *l* that comes from the east
28: 3 His appearance was like *l*,
Lk 10:18 "I saw Satan fall like *l* from heaven.
Rev 4: 5 From the throne came flashes of *l*,

LIGHTS (LIGHT)
Ge 1:14 "Let there be *l* in the expanse
Lk 8:16 No one *l* a lamp and hides it in a jar

LIKE-MINDED* (MIND)
Php 2: 2 make my joy complete by being *l*,

LIKENESS
Ge 1:26 man in our image, in our *l*,
Ps 17:15 I will be satisfied with seeing your *l*
Isa 52:14 his form marred beyond human *l*—
Ro 8: 3 Son in the *l* of sinful man
8:29 to be conformed to the *l* of his Son,
2Co 3:18 his *l* with ever-increasing glory,
Php 2: 7 being made in human *l*.
Jas 3: 9 who have been made in God's *l*.

LILIES (LILY)
Lk 12:27 "Consider how the *l* grow.

LILY (LILIES)
SS 2: 1 a *l* of the valleys.
2: 2 *Lover* Like a *l* among thorns

LIMIT
Ps 147: 5 his understanding has no *l*.
Jn 3:34 for God gives the Spirit without *l*.

LINEN
Lev 16: 4 He is to put on the sacred *l* tunic,
Pr 31:22 she is clothed in fine *l* and purple.
31:24 She makes *l* garments
Mk 15:46 So Joseph bought some *l* cloth,
Jn 20: 6 He saw the strips of *l* lying there,
Rev 15: 6 shining *l* and wore golden sashes
19: 8 Fine *l*, bright and clean,

LINGER
Hab 2: 3 Though it *l*, wait for it;

LION (LION'S LIONS')
Jdg 14: 6 power so that he tore the *l* apart
1Sa 17:34 When a *l* or a bear came
Isa 11: 7 and the *l* will eat straw like the ox.
65:25 and the *l* will eat straw like the ox,
Eze 1:10 right side each had the face of a *l*,
10:14 the third the face of a *l*,
Da 7: 4 "The first was like a *l*,
1Pe 5: 8 around like a roaring *l* looking
Rev 4: 7 The first living creature was like a *l*
5: 5 See, the *L* of the tribe of Judah,

LION'S (LION)
Ge 49: 9 You are a *l* cub, O Judah;

LIONS' (LION)
Da 6: 7 shall be thrown into the *l* den.

LIPS
Ps 8: 2 From the *l* of children and infants
34: 1 his praise will always be on my *l*.
40: 9 I do not seal my *l*,
63: 3 my *l* will glorify you.
119:171 May my *l* overflow with praise,
140: 3 the poison of vipers is on their *l*.
141: 3 keep watch over the door of my *l*.
Pr 10:13 on the *l* of the discerning,
10:18 who conceals his hatred has lying *l*,
10:32 *l* of the righteous know what is
12:22 The LORD detests lying *l*,
13: 3 He who guards his *l* guards his life,
14: 7 will not find knowledge on his *l*.
24:26 is like a kiss on the *l*.
26:23 are fervent *l* with an evil heart.
27: 2 someone else, and not your own *l*.
Isa 6: 5 For I am a man of unclean *l*,
28:11 with foreign *l* and strange tongues
29:13 and honor me with their *l*,
Mal 2: 7 "For the *l* of a priest ought
Mt 15: 8 These people honor me with their *l*
21:16 " 'From the *l* of children
Lk 4:22 words that came from his *l*.
Ro 3:13 "The poison of vipers is on their *l*."
Col 3: 8 and filthy language from your *l*.
Heb 13:15 the fruit of *l* that confess his name.
1Pe 3:10 and his *l* from deceitful speech.

LISTEN (LISTENED LISTENING LISTENS)
Dt 18:15 You must *l* to him.
30:20 *l* to his voice, and hold fast to him.
1Ki 4:34 came to *l* to Solomon's wisdom,
2Ki 21: 9 But the people did not *l*.
Pr 1: 5 let the wise *l* and add
Ecc 5: 1 Go near to *l* rather
Eze 2: 5 And whether they *l* or fail to *l*—
Mt 12:42 earth to *l* to Solomon's wisdom,
Mk 9: 7 *L* to him!" Suddenly,
Jn 10:27 My sheep *l* to my voice; I know
Ac 3:22 you must *l* to everything he tells
Jas 1:19 Everyone should be quick to *l*,
1:22 Do not merely *l* to the word,
1Jn 4: 6 not from God does not *l* to us.

LISTENED (LISTEN)
Ne 8: 3 And all the people *l* attentively
Isa 66: 4 when I spoke, no one *l*.
Da 9: 6 We have not *l* to your servants

LISTENING (LISTEN)
1Sa 3: 9 Speak, LORD, for your servant is *l*
Pr 18:13 He who answers before *l*—
Lk 10:39 at the Lord's feet *l* to what he said.

LISTENS (LISTEN)
Pr 12:15 but a wise man *l* to advice.
Lk 10:16 "He who *l* to you *l*
1Jn 4: 6 and whoever knows God *l* to us;

LIVE (ALIVE LIFE LIFETIME LIVES LIVING)
Ge 3:22 tree of life and eat, and *l* forever."
Ex 20:12 so that you may *l* long
33:20 for no one may see me and *l*."
Nu 21: 8 who is bitten can look at it and *l*."
Dt 5:24 we have seen that a man can *l*
6: 2 as you *l* by keeping all his decrees
8: 3 to teach you that man does not *l*
Job 14:14 If a man dies, will he *l* again?
Ps 15: 1 Who may *l* on your holy hill?
24: 1 the world, and all who *l* in it;
26: 8 I love the house where you *l*,
119:175 Let me *l* that I may praise you,
Pr 21: 9 Better to *l* on a corner of the roof
21:19 Better to *l* in a desert
Ecc 9: 4 a *l* dog is better off than a dead lion
Isa 26:19 But your dead will *l*;
55: 3 hear me, that your soul may *l*.
Eze 17:19 LORD says: As surely as I *l*,
20:11 for the man who obeys them will *l*
37: 3 can these bones *l*?" I said,
Am 5: 6 Seek the LORD and *l*,
Hab 2: 4 but the righteous will *l* by his faith
Zec 2:11 I will *l* among you and you will
Mt 4: 4 'Man does not *l* on bread alone,
Lk 4: 4 'Man does not *l* on bread alone.' "
Jn 14:19 Because I *l*, you also will *l*.
Ac 17:24 does not *l* in temples built by hands
17:28 'For in him we *l* and move
Ro 1:17 "The righteous will *l* by faith."
2Co 5: 7 We *l* by faith, not by sight.
6:16 "I will *l* with them and walk
Gal 2:20 The life I *l* in the body, I *l* by faith
3:11 "The righteous will *l* by faith."
5:25 Since we *l* by the Spirit, let us keep

Eph 4:17 that you must no longer *l*
Php 1:21 to *l* is Christ and to die is gain.
Col 1:10 order that you may *l* a life worthy
1Th 4: 1 we instructed you how to *l* in order
5:13 *L* in peace with each other.
1Ti 2: 2 that we may *l* peaceful
2Ti 3:12 who wants to *l* a godly life
Tit 2:12 and to *l* self-controlled, upright
Heb 10:38 But my righteous one will *l* by faith
12:14 Make every effort to *l* in peace
1Pe 1:17 *l* your lives as strangers here
3: 8 *l* in harmony with one another;

LIVES (LIVE)
Ge 45: 7 and to save your *l* by a great
Job 19:25 I know that my Redeemer *l*,
Pr 1:19 it takes away the *l*
Isa 57:15 he who *l* forever, whose name is
Da 3:28 to give up their *l* rather than serve
Jn 14:17 for he *l* with you and will be in you.
Ro 6:10 but the life he *l*, he *l* to God.
7:18 I know that nothing good *l* in me,
8: 9 if the Spirit of God *l* in you.
14: 7 For none of us *l* to himself alone
1Co 3:16 and that God's Spirit *l* in you?
Gal 2:20 I no longer live, but Christ *l* in me.
1Th 2: 8 only the gospel of God but our *l*
1Ti 2: 2 quiet *l* in all godliness and holiness.
Tit 2:12 and godly *l* in this present age,
Heb 7:24 but because Jesus *l* forever,
13: 5 Keep your *l* free from the love
1Pe 3: 2 the purity and reverence of your *l*.
2Pe 3:11 You ought to live holy and godly *l*
1Jn 3:16 to lay down our *l* for our brothers.
4:16 Whoever *l* in love *l* in God,

LIVING (LIVE)
Ge 2: 7 and the man became a *l* being.
1Sa 17:26 defy the armies of the *l* God?"
Isa 53: 8 cut off from the land of the *l*;
Jer 2:13 the spring of *l* water,
Eze 1: 5 what looked like four *l* creatures.
Zec 14: 8 On that day *l* water will flow out
Mt 22:32 the God of the dead but of the *l*."
Jn 4:10 he would have given you *l* water."
6:51 I am the *l* bread that came
7:38 streams of *l* water will flow
Ro 8:11 Jesus from the dead is *l* in you,
12: 1 to offer your bodies as *l* sacrifices,
1Co 9:14 the gospel should receive their *l*
Heb 4:12 For the word of God is *l* and active.
10:20 and *l* way opened for us
10:31 to fall into the hands of the *l* God.
1Pe 1:23 through the *l* and enduring word
Rev 1:18 I am the *L* One; I was dead,
4: 6 the throne, were four *l* creatures,
7:17 to springs of *l* water.

LOAD (LOADS)
Gal 6: 5 for each one should carry his own *l*.

LOADS (LOAD)
Mt 23: 4 They tie up heavy *l* and put them

LOAF (LOAVES)
1Co 10:17 for we all partake of the one *l*.

LOAVES (LOAF)
Mk 6:41 Taking the five *l* and the two fish
8: 6 When he had taken the seven *l*
Lk 11: 5 'Friend, lend me three *l* of bread,

LOCKED
Jn 20:26 the doors were *l*, Jesus came
Gal 3:23 *l* up until faith should be revealed.

LOCUSTS
Ex 10: 4 I will bring *l* into your country
Joel 2:25 you for the years the *l* have eaten—
Mt 3: 4 His food was *l* and wild honey.
Rev 9: 3 And out of the smoke *l* came

LOFTY
Ps 139: 6 too *l* for me to attain.
Isa 57:15 is what the high and *l* One says—

LONELY
Ps 68: 6 God sets the *l* in families,
Lk 5:16 Jesus often withdrew to *l* places

LONG (LENGTH LENGTHY LONGED LONGING LONGINGS LONGS)
Ex 17:11 As *l* as Moses held up his hands,
Nu 6: 5 the hair of his head grow *l*.
1Ki 18:21 "How *l* will you waver
Ps 119: 97 I meditate on it all day *l*.
119:174 I *l* for your salvation, O LORD,
Hos 7:13 I *l* to redeem them
Am 5:18 Why do you *l* for the day
Mt 25: 5 The bridegroom was a *l* time
Jn 9: 4 As *l* as it is day, we must do
1Co 11:14 that if a man has *l* hair,
Eph 3:18 to grasp how wide and *l* and high
Php 1: 8 God can testify how I *l* for all
1Pe 1:12 Even angels *l* to look

LONGED (LONG)
Mt 13:17 righteous men *l* to see what you see
23:37 how often I have *l*
Lk 13:34 how often I have *l*
2Ti 4: 8 to all who have *l* for his appearing.

LONGING* (LONG)
Dt 28:65 with *l*, and a despairing heart.
Job 7: 2 Like a slave *l* for the evening
Ps 119: 20 My soul is consumed with *l*
119: 81 with *l* for your salvation,
119:131 *l* for your commands.
143: 7 my spirit faints with *l*.
Pr 13:12 but a *l* fulfilled is a tree of life.
13:19 A *l* fulfilled is sweet to the soul,
Eze 23:27 look on these things with *l*
Lk 16:21 and *l* to eat what fell from the rich
Ro 15:23 since I have been *l* for many years
2Co 5: 2 *l* to be clothed with our heavenly
7: 7 He told us about your *l* for me,
7:11 what alarm, what *l*, what concern,
1Th 2:17 out of our intense *l* we made every
Heb 11:16 they were *l* for a better country—

LONGINGS* (LONG)
Ps 38: 9 All my *l* lie open before you,
112: 10 the *l* of the wicked will come

LONGS* (LONG)
Ps 63: 1 my body *l* for you,
Isa 26: 9 in the morning my spirit *l* for you.
30:18 Yet the LORD *l* to be gracious
Php 2:26 For he *l* for all of you and is

LOOK (LOOKED LOOKING LOOKS)
Ge 19:17 "Flee for your lives! Don't *l* back,
Ex 3: 6 because he was afraid to *l* at God.
Nu 21: 8 anyone who is bitten can *l* at it
32: 8 Kadesh Barnea to *l* over the land.
Dt 4:29 you will find him if you *l* for him
1Sa 16: 7 The LORD does not *l*
Job 31: 1 not to *l* lustfully at a girl.
Ps 34: 5 Those who *l* to him are radiant;
105: 4 *L* to the LORD and his strength;
113: 6 who stoops down to *l*
123: 2 As the eyes of slaves *l* to the hand
Pr 1:28 they will *l* for me but will not find
4:25 Let your eyes *l* straight ahead,
15:30 A cheerful *l* brings joy to the heart,
Isa 17: 7 In that day men will *l*
31: 1 do not *l* to the Holy One of Israel,
40:26 Lift your eyes and *l* to the heavens:
60: 5 Then you will *l* and be radiant,
Jer 3: 3 Yet you have the brazen *l*
6:16 "Stand at the crossroads and *l*;
Eze 34:11 for my sheep and *l* after them.
Hab 1:13 Your eyes are too pure to *l* on evil;
Zec 12:10 They will *l* on me, the one they
Mt 18:10 "See that you do not *l* down on one
18:12 go to *l* for the one that wandered
23:27 which *l* beautiful on the outside
Mk 13:21 '*L*, here is the Christ!' or, '*L*,
Lk 6:41 "Why do you *l* at the speck
24:39 *L* at my hands and my feet.
Jn 1:36 he said, "*L*, the Lamb of God!"
4:35 open your eyes and *l* at the fields!
19:37 "They will *l* on the one they have
Ro 14:10 why do you *l* down on your brother
Php 2: 4 Each of you should *l* not only
1Ti 4:12 Don't let anyone *l* down on you
Jas 1:27 to *l* after orphans and widows
1Pe 1:12 long to *l* into these things.
2Pe 3:12 as you *l* forward to the day of God

LOOKED (LOOK)
Ge 19:26 Lot's wife *l* back, and she became
Ex 2:25 So God *l* on the Israelites
1Sa 6:19 because they had *l* into the ark
SS 3: 1 I *l* for the one my heart loves;
Eze 22:30 "I *l* for a man among them who
34: 6 and no one searched or *l* for them.
44: 4 I *l* and saw the glory
Da 7: 9 "As I *l*,
10: 5 I *l* up and there before me was
Hab 3: 6 he *l*, and made the nations tremble.
Mt 25:36 I was sick and you *l* after me,
Lk 18: 9 and *l* down on everybody else,
22:61 The Lord turned and *l* straight
1Jn 1: 1 which we have *l* at and our hands

LOOKING (LOOK)
Ps 69: 3 *l* for my God.
119: 82 My eyes fail, *l* for your promise;
119:123 My eyes fail, *l* for your salvation,
Mk 16: 6 "You are *l* for Jesus the Nazarene,
2Co 10: 7 You are *l* only on the surface
Php 4:17 Not that I am *l* for a gift,
1Th 2: 6 We were not *l* for praise from men,
2Pe 3:13 with his promise we are *l* forward
Rev 5: 6 I saw a Lamb, *l* as if it had been

LOOKS (LOOK)
1Sa 16: 7 Man *l* at the outward appearance,
Ezr 8:22 is on everyone who *l* to him,
Ps 104: 32 who *l* at the earth, and it trembles;
138: 6 on high, he *l* upon the lowly,
Pr 27:18 he who *l* after his master will be
Eze 34:12 As a shepherd *l* after his scattered
Mt 5:28 But I tell you that anyone who *l*
16: 4 and adulterous generation *l*
Lk 9:62 and *l* back is fit for service
Jn 6:40 Father's will is that everyone who *l*
12:45 When he *l* at me, he sees the one
Php 2:21 For everyone *l* out
Jas 1:25 But the man who *l* intently

LOOSE
Isa 33:23 Your rigging hangs *l*:
Mt 16:19 and whatever you *l* on earth will be
18:18 and whatever you *l* on earth will be

LORD† (LORD'S† LORDED LORDING)
Ge 18:27 been so bold as to speak to the *L*,
Ex 15:17 O *L*, your hands established.
Nu 16:13 now you also want to *l* it over us?
Dt 10:17 God of gods and *L* of lords,
Jos 3:13 the *L* of all the earth—set foot
1Ki 3:10 *L* was pleased that Solomon had
Ne 4:14 Remember the *L*, who is great
Job 28:28 'The fear of the *L*—that is wisdom,
Ps 37:13 but the *L* laughs at the wicked,
38:22 O *L* my Savior.
54: 4 the *L* is the one who sustains me.
62:12 and that you, O *L*, are loving.
69: 6 O *L*, the LORD Almighty;
86: 5 You are forgiving and good, O *L*,
86: 8 gods there is none like you, O *L*;
89:49 O *L*, where is your former great
110: 1 The LORD says to my *L*:
110: 5 The *L* is at your right hand;
130: 3 O *L*, who could stand?
135: 5 that our *L* is greater than all gods.
136: 3 Give thanks to the *L* of lords:
147: 5 Great is our *L* and mighty in power
Isa 6: 1 I saw the *L* seated on a throne,
Da 2:47 and the *L* of kings and a revealer
9: 4 "O *L*, the great and awesome God,
9: 7 "*L*, you are righteous,
9: 9 The *L* our God is merciful
9:19 O *L*, listen! O *L*, forgive! O *L*,
Mt 3: 3 'Prepare the way for the *L*,
4: 7 'Do not put the *L* your God
4:10 'Worship the *L* your God,
7:21 "Not everyone who says to me, '*L*,
9:38 Ask the *L* of the harvest, therefore,
12: 8 Son of Man is *L* of the Sabbath."
20:25 of the Gentiles *l* it over them,
21: 9 comes in the name of the *L*!"
22:37 " 'Love the *L* your God
22:44 For he says, " 'The *L* said to my *L*:
23:39 comes in the name of the *L*.' "
Mk 1: 3 'Prepare the way for the *L*,
12:11 the *L* has done this,
12:29 the *L* our God, the *L* is one.
12:30 Love the *L* your God
Lk 2: 9 glory of the *L* shone around them,
6: 5 The Son of Man is *L* of the Sabbath
6:46 "Why do you call me, '*L*, *L*,'
10:27 " 'Love the *L* your God
11: 1 one of his disciples said to him, "*L*,
24:34 The *L* has risen and has appeared
Jn 1:23 'Make straight the way for the *L*.' "
Ac 2:21 on the name of the *L* will be saved.'
2:25 " 'I saw the *L* always before me.
2:34 " 'The *L* said to my *L*:
8:16 into the name of the *L* Jesus.
9: 5 "Who are you, *L*?" Saul asked.
10:36 through Jesus Christ, who is *L*
11:23 true to the *L* with all their hearts.
16:31 replied, "Believe in the *L* Jesus,
Ro 4:24 in him who raised Jesus our *L*
5:11 in God through our *L* Jesus Christ,
6:23 life in Christ Jesus our *L*.
8:39 of God that is in Christ Jesus our *L*.
10: 9 with your mouth, "Jesus is *L*,"
10:13 on the name of the *L* will be saved
10:16 *L*, who has believed our message?"
11:34 Who has known the mind of the *L*?
12:11 your spiritual fervor, serving the *L*.
13:14 yourselves with the *L* Jesus Christ,
14: 4 for the *L* is able to make him stand.
14: 8 we live to the *L*; and if we die,
1Co 1:31 Let him who boasts boast in the *L*."

1Co 3: 5 the L has assigned to each his task.
4: 5 time; wait till the L comes.
6:13 for the L, and the L for the body.
6:14 By his power God raised the L
7:32 affairs—how he can please the L.
7:34 to be devoted to the L in both body
7:35 in undivided devotion to the L.
7:39 but he must belong to the L.
8: 6 and there is but one L, Jesus Christ,
10: 9 We should not test the L,
11:23 For I received from the L what I
12: 3 "Jesus is L," except by the Holy
15:57 victory through our L Jesus Christ.
15:58 fully to the work of the L,
16:22 If anyone does not love the L—
2Co 1:24 Not that we l it over your faith,
2:12 found that the L had opened a door
3:17 Now the L is the Spirit,
4: 5 but Jesus Christ as L, and ourselves
5: 6 in the body we are away from the L
8: 5 they gave themselves first to the L
8:21 not only in the eyes of the L but
10:17 Let him who boasts boast in the L."
10:18 but the one whom the L commends
13:10 the authority the L gave me
Gal 6:14 in the cross of our L Jesus Christ,
Eph 4: 5 one L, one faith, one baptism;
5: 8 but now you are light in the L.
5:10 and find out what pleases the L.
5:19 make music in your heart to the L,
5:22 submit to your husbands as to the L
6: 1 obey your parents in the L,
6: 7 as if you were serving the L,
6: 8 know that the L will reward
6:10 in the L and in his mighty power.
Php 2:11 confess that Jesus Christ is L,
3: 1 my brothers, rejoice in the L!
3: 8 of knowing Christ Jesus my L,
4: 1 you should stand firm in the L,
4: 4 Rejoice in the L always.
4: 5 The L is near.
Col 1:10 you may live a life worthy of the L
2: 6 as you received Christ Jesus as L,
3:13 Forgive as the L forgave you.
3:17 do it all in the name of the L Jesus,
3:18 your husbands, as is fitting in the L.
3:20 in everything, for this pleases the L
3:23 as working for the L, not for men,
3:24 It is the L Christ you are serving.
3:24 receive an inheritance from the L
4:17 work you have received in the L."
1Th 3: 8 since you are standing firm in the L
3:12 May the L make your love increase
4: 1 and urge you in the L Jesus
4: 6 The L will punish men
4:15 who are left till the coming of the L
5: 2 day of the L will come like a thief
5:23 at the coming of our L Jesus Christ.
2Th 1: 7 when the L Jesus is revealed
1:12 of our L Jesus may be glorified
2: 1 the coming of our L Jesus Christ
2: 8 whom the L Jesus will overthrow
3: 3 L is faithful, and he will strengthen
3: 5 May the L direct your hearts
1Ti 6:15 the King of kings and L of lords,
2Ti 1: 8 ashamed to testify about our L,
2:19 "The L knows those who are his,"
4: 8 which the L, the righteous Judge,
4:17 But the L stood at my side
Heb 1:10 O L, you laid the foundations
10:30 "The L will judge his people."
12:14 holiness no one will see the L.
13: 6 L is my helper; I will not be afraid.
Jas 3: 9 With the tongue we praise our L
4:10 Humble yourselves before the L,
5:11 The L is full of compassion
1Pe 1:25 the word of the L stands forever."
2: 3 you have tasted that the L is good.
3:12 eyes of the L are on the righteous
3:15 in your hearts set apart Christ as L.
2Pe 1:11 into the eternal kingdom of our L
1:16 and coming of our L Jesus Christ,
2: 1 the sovereign L who bought
2: 9 then the L knows how
3: 9 The L is not slow in keeping his
3:18 and knowledge of our L and Savior
Jude :14 the L is coming with thousands
Rev 4: 8 holy, holy is the L God Almighty,
4:11 "You are worthy, our L and God,
11:15 has become the kingdom of our L
17:14 he is L of lords and King of kings—
19:16 KINGS AND L OF LORDS.
22: 5 for the L God will give them light.
22:20 Come, L Jesus.

LORD'S† (LORD†)
Lk 1:38 "I am the L servant," Mary
Ac 11:21 The L hand was with them,
21:14 and said, "The L will be done."
1Co 7:32 is concerned about the L affairs—
10:26 "The earth is the L, and everything
11:26 you proclaim the L death
2Co 3:18 faces all reflect the L glory,
Eph 5:17 but understand what the L will is.
2Ti 2:24 And the L servant must not quarrel
Heb 12: 5 light of the L discipline,
Jas 4:15 you ought to say, "If it is the L will,
5: 8 because the L coming is near.
1Pe 2:13 Submit yourselves for the L sake

LORDED* (LORD†)
Ne 5:15 Their assistants also l it

LORDING* (LORD†)
1Pe 5: 3 not l it over those entrusted to you,

LORD‡ (LORD'S†)
Ge 2: 4 When the L God made the earth
2: 7 the L God formed the man
2:22 Then the L God made a woman
3:21 The L God made garments of skin
3:23 So the L God banished him
4: 4 The L looked with favor on Abel
4:26 began to call on the name of the L.
6: 7 So the L said, "I will wipe mankind
7:16 Then the L shut him in.
9:26 Blessed be the L, the God of Shem!
11: 9 there the L confused the language
12: 1 L had said to Abram, "Leave your
15: 6 Abram believed the L,
15:18 On that day the L made a covenant
17: 1 the L appeared to him and said,
18: 1 The L appeared to Abraham
18:14 Is anything too hard for the L?
18:19 way of the L by doing what is right
21: 1 Now the L was gracious to Sarah
22:14 that place The L Will Provide.
24: 1 the L had blessed him in every way
26: 2 The L appeared to Isaac and said,
28:13 There above it stood the L,
31:49 "May the L keep watch
39: 2 The L was with Joseph
39:21 in the prison, the L was with him;
Ex 3: 2 the angel of the L appeared to him
4:11 Is it not I, the L? Now go;
4:31 heard that the L was concerned
6: 2 also said to Moses, "I am the L.
9:12 the L hardened Pharaoh's heart
12:27 'It is the Passover sacrifice to the L,
12:43 The L said to Moses and Aaron,
13: 9 For the L brought you out of Egypt
13:21 By day the L went ahead of them
14:13 the deliverance the L will bring
14:30 That day the L saved Israel
15: 3 The L is a warrior;
15:11 among the gods is like you, O L?
15:26 for I am the L, who heals you."
16:12 know that I am the L your God.' "
16:23 day of rest, a holy Sabbath to the L.
17:15 and called it The L is my Banner.
19: 8 will do everything the L has said."
19:20 The L descended to the top
20: 2 "I am the L your God, who
20: 5 the L your God, am a jealous God,
20: 7 for the L will not hold anyone
20:10 a Sabbath to the L your God.
20:11 in six days the L made the heavens
20:12 in the land the L your God is giving
23:25 Worship the L your God,
24: 3 "Everything the L has said we will
24:12 The L said to Moses, "Come up
24:16 and the glory of the L settled
25: 1 The L said to Moses, "Tell
28:36 HOLY TO THE L.
30:11 Then the L said to Moses,
31:13 so you may know that I am the L,
31:18 When the L finished speaking
33:11 The L would speak to Moses face
33:19 And the L said, "I will cause all my
34: 1 L said to Moses, "Chisel out two
34: 6 proclaiming, "The L, the L,
34:10 awesome is the work that I, the L,
34:29 because he had spoken with the L.
40:34 glory of the L filled the tabernacle.
40:38 So the cloud of the L was
Lev 8:36 did everything the L commanded
9:23 and the glory of the L appeared
10: 2 and they died before the L.
19: 2 'Be holy because I, the L your God,
20: 8 I am the L, who makes you holy.
20:26 to be holy to me because I, the L,
23:40 and rejoice before the L your God
Nu 6:24 Say to them: " ' "The L bless you
8: 5 L said to Moses: "Take the Levites
11: 1 hardships in the hearing of the L,
14:14 O L, have been seen face to face,
14:18 you have declared: 'The L is slow
14:21 glory of the L fills the whole earth,
21: 6 Then the L sent venomous snakes
22:31 Then the L opened Balaam's eyes,
23:12 "Must I not speak what the L puts
30: 2 When a man makes a vow to the L
32:12 followed the L wholeheartedly.'
Dt 1:21 and take possession of it as the L,
2: 7 forty years the L your God has
4:29 there you seek the L your God,
5: 6 And he said: "I am the L your God,
5: 9 the L your God, am a jealous God,
6: 4 The L our God, the L is one.
6: 5 Love the L your God
6:16 Do not test the L your God
6:25 law before the L our God,
7: 1 When the L your God brings you
7: 6 holy to the L your God.
7: 8 But it was because the L loved you
7: 9 that the L your God is God;
7:12 then the L your God will keep his
8: 5 so the L your God disciplines you.
9:10 The L gave me two stone tablets
10:12 but to fear the L your God,
10:14 To the L your God belong
10:17 For the L your God is God of gods
10:20 Fear the L your God and serve him
10:22 now the L your God has made you
11: 1 Love the L your God and keep his
11:13 to love the L your God
16: 1 the Passover of the L your God,
17:15 the king the L your God chooses.
28: 1 If you fully obey the L your God
28:15 if you do not obey the L your God
29: 1 covenant the L commanded Moses
29:29 things belong to the L our God,
30: 4 from there the L your God will
30: 6 L your God will circumcise your
30:10 if you obey the L your God
30:16 today to love the L your God,
30:20 For the L is your life, and he will
31: 6 for the L your God goes with you;
34: 5 of the L died there in Moab,
Jos 10:14 a day when the L listened to a man.
22: 5 to love the L your God, to walk
23:11 careful to love the L your God.
24:15 my household, we will serve the L
24:18 We too will serve the L,
Jdg 2:12 They forsook the L, the God
Ru 1: 8 May the L show kindness to you,
4:13 And the L enabled her to conceive,
1Sa 1:11 him to the L for all the days
1:15 I was pouring out my soul to the L.
1:28 So now I give him to the L.
2: 2 "There is no one holy like the L;
2:25 but if a man sins against the L,
2:26 in favor with the L and with men.
3: 9 L, for your servant is listening.' "
3:19 The L was with Samuel
7:12 "Thus far has the L helped us."
9:17 sight of Saul, the L said to him,
11:15 as king in the presence of the L.
12:18 all the people stood in awe of the L
12:22 his great name the L will not reject
12:24 But be sure to fear the L
13:14 the L has sought out a man
14: 6 Nothing can hinder the L
15:22 "Does the L delight
16:13 Spirit of the L came upon David
17:45 you in the name of the L Almighty,
2Sa 6:14 danced before the L
7:22 How great you are, O Sovereign L!
8: 6 L gave David victory everywhere
12: 7 This is what the L, the God
22: 2 "The L is my rock, my fortress
22:29 You are my lamp, O L;
22:31 the word of the L is flawless.
1Ki 1:30 today what I swore to you by the L,
2: 3 and observe what the L your God
3: 7 O L my God, you have made your
5: 5 for the Name of the L my God,
5:12 The L gave Solomon wisdom,
8:11 the glory of the L filled his temple.
8:23 toward heaven and said: "O L,
8:61 fully committed to the L our God,
9: 3 The L said to him: "I have heard
10: 9 Praise be to the L your God,
15:14 committed to the L all his life.
18:21 If the L is God, follow him;
18:36 "O L, God of Abraham, Isaac
18:39 "The L— he is God! The L—
21:23 also concerning Jezebel the L says:

‡This entry represents the translation of the Hebrew name for God, *Yahweh,* always indicated in the NIV by LORD. For Lord, see the concordance entries **LORD†** and **LORD'S†**.

2Ki 13:23 But the *L* was gracious to them
17:18 So the *L* was very angry with Israel
18: 5 Hezekiah trusted in the *L*,
19: 1 and went into the temple of the *L*.
20:11 *L* made the shadow go back the ten
21:12 Therefore this is what the *L*,
22: 2 right in the eyes of the *L*
22: 8 of the Law in the temple of the *L*."
23: 3 to follow the *L* and keep his
23:21 the Passover to the *L* your God,
23:25 a king like him who turned to the *L*
24: 2 The *L* sent Babylonian, Aramean,
24: 4 and the *L* was not willing to forgive
1Ch 10:13 because he was unfaithful to the *L*;
11: 3 with them at Hebron before the *L*,
11: 9 the *L* Almighty was with him.
13: 6 from there the ark of God the *L*, who
16: 8 Give thanks to the *L*, call
16:11 Look to the *L* and his strength;
16:14 He is the *L* our God;
16:23 Sing to the *L*, all the earth;
17: 1 covenant of the *L* is under a tent."
21:24 take for the *L* what is yours,
22: 5 to be built for the *L* should be
22:11 build the house of the *L* your God,
22:13 and laws that the *L* gave Moses
22:16 Now begin the work, and the *L* be
22:19 soul to seeking the *L* your God.
25: 7 and skilled in music for the *L*—
28: 9 for the *L* searches every heart
28:20 for the *L* God, my God, is with you
29: 1 not for man but for the *L* God.
29:11 O *L*, is the greatness and the power
29:18 O *L*, God of our fathers Abraham,
29:25 The *L* highly exalted Solomon
2Ch 1: 1 for the *L* his God was with him
5:13 to give praise and thanks to the *L*.
5:14 the glory of the *L* filled the temple
6:16 "Now *L*, God of Israel, keep
6:41 O *L* God, and come
6:42 O *L* God, do not reject your
7: 1 the glory of the *L* filled the temple.
7:12 the *L* appeared to him at night
7:21 'Why has the *L* done such a thing
9: 8 as king to rule for the *L* your God.
13:12 do not fight against the *L*,
14: 2 right in the eyes of the *L* his God.
15:14 to the *L* with loud acclamation,
16: 9 of the *L* range throughout the earth
17: 9 the Book of the Law of the *L*;
18:13 said, "As surely as the *L* lives,
19: 6 judging for man but for the *L*,
19: 9 wholeheartedly in the fear of the *L*.
20:15 This is what the *L* says to you:
20:20 Have faith in the *L* your God
20:21 appointed men to sing to the *L*
26: 5 As long as he sought the *L*,
26:16 He was unfaithful to the *L* his God,
29:30 to praise the *L* with the words
30: 9 for the *L* your God is gracious
31:20 and faithful before the *L* his God.
32: 8 with us is the *L* our God to help us
34:14 Law of the *L* that had been given
34:31 to follow the *L* and keep his
Ezr 3:10 foundation of the temple of the *L*,
7: 6 for the hand of the *L* his God was
7:10 observance of the Law of the *L*,
9: 5 hands spread out to the *L* my God
9: 8 the *L* our God has been gracious
9:15 O *L*, God of Israel, you are
Ne 1: 5 Then I said: "O *L*, God of heaven,
8: 1 which the *L* had commanded
9: 6 You alone are the *L*.
Job 1: 6 to present themselves before the *L*,
1:21 *L* gave and the *L* has taken away;
38: 1 the *L* answered Job out
42: 9 and the *L* accepted Job's prayer.
42:12 The *L* blessed the latter part
Ps 1: 2 But his delight is in the law of the *L*
1: 6 For the *L* watches over the way
4: 6 of your face shine upon us, O *L*.
4: 8 for you alone, O *L*,
5: 3 In the morning, O *L*,
6: 1 O *L*, do not rebuke me
8: 1 O *L*, our Lord,
9: 9 The *L* is a refuge for the oppressed,
9:19 Arise, O *L*, let not man triumph;
10:16 The *L* is King for ever and ever;
12: 6 And the words of the *L* are flawless
16: 5 *L*, you have assigned me my
16: 8 I have set the *L* always before me.
18: 1 I love you, O *L*, my strength.
18: 6 In my distress I called to the *L*;
18:30 the word of the *L* is flawless.
19: 7 The law of the *L* is perfect,
19:14 O *L*, my Rock and my Redeemer.
20: 5 May the *L* grant all your requests.
20: 7 in the name of the *L* our God.
22: 8 let the *L* rescue him.

Ps 23: 1 The *L* is my shepherd, I shall
23: 6 I will dwell in the house of the *L*
24: 3 Who may ascend the hill of the *L*?
24: 8 The *L* strong and mighty,
25:10 All the ways of the *L* are loving
27: 1 The *L* is my light and my salvation
27: 4 to gaze upon the beauty of the *L*
27: 6 I will sing and make music to the *L*.
29: 1 Ascribe to the *L*, O mighty ones,
29: 4 The voice of the *L* is powerful;
30: 4 Sing to the *L*, you saints of his;
31: 5 redeem me, O *L*, the God of truth.
32: 2 whose sin the *L* does not count
33: 1 joyfully to the *L*, you righteous;
33: 6 of the *L* were the heavens made,
33:12 is the nation whose God is the *L*,
33:18 But the eyes of the *L* are
34: 1 I will extol the *L* at all times;
34: 3 Glorify the *L* with me;
34: 4 I sought the *L*, and he answered me
34: 7 The angel of the *L* encamps
34: 8 Taste and see that the *L* is good;
34: 9 Fear the *L*, you his saints,
34:15 The eyes of the *L* are
34:18 The *L* is close to the brokenhearted
37: 4 Delight yourself in the *L*
37: 5 Commit your way to the *L*;
39: 4 "Show me, O *L*, my life's end
40: 1 I waited patiently for the *L*;
40: 5 Many, O *L* my God,
46: 8 Come and see the works of the *L*,
47: 2 How awesome is the *L* Most High,
48: 1 Great is the *L*, and most worthy
50: 1 The Mighty One, God, the *L*,
55:22 Cast your cares on the *L*
59: 8 But you, O *L*, laugh at them;
68: 4 his name is the *L*—
68:18 O *L* God, might dwell there.
68:20 from the Sovereign *L* comes escape
69:31 This will please the *L* more
72:18 Praise be to the *L* God, the God
75: 8 In the hand of the *L* is a cup
78: 4 the praiseworthy deeds of the *L*,
84: 8 my prayer, O *L* God Almighty;
84:11 For the *L* God is a sun and shield;
85: 7 Show us your unfailing love, O *L*,
86:11 Teach me your way, O *L*,
87: 2 the *L* loves the gates of Zion
89: 5 heavens praise your wonders, O *L*,
89: 8 O *L* God Almighty, who is like you
91: 2 I will say of the *L*, "He is my refuge
92: 1 It is good to praise the *L*
92: 4 by your deeds, O *L*;
92:13 planted in the house of the *L*,
93: 1 The *L* reigns, he is robed in majesty
93: 5 house for endless days, O *L*.
94: 1 O *L*, the God who avenges,
94:12 is the man you discipline, O *L*,
94:18 your love, O *L*, supported me.
95: 1 Come, let us sing for joy to the *L*;
95: 3 For the *L* is the great God,
95: 6 let us kneel before the *L* our Maker
96: 1 Sing to the *L* a new song;
96: 5 but the *L* made the heavens.
96: 8 to the *L* the glory due his name;
96: 9 Worship the *L* in the splendor
96:13 they will sing before the *L*,
97: 1 The *L* reigns, let the earth be glad;
97: 9 O *L*, are the Most High
98: 1 Sing to the *L* a new song,
98: 2 *L* has made his salvation known
98: 4 Shout for joy to the *L*, all the earth,
99: 1 The *L* reigns,
99: 2 Great is the *L* in Zion;
99: 5 Exalt the *L* our God
99: 9 Exalt the *L* our God
100: 1 Shout for joy to the *L*, all the earth.
100: 2 Worship the *L* with gladness;
100: 3 Know that the *L* is God.
100: 5 For the *L* is good and his love
101: 1 to you, O *L*, I will sing praise.
102: 12 But you, O *L*, sit enthroned forever
103: 1 Praise the *L*, O my soul;
103: 8 The *L* is compassionate
103: 19 The *L* has established his throne
104: 1 O *L* my God, you are very great;
104: 24 How many are your works, O *L*!
104: 33 I will sing to the *L* all my life;
105: 4 Look to the *L* and his strength;
105: 7 He is the *L* our God;
106: 2 proclaim the mighty acts of the *L*
107: 1 Give thanks to the *L*, for he is good
107: 8 to the *L* for his unfailing love
107: 21 to the *L* for his unfailing love
107: 43 and consider the great love of the *L*
108: 3 I will praise you, O *L*,
109: 26 Help me, O *L* my God;
110: 1 The *L* says to my Lord:
110: 4 The *L* has sworn

Ps 111: 2 Great are the works of the *L*;
111: 4 *L* is gracious and compassionate.
111: 10 The fear of the *L* is the beginning
112: 1 Blessed is the man who fears the *L*,
113: 1 Praise, O servants of the *L*,
113: 2 Let the name of the *L* be praised,
113: 4 *L* is exalted over all the nations,
113: 5 Who is like the *L* our God,
115: 1 Not to us, O *L*, not to us
115: 18 it is we who extol the *L*,
116: 12 How can I repay the *L*
116: 15 Precious in the sight of the *L*
117: 1 Praise the *L*, all you nations;
118: 1 Give thanks to the *L*, for he is good
118: 5 In my anguish I cried to the *L*,
118: 8 It is better to take refuge in the *L*
118: 18 The *L* has chastened me severely,
118: 23 the *L* has done this,
118: 24 This is the day the *L* has made;
118: 26 comes in the name of the *L*.
119: 1 to the law of the *L*.
119: 64 with your love, O *L*;
119: 89 Your word, O *L*, is eternal;
119:126 It is time for you to act, O *L*;
119:159 O *L*, according to your love.
120: 1 I call on the *L* in my distress,
121: 2 My help comes from the *L*,
121: 5 The *L* watches over you—
121: 8 the *L* will watch over your coming
122: 1 "Let us go to the house of the *L*."
123: 2 so our eyes look to the *L* our God,
124: 1 If the *L* had not been on our side—
124: 8 Our help is in the name of the *L*,
125: 2 so the *L* surrounds his people
126: 3 The *L* has done great things for us,
126: 4 Restore our fortunes, O *L*,
127: 1 Unless the *L* builds the house,
127: 3 Sons are a heritage from the *L*,
128: 1 Blessed are all who fear the *L*,
130: 1 O *L*; O Lord, hear my voice.
130: 3 If you, O *L*, kept a record of sins,
130: 5 I wait for the *L*, my soul waits,
131: 3 O Israel, put your hope in the *L*
132: 1 O *L*, remember David
132: 13 For the *L* has chosen Zion,
133: 3 For there the *L* bestows his
134: 3 May the *L*, the Maker of heaven
135: 4 For the *L* has chosen Jacob
135: 6 The *L* does whatever pleases him,
136: 1 Give thanks to the *L*, for he is good
137: 4 How can we sing the songs of the *L*
138: 1 I will praise you, O *L*,
138: 8 The *L* will fulfill his purpose
139: 1 O *L*, you have searched me
140: 1 Rescue me, O *L*, from evil men;
141: 1 O *L*, I call to you; come quickly
141: 3 Set a guard over my mouth, O *L*;
142: 5 I cry to you, O *L*;
143: 9 Rescue me from my enemies, O *L*,
144: 3 O *L*, what is man that you care
145: 3 Great is the *L* and most worthy
145: 8 *L* is gracious and compassionate,
145: 9 The *L* is good to all;
145: 17 The *L* is righteous in all his ways
145: 18 The *L* is near to all who call on him
146: 5 whose hope is in the *L* his God,
146: 7 The *L* sets prisoners free,
147: 2 The *L* builds up Jerusalem;
147: 7 Sing to the *L* with thanksgiving;
147: 11 *L* delights in those who fear him,
147: 12 Extol the *L*, O Jerusalem;
148: 1 Praise the *L* from the heavens,
148: 7 Praise the *L* from the earth,
149: 4 For the *L* takes delight
150: 1 Praise the *L*.
150: 6 that has breath praise the *L*.
Pr 1: 7 The fear of the *L* is the beginning
1:29 and did not choose to fear the *L*,
2: 5 will understand the fear of the *L*
2: 6 For the *L* gives wisdom,
3: 5 Trust in the *L* with all your heart
3: 7 fear the *L* and shun evil.
3: 9 Honor the *L* with your wealth,
3:12 the *L* disciplines those he loves,
3:19 By wisdom the *L* laid the earth's
5:21 are in full view of the *L*,
6:16 There are six things the *L* hates,
8:13 To fear the *L* is to hate evil;
9:10 "The fear of the *L* is the beginning
10:27 The fear of the *L* adds length to life
11: 1 The *L* abhors dishonest scales,
12:22 The *L* detests lying lips,
14: 2 whose walk is upright fears the *L*,
14:26 He who fears the *L* has a secure
14:27 The fear of the *L* is a fountain
15: 3 The eyes of the *L* are everywhere,
15:16 Better a little with the fear of the *L*
15:33 of the *L* teaches a man wisdom,
16: 2 but motives are weighed by the *L*.

Pr 16: 3 Commit to the *L* whatever you do,
16: 4 The *L* works out everything
16: 5 The *L* detests all the proud of heart
16: 9 but the *L* determines his steps.
16:33 but its every decision is from the *L*.
18:10 The name of the *L* is a strong tower
18:22 and receives favor from the *L*.
19:14 but a prudent wife is from the *L*.
19:17 to the poor lends to the *L*,
19:23 The fear of the *L* leads to life:
20:10 the *L* detests them both.
21: 2 but the *L* weighs the heart.
21: 3 to the *L* than sacrifice.
21:30 that can succeed against the *L*.
21:31 but victory rests with the *L*.
22: 2 The *L* is the Maker of them all.
22:23 for the *L* will take up their case
23:17 for the fear of the *L*.
24:18 or the *L* will see and disapprove
24:21 Fear the *L* and the king, my son,
25:22 and the *L* will reward you.
28:14 is the man who always fears the *L*,
29:26 from the *L* that man gets justice.
30: 7 "Two things I ask of you, O *L*;
31:30 a woman who fears the *L* is
Isa 2: 3 up to the mountain of the *L*,
2:10 the ground from dread of the *L*
3:17 the *L* will make their scalps bald."
4: 2 of the *L* will be beautiful
5:16 the *L* Almighty will be exalted
6: 3 holy, holy is the *L* Almighty;
9: 7 The zeal of the *L* Almighty
11: 2 The Spirit of the *L* will rest on him
11: 9 full of the knowledge of the *L*
12: 2 The *L*, the *L*, is my strength
18: 7 of the Name of the *L* Almighty.
24: 1 the *L* is going to lay waste the earth
25: 1 O *L*, you are my God;
25: 6 this mountain the *L* Almighty will
25: 8 The Sovereign *L* will wipe away
26: 4 Trust in the *L* forever,
26: 8 *L*, walking in the way of your laws,
26:13 O *L*, our God, other lords
26:21 the *L* is coming out of his dwelling
27: 1 the *L* will punish with his sword,
27:12 In that day the *L* will thresh
28: 5 In that day the *L* Almighty
29: 6 the *L* Almighty will come
29:15 to hide their plans from the *L*,
30:18 For the *L* is a God of justice.
30:26 when the *L* binds up the bruises
30:27 the Name of the *L* comes from afar
30:30 The *L* will cause men
33: 2 O *L*, be gracious to us;
33: 6 the fear of the *L* is the key
33:22 For the *L* is our judge,
34: 2 The *L* is angry with all nations;
35: 2 they will see the glory of the *L*,
35:10 the ransomed of the *L* will return.
38: 7 to you that the *L* will do what he
40: 3 the way for the *L*;
40: 5 the glory of the *L* will be revealed,
40: 7 the breath of the *L* blows on them.
40:10 the Sovereign *L* comes with power,
40:14 Whom did the *L* consult
40:28 The *L* is the everlasting God,
40:31 but those who hope in the *L*
41:14 will help you," declares the *L*,
41:20 that the hand of the *L* has done this
42: 6 the *L*, have called you
42: 8 "I am the *L*; that is my name!
42:13 The *L* will march out like a mighty
42:21 It pleased the *L*
43: 3 For I am the *L*, your God,
43:11 I, even I, am the *L*,
44: 6 "This is what the *L* says—
44:24 I am the *L*,
45: 5 I am the *L*, and there is no other;
45: 7 I, the *L*, do all these things.
45:21 Was it not I, the *L*?
48:17 "I am the *L* your God,
50: 4 Sovereign *L* has given me
50:10 Who among you fears the *L*
51: 1 and who seek the *L*:
51:11 The ransomed of the *L* will return.
51:15 the *L* Almighty is his name.
53: 1 the arm of the *L* been revealed?
53: 6 and the *L* has laid on him
53:10 and the will of the *L* will prosper
54: 5 the *L* Almighty is his name—
55: 6 Seek the *L* while he may be found;
55: 7 to the *L*, and he will have mercy
56: 6 who bind themselves to the *L*
58: 8 of the *L* will be your rear guard.
58:11 The *L* will guide you always;
59: 1 the arm of the *L* is not too short
60: 1 the glory of the *L* rises upon you.
60:16 Then you will know that I, the *L*,
60:20 the *L* will be your everlasting light,
Isa 61: 1 Spirit of the Sovereign *L* is on me,
61: 3 a planting of the *L*
61:10 I delight greatly in the *L*;
61:11 so the Sovereign *L* will make
62: 4 for the *L* will take delight in you,
63: 7 I will tell of the kindnesses of the *L*,
64: 8 Yet, O *L*, you are our Father.
66:15 See, the *L* is coming with fire,
Jer 1: 9 Then the *L* reached out his hand
2:19 when you forsake the *L* your God
3:25 sinned against the *L* our God,
4: 4 Circumcise yourselves to the *L*,
8: 7 the requirements of the *L*.
9:24 I am the *L*, who exercises kindness,
10: 6 No one is like you, O *L*;
10:10 But the *L* is the true God;
12: 1 You are always righteous, O *L*,
14: 7 O *L*, do something for the sake
14:20 O *L*, we acknowledge our
16:15 will say, 'As surely as the *L* lives,
16:19 O *L*, my strength and my fortress,
17: 7 is the man who trusts in the *L*,
17:10 "I the *L* search the heart
20:11 *L* is with me like a mighty warrior;
23: 6 The *L* Our Righteousness.
24: 7 heart to know me, that I am the *L*.
28: 9 as one truly sent by the *L* only
31:11 For the *L* will ransom Jacob
31:22 The *L* will create a new thing
31:34 his brother, saying, 'Know the *L*,'
32:27 I am the *L*, the God of all mankind.
33:16 The *L* Our Righteousness.'
36: 6 the words of the *L* that you wrote
40: 3 now the *L* has brought it about;
42: 3 Pray that the *L* your God will tell
42: 4 I will tell you everything the *L* says
42: 6 we will obey the *L* our God,
50: 4 go in tears to seek the *L* their God.
51:10 " 'The *L* has vindicated us;
51:56 For the *L* is a God of retribution;
La 3:24 to myself, "The *L* is my portion;
3:25 *L* is good to those whose hope is
3:40 and let us return to the *L*.
Eze 1: 3 the word of the *L* came
1:28 of the likeness of the glory of the *L*.
4:14 Sovereign *L*! I have never defiled
10: 4 Then the glory of the *L* rose
15: 7 you will know that I am the *L*.
30: 3 the day of the *L* is near—
36:23 nations will know that I am the *L*,
37: 4 'Dry bones, hear the word of the *L*!
43: 4 glory of the *L* entered the temple
44: 4 LORD filling the temple of the *L*,
Da 9: 2 to the word of the *L* given
Hos 1: 7 horsemen, but by the *L* their God."
2:20 and you will acknowledge the *L*.
3: 1 as the *L* loves the Israelites,
3: 5 They will come trembling to the *L*
6: 1 "Come, let us return to the *L*.
6: 3 Let us acknowledge the *L*;
10:12 for it is time to seek the *L*,
12: 5 the *L* is his name of renown!
14: 1 O Israel, to the *L* your God.
Joel 1: 1 The word of the *L* that came
1:15 For the day of the *L* is near;
2: 1 for the day of the *L* is coming.
2:11 The day of the *L* is great;
2:13 Return to the *L* your God,
2:23 rejoice in the *L* your God,
2:31 the great and dreadful day of the *L*.
2:32 on the name of the *L* will be saved;
3:14 For the day of the *L* is near
3:16 the *L* will be a refuge for his people,
Am 4:13 the *L* God Almighty is his name.
5: 6 Seek the *L* and live,
5:15 Perhaps the *L* God Almighty will
5:18 long for the day of the *L*?
7:15 *L* took me from tending the flock
8:12 searching for the word of the *L*,
9: 5 The Lord, the *L* Almighty,
Ob :15 "The day of the *L* is near
Jnh 1: 3 But Jonah ran away from the *L*
1: 4 the *L* sent a great wind on the sea,
1:17 But the *L* provided a great fish
2: 9 Salvation comes from the *L*."
4: 2 He prayed to the *L*, "O *L*,
4: 6 Then the *L* God provided a vine
Mic 1: 1 The word of the *L* that came to Micah
4: 2 up to the mountain of the *L*,
5: 4 flock in the strength of the *L*,
6: 2 For the *L* has a case
6: 8 And what does the *L* require of you
7: 7 as for me, I watch in hope for the *L*,
Na 1: 2 The *L* takes vengeance on his foes
1: 3 The *L* is slow to anger
Hab 2:14 knowledge of the glory of the *L*,
2:20 But the *L* is in his holy temple;
3: 2 I stand in awe of your deeds, O *L*.
Zep 1: 1 The word of the *L* that came
Zep 1: 7 for the day of the *L* is near.
3:17 The *L* your God is with you,
Hag 1: 1 the word of the *L* came
1: 8 and be honored," says the *L*.
2:23 that day,' declares the *L* Almighty,
Zec 1: 1 the word of the *L* came
1:17 and the *L* will again comfort Zion
3: 1 standing before the angel of the *L*,
4: 6 by my Spirit,' says the *L* Almighty.
6:12 and build the temple of the *L*.
8:21 the *L* and seek the *L* Almighty.
9:16 The *L* their God will save them
14: 5 Then the *L* my God will come,
14: 9 The *L* will be king
14:16 the *L* Almighty, and to celebrate
Mal 1: 1 The word of the *L* to Israel
3: 6 "I the *L* do not change.
4: 5 and dreadful day of the *L* comes.

LORD'S‡ (LORD‡)

Ex 4:14 the *L* anger burned against Moses
12:11 Eat it in haste; it is the *L* Passover.
34:34 he entered the *L* presence
Lev 23: 4 " 'These are the *L* appointed feasts,
Nu 9:23 At the *L* command they encamped
14:41 you disobeying the *L* command?
32:13 The *L* anger burned against Israel
Dt 6:18 is right and good in the *L* sight,
10:13 and to observe the *L* commands
32: 9 For the *L* portion is his people,
Jos 21:45 Not one of all the *L* good promises
1Sa 24:10 because he is the *L* anointed.'
1Ki 10: 9 Because of the *L* eternal love
Ps 24: 1 The earth is the *L*, and everything
32:10 but the *L* unfailing love
89: 1 of the *L* great love forever;
103: 17 *L* love is with those who fear him,
118: 15 "The *L* right hand has done mighty
Pr 3:11 do not despise the *L* discipline
19:21 but it is the *L* purpose that prevails.
Isa 24:14 west they acclaim the *L* majesty.
30: 9 to listen to the *L* instruction.
49: 4 Yet what is due me is in the *L* hand
53:10 Yet it was the *L* will to crush him
55:13 This will be for the *L* renown,
61: 2 to proclaim the year of the *L* favor
62: 3 of splendor in the *L* hand,
Jer 25:17 So I took the cup from the *L* hand
48:10 lax in doing the *L* work!
51: 7 was a gold cup in the *L* hand;
La 3:22 of the *L* great love we are not
Eze 7:19 them in the day of the *L* wrath.
Joel 3:18 will flow out of the *L* house
Ob :21 And the kingdom will be the *L*.
Mic 4: 1 of the *L* temple will be established
6: 2 O mountains, the *L* accusation;
Hab 2:16 from the *L* right hand is coming
Zep 2: 3 sheltered on the day of the *L* anger.

LOSE (LOSES LOSS LOST)

Dt 1:28 Our brothers have made us *l* heart.
1Sa 17:32 "Let no one *l* heart on account
Isa 7: 4 Do not *l* heart because of these two
Mt 10:39 Whoever finds his life will *l* it,
Lk 9:25 and yet *l* or forfeit his very self?
Jn 6:39 that I shall *l* none of all that he has
2Co 4: 1 this ministry, we do not *l* heart.
4:16 Therefore we do not *l* heart.
Heb 12: 3 will not grow weary and *l* heart.
12: 5 do not *l* heart when he rebukes you
2Jn : 8 that you do not *l* what you have

LOSES (LOSE)

Mt 5:13 But if the salt *l* its saltiness,
Lk 15: 4 you has a hundred sheep and *l* one
15: 8 has ten silver coins and *l* one.

LOSS (LOSE)

Ro 11:12 and their *l* means riches
1Co 3:15 he will suffer *l*; he himself will be
Php 3: 8 I consider everything a *l* compared

LOST (LOSE)

Ps 73: 2 I had nearly *l* my foothold.
Jer 50: 6 "My people have been *l* sheep;
Eze 34: 4 the strays or searched for the *l*.
34:16 for the *l* and bring back the strays.
Mt 18:14 any of these little ones should be *l*.
Lk 15: 4 go after the *l* sheep until he finds it?
15: 6 with me; I have found my *l* sheep.'
15: 9 with me; I have found my *l* coin.'
15:24 is alive again; he was *l* and is found
19:10 to seek and to save what was *l*."
Php 3: 8 for whose sake I have *l* all things.

LOT (LOTS)

Nephew of Abraham (Ge 11:27; 12:5). Chose to live in Sodom (Ge 13). Rescued from four kings (Ge 14). Rescued from Sodom (Ge 19:1-29; 2Pe 2:7). Fathered Moab and Ammon by his daughters (Ge 19:30-38).

Est 3: 7 the *l*) in the presence of Haman
9:24 the *l*) for their ruin and destruction.
Pr 16:33 The *l* is cast into the lap,
18:18 Casting the *l* settles disputes
Ecc 3:22 his work, because that is his *l*.
Ac 1:26 Then they cast lots, and the *l* fell

LOTS (LOT)

Jos 18:10 Joshua then cast *l* for them
Ps 22:18 and cast *l* for my clothing.
Joel 3: 3 They cast *l* for my people
Ob :11 and cast *l* for Jerusalem,
Mt 27:35 divided up his clothes by casting *l*.
Ac 1:26 Then they cast *l*, and the lot fell

LOVE* (BELOVED LOVED LOVELY LOVER LOVER'S LOVERS LOVES LOVING LOVING-KINDNESS)

Ge 20:13 'This is how you can show your *l*
22: 2 your only son, Isaac, whom you *l*,
29:18 Jacob was in *l* with Rachel and said
29:20 days to him because of his *l* for her.
29:32 Surely my husband will *l* me now."
Ex 15:13 "In your unfailing *l* you will lead
20: 6 showing *l* to a thousand generations
20: 6 of those who *l* me
21: 5 'I *l* my master and my wife
34: 6 abounding in *l* and faithfulness,
34: 7 maintaining *l* to thousands,
Lev 19:18 but *l* your neighbor as yourself.
19:34 *L* him as yourself,
Nu 14:18 abounding in *l* and forgiving sin
14:19 In accordance with your great *l*,
Dt 5:10 showing *l* to a thousand generations
5:10 of those who *l* me
6: 5 *L* the LORD your God
7: 9 generations of those who *l* him
7: 9 keeping his covenant of *l*
7:12 God will keep his covenant of *l*
7:13 He will *l* you and bless you
10:12 to walk in all his ways, to *l* him,
10:19 you are to *l* those who are aliens,
11: 1 *L* the LORD your God
11:13 to *l* the LORD your God
11:22 to *l* the LORD your God,
13: 3 you *l* him with all your heart
13: 6 wife you *l*, or your closest friend
19: 9 to *l* the LORD your God
21:15 the son of the wife he does not *l*,
21:16 the son of the wife he does not *l*.
30: 6 so that you may *l* him
30:16 today to *l* the LORD your God,
30:20 and that you may *l* the LORD your
33: 3 Surely it is you who *l* the people;
Jos 22: 5 to *l* the LORD your God, to walk
23:11 careful to *l* the LORD your God.
Jdg 5:31 may they who *l* you be like the sun
14:16 You hate me! You don't really *l* me
16: 4 he fell in *l* with a woman
16:15 "How can you say, 'I *l* you,'
1Sa 18:20 Saul's daughter Michal was in *l*
20:17 had David reaffirm his oath out of *l*
2Sa 1:26 Your *l* for me was wonderful,
7:15 But my *l* will never be taken away
13: 1 son of David fell in *l* with Tamar,
13: 4 said to him, "I'm in *l* with Tamar,
16:17 "Is this the *l* you show your friend?
19: 6 You *l* those who hate you
19: 6 hate you and hate those who *l* you.
1Ki 3: 3 Solomon showed his *l*
8:23 you who keep your covenant of *l*
10: 9 of the LORD's eternal *l* for Israel,
11: 2 Solomon held fast to them in *l*.
1Ch 16:34 his *l* endures forever.
16:41 "for his *l* endures forever."
17:13 I will never take my *l* away
2Ch 5:13 his *l* endures forever."
6:14 you who keep your covenant of *l*
6:42 Remember the great *l* promised
7: 3 his *l* endures forever."
7: 6 saying, "His *l* endures forever."
9: 8 Because of the *l* of your God
19: 2 and *l* those who hate the LORD?
20:21 for his *l* endures forever."
Ezr 3:11 his *l* to Israel endures forever."
Ne 1: 5 covenant of *l* with those who *l* him
9:17 slow to anger and abounding in *l*.
9:32 who keeps his covenant of *l*,
13:22 to me according to your great *l*.
Job 15:34 of those who *l* bribes.
19:19 those I *l* have turned against me.
37:13 or to water his earth and show his *l*.
Ps 4: 2 How long will you *l* delusions
5:11 that those who *l* your name may
6: 4 save me because of your unfailing *l*.
11: 5 wicked and those who *l* violence
13: 5 But I trust in your unfailing *l*;
17: 7 Show the wonder of your great *l*,
Ps 18: 1 I *l* you, O LORD, my strength.
21: 7 through the unfailing *l*
23: 6 Surely goodness and *l* will follow
25: 6 O LORD, your great mercy and *l*,
25: 7 according to your *l* remember me,
26: 3 for your *l* is ever before me,
26: 8 I *l* the house where you live,
31: 7 I will be glad and rejoice in your *l*,
31:16 save me in your unfailing *l*.
31:21 for he showed his wonderful *l*
31:23 *L* the LORD, all his saints!
32:10 but the LORD's unfailing *l*
33: 5 the earth is full of his unfailing *l*.
33:18 whose hope is in his unfailing *l*,
33:22 May your unfailing *l* rest upon us,
36: 5 Your *l*, O LORD, reaches
36: 7 How priceless is your unfailing *l*!
36:10 Continue your *l* to those who know
40:10 I do not conceal your *l*
40:11 may your *l* and your truth always
40:16 may those who *l* your salvation
42: 8 By day the LORD directs his *l*,
44:26 of your unfailing *l*.
45: 7 You *l* righteousness and hate
48: 9 we meditate on your unfailing *l*.
51: 1 according to your unfailing *l*;
52: 3 You *l* evil rather than good,
52: 4 You *l* every harmful word,
52: 8 I trust in God's unfailing *l*
57: 3 God sends his *l* and his faithfulness
57:10 For great is your *l*, reaching
59:16 in the morning I will sing of your *l*;
60: 5 that those you *l* may be delivered.
61: 7 appoint your *l* and faithfulness
63: 3 Because your *l* is better than life,
66:20 or withheld his *l* from me!
69:13 in your great *l*, O God,
69:16 out of the goodness of your *l*;
69:36 and those who *l* his name will dwell
70: 4 may those who *l* your salvation
77: 8 Has his unfailing *l* vanished forever
85: 7 Show us your unfailing *l*, O LORD
85:10 *L* and faithfulness meet together;
86: 5 abounding in *l* to all who call
86:13 For great is your *l* toward me;
86:15 abounding in *l* and faithfulness.
88:11 Is your *l* declared in the grave,
89: 1 of the LORD's great *l* forever;
89: 2 declare that your *l* stands firm
89:14 *l* and faithfulness go before you.
89:24 My faithful *l* will be with him,
89:28 I will maintain my *l* to him forever,
89:33 but I will not take my *l* from him,
89:49 where is your former great *l*,
90:14 with your unfailing *l*,
92: 2 to proclaim your *l* in the morning
94:18 your *l*, O LORD, supported me.
97:10 Let those who *l* the LORD hate
98: 3 He has remembered his *l*
100: 5 is good and his *l* endures forever;
101: 1 I will sing of your *l* and justice;
103: 4 crowns you with *l* and compassion.
103: 8 slow to anger, abounding in *l*.
103: 11 so great is his *l* for those who fear
103: 17 LORD's *l* is with those who fear
106: 1 his *l* endures forever.
106: 45 and out of his great *l* he relented.
107: 1 his *l* endures forever.
107: 8 to the LORD for his unfailing *l*
107: 15 to the LORD for his unfailing *l*
107: 21 to the LORD for his unfailing *l*
107: 31 to the LORD for his unfailing *l*
107: 43 consider the great *l* of the LORD.
108: 4 For great is your *l*, higher
108: 6 that those you *l* may be delivered.
109: 21 out of the goodness of your *l*,
109: 26 save me in accordance with your *l*.
115: 1 because of your *l* and faithfulness.
116: 1 I *l* the LORD, for he heard my
117: 2 For great is his *l* toward us,
118: 1 his *l* endures forever.
118: 2 "His *l* endures forever."
118: 3 "His *l* endures forever."
118: 4 "His *l* endures forever."
118: 29 his *l* endures forever.
119: 41 May your unfailing *l* come to me,
119: 47 because I *l* them.
119: 48 to your commands, which I *l*,
119: 64 The earth is filled with your *l*,
119: 76 May your unfailing *l* be my
119: 88 my life according to your *l*,
119: 97 Oh, how I *l* your law!
119:113 but I *l* your law.
119:119 therefore I *l* your statutes.
119:124 your servant according to your *l*
119:127 Because I *l* your commands
119:132 to those who *l* your name.
119:149 in accordance with your *l*;
119:159 O LORD, according to your *l*.
Ps 119:159 See how I *l* your precepts;
119:163 but I *l* your law.
119:165 peace have they who *l* your law,
119:167 for I *l* them greatly.
122: 6 "May those who *l* you be secure.
130: 7 for with the LORD is unfailing *l*
136: 1 -26 *His l endures forever.*
138: 2 for your *l* and your faithfulness,
138: 8 your *l*, O LORD, endures forever
143: 8 of your unfailing *l*,
143: 12 In your unfailing *l*, silence my
145: 8 slow to anger and rich in *l*.
145: 20 over all who *l* him,
147: 11 who put their hope in his unfailing *l*
Pr 1:22 you simple ones *l* your simple
3: 3 Let *l* and faithfulness never leave
4: 6 *l* her, and she will watch over you.
5:19 you ever be captivated by her *l*.
7:18 let's drink deep of *l* till morning;
7:18 let's enjoy ourselves with *l*!
8:17 I *l* those who *l* me,
8:21 wealth on those who *l* me
8:36 all who hate me *l* death."
9: 8 rebuke a wise man and he will *l* you
10:12 but *l* covers over all wrongs.
14:22 those who plan what is good find *l*
15:17 of vegetables where there is *l*
16: 6 Through *l* and faithfulness sin is
17: 9 over an offense promotes *l*,
18:21 and those who *l* it will eat its fruit.
19:22 What a man desires is unfailing *l*;
20: 6 claims to have unfailing *l*,
20:13 Do not *l* sleep or you will grow
20:28 *L* and faithfulness keep a king safe;
20:28 through *l* his throne is made secure
21:21 who pursues righteousness and *l*
27: 5 rebuke than hidden *l*.
Ecc 3: 8 a time to *l* and a time to hate,
9: 1 but no man knows whether *l*
9: 6 Their *l*, their hate
9: 9 life with your wife, whom you *l*,
SS 1: 2 for your *l* is more delightful
1: 3 No wonder the maidens *l* you!
1: 4 we will praise your *l* more
1: 7 you whom I *l*, where you graze
2: 4 and his banner over me is *l*.
2: 5 for I am faint with *l*.
2: 7 Do not arouse or awaken *l*
3: 5 Do not arouse or awaken *l*
4:10 How delightful is your *l*, my sister,
4:10 How much more pleasing is your *l*
5: 8 Tell him I am faint with *l*.
7: 6 O *l*, with your delights!
7:12 there I will give you my *l*.
8: 4 Do not arouse or awaken *l*
8: 6 for *l* is as strong as death,
8: 7 Many waters cannot quench *l*;
8: 7 all the wealth of his house for *l*,
Isa 1:23 they all *l* bribes
5: 1 I will sing for the one I *l*
16: 5 In *l* a throne will be established;
38:17 In your *l* you kept me
43: 4 and because I *l* you,
54:10 yet my unfailing *l* for you will not
55: 3 my faithful *l* promised to David.
56: 6 to *l* the name of the LORD,
56:10 they *l* to sleep.
57: 8 a pact with those whose beds you *l*,
61: 8 "For I, the LORD, *l* justice;
63: 9 In his *l* and mercy he redeemed
66:10 all you who *l* her;
Jer 2:25 I *l* foreign gods,
2:33 How skilled you are at pursuing *l*!
5:31 and my people *l* it this way.
12: 7 I will give the one I *l*
14:10 "They greatly *l* to wander;
16: 5 my *l* and my pity from this people
31: 3 you with an everlasting *l*;
32:18 You show *l* to thousands
33:11 his *l* endures forever."
La 3:22 of the LORD's great *l* we are not
3:32 so great is his unfailing *l*.
Eze 16: 8 saw that you were old enough for *l*,
23:17 of *l*, and in their lust they defiled
33:32 more than one who sings *l* songs
Da 9: 4 covenant of *l* with all who *l* him
Hos 1: 6 for I will no longer show *l*
1: 7 Yet I will show *l* to the house
2: 4 I will not show my *l* to her children
2:19 in *l* and compassion.
2:23 I will show my *l* to the one I called
3: 1 Go, show your *l* to your wife again,
3: 1 and *l* the sacred raisin cakes."
3: 1 *L* her as the LORD loves
4: 1 "There is no faithfulness, no *l*,
4:18 their rulers dearly *l* shameful ways.
6: 4 Your *l* is like the morning mist,
9: 1 you *l* the wages of a prostitute
9:15 I will no longer *l* them;

Hos 10:12 reap the fruit of unfailing *l,*
11: 4 with ties of *l;*
12: 6 maintain *l* and justice,
14: 4 and *l* them freely,
Joel 2:13 slow to anger and abounding in *l,*
Am 4: 5 for this is what you *l* to do,"
5:15 Hate evil, *l* good;
Jnh 4: 2 slow to anger and abounding in *l,*
Mic 3: 2 you who hate good and *l* evil;
6: 8 To act justly and to *l* mercy
Zep 3:17 he will quiet you with his *l,*
Zec 8:17 and do not *l* to swear falsely.
8:19 Therefore *l* truth and peace."
Mt 3:17 "This is my Son, whom I *l;*
5:43 '*L* your neighbor and hate your
5:44 *L* your enemies and pray
5:46 you *l* those who *l* you, what reward
6: 5 for they *l* to pray standing
6:24 he will hate the one and *l* the other,
12:18 the one I *l,* in whom I delight;
17: 5 "This is my Son, whom I *l;*
19:19 and '*l* your neighbor as yourself.' "
22:37 " '*L* the Lord your God
22:39 '*L* your neighbor as yourself.'
23: 6 they *l* the place of honor
23: 7 they *l* to be greeted
24:12 the *l* of most will grow cold,
Mk 1:11 "You are my Son, whom I *l;*
9: 7 "This is my Son, whom I *l.*
12:30 *L* the Lord your God
12:31 '*L* your neighbor as yourself.'
12:33 To *l* him with all your heart,
12:33 and to *l* your neighbor
Lk 3:22 "You are my Son, whom I *l;*
6:27 you who hear me: *L* your enemies,
6:32 Even 'sinners' *l* those who *l* them.
6:32 you *l* those who *l* you, what credit
6:35 *l* your enemies, do good to them,
7:42 which of them will *l* him more?"
10:27 and, '*L* your neighbor as yourself
10:27 " '*L* the Lord your God
11:42 you neglect justice and the *l* of God
11:43 you *l* the most important seats
16:13 he will hate the one and *l* the other,
20:13 whom I *l;* perhaps they will respect
20:46 *l* to be greeted in the marketplaces
Jn 5:42 I know that you do not have the *l*
8:42 were your Father, you would *l* me,
11: 3 "Lord, the one you *l* is sick."
13: 1 them the full extent of his *l.*
13:34 I give you: *L* one another.
13:34 so you must *l* one another.
13:35 disciples, if you *l* one another."
14:15 "If you *l* me, you will obey what I
14:21 I too will *l* him and show myself
14:23 My Father will *l* him, and we will
14:24 He who does not *l* me will not obey
14:31 world must learn that I *l* the Father
15: 9 Now remain in my *l.*
15:10 commands and remain in his *l.*
15:10 you will remain in my *l,*
15:12 *L* each other as I have loved you.
15:13 Greater *l* has no one than this,
15:17 This is my command: *L* each other.
15:19 to the world, it would *l* you
17:26 known in order that the *l* you have
21:15 do you truly *l* me more than these
21:15 he said, "you know that I *l* you."
21:16 Yes, Lord, you know that I *l* you."
21:16 do you truly *l* me?" He answered,
21:17 all things; you know that I *l* you."
21:17 "Do you *l* me?" He said, "Lord,
21:17 "Simon son of John, do you *l* me?"
Ro 5: 5 because God has poured out his *l*
5: 8 God demonstrates his own *l* for us
8:28 for the good of those who *l* him,
8:35 us from the *l* of Christ?
8:39 us from the *l* of God that is
12: 9 *L* must be sincere.
12:10 to one another in brotherly *l.*
13: 8 continuing debt to *l* one another,
13: 9 "*L* your neighbor as yourself."
13:10 Therefore *l* is the fulfillment
13:10 *L* does no harm to its neighbor.
14:15 you are no longer acting in *l.*
15:30 and by the *l* of the Spirit,
16: 8 Greet Ampliatus, whom I *l*
1Co 2: 9 prepared for those who *l* him"—
4:17 my son whom I *l,* who is faithful
4:21 or in *l* and with a gentle spirit?
8: 1 Knowledge puffs up, but *l* builds up
13: 1 have not *l,* I am only a resounding
13: 2 but have not *l,* I am nothing.
13: 3 but have not *l,* I gain nothing.
13: 4 Love is patient, *l* is kind.
13: 4 *L* is patient, love is kind.
13: 6 *L* does not delight in evil
13: 8 *L* never fails.
13:13 But the greatest of these is *l.*
1Co 13:13 three remain: faith, hope and *l.*
14: 1 way of *l* and eagerly desire spiritual
16:14 Do everything in *l.*
16:22 If anyone does not *l* the Lord—
16:24 My *l* to all of you in Christ Jesus.
2Co 2: 4 to let you know the depth of my *l*
2: 8 therefore, to reaffirm your *l* for him
5:14 For Christ's *l* compels us,
6: 6 in the Holy Spirit and in sincere *l;*
8: 7 complete earnestness and in your *l*
8: 8 sincerity of your *l* by comparing it
8:24 show these men the proof of your *l*
11:11 Why? Because I do not *l* you?
12:15 If I *l* you more, will you *l* me less?
13:11 And the God of *l* and peace will be
13:14 of the Lord Jesus Christ, and the *l*
Gal 5: 6 is faith expressing itself through *l.*
5:13 rather, serve one another in *l.*
5:14 "*L* your neighbor as yourself."
5:22 But the fruit of the Spirit is *l,* joy,
Eph 1: 4 In *l* he predestined us
1:15 and your *l* for all the saints,
2: 4 But because of his great *l* for us,
3:17 being rooted and established in *l,*
3:18 and high and deep is the *l* of Christ,
3:19 and to know this *l* that surpasses
4: 2 bearing with one another in *l.*
4:15 Instead, speaking the truth in *l,*
4:16 grows and builds itself up in *l,*
5: 2 loved children and live a life of *l,*
5:25 *l* your wives, just as Christ loved
5:28 husbands ought to *l* their wives
5:33 each one of you also must *l* his wife
6:23 *l* with faith from God the Father
6:24 Christ with an undying *l.*
6:24 to all who *l* our Lord Jesus Christ
Php 1: 9 that your *l* may abound more
1:16 so in *l,* knowing that I am put here
2: 1 from his *l,* if any fellowship
2: 2 having the same *l,* being one
4: 1 you whom I *l* and long for,
Col 1: 4 of the *l* you have for all the saints—
1: 5 *l* that spring from the hope that is
1: 8 also told us of your *l* in the Spirit.
2: 2 in heart and united in *l,*
3:14 And over all these virtues put on *l,*
3:19 *l* your wives and do not be harsh
1Th 1: 3 your labor prompted by *l,*
3: 6 good news about your faith and *l.*
3:12 May the Lord make your *l* increase
4: 9 about brotherly *l* we do not need
4: 9 taught by God to *l* each other.
4:10 you do *l* all the brothers
5: 8 on faith and *l* as a breastplate,
5:13 them in the highest regard in *l*
2Th 1: 3 and the *l* every one of you has
2:10 because they refused to *l* the truth
3: 5 direct your hearts into God's *l*
1Ti 1: 5 The goal of this command is *l,*
1:14 and *l* that are in Christ Jesus.
2:15 *l* and holiness with propriety.
4:12 in life, in *l,* in faith and in purity.
6:10 For the *l* of money is a root
6:11 faith, *l,* endurance and gentleness.
2Ti 1: 7 of power, of *l* and of self-discipline.
1:13 with faith and *l* in Christ Jesus.
2:22 and pursue righteousness, faith, *l*
3: 3 unholy, without *l,* unforgiving,
3:10 faith, patience, *l,* endurance,
Tit 2: 2 in faith, in *l* and in endurance.
2: 4 women to *l* their husbands
3: 4 and *l* of God our Savior appeared,
3:15 Greet those who *l* us in the faith.
Phm : 5 and your *l* for all the saints.
: 7 Your *l* has given me great joy
: 9 yet I appeal to you on the basis of *l.*
Heb 6:10 and the *l* you have shown him
10:24 may spur one another on toward *l*
13: 5 free from the *l* of money
Jas 1:12 promised to those who *l* him.
2: 5 he promised those who *l* him?
2: 8 "*L* your neighbor as yourself,"
1Pe 1: 8 you have not seen him, you *l* him;
1:22 the truth so that you have sincere *l*
1:22 *l* one another deeply,
2:17 *L* the brotherhood of believers,
3: 8 be sympathetic, *l* as brothers,
3:10 "Whoever would *l* life
4: 8 Above all, *l* each other deeply,
4: 8 *l* covers over a multitude of sins.
5:14 Greet one another with a kiss of *l.*
2Pe 1: 7 and to brotherly kindness, *l.*
1:17 "This is my Son, whom I *l;*
1Jn 2: 5 God's *l* is truly made complete
2:15 Do not *l* the world or anything
2:15 the *l* of the Father is not in him.
3: 1 How great is the *l* the Father has
3:10 anyone who does not *l* his brother.
3:11 We should *l* one another.
1Jn 3:14 Anyone who does not *l* remains
3:14 because we *l* our brothers.
3:16 This is how we know what *l* is:
3:17 how can the *l* of God be in him?
3:18 let us not *l* with words or tongue
3:23 to *l* one another as he commanded
4: 7 Dear friends, let us *l* one another,
4: 7 for *l* comes from God.
4: 8 Whoever does not *l* does not know
4: 8 not know God, because God is *l.*
4: 9 This is how God showed his *l*
4:10 This is *l:* not that we loved God,
4:11 we also ought to *l* one another.
4:12 seen God; but if we *l* one another,
4:12 and his *l* is made complete in us.
4:16 God is *l.*
4:16 Whoever lives in *l* lives in God,
4:16 and rely on the *l* God has for us.
4:17 *l* is made complete among us
4:18 But perfect *l* drives out fear,
4:18 There is no fear in *l.*
4:18 who fears is not made perfect in *l.*
4:19 We *l* because he first loved us.
4:20 If anyone says, "I *l* God,"
4:20 anyone who does not *l* his brother,
4:20 whom he has seen, cannot *l* God,
4:21 loves God must also *l* his brother.
5: 2 we know that we *l* the children
5: 3 This is *l* for God: to obey his
2Jn : 1 whom I *l* in the truth—
: 3 will be with us in truth and *l.*
: 5 I ask that we *l* one another.
: 6 his command is that you walk in *l.*
: 6 this is *l:* that we walk in obedience
3Jn : 1 To my dear friend Gaius, whom I *l*
: 6 have told the church about your *l.*
Jude : 2 peace and *l* be yours in abundance.
:12 men are blemishes at your *l* feasts,
:21 Keep yourselves in God's *l*
Rev 2: 4 You have forsaken your first *l.*
2:19 I know your deeds, your *l* and faith
3:19 Those whom I *l* I rebuke
12:11 they did not *l* their lives so much

LOVED* (LOVE)

Ge 24:67 she became his wife, and he *l* her;
25:28 *l* Esau, but Rebekah *l* Jacob.
29:30 and he *l* Rachel more than Leah.
29:31 the LORD saw that Leah was not *l,*
29:33 the LORD heard that I am not *l,*
34: 3 and he *l* the girl and spoke tenderly
37: 3 Now Israel *l* Joseph more than any
37: 4 saw that their father *l* him more
Dt 4:37 Because he *l* your forefathers
7: 8 But it was because the LORD *l* you
10:15 on your forefathers and *l* them,
1Sa 1: 5 a double portion because he *l* her,
18: 1 in spirit with David, and he *l* him
18: 3 with David because he *l* him
18:16 But all Israel and Judah *l* David,
18:28 that his daughter Michal *l* David,
20:17 because he *l* him as he *l* himself.
2Sa 1:23 in life they were *l* and gracious,
12:24 The LORD *l* him; and
12:25 and because the LORD *l* him,
13:15 hated her more than he had *l* her.
1Ki 11: 1 *l* many foreign women
2Ch 11:21 Rehoboam *l* Maacah daughter
26:10 in the fertile lands, for he *l* the soil.
Ne 13:26 He was *l* by his God, and God
Ps 44: 3 light of your face, for you *l* them.
47: 4 the pride of Jacob, whom he *l.*
78:68 Mount Zion, which he *l.*
88:18 taken my companions and *l* ones
109: 17 He *l* to pronounce a curse—
Isa 5: 1 My *l* one had a vineyard
Jer 2: 2 how as a bride you *l* me
8: 2 which they have *l* and served
31: 3 "I have *l* you with an everlasting
Eze 16:37 those you *l* as well as those you
Hos 2: 1 and of your sisters, 'My *l* one.'
2:23 to the one I called 'Not my *l* one.'
3: 1 though she is *l* by another
9:10 became as vile as the thing they *l.*
11: 1 "When Israel was a child, I *l* him,
Mal 1: 2 "But you ask, 'How have you *l* us?'
1: 2 "I have *l* you," says the LORD.
1: 2 "Yet I have *l* Jacob, but Esau I
Mk 10:21 Jesus looked at him and *l* him.
12: 6 left to send, a son, whom he *l.*
Lk 7:47 been forgiven—for she *l* much.
16:14 The Pharisees, who *l* money,
Jn 3:16 so *l* the world that he gave his one
3:19 but men *l* darkness instead of light
11: 5 Jesus *l* Martha and her sister
11:36 "See how he *l* him!" But some
12:43 for they *l* praise from men more
13: 1 Having *l* his own who were
13:23 the disciple whom Jesus *l,*

Jn 13:34 As I have *l* you, so you must love
14:21 He who loves me will be *l*
14:28 If you *l* me, you would be glad that
15: 9 the Father has *l* me, so have I *l* you.
15:12 Love each other as I have *l* you.
16:27 loves you because you have *l* me
17:23 have *l* them even as you have *l* me.
17:24 you *l* me before the creation
19:26 the disciple whom he *l* standing
20: 2 one Jesus *l*, and said, "They have
21: 7 the disciple whom Jesus *l* said
21:20 whom Jesus *l* was following
Ro 1: 7 To all in Rome who are *l* by God
8:37 conquerors through him who *l* us.
9:13 "Jacob I *l*, but Esau I hated."
9:25 her 'my *l* one' who is not my *l* one,"
11:28 they are *l* on account
Gal 2:20 who *l* me and gave himself for me.
Eph 5: 1 as dearly *l* children and live a life
5: 2 as Christ *l* us and gave himself up
5:25 just as Christ *l* the church
Col 3:12 and dearly *l*, clothe yourselves
1Th 1: 4 For we know, brothers *l* by God,
2: 8 We *l* you so much that we were
2Th 2:13 for you, brothers *l* by the Lord,
2:16 who *l* us and by his grace gave us
2Ti 4:10 for Demas, because he *l* this world,
Heb 1: 9 You have *l* righteousness
2Pe 2:15 who *l* the wages of wickedness.
1Jn 4:10 This is love: not that we *l* God,
4:10 but that he *l* us and sent his Son
4:11 Dear friends, since God so *l* us,
4:19 We love because he first *l* us.
Jude : 1 who are *l* by God the Father
Rev 3: 9 and acknowledge that I have *l* you.

LOVELY* (LOVE)
Ge 29:17 but Rachel was *l* in form,
Est 1:11 and nobles, for she was *l* to look at.
2: 7 was *l* in form and features,
Ps 84: 1 How *l* is your dwelling place,
SS 1: 5 Dark am I, yet *l*,
2:14 and your face is *l*.
4: 3 your mouth is *l*.
5:16 he is altogether *l*.
6: 4 *l* as Jerusalem,
Am 8:13 *l* young women and strong young
Php 4: 8 whatever is *l*, whatever is

LOVER* (LOVE)
SS 1:13 My *l* is to me a sachet of myrrh
1:14 My *l* is to me a cluster
1:16 How handsome you are, my *l*!
2: 3 is my *l* among the young men.
2: 8 Listen! My *l*!
2: 9 My *l* is like a gazelle or a young
2:10 My *l* spoke and said to me,
2:16 *Beloved* My *l* is mine and I am his;
2:17 turn, my *l*,
4:16 Let my *l* come into his garden
5: 2 Listen! My *l* is knocking:
5: 4 My *l* thrust his hand
5: 5 I arose to open for my *l*,
5: 6 I opened for my *l*,
5: 6 but my *l* had left; he was gone.
5: 8 if you find my *l*,
5:10 *Beloved* My *l* is radiant and ruddy,
5:16 This is my *l*, this my friend,
6: 1 Where has your *l* gone,
6: 1 Which way did your *l* turn,
6: 2 *Beloved* My *l* has gone
6: 3 I am my lover's and my *l* is mine;
7: 9 May the wine go straight to my *l*,
7:10 I belong to my *l*,
7:11 my *l*, let us go to the countryside,
7:13 that I have stored up for you, my *l*.
8: 5 leaning on her *l*?
8:14 *Beloved* Come away, my *l*,
1Ti 3: 3 not quarrelsome, not a *l* of money.

LOVER'S* (LOVE)
SS 6: 3 I am my *l* and my lover is mine;

LOVERS* (LOVE)
SS 5: 1 drink your fill, O *l*.
Jer 3: 1 as a prostitute with many *l*—
3: 2 the roadside you sat waiting for *l*,
4:30 Your *l* despise you;
La 1: 2 Among all her *l*
Eze 16:33 but you give gifts to all your *l*,
16:36 in your promiscuity with your *l*,
16:37 I am going to gather all your *l*,
16:39 Then I will hand you over to your *l*,
16:41 and you will no longer pay your *l*.
23: 5 she lusted after her *l*, the Assyrians
23: 9 I handed her over to her *l*,
23:20 There she lusted after her *l*,
23:22 I will stir up your *l* against you,
Hos 2: 5 She said, 'I will go after my *l*,
2: 7 She will chase after her *l*
2:10 lewdness before the eyes of her *l*;
2:12 she said were her pay from her *l*;
2:13 and went after her *l*,
8: 9 Ephraim has sold herself to *l*.
2Ti 3: 2 People will be *l* of themselves,
3: 2 *l* of money, boastful, proud,
3: 3 without self-control, brutal, not *l*
3: 4 *l* of pleasure rather than *l* of God—

LOVES* (LOVE)
Ge 44:20 sons left, and his father *l* him.'
Dt 10:18 and *l* the alien, giving him food
15:16 because he *l* you and your family
21:15 and he *l* one but not the other,
21:16 son of the wife he *l* in preference
23: 5 because the LORD your God *l* you
28:54 wife he *l* or his surviving children,
28:56 will begrudge the husband she *l*
33:12 and the one the LORD *l* rests
Ru 4:15 who *l* you and who is better to you
2Ch 2:11 "Because the LORD *l* his people,
Ps 11: 7 he *l* justice;
33: 5 The LORD *l* righteousness
34:12 Whoever of you *l* life
37:28 For the LORD *l* the just
87: 2 the LORD *l* the gates of Zion
91:14 Because he *l* me," says the LORD,
99: 4 The King is mighty, he *l* justice—
119:140 and your servant *l* them.
127: 2 for he grants sleep to those he *l*.
146: 8 the LORD *l* the righteous.
Pr 3:12 the LORD disciplines those he *l*,
12: 1 Whoever *l* discipline *l* knowledge,
13:24 he who *l* him is careful
15: 9 he *l* those who pursue
17:17 A friend *l* at all times,
17:19 He who *l* a quarrel *l* sin;
19: 8 He who gets wisdom *l* his own soul
21:17 He who *l* pleasure will become
21:17 whoever *l* wine and oil will never
22:11 He who *l* a pure heart and whose
29: 3 A man who *l* wisdom brings joy
Ecc 5:10 Whoever *l* money never has
5:10 whoever *l* wealth is never satisfied
SS 3: 1 I looked for the one my heart *l*;
3: 2 I will search for the one my heart *l*.
3: 3 "Have you seen the one my heart *l*
3: 4 when I found the one my heart *l*.
Hos 3: 1 as the LORD *l* the Israelites,
10:11 that *l* to thresh;
12: 7 he *l* to defraud.
Mal 2:11 the sanctuary the LORD *l*,
Mt 10:37 anyone who *l* his son or daughter
10:37 "Anyone who *l* his father
Lk 7: 5 because he *l* our nation
7:47 has been forgiven little *l* little."
Jn 3:35 Father *l* the Son and has placed
5:20 For the Father *l* the Son
10:17 reason my Father *l* me is that I lay
12:25 The man who *l* his life will lose it,
14:21 He who *l* me will be loved
14:21 obeys them, he is the one who *l* me.
14:23 Jesus replied, "If anyone *l* me,
16:27 the Father himself *l* you
Ro 13: 8 for he who *l* his fellowman has
1Co 8: 3 But the man who *l* God is known
2Co 9: 7 for God *l* a cheerful giver.
Eph 1: 6 has freely given us in the One he *l*.
5:28 He who *l* his wife *l* himself.
5:33 must love his wife as he *l* himself,
Col 1:13 us into the kingdom of the Son he *l*,
Tit 1: 8 one who *l* what is good, who is
Heb 12: 6 the Lord disciplines those he *l*,
1Jn 2:10 Whoever *l* his brother lives
2:15 If anyone *l* the world, the love
4: 7 Everyone who *l* has been born
4:21 Whoever *l* God must also love his
5: 1 who *l* the father *l* his child
3Jn : 9 but Diotrephes, who *l* to be first,
Rev 1: 5 To him who *l* us and has freed us
20: 9 camp of God's people, the city he *l*.
22:15 and everyone who *l* and practices

LOVING* (LOVE)
Ps 25:10 All the ways of the LORD are *l*
59:10 my *l* God.
59:17 O God, are my fortress, my *l* God.
62:12 and that you, O Lord, are *l*.
144: 2 He is my *l* God and my fortress,
145: 13 and *l* toward all he has made.
145: 17 and *l* toward all he has made.
Pr 5:19 A *l* doe, a graceful deer—
Heb 13: 1 Keep on *l* each other as brothers.
1Jn 5: 2 by *l* God and carrying out his

LOVING-KINDNESS* (LOVE)
Jer 31: 3 I have drawn you with *l*.

LOWER
Ps 8: 5 You made him a little *l*
2Co 11: 7 a sin for me to *l* myself in order
Heb 2: 7 You made him a little *l*

LOWING
1Sa 15:14 What is this *l* of cattle that I hear?"

LOWLY
Job 5:11 The *l* he sets on high,
Ps 138: 6 on high, he looks upon the *l*,
Pr 29:23 but a man of *l* spirit gains honor.
Isa 57:15 also with him who is contrite and *l*
Eze 21:26 *l* will be exalted and the exalted
1Co 1:28 He chose the *l* things of this world

LOYAL
1Ch 29:18 and keep their hearts *l* to you.
Ps 78: 8 whose hearts were not *l* to God,

LUKE*
Co-worker with Paul (Col 4:14; 2Ti 4:11; Phm 24).

LUKEWARM*
Rev 3:16 So, because you are *l*— neither hot

LUST (LUSTED LUSTS)
Pr 6:25 Do not *l* in your heart
Eze 20:30 and *l* after their vile images?
Col 3: 5 sexual immorality, impurity, *l*,
1Th 4: 5 not in passionate *l* like the heathen,
1Pe 4: 3 in debauchery, *l*, drunkenness,
1Jn 2:16 the *l* of his eyes and the boasting

LUSTED (LUST)
Eze 23: 5 she *l* after her lovers, the Assyrians

LUSTS* (LUST)
Nu 15:39 yourselves by going after the *l*
Ro 1:26 God gave them over to shameful *l*.

LUXURY
Jas 5: 5 You have lived on earth in *l*

LYDIA'S*
Ac 16:40 went to *L* house, where they met

LYING (LIE)
Pr 6:17 a *l* tongue,
12:22 The LORD detests *l* lips,
21: 6 A fortune made by a *l* tongue
26:28 A *l* tongue hates those it hurts,

MACEDONIA
Ac 16: 9 "Come over to *M* and help us."

MAD
Dt 28:34 The sights you see will drive you *m*

MADE (MAKE)
Ge 1: 7 So God *m* the expanse
1:16 God *m* two great lights—
1:16 He also *m* the stars.
1:25 God *m* the wild animals according
1:31 God saw all that he had *m*,
2:22 Then the LORD God *m* a woman
6: 6 was grieved that he had *m* man
9: 6 has God *m* man.
15:18 that day the LORD *m* a covenant
Ex 20:11 six days the LORD *m* the heavens
20:11 the Sabbath day and *m* it holy.
24: 8 the covenant that the LORD has *m*
32: 4 *m* it into an idol cast in the shape
Lev 16:34 Atonement is to be *m* once a year
Dt 32: 6 who *m* you and formed you?
Jos 24:25 On that day Joshua *m* a covenant
2Ki 19:15 You have *m* heaven and earth.
2Ch 2:12 the God of Israel, who *m* heaven
Ne 9: 6 You *m* the heavens,
9:10 You *m* a name for yourself,
Ps 33: 6 of the LORD were the heavens *m*,
95: 5 The sea is his, for he *m* it,
96: 5 but the LORD *m* the heavens.
100: 3 It is he who *m* us, and we are his;
118: 24 This is the day the LORD has *m*;
136: 7 who *m* the great lights—
139: 14 I am fearfully and wonderfully *m*;
Ecc 3:11 He has *m* everything beautiful
Isa 43: 7 whom I formed and *m*."
45:12 It is I who *m* the earth
45:18 he who fashioned and *m* the earth,
66: 2 Has not my hand *m* all these things
Jer 10:12 But God *m* the earth by his power;
27: 5 and outstretched arm I *m* the earth
32:17 you have *m* the heavens
33: 2 LORD says, he who *m* the earth,
51:15 "He *m* the earth by his power;
Eze 3:17 I have *m* you a watchman
33: 7 I have *m* you a watchman
Am 5: 8 (he who *m* the Pleiades and Orion,

Jnh 1: 9 who *m* the sea and the land."
Mk 2:27 "The Sabbath was *m* for man,
Jn 1: 3 Through him all things were *m*;
Ac 17:24 "The God who *m* the world
1Co 3: 6 watered it, but God *m* it grow.
Heb 1: 2 through whom he *m* the universe.
Jas 3: 9 who have been *m* in God's likeness
Rev 14: 7 Worship him who *m* the heavens,

MAGDALENE
Lk 8: 2 Mary (called *M)* from whom seven

MAGI
Mt 2: 1 *M* from the east came to Jerusalem

MAGIC (MAGICIANS)
Eze 13:20 I am against your *m* charms
Rev 21: 8 those who practice *m* arts,
22:15 those who practice *m* arts,

MAGICIANS (MAGIC)
Ex 7:11 the Egyptian *m* also did the same
Da 2: 2 So the king summoned the *m*,

MAGNIFICENCE* (MAGNIFICENT)
1Ch 22: 5 for the LORD should be of great *m*

MAGNIFICENT (MAGNIFICENCE)
1Ki 8:13 I have indeed built a *m* temple
Isa 28:29 in counsel and *m* in wisdom.
Mk 13: 1 stones! What *m* buildings!"

MAGOG
Eze 38: 2 of the land of *M*, the chief prince
39: 6 I will send fire on *M*
Rev 20: 8 and *M*— to gather them for battle.

MAIDEN (MAIDENS)
Pr 30:19 and the way of a man with a *m*.
Isa 62: 5 As a young man marries a *m*,
Jer 2:32 Does a *m* forget her jewelry,

MAIDENS (MAIDEN)
SS 1: 3 No wonder the *m* love you!

MAIMED
Mt 18: 8 It is better for you to enter life *m*

MAINTAIN (MAINTAINING)
Ps 82: 3 *m* the rights of the poor
106: 3 Blessed are they who *m* justice,
Hos 12: 6 *m* love and justice,
Am 5:15 *m* justice in the courts.
Ro 3:28 For we *m* that a man is justified

MAINTAINING* (MAINTAIN)
Ex 34: 7 faithfulness, *m* love to thousands,

MAJESTIC* (MAJESTY)
Ex 15: 6 was *m* in power.
15:11 *m* in holiness,
Job 37: 4 he thunders with his *m* voice.
Ps 8: 1 how *m* is your name in all the earth
8: 9 how *m* is your name in all the earth
29: 4 the voice of the LORD is *m*.
68:15 of Bashan are *m* mountains;
76: 4 more *m* than mountains rich
111: 3 Glorious and *m* are his deeds,
SS 6: 4 *m* as troops with banners.
6:10 *m* as the stars in procession?
Isa 30:30 men to hear his *m* voice
Eze 31: 7 It was *m* in beauty,
2Pe 1:17 came to him from the *M* Glory,

MAJESTY* (MAJESTIC)
Ex 15: 7 In the greatness of your *m*
Dt 5:24 has shown us his glory and his *m*,
11: 2 his *m*, his mighty hand, his
33:17 In *m* he is like a firstborn bull;
33:26 and on the clouds in his *m*.
1Ch 16:27 Splendor and *m* are before him;
29:11 and the *m* and the splendor,
Est 1: 4 the splendor and glory of his *m*.
7: 3 if it pleases your *m*, grant me my
Job 37:22 God comes in awesome *m*.
40:10 and clothe yourself in honor and *m*
Ps 21: 5 on him splendor and *m*.
45: 3 with splendor and *m*.
45: 4 In your *m* ride forth victoriously
68:34 whose *m* is over Israel,
93: 1 The LORD reigns, he is robed in *m*
93: 1 the LORD is robed in *m*
96: 6 Splendor and *m* are before him;
104: 1 clothed with splendor and *m*.
110: 3 Arrayed in holy *m*,
145: 5 of the glorious splendor of your *m*,
Isa 2:10 and the splendor of his *m*!
2:19 and the splendor of his *m*,
2:21 and the splendor of his *m*,
24:14 west they acclaim the LORD's *m*.
26:10 and regard not the *m* of the LORD.
Isa 53: 2 or *m* to attract us to him,
Eze 31: 2 can be compared with you in *m*?
31:18 with you in splendor and *m*?
Da 4:30 and for the glory of my *m*?"
Mic 5: 4 in the *m* of the name
Zec 6:13 and he will be clothed with *m*
Ac 19:27 will be robbed of her divine *m*."
25:26 to write to His *M* about him.
2Th 1: 9 and from the *m* of his power
Heb 1: 3 hand of the *M* in heaven.
8: 1 of the throne of the *M* in heaven,
2Pe 1:16 but we were eyewitnesses of his *m*.
Jude :25 only God our Savior be glory, *m*,

MAKE (MADE MAKER MAKERS MAKES MAKING MAN-MADE)
Ge 1:26 "Let us *m* man in our image,
2:18 I will *m* a helper suitable for him."
6:14 *m* yourself an ark of cypress wood;
12: 2 "I will *m* you into a great nation
Ex 22: 3 thief must certainly *m* restitution,
25: 9 *M* this tabernacle and all its
25:40 See that you *m* them according
Nu 6:25 the LORD *m* his face shine
2Sa 7: 9 Now I will *m* your name great,
Job 7:17 "What is man that you *m* so much
Ps 4: 8 *m* me dwell in safety.
20: 4 and *m* all your plans succeed.
108: 1 *m* music with all my soul.
110: 1 hand until I *m* your enemies
119:165 and nothing can *m* them stumble.
Pr 3: 6 and he will *m* your paths straight.
4:26 *M* level paths for your feet
20:18 *M* plans by seeking advice;
Isa 14:14 I will *m* myself like the Most High
29:16 "He did not *m* me"?
55: 3 I will *m* an everlasting covenant
61: 8 and *m* an everlasting covenant
Jer 31:31 "when I will *m* a new covenant
Eze 37:26 I will *m* a covenant of peace
Mt 3: 3 *m* straight paths for him.' "
28:19 and *m* disciples of all nations,
Mk 1:17 "and I will *m* you fishers of men."
Lk 13:24 "*M* every effort to enter
14:23 country lanes and *m* them come in,
Ro 14:19 *m* every effort to do what leads
2Co 5: 9 So we *m* it our goal to please him,
Eph 4: 3 *M* every effort to keep the unity
Col 4: 5 *m* the most of every opportunity.
1Th 4:11 *M* it your ambition
Heb 4:11 *m* every effort to enter that rest,
8: 5 it that you *m* everything according
12:14 *M* every effort to live in peace
2Pe 1: 5 *m* every effort to add
3:14 *m* every effort to be found spotless,

MAKER* (MAKE)
Job 4:17 Can a man be more pure than his *M*
9: 9 He is the *M* of the Bear and Orion,
32:22 my *M* would soon take me away.
35:10 no one says, 'Where is God my *M*,
36: 3 I will ascribe justice to my *M*.
40:19 yet his *M* can approach him
Ps 95: 6 kneel before the LORD our *M*;
115: 15 the *M* of heaven and earth.
121: 2 the *M* of heaven and earth.
124: 8 the *M* of heaven and earth.
134: 3 the *M* of heaven and earth.
146: 6 the *M* of heaven and earth,
149: 2 Let Israel rejoice in their *M*;
Pr 14:31 poor shows contempt for their *M*,
17: 5 poor shows contempt for their *M*;
22: 2 The LORD is the *M* of them all.
Ecc 11: 5 the *M* of all things.
Isa 17: 7 that day men will look to their *M*
27:11 so their *M* has no compassion
45: 9 to him who quarrels with his *M*,
45:11 the Holy One of Israel, and its *M*:
51:13 that you forget the LORD your *M*,
54: 5 For your *M* is your husband—
Jer 10:16 for he is the *M* of all things,
51:19 for he is the *M* of all things,
Hos 8:14 Israel has forgotten his *M*

MAKERS* (MAKE)
Isa 45:16 All the *m* of idols will be put

MAKES (MAKE)
Ps 23: 2 *m* me lie down in green pastures,
Pr 13:12 Hope deferred *m* the heart sick,
1Co 3: 7 but only God, who *m* things grow.

MAKING (MAKE)
Ps 19: 7 *m* wise the simple.
Ecc 12:12 Of *m* many books there is no end,
Jn 5:18 *m* himself equal with God.
Eph 5:16 *m* the most of every opportunity,

MALACHI*
Mal 1: 1 of the LORD to Israel through *M*.

MALE
Ge 1:27 *m* and female he created them.
Ex 13: 2 to me every firstborn *m*.
Nu 8:16 the first *m* offspring
Mt 19: 4 the Creator 'made them *m*
Gal 3:28 slave nor free, *m* nor female,

MALICE (MALICIOUS)
Mk 7:22 adultery, greed, *m*, deceit,
Ro 1:29 murder, strife, deceit and *m*.
1Co 5: 8 the yeast of *m* and wickedness,
Eph 4:31 along with every form of *m*.
Col 3: 8 *m*, slander, and filthy language
1Pe 2: 1 rid yourselves of all *m*

MALICIOUS (MALICE)
Pr 26:24 A *m* man disguises himself
1Ti 3:11 not *m* talkers but temperate
6: 4 *m* talk, evil suspicions

MALIGN
Tit 2: 5 so that no one will *m* the word

MAN (MAN'S MANKIND MEN MEN'S WOMAN WOMEN)
Ge 1:26 "Let us make *m* in our image,
2: 7 God formed the *m* from the dust
2: 8 *m* became a living being
2:15 God took the *m* and put
2:18 for the *m* to be alone
2:20 *m* gave names to all the
2:23 she was taken out of *m*.
2:25 *m* and his wife were both
3: 9 God called to the *m*,
3:22 *m* has now become like
4: 1 I have brought forth a *m*.
6: 3 not contend with *m* forever,
6: 6 grieved that he had made *m*
9: 6 Whoever sheds the blood of *m*,
Dt 8: 3 *m* does not live on bread
1Sa 13:14 a *m* after his own heart
15:29 he is not a *m* that he
16: 7 at the things *m* looks at.
Job 14: 1 *M* born of woman is of few
14:14 If a *m* dies, will he live
Ps 1: 1 Blessed is the *m* who does
8: 4 what is *m* that you are
32: 2 Blessed is the *m* whose sin
40: 4 Blessed is the *m* who makes
84:12 blessed is the *m* who trusts
103: 15 As for *m*, his days are
112: 1 Blessed is the *m* who fears
119: 9 can a young *m* keep his
127: 5 Blessed is the *m* whose quiver
144: 3 what is *m* that you care
Pr 3:13 Blessed is the *m* who finds
9: 9 Instruct a wise *m*
14:12 that seems right to a *m*,
30:19 way of a *m* with a maiden.
Isa 53: 3 a *m* of sorrows,
Jer 17: 5 the one who trusts in *m*,
17: 7 blessed is the *m* who trusts
Eze 22:30 I looked for a *m*
Mt 4: 4 *M* does not live on bread
19: 5 a *m* will leave his father
Mk 8:36 What good is it for a *m*
Lk 4: 4 '*M* does not live on bread
Ro 5:12 entered the world through one *m*
1Co 2:15 spiritual *m* makes judgments
3:12 If any *m* builds on this
7: 1 good for a *m* not to marry.
7: 2 each *m* should have his own
11: 3 head of every *m* is Christ,
11: 3 head of woman is *m*
13:11 When I became a *m*,
15:21 death came through a *m*,
15:45 first *m* Adam became a
15:47 the second *m* from heaven
2Co 12: 2 I know a *m* in Christ
Eph 2:15 create in himself one new *m*
5:31 a *m* will leave his father
Php 2: 8 found in appearance as a *m*,
1Ti 2: 5 the *m* Christ Jesus,
2:11 have authority over a *m*;
2Ti 3:17 that the *m* of God may be
Heb 2: 6 what is *m* that you are
9:27 as *m* is destined to die

MAN'S (MAN)
Pr 20:24 A *m* steps are directed by
Jer 10:23 a *m* life is not his own;
1Co 1:25 is wiser than *m* wisdom,

MAN-MADE (MAKE)
Heb 9:11 perfect tabernacle that is not *m*,
9:24 not enter a *m* sanctuary that was

MANAGE (MANAGER)
Jer 12: 5 how will you *m* in the thickets
1Ti 3: 4 He must *m* his own family well
3:12 one wife and must *m* his children
5:14 to *m* their homes and to give

MANAGER (MANAGE)
Lk 12:42 Who then is the faithful and wise *m*
16: 1 a rich man whose *m* was accused

MANASSEH
1. Firstborn of Joseph (Ge 41:51; 46:20). Blessed by Jacob but not firstborn (Ge 48). Tribe of blessed (Dt 33:17), numbered (Nu 1:35; 26:34), half allotted land east of Jordan (Nu 32; Jos 13: 8-33), half west (Jos 17; Eze 48:4), failed to fully possess (Jos 17:12-13; Jdg 1:27), 12,000 from (Rev 7:6).
2. Son of Hezekiah; king of Judah (2Ki 21:1-18; 2Ch 33:1-20). Judah exiled for his detestable sins (2Ki 21:10-15). Repentance (2Ch 33:12-19).

MANDRAKES
Ge 30:14 give me some of your son's *m*."

MANGER
Lk 2:12 in strips of cloth and lying in a *m*."

MANIFESTATION*
1Co 12: 7 to each one the *m* of the Spirit is

MANKIND (MAN)
Ge 6: 7 I will wipe *m*, whom I have created
Ps 33:13 and sees all *m*;
Pr 8:31 and delighting in *m*.
Ecc 7:29 God made *m* upright,
Isa 40: 5 and all *m* together will see it.
45:12 and created *m* upon it.
Jer 32:27 "I am the LORD, the God of all *m*.
Zec 2:13 Be still before the LORD, all *m*,
Lk 3: 6 And all *m* will see God's salvation

MANNA
Ex 16:31 people of Israel called the bread *m*.
Dt 8:16 He gave you *m* to eat in the desert,
Jn 6:49 Your forefathers ate the *m*
Rev 2:17 I will give some of the hidden *m*.

MANNER
1Co 11:27 in an unworthy *m* will be guilty
Php 1:27 conduct yourselves in a *m* worthy

MANSIONS*
Ps 49:14 far from their princely *m*.
Isa 5: 9 the fine *m* left without occupants.
Am 3:15 and the *m* will be demolished,"
5:11 though you have built stone *m*,

MARCH
Jos 6: 4 *m* around the city seven times,
Isa 42:13 LORD will *m* out like a mighty

MARITAL* (MARRY)
Ex 21:10 of her food, clothing and *m* rights.
Mt 5:32 except for *m* unfaithfulness,
19: 9 except for *m* unfaithfulness,
1Co 7: 3 husband should fulfill his *m* duty

MARK (MARKS)
Cousin of Barnabas (Col 4:10; 2Ti 4:11; Phm 24; 1Pe 5:13), see JOHN.
Ge 4:15 Then the LORD put a *m* on Cain
Rev 13:16 to receive a *m* on his right hand

MARKET (MARKETPLACE MARKETPLACES)
Jn 2:16 turn my Father's house into a *m*!"

MARKETPLACE (MARKET)
Lk 7:32 are like children sitting in the *m*

MARKETPLACES (MARKET)
Mt 23: 7 they love to be greeted in the *m*

MARKS (MARK)
Jn 20:25 Unless I see the nail *m* in his hands
Gal 6:17 bear on my body the *m* of Jesus.

MARRED
Isa 52:14 his form *m* beyond human likeness

MARRIAGE (MARRY)
Mt 22:30 neither marry nor be given in *m*;
24:38 marrying and giving in *m*,
Ro 7: 2 she is released from the law of *m*.
Heb 13: 4 by all, and the *m* bed kept pure,

MARRIED (MARRY)
Dt 24: 5 happiness to the wife he has *m*.
Ezr 10:10 you have *m* foreign women,
Pr 30:23 an unloved woman who is *m*,
Mt 1:18 pledged to be *m* to Joseph,
Mk 12:23 since the seven were *m* to her?"
Ro 7: 2 by law a *m* woman is bound
1Co 7:27 Are you *m*? Do not seek a divorce.
7:33 But a *m* man is concerned about
7:36 They should get *m*.

MARRIES (MARRY)
Mt 5:32 anyone who *m* the divorced woman
19: 9 and *m* another woman commits
Lk 16:18 the man who *m* a divorced woman

MARROW
Heb 4:12 joints and *m*; it judges the thoughts

MARRY (INTERMARRY MARITAL MARRIAGE MARRIED MARRIES)
Dt 25: 5 brother shall take her and *m* her
Mt 22:30 resurrection people will neither *m*
1Co 7: 1 It is good for a man not to *m*.
7: 9 control themselves, they should *m*,
7:28 if you do *m*, you have not sinned;
1Ti 4: 3 They forbid people to *m*
5:14 So I counsel younger widows to *m*,

MARTHA*
Sister of Mary and Lazarus (Lk 10:38-42; Jn 11; 12:2).

MARVELED* (MARVELOUS)
Lk 2:33 mother *m* at what was said about
2Th 1:10 and to be *m* at among all those who

MARVELING* (MARVELOUS)
Lk 9:43 While everyone was *m*

MARVELOUS* (MARVELED MARVELING)
1Ch 16:24 his *m* deeds among all peoples.
Job 37: 5 God's voice thunders in *m* ways;
Ps 71:17 to this day I declare your *m* deeds.
72:18 who alone does *m* deeds.
86:10 For you are great and do *m* deeds;
96: 3 his *m* deeds among all peoples.
98: 1 for he has done *m* things;
118: 23 and it is *m* in our eyes.
Isa 25: 1 you have done *m* things,
Zec 8: 6 but will it seem *m* to me?"
8: 6 "It may seem *m* to the remnant
Mt 21:42 and it is *m* in our eyes'?
Mk 12:11 and it is *m* in our eyes'?"
Rev 15: 1 in heaven another great and *m* sign
15: 3 "Great and *m* are your deeds,

MARY
1. Mother of Jesus (Mt 1:16-25; Lk 1:27-56; 2: 1-40). With Jesus at temple (Lk 2:41-52), at the wedding in Cana (Jn 2:1-5), questioning his sanity (Mk 3:21), at the cross (Jn 19:25-27). Among disciples after Ascension (Ac 1:14).
2. Magdalene; former demoniac (Lk 8:2). Helped support Jesus' ministry (Lk 8:1-3). At the cross (Mt 27:56; Mk 15:40; Jn 19:25), burial (Mt 27:61; Mk 15:47). Saw angel after resurrection (Mt 28:1-10; Mk 16:1-9; Lk 24:1-12); also Jesus (Jn 20: 1-18).
3. Sister of Martha and Lazarus (Jn 11). Washed Jesus' feet (Jn 12:1-8).

MASQUERADES*
2Co 11:14 for Satan himself *m* as an angel

MASTER (MASTER'S MASTERED MASTERS MASTERY)
Ge 4: 7 to have you, but you must *m* it."
Hos 2:16 you will no longer call me 'my *m*.'
Mal 1: 6 If I am a *m*, where is the respect
Mt 10:24 nor a servant above his *m*.
23: 8 for you have only one *M*
24:46 that servant whose *m* finds him
25:21 "His *m* replied, 'Well done,
25:23 "His *m* replied, 'Well done,
Ro 6:14 For sin shall not be your *m*,
14: 4 To his own *m* he stands or falls.
Col 4: 1 you know that you also have a *M*
2Ti 2:21 useful to the *M* and prepared

MASTER'S (MASTER)
Mt 25:21 Come and share your *m* happiness

MASTERED* (MASTER)
1Co 6:12 but I will not be *m* by anything.
2Pe 2:19 a slave to whatever has *m* him.

MASTERS (MASTER)
Pr 25:13 he refreshes the spirit of his *m*.
Mt 6:24 "No one can serve two *m*.
Lk 16:13 "No servant can serve two *m*.
Eph 6: 5 obey your earthly *m* with respect
6: 9 And *m*, treat your slaves
Col 3:22 obey your earthly *m* in everything;
4: 1 *M*, provide your slaves
1Ti 6: 1 should consider their *m* worthy
6: 2 who have believing *m* are not
Tit 2: 9 subject to their *m* in everything,
1Pe 2:18 to your *m* with all respect,

MASTERY* (MASTER)
Ro 6: 9 death no longer has *m* over him.

MAT
Mk 2: 9 'Get up, take your *m* and walk'?
Ac 9:34 Get up and take care of your *m*."

MATCHED*
2Co 8:11 do it may be *m* by your completion

MATTHEW*
Apostle; former tax collector (Mt 9:9-13; 10:3; Mk 3:18; Lk 6:15; Ac 1:13). Also called Levi (Mk 2:14-17; Lk 5:27-32).

MATTHIAS
Ac 1:26 the lot fell to *M*; so he was added

MATURE* (MATURITY)
Lk 8:14 and pleasures, and they do not *m*.
1Co 2: 6 a message of wisdom among the *m*,
Eph 4:13 of the Son of God and become *m*,
Php 3:15 of us who are *m* should take such
Col 4:12 firm in all the will of God, *m*
Heb 5:14 But solid food is for the *m*,
Jas 1: 4 work so that you may be *m*

MATURITY* (MATURE)
Heb 6: 1 about Christ and go on to *m*,

MEAL
Pr 15:17 Better a *m* of vegetables where
1Co 10:27 some unbeliever invites you to a *m*
Heb 12:16 for a single *m* sold his inheritance

MEANING
Ne 8: 8 and giving the *m* so that the people

MEANINGLESS
Ecc 1: 2 "*M*! *M*!" says the Teacher.
1Ti 1: 6 from these and turned to *m* talk.

MEANS
1Co 9:22 by all possible *m* I might save some

MEASURE (MEASURED MEASURES)
Ps 71:15 though I know not its *m*.
Eze 45: 3 In the sacred district, *m*
Zec 2: 2 He answered me, "To *m* Jerusalem
Lk 6:38 A good *m*, pressed
Eph 3:19 to the *m* of all the fullness of God.
4:13 to the whole *m* of the fullness
Rev 11: 1 "Go and *m* the temple of God

MEASURED (MEASURE)
Isa 40:12 Who has *m* the waters
Jer 31:37 if the heavens above can be *m*

MEASURES (MEASURE)
Dt 25:14 Do not have two differing *m*
Pr 20:10 Differing weights and differing *m*

MEAT
Pr 23:20 or gorge themselves on *m*,
Ro 14: 6 He who eats *m*, eats to the Lord,
14:21 It is better not to eat *m*
1Co 8:13 I will never eat *m* again,
10:25 *m* market without raising questions

MEDDLER* (MEDDLES)
1Pe 4:15 kind of criminal, or even as a *m*.

MEDDLES* (MEDDLER)
Pr 26:17 is a passer-by who *m*

MEDIATOR
1Ti 2: 5 and one *m* between God and men,
Heb 8: 6 of which he is *m* is superior
9:15 For this reason Christ is the *m*
12:24 to Jesus the *m* of a new covenant,

MEDICINE*
Pr 17:22 A cheerful heart is good *m*,

MEDITATE* (MEDITATED MEDITATES MEDITATION)
Ge 24:63 out to the field one evening to *m*,
Jos 1: 8 from your mouth; *m* on it day
Ps 48: 9 we *m* on your unfailing love.
77:12 I will *m* on all your works
119: 15 I *m* on your precepts
119: 23 your servant will *m*
119: 27 then I will *m* on your wonders.
119: 48 and I *m* on your decrees.
119: 78 but I will *m* on your precepts.
119: 97 I *m* on it all day long.
119: 99 for I *m* on your statutes.

Ps 119:148 that I may *m* on your promises.
143: 5 I *m* on all your works
145: 5 I will *m* on your wonderful works.

MEDITATED* (MEDITATE)
Ps 39: 3 and as I *m*, the fire burned;

MEDITATES* (MEDITATE)
Ps 1: 2 and on his law he *m* day and night.

MEDITATION* (MEDITATE)
Ps 19:14 of my mouth and the *m* of my heart
104: 34 May my *m* be pleasing to him,

MEDIUM
Lev 20:27 " 'A man or woman who is a *m*

MEEK* (MEEKNESS)
Ps 37:11 But the *m* will inherit the land
Zep 3:12 the *m* and humble,
Mt 5: 5 Blessed are the *m*,

MEEKNESS* (MEEK)
2Co 10: 1 By the *m* and gentleness of Christ,

MEET (MEETING MEETINGS MEETS)
Ps 42: 2 When can I go and *m* with God?
85:10 Love and faithfulness *m* together;
Am 4:12 prepare to *m* your God, O Israel."
1Co 11:34 when you *m* together it may not
1Th 4:17 them in the clouds to *m* the Lord

MEETING (MEET)
Ex 40:34 the cloud covered the Tent of *M*,
Heb 10:25 Let us not give up *m* together,

MEETINGS* (MEET)
1Co 11:17 for your *m* do more harm

MEETS (MEET)
Heb 7:26 Such a high priest *m* our need—

MELCHIZEDEK
Ge 14:18 *M* king of Salem brought out bread
Ps 110: 4 in the order of *M*."
Heb 7:11 in the order of *M*, not in the order

MELT (MELTS)
2Pe 3:12 and the elements will *m* in the heat.

MELTS (MELT)
Am 9: 5 he who touches the earth and it *m*,

MEMBER (MEMBERS)
Ro 12: 5 each *m* belongs to all the others.

MEMBERS (MEMBER)
Mic 7: 6 a man's enemies are the *m*
Mt 10:36 a man's enemies will be the *m*
Ro 7:23 law at work in the *m* of my body,
12: 4 of us has one body with many *m*,
1Co 6:15 not know that your bodies are *m*
12:24 But God has combined the *m*
Eph 3: 6 *m* together of one body,
4:25 for we are all *m* of one body.
5:30 for we are *m* of his body.
Col 3:15 as *m* of one body you were called

MEMORABLE* (MEMORY)
Eze 39:13 day I am glorified will be a *m* day

MEMORIES* (MEMORY)
1Th 3: 6 us that you always have pleasant *m*

MEMORY (MEMORABLE MEMORIES)
Pr 10: 7 *m* of the righteous will be
Mt 26:13 she has done will also be told, in *m*

MEN (MAN)
Ge 6: 2 daughter of *m* were beautiful,
6: 4 heroes of old, *m* of renown
Ps 9:20 nations know they are but *m*.
11: 4 He observes the sons of *m*;
Mt 4:19 will make you fishers of *m*
5:16 your light shine before *m*
6:14 if you forgive *m* when
10:32 acknowledges me before *m*
12:31 blasphemy will be forgiven *m*,
12:36 *m* will have to give account
23: 5 is done for *m* to see:
Mk 7: 7 are but rules taught by *m*.
Lk 6:22 Blessed are you when *m*
6:26 Woe to you when all *m*
Jn 1: 4 life was the light of *m*.
2:24 for he knew all *m*.
3:19 *m* loved darkness instead
12:32 will draw all *m* to myself
13:35 all *m* will know that you
Ac 5:29 obey God rather than *m*!
Ro 1:18 wickedness of *m*
1:27 indecent acts with other *m*,
5:12 death came to all *m*,
1Co 2:11 among *m* knows the thoughts
3: 3 acting like mere *m*?
3:21 no more boasting about *m*!
9:22 all things to all *m*
13: 1 tongues of *m* and of angels
16:13 be *m* of courage;
16:18 Such *m* deserve recognition.
2Co 5:11 we try to persuade *m*.
8:21 but also in the eyes of *m*.
Gal 1: 1 sent not from *m* nor
1:10 to win approval of *m*, or
Eph 4: 8 and gave gifts to *m*.
1Th 2: 4 as *m* approved by God
2:13 not as the word of *m*,
1Ti 2: 4 wants all *m* to be saved
2: 6 as a ransom for all *m*—
4:10 the Savior of all *m*
5: 2 younger *m* as brothers
2Ti 2: 2 entrust to reliable *m*
Tit 2:11 has appeared to all *m*.
Heb 5: 1 is selected from among *m*
7:28 high priests *m* who are weak;
2Pe 1:21 but *m* spoke from God
Rev 21: 3 dwelling of God is with *m*,

MEN'S (MAN)
2Ki 19:18 fashioned by *m* hands.
2Ch 32:19 the work of *m* hands.
1Co 2: 5 not rest on *m* wisdom,

MENAHEM*
King of Israel (2Ki 15:17-22).

MENE
Da 5:25 that was written: *M, M*,

MEPHIBOSHETH
Son of Jonathan shown kindness by David (2Sa 4:4; 9; 21:7). Accused of siding with Absalom (2Sa 16:1-4; 19:24-30).

MERCHANT
Pr 31:14 She is like the *m* ships,
Mt 13:45 of heaven is like a *m* looking

MERCIFUL (MERCY)
Dt 4:31 the LORD your God is a *m* God;
Ne 9:31 for you are a gracious and *m* God.
Ps 77: 9 Has God forgotten to be *m*?
78:38 Yet he was *m*;
Jer 3:12 for I am *m*,' declares the LORD,
Da 9: 9 The Lord our God is *m*
Mt 5: 7 Blessed are the *m*,
Lk 1:54 remembering to be *m*
6:36 Be *m*, just as your Father is *m*.
Heb 2:17 in order that he might become a *m*
Jas 2:13 to anyone who has not been *m*.
Jude :22 Be *m* to those who doubt; snatch

MERCY (MERCIFUL)
Ex 33:19 *m* on whom I will have *m*,
2Sa 24:14 of the LORD, for his *m* is great;
1Ch 21:13 for his *m* is very great;
Ne 9:31 But in your great *m* you did not put
Ps 25: 6 O LORD, your great *m* and love,
28: 6 for he has heard my cry for *m*.
57: 1 Have *m* on me, O God, have *m*
Pr 28:13 renounces them finds *m*.
Isa 63: 9 and *m* he redeemed them;
Da 9:18 but because of your great *m*.
Hos 6: 6 For I desire *m*, not sacrifice,
Am 5:15 LORD God Almighty will have *m*
Mic 6: 8 To act justly and to love *m*
7:18 but delight to show *m*.
Hab 3: 2 in wrath remember *m*.
Zec 7: 9 show *m* and compassion
Mt 5: 7 for they will be shown *m*.
9:13 learn what this means: 'I desire *m*,
12: 7 'I desire *m*, not sacrifice,' you
18:33 Shouldn't you have had *m*
23:23 justice, *m* and faithfulness.
Lk 1:50 His *m* extends to those who fear
Ro 9:15 "I will have *m* on whom I have *m*,
9:18 Therefore God has *m*
11:32 so that he may have *m* on them all.
12: 1 brothers, in view of God's *m*,
12: 8 if it is showing *m*, let him do it
Eph 2: 4 who is rich in *m*, made us alive
1Ti 1:13 I was shown *m* because I acted
1:16 for that very reason I was shown *m*
Tit 3: 5 we had done, but because of his *m*.
Heb 4:16 so that we may receive *m*
Jas 2:13 judgment without *m* will be shown
2:13 *M* triumphs over judgment!
3:17 submissive, full of *m* and good fruit
5:11 full of compassion and *m*.
1Pe 1: 3 In his great *m* he has given us new
2:10 once you had not received *m*,
Jude :23 to others show *m*, mixed with fear

MERRY
Lk 12:19 Take life easy; eat, drink and be *m*

MESHACH
Hebrew exiled to Babylon; name changed from Mishael (Da 1:6-7). Refused defilement by food (Da 1:8-20). Refused to worship idol (Da 3:1-18); saved from furnace (Da 3:19-30).

MESSAGE (MESSENGER)
Isa 53: 1 Who has believed our *m*
Jn 12:38 "Lord, who has believed our *m*
Ac 5:20 "and tell the people the full *m*
10:36 You know the *m* God sent
17:11 for they received the *m*
Ro 10:16 who has believed our *m*?"
10:17 faith comes from hearing the *m*,
1Co 1:18 For the *m* of the cross is
2: 4 My *m* and my preaching were not
2Co 5:19 to us the *m* of reconciliation.
2Th 3: 1 pray for us that the *m*
Tit 1: 9 firmly to the trustworthy *m*
Heb 4: 2 the *m* they heard was of no value
1Pe 2: 8 because they disobey the *m*—

MESSENGER (MESSAGE)
Pr 25:13 is a trustworthy *m*
Mal 3: 1 I will send my *m*, who will prepare
Mt 11:10 " 'I will send my *m* ahead of you,
2Co 12: 7 a *m* of Satan, to torment me.

MESSIAH*
Jn 1:41 "We have found the *M*" (that is,
4:25 "I know that *M*" (called Christ) "is

METHUSELAH
Ge 5:27 Altogether, *M* lived 969 years,

MICAH
1. Idolater from Ephraim (Jdg 17-18).
2. Prophet from Moresheth (Jer 26:18-19; Mic 1:1).

MICAIAH
Prophet of the LORD who spoke against Ahab (1Ki 22:1-28; 2Ch 18:1-27).

MICHAEL
Archangel (Jude 9); warrior in angelic realm, protector of Israel (Da 10:13, 21; 12:1; Rev 12:7).

MICHAL
Daughter of Saul, wife of David (1Sa 14:49; 18:20-28). Warned David of Saul's plot (1Sa 19). Saul gave her to Paltiel (1Sa 25:44); David retrieved her (2Sa 3:13-16). Criticized David for dancing before the ark (2Sa 6:16-23); 1Ch 15:29).

MIDIAN
Ex 2:15 Pharaoh and went to live in *M*,
Jdg 7: 2 me to deliver *M* into their hands.

MIDWIVES
Ex 1:17 The *m*, however, feared God

MIGHT (ALMIGHTY MIGHTIER MIGHTY)
Jdg 16:30 Then he pushed with all his *m*,
2Sa 6: 5 with all their *m* before the LORD,
6:14 before the LORD with all his *m*,
2Ch 20: 6 Power and *m* are in your hand,
Ps 21:13 we will sing and praise your *m*.
54: 1 vindicate me by your *m*.
Isa 63:15 Where are your zeal and your *m*?
Mic 3: 8 and with justice and *m*,
Zec 4: 6 'Not by *m* nor by power,
Col 1:11 power according to his glorious *m*
1Ti 6:16 To him be honor and *m* forever.

MIGHTIER (MIGHT)
Ps 93: 4 *M* than the thunder

MIGHTY (MIGHT)
Ge 49:24 of the hand of the *M* One of Jacob,
Ex 6: 1 of my *m* hand he will drive them
13: 3 out of it with a *m* hand.
Dt 5:15 out of there with a *m* hand
7: 8 he brought you out with a *m* hand
10:17 the great God, *m* and awesome,
34:12 one has ever shown the *m* power
2Sa 1:19 How the *m* have fallen!
23: 8 the names of David's *m* men:
Ne 9:32 the great, *m* and awesome God,
Job 36: 5 God is *m*, but does not despise men
Ps 24: 8 The LORD strong and *m*,
45: 3 upon your side, O *m* one;
50: 1 The *M* One, God, the LORD,
62: 7 he is my *m* rock, my refuge.
68:33 who thunders with *m* voice.
71:16 proclaim your *m* acts,
77:12 and consider all your *m* deeds.
77:15 With your *m* arm you redeemed

Ps 89: 8 You are *m*, O LORD,
93: 4 the LORD on high is *m*.
99: 4 The King is *m*, he loves justice—
110: 2 LORD will extend your *m* scepter
118: 15 right hand has done *m* things!
136: 12 with a *m* hand and outstretched
145: 4 they will tell of your *m* acts.
145: 12 all men may know of your *m* acts
147: 5 Great is our Lord and *m* in power;
SS 8: 6 like a *m* flame.
Isa 9: 6 Wonderful Counselor, *M* God,
60:16 your Redeemer, the *M* One
63: 1 *m* to save."
Jer 10: 6 and your name is *m* in power.
20:11 with me like a *m* warrior;
32:19 your purposes and *m* are your
Eze 20:33 I will rule over you with a *m* hand
Zep 3:17 he is *m* to save.
Mt 26:64 at the right hand of the *M* One
Eph 1:19 like the working of his *m* strength,
6:10 in the Lord and in his *m* power.
1Pe 5: 6 therefore, under God's *m* hand,

MILE*
Mt 5:41 If someone forces you to go one *m*,

MILK
Ex 3: 8 a land flowing with *m* and honey—
23:19 a young goat in its mother's *m*.
Pr 30:33 as churning the *m* produces butter,
Isa 55: 1 Come, buy wine and *m*
1Co 3: 2 I gave you *m*, not solid food,
Heb 5:12 You need *m*, not solid food!
1Pe 2: 2 babies, crave pure spiritual *m*,

MILLSTONE (STONE)
Lk 17: 2 sea with a *m* tied around his neck

MIND (DOUBLE-MINDED LIKE-MINDED MINDED MINDFUL MINDS)
Nu 23:19 that he should change his *m*.
Dt 28:65 LORD will give you an anxious *m*,
1Sa 15:29 Israel does not lie or change his *m*;
1Ch 28: 9 devotion and with a willing *m*,
2Ch 30:12 the people to give them unity of *m*
Ps 26: 2 examine my heart and my *m*;
110: 4 and will not change his *m*:
Isa 26: 3 him whose *m* is steadfast,
Jer 17:10 and examine the *m*,
Mt 22:37 all your soul and with all your *m*.'
Mk 12:30 with all your *m* and with all your
Lk 10:27 your strength and with all your *m*';
Ac 4:32 believers were one in heart and *m*.
Ro 1:28 he gave them over to a depraved *m*
7:25 I myself in my *m* am a slave
8: 6 The *m* of sinful man is death,
8: 7 the sinful *m* is hostile to God.
12: 2 by the renewing of your *m*.
14:13 make up your *m* not
1Co 1:10 you may be perfectly united in *m*
2: 9 no *m* has conceived
14:14 spirit prays, but my *m* is unfruitful.
2Co 13:11 be of one *m*, live in peace.
Php 3:19 Their *m* is on earthly things.
Col 2:18 and his unspiritual *m* puffs him up
1Th 4:11 to *m* your own business
Heb 7:21 and will not change his *m*:

MINDED* (MIND)
1Pe 4: 7 be clear *m* and self-controlled

MINDFUL* (MIND)
Ps 8: 4 what is man that you are *m* of him,
Lk 1:48 God my Savior, for he has been *m*
Heb 2: 6 What is man that you are *m* of him,

MINDS (MIND)
Dt 11:18 of mine in your hearts and *m*;
Ps 7: 9 who searches *m* and hearts,
Jer 31:33 "I will put my law in their *m*
Lk 24:38 and why do doubts rise in your *m*?
24:45 Then he opened their *m*
Ro 8: 5 to the sinful nature have their *m* set
2Co 4: 4 god of this age has blinded the *m*
Eph 4:23 new in the attitude of your *m*;
Col 3: 2 Set your *m* on things above,
Heb 8:10 I will put my laws in their *m*
10:16 and I will write them on their *m*."
1Pe 1:13 prepare your *m* for action;
Rev 2:23 I am he who searches hearts and *m*,

MINISTER (MINISTERING MINISTERS MINISTRY)
Ps 101: 6 will *m* to me.
1Ti 4: 6 you will be a good *m*

MINISTERING (MINISTER)
Heb 1:14 Are not all angels *m* spirits sent

MINISTERS (MINISTER)
2Co 3: 6 as *m* of a new covenant—

MINISTRY (MINISTER)
Ac 6: 4 to prayer and the *m* of the word."
Ro 11:13 I make much of my *m*
2Co 4: 1 God's mercy we have this *m*,
5:18 gave us the *m* of reconciliation:
6: 3 so that our *m* will not be
Gal 2: 8 who was at work in the *m* of Peter
2Ti 4: 5 discharge all the duties of your *m*.
Heb 8: 6 But the *m* Jesus has received is

MIRACLE* (MIRACLES MIRACULOUS)
Ex 7: 9 'Perform a *m*,' then say to Aaron,
Mk 9:39 "No one who does a *m*
Lk 23: 8 hoped to see him perform some *m*.
Jn 7:21 "I did one *m*, and you are all
Ac 4:16 they have done an outstanding *m*,

MIRACLES* (MIRACLE)
1Ch 16:12 his *m*, and the judgments he
Ne 9:17 to remember the *m* you performed
Job 5: 9 *m* that cannot be counted.
9:10 *m* that cannot be counted.
Ps 77:11 I will remember your *m* of long ago
77:14 You are the God who performs *m*;
78:12 He did *m* in the sight
105: 5 his *m*, and the judgments he
106: 7 they gave no thought to your *m*;
106: 22 *m* in the land of Ham
Mt 7:22 out demons and perform many *m*?'
11:20 most of his *m* had been performed,
11:21 If the *m* that were performed
11:23 If the *m* that were performed
13:58 And he did not do many *m* there
24:24 and perform great signs and *m*
Mk 6: 2 does *m*! Isn't this the carpenter?
6: 5 He could not do any *m* there,
13:22 and *m* to deceive the elect—
Lk 10:13 For if the *m* that were performed
19:37 for all the *m* they had seen:
Jn 7: 3 disciples may see the *m* you do.
10:25 *m* I do in my Father's name speak
10:32 "I have shown you many great *m*
10:38 do not believe me, believe the *m*,
14:11 the evidence of the *m* themselves.
15:24 But now they have seen these *m*,
Ac 2:22 accredited by God to you by *m*,
8:13 by the great signs and *m* he saw.
19:11 God did extraordinary *m*
Ro 15:19 by the power of signs and *m*,
1Co 12:28 third teachers, then workers of *m*,
12:29 Are all teachers? Do all work *m*?
2Co 12:12 and *m*— were done among you
Gal 3: 5 work *m* among you because you
2Th 2: 9 in all kinds of counterfeit *m*,
Heb 2: 4 it by signs, wonders and various *m*,

MIRACULOUS (MIRACLE)
Dt 13: 1 and announces to you a *m* sign
Mt 12:39 generation asks for a *m* sign!
13:54 this wisdom and these *m* powers?"
Jn 2:11 This, the first of his *m* signs,
2:23 people saw the *m* signs he was
3: 2 could perform the *m* signs you are
4:48 "Unless you people see *m* signs
7:31 will he do more *m* signs
9:16 "How can a sinner do such *m* signs
12:37 Jesus had done all these *m* signs
20:30 Jesus did many other *m* signs
Ac 2:43 *m* signs were done by the apostles.
5:12 apostles performed many *m* signs
1Co 1:22 Jews demand *m* signs and Greeks
12:10 to another *m* powers,

MIRE
Ps 40: 2 out of the mud and *m*;
Isa 57:20 whose waves cast up *m* and mud.

MIRIAM
Sister of Moses and Aaron (Nu 26:59). Led dancing at Red Sea (Ex 15:20-21). Struck with leprosy for criticizing Moses (Nu 12). Death (Nu 20:1).

MIRROR
1Co 13:12 but a poor reflection as in a *m*;
Jas 1:23 a man who looks at his face in a *m*

MISDEEDS*
Ps 99: 8 though you punished their *m*.
Ro 8:13 put to death the *m* of the body,

MISERY
Ex 3: 7 "I have indeed seen the *m*
Jdg 10:16 he could bear Israel's *m* no longer.
Hos 5:15 in their *m* they will earnestly seek
Ro 3:16 ruin and *m* mark their ways,
Jas 5: 1 of the *m* that is coming upon you.

MISFORTUNE
Ob :12 brother in the day of his *m*,

MISLEAD (MISLED)
Isa 47:10 wisdom and knowledge *m* you

MISLED (MISLEAD)
1Co 15:33 Do not be *m*: "Bad company

MISS (MISSES)
Pr 19: 2 nor to be hasty and *m* the way.

MISSES (MISS)
Heb 12:15 See to it that no one *m* the grace

MIST
Hos 6: 4 Your love is like the morning *m*,
Jas 4:14 You are a *m* that appears for a little

MISTREAT (MISTREATED)
Ex 22:21 "Do not *m* an alien or oppress him,
Eze 22:29 and needy and *m* the alien,
Lk 6:28 pray for those who *m* you.

MISTREATED (MISTREAT)
Eze 22: 7 *m* the fatherless and the widow.
Heb 11:25 to be *m* along with the people
11:37 destitute, persecuted and *m*—
13: 3 who are *m* as if you yourselves

MISUSE* (MISUSES)
Ex 20: 7 "You shall not *m* the name
Dt 5:11 "You shall not *m* the name
Ps 139: 20 your adversaries *m* your name.

MISUSES* (MISUSE)
Ex 20: 7 anyone guiltless who *m* his name.
Dt 5:11 anyone guiltless who *m* his name.

MIXED (MIXING)
Da 2:41 even as you saw iron *m* with clay.

MIXING (MIXED)
Isa 5:22 and champions at *m* drinks,

MOAB (MOABITESS)
Ge 19:37 she named him *M*; he is the father
Dt 34: 6 He buried him in *M*, in the valley
Ru 1: 1 live for a while in the country of *M*.
Isa 15: 1 An oracle concerning *M*:
Jer 48:16 "The fall of *M* is at hand;
Am 2: 1 "For three sins of *M*,

MOABITESS (MOAB)
Ru 1:22 accompanied by Ruth the *M*,

MOAN
Ps 90: 9 we finish our years with a *m*.

MOCK (MOCKED MOCKER MOCKERS MOCKING MOCKS)
Ps 22: 7 All who see me *m* me;
119: 51 The arrogant *m* me
Pr 1:26 I will *m* when calamity overtakes
14: 9 Fools *m* at making amends for sin,
Mk 10:34 who will *m* him and spit on him,

MOCKED (MOCK)
Ps 89:51 with which they have *m* every step
Mt 27:29 knelt in front of him and *m* him.
27:41 of the law and the elders *m* him.
Gal 6: 7 not be deceived: God cannot be *m*.

MOCKER (MOCK)
Pr 9: 7 corrects a *m* invites insult;
9:12 if you are a *m*, you alone will suffer
20: 1 Wine is a *m* and beer a brawler;
22:10 Drive out the *m*, and out goes strife

MOCKERS (MOCK)
Ps 1: 1 or sit in the seat of *m*.
Pr 29: 8 *M* stir up a city,

MOCKING (MOCK)
Isa 50: 6 face from *m* and spitting.

MOCKS (MOCK)
Pr 17: 5 He who *m* the poor shows
30:17 "The eye that *m* a father,

MODEL*
Eze 28:12 " 'You were the *m* of perfection,
1Th 1: 7 And so you became a *m*
2Th 3: 9 to make ourselves a *m* for you

MODESTY*
1Co 12:23 are treated with special *m*,

MOLDED*
Job 10: 9 Remember that you *m* me like clay

MOLDY
Jos 9: 5 of their food supply was dry and *m.*

MOLECH
Lev 20: 2 of his children to *M* must be put
1Ki 11:33 and *M* the god of the Ammonites,

MOMENT (MOMENTARY)
Job 20: 5 the joy of the godless lasts but a *m.*
Ps 2:12 for his wrath can flare up in a *m.*
30: 5 For his anger lasts only a *m,*
Pr 12:19 but a lying tongue lasts only a *m.*
Isa 54: 7 "For a brief *m* I abandoned you,
66: 8 or a nation be brought forth in a *m?*
Gal 2: 5 We did not give in to them for a *m,*

MOMENTARY* (MOMENT)
2Co 4:17 and *m* troubles are achieving

MONEY
Pr 13:11 Dishonest *m* dwindles away,
Ecc 5:10 Whoever loves *m* never has *m*
Isa 55: 1 and you who have no *m,*
Mt 6:24 You cannot serve both God and *M.*
27: 5 Judas threw the *m* into the temple
Lk 3:14 "Don't extort *m* and don't accuse
9: 3 no bread, no *m,* no extra tunic.
16:13 You cannot serve both God and *M*
Ac 5: 2 part of the *m* for himself,
1Co 16: 2 set aside a sum of *m* in keeping
1Ti 3: 3 not quarrelsome, not a lover of *m.*
6:10 For the love of *m* is a root
2Ti 3: 2 lovers of *m,* boastful, proud,
Heb 13: 5 free from the love of *m*
1Pe 5: 2 not greedy for *m,* but eager to serve

MONEYLENDER* (LEND)
Ex 22:25 not be like a *m;* charge him no
Lk 7:41 men owed money to a certain *m.*

MONTH (MONTHS)
Ex 12: 2 "This *m* is to be for you the first
Eze 47:12 Every *m* they will bear,
Rev 22: 2 of fruit, yielding its fruit every *m.*

MONTHS (MONTH)
Gal 4:10 and *m* and seasons and years!
Rev 11: 2 trample on the holy city for 42 *m.*
13: 5 his authority for forty-two *m.*

MOON
Jos 10:13 and the *m* stopped,
Ps 8: 3 the *m* and the stars,
74:16 you established the sun and *m.*
89:37 be established forever like the *m,*
104: 19 The *m* marks off the seasons,
121: 6 nor the *m* by night.
136: 9 the *m* and stars to govern the night;
148: 3 Praise him, sun and *m,*
SS 6:10 fair as the *m,* bright as the sun,
Joel 2:31 and the *m* to blood
Hab 3:11 and *m* stood still in the heavens
Mt 24:29 and the *m* will not give its light;
Ac 2:20 and the *m* to blood
1Co 15:41 *m* another and the stars another;
Col 2:16 a New *M* celebration or a Sabbath
Rev 6:12 the whole *m* turned blood red,
21:23 city does not need the sun or the *m*

MORAL*
Jas 1:21 rid of all *m* filth and the evil that is

MORDECAI
Benjamite exile who raised Esther (Est 2:5-15). Exposed plot to kill Xerxes (Est 2:19-23). Refused to honor Haman (Est 3:1-6; 5:9-14). Charged Esther to foil Haman's plot against the Jews (Est 4). Xerxes forced Haman to honor Mordecai (Est 6). Mordecai exalted (Est 8-10). Established Purim (Est 9:18-32).

MORIAH*
Ge 22: 2 and go to the region of *M.*
2Ch 3: 1 LORD in Jerusalem on Mount *M,*

MORNING
Ge 1: 5 and there was *m*— the first day.
Dt 28:67 In the *m* you will say, "If only it
2Sa 23: 4 he is like the light of *m* at sunrise
Ps 5: 3 In the *m,* O LORD,
Pr 27:14 blesses his neighbor early in the *m,*
Isa 14:12 O *m* star, son of the dawn!
La 3:23 They are new every *m;*
2Pe 1:19 and the *m* star rises in your hearts.
Rev 2:28 I will also give him the *m* star.
22:16 of David, and the bright *M* Star."

MORTAL
Ge 6: 3 for he is *m;* his days will be
Job 10: 4 Do you see as a *m* sees?
Ro 8:11 also give life to your *m* bodies
1Co 15:53 and the *m* with immortality.
2Co 5: 4 that what is *m* may be swallowed

MOSES
Levite; brother of Aaron (Ex 6:20; 1Ch 6:3). Put in basket into Nile; discovered and raised by Pharaoh's daughter (Ex 2:1-10). Fled to Midian after killing Egyptian (Ex 2:11-15). Married to Zipporah, fathered Gershom (Ex 2:16-22).

Called by the LORD to deliver Israel (Ex 3-4). Pharaoh's resistance (Ex 5). Ten plagues (Ex 7-11). Passover and Exodus (Ex 12-13). Led Israel through Red Sea (Ex 14). Song of deliverance (Ex 15:1-21). Brought water from rock (Ex 17:1-7). Raised hands to defeat Amalekites (Ex 17:8-16). Delegated judges (Ex 18; Dt 1:9-18).

Received Law at Sinai (Ex 19-23; 25-31; Jn 1:17). Announced Law to Israel (Ex 19:7-8; 24; 35). Broke tablets because of golden calf (Ex 32; Dt 9). Saw glory of the LORD (Ex 33-34). Supervised building of tabernacle (Ex 36-40). Set apart Aaron and priests (Lev 8-9). Numbered tribes (Nu 1-4; 26). Opposed by Aaron and Miriam (Nu 12). Sent spies into Canaan (Nu 13). Announced forty years of wandering for failure to enter land (Nu 14). Opposed by Korah (Nu 16). Forbidden to enter land for striking rock (Nu 20:1-13; Dt 1:37). Lifted bronze snake for healing (Nu 21:4-9; Jn 3:14). Final address to Israel (Dt 1-33). Succeeded by Joshua (Nu 27:12-23; Dt 34). Death (Dt 34:5-12).

"Law of Moses" (1Ki 2:3; Ezr 3:2; Mk 12:26; Lk 24:44). "Book of Moses" (2Ch 25:12; Ne 13:1). "Song of Moses" (Ex 15:1-21; Rev 15:3). "Prayer of Moses" (Ps 90).

MOTH
Mt 6:19 where *m* and rust destroy,

MOTHER (GRANDMOTHER MOTHER-IN-LAW MOTHER'S)
Ge 2:24 and *m* and be united to his wife,
3:20 because she would become the *m*
Ex 20:12 "Honor your father and your *m,*
Lev 20: 9 " 'If anyone curses his father or *m,*
Dt 5:16 "Honor your father and your *m,*
21:18 who does not obey his father and *m*
27:16 who dishonors his father or his *m.*"
Jdg 5: 7 arose a *m* in Israel.
1Sa 2:19 Each year his *m* made him a little
Ps 113: 9 as a happy *m* of children.
Pr 10: 1 but a foolish son grief to his *m.*
23:22 do not despise your *m*
23:25 May your father and *m* be glad;
29:15 a child left to himself disgraces his *m.*
30:17 that scorns obedience to a *m,*
31: 1 an oracle his *m* taught him:
Isa 49:15 "Can a *m* forget the baby
66:13 As a *m* comforts her child,
Jer 20:17 with my *m* as my grave,
Mic 7: 6 a daughter rises up against her *m,*
Mt 10:35 a daughter against her *m,*
10:37 or *m* more than me is not worthy
12:48 He replied to him, "Who is my *m,*
15: 4 'Honor your father and *m*'
19: 5 and *m* and be united to his wife,
19:19 honor your father and *m,*'
Mk 7:10 'Honor your father and your *m,*' and,
10:19 honor your father and *m.*' "
Lk 11:27 "Blessed is the *m* who gave you
12:53 daughter and daughter against *m,*
18:20 honor your father and *m.*' "
Jn 19:27 to the disciple, "Here is your *m.*"
Gal 4:26 is above is free, and she is our *m.*
Eph 5:31 and *m* and be united to his wife,
6: 2 "Honor your father and *m*"—
1Th 2: 7 like a *m* caring for her little
2Ti 1: 5 and in your *m* Eunice and,

MOTHER-IN-LAW (MOTHER)
Ru 2:19 Ruth told her *m* about the one
Mt 10:35 a daughter-in-law against her *m*—

MOTHER'S (MOTHER)
Job 1:21 "Naked I came from my *m* womb,
Pr 1: 8 and do not forsake your *m* teaching
Ecc 5:15 from his *m* womb,
11: 5 the body is formed in a *m* womb,
Jn 3: 4 time into his *m* womb to be born!"

MOTIVE* (MOTIVES)
1Ch 28: 9 and understands every *m*

MOTIVES* (MOTIVE)
Pr 16: 2 but *m* are weighed by the LORD.
1Co 4: 5 will expose the *m* of men's hearts.
Php 1:18 whether from false *m* or true,
1Th 2: 3 spring from error or impure *m,*
Jas 4: 3 because you ask with wrong *m,*

MOUNT (MOUNTAIN MOUNTAINS MOUNTAINTOPS)
Ps 89: 9 when its waves *m* up, you still them
Isa 14:13 enthroned on the *m* of assembly,
Eze 28:14 You were on the holy *m* of God;
Zec 14: 4 stand on the *M* of Olives,

MOUNTAIN (MOUNT)
Ge 22:14 "On the *m* of the LORD it will be
Ex 24:18 And he stayed on the *m* forty days
Dt 5: 4 face to face out of the fire on the *m.*
Job 14:18 "But as a *m* erodes and crumbles
Ps 48: 1 in the city of our God, his holy *m.*
Isa 40: 4 every *m* and hill made low;
Mic 4: 2 let us go up to the *m* of the LORD,
Mt 4: 8 the devil took him to a very high *m*
17:20 say to this *m,* 'Move from here
Mk 9: 2 with him and led them up a high *m,*
Lk 3: 5 every *m* and hill made low.
Jn 4:21 the Father neither on this *m*
2Pe 1:18 were with him on the sacred *m.*

MOUNTAINS (MOUNT)
Ps 36: 6 righteousness is like the mighty *m,*
46: 2 the *m* fall into the heart of the sea,
90: 2 Before the *m* were born
Isa 52: 7 How beautiful on the *m*
54:10 Though the *m* be shaken
55:12 the *m* and hills
Eze 34: 6 My sheep wandered over all the *m*
Mt 24:16 are in Judea flee to the *m.*
Lk 23:30 they will say to the *m,* "Fall on us!"
1Co 13: 2 if I have a faith that can move *m,*
Rev 6:16 They called to the *m* and the rocks,

MOUNTAINTOPS (MOUNT)
Isa 42:11 let them shout from the *m.*

MOURN (MOURNING MOURNS)
Ecc 3: 4 a time to *m* and a time to dance,
Isa 61: 2 to comfort all who *m,*
Mt 5: 4 Blessed are those who *m,*
Ro 12:15 *m* with those who *m.*

MOURNING (MOURN)
Isa 61: 3 instead of *m,*
Jer 31:13 I will turn their *m* into gladness;
Rev 21: 4 There will be no more death or *m*

MOURNS (MOURN)
Zec 12:10 as one *m* for an only child,

MOUTH (MOUTHS)
Nu 22:38 only what God puts in my *m.*"
Dt 8: 3 comes from the *m* of the LORD.
18:18 I will put my words in his *m,*
30:14 it is in your *m* and in your heart
Jos 1: 8 of the Law depart from your *m;*
2Ki 4:34 *m* to *m,* eyes to eyes, hands
Ps 10: 7 His *m* is full of curses and lies
17: 3 resolved that my *m* will not sin.
19:14 May the words of my *m*
37:30 *m* of the righteous man utters
40: 3 He put a new song in my *m,*
71: 8 My *m* is filled with your praise,
119:103 sweeter than honey to my *m!*
141: 3 Set a guard over my *m,* O LORD;
Pr 2: 6 and from his *m* come knowledge
4:24 Put away perversity from your *m;*
10:11 The *m* of the righteous is a fountain
10:31 *m* of the righteous brings forth
16:23 A wise man's heart guides his *m,*
26:28 and a flattering *m* works ruin.
27: 2 praise you, and not your own *m;*
Ecc 5: 2 Do not be quick with your *m,*
SS 1: 2 with the kisses of his *m*—
5:16 His *m* is sweetness itself;
Isa 29:13 come near to me with their *m*
40: 5 For the *m* of the LORD has spoken
45:23 my *m* has uttered in all integrity
51:16 I have put my words in your *m*
53: 7 so he did not open his *m.*
55:11 my word that goes out from my *m:*
59:21 *m* will not depart from your *m,*
Eze 3: 2 So I opened my *m,* and he gave me
Mal 2: 7 and from his *m* men should seek
Mt 4: 4 comes from the *m* of God.' "
12:34 overflow of the heart the *m* speaks.
15:11 into a man's *m* does not make him
15:18 out of the *m* come from the heart,
Lk 6:45 overflow of his heart his *m* speaks.
Ro 10: 9 That if you confess with your *m,*
15: 6 and *m* you may glorify the God
1Pe 2:22 and no deceit was found in his *m.*"
Rev 1:16 and out of his *m* came a sharp
2:16 them with the sword of my *m.*
3:16 I am about to spit you out of my *m.*
19:15 Out of his *m* comes a sharp sword

MOUTHS (MOUTH)
Ps 78:36 would flatter him with their *m*,
Eze 33:31 With their *m* they express devotion
Ro 3:14 "Their *m* are full of cursing
Eph 4:29 talk come out of your *m*,
Jas 3: 3 bits into the *m* of horses

MOVE (MOVED MOVES)
Dt 19:14 Do not *m* your neighbor's
Pr 23:10 Do not *m* an ancient boundary
Ac 17:28 and *m* and have our being.'
1Co 13: 2 have a faith that can *m* mountains,
15:58 Let nothing *m* you.

MOVED (MOVE)
Ex 35:21 and whose heart *m* him came
2Ch 36:22 the LORD *m* the heart
Ezr 1: 5 everyone whose heart God had *m*
Ps 93: 1 it cannot be *m*.
Jn 11:33 he was deeply *m* in spirit
Col 1:23 not *m* from the hope held out

MOVES (MOVE)
Dt 23:14 For the LORD your God *m* about

MUD (MUDDIED)
Ps 40: 2 out of the *m* and mire;
Isa 57:20 whose waves cast up mire and *m*.
Jn 9: 6 made some *m* with the saliva,
2Pe 2:22 back to her wallowing in the *m*."

MUDDIED (MUD)
Pr 25:26 Like a *m* spring or a polluted well
Eze 32:13 or *m* by the hoofs of cattle.

MULBERRY*
Lk 17: 6 you can say to this *m* tree,

MULTITUDE (MULTITUDES)
Isa 31: 1 who trust in the *m* of their chariots
Jas 5:20 and cover over a *m* of sins.
1Pe 4: 8 love covers over a *m* of sins.
Rev 7: 9 me was a great *m* that no one could
19: 1 of a great *m* in heaven shouting:

MULTITUDES (MULTITUDE)
Ne 9: 6 and the *m* of heaven worship you.
Da 12: 2 *M* who sleep in the dust
Joel 3:14 *M*, *m* in the valley of decision!

MURDER (MURDERED MURDERER MURDERERS)
Ex 20:13 "You shall not *m*.
Dt 5:17 "You shall not *m*.
Pr 28:17 A man tormented by the guilt of *m*
Mt 5:21 'Do not *m*, and anyone who
15:19 *m*, adultery, sexual immorality,
Ro 1:29 *m*, strife, deceit and malice.
13: 9 "Do not *m*," "Do not steal,"
Jas 2:11 adultery," also said, "Do not *m*."

MURDERED (MURDER)
Mt 23:31 of those who *m* the prophets.
Ac 7:52 now you have betrayed and *m* him
1Jn 3:12 to the evil one and *m* his brother.

MURDERER (MURDER)
Nu 35:16 he is a *m*; the *m* shall be put
Jn 8:44 He was a *m* from the beginning,
1Jn 3:15 who hates his brother is a *m*,

MURDERERS (MURDER)
1Ti 1: 9 for *m*, for adulterers and perverts,
Rev 21: 8 the *m*, the sexually immoral,
22:15 the sexually immoral, the *m*,

MUSIC* (MUSICAL MUSICIAN MUSICIANS)
Ge 31:27 singing to the *m* of tambourines
Jdg 5: 3 I will make *m* to the LORD,
1Ch 6:31 put in charge of the *m* in the house
6:32 They ministered with *m*
25: 6 fathers for the *m* of the temple
25: 7 and skilled in *m* for the LORD—
Ne 12:27 and with the *m* of cymbals,
Job 21:12 They sing to the *m* of tambourine
Ps 27: 6 and make *m* to the LORD.
33: 2 make *m* to him on the ten-stringed
45: 8 the *m* of the strings makes you glad
57: 7 I will sing and make *m*.
81: 2 Begin the *m*, strike the tambourine,
87: 7 As they make *m* they will sing,
92: 1 and make *m* to your name,
92: 3 to the *m* of the ten-stringed lyre
95: 2 and extol him with *m* and song.
98: 4 burst into jubilant song with *m*;
98: 5 make *m* to the LORD
108: 1 make *m* with all my soul.
144: 9 the ten-stringed lyre I will make *m*
147: 7 make *m* to our God on the harp.
149: 3 make *m* to him with tambourine
Isa 30:32 will be to the *m* of tambourines
La 5:14 young men have stopped their *m*.
Eze 26:13 *m* of your harps will be heard no
Da 3: 5 lyre, harp, pipes and all kinds of *m*,
3: 7 and all kinds of *m*, all the peoples,
3:10 and all kinds of *m* must fall down
3:15 lyre, harp, pipes and all kinds of *m*,
Am 5:23 to the *m* of your harps.
Hab 3:19 For the director of *m*.
Lk 15:25 came near the house, he heard *m*
Eph 5:19 make *m* in your heart to the Lord,
Rev 18:22 The *m* of harpists and musicians,

MUSICAL* (MUSIC)
1Ch 15:16 accompanied by *m* instruments:
23: 5 with the *m* instruments I have
2Ch 7: 6 with the LORD's *m* instruments,
23:13 with *m* instruments were leading
34:12 skilled in playing *m* instruments—
Ne 12:36 with *m* instruments prescribed
Am 6: 5 and improvise on *m* instruments.

MUSICIAN* (MUSIC)
1Ch 6:33 Heman, the *m*, the son of Joel,

MUSICIANS* (MUSIC)
1Ki 10:12 to make harps and lyres for the *m*.
1Ch 9:33 Those who were *m*, heads
15:19 The *m* Heman, Asaph
2Ch 5:12 All the Levites who were *m*—
9:11 to make harps and lyres for the *m*.
35:15 The *m*, the descendants of Asaph,
Ps 68:25 are the singers, after them the *m*;
Rev 18:22 The music of harpists and *m*,

MUSTARD
Mt 13:31 kingdom of heaven is like a *m* seed,
17:20 you have faith as small as a *m* seed,
Mk 4:31 It is like a *m* seed, which is

MUTILATORS*
Php 3: 2 those men who do evil, those *m*

MUTUAL* (MUTUALLY)
Ro 14:19 leads to peace and to *m* edification.
1Co 7: 5 by *m* consent and for a time,

MUTUALLY* (MUTUAL)
Ro 1:12 and I may be *m* encouraged

MUZZLE*
Dt 25: 4 Do not *m* an ox while it is treading
Ps 39: 1 I will put a *m* on my mouth
1Co 9: 9 "Do not *m* an ox while it is
1Ti 5:18 "Do not *m* the ox while it is

MYRRH
Ps 45: 8 All your robes are fragrant with *m*
SS 1:13 My lover is to me a sachet of *m*
Mt 2:11 of gold and of incense and of *m*.
Mk 15:23 offered him wine mixed with *m*,
Jn 19:39 Nicodemus brought a mixture of *m*
Rev 18:13 of incense, *m* and frankincense,

MYSTERIES* (MYSTERY)
Job 11: 7 "Can you fathom the *m* of God?
Da 2:28 a God in heaven who reveals *m*.
2:29 of *m* showed you what is going
2:47 Lord of kings and a revealer of *m*,
1Co 13: 2 can fathom all *m* and all knowledge
14: 2 he utters *m* with his spirit.

MYSTERY* (MYSTERIES)
Da 2:18 God of heaven concerning this *m*,
2:19 the night the *m* was revealed
2:27 to the king the *m* he has asked
2:30 this *m* has been revealed to me,
2:47 for you were able to reveal this *m*."
4: 9 and no *m* is too difficult for you.
Ro 11:25 you to be ignorant of this *m*,
16:25 to the revelation of the *m* hidden
1Co 15:51 I tell you a *m*: We will not all sleep,
Eph 1: 9 to us the *m* of his will according
3: 3 the *m* made known to me
3: 4 insight into the *m* of Christ,
3: 6 This *m* is that through the gospel
3: 9 the administration of this *m*,
5:32 This is a profound *m*—
6:19 I will fearlessly make known the *m*
Col 1:26 the *m* that has been kept hidden
1:27 the glorious riches of this *m*,
2: 2 in order that they may know the *m*
4: 3 so that we may proclaim the *m*
1Ti 3:16 the *m* of godliness is great:
Rev 1:20 *m* of the seven stars that you saw
10: 7 the *m* of God will be accomplished,
17: 5 written on her forehead: *M*
17: 7 explain to you the *m* of the woman

MYTHS*
1Ti 1: 4 nor to devote themselves to *m*
4: 7 Have nothing to do with godless *m*
2Ti 4: 4 from the truth and turn aside to *m*.
Tit 1:14 will pay no attention to Jewish *m*

NAAMAN
Aramean general whose leprosy was cleansed by Elisha (2Ki 5).

NABAL
Wealthy Carmelite the LORD killed for refusing to help David (1Sa 25). David married Abigail, his widow (1Sa 25:39-42).

NABOTH*
Jezreelite killed by Jezebel for his vineyard (1Ki 21). Ahab's family destroyed for this (1Ki 21:17-24; 2Ki 9:21-37).

NADAB
1. Firstborn of Aaron (Ex 6:23); killed with Abihu for offering unauthorized fire (Lev 10; Nu 3:4).
2. Son of Jeroboam I; king of Israel (1Ki 15:25-32).

NAHUM
Prophet against Nineveh (Na 1:1).

NAIL* (NAILING)
Jn 20:25 "Unless I see the *n* marks

NAILING* (NAIL)
Ac 2:23 him to death by *n* him to the cross.
Col 2:14 he took it away, *n* it to the cross.

NAIVE
Ro 16:18 they deceive the minds of *n* people.

NAKED
Ge 2:25 The man and his wife were both *n*,
Job 1:21 *N* I came from my mother's womb,
Isa 58: 7 when you see the *n*, to clothe him,
2Co 5: 3 are clothed, we will not be found *n*.

NAME (NAMES)
Ge 2:19 man to see what he would *n* them;
4:26 to call on the *n* of the LORD.
11: 4 so that we may make a *n*
12: 2 I will make your *n* great,
32:29 Jacob said, "Please tell me your *n*."
Ex 3:15 This is my *n* forever, the *n*
20: 7 "You shall not misuse the *n*
34:14 for the LORD, whose *n* is Jealous,
Lev 24:11 Israelite woman blasphemed the *N*
Dt 5:11 "You shall not misuse the *n*
12:11 choose as a dwelling for his *N*—
18: 5 minister in the LORD's *n* always.
25: 6 carry on the *n* of the dead brother
28:58 this glorious and awesome *n*—
Jos 7: 9 do for your own great *n*?"
Jdg 13:17 "What is your *n*, so that we may
1Sa 12:22 of his great *n* the LORD will not
2Sa 6: 2 which is called by the *N*, the name
7: 9 Now I will make your *n* great,
1Ki 5: 5 will build the temple for my *N*.'
8:29 you said, 'My *N* shall be there,'
1Ch 17: 8 I will make your *n* like the names
2Ch 7:14 my people, who are called by my *n*,
Ne 9:10 You made a *n* for yourself,
Ps 8: 1 how majestic is your *n*
9:10 Those who know your *n* will trust
20: 7 in the *n* of the LORD our God.
29: 2 to the LORD the glory due his *n*;
34: 3 let us exalt his *n* together.
44:20 If we had forgotten the *n*
66: 2 Sing the glory of his *n*;
68: 4 Sing to God, sing praise to his *n*,
79: 9 for the glory of your *n*;
96: 8 to the LORD the glory due his *n*;
103: 1 my inmost being, praise his holy *n*.
115: 1 but to your *n* be the glory,
138: 2 your *n* and your word.
145: 1 I will praise your *n* for ever
147: 4 and calls them each by *n*.
Pr 3: 4 you will win favor and a good *n*
18:10 *n* of the LORD is a strong tower;
22: 1 A good *n* is more desirable
30: 4 What is his *n*, and the *n* of his son?
Ecc 7: 1 A good *n* is better
SS 1: 3 your *n* is like perfume poured out.
Isa 12: 4 thanks to the LORD, call on his *n*;
26: 8 your *n* and renown
40:26 and calls them each by *n*.
42: 8 "I am the LORD; that is my *n*!
56: 5 I will give them an everlasting *n*
57:15 who lives forever, whose *n* is holy:
63:14 to make for yourself a glorious *n*.
Jer 14: 7 do something for the sake of your *n*
15:16 for I bear your *n*,

Eze 20: 9 of my *n* I did what would keep it
20:14 of my *n* I did what would keep it
20:22 of my *n* I did what would keep it
Da 12: 1 everyone whose *n* is found written
Hos 12: 5 the LORD is his *n* of renown!
Joel 2:32 on the *n* of the LORD will be saved
Mic 5: 4 in the majesty of the *n*
Zep 3: 9 call on the *n* of the LORD
Zec 6:12 is the man whose *n* is the Branch,
14: 9 one LORD, and his *n* the only *n*.
Mal 1: 6 O priests, who show contempt for my *n*.
Mt 1:21 and you are to give him the *n* Jesus,
6: 9 hallowed be your *n*,
18:20 or three come together in my *n*,
24: 5 For many will come in my *n*,
28:19 them in the *n* of the Father
Mk 9:41 gives you a cup of water in my *n*
Lk 11: 2 hallowed be your *n*,
Jn 10: 3 He calls his own sheep by *n*
14:13 I will do whatever you ask in my *n*,
16:24 asked for anything in my *n*.
Ac 2:21 on the *n* of the Lord will be saved.'
4:12 for there is no other *n*
Ro 10:13 "Everyone who calls on the *n*
Php 2: 9 him the *n* that is above every *n*,
2:10 at the *n* of Jesus every knee should
Col 3:17 do it all in the *n* of the Lord Jesus,
Heb 1: 4 as the *n* he has inherited is superior
Jas 5:14 him with oil in the *n* of the Lord.
1Jn 5:13 believe in the *n* of the Son of God
Rev 2:17 stone with a new *n* written on it,
3: 5 I will never blot out his *n*
3:12 I will also write on him my new *n*.
19:13 and his *n* is the Word of God.
20:15 If anyone's *n* was not found written

NAMES (NAME)
Ex 28: 9 engrave on them the *n* of the sons
Lk 10:20 but rejoice that your *n* are written
Php 4: 3 whose *n* are in the book of life.
Heb 12:23 whose *n* are written in heaven.
Rev 21:27 but only those whose *n* are written

NAOMI
Wife of Elimelech, mother-in-law of Ruth (Ru 1: 2, 4). Left Bethlehem for Moab during famine (Ru 1:1). Returned a widow, with Ruth (Ru 1:6-22). Advised Ruth to seek marriage with Boaz (Ru 2: 17-3:4). Cared for Ruth's son Obed (Ru 4:13-17).

NAPHTALI
Son of Jacob by Bilhah (Ge 30:8; 35:25; 1Ch 2: 2). Tribe of blessed (Ge 49:21; Dt 33:23), numbered (Nu 1:43; 26:50), allotted land (Jos 19:32-39; Eze 48:3), failed to fully possess (Jdg 1:33), supported Deborah (Jdg 4:10; 5:18), David (1Ch 12: 34), 12,000 from (Rev 7:6).

NARROW
Mt 7:13 "Enter through the *n* gate.
7:14 and *n* the road that leads to life,

NATHAN
Prophet and chronicler of Israel's history (1Ch 29:29; 2Ch 9:29). Announced the Davidic covenant (2Sa 7; 1Ch 17). Denounced David's sin with Bathsheba (2Sa 12). Supported Solomon (1Ki 1).

NATHANAEL*
Apostle (Jn 1:45-49; 21:2). Probably also called Bartholomew (Mt 10:3).

NATION (NATIONS)
Ge 12: 2 "I will make you into a great *n*
Ex 19: 6 a kingdom of priests and a holy *n*.'
Dt 4: 7 What other *n* is so great
Jos 5: 8 And after the whole *n* had been
2Sa 7:23 one *n* on earth that God went out
Ps 33:12 Blessed is the *n* whose God is
Pr 11:14 For lack of guidance a *n* falls,
14:34 Righteousness exalts a *n*,
Isa 2: 4 *N* will not take up sword
26: 2 that the righteous *n* may enter,
60:12 For the *n* or kingdom that will not
65: 1 To a *n* that did not call on my name
66: 8 a *n* be brought forth in a moment?
Mic 4: 3 *N* will not take up sword
Mt 24: 7 *N* will rise against *n*,
Mk 13: 8 *N* will rise against *n*,
1Pe 2: 9 a royal priesthood, a holy *n*,
Rev 5: 9 and language and people and *n*.
7: 9 from every *n*, tribe, people
14: 6 to every *n*, tribe, language

NATIONS (NATION)
Ge 17: 4 You will be the father of many *n*.
18:18 and all *n* on earth will be blessed
Ex 19: 5 of all *n* you will be my treasured
Lev 20:26 apart from the *n* to be my own.
Dt 7: 1 drives out before you many *n*—
15: 6 You will rule over many *n*
Jdg 3: 1 These are the *n* the LORD left
2Ch 20: 6 rule over all the kingdoms of the *n*.
Ne 1: 8 I will scatter you among the *n*,
Ps 2: 1 Why do the *n* conspire
2: 8 I will make the *n* your inheritance,
9: 5 You have rebuked the *n*
22:28 and he rules over the *n*.
46:10 I will be exalted among the *n*,
47: 8 God reigns over the *n*;
66: 7 his eyes watch the *n*—
67: 2 your salvation among all *n*.
68:30 Scatter the *n* who delight in war.
72:17 All *n* will be blessed through him,
96: 3 Declare his glory among the *n*,
99: 2 he is exalted over all the *n*.
106: 35 but they mingled with the *n*
110: 6 He will judge the *n*, heaping up
113: 4 The LORD is exalted over all the *n*
Isa 2: 2 and all *n* will stream to it.
11:10 the *n* will rally to him,
12: 4 among the *n* what he has done,
40:15 Surely the *n* are like a drop
42: 1 and he will bring justice to the *n*.
51: 4 justice will become a light to the *n*.
52:15 so will he sprinkle many *n*,
56: 7 a house of prayer for all *n*."
60: 3 *N* will come to your light,
66:18 and gather all *n* and tongues,
Jer 1: 5 you as a prophet to the *n*."
3:17 and all *n* will gather in Jerusalem
31:10 "Hear the word of the LORD, O *n*;
33: 9 and honor before all *n*
46:28 I completely destroy all the *n*
Eze 22: 4 you an object of scorn to the *n*
34:13 I will bring them out from the *n*
36:23 *n* will know that I am the LORD,
37:22 and they will never again be two *n*
39:21 I will display my glory among the *n*
Hos 7: 8 "Ephraim mixes with the *n*;
Joel 2:17 a byword among the *n*.
3: 2 I will gather all *n*
Am 9:12 and all the *n* that bear my name,"
Zep 3: 8 I have decided to assemble the *n*,
Hag 2: 7 and the desired of all *n* will come,
Zec 8:13 an object of cursing among the *n*,
8:23 *n* will take firm hold of one Jew
9:10 He will proclaim peace to the *n*.
14: 2 I will gather all the *n* to Jerusalem
Mt 12:18 he will proclaim justice to the *n*.
24: 9 and you will be hated by all *n*
24:14 whole world as a testimony to all *n*,
25:32 All the *n* will be gathered
28:19 and make disciples of all *n*,
Mk 11:17 a house of prayer for all *n*'?
Ac 4:25 " 'Why do the *n* rage
Ro 15:12 who will arise to rule over the *n*;
Gal 3: 8 All *n* will be blessed through you."
1Ti 3:16 was preached among the *n*,
Rev 15: 4 All *n* will come
21:24 The *n* will walk by its light,
22: 2 are for the healing of the *n*.

NATURAL (NATURE)
Ro 6:19 you are weak in your *n* selves.
1Co 15:44 If there is a *n* body, there is

NATURE (NATURAL)
Ro 1:20 his eternal power and divine *n*—
7:18 lives in me, that is, in my sinful *n*.
8: 4 do not live according to the sinful *n*
8: 5 to the sinful *n* have their minds set
8: 8 by the sinful *n* cannot please God.
13:14 to gratify the desires of the sinful *n*.
Gal 5:13 freedom to indulge the sinful *n*;
5:19 The acts of the sinful *n* are obvious:
5:24 Jesus have crucified the sinful *n*
Php 2: 6 Who, being in very *n* God,
Col 3: 5 whatever belongs to your earthly *n*
2Pe 1: 4 you may participate in the divine *n*

NAZARENE* (NAZARETH)
Mt 2:23 prophets: "He will be called a *N*."
Mk 14:67 "You also were with that *N*, Jesus,"
16: 6 "You are looking for Jesus the *N*,
Ac 24: 5 He is a ringleader of the *N* sect and

NAZARETH (NAZARENE)
Mt 4:13 Leaving *N*, he went and lived
Lk 4:16 to *N*, where he had been brought
Jn 1:46 "*N*! Can anything good come

NAZIRITE
Nu 6: 2 of separation to the LORD as a *N*,
Jdg 13: 7 because the boy will be a *N* of God

NEBO
Dt 34: 1 Then Moses climbed Mount *N*

NEBUCHADNEZZAR
Babylonian king. Subdued and exiled Judah (2Ki 24-25; 2Ch 36; Jer 39). Dreams interpreted by Daniel (Da 2; 4). Worshiped God (Da 3:28-29; 4:34-37).

NECESSARY*
Ac 1:21 Therefore it is *n* to choose one
Ro 13: 5 it is *n* to submit to the authorities,
2Co 9: 5 I thought it *n* to urge the brothers
Php 1:24 it is more *n* for you that I remain
2:25 But I think it is *n* to send back
Heb 8: 3 and so it was *n* for this one
9:16 it is *n* to prove the death
9:23 It was *n*, then, for the copies

NECK (STIFF-NECKED)
Pr 3:22 an ornament to grace your *n*.
6:21 fasten them around your *n*.
Mt 18: 6 a large millstone hung around his *n*

NECO
Pharaoh who killed Josiah (2Ki 23:29-30; 2Ch 35:20-22), deposed Jehoahaz (2Ki 23:33-35; 2Ch 36:3-4).

NEED (NEEDS NEEDY)
1Ki 8:59 Israel according to each day's *n*,
Ps 79: 8 for we are in desperate *n*.
116: 6 when I was in great *n*, he saved me.
142: 6 for I am in desperate *n*;
Mt 6: 8 for your Father knows what you *n*
Lk 15:14 country, and he began to be in *n*.
Ac 2:45 they gave to anyone as he had *n*.
Ro 12:13 with God's people who are in *n*.
1Co 12:21 say to the hand, "I don't *n* you!"
Eph 4:28 something to share with those in *n*.
1Ti 5: 3 to those widows who are really in *n*
Heb 4:16 grace to help us in our time of *n*.
1Jn 3:17 sees his brother in *n* but has no pity

NEEDLE
Mt 19:24 go through the eye of a *n*

NEEDS (NEED)
Isa 58:11 he will satisfy your *n*
Php 2:25 sent to take care of my *n*.
4:19 God will meet all your *n* according
Jas 2:16 does nothing about his physical *n*,

NEEDY (NEED)
Dt 15:11 toward the poor and *n* in your land.
1Sa 2: 8 and lifts the *n* from the ash heap;
Ps 35:10 and *n* from those who rob them."
69:33 The LORD hears the *n*
72:12 he will deliver the *n* who cry out,
140: 12 and upholds the cause of the *n*.
Pr 14:21 blessed is he who is kind to the *n*.
14:31 to the *n* honors God.
22:22 and do not crush the *n* in court,
31: 9 defend the rights of the poor and *n*
31:20 and extends her hands to the *n*.
Mt 6: 2 "So when you give to the *n*,

NEGLECT* (NEGLECTED)
Dt 12:19 Be careful not to *n* the Levites
14:27 And do not *n* the Levites living
Ezr 4:22 Be careful not to *n* this matter.
Ne 10:39 We will not *n* the house of our God
Est 6:10 Do not *n* anything you have
Ps 119: 16 I will not *n* your word.
Lk 11:42 you *n* justice and the love of God.
Ac 6: 2 for us to *n* the ministry of the word
1Ti 4:14 Do not *n* your gift, which was

NEGLECTED (NEGLECT)
Mt 23:23 But you have *n* the more important

NEHEMIAH
Cupbearer of Artaxerxes (Ne 2:1); governor of Israel (Ne 8:9). Returned to Jerusalem to rebuild walls (Ne 2-6). With Ezra, reestablished worship (Ne 8). Prayer confessing nation's sin (Ne 9). Dedicated wall (Ne 12).

NEIGHBOR (NEIGHBOR'S)
Ex 20:16 give false testimony against your *n*.
20:17 or anything that belongs to your *n*
Lev 19:13 Do not defraud your *n* or rob him.
19:17 Rebuke your *n* frankly
19:18 but love your *n* as yourself.
Ps 15: 3 who does his *n* no wrong
Pr 3:29 Do not plot harm against your *n*,
11:12 who lacks judgment derides his *n*,
14:21 He who despises his *n* sins,
16:29 A violent man entices his *n*
24:28 against your *n* without cause,
25:18 gives false testimony against his *n*.
27:10 better a *n* nearby than a brother far
27:14 If a man loudly blesses his *n*
29: 5 Whoever flatters his *n*

Jer 31:34 No longer will a man teach his *n*,
Zec 8:17 do not plot evil against your *n*,
Mt 5:43 Love your *n* and hate your enemy.'
19:19 and 'love your *n* as yourself.' "
Mk 12:31 The second is this: 'Love your *n*
Lk 10:27 and, 'Love your *n* as yourself.' "
10:29 who is my *n*?" In reply Jesus said:
Ro 13: 9 "Love your *n* as yourself."
13:10 Love does no harm to its *n*.
15: 2 Each of us should please his *n*
Gal 5:14 "Love your *n* as yourself."
Eph 4:25 and speak truthfully to his *n*,
Heb 8:11 No longer will a man teach his *n*,
Jas 2: 8 "Love your *n* as yourself,"

NEIGHBOR'S (NEIGHBOR)
Ex 20:17 You shall not covet your *n* wife,
Dt 5:21 not set your desire on your *n* house
19:14 not move your *n* boundary stone
27:17 who moves his *n* boundary stone."
Pr 25:17 Seldom set foot in your *n* house—

NESTS
Mt 8:20 and birds of the air have *n*,

NET (NETS)
Pr 1:17 How useless to spread a *n*
Hab 1:15 he catches them in his *n*,
Mt 13:47 of heaven is like a *n* that was let
Jn 21: 6 "Throw your *n* on the right side

NETS (NET)
Ps 141: 10 Let the wicked fall into their own *n*
Mt 4:20 At once they left their *n*
Lk 5: 4 and let down the *n* for a catch."

NEVER-FAILING*
Am 5:24 righteousness like a *n* stream!

NEW
Ps 40: 3 He put a *n* song in my mouth,
98: 1 Sing to the LORD a *n* song,
Ecc 1: 9 there is nothing *n* under the sun.
Isa 42: 9 and *n* things I declare;
62: 2 you will be called by a *n* name
65:17 *n* heavens and a *n* earth.
66:22 "As the *n* heavens and the *n* earth
Jer 31:31 "when I will make a *n* covenant
La 3:23 They are *n* every morning;
Eze 11:19 undivided heart and put a *n* spirit
18:31 and get a *n* heart and a *n* spirit.
36:26 give you a *n* heart and put a *n* spirit
Zep 3: 5 and every *n* day he does not fail,
Mt 9:17 Neither do men pour *n* wine
Mk 16:17 they will speak in *n* tongues;
Lk 5:39 after drinking old wine wants the *n*
22:20 "This cup is the *n* covenant
Jn 13:34 "A *n* commandment I give you:
Ac 5:20 the full message of this *n* life."
Ro 6: 4 the Father, we too may live a *n* life.
1Co 5: 7 old yeast that you may be a *n* batch
11:25 "This cup is the *n* covenant
2Co 3: 6 as ministers of a *n* covenant—
5:17 he is a *n* creation; the old has gone,
Gal 6:15 what counts is a *n* creation.
Eph 4:23 to be made *n* in the attitude
4:24 and to put on the *n* self, created
Col 3:10 and have put on the *n* self,
Heb 8: 8 when I will make a *n* covenant
9:15 is the mediator of a *n* covenant,
10:20 by a *n* and living way opened for us
12:24 Jesus the mediator of a *n* covenant,
1Pe 1: 3 great mercy he has given us *n* birth
2Pe 3:13 to a *n* heaven and a *n* earth,
1Jn 2: 8 Yet I am writing you a *n* command;
Rev 2:17 stone with a *n* name written on it,
3:12 the *n* Jerusalem, which is coming
21: 1 I saw a *n* heaven and a *n* earth,

NEWBORN (BEAR)
1Pe 2: 2 Like *n* babies, crave pure spiritual

NEWS
2Ki 7: 9 This is a day of good *n*
Ps 112: 7 He will have no fear of bad *n*;
Pr 15:30 good *n* gives health to the bones.
25:25 is good *n* from a distant land.
Isa 52: 7 the feet of those who bring good *n*,
61: 1 me to preach good *n* to the poor.
Na 1:15 the feet of one who brings good *n*,
Mt 4:23 preaching the good *n*
9:35 preaching the good *n*
11: 5 the good *n* is preached to the poor.
Mk 1:15 Repent and believe the good *n*!"
16:15 preach the good *n* to all creation.
Lk 1:19 and to tell you this good *n*.
2:10 I bring you good *n*
3:18 and preached the good *n* to them.
4:43 "I must preach the good *n*
8: 1 proclaiming the good *n*
16:16 the good *n* of the kingdom
Ac 5:42 proclaiming the good *n* that Jesus
10:36 telling the good *n* of peace
14: 7 continued to preach the good *n*.
14:21 They preached the good *n*
17:18 preaching the good *n* about Jesus
Ro 10:15 feet of those who bring good *n*!"

NICODEMUS*
Pharisee who visted Jesus at night (Jn 3). Argued fair treatment of Jesus (Jn 7:50-52). With Joseph, prepared Jesus for burial (Jn 19:38-42).

NIGHT (NIGHTS NIGHTTIME)
Ge 1: 5 and the darkness he called "*n*."
1:16 and the lesser light to govern the *n*.
Ex 13:21 and by *n* in a pillar of fire
14:24 During the last watch of the *n*.
Dt 28:66 filled with dread both *n* and day,
Jos 1: 8 and *n*, so that you may be careful
Job 35:10 who gives songs in the *n*,
Ps 1: 2 on his law he meditates day and *n*.
19: 2 *n* after *n* they display knowledge.
42: 8 at *n* his song is with me—
63: 6 of you through the watches of the *n*
77: 6 I remembered my songs in the *n*.
90: 4 or like a watch in the *n*.
91: 5 You will not fear the terror of *n*,
119: 148 through the watches of the *n*,
121: 6 nor the moon by *n*.
136: 9 the moon and stars to govern the *n*;
Pr 31:18 and her lamp does not go out at *n*.
Isa 21:11 Watchman, what is left of the *n*?"
58:10 and your *n* will become like
Jer 33:20 and my covenant with the *n*,
Lk 2: 8 watch over their flocks at *n*.
6:12 and spent the *n* praying to God.
Jn 3: 2 He came to Jesus at *n* and said,
9: 4 *N* is coming, when no one can work
1Th 5: 2 Lord will come like a thief in the *n*.
5: 5 We do not belong to the *n*
Rev 21:25 for there will be no *n* there.

NIGHTS (NIGHT)
Jnh 1:17 the fish three days and three *n*.
Mt 4: 2 After fasting forty days and forty *n*
12:40 three *n* in the belly of a huge fish,
2Co 6: 5 in hard work, sleepless *n*

NIGHTTIME* (NIGHT)
Zec 14: 7 or *n*— a day known to the LORD.

NIMROD
Ge 10: 9 "Like *N*, a mighty hunter

NINEVEH
Jnh 1: 2 "Go to the great city of *N*
Na 1: 1 An oracle concerning *N*.
Mt 12:41 The men of *N* will stand up

NOAH
Righteous man (Eze 14:14, 20) called to build ark (Ge 6-8; Heb 11:7; 1Pe 3:20; 2Pe 2:5). God's covenant with (Ge 9:1-17). Drunkenness of (Ge 9:18-23). Blessed sons, cursed Canaan (Ge 9:24-27).

NOBLE
Ru 3:11 you are a woman of *n* character.
Ps 45: 1 My heart is stirred by a *n* theme
Pr 12: 4 of *n* character is her husband's
31:10 A wife of *n* character who can find?
31:29 "Many women do *n* things,
Isa 32: 8 But the *n* man makes *n* plans,
Lk 8:15 good soil stands for those with a *n*
Ro 9:21 of clay some pottery for *n* purposes
Php 4: 8 whatever is *n*, whatever is right,
2Ti 2:20 some are for *n* purposes

NOSTRILS
Ge 2: 7 and breathed into his *n* the breath
Ex 15: 8 By the blast of your *n*
Ps 18:15 at the blast of breath from your *n*.

NOTE
Ac 4:13 and they took *n* that these men had
Php 3:17 take *n* of those who live according

NOTHING
2Sa 24:24 offerings that cost me *n*."
Ne 9:21 in the desert; they lacked *n*,
Ps 73:25 earth has *n* I desire besides you
Jer 32:17 *N* is too hard for you
Jn 15: 5 apart from me you can do *n*.

NOURISH
Pr 10:21 The lips of the righteous *n* many,

NULLIFY
Mt 15: 6 Thus you *n* the word of God
Ro 3:31 Do we, then, *n* the law by this faith

OATH
Ex 33: 1 up to the land I promised on *o*
Nu 30: 2 or takes an *o* to obligate himself
Dt 6:18 promised on *o* to your forefathers,
7: 8 and kept the *o* he swore
29:12 you this day and sealing with an *o*,
Ps 95:11 So I declared on *o* in my anger,
119: 106 I have taken an *o* and confirmed it,
132: 11 The LORD swore an *o* to David,
Ecc 8: 2 because you took an *o* before God.
Mt 5:33 'Do not break your *o*, but keep
Heb 7:20 And it was not without an *o*!

OBADIAH
1. Believer who sheltered 100 prophets from Jezebel (1Ki 18:1-16).
2. Prophet against Edom (Ob 1).

OBEDIENCE* (OBEY)
Ge 49:10 and the *o* of the nations is his.
Jdg 2:17 of *o* to the LORD's commands.
1Ch 21:19 So David went up in *o*
2Ch 31:21 in *o* to the law and the commands,
Pr 30:17 that scorns *o* to a mother,
Lk 23:56 Sabbath in *o* to the commandment.
Ac 21:24 but that you yourself are living in *o*
Ro 1: 5 to the *o* that comes from faith.
5:19 also through the *o* of the one man
6:16 to *o*, which leads to righteousness?
16:19 Everyone has heard about your *o*,
2Co 9:13 for the *o* that accompanies your
10: 6 once your *o* is complete.
Phm :21 Confident of your *o*, I write to you,
Heb 5: 8 he learned *o* from what he suffered
1Pe 1: 2 for *o* to Jesus Christ and sprinkling
2Jn : 6 that we walk in *o* to his commands.

OBEDIENT* (OBEY)
Dt 30:17 heart turns away and you are not *o*,
Isa 1:19 If you are willing and *o*,
Lk 2:51 with them and was *o* to them.
Ac 6: 7 of priests became *o* to the faith.
2Co 2: 9 if you would stand the test and be *o*
7:15 he remembers that you were all *o*,
10: 5 thought to make it *o* to Christ.
Php 2: 8 and became *o* to death—
Tit 3: 1 to be *o*, to be ready
1Pe 1:14 As *o* children, do not conform

OBEY (OBEDIENCE OBEDIENT OBEYED OBEYING OBEYS)
Ex 12:24 "*O* these instructions as a lasting
19: 5 Now if you *o* me fully and keep my
24: 7 the LORD has said; we will *o*."
Lev 18: 4 You must *o* my laws and be careful
25:18 and be careful to *o* my laws,
Nu 15:40 remember to *o* all my commands
Dt 5:27 We will listen and *o*."
6: 3 careful to *o* so that it may go well
6:24 us to *o* all these decrees
11:13 if you faithfully *o* the commands I
12:28 to *o* all these regulations I am
13: 4 Keep his commands and *o* him;
21:18 son who does not *o* his father
28: 1 If you fully *o* the LORD your God
28:15 if you do not *o* the LORD your
30: 2 and *o* him with all your heart
30:10 if you *o* the LORD your God
30:14 and in your heart so you may *o* it.
32:46 children to *o* carefully all the words
Jos 1: 7 to *o* all the law my servant Moses
22: 5 in all his ways, to *o* his commands,
24:24 the LORD our God and *o* him."
1Sa 15:22 To *o* is better than sacrifice,
1Ki 8:61 by his decrees and *o* his commands
2Ki 17:13 that I commanded your fathers to *o*
2Ch 34:31 and to *o* the words of the covenant
Ne 1: 5 who love him and *o* his commands,
Ps 103: 18 and remember to *o* his precepts.
103: 20 who *o* his word.
119: 17 I will *o* your word.
119: 34 and *o* it with all my heart.
119: 57 I have promised to *o* your words.
119: 67 but now I *o* your word.
119: 100 for I *o* your precepts.
119: 129 therefore I *o* them.
119: 167 I *o* your statutes,
Pr 5:13 I would not *o* my teachers
Jer 7:23 I gave them this command: *O* me,
11: 4 '*O* me and do everything I
11: 7 and again, saying, "*O* me."
42: 6 we will *o* the LORD our God,
Da 9: 4 who love him and *o* his commands,
Mt 8:27 the winds and the waves *o* him!"
19:17 to enter life, *o* the commandments
28:20 to *o* everything I have commanded
Lk 11:28 hear the word of God and *o* it."
Jn 14:15 you will *o* what I command.
14:23 loves me, he will *o* my teaching.

Jn 14:24 not love me will not *o* my teaching.
15:10 If you *o* my commands, you will
Ac 5:29 "We must *o* God rather than men!
5:32 given to those who *o* him."
Ro 2:13 it is those who *o* the law who will
6:12 body so that you *o* its evil desires.
6:16 slaves to the one whom you *o*—
6:16 yourselves to someone to *o* him
15:18 in leading the Gentiles to *o* God
16:26 nations might believe and *o* him—
Gal 5: 3 obligated to *o* the whole law.
Eph 6: 1 *o* your parents in the Lord,
6: 5 *o* your earthly masters with respect
Col 3:20 *o* your parents in everything,
3:22 *o* your earthly masters
2Th 3:14 anyone does not *o* our instruction
1Ti 3: 4 and see that his children *o* him
Heb 5: 9 eternal salvation for all who *o* him
13:17 *O* your leaders and submit
1Pe 4:17 for those who do not *o* the gospel
1Jn 3:24 Those who *o* his commands live
5: 3 love for God: to *o* his commands.
Rev 12:17 those who *o* God's commandments
14:12 the saints who *o* God's

OBEYED (OBEY)
Ge 22:18 blessed, because you have *o* me."
Jos 1:17 we fully *o* Moses, so we will obey
Ps 119: 4 that are to be fully *o*.
Da 9:10 we have not *o* the LORD our God
Jnh 3: 3 Jonah *o* the word of the LORD
Mic 5:15 the nations that have not *o* me."
Jn 15:10 as I have *o* my Father's commands
15:20 If they *o* my teaching, they will
17: 6 and they have *o* your word.
Ac 7:53 through angels but have not *o* it."
Ro 6:17 you wholeheartedly *o* the form
Php 2:12 as you have always *o*— not only
Heb 11: 8 *o* and went, even though he did not
1Pe 3: 6 who *o* Abraham and called him her

OBEYING (OBEY)
1Sa 15:22 as in *o* the voice of the LORD?
Ps 119: 5 steadfast in *o* your decrees!
Gal 5: 7 and kept you from *o* the truth?
1Pe 1:22 purified yourselves by *o* the truth

OBEYS (OBEY)
Lev 18: 5 for the man who *o* them will live
Pr 19:16 He who *o* instructions guards his
Eze 20:11 for the man who *o* them will live
Jn 14:21 has my commands and *o* them,
Ro 2:27 and yet *o* the law will condemn you
1Jn 2: 5 if anyone *o* his word, God's love is

OBLIGATED (OBLIGATION)
Ro 1:14 I am *o* both to Greeks
Gal 5: 3 himself be circumcised that he is *o*

OBLIGATION (OBLIGATED)
Ro 8:12 Therefore, brothers, we have an *o*

OBSCENITY*
Eph 5: 4 Nor should there be *o*, foolish talk

OBSCURES*
Job 42: 3 'Who is this that *o* my counsel

OBSERVE (OBSERVING)
Ex 31:13 'You must *o* my Sabbaths.
Lev 25: 2 the land itself must *o* a sabbath
Dt 4: 6 *O* them carefully, for this will show
5:12 "*O* the Sabbath day
8: 6 *O* the commands of the LORD
11:22 If you carefully *o* all these
26:16 carefully *o* them with all your heart
Ps 37:37 the blameless, *o* the upright;

OBSERVING (OBSERVE)
Ro 3:27 principle? On that of *o* the law?
Gal 2:16 a man is not justified by *o* the law,
3: 2 you receive the Spirit by *o* the law,
3:10 All who rely on *o* the law are

OBSOLETE
Heb 8:13 he has made the first one *o*;

OBSTACLE* (OBSTACLES)
Ro 14:13 or *o* in your brother's way.

OBSTACLES (OBSTACLE)
Ro 16:17 put *o* in your way that are contrary

OBSTINATE
Isa 65: 2 hands to an *o* people,
Ro 10:21 to a disobedient and *o* people."

OBTAIN (OBTAINED OBTAINS)
Ro 11: 7 sought so earnestly it did not *o*,
2Ti 2:10 they too may *o* the salvation that

OBTAINED (OBTAIN)
Ro 9:30 not pursue righteousness, have *o* it,
Php 3:12 Not that I have already *o* all this,
Heb 9:12 having *o* eternal redemption.

OBTAINS* (OBTAIN)
Pr 12: 2 A good man *o* favor

OBVIOUS*
Mt 6:18 so that it will not be *o*
Gal 5:19 The acts of the sinful nature are *o*:
1Ti 5:24 The sins of some men are *o*,
5:25 In the same way, good deeds are *o*,

OCCASIONS
Eph 6:18 in the Spirit on all *o* with all kinds

OFFENDED (OFFENSE)
Pr 18:19 An *o* brother is more unyielding

OFFENDERS* (OFFENSE)
1Co 6: 9 nor homosexual *o* nor thieves

OFFENSE (OFFENDED OFFENDERS OFFENSES OFFENSIVE)
Pr 17: 9 over an *o* promotes love,
19:11 it is to his glory to overlook an *o*.
Gal 5:11 In that case the *o* of the cross has

OFFENSES (OFFENSE)
Isa 44:22 swept away your *o* like a cloud,
59:12 For our *o* are many in your sight,
Eze 18:30 Repent! Turn away from all your *o*;
33:10 "Our *o* and sins weigh us down,

OFFENSIVE (OFFENSE)
Ps 139: 24 See if there is any *o* way in me,

OFFER (OFFERED OFFERING OFFERINGS OFFERS)
Ps 4: 5 *O* right sacrifices
Ro 6:13 Do not *o* the parts of your body
12: 1 to *o* your bodies as living sacrifices,
Heb 9:25 he enter heaven to *o* himself again
13:15 therefore, let us continually *o*

OFFERED (OFFER)
Isa 50: 6 I *o* my back to those who beat me,
1Co 9:13 share in what is *o* on the altar?
10:20 of pagans are *o* to demons,
Heb 7:27 once for all when he *o* himself.
9:14 the eternal Spirit *o* himself
11: 4 By faith Abel *o* God a better
11:17 when God tested him, *o* Isaac
Jas 5:15 prayer *o* in faith will make the sick

OFFERING (OFFER)
Ge 4: 3 of the soil as an *o* to the LORD.
22: 2 a burnt *o* on one of the mountains I
22: 8 provide the lamb for the burnt *o*,
Ex 29:24 before the LORD as a wave *o*.
29:40 quarter of a hin of wine as a drink *o*.
Lev 1: 3 If the *o* is a burnt *o* from the herd,
2: 4 " 'If you bring a grain *o* baked
3: 1 " 'If someone's *o* is a fellowship *o*,
4: 3 a sin *o* for the sin he has committed
5:15 It is a guilt *o*.
7:37 ordination *o* and the fellowship *o*,
9:24 and consumed the burnt *o*
22:18 to fulfill a vow or as a freewill *o*,
22:21 a special vow or as a freewill *o*,
1Sa 13: 9 And Saul offered up the burnt *o*.
1Ch 21:26 from heaven on the altar of burnt *o*.
2Ch 7: 1 and consumed the burnt *o*
Ps 40: 6 Sacrifice and *o* you did not desire,
116: 17 I will sacrifice a thank *o* to you
Isa 53:10 the LORD makes his life a guilt *o*,
Mt 5:23 if you are *o* your gift at the altar
Ro 8: 3 likeness of sinful man to be a sin *o*.
Eph 5: 2 as a fragrant *o* and sacrifice to God.
Php 2:17 I am being poured out like a drink *o*
4:18 are a fragrant *o*, an acceptable
2Ti 4: 6 being poured out like a drink *o*,
Heb 10: 5 "Sacrifice and *o* you did not desire,
1Pe 2: 5 *o* spiritual sacrifices acceptable

OFFERINGS (OFFER)
1Sa 15:22 Does the LORD delight in burnt *o*
2Ch 35: 7 and goats for the Passover *o*,
Isa 1:13 Stop bringing meaningless *o*!
Hos 6: 6 of God rather than burnt *o*.
Mal 3: 8 do we rob you?' "In tithes and *o*.
Mk 12:33 is more important than all burnt *o*
Heb 10: 8 First he said, "Sacrifices and *o*,

OFFERS (OFFER)
Heb 10:11 and again he *o* the same sacrifices,

OFFICER (OFFICIALS)
2Ti 2: 4 wants to please his commanding *o*.

OFFICIALS (OFFICER)
Ex 5:21 a stench to Pharaoh and his *o*.
Pr 17:26 or to flog *o* for their integrity.
29:12 all his *o* become wicked.

OFFSPRING
Ge 3:15 and between your *o* and hers;
12: 7 "To your *o* I will give this land."
13:16 I will make your *o* like the dust
26: 4 and through your *o* all nations
28:14 blessed through you and your *o*.
Ex 13: 2 The first *o* of every womb
Ru 4:12 Through the *o* the LORD gives
Isa 44: 3 I will pour out my Spirit on your *o*,
53:10 he will see his *o* and prolong his
Ac 3:25 'Through your *o* all peoples
17:28 own poets have said, 'We are his *o*.'
17:29 "Therefore since we are God's *o*,
Ro 4:18 said to him, "So shall your *o* be."
9: 8 who are regarded as Abraham's *o*.

OG
Nu 21:33 *O* king of Bashan and his whole
Ps 136: 20 and *O* king of Bashan—

OIL
Ex 29: 7 Take the anointing *o* and anoint
30:25 It will be the sacred anointing *o*.
Dt 14:23 tithe of your grain, new wine and *o*,
1Sa 10: 1 Then Samuel took a flask of *o*
16:13 So Samuel took the horn of *o*
1Ki 17:16 and the jug of *o* did not run dry,
2Ki 4: 6 Then the *o* stopped flowing.
Ps 23: 5 You anoint my head with *o*;
45: 7 by anointing you with the *o* of joy.
104: 15 *o* to make his face shine,
133: 2 It is like precious *o* poured
Pr 21:17 loves wine and *o* will never be
Isa 1: 6 or soothed with *o*.
61: 3 the *o* of gladness
Mt 25: 3 but did not take any *o* with them.
Heb 1: 9 by anointing you with the *o* of joy."

OLIVE (OLIVES)
Ge 8:11 beak was a freshly plucked *o* leaf!
Jdg 9: 8 said to the *o* tree, 'Be our king.'
Jer 11:16 LORD called you a thriving *o* tree
Zec 4: 3 Also there are two *o* trees by it,
Ro 11:17 and you, though a wild *o* shoot,
11:24 of an *o* tree that is wild by nature,
Rev 11: 4 These are the two *o* trees

OLIVES (OLIVE)
Zec 14: 4 stand on the Mount of *O*,
Mt 24: 3 sitting on the Mount of *O*,
Jas 3:12 a fig tree bear *o*, or a grapevine bear

OMEGA*
Rev 1: 8 "I am the Alpha and the *O*,"
21: 6 I am the Alpha and the *O*,
22:13 I am the Alpha and the *O*,

OMIT*
Jer 26: 2 I command you; do not *o* a word.

OMRI
King of Israel (1Ki 16:21-26).

ONESIMUS*
Col 4: 9 He is coming with *O*, our faithful
Phm :10 I appeal to you for my son *O*,

ONESIPHORUS*
2Ti 1:16 mercy to the household of *O*,
4:19 Aquila and the household of *O*.

ONIONS*
Nu 11: 5 melons, leeks, *o* and garlic.

ONYX
Ex 28: 9 "Take two *o* stones and engrave
28:20 in the fourth row a chrysolite, an *o*

OPENHANDED* (HAND)
Dt 15: 8 Rather be *o* and freely lend him
15:11 you to be *o* toward your brothers

OPINIONS*
1Ki 18:21 will you waver between two *o*?
Pr 18: 2 but delights in airing his own *o*.

OPPONENTS (OPPOSE)
Pr 18:18 and keeps strong *o* apart.

OPPORTUNE (OPPORTUNITY)
Lk 4:13 he left him until an *o* time.

OPPORTUNITY* (OPPORTUNE)
1Sa 18:21 "Now you have a second *o*
Jer 46:17 he has missed his *o*.'
Mt 26:16 watched for an *o* to hand him over.

Mk 14:11 So he watched for an *o* to hand him
Lk 22: 6 and watched for an *o* to hand Jesus
Ac 25:16 and has had an *o* to defend himself
Ro 7: 8 seizing the *o* afforded
7:11 seizing the *o* afforded
1Co 16:12 but he will go when he has the *o*.
2Co 5:12 are giving you an *o* to take pride
11:12 from under those who want an *o*
Gal 6:10 as we have *o*, let us do good
Eph 5:16 making the most of every *o*,
Php 4:10 but you had no *o* to show it.
Col 4: 5 make the most of every *o*.
1Ti 5:14 to give the enemy no *o* for slander.
Heb 11:15 they would have had *o* to return.

OPPOSE (OPPONENTS OPPOSED OPPOSES OPPOSING OPPOSITION)
Ex 23:22 and will *o* those who *o* you.
1Sa 2:10 those who *o* the LORD will be
Job 23:13 he stands alone, and who can *o* him
Ac 11:17 I to think that I could *o* God?"
2Ti 2:25 Those who *o* him he must gently
Tit 1: 9 doctrine and refute those who *o* it.
2: 8 so that those who *o* you may be

OPPOSED (OPPOSE)
Gal 2:11 to Antioch, I *o* him to his face,
3:21 therefore, *o* to the promises of God

OPPOSES (OPPOSE)
Jas 4: 6 "God *o* the proud
1Pe 5: 5 because, "God *o* the proud

OPPOSING (OPPOSE)
1Ti 6:20 the *o* ideas of what is falsely called

OPPOSITION (OPPOSE)
Heb 12: 3 Consider him who endured such *o*

OPPRESS (OPPRESSED OPPRESSES OPPRESSION OPPRESSOR)
Ex 1:11 masters over them to *o* them
22:21 "Do not mistreat an alien or *o* him,
Isa 3: 5 People will *o* each other—
Eze 22:29 they *o* the poor and needy
Da 7:25 the Most High and *o* his saints
Am 5:12 You *o* the righteous and take bribes
Zec 7:10 Do not *o* the widow
Mal 3: 5 who *o* the widows

OPPRESSED (OPPRESS)
Jdg 2:18 as they groaned under those who *o*
Ps 9: 9 The LORD is a refuge for the *o*,
82: 3 the rights of the poor and *o*.
146: 7 He upholds the cause of the *o*
Pr 16:19 in spirit and among the *o*
31: 5 and deprive all the *o* of their rights.
Isa 1:17 encourage the *o*.
53: 7 He was *o* and afflicted,
58:10 and satisfy the needs of the *o*,
Zec 10: 2 *o* for lack of a shepherd.
Lk 4:18 to release the *o*,

OPPRESSES (OPPRESS)
Pr 14:31 He who *o* the poor shows contempt
22:16 He who *o* the poor
Eze 18:12 He *o* the poor and needy.

OPPRESSION (OPPRESS)
Ps 12: 5 "Because of the *o* of the weak
72:14 He will rescue them from *o*
119:134 Redeem me from the *o* of men,
Isa 53: 8 By *o* and judgment he was taken
58: 9 "If you do away with the yoke of *o*,

OPPRESSOR (OPPRESS)
Ps 72: 4 he will crush the *o*.
Isa 51:13 For where is the wrath of the *o*?
Jer 22: 3 hand of his *o* the one who has been

ORDAINED
Ps 8: 2 you have *o* praise
111: 9 he *o* his covenant forever—
139: 16 All the days *o* for me
Eze 28:14 for so I *o* you.
Hab 1:12 you have *o* them to punish.
Mt 21:16 you have *o* praise'?"

ORDER (ORDERLY ORDERS)
Nu 9:23 They obeyed the LORD's *o*,
Ps 110: 4 in the *o* of Melchizedek."
Heb 5:10 priest in the *o* of Melchizedek.
9:10 until the time of the new *o*.
Rev 21: 4 for the old *o* of things has passed

ORDERLY (ORDER)
1Co 14:40 done in a fitting and *o* way.
Col 2: 5 and delight to see how *o* you are

ORDERS (ORDER)
Mk 1:27 He even gives *o* to evil spirits
Mk 3:12 But he gave them strict *o* not
9: 9 Jesus gave them *o* not

ORDINARY
Ac 4:13 that they were unschooled, *o* men,

ORGIES*
Ro 13:13 not in *o* and drunkenness,
Gal 5:21 drunkenness, *o*, and the like.
1Pe 4: 3 *o*, carousing and detestable

ORIGIN (ORIGINATE ORIGINS)
2Pe 1:21 For prophecy never had its *o*

ORIGINATE* (ORIGIN)
1Co 14:36 Did the word of God *o* with you?

ORIGINS* (ORIGIN)
Mic 5: 2 whose *o* are from of old,

ORNAMENT* (ORNAMENTED)
Pr 3:22 an *o* to grace your neck.
25:12 of gold or an *o* of fine gold

ORNAMENTED (ORNAMENT)
Ge 37: 3 and he made a richly *o* robe for him

ORPHAN* (ORPHANS)
Ex 22:22 advantage of a widow or an *o*.

ORPHANS (ORPHAN)
Jn 14:18 will not leave you as *o*; I will come
Jas 1:27 to look after *o* and widows

OTHNIEL
Nephew of Caleb (Jos 15:15-19; Jdg 1:12-15). Judge who freed Israel from Aram (Jdg 3:7-11).

OUTBURSTS*
2Co 12:20 jealousy, *o* of anger, factions,

OUTCOME
Heb 13: 7 Consider the *o* of their way of life
1Pe 4:17 what will the *o* be for those who do

OUTNUMBER
Ps 139: 18 they would *o* the grains of sand.

OUTSIDERS*
Col 4: 5 wise in the way you act toward *o*;
1Th 4:12 daily life may win the respect of *o*
1Ti 3: 7 also have a good reputation with *o*,

OUTSTANDING
SS 5:10 *o* among ten thousand.
Ro 13: 8 no debt remain *o*,

OUTSTRETCHED
Ex 6: 6 and will redeem you with an *o* arm
Dt 4:34 by a mighty hand and an *o* arm,
5:15 with a mighty hand and an *o* arm.
1Ki 8:42 your mighty hand and your *o* arm
Ps 136: 12 with a mighty hand and *o* arm;
Jer 27: 5 and *o* arm I made the earth
32:17 by your great power and *o* arm.
Eze 20:33 an *o* arm and with outpoured wrath

OUTWEIGHS (WEIGH)
2Co 4:17 an eternal glory that far *o* them all.

OUTWIT*
2Co 2:11 in order that Satan might not *o* us.

OVERAWED* (AWE)
Ps 49:16 Do not be *o* when a man grows rich

OVERBEARING*
Tit 1: 7 not *o*, not quick-tempered,

OVERCAME (OVERCOME)
Rev 3:21 as I *o* and sat down with my Father
12:11 They *o* him

OVERCOME (OVERCAME OVERCOMES)
Mt 16:18 and the gates of Hades will not *o* it.
Mk 9:24 I do believe; help me *o* my unbelief
Lk 10:19 to *o* all the power of the enemy;
Jn 16:33 But take heart! I have *o* the world."
Ro 12:21 Do not be *o* by evil, but *o* evil
2Pe 2:20 and are again entangled in it and *o*,
1Jn 2:13 because you have *o* the evil one.
4: 4 are from God and have *o* them,
5: 4 is the victory that has *o* the world,
Rev 17:14 but the Lamb will *o* them

OVERCOMES* (OVERCOME)
1Jn 5: 4 born of God *o* the world.
5: 5 Who is it that *o* the world?
Rev 2: 7 To him who *o*, I will give the right
2:11 He who *o* will not be hurt at all
2:17 To him who *o*, I will give some
2:26 To him who *o* and does my will
Rev 3: 5 He who *o* will, like them, be
3:12 Him who *o* I will make a pillar
3:21 To him who *o*, I will give the right
21: 7 He who *o* will inherit all this,

OVERFLOW (OVERFLOWING OVERFLOWS)
Ps 65:11 and your carts *o* with abundance.
119:171 May my lips *o* with praise,
La 1:16 and my eyes *o* with tears.
Mt 12:34 out of the *o* of the heart the mouth
Lk 6:45 out of the *o* of his heart his mouth
Ro 5:15 Jesus Christ, *o* to the many! Again,
15:13 so that you may *o* with hope
2Co 4:15 to *o* to the glory of God.
1Th 3:12 *o* for each other and for everyone

OVERFLOWING (OVERFLOW)
Pr 3:10 then your barns will be filled to *o*,
2Co 8: 2 their *o* joy and their extreme
9:12 *o* in many expressions of thanks
Col 2: 7 as you were taught, and *o*

OVERFLOWS* (OVERFLOW)
Ps 23: 5 my cup *o*.
2Co 1: 5 also through Christ our comfort *o*.

OVERJOYED* (JOY)
Da 6:23 The king was *o* and gave orders
Mt 2:10 they saw the star, they were *o*.
Jn 20:20 The disciples were *o*
Ac 12:14 she was so *o* she ran back
1Pe 4:13 so that you may be *o*

OVERLOOK
Pr 19:11 it is to his glory to *o* an offense.

OVERSEER* (OVERSEERS)
Pr 6: 7 no *o* or ruler,
1Ti 3: 1 anyone sets his heart on being an *o*,
3: 2 Now the *o* must be above reproach,
Tit 1: 7 Since an *o* is entrusted
1Pe 2:25 returned to the Shepherd and *O*

OVERSEERS* (OVERSEER)
Ac 20:28 the Holy Spirit has made you *o*.
Php 1: 1 together with the *o* and deacons:
1Pe 5: 2 as *o*— not because you must,

OVERSHADOW* (OVERSHADOWING)
Lk 1:35 power of the Most High will *o* you.

OVERSHADOWING (OVERSHADOW)
Ex 25:20 wings spread upward, *o* the cover
Heb 9: 5 the glory, *o* the atonement cover.

OVERTHROW (OVERTHROWS)
2Th 2: 8 whom the Lord Jesus will *o*

OVERTHROWS (OVERTHROW)
Pr 13: 6 but wickedness *o* the sinner.
Isa 44:25 who *o* the learning of the wise

OVERWHELMED (OVERWHELMING)
2Sa 22: 5 the torrents of destruction *o* me.
1Ki 10: 5 temple of the LORD, she was *o*.
Ps 38: 4 My guilt has *o* me
65: 3 When we were *o* by sins,
Mt 26:38 "My soul is *o* with sorrow
Mk 7:37 People were *o* with amazement.
9:15 they were *o* with wonder
2Co 2: 7 so that he will not be *o*

OVERWHELMING (OVERWHELMED)
Pr 27: 4 Anger is cruel and fury *o*,
Isa 10:22 *o* and righteous.
28:15 When an *o* scourge sweeps by,

OWE
Ro 13: 7 If you *o* taxes, pay taxes; if revenue
Phm :19 to mention that you *o* me your very

OWNER'S (OWNERSHIP)
Isa 1: 3 the donkey his *o* manger,

OWNERSHIP* (OWNER'S)
2Co 1:22 He anointed us, set his seal of *o*

OX (OXEN)
Dt 25: 4 Do not muzzle an *o*
Isa 11: 7 and the lion will eat straw like the *o*
Eze 1:10 and on the left the face of an *o*;
Lk 13:15 of you on the Sabbath untie his *o*
1Co 9: 9 "Do not muzzle an *o*
1Ti 5:18 "Do not muzzle the *o*
Rev 4: 7 second was like an *o*, the third had

OXEN (OX)
1Ki 19:20 Elisha then left his *o* and ran
Lk 14:19 'I have just bought five yoke of *o*,

PAGAN (PAGANS)
Mt 18:17 as you would a *p* or a tax collector.

Lk 12:30 For the *p* world runs

PAGANS* (PAGAN)
Isa 2: 6 and clasp hands with *p*.
Mt 5:47 Do not even *p* do that? Be perfect,
6: 7 do not keep on babbling like *p*,
6:32 For the *p* run after all these things,
1Co 5: 1 that does not occur even among *p*:
10:20 but the sacrifices of *p* are offered
12: 2 You know that when you were *p*,
1Pe 2:12 such good lives among the *p* that,
4: 3 in the past doing what *p* choose
3Jn : 7 receiving no help from the *p*.

PAID (PAY)
Isa 40: 2 that her sin has been *p* for,
Zec 11:12 So they *p* me thirty pieces of silver.

PAIN (PAINFUL PAINS)
Ge 3:16 with *p* you will give birth
6: 6 and his heart was filled with *p*.
Job 6:10 my joy in unrelenting *p*—
33:19 may be chastened on a bed of *p*
Jer 4:19 I writhe in *p*.
15:18 Why is my *p* unending
Mt 4:24 suffering severe *p*,
Jn 16:21 woman giving birth to a child has *p*
1Pe 2:19 up under the *p* of unjust suffering
Rev 21: 4 or mourning or crying or *p*,

PAINFUL (PAIN)
Ge 3:17 through *p* toil you will eat of it
5:29 and *p* toil of our hands caused
Job 6:25 How *p* are honest words!
Eze 28:24 neighbors who are *p* briers
2Co 2: 1 I would not make another *p* visit
Heb 12:11 seems pleasant at the time, but *p*.
1Pe 4:12 at the *p* trial you are suffering,

PAINS (PAIN)
Ge 3:16 "I will greatly increase your *p*
Mt 24: 8 these are the beginning of birth *p*.
Ro 8:22 as in the *p* of childbirth right up
Gal 4:19 again in the *p* of childbirth
1Th 5: 3 as labor *p* on a pregnant woman,

PAIRS
Ge 7: 8 *P* of clean and unclean animals,

PALACE (PALACES)
2Sa 7: 2 "Here I am, living in a *p* of cedar,
Jer 22: 6 is what the LORD says about the *p*
22:13 "Woe to him who builds his *p*

PALACES (PALACE)
Mt 11: 8 wear fine clothes are in kings' *p*.
Lk 7:25 and indulge in luxury are in *p*.

PALE
Isa 29:22 no longer will their faces grow *p*.
Jer 30: 6 every face turned deathly *p*?
Da 10: 8 my face turned deathly *p*
Rev 6: 8 and there before me was a *p* horse!

PALM (PALMS)
Jn 12:13 They took *p* branches and went out
Rev 7: 9 and were holding *p* branches

PALMS (PALM)
Isa 49:16 you on the *p* of my hands;

PAMPERS*
Pr 29:21 If a man *p* his servant from youth,

PANIC
Dt 20: 3 or give way to *p* before them.
1Sa 14:15 It was a *p* sent by God.
Eze 7: 7 there is *p*, not joy,
Zec 14:13 by the LORD with great *p*.

PANTS
Ps 42: 1 As the deer *p* for streams of water,

PARABLES
See also JESUS: PARABLES
Ps 78: 2 I will open my mouth in *p*,
Mt 13:35 "I will open my mouth in *p*,
Lk 8:10 but to others I speak in *p*, so that,

PARADISE*
Lk 23:43 today you will be with me in *p*."
2Co 12: 4 God knows—was caught up to *p*.
Rev 2: 7 of life, which is in the *p* of God.

PARALYTIC
Mt 9: 2 Some men brought to him a *p*,
Mk 2: 3 bringing to him a *p*, carried by four
Ac 9:33 a *p* who had been bedridden

PARCHED
Ps 143: 6 my soul thirsts for you like a *p* land.

PARCHMENTS*
2Ti 4:13 and my scrolls, especially the *p*.

PARDON* (PARDONED PARDONS)
2Ch 30:18 *p* everyone who sets his heart
Job 7:21 Why do you not *p* my offenses
Isa 55: 7 and to our God, for he will freely *p*.
Joel 3:21 I will *p*."

PARDONED* (PARDON)
Nu 14:19 as you have *p* them from the time
Joel 3:21 bloodguilt, which I have not *p*,

PARDONS* (PARDON)
Mic 7:18 who *p* sin and forgives

PARENTS
Pr 17: 6 and *p* are the pride of their children
19:14 wealth are inherited from *p*,
Mt 10:21 children will rebel against their *p*
Lk 18:29 left home or wife or brothers or *p*
21:16 You will be betrayed even by *p*, brothers,
Jn 9: 3 Neither this man nor his *p* sinned,"
Ro 1:30 they disobey their *p*; they are
2Co 12:14 for their *p*, but *p* for their children.
Eph 6: 1 Children, obey your *p* in the Lord,
Col 3:20 obey your *p* in everything,
1Ti 5: 4 repaying their *p* and grandparents,
2Ti 3: 2 disobedient to their *p*, ungrateful,

PARTAKE*
1Co 10:17 for we all *p* of the one loaf.

PARTIAL* (PARTIALITY)
Pr 18: 5 It is not good to be *p* to the wicked

PARTIALITY (PARTIAL)
Lev 19:15 do not show *p* to the poor
Dt 1:17 Do not show *p* in judging;
10:17 who shows no *p* and accepts no
16:19 Do not pervert justice or show *p*.
2Ch 19: 7 our God there is no injustice or *p*
Job 32:21 I will show *p* to no one,
34:19 who shows no *p* to princes
Pr 24:23 To show *p* in judging is not good:
Mal 2: 9 have shown *p* in matters of the law
Lk 20:21 and that you do not show *p*
1Ti 5:21 keep these instructions without *p*,

PARTICIPANTS (PARTICIPATE)
1Co 10:20 you to be *p* with demons.

PARTICIPATE (PARTICIPANTS PARTICIPATION)
1Pe 4:13 rejoice that you *p* in the sufferings
2Pe 1: 4 that through them you may *p*

PARTICIPATION (PARTICIPATE)
1Co 10:16 is not the bread that we break a *p*

PARTNER (PARTNERS PARTNERSHIP)
Pr 2:17 who has left the *p* of her youth
Mal 2:14 though she is your *p*, the wife
1Pe 3: 7 them with respect as the weaker *p*

PARTNERS (PARTNER)
Eph 5: 7 Therefore do not be *p* with them.

PARTNERSHIP* (PARTNER)
Php 1: 5 because of your *p* in the gospel

PASS (PASSED PASSER-BY PASSING)
Ex 12:13 and when I see the blood, I will *p*
33:19 goodness to *p* in front of you,
1Ki 9: 8 all who *p* by will be appalled
19:11 for the LORD is about to *p* by."
Ps 90:10 for they quickly *p*, and we fly away.
105: 19 till what he foretold came to *p*,
Isa 31: 5 he will '*p* over' it and will rescue it
43: 2 When you *p* through the waters,
62:10 *P* through, *p* through the gates!
Jer 22: 8 "People from many nations will *p*
La 1:12 to you, all you who *p* by?
Da 7:14 dominion that will not *p* away,
Am 5:17 for I will *p* through your midst,"
Mt 24:34 will certainly not *p* away
24:35 Heaven and earth will *p* away,
Mk 13:31 Heaven and earth will *p* away,
Lk 21:33 Heaven and earth will *p* away,
1Co 13: 8 there is knowledge, it will *p* away.
Jas 1:10 he will *p* away like a wild flower.
1Jn 2:17 The world and its desires *p* away,

PASSED (PASS)
Ge 15:17 a blazing torch appeared and *p*
Ex 33:22 you with my hand until I have *p* by.
2Ch 21:20 He *p* away, to no one's regret,
Ps 57: 1 wings until the disaster has *p*.
Lk 10:32 saw him, *p* by on the other side.
1Co 15: 3 For what I received I *p* on to you

Heb 11:29 By faith the people *p*

PASSER-BY* (PASS)
Pr 26:10 is he who hires a fool or any *p*.
26:17 is a *p* who meddles

PASSING (PASS)
1Co 7:31 world in its present form is *p* away.
1Jn 2: 8 because the darkness is *p*

PASSION* (PASSIONATE PASSIONS)
Hos 7: 6 Their *p* smolders all night;
1Co 7: 9 better to marry than to burn with *p*.

PASSIONATE* (PASSION)
1Th 4: 5 not in *p* lust like the heathen,

PASSIONS* (PASSION)
Ro 7: 5 the sinful *p* aroused
Gal 5:24 crucified the sinful nature with its *p*
Tit 2:12 to ungodliness and worldly *p*,
3: 3 and enslaved by all kinds of *p*

PASSOVER
Ex 12:11 Eat it in haste; it is the LORD's *P*.
Nu 9: 2 Have the Israelites celebrate the *P*
Dt 16: 1 celebrate the *P* of the LORD your
Jos 5:10 the Israelites celebrated the *P*.
2Ki 23:21 "Celebrate the *P* to the LORD
Ezr 6:19 the exiles celebrated the *P*.
Mk 14:12 customary to sacrifice the *P* lamb,
Lk 22: 1 called the *P*, was approaching,
1Co 5: 7 our *P* lamb, has been sacrificed.
Heb 11:28 he kept the *P* and the sprinkling

PAST
Isa 43:18 do not dwell on the *p*.
65:16 For the *p* troubles will be forgotten
Ro 15: 4 in the *p* was written to teach us,
16:25 the mystery hidden for long ages *p*,
Eph 3: 9 which for ages *p* was kept hidden
Heb 1: 1 In the *p* God spoke

PASTORS*
Eph 4:11 and some to be *p* and teachers,

PASTURE (PASTURES)
Ps 37: 3 dwell in the land and enjoy safe *p*.
95: 7 and we are the people of his *p*,
100: 3 we are his people, the sheep of his *p*
Jer 50: 7 against the LORD, their true *p*,
Eze 34:13 I will *p* them on the mountains
Zec 11: 4 "*P* the flock marked for slaughter.
Jn 10: 9 come in and go out, and find *p*.

PASTURES (PASTURE)
Ps 23: 2 He makes me lie down in green *p*,

PATCH
Jer 10: 5 Like a scarecrow in a melon *p*,
Mt 9:16 No one sews a *p* of unshrunk cloth

PATH (PATHS)
Ps 16:11 known to me the *p* of life;
27:11 lead me in a straight *p*
119: 32 I run in the *p* of your commands,
119:105 and a light for my *p*.
Pr 2: 9 and fair—every good *p*.
12:28 along that *p* is immortality.
15:10 awaits him who leaves the *p*;
15:19 the *p* of the upright is a highway.
15:24 The *p* of life leads upward
21:16 from the *p* of understanding
Isa 26: 7 The *p* of the righteous is level;
Jer 31: 9 on a level *p* where they will not
Mt 13: 4 fell along the *p*, and the birds came
Lk 1:79 to guide our feet into the *p* of peace
2Co 6: 3 no stumbling block in anyone's *p*,

PATHS (PATH)
Ps 23: 3 He guides me in *p* of righteousness
25: 4 teach me your *p*;
Pr 2:13 who leave the straight *p*
3: 6 and he will make your *p* straight.
4:11 and lead you along straight *p*.
4:26 Make level *p* for your feet
5:21 and he examines all his *p*.
8:20 along the *p* of justice,
22: 5 In the *p* of the wicked lie thorns
Isa 2: 3 so that we may walk in his *p*."
Jer 6:16 ask for the ancient *p*,
Mic 4: 2 so that we may walk in his *p*."
Mt 3: 3 make straight *p* for him.'"
Ac 2:28 to me the *p* of life;
Ro 11:33 and his *p* beyond tracing out!
Heb 12:13 "Make level *p* for your feet,"

PATIENCE* (PATIENT)
Pr 19:11 A man's wisdom gives him *p*;
25:15 Through *p* a ruler can be persuaded
Ecc 7: 8 and *p* is better than pride.

Isa 7:13 Is it not enough to try the p of men?
7:13 Will you try the p of my God also?
Ro 2: 4 and p, not realizing that God's
9:22 bore with great p the objects
2Co 6: 6 understanding, p and kindness;
Gal 5:22 joy, peace, p, kindness, goodness,
Col 1:11 may have great endurance and p,
3:12 humility, gentleness and p.
1Ti 1:16 Jesus might display his unlimited p
2Ti 3:10 my purpose, faith, p, love,
4: 2 with great p and careful instruction
Heb 6:12 p inherit what has been promised.
Jas 5:10 as an example of p in the face
2Pe 3:15 that our Lord's p means salvation,

PATIENT* (PATIENCE PATIENTLY)

Ne 9:30 For many years you were p
Job 6:11 What prospects, that I should be p?
Pr 14:29 A p man has great understanding,
15:18 but a p man calms a quarrel.
16:32 Better a p man than a warrior,
Mt 18:26 'Be p with me,' he begged,
18:29 'Be p with me, and I will pay you
Ro 12:12 Be joyful in hope, p in affliction,
1Co 13: 4 Love is p, love is kind.
2Co 1: 6 produces in you p endurance
Eph 4: 2 humble and gentle; be p,
1Th 5:14 help the weak, be p with everyone.
Jas 5: 7 Be p, then, brothers,
5: 7 and how p he is for the autumn
5: 8 You too, be p and stand firm,
2Pe 3: 9 He is p with you, not wanting
Rev 1: 9 p endurance that are ours in Jesus,
13:10 This calls for p endurance
14:12 This calls for p endurance

PATIENTLY* (PATIENT)

Ps 37: 7 still before the LORD and wait p
40: 1 I waited p for the LORD;
Isa 38:13 I waited p till dawn,
Hab 3:16 Yet I will wait p for the day
Ac 26: 3 I beg you to listen to me p.
Ro 8:25 we do not yet have, we wait for it p.
Heb 6:15 after waiting p, Abraham received
1Pe 3:20 ago when God waited p in the days
Rev 3:10 kept my command to endure p,

PATTERN

Ex 25:40 according to the p shown you
Ro 5:14 who was a p of the one to come.
12: 2 longer to the p of this world,
2Ti 1:13 keep as the p of sound teaching,
Heb 8: 5 according to the p shown you

PAUL

Also called Saul (Ac 13:9). Pharisee from Tarsus (Ac 9:11; Php 3:5). Apostle (Gal 1). At stoning of Stephen (Ac 8:1). Persecuted Church (Ac 9:1-2; Gal 1:13). Vision of Jesus on road to Damascus (Ac 9:4-9; 26:12-18). In Arabia (Gal 1:17). Preached in Damascus; escaped death through the wall in a basket (Ac 9:19-25). In Jerusalem; sent back to Tarsus (Ac 9:26-30).

Brought to Antioch by Barnabas (Ac 11:22-26). First missionary journey to Cyprus and Galatia (Ac 13-14). Stoned at Lystra (Ac 14:19-20). At Jerusalem council (Ac 15). Split with Barnabas over Mark (Ac 15:36-41).

Second missionary journey with Silas (Ac 16-20). Called to Macedonia (Ac 16:6-10). Freed from prison in Philippi (Ac 16:16-40). In Thessalonica (Ac 17:1-9). Speech in Athens (Ac 17:16-33). In Corinth (Ac 18). In Ephesus (Ac 19). Return to Jerusalem (Ac 20). Farewell to Ephesian elders (Ac 20:13-38). Arrival in Jerusalem (Ac 21:1-26). Arrested (Ac 21:27-36). Addressed crowds (Ac 22), Sanhedrin (Ac 23:1-11). Transferred to Caesarea (Ac 23:12-35). Trial before Felix (Ac 24), Festus (Ac 25:1-12). Before Agrippa (Ac 25:13-26:32). Voyage to Rome; shipwreck (Ac 27). Arrival in Rome (Ac 28).

Epistles: Romans, 1 and 2 Corinthians, Galatians, Ephesians, Philippians, Colossians, 1 and 2 Thessalonians, 1 and 2 Timothy, Titus, Philemon.

PAVEMENT

Jn 19:13 as the Stone P (which

PAY (PAID PAYMENT PAYS REPAID REPAY REPAYING)

Lev 26:43 They will p for their sins
Dt 7:12 If you p attention to these laws
Pr 4: 1 p attention and gain understanding
4:20 My son, p attention to what I say;
5: 1 My son, p attention to my wisdom,
6:31 if he is caught, he must p sevenfold,
19:19 man must p the penalty;
22:17 P attention and listen
24:29 I'll p that man back for what he did
Eze 40: 4 and p attention to everything I am
Zec 11:12 give me my p; but if not, keep it."
Mt 20: 2 He agreed to p them a denarius
22:16 you p no attention to who they are.
22:17 Is it right to p taxes to Caesar
Lk 3:14 falsely—be content with your p."
19: 8 I will p back four times the amount
Ro 13: 6 This is also why you p taxes,
2Pe 1:19 you will do well to p attention to it,

PAYMENT (PAY)

Ps 49: 8 no p is ever enough—
Php 4:18 I have received full p and

PAYS (PAY)

Pr 17:13 If a man p back evil for good,
1Th 5:15 sure that nobody p back wrong

PEACE (PEACEABLE PEACEFUL PEACEMAKERS)

Lev 26: 6 " 'I will grant p in the land,
Nu 6:26 and give you p." '
25:12 him I am making my covenant of p
Dt 20:10 make its people an offer of p.
Jdg 3:11 So the land had p for forty years,
3:30 and the land had p for eighty years.
5:31 Then the land had p forty years.
6:24 and called it The LORD is P.
8:28 the land enjoyed p forty years.
1Sa 7:14 And there was p between Israel
2Sa 10:19 they made p with the Israelites
1Ki 2:33 may there be the LORD's p forever
22:44 also at p with the king of Israel.
2Ki 9:17 come in p?' " The horseman rode
1Ch 19:19 they made p with David
22: 9 and I will grant Israel p
2Ch 14: 1 and in his days the country was at p
20:30 kingdom of Jehoshaphat was at p,
Job 3:26 I have no p, no quietness;
22:21 to God and be at p with him;
Ps 29:11 LORD blesses his people with p.
34:14 seek p and pursue it.
37:11 and enjoy great p.
37:37 there is a future for the man of p.
85:10 righteousness and p kiss each other
119:165 Great p have they who love your
120: 7 I am a man of p;
122: 6 Pray for the p of Jerusalem:
147: 14 He grants p to your borders
Pr 12:20 but joy for those who promote p.
14:30 A heart at p gives life to the body,
16: 7 his enemies live at p with him.
17: 1 Better a dry crust with p and quiet
Ecc 3: 8 a time for war and a time for p.
Isa 9: 6 Everlasting Father, Prince of P.
14: 7 All the lands are at rest and at p;
26: 3 You will keep in perfect p
32:17 The fruit of righteousness will be p;
48:18 your p would have been like a river,
48:22 "There is no p," says the LORD,
52: 7 who proclaim p,
53: 5 punishment that brought us p was
54:10 nor my covenant of p be removed,"
55:12 and be led forth in p;
57: 2 enter into p;
57:19 P, p, to those far and near,"
57:21 "There is no p," says my God,
59: 8 The way of p they do not know;
Jer 6:14 'P, p,' they say,
8:11 "P, p," . . . there is no p.
30:10 Jacob will again have p
46:27 Jacob will again have p
Eze 13:10 "P," when there is no p,
34:25 " 'I will make a covenant of p
37:26 I will make a covenant of p
Mic 5: 5 And he will be their p.
Zec 8:19 Therefore love truth and p."
9:10 He will proclaim p to the nations.
Mal 2: 5 a covenant of life and p,
2: 6 He walked with me in p
Mt 10:34 I did not come to bring p,
Mk 9:50 and be at p with each other."
Lk 1:79 to guide our feet into the path of p
2:14 on earth p to men on whom his
19:38 "P in heaven and glory
Jn 14:27 P I leave with you; my p
16:33 so that in me you may have p.
Ro 1: 7 and p to you from God our Father
2:10 and p for everyone who does good:
5: 1 we have p with God
8: 6 by the Spirit is life and p;
12:18 on you, live at p with everyone.
14:19 effort to do what leads to p
1Co 7:15 God has called us to live in p.
14:33 a God of disorder but of p.
2Co 13:11 be of one mind, live in p.
Gal 5:22 joy, p, patience, kindness,
Eph 2:14 he himself is our p, who has made
2:15 thus making p, and in this one body
Eph 2:17 and p to those who were near.
6:15 comes from the gospel of p.
Php 4: 7 the p of God, which transcends all
Col 1:20 by making p through his blood,
3:15 Let the p of Christ rule
3:15 of one body you were called to p.
1Th 5: 3 While people are saying, "P
5:13 Live in p with each other.
5:23 the God of p, sanctify you through
2Th 3:16 the Lord of p himself give you p
2Ti 2:22 righteousness, faith, love and p,
Heb 7: 2 "king of Salem" means "king of p."
12:11 p for those who have been trained
12:14 effort to live in p with all men
13:20 May the God of p, who
1Pe 3:11 he must seek p and pursue it.
2Pe 3:14 blameless and at p with him.
Rev 6: 4 power to take p from the earth

PEACEABLE* (PEACE)

Tit 3: 2 to slander no one, to be p

PEACEFUL (PEACE)

1Ti 2: 2 that we may live p and quiet lives

PEACE-LOVING

Jas 3:17 then p, considerate

PEACEMAKERS* (PEACE)

Mt 5: 9 Blessed are the p,
Jas 3:18 P who sow in peace raise a harvest

PEARL* (PEARLS)

Rev 21:21 each gate made of a single p.

PEARLS (PEARL)

Mt 7: 6 do not throw your p to pigs.
13:45 like a merchant looking for fine p,
1Ti 2: 9 or gold or p or expensive clothes,
Rev 21:21 The twelve gates were twelve p,

PEDDLE*

2Co 2:17 we do not p the word of God

PEG

Jdg 4:21 She drove the p through his temple

PEKAH

King of Israel (2Ki 15:25-31; Isa 7:1).

PEKAHIAH*

Son of Menahem; king of Israel (2Ki 15:22-26).

PEN

Ps 45: 1 my tongue is the p
Mt 5:18 letter, not the least stroke of a p,
Jn 10: 1 who does not enter the sheep p

PENETRATES*

Heb 4:12 it p even to dividing soul and spirit,

PENNIES* (PENNY)

Lk 12: 6 not five sparrows sold for two p?

PENNY* (PENNIES)

Mt 5:26 out until you have paid the last p.
10:29 Are not two sparrows sold for a p?
Mk 12:42 worth only a fraction of a p.
Lk 12:59 out until you have paid the last p."

PENTECOST*

Ac 2: 1 of P came, they were all together
20:16 if possible, by the day of P.
1Co 16: 8 I will stay on at Ephesus until P,

PEOPLE (PEOPLES)

Ge 11: 6 as one p speaking the same
Ex 5: 1 Let my p go,
6: 7 take you as my own p,
8:23 between my p and your p.
15:13 the p you have redeemed.
19: 8 The p all responded together,
24: 3 Moses went and told the p
32: 1 When the p saw that Moses
32: 9 they are a stiff-necked p.
33:13 this nation is your p.
Lev 9: 7 for yourself and the p;
16:24 the burnt offering for the p,
26:12 and you will be my p.
Nu 11:11 burden of all these p on
14:11 p treat me with contempt?
14:19 forgive the sin of these p,
22: 5 A p has come out of Egypt
Dt 4: 6 a wise and understanding p.
4:20 the p of his inheritance,
5:28 what this p said to you.
7: 6 a p holy to the LORD
26:18 that you are his p,
31: 7 you must go with this p
31:16 these p will soon prostitute
32: 9 the LORD's portion is his p,

Dt 32:43 atonement for his land and p.
33:29 a p saved by the LORD?
Jos 1: 6 you will lead this p
24:24 the p said to Joshua,
Jdg 2: 7 p served the LORD throughout
Ru 1:16 Your p will be my p
1Sa 8: 7 the p are saying to you;
12:22 LORD will not reject his p,
2Sa 5: 2 will shepherd my p Israel
7:10 provide a place for my p
1Ki 3: 8 among the p you have chosen,
8:30 your p Israel when they pray
8:56 has given rest to his p
18:39 when all the p saw this,
2Ki 23: 3 all the p pledged themselves
1Ch 17:21 to redeem p for himself
29:17 how willingly your p who are
2Ch 2:11 Because the LORD loves his p,
7: 5 p dedicated the temple
7:14 if my p, who are called
30: 6 "P of Israel, return to
36:16 was aroused against his p
Ezr 2: 1 These are the p of the
3: 1 p assembled as one man
Ne 1:10 your p, whom you redeemed
4: 6 p worked with all their heart
8: 1 p assembled as one man
Est 3: 6 to destroy all Mordecai's p,
Job 12: 2 Doubtless you are the p,
Ps 29:11 gives strength to his p;
33:12 p he chose for his inheritance
50: 4 that he may judge his p
53: 6 restores the fortunes of his p,
81:13 If my p would but listen
94:14 LORD will not reject his p;
95: 7 we are the p of his pasture,
95:10 a p whose hearts go astray,
125: 2 the LORD surrounds his p
135: 14 LORD will vindicate his p
144: 15 p whose God is the LORD.
Pr 14:34 sin is a disgrace to any p.
29: 2 righteous thrive, the p rejoice
29:18 the p cast off restraint
Isa 1: 3 my p do not understand.
1: 4 a p loaded with guilt,
5:13 my p will go into exile
6:10 the heart of this p calloused;
9: 2 the p walking in darkness
12:12 will assemble the scattered p
19:25 Blessed be Egypt my p,
25: 8 remove the disgrace of his p
29:13 These p come near to me
40: 1 Comfort, comfort my p
40: 7 Surely the p are grass.
42: 6 a covenant for the p
49:13 the LORD comforts his p
51: 4 "Listen to me, my p;
52: 6 my p will know my name;
53: 8 for the transgression of my p
60:21 will all your p be righteous
62:12 will be called the Holy P,
65:23 they will be a p blessed
Jer 2:11 my p have exchanged their
2:13 p have committed two sins:
2:32 my p have forgotten me,
4:22 My p are fools;
5:14 Because the p have spoken
5:31 my p love it this way
7:16 do not pray for this p
18:15 my p have forgotten me;
25: 7 They will be my p,
30: 3 I will bring my p Israel
Eze 13:23 I will save my p from
36: 8 fruit for my p Israel,
36:28 you will be my p,
36:38 be filled with flocks of p.
37:13 Then you, my p, will know
38:14 p Israel are living in safety
39: 7 name among my p Israel.
Da 7:27 saints, the p of the Most High.
8:24 mighty men and the holy p
9:19 your p bear your name
9:24 are decreed for your p
9:26 p of the ruler who will come
10:14 will happen to your p
11:32 p who know their God will
12: 1 prince who protects your p.
Hos 1:10 'You are not my p,'
2:23 'You are my p';
4:14 a p without understanding
Joel 2:18 and take pity on his p.
3:16 be a refuge for his p,
Am 9:14 back my exiled p Israel;
Mic 6: 2 a case against his p;
7:14 Shepherd your p with
Hag 1:12 remnant of the p obeyed
Zec 2:11 and will become my p.
8: 7 I will save my p
13: 9 will say, 'They are my p,'

Mk 7: 6 p honor me with their lips
8:27 "Who do p say I am?"
Lk 1:17 make ready a p prepared
1:68 and has redeemed his p.
2:10 joy that will be for all the p.
21:23 and wrath against this p.
Jn 11:50 one man die for the p
18:14 if one man died for the p.
Ac 15:14 from the Gentiles a p.
18:10 have many p in this city.
Ro 9:25 will call them 'my p.'
11: 1 Did God reject his p?
15:10 O Gentiles, with his p."
2Co 6:16 and they will be my p."
Tit 2:14 a p that are his very own,
Heb 2:17 for the sins of the p.
4: 9 a Sabbath-rest for the p
5: 3 for the sins of the p.
10:30 Lord will judge his p.
11:25 mistreated along with the p
13:12 to make the p holy
1Pe 2: 9 you are a chosen p,
2:10 Once you were not a p,
2:10 you are the p of God;
2Pe 2: 1 false prophets among the p,
3:11 kind of p ought you to be?
Rev 18: 4 "Come out of her, my p,
21: 3 They will be his p,

PEOPLES (PEOPLE)

Ge 17:16 kings of p will come from her
25:23 two p from within you will
27:29 and p bow down to you
28: 3 become a community of p.
48: 4 you a community of p,
Dt 14: 2 of all the p on the face of
28:10 Then all the p on earth
32: 8 set up boundaries for the p
Jos 4:24 all the p of the earth might
1Ki 8:43 all the p of the earth may
2Ch 7:20 of ridicule among all p.
Ps 9: 8 he will govern the p
67: 5 may all the p praise you.
87: 6 in the register of the p:
96:10 he will judge the p
Isa 2: 4 settle disputes for many p.
17:12 Oh, the uproar of the p—
25: 6 of rich food for all p,
34: 1 pay attention, you p!
55: 4 him a witness to the p,
Jer 10: 3 customs of the p are worthless
Da 7:14 all p, nations and men
Mic 4: 1 and p will stream to it.
4: 3 will judge between many p
5: 7 in the midst of many p
Zep 3: 9 purify the lips of the p,
3:20 among all the p of the
Zec 8:20 Many p and the inhabitants
12: 2 all the surrounding p reeling.
Rev 10:11 prophesy again about many p,
17:15 the prostitute sits, are p,

PEOR

Nu 25: 3 joined in worshiping the Baal of P.
Dt 4: 3 who followed the Baal of P,

PERCEIVE (PERCEIVING)

Ps 139: 2 you p my thoughts from afar.
Pr 24:12 not he who weighs the heart p it?

PERCEIVING* (PERCEIVE)

Isa 6: 9 be ever seeing, but never p.'
Mt 13:14 you will be ever seeing but never p.
Mk 4:12 may be ever seeing but never p,
Ac 28:26 you will be ever seeing but never p

PERFECT* (PERFECTER PERFECTING PERFECTION)

Dt 32: 4 He is the Rock, his works are p,
2Sa 22:31 "As for God, his way is p;
22:33 and makes my way p.
Job 36: 4 one p in knowledge is with you.
37:16 of him who is p in knowledge?
Ps 18:30 As for God, his way is p;
18:32 and makes my way p.
19: 7 The law of the LORD is p,
50: 2 From Zion, p in beauty,
64: 6 "We have devised a p plan!"
SS 6: 9 but my dove, my p one, is unique,
Isa 25: 1 for in p faithfulness
26: 3 You will keep in p peace
Eze 16:14 had given you made your beauty p,
27: 3 "I am p in beauty."
28:12 full of wisdom and p in beauty.
Mt 5:48 Do not even pagans do that? Be p,
5:48 as your heavenly Father is p.
19:21 answered, "If you want to be p,
Ro 12: 2 his good, pleasing and p will.
2Co 12: 9 for my power is made p

Php 3:12 or have already been made p,
Col 1:28 so that we may present everyone p
3:14 binds them all together in p unity.
Heb 2:10 the author of their salvation p
5: 9 what he suffered and, once made p,
7:19 useless (for the law made nothing p
7:28 who has been made p forever.
9:11 and more p tabernacle that is not
10: 1 make p those who draw
10:14 he has made p forever those who
11:40 with us would they be made p.
12:23 spirits of righteous men made p,
Jas 1:17 Every good and p gift is from above
1:25 into the p law that gives freedom,
3: 2 he is a p man, able
1Jn 4:18 But p love drives out fear,
4:18 The one who fears is not made p

PERFECTER* (PERFECT)

Heb 12: 2 the author and p of our faith,

PERFECTING* (PERFECT)

2Co 7: 1 p holiness out of reverence for God

PERFECTION* (PERFECT)

Ps 119: 96 To all p I see a limit;
La 2:15 the p of beauty,
Eze 27: 4 builders brought your beauty to p.
27:11 they brought your beauty to p.
28:12 " 'You were the model of p,
1Co 13:10 but when p comes, the imperfect
2Co 13: 9 and our prayer is for your p.
13:11 Aim for p, listen to my appeal,
Heb 7:11 If p could have been attained

PERFORM (PERFORMED PERFORMS)

Ex 3:20 with all the wonders that I will p
2Sa 7:23 to p great and awesome wonders
Jn 3: 2 no one could p the miraculous

PERFORMED (PERFORM)

Mt 11:21 If the miracles that were p
Jn 10:41 John never p a miraculous

PERFORMS (PERFORM)

Ps 77:14 You are the God who p miracles;

PERFUME

Ecc 7: 1 A good name is better than fine p,
SS 1: 3 your name is like p poured out.
Mk 14: 3 jar of very expensive p,

PERIL

2Co 1:10 us from such a deadly p,

PERISH (PERISHABLE PERISHED PERISHES PERISHING)

Ge 6:17 Everything on earth will p.
Est 4:16 And if I p, I p."
Ps 1: 6 but the way of the wicked will p.
37:20 But the wicked will p:
73:27 Those who are far from you will p;
102: 26 They will p, but you remain;
Pr 11:10 when the wicked p, there are
19: 9 and he who pours out lies will p.
21:28 A false witness will p,
28:28 when the wicked p, the righteous
Isa 1:28 who forsake the LORD will p.
29:14 the wisdom of the wise will p,
60:12 that will not serve you will p;
Zec 11: 9 the dying die, and the perishing p.
Lk 13: 3 unless you repent, you too will all p
13: 5 unless you repent, you too will all p
21:18 But not a hair of your head will p.
Jn 3:16 whoever believes in him shall not p
10:28 eternal life, and they shall never p;
Ro 2:12 apart from the law will also p apart
Col 2:22 These are all destined to p with use,
2Th 2:10 They p because they refused
Heb 1:11 They will p, but you remain;
1Pe 1: 4 into an inheritance that can never p
2Pe 3: 9 not wanting anyone to p,

PERISHABLE (PERISH)

1Co 15:42 The body that is sown is p,
1Pe 1:18 not with p things such
1:23 not of p seed, but of imperishable,

PERISHED (PERISH)

Ps 119: 92 I would have p in my affliction.

PERISHES (PERISH)

Job 8:13 so p the hope of the godless.
1Pe 1: 7 which p even though refined by fire

PERISHING (PERISH)

1Co 1:18 foolishness to those who are p,
2Co 2:15 being saved and those who are p.
4: 3 it is veiled to those who are p.

PERJURERS* (PERJURY)
Mal 3: 5 and *p*, against those who defraud
1Ti 1:10 for slave traders and liars and *p*—

PERJURY* (PERJURERS)
Jer 7: 9 murder, commit adultery and *p*,

PERMANENT
Heb 7:24 lives forever, he has a *p* priesthood.

PERMISSIBLE (PERMIT)
1Co 6:12 "Everything is *p* for me"—
10:23 "Everything is *p*"— but not

PERMIT (PERMISSIBLE PERMITTED)
Hos 5: 4 "Their deeds do not *p* them
1Ti 2:12 I do not *p* a woman to teach

PERMITTED (PERMIT)
Mt 19: 8 Moses *p* you to divorce your wives
2Co 12: 4 things that man is not *p* to tell.

PERSECUTE (PERSECUTED PERSECUTION PERSECUTIONS)
Ps119: 86 for men *p* me without cause.
Mt 5:11 *p* you and falsely say all kinds
5:44 and pray for those who *p* you,
Jn 15:20 they persecuted me, they will *p* you
Ac 9: 4 why do you *p* me?" "Who are you,
Ro 12:14 Bless those who *p* you; bless

PERSECUTED (PERSECUTE)
Mt 5:10 Blessed are those who are *p*
5:12 same way they *p* the prophets who
Jn 15:20 If they *p* me, they will persecute
1Co 4:12 when we are *p*, we endure it;
15: 9 because I *p* the church of God.
2Co 4: 9 in despair; *p*, but not abandoned;
1Th 3: 4 kept telling you that we would be *p*.
2Ti 3:12 life in Christ Jesus will be *p*,
Heb 11:37 destitute, *p* and mistreated—

PERSECUTION (PERSECUTE)
Mt 13:21 When trouble or *p* comes
Ro 8:35 or hardship or *p* or famine

PERSECUTIONS (PERSECUTE)
Mk 10:30 and with them, *p*) and in the age
2Co 12:10 in hardships, in *p*, in difficulties.
2Th 1: 4 faith in all the *p* and trials you are
2Ti 3:11 love, endurance, *p*, sufferings—

PERSEVERANCE* (PERSEVERE)
Ro 5: 3 we know that suffering produces *p*;
5: 4 *p*, character; and character, hope.
2Co 12:12 were done among you with great *p*.
2Th 1: 4 churches we boast about your *p*
3: 5 into God's love and Christ's *p*.
Heb 12: 1 run with *p* the race marked out
Jas 1: 3 the testing of your faith develops *p*.
1: 4 *P* must finish its work
5:11 You have heard of Job's *p*
2Pe 1: 6 *p*; and to *p*, godliness;
Rev 2: 2 your hard work and your *p*.
2:19 and faith, your service and *p*,

PERSEVERE* (PERSEVERANCE PERSEVERED PERSEVERES PERSEVERING)
1Ti 4:16 *P* in them, because if you do,
Heb 10:36 You need to *p* so that

PERSEVERED* (PERSEVERE)
Heb 11:27 he *p* because he saw him who is
Jas 5:11 consider blessed those who have *p*.
Rev 2: 3 You have *p* and have endured

PERSEVERES* (PERSEVERE)
1Co 13: 7 trusts, always hopes, always *p*.
Jas 1:12 Blessed is the man who *p*

PERSEVERING* (PERSEVERE)
Lk 8:15 retain it, and by *p* produce a crop.

PERSIANS
Da 6:15 law of the Medes and *P* no decree

PERSISTENCE*
Ro 2: 7 To those who by *p*

PERSUADE (PERSUADED PERSUASIVE)
Ac 18: 4 trying to *p* Jews and Greeks.
2Co 5:11 is to fear the Lord, we try to *p* men.

PERSUADED (PERSUADE)
Ro 4:21 being fully *p* that God had power

PERSUASIVE (PERSUADE)
1Co 2: 4 not with wise and *p* words,

PERVERSION* (PERVERT)
Lev 18:23 sexual relations with it; that is a *p*.
20:12 What they have done is a *p*;
Ro 1:27 the due penalty for their *p*.
Jude : 7 up to sexual immorality and *p*.

PERVERT (PERVERSION PERVERTED PERVERTS)
Ex 23: 2 do not *p* justice by siding
Dt 16:19 Do not *p* justice or show partiality.
Job 34:12 that the Almighty would *p* justice.
Pr 17:23 to *p* the course of justice.
Gal 1: 7 are trying to *p* the gospel of Christ.

PERVERTED (PERVERT)
1Sa 8: 3 and accepted bribes and *p* justice.

PERVERTS* (PERVERT)
1Ti 1:10 for murderers, for adulterers and *p*,

PESTILENCE (PESTILENCES)
Ps 91: 6 nor the *p* that stalks in the darkness

PESTILENCES (PESTILENCE)
Lk 21:11 famines and *p* in various places,

PETER
Apostle, brother of Andrew, also called Simon (Mt 10:2; Mk 3:16; Lk 6:14; Ac 1:13), and Cephas (Jn 1:42). Confession of Christ (Mt 16:13-20; Mk 8:27-30; Lk 9:18-27). At transfiguration (Mt 17:1-8; Mk 9:2-8; Lk 9:28-36; 2Pe 1:16-18). Caught fish with coin (Mt 17:24-27). Denial of Jesus predicted (Mt 26:31-35; Mk 14:27-31; Lk 22:31-34; Jn 13:31-38). Denied Jesus (Mt 26:69-75; Mk 14:66-72; Lk 22:54-62; Jn 18:15-27). Commissioned by Jesus to shepherd his flock (Jn 21:15-23).
Speech at Pentecost (Ac 2). Healed beggar (Ac 3:1-10). Speech at temple (Ac 3:11-26), before Sanhedrin (Ac 4:1-22). In Samaria (Ac 8:14-25). Sent by vision to Cornelius (Ac 10). Announced salvation of Gentiles in Jerusalem (Ac 11; 15). Freed from prison (Ac 12). Inconsistency at Antioch (Gal 2:11-21). At Jerusalem Council (Ac 15).
Epistles: 1-2 Peter.

PETITION (PETITIONS)
1Ch 16: 4 to make *p*, to give thanks,
Php 4: 6 by prayer and *p*, with thanksgiving,

PETITIONS (PETITION)
Heb 5: 7 he offered up prayers and *p*

PHANTOM*
Ps 39: 6 Man is a mere *p* as he goes to

PHARAOH (PHARAOH'S)
Ge 12:15 her to *P*, and she was taken
41:14 So *P* sent for Joseph, and he was
Ex 14: 4 glory for myself through *P*
14:17 And I will gain glory through *P*

PHARAOH'S (PHARAOH)
Ex 7: 3 But I will harden *P* heart, and

PHARISEE (PHARISEES)
Ac 23: 6 brothers, I am a *P*, the son of a *P*.
Php 3: 5 in regard to the law, a *P*; as for zeal,

PHARISEES (PHARISEE)
Mt 5:20 surpasses that of the *P*
16: 6 guard against the yeast of the *P*
23:13 of the law and *P*, you hypocrites!
Jn 3: 1 a man of the *P* named Nicodemus,

PHILADELPHIA
Rev 3: 7 the angel of the church in *P* write:

PHILEMON*
Phm : 1 To *P* our dear friend and fellow

PHILIP
1. Apostle (Mt 10:3; Mk 3:18; Lk 6:14; Jn 1:43-48; 14:8; Ac 1:13).
2. Deacon (Ac 6:1-7); evangelist in Samaria (Ac 8:4-25), to Ethiopian (Ac 8:26-40).

PHILIPPI
Ac 16:12 From there we traveled to *P*,
Php 1: 1 To all the saints in Christ Jesus at *P*

PHILISTINE (PHILISTINES)
Jos 13: 3 of the five *P* rulers in Gaza,
1Sa 14: 1 let's go over to the *P* outpost
17:26 is this uncircumcised *P* that he
17:37 me from the hand of this *P*."

PHILISTINES (PHILISTINE)
Jdg 10: 7 them into the hands of the *P*
13: 1 the hands of the *P* for forty years.
16: 5 The rulers of the *P* went to her
1Sa 4: 1 at Ebenezer, and the *P* at Aphek.
5: 8 together all the rulers of the *P*
13:23 a detachment of *P* had gone out
17: 1 the *P* gathered their forces for war
23: 1 the *P* are fighting against Keilah
27: 1 is to escape to the land of the *P*.
31: 1 Now the *P* fought against Israel;
2Sa 5:17 When the *P* heard that David had
8: 1 David defeated the *P* and subdued
21:15 there was a battle between the *P*
2Ki 18: 8 he defeated the *P*, as far as Gaza
Am 1: 8 Ekron till the last of the *P* is dead,"

PHILOSOPHER* (PHILOSOPHY)
1Co 1:20 Where is the *p* of this age?

PHILOSOPHY* (PHILOSOPHER)
Col 2: 8 through hollow and deceptive *p*,

PHINEHAS
Nu 25: 7 When *P* son of Eleazar, the son
Ps106: 30 But *P* stood up and intervened,

PHOEBE*
Ro 16: 1 I commend to you our sister *P*,

PHYLACTERIES*
Mt 23: 5 They make their *p* wide

PHYSICAL
Ro 2:28 merely outward and *p*.
Col 1:22 by Christ's *p* body through death
1Ti 4: 8 For *p* training is of some value,
Jas 2:16 but does nothing about his *p* needs,

PICK (PICKED)
Mk 16:18 they will *p* up snakes

PICKED (PICK)
Lk 14: 7 noticed how the guests *p* the places
Jn 5: 9 he *p* up his mat and walked.

PIECE (PIECES)
Jn 19:23 woven in one *p* from top to bottom.

PIECES (PIECE)
Ge 15:17 and passed between the *p*.
Jer 34:18 and then walked between its *p*.
Zec 11:12 So they paid me thirty *p* of silver.
Mt 14:20 of broken *p* that were left over.

PIERCE (PIERCED)
Ex 21: 6 and *p* his ear with an awl.
Pr 12:18 Reckless words *p* like a sword,
Lk 2:35 a sword will *p* your own soul too."

PIERCED (PIERCE)
Ps 22:16 they have *p* my hands and my feet.
40: 6 but my ears you have *p*;
Isa 53: 5 But he was *p* for our transgressions,
Zec 12:10 look on me, the one they have *p*,
Jn 19:37 look on the one they have *p*."
Rev 1: 7 even those who *p* him;

PIG'S (PIGS)
Pr 11:22 Like a gold ring in a *p* snout

PIGEONS
Lev 5:11 afford two doves or two young *p*,
Lk 2:24 "a pair of doves or two young *p*."

PIGS (PIG'S)
Mt 7: 6 do not throw your pearls to *p*.
Mk 5:11 A large herd of *p* was feeding on

PILATE
Governor of Judea. Questioned Jesus (Mt 27:1-26; Mk 15:15; Lk 22:66-23:25; Jn 18:28-19:16); sent him to Herod (Lk 23:6-12); consented to his crucifixion when crowds chose Barabbas (Mt 27:15-26; Mk 15:6-15; Lk 23:13-25; Jn 19:1-10).

PILLAR (PILLARS)
Ge 19:26 and she became a *p* of salt.
Ex 13:21 ahead of them in a *p* of cloud
1Ti 3:15 the *p* and foundation of the truth.
Rev 3:12 who overcomes I will make a *p*

PILLARS (PILLAR)
Gal 2: 9 and John, those reputed to be *p*,

PINIONS
Dt 32:11 and carries them on its *p*.

PISGAH
Dt 3:27 Go up to the top of *P* and look west

PIT
Ps 7:15 falls into the *p* he has made.
40: 2 He lifted me out of the slimy *p*,
103: 4 who redeems your life from the *p*
Pr 23:27 for a prostitute is a deep *p*

Pr 26:27 If a man digs a *p*, he will fall into it;
Isa 24:17 Terror and *p* and snare await you,
38:17 me from the *p* of destruction;
Mt 15:14 a blind man, both will fall into a *p*."

PITCH
Ge 6:14 and coat it with *p* inside and out.
Ex 2: 3 and coated it with tar and *p*.

PITIED (PITY)
1Co 15:19 we are to be *p* more than all men.

PITY (PITIED)
Ps 72:13 He will take *p* on the weak
Ecc 4:10 But *p* the man who falls
Lk 10:33 when he saw him, he took *p* on him

PLAGUE (PLAGUED PLAGUES)
2Ch 6:28 "When famine or *p* comes
Ps 91: 6 nor the *p* that destroys at midday.

PLAGUED* (PLAGUE)
Ps 73: 5 they are not *p* by human ills.
73:14 All day long I have been *p*;

PLAGUES (PLAGUE)
Hos 13:14 Where, O death, are your *p*?
Rev 21: 9 full of the seven last *p* came
22:18 to him the *p* described in this book.

PLAIN
Isa 40: 4 the rugged places a *p*.
Ro 1:19 what may be known about God is *p*

PLAN (PLANNED PLANS)
Ex 26:30 according to the *p* shown you
Job 42: 2 no *p* of yours can be thwarted.
Pr 14:22 those who *p* what is good find love
21:30 is no wisdom, no insight, no *p*
Am 3: 7 nothing without revealing his *p*
Eph 1:11 predestined according to the *p*

PLANK
Mt 7: 3 attention to the *p* in your own eye?
Lk 6:41 attention to the *p* in your own eye?

PLANNED (PLAN)
Ps 40: 5 The things you *p* for us
Isa 14:24 "Surely, as I have *p*, so it will be,
23: 9 The LORD Almighty *p* it,
46:11 what I have *p*, that will I do.
Heb 11:40 God had *p* something better for us

PLANS (PLAN)
Ps 20: 4 and make all your *p* succeed.
33:11 *p* of the LORD stand firm forever,
Pr 15:22 *P* fail for lack of counsel,
16: 3 and your *p* will succeed.
19:21 Many are the *p* in a man's heart,
20:18 Make *p* by seeking advice;
Isa 29:15 to hide their *p* from the LORD,
30: 1 those who carry out *p* that are not
32: 8 But the noble man makes noble *p*,
2Co 1:17 Or do I make my *p* in a worldly

PLANT (PLANTED PLANTING PLANTS)
Am 9:15 I will *p* Israel in their own land,
Mt 15:13 "Every *p* that my heavenly Father

PLANTED (PLANT)
Ge 2: 8 the LORD God had *p* a garden
Ps 1: 3 He is like a tree *p* by streams
Jer 17: 8 He will be like a tree *p* by the water
Mt 15:13 Father has not *p* will be pulled
21:33 was a landowner who *p* a vineyard.
Lk 13: 6 "A man had a fig tree, *p*
1Co 3: 6 I *p* the seed, Apollos watered it,
Jas 1:21 humbly accept the word *p* in you,

PLANTING (PLANT)
Isa 61: 3 a *p* of the LORD

PLANTS (PLANT)
Pr 31:16 out of her earnings she *p* a vineyard
1Co 3: 7 So neither he who *p* nor he who
9: 7 Who *p* a vineyard and does not eat

PLATTER
Mk 6:25 head of John the Baptist on a *p*."

PLAY (PLAYED)
1Sa 16:23 David would take his harp and *p*.
Isa 11: 8 The infant will *p* near the hole

PLAYED (PLAY)
Lk 7:32 " 'We *p* the flute for you,
1Co 14: 7 anyone know what tune is being *p*

PLEA (PLEAD PLEADED PLEADS)
1Ki 8:28 to your servant's prayer and his *p*
Ps 102: 17 he will not despise their *p*.
La 3:56 You heard my *p*: "Do not close

PLEAD (PLEA)
Isa 1:17 *p* the case of the widow.

PLEADED (PLEA)
2Co 12: 8 Three times I *p* with the Lord

PLEADS (PLEA)
Job 16:21 on behalf of a man he *p* with God

PLEASANT (PLEASE)
Ge 49:15 and how *p* is his land,
Ps 16: 6 for me in *p* places;
133: 1 How good and *p* it is
135: 3 sing praise to his name, for that is *p*
147: 1 how *p* and fitting to praise him!
Pr 2:10 knowledge will be *p* to your soul.
3:17 Her ways are *p* ways,
16:21 and *p* words promote instruction.
16:24 *P* words are a honeycomb,
Isa 30:10 Tell us *p* things,
1Th 3: 6 that you always have *p* memories
Heb 12:11 No discipline seems *p* at the time,

PLEASANTNESS* (PLEASE)
Pr 27: 9 the *p* of one's friend springs

PLEASE (PLEASANT PLEASANTNESS PLEASED PLEASES PLEASING PLEASURE PLEASURES)
Ps 69:31 This will *p* the LORD more
Pr 20:23 and dishonest scales do not *p* him.
Isa 46:10 and I will do all that I *p*.
Jer 6:20 your sacrifices do not *p* me."
27: 5 and I give it to anyone I *p*.
Jn 5:30 for I seek not to *p* myself
Ro 8: 8 by the sinful nature cannot *p* God.
15: 1 of the weak and not to *p* ourselves.
15: 2 Each of us should *p* his neighbor
1Co 7:32 affairs—how he can *p* the Lord.
10:33 I try to *p* everybody in every way.
2Co 5: 9 So we make it our goal to *p* him,
Gal 1:10 or of God? Or am I trying to *p* men
6: 8 the one who sows to *p* the Spirit,
Col 1:10 and may *p* him in every way:
1Th 2: 4 We are not trying to *p* men
4: 1 how to live in order to *p* God,
2Ti 2: 4 wants to *p* his commanding officer.
Tit 2: 9 to try to *p* them, not to talk back
Heb 11: 6 faith it is impossible to *p* God,

PLEASED (PLEASE)
Dt 28:63 as it *p* the LORD to make you
1Sa 12:22 LORD was *p* to make you his own.
1Ki 3:10 The Lord was *p* that Solomon had
1Ch 29:17 that you test the heart and are *p*
Mic 6: 7 Will the LORD be *p*
Mal 1:10 I am not *p* with you," says
Mt 3:17 whom I love; with him I am well *p*
17: 5 whom I love; with him I am well *p*.
Mk 1:11 whom I love; with you I am well *p*
Lk 3:22 whom I love; with you I am well *p*
1Co 1:21 God was *p* through the foolishness
Col 1:19 For God was *p* to have all his
Heb 10: 6 you were not *p*.
10: 8 nor were you *p* with them"
10:38 I will not be *p* with him."
11: 5 commended as one who *p* God.
13:16 for with such sacrifices God is *p*.
2Pe 1:17 whom I love; with him I am well *p*

PLEASES (PLEASE)
Job 23:13 He does whatever he *p*.
Ps 115: 3 he does whatever *p* him.
135: 6 The LORD does whatever *p* him,
Pr 15: 8 but the prayer of the upright *p* him.
21: 1 it like a watercourse wherever he *p*.
Ecc 2:26 To the man who *p* him, God gives
7:26 man who *p* God will escape her,
Da 4:35 He does as he *p*
Jn 3: 8 The wind blows wherever it *p*.
8:29 for I always do what *p* him."
Eph 5:10 truth) and find out what *p* the Lord
Col 3:20 in everything, for this *p* the Lord.
1Ti 2: 3 This is good, and *p* God our Savior,
1Jn 3:22 his commands and do what *p* him.

PLEASING (PLEASE)
Ge 2: 9 trees that were *p* to the eye
Lev 1: 9 an aroma *p* to the LORD.
Ps 19:14 be *p* in your sight,
104: 34 May my meditation be *p* to him,
Pr 15:26 but those of the pure are *p* to him.
16: 7 When a man's ways are *p*
SS 1: 3 *P* is the fragrance of your perfumes
4:10 How much more *p* is your love
7: 6 How beautiful you are and how *p*,
Ro 12: 1 *p* to God—this is your spiritual
14:18 Christ in this way is *p* to God
Php 4:18 an acceptable sacrifice, *p* to God.

1Ti 5: 4 grandparents, for this is *p* to God.
Heb 13:21 may he work in us what is *p* to him,

PLEASURE (PLEASE)
Ps 5: 4 You are not a God who takes *p*
51:16 you do not take *p* in burnt offerings
147: 10 His *p* is not in the strength
Pr 10:23 A fool finds *p* in evil conduct,
18: 2 A fool finds no *p* in understanding
21:17 He who loves *p* will become poor;
Isa 1:11 I have no *p*
Jer 6:10 they find no *p* in it.
Eze 18:23 Do I take any *p* in the death
18:32 For I take no *p* in the death
33:11 I take no *p* in the death
Lk 10:21 Father, for this was your good *p*.
Eph 1: 5 in accordance with his *p* and will—
1: 9 of his will according to his good *p*,
1Ti 5: 6 the widow who lives for *p* is dead
2Ti 3: 4 lovers of *p* rather than lovers
2Pe 2:13 Their idea of *p* is to carouse

PLEASURES* (PLEASE)
Ps 16:11 with eternal *p* at your right hand.
Lk 8:14 and *p*, and they do not mature.
Tit 3: 3 by all kinds of passions and *p*.
Heb 11:25 rather than to enjoy the *p* of sin
Jas 4: 3 may spend what you get on your *p*.
2Pe 2:13 reveling in their *p* while they feast

PLEDGE
Dt 24:17 take the cloak of the widow as a *p*.
1Pe 3:21 but the *p* of a good conscience

PLEIADES
Job 38:31 "Can you bind the beautiful *P*?
Am 5: 8 (he who made the *P* and Orion,

PLENTIFUL (PLENTY)
Mt 9:37 harvest is *p* but the workers are
Lk 10: 2 harvest is *p*, but the workers are

PLENTY (PLENTIFUL)
2Co 8:14 the present time your *p* will supply
Php 4:12 whether living in *p* or in want.

PLOT (PLOTS)
Est 2:22 Mordecai found out about the *p*
Ps 2: 1 and the peoples *p* in vain?
Pr 3:29 not *p* harm against your neighbor,
Zec 8:17 do not *p* evil against your neighbor,
Ac 4:25 and the peoples *p* in vain?

PLOTS (PLOT)
Pr 6:14 who *p* evil with deceit in his heart

PLOW (PLOWMAN PLOWSHARES)
Lk 9:62 "No one who puts his hand to the *p*

PLOWMAN (PLOW)
1Co 9:10 because when the *p* plows

PLOWSHARES (PLOW)
1Sa 13:20 to the Philistines to have their *p*,
Isa 2: 4 They will beat their swords into *p*
Joel 3:10 Beat your *p* into swords
Mic 4: 3 They will beat their swords into *p*

PLUCK
Mk 9:47 your eye causes you to sin, *p* it out.

PLUNDER (PLUNDERED)
Ex 3:22 And so you will *p* the Egyptians."
Est 3:13 of Adar, and to *p* their goods.
8:11 to *p* the property of their enemies.
9:10 did not lay their hands on the *p*.
Pr 22:23 and will *p* those who *p* them.
Isa 3:14 the *p* from the poor is

PLUNDERED (PLUNDER)
Eze 34: 8 lacks a shepherd and so has been *p*

PLUNGE
1Ti 6: 9 and harmful desires that *p* men
1Pe 4: 4 think it strange that you do not *p*

PODS
Lk 15:16 with the *p* that the pigs were eating,

POINT
Mt 4: 5 on the highest *p* of the temple.
26:38 with sorrow to the *p* of death.
Jas 2:10 yet stumbles at just one *p* is guilty
Rev 2:10 Be faithful, even to the *p* of death,

POISON
Ps 140: 3 the *p* of vipers is on their lips.
Mk 16:18 and when they drink deadly *p*,
Ro 3:13 "The *p* of vipers is on their lips."
Jas 3: 8 It is a restless evil, full of deadly *p*.

POLE (POLES)
Nu 21: 8 "Make a snake and put it up on a *p*;
Dt 16:21 not set up any wooden Asherah *p*

POLES (POLE)
Ex 25:13 Then make *p* of acacia wood

POLISHED
Isa 49: 2 he made me into a *p* arrow

POLLUTE* (POLLUTED POLLUTES)
Nu 35:33 " 'Do not *p* the land where you are.
Jude : 8 these dreamers *p* their own bodies,

POLLUTED* (POLLUTE)
Ezr 9:11 entering to possess is a land *p*
Pr 25:26 Like a muddied spring or a *p* well
Ac 15:20 to abstain from food *p* by idols,
Jas 1:27 oneself from being *p* by the world.

POLLUTES* (POLLUTE)
Nu 35:33 Bloodshed *p* the land,

PONDER (PONDERED)
Ps 64: 9 and *p* what he has done.
119: 95 but I will *p* your statutes.

PONDERED (PONDER)
Ps 111: 2 they are *p* by all who delight
Lk 2:19 up all these things and *p* them

POOR (POVERTY)
Lev 19:10 Leave them for the *p* and the alien.
23:22 Leave them for the *p* and the alien.
27: 8 If anyone making the vow is too *p*
Dt 15: 4 there should be no *p* among you,
15: 7 is a *p* man among your brothers
15:11 There will always be *p* people
24:12 If the man is *p*, do not go to sleep
24:14 advantage of a hired man who is *p*
Job 5:16 So the *p* have hope,
24: 4 force all the *p* of the land
Ps 14: 6 frustrate the plans of the *p*,
34: 6 This *p* man called, and the LORD
35:10 You rescue the *p* from those too
40:17 Yet I am *p* and needy;
68:10 O God, you provided for the *p*.
82: 3 maintain the rights of the *p*
112: 9 scattered abroad his gifts to the *p*,
113: 7 He raises the *p* from the dust
140: 12 the LORD secures justice for the *p*
Pr 10: 4 Lazy hands make a man *p*,
13: 7 to be *p*, yet has great wealth.
14:20 The *p* are shunned
14:31 oppresses the *p* shows contempt
17: 5 who mocks the *p* shows contempt
19: 1 Better a *p* man whose walk is
19:17 to the *p* lends to the LORD,
19:22 better to be *p* than a liar.
20:13 not love sleep or you will grow *p*;
21:13 to the cry of the *p*,
21:17 who loves pleasure will become *p*;
22: 2 Rich and *p* have this in common:
22: 9 for he shares his food with the *p*.
22:22 not exploit the *p* because they are *p*
28: 6 Better a *p* man whose walk is
28:27 to the *p* will lack nothing,
29: 7 care about justice for the *p*,
31: 9 defend the rights of the *p*
31:20 She opens her arms to the *p*
Ecc 4:13 Better a *p* but wise youth
Isa 3:14 the plunder from the *p* is
10: 2 to deprive the *p* of their rights
14:30 of the *p* will find pasture,
25: 4 You have been a refuge for the *p*,
32: 7 schemes to destroy the *p* with lies,
61: 1 me to preach good news to the *p*.
Jer 22:16 He defended the cause of the *p*
Eze 18:12 He oppresses the *p* and needy.
Am 2: 7 They trample on the heads of the *p*
4: 1 you women who oppress the *p*
5:11 You trample on the *p*
Zec 7:10 or the fatherless, the alien or the *p*.
Mt 5: 3 saying: "Blessed are the *p* in spirit,
11: 5 the good news is preached to the *p*.
19:21 your possessions and give to the *p*,
26:11 The *p* you will always have
Mk 12:42 But a *p* widow came and put
14: 7 The *p* you will always have
Lk 4:18 me to preach good news to the *p*.
6:20 "Blessed are you who are *p*,
11:41 is inside the dish, to the *p*,
14:13 invite the *p*, the crippled, the lame,
21: 2 also saw a *p* widow put
Jn 12: 8 You will always have the *p*
Ac 9:36 doing good and helping the *p*.
10: 4 and gifts to the *p* have come up
24:17 to bring my people gifts for the *p*
Ro 15:26 for the *p* among the saints
1Co 13: 3 If I give all I possess to the *p*
2Co 6:10 sorrowful, yet always rejoicing; *p*,
8: 9 yet for your sakes he became *p*,
Gal 2:10 continue to remember the *p*,
Jas 2: 2 and a *p* man in shabby clothes
2: 5 not God chosen those who are *p*
2: 6 But you have insulted the *p*.

POPULATION*
Pr 14:28 A large *p* is a king's glory,

PORTION
Nu 18:29 as the LORD's *p* the best
Dt 32: 9 For the LORD's *p* is his people,
1Sa 1: 5 But to Hannah he gave a double *p*
2Ki 2: 9 "Let me inherit a double *p*
Ps 73:26 and my *p* forever.
119: 57 You are my *p*, O LORD;
Isa 53:12 Therefore I will give him a *p*
Jer 10:16 He who is the *P* of Jacob is not like
La 3:24 to myself, "The LORD is my *p*;
Zec 2:12 LORD will inherit Judah as his *p*

PORTRAIT
Lk 20:24 Whose *p* and inscription are on it?"

PORTRAYED
Gal 3: 1 very eyes Jesus Christ was clearly *p*

POSITION (POSITIONS)
Ro 12:16 to associate with people of low *p*.
Jas 1: 9 ought to take pride in his high *p*.
2Pe 3:17 and fall from your secure *p*.

POSITIONS (POSITION)
2Ch 20:17 Take up your *p*; stand firm
Jude : 6 the angels who did not keep their *p*

POSSESS (POSSESSED POSSESSING POSSESSION POSSESSIONS)
Nu 33:53 for I have given you the land to *p*.
Dt 4:14 you are crossing the Jordan to *p*.
Pr 8:12 I *p* knowledge and discretion.
Jn 5:39 that by them you *p* eternal life.

POSSESSED (POSSESS)
Jn 10:21 the sayings of a man *p* by a demon.

POSSESSING* (POSSESS)
2Co 6:10 nothing, and yet *p* everything.

POSSESSION (POSSESS)
Ge 15: 7 to give you this land to take *p* of it
Ex 6: 8 I will give it to you as a *p*.
19: 5 nations you will be my treasured *p*.
Nu 13:30 "We should go up and take *p*
Dt 7: 6 to be his people, his treasured *p*.
Jos 1:11 take *p* of the land the LORD your
Ps 2: 8 the ends of the earth your *p*.
135: 4 Israel to be his treasured *p*.
Eph 1:14 of those who are God's *p*—

POSSESSIONS (POSSESS)
Mt 19:21 go, sell your *p* and give to the poor,
Lk 11:21 guards his own house, his *p* are safe
12:15 consist in the abundance of his *p*."
19: 8 now I give half of my *p* to the poor,
Ac 4:32 any of his *p* was his own,
2Co 12:14 what I want is not your *p* but you.
Heb 10:34 yourselves had better and lasting *p*.
1Jn 3:17 If anyone has material *p*

POSSIBLE
Mt 19:26 but with God all things are *p*."
26:39 if it is *p*, may this cup be taken
Mk 9:23 "Everything is *p* for him who
10:27 all things are *p* with God."
14:35 prayed that if *p* the hour might pass
Ro 12:18 If it is *p*, as far as it depends on you,
1Co 6: 5 Is it *p* that there is nobody
9:19 to everyone, to win as many as *p*.
9:22 by all *p* means I might save some.

POT (POTSHERD POTTER POTTER'S POTTERY)
2Ki 4:40 there is death in the *p*!"
Jer 18: 4 But the *p* he was shaping

POTIPHAR*

Egyptian who bought Joseph (Ge 37:36), set him over his house (Ge 39:1-6), sent him to prison (Ge 39:7-30).

POTSHERD (POT)
Isa 45: 9 a *p* among the potsherds

POTTER (POT)
Isa 29:16 Can the pot say of the *p*,
45: 9 Does the clay say to the *p*,
64: 8 We are the clay, you are the *p*;
Jer 18: 6 "Like clay in the hand of the *p*,
Zec 11:13 it to the *p*"— the handsome price
Ro 9:21 Does not the *p* have the right

POTTER'S (POT)
Mt 27: 7 to use the money to buy the *p* field

POTTERY (POT)
Ro 9:21 of clay some *p* for noble purposes

POUR (POURED POURS)
Ps 62: 8 *p* out your hearts to him,
Isa 44: 3 I will *p* out my Spirit
Eze 20: 8 So I said I would *p* out my wrath
39:29 for I will *p* out my Spirit
Joel 2:28 I will *p* out my Spirit on all people.
Zec 12:10 I will *p* out on the house of David
Mal 3:10 *p* out so much blessing that you
Ac 2:17 I will *p* out my Spirit on all people.

POURED (POUR)
Ps 22:14 I am *p* out like water,
Isa 32:15 till the Spirit is *p* upon us
Mt 26:28 which is *p* out for many
Lk 22:20 in my blood, which is *p* out for you.
Ac 2:33 and has *p* out what you now see
10:45 of the Holy Spirit had been *p* out
Ro 5: 5 because God has *p* out his love
Php 2:17 even if I am being *p* out like a drink
2Ti 4: 6 I am already being *p* out like
Tit 3: 6 whom he *p* out on us generously
Rev 16: 2 and *p* out his bowl on the land,

POURS (POUR)
Lk 5:37 And no one *p* new wine

POVERTY* (POOR)
Dt 28:48 and thirst, in nakedness and dire *p*,
1Sa 2: 7 The LORD sends *p* and wealth;
Pr 6:11 *p* will come on you like a bandit
10:15 but *p* is the ruin of the poor.
11:24 withholds unduly, but comes to *p*.
13:18 who ignores discipline comes to *p*
14:23 but mere talk leads only to *p*.
21: 5 as surely as haste leads to *p*.
22:16 to the rich—both come to *p*.
24:34 *p* will come on you like a bandit
28:19 fantasies will have his fill of *p*.
28:22 and is unaware that *p* awaits him.
30: 8 give me neither *p* nor riches,
31: 7 let them drink and forget their *p*
Ecc 4:14 born in *p* within his kingdom.
Mk 12:44 out of her *p*, put in everything—
Lk 21: 4 she out of her *p* put in all she had
2Co 8: 2 and their extreme *p* welled up
8: 9 through his *p* might become rich.
Rev 2: 9 I know your afflictions and your *p*

POWER (POWERFUL POWERS)
Ex 15: 6 was majestic in *p*.
32:11 out of Egypt with great *p*
Dt 8:17 "My *p* and the strength
34:12 one has ever shown the mighty *p*
1Sa 10: 6 LORD will come upon you in *p*,
10:10 Spirit of God came upon him in *p*,
11: 6 Spirit of God came upon him in *p*,
16:13 the LORD came upon David in *p*.
1Ch 29:11 LORD, is the greatness and the *p*
2Ch 20: 6 *P* and might are in your hand,
32: 7 for there is a greater *p* with us
Job 9: 4 wisdom is profound, his *p* is vast.
36:22 "God is exalted in his *p*.
37:23 beyond our reach and exalted in *p*;
Ps 20: 6 with the saving *p* of his right hand.
63: 2 and beheld your *p* and your glory.
66: 3 So great is your *p*
68:34 Proclaim the *p* of God,
77:14 you display your *p*
89:13 Your arm is endued with *p*;
145: 6 of the *p* of your awesome works,
147: 5 Great is our Lord and mighty in *p*;
150: 2 Praise him for his acts of *p*;
Pr 3:27 when it is in your *p* to act.
18:21 The tongue has the *p* of life
24: 5 A wise man has great *p*,
Isa 11: 2 the Spirit of counsel and of *p*,
40:10 the Sovereign LORD comes with *p*
40:26 of his great *p* and mighty strength,
63:12 who sent his glorious arm of *p*
Jer 10: 6 and your name is mighty in *p*.
10:12 But God made the earth by his *p*;
27: 5 With my great *p* and outstretched
32:17 and the earth by your great *p*
Hos 13:14 from the *p* of the grave;
Na 1: 3 to anger and great in *p*;
Zec 4: 6 nor by *p*, but by my Spirit,'
Mt 22:29 do not know the Scriptures or the *p*
24:30 on the clouds of the sky, with *p*
Lk 1:35 and the *p* of the Most High will
4:14 to Galilee in the *p* of the Spirit,
9: 1 he gave them *p* and authority
10:19 to overcome all the *p* of the enemy;

Lk 24:49 clothed with *p* from on high."
Ac 1: 8 you will receive *p* when the Holy
4:28 They did what your *p* and will had
4:33 With great *p* the apostles
10:38 with the Holy Spirit and *p*,
26:18 and from the *p* of Satan to God,
Ro 1:16 it is the *p* of God for the salvation
1:20 his eternal *p* and divine nature—
4:21 fully persuaded that God had *p*
9:17 that I might display my *p* in you
15:13 overflow with hope by the *p*
15:19 through the *p* of the Spirit.
1Co 1:17 cross of Christ be emptied of its *p*.
1:18 to us who are being saved it is the *p*
2: 4 a demonstration of the Spirit's *p*,
6:14 By his *p* God raised the Lord
15:24 all dominion, authority and *p*.
15:56 of death is sin, and the *p*
2Co 4: 7 to show that this all-surpassing *p* is
6: 7 in truthful speech and in the *p*
10: 4 they have divine *p*
12: 9 for my *p* is made perfect
13: 4 weakness, yet he lives by God's *p*.
Eph 1:19 and his incomparably great *p*
3:16 you with *p* through his Spirit
3:20 according to his *p* that is at work
6:10 in the Lord and in his mighty *p*.
Php 3:10 and the *p* of his resurrection
3:21 by the *p* that enables him
Col 1:11 strengthened with all *p* according
2:10 who is the head over every *p*
1Th 1: 5 also with *p*, with the Holy Spirit
2Ti 1: 7 but a spirit of *p*, of love
3: 5 form of godliness but denying its *p*.
Heb 2:14 might destroy him who holds the *p*
7:16 of the *p* of an indestructible life.
1Pe 1: 5 by God's *p* until the coming
2Pe 1: 3 His divine *p* has given us
Jude :25 *p* and authority, through Jesus
Rev 4:11 to receive glory and honor and *p*,
5:12 to receive *p* and wealth
11:17 you have taken your great *p*
19: 1 and glory and *p* belong to our God,
20: 6 The second death has no *p*

POWERFUL (POWER)

2Ch 27: 6 Jotham grew *p* because he walked
Est 9: 4 and he became more and more *p*.
Ps 29: 4 The voice of the LORD is *p*;
Jer 32:18 *p* God, whose name is the LORD
Zec 8:22 *p* nations will come to Jerusalem
Mk 1: 7 "After me will come one more *p*
Lk 24:19 *p* in word and deed before God
2Th 1: 7 in blazing fire with his *p* angels.
Heb 1: 3 sustaining all things by his *p* word.
Jas 5:16 The prayer of a righteous man is *p*

POWERLESS

Ro 5: 6 when we were still *p*, Christ died
8: 3 For what the law was *p* to do

POWERS (POWER)

Da 4:35 pleases with the *p* of heaven
Ro 8:38 nor any *p*, neither height nor depth
1Co 12:10 to another miraculous *p*,
Eph 6:12 against the *p* of this dark world
Col 1:16 whether thrones or *p* or rulers
2:15 And having disarmed the *p*
Heb 6: 5 and the *p* of the coming age,
1Pe 3:22 and *p* in submission to him.

PRACTICE (PRACTICED PRACTICES)

Lev 19:26 " 'Do not *p* divination or sorcery.
Ps 119: 56 This has been my *p*:
Eze 33:31 but they do not put them into *p*.
Mt 7:24 into *p* is like a wise man who built
23: 3 for they do not *p* what they preach.
Lk 8:21 hear God's word and put it into *p*."
Ro 12:13 *P* hospitality.
Php 4: 9 or seen in me—put it into *p*.
1Ti 5: 4 to put their religion into *p* by caring

PRACTICED (PRACTICE)

Mt 23:23 You should have *p* the latter,

PRACTICES (PRACTICE)

Ps 101: 7 No one who *p* deceit
Mt 5:19 but whoever *p* and teaches these
Col 3: 9 taken off your old self with its *p*

PRAISE (PRAISED PRAISES PRAISEWORTHY PRAISING)

Ex 15: 2 He is my God, and I will *p* him,
Dt 10:21 He is your *p*; he is your God,
26:19 declared that he will set you in *p*,
32: 3 Oh, *p* the greatness of our God!
Ru 4:14 said to Naomi: "*P* be to the LORD,
2Sa 22: 4 to the LORD, who is worthy of *p*,
22:47 The LORD lives! *P* be to my Rock
1Ch 16:25 is the LORD and most worthy of *p*;
1Ch 16:35 that we may glory in your *p*."
23: 5 four thousand are to *p* the LORD
29:10 "*P* be to you, O LORD,
2Ch 5:13 they raised their voices in *p*
20:21 and to *p* him for the splendor
29:30 to *p* the LORD with the words
Ezr 3:10 took their places to *p* the LORD,
Ne 9: 5 and *p* the LORD your God,
Ps 8: 2 you have ordained *p*
9: 1 I will *p* you, O LORD,
16: 7 I will *p* the LORD, who counsels
26: 7 proclaiming aloud your *p*
30: 4 *p* his holy name.
33: 1 it is fitting for the upright to *p* him.
34: 1 his *p* will always be on my lips.
40: 3 a hymn of *p* to our God.
42: 5 for I will yet *p* him,
43: 5 for I will yet *p* him,
45:17 the nations will *p* you for ever
47: 7 sing to him a psalm of *p*.
48: 1 the LORD, and most worthy of *p*,
51:15 and my mouth will declare your *p*.
56: 4 In God, whose word I *p*,
57: 9 I will *p* you, O Lord,
63: 4 I will *p* you as long as I live,
65: 1 *P* awaits you, O God, in Zion;
66: 2 make his *p* glorious.
66: 8 *P* our God, O peoples,
68:19 *P* be to the Lord, to God our Savior
68:26 *p* the LORD in the assembly
69:30 I will *p* God's name in song
69:34 Let heaven and earth *p* him,
71: 8 My mouth is filled with your *p*,
71:14 I will *p* you more and more.
71:22 I will *p* you with the harp
74:21 the poor and needy *p* your name.
86:12 I will *p* you, O Lord my God,
89: 5 The heavens *p* your wonders,
92: 1 It is good to *p* the LORD
96: 2 Sing to the LORD, *p* his name;
100: 4 and his courts with *p*;
101: 1 to you, O LORD, I will sing *p*.
102: 18 not yet created may *p* the LORD:
103: 1 *P* the LORD, O my soul;
103: 20 *P* the LORD, you his angels,
104: 1 *P* the LORD, O my soul.
105: 2 Sing to him, sing *p* to him;
106: 1 *P* the LORD.
108: 3 I will *p* you, O LORD,
111: 1 *P* the LORD.
113: 1 *P* the LORD.
117: 1 *P* the LORD, all you nations;
119:175 Let me live that I may *p* you,
135: 1 *P* the LORD.
135: 20 you who fear him, *p* the LORD.
138: 1 I will *p* you, O LORD,
139: 14 I *p* you because I am fearfully
144: 1 *P* be to the LORD my Rock,
145: 3 is the LORD and most worthy of *p*;
145: 10 All you have made will *p* you,
145: 21 Let every creature *p* his holy name
146: 1 *P* the LORD, O my soul.
147: 1 how pleasant and fitting to *p* him!
148: 1 *P* the LORD from the heavens,
148: 13 Let them *p* the name of the LORD,
149: 1 his *p* in the assembly of the saints.
149: 6 May the *p* of God be
149: 9 *P* the LORD.
150: 2 *p* him for his surpassing greatness.
150: 6 that has breath *p* the LORD.
Pr 27: 2 Let another *p* you, and not your
27:21 man is tested by the *p* he receives.
31:31 let her works bring her *p*
SS 1: 4 we will *p* your love more than wine
Isa 12: 1 "I will *p* you, O LORD.
42:10 his *p* from the ends of the earth,
61: 3 and a garment of *p*
Jer 33: 9 *p* and honor before all nations
Da 2:20 "*P* be to the name of God for ever
4:37 *p* and exalt and glorify the King
Mt 5:16 and *p* your Father in heaven.
21:16 you have ordained *p*'?"
Lk 19:37 to *p* God in loud voices
Jn 5:44 effort to obtain the *p* that comes
12:43 for they loved *p* from men more
Ro 2:29 Such a man's *p* is not from men,
15: 7 in order to bring *p* to God.
2Co 1: 3 *P* be to the God and Father
Eph 1: 3 *P* be to the God and Father
1: 6 to the *p* of his glorious grace,
1:12 might be for the *p* of his glory.
1:14 to the *p* of his glory.
1Th 2: 6 We were not looking for *p*
Heb 13:15 offer to God a sacrifice of *p*—
Jas 3: 9 With the tongue we *p* our Lord
5:13 happy? Let him sing songs of *p*.
Rev 5:13 be *p* and honor and glory
7:12 *P* and glory

PRAISED (PRAISE)

1Ch 29:10 David *p* the LORD in the presence
Ne 8: 6 Ezra *p* the LORD, the great God;
Job 1:21 may the name of the LORD be *p*."
Ps 113: 2 Let the name of the LORD be *p*,
Pr 31:30 who fears the LORD is to be *p*.
Isa 63: 7 the deeds for which he is to be *p*,
Da 2:19 Then Daniel *p* the God of heaven
4:34 Then I *p* the Most High; I honored
Lk 18:43 the people saw it, they also *p* God.
23:47 seeing what had happened, *p* God
Ro 9: 5 who is God over all, forever *p*!
Gal 1:24 And they *p* God because of me.
1Pe 4:11 that in all things God may be *p*

PRAISES (PRAISE)

2Sa 22:50 I will sing *p* to your name.
Ps 18:49 I will sing *p* to your name.
47: 6 Sing *p* to God, sing *p*;
147: 1 How good it is to sing *p* to our God,
Pr 31:28 her husband also, and he *p* her:
1Pe 2: 9 that you may declare the *p*

PRAISEWORTHY* (PRAISE)

Ps 78: 4 the *p* deeds of the LORD,
Php 4: 8 if anything is excellent or *p*—

PRAISING (PRAISE)

Lk 2:13 *p* God and saying, "Glory to God
2:20 *p* God for all the things they had
Ac 2:47 *p* God and enjoying the favor
10:46 speaking in tongues and *p* God.
1Co 14:16 If you are *p* God with your spirit,

PRAY (PRAYED PRAYER PRAYERS PRAYING PRAYS)

Dt 4: 7 is near us whenever we *p* to him?
1Sa 12:23 the LORD by failing to *p* for you.
1Ki 8:30 when they *p* toward this place.
2Ch 7:14 will humble themselves and *p*
Ezr 6:10 and *p* for the well-being of the king
Job 42: 8 My servant Job will *p* for you,
Ps 5: 2 for to you I *p*.
32: 6 let everyone who is godly *p*
122: 6 *P* for the peace of Jerusalem:
Jer 29: 7 *P* to the LORD for it,
29:12 upon me and come and *p* to me,
42: 3 *P* that the LORD your God will
Mt 5:44 and *p* for those who persecute you,
6: 5 "And when you *p*, do not be like
6: 9 "This, then, is how you should *p*:
14:23 up on a mountainside by himself to *p*.
19:13 hands on them and *p* for them.
26:36 Sit here while I go over there and *p*
Lk 6:28 *p* for those who mistreat you.
11: 1 us to *p*, just as John taught his
18: 1 them that they should always *p*
22:40 "*P* that you will not fall
Jn 17:20 I *p* also for those who will believe
Ro 8:26 do not know what we ought to *p* for,
1Co 14:13 in a tongue should *p* that he may
Eph 1:18 I *p* also that the eyes
3:16 I *p* that out of his glorious riches he
6:18 And *p* in the Spirit on all occasions
Col 1:10 we *p* this in order that you may live
4: 3 *p* for us, too, that God may open
1Th 5:17 Be joyful always; *p* continually;
2Th 1:11 in mind, we constantly *p* for you,
Jas 5:13 one of you in trouble? He should *p*.
5:16 *p* for each other so that you may be
1Pe 4: 7 self-controlled so that you can *p*.
Jude :20 up in your most holy faith and *p*

PRAYED (PRAY)

1Sa 1:27 I *p* for this child, and the LORD
1Ki 18:36 Elijah stepped forward and *p*:
19: 4 under it and *p* that he might die.
2Ki 6:17 And Elisha *p*, "O LORD,
2Ch 30:18 But Hezekiah *p* for them, saying,
Ne 4: 9 we *p* to our God and posted a guard
Job 42:10 After Job had *p* for his friends,
Da 6:10 got down on his knees and *p*,
9: 4 I *p* to the LORD my God
Jnh 2: 1 From inside the fish Jonah *p*
Mt 26:39 with his face to the ground and *p*,
Mk 1:35 off to a solitary place, where he *p*.
14:35 *p* that if possible the hour might
Lk 22:41 knelt down and *p*, "Father,
Jn 17: 1 he looked toward heaven and *p*:
Ac 4:31 After they *p*, the place where they
6: 6 who *p* and laid their hands on them
8:15 they *p* for them that they might
13: 3 So after they had fasted and *p*,

PRAYER (PRAY)

2Ch 30:27 for their *p* reached heaven,
Ezr 8:23 about this, and he answered our *p*.
Ps 4: 1 be merciful to me and hear my *p*.
6: 9 the LORD accepts my *p*.

Ps 17: 1 Give ear to my *p*—
17: 6 give ear to me and hear my *p*.
65: 2 O you who hear *p*,
66:20 who has not rejected my *p*
86: 6 Hear my *p*, O LORD;
Pr 15: 8 but the *p* of the upright pleases him
15:29 but he hears the *p* of the righteous.
Isa 56: 7 a house of *p* for all nations."
Mt 21:13 house will be called a house of *p*,'
21:22 receive whatever you ask for in *p*."
Mk 9:29 This kind can come out only by *p*."
11:24 whatever you ask for in *p*,
Jn 17:15 My *p* is not that you take them out
Ac 1:14 all joined together constantly in *p*,
2:42 to the breaking of bread and to *p*.
6: 4 and will give our attention to *p*
10:31 has heard your *p* and remembered
16:13 expected to find a place of *p*.
Ro 12:12 patient in affliction, faithful in *p*.
1Co 7: 5 you may devote yourselves to *p*.
2Co 13: 9 and our *p* is for your perfection.
Php 1: 9 this is my *p*: that your love may
4: 6 but in everything, by *p* and petition
Col 4: 2 yourselves to *p*, being watchful
1Ti 2: 8 to lift up holy hands in *p*,
4: 5 by the word of God and *p*.
Jas 5:15 *p* offered in faith will make the sick
1Pe 3:12 and his ears are attentive to their *p*,

PRAYERS (PRAY)
1Ch 5:20 He answered their *p*, because they
Isa 1:15 even if you offer many *p*,
Mk 12:40 and for a show make lengthy *p*.
2Co 1:11 as you help us by your *p*.
Eph 6:18 on all occasions with all kinds of *p*
1Ti 2: 1 then, first of all, that requests, *p*,
1Pe 3: 7 so that nothing will hinder your *p*.
Rev 5: 8 which are the *p* of the saints.
8: 3 with the *p* of all the saints,

PRAYING (PRAY)
Ge 24:45 "Before I finished *p* in my heart,
1Sa 1:12 As she kept on *p* to the LORD,
Mk 11:25 And when you stand *p*,
Lk 3:21 as he was *p*, heaven was opened
6:12 and spent the night *p* to God.
9:29 As he was *p*, the appearance
Jn 17: 9 I am not *p* for the world,
Ac 9:11 from Tarsus named Saul, for he is *p*
16:25 and Silas were *p* and singing hymns
Ro 15:30 in my struggle by *p* to God for me.
Eph 6:18 always keep on *p* for all the saints.

PRAYS (PRAY)
1Co 14:14 my spirit *p*, but my mind is

PREACH (PREACHED PREACHING)
Isa 61: 1 me to *p* good news to the poor.
Mt 10: 7 As you go, *p* this message:
23: 3 they do not practice what they *p*.
Mk 16:15 and *p* the good news to all creation.
Lk 4:18 me to *p* good news to the poor.
Ac 9:20 At once he began to *p*
16:10 us to *p* the gospel to them.
Ro 1:15 am so eager to *p* the gospel
10:15 how can they *p* unless they are sent
15:20 to *p* the gospel where Christ was
1Co 1:17 to *p* the gospel—not with words
1:23 wisdom, but we *p* Christ crucified:
9:14 that those who *p* the gospel should
9:16 Woe to me if I do not *p* the gospel!
2Co 4: 5 For we do not *p* ourselves,
10:16 so that we can *p* the gospel
Gal 1: 8 from heaven should *p* a gospel
2Ti 4: 2 I give you this charge: *P* the Word;

PREACHED (PREACH)
Mt 24:14 gospel of the kingdom will be *p*
Mk 6:12 and *p* that people should repent.
13:10 And the gospel must first be *p*
14: 9 wherever the gospel is *p*
Ac 8: 4 had been scattered *p* the word
28:31 hindrance he *p* the kingdom
1Co 9:27 so that after I have *p* to others,
15: 1 you of the gospel I *p* to you,
2Co 11: 4 other than the Jesus we *p*,
Gal 1: 8 other than the one we *p* to you,
Eph 2:17 *p* peace to you who were far away
Php 1:18 false motives or true, Christ is *p*.
1Ti 3:16 was *p* among the nations,
1Pe 1:25 this is the word that was *p* to you.
3:19 and *p* to the spirits in prison who

PREACHING (PREACH)
Lk 9: 6 *p* the gospel and healing people
Ac 18: 5 devoted himself exclusively to *p*,
Ro 10:14 hear without someone *p* to them?
1Co 2: 4 and my *p* were not with wise
9:18 in *p* the gospel I may offer it free
Gal 1: 9 If anybody is *p* to you a gospel
1Ti 4:13 the public reading of Scripture, to *p*
5:17 especially those whose work is *p*

PRECEDE*
1Th 4:15 will certainly not *p* those who have

PRECEPTS*
Dt 33:10 He teaches your *p* to Jacob
Ps 19: 8 The *p* of the LORD are right,
103: 18 and remember to obey his *p*.
105: 45 that they might keep his *p*
111: 7 all his *p* are trustworthy.
111: 10 who follow his *p* have good
119: 4 You have laid down *p*
119: 15 I meditate on your *p*
119: 27 understand the teaching of your *p*;
119: 40 How I long for your *p*!
119: 45 for I have sought out your *p*.
119: 56 I obey your *p*.
119: 63 to all who follow your *p*.
119: 69 I keep your *p* with all my heart.
119: 78 but I will meditate on your *p*.
119: 87 but I have not forsaken your *p*.
119: 93 I will never forget your *p*,
119: 94 I have sought out your *p*.
119:100 for I obey your *p*.
119:104 I gain understanding from your *p*;
119:110 but I have not strayed from your *p*.
119:128 because I consider all your *p* right,
119:134 that I may obey your *p*.
119:141 I do not forget your *p*.
119:159 See how I love your *p*;
119:168 I obey your *p* and your statutes,
119:173 for I have chosen your *p*.

PRECIOUS
Ps 19:10 They are more *p* than gold,
72:14 for *p* is their blood in his sight.
116: 15 *P* in the sight of the LORD
119: 72 from your mouth is more *p* to me
139: 17 How *p* to me are your thoughts,
Pr 8:11 for wisdom is more *p* than rubies,
Isa 28:16 a *p* cornerstone for a sure
1Pe 1:19 but with the *p* blood of Christ,
2: 4 but chosen by God and *p* to him—
2: 6 a chosen and *p* cornerstone,
2Pe 1: 1 Christ have received a faith as *p*
1: 4 us his very great and *p* promises,

PREDESTINED* (DESTINY)
Ro 8:29 *p* to be conformed to the likeness
8:30 And those he *p*, he also called;
Eph 1: 5 In love he *p* us to be adopted
1:11 having been *p* according

PREDICTED (PREDICTION)
1Sa 28:17 The LORD has done what he *p*
Ac 7:52 killed those who *p* the coming
1Pe 1:11 when he *p* the sufferings of Christ

PREDICTION* (PREDICTED PREDICTIONS)
Jer 28: 9 only if his *p* comes true."

PREDICTIONS (PREDICTION)
Isa 44:26 and fulfills the *p* of his messengers,

PREGNANT
Ex 21:22 who are fighting hit a *p* woman
Mt 24:19 be in those days for *p* women
1Th 5: 3 as labor pains on a *p* woman,

PREPARE (PREPARED)
Ps 23: 5 You *p* a table before me
Isa 25: 6 the LORD Almighty will *p*
40: 3 "In the desert *p*
Am 4:12 *p* to meet your God, O Israel."
Mal 3: 1 who will *p* the way before me.
Mt 3: 3 '*P* the way for the Lord,
Jn 14: 2 there to *p* a place for you.
Eph 4:12 to *p* God's people for works
1Pe 1:13 Therefore, *p* your minds for action;

PREPARED (PREPARE)
Ex 23:20 to bring you to the place I have *p*.
Mt 25:34 the kingdom *p* for you
Ro 9:22 of his wrath—*p* for destruction?
1Co 2: 9 what God has *p* for those who love
Eph 2:10 which God *p* in advance for us
2Ti 2:21 and *p* to do any good work.
4: 2 be *p* in season and out of season;
1Pe 3:15 Always be *p* to give an answer

PRESCRIBED
Ezr 7:23 Whatever the God of heaven has *p*,

PRESENCE (PRESENT)
Ex 25:30 Put the bread of the *P* on this table
33:14 The LORD replied, "My *P* will go
Nu 4: 7 "Over the table of the *P* they are
1Sa 6:20 in the *p* of the LORD, this
21: 6 of the *P* that had been removed
2Sa 22:13 Out of the brightness of his *p*
2Ki 17:23 LORD removed them from his *p*,
23:27 also from my *p* as I removed Israel,
Ezr 9:15 one of us can stand in your *p*."
Ps 16:11 you will fill me with joy in your *p*,
21: 6 with the joy of your *p*.
23: 5 in the *p* of my enemies.
31:20 the shelter of your *p* you hide them
41:12 and set me in your *p* forever.
51:11 Do not cast me from your *p*
52: 9 in the *p* of your saints.
89:15 who walk in the light of your *p*,
90: 8 our secret sins in the light of your *p*
114: 7 O earth, at the *p* of the Lord,
139: 7 Where can I flee from your *p*?
Isa 26:17 so were we in your *p*, O LORD.
Jer 5:22 "Should you not tremble in my *p*?
Eze 38:20 of the earth will tremble at my *p*.
Hos 6: 2 that we may live in his *p*.
Na 1: 5 The earth trembles at his *p*,
Mal 3:16 in his *p* concerning those who
Ac 2:28 you will fill me with joy in your *p*.'
1Th 3: 9 have in the *p* of our God
3:13 and holy in the *p* of our God
2Th 1: 9 and shut out from the *p* of the Lord
Heb 9:24 now to appear for us in God's *p*.
1Jn 3:19 rest in his *p* whenever our hearts
Jude :24 before his glorious *p* without fault

PRESENT (PRESENCE)
1Co 3:22 life or death or the *p* or the future—
7:26 of the *p* crisis, I think that it is good
2Co 11: 2 so that I might *p* you as a pure
Eph 5:27 and to *p* her to himself
1Ti 4: 8 holding promise for both the *p* life
2Ti 2:15 Do your best to *p* yourself to God
Jude :24 and to *p* you before his glorious

PRESERVE
Lk 17:33 and whoever loses his life will *p* it.

PRESERVES
Ps 119:50 Your promise *p* my life.

PRESS (PRESSED PRESSURE)
Php 3:12 but I *p* on to take hold of that
3:14 I *p* on toward the goal

PRESSED (PRESS)
Lk 6:38 *p* down, shaken together

PRESSURE (PRESS)
2Co 1: 8 We were under great *p*, far
11:28 I face daily the *p* of my concern

PRETENDED
1Sa 21:13 So he *p* to be insane

PREVAILS
1Sa 2: 9 "It is not by strength that one *p*;
Pr 19:21 but it is the LORD's purpose that *p*

PRICE (PRICELESS)
Job 28:18 the *p* of wisdom is beyond rubies.
1Co 6:20 your own; you were bought at a *p*.
7:23 bought at a *p*; do not become slaves

PRICELESS* (PRICE)
Ps 36: 7 How *p* is your unfailing love!

PRIDE (PROUD)
Pr 8:13 I hate *p* and arrogance,
11: 2 When *p* comes, then comes
13:10 *P* only breeds quarrels,
16:18 *P* goes before destruction,
29:23 A man's *p* brings him low,
Isa 25:11 God will bring down their *p*
Da 4:37 And those who walk in *p* he is able
Am 8: 7 The LORD has sworn by the *P*
2Co 5:12 giving you an opportunity to take *p*
7: 4 in you; I take great *p* in you.
8:24 and the reason for our *p* in you,
Gal 6: 4 Then he can take *p* in himself,
Jas 1: 9 ought to take *p* in his high position.

PRIEST (PRIESTHOOD PRIESTLY PRIESTS)
Ge 14:18 He was *p* of God Most High,
Nu 5:10 to the *p* will belong to the *p*.'"
2Ch 13: 9 and seven rams may become a *p*
Ps 110: 4 "You are a *p* forever,
Heb 2:17 faithful high *p* in service to God,
3: 1 and high *p* whom we confess.
4:14 have a great high *p* who has gone
4:15 do not have a high *p* who is unable
5: 6 "You are a *p* forever,
6:20 He has become a high *p* forever,
7: 3 Son of God he remains a *p* forever.
7:15 clear if another *p* like Melchizedek
7:26 Such a high *p* meets our need—
8: 1 We do have such a high *p*,
10:11 Day after day every *p* stands

Heb 13:11 The high *p* carries the blood

PRIESTHOOD (PRIEST)
Heb 7:24 lives forever, he has a permanent *p*.
1Pe 2: 5 into a spiritual house to be a holy *p*,
2: 9 you are a chosen people, a royal *p*,

PRIESTLY (PRIEST)
Ro 15:16 to the Gentiles with the *p* duty

PRIESTS (PRIEST)
Ex 19: 6 you will be for me a kingdom of *p*
Lev 21: 1 "Speak to the *p*, the sons of Aaron,
Eze 42:13 where the *p* who approach
46: 2 *p* are to sacrifice his burnt offering
Mal 1: 6 O *p*, who show contempt for my name.
Rev 5:10 to be a kingdom and *p*
20: 6 but they will be *p* of God

PRIME
Isa 38:10 recovery: I said, "In the *p* of my life

PRINCE (PRINCES PRINCESS)
Isa 9: 6 Everlasting Father, *P* of Peace.
Eze 34:24 and my servant David will be *p*
37:25 my servant will be their *p* forever.
Da 8:25 stand against the *P* of princes.
Jn 12:31 now the *p* of this world will be
Ac 5:31 as *P* and Savior that he might give

PRINCES (PRINCE)
Ps 118: 9 than to trust in *p*.
148: 11 you *p* and all rulers on earth,
Isa 40:23 He brings *p* to naught

PRINCESS* (PRINCE)
Ps 45:13 All glorious is the *p*

PRISCILLA*
Wife of Aquila; co-worker with Paul (Ac 18; Ro 16:3; 1Co 16:19; 2Ti 4:19); instructor of Apollos (Ac 18:24-28).

PRISON (PRISONER PRISONERS)
Ps 66:11 You brought us into *p*
142: 7 Set me free from my *p*,
Isa 42: 7 to free captives from *p*
Mt 25:36 I was in *p* and you came to visit me
2Co 11:23 been in *p* more frequently,
Heb 11:36 others were chained and put in *p*.
13: 3 Remember those in *p*
1Pe 3:19 spirits in *p* who disobeyed long ago
Rev 20: 7 Satan will be released from his *p*

PRISONER (PRISON)
Ro 7:23 and making me a *p* of the law of sin
Gal 3:22 declares that the whole world is a *p*
Eph 3: 1 the *p* of Christ Jesus for the sake

PRISONERS (PRISON)
Ps 68: 6 he leads forth the *p* with singing;
79:11 groans of the *p* come before you;
107: 10 *p* suffering in iron chains,
146: 7 The LORD sets *p* free,
Zec 9:12 to your fortress, O *p* of hope;
Lk 4:18 me to proclaim freedom for the *p*
Gal 3:23 we were held *p* by the law,

PRIVILEGE*
2Co 8: 4 pleaded with us for the *p* of sharing

PRIZE*
1Co 9:24 Run in such a way as to get the *p*.
9:24 but only one gets the *p*? Run
9:27 will not be disqualified for the *p*.
Php 3:14 on toward the goal to win the *p*
Col 2:18 of angels disqualify you for the *p*.

PROBE
Job 11: 7 Can you *p* the limits
Ps 17: 3 Though you *p* my heart

PROCEDURE
Ecc 8: 6 For there is a proper time and *p*

PROCESSION
Ps 68:24 Your *p* has come into view, O God,
118: 27 boughs in hand, join in the festal *p*
1Co 4: 9 on display at the end of the *p*,
2Co 2:14 us in triumphal *p* in Christ

PROCLAIM (PROCLAIMED PROCLAIMING PROCLAIMS PROCLAMATION)
Ex 33:19 and I will *p* my name, the LORD,
Lev 25:10 and *p* liberty throughout the land
Dt 30:12 and *p* it to us so we may obey it?"
2Sa 1:20 *p* it not in the streets of Ashkelon,
1Ch 16:23 *p* his salvation day after day.
Ne 8:15 and that they should *p* this word
Ps 2: 7 I will *p* the decree of the LORD:
9:11 *p* among the nations what he has
Ps 19: 1 the skies *p* the work of his hands.
22:31 They will *p* his righteousness
40: 9 I *p* righteousness in the great
50: 6 the heavens *p* his righteousness,
64: 9 they will *p* the works of God
68:34 *P* the power of God,
71:16 I will come and *p* your mighty acts,
92: 2 to *p* your love in the morning
96: 2 *p* his salvation day after day.
97: 6 The heavens *p* his righteousness,
106: 2 Who can *p* the mighty acts
118: 17 will *p* what the LORD has done.
145: 6 and I will *p* your great deeds.
Isa 12: 4 and *p* that his name is exalted.
42:12 and *p* his praise in the islands.
52: 7 who *p* salvation,
61: 1 to *p* freedom for the captives
66:19 They will *p* my glory
Jer 7: 2 house and there *p* this message:
50: 2 lift up a banner and *p* it;
Hos 5: 9 I *p* what is certain.
Zec 9:10 He will *p* peace to the nations.
Mt 10:27 in your ear, *p* from the roofs.
12:18 and he will *p* justice to the nations.
Lk 4:18 me to *p* freedom for the prisoners
9:60 you go and *p* the kingdom of God."
Ac 17:23 unknown I am going to *p*
20:27 hesitated to *p* to you the whole will
1Co 11:26 you *p* the Lord's death
Col 1:28 We *p* him, admonishing
4: 4 Pray that I may *p* it clearly,
1Jn 1: 1 this we *p* concerning the Word

PROCLAIMED (PROCLAIM)
Ex 9:16 and that my name might be *p*
34: 5 there with him and *p* his name,
Ps 68:11 was the company of those who *p* it:
Ro 15:19 I have fully *p* the gospel of Christ.
Col 1:23 that has been *p* to every creature
2Ti 4:17 me the message might be fully *p*

PROCLAIMING (PROCLAIM)
Ps 26: 7 *p* aloud your praise
92:15 *p*, "The LORD is upright;
Ac 5:42 and *p* the good news that Jesus is
Ro 10: 8 the word of faith we are *p*:

PROCLAIMS (PROCLAIM)
Dt 18:22 If what a prophet *p* in the name

PROCLAMATION (PROCLAIM)
Isa 62:11 The LORD has made *p*

PRODUCE (PRODUCES)
Mt 3: 8 *P* fruit in keeping with repentance.
3:10 tree that does not *p* good fruit will

PRODUCES (PRODUCE)
Pr 30:33 so stirring up anger *p* strife."
Ro 5: 3 that suffering *p* perseverance;
Heb 12:11 it *p* a harvest of righteousness

PROFANE (PROFANED)
Lev 19:12 and so *p* the name of your God.
22:32 Do not *p* my holy name.
Mal 2:10 Why do we *p* the covenant

PROFANED (PROFANE)
Eze 36:20 the nations they *p* my holy name,

PROFESS*
1Ti 2:10 for women who *p* to worship God.
Heb 4:14 let us hold firmly to the faith we *p*.
10:23 unswervingly to the hope we *p*,

PROFIT (PROFITABLE)
Pr 14:23 All hard work brings a *p*,
21: 5 The plans of the diligent lead to *p*
Isa 44:10 which can *p* him nothing?
2Co 2:17 not peddle the word of God for *p*.
Php 3: 7 was to my *p* I now consider loss

PROFITABLE* (PROFIT)
Pr 3:14 for she is more *p* than silver
31:18 She sees that her trading is *p*,
Tit 3: 8 These things are excellent and *p*

PROFOUND
Job 9: 4 His wisdom is *p*, his power is vast.
Ps 92: 5 how *p* your thoughts!
Eph 5:32 This is a *p* mystery—but I am

PROGRESS
Php 1:25 continue with all of you for your *p*
1Ti 4:15 so that everyone may see your *p*.

PROLONG*
Dt 5:33 *p* your days in the land that you
Ps 85: 5 Will you *p* your anger
Pr 3: 2 for they will *p* your life many years
Isa 53:10 will see his offspring and *p* his days,
La 4:22 he will not *p* your exile.

PROMISE (PROMISED PROMISES)
Nu 23:19 Does he *p* and not fulfill?
Jos 23:14 Every *p* has been fulfilled;
2Sa 7:25 keep forever the *p* you have made
1Ki 8:20 The LORD has kept the *p* he made
8:24 You have kept your *p*
Ne 5:13 man who does not keep this *p*.
9: 8 have kept your *p* because you are
Ps 77: 8 Has his *p* failed for all time?
119: 41 your salvation according to your *p*;
119: 50 Your *p* preserves my life.
119: 58 to me according to your *p*.
119: 162 I rejoice in your *p*
Ac 2:39 The *p* is for you and your children
Ro 4:13 offspring received the *p* that he
4:20 unbelief regarding the *p* of God,
Gal 3:14 that by faith we might receive the *p*
Eph 2:12 foreigners to the covenants of the *p*
1Ti 4: 8 holding *p* for both the present life
Heb 6:13 When God made his *p* to Abraham
11:11 him faithful who had made the *p*.
2Pe 3: 9 Lord is not slow in keeping his *p*,
3:13 with his *p* we are looking forward

PROMISED (PROMISE)
Ge 21: 1 did for Sarah what he had *p*.
24: 7 who spoke to me and *p* me on oath,
Ex 3:17 And I have *p* to bring you up out
Nu 10:29 for the LORD has *p* good things
Dt 15: 6 your God will bless you as he has *p*,
26:18 his treasured possession as he *p*,
2Sa 7:28 and you have *p* these good things
1Ki 9: 5 I *p* David your father when I said,
2Ch 6:15 with your mouth you have *p*
Ps 119: 57 I have *p* to obey your words.
Lk 24:49 to send you what my Father has *p*;
Ac 1: 4 but wait for the gift my Father *p*,
13:32 What God *p* our fathers he has
Ro 4:21 power to do what he had *p*.
Tit 1: 2 *p* before the beginning of time,
Heb 10:23 for he who *p* is faithful.
10:36 you will receive what he has *p*.
Jas 1:12 the crown of life that God has *p*
2: 5 the kingdom he *p* those who love
2Pe 3: 4 "Where is this 'coming' he *p*?
1Jn 2:25 And this is what he *p* us—

PROMISES (PROMISE)
Jos 21:45 one of all the LORD's good *p*
23:14 of all the good *p* the LORD your
1Ki 8:56 failed of all the good *p* he gave
1Ch 17:19 and made known all these great *p*.
Ps 85: 8 he *p* peace to his people, his saints
106: 12 Then they believed his *p*
119: 140 Your *p* have been thoroughly
119: 148 that I may meditate on your *p*.
145: 13 The LORD is faithful to all his *p*
Ro 9: 4 the temple worship and the *p*.
2Co 1:20 matter how many *p* God has made,
7: 1 Since we have these *p*, dear friends,
Heb 8: 6 and it is founded on better *p*.
2Pe 1: 4 us his very great and precious *p*,

PROMOTE (PROMOTES)
Pr 12:20 but joy for those who *p* peace.
16:21 and pleasant words *p* instruction.
1Ti 1: 4 These *p* controversies rather

PROMOTES (PROMOTE)
Pr 17: 9 over an offense *p* love,

PROMPTED
1Th 1: 3 your labor *p* by love, and your
2Th 1:11 and every act *p* by your faith.

PRONOUNCE (PRONOUNCED)
1Ch 23:13 to *p* blessings in his name forever.

PRONOUNCED (PRONOUNCE)
1Ch 16:12 miracles, and the judgments he *p*,

PROOF (PROVE)
Ac 17:31 He has given *p* of this to all men
2Co 8:24 Therefore show these men the *p*

PROPER
Ps 104: 27 give them their food at the *p* time.
145: 15 give them their food at the *p* time.
Ecc 5:18 Then I realized that it is good and *p*
8: 5 the wise heart will know the *p* time
Mt 24:45 give them their food at the *p* time?
Lk 1:20 which will come true at their *p* time
1Co 11:13 Is it *p* for a woman to pray to God
Gal 6: 9 at the *p* time we will reap a harvest
1Ti 2: 6 the testimony given in its *p* time.
1Pe 2:17 Show *p* respect to everyone:

PROPERTY
Heb 10:34 the confiscation of your *p*,

PROPHECIES (PROPHESY)
1Co 13: 8 where there are *p*, they will cease;
1Th 5:20 do not treat *p* with contempt.

PROPHECY (PROPHESY)
Da 9:24 to seal up vision and *p*
1Co 12:10 miraculous powers, to another *p*,
13: 2 of *p* and can fathom all mysteries
14: 1 gifts, especially the gift of *p*.
14: 6 or *p* or word of instruction?
14:22 *p*, however, is for believers,
2Pe 1:20 you must understand that no *p*
Rev 22:18 the words of the *p* of this book:

PROPHESIED (PROPHESY)
Nu 11:25 the Spirit rested on them, they *p*,
1Sa 19:24 and also *p* in Samuel's presence.
Jn 11:51 that year he *p* that Jesus would
Ac 19: 6 and they spoke in tongues and *p*.
21: 9 four unmarried daughters who *p*.

PROPHESIES (PROPHESY)
Jer 28: 9 the prophet who *p* peace will be
Eze 12:27 and he *p* about the distant future.'
1Co 11: 4 *p* with his head covered dishonors
14: 3 But everyone who *p* speaks to men

PROPHESY (PROPHECIES PROPHECY PROPHESIED PROPHESIES PROPHESYING PROPHET PROPHET'S PROPHETESS PROPHETS)
1Sa 10: 6 and you will *p* with them;
Eze 13: 2 Say to those who *p* out
13:17 daughters of your people who *p* out
34: 2 *p* against the shepherds of Israel;
37: 4 "*P* to these bones and say to them,
Joel 2:28 Your sons and daughters will *p*,
Mt 7:22 Lord, did we not *p* in your name,
Ac 2:17 Your sons and daughters will *p*,
1Co 13: 9 know in part and we *p* in part,
14:39 my brothers, be eager to *p*,
Rev 11: 3 and they will *p* for 1,260 days,

PROPHESYING (PROPHESY)
1Ch 25: 1 and Jeduthun for the ministry of *p*,
Ro 12: 6 If a man's gift is *p*, let him use it

PROPHET (PROPHESY)
Ex 7: 1 your brother Aaron will be your *p*.
Nu 12: 6 "When a *p* of the LORD is
Dt 13: 1 If a *p*, or one who foretells
18:18 up for them a *p* like you
18:22 If what a *p* proclaims in the name
1Sa 3:20 that Samuel was attested as a *p*
9: 9 because the *p* of today used
1Ki 1: 8 son of Jehoiada, Nathan the *p*,
18:36 the *p* Elijah stepped forward
2Ki 5: 8 and he will know that there is a *p*
6:12 "but Elisha, the *p* who is in Israel,
20: 1 The *p* Isaiah son of Amoz went
2Ch 35:18 since the days of the *p* Samuel;
36:12 himself before Jeremiah the *p*,
Ezr 5: 1 Haggai the *p* and Zechariah the *p*,
Eze 2: 5 they will know that a *p* has been
33:33 they will know that a *p* has been
Hos 9: 7 the *p* is considered a fool,
Am 7:14 "I was neither a *p* nor a prophet's
Hab 1: 1 that Habakkuk the *p* received.
Hag 1: 1 came through the *p* Haggai
Zec 1: 1 to the *p* Zechariah son of Berekiah,
13: 4 that day every *p* will be ashamed
Mal 4: 5 I will send you the *p* Elijah
Mt 10:41 Anyone who receives a *p*
11: 9 what did you go out to see? A *p*?
12:39 except the sign of the *p* Jonah.
Lk 1:76 will be called a *p* of the Most High;
4:24 "no *p* is accepted in his hometown.
7:16 A great *p* has appeared among us,"
24:19 "He was a *p*, powerful in word
Jn 1:21 "Are you the *P*?" He answered,
Ac 7:37 'God will send you a *p* like me
21:10 a *p* named Agabus came
1Co 14:37 If anybody thinks he is a *p*
Rev 16:13 and out of the mouth of the false *p*.

PROPHET'S (PROPHESY)
2Pe 1:20 about by the *p* own interpretation.

PROPHETESS (PROPHESY)
Ex 15:20 Then Miriam the *p*, Aaron's sister,
Jdg 4: 4 a *p*, the wife of Lappidoth,
Isa 8: 3 I went to the *p*, and she conceived
Lk 2:36 a *p*, Anna, the daughter of Phanuel,

PROPHETS (PROPHESY)
Nu 11:29 that all the LORD's people were *p*
1Sa 10:11 Is Saul also among the *p*?"
1Sa 28: 6 him by dreams or Urim or *p*.
1Ki 19:10 put your *p* to death with the sword.
1Ch 16:22 do my *p* no harm."
Ps 105: 15 do my *p* no harm."
Jer 23: 9 Concerning the *p*:
23:30 "I am against the *p* who steal
Eze 13: 2 prophesy against the *p*
Mt 5:17 come to abolish the Law or the *P*;
7:12 for this sums up the Law and the *P*.
7:15 "Watch out for false *p*.
22:40 and the *P* hang on these two
23:37 you who kill the *p* and stone those
24:24 false Christs and false *p* will appear
26:56 of the *p* might be fulfilled."
Lk 10:24 For I tell you that many *p*
11:49 'I will send them *p* and apostles,
24:25 believe all that the *p* have spoken!
24:44 me in the Law of Moses, the *P*
Ac 3:24 "Indeed, all the *p* from Samuel on,
10:43 All the *p* testify about him that
13: 1 the church at Antioch there were *p*
26:22 nothing beyond what the *p*
28:23 the Law of Moses and from the *P*.
Ro 1: 2 through his *p* in the Holy
3:21 to which the Law and the *P* testify.
11: 3 they have killed your *p*
1Co 12:28 second *p*, third teachers, then
12:29 Are all *p*? Are all teachers?
14:32 The spirits of *p* are subject
Eph 2:20 foundation of the apostles and *p*,
3: 5 Spirit to God's holy apostles and *p*.
4:11 some to be *p*, some
Heb 1: 1 through the *p* at many times
1Pe 1:10 Concerning this salvation, the *p*,
2Pe 1:19 word of the *p* made more certain,
3: 2 spoken in the past by the holy *p*
1Jn 4: 1 because many false *p* have gone out
Rev 11:10 these two *p* had tormented those
18:20 Rejoice, saints and apostles and *p*!

PROPORTION
Dt 16:10 by giving a freewill offering in *p*
16:17 Each of you must bring a gift in *p*

PROPRIETY*
1Ti 2: 9 with decency and *p*,
2:15 in faith, love and holiness with *p*.

PROSPECT*
Pr 10:28 The *p* of the righteous is joy,

PROSPER (PROSPERED PROSPERITY PROSPEROUS PROSPERS)
Dt 5:33 so that you may live and *p*
28:63 pleased the LORD to make you *p*
29: 9 that you may *p* in everything you
1Ki 2: 3 so that you may *p* in all you do
Ezr 6:14 and *p* under the preaching
Pr 11:10 When the righteous *p*, the city
11:25 A generous man will *p*;
17:20 A man of perverse heart does not *p*
28:13 who conceals his sins does not *p*,
28:25 he who trusts in the LORD will *p*.
Isa 53:10 of the LORD will *p* in his hand.
Jer 12: 1 Why does the way of the wicked *p*?

PROSPERED (PROSPER)
Ge 39: 2 was with Joseph and he *p*,
2Ch 14: 7 So they built and *p*.
31:21 And so he *p*.

PROSPERITY (PROSPER)
Dt 28:11 will grant you abundant *p*—
30:15 I set before you today life and *p*,
Job 36:11 will spend the rest of their days in *p*
Ps 73: 3 when I saw the *p* of the wicked.
122: 9 I will seek your *p*.
128: 2 blessings and *p* will be yours.
Pr 3: 2 and bring you *p*.
13:21 but *p* is the reward of the righteous.
21:21 finds life, *p* and honor.
Isa 45: 7 I bring *p* and create disaster;

PROSPEROUS (PROSPER)
Dt 30: 9 your God will make you most *p*
Jos 1: 8 Then you will be *p* and successful.
Job 42:10 the LORD made him *p* again

PROSPERS (PROSPER)
Ps 1: 3 Whatever he does *p*.
Pr 16:20 gives heed to instruction *p*,
19: 8 he who cherishes understanding *p*.

PROSTITUTE (PROSTITUTES PROSTITUTION)
Lev 20: 6 and spiritists to *p* himself
Nu 15:39 and not *p* yourselves by going
Jos 2: 1 the house of a *p* named Rahab
Pr 6:26 for the *p* reduces you to a loaf
7:10 like a *p* and with crafty intent.
Pr 23:27 for a *p* is a deep pit
Eze 16:15 and used your fame to become a *p*.
23: 7 a *p* to all the elite of the Assyrians
Hos 3: 3 you must not be a *p* or be intimate
1Co 6:15 of Christ and unite them with a *p*?
6:16 with a *p* is one with her in body?
Rev 17: 1 you the punishment of the great *p*,

PROSTITUTES (PROSTITUTE)
Pr 29: 3 of *p* squanders his wealth.
Mt 21:31 and the *p* are entering the kingdom
Lk 15:30 property with *p* comes home,
1Co 6: 9 male *p* nor homosexual offenders

PROSTITUTION (PROSTITUTE)
Eze 16:16 where you carried on your *p*.
23: 3 engaging in *p* from their youth.
Hos 4:10 engage in *p* but not increase,

PROSTRATE
Dt 9:18 again I fell *p* before the LORD
1Ki 18:39 they fell *p* and cried, "The LORD

PROTECT (PROTECTED PROTECTION PROTECTS)
Dt 23:14 about in your camp to *p* you
Ps 25:21 integrity and uprightness *p* me,
32: 7 you will *p* me from trouble
40:11 your truth always *p* me.
41: 2 The LORD will *p* him
91:14 I will *p* him, for he acknowledges
140: 1 *p* me from men of violence,
Pr 2:11 Discretion will *p* you,
4: 6 forsake wisdom, and she will *p* you;
Jn 17:11 *p* them by the power of your name
17:15 that you *p* them from the evil one.
2Th 3: 3 and *p* you from the evil one.

PROTECTED (PROTECT)
Jos 24:17 He *p* us on our entire journey
1Sa 30:23 He has *p* us and handed
Ps 37:28 They will be *p* forever,
Jn 17:12 I *p* them and kept them safe

PROTECTION (PROTECT)
Ezr 9: 9 he has given us a wall of *p* in Judah
Ps 5:11 Spread your *p* over them,

PROTECTS (PROTECT)
Ps 116: 6 The LORD *p* the simplehearted;
Pr 2: 8 and *p* the way of his faithful ones.
1Co 13: 7 It always *p*, always trusts,

PROUD (PRIDE)
Ps 31:23 but the *p* he pays back in full.
101: 5 has haughty eyes and a *p* heart,
138: 6 but the *p* he knows from afar.
Pr 3:34 He mocks *p* mockers
16: 5 The LORD detests all the *p*
16:19 than to share plunder with the *p*.
18:12 his downfall a man's heart is *p*,
21: 4 Haughty eyes and a *p* heart,
Isa 2:12 store for all the *p* and lofty,
Ro 12:16 Do not be *p*, but be willing
1Co 13: 4 it does not boast, it is not *p*.
2Ti 3: 2 lovers of money, boastful, *p*,
Jas 4: 6 "God opposes the *p*
1Pe 5: 5 because, "God opposes the *p*

PROVE (PROOF PROVED PROVING)
Pr 29:25 Fear of man will *p* to be a snare,
Jn 8:46 Can any of you *p* me guilty of sin?
Ac 26:20 *p* their repentance by their deeds.
1Co 4: 2 been given a trust must *p* faithful.

PROVED (PROVE)
Ps 51: 4 so that you are *p* right
Mt 11:19 wisdom is *p* right by her actions."
Ro 3: 4 "So that you may be *p* right
1Pe 1: 7 may be *p* genuine and may result

PROVIDE (PROVIDED PROVIDES PROVISION)
Ge 22: 8 "God himself will *p* the lamb
22:14 that place "The LORD will *P*."
Isa 43:20 because I *p* water in the desert
61: 3 and *p* for those who grieve in Zion
1Co 10:13 *p* a way out so that you can stand
1Ti 5: 8 If anyone does not *p*
Tit 3:14 in order that they may *p*

PROVIDED (PROVIDE)
Ps 68:10 O God, you *p* for the poor.
111: 9 He *p* redemption for his people;
Jnh 1:17 But the LORD *p* a great fish
4: 6 Then the LORD God *p* a vine
4: 7 dawn the next day God *p* a worm,
4: 8 God *p* a scorching east wind,
Gal 4:18 to be zealous, *p* the purpose is good
Heb 1: 3 After he had *p* purification for sins,

PROVIDES (PROVIDE)
Ps 111: 5 He *p* food for those who fear him;
Pr 31:15 she *p* food for her family
Eze 18: 7 and *p* clothing for the naked.
1Ti 6:17 who richly *p* us with everything
1Pe 4:11 it with the strength God *p*,

PROVING* (PROVE)
Ac 9:22 by *p* that Jesus is the Christ.
17: 3 and *p* that the Christ had to suffer
18:28 *p* from the Scriptures that Jesus

PROVISION (PROVIDE)
Ro 5:17 who receive God's abundant *p*

PROVOKED
Ecc 7: 9 Do not be quickly *p* in your spirit,
Jer 32:32 Judah have *p* me by all the evil they

PROWLS
1Pe 5: 8 Your enemy the devil *p*

PRUDENCE* (PRUDENT)
Pr 1: 4 for giving *p* to the simple,
8: 5 You who are simple, gain *p*;
8:12 "I, wisdom, dwell together with *p*;
15: 5 whoever heeds correction shows *p*.
19:25 and the simple will learn *p*;

PRUDENT* (PRUDENCE)
Pr 1: 3 acquiring a disciplined and *p* life,
12:16 but a *p* man overlooks an insult.
12:23 A *p* man keeps his knowledge
13:16 Every *p* man acts out of knowledge
14: 8 The wisdom of the *p* is
14:15 a *p* man gives thought to his steps.
14:18 the *p* are crowned with knowledge.
19:14 but a *p* wife is from the LORD.
22: 3 *p* man sees danger and takes
27:12 The *p* see danger and take refuge,
Jer 49: 7 Has counsel perished from the *p*?
Am 5:13 Therefore the *p* man keeps quiet

PRUNES (PRUNING)
Jn 15: 2 that does bear fruit he *p*

PRUNING (PRUNES)
Isa 2: 4 and their spears into *p* hooks.
Joel 3:10 and your *p* hooks into spears.

PSALMS
Eph 5:19 Speak to one another with *p*,
Col 3:16 and as you sing *p*, hymns

PUBLICLY
Ac 20:20 have taught you *p* and from house
1Ti 5:20 Those who sin are to be rebuked *p*,

PUFFS
1Co 8: 1 Knowledge *p* up, but love builds up

PULLING
2Co 10: 8 building you up rather than *p* you

PUNISH (PUNISHED PUNISHES PUNISHMENT)
Ge 15:14 But I will *p* the nation they serve
Ex 32:34 I will *p* them for their sin."
Pr 17:26 It is not good to *p* an innocent man,
23:13 if you *p* him with the rod, he will
Isa 13:11 I will *p* the world for its evil,
Jer 2:19 Your wickedness will *p* you;
21:14 I will *p* you as your deeds deserve,
Zep 1:12 and *p* those who are complacent,
Ac 7: 7 But I will *p* the nation they serve
2Th 1: 8 He will *p* those who do not know
1Pe 2:14 by him to *p* those who do wrong

PUNISHED (PUNISH)
Ezr 9:13 you have *p* us less than our sins
Ps 99: 8 though you *p* their misdeeds.
La 3:39 complain when *p* for his sins?
Mk 12:40 Such men will be *p* most severely."
Lk 23:41 the same sentence? We are *p* justly,
2Th 1: 9 be *p* with everlasting destruction
Heb 10:29 to be *p* who has trampled the Son

PUNISHES (PUNISH)
Heb 12: 6 and he *p* everyone he accepts

PUNISHMENT (PUNISH)
Isa 53: 5 the *p* that brought us peace was
Jer 4:18 This is your *p*.
Mt 25:46 Then they will go away to eternal *p*
Lk 12:48 and does things deserving *p* will be
21:22 For this is the time of *p*
Ro 13: 4 wrath to bring *p* on the wrongdoer.
Heb 2: 2 disobedience received its just *p*,
2Pe 2: 9 while continuing their *p*.

PURCHASED
Ps 74: 2 Remember the people you *p* of old,
Rev 5: 9 with your blood you *p* men for God

PURE (PURIFICATION PURIFIED PURIFIES PURIFY PURITY)
2Sa 22:27 to the *p* you show yourself *p*,
Job 14: 4 Who can bring what is *p*
Ps 19: 9 The fear of the LORD is *p*,
24: 4 who has clean hands and a *p* heart,
51:10 Create in me a *p* heart, O God,
119: 9 can a young man keep his way *p*?
Pr 15:26 those of the *p* are pleasing to him.
20: 9 can say, "I have kept my heart *p*;
Isa 52:11 Come out from it and be *p*,
Hab 1:13 Your eyes are too *p* to look on evil;
Mt 5: 8 Blessed are the *p* in heart,
2Co 11: 2 I might present you as a *p* virgin
Php 4: 8 whatever is *p*, whatever is lovely,
1Ti 1: 5 which comes from a *p* heart
5:22 Keep yourself *p*.
2Ti 2:22 call on the Lord out of a *p* heart.
Tit 1:15 To the *p*, all things are *p*,
2: 5 to be self-controlled and *p*,
Heb 7:26 blameless, *p*, set apart from sinners
13: 4 and the marriage bed kept *p*,
Jas 1:27 that God our Father accepts as *p*
3:17 comes from heaven is first of all *p*;
1Jn 3: 3 him purifies himself, just as he is *p*.

PURGE
Pr 20:30 and beatings *p* the inmost being.

PURIFICATION (PURE)
Heb 1: 3 After he had provided *p* for sins,

PURIFIED (PURE)
Ac 15: 9 for he *p* their hearts by faith.
1Pe 1:22 Now that you have *p* yourselves

PURIFIES* (PURE)
1Jn 1: 7 of Jesus, his Son, *p* us from all sin.
3: 3 who has this hope in him *p* himself,

PURIFY (PURE)
Nu 19:12 He must *p* himself with the water
2Co 7: 1 us *p* ourselves from everything that
Tit 2:14 to *p* for himself a people that are
Jas 4: 8 you sinners, and *p* your hearts,
1Jn 1: 9 and *p* us from all unrighteousness.

PURIM
Est 9:26 Therefore these days were called *P*

PURITY* (PURE)
Hos 8: 5 long will they be incapable of *p*?
2Co 6: 6 in *p*, understanding, patience
1Ti 4:12 in life, in love, in faith and in *p*.
5: 2 as sisters, with absolute *p*.
1Pe 3: 2 when they see the *p* and reverence

PURPLE
Pr 31:22 she is clothed in fine linen and *p*.
Mk 15:17 They put a *p* robe on him, then

PURPOSE (PURPOSED PURPOSES)
Ex 9:16 I have raised you up for this very *p*,
Job 36: 5 he is mighty, and firm in his *p*.
Pr 19:21 but it is the LORD's *p* that prevails
Isa 46:10 I say: My *p* will stand,
55:11 and achieve the *p* for which I sent it
Ac 2:23 handed over to you by God's set *p*
Ro 8:28 have been called according to his *p*.
9:11 in order that God's *p*
9:17 "I raised you up for this very *p*,
1Co 3: 8 the man who waters have one *p*,
2Co 5: 5 who has made us for this very *p*
Gal 4:18 be zealous, provided the *p* is good,
Eph 1:11 in conformity with the *p* of his will,
3:11 according to his eternal *p* which he
Php 2: 2 love, being one in spirit and *p*.
2:13 and to act according to his good *p*.
2Ti 1: 9 but because of his own *p* and grace.

PURPOSED (PURPOSE)
Isa 14:24 and as I have *p*, so it will stand.
14:27 For the LORD Almighty has *p*,
Eph 1: 9 which he *p* in Christ, to be put

PURPOSES (PURPOSE)
Ps 33:10 he thwarts the *p* of the peoples.
Jer 23:20 the *p* of his heart.
32:19 great are your *p* and mighty are

PURSE (PURSES)
Hag 1: 6 to put them in a *p* with holes in it."
Lk 10: 4 Do not take a *p* or bag or sandals;
22:36 "But now if you have a *p*, take it,

PURSES (PURSE)
Lk 12:33 Provide *p* for yourselves that will

PURSUE (PURSUES)
Ps 34:14 seek peace and *p* it.
Pr 15: 9 he loves those who *p* righteousness
Ro 9:30 who did not *p* righteousness,
1Ti 6:11 and *p* righteousness, godliness,
2Ti 2:22 and *p* righteousness, faith,
1Pe 3:11 he must seek peace and *p* it.

PURSUES (PURSUE)
Pr 21:21 He who *p* righteousness and love
28: 1 wicked man flees though no one *p*,

QUAIL
Ex 16:13 That evening *q* came and covered
Nu 11:31 and drove *q* in from the sea.

QUALITIES* (QUALITY)
Da 6: 3 by his exceptional *q* that the king
Ro 1:20 of the world God's invisible *q*—
2Pe 1: 8 For if you possess these *q*

QUALITY (QUALITIES)
1Co 3:13 and the fire will test the *q*

QUARREL (QUARRELING QUARRELS QUARRELSOME)
Pr 15:18 but a patient man calms a *q*.
17:14 Starting a *q* is like breaching a dam;
17:19 He who loves a *q* loves sin;
20: 3 but every fool is quick to *q*.
26:17 in a *q* not his own.
26:20 without gossip a *q* dies down.
2Ti 2:24 And the Lord's servant must not *q*;
Jas 4: 2 You *q* and fight.

QUARRELING (QUARREL)
1Co 3: 3 For since there is jealousy and *q*
2Ti 2:14 before God against *q* about words;

QUARRELS (QUARREL)
Pr 13:10 Pride only breeds *q*,
Isa 45: 9 Woe to him who *q* with his Maker,
2Ti 2:23 because you know they produce *q*.
Jas 4: 1 What causes fights and *q*

QUARRELSOME (QUARREL)
Pr 19:13 a *q* wife is like a constant dripping.
21: 9 than share a house with a *q* wife.
26:21 so is a *q* man for kindling strife.
1Ti 3: 3 not violent but gentle, not *q*,

QUEEN
1Ki 10: 1 When the *q* of Sheba heard about
2Ch 9: 1 When the *q* of Sheba heard
Mt 12:42 The *Q* of the South will rise

QUENCH (QUENCHED)
SS 8: 7 Many waters cannot *q* love;

QUENCHED (QUENCH)
Isa 66:24 nor will their fire be *q*,
Mk 9:48 and the fire is not *q*.'

QUICK-TEMPERED* (TEMPER)
Pr 14:17 A *q* man does foolish things,
14:29 but a *q* man displays folly.
Tit 1: 7 not *q*, not given to drunkenness,

QUIET (QUIETNESS)
Ps 23: 2 he leads me beside *q* waters,
Pr 17: 1 Better a dry crust with peace and *q*
Ecc 9:17 The *q* words of the wise are more
Am 5:13 Therefore the prudent man keeps *q*
Zep 3:17 he will *q* you with his love,
Lk 19:40 he replied, "if they keep *q*,
1Th 4:11 it your ambition to lead a *q* life,
1Ti 2: 2 we may live peaceful and *q* lives
1Pe 3: 4 beauty of a gentle and *q* spirit,

QUIETNESS (QUIET)
Isa 30:15 in *q* and trust is your strength,
32:17 the effect of righteousness will be *q*
1Ti 2:11 A woman should learn in *q*

QUIVER
Ps 127: 5 whose *q* is full of them.

RACE
Ecc 9:11 The *r* is not to the swift
Ac 20:24 if only I may finish the *r*
1Co 9:24 that in a *r* all the runners run,
Gal 2: 2 that I was running or had run my *r*
5: 7 You were running a good *r*.
2Ti 4: 7 I have finished the *r*, I have kept
Heb 12: 1 perseverance the *r* marked out

RACHEL
Daughter of Laban (Ge 29:16); wife of Jacob (Ge

29:28); bore two sons (Ge 30:22-24; 35:16-24; 46: 19). Stole Laban's gods (Ge 31:19, 32-35). Death (Ge 35:19-20).

RADIANCE (RADIANT)
Eze 1:28 so was the *r* around him.
Heb 1: 3 The Son is the *r* of God's glory

RADIANT (RADIANCE)
Ex 34:29 he was not aware that his face was *r*
Ps 34: 5 Those who look to him are *r*;
SS 5:10 *Beloved* My lover is *r* and ruddy,
Isa 60: 5 Then you will look and be *r*,
Eph 5:27 her to himself as a *r* church,

RAGE
Ac 4:25 " 'Why do the nations *r*
Col 3: 8 *r*, malice, slander, and filthy

RAGS
Isa 64: 6 our righteous acts are like filthy *r*;

RAHAB
Prostitute of Jericho who hid Israelite spies (Jos 2; 6:22-25; Heb 11:31; Jas 2:25). Mother of Boaz (Mt 1:5).

RAIN (RAINBOW)
Ge 7: 4 from now I will send *r* on the earth
1Ki 17: 1 nor *r* in the next few years
18: 1 and I will send *r* on the land."
Mt 5:45 and sends *r* on the righteous
Jas 5:17 it did not *r* on the land for three
Jude :12 They are clouds without *r*,

RAINBOW (RAIN)
Ge 9:13 I have set my *r* in the clouds,

RAISE (RISE)
Jn 6:39 but *r* them up at the last day.
1Co 15:15 he did not *r* him if in fact the dead

RAISED (RISE)
Isa 52:13 he will be *r* and lifted up
Mt 17:23 on the third day he will be *r* to life
Lk 7:22 the deaf hear, the dead are *r*,
Ac 2:24 But God *r* him from the dead,
Ro 4:25 was *r* to life for our justification.
6: 4 as Christ was *r* from the dead
8:11 And if the Spirit of him who *r* Jesus
10: 9 in your heart that God *r* him
1Co 15: 4 that he was *r* on the third day
15:20 But Christ has indeed been *r*

RALLY*
Isa 11:10 the nations will *r* to him,

RAM (RAMS)
Ge 22:13 there in a thicket he saw a *r* caught
Da 8: 3 before me was a *r* with two horns,

RAMPART*
Ps 91: 4 will be your shield and *r*.

RAMS (RAM)
1Sa 15:22 to heed is better than the fat of *r*.
Mic 6: 7 pleased with thousands of *r*,

RAN (RUN)
Jnh 1: 3 But Jonah *r* away from the LORD

RANSOM (RANSOMED)
Isa 50: 2 Was my arm too short to *r* you?
Hos 13:14 "I will *r* them from the power
Mt 20:28 and to give his life as a *r* for many."
Mk 10:45 and to give his life as a *r* for many."
1Ti 2: 6 who gave himself as a *r* for all men
Heb 9:15 as a *r* to set them free

RANSOMED (RANSOM)
Isa 35:10 and the *r* of the LORD will return.

RARE
Pr 20:15 that speak knowledge are a *r* jewel.

RAVEN (RAVENS)
Ge 8: 7 made in the ark and sent out a *r*,
Job 38:41 Who provides food for the *r*

RAVENS (RAVEN)
1Ki 17: 6 The *r* brought him bread
Ps 147: 9 and for the young *r* when they call.
Lk 12:24 Consider the *r*: They do not sow

READ (READING READS)
Dt 17:19 he is to *r* it all the days of his life
Jos 8:34 Joshua *r* all the words of the law—
2Ki 23: 2 He *r* in their hearing all the words
Ne 8: 8 They *r* from the Book of the Law
Jer 36: 6 and *r* to the people from the scroll
2Co 3: 2 known and *r* by everybody.

READING (READ)
1Ti 4:13 to the public *r* of Scripture,

READS (READ)
Rev 1: 3 Blessed is the one who *r* the words

REAFFIRM
2Co 2: 8 therefore, to *r* your love for him.

REAL* (REALITIES REALITY)
Jn 6:55 is *r* food and my blood is *r* drink.
1Jn 2:27 all things and as that anointing is *r*,

REALITIES* (REAL)
Heb 10: 1 are coming—not the *r* themselves.

REALITY* (REAL)
Col 2:17 the *r*, however, is found in Christ.

REALM (REALMS)
Hab 2: 9 "Woe to him who builds his *r*

REALMS (REALM)
Eph 1: 3 the heavenly *r* with every spiritual
2: 6 in the heavenly *r* in Christ Jesus,

REAP (REAPER REAPS)
Job 4: 8 and those who sow trouble *r* it.
Ps 126: 5 will *r* with songs of joy.
Hos 8: 7 and *r* the whirlwind.
10:12 *r* the fruit of unfailing love,
Jn 4:38 you to *r* what you have not worked
Ro 6:22 the benefit you *r* leads to holiness,
2Co 9: 6 generously will also *r* generously.
Gal 6: 8 from that nature will *r* destruction;

REAPER (REAP)
Jn 4:36 and the *r* may be glad together.

REAPS (REAP)
Pr 11:18 who sows righteousness *r* a sure
22: 8 He who sows wickedness *r* trouble,
Gal 6: 7 A man *r* what he sows.

REASON (REASONED)
Ge 2:24 For this *r* a man will leave his
Isa 1:18 "Come now, let us *r* together,"
Mt 19: 5 'For this *r* a man will leave his
Jn 12:27 it was for this very *r* I came
15:25 'They hated me without *r*.'
1Pe 3:15 to give the *r* for the hope that you
2Pe 1: 5 For this very *r*, make every effort

REASONED (REASON)
1Co 13:11 thought like a child, I *r* like a child.

REBEKAH
Sister of Laban, secured as bride for Isaac (Ge 24). Mother of Esau and Jacob (Ge 25:19-26). Taken by Abimelech as sister of Isaac; returned (Ge 26:1-11). Encouraged Jacob to trick Isaac out of blessing (Ge 27:1-17).

REBEL (REBELLED REBELLION REBELS)
Nu 14: 9 Only do not *r* against the LORD.
1Sa 12:14 and do not *r* against his commands,
Mt 10:21 children will *r* against their parents

REBELLED (REBEL)
Ps 78:56 and *r* against the Most High;
Isa 63:10 Yet they *r*

REBELLION (REBEL)
Ex 34: 7 and forgiving wickedness, *r* and sin
Nu 14:18 in love and forgiving sin and *r*.
1Sa 15:23 For *r* is like the sin of divination,
2Th 2: 3 will not come, until the *r* occurs

REBELS (REBEL)
Ro 13: 2 he who *r* against the authority is
1Ti 1: 9 but for lawbreakers and *r*,

REBIRTH* (BEAR)
Tit 3: 5 us through the washing of *r*

REBUILD (BUILD)
Ezr 5: 2 set to work to *r* the house of God
Ne 2:17 let us *r* the wall of Jerusalem,
Ps 102: 16 For the LORD will *r* Zion
Da 9:25 and *r* Jerusalem until the Anointed
Am 9:14 they will *r* the ruined cities
Ac 15:16 Its ruins I will *r*,

REBUILT (BUILD)
Zec 1:16 and there my house will be *r*.

REBUKE (REBUKED REBUKES REBUKING)
Lev 19:17 *R* your neighbor frankly
Ps 141: 5 let him *r* me—it is oil on my head.
Pr 3:11 and do not resent his *r*,
9: 8 *r* a wise man and he will love you.
15:31 He who listens to a life-giving *r*
17:10 A *r* impresses a man
19:25 *r* a discerning man, and he will gain
25:12 is a wise man's *r* to a listening ear.
27: 5 Better is open *r*
30: 6 or he will *r* you and prove you a liar
Ecc 7: 5 It is better to heed a wise man's *r*
Isa 54: 9 never to *r* you again.
Jer 2:19 your backsliding will *r* you.
Lk 17: 3 "If your brother sins, *r* him,
1Ti 5: 1 Do not *r* an older man harshly,
2Ti 4: 2 correct, *r* and encourage—
Tit 1:13 Therefore, *r* them sharply,
2:15 Encourage and *r* with all authority.
Rev 3:19 Those whom I love I *r*

REBUKED (REBUKE)
Mk 16:14 he *r* them for their lack of faith
1Ti 5:20 Those who sin are to be *r* publicly,

REBUKES (REBUKE)
Job 22: 4 "Is it for your piety that he *r* you
Pr 28:23 He who *r* a man will
29: 1 remains stiff-necked after many *r*
Heb 12: 5 do not lose heart when he *r* you,

REBUKING (REBUKE)
2Ti 3:16 *r*, correcting and training

RECEIVE (RECEIVED RECEIVES)
Mt 10:41 a righteous man will *r* a righteous
Mk 10:15 anyone who will not *r* the kingdom
Jn 20:22 and said, "*R* the Holy Spirit.
Ac 1: 8 you will *r* power when the Holy
2:38 you will *r* the gift of the Holy Spirit
19: 2 "Did you *r* the Holy Spirit
20:35 'It is more blessed to give than to *r*
1Co 9:14 the gospel should *r* their living
2Co 6:17 and I will *r* you."
1Ti 1:16 believe on him and *r* eternal life.
Jas 1: 7 should not think he will *r* anything
2Pe 1:11 and you will *r* a rich welcome
1Jn 3:22 and *r* from him anything we ask,
Rev 4:11 to *r* glory and honor and power,
5:12 to *r* power and wealth and wisdom

RECEIVED (RECEIVE)
Mt 6: 2 they have *r* their reward in full.
10: 8 Freely you have *r*, freely give.
Mk 11:24 believe that you have *r* it,
Jn 1:12 Yet to all who *r* him,
1:16 his grace we have all *r* one blessing
Ac 8:17 and they *r* the Holy Spirit.
10:47 They have *r* the Holy Spirit just
Ro 8:15 but you *r* the Spirit of sonship.
1Co 11:23 For I *r* from the Lord what I
2Co 1: 4 the comfort we ourselves have *r*
Col 2: 6 just as you *r* Christ Jesus as Lord,
1Pe 4:10 should use whatever gift he has *r*

RECEIVES (RECEIVE)
Pr 18:22 and *r* favor from the LORD.
27:21 but man is tested by the praise he *r*.
Mt 7: 8 everyone who asks *r*; he who seeks
10:40 he who *r* me *r* the one who sent me.
10:40 "He who *r* you *r* me, and he who
Ac 10:43 believes in him *r* forgiveness of sins

RECITE
Ps 45: 1 as I *r* my verses for the king;

RECKLESS
Pr 12:18 *R* words pierce like a sword,
14:16 but a fool is hotheaded and *r*.

RECKONING
Isa 10: 3 What will you do on the day of *r*,
Hos 9: 7 the days of *r* are at hand.

RECLAIM* (CLAIM)
Isa 11:11 time to *r* the remnant that is left

RECOGNITION (RECOGNIZE)
1Co 16:18 Such men deserve *r*.
1Ti 5: 3 Give proper *r* to those widows who

RECOGNIZE (RECOGNITION RECOGNIZED)
Mt 7:16 By their fruit you will *r* them.
1Jn 4: 2 This is how you can *r* the Spirit
4: 6 This is how we *r* the Spirit of truth

RECOGNIZED (RECOGNIZE)
Mt 12:33 for a tree is *r* by its fruit.
Ro 7:13 in order that sin might be *r* as sin,

RECOMPENSE*
Isa 40:10 and his *r* accompanies him.
62:11 and his *r* accompanies him.' "

RECONCILE* (RECONCILED RECONCILIATION RECONCILING)
Ac 7:26 He tried to *r* them by saying, 'Men,
Eph 2:16 in this one body to *r* both of them
Col 1:20 him to *r* to himself all things,

RECONCILED* (RECONCILE)
Mt 5:24 First go and be *r* to your brother;
Lk 12:58 try hard to be *r* to him on the way,
Ro 5:10 how much more, having been *r*,
5:10 we were *r* to him through the death
1Co 7:11 or else be *r* to her husband.
2Co 5:18 who *r* us to himself through Christ
5:20 you on Christ's behalf: Be *r* to God.
Col 1:22 he has *r* you by Christ's physical

RECONCILIATION* (RECONCILE)
Ro 5:11 whom we have now received *r*.
11:15 For if their rejection is the *r*
2Co 5:18 and gave us the ministry of *r*:
5:19 committed to us the message of *r*.

RECONCILING* (RECONCILE)
2Co 5:19 that God was *r* the world to himself

RECORD (RECORDED)
Ps 130: 3 If you, O LORD, kept a *r* of sins,
Hos 13:12 his sins are kept on *r*.
1Co 13: 5 is not easily angered, it keeps no *r*

RECORDED (RECORD)
Job 19:23 "Oh, that my words were *r*,
Jn 20:30 which are not *r* in this book.

RECOUNT*
Ps 40: 5 no one can *r* to you;
79:13 we will *r* your praise.
119: 13 With my lips I *r*

RED
Ex 15: 4 are drowned in the *R* Sea.
Ps 106: 9 He rebuked the *R* Sea,
Pr 23:31 Do not gaze at wine when it is *r*,
Isa 1:18 though they are *r* as crimson,

REDEEM (KINSMAN-REDEEMER REDEEMED REDEEMER REDEEMS REDEMPTION)
Ex 6: 6 will *r* you with an outstretched arm
2Sa 7:23 on earth that God went out to *r*
Ps 44:26 *r* us because of your unfailing love.
49: 7 No man can *r* the life of another
49:15 God will *r* my life from the grave;
130: 8 He himself will *r* Israel
Hos 13:14 I will *r* them from death.
Gal 4: 5 under law, to *r* those under law,
Tit 2:14 for us to *r* us from all wickedness

REDEEMED (REDEEM)
Job 33:28 He *r* my soul from going
Ps 71:23 I, whom you have *r*.
107: 2 Let the *r* of the LORD say this—
Isa 35: 9 But only the *r* will walk there,
63: 9 In his love and mercy he *r* them;
Gal 3:13 Christ *r* us from the curse
1Pe 1:18 or gold that you were *r*

REDEEMER (REDEEM)
Job 19:25 I know that my *R* lives,
Ps 19:14 O LORD, my Rock and my *R*.
Isa 44: 6 and *R*, the LORD Almighty:
48:17 your *R*, the Holy One of Israel:
59:20 "The *R* will come to Zion,

REDEEMS (REDEEM)
Ps 34:22 The LORD *r* his servants;
103: 4 he *r* my life from the pit

REDEMPTION (REDEEM)
Ps 130: 7 and with him is full *r*.
Lk 21:28 because your *r* is drawing near."
Ro 3:24 grace through the *r* that came
8:23 as sons, the *r* of our bodies.
1Co 1:30 our righteousness, holiness and *r*.
Eph 1: 7 In him we have *r* through his blood
1:14 until the *r* of those who are God's
4:30 you were sealed for the day of *r*.
Col 1:14 in whom we have *r*, the forgiveness
Heb 9:12 having obtained eternal *r*.

REED
Isa 42: 3 A bruised *r* he will not break,
Mt 12:20 A bruised *r* he will not break,

REFINE*
Jer 9: 7 "See, I will *r* and test them,
Zec 13: 9 I will *r* them like silver
Mal 3: 3 and *r* them like gold and silver.

REFLECT (REFLECTS)
2Co 3:18 unveiled faces all *r* the Lord's

REFLECTS (REFLECT)
Pr 27:19 As water *r* a face,

REFRESH (REFRESHED REFRESHING)
Phm :20 in the Lord; *r* my heart in Christ.

REFRESHED (REFRESH)
Pr 11:25 refreshes others will himself be *r*.

REFRESHING* (REFRESH)
Ac 3:19 that times of *r* may come

REFUGE
Nu 35:11 towns to be your cities of *r*,
Dt 33:27 The eternal God is your *r*,
Jos 20: 2 to designate the cities of *r*,
Ru 2:12 wings you have come to take *r*."
2Sa 22: 3 God is my rock, in whom I take *r*,
22:31 a shield for all who take *r* in him.
Ps 2:12 Blessed are all who take *r* in him.
5:11 But let all who take *r* in you be glad
9: 9 The LORD is a *r* for the oppressed,
16: 1 for in you I take *r*.
17: 7 those who take *r* in you
18: 2 God is my rock, in whom I take *r*.
31: 2 be my rock of *r*,
34: 8 blessed is the man who takes *r*
36: 7 find *r* in the shadow of your wings.
46: 1 God is our *r* and strength,
62: 8 for God is our *r*.
71: 1 In you, O LORD, I have taken *r*;
91: 2 "He is my *r* and my fortress,
144: 2 my shield, in whom I take *r*,
Pr 14:26 and for his children it will be a *r*.
30: 5 a shield to those who take *r* in him.
Na 1: 7 a *r* in times of trouble.

REFUSE (REFUSED)
Jn 5:40 yet you *r* to come to me to have life

REFUSED (REFUSE)
2Th 2:10 because they *r* to love the truth
Rev 16: 9 but they *r* to repent and glorify him

REGARD (REGARDS)
1Th 5:13 Hold them in the highest *r* in love

REGARDS (REGARD)
Ro 14:14 But if anyone *r* something

REGRET
2Co 7:10 leads to salvation and leaves no *r*,

REHOBOAM
Son of Solomon (1Ki 11:43; 1Ch 3:10). Harsh treatment of subjects caused divided kingdom (1Ki 12:1-24; 14:21-31; 2Ch 10-12).

REIGN (REIGNED REIGNS)
Ex 15:18 The LORD will *r*
Ps 68:16 mountain where God chooses to *r*,
Isa 9: 7 He will *r* on David's throne
24:23 for the LORD Almighty will *r*
32: 1 See, a king will *r* in righteousness
Jer 23: 5 a King who will *r* wisely
Lk 1:33 and he will *r* over the house
Ro 6:12 Therefore do not let sin *r*
1Co 15:25 For he must *r* until he has put all
2Ti 2:12 we will also *r* with him.
Rev 11:15 and he will *r* for ever and ever."
20: 6 will *r* with him for a thousand years
22: 5 And they will *r* for ever and ever.

REIGNED (REIGN)
Ro 5:21 so that, just as sin *r* in death,
Rev 20: 4 and *r* with Christ a thousand years.

REIGNS (REIGN)
Ps 9: 7 The LORD *r* forever;
47: 8 God *r* over the nations;
93: 1 The LORD *r*, he is robed
96:10 among the nations, "The LORD *r*
97: 1 The LORD *r*, let the earth be glad;
99: 1 The LORD *r*, / let the nations tremble;
146: 10 The LORD *r* forever,
Isa 52: 7 "Your God *r*!"
Rev 19: 6 For our Lord God Almighty *r*.

REIN
Jas 1:26 and yet does not keep a tight *r*

REJECT (REJECTED REJECTION REJECTS)
Ps 94:14 For the LORD will not *r* his people
Ro 11: 1 I ask then: Did God *r* his people?

REJECTED (REJECT)
1Sa 8: 7 it is not you they have *r*,
1Ki 19:10 The Israelites have *r* your covenant
2Ki 17:15 They *r* his decrees
Ps 66:20 who has not *r* my prayer
118: 22 The stone the builders *r*
Isa 5:24 for they have *r* the law
41: 9 chosen you and have not *r* you.
53: 3 He was despised and *r* by men,
Jer 8: 9 Since they have *r* the word
Mt 21:42 " 'The stone the builders *r*
1Ti 4: 4 nothing is to be *r* if it is received
1Pe 2: 4 *r* by men but chosen by God
2: 7 "The stone the builders *r*

REJECTION* (REJECT)
Ro 11:15 For if their *r* is the reconciliation

REJECTS (REJECT)
Lk 10:16 but he who *r* me *r* him who sent me
Jn 3:36 whoever *r* the Son will not see life,
1Th 4: 8 he who *r* this instruction does not

REJOICE (JOY)
Dt 12: 7 shall *r* in everything you have put
1Ch 16:10 of those who seek the LORD *r*.
16:31 Let the heavens *r*, let the earth be
Ps 2:11 and *r* with trembling.
5:11 those who love your name may *r*
9:14 and there *r* in your salvation.
34: 2 let the afflicted hear and *r*.
63:11 But the king will *r* in God;
66: 6 come, let us *r* in him.
68: 3 and *r* before God;
105: 3 of those who seek the LORD *r*.
118: 24 let us *r* and be glad in it.
119: 14 I *r* in following your statutes
119:162 I *r* in your promise
149: 2 Let Israel *r* in their Maker;
Pr 5:18 may you *r* in the wife of your youth
23:25 may she who gave you birth *r*!
24:17 stumbles, do not let your heart *r*,
Isa 9: 3 as men *r*
35: 1 the wilderness will *r* and blossom.
61: 7 they will *r* in their inheritance;
62: 5 so will your God *r* over you.
Jer 31:12 they will *r* in the bounty
Zep 3:17 he will *r* over you with singing."
Zec 9: 9 *R* greatly, O Daughter of Zion!
Lk 6:23 "*R* in that day and leap for joy,
10:20 but *r* that your names are written
15: 6 '*R* with me; I have found my lost
15: 9 '*R* with me; I have found my lost
Ro 5: 2 And we *r* in the hope of the glory
12:15 Rejoice with those who *r*; mourn
Php 2:17 I am glad and *r* with all of you.
3: 1 Finally, my brothers, *r* in the Lord!
4: 4 *R* in the Lord always.
1Pe 4:13 But *r* that you participate
Rev 19: 7 Let us *r* and be glad

REJOICES (JOY)
Ps 13: 5 my heart *r* in your salvation.
16: 9 my heart is glad and my tongue *r*;
Isa 61:10 my soul *r* in my God.
62: 5 as a bridegroom *r* over his bride,
Lk 1:47 and my spirit *r* in God my Savior,
Ac 2:26 my heart is glad and my tongue *r*;
1Co 12:26 if one part is honored, every part *r*
13: 6 delight in evil but *r* with the truth.

REJOICING (JOY)
2Sa 6:12 to the City of David with *r*.
Ne 12:43 *r* because God had given them
Ps 30: 5 but *r* comes in the morning.
Lk 15: 7 in the same way there will be more *r*
Ac 5:41 *r* because they had been counted
2Co 6:10 sorrowful, yet always *r*; poor,

RELATIVES
Pr 19: 7 A poor man is shunned by all his *r*
Mk 6: 4 among his *r* and in his own house is
Lk 21:16 betrayed even by parents, brothers, *r*
1Ti 5: 8 If anyone does not provide for his *r*

RELEASE (RELEASED)
Isa 61: 1 and *r* from darkness,
Lk 4:18 to *r* the oppressed,

RELEASED (RELEASE)
Ro 7: 6 we have been *r* from the law
Rev 20: 7 Satan will be *r* from his prison

RELENTED (RELENTS)
Ex 32:14 the LORD *r* and did not bring
Ps 106: 45 and out of his great love he *r*.

RELENTS* (RELENTED)
Joel 2:13 and he *r* from sending calamity.
Jnh 4: 2 a God who *r* from sending calamity

RELIABLE (RELY)
Pr 22:21 teaching you true and *r* words,

Jn 8:26 But he who sent me is *r*,
2Ti 2: 2 witnesses entrust to *r* men who will

RELIANCE* (RELY)
Pr 25:19 is *r* on the unfaithful in times

RELIED (RELY)
2Ch 13:18 were victorious because they *r*
16: 8 Yet when you *r* on the LORD,
Ps 71: 6 From birth I have *r* on you;

RELIEF
Job 35: 9 they plead for *r* from the arm
Ps 94:13 you grant him *r* from days
143: 1 come to my *r*.
La 3:49 without *r*,
3:56 to my cry for *r*."
2Th 1: 7 and give *r* to you who are troubled,

RELIGION* (RELIGIOUS)
Ac 25:19 dispute with him about their own *r*
26: 5 to the strictest sect of our *r*,
1Ti 5: 4 all to put their *r* into practice
Jas 1:26 himself and his *r* is worthless.
1:27 *R* that God our Father accepts

RELIGIOUS (RELIGION)
Jas 1:26 If anyone considers himself *r*

RELY (RELIABLE RELIANCE RELIED)
Isa 50:10 and *r* on his God.
Eze 33:26 you then possess the land? You *r*
2Co 1: 9 this happened that we might not *r*
Gal 3:10 All who *r* on observing the law are
1Jn 4:16 and *r* on the love God has for us.

REMAIN (REMAINS)
Nu 33:55 allow to *r* will become barbs
Ps 102: 27 But you *r* the same,
Jn 1:32 from heaven as a dove and *r* on him
15: 4 *R* in me, and I will *r* in you.
15: 7 If you *r* in me and my words
15: 9 Now *r* in my love.
Ro 13: 8 Let no debt *r* outstanding,
1Co 13:13 And now these three *r*: faith,
2Ti 2:13 he will *r* faithful,
Heb 1:11 They will perish, but you *r*;
1Jn 2:27 just as it has taught you, *r* in him.

REMAINS (REMAIN)
Ps 146: 6 the LORD, who *r* faithful forever.
Heb 7: 3 Son of God he *r* a priest forever.

REMEDY
Isa 3: 7 "I have no *r*.

REMEMBER (REMEMBERED REMEMBERS REMEMBRANCE)
Ge 9:15 I will *r* my covenant between me
Ex 20: 8 "*R* the Sabbath day
33:13 *R* that this nation is your people."
Dt 5:15 *R* that you were slaves in Egypt
1Ch 16:12 *R* the wonders he has done,
Job 36:24 *R* to extol his work,
Ps 25: 6 *R*, O LORD, your great mercy
63: 6 On my bed I *r* you;
74: 2 *R* the people you purchased of old,
77:11 I will *r* the deeds of the LORD;
Ecc 12: 1 *R* your Creator
Isa 46: 8 "*R* this, fix it in mind,
Jer 31:34 and will *r* their sins no more."
Hab 3: 2 in wrath *r* mercy.
Lk 1:72 and to *r* his holy covenant,
Gal 2:10 we should continue to *r* the poor,
Php 1: 3 I thank my God every time I *r* you.
2Ti 2: 8 *R* Jesus Christ, raised
Heb 8:12 and will *r* their sins no more."

REMEMBERED (REMEMBER)
Ex 2:24 he *r* his covenant with Abraham,
3:15 am to be *r* from generation
Ps 98: 3 He has *r* his love
106: 45 for their sake he *r* his covenant
111: 4 He has caused his wonders to be *r*;
136: 23 to the One who *r* us
Isa 65:17 The former things will not be *r*,
Eze 18:22 offenses he has committed will be *r*
33:13 things he has done will be *r*;

REMEMBERS (REMEMBER)
Ps 103: 14 he *r* that we are dust.
111: 5 he *r* his covenant forever.
Isa 43:25 and *r* your sins no more.

REMEMBRANCE (REMEMBER)
Lk 22:19 given for you; do this in *r* of me."
1Co 11:24 which is for you; do this in *r* of me
11:25 whenever you drink it, in *r* of me."

REMIND
Jn 14:26 will *r* you of everything I have said
2Pe 1:12 I will always *r* you of these things,

REMNANT
Ezr 9: 8 has been gracious in leaving us a *r*
Isa 11:11 time to reclaim the *r* that is left
Jer 23: 3 "I myself will gather the *r*
Zec 8:12 inheritance to the *r* of this people.
Ro 11: 5 the present time there is a *r* chosen

REMOVED
Ps 30:11 you *r* my sackcloth and clothed me
103: 12 so far has he *r* our transgressions
Jn 20: 1 and saw that the stone had been *r*

REND
Joel 2:13 *R* your heart

RENEW (RENEWAL RENEWED RENEWING)
Ps 51:10 and *r* a steadfast spirit within me.
Isa 40:31 will *r* their strength.

RENEWAL (RENEW)
Isa 57:10 You found *r* of your strength,
Tit 3: 5 of rebirth and *r* by the Holy Spirit,

RENEWED (RENEW)
Ps 103: 5 that your youth is *r* like the eagle's.
2Co 4:16 yet inwardly we are being *r* day

RENEWING* (RENEW)
Ro 12: 2 transformed by the *r* of your mind.

RENOUNCE (RENOUNCED RENOUNCES)
Da 4:27 *R* your sins by doing what is right,

RENOUNCED (RENOUNCE)
2Co 4: 2 we have *r* secret and shameful

RENOUNCES (RENOUNCE)
Pr 28:13 confesses and *r* them finds

RENOWN*
Ge 6: 4 were the heroes of old, men of *r*.
Ps 102: 12 *r* endures through all generations.
135: 13 *r*, O LORD, through all
Isa 26: 8 your name and *r*
55:13 This will be for the LORD's *r*,
63:12 to gain for himself everlasting *r*,
Jer 13:11 to be my people for my *r* and praise
32:20 have gained the *r* that is still yours.
33: 9 Then this city will bring me *r*, joy,
49:25 the city of *r* not been abandoned,
Eze 26:17 How you are destroyed, O city of *r*,
Hos 12: 5 the LORD is his name of *r*!

REPAID (PAY)
Lk 6:34 to 'sinners,' expecting to be *r* in full
14:14 you will be *r* at the resurrection
Col 3:25 Anyone who does wrong will be *r*

REPAY (PAY)
Dt 7:10 But those who hate him he will *r*
32:35 It is mine to avenge; I will *r*.
Ru 2:12 May the LORD *r* you
Ps 103: 10 or *r* us according to our iniquities.
116: 12 How can I *r* the LORD
Jer 25:14 I will *r* them according
Ro 12:17 Do not *r* anyone evil for evil.
12:19 "It is mine to avenge; I will *r*,"
1Pe 3: 9 Do not *r* evil with evil

REPAYING (PAY)
2Ch 6:23 *r* the guilty by bringing
1Ti 5: 4 so *r* their parents and grandparents

REPEATED
Heb 10: 1 the same sacrifices *r* endlessly year

REPENT (REPENTANCE REPENTED REPENTS)
1Ki 8:47 *r* and plead with you in the land
Job 36:10 commands them to *r* of their evil.
42: 6 and *r* in dust and ashes."
Jer 15:19 "If you *r*, I will restore you
Eze 18:30 *R*! Turn away from all your
18:32 *R* and live! "Take up a lament
Mt 3: 2 "*R*, for the kingdom of heaven is
4:17 "*R*, for the kingdom of heaven is
Mk 6:12 and preached that people should *r*.
Lk 13: 3 unless you *r*, you too will all perish.
Ac 2:38 Peter replied, "*R* and be baptized,
3:19 *R*, then, and turn to God,
17:30 all people everywhere to *r*.
26:20 also, I preached that they should *r*
Rev 2: 5 *R* and do the things you did at first.

REPENTANCE (REPENT)
Isa 30:15 "In *r* and rest is your salvation,
Mt 3: 8 Produce fruit in keeping with *r*.
Mk 1: 4 a baptism of *r* for the forgiveness
Lk 3: 8 Produce fruit in keeping with *r*.
5:32 call the righteous, but sinners to *r*."
24:47 and *r* and forgiveness of sins will be
Ac 20:21 that they must turn to God in *r*
26:20 and prove their *r* by their deeds.
Ro 2: 4 kindness leads you toward *r*?
2Co 7:10 Godly sorrow brings *r* that leads
2Pe 3: 9 but everyone to come to *r*.

REPENTED (REPENT)
Mt 11:21 they would have *r* long ago

REPENTS (REPENT)
Lk 15: 7 in heaven over one sinner who *r*
15:10 of God over one sinner who *r*."
17: 3 rebuke him, and if he *r*, forgive him

REPORTS
Ex 23: 1 "Do not spread false *r*.

REPOSES*
Pr 14:33 Wisdom *r* in the heart

REPRESENTATION*
Heb 1: 3 and the exact *r* of his being,

REPROACH
Job 27: 6 my conscience will not *r* me
Isa 51: 7 Do not fear the *r* of men
1Ti 3: 2 Now the overseer must be above *r*,

REPUTATION
1Ti 3: 7 also have a good *r* with outsiders,

REQUESTS
Ps 20: 5 May the LORD grant all your *r*.
Php 4: 6 with thanksgiving, present your *r*

REQUIRE (REQUIRED REQUIRES)
Mic 6: 8 And what does the LORD *r* of you

REQUIRED (REQUIRE)
1Co 4: 2 it is *r* that those who have been

REQUIRES (REQUIRE)
1Ki 2: 3 what the LORD your God *r*:
Heb 9:22 the law *r* that nearly everything be

RESCUE (RESCUED RESCUES)
Ps 22: 8 let the LORD *r* him.
31: 2 come quickly to my *r*;
69:14 *R* me from the mire,
91:14 says the LORD, "I will *r* him;
143: 9 *R* me from my enemies, O LORD,
Da 6:20 been able to *r* you from the lions?"
Ro 7:24 Who will *r* me from this body
Gal 1: 4 himself for our sins to *r* us
2Pe 2: 9 how to *r* godly men from trials

RESCUED (RESCUE)
Ps 18:17 He *r* me from my powerful enemy,
Pr 11: 8 The righteous man is *r*
Col 1:13 For he has *r* us from the dominion

RESCUES (RESCUE)
Da 6:27 He *r* and he saves;
1Th 1:10 who *r* us from the coming wrath.

RESENT* (RESENTFUL RESENTS)
Pr 3:11 and do not *r* his rebuke,

RESENTFUL* (RESENT)
2Ti 2:24 to everyone, able to teach, not *r*.

RESENTS* (RESENT)
Pr 15:12 A mocker *r* correction;

RESERVE (RESERVED)
1Ki 19:18 Yet I *r* seven thousand in Israel—

RESERVED (RESERVE)
Ro 11: 4 "I have *r* for myself seven

RESIST (RESISTED RESISTS)
Da 11:32 know their God will firmly *r* him.
Mt 5:39 I tell you, Do not *r* an evil person.
Lk 21:15 of your adversaries will be able to *r*
Jas 4: 7 *R* the devil, and he will flee
1Pe 5: 9 *R* him, standing firm in the faith,

RESISTED (RESIST)
Job 9: 4 Who has *r* him and come out

RESISTS* (RESIST)
Ro 9:19 For who *r* his will?" But who are

RESOLVED
Ps 17: 3 I have *r* that my mouth will not sin.
Da 1: 8 But Daniel *r* not to defile himself
1Co 2: 2 For I *r* to know nothing while I was

RESOUNDING*
Ps 150: 5 praise him with *r* cymbals.
1Co 13: 1 I am only a *r* gong or a clanging

RESPECT (RESPECTABLE RESPECTED RESPECTS)
Lev 19: 3 " 'Each of you must *r* his mother
19:32 show *r* for the elderly and revere
Pr 11:16 A kindhearted woman gains *r*,
Mal 1: 6 where is the *r* due me?" says
Eph 5:33 and the wife must *r* her husband.
6: 5 obey your earthly masters with *r*
1Th 4:12 so that your daily life may win the *r*
5:12 to *r* those who work hard
1Ti 3: 4 children obey him with proper *r*.
3: 8 are to be men worthy of *r*, sincere,
3:11 are to be women worthy of *r*,
6: 1 their masters worthy of full *r*,
Tit 2: 2 worthy of *r*, self-controlled,
1Pe 2:17 Show proper *r* to everyone:
3: 7 them with *r* as the weaker partner
3:16 But do this with gentleness and *r*,

RESPECTABLE* (RESPECT)
1Ti 3: 2 self-controlled, *r*, hospitable,

RESPECTED (RESPECT)
Pr 31:23 Her husband is *r* at the city gate,

RESPECTS (RESPECT)
Pr 13:13 he who *r* a command is rewarded.

RESPLENDENT*
Ps 76: 4 You are *r* with light,
132: 18 but the crown on his head will be *r*

RESPOND
Ps 102: 17 He will *r* to the prayer
Hos 2:21 "I will *r* to the skies,

RESPONSIBILITY (RESPONSIBLE)
Ac 18: 6 your own heads! I am clear of my *r*.

RESPONSIBLE (RESPONSIBILITY)
Nu 1:53 The Levites are to be *r* for the care
1Co 7:24 Brothers, each man, as *r* to God,

REST (RESTED RESTS SABBATH-REST)
Ex 31:15 the seventh day is a Sabbath of *r*,
33:14 go with you, and I will give you *r*."
Lev 25: 5 The land is to have a year of *r*.
Dt 31:16 going to *r* with your fathers,
Jos 14:15 Then the land had *r* from war.
21:44 The LORD gave them *r*
1Ki 5: 4 The LORD my god has given me *r*
1Ch 22: 9 who will be a man of peace and *r*,
Job 3:17 and there the weary are at *r*.
Ps 16: 9 my body also will *r* secure,
33:22 May your unfailing love *r* upon us,
62: 1 My soul finds *r* in God alone;
62: 5 Find *r*, O my soul, in God alone;
90:17 of the Lord our God *r* upon us;
91: 1 will *r* in the shadow
95:11 "They shall never enter my *r*."
Pr 6:10 a little folding of the hands to *r*—
Isa 11: 2 Spirit of the LORD will *r* on him—
11:10 and his place of *r* will be glorious.
30:15 "In repentance and *r* is your
32:18 in undisturbed places of *r*.
57:20 which cannot *r*,
Jer 6:16 and you will find *r* for your souls.
47: 6 'how long till you *r*?
Mt 11:28 and burdened, and I will give you *r*.
2Co 12: 9 so that Christ's power may *r* on me
Heb 3:11 'They shall never enter my *r*.' "
4: 3 'They shall never enter my *r*.' "
4:10 for anyone who enters God's *r*
Rev 14:13 "they will *r* from their labor,

RESTED (REST)
Ge 2: 2 so on the seventh day he *r*
Heb 4: 4 "And on the seventh day God *r*

RESTITUTION
Ex 22: 3 "A thief must certainly make *r*,
Lev 6: 5 He must make *r* in full, add a fifth
Nu 5: 8 the *r* belongs to the LORD

RESTORE (RESTORES)
Ps 51:12 *R* to me the joy of your salvation
80: 3 *R* us, O God;
126: 4 *R* our fortunes, O LORD,
Jer 31:18 *R* me, and I will return,
La 5:21 *R* us to yourself, O LORD,
Da 9:25 From the issuing of the decree to *r*
Na 2: 2 The LORD will *r* the splendor
Gal 6: 1 are spiritual should *r* him gently.
1Pe 5:10 will himself *r* you and make you

RESTORES (RESTORE)
Ps 23: 3 he *r* my soul.

RESTRAINED (RESTRAINT)
Ps 78:38 Time after time he *r* his anger

RESTRAINING (RESTRAINT)
Pr 27:16 *r* her is like *r* the wind
Col 2:23 value in *r* sensual indulgence.

RESTRAINT (RESTRAINED RESTRAINING)
Pr 17:27 of knowledge uses words with *r*,
23: 4 have the wisdom to show *r*.
29:18 no revelation, the people cast off *r*;

RESTS (REST)
Dt 33:12 and the one the LORD loves *r*
Pr 19:23 one *r* content, untouched
Lk 2:14 to men on whom his favor *r*."

RESULT
Lk 21:13 This will *r* in your being witnesses
Ro 6:22 to holiness, and the *r* is eternal life.
11:31 as a *r* of God's mercy to you.
2Co 3: 3 from Christ, the *r* of our ministry,
2Th 1: 5 as a *r* you will be counted worthy
1Pe 1: 7 may be proved genuine and may *r*

RESURRECTION*
Mt 22:23 who say there is no *r*, came to him
22:28 at the *r*, whose wife will she be
22:30 At the *r* people will neither marry
22:31 But about the *r* of the dead—
27:53 and after Jesus' *r* they went
Mk 12:18 who say there is no *r*, came to him
12:23 At the *r* whose wife will she be,
Lk 14:14 repaid at the *r* of the righteous."
20:27 who say there is no *r*, came to Jesus
20:33 at the *r* whose wife will she be,
20:35 in the *r* from the dead will neither
20:36 since they are children of the *r*.
Jn 11:24 again in the *r* at the last day."
11:25 Jesus said to her, "I am the *r*
Ac 1:22 become a witness with us of his *r*."
2:31 he spoke of the *r* of the Christ,
4: 2 in Jesus the *r* of the dead.
4:33 to testify to the *r* of the Lord Jesus,
17:18 good news about Jesus and the *r*.
17:32 When they heard about the *r*
23: 6 of my hope in the *r* of the dead."
23: 8 Sadducees say that there is no *r*,
24:15 that there will be a *r*
24:21 'It is concerning the *r*
Ro 1: 4 Son of God by his *r* from the dead:
6: 5 also be united with him in his *r*.
1Co 15:12 some of you say that there is no *r*
15:13 If there is no *r* of the dead,
15:21 the *r* of the dead comes
15:29 if there is no *r*, what will those do
15:42 So will it be with the *r* of the dead.
Php 3:10 power of his *r* and the fellowship
3:11 to attain to the *r* from the dead.
2Ti 2:18 say that the *r* has already taken
Heb 6: 2 on of hands, the *r* of the dead,
11:35 so that they might gain a better *r*.
1Pe 1: 3 hope through the *r* of Jesus Christ
3:21 It saves you by the *r* of Jesus Christ
Rev 20: 5 This is the first *r*.
20: 6 those who have part in the first *r*.

RETALIATE*
1Pe 2:23 he did not *r*; when he suffered,

RETRIBUTION
Ps 69:22 may it become *r* and a trap.
Jer 51:56 For the LORD is a God of *r*;
Ro 11: 9 a stumbling block and a *r* for them.

RETURN (RETURNED RETURNS)
Ge 3:19 and to dust you will *r*."
2Sa 12:23 go to him, but he will not *r* to me."
2Ch 30: 9 If you *r* to the LORD, then your
Ne 1: 9 but if you *r* to me and obey my
Job 10:21 joy before I go to the place of no *r*,
16:22 before I go on the journey of no *r*.
22:23 If you *r* to the Almighty, you will
Ps 80:14 *R* to us, O God Almighty!
126: 6 will *r* with songs of joy,
Isa 10:21 A remnant will *r*, a remnant
35:10 the ransomed of the LORD will *r*.
55:11 It will not *r* to me empty,
Jer 24: 7 for they will *r* to me
31: 8 a great throng will *r*.
La 3:40 and let us *r* to the LORD.
Hos 6: 1 "Come, let us *r* to the LORD.
12: 6 But you must *r* to your God;
14: 1 *R*, O Israel, to the LORD your
Joel 2:12 "*r* to me with all your heart,
Zec 1: 3 '*R* to me,' declares the LORD
10: 9 and they will *r*.

RETURNED (RETURN)
Ps 35:13 When my prayers *r*
Am 4: 6 yet you have not *r* to me,"
1Pe 2:25 now you have *r* to the Shepherd

RETURNS (RETURN)
Pr 3:14 and yields better *r* than gold.
Isa 52: 8 When the LORD *r* to Zion,
Mt 24:46 finds him doing so when he *r*.

REUBEN
Firstborn of Jacob by Leah (Ge 29:32; 46:8; 1Ch 2:1). Attempted to rescue Joseph (Ge 37:21-30). Lost birthright for sleeping with Bilhah (Ge 35:22; 49:4). Tribe of blessed (Ge 49:3-4; Dt 33:6), numbered (Nu 1:21; 26:7), allotted land east of Jordan (Nu 32; 34:14; Jos 13:15), west (Eze 48:6), failed to help Deborah (Jdg 5:15-16), supported David (1Ch 12:37), 12,000 from (Rev 7:5).

REVEAL (REVEALED REVEALS REVELATION REVELATIONS)
Mt 11:27 to whom the Son chooses to *r* him.
Gal 1:16 was pleased to *r* his Son in me

REVEALED (REVEAL)
Dt 29:29 but the things *r* belong to us
Isa 40: 5 the glory of the LORD will be *r*,
43:12 I have *r* and saved and proclaimed
53: 1 the arm of the LORD been *r*?
65: 1 I *r* myself to those who did not ask
Mt 11:25 and *r* them to little children.
Jn 12:38 the arm of the Lord been *r*?"
17: 6 "I have *r* you to those whom you
Ro 1:17 a righteousness from God is *r*,
8:18 with the glory that will be *r* in us.
10:20 I *r* myself to those who did not ask
16:26 but now *r* and made known
1Co 2:10 but God has *r* it to us by his Spirit.
2Th 1: 7 happen when the Lord Jesus is *r*
2: 3 and the man of lawlessness is *r*,
1Pe 1: 7 and honor when Jesus Christ is *r*.
1:20 but was *r* in these last times
4:13 overjoyed when his glory is *r*.

REVEALS* (REVEAL)
Nu 23: 3 Whatever he *r* to me I will tell you
Job 12:22 He *r* the deep things of darkness
Da 2:22 He *r* deep and hidden things;
2:28 a God in heaven who *r* mysteries.
Am 4:13 and *r* his thoughts to man,

REVELATION* (REVEAL)
2Sa 7:17 David all the words of this entire *r*.
1Ch 17:15 David all the words of this entire *r*.
Pr 29:18 Where there is no *r*, the people cast
Da 10: 1 a *r* was given to Daniel (who was
Hab 2: 2 "Write down the *r*
2: 3 For the *r* awaits an appointed time;
Lk 2:32 a light for *r* to the Gentiles
Ro 16:25 according to the *r*
1Co 14: 6 I bring you some *r* or knowledge
14:26 a *r*, a tongue or an interpretation.
14:30 And if a *r* comes to someone who is
Gal 1:12 I received it by *r* from Jesus Christ.
2: 2 I went in response to a *r*
Eph 1:17 you the Spirit of wisdom and *r*,
3: 3 mystery made known to me by *r*,
Rev 1: 1 *r* of Jesus Christ, which God gave

REVELATIONS* (REVEAL)
2Co 12: 1 on to visions and *r* from the Lord.
12: 7 of these surpassingly great *r*,

REVELED* (REVELRY)
Ne 9:25 they *r* in your great goodness.

REVELRY (REVELED)
Ex 32: 6 drink and got up to indulge in *r*.
1Co 10: 7 and got up to indulge in pagan *r*."

REVENGE (VENGEANCE)
Lev 19:18 " 'Do not seek *r* or bear a grudge
Ro 12:19 Do not take *r*, my friends,

REVERE* (REVERENCE REVERENT REVERING)
Lev 19:32 for the elderly and *r* your God.
Dt 4:10 so that they may learn to *r* me
13: 4 must follow, and him you must *r*.
14:23 to *r* the LORD your God always.
17:19 learn to *r* the LORD his God
28:58 and do not *r* this glorious
Job 37:24 Therefore, men *r* him,
Ps 22:23 *R* him, all you descendants
33: 8 let all the people of the world *r* him
102: 15 of the earth will *r* your glory.
Ecc 3:14 God does it so that men will *r* him.
Isa 25: 3 cities of ruthless nations will *r* you.
59:19 of the sun, they will *r* his glory.
63:17 hearts so we do not *r* you?
Jer 10: 7 Who should not *r* you,
Hos 10: 3 because we did not *r* the LORD.
Mal 4: 2 But for you who *r* my name,

REVERENCE (REVERE)
Lev 19:30 and have *r* for my sanctuary.
Ne 5:15 of *r* for God I did not act like that.
Ps 5: 7 in *r* will I bow down
Da 6:26 people must fear and *r* the God
2Co 7: 1 perfecting holiness out of *r* for God
Eph 5:21 to one another out of *r* for Christ.
Col 3:22 of heart and *r* for the Lord.
1Pe 3: 2 when they see the purity and *r*
Rev 11:18 and those who *r* your name,

REVERENT* (REVERE)
Ecc 8:12 with God-fearing men, who are *r*
Tit 2: 3 women to be *r* in the way they live,
Heb 5: 7 because of his *r* submission.
1Pe 1:17 as strangers here in *r* fear.

REVERING* (REVERE)
Dt 8: 6 walking in his ways and *r* him.
Ne 1:11 who delight in *r* your name.

REVERSE*
Isa 43:13 When I act, who can *r* it?"

REVIVE* (REVIVING)
Ps 80:18 *r* us, and we will call on your name.
85: 6 Will you not *r* us again,
Isa 57:15 and to *r* the heart of the contrite.
57:15 to *r* the spirit of the lowly
Hos 6: 2 After two days he will *r* us;

REVIVING* (REVIVE)
Ps 19: 7 *r* the soul.

REVOKED
Isa 45:23 a word that will not be *r*:

REWARD (REWARDED REWARDING REWARDS)
Ge 15: 1 your very great *r*."
1Sa 24:19 May the LORD *r* you well
Ps 19:11 in keeping them there is great *r*.
62:12 Surely you will *r* each person
127: 3 children a *r* from him.
Pr 9:12 are wise, your wisdom will *r* you;
11:18 sows righteousness reaps a sure *r*.
13:21 prosperity is the *r* of the righteous.
19:17 he will *r* him for what he has done.
25:22 and the LORD will *r* you.
31:31 Give her the *r* she has earned,
Isa 40:10 See, his *r* is with him,
49: 4 and my *r* is with my God."
61: 8 In my faithfulness I will *r* them
62:11 See, his *r* is with him,
Jer 17:10 to *r* a man according to his conduct
32:19 you *r* everyone according
Mt 5:12 because great is your *r* in heaven,
6: 1 you will have no *r*
6: 5 they have received their *r* in full.
10:41 a prophet will receive a prophet's *r*,
16:27 and then he will *r* each person
Lk 6:23 because great is your *r* in heaven.
6:35 Then your *r* will be great,
1Co 3:14 built survives, he will receive his *r*.
Eph 6: 8 know that the Lord will *r* everyone
Col 3:24 an inheritance from the Lord as a *r*.
Heb 11:26 he was looking ahead to his *r*.
Rev 22:12 I am coming soon! My *r* is with me

REWARDED (REWARD)
Ru 2:12 May you be richly *r* by the LORD,
2Sa 22:21 of my hands he has *r* me.
2Ch 15: 7 for your work will be *r*."
Ps 18:24 The LORD has *r* me according
Pr 13:13 he who respects a command is *r*.
14:14 and the good man *r* for his.
Jer 31:16 for your work will be *r*,"
1Co 3: 8 and each will be *r* according
Heb 10:35 your confidence; it will be richly *r*.
2Jn : 8 but that you may be *r* fully.

REWARDING* (REWARD)
Rev 11:18 for *r* your servants the prophets

REWARDS (REWARD)
1Sa 26:23 The LORD *r* every man
Pr 12:14 the work of his hands *r* him.
Heb 11: 6 that he *r* those who earnestly seek

RIBS
Ge 2:21 he took one of the man's *r*

RICH (RICHES RICHEST)
Job 34:19 does not favor the *r* over the poor,
Ps 49:16 overawed when a man grows *r*,
145: 8 slow to anger and *r* in love.
Pr 21:17 loves wine and oil will never be *r*.
22: 2 *R* and poor have this in common:
23: 4 Do not wear yourself out to get *r*;
28: 6 than a *r* man whose ways are
Pr 28:20 to get *r* will not go unpunished.
28:22 A stingy man is eager to get *r*
Ecc 5:12 but the abundance of a *r* man
Isa 33: 6 a *r* store of salvation and wisdom
53: 9 and with the *r* in his death,
Jer 9:23 or the *r* man boast of his riches,
Zec 3: 4 and I will put *r* garments on you."
Mt 19:23 it is hard for a *r* man
Lk 1:53 but has sent the *r* away empty.
6:24 "But woe to you who are *r*,
12:21 for himself but is not *r* toward God
16: 1 "There was a *r* man whose
21: 1 Jesus saw the *r* putting their gifts
2Co 6:10 yet making many *r*; having nothing
8: 2 poverty welled up in *r* generosity.
8: 9 he was *r*, yet for your sakes he
9:11 You will be made *r* in every way
Eph 2: 4 love for us, God, who is *r* in mercy,
1Ti 6: 9 want to get *r* fall into temptation
6:17 Command those who are *r*
6:18 to do good, to be *r* in good deeds,
Jas 1:10 the one who is *r* should take pride
2: 5 the eyes of the world to be *r* in faith
5: 1 you *r* people, weep and wail
Rev 2: 9 and your poverty—yet you are *r*!
3:18 you can become *r*; and white

RICHES (RICH)
Job 36:18 that no one entices you by *r*;
Ps 49: 6 and boast of their great *r*?
49:12 despite his *r*, does not endure;
62:10 though your *r* increase,
119: 14 as one rejoices in great *r*.
Pr 3:16 in her left hand are *r* and honor.
11:28 Whoever trusts in his *r* will fall,
22: 1 is more desirable than great *r*;
27:24 for *r* do not endure forever,
30: 8 give me neither poverty nor *r*,
Isa 10: 3 Where will you leave your *r*?
60: 5 to you the *r* of the nations will
Jer 9:23 or the rich man boast of his *r*,
Lk 8:14 *r* and pleasures, and they do not
Ro 9:23 to make the *r* of his glory known
11:33 the depth of the *r* of the wisdom
Eph 2: 7 he might show the incomparable *r*
3: 8 to the Gentiles the unsearchable *r*
Col 1:27 among the Gentiles the glorious *r*
2: 2 so that they may have the full *r*

RICHEST (RICH)
Isa 55: 2 and your soul will delight in the *r*

RID
Ge 21:10 "Get *r* of that slave woman
1Co 5: 7 Get *r* of the old yeast that you may
Gal 4:30 "Get *r* of the slave woman

RIDE (RIDER RIDING)
Ps 45: 4 In your majesty *r* forth victoriously

RIDER (RIDE)
Rev 6: 2 was a white horse! Its *r* held a bow,
19:11 whose *r* is called Faithful and True.

RIDING (RIDE)
Zec 9: 9 gentle and *r* on a donkey,
Mt 21: 5 gentle and *r* on a donkey,

RIGGING
Isa 33:23 Your *r* hangs loose:

RIGHT (RIGHTS)
Ge 4: 7 But if you do not do what is *r*,
18:19 of the LORD by doing what is *r*
18:25 the Judge of all the earth do *r*?"
48:13 on his left toward Israel's *r* hand,
Ex 15: 6 Your *r* hand, O LORD,
15:26 and do what is *r* in his eyes,
Dt 5:32 do not turn aside to the *r*
6:18 Do what is *r* and good
13:18 and doing what is *r* in his eyes.
Jos 1: 7 do not turn from it to the *r*
1Sa 12:23 you the way that is good and *r*.
1Ki 3: 9 to distinguish between *r* and wrong
15: 5 For David had done what was *r*
2Ki 7: 9 to each other, "We're not doing *r*.
Ne 9:13 and laws that are just and *r*,
Ps 16: 8 Because he is at my *r* hand,
16:11 eternal pleasures at your *r* hand.
17: 7 you who save by your *r* hand
18:35 and your *r* hand sustains me;
19: 8 The precepts of the LORD are *r*,
25: 9 He guides the humble in what is *r*
33: 4 For the word of the LORD is *r*
44: 3 it was your *r* hand, your arm,
45: 4 let your *r* hand display awesome
51: 4 so that you are proved *r*
63: 8 your *r* hand upholds me.
73:23 you hold me by my *r* hand.
91: 7 ten thousand at your *r* hand,
Ps 98: 1 his *r* hand and his holy arm
106: 3 who constantly do what is *r*.
110: 1 "Sit at my *r* hand
118: 15 LORD's *r* hand has done mighty
119:144 Your statutes are forever *r*;
137: 5 may my *r* hand forget its skill.
139: 10 your *r* hand will hold me fast."
Pr 1: 3 doing what is *r* and just and fair;
4:27 Do not swerve to the *r* or the left;
14:12 There is a way that seems *r*
18:17 The first to present his case seems *r*
Ecc 7:20 who does what is *r* and never sins.
SS 1: 4 How *r* they are to adore you!
Isa 1:17 learn to do *r*!
7:15 reject the wrong and choose the *r*.
30:10 us no more visions of what is *r*!
30:21 Whether you turn to the *r*
41:10 you with my righteous *r* hand.
41:13 who takes hold of your *r* hand
48:13 my *r* hand spread out the heavens;
64: 5 to the help of those who gladly do *r*
Jer 23: 5 and do what is just and *r* in the land
Eze 18: 5 who does what is just and *r*.
18:21 and does what is just and *r*,
33:14 and does what is just and *r*—
Hos 14: 9 The ways of the LORD are *r*;
Mt 5:29 If your *r* eye causes you to sin,
6: 3 know what your *r* hand is doing,
22:44 "Sit at my *r* hand
25:33 He will put the sheep on his *r*
Jn 1:12 he gave the *r* to become children
Ac 2:34 "Sit at my *r* hand
7:55 Jesus standing at the *r* hand of God
Ro 3: 4 "So that you may be proved *r*
8:34 is at the *r* hand of God and is
9:21 Does not the potter have the *r*
12:17 careful to do what is *r* in the eyes
1Co 9: 4 Don't we have the *r* to food
2Co 8:21 we are taking pains to do what is *r*,
Eph 1:20 and seated him at his *r* hand
6: 1 parents in the Lord, for this is *r*.
Php 4: 8 whatever is *r*, whatever is pure,
2Th 3:13 never tire of doing what is *r*.
Heb 1: 3 down at the *r* hand of the Majesty
Jas 2: 8 as yourself," you are doing *r*.
1Pe 3:14 if you should suffer for what is *r*,
1Jn 2:29 who does what is *r* has been born
Rev 2: 7 I will give the *r* to eat from the tree
3:21 I will give the *r* to sit with me
22:11 let him who does *r* continue to do *r*

RIGHTEOUS (RIGHTEOUSLY RIGHTEOUSNESS)
Ge 6: 9 Noah was a *r* man, blameless
18:23 "Will you sweep away the *r*
Nu 23:10 Let me die the death of the *r*,
Ne 9: 8 your promise because you are *r*.
Job 36: 7 He does not take his eyes off the *r*;
Ps 1: 5 nor sinners in the assembly of the *r*.
5:12 O LORD, you bless the *r*;
11: 7 For the LORD is *r*,
15: 2 and who does what is *r*,
34:15 The eyes of the LORD are on the *r*
37:16 Better the little that the *r* have
37:21 but the *r* give generously;
37:25 yet I have never seen the *r* forsaken
37:30 of the *r* man utters wisdom,
55:22 he will never let the *r* fall.
64:10 Let the *r* rejoice in the LORD
68: 3 But may the *r* be glad
112: 4 compassionate and *r* man.
118: 20 through which the *r* may enter.
119: 7 as I learn your *r* laws.
119:137 *R* are you, O LORD,
140: 13 Surely the *r* will praise your name
143: 2 for no one living is *r* before you.
145: 17 The LORD is *r* in all his ways
Pr 3:33 but he blesses the home of the *r*.
4:18 of the *r* is like the first gleam
10: 7 of the *r* will be a blessing,
10:11 The mouth of the *r* is a fountain
10:16 The wages of the *r* bring them life,
10:20 The tongue of the *r* is choice silver,
10:24 what the *r* desire will be granted.
10:28 The prospect of the *r* is joy,
10:32 of the *r* know what is fitting,
11:23 The desire of the *r* ends only
11:30 The fruit of the *r* is a tree of life,
12:10 A *r* man cares for the needs
12:21 No harm befalls the *r*,
13: 9 The light of the *r* shines brightly,
15:28 of the *r* weighs its answers,
15:29 but he hears the prayer of the *r*.
16:31 it is attained by a *r* life.
18:10 the *r* run to it and are safe.
20: 7 The *r* man leads a blameless life;
21:15 justice is done, it brings joy to the *r*
23:24 The father of a *r* man has great joy;
28: 1 but the *r* are as bold as a lion.

Pr 29: 6 but a *r* one can sing and be glad.
29: 7 The *r* care about justice
29:27 The *r* detest the dishonest;
Ecc 7:20 There is not a *r* man on earth
Isa 26: 7 The path of the *r* is level;
41:10 you with my *r* right hand.
45:21 a *r* God and a Savior;
53:11 his knowledge my *r* servant will
64: 6 and all our *r* acts are like filthy rags
Jer 23: 5 up to David a *r* Branch,
Eze 3:20 when a *r* man turns
18: 5 "Suppose there is a *r* man
18:20 of the *r* man will be credited
33:12 The *r* man, if he sins, will not be
Da 9:18 requests of you because we are *r*,
Hab 2: 4 but the *r* will live by his faith—
Zec 9: 9 *r* and having salvation,
Mal 3:18 see the distinction between the *r*
Mt 5:45 rain on the *r* and the unrighteous.
9:13 For I have not come to call the *r*,
10:41 and anyone who receives a *r* man
13:43 Then the *r* will shine like the sun
13:49 and separate the wicked from the *r*
25:37 "Then the *r* will answer him, 'Lord,
25:46 to eternal punishment, but the *r*
Ac 24:15 will be a resurrection of both the *r*
Ro 1:17 as it is written: "The *r* will live
2: 5 when his *r* judgment will be
2:13 the law who will be declared *r*.
3:10 "There is no one *r*, not even one;
3:20 Therefore no one will be declared *r*
5:19 one man the many will be made *r*.
Gal 3:11 because, "The *r* will live by faith."
1Ti 1: 9 that law is made not for the *r*
2Ti 4: 8 which the Lord, the *r* Judge,
Tit 3: 5 because of *r* things we had done,
Heb 10:38 But my *r* one will live by faith.
Jas 5:16 The prayer of a *r* man is powerful
1Pe 3:12 the eyes of the Lord are on the *r*
3:18 the *r* for the unrighteous,
4:18 "If it is hard for the *r* to be saved,
1Jn 2: 1 defense—Jesus Christ, the *R* One.
3: 7 does what is right is *r*, just as he is *r*.
Rev 19: 8 stands for the *r* acts of the saints.)

RIGHTEOUSLY* (RIGHTEOUS)
Ps 9: 4 on your throne, judging *r*.
Isa 33:15 He who walks *r*
Jer 11:20 LORD Almighty, you who judge *r*

RIGHTEOUSNESS (RIGHTEOUS)
Ge 15: 6 and he credited it to him as *r*.
Dt 9: 4 of this land because of my *r*."
1Sa 26:23 LORD rewards every man for his *r*
1Ki 10: 9 to maintain justice and *r*."
Job 37:23 great *r*, he does not oppress.
Ps 7:17 to the LORD because of his *r*
9: 8 He will judge the world in *r*;
17:15 And I—in *r* I will see your face;
23: 3 He guides me in paths of *r*
33: 5 The LORD loves *r* and justice;
35:28 My tongue will speak of your *r*
36: 6 Your *r* is like the mighty
37: 6 He will make your *r* shine like
40: 9 I proclaim *r* in the great assembly;
45: 4 in behalf of truth, humility and *r*;
45: 7 You love *r* and hate wickedness;
48:10 your right hand is filled with *r*.
65: 5 us with awesome deeds of *r*,
71: 2 Rescue me and deliver me in your *r*
71:15 My mouth will tell of your *r*,
71:19 Your *r* reaches to the skies, O God,
85:10 *r* and peace kiss each other.
89:14 *R* and justice are the foundation
96:13 He will judge the world in *r*
98: 9 He will judge the world in *r*
103: 6 The LORD works *r*
103: 17 his *r* with their children's children
106: 31 This was credited to him as *r*
111: 3 and his *r* endures forever.
118: 19 Open for me the gates of *r*;
132: 9 May your priests be clothed with *r*;
145: 7 and joyfully sing of your *r*.
Pr 11: 5 *r* of the blameless makes a straight
11:18 he who sows *r* reaps a sure reward.
13: 6 *R* guards the man of integrity,
14:34 *R* exalts a nation,
16: 8 Better a little with *r*
16:12 a throne is established through *r*.
21:21 He who pursues *r* and love
Isa 5:16 will show himself holy by his *r*.
9: 7 it with justice and *r*
11: 4 but with *r* he will judge the needy,
16: 5 and speeds the cause of *r*.
26: 9 the people of the world learn *r*.
32:17 The fruit of *r* will be peace;
42: 6 "I, the LORD, have called you in *r*;
42:21 the LORD for the sake of his *r*
45: 8 "You heavens above, rain down *r*;
Isa 51: 1 "Listen to me, you who pursue *r*
51: 6 my *r* will never fail.
51: 8 But my *r* will last forever,
58: 8 then your *r* will go before you,
59:17 He put on *r* as his breastplate,
61:10 and arrayed me in a robe of *r*,
63: 1 "It is I, speaking in *r*,
Jer 9:24 justice and *r* on earth,
23: 6 The LORD Our *R*.
Eze 3:20 a righteous man turns from his *r*
14:20 save only themselves by their *r*.
18:20 The *r* of the righteous man will be
33:12 *r* of the righteous man will not save
Da 9:24 to bring in everlasting *r*,
12: 3 and those who lead many to *r*,
Hos 10:12 Sow for yourselves *r*,
Am 5:24 *r* like a never-failing stream!
Mic 7: 9 I will see his *r*.
Zep 2: 3 Seek *r*, seek humility;
Mal 4: 2 the sun of *r* will rise with healing
Mt 5: 6 those who hunger and thirst for *r*,
5:10 who are persecuted because of *r*,
5:20 unless your *r* surpasses that
6: 1 to do your 'acts of *r*' before men,
6:33 But seek first his kingdom and his *r*
Jn 16: 8 world of guilt in regard to sin and *r*
Ac 24:25 Paul discoursed on *r*, self-control
Ro 1:17 For in the gospel a *r* from God is
3: 5 brings out God's *r* more clearly,
3:22 This *r* from God comes
4: 3 and it was credited to him as *r*."
4: 5 wicked, his faith is credited as *r*.
4: 6 man to whom God credits *r* apart
4: 9 faith was credited to him as *r*.
4:13 through the *r* that comes by faith.
4:22 why "it was credited to him as *r*."
5:18 of *r* was justification that brings life
6:13 body to him as instruments of *r*.
6:16 or to obedience, which leads to *r*?
6:18 and have become slaves to *r*.
6:19 in slavery to *r* leading to holiness.
8:10 yet your spirit is alive because of *r*.
9:30 did not pursue *r*, have obtained it,
10: 3 they did not know the *r* that comes
14:17 but of *r*, peace and joy
1Co 1:30 our *r*, holiness and redemption.
2Co 3: 9 is the ministry that brings *r*!
5:21 that in him we might become the *r*
6: 7 with weapons of *r* in the right hand
6:14 For what do *r* and wickedness have
9: 9 his *r* endures forever."
Gal 2:21 for if *r* could be gained
3: 6 and it was credited to him as *r*."
3:21 then *r* would certainly have come
Eph 4:24 created to be like God in true *r*
5: 9 *r* and truth) and find out what
6:14 with the breastplate of *r* in place,
Php 1:11 filled with the fruit of *r* that comes
3: 6 as for legalistic *r*, faultless.
3: 9 not having a *r* of my own that
1Ti 6:11 and pursue *r*, godliness, faith, love,
2Ti 2:22 and pursue *r*, faith, love and peace,
3:16 correcting and training in *r*,
4: 8 is in store for me the crown of *r*,
Heb 1: 8 and *r* will be the scepter
5:13 with the teaching about *r*.
7: 2 his name means "king of *r*";
11: 7 became heir of the *r* that comes
12:11 it produces a harvest of *r*
Jas 2:23 and it was credited to him as *r*,"
3:18 sow in peace raise a harvest of *r*.
1Pe 2:24 die to sins and live for *r*;
2Pe 2:21 not to have known the way of *r*,
3:13 and a new earth, the home of *r*.

RIGHTS (RIGHT)
Ps 82: 3 maintain the *r* of the poor
Pr 31: 8 for the *r* of all who are destitute.
Isa 10: 2 to deprive the poor of their *r*
La 3:35 to deny a man his *r*
Gal 4: 5 that we might receive the full *r*

RING
Pr 11:22 Like a gold *r* in a pig's snout
Lk 15:22 Put a *r* on his finger and sandals

RIOTS
2Co 6: 5 imprisonments and *r*; in hard work,

RIPE
Joel 3:13 for the harvest is *r*.
Am 8: 1 showed me: a basket of *r* fruit.
Jn 4:35 at the fields! They are *r* for harvest.
Rev 14:15 for the harvest of the earth is *r*."

RISE (RAISE RAISED RISEN ROSE)
Lev 19:32 " '*R* in the presence of the aged,
Nu 24:17 a scepter will *r* out of Israel.
Isa 26:19 their bodies will *r*.
Mal 4: 2 of righteousness will *r* with healing
Mt 27:63 'After three days I will *r* again.'
Mk 8:31 and after three days *r* again.
Lk 18:33 On the third day he will *r* again."
Jn 5:29 those who have done good will *r*
20: 9 had to *r* from the dead.)
Ac 17: 3 had to suffer and *r* from the dead.
1Th 4:16 and the dead in Christ will *r* first.

RISEN (RISE)
Mt 28: 6 He is not here; he has *r*, just
Mk 16: 6 He has *r*! He is not here.
Lk 24:34 The Lord has *r* and has appeared

RIVER (RIVERS)
Ps 46: 4 There is a *r* whose streams make
Isa 66:12 "I will extend peace to her like a *r*,
Eze 47:12 grow on both banks of the *r*.
Rev 22: 1 Then the angel showed me the *r*

RIVERS (RIVER)
Ps 137: 1 By the *r* of Babylon we sat

ROAD (CROSSROADS ROADS)
Mt 7:13 and broad is the *r* that leads

ROADS (ROAD)
Lk 3: 5 crooked *r* shall become straight,

ROARING
1Pe 5: 8 prowls around like a *r* lion looking

ROB (ROBBERS ROBBERY ROBS)
Mal 3: 8 "Will a man *r* God? Yet you *r* me.

ROBBERS (ROB)
Jer 7:11 become a den of *r* to you?
Mk 15:27 They crucified two *r* with him,
Lk 19:46 but you have made it 'a den of *r*.' "
Jn 10: 8 came before me were thieves and *r*,

ROBBERY (ROB)
Isa 61: 8 I hate *r* and iniquity.

ROBE (ROBED ROBES)
Ge 37: 3 and he made a richly ornamented *r*
Isa 6: 1 the train of his *r* filled the temple.
61:10 arrayed me in a *r* of righteousness,
Rev 6:11 each of them was given a white *r*,

ROBED (ROBE)
Ps 93: 1 the LORD is *r* in majesty
Isa 63: 1 Who is this, *r* in splendor,

ROBES (ROBE)
Ps 45: 8 All your *r* are fragrant with myrrh
Rev 7:13 "These in white *r*— who are they,

ROBS* (ROB)
Pr 19:26 He who *r* his father and drives out
28:24 He who *r* his father or mother

ROCK
Ge 49:24 of the Shepherd, the *R* of Israel,
Ex 17: 6 Strike the *r*, and water will come
Nu 20: 8 Speak to that *r* before their eyes
Dt 32: 4 He is the *R*, his works are perfect,
32:13 him with honey from the *r*,
2Sa 22: 2 "The LORD is my *r*, my fortress
Ps 18: 2 The LORD is my *r*, my fortress
19:14 O LORD, my *R* and my Redeemer
40: 2 he set my feet on a *r*
61: 2 lead me to the *r* that is higher
92:15 he is my *R*, and there is no
Isa 26: 4 the LORD, is the *R* eternal.
51: 1 to the *r* from which you were cut
Da 2:34 you were watching, a *r* was cut out,
Mt 7:24 man who built his house on the *r*.
16:18 and on this *r* I will build my church
Ro 9:33 and a *r* that makes them fall,
1Co 10: 4 the spiritual *r* that accompanied
1Pe 2: 8 and a *r* that makes them fall."

ROD (RODS)
2Sa 7:14 I will punish him with the *r* of men,
Ps 23: 4 your *r* and your staff,
Pr 13:24 He who spares the *r* hates his son,
22:15 the *r* of discipline will drive it far
23:13 if you punish him with the *r*,
29:15 *r* of correction imparts wisdom,
Isa 11: 4 the earth with the *r* of his mouth;

RODS (ROD)
2Co 11:25 Three times I was beaten with *r*,

ROLL (ROLLED)
Mk 16: 3 "Who will *r* the stone away

ROLLED (ROLL)
Lk 24: 2 They found the stone *r* away

ROMAN
Ac 16:37 even though we are *R* citizens,
22:25 you to flog a *R* citizen who hasn't

ROOF (ROOFS)
Pr 21: 9 Better to live on a corner of the *r*

ROOFS
Mt 10:27 in your ear, proclaim from the *r*.

ROOM (ROOMS)
Mt 6: 6 But when you pray, go into your *r*,
Mk 14:15 He will show you a large upper *r*,
Lk 2: 7 there was no *r* for them in the inn.
Jn 8:37 because you have no *r* for my word
21:25 the whole world would not have *r*
2Co 7: 2 Make *r* for us in your hearts.

ROOMS (ROOM)
Jn 14: 2 In my Father's house are many *r*;

ROOSTER
Mt 26:34 this very night, before the *r* crows,

ROOT (ROOTED ROOTS)
Isa 11:10 In that day the *R* of Jesse will stand
53: 2 and like a *r* out of dry ground.
Mt 3:10 already at the *r* of the trees,
13:21 But since he has no *r*, he lasts only
Ro 11:16 if the *r* is holy, so are the branches.
15:12 "The *R* of Jesse will spring up,
1Ti 6:10 of money is a *r* of all kinds of evil.
Rev 5: 5 the *R* of David, has triumphed.
22:16 I am the *R* and the Offspring

ROOTED (ROOT)
Eph 3:17 being *r* and established in love,

ROOTS (ROOT)
Isa 11: 1 from his *r* a Branch will bear fruit.

ROSE (RISE)
SS 2: 1 I am a *r* of Sharon,
1Th 4:14 believe that Jesus died and *r* again

ROTS
Pr 14:30 but envy *r* the bones.

ROUGH
Isa 42:16 and make the *r* places smooth.
Lk 3: 5 the *r* ways smooth.

ROUND
Ecc 1: 6 *r* and *r* it goes,

ROYAL
Ps 45: 9 at your right hand is the *r* bride
Da 1: 8 not to defile himself with the *r* food
Jas 2: 8 If you really keep the *r* law found
1Pe 2: 9 a *r* priesthood, a holy nation,

RUBBISH*
Php 3: 8 I consider them *r*, that I may gain

RUBIES
Job 28:18 the price of wisdom is beyond *r*.
Pr 3:15 She is more precious than *r*;
8:11 for wisdom is more precious than *r*,
31:10 She is worth far more than *r*.

RUDDER*
Jas 3: 4 by a very small *r* wherever the pilot

RUDDY
1Sa 16:12 He was *r*, with a fine appearance
SS 5:10 *Beloved* My lover is radiant and *r*,

RUDE*
1Co 13: 5 It is not *r*, it is not self-seeking,

RUIN (RUINED RUINING RUINS)
Pr 10: 8 but a chattering fool comes to *r*.
10:10 and a chattering fool comes to *r*.
10:14 but the mouth of a fool invites *r*.
10:29 but it is the *r* of those who do evil.
18:24 many companions may come to *r*,
19:13 A foolish son is his father's *r*,
26:28 and a flattering mouth works *r*.
SS 2:15 that *r* the vineyards,
Eze 21:27 A *r!* A *r!* I will make it a *r!*
1Ti 6: 9 desires that plunge men into *r*

RUINED (RUIN)
Isa 6: 5 "I am *r!* For I am a man
Mt 9:17 and the wineskins will be *r*.
12:25 divided against itself will be *r*,

RUINING* (RUIN)
Tit 1:11 they are *r* whole households

RUINS (RUIN)
Pr 19: 3 A man's own folly *r* his life,
Ecc 4: 5 and *r* himself.
2Ti 2:14 and only *r* those who listen.

RULE (RULER RULERS RULES)
Ge 1:26 let them *r* over the fish of the sea
3:16 and he will *r* over you."
Jdg 8:22 said to Gideon, "*R* over us—
1Sa 12:12 'No, we want a king to *r* over us'—
Ps 2: 9 You will *r* them with an iron
67: 4 for you *r* the peoples justly
119:133 let no sin *r* over me.
Pr 17: 2 A wise servant will *r*
Isa 28:10 *r* on *r*, *r* on *r*;
Eze 20:33 I will *r* over you with a mighty
Zec 6:13 and will sit and *r* on his throne.
9:10 His *r* will extend from sea to sea
Ro 13: 9 are summed up in this one *r*:
15:12 arise to *r* over the nations;
1Co 7:17 This is the *r* I lay down in all
Gal 6:16 and mercy to all who follow this *r*,
Eph 1:21 far above all *r* and authority,
Col 3:15 the peace of Christ *r* in your hearts,
2Th 3:10 we gave you this *r*: "If a man will
Rev 2:27 He will *r* them with an iron scepter;
12: 5 who will *r* all the nations
19:15 He will *r* them with an iron scepter

RULER (RULE)
Ps 8: 6 You made him *r* over the works
Pr 19: 6 Many curry favor with a *r*,
23: 1 When you sit to dine with a *r*,
25:15 Through patience a *r* can be
29:26 Many seek an audience with a *r*,
Isa 60:17 and righteousness your *r*.
Da 9:25 the *r*, comes, there will be seven
Mic 5: 2 one who will be *r* over Israel,
Mt 2: 6 for out of you will come a *r*
Eph 2: 2 of the *r* of the kingdom of the air,
1Ti 6:15 God, the blessed and only *R*,
Rev 1: 5 and the *r* of the kings of the earth.

RULERS (RULE)
Ps 2: 2 and the *r* gather together
119:161 *R* persecute me without cause,
Isa 40:23 reduces the *r* of this world
Da 7:27 and all *r* will worship and obey him
Mt 20:25 "You know that the *r*
Ac 13:27 and their *r* did not recognize Jesus,
Ro 13: 3 For *r* hold no terror
1Co 2: 6 of this age or of the *r* of this age,
Eph 3:10 should be made known to the *r*
6:12 the *r*, against the authorities,
Col 1:16 or powers or *r* or authorities;

RULES (RULE)
Nu 15:15 is to have the same *r* for you
2Sa 23: 3 when he *r* in the fear of God,
Ps 22:28 and he *r* over the nations.
66: 7 He *r* forever by his power,
103: 19 and his kingdom *r* over all.
Isa 29:13 is made up only of *r* taught by men.
40:10 and his arm *r* for him.
Mt 15: 9 their teachings are but *r* taught
Lk 22:26 one who *r* like the one who serves.
2Ti 2: 5 he competes according to the *r*.

RUMORS
Jer 51:46 afraid when *r* are heard in the land;
Mt 24: 6 You will hear of wars and *r* of wars,

RUN (RAN RUNNERS RUNNING RUNS)
Ps 19: 5 champion rejoicing to *r* his course.
Pr 4:12 when you *r*, you will not stumble.
18:10 the righteous *r* to it and are safe.
Isa 10: 3 To whom will you *r* for help?
40:31 they will *r* and not grow weary,
Joel 3:18 ravines of Judah will *r* with water.
Hab 2: 2 so that a herald may *r* with it.
1Co 9:24 *R* in such a way as to get the prize.
Gal 2: 2 that I was running or had *r* my race
Php 2:16 on the day of Christ that I did not *r*
Heb 12: 1 let us *r* with perseverance the race

RUNNERS* (RUN)
1Co 9:24 that in a race all the *r* run,

RUNNING (RUN)
Ps 133: 2 *r* down on Aaron's beard,
Lk 17:23 Do not go *r* off after them.
1Co 9:26 I do not run like a man *r* aimlessly;
Gal 5: 7 You were *r* a good race.

RUNS (RUN)
Jn 10:12 he abandons the sheep and *r* away.

RUSH
Pr 1:16 for their feet *r* into sin,
6:18 feet that are quick to *r* into evil,
Isa 59: 7 Their feet *r* into sin;

RUST
Mt 6:19 where moth and *r* destroy,

RUTH*
Moabitess; widow who went to Bethlehem with mother-in-law Naomi (Ru 1). Gleaned in field of Boaz; shown favor (Ru 2). Proposed marriage to Boaz (Ru 3). Married (Ru 4:1-12); bore Obed, ancestor of David (Ru 4:13-22), Jesus (Mt 1:5).

RUTHLESS
Pr 11:16 but *r* men gain only wealth.
Ro 1:31 are senseless, faithless, heartless, *r*.

SABBATH (SABBATHS)
Ex 20: 8 "Remember the *S* day
31:14 " 'Observe the *S*, because it is holy
Lev 25: 2 the land itself must observe a *s*
Dt 5:12 "Observe the *S* day
Isa 56: 2 keeps the *S* without desecrating it,
56: 6 all who keep the *S*
58:13 if you call the *S* a delight
Jer 17:21 not to carry a load on the *S* day
Mt 12: 1 through the grainfields on the *S*.
Lk 13:10 On a *S* Jesus was teaching in one
Col 2:16 a New Moon celebration or a *S* day

SABBATH-REST* (REST)
Heb 4: 9 then, a *S* for the people of God;

SABBATHS (SABBATH)
2Ch 2: 4 evening and on *S* and New Moons
Eze 20:12 Also I gave them my *S*

SACKCLOTH
Ps 30:11 you removed my *s* and clothed me
Da 9: 3 in fasting, and in *s* and ashes.
Mt 11:21 would have repented long ago in *s*

SACRED
Lev 23: 2 are to proclaim as *s* assemblies.
Mt 7: 6 "Do not give dogs what is *s*;
Ro 14: 5 One man considers one day more *s*
1Co 3:17 for God's temple is *s*, and you are
2Pe 1:18 were with him on the *s* mountain.
2:21 on the *s* command that was

SACRIFICE (SACRIFICED SACRIFICES)
Ge 22: 2 *S* him there as a burnt offering
Ex 12:27 'It is the Passover *s* to the LORD,
1Sa 15:22 To obey is better than *s*,
1Ki 18:38 the LORD fell and burned up the *s*,
1Ch 21:24 or *s* a burnt offering that costs me
Ps 40: 6 *S* and offering you did not desire,
50:14 *S* thank offerings to God,
51:16 You do not delight in *s*,
54: 6 I will *s* a freewill offering to you;
107: 22 Let them *s* thank offerings
141: 2 of my hands be like the evening *s*.
Pr 15: 8 The LORD detests the *s*
21: 3 to the LORD than *s*.
Da 9:27 the 'seven' he will put an end to *s*
12:11 time that the daily *s* is abolished
Hos 6: 6 For I desire mercy, not *s*,
Mt 9:13 this means: 'I desire mercy, not *s*.'
Ro 3:25 God presented him as a *s*
Eph 5: 2 as a fragrant offering and *s* to God.
Php 4:18 an acceptable *s*, pleasing to God.
Heb 9:26 away with sin by the *s* of himself.
10: 5 "*S* and offering you did not desire,
10:10 holy through the *s* of the body
10:14 by one *s* he has made perfect
10:18 there is no longer any *s* for sin.
11: 4 faith Abel offered God a better *s*
13:15 offer to God a *s* of praise—
1Jn 2: 2 He is the atoning *s* for our sins,
4:10 as an atoning *s* for our sins.

SACRIFICED (SACRIFICE)
Ac 15:29 are to abstain from food *s* to idols,
1Co 5: 7 our Passover lamb, has been *s*.
8: 1 Now about food *s* to idols:
Heb 7:27 He *s* for their sins once for all
9:28 so Christ was *s* once

SACRIFICES (SACRIFICE)
Ps 51:17 The *s* of God are a broken spirit;
Mk 12:33 than all burnt offerings and *s*."
Ro 12: 1 to offer your bodies as living *s*,
Heb 9:23 with better *s* than these.
13:16 for with such *s* God is pleased.
1Pe 2: 5 offering spiritual *s* acceptable

SAD
Lk 18:23 he heard this, he became very *s*,

SADDUCEES
Mt 16: 6 the yeast of the Pharisees and *S*."
Mk 12:18 *S*, who say there is no resurrection,
Ac 23: 8 *S* say that there is no resurrection,

SAFE (SAVE)
Ps 27: 5 he will keep me *s* in his dwelling;
37: 3 in the land and enjoy *s* pasture.
Pr 18:10 the righteous run to it and are *s.*
28:26 he who walks in wisdom is kept *s.*
29:25 in the LORD is kept *s.*
Jer 12: 5 If you stumble in *s* country,
Jn 17:12 kept them *s* by that name you gave
1Jn 5:18 born of God keeps him *s,*

SAFETY (SAVE)
Ps 4: 8 make me dwell in *s.*
Hos 2:18 so that all may lie down in *s.*
1Th 5: 3 people are saying, "Peace and *s,*"

SAINTS
1Sa 2: 9 He will guard the feet of his *s,*
Ps 16: 3 As for the *s* who are in the land,
30: 4 Sing to the LORD, you *s* of his;
31:23 Love the LORD, all his *s!*
34: 9 Fear the LORD, you his *s,*
116: 15 is the death of his *s.*
149: 1 his praise in the assembly of the *s.*
149: 5 Let the *s* rejoice in this honor
Da 7:18 the *s* of the Most High will receive
Ro 8:27 intercedes for the *s* in accordance
1Co 6: 2 not know that the *s* will judge
Eph 1:15 Jesus and your love for all the *s,*
1:18 of his glorious inheritance in the *s,*
6:18 always keep on praying for all the *s*
Phm : 7 have refreshed the hearts of the *s.*
Rev 5: 8 which are the prayers of the *s.*
19: 8 for the righteous acts of the *s.)*

SAKE (SAKES)
1Sa 12:22 For the *s* of his great name
Ps 23: 3 righteousness for his name's *s.*
44:22 Yet for your *s* we face death all day
106: 8 Yet he saved them for his name's *s,*
Isa 42:21 for the *s* of his righteousness
43:25 your transgressions, for my own *s,*
48: 9 For my own name's *s* I delay my
48:11 For my own *s,* for my own *s,*
Jer 14: 7 for the *s* of your name.
14:21 For the *s* of your name do not
Eze 20: 9 But for the *s* of my name I did what
20:14 But for the *s* of my name I did what
20:22 and for the *s* of my name I did what
36:22 but for the *s* of my holy name,
Da 9:17 For your *s,* O Lord, look with favor
Mt 10:39 life for my *s* will find it.
19:29 for my *s* will receive a hundred
1Co 9:23 I do all this for the *s* of the gospel,
2Co 12:10 for Christ's *s,* I delight
Php 3: 7 loss for the *s* of Christ.
Heb 11:26 He regarded disgrace for the *s*
1Pe 2:13 for the Lord's *s* to every authority
3Jn : 7 was for the *s* of the Name that they

SAKES* (SAKE)
2Co 8: 9 yet for your *s* he became poor,

SALEM
Ge 14:18 king of *S* brought out bread
Heb 7: 2 "king of *S*" means "king of peace."

SALT
Ge 19:26 and she became a pillar of *s.*
Nu 18:19 covenant of *s* before the LORD
Mt 5:13 "You are the *s* of the earth.
Col 4: 6 with *s,* so that you may know how
Jas 3:11 *s* water flow from the same spring?

SALVATION* (SAVE)
Ex 15: 2 he has become my *s.*
2Sa 22: 3 my shield and the horn of my *s.*
23: 5 Will he not bring to fruition my *s*
1Ch 16:23 proclaim his *s* day after day.
2Ch 6:41 O LORD God, be clothed with *s,*
Ps 9:14 and there rejoice in your *s.*
13: 5 my heart rejoices in your *s.*
14: 7 that *s* for Israel would come out
18: 2 is my shield and the horn of my *s,*
27: 1 The LORD is my light and my *s*—
28: 8 a fortress of *s* for his anointed one.
35: 3 "I am your *s.*"
35: 9 and delight in his *s.*
37:39 The *s* of the righteous comes
40:10 I speak of your faithfulness and *s.*
40:16 those who love your *s* always say,
50:23 way so that I may show him the *s*
51:12 Restore to me the joy of your *s*
53: 6 that *s* for Israel would come out
62: 1 my *s* comes from him.
62: 2 He alone is my rock and my *s;*
62: 6 He alone is my rock and my *s;*
62: 7 My *s* and my honor depend
67: 2 your *s* among all nations.
69:13 answer me with your sure *s.*
Ps 69:27 do not let them share in your *s.*
69:29 may your *s,* O God, protect me.
70: 4 those who love your *s* always say,
71:15 of your *s* all day long,
74:12 you bring *s* upon the earth.
85: 7 and grant us your *s.*
85: 9 Surely his *s* is near those who fear
91:16 and show him my *s.*"
95: 1 to the Rock of our *s.*
96: 2 proclaim his *s* day after day.
98: 1 have worked *s* for him.
98: 2 The LORD has made his *s* known
98: 3 the *s* of our God.
116: 13 I will lift up the cup of *s*
118: 14 he has become my *s.*
118: 21 you have become my *s.*
119: 41 your *s* according to your promise;
119: 81 with longing for your *s,*
119:123 My eyes fail, looking for your *s,*
119:155 *S* is far from the wicked,
119:166 I wait for your *s,* O LORD,
119:174 I long for your *s,* O LORD,
132: 16 I will clothe her priests with *s,*
149: 4 he crowns the humble with *s.*
Isa 12: 2 Surely God is my *s;*
12: 2 he has become my *s.*"
12: 3 from the wells of *s.*
25: 9 let us rejoice and be glad in his *s.*"
26: 1 God makes *s*
26:18 We have not brought *s* to the earth;
30:15 "In repentance and rest is your *s,*
33: 2 our *s* in time of distress.
33: 6 a rich store of *s* and wisdom
45: 8 let *s* spring up,
45:17 the LORD with an everlasting *s;*
46:13 I will grant *s* to Zion,
46:13 and my *s* will not be delayed.
49: 6 that you may bring my *s*
49: 8 and in the day of *s* I will help you;
51: 5 my *s* is on the way,
51: 6 But my *s* will last forever,
51: 8 my *s* through all generations."
52: 7 who proclaim *s,*
52:10 the *s* of our God.
56: 1 for my *s* is close at hand
59:16 so his own arm worked *s* for him,
59:17 and the helmet of *s* on his head;
60:18 but you will call your walls *S*
61:10 me with garments of *s*
62: 1 her *s* like a blazing torch.
63: 5 so my own arm worked *s* for me,
Jer 3:23 is the *s* of Israel.
La 3:26 quietly for the *s* of the LORD.
Jnh 2: 9 *S* comes from the LORD."
Zec 9: 9 righteous and having *s,*
Lk 1:69 He has raised up a horn of *s* for us
1:71 of long ago), *s* from our enemies
1:77 give his people the knowledge of *s*
2:30 For my eyes have seen your *s,*
3: 6 And all mankind will see God's *s*
19: 9 "Today *s* has come to this house,
Jn 4:22 for *s* is from the Jews.
Ac 4:12 *S* is found in no one else,
13:26 message of *s* has been sent.
13:47 that you may bring *s* to the ends
28:28 to know that God's *s* has been sent
Ro 1:16 for the *s* of everyone who believes:
11:11 *s* has come to the Gentiles
13:11 because our *s* is nearer now
2Co 1: 6 it is for your comfort and *s;*
6: 2 and in the day of *s* I helped you."
6: 2 of God's favor, now is the day of *s.*
7:10 brings repentance that leads to *s*
Eph 1:13 word of truth, the gospel of your *s.*
6:17 Take the helmet of *s* and the sword
Php 2:12 to work out your *s* with fear
1Th 5: 8 and the hope of *s* as a helmet.
5: 9 to receive *s* through our Lord Jesus
2Ti 2:10 they too may obtain the *s* that is
3:15 wise for *s* through faith
Tit 2:11 of God that brings *s* has appeared
Heb 1:14 to serve those who will inherit *s?*
2: 3 This *s,* which was first announced
2: 3 escape if we ignore such a great *s?*
2:10 of their *s* perfect through suffering.
5: 9 of eternal *s* for all who obey him
6: 9 case—things that accompany *s.*
9:28 to bring *s* to those who are waiting
1Pe 1: 5 the coming of the *s* that is ready
1: 9 of your faith, the *s* of your souls.
1:10 Concerning this *s,* the prophets,
2: 2 by it you may grow up in your *s,*
2Pe 3:15 that our Lord's patience means *s,*
Jude : 3 to write to you about the *s* we share
Rev 7:10 "*S* belongs to our God,
12:10 have come the *s* and the power
19: 1 *S* and glory and power belong

SAMARIA (SAMARITAN)
1Ki 16:24 He bought the hill of *S*
2Ki 17: 6 the king of Assyria captured *S*
Jn 4: 4 Now he had to go through *S.*
4: 5 came to a town in *S* called Sychar,

SAMARITAN (SAMARIA)
Lk 10:33 But a *S,* as he traveled, came where
17:16 and thanked him—and he was a *S.*
Jn 4: 7 When a *S* woman came

SAMSON
Danite judge. Birth promised (Jdg 13). Married to Philistine, but wife given away (Jdg 14). Vengeance on Philistines (Jdg 15). Betrayed by Delilah (Jdg 16:1-22). Death (Jdg 16:23-31). Feats of strength: killed lion (Jdg 14:6), 30 Philistines (Jdg 14:19), 1,000 Philistines with jawbone (Jdg 15: 13-17), carried off gates of Gaza (Jdg 16:3), pushed down temple of Dagon (Jdg 16:25-30).

SAMUEL
Ephraimite judge and prophet (Heb 11:32). Birth prayed for (1Sa 1:10-18). Dedicated to temple by Hannah (1Sa 1:21-28). Raised by Eli (1Sa 2: 11, 18-26). Called as prophet (1Sa 3). Led Israel to victory over Philistines (1Sa 7). Asked by Israel for a king (1Sa 8). Anointed Saul as king (1Sa 9-10). Farewell speech (1Sa 12). Rebuked Saul for sacrifice (1Sa 13). Announced rejection of Saul (1Sa 15). Anointed David as king (1Sa 16). Protected David from Saul (1Sa 19:18-24). Death (1Sa 25:1). Returned from dead to condemn Saul (1Sa 28).

SANBALLAT
Led opposition to Nehemiah's rebuilding of Jerusalem (Ne 2:10, 19; 4; 6).

SANCTIFIED* (SANCTIFY)
Jn 17:19 that they too may be truly *s.*
Ac 20:32 among all those who are *s.*
26:18 among those who are *s* by faith
Ro 15:16 to God, *s* by the Holy Spirit.
1Co 1: 2 to those *s* in Christ Jesus
6:11 But you were washed, you were *s,*
7:14 and the unbelieving wife has been *s*
7:14 the unbelieving husband has been *s*
1Th 4: 3 It is God's will that you should be *s*
Heb 10:29 blood of the covenant that *s* him,

SANCTIFY* (SANCTIFIED SANCTIFYING)
Jn 17:17 *S* them by the truth; your word is
17:19 For them I *s* myself, that they too
1Th 5:23 *s* you through and through.
Heb 9:13 are ceremonially unclean *s* them

SANCTIFYING* (SANCTIFY)
2Th 2:13 through the *s* work of the Spirit
1Pe 1: 2 through the *s* work of the Spirit,

SANCTUARY
Ex 25: 8 "Then have them make a *s* for me,
Lev 19:30 and have reverence for my *s,*
Ps 15: 1 LORD, who may dwell in your *s?*
63: 2 I have seen you in the *s*
68:24 of my God and King into the *s.*
68:35 are awesome, O God, in your *s;*
73:17 me till I entered the *s* of God;
102: 19 looked down from his *s* on high,
134: 2 Lift up your hands in the *s*
150: 1 Praise God in his *s;*
Eze 37:26 I will put my *s* among them forever
41: 1 the man brought me to the outer *s*
Da 9:26 will destroy the city and the *s.*
Heb 6:19 It enters the inner *s*
8: 2 in the *s,* the true tabernacle set up
8: 5 They serve at a *s* that is a copy
9:24 enter a man-made *s* that was only

SAND
Ge 22:17 and as the *s* on the seashore.
Mt 7:26 man who built his house on *s.*

SANDAL (SANDALS)
Ru 4: 7 one party took off his *s*

SANDALS (SANDAL)
Ex 3: 5 off your *s,* for the place where you
Dt 25: 9 take off one of his *s,* spit in his face
Jos 5:15 off your *s,* for the place where you
Mt 3:11 whose *s* I am not fit to carry.

SANG (SING)
Ex 15: 1 and the Israelites *s* this song
15:21 Miriam *s* to them:
Nu 21:17 Then Israel *s* this song:
Jdg 5: 1 Barak son of Abinoam *s* this song:
1Sa 18: 7 As they danced, they *s:*
2Sa 22: 1 David *s* to the LORD the words
2Ch 5:13 in praise to the LORD and *s:*

2Ch 29:30 So they *s* praises with gladness
Ezr 3:11 thanksgiving they *s* to the LORD:
Job 38: 7 while the morning stars *s* together
Ps 106: 12 and *s* his praise.
Rev 5: 9 And they *s* a new song:
5:12 In a loud voice they *s*:
14: 3 they *s* a new song before the throne
15: 3 and *s* the song of Moses the servant

SAP
Ro 11:17 share in the nourishing *s*

SAPPHIRA*
Ac 5: 1 together with his wife *S*,

SARAH
Wife of Abraham, originally named Sarai; barren (Ge 11:29-31; 1Pe 3:6). Taken by Pharaoh as Abraham's sister; returned (Ge 12:10-20). Gave Hagar to Abraham; sent her away in pregnancy (Ge 16). Name changed; Isaac promised (Ge 17:15-21; 18:10-15; Heb 11:11). Taken by Abimelech as Abraham's sister; returned (Ge 20). Isaac born; Hagar and Ishmael sent away (Ge 21:1-21; Gal 4:21-31). Death (Ge 23).

SARDIS
Rev 3: 1 the angel of the church in *S* write:

SASH (SASHES)
Rev 1:13 with a golden *s* around his chest.

SASHES (SASH)
Rev 15: 6 wore golden *s* around their chests.

SAT (SIT)
Ps 137: 1 By the rivers of Babylon we *s*
Mk 16:19 and he *s* at the right hand of God.
Lk 10:39 who *s* at the Lord's feet listening
Heb 1: 3 he *s* down at the right hand
8: 1 who *s* down at the right hand
10:12 he *s* down at the right hand of God.
12: 2 and *s* down at the right hand

SATAN
Job 1: 6 and *S* also came with them.
Zec 3: 2 said to *S*, "The LORD rebuke you,
Mt 12:26 If *S* drives out *S*, he is divided
16:23 *S*! You are a stumbling block to me;
Mk 4:15 *S* comes and takes away the word
Lk 10:18 "I saw *S* fall like lightning
22: 3 *S* entered Judas, called Iscariot,
Ro 16:20 The God of peace will soon crush *S*
1Co 5: 5 is present, hand this man over to *S*,
2Co 11:14 for *S* himself masquerades
12: 7 a messenger of *S*, to torment me.
1Ti 1:20 handed over to *S* to be taught not
Rev 12: 9 serpent called the devil, or *S*,
20: 2 or *S*, and bound him for a thousand
20: 7 *S* will be released from his prison

SATISFIED (SATISFY)
Ps 17:15 I will be *s* with seeing your likeness
22:26 The poor will eat and be *s*;
63: 5 My soul will be *s* as with the richest
104: 28 they are *s* with good things.
105: 40 *s* them with the bread of heaven.
Pr 13: 4 the desires of the diligent are fully *s*
30:15 are three things that are never *s*,
Ecc 5:10 whoever loves wealth is never *s*
Isa 53:11 he will see the light of life and be *s*
Mt 14:20 They all ate and were *s*,
Lk 6:21 for you will be *s*.

SATISFIES* (SATISFY)
Ps 103: 5 who *s* your desires with good things,
107: 9 for he *s* the thirsty
147: 14 and *s* you with the finest of wheat.

SATISFY (SATISFIED SATISFIES)
Ps 90:14 *S* us in the morning
145: 16 *s* the desires of every living thing.
Pr 5:19 may her breasts *s* you always,
Isa 55: 2 and your labor on what does not *s*?
58:10 and *s* the needs of the oppressed,

SAUL
1. Benjamite; anointed by Samuel as first king of Israel (1Sa 9-10). Defeated Ammonites (1Sa 11). Rebuked for offering sacrifice (1Sa 13:1-15). Defeated Philistines (1Sa 14). Rejected as king for failing to annihilate Amalekites (1Sa 15). Soothed from evil spirit by David (1Sa 16:14-23). Sent David against Goliath (1Sa 17). Jealousy and attempted murder of David (1Sa 18:1-11). Gave David Michal as wife (1Sa 18:12-30). Second attempt to kill David (1Sa 19). Anger at Jonathan (1Sa 20:26-34). Pursued David: killed priests at Nob (1Sa 22), went to Keilah and Ziph (1Sa 23), life spared by David at En Gedi (1Sa 24) and in his tent (1Sa 26). Rebuked by Samuel's spirit for consulting witch at Endor (1Sa 28). Wounded by Philistines; took his own life (1Sa 31; 1Ch 10). Lamented by David (2Sa 1:17-27). Children (1Sa 14:49-51; 1Ch 8).
2. See PAUL

SAVAGE
Ac 20:29 *s* wolves will come in among you

SAVE (SAFE SAFETY SALVATION SAVED SAVES SAVIOR)
Ge 45: 5 to *s* lives that God sent me ahead
1Ch 16:35 Cry out, "*S* us, O God our Savior;
Job 40:14 that your own right hand can *s* you.
Ps 17: 7 you who *s* by your right hand
18:27 You *s* the humble
28: 9 *S* your people and bless your
31:16 *s* me in your unfailing love.
69:35 for God will *s* Zion
71: 2 turn your ear to me and *s* me.
72:13 and *s* the needy from death.
89:48 or *s* himself from the power
91: 3 Surely he will *s* you
109: 31 to *s* his life from those who
146: 3 in mortal men, who cannot *s*.
Pr 2:16 will *s* you also from the adulteress,
Isa 35: 4 he will come to *s* you."
38:20 The LORD will *s* me,
46: 7 it cannot *s* him from his troubles.
59: 1 of the LORD is not too short to *s*,
63: 1 mighty to *s*."
Jer 17:14 *s* me and I will be saved,
Eze 3:18 ways in order to *s* his life,
7:19 able to *s* them in the day
14:14 they could *s* only themselves
33:12 of the righteous man will not *s* him
34:22 I will *s* my flock, and they will no
Da 3:17 the God we serve is able to *s* us
Hos 1: 7 and I will *s* them—not by bow,
Zep 1:18 will be able to *s* them
3:17 he is mighty to *s*.
Zec 8: 7 "I will *s* my people
Mt 1:21 he will *s* his people from their sins
16:25 wants to *s* his life will lose it,
Lk 19:10 to seek and to *s* what was lost."
Jn 3:17 but to *s* the world through him.
12:47 come to judge the world, but to *s* it.
Ro 11:14 people to envy and *s* some of them.
1Co 7:16 whether you will *s* your husband?
1Ti 1:15 came into the world to *s* sinners—
Heb 7:25 to *s* completely those who come
Jas 5:20 of his way will *s* him from death
Jude :23 others from the fire and *s* them;

SAVED (SAVE)
Ps 22: 5 They cried to you and were *s*;
33:16 No king is *s* by the size of his army;
34: 6 he *s* him out of all his troubles.
106: 21 They forgot the God who *s* them,
116: 6 when I was in great need, he *s* me.
Isa 25: 9 we trusted in him, and he *s* us.
45:22 "Turn to me and be *s*,
64: 5 How then can we be *s*?
Jer 4:14 from your heart and be *s*.
8:20 and we are not *s*."
Eze 3:19 but you will have *s* yourself.
33: 5 warning, he would have *s* himself.
Joel 2:32 on the name of the LORD will be *s*;
Mt 10:22 firm to the end will be *s*.
24:13 firm to the end will be *s*.
Mk 13:13 firm to the end will be *s*.
16:16 believes and is baptized will be *s*,
Jn 10: 9 enters through me will be *s*.
Ac 2:21 on the name of the Lord will be *s*.'
2:47 daily those who were being *s*.
4:12 to men by which we must be *s*."
15:11 of our Lord Jesus that we are *s*,
16:30 do to be *s*?" They replied,
Ro 5: 9 how much more shall we be *s*
9:27 only the remnant will be *s*.
10: 1 the Israelites is that they may be *s*.
10: 9 him from the dead, you will be *s*.
10:13 on the name of the Lord will be *s*."
11:26 so all Israel will be *s*, as it is written:
1Co 1:18 to us who are being *s* it is the power
3:15 will suffer loss; he himself will be *s*,
5: 5 his spirit *s* on the day of the Lord.
10:33 of many, so that they may be *s*.
15: 2 By this gospel you are *s*,
Eph 2: 5 it is by grace you have been *s*.
2: 8 For it is by grace you have been *s*,
2Th 2:13 you to be *s* through the sanctifying
1Ti 2: 4 who wants all men to be *s*
2:15 But women will be *s*
2Ti 1: 9 who has *s* us and called us
Tit 3: 5 He *s* us through the washing
Heb 10:39 but of those who believe and are *s*.

SAVES (SAVE)
Ps 7:10 who *s* the upright in heart.
68:20 Our God is a God who *s*;
145: 19 he hears their cry and *s* them.
1Pe 3:21 It *s* you by the resurrection

SAVIOR* (SAVE)
Dt 32:15 and rejected the Rock his *S*.
2Sa 22: 3 stronghold, my refuge and my *s*—
22:47 Exalted be God, the Rock, my *S*!
1Ch 16:35 Cry out, "Save us, O God our *S*;
Ps 18:46 Exalted be God my *S*!
24: 5 and vindication from God his *S*.
25: 5 for you are God my *S*,
27: 9 O God my *S*.
38:22 O Lord my *S*.
42: 5 my *S* and
42:11 my *S* and my God.
43: 5 my *S* and my God.
65: 5 O God our *S*,
68:19 Praise be to the Lord, to God our *S*,
79: 9 Help us, O God our *S*,
85: 4 Restore us again, O God our *S*,
89:26 my God, the Rock my *S*.'
Isa 17:10 You have forgotten God your *S*;
19:20 he will send them a *s* and defender,
43: 3 the Holy One of Israel, your *S*;
43:11 and apart from me there is no *s*.
45:15 O God and *S* of Israel.
45:21 a righteous God and a *S*;
49:26 that I, the LORD, am your *S*,
60:16 know that I, the LORD, am your *S*,
62:11 'See, your *S* comes!
63: 8 and so he became their *S*.
Jer 14: 8 its *S* in times of distress,
Hos 13: 4 no *S* except me.
Mic 7: 7 I wait for God my *S*;
Hab 3:18 I will be joyful in God my *S*.
Lk 1:47 and my spirit rejoices in God my *S*,
2:11 of David a *S* has been born to you;
Jn 4:42 know that this man really is the *S*
Ac 5:31 *S* that he might give repentance
13:23 God has brought to Israel the *S*
Eph 5:23 his body, of which he is the *S*.
Php 3:20 we eagerly await a *S* from there,
1Ti 1: 1 by the command of God our *S*
2: 3 This is good, and pleases God our *S*
4:10 who is the *S* of all men,
2Ti 1:10 through the appearing of our *S*,
Tit 1: 3 me by the command of God our *S*,
1: 4 the Father and Christ Jesus our *S*.
2:10 about God our *S* attractive.
2:13 appearing of our great God and *S*,
3: 4 and love of God our *S* appeared,
3: 6 through Jesus Christ our *S*,
2Pe 1: 1 *S* Jesus Christ have received a faith
1:11 eternal kingdom of our Lord and *S*
2:20 and *S* Jesus Christ and are again
3: 2 and *S* through your apostles.
3:18 and knowledge of our Lord and *S*
1Jn 4:14 Son to be the *S* of the world.
Jude :25 to the only God our *S* be glory,

SCALE (SCALES)
Ps 18:29 with my God I can *s* a wall.

SCALES (SCALE)
Lev 11: 9 may eat any that have fins and *s*.
19:36 Use honest *s* and honest weights,
Pr 11: 1 The LORD abhors dishonest *s*,
Da 5:27 You have been weighed on the *s*
Rev 6: 5 Its rider was holding a pair of *s*

SCAPEGOAT (GOAT)
Lev 16:10 by sending it into the desert as a *s*.

SCARECROW*
Jer 10: 5 Like a *s* in a melon patch,

SCARLET
Jos 2:21 she tied the *s* cord in the window.
Isa 1:18 "Though your sins are like *s*,
Mt 27:28 They stripped him and put a *s* robe

SCATTER (SCATTERED SCATTERS)
Dt 4:27 The LORD will *s* you
Ne 1: 8 I will *s* you among the nations,
Jer 9:16 I will *s* them among nations that
30:11 the nations among which I *s* you,
Zec 10: 9 I *s* them among the peoples,

SCATTERED (SCATTER)
Isa 11:12 he will assemble the *s* people
Jer 31:10 'He who *s* Israel will gather them
Zec 2: 6 "for I have *s* you to the four winds
13: 7 and the sheep will be *s*,
Mt 26:31 and the sheep of the flock will be *s*.'
Jn 11:52 but also for the *s* children of God,
Ac 8: 4 who had been *s* preached the word
Jas 1: 1 To the twelve tribes *s*

1Pe 1: 1 *s* throughout Pontus, Galatia,

SCATTERS (SCATTER)
Mt 12:30 he who does not gather with me *s*.

SCEPTER
Ge 49:10 The *s* will not depart from Judah,
Nu 24:17 a *s* will rise out of Israel.
Ps 2: 9 You will rule them with an iron *s*;
45: 6 a *s* of justice will be the *s*
Heb 1: 8 and righteousness will be the *s*
Rev 2:27 'He will rule them with an iron *s*;
12: 5 rule all the nations with an iron *s*.
19:15 "He will rule them with an iron *s*."

SCHEMES
Pr 6:18 a heart that devises wicked *s*,
24: 9 The *s* of folly are sin,
2Co 2:11 For we are not unaware of his *s*.
Eph 6:11 stand against the devil's *s*.

SCHOLAR*
1Co 1:20 Where is the *s*? Where is

SCOFFERS
2Pe 3: 3 that in the last days *s* will come,

SCORN (SCORNED SCORNING SCORNS)
Ps 69: 7 For I endure *s* for your sake,
69:20 *S* has broken my heart
89:41 he has become the *s*
109: 25 I am an object of *s* to my accusers;
119: 22 Remove from me *s* and contempt,
Mic 6:16 you will bear the *s* of the nations."

SCORNED (SCORN)
Ps 22: 6 *s* by men and despised

SCORNING (SCORN)
Heb 12: 2 him endured the cross, *s* its shame,

SCORNS (SCORN)
Pr 13:13 He who *s* instruction will pay for it,
30:17 that *s* obedience to a mother,

SCORPION
Lk 11:12 will give him a *s*? If you then,
Rev 9: 5 sting of a *s* when it strikes a man.

SCOUNDREL
Pr 6:12 A *s* and villain,

SCRIPTURE (SCRIPTURES)
Jn 2:22 Then they believed the *S*
7:42 Does not the *S* say that the Christ
10:35 and the *S* cannot be broken—
Ac 8:32 was reading this passage of *S*:
1Ti 4:13 yourself to the public reading of *S*,
2Ti 3:16 All *S* is God-breathed
2Pe 1:20 that no prophecy of *S* came about

SCRIPTURES (SCRIPTURE)
Mt 22:29 because you do not know the *S*
Lk 24:27 said in all the *S* concerning himself.
24:45 so they could understand the *S*.
Jn 5:39 These are the *S* that testify about
Ac 17:11 examined the *S* every day to see
2Ti 3:15 you have known the holy *S*,
2Pe 3:16 as they do the other *S*,

SCROLL
Ps 40: 7 it is written about me in the *s*.
Isa 34: 4 and the sky rolled up like a *s*;
Eze 3: 1 eat what is before you, eat this *s*;
Heb 10: 7 it is written about me in the *s*—
Rev 6:14 The sky receded like a *s*, rolling up,
10: 8 take the *s* that lies open in the hand

SCUM
1Co 4:13 this moment we have become the *s*

SEA (SEASHORE)
Ex 14:16 go through the *s* on dry ground.
Dt 30:13 "Who will cross the *s* to get it
1Ki 7:23 He made the *S* of cast metal,
Job 11: 9 and wider than the *s*.
Ps 93: 4 mightier than the breakers of the *s*
95: 5 The *s* is his, for he made it,
Ecc 1: 7 All streams flow into the *s*,
Isa 57:20 the wicked are like the tossing *s*,
Jnh 1: 4 LORD sent a great wind on the *s*,
Mic 7:19 iniquities into the depths of the *s*.
Hab 2:14 as the waters cover the *s*.
Zec 9:10 His rule will extend from *s* to *s*
Mt 18: 6 drowned in the depths of the *s*.
1Co 10: 1 that they all passed through the *s*.
Jas 1: 6 who doubts is like a wave of the *s*,
Jude :13 They are wild waves of the *s*,
Rev 10: 2 He planted his right foot on the *s*
13: 1 I saw a beast coming out of the *s*.
20:13 The *s* gave up the dead that were

Rev 21: 1 and there was no longer any *s*.

SEAL (SEALED SEALS)
Ps 40: 9 I do not *s* my lips,
SS 8: 6 Place me like a *s* over your heart,
Da 12: 4 and *s* the words of the scroll
Jn 6:27 God the Father has placed his *s*
1Co 9: 2 For you are the *s* of my apostleship
2Co 1:22 set his *s* of ownership on us,
Eph 1:13 you were marked in him with a *s*,
Rev 6: 3 the Lamb opened the second *s*,
6: 5 When the Lamb opened the third *s*,
6: 7 the Lamb opened the fourth *s*,
6: 9 When he opened the fifth *s*,
6:12 I watched as he opened the sixth *s*.
8: 1 When he opened the seventh *s*,
9: 4 people who did not have the *s*
22:10 "Do not *s* up the words

SEALED (SEAL)
Eph 4:30 with whom you were *s* for the day
2Ti 2:19 solid foundation stands firm, *s*
Rev 5: 1 on both sides and *s* with seven seals

SEALS (SEAL)
Rev 5: 2 "Who is worthy to break the *s*
6: 1 opened the first of the seven *s*.

SEAMLESS*
Jn 19:23 This garment was *s*, woven

SEARCH (SEARCHED SEARCHES SEARCHING)
Ps 4: 4 *s* your hearts and be silent.
139: 23 *S* me, O God, and know my heart;
Pr 2: 4 and *s* for it as for hidden treasure,
25: 2 to *s* out a matter is the glory
SS 3: 2 I will *s* for the one my heart loves.
Jer 17:10 "I the LORD *s* the heart
Eze 34:11 I myself will *s* for my sheep
34:16 I will *s* for the lost and bring back
Lk 15: 8 and *s* carefully until she finds it?

SEARCHED (SEARCH)
Ps 139: 1 O LORD, you have *s* me
Ecc 12:10 The Teacher *s* to find just the right
1Pe 1:10 *s* intently and with the greatest

SEARCHES (SEARCH)
1Ch 28: 9 for the LORD *s* every heart
Ps 7: 9 who *s* minds and hearts,
Pr 11:27 but evil comes to him who *s* for it.
20:27 The lamp of the LORD *s* the spirit
Ro 8:27 And he who *s* our hearts knows
1Co 2:10 The Spirit *s* all things,
Rev 2:23 will know that I am he who *s* hearts

SEARCHING (SEARCH)
Jdg 5:15 there was much *s* of heart.
Am 8:12 *s* for the word of the LORD,

SEARED
1Ti 4: 2 whose consciences have been *s*

SEASHORE (SEA)
Jos 11: 4 as numerous as the sand on the *s*.
1Ki 4:29 as measureless as the sand on the *s*.

SEASON (SEASONED SEASONS)
Lev 26: 4 I will send you rain in its *s*,
Ps 1: 3 which yields its fruit in *s*
2Ti 4: 2 be prepared in *s* and out of *s*;

SEASONED* (SEASON)
Col 4: 6 full of grace, *s* with salt,

SEASONS (SEASON)
Ge 1:14 signs to mark *s* and days and years,
Gal 4:10 and months and *s* and years!

SEAT (SEATED SEATS)
Ps 1: 1 or sit in the *s* of mockers.
Pr 31:23 where he takes his *s*
Da 7: 9 and the Ancient of Days took his *s*.
Lk 14: 9 say to you, 'Give this man your *s*.'
2Co 5:10 before the judgment *s* of Christ,

SEATED (SEAT)
Ps 47: 8 God is *s* on his holy throne.
Isa 6: 1 I saw the Lord *s* on a throne,
Lk 22:69 of Man will be *s* at the right hand
Eph 1:20 and *s* him at his right hand
2: 6 and *s* us with him in the heavenly
Col 3: 1 where Christ is *s* at the right hand
Rev 14:14 *s* on the cloud was one "like a son
20:11 white throne and him who was *s*

SEATS (SEAT)
Lk 11:43 you love the most important *s*

SECLUSION*
Lk 1:24 and for five months remained in *s*.

SECRET (SECRETLY SECRETS)
Dt 29:29 The *s* things belong
Jdg 16: 6 Tell me the *s* of your great strength
Ps 90: 8 our *s* sins in the light
139: 15 when I was made in the *s* place.
Pr 11:13 but a trustworthy man keeps a *s*.
21:14 A gift given in *s* soothes anger,
Jer 23:24 Can anyone hide in *s* places
Mt 6: 4 so that your giving may be in *s*.
6:18 who sees what is done in *s*,
Mk 4:11 "The *s* of the kingdom
1Co 2: 7 No, we speak of God's *s* wisdom,
4: 1 entrusted with the *s* things of God.
2Co 4: 2 we have renounced *s* and shameful
Eph 5:12 what the disobedient do in *s*.
Php 4:12 I have learned the *s*

SECRETLY (SECRET)
2Pe 2: 1 They will *s* introduce destructive
Jude : 4 about long ago have *s* slipped

SECRETS (SECRET)
Ps 44:21 since he knows the *s* of the heart?
Ro 2:16 day when God will judge men's *s*
1Co 14:25 the *s* of his heart will be laid bare.
Rev 2:24 Satan's so-called deep *s* (I will not

SECURE (SECURITY)
Dt 33:12 beloved of the LORD rest *s* in him,
Ps 16: 5 you have made my lot *s*.
16: 9 my body also will rest *s*,
112: 8 His heart is *s*, he will have no fear;
Pr 14:26 fears the LORD has a *s* fortress,
Heb 6:19 an anchor for the soul, firm and *s*.
2Pe 3:17 and fall from your *s* position.

SECURITY (SECURE)
Job 31:24 or said to pure gold, 'You are my *s*,'

SEED (SEEDS SEEDTIME)
Ge 1:11 on the land that bear fruit with *s*
Isa 55:10 so that it yields *s* for the sower
Mt 13: 3 "A farmer went out to sow his *s*.
13:31 of heaven is like a mustard *s*,
17:20 have faith as small as a mustard *s*,
Lk 8:11 of the parable: The *s* is the word
1Co 3: 6 I planted the *s*, Apollos watered it,
2Co 9:10 he who supplies *s* to the sower
Gal 3:29 then you are Abraham's *s*,
1Pe 1:23 not of perishable *s*,
1Jn 3: 9 because God's *s* remains in him;

SEEDS (SEED)
Jn 12:24 But if it dies, it produces many *s*.
Gal 3:16 Scripture does not say "and to *s*,"

SEEDTIME* (SEED)
Ge 8:22 *s* and harvest,

SEEK (SEEKING SEEKS SELF-SEEKING SOUGHT)
Lev 19:18 Do not *s* revenge or bear a grudge
Dt 4:29 if from there you *s* the LORD your
1Ki 22: 5 "First *s* the counsel of the LORD."
1Ch 28: 9 If you *s* him, he will be found
2Ch 7:14 themselves and pray and *s* my face
15: 2 If you *s* him, he will be found
Ps 34:10 those who *s* the LORD lack no
105: 3 of those who *s* the LORD rejoice.
105: 4 *s* his face always.
119: 2 and *s* him with all their heart.
119: 10 I *s* you with all my heart;
119:176 *S* your servant,
Pr 8:17 and those who *s* me find me.
18:15 the ears of the wise *s* it out.
25:27 is it honorable to *s* one's own honor
28: 5 those who *s* the LORD understand
Isa 55: 6 *S* the LORD while he may be
65: 1 found by those who did not *s* me.
Jer 29:13 You will *s* me and find me
Hos 10:12 for it is time to *s* the LORD,
Am 5: 4 "*S* me and live;
Zep 2: 3 *S* the LORD, all you humble
Mt 6:33 But *s* first his kingdom
7: 7 and it will be given to you; *s*
Lk 12:31 *s* his kingdom, and these things will
19:10 For the Son of Man came to *s*
Jn 5:30 for I *s* not to please myself
Ro 10:20 found by those who did not *s* me;
1Co 7:27 you married? Do not *s* a divorce.
10:24 Nobody should *s* his own good,
Heb 11: 6 rewards those who earnestly *s* him.
1Pe 3:11 he must *s* peace and pursue it.

SEEKING (SEEK)
2Ch 30:19 who sets his heart on *s* God—
Pr 20:18 Make plans by *s* advice;

Mal 3: 1 the Lord you are *s* will come
Jn 8:50 I am not *s* glory for myself;
1Co 10:33 For I am not *s* my own good

SEEKS (SEEK)
Pr 11:27 He who *s* good finds good will,
Mt 7: 8 he who *s* finds; and to him who
Jn 4:23 the kind of worshipers the Father *s*.
Ro 3:11 no one who *s* God.

SEER
1Sa 9: 9 of today used to be called a *s*.)

SELF-CONTROL* (CONTROL)
Pr 25:28 is a man who lacks *s*.
Ac 24:25 *s* and the judgment to come,
1Co 7: 5 you because of your lack of *s*.
Gal 5:23 faithfulness, gentleness and *s*.
2Ti 3: 3 slanderous, without *s*, brutal,
2Pe 1: 6 and to knowledge, *s*; and to *s*,

SELF-CONTROLLED* (CONTROL)
1Th 5: 6 are asleep, but let us be alert and *s*.
5: 8 let us be *s*, putting on faith and love
1Ti 3: 2 *s*, respectable, hospitable,
Tit 1: 8 who is *s*, upright, holy
2: 2 worthy of respect, *s*, and sound
2: 5 to be *s* and pure, to be busy at home
2: 6 encourage the young men to be *s*.
2:12 to live *s*, upright and godly lives
1Pe 1:13 prepare your minds for action; be *s*;
4: 7 and *s* so that you can pray.
5: 8 Be *s* and alert.

SELF-DISCIPLINE* (DISCIPLINE)
2Ti 1: 7 a spirit of power, of love and of *s*.

SELF-INDULGENCE*
Mt 23:25 inside they are full of greed and *s*.
Jas 5: 5 lived on earth in luxury and *s*.

SELF-SEEKING* (SEEK)
Ro 2: 8 But for those who are *s*
1Co 13: 5 it is not *s*, it is not easily angered,

SELFISH*
Ps 119: 36 and not toward *s* gain.
Pr 18: 1 An unfriendly man pursues *s* ends;
Gal 5:20 fits of rage, *s* ambition, dissensions,
Php 1:17 preach Christ out of *s* ambition,
2: 3 Do nothing out of *s* ambition
Jas 3:14 and *s* ambition in your hearts,
3:16 you have envy and *s* ambition,

SELL (SELLING SELLS SOLD)
Ge 25:31 "First *s* me your birthright."
Mk 10:21 *s* everything you have
Rev 13:17 or *s* unless he had the mark,

SELLING (SELL)
Lk 17:28 buying and *s*, planting and building

SELLS (SELL)
Pr 31:24 makes linen garments and *s* them,

SEND (SENDING SENDS SENT)
Ps 43: 3 *S* forth your light and your truth,
Isa 6: 8 *S* me!" He said, "Go and tell this
Mal 3: 1 "See, I will *s* my messenger,
Mt 9:38 to *s* out workers into his harvest
24:31 And he will *s* his angels
Mk 1: 2 I will *s* my messenger ahead of you,
Lk 20:13 I will *s* my son, whom I love;
Jn 3:17 For God did not *s* his Son
16: 7 but if I go, I will *s* him to you.
1Co 1:17 For Christ did not *s* me to baptize,

SENDING (SEND)
Mt 10:16 I am *s* you out like sheep
Jn 20:21 Father has sent me, I am *s* you."
Ro 8: 3 God did by *s* his own Son

SENDS (SEND)
Ps 57: 3 God *s* his love and his faithfulness.

SENNACHERIB
Assyrian king whose siege of Jerusalem was overthrown by the LORD following prayer of Hezekiah and Isaiah (2Ki 18:13-19:37; 2Ch 32:1-21; Isa 36-37).

SENSES*
Lk 15:17 "When he came to his *s*, he said,
1Co 15:34 Come back to your *s* as you ought,
2Ti 2:26 and that they will come to their *s*

SENSITIVITY*
Eph 4:19 Having lost all *s*, they have given

SENSUAL* (SENSUALITY)
Col 2:23 value in restraining *s* indulgence.
1Ti 5:11 For when their *s* desires overcome

SENSUALITY* (SENSUAL)
Eph 4:19 have given themselves over to *s*

SENT (SEND)
Ex 3:14 to the Israelites: 'I AM has *s* me
Isa 55:11 achieve the purpose for which I *s* it.
61: 1 He has *s* me to bind up
Jer 28: 9 as one truly *s* by the LORD only
Mt 10:40 me receives the one who *s* me.
Mk 6: 7 he *s* them out two by two
Lk 4:18 He has *s* me to proclaim freedom
9: 2 and he *s* them out to preach
10:16 rejects me rejects him who *s* me."
Jn 1: 6 There came a man who was *s*
4:34 "is to do the will of him who *s* me
5:24 believes him who *s* me has eternal
8:16 I stand with the Father, who *s* me.
9: 4 must do the work of him who *s* me.
16: 5 "Now I am going to him who *s* me,
17: 3 and Jesus Christ, whom you have *s*.
17:18 As you *s* me into the world,
20:21 As the Father has *s* me, I am
Ro 10:15 can they preach unless they are *s*?
Gal 4: 4 God *s* his Son, born of a woman,
1Jn 4:10 but that he loved us and *s* his Son

SENTENCE
2Co 1: 9 in our hearts we felt the *s* of death.

SEPARATE (SEPARATED SEPARATES SEPARATION)
Mt 19: 6 has joined together, let man not *s*."
Ro 8:35 Who shall *s* us from the love
1Co 7:10 wife must not *s* from her husband.
2Co 6:17 and be *s*, says the Lord.
Eph 2:12 at that time you were *s* from Christ,

SEPARATED (SEPARATE)
Isa 59: 2 But your iniquities have *s*
Eph 4:18 in their understanding and *s*

SEPARATES (SEPARATE)
Pr 16:28 and a gossip *s* close friends.
17: 9 repeats the matter *s* close friends.
Mt 25:32 as a shepherd *s* the sheep

SEPARATION (SEPARATE)
Nu 6: 2 a vow of *s* to the LORD

SERAPHS*
Isa 6: 2 Above him were *s*, each
6: 6 Then one of the *s* flew to me

SERIOUSNESS*
Tit 2: 7 *s* and soundness of speech that

SERPENT (SERPENT'S)
Ge 3: 1 the *s* was more crafty than any
Isa 27: 1 Leviathan the coiling *s*;
Rev 12: 9 that ancient *s* called the devil
20: 2 that ancient *s*, who is the devil,

SERPENT'S (SERPENT)
2Co 11: 3 Eve was deceived by the *s* cunning,

SERVANT (SERVANTS)
Ex 14:31 trust in him and in Moses his *s*.
21: 2 "If you buy a Hebrew *s*, he is
1Sa 3:10 "Speak, for your *s* is listening."
2Sa 7:19 the future of the house of your *s*.
1Ki 20:40 While your *s* was busy here
Job 1: 8 "Have you considered my *s* Job?
Ps 19:11 By them is your *s* warned;
19:13 Keep your *s* also from willful sins;
31:16 Let your face shine on your *s*;
89: 3 I have sworn to David my *s*,
Pr 14:35 A king delights in a wise *s*,
17: 2 wise *s* will rule over a disgraceful
22: 7 and the borrower is *s* to the lender.
31:15 and portions for her *s* girls.
Isa 41: 8 "But you, O Israel, my *s*,
49: 3 He said to me, "You are my *s*,
53:11 my righteous *s* will justify
Zec 3: 8 going to bring my *s*, the Branch.
Mal 1: 6 his father, and a *s* his master.
Mt 8:13 his *s* was healed at that very hour.
20:26 great among you must be your *s*,
24:45 Who then is the faithful and wise *s*,
25:21 'Well done, good and faithful *s*!
Lk 1:38 I am the Lord's *s*," Mary answered.
16:13 "No *s* can serve two masters.
Jn 12:26 and where I am, my *s* also will be.
Ro 1: 1 a *s* of Christ Jesus, called
13: 4 For he is God's *s* to do you good.
Php 2: 7 taking the very nature of a *s*,
Col 1:23 of which I, Paul, have become a *s*.
2Ti 2:24 And the Lord's *s* must not quarrel;

SERVANTS (SERVANT)
Lev 25:55 for the Israelites belong to me as *s*.
2Ki 17:13 to you through my *s* the prophets."
Ezr 5:11 "We are the *s* of the God of heaven
Ps 34:22 The LORD redeems his *s*;
103: 21 you his *s* who do his will.
104: 4 flames of fire his *s*.
Isa 44:26 who carries out the words of his *s*
65: 8 so will I do in behalf of my *s*;
65:13 my *s* will drink,
Lk 17:10 should say, 'We are unworthy *s*;
Jn 15:15 longer call you *s*, because a servant
Ro 13: 6 for the authorities are God's *s*,
1Co 3: 5 And what is Paul? Only *s*,
Heb 1: 7 his *s* flames of fire."

SERVE (SERVED SERVES SERVICE SERVING)
Dt 10:12 to *s* the LORD your God
11:13 and to *s* him with all your heart
13: 4 *s* him and hold fast to him.
28:47 you did not *s* the LORD your
Jos 22: 5 and to *s* him with all your heart
24:15 this day whom you will *s*,
24:18 We too will *s* the LORD,
1Sa 7: 3 to the LORD and *s* him only,
12:20 but *s* the LORD with all your heart
12:24 *s* him faithfully with all your heart;
2Ch 19: 9 "You must *s* faithfully
Job 36:11 If they obey and *s* him,
Ps 2:11 *S* the LORD with fear
Da 3:17 the God we *s* is able to save us
Mt 4:10 Lord your God, and *s* him only.'"
6:24 "No one can *s* two masters.
20:28 but to *s*, and to give his life
Ro 12: 7 If it is serving, let him *s*;
Gal 5:13 rather, *s* one another in love.
Eph 6: 7 *S* wholeheartedly,
1Ti 6: 2 they are to *s* them even better,
Heb 9:14 so that we may *s* the living God!
1Pe 4:10 gift he has received to *s* others,
5: 2 greedy for money, but eager to *s*;
Rev 5:10 kingdom and priests to *s* our God,

SERVED (SERVE)
Mt 20:28 Son of Man did not come to be *s*,
Jn 12: 2 Martha *s*, while Lazarus was
Ac 17:25 And he is not *s* by human hands,
Ro 1:25 and *s* created things rather
1Ti 3:13 Those who have *s* well gain

SERVES (SERVE)
Lk 22:26 one who rules like the one who *s*.
22:27 But I am among you as one who *s*.
Jn 12:26 Whoever *s* me must follow me;
Ro 14:18 because anyone who *s* Christ
1Pe 4:11 If anyone *s*, he should do it

SERVICE (SERVE)
Lk 9:62 fit for *s* in the kingdom
12:35 "Be dressed ready for *s*
Ro 15:17 in Christ Jesus in my *s* to God.
1Co 12: 5 There are different kinds of *s*,
16:15 themselves to the *s* of the saints.
2Co 9:12 This *s* that you perform is not only
Eph 4:12 God's people for works of *s*,
Rev 2:19 and faith, your *s* and perseverance,

SERVING (SERVE)
Jos 24:15 if *s* the LORD seems undesirable
2Ch 12: 8 learn the difference between *s* me
Ro 12: 7 If it is *s*, let him serve;
12:11 your spiritual fervor, *s* the Lord.
16:18 people are not *s* our Lord Christ,
Eph 6: 7 as if you were *s* the Lord, not men,
Col 3:24 It is the Lord Christ you are *s*.
2Ti 2: 4 No one *s* as a soldier gets involved

SETH
Ge 4:25 birth to a son and named him *S*,

SETTLE
Mt 5:25 "*S* matters quickly
2Th 3:12 in the Lord Jesus Christ to *s* down

SEVEN (SEVENS SEVENTH)
Ge 7: 2 Take with you *s* of every kind
Jos 6: 4 march around the city *s* times,
1Ki 19:18 Yet I reserve *s* thousand in Israel—
Pr 6:16 *s* that are detestable to him:
24:16 a righteous man falls *s* times,
Isa 4: 1 In that day *s* women
Da 9:25 comes, there will be *s* 'sevens,'
Mt 18:21 Up to *s* times?" Jesus answered,
Lk 11:26 takes *s* other spirits more wicked
Ro 11: 4 for myself *s* thousand who have not
Rev 1: 4 To the *s* churches in the province
6: 1 opened the first of the *s* seals.
8: 2 and to them were given *s* trumpets.
10: 4 And when the *s* thunders spoke,
15: 7 to the *s* angels *s* golden bowls filled

SEVENS* (SEVEN)
Da 9:24 "Seventy *'s'* are decreed
9:25 will be seven *'s,'* and sixty-two *'s.'*
9:26 the sixty-two *'s,'* the Anointed

SEVENTH (SEVEN)
Ge 2: 2 By the *s* day God had finished
Ex 20:10 but the *s* day is a Sabbath
23:11 but during the *s* year let the land lie
23:12 but on the *s* day do not work,
Heb 4: 4 "And on the *s* day God rested

SEVERE
2Co 8: 2 Out of the most *s* trial, their
1Th 1: 6 of the Lord; in spite of *s* suffering,

SEWED (SEWS)
Ge 3: 7 so they *s* fig leaves together

SEWS (SEWED)
Mt 9:16 No one *s* a patch of unshrunk cloth

SEXUAL (SEXUALLY)
Ex 22:19 "Anyone who has *s* relations
Lev 18: 6 relative to have *s* relations.
18: 7 father by having *s* relations
18:20 Do not have *s* relations with
Mt 15:19 murder, adultery, *s* immorality,
Ac 15:20 by idols, from *s* immorality,
1Co 5: 1 reported that there is *s* immorality
6:13 body is not meant for *s* immorality,
6:18 Flee from *s* immorality.
10: 8 should not commit *s* immorality,
2Co 12:21 *s* sin and debauchery
Gal 5:19 *s* immorality, impurity
Eph 5: 3 even a hint of *s* immorality,
Col 3: 5 *s* immorality, impurity, lust,
1Th 4: 3 that you should avoid *s* immorality

SEXUALLY (SEXUAL)
1Co 5: 9 to associate with *s* immoral people
6: 9 Neither the *s* immoral nor idolaters
6:18 he who sins *s* sins against his own
Heb 12:16 See that no one is *s* immoral,
13: 4 the adulterer and all the *s* immoral.
Rev 21: 8 the murderers, the *s* immoral,

SHADE
Ps 121: 5 the LORD is your *s*
Isa 25: 4 and a *s* from the heat.

SHADOW
Ps 17: 8 hide me in the *s* of your wings
23: 4 through the valley of the *s* of death,
36: 7 find refuge in the *s* of your wings.
91: 1 will rest in the *s* of the Almighty.
Isa 51:16 covered you with the *s* of my hand
Col 2:17 These are a *s* of the things that
Heb 8: 5 and *s* of what is in heaven.
10: 1 The law is only a *s*

SHADRACH
Hebrew exiled to Babylon; name changed from Hananiah (Da 1:6-7). Refused defilement by food (Da 1:8-20). Refused to worship idol (Da 3:1-18); saved from furnace (Da 3:19-30).

SHAKE (SHAKEN SHAKING)
Ps 64: 8 all who see them will *s* their heads
99: 1 let the earth *s*.
Hag 2: 6 I will once more *s* the heavens
Heb 12:26 "Once more I will *s* not only

SHAKEN (SHAKE)
Ps 16: 8 I will not be *s*.
30: 6 "I will never be *s*."
62: 2 he is my fortress, I will never be *s*.
112: 6 Surely he will never be *s*;
Isa 54:10 Though the mountains be *s*
Mt 24:29 and the heavenly bodies will be *s*.'
Lk 6:38 *s* together and running over,
Ac 2:25 I will not be *s*.
Heb 12:27 that what cannot be *s* may remain.

SHAKING* (SHAKE)
Ps 22: 7 they hurl insults, *s* their heads:
Mt 27:39 insults at him, *s* their heads
Mk 15:29 *s* their heads and saying, "So!

SHALLUM
King of Israel (2Ki 15:10-16).

SHAME (ASHAMED SHAMED SHAMEFUL)
Ps 25: 3 will ever be put to *s*,
34: 5 their faces are never covered with *s*
69: 6 not be put to *s* because of me,
Pr 13:18 discipline comes to poverty and *s*,
18:13 that is his folly and his *s*.
Jer 8: 9 The wise will be put to *s*;
8:12 No, they have no *s* at all;
Ro 9:33 trusts in him will never be put to *s*."
Ro 10:11 trusts in him will never be put to *s*."
1Co 1:27 things of the world to *s* the wise;
Heb 12: 2 endured the cross, scorning its *s*,

SHAMED (SHAME)
Jer 10:14 every goldsmith is *s* by his idols.
Joel 2:26 never again will my people be *s*.

SHAMEFUL (SHAME)
2Co 4: 2 have renounced secret and *s* ways;
2Pe 2: 2 Many will follow their *s* ways
Rev 21:27 nor will anyone who does what is *s*

SHAMGAR
Judge; killed 600 Philistines (Jdg 3:31).

SHAPE (SHAPES SHAPING)
Job 38:14 The earth takes *s* like clay

SHAPES (SHAPE)
Isa 44:10 Who *s* a god and casts an idol,

SHAPING (SHAPE)
Jer 18: 4 the pot he was *s* from the clay was

SHARE (SHARED SHARERS SHARES SHARING)
Ge 21:10 that slave woman's son will never *s*
Lev 19:17 frankly so you will not *s* in his guilt.
Dt 10: 9 That is why the Levites have no *s*
1Sa 30:24 All will *s* alike."
Eze 18:20 The son will not *s* the guilt
Mt 25:21 and *s* your master's happiness!'
Lk 3:11 "The man with two tunics should *s*
Ro 8:17 if indeed we *s* in his sufferings
12:13 *S* with God's people who are
2Co 1: 7 as you *s* in our sufferings,
Gal 4:30 the slave woman's son will never *s*
6: 6 in the word must *s* all good things
Eph 4:28 something to *s* with those in need.
Col 1:12 you to *s* in the inheritance
2Th 2:14 that you might *s* in the glory
1Ti 5:22 and do not *s* in the sins of others.
6:18 and to be generous and willing to *s*.
2Ti 2: 6 the first to receive a *s* of the crops.
Heb 12:10 that we may *s* in his holiness.
13:16 to do good and to *s* with others,
Rev 22:19 from him his *s* in the tree of life

SHARED (SHARE)
Ps 41: 9 he who *s* my bread,
Ac 4:32 but they *s* everything they had.
Heb 2:14 he too *s* in their humanity so that

SHARERS* (SHARE)
Eph 3: 6 and *s* together in the promise

SHARES (SHARE)
Pr 22: 9 for he *s* his food with the poor.
Jn 13:18 'He who *s* my bread has lifted up

SHARING (SHARE)
1Co 9:10 so in the hope of *s* in the harvest.
2Co 9:13 for your generosity in *s* with them
Php 3:10 the fellowship of *s* in his sufferings,
Phm : 6 you may be active in *s* your faith,

SHARON
SS 2: 1 I am a rose of *S*,

SHARP (SHARPENED SHARPENS SHARPER)
Pr 5: 4 *s* as a double-edged sword.
Isa 5:28 Their arrows are *s*,
Rev 1:16 came a *s* double-edged sword.
19:15 Out of his mouth comes a *s* sword

SHARPENED (SHARP)
Eze 21: 9 *s* and polished—

SHARPENS* (SHARP)
Pr 27:17 As iron *s* iron,
27:17 so one man *s* another.

SHARPER* (SHARP)
Heb 4:12 *S* than any double-edged sword,

SHATTER (SHATTERED SHATTERS)
Jer 51:20 with you I *s* nations,

SHATTERED (SHATTER)
1Sa 2:10 who oppose the LORD will be *s*.
Job 16:12 All was well with me, but he *s* me;
17:11 days have passed, my plans are *s*,
Ecc 12: 6 before the pitcher is *s* at the spring,

SHATTERS (SHATTER)
Ps 46: 9 he breaks the bow and *s* the spear,

SHAVED
Jdg 16:17 my head were *s*, my strength would
1Co 11: 5 it is just as though her head were *s*.

SHEAF (SHEAVES)
Lev 23:11 is to wave the *s* before the LORD

SHEARER* (SHEARERS)
Ac 8:32 and as a lamb before the *s* is silent,

SHEARERS (SHEARER)
Isa 53: 7 and as a sheep before her *s* is silent,

SHEAVES (SHEAF)
Ge 37: 7 while your *s* gathered around mine
Ps 126: 6 carrying *s* with him.

SHEBA
1. Benjamite who rebelled against David (2Sa 20).
2. See QUEEN.

SHECHEM
1. Raped Jacob's daughter Dinah; killed by Simeon and Levi (Ge 34).
2. City where Joshua renewed the covenant (Jos 24).

SHED (SHEDDING SHEDS)
Ge 9: 6 by man shall his blood be *s*;
Pr 6:17 hands that *s* innocent blood,
Ro 3:15 "Their feet are swift to *s* blood;
Col 1:20 through his blood, *s* on the cross.

SHEDDING (SHED)
Heb 9:22 without the *s* of blood there is no

SHEDS (SHED)
Ge 9: 6 "Whoever *s* the blood of man,

SHEEP (SHEEP'S SHEEPSKINS)
Nu 27:17 LORD's people will not be like *s*
Dt 17: 1 a *s* that has any defect or flaw in it,
1Sa 15:14 "What then is this bleating of *s*
Ps 44:22 we are considered as *s*
78:52 led them like *s* through the desert.
100: 3 we are his people, the *s*
119:176 I have strayed like a lost *s*.
SS 4: 2 teeth are like a flock of *s* just shorn,
Isa 53: 6 We all, like *s*, have gone astray,
53: 7 as a *s* before her shearers is silent,
Jer 50: 6 "My people have been lost *s*;
Eze 34:11 I myself will search for my *s*
Zec 13: 7 and the *s* will be scattered,
Mt 9:36 helpless, like *s* without a shepherd.
10:16 I am sending you out like *s*
12:11 "If any of you has a *s* and it falls
18:13 he is happier about that one *s*
25:32 as a shepherd separates the *s*
Jn 10: 1 man who does not enter the *s* pen
10: 3 He calls his own *s* by name
10: 7 the truth, I am the gate for the *s*.
10:15 and I lay down my life for the *s*.
10:27 My *s* listen to my voice; I know
21:17 Jesus said, "Feed my *s*.
1Pe 2:25 For you were like *s* going astray,

SHEEP'S* (SHEEP)
Mt 7:15 They come to you in *s* clothing,

SHEEPSKINS* (SHEEP)
Heb 11:37 They went about in *s* and goatskins

SHEKEL
Ex 30:13 This half *s* is an offering

SHELTER
Ps 27: 5 me in the *s* of his tabernacle
31:20 In the *s* of your presence you hide
55: 8 I would hurry to my place of *s*,
61: 4 take refuge in the *s* of your wings.
91: 1 in the *s* of the Most High
Ecc 7:12 Wisdom is a *s*
Isa 4: 6 It will be a *s* and shade
25: 4 a *s* from the storm
32: 2 Each man will be like a *s*
58: 7 the poor wanderer with *s*—

SHEM
Son of Noah (Ge 5:32; 6:10). Blessed (Ge 9:26). Descendants (Ge 10:21-31; 11:10-32).

SHEPHERD (SHEPHERDS)
Ge 48:15 the God who has been my *s*
49:24 because of the *S*, the Rock of Israel
Nu 27:17 will not be like sheep without a *s*."
2Sa 7: 7 commanded to *s* my people Israel,
1Ki 22:17 on the hills like sheep without a *s*,
Ps 23: 1 LORD is my *s*, I shall not be in want.
28: 9 be their *s* and carry them forever.
80: 1 Hear us, O *S* of Israel,
Isa 40:11 He tends his flock like a *s*:
Jer 31:10 will watch over his flock like a *s*.'
Eze 34: 5 scattered because there was no *s*,
34:12 As a *s* looks after his scattered

Zec 11: 9 and said, "I will not be your *s*.
11:17 "Woe to the worthless *s*,
13: 7 "Strike the *s*,
Mt 2: 6 who will be the *s* of my people
9:36 and helpless, like sheep without a *s*.
26:31 " 'I will strike the *s*,
Jn 10:11 The good *s* lays down his life
10:14 "I am the good *s*; I know my sheep
10:16 there shall be one flock and one *s*.
Heb 13:20 that great *S* of the sheep, equip you
1Pe 5: 4 And when the Chief *S* appears,
Rev 7:17 of the throne will be their *s*;

SHEPHERDS (SHEPHERD)
Jer 23: 1 "Woe to the *s* who are destroying
50: 6 their *s* have led them astray
Eze 34: 2 prophesy against the *s* of Israel;
Lk 2: 8 there were *s* living out in the fields
Ac 20:28 Be *s* of the church of God,
1Pe 5: 2 Be *s* of God's flock that is
Jude :12 *s* who feed only themselves.

SHIBBOLETH*
Jdg 12: 6 No," they said, "All right, say '*S*.' "

SHIELD (SHIELDED SHIELDS)
Ge 15: 1 I am your *s*,
2Sa 22: 3 my *s* and the horn of my salvation.
22:36 You give me your *s* of victory;
Ps 3: 3 But you are a *s* around me,
5:12 with your favor as with a *s*.
7:10 My *s* is God Most High,
18: 2 He is my *s* and the horn
28: 7 LORD is my strength and my *s*;
33:20 he is our help and our *s*.
84:11 For the LORD God is a sun and *s*;
91: 4 his faithfulness will be your *s*
115: 9 he is their help and *s*.
119:114 You are my refuge and my *s*;
144: 2 my *s*, in whom I take refuge,
Pr 2: 7 he is a *s* to those whose walk is
30: 5 he is a *s* to those who take refuge
Eph 6:16 to all this, take up the *s* of faith,

SHIELDED (SHIELD)
1Pe 1: 5 through faith are *s* by God's power

SHIELDS (SHIELD)
Dt 33:12 for he *s* him all day long,

SHIFTLESS*
Pr 19:15 and the *s* man goes hungry.

SHIMEI
Cursed David (2Sa 16:5-14); spared (2Sa 19:16-23). Killed by Solomon (1Ki 2:8-9, 36-46).

SHINE (SHINES SHINING SHONE)
Nu 6:25 the LORD make his face *s*
Job 33:30 that the light of life may *s* on him.
Ps 4: 6 Let the light of your face *s* upon us,
37: 6 make your righteousness *s* like
67: 1 and make his face *s* upon us; *Selah*
80: 1 between the cherubim, *s* forth
118: 27 and he has made his light *s* upon us.
Isa 60: 1 "Arise, *s*, for your light has come,
Da 12: 3 are wise will *s* like the brightness
Mt 5:16 let your light *s* before men,
13:43 the righteous will *s* like the sun
2Co 4: 6 made his light *s* in our hearts
Eph 5:14 and Christ will *s* on you."
Php 2:15 in which you *s* like stars

SHINES (SHINE)
Ps 50: 2 God *s* forth.
Pr 13: 9 The light of the righteous *s* brightly
Jn 1: 5 The light *s* in the darkness,

SHINING (SHINE)
Pr 4:18 *s* ever brighter till the full light
2Pe 1:19 as to a light *s* in a dark place,
Rev 1:16 His face was like the sun *s*

SHIPS
Pr 31:14 She is like the merchant *s*,

SHIPWRECKED*
2Co 11:25 I was stoned, three times I was *s*,
1Ti 1:19 and so have *s* their faith.

SHISHAK
1Ki 14:25 *S* king of Egypt attacked Jerusalem
2Ch 12: 2 *S* king of Egypt attacked Jerusalem

SHOCKING*
Jer 5:30 "A horrible and *s* thing

SHONE (SHINE)
Mt 17: 2 His face *s* like the sun,
Lk 2: 9 glory of the Lord *s* around them,
Rev 21:11 It *s* with the glory of God,

SHOOT
Isa 53: 2 up before him like a tender *s*,
Ro 11:17 and you, though a wild olive *s*,

SHORE
Lk 5: 3 asked him to put out a little from *s*.

SHORT (SHORTENED)
Nu 11:23 "Is the LORD's arm too *s*?
Isa 50: 2 Was my arm too *s* to ransom you?
59: 1 of the LORD is not too *s* to save,
Mt 24:22 If those days had not been cut *s*,
Ro 3:23 and fall *s* of the glory of God,
1Co 7:29 brothers, is that the time is *s*.
Heb 4: 1 of you be found to have fallen *s* of it
Rev 20: 3 he must be set free for a *s* time.

SHORTENED (SHORT)
Mt 24:22 of the elect those days will be *s*.

SHOULDER (SHOULDERS)
Zep 3: 9 and serve him *s* to *s*.

SHOULDERS (SHOULDER)
Dt 33:12 LORD loves rests between his *s*."
Isa 9: 6 and the government will be on his *s*
Lk 15: 5 he joyfully puts it on his *s*

SHOUT (SHOUTED)
Ps 47: 1 *s* to God with cries of joy.
66: 1 *S* with joy to God, all the earth!
95: 1 let us *s* aloud to the Rock
98: 4 *S* for joy to the LORD, all the earth
100: 1 *S* for joy to the LORD, all the earth
Isa 12: 6 *S* aloud and sing for joy, people
26:19 wake up and *s* for joy.
35: 6 the mute tongue *s* for joy.
40: 9 lift up your voice with a *s*,
42: 2 He will not *s* or cry out,
44:23 *s* aloud, O earth beneath.
54: 1 burst into song, *s* for joy,
Zec 9: 9 *S*, Daughter of Jerusalem!

SHOUTED (SHOUT)
Job 38: 7 and all the angels *s* for joy?

SHOW (SHOWED)
Ex 18:20 and *s* them the way to live
33:18 Moses said, "Now *s* me your glory
2Sa 22:26 the faithful you *s* yourself faithful,
1Ki 2: 2 "So be strong, *s* yourself a man,
Ps 17: 7 *S* the wonder of your great love,
25: 4 *S* me your ways, O LORD,
39: 4 "*S* me, O LORD, my life's end
85: 7 *S* us your unfailing love, O LORD,
143: 8 *S* me the way I should go,
Pr 23: 4 have the wisdom to *s* restraint.
SS 2:14 *s* me your face,
Isa 5:16 the holy God will *s* himself holy
30:18 he rises to *s* you compassion.
Eze 28:25 I will *s* myself holy among them
Joel 2:30 I will *s* wonders in the heavens
Zec 7: 9 *s* mercy and compassion
Ac 2:19 I will *s* wonders in the heaven
10:34 it is that God does not *s* favoritism
1Co 12:31 now I will *s* you the most excellent
Eph 2: 7 ages he might *s* the incomparable
Tit 2: 7 In your teaching *s* integrity,
Jas 2:18 I will *s* you my faith by what I do.
Jude :23 to others *s* mercy, mixed with fear

SHOWED (SHOW)
1Ki 3: 3 Solomon *s* his love for the LORD
Lk 24:40 he *s* them his hands and feet.
1Jn 4: 9 This is how God *s* his love

SHOWERS
Eze 34:26 in season; there will be *s* of blessing
Hos 10:12 and *s* righteousness on you.

SHREWD
2Sa 22:27 to the crooked you show yourself *s*.
Mt 10:16 Therefore be as *s* as snakes and

SHRINK (SHRINKS)
Heb 10:39 But we are not of those who *s* back

SHRINKS* (SHRINK)
Heb 10:38 And if he *s* back,

SHRIVEL
Isa 64: 6 we all *s* up like a leaf,

SHUDDER
Eze 32:10 and their kings will *s* with horror

SHUHITE
Job 2:11 Bildad the *S* and Zophar

SHUN* (SHUNS)
Job 28:28 and to *s* evil is understanding.' "
Pr 3: 7 fear the LORD and *s* evil.

SHUNS (SHUN)
Job 1: 8 a man who fears God and *s* evil."
Pr 14:16 man fears the LORD and *s* evil,

SHUT
Ge 7:16 Then the LORD *s* him in.
Isa 22:22 what he opens no one can *s*,
60:11 they will never be *s*, day or night,
Da 6:22 and he *s* the mouths of the lions.
Heb 11:33 who *s* the mouths of lions,
Rev 3: 7 no one can *s*, and what he shuts
21:25 On no day will its gates ever be *s*,

SICK (SICKNESS)
Pr 13:12 Hope deferred makes the heart *s*,
Eze 34: 4 or healed the *s* or bound up
Mt 9:12 who need a doctor, but the *s*.
10: 8 Heal the *s*, raise the dead, cleanse
25:36 I was *s* and you looked after me,
1Co 11:30 many among you are weak and *s*,
Jas 5:14 of you *s*? He should call the elders

SICKBED* (BED)
Ps 41: 3 LORD will sustain him on his *s*

SICKLE
Joel 3:13 Swing the *s*,
Rev 14:14 gold on his head and a sharp *s*

SICKNESS (SICK)
Mt 4:23 and healing every disease and *s*

SIDE (SIDES)
Ps 91: 7 A thousand may fall at your *s*,
124: 1 If the LORD had not been on our *s*
Jn 18:37 Everyone on the *s* of truth listens
20:20 he showed them his hands and *s*.
2Ti 4:17 But the Lord stood at my *s*
Heb 10:33 at other times you stood *s* by *s*

SIDES (SIDE)
Nu 33:55 in your eyes and thorns in your *s*.

SIFT
Lk 22:31 Satan has asked to *s* you as wheat.

SIGHING
Isa 35:10 and sorrow and *s* will flee away.

SIGHT
Ps 51: 4 and done what is evil in your *s*,
90: 4 For a thousand years in your *s*
116: 15 Precious in the *s* of the LORD
Pr 3: 4 in the *s* of God and man.
Mt 11: 5 The blind receive *s*, the lame walk,
Ac 4:19 right in God's *s* to obey you rather
1Co 3:19 this world is foolishness in God's *s*.
2Co 5: 7 We live by faith, not by *s*.
1Pe 3: 4 which is of great worth in God's *s*.

SIGN (SIGNS)
Ge 9:12 "This is the *s* of the covenant I am
17:11 and it will be the *s* of the covenant
Isa 7:14 the Lord himself will give you a *s*:
55:13 for an everlasting *s*,
Eze 20:12 I gave them my Sabbaths as a *s*
Mt 12:38 to see a miraculous *s* from you."
24: 3 what will be the *s* of your coming
24:30 "At that time the *s* of the Son
Lk 2:12 This will be a *s* to you: You will
11:29 It asks for a miraculous *s*,
Ro 4:11 he received the *s* of circumcision,
1Co 11:10 to have a *s* of authority on her head
14:22 are a *s*, not for believers

SIGNS (SIGN)
Ge 1:14 let them serve as *s* to mark seasons
Ps 78:43 day he displayed his miraculous *s*
105: 27 They performed his miraculous *s*
Da 6:27 he performs *s* and wonders
Mt 24:24 and perform great *s* and miracles
Mk 16:17 these *s* will accompany those who
Jn 3: 2 perform the miraculous *s* you are
20:30 Jesus did many other miraculous *s*
Ac 2:19 and *s* on the earth below,
1Co 1:22 Jews demand miraculous *s*
2Co 12:12 *s*, wonders and miracles—
2Th 2: 9 *s* and wonders, and in every sort

SIHON
Nu 21:21 to say to *S* king of the Amorites:
Ps 136: 19 *S* king of the Amorites

SILAS*
Prophet (Ac 15:22-32); co-worker with Paul on second missionary journey (Ac 16-18; 2Co 1:19). Co-writer with Paul (1Th 1:1; 2Th 1:1); Peter (1Pe 5:12).

SILENCE (SILENCED SILENT)
1Pe 2:15 good you should *s* the ignorant talk
Rev 8: 1 there was *s* in heaven

SILENCED (SILENCE)
Ro 3:19 so that every mouth may be *s*
Tit 1:11 They must be *s*, because they are

SILENT (SILENCE)
Est 4:14 For if you remain *s* at this time,
Ps 30:12 to you and not be *s*.
32: 3 When I kept *s*,
39: 2 But when I was *s* and still,
Pr 17:28 a fool is thought wise if he keeps *s*,
Ecc 3: 7 a time to be *s* and a time to speak,
Isa 53: 7 as a sheep before her shearers is *s*,
62: 1 For Zion's sake I will not keep *s*,
Hab 2:20 let all the earth be *s* before him."
Ac 8:32 and as a lamb before the shearer is *s*
1Co 14:34 women should remain *s*
1Ti 2:12 over a man; she must be *s*.

SILVER
Ps 12: 6 like *s* refined in a furnace of clay,
66:10 you refined us like *s*.
Pr 2: 4 and if you look for it as for *s*
3:14 for she is more profitable than *s*
8:10 Choose my instruction instead of *s*,
22: 1 to be esteemed is better than *s*
25: 4 Remove the dross from the *s*,
25:11 is like apples of gold in settings of *s*.
Isa 48:10 I have refined you, though not as *s*;
Eze 22:18 They are but the dross of *s*.
Da 2:32 its chest and arms of *s*, its belly
Hag 2: 8 'The *s* is mine and the gold is mine,'
Zec 13: 9 I will refine them like *s*
Ac 3: 6 Peter said, "*S* or gold I do not have,
1Co 3:12 *s*, costly stones, wood, hay or straw
1Pe 1:18 not with perishable things such as *s*

SILVERSMITH
Ac 19:24 A *s* named Demetrius, who made

SIMEON
Son of Jacob by Leah (Ge 29:33; 35:23; 1Ch 2:1). With Levi killed Shechem for rape of Dinah (Ge 34:25-29). Held hostage by Joseph in Egypt (Ge 42:24-43:23). Tribe of blessed (Ge 49:5-7), numbered (Nu 1:23; 26:14), allotted land (Jos 19:1-9; Eze 48:24), 12,000 from (Rev 7:7).

SIMON
1. See PETER.
2. Apostle, called the Zealot (Mt 10:4; Mk 3:18; Lk 6:15; Ac 1:13).
3. Samaritan sorcerer (Ac 8:9-24).

SIMPLE
Ps 19: 7 making wise the *s*.
119:130 it gives understanding to the *s*.
Pr 8: 5 You who are *s*, gain prudence;
14:15 A *s* man believes anything,

SIMPLEHEARTED* (HEART)
Ps 116: 6 The LORD protects the *s*;

SIN (SINFUL SINNED SINNER SINNERS SINNING SINS)
Ge 4: 7 *s* is crouching at your door;
Ex 32:32 please forgive their *s*—but if not,
Nu 5: 7 and must confess the *s* he has
32:23 be sure that your *s* will find you
Dt 24:16 each is to die for his own *s*.
1Sa 12:23 it from me that I should *s*
15:23 For rebellion is like the *s*
1Ki 8:46 for there is no one who does not *s*
2Ch 7:14 and will forgive their *s* and will heal
Job 1:22 Job did not *s* by charging God
Ps 4: 4 In your anger do not *s*;
17: 3 resolved that my mouth will not *s*.
32: 2 whose *s* the LORD does not count
32: 5 Then I acknowledged my *s* to you
36: 2 too much to detect or hate his *s*.
38:18 I am troubled by my *s*.
39: 1 and keep my tongue from *s*;
51: 2 and cleanse me from my *s*.
66:18 If I had cherished *s* in my heart,
119: 11 that I might not *s* against you.
119:133 let no *s* rule over me.
Pr 5:22 the cords of his *s* hold him fast.
10:19 words are many, *s* is not absent,
14: 9 Fools mock at making amends for *s*
16: 6 faithfulness *s* is atoned for;
17:19 He who loves a quarrel loves *s*;
20: 9 I am clean and without *s*"?
Isa 3: 9 they parade their *s* like Sodom;
6: 7 is taken away and your *s* atoned
64: 5 But when we continued to *s*
Jer 31:30 everyone will die for his own *s*;
Eze 3:18 that wicked man will die for his *s*,
18:26 his righteousness and commits *s*,
33: 8 that wicked man will die for his *s*,
Am 4: 4 "Go to Bethel and *s*;
Mic 6: 7 of my body for the *s* of my soul?
7:18 who pardons *s* and forgives
Zec 3: 4 "See, I have taken away your *s*,
Mt 18: 6 little ones who believe in me to *s*,
Mk 3:29 he is guilty of an eternal *s*."
9:43 If your hand causes you to *s*,
Lk 17: 1 people to *s* are bound to come,
Jn 1:29 who takes away the *s* of the world!
8: 7 "If any one of you is without *s*,
8:34 everyone who sins is a slave to *s*.
8:46 Can any of you prove me guilty of *s*
Ro 2:12 All who *s* apart from the law will
5:12 as *s* entered the world
5:20 where *s* increased, grace increased
6: 2 By no means! We died to *s*;
6:11 count yourselves dead to *s*
6:14 For *s* shall not be your master,
6:23 For the wages of *s* is death,
7: 7 I would not have known what *s* was
7:25 sinful nature a slave to the law of *s*.
14:23 that does not come from faith is *s*.
1Co 8:12 When you *s* against your brothers
15:56 The sting of death is *s*,
2Co 5:21 God made him who had no *s* to be *s*
Gal 6: 1 if someone is caught in a *s*,
1Ti 5:20 Those who *s* are to be rebuked
Heb 4:15 just as we are—yet was without *s*.
9:26 to do away with *s* by the sacrifice
11:25 the pleasures of *s* for a short time.
12: 1 and the *s* that so easily entangles,
Jas 1:15 it gives birth to *s*; and *s*,
1Pe 2:22 "He committed no *s*,
1Jn 1: 7 his Son, purifies us from all *s*.
1: 8 If we claim to be without *s*,
2: 1 But if anybody does *s*, we have one
3: 4 in fact, *s* is lawlessness.
3: 5 And in him is no *s*.
3: 6 No one who continues to *s* has
3: 9 born of God will continue to *s*,
5:16 There is a *s* that leads to death.
5:17 All wrongdoing is *s*, and there is *s*
5:18 born of God does not continue to *s*;

SINAI
Ex 19:20 descended to the top of Mount *S*
31:18 speaking to Moses on Mount *S*,
Ps 68:17 from *S* into his sanctuary.

SINCERE* (SINCERITY)
Da 11:34 many who are not *s* will join them.
Ac 2:46 ate together with glad and *s* hearts,
Ro 12: 9 Love must be *s*.
2Co 6: 6 in the Holy Spirit and in *s* love;
11: 3 somehow be led astray from your *s*
1Ti 1: 5 a good conscience and a *s* faith.
3: 8 *s*, not indulging in much wine,
2Ti 1: 5 have been reminded of your *s* faith,
Heb 10:22 near to God with a *s* heart
Jas 3:17 and good fruit, impartial and *s*.
1Pe 1:22 the truth so that you have *s* love

SINCERITY* (SINCERE)
1Co 5: 8 bread without yeast, the bread of *s*
2Co 1:12 in the holiness and *s* that are
2:17 speak before God with *s*,
8: 8 but I want to test the *s* of your love
Eph 6: 5 and with *s* of heart, just
Col 3:22 but with *s* of heart and reverence

SINFUL (SIN)
Ps 51: 5 Surely I was *s* at birth,
51: 5 *s* from the time my mother
Lk 5: 8 from me, Lord; I am a *s* man!"
Ro 7: 5 we were controlled by the *s* nature,
7:18 lives in me, that is, in my *s* nature.
7:25 but in the *s* nature a slave to the law
8: 3 Son in the likeness of *s* man
8: 4 not live according to the *s* nature
8: 7 the *s* mind is hostile to God.
8: 8 by the *s* nature cannot please God.
8: 9 are controlled not by the *s* nature
8:13 if you live according to the *s* nature
13:14 to gratify the desires of the *s* nature
1Co 5: 5 so that the *s* nature may be
Gal 5:13 freedom to indulge the *s* nature;
5:16 gratify the desires of the *s* nature.
5:19 The acts of the *s* nature are obvious
5:24 Jesus have crucified the *s* nature
6: 8 sows to please his *s* nature,
Col 2:11 in the putting off of the *s* nature,
Heb 3:12 brothers, that none of you has a *s*,
1Pe 2:11 abstain from *s* desires, which war
1Jn 3: 8 He who does what is *s* is

SING (SANG SINGER SINGING SINGS SONG SONGS SUNG)
Ex 15: 1 "I will *s* to the LORD,
Ps 5:11 let them ever *s* for joy.
13: 6 I will *s* to the LORD,
30: 4 *S* to the LORD, you saints of his;
33: 1 *S* joyfully to the LORD, you
47: 6 *S* praises to God, *s* praises;
57: 7 I will *s* and make music.
59:16 But I will *s* of your strength,
63: 7 I *s* in the shadow of your wings.
66: 2 *S* to the glory of his name;
89: 1 I will *s* of the LORD's great love
95: 1 Come, let us *s* for joy to the LORD
96: 1 *S* to the LORD a new song;
98: 1 *S* to the LORD a new song,
101: 1 I will *s* of your love and justice;
108: 1 I will *s* and make music
137: 3 "*S* us one of the songs of Zion!"
147: 1 is to *s* praises to our God,
149: 1 *S* to the LORD a new song,
Isa 54: 1 "*S*, O barren woman,
1Co 14:15 also pray with my mind; I will *s*
Eph 5:19 *S* and make music in your heart
Col 3:16 and as you *s* psalms, hymns
Jas 5:13 Is anyone happy? Let him *s* songs

SINGER* (SING)
2Sa 23: 1 Israel's *s* of songs:

SINGING (SING)
Ps 63: 5 with *s* lips my mouth will praise
68: 6 he leads forth the prisoners with *s*;
98: 5 with the harp and the sound of *s*,
Isa 35:10 They will enter Zion with *s*;
Zep 3:17 he will rejoice over you with *s*."
Ac 16:25 Silas were praying and *s* hymns
Rev 5:13 on the sea, and all that is in them, *s*:

SINGLE
Ex 23:29 I will not drive them out in a *s* year,
Mt 6:27 you by worrying can add a *s* hour
Gal 5:14 law is summed up in a *s* command:

SINGS (SING)
Eze 33:32 more than one who *s* love songs

SINNED (SIN)
Lev 5: 5 confess in what way he has *s*
1Sa 15:24 Then Saul said to Samuel, "I have *s*
2Sa 12:13 "I have *s* against the LORD."
24:10 I have *s* greatly in what I have done
2Ch 6:37 'We have *s*, we have done wrong
Job 1: 5 "Perhaps my children have *s*
33:27 'I *s*, and perverted what was right,
Ps 51: 4 Against you, you only, have I *s*
Jer 2:35 because you say, 'I have not *s*.'
14:20 we have indeed *s* against you.
Da 9: 5 we have *s* and done wrong.
Mic 7: 9 Because I have *s* against him,
Mt 27: 4 "I have *s*," he said,
Lk 15:18 I have *s* against heaven
Ro 3:23 for all have *s* and fall short
5:12 all *s*—for before the law was given,
2Pe 2: 4 did not spare angels when they *s*,
1Jn 1:10 claim we have not *s*, we make him

SINNER (SIN)
Ecc 9:18 but one *s* destroys much good.
Lk 15: 7 in heaven over one *s* who repents
18:13 'God, have mercy on me, a *s*.'
1Co 14:24 convinced by all that he is a *s*
Jas 5:20 Whoever turns a *s* from the error
1Pe 4:18 become of the ungodly and the *s*?"

SINNERS (SIN)
Ps 1: 1 or stand in the way of *s*
37:38 But all *s* will be destroyed;
Pr 1:10 My son, if *s* entice you,
23:17 Do not let your heart envy *s*,
Mt 9:13 come to call the righteous, but *s*."
Ro 5: 8 While we were still *s*, Christ died
Gal 2:17 evident that we ourselves are *s*,
1Ti 1:15 came into the world to save *s*—
Heb 7:26 set apart from *s*, exalted

SINNING (SIN)
Ex 20:20 be with you to keep you from *s*."
1Co 15:34 stop *s*; for there are some who are
Heb 10:26 If we deliberately keep on *s*
1Jn 3: 6 No one who lives in him keeps on *s*
3: 9 go on *s*, because he has been born

SINS (SIN)
Lev 5: 1 " 'If a person *s* because he does not
16:30 you will be clean from all your *s*.
26:40 " 'But if they will confess their *s*
Nu 15:30 " 'But anyone who *s* defiantly,
1Sa 2:25 If a man *s* against another man,
2Ki 14: 6 each is to die for his own *s*."

Ezr 9: 6 our *s* are higher than our heads
9:13 less than our *s* have deserved
Ps 19:13 your servant also from willful *s*;
32: 1 whose *s* are covered.
51: 9 Hide your face from my *s*
79: 9 deliver us and forgive our *s*
85: 2 and covered all their *s*.
103: 3 who forgives all your *s*
103: 10 does not treat us as our *s* deserve
130: 3 O LORD, kept a record of *s*,
Pr 14:21 He who despises his neighbor *s*,
28:13 who conceals his *s* does not
29:22 one commits many *s*.
Ecc 7:20 who does what is right and never *s*.
Isa 1:18 "Though your *s* are like scarlet,
38:17 you have put all my *s*
43:25 and remembers your *s* no more.
59: 2 your *s* have hidden his face
64: 6 like the wind our *s* sweep us away.
Jer 31:34 and will remember their *s* no more
La 3:39 complain when punished for his *s*?
Eze 18: 4 soul who *s* is the one who will die.
33:10 Our offenses and *s* weigh us down,
36:33 day I cleanse you from all your *s*,
Hos 14: 1 Your *s* have been your downfall!
Mt 1:21 he will save his people from their *s*
6:15 if you do not forgive men their *s*,
9: 6 authority on earth to forgive *s* . . . . . "
18:15 "If your brother *s* against you,
26:28 for many for the forgiveness of *s*.
Lk 5:24 authority on earth to forgive *s* . . . . . "
11: 4 Forgive us our *s*,
17: 3 "If your brother *s*, rebuke him,
Jn 8:24 you will indeed die in your *s*."
20:23 If you forgive anyone his *s*,
Ac 2:38 for the forgiveness of your *s*.
3:19 so that your *s* may be wiped out,
10:43 forgiveness of *s* through his name."
22:16 be baptized and wash your *s* away,
26:18 they may receive forgiveness of *s*
Ro 4: 7 whose *s* are covered.
4:25 delivered over to death for our *s*
1Co 15: 3 died for our *s* according
2Co 5:19 not counting men's *s* against them.
Gal 1: 4 himself for our *s* to rescue us
Eph 2: 1 dead in your transgressions and *s*,
Col 2:13 us all our *s*, having canceled
1Ti 5:22 and do not share in the *s* of others.
Heb 1: 3 he had provided purification for *s*,
2:17 atonement for the *s* of the people.
7:27 He sacrificed for their *s* once for all
8:12 and will remember their *s* no more
9:28 to take away the *s* of many people;
10: 4 of bulls and goats to take away *s*.
10:12 for all time one sacrifice for *s*,
10:26 of the truth, no sacrifice for *s* is left,
Jas 4:17 ought to do and doesn't do it, *s*.
5:16 Therefore confess your *s*
5:20 and cover over a multitude of *s*.
1Pe 2:24 He himself bore our *s* in his body
3:18 For Christ died for *s* once for all,
4: 8 love covers over a multitude of *s*.
1Jn 1: 9 If we confess our *s*, he is faithful
2: 2 He is the atoning sacrifice for our *s*,
3: 5 so that he might take away our *s*.
4:10 as an atoning sacrifice for our *s*.
Rev 1: 5 has freed us from our *s* by his blood

SISERA
Jdg 4: 2 The commander of his army was *S*,
5:26 She struck *S*, she crushed his head,

SISTER (SISTERS)
Lev 18: 9 have sexual relations with your *s*,
Mk 3:35 does God's will is my brother and *s*

SISTERS (SISTER)
Mt 19:29 or brothers or *s* or father or mother
1Ti 5: 2 as *s*, with absolute purity.

SIT (SAT SITS SITTING)
Dt 6: 7 them when you *s* at home
1Ki 8:25 fail to have a man to *s* before me
Ps 1: 1 or *s* in the seat of mockers.
26: 5 and refuse to *s* with the wicked.
80: 1 you who *s* enthroned
110: 1 "*S* at my right hand
139: 2 You know when I *s* and when I rise
SS 2: 3 I delight to *s* in his shade,
Isa 16: 5 in faithfulness a man will *s* on it—
Mic 4: 4 Every man will *s* under his own
Mt 20:23 to *s* at my right or left is not for me
22:44 "*S* at my right hand
Lk 22:30 in my kingdom and *s* on thrones,
Heb 1:13 "*S* at my right hand
Rev 3:21 right to *s* with me on my throne,

SITS (SIT)
Ps 99: 1 *s* enthroned between the cherubim,
Isa 40:22 He *s* enthroned above the circle
Mt 19:28 of Man *s* on his glorious throne,
Rev 4: 9 thanks to him who *s* on the throne

SITTING (SIT)
Est 2:19 Mordecai was *s* at the king's gate.
Mt 26:64 the Son of Man *s* at the right hand
Rev 4: 2 in heaven with someone *s* on it.

SITUATION (SITUATIONS)
1Co 7:24 remain in the *s* God called him
Php 4:12 of being content in any and every *s*,

SITUATIONS* (SITUATION)
2Ti 4: 5 head in all *s*, endure hardship,

SKIES (SKY)
Ps 19: 1 the *s* proclaim the work
71:19 Your righteousness reaches to the *s*
108: 4 your faithfulness reaches to the *s*.

SKILL (SKILLED SKILLFUL)
Ps 137: 5 may my right hand forget its *s*.
Ecc 10:10 but *s* will bring success.

SKILLED (SKILL)
Pr 22:29 Do you see a man *s* in his work?

SKILLFUL (SKILL)
Ps 45: 1 my tongue is the pen of a *s* writer.
78:72 with *s* hands he led them.

SKIN (SKINS)
Job 19:20 with only the *s* of my teeth.
19:26 And after my *s* has been destroyed,
Jer 13:23 Can the Ethiopian change his *s*

SKINS (SKIN)
Ex 25: 5 ram *s* dyed red and hides
Lk 5:37 the new wine will burst the *s*,

SKULL
Mt 27:33 (which means The Place of the *S*).

SKY (SKIES)
Ge 1: 8 God called the expanse "*s*."
Pr 30:19 the way of an eagle in the *s*,
Isa 34: 4 and the *s* rolled up like a scroll;
Jer 33:22 stars of the *s* and as measureless
Mt 24:29 the stars will fall from the *s*,
24:30 coming on the clouds of the *s*,
Rev 20:11 Earth and *s* fled from his presence,

SLACK*
Pr 18: 9 One who is *s* in his work

SLAIN (SLAY)
1Sa 18: 7 "Saul has *s* his thousands,
Eze 37: 9 into these *s*, that they may live.'"
Rev 5: 6 as if it had been *s*, standing
5:12 "Worthy is the Lamb, who was *s*,
6: 9 the souls of those who had been *s*

SLANDER (SLANDERED SLANDERER SLANDERERS SLANDEROUS)
Lev 19:16 "'Do not go about spreading *s*
Ps 15: 3 and has no *s* on his tongue,
Pr 10:18 and whoever spreads *s* is a fool.
2Co 12:20 outbursts of anger, factions, *s*,
Eph 4:31 rage and anger, brawling and *s*,
1Ti 5:14 the enemy no opportunity for *s*.
Tit 3: 2 to *s* no one, to be peaceable
1Pe 3:16 in Christ may be ashamed of their *s*
2Pe 2:10 afraid to *s* celestial beings;

SLANDERED (SLANDER)
1Co 4:13 when we are *s*, we answer kindly.

SLANDERER (SLANDER)
1Co 5:11 an idolater or a *s*, a drunkard

SLANDERERS (SLANDER)
Ro 1:30 They are gossips, *s*, God-haters,
1Co 6:10 nor the greedy nor drunkards nor *s*
Tit 2: 3 not to be *s* or addicted

SLANDEROUS (SLANDER)
2Ti 3: 3 unforgiving, *s*, without self-control
2Pe 2:11 do not bring *s* accusations

SLAUGHTER (SLAUGHTERED)
Isa 53: 7 he was led like a lamb to the *s*,
Jer 11:19 been like a gentle lamb led to the *s*;
Ac 8:32 "He was led like a sheep to the *s*,

SLAUGHTERED (SLAUGHTER)
Ps 44:22 we are considered as sheep to be *s*.
Ro 8:36 we are considered as sheep to be *s*

SLAVE (ENSLAVED SLAVERY SLAVES)
Ge 21:10 "Get rid of that *s* woman
Mt 20:27 wants to be first must be your *s*—
Jn 8:34 everyone who sins is a *s* to sin.
Ro 7:14 I am unspiritual, sold as a *s* to sin.
1Co 7:21 Were you a *s* when you were called
12:13 whether Jews or Greeks, *s* or free
Gal 3:28 *s* nor free, male nor female,
4: 7 So you are no longer a *s*, but a son;
4:30 Get rid of the *s* woman and her son
Col 3:11 barbarian, Scythian, *s* or free,
1Ti 1:10 for *s* traders and liars and perjurers
Phm :16 no longer as a *s*, but better than a *s*,
2Pe 2:19 a man is a *s* to whatever has

SLAVERY (SLAVE)
Ex 2:23 The Israelites groaned in their *s*
Ro 6:19 parts of your body in *s* to impurity
Gal 4: 3 were in *s* under the basic principles
1Ti 6: 1 of *s* should consider their masters

SLAVES (SLAVE)
Ps 123: 2 As the eyes of *s* look to the hand
Ecc 10: 7 I have seen *s* on horseback,
Ro 6: 6 that we should no longer be *s* to sin
6:16 you are *s* to sin, which leads
6:22 and have become *s* to God,
Gal 2: 4 in Christ Jesus and to make us *s*.
4: 8 you were *s* to those who
Eph 6: 5 *S*, obey your earthly masters
Col 3:22 *S*, obey your earthly masters
4: 1 provide your *s* with what is right
Tit 2: 9 Teach *s* to be subject

SLAY (SLAIN)
Job 13:15 Though he *s* me, yet will I hope

SLEEP (ASLEEP SLEEPER SLEEPING SLEEPS)
Ge 2:21 the man to fall into a deep *s*;
15:12 Abram fell into a deep *s*,
28:11 it under his head and lay down to *s*.
Ps 4: 8 I will lie down and *s* in peace,
121: 4 will neither slumber nor *s*.
127: 2 for he grants *s* to those he loves.
Pr 6: 9 When will you get up from your *s*?
Ecc 5:12 The *s* of a laborer is sweet,
1Co 15:51 We will not all *s*, but we will all be
1Th 5: 7 For those who *s*, *s* at night,

SLEEPER (SLEEP)
Eph 5:14 "Wake up, O *s*,

SLEEPING (SLEEP)
Mk 13:36 suddenly, do not let him find you *s*.

SLEEPLESS*
2Co 6: 5 in hard work, *s* nights and hunger;

SLEEPS (SLEEP)
Pr 10: 5 he who *s* during harvest is

SLIMY
Ps 40: 2 He lifted me out of the *s* pit,

SLING
1Sa 17:50 over the Philistine with a *s*

SLIP (SLIPPING)
Dt 4: 9 let them *s* from your heart as long
Ps 121: 3 He will not let your foot *s*—

SLIPPING (SLIP)
Ps 66: 9 and kept our feet from *s*.

SLOW
Ex 34: 6 and gracious God, *s* to anger,
Jas 1:19 *s* to speak and *s* to become angry,
2Pe 3: 9 The Lord is not *s* in keeping his

SLUGGARD
Pr 6: 6 Go to the ant, you *s*;
13: 4 The *s* craves and gets nothing,
20: 4 A *s* does not plow in season;
26:15 The *s* buries his hand in the dish;

SLUMBER
Ps 121: 3 he who watches over you will not *s*;
Pr 6:10 A little sleep, a little *s*,
Ro 13:11 for you to wake up from your *s*,

SLUR
Ps 15: 3 and casts no *s* on his fellow man,

SMELL
Ecc 10: 1 As dead flies give perfume a bad *s*,
2Co 2:16 To the one we are the *s* of death;

SMITTEN
Isa 53: 4 *s* by him, and afflicted.

SMOKE
Ex 19:18 Mount Sinai was covered with *s*,
Ps 104: 32 touches the mountains, and they *s*.
Isa 6: 4 and the temple was filled with *s*.
Joel 2:30 blood and fire and billows of *s*.
Ac 2:19 blood and fire and billows of *s*.
Rev 15: 8 filled with *s* from the glory

SMYRNA
Rev 2: 8 the angel of the church in *S* write:

SNAKE (SNAKES)
Nu 21: 8 "Make a *s* and put it up on a pole;
Pr 23:32 In the end it bites like a *s*
Jn 3:14 Moses lifted up the *s* in the desert,

SNAKES (SNAKE)
Mt 10:16 as shrewd as *s* and as innocent
Mk 16:18 they will pick up *s* with their hands;

SNARE (ENSNARE ENSNARED SNARED)
Dt 7:16 for that will be a *s* to you.
Ps 69:22 before them become a *s*;
91: 3 from the fowler's *s*
Pr 29:25 Fear of man will prove to be a *s*,
Ro 11: 9 "May their table become a *s*

SNARED (SNARE)
Pr 3:26 will keep your foot from being *s*.

SNATCH
Jn 10:28 no one can *s* them out of my hand.
Jude :23 *s* others from the fire and save

SNOUT
Pr 11:22 Like a gold ring in a pig's *s*

SNOW
Ps 51: 7 and I will be whiter than *s*.
Isa 1:18 they shall be as white as *s*;

SNUFF (SNUFFED)
Isa 42: 3 a smoldering wick he will not *s* out.
Mt 12:20 a smoldering wick he will not *s* out,

SNUFFED (SNUFF)
Pr 13: 9 but the lamp of the wicked is *s* out.

SOAP
Mal 3: 2 a refiner's fire or a launderer's *s*.

SOAR (SOARED)
Isa 40:31 They will *s* on wings like eagles;

SOARED (SOAR)
2Sa 22:11 He *s* on the wings of the wind.

SOBER
Ro 12: 3 think of yourself with *s* judgment,

SODOM
Ge 13:12 and pitched his tents near *S*.
19:24 rained down burning sulfur on *S*
Isa 1: 9 we would have become like *S*,
Lk 10:12 on that day for *S* than for that town
Ro 9:29 we would have become like *S*,
Rev 11: 8 which is figuratively called *S*

SOIL
Ge 4: 2 kept flocks, and Cain worked the *s*.
Mt 13:23 on good *s* is the man who hears

SOLD (SELL)
1Ki 21:25 who *s* himself to do evil in the eyes
Mt 10:29 Are not two sparrows *s* for a penny
13:44 then in his joy went and *s* all he had
Ro 7:14 I am unspiritual, *s* as a slave to sin.

SOLDIER
1Co 9: 7 as a *s* at his own expense?
2Ti 2: 3 with us like a good *s* of Christ Jesus

SOLE
Dt 28:65 place for the *s* of your foot.
Isa 1: 6 From the *s* of your foot to the top

SOLID
2Ti 2:19 God's *s* foundation stands firm,
Heb 5:12 You need milk, not *s* food!

SOLOMON
Son of David by Bathsheba; king of Judah (2Sa 12:24; 1Ch 3:5, 10). Appointed king by David (1Ki 1); adversaries Adonijah, Joab, Shimei killed by Benaiah (1Ki 2). Asked for wisdom (1Ki 3; 2Ch 1). Judged between two prostitutes (1Ki 3:16-28). Built temple (1Ki 5-7; 2Ch 2-5); prayer of dedication (1Ki 8; 2Ch 6). Visited by Queen of Sheba (1Ki 10; 2Ch 9). Wives turned his heart from God (1Ki 11:1-13). Jeroboam rebelled against (1Ki 11:26-40). Death (1Ki 11:41-43; 2Ch 9:29-31).
Proverbs of (1Ki 4:32; Pr 1:1; 10:1; 25:1); psalms of (Ps 72; 127); song of (SS 1:1).

SON (SONS SONSHIP)
Ge 17:19 your wife Sarah will bear you a *s*,
21:10 rid of that slave woman and her *s*,
22: 2 "Take your *s*, your only *s*, Isaac,
Ex 11: 5 Every firstborn *s* in Egypt will die,
Dt 1:31 father carries his *s*, all the way you
6:20 In the future, when your *s* asks you,
8: 5 as a man disciplines his *s*,
21:18 rebellious *s* who does not obey his
2Sa 7:14 be his father, and he will be my *s*.
1Ki 3:20 and put her dead *s* by my breast.
Ps 2: 7 He said to me, "You are my *S*;
2:12 Kiss the *S*, lest he be angry
8: 4 the *s* of man that you care for him?
Pr 3:12 as a father the *s* he delights in.
6:20 My *s*, keep your father's
10: 1 A wise *s* brings joy to his father,
13:24 He who spares the rod hates his *s*,
29:17 Discipline your *s*, and he will give
Isa 7:14 with child and will give birth to a *s*,
Eze 18:20 The *s* will not share the guilt
Da 3:25 the fourth looks like a *s* of the gods
7:13 before me was one like a *s* of man,
Hos 11: 1 and out of Egypt I called my *s*.
Am 7:14 neither a prophet nor a prophet's *s*,
Mt 1: 1 of Jesus Christ the *s* of David,
1:21 She will give birth to a *s*,
2:15 "Out of Egypt I called my *s*."
3:17 "This is my *S*, whom I love;
4: 3 "If you are the *S* of God, tell these
8:20 but the *S* of Man has no place
11:27 one knows the *S* except the Father,
12: 8 For the *S* of Man is Lord
12:32 a word against the *S* of Man will be
12:40 so the *S* of Man will be three days
13:41 *S* of Man will send out his angels,
13:55 "Isn't this the carpenter's *s*?
14:33 "Truly you are the *S* of God."
16:16 "You are the Christ, the *S*
16:27 For the *S* of Man is going to come
17: 5 "This is my *S*, whom I love;
19:28 when the *S* of Man sits
20:18 and the *S* of Man will be betrayed
20:28 as the *S* of Man did not come
21: 9 "Hosanna to the *S* of David!"
22:42 Whose *s* is he?" "The *s* of David,"
24:27 so will be the coming of the *S*
24:30 They will see the *S* of Man coming
24:44 the *S* of Man will come at an hour
25:31 "When the *S* of Man comes
26:63 if you are the Christ, the *S* of God."
27:54 "Surely he was the *S* of God!"
28:19 and of the *S* and of the Holy Spirit,
Mk 1:11 "You are my *S*, whom I love;
2:28 So the *S* of Man is Lord
8:38 the *S* of Man will be ashamed
9: 7 "This is my *S*, whom I love.
10:45 even the *S* of Man did not come
13:32 nor the *S*, but only the Father.
14:62 you will see the *S* of Man sitting
Lk 1:32 and will be called the *S*
2: 7 she gave birth to her firstborn, a *s*.
3:22 "You are my *S*, whom I love;
9:35 This is my *S*, whom I have chosen;
9:58 but the *S* of Man has no place
12: 8 the *S* of Man will also acknowledge
15:20 he ran to his *s*, threw his arms
18: 8 when the *S* of Man comes,
18:31 written by the prophets about the *S*
19:10 For the *S* of Man came to seek
Jn 1:34 I testify that this is the *S* of God."
3:14 so the *S* of Man must be lifted up,
3:16 that he gave his one and only *S*,
3:36 believes in the *S* has eternal life,
5:19 the *S* can do nothing by himself;
6:40 is that everyone who looks to the *S*
11: 4 so that God's *S* may be glorified
17: 1 Glorify your *S*, that your *S* may
Ac 7:56 and the *S* of Man standing
13:33 " 'You are my *S*;
Ro 1: 4 with power to be the *S* of God
5:10 to him through the death of his *S*,
8: 3 did by sending his own *S*
8:29 conformed to the likeness of his *S*,
8:32 He who did not spare his own *S*,
1Co 15:28 then the *S* himself will be made
Gal 2:20 I live by faith in the *S* of God,
4: 4 God sent his *S*, born of a woman,
4:30 rid of the slave woman and her *s*,
1Th 1:10 and to wait for his *S* from heaven,
Heb 1: 2 days he has spoken to us by his *S*,
1: 5 "You are my *S*;
2: 6 the *s* of man that you care for him?
4:14 Jesus the *S* of God, let us hold
5: 5 "You are my *S*;
7:28 appointed the *S*, who has been
10:29 punished who has trampled the *S*
Heb 12: 6 everyone he accepts as a *s*."
2Pe 1:17 saying, "This is my *S*, whom I love;
1Jn 1: 3 is with the Father and with his *S*,
1: 7 his *S*, purifies us from all sin.
2:23 whoever acknowledges the *S* has
3: 8 reason the *S* of God appeared was
4: 9 only *S* into the world that we might
4:14 that the Father has sent his *S*
5: 5 he who believes that Jesus is the *S*
5:11 eternal life, and this life is in his *S*.
Rev 1:13 lampstands was someone "like a *s*
14:14 on the cloud was one "like a *s*

SONG (SING)
Ex 15: 2 LORD is my strength and my *s*;
Ps 40: 3 He put a new *s* in my mouth,
69:30 I will praise God's name in *s*
96: 1 Sing to the LORD a new *s*;
98: 4 burst into jubilant *s* with music;
119: 54 Your decrees are the theme of my *s*
149: 1 Sing to the LORD a new *s*,
Isa 49:13 burst into *s*, O mountains!
55:12 will burst into *s* before you,
Rev 5: 9 And they sang a new *s*:
15: 3 and sang the *s* of Moses the servant

SONGS (SING)
2Sa 23: 1 Israel's singer of *s*:
Job 35:10 who gives *s* in the night,
Ps 100: 2 come before him with joyful *s*.
126: 6 will return with *s* of joy,
137: 3 "Sing us one of the *s* of Zion!"
Eph 5:19 with psalms, hymns and spiritual *s*.
Jas 5:13 Is anyone happy? Let him sing *s*

SONS (SON)
Ge 6: 2 the *s* of God saw that the daughters
10:20 These are the *s* of Ham
Ru 4:15 who is better to you than seven *s*,
Ps 127: 3 *S* are a heritage from the LORD,
132: 12 if your *s* keep my covenant
Hos 1:10 they will be called *'s*
Joel 2:28 Your *s* and daughters will prophesy
Mt 5: 9 for they will be called *s* of God.
Lk 6:35 and you will be *s* of the Most High,
Jn 12:36 so that you may become *s* of light."
Ro 8:14 by the Spirit of God are *s* of God.
9:26 they will be called *'s*
2Co 6:18 and you will be my *s* and daughters
Gal 3:26 You are all *s* of God through faith
4: 5 we might receive the full rights of *s*.
4: 6 Because you are *s*, God sent
Heb 12: 7 discipline; God is treating you as *s*.

SONSHIP* (SON)
Ro 8:15 but you received the Spirit of *s*.

SORCERY
Lev 19:26 " 'Do not practice divination or *s*.

SORROW (SORROWS)
Ps 6: 7 My eyes grow weak with *s*;
116: 3 I was overcome by trouble and *s*.
Isa 60:20 and your days of *s* will end.
Jer 31:12 and they will *s* no more.
Ro 9: 2 I have great *s* and unceasing
2Co 7:10 Godly *s* brings repentance that

SORROWS (SORROW)
Isa 53: 3 a man of *s*, and familiar

SOUGHT (SEEK)
2Ch 26: 5 As long as he *s* the LORD,
31:21 he *s* his God and worked
Ps 34: 4 I *s* the LORD, and he answered me
119: 58 I have *s* your face with all my heart;

SOUL (SOULS)
Dt 6: 5 with all your *s* and with all your
10:12 all your heart and with all your *s*,
30: 6 all your heart and with all your *s*,
Jos 22: 5 with all your heart and all your *s*."
2Ki 23:25 and with all his *s* and with all his
Ps 23: 3 he restores my *s*.
34: 2 My *s* will boast in the LORD;
42: 1 so my *s* pants for you, O God.
42:11 Why are you downcast, O my *s*?
62: 5 Find rest, O my *s*, in God alone;
63: 8 My *s* clings to you;
94:19 consolation brought joy to my *s*.
103: 1 Praise the LORD, O my *s*;
Pr 13:19 A longing fulfilled is sweet to the *s*,
16:24 sweet to the *s* and healing
22: 5 he who guards his *s* stays far
Isa 55: 2 your *s* will delight in the richest
La 3:20 and my *s* is downcast within me.
Eze 18: 4 For every living *s* belongs to me,
Mt 10:28 kill the body but cannot kill the *s*.
16:26 yet forfeits his *s*? Or what can
22:37 with all your *s* and with all your

Heb 4:12 even to dividing *s* and spirit,
3Jn :2 even as your *s* is getting along well.

SOULS (SOUL)
Pr 11:30 and he who wins *s* is wise.
Jer 6:16 and you will find rest for your *s*.
Mt 11:29 and you will find rest for your *s*.

SOUND (FINE-SOUNDING)
Ge 3:8 and his wife heard the *s*
Pr 3:21 preserve *s* judgment
Eze 3:12 I heard behind me a loud rumbling *s*
Jn 3:8 You hear its *s*, but you cannot tell
Ac 2:2 Suddenly a *s* like the blowing
1Co 14:8 if the trumpet does not *s* a clear call
15:52 the trumpet will *s*, the dead will
1Ti 1:10 to the *s* doctrine that conforms
2Ti 4:3 men will not put up with *s* doctrine.
Tit 1:9 can encourage others by *s* doctrine
2:1 is in accord with *s* doctrine.

SOUR
Eze 18:2 " 'The fathers eat *s* grapes,

SOURCE
Heb 5:9 became the *s* of eternal salvation

SOVEREIGN (SOVEREIGNTY)
Ge 15:2 But Abram said, "O *S* LORD,
2Sa 7:18 O *S* LORD, and what is my family,
Ps 71:16 your mighty acts, O *S* LORD;
Isa 25:8 *S* LORD will wipe away the tears
40:10 the *S* LORD comes with power,
50:4 *S* LORD has given me
61:1 The Spirit of the *S* LORD is on me,
61:11 so the *S* LORD will make
Jer 32:17 to the LORD: "Ah, *S* LORD,
Eze 12:28 fulfilled, declares the *S* LORD.' "
Da 4:25 that the Most High is *s*
2Pe 2:1 denying the *s* Lord who bought
Jude :4 and deny Jesus Christ our only *S*

SOVEREIGNTY (SOVEREIGN)
Da 7:27 Then the *s*, power and greatness

SOW (SOWER SOWN SOWS)
Job 4:8 and those who *s* trouble reap it.
Ps 126:5 Those who *s* in tears
Hos 8:7 "They *s* the wind
10:12 *S* for yourselves righteousness,
Mt 6:26 they do not *s* or reap or store away
13:3 "A farmer went out to *s* his seed.
1Co 15:36 What you *s* does not come to life
Jas 3:18 Peacemakers who *s*
2Pe 2:22 and, "A *s* that is washed goes back

SOWER (SOW)
Isa 55:10 so that it yields seed for the *s*
Mt 13:18 to what the parable of the *s* means:
Jn 4:36 so that the *s* and the reaper may be
2Co 9:10 Now he who supplies seed to the *s*

SOWN (SOW)
Mt 13:8 sixty or thirty times what was *s*.
Mk 4:15 along the path, where the word is *s*.
1Co 15:42 The body that is *s* is perishable,

SOWS (SOW)
Pr 11:18 he who *s* righteousness reaps a sure
22:8 He who *s* wickedness reaps trouble
2Co 9:6 Whoever *s* sparingly will
Gal 6:7 A man reaps what he *s*.

SPARE (SPARES SPARING)
Est 7:3 *s* my people—this is my request.
Ro 8:32 He who did not *s* his own Son,
11:21 natural branches, he will not *s* you
2Pe 2:4 For if God did not *s* angels
2:5 if he did not *s* the ancient world

SPARES (SPARE)
Pr 13:24 He who *s* the rod hates his son,

SPARING (SPARE)
Pr 21:26 but the righteous give without *s*.

SPARKLE
Zec 9:16 They will *s* in his land

SPARROW (SPARROWS)
Ps 84:3 Even the *s* has found a home,

SPARROWS (SPARROW)
Mt 10:29 Are not two *s* sold for a penny?

SPEAR (SPEARS)
1Sa 19:10 as Saul drove the *s* into the wall.
Ps 46:9 breaks the bow and shatters the *s*,

SPEARS (SPEAR)
Isa 2:4 and their *s* into pruning hooks.
Joel 3:10 and your pruning hooks into *s*.
Mic 4:3 and their *s* into pruning hooks.

SPECIAL
Jas 2:3 If you show *s* attention

SPECK
Mt 7:3 look at the *s* of sawdust

SPECTACLE
1Co 4:9 We have been made a *s*
Col 2:15 he made a public *s* of them,

SPEECH
Ps 19:3 There is no *s* or language
Pr 22:11 pure heart and whose *s* is gracious
2Co 8:7 in faith, in *s*, in knowledge,
1Ti 4:12 set an example for the believers in *s*

SPEND (SPENT)
Pr 31:3 do not *s* your strength on women,
Isa 55:2 Why *s* money on what is not bread,
2Co 12:15 So I will very gladly *s*

SPENT (SPEND)
Mk 5:26 many doctors and had *s* all she had,
Lk 6:12 and *s* the night praying to God.
15:14 After he had *s* everything,

SPIN
Mt 6:28 They do not labor or *s*.

SPIRIT (SPIRIT'S SPIRITS SPIRITUAL SPIRITUALLY)
Ge 1:2 and the *S* of God was hovering
6:3 "My *S* will not contend
Ex 31:3 I have filled him with the *S* of God,
Nu 11:25 and put the *S* on the seventy elders.
Dt 34:9 filled with the *s* of wisdom
Jdg 6:34 Then the *S* of the LORD came
11:29 Then the *S* of the LORD came
13:25 and the *S* of the LORD began
1Sa 10:10 the *S* of God came upon him
16:13 day on the *S* of the LORD came
16:14 the *S* of the LORD had departed
2Sa 23:2 "The *S* of the LORD spoke
2Ki 2:9 inherit a double portion of your *s*,"
Ne 9:20 You gave your good *S*
9:30 By your *S* you admonished them
Job 33:4 The *S* of God has made me;
Ps 31:5 Into your hands I commit my *s*;
34:18 saves those who are crushed in *s*.
51:10 and renew a steadfast *s* within me.
51:11 or take your Holy *S* from me.
51:17 sacrifices of God are a broken *s*;
106:33 rebelled against the *S* of God,
139:7 Where can I go from your *S*?
143:10 may your good *S*
Isa 11:2 The *S* of the LORD will rest
30:1 an alliance, but not by my *S*,
32:15 till the *S* is poured upon us
44:3 I will pour out my *S*
57:15 him who is contrite and lowly in *s*,
61:1 The *S* of the Sovereign LORD is
63:10 and grieved his Holy *S*.
Eze 11:19 an undivided heart and put a new *s*
13:3 prophets who follow their own *s*
36:26 you a new heart and put a new *s*
Da 4:8 and the *s* of the holy gods is in him
Joel 2:28 I will pour out my *S* on all people.
Zec 4:6 but by my *S*,' says the LORD
Mt 1:18 to be with child through the Holy *S*
3:11 will baptize you with the Holy *S*
3:16 he saw the *S* of God descending
4:1 led by the *S* into the desert
5:3 saying: "Blessed are the poor in *s*,
10:20 but the *S* of your Father speaking
12:31 against the *S* will not be forgiven.
26:41 *s* is willing, but the body is weak."
28:19 and of the Son and of the Holy *S*,
Mk 1:8 he will baptize you with the Holy *S*
Lk 1:35 "The Holy *S* will come upon you,
1:80 child grew and became strong in *s*;
3:16 will baptize you with the Holy *S*
4:18 "The *S* of the Lord is on me,
11:13 Father in heaven give the Holy *S*
23:46 into your hands I commit my *s*."
Jn 1:33 who will baptize with the Holy *S*.'
3:5 a man is born of water and the *S*,
4:24 God is *s*, and his worshipers must
6:63 The *S* gives life; the flesh counts
7:39 Up to that time the *S* had not been
14:26 But the Counselor, the Holy *S*,
16:13 But when he, the *S* of truth, comes,
20:22 and said, "Receive the Holy *S*.
Ac 1:5 will be baptized with the Holy *S*."
1:8 when the Holy *S* comes on you;
2:4 of them were filled with the Holy *S*
2:17 I will pour out my *S* on all people.
2:38 will receive the gift of the Holy *S*.
4:31 they were all filled with the Holy *S*
5:3 that you have lied to the Holy *S*
6:3 who are known to be full of the *S*
8:15 that they might receive the Holy *S*,
9:17 and be filled with the Holy *S*."
11:16 will be baptized with the Holy *S*.'
13:2 and fasting, the Holy *S* said,
19:2 "Did you receive the Holy *S*
Ro 8:4 nature but according to the *S*.
8:5 set on what the *S* desires.
8:9 And if anyone does not have the *S*
8:13 but if by the *S* you put
8:16 The *S* himself testifies
8:23 who have the firstfruits of the *S*,
8:26 the *S* helps us in our weakness.
1Co 2:10 God has revealed it to us by his *S*.
2:14 man without the *S* does not accept
5:3 present, I am with you in *s*.
6:19 body is a temple of the Holy *S*,
12:13 baptized by one *S* into one body—
2Co 1:22 and put his *S* in our hearts
3:3 but with the *S* of the living God,
3:6 the letter kills, but the *S* gives life.
3:17 Now the Lord is the *S*,
5:5 and has given us the *S* as a deposit,
7:1 that contaminates body and *s*,
Gal 3:2 Did you receive the *S*
5:16 by the *S*, and you will not gratify
5:22 But the fruit of the *S* is love, joy,
5:25 let us keep in step with the *S*.
6:8 from the *S* will reap eternal life.
Eph 1:13 with a seal, the promised Holy *S*,
2:22 in which God lives by his *S*.
4:4 There is one body and one *S*—
4:30 do not grieve the Holy *S* of God,
5:18 Instead, be filled with the *S*.
6:17 of salvation and the sword of the *S*,
Php 2:2 being one in *s* and purpose.
1Th 5:23 May your whole *s*, soul
2Th 2:13 the sanctifying work of the *S*
1Ti 3:16 was vindicated by the *S*,
2Ti 1:7 For God did not give us a *s*
Heb 2:4 of the Holy *S* distributed according
4:12 even to dividing soul and *s*,
10:29 and who has insulted the *S* of grace
1Pe 3:4 beauty of a gentle and quiet *s*,
2Pe 1:21 carried along by the Holy *S*.
1Jn 3:24 We know it by the *S* he gave us.
4:1 Dear friends, do not believe every *s*
4:13 because he has given us of his *S*.
Jude :20 holy faith and pray in the Holy *S*.
Rev 2:7 let him hear what the *S* says

SPIRIT'S* (SPIRIT)
1Co 2:4 a demonstration of the *S* power,
1Th 5:19 not put out the *S* fire; do not treat

SPIRITS (SPIRIT)
1Co 12:10 to another distinguishing between *s*,
14:32 The *s* of prophets are subject
1Jn 4:1 test the *s* to see whether they are

SPIRITUAL (SPIRIT)
Ro 12:1 to God—this is your *s* act of worship.
12:11 but keep your *s* fervor, serving
1Co 2:13 expressing *s* truths in *s* words.
3:1 I could not address you as *s* but
12:1 Now about *s* gifts, brothers,
14:1 of love and eagerly desire *s* gifts,
15:44 a natural body, it is raised a *s* body.
Gal 6:1 you who are *s* should restore him
Eph 1:3 with every *s* blessing in Christ.
5:19 with psalms, hymns and *s* songs.
6:12 and against the *s* forces of evil
1Pe 2:2 newborn babies, crave pure *s* milk,
2:5 are being built into a *s* house

SPIRITUALLY (SPIRIT)
1Co 2:14 because they are *s* discerned.

SPIT
Mt 27:30 They *s* on him, and took the staff
Rev 3:16 I am about to *s* you out

SPLENDOR
1Ch 16:29 the LORD in the *s* of his holiness.
29:11 the glory and the majesty and the *s*,
Job 37:22 of the north he comes in golden *s*;
Ps 29:2 in the *s* of his holiness.
45:3 clothe yourself with *s* and majesty.
96:6 *S* and majesty are before him;
96:9 in the *s* of his holiness;
104:1 you are clothed with *s* and majesty.
145:5 of the glorious *s* of your majesty,
145:12 and the glorious *s* of your kingdom.
148:13 his *s* is above the earth
Pr 4:9 and present you with a crown of *s*."
16:31 Gray hair is a crown of *s*;
20:29 gray hair the *s* of the old.
Isa 55:5 for he has endowed you with *s*."
60:21 for the display of my *s*.

Isa 61: 3 the LORD for the display of his s.
63: 1 Who is this, robed in s,
Hab 3: 4 His s was like the sunrise;
Mt 6:29 in all his s was dressed like one
Lk 9:31 appeared in glorious s, talking
2Th 2: 8 and destroy by the s of his coming.

SPOIL (SPOILS)
Ps 119:162 like one who finds great s.

SPOILS (SPOIL)
Isa 53:12 he will divide the s with the strong,
Jn 6:27 Do not work for food that s,

SPONTANEOUS*
Phm :14 so that any favor you do will be s

SPOTLESS
2Pe 3:14 make every effort to be found s,

SPOTS (SPOTTED)
Jer 13:23 or the leopard its s?

SPOTTED (SPOTS)
Ge 30:32 and every s or speckled goat.

SPREAD (SPREADING SPREADS)
Ps 78:19 "Can God s a table in the desert?
Ac 6: 7 So the word of God s.
12:24 of God continued to increase and s.
13:49 of the Lord s through the whole
19:20 the word of the Lord s widely
2Th 3: 1 message of the Lord may s rapidly

SPREADING (SPREAD)
Pr 29: 5 is s a net for his feet.
1Th 3: 2 God's fellow worker in s the gospel

SPREADS (SPREAD)
Pr 10:18 and whoever s slander is a fool.

SPRING (SPRINGS WELLSPRING)
Jer 2:13 the s of living water,
Jn 4:14 in him a s of water welling up
Jas 3:12 can a salt s produce fresh water.

SPRINGS (SPRING)
2Pe 2:17 These men are s without water

SPRINKLE (SPRINKLED SPRINKLING)
Lev 16:14 and with his finger s it on the front

SPRINKLED (SPRINKLE)
Heb 10:22 having our hearts s to cleanse us

SPRINKLING (SPRINKLE)
1Pe 1: 2 to Jesus Christ and s by his blood:

SPROUT
Pr 23: 5 for they will surely s wings
Jer 33:15 I will make a righteous Branch s

SPUR*
Heb 10:24 how we may s one another

SPURNS*
Pr 15: 5 A fool s his father's discipline,

SPY
Gal 2: 4 ranks to s on the freedom we have

SQUANDERED (SQUANDERS)
Lk 15:13 there s his wealth in wild living.

SQUANDERS* (SQUANDERED)
Pr 29: 3 of prostitutes s his wealth.

SQUARE
Rev 21:16 The city was laid out like a s,

STABILITY*
Pr 29: 4 By justice a king gives a country s,

STAFF
Ge 49:10 the ruler's s from between his feet,
Ex 7:12 Aaron's s swallowed up their staffs.
Nu 17: 6 and Aaron's s was among them.
Ps 23: 4 your rod and your s,

STAIN (STAINED)
Eph 5:27 without s or wrinkle or any other

STAINED (STAIN)
Isa 63: 1 with his garments s crimson?

STAKES
Isa 54: 2 strengthen your s.

STAND (STANDING STANDS STOOD)
Ex 14:13 S firm and you will see
Jos 10:12 "O sun, s still over Gibeon,
2Ch 20:17 s firm and see the deliverance
Job 19:25 in the end he will s upon the earth.
Ps 1: 1 or s in the way of sinners
1: 5 Therefore the wicked will not s
24: 3 Who may s in his holy place?
33:11 of the LORD s firm forever,
40: 2 and gave me a firm place to s.
76: 7 Who can s before you
93: 5 Your statutes s firm;
119:120 I s in awe of your laws.
130: 3 O Lord, who could s?
Ecc 5: 7 Therefore s in awe of God.
Isa 7: 9 If you do not s firm in your faith,
29:23 will s in awe of the God of Israel.
Eze 22:30 s before me in the gap on behalf
Hab 3: 2 I s in awe of your deeds, O LORD.
Zec 14: 4 On that day his feet will s
Mal 3: 2 Who can s when he appears?
Mt 12:25 divided against itself will not s.
Ro 14: 4 for the Lord is able to make him s.
14:10 we will all s before God's judgment
1Co 10:13 out so that you can s up under it.
15:58 Therefore, my dear brothers, s firm
16:13 Be on your guard; s firm in the faith
Gal 5: 1 S firm, then, and do not let
Eph 6:14 S firm then, with the belt
2Th 2:15 s firm and hold to the teachings we
Jas 5: 8 You too, be patient and s firm,
Rev 3:20 Here I am! I s at the door

STANDING (STAND)
Ex 3: 5 where you are s is holy ground."
Jos 5:15 the place where you are s is holy."
Ru 2: 1 a man of s, whose name was Boaz.
4:11 May you have s in Ephrathah
Lk 21:19 By s firm you will gain life.
1Ti 3:13 have served well gain an excellent s
1Pe 5: 9 Resist him, s firm in the faith,

STANDS (STAND)
Ps 89: 2 that your love s firm forever,
119: 89 it s firm in the heavens.
Pr 12: 7 the house of the righteous s firm.
Isa 40: 8 but the word of our God s forever."
Mt 10:22 but he who s firm to the end will be
2Ti 2:19 God's solid foundation s firm,
1Pe 1:25 but the word of the Lord s forever

STAR (STARS)
Nu 24:17 A s will come out of Jacob;
Isa 14:12 O morning s, son of the dawn!
Mt 2: 2 We saw his s in the east
2Pe 1:19 the morning s rises in your hearts.
Rev 2:28 I will also give him the morning s.
22:16 and the bright Morning S."

STARS (STAR)
Ge 1:16 He also made the s.
Job 38: 7 while the morning s sang together
Da 12: 3 like the s for ever and ever.
Php 2:15 in which you shine like s

STATURE
1Sa 2:26 boy Samuel continued to grow in s
Lk 2:52 And Jesus grew in wisdom and s,

STATUTES
Ps 19: 7 s of the LORD are trustworthy,
93: 5 Your s stand firm;
119: 2 Blessed are they who keep his s
119: 14 I rejoice in following your s
119: 24 Your s are my delight;
119: 36 Turn my heart toward your s
119: 99 for I meditate on your s.
119:111 Your s are my heritage forever;
119:125 that I may understand your s.
119:129 Your s are wonderful;
119:138 The s you have laid
119:152 Long ago I learned from your s
119:167 I obey your s,

STEADFAST*
Ps 51:10 and renew a s spirit within me.
57: 7 My heart is s, O God,
57: 7 my heart is s;
108: 1 My heart is s, O God;
111: 8 They are s for ever and ever,
112: 7 his heart is s, trusting in the LORD
119: 5 Oh, that my ways were s
Isa 26: 3 him whose mind is s,
1Pe 5:10 and make you strong, firm and s.

STEADY
Isa 35: 3 s the knees that give way;

STEAL (STOLEN)
Ex 20:15 "You shall not s.
Lev 19:11 " 'Do not s.
Dt 5:19 "You shall not s.
Mt 19:18 do not s, do not give false
Ro 13: 9 "Do not s," "Do not covet,"
Eph 4:28 has been stealing must s no longer,

STEP (FOOTSTEPS STEPS)
Job 34:21 he sees their every s.
Gal 5:25 let us keep in s with the Spirit.

STEPHEN
Deacon (Ac 6:5). Arrested (Ac 6:8-15). Speech to Sanhedrin (Ac 7). Stoned (Ac 7:54-60; 22:20).

STEPS (STEP)
Ps 37:23 he makes his s firm;
Pr 14:15 prudent man gives thought to his s.
16: 9 but the LORD determines his s.
20:24 A man's s are directed
Jer 10:23 it is not for man to direct his s.
1Pe 2:21 that you should follow in his s.

STERN (STERNNESS)
Pr 15:10 S discipline awaits him who leaves

STERNNESS* (STERN)
Ro 11:22 and s of God: s to those who fell,

STICKS
Pr 18:24 there is a friend who s closer

STIFF-NECKED (NECK)
Ex 34: 9 Although this is a s people,
Pr 29: 1 A man who remains s

STILL
Jos 10:13 So the sun stood s,
Ps 37: 7 Be s before the LORD
46:10 "Be s, and know that I am God;
89: 9 its waves mount up, you s them.
Zec 2:13 Be s before the LORD, all mankind
Mk 4:39 said to the waves, "Quiet! Be s!"

STIMULATE*
2Pe 3: 1 as reminders to s you

STING
1Co 15:55 Where, O death, is your s?"

STINGY
Pr 28:22 A s man is eager to get rich

STIRRED (STIRS)
Ps 45: 1 My heart is s by a noble theme

STIRS (STIRRED)
Pr 6:19 and a man who s up dissension
10:12 Hatred s up dissension,
15: 1 but a harsh word s up anger.
15:18 hot-tempered man s up dissension,
16:28 A perverse man s up dissension,
28:25 A greedy man s up dissension,
29:22 An angry man s up dissension,

STOLEN (STEAL)
Lev 6: 4 he must return what he has s
SS 4: 9 You have s my heart, my sister,

STOMACH
1Co 6:13 Food for the s and the s for food"—
Php 3:19 their god is their s, and their glory

STONE (CAPSTONE CORNERSTONE MILLSTONE STONED STONES)
Ex 24: 4 set up twelve s pillars representing
28:10 on one s and the remaining six
34: 1 "Chisel out two s tablets like
Dt 4:13 then wrote them on two s tablets.
19:14 your neighbor's boundary s set up
1Sa 17:50 the Philistine with a sling and a s;
Ps 91:12 will not strike your foot against a s.
118: 22 The s the builders rejected
Pr 22:28 not move an ancient boundary s
Isa 8:14 a s that causes men to stumble
28:16 "See, I lay a s in Zion,
Eze 11:19 remove from them their heart of s
36:26 remove from you your heart of s
Mt 7: 9 will give him a s? Or if he asks
21:42 " 'The s the builders rejected
24: 2 not one s here will be left
Mk 16: 3 "Who will roll the s away
Lk 4: 3 tell this s to become bread."
Jn 8: 7 the first to throw a s at her."
Ac 4:11 " 'the s you builders rejected,
Ro 9:32 stumbled over the "stumbling s."
2Co 3: 3 not on tablets of s but on tablets
1Pe 2: 6 "See, I lay a s in Zion,
Rev 2:17 also give him a white s

STONED (STONE)
2Co 11:25 once I was s, three times I was
Heb 11:37 They were s; they were sawed

STONES (STONE)
Ex 28:21 are to be twelve s, one for each
Jos 4: 3 to take up twelve s from the middle
1Sa 17:40 chose five smooth s

Mt 3: 9 out of these s God can raise up
1Co 3:12 silver, costly s, wood, hay or straw,
1Pe 2: 5 also, like living s, are being built

STOOD (STAND)
Jos 10:13 So the sun s still,
Lk 22:28 You are those who have s by me
2Ti 4:17 But the Lord s at my side
Jas 1:12 because when he has s the test,

STOOP (STOOPS)
2Sa 22:36 you s down to make me great.

STOOPS (STOOP)
Ps 113: 6 who s down to look

STOP
Job 37:14 s and consider God's wonders.
Isa 1:13 S bringing meaningless offerings!
1:16 S doing wrong,
2:22 S trusting in man,
Jer 32:40 I will never s doing good to them,
Mk 9:39 "Do not s him," Jesus said.
Jn 6:43 "S grumbling among yourselves,"
7:24 S judging by mere appearances,
20:27 S doubting and believe."
Ro 14:13 Therefore let us s passing judgment
1Co 14:20 Brothers, s thinking like children.

STORE (STORED)
Pr 2: 1 and s up my commands within you,
7: 1 and s up my commands within you.
10:14 Wise men s up knowledge,
Isa 33: 6 a rich s of salvation and wisdom
Mt 6:19 not s up for yourselves treasures
6:26 or reap or s away in barns,
2Ti 4: 8 Now there is in s for me the crown

STORED (STORE)
Lk 6:45 out of the good s up in his heart,
Col 1: 5 from the hope that is s up for you

STOREHOUSE (HOUSE)
Mal 3:10 Bring the whole tithe into the s,

STORIES*
2Pe 1:16 did not follow cleverly invented s
2: 3 you with s they have made up.

STORM
Job 38: 1 LORD answered Job out of the s.
Ps 107: 29 He stilled the s to a whisper;
Lk 8:24 the s subsided, and all was calm.

STOUTHEARTED* (HEART)
Ps 138: 3 you made me bold and s.

STRAIGHT
Ps 27:11 lead me in a s path
107: 7 He led them by a s way
Pr 2:13 who leave the s paths
3: 6 and he will make your paths s.
4:11 and lead you along s paths.
4:25 Let your eyes look s ahead,
11: 5 of the blameless makes a s way
15:21 of understanding keeps a s course.
Isa 40: 3 make s in the wilderness
Mt 3: 3 make s paths for him.'"
Jn 1:23 'Make s the way for the Lord.'"
2Pe 2:15 They have left the s way

STRAIN (STRAINING)
Mt 23:24 You s out a gnat but swallow

STRAINING (STRAIN)
Php 3:13 and s toward what is ahead,

STRANGE (STRANGER STRANGERS)
Isa 28:11 with foreign lips and s tongues
1Co 14:21 "Through men of s tongues
1Pe 4: 4 They think it s that you do not

STRANGER (STRANGE)
Ps 119: 19 I am a s on earth;
Mt 25:35 I was a s and you invited me in,
Jn 10: 5 But they will never follow a s;

STRANGERS (STRANGE)
Heb 13: 2 Do not forget to entertain s,
1Pe 2:11 as aliens and s in the world,

STRAW
Isa 11: 7 and the lion will eat s like the ox.
1Co 3:12 silver, costly stones, wood, hay or s

STRAYED (STRAYS)
Ps 119: 176 I have s like a lost sheep.
Jer 31:19 After I s,

STRAYS (STRAYED)
Pr 21:16 A man who s from the path
Eze 34:16 for the lost and bring back the s.

STREAM (STREAMS)
Am 5:24 righteousness like a never-failing s!

STREAMS (STREAM)
Ps 1: 3 He is like a tree planted by s
46: 4 is a river whose s make glad
Ecc 1: 7 All s flow into the sea,
Jn 7:38 s of living water will flow

STREET
Mt 6: 5 on the s corners to be seen by men.
22: 9 Go to the s corners and invite
Rev 21:21 The great s of the city was of pure gold,

STRENGTH (STRONG)
Ex 15: 2 The LORD is my s and my song;
Dt 4:37 by his Presence and his great s,
6: 5 all your soul and with all your s.
Jdg 16:15 told me the secret of your great s."
2Sa 22:33 It is God who arms me with s
2Ki 23:25 with all his soul and with all his s,
1Ch 16:11 Look to the LORD and his s;
16:28 ascribe to the LORD glory and s,
29:12 In your hands are s and power
Ne 8:10 for the joy of the LORD is your s."
Ps 18: 1 I love you, O LORD, my s.
21:13 Be exalted, O LORD, in your s;
28: 7 The LORD is my s and my shield;
29:11 The LORD gives s to his people;
33:16 no warrior escapes by his great s.
46: 1 God is our refuge and s,
59:17 O my S, I sing praise to you;
65: 6 having armed yourself with s,
73:26 but God is the s of my heart
84: 5 Blessed are those whose s is in you,
96: 7 ascribe to the LORD glory and s.
105: 4 Look to the LORD and his s;
118: 14 The LORD is my s and my song;
147: 10 not in the s of the horse,
Pr 24: 5 a man of knowledge increases s;
30:25 Ants are creatures of little s,
Isa 12: 2 the LORD, is my s and my song;
31: 1 and in the great s of their horsemen
40:26 of his great power and mighty s,
40:31 will renew their s.
63: 1 forward in the greatness of his s?
Jer 9:23 or the strong man boast of his s
Mic 5: 4 flock in the s of the LORD,
Hab 3:19 The Sovereign LORD is my s;
Mk 12:30 all your mind and with all your s.'
1Co 1:25 of God is stronger than man's s.
Eph 1:19 is like the working of his mighty s,
Php 4:13 through him who gives me s.
Heb 11:34 whose weakness was turned to s;
1Pe 4:11 it with the s God provides,

STRENGTHEN (STRONG)
2Ch 16: 9 to s those whose hearts are fully
Ps 119: 28 s me according to your word.
Isa 35: 3 S the feeble hands,
41:10 I will s you and help you;
Lk 22:32 have turned back, s your brothers."
Eph 3:16 of his glorious riches he may s you
1Th 3:13 May he s your hearts
2Th 2:17 and s you in every good deed
Heb 12:12 s your feeble arms and weak knees.

STRENGTHENED (STRONG)
Col 1:11 being s with all power according
Heb 13: 9 good for our hearts to be s by grace,

STRENGTHENING (STRONG)
1Co 14:26 done for the s of the church.

STRETCHES
Ps 104: 2 he s out the heavens like a tent

STRICKEN (STRIKE)
Isa 53: 8 of my people he was s.

STRICT
1Co 9:25 in the games goes into s training.

STRIFE (STRIVE)
Pr 17: 1 than a house full of feasting, with s.
20: 3 It is to a man's honor to avoid s,
22:10 out the mocker, and out goes s;
30:33 so stirring up anger produces s."
1Ti 6: 4 s, malicious talk, evil suspicions

STRIKE (STRIKES STROKE)
Ge 3:15 and you will s his heel."
Zec 13: 7 "S the shepherd,
Mt 4: 6 so that you will not s your foot
26:31 "'I will s the shepherd,

STRIKES (STRIKE)
Mt 5:39 If someone s you on the right

STRIPS
Lk 2:12 You will find a baby wrapped in s
Jn 20: 5 in at the s of linen lying there

STRIVE* (STRIFE)
Ac 24:16 I s always to keep my conscience
1Ti 4:10 (and for this we labor and s),

STROKE (STRIKE)
Mt 5:18 the smallest letter, not the least s

STRONG (STRENGTH STRENGTHEN STRENGTHENED STRENGTHENING STRONGER)
Dt 3:24 your greatness and your s hand.
31: 6 Be s and courageous.
Jos 1: 6 "Be s and courageous,
Jdg 5:21 March on, my soul; be s!
2Sa 10:12 Be s and let us fight bravely
1Ki 2: 2 "So be s, show yourself a man,
1Ch 28:20 "Be s and courageous,
2Ch 32: 7 them with these words: "Be s
Ps 24: 8 The LORD s and mighty,
31: 2 a s fortress to save me.
62:11 that you, O God, are s,
Pr 18:10 The name of the LORD is a s tower
31:17 her arms are s for her tasks.
Ecc 9:11 or the battle to the s,
SS 8: 6 for love is as s as death,
Isa 35: 4 "Be s, do not fear;
53:12 he will divide the spoils with the s,
Jer 9:23 or the s man boast of his strength
50:34 Yet their Redeemer is s;
Hag 2: 4 Be s, all you people of the land,'
Mt 12:29 can anyone enter a s man's house
Lk 2:40 And the child grew and became s;
Ro 15: 1 We who are s ought to bear
1Co 1: 8 He will keep you s to the end,
1:27 things of the world to shame the s.
16:13 in the faith; be men of courage; be s
2Co 12:10 For when I am weak, then I am s.
Eph 6:10 be s in the Lord and in his mighty
2Ti 2: 1 be s in the grace that is
1Pe 5:10 restore you and make you s,

STRONGER (STRONG)
Dt 4:38 before you nations greater and s
1Co 1:25 of God is s than man's strength.

STRONGHOLD (STRONGHOLDS)
2Sa 22: 3 He is my s, my refuge and my
Ps 9: 9 a s in times of trouble.
18: 2 the horn of my salvation, my s.
27: 1 The LORD is the s of my life—
144: 2 my s and my deliverer,

STRONGHOLDS (STRONGHOLD)
Zep 3: 6 their s are demolished.
2Co 10: 4 have divine power to demolish s.

STRUGGLE (STRUGGLED STRUGGLING)
Ro 15:30 me in my s by praying to God
Eph 6:12 For our s is not against flesh
Heb 12: 4 In your s against sin, you have not

STRUGGLED (STRUGGLE)
Ge 32:28 because you have s with God

STRUGGLING* (STRUGGLE)
Col 1:29 To this end I labor, s
2: 1 to know how much I am s for you

STUDENT (STUDY)
Mt 10:24 "A s is not above his teacher,

STUDY (STUDENT)
Ezr 7:10 Ezra had devoted himself to the s
Ecc 12:12 and much s wearies the body.
Jn 5:39 You diligently s the Scriptures

STUMBLE (STUMBLES STUMBLING)
Ps 37:24 though he s, he will not fall,
119: 165 and nothing can make them s.
Pr 3:23 and your foot will not s;
Isa 8:14 a stone that causes men to s
Jer 13:16 before your feet s
31: 9 a level path where they will not s,
Eze 7:19 for it has made them s into sin.
Hos 14: 9 but the rebellious s in them.
Mal 2: 8 teaching have caused many to s;
Jn 11: 9 A man who walks by day will not s,
Ro 9:33 in Zion a stone that causes men to s
14:20 that causes someone else to s.
1Co 10:32 Do not cause anyone to s,
Jas 3: 2 We all s in many ways.
1Pe 2: 8 and, "A stone that causes men to s
1Jn 2:10 nothing in him to make him s.

STUMBLES (STUMBLE)
Pr 24:17 when he s, do not let your heart

Jn 11:10 is when he walks by night that he *s*,
Jas 2:10 and yet *s* at just one point is guilty

STUMBLING (STUMBLE)
Lev 19:14 put a *s* block in front of the blind,
Ps 56:13 and my feet from *s*,
Mt 16:23 Satan! You are a *s* block to me;
Ro 9:32 They stumbled over the "*s* stone."
11: 9 a *s* block and a retribution for them
14:13 up your mind not to put any *s* block
1Co 1:23 a *s* block to Jews and foolishness
8: 9 freedom does not become a *s* block
2Co 6: 3 We put no *s* block in anyone's path,

STUMP
Isa 6:13 so the holy seed will be the *s*
11: 1 up from the *s* of Jesse;

STUPID
Pr 12: 1 but he who hates correction is *s*.
2Ti 2:23 to do with foolish and *s* arguments,

STUPOR
Ro 11: 8 "God gave them a spirit of *s*,

SUBDUE (SUBDUED)
Ge 1:28 in number; fill the earth and *s* it.

SUBDUED (SUBDUE)
Jos 10:40 So Joshua *s* the whole region,
Ps 47: 3 He *s* nations under us,

SUBJECT (SUBJECTED)
Mt 5:22 angry with his brother will be *s*
1Co 14:32 of prophets are *s* to the control
15:28 then the Son himself will be made *s*
Tit 2: 5 and to be *s* to their husbands,
2: 9 slaves to be *s* to their masters
3: 1 Remind the people to be *s* to rulers

SUBJECTED (SUBJECT)
Ro 8:20 For the creation was *s*

SUBMISSION (SUBMIT)
1Co 14:34 but must be in *s*, as the Law says.
1Ti 2:11 learn in quietness and full *s*.

SUBMISSIVE (SUBMIT)
Jas 3:17 then peace-loving, considerate, *s*,
1Pe 3: 1 in the same way be *s*
5: 5 in the same way be *s*

SUBMIT (SUBMISSION SUBMISSIVE SUBMITS)
Ro 13: 1 Everyone must *s* himself
13: 5 necessary to *s* to the authorities,
1Co 16:16 to *s* to such as these
Eph 5:21 *S* to one another out of reverence
Col 3:18 Wives, *s* to your husbands,
Heb 12: 9 How much more should we *s*
13:17 Obey your leaders and *s*
Jas 4: 7 *S* yourselves, then, to God.
1Pe 2:18 *s* yourselves to your masters

SUBMITS* (SUBMIT)
Eph 5:24 Now as the church *s* to Christ,

SUBTRACT*
Dt 4: 2 what I command you and do not *s*

SUCCEED (SUCCESS SUCCESSFUL)
Ps 20: 4 and make all your plans *s*.
Pr 15:22 but with many advisers they *s*.
16: 3 and your plans will *s*.
21:30 that can *s* against the LORD.

SUCCESS (SUCCEED)
Ge 39:23 and gave him *s* in whatever he did.
1Sa 18:14 In everything he did he had great *s*,
1Ch 12:18 *S*, *s* to you, and *s*
22:13 you will have *s* if you are careful
2Ch 26: 5 the LORD, God gave him *s*.
Ecc 10:10 but skill will bring *s*.

SUCCESSFUL (SUCCEED)
Jos 1: 7 that you may be *s* wherever you go.
2Ki 18: 7 he was *s* in whatever he undertook.
2Ch 20:20 in his prophets and you will be *s*."

SUFFER (SUFFERED SUFFERING SUFFERINGS SUFFERS)
Job 36:15 those who *s* he delivers
Isa 53:10 to crush him and cause him to *s*,
Mk 8:31 the Son of Man must *s* many things
Lk 24:26 the Christ have to *s* these things
24:46 The Christ will *s* and rise
2Co 1: 6 of the same sufferings we *s*.
Php 1:29 to *s* for him, since you are going
Heb 2:18 would have him to *s* many times
1Pe 3:17 to *s* for doing good
4:16 However, if you *s* as a Christian,

SUFFERED (SUFFER)
Heb 2: 9 and honor because he *s* death,
2:18 Because he himself *s*
1Pe 2:21 Christ *s* for you, leaving you
4: 1 he who has *s* in his body is done

SUFFERING (SUFFER)
Job 36:15 who suffer he delivers in their *s*;
Ps 22:24 the *s* of the afflicted one;
Isa 53: 3 of sorrows, and familiar with *s*.
53:11 After the *s* of his soul,
La 1:12 Is any *s* like my *s*
Ac 5:41 worthy of *s* disgrace for the Name.
Ro 5: 3 know that *s* produces
2Ti 1: 8 But join with me in *s* for the gospel,
Heb 2:10 of their salvation perfect through *s*.
13: 3 as if you yourselves were *s*.
1Pe 4:12 at the painful trial you are *s*,

SUFFERINGS (SUFFER)
Ro 5: 3 but we also rejoice in our *s*,
8:17 share in his *s* in order that we may
8:18 that our present *s* are not worth
2Co 1: 5 as the *s* of Christ flow
Php 3:10 the fellowship of sharing in his *s*,
1Pe 4:13 rejoice that you participate in the *s*
5: 9 are undergoing the same kind of *s*.

SUFFERS (SUFFER)
Pr 13:20 but a companion of fools *s* harm.
1Co 12:26 If one part *s*, every part *s* with it;

SUFFICIENT
2Co 12: 9 said to me, "My grace is *s* for you,

SUITABLE
Ge 2:18 I will make a helper *s* for him."

SUMMED* (SUMS)
Ro 13: 9 there may be, are *s* up
Gal 5:14 The entire law is *s* up

SUMMONS
Ps 50: 1 speaks and *s* the earth
Isa 45: 3 God of Israel, who *s* you by name.

SUMS* (SUMMED)
Mt 7:12 for this *s* up the Law

SUN (SUNRISE)
Jos 10:13 So the *s* stood still,
Jdg 5:31 may they who love you be like the *s*
Ps 84:11 For the LORD God is a *s*
121: 6 the *s* will not harm you by day,
136: 8 the *s* to govern the day,
Ecc 1: 9 there is nothing new under the *s*.
Isa 60:19 The *s* will no more be your light
Mal 4: 2 the *s* of righteousness will rise
Mt 5:45 He causes his *s* to rise on the evil
13:43 the righteous will shine like the *s*
17: 2 His face shone like the *s*,
Lk 23:45 for the *s* stopped shining.
Eph 4:26 Do not let the *s* go
Rev 1:16 His face was like the *s* shining
21:23 The city does not need the *s*

SUNG (SING)
Mt 26:30 When they had *s* a hymn, they

SUNRISE (SUN)
2Sa 23: 4 he is like the light of morning at *s*
Hab 3: 4 His splendor was like the *s*;

SUPERIOR
Heb 1: 4 he became as much *s* to the angels
8: 6 ministry Jesus has received is as *s*

SUPERVISION
Gal 3:25 longer under the *s* of the law.

SUPPER
Lk 22:20 after the *s* he took the cup, saying,
1Co 11:25 after *s* he took the cup,
Rev 19: 9 to the wedding *s* of the Lamb!' "

SUPPLIED (SUPPLY)
Ac 20:34 of mine have *s* my own needs
Php 4:18 and even more; I am amply *s*,

SUPPLY (SUPPLIED SUPPLYING)
2Co 8:14 your plenty will *s* what they need,
1Th 3:10 and *s* what is lacking in your faith.

SUPPLYING* (SUPPLY)
2Co 9:12 you perform is not only *s* the needs

SUPPORT (SUPPORTED SUPPORTING)
Ps 18:18 but the LORD was my *s*.
Ro 11:18 consider this: You do not *s* the root
1Co 9:12 If others have this right of *s*

SUPPORTED (SUPPORT)
Ps 94:18 your love, O LORD, *s* me.
Col 2:19 *s* and held together by its ligaments

SUPPORTING (SUPPORT)
Eph 4:16 held together by every *s* ligament,

SUPPRESS*
Ro 1:18 wickedness of men who *s* the truth

SUPREMACY* (SUPREME)
Col 1:18 in everything he might have the *s*.

SUPREME (SUPREMACY)
Pr 4: 7 Wisdom is *s*; therefore get wisdom.

SURE
Nu 28:31 Be *s* the animals are without defect
32:23 you may be *s* that your sin will find
Dt 6:17 Be *s* to keep the commands
14:22 Be *s* to set aside a tenth
29:18 make *s* there is no root
Jos 23:13 then you may be *s* that the LORD
1Sa 12:24 But be *s* to fear the LORD
Ps 19: 9 The ordinances of the LORD are *s*
132: 11 a *s* oath that he will not revoke:
Pr 27:23 Be *s* you know the condition
Isa 28:16 cornerstone for a *s* foundation;
Eph 5: 5 of this you can be *s*: No immoral,
Heb 11: 1 faith is being *s* of what we hope for
2Pe 1:10 to make your calling and election *s*.

SURFACE
2Co 10: 7 You are looking only on the *s*

SURPASS* (SURPASSED SURPASSES SURPASSING)
Pr 31:29 but you *s* them all."

SURPASSED* (SURPASS)
Jn 1:15 'He who comes after me has *s* me
1:30 man who comes after me has *s* me

SURPASSES* (SURPASS)
Pr 8:19 what I yield *s* choice silver.
Mt 5:20 unless your righteousness *s* that
Eph 3:19 to know this love that *s* knowledge

SURPASSING* (SURPASS)
Ps 150: 2 praise him for his *s* greatness.
2Co 3:10 in comparison with the *s* glory.
9:14 of the *s* grace God has given you.
Php 3: 8 the *s* greatness of knowing Christ

SURPRISE (SURPRISED)
1Th 5: 4 that this day should *s* you like

SURPRISED (SURPRISE)
1Pe 4:12 do not be *s* at the painful trial you
1Jn 3:13 Do not be *s*, my brothers,

SURRENDER
1Co 13: 3 and *s* my body to the flames,

SURROUND (SURROUNDED SURROUNDS)
Ps 5:12 you *s* them with your favor
32: 7 and *s* me with songs of deliverance.
89: 7 awesome than all who *s* him.
125: 2 As the mountains *s* Jerusalem,
Jer 31:22 a woman will *s* a man."

SURROUNDED (SURROUND)
Heb 12: 1 since we are *s* by such a great cloud

SURROUNDS* (SURROUND)
Ps 32:10 *s* the man who trusts in him.
89: 8 and your faithfulness *s* you.
125: 2 so the LORD *s* his people

SUSA
Ezr 4: 9 and Babylon, the Elamites of *S*,
Ne 1: 1 while I was in the citadel of *S*,

SUSPENDS*
Job 26: 7 he *s* the earth over nothing.

SUSPICIONS*
1Ti 6: 4 evil *s* and constant friction

SUSTAIN (SUSTAINING SUSTAINS)
Ps 55:22 and he will *s* you;
Isa 46: 4 I am he, I am he who will *s* you.

SUSTAINING* (SUSTAIN)
Heb 1: 3 *s* all things by his powerful word.

SUSTAINS (SUSTAIN)
Ps 18:35 and your right hand *s* me;
146: 9 and *s* the fatherless and the widow,
147: 6 The LORD *s* the humble
Isa 50: 4 to know the word that *s* the weary.

SWALLOW (SWALLOWED)
Isa 25: 8 he will *s* up death forever.
Jnh 1:17 provided a great fish to *s* Jonah,
Mt 23:24 You strain out a gnat but *s* a camel.

SWALLOWED (SWALLOW)
1Co 15:54 "Death has been *s* up in victory."
2Co 5: 4 so that what is mortal may be *s* up

SWAYED
Mt 11: 7 A reed *s* by the wind? If not,
22:16 You aren't *s* by men, because you
2Ti 3: 6 are *s* by all kinds of evil desires,

SWEAR (SWORE SWORN)
Lev 19:12 " 'Do not *s* falsely by my name
Ps 24: 4 or *s* by what is false.
Isa 45:23 by me every tongue will *s*.
Mt 5:34 Do not *s* at all: either by heaven,
Jas 5:12 Above all, my brothers, do not *s*—

SWEAT*
Ge 3:19 By the *s* of your brow
Lk 22:44 his *s* was like drops of blood falling

SWEET (SWEETER SWEETNESS)
Job 20:12 "Though evil is *s* in his mouth
Ps 119:103 How *s* are your words
Pr 9:17 "Stolen water is *s*;
13:19 A longing fulfilled is *s* to the soul,
16:24 *s* to the soul and healing
20:17 by fraud tastes *s* to a man,
24:14 also that wisdom is *s* to your soul;
Ecc 5:12 The sleep of a laborer is *s*,
Isa 5:20 and *s* for bitter.
Eze 3: 3 it tasted as *s* as honey in my mouth.
Rev 10:10 It tasted as *s* as honey in my mouth

SWEETER (SWEET)
Ps 19:10 they are *s* than honey,
119:103 *s* than honey to my mouth!

SWEETNESS* (SWEET)
SS 4:11 Your lips drop *s* as the honeycomb,
5:16 His mouth is *s* itself;

SWEPT
Mt 12:44 finds the house unoccupied, *s* clean

SWERVE*
Pr 4: 5 do not forget my words or *s*
4:27 Do not *s* to the right or the left;

SWIFT
Pr 1:16 they are *s* to shed blood.
Ecc 9:11 The race is not to the *s*
Isa 59: 7 they are *s* to shed innocent blood.
Ro 3:15 "Their feet are *s* to shed blood;
2Pe 2: 1 bringing *s* destruction

SWINDLER* (SWINDLERS)
1Co 5:11 or a slanderer, a drunkard or a *s*.

SWINDLERS* (SWINDLER)
1Co 5:10 or the greedy and *s*, or idolaters.
6:10 *s* will inherit the kingdom of God.

SWORD (SWORDS)
Ge 3:24 and a flaming *s* flashing back
Dt 32:41 when I sharpen my flashing *s*
Jos 5:13 of him with a drawn *s* in his hand.
1Sa 17:45 "You come against me with *s*
17:47 here will know that it is not by *s*
31: 4 so Saul took his own *s* and fell on it.
2Sa 12:10 therefore, the *s* will never depart
Ps 44: 6 my *s* does not bring me victory;
45: 3 Gird your *s* upon your side,
Pr 12:18 Reckless words pierce like a *s*,
Isa 2: 4 Nation will not take up *s*
Mic 4: 3 Nation will not take up *s*
Mt 10:34 come to bring peace, but a *s*.
26:52 all who draw the *s* will die by the *s*.
Lk 2:35 a *s* will pierce your own soul too."
Ro 13: 4 for he does not bear the *s*
Eph 6:17 of salvation and the *s* of the Spirit,
Heb 4:12 Sharper than any double-edged *s*,
Rev 1:16 came a sharp double-edged *s*.
19:15 Out of his mouth comes a sharp *s*

SWORDS (SWORD)
Ps 64: 3 who sharpen their tongues like *s*
Isa 2: 4 They will beat their *s*
Joel 3:10 Beat your plowshares into *s*

SWORE (SWEAR)
Heb 6:13 for him to swear by, he *s* by himself

SWORN (SWEAR)
Ps 110: 4 The LORD has *s*
Eze 20:42 the land I had *s* with uplifted hand
Heb 7:21 "The Lord has *s*

SYCAMORE-FIG (FIG)
Am 7:14 and I also took care of *s* trees.
Lk 19: 4 and climbed a *s* tree to see him,

SYMBOLIZES*
1Pe 3:21 this water *s* baptism that now saves

SYMPATHETIC* (SYMPATHY)
1Pe 3: 8 in harmony with one another; be *s*,

SYMPATHIZED* (SYMPATHY)
Heb 10:34 You *s* with those in prison

SYMPATHY (SYMPATHETIC SYMPATHIZED)
Ps 69:20 I looked for *s*, but there was none,

SYNAGOGUE
Lk 4:16 the Sabbath day he went into the *s*,
Ac 17: 2 custom was, Paul went into the *s*,

TABERNACLE (TABERNACLES)
Ex 40:34 the glory of the LORD filled the *t*.
Heb 8: 2 the true *t* set up by the Lord,
9:11 and more perfect *t* that is not
9:21 sprinkled with the blood both the *t*
Rev 15: 5 that is, the *t* of the Testimony,

TABERNACLES (TABERNACLE)
Lev 23:34 the LORD's Feast of *T* begins,
Dt 16:16 Feast of Weeks and the Feast of *T*.
Zec 14:16 and to celebrate the Feast of *T*.

TABLE (TABLES)
Ex 25:23 "Make a *t* of acacia wood—
Ps 23: 5 You prepare a *t* before me

TABLES (TABLE)
Jn 2:15 changers and overturned their *t*.
Ac 6: 2 word of God in order to wait on *t*.

TABLET (TABLETS)
Pr 3: 3 write them on the *t* of your heart.
7: 3 write them on the *t* of your heart.

TABLETS (TABLET)
Ex 31:18 he gave him the two *t*
Dt 10: 5 and put the *t* in the ark I had made,
2Co 3: 3 not on *t* of stone but on *t*

TAKE (TAKEN TAKES TAKING TOOK)
Ge 15: 7 land to *t* possession of it."
22:17 Your descendants will *t* possession
Ex 3: 5 "*T* off your sandals,
21:23 you are to *t* life for life, eye for eye,
22:22 "Do not *t* advantage of a widow
Lev 10:17 given to you to *t* away the guilt
25:14 do not *t* advantage of each other.
Nu 13:30 and *t* possession of the land,
Dt 1: 8 and *t* possession of the land that
12:32 do not add to it or *t* away from it.
31:26 "*T* this Book of the Law
1Sa 8:11 He will *t* your sons and make them
1Ch 17:13 I will never *t* my love away
Job 23:10 But he knows the way that I *t*;
Ps 2:12 Blessed are all who *t* refuge in him.
25:18 and *t* away all my sins.
27:14 be strong and *t* heart
31:24 Be strong and *t* heart,
49:17 for he will *t* nothing with him
51:11 or *t* your Holy Spirit from me.
73:24 afterward you will *t* me into glory.
118: 8 It is better to *t* refuge in the LORD
Pr 22:23 for the LORD will *t* up their case
Isa 62: 4 for the LORD will *t* delight in you,
Eze 3:10 and *t* to heart all the words I speak
33:11 I *t* no pleasure in the death
Mt 10:38 anyone who does not *t* his cross
11:29 *T* my yoke upon you and learn
16:24 deny himself and *t* up his cross
26:26 saying, "*T* and eat; this is my body
Mk 14:36 *T* this cup from me.
1Ti 6:12 *T* hold of the eternal life

TAKEN (TAKE)
Ge 2:23 for she was *t* out of man."
Lev 6: 4 must return what he has stolen or *t*
Nu 8:16 I have *t* them as my own in place
19: 3 it is to be *t* outside the camp
Ecc 3:14 added to it and nothing *t* from it.
Isa 6: 7 your guilt is *t* away and your sin
Zec 3: 4 "See, I have *t* away your sin,
Mt 13:12 even what he has will be *t* from him
24:40 one will be *t* and the other left.
26:39 may this cup be *t* from me.
Mk 16:19 he was *t* up into heaven
Ac 1: 9 he was *t* up before their very eyes,
Ro 5:13 But sin is not *t* into account
1Ti 3:16 was *t* up in glory.

TAKES (TAKE)
1Ki 20:11 should not boast like one who *t* it
Ps 5: 4 You are not a God who *t* pleasure
34: 8 blessed is the man who *t* refuge
Lk 6:30 and if anyone *t* what belongs to you
Jn 1:29 who *t* away the sin of the world!
10:18 No one *t* it from me, but I lay it
Rev 22:19 And if anyone *t* words away

TAKING (TAKE)
Ac 15:14 by *t* from the Gentiles a people
Php 2: 7 *t* the very nature of a servant,

TALENT
Mt 25:15 to another one *t*, each according

TALES*
1Ti 4: 7 with godless myths and old wives' *t*

TALL
1Sa 17: 4 He was over nine feet *t*.
1Ch 11:23 who was seven and a half feet *t*.

TAMAR
1. Wife of Judah's sons Er and Onan (Ge 38:1-10). Tricked Judah into fathering children when he refused her his third son (Ge 38:11-30).
2. Daughter of David, raped by Amnon (2Sa 13).

TAMBOURINE
Ps 150: 4 praise him with *t* and dancing,

TAME* (TAMED)
Jas 3: 8 but no man can *t* the tongue.

TAMED* (TAME)
Jas 3: 7 the sea are being *t* and have been *t*

TARSHISH
Jnh 1: 3 from the LORD and headed for *T*.

TARSUS
Ac 9:11 ask for a man from *T* named Saul,

TASK (TASKS)
1Ch 29: 1 The *t* is great, because this palatial
Mk 13:34 each with his assigned *t*,
Ac 20:24 complete the *t* the Lord Jesus has
1Co 3: 5 the Lord has assigned to each his *t*.
2Co 2:16 And who is equal to such a *t*?
1Ti 3: 1 an overseer, he desires a noble *t*.

TASKS (TASK)
Pr 31:17 her arms are strong for her *t*.

TASTE (TASTED TASTY)
Ps 34: 8 *T* and see that the LORD is good;
119:103 sweet are your words to my *t*,
Pr 24:13 from the comb is sweet to your *t*.
SS 2: 3 and his fruit is sweet to my *t*.
Col 2:21 Do not *t*! Do not touch!"?
Heb 2: 9 the grace of God he might *t* death

TASTED (TASTE)
Eze 3: 3 it *t* as sweet as honey in my mouth.
1Pe 2: 3 now that you have *t* that the Lord
Rev 10:10 It *t* as sweet as honey in my mouth,

TASTY (TASTE)
Ge 27: 4 Prepare me the kind of *t* food I like

TATTOO*
Lev 19:28 or put *t* marks on yourselves.

TAUGHT (TEACH)
1Ki 4:33 He also *t* about animals and birds,
2Ki 17:28 *t* them how to worship the LORD.
2Ch 17: 9 They *t* throughout Judah,
Ps 119:102 for you yourself have *t* me.
Pr 4: 4 he *t* me and said,
31: 1 an oracle his mother *t* him:
Isa 29:13 is made up only of rules *t* by men.
50: 4 ear to listen like one being *t*.
Mt 7:29 he *t* as one who had authority,
15: 9 their teachings are but rules *t*
Lk 4:15 He *t* in their synagogues,
Ac 20:20 have *t* you publicly and from house
1Co 2:13 but in words *t* by the Spirit,
Gal 1:12 nor was I *t* it; rather, I received it
1Ti 1:20 to Satan to be *t* not to blaspheme.
1Jn 2:27 just as it has *t* you, remain in him.

TAX (TAXES)
Mt 11:19 a friend of *t* collectors and "sinners
17:24 of the two-drachma *t* came to Peter

TAXES (TAX)
Mt 22:17 Is it right to pay *t* to Caesar or not
Ro 13: 7 If you owe *t*, pay *t*; if revenue,

TEACH (TAUGHT TEACHER TEACHERS TEACHES TEACHING TEACHINGS)
Ex 4:12 and will *t* you what to say."
18:20 *T* them the decrees and laws,
33:13 *t* me your ways so I may know you
Lev 10:11 and you must *t* the Israelites all
Dt 4: 9 *T* them to your children
6: 1 me to *t* you to observe
8: 3 to *t* you that man does not live
11:19 *T* them to your children, talking
1Sa 12:23 I will *t* you the way that is good
1Ki 8:36 *T* them the right way to live,
Job 12: 7 ask the animals, and they will *t* you
Ps 32: 8 *t* you in the way you should go;
34:11 I will *t* you the fear of the LORD.
51:13 I will *t* transgressors your ways,
78: 5 forefathers to *t* their children,
90:12 *T* us to number our days aright,
119: 33 *T* me, O LORD, to follow your
143: 10 *T* me to do your will,
Pr 9: 9 *t* a righteous man and he will add
Jer 31:34 No longer will a man *t* his neighbor
Mic 4: 2 He will *t* us his ways,
Lk 11: 1 said to him, "Lord, *t* us to pray,
12:12 for the Holy Spirit will *t* you
Jn 14:26 will *t* you all things and will remind
Ro 2:21 who *t* others, do you not *t* yourself?
15: 4 in the past was written to *t* us,
1Ti 2:12 I do not permit a woman to *t*
3: 2 respectable, hospitable, able to *t*,
2Ti 2: 2 also be qualified to *t* others.
2:24 kind to everyone, able to *t*,
Tit 2: 1 You must *t* what is in accord
2:15 then, are the things you should *t*.
Heb 8:11 No longer will a man *t* his neighbor
Jas 3: 1 know that we who *t* will be judged
1Jn 2:27 you do not need anyone to *t* you.

TEACHER (TEACH)
Ecc 1: 1 The words of the *T*, son of David,
Mt 10:24 "A student is not above his *t*,
13:52 "Therefore every *t*
23:10 Nor are you to be called '*t*,'
Lk 6:40 A student is not above his *t*,
Jn 3: 2 we know you are a *t* who has come
13:14 and *T*, have washed your feet,

TEACHERS (TEACH)
Ps 119: 99 I have more insight than all my *t*,
Pr 5:13 I would not obey my *t*
Lk 20:46 "Beware of the *t* of the law.
1Co 12:28 third *t*, then workers of miracles,
Eph 4:11 and some to be pastors and *t*,
2Ti 4: 3 around them a great number of *t*
Heb 5:12 by this time you ought to be *t*,
Jas 3: 1 of you should presume to be *t*,
2Pe 2: 1 as there will be false *t* among you.

TEACHES (TEACH)
Ps 25: 9 and *t* them his way.
94:10 Does he who *t* man lack
Pr 15:33 of the LORD *t* a man wisdom,
Isa 48:17 who *t* you what is best for you,
Mt 5:19 *t* these commands will be called
1Ti 6: 3 If anyone *t* false doctrines
Tit 2:12 It *t* us to say "No" to ungodliness
1Jn 2:27 his anointing *t* you about all things

TEACHING (TEACH)
Ezr 7:10 to *t* its decrees and laws in Israel.
Pr 1: 8 and do not forsake your mother's *t*.
3: 1 My son, do not forget my *t*,
6:23 this *t* is a light,
Mt 28:20 *t* them to obey everything I have
Jn 7:17 whether my *t* comes from God or
8:31 to my *t*, you are really my disciples.
14:23 loves me, he will obey my *t*.
Ac 2:42 themselves to the apostles' *t*
Ro 12: 7 let him serve; if it is *t*, let him teach;
Eph 4:14 and there by every wind of *t*
2Th 3: 6 to the *t* you received from us.
1Ti 4:13 of Scripture, to preaching and to *t*.
5:17 whose work is preaching and *t*.
6: 3 Lord Jesus Christ and to godly *t*,
2Ti 3:16 is God-breathed and is useful for *t*,
Tit 1:11 by *t* things they ought not
2: 7 In your *t* show integrity,
Heb 5:13 with the *t* about righteousness.
2Jn : 9 and does not continue in the *t*

TEACHINGS (TEACH)
Pr 7: 2 guard my *t* as the apple of your eye.
2Th 2:15 hold to the *t* we passed on to you,
Heb 6: 1 leave the elementary *t* about Christ

TEAR (TEARS)
Rev 7:17 God will wipe away every *t*
21: 4 He will wipe every *t*

TEARS (TEAR)
Ps 126: 5 Those who sow in *t*
Isa 25: 8 LORD will wipe away the *t*
Jer 31:16 and your eyes from *t*,
50: 4 in *t* to seek the LORD their God.
Lk 7:38 she began to wet his feet with her *t*.
2Co 2: 4 anguish of heart and with many *t*,
Php 3:18 and now say again even with *t*,

TEETH (TOOTH)
Job 19:20 with only the skin of my *t*.
Ps 35:16 they gnashed their *t* at me.
Jer 31:29 and the children's *t* are set on edge
Mt 8:12 will be weeping and gnashing of *t*."

TEMPER (EVEN-TEMPERED HOT-TEMPERED ILL-TEMPERED QUICK-TEMPERED)
Pr 16:32 a man who controls his *t*

TEMPERANCE see SELF-CONTROL

TEMPERATE*
1Ti 3: 2 *t*, self-controlled, respectable,
3:11 not malicious talkers but *t*
Tit 2: 2 Teach the older men to be *t*,

TEMPEST
Ps 50: 3 and around him a *t* rages.
55: 8 far from the *t* and storm."

TEMPLE (TEMPLES)
1Ki 6: 1 began to build the *t* of the LORD.
6:38 the *t* was finished in all its details
8:10 the cloud filled the *t* of the LORD.
8:27 How much less this *t* I have built!
2Ch 36:19 They set fire to God's *t*
36:23 me to build a *t* for him at Jerusalem
Ezr 6:14 finished building the *t* according
Ps 27: 4 and to seek him in his *t*.
Isa 6: 1 and the train of his robe filled the *t*.
Eze 10: 4 cloud filled the *t*, and the court was
43: 4 glory of the LORD entered the *t*
Hab 2:20 But the LORD is in his holy *t*;
Mt 12: 6 that one greater than the *t* is here.
26:61 'I am able to destroy the *t* of God
27:51 of the *t* was torn in two from top
Lk 21: 5 about how the *t* was adorned
Jn 2:14 In the *t* courts he found men selling
1Co 3:16 that you yourselves are God's *t*
6:19 you not know that your body is a *t*
2Co 6:16 For we are the *t* of the living God.
Rev 21:22 I did not see a *t* in the city,

TEMPLES (TEMPLE)
Ac 17:24 does not live in *t* built by hands.

TEMPORARY
2Co 4:18 what is seen is *t*, but what is unseen

TEMPT* (TEMPTATION TEMPTED TEMPTER TEMPTING)
1Co 7: 5 again so that Satan will not *t* you
Jas 1:13 does he *t* anyone; but each one is

TEMPTATION* (TEMPT)
Mt 6:13 And lead us not into *t*,
26:41 pray so that you will not fall into *t*.
Mk 14:38 pray so that you will not fall into *t*.
Lk 11: 4 And lead us not into *t*.' "
22:40 "Pray that you will not fall into *t*."
22:46 pray so that you will not fall into *t*
1Co 10:13 No *t* has seized you except what is
1Ti 6: 9 want to get rich fall into *t*

TEMPTED* (TEMPT)
Mt 4: 1 into the desert to be *t* by the devil.
Mk 1:13 was in the desert forty days, being *t*
Lk 4: 2 for forty days he was *t* by the devil.
1Co 10:13 But when you are *t*, he will
10:13 he will not let you be *t*
Gal 6: 1 yourself, or you also may be *t*.
1Th 3: 5 way the tempter might have *t* you
Heb 2:18 able to help those who are being *t*.
2:18 he himself suffered when he was *t*,
4:15 but we have one who has been *t*
Jas 1:13 For God cannot be *t* by evil,
1:13 When *t*, no one should say,
1:14 each one is *t* when, by his own evil

TEMPTER* (TEMPT)
Mt 4: 3 The *t* came to him and said,
1Th 3: 5 some way the *t* might have

TEMPTING* (TEMPT)
Lk 4:13 the devil had finished all this *t*,
Jas 1:13 no one should say, "God is *t* me."

TEN (TENTH TITHE TITHES)
Ex 34:28 covenant—the *T* Commandments.
Lev 26: 8 of you will chase *t* thousand,
Dt 4:13 covenant, the *T* Commandments,
10: 4 The *T* Commandments he had
Ps 91: 7 *t* thousand at your right hand,
Da 7:24 *t* horns are *t* kings who will come
Mt 25: 1 will be like *t* virgins who took
25:28 it to the one who has the *t* talents.
Lk 15: 8 suppose a woman has *t* silver coins
Rev 12: 3 and *t* horns and seven crowns

TENANTS
Mt 21:34 servants to the *t* to collect his fruit.

TEND
Jer 23: 2 to the shepherds who *t* my people:
Eze 34:14 I will *t* them in a good pasture,

TENDERNESS*
Isa 63:15 Your *t* and compassion are
Php 2: 1 fellowship with the Spirit, if any *t*

TENT (TENTMAKER TENTS)
Ex 27:21 In the *T* of Meeting,
40: 2 "Set up the tabernacle, the *T*
Isa 54: 2 "Enlarge the place of your *t*,
2Co 5: 1 that if the earthly *t* we live
2Pe 1:13 as long as I live in the *t* of this body,

TENTH (TEN)
Ge 14:20 Abram gave him a *t* of everything.
Nu 18:26 you must present a *t* of that tithe
Dt 14:22 Be sure to set aside a *t*
1Sa 8:15 He will take a *t* of your grain
Lk 11:42 you give God a *t* of your mint,
18:12 I fast twice a week and give a *t*
Heb 7: 4 patriarch Abraham gave him a *t*

TENTMAKER* (TENT)
Ac 18: 3 and because he was a *t* as they were

TENTS (TENT)
Ge 13:12 and pitched his *t* near Sodom.
Ps 84:10 than dwell in the *t* of the wicked.

TERAH
Ge 11:31 *T* took his son Abram, his

TERRIBLE (TERROR)
2Ti 3: 1 There will be *t* times

TERRIFIED (TERROR)
Dt 7:21 Do not be *t* by them,
20: 3 do not be *t* or give way to panic
Ps 90: 7 and *t* by your indignation.
Mt 14:26 walking on the lake, they were *t*.
17: 6 they fell facedown to the ground, *t*.
27:54 they were *t*, and exclaimed,
Mk 4:41 They were *t* and asked each other,

TERRIFYING (TERROR)
Heb 12:21 The sight was so *t* that Moses said,

TERRITORY
2Co 10:16 done in another man's *t*.

TERROR (TERRIBLE TERRIFIED TERRIFYING)
Dt 2:25 very day I will begin to put the *t*
28:67 of the *t* that will fill your hearts
Job 9:34 so that his *t* would frighten me no
Ps 91: 5 You will not fear the *t* of night,
Pr 21:15 but *t* to evildoers.
Isa 13: 8 *T* will seize them,
24:17 *T* and pit and snare await you,
51:13 live in constant *t* every day
54:14 *T* will be far removed;
Lk 21:26 Men will faint from *t*, apprehensive
Ro 13: 3 For rulers hold no *t*

TEST (TESTED TESTING TESTS)
Dt 6:16 Do not *t* the LORD your God
Jdg 3: 1 to *t* all those Israelites who had not
1Ki 10: 1 came to *t* him with hard questions.
1Ch 29:17 that you *t* the heart and are pleased
Ps 26: 2 *T* me, O LORD, and try me,
78:18 They willfully put God to the *t*
106: 14 wasteland they put God to the *t*.
139: 23 *t* me and know my anxious
Jer 11:20 and *t* the heart and mind,
Lk 4:12 put the Lord your God to the *t*.' "
Ac 5: 9 How could you agree to *t* the Spirit
Ro 12: 2 Then you will be able to *t*
1Co 3:13 and the fire will *t* the quality
10: 9 We should not *t* the Lord,
2Co 13: 5 unless, of course, you fail the *t*?
1Th 5:21 *T* everything.
Jas 1:12 because when he has stood the *t*,
1Jn 4: 1 *t* the spirits to see whether they are

TESTED (TEST)
Ge 22: 1 Some time later God *t* Abraham.
Job 23:10 when he has *t* me, I will come forth
34:36 that Job might be *t* to the utmost
Ps 66:10 For you, O God, *t* us;
Pr 27:21 man is *t* by the praise he receives.
Isa 28:16 a *t* stone,
48:10 I have *t* you in the furnace
1Ti 3:10 They must first be *t*; and then
Heb 11:17 By faith Abraham, when God *t* him

TESTIFIES (TESTIFY)
Jn 5:32 There is another who *t* in my favor,
Ro 8:16 The Spirit himself *t*

TESTIFY (TESTIFIES TESTIMONY)
Pr 24:28 Do not *t* against your neighbor
Jn 1: 7 a witness to *t* concerning that light,
1:34 and I *t* that this is the Son of God."
5:39 are the Scriptures that *t* about me,
7: 7 because I *t* that what it does is evil.
15:26 he will *t* about me. And you
Ac 4:33 continued to *t* to the resurrection
10:43 All the prophets *t* about him that
2Ti 1: 8 ashamed to *t* about our Lord,
1Jn 4:14 *t* that the Father has sent his Son
5: 7 For there are three that *t*: the Spirit

TESTIMONY (TESTIFY)
Ex 20:16 "You shall not give false *t*
31:18 gave him the two tablets of the *T*,
Nu 35:30 only on the *t* of witnesses.
Dt 19:18 giving false *t* against his brother,
Pr 12:17 A truthful witness gives honest *t*,
Isa 8:20 and to the *t*! If they do not speak
Mt 15:19 sexual immorality, theft, false *t*,
24:14 preached in the whole world as a *t*
Lk 18:20 not give false *t*, honor your father
Jn 2:25 He did not need man's *t* about man
21:24 We know that his *t* is true.
1Jn 5: 9 but God's *t* is greater because it is
Rev 12:11 and by the word of their *t*;

TESTING (TEST)
Lk 8:13 but in the time of *t* they fall away.
Heb 3: 8 during the time of *t* in the desert,
Jas 1: 3 because you know that the *t*

TESTS (TEST)
Pr 17: 3 but the LORD *t* the heart.
1Th 2: 4 but God, who *t* our hearts.

THADDAEUS
Apostle (Mt 10:3; Mk 3:18); probably also known as Judas son of James (Lk 6:16; Ac 1:13).

THANK (THANKFUL THANKFULNESS THANKS THANKSGIVING)
Php 1: 3 I *t* my God every time I remember
1Th 3: 9 How can we *t* God enough for you

THANKFUL (THANK)
Col 3:15 And be *t*.
Heb 12:28 let us be *t*, and so worship God

THANKFULNESS (THANK)
1Co 10:30 If I take part in the meal with *t*,
Col 2: 7 taught, and overflowing with *t*.

THANKS (THANK)
1Ch 16: 8 Give *t* to the LORD, call
Ne 12:31 assigned two large choirs to give *t*.
Ps 7:17 I will give *t* to the LORD
28: 7 and I will give *t* to him in song.
30:12 my God, I will give you *t* forever.
35:18 I will give you *t* in the great
75: 1 we give *t*, for your Name is near;
100: 4 give *t* to him and praise his name.
107: 1 Give *t* to the LORD, for he is good;
118: 28 are my God, and I will give you *t*;
136: 1 Give *t* to the LORD, for he is good.
Ro 1:21 as God nor gave *t* to him,
1Co 11:24 when he had given *t*, he broke it
15:57 *t* be to God! He gives us the victory
2Co 2:14 *t* be to God, who always leads us
9:15 *T* be to God for his indescribable
1Th 5:18 give *t* in all circumstances,
Rev 4: 9 and *t* to him who sits on the throne

THANKSGIVING (THANK)
Ps 95: 2 Let us come before him with *t*
100: 4 Enter his gates with *t*
1Co 10:16 cup of *t* for which we give thanks
Php 4: 6 by prayer and petition, with *t*,
1Ti 4: 3 created to be received with *t*

THEFT (THIEF)
Mt 15:19 sexual immorality, *t*, false

THEFTS* (THIEF)
Rev 9:21 their sexual immorality or their *t*.

THEME*
Ps 45: 1 My heart is stirred by a noble *t*
119: 54 Your decrees are the *t* of my song

THIEF (THEFT THEFTS THIEVES)
Ex 22: 3 A *t* must certainly make restitution
Pr 6:30 Men do not despise a *t* if he steals
Lk 12:39 at what hour the *t* was coming,
1Th 5: 2 day of the Lord will come like a *t*
1Pe 4:15 or *t* or any other kind of criminal,
Rev 16:15 I come like a *t*! Blessed is he who

THIEVES (THIEF)
Mt 6:19 and where *t* break in and steal.
Jn 10: 8 who ever came before me were *t*
1Co 6:10 nor homosexual offenders nor *t*

THINK (THINKING THOUGHT THOUGHTS)
Ps 63: 6 I *t* of you through the watches
Isa 44:19 No one stops to *t*,
Mt 22:42 "What do you *t* about the Christ?
Ro 12: 3 Do not *t* of yourself more highly
Php 4: 8 praiseworthy—*t* about such things

THINKING (THINK)
Pr 23: 7 who is always *t* about the cost.
1Co 14:20 Brothers, stop *t* like children.
2Pe 3: 1 to stimulate you to wholesome *t*.

THIRST (THIRSTS THIRSTY)
Ps 69:21 and gave me vinegar for my *t*.
Mt 5: 6 Blessed are those who hunger and *t*
Jn 4:14 the water I give him will never *t*.
2Co 11:27 I have known hunger and *t*
Rev 7:16 never again will they *t*.

THIRSTS (THIRST)
Ps 42: 2 My soul *t* for God,

THIRSTY (THIRST)
Ps 107: 9 for he satisfies the *t*
Pr 25:21 if he is *t*, give him water to drink.
Isa 55: 1 "Come, all you who are *t*,
Mt 25:35 I was *t* and you gave me something
Jn 7:37 "If anyone is *t*, let him come to me
Ro 12:20 if he is *t*, give him something
Rev 21: 6 To him who is *t* I will give to drink
22:17 Whoever is *t*, let him come;

THOMAS
Apostle (Mt 10:3; Mk 3:18; Lk 6:15; Jn 11:16; 14:5; 21:2; Ac 1:13). Doubted resurrection (Jn 20: 24-28).

THONGS
Mk 1: 7 *t* of whose sandals I am not worthy

THORN (THORNBUSHES THORNS)
2Co 12: 7 there was given me a *t* in my flesh,

THORNBUSHES (THORN)
Lk 6:44 People do not pick figs from *t*,

THORNS (THORN)
Ge 3:18 It will produce *t* and thistles
Nu 33:55 in your eyes and *t* in your sides.
Mt 13: 7 fell among *t*, which grew up
27:29 and then twisted together a crown of *t*
Heb 6: 8 But land that produces *t*

THOUGHT (THINK)
Pr 14:15 a prudent man gives *t* to his steps.
21:29 an upright man gives *t* to his ways.
1Co 13:11 I talked like a child, I *t* like a child,

THOUGHTS (THINK)
1Ch 28: 9 every motive behind the *t*.
Ps 94:11 The LORD knows the *t* of man;
139: 23 test me and know my anxious *t*.
Isa 55: 8 "For my *t* are not your *t*,
Mt 15:19 For out of the heart come evil *t*,
1Co 2:11 among men knows the *t* of a man
Heb 4:12 it judges the *t* and attitudes

THREE
Ge 6:10 Noah had *t* sons: Shem, Ham
Ex 23:14 "*T* times a year you are
Dt 19:15 the testimony of two or *t* witnesses.
2Sa 23: 8 a Tahkemonite, was chief of the *T*;
Pr 30:15 "There are *t* things that are never
30:18 "There are *t* things that are too
30:21 "Under *t* things the earth trembles,
30:29 "There are *t* things that are stately
Ecc 4:12 of *t* strands is not quickly broken.
Da 3:24 "Weren't there *t* men that we tied up
Am 1: 3 "For *t* sins of Damascus,
Jnh 1:17 inside the fish *t* days and *t* nights.
Mt 12:40 so the Son of Man will be *t* days
12:40 *t* nights in the belly of a huge fish,
12:40 *t* nights in the heart of the earth.
17: 4 I will put up *t* shelters—one
18:20 or *t* come together in my name,
26:34 you will disown me *t* times."
26:75 you will disown me *t* times."
27:63 'After *t* days I will rise again.'
Mk 8:31 and after *t* days rise again.
9: 5 Let us put up *t* shelters—one
14:30 yourself will disown me *t* times."
Jn 2:19 and I will raise it again in *t* days."
1Co 13:13 And now these *t* remain: faith,
14:27 or at the most *t*— should speak,
2Co 13: 1 testimony of two or *t* witnesses."
1Jn 5: 7 For there are *t* that testify:

THRESHER* (THRESHING)
1Co 9:10 plowman plows and the *t* threshes,

THRESHING (THRESHER)
Ru 3: 6 So she went down to the *t* floor
2Sa 24:18 an altar to the LORD on the *t* floor
Lk 3:17 is in his hand to clear his *t* floor

THREW (THROW)
Da 6:16 and *t* him into the lions' den.
Jnh 1:15 took Jonah and *t* him overboard,

THRIVE
Pr 29: 2 When the righteous *t*, the people

THROAT (THROATS)
Ps 5: 9 Their *t* is an open grave;
Pr 23: 2 and put a knife to your *t*

THROATS (THROAT)
Ro 3:13 "Their *t* are open graves;

THROB*
Isa 60: 5 your heart will *t* and swell with joy;

THRONE (ENTHRONED ENTHRONES THRONES)
2Sa 7:16 your *t* will be established forever
1Ch 17:12 and I will establish his *t* forever.
Ps 11: 4 the LORD is on his heavenly *t*.
45: 6 Your *t*, O God, will last for ever
47: 8 God is seated on his holy *t*.
89:14 justice are the foundation of your *t*;
Isa 6: 1 I saw the Lord seated on a *t*,
66: 1 "Heaven is my *t*,
Eze 28: 2 I sit on the *t* of a god
Da 7: 9 His *t* was flaming with fire,
Mt 19:28 Son of Man sits on his glorious *t*,
Ac 7:49 prophet says: " 'Heaven is my *t*,
Heb 1: 8 "Your *t*, O God, will last for ever
4:16 Let us then approach the *t* of grace
12: 2 at the right hand of the *t* of God.
Rev 3:21 sat down with my Father on his *t*.
3:21 the right to sit with me on my *t*,
4: 2 there before me was a *t* in heaven
4:10 They lay their crowns before the *t*
20:11 Then I saw a great white *t*
22: 3 *t* of God and of the Lamb will be

THRONES (THRONE)
Mt 19:28 me will also sit on twelve *t*,
Rev 4: 4 throne were twenty-four other *t*,

THROW (THREW)
Jn 8: 7 the first to *t* a stone at her."
Heb 10:35 So do not *t* away your confidence;
12: 1 let us *t* off everything that hinders

THUNDER (THUNDERS)
Ps 93: 4 Mightier than the *t*
Mk 3:17 which means Sons of *T*); Andrew,

THUNDERS (THUNDER)
Job 37: 5 God's voice *t* in marvelous ways;
Ps 29: 3 the God of glory *t*,
Rev 10: 3 the voices of the seven *t* spoke.

THWART* (THWARTED)
Isa 14:27 has purposed, and who can *t* him?

THWARTED (THWART)
Job 42: 2 no plan of yours can be *t*.

THYATIRA
Rev 2:18 the angel of the church in *T* write:

TIBNI
King of Israel (1Ki 16:21-22).

TIDINGS
Isa 40: 9 You who bring good *t* to Jerusalem
52: 7 who bring good *t*,

TIES
Hos 11: 4 with *t* of love;

Mt 12:29 unless he first *t* up the strong man?

TIGHT*
Jas 1:26 and yet does not keep a *t* rein

TIGHTFISTED*
Dt 15: 7 or *t* toward your poor brother.

TIME (TIMES)
Est 4:14 come to royal position for such a *t*
Ecc 3: 1 There is a *t* for everything,
8: 5 wise heart will know the proper *t*
Da 7:25 to him for a *t*, times and half a *t*.
12: 7 "It will be for a *t*, times and half a *t*.
Hos 10:12 for it is *t* to seek the LORD,
Jn 2: 4 Jesus replied, "My *t* has not yet
17: 1 prayed: "Father, the *t* has come.
Ro 9: 9 "At the appointed *t* I will return,
13:11 understanding the present *t*.
1Co 7:29 brothers, is that the *t* is short.
2Co 6: 2 now is the *t* of God's favor,
2Ti 1: 9 Jesus before the beginning of *t*,
Tit 1: 2 promised before the beginning of *t*,
Heb 9:28 and he will appear a second *t*,
10:12 for all *t* one sacrifice for sins,
1Pe 4:17 For it is *t* for judgment to begin

TIMES (TIME)
Ps 9: 9 a stronghold in *t* of trouble.
31:15 My *t* are in your hands;
62: 8 Trust in him at all *t*, O people;
Pr 17:17 A friend loves at all *t*,
Isa 46:10 from ancient *t*, what is still to come
Am 5:13 for the *t* are evil.
Mt 16: 3 cannot interpret the signs of the *t*.
18:21 how many *t* shall I forgive my
Ac 1: 7 "It is not for you to know the *t*
Rev 12:14 *t* and half a time, out

TIMID (TIMIDITY)
1Th 5:14 encourage the *t*, help the weak,

TIMIDITY* (TIMID)
2Ti 1: 7 For God did not give us a spirit of *t*

TIMOTHY
Believer from Lystra (Ac 16:1). Joined Paul on second missionary journey (Ac 16-20). Sent to settle problems at Corinth (1Co 4:17; 16:10). Led church at Ephesus (1Ti 1:3). Co-writer with Paul (1Th 1:1; 2Th 1:1; Phm 1).

TIP
Job 33: 2 my words are on the *t* of my tongue

TIRE (TIRED)
2Th 3:13 never *t* of doing what is right.

TIRED (TIRE)
Ex 17:12 When Moses' hands grew *t*,
Isa 40:28 He will not grow *t* or weary,

TITHE (TEN)
Lev 27:30 " 'A *t* of everything from the land,
Dt 12:17 eat in your own towns the *t*
Mal 3:10 the whole *t* into the storehouse,

TITHES (TEN)
Nu 18:21 give to the Levites all the *t* in Israel
Mal 3: 8 'How do we rob you?' "In *t*

TITUS*
Gentile co-worker of Paul (Gal 2:1-3; 2Ti 4:10); sent to Corinth (2Co 2:13; 7-8; 12:18), Crete (Tit 1:4-5).

TODAY
Ps 2: 7 *t* I have become your Father.
95: 7 *T*, if you hear his voice,
Mt 6:11 Give us *t* our daily bread.
Lk 2:11 *T* in the town of David a Savior has
23:43 *t* you will be with me in paradise."
Ac 13:33 *t* I have become your Father.'
Heb 1: 5 *t* I have become your Father"?
3: 7 "*T*, if you hear his voice,
3:13 daily, as long as it is called *T*,
5: 5 *t* I have become your Father."
13: 8 Christ is the same yesterday and *t*

TOIL (TOILED TOILING)
Ge 3:17 through painful *t* you will eat of it

TOILED (TOIL)
2Co 11:27 and *t* and have often gone

TOILING (TOIL)
2Th 3: 8 *t* so that we would not be a burden

TOLERANCE* (TOLERATE)
Ro 2: 4 for the riches of his kindness, *t*

TOLERATE (TOLERANCE)
Hab 1:13 you cannot *t* wrong.
Rev 2: 2 that you cannot *t* wicked men,

TOMB
Mt 27:65 make the *t* as secure as you know
Lk 24: 2 the stone rolled away from the *t*,

TOMORROW
Pr 27: 1 Do not boast about *t*,
Isa 22:13 "for *t* we die!"
Mt 6:34 Therefore do not worry about *t*,
1Co 15:32 for *t* we die."
Jas 4:13 "Today or *t* we will go to this

TONGUE (TONGUES)
Ex 4:10 I am slow of speech and *t*."
Job 33: 2 my words are on the tip of my *t*.
Ps 5: 9 with their *t* they speak deceit.
34:13 keep your *t* from evil
37:30 and his *t* speaks what is just.
39: 1 and keep my *t* from sin;
51:14 my *t* will sing of your righteousness
52: 4 O you deceitful *t*!
71:24 My *t* will tell of your righteous acts
119:172 May my *t* sing of your word,
137: 6 May my *t* cling to the roof
139: 4 Before a word is on my *t*
Pr 6:17 a lying *t*,
10:19 but he who holds his *t* is wise.
12:18 but the *t* of the wise brings healing.
15: 4 The *t* that brings healing is a tree
17:20 he whose *t* is deceitful falls
21:23 He who guards his mouth and his *t*
25:15 and a gentle *t* can break a bone.
26:28 A lying *t* hates those it hurts,
28:23 than he who has a flattering *t*.
31:26 and faithful instruction is on her *t*.
SS 4:11 milk and honey are under your *t*.
Isa 32: 4 and the stammering *t* will be fluent
45:23 by me every *t* will swear.
50: 4 has given me an instructed *t*,
59: 3 and your *t* mutters wicked things.
Lk 16:24 of his finger in water and cool my *t*,
Ro 14:11 every *t* will confess to God.' "
1Co 14: 2 speaks in a *t* does not speak to men
14: 4 He who speaks in a *t* edifies himself
14: 9 intelligible words with your *t*,
14:13 in a *t* should pray that he may
14:19 than ten thousand words in a *t*.
14:26 revelation, a *t* or an interpretation.
14:27 If anyone speaks in a *t*, two—
Php 2:11 every *t* confess that Jesus Christ is
Jas 1:26 does not keep a tight rein on his *t*,
3: 5 Likewise the *t* is a small part
3: 8 but no man can tame the *t*.
1Jn 3:18 or *t* but with actions and in truth.

TONGUES (TONGUE)
Ps 12: 4 "We will triumph with our *t*;
126: 2 our *t* with songs of joy.
Isa 28:11 with foreign lips and strange *t*
66:18 and gather all nations and *t*,
Jer 23:31 the prophets who wag their own *t*
Mk 16:17 in new *t*; they will pick up snakes
Ac 2: 3 to be *t* of fire that separated
2: 4 and began to speak in other *t*
10:46 For they heard them speaking in *t*
19: 6 and they spoke in *t* and prophesied
Ro 3:13 their *t* practice deceit."
1Co 12:10 still another the interpretation of *t*.
12:28 speaking in different kinds of *t*.
12:30 Do all speak in *t*? Do all interpret?
13: 1 If I speak in the *t* of men
13: 8 where there are *t*, they will be
14: 5 greater than one who speaks in *t*,
14:18 speak in *t* more than all of you.
14:21 "Through men of strange *t*
14:39 and do not forbid speaking in *t*.

TOOK (TAKE)
Isa 53: 4 Surely he *t* up our infirmities
Mt 8:17 "He *t* up our infirmities
26:26 they were eating, Jesus *t* bread,
26:27 Then he *t* the cup, gave thanks
1Co 11:23 the night he was betrayed, *t* bread,
11:25 after supper he *t* the cup, saying,
Php 3:12 for which Christ Jesus *t* hold of me.

TOOTH (TEETH)
Ex 21:24 eye for eye, *t* for *t*, hand for hand,
Mt 5:38 'Eye for eye, and *t* for *t*.'

TOP
Dt 28:13 you will always be at the *t*,
Isa 1: 6 of your foot to the *t* of your head
Mt 27:51 torn in two from *t* to bottom.

TORMENT (TORMENTED TORMENTORS)
Lk 16:28 also come to this place of *t*.'
2Co 12: 7 a messenger of Satan, to *t* me.

TORMENTED (TORMENT)
Rev 20:10 They will be *t* day and night

TORMENTORS (TORMENT)
Ps 137: 3 our *t* demanded songs of joy;

TORN
Gal 4:15 you would have *t* out your eyes
Php 1:23 I do not know! I am *t*

TORTURED*
Mt 18:34 turned him over to the jailers to be *t*,
Heb 11:35 Others were *t* and refused

TOSSED (TOSSING)
Eph 4:14 *t* back and forth by the waves,
Jas 1: 6 of the sea, blown and *t* by the wind.

TOSSING (TOSSED)
Isa 57:20 But the wicked are like the *t* sea,

TOUCH (TOUCHED TOUCHES)
Ge 3: 3 you must not *t* it, or you will die.' "
Ex 19:12 go up the mountain or *t* the foot
Ps 105: 15 "Do not *t* my anointed ones;
Mt 9:21 If I only *t* his cloak, I will be healed
Lk 18:15 babies to Jesus to have him *t* them.
24:39 It is I myself! *T* me and see;
2Co 6:17 *T* no unclean thing,
Col 2:21 Do not taste! Do not *t*!"?

TOUCHED (TOUCH)
1Sa 10:26 men whose hearts God had *t*.
Isa 6: 7 With it he *t* my mouth and said,
Mt 14:36 and all who *t* him were healed.
Lk 8:45 "Who *t* me?" Jesus asked.
1Jn 1: 1 looked at and our hands have *t*—

TOUCHES (TOUCH)
Ex 19:12 Whoever *t* the mountain shall
Zec 2: 8 for whoever *t* you *t* the apple

TOWER
Ge 11: 4 with a *t* that reaches to the heavens
Pr 18:10 of the LORD is a strong *t*;

TOWN (TOWNS)
Mt 2:23 and lived in a *t* called Nazareth.

TOWNS (TOWN)
Nu 35: 2 to give the Levites *t* to live
35:15 These six *t* will be a place of refuge
Jer 11:13 as many gods as you have *t*,
Mt 9:35 Jesus went through all the *t*

TRACING*
Ro 11:33 and his paths beyond *t* out!

TRACK
Job 14:16 but not keep *t* of my sin.

TRADERS (TRADING)
1Ti 1:10 for slave *t* and liars and perjurers—

TRADING (TRADERS)
1Ki 10:22 The king had a fleet of *t* ships at sea
Pr 31:18 She sees that her *t* is profitable,

TRADITION (TRADITIONS)
Mt 15: 2 "Why do your disciples break the *t*
15: 6 word of God for the sake of your *t*.
Mk 7:13 by your *t* that you have handed
Col 2: 8 which depends on human *t*

TRADITIONS (TRADITION)
Mk 7: 8 are holding on to the *t* of men."
Gal 1:14 zealous for the *t* of my fathers.

TRAIL
1Ti 5:24 the sins of others *t* behind them.

TRAIN* (TRAINED TRAINING)
Ps 68:18 you led captives in your *t*;
Pr 22: 6 *T* a child in the way he should go,
Isa 2: 4 nor will they *t* for war anymore.
6: 1 the *t* of his robe filled the temple.
Mic 4: 3 nor will they *t* for war anymore.
Eph 4: 8 he led captives in his *t*
1Ti 4: 7 rather, *t* yourself to be godly.
Tit 2: 4 they can *t* the younger women

TRAINED (TRAIN)
Lk 6:40 everyone who is fully *t* will be like
Ac 22: 3 Under Gamaliel I was thoroughly *t*
2Co 11: 6 I may not be a *t* speaker,
Heb 5:14 by constant use have *t* themselves
12:11 for those who have been *t* by it.

TRAINING* (TRAIN)
1Co 9:25 in the games goes into strict *t.*
Eph 6: 4 up in the *t* and instruction
1Ti 4: 8 For physical *t* is of some value,
2Ti 3:16 correcting and *t* in righteousness,

TRAITOR (TRAITORS)
Lk 6:16 and Judas Iscariot, who became a *t.*
Jn 18: 5 Judas the *t* was standing there

TRAITORS (TRAITOR)
Ps 59: 5 show no mercy to wicked *t.*

TRAMPLE (TRAMPLED)
Joel 3:13 Come, *t* the grapes,
Am 2: 7 They *t* on the heads of the poor
5:11 You *t* on the poor
8: 4 Hear this, you who *t* the needy
Mt 7: 6 they may *t* them under their feet,
Lk 10:19 I have given you authority to *t*

TRAMPLED (TRAMPLE)
Isa 63: 6 I *t* the nations in my anger;
Lk 21:24 Jerusalem will be *t*
Heb 10:29 to be punished who has *t* the Son
Rev 14:20 They were *t* in the winepress

TRANCE*
Ac 10:10 was being prepared, he fell into a *t.*
11: 5 and in a *t* I saw a vision.
22:17 into a *t* and saw the Lord speaking.

TRANQUILLITY*
Ecc 4: 6 Better one handful with *t*

TRANSACTIONS*
Ru 4: 7 method of legalizing *t* in Israel.)

TRANSCENDS*
Php 4: 7 which *t* all understanding,

TRANSFIGURED*
Mt 17: 2 There he was *t* before them.
Mk 9: 2 There he was *t* before them.

TRANSFORM* (TRANSFORMED)
Php 3:21 will *t* our lowly bodies

TRANSFORMED (TRANSFORM)
Ro 12: 2 be *t* by the renewing of your mind.
2Co 3:18 are being *t* into his likeness

TRANSGRESSED* (TRANSGRESSION)
Da 9:11 All Israel has *t* your law

TRANSGRESSION* (TRANSGRESSED TRANSGRESSIONS TRANSGRESSORS)
Ps 19:13 innocent of great *t.*
Isa 53: 8 for the *t* of my people he was
Da 9:24 and your holy city to finish *t,*
Mic 1: 5 All this is because of Jacob's *t,*
1: 5 What is Jacob's *t?*
3: 8 to declare to Jacob his *t,*
6: 7 Shall I offer my firstborn for my *t,*
7:18 who pardons sin and forgives the *t*
Ro 4:15 where there is no law there is no *t.*
11:11 Rather, because of their *t,*
11:12 if their *t* means riches for the world

TRANSGRESSIONS* (TRANSGRESSION)
Ps 32: 1 whose *t* are forgiven,
32: 5 my *t* to the LORD"—
39: 8 Save me from all my *t;*
51: 1 blot out my *t.*
51: 3 For I know my *t,*
65: 3 you forgave our *t.*
103: 12 so far has he removed our *t* from us
Isa 43:25 your *t,* for my own sake,
50: 1 of your *t* your mother was sent
53: 5 But he was pierced for our *t,*
Mic 1:13 for the *t* of Israel
Ro 4: 7 whose *t* are forgiven,
Gal 3:19 because of *t* until the Seed to whom
Eph 2: 1 you were dead in your *t* and sins,
2: 5 even when we were dead in *t*—

TRANSGRESSORS* (TRANSGRESSION)
Ps 51:13 Then I will teach *t* your ways,
Isa 53:12 and made intercession for the *t.*
53:12 and was numbered with the *t.*
Lk 22:37 'And he was numbered with the *t*';

TRAP (TRAPPED TRAPS)
Ps 69:22 may it become retribution and a *t.*
Pr 20:25 a *t* for a man to dedicate something
28:10 will fall into his own *t,*
Isa 8:14 a *t* and a snare.
Mt 22:15 and laid plans to *t* him in his words.
Lk 21:34 close on you unexpectedly like a *t.*
Ro 11: 9 their table become a snare and a *t,*
1Ti 3: 7 into disgrace and into the devil's *t.*
1Ti 6: 9 and a *t* and into many foolish
2Ti 2:26 and escape from the *t* of the devil,

TRAPPED (TRAP)
Pr 6: 2 if you have been *t* by what you said
12:13 An evil man is *t* by his sinful talk,

TRAPS (TRAP)
Jos 23:13 they will become snares and *t*
La 4:20 was caught in their *t.*

TRAVEL (TRAVELER)
Pr 4:15 Avoid it, do not *t* on it;
Mt 23:15 You *t* over land and sea

TRAVELER (TRAVEL)
Job 31:32 door was always open to the *t*—
Jer 14: 8 like a *t* who stays only a night?

TREACHEROUS (TREACHERY)
Ps 25: 3 who are *t* without excuse.
2Ti 3: 4 not lovers of the good, *t,* rash,

TREACHERY (TREACHEROUS)
Isa 59:13 rebellion and *t* against the LORD,

TREAD (TREADING TREADS)
Ps 91:13 You will *t* upon the lion

TREADING (TREAD)
Dt 25: 4 an ox while it is *t* out the grain.
1Co 9: 9 an ox while it is *t* out the grain."
1Ti 5:18 the ox while it is *t* out the grain,"

TREADS (TREAD)
Rev 19:15 He *t* the winepress of the fury

TREASURE (TREASURED TREASURES TREASURY)
Pr 2: 4 and search for it as for hidden *t,*
Isa 33: 6 of the LORD is the key to this *t.*
Mt 6:21 For where your *t* is, there your
13:44 of heaven is like *t* hidden in a field.
Lk 12:33 a *t* in heaven that will not be
2Co 4: 7 But we have this *t* in jars of clay
1Ti 6:19 In this way they will lay up *t*

TREASURED (TREASURE)
Ex 19: 5 you will be my *t* possession.
Dt 7: 6 to be his people, his *t* possession.
26:18 his *t* possession as he promised,
Job 23:12 I have *t* the words
Mal 3:17 when I make up my *t* possession.
Lk 2:19 But Mary *t* up all these things
2:51 But his mother *t* all these things

TREASURES (TREASURE)
1Ch 29: 3 my God I now give my personal *t*
Pr 10: 2 Ill-gotten *t* are of no value,
Mt 6:19 up for yourselves *t* on earth,
13:52 out of his storeroom new *t*
Col 2: 3 in whom are hidden all the *t*
Heb 11:26 of greater value than the *t* of Egypt,

TREASURY (TREASURE)
Mk 12:43 more into the *t* than all the others.

TREAT (TREATED TREATING TREATMENT)
Lev 22: 2 sons to *t* with respect the sacred
Ps 103: 10 he does not *t* us as our sins deserve
Mt 18:17 *t* him as you would a pagan
18:35 my heavenly Father will *t* each
Eph 6: 9 *t* your slaves in the same way.
1Th 5:20 do not *t* prophecies with contempt.
1Ti 5: 1 *T* younger men as brothers,
1Pe 3: 7 and *t* them with respect

TREATED (TREAT)
Lev 19:34 The alien living with you must be *t*
25:40 He is to be *t* as a hired worker
1Sa 24:17 "You have *t* me well, but I have
Heb 10:29 who has *t* as an unholy thing

TREATING (TREAT)
Ge 18:25 *t* the righteous and the wicked
Heb 12: 7 as discipline; God is *t* you as sons.

TREATMENT (TREAT)
Col 2:23 and their harsh *t* of the body,

TREATY
Ex 34:12 not to make a *t* with those who live
Dt 7: 2 Make no *t* with them, and show
23: 6 Do not seek a *t* of friendship with them

TREE (TREES)
Ge 2: 9 and the *t* of the knowledge of good
2: 9 of the garden were the *t* of life
Dt 21:23 hung on a *t* is under God's curse.
2Sa 18: 9 Absalom's head got caught in the *t.*
1Ki 14:23 and under every spreading *t.*
Ps 1: 3 He is like a *t* planted by streams
52: 8 But I am like an olive *t*
92:12 righteous will flourish like a palm *t,*
Pr 3:18 She is a *t* of life to those who
11:30 of the righteous is a *t* of life,
27:18 He who tends a fig *t* will eat its fruit
Isa 65:22 For as the days of a *t,*
Jer 17: 8 He will be like a *t* planted
Eze 17:24 I the LORD bring down the tall *t*
Da 4:10 before me stood a *t* in the middle
Mic 4: 4 and under his own fig *t,*
Zec 3:10 to sit under his vine and fig *t,*'
Mt 3:10 every *t* that does not produce good
12:33 for a *t* is recognized by its fruit.
Lk 19: 4 climbed a sycamore-fig *t* to see him
Ac 5:30 killed by hanging him on a *t.*
Ro 11:24 be grafted into their own olive *t!*
Gal 3:13 is everyone who is hung on a *t.*"
Jas 3:12 My brothers, can a fig *t* bear olives,
1Pe 2:24 sins in his body on the *t,*
Rev 2: 7 the right to eat from the *t* of life,
22: 2 side of the river stood the *t* of life,
22:14 they may have the right to the *t*
22:19 from him his share in the *t* of life

TREES (TREE)
Jdg 9: 8 One day the *t* went out
Ps 96:12 Then all the *t* of the forest will sing
Isa 55:12 and all the *t* of the field
Mt 3:10 The ax is already at the root of the *t*
Mk 8:24 they look like *t* walking around."
Jude :12 autumn *t,* without fruit

TREMBLE (TREMBLED TREMBLES TREMBLING)
Ex 15:14 The nations will hear and *t;*
1Ch 16:30 *T* before him, all the earth!
Ps 114: 7 *T,* O earth, at the presence
Jer 5:22 "Should you not *t* in my presence?
Eze 38:20 of the earth will *t* at my presence.
Joel 2: 1 Let all who live in the land *t,*
Hab 3: 6 he looked, and made the nations *t.*

TREMBLED (TREMBLE)
Ex 19:16 Everyone in the camp *t.*
20:18 in smoke, they *t* with fear.
2Sa 22: 8 "The earth *t* and quaked,
Ac 7:32 Moses *t* with fear and did not dare

TREMBLES (TREMBLE)
Ps 97: 4 the earth sees and *t.*
104: 32 he who looks at the earth, and it *t,*
Isa 66: 2 and *t* at my word.
Jer 10:10 When he is angry, the earth *t;*
Na 1: 5 The earth *t* at his presence,

TREMBLING (TREMBLE)
Ps 2:11 and rejoice with *t.*
Da 10:10 set me *t* on my hands and knees.
Php 2:12 out your salvation with fear and *t,*
Heb 12:21 terrifying that Moses said, "I am *t*

TRESPASS* (TRESPASSES)
Ro 5:15 But the gift is not like the *t.*
5:15 died by the *t* of the one man,
5:17 For if, by the *t* of the one man,
5:18 result of one *t* was condemnation
5:20 added so that the *t* might increase.

TRESPASSES* (TRESPASS)
Ro 5:16 but the gift followed many *t*

TRIAL (TRIALS)
Ps 37:33 condemned when brought to *t.*
Mk 13:11 you are arrested and brought to *t,*
2Co 8: 2 most severe *t,* their overflowing
Jas 1:12 is the man who perseveres under *t,*
1Pe 4:12 at the painful *t* you are suffering,
Rev 3:10 you from the hour of *t* that is going

TRIALS* (TRIAL)
Dt 7:19 saw with your own eyes the great *t,*
29: 3 own eyes you saw those great *t,*
Lk 22:28 who have stood by me in my *t.*
1Th 3: 3 one would be unsettled by these *t.*
2Th 1: 4 the persecutions and *t* you are
Jas 1: 2 whenever you face *t* of many kinds,
1Pe 1: 6 had to suffer grief in all kinds of *t.*
2Pe 2: 9 how to rescue godly men from *t*

TRIBE (HALF-TRIBE TRIBES)
Heb 7:13 no one from that *t* has ever served
Rev 5: 5 See, the Lion of the *t* of Judah,
5: 9 God from every *t* and language
11: 9 men from every people, *t,*
14: 6 to every nation, *t,* language

TRIBES (TRIBE)
Ge 49:28 All these are the twelve *t* of Israel,
Mt 19:28 judging the twelve *t* of Israel.

TRIBULATION*
Rev 7:14 who have come out of the great *t*;

TRICKERY*
Ac 13:10 full of all kinds of deceit and *t*.
2Co 12:16 fellow that I am, I caught you by *t*!

TRIED (TRY)
Ps 73:16 When I *t* to understand all this,
95: 9 where your fathers tested and *t* me,
Heb 3: 9 where your fathers tested and *t* me

TRIES (TRY)
Lk 17:33 Whoever *t* to keep his life will lose

TRIMMED
Mt 25: 7 virgins woke up and *t* their lamps.

TRIUMPH (TRIUMPHAL TRIUMPHED TRIUMPHING TRIUMPHS)
Ps 25: 2 nor let my enemies *t* over me.
54: 7 my eyes have looked in *t*
112: 8 in the end he will look in *t*
118: 7 I will look in *t* on my enemies.
Pr 28:12 When the righteous *t*, there is great
Isa 42:13 and will *t* over his enemies.

TRIUMPHAL* (TRIUMPH)
Isa 60:11 their kings led in *t* procession.
2Co 2:14 us in *t* procession in Christ

TRIUMPHED (TRIUMPH)
Rev 5: 5 of Judah, the Root of David, has *t*.

TRIUMPHING* (TRIUMPH)
Col 2:15 of them, *t* over them by the cross.

TRIUMPHS* (TRIUMPH)
Jas 2:13 Mercy *t* over judgment! What

TROUBLE (TROUBLED TROUBLES)
Ge 41:51 God has made me forget all my *t*
Jos 7:25 Why have you brought this *t* on us?
Job 2:10 good from God, and not *t*?"
5: 7 Yet man is born to *t*
14: 1 is of few days and full of *t*.
42:11 him over all the *t* the LORD had
Ps 7:14 conceives *t* gives birth
7:16 The *t* he causes recoils on himself;
9: 9 a stronghold in times of *t*.
10:14 But you, O God, do see *t* and grief;
22:11 for *t* is near
27: 5 For in the day of *t*
32: 7 you will protect me from *t*
37:39 he is their stronghold in time of *t*.
41: 1 LORD delivers him in times of *t*.
46: 1 an ever-present help in *t*.
50:15 and call upon me in the day of *t*;
59:16 my refuge in times of *t*.
66:14 spoke when I was in *t*.
86: 7 In the day of my *t* I will call to you,
91:15 I will be with him in *t*,
107: 6 to the LORD in their *t*,
107: 13 they cried to the LORD in their *t*,
116: 3 I was overcome by *t* and sorrow.
119:143 *T* and distress have come upon me,
138: 7 Though I walk in the midst of *t*,
143: 11 righteousness, bring me out of *t*.
Pr 11: 8 righteous man is rescued from *t*,
11:17 a cruel man brings *t* on himself
11:29 He who brings *t* on his family will
12:13 but a righteous man escapes *t*.
12:21 but the wicked have their fill of *t*.
15:27 A greedy man brings *t* to his family
19:23 one rests content, untouched by *t*.
22: 8 He who sows wickedness reaps *t*,
24:10 If you falter in times of *t*,
25:19 on the unfaithful in times of *t*.
28:14 he who hardens his heart falls into *t*
Jer 30: 7 It will be a time of *t* for Jacob,
Na 1: 7 a refuge in times of *t*.
Zep 1:15 a day of *t* and ruin,
Mt 6:34 Each day has enough *t* of its own.
13:21 When *t* or persecution comes
Jn 16:33 In this world you will have *t*.
Ro 8:35 Shall *t* or hardship or persecution
2Co 1: 4 those in any *t* with the comfort we
2Th 1: 6 *t* to those who *t* you
Jas 5:13 one of you in *t*? He should pray.

TROUBLED (TROUBLE)
Ps 38:18 I am *t* by my sin.
Isa 38:14 I am *t*; O Lord, come to my aid!"
Mk 14:33 began to be deeply distressed and *t*.
Jn 14: 1 "Do not let your hearts be *t*.
14:27 Do not let your hearts be *t*
2Th 1: 7 and give relief to you who are *t*,

TROUBLES (TROUBLE)
Ps 34: 6 he saved him out of all his *t*.
34:17 he delivers them from all their *t*.
34:19 A righteous man may have many *t*,
40:12 For *t* without number surround me
54: 7 he has delivered me from all my *t*,
1Co 7:28 those who marry will face many *t*
2Co 1: 4 who comforts us in all our *t*,
4:17 and momentary *t* are achieving
6: 4 in *t*, hardships and distresses;
7: 4 in all our *t* my joy knows no bounds
Php 4:14 good of you to share in my *t*.

TRUE (TRUTH)
Nu 11:23 not what I say will come *t* for you."
12: 7 this is not *t* of my servant Moses;
Dt 18:22 does not take place or come *t*,
Jos 23:15 of the LORD your God has come *t*
1Sa 9: 6 and everything he says comes *t*.
1Ki 10: 6 and your wisdom is *t*.
2Ch 6:17 your servant David come *t*.
15: 3 was without the *t* God,
Ps 33: 4 of the LORD is right and *t*;
119:142 and your law is *t*.
119:151 and all your commands are *t*.
119:160 All your words are *t*;
Pr 8: 7 My mouth speaks what is *t*,
22:21 teaching you *t* and reliable words,
Jer 10:10 But the LORD is the *t* God;
28: 9 only if his prediction comes *t*."
Eze 33:33 "When all this comes *t*—
Lk 16:11 who will trust you with *t* riches?
Jn 1: 9 The *t* light that gives light
4:23 when the *t* worshipers will worship
6:32 Father who gives you the *t* bread
7:28 on my own, but he who sent me is *t*
15: 1 "I am the *t* vine, and my Father is
17: 3 the only *t* God, and Jesus Christ,
19:35 testimony, and his testimony is *t*.
21:24 We know that his testimony is *t*.
Ac 10:34 "I now realize how *t* it is that God
11:23 all to remain *t* to the Lord
14:22 them to remain *t* to the faith.
17:11 day to see if what Paul said was *t*.
Ro 3: 4 Let God be *t*, and every man a liar.
Php 4: 8 whatever is *t*, whatever is noble,
1Jn 2: 8 and the *t* light is already shining.
5:20 He is the *t* God and eternal life.
Rev 19: 9 "These are the *t* words of God."
22: 6 These words are trustworthy and *t*.

TRUMPET (TRUMPETS)
Isa 27:13 And in that day a great *t* will sound
Eze 33: 5 Since he heard the sound of the *t*
Zec 9:14 Sovereign LORD will sound the *t*;
Mt 24:31 send his angels with a loud *t* call,
1Co 14: 8 if the *t* does not sound a clear call,
15:52 For the *t* will sound, the dead will
1Th 4:16 and with the *t* call of God,
Rev 8: 7 The first angel sounded his *t*,

TRUMPETS (TRUMPET)
Jdg 7:19 They blew their *t* and broke the jars
Rev 8: 2 and to them were given seven *t*.

TRUST* (ENTRUST ENTRUSTED TRUSTED TRUSTFULLY TRUSTING TRUSTS TRUSTWORTHY)
Ex 14:31 put their *t* in him and in Moses his
19: 9 and will always put their *t* in you."
Nu 20:12 "Because you did not *t*
Dt 1:32 you did not *t* in the LORD your
9:23 You did not *t* him or obey him.
28:52 walls in which you *t* fall down.
Jdg 11:20 did not *t* Israel to pass
2Ki 17:14 who did not *t* in the LORD their
18:30 to *t* in the LORD when he says,
1Ch 9:22 to their positions of *t* by David
Job 4:18 If God places no *t* in his servants,
15:15 If God places no *t* in his holy ones,
31:24 "If I have put my *t* in gold
39:12 Can you *t* him to bring
Ps 4: 5 and *t* in the LORD.
9:10 Those who know your name will *t*
13: 5 But I *t* in your unfailing love;
20: 7 Some *t* in chariots and some
20: 7 we *t* in the name of the LORD our
22: 4 In you our fathers put their *t*;
22: 9 you made me *t* in you
25: 2 I lift up my soul; in you I *t*,
31: 6 I *t* in the LORD.
31:14 But I *t* in you, O LORD;
33:21 for we *t* in his holy name.
37: 3 *T* in the LORD and do good;
37: 5 *t* in him and he will do this:
40: 3 and put their *t* in the LORD.
40: 4 who makes the LORD his *t*,
44: 6 I do not *t* in my bow,
49: 6 those who *t* in their wealth
49:13 of those who *t* in themselves,
52: 8 I *t* in God's unfailing love
Ps 55:23 But as for me, I *t* in you.
56: 3 I will *t* in you.
56: 4 in God I *t*; I will not be afraid.
56:11 in God I *t*; I will not be afraid.
62: 8 *T* in him at all times, O people;
62:10 Do not *t* in extortion
78: 7 Then they would put their *t* in God
78:22 or *t* in his deliverance.
91: 2 my God, in whom I *t*."
115: 8 and so will all who *t* in them.
115: 9 O house of Israel, *t* in the LORD—
115: 10 O house of Aaron, *t* in the LORD
115: 11 You who fear him, *t* in the LORD
118: 8 than to *t* in man.
118: 9 than to *t* in princes.
119: 42 for I *t* in your word.
125: 1 Those who *t* in the LORD are like
135: 18 and so will all who *t* in them.
143: 8 for I have put my *t* in you.
146: 3 Do not put your *t* in princes,
Pr 3: 5 *T* in the LORD with all your heart
21:22 the stronghold in which they *t*.
22:19 So that your *t* may be in the LORD
Isa 8:17 I will put my *t* in him.
12: 2 I will *t* and not be afraid.
26: 4 *T* in the LORD forever,
30:15 in quietness and *t* is your strength,
31: 1 who *t* in the multitude
36:15 to *t* in the LORD when he says,
42:17 But those who *t* in idols,
50:10 *t* in the name of the LORD
Jer 2:37 LORD has rejected those you *t*;
5:17 the fortified cities in which you *t*.
7: 4 Do not *t* in deceptive words
7:14 the temple you *t* in, the place I gave
9: 4 do not *t* your brothers.
12: 6 Do not *t* them,
28:15 you have persuaded this nation to *t*
39:18 you *t* in me, declares the LORD.'"
48: 7 Since you *t* in your deeds
49: 4 you *t* in your riches and say,
49:11 Your widows too can *t* in me."
Mic 7: 5 Do not *t* a neighbor;
Na 1: 7 He cares for those who *t* in him,
Zep 3: 2 She does not *t* in the LORD,
3:12 who *t* in the name of the LORD.
Lk 16:11 who will *t* you with true riches?
Jn 12:36 Put your *t* in the light
14: 1 *T* in God; *t* also in me.
Ac 14:23 Lord, in whom they had put their *t*.
Ro 15:13 you with all joy and peace as you *t*
1Co 4: 2 been given a *t* must prove faithful.
9:17 discharging the *t* committed
2Co 13: 6 I *t* that you will discover that we
Heb 2:13 "I will put my *t* in him."

TRUSTED* (TRUST)
1Sa 27:12 Achish *t* David and said to himself,
2Ki 18: 5 Hezekiah *t* in the LORD, the God
1Ch 5:20 their prayers, because they *t*
Job 12:20 He silences the lips of *t* advisers
Ps 5: 9 from their mouth can be *t*;
22: 4 they *t* and you delivered them.
22: 5 in you they *t* and were not
26: 1 I have *t* in the LORD
41: 9 Even my close friend, whom I *t*,
52: 7 but *t* in his great wealth
Isa 20: 5 Those who *t* in Cush and boasted
25: 9 This is the LORD, we *t* in him;
25: 9 we *t* in him, and he saved us.
47:10 You have *t* in your wickedness
Jer 13:25 and *t* in false gods.
38:22 those *t* friends of yours.
48:13 ashamed when they *t* in Bethel.
Eze 16:15 " 'But you *t* in your beauty
Da 3:28 They *t* in him and defied the king's
6:23 because he had *t* in his God.
Lk 11:22 the armor in which the man *t*
16:10 *t* with very little can also be *t*
Ac 12:20 a *t* personal servant of the king,
Tit 2:10 but to show that they can be fully *t*,
3: 8 so that those who have *t*

TRUSTFULLY* (TRUST)
Pr 3:29 who lives *t* near you.

TRUSTING* (TRUST)
Job 15:31 by *t* what is worthless,
Ps 112: 7 his heart is steadfast, *t*
Isa 2:22 Stop *t* in man,
Jer 7: 8 you are *t* in deceptive words that

TRUSTS* (TRUST)
Job 8:14 What he *t* in is fragile;
Ps 21: 7 For the king *t* in the LORD;
22: 8 "He *t* in the LORD;
28: 7 my heart *t* in him, and I am helped.
32:10 surrounds the man who *t* in him.
84:12 blessed is the man who *t* in you.

Ps 86: 2 who *t* in you.
Pr 11:28 Whoever *t* in his riches will fall,
16:20 blessed is he who *t* in the LORD.
28:25 he who *t* in the LORD will prosper.
28:26 He who *t* in himself is a fool,
29:25 whoever *t* in the LORD is kept safe
Isa 26: 3 because he *t* in you.
28:16 one who *t* will never be dismayed.
Jer 17: 5 "Cursed is the one who *t* in man,
17: 7 blessed is the man who *t*
Eze 33:13 but then he *t* in his righteousness
Hab 2:18 For he who makes it *t*
Mt 27:43 He *t* in God.
Ro 4: 5 but *t* God who justifies the wicked,
9:33 one who *t* in him will never be put
10:11 "Anyone who *t* in him will never
1Co 13: 7 always protects, always *t*,
1Pe 2: 6 and the one who *t* in him

TRUSTWORTHY* (TRUST)
Ex 18:21 *t* men who hate dishonest gain—
2Sa 7:28 you are God! Your words are *t*,
Ne 13:13 these men were considered *t*.
Ps 19: 7 The statutes of the LORD are *t*,
111: 7 all his precepts are *t*.
119: 86 All your commands are *t*;
119:138 they are fully *t*.
Pr 11:13 but a *t* man keeps a secret.
13:17 but a *t* envoy brings healing.
25:13 is a *t* messenger to those who send
Da 2:45 and the interpretation is *t*."
6: 4 he was *t* and neither corrupt
Lk 16:11 So if you have not been *t*
16:12 And if you have not been *t*
19:17 'Because you have been *t*
1Co 7:25 one who by the Lord's mercy is *t*.
1Ti 1:15 Here is a *t* saying that deserves full
3: 1 Here is a *t* saying: If anyone sets his
3:11 but temperate and *t* in everything.
4: 9 This is a *t* saying that deserves full
2Ti 2:11 Here is a *t* saying:
Tit 1: 9 must hold firmly to the *t* message
3: 8 This is a *t* saying.
Rev 21: 5 for these words are *t* and true."
22: 6 "These words are *t* and true.

TRUTH* (TRUE TRUTHFUL TRUTHFULNESS TRUTHS)
Ge 42:16 tested to see if you are telling the *t*.
1Ki 17:24 LORD from your mouth is the *t*."
22:16 the *t* in the name of the LORD?"
2Ch 18:15 the *t* in the name of the LORD?"
Ps 15: 2 who speaks the *t* from his heart
25: 5 guide me in your *t* and teach me,
26: 3 and I walk continually in your *t*.
31: 5 redeem me, O LORD, the God of *t*
40:10 do not conceal your love and your *t*
40:11 your *t* always protect me.
43: 3 Send forth your light and your *t*,
45: 4 victoriously in behalf of *t*, humility
51: 6 Surely you desire *t*
52: 3 than speaking the *t*.
86:11 and I will walk in your *t*;
96:13 and the peoples in his *t*.
119: 30 I have chosen the way of *t*;
119: 43 of *t* from my mouth,
145: 18 to all who call on him in *t*.
Pr 16:13 they value a man who speaks the *t*.
23:23 Buy the *t* and do not sell it;
Isa 45:19 I, the LORD, speak the *t*;
48: 1 but not in *t* or righteousness—
59:14 *t* has stumbled in the streets,
59:15 *T* is nowhere to be found,
65:16 will do so by the God of *t*;
65:16 will swear by the God of *t*.
Jer 5: 1 who deals honestly and seeks the *t*,
5: 3 do not your eyes look for *t*?
7:28 *T* has perished; it has vanished
9: 3 it is not by *t*
9: 5 and no one speaks the *t*.
26:15 for in *t* the LORD has sent me
Da 8:12 and *t* was thrown to the ground.
9:13 and giving attention to your *t*.
10:21 what is written in the Book of *T*.
11: 2 "Now then, I tell you the *t*:
Am 5:10 and despise him who tells the *t*.
Zec 8: 3 will be called the City of *T*,
8:16 are to do: Speak the *t* to each other,
8:19 Therefore love *t* and peace."
Mt 5:18 I tell you the *t*, until heaven
5:26 I tell you the *t*, you will not get out
6: 2 I tell you the *t*, they have received
6: 5 I tell you the *t*, they have received
6:16 I tell you the *t*, they have received
8:10 "I tell you the *t*, I have not found
10:15 I tell you the *t*, it will be more
10:23 I tell you the *t*, you will not finish
10:42 I tell you the *t*, he will certainly not
11:11 I tell you the *t*: Among those born
Mt 13:17 For I tell you the *t*, many prophets
16:28 I tell you the *t*, some who are
17:20 I tell you the *t*, if you have faith
18: 3 And he said: "I tell you the *t*,
18:13 And if he finds it, I tell you the *t*,
18:18 "I tell you the *t*, whatever you bind
19:23 to his disciples, "I tell you the *t*,
19:28 "I tell you the *t*, at the renewal
21:21 Jesus replied, "I tell you the *t*,
21:31 Jesus said to them, "I tell you the *t*,
22:16 of God in accordance with the *t*.
23:36 I tell you the *t*, all this will come
24: 2 "I tell you the *t*, not one stone here
24:34 I tell you the *t*, this generation will
24:47 I tell you the *t*, he will put him
25:12 'I tell you the *t*, I don't know you.'
25:40 The King will reply, 'I tell you the *t*
25:45 "He will reply, 'I tell you the *t*,
26:13 tell you the *t*, wherever this gospel
26:21 "I tell you the *t*, one
26:34 "I tell you the *t*," Jesus answered,
Mk 3:28 I tell you the *t*, all the sins
5:33 with fear, told him the whole *t*.
8:12 I tell you the *t*, no sign will be given
9: 1 he said to them, "I tell you the *t*,
9:41 I tell you the *t*, anyone who gives
10:15 I tell you the *t*, anyone who will not
10:29 "I tell you the *t*," Jesus replied,
11:23 "I tell you the *t*, if anyone says
12:14 of God in accordance with the *t*.
12:43 Jesus said, "I tell you the *t*,
13:30 I tell you the *t*, this generation will
14: 9 I tell you the *t*, wherever the gospel
14:18 "I tell you the *t*, one
14:25 "I tell you the *t*, I will not drink
14:30 "I tell you the *t*," Jesus answered,
Lk 4:24 "I tell you the *t*," he continued,
9:27 I tell you the *t*, some who are
12:37 I tell you the *t*, he will dress himself
12:44 I tell you the *t*, he will put him
18:17 I tell you the *t*, anyone who will not
18:29 I tell you the *t*," Jesus said to them,
20:21 of God in accordance with the *t*.
21: 3 "I tell you the *t*," he said, "this
21:32 tell you the *t*, this generation will
23:43 answered him, "I tell you the *t*,
Jn 1:14 from the Father, full of grace and *t*.
1:17 and *t* came through Jesus Christ.
1:51 "I tell you the *t*, you shall see
3: 3 "I tell you the *t*, no one can see
3: 5 Jesus answered, "I tell you the *t*,
3:11 I tell you the *t*, we speak
3:21 But whoever lives by the *t* comes
4:23 worship the Father in spirit and *t*,
4:24 must worship in spirit and in *t*."
5:19 "I tell you the *t*, the Son can do
5:24 "I tell you the *t*, whoever hears my
5:25 I tell you the *t*, a time is coming
5:33 and he has testified to the *t*.
6:26 "I tell you the *t*, you are looking
6:32 Jesus said to them, "I tell you the *t*,
6:47 I tell you the *t*, he who believes has
6:53 Jesus said to them, "I tell you the *t*,
7:18 the one who sent him is a man of *t*;
8:32 Then you will know the *t*,
8:32 and the *t* will set you free."
8:34 Jesus replied, "I tell you the *t*,
8:40 who has told you the *t* that I heard
8:44 to the *t*, for there is no *t* in him.
8:45 I tell the *t*, you do not believe me!
8:46 I am telling the *t*, why don't you
8:51 I tell you the *t*, if anyone keeps my
8:58 "I tell you the *t*," Jesus answered,
10: 1 "I tell you the *t*, the man who does
10: 7 "I tell you the *t*, I am the gate
12:24 I tell you the *t*, unless a kernel
13:16 I tell you the *t*, no servant is greater
13:20 tell you the *t*, whoever accepts
13:21 "I tell you the *t*, one of you is going
13:38 I tell you the *t*, before the rooster
14: 6 I am the way and the *t* and the life.
14:12 I tell you the *t*, anyone who has
14:17 with you forever—the Spirit of *t*.
15:26 the Spirit of *t* who goes out
16: 7 But I tell you the *t*: It is
16:13 But when he, the Spirit of *t*, comes,
16:13 comes, he will guide you into all *t*.
16:20 I tell you the *t*, you will weep
16:23 I tell you the *t*, my Father will give
17:17 them by the *t*; your word is *t*.
18:23 if I spoke the *t*, why did you strike
18:37 into the world, to testify to the *t*.
18:37 on the side of *t* listens to me."
18:38 "What is *t*?" Pilate asked.
19:35 He knows that he tells the *t*,
21:18 I tell you the *t*, when you were
Ac 20:30 and distort the *t* in order
21:24 everybody will know there is no *t*
21:34 commander could not get at the *t*
Ac 24: 8 able to learn the *t* about all these
28:25 "The Holy Spirit spoke the *t*
Ro 1:18 of men who suppress the *t*
1:25 They exchanged the *t* of God
2: 2 who do such things is based on *t*.
2: 8 who reject the *t* and follow evil,
2:20 embodiment of knowledge and *t*—
9: 1 I speak the *t* in Christ—I am not
15: 8 of the Jews on behalf of God's *t*,
1Co 5: 8 the bread of sincerity and *t*.
13: 6 in evil but rejoices with the *t*.
2Co 4: 2 setting forth the *t* plainly we
11:10 As surely as the *t* of Christ is in me,
12: 6 because I would be speaking the *t*.
13: 8 against the *t*, but only for the *t*.
Gal 2: 5 so that the *t* of the gospel might
2:14 in line with the *t* of the gospel,
4:16 enemy by telling you the *t*?
5: 7 and kept you from obeying the *t*?
Eph 1:13 when you heard the word of *t*,
4:15 Instead, speaking the *t* in love,
4:21 him in accordance with the *t* that is
5: 9 and *t*) and find out what pleases
6:14 with the belt of *t* buckled
Col 1: 5 heard about in the word of *t*,
1: 6 understood God's grace in all its *t*.
2Th 2:10 because they refused to love the *t*
2:12 who have not believed the *t*
2:13 and through belief in the *t*.
1Ti 2: 4 to come to a knowledge of the *t*.
2: 7 I am telling the *t*, I am not lying—
3:15 the pillar and foundation of the *t*.
4: 3 who believe and who know the *t*.
6: 5 who have been robbed of the *t*
2Ti 2:15 correctly handles the word of *t*.
2:18 have wandered away from the *t*.
2:25 them to a knowledge of the *t*,
3: 7 never able to acknowledge the *t*.
3: 8 so also these men oppose the *t*—
4: 4 will turn their ears away from the *t*
Tit 1: 1 the knowledge of the *t* that leads
1:14 of those who reject the *t*.
Heb 10:26 received the knowledge of the *t*,
Jas 1:18 birth through the word of *t*,
3:14 do not boast about it or deny the *t*.
5:19 of you should wander from the *t*
1Pe 1:22 by obeying the *t* so that you have
2Pe 1:12 established in the *t* you now have.
2: 2 the way of *t* into disrepute.
1Jn 1: 6 we lie and do not live by the *t*.
1: 8 deceive ourselves and the *t* is not
2: 4 commands is a liar, and the *t* is not
2: 8 its *t* is seen in him and you,
2:20 and all of you know the *t*.
2:21 because no lie comes from the *t*.
2:21 because you do not know the *t*,
3:18 or tongue but with actions and in *t*.
3:19 we know that we belong to the *t*,
4: 6 is how we recognize the Spirit of *t*
5: 6 testifies, because the Spirit is the *t*.
2Jn : 1 whom I love in the *t*—
: 2 who know the *t*—because of the *t*,
: 3 will be with us in *t* and love.
: 4 of your children walking in the *t*,
3Jn : 1 friend Gaius, whom I love in the *t*.
: 3 how you continue to walk in the *t*.
: 3 tell about your faithfulness to the *t*
: 4 my children are walking in the *t*.
: 8 we may work together for the *t*.
:12 everyone—and even by the *t* itself.

TRUTHFUL* (TRUTH)
Pr 12:17 A *t* witness gives honest testimony,
12:19 *T* lips endure forever,
12:22 but he delights in men who are *t*.
14: 5 A *t* witness does not deceive,
14:25 A *t* witness saves lives,
Jer 4: 2 and if in a *t*, just and righteous way
Jn 3:33 it has certified that God is *t*.
2Co 6: 7 in *t* speech and in the power

TRUTHFULNESS* (TRUTH)
Ro 3: 7 "If my falsehood enhances God's *t*

TRUTHS* (TRUTH)
1Co 2:13 expressing spiritual *t*
1Ti 3: 9 hold of the deep *t* of the faith
4: 6 brought up in the *t* of the faith
Heb 5:12 to teach you the elementary *t*

TRY (TRIED TRIES TRYING)
Ps 26: 2 Test me, O LORD, and *t* me,
Isa 7:13 enough to *t* the patience of men?
Lk 12:58 *t* hard to be reconciled to him
13:24 will *t* to enter and will not be able
1Co 10:33 even as I *t* to please everybody
14:12 *t* to excel in gifts that build up
2Co 5:11 is to fear the Lord, we *t*
1Th 5:15 always *t* to be kind to each other

Tit 2: 9 to *t* to please them, not to talk back

TRYING (TRY)
2Co 5:12 We are not *t* to commend ourselves
Gal 1:10 If I were still *t* to please men,
1Th 2: 4 We are not *t* to please men but God
1Pe 1:11 *t* to find out the time
1Jn 2:26 things to you about those who are *t*

TUMORS
1Sa 5: 6 them and afflicted them with *t*.

TUNE
1Co 14: 7 anyone know what *t* is being

TUNIC (TUNICS)
Lk 6:29 do not stop him from taking your *t*.

TUNICS (TUNIC)
Lk 3:11 "The man with two *t* should share

TURMOIL
Ps 65: 7 and the *t* of the nations.
Pr 15:16 than great wealth with *t*.

TURN (TURNED TURNING TURNS)
Ex 32:12 *T* from your fierce anger; relent
Nu 32:15 If you *t* away from following him,
Dt 5:32 do not *t* aside to the right
28:14 Do not *t* aside from any
30:10 and *t* to the LORD your God
Jos 1: 7 do not *t* from it to the right
1Ki 8:58 May he *t* our hearts to him,
2Ch 7:14 and *t* from their wicked ways,
30: 9 He will not *t* his face from you
Job 33:30 to *t* back his soul from the pit,
Ps 28: 1 do not *t* a deaf ear to me.
34:14 *T* from evil and do good;
51:13 and sinners will *t* back to you.
78: 6 they in *t* would tell their children.
119: 36 *T* my heart toward your statutes
119:132 *T* to me and have mercy on me,
Pr 22: 6 when he is old he will not *t* from it.
Isa 17: 7 *t* their eyes to the Holy One
28: 6 to those who *t* back the battle
29:16 You *t* things upside down,
30:21 Whether you *t* to the right
45:22 "*T* to me and be saved,
55: 7 Let him *t* to the LORD,
Jer 31:13 I will *t* their mourning
Eze 33: 9 if you do warn the wicked man to *t*
33:11 *T*! *T* from your evil ways!
Jnh 3: 9 and with compassion *t*
Mal 4: 6 He will *t* the hearts of the fathers
Mt 5:39 you on the right cheek, *t*
10:35 For I have come to *t*
Lk 1:17 to *t* the hearts of the fathers
Jn 12:40 nor *t*— and I would heal them."
16:20 but your grief will *t* to joy.
Ac 3:19 Repent, then, and *t* to God,
26:18 and *t* them from darkness to light,
1Co 14:31 For you can all prophesy in *t*
15:23 But each in his own *t*: Christ,
1Ti 6:20 *T* away from godless chatter
1Pe 3:11 He must *t* from evil and do good;

TURNED (TURN)
Dt 23: 5 *t* the curse into a blessing for you,
1Ki 11: 4 his wives *t* his heart
2Ch 15: 4 But in their distress they *t*
Est 9: 1 but now the tables were *t*
9:22 when their sorrow was *t* into joy
Ps 14: 3 All have *t* aside,
30:11 You *t* my wailing into dancing;
40: 1 he *t* to me and heard my cry.
Isa 9:12 for all this, his anger is not *t* away,
53: 6 each of us has *t* to his own way;
Hos 7: 8 Ephraim is a flat cake not *t* over.
Joel 2:31 The sun will be *t* to darkness
Lk 22:32 And when you have *t* back,
Ro 3:12 All have *t* away,

TURNING (TURN)
2Ki 21:13 wiping it and *t* it upside down.
Pr 2: 2 *t* your ear to wisdom
14:27 *t* a man from the snares of death.

TURNS (TURN)
2Sa 22:29 the LORD *t* my darkness into light
Pr 15: 1 A gentle answer *t* away wrath,
Isa 44:25 and *t* it into nonsense,
Jas 5:20 Whoever *t* a sinner from the error

TWELVE
Ge 35:22 Jacob had *t* sons: The sons of Leah:
49:28 All these are the *t* tribes of Israel,
Mt 10: 1 He called his *t* disciples to him
Lk 9:17 the disciples picked up *t* basketfuls
Rev 21:12 the names of the *t* tribes of Israel.
21:14 of the *t* apostles of the Lamb.

TWIN (TWINS)
Ge 25:24 there were *t* boys in her womb.

TWINKLING*
1Co 15:52 in a flash, in the *t* of an eye,

TWINS (TWIN)
Ro 9:11 before the *t* were born

TWISTING* (TWISTS)
Pr 30:33 and as *t* the nose produces blood,

TWISTS (TWISTING)
Ex 23: 8 and *t* the words of the righteous.

TYRANNICAL*
Pr 28:16 A *t* ruler lacks judgment,

TYRE
Eze 28:12 a lament concerning the king of *T*
Mt 11:22 it will be more bearable for *T*

UNAPPROACHABLE*
1Ti 6:16 immortal and who lives in *u* light,

UNASHAMED*
1Jn 2:28 and *u* before him at his coming.

UNBELIEF* (UNBELIEVER UNBELIEVERS UNBELIEVING)
Mk 9:24 help me overcome my *u*!"
Ro 4:20 through *u* regarding the promise
11:20 they were broken off because of *u*,
11:23 And if they do not persist in *u*,
1Ti 1:13 because I acted in ignorance and *u*.
Heb 3:19 able to enter, because of their *u*.

UNBELIEVER* (UNBELIEF)
1Co 7:15 But if the *u* leaves, let him do so.
10:27 If some *u* invites you to a meal
14:24 if an *u* or someone who does not
2Co 6:15 have in common with an *u*?
1Ti 5: 8 the faith and is worse than an *u*.

UNBELIEVERS* (UNBELIEF)
Lk 12:46 and assign him a place with the *u*.
Ro 15:31 rescued from the *u* in Judea
1Co 6: 6 another—and this in front of *u*!
14:22 however, is for believers, not for *u*.
14:22 not for believers but for *u*;
14:23 do not understand or some *u* come
2Co 4: 4 this age has blinded the minds of *u*,
6:14 Do not be yoked together with *u*.

UNBELIEVING* (UNBELIEF)
Mt 17:17 "O *u* and perverse generation,"
Mk 9:19 "O *u* generation," Jesus replied,
Lk 9:41 "O *u* and perverse generation,"
1Co 7:14 For the *u* husband has been
7:14 and the *u* wife has been sanctified
Heb 3:12 *u* heart that turns away
Rev 21: 8 But the cowardly, the *u*, the vile,

UNBLEMISHED*
Heb 9:14 the eternal Spirit offered himself *u*

UNCEASING
Ro 9: 2 and *u* anguish in my heart.

UNCERTAIN*
1Ti 6:17 which is so *u*, but to put their hope

UNCHANGEABLE* (UNCHANGING)
Heb 6:18 by two *u* things in which it is

UNCHANGING* (UNCHANGEABLE)
Heb 6:17 wanted to make the *u* nature

UNCIRCUMCISED
Lev 26:41 when their *u* hearts are humbled
1Sa 17:26 Who is this *u* Philistine that he
Jer 9:26 house of Israel is *u* in heart."
Ac 7:51 stiff-necked people, with *u* hearts
Ro 4:11 had by faith while he was still *u*.
1Co 7:18 Was a man *u* when he was called?
Col 3:11 circumcised or *u*, barbarian,

UNCIRCUMCISION
1Co 7:19 is nothing and *u* is nothing.
Gal 5: 6 neither circumcision nor *u* has any

UNCLEAN
Ge 7: 2 and two of every kind of *u* animal,
Lev 10:10 between the *u* and the clean,
11: 4 it is ceremonially *u* for you.
17:15 he will be ceremonially *u* till evening.
Isa 6: 5 ruined! For I am a man of *u* lips,
52:11 Touch no *u* thing!
Mt 15:11 mouth does not make him '*u*,'
Ac 10:14 never eaten anything impure or *u*."
Ro 14:14 fully convinced that no food is *u*
2Co 6:17 Touch no *u* thing,

UNCLOTHED*
2Co 5: 4 because we do not wish to be *u*

UNCONCERNED*
Eze 16:49 were arrogant, overfed and *u*;

UNCOVERED
Ru 3: 7 Ruth approached quietly, *u* his feet
1Co 11: 5 with her head *u* dishonors her head
11:13 to pray to God with her head *u*?
Heb 4:13 Everything is *u* and laid bare

UNDERGOES* (UNDERGOING)
Heb 12: 8 (and everyone *u* discipline),

UNDERGOING* (UNDERGOES)
1Pe 5: 9 the world are *u* the same kind

UNDERSTAND (UNDERSTANDING UNDERSTANDS UNDERSTOOD)
Ne 8: 8 the people could *u* what was being
Job 38: 4 Tell me, if you *u*.
42: 3 Surely I spoke of things I did not *u*,
Ps 14: 2 men to see if there are any who *u*,
73:16 When I tried to *u* all this,
119: 27 Let me *u* the teaching
119:125 that I may *u* your statutes.
Pr 2: 5 then you will *u* the fear
2: 9 Then you will *u* what is right
30:18 four that I do not *u*:
Ecc 7:25 to *u* the stupidity of wickedness
11: 5 so you cannot *u* the work of God,
Isa 6:10 *u* with their hearts,
44:18 know nothing, they *u* nothing;
52:15 they have not heard, they will *u*.
Jer 17: 9 Who can *u* it?
31:19 after I came to *u*,
Da 9:25 and *u* this: From the issuing
Hos 14: 9 Who is discerning? He will *u* them.
Mt 13:15 *u* with their hearts
24:15 Daniel—let the reader *u*—
Lk 24:45 so they could *u* the Scriptures.
Ac 8:30 "Do you *u* what you are reading?"
Ro 7:15 I do not *u* what I do.
15:21 those who have not heard will *u*."
1Co 2:12 that we may *u* what God has freely
2:14 and he cannot *u* them,
14:16 those who do not *u* say "Amen"
Eph 5:17 but *u* what the Lord's will is.
Heb 11: 3 By faith we *u* that the universe was
2Pe 1:20 you must *u* that no prophecy
3: 3 you must *u* that in the last days
3:16 some things that are hard to *u*,

UNDERSTANDING (UNDERSTAND)
1Ki 4:29 and a breadth of *u* as measureless
Job 12:12 Does not long life bring *u*?
28:12 Where does *u* dwell?
28:28 and to shun evil is *u*.' "
32: 8 of the Almighty, that gives him *u*.
36:26 How great is God—beyond our *u*!
37: 5 he does great things beyond our *u*.
Ps 111: 10 follow his precepts have good *u*.
119: 34 Give me *u*, and I will keep your law
119:100 I have more *u* than the elders,
119:104 I gain *u* from your precepts;
119:130 it gives *u* to the simple.
136: 5 who by his *u* made the heavens,
147: 5 his *u* has no limit.
Pr 2: 2 and applying your heart to *u*,
2: 6 his mouth come knowledge and *u*.
3: 5 and lean not on your own *u*;
3:13 the man who gains *u*,
4: 5 Get wisdom, get *u*;
4: 7 Though it cost all you have, get *u*.
7: 4 and call *u* your kinsman;
9:10 knowledge of the Holy One is *u*.
10:23 but a man of *u* delights in wisdom.
11:12 but a man of *u* holds his tongue.
14:29 A patient man has great *u*,
15:21 a man of *u* keeps a straight course.
15:32 whoever heeds correction gains *u*.
16:16 to choose *u* rather than silver!
16:22 *U* is a fountain of life
17:27 and a man of *u* is even-tempered.
18: 2 A fool finds no pleasure in *u*
19: 8 he who cherishes *u* prospers.
20: 5 but a man of *u* draws them out.
23:23 get wisdom, discipline and *u*.
Isa 11: 2 the Spirit of wisdom and of *u*,
40:28 and his *u* no one can fathom.
56:11 They are shepherds who lack *u*;
Jer 3:15 you with knowledge and *u*.
10:12 stretched out the heavens by his *u*.
Da 5:12 a keen mind and knowledge and *u*,
10:12 that you set your mind to gain *u*
Hos 4:11 which take away the *u*
Mk 4:12 and ever hearing but never *u*;
12:33 with all your *u* and with all your

Lk 2:47 who heard him was amazed at his *u*
2Co 6: 6 in purity, *u*, patience and kindness;
Eph 1: 8 on us with all wisdom and *u*.
Php 4: 7 of God, which transcends all *u*,
Col 1: 9 through all spiritual wisdom and *u*.
2: 2 have the full riches of complete *u*,
1Jn 5:20 God has come and has given us *u*,

UNDERSTANDS (UNDERSTAND)
1Ch 28: 9 and *u* every motive
Jer 9:24 that he *u* and knows me,
Mt 13:23 man who hears the word and *u* it.
Ro 3:11 there is no one who *u*,
1Ti 6: 4 he is conceited and *u* nothing.

UNDERSTOOD (UNDERSTAND)
Ne 8:12 they now *u* the words that had
Ps 73:17 then I *u* their final destiny.
Isa 40:13 Who has *u* the mind of the LORD,
40:21 Have you not *u* since the earth was
Jn 1: 5 but the darkness has not *u* it.
Ro 1:20 being *u* from what has been made,

UNDESIRABLE*
Jos 24:15 But if serving the LORD seems *u*

UNDIVIDED*
1Ch 12:33 to help David with *u* loyalty—
Ps 86:11 give me an *u* heart,
Eze 11:19 I will give them an *u* heart
1Co 7:35 way in *u* devotion to the Lord.

UNDOING
Pr 18: 7 A fool's mouth is his *u*,

UNDYING*
Eph 6:24 Lord Jesus Christ with an *u* love.

UNEQUALED*
Mt 24:21 *u* from the beginning of the world
Mk 13:19 of distress *u* from the beginning,

UNFADING*
1Pe 3: 4 the *u* beauty of a gentle

UNFAILING*
Ex 15:13 "In your *u* love you will lead
1Sa 20:14 But show me *u* kindness like that
2Sa 22:51 he shows *u* kindness
Ps 6: 4 save me because of your *u* love.
13: 5 But I trust in your *u* love;
18:50 he shows *u* kindness
21: 7 through the *u* love
31:16 save me in your *u* love.
32:10 but the LORD's *u* love
33: 5 the earth is full of his *u* love.
33:18 those whose hope is in his *u* love,
33:22 May your *u* love rest upon us,
36: 7 How priceless is your *u* love!
44:26 redeem us because of your *u* love.
48: 9 we meditate on your *u* love.
51: 1 according to your *u* love;
52: 8 I trust in God's *u* love
77: 8 Has his *u* love vanished forever?
85: 7 Show us your *u* love, O LORD,
90:14 in the morning with your *u* love,
107: 8 thanks to the LORD for his *u* love
107: 15 thanks to the LORD for his *u* love
107: 21 to the LORD for his *u* love
107: 31 to the LORD for his *u* love
119: 41 May your *u* love come to me,
119: 76 May your *u* love be my comfort,
130: 7 for with the LORD is *u* love
143: 8 bring me word of your *u* love,
143: 12 In your *u* love, silence my enemies;
147: 11 who put their hope in his *u* love.
Pr 19:22 What a man desires is *u* love;
20: 6 Many a man claims to have *u* love,
Isa 54:10 yet my *u* love for you will not be
La 3:32 so great is his *u* love.
Hos 10:12 reap the fruit of *u* love,

UNFAITHFUL (UNFAITHFULNESS)
Lev 6: 2 is *u* to the LORD by deceiving his
Nu 5: 6 and so is *u* to the LORD,
1Ch 10:13 because he was *u* to the LORD;
Pr 11: 6 the *u* are trapped by evil desires.
13: 2 the *u* have a craving for violence.
13:15 but the way of the *u* is hard.
22:12 but he frustrates the words of the *u*.
23:28 and multiplies the *u* among men.
25:19 is reliance on the *u* in times
Jer 3:20 But like a woman *u* to her husband,

UNFAITHFULNESS (UNFAITHFUL)
1Ch 9: 1 to Babylon because of their *u*.
Mt 5:32 except for marital *u*, causes her
19: 9 for marital *u*, and marries another

UNFIT*
Tit 1:16 and *u* for doing anything good.

UNFOLDING
Ps 119:130 the *u* of your words gives light;

UNFORGIVING*
2Ti 3: 3 unholy, without love, *u*, slanderous

UNFRIENDLY*
Pr 18: 1 An *u* man pursues selfish ends;

UNFRUITFUL
1Co 14:14 my spirit prays, but my mind is *u*.

UNGODLINESS (UNGODLY)
Tit 2:12 It teaches us to say "No" to *u*

UNGODLY (UNGODLINESS)
Ro 5: 6 powerless, Christ died for the *u*.
1Ti 1: 9 the *u* and sinful, the unholy
2Ti 2:16 in it will become more and more *u*.
2Pe 2: 6 of what is going to happen to the *u*;
Jude :15 and to convict all the *u*

UNGRATEFUL*
Lk 6:35 he is kind to the *u* and wicked.
2Ti 3: 2 disobedient to their parents, *u*,

UNHOLY*
1Ti 1: 9 and sinful, the *u* and irreligious;
2Ti 3: 2 ungrateful, *u*, without love,
Heb 10:29 as an *u* thing the blood

UNINTENTIONALLY
Lev 4: 2 'When anyone sins *u* and does
Nu 15:22 " 'Now if you *u* fail to keep any
Dt 4:42 flee if he had *u* killed his neighbor

UNIT
1Co 12:12 body is a *u*, though it is made up

UNITE (UNITED UNITY)
1Co 6:15 and *u* them with a prostitute?

UNITED (UNITE)
Ge 2:24 and mother and be *u* to his wife,
Mt 19: 5 and mother and be *u* to his wife,
Ro 6: 5 If we have been *u* with him like this
Eph 5:31 and mother and be *u* to his wife,
Php 2: 1 from being *u* with Christ,
Col 2: 2 encouraged in heart and *u* in love,

UNITY* (UNITE)
2Ch 30:12 the people to give them *u* of mind
Ps 133: 1 is when brothers live together in *u*!
Jn 17:23 May they be brought to complete *u*
Ro 15: 5 a spirit of *u* among yourselves
Eph 4: 3 effort to keep the *u* of the Spirit
4:13 up until we all reach *u* in the faith
Col 3:14 them all together in perfect *u*.

UNIVERSE*
1Co 4: 9 made a spectacle to the whole *u*,
Eph 4:10 in order to fill the whole *u*.)
Php 2:15 which you shine like stars in the *u*
Heb 1: 2 and through whom he made the *u*.
11: 3 understand that the *u* was formed

UNJUST
Ro 3: 5 That God is *u* in bringing his wrath
9:14 What then shall we say? Is God *u*?
1Pe 2:19 up under the pain of *u* suffering

UNKNOWN
Ac 17:23 TO AN *U* GOD.

UNLEAVENED
Ex 12:17 "Celebrate the Feast of *U* Bread,
Dt 16:16 at the Feast of *U* Bread, the Feast

UNLIMITED*
1Ti 1:16 Jesus might display his *u* patience

UNLOVED
Pr 30:23 an *u* woman who is married,

UNMARRIED
1Co 7: 8 It is good for them to stay *u*,
7:27 Are you *u*? Do not look for a wife.
7:32 An *u* man is concerned about

UNPLOWED
Ex 23:11 the seventh year let the land lie *u*
Hos 10:12 and break up your *u* ground;

UNPRODUCTIVE
Tit 3:14 necessities and not live *u* lives.
2Pe 1: 8 and *u* in your knowledge

UNPROFITABLE
Tit 3: 9 because these are *u* and useless.

UNPUNISHED
Ex 34: 7 Yet he does not leave the guilty *u*;
Pr 6:29 no one who touches her will go *u*.
11:21 of this: The wicked will not go *u*,
19: 5 A false witness will not go *u*,

UNQUENCHABLE
Lk 3:17 he will burn up the chaff with *u* fire

UNREPENTANT*
Ro 2: 5 stubbornness and your *u* heart,

UNRIGHTEOUS*
Zep 3: 5 yet the *u* know no shame.
Mt 5:45 rain on the righteous and the *u*.
1Pe 3:18 the righteous for the *u*, to bring you
2Pe 2: 9 and to hold the *u* for the day

UNSEARCHABLE
Ro 11:33 How *u* his judgments,
Eph 3: 8 preach to the Gentiles the *u* riches

UNSEEN*
Mt 6: 6 and pray to your Father, who is *u*.
6:18 who is *u*; and your Father,
2Co 4:18 on what is seen, but on what is *u*.
4:18 temporary, but what is *u* is eternal.

UNSETTLED*
1Th 3: 3 so that no one would be *u*
2Th 2: 2 not to become easily *u*

UNSHRUNK
Mt 9:16 patch of *u* cloth on an old garment,

UNSPIRITUAL*
Ro 7:14 but I am *u*, sold as a slave to sin.
Col 2:18 and his *u* mind puffs him up
Jas 3:15 down from heaven but is earthly, *u*,

UNSTABLE*
Jas 1: 8 he is a double-minded man, *u*
2Pe 2:14 they seduce the *u*; they are experts
3:16 ignorant and *u* people distort,

UNTHINKABLE*
Job 34:12 It is *u* that God would do wrong,

UNTIE
Mk 1: 7 worthy to stoop down and *u*.
Lk 13:15 each of you on the Sabbath *u* his ox

UNVEILED*
2Co 3:18 with *u* faces all reflect the Lord's

UNWHOLESOME*
Eph 4:29 Do not let any *u* talk come out

UNWISE
Eph 5:15 how you live—not as *u* but as wise,

UNWORTHY*
Ge 32:10 I am *u* of all the kindness
Job 40: 4 "I am *u*— how can I reply to you?
Lk 17:10 should say, 'We are *u* servants;
1Co 11:27 Lord in an *u* manner will be guilty

UPHOLD (UPHOLDS)
Isa 41:10 I will *u* you with my righteous right
Ro 3:31 Not at all! Rather, we *u* the law.

UPHOLDS* (UPHOLD)
Ps 37:17 but the LORD *u* the righteous.
37:24 for the LORD *u* him with his hand.
63: 8 your right hand *u* me.
140: 12 and *u* the cause of the needy.
145: 14 The LORD *u* all those who fall
146: 7 He *u* the cause of the oppressed

UPRIGHT
Dt 32: 4 *u* and just is he.
Job 1: 1 This man was blameless and *u*;
Ps 7:10 who saves the *u* in heart.
11: 7 *u* men will see his face.
25: 8 Good and *u* is the LORD;
33: 1 it is fitting for the *u* to praise him.
64:10 let all the *u* in heart praise him!
92:15 proclaiming, "The LORD is *u*;
97:11 and joy on the *u* in heart.
119: 7 I will praise you with an *u* heart
Pr 2: 7 He holds victory in store for the *u*,
3:32 but takes the *u* into his confidence.
14: 2 whose walk is *u* fears the LORD,
15: 8 but the prayer of the *u* pleases him.
21:29 an *u* man gives thought to his ways.
Isa 26: 7 O *u* One, you make the way
Tit 1: 8 who is self-controlled, *u*, holy
2:12 *u* and godly lives in this present

UPROOTED
Dt 28:63 You will be *u* from the land you are

Jer 31:40 The city will never again be *u*
Jude :12 without fruit and *u*— twice dead.

UPSET
Lk 10:41 are worried and *u* about many

URIAH
Hittite husband of Bathsheba, killed by David's order (2Sa 11).

USEFUL
Eph 4:28 doing something *u*
2Ti 2:21 *u* to the Master and prepared
3:16 Scripture is God-breathed and is *u*
Phm :11 now he has become *u* both to you

USELESS
1Co 15:14 our preaching is *u*
Tit 3: 9 these are unprofitable and *u*.
Phm :11 Formerly he was *u* to you,
Heb 7:18 *u* (for the law made nothing perfect
Jas 2:20 faith without deeds is *u?*

USURY
Ne 5:10 But let the exacting of *u* stop!
Ps 15: 5 who lends his money without *u*

UTMOST
Job 34:36 that Job might be tested to the *u*

UTTER (UTTERS)
Ps 78: 2 I will *u* hidden things, things from of old—
Mt 13:35 I will *u* things hidden

UTTERS (UTTER)
1Co 14: 2 he *u* mysteries with his spirit.

UZZIAH
Son of Amaziah; king of Judah also known as Azariah (2Ki 15:1-7; 1Ch 6:24; 2Ch 26). Struck with leprosy because of pride (2Ch 26:16-23).

VAIN
Ps 33:17 A horse is a *v* hope for deliverance;
73:13 in *v* have I kept my heart pure;
127: 1 its builders labor in *v*.
Isa 65:23 They will not toil in *v*
1Co 15: 2 Otherwise, you have believed in *v*.
15:58 labor in the Lord is not in *v*.
2Co 6: 1 not to receive God's grace in *v*.
Gal 2: 2 running or had run my race in *v*.

VALIANT
1Sa 10:26 by *v* men whose hearts God had

VALID
Jn 8:14 my own behalf, my testimony is *v*,

VALLEY (VALLEYS)
Ps 23: 4 walk through the *v* of the shadow
Isa 40: 4 Every *v* shall be raised up,
Joel 3:14 multitudes in the *v* of decision!

VALLEYS (VALLEY)
SS 2: 1 a lily of the *v*.

VALUABLE (VALUE)
Lk 12:24 And how much more *v* you are

VALUE (VALUABLE VALUED)
Lev 27: 3 set the *v* of a male between the ages
Pr 16:13 they *v* a man who speaks the truth.
31:11 and lacks nothing of *v*.
Mt 13:46 When he found one of great *v*,
1Ti 4: 8 For physical training is of some *v*,
Heb 11:26 as of greater *v* than the treasures

VALUED (VALUE)
Lk 16:15 What is highly *v* among men is

VANISHES
Jas 4:14 appears for a little while and then *v*.

VASHTI*
Queen of Persia replaced by Esther (Est 1-2).

VAST
Ge 2: 1 completed in all their *v* array.
Dt 1:19 of the Amorites through all that *v*
8:15 He led you through the *v*
Ps 139: 17 How *v* is the sum of them!

VEGETABLES
Pr 15:17 of *v* where there is love
Ro 14: 2 whose faith is weak, eats only *v*.

VEIL
Ex 34:33 to them, he put a *v* over his face.
2Co 3:14 for to this day the same *v* remains

VENGEANCE (AVENGE AVENGER AVENGES AVENGING REVENGE)
Nu 31: 3 to carry out the LORD's *v* on them
Isa 34: 8 For the LORD has a day of *v*,
Na 1: 2 The LORD takes *v* on his foes

VERDICT
Jn 3:19 This is the *v:* Light has come

VICTOR'S* (VICTORY)
2Ti 2: 5 he does not receive the *v* crown

VICTORIES* (VICTORY)
2Sa 22:51 He gives his king great *v;*
Ps 18:50 He gives his king great *v;*
21: 1 great is his joy in the *v* you give!
21: 5 Through the *v* you gave, his glory is
44: 4 who decrees *v* for Jacob.

VICTORIOUS (VICTORY)
Ps 20: 5 for joy when you are *v*

VICTORIOUSLY* (VICTORY)
Ps 45: 4 In your majesty ride forth *v*

VICTORY (VICTOR'S VICTORIES VICTORIOUS VICTORIOUSLY)
2Sa 8: 6 gave David *v* wherever he
Ps 44: 6 my sword does not bring me *v;*
60:12 With God we will gain the *v*,
129: 2 they have not gained the *v* over me.
Pr 11:14 but many advisers make *v* sure.
1Co 15:54 "Death has been swallowed up in *v*
15:57 He gives us the *v* through our Lord
1Jn 5: 4 This is the *v* that has overcome

VIEW
Pr 5:21 are in full *v* of the LORD,
2Ti 4: 1 and in *v* of his appearing

VILLAGE
Mk 6: 6 went around teaching from *v* to *v*.

VINDICATED (VINDICATION)
Job 13:18 I know I will be *v*.
1Ti 3:16 was *v* by the Spirit,

VINDICATION (VINDICATED)
Ps 24: 5 and *v* from God his Savior.

VINE (VINEYARD)
Ps 128: 3 Your wife will be like a fruitful *v*
Isa 36:16 one of you will eat from his own *v*
Jnh 4: 6 Jonah was very happy about the *v*.
Jn 15: 1 "I am the true *v*, and my Father is

VINEGAR
Pr 10:26 As *v* to the teeth and smoke
Mk 15:36 filled a sponge with wine *v*,

VINEYARD (VINE)
1Ki 21: 1 an incident involving a *v* belonging
Pr 31:16 out of her earnings she plants a *v*.
SS 1: 6 my own *v* I have neglected.
Isa 5: 1 My loved one had a *v*
1Co 9: 7 Who plants a *v* and does not eat

VIOLATION
Heb 2: 2 every *v* and disobedience received

VIOLENCE (VIOLENT)
Ge 6:11 in God's sight and was full of *v*.
Isa 53: 9 though he had done no *v*,
60:18 No longer will *v* be heard
Eze 45: 9 Give up your *v* and oppression
Joel 3:19 of *v* done to the people of Judah,
Jnh 3: 8 give up their evil ways and their *v*.

VIOLENT (VIOLENCE)
Eze 18:10 "Suppose he has a *v* son, who sheds
1Ti 1:13 and a persecutor and a *v* man,
3: 3 not *v* but gentle, not quarrelsome,
Tit 1: 7 not *v*, not pursuing dishonest gain.

VIPERS
Ps 140: 3 the poison of *v* is on their lips.
Lk 3: 7 "You brood of *v!* Who warned you
Ro 3:13 "The poison of *v* is on their lips."

VIRGIN (VIRGINS)
Dt 22:15 shall bring proof that she was a *v*
Isa 7:14 The *v* will be with child
Mt 1:23 "The *v* will be with child
Lk 1:34 I am a *v?*" The angel answered,
2Co 11: 2 that I might present you as a pure *v*

VIRGINS (VIRGIN)
Mt 25: 1 will be like ten *v* who took their
1Co 7:25 Now about *v:* I have no command

VIRTUES*
Col 3:14 And over all these *v* put on love,

VISIBLE
Eph 5:13 exposed by the light becomes *v*,
Col 1:16 and on earth, *v* and invisible,

VISION (VISIONS)
Da 9:24 to seal up *v* and prophecy
Ac 26:19 disobedient to the *v* from heaven.

VISIONS (VISION)
Nu 12: 6 I reveal myself to him in *v*,
Joel 2:28 your young men will see *v*.
Ac 2:17 your young men will see *v*,

VOICE
Dt 30:20 listen to his *v*, and hold fast to him.
1Sa 15:22 as in obeying the *v* of the LORD?
Job 40: 9 and can your *v* thunder like his?
Ps 19: 4 Their *v* goes out into all the earth,
29: 3 The *v* of the LORD is
66:19 and heard my *v* in prayer.
95: 7 Today, if you hear his *v*,
Pr 8: 1 Does not understanding raise her *v*
Isa 30:21 your ears will hear a *v* behind you,
40: 3 A *v* of one calling:
Mk 1: 3 "a *v* of one calling in the desert,
Jn 5:28 are in their graves will hear his *v*
10: 3 and the sheep listen to his *v*.
Ro 10:18 "Their *v* has gone out
Heb 3: 7 "Today, if you hear his *v*,
Rev 3:20 If anyone hears my *v* and opens

VOMIT
Lev 18:28 it will *v* you out as it vomited out
Pr 26:11 As a dog returns to its *v*,
2Pe 2:22 "A dog returns to its *v*," and,

VOW (VOWS)
Nu 6: 2 a *v* of separation to the LORD
30: 2 When a man makes a *v*
Jdg 11:30 Jephthah made a *v* to the LORD:

VOWS (VOW)
Ps 116: 14 I will fulfill my *v* to the LORD
Pr 20:25 and only later to consider his *v*.

VULTURES
Mt 24:28 is a carcass, there the *v* will gather.

WAGE (WAGES WAGING)
2Co 10: 3 we do not *w* war as the world does.

WAGES (WAGE)
Mal 3: 5 who defraud laborers of their *w*,
Lk 10: 7 for the worker deserves his *w*.
Ro 4: 4 his *w* are not credited to him
6:23 For the *w* of sin is death,
1Ti 5:18 and "The worker deserves his *w*."

WAGING (WAGE)
Ro 7:23 *w* war against the law of my mind

WAILING
Ps 30:11 You turned my *w* into dancing;

WAIST
2Ki 1: 8 and with a leather belt around his *w*."
Mt 3: 4 he had a leather belt around his *w*.

WAIT (AWAITS WAITED WAITING WAITS)
Ps 27:14 *W* for the LORD;
130: 5 I *w* for the LORD, my soul waits,
Isa 30:18 Blessed are all who *w* for him!
Ac 1: 4 *w* for the gift my Father promised,
Ro 8:23 as we *w* eagerly for our adoption
1Th 1:10 and to *w* for his Son from heaven,
Tit 2:13 while we *w* for the blessed hope—

WAITED (WAIT)
Ps 40: 1 I *w* patiently for the LORD;

WAITING (WAIT)
Heb 9:28 to those who are *w* for him.

WAITS (WAIT)
Ro 8:19 creation *w* in eager expectation

WAKE (AWAKE WAKENS)
Eph 5:14 "*W* up, O sleeper,

WAKENS* (WAKE)
Isa 50: 4 He *w* me morning by morning,
50: 4 *w* my ear to listen like one being

WALK (WALKED WALKING WALKS)
Lev 26:12 I will *w* among you and be your
Dt 5:33 *W* in all the way that the LORD
6: 7 and when you *w* along the road,
10:12 to *w* in all his ways, to love him,
11:19 and when you *w* along the road,

Dt 11:22 to *w* in all his ways and to hold fast
26:17 and that you will *w* in his ways,
Jos 22: 5 to *w* in all his ways,
Ps 1: 1 who does not *w* in the counsel
15: 2 He whose *w* is blameless
23: 4 Even though I *w*
84:11 from those whose *w* is blameless.
89:15 who *w* in the light of your presence
119: 45 I will *w* about in freedom,
Pr 4:12 When you *w*, your steps will not be
6:22 When you *w*, they will guide you;
Isa 2: 3 so that we may *w* in his paths."
2: 5 let us *w* in the light of the LORD.
30:21 saying, "This is the way; *w* in it."
40:31 they will *w* and not be faint.
57: 2 Those who *w* uprightly
Jer 6:16 ask where the good way is, and *w*
Da 4:37 And those who *w* in pride he is able
Am 3: 3 Do two *w* together
Mic 4: 5 All the nations may *w*
6: 8 and to *w* humbly with your God.
Mk 2: 9 'Get up, take your mat and *w*'?
Jn 8:12 Whoever follows me will never *w*
1Jn 1: 6 with him yet *w* in the darkness,
1: 7 But if we *w* in the light,
2Jn : 6 his command is that you *w* in love.

WALKED (WALK)
Ge 5:24 Enoch *w* with God; then he was no
Jos 14: 9 which your feet have *w* will be your
Mt 14:29 *w* on the water and came toward Jesus.

WALKING (WALK)
1Ki 3: 3 love for the LORD by *w* according
Da 3:25 I see four men *w* around in the fire,
2Jn : 4 of your children *w* in the truth,

WALKS (WALK)
Pr 10: 9 The man of integrity *w* securely,
13:20 He who *w* with the wise grows wise
Isa 33:15 He who *w* righteously
Jn 11: 9 A man who *w* by day will not

WALL (WALLS)
Jos 6:20 *w* collapsed; so every man charged
Ne 2:17 let us rebuild the *w* of Jerusalem,
Eph 2:14 the dividing *w* of hostility,
Rev 21:12 It had a great, high *w*

WALLOWING
2Pe 2:22 back to her *w* in the mud."

WALLS (WALL)
Isa 58:12 be called Repairer of Broken *W*,
60:18 but you will call your *w* Salvation
Heb 11:30 By faith the *w* of Jericho fell,

WANDER (WANDERED)
Nu 32:13 he made them *w* in the desert forty
Jas 5:19 one of you should *w* from the truth

WANDERED (WANDER)
Eze 34: 6 My sheep *w* over all the mountains
Mt 18:12 go to look for the one that *w* off?
1Ti 6:10 have *w* from the faith and pierced
2Ti 2:18 who have *w* away from the truth.

WANT (WANTED WANTING WANTS)
1Sa 8:19 "We *w* a king over us.
Mt 19:21 Jesus answered, "If you *w*
Lk 19:14 'We don't *w* this man to be our king
Ro 7:15 For what I *w* to do I do not do,
13: 3 Do you *w* to be free from fear
2Co 12:14 what I *w* is not your possessions
Php 3:10 I *w* to know Christ and the power

WANTED (WANT)
1Co 12:18 of them, just as he *w* them to be.
Heb 6:17 Because God *w* to make

WANTING (WANT)
Da 5:27 weighed on the scales and found *w*.
2Pe 3: 9 with you, not *w* anyone to perish,

WANTS (WANT)
Mt 5:42 from the one who *w* to borrow
20:26 whoever *w* to become great
Mk 8:35 For whoever *w* to save his life will
10:43 whoever *w* to become great
Ro 9:18 he hardens whom he *w* to harden.
1Ti 2: 4 who *w* all men to be saved
1Pe 5: 2 you are willing, as God *w* you to be;

WAR (WARRIOR WARS)
Jos 11:23 Then the land had rest from *w*.
1Sa 15:18 make *w* on them until you have
Ps 68:30 the nations who delight in *w*.
120: 7 but when I speak, they are for *w*.
144: 1 who trains my hands for *w*,
Isa 2: 4 nor will they train for *w* anymore.
Da 9:26 *W* will continue until the end,
Ro 7:23 waging *w* against the law
2Co 10: 3 we do not wage *w* as the world does
1Pe 2:11 which *w* against your soul.
Rev 12: 7 And there was *w* in heaven.
19:11 With justice he judges and makes *w*

WARN* (WARNED WARNING WARNINGS)
Ex 19:21 *w* the people so they do not force
Nu 24:14 let me *w* you of what this people
1Sa 8: 9 but *w* them solemnly and let them
1Ki 2:42 swear by the LORD and *w* you,
2Ch 19:10 you are to *w* them not to sin
Ps 81: 8 O my people, and I will *w* you—
Jer 42:19 I *w* you today that you made a fatal
Eze 3:18 and you do not *w* him or speak out
3:19 But if you do *w* the wicked man
3:20 Since you did not *w* him, he will die
3:21 if you do *w* the righteous man not
33: 3 blows the trumpet to *w* the people,
33: 6 blow the trumpet to *w* the people
33: 9 if you do *w* the wicked man to turn
Lk 16:28 Let him *w* them, so that they will
Ac 4:17 we must *w* these men
1Co 4:14 but to *w* you, as my dear children.
Gal 5:21 I *w* you, as I did before, that those
1Th 5:14 brothers, *w* those who are idle,
2Th 3:15 an enemy, but *w* him as a brother.
2Ti 2:14 *W* them before God
Tit 3:10 and then *w* him a second time.
3:10 *W* a divisive person once,
Rev 22:18 I *w* everyone who hears the words

WARNED (WARN)
2Ki 17:13 The LORD *w* Israel and Judah
Ps 19:11 By them is your servant *w*;
Jer 22:21 I *w* you when you felt secure,
Mt 3: 7 Who *w* you to flee
1Th 4: 6 have already told you and *w* you.
Heb 11: 7 when *w* about things not yet seen,
12:25 they refused him who *w* them

WARNING (WARN)
Jer 6: 8 Take *w*, O Jerusalem,
1Ti 5:20 so that the others may take *w*.

WARNINGS (WARN)
1Co 10:11 and were written down as *w* for us,

WARRIOR (WAR)
Ex 15: 3 The LORD is a *w*;
1Ch 28: 3 you are a *w* and have shed blood.'
Pr 16:32 Better a patient man than a *w*,

WARS (WAR)
Ps 46: 9 He makes *w* cease to the ends
Mt 24: 6 You will hear of *w* and rumors of *w*,

WASH (WASHED WASHING)
Ps 51: 7 *w* me, and I will be whiter
Jer 4:14 *w* the evil from your heart
Jn 13: 5 and began to *w* his disciples' feet,
Ac 22:16 be baptized and *w* your sins away,
Jas 4: 8 *W* your hands, you sinners,
Rev 22:14 Blessed are those who *w* their robes

WASHED (WASH)
Ps 73:13 in vain have I *w* my hands
1Co 6:11 you were *w*, you were sanctified,
Heb 10:22 and having our bodies *w*
2Pe 2:22 and, "A sow that is *w* goes back
Rev 7:14 they have *w* their robes

WASHING (WASH)
Eph 5:26 cleansing her by the *w* with water
1Ti 5:10 showing hospitality, *w* the feet
Tit 3: 5 us through the *w* of rebirth

WASTED (WASTING)
Jn 6:12 Let nothing be *w*."

WASTING (WASTED)
2Co 4:16 Though outwardly we are *w* away,

WATCH (WATCHER WATCHES WATCHING WATCHMAN)
Ge 31:49 "May the LORD keep *w*
Ps 90: 4 or like a *w* in the night.
141: 3 keep *w* over the door of my lips.
Pr 4: 6 love her, and she will *w* over you.
6:22 when you sleep, they will *w*
Jer 31:10 will *w* over his flock like a shepherd
Mic 7: 7 I *w* in hope for the LORD,
Mt 24:42 "Therefore keep *w*, because you do
26:41 *W* and pray so that you will not fall
Mk 13:35 "Therefore keep *w* because you do
Lk 2: 8 keeping *w* over their flocks at night
1Ti 4:16 *W* your life and doctrine closely.
Heb 13:17 They keep *w* over you

WATCHER* (WATCH)
Job 7:20 O *w* of men?

WATCHES* (WATCH)
Nu 19: 5 While he *w*, the heifer is
Job 24:15 The eye of the adulterer *w* for dusk;
Ps 1: 6 For the LORD *w* over the way
33:14 from his dwelling place he *w*
63: 6 of you through the *w* of the night.
119:148 through the *w* of the night,
121: 3 he who *w* over you will not slumber
121: 4 indeed, he who *w* over Israel
121: 5 The LORD *w* over you—
127: 1 Unless the LORD *w* over the city,
145: 20 LORD *w* over all who love him,
146: 9 The LORD *w* over the alien
Pr 31:27 She *w* over the affairs
Ecc 11: 4 Whoever *w* the wind will not plant;
La 2:19 as the *w* of the night begin;
4:16 he no longer *w* over them.

WATCHING (WATCH)
Lk 12:37 whose master finds them *w*

WATCHMAN (WATCH)
Eze 3:17 I have made you a *w* for the house
33: 6 but I will hold the *w* accountable

WATER (WATERED WATERING WATERS WELL-WATERED)
Ex 7:20 all the *w* was changed into blood.
17: 1 but there was no *w* for the people
Nu 20: 2 there was no *w* for the community,
Ps 1: 3 like a tree planted by streams of *w*,
22:14 I am poured out like *w*,
42: 1 As the deer pants for streams of *w*,
Pr 25:21 if he is thirsty, give him *w* to drink.
Isa 12: 3 With joy you will draw *w*
30:20 of adversity and the *w* of affliction,
32: 2 like streams of *w* in the desert
49:10 and lead them beside springs of *w*.
Jer 2:13 broken cisterns that cannot hold *w*.
17: 8 will be like a tree planted by the *w*
31: 9 I will lead them beside streams of *w*
Eze 36:25 I will sprinkle clean *w* on you,
Zec 14: 8 On that day living *w* will flow out
Mt 14:29 walked on the *w* and came toward Jesus.
Mk 9:41 anyone who gives you a cup of *w*
Lk 5: 4 to Simon, "Put out into deep *w*,
Jn 3: 5 unless he is born of *w* and the Spirit.
4:10 he would have given you living *w*."
7:38 streams of living *w* will flow
Eph 5:26 washing with *w* through the word,
Heb 10:22 our bodies washed with pure *w*.
1Pe 3:21 this *w* symbolizes baptism that now
2Pe 2:17 These men are springs without *w*
1Jn 5: 6 This is the one who came by *w*
5: 6 come by *w* only, but by *w*
5: 8 the Spirit, the *w* and the blood;
Rev 7:17 to springs of living *w*.
21: 6 cost from the spring of the *w* of life.

WATERED (WATER)
1Co 3: 6 I planted the seed, Apollos *w* it,

WATERING (WATER)
Isa 55:10 it without *w* the earth

WATERS (WATER)
Ps 23: 2 he leads me beside quiet *w*,
Ecc 11: 1 Cast your bread upon the *w*,
SS 8: 7 Many *w* cannot quench love;
Isa 11: 9 as the *w* cover the sea.
43: 2 When you pass through the *w*,
55: 1 come to the *w*;
58:11 like a spring whose *w* never fail.
Hab 2:14 as the *w* cover the sea.
1Co 3: 7 plants nor he who *w* is anything,

WAVE (WAVES)
Lev 23:11 He is to *w* the sheaf
Jas 1: 6 he who doubts is like a *w* of the sea,

WAVER*
1Ki 18:21 "How long will you *w*
Ro 4:20 Yet he did not *w* through unbelief

WAVES (WAVE)
Isa 57:20 whose *w* cast up mire and mud.
Mt 8:27 Even the winds and the *w* obey him
Eph 4:14 tossed back and forth by the *w*,

WAY (WAYS)
Ex 13:21 of cloud to guide them on their *w*
18:20 and show them the *w* to live
Dt 1:33 to show you the *w* you should go.
32: 6 Is this the *w* you repay the LORD,
1Sa 12:23 I will teach you the *w* that is good
2Sa 22:31 "As for God, his *w* is perfect;
1Ki 8:23 wholeheartedly in your *w*.
8:36 Teach them the right *w* to live,
Job 23:10 But he knows the *w* that I take;

Ps 1: 1 or stand in the *w* of sinners
32: 8 teach you in the *w* you should go;
37: 5 Commit your *w* to the LORD;
86:11 Teach me your *w*, O LORD,
119: 9 can a young man keep his *w* pure?
139: 24 See if there is any offensive *w* in me
Pr 4:11 I guide you in the *w* of wisdom
12:15 The *w* of a fool seems right to him,
14:12 There is a *w* that seems right
16:17 he who guards his *w* guards his life.
19: 2 nor to be hasty and miss the *w*.
22: 6 Train a child in the *w* he should go,
30:19 and the *w* of a man with a maiden.
Isa 30:21 saying, "This is the *w*; walk in it."
35: 8 it will be called the *W* of Holiness.
40: 3 the *w* for the LORD;
48:17 you in the *w* you should go.
53: 6 each of us has turned to his own *w*;
55: 7 Let the wicked forsake his *w*
Jer 5:31 and my people love it this *w*.
Mal 3: 1 who will prepare the *w* before me.
Mt 3: 3 'Prepare the *w* for the Lord,
Lk 7:27 who will prepare your *w* before you
Jn 14: 6 "I am the *w* and the truth
Ac 1:11 in the same *w* you have seen him go
9: 2 any there who belonged to the *W*,
24:14 of the *W*, which they call a sect.
1Co 10:13 also provide a *w* out so that you can
12:31 will show you the most excellent *w*.
14: 1 Follow the *w* of love and eagerly
Col 1:10 and may please him in every *w*:
Tit 2:10 that in every *w* they will make
Heb 4:15 who has been tempted in every *w*,
9: 8 was showing by this that the *w*
10:20 and living *w* opened for us
13:18 desire to live honorably in every *w*.

WAYS (WAY)
Ex 33:13 teach me your *w* so I may know
Dt 10:12 to walk in all his *w*, to love him,
26:17 and that you will walk in his *w*,
30:16 in his *w*, and to keep his commands
32: 4 and all his *w* are just.
Jos 22: 5 in all his *w*, to obey his commands,
2Ch 11:17 walking in the *w* of David
Job 34:21 "His eyes are on the *w* of men;
Ps 25: 4 Show me your *w*, O LORD,
25:10 All the *w* of the LORD are loving
37: 7 fret when men succeed in their *w*,
51:13 I will teach transgressors your *w*,
77:13 Your *w*, O God, are holy.
119: 59 I have considered my *w*
139: 3 you are familiar with all my *w*.
145: 17 The LORD is righteous in all his *w*
Pr 3: 6 in all your *w* acknowledge him,
4:26 and take only *w* that are firm.
5:21 For a man's *w* are in full view
16: 2 All a man's *w* seem innocent
16: 7 When a man's *w* are pleasing
Isa 2: 3 He will teach us his *w*,
55: 8 neither are your *w* my *w*,"
Eze 28:15 You were blameless in your *w*
33: 8 out to dissuade him from his *w*,
Hos 14: 9 The *w* of the LORD are right;
Ro 1:30 they invent *w* of doing evil;
Jas 3: 2 We all stumble in many *w*.

WEAK (WEAKER WEAKNESS WEAKNESSES)
Ps 41: 1 is he who has regard for the *w*;
72:13 He will take pity on the *w*
82: 3 Defend the cause of the *w*
Eze 34: 4 You have not strengthened the *w*
Mt 26:41 spirit is willing, but the body is *w*."
Ac 20:35 of hard work we must help the *w*,
Ro 14: 1 Accept him whose faith is *w*,
15: 1 to bear with the failings of the *w*
1Co 1:27 God chose the *w* things
8: 9 become a stumbling block to the *w*.
9:22 To the *w* I became *w*, to win the *w*.
11:30 That is why many among you are *w*
2Co 12:10 For when I am *w*, then I am strong.
1Th 5:14 help the *w*, be patient
Heb 12:12 your feeble arms and *w* knees.

WEAK-WILLED (WILL)
2Ti 3: 6 and gain control over *w* women,

WEAKER* (WEAK)
2Sa 3: 1 the house of Saul grew *w* and *w*.
1Co 12:22 seem to be *w* are indispensable,
1Pe 3: 7 them with respect as the *w* partner

WEAKNESS* (WEAK)
La 1: 6 in *w* they have fled
Ro 8:26 the Spirit helps us in our *w*.
1Co 1:25 and the *w* of God is stronger
2: 3 I came to you in *w* and fear,
15:43 it is sown in *w*, it is raised in power;
2Co 11:30 boast of the things that show my *w*.
12: 9 for my power is made perfect in *w*
13: 4 he was crucified in *w*, yet he lives
Heb 5: 2 since he himself is subject to *w*.
11:34 whose *w* was turned to strength;

WEAKNESSES* (WEAK)
2Co 12: 5 about myself, except about my *w*.
12: 9 all the more gladly about my *w*,
12:10 I delight in *w*, in insults,
Heb 4:15 unable to sympathize with our *w*,

WEALTH
Dt 8:18 gives you the ability to produce *w*,
2Ch 1:11 and you have not asked for *w*,
Ps 39: 6 he heaps up *w*, not knowing who
Pr 3: 9 Honor the LORD with your *w*,
10: 4 but diligent hands bring *w*.
11: 4 *W* is worthless in the day of wrath,
13: 7 to be poor, yet has great *w*.
15:16 than great *w* with turmoil.
22: 4 bring *w* and honor and life.
Ecc 5:10 whoever loves *w* is never satisfied
5:13 *w* hoarded to the harm of its owner,
SS 8: 7 all the *w* of his house for love,
Mt 13:22 and the deceitfulness of *w* choke it,
Mk 10:22 away sad, because he had great *w*.
12:44 They all gave out of their *w*; but she
Lk 15:13 and there squandered his *w*
1Ti 6:17 nor to put their hope in *w*,
Jas 5: 2 Your *w* has rotted, and moths have
5: 3 You have hoarded *w*

WEAPON (WEAPONS)
Ne 4:17 work with one hand and held a *w*

WEAPONS (WEAPON)
Ecc 9:18 Wisdom is better than *w* of war,
2Co 6: 7 with *w* of righteousness
10: 4 The *w* we fight with are not

WEAR (WEARING)
Dt 8: 4 Your clothes did not *w* out
22: 5 nor a man *w* women's clothing,
Ps 102: 26 they will all *w* out like a garment.
Pr 23: 4 Do not *w* yourself out to get rich;
Isa 51: 6 the earth will *w* out like a garment
Heb 1:11 they will all *w* out like a garment.
Rev 3:18 and white clothes to *w*,

WEARIES (WEARY)
Ecc 12:12 and much study *w* the body.

WEARING (WEAR)
Jn 19: 5 When Jesus came out *w* the crown
Jas 2: 3 attention to the man *w* fine clothes
1Pe 3: 3 as braided hair and the *w*
Rev 7: 9 They were *w* white robes

WEARY (WEARIES)
Isa 40:28 He will not grow tired or *w*,
40:31 they will run and not grow *w*,
50: 4 know the word that sustains the *w*.
Mt 11:28 all you who are *w* and burdened,
Gal 6: 9 Let us not become *w* in doing good,
Heb 12: 3 so that you will not grow *w*
Rev 2: 3 my name, and have not grown *w*.

WEDDING
Mt 22:11 who was not wearing *w* clothes.
Rev 19: 7 For the *w* of the Lamb has come,

WEEDS
Mt 13:25 and sowed *w* among the wheat,

WEEK
Mt 28: 1 at dawn on the first day of the *w*,
1Co 16: 2 On the first day of every *w*,

WEEP (WEEPING WEPT)
Ecc 3: 4 a time to *w* and a time to laugh,
Lk 6:21 Blessed are you who *w* now,
23:28 *w* for yourselves and for your

WEEPING (WEEP)
Ps 30: 5 *w* may remain for a night,
126: 6 He who goes out *w*,
Jer 31:15 Rachel *w* for her children
Mt 2:18 Rachel *w* for her children
8:12 where there will be *w* and gnashing

WEIGH (OUTWEIGHS WEIGHED WEIGHS WEIGHTIER WEIGHTS)
1Co 14:29 others should *w* carefully what is

WEIGHED (WEIGH)
Job 28:15 nor can its price be *w* in silver.
Da 5:27 You have been *w* on the scales
Lk 21:34 or your hearts will be *w*

WEIGHS (WEIGH)
Pr 12:25 An anxious heart *w* a man down,
15:28 of the righteous *w* its answers,
21: 2 but the LORD *w* the heart.
24:12 not he who *w* the heart perceive

WEIGHTIER* (WEIGH)
Jn 5:36 "I have testimony *w* than that

WEIGHTS (WEIGH)
Lev 19:36 Use honest scales and honest *w*,
Dt 25:13 Do not have two differing *w*
Pr 11: 1 but accurate *w* are his delight.

WELCOME (WELCOMES)
Mk 9:37 welcomes me does not *w* me
2Pe 1:11 and you will receive a rich *w*

WELCOMES (WELCOME)
Mt 18: 5 whoever *w* a little child like this
2Jn :11 Anyone who *w* him shares

WELL (WELLED WELLING WELLS)
Mt 15:31 crippled made *w*, the lame walking
Lk 14: 5 falls into a *w* on the Sabbath day,
17:19 your faith has made you *w*."
Jas 5:15 in faith will make the sick person *w*

WELL-WATERED (WATER)
Isa 58:11 You will be like a *w* garden,

WELLED* (WELL)
2Co 8: 2 and their extreme poverty *w* up

WELLING* (WELL)
Jn 4:14 of water *w* up to eternal life."

WELLS (WELL)
Isa 12: 3 from the *w* of salvation.

WELLSPRING* (SPRING)
Pr 4:23 for it is the *w* of life.

WEPT (WEEP)
Ps 137: 1 of Babylon we sat and *w*
Lk 22:62 And he went outside and *w* bitterly
Jn 11:35 Jesus *w*.

WEST
Ps 103: 12 as far as the east is from the *w*,
107: 3 from east and *w*, from north

WHEAT
Mt 3:12 gathering his *w* into the barn
13:25 and sowed weeds among the *w*,
Lk 22:31 Satan has asked to sift you as *w*.
Jn 12:24 a kernel of *w* falls to the ground

WHEELS
Eze 1:16 appearance and structure of the *w*:

WHIRLWIND (WIND)
2Ki 2: 1 to take Elijah up to heaven in a *w*,
Hos 8: 7 and reap the *w*.
Na 1: 3 His way is in the *w* and the storm,

WHISPER (WHISPERED)
1Ki 19:12 And after the fire came a gentle *w*.
Job 26:14 how faint the *w* we hear of him!
Ps 107: 29 He stilled the storm to a *w*;

WHISPERED (WHISPER)
Mt 10:27 speak in the daylight; what is *w*

WHITE (WHITER)
Isa 1:18 they shall be as *w* as snow;
Da 7: 9 His clothing was as *w* as snow;
7: 9 the hair of his head was *w* like wool
Mt 28: 3 and his clothes were *w* as snow.
Rev 1:14 hair were *w* like wool, as *w* as snow,
3: 4 dressed in *w*, for they are worthy.
6: 2 and there before me was a *w* horse!
7:13 "These in *w* robes—who are they,
19:11 and there before me was a *w* horse,
20:11 Then I saw a great *w* throne

WHITER (WHITE)
Ps 51: 7 and I will be *w* than snow.

WHOLE
Ge 1:29 plant on the face of the *w* earth
2: 6 and watered the *w* surface
11: 1 Now the *w* world had one language
Ex 12:47 The *w* community
19: 5 Although the *w* earth is mine,
Lev 16:17 and the *w* community of Israel.
Nu 14:21 of the LORD fills the *w* earth,
32:13 until the *w* generation
Dt 13:16 *w* burnt offering to the LORD your
19: 8 gives you the *w* land he promised
Jos 2: 3 come to spy out the *w* land."
1Sa 1:28 For his *w* life he will be given

1Sa 17:46 the *w* world will know that there is
1Ki 10:24 The *w* world sought audience
2Ki 21: 8 and will keep the *w* Law that my
Ps 72:19 may the *w* earth be filled
Pr 4:22 and health to a man's *w* body.
8:31 rejoicing in his *w* world
Ecc 12:13 for this is the *w* duty of man.
Isa 1: 5 Your *w* head is injured,
6: 3 the *w* earth is full of his glory."
14:26 plan determined for the *w* world;
Eze 34: 6 were scattered over the *w* earth,
37:11 these bones are the *w* house
Da 2:35 mountain and filled the *w* earth.
Zep 1:18 the *w* world will be consumed,
Zec 14: 9 will be king over the *w* earth.
Mal 3:10 the *w* tithe into the storehouse,
Mt 5:29 than for your *w* body to be thrown
6:22 your *w* body will be full of light.
16:26 for a man if he gains the *w* world,
24:14 will be preached in the *w* world
Lk 21:35 live on the face of the *w* earth.
Jn 12:19 Look how the *w* world has gone
13:10 to wash his feet; his *w* body is clean
21:25 the *w* world would not have room
Ac 17:26 they should inhabit the *w* earth;
20:27 proclaim to you the *w* will of God.
Ro 1: 9 whom I serve with my *w* heart
3:19 and the *w* world held accountable
8:22 know that the *w* creation has been
1Co 4: 9 made a spectacle to the *w* universe,
12:17 If the *w* body were an ear,
Gal 3:22 declares that the *w* world is
5: 3 obligated to obey the *w* law.
Eph 4:10 in order to fill the *w* universe.)
4:13 attaining to the *w* measure
1Th 5:23 May your *w* spirit, soul
Jas 2:10 For whoever keeps the *w* law
1Jn 2: 2 but also for the sins of the *w* world.
Rev 3:10 going to come upon the *w* world

WHOLEHEARTED* (HEART)
2Ki 20: 3 you faithfully and with *w* devotion
1Ch 28: 9 and serve him with *w* devotion
29:19 my son Solomon the *w* devotion
Isa 38: 3 you faithfully and with *w* devotion

WHOLEHEARTEDLY* (HEART)
Nu 14:24 a different spirit and follows me *w*,
32:11 they have not followed me *w*,
32:12 for they followed the LORD *w*.'
Dt 1:36 because he followed the LORD *w*
Jos 14: 8 followed the LORD my God *w*.
14: 9 followed the LORD my God *w*.'
14:14 the LORD, the God of Israel, *w*.
1Ki 8:23 with your servants who continue *w*
1Ch 29: 9 for they had given freely and *w*
2Ch 6:14 with your servants who continue *w*
15:15 oath because they had sworn it *w*.
19: 9 and *w* in the fear of the LORD.
25: 2 in the eyes of the LORD, but not *w*
31:21 he sought his God and worked *w*.
Ro 6:17 you *w* obeyed the form of teaching
Eph 6: 7 Serve *w*, as if you were serving

WHOLESOME*
2Ki 2:22 And the water has remained *w*
2Pe 3: 1 to stimulate you to *w* thinking.

WICK
Isa 42: 3 a smoldering *w* he will not snuff out
Mt 12:20 a smoldering *w* he will not snuff out

WICKED (WICKEDNESS)
Ge 13:13 Now the men of Sodom were *w*
39: 9 How then could I do such a *w* thing
Ex 23: 1 Do not help a *w* man
Nu 14:35 things to this whole *w* community,
Dt 15: 9 not to harbor this *w* thought:
Jdg 19:22 some of the *w* men
1Sa 2:12 Eli's sons were *w* men; they had no
15:18 completely destroy those *w* people,
25:17 He is such a *w* man that no one can
2Sa 13:12 in Israel! Don't do this *w* thing.
2Ki 17:11 They did *w* things that provoked
2Ch 7:14 and turn from their *w* ways,
19: 2 "Should you help the *w*
Ne 13:17 "What is this *w* thing you are doing
Ps 1: 1 walk in the counsel of the *w*
1: 5 Therefore the *w* will not stand
7: 9 to an end the violence of the *w*
10:13 Why does the *w* man revile God?
11: 5 the *w* and those who love violence
12: 8 The *w* freely strut about
26: 5 and refuse to sit with the *w*.
32:10 Many are the woes of the *w*,
36: 1 concerning the sinfulness of the *w*:
37:13 but the Lord laughs at the *w*,
49: 5 when *w* deceivers surround me—
50:16 But to the *w*, God says:
58: 3 Even from birth the *w* go astray;
73: 3 when I saw the prosperity of the *w*.
82: 2 and show partiality to the *w*? *Selah*
112: 10 the longings of the *w* will come
119: 61 Though the *w* bind me with ropes,
119:155 Salvation is far from the *w*,
140: 8 do not grant the *w* their desires,
141: 10 Let the *w* fall into their own nets,
146: 9 but he frustrates the ways of the *w*.
Pr 2:12 you from the ways of *w* men,
4:14 Do not set foot on the path of the *w*
6:18 a heart that devises *w* schemes,
9: 7 whoever rebukes a *w* man incurs
10:20 the heart of the *w* is of little value.
10:28 the hopes of the *w* come to nothing
11: 5 *w* are brought down by their own
11:10 when the *w* perish, there are shouts
11:21 The *w* will not go unpunished,
12: 5 but the advice of the *w* is deceitful.
12:10 the kindest acts of the *w* are cruel.
14:19 the *w* at the gates of the righteous.
15: 3 keeping watch on the *w*
15:26 detests the thoughts of the *w*,
21:10 The *w* man craves evil;
21:29 A *w* man puts up a bold front,
28: 1 *w* man flees though no one pursues,
28: 4 who forsake the law praise the *w*,
29: 7 but the *w* have no such concern.
29:16 When the *w* thrive, so does sin,
29:27 the *w* detest the upright.
Isa 11: 4 breath of his lips he will slay the *w*.
13:11 the *w* for their sins.
26:10 Though grace is shown to the *w*,
48:22 says the LORD, "for the *w*."
53: 9 He was assigned a grave with the *w*
55: 7 Let the *w* forsake his way
57:20 But the *w* are like the tossing sea,
Jer 35:15 of you must turn from your *w* ways
Eze 3:18 that *w* man will die for his sin,
13:22 you encouraged the *w* not to turn
14: 7 and puts a *w* stumbling block
18:21 "But if a *w* man turns away
18:23 pleasure in the death of the *w*?
21:25 " 'O profane and *w* prince of Israel,
33: 8 When I say to the *w*, 'O *w* man,
33:11 pleasure in the death of the *w*,
33:14 to the *w* man, 'You will surely die,'
33:19 And if a *w* man turns away
Da 12:10 but the *w* will continue to be *w*.
Mt 12:39 *w* and adulterous generation asks
12:45 be with this *w* generation."
12:45 with it seven other spirits more *w*
Lk 6:35 he is kind to the ungrateful and *w*.
Ac 2:23 and you, with the help of *w* men,
Ro 4: 5 but trusts God who justifies the *w*,
1Co 5:13 "Expel the *w* man from among you
6: 9 not know that the *w* will not inherit
Rev 2: 2 that you cannot tolerate *w* men,

WICKEDNESS (WICKED)
Ge 6: 5 The LORD saw how great man's *w*
Ex 34: 7 and forgiving *w*, rebellion and sin.
Lev 16:21 and confess over it all the *w*
19:29 to prostitution and be filled with *w*.
Dt 9: 4 it is on account of the *w*
Ne 9: 2 and confessed their sins and the *w*
Ps 45: 7 You love righteousness and hate *w*;
92:15 he is my Rock, and there is no *w*
Pr 13: 6 but *w* overthrows the sinner.
Jer 3: 2 land with your prostitution and *w*.
8: 6 No one repents of his *w*,
14:20 O LORD, we acknowledge our *w*
Eze 18:20 the *w* of the wicked will be charged
28:15 created till *w* was found in you.
33:19 wicked man turns away from his *w*
Da 4:27 and your *w* by being kind
9:24 to atone for *w*, to bring
Jnh 1: 2 its *w* has come up before me."
Mt 24:12 Because of the increase of *w*,
Lk 11:39 inside you are full of greed and *w*.
Ac 1:18 (With the reward he got for his *w*,
Ro 1:18 who suppress the truth by their *w*,
1Co 5: 8 the yeast of malice and *w*,
2Co 6:14 what do righteousness and *w* have
2Ti 2:19 of the Lord must turn away from *w*
Tit 2:14 for us to redeem us from all *w*
Heb 1: 9 loved righteousness and hated *w*;
8:12 For I will forgive their *w*
2Pe 2:15 who loved the wages of *w*.

WIDE
Ps 81:10 Open *w* your mouth and I will fill it
Isa 54: 2 stretch your tent curtains *w*,
Mt 7:13 For *w* is the gate and broad is
2Co 6:13 my children—open *w* your hearts
Eph 3:18 to grasp how *w* and long and high

WIDOW (WIDOWS)
Ex 22:22 "Do not take advantage of a *w*
Dt 10:18 cause of the fatherless and the *w*,
Ps 146: 9 sustains the fatherless and the *w*,
Isa 1:17 plead the case of the *w*.
Lk 21: 2 saw a poor *w* put in two very small
1Ti 5: 4 But if a *w* has children

WIDOWS (WIDOW)
Ps 68: 5 to the fatherless, a defender of *w*,
Ac 6: 1 their *w* were being overlooked
1Co 7: 8 to the unmarried and the *w* I say:
1Ti 5: 3 to those *w* who are really
Jas 1:27 look after orphans and *w*

WIFE (WIVES WIVES')
Ge 2:24 and mother and be united to his *w*,
19:26 But Lot's *w* looked back,
24:67 she became his *w*, and he loved her;
Ex 20:17 shall not covet your neighbor's *w*,
Lev 20:10 adultery with another man's *w*—
Dt 5:21 shall not covet your neighbor's *w*.
24: 5 happiness to the *w* he has married.
Ru 4:13 took Ruth and she became his *w*.
Pr 5:18 in the *w* of your youth.
12: 4 *w* of noble character is her
18:22 He who finds a *w* finds what is
19:13 quarrelsome *w* is like a constant
31:10 *w* of noble character who can find?
Hos 1: 2 take to yourself an adulterous *w*
Mal 2:14 the witness between you and the *w*
Mt 1:20 to take Mary home as your *w*,
19: 3 for a man to divorce his *w* for any
Lk 17:32 Remember Lot's *w*! Whoever tries
18:29 or *w* or brothers or parents
1Co 7: 2 each man should have his own *w*,
7:33 how he can please his *w*—
Eph 5:23 the husband is the head of the *w*
5:33 must love his *w* as he loves himself,
1Ti 3: 2 husband of but one *w*, temperate,
Rev 21: 9 I will show you the bride, the *w*

WILD
Ge 1:25 God made the *w* animals according
8: 1 Noah and all the *w* animals
Lk 15:13 squandered his wealth in *w* living.
Ro 11:17 and you, though a *w* olive shoot,

WILL (WEAK-WILLED WILLFUL WILLING WILLINGNESS)
Ps 40: 8 I desire to do your *w*, O my God;
143: 10 Teach me to do your *w*,
Isa 53:10 Yet it was the LORD's *w*
Mt 6:10 your *w* be done
7:21 who does the *w* of my Father
10:29 apart from the *w* of your Father.
12:50 does the *w* of my Father
26:39 Yet not as I *w*, but as you *w*."
26:42 I drink it, may your *w* be done."
Jn 6:38 but to do the *w* of him who sent me.
7:17 If anyone chooses to do God's *w*,
Ac 20:27 to you the whole *w* of God.
Ro 12: 2 and approve what God's *w* is—
1Co 7:37 but has control over his own *w*,
Eph 5:17 understand what the Lord's *w* is.
Php 2:13 for it is God who works in you to *w*
1Th 4: 3 God's *w* that you should be sanctified:
5:18 for this is God's *w* for you
2Ti 2:26 has taken them captive to do his *w*.
Heb 2: 4 distributed according to his *w*.
9:16 In the case of a *w*, it is necessary
10: 7 I have come to do your *w*, O God
13:21 everything good for doing his *w*,
Jas 4:15 "If it is the Lord's *w*,
1Pe 3:17 It is better, if it is God's *w*,
4: 2 but rather for the *w* of God.
2Pe 1:21 never had its origin in the *w*
1Jn 5:14 we ask anything according to his *w*,
Rev 4:11 and by your *w* they were created

WILLFUL (WILL)
Ps 19:13 Keep your servant also from *w* sins;

WILLING (WILL)
1Ch 28: 9 devotion and with a *w* mind,
29: 5 who is *w* to consecrate himself
Ps 51:12 grant me a *w* spirit, to sustain me.
Da 3:28 were *w* to give up their lives rather
Mt 18:14 Father in heaven is not *w* that any
23:37 her wings, but you were not *w*.
26:41 The spirit is *w*, but the body is weak
1Ti 6:18 and to be generous and *w* to share.
1Pe 5: 2 but because you are *w*,

WILLINGNESS* (WILL)
2Co 8:11 so that your eager *w*
8:12 For if the *w* is there, the gift is

WIN (WINS WON)
1Co 9:19 myself a slave to everyone, to *w*
Php 3:14 on toward the goal to *w* the prize
1Th 4:12 your daily life may *w* the respect

WIND (WHIRLWIND WINDS)
Ps 1: 4 that the *w* blows away.
Ecc 2:11 meaningless, a chasing after the *w*;
Hos 8: 7 "They sow the *w*
Mk 4:41 Even the *w* and the waves obey
Jn 3: 8 The *w* blows wherever it pleases.
Eph 4:14 and there by every *w* of teaching
Jas 1: 6 blown and tossed by the *w*.

WINDOW
Jos 2:21 she tied the scarlet cord in the *w*.
Ac 20: 9 in a *w* was a young man named
2Co 11:33 in a basket from a *w* in the wall

WINDS (WIND)
Ps 104: 4 He makes *w* his messengers,
Mt 24:31 gather his elect from the four *w*,
Heb 1: 7 "He makes his angels *w*,

WINE
Ps 104: 15 *w* that gladdens the heart of man,
Pr 20: 1 *W* is a mocker and beer a brawler;
23:20 join those who drink too much *w*
23:31 Do not gaze at *w* when it is red,
31: 6 *w* to those who are in anguish;
SS 1: 2 your love is more delightful than *w*.
Isa 28: 7 And these also stagger from *w*
55: 1 Come, buy *w* and milk
Mt 9:17 Neither do men pour new *w*
Lk 23:36 They offered him *w* vinegar
Jn 2: 3 When the *w* was gone, Jesus'
Ro 14:21 not to eat meat or drink *w*
Eph 5:18 on *w*, which leads to debauchery.
1Ti 5:23 a little *w* because of your stomach
Rev 16:19 with the *w* of the fury of his wrath.

WINEPRESS
Isa 63: 2 like those of one treading the *w*?
Rev 19:15 He treads the *w* of the fury

WINESKINS
Mt 9:17 do men pour new wine into old *w*.

WINGS
Ex 19: 4 and how I carried you on eagles' *w*
Ru 2:12 under whose *w* you have come
Ps 17: 8 hide me in the shadow of your *w*
91: 4 under his *w* you will find refuge;
Isa 6: 2 him were seraphs, each with six *w*:
40:31 They will soar on *w* like eagles;
Eze 1: 6 of them had four faces and four *w*.
Zec 5: 9 in their *w*! They had *w* like those
Mal 4: 2 rise with healing in its *w*.
Lk 13:34 hen gathers her chicks under her *w*,
Rev 4: 8 the four living creatures had six *w*

WINS (WIN)
Pr 11:30 and he who *w* souls is wise.

WINTER
Mk 13:18 that this will not take place in *w*,

WIPE (WIPED)
Isa 25: 8 The Sovereign LORD will *w* away
Rev 7:17 God will *w* away every tear
21: 4 He will *w* every tear

WIPED (WIPE)
Lk 7:38 Then she *w* them with her hair,
Ac 3:19 so that your sins may be *w* out,

WISDOM (WISE)
Ge 3: 6 and also desirable for gaining *w*,
1Ki 4:29 God gave Solomon *w* and very
2Ch 1:10 Give me *w* and knowledge,
Ps 51: 6 you teach me *w* in the inmost place
111: 10 of the LORD is the beginning of *w*;
Pr 2: 6 For the LORD gives *w*,
3:13 Blessed is the man who finds *w*,
4: 7 *W* is supreme; therefore get
8:11 for *w* is more precious than rubies,
11: 2 but with humility comes *w*.
13:10 *w* is found in those who take advice
23:23 get *w*, discipline and understanding
29: 3 A man who loves *w* brings joy
29:15 The rod of correction imparts *w*,
31:26 She speaks with *w*,
Isa 11: 2 Spirit of *w* and of understanding,
28:29 in counsel and magnificent in *w*.
Jer 10:12 he founded the world by his *w*
Mic 6: 9 and to fear your name is *w*—
Mt 11:19 But *w* is proved right by her actions
Lk 2:52 And Jesus grew in *w* and stature,
Ac 6: 3 known to be full of the Spirit and *w*.
Ro 11:33 the depth of the riches of the *w*
1Co 1:17 not with words of human *w*,
1:30 who has become for us *w* from God
12: 8 through the Spirit the message of *w*
Eph 1:17 may give you the Spirit of *w*
Col 2: 3 are hidden all the treasures of *w*
Col 2:23 indeed have an appearance of *w*,
Jas 1: 5 of you lacks *w*, he should ask God,
3:13 in the humility that comes from *w*.
Rev 5:12 and wealth and *w* and strength

WISE (WISDOM WISER)
1Ki 3:12 give you a *w* and discerning heart,
Job 5:13 He catches the *w* in their craftiness
Ps 19: 7 making *w* the simple.
Pr 3: 7 Do not be *w* in your own eyes;
9: 8 rebuke a *w* man and he will love
10: 1 A *w* son brings joy to his father,
11:30 and he who wins souls is *w*.
13: 1 A *w* son heeds his father's
13:20 He who walks with the *w* grows *w*,
16:23 A *w* man's heart guides his mouth,
17:28 Even a fool is thought *w*
Ecc 9:17 The quiet words of the *w* are more
Jer 9:23 "Let not the *w* man boast
Eze 28: 6 " 'Because you think you are *w*,
Da 2:21 He gives wisdom to the *w*
12: 3 Those who are *w* will shine like
Mt 11:25 hidden these things from the *w*
25: 2 them were foolish and five were *w*.
1Co 1:19 I will destroy the wisdom of the *w*;
1:27 things of the world to shame the *w*;
3:19 He catches the *w* in their craftiness
Eph 5:15 but as *w*, making the most
2Ti 3:15 able to make you *w* for salvation
Jas 3:13 Who is *w* and understanding

WISER (WISE)
Pr 9: 9 a wise man and he will be *w* still;
1Co 1:25 of God is *w* than man's wisdom,

WISH (WISHES)
Jn 15: 7 ask whatever you *w*, and it will be
Ro 9: 3 For I could *w* that I myself were
Rev 3:15 I *w* you were either one

WISHES (WISH)
Rev 22:17 let him come; and whoever *w*,

WITCHCRAFT
Dt 18:10 engages in *w*, or casts spells,
Gal 5:20 idolatry and *w*; hatred, discord,

WITHDREW
Lk 5:16 But Jesus often *w* to lonely places

WITHER (WITHERS)
Ps 1: 3 and whose leaf does not *w*.
37:19 In times of disaster they will not *w*;

WITHERS (WITHER)
Isa 40: 7 The grass *w* and the flowers fall,
1Pe 1:24 the grass *w* and the flowers fall,

WITHHELD (WITHHOLD)
Ge 22:12 you have not *w* from me your son,

WITHHOLD (WITHHELD WITHHOLDS)
Ps 84:11 no good thing does he *w*
Pr 23:13 Do not *w* discipline from a child;

WITHHOLDS (WITHHOLD)
Dt 27:19 "Cursed is the man who *w* justice

WITNESS (EYEWITNESSES WITNESSES)
Pr 12:17 truthful *w* gives honest testimony,
19: 9 A false *w* will not go unpunished,
Jn 1: 8 he came only as a *w* to the light.

WITNESSES (WITNESS)
Dt 19:15 by the testimony of two or three *w*.
Mt 18:16 by the testimony of two or three *w*.'
Ac 1: 8 and you will be my *w* in Jerusalem,

WIVES (WIFE)
Eph 5:22 *W*, submit to your husbands
5:25 love your *w*, just as Christ loved
1Pe 3: 1 words by the behavior of their *w*,

WIVES' (WIFE)
1Ti 4: 7 with godless myths and old *w* tales

WOE
Isa 6: 5 "*W* to me!" I cried.
Eze 34: 2 *W* to the shepherds
Mt 18: 7 "*W* to the world
23:13 "*W* to you, teachers of the law
Jude :11 *W* to them! They have taken

WOLF (WOLVES)
Isa 65:25 *w* and the lamb will feed together,

WOLVES (WOLF)
Mt 10:16 you out like sheep among *w*.

WOMAN (MAN)
Ge 2:22 God made a *w* from
2:23 she shall be called '*w*,'
3: 6 *w* saw that the fruit
3:12 The *w* you put here with
3:15 between you and the *w*,
3:16 To the *w* he said,
12:11 a beautiful *w* you are.
20: 3 because of the *w* you have
24: 5 if the *w* is unwilling
Ex 2: 1 married a Levite *w*
3:22 Every *w* is to ask her
21:10 If he marries another *w*
21:22 hit a pregnant *w*
Lev 12: 2 *w* who becomes pregnant
15:19 *w* has her regular flow
15:25 a *w* has a discharge
18:17 sexual relations with both a *w*
20:13 as one lies with a *w*,
Nu 5:29 when a *w* goes astray
30: 3 young *w* still living in
30: 9 by a widow or divorced *w*
30:10 *w* living with her husband
Dt 20: 7 become pledged to a *w*
21:11 the captives a beautiful *w*
22: 5 *w* must not wear men's
22:13 married this *w* but when
Jdg 4: 9 hand Sisera over to a *w*.
13: 6 the *w* went to her husband
14: 2 have seen a Philistine *w*
16: 4 he fell in love with a *w*
20: 4 husband of the murdered *w*
Ru 3:11 a *w* of noble character
1Sa 1:15 a *w* who is deeply troubled
25: 3 intelligent and beautiful *w*,
28: 7 a *w* who is a medium,
2Sa 11: 2 he saw a *w* bathing
13:17 "Get this *w* out of here
14: 2 had a wise *w* brought
20:16 a wise *w* called from
1Ki 3:18 this *w* also had a baby.
17:24 the *w* said to Elijah,
2Ki 4: 8 a well-to-do *w* was there,
8: 1 Elisha had said to the *w*
9:34 "Take care of that cursed *w*,"
Job 14: 1 Man born of *w* is of few
Pr 11:16 A kindhearted *w* gains respect,
11:22 a beautiful *w* who shows no
14: 1 a wise *w* builds her house,
30:23 unloved *w* who is married,
31:30 a *w* who fears the LORD
Isa 54: 1 O barren *w*, you who never
Mt 5:28 looks at a *w* lustfully
9:20 a *w* who had been subject
15:28 *W* you have great faith!
26: 7 a *w* came to him with
Mk 5:25 a *w* was there who had
7:25 a *w* whose little daughter
Lk 7:39 what kind of a *w* she is
10:38 a *w* named Martha opened
13:12 "*W*, you are set free
15: 8 suppose a *w* has ten silver
Jn 2: 4 *w*, why do you involve
4: 7 a Samaritan *w* came
8: 3 a *w* caught in adultery.
19:26 *w*, here is your son,"
20:15 *W*, 'he said, "Why are you crying?
Ac 9:40 Turning toward the dead *w*,
16:14 was a *w* named Lydia,
Ro 7: 2 a married *w* is bound to
1Co 7: 2 each *w* her own husband
7:15 a believing man or *w* is
7:34 an unmarried *w* or virgin
7:39 *w* is bound to her husband
11: 3 the head of the *w* is man,
11: 7 the *w* is the glory of man
11:13 a *w* to pray to God with
Gal 4: 4 his Son, born of a *w*,
4:31 not children of the slave *w*,
1Ti 2:11 A *w* should learn in
5:16 any *w* who is a believer
Rev 2:20 You tolerate that *w* Jezebel,
12: 1 a *w* clothed with the sun
12:13 he pursued the *w* who had
17: 3 a *w* sitting on a scarlet

WOMEN (MAN)
Mt 11:11 among those born of *w*,
28: 5 The angel said to the *w*,
Mk 15:41 Many other *w* who had come
Lk 1:42 Blessed are you among *w*,
8: 2 also some *w* who had been
23:27 *w* who mourned and wailed
24:11 they did not believe the *w*,
Ac 1:14 along with the *w* and Mary
16:13 speak to the *w* who had
17: 4 not a few prominent *w*.
Ro 1:26 *w* exchanged natural relations
1Co 14:34 *w* should remain silent in
Php 4: 3 help these *w* who have
1Ti 2: 9 want *w* to dress modestly
5: 2 older *w* as mothers,

Tit 2: 3 teach the older *w* to be
2: 4 train the younger *w* to love
Heb 11:35 *W* received back their dead
1Pe 3: 5 the holy *w* of the past

WOMB
Job 1:21 Naked I came from my mother's *w*,
Ps 139: 13 in my mother's *w*.
Pr 31: 2 "O my son, O son of my *w*,
Jer 1: 5 you in the *w* I knew you,
Lk 1:44 the baby in my *w* leaped for joy.
Jn 3: 4 into his mother's *w* to be born!"

WON (WIN)
1Pe 3: 1 they may be *w* over without words

WONDER (WONDERFUL WONDERS)
Ps 17: 7 Show the *w* of your great love,
SS 1: 3 No *w* the maidens love you!

WONDERFUL* (WONDER)
2Sa 1:26 Your love for me was *w*,
1:26 more *w* than that of women.
1Ch 16: 9 tell of all his *w* acts.
Job 42: 3 things too *w* for me to know.
Ps 26: 7 and telling of all your *w* deeds.
31:21 for he showed his *w* love to me
75: 1 men tell of your *w* deeds.
105: 2 tell of all his *w* acts.
107: 8 and his *w* deeds for men,
107: 15 and his *w* deeds for men,
107: 21 and his *w* deeds for men.
107: 24 his *w* deeds in the deep.
107: 31 and his *w* deeds for men.
119: 18 *w* things in your law.
119:129 Your statutes are *w*;
131: 1 or things too *w* for me.
139: 6 Such knowledge is too *w* for me,
139: 14 your works are *w*,
145: 5 I will meditate on your *w* works.
Isa 9: 6 *W* Counselor, Mighty God,
28:29 *w* in counsel and magnificent
Mt 21:15 of the law saw the *w* things he did
Lk 13:17 with all the *w* things he was doing.
1Pe 2: 9 out of darkness into his *w* light.

WONDERS (WONDER)
Ex 3:20 with all the *w* that I will perform
Dt 10:21 and awesome *w* you saw
2Sa 7:23 awesome *w* by driving out nations
Job 37:14 stop and consider God's *w*.
Ps 9: 1 I will tell of all your *w*.
89: 5 The heavens praise your *w*,
119: 27 then I will meditate on your *w*.
Joel 2:30 I will show *w* in the heavens
Ac 2:11 we hear them declaring the *w*
2:19 I will show *w* in the heaven above
5:12 many miraculous signs and *w*
2Co 12:12 that mark an apostle—signs, *w*
2Th 2: 9 and *w*, and in every sort
Heb 2: 4 also testified to it by signs, *w*

WOOD
Isa 44:19 Shall I bow down to a block of *w*?"
1Co 3:12 costly stones, *w*, hay or straw,

WOOL
Pr 31:13 She selects *w* and flax
Isa 1:18 they shall be like *w*.
Da 7: 9 hair of his head was white like *w*.
Rev 1:14 and hair were white like *w*,

WORD (BYWORD WORDS)
Nu 30: 2 he must not break his *w*
Dt 8: 3 but on every *w* that comes
2Sa 22:31 the *w* of the LORD is flawless.
Ps 56: 4 In God, whose *w* I praise,
119: 9 By living according to your *w*.
119: 11 I have hidden your *w* in my heart
119:105 Your *w* is a lamp to my feet
Pr 12:25 but a kind *w* cheers him up.
15: 1 but a harsh *w* stirs up anger.
25:11 A *w* aptly spoken
30: 5 "Every *w* of God is flawless;
Isa 55:11 so is my *w* that goes out
Jer 23:29 "Is not my *w* like fire," declares
Mt 4: 4 but on every *w* that comes
12:36 for every careless *w* they have
15: 6 Thus you nullify the *w* of God
Mk 4:14 parable? The farmer sows the *w*.
Jn 1: 1 was the *W*, and the *W* was
1:14 The *W* became flesh and made his
17:17 them by the truth; your *w* is truth.
Ac 6: 4 and the ministry of the *w*."
2Co 2:17 we do not peddle the *w* of God
4: 2 nor do we distort the *w* of God.
Eph 6:17 of the Spirit, which is the *w* of God.
Php 2:16 as you hold out the *w* of life—
Col 3:16 Let the *w* of Christ dwell
2Ti 2:15 and who correctly handles the *w*
Heb 4:12 For the *w* of God is living
Jas 1:22 Do not merely listen to the *w*,
2Pe 1:19 And we have the *w* of the prophets

WORDS (WORD)
Dt 11:18 Fix these *w* of mine in your hearts
Ps 12: 6 the *w* of the LORD are flawless,
119:103 How sweet are your *w* to my taste,
119:130 The unfolding of your *w* gives light;
119:160 All your *w* are true;
Pr 2: 1 My son, if you accept my *w*
10:19 When *w* are many, sin is not absent
16:24 Pleasant *w* are a honeycomb,
30: 6 Do not add to his *w*,
Ecc 12:11 The *w* of the wise are like goads,
Jer 15:16 When your *w* came, I ate them;
Mt 24:35 but my *w* will never pass away.
Lk 6:47 and hears my *w* and puts them
Jn 6:68 You have the *w* of eternal life.
15: 7 in me and my *w* remain in you,
1Co 2:13 but in *w* taught by the Spirit,
14:19 rather speak five intelligible *w*
Rev 22:19 And if anyone takes *w* away

WORK (WORKED WORKER WORKERS WORKING WORKMAN WORKMANSHIP WORKS)
Ge 2: 2 day he rested from all his *w*.
Ex 23:12 "Six days do your *w*,
Nu 8:11 ready to do the *w* of the LORD.
Dt 5:14 On it you shall not do any *w*,
Ps 19: 1 the skies proclaim the *w*
Ecc 5:19 his lot and be happy in his *w*—
Jer 48:10 lax in doing the LORD's *w*!
Mt 20: 1 to hire men to *w* in his vineyard.
Jn 6:27 Do not *w* for food that spoils,
9: 4 we must do the *w* of him who sent
Ac 13: 2 for the *w* to which I have called
1Co 3:13 test the quality of each man's *w*.
4:12 We *w* hard with our own hands.
Eph 4:16 up in love, as each part does its *w*.
Php 1: 6 that he who began a good *w*
2:12 continue to *w* out your salvation
Col 3:23 Whatever you do, *w* at it
1Th 4:11 and to *w* with your hands,
5:12 to respect those who *w* hard
2Th 3:10 If a man will not *w*, he shall not eat
2Ti 3:17 equipped for every good *w*.
Heb 6:10 he will not forget your *w*
2Jn :11 him shares in his wicked *w*.
3Jn : 8 men so that we may *w* together

WORKED (WORK)
1Co 15:10 No, I *w* harder than all of them—
2Th 3: 8 On the contrary, we *w* night

WORKER (WORK)
Lk 10: 7 for the *w* deserves his wages.
1Ti 5:18 and "The *w* deserves his wages."

WORKERS (WORK)
Mt 9:37 is plentiful but the *w* are few.
1Co 3: 9 For we are God's fellow *w*;

WORKING (WORK)
Col 3:23 as *w* for the Lord, not for men,

WORKMAN (WORK)
2Ti 2:15 a *w* who does not need

WORKMANSHIP* (WORK)
Eph 2:10 For we are God's *w*, created

WORKS (WORK)
Ps 66: 5 how awesome his *w* in man's behalf
145: 6 of the power of your awesome *w*,
Pr 8:22 As the first of his *w*,
31:31 let her *w* bring her praise
Ro 4: 2 in fact, Abraham was justified by *w*
8:28 in all things God *w* for the good
Eph 2: 9 not by *w*, so that no one can boast.
4:12 to prepare God's people for *w*

WORLD (WORLDLY)
Ps 9: 8 He will judge the *w*
50:12 for the *w* is mine, and all that is in it
96:13 He will judge the *w*
Pr 8:23 before the *w* began.
Isa 13:11 I will punish the *w* for its evil,
Zep 1:18 the whole *w* will be consumed,
Mt 5:14 "You are the light of the *w*.
16:26 for a man if he gains the whole *w*,
Mk 16:15 into all the *w* and preach the good
Jn 1:29 who takes away the sin of the *w*!
3:16 so loved the *w* that he gave his one
8:12 he said, "I am the light of the *w*.
15:19 As it is, you do not belong to the *w*,
16:33 In this *w* you will have trouble.
17: 5 had with you before the *w* began.
17:14 not of the *w* any more than I am
Jn 18:36 "My kingdom is not of this *w*.
Ac 17:24 "The God who made the *w*
Ro 3:19 and the whole *w* held accountable
10:18 their words to the ends of the *w*."
1Co 1:27 things of the *w* to shame the strong.
3:19 the wisdom of this *w* is foolishness
6: 2 that the saints will judge the *w*?
2Co 5:19 that God was reconciling the *w*
10: 3 For though we live in the *w*,
1Ti 6: 7 For we brought nothing into the *w*,
Heb 11:38 the *w* was not worthy of them.
Jas 2: 5 poor in the eyes of the *w* to be rich
4: 4 with the *w* is hatred toward God?
1Pe 1:20 before the creation of the *w*,
1Jn 2: 2 but also for the sins of the whole *w*.
2:15 not love the *w* or anything in the *w*.
5: 4 born of God overcomes the *w*.
Rev 13: 8 slain from the creation of the *w*.

WORLDLY (WORLD)
1Co 3: 1 address you as spiritual but as *w*—
Tit 2:12 to ungodliness and *w* passions,

WORM
Mk 9:48 " 'their *w* does not die,

WORRY (WORRYING)
Mt 6:25 I tell you, do not *w* about your life,
10:19 do not *w* about what to say

WORRYING (WORRY)
Mt 6:27 of you by *w* can add a single hour

WORSHIP (WORSHIPED WORSHIPS)
Jos 22:27 that we will *w* the LORD
2Ki 17:36 arm, is the one you must *w*.
1Ch 16:29 *w* the LORD in the splendor
Ps 95: 6 Come, let us bow down in *w*,
100: 2 *w* the LORD with gladness;
Zec 14:17 up to Jerusalem to *w* the King,
Mt 2: 2 and have come to *w* him."
4: 9 "if you will bow down and *w* me."
Jn 4:24 and his worshipers must *w* in spirit
Ro 12: 1 to God—this is your spiritual act of *w*.
Heb 10: 1 perfect those who draw near to *w*.

WORSHIPED (WORSHIP)
2Ch 29:30 and bowed their heads and *w*.
Mt 28: 9 clasped his feet and *w* him.

WORSHIPS (WORSHIP)
Isa 44:15 But he also fashions a god and *w* it;

WORTH (WORTHY)
Job 28:13 Man does not comprehend its *w*;
Pr 31:10 She is *w* far more than rubies.
Mt 10:31 are *w* more than many sparrows.
Ro 8:18 sufferings are not *w* comparing
1Pe 1: 7 of greater *w* than gold,
3: 4 which is of great *w* in God's sight.

WORTHLESS
Pr 11: 4 Wealth is *w* in the day of wrath,
Jas 1:26 himself and his religion is *w*.

WORTHY (WORTH)
1Ch 16:25 For great is the LORD and most *w*
Mt 10:37 more than me is not *w* of me;
Lk 15:19 I am no longer *w* to be called your
Eph 4: 1 to live a life *w* of the calling you
Php 1:27 in a manner *w* of the gospel
Col 1:10 in order that you may live a life *w*
1Ti 3: 8 are to be men *w* of respect, sincere,
Heb 3: 3 Jesus has been found *w*
3Jn : 6 on their way in a manner *w* of God.
Rev 5: 2 "Who is *w* to break the seals

WOUND (WOUNDS)
1Co 8:12 and *w* their weak conscience,

WOUNDS (WOUND)
Pr 27: 6 *w* from a friend can be trusted
Isa 53: 5 and by his *w* we are healed.
Zec 13: 6 'What are these *w* on your body?'
1Pe 2:24 by his *w* you have been healed.

WRAPS
Ps 104: 2 He *w* himself in light

WRATH
2Ch 36:16 scoffed at his prophets until the *w*
Ps 2: 5 and terrifies them in his *w*, saying,
76:10 Surely your *w* against men brings
Pr 15: 1 A gentle answer turns away *w*,
Isa 13:13 at the *w* of the LORD Almighty,
51:17 the cup of his *w*,
Jer 25:15 filled with the wine of my *w*
Eze 5:13 my *w* against them will subside,
20: 8 So I said I would pour out my *w*
Am 1: 3 I will not turn back my *w*,
Na 1: 2 maintains his *w* against his enemies

Zep 1:15 That day will be a day of *w*,
Jn 3:36 for God's *w* remains on him."
Ro 1:18 The *w* of God is being revealed
2: 5 you are storing up *w*
5: 9 saved from God's *w* through him!
9:22 choosing to show his *w*
1Th 5: 9 God did not appoint us to suffer *w*
Rev 6:16 and from the *w* of the Lamb!
19:15 the fury of the *w* of God Almighty.

WRESTLED
Ge 32:24 and a man *w* with him till daybreak

WRITE (WRITER WRITING WRITTEN WROTE)
Dt 6: 9 *W* them on the doorframes
10: 2 I will *w* on the tablets the words
Pr 7: 3 *w* them on the tablet of your heart.
Jer 31:33 and *w* it on their hearts.
Heb 8:10 and *w* them on their hearts.
Rev 3:12 I will also *w* on him my new name.

WRITER* (WRITE)
Ps 45: 1 my tongue is the pen of a skillful *w*.

WRITING (WRITE)
1Co 14:37 him acknowledge that what I am *w*

WRITTEN (WRITE)
Dt 28:58 which are *w* in this book,
Jos 1: 8 careful to do everything *w* in it.
23: 6 to obey all that is *w* in the Book
Ps 40: 7 it is *w* about me in the scroll.
Da 12: 1 everyone whose name is found *w*
Mal 3:16 A scroll of remembrance was *w*
Lk 10:20 but rejoice that your names are *w*
24:44 must be fulfilled that is *w* about me
Jn 20:31 these are *w* that you may believe
21:25 for the books that would be *w*.
Ro 2:15 of the law are *w* on their hearts,
1Co 4: 6 "Do not go beyond what is *w*."
10:11 as examples and were *w* down
2Co 3: 3 *w* not with ink but with the Spirit
Col 2:14 having canceled the *w* code,
Heb 10: 7 it is *w* about me in the scroll—
12:23 whose names are *w* in heaven.
Rev 21:27 but only those whose names are *w*

WRONG (WRONGDOING WRONGED WRONGS)
Ex 23: 2 Do not follow the crowd in doing *w*
Nu 5: 7 must make full restitution for his *w*,
Dt 32: 4 A faithful God who does no *w*,
Job 34:12 unthinkable that God would do *w*,
Ps 5: 5 you hate all who do *w*.
Gal 2:11 to his face, because he was clearly in the *w*.
1Th 5:15 that nobody pays back *w* for *w*,

WRONGDOING (WRONG)
Job 1:22 sin by charging God with *w*.
1Jn 5:17 All *w* is sin, and there is sin that

WRONGED (WRONG)
1Co 6: 7 not rather be *w*? Why not rather

WRONGS (WRONG)
Pr 10:12 but love covers over all *w*.
1Co 13: 5 angered, it keeps no record of *w*.

WROTE (WRITE)
Ex 34:28 And he *w* on the tablets the words
Jn 5:46 for he *w* about me.
8: 8 down and *w* on the ground.

XERXES
King of Persia, husband of Esther. Deposed Vashti; replaced her with Esther (Est 1-2). Sealed Haman's edict to annihilate the Jews (Est 3). Received Esther without having called her (Est 5:1-8). Honored Mordecai (Est 6). Hanged Haman (Est 7). Issued edict allowing Jews to defend themselves (Est 8). Exalted Mordecai (Est 8:1-2, 15; 9:4; 10).

YEAR (YEARS)
Ex 34:23 Three times a *y* all your men are
Lev 16:34 to be made once a *y* for all the sins
25: 4 But in the seventh *y* the land is
25:11 The fiftieth *y* shall be a jubilee
Heb 10: 1 repeated endlessly *y* after *y*,

YEARS (YEAR)
Ge 1:14 to mark seasons and days and *y*,
Ex 12:40 lived in Egypt was 430 *y*.
16:35 The Israelites ate manna forty *y*,
Job 36:26 of his *y* is past finding out.
Ps 90: 4 For a thousand *y* in your sight
90:10 The length of our days is seventy *y*
Pr 3: 2 they will prolong your life many *y*
Lk 3:23 Jesus himself was about thirty *y* old
2Pe 3: 8 the Lord a day is like a thousand *y*,
Rev 20: 2 and bound him for a thousand *y*.

YEAST
Ex 12:15 are to eat bread made without *y*.
Mt 16: 6 guard against the *y* of the Pharisees
1Co 5: 6 you know that a little *y* works

YESTERDAY
Heb 13: 8 Jesus Christ is the same *y*

YOKE (YOKED)
1Ki 12: 4 and the heavy *y* he put on us,
Mt 11:29 Take my *y* upon you and learn
Gal 5: 1 be burdened again by a *y*

YOKED (YOKE)
2Co 6:14 Do not be *y* together

YOUNG (YOUNGER YOUTH)
2Ch 10:14 he followed the advice of the *y* men
Ps 37:25 I was *y* and now I am old,
119: 9 How can a *y* man keep his way
Pr 20:29 The glory of *y* men is their strength
Isa 40:11 he gently leads those that have *y*.
Joel 2:28 your *y* men will see visions.
Ac 2:17 your *y* men will see visions,
7:58 at the feet of a *y* man named Saul.
1Ti 4:12 down on you because you are *y*,
Tit 2: 6 encourage the *y* men
1Pe 5: 5 *Y* men, in the same way be
1Jn 2:13 I write to you, *y* men,

YOUNGER (YOUNG)
1Ti 5: 1 Treat *y* men as brothers, older
Tit 2: 4 Then they can train the *y* women

YOUTH (YOUNG)
Ps 103: 5 so that your *y* is renewed like
Ecc 12: 1 Creator in the days of your *y*,
2Ti 2:22 Flee the evil desires of *y*,

ZACCHAEUS
Lk 19: 2 A man was there by the name of *Z*;

ZEAL (ZEALOUS)
Ps 69: 9 for *z* for your house consumes me,
Pr 19: 2 to have *z* without knowledge,
Isa 59:17 and wrapped himself in *z*
Jn 2:17 "*Z* for your house will consume me
Ro 10: 2 their *z* is not based on knowledge.
12:11 Never be lacking in *z*,

ZEALOUS (ZEAL)
Nu 25:13 he was *z* for the honor of his God
Pr 23:17 always be *z* for the fear
Eze 39:25 and I will be *z* for my holy name.
Gal 4:18 fine to be *z*, provided the purpose is

ZEBULUN
Son of Jacob by Leah (Ge 30:20; 35:23; 1Ch 2:1). Tribe of blessed (Ge 49:13; Dt 33:18-19), numbered (Nu 1:31; 26:27), allotted land (Jos 19:10-16; Eze 48:26), failed to fully possess (Jdg 1:30), supported Deborah (Jdg 4:6-10; 5:14, 18), David (1Ch 12:33), 12,000 from (Rev 7:8).

ZECHARIAH
1. Son of Jeroboam II; king of Israel (2Ki 15:8-12).
2. Post-exilic prophet who encouraged rebuilding of temple (Ezr 5:1; 6:14; Zec 1:1).

ZEDEKIAH
1. False prophet (1Ki 22:11-24; 2Ch 18:10-23).
2. Mattaniah, son of Josiah (1Ch 3:15), made king of Judah by Nebuchadnezzar (2Ki 24:17-25:7; 2Ch 36:10-14; Jer 37-39; 52:1-11).

ZEPHANIAH
Prophet; descendant of Hezekiah (Zep 1:1).

ZERUBBABEL
Descendant of David (1Ch 3:19; Mt 1:3). Led return from exile (Ezr 2:2; Ne 7:7). Governor of Israel; helped rebuild altar and temple (Ezr 3; Hag 1-2; Zec 4).

ZILPAH
Servant of Leah, mother of Jacob's sons Gad and Asher (Ge 30:9-12; 35:26, 46:16-18).

ZIMRI
King of Israel (1Ki 16:9-20).

ZION
2Sa 5: 7 David captured the fortress of *Z*,
Ps 2: 6 King on *Z*, my holy hill."
9:11 to the LORD, enthroned in *Z*;
74: 2 Mount *Z*, where you dwelt.
87: 2 the LORD loves the gates of *Z*
102: 13 and have compassion on *Z*,
Ps 137: 3 "Sing us one of the songs of *Z*!"
Isa 2: 3 The law will go out from *Z*,
28:16 "See, I lay a stone in *Z*,
51:11 They will enter *Z* with singing;
52: 8 When the LORD returns to *Z*,
Jer 50: 5 They will ask the way to *Z*
Joel 3:21 The LORD dwells in *Z*!
Am 6: 1 to you who are complacent in *Z*,
Mic 4: 2 The law will go out from *Z*,
Zec 9: 9 Rejoice greatly, O Daughter of *Z*!
Ro 9:33 I lay in *Z* a stone that causes men
11:26 "The deliverer will come from *Z*;
Heb 12:22 But you have come to Mount *Z*,
Rev 14: 1 standing on Mount *Z*,

ZIPPORAH*
Daughter of Reuel; wife of Moses (Ex 2:21-22; 4:20-26; 18:1-6).

ZOPHAR
One of Job's friends (Job 11; 20).

Index to Color Maps

Map 1: WORLD OF THE PATRIARCHS

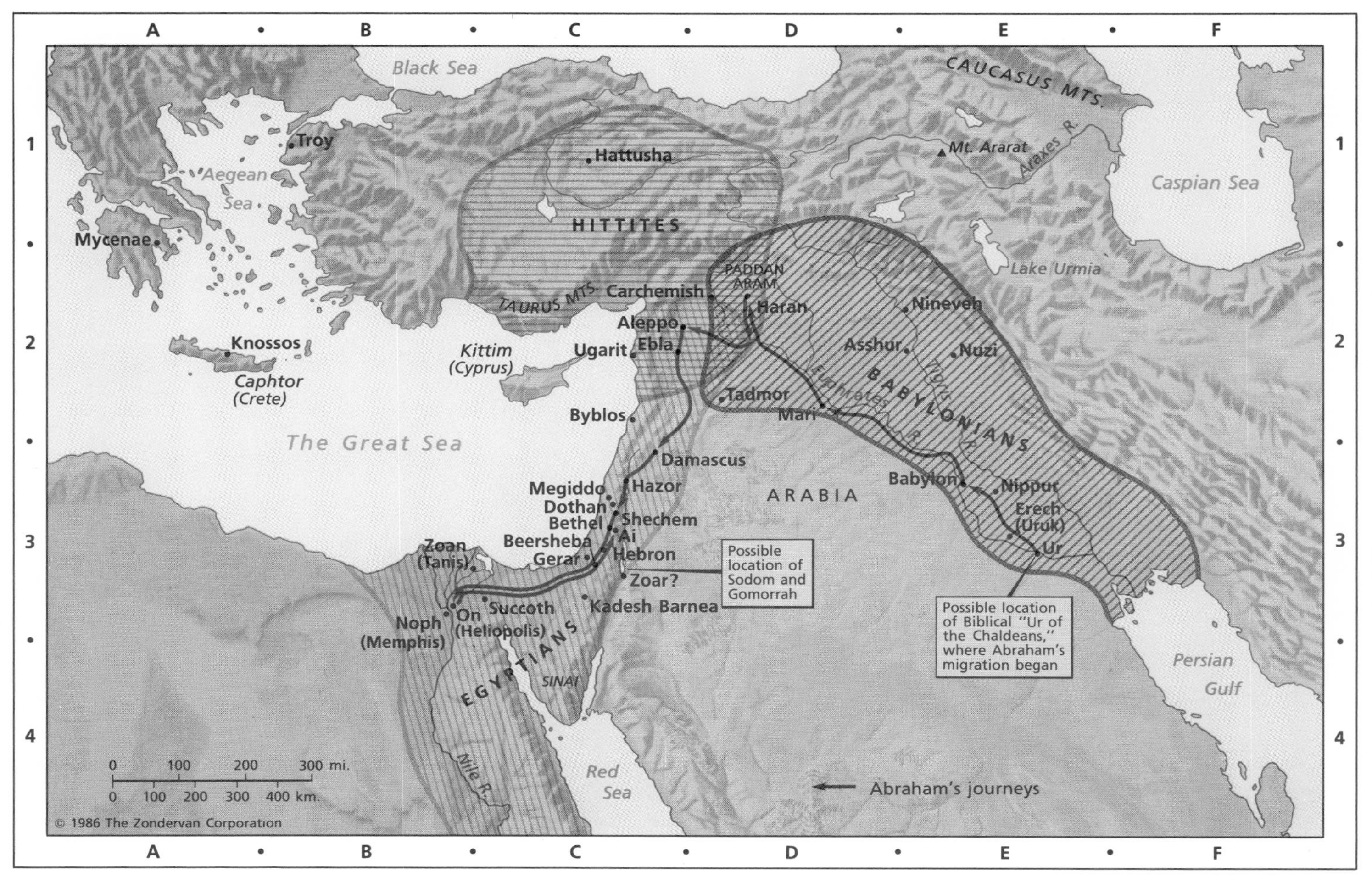

Map 2: **PALESTINE AND SINAI**

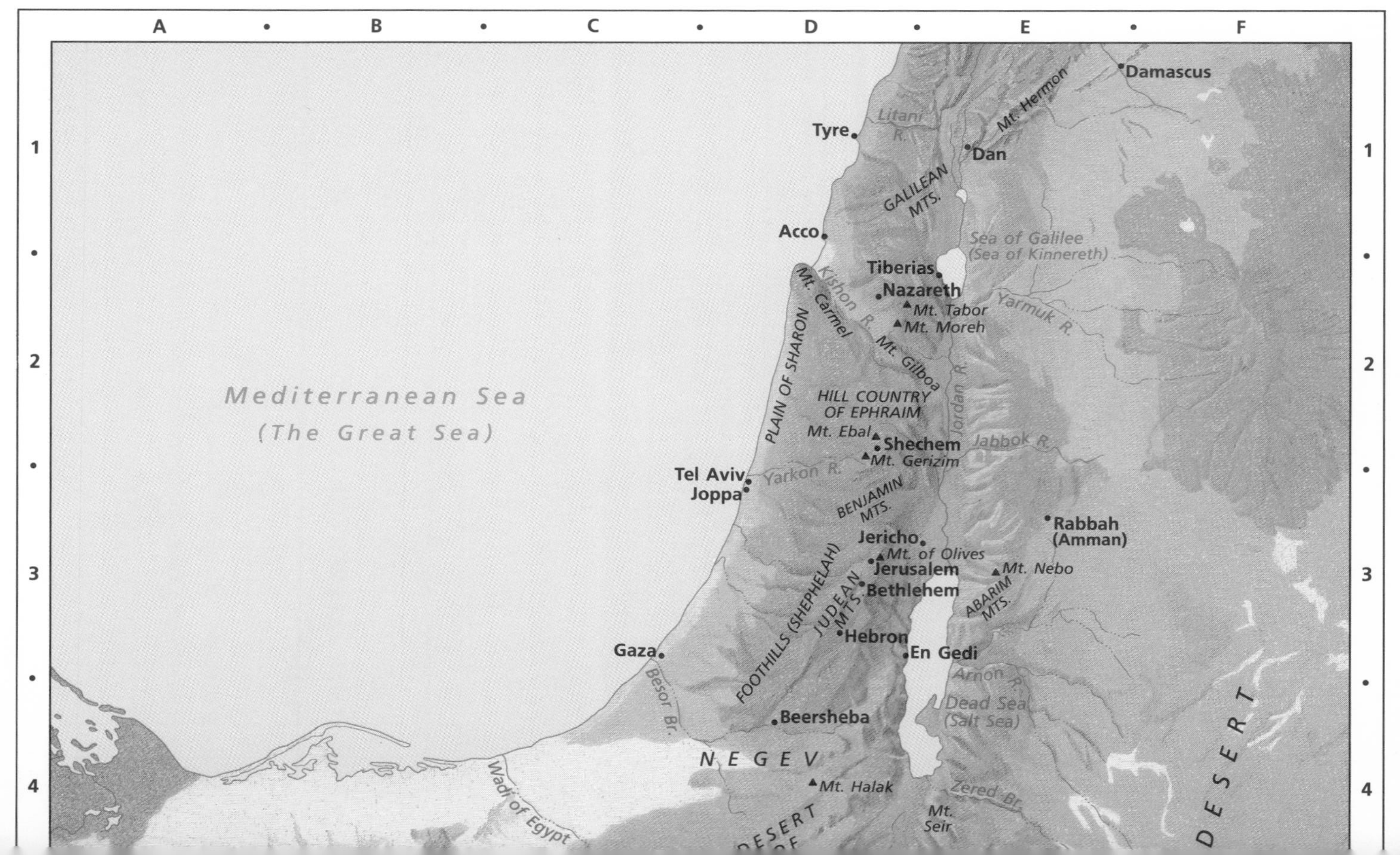

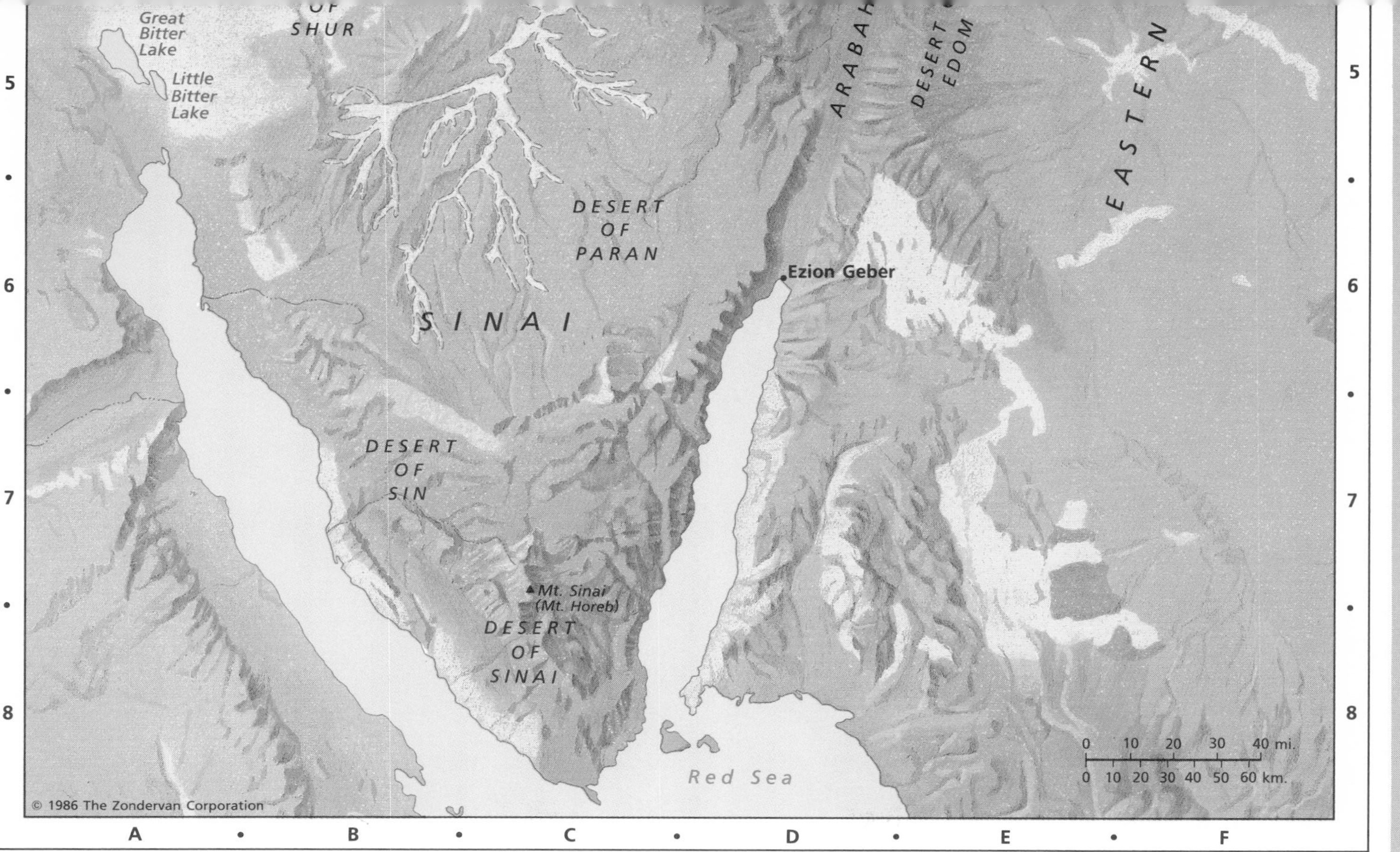
Great Bitter Lake
Little Bitter Lake
SHUR
DESERT OF PARAN
SINAI
ARABAH
DESERT EDOM
EASTERN
Ezion Geber
DESERT OF SIN
Mt. Sinai (Mt. Horeb)
DESERT OF SINAI
Red Sea
0 10 20 30 40 mi.
0 10 20 30 40 50 60 km.
A B C D E F
5 6 7 8

Map 3: **EXODUS AND CONQUEST OF CANAAN**

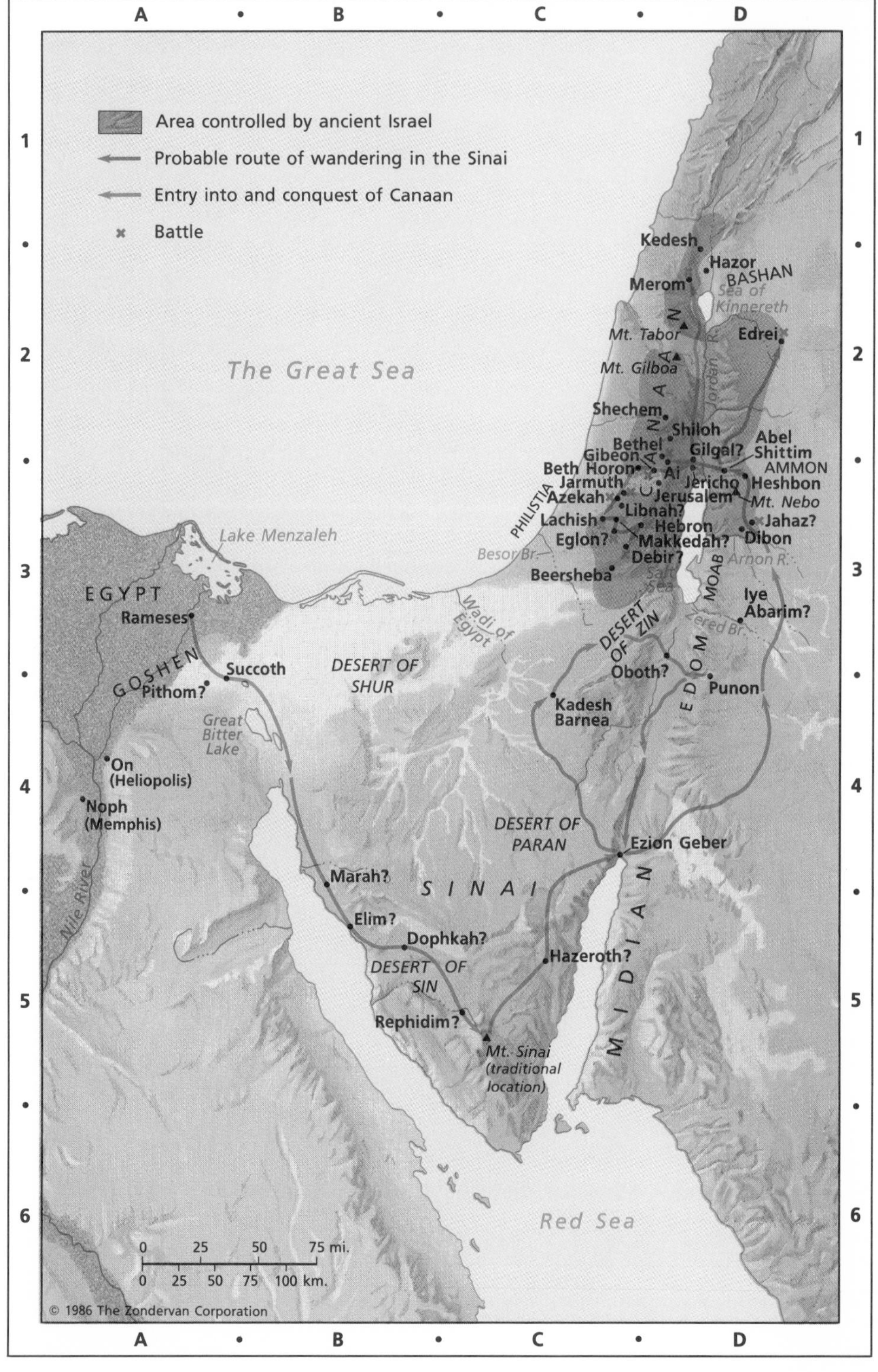
A • B • C • D
1 • 2 • 3 • 4 • 5 • 6
Area controlled by ancient Israel
Probable route of wandering in the Sinai
Entry into and conquest of Canaan
Battle
The Great Sea
Kedesh
Hazor
BASHAN
Merom
Sea of Kinnereth
Mt. Tabor
Edrei
Mt. Gilboa
CANAAN
Jordan R.
Shechem
Shiloh
Bethel
Gibeon
Gilgal?
Abel Shittim
Beth Horon
Ai
AMMON
Jarmuth
Jericho
Heshbon
Azekah
Jerusalem
Mt. Nebo
PHILISTIA
Libnah?
Lachish
Hebron
Jahaz?
Eglon?
Makkedah?
Dibon
Besor Br.
Debir?
Arnon R.
Beersheba
Salt Sea
MOAB
Lake Menzaleh
EGYPT
Rameses
Wadi of Egypt
Iye Abarim?
DESERT OF ZIN
Zered Br.
GOSHEN
Succoth
DESERT OF SHUR
Oboth?
EDOM
Pithom?
Punon
Kadesh Barnea
Great Bitter Lake
On (Heliopolis)
Noph (Memphis)
DESERT OF PARAN
Ezion Geber
Marah?
SINAI
Nile River
Elim?
Dophkah?
MIDIAN
Hazeroth?
DESERT OF SIN
Rephidim?
Mt. Sinai (traditional location)
Red Sea
0 25 50 75 mi.
0 25 50 75 100 km.
© 1986 The Zondervan Corporation

Map 4: **LAND OF THE TWELVE TRIBES**

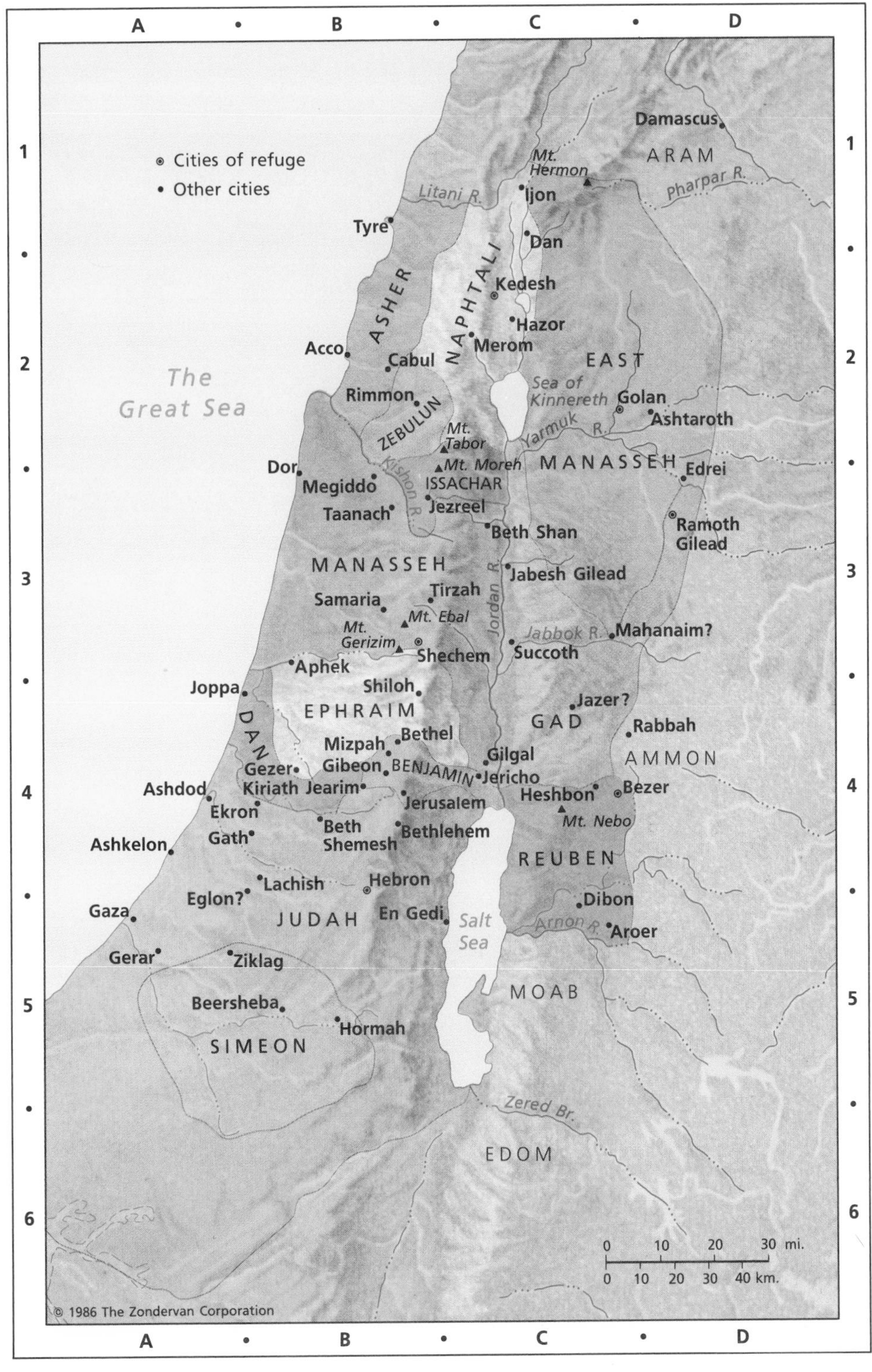

Map 5: **KINGDOM OF DAVID AND SOLOMON**

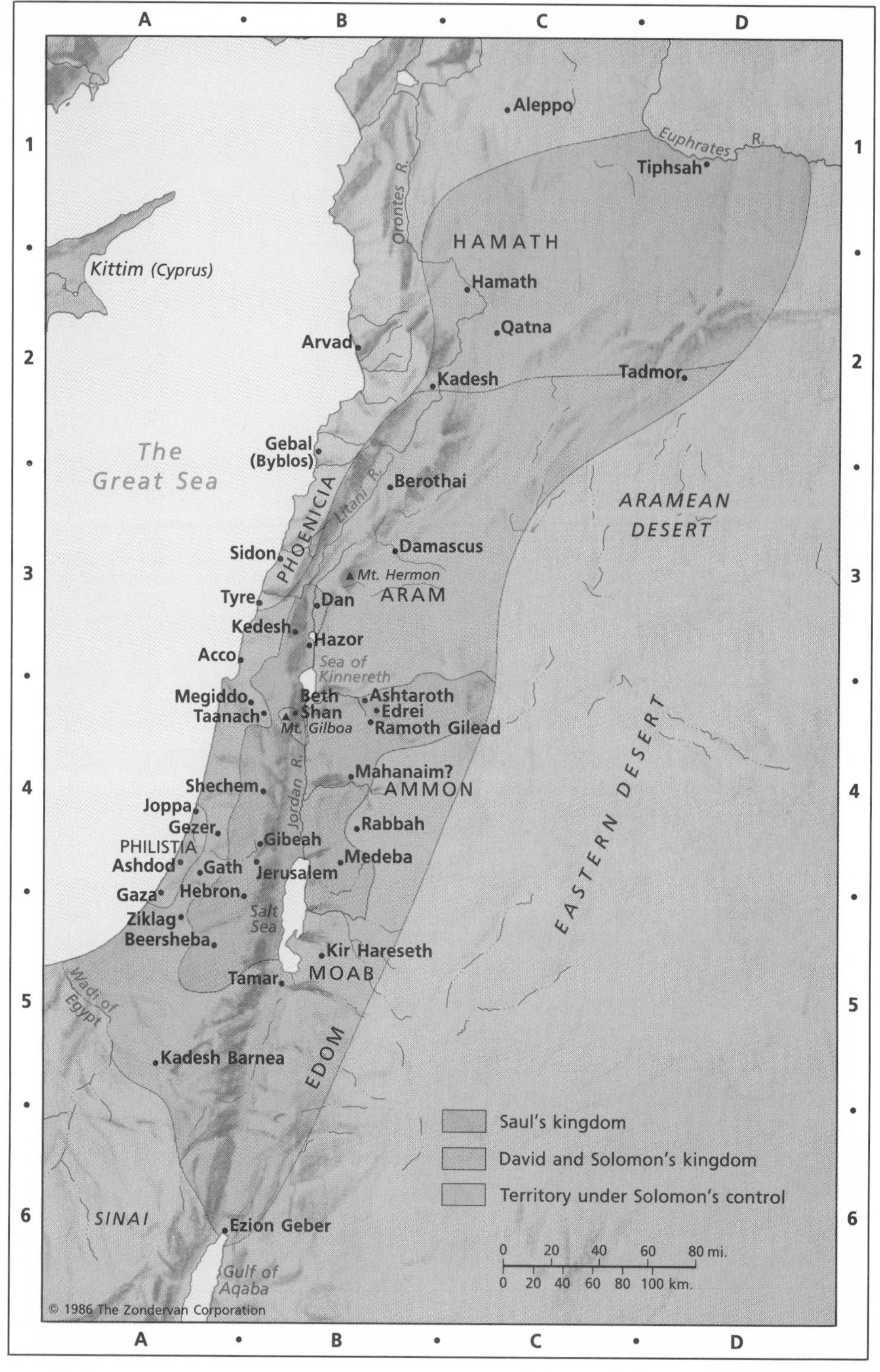
A
B
C
D
1
2
3
4
5
6
Aleppo
Euphrates R.
Tiphsah
Orontes R.
HAMATH
Hamath
Qatna
Kittim (Cyprus)
Arvad
Kadesh
Tadmor
The Great Sea
Gebal (Byblos)
PHOENICIA
Litani R.
Berothai
ARAMEAN DESERT
Damascus
Sidon
Mt. Hermon
ARAM
Tyre
Dan
Kedesh
Hazor
Acco
Sea of Kinnereth
Megiddo
Taanach
Beth Shan
Mt. Gilboa
Ashtaroth
Edrei
Ramoth Gilead
Shechem
Jordan R.
Mahanaim?
AMMON
Joppa
Gezer
PHILISTIA
Gibeah
Rabbah
Ashdod
Gath
Jerusalem
Medeba
Gaza
Hebron
Salt Sea
Ziklag
Beersheba
Kir Hareseth
EASTERN DESERT
Tamar
MOAB
Wadi of Egypt
Kadesh Barnea
EDOM
Saul's kingdom
David and Solomon's kingdom
Territory under Solomon's control
SINAI
Ezion Geber
0 20 40 60 80 mi.
0 20 40 60 80 100 km.
Gulf of Aqaba
© 1986 The Zondervan Corporation

Map 6: PROPHETS IN ISRAEL AND JUDAH

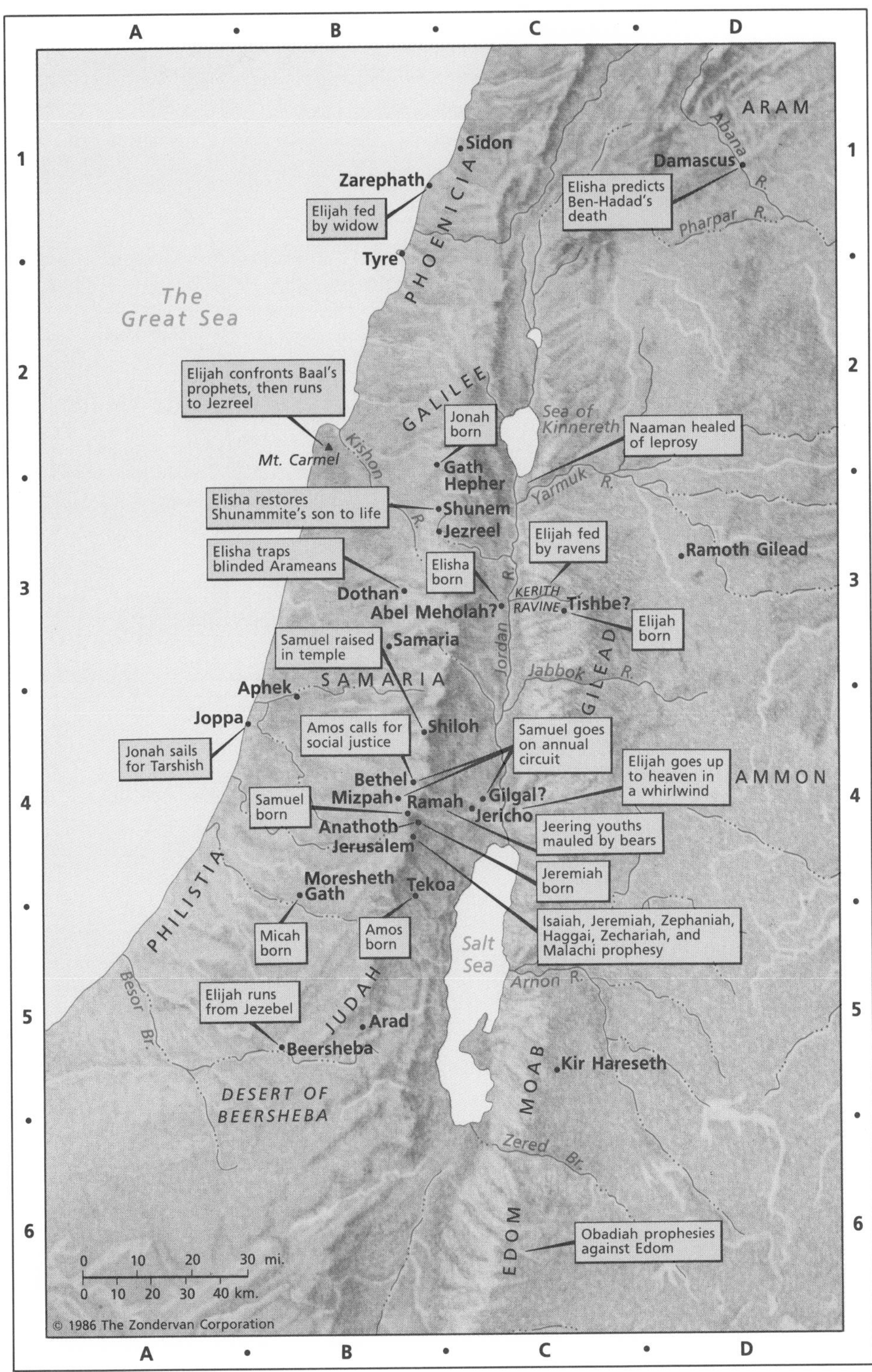
A • B • C • D
1
2
3
4
5
6
ARAM
Abana R.
Sidon
Damascus
Zarephath
Elijah fed by widow
Elisha predicts Ben-Hadad's death
Pharpar R.
Tyre
PHOENICIA
The Great Sea
Elijah confronts Baal's prophets, then runs to Jezreel
GALILEE
Jonah born
Sea of Kinnereth
Naaman healed of leprosy
Mt. Carmel
Kishon R.
Gath Hepher
Yarmuk R.
Elisha restores Shunammite's son to life
Shunem
Jezreel
Elijah fed by ravens
Ramoth Gilead
Elisha traps blinded Arameans
Elisha born
Jordan R.
Dothan
KERITH RAVINE
Abel Meholah?
Tishbe?
Elijah born
Samuel raised in temple
Samaria
GILEAD
Jabbok R.
SAMARIA
Aphek
Joppa
Jonah sails for Tarshish
Amos calls for social justice
Shiloh
Samuel goes on annual circuit
Elijah goes up to heaven in a whirlwind
AMMON
Bethel
Samuel born
Mizpah
Ramah
Gilgal?
Jericho
Anathoth
Jeering youths mauled by bears
Jerusalem
Jeremiah born
PHILISTIA
Moresheth Gath
Tekoa
Isaiah, Jeremiah, Zephaniah, Haggai, Zechariah, and Malachi prophesy
Micah born
Amos born
Salt Sea
Arnon R.
Besor Br.
JUDAH
Elijah runs from Jezebel
Arad
Beersheba
MOAB
Kir Hareseth
DESERT OF BEERSHEBA
Zered Br.
EDOM
Obadiah prophesies against Edom
0 10 20 30 mi.
0 10 20 30 40 km.
© 1986 The Zondervan Corporation

Map 7: ASSYRIAN AND BABYLONIAN EMPIRES

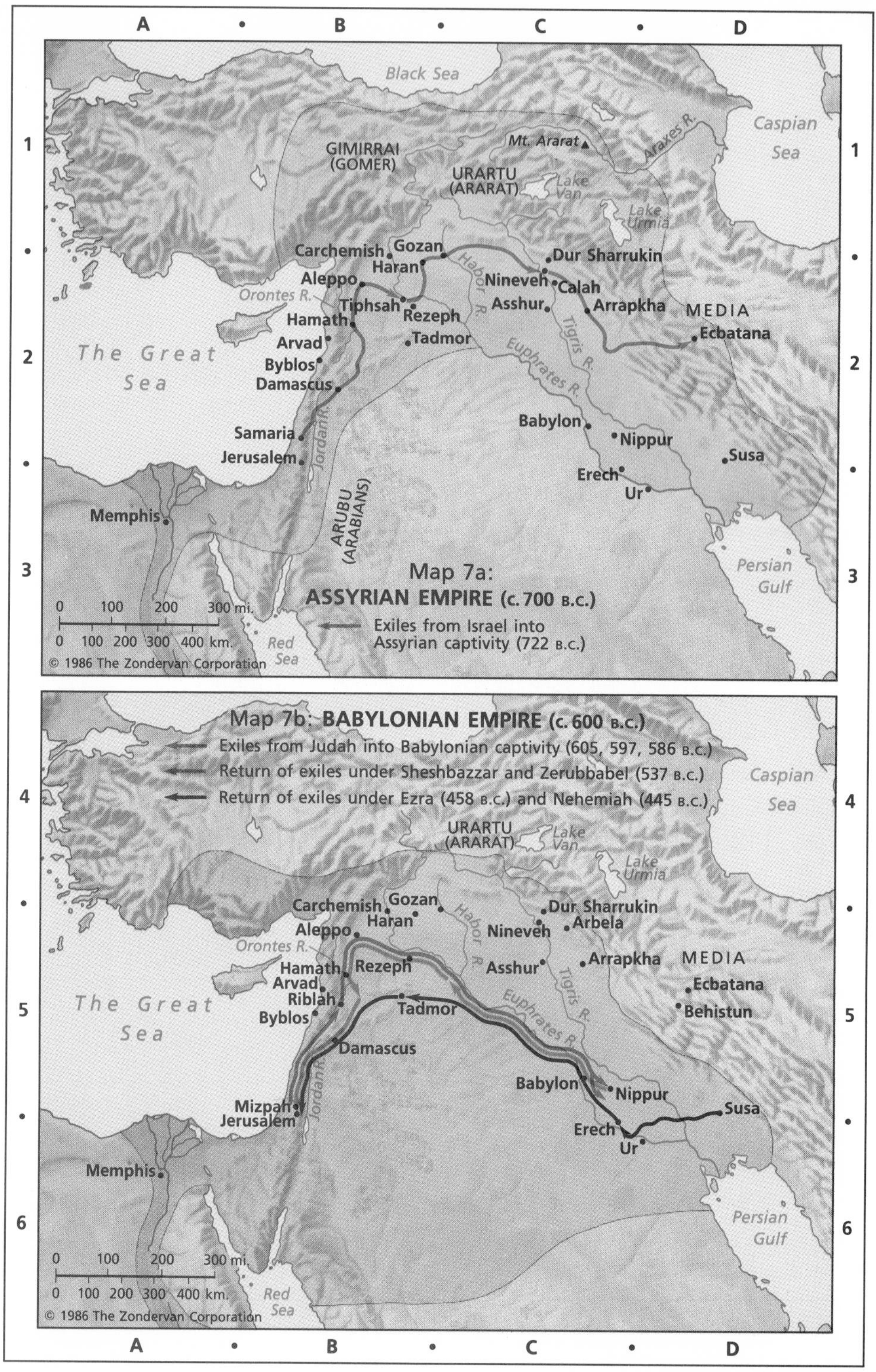

Map 8: **JERUSALEM IN JESUS' TIME**

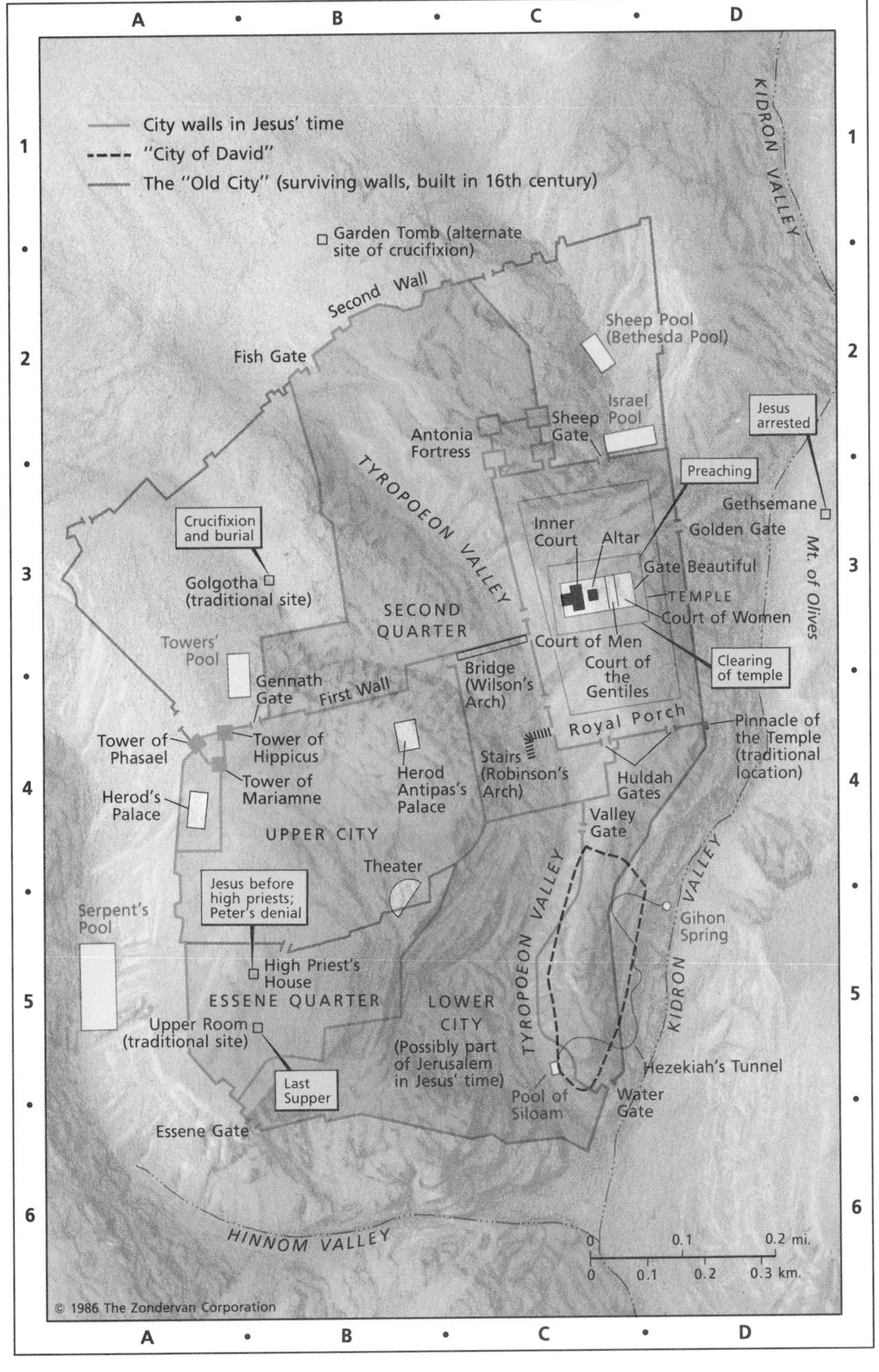

A
B
C
D
1
2
3
4
5
6
City walls in Jesus' time
"City of David"
The "Old City" (surviving walls, built in 16th century)
KIDRON VALLEY
Garden Tomb (alternate site of crucifixion)
Second Wall
Sheep Pool (Bethesda Pool)
Fish Gate
Israel Pool
Sheep Gate
Antonia Fortress
Jesus arrested
Preaching
TYROPOEON VALLEY
Gethsemane
Golden Gate
Crucifixion and burial
Inner Court
Altar
Mt. of Olives
Gate Beautiful
Golgotha (traditional site)
TEMPLE
SECOND QUARTER
Court of Women
Towers' Pool
Court of Men
Clearing of temple
Court of the Gentiles
Gennath Gate
First Wall
Bridge (Wilson's Arch)
Royal Porch
Pinnacle of the Temple (traditional location)
Tower of Phasael
Tower of Hippicus
Stairs (Robinson's Arch)
Herod Antipas's Palace
Huldah Gates
Tower of Mariamne
Herod's Palace
Valley Gate
UPPER CITY
Theater
Jesus before high priests; Peter's denial
Serpent's Pool
Gihon Spring
TYROPOEON VALLEY
KIDRON VALLEY
High Priest's House
ESSENE QUARTER
LOWER CITY
(Possibly part of Jerusalem in Jesus' time)
Upper Room (traditional site)
Last Supper
Hezekiah's Tunnel
Pool of Siloam
Water Gate
Essene Gate
HINNOM VALLEY
0
0.1
0.2 mi.
0
0.1
0.2
0.3 km.

Map 9: JESUS' MINISTRY

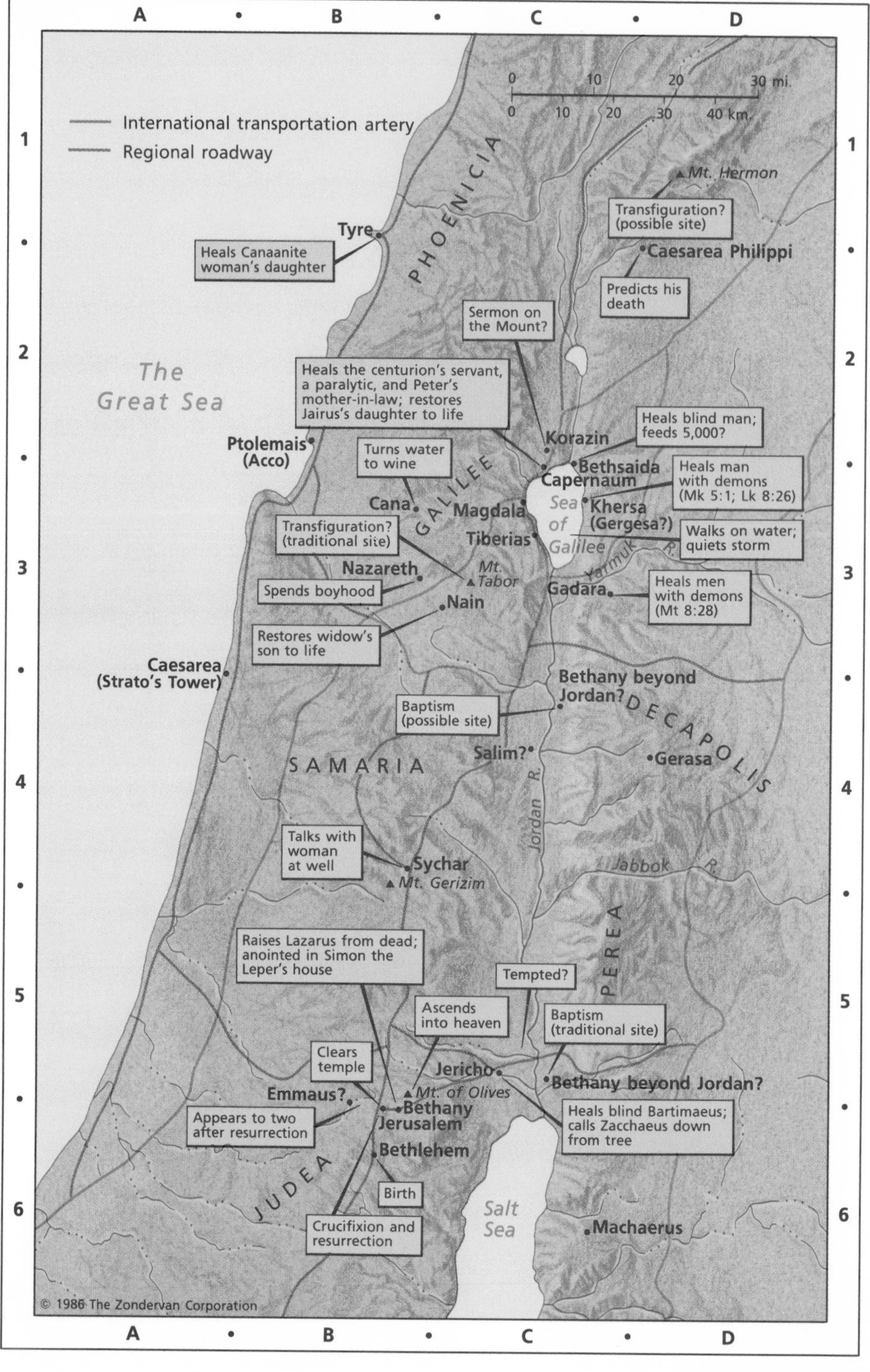

A
B
C
D
1
2
3
4
5
6
International transportation artery
Regional roadway
0 10 20 30 mi.
0 10 20 30 40 km.
The Great Sea
PHOENICIA
Mt. Hermon
Transfiguration? (possible site)
Caesarea Philippi
Predicts his death
Tyre
Heals Canaanite woman's daughter
Sermon on the Mount?
Heals the centurion's servant, a paralytic, and Peter's mother-in-law; restores Jairus's daughter to life
Korazin
Heals blind man; feeds 5,000?
Bethsaida
Capernaum
Heals man with demons (Mk 5:1; Lk 8:26)
Ptolemais (Acco)
Turns water to wine
GALILEE
Cana
Magdala
Sea of Galilee
Khersa (Gergesa?)
Walks on water; quiets storm
Transfiguration? (traditional site)
Tiberias
Yarmuk R.
Nazareth
Mt. Tabor
Gadara
Heals men with demons (Mt 8:28)
Spends boyhood
Nain
Restores widow's son to life
Caesarea (Strato's Tower)
Bethany beyond Jordan?
DECAPOLIS
Baptism (possible site)
Salim?
Gerasa
SAMARIA
Jordan R.
Talks with woman at well
Sychar
Mt. Gerizim
Jabbok R.
PEREA
Raises Lazarus from dead; anointed in Simon the Leper's house
Tempted?
Ascends into heaven
Baptism (traditional site)
Clears temple
Jericho
Bethany beyond Jordan?
Emmaus?
Mt. of Olives
Bethany
Jerusalem
Appears to two after resurrection
Heals blind Bartimaeus; calls Zacchaeus down from tree
Bethlehem
JUDEA
Birth
Salt Sea
Machaerus
Crucifixion and resurrection

Map 10: **APOSTLES' EARLY TRAVELS**

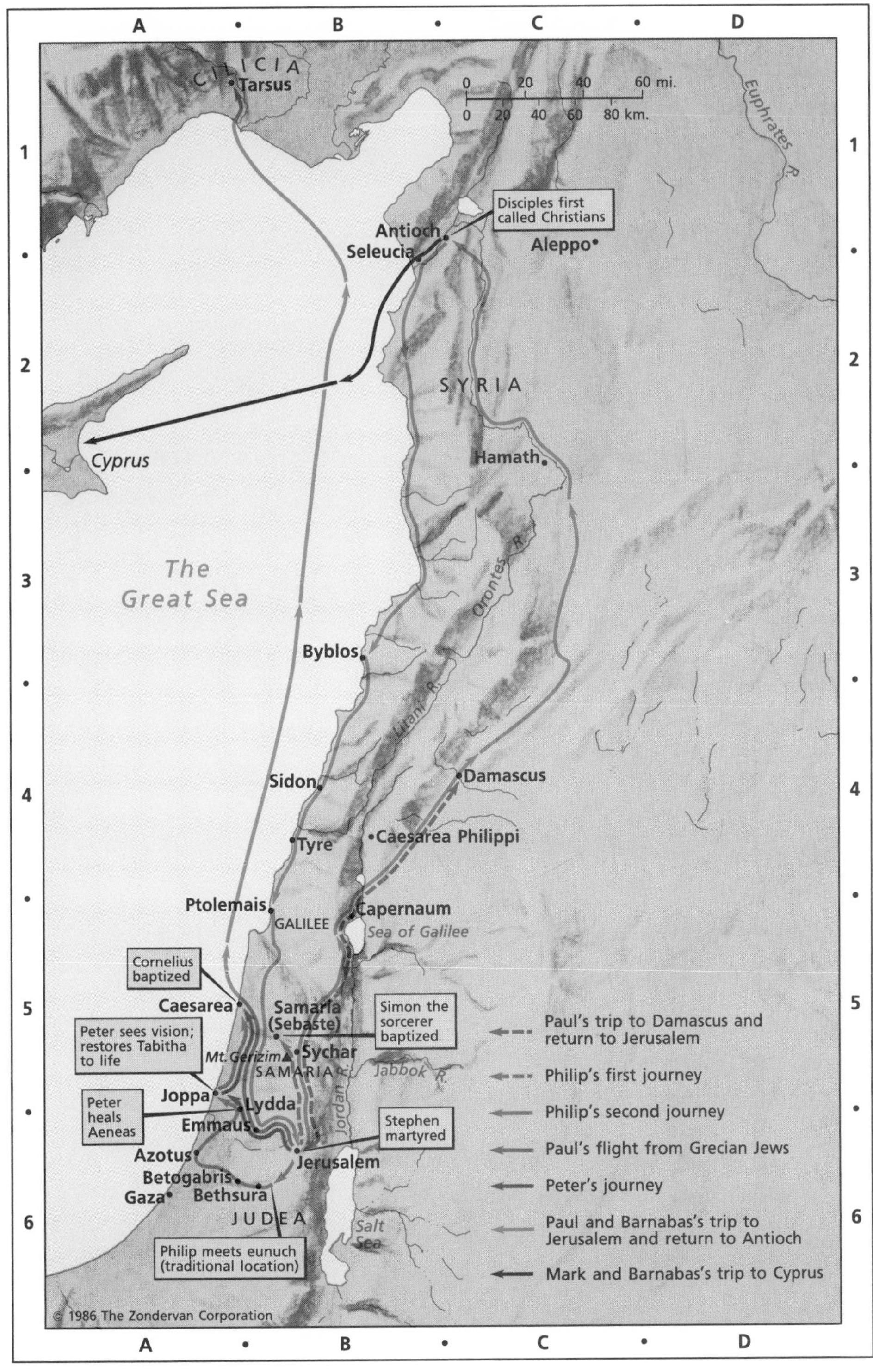
A
B
C
D
1
2
3
4
5
6
CILICIA
Tarsus
0 20 40 60 mi.
0 20 40 60 80 km.
Euphrates R.
Disciples first called Christians
Antioch
Seleucia
Aleppo
SYRIA
Cyprus
Hamath
The Great Sea
Orontes R.
Byblos
Litani R.
Sidon
Damascus
Tyre
Caesarea Philippi
Ptolemais
Capernaum
GALILEE
Sea of Galilee
Cornelius baptized
Caesarea
Samaria (Sebaste)
Simon the sorcerer baptized
Peter sees vision; restores Tabitha to life
Mt. Gerizim
Sychar
SAMARIA
Jabbok R.
Joppa
Lydda
Peter heals Aeneas
Emmaus
Jordan
Stephen martyred
Azotus
Jerusalem
Betogabris
Gaza
Bethsura
JUDEA
Salt Sea
Philip meets eunuch (traditional location)
Paul's trip to Damascus and return to Jerusalem
Philip's first journey
Philip's second journey
Paul's flight from Grecian Jews
Peter's journey
Paul and Barnabas's trip to Jerusalem and return to Antioch
Mark and Barnabas's trip to Cyprus
© 1986 The Zondervan Corporation

Map 11: **PAUL'S MISSIONARY JOURNEYS**

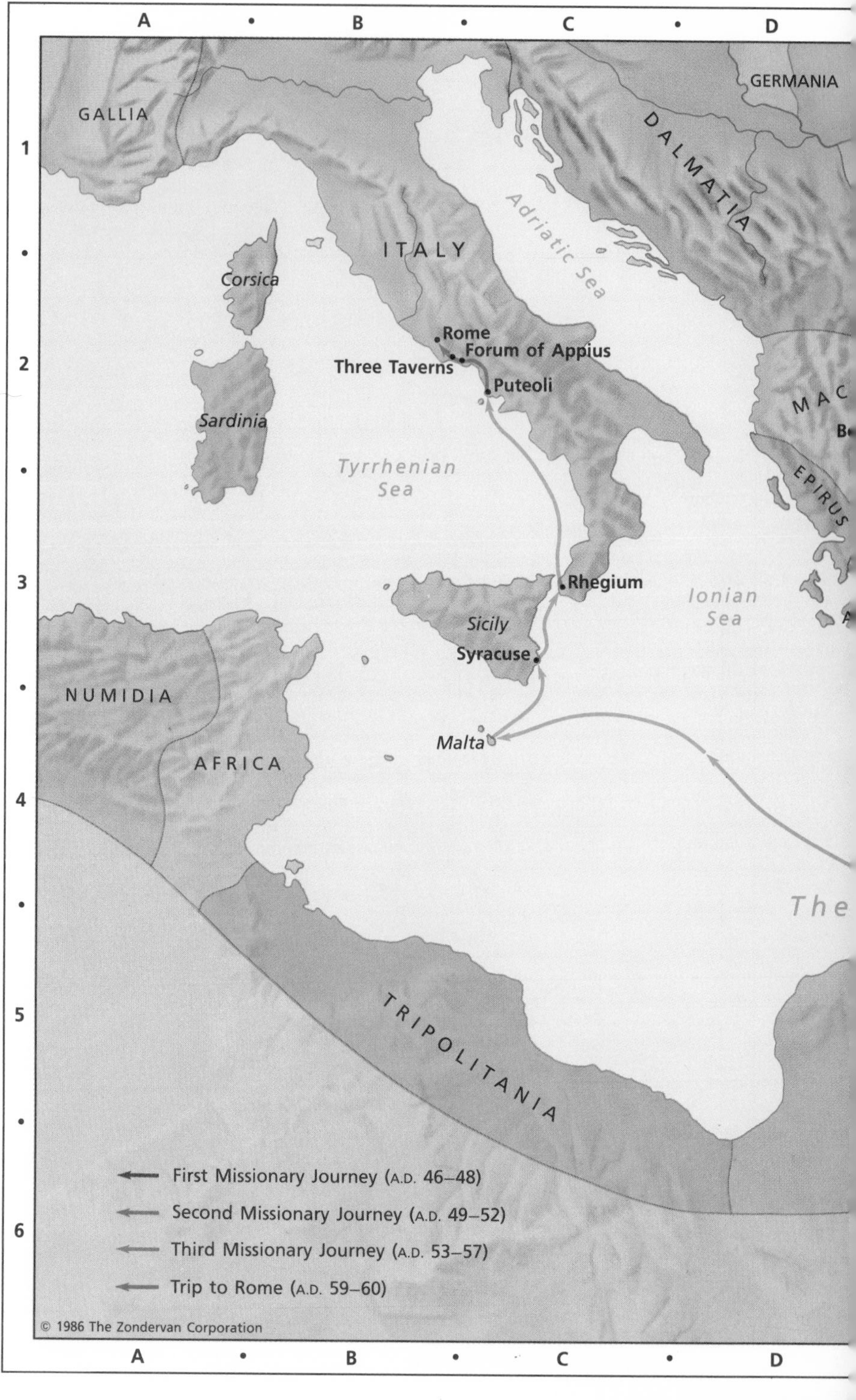
A
B
C
D
1
2
3
4
5
6
GALLIA
GERMANIA
DALMATIA
Adriatic Sea
ITALY
Corsica
Sardinia
Rome
Forum of Appius
Three Taverns
Puteoli
Tyrrhenian Sea
MAC
EPIRUS
Rhegium
Ionian Sea
Sicily
Syracuse
NUMIDIA
Malta
AFRICA
TRIPOLITANIA
First Missionary Journey (A.D. 46–48)
Second Missionary Journey (A.D. 49–52)
Third Missionary Journey (A.D. 53–57)
Trip to Rome (A.D. 59–60)
© 1986 The Zondervan Corporation

E
F
G
H
1
2
3
4
5
6
DACIA
Black Sea
MOESIA
THRACE
Philippi
Neapolis
Apollonia
Samothrace
Thessalonica
Olympus
Troas
Assos
Aegean Sea
Mitylene
Kios
MYSIA
Pergamum
Thyatira
ASIA
Sardis
Philadelphia
Smyrna
LYDIA
Ephesus
Samos
Athens
Laodicea
Colosse
Miletus
Patmos
Cos
Cnidus
LYCIA
Patara
Myra
Rhodes
Crete
Lasea
Salmone
Fair Havens
Great Sea
BITHYNIA AND PONTUS
GALATIA
CAPPADOCIA
COMMAGENE
LYCAONIA
Pisidian Antioch
PHRYGIA
PISIDIA
Iconium
Lystra
Derbe
CILICIA
Tarsus
Issus
Euphrates R.
Aleppo
Antioch
Seleucia
Attalia
PAMPHYLIA
Perga
SYRIA
Cyprus
Salamis
Paphos
PHOENICIA
ABILENE
Sidon
Damascus
Tyre
Ptolemais
Caesarea
JUDEA
Jordan R.
Jerusalem
Salt Sea
ARABIA
CYRENAICA
EGYPT
Nile R.
Red Sea
0
100
200 mi.
0
100
200
300 km.

Map 12: CHRISTIANITY IN THE WORLD TODAY

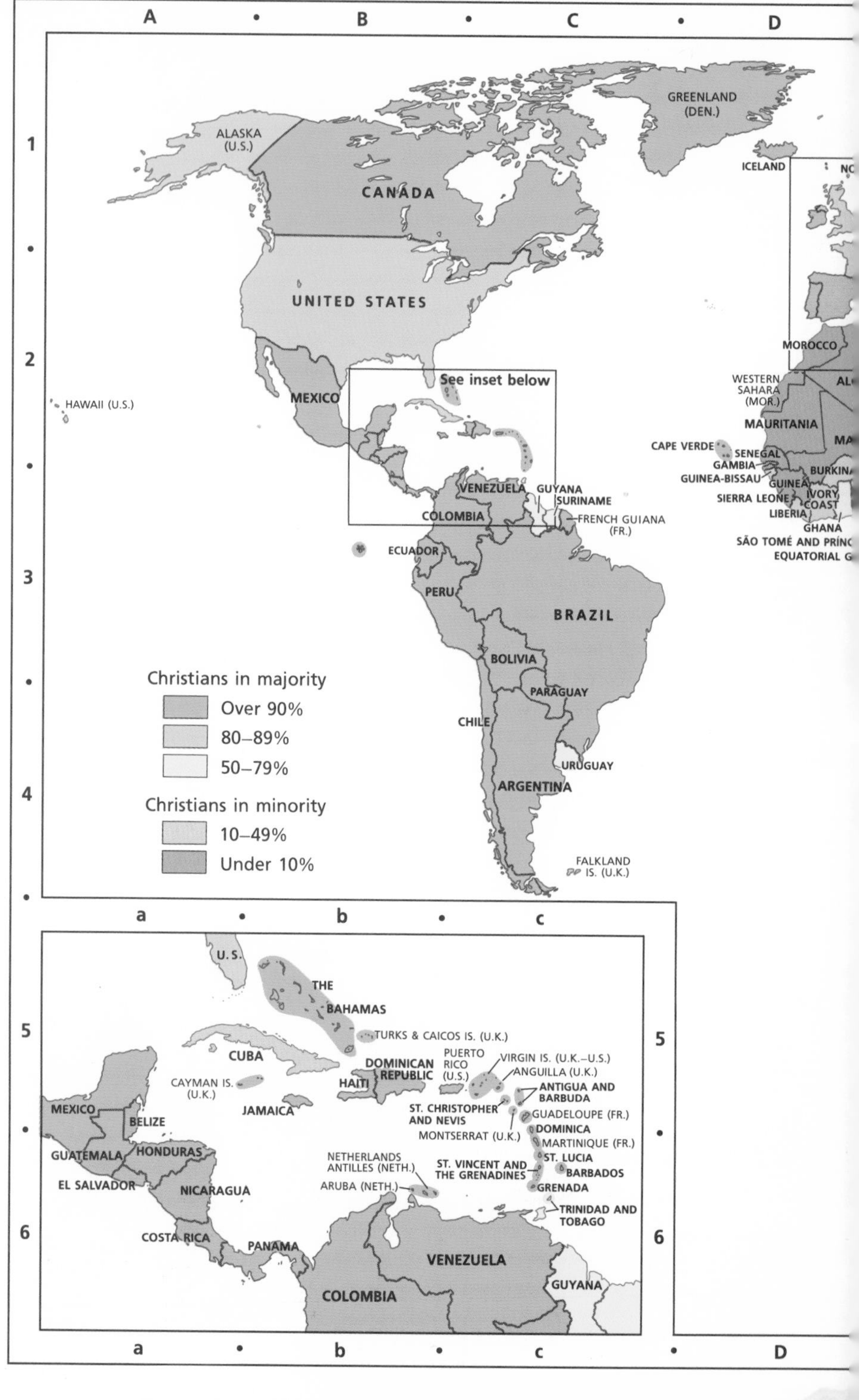

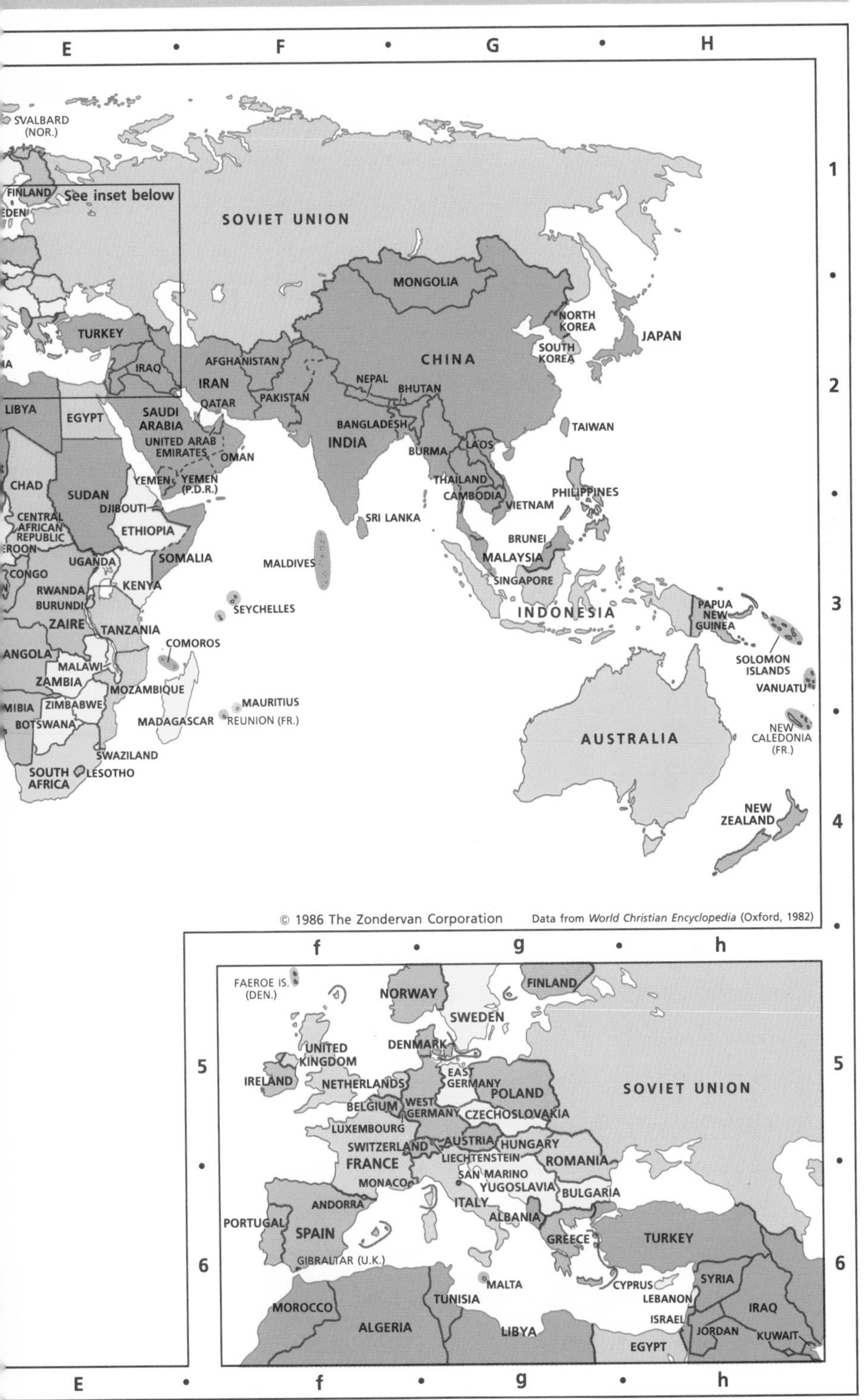

Data from *World Christian Encyclopedia* (Oxford, 1982)

Map 13: ROMAN EMPIRE

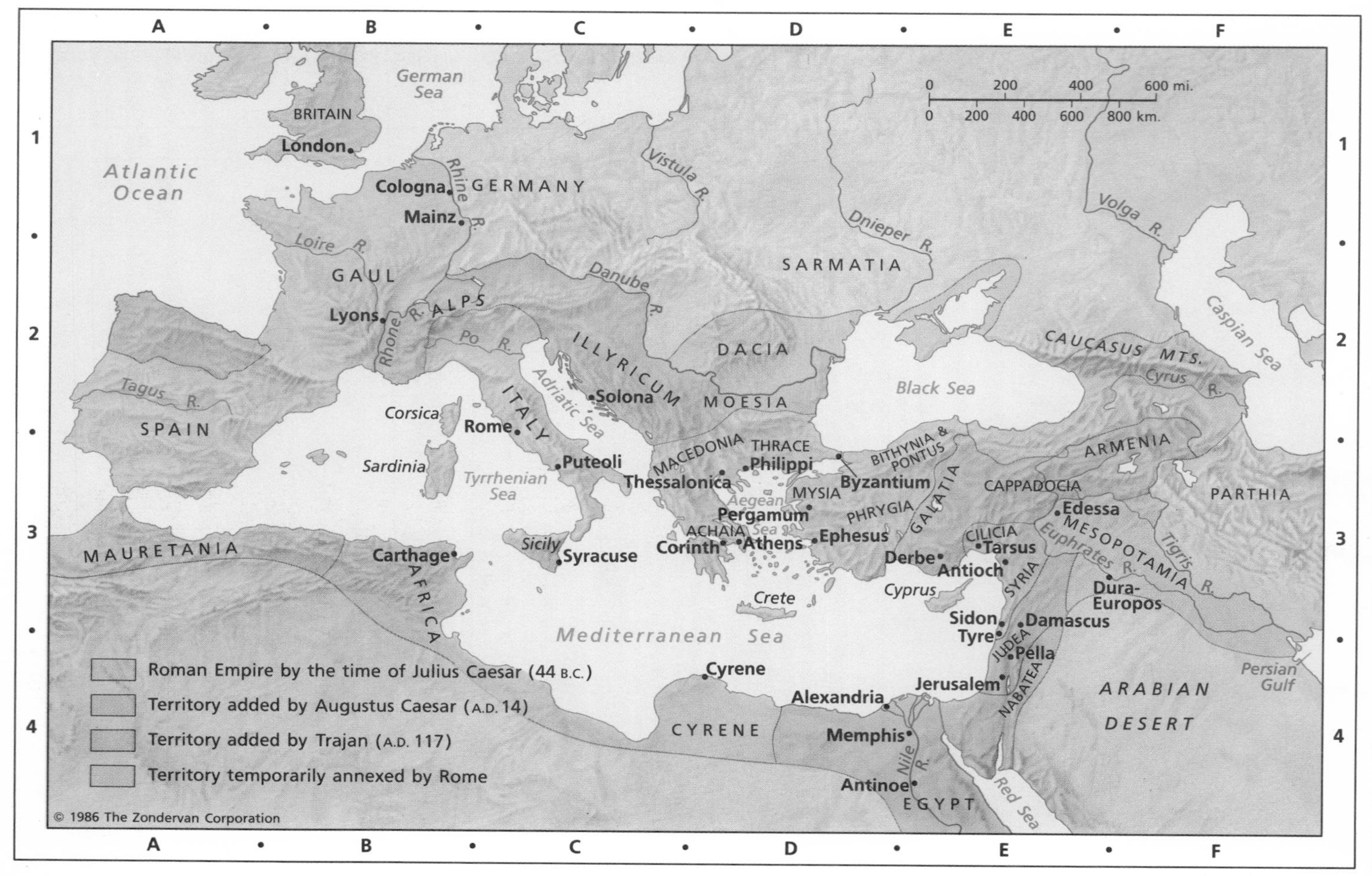